SUPPLEMENT XXI
Neith Boyce to Ira Wolfert

American Writers
A Collection of Literary Biographies

JAY PARINI
Editor in Chief

SUPPLEMENT XXI
Neith Boyce to Ira Wolfert

CHARLES SCRIBNER'S SONS
A part of Gale, Cengage Learning

GALE
CENGAGE Learning

Detroit • New York • San Francisco • New Haven, Conn • Waterville, Maine • London

GALE
CENGAGE Learning™

American Writers Supplement XXI

Editor in Chief: Jay Parini

Project Editor: Lisa Kumar

Permissions: Sari Gordon, Tracie Richardson, Jhanay Williams

Composition and Electronic Capture: Gary Leach

Manufacturing: Cynde Lentz

Publisher: Jim Draper

Product Manager: Janet Witalec

© 2011 Charles Scribner's Sons, a part of Gale, Cengage Learning

For product information and technology assistance, contact us at **Gale Customer Support, 1-800-877-4253.**
For permission to use material from this text or product, submit all requests online at **www.cengage.com/permissions**
Further permissions questions can be emailed to **permissionrequest@cengage.com**

While every effort has been made to ensure the reliability of the information presented in this publication, Gale, a part of Cengage Learning, does not guarantee the accuracy of the data contained herein. Gale accepts no payment for listing; and inclusion in the publication of any organization, agency, institution, publication, service, or individual does not imply endorsement of the editors or publisher. Errors brought to the attention of the publisher and verified to the satisfaction of the publisher will be corrected in future editions.

EDITORIAL DATA PRIVACY POLICY. Does this publication contain information about you as an individual? If so, for more information about our editorial data privacy policies, please see our Privacy Statement at www.gale.cengage.com

LIBRARY OF CONGRESS CATALOGING-IN-PUBLICATION DATA

American writers: a collection of literary biographies / Leonard Unger, editor in chief.
    p. cm.
    The 4-vol. main set consists of 97 of the pamphlets originally published as the University of Minnesota pamphlets on American writers; some have been rev. and updated. The supplements cover writers not included in the original series.
    Supplement 2, has editor in chief, A. Walton Litz; Retrospective suppl. 1, c1998, was edited by A. Walton Litz & Molly Weigel; Suppl. 5–7 have as editor-in-chief, Jay Parini.
    Includes bibliographies and index.
    Contents: v. 1. Henry Adams to T.S. Eliot — v. 2. Ralph Waldo Emerson to Carson McCullers — v. 3. Archibald MacLeish to George Santayana — v. 4. Isaac Bashevis Singer to Richard Wright — Supplement\[s\]: 1, pt. 1. Jane Addams to Sidney Lanier. 1, pt. 2. Vachel Lindsay to Elinor Wylie. 2, pt. 1. W.H. Auden to O. Henry. 2, pt. 2. Robinson Jeffers to Yvor Winters. — 4, pt. 1. Maya Angelou to Linda Hogan. 4, pt. 2. Susan Howe to Gore Vidal — Suppl. 5. Russell Banks to Charles Wright — Suppl. 6. Don DeLillo to W. D. Snodgrass — Suppl. 7. Julia Alvarez to Tobias Wolff — Suppl. 8. T.C. Boyle to August Wilson. — Suppl. 11 Toni Cade Bambara to Richard Yates.
    ISBN 0-684-19785-5 (set) — ISBN 0-684-13662-7
    1. American literature—History and criticism. 2. American literature—Bio-bibliography. 3. Authors, American—Biography. I. Unger, Leonard. II. Litz, A. Walton. III. Weigel, Molly. IV. Parini, Jay. V. University of Minnesota pamphlets on American writers.

PS129 .A55
810'.9
\[B\]   73-001759

ISBN-13: 978-0-684-31596-6
ISBN-10: 0-684-31596-3

Gale
27500 Drake Rd.
Farmington Hills, MI, 48331-3535

Printed in Mexico
1 2 3 4 5 6 7 14 13 12 11 10

Acknowledgments

List of Subjects

Introduction   ix

List of Contributors   xi

NEITH BOYCE   1
  Carol DeBoer-Langworthy

WILLIAM BRONK   17
  Guy Rotella

LARRY BROWN   35
  James H. Watkins

BILLY COLLINS   51
  Angela Garcia

MICHAEL CONNELLY   67
  Scott Earle

WILLIAM VIRGIL DAVIS   83
  H. L. Hix

RHINA P. ESPAILLAT   97
  Alfred Nicol

AMY HEMPEL   115
  Amanda Fields

LYNDA HULL   129
  April Ossmann

DAVID HENRY HWANG   143
  L. Bailey McDaniel

C. L. R. JAMES   159
  Stephen Soitos

JHUMPA LAHIRI   175
  Patricia J. Ferreira

SAM PICKERING   191
  John Gatta

MARILYNNE ROBINSON   209
  Joseph Dewey

GILBERT SORRENTINO   225
  John Domini

NATASHA TRETHEWEY   243
  Joan Wylie Hall

IRA WOLFERT   261
  Joseph G. Ramsey

Cumulative Index   281

Authors List   563

Introduction

Writers believe passionately in what lies before them, the task of making a novel, a poem, a play, an essay, a memoir. In his Nobel Prize acceptance speech, William Faulkner put the matter well, saying that the writer must commit to such lofty ideals as "love and honor and pity and pride and compassion and sacrifice." This is a heady calling, but what always seems astonishing is that so many fine writers come forward in each generation, committing themselves again and again to this ideals, creating memorable work in language that remains fresh, decade after decade.

In this twenty-first supplement of *American Writers,* we look closely at a range of writers who have committed to these ideals that Faulkner speaks of, always within the context of his or her time. These are all accomplished writers with major reputations in a variety of genres, and yet none of them has yet been featured in our series. These articles should prove helpful to readers who wish to dig more thoroughly into their work, to understand the shape of the career and its situation within the American literary landscape. We hope these articles will demonstrate how each—in his or her way—has added something of considerable value to American culture.

This series had its origin in a popular series of critical and biographical monographs that appeared between 1959 and 1972. *The Minnesota Pamphlets on American Writers* were incisively written and informative, treating ninety-seven American writers in a format and style that attracted a devoted following of readers over the years. The series proved invaluable to a generation of students and teachers, who could depend on these reliable, deeply thoughtful, often penetrating critiques of major figures. The idea of reprinting these essays occurred to Charles Scribner, Jr. (1921-1995), the well-known publisher. The series appeared in four volumes entitled *American Writers: A Collection of Literary Biographies* (1974).

Since then, twenty supplements have appeared, treating well over two hundred American writers in any number of genres. The idea has been consistent with the original series: to provide clear, informative essays aimed at the general reader, which includes students in high school and college. As anyone looking through this volume will notice, these essays often rise to a high level of craft and critical vision, yet they aim to introduce a writer of note in the history of American literature, offering a sense of the scope and nature of the career under review. The relevant biographical and historical backgrounds are also provided, thus placing the work itself in a living context.

The authors of these critical articles have published any number of books and articles in their field, and several are well-known writers of poetry or fiction as well as critics. As anyone glancing through this volume will observe, they have been held to the highest standards of good writing and intelligent scholarship. The essays each conclude with a select bibliography intended to direct the reading of those should want to pursue the subject further.

The writers studied in this supplement mostly contemporary, although a few of them—Neith Boyce, Ira Wolfert, and C. L. R. James—were writers mainly active in the mid-twentieth century. William Bronk, Billy Collins, William Virgil Davis, Rhina Espaillat, Lynda Hull, and Natasha Trethewey are mainly poets by trade, though some of them have also worked in other areas as well. (Davis, for instance, is a critic and scholar of poetry as well as a poet.) Among recent fiction writers, we examine the careers of

Larry Brown, Michael Connelly, Amy Hempel, Jhumpa Lahiri, Marilynne Robinson, and Gilbert Sorrentino. David Henry Hwang is a major contemporary playwright, while Sam Pickering is an essayist and memoirist whose singular, wry voice has filled over twenty volumes over the past thirty years or more.

While each of the writers discussed in this volume has already found an audience and, in some cases, won major prizes, few of them have yet to receive the kind of sustained attain they deserve, although each has been reviewed at length in periodicals. The hope is that these articles will form a baseline of sorts, a beginning, and that further criticism and scholarship will follow.

Context is crucial when it comes to understanding a writer's world, and every effort has been made to locate these authors in their specific time and place. The hope is that this supplement performs a valuable service in doing so, offering substantial introductions to American writers who have had a significant impact on our culture, living up to the standards put forward so memorably by William Faulkner when he spoke in Stockholm about "the old universal truths" that must never be forgotten or ignored.

—*JAY PARINI*

Contributors

Carol DeBoer-Langworthy. Carol DeBoer-Langworthy teaches in the Nonfiction Writing Program at Brown University. She did her master's and doctoral theses on Neith Boyce and published an edition of Boyce's autobiographical writings in 2003. Her critical essays on Boyce have appeared in *Documentary Editing and Resources for American Literary Study.* Neith Boyce

Joseph Dewey. Joseph Dewey is an Associate Professor of American Literature and Culture at the University of Pittsburgh. He is the author of *In a Dark Time: The Apocalyptic Temper of the American Novel since Hiroshima; Novels from Reagan's America: A New Realism; Understanding Richard Powers,* and *Beyond Grief and Nothing: A Reading of Don DeLillo,* in addition to editing casebooks on Henry James and on DeLillo's *Underworld* and most recently on *The Catcher in the Rye.* His articles and reviews have appeared in numerous journals and casebooks. Marilynne Robinson

John Domini. John Domini has worked as a visiting writer at many universities, including Harvard and Northwestern. He is the author of three novels, including *A Tomb on the Periphery* (Gival Press, 2008), and two books of stories. His first collection of criticism, *The Sea-God's Herb: Selected Work on the Postmodern Project,* was published in 2010 by the Red Hen Press. He has won awards in all genres, and has published short fiction in the *Paris Review* and elsewhere, as well as critical work in the *New York Times* and other journals (including Italian publications). Gilbert Sorrentino

Scott Earle. After two years of teaching English in a Japanese fishing village, Scott Earle earned a doctorate from the University of Arkansas. He now teaches at Tacoma Community College and is raising a family by the waters of Puget Sound. Michael Connelly

Patricia J. Ferreira. Patricia J. Ferreira is an Associate Professor of English at Norwich University, where she teaches courses on American cultural and ethnic literature. She has published essays on Frederick Douglass's travels in Ireland, appeared in the documentary "Frederick Douglass and the White Negro," and has been a guest on Public Radio International's *Tavis Smiley Program.* Jhumpa Lahiri

Amanda Fields. Amanda Fields received an M.F.A. in creative writing from the University of Minnesota and an M.A. in English from Iowa State University. Her work has appeared in *Indiana Review* 29.1 and *Brevity* 30. Her short story, "Boiler Room," was nominated for a Pushcart Prize, and she received an Artist Initia-

tive grant from the Minnesota State Arts Board in 2006. She taught writing at the American University in Cairo, Egypt before beginning work on a Ph.D. in rhetoric and composition at the University of Arizona. Amy Hempel

Angela Garcia. Angela Garcia teaches English Language Development at Linn-Benton Community College and in the public school system in Corvallis, Oregon. She received degrees in English from the University of California, Davis and University of California, Berkeley, where she specialized in the study and writing of poetry. Billy Collins

John Gatta. John Gatta is the Dean of the College of Arts and Sciences and Professor of English at Sewanee, The University of the South. He is the author of *Making Nature Sacred: Literature, Religion, and Environment in American from the Puritans to the Present* (2004), as well as other books and numerous articles related to American literary culture and religion. Much of his work has been devoted to critical commentary on Hawthorne, Thoreau, Whitman, Stowe, and colonial New England writing. Sam Pickering

Joan Wylie Hall. Joan Wylie Hall is a lecturer in English at the University of Mississippi. She is the author of *Shirley Jackson: A Study of the Short Fiction* and editor of *Conversations with Audre Lorde.* She has published articles on Willa Cather, Anna Deavere Smith, Josephine Humphreys, Eudora Welty, and other American women writers. Her essays on Ann Patchett and Janisse Ray appeared in previous volumes of the *American Writers Supplement.* Natasha Trethewey

H. L. Hix. H. L. Hix teaches in the creative writing M.F.A. program at the University of Wyoming. His poetry books include *Incident Light,* a verse biography of the artist Petra Soesemann, and *Chromatic,* a finalist for the 2006 National Book Award. His critical work includes monographs on the poet W. S. Merwin and the fiction writer William H. Gass. William Virgil Davis

L. Bailey McDaniel. L. Bailey McDaniel teaches post-colonial and U.S. literature at Oakland University. Her work explores the hegemonic inter-dependencies between categories of race, class, sexuality, and gender in modern drama. Her most recent project investigates performances of motherhood in twentieth-century American drama. David Henry Hwang

Alfred Nicol. Alfred Nicol is a poet whose first book of poems, *Winter Light,* received the 2004 Richard Wilbur Award. In addition, his poetry manuscript, *Elegy for Everyone,* was chosen for

the first Anita Dorn Memorial Prize and was published in 2010. He edited the *Powow River Anthology,* published in 2006, and his poems have appeared in *Poetry, The New England Review, Dark Horse, First Things, Atlanta Review, Commonweal, Crisis, The Formalist, Light, The Hopkins Review,* and other literary journals. RHINA P. ESPAILLAT

April Ossmann. April Ossmann has taught courses at the University of Maine, Farmington, and seminars for the Stonecoast M.F.A. Program in Creative Writing. She is the author of *Anxious Music* (Four Way Books, 2007), and has published poems widely in magazines and anthologies. Formerly a publisher, she owns a consulting business offering manuscript editing and publishing advice to poets; and teaches workshops using a method she developed to teach poets to revise their work objectively. LYNDA HULL

Joseph G. Ramsey. Joseph G. Ramsey teaches English and American Literature at Quincy College. His essays, which explore interconnections between U.S. mass/popular culture and radical politics, have appeared in the journals *Minnesota Review, Socialism and Democracy,* and *Reconstruction: Studies in Contemporary Culture,* as well as in a previous volume of the *American Writers* Series. He is a member of the editorial board of *Cultural Logic: An Electronic Journal of Marxist Theory and Practice,* and is currently editing a special issue titled 'Culture and Crisis,' which will appear in the Winter of 2010-2011 at http://www.clogic.eserver.org IRA WOLFERT

Guy Rotella. Guy Rotella teaches modern and postmodern poetry at Northeastern University. His books include *Reading and Writing Nature* (on Frost, Stevens, Moore, and Bishop) and *Castings* (on monuments and monumentality in poems by Bishop, Lowell, Merrill, Heaney, and Walcott). His essays have appeared in *American Literature, Contemporary Literature, Literary Imagination,* and many other journals. From 1984 through 2009 he edited the Morse Poetry Prize. WILLIAM BRONK

Stephen Soitos. Stephen Soitos is an artist and writer living in western Massachusetts. He is the author of *Blues Detective: A Study of African-American Detective Fiction* (1996). His essay on Chester Himes was recently published in *Wiley-Blackwell's Companion to Crime Fiction* (2010). He is the author of many essays on African-American art, writers, and culture. C. L. R. JAMES

James H. Watkins. James H. Watkins is an associate professor of English at Berry College in Rome, Georgia. He is the editor of *Southern Selves: A Collection of Autobiographical Writing* (Vintage 1998) and his work on U.S. southern autobiography has appeared in *The Southern Quarterly, The Indian American Culture and Research Journal, The North Carolina Literary Review,* and other journals and books. He is co-director of the biennial Southern Women Writers Conference at Berry College. LARRY BROWN.

SUPPLEMENT XXI
Neith Boyce to Ira Wolfert

NEITH BOYCE

(1872—1951)

Carol DeBoer-Langworthy

IN THE EARLY years of the twentieth century Neith Boyce was well known as a writer of short stories and novels. She was also a feminist, an anarchist, a "part-time bohemian"—and a mother of four, narrative historian, playwright, documentary editor, and hooker of rugs. At present, however, the world knows Neith Boyce largely as the wife in a marriage famous in the Progressive Era. Neith Boyce and her partner of some forty-five years, the radical journalist Hutchins Hapgood (1869–1944), were rediscovered by scholars in the late 1960s—he for his literary journalism, and she for her feminism as second-wave feminism sought its nineteenth- and early twentieth-century origins. Only since the late 1990s has Neith's writing begun to receive scholarly assessment as literature.

Neith's short stories in popular and serious mass-circulation magazines articulated the emotional and practical dilemmas of the New Woman at the turn of the twentieth century. Starting with small pieces of girlhood verse and then prose in her father's newspapers in California, Neith made a national mark with her naturalistic short stories appearing in the *Chap-Book,* published in Chicago in the mid-1890s. Initially supplementing her income as a young newspaperwoman in Greenwich Village, she published stories in national mass circulation magazines throughout the first two decades of the twentieth century. As June Sochen noted in *Movers and Shakers,* the implications of Neith's stories and novels were largely ignored at the time. Furthermore, Neith's feminism was nuanced with a tragic disbelief in Progress. Neith's underlying literary theme may have been larger than love, marriage, and women's lives. To understand this, we must detach Neith Boyce from her husband to assess her literature independently.

EARLY LIFE

Neith Boyce was born in Franklin, Indiana, on March 22, 1872, to parents whose first child, a son, had been born out of wedlock. Her father, Henry Harrison Boyce (1841–1903) had been a married schoolteacher in Illinois when he enlisted in the Union Army following Lincoln's second call for troops in 1861. Henry Boyce distinguished himself as an artilleryman during the Civil War, was wounded twice, and discharged as a captain at age twenty-three, although he may have been brevetted to major in the field. After the war, still married, he was superintendent of schools in Lake Forest, Illinois, where he met Mary Ella Smith (1845–1937), a teacher grieving the death of her fiancé. The two had a son together in 1869 and had to leave town for Gosport, Indiana. After Henry's divorce from his first wife, Martha Chapin, in June 1870, Henry and Mary Ella married that August in Vincennes, Indiana.

In Franklin, Indiana, Henry distinguished himself as superintendent of schools, creating and heading the high school. Mary was its principal and taught classical languages. Deeply educated in the classical world and probably influenced by John Ruskin, Mary named her first daughter for the chthonic Egyptian goddess Neith. But shortly after Neith was born in 1872, something in the Boyces' background was exposed and both parents were fired. The family left Franklin in 1873, and Mary and Henry left the field of teaching forever. Thus began a pattern of starting over and being on the run from scandal that would continue throughout their lifetimes and influence their daughter's life as well.

By 1880 the Boyces had five children, and Henry was working as a traveling representative

for a book publisher in Milwaukee. That year, diphtheria struck the city. As Neith wrote in her autobiography (a memoir written, interestingly, in the third person and using pseudonyms):

> Trouble came into the house: first one, then another of the children sickened; then they were all upstairs except Iras [Neith]. There were strange nurses. Iras [Neith] never saw her father or mother, they were up there with the other children, they never came downstairs.... No one had time or inclination to talk to her, she knew nothing, yet she knew all. She had a feeling like death.
>
> (*Modern World*, p. 47)

One day Martha Smith, Mary's mother and Neith's grandmother, received from her daughter this message, probably by telegraph: "Carl dead and buried, Etha dead; Paul dying. Come. Mary." Neith's four siblings had died. This episode initiated Neith's lifelong isolation and a tragic, fatalistic view of the universe, which also would color her view of Progressive reform. Neith feared intimacy, apprehensive that others she loved might suffer and die early. As Neith herself admitted, early on she began "walling herself up" to avoid becoming too close to people.

After the Milwaukee tragedy, the remaining three Boyces settled in Los Angeles, California. Soon Neith's creative parents became leading citizens in the newly Anglo city. Mary Boyce established the Ruskin Art Club and brought the first exhibit of engravings from Paris to U.S. shores in 1891. She also founded the Flower Festival Society, which survives as the Rose Bowl football game and Rose Parade in Pasadena. Henry Boyce founded a major bank and an "immigration society" that helped create the myth of California as the land of sun and promise—as well as cofounding the *Los Angeles Times* in 1884. In that newspaper, Neith began publishing poetry and other "small pieces" (*Modern World*, p. 80).

As a teenager Neith Boyce belonged to a bohemian group in Los Angeles and began publishing short stories in little magazines. These stories often had an unusual empathy for the prior rulers of the land before Eastern settlement: the old Hispanic families and the Native Americans confronting a vast social change. One was

published by Herbert S. Stone and Ingalls Wilder's *Chap-Book* in 1896 and included in its printed annual volume that same year.

By then Neith and her family (now including two younger sisters) were living in Boston and, later, New York. Scandal (again) and an economic collapse had driven her parents to the East. The economic collapse of Los Angeles would become the backdrop for her first novel, *The Forerunner* (1903). Neith had hoped to attend one of the private women's colleges in the East and managed one year as a boarder at Los Angeles College in 1886–1887. But the family fortunes were so low that she began working alongside her parents in their editorial endeavors. As a young woman, Neith taught herself French, read the classics, and remained all her life a deep reader in many genres, including history.

In New York, Mary Boyce began working on the *Woman's Cycle,* the national magazine of the General Federation of Women's Clubs. When named its chief editor, Mary renamed it *Lotos* and dedicated it to arts and culture as well as women's suffrage. Beginning in 1895 Neith published poetry, short stories, and literary journalism in *Lotos*. She also wrote a monthly column called "Book Notes and News," which offered her opinions about the need for a genuine American novel form. After its merger into the *Bookman*, the magazine was a forum for her work for years, with such articles as "The News Element in Modern Fiction" in the April 1901 issue. Advertisements for her novels would run in this magazine through 1910.

By the time her family swept through Manhattan and on to Mount Vernon, New York, Neith was having success selling short stories and poems to Saturday supplements and magazines. Josephine Redding (d. 1922), founding editor of *Vogue,* took an interest in Neith and introduced her to Norman Hapgood (1868–1937), then a reporter on the New York *Commercial Advertiser,* where Lincoln Steffens was city editor. Neith was hired as a reporter in 1897. On the strength of this job, she moved into a one-room "apartment" in the Judson Hotel on Washington Square in Greenwich Village and began what was probably the happiest period of her life. Her joyous

existence as an independent worker in the writing trade is portrayed lyrically in her autobiography. She befriended artists, activists, and writers, often for life. On the job, Steffens, Abraham Cahan (1860–1951), and Pitts Duffield (1869–1938) would become lifelong friends, Duffield serving as her initial book publisher and Cahan promoting her works through blurbs.

Steffens quickly realized Neith's editorial aptitude and put her on "the desk," correcting and smoothing the copy of other writers. One reporter whose writing she improved was Hutchins Hapgood, younger brother of Norman. According to his autobiography, he fell in love with her at first sight, decided that she was the right mate for him, and pursued her ardently.

Their relationship perhaps verifies the old adage that opposites attract. Neith was a disciplined writer, self-possessed, and ambitious. Hutchins was voluble, sociable, and prone both to drink and to what he called "confession." At the time, Neith was publishing nine "papers" under the rubric of "The Bachelor Girl" in *Vogue*—a sardonic running account of being a single working female in New York. It offered a biting critique of marriage, which was thinning the ranks of the author's compatriots even while she acknowledged that young women had few other good prospects for a middle-class life.

After agonizing over whether to marry or not, Neith agreed to Hapgood's offer. She revised her life plan to include marriage and children, but without giving up Art. Neith insisted that their union was to be "tentative, it was not to be till death did them part. If either of them didn't like it, retreat must be easy" (*Modern World,* p. 186). It was to be egalitarian, based on New Womanhood principles of equality between the sexes in standards of personal behavior, particularly sexual behavior, alongside respect for individual autonomy. This all stemmed from the nineteenth-century free love movement, which promulgated not sexual profligacy but a belief that love, not necessarily marriage, should be the basis for sexual relationships. Also in play were anarchist-libertarian ideals of freedom from the social control of personal relations. These "new" proposed sexual patterns also built on the peren-

nial American interest in perfectionism: finding the perfect solution to a problem, in this case solving contradictions such as inequality between the sexes, differing power balances for males and females in society, and resolving conflict. The conflict called at the time "sex antagonism" would become a stated topic of Hutch and a perennial theme for Neith. Resolving this in their marriage proved harder to implement than to theorize.

Even so, as her husband acknowledged in *The Story of a Lover* (published anonymously in 1919), Neith was actually far more radical than he. As Hapgood wrote in this breathless memoir of their intimate relationship, she had: "a deeper nature, a nature more unconventional than mine, and less theoretical. She tended more than I to put into thorough practice what she had once mentally accepted" (p. 109).

In an 1898 letter to his grandmother about their engagement, Hapgood describes Neith:

> She will be 25 years old in March, is [fair-skinned] with dark red hair, slight in figure. She is very independent and rigorous in character. Has been making her own living of late and is a clever writer for the newspaper and magazines. She has many literary schemes in her head, is now writing a novel and hopes soon to write a play.

Marrying Hutch in 1899, Neith would spend the rest of her life working out the fine print in their marriage contract.

NEGOTIATING MARRIAGE

As a married woman, Neith fought hard to maintain her autonomy, a major source of contention in their relationship—Hutch claiming that Neith never really acknowledged him and Neith resisting his overwhelming neediness. This battle soon took over her literature as well as life. According to Hapgood, an emotional crisis loomed when Neith discovered she was pregnant. Initially fearing motherhood, Neith soon fell in love with her first son, Boyce Hapgood, born in 1901, and would go on to bear three more children. But their lives were far from a picture of domestic tranquility.

Thanks to some Hapgood family money (his father was a millionaire Midwestern manufacturer of farm implements), the couple could live comfortably abroad on occasion. They developed a pattern of going to Italy when a book needed finishing, and the year 1903 found the young family settled into a villa outside Florence, where Neith completed her first novel, *The Forerunner.*

The accidental death of her beloved father later that year brought them back to New York. She returned from Europe pregnant with Charles H. Hapgood II, who was born in New York in May 1904. That fall the newly enlarged family moved to Chicago, where Hapgood's best friend Arthur Bentley (1870–1957) set him up with work on the *Chicago Evening News,* and Hapgood began exploring anarchism and the labor movement. Part of that exploration included his embrace of "varietism," a version of anarchism that, in his formulation, at least, held that relationships outside of marriage would enhance the primary one. Thus Neith's new social circle in Chicago included not only anarchists such as Terry Carlin and Hippolyte Havel but also the various women her husband took as lovers. Although Neith would eventually accede to Hapgood's pleas that they both experiment with living and loving arrangements, initially she was not interested, and, perhaps not coincidentally, she and the children soon were living with her mother in New York and in-laws in Seal Harbor, Maine—a Hapgood extended-family summer tradition.

The couple maintained a peripatetic lifestyle, often separated by choice or circumstance, with Hapgood off in pursuit of "stories" while Neith stayed at home with the children and tried to write. Her mother often lived near or with them and helped care for the children, and Neith's sister Margaret Bonnell and her daughter Alice often spent time at their home when Hapgood was away. The couple brought servants back with them from Italy and occasionally employed various anarchists such as Hippolyte Havel as cooks. But Hapgood was never satisfied with Neith's housekeeping or independence and tried to reform her into something akin to Maggie, the wife of the Chicago labor organizer Anton Jo-

hannsen, subject of his *The Spirit of Labor* (1907): a good mother who kept the house clean and did not challenge her husband's varietist ideas or multiple sexual partners. Neith's reasons for staying with Hapgood have puzzled several scholars. In a letter to her mother in 1907, Neith's good friend Mary Smith Berenson, the art connoisseur and historian, perhaps comes closest to explaining the situation:

> I could not have believed it if I hadn't heard it from her own lips—… Neith loves her husband *because* of his unreasonableness & brutality & selfishness— yes & his dissipation. She thinks it is glorious & manly to get drunk with ruffians & to do all sorts of wild & reckless things, & she *admires* him when he comes home & … is as cross as a bear. She despises "reasonable" men, "good" men, "sensible" men: she thinks nothing is so fascinating as great unruly unreflecting passions that drown reason & conscience & common sense. This is what she calls "Life," and Hutchins embodies it for her, & she adores him for it.

(Mary Berenson to Hannah Whitall Smith, March 9, 1907)

Especially during their periods of separation, the couple examined and negotiated their relationship in frequent letters. The result is a rich vein of correspondence now held in the Hapgood Family Papers at Yale's Beinecke Rare Book and Manuscript Library. As Christine Stansell wrote of this remarkable collection, the couple "used the letters to adjudicate practical matters about children's shoes and doctors' bills, publishers' advances and repairs on the house—and to enact their erotic connection" (*American Moderns,* p. 291). Neith managed to keep Hapgood alert through her intellectual challenges. But the rules of the relationship were that the couple's sexual engagements were to be common property. Stansell believes that "Disclosure was the turn-on" (p. 292). During Hapgood's many affairs, Neith fought hard to maintain not only her primary role in Hutch's affection but to sustain the family. One initial strategy was to affect indifference to Hapgood's behavior. On occasion, however, her ruse failed. True frankness occurred only much later in their relationship. In the meantime, her real feelings perhaps came out only in her literature.

All of these volatile undercurrents in the marriage erupted when, soon after her novel about

the expatriate colony in Florence, *The Eternal Spring,* appeared in January 1906, the couple returned to Europe. Heading first for Italy, they moved into Villa Linda near the home of Bernard and Mary Berenson. After the birth of daughter Miriam in a hotel along the Arno in late November, Neith maintained the household while Hapgood traveled to Germany, France, and England on projects. In June 1907 they moved to a house in Champery, Switzerland, then in October moved to Paris, in December taking a house in St. Cloud outside Paris for six months. Apparently during this time, the couple began experimenting—"swapping" sexual partners with Arthur and Anna Bentley while Neith was working on her novel about varietism in marriage. Complications ensued when Arthur, Hapgood's best friend, fell deeply in love with Neith, and she with him. Hapgood, apparently more comfortable with the theory of varietism than with its practice, became jealous.

Bentley and his wife had come to Europe to help him recover from completing his major book, *The Process of Government.* Neith's *The Bond* appeared in the United States while the Bentleys spent the month of April 1908 with the Hapgoods in St. Cloud; this stay seems to have precipitated a crisis that sent the Hapgoods scurrying back to the United States—and Hutch to Chicago to interview Terry Carlin and "Marie," she the model for his *An Anarchist Woman.* Bentley also returned to the United States and came to press his case with and for Neith. Hutch at some point gave Neith an ultimatum: me and the children, or Arthur. Over the winter of 1908–1909 Neith suffered a nervous breakdown while the family lived in Indianapolis. After time in a sanatorium, she recovered further in the home of the Robert Morss Lovetts in Chicago. That spring Hapgood commissioned a bucolic photograph in Indiana of Neith dressed in white, her head covered by a shawl and surrounded by her three children also in white, and sent copies to friends around the world: Neith had chosen him and the children. Bentley, meanwhile, also had a nervous breakdown and retreated from Chicago to a farm in Indiana, where he spent the remainder of his

life writing books of political and semantic philosophy only now being appreciated.

This marital crisis eventually found its way into the book Hapgood published anonymously in 1919, *The Story of a Lover.* Although Neith had originally suggested a ménage à quatre so that she could bear Arthur's child, in his book Hapgood reported it as a ménage à trois, thereby claiming the role of wronged spouse. He reported that after this episode, Neith had at last given up the "great illusion" (romantic love) and settled for family life. Nonetheless, Neith wrote to Lincoln Steffens that she was glad the book was published but "Hutch's truth is not my truth."

PROVINCETOWN

Whatever her feelings about her break with Bentley at the time, spring 1910 found the Hapgoods back on the East Coast, where Hapgood worked as an editorial writer for the *New York Post* and Neith gave birth to her fourth and last child, Beatrix, in Spring Lake, New Jersey. Hapgood's father, perhaps alarmed at the family's erratic lifestyle, bought them (sight unseen) a large house in Dobbs Ferry, New York, in 1911. From here Neith kept at her writing while Hutch was a columnist for the *New York Globe.* That summer, lured by the labor journalist Mary Heaton Vorse (1874–1966), the family spent their first summer season in Provincetown, Massachusetts. Ultimately they would own four houses in what has been termed the birthplace of the little theater movement in America, establishing a family connection that still persists. Soon they were joined by Susan Glaspell and George Cram ("Jig") Cook; Wilbur Daniel Steele and his wife Margaret, a painter; and Mary's new husband, Joe O'Brien. These four couples, the "regulars," were the bedrock from which sprang the Provincetown Players.

In mid-July 1914 Neith and her good friend Mabel Dodge (1879–1962), along with Mabel's "nurse," Frances Galvin, and their children Boyce, Beatrix, and John departed for Italy. Joined there by Carl Van Vechten, they were nearly trapped as war spread over Europe. Neith's

"War Diary" details this experience. Neith, the children, and Van Vechten made it back to the United States on the *Stampalia*. The war soon brought to Provincetown a larger contingent of artists, writers, and thinkers, including John Reed, birth control advocate Margaret Sanger, Polly Holladay and Hippolyte Havel, Max Eastman and Ida Rauh, artists B. J. O. Nordfeldt and Margaret Nordfeldt, stage designers Lee Simonson and Robert Edmond Jones, visual artists Andrew Dasburg, Stuart Davis, and Charles Demuth, and the author and critic Floyd Dell, among others. Mary Heaton Vorse made an offer to buy Lewis Wharf, a fishing wharf jutting out into Cape Cod Bay. All of this set the scene for the summer of 1915, when Neith was crucial to the founding of the Provincetown Players.

Brenda Murphy opens her book on this group and modernism with a discussion of the "mythology" that surrounds the founding of the group in 1915. Influenced by ideas of the New Stagecraft from Gordon Craig (1872–1966)—whom Neith had known earlier in Florence and with whom Mary Berenson had encouraged a flirtation—this new way of producing theater involved a simpler stage setting, a version of impressionism in theater. Dialogue was to mimic vernacular conversation rather than the ponderous "speeches" of nineteenth-century drama. Some plays by Neith, rejected by the Washington Square Players founded in 1914, were ready for production when she began promoting the idea of writing and producing their own plays in Provincetown that summer of 1915.

Her *Constancy* opened at 10 p.m. on July 15, 1915, in the home the Hapgoods were renting at the time, the Bissell Cottage at 621 Commercial Street in Provincetown. Neith directed and took the lead role of Moira opposite Joe O'Brien as Rex in a setting created by Robert Edmond Jones. A satire of Mabel Dodge's affair with John Reed, the play was primarily a vehicle for Neith to ponder a woman's response to male infidelity. The other offering was Glaspell and Cook's *Suppressed Desires,* a satire of the trend toward psychoanalysis. Later that summer, the two plays were restaged on Lewis Wharf, and the Players

coalesced around anarchist principles the following summer.

Not only was Neith in on the beginning of this group, she possibly *was* the beginning. Leona Egan, Cheryl Black, Judith Barlow, J. Ellen Gainor, and Jeffery Kennedy are among the scholars now revising the mythology of the group and exploring Neith's role in its genesis. According to Susan Glaspell's memoir *The Road to the Temple* (1926), her husband, George Cram (Jig) Cook, who is usually called the founder of the Provincetown Players, and Neith talked through the group's anarchistic statement of purpose together in 1916. "He and Neith Boyce said it together. He came home and wrote it down as an affirmation of faith" (Glaspell, p. 203). Edna Kenton's brief history of the group confirms this, stating that although the original document is in Jig's handwriting, the articulation of the group's artistic vision was jointly "formulated" with Neith (Kenton, p. 14). Mary Heaton Vorse, one of Neith's best friends and the person who looked after her when she was dying, agreed. Neith herself is remarkably silent on the topic, perhaps because, as a good anarchist, she was considering the group's welfare. Was the group conscience more important to her than individual fame?

In 1968–1969, Charles H. Hapgood II, Neith's younger son, laid out Neith's role in the group's creation to Louis Sheaffer, one of Eugene O'Neill's early biographers. In an interview, he said that the idea for the groundbreaking theater group had been his mother's:

> The Provincetown Players was originally my mother's idea, she had written plays, done quite a bit of writing, and thought no use to wait for Broadway to produce their work but should do it themselves.... She was the one who urged it. She was the builder type, kept after things, didn't let them drop ... organizer and builder, felt very strongly about this ... she sold the idea to Jig Cook, who grabbed it. (Ellipses in original transcript.)

Today Neith is gauged second only to her good friend Susan Glaspell, who is ranked second only to Eugene O'Neill, in importance as a playwright within that movement. Neith's plays were part of those six formative seasons in the Players' history (1916–1922), when the group staged ninety-

seven plays by forty-seven American authors, including O'Neill and Glaspell. As the distinguished scholar Robert K. Sarlós has noted, this company was "the single most fruitful American theatre prior to the Second World War: it introduced more native playwrights, had a greater impact on audiences and critics, and a longer life than any other similar group" (p. 160). Its contributions include the development of a noncommercial theatrical tradition (surviving as the Off-Broadway theater), racially integrated casts, the discovery of two major playwrights (Glaspell and O'Neill), an attempt at nonhierarchical organizational structure in theater companies, and numerous scenic innovations called the "New Stagecraft."

Three of Neith's plays, *Winter's Night*, *Constancy*, and *Enemies*, were performed by the officially named group in the summer of 1916 at Lewis Wharf. Her *The Two Sons*, along with *Constancy* and *Winter's Night*, were performed subsequently as part of the group's winter season of 1916–1917 at the Playwrights Theater at 139 Macdougal Street in New York's Greenwich Village. This marks the end of her direct involvement with the group, perhaps because marital stresses once again threatened to overwhelm her.

In September 1917 Neith and her four children took up residence separate from Hapgood on a rented farm outside Norwich, Vermont. This separation—ostensibly to help the elder son, Boyce (nicknamed "Harry"), complete high school—probably was intended to be permanent. John Pyne, the younger brother of actress Mary Pyne (1894?–1919), with whom Hapgood was having an affair in New York, joined their household in Vermont, and then went west with Harry in August 1918. After Harry died in New Mexico in the 1918 influenza pandemic, Neith and Hutch were reunited. Neith suffered a profound depression, blaming herself for allowing Harry to pursue his dream of the cowboy life. In 1919 Neith sought relief from her grief by holding séances with her dead son, managed by a medium and sometimes with her second son, Charles, as the intermediary. Her memoir of the year in Vermont, *Harry, A Portrait,* appeared in 1923, the same year as the novel on which she

had worked in Vermont, *Proud Lady*. Thereafter her publishing career diminished, but she kept writing and seeking publication until the end of her life.

BETWEEN THE WARS

Although Hapgood's account of their 1906–1908 marital crisis, *The Story of a Lover,* was published anonymously in 1919, he was "outed" as the author in print, whereupon the book was suppressed by the censor for indecency. A court case in 1920 ruled otherwise, but most copies of the book had been pulped. In 1922 the couple sold their Dobbs Ferry home and left for another extended stay in Europe. After a summer in Provincetown, they traveled to London, Paris, and Switzerland, where they attended the Conference of Lausanne as observers and witnessed the birth of the Republic of Turkey. This peace conference ending World War I was covered by old friends Steffens and Guy Hickok. Neith and her daughter Miriam met a young reporter also covering the conference, Ernest Hemingway. The family reunited for the summer of 1923 in Cavalaire, France, then went on to Paris. The end of that year brought Neith, Beatrix, and Hapgood to the Berensons' Villa Corbignano in Settignano outside Florence.

Early 1924 took them to the south of France: Cannes, Monte Carlo, and Vence. In spring 1924 Neith, Beatrix, and Charles returned to the United States while Hapgood and his favorite daughter, Miriam, resided in Paris and visited Jo Davidson's studio (for a life bust of Hapgood), Gertrude Stein's salon, the Bullitts, and James Joyce and family. Back in the United States, Neith began looking for a farm and in 1925 bought the Wheeler Farm outside Richmond, New Hampshire, with funds from her royalties. The peripatetic waltz continued, with various family members spending winters in rented apartments in New York or in Cambridge, Massachusetts, while son Charles was at Harvard. Neith demonstrated the Boyce family skill in real estate, also organizing purchases of other houses in Provincetown. This property would tide them

over during the coming Depression. In 1928 she began buying and selling stocks, at a small profit. Along with her daughter Miriam and son Charles, she visited her old friend Mabel Dodge (now Luhan) in Taos, New Mexico—Miriam stayed on, with Hapgood buying her a house there.

But nothing could protect Neith from the Crash of 1929. Tempted by a Harvard classmate's offer to double his money quickly, Hapgood invested his inherited fortune in a scheme that failed with the market drop in October 1929. The next year the couple sold one of their properties, the Cavalier cottage in Provincetown, and began living in diminished circumstances. They could spend winters in New York or Key West, summering in Provincetown or on her farm. In 1930 Neith wrote the first draft of *The Sea Lady,* a play in eight scenes she adapted from the fantasy novel by H. G. Wells. Over the next five years she labored on this adaptation for the Broadway stage, with talk of a film version, only to have it pulled at the last minute owing to rights issues. She also worked on a "murder play" and a one-act called *All in the Family.* Perhaps motivated by real financial need, Neith was remarkably productive during the 1930s, retaining an agent, visiting theater producers in New York, and entering writing contests. Intrigued by local New Hampshire history, she wrote a historical pageant about the town of Winchester titled "Two Hundred Years in an Hour" for the town's 200th anniversary in 1932. A book of local history infused with what we now call postmodern mourning, *The Town in the Forest: Life Story of Richmond, New Hampshire,* would see print only in 1992 as edited by her daughter Beatrix Hapgood Faust. Neith also became interested in local arts and crafts, collecting antiques for her farmhouse and hooking rugs, as that area of New Hampshire sheltered a number of artists from the Depression. Meanwhile, Hapgood labored on what he called his booze book, "My Forty Years of Drink," which never saw publication.

In 1933 Carl Van Vechten photographed Neith and Hutchins and Beatrix, who lived with them, eschewing college. In 1934 the couple began wintering in Key West near their friends Katy and John Dos Passos and Hemingway. That winter Neith began typing up some old family letters from a stash that Hapgood's father had left in their Dobbs Ferry house. By this time the couple had renegotiated their friendships with former lovers. In 1936 Neith and Hutch summered at the farm near Richmond, New Hampshire, then visited John and perhaps Lucy Wood Collier in Alabama on their drive to Key West for the winter, also stopping in St. Augustine, Florida, to visit Arthur Bentley and his second wife. By this time John Collier (1884-1968) was the Commissioner of Indian Affairs under Franklin D. Roosevelt. Presumably, Hutch's long-term affair with Lucy (b. 1886) had ended. The Colliers divorced in 1943.

During these winters Neith worked on a long but eventually unpublished novel about Key West, "The Doomed City," which she sent to an *Atlantic Monthly* contest in 1938. She also urged Hapgood to write his autobiography after a friend interceded with a publisher for a contract. She took on the role of amanuensis during Hapgood's three-month recuperation from prostate surgery in New York, interviewing him at bedside, going over his old correspondence, and reviewing his works, taking down his words by typewriter. After Hapgood marked up the copy, she retyped it again. *A Victorian in the Modern World,* now considered a classic of cultural history, appeared in 1939 and has persisted as a major source for scholars seeking a sense of life in America before World War I.

Perhaps inspired by Hapgood's success, Neith wrote her own autobiography in Key West the winter of 1939–1940. Written in the third person, it assigns pseudonyms to everyone except her mother, "Mary." It stops at the marriage bed, although she later typed up the manuscript to precede another major document, the "Diary–1903," covering her first stay in Italy. Together, Neith and Hapgood began work on a family letters project—Neith typing up transcripts of family correspondence, largely from Hapgood forebears going back some 250 years. This is the project she worked on during the last ten years of her life, with private publication occurring the summer before she died in 1951. It was cutting-edge in approach: a documentary history of the

United States using private (Hapgood and Boyce) family letters with public documents to comment on the American experiment. Her individualist anarchism shines through, as she argues that yeomanry is necessary for democracy. This textual fusion was too far ahead of most editors.

FINAL YEARS

In 1944 Hapgood died in their home at 583 Commercial Street, Provincetown. According to family legend, Neith looked up from the deathbed at her second daughter and said, "I want to be with you." She sold the Provincetown house and purchased another in Wellfleet, which she shared with Beatrix and Luke Faust and their children. One of her old friends later told the present writer that Neith also sought surcease from the FBI, which was hounding her—not understanding the difference between an anarchist and a communist.

After the Fausts left Wellfleet in 1951, her daughters arranged for Neith to live in a small walk-up apartment at 462 Commercial Street, Provincetown. She had begun having small strokes and was bedridden and speechless the last months of her life. Monitored by her good friend next door, Mary Heaton Vorse, Neith had Rachel Kelly as a nurse. In fall 1951 she received a carton of the family history book, *The Story of an American Family: Letters of the Hapgood Family, 1648–1917* after it was privately printed. She died on December 2, 1951. A funeral was held in the First Unitarian Church in Petersham, Massachusetts, ancestral home of the Hapgoods. She was buried at the foot of Hapgood's grave in the East Cemetery of that city. At her request, her father's favorite song from the Civil War, "We're Tenting Tonight on the Old Campground," was read at her funeral.

APPROACH TO WRITING AND EARLY WORKS

In her writing, Neith refashioned all of these emotional dynamics, along with her family history, characters she met, and settings important in her own life. She also critiqued traditional politics and seems to have been loyal to anar-

chism (individually interpreted) throughout her long life. In Boston, where Neith worked alongside her mother on the socialist *Arena* magazine, she probably knew of, or met, the anarchist Benjamin R. Tucker. Tucker's ideas, later termed "Boston anarchism," included a main tenet that one's individual conscience and pursuit of self-interest was not to be impeded by any collective body or authority. This nexus of ideas of personal freedom included holding private property, even while believing that all conflict could be worked out through group process.

In 1892 the Arena Publishing Company brought out Neith's first book, a volume of poetry, *Songs,* with drawings by her girlhood friend in Los Angeles. That volume includes "Prisoned Love," which perhaps reveals her dilemma about emotional attachment to persons:

And I shut the gate of my heart
Crying, "Thou Shalt not go!
I will hold thee, Love, till thou
A willing prisoner art!"
And now, shaken with dread,
In the silence drear I wait
Afraid to open the gate
Lest love be dead!

[15]

She also developed a pattern of masking potentially embarrassing details in the public version of herself, whether in print or live. Even so, the issues over which she felt shame came out in her literature. She also tackled epic family struggles, the naturalistic effects of world events and nature upon individual humans, and stifling patterns of social convention. As her husband sometimes accused her, marriage was not all that important to her. In actuality, she had a deep understanding of all the power dynamics embodied in marriage and how it operated as a social institution far beyond "romance."

Sternly disciplined, she could withdraw into her mental pursuits, becoming remote to others. Even as a child, she admitted this as a fault. In her autobiography she recalled creating an alternate, less admirable personage, "You," and deriding it for making social blunders, being unable to socialize with others. As a child she had a

nightmare vision of a cruel Fate that made life-and-death decisions regardless of an individual's merit. As an adult she attempted to change her views, as demanded by Hapgood, but with limited success. Her ability to concentrate allowed her to work at writing while in the midst of a sometimes chaotic marriage and to rear four children while moving around the United States and Europe. From time to time she suffered mysterious illnesses, probably brought on by stress: she would stop eating and smoke even more than usual. Her daughters reported heavy drinking, especially after Hapgood's death.

As noted, her early short poems appeared in magazines and newspapers throughout the country, with Neith publishing in perhaps hundreds of magazines and newspapers around the country before her marriage, and private poetry for family members thereafter. This private poetry often commemorated events such as birthdays, and now serves as a sort of barometer of the temperature of the marriage. Unlike much newspaper poetry of the time, however, her early newspaper poetry seldom references current events.

Short stories were, literally, her bread and butter while working on the *Commercial Advertiser*: her salary covered only the rent, not food or carfare. As Neith later wrote of herself then, "She withdrew into herself emotionally and felt almost nothing; except a perennial interest in the surface of life, in watching and recording it, finding it amusing and good material, and even entering into the emotions of her characters enough to be able to record those.… In fact the warmth sealed up in [Neith], which had no other outward expression, must have gone into these stories" (*Modern World*, p. 121). They appeared in the newspaper's Saturday supplements, prompting Steffens once to ask, with a chuckle, "Why don't you have some happy endings?" (p. 155).

Neith's stories depict the dilemmas of the New Woman, who was supposed to have a lot of new freedoms but often found herself encountering other kinds of restraints. Often the female protagonist is not particularly noble, and the problem of the story revolves around her ignorance of or lack of empathy for a man. Other stories depict a long-suffering heroine who puts her husband's welfare, and self-actualization, above her own. Although on the surface these seem to uphold the status quo of expectations for females, they also contain a critique of a society that demands such sacrifice to male supremacy. Most of her heroines, however, get into trouble for not being true to themselves: choosing to marry for convenience or just because they said they would (*Proud Lady*). Others misjudge or challenge some parameter of the rules of the institution of marriage, or unwisely submit to those rules. In "A Provident Woman," a long short story she called a novelette and collected in her third book, *The Folly of Others* (1904), her working girl heroine Cecilia Clayber makes the error of marrying an older man (her boss) in order to provide for her younger siblings—who disdain her for her sacrifice.

Neith seems to have been able to calibrate her stories to the various magazine markets. "My Dear Niece" (*Good Housekeeping,* 1911) depicts an older woman's sympathy for the niece's railing against women's lot. Her "Undertow," a long story that appeared in *Lippincott's Monthly Magazine* in August 1914, argues for young women to have a period of sexual experimentation without penalty, as do young men. But another set of stories, what Neith called her "Wives" series, almost parodies the stock plot of what were called women's stories.

NOVELS

Her first and arguably best novel, *The Forerunner* (1903), was completed and published during Neith's first stay in Italy. Initially laid in Los Angeles in the late 1880s, this naturalistic novel contemplates the corrosive effects of money-getting and -losing, starting with the city's economic boom and bust of 1886–1887. Moving on to New York, it shows subtle class and regional markers through detailed social interactions. It ends in Wyoming, where a copper mine is being set up by Daniel Devin, a creative businessman much like Neith's father. Again we have a heroine, Anna Quartermain, who is less than perfect even while technically completely within society's rules. A gifted near-professional

singer, she is a bit heartless and self-absorbed; as dedicated to her passion, singing, as her husband is to the art of business. Her husband dies of pneumonia (or a broken heart?) when his business venture starts to unravel. Perhaps unusual for the times is Neith's empathetic portrayal of Jewish characters as outsiders with special insight into a society. An anonymous reviewer of this book compared it "with the work of Mrs. [Edith] Wharton and Mrs. Mary E. Wilkins Freeman ... and with that of the late Frank Norris" (Scrapbook 1903-1906). "California Naturalism" is probably the best genre category for this novel.

Neith's next novel, *The Eternal Spring* (1906), uses the Florentine villa of the art historians Bernard and Mary Berenson as backdrop for a psychological study of mental illness. Forecasting F. Scott Fitzgerald's *Tender Is the Night,* it depicts a young woman haunted by a family prediction of instability. Its male protagonist, Barry Carleton, resembles Bentley: an exhausted Chicago newspaperman able to live in Florence through recent canny stock investments. He returns to the villa of Elizabeth Craven, an American and recently the widow of a famous art connoisseur (based on B.B.), to ask her to marry him. Soon, however, he is attracted to Elizabeth's guest, Clara Langham. The character Clara is based on the life of the world beauty Gladys Deacon, who resided in Italy occasionally, "chaperoned" by her mother, who had been disgraced by her husband's murder of her lover. Mama seeks a good marriage for her daughter, a talented pianist who is subject to fits of nerves. Carleton becomes intrigued by the family dishonor, feeling there is a connection to Clara's illness. A newspaperman, he investigates the murder and the mental condition (by letter from the United States) and determines to intervene in the situation. He informs Clara of her mother's perfidy, also confronting Mama. Truth resolves all, and Clara and Barry decide to live in the United States after their wedding. The real Gladys Deacon, however, submitted to Mama's wishes and married the Duke of Marlborough. Perhaps what makes the novel unusual is its depiction of a male's feelings of falling in love.

Neith's next novel, *The Bond* (1908), appeared while she and Hutch were deep in negotiation about their relationship. It reflects an earlier phase of their struggles with varietism, a subset of anarchism that promulgated multiple sexual partners as a way to avoid considering one's partner as "property." As Neith's biographer, the present writer reads this book as a deeply coded account of a major crisis in their famous, forty-five-year-long marriage. On the surface a questioning of the double standard of sexual behavior between men and women, the novel actually is a subtle discussion of some contradictions within New Womanhood as well as varietism. By tackling the hot potato of sex and questioning traditional monogamy, *The Bond* provides a window on the radicalisms alive in Greenwich Village in the early part of the twentieth century. The book portrays persons struggling to redefine the relationships between men and women—especially the role of sex in the early era of Freud—and the role of personal autonomy in the era of feminism. It also introduces a thread that runs through much of her literature: alcoholism. In this novel, as in others, a male character who is sympathetic to the female protagonist (sometimes in love with her) is portrayed as a chronic inebriate—without judgment. That person sometimes functions as an interlocutor, saying out loud what others cannot. In short, accurate human communication is impossible; therefore "real" honesty between men and women is unfeasible.

Teresa, a sculptor, resists her growing emotional and financial dependence on her husband, Basil, a painter. Imperfect communication between the major protagonists leads the wife to suspect the husband of sexual activity that may or may not have occurred, and he refuses to share that information (although they have an agreement to share all). When Teresa has a flirtation in revenge, Basil becomes jealous and demands information, assuming consummation of the affair because her ostensible lover signs a letter with his first name. Teresa tells all (while Basil does not), in order to save the marriage. This rather depressing saga of female acquiescence ends the book, but not before Teresa tells Basil:

"We're good friends, anyway. I think we always shall be, and like each other best of all. It doesn't matter if we amuse ourselves a little by the way. There—that's the point of view I'm striving to reach."

"You are? Well, I thought you'd *always* had that point of view."

"In a purely abstract way, but I want to *feel* it—I want to put it into practice. I hate mere theories."

(The Bond, p. 163)

What Ellen Kay Trimberger calls the couple's "sexualized warfare"—mixture of aggression and passion—is displayed in a scene when Teresa and Basil have been arguing:

> He [Basil] made an effort to hold his position. "You won't do a thing I ask you to! You won't even stop reading, though you're spoiling your eyes.... You don't care anything about me, that's the real truth! If you did, you—"
>
> She [Teresa] drew his head down and kissed him.
>
> "Idiot!" she murmured.
>
> His arms went round her, caught her up, held her close.
>
> "How I love you!" he said angrily.

(p. 85)

Ross Wetzsteon called this novel "pedestrian" for its excessive discussion of theories, although a "genuine attempt to explore a modern marriage, to establish a balance of power between men and women, to find some psychic equilibrium between love and work, domesticity and creativity, intimacy and autonomy, submission and independence"(p. 186). None of the novel's reviewers noticed that it questioned the double standard of sexual behavior, preferring instead to mock and misunderstand her project.

Neith's last published novel, *Proud Lady* (1923), is laid in what seems to be her mother's hometown of Sycamore, Illinois, just after the Civil War and parallels her parents' dilemma even while giving its male protagonist—a Civil War survivor—what we now might term post-traumatic stress disorder. Its rather stiff-necked heroine (perhaps modeled on her grandmother, Martha Lowell Smith) realizes—only after her husband's premature death—that (1) she should not have married him, but (2) having done so, she should have set him free to maintain his second family with a lower-class lover. In this novel, Neith explores the destructive self-righteousness of the "good" woman, even while sympathizing with the woman's high-minded quest for Truth. Neith also nonjudgmentally portrays a pattern of males with multiple wives.

PLAYS

By helping to found the Provincetown Players on Cape Cod, Neith was part of the revolution in staging, dialogue, and theme that the "little theater" movement brought to American and international theater. Robert Károly Sarlós has stated that accounts of the origin of this seminal group, "even by participants, are contradictory" (p. 9). Theater would be the medium in which Neith perhaps achieved her greatest innovation and artistic impact. During the first two official years of this group, it performed three works written by Neith and another cowritten with Hutchins. She wrote, acted in, and directed its first play, *Constancy,* in the couple's Provincetown cottage in the summer of 1915, with its "set" designed by Robert Edmond Jones. This satire on the relationship of John Reed and Mabel Dodge, one of Neith's best friends, has, like many of her short stories and novels, a distinct feminism that is often overlooked. It doesn't have a "resolution," but one admires the lead character's force of will in sending a philanderer away. Called a "curtain-raiser" by Arthur and Barbara Gelb, this play was repeated in the summer of 1916 in Provincetown, when Eugene O'Neill joined the group (p. 495).

That 1916 summer also saw production of Neith's *Winter's Night,* now considered a classic one-act play of naturalism. Its biblically named three characters (Sarah, Rachel, and Jacob) inhabit a Midwestern winter scene similar to Glaspell's later *Trifles*—a farm household on the day of the funeral of Daniel Wescott, husband to Rachel. Jacob, Daniel's bachelor brother, tells

Rachel that he never married and stayed on the farm because of his love for her. Appalled, she rejects his offer of marriage, articulating her long-held dream of moving to the city to work as a seamstress with colorful fabrics that symbolize life. A neighbor, Sarah (played by Mary Heaton Vorse), interrupts this debate as she arrives to spend the night with the newly widowed Rachel. Jacob leaves the house with a loaded gun to kill a fox that has been harrying the chicken coop. A shot is heard, followed by Sarah's scream offstage: suicide. Sarlós and other scholars have noted the intertextuality of this work with that of O'Neill. Both playwrights often feature a love triangle: two persons in love with a third. O'Neill's first full-length play, *Beyond the Horizon* (1918), echoes her *Winter's Night* dynamic, with an older brother giving up a beloved to a younger brother. Neith's *The Two Sons* is another one-act with a love triangle—this time of siblings Karl and Paul quarreling over a mother's love. Arnold Goldman has noted that Karl's drunken confession of fraternal love and jealousy is "remarkably similar" to Jamie Tyrone's analogous admission in O'Neill's much later *Long Day's Journey into Night.*

Most studied, however, is Neith's *Enemies,* which she cowrote and performed with Hutchins—she as She and he as He. This play has been interpreted as depicting the couple's fraught relationship. He decries She's "spiritual infidelity" by having a nonsexual relationship with another man, while his own relationships with other women are mere "physical intimacies." The play ends with their armed truce—a standard denouement in a number of Neith's artistic efforts.

These three plays (*Enemies, Winter's Night,* and *The Two Sons*) for the Provincetown Players went into print as well as production at the Playwrights Theater on 139 Macdougal Street in New York's Greenwich Village for the 1916–1917 season. In addition, Neith's papers in the Hapgood Family Papers at Yale contain working versions of some twenty others. During the 1930s, after Hapgood had lost much of his inheritance in the Crash, Neith worked hard on commercially viable plays, entering them in contests and seeking production. None except a local history pageant in New Hampshire was staged, but a 1938 radio play, *Hurricane*—justifying armed resistance to fascism—may have been aired. This play denotes her intellectual movement away from pacifism.

Anarchism was important in the Players' nonhierarchical approach, along with their belief that theater should be a unifying cultural force. Neith served on the group's early "revision" committee, which was soon ignored as the theater became more commercial. Like many of the women involved with the group, she moved on to other venues (or was forced out?). A whiff of her anarchism survives in the last major play she crafted, *The Sea Lady.* At the end of this comedic critique of the British class system, the mermaid and male protagonist swim off together, each wearing a Phrygian cap, the symbol of liberty.

NONFICTION

Neith's *Harry: A Portrait* (1923) sets out every mother's dream, to see a child achieve love and fulfilling work; it also catalogs every mother's worst nightmare: loss of her child. This memoir recounts the year October 1917 to October 1918 as a time "clear and perfect in every detail." Nonetheless, this book has a deliberately dream-like quality, with no names—certainly not last names—of people or even that of this small Vermont town whose life so enchants Neith while she lives apart from Hapgood. She falls in love with the farm, its picket fence, the village of a thousand, and the contented family life it all affords. She writes:

> This place was the only real community I had ever lived in; it actually came nearer to a certain social ideal—I might call it the anarchistic ideal, or the old American ideal—than any other I had known. Equality prevailed (of a sort)—and fraternity too, with human limitations—and perhaps liberty, as much as can be expected.
>
> (*Harry,* p. 57)

Obscuring her estrangement from Hapgood at this time, she chronicles a year of seeing her firstborn son achieve maturity, find a lover (her best friend, a nearby matron), and achieve his

career dream as a "rider" or cowboy. It negotiates the tricky terrain of mother-son love and is quietly and determinedly antiwar.

It also opens new ground in what is now called creative nonfiction. The novelist Abraham Cahan, a former colleague on the New York *Commercial Advertiser,* wrote Neith after seeing the book in manuscript: "The story is so full of color, so subtle, so truly charming. A true tale like this is more valuable to literature than carloads of the best-paid fiction." The novelist Robert Herrick (1868–1938), with whom Neith had argued about the war, wrote the book's publisher in 1921: "I have long been of the opinion that the novel, in its conventionalized form, is likely to become merged into imaginative biography and autobiography and Mrs. Hapgood's picture of Harry carries out this theory.... I like this much the best of all Mrs. Hapgood's writing." In his autobiography, Hutch later opined: "The purest literature is seldom recognized as literature at all.... Neith's book, which she wrote about Boyce, *Harry,* was so much beyond literature as most people understood the word, that few could understand its relationship. It was not so much about her son as about the son of all womankind" (*A Victorian in the Modern World,* p. 441).

In her own autobiography, which was crafted in 1939–1940 but printed only in 2003, Neith is similarly obscure, even while achieving some universality. As stated earlier, she reveals no details of her parents' initial relationship. (Nor were these details ever revealed to her own children.) Written in the third person, with Neith calling herself "Iras," the autobiography is the saga of an American family's struggles with life on its way to solid middle-class respectability. Neith's pseudonym for her family name is "Carolan," probably borrowed from that of the anarchist Terry Carlin (1854–1934), whom she met in Chicago and knew well. This document confirms one early belief of its heroine, Iras:

> There was one bond she felt, though—that of the family. That was something different from individual relationships. You didn't choose the family, it happened, and it was more than the sum of its parts. It didn't matter whether you liked or disliked individual members of it; in trouble the family would rally round.
>
> (*Modern World,* p. 171)

Neith's final thoughts on marriage and family, as well as anarchism, appear in her last published work (1951). This privately published documentary history—a collection of family letters and public documents, with commentary—finds a consistent thread in American history from colonial times through the cultural revolution of the early twentieth century. The story is removed from the petty personal feelings of humans, who are portrayed as characters in a war game or drama seen from a theater box. It argues for yeomanry—small communities of freeholders—as the basis of democracy, in keeping with individualist anarchism. It also shows Neith's continued allegiance to that interlocking nexus of ideas of personal freedom that included holding private property.

Titled *The Story of an American Family: Letters of the Hapgood Family, 1648–1917,* the work occupied Neith for the last ten years of her life. As she wrote:

> The family is the first social unit; and represents, at least in humanities and perhaps through the animal and insect kingdoms, the first feeling of solidarity between individuals. It might be called indeed the first socialism, if the wider instinct for solidarity prove to be of sufficient vitality, so that the family solidarity may no longer be so important a factor; but that is certainly a long way off.
>
> (Version A 1)

Innovative but flawed in presentation, the manuscript was misunderstood by all publishers who looked at it. But it demonstrates the continued creativity and experimentation with form of this modernist writer until the very end of her life.

CONCLUSION

This founding member of the Provincetown Players lived and worked into the mid-twentieth century, largely as an innovator without honor. She had an uncanny instinct for the new—whether in literary style, ways and places to live, or self-presentation—and attempted to apply new

theories to her life and literature. Her short stories portray a new psychological reality for women in the twentieth century. Her plays are part of the new voice and staging of what would become American theater. Her novels discuss the power structure of emotional relationships. Her final work of history forecast what we now call social and cultural history. Neith Boyce was an important member of the large group of people whose ideas and literary techniques are now branded as modernism. At very least, her career is worthy of examination as a window into this larger movement. At most, her literature achieves greatness as we empathize with her characters pondering ethical aspects of their personal relationships. Some things never change.

Selected Bibliography

WORKS OF NEITH BOYCE

FICTION, NONFICTION, AND POETRY

Songs. Boston: Arena, 1892.

The Forerunner. New York: Fox, Duffield, 1903. (Also available through Kessinger Publishing Legacy Reprints.)

The Folly of Others. New York: Fox, Duffield, 1904.

The Eternal Spring. New York: Fox, Duffield, 1906.

The Bond. New York: Fox, Duffield, 1908. (Also available through Kessinger Publishing Legacy Reprints.)

Harry: A Portrait. New York: Thomas Seltzer, 1923.

Proud Lady. New York: Thomas Seltzer, 1923.

The Story of an American Family: Letters and Commentary on the Hapgood Family, 1648–1917. Chicopee, Mass.: Brown-Murphy, 1951.

The Town in the Forest: Life Story of Richmond, New Hampshire. Edited by Beatrix Hapgood Faust. Richmond: Richmond, New Hampshire Archives, 1992.

The Modern World of Neith Boyce: Autobiography and Diaries. Edited by Carol DeBoer-Langworthy. Albuquerque: University of New Mexico Press, 2003.

PLAYS

"Constancy." In *1915, The Cultural Moment: The New Politics, the New Woman, the New Psychology, the New Art, & the New Theatre in America.* Edited by Adele Heller and Lois Rudnick. New Brunswick, N.J.: Rutgers University Press, 1991. Pp. 274–280.

"Winter's Night." In *Fifty More Contemporary One-Act Plays.* Edited by Frank Shay. New York: D. Appleton, 1928. Pp. 39–46. Also in *A Century of Plays by American Women.* Edited by Rachel France. New York: Richard Rosen Press, 1979. Pp. 79–85. Most authoritatively in *Women Writers of the Provincetown Players: A Collection of Short Works.* Edited by Judith E. Barlow. Albany: State University of New York Press, 2009. Pp. 33–46.

"Enemies." (With Hutchins Hapgood.) In *The Provincetown Plays.* Edited by George Cram Cook and Frank Shay. Cincinnati: Stewart Kidd, 1921. Pp. 117–136. Also in *Intimate Warriors: Portraits of a Modern Marriage, 1899–1944. Selected Works by Neith Boyce and Hutchins Hapgood.* Edited by Ellen Kay Trimberger. New York: Feminist Press, 1991. Pp. 186–195.

"The Two Sons." In *The Provincetown Plays.* Third series. Edited by Frank Shay. New York: Frank Shay, 1916. Pp. 147–169. (Also available through Kessinger Publishing Legacy Reprints.)

SHORT STORIES AND LITERARY JOURNALISM

"In a Garden." In *Stories from the Chap-Book.* Chicago: Herbert S. Stone, 1896. Pp. 29–43.

"The Bachelor Girl," nine "papers" in *Vogue,* May 5, 1898–November 3, 1898.

"The Sands of the Green River." In *New Stories from the Chap-Book.* Chicago: Herbert S. Stone, 1898. Pp. 3–18. (Also available through Kessinger Publishing Legacy Reprints.)

"A Provident Woman." *Lippincott's Magazine* 73: 259–317 (March 1904).

"My Dear Niece." *Good Housekeeping* 53: 33–41 (July 1911).

"The Undertow." *Lippincott's Monthly Magazine* 560: 129–176 (August 1914).

CRITICAL AND BIOGRAPHICAL STUDIES

Barlow, Judith E., ed. *Women Writers of the Provincetown Players: A Collection of Short Works.* Albany: State University of New York Press, 2009.

Black, Cheryl. *The Women of Provincetown, 1915–1922.* Tuscaloosa: University of Alabama Press, 2002.

DeBoer-Langworthy, Carol. "Not a Bourgeois Project: Neith Boyce's *The Story of an American Family.*" In *Resources for American Literary Study* 32. New York: AMS Press, 2009. Pp. 49–83.

Fishbein, Leslie. *Rebels in Bohemia: The Radicals of The Masses, 1911–1917.* Chapel Hill: University of North Carolina Press, 1982.

Glaspell, Susan. *The Road to the Temple: A Biography of George Cram Cook.* Edited and introduced by Linda Ben-Zvi. Jefferson, N.C.: McFarland, 2005.

Goldman, Arnold. "The Culture of the Provincetown Players." *Journal of American Studies* 12, no. 3: 291–310 (December 1978).

Heller, Adele, and Lois Rudnick, eds. *1915, The Cultural Moment: The New Politics, the New Woman, the New Psychology, the New Art, & the New Theatre in America.* New Brunswick, N.J.: Rutgers University Press, 1991.

Kennedy, Jeffery. "The Artistic Legacy of the Provincetown Playhouse, 1918–1922." Ph.D. dissertation, New York University, 2007. Ann Arbor: UMI, 2007.

Kenton, Edna. *The Provincetown Players and the Playwrights' Theatre, 1915–1922.* Edited by Travis Bogard and Jackson R. Bryer. Jefferson, N.C.: McFarland, 2004.

Murphy, Brenda. *The Provincetown Players and the Culture of Modernity.* Cambridge, U.K., and New York: Cambridge University Press, 2005.

Sarlós, Robert Károly. *Jig Cook and the Provincetown Players: Theatre in Ferment.* Amherst: University of Massachusetts Press, 1982.

Sochen, June. *The New Woman: Feminism in Greenwich Village, 1910–1920.* New York: Quadrangle, 1972.

———. *Movers and Shakers: American Women Thinkers and Activists, 1900–1970.* New York: Quadrangle, 1973.

Stansell, Christine. *American Moderns: Bohemian New York and the Creation of a New Century.* New York: Henry Holt, 2000.

Tancheva, Kornelia. "'I Do Not Participate in Liberations': Female Dramatic and Theatrical Modernism in the 1910s and 1930s." In *Unmanning Modernism: Gendered Re-Readings.* Edited by Elizabeth Jane Harrison and Shirley Peterson. Knoxville: University of Tennessee Press, 1997. Pp. 153–167.

Trimberger, Ellen Kay, ed. *Intimate Warriors: Portraits of a Modern Marriage, 1899–1944. Selected Works by Neith Boyce and Hutchins Hapgood.* New York: Feminist Press, 1991.

Wetzsteon, Ross. *Republic of Dreams: Greenwich Village, The American Bohemia, 1910–1960.* New York: Simon & Schuster, 2002.

BOOKS BY HUTCHINS HAPGOOD

The Spirit of the Ghetto: Studies of the Jewish Quarter of New York. New York: Funk & Wagnalls, 1902. Reprint, edited by Moses Rischin, Cambridge, Mass: Belknap Press, 1967. Rev. ed. with an introduction by Irving Howe, New York: Schocken Books, 1976.

The Story of a Lover. New York: Boni & Liveright, 1919. (Also available through Kessinger Publishing Legacy Reprints.)

A Victorian in the Modern World. New York: Harcourt, Brace, 1939. Reprint, edited by Robert Allen Skotheim, Seattle: University of Washington Press, Americana Library Edition, 1972.

PAPERS

Arthur F. Bentley Mss and Bentley Mss II. Lilly Library. Indiana University, Bloomington, Ind.

Eugene O'Neill / Louis Sheaffer Collection. Charles E. Shain Library. Connecticut College, New London, Conn.

Hannah Whitall Smith Mss. Lilly Library. Indiana University, Bloomington, Ind.

Hapgood Family Papers. Yale Collection of American Literature. Beinecke Rare Book and Manuscript Library, New Haven, Conn.

Mabel Dodge Luhan Papers. Yale Collection of American Literature. Beinecke Rare Book and Manuscript Library, New Haven, Conn.

Miriam Hapgood DeWitt Papers. Yale Collection of American Literature. Beinecke Rare Book and Manuscript Library, New Haven, Conn.

LETTERS AND OTHER WORKS CITED

Berenson, Mary, to Hannah Whitall Smith, March 9, 1907. Hannah Whitall Smith Mss., Lilly Library. Indiana University, Bloomington, Ind.

Boyce, Neith, to Lincoln Steffens, January 8 [1920?]. Hapgood Family Papers. Yale Collection of American Literature. Beinecke Rare Book and Manuscript Library, New Haven, Conn.

Cahan, Abraham, to Neith Boyce, May 26, 1921. Hapgood Family Papers. Yale Collection of American Literature. Beinecke Rare Book and Manuscript Library, New Haven, Conn.

Gelb, Arthur and Barbara Gelb, *O'Neill: Life with Monte Cristo.* New York: Applause, 2002

Hapgood, Charles H., II, interviewed by Lou Sheaffer, circa late 1968/1969. Transcript. Sheaffer-O'Neill Collection. Connecticut College, New London, Conn.

Hapgood, Hutchins, to Lydia Seaver (Wilson) Hapgood, November 1898. Hapgood Family Papers. Yale Collection of American Literature. Beinecke Rare Book and Manuscript Library, New Haven, Conn.

Herrick, Robert, to Thomas Seltzer, [December?] 12, 1921. Hapgood Family Papers. Yale Collection of American Literature. Beinecke Rare Book and Manuscript Library, New Haven, Conn.

"Scrapbook 1903-06." in Miriam Hapgood DeWitt Papers, Hapgood Family Papers. Yale Collection of American Literature. Beinecke Rare Book and Manuscript Library, New Haven, Conn.

Version A1 of "The Story of an American Family." Hapgood Family Papers. Yale Collection of American Literature. Beinecke Rare Book and Manuscript Library, New Haven, Conn.

WILLIAM BRONK

(1918—1999)

Guy Rotella

WILLIAM BRONK WAS intensely committed to a poetry of ideas, yet he sometimes contradicted this notion in his work. Bronk was equally committed to poetry as a way of life, a nearly religious vocation, yet in a letter to the poet Samuel French Morse he uttered heresy, saying "poetry is what we don't read" (quoted in Rotella, p. 15). From these and other oddly matched and competing commitments, creeds, and countercreeds, Bronk concocted a distinctive life and a distinguished body of work. He did so whether he considered the conflicting strains in his thinking and feeling as contradictions or as paradoxes, and whether he experienced them as foreseeable or shocking, and whether he reacted to them with humor or alarm, resignation, resolve, or despair.

Bronk's great subject—he returned to it with an apt and admirably disciplined persistence that can sometimes seem relentless, even obsessive—is humanity's fundamental but fundamentally hopeless desire to discover or create a meaningful version of the world that is fully commensurate with the world as it actually is. Bronk's most characteristic poems put that desire in motion and then bear witness to its failure, so that recognitions, demonstrations, and assertions of a radical misfit between what we say about reality and reality itself regularly center (and decenter) Bronk's work. The few poems that do not address the matter outright address it indirectly. They are offshoots, not alternatives, and Bronk's verses of every kind—poems on music, sculpture, and archaeology, painstakingly precise descriptions of natural scenes and seasons, explorations of cultural relativism with a distinctly postmodern and postcolonial feel, and emotionally intense or deliberately arid considerations of love, the nature of the self, the limitations of language, and the questionable virtue or value of any and all human aspiration, activity, and achievement (especially when set against less "humanist," more macro-, micro- or otherwise cosmic scales)—all of these turn on observations of the unbridgeable gulf between what we claim to know about the world and our profound ignorance of it.

Bronk is a great poet of negation. Again and again in his work, the human drive to meaning encounters evidence that there is no meaning. For Bronk, no matter what pattern of significance people describe, ascribe, or create in response to their need for order, that pattern is never *the* world but only *a* world, imprecise, incomplete, and wrong, whether it's expressed in Mayan calendars, Bible stories, Einstein's physics, prosodic conventions, or any of the other varied and varying mythological, religious, philosophical, political, artistic, or scientific systems of "truth" that individuals or cultures produce and rely on in any time or place. This radically relativistic, antifoundational sense that we cannot have what we most naturally need and want is Bronk's foundational certainty, his absolute. He was sure that the human desire for order and truth is essential, but he was just as sure that every version of reality created to satisfy that desire is inessential and ultimately unsatisfying, a failed equivalent to reality, an illusion, delusion, or lie.

Bronk was confident (however inexact that faithful word might seem here) that the gap between the always only virtual worlds we construe and construct and the real or actual world has never been and never can be closed. Meanwhile, if a sometimes solipsist Bronk sometimes wondered whether the real exists at all, he was wholly sure that in any case we cannot know it. Assertions of radical ignorance are a Bronk signature, as are refusals, rejections, and

denials of past and present (even future) cultural assumptions and consolations. At the same time, however, Bronk's faithfulness to his own experience included fidelity to the depth and intensity of his own needs for certainty, order, truth, and enduring love. This helped him sometimes to sympathize with the consolations other people find and accept, even though he could not find or accept them himself. It also encouraged him to think (rather mystically, for so committed a skeptic) that our inability to know the real is the one sure sign that the real exists, and to think as well that the selfishness alienating people from one another (whether as an outcome of biology or psychology or of competing cultural dispensations within or across locations in time and place) guarantees our common humanity. It's as though the sum of negations is sometimes affirmation, as some mathematics have it, as if, in Bronk, reverence and heresy combined, and Plato, the transcendentalists, and certain saints were crossed with Nietzsche, as if desire's inevitable failures clinch and confirm desire as fact, however counterfactual desire's realizations. Meanwhile, even such constricted affirmations in Bronk's work are harshly beset and vanishingly narrow. His ultimate vision is nearest Samuel Beckett's: the conviction, in the theater critic John Lahr's fine formulation, that the only meaning humans have is the compulsion to relate our lack of meaning.

Bronk compulsively relates it. His bleak persistence is a paradoxical, almost religious tribute to the intense human need somehow to know, understand, and assent, a need that no evidence, experience, or belief can fulfill but that no defeat can entirely quench. Bronk rarely departs from this thematic focus; therefore, his work involves considerable repetition, redundancy even. At the same time, however, Bronk finds remarkably many ways in which to approach his central theme. As a result, he provides considerable variety of circumstance, tone, and treatment (for example, and again like Beckett, his responses to barren circumstance can be comic as well as despairing, wistful or tender as well as acerbic). Sameness and variety mark Bronk's use of form as well. If in his late poems Bronk sometimes works with what Edward Foster

has neatly termed the ruins of poetic form, most of his poems are written in flexible but conventional five-stress, more or less iambic lines arranged in traditional-looking stanzas. And yet the poems' commitment to treating philosophical abstraction in a colloquial language of plainspoken accuracy, their often brilliant handling of caesuras and enjambment, and their remarkable variety of discursive and other situations lends their formal similarity considerable texture and range. By the way, Bronk's poetry is almost always unrhymed, perhaps in order to challenge and subvert his roughly regular metrics by stressing the dissonance rather than consonance between human forms and the world they seek to shape or contain—the world that, in Bronk's view, they always falsify in the process. (One further point on Bronk's forms: in the 1970s and very early 1980s, he worked with arbitrary restrictions on length, publishing volumes composed entirely of fourteen-, eight-, four-, three-, and then twenty-line poems, respectively.)

As for Bronk's proclivity for abstraction, while he always wrote poetry with an unusually high proportion of ideational statements, tension between and among those statements (Bronk multiplies and combines them in ways that urge balance and also upend it) creates concrete and emotional as well as more abstruse intellectual dramas. Meanwhile, Bronk's late poems try to make poetry while discarding imagery and figurative language almost completely, as if to deny the very substance of poetry itself. On the other hand, an emphasis on ideas apart from their embodiments is well within poetry's traditional circuit, and the late poems' intensified turn toward epigram, apothegm, or pensée may be seen not so much to oppose poetry as to oppose poetry's more familiar emphases on figuration and ornament. In any case, for all their intellectual abstraction, Bronk's poems, early and late, nearly always imbue ideas with feeling. Bronk came of age as a poet during the revival of interest in metaphysical poetry and its tense mergers of intellection and emotion; "It is to feel," he said in a poem, defining something fundamental; and in his best work ideas and emotions are aspects of one another, in keeping with E. L.

Doctorow's principle that good writing evokes sensation in the reader: not the fact that it is raining but the feeling of being rained on. For all his emphasis on ideas or abstraction, then, Bronk is also a powerful poet of emotions. Within his range, he got himself pretty fully expressed or stated, as Virginia Woolf said a writer ought to do.

Bronk's insistence that ideologies, knowledge systems, worldviews, and faiths of every kind are fraudulent constructions created in response to human need and imposed upon reality rather than discovered in it, along with his cultural relativism, commitment to indeterminacy, distrust of language, and sense of the self as multiple and fluid rather than stable and consistent, all connect his work to poststructuralist and postmodernist thought as well as to such developments in science as quantum mechanics, the uncertainty principle, and Kurt Gödel's incompleteness theorem, with their disruptions of common sense, conventional logic, and objectivity and certitude. But Bronk is less concerned with analyzing the relation of, say, knowledge systems to hegemonic power than many postmodernists are, and he is less concerned with salvaging partial objectivity and probable truth than are many scientists and mathematicians confronting indeterminacy and other obstacles to wholly certain knowledge. Where most scientists, theorists, or poets seek and find more accurate (or more just) systems to replace the ones they reject (developing ways to make advances or to make do), for Bronk, replacement systems do not so much correct or reduce prior errors as replicate in new or different terms the error inherent in every system.

Bronk's worldview is absolutely relative, then, a form of radical idealism in its complete refusal to compromise. It precludes progress, and whatever his relations to postmodern theory and self-critical science, his literary influences extend to the Bible, Shakespeare, such premodern writers as Emily Dickinson, Herman Melville, and Henry David Thoreau, and the modernist poets Robert Frost and Wallace Stevens, as well as to Marcel Proust, so that he can be unusually tricky to "place." For instance, his much-discussed connections with early postmodern poets like Charles Olson and George Oppen, while important, are less definitive than they are sometimes made to seem, largely because Olson's and Oppen's ideological faiths in amelioration or transformation were wholly alien to Bronk.

Meanwhile, for the career of a significant poet, Bronk's had a somewhat irregular shape. He began with a work of imaginative and contrarian literary history, and neither it nor his first book of poems was published until many years after it was written. A fine early poem was published in the *New Yorker,* but he could never place another there, and most of Bronk's books were brought out by small, barely visible, even obscure presses (although sometimes in beautifully designed and printed editions). Even after the breakthrough publication in 1981 of *Life Supports: New and Collected Poems* (which was put out by the highly regarded North Point Press, received the 1982 American Book Award for Poetry, and was widely reviewed and admired), Bronk's public profile, his "reputation," did not change much. He could still encounter publishing difficulties: North Point rejected one later book (although it published four additional collections, one of prose), and after North Point ceased operations Bronk was again dependent on small publishers with limited distribution. A decade after his death, a long-promised volume collecting his later poems had yet to appear. Similarly, for reasons of temperament, and because he spent most of his life in relatively out-of-the-way Hudson Falls, New York, Bronk was never fully part of any of the mainstream or avant-garde literary movements or schools of his day. Through his Dartmouth College teacher, mentor, and friend Sidney Cox, he met Frost and was strongly influenced by him, as he was by Stevens' poetry of ideas (if not by his essential gaudiness), but those poets were of another generation. Slightly older Dartmouth classmates, Reuel Denney and Samuel French Morse, may have been more important to him at least he said they were; they are seen now as minor poets. On the other hand, Bronk's relationships with then marginal, eventually famous little magazines, especially *Origin* and *Black Mountain Review*, were real; he sometimes read his work in important venues

(crustily rejecting other chances to do so); and in his own way he became the host of a rusticated or homespun intellectual and artistic salon and an influence on writers as diverse as Paul Auster and Kay Ryan. Working at and from the margins, with occasional forays to the center, Bronk was an American original. The thematic core of his poems is as bleakly grave and compellingly attractive as a black hole in space; the dark integrity and intensity of its poetic telling are bracing if never consoling; his best poems produce scouring clarifications and refreshments.

BIOGRAPHY

A descendent of Jonas Bronck, for whom the Bronx was named, William Bronk was born on February 17, 1918, in Fort Edward, New York (his parents were away from the family home in Hudson Falls while his father supervised a construction job at the time of his birth). When Bronk was a baby, the family returned to Hudson Falls, and aside from college, a stint in the army, and vacation travel, Bronk spent most of his life in the village, where he lived in the large Victorian family home at 57 Pearl Street. As the term "village" fails to convey, Hudson Falls (named for the cascade where the Hudson River turns south after flowing eastward from the Adirondacks) had experienced a period of importance as a center of pulp and lumber mills. But that era was receding into the past during Bronk's lifetime, when Hudson Falls grew quieter and more peripheral. Bronk's father, William M. Bronk, Sr., had participated in the village's prosperity as a banker (although the bank failed during the Great Depression) and as proprietor of the Bronk Coal (later, Fuel) & Lumber Company. A community leader and a businessman through and through, aloof, laconic, and stern in the parental style of his era, Bronk's father was confounded by his son's artistic leanings, treating them with incomprehension, impatience, or indifference rather than encouragement. Bronk's strong-willed mother, Ethel, saw herself as something of a "grand dame." Much aware of her social position and importance and widely involved in women's volunteer community

groups, she had some reputation as a gossip; her son inherited her imperiousness as well as her intense interest in neighborhood dramas and scandals. By Bronk's own report, his childhood household, shared with his two older sisters, felt oppressively lonely and silent. His parents seemed to him angry with and estranged from one another rather than affectionate or loving: perhaps their belonging to different churches was an outward sign that the two were ill-matched.

According to his biographer, Lyman Gilmore, Bronk experienced alienation and a lack of empathy as a child, and a dour, sometimes depressed diffidence toward life's ordinary as well as loftier social, religious, or philosophical consolations stayed with him all his days. But that distrust was equally an honest report of his own emotional and intellectual experiences, of his lifelong, always frustrated search for meaning in the world itself and in the supposedly containing or consoling versions of reality offered by other people and by his own and other cultures. Still, for all of that, Bronk's adolescence seems typical enough. He played fife in the high school band, was a leading member of a literary-minded clique, and became the protégé of an enthusiastic young English teacher, Elizabeth Clark, who introduced him to modern poets and to the possibility of art as a valid and valuable way of life. Expectant searches for mentors and for membership in elite artistic communities would become a pattern in Bronk's college years and after. When met, his expectations produced occasional elation; when, as far more often, his expectations were disappointed, he felt resentment, depression, and despair. At the same time, Bronk could face either outcome with wry, sometimes self-deprecating wit, a quality that, with his appreciation of nature and of music, his talents for intimate friendship and witty conversation, and his taste for good food and drink, softened his accurate, if also arrogant sense of himself as exceptional, his characteristic bluntness, and his temperamental and conceptual attractions to life's grimmer facts.

Bronk entered Dartmouth College at the age of sixteen in 1934. His father had doubts about

his choice: he thought the liberal arts curriculum there unlikely to prepare his son for the practical life of commercial success he envisioned for him. Nonetheless, he permitted the boy to enroll. Meanwhile, Bronk had his own ideas. When he visited the school before attending, he wrote to friends about the José Clemente Orozco murals and the atmosphere of intellectual openness and artistic experiment on campus—implying a clear, attractive alternative to the conservative stodginess of the family home, hometown, and business. Bronk was happy at Dartmouth. Early on he met the charismatic English teacher Sidney Cox and, repeating his high school experience with Elizabeth Clark, became a leading member of Cox's coterie of favored students. Cox closely guided Bronk's formal and informal studies and became a vital mentor. During part of his undergraduate career, Bronk boarded with Cox and his wife, and he continued to visit them after he graduated. Cox encouraged Bronk's writing, praising it to others. He instilled confidence in his student and helped inculcate in him lifelong commitments to the clear, colloquial, and forthright expression of his own ideas and feelings, without concern for their fit or misfit to the assumptions, beliefs, or expectations of others. Cox later set down those values in *Indirections* (1947), a book on writing he implicitly addressed to Bronk, and the two remained intimate friends, exchanging poems, ideas, and gossip, until Cox's death in 1952. They did so despite their disagreements about World War II (Bronk was isolationist; Cox favored American intervention) and despite the clash between Cox's sunny sincerity and Bronk's bleaker outlook. Bronk's success at Dartmouth was capped by his winning the Grimes and Perkins prizes in his senior year and being chosen to deliver the college's commencement address. He and Cox were sure of its brilliance and certain that audience members mystified by its remarks on poetry and life were philistines.

Dartmouth nurtured and confirmed Bronk's talent and sense of vocation; Harvard, where he went on to graduate school in the fall of 1939, undid them, or threatened to. The congenially personal and subjective approach to literature he had enjoyed in Hanover, New Hampshire, was supplanted in Cambridge, Massachusetts, by historicist and New Critical approaches in which objective analysis rebuked, even derided, impressionistic appreciation. Bronk disliked the difference intensely. At Harvard, he found no approving mentor. He felt the university was cold, impersonal, and rude. He seemed overawed by its institutional size and complexity, and he was wholly out of sympathy with the "scientific" approach to literary study he encountered there. After one semester, he withdrew, declared his independence, and retreated to Norwich, Vermont, near enough to his alma mater for comfort but not so near as to court embarrassment at having dropped out of Harvard. There, Bronk began the book on Thoreau, Walt Whitman, and Melville he eventually called *The Brother in Elysium: Ideas of Friendship and Society in the United States* (1980). This volume was both a reflection of and a riposte to doings in Cambridge. It mirrored the reassessment of the American literary tradition then being brilliantly performed by Harvard's F. O. Matthiessen, for instance, but rejected its method: where Matthiessen and others concerned themselves with precise intellectual and cultural placement and with judgments supported by detailed analysis and rigorous argument, Bronk constructed a cento of quotations linked by description, narrative, and assertion. His aim was not literary history or interpretative scholarship but rather the discovery and working out of his own thoughts and feelings through encounters with the thoughts and feelings of others; if that meant their words were subjectively selected and arranged to speak for him, so be it. Academic fashions aside, when completed by the addition of the Melville section some years later in 1946, Bronk's book (which remained unpublished until 1980) proved a remarkable piece of writing for a young man; it bears comparison to a similarly anti-academic work on related material, written by another disgruntled Harvard graduate student of the time, Charles Olson's 1947 *Call Me Ishmael* (although Bronk's concerns with individuality and with the limitations of knowledge and language in a probably meaningless world are far from Olson's progressive romance of the spatial sublime).

WILLIAM BRONK

Bronk's withdrawal from Harvard was no doubt bracing, but it must also have sometimes felt like defeat to the young man who had left Hudson Falls wearing an aura of gleaming promise, succeeded brilliantly at Dartmouth, and lacked experience of failure—especially when he thought about returning home after the rejection of all his post-Harvard attempts to find a teaching position or admission to another graduate school. Perhaps Bronk took some solace from the invitation he'd received from Kathleen Frazier to spend the entire summer of 1939 in residence at the artists' colony she conducted in western Massachusetts, the Cummington School for the Arts. Bronk had spent a week at Cummington during the previous summer, and he relished the atmosphere of serious work and easy conversation among artists, writers, composers, and dancers he had found there. During his longer stay, he worked on poems and on the Thoreau essay he'd begun in Norwich; renewed acquaintance with two painters who became lifelong friends, Herman Maril and Eugene Canadé; and met the documentary filmmaker Shirley Clark and the dancer Al Pew (later called Albert Brooks). The experience must have re-created for a time the sort of congenial, supportive, and encouraging atmosphere he'd known at Dartmouth. But when the Cummington session was over, not wanting to return to Hanover or Hudson Falls, Bronk moved to Greenwich Village. He sounds lost and dejected there in a letter to a Dartmouth classmate. In Gilmore's biography, he calls himself "a poor bewildered creature," with no sense of what he wants to do or of how to find a job beyond the unsatisfying one of selling clothes as a temporary department store clerk hired for the Christmas rush. Even the Red Cross had turned him down.

In January 1940, Bronk was back in Hudson Falls. Planning to stay for a month, he lingered for more than a year, until his induction into the army. During that period, he vacillated between practical efforts to change his situation and the lethargic, perhaps depressive passivity he would experience at times throughout his life. He wrote poems, worked on the Whitman section of *The Brother in Elysium*, and began to develop some

of the philosophical positions that would characterize his verse: skepticism about assertions of truth, for instance, and the suggestion that disappointments and negations can have an affirming or refreshing effect. He also began to take long walks in the fields and forests and along the canals of Hudson Falls. Those activities became a staple of his adult life and provided the closely observed, precisely described experiences of the natural world essential to many of his poems.

Bronk had triumphed at Dartmouth, fled Harvard, flourished briefly at Cummington, and been lost in New York. Now he was alternately productive or idle in Hudson Falls. This period, whether retreat, reverie, or recuperation, was interrupted when Bronk was conscripted into the U.S. Army. Inducted in March 1941, he was at first resentful, but over time his experience came to seem useful. He met and learned to get along with people outside the elite academic circles where he had felt either comfortable (at Dartmouth) or abused (at Harvard); he discovered in himself a capacity for leadership, going to officer candidate school and becoming an officer; he mastered the arcane matter of signal corps work (perhaps it gave him his frequent image of the self as a receiving instrument); and he served in diverse, sometimes beautiful locations: Virginia, Bermuda, Florida, and New York. Bronk's poems of the period begin to reflect his mature belief that reality is marked by incompatible conditions for which no resolution or consolation can be found.

In the fall of 1945, with the war over, Bronk was discharged and, with Cox's help, was hired to teach English and serve as a dormitory proctor at Union College in Schenectady, New York. Apparently successful there, he was offered the chance to continue after his first year, but he chose instead to return to Pearl Street and Hudson Falls and to a life working at and eventually running the family business (he claimed to hate the work or to find it unbearably dull, but he stayed on there for more than thirty years, until he liquidated the firm and retired in 1978).

The reasons for Bronk's decision to go home after his Union College year are murky: although he enjoyed conversation with customers and sales representatives, he always disliked the business

side of business. Perhaps the lassitude that could haunt him took over. He may have felt a sense of family obligation. (His father had died in 1941; Bronk's only published reaction is the poem "My Father Photographed with Friends," a beautifully restrained lyric conveying a son's mostly thwarted search for paternal contact and resemblance.) He might have thought the coal and lumber yard would give him a surer income and greater freedom and time to write than college teaching could. Perhaps his struggles at Harvard and in New York made the homely and familiar seem newly attractive or simply safe. Perhaps he knew he throve some on being balked or beset by limitation. In any case, Bronk returned to his boyhood home and stayed there. He took vacation trips to Europe, the Caribbean, and Central and South America (often with his sister Betty), and he rode buses or trains to concerts, shows, and exhibitions in New York and elsewhere (Bronk never drove a car). But those things aside, Hudson Falls became his world. He shared the Pearl Street house with his mother until she died in 1982, and he went on living there until his own death in 1999, never updating wiring or plumbing and continuing to use the coal stove that had been there for years. He saw the graceful elms that lined the street and arched above the house succumb to blight and come down, and houses and carefully set out trees would serve as central images for Bronk's characteristic expressions of the decay, decrepitude, and frustration shadowing the structures humans build to order and shape the world.

Meanwhile, Bronk gradually worked out the patterns that characterized his adult life. Grudgingly or patiently, he did business at the office, but he also read and wrote poems at work as well as at home, scandalizing his commercially oriented uncle. Alone or with friends, he took long walks in the Hudson Falls countryside, observing animals, plants, and the swing and sway of the seasons, as well as jotting notes for poems on scraps of paper he carried with him (sheets torn from pads advertising Glens Falls Portland Cement, for instance) and sunning beside or swimming nude in the abandoned local canals. He became a fine host and an accomplished cook, sending away for prime ingredients for gourmet meals or cocktails and welcoming local friends as well as writers and artists who sought him out from farther away. But Bronk was also often severely depressed and lonely at home, and subject to bouts of rage and despair. Homosexual, he was ill at ease with his desires early on and mostly repressed them (by his own admission he typically pursued, attracted, and then harshly rejected potential lovers). On the other hand, after the Stonewall riots in 1968, Bronk's self-repression relaxed, and he found his way to fulfilling if sometimes troubled erotic relationships with several men as well as with his old friend, then intimate companion, Laura Greenlaw. (Gilmore provides the details.)

Bronk was also a skilled and voluminous letter writer. His supposed isolation aside (he might have agreed with Frost who, when asked if he didn't miss living in the city where everything went on, answered, where I am, *I* go on), Bronk conducted energetic epistolary relationships with a wide community of poets, painters, editors, and friends, many of whom he saw in person only rarely, if at all. Bronk's letters to Cid Corman, Robert Creeley, Charles Olson, George Oppen, James Weil, Robert Meyer, Samuel French Morse, Eugene Canadé, Herman Maril, and many others, are housed in Columbia University's Bronk collection and other archives. Witty, elegant, and informative (and sometimes despairing, vituperative, and scatological, as well), they provided a version of the membership in a likeminded and talented coterie Bronk had relished in school; they are essential to understanding the poet's life and work.

Perhaps this is the place for further comment on Bronk's personality. An indefatigable writer, he was startlingly intelligent and deeply if unsystematically read in aesthetics, history, and science as well as literature. He was unusually sure of his own convictions and brutally or refreshingly frank in enunciating them, as he also was in describing his emotional or sexual responses to others. Prickly, sometimes cranky, deeply sensitive to real or imagined slights, and often tart, even acerbic in letters, he was by all reports congenial, impassioned, and compassionate in

person, a kind, sympathetic, and generous friend—although quick to anger when he felt his openness had been abused. As noted earlier, he sometimes suffered periods of debilitating depression and experienced, too, moments of perhaps complementary elation. Late in his life he was treated with antidepressant medications. For most of his days an inveterate walker, frequent swimmer, sometime cross-country skier, and occasional exuberant dancer, in his last years Bronk suffered from pancreatitis, asthma, and emphysema. Eventually he was tethered to an oxygen tank that kept him mostly indoors, although a lengthy supply hose let him move about the house. Bronk's life had long ago settled into the routines of business, retirement, writing, hosting, and occasional travel mentioned above when (just after his eighty-first birthday, on February 22, 1999) he died, apparently from complications of emphysema. Prolific until the end, he left a final poem on the table beside the chair in which he customarily sat to write.

After years of relative obscurity, and although he never quite recovered from early neglect, Bronk had become somewhat better known in his later years. He received the American Book Award in 1982, wrote a commissioned poem for Mario Cuomo's inauguration as governor of New York, gave more frequent public readings, recorded his work for posterity, and saw his writing become the subject of academic interest (a symposium with its papers later published as a special issue of a journal, for instance). The composer Robert Gogan set some of his verses for piano and voice; Bronk found a welcoming home for his art collection at a local college; and he won the thirty-five-thousand-dollar Lannan Foundation Literary Award in 1991. Meanwhile, New Directions published a volume of his selected poems, and he became the focal point of a circle of younger writers, artists, scholars, and appreciative friends, many of whom visited him at home in Hudson Falls. Yet, at the time of his death, Bronk remained more or less on the margins of evaluative, literary historical, and anthology accounts of his period's poetry and poetics. Fuller estimates of his place in the poetry of the second half of the twentieth century—

Gilmore's biography, a second collection of essays, and fine critical studies by Bert Kimmelman, David Clippinger, and Henry Weinfield—have since emerged. A collected edition of the later poems and a selection from the letters were said to be in the offing as of the year 2010. (Other important scholars of Bronk's work include Norman Finkelstein, Burton Hatlen, Louise Chawla, John Ernest, Thomas Lisk, and Ronald Collins; the last is especially good on Bronk and science.)

Finally, whether one is suspicious of or seduced by biographical explanations of intellectual and artistic predilections, two aspects of Bronk's life seem certain to have had significant bearing on the ideas that inform his work. Again and again, Bronk's travels to other cultures (along with his studies in the histories of art and science and of civilizations) suggested to him that human beliefs, explanations, and arrangements—the small or greater "truths" people and cultures live by—are always partial, arbitrary, and contingent, constructed and imposed rather than discovered, known for sure, and permanent. This helped to make Bronk, to repeat a phrase, the absolute relativist he was. Similarly, and perhaps still more profoundly, Bronk's being homosexual in a cultural moment that condemned, criminalized, and punished as unnatural and perverse the expression of desires he knew to be naturally his own may have made him especially sensitive to the gulf between what we say about reality and reality itself, the gulf from which, for all sorts of good reasons, he created his poems.

PROSE

Bronk's prose writings are collected in 1983's *Vectors and Smoothable Curves,* which is supplemented by two important Elizabeth Press pamphlets (one, *The Attendant,* reprints the essay originally called "The Lens of Poetry"; the other, *As David Danced,* provides the text of Bronk's American Book Award acceptance speech). Earthy and exquisite at once, abstruse and colloquial, written with the startling clarity and crisp exactitude of sentiment and thought that typify his poems, Bronk's prose is a highly readable and efficient guide to the poet's main concerns. For instance, in addition to its strenuous ho-

mosocial subtext and its implicit critique of "objective" or "scientific" literary scholarship, *The Brother in Elysium* affirms Bronk's thoroughgoing commitment to individual experience, no matter how ill-aligned its varied implications may be to one another or to cultural assumptions and expectations. In the lives and writings of Thoreau and Melville, Bronk finds examples of the open-minded fortitude individuals require if they are to rely on their own experience and face the inconsistencies experience reveals: the only partial usefulness and ultimate insufficiency of all human solutions to the problems of living, for instance, or the inextricability of good from evil in ideas, actions, or political and judicial systems conventionally presumed to be wholly just or unjust, right or wrong. Bronk also finds a further strength in his nineteenth-century forebears: the sterner stuff required to trust experience and its vagaries while also refusing to accept any particular experience as final, so that the impetus experience might give to someone to make corrections, say, or to claim righteousness, is always trumped by reconsideration. Bronk presents Whitman as a nearly negative example of all of this: that poet, he thinks, is apt to insist so forcefully on unity, coherence, and form (albeit by way of an apparent faith in multiplicity, irrationality, and formlessness) that he willfully destroys them. As is usual with Bronk, the ideas on offer do not involve clear-cut choices between paired opposites in diametrical conflict; instead, they are irresolvably many and unevenly angled. Additive without summation, they promote corrosive and lively rethinking rather than finality or contentment; they urge restless, disruptive seeking, not complacent restfulness in the achieved comforts of some confidently held knowledge or faith. Characteristically, Bronk praises Melville's hard-earned belief in "sacred uncertainty," saying he clutched it like a golden bough. Bronk leaves uncertainty's role woozily indeterminate: is it a tool permitting the exhausted wanderer (some Aeneas, say) to pause, take stock, and then return to the quest, or a passport to hell? In any case, Bronk clutched uncertainty, too, and held it sacred: the awe he felt before it promoted modesty as well as boldly radical doubt.

Vectors and Smoothable Curves also collects the essays Bronk first published in his 1974 book *The New World*. Based on his travels to South and Central America and his related studies of Incan and Mayan civilizations, these pieces function as forms of comparative archaeology. Describing sites at Machu Picchu, Tikal, Palenque, and Copan, they show how old and civilized the "new" world really was before the European "discovery." Implicitly, they reveal the illusions, projections, and will to power underlying colonialist versions of the Americas as unpopulated, uncivilized, or savage, a blank space in need of settlement, inscription, or conversion—those code words for appropriation and exploitation. The essays also avoid the sense of contemporary cultural superiority that often gives a condescending air to even admiring accounts of civilizations in ruins. Bronk's finely tuned descriptions of Incan and Mayan monuments, artifacts, and rituals, and of the cosmologies that once supported them, show full respect for the human inventiveness and energy that created those cultures and permitted them to prosper for centuries by giving ritualistic shape to disorderly life and death; by giving, in calendars and architecture, stable, predictable structures to fluid time and space.

Meanwhile, though, Bronk's archeological essays also avoid the frequent postcolonial tendency to valorize lost, destroyed, or defeated cultures, or to treat them as innocent victims. Instead, for all his praise of their severe or intricate beauties, Bronk sees Incan and Mayan cultures as wholly of a piece with every other culture, past, present, and future. He presents them as equivalent to other civilizations in their drive to power and control, their need to impose, enforce, and perpetuate some particular but necessarily partial and falsifying order. And he also presents them as equal to other cultures in their inevitable decline and dissolution, the fate of every civilization, whether that fate is brought about by failures of conviction from within (when once-sufficient satisfactions wither) or by destruction or conquest from without. Honoring the alterity and strangeness as well as the beauty and power of Incan and Mayan cultures (he is typi-

cally thrilled by the potential for variety and invention that cultural difference signals and just as typically chastened by the limitations of knowledge and understanding it reveals), Bronk exalts and exults in the creative energy of human attempts to compose reality. At the same time, his confidence that every composition is partial and fated eventually to fail counsels caution and despair, as examples of once-potent civilizations all but lost in hidden mountain valleys or depths of jungle growth well might. All of this is Bronk's version of the "Ozymandias" effect. Meditating on ruins, Bronk joins Shelley in treating civilizations as organisms with life spans rather than as monuments; thus, he levels cultural hierarchies, but he does so without Shelley's compensatory hope for progressive political transformation. Instead, he shares Stevens' sense that the rage for order is blasted as well as blessed, and Frost's sense that whatever history is, it is not progress.

Four additional, very brief essays complete Bronk's published prose. Two, "Costume as Metaphor" and "Desire and Denial," were originally paired in the pamphlet *A Partial Glossary* and round out *Vectors and Smoothable Curves*; the others are "The Attendant" and the award acceptance speech. Again, these pieces provide guidance for reading Bronk's verse. The first of them has this to say about "costume," a term that in the present instance ought to be understood as construing not only clothing but any outfit we put on in order to organize ourselves and the world: a set of beliefs, a political ideology, a worldview or cultural system: "How hopeless it is to pose in any particular costume when all we are is limitless [capable of sporting endless costumes] and costume denies that, limits us in a role" (p. 48). This approaches Bronk's fundamental insight: we need the clothes (the faiths, the laws, the epistemes) we don to protect us from the world; they alienate and isolate us from it, too, and end up worn out, reduced to rags, discarded. Bronk says the same for languages: the arbitrary sets of conjugations and declensions, of rules for person, number, and syntax of any particular language, both shape our experience and distort it; whatever language we speak, it

speaks (and limits) us as we speak it. "Desire and Denial" has this uneasy and many-layered conclusion to convey: "we are denied those shapes and spaces of desire by our desire which rejects them" (p. 51). And the essay repeats what its companion piece implies about human identity when it describes our capacity for endless posing: the self can vary so that it is "[s]hapeless and impalpable" (p. 51).

"The Attendant" and "As David Danced" address poetry directly. The first offers this disarmingly gnomic utterance as definition: "Poetry is about reality in the way that a lens is about light" (p. 7). The second returns to the figure of attire. More explicit and exhortatory than gnomic, it still conveys enough of Bronk's multi-angled and mysterious precision to lead us (by way of its own spiral staircase of competing commitments, claims, and counterclaims) both directly and by twists and turns to Bronk's resolute, unresolved poetry and its dramas of desire and denial:

> In our thinking and in our feeling we are not often open. Custom and costume cover us; we wear them as forms of protective clothing against the threats and dangers of experience to which we refuse to open ourselves because that experience really is dangerous and threatening. It is destructive and can kill us. Religious and social and intellectual forms of many kinds deny our experience and protect us from it, closing our openness. But the true reader opens himself to the experience of the work and so honors it.... It is the nature of poetry not to deny experience.
>
> (p. 1)

POETRY TO 1981

The first and major phase of Bronk's poetic career begins a little uncertainly with the book *My Father Photographed with Friends*, which was completed by 1945, although it was not published until 1976. Not quite juvenilia, it is nonetheless youthful, apprentice work, more marked by promise than achievement. The collection has limp imitations of poems by Frost and Marianne Moore (his "Two Look at Two" and "Acquainted with the Night"; her "The Fish"), and it features inert rhymes and flat, antipoetic statements (a flaw Bronk later converts to a strength). Nonethe-

less, the book shows signs of the poetic vigor to come. It includes the excellent title poem mentioned above, which establishes an important Bronk theme: our always balked desire to know other people, including the ones we are closest to. "Some Birds on a Dun Field" captures Bronk's characteristic sense of desolation in sparse, nearly colorless images. "Home Address" is among the first of Bronk's many eloquent portrayals of dwellings that house us all too awkwardly. And "Joe's Jitters" leavens despondency with jaunty wit; there are instances here and there of vigilant phrasing. Meanwhile, "The Woods, New York" points toward Bronk's archaeological subject, saying that America's largest city will one day join Babylon and Thebes as a ruin subjected to confused investigation. For all of this, however, Bronk's first fully realized book is his second (and first published), *Light and Dark*.

As already noted, the *New Yorker* printed an early Bronk poem; a few others appeared in minor journals early on, but Bronk's most important initial publishing success came in Cid Corman's innovative journal *Origin*. In 1950, Corman told the poet Sam Morse (Bronk's friend and Dartmouth College classmate) that Robert Creeley was looking for poems to include in a magazine he planned to start. Morse recommended Bronk. Creeley and Corman were impressed by his work, and when Creeley's plans fell through, several of Bronk's poems came out in the first numbers of *Origin*, beginning in 1951. Bronk's work appeared in every series of the journal (the editor later called him the thread that bound the issues together). Corman and *Origin* gave Bronk his first real audience. They provided vital encouragement at a time when he felt alone, unread, and unappreciated.

Literary historians typically separate the poets of Bronk's era into academic traditionalists and avant-garde experimenters, but Bronk appeared in *Origin* with formalists like Morse and James Merrill as well as with so-called open, anti-academic poets like Olson, Creeley, and Oppen. This reminds us that literary history involves retrospective oversimplification as well as the corrective lens of hindsight. Bronk's work

melds traditional metrics with postmodern themes in ways no oppositional taxonomy can rightly represent, not least because his radical skepticism about identity, language, and human systems of organization also involves aspects of epistemological and ethical idealism. Most often framed in statement-rich blank verse, Bronk's poems can seem both in and out of tune with poetics that claim to discard absolutes along with metrics and to go in fear of abstraction. In a letter to Morse, Bronk said he did not think that he and Creeley, Oppen, and others were after the same thing at all. On the other hand, Bronk's intense individualism made him unusually suspicious of even the best supported claims of resemblance.

Corman's Origin Press published Bronk's *Light and Dark* in 1956 (James Weil's Elizabeth Press reissued it in 1975). A bit uneven, and barely reviewed, the book conveys Bronk's central themes in his mature manner. The fine opening poem is characteristic. "Some Musicians Play Chamber Music for Us" addresses music, of course, a subject Bronk returns to often, and the poem borrows from composition and performance practices patterns of sequenced, layered, and counterpointed statements, variations, restatements, and responses: assents, rebuttals, doubts. Those patterns become Bronk's principle procedure for organizing statements in his poems while also keeping the poems off-center (the poems conclude, of course, but they only rarely resolve, in the musical or other senses). "Some Musicians Play Chamber Music for Us" imitates the patterns it describes. The shifting among longer and shorter phrases, the modulated play between enjambed and end-stopped lines (reflecting the way musical phrases coincide with bar lines or lightly or forcefully overrun them), and the variously placed caesuras in the poem all give Bronk's statements a physical, syntactical, emotional, and ideational suppleness his earliest poems lack. It is a thematic as well as technical matter. Bronk notes that it is the task of the artist to address the fragmentary nature of music. Fragments are not whole; traps contain only by artifice, force, and damage. The poem's competing ideas and statements, like music, like its own line ends, pauses,

and phrases, go in and out of kilter; they define in more than one direction.

On the strength of this and related poems in *Light and Dark*, Henry Weinfield argues that Bronk's second volume benefits from his abandonment of Frost for Stevens. It is true that the new influence of Stevens was salutary for Bronk. He learned much from Stevens' deft incorporation into poems of philosophical statements and from his skilled handling of blank verse (for this and the next several volumes, his most important ones, blank verse is Bronk's most typical form). And one of *Light and Dark*'s important poems, "The Acts of the Apostles," is an effective if riskily close imitation of Stevens' "Sunday Morning." (Like Stevens, Bronk recalls religious faith nostalgically while bluntly denying its truth; like Stevens, he responds to the loss of faith by defining humanity's descent into knowledge as a secular version of the fortunate fall; and like Stevens, he uses images of soaring birds to announce that the drop from belief into emptiness can yield up briefly sustaining although not redemptive flights of imagination.) But Weinfield's distinction is too stark: Bronk did not abandon Frost for Stevens; he added one influence to the other.

The Frost whom Bronk met and learned from in the 1930s had already moved from his earlier dramatic and character-driven verse to far more direct and unresolved engagements with contradictory, competing, and complementary ideas or statements, often in blank verse and epigrammatic poems (Frost's own versions of definitions that move in more than one direction). And throughout his career Bronk used Frost's colloquial bent to chasten Stevens' verbal flash and conceptual and textural dandyism. More important, Bronk shares with Stevens *and* Frost a fundamental belief that all human faiths and structures are imposed constructions, not descriptions (this is the view the qualifying word "momentary" conveys in Frost's definition of poetry as "a momentary stay against confusion"; it is part of what Stevens means by the term "violence" when he calls poetry a violence from within protecting us against a greater violence from without). Meanwhile, there is, or comes to

be, a key difference between Bronk and *both* Frost and Stevens. Bronk's predecessors typically see poetry as continuous with other human efforts to shape the world and make it meaningful (Frost in his sociable willingness to temper what he called formity with conformity; Stevens in his more private effort to provide his fellows with supreme fictions that can "replace" expired truths). Bronk only sometimes does so. Increasingly as his work develops, Bronk seeks to *separate* poetry from other always only palliative and illusory forms of consolation and to make it chastise, contradict, and exhaust them; he aims, that is, to keep poetry (in the terms laid out in "As David Danced") the one thing wholly open to experience's emptiness rather than a partially solacing stay against or a fictive protection from it.

In any case, beginning with *Light and Dark,* and increasingly in the volumes to follow, Bronk moves beyond influence and into his own voice and vision. Perhaps the analysis in this essay has made that vision seem too dark; after all, the title of the volume under discussion at the present names light, as well, and several poems in the book emphasize compensatory comforts in darkened situations. For instance, without covering up the bare stubs of sumac's December nakedness, "A Winter Shrub" momentarily restores the bush's summer and autumn clothes. As "The Mind's Landscape on an Early Winter Day" paradoxically has it, however blind we are, we nevertheless attempt to make our way through the darkness.

Light and Dark was published at the time when Bronk was making his first trips to visit Mayan ruins. The book's finest and final poem, "At Tikal," reflects those journeys. The poem's elegant handling of statements in counterpoint (and of varied phrasal lengths, shifting caesuras, and variously enjambed and end-stopped lines) is vintage Bronk, as is its finely realized archaeological argument. "At Tikal" describes a people as they developed a culture or civilization. The ancient Mayans, living in what is now Guatemala, were discontent with the slash and burn of subsistence agriculture. They wanted more, and by means of imagination, they achieved it. Fram-

ing time and space with calendars and buildings, they carved out the stone dating systems and raised the step-pyramid temples and associated sacrificial rites that made their world predictable and brought it under control. Or so it seemed to them. Bronk's depiction combines admiring praise for the attainments of Mayan culture with deprecation for its presumptions to truth and permanence. The stars are stranger and more remote than Mayan astronomy captured; rain, like the other things of nature, is not a pet, a domesticated creature obedient to human commands to come or go or stay. Tikal is a ruin now; the city's confident and self-regarding orders are overthrown and overgrown. Bronk dramatizes Tikal's sudden collapse back into jungle by means of an abrupt shift from the past to the present tense. This disruptive chronological maneuver replicates the way time itself upset the stable city and wrecked the rigid rituals its people had designed to measure, control, and conquer time: eventually, the structures people impose on reality fail, nature overwhelms culture, and the ungovernable wild takes back what once seemed safely tamed.

With his usual commitment to clear argument and transparent statement, Bronk adds a second stanza to "At Tikal"; it renders the implications of the Mayan experience explicit; it also insists that the lessons this single city in ruins teaches are general or universal rather than merely specific. The fall of Tikal does not represent some particular cultural failure to which we might be immune or feel superior. Rather, the Mayan condition is the human condition, and the Mayan response is equivalent to every human endeavor to formulate reality, to give it pattern and meaning. Our common circumstance is hard: we lack a coherent world. As with the Mayans, our imaginative reaction to this deprivation is often noble: we create an orderly world. But noble or not, the result is always a wall or a cage. For a while, the structure we put in place keeps danger in or out, or feels as though it does; it is also an obstacle or a snare. What comforts us distorts, contains, and constrains us, too. And when, as it must, the wall falls or the cage col-

lapses, we begin the process anew, unable to do without it.

Two features of Bronk's mature voice as it appears in *Light and Dark* deserve particular mention here. One is his use of exclamations like "ah" and "oh." Bronk renovates these supposedly archaic or passé poeticisms, as in the last line of "At Tikal", where the word "oh" conveys lamentation (as if to say, "alas"); it conveys, too, the elation or exaltation that sometimes accompanies such extreme or sublime states as utter desolation; but it also conveys the uninflected flatness of a fully foreknown and always anticipated deflation. This sort of layering of feeling and thought, of competing moods and positions, gives Bronk's work its special tartness and tang, the flavor of hope and hope discarded, of vitality and vitiation and all the points between. The second feature apparent here and persisting throughout Bronk's career is his frequent use of the first-person-plural pronoun. Unusual in poets of Bronk's era, more common in periods when knowledge is more confidently held and more generally shared (and a sign of humility, too), the "we" that speaks in so many Bronk poems communicates his paradoxical sense that individuals, like cultures or civilizations, are unified precisely by their shared circumstance of extreme privacy and perceptual and conceptual limitation. This has the unexpected effect of permitting the alien and alienated poet to speak representatively for his time and place, to speak for and to a community of alien and alienated others.

Bronk's next and arguably strongest book, *The World, the Worldless,* appeared in 1964, when the poet was forty-six and after a difficult eight-year period when, despite his own efforts and those of several friends on his behalf, Bronk's work was routinely rejected by book and magazine editors alike (except for Corman at *Origin*). Eventually, *The World, the Worldless* was jointly published by James Laughlin's New Directions press in cooperation with the *San Francisco Review.* (June Degnan, the sister of the poet George Oppen, was an editor at the West Coast journal, and Oppen had brought Bronk to her attention, based on his admiration for *Light and Dark*.) The publication process involved a

number of false starts, and those exacerbated Bronk's characteristic diffidence toward the poetry business—perhaps rightly, since, although the book was well received, after its appearance Bronk would again be without a commercial publisher until 1981. However that might be, and to repeat, *The World, the Worldless* may well be Bronk's best individual book. His themes of denial and desire find fully convincing expression in it; neither aspect finally dominates the other.

"Blue Spruces in Pairs, a Bird Bath Between" begins mildly. In a mood of domestic tranquility, even nostalgia, it describes an outdated fad in ornamental planting. But the poem's close is caustic. Not just lawn layouts and houses but all human attempts to know, shape, and control the world: astronomy, say, or religions and their promise of heavenly afterlife, even the enterprise of civilization building itself, are reduced to a hollow sequence of fleeting and arbitrary fashions with no essential grounding in or connection to the real—such diminishment leaves us stranded. Meanwhile, several poems in *The World, the Worldless* celebrate as well as chastise the ingenuity and power of the structures we create to house ourselves against such crippling vacancy. In the opening lines of "In Navaho Country" such celebration, heartfelt though it is, is a companion to chastening, which is typical of Bronk. The proliferation of "Hogan"-like words beginning with the letters "ho" or "h" elegantly enacts what the stanza describes: the imagination's strenuous capacity to propagate itself and expand a germ of shape into cosmic structures that protectively organize and domesticate the world. But ultimately the stanza's insistent patterning is overdone; it deliberately becomes less grand than grandiose, parody as well as praise. The last line quoted names the rub: any starting point would deliver an equivalent result. As the rest of the poem specifies, whatever patterns we make are arbitrary; worse, they depend for their existence upon the very un-patterned emptiness they mean to organize. It follows that any particular pattern on offer is fraudulent—our versions, whether based on hogans, houses of different sorts, or other enclosed spaces (rooms or architectural pattern books or Bibles, perhaps), are always wrong, with no foundation to stand on. It goes like this. We want a place of meaning, not a void. We loft up house plans or other shapes to create one. Doing so, we deceive ourselves, treating impositions as descriptions. The deception consoles us for a while, but eventually its delusiveness shows through. The void permits the hogans to be erected and multiplied; it ensures their demolition.

Those are bleak conclusions, but the meaning of a poem comes from its entire texture, not its conclusions. In Bronk's case, that texture involves, among other things, competing statements that define in multiple directions: affirming and negating while doubting the rightness of either response, and while also trying out additional, more finely modulated postures. To put it another way, Bronk composed not individual notes but chords, orchestrating layered tonalities that create meanings resistant to paraphrase and alive with mixed feeling as well as ideas and argument. And chords and counterpoint and their allies occur not only within poems but also in dissonant or consonant relationships between and among them, for if some poems are mostly dark, others more nearly affirm. In "My House New-Painted," for instance, Bronk challenges his habitual contempt for compromise to praise limited but nonetheless real domestic satisfactions. "The Annihilation of Matter" is threateningly titled but sings a hymn to light, as does "Metonymy as an Approach to the Real World," where beauty concedes nothing at all to the conceded fact that nothing is absolute. "Certain Beasts, Like Cats" also confirms the loveliness of the world, as does "Midsummer"; and "Boolean Algebra: $X^2=X$" catalogs mathematical error and imprecision only to end in astonished joy at the artistry and vigor of probably pointless human endeavors to apprehend reality's shape. At the same time, poems like those are set off or offset by other, more nearly desolate, ones—"The Belief in the Self Abandoned," for example.

Among the best poems in *The World, the Worldless* are those in which a delicate tenderness tempers desolation, denial, or abnegation. "Virgin and Child with Music and Numbers" (*Life*

Supports, pp. 52–53) achieves this in religious terms. Faithless itself, perhaps, and fully aware of all that militates against belief in the miraculous (the fear of crucifixion, especially, but other dangers, too), the poem nevertheless concludes in hedged but gentle prayer or imploration. "Skunk Cabbage" (*Life Supports*, p. 56) attains a similar effect in terms of the natural world. Describing with botanical precision the early spring plant named in the title, the poem refuses to prettify: as the plant's name says, skunk cabbage is fetid; the elements rub it raw; it stinks. But "it stinks of livingness." "It looks like tenderness, the way it curves / upward and breaks over to cover within." It seems to be no coincidence that the intimate shape these lines describe recalls a Madonna and child in outline.

Finally, Bronk's archaeological concerns also appear often in *The World, the Worldless*, in "A Postcard to Send to Sumer," "Tenochtitlan," and "A Black Clay Fish from Oaxaca" but most importantly in "The Beautiful Wall, Machu Picchu." This last is an elegant *ars poetica* (or theory of poetry) in which Bronk sets Greek sculpture and willingly yields to the hand that shapes it, against the austerities of Incan stonework, which (like Bronk's own layered or stacked up statements) respects the world's intractable indifference while nonetheless loving the soundness of its own construction.

The World, the Worldless received strong reviews from the poet Hayden Carruth and others, but it did not launch Bronk's career. His subsequent work was rescued from a new round of repeated rejections by the intervention of the poet and publisher James L. Weil, who brought out Bronk's next several books in superbly designed editions elegantly printed on fine Italian paper. If their audience was small, they honored the author and his work. Bronk was deeply grateful, and Bronk and Weil became close friends. The books published by Weil's Elizabeth Press (in addition to the reissue of *Light and Dark* and the early works *My Father Photographed with Friends* and *The Brother in Elysium* and the essay collection *The New World*) are *The Empty Hands* (1969), *That Tantalus* (1971), *To Praise the Music* (1972), *Silence and Metaphor* (1975),

The Meantime (1976), *Finding Losses* (1976), *The Force of Desire* (1978), and a limited edition of *Life Supports* (1981). These several books consolidate the thematic and technical achievements of *Light and Dark* and *The World, the Worldless* and in some ways can be treated as a group.

The work they offer includes poems based on Bronk's travels, as well as poems on familiar philosophical considerations ("On *Credo Ut Intelligam*"; "Ergo Non Sum. Est."), on the limitations of language and the elusiveness of the self ("On the Failure of Meaning in the Absence of Objective Analogs"; "The Plainest Narrative"), and on archaeological subjects ("The Smile on the Face of a Kouros," "The Mayan Glyphs Unread," "The Greeks, the Chinese, or Say the Mayans," "Beatific Effigies"). There are poems featuring dry humor: "Go Ahead; Goodbye; Good Luck; and Watch Out," for instance, whose over-determined title forecasts a subversively comic yet tolerant take on the quest for balm in Gilead. And there are fine poems on the beauties and limitations of mathematical and scientific explanations of reality: "Euclidean Spaces: Linear Time" and "On Divers Geometries," for example.

As that catalog suggests, Bronk's characteristic subject matter persists in the books from *The Empty Hands* through *Life Supports*; in technical terms, a flexible five-beat, roughly iambic line remains his mainstay. On the other hand, these books also present new subjects and considerable formal experiment. There are a number of love poems, variously tender, wry, and acerbic: "Colloquy on a Bed," "The Wall," "Yes: I Mean So OK–Love," and "Love as a Great Power," for instance. Several poems consider, sometimes comically, the prevalence in human affairs of ignorance and error (for examples, see "Conjectural Reading," "I Thought It Was Harry," and "The Ignorant Lust after Knowledge"). There are poems on aging ("At Fifty"), and the beautiful pastoral elegy called "The Elms Dying—And My Friend, Lew Stillwell, Dead" (which is actually an *anti*-pastoral elegy: it lacks the mode's conventional—and crucial—turn to consolation). And there are several poems addressing subjects increasingly central in Bronk's late work: the ir-

relevance on any cosmic scale of human efforts and achievements, including poetry itself ("Something Matters but We Don't," "On the Death of Cardinal Tisserant," "The Defence of Poesie"); the lack of clear distinctions between good and evil when they are seen from the point of view of eternity ("Not to Be Satan nor to Deal with Him"); and the sense that we do not so much live life as we are lived by it ("Evaluation").

As noted, blank verse persists as the dominant meter in these books, but there is considerable formal variety in them as well. A few poems experiment with sharply truncated lines, and the proportion of colloquial voicing and demotic vocabulary greatly increases, as does the amount of private material and of local references included (the paired poems "The Aggrandizement" and "The Use-Unuse of Us" can serve as examples of those features). But the major technical development of these books, perhaps reflecting an attempt by Bronk to use formal experimentation to keep his potentially too-consistent thematic concerns both varied and engaging, is his choice in several of them to work with arbitrary restrictions on length, so that the poems of *To Praise the Music* all have fourteen lines; those of *Silence and Metaphor* have eight; of *Finding Losses,* four; of *The Force of Desire,* three; and (expansion following contraction) of the new poems gathered in *Life Supports,* twenty. The technical virtuosity on display in these books is remarkable, perhaps most especially in *To Praise the Music,* where Bronk exploits the thematic and formal potential of the many structural arrangements available for shaping fourteen-line poems into stanzas. He makes form an extension of content with great technical mastery in these unrhymed experiments in and against the grain of the sonnet.

Such generalizations aside, these books have many first-rate poems. A too-short list would include "The Strong Room of the House," which returns to Bronk's domestic metaphor with great success; the valedictory meditation "The Rumination of Rivers"; and many others. Among them, "The Abnegation" is a sturdy and wholly characteristic poem of refusal. Its stringent abstraction gains great emotional intensity from the large

quantum of desire it has to repress in order to claim its denial. Fine among the briefer poems, "The World," whether it addresses a god or a lover, matches a yearning for stability and safety with full recognition of the threats of vacancy, danger, and drift. Finally, one of Bronk's greatest poems, "The Real Surrounding: On Canaletto's Venice," revisits the theme and method of "The Beautiful Wall, Machu Picchu." Contrasting the painters J. M. W. Turner and Canaletto, it chooses against the glorious dazzle and bedazzlement conveyed by the English artist to cast its lot instead with the Italian's meticulously representational rendering of reality, a rendering that, somewhat surprisingly, includes reality's actual emptiness.

LATER POEMS

The later stage of Bronk's career is difficult to estimate, since, following the major achievement of *Life Supports,* the late work is remarkably uneven as well as unusually prolific. Bronk published ten books between 1981 and his death in 1999. Red Ozier brought out *Careless Love and Its Apostrophes* in 1985; North Point published *Manifest; and Furthermore* in 1987, *Death Is the Place* in 1989, and *Living Instead* in 1991; Moyer Bell issued *Some Words* in 1992; and Edward Foster's Talisman House published *The Mild Day* in 1993, *Our Selves* in 1994, *The Cage of Age* in 1996, *All of What We Loved* in 1998, and (posthumously) *Metaphor of Trees and Last Poems* in 1999, the year Bronk died. (In 1997, Talisman House also reissued *Life Supports* and *Vectors and Smoothable Curves.*) The printing of so many books at such brief intervals might suggest poems more fragmentary, rough, and improvised than carefully crafted and revised. In Bronk's case, the suggestion seems right, and the typical late Bronk poem is more diarylike or aphoristic than conventionally poetic, in part because Bronk largely abandons in his later work the five-beat metrical base and the intricate and unresolved layering of competing statements that give his mature poems their distinctive flavor. Thematically, the poems of Bronk's last phase continue to treat the ideas and attitudes discussed

above, but now they do so more often by stating conclusions than by moving toward and resisting them dramatically while permitting the reader to experience or witness the process. To some tastes, this involves a considerable falling off in quality, as does the tendency of the late poems toward abrupt refusals of refinement or "finish" (however unresolved or inconclusive that finish might have been). Sometimes, those refusals imply impatience, irritation, even disgust with poetry itself, as though the hard-earned and dramatically presented abjurations of the earlier work had become little more than automatic responses. At worst, this results in starkly unmediated utterances lacking the "unmortared" but "interlocked" "just joint" of desire and denial that makes the earlier poems so memorable. At best, it results in an uncompromising wisdom literature, less poetry than adage perhaps, in which stern, occasionally humorous, sometimes strident refusals of any and every fraudulent consolation provide what sips or swigs of refreshment there are.

Some scholars and critics, however—Norman Finkelstein and Edward Foster among them—have thought that Bronk's late work invigorates poetry precisely by doing without the amelioration that poetry as an act of composition still can offer after it abandons every other consolation. They imply that in the later work Bronk boldly chastises even the (falsely) comforting patterns of sound and sense poetry usually provides, no matter how desperate its ideas have become. Another perspective, by comparison, is nearer Henry Weinfield's. He considers Bronk's late work a kind of coda, in which the impasse adumbrated in the most condensed poems of *Life Supports* (where antiessentialist belief confronts essentialist form, and where the urge to compression and completeness runs up against Bronk's proclivity to generate endlessly additive but forever incomplete particulars) finally becomes an insuperable obstacle to effective and affecting verse. In any case, Bronk's last books have many poems that could be characterized as unrealized and unsettled. On the other hand, there are many successful poems in Bronk's new mode—the minimalist "Bursts of Light," for instance. In this poem, the contrasting impulses to fulfillment and violent desolation are movingly conjoined, their dramatic encounter underscored by the poem's attractive uncertainty about who (or what) it wants to act or be acted upon. Meanwhile, the implied narrative running throughout Bronk's late poems of an appetitive self detaching itself from the things of this world has its own documentary power. Even so, however, the cumulative effective of the later work often makes Bronk seem too much like what Gertrude Stein called Ezra Pound: a village explainer. Fine, as she said, if one is a village; if not, not.

That said, there are many pleasures to be had in Bronk's late work. The aphoristic strain can gratify, as in these examples: "We come to learn hopelessness, / to not need hope for longer" (*Careless Love and Its Apostrophes*, p. 32); "the absurd is all of truth" ("Another Look," *Our Selves*, p. 45). And several times, the slipperiness of language proves a resource as well as a burden. In the poem "Gulliver Found," for instance, Bronk wittily deploys the ambiguity lurking in prepositions to encourage second thoughts about a line's apparent sense. In "Compensation," he uses a syntactical pun to remove and restore compensation in equal portions. And the ambivalent title Bronk gives to the poem "Doubtful Creed" erases and reinscribes its summary line.

Related ideas touched on in several earlier poems, that the world is a stage and that the self is a shifting, contingent role and not a stable essence, recur frequently in the later work to good effect, as does the application to all human shapes and structures of Gödel's theory that mathematical systems are grounded only on themselves and not on external reality. Bronk's mystical view that nothingness may be a kind of fulfillment occasionally appears as well: for instance, when he advises the reader to "Go emptied into the world" ("Smart Move," *The Cage of Age*, p. 8). Some poems convey in their vibrant phrasing the solace that natural beauty sometimes provides in a meaningless world, as in these lines from "Winter Sacrament": "barked hawthorn brassed / in the sun" (*Careless Love and Its Apostrophes*, p. 9). Several poems—"Period Metaphor" and "Knowledge of Plates," for example—employ figures of

speech from sources as seemingly divorced from one another as the Bible and the science of plate tectonics to stress the instability and drift of every personal or cultural system or belief, and of reality itself. And "The House That Doesn't House" attempts to move beyond Bronk's fundamental impasse: his certainty that every shaping structure is also an obstacle or cage. In that poem, he seeks a place of shelter that is not also a barrier. As sure as always that there is no such place to be found or had, this, too, as much else in Bronk's late work, makes us feel again the uplift and downdraft mutually produced by our always facing a world in which our desires for order, knowledge, permanence, and truth are both inspired and denied. In Bronk's work, early and late, cold comfort, as the words imply, does more than merely chill.

Selected Bibliography

WORKS OF WILLIAM BRONK

POETRY

Light and Dark. Origin Press, 1956. Reprinted, New Rochelle, N.Y.: Elizabeth Press, 1975.

The World, the Worldless. New York: New Directions Press, 1964.

My Father Photographed With Friends: And Other Pictures. New Rochelle, N.Y.: Elizabeth Press, 1976.

Life Supports: New and Collected Poems. San Francisco: North Point Press, 1981.

Careless Love and Its Apostrophes. New York: Red Ozier Press, 1985.

Manifest; and Furthermore. San Francisco: North Point Press, 1987.

Death Is the Place. San Francisco: North Point Press, 1989.

Living Instead. San Francisco: North Point Press, 1991.

Some Words. Mount Kisco, N.Y., and London: Moyer Bell, 1992.

The Mild Day. Hoboken, N.J.: Talisman House, 1993.

Our Selves. Hoboken, N.J.: Talisman House, 1994.

The Cage of Age. Jersey City, N.J.: Talisman House, 1996.

All of What We Loved. Jersey City, N.J.: Talisman House, 1998.

Metaphor of Trees and Last Poems. Jersey City, N.J.: Talisman House, 1999.

PROSE

Vectors and Smoothable Curves: Collected Essays. San Francisco: North Point Press, 1983. (Includes *The Brother in Elysium* and *The New World,* along with other prose.)

As David Danced. New Rochelle, N.Y.: James L. Weil, 1983.

The Attendant. New Rochelle, N.Y.: James L. Weil, 1984.

BIOGRAPHICAL AND CRITICAL STUDIES

Clippinger, David. *The Mind's Landscape: William Bronk and Twentieth Century American Poetry.* Newark, N.J.: University of Delaware Press, 2006.

————, ed. *The Body of This Life: Reading William Bronk.* Jersey City, N.J.: Talisman House, 2001.

Corman, Cid. *William Bronk: An Essay.* Carrboro, N.C.: Truck Press, 1976.

Ernest, John. "Fossilized Fish and the World of Unknowing: John Ashbery and William Bronk." In *The Tribe of John: Ashbery and Contemporary Poetry.* Edited by Susan M. Schultz. Tuscaloosa and London: University of Alabama Press, 1995.

Finkelstein, Norman M. "The World as Desire." *Contemporary Literature* 23, no. 4:480–492 (1982).

Foster, Edward. *Answerable to None: Berrigan, Bronk, and the American Real.* New York: Spuyten Duyvil, 1999.

Gilmore, Lyman. *The Force of Desire: A Life of William Bronk.* Jersey City, N.J.: Talisman House, 2006.

Kimmelman, Burt, and Henry Weinfield, eds. *Sagetrieb* 7, no. 3:5–160 (winter 1988; William Bronk special issue).

Kimmelman, Burt. *The "Winter Mind": William Bronk and American Letters.* Cranbury, N.J.: Associated University Presses, 1998.

Lisk, Thomas. "William Bronk's Path among the Forms." *Jacket* (http://jacketmagazine.com/29/lisk-bronk.html), April 2006.

Morse, Samuel French. "Life Supports." *Poetry* 141: 105–110 (November 1982).

Rotella, Guy. "What We Don't Read: Letters from William Bronk to Samuel French Morse." *Literary Imagination* 9, no. 1:15–28 (2007).

Weinfield, Henry. *The Music of Thought in the Poetry of George Oppen and William Bronk.* Iowa City: University of Iowa Press, 2009.

LARRY BROWN

(1951—2004)

James H. Watkins

FEW IMAGES OF the American South have been as durable or colorful as that of the backwoods poor white. From William Byrd of Westover's early eighteenth-century descriptions of degenerate North Carolinians who eat so much pork that they "seem to Grunt rather than Speak" (*Secret History*, p. 55) to Erskine Caldwell's depraved residents of *Tobacco Road* (1932) and James Dickey's hillbilly rapists in *Deliverance* (1970), rural working-class white southerners have prominently populated narratives of the American South, serving alternately—sometimes simultaneously—as objects of pity or occasions for laughter. Only in the last decades of the twentieth century have writers from blue-collar backgrounds in the southeastern United States stepped up to offer their own stories of life in what the documentary filmmaker Gary Hawkins has termed the "Rough South." In an all too brief literary career that spanned less than twenty-five years, the largely self-taught novelist, short story writer, and essayist Larry Brown established himself as an important voice in American fiction by reworking the familiar tropes of the southern gothic tradition, producing a critically acclaimed body of work inhabited by rural white southerners whose intimate familiarity with violence, alcoholism, poverty, and ignorance makes them resemble at first glance the stereotypical white trash characters of earlier eras. However, in sparse, exact prose stripped of any trace of sentimentality, Brown reveals his characters' tenacity of spirit as they struggle to make the best choices they can within their severely constrained circumstances, affirming their humanity and in so doing forcing his readers to acknowledge their own kinship with individuals whom they might otherwise feel more comfortable regarding with contempt, fear, or pity. Although

a handful of blue-collar southern writers with similar concerns and styles preceded Brown in the 1970s, most notably the Florida novelist Harry Crews, no writer deserves more credit than Brown for helping to raise the so-called Grit Lit school of southern literature to a level of critical respectability.

Brown's unconventional path to literary success earned him almost as much admiration as his writing itself. At age twenty-nine, saddled with the considerable financial challenge of providing for a wife and three children and with no education beyond high school, no encouragement from anyone he knew, and no familiarity whatsoever with the vicissitudes of the publishing world, he abruptly decided to try his hand at becoming a serious writer. In the latter half of his short-lived career, in his essays and in remarks he made on the college lecture circuit and in numerous published interviews, Brown repeatedly gave humble testimony to his demanding personal work ethic and its relationship to his development as an artist. Dismissing romantic associations between genius and talent, he spoke with an almost sacramental reverence of the craft of writing and the self-discipline required to master it. He wrote, by his own estimation, more than a hundred stories and three novels—all the while working full time as a firefighter and doing additional odd jobs to support his family—before finally placing a story in a serious literary journal. In one of his first addresses at a literary event, Brown told an audience at the Fifth Biennial Conference on Southern Literature in Chattanooga, Tennessee, in 1989 that "it took me a long time to understand what literature was, and why it was so hard to write, and what it could do to you once you understood it. For me, very simply it meant that I could meet people on the

page who were as real as the people I knew in my own life" ("A Late Start," p. 245).

Adding to Brown's mythos is the fact that he was born in William Faulkner's hometown of Oxford, Mississippi, the model for Faulkner's fictional Yoknapatawpha County, and, with the exception of a decade in Memphis during his youth and a two-year stint in the Marines, he lived his entire life just a few miles outside of Oxford in rural areas of Lafayette County. Although the two writers shared some important thematic concerns—their work is informed by a strong identification with place, they both wrote about the encroachment of civilization on nature, and they both were primarily interested in how their characters measure up to a common definition of personal honor—stylistically, they were near opposites: Brown's minimalist prose bears little resemblance to Faulkner's extravagant verbosity and suggests instead the strong influence of Raymond Carver and Ernest Hemingway. Regarding the inevitable comparisons to Faulkner, whose work he deeply admired, Brown observed, "this is something I didn't want that I knew was going to happen anyway. I also knew there wouldn't be anything I could do about it.... People just naturally expect a lot out of me as a writer because I was born in Oxford. But I try not to worry about it, and just go on and do my work" ("A Late Start," p. 239).

AN ORDINARY LIFE

When he was born on July 9, 1951, nothing in William Larry Brown's circumstances suggested that one day he would achieve critical acclaim as a major voice in American fiction. The third child of Knox and Leona Brown, both of whom had roots in rural Lafayette County, Mississippi, Brown was brought home from the hospital in Oxford to the shack on the property his father worked as a sharecropper, where the Browns would live for the next three years before moving to Memphis. Knox Brown was a combat veteran of World War II whose fortunes failed to materialize, in large part owing to his alcoholism and consequent inability to hold a steady job. Like Virgil Davis, the broken patriarch in

Brown's novel *Father and Son* (1996), Knox Brown was deeply traumatized by his combat experience—according to Brown he fought in the Battle of the Bulge—and his frequent bouts of heavy drinking often devolved into tearful recollections of the brutality he had witnessed on the battlefield. "The stories he told were terrible, frightening things about the friends he had seen killed, and the cold they fought in, and the overwhelming amount of death he had seen on both sides," Brown recalled ("A Late Start," p. 240). Witnessing his father's struggles to free himself of his personal demons and recognizing in those struggles a refusal to sink into utter hopelessness left a deep impression on Brown that would manifest itself years later in the painfully realistic yet ultimately sympathetic manner in which he depicted many of his most luckless characters.

Brown's mother did her best to provide some stability in the lives of her four children while steadfastly standing by her husband through all of his difficulties. (The two would remain married until Knox's death from a heart attack in 1968.) She also gave to her children a love of reading, which she modeled for them throughout their childhood, even during the toughest of times. Brown told the interviewer Kay Bonetti, "One of my earliest memories is of seeing [his mother] reading. There were always books in our house. I just grew to love it real early, I guess—escaping into stories and other worlds" (Watson, ed., p. 80). He recalls that because his mother's reading bothered his father, who had little patience for books, she often resorted to hiding her magazines from him in order to avoid his displeasure. He also recalls her buying a set of encyclopedias and other books for the family, and they regularly made use of the public libraries, wherever they happened to live at the time. In an interview with Tom Rankin, Brown remembers responding very strongly in his childhood to the *Iliad* and the *Odyssey* as well as other stories from mythology in a set of classics his mother bought, but he was more often drawn to westerns and boy's literature with outdoor settings (Watson, ed., p. 100).

The Browns' years in Memphis were marked by declining fortunes and narrowing hopes as Knox lost job after job because of his drinking problem and the family was forced to move repeatedly from one rental house to the next, each in a dingier neighborhood than the one before. The family eventually moved back to Tula, in rural Lafayette County, Mississippi, in 1964. Although he spent most of his formative years in Memphis, Brown repeatedly characterized his time there as uninspiring and ultimately unimportant to his development as an author. It was the Mississippi woods, which he had visited regularly in his early childhood during the family's frequent trips sixty miles south to visit kin and where he roamed extensively during his high school years in Tula, that charged his imagination. Brown's love of the outdoors, not his geographical proximity to the fictional Yoknapatawpha County, prompted the sixteen-year-old to appreciate William Faulkner's fiction. Recalling finding the story "The Bear" in a copy of *Big Woods* (1955) loaned to him by a buddy, Brown was astounded at the discovery: "There was so much in there that touched me: the brooding wilderness and what it looked like, the quest for one dog that could bay and hold the great bear until the men could arrive with the guns, the steady encroaching of civilization into the wild place that the boy Ike McCaslin knew like the back of his hand.... And just imagine, I thought: a man made up that story" ("Tribute to William Faulkner," p. 269). Despite his love of reading, Brown never excelled in his studies. He failed high school English in his senior year and had to attend summer school before receiving his diploma months after his peers had graduated from Lafayette High School earlier in the summer of 1969.

After graduating he took a job at the stove factory in Oxford where his father had been working at the time of his death the year before. In 1970, with the U.S. war in Vietnam escalating and the prospect of a draft notice in the mail becoming more and more likely, Brown opted to enlist in the Marines in hopes that he might have more of a choice in where he was deployed than if he waited to be drafted into the army. After

training in Parris Island, South Carolina, and a brief assignment at Camp Lejeune in North Carolina, Brown was stationed for two years beginning in 1971 at the Marine Barracks in Philadelphia, where, at the NCO club on the base, he associated with the wounded soldiers returning from Vietnam who would later inspire him to write his first published novel, *Dirty Work* (1989).

When he was discharged from the Marines in 1972 Brown returned to Tula and resumed working at the stove factory. He took a job a year later at the Oxford Fire Department, where he would work for sixteen years, eventually earning the rank of captain before retiring in 1990 to pursue writing as a full-time career. In 1974, at the age of twenty, Brown married Mary Annie Coleman, whom he had met immediately upon his return when he was celebrating his discharge from the Marines, and the two settled into a mobile home on Mary Annie's parents' property. They began a family soon thereafter, with Billy Ray born the following year and another son, Shane, in 1979. A daughter, LeAnne, was born in 1982. Throughout the early years of the marriage, Brown supplemented his income from the Fire Department by working odd jobs painting, doing carpentry and farm work, installing fences—whatever would help put food on the table. One particularly distasteful job involved thinning out second-growth pine stands by injecting the selected trees with poison to create more room for the other trees to grow, a process he would describe in stark detail in his novel *Joe* (1991), whose eponymous hard-drinking protagonist is employed in the same grim method of deforestation.

APPRENTICESHIP AND ACHIEVEMENT

In 1980, after years of juggling sometimes two or three part-time jobs along with his fireman's job, as his thirtieth birthday loomed on the horizon, Brown began to realize that his bread-winning efforts were barely meeting the family's expenses, and the prospect of continuing to labor away at so many jobs with no end point in sight was sobering. Knowing he had an aptitude for figuring out how to build things, and reflecting

on his lifelong enjoyment of reading, Brown's thoughts turned to the possibility of a career change.

> I wondered what it took to be a writer, and I wondered if just anybody could do it. I wondered if it might be like learning how to build houses, or lay brick, or even fight fires, for that matter. I knew that some writers make a lot of money. I was a big fan of Stephen King, and I knew that his books sold well. The main question was, could a person teach himself how to do it by doing it? It seemed a logical question to me. I had absolutely no idea of the odds against me when I decided to try it.
>
> ("A Late Start," p. 242)

Brown secluded himself in the back of the house during virtually every moment of his off hours and in seven months produced an amateurish novel about a man-eating bear on a rampage in Yellowstone National Park, but he was unable to find a publisher for the book. "The main reason they didn't want it," he recalls, "is because it was horrible. You would not believe how horrible" (p. 242). Undaunted, he shifted his attention to mastering the short story form, writing more than seventy pieces of short fiction, to his reckoning, before publishing a story about some marijuana farmers in *Easyriders* magazine, a lowbrow publication targeting bikers (i.e., motorcycle enthusiasts).

Throughout the first two years of his apprenticeship, Brown's motivation was primarily financial in nature, but as the constant rejections pushed him to seek ways to improve his writing and he took to reading more serious literature with an eye to replicating the motifs and structural devices he found there, he became less concerned with garnering popular and financial success and aspired instead to simply master the art of writing and produce quality fiction like that he admired. As the *New York Times* reporter Peter Applebome described it in his profile on Brown in 1990, "Having begun with visions of being the next Stephen King, he decided he would rather be the next Flannery O'Connor." One writer he rediscovered at that time was William Faulkner, whose narrative sophistication and mythic themes Brown was now able to appreciate more fully. Upon learning of Faulkner's own academic underperformance in high school and subsequent self-education as a writer, Brown also found a role model. Other writers Brown discovered and sought to emulate at the time include Cormac McCarthy and someone who would become a mentor and one of his most vocal and influential champions, Harry Crews.

During this time Brown also met the Mississippi novelist Barry Hannah, who had just taken a position on the creative writing faculty at the University of Mississippi. Hannah was unimpressed with Brown's potential as a writer when they first met. He recalls that Brown pushed stories on him to read "that were so bad, I'd duck out of the bar when I saw him coming down the walk with the inevitable brown manila envelope. I couldn't stand hurting his feelings. I loved his sincerity. [But] I didn't give him a cold prayer in hell as to a future in literature" ("Larry Brown: Passion to Brilliance," p. x). At Hannah's less-than-enthusiastic encouragement, Brown took the novelist Ellen Douglas' graduate-level fiction writing workshop at the University of Mississippi in the spring 1982 term, for which he had to apply as a special-status student, since he had never taken an undergraduate college course, let alone received a degree. According to Douglas, "The main thing I did was point him in the direction of writers he needed to read. He already knew how to write a sentence" (quoted in Cash, "Apprenticeship" p. 114).

Undeterred by the mounting stack of rejection notices, Brown continued to hone his craft, writing by his own estimation thirty-nine stories in 1983. Finally, in 1984 he received word that the journal *Fiction International* had accepted his story "Boy and Dog." That year he enrolled in a fiction writing workshop held in the Memphis Public Library, requiring a weekly 120-mile round trip, and started work on the manuscript that would become *Joe*.

Brown's persistence finally started paying dividends in 1985 when the *Mississippi Review* editor Frederick Barthelme notified him that his story "Facing the Music" had been accepted for publication, though it would take over a year, when the issue was finally published, before he would reap the benefits of the attention it

garnered. The story, about a man who drinks himself into a stupor while watching Ray Milland's alcoholic character in the film *The Lost Weekend* on TV so that he can postpone making love with his wife, who has recently received a mastectomy, had been rejected seven times. A few months after hearing from Barthelme, Brown was promoted to captain at the Fire Department, and during his days off in the spring and summer of 1986 he and some friends built a new house for the family near the community of Yocona, a few miles from Tula. Brown designed the house and made sure to include a separate space on the other side of the carport for a study where he could work undisturbed. The month he completed construction of the house he began work on the manuscript for *Dirty Work*.

When the *Mississippi Review* published "Facing the Music" in the spring of 1987, Shannon Ravenel, senior editor at Algonquin Books of Chapel Hill, read the story and was surprised not to recognize the author's name because, she recalled, "the story was so good, so accomplished, so sure-footed, I figured it had to be by some established writer" (quoted in Cash, "Apprenticeship," p. 123). At Algonquin in the late 1980s, Ravenel was assembling an impressive list of authors, publishing first works and helping launch the careers of such talented southern writers as Clyde Edgerton, Kaye Gibbons, and Jill McCorkle. When she contacted Brown in the spring of 1987 about the possibility of publishing a collection of his short fiction she asked him if he had enough stories for a book. Brown recalled to the *Washington Post* interviewer Judith Weinraub that he wrote back to Ravenel, "I've got a hundred. How many do you want to see?" ("Apprenticeship," p. 124). After reading the stories he sent her, Ravenel wrote back with an offer for a book deal and closed by saying, "I would love to be your editor and have the pleasure of watching over your work for as long as that seems useful to you" ("Apprenticeship," p. 125). Algonquin published *Facing the Music* the following year and would publish all but one of the other nine books Brown would write.

The door of opportunity finally had opened for Brown. His novel *Dirty Work* appeared the following year, with a promotional tour that culminated in an interview with Jane Pauley on the *Today Show*. One of the stories from *Facing the Music,* "Kubuku Rides (This Is It)," about an alcoholic housewife, was chosen by Margaret Atwood for inclusion in *Best American Short Stories 1989*. On the basis of these early achievements, he was invited as a featured speaker to the Chattanooga Conference on Southern Literature. In his essay "Chattanooga Nights," Brown recalls that "the conference was the first well-paying gig I ever had, and the money they were giving me was a lot more than a whole month's salary at the fire department" (*Billy Ray's Farm,* p. 30). Even more important, though, was the prospect of "hang[ing] around some other writers for three days. I would have gone for nothing just to have been able to do that." Ultimately, the talk in Chattanooga represented a rite of passage for him, a moment to acknowledge to himself his arrival: "It had been almost nine years since I'd decided I wanted to write.... I'd come to know that the writer had to just keep on writing, ignore the rejections, and work toward the day when the work would be good. I felt like I'd finally reached that day" (p. 30). In January 1990, shortly after the Chattanooga conference, Brown retired from his position at the fire department to write full time. Until his death fourteen years later, he would maintain his strict work ethic, producing a body of award-winning work, lecturing and leading workshops at Bread Loaf and other prestigious writers conferences, and teaching creative writing in residencies across the country, including a semester at the University of Mississippi. In 2000 the filmmaker Gary Hawkins' documentary *The Rough South of Larry Brown* was released, followed in 2001 by the director-actor Arliss Howard's film *Big Bad Love,* an adaptation of several of the stories in Brown's second collection of the same name published in 1990. Remembering his own frustrations during his apprenticeship years, Brown went out of his way to offer guidance and support to aspiring writers and was well known in the Oxford area for his generosity of spirit and genuine humility. He was nearing completion of the manuscript for his sixth novel, *A Miracle of Catfish* (2007), when

he suffered a sudden heart attack and died on November 24, 2004, at age fifty-three.

MAJOR THEMES

In the two collections of short fiction and five novels Brown published in his lifetime and the posthumously published *A Miracle of Catfish,* Brown evokes a dystopian landscape populated by down-and-out drifters, religious fanatics, worn-out farmers, good old boys and girls, long-suffering wives and mothers, and tough-as-nails law officers. Alcohol flows freely in this world, and a good bit of marijuana is smoked as well. All of his stories and all but one of his novels—*Father and Son* (1996), set in 1968—have contemporary settings. With the exception of a few stories and *Dirty Work* (1989), which is set in a Veterans Administration hospital, and *The Rabbit Factory* (2003), set mostly in Memphis, they feature rural and small-town southern locales where most of the inhabitants seem to have missed out on the so-called Sunbelt era of economic progress in the region during the 1970s and 1980s. His protagonists are typically middle-aged men trying to contend with forces over which they have little to no control and turning to alcohol as an anodyne for the pain and frustration they face. (A heavy drinker himself, Brown seems to have avoided most of the personal problems his alcoholic characters experience.) Despite their limitations, they are endowed with a basic decency and sense of personal honor that affords them, if for some only temporarily, the means of avoiding the pull into the moral abysses that surround them.

In Brown's fictive world, danger lies lurking most anywhere, and violence is unleashed in the blink of an eye: an ill-spirited monkey leaps from ten feet away onto Glen Davis, the tortured antihero of *Father and Son,* deeply lacerating Glen's hand and arm before he pummels the monkey to death and leaves its lifeless, mangled body on a bar, its owner lying bleeding and nearly lifeless nearby; a friendly stranger who has taken in a homeless seventeen-year-old, the eponymous heroine of *Fay* (2000), drives her to an isolated stretch of beach, suddenly pulls a sharpshooter's rifle out of his trunk and shoots down a single-engine aircraft to exact revenge on the pilot, who had raped Fay the week before; a backsliding faith healer in "A Roadside Resurrection" (1991) is left to be torn apart by a monstrous hairy-tailed idiot man-child when his parents, hoping for a miracle cure, lead the fallen preacher into the cellar where they have kept their son locked up his entire adult life. Harry Crews and Cormac McCarthy are two writers whose work Brown has cited as inspirations for his excavations of humankind's propensity to violence. In an essay paying tribute to Crews, he recalls the shock of surprise and delight he experienced when, at about the time he started writing, a friend gave him a copy of Crews's *A Feast of Snakes* (1976), about a washed-up former high school football star who goes on a shooting rampage during his small town's annual rattle-snake roundup festival: "I remember how that book moved me, shook me, riveted me. I'd never read anything like it and didn't know such things could be done in a book.... It was an unearthly combination of hilarity and stark reality and beauty and sadness, and I could only shake my head over the power of imagination that created it" ("Harry Crews: Mentor and Friend," p. 3). A decade later, when Crews wrote a laudatory review in 1990 of *Big Bad Love* for the *Los Angeles Times Book Review,* the two corre-sponded and began a friendship. Brown paid homage to the support and inspiration he received from his mentor by dedicating *Fay* to him, writ-ing, "For my uncle in all ways but blood: Harry Crews."

Acknowledging the brutality and utter de-pravity of many of Brown's characters, the novel-ist and essayist Rick Bass expresses concern that readers may seize on these details at the expense of overlooking the deep concern with morality that pervades Brown's fiction: "[His] novels are novels of manners, of deeply moral values, works in which every action has profound consequence and in which every description is either laced—if not fraught—with beauty or laments the absence thereof" ("Tribute to Larry Brown," in Cash and Perry, eds., p. vii). In "A Late Start," Brown echoes Bass's concern, expressing his "strong

belief in the resiliency of the human spirit" and observing that "as a writer, it bothers me to be accused of brutality, of cruelty, of hardheartedness, of a lack of compassion." Noting "a certain uneasy feeling" his work has evoked in some reviewers, he speculates,

> I wonder if this is because I make them look a little too deeply into my characters' lives. Maybe I make them know more than they want to about the poor, or the unfortunate, or the alcoholic. But a sensible writer writes what he or she knows best, and draws on the material that's closest, and the lives that are observed. I try to write as close as I can to the heart of the matter. I write out of experience and imagination, toward blind faith and hope.
>
> ("A Late Start," p. 240)

Linked to this theme of redemption is the recurring theme of human connection, through blood ties (the importance of family is underscored repeatedly throughout his corpus), marriage, or, quite frequently, surrogate fraternal and paternal relationships. Whether in its negative form, as in "Facing the Music," where the narrator's dread of physical contact with his emotionally needy wife belies the achingly deep love he still feels for her, or in its more positive forms, as in *Joe,* when the womanizing alcoholic ex-con protagonist Joe Ransom becomes the unlikely father figure to Gary Jones, a teenager from a family so backward and poor that he doesn't even know how to use a toothbrush, Brown casts the need for relationships, however flawed by miscommunication and misaligned expectations or haunted by crimes of the past, as a fundamental need.

Brown's fiction is also marked by a keen attention to how gender is constructed and how shifting definitions of masculinity and femininity impede intimacy and personal happiness. Nevertheless, although the testosterone level runs high, Brown's concerns with gender run deep. As the writer Darlin' Neal observes in her essay "*Facing the Music*: What's Wrong with All Those Happy Endings": "In piercing [the] macho armor, he does not represent female otherness as a threat to be conquered along the way to story resolve, nor do male characters sweep women aside as objects obstructing the path toward male honor" (Cash

and Perry, eds., p. 3). Although some of his novels do seem at first glance to contradict Neal's assertion (which is restricted simply to the stories in *Facing the Music*), Brown uses these tropes to deconstruct mythologies of patriarchal power. For instance, in *Father and Son,* Jewel Coleman is romantically involved with the novel's two primary characters, Sheriff Bobby Blanchard and his outlaw half-brother Glen Davis, with whom she had had a son before Glen was sent to prison for vehicular homicide. As Thomas Aervold Bjerre points out in his essay "The White Trash Cowboys of *Father and Son,*" although Brown creates the expectation of a High Noon resolution of the conflict with Jewel as the prize, he grants Mary Blanchard, Bobby's mother, and Jewel more agency in the matter than is ultimately given to Bobby and Glen, thus undermining the masculinist conventions of personal honor that seem to structure the novel (Cash and Perry, eds., pp. 69–70). In this novel, as in most of Brown's others, female subjectivity offers a rational counterbalance to the contested masculinity of his male protagonists.

Brown's work also shows a strong concern for the impact of economic and technological change on the southern rural landscape and the people who inhabit it. In *On Fire* (1994) he expresses his disgust over the degradation of the southern hardwood forests and their replacement by the monoculture of commercial pines, noting, "Faulkner was right. He said the land would accomplish its own revenge on the people. I just wish it hadn't happened in my time" (p. 64). The rural landscape undergoes rapid change, as in one memorable scene in *Fay,* when the young runaway persuades her lover to drive her hundreds of miles back to the shack in the woods she ran away from only months before. When they finally arrive at the site the shack is gone: "It was only by looking at a big cedar tree that had stood at the rear of the house that she knew she was in the right place. But there was nothing left of the house, only a chewed patch of ground, a few shattered stumps" (p. 355). As Brown makes clear here, "progress" too often comes at the expense of losing one's connection to the

past, and even a painful past is better than none at all.

Compared to an earlier era of southern literature, when race was the overriding concern of writers from the region, Brown's work reflects a broader trend in which this theme has diminished in importance. This is not to say that he bypasses the subject but rather that he expresses optimism about the lessening of racial tensions a generation after the fall of Jim Crow. Brown came of age amidst the passing of segregation, and even though the Browns were still living in Memphis in 1962, when James Meredith's admission to the University of Mississippi sparked one of the most violent clashes of the civil rights movement, he certainly would have been keenly aware that this battle was raging in the place they still regarded as home. Given the manner in which his fiction characterizes a past filled with racial violence and abject discrimination, as in Braiden Chaney's traumatic memories of his Mississippi childhood in *Dirty Work,* one can safely assume that, like the vast majority of white Mississippians today, Brown came to regard the social and political changes in the wake of segregation as an improvement, even if he may have held little sympathy for the protesters during the 1960s, as his circumspection on such an important historical moment in his own backyard probably suggests. White racial privilege persists in Brown's fiction, as in the rest of the United States, but Brown was more concerned with how an array of color-blind social forces create and maintain an underclass of forgotten others.

SHORT FICTION

Brown honed his terse, hard-edged style by working primarily in the short story form, a genre in which directness and compression of meaning are at a premium. Although he would turn early in his publishing career from writing stories to writing novels and nonfiction exclusively, his two collections of short fiction, *Facing the Music* (1988) and *Big Bad Love* (1990), contain some of his finest work. He published only a handful of stories after these collections, most notably "A Roadside Resurrection," which appeared in the

Paris Review in 1991. Owing in large part to Algonquin's savvy marketing of *Facing the Music,* which capitalized on Brown's colorful biography, most critics seemed more in awe of his firefighting job and his connection to Faulkner through geographical coincidence than of his writing prowess. As Keith Ronald Perry details in his essay "'Building' Larry Brown(s) at Algonquin Books of Chapel Hill," one reviewer writing for the *Orlando Sentinel* barely mentioned the stories, dwelling on Brown's other job instead, though he did note that "Fireman Brown has made himself into a very good short story writer. In fact, if his first book … were itself a fire, it would require five alarms. The stories are that strong" (Cash and Perry, eds., p. 134). Another reviewer, this one from the *Cleveland Plain Dealer,* offered backhanded praise to Brown for "hurl[ing] himself into his writing with all the eager recklessness of a rookie battling his first apartment house blaze. Readers may come away from *Facing the Music* feeling a little scorched themselves" (Cash and Perry, eds., p. 134). Many of these same reviewers referenced Oxford and its more famous literary resident. However, a few dismissed comparisons to Faulkner as ultimately irrelevant to the matter at hand, if not injurious to Brown. Writing for the *Winston-Salem Journal,* Betty Leighton asked, "Why not allow Larry Brown to be Larry Brown, not a contender thrust into the ring with one of the heavyweights in American literature?" (Cash and Perry, eds., p. 135). Positive reviews that focused on the fiction itself appeared in the *Village Voice,* the *Antioch Review,* and *Publishers Weekly,* among others.

Of the eleven stories in *Facing the Music,* the title story, along with "Boy and Dog," and "Kubuku Rides (This Is It)," drew the most praise and stand out as most worthy of critical attention. "Kubuku Rides," the story Atwood selected to include in the *Best American Short Stories 1989,* is about an African American housewife, ironically named Angel, who is a far cry from the Victorian feminine ideal of the angel in the house. An alcoholic who is failing miserably at taking control of her problem, she makes ineffectual attempts to hide her drinking from her husband and children. Oddly, Brown chose to have the

story narrated in third person in African American dialect, but focalized through Angel's point of view, resulting in a curiously effective mode of storytelling, as if she is standing outside of herself and watching the actions of a stranger who inhabits her body. In an interview with Dorie LaRue, Brown explained that Kubuku, not Angel, is the narrator, and that Kubuku is a sort of spirit presence rather than an actual character (Watson, ed., *Conversations,* p. 51). When Angel's husband comes home expecting dinner and notices she is drunk she tries to deny it: "'This just my first one,' she say, but she lying. She done had five and ain't even took nothing out the deep freeze" (p. 12). Trapped in her loneliness and contemplating suicide, she "worries all day about drinking, then in the evening she done worried so much about *not* drinking she starts *in* drinking. She in one of them vicious circles" (p. 12). But the circle is spiraling out of control as, at the end of the story, she appears to have burned the last bridge connecting her to the relative safety of her marriage and home.

Brown presents another marriage in serious danger of running aground in "Facing the Music," whose considerable narrative power derives as much from the flat, affectless voice of the unnamed narrator as it does from the painful situation in which he and his wife are trapped. When he recalls a callous comment he made to her in order to rebuff her sexual advances, he thinks, "I don't know why I have to be so mean to her, like it's her fault. She asks me if I want some more ice. I'm drinking whiskey. She knows it helps me. I'm not so much of a bastard that I don't know she loves me" (p. 2). Sexual tension pervades the room as he drinks in bed and watches the late-night TV broadcast of Billy Wilder's 1945 film *The Lost Weekend* while his sexually neglected wife bustles about for attention. Feeling his masculinity threatened because of his inability to perform sexually for her as a result of his revulsion over her disfigurement from the mastectomy, he distances himself from the immediate situation by identifying with the doomed heroism of Don Birnam, Ray Milland's character in the film, an alcoholic writer whose sole remaining possessions are his

typewriter and a briefcase containing the manuscript of his unfinished novel. In a subtle shift of tone on the last page of the story, as his wife completes her preparations for bed and starts turning out the lights, the narrator's self-pitying identification with Birnam's struggles ironically gives way to his identification with Birnam's acceptance of responsibility: "Ray is typing with two fingers somewhere, just the title and his name. I can hear the pecking of his keys. The old boy, he's trying to do what he knows he should. He has responsibilities to people who love him and need him, he can't let them down. But he's scared to death. He doesn't know where to start" (p. 9). The story ends on an obliquely positive note. Fondly recalling the way his wife gave herself to him completely when they made love on their honeymoon twenty-two years earlier, he admits, "Nothing's changed." In the darkness they "reach to find each other in the darkness like people who are blind" (p. 9).

In a very different vein, "Boy and Dog," which had been Brown's first published piece of serious fiction, is remarkable for its eccentric form and its powerful minimalism. Written in stanzaic form, each line a sentence containing five words, it is told in deadpan style from the point of view of an eight-year-old boy whose impulsive act of revenge against the driver who ran over his dog initiates a calamitous chain of errors whose initial comedic power is unaffected—perhaps accentuated—by the fatal consequences of the act. When the Mustang driver's car circles back, leaning his head out the window to find the hubcap that came off when he hit the dog, the boy throws a brick, hitting him in the head and knocking him unconscious. The car careens into a tree and is quickly consumed in flames as the helpless youngster stares in disbelief. When a passing driver tries to pull the man from the burning car, his hand becomes bonded to the red hot door handle and he too catches fire before he can wrench his hand away from the door. Brown writes,

The kid watched all this.
The hero flailed the grass.
Somebody needed to get help.
But of course nobody did.

Some people won't get involved.
The car was fully involved.

(p. 65)

When a fire truck finally arrives, a panicked novice firefighter neglects to lock the brakes, causing the truck to roll backward into a ditch when the hose pump is turned on. By the time they can muster the wherewithal to grab some fire extinguishers, a news crew has arrived and set up its cameras, filming the firefighters as they empty their extinguishers to no apparent effect on the fire. While the story lacks the depth of characterization that typifies much of Brown's work, its slapstick comedy and ironic point of view are held in tension with the horrific events that unfold, underscoring the story's theme of the sudden unpredictability of death.

Although the publication of *Big Bad Love* was met with less enthusiastic acclaim than his previous work, it still received generally positive reviews. Many noted a growing degree of pessimism in this new volume of stories while others looked beyond the bleakness to praise the manner in which he unveils his characters' emotional needs. One such reviewer, Clancy Sigal, writing for the *Washington Post Book World*, observed that, "in a sense, Brown is the beneficiary of an uneasy feeling among critics and editors that attenuating middle-class angst, the keynote of so much recent fiction, is simply not enough. Larry Brown, poet of the southern white underclass, was there when we needed him" (Cash, "Saving Them from Their Lives," in Cash and Perry, eds., p. 36). In what he regarded as a signal moment in his career, Brown was overjoyed to learn that his hero Harry Crews had written a highly positive review of the book. Praising the stories as "all rather like some perfect object one has come across in the wilderness like a perfectly shaped stone," he ended the review by expressing the hope that Brown's career would be "prolific," adding, "My hope that he will write a lot is entirely selfish, because whatever he writes, I will read" (p. 37).

The stories in *Big Bad Love* are arranged in three parts: part 1 comprises eight stories of similar brevity; part 2 is composed of a single longer story, "Discipline"; and part 3 is a novella

over sixty pages in length titled "92 Days." With the exception of "Discipline," they all are set in the same area of Mississippi where Brown lived. A common theme running through these stories is frustrated love and unfulfilling sex. In the title story, the narrator seems to be more upset about the death of his hunting dog than the dissolution of his marriage. In "Wild Thing," a philandering good old boy looking for excitement outside of his marriage finds himself in a self-destructive relationship with a younger woman whose husband may be preparing to kill him, although he seems to get little emotional sustenance from the illicit relationship other than the thrill of danger. "Waiting for the Ladies" depicts yet another bored and frustrated married man who experiences a kind of emotional reawakening when he learns that an exhibitionist has flashed his wife at the local dump. Armed and obsessed with thoughts of revenge, he tracks the culprit to his home after a high-speed auto chase, only to break down and tell the man and his mother about his woes. "Discipline" stands out from the realism of the other stories in the book and must have provided considerable amusement for Brown when he wrote it. Its farcical plot involves a writer seeking early parole from prison, where he apparently has been sent for plagiarism. But when he is asked to read to the parole board from his most recent work in order to demonstrate his rehabilitation, the writing is so obviously derivative of Faulkner that he is shouted down. Like "Discipline," the novella "92 Days" is highly self-reflexive in its focus on writing matters, though it is much more autobiographical in nature than any other work in the collection. The narrator, Leon Barlow, has lost his marriage and is on the verge of losing his sanity because of his monomaniacal, but so far unsuccessful, drive to become a published writer. The last straw that threatens to take him over the edge occurs near the beginning of the story when he receives a rejection notice for a novel. In the letter the editor praises his work extensively for its literary merit before adding that, unfortunately, few readers are interested in "novels about drunk pulpwood haulers and rednecks and deer hunting" (p. 143). The letter sets off an especially ugly bout

of despair, yet by the end of the story Barlow remains unswayed, vowing, "I knew I had to keep going on. I had chosen my own path. Nothing could turn me from it" (p. 193).

NOVELS

Brown's first published novel, *Dirty Work* (1989), was received even more favorably than *Facing the Music* had been the year before. In a review in the *New York Times,* Rick Bass described the novel as "unforgettable" ("In the Hospital"). Reminiscent of Dalton Trumbo's antiwar novel *Johnny Got His Gun* (1939), Braiden Chaney, an African American Vietnam veteran, lost all of his limbs in combat and has languished in a Memphis Veterans Administration hospital for over two decades until Walter James, a white man who hails from Chaney's home state of Mississippi, is placed in the bed next to him. A wound he had received in Vietnam left Walter's face disfigured and he now awaits treatment for the seizures that have been growing in frequency and severity over the years.

The book alternates between the two men's points of view, and Braiden's sections are especially dazzling in their inventiveness, often involving long fantasies in which he escapes into his imaginary worlds, hunting lions in Africa, eating his mother's biscuits in his childhood home, conversing with Jesus. In one such scene, a startlingly human Jesus appears at Braiden's bedside, commiserates with him about the wickedness of the world, bums a cigarette off of Braiden and asks him if he would like one too: "He got His going and got me one going and then sat there holding it for me while I smoked. You could tell He had a lot on His mind" (pp. 92–93). What Braiden wants Jesus cannot give him, but Jesus implies that Walter may be the savior Braiden has been looking for. Much of the novel involves Braiden's efforts to forge a bond with Walter so that he will perform the mercy killing that Braiden prays will come soon.

In their conversations the two men find they have a shared background of poverty in rural Mississippi that ameliorates the racial tensions that hamper their initial efforts at friendship. But it is their common experience of physical disfigurement and psychological trauma from combat that ultimately creates the bond between the two. Verbie Lovorn Prevost argues in "Larry Brown's *Dirty Work*: A Study of Man's Responsibility for Suffering" that most of the book's reviewers have been so taken with its antiwar theme that they have overlooked the fact that "the effects of the Vietnam War merely serve as a scaffolding for the real concern/issue of the novel, the larger question, which is: What is the nature of suffering in the world?" (p. 22). Gradually, perhaps through Braiden's subtle machinations, their conversations narrow down to essentially theological arguments about grace, redemption, and moral responsibility, in particular how they can possibly take responsibility for their own moral conditions given their ruined physical conditions. By the end of the novel, each has come to a resolution about how he must act in a flawed world.

Brown's second novel, *Joe* (1991), winner of the 1992 Southern Book Critics Circle award for Fiction, is considered by many his best work. An anonymous reviewer in *Publishers Weekly* announced that Brown "comes into his own as a writer" and praised him for "never condescend-[ing] to his uneducated, gambling-addicted, casually promiscuous characters" (July 19, 1991, p. 46). While most would question Rick Bass's assertion in his tribute piece written after Brown's death that *Joe* deserves to be regarded as "one of a small handful of great American novels" (Cash and Perry, eds., p. xiv), it does offer a memorable portrait of a blue-collar Everyman whose fumbling attempts to contend with the impersonal economic forces that thrust disruptive social and ecological change on rural America achieve an iconic status. Demonstrating an increased confidence in his storytelling abilities, Brown expands his scope to a parallel plot involving Joe Ransom, a hard-drinking middle-aged divorcé who has spent a couple of years in jail and now works as a foreman for a deforestation crew, and the family of the malevolent Wade Jones, poor whites who have drifted into the area. When Wade's teenage son Gary wanders into an area where Joe's crew is working, he asks for a job and is

hired, then befriended by Joe, setting in motion a surrogate father-and-son relationship that serves as the primary action of the novel.

Gary has grown up in a familial environment in which the notion of personal honor is utterly foreign and unfamiliar. Gary's father, the despicable Wade Jones, descends from a long line of sociopathic outcasts that extends at least as far back as Twain's Pap Finn, although it is abundantly clear that the family line has degenerated since Pap's time. Having dragged his family throughout the South for migrant labor work, he has brought them to the squalid cabin in the woods they now occupy. Willing to do anything for beer money, including selling an infant daughter to a couple, pimping another daughter, and murdering a wino for pocket change, he regularly beats his wife and children. By juxtaposing the Jones family's abject poverty and depravity against Joe's lower-middle-class sensibilities and standard of living, Brown creates a more nuanced socioeconomic depiction of the Rough South than readers are accustomed to finding.

Brown foregrounds the relationship between Joe and Gary against a backdrop of environmental destruction driven by rapacious corporate greed. In order to clear property of less profitable timber so a single species of commercial timber can be planted for a giant pulp wood and paper corporation, Joe's crew injects poison into the healthy trees, which will die and fall over in a few years, replacing a relatively ecologically diverse forest with a monoculture that provides an inferior habitat for the other species that inhabit the area. The effect of the herbicide is almost instantaneous: "Joe raised his head and looked far down the tract to the dying trees they'd injected three days before. It was as if a blight had grown across the emerald tops of the forest and was trying to catch up to where they stood" (p. 22). In his essay "Economics of the Cracker Landscape: Poverty as an Environmental Issue in Larry Brown's *Joe*," Jay Watson argues that the novel highlights the inseparability of economic forces and destruction of natural areas, an aspect of environmentalism that is especially pertinent to the southeastern United States, where population

density is much greater than in other heavily wooded areas of the country (Cash and Perry, eds., p. 49).

While Brown clearly wants us to view Joe's form of labor in a negative light, there are plenty of other problems in his life that ultimately take a greater toll on him. Despite his essential goodness, Joe's attempts at redeeming his life prove unsuccessful by the end of the novel. Corresponding with Joe's gradually downward spiral, Gary apparently manages to escape the life of abject poverty and the malignant influence of his biological father, which would not have been possible without Joe's intervention and guidance. Thus, Gary's reclaimed life represents a partial victory for Joe, who cannot reimagine his own personal choices beyond the honor-bound constructions of working-class white southern masculinity that constrain him.

Brown's third novel, *Father and Son* (1996), earned the author his second Southern Book Critics Circle Award and pleased most reviewers. One anonymous reviewer for *Publishers Weekly* described it as Brown's "most wise, humane, and haunting work to date" (June 24, 1996, p. 44). Referring to it as the "work of a writer absolutely confident of his own voice," Anthony Quinn, writing for the *New York Times,* expressed particular admiration for the apparent timelessness of the story, asserting, "What adds even more intensity to the novel's mythic resonance is its almost complete exclusion of contemporary history. One would hardly know it is set in the 60's" ("Summer of Hate"). Inspired by an actual incident that took place in Lafayette County before Brown was born, it traces a five-day sequence of events centering around Glen Davis, who is fresh out of prison and looking to settle some old scores. His father, Virgil, a broken-down alcoholic war veteran who has grown close to Glen's son, David, and David's mother, Jewel, in the three years since Glen's imprisonment, has hopes of re-creating the model family by reuniting Glen and David, but Glen makes clear that Virgil's mistreatment of his recently deceased mother has obliterated any chance of such domestic peace. Sheriff Bobby Blanchard is the novel's protagonist, providing the moral compass

throughout the story, though Brown gives equal time to Glen. During Glen's absence, Bobby and Jewel developed a romantic relationship that is now on hold as Jewel, who has matured considerably in the last three years, sorts out her feelings.

More than a few critics have commented on the somewhat formulaic plot structure, which clearly evokes the classic lawman/outlaw westerns of film and middlebrow literature. Acknowledging this motif, Thomas Aervold Bjerre argues that Brown subverts the conventions of the western in order to expose the damaging nature of what are primarily southern codes of masculine honor, something Brown accomplishes by granting more agency to the female characters than to the males. As readers will discover, perhaps even more integral to the novel's concerns is the question of paternity. Bobby's mother, Mary, has never married and has never divulged to Bobby the identity of the man who got her pregnant. Jewel has grown up from the thrill-seeking girl who was once attracted to Glen and is now interested in finding a suitable father for David. Meanwhile, Virgil longs for a second chance at the role he cast aside in his younger days.

Concerns about family ties inform Brown's fourth novel, *Fay* (2000), as well. A sequel of sorts to *Joe* (Fay is the seventeen-year-old sister of Gary Jones), this is Brown's last novel to receive overwhelmingly positive reviews. An anonymous reviewer in *Publishers Weekly* expressed some impatience with the initially slow-moving plot but concluded by calling the book "a triumph of realism and humane imagination" (January 10, 2000, p. 43). In *Kirkus Reviews* another anonymous reviewer called it "close to a masterpiece" and declared, "The search for love and family has seldom been portrayed with such harsh realism as in this almost literally stunning fourth novel" (January 15, 2000). Brown begins the novel at exactly the same point of action where we last see Fay in *Joe,* as she is slipping away in the night to run away from her abusive father, though now the point of view is focalized through her eyes as she picks her way along the unlighted gravel road in search of refuge. On her journey she meets a few decent people—most notably state trooper Sam Harris—and a lot of bad ones. Although she is clearly a decent person, she attracts serious, sometimes fatal, trouble to those who take her in.

Fay seems completely innocent and naive as she begins her journey, but her instinct for survival is strong as well, and these two opposing facets of her personality give her character a degree of moral complexity that Brown chooses to leave unexplored. Robert Beuka, in his essay "Hard Traveling: *Fay*'s Deep South Landscape of Violence," notes the ambiguous "extent of Fay's complicity" in the deaths and other damage she leaves in her wake: "Is she a young innocent at the mercy of the men she encounters, or does she craftily use her sexuality to advance beyond her dirt-poor background?" (Cash and Perry, eds., p. 79). The only answer Brown gives to that question is a one-page epilogue, set in the New Orleans French Quarter in an undisclosed time—whether the same summer or years later, we have no way of knowing. When Fay approaches the entrance to a strip club, the barker calls her by name as she enters.

Although Brown sustained his pace of productivity after the publication of *Fay,* his last two novels, *The Rabbit Factory* (2003) and the posthumously published *A Miracle of Catfish* (2007), reflect a turning away from the relatively conventional, unified plot structures that typified his previous novels in favor of a more ambitious, fragmented form. Some reviewers expressed frustration with what seemed a haphazard, poorly organized structure in *The Rabbit Factory,* but this may well have been as much a result of Brown's departure from a mode of storytelling they had come to expect from him. In *"The Rabbit Factory:* Escaping the Isolation of the Cage," Richard Gaughran quotes several examples of this negative critical response, such as Jeff Kunerth's assertion in the *Detroit Free-Press* that, "In essence, the book is six short stories chopped into pieces and sewn back together in alternating order" (Cash and Perry, eds., p. 99). David Finkle made a similar assessment in the *New York Times,* calling the book "essentially a series of short stories peopled by loosely connected characters," though he expressed no displeasure with the book (p. 99). Opposing this view in his essay, Gaugh-

ran maintains that the book's "structure is anything but accidental" (p. 99). However, critics of the book's apparently disjointed structure may be unpersuaded by Gaughran's argument that Brown means to use his characters' obliviousness to their accidental interconnections in order to "celebrate[ ] the basic human desire for connection" while simultaneously "acknowledg[ing] the profound obstacles that can make such connections, love utmost among them, difficult to achieve" (p. 100).

Although the plot structure of *A Miracle of Catfish* is less fragmented than that of *The Rabbit Factory,* it also features a loosely assembled cast of characters, all tied in some way to Cortez Sharp, whose personal quest to create the perfect catfish pond results in the presence there of Ursula, the titular miraculous fish. Most of the action is limited to the area contained in Brown's hand-drawn map of Sharp's property and the adjoining tracts of land in the rural neighborhood, and this visual representation underscores the considerable attention Brown gives in the novel to the land itself and to the labor and leisure that connect most of the characters to it. Nine-year-old Jimmy, who longs for attention from his ne'er-do-well father, lives in a run-down trailer on a property adjacent to Sharp's, and the boy's search for connection with the absent father provides another familiar plot thread.

One problem reviewers faced in assessing this work is summed up neatly in the book's subtitle: "A Novel in Progress." How much would Brown have trimmed down the 455-page novel had he lived to complete the manuscript? Did Ravenel take out any important material when she removed 33,000 words from the original manuscript? Most importantly, given the absence of a conclusion, how would he have ended it? Beverly Lowry, writing for the *New York Times,* expressed more bemusement than frustration over the missing conclusion, observing that "while a book without an ending is a little like a joke without a punchline, in this case I expect we should be glad for what we have." Given this significant shortcoming, along with the numerous bracketed ellipses indicating Ravenel's excisions and the novel's meandering,

at times apparently aimless, forward momentum, this book is likely to be of interest primarily to scholars of his work and serious fans of his early writings.

NONFICTION

Brown's two books of nonfiction, *On Fire* (1994) and *Billy Ray's Farm: Essays from a Place Called Tula* (2001), never received as much acclaim as his fiction. However, while these books are of primary interest to readers of Brown's fiction who wish for insights into the nature of his art, they also stand on their own as well-wrought meditations on the meaning of work, both manual and intellectual. Ironically, readers may gain more appreciation of Brown's fiction through his meditations on firefighting (*On Fire*) and farm work and building (*Billy Ray's Farm*) than through the sections of the book that address writing directly.

Published after Brown had established his reputation for gritty, hard-nosed realism in two books of stories and two novels, *On Fire* was met with some disappointment for its failure to deliver the same kind of punch many readers had come to expect. As summarized by Robert G. Barrier in his essay "Home and the Open Road: The Nonfiction of Larry Brown," one reviewer for the *Village Voice* complained that it lacked the hard-edged, masculine power of his fiction and asserted that "sentimentality has replaced the hell-bent smoke-eater swagger. So do something for [Brown]: buy a smoke alarm but not this idiot-savant schtick" (Cash and Perry, eds., p. 88). Others, such as a reviewer for the *Hartford Courant* who observed that it "has the feel of an overdone pamphlet" (p. 88), complained about the book's brevity and apparent lack of substance. However, the novelist Madison Smartt Bell, writing for the *New York Times,* offered a more positive reaction, writing, "At first glance it seems to be a grab bag of nearly random observations and anecdotes, but on closer inspection it turns into a work of great thematic integrity that reveals itself as much between the lines as in them" (p. 88). Echoing and elaborating on Bell's reaction, Barrier argues in his essay that both *On Fire* and

Billy Ray's Farm reflect Brown's long-standing "empathy for working-class Southerners" but also "his overall appreciation of craftsmanship, of studied, hard-won expertise" (p. 87).

When Brown begins *On Fire* by describing his great affection for the tools he uses in his work and the comfort he takes from knowing he can depend on them in order to do the job right, he offers a glimpse into the aesthetic importance he places on structural integrity as well. "You have to believe in the bowline," he declares, "before you can believe you can rappel" (p. 1). In a similar vein, as he describes the necessity of detachment in emergency rescue work, we come to understand his ability as a novelist to look at suffering without averting his gaze and to describe it without sentimentality. "You cannot think about a person's pain and do your most efficient job," he explains. "If your feelings about his feelings are weighing on your mind more than how best to remove the crumpled car door from around his body, you're not doing him any good" (p. 47).

Brown devotes as much attention in *On Fire* to the easy camaraderie between the men during their leisure time and between calls at the fire hall as he does to the dangerous work itself. The bonds of affection he describes are the kind one hears in the accounts of combat veterans. At the end of the book, as he turns from this line of work to assume his full-time work as a writer, he declares, "I have left all that now forever, even though in my heart I am still one of them" (p. 182). While the powers of observation required of a writer necessitate a degree of detachment and objectivity, Brown makes clear that he still identifies with the working-class folks he has known and worked with most of his life, and this quality is perhaps the most distinctive and appealing aspect of his fiction.

Comprising mostly previously published essays, *Billy Ray's Farm* lacks the coherence and thematic unity of *On Fire*. But it too speaks in metaphorical terms about Brown's artistic insistence on the well-wrought thing while also making a convincing case for the ingenuity and resourcefulness required of the ordinary farmer. The title is taken from an essay about the cattle enterprise his oldest son began in 4-H during his high school years and the dream Billy Ray has of operating an actual working farm. In reading Brown's description in that essay of a nightmarish situation in which he had to save single-handedly one of Billy Ray's cows that had fallen and become trapped during a difficult delivery of a calf, we learn that raising cattle can require almost the same degree of ingenuity and patience as fire rescue work. In another essay, "Shack," Brown draws implicit and explicit comparisons to *Walden* as he takes a Thoreauvian approach to the design and construction of a small house he situated on his property next to his catfish pond for a work space. As Barrier notes, ironically, Brown died just after completing all but the electrical wiring for the cabin (Cash and Perry, eds., p. 97).

CONCLUSION

Brown's work has been praised with good justification for the manner in which he lifted the blue-collar white southerner from the level of stereotype to the fully realized, three-dimensional literary character whose struggles and passions are shown to be not so different from anyone else's, and for this he will rightly be remembered. The most self-evident reason he was able to achieve that is because he wrote about a world he knew intimately. Paradoxically, he could never have achieved that level of empathy without his remarkable capacity for brutal honesty.

Selected Bibliography

WORKS OF LARRY BROWN

NOVELS

Dirty Work. Chapel Hill, N.C.: Algonquin, 1989.

Joe. Chapel Hill, N.C.: Algonquin, 1991.

Father and Son. Chapel Hill, N.C.: Algonquin, 1996.

Fay. Chapel Hill, N.C.: Algonquin, 2000.

The Rabbit Factory. New York: Free Press/Simon & Schuster, 2003.

A Miracle of Catfish: A Novel in Progress. Chapel Hill, N.C.: Algonquin, 2007.

SHORT FICTION

Facing the Music. Chapel Hill, N.C.: Algonquin, 1988.

Big Bad Love. Chapel Hill, N.C.: Algonquin, 1990.

NONFICTION

A Late Start. (Eight-page pamphlet.) Chapel Hill: Algonquin, 1989. Reprinted in his *Dirty Work,* Chapel Hill, N.C.: Algonquin, 2007.

On Fire. Chapel Hill, N.C.:Algonquin, 1994.

"A Tribute to William Faulkner." In *Faulkner at 100: Retrospect and Prospect.* Edited by Donald M. Kartiganer and Ann J. Abadie. Jackson: University Press of Mississippi, 2000. Pp. 267–271.

Billy Ray's Farm: Essays from a Place Called Tula. Chapel Hill, N.C.: Algonquin, 2001.

"Harry Crews: Mentor and Friend" in Bledsoe, Erik, *Perspectives on Harry Crews,* University of Mississippi, 2001.

CRITICAL AND BIOGRAPHICAL STUDIES

Brown's papers, including original manuscripts, galleys, and promotional materials relating to his work, are collected at the University of Mississippi's J.D. Williams Library, Department of Archives and Special Collections. Early drafts of *Joe* are housed in the University of North Carolina-Chapel Hill's Southern Historical Collection at the Louis Round Wilson Special Collections Library.

Applebome, Peter. "Larry Brown's Long and Rough Road to Becoming a Writer." *New York Times,* March 5, 1990. Available online (http://www.nytimes.com/1990/03/05/books/larry-brown-s-long-and-rough-road-to-becoming-a-writer.html?pagewanted=all).

Bass, Rick. "In the Hospital, Waiting for a Savior." *New York Times,* October 1, 1989. Available online (http://www.nytimes.com/1989/10/01/books/in-the-hospital-waiting-for-a-savior.html?pagewanted=1). (Review of *Dirty Work.*)

Brooks, Cleanth. *An Affair of Honor: Larry Brown's Joe: An Essay.* Chapel Hill, N.C.: Algonquin, 1991.

Byrd, William. "The Secret History of the Line." In his *Histories of the Dividing Line Betwixt Virginia and North Carolina.* New York: Dover, 1967.

Cash, Jean W. "Larry Brown's Literary Apprenticeship: 1980–1988." *Studies in American Culture* 30, no. 1: 95–128 (October 2007).

Cash, Jean W., and Keith Ronald Perry, eds. *Larry Brown and the Blue-Collar South.* Jackson: University Press of Mississippi, 2008.

Farmer, Joy A. "The Sound and the Fury of Larry Brown's 'Waiting for the Ladies.'" *Studies in Short Fiction* 29, no. 3: 315–322 (1992).

Hannah, Barry. "Larry Brown: Passion to Brilliance." In *A Miracle of Catfish: A Novel in Progress.* Chapel Hill, N.C.: Algonquin, 2007. Pp. vii–xi.

Jones, Suzanne W. "Refighting Old Wars: Race Relations and Masculine Conventions in Fiction by Larry Brown and Madison Smartt Bell." In *The Southern State of Mind.* Edited by Jan Nordby Gretlund. Columbia: University of South Carolina Press, 1999. Pp. 107–120.

Lowry, Beverly. "The One That Got Away." *New York Times,* April 29, 2007. Available online (http://www.nytimes.com/2007/04/29/books/review/Lowry.t.html?pagewanted=print). (Review of *A Miracle of Cat-fish.*)

Lyons, Paul. "Larry Brown's *Joe* and the Uses and Abuses of the 'Region' Concept." *Studies in American Fiction* 25, no. 1: 101–124 (1997).

Prevost, Verbie Lovorn. "Larry Brown's *Dirty Work*: A Study of Man's Responsibility for Suffering." *Tennessee Philological Bulletin: Proceedings from the Annual Meeting of the Tennessee Philological Association* 30: 21–27 (1993).

Quinn, Anthony. "The Summer of Hate." *New York Times,* September 22, 1996. Available online (http://www.nytimes.com/1996/09/22/books/the-summer-of-hate.html?pagewanted=1). (Review of *Father and Son.*)

Staunton, John A. "Shadowing Grace in the Post-Southern South: 'A Roadside Resurrection' and Larry Brown's Narratives of Witness." *Religion & Literature* 33, no. 1: 43–74 (2001).

Wyatt, Edward. "Larry Brown, Author of Spare, Dark Stories, Dies at 53." *New York Times,* November 26, 2004. Available online (http://www.nytimes.com/2004/11/26/books/26brown.html?ex=1259211600&en=6c93d3b854c37cd3&ei=5090&partner=rssuserland). (Obituary.)

INTERVIEWS

Manley, Michael S. "Telling Stories: An Interview with Larry Brown." In *Delicious Imaginations: Conversations with Contemporary Writers.* Edited by Sarah Griffiths and Kevin J. Kehrwald. West Lafayette, Ind.: Notabell Books, 1998. Pp. 117–128.

Watson, Jay, ed. *Conversations with Larry Brown.* Jackson: University Press of Mississippi, 2007.

FILMS BASED ON THE WORKS OF LARRY BROWN

The Rough South of Larry Brown. Directed and written by Gary Hawkins. Blue Moon Film Productions and Down Home Entertainment, 2002.

Big Bad Love. Directed by Arliss Howard. Big Bad Love LLC, Pieface Productions, Rocking S, and Sun Moon & Stars Productions, 2001.

BILLY COLLINS

(1941—)

Angela Garcia

As DESIGNATED POET of the everyman and master at delivering his often dry and witty pieces, William J. (Billy) Collins has presented the American public with immensely popular poetry and gained critical acclaim in the process. The comic element is rare in contemporary, self-serious verse, and Collins' poetry has offered an antidote: a dry, acerbic, understated Irish wit as an intrinsic part of his poetry's whole. These lyric poems often rely on humor—what many consider hilarious takes on ordinary situations, or simply absurdist scenarios rooted in daily life—as their foundation.

The best examples of his work typically intrigue and seduce the reader from the introductory lines by presenting the regular domestic routine—coffee cup or morning stroll—as an open door. Gradually, even as the poem takes quasi-logical steps toward its shift into a deeper truth, it awakens a sense of the absurd in the reader. Poetic themes throughout his career have leaned toward the classic mysteries of the passage of time and death—again, usually crystallized from a moment of ordinary experience. These are conveyed through the poet's sometimes searching, sometimes mocking, but always plain-spoken style. Collins' poetry has drawn comparisons to Robert Frost's for its seemingly simple yet artful appeal.

This refusal to be deliberately obscure in his work, and his sarcastic wit targeting those who practice this opaqueness, is indeed part of what makes Collins' persona so popular. It is no accident that his friend Bill Murray, a comedian who specializes in similar deadpan delivery, introduces his compact disc *Billy Collins Live: A Performance at the Peter Norton Symphony Space April 20, 2005.*

Undoubtedly Collins' greatest achievement is bringing people to poetry, notably as eleventh poet laureate of the United States from 2001 to 2003. Through this work, creating what he has termed a "poetry jukebox" for schools, Collins has introduced the pleasures of poetry to tens of thousands of readers and listeners who had previously shied away from the typical high school curriculum of difficult pieces—whether Shakespearean or metaphysical, Romantic or modernist—attached to, and sometimes dependent upon, lengthy interpretation.

Collins' own career is a reminder of how readers or listeners can slow down and truly enjoy the moment through a poem; as George Carlin noted, the mind is never so open to new ideas as in the moment when you make a person laugh. In this respect Collins, both as an exceptionally popular, even record-breaking poet and as a comedy performer, has revived an interest in the art of poetry overall and shattered the walls enclosing an admittedly elite market.

Instead, by demystifying poetry and making it accessible to a wide readership, Collins has placed himself in a pantheon of popular poets such as Henry Wadsworth Longfellow, Edgar Allen Poe, and the Canadian poet Robert Service. The difference is that these poets worked within a strong traditional meter, and the poems spread in popularity in part because their rhythms and rhymes were so memorable, through the poems' mnemonics. Listeners as young as four years old once memorized excerpts from *The Song of Hiawatha,* or "The Raven," and recited the verses. Critics have also compared Collins to Ogden Nash because they both relish the nonsensical, although Nash used traditional forms.

Yet while he delivers his work with admirable pitch, timing, and finesse, Collins' poetry employs a more conversational cadence, a feature typical of contemporary verse in English for decades.

Sound is important, but sense—the substance of the meditation or observation, its imagery and metaphor—is placed in the foreground. While some of his poems do take on a whimsical academic bent, the point of view seems that of a passerby/hobbyist rather than professor: a poem might explore anything from a turn of phrase to a tidbit of information such as the number of sheep's hides needed to produce a bound work of vellum. Religious commonplaces about angels or the dead are turned, examined, and viewed with different angles to the light. Any verbal ephemera may serve as springboard to musings on mutability or mortality.

But the runaway commercial success of Collins' books of poems may have played a part in fueling critical skepticism. Beginning around 2001, some critics began to express disappointment with the pedestrian, monotonous quality they found Collins' poems. They argue that, like many contemporary pieces, the observational, wit-laced Collins poem is funny when read but does not lend itself to the multiple interpretations afforded by the poems Collins holds up as influences—among them, Coleridge's conversational poems such as "This Lime-Tree Bower My Prison." And so a handful of academics, usually in journal articles, have publicly cast their doubts upon the question of whether the poems—in spite of their commercial success—will endure. Some have also questioned whether the poet's style has effectively changed or developed through two decades and eight core collections.

Collins, thus, has deflated the idea of literary permanence by, in typical self-deprecating style, devaluing his own status as a poet and naming influences—poetry prodigies such as Emily Dickinson—whose poems make him infuriate him with their skill. At the same time, using the same example, he derides the idea of poetic development, in essence defending his work against the claim that the poems continue to rely on the same poetic formula. "Development is overrated," he said in a 2008 interview with James Mustich. "Dickinson never developed."

Instead, Collins vows to rely on the same formula while varying the topics in his work. Although a professor himself, he seems to enjoy

parrying with establishment critics—maddening them with his commercial success while deflecting their blows. Earning the average reader's or listener's critical acclaim seems the foremost priority for the poet.

Collins, who arguably claims the title of premier poetic satirist, in turn has parodied the academic-poetic world by riffing on literary-academic events from workshopping a poem to introducing a poem at a reading. These spoofs have been widely recognized and warmly received, at least to readers familiar with that enclosed universe. Throughout his career, he has parodied traditional verse forms as well as trained his powers of ironic observation upon human tendencies such as self-consolation, forgetfulness, and nostalgia.

BIOGRAPHY

Collins is an only child, born on March 22, 1941, in New York City, to William S. and Katherine Collins, both of whom were thirty-nine at his birth; his parents doted on him as he attended schools in Jackson Heights, Queens. The poet has repeatedly named his parents as powerful literary influences and has dedicated several collections to them or to their memories. His mother, a nurse, memorized and recited poetry prodigiously, and he has often cited Mother Goose as his (and everyone's) first major influence. From his father, an electrician, Collins inherited his sense of humor.

When Collins was a teenager, his father became an insurance broker and moved the family to Westchester County. His father was the family joker, master of the formal joke, the zinger, and the practical joke—even in his Wall Street office. So his father had jokes to suit every moment, while his mother was able to provide a few lines of poetry for every occasion. This dual influence definitively shaped, and continues to shape, his style. Collins' humor, in particular, ranges from whimsical to ironic to wickedly mocking.

Collins enjoyed his parents' attention, and they in turn encouraged his creative bent. He has

recalled perusing the encyclopedia at age five to impress house guests, and at seven or so writing his first observational poem about a sailboat he had sighted as he rode in the family car. As he grew older his father reportedly brought back issues of *Poetry* from his office for the boy to study (Collins).

Collins was enrolled in Catholic schools throughout his childhood. In high school, influences inside the classroom featured such antique pieces as Longfellow's *Hiawatha.* However, outside the classroom was another story. Collins discovered Beat writers and poets such as Lawrence Ferlinghetti and his collection *Coney Island of the Mind,* encountering subjects and styles he had not known existed. (These experiences spurred him, as poet laureate, to bring contemporary poetry to today's high schoolers.)

These iconoclastic voices appealed to the young Billy Collins and drew him to try his hand at finding his own voice, shaping his own craft. Eventually he joined the staff of his High School literary magazine (Collins), where he wrote pieces decrying capitalism and the social order. Like all young people, he was vulnerable to teachers' remarks and could remain wounded by them. Collins has remarked in interviews that approval never affected him as much as criticism did. The criticisms of a few teachers who (he admits, probably rightfully) dismissed his teenage verse stayed with him the longest and goaded him to succeed in spite of their dismissal of his work.

In 1963 the poet graduated from College of the Holy Cross, a Jesuit institution in Worcester, Massachusetts, with a B.A. in English. Collins went on to earn a master's degree in English (1965) and a Ph.D. in romantic poetry from the University of California–Riverside (1971), always writing poems on the side. In the 1970s Collins' poems began to appear in *Rolling Stone,* drawing comparisons to Richard Brautigan's terse, sardonic, and sometimes irreverent style. Like many of his generation, Collins continued to call on the Beat poets—Allen Ginsberg, Gregory Corso, Ferlinghetti—as well as Jack Kerouac's *On the Road* as influences.

In 1969 Collins began teaching literature and composition as an assistant professor of English at Lehman College of the City University of New York. In 1975 he cofounded the *Mid Atlantic Review.* Two early works published by small presses in 1977 and 1980, *Video Poems* and *Pokerface,* already signaled his signature wit, absurdist humor, and casual diction.

However, Collins began to earn serious literary notice beginning with his collection *The Apple That Astonished Paris* in 1988, published when he was forty-seven. He had sent poems to an editor at University of Arkansas Press, Miller Williams, who selected several of his poems as representative of the type of high quality poetry he would publish. Williams suggested to Collins that when he wrote more poems on the level of those few, he would have his book. After *The Apple That Astonished Paris,* seven collections and two compact discs followed, which would enjoy wide popular and commercial success.

The poet has done much to engage readers through his readings and recordings. As a gifted comedian and tireless reader of his own poems on the poetry circuit, Collins has attracted enthusiasm and delight among all ages in presenting and engaging listeners through his hilarious and enlightening scenarios. National Public Radio appearances, in interviews on *Fresh Air* and especially as a reader on Garrison Keillor's *Prairie Home Companion,* proved pivotal in attracting nationwide attention and enthusiastic reviews. Collins' doggedly unpretentious style proved a good match for Keillor's down-home variety show programming, and his numerous appearances over the years have included special programs such as New Year's Eve. On college campuses and in other venues, the poet has routinely attracted several hundred or even a few thousand listeners to a poetry reading, a highly unusual turnout for what is generally a rarefied event. (Many fans, national and international, agree that "live" is the best way to appreciate Billy Collins and to savor his poetry.)

In 1999, two years before Collins was named poet laureate, his publishing house, University of Pittsburgh Press, underwent a highly publicized tug-of-war with Random House over rights to

several poems. Collins' soaring book sales and critical accolades had spurred a much-hyped six-figure advance (actually rumored to be a million-dollar advance) on a three-book deal for Random House; this deal, unheard of for a book of poetry, provoked no small amount of interest, awe, and envy that reverberated through the publishing world and took the poetry world by storm. Ultimately several of the poet's collections, including *Questions About Angels* (1988), *The Art of Drowning* (1995), and *Picnic, Lightning* (1998) would sell more than fifty thousand copies each—a phenomenal figure in the poetry market. *Sailing Alone Around the Room: New and Selected Poems* (2001)—which includes pieces from four books from 1988 to 1998 as well as twenty new poems—would sell more than 160,000 copies in the next decade.

Although the irony and light touch in his poems obviously contributed much to his growing popular appeal, his work was also recognized for its underlying seriousness of purpose and its grace, its tact. Thus Collins definitively entered the radar of the American poetry world when he was named poet laureate of the United States in 2001, following Stanley Kunitz. (Collins was reelected to a second term in 2002). Using this post, the poet worked determinedly to expand poetic readership. As laureate he launched and promoted the Poetry 180 Web site, designed to bring one accessible poem per day to a high school audience. Each poem, selected by Collins for its accessibility, would be read aloud, allowing it simply to be heard and to wash over students. This way the poetry could be absorbed and experienced without being explicated, analyzed, or assigned as part of the curriculum by a literature teacher, for example, perhaps fishing for a particular interpretation.

As laureate, he also composed and presented a poem in memory of the victims of the September 11 World Trade Center attacks, "The Names." He was invited to read the poem to a special Joint Session of Congress in September 2002. He published a children's book, *Daddy's Little Boy,* in 2004. Collins also served as poet laureate of New York State from 2005 to 2007.

Besides his poetry readings, Collins conducted poetry workshops for several summers in Ireland, regularly working at universities and summer schools from Galway to the Poets' House in Donegal; in summer 2008 he worked with the John Hewitt Summer School in Armagh. The poet has read for many enthusiastic Irish audiences there as well, and has read with the Nobel laureate Seamus Heaney.

Collins has won numerous honors. He has received fellowships from the Guggenheim Foundation, the National Endowment of the Arts, and the New York Foundation for the Arts. Other awards include the Bess Hokin Award, the Oscar Blumenthal Award, the Frederick Bock Prize, and the Levinson Prize sponsored by *Poetry* magazine. His early collection *Questions About Angels* was a selection for the National Poetry Series. In 1992 Collins was named a "Literary Lion" of the New York Public Library.

He is the editor of two anthologies, *Poetry 180: A Turning Back to Poetry* (2003) and *180 More: Extraordinary Poems for Every Day* (2005), books connected to the Poetry 180 teacher-friendly Web site he launched as poet laureate of the United States, the latter receiving the stronger reviews. His essay "Poetry, Pleasure, and the Hedonist Reader" was included in *The Eye of the Poet: Six Views of the Art and Craft of Poetry* (2002). Finally, Collins was guest editor of *The Best American Poetry 2006.*

For forty years he has taught creative writing, literature, and composition courses to students at Lehman College, City University of New York, in the Bronx, where he was named Distinguished Professor of English in 2001. He was a visiting writer at Sarah Lawrence College. He was also appointed the Irving Bacheller Chair of Creative Writing at Rollins College in Winter Park, Florida; the poet has been named a visiting scholar with the Winter Park Institute. Collins lives with his wife, Diane, an architect, in Somers, Westchester County, New York; they were married in 1979.

AUDIENCE AND INTRODUCTIONS

Collins prizes his relationship with his audience. Most of his book collections begin with an

introductory poem addressed explicitly to the reader—an invitation, essentially, to engage in conversation with the speaker—but never more flippantly than in "A Portrait of the Reader with a Bowl of Cereal" (*Picnic, Lightning*). Here he deliberately subverts any formality established by modernist poets such as W. B. Yeats (quoted in the epigraph as refusing to speak to the reader directly in poems "as to someone at the breakfast table"[p. 3]). In doing so Collins seeks to demystify the poetic process and product both: he provides an assurance that the reader need not fear difficulty or obscurity and instead offers the promise of a clear and accessible contemporary poem.

Collins has called his reaching out to readers a type of lasso, and he certainly ropes them in—but gently. *Nine Horses* (2002) opens with "Night Letter to the Reader," and *The Trouble with Poetry and Other Poems* (2005) likewise begins with "You, Reader." Both establish the domestic setting—in the former, the imagery of goldfish, salt and pepper shakers, a bowl of pears; in the latter, the lawn, the speaker in pajamas, the dog.

And so the informal tone is irrevocably and rebelliously set for the work—and the works to come, for few other settings can be less ceremonious, more informal and even, finally, more intimate than sitting down in one's pajamas or bathrobe to eat cereal with another human being before either is quite awake—a scene usually reserved for a parent, sibling, roommate, lover, spouse, and their silences. The poet essentially shouts out his break with Yeatsian tradition and, like poets from William Carlos Williams to the Beats, expresses his preference for the informal diction and meter that most contemporary poets favor. Delighting in shifts of logic, the speaker claims his tablemate (the reader, or *you*) is invisible and yet, when he has something to say, sees that "you will look up, as always, / your spoon dripping milk, ready to listen" (*Picnic, Lightning*, p. 4).

In interviews and readings alike, Collins has repeatedly emphasized the movement of his poem as going from simple and everyday observation and shifting gradually, by the end of the poem, to transcendence: "down the rabbit hole." The writer has referred to this as typical progress for all poetry—its antithesis being a poem that begins obscurely so that the reader must enter a no-man's-land with no bearings or signposts. That Collins deliberately begins with an ordinary moment and ends the poem with a sort of transcendence or mystery is key to his individual poetics. The conversational quality of his work has occasionally been debated, but he has defended himself against accusations of his poetry as cut up prose.

STYLE AND INFLUENCE: THE WORD AS WELLSPRING

Billy Collins has admitted that he did write opaquely for a period, in attempts to emulate modernist poets. He was a "Wallace Stevens acolyte" but gradually experienced a shift in his poetry writing from tangles of imitative obscurity, where even he didn't know what he was trying to say, to lucidity. His anthology *The New Poetry* would serve as a revelation for the young Billy Collins.

Still, the writer has pronounced Samuel Taylor Coleridge his biggest influence, from his dreamlike and mysterious visions to what Collins calls his conversation poems. "This Lime-Tree Bower My Prison," which observes the dappled leaves and conveys nature's power to soothe and comfort (framed in a conversation or letter to his absent friend Charles) ends by passionately proclaiming: "No sound is dissonant which tells of Life."

For Collins, the true inspiration for any poet is other poems, which goad the artist toward creating greater art. Indeed, the written word stands out as prime catalyst for much of Collins' work, beginning with his roots in reading within poems such as "Books" (*The Apple That Astonished Paris*). Ending with an evocation of "Hansel and Gretel," the poem is a meditation on fairy tales and the mother reading to child as a path to a magical world. Collins has repeatedly cited Mother Goose as our true first influence.

"First Reader" (*Questions About Angels*) looks at the early Dick and Jane books of school

but resists easy derision of these texts. Instead, the poem rues what is lost when one learns to read, focusing diligently on the fine print. The speaker conveys that in succumbing to the world of systematized literacy, we ourselves are lost to an academic system, perhaps losing our preliterate, primordial individuality and ways of looking and being: "Alphabetical ourselves in the rows of classroom desks, / we were forgetting how to look, learning how to read" (p. 21).

Stylistically then, in many Collins poems, the speaker's device—in order to create a theme—is to use a word, phrase, or in this case a quotation as springboard or inspiration. Several poems grasp at a dictionary word, encyclopedic tidbit or the like and, from this strand, weave a narrative from it: an entire scenario of often exaggerated, surreal extremes conceptualized simply in order to see where the poem takes the speaker. Others play with the language and concoct variations for amusing results. The best of these poems, such as "The Lanyard" (*The Trouble with Poetry*), emerge as an autonomous whole from this verbal launching pad, essentially freeing themselves through a completeness of lyric or narrative imagination.

The poems differ in their openings, and though some do appear similar in formula, they offer a variety of styles. Some seem to take on the surrealist Latin American tone of Pablo Neruda's odes through their wild, speculative imaginings, their twists and dark irrational turns. Still others evoke a plainspoken Zen style. Collins has often stated the influence of these poets. He connects the haiku to the celebration of the minutiae that he aspires to in his work. Indeed, he directly devotes a poem to celebrating the muted grace, simplicity, and mnemonic quality of haiku with "Japan." The wondrousness of this particular haiku to the speaker is evident in his mouthing and whispering and thinking it, in its compact perfection: the mystery inherent in the expression of a moth lightly resting on a heavy iron temple bell. As he repeats line openings, the poem continues to mesmerize. Finally, the speaker becomes or inhabits the different elements in the poem. After a subtle shift the poem ends erotically (rare in a Collins poem), as if to

culminate all these different versions of saying, of self-meditation and religious chanting:

When I say it at the window,
the bell is the world
and I am the moth resting there.

When I say it into the mirror,
I am the heavy bell
and the moth is life with its papery wings.

And later, when I say it to you in the dark,
you are the bell,
and I am the tongue of the bell, ringing you,

and the moth has flown
from its line
and moves like a hinge in the air above our bed.

(*Picnic, Lightning*, p. 52)

The final line may be a bit of a visual puzzle, but nonetheless the poem retains its power, melding aesthetic, spiritual, and sexual realms.

Included among the new poems in *Sailing Alone Around the Room* is one with the apt and metacognitive title "Reading an Anthology of Chinese Poems of the Sung Dynasty, I Pause to Admire the Length and Clarity of Their Titles." Collins admires how the ancient Chinese poets use titles to let the reader know the bearings of the poem, and often these titles patiently lay out the details of the poet's setting.

On the other hand, poems such as "Litany" (*Nine Horses*), though playful and whimsical, may rely too heavy-handedly on the featured epigraph, as if Collins were carrying out a self-assigned exercise for composing a poem. Simply put, the poem fails to transform the ideas of the epigraph into anything more substantial. Instead the speaker ironically riffs on the expression, cataloging what "you" are and what you are not, in a clever but thematically limited response. Ultimately, in this instance, the admittedly blazing wit or sarcasm—which rates highly in a reading—may not bring readers any closer to the kind of truth or enlightenment they may seek in a poem. Instead, the intended tribute to the beloved at the end of the poem—intimations of the sacred through images of bread and knife, the crystal goblet and wine—is undercut by the arch diction

and images intended merely for comic effect, weakening the seriousness of tone attempted in the concluding lines. It may be difficult for the reader to readjust the mood for a sudden shift to solemnity. This is a pattern repeated in other Collins poems, in which the air of mystery or universality inserted toward the end of the poem appears forced and difficult to salvage. The overall effect can be one of smugness or self-satisfaction.

However, the mild-mannered tone so prevalent in Collins' work continues to offer instant invitation (if not interpretation) as the poems that often introduce his collections stretch out a hand to invite the reader to take a dip in the pool, so to speak. The poem that opens even an early collection such as *The Apple That Astonished Paris* exemplifies this offer of trust.

HOW TO TREAT A POEM

Many Collins poems contain an ulterior motive: they work to deflate the popular aversion toward the opaque poem. His more popular meditations on poetry itself, and what it should not be, include "Introduction to Poetry" (*The Apple That Astonished Paris*) as well as the title poem from *The Trouble with Poetry*.

Although Collins has been employed for decades as a literature professor, he has spoken in interviews of the danger of the critical interpretation replacing the poem, mainly by confining the reading to a dissection of its meaning. Indeed, the poet views too much interpretation of what a poem "means" or is "trying to say"—sad terms he sees as overused by teachers and textbooks—as sheer, needless destruction of the poem itself. He has suggested that close reading offers alternative ways to experience a poem, or to teach others to experience it: readers might try examining the tonal shifts within the poem, for example, or, explore the space within the poem, as he recommends in "Introduction to Poetry."

Collins frequently ends his books with a poem about poetry itself. His collection *Ballistics* (2008) sends his book out into the world with

"Envoy," in which the poem is viewed as missive, spreading the word as part of a faith, a mission.

THE POET AS SATIRIST

Already in "The History Teacher" and "Nostalgia" (*Questions About Angels*, pp. 90, 104), Collins evinces his trademark wit, targeting on the one hand the dumbing down or whitewashing of texts for students and, on the other, the human tendency to look back at previous decades (here, historical periods) with seemingly lunatic, distorted sentimentality. "Remember the 1340s? ... Where has the summer of 1572 gone?" he announces to peals of laughter on his compact disc recording. Collins takes up this theme again in "Lines Composed Over Three Thousand Miles from Tintern Abbey" (*Picnic, Lightning*), where he mocks poets' attraction to this commonplace wistfulness, from Wordsworth and other Romantics to contemporary poets:

he could be moping through the shadows
of a dark Bavarian forest,
a wedge of cheese and a volume of fairy tales
tucked into his rucksack.

But the feeling is always the same.
It was better the first time.
This time is not nearly as good.
I'm not feeling as chipper as I did back then.

Something is always missing—
swans, a glint on the surface of a lake,
some minor but essential touch.
Or the quality of things has diminished.

The sky was a deeper, more dimensional blue,
clouds were more cathedral-like,
and water rushed over rock
with greater effervescence.

(p. 61)

This excerpt typifies some of the strengths and weaknesses of Collins' work. Again, he evokes a literary, in this case, poetic reference in placing himself as a writer so many thousands of miles away from Wordsworth's famous locale. And he deflates or diminishes Wordsworth's original

yearning by generalizing on these poets' Romantic sentimentality. Stylistically, the short abrupt lines ("But the feeling is always the same") add a comical veneer; however, the passive verbs and abstract thought processes of the speaker—along with the somewhat clichéd imagery—eventually weaken the feeling that the poem claims the reader eventually inherits himself through reading it: "Something will be missing.... Nothing will be as it was / a few hours ago, back in the glorious past / before our naps, back in that Golden Age" (pp. 62–63). The self-mockery rings a bit hollow, somewhat fatigued and diluted by the final lines.

The theme of memory, or rather its loss, reemerges in "Forgetfulness" (*Questions About Angels*). In it, Collins gently pokes fun at our dwindling faculties as we age. Evocative of Elizabeth Bishop's famous villanelle "One Art" ("The art of losing isn't hard to master ..."), Collins' poem begins as a quirky catalog of lost data in the brain ("the capital of Paraguay," p. 20) but maintains a poignant compassion, even affection, for human foibles that resounds in its more settled concluding lines: "No wonder the moon in the window seems to have drifted / out of a love poem that you used to know by heart" (p. 21). The overall tone is one of familiar and fond reassurance about our plunge into vagueness, this middle-aged eroding.

Questions About Angels also showcases Collins' mimicry of other poets, in this case taking on pared-down, goddess-like poems of self-victimization. In an extreme and masculine version reminiscent of Sylvia Plath's *Ariel* (though of course, in parody, it gives up any semblance of that poetic power), the speaker strips down, methodically removing flesh and organs. He describes this, absurdly, as a regular routine ("weekdays, particularly Wednesdays. / This is how I go about it: / ... I should mention that sometimes I leave my penis on," p. 41). Collins has been called a stand-up poet, and this would be an example of the line that gets a laugh. The juxtaposition of an extreme version of artistic purity and the conversational style makes the idea of such extreme self-purification as part of the writing process seem supremely foolish indeed.

"My Heart" (*The Art of Drowning*) mines a similar stylistic vein in its working of a conceit. In it, the poet elaborately conveys the metaphor of his own heart as religious relic, and, taking this terminology *ad extremum,* presents the reader with the picture of his heart as dead or numb, an object for autopsy or archaeology. Apparently the heart has been sacrificed, or sacrifices itself for someone or something. Collins cleverly works in his Irish heritage and birth year. So the influence of poets of the past cuts both ways in his work, at times as a subject for parody but more often as a stylistic influence.

Poems that do function brilliantly as sheer parody, blatant and often hilarious, are generally among the most popular, and most recited, of Collins' work. "Paradelle for Susan" (*Picnic, Lightning*) may be the prime example. Collins' coining of the word "paradelle" brazenly sweeps up the villanelle, the sonnet, and every other strict traditional verse form with complex rhymes and repetitions as targets for his learned wit. In painstaking imitation of poets in the traditional verse camp, Collins' convoluted footnoted explanation of his work agonizingly lays out all the rules of the "paradelle." The lengthy footnote perfectly captures and capitalizes on this dying trend: "Similarly, the final stanza must use *every* word from *all* the preceding stanzas and *only* those words." This is all that Collins' style ventures to counter.

The poem itself, which the reader gradually recognizes as a tortured mathematical puzzle, brilliantly satirizes traditional verse and is a masterpiece of forced endings, its lines tailing off with leftover words in order to squeeze itself into the purported form. Thus the speaker dutifully ends his verses in muted incoherent uproar: "Always nervous, I perched on your highest bird the." And finally, "Darken the mountain, time and find was my into it was with to to" (p. 64). The speaker's talent is for finding the most ridiculous sequence possible to the point of absurdity.

Similarly, one of Collins' longest pieces, "Victoria's Secret" (*Picnic, Lightning*) dryly

mimics the style and content of the Victoria's Secret lingerie catalog. The speaker meticulously describes the models' clothing in the catalog's detailed and sometimes ridiculous terminology ("my organza-trimmed / whisperweight camisole with / keyhole closure," p. 55). He also delineates facial expressions (usually pouts) and surmises reasons for their displeasure: "Perhaps her ice cream has tumbled / out of its cone onto the parquet floor. / Perhaps she has been waiting all day / for a new sofa to be delivered" (pp. 57–58). He puts words into the women's mouths. Clearly the speaker is intrigued by the figures he has graciously or playfully elevated to Correggio's voluptuous Renaissance models, but the tone slyly ducks any intimation of sexual seriousness, comfortable in the lighter mocking. As sometimes occurs with Collins' satires, the poem stumbles on its way to resolution when the speaker leaves the comfort zone of his riff on the catalog and forces a transcendence that does not quite arrive: "I ride to sleep, my closed eyes / still burning from all the glossy lights of day" (p. 58).

"Pinup" (*The Art of Drowning*) strives for a similar, though more titillating, effect—again, working within self-imposed guidelines of what is acceptable, maintaining a certain innocence, and always just this side of lasciviousness. With "Taking Off Emily Dickinson's Clothes" (*Picnic, Lightning*), the speaker bends these rules somewhat. Here the speaker seems to relish breaking a taboo associated with Dickinson's reputation for eccentricity, virginity, and white clothing as he takes on the traditional male role of the undresser or stripper of women, this time a desexualized and iconic literary giant. Although the subject does not resist, and merely "close[s] her eyes to the orchard," all of the liberties taken, the actions executed, are by the speaker:

and I proceeded like a polar explorer
through clips, clasps, and moorings,
catches, straps, and whalebone stays,
sailing toward the iceberg of her nakedness.

(p. 74)

Perhaps it is merely the feminists' turn to be goaded. In the same way that the speaker states "there were sudden dashes / whenever we spoke," the concluding lines devolve toward a parroting of Dickinson's most famous lines, rather cheaply—a "greatest hits" compilation not as original as the rest of Collins' poem, and wooden as a poetic denouement of the established narrative. What keeps the poem stubbornly in its place as a parody, or what some critics have deemed a "joke poem," also keeps it on the surface, without much depth or any reflection on Dickinson's work. At the same time, Collins has often stated how much he admires her work, and how much envy her poems inspire in him.

It is notable in a Collins poem when irony is absent; however, a marked seriousness of purpose underlies the seeming whimsy of other poems. Collins has stated that the closest thing to an elegy for his father that he has written is the paean "The Death of the Hat" (*Picnic, Lightning*). Rather than mocking nostalgia, the poem succumbs affectionately to it, saluting the era of the hat, when everyone wore one. This in turn leads the speaker to muse on the hat his father wore to the office every day and the hat he wears now, after a life of work: "a hat of earth, / and on top of that, / a lighter one of cloud and sky—a hat of wind" (p. 82).

SPIRIT, TRAVEL, ART, AND MUSIC

As much as death stands as a central theme of Collins' poetry, art—visual arts, music, and especially writing—emerge as metaphors (sometimes merging with ideas of death, time, or timelessness) in nearly all of Collins' work. They enable the speaker in the poems to see and notice his surroundings more deeply, and to be moved by them in the face of limited days and hours.

Questions About Angels balances a playful nonchalance and a genuine interest in answers as it asks some childlike theological questions about how angels pass the time, if they fly or swing, the fabric of their robes, how they sleep, and what they think. These are distilled into the image of an angel (or woman) dancing in front of a jazz combo, perhaps the speaker's idea of heaven. The love of jazz is a repeated motif throughout the books.

Picnic, Lightning offers another tongue-in-cheek spiritual exploration in "Shoveling Snow with Buddha." Its tone is not unlike the dry, comic take on an icon that characterizes "Taking Off Emily Dickinson's Clothes"—a tone that, in some sense, implies the taking down of an icon. While the Buddha poem echoes and caricatures Wallace Stevens' visions of enigmatic nothingness such as "The Snow Man," it also breaks into the reader's consciousness more rawly, taking the form of a casual conversation between the speaker and Buddha as they shovel snow on the driveway together. In fact, Collins depicts a one-sided conversation by the speaker until Buddha, like a small child speaking to a parent, breaks the silence to ask if they can play cards afterward—the god as subordinate. The hot chocolate and cards scenario they envision, the warmth after the cold and singular purpose of the Zen shoveling, presents its own bliss.

The pleasures of travel make their mark in *Nine Horses* with "Istanbul," a bathhouse experience, and "Paris," a longer lyric beginning in the domestic again, this time a foreign apartment, drifting to the ritual of newspaper and coffee and then visually anticipating a day to explore a foreign city, the museums, the cheese, the landscape, the river. In this imagining, filled with sumptuously rendered detail, Collins enjoys wondering about the bountiful future pleasure the day extends to him. *Nine Horses* also ricochets the reader from a decadent poolside atmosphere in Siracusa, Italy—where the speaker, drink in hand, playfully imitates a foreigner's English—to New Orleans, for a more metaphysical but nevertheless offhand take on the speaker's death.

Poems about painters and paintings figure prominently in Collins' work. In examining American and European paintings, the speaker places himself, sometimes explicitly, at museums, such as in "Musée des Beaux Arts Revisited" (*Picnic, Lightning*)—a takeoff on W. H. Auden's classic poem on the painting of Icarus' fall. Elsewhere, poems in *Questions About Angels* depict the speaker entering into paintings of Constable's clouds ("Student of Clouds") or imagining Victor Goya's life as a painter, meeting him at the door ("Candle Hat"). In *Nine Horses* he liberally refers to art in his themes; the book title itself refers to a painting given the speaker by his wife, on the occasion of his birthday; the horses' meditative expressions recall for the speaker a pagan godliness or iconic quality. Strangely for a title poem, it ends with a somewhat facile metaphor of the bridle and the cinch, dissolving, as many of the poems do, into a sudden mourning for time's constant passing, death's gentle chariot, in the final image.

In both "Trompe L'Oeil" and "Study in Orange and White," art enters life—in the first, through the aesthetically pleasing bunch of asparagus sitting in a bowl of water. Collins delves into the hedonistic pleasures of good food, likewise, in "Osso Bucco" (*The Art of Drowning*), which unabashedly celebrates the spectacularly rendered meal, the full stomach. In these poems the lyric is reminiscent of Robert Hass, another contemporary poet and former poet laureate, celebrating the sensuality of blackberries (the fruit and the word or sound sense) in "Meditation at Lagunitas" (*Praise*).

Several poems, especially in later collections, rhapsodize about the artistry of jazz, offhandedly naming the artist and song heard at the moment, for example, in "I Chop Some Parsley While Listening to Art Blakey's Version of 'Three Blind Mice'" (*Picnic, Lightning*). The speaker is moved to tears. In *The Art of Drowning*, "Nightclub" flips through clever variations of "beautiful" and "foolish" in song lyrics, an homage to the vocals of Johnny Hartman, and "Sunday Morning with the Sensational Nightingales" delves into the beauty of gospel music and glories in the positive, energetic "high" it imparts.

TIME AND BLESSING; "THE NAMES"

Although he returns again and again to what he has named the central theme of all poetry, death, Collins is also riveted by mutability, a theme supported by a kind of innocent and abstract love that finds unexpected beauty in the smallest things. Life's inevitable changes come to serve less as a topic for parody ("Nostalgia") and instead as an occasion for chastened wonder.

Nine Horses as a volume accelerates its mourning of the passing hours in the title poem as well as several other lyrics, among them images recalling and memorializing his parents. In "No Time," the speaker greets his parents, who have passed away, with a beeping horn as he drives past the cemetery. Consequently he imagines his father "rising up" (p. 101), an expression of stern admonition on his face, in response to his son's transgression upon the boundaries of appropriate behavior. The effect in reviving their lifelike gestures is gently humorous and affectionate.

"Velocity" mourns the invisible passages of time in imagining and drawing "speed lines" trailing behind us even as we are motionless, as we relentlessly move through the limited hours of our given lives—a difficult but original metaphor. Death combined with domestic themes, echoes of Emily Dickinson, is the motif called up in "Rooms," which examines and whimsically weighs the choices—study, kitchen, or dining room—for deciding which might serve best at life's end. The lyric ends with an image of a hidden nest of mice; as in the title poem "Nine Horses," we are presented with mutability as a kind of languid afterthought.

Consequently, the speaker seizes the day. In the aptly named "Aimless Love," the speaker falls for a wren, mouse, seamstress, chestnut, and finally the soap he uses to wash his hands—a kind of disinterested and yet affectionate verbal caress one finds in the odes of Pablo Neruda, who famously celebrated the tomato, the potato, and other mundane or everyday instances of beauty.

Similarly, in "Love," Collins again evokes the moment of being, this time on a train, illuminating a male face in awe at a young lady lifting a cello case onto an overhead rack. Whether he is brother or lover is not clear, only that his face bears an expression of almost religious devotion.

In a possible Catholic twist on this theme, the speaker imaginatively punishes himself for not stopping to smell the roses in "Roadside Flowers." Rather than roses, it is a bunch of wild phlox he has not lingered to sniff or admire, and as penance he carries around with him the entire day the weight of his regret. The speaker makes up for this sin by writing about the phlox in his notebook, effectively releasing the heavy burden. The poet suggests the act of writing as a type of absolution for an aesthetic violation, or sin of omission.

Although Collins' meditations on death are often leavened by his particular brand of dark whimsy, the gravest of national events naturally inspired an entirely different kind of lyric from the then poet laureate. The responsibility of composing a national poem in honor of a public event or ceremony has fallen more often on the shoulders of British poets laureate than those of the United States; however, Collins responded to the nationally traumatizing World Trade Center attack, a difficult task to encapsulate in poetry, with aplomb.

"The Names" immediately recalls another national and fiercely nationalistic poet who felt the duty of responding to a historical rebellion in his own nation: W. B. Yeats in "Easter 1916," his famous poem about the patriots who perished during the Easter Uprising at Dublin's General Post Office against English imperialism. Yeats names the patriots in his poem, and as he does so, he tells the reader he is naming them:

That is Heaven's part, our part
To murmur name upon name,
As a mother names her child
When sleep at last has come
On limbs that had run wild.
...
We know their dream; enough
To know they dreamed and are dead;
And what if excess of love
Bewildered them till they died?
I write it out in a verse—
MacDonagh and MacBride
And Connolly and Pearse
Now and in time to be,
Wherever green is worn,
Are changed, changed utterly.
A terrible beauty is born.

Collins, unlike Yeats, does not necessarily make martyrs out of the dead; the victims were not leaders of a citizen rebellion. However, he too

memorializes his compatriots by naming. Collins waxes less fierce and passionate, more grieving, as he depicts the names as imprinted permanently on nature. What is striking is the multicultural-ism represented in the names, from Medina, Ishikawa and Torres to Kelly and Lee. He names one last name for each letter of the alphabet save X, harking back again to the roots of writing in a moving piece of verse memorializing daughters and sons.

There is something holy in the secular-seeming diction of this uncharacteristically but necessarily grave poem. These poets, both Catholics, have lived and breathed an atmosphere of rites and holy sacraments that have for centuries included—even highlighted—naming, as integral as baptism and the rites of death. In fact, Collins served as an altar boy in the Latin mass and has cited the magic of language in the repetition of ancient Latin phrases, words he did not understand, as inspiring his career. The act of writing, like the Catholic mass, like the act of memorializing, honors the human need for ceremony, and this poem ritualizes the grieving for the September 11 victims. Like the poets who read at presidential inaugurations, as Robert Frost notably read at John F. Kennedy's ceremony and Elizabeth Alexander read at Barack Obama's, the poet laureate is honored to compose these weighted poems of ceremony as a rite of celebration, or in Collins' case, of death, remembering and thus beginning to heal a nation.

This elegy, fixed as it is on a national, political event, stands apart from the bulk of Collins' work, which famously homes in on small daily miracles, or sacraments of life—seeing the sacred in the seemingly trivial moment. However, in its implicit grief for the preciousness and beauty of life, as well as its brevity, it continues the thematic patterns of Collins' earlier lyrics.

THE TROUBLE WITH POETRY *AND* BALLISTICS

The risk of all career poets is to begin to parody themselves. Many critics have continued to review Collins' work favorably. However, beginning with his collection *Sailing Alone Around the Room* (2001) and continuing with the next two books, some critics began to grow disenchanted with the repetitious formula they saw in his domestically centered poems. These were readers who understood the in-jokes but instead wished to be challenged; they felt that the poet was playing it safe in his collusion, the wink and the smile from writer to reader, by not risking heavier subjects or by refusing to alter his traditional tercets and conversational style in order to retain popularity.

As early as the publication of *Nine Horses,* critics began to note the lack of tension in the poems and to object to their seeming lack of complexity. Perhaps one of the most vocal and daring critics was David Orr in the *New York Times Book Review,* writing on *The Trouble with Poetry,* who analyzed the poet's shortcomings in a parody of a Collins poem. As though considering Coleridge's dictum "No sound is dissonant which tells of Life," a growing circle of critics (joined subsequently by bloggers) have been squirming, calling for more tension, more complexity, more dissonance from their everyman poet.

"THE LANYARD"

Despite its mixed critical reception, *The Trouble with Poetry* produced a runaway hit with "The Lanyard," a much-acclaimed poem—both in spoken and written form—that has drawn more notice than the rest. Listeners were first drawn to the poem when Collins introduced it on a New Year's Eve broadcast of Garrison Keillor's *Prairie Home Companion* radio program. The poem has been admired and quoted ever since by readers who find it exceptionally moving, which begs the question, Why does this lyric seem to stand out, to be placed on a higher shelf than the others? It may be that structure, style, and content combine to make this poem, while witty, a weightier work than those poems that seem contained on the page by their inside jokes.

Like some other Collins works, the poem begins innocently with a word from the dictio-

nary, "lanyard"—in this case one of those little braided cords children make in arts and crafts class for Mom to wear around her neck. Out of this Collins weaves a poem that deals with a relationship that we all have a stake in: the mother-child relationship. With mounting absurdity, the speaker amusedly recounts, and then somewhat bemoans his childhood innocence, when, as a boy in camp, he fashioned this most useless and seemingly nonpoetic of ordinary objects.

Using an increasingly comic discrepancy as its paradigm, in the magnanimous gifts of the generous mother and the timeworn offering of the automatically receiving child, the poem creates a series of extreme and uproarious comparisons—recognizable for their truth. The poem achieves the transparency Collins aims for yet also a complexity and ambiguity. It also manages a certain transcendence by the end of the piece, when the speaker looks back at his boyhood self and, somewhat humbled, admits how wildly the lanyard fell short—and *he* fell short—in taking his mother's gifts for granted.

The poem climaxes with hyperbole and repetition:

> She gave me life and milk from her breasts,
> and I gave her a lanyard.
> She nursed me in many a sickroom,
> lifted teaspoons of medicine to my lips,
> set cold face-cloths on my forehead,
> and then led me out into the airy light
>
> and taught me to walk and swim,
> and I, in turn, presented her with a lanyard.
> Here are thousands of meals, she said,
> and here is clothing and a good education.
> And here is your lanyard, I replied,
> which I made with a little help from a counselor.
>
> Here is a breathing body and a beating heart,
> strong legs, bones and teeth,
> and two clear eyes to read the world, she whispered,
> and here, I said, is the lanyard I made at camp.

Collins ends the poem not with the ringing truth "that you can never repay your mother" but with an awakening from delusion:

> I was sure as a boy could be
> that this useless, worthless thing I wove
> out of boredom would be enough to make us even.

(pp. 45–46)

Overriding both mother's and son's voices is nobility of sentiment—the recognition that they would never be even—and this is no small part of the poem's attraction. As the mother nurtures with "milk from her breasts" and all the other fundamentals of life, the speaker mimics the simple innocence of the child and his entitlements in the face of all this.

In terms of poetics, Collins weaves the little boy's tiny object with the greater truth of the mother's sacrifice until it becomes a kind of chant. The mesmerizing alternation of "she" counterbalanced with "I" emphasize the huge and meager actions and provisions of the mother and son: "she gave me," "I gave her," "she nursed me," "I, in turn presented her." Repetition too—"here are," "here is," and the bizarre word "lanyard"—make up a great part of the appeal. The line "And here, I wish to say to her now, is a smaller gift" serves as a bridge that connects past to future, the boy with the man.

Just as with the nursery rhymes Collins cites as intrinsic to his love of poetry, sound as much as sense satisfies the reader of the poem, which is composed largely of iambs and dactyls. From the first lovely and evocative verb "ricocheting" to convey the puttering from one object or activity in the room to another, and its echo in "pale," poetic assonance provides echoes between words and their meanings: "strand" and "lanyard" and "past," "counselor" and "thousands of meals."

The chant, in its final lines, leads the reader to illumination. Redemption, while late and flawed, comes through the realization and late gratitude of the now grown-up son. Also, in a challenge to the reader, the speaker offers this confession (based on primary school logic) as a "smaller gift." It seems that this enlightened, truthful viewpoint is what makes the small, obviously pardonable child's mistake now an adult gift—its substance or importance held in higher esteem because of the spirit in which it was offered. In spite of its naiveté, or maybe because

63

of it, the child's gift proves weightier, and catchier.

So it is interesting that "The Lanyard," a nativity poem of sorts, has emerged as a much larger and more resonant boyhood poem, perhaps because it looks outside itself to the mother, in contrast to, for example, poems such as "On Turning Ten" from *The Art of Drowning* (marred in the first three of the four stanzas by an ultimately debilitating sarcasm—a confusing mixture of tone) or even "Boyhood," a model-train-in-the-basement, little-boy poem that seems more facile and self-centered in retrospect— perhaps fatally so. Still, readers recognize its magical quality.

Thus the poet who has diligently mocked sentimental nostalgia produces a tribute to his mother, albeit subversively, through its antithesis: the image of the everyday, ungrateful child. Following Emily Dickinson's advice, he tells the truth but tells it slant. And the sarcasm? It serves a greater good, in magnifying the crucial gifts of the archetypal mother, milk and all.

CAREER-LONG WHISPERS OF MORTALITY

The mystery of death comes into play throughout all of Collins' books, not merely frisking around the edges of poems as in *Questions About Angels* but starring in them. Sometimes mortality, and the uncertainty of its timetable, is faced head on, as when personified as the Grim Reaper who prowls the neighborhood and eventually comes to call on the speaker in "My Number" (*The Apple That Astonished Paris,* p. 54). Here Death is the protagonist, a Grinch-like but all-powerful and devious criminal. At the end, he is parked at the end of the speaker's road, at which point the speaker tries to avoid the inevitable. And so Collins speaks for his poetry, which—like all art—is trying to charm its way out of death or evade death, and by deceiving time, to gain the permanence of art explored within John Keats's "Ode on a Grecian Urn" or his sonnet "On First Looking Into Chapman's Homer."

In "The Dead" (*Questions About Angels*) the speaker responds to the storied dead looking over us, rowing in their boats and, in a slightly sinister turn, "wait[ing], like parents, for us to close our eyes" (p. 49). In "The Wires of the Night," the speaker struggles to conceptualize and absorb a beloved person's death and creates a numb, mechanized metaphor from it. He sees the death, in turn, as a room or hall, as a body with clothing, as a door, and as a car. Mainly he sees it as a house, but a house that is somehow uninhabitable, slippery to grasp. The speaker lies awake, in painful awareness of the hours to follow:

In the freakish pink and gray of dawn I took
his death to bed with me and his death was my bed
and in every corner of the room it hid from the light,

and then it was the light of day and the next day
and all the days to follow, and it moved into the
  future
like the sharp tip of a pen moving across an empty
  page.

(p. 73)

The title poem in *Picnic, Lightning* refers to Vladimir Nabokov's dismissal of Humbert's mother in his famous novel. Parenthetically and with admirable nonchalance, the author kills her off, his laissez-faire attitude initially echoed in Collins' tone but surmounted by a sincere wonderment, then meditation on the fearful suddenness of death; this poem sits apart from the purely whimsical takes on death, settling as it does on a particularly solemn viewpoint.

While beginning with a gloss on Nabokov's rare or oddball way of dying, the speaker catalogs others: meteors, safes falling from roofs onto the random pedestrian. He elaborates on the imagined picnic surprised by lightning: "the thermos toppling over, / spilling out on the grass" (p. 24). The lyric continues with a litany of possible deaths: irreversible damage to the organs—how the heart quits, a blood clot forms ("a tiny dark ship is unmoored / into the flow of the body's rivers") or the how the brain stands so vulnerable ("a monastery, / defenseless on the shore").

Finally, by depicting the speaker as immersed in perhaps the most mundane of gardening work, shoveling compost into a wheelbarrow and trying to beautify flower boxes with red impatiens (an

echo of the red blood and organs), the poem effectively juxtaposes the mundane and the metaphysical. But death always awaits on the sidelines. Suddenly, for the speaker, the simplest things in nature brighten and come into focus as never before: the earth is fantastical with its "bits of leaf like flakes off a fresco" (p. 25). Reminiscent of Virginia Woolf's moments of being, even the colors, the blues and whites, come alive and deepen his consciousness.

While the edge of the spade scrapes a rock, small plants begin "singing" and time continues to pass through the image of the sundial in the garden: "one hour sweeps into the next" (p. 24). Here the sense of the surreal gently intercedes, as these preternaturally enhanced visions stem from a musing on the terrible spinning wheel of death. The sundial, like the absent god in the poem, suggests stony indifference.

This is the dilemma that continues to plague Collins' poetry, the universal theme that remains insoluble and thus has driven so many poets' dark obsessions. Initially drawn by the freak accident so understated in the novel, its sketched lines hardly traceable, the poet takes a fleeting literary reference to its logical and frightening conclusion. And this chink in the sometimes too-witty armor allows for a greater richness in the poetry; indeed, the macabre takes on real resonance as embodied by the puttering speaker who dares to imagine the risk of real death. Readers too find themselves enveloped in the sharp edges of the garden.

In *Nine Horses,* Collins' style of wry observation amplifies the theme of death, which re-emerges with increasing regularity, for example, by way of the obituary page of the newspaper (the famous names suggesting the *New York Times*) in "Obituaries." Collins' droll twist turns on the strange incongruity of the deceased's careers in their seemingly random occurrences. The poem expresses sheer awe at the numbers who die daily, famous or not-so-famous who are spared life's continuous forward march. The tone shifts from sardonic to humbled.

The title poem of *Ballistics* (2008) begins with an offhand evocation of a photograph the speaker has witnessed that depicts a bullet entering a book—the title of which the speaker cannot ascertain and so humorously speculates is a book of poems. In his imagination the bullet pierces even the back flap of the title, penetrating the writing. With Collins' wry description of the photograph on the back flap, one can already hear the hundreds of varieties of laughter erupting from the audience as they empathize with human spitefulness. In Collins' poems, the spirit of revenge often provides for even greater panache than usual. But throughout *Ballistics,* several imagined deaths sound among the poems, some fanciful and detached, some with the fear palpable within their scenes. Readers, as they age, will continue to find solace in these lyrics influenced by one's own impending death.

The legacy Billy Collins leaves is one of unpretentiousness and wisdom, and not least of all a life's work dedicated to returning poetry to the people. While his work may continue to excite vehemence and debate, the poet has established a primal connection to the audience that is vital for poets and poetry to continue to nurture through the generations.

Selected Bibliography

WORKS OF BILLY COLLINS

POETRY

Pokerface. [s.l.]: Kenmore Press, 1977.

Video Poems, Long Beach, Calif.: Applezaba Press, 1980.

The Apple That Astonished Paris. Fayetteville: University of Arkansas Press, 1988.

Questions About Angels. New York: Qwill/William Morrow, 1991. Reprinted, Pittsburgh: University of Pittsburgh Press, 1999.

The Art of Drowning. Pittsburgh: University of Pittsburgh Press, 1995.

Picnic, Lightning. Pittsburgh: University of Pittsburgh Press, 1998.

Sailing Alone Around the Room: New and Selected Poems. New York: Random House, 2001.

"The Names." Available online (http://www.billy-collins.com/2005/06/the_names_billy.html). 2002.

Nine Horses. New York: Random House, 2002.

The Trouble with Poetry and Other Poems. New York: Random House, 2005.

Ballistics. New York: Random House, 2008.

COMPACT DISCS

Billy Collins Live: A Performance at the Peter Norton Symphony Space, April 20, 2005. Random House Audio, 2005.

The Best Cigarette, 1997. Reissued, Cielo Vivo/Small Good Press, 2005.

OTHER WORKS

"Poetry, Pleasure, and the Hedonist Reader." In *The Eye of the Poet: Six Views of the Art and Craft of Poetry.* Edited by David Citino. New York: Oxford University Press, 2002. Pp. 1–33.

Daddy's Little Boy. New York: HarperCollins, 2004. (Children's book.)

EDITED ANTHOLOGIES

Poetry 180: A Turning Back to Poetry. New York: Random House, 2003.

180 More: Extraordinary Poems for Every Day. New York: Random House, 2005.

The Best American Poetry, 2006. New York: Simon & Schuster, 2006.

Bright Wings: An Illustrated Anthology of Poems About Birds. New York: Columbia University Press, 2010.

CRITICAL AND BIOGRAPHICAL STUDIES

Alleva, Richard. "A Major Minor Poet: Billy Collins Isn't Just Funny." *Commonweal,* January 11, 2002, pp. 21–22.

"Collins, Billy." *Encyclopedia of World Biography.* 2nd ed. Vol. 28. Detroit: Gale, 2008. pp. 83-85.

Garbett, Ann D. "Billy Collins." In *Critical Survey of Poetry.* 2nd rev. ed. Edited by Philip K. Jason. Pasadena, Calif.: Salem Press, 2003.

Garner, Dwight. "Stand-Up Poet." *New York Times Book Review,* September 23, 2001. Available online (http://www.nytimes.com/2001/09/23/books/stand-up-poet.html?pagewanted=2).

Hilbert, Ernest. "Wages of Fame: The Case of Billy Collins." *Contemporary Poetry Review* (http://www.cprw.com/Hilbert/collins2.htm).

Orr, David. "Charming Billy." *New York Times,* January 8, 2006. Available online (http://www.nytimes.com/2006/01/08/books/review/08orr.html). (Review of *The Trouble with Poetry.*)

Riggott, Julie. "From Victoria's Secret to Emily Dickinson's clothes." *Pasadena Weekly,* April 20, 2006. Available online (http://www.pasadenaweekly.com/cms/story/detail/from_victorias_secret_to_emily_dickinsons_clothes/3339/).

Stonecipher, Donna. "Billy Collins Flatters Poetry Readers and They Flock to Him." *Seattle Post-Intelligencer,* January 9, 2004. Available online (http://www.seattlepi.com/books/155824_book09.html).

INTERVIEWS

"A Brisk Walk: An Interview with Billy Collins." *Guernica* (http://www.guernicamag.com/interviews/185/a_brisk_walk/), June 2006.

"Experts: Billy Collins." *Big Think* (http://bigthink.com/billycollins).

Leung, Rebecca. "Billy Collins: America's Poet." *CBS News,* July 2, 2003. Available online (http://www.cbsnews.com/stories/2003/06/30/60II/main561047.shtml).

Mustich, James. "Billy Collins: Ballistics." *Barnes & Nobel Review* (http://bnreview.barnesandnoble.com/t5/Interview/Billy-Collins-Ballistics/ba-p/758), December 1, 2008.

Van de Kamp, Alexandra. "Felicitous Spaces: An Interview with U.S. Poet Laureate Billy Collins." *Terra Incognita* (http://www.terraincognita.50megs.com/interview.html), January 2001.

OTHER WORKS

The Collected Poems of W.B. Yeats, Wordsworth Editions Limited, Hertfordshire. 1994. Additional material incorporated 2000. pp. 153-154.

MICHAEL CONNELLY

(1956—)

Scott Earle

IF THE COURSE of a young man's life can be said to hinge on a single incident, Michael Connelly's direction was set one evening when, driving home from work, he saw a running man peel off his shirt and try to hide a gun. Sixteen-year-old Michael did the right thing and went to the police. They assembled a lineup for him, but he could not identify the suspect. One detective took this not as a sign to continue the investigation but as a moral failure on Connelly's part: the boy had wilted under pressure, failed to deliver. Connelly himself, recording this incident in his introduction to the collection *Crime Beat* (2004), was left impressed by the gruff detective who never believed him.

Connelly, born July 21, 1956, in Philadelphia, son of W. Michael and Mary Connelly, grew up in Devon, Pennsylvania, in a home his father had built. The family moved to Florida when he was a young teen, and later he would attend the University of Florida, where he graduated in 1980. By that time, he had already decided to use journalism as a springboard to the writing of crime fiction. In his career as a journalist, he covered the violence that erupted in southern Florida as the result of the cocaine trade, and in 1986 was shortlisted, along with another journalist, for a Pulitzer Prize for his reporting on a plane crash.

That distinction gave him the opportunity to interview for a job in Los Angeles. Asked to write a follow-up to the story of a real-life bank heist involving L.A.'s sewers, he met expectations—and would return to the heist as material for his first novel, *The Black Echo* (1992). His personal life paralleled this professional direction: in 1984 he married Linda McCaleb, a literary manager, and the couple would have a daughter, Callie.

INFLUENCES AND EARLY WORK

Michael Connelly has granted over one hundred interviews since entering the field of crime fiction. Although he works to make himself accessible to his fans and to the press, his interviews seldom move into areas such as family life; he prefers to focus on craft. In doing so, he speaks openly of the joys and struggles of writing, his literary influences, and, where relevant, the events in his life that helped him choose this path. The two most helpful print sources for understanding the relationship between Connelly's life and work are *Crime Beat* and *The Lineup* (2009). The former collects his articles as a journalist working in Florida and Los Angeles, but Connelly's introduction is most instructive here in outlining lessons learned on the beat and applied to his fiction—for example, the way he works as a novelist to capture the telling details that show crime's effect on the cops who combat it. In *The Lineup*—subtitled "The World's Greatest Crime Writers Tell the Inside Story of Their Greatest Detectives"—Connelly discusses the creation of Harry Bosch and more generally Connelly's interest in other writers of crime fiction. Authors he lists as mentors include Raymond Chandler, Ross Macdonald, and Joseph Wambaugh, as well as James Lee Burke, Lawrence Block, and Thomas Harris. At one point he quotes a line of Raymond Chandler's concerning the personality and code of a fictional detective (p. 58), contextualized here:

> But down these mean streets a man must go who is not himself mean, who is neither tarnished nor afraid. The detective in this kind of story must be such a man. He is the hero, he is everything. He must be a complete man and a common man and yet an unusual man. He must be, to use a rather weathered phrase, a man of honor, by instinct, by inevitability, without thought of it, and certainly

without saying it. He must be the best man in his world and a good enough man for any world.

(Chandler, "The Simple Art of Murder")

Chandler's evocative depictions of L.A. had helped inspire Connelly to become a writer, and this creed would help Connelly formulate the character of Hieronymus ("Harry") Bosch, the central character of Connelly's corpus. Harry's code of honor is simple: everyone counts or no one counts.

Harry Bosch springs into life already fully realized in Connelly's first completed novel, *The Black Echo*, which won the Edgar Allan Poe Award for best first novel from the Mystery Writers of America. A Vietnam veteran who endured bitter tunnel fighting, Bosch has already seen success and scandal as a detective in L.A.: he has inspired a television movie and a TV series and used his windfall to buy a one-bedroom cantilever house on a hill overlooking Universal Studios. He has also been transferred from the elite Robbery-Homicide Division to Hollywood, the lowest of the low, owing to procedural issues regarding the shooting death of a serial killer named the Dollmaker. Bosch is an orphan; he is an institutional man who has gone from the foster care system to the army to the police force. He is a perpetual outsider forced to work with others and enjoys the lonely beauty and sorrow of jazz. We learn all this and more as the novel begins, and yet the city itself almost proves the equal of Bosch as a character. A possible murder scene by the reservoir opens the novel:

To [Harry's] back was the blue-green expanse of the Hollywood reservoir, 60 million gallons of the city's drinking water trapped by the venerable old dam in a canyon between two of the Hollywood Hills. A six-foot band of dried clay ran the length of the shoreline, a reminder that L.A. was in its fourth year of drought.

(p. 9)

Reading this book and the ones to follow provides an introduction to Los Angeles in all its contradictions. We see its beauty and its vulnerability paired side by side.

Nearby, a coroner's technician works the limbs of a hype's (heroin addict's) corpse, at-tempting to formulate time of death for Bosch: "Bosch knew rigor mortis worked its way from the head through the body and then into the extremities" (p. 15). Connelly seems a natural teacher—his Bosch books provide an education concerning the world of the detective—and thus his work is often placed into the subgenre of crime fiction known as the police procedural. Using other protagonists, Connelly will also write books that satisfy the requirements of the suspense novel or thriller.

Harry recognizes the dead man as a fellow "tunnel rat" from Vietnam and begins to reach for the unseen threads that brought the two together. Turning to his partner, Jerry Edgar, Bosch asks if he believes in coincidence. Before Edgar can really reply, Bosch asserts, "There are no coincidences" (p. 26). This conviction, which Bosch reiterates through the series, is an old one in detective literature. As a suspect exclaims to "The Continental Op" in Dashiell Hammett's "Arson Plus," "The coincidence of the Coonses stumbling into my uncle's house is, I fancy, too much for your detecting instincts" (p. 16).

Putting the case aside for a few hours, Bosch contemplates the city he loves. "The setting sun burned the sky pink and orange in the same bright hues as surfers' bathing suits. It was beautiful deception, Bosch thought, as he drove north on the Hollywood Freeway to home. Sunsets did that here. Made you forget that it was the smog that made their colors so brilliant, that behind every pretty picture there could be an ugly story" (p. 70). At home he reflects on his past, specifically his time in Vietnam with the hype—a man whose personal courage Bosch once admired and whose ability to survive was legendary. Both of them had been among the "young men who had dropped down into hell and come back to smile into the camera. Out of the blue and into the black is what they called going into a tunnel. Each one was a black echo. Nothing but death in there. But, still, they went" (p. 76). In *The Lineup*, Connelly talks at length about the neighborhood tunnel, visible from his childhood home, that dominated many an uneasy dream. Walking it was a rite of passage; once done, the triumphant boy could jeer all those without the courage to

follow. As an adult, Connelly would use the tunnel not only as a metaphor for life and death but also as characterization. Bosch has the confident, jaded air of a survivor.

Eleanor Wish, FBI agent and unlikely criminal mastermind, is a femme fatale for the late twentieth century. The type—powerful, independent, manipulative, sexually attractive, and amoral—emerged on the silver screen during and after World War II in the heyday of film noir, as men returned home from war to discover "Rosie the Riveter" working alongside them in America's factories. Wish's characterization reflects some of those elements combined with a vulnerability that recalls L.A. itself, teetering on the edge of both natural and manmade disasters. Wish makes a strong first impression that Bosch will never quite be able to shake, though he senses something dark about her even so: "A nice tan and little makeup. She looked hard-shell and maybe a little weary for so early in the day, the way lady cops and hookers get" (p. 85). Connelly makes skillful use of Eleanor to characterize Bosch by allowing the reader to see him through the eyes of others. She confides to him, "You were cleared early on. At first we got excited. I mean, we look through the files of people with tunnel experience in Vietnam and there sitting on the top was the famous Harry Bosch, detective superstar, a couple books written about his cases. TV movie, a spin-off series" (p. 109). Their working relationship eventually becomes personal, enough so that Eleanor invites him to her home, where he sees a print of Edward Hopper's *Nighthawks*. Like jazz, it evokes an era but also a state of mind: "I am the loner," he thinks. "I am the nighthawk" (p. 234).

After Harry and Eleanor make love for the first time, he goes out on her balcony to see the jacaranda trees shedding flowers "fallen like a violet snow on the ground" (p. 248). She joins him and tells a story about how she picked up a scar on Highland Avenue, in Pennsylvania, where she grew up. (According to Connelly's essay in *The Lineup*, "Highland" was the name of the street where he had lived in the house by the tunnel.)

The intricately crafted plot builds upon the true crime served up to Connelly as a test when he interviewed for the *Los Angeles Times*. It involves a daring series of bank heists making use of the city's labyrinthine sewer network. Bosch, the tunnel rat, must go into the black again to stop a corrupt FBI agent—Wish's partner, whom she betrays to save Bosch—and then convince Eleanor to turn herself in.

A reporter named Joel Bremmer provokes some of the more interesting questions to arise from this book. Here he is presented as a trusted veteran able to negotiate the sometimes tricky divide between the LAPD and the *L.A. Times;* he counts Bosch himself as a source. By the third novel, he will be revealed as a serial killer in his own right, dubbed the Follower. But was he conceived as a killer from the beginning? Connelly's novels are intricately plotted, and so it seems reasonable to assume that he plans ahead. But how far ahead? And does he leave room for the kind of improvisation that Bosch so enjoys in jazz?

CONNELLY'S UNIVERSE

Michael Connelly over the course of twenty-one novels has crafted a universe all his own. It is self-referential, filled with interwoven strands, a tapestry seamlessly executed. It is not metafiction. It is timely rather than timeless, filled with topical references, a reflection of the writer's roots in the immediacy of daily reporting. It is recognizably our own universe—more or less realistic, but with lurid elements given prominent attention. It rewards readers' loyalty and diligent observation (qualities Bosch and, likely, Connelly himself possess in abundance), as fans are able to follow Harry while also catching glimpses of favorite characters from books past. Connelly drops allusions like bread crumbs to help readers track the course of these characters' lives. He himself calls his work a canvas, citing Harry's namesake, the painter Hieronymus Bosch, and his densely peopled triptychs. This helps to explain why so many of Connelly's characters appear in the Bosch novels. More flattering is the fact that Harry Bosch has begun showing up as

an iconic reference in the work of other novelists, with Connelly's permission (Nolan, p. D8). Paula L. Woods' *Strange Bedfellows* has Bosch appear in front of police headquarters and in the thoughts of protagonist Charlotte Justice. In Joe Gores' *Cons, Scams, and Grifts,* Bosch is mentioned as a possible resource as cops pursue a case across jurisdictional boundaries. And in Robert Crais' *The Last Detective*, Elvis Cole talks to Bosch at the Hollywood police station.

The Black Ice (1993) is the second Bosch novel and continues the theme of corruption, only this time in the police force. How can a policeman "cross" and live with himself? This question takes on new meaning depending on the page number, because the novel goes through several plot twists. Early on, the antagonist, a cop named Cal Moore, updates Bosch on the drug wars: "Basically, black ice and glass are the same thing.... Basically, somebody took coke, heroin and PCP and rocked 'em all up together. A powerful little rock. It's supposed to do everything. It's got a crack high but the heroin also gives it legs" (pp. 27–28). Moore, unknown to Bosch at the time, has "gone over" to the criminal world and become a drug kingpin in Mexico, taking his half-brother's place. But can he really face the loss of his ideals? At novel's end, the question is answered when Moore sets himself up for Bosch to shoot him: suicide by cop.

The Concrete Blonde (1994) is one of the strongest entries in the series. Dipping into Bosch's backstory again, we are presented with that moment when he collides with the Dollmaker. "Bosch fired one shot, his gun kicking up in his two-handed grasp. The naked man jerked upright and backward. He hit the wood-paneled wall behind him, then bounced forward and fell across the bed thrashing and gagging. Bosch quickly moved into the room and to the bed" (p. 4). The episode becomes relevant when Bosch is sued by the man's widow, who claims he had been innocent and Bosch a cowboy and vigilante. Complicating matters immensely, a new victim, "the concrete blonde," has been found slain in a manner exactly matching the Dollmaker's pattern. Bosch's partner Jerry is a competent cop, but he "never seemed to understand that the homicide squad wasn't a job. It was a mission" (p. 52). Thus Connelly isolates Bosch; though he has a partner, he faces this crisis essentially on his own.

Even while under tremendous pressure—legal, professional, and political—Bosch keeps his analytical cool. Of the concrete blonde, he says, "It was either him [the Dollmaker] or a copycat ... or maybe he had a partner we didn't know about" (p. 57). Interestingly, Connelly will explore permutations like these when using serial killers in future books. Bosch may retain a certain cool under fire, but he is not even close to perfect; Connelly didn't design him to be. He seems quick to judge his fellow officers, or at least willing to ascribe to them motives that are less than pure: "He's fucking me because he didn't get to shoot Church himself" (p. 73) Bosch says of a colleague who is testifying on the witness stand.

The book is notable for the tension or "dramatic sense" of its plot. The plaintiff's attorney, Honey (dubbed "Money") Chandler, in going after Bosch in court, paints a devastatingly plausible picture of a man intent on avenging slain sex workers (the Dollmaker's preferred victim). She asks the chief of police if he knows that Bosch's mother herself had been a prostitute, and further that she had been murdered by an as yet unknown killer. (This revelation in trial points the way to the plot of the next novel, *The Last Coyote*.)

Later, departmental adversary Irvin Irving softens toward Bosch, who had always instinctively resisted becoming a team player, leading to antagonism between the men. Now Irving praises Bosch's work on the case and finally confides that he had been the one to find Bosch's mother—he had been the beat cop to find her body. They will be at odds again, as for example when Irving blames Bosch personally for the escape of the Echo Park Bagman.

Connelly tries to enliven the teaching component of the police procedural in the following passage, as Bremmer explains the unspoken truth behind Chandler's strategy: "In a civil rights case, if the plaintiff wins ... then the defendant—in this case the city is paying your tab—has to pay the

lawyer's fees" even if the jury awards a symbolic verdict of a dollar in damages (p. 297). The person educating Harry about this legal scam will soon be exposed as the Follower. Twists in the case take the reader's list of suspects from a vice cop with pedophiliac tendencies to a consulting psychologist on the Dollmaker investigations to the true killer, Bremmer. And while Bosch believes his lover Sylvia Moore (the widow of the cop he had slain in *The Black Ice*) is in danger, in reality "Money" Chandler has been targeted. She will become Bremmer's last victim before Bosch brings him in.

In *The Last Coyote* (1995), the reader finds Bosch placed on involuntary leave and undergoing a mandatory psychological evaluation given by a strong character named Dr. Carmen Hinojos. Bosch will take the opportunity, long delayed, to look into the death of his mother Marjorie Lowe, ignoring the doctor's concerns that this will put him under even more stress. Connelly throws the reader multiple red herrings before Bosch finds the unlikeliest of killers: Meredith Roman, his mother's best friend. A deputy district attorney named Conklin, whom both women loved, had promised to marry Marjorie and go away with her, even at the cost of his career (p. 392). And this heartbreak—even betrayal, from Meredith's point of view—she could not stand. Bosch concludes that she killed Marjorie in "a cat fight between whores" (p. 482). It says something about his world that he is able to put his thoughts into these words.

Connelly actually found inspiration for the plot in the real-life story of the author James Ellroy (*The Lineup*, pp. 53–54). Like Ellroy, Bosch attempts to find, in his work, a kind of therapy to ease him past his mother's death.

FROM POLICE PROCEDURALS TO THRILLERS

Connelly's next book, *The Poet* (1996), was important to his maturation as a writer and, in expanding his audience, greatly stimulated his career. He introduces a new protagonist, crime beat reporter Jack McEvoy, whose name suggests Jack Burden. (Appearing again as a protagonist in *The Scarecrow* years later, Jack uses a line from *All the President's Men*: "Run that baby," then calls it "one of the greatest reporter stories ever told" [*Scarecrow*, p. 61].) In *The Poet*, Jack's brother is murdered by the eponymous serial killer, and Jack—along with FBI agent Rachel Walling, with whom he has a taboo relationship—must track the Poet down across a broad landscape of American law enforcement, for law enforcement officers are the killer's targets.

Not only has Connelly introduced a new protagonist but also the first-person point of view. Jack and Rachel's first night together provides us with an example of its immediacy:

"Always keep one for emergencies," she said with a smile in her voice.

We made love after that. Slowly, smiling in the shadows of the room. I think of it now as a wonderful moment, perhaps the most erotic and passionate hour of my life.

(p. 275)

But the dispassionate observer of human nature in Jack knows that he is romanticizing the scene. Rachel Walling will eventually be exiled to FBI purgatory for her lapse in judgment, a move foreshadowed in her conversations with Jack. Their relationship will be revisited in *The Scarecrow*.

Fairly late in the novel, the reader enjoys an action scene ending in the death of a serial killer—but with pages left to turn, could this be the Poet?

Gladden sat up as I got to him and we both lunged for the gun, our hands reaching it at the same time. We fought for control and rolled over each other. My thought was to get to the trigger and just start firing. It didn't matter if I hit him, as long as I didn't hit myself.... The gun discharged and I felt a sharp pain as the bullet clipped the webbing between my thumb and palm and the escaping gases scorched my hand.

(p. 413)

Jack has slain a giant, only one who has been set up by the Machiavellian Poet, the FBI agent Bob Backus. In the true climax of the novel, Jack almost falls prey to the Poet's psychosexual rage before Rachel saves him; the killer escapes, badly wounded, to reappear later in *The Narrows*.

Connelly says of his success with thrillers like *The Poet:* "I didn't consciously switch genres. I just write the kinds of stories I want to read, and they get classified—by publishers, reviewers, and everybody. Some are seen as police procedurals, some are seen as thrillers, whatever. The constant dilemma for me as a writer is how to keep from getting stale" (Anderson). He adds that the publishing industry just does a better job marketing thrillers; it is a formula they understand and know how to exploit. Later, Connelly will show equal aptitude for the subgenre known as the legal thriller.

Trunk Music (1997) marks the return of Harry Bosch, who seems invigorated by Connelly's break in attention. Here he gets thrown together with the memorable FBI agent Roy Lindell, a huge man working undercover as a mobster when the two first meet. Thus Lindell plays against type in the Connelly universe: he begins the story as a criminal and ends it on the right side of "the blue line," his character arc being the opposite of Connelly's agents thus far. Lindell will appear again in *Angels Flight* and *Lost Light*.

What Bosch finds is a murder disguised as a mob hit and an adulterous tangle of sexual and financial motivations for his suspects. The ultimate score reads as follows: dirty cop Ray Powers had killed Tony Aliso, a money launderer for the mob, on behalf of his lover, the victim's wife. Tony, in turn, had been carrying on an affair with a stripper named Layla (aka Gretchen) with a strongly incestuous connection to the much older Tony. By the end of the novel, all are dead but for the stripper, and Bosch lets her go. In a surprise twist, he has just gotten married to Eleanor Wish, and a honeymoon is a poor time for police work. Connelly, a highly allusive writer, may have created the name Powers as a subtle reference to Powers Boothe, the actor who once played the role of Chandler's iconic detective Philip Marlowe.

In *Blood Work* (1998) Connelly introduces his second new protagonist, the FBI profiler Terry McCaleb (named, perhaps, in honor of Connelly's wife). The plot sees McCaleb take down the serial killer dubbed the Code Killer, who had tried to "help" him by murdering an appropriate donor for Terry's new heart; the germ for Terry's remorse came from a real heart transplant for one of Connelly's friends. During the investigation, Terry runs into an L.A. cop whose contempt for the *L.A. Times* is casually evident: "Didn't I read about you recently? Something in the *Slimes,* right?" (p. 40). This comment embodies the mutual animosity between the two Los Angeles institutions.

Connelly drops in another allusion when describing McCaleb as poorly dressed for a date: "McCaleb was in shorts, sandals and a T-shirt that said Robicheaux's Dock & Baitshop on it" (p. 121). Dave Robicheaux, of course, is the protagonist of James Lee Burke, who proves more than willing to return Connelly's admiration.

With *Angels Flight* (1999), Connelly tackles race in Los Angeles. Bosch is called into a politically sensitive case because he is politically expendable—and very good at what he does. A famous civil rights attorney lies slain on the floor of a tourist tram called Angels Flight, his murder made to look quite personal. But was it? And was the shooter a member of the LAPD, with whom the victim had clashed so many times? This book, which ends in a truncated riot, allows Connelly to comment on the Rodney King riots of 1992 and on the distrust of the LAPD in the African American community. At the same time, Connelly continues interweaving the narrative strands of his universe, as for example when Harry Bosch looks at a sunshade used for ads: "On the one Bosch could see there was an ad for an Eastwood picture called *Blood Work*. The movie was based on a true story about a former FBI agent Bosch was acquainted with" (p. 86). Harry must suffer through trauma of his own when he finds that Eleanor is leaving him; the news recalls, for him, the day he heard of his mother's death and dove to the bottom of a swimming pool and screamed. As the reader finds out later, Eleanor is pregnant with his child—a daughter—and will not disappear entirely from Bosch's life until she is gunned down in *Nine Dragons*.

At the end, we have a rough form of justice—street justice—as a mob pulls the corrupt Internal

Affairs Division detective John Chastain out of Bosch's car and kills him (p. 448). It was Chastain who had primed the pump for this riot by shooting to death the attorney, Howard Elias, over fear that his corruption would be exposed.

Void Moon (2000) introduces Connelly's fourth protagonist, albeit the first woman and the first thief—the first time we have crossed the blue line to empathize with a criminal. Cassie Black's standing is helped by the company she keeps; the antagonist here is one of Connelly's best, the psychopathic detective and mob "fixer" Jack Karch, whose sins are so pervasive and so black that Cassie comes across, by contrast, as a relatively likeable protagonist. Cassie conveys the idea of crime as adrenaline rush: "[She] felt herself getting excited. Keeping up through electronics magazines was one thing, but actually seeing the equipment was dipping the hot wire into her blood. She could feel the blood pounding in her temples" (p. 96). Connelly will make extensive use of this metaphor for Cassie Black, but it appears in variations for other characters throughout Connelly's corpus.

Booklist said of the novel's antagonist, "Jack Karch, the pit bull, is not only a chilling sicko, but also an incredibly skilled investigator" (Gaughan and Taylor, p. 308). We see evidence of this throughout the book, as Karch combines the mental acuity of a con man with the experience of years tracking down people who don't want to be found. Here he scams a hapless representative of a cell phone company:

> "Okay, sir. Do you want to wait on the address change, too?"
>
> Karch smiled. It always worked best when the victim prompted the con.
>
> "No, let's do—tell you what, maybe I should wait. My mail's being forwarded from my old place anyway. But wait a minute, I forget offhand, which address does the bill go to? My home or office?"
>
> "I don't know, sir. Four thousand Warner Boulevard, number five-twenty. Which is that?"
>
> (pp. 268–269)

Cassie cannot prevent Karch's finding her; it will take all her ingenuity and all her luck (the novel's setting is Las Vegas, after all) to prevent his killing her and her little girl.

In *A Darkness More Than Night* (2001), for the first time, Bosch is set up as the prime suspect in a murder. Terry McCaleb himself follows the clues to Bosch's feet, led by an owl placed at the scene of a murder: an allusion to the owls sitting in judgment in the paintings of Hieronymus Bosch. McCaleb, ever the profiler, pegs Bosch as an "avenging angel" in mentality, so it's entirely possible that he could have done it, crossing the line into vigilante territory (as "Money" Chandler had accused him of doing, years before)—the victim had been a man named Edward Gunn who himself had killed a prostitute.

This novel, named one of the Best Books of the Year by the *Los Angeles Times,* is as hard-boiled as any in Connelly's fiction; nevertheless, it has moments of poetry, as in this description of saltwater from Terry's point of view: "The water the bow cut through was flat and as blue-black as a marlin's skin" (p. 56). Terry realizes Bosch has been framed, and the two begin to work together: Bosch saves Terry from an LAPD cop-turned-bail-bondsman named Rudy Tafero, and Terry returns the favor by saving Bosch from Rudy's brother.

Hollywood is a consistent source of villains in Connelly's universe. In this case, the villain pulling the strings is a Hollywood director, David Storey. He is on trial for the murder of a starlet, and his case draws fairly obvious comparisons to famous L.A. cases such as that of the Menendez brothers. Jack McEvoy makes an appearance in his capacity as a reporter covering the trial for the papers, though he plays no role in the plot: just another example of an interwoven thread, a reward for loyal fans. Storey had hatched the idea of framing Bosch from his jail cell, but the arrogant director is forced to plead guilty to avoid a possible death sentence when faced with evidence of his collusion with Tafero.

This book gives us perhaps our best snapshot of Harry Bosch: "McCaleb appraised him. His hair was shorter than McCaleb had remembered it. More gray but that was to be expected. He still had the mustache and the eyes. They reminded him of Graciela's, so dark there was

almost no delineation between iris and pupil. But Bosch's eyes were weary and slightly hooded by wrinkles at the corners. Still, they were always moving, observing" (pp. 89–90). A more clouded picture emerges of Bosch the inner man, as a revelation at novel's end shakes our view of him: he had actually anticipated the murder of Gunn and allowed it to happen as a kind of rough justice for the slain prostitute. That is enough for Terry McCaleb to dissolve their friendship. After he leaves, Bosch looks down at his city:

> Slowly, his eyes came up and he looked through the kitchen window and out through the Cahuenga Pass. The lights of Hollywood glimmered in the cut, a mirror reflection of the stars of all galaxies everywhere. He thought about all that was bad out there. A city with more things wrong than right.... A city of lost light. His city. It was all of that and, still, always still, a place to begin again. His city. The city of the second chance.
>
> (p. 466)

Bosch hopes for redemption and will have opportunities to find it; this is an important new theme in Connelly's work, echoed most strongly at the end of *Nine Dragons*.

The next year 2002 saw the release of the film *Blood Work* based on Connelly's novel. Directed by Clint Eastwood, the film is a reminder of why writers find their work so often transformed on the big screen. In the novel, McCaleb develops heart problems for a fairly subtle reason: he cares too much about the victims of the killers he sought to put away. Apparently, that would not play in the new medium; the film has him suffer a heart attack while chasing the Code Killer on foot. The characters of Buddy Lockridge and Graciela are also changed, the former beyond recognition—he *is* the Code Killer—the latter in a way that gives her a harder edge: she helps kill him. Connelly sounds realistic when contemplating Hollywood as a consumer of a writer's work: According to *The Encyclopedia of World Biography,* "Even before [Connelly] wrote the book, he told *Sarasota Herald Tribune* writer John Griffin that a fellow author had 'said that when you sell your books to Hollywood, it's like selling them a car, and it's their turn to drive it and they might hit a wall or something, but it's their car now.'"

Also appearing in 2002, the novel *Chasing the Dime* presented a brand-new protagonist, a young tech hotshot and incipient world-changer named Henry Pierce (interestingly, Connelly originally assigned the name Pierce to the character who would become Harry Bosch [*The Lineup,* p. 52]). Like Bosch, Pierce has lost a female family member to violence. And, like Bosch, Pierce is the victim of an attempted frame for murder. Because of his past—his sister Isabelle ran away from home, only to be murdered by the Dollmaker—he is easily lured into the world of the sex trade in L.A., a world of escorts, porn, and murder. Cody Zeller, an old friend, surfer dude, and fellow genius, is the antagonist here. Pierce's invention Proteus promises to transform world tech by providing the energy for tomorrow's molecular computers, and Zeller wants it. Connelly has a fascination with tech: glimpses of it can be seen in the Bosch novels, it is expressed more fully in *Void Moon,* and it reaches its fullest expression here and in *The Scarecrow.*

City of Bones (2002) brings light to the devastating cycle of abuse in the American family. When a father sexually abuses his daughter, she takes it out on her little brother, beating him routinely to the point of breaking bones. When he runs away, he still can't escape victimhood, as he is murdered for his skateboard. Decades later, Bosch takes on this "cold case" and learns the depth and breadth of the boy's suffering. Sampling the coroner's lengthy report, we find that "the right humerus shows two separate and healed fractures. The breaks are longitudinal. This tells us the fractures are the result of the twisting of the arm with great force. It happened to him once and then it happened again" (p. 57). Broken legs, ribs, and a fractured skull add to this total: the boy suffered throughout his short life. Later, Bosch, having injured himself reaching the boy's body and now sitting in the car with Edgar, reacts: "[He] just sat there for a moment before starting the engine. Finally, he hit the steering wheel hard with the heel of his palm, sending a shock down the injured side of his chest" (p. 63). In his introduction to *The*

Blue Religion, Connelly talks about "an adage attributed to Joseph Wambaugh, the great writer of police stories, that informs our efforts here. It is as simple as it is true. It holds that the best story about the badge is not about how a cop works on a case. It is about how the case works on the cop" (p. viii).

Bosch's new love interest, a cop named Julia Brascher, seems too good to be true. She admires Bosch, wants to emulate him, and willingly sleeps with him. But she proves mentally unstable, and their relationship is cut tragically short by her death on the job; she had been apprehending a suspect and died by her own gun. The really interesting question is whether it might have been intentional.

Irving confronts Bosch in a somber scene following Brascher's death. Even though Irving is an unsympathetic figure, his words have a ring of truth:

> "Detective, there are some officers in this department they call 'shit magnets.' I am sure you have heard the term. Personally, I find the phrase distasteful. But its meaning is that things always seem to happen to these particular officers. Bad things. Repeatedly. Always."

> Bosch waited in the dark for what he knew was coming.

> "Unfortunately, Detective Bosch, you are one of those officers."
>
> (p. 273)

Irving's speech notwithstanding, Harry is reassigned to the Robbery-Homicide Division, bringing his story back full circle to the time before he took the fall from RHD for killing the Dollmaker. However, he decides to retire rather than accept the transfer.

Lost Light introduces Bosch as a private investigator and showcases his voice in the first person. *Lost Light* was published in 2003 and named one of the Best Books of the year by the *Los Angeles Times.* One of the things retirement has brought Harry is the opportunity to play jazz, not just listen to it, and he has found an excellent teacher in one of his old heroes. "Sugar Ray was a good teacher because he didn't know how to

teach. He told me stories and told me how to love the instrument, how to draw from it the sounds of life.... As I played, Sugar Ray watched my finger work and nodded approvingly. Halfway through the ballad he closed his eyes and just listened, nodding his head with the beats. It was a high compliment" (pp. 82–83). The first-person narrative allows for this more intimate look at Bosch; further, it connects Connelly to the long tradition of first-person narration in the crime novel.

Given Connelly's interest in tech, it should come as no surprise that his Web site serves as more than mere window dressing. It carries an impressive number of links to interviews, announcements, videos, and more. But one of its more intriguing sections has to do with music. There, Connelly lists the songs referenced in his books and introduces the CD *Dark Sacred Night* by commenting, in part, on the connections he finds between improvisation in jazz and his own writing. The improvisations Connelly mentions could be put another way: they are variations on a theme. Analyzing Connelly's books back-to-back reveals this basic writing technique. For example, the theme of police corruption (at the local, state, or federal level) appears in *The Black Echo, The Black Ice, Trunk Music, Angels Flight,* and many more books. In *Lost Light* it takes the form of both corrupt police and corrupt FBI agents or—to be generous—overzealous Homeland Security agents all too willing to cut corners in the name of national security.

Agent Roy Lindell appears and again helps Bosch, but not without sparks flying between them. Lindell's former lover, a fellow FBI agent, had been murdered, and Bosch stumbles into her case while pursuing another. Harry has to blackmail the FBI with an incriminating tape to keep the feds off his case as he pursues a trail laid down by cops with everything to hide. At one point, he just wants to know what is going on, allowing Connelly to address a major topical issue:

> I pulled to the side of San Vicente. We were a couple blocks from where Marilyn Monroe had

OD'd, one of the city's lasting scandals and mysteries.

"Then what, Roy? I'm tired of talking to myself."

Lindell nodded and then looked over at me.

"Homeland security, baby."

(p. 112)

While answers are slow to come in his professional life, Bosch struggles to accommodate a new revelation in his personal life: he finds himself to be a father, with Eleanor, of a little girl named Maddie. "I stepped forward and squatted down in front of the girl. I knew from dealing with young witnesses that it was best to approach them on their level.... I leaned forward and raised her tiny fists and held them against my closed eyes" (p. 384–385).

The Narrows (2004) reintroduces Connelly's most popular antagonist, the Poet; and once again, FBI Agent Rachel Walling will track Backus, her old mentor. "She could feel the juice begin moving within her blood again, turning it a darker red. Almost black" (p. 6). The reader discovers that Terry McCaleb is dead, a realization that carries real punch because of the depth of Connelly's characterizations. Bosch is asked by Terry's widow, Graciela, to solve his apparent murder, a case that will eventually unite him with Rachel in pursuit of Backus. This is the second novel in which Bosch speaks in the first person: "I thought about the daughter. I had never seen her but Terry had told me about her. He'd told me her name and why he had named her. I wondered if Graciela knew that story" (p. 15). It was the story of how Bosch and McCaleb first met, working together to take down a budding serial killer. Later, going through Terry's notes with his widow's permission, Bosch finds "a file with seemingly prescient notes on Elizabeth Smart, a child kidnapped in Utah who was found and returned after nearly a year. He correctly wrote 'alive' under one of the newspaper photos of the young girl" (p. 102). By evoking this actual 2002–2003 case, Connelly the newspaper reporter once again informs Connelly the novelist, ensuring that the fiction remains timely and well grounded in the details of our world.

Every good cop or private investigator seems to have a certain capacity for duplicity. It proves useful for Harry Bosch when he manages to tease information from a reporter without alerting her to his own investigation:

"Is there an official investigation?"

"No. That would be like asking the CIA to investigate the Kennedy assassination. The third one. It would just be a cover-up."

"What are you talking about? The third what?"

"The third Kennedy. The son. John-John. You think his plane just dove into the water like they said?"

(pp. 139–140)

Of course, the reporter dismisses him as a conspiracy nut, which was exactly his plan. Later, Bosch inquires about who had been to Terry McCaleb's funeral, an opportunity for Connelly, again, to connect his universe to our own. "There were a few [agents] and there were some cops and family and friends. Clint Eastwood was there. I think he took his own helicopter out" (p. 170).

For chapter 41, Connelly does an unusual thing: he picks up the plot through Rachel Walling's narrative voice. It strikes the reader as unusual not because the character is female—Cassie Black was the protagonist of *Void Moon*, after all—but because Bosch seldom shares storytelling duties. Then Connelly decides to go one stratagem better: he alternates narrative voices the rest of the way, with each character taking a turn for a short scene. Working together, they bring down the Poet once and for all. One has the feeling that Connelly was trying to challenge himself as a writer here, to test the breadth of his abilities, like a juggler moving from three balls to four.

Connelly's next Harry Bosch novel, *The Closers,* was published in May 2005 and debuted at number one on the *New York Times* best-seller list. Bosch comes out of retirement to rejoin the force and becomes part of a "cold case" unit; as a cop again, he gives up the intimate first-person narration of the private investigator. Harry's new supervisor warns him: "With fresh kills it is clinical because things move fast. With old cases it is

emotional. You are going to see the toll of violence over time. Be prepared for it" (p. 18). That turns out to be good advice; as with *City of Bones,* this cold case leads to heightened, not dulled, emotion. At the end of the novel we see the proof. Robert Verloren, the victim's father, cared enough about his daughter's death that he gets himself thrown in jail just for the opportunity to assassinate the murderer.

With *The Lincoln Lawyer* (2005), Connelly introduces perhaps the most successfully realized non-Bosch protagonist to date. Mickey Haller is Bosch's half-brother, as it turns out, though that information is not immediately clear. Mickey is a cynical and devastatingly effective defense attorney with one eye on the California bar and the other on everyone else. He has two ex-wives, the legacy of a famous father, and the first faint stirrings of conscience with which to contend. At the time of the novel's release Adam Woog of the *Seattle Times* wrote that "Mickey is a terrific character" and Carol Memmott of *USA Today* called *The Lincoln Lawyer* one of Connelly's best novels, "if not *the* best."

Mickey dominates this legal thriller, always one step ahead of the game—at least, until the novel's climax, when events catch up to him. Early on, he projects confidence in contemplating an upcoming trial: "If they told the truth, I had them. If they lied, I had them. I don't relish the idea of embarrassing law enforcement officers in open court, but my hope was that they would lie. If a jury sees a cop lie on the witness stand, then the case might as well end right there" (p. 14). Mickey's client would skate on a technicality— namely that the surveillance copter used to gather incriminating evidence violated his civil rights by flying under the legal floor for aircraft.

Candid in his interior monologue, Mickey thinks about the law: "There was nothing about [it] that I cherished anymore. The law school notions about the virtue of the adversarial system, of the system's checks and balances, of the search for truth had long since eroded like the faces of statues from earlier civilizations. The law was not about truth. It was about negotiation, amelioration, manipulation" (p. 30). Like the Lincoln Town Cars that collectively comprise Mickey's

"office," he is always on the move, a sophist ready and willing to follow the money.

What principles he does have he seems to have inherited from his father, and even they seem dubious. Of his father's relationships with prostitutes, Mickey notes that "he defended many and charged few. Maybe I was just continuing a family tradition" (p. 58). This reference applies to Bosch's mother Marjorie, as long before she fell for a prosecuting attorney, she fell for a brilliant defense attorney. Mickey's father was also Harry's.

Both here and in *Echo Park,* we have a parent nurturing, even enabling, a psychopathic child. In this case, the mother nearly kills Haller before he shoots her dead.

A FASCINATION WITH SERIAL KILLERS

Echo Park, from 2006, combines this notion of a parent's misguided love with the reliable trope of a serial killer. Harry Bosch enters the picture still intent on solving a murder that frustrated him years ago. As we have seen, Bosch engages in creative falsehood when it helps his case. Here he lies by omission to test an apartment manager's alibi:

"I wasn't here. I was on vacation in Italy."

Bosch smiled.

"I love Italy. Where'd you go?"

Kay's face brightened.

"I went up to Lake Como and then over to a small hill town called Asolo. It's where Robert Browning lived."

Bosch nodded like he knew the places and knew who Robert Browning was.

(pp. 10–11)

Micky Haller's name comes up as someone who once represented serial killer Raynard Waits. FBI profiler Rachel Walling also makes an appearance, with Bosch briefly recalling their one night stand in Las Vegas (p. 74) before they resume

their relationship. When Waits, aka the Echo Park Butcher or simply the Bagman, agrees to lead Bosch to the body of the victim whose case he had been trying to close, Bosch reluctantly agrees. But the Bagman escapes because other officers don't do their jobs, and some of them pay with their lives. Comforting wounded partner Kiz Rider in the hospital, Bosch listens uncomfortably as she berates herself. "If you had been up top instead of me none of this would've happened. Because you wouldn't have hesitated, Harry. You would've blown his shit away" (p. 228). And that is exactly what Harry does when he tracks the monster to his lair—appropriately enough for Harry, in a tunnel.

What is the psychology of a serial killer? Connelly seems as fascinated by this question as any writer; remember that Thomas Harris is among those he has listed as mentors. At one point in reference to the Bagman, an attorney complains, "He's a stone-cold killer and he's in there vamping like Hannibal Lecter" (*Echo Park,* p. 141). We see this "vamping" later when the killer exclaims, "I always say a woman is at her best when she is dead but still warm" (p. 146). It's one of the most chilling lines to be found anywhere in Connelly, except that, in the case of this particular murder, it is a lie—the Bagman is covering for someone else, all in the hopes that he could lead investigators to a spot so rugged that he might effect an escape. And that is what he does, echoing Lecter's famous escape in *The Silence of the Lambs,* though in a far more prosaic way.

Connelly's readers have ample opportunity to contemplate this pathology. Given the almost unfathomable nature of the subject, such contemplation can meander across a very broad, very bleak plain. Serial killers are born the way they are; no, *The Poet* suggests, they are formed through abuse, morphing from victim to victimizer. They are loners; or, as in *The Scarecrow,* they connect with others of like mind through the Internet, working as mentor and protégé. They rely on the shadows to hide their actions; they carry huge egos that compel attention, ultimately bringing them down, as with the Follower from *The Concrete Blonde.* They haunt a single locale, hunkering down in a place like the Bagman's "foxhole"; they travel the country as Backus does searching for victims. A list of Connelly's stable of serial killers is best given by appellation: the Dollmaker, the Follower, the Poet, the Cemetery Man, the Code Killer, the Bagman, the Scarecrow, and so on (the psychopathic Las Vegas "fixer" Jack Karch is at home in this company, and his nickname particularly fits his locale: the Jack of Spades). Such appellations capture the essence of these men better than any legal or given name ever could.

Unique in Connelly's corpus, *The Overlook* (2007) is a novel with portions serialized in the *New York Times Magazine* in 2006, prior to hardcover publication. Fears of a possible radiation leak or even a "dirty bomb" elevate the level of suspense in this murder mystery. Once again Connelly addresses a timely theme in our society, in this case terrorism, in his tightest, most streamlined novel to date.

Bosch and Rachel Walling are thrown together again and view a murder scene. With experience and insight, Rachel explains why a victim killed executioner-style might have soda stains on his clothing and why no one heard the shots: the killer used "an improvised silencer to dampen the sound.... You tape an empty plastic liter Coke bottle to the muzzle of the weapon and the sound of the shot is significantly reduced as sound waves are projected into the bottle rather than the open air" (p. 19). But what Rachel does not know is that her own partner has done the killing, in this case for love of a woman, the victim's selfish wife. Once again, variations on a theme: in Connelly, love (or lust) will trump a man's honor. That's not true for Bosch, but it holds for lesser men.

Mickey Haller returns in *The Brass Verdict* (2008), this time teaming with Bosch to create a formidable, if adversarial, duo. At novel's end Mickey (and readers new to Connelly) realize that the two are actually half-brothers. The novel topped the *New York Times* best-seller list and was named one of the Best Books of the Year by *Publishers Weekly* while garnering strong reviews. Haller, speaking in the first person as in *The Lincoln Lawyer,* echoes that book with these

opening lines: "Everybody lies. Cops lie. Lawyers lie. Witnesses lie. The victims lie. A trial is a contest of lies" (p. 3). His cynicism surpasses that of his half-brother Harry, who may be cynical about aspects of the justice system and distrustful of others—even other cops—but who seems against all experience to retain the hope of a believer in his heart.

Hollywood provides the villain again, this time in the person of a movie producer, Walter Elliot. As his defense attorney, Haller reminds him, "The prosecution will simply say that you did know Johan Rilz was your wife's lover, and they'll trot out evidence and testimony that will indicate that a divorce forced by your wife's infidelity would cost you in excess of a hundred million dollars and possibly dilute your control of the studio" (p. 179). As it so happened, those facts were sufficient motivation for Elliot to murder them both. Colluding with Elliot, in some ways the greater evil, is a judge with an impeccable reputation; but by novel's end Mickey has seen through her machinations.

> "I wanted you to know that I know. And soon enough everybody else will as well."
>
> "I am sure I don't know what you are talking about. What do you know, Mr. Haller?"
>
> "I know that you are for sale and that you tried to have me killed."
>
> (p. 525)

Haller's cynicism about liars at novel's beginning was, thus, insufficient to the reality, for he had failed to list judges. Now his list is complete.

In *The Scarecrow* (2009), a new and brilliant serial killer stalks reporter Jack McEvoy and FBI agent Rachel Walling, once again pitting these two against a psychopath. The twist here—the variation on a theme—is that there are two killers, both computer geniuses, both adept at using computers to identify and isolate their victims.

Having just been downsized from the *Los Angeles Times,* Jack tries to do the right thing by teaching his replacement the ways of the crime beat. Of cops, he says, "They have a hidden nobility. The good ones, I mean. And if you can somehow get that into your stories, you will win them over every time. So look for the telling details, the little moments of nobility" (p. 31). His mention of the "little moments" recalls Connelly's own study of police officers as recounted in *Crime Beat* (p. 3).

Connelly is interested here in commenting not only on technology's dangers for the newspaper industry—Jack's downsizing seems a direct result of online news and "tweets"—but also of the dangers inherent to social networking sites. The Scarecrow, given name Wesley Carver, muses on this phenomenon: "It was always amazing to Carver how trusting or naïve young people were. They didn't believe that anybody could connect the dots. They believed that they could bare their souls on the Internet, post photos and information at will, and not expect any consequences" (p. 113). Janet Maslin, writing for the *New York Times,* praised the novel: "*The Scarecrow* ... pivots energetically among its subplots, often returning affectionately to the newspaper world."

This novel marks the second time Connelly has used Jack as a protagonist, something he had done previously with Terry McCaleb and Mickey Haller. But none have gone beyond two books, as if obeying an unwritten rule of Connelly's universe: that Harry Bosch must lie at its center as the sole series protagonist. (Should Harry age beyond mandatory retirement age, Connelly will have options ready-to-hand as replacements.)

Indeed, prior to Harry's next novelistic outing, *Nine Dragons* (2009), he makes an appearance in "Father's Day," a short story Connelly contributed to a collection titled *The Blue Religion* (2008), one of several anthologies Connelly has edited in association with organizations such as the Mystery Writers of America, for which he served as president in 2003–2004. In "Father's Day" we find that Bosch's newest partner Ignacio Ferras "had become a father for the first time six months earlier. Bosch knew this. The experience had made him a professional dad, and every Monday he came in to the squad with a new batch of photos" (p. 351). The plot of the story is grating—it concerns the murder of a toddler—and the reader who goes on to read *Nine*

Dragons learns that within about a year Ferras too will be dead. Nevertheless, the story ends on a hopeful note as Bosch calls his daughter overseas and they build upon the bond forged that day he put her tiny fists against his eyes.

In *Nine Dragons,* Bosch finds himself flying to Hong Kong to rescue his daughter from kidnappers. Mistakenly, he believes she has been abducted by the triads because of a case Harry had been working in Los Angeles. Bosch attempts to comfort Robert Li, one of the actual perpetrators of a murder plot, when he promises him justice for his slain father. He references the night twelve years before when a mini-riot left one cop dead and Bosch a lucky survivor finding comfort at the hands of the elder Li, events first recorded in *Angels Flight*. Connelly is always topical: Robert Li, though dissembling in a later interview with Bosch, tells the truth in this at least: "We expanded at the wrong time—right before the downturn. The banks get the government bailout but not us. We could lose everything" (p. 62).

In one of her last conversations, Eleanor Wish foreshadows the real reason for their daughter's disappearance: "She stayed with a friend all night to 'teach me a lesson,'" she says. "I called the police then and it was all very embarrassing because they found her at her friend's. I'm sorry I didn't tell you. But she and I have been having problems" (p. 132). In a gamble more desperate than any her mother ever took, Maddie faked her kidnapping because she knew it would bring her father to save her. The charade becomes real when she falls into the hands of the Chinese black market, people who view her as a human factory ready to be harvested for her organs. And she really does need Harry to save her. In a novel blending the police procedural with martial arts action, Eleanor Wish is killed and Bosch gets his daughter back, leaving a trail of bodies in his wake. At the end, father and daughter feel they are both responsible for Eleanor's death, and Bosch loses his first partner in the line of duty. Ignacio Ferras joins Eleanor Wish as the second notable character in the novel to die. As with *A Darkness More Than Night,* we have only a faint hope of redemption in the promise of future action.

CONNELLY'S PLACE IN LITERARY CULTURE

Not all Connelly novels may be remembered by fans with the reverence they reserve for *The Black Echo* and *The Concrete Blonde*. What is clear, however, is that Connelly has managed to maintain the prolific production of a newspaperman while still producing work of quality, a combination that has paid off handsomely.

According to his Web site, Connelly's books have been translated into thirty-five languages and have won numerous awards including the Edgar Award, Anthony Award, Macavity Award, Los Angeles Times Best Mystery/Thriller Award, Shamus Award, Dilys Award, Nero Award, Barry Award, Audie Award, Ridley Award, Maltese Falcon Award (Japan), .38 Caliber Award (France), Grand Prix Award (France), Premio Bancarella Award (Italy), and Pepe Carvalho Award (Spain).

For all his popular acclaim, however, genre fiction traditionally has been poorly represented in the literary canon, which, practically speaking, can be viewed as a body of literature that editors, professors, book critics, librarians, and others label the best, or possessing the highest quality. Michael Connelly has mastered the crime novel, but does that qualify him as someone worth serious study? Are his insights about human nature, for example, such that graduate students ought to be writing papers—if not dissertations—on his work?

James Lee Burke, giving an interview to Danuta Kean for Orionbooks, suggests that crime fiction has become popular because it reflects what is going on in society. "The crime novel has replaced the sociological novel of the '20s and '30s." This point is debatable, but many would agree that the best crime fiction belongs in the canon. Further, it is possible to argue that writers like Michael Connelly transcend genre. If so, their place in our literature—Connelly's place—is secure.

Selected Bibliography

WORKS OF MICHAEL CONNELLY

NOVELS

The Black Echo. Boston: Little, Brown, 1992. New York: Grand, 2002.

The Black Ice. Boston: Little, Brown, 1993; New York: Vision, 1993.

The Concrete Blonde. Boston: Little, Brown, 1994. New York: Grand, 2007.

The Last Coyote. Boston: Little, Brown, 1995. New York: Grand, 2007.

The Poet. Boston: Little, Brown, 1996. New York: Warner, 1997.

Trunk Music. Boston: Little, Brown, 1997. New York: Grand, 2008.

Blood Work. Boston: Little, Brown, 1998. New York: Warner, 2002.

Angels Flight. Boston: Little, Brown, 1999. (Quotations from edition: New York: Warner Books, March, 2003.)

Void Moon. Boston: Little, Brown, 2000. New York: Grand, 2003.

A Darkness More Than Night. Boston: Little, Brown, 2001. New York: Grand, 2003.

Chasing the Dime. Boston: Little, Brown, 2002. New York: Vision, 2003.

City of Bones. Boston: Little, Brown, 2002. New York: Warner, 2003.

Lost Light. Boston: Little, Brown, 2003. New York: Vision, 2004.

The Narrows. New York: Little, Brown, 2004. New York: Warner, 2005.

The Closers. New York: Little, Brown, 2005. New York: Grand, 2006.

The Lincoln Lawyer. New York: Little, Brown, 2005. New York: Grand, 2006.

Echo Park. New York: Little, Brown, 2006. New York: Warner 2007.

The Overlook. New York: Little, Brown, 2007. (Portions were serialized in the *New York Times Magazine* in 2006.)

The Brass Verdict. New York: Little, Brown, 2008. New York: Grand, 2009.

Nine Dragons. New York: Little, Brown, 2009.

The Scarecrow. New York: Little, Brown, 2009.

SHORT FICTION

"Cahoots." In *Measures of Poison*. Edited by Dennis McMillan. New York: Dennis McMillan, 2002.

"Two-Bagger." In *The Best American Mystery Stories 2002*.

Edited by Otto Penzler. New York: Houghton Mifflin, 2002.

"Christmas Even." In *Murder and All That Jazz*. Edited by Robert J. Randisi. New York: Signet, 2004.

"After Midnight." In *Men from Boys*. Edited by John Harvey. London: Heinemann, 2003; New York: HarperCollins, 2005.

"Angle of Investigation." In *Plots with Guns*. Edited by Anthony Neil Smith. New York: Dennis McMillan, 2005.

"Cielo Azul." In *Dangerous Women*. Edited by Otto Penzler. New York: Mysterious Press, 2005.

"One Dollar Jackpot." In *Dead Man's Hand: Crime Fiction at the Poker Table*. Edited by Otto Penzler. New York: Harcourt, 2007.

"Suicide Run." In *Hollywood and Crime*. Edited by Robert J. Randisi. New York: Pegasus, 2007.

"Father's Day." In *Mystery Writers of America Presents The Blue Religion: New Stories About Cops, Criminals, and the Chase*. Edited by Michael Connelly. New York: Little, Brown, 2008. Pp. 348–366.

"Mulholland Dive." In *The Best American Mystery Stories 2008*. Edited by George Pelecanos. New York: Houghton Mifflin, 2008.

NONFICTION

Crime Beat: A Decade of Covering Cops and Killers. New York: Little, Brown, 2006. New York: Back, 2007.

"Hieronymus Bosch." In *The Lineup*. Edited by Otto Penzler. New York: Little, Brown, 2009.

"When Fact Meets Fiction, the Cases Are Harder to Solve." CNN (http://www.cnn.com/2009/CRIME/10/29/michael. connelly.fact.fiction/index.html), October 29, 2009.

AS EDITOR

International Association of Crime Writers Presents Murder in Vegas: New Crime Tales of Gambling and Desperation. New York: Forge, 2005; Doherty, 2006.

Mystery Writers of America Presents The Blue Religion: New Stories About Cops, Criminals, and the Chase. New York: Little, Brown, 2008.

Mystery Writers of America Presents In the Shadow of the Master. New York: Morrow, 2009.

CRITICAL STUDIES AND REVIEWS

Gaughan, Thomas, and Gilbert Taylor. "Void Moon." *Booklist,* October 1, 1999, p. 308.

Maslin, Janet. "Print Reporter vs. Web, and Sinister Webmaster." *New York Times,* May 20, 2009. Available online (http://www.nytimes.com/2009/05/21/books/21masl.html).

Memmott, Carol. "'Lincoln' Navigates Crime Curves at Breakneck Speed." *USA Today,* October 3, 2005. Avail-

able online (http://www.usatoday.com/life/books/reviews/2005-10-03-lincoln-lawyer_x.htm).

"Michael Connelly." *Encyclopedia of World Biography* (http://www.notablebiographies.com/newsmakers2/2007-A-Co/Connelly-Michael.html), 2008.

Michael Connelly Web site (www.michaelconnelly.com). Created and managed by Jane Davis.

Nolan, Tom. "Connelly's Lt. Bosch Moonlights—In Other Writers' Books." *Wall Street Journal,* April 4, 2006, p. D8.

Woog, Adam. "A Backseat Attorney in a Top-Notch Mystery." *Seattle Times,* October 5, 2005. Available online (http://community.seattletimes.nwsource.com/archive/?date=20051005&slug=connelly05).

INTERVIEWS

Anderson, Karen. "Living Two Lives." *January Magazine* (http://januarymagazine.com/profiles/connelly.html), February 1999.

"Author Talk." Bookreporter.com (http://www.bookreporter.com/authors/au-connelly-michael.asp), October 16, 2009.

"Michael Connelly Talks to Danuta Kean About How Having Children Has Affected His Crime Writing." Orion Publishing Group (http://www.orionbooks.co.uk/interview.aspx?ID=4677), 2007.

FILM BASED ON THE WORK OF MICHAEL CONNELLY

Blood Work. Directed by Clint Eastwood. Warner Brothers, 2002.

OTHER SOURCES

Chandler, Raymond. "The Simple Art of Murder." 1950. Available online (http://www.en.utexas.edu/amlit/amlitprivate/scans/chandlerart.html).

Dunn, Adam. "Joseph Wambaugh Sounds Off." CNN (http://archives.cnn.com/2000/books/news/10/13/wambaugh.qanda/), October 13, 2000.

Hammett, Dashiell. "Arson Plus." In *Crime Stories and Other Writings*. Edited by Steven Marcus. New York: Library of America, 2001.

"James Lee Burke Talks with Danuta Kean About the Big Moral and Political Issues Which Underpin His Novels." Orion Publishing Group (http://www.orionbooks.co.uk/interview.aspx?ID=4559), 2007.

WILLIAM VIRGIL DAVIS

(1940—)

H. L. Hix

WILLIAM VIRGIL DAVIS' poetic career has been distinctive in various ways: though he has published poetry in journals prodigiously, Davis has gathered only a small number of those poems into collections; his poetry is particular and personal in its explicit subject matter, but it operates within a framework of universal and metaphysical concerns informed by his training in theology; and his poetic career is inseparable from a distinguished scholarly career as a leading expert on the work of Robert Bly and of R. S. Thomas. Davis' work sums to a confession, not in the sense typically intended by the term "confessional poetry," of confession as psychological autobiography with therapeutic aims, but in the centuries-old sense, used by Saint Augustine and Jean-Jacques Rousseau, of confession as *spiritual* autobiography with redemptive aims.

LIFE

Born on May 26, 1940, William Virgil Davis was raised in Canton, Ohio, by his parents, Virgil Sanor and Anna Bertha (Orth) Davis. In 1971 he married Carol Ann Demske; they have one son, William. Davis attended Ohio University, earning an AB degree in 1962, an MA in 1965, and a PhD in American literature in 1967. He also holds a master of divinity degree, earned in 1965 from Pittsburgh Theological Seminary, and in 1971 he was ordained a Presbyterian minister.

Davis held short teaching positions at Ohio University, Central Connecticut State University, and Tunxis Community College (Farmington, Connecticut) before teaching as assistant professor in the English Department at the University of Illinois at Chicago Circle from 1972 to 1977. In 1977 he was hired by Baylor University in Waco, Texas, where he has taught since, as associate professor from 1977 to 1979 and as professor of English and writer in residence from 1979 to the present. Over the years, Davis has held various visiting appointments, three of them Fulbrights, at the University of Vienna, the University of Montana, the University of Wales, University College of Swansea, and the University of Copenhagen. His two full-length poetry collections were published as a result of winning major national awards: *One Way to Reconstruct the Scene* won the 1979 Yale Series of Younger Poets Award, and *Landscape and Journey* the 2009 New Criterion Poetry Prize. Davis and his wife live in Waco, Texas.

AN APPROACH TO DAVIS' WORK

His having earned in the same year a master of divinity degree from one institution and master of arts from another suggests something that his later career confirms, namely that Davis possesses an ability to "multitask," to maintain and coordinate simultaneous labors. Though best known as a poet, Davis has been a prolific scholar as well, having authored or edited several books of criticism, in addition to numerous articles on various writers, mostly contemporary poets but including also such fiction writers as William Faulkner and Katherine Anne Porter and such "great books" authors as Aeschylus and Edmund Spenser. His scholarship has focused primarily on two poets, the American poet and provocateur Robert Bly (b. 1926) and the Welsh poet and priest R. S. Thomas (1913–2000); he has authored or edited three books on Bly and two on Thomas. This essay will examine Davis' scholarship on those two poets before considering his own poetry, for two reasons: first, because in both cases Davis is the leading authority on that poet's work, so his

scholarship, valid in its own right, is a part of his work that merits survey; and second, because Davis' intensive study of those two poets could not but influence his own poetry, nor could his statements about those two poets' work be without relevance to his own poetry.

After an overview of his scholarship, this essay will turn to Davis' poetry, focusing on what he has gathered into his four collections: two chapbooks and two full-length books. His oeuvre as collected in books is unusually slender for a poet of his stature (in that regard rather like the oeuvres of Elizabeth Bishop or Philip Larkin), despite the fact that his oeuvre as published in magazines and journals is unusually large, over a thousand individual poems. The rationale for giving more attention to the few poems in his books than to the many he has published in journals comes from Davis himself. At one point in his *Robert Bly: The Poet and His Critics* (1994), Davis contrasts books of "collected" poems with books of "selected" poems. "Collected poems," he says, "usually contain all of a writer's published poems," and by virtue of that "are definitive." In contrast, selected poems, "especially when the poems are selected by the writer personally, are, by definition incomplete, and they are often unevenly balanced across the canon … Such books insist that a writer is still alive, well, still writing" (p. 70). Though made in regard to Bly's poems, the contrast might be extended to Davis' own. By publishing so many poems in journals and so few in books, Davis has elected a course of publication different from that taken by most poets. Because he has treated journals the way many poets treat books, as the authoritative publication venue, each of his poetry books and chapbooks has taken on the character of a slender "selected," with the result that, even at the point in a long and distinguished career when many poets have begun to pursue the "definitive," or to let others impose it on their work, Davis' books, like books of selected poems, insist that he "is still alive, well, still writing." This essay will attempt to honor that aspect of Davis' work by seeking not definitiveness but rather ways of regarding Davis' existing work that remain open to what may yet come from a poet who is still alive and well, still writing actively.

SCHOLARSHIP ON ROBERT BLY

In the short (one-paragraph) preface to his 1988 monograph *Understanding Robert Bly*, Davis gives a simple reason for writing about Robert Bly: he is interested in Bly's work. Having a simple motivation for deciding to write about Bly, though, does not make any easier the acting out of that decision. Writing about Bly is intriguing and challenging, Davis observes, in part because Bly has produced a large body of work that defies categorization. Though the ideas—the results of Bly's inquiries—may be unsystematic, Davis nonetheless sees Bly's ideas as providing a consistent method through which Bly arrives at the various unsystematic results (p. 7). His noting in Bly a consistent method frees Davis from the need to categorize Bly's work: if Bly's poems from a given period reflect, and are reflected in, his cultural-philosophical inquiries of the same period, Davis can adopt as his method of reading Bly the correlation of Bly's poems and inquiries, elucidating the work by such comparison rather than by an artificially imposed categorization.

Just as their being unsystematic does not prevent Bly's ideas from sharing a method, so their being unsystematic does not prevent them from sharing a common focus, which Davis identifies as inwardness, an obsession that "has been present in Bly from the beginning" (p. 11) and that remains a constant with Bly throughout his career. Noting how frequently inwardness recurs in Bly's work, Davis treats it as a defining presence. It is central to "Where We Must Look for Help," the "only unrevised poem from his MA thesis" (p. 18) that Bly included in his first book, *Silence in the Snowy Fields* (1962) and the first poem Davis discusses. The poem's point, Davis contends, is that "one must awaken to the inward man" (p. 20). Inwardness continues as a central theme in Bly's second book, *The Light Around the Body* (1967), as for example in "Moving Inward at Last," which Davis calls "one of the most important poems" in the book, a poem that "points to a movement 'inward,' the direc-

tion that both this book and most of Bly's remaining work will take"; in this way, it "climaxes the dominant thematic movement of *Light*" (p. 64). Continuing the theme, *Sleepers Joining Hands* (1973) is "a book not about 'the light around the body' but a book about the light within" (p. 95). "The Pail," in *This Body Is Made of Camphor and Gopherwood* (1977), continues to deploy "the Boehmean dichotomy of inner and outer" (p. 125). In thus exerting thematic centrality, inwardness performs at least two roles for Bly. First, it offers a moral-spiritual-existential ideal for humans (for Bly himself, and for his readers), and secondly, inwardness functions as an aesthetic ideal for the poems themselves. In other words, Bly's poems themselves seek inwardness, but they also recommend inwardness to us.

Davis sees their pursuit of inwardness as giving Bly's poems the attribute of meditativeness, an insight in support of which Davis appeals to scholar Louis Martz's analysis of meditative verse. Davis finds Martz's explication of interiority useful in construing Bly's attempts to move inward. He quotes Martz's claim that the typical meditative poem "creates an interior drama … by some form of self-address, and concludes with a moment of illumination, where the speaker's self has, for a time, found an answer to its conflicts"; the poem creates that interior drama through language "heightened by a voice that is at once that of a unique individual and yet still the voice of a man searching inwardly in common ways for the common bond of mankind" (as quoted by Davis, pp. 125–126). Davis takes Bly as a unique individual and his voice as that of a man thus inwardly searching.

In *Understanding Robert Bly*, then, Davis portrays Bly as at heart a lyric poet, calling the voice of *Silence in the Snowy Fields* both "Bly's first voice" and "his most authentic voice, the one he keeps coming back to." The originality and authenticity of its voice leads Davis to assert *Silence in the Snowy Fields* as Bly's "most important book" (p. 17). The contrast by which Davis makes his point is a formal one: a preference for the shorter, more concentrated lyric that Bly introduced in *Silence* and returns to repeatedly throughout his oeuvre, over the longer,

looser narrative poem that periodically occurs in the collections that have followed *Silence in the Snowy Fields*. "Bly has seldom been interested in or successful with long narrative poems," Davis says; "his temperament seems to be more attuned to the lyric, and, even in the prose poem, when he stays closest to the lyric he is most successful" (p. 107).

In Davis' other monograph on Bly, *Robert Bly: The Poet and His Critics*, the contrast is different, and its resolution, though still favoring lyric, more ambiguous. In the later book, Davis still treats "the dichotomy represented by these two early books" (*Silence in the Snowy Fields* and *The Light Around the Body*) as continuing "to define Bly's career," and describes "both his lyrical voice and his controversial stands on social and political issues" as having "continued throughout the years, though they are often curiously mixed together" (p. x). But the formal contrast in Davis' first Bly book—short lyric, long narrative—is sharper than the thematic contrast in his second Bly book—lyrical versus political—so the latter distinction leaves Davis' evaluation of the poems more qualified, without preventing lyricality from remaining an important criterion for evaluation. The sociopolitical poems, Davis implies, have and retain value in large part according to how much room they allow in themselves for the lyrical voice.

Like sociopolitical poems, the prose poem continues, in Davis' second book on Bly no less than in the first, to be justified primarily by its proximity to lyric. In his "turn to the prose poem," Davis notes, Bly "seemed to be suggesting that prose poems begin to appear at specific times and in specific places as a kind of poetic stay against the extinction of poetry per se in such times and places" (p. 34). Davis lists numerous features that Bly identifies as virtues of prose poems: they "absorb details better than lined poems, allow the poem to give equal and individual space to many 'separate events,' permit a return to 'original perceptions,' help to make immediate intimacy, celebrate 'what takes place only once,' and"—the virtue Davis most highly values—"are spoken by a man or woman 'talking not before a crowd but in a low voice to

someone he is sure is listening'" (p. 35). That last feature in particular fulfills the basic evaluative contrast of Davis' book, the contrast between Bly's first and most authentic voice, the lyric voice in which Bly speaks quietly and succinctly to someone he is sure is listening, and Bly's later political voice, in Davis' view less authentic, that speaks loudly, at length, and to a crowd.

Lyric as a genre antedates recorded history, so the lyric quality in Bly's best work is traditional, surely, but it is also used, Davis believes, to novel effect. Davis cites the poet Donald Hall's application to Bly's work of Bly's own term, "new imagination," a term "Bly had used in his first published essay on poetry" to name a "kind of imagination new to American poetry" that Hall thinks Bly's work exemplifies, a kind of imagination that enables Bly's poetry to be "subjective but not autobiographical" (as quoted in *Robert Bly: The Poet and His Critics*, p. 1). This new imagination, Davis implies, gives Bly's poetry, at least that written in his early, authentic, lyric voice, "a 'profound subjectivity' that, as [Howard] Nelson argues, might finally be taken as a 'description of intuition itself'" (p. 1). The consensus about Bly's work that Davis is recording, and in which he joins Hall and Nelson, is that the profundity—the depth—of Bly's poetry derives from the degree of its subjectivity, from its being so unreservedly subjective, so unburdened by objectivity, that it arrives at a space of intuition otherwise inaccessible.

ON R. S. THOMAS

In his *R. S. Thomas: Poetry and Theology* (2007), Davis approaches the poetry of R. S. Thomas with a recognition similar to his recognition about the concurrence of Bly's poetry and philosophical speculations but with the difference that for Thomas, the concurrent speculation is theological rather than philosophical, in accord with Thomas' other vocation (in addition to his being a poet), his vocation as an Anglican priest. This difference leads Davis to qualify and limit the comparison: "it seems necessary to accept Thomas, *as poet*, on poetry's terms exclusively—even when he deals with religious themes and, especially so,

even when the poems seem to contradict the theological position espoused by the priest" (p. 7). In Bly, the seeming self-contradictions occur between the various philosophical speculations, and thus primarily trouble the speculations themselves, rather than troubling the concurrence between the speculations and the poetry; in Thomas, the seeming self-contradictions occur between the poetic and theological vocations, and thus trouble the concurrence between them. Any expectation of concurrence, though, comes from us, the readers: *we* expects priests to write poetry that concurs with their religious beliefs, though nothing about poetry itself (and possibly nothing about priesthood, either) obliges them to do so. Davis' point is that in Bly, the poetry and the ideas seem consistently to concur, though the ideas themselves are unsystematic; in Thomas the ideas themselves are more systematic, more consistent with one another, but the poems do not always concur with them. When they do not concur, Davis recommends that we let go of expectations about how priests ought to write, so that we may treat Thomas' poetry on its own terms. It is not self-evident that we should grant so clear a distinction between the poetry and the theology; David C. Mahan, for instance, reminds us that Thomas was "far from consistent" in maintaining the distinction himself, and he asks how "we assimilate the ways that Thomas *conflates* religion and poetry," citing Thomas' aphorism that "poetry is religion, religion is poetry" (p. 536). Still, Davis believes that granting Thomas' poetry autonomy underwrites its attempt to work out its own salvation in fear and trembling, and it underwrites a reader's arriving at the richest available understanding of the poems.

Another difference between Bly and Thomas helps Davis make the transition from the one to the other in the very first words of the preface to *R. S. Thomas: Poetry and Theology*. In his books on Bly, Davis has been careful to note Bly's focus on the unconscious, as when, drawing on Jungian psychology, Bly asserts that "poets should develop their 'underneath,' their 'inferior' functions, which are their 'link to all the rest of humanity'" (*Robert Bly: The Poet and His Crit-*

ics, p. 28), so it is difficult not to see the opening of the preface to his Thomas book as an attempt by Davis to mark a transition from Bly as unconscious pilgrim to Thomas as conscious pilgrim. Having noted already that for Bly the journey, an inward one, fulfills an ideal of subjectivity, Davis chooses different words to describe Thomas' pilgrimage, thus marking a different journey. Those words distinguish Thomas, the conscious pilgrim, from Bly, the unconscious pilgrim, by declaring attention more essential than intuition.

Bly and Thomas resemble one another, though, in the definitiveness of lyric to the sensibility of each. Davis concedes that some poets (such as Dante and John Milton), write long poems, but for lyric poets, the pilgrimage does not follow a straight line. They let themselves be directed more by immediate experience than by an overarching plan. Having described Bly as such a lyric poet, Davis describes Thomas as one of those rare poets who is a synthesis of the two types. Thus, Thomas' individual poems, as Davis sees them, operate as both individual works and parts of a larger whole.

Davis, though careful not to reduce Thomas' poetry to any one of its dimensions, adeptly offers succinct characterizations of important aspects of Thomas' poetry, one of which is its communicative purpose and structure. For Thomas, Davis claims in *R. S. Thomas: Poetry and Theology*, every poem "fills in a gap, both in knowledge and in experience. In so filling in a space where otherwise there would have been nothing, the poem becomes the means of voiding the void, of closing the gaps—both between God and man and between man and man" (p. 90). Its filling in a gap in this way gives the poem a double charge: "the poem communicates by its structure and by its statement, both by its being and by its saying. And furthermore, the poem itself fills up this gap between God and man, this void—even if, before it was written or spoken, the void had gone unnoticed." No one poem, though, can fill in the gap once and for all; the lyric must recur repeatedly, "so Thomas, again and again, presents us with one man, alone, lonely for and before God, calling across the gapped void between them," without an *expectation*, but with a *hope*, "that, somehow, God will hear his 'verbal hunger' and be moved—if not to respond, at least to listen." This, Davis claims, "is Thomas' constant theme, expressed and explored throughout his work" (p. 90). If Bly's poetry tries to fill an inward gap, the gap between oneself and the transcendent within oneself, Thomas tries to fill an outward gap, the gap between oneself and the transcendent outside or beyond oneself. Bly in his poetry wants to dig down; Thomas in his wants to dig out. Davis, in his own poetry, will seek to fulfill both impulses.

DAVIS' POETRY

Davis' criticism and poetry are not entirely independent; each informs the other. His poetic obsessions steer him toward subjects of critical investigation, and the critical work offers him models for pursuing those obsessions, models that clarify his thinking about, and enliven his practice of, poetry.

Davis himself affirms the interrelatedness of his criticism and his poetry when, in *Robert Bly: The Poet and His Critics*, he cites approvingly William Matthews' assertion "that 'poets who are also critics always,' when writing about poems by other poets, also write, 'in an elaborate code,' about their own poems—'both those they have written and those they aspire to write.'" Davis opines that "Matthews, himself a poet, is without a doubt right" (p. 12). He adds confirmation of the point in his work on R. S. Thomas, when he claims to have "attempted to follow Thomas in his pilgrimage through his life and work and to make his journey my own" (p. 158). But any journey travels through one landscape and toward another, and Davis, while recognizing Thomas' career "as a pilgrimage to, or toward, a sacred place" (p. 17), also observes that Thomas' sense of affinity with other poets sometimes finds its basis in place, as with Thomas' love of Robinson Jeffers' poetry, which is grounded in the similarity between "the landscape of Jeffers's California coast" and the landscape near Thomas' Welsh coast at Aberdaron, as Davis points out in his 2008 article "The Lame Feet of Salvation"

(p. 167). So in making Thomas' journey his own, Davis will also be making Thomas' landscape(s) his own, or at least affirming the importance of grounding one's poetry in a landscape. Davis' most recent collection reflects in its title, *Landscape and Journey*, this double aspect of pilgrimage.

DAVIS' POETRY AS A JOURNEY

His foregrounding of the pilgrimage as a metaphor suggests that one way to read Davis' poetry is to traverse it, to take a journey through it, moving chronologically from book to book, beginning with the earliest.

Even though the title poem of Davis' first poetry collection depicts an incomplete, tragically aborted journey, its central placement in the book (pages 30 and 31 of a book with sixty-two pages of poetry) and its status as the title poem imply its importance to the whole collection. One way to employ the title poem as a key to the whole collection can be derived from a statement Davis made in his *Understanding Robert Bly*. There, speaking of Bly's poem "Kneeling Down to Look into a Culvert," Davis says, "the opening line of the second stanza, 'I kneel near floating shadowy water,' containing four of his most definitive value words, may be the most succinct, quintessential line in all of Bly" (p. 150). An analogous observation might nominate the first two lines of "One Way to Reconstruct the Scene" as succinct and quintessential Davis. Those two lines contain several of Davis' most definitive value words: moon, snow, trees, glass, blue. Those words recur within this one poem itself but also recur repeatedly throughout the book.

The scene being reconstructed in the poem is that of a one-vehicle car crash. We view the scene some time after the wreck. We are shown certain key features about the car and also shown important facts about the two victims of the crash. The scene itself reveals some information about the wreck; for example, the location of the tree against which the car rests implies the path of the car, since the tree stands at a specific point near a curve in the road.

However, neither narrator nor reader occupies a clear and stable position in regard to the scene. The poem makes no attempt to establish just who the narrator is. He or she at certain moments resembles an omniscient narrator, with access to information that mere observation of the scene could not provide. For example, the narrator knows that before the unfortunate drive that resulted in the crash, the girl had been waiting for the man for a while and that they had been sitting together. The narrator even knows such background information as the origins of the bridge and its connection to the scene. The narrator knows that the crash was precipitated when, without warning, something blocked the driver's view.

Yet the narrator is *not* omniscient. Sometimes he or she must guess or speculate. The narrator speaks from an indefinite present about the crash as an event in an indefinite past. So the moon *looked* blue, it *was* winter, and so on. That indefiniteness magnifies the incompleteness and ambiguity of the narrator's report. For instance, one of the two people involved in the wreck is referred to as a girl, and the other as a man, but the nature of their relationship is not made clear. We the readers do not know, though presumably the narrator does, whether the man and girl are father and daughter, husband and wife, friends, or lovers. Similarly, the reader is told how the girl lays but does not reveal if she is dead or alive. Neither of the later variations, resolves the question, so the reader knows neither the fact itself nor whether the narrator knows the fact. All of which conspires to make Davis' *re*construction of the scene also a *de*construction of it, an artful placing of the reader into the epistemological position attributed to the man and the girl.

Structurally, "One Way to Reconstruct the Scene" replicates in miniature the observation visible in Davis' larger body of poetry, the one he notes in both Bly and Thomas, that of return to beginnings. The last two lines echo the first two, returning the reader to beginning of the poem, using the word reconstructed. The poem represents both a landscape and a journey. It depicts a static landscape, in which only the light snow and the moon move, but one in which a

journey (though an abruptly ended one) is implied, a journey that (like Wallace Stevens' jar in Tennessee) organizes the landscape around it.

As if in echo of Davis' implication, made in regard to Thomas, that the lyric act must recur repeatedly, the fact that the repeated words in the first pair and the last pair of lines of "One Way to Reconstruct the Scene" (moon, snow, trees, glass, blue) are fairly abstract nouns—"tree" and "trees" are each used several times in the poem, but "maple" only once—gives a clue to the way, across his whole body of work, not only in this poem, Davis treats the lyric act as recurring, rather than as once and for all. Rather than trying to individuate each instance of the use of those key words, Davis lets the connotations of each word add up, creating connections across poems and adding resonances to the imagery. So snow, for instance, does not achieve its full meaning by being specified and particularized in any one poem, but by gathering associations through repeated use in multiple poems.

Among the many poems from *One Way to Reconstruct the Scene* in which the moon figures prominently is "Driving Alone in Winter" (p. 14). Even in this short (ten-line) poem, others of Davis' value words appear—"snow" once and "trees" twice—but it is the moon that has so active a part that it becomes one of the characters in the poem. The speaker contextualizes himself as driving alone and establishes that aloneness through what Kenneth Burke calls the "scene/agent ratio," namely that the landscape reflects the speaker's aloneness: the land is empty, the road rutted (itself a signal of desolation, since only an unpaved road would have ruts). The speaker's aloneness prompts memories of other times in the car in similar landscapes, with the company of family members, but with the same external physical details marking the journeys.

Already, even after a comparison of only two poems, "One Way to Reconstruct the Scene" and "Driving Alone in Winter," the summative usage of general nouns in Davis' poetry begins to operate. The moon presides over the scene in both poems, serves in both poems as an objective correlative for the characters, and figures as an

agent of memory, ushering speaker and reader from the present into the past.

"Snow" is the most frequently used of the value words in Davis. At least a dozen of the poems in *One Way to Reconstruct the Scene* feature that word. One in which it seems peculiarly important is "January" (p. 24). In it, the snow, normally external to oneself, a feature of the outside world, has become a part of the speaker's own body. The first sentence recalls Franz Kafka's *Metamorphosis*: "One morning I awoke and found that it had been snowing all night inside my body." But unlike Kafka's Gregor Samsa, the speaker in "January" had not been transformed so much as he had been inhabited, possessed. He describes the snow as having continued after he awakened, "still falling, filtering down through my ribs, filling in my arms and legs." The result of the internal snowfall was paralysis. "I could no longer move," he says, because his "legs were too heavy, weighted with the snow." By swelling his tongue and freezing his mouth shut, the snow had imposed the specific paralysis of silence. Unable to move or speak, he had also been unable to fulfill his promise to visit "a young woman who lived alone in one room above a garage," of whom he mentions only two attributes, that she "had long black hair" and that she "never laughed." He makes it clear that some time has passed since this occasion and that the breach between him and her, the one occasioned by the internal snowfall, was never overcome, when he concludes by remarking that "She must be wondering what happened to me."

Another "snow" poem employs the word as its title. In "Snow" the speaker himself, not another person, is left trying to determine his place in the world. Cause for such wondering begins early, with the uncanny anticipation of reality by dream. Seeking to locate the world's going and his own going with it, the speaker tries to elicit a response from the world by saying his name to the mountain and waiting for an echo, but the world ignores him.

As with Davis' use of "moon," so with his use of "snow," the instances accrue, establishing associations and adding layers of meaning. In

"January," the speaker tries to speak and cannot, because of one effect of the snow, and in "Snow," the speaker speaks but to no effect, seeking but not receiving an echo. In "January," the speaker tries to move but cannot, because of the snow's weight; in "Snow," the speaker moves but the record of his movement is quickly erased by the snow. Similarly, the snow in both "January" and "Snow" creates associations with "Driving Alone in Winter" (the absent brothers and parents in "Driving Alone in Winter" recalling the absent woman in "January" and the speaker's absent self in "Snow") and with "One Way to Reconstruct the Scene" (in which, as in the other poems, the falling of the snow exemplifies the pervasive and ongoing agency of nature, its indifference to human doings).

Trees figure prominently in "Winter Light" (p. 13), performing there a dual function, a mediation reminiscent of Thomas' assignment to poetry of the task of bridging the gap between God and humans. In the first (short, three-line) stanza, the trees—specifically their "dead limbs"—capture the mysterious elements and aspects of nature coming down from above: darkness falling through itself, water destined to freeze, and "the hard light of winter." Then in the second stanza, the trees offer a figure for the self-understanding of the human speaker, who reports that on his early morning walk "I stop, / stoop, stare at my own reflection, / bent like a branch is bent by water." The tree, in other words, is figuratively both transcendent and immanent, both human and divine. This is not Matthew Arnold's temporal entrapment, "Wandering between two worlds, one dead, / The other powerless to be born," but something closer to Wendell Berry's simultaneous reality of earthly life and the Great Economy, the subjection of the former to the latter.

Trees also figure importantly in "That House, This Room" (p. 54), in this case by embodying memory. The speaker addresses an unnamed other who shares with him an ambiguous moment, most often referred to in the present tense, but once referred to as having passed. The trees have a place in a series of mysterious transformations. By its part in these metamorphoses, the tree gives physical form to the insubstantial (the wind) and also gives (by remembering) the past to the present and the present to the past. "That House, This Room" employs the phrase "There is nothing to know" with a different sense than the sense given by the nearly identical phrase "There was nothing to know" in "One Way to Reconstruct the Scene." There, the phrase meant something like "nothing was available as an object of knowledge, that which is to be known"; here, because it continues onto the last line with no intervening punctuation, it means something like "nothing was available as the subject, that which does the knowing." In "One Way to Reconstruct the Scene," the "present absence" is the known; in "That House, This Room," the present absence is the knower.

Glass has thematic importance in the poem that opens the book, "Another Night with Snow" (pp. 3–4). Others of Davis' recurring value words, "snow" and "trees," appear first, as the speaker begins to describe the setting:

It is March, 1940. I am not born.
It snows all night. Snow more than a foot
deep between the houses. Trees

holding it along their arms' length.

Speaker and chronology both are complicated by the present tense: the speaker is simultaneously an unborn child whose mother, pregnant with him, will appear within the scene, and the adult that unborn child will become (has become), looking back at and down on the scene. The father is described as walking home from the factory where he works, carrying his lunch box under his arm, as the mother, "big with me, waits / behind the window." The glass thus simultaneously makes the husband present to the wife and separates him from her, and does the same in reverse, makes her present to him and separates her from him: "Her breath blossoms, / flowers the glass." The window, anticipating the terms Davis will make explicit in *Landscape and Journey*—the title to his 2009 book, published thirty years after *One Way to Reconstruct the Scene*—frames the father's journey (his walk home) as a landscape for the mother as she stands watching

him walk home, but it also makes equivalent the journey and the landscape for the speaker, and indeed for all the characters, in the poem's last two lines, after the father has stopped to buy a loaf of bread and after he has entered the house and kissed his wife. Then "we"—at least the speaker as an unborn child, the speaker's mother, and the speaker's father, but possibly also the speaker as an adult and even the reader of the poem—"stand at the window and watch / the snow fall slowly through the years."

"Blue," the last of the value words highlighted in the opening two lines of the title poem, colors Davis' "A Late Elegy for John Berryman" (pp. 22–23), by appearing not within the poem itself but in the Peter Davison epigraph appended to it. In the poem itself, the one explicitly named color is red, but the red lights in the poem serve as a contrast, to emphasize the much more extensive presence of blue in the scene. Though the blue, unlike the red, is implicit, it is (also unlike the red) not localized but distributed widely throughout the scene: in ice floes on the Chicago River; in the spot of light under a light pole; in the breath of the old man walking along Wacker Drive; in his face, exposed to the bitter wind; and in the snow. But "blue" in its figurative usage, to describe an emotional state, is also present: the poem is an elegy for a poet who committed suicide after years of alcoholism and depression, and the other persons present in the poem, the old man and the speaker, also seem metaphorically blue.

In one of the most unfavorable reviews of *One Way to Reconstruct the Scene*, T. R. Hummer criticizes the poems for promising more than they deliver. Hummer argues that Davis consistently ends the poems too neatly and too soon. Hummer prefers Davis' longer poems to his shorter ones. Even though he believes that in general Davis is pleased when his poems end quickly and succinctly, Hummer finds the longer poems such as "Another Night with Snow" and the title poem more successful. This assessment contrasts sharply with Davis' own assessment of Bly: Davis prefers Bly's shorter poems, Hummer prefers Davis' longer ones. One counter to Hummer's assessment, and a way of reconciling it with Davis' expressed preference for shorter poems, is Glenn R. Swetman's summation of *One Way to Reconstruct the Scene*: "the entire book, every poem, concerns itself in some way with the interplay between memory, the imagination, and present reality" (p. 77). Because Davis' value words—"snow," "trees," "moon," and so forth—are abstract nouns, their particularity, specificity, and robustness will derive, then, from their recurrence in poems thus thematically united. "Snow," for instance, will have its richest meaning in Davis not in a short poem taken by itself but rather in a long poem in which it recurs often enough to take on particularity by repetition, or in a short poem taken not separately but in the context of the other poems in the book, when the various instances of snow have accumulated under the influence of the overarching theme. Which means, by extension, that *One Way to Reconstruct the Scene* will enrich its meaning as Davis' books (like snow) accumulate or as his journey continues to progress.

It is instructive to attend to the value words "moon," "snow," "trees," "blue," and "glass," but attending exclusively to them would leave out the third section of *One Way to Reconstruct the Scene*. Nearly every page of the first, second, and fourth sections of the book includes at least one of those value words, yet those words are almost entirely absent from the third section, where the key word is "bones." That third section, then, offers a transition to Davis' first chapbook, *The Dark Hours* (1984), which shares its governing conceit.

The Dark Hours opens with a long epigraph from the biblical book of Ezekiel, chapter 37, presented in lines. The version Davis presents is fairly close to the New American Standard version, but it is divided into lines, in contrast to all the major translations, which present chapter 37 in prose. Davis' use of this passage of Ezekiel as his epigraph presages the prophetic tenor of the poems to follow. In his 1980 study *The Language and Imagery of the Bible*. G. B. Caird notes that a translator of Ezekiel 37:1–14 faces "insoluble problems" because the English word "spirit" cannot "do all that is done with *ruah* in Hebrew or *pneuma* in Greek, both of which can mean

'spirit', 'breath' and 'wind' ... with 'point of the compass' thrown in for good measure" (Philadelphia: Westminster Press, pp. 43–44). Janet McCann notes of this epigraph that "these living dead from Ezekiel become an image of awareness of death and the individual's attempts to cope with this awareness" (p. 109), but she notes also that "mingled with the sadness of heavy awareness of mortality is a suggestion of the kind of ambiguous, apocalyptic prophecy that characterizes Ezekiel" (p. 110). Like the biblical book from which its epigraph is taken, then, and like Davis' own earlier book, *The Dark Hours* achieves its oracular quality in part by the multiplicity of tenors borne by the vehicles of its metaphors, the multiplicity of meanings borne by its words, and gathered in part by the repetition of those words.

In "Where the Bones Move" (p. 11), the speaker sees himself as mirrored by his bones. The bones take on the role of alter ego for the speaker, identical in certain respects but opposed in other respects. They are identical, for example, in repeating the speaker's movements, but opposed by being inverted, and by being plural in contrast to the singular speaker. The bones inhabit and exude darkness. The speaker seeks the bones' darkness, the dark currents they inhabit and the dark words that seep from them.

Winter Light returns from "bones" to the other value words ("moon," "snow," and so forth), but it arrives by means of these at the words that become the title of Davis' second full-length book, "landscape" and "journey." In the first part of *Winter Light*, the value words from *One Way to Reconstruct the Scene* figure prominently. So, for example, in the first poem, glass is implicitly present when "the light in the opened window burns / your eyes" (p. 109); in the second, it is snow, which "fell deep and slow" (p. 110); in the third, both trees *and* snow appear: "The barren trees / in the small woods, with snow along // their limbs" (p. 111). The most obvious form of continuity, though, is through the title poem, "Winter Light," which was included in *One Way to Reconstruct the Scene* before its inclusion in *Winter Light*. "Winter Light" also offers continuity with *The Dark Hours*, by reiterating the im-age of the speaker staring down at his reflection beneath him. In "Where the Bones Move," from *The Dark Hours*, the bones are his alter ego; in "Winter Light," the trees have that role.

The continuity extends backward, then, but also forward. By the end of the book we have moved to the key terms of the second full-length collection, "landscape" and "journey." In "An Evening in Advent" (p. 126), for instance, one leads to the other. We begin with a (very quiet) landscape, in which occur such miracles as moonlight having "lifted the water from the well." In this landscape, detail shows itself clearly:

every pebble shows, grows whole.
The corn stubble still stands in its even rows.
Each tree can be seen individually.

But the survey of the landscape culminates in a journey: "we walk out alone," feeling "blessed, even among our own shadows." Similarly, in the final poem in the book, "Winter Walk" (p. 128), a landscape ("Now the moonlight // runs her smooth hand over the land / and the wind whispers above it") prepares for a journey, "the small sound of my going."

The terms "landscape" and "journey" in the title of Davis' 2009 collection contrast with one another, in the sense that the former seems essentially static and synchronic, the latter essentially dynamic and diachronic. But they also depend on one another, since after all a journey must traverse a landscape, and perhaps in doing so define that landscape. Davis draws attention especially to that mutual dependency by posting as his epigraph to the book a passage from W. G. Sebald that concludes by referring to "the landscape, now almost immersed in oblivion, through which my journey had taken me." The emphasis on dependency and interrelatedness, rather than exclusion or contrast, is furthered by Davis' structuring the book in three sections, rather than two, so that there is no easy or straightforward mimicking of the titles; the book, in other words, is not divided into one section of landscape poems and another section of journey poems.

Transition from his previous books occurs in various ways, such as thematic and lexical continuities. Additionally, transition from *Winter Light* to *Landscape and Journey* is advanced by the repetition of several poems, including "Vigil at Heiligenkreuz," in both books. Indeed, when the speaker asks "Do I drowse?" a continuity is established across all of Davis' books, from the "She seemed to be sleeping" of the title poem in *One Way to Reconstruct the Scene,* through "Their Sleep" in *The Dark Hours,* to "Vigil at Heiligenkreuz" (p. 17), with its appearance in the two most recent books. In "Vigil," set in Heiligenkreuz, an abbey near Vienna, and the oldest continuously active Cistercian abbey, landscape and journey meet. The speaker is "sitting half-asleep in the long dark" of the abbey, observing its interior landscape (as well, one assumes, since it is a vigil, as his own interior landscape), when "a young monk slips past so quickly / I almost miss him." The monk is on his journey through this close landscape, "hurrying to service / with his brothers." Though the speaker's landscape and the monk's journey meet literally in a brief moment, the poem, in a gesture representative of Davis' poetry, places that fleeting, literal, mundane present into the perpetual, transcendent present we sometimes name eternity: the speaker observes, and the monk walks down, "the cold aisle / of the centuries / where we both serve."

Such continuity across books is the continuity not only of Davis' own imperative, tendered in connection with R. S. Thomas' poetry, that lyric, to achieve its aim of filling the gap between human and God, must recur repeatedly; it is also the continuity of the step after step of a pilgrim on his journey. The continuity, of course, is not confined to "Vigil at Heiligenkreuz." "Stave Church" (p. 18), just across the page, also depicts the intersection of a landscape with a journey. As in "Vigil," the speaker in "Stave Church" is visiting a sacred interior landscape. The journey in this case is the speaker's own, rather than someone else's; instead of the journey passing through the sacred landscape, the journey is to the sacred landscape and back. Inside the stave church, the speaker observes the interior landscape as the speaker in "Vigil" had done in the

abbey. Lyric continuity is established in various ways: the identity of this landscape with others and of this journey with others; resonance with the lyrics of other poets (for example, with Philip Larkin's "Church Going," which asks, also of a visit to a church, questions very like Davis' "What do we hope to find?"); and resonance with his own poems, as when the speaker's trail of footprints to the church evokes the covered-over tracks in Davis' "Snow" from *One Way to Reconstruct the Scene.*

DAVIS' POETRY AS A LANDSCAPE

If Davis' identification with the pilgrimage suggests one approach to reading his poetry, namely to journey through it from book to book, from beginning to end (or, to fulfill his observation about both Bly and Thomas, from beginning to new beginning), the title of his 2009 collection suggests an opposite, but equally apposite, approach. One might journey through the poetry, but one might also treat it as a landscape; one might, in other words, survey it. Since this essay has made a point of taking Davis at his word when he says that poets when writing about others' poems are also writing about their own, it will base its survey of Davis' own poetry on features that Davis has noted in the work of Bly and Thomas.

This essay has already suggested that Davis' poetry can be viewed as a *spiritual* autobiography with redemptory aims. This quality appears most obviously when the chosen landscape of the poem itself claims connection to spirituality, as in "Vigil at Heiligenkreuz" and "Stave Church," but the spirituality need not be quite so explicit. For example, in *Winter Light,* "Legacy" (p. 110) occupies not a church but a family dwelling. This seemingly mundane topos, though, is made sacred by the winter weather that encloses the house, nestling the family within it. Thus enclosed, their most ordinary actions become spiritual. Their attitudes and perceptions, too, are altered. But that past transformation of experience from the mundane into the spiritual extends also into the present, so that when the family members again experience similar nights their

memories transfer them from the temporal into the eternal realm. The enclosed spaces in Davis' poetry—the car in "Driving Alone in Winter," the house in "Legacy," the church in "Stave Church"—all become sacred, as provocations to memory and as places for the infinite and finite to meet.

The spiritual tenor of the autobiography in Davis' poetry appears indirectly but plainly in the brief anecdote of "In the Cold Air Register" (*Landscape and Journey*, p. 4). The speaker recounts how, when he was a child, his father would hold him by the legs, upside down, into the cold air register, so that he, the boy, could recover the item lost in the vent. A poem with a different purpose might emphasize, for instance, the items that occasionally fell into the register: coins or bobby pins or keys, each of which might betoken some specific memory. But in Davis' actual poem, what gets emphasized is not the object to be recuperated but the fact of the speaker's descent, dependency, and restoration to light, three elements typical of narratives of spiritual journeys. Like Odysseus or like Christ harrowing hell, the boy descends; like Christian in *Pilgrim's Progress,* he is dependent on the father (allegorically in John Bunyan, literally in Davis); and like the unbound one in Plato's allegory of the cave, he is led up to the light. The boy's internal state comes to correspond with the external environment (the room that, compared to the dark register, is brightly lit).

When Davis speaks of inwardness in Robert Bly's work, he notes four different ways in which it manifests itself: as a "personalized private mysticism," through "outward, public protest poems," as an "attempt to plumb universal mythic consciousness," and by "search[ing] out the 'ancestors,' both literal and psychological, which haunt his past, inhabit his memories, and continue to people his present world" (*Understanding Robert Bly*, p. 11). Though nothing in Davis' work parallels the public protest poems, the other forms of inwardness recur in Davis' own poetry just as they do in Bly's.

Each of the three forms of inwardness manifests itself in various ways in various of Davis' poems, but "October: With Rain" (*Land-scape and Journey*, p. 15) seems an especially vivid example of the private mysticism. The poem begins with a perceptual observation about the way daylight appears through a windowpane, but the observation leads to an association that is personalized—the speaker thinks about his son and about his own age—and private insofar as the speaker makes no attempt to justify or explain it. The speaker and his son try to make sense of things at the same time and place, in one another's presence, but each keeps his musings personalized and private.

"Personalized private mysticism" might seem incompatible with "universal mythic consciousness," but nothing prevents their sustaining, rather than contradicting, one another. "Winter Roses" (*Landscape and Journey*, p. 30) signals its inclination toward the universal by its use of the second person. It is "you," not "I," who is said to "stand and stare" from "the small / balcony," and whose "coffee cools in the tiny / china cup." Like the abstract nouns that Davis employs throughout his work (and which continue their work here, as in the observation that "the whole hillside" is "filled with snow"), the second person flexibly accommodates more than one particular: "you" does not refer only to one reader, but to any reader. That the speaker in "October: With Rain" can think he and his son are thinking out the same thing is reasonable in part because a personal and private mysticism might not be idiotic (in the etymological sense, unique to oneself) but might derive from a universal mythic consciousness—as Davis can count on the roses doing here in "Winter Roses." So Davis need not explicitly link roses to birth and death, as for instance Sor Juana Inés de la Cruz does in her Sonnet 147, calling the rose one "in whose one being nature has united / the joyful cradle and the mournful grave" (in *The Golden Age: Poems of the Spanish Renaissance,* translated by Edith Grossman, New York: W. W. Norton, 2006, p. 195), in order to rely on the reader to make that universal mythic association. So Davis in "Winter Roses" can allude to birth and youth without naming either and do the same with death. Davis himself seems to affirm the ultimate unity of the personal private mysticism

with the universal mythic consciousness when he takes note, in *Robert Bly: The Poet and His Critics*, of Howard Nelson's attribution to Bly of "a 'profound subjectivity'"—a complete privacy— "that … might finally be taken as a 'description of intuition itself'"—a complete universality (p. 1).

Similarly, inwardness as a searching out of the ancestors recurs throughout Davis' poetry, as for example in elegies to his parents and homages to older poets such as James Wright and John Berryman. The searching out of ancestors is especially prominent, though, in "Scenes from Childhood" (*Landscape and Journey*, pp. 9–11), which might also have been aptly named "Characters from Childhood." Each of the four numbered sections gives a condensed description of one such character: the coalman, the breadman, the iceman, and the man who sharpened knives and scissors. Though these might seem unlikely choices for a poet to claim as "ancestors," each is recalled by the speaker for some key feature that can be taken literally but also allegorically or metaphorically, so for instance the iceman has a playful side to balance his resilience in labor. From the iceman's example of infusing his labor with humor, and from his gift of slivers of ice in summer, the speaker has absorbed a spiritual value, of embracing one's actual circumstances, as embodied in the chilren's love of the cold ice.

In his 1988 discussion of Bly, Davis quotes the poet W. S. Merwin: "Tell me what you see vanishing and I / Will tell you who you are" (*Understanding Robert Bly*, pp. 33–34). Then in discussing Thomas, Davis quotes the poet Charles Wright: "It's what we forget that defines us" (*R. S. Thomas*, p. 158). Attention to what they see vanishing and what they forget helps Davis see the poetry of Bly and Thomas more clearly, and attention to what he sees vanishing and what he forgets helps elucidate Davis' poetry more clearly. The forgetting, in particular, cannot but be connected to Davis' ongoing preoccupation with memory.

Davis' poems see things vanishing, and see things *as* vanishing, persistently. The landscapes often are shrouded in, and the journeys often pass through, fog or mist or snow. The settings are often in twilight or at night, in darkness that is gathering or has gathered. The people are often those who have vanished. Often, even the destinations have already vanished, as in "Pilgrimage" (*Landscape and Journey,* p. 57), in which this vanishing, this already having forgotten even before the experience, tells the speaker who he is.

No poem, though, could better exemplify this feature of Davis' work than the poem that currently holds pride of place as the last poem in *Landscape and Journey*, "Border View, Hot Springs, Texas" (,p. 78). The speaker recalls a few particular details of a house, but then concedes that they are mostly forgotten. And this act of remembering what it has seen vanishing is paradoxically also a forgetting. The remembered house does not fill the speaker's mind, but is only vaguely present in his consciousness. And in this case at least, the speaker, by telling himself what he sees vanishing, can tell himself who he is, because he is what is vanishing: when the house that has vanished floats into the vacant room of his mind, it tells the speaker that *everything*, including himself, is capable of disappearing.

POET OF QUESTIONS

Davis identifies Thomas as "a poet of questions and of quests. He is a patient poet, given to the 'interrogation of silence,' but he is not a poet of answers" (*R. S. Thomas*, p. 52). Or, again: "Poems, for Thomas, seem always to end in questions—demanding more poems" (p. 95). Similarly, Davis is also a poet of questions, whose work does not give answers but gives questions that demand more poems. His being a poet of questions is literal: he asks questions on page after page of the books. For example, in "Property of Loss" he inquires:

When you reach and take your handkerchief
from your pocket, will you notice
how the image imprinted on it,
[…] fits perfectly
against the confines of your face?
                    (*One Way to Reconstruct the Scene*, p. 17)

Davis is also, though, a poet of questions more figuratively. Questions pervade his poems

whether or not they take the grammatical form of a question or are punctuated by a question mark. In "View from the Backyard" (*One Way to Reconstruct the Scene*, pp. 8–9) the speaker and his wife and son watch birds gathering at dusk; after the wife's offering a speculation about why the birds gather in that way, the speaker lets the question stay open, without resolution. Her answer is "as good as any guess I have and so we let it go at that, not really wanting to know." In "Following the Bones" (*One Way to Reconstruct the Scene*, p. 37), the speaker's last two lines are grammatically a declaration, but they still identify a question: "I've followed them / even though I do not know where they're going."

The many questions in Davis' own poems are, on at least one occasion, explicitly connected with R. S. Thomas, the poet Davis called a poet of questions. In "A Visit to Manafon" (*Landscape and Journey*, pp. 20–22), a poem dedicated to Thomas, the speaker asks the warden of the chapel there if she remembered Thomas, to which question she replies with a question of her own. More often, though, the questions in Davis' poetry are simply questions about the same things Thomas' poems inquire to: divinity, mortality, family, the universal questions of meaning in human life.

ISOLATED AND INDEPENDENT

Davis clearly values poems as "isolated and independent" entities (to recall once more Davis' own descriptive words about the work of R. S. Thomas); in the absence of such a valuation, it is hard to explain his prolific journal publication of more than a thousand individual poems. But the recurring vocabulary and imagery (snow, trees, winter, darkness, bones, and so on), the persistent preoccupations (such as memory), the ongoing autobiographical exploration, the overarching frameworks of landscape and journey, the theological undercurrent, the occasional repetition and recontextualization of a poem by publishing it in two collections, all suggest that Davis also construes these many, many "isolated and independent" poems also (again as with Thomas'

work) as "related segments of a much larger project," an ongoing project in which he has been engaged since the inception of his writing career and a project still very much in progress.

Selected Bibliography

WORKS OF WILLIAM VIRGIL DAVIS

POETRY
One Way to Reconstruct the Scene. New Haven, Conn.: Yale University Press, 1980.
The Dark Hours. Austin, Texas: Calliope Press, 1984.
Winter Light. In *Texas Poets in Concert: A Quartet*. Denton: University of North Texas Press, 1990. Pp. 106–128.
Landscape and Journey. Chicago: Ivan R. Dee, 2009.

CRITICISM AND OTHER WORK
Understanding Robert Bly. Columbia: University of South Carolina Press, 1988.
Critical Essays on Robert Bly. (Editor.) New York: G. K. Hall, 1992.
Miraculous Simplicity: Essays on R. S. Thomas. (Editor.) Fayetteville: University of Arkansas Press, 1993.
Robert Bly: The Poet and His Critics. Columbia, S.C.: Camden House, 1994.
"'Talked to by Silence': Apocalyptic Yearnings in Louise Glück's *The Wild Iris*." *Christianity and Literature* 52, no. 1: 47–56 (autumn 2002).
R. S. Thomas: Poetry and Theology. Waco, Tex.: Baylor University Press, 2007.
"'The Lame Feet of Salvation': A Reading of R. S. Thomas and Robinson Jeffers." *Renascence* 60, no. 2:161–176 (winter 2008).

BIOGRAPHICAL AND CRITICAL STUDIES
Hummer, T. R. Untitled review of *One Way to Reconstruct the Scene. Rocky Mountain Review of Language and Literature* 35, no. 2:160–162 (1981).
Mahan, David C. Untitled review of *R. S. Thomas: Poetry and Theology. Christianity and Literature* 58, no. 3:534–537 (spring 2009).
McCann, Janet. Untitled review of *The Dark Hours. South Central Review* 2, no. 4:108–111 (winter 1985).
Swetman, Glenn R. Untitled review of *One Way to Reconstruct the Scene. South Central Bulletin* 41, no. 3:77 (autumn 1981).

RHINA P. ESPAILLAT

(1932—)

Alfred Nicol

RHINA P. ESPAILLAT is a bilingual poet whose verse gained wide readership and influence toward the close of the twentieth century. Often associated with New Formalism, Espaillat began writing in received forms before it was out of fashion to do so. Her poetry is admired—and occasionally, if improbably, criticized—for its graciousness and warmth of humanity, as well as for its seamless match of conversational tone and meter. No avant-gardist, Espaillat is a contemporary master of traditionalist poetics. Though her techniques are those of four centuries of English and Spanish poets, her concerns are those of a woman of her own time: the immigrant daughter of an exiled Latin American diplomat, she taught for fifteen years in the New York City school system. She is all the more a woman of her time for carrying with her remnants of another time. The simple Catholic faith she experienced in her native Dominican Republic is never entirely displaced by the skepticism she acquired later in life; both ways of perceiving the world inform her poetry. Her childhood experience of hearing poetry read aloud to music in her grandmother's living room gave rise to her lifelong promotion of poetry as a way of bringing people together; her major literary and political concerns are centered on the idea of inclusiveness.

LIFE

Even without including the fictional personae Rhina Espaillat has created, the many speakers of her poems present the reader with an entire life, a woman's life fully experienced. Though she was not born in the United States, it is a particularly American life that the voices in her poems recite. She is the immigrant daughter of an exiled Latin American diplomat; she is a delivery girl in the city, running errands for her mother, a dressmaker; she is the young bride of a returning soldier and his helpmate as he works to organize the New York City teacher's union; she is herself a schoolteacher for fifteen years, the mother of three sons and finally a loving grandmother full of affection, concern, and cautious hope for the future.

Rhina Polonia Espaillat was born January 20, 1932, in Santo Domingo, the capital of the Dominican Republic, the only child of Carlos Manuel Homero Espaillat and Dulce María Batista. Espaillat's earliest memories include the pleasurable one of hearing poetry recited in her home to the sound of guitars and the piano. Her grandmother, herself a poet, would invite other poets and musicians to the house for recitals. Though as a child she could not understand what was being said, she understood immediately an essential thing about how it was said: music came from the spoken words as well as from the instruments. As she once said during a spoken introduction to Melopoeia at the West Chester Poetry Conference, "These people were having fun."

The muse visited Rhina Espaillat very early in life. Before she had even learned to write, Espaillat made up poems in Spanish which her grandmother wrote down for her.

Her family moved to New York City in 1939, when Rhina was seven years old. Two years earlier, Rhina's great-uncle, Rafael Brache, a high-ranking diplomat in the Dominican Republic, had been sent into exile by Rafael Trujillo, the dictator responsible for the brutal massacre of thousands of Haitians on the Dominican/Haitian border in October 1937. At the time, her father was serving in Washington, D.C., as secretary to the Dominican delegation. Brache repudiated

Trujillo in a letter condemning the massacre as a "criminal act," which resulted in immediate exile for the entire delegation.

Espaillat's parents rented an apartment on West Forty-ninth Street in Manhattan. Young Rhina stayed with her father's mother in the city of La Vega, in the central valley of the Dominican Republic, until her parents found steady employment and saved enough to send for her, not an easy task in those years of the Great Depression. Her father found work as a porter, doing odd jobs, until he was hired at a mannequin factory, where eventually he became bookkeeper. Her mother worked at home as a dressmaker. They were able to send for her in early May 1939. The young poet boarded the *Leif Erickson* with a friend of her aunt and arrived at New York City five days later.

One might conceivably locate the source of almost all the major themes of Espaillat's poetry in the circumstances of her family's removal from their native country to the United States. Always in her work there is the sense of Everyman's hidden nobility, for which her experience provided the image of her father working to assemble mannequins for department stores. There is the conscious love of family members, which is distinct from the natural, semiconscious love of family almost everyone feels, in this one particular: its apprehension that our loved ones can be taken from us suddenly. Often in Espaillat's poetry, we find characters sympathetically portrayed with the alertness to telling detail that is awakened when we see someone for the first—or for the last—time. There is also her insight into the immigrant experience, which she has learned firsthand. A related theme, perhaps the defining theme of Espaillat's work, is her attention to the life of the mind as it journeys this way and back across the border between different languages.

For Espaillat the poet, the next important occurrence took place at Julia Richman High School in Manhattan. One of her English teachers there was Catherine Haydon Jacobs, a poet whose work had appeared in magazines during the 1940s and 1950s. She sent some of the fifteen-year-old Espaillat's poems to *Ladies' Home Journal,* which accepted three of them for publication in 1947. Jacobs also showed Espaillat's poems to the Poetry Society of America; at the age of sixteen, she became the youngest person ever accepted to the society. A second publication came about when, in January 1950, a feature article in the *New York Sun,* "Teen Poet Wins Honors," quoted one of young Espaillat's poems, "The Pigeons," in its entirety.

Espaillat attended Hunter College of the City University of New York, graduating in 1953 with a B.A. in English Literature. During her senior year at the college, three eminent poets, W. H. Auden, Marianne Moore, and Karl Shapiro, were asked to edit a volume of poetry written by students enrolled in New York colleges and universities. They chose three of Espaillat's poems to include in the collection, *Riverside Poetry, 1953.*

On June 28, 1952, Espaillat married Alfred Moskowitz, who had returned from World War II in March 1946, having fought in the Battle of the Bulge and the Rhine Crossing. Her husband, who later in life would become a respected and prolific sculptor, at that time taught industrial arts in the New York City junior high schools. After her graduation from Hunter College, Espaillat also taught at the junior high school level until her first son, Philip, was born in 1954; a second son, Warren, was born in 1957. She spent the next years at home raising her two young sons, then returned to school herself, earning an M.S.E. degree from Queens College in 1965. She then taught English in Jamaica High School for fifteen years. A foster son, Gaston W. Dubois (b. 1952) became part of the family in 1968.

Since her retirement from high-school teaching in 1980, Espaillat's gift for teaching young people has continued to bring invitations to conduct classes and seminars at colleges around the country, including five colleges of the City University of New York, Dartmouth College, Syracuse University, Assumption, Mount Holyoke, University of Evansville, and Sarah Lawrence College, and for many years she has been part of the teaching staff at the West Chester Poetry Conference in Pennsylvania. The teacherly aspect of Espaillat's personality is evident in her insistence that poetry not only

express the poet's thought and feeling but communicate as well. Her own poetry, while not lacking in subtlety, is never opaque or hermetic. The time she has spent in the classroom also makes itself evident in her willingness on occasion to risk writing in a genre abandoned by most contemporary poets, the didactic poem. When Espaillat consciously sets out to do so, she often succeeds in making new a genre long fallen out of fashion. "Guidelines," a poem included in her 2008 book *Her Place in These Designs,* prescribes a radically simple way of life.

Espaillat wrote very little during the years spent raising her children and teaching high school. Unlike some writers who chafe under the constraint of having to devote too much time to domestic responsibilities at the expense of their literary work, this poet chooses to celebrate those years, not only for the joys and sorrows they brought her but for the direction they gave her poetry:

> I raised three sons: two born to me, and a foster-son. They have been a joy to me all their lives. Of course raising them took time but it was time well spent and worth any number of poems. I think that all the things a woman does that keep her from writing may frustrate her in the short run, but in the long run they contribute to the poems that she may write eventually. They provide the roots in daily living that keep poetry—all writing—from being self-referential and esoteric.
>
> (Letter to Silvio Torres-Saillant)

When she does allow herself to complain about having her writing time interrupted, it is done with a light touch, as in the humorous poem "The Poet's Husband Engages in Gourmet Cooking."

Returning to her writing after long absence, Espaillat gathered about her other poets, helping to organize a poetry workshop known as the Fresh Meadows Poets in Queens, New York, which continues to meet. Its members have included Yala Korwin and Michael Burch. Thus having worked to build a camaraderie among poets and a nascent readership, Espaillat set to work creating a corpus whose magnitude is astonishing when one considers that her first book, *Lapsing to Grace,* appeared in 1992 when she was sixty years old. It would be followed by

five full-length collections, three chapbooks, a bilingual book of prose and poetry, and a bilingual collection of short stories. Recognition of her extraordinary talent came quickly. In 1998 she received the T. S. Eliot Award for her second collection, *Where Horizons Go.* Her third collection, *Rehearsing Absence,* won the 2001 Richard Wilbur Award. Espaillat was invited to participate in the National Book Festival sponsored by the Library of Congress and First Lady Laura Bush in 2003. She was one of eleven living poets whom Dana Gioia chose to include in the anthology *100 Great Poets of the English Language* (Longman, 2004).

At the time of her first book's publication, Espaillat had already moved with her husband from New York City to Newburyport, Massachusetts. Once again she went about gathering a "workshop" of poets, this one known as the Powow River Poets. Having been invited by Len Krisak to participate in a reading series he hosted in Newton, Massachusetts, Espaillat invited Krisak to join the workshop. Not long afterward, the two of them initiated the Powow River Poets Reading Series, which brought many of the nation's best poets to present their works at the seaside town. The reading series, together with the considerable talents and accomplishments of the poets who gathered once a month to show and critique new poems, gained the workshop a national reputation.

Well into her seventies, Espaillat's literary production and innovation show no sign of flagging. Here again the distinguishing characteristic of her work is in its easy crossing over from Spanish to English and back again, in its fruitful exchange between the culture of the Dominican Republic where she was born and that of the United States where she has lived most of her life. A tariff-free commerce enriches both of these states of mind. Having translated a number of the poems of the Spanish mystic and Carmelite friar San Juan de la Cruz (1542–1591) into English, she then immersed herself in translating the poems of Robert Frost into Spanish. She has completed Spanish versions of forty of his best-known poems. With the classical guitarist John Tavano, she brought the performance of *Melo-*

poeia to New England, introducing the art form she had first experienced in her grandmother's home in La Vega to audiences north of Boston, who found themselves delighted to hear the poems of Federico García Lorca, Pablo Neruda, and Espaillat's fellow Dominican poet in New England, César Sánchez Beras, read to the accompaniment of Francisco Tárrega, Antônio Carlos Jobim, and other Spanish and Latin American composers. Audiences discovered a new way of hearing poetry, allowing them to find enjoyment even in poetry written in a language they might not understand. Espaillat's principal contribution to poetry in Spanish, a poetry known for its emotional and sensuous imagery, may be her bringing to it the philosophic introspection associated with the poetry of New England, both in her translations of Robert Frost and others and in her own poems in Spanish.

TRADITIONALIST POETICS

Often associated with New Formalism, Espaillat, born in the early 1930s, began writing in received forms before it was out of fashion to do so. Espaillat thus found herself "in the forefront of a movement she never had to 'join'" (Krisak). Be that as it may, Espaillat's arrival "in the forefront," even if accidental like that of Charlie Chaplin's character in the movie *Modern Times,* situated her precisely at the center of a strongly contested battle over the merit of traditionalist poetics. As she began to publish her work, around 1985, in those few literary journals that were then willing to consider metrical poetry, New Formalism began to gain adherents while at the same time attracting harsh criticism. Ira Sadoff's essay "Neo-Formalism: A Dangerous Nostalgia" appeared in the *American Poetry Review* in 1990. The poem "Changeling" marked Espaillat's first appearance in *Poetry* in August 1991; her first collection, *Lapsing to Grace,* appeared in 1992.

Though Espaillat is no polemicist, her work in poetry, her outlook, and her very person stood in contradiction to Sadoff's chief claims against the New Formalists, who were supposed to have "a social as well as a linguistic agenda" (p. 7). That agenda was said to be a conservative one, driven by "a nostalgia for moral and linguistic certainty" (p. 7). Sadoff saw in neo-formalism a reaction to democratic relativism. He even suspected that racism lurked beneath the surface of the formalists' aesthetic: "The neo-formalists' perhaps unconscious exaltation of the iamb veils their attempt to privilege prevailing white Anglo-Saxon rhythms and culture" (p. 8).

The emergence of Rhina Espaillat in the late 1980s and early 1990s revealed a poet for whom "democratic relativism" was the closest thing to an article of faith, a lifelong liberal Democrat who could hardly have intended to privilege Anglo-Saxon rhythms at the expense of her own Latin heritage, a poet who would bring to North America a polyrhythmic sound she had first heard in her grandmother's living room in La Vega, where she heard poetry read aloud to the accompaniment of classical guitar. Yet Espaillat wrote not only in meter but in form. Not only did she write sonnets, villanelles, sestinas, and pantoums; she made use of Spanish forms such as the *décima,* the *glosa,* and the *ovillejo.*

As a child, Espaillat actually believed that she had invented prosody! (Scheele). Of course her claim was the innocent mistake of a gifted child excited by an intellectual discovery, but the dexterity with which she handles meter even in her first volume of poems shows how naturally versification comes to this poet. She is so adept with traditionalist poetics as to bring a certain *sprezzatura* to her use of them: she employs Frost's model of laying the rhythms of common speech over a grid of iambic pentameter, bending without breaking the meter; often she uses enjambment to half-muffle end rhyme. Much of her art is in concealing her art; what is noticed at first glance is the tip of the iceberg.

The very first poem in Espaillat's first book of poems, "Highway Apple Trees," establishes both the democratic and the formalist sensibilities of the poet, brought together with what seems an instinctual grasp of metric possibility.

Nobody seeds this harvest, it just grows,
miraculous, above old caps and cans.
These apples may be sweet. Nobody knows

if they were meant to ripen under those
slow summer clouds, cooled by their small green
  fans.
Nobody seeds this harvest, it just grows,

nodding assent to every wind that blows,
uselessly safe, far from our knives and pans.
These apples may be sweet. Nobody knows

what future orchards live in cores one throws
from glossy limousines or battered vans.
Nobody seeds this harvest; it just grows,

denied the gift of purpose we suppose
would give it worth, conferred by human hands.
These apples, maybe sweet (nobody knows),

soften and fall, as autumn comes and goes,
into a sleep well-earned as any man's.
Nobody seeds this harvest, it just grows.
These apples may be sweet. Nobody knows.

The poem is written in iambic pentameter, but the first metrical foot is a trochee.

x - / - x / - x / - - / - x
Nobody seeds this harvest, it just grows.

This simple inversion serves at least two purposes. It gets the poem off to a running start—the speaker of the poem is traveling on the highway—and the two unstressed syllables preceding the word "seeds" subtly increase the emphasis on that word, the most important word in the poem, for in the absence of someone to do the planting, or seeding, the seeds must establish themselves as best they can on their own. Because Espaillat substitutes a pyrrhic in the fourth foot which is cut in half by the caesura, the two unstressed syllables before the word "grows" create a similar effect. So, like a master drummer, the poet begins with a line of iambic pentameter in which can be heard two anapest-like runs that succinctly deliver the message of the poem. The "harvest" this poem celebrates is not planned or pre-ordained; "Nobody seeds, ... it just grows."

What the poet pronounces "miraculous" is the triumph of the haphazard, the disorderly way life has of coming alive. And she truly does celebrate. The lines of her poem dance to a syncopated rhythm. Though every line is of course made up of five iambic feet, the caesuras fall in different places, so that the ear hears phrases of varying lengths. A caesura separates the second line into two parts, of two feet and of three feet. The opposite occurs in the third line, where the three-foot section comes first, after which the lines are enjambed so that there is no natural stop till the comma creates a caesura in line five. In reading a poem as rhythmically sophisticated as this one, it may be useful for the reader to imagine playing a saxophone, using the punctuation as an indication of where to draw in new breath—where each line is of ten syllables, yet the phrases are as long as twenty-eight syllables. That's quite a riff.

And the whole is quite an improvisation, as it should be in a poem whose theme is the provisional, make-do nature of existence, where there is no hierarchical imposition of relevance or irrelevance. "Nobody knows / what future orchards live in cores one throws / from glossy limousines or battered vans." The "Highway" of the poem's title is an American highway, which the poet knows very well, having visited all but seven states by way of automobile during the summers of the years in which she raised her family, viewing her surroundings with the alertness of one "not from these parts." The blessed seeming aimlessness of the American experience is a long way from the authoritarian rule of a man like Rafael Trujillo.

The typical way of life in a democracy is to make one's own way. The value of an individual's life depends on its adherence to a purpose not given but discovered. And one has to look around to discover; one has to do what "Highway Apple Trees" does in looking to the left and to the right, looking above and below. Espaillat's poetic craftsmanship, never separate from her poetic vision, serves to emphasize this way of bringing things to focus. Whether they were "meant to" or not, she writes, the apples ripen under

slow summer clouds, cooled by their small green
  fans.

Of the ten syllables of this line of iambic pentameter, seven are stressed, slowing the line

down to the pace of those great white clouds that cross the sky in late August, when apples begin to color. In this near-stillness, the poet's eyes are able to take in the entire event, noting how the very wind that works so hard to push the clouds above makes rapid little fans of the apple leaves below. What a moment of seeing. And it is only a moment—remember, the speaker of this poem is traveling by automobile.

Had she hesitated to accept what her circumstance made present to her, had she attempted to filter the experience with reference to an ideology, she would have missed it altogether. Her only recourse is to take it all in irrespective of its apparent worth,

> nodding assent to every wind that blows,
> uselessly safe, far from our knives and pans.

Note how Espaillat uses a metrical device here again to charge her words with meaning. Both lines begin with an inverted first foot and thus echo one another rhythmically:

> "Nodding assent …"
> "Uselessly safe …"

The poet feels she can afford the indulgence of nodding assent to every even contrary wind. She can afford that indulgence because she is "uselessly safe," which is a strange and accurate thing to say. She is safest precisely when she is of least use to those who would make use of a person, who would rally or coerce her to narrow her vision to a prescribed way of seeing. She can keep nodding her assent because she has not subscribed to a mass disapproval of something or someone. She rightly suspects that those who would make use of her have knives at their disposal.

She will use the same metrical device once again in the poem, heightening the effect of "soften and fall" by having it immediately preceded by the parenthetical "nobody knows." She imagines a peaceful end for these roadside apples, which will "soften and fall" rather be made use of, peeled and pared. "A sleep well-earned as any man's" is what she wishes for them, and for those who travel with her.

"Nobody knows." Those are the poem's final words, and because this is a villanelle, a form in which two lines of the first stanza are repeated throughout the poem, this is not the first iteration of the phrase. With each repetition its significance is altered slightly; the suggested meanings do not drop away but accumulate. The effect is like what happens in a church choir, where one voice may be a touch flat, another a bit sharp, so that together the many voices thicken the notes they sing. By the closing line of this villanelle, the phrase "nobody knows" has been "thickened"; it is carrying some weight. Nobody knows if these apples are sweet; nobody knows ahead of time what the significance of an individual life may be; nobody knows what effect our lives may have on those who come after us; nobody knows whether we will fall naturally into "a sleep well-earned" or whether our lives may end in violence; and nobody knows if any person's final end is "a sleep well-earned" or something as yet unimagined. Nobody knows.

If a poem by Rhina Espaillat ever expresses a nostalgia for any kind of certainty, it is acknowledged as nostalgia only; she goes in dread of the kind of authoritarian mind that would declare final certainty while forbidding those with questions the right to speak.

Espaillat is certainly not dogmatic in her decision to write metric rather than free verse. For all her skill with traditionalist poetics, she finds much to admire in the free verse of others, especially that of her great favorite Stanley Kunitz. She has written a number of highly successful poems in free verse, including "Dreaming Water" (*The Shadow I Dress In*), "When We Sold the Tent" (*Playing at Stillness*), and a poem ironically titled "Prosody" (*Shadow,* p. 96):

Finally, the sound of language is the important thing in poetry; the music of language is what makes it poetry. All of the tools in the traditionalist's toolbox are of use in making language sing, which is the poet's first responsibility; she would be most reluctant to have any of those tools taken from her. Her abiding concern for craft should not be confused with any kind of clerkly obsession, however; as the title of one of her poems tells us, "Dancers Work by Forgetting." Espaillat writes entirely "by ear"; if she is writing a sonnet, the fourteen lines of

her first draft are composed before she sets pen to paper. She has spoken of three elements that make a poem possible for her: "a feeling, a beat, and an image" (Poetry Workshop). A feeling and a beat—that might be a blues man talking. Though Espaillat will not allow herself to write poems that frustrate the reader's genuine attempt to understand, always the music comes first.

BILINGUAL/BILINGÜE

Certainly there are many poets who speak more than one language and some who write in a language other than that first spoken at home. Espaillat's bilingualism is important to a consideration of her work not only because she continued to write in both Spanish and English throughout her career, but because bilingualism itself is central to her conception of what it means to be a poet. She makes this connection emphatically in an essay called "Bilingual/*Bilingüe*" included in her second book of poems, *Where Horizons Go.*

After her family moved from Santo Domingo to New York when she was seven, her father forbade English to be spoken at home, and he demanded that both the Spanish spoken inside the home and the English spoken outside be used correctly. Espaillat's concept of bilingualism derives from this concern of her father's: "I mean by bilingualism ... what my father meant by it: the complete mastery of two languages" (Cruz-Hacker, "Dominican-Americans from Here and from There," p. 25). As one of the speakers in Espaillat's "An Imaginary Dialogue," her father complains about the advent of so-called Spanglish. He says that young people will lose out, as they will "finally find themselves without mastery of a single language, having wasted the magnificent opportunity to master two"(Torres-Saillant, "Answering to the Music," p. 11).

Certainly Espaillat has mastered both her native Spanish and her adopted English. In reviewing Espaillat's second book for *Poetry,* Bill Christophersen wrote, "English is Espaillat's second language the way it was Conrad's: she enriches it with every line she writes" (p. 348). Most of Espaillat's work in poetry has been done in this

"second language"; its eloquence is all the more remarkable for it. In an interview with Roy Scheele, Espaillat spoke of the advantage to a writer of being bilingual:

> The thing that bilingualism does for all of us who are bilingual is that it severs an intimate connection that we have with language. If you speak only one language, you feel that this is the only one there is; all the others are translations of it, but its words are the real names for things. But once you learn to live in another language, and think in it, the way I think in English, you are undeceived of that, and you understand that all language is arbitrary, that there is no language that reality speaks—reality is mute. Each language is as valid as all the others— and as useless, in the long run, because not one of them captures the whole of what we're looking for. So it just breaks that illusion you have in childhood that when you say "tree" you are naming something. You are not.
>
> (Scheele p. 36)

It is easy to hear in Espaillat's explanation of the benefits of speaking more than one language yet another expression of her vigilance against false certainty and the prejudice that follows from it. She does not merely tell us that different languages are equally good in their different ways; she says that, finally, none of them is quite good enough. She reminds us that a poet's work is never finished. The ineffable remains the ineffable, no matter how many towers of Babel are constructed out of rickety metaphor, because, as Espaillat's acknowledged master poet, Robert Frost, taught us, all metaphor breaks down at some point.

This respect for the limits of what language can do equates with a respect for persons. Writing about her parents in an essay called "A Recollection and Perhaps a Tribute," Espaillat reminds herself, "All these small truths are snippets, appearances, inconsistencies; what's hard is grasping the whole being, the essence of that person hidden behind all the stories and at last in the grave" (*Agua de dos ríos,* p. 84). One senses an ambivalence in the poet's attitude toward language. She believes that literature is "an art intimately linked to the integrity of language" (p. 104); it is incumbent upon her as poet to use her skill to make language present reality to the

reader as best she can. But she is not altogether disappointed to find that the greater part of reality slips away, uncontained. There is always that which "nobody knows," which nobody can say, which escapes certainty.

Espaillat's experience of leaving home at a young age to live where at first she could not understand the language spoken is shared by a great many American citizens, of course. One of her best-known poems, also titled "Bilingual/Bilingüe," depicts the emotional struggle and the intellectual excitement she experienced when she first encountered English, "this rich, electric language with its heavy beat and its flavor of violence" (*Agua de dos ríos,* p. 80). It records the unconscious triumph of a youthful spirit strong enough to reconcile a world of contradiction.

Espaillat has thrown herself wholeheartedly into the essential work of translation. Because Espaillat feels "at home" in both languages, she is ideally suited to the difficult, if not impossible, task of translation. As Robert Frost famously remarked, "poetry is what is lost in translation." Her translations into English of poems written in Spanish include those of San Juan de la Cruz, Quiterio Berroa y Canelo, Fray Miguel de Guevara, Sor Juana Inés de la Cruz, Miguel Hernández, Manuel del Cabral, César Sánchez Beras, and Juan Matos. She also has dedicated herself to the great project of translating Robert Frost into Spanish. Over a period of five years, she has produced Spanish versions of forty of Frost's best poems. Her ambition is to correct a perspective she finds too limited: "For Latin readers, Walt Whitman is *the* voice of America." She would like to make poems by Frost and Dickinson available to Spanish readers. In translating, she explains, "we can only reconcile ourselves to the fact that something will be lost and strive to lose as little as possible" ("Translating Frost")

One should not overlook Espaillat's translations of her own poems. Included in her first collection, *Lapsing to Grace,* were four poems in Spanish that she left untranslated, perhaps as a tease to her English readers, or perhaps as a nod to the Spanish readers she trusted her poems might find (for in fact, her first introduction to

readers of Hispanic literature did not come until her inclusion in an anthology titled *In Other Words: Literature by Latinas of the United States,* published in 1994). Her second book, *Where Horizons Go* (1998), had in it one poem written in Spanish, "Para Mi Tataranieto El Astropionero," for which Espaillat supplied her own translation on the facing page. This poem, in both its Spanish and English versions, was reprinted in the chapbook *Mundo y Palabra* (2001). The chapbook also included one of those four Spanish poems from *Lapsing to Grace,* "Resignación," this time side by side with Len Krisak's translation.

In 2006 the National Press of the Dominican Republic published *Agua de dos ríos / Water from Two Rivers,* for which Silvio Torres-Saillant of Syracuse University provided a scholarly introduction in Spanish. The book showcases Espaillat's bilingualism. The first section contains a dozen poems originally composed in Spanish, including the five already mentioned, with Espaillat's translations of all but the one translated by Krisak. Section 2 presents six poems written in English which the poet has translated into Spanish. Section 3 is made up of essays written in both languages. Section 4 is a selection of Espaillat's poems in English, and section 5 a selection of her translations from poems in Spanish into English, including poems by Sor Juana Inés de la Cruz, Fray Miguel de Guevara, Quiterio Berroa y Canelo, Manuel del Cabral, San Juan de la Cruz, Juan de Tasis, César Sánchez Beras, and Juan Matos. The last section contains Spanish translations of English poems by Len Krisak and the author.

The following year, a second book written by Espaillat was published in the Dominican Republic, this one a bilingual collection of short stories, *El olor de la memoria / The Scent of Memory.*

Her Place in These Designs (2008) includes two new poems composed in Spanish, with the poet's own translations. Naturally, because the book appeared at a time when so much of her energy was devoted to the project of translating Robert Frost, two poems in the collection address that essential, impossible subject of translation itself.

RHINA P. ESPAILLAT

DOMESTICITY AND COMMUNITY

The poet-critic Jan Schreiber notes that the range of poetry's acceptable subject matter broadened in the twentieth century, and attributes this at least partly to the greater number of women poets who came to prominence. Not only were these women "well acquainted with household chores," but "perhaps less ready to equate broad general statements with wisdom" (p. 39). Certainly Rhina Espaillat's attitude concerning her own experience as poet and housewife and mother supports this idea. She resists the commonly held belief that domestic responsibilities have an oppressive and entirely negative effect on the creative spirit. In a letter to Silvio Torres-Saillant she wrote, "My poems are full of cooking and laundry and ordinary loves and losses, and I don't regret that."

Of course there is an act of defiance hidden in Espaillat's apparent acceptance of things as they are, and in her refusal to regret that her poems are full of the things that fill her days. To write a Shakespearean sonnet on helping a grandson with his homework is to say that this act of mentoring is as worthy of inclusion in the great tradition as are the things young people do when first in love. The poet will not hedge her bet: "My poems are full of ... ordinary loves—I don't regret that."

"Ordinary loves" is itself a remarkable phrase. Is the teenaged Romeo's love for Juliet something out of the ordinary? What makes Abelard's love for Heloise extraordinary is that it survives the consequence it brings upon itself. All loves that outlast the initial infatuation bring consequences, at the very least things like cooking and laundry and paying the rent; perhaps children and grandchildren; teenagers and in-laws. Any love that lasts is extraordinary in laying itself open to what may come of it, which is the stuff of life and everything that any writer has ever had to write about.

In tacitly equating her "ordinary loves" with those the great masters took as subjects, Espaillat is traversing an invisible border. For those who know the power of imagination, it is no small thing to cross an imaginary line. Espaillat hesitated taking her first steps toward writing the poems that were given her to write. In a poem called "Workshop," she tells of her inability to answer when, with good intentions, an old friend who is a poet asks what she has been up to. She suspects that she will disappoint in admitting that she has not been up to "literature":

"Where have you been," says my old friend the poet,
"and what have you been doing?" The question
weighs and measures me like an unpaid bill,
hangs in the air, waiting for some remittance.

Well, I've been coring apples, layering them
in raisins and brown sugar; I've been finding
what's always lost, mending and brushing,
pruning houseplants, remembering birthdays.

The wisdom of others thunders past me
like sonic booming; what I know of the world
fits easily in the palm of one hand
and lies quietly there, like a child's cheek.

Spoon-fed to me each evening, history
puts on my children's faces, because they
are the one alphabet all of me reads.
I've been setting the table for the dead,

rehearsing the absence of the living,
seasoning age with names for the unborn.
I've been putting a life together, like
supper, like a poem, with what I have.

(Rehearsing Absence, p. 34)

By her own admission, Espaillat wrote very little during the years spent teaching and raising her children. Because the poem is titled "Workshop," we may conjecture that the lack of confidence the speaker experiences at first comes from her uncertainty that she still belongs in a gathering of poets. Her friend's question only brings to focus the question she must be asking herself as she begins to write again after a long hiatus. The question is not only "What have you been doing?" but "What will you do now?" or "How will you go about doing what you hope to do?" Though initially at a loss for words to respond, Espaillat finally arrives at what amounts to an *ars poetica*. From here on she will put her poems together the way she has been putting suppers together, "with what I have."

What she has, finally, are the people who live with her and those with whom she makes some

connection, even those who come into her life only briefly; she has a sense of belonging. Taken as a whole, her work in poetry, while it is sophisticated, eloquent, and wise, is yet not unlike the song of a very young child in its crib, naming the ones she loves and who love her. There is her husband, the sculptor Alfred Moskowitz; they have been married over fifty-seven years: "He has forgotten wedding, bride / in favor of my aging face" (*The Shadow I Dress In,* p. 12). Espaillat counts herself among the fortunate, happy in her marriage; she does not take intimacy that has lasted a half-century for granted. She still looks at her lifelong companion with a sense of wonder. Espaillat celebrates the mystery of desire itself in a poem called "Current," and in other poems acknowledges that man and woman remain a mystery to one another: she does not lose sight of the times when even the happiest of marriages are but two solitudes side by side. In her poem "Rainy Sunday," Espaillat captures how even what cannot be shared between two people becomes part of a life lived together.

"What are you thinking?" he asked. We had not
  spoken.
"Nothing," I said, and it was partly true.
For thought was not the silence he had broken,
But slow rains drifting earthward. Cold and blue,
A dog was barking in my memory …
Another … and another. My sad town
Filtered its tattered twilight over me;
Regrets, like odors, sifted softly down
And blew the world away. He could not know
That in a web of lamplight, as in bars
I was a child caught in the long ago
And pinioned to the wake of alien stars.
The dead were with me, chanting their old wrongs,
Scratchy with use, trapped in a dusty groove.
Far off I heard the present sing its songs
And watched the world retreat, and could not move.
Fearful at last, and hungry for my kind,
I thrust the dead away by force of will
And sighed, how blessed it is to leave behind
All but this living world that knows me still!
And then I saw his eyes, opaque with thought
And dark with silences where I was not.

                  (*Where Horizons Go,* p. 37)

The novelist and storyteller Isaac Bashevis Singer has written that no person ever really knows another. To pretend otherwise is a kind of impudence. Respect for human dignity requires that we sometimes keep a loving distance. Though Rhina's family members often appear in her poems, there is never any rush to unveil their secrets. In a poem called "Minefields" (*Rehearsing Absence,* p. 51), the poet's husband, a veteran of the Second World War, mentions a fellow soldier killed "when a mine blew up his jeep." The highway on which the couple is traveling passes the town where the young man had lived. On their return trip, her husband again brings up the soldier's name as they pass his hometown, using almost the exact same few words to say what had happened in Belgium so long ago. He does not elaborate, and she does not press him to say more. She knows very well what stores of emotion lie hidden beneath the spoken phrases. She knows very well how much she cannot know.

Espaillat has given her readers loving portraits of her children and grandchildren in poems whose very titles—"Rat in the Engine," "Canticle of Her Coming and Going"—assure the reader that the author, doting parent though she may be, is a true poet who brings all her art to the task. She has also written poems in which her anguish at losing her mother to Alzheimer's finds expression. In a villanelle called "Song" (*Where Horizons Go,* p. 26), she uses as her method of composition the erratic, associative word selection forced upon her mother by her illness:

From hair to horse to house to rose,
her tongue unfastened like her gait,
her gaze, her guise, her ghost, she goes.

The poem is an act of stealing back what has been stolen. Her mother, no longer able to "name the thing she knows," substitutes one word for another seemingly at random. The poet/daughter whom she first taught to speak now takes her example again, making sense of the associative leaps from one word to the next. Her mother's distracted "gaze" is a "guise," not her true face; it is her "ghost" we see as she "goes": the real

woman of flesh and blood will not return. But the poet has repaired her mother's broken language so that it may carry meaning again. She gives language back to the one who gave it to her.

The poems for her father are no less complex and moving. Her loving criticism of the man finds its way to praise: "Less practical than wise, / less wise than good" (*The Shadow I Dress In,* p. 50). Two of Espaillat's poems, "Encounter" and "I Dreamt You Young," published twelve years apart, tell of meeting her father in dreams, as though the distance between this world and the next were as easily crossed as that between a young woman and her outwardly stern father. In the poems for her father, too, language itself is of central importance. In the earlier of the two dream poems, the poet says ruefully, "I thought I knew / what words would heal the hurt" (*Lapsing to Grace,* p. 33). In another poem, "Learning Bones," she applies herself to memorizing the words that might bring her closer to her father, studying the Latin names in a book of anatomy: "I'm learning bones to please my father's ghost," she writes. Later in the poem, however, she acknowledges that there will be "no returning, / and no soft speech will bring soft answer back" (*Lapsing,* pp. 34–35).

Espaillat often speaks of language in speaking of the "ordinary loves" that fill her poetry. For example, she has written a poem called "Remembering My Parents Remembering the Books They Read" (*Her Place in These Designs,* p. 5). The felt connection between these two means of connecting with others, love and language, receives perhaps its fullest expression in her poem "Translation" (*The Shadow I Dress In,* p. 34). The poet recognizes the importance of the question because it is understood that love needs a language to work in. If, as Robert Frost wrote, "earth is the right place for love," human speech is the right medium for it.

Because of her focus on connecting with the people around her through loving communication and of encouraging new connections between people, Espaillat's poems, though domestic, are not insular. Where Blake urged his readers to see eternity in a grain of sand, Espaillat wants to show us how many of the world's peoples rub elbows in a kitchen where a single family gathers. In a poem called "Cartography" (*Shadow,* p. 31) she and her grandchildren study a map spread out on the table before they go to bed. She notes that, in the town where they live, all the small streets along the harbor are named to honor the dead.

The poet refers to a certain connectedness that finally includes all the nations of the world; it is Isaiah's vision, down to the very detail that the "knitting" takes place in the bones of a sleeping child: "The wolf also shall dwell with the lamb, and the leopard shall lie down with the kid; and the calf and the young lion and the fatling together; and a little child shall lead them" (Isaiah 11:6).

In an essay written in Spanish, "La casa solariega" ("The Family Mansion"), Espaillat again gives expression to this visionary idea: "A certain secret and eternal intuition tells us that we are one single family" (*Agua de dos ríos,* p. 90). It is a simple idea with profound moral significance in a world where so many are displaced and homeless, set adrift, seeking refuge. While lamenting the pain that comes of violence and upheaval, Espaillat welcomes the intermingling of peoples, which is always a family reunion, always an occasion both of sadness and of rejoicing. She speaks of migration as part of the human condition: "That's what they've always done, all the children of Adam and Eve, tireless travelers, friends of change, victims of change, eternal exiles, whether because of politics, poverty, climate, prejudice, or the simple desire to explore the other shore, the other side of the mountain" (p. 90). Her own experience makes it impossible to regard the newcomer as an outsider. Her impulse is to include the one she doesn't quite recognize among the "cousins from home ... practicing their English."

This idea rooted in the prophecy of Isaiah is also a quintessentially American idea. Simply by looking around at her neighbors, the poet from the town of La Vega was able to see she belonged in her adopted country. As she told Alba Cruz-Hacker in an interview,

I think of myself as a typical person of the U.S.: that is, a person with a foreign background who grew up speaking English and some other "mother tongue," who has relatives elsewhere and profound emotional ties to some other place, but who is mostly wholly "home" in the United States, in its language and ideals. I grew up in New York City among such people, from 1939 and through the 40s and 50s, and we all knew that we had someone at home who spoke only Polish or Yiddish, Spanish or Chinese or Italian or Greek.

("Dominican-Americans from Here and From There," p. 8)

Espaillat's natural inclination is to celebrate cultural differences; every new instance of "otherness" has a familiar feeling to her. Silvio Torres-Saillant writes that "Where ethnicity is concerned, then, Espaillat thinks that 'more is better' because the larger the group into which you feel you belong, the smaller the number of those you can marginalize through exclusionary othering" ("Answering to the Music," p. 51). In "Purim Parade" she takes delight in listing the various participants in a Jewish holiday event.

Mischievously, the poet describes this very American scene in haiku stanzas, including yet one more different cultural influence in the mix, and not one chosen at random, either, for the Japanese form requires not just the counting of syllables but the juxtaposition of strikingly different images. The form does what the parade does, combining disparate elements in a way that works, such as getting the Celtic bagpipes to play Israel's national anthem.

Espaillat's poem makes of the Purim parade a ritual enactment of the American ideal. She is so interested in making sure that nobody is left out of such an occasion that she is alert to notice anyone who is pushed to the margins of human society, forced to watch from the sidelines. She is quick to recognize "the family trait" in the one whose outsider status or physical appearance or quirky behavior make him less than welcome at the reunion, or whose personal demons cause him to rip up the invitation. Some of her best poetry takes as its subject the marginalized person. There is the blind man with his cane about whom she writes "Swinging an Arc Before Him As He Goes," and another man of whom she writes "He Lives On the Landing." There is

her delightfully forgiving poem "For the Lady in the Black Raincoat Who Slept Through an Entire Poetry Reading" and her unforgiving masterpiece "The Ballad of San Isidro."

It is not pity alone that makes her refuse to avert her eyes; her interest in the outcast is exactly that—interest. She welcomes such a person to the family gathering not only so he may share in the feast but so she can find out what he brings to the table. Her poem "There is a Man" begins in compassion but ends in admiration:

There is a man goes stumbling through this town,
his left side trembling as if touched by stroke
or palsy, maybe, and he wears a face
that says, "I want this," looking steady, down
where feet must totter straight. We never spoke,
I do not know him, but in all this place
nobody says so surely or so clear,
Desire is all there is to keep us here.

How easy—irresistible, for me—
in the ungainly shoes he drags with such
tenacity, to falter, to let be,
let go. Just once, I think, release your touch
on that hard substance, life, and you go free.
How wonderful to want it all that much.

(*Rehearsing Absence*, p. 52)

"There is a Man" is a deceptively simple title. It is chameleon-like in that it changes color—it takes on a different shade of meaning—depending on which of its four syllables is accented. In the body of the poem, where the phrase serves as the lead-in to a story or anecdote, the main accent falls on the second syllable with a lesser accent falling on the fourth:

There *is* a *man*

If the emphasis is placed on the first syllable, a contrast is implied:

There is a *man*

That is to say, now there is a singular example of the human species, this individual who persists in struggling through hardship. This person's unquenchable desire distinguishes him from so many others who lead tepid, complacent lives.

(The poet even accuses herself of belonging to the lukewarm party.)

Yet another way of phrasing these four syllables conveys something of importance, when equal emphasis is given to the first and fourth syllables:

There is a *man*

Read this way, the statement is an act of recognition. It is to say, "That one looks familiar to me. I see that he is someone like myself; he is a human being. I do not know his name; I may never know him completely—that mystery too I recognize as essential to his humanity—but I can say this much. *There* is a *man*."

Recognized as a human being, this *man* belongs to the family of man and is welcome at the family table, with all the other "cousins." What is more, of all those gathered there, "in all this place / nobody says so surely or so clear" what he is able to say through the gesture of dragging his ungainly shoes along the street.

Acts of recognition like this one, the antithesis of prejudice and discrimination, define the art of poetry as Rhina Espaillat understands and practices it: "Poetry, the art I know most intimately, invit[es] us one by one, word by word, poem by poem, into an eternal dialogue with all the inhabitants of the planet, in every century, teaching us how closely we resemble those different relatives we will never meet, how similar to La Vega every town is in which people are born, work, dream, love, suffer and die"(*Agua de dos ríos*, p. 90).

A QUARREL WITH GOD

Espaillat's poems often side with the beleaguered family of man in its quarrel with a paternal God viewed as too distant and hardly trustworthy. In a letter to Silvio Torres-Saillant, she complains of "the inexplicable callousness of a deity we're told is our loving father" (e-mail to Torres-Saillant, August 16, 2009). Yet she can never call it quits between God and herself. God, or at least the idea of God, is a constant in her poems, though faith in him is not a given but something

desirable placed just beyond the poet's reach. "How hard a thing it is / to pray against the wind and go unheard," she writes ("Recollection," *Lapsing to Grace*, p. 20).

The poet's skepticism never results in an utter and complete loss of faith—unbelief too might be considered a desirable thing placed just out of reach—which sometimes makes for a plaintive, irrational poetry not terribly different from that of a "religious" poet such as George Herbert when he is most beset by doubt: "Ah, my dear God! though I am clean forgot, / Let me not love Thee, if I love Thee not" (Herbert, p. 48). Herbert's prayer to be released from his faith would not be out of place in Espaillat's verse; there too, though, it would most likely go unanswered, leaving the poet to pray again without conviction that her words will reach the One to whom they are addressed.

Father, you must not fail, although I may:
Be here, be real, absence I whisper to....
(*Lapsing to Grace,* p. 48)

In her sonnet "Breath," she envies Herbert's ability to sing his resignation to God's will, where her own doubt remains unresigned.

How hard and with what patience have I tried
to sing like you, George Herbert, make of prayer
a song of praise in which to bless, confide,
surrender without blame, like you, who bare
yourself to God and lie down in His hand
as on a bed that Love prepares for you.
You never question, rage to understand
the secrets He withholds from us. I do, ...
(*Rehearsing Absence,* p. 59)

Perhaps the poet with whom Espaillat has the deepest correspondence in this matter is Thomas Hardy. In her work, as in his, grief attaches to the inability to put one's faith in God. At times she would seem to prefer that God come out and declare himself an enemy, as Hardy wished he would: "If but some vengeful god would call to me / From up the sky, and laugh ..." (Hardy, p. 6). At least then one could know that he exists, and even his declared malevolence would be better than his apparent indifference toward human

injustice and the seemingly random, destructive forces of nature.

Espaillat describes her poem sequence "The Story Teller's Hour" as "a meditation on the unforeseen, the disconnect between intention and result, the dreadful insecurity in which human life is lived, and the absurdity of the role love plays in all of it" (e-mail to Torres-Saillant). Love plays an absurd role because it is merely human, and is of no avail in the face of divine indifference. One poem in the sequence particularly underscores Espaillat's refusal to consider God a trustworthy overseer of his work. The poem, based on a newspaper account, tells of a man "who visits a friend with cancer to pray with her" but the friend dozes off while the man is in another room, the candle sets fire to the bedsheets, and both perish when the house goes up in flames. It is an unflinching portrayal of an unsympathetic deity whose actions speak louder than his silence. Because the two friends had gathered together in his name to pray, and because the fire began with the toppling of a devotional candle, it is as though the answer to their prayer is the derisive laughter of the vengeful God that Hardy invoked.

If indeed God is that kind of god, it would be more than justifiable to take a stand against him. Espaillat knows that she is not herself "of the devil's party," as Blake said of Milton, but she does not look on those defeated, darker angels without sympathy. In "Michael's Veterans Remember" (*Playing at Stillness,* p. 66), the victorious angels barely suppress their second thoughts, having overthrown their brothers. What they have witnessed in the heat of battle did not appear anything like a father's love. A dissonant chord sounds in their continued hymn to God's majesty. Like fearful party members after a purge, they redouble their efforts to believe correctly.

Ever faithful to her art, Espaillat arranges what may be the most passionate outburst in her quarrel with God in the fourteen lines of a sonnet, "You Who Sleep Soundly Through Our Bleakest Hour":

The Jewish theologian Abraham Heschel made a distinction between asking a question and facing a problem: "To ask a question is an act of the intellect; to face a problem is a situation involving the whole person. A question is the result of thirst for knowledge; a problem reflects a state of perplexity, or even distress. A question calls for an answer, a problem calls for a solution" (p. 1).

Though a giant question mark hovers over Espaillat's sonnet, the poem itself is comprised of one long imperative sentence; no question is asked. The words of the poem, though artfully put together, are not the words of a person using her intellect to find something out. They are evidence of a person "in a state of perplexity, or even distress." The poet has summoned her courage to face a problem, and the form of the poem mirrors the state in which the person finds herself. It is an Elizabethan sonnet, three quatrains of which address directly a deity described as indifferent, hostile in his absence, complicit; demanding that he look and see the one who presents herself before him. The ending couplet makes the reader do just that; the *volta,* or "turn" of the sonnet, turns the reader's attention to the speaker of the poem. As the use of the second person indicates, God himself is the first intended reader of this sonnet; if he were an attentive reader, he would now turn to see the poet who stands uncovered, letting her guard down, baring her thoughts. The poem, in both its form and its content, is the very embodiment of what Heschel called a problem.

Though clearly, for Espaillat, faith in God would be a good thing if it were possible, she is adamant in rejecting the fanatic's certainty. She says admiringly of her favorite poet, "In a poem by Robert Frost, there is no such thing as complete confidence" ("Translating Frost"). She is ever wary of "true believers" who use dogma to exclude those who differ with them. But she is wise to the reality that skepticism may present a view of the world as narrow as that of any creed. She will not allow herself a skeptic's self-congratulation; Espaillat's doubt is itself subject to doubt. In an early poem, "Slum Church" (*Lapsing to Grace,* p. 42), she describes the look of tender compassion that an angel carved in stone bestows on the grimy city. At first she tells herself that only a mortal sculptor could have the

understanding of human experience necessary to impart to the angel her kindly, pensive look. Then, however, the question arises: Would that be possible had the sculptor not first received a gift from his own maker? This questioning realization is made all the more poignant when one considers that the poet too, like the sculptor, has rendered for us the angel's stone face in which "a spirit moves."

Taken as a whole, Espaillat's work does not so much deny spiritual truths as weigh them against the experience of mortal men and women in an attempt to bring the two sides of the scale into balance. Not for her are the flights of idealistic poets. In a poem called "Body's Weight" (*Her Place in These Designs,* p. 56), she takes issue with lines a friend has written, which she makes the poem's epigraph.

Espaillat is glad to have the body's prompts. She would have found an ally in the great French essayist Michel de Montaigne, who wrote that "Those exquisite subtleties are only good for sermons: they are themes which seek to drive us into the next world like donkeys. But life is material motion in the body, an activity, by its very essence, imperfect and unruly: I work to serve it on its own terms" (Kramer, p. 40). The argument is one that her poems insist on. In one poem she writes:

> Guilty, guilty, and gladly! Take those wings
> away, that halo: dressed for earth, I stand
> convicted of no saintly taste at all
> for spirit's leanness.
>
> (*The Shadow I Dress In,* p. 15)

Another poem praises the human body at the very moment when it is most likely to be criticized, when the poet is standing on the scale. In "Weighing In," the poet takes pleasure in noting the parallel between gaining weight and gaining experience.

While Espaillat, like Montaigne, has no use for "exquisite subtleties," her own thought is subtle enough. It is important to consider that her own religious heritage is a Catholic one; that for Catholics the line between spirit and matter is permeable. In the sacrament of the Eucharist the bread *becomes* the body of Christ. It would be difficult if not impossible to distinguish between "creature comforts" and signs of the spirit in an old-fashioned Catholic home like the one in which Espaillat was raised, where religious images hang on the walls of the rooms in which the family gathers, where the face of the saint is right there beside the face of the cousin, just over his shoulder. There is that in religious faith which is itself part of what the body knows.

In section 5 of her poem "Snapshots in an Album," Espaillat describes with profound tenderness and sympathy the Catholic home of her childhood, where, of course, a Marian icon held a central place:

Jan Schreiber has written with regard to the religious sentiment in Espaillat's poetry, "For most poets nowadays, religious conviction amounts to only a memory of a memory. Espaillat recognizes this, yet she attempts to invoke the feeling of a remembered religious heritage while retaining the skepticism and ironic detachment that shape her primary perceptions" (p. 40). Here, Shreiber, though he is an insightful reader of Espaillat's work, ascribes to her religious poetry more artifice than is really there. Espaillat describes her inability to suppress the truth when writing poems as an "occupational hazard": she would be incapable of dissembling the problematic yearning toward faith evident in so many of her poems. For Espaillat, religious conviction, while not readily available, amounts to something more than a memory of a memory. Writing about an ordinary "snapshot," she presents her reader with a lovingly rendered, painterly image; the poet who can give us so vivid a description of prayer is unlikely ever to distance herself very far from the person who prays.

Indeed, this poet who is so adamant in refusing to trade the human condition for something more spiritual finds herself pleasantly surprised to catch a glimpse of the Christian god-made-man in a human context. In a poem called "For an Old Friend Encountered Unexpectedly" (*Playing at Stillness,* p. 58), the title refers to Christ himself, nailed to a silver cross and dangling from the ear of a young girl at the supermarket. She speaks to him as she would any old friend,

but says she was unable to find him there. Now, though, she is delighted to run into him by chance. And as happens so often when old friends meet after long separation, the one is immediately reminded of the essential quality of the other, shocked into glad recognition. What occurs to her to say includes references to things she remembers hearing him say; her tone is at once chiding and admiring:

To say that one never knows "where is holy ground" is to say that it could be anywhere. That expresses perfectly a religious perception of reality. To think that way affects the way one walks. By the same token, Christian prayer might well be defined as speaking to God as one would speak to a friend. That is what Espaillat does, not only in this poem but in others, including "On the Avenue" (*Playing at Stillness,* pp. 69–71), where again she finds God in the marketplace and strikes up a conversation. For this once, at least, it is a two-way conversation. She casually brings up the usual grievances, to which he responds with brilliant non sequiturs and evasions, altogether preferable to his usual silence. The "problem" that Espaillat so clearly outlined in her powerful sonnet is at least momentarily resolved:

> He turned to face me, and His mouth
> released a spate of starlings, and a peal
> of bells, and tiers of dressy shoes, and stacks
> of books on sale at Doubleday, and rows
> of steaming carts with shish kebabs, meat pies
> and every meretricious face The Good
> has ever worn.
>
> ...
>
> So I let it pass,
> indulged Him as He uttered fountains, grass,
> Johann Sebastian on steel drums, and more
> genial evasions.
>
> We resumed our walk,
> trading impressions through the darkening air,
> to the amusement of some two or three
> who, disbelieving what the eye can't see,
> missed God in the clear robe of His disguise
> and, skeptical of solitary talk,
> enjoyed my gestures, thinking me alone

above those skaters on their lake of stone.

"On the Avenue" represents a rare truce in Espaillat's ongoing quarrel with God, but it is wonderful that she finds him willing to meet her on her own ground, in the heart of her beloved New York City, hardly the place for "exquisite subtleties." A return to Abraham Heschel's distinction between a question and a problem brings into relief something even more remarkable about the meeting, which is that God brushes aside the poet's questions. These acts of the intellect are beside the point. Both parties understand that the real problem involves the whole person, to whom God turns, responding with as much of himself as may be perceived by someone who believes what the eye can't see. The maker of poems and the Maker find they have quite a lot in common to talk about.

CONCLUSION

Rhina Espaillat's good nature and geniality are as evident in her writing as in her person; they go a long way toward diverting the reader's attention from the darker elements that have always been part of her work. A terrible sadness finds expression in poems like "Old House," from *Playing at Stillness,* published in 2005.

> Old house where I ceased to live, where I live forever
> caught as in amber, trapped as the dead remember,
> wearing my father's death and my mother's hunger
> like a coat made over,
>
> strip it away: I am tired of piety. Sever
> the long tight bloodlines from weaver to weaver
> unbroken, from giver to giver.
> Peel away anger
>
> borne in the bones like death; let me discover
> the small bright coin of myself in the purse of some
>   other.
> Old house where I never lived, where I die forever,
> let it be over.
>
> (p. 80)

In an essay included in *Agua de dos ríos,* Espaillat described the family mansion her aunt dreamed of building, with many windows and

many rooms to house all of her relatives, whom she imagined returning often to rest there. Espaillat likened her aunt's dream to the reality of poetry and the arts, "the family mansion of the human race" (p. 90). In this poem, however, the poet seems to want to evict herself from that mansion. An overwhelming fatigue has taken hold of her: "I am tired of piety." She is not speaking here of religious observance; she is echoing Wordsworth, who wrote of generations "bound each to each / by natural piety" (p. 139). But the poet only wants to get out from under the heaviness of so much human interdependence; she feels "caught as in amber." She would sever the ties that too literally bind her. To be "trapped as the dead remember" is to have your self-image limited to what has been reflected back by persons no longer able to change what they think of you. It is to lose the ability to grow; it is to suffocate. In her panic at the lack of air to breathe, the poet would even willingly relinquish the one thing central to her work in poetry, the sense of the interconnectedness of all peoples, the vision of "an endless knitting" that takes place in the blood. "Sever / the long tight bloodlines from weaver to weaver." The poem is reckless in its awful willingness to abandon the family mansion, to let the roof collapse. For once, the visionary poet's faith in the power of her art seems exhausted. Yet Espaillat makes searing poetry even of this crisis of faith.

All of Espaillat's full-length books comprise poems both old and new, mixing her most recent poems with those written throughout her life. This poem, though included in one of the later collections, was written thirty years earlier, at a time when she wrote very little and did not publish. Composed during a period of great emotional duress after her mother's near-successful attempt to end her own life, the poem strikes out against everything that is held most dear in the larger body of her work. It represents a personal nadir, and makes painfully evident that the vision which informs her poetry is one not conjured out of thin air, but arises from a profound sense of what it means to be fully human. It is a knowledge acquired in the act of making whole what had been broken. "Old

House" is one of the first poems that Espaillat wrote when she decided she must write again, one of the first stones she laid down. She had to build up from there.

Selected Bibliography

WORKS OF RHINA P. ESPAILLAT

POETRY

Lapsing to Grace. East Lansing, Mich.: Bennett & Kitchel, 1992.

Where Horizons Go. Kirksville, Mo.: New Odyssey Press, 1998.

Mundo y Palabra: The World & the Word. Durham, N.H.: Oyster River Press, 2001.

Rehearsing Absence. Evansville, Ind.: University of Evansville Press, 2001.

Greatest Hits 1942–2001. Johnstown, Ohio: Pudding House Publications, 2003.

The Story-teller's Hour. Louisville, Ky.: Scienter Press, 2004.

The Shadow I Dress In. Cincinnati: David Robert Books, 2004.

Playing at Stillness. Kirksville, Mo.: Truman State University Press, 2005.

Her Place in These Designs. Kirksville, Mo.: Truman State University Press, 2008.

OTHER WORKS

Trovas del mar / Troves of the Sea, by César Sánchez Beras. Santo Domingo, Dominican Republic: Editora Búho, 2002. (Translation, with Len Krisak.)

Agua de dos ríos / Water from Two Rivers. Santo Domingo, Dominican Republic: Editora Nacional, 2006. (Essays, poems, stories, and translations.)

El olor de la memoria / The Scent of Memory. Santo Domingo, Dominican Republic: Ediciones Cedibil, 2007. (Short stories in English and Spanish.)

CD RECORDING

Melopoeia. With Alfred Nicol and John Tavano. Thomas Eaton Recording, 2009.

UNPUBLISHED CORRESPONDENCE AND LECTURE

Letter to Silvio Torres-Saillant. February 17, 2000.

E-mail to Silvio Torres-Saillant. August 16, 2006. (Document provided by the author.)

"Translating Frost." A talk given at the Frost House in Derry, New Hampshire, August 2, 2009.

Poetry Workshop with Rhina P. Espaillat at Powow River Poetry Conference. Newburyport, Mass. January 9, 2010.

CRITICAL AND BIOGRAPHICAL STUDIES

Christophersen, Bill. "Spruce but Loose: Formalism in the Nineties." *Poetry* 174, no. 6: 345–351 (September 1999).

Cruz-Hacker, Alba. "Dominican-Americans from Here and from There: Rhina P. Espaillat's Articulations of Dual Ethnic Identity." Presented at the 2005 Hawaii International Conference on Arts & Humanities. January 13-16, 2005.

———. "With One Foot Here and the Other One There: Blurring the Boundaries Between Home and Exile." *Soundings: A Journal of Exploratory Research and Analysis* 2 (2005). Available online: (http://honors.csustan.edu/journals/Soundings/Cruz-Hacker.pdf)

Dorn, Alfred. "A Questioning Muse." *Iambs & Trochees* 1, no. 2. (fall–winter 2002). Pp. 108-114.

Dowling, Gregory. "Review of *Playing at Stillness* by Rhina P. Espaillat." *Semicerchio* 34: 95 (2006).

Kennedy, X. J. "Introduction: 'The Breathing of the Muse.'" In *The Powow River Anthology*. Edited by Alfred Nicol. Flagler Beach, Fla.: Ocean Publishing, 2006.

Kramer, Jane. "Me, Myself and I: What Made Michel de Montaigne the First Modern Man?" *New Yorker,* September 7, 2009, pp. 34–41.

Krisak, Len. "Rhina P. Espaillat." In *Dictionary of Literary Biography, Vol. 282: New Formalist Poets.* Edited by Jonathan N. Barron. Detroit: Gale Group, 2003. Pp. 78–82.

Makuck, Peter, "Heartlands." *Hudson Review* 58, no. 3: 498–506 (autumn 2005).

Marinez, Sophie. "Espaillat, Rhina." In *The Oxford Encyclopedia of Latinos and Latinas in the United States.* Vol 2. Edited by Suzanne Oboler and Deena J. González. New York: Oxford University Press, 2005.

Murphy, Tim. "Lost in Translation." *First Things,* December 14, 2007. Available online: (http://www.firstthings.com/onthesquare/2007/12/lost-in-translation).

Ramirez, Luz Elena, Ed. "*Lapsing to Grace:* Rhina P. Espaillat." In *Encyclopedia of Hispanic-American Literature.* Infobase Publishing, 2008.

———. "Rhina P. Espaillat: A Dominican-American Poet." *Encyclopedia of Hispanic-American Literature.* Infobase Publishing, 2008.

———. "*Where Horizons Go:* Rhina P. Espaillat" *Encyclopedia of Hispanic-American Literature.* Infobase Publishing, 2008.

Sadoff, Ira. "New Formalism: A Dangerous Nostalgia." *American Poetry Review,* January–February 1990. Pp. 7-13.

Salemi, Joseph S. "The Poetry of Nicey-Nice." *Expansive Poetry & Music Online* (http://www.n2hos.com/acm/archives.html), March 2002.

Schreiber, Jan. "*Rehearsing Absence* by Rhina Espaillat." *Edge City Review* 6, no. 1: 39–41 (September 2002).

Shaw, Robert B. "Straws in the Wind." *Poetry* 180, no. 6: 345–354 (September 2002).

Stoner, Julie. "Rhina P. Espaillat: Her Place in These Designs." Able Muse. Available online: (http://www.ablemuse.com/v8/book-review/julie-stoner/her-place-these-designs-espaillat).

Torres-Saillant, Silvio. "Answering to the Music: The Poetry of Rhina P. Espaillat." Unpublished manuscript.

———. "Espaillat, Rhina P." In *Making It in America: A Sourcebook on Eminent Ethnic Americans.* Edited by Elliott Robert Barkan. Santa Barbara, Calif.: ABC-CLIO, 2001. Pp. 115–116.

———. "Formalismo y credo musical: Introducción a la poesía de Rhina P. Espaillat." In *Agua de dos ríos / Water from Two Rivers.* Santo Domingo, Dominican Republic: Editora Nacional, 2006.

Torres-Saillant, Silvio, and Ramona Hernández. *The Dominican Americans.* Westport, Conn.: Greenwood Press, 1998.

Vartabedian, Sonya. "Bridging Poetry." *Daily News* (Newburyport, Mass.), January 8, 2001, pp. B1–2.

Wilbur, Richard. Foreword to *Landscapes with Women: Four American Poets.* Canton, Conn.: Singular Speech Press, 1999.

INTERVIEWS

Kotzin, Miriam. "Rhina Espaillat: The Per Contra Interview with Miriam Kotzin." *Per Contra* (http://www.percontra.net/11espaillatinterview.htm), summer 2008.

Monsour, Leslie. "The Art of Memory: My Visit with Rhina Espaillat." *Mezzo Cammin* 2, no. 1, 2007 (http://www.mezzocammin.com/iambic.php?amp;vol=2007&iss=1&cat=about&page=about).

Scheele, Roy. "A Conversation with Poet Rhina P. Espaillat." *Texas Poetry Journal* 2, no. 1: 25–47 (spring 2006).

OTHER SOURCES CITED

Hardy, Thomas. *The Works of Thomas Hardy in Prose and Verse.* Volume 1: Verse. London.: Macmillan & Co., 1920.

Herbert, George. *The Works of George Herbert.* London: Oxford University Press, 1972.

Heschel, Abraham J. *Who is Man?* Stanford, Calif.: Stanford University Press, 1965.

Wordsworth, William. *The Essential Wordsworth.* New York: Gallahad Books, 1993.

AMY HEMPEL

(1951—)

Amanda Fields

KNOWN FOR THE lyrical precision of her prose, the short story writer Amy Hempel was born on December 14, 1951, in Chicago, to Gardiner and Gloria Hempel. She grew up in Chicago and Denver before moving to San Francisco at age sixteen. Her mother was a guide at an art museum, and her father was an executive in the field of information-handling systems. Her parents encouraged reading from an early age, and they stocked their homes with books.

When Hempel was nineteen, her mother committed suicide, and her maternal aunt committed suicide shortly after that. Hempel's life has been marked by other jarring events, such as grave motorcycle and car accidents. In addition, one of her best friends died from leukemia. Events such as these have repeatedly found their way into Hempel's stories, though she often points out in interviews that real-life events are merely places to begin, that the stories always lead elsewhere, beyond nonfiction.

WRITING CAREER

Hempel attended five different California universities, doing course work in such fields as pre-med and journalism, but did not receive an academic degree. In the 1980s she moved to New York City, where she studied under the writer and Knopf editor Gordon Lish at Columbia University in his Tactics of Fiction workshops. She also worked at publishing houses and as a veterinary surgical assistant as she was becoming a short story writer. Gordon Lish ushered such writers as Raymond Carver and Mary Robison into publication and recognition and Hempel benefited from his tutelage as well. Lish's workshops were known for their intensity and for Lish's insistence that the participating writers do something new or do nothing at all.

In Lish's workshop Hempel produced the first short story she had ever written, "In the Cemetery Where Al Jolson Is Buried." The assignment was to write a story about a terrible secret that the writer deeply regretted, something that would pull apart the writer's sense of identity. Hempel chose to write about her response to the terminal illness and death of a friend, Jessica Wolfson, who died from leukemia. First published in 1983 in the literary journal *TriQuarterly* and later widely anthologized, "In the Cemetery Where Al Jolson Is Buried" remains Hempel's most famous work. Another story, "Nashville Gone to Ashes," was produced when Lish's workshop participants were asked to write from the point of view of a character whose perspective is fundamentally different than that of the writer. Both of these stories appeared in Hempel's first collection, *Reasons to Live,* published in 1985.

Three more short story collections followed. In 1990 Hempel published *At the Gates of the Animal Kingdom,* which contains another of her best-known stories, "The Harvest." The 1997 collection *Tumble Home* includes a novella of that title as well as stories. *The Dog of the Marriage* was published in 2005. In 2006 all four collections were published by Scribner in *The Collected Stories of Amy Hempel.* The collection of forty-eight stories won the 2007 Ambassador Book Award and was named by the *New York Times* as one of the Ten Best Books of the year. In addition, in 1995 Hempel coedited with Jim Shepard a collection of poetry titled *Unleashed: Poems By Writers' Dogs,* for which writers such as John Irving and Arthur Miller wrote poems from the point of view of dogs. Further, Hempel has frequently published stories in such magazines as *Harper's, GQ,* and *Vanity Fair.*

Hempel is a well-known member of the minimalist generation of short story writers that

includes Raymond Carver and Mary Robison. Generally, minimalist fiction may have disparate parts that all demonstrate a theme threaded throughout the piece. Every character and movement in the piece is significant, so the writing is often spare and concise. Minimalists demonstrate the beauty and significance of the single detail in relationship to the meaning and feeling that emerges from the story. Chuck Palahniuk, the author of *Fight Club,* wrote in *LA Weekly* that what he likes about Amy Hempel's minimalist stories is that "You don't have to hold readers by both ears and ram every moment down their throats. Instead, a story can be a succession of tasty, smelly, touchable details.... each story [of Hempel's] is so tight, so boiled to bare facts, that all you can do is lie on the floor, face down, and praise it." This description takes readers beyond some conventional definitions of minimalism, for Hempel's writing is precise and its tone is affective rather than "affectless," the charge often levied against minimalists.

While praise for Amy Hempel's work is easy to find, not everyone loves minimalists or Amy Hempel. John Updike did not approve of the minimalist style, considering it a fad that would not make sense to readers in the future. In a review of *The Dog of the Marriage* in the *Observer,* Adam Mars-Jones writes of Hempel's style that it "sometimes requires a disproportionate effort from the reader." In addition, some of Hempel's more fragmented stories might appear to have a lack of organization weakened by what could be seen as flippant or random observations that could be placed anywhere in the story. Minimalism, and the way Hempel uses it, in short, is not always praised by those who desire more meat in the story and greater clarity in form and tone. However, Hempel's supporters would argue for her pristine sentences, concision, and wit.

Hempel is one of the few contemporary writers focusing almost solely on short stories and has received many awards and critical recognition for her work in the genre, including a Guggenheim Fellowship, a USA Fellowship grant, and the Hobson Award. She received the Rea Award for the Short Story in 2008 and the PEN/Malamud Award for Short Fiction in 2009.

Hempel lives in New York City and teaches fiction at Brooklyn College, where she is the program coordinator of the graduate program in fiction. She also has taught at the New School, Bennington College's low residency M.F.A. program, Princeton University, and Columbia University. In fall 2009, she began her tenure as a Briggs-Copeland Lecturer on English at Harvard College.

In spite of not completing a degree, Hempel continues to be drawn to academic study. Hempel has taken classes in forensics, criminology, and psychology. She says that her interest in criminology is not so far from the interest of a fiction writer. At one point she took an anatomy course that allowed her to observe autopsies, and she has suggested that experiences such as this have encouraged her to confront a fear of death that resonates as a theme in many of her stories.

Additionally, she works as a puppy raiser for dogs that will eventually become seeing-eye guides. Her experiences have left her with respect for the personalities and idiosyncrasies of individual dogs. The frequent inclusion of dogs in her stories attests to an abiding relationship with these animals. Reviewers have suggested that the dogs often serve as a counterpoint to the human characters—the dogs somehow wise, patient, and loving in ways that the main characters fail to be.

Several other themes and images recur in Hempel's stories, such as water and oceans, graveyards, an ambivalence toward children, the loss of relationships, grief, and intimacy (or lack thereof). Hempel also focuses on reflecting the everydayness of life, of just going on and surviving, and she has noted that incidents from her life are sometimes transformed in story. Her mother's and aunt's suicides may have figured prominently, for instance, in stories such as "Tom-Rock Through Eels," "The Most Girl Part of You," and "Tumble Home." In an interview on the *Cult* Web site, she says, "I have drawn a lot from my experience, though it ends up altered on the page (sometimes not very much, sometimes a good deal). I've found that nearly every time I've written about something that happened, I've

had to tamp it down, cut it in half, to make it as credible as fiction" (Hart).

Characters in Hempel's pieces are often working through a conflict that is lodged deeply within them, something that has no easy answer, something that feels both mysterious and real. As D. T. Max writes in a 2005 review of *The Dog of the Marriage,* Hempel's stories "tell us not just what life is like but the authentic way to see it." Hempel, states Max, is in good company with a group of writers known as "'dirty realists,'" who "approached modern reality with an affectless tone that was later much derided." These writers incorporated the elements of American popular and advertising culture and cultivated an "antiromantic" tone that left some critics wondering if this type of writing would sew itself firmly into the canvas of classic American literature.

While this is yet to be determined, the characters in Hempel's stories certainly reflect unforgettable aspects of American culture. Characters drive endless highways, from one coast to another. A family is stuck in traffic on the Golden Gate Bridge on their way to a gas station that has maintained its original features, such as pumps, but is now a popular hamburger restaurant. People love their pets and often treat them with more care than they show toward their human family members. Characters cite the soothing terminology of pop psychology. They are distanced from each other in various ways, physically and mentally. Life is broken into a series of fragments, each one contributing to the postmodern sensibility that words, actions, and feelings have become disjointed. In a *New York Times* book review, Erica Wagner writes that "Hempel's narrators are smart, damaged loners whose lives have a sense of being salvaged from a wreck. The humor is mordant, rather than what is commonly called redemptive...." Hempel's characters step back from the wreck of their lives and examine them with dark humor and a biting sense of sadness.

Even though Hempel often discusses the conversational give-and-take between reading and writing, as well as the ways that stories by her contemporaries inspire and dialogue with her own, her work is seen by many as unique despite being placed within a style whose parameters are sometimes too simply defined. Moody's introduction to the *Collected Stories* points to what makes Hempel distinctive. He recalls picking up her first book, *Reasons to Live,* at a time when he was tired of the "*masculine* examples of contemporary fiction.... I had never punched another man, nor shot a bird from the sky, nor had I fact-checked among the coke-snorting glitterati. And these narratives by male writers seemed to *require* complicity with their larger-than-life protagonists" (p. xii). By contrast, Moody points to Hempel's sentences, which "do not rage or posture the way the men of the minimalist realist period did. They ache" (p. xii). Moody and others believe that Hempel's work reflects an important characteristic of the best contemporary women writers.

Her stories are filled with wit, and her characters may seem to have flippant attitudes, but it is nevertheless greatly apparent that Hempel cares about these individuals. Her presentation of these characters is an exploration of the formulas of life and language that are too artificial and constrained to be meaningful. For instance, in "Today Will Be a Quiet Day," readers may infer that there is something problematic about the relationship and interactions between a father and his two children, who are spending the day together after the father decided that "He wanted to know how they were, is all" (p. 89). Through the story, the characters seem distanced from each other; the father's desire to see how his children are seems more out of a sense of obligation based on the father's tone, since a friend of his son's recently committed suicide. But the details and gestures in the piece speak to a deep love he has for his children and their welfare. This is part of what is so effective about Hempel's sentences; she emphasizes the power of significant, active details over explanation. As the daughter in the story says, "You can't explain after the punchline ... and have it still be funny" (p. 92). Hempel's stories tend to hold to the idea that readers do not desire explanation, because the details and actions will convey all they need to convey.

AMY HEMPEL

STYLE AND PROCESS

The word "miniaturist" pops up in many reviews of Hempel's stories, suggesting that she is adept at creating concise stories that capture significant details, much like a miniature painting. Her prose is often spare and almost always exact. For instance, in "Tom-Rock Through The Eels," the protagonist tries to think about her mother, who committed suicide. She tries to piece together the right words to say because so many of her friends seem to have mothers who can be defined in a few lines, such as the welcoming Mrs. Price, "who told me I didn't have to ring their doorbell" (p. 185). The narrator characterizes her own mother oddly, completely, and originally with the following concise line: "When I have to say something, here is what I can say—that when I was born, my mother wore me like a fur" (p. 185). In regard to descriptions of her style, Hempel eventually became amenable to a term Raymond Carver used: precisionist. The lines are precise and suggestive; the stories are taut yet thick with feeling. The difficulties of emotional authenticity plague many of her characters, and the ways they make use of language are the most significant evidence of that conflict.

Even in her shortest story, a one-liner from *The Dog of the Marriage,* she suggests an elaborate amount of detail about the speaker's character. The story, titled "Memoir," reads: "Just once in my life—oh, when have I ever wanted anything just once in my life?" (p. 373). The sentence suggests an epiphany for the speaker and deconstructs a common phrase. How many people have specifically yearned for something "just once" and have verbally stated that, only to want it again and to put it into the same linguistic configuration? The tone is a bit melancholy and a bit relieved. One line conveys all of that.

Like many successful writers, Hempel is often asked about her writing process. She claims to begin most stories with the last line. Since Hempel does not believe that good stories begin with abstract ideas, these final lines are usually concrete, such as a visceral image or a striking piece of conversation she has overheard. Hempel then writes toward the final line that initiated the story. In creating sentences, she says, "I'll turn a sentence over endlessly in my head before it hits the page.... So much revision happens before the writing starts" (Sherman). She also considers her audience and, like many writers, asks herself what kind of reader she wants and whom she is writing for. Unlike writers who call parts of the process playful, however, Hempel says, "Play? There's no play to it at all. I mean, I'm glad it can read that way sometimes. It's hard work" (Sherman). She approaches stories with the consciousness of a poet, and it is telling that she also incorporates the reading of poetry into her fiction courses.

Often, Hempel's stories begin after something significant has occurred in the main character's life, such as after her mother dies in "San Francisco." The two-page story consists of the main character speculating about whether or not an earthquake caused her mother's watch to roll off a dresser and disappear. The main character's sister has accused her of taking their deceased mother's watch. Rather than focusing on the tragedy of the mother dying, Hempel focuses on the pettiness of the family after the mother has died. Hempel's work frequently delves into characters' lives after the death of someone they love, such as the deceased husband in "Nashville Gone to Ashes" or the mother in "Tom-Rock Through Eels." Hempel has said, "I like the moment the thing changes. I like the aftermath of the big event more than I like to portray the event itself" (Welch).

In an interview with Dave Welch on Powells. com, Hempel calls her writing a "call-and-response proposition." As an example, she explains that Grace Paley's "Subject of Childhood" and Mary Robison's "Widower" "called up something in [her]" which resulted in "Today Will Be a Quiet Day," the final story in *Reasons to Live*. She cites the work of many of her contemporaries as part of this call-and-response, including Ann Beattie, Raymond Carver, Barry Hannah, and Denis Johnson.

Hempel's continued success as a short story writer comes at a time when emerging fiction writers find it increasingly more difficult to pitch short story collections to literary agents and publishers. Many writers claim that it is more

difficult to get short stories published and that they are pressured to produce a novel. But Hempel believes that short story writers do not necessarily have to become novelists, or vice versa. Hempel's unbending perspective about the distinctions between the genres of fiction may be heartening to those writers who feel as if they must write in a particular form or multiple forms in order to be published. She is an example of a writer whose devotion to genre seems to go beyond the marketing demands of the publishing industry.

REASONS TO LIVE (1985)

One of the main features of "In a Tub," the collection's opening story, is its sense of lyricism, which contributes to its pulse, defined by the writer Sandra Scofield as the "vibrancy in a story [that] makes the scene live on the page and makes it matter to the reader" (p. 17). Further, the "pulse is emotional, an attitude, a state of desire or need" (p. 18). Hempel's work is both poetic and taut, while laden with the emotion that shows desire. At first one might say that her work is efficient, but the term is too caught up in a sense of tidiness that does not befit the overall sensibility of Hempel's work. We often say of minimalism that it is efficient, and this can bring us to a sense about the writer's class—Raymond Carver is an example of a writer whose socioeconomic class is frequently discussed in relationship to his writing. It has even been suggested that his lack of time, as a working-class writer, contributed to the economy of his sentences. But "economy" is also a term that raises too many connotations about our time-crunched world. Hempel's sentences are efficient, but they are not so precious as to lose intensity. Instead, like lines of poetry, Hempel's sentences succinctly capture the complexities of life.

The story is broken into vignettes that read almost like the accumulated imagery of a poem. The narrator's main desire is to find a place where she can hear the beat of her heart, which she is convinced has stopped. The first place she tries is a silent church ("I got in my car and headed for God"). At one point in the story, the narrator watches her cat sleeping on the other side of a window. She taps on the glass, but the cat does not acknowledge her. Hempel writes, "The sound that I make is not food" (p. 3). Later in the story, readers can begin to understand the importance of this small detail, for it seems that every detail in Hempel's stories is significant and threaded to the next detail. The cat knows what to listen to in ways that the narrator does not; the cat knows where to find the beat of its heart and the essence of its life. The cat understands when it is important to hear and acknowledge and when it isn't. This is the narrator's conflict. It is a subtle conflict, one that, placed in the hands of a writer less deft, would become heavily moral. This lack of heavy-handed morality is another strength of Hempel's work, as the pulse generated from these apt images emerges like a fish momentarily breaking through the surface of water.

The story contains a resolution that feels momentary and realistic: the narrator suggests that one should sink into a tub, wait for the water to still, "slide your head under, and listen for the playfulness of your heart" (p. 4). She begins and ends with the image of the heart—the heart stopping at the beginning and being playful at the end. It is clear that the narrator has gone through a transformation after she has searched through and mined these images and memories—the church, the cat, sneaking out as a child and sinking into a concrete-mixing tub, and, finally, sinking into her own tub at home. It is here that the literal pulse of the narrator's heart is mentioned. She has been looking for her heart all along, thinking it had stopped. What she finds is that she really needs a space where she can listen to it, and the best place is under the water in the tub, waiting for the water to still, holding one's breath, and listening.

The narrator of "In the Tub" has an intense desire to listen, fully, to the self. It is the first story in *Reasons to Live* and a fitting opening to the collected stories, for it often seems as if Hempel is urging readers to listen, as if her characters are trying to listen to themselves and failing. She describes a lack of words and language through an expert use of language. Her characters are looking for a way to listen even if

it feels as if somehow their very hearts are failing them.

The story "Nashville Gone to Ashes" underscores the complexity of intimate relationships through an eccentric set of circumstances. The widow of a veterinarian named F. Lee Forest, shortened verbally to Flea, has decided it is time to find new owners for all of the animals Flea had kept at home as pets. She is allergic to animals, but she helped Flea start his medical practice with money from her family's applesauce business. The Nashville of the title is a saluki, Flea's favorite, and Flea's death initiates a show of grief on Nashville's part that leads her to waste away to the point that the narrator must put her to sleep.

The narrator loved her husband but was constantly baffled by what love meant, because it seemed that his love for the animals was truer than his love for her. She cites Will Rogers' statement that vets are noble because they have to love their patients, who cannot directly say what is wrong with them, in order to treat them. This is what the narrator's husband did and felt. This utter love for animals stood in the way of his love for his wife. She claims, "I think it was that love that I loved. That kind of involvement was reassuring; I felt it would extend to me, as well. That it did not or that it did, but only as much and no more, was confusing at first…. But the furious care he gave the animals gave me hope and kept me waiting" (p. 18).

Flea's unconditional love for the animals is juxtaposed with the narrator's complicated feelings about what love is and what it means. She cannot help but compare the love of her marriage with the love Flea had for the animals. But Flea is revealed as having a more simplistic view of animals: "Animals are pure, Flea used to say. There is nothing deceptive about them" (p. 21). At this point in the story, Hempel makes another turn: "I would argue: Think about cats. They stumble and fall, then quickly begin to wash—I *meant* to do that. Pretense is deception, and cats pretend: Who, me? They move in next door where the food is better and meet you on the street and don't know your name, or *their* name" (pp. 21–22). Hempel does not stop there, though;

she takes a striking turn into the unexpected: "But in the morning Chuck [one of Flea's cats] purrs against my throat, and it feels like prayer. In the morning is when I pray" (p. 22).

The story is filled with moments such as these, where the narrator's viewpoint is complicated by the actions of animals and her responses to them, and these interactions are ticks of grief about the loss of her husband. Though the narrator knows that Chuck the cat is not trying to comfort her, what matters at that moment in the morning is that it *feels* like it. It feels as if there is a sense of spirituality in her relationship with Chuck. And this was all she ever really wanted from her husband. It is not what things actually mean but what they should mean that matters. Characters in Hempel's stories often respond in detached ways, but her writing is unique in that their detachment demonstrates their intense connections to their feelings and their confusion about how to say and do what they actually mean. Although some writers who employ detached irony and wit might be accused of not caring about their characters, Hempel's work resonates with depth and emotion in spite of her characters' emotional incapacities. For instance: "After F. Lee's death, someone asked me how I was. I said that I finally had enough hangers in the closet. I don't think that that is what I meant to say. Or maybe it is" (p. 23). While the narrator ponders her reaction, she recalls that Nashville the dog stopped eating, got an infection, and had to be put to sleep: "Nashville *died* of *her* broken heart" (p. 23). Yet the emphasis on "her" reiterates the narrator's grief, reminding us that there are two broken hearts to be considered, even though the narrator "felt upstaged by the dog" (p. 23).

True to her style throughout *Reasons to Live,* Hempel mixes wit here with a potent sense of sadness. In the final scene of the story, the narrator receives flowers from Flea on their anniversary and learns from the florist that he had a standing order each year in case he forgot. Stunned and "spooked," she takes a walk, running into a beggar whose dog holds a sign and a dish asking for food. She buys ground beef to give to the dog. She feels good until she sees another man with an empty cup across the street.

This man doesn't have a dog, and she has not given him anything. "How far do you take a thing like this?" she wonders. "I think you take it all the way to heart. We give what we can—that's as far as the heart can go" (p. 25). Then she runs back home, back to the place where, presumably, Flea gave her all he could.

The sense that authenticity has been lost seems to characterize *Reasons to Live,* and no other story emphasizes that more than "In the Cemetery Where Al Jolson Is Buried," Hempel's first and best-known work of fiction. The story follows a narrator visiting a friend who is dying from a long-term illness in a hospital near Hollywood in California. It is the narrator's only visit to her friend in the hospital.

The story begins with dialogue—the narrator's ill friend requests that she tell her "useless stuff" (p. 29). The narrator tells her friend intriguing lies, such as that "the shape of the moon is like a banana—you see it looking full, you're seeing it end-on" (p. 29). It doesn't matter whether it's true or not. But the stories aren't useless; they're entertaining, and they seem to be a way for the narrator to show her love for her sick friend in an unconventional way. Both the narrator and the friend find it difficult to talk about the illness, and the story is about the narrator's capacity for grief and her fear of death. The narrator feels guilty for neglecting her friend, and desperate, and her responses to the ill friend demonstrate this sadness. She desperately wishes she were a better friend, and she tries: "She laughs, and I cling to the sound the way someone dangling above a ravine holds fast to the thrown rope" (p. 32). In that image we see the way the narrator is terrified of mortality and regretful of her incapacity to help see her friend through this illness.

There is a dedication at the end of the story to Jessica Wolfson, a friend of Hempel's who died of leukemia. Hempel wrote this piece when assigned in Gordon Lish's workshop to write about her most terrible secret. The piece certainly has the feeling of a nonfiction piece—where the narrator is questioning how to tell the story, which details to include, and whether she can lie about it since no one else knows what really

happened. The story does not detail the sickness; it details the fear of the sickness and the inarticulateness of grief. The narrator, however, does find a way to articulate her grief. She says she remembers "only the useless things [she] hear[s]" (p. 39). She says she will "review those things that will figure in the retelling: a kiss through surgical gauze, the pale hand correcting the position of the wig. I noted these gestures as they happened, not in any retrospect—though I don't know why looking back should show us more than looking *at*" (p. 39). For it is the "looking at" that the narrator finds more difficult than anything else.

At the end, the protagonist returns to the story of a chimp, taken from the real chimpanzee, Koko, that she had told her friend about. For her friend, she had culled sad details, the details her friend did not want to hear. Her friend does not want to hear certain things just as the narrator does not want to see the shocking details of her friend's illness; she can hardly look when her friend's wasted leg is exposed from under a blanket. At the end of the story, though, the narrator is finally able to reveal something that is sad and most certainly not useless; her friend is no longer alive to resist this sort of telling. She reflects on the chimp, the one that was taught sign language. She speculates about the kind of things the chimp signed to her baby, consisting of orders such as "Baby, drink milk." Hempel writes, "And when the baby died, the mother stood over the body, her wrinkled hands moving with animal grace, forming again and again the words: Baby, come hug, Baby, come hug, fluent now in the language of grief" (p. 40). Ultimately, the fact that the protagonist and her friend cannot talk about the grief or the inevitability of death is compounded by the chimp's moving capacity to speak grief's language.

What lifts and characterizes this story is Hempel's capacity to demonstrate the deep and complex sadness of her characters even as they succumb to irony and to the discourse they are left with—the inadequate language of American popular culture. The way Hempel does this is incomparable. This theme pervades much of contemporary American literature, where charac-

ters cannot feel and desperately want to, where they fall into irony and flatness. This sort of fiction fails when readers are left with the sense that the writer doesn't care about the characters, that the writer is simply walking characters about in order to show a witty sense of detachment and to parody the emotional distance lamented in American life, that the writer is using the characters for purposes other than to elicit a response to their humanity. Hempel's characters are cared about, though, deeply, and one could argue that the reason "In the Cemetery Where Al Jolson Is Buried" is so popular is because the narrator's inability to handle the situation of her friend's death and dying with anything but irony is written in such a way that we cannot help but feel the intensity of her grief. Perhaps the narrator is more fluent in the language of grief than she realizes. Hempel's collection shows a deep care and concern for people who are unable to cope in a culture that does not instill in them the tools and appropriate forms of discourse to do so. Perhaps this is why Hempel's first collection of stories remains one of the most beloved.

AT THE GATES OF THE ANIMAL KINGDOM (1990)

"The Harvest," another of Hempel's best-known works, has become a popular story in writing workshops. It is structured in two parts. In the first part, the narrator has been in a car accident with a married man whom she doesn't see again, and she must go through rehabilitation and deal with the physical ailments that will never go away. Her identity is questioned and seems to come to a halt. She says, "I moved through the days like a severed head that finishes a sentence" (p. 106). The statement expresses her feeling that, post-accident and post-recovery, she still feels dead. But the phrase "severed head" is so apt because it stops the reader in the middle of the paragraph. The idea of a severed head finishing a sentence is difficult to grasp. And then, suddenly, it isn't. Suddenly, a reader will understand the feeling. This is typical of Hempel's stories.

But then the story takes another turn. There is a space break, and the narrator begins to discuss what is left out in truth-telling and in storytelling. She breaks down moments in "The Harvest" that she has made up until now. For instance, the man she was with in the car accident was not actually married. "But when you thought he had a wife," she asks, "wasn't I liable to do anything? And didn't I have it coming?" (p. 108). The narrator addresses the reader and challenges the ways that certain details would change the reader's response in ways that would not show the emotional truth of the story. Metafiction such as this deliberately interferes with the relationship between the writer and the reader, creating another relationship between them, where the writer becomes a character and where the narrator can be confused with the writer. A reader could mistake the second half of the story as the "real" story, the one experienced by Amy Hempel, who has been in a few terrible accidents. But that would miss the point. Hempel does in this story what Tim O'Brien does in *The Things They Carried:* she sets out to challenge readers' opinions about truth and storytelling. Telling the story, whether it is true or not, changes it. Putting it into words transforms it. Some facts, when distorted, create a more compelling story. At the same time, readers' assumptions about facts can lull them into too much comfort with the context of a story. For instance, it makes a difference to most readers when they learn that Amy Hempel's mother committed suicide; it creates a sense of intimacy with the stories, as if she may be using them to express her own relationship with grief. But stories such as "The Harvest" are a reminder that too much emphasis on what is real and what is not can cause the audience to miss the power of art.

Hempel has also said that "The Harvest" acknowledges the tendency toward "personal mythmaking" (Welch). The stitches the main character gets in the hospital could be anywhere from three hundred to five hundred because she reveals different numbers at different times in the story and, each time, admits to exaggerating "because nothing is ever quite as bad as it *could* be" (p. 103). Although this is the main character's rationale, readers see by the end of the story that the overarching point is that stories are vehicles:

they move us from place to place, and movement itself transforms, alters, and shifts, even if only temporarily.

In the story "Rapture of the Deep," the narrator works for a temp agency that has sent her to stay with a Miss Locey on Halloween night. Miss Locey threw out her back and cannot hand out candy, so she is afraid that trick-or-treaters will retaliate. She became incapacitated on an exercise bike shortly after she struck a deal with God that she would exercise more if it turned out that she was *not* pregnant. She is on muscle relaxants. She also wears rings on every finger, revealing to the narrator that they are her deceased mother's rings, and believes in the power of each type of stone just as she believes in the healing effects of the medicine prescribed by her doctor. She says that topaz is her favorite: "It cures madness and brightens the wit. Powdered and put in wine, it cures insomnia. It was used by mariners without a moon" (p. 126). The narrator, up until this point skeptical, is struck by "mariners without a moon" and repeats it as Miss Locey takes her hand and looks at the gold band the narrator wears. The ring was given to the narrator by her fiancé, who died while scuba diving.

The protagonist tells Miss Locey that she needed to hear from God after he had betrayed her by letting her fiancé die. Hempel writes, "I needed for [God] to have to tilt his head way back to look up to me, exposing his throat" (p. 127). The text is powerful here because the conventional ways of communicating with God—bargaining, pleading, threatening—are thwarted. Miss Locey's deal with God about pregnancy pales in comparison with the narrator's demand that God look up at her so that his throat, that most vulnerable of places on the human body, is exposed. Again, Hempel looks for a place on or in the body to describe pain and loss, and this time she incarnates the entity of God, in turn showing that the protagonist needs God to have remorse for what has happened, enough remorse to become vulnerable to a human being. In the end, though, the sense of betrayal the narrator feels toward God is not meant to be elevated above that of others. She says of Miss Locey's television, which will be turned on when Miss

Locey awakens in the morning, still bedridden, that "She would open her eyes to women in colored tights, all still working out their sides of deals with God" (p. 128).

The term "rapture of the deep," as revealed in the story, is something that can occur when a scuba diver goes down too deep and cannot get back up. The narrator and Miss Locey marvel over the beauty of the phrase and how unfortunate it is that it describes something so tragic. It reflects too the depth of sadness that so many of Hempel's characters must reach, places that they cannot go too far into for fear of not coming back out.

"Tom-Rock Through the Eels" begins with the protagonist looking for peat. She is going to create a rock garden specifically because she needs a place to put a rock she dove for in Lake Ontario. She had seen through thirty feet of water that the word "Tom" was painted on the rock. We learn that her mother insisted she dive for the rock.

We learn later that the narrator's mother committed suicide. When the narrator's father is out of town, she sleeps in her parents' bed, on the same side her mother did, and she awakes to "find [herself] in the pose [her] mother died in—lying on her side, her arm reaching from under her head as though she were doing the sidestroke in a pool, the pills she had swallowed weighing her down like so many pebbles in her pockets" (p. 182). It seems that the narrator is somehow trying to work through grief in her sleep.

The protagonist's grandmother has to take sleeping pills to deal with her daughter's suicide, and it causes her to forget details small and large. "What is the word I want?" asks the grandmother (p. 183). The narrator remembers her own mother's response to forgetting what one had wanted to say: "Then it must have been a lie" (p. 184). She lists several mothers of her friends when she was younger, devoting about a paragraph to each one. "Roll all of the mothers up into one and The Good Times with My Mother would not get me into even enough water to soak a box of prunes," Hempel writes (p. 188). At the end of the story, the narrator is meeting her grandmother out on a train platform and forgets

what she wanted to say to her. Her mother's words, "Then it must have been a lie," echo in her head.

In this story, the language of grief is trapped. Its verbal expressions are covered over in a haze of pills. And grief is reflected in actions. The grandmother sleeps beneath a framed picture of her daughter that is hung on the wall. She does this in California, where the fear of earthquakes causes most people to avoid hanging things above beds. The narrator finds herself awakening in the position her mother died in after overdosing on pills. She deliberately sleeps on her mother's side of the bed. These actions and physical responses are more powerful indicators of grief than if the characters had remembered what they were going to say.

TUMBLE HOME (1997)

This brief collection contains Hempel's longest piece, the titular novella, as well as a short story, "Housewife," that consists of one sentence. The collection opens with "Weekend," one of the few stories told in third-person omniscient. The situation, like many in Hempel's fiction, is both realistic and rather absurd. On a typical summer day, a family gathers for an impromptu baseball game that is interrupted by a group of dogs that run to third base. A girl named Joy, whose leg is in a cast, hits the ball, and her cousin Zeke runs for her to first base with a glass of gin and tonic in his hand. The game is called, and one of the dogs grabs a foul ball and heads toward the river, followed by the rest of the dogs. There is a space break, and then, in the second part, the family that has gathered for the weekend has dinner and plays horseshoes until the sun goes down. The children are sent to bed, and the men, women, and dogs lounge on the porch. They pick ticks off the dogs and smoke. The story ends lovingly: "And when the men kissed the women good night, and their weekend whiskers scratched the women's cheeks, the women did not think *shave,* they thought: *stay*" (p. 200). In this final line, readers might sense the fullness of longing and its inability to be sated. They might feel appreciation and sadness, a mishmash of emotions, as the

characters in the story seem to feel. The weekend, after all, is temporary; the moments of the day fleeting before the upcoming week in its daily routines. This temporary happiness is a fitting opener for the stories that follow, which culminate in the titular novella.

The narrator of "Tumble Home" is in a mental institution, and the story is written in the form of a letter that she is writing to a famous artist she met once while having tea. Since she does not know the artist well, she often asks questions and provides logistical details such as the fact that her mother committed suicide. However, there is an intimacy to the letter format: it is informal and lengthy, written over the course of several days. The narrator is reaching out to a stranger, with an interest in him but with an intense need to explain herself, somehow, in terms that are common to many of Hempel's narrators. The story begins:

> I have written letters that are failures, but I have written few, I think, that are lies. Trying to reach a person means asking the same question over and again: Is this the truth, or not? I begin this letter to you, then, in the western tradition. If I understand it, the western tradition is: Put your cards on the table.
>
> This is easier, I think, when your life has been tipped over and poured out. Things matter less; there is the joy of being less polite, and of being less—not more—careful. We can say everything.
>
> Although maybe not. Like in fishing? The lighter the line, the easier it is to get your lure down deep. Having delivered myself of the manly analogy, I see it to be not a failure, but a lie. How can I possibly put an end to this when it feels so good to pull sounds out of my body and show them to you. These sounds—this letter—it is my lipstick, my lingerie, my high heels.
>
> Writing to you fills the days in this place. And sometimes I long for days when nothing happens.
>
> (pp. 233–234)

A reader might note that the introduction to "Tumble Home" is slightly different from most of Hempel's beginnings. This approach may have to do with the process she describes in writing a novella or a novel—pulling several elements

forward at once may have required more of a sense of purpose in the beginning. In this case, someone is being written to and for particular reasons. Hempel has said that it took a long time for the letter format to emerge, but when it did she knew it was the right one. The letter format provides a scaffolding for the fragmentary nature of the story—the narrator observes and interacts with her peers at the mental institution, reflects upon her past, and presents seemingly random thoughts as one might do when writing a long letter over the course of many days. Yet there are particular themes that pull the reader along—the narrator's curiosity about the artist she is writing to, the mention of her mother who committed suicide, interactions with her peers at the institution. Hempel threads these themes together so that they read like a letter to the self, a format that allows for digression.

The introductory paragraphs present reasons for writing the letter, but these reasons differ from each other and are not ultimately settled upon; the narrator reflects and ponders on the page, allowing contradictions to emerge in her ways of viewing the process. She suggests that, because her life has "been tipped over and poured out," she "can say everything" (p. 233). In the next paragraph, she speculates that perhaps it isn't true that she is capable of revealing so much. Her fishing analogy serves as a thematic representation of many of Hempel's stories: the seeming lightness of her sentences often has a more profound effect than originally anticipated: "The lighter the line, the easier it is to get your lure down deep" (p. 233). Yet the narrator is not sure that this is true either. In attempting to lay her cards on the table, she discovers, perhaps, that she still needs to sort through them, and she must acknowledge that they are juxtaposed in such a way that they cannot be entirely explained. Nonetheless, she keeps writing; like so many of Hempel's narrators, she soldiers on.

And, like many of the characters, this narrator is less interested in assigning meaning to images and memories than in reveling in them, in feeling their significance without having to spell out their meanings. It is in the structure of Hempel's texts and the composition of her sentences, rather than in trying to find the overall meaning, that readers can discover profundity. As the narrator writes in "Tumble Home,"

> Always, we are asking here, what does a thing mean? And being asked back, What do you mean? Whereas I like to say things just to say them, because they are pleasing to say, to remember and say, "There is a tiny cove on a lake in the Sierras and I sat in its sand one late summer night when the air didn't move but was clear and dry and the lake barely lapped and the only thing that moved was a passenger ferry set forth from the other side that was strung with lights like a flirty Parisian barge and made no noise but kept coming closer," a consolation then, and now.
>
> (p. 283)

In both addressing an artist (the man to whom the protagonist is writing) and working in the form of a letter, Hempel also confronts the act of writing and its relationship to reality. At some point the narrator writes in her diary an excerpt from a transcript of the artist, whose name is Arthur Brookmyer, "about the importance of an artist's capacity to absorb 'the shocks of reality' and to 'reassert himself in the face of such shocks, as when a dog shakes off water after emerging from the sea'" (p. 295). Once again the images of dogs and water become significant aspects. Most importantly, the validity and significance of art is crystallized in this passage. Hempel's view of the alterations inherent in the medium of storytelling is further supported by the quote. In interviews, Hempel attributes this quote to a real artist, Robert Motherwell, but has stated that the artist in "Tumble Home" is not meant to reflect Motherwell.

The protagonist defines "tumble home" as "the place on a ship that is … the widest part of the bow before it narrows to cut through water—it is the point where the water parts and goes to one side of the ship or the other. To me, tumble home is the place where nothing can touch you" (p. 246). Most of Hempel's characters seem to be seeking a place like that, where the waters part, where nothing can touch them, where they can cut through the complexity of the world like a blade.

AMY HEMPEL

THE DOG OF THE MARRIAGE *(2005)*

Among the notable stories in this collection is "What Were the White Things?" It opens with an artist's presentation, which the protagonist is attending in a church after being attracted to an advertisement that reads: "Finding the Mystery in Clarity" (p. 343). The protagonist had been on her way to see a radiologist for what she suspects will be bad news, and she interrupts her journey to watch the presentation. The artist paints pieces of crockery, and he is giving a history of these paintings through a slideshow. The artist begins to philosophize about the meanings of his paintings, discussing what is there and what isn't. The audience nods and accepts his statements. Then someone in the audience, referring to indefinable images in several of the paintings throughout the slideshow, asks, "What were the white things?" (p. 344). The artist refuses to answer.

The protagonist then reveals that her mother, before dying, had told her to claim everything in the house she wanted to keep because she was going to give the rest away. Whenever the protagonist tried to claim something, her mother told her that it had already been claimed by someone else. Once the protagonist leaves the artist's lecture, she tries to recall the things of her mother's that she had wanted to keep, and all she can think of is that they were white. She then goes to the radiologist, late. When the films come back, the doctor explains to her what has been found. There are white spots on the films that represent her illness. When the doctor asks if she understands, she says yes, then asks what the white things are. He explains again. She asks again. The story ends there.

Perhaps the white things are the things that are so secret that the characters in these stories cannot look at them full on. Perhaps the white things are the things that cannot be articulated. Perhaps the white things are the very things we try to make meaning for when we are the audience, the very things, perhaps, we do not need to make meaning for. The story suggests—through the accepting audience, the radiologist, the narrator's denial—that our desire to make meaning is often contrived rather than innate.

This story also seems to be about the inability to completely comprehend the extent of something. The narrator, in looking at the white spots on the films, cannot comprehend the reality of the situation. In this case, it is an illness. Hempel puts together the seriousness of this illness with another symbolic, and less grave, event—the artist's "white things." She threads seemingly disparate images and events, which is one aspect of minimalism.

"Offertory" is the final story of *The Dog of the Marriage* and thus of *The Collected Stories*. This story picks up with the narrator from "Tumble Home," who wrote a confessional letter to a famous artist she had met just once. She is out of the mental institution she had stayed in for a year, and she has moved to a home on a lake with the intentions of swimming each day to the other side with her dog. She finds out quickly that the place she has moved is a place of rules, including no dogs on the beach or in the lake. In the midst of this adjustment, she receives a letter from the famous artist she wrote to. He wants to meet her.

They become lovers, and soon he is obsessive about a story she tells him. She used to partner up with a husband and wife. The artist wants to hear about every sexual encounter she had with them. He makes her draw out every detail, and he asks explicit questions. As time goes on, she begins to make up many of the details, and she is bored in the telling. But the artist doesn't relent in his need for these details.

Even as the narrator is fatigued and, at times, disgusted by her lover's need to know about the threesome, there are many things that continue to draw her toward him. At an art exhibition, for instance, they have a similar response to the weaknesses in another artist's work. And the two of them move into a phase in which they decide, as she had proposed in her letter from "Tumble Home," to lay their cards on the table. They decide to tell each other everything, to leave nothing out. In spite of this agreement, the things that interest the narrator in telling about her sexual encounters with the husband and wife are not the things that interest the artist. Their desire for certain types of details—the dissonance in

this—works against their agreement to say everything they can.

Yet whenever there are moments of dissonance and doubt for the narrator as she regards her relationship with the artist, something happens to bring it back into balance. For instance, she arrives at the artist's loft one night, and he plays a pornographic film for her that makes her very uncomfortable. As he remarks on the film, he doesn't seem to realize her discomfort. Just when she is most perturbed by the film, he mutes it and turns his attention fully to her. "This quality of attention righted things between us," Hempel writes (p. 391). They whisper the word "harmony" to each other. There is harmony in dissonance, just as "there is an almost unbridgeable gulf between what an artist sees and what an artist paints" (p. 391). Again, Hempel's view that a story, whether it is true or not, transforms in the telling, is emphasized. The artist, the narrator realizes, "said he wanted to see everything, but did he, really? Does a person want to know the thing he is asking you to tell him?" (p. 398). Despite her frustration with his desire for truth, but only if it is a certain kind of truth, the protagonist also feels that she is "never more [herself] than when [she] was lying in this man's arms" (p. 402). The verb "lying" can be seen, in this case, as both the physical act of lying down with a person and the verbal act of distortion. In the end, the protagonist comes to realize, and we come to realize as readers, that the story we have here is the best we can get. The stories of our lives are what we can do. There is harmony to this sentiment.

In a collection that is full of loss, this final story leaves readers with a kind of spiritual offering that is suggested in its title ("Offertory"). In the Christian Eucharist, the bread and wine are offered as symbols of the tangible pain of Jesus Christ, and to many Christians these symbols are literally transformed into the body and blood of Jesus Christ. Though readers expect more offerings from Amy Hempel, the idea of the "offertory" emphasizes the essence of most of her work: the concrete details, the physical aspects of the body and the life, *are* the feelings. While these feelings peel away from physicality, and

while Hempel's characters experience these disjunctions, readers are left, like the poet, with images, with the tangible. Rather than being a minimalist, after all, Hempel is a poet. It seems that most good writers are.

Selected Bibliography

WORKS OF AMY HEMPEL

SHORT FICTION
Reasons to Live. New York: Knopf, 1985.
At the Gates of the Animal Kingdom. New York: Knopf, 1990.
Tumble Home. New York: Scribner, 1997.
The Dog of the Marriage. New York: Scribner, 2005.
The Collected Stories of Amy Hempel. New York: Scribner, 2006. (Page citations to Hempel's works refer to this volume.)

AS EDITOR
Unleashed: Poems by Writers' Dogs. With Jim Shepard. New York: Crown, 1995.

CRITICAL STUDIES AND REVIEWS

Mars-Jones, Adam. "Is There an Original Voice in There?" *Observer,* March 16, 2008. Available online (http://www.guardian.co.uk/books/2008/mar/16/fiction.reviews).

Max, D. T. "Isn't It Antiromantic?" *New York Times Book Review,* April 10, 2005. Available online (http://www.nytimes.com/2005/04/10/books/review/10MAXL.html).

Moody, Rick. Introduction to *The Collected Stories of Amy Hempel.* New York: Scribner, 2006.

Palahniuk, Chuck. "She Breaks Your Heart." *LA Weekly,* September 26, 2002. Available online (http://www.laweekly.com/2002-09-26/art-books/she-breaks-your-heart).

Scofield, Sandra. *The Scene Book: A Primer for the Fiction Writer.* New York: Penguin, 2007.

Sherman, Suzan. "Amy Hempel." *Bomb* 59 (spring 1997). Available online (http://www.bombsite.com/issues/59/articles/2058).

Wagner, Erica. "Little Earthquakes." *New York Times,* May 21, 2006. Available online (http://www.nytimes.com/2006/05/21/books/review/21wagner.html).

INTERVIEWS

Hart, Rob. "A Long Time Coming." *The Cult* (http://chuckpalahniuk.net/interviews/authors/amy-hempel-interview), August 27, 2008.

Murphy, Jessica. "Sentence by Sentence." *Atlantic Online* (http://www.theatlantic.com/doc/200604u/hempel-interview), April 17, 2006.

Welch, Dave. "Forty-Eight Ways of Looking at Amy Hempel." Powells.com (http://www.powells.com/authors/hempel.html), April 27, 2006.

LYNDA HULL

(1954—1994)

April Ossmann

LYNDA HULL'S CAREER as a poet was brief but brilliant. Superlatives such as "great" and "genius" have commonly been used to describe her. Poets as various as Yusef Komunyakaa, Mark Doty, and David Jauss have recorded accolades for her work. Jauss, in a 2009 interview, writes that she is "one of the greatest poets of her generation. Hers is one of the most lyrical voices in our poetry, and she married that lyricism to narrative in a way that few other poets have ever managed." Hull published two books during her life, *Ghost Money* (1986) and *Star Ledger* (1991), and her third, *The Only World,* was published shortly after her death. Since then, one other collection of her work has been published, *Lynda Hull: Collected Poems* (2006), which preserves her first three books in their entirety. (Page citations in this essay refer to this collection.)

Hull mastered a style so lavishly decorated as to be fairly described as baroque, but also finely honed, both elevated and colloquial in its diction, and elevated and gritty in its scenery and in the harrowing street and underworld lives it describes. In Betsy Sholl's words, "She is a master of diction and syntax, of stunning verbs [including verbs created from nouns and other parts of speech], metaphors, [and] adjective/noun pairings. And her syntax as conduit for voice, for the sinuous meanderings of memory and its relation to the present is utterly masterful" (2009 interview).

LIFE

Lynda Hull was born to Gene and Christine Hull, in Glen Ridge, New Jersey, on December 4, 1954. According to Christine (2009 interview), Lynda was so uncomfortable with her upper-middle-class existence that for her whole life she told people that she was born in Newark (the begin-

ning, perhaps, of the personae she created for herself in her poetry and life). Lynda grew up in Upper Montclair, New Jersey; Florida; upstate New York; Pittsburgh (and Montclair again, during her teens). Gene Hull was a salesman, primarily of carpets and floor coverings, and Christine was a regional head dietitian for New Jersey state mental hospitals. Lynda was the oldest of their four children, having a younger sister, Mary, and two younger brothers, Eugene ("Chip"), and Jon Christopher. She was particularly close to Mary, whom her mother says she "always looked after." Lynda identified strongly with underdogs (including underdog cities, like Newark), and according to her mother, she thoroughly disliked material things and wanted to be poor. From early childhood she identified with children who had suffered harm or were "different" in some way, and in second grade she befriended a boy who had cerebral palsy, walking him to school and carrying his books; compassionate behavior typical of Lynda throughout her childhood and adult life.

Lynda's lifelong love affair with reading began with her nursery school books, and Christine remembers her accepting her brothers' invitation to play outdoors by climbing a tree and reading while her brothers played below. In fourth grade she was introduced to haiku, and it was a transforming experience, inspiring her passion for poetry. She was quite close to her paternal grandmother, who was a teacher and also had a love of poetry, which they read together. In addition to reading, Lynda loved flowers and horses; she owned a succession of horses over a period of six to eight years, feeding, grooming, and caring for them herself, and became a very accomplished horsewoman, with a particular talent for jumping.

She wrote both poems and stories as a child (Christine says she was always writing in her notebook, on car trips and the like). She shared her stories but refused to share her poetry with her family, much to her mother's dismay. Christine remembers an early short story Lynda wrote about what she imagined as the terrible sterility of apartment life in the neighborhood surrounding Princeton University, which they visited when college shopping for Lynda. Christine recalls her being a brilliant student with a photographic memory, able to correctly identify page numbers for random passages in books, and with a remarkable facility for languages. Christine and Gene wanted to send her to private school because the local public high school was troubled by race riots and interracial bullying, but Lynda (despite being afraid for her own safety), refused to change schools. She had a horror of being associated with people she considered snobs and didn't want to leave her three close friends in high school—all troubled girls, the "underdog" types to whom she was so drawn and who Christine felt were a part of the reason her honor student daughter began to get into trouble, including using drugs.

On the occasion of her sixteenth birthday, Lynda's parents celebrated by giving her a big party; much to their shock, she ran away the next day (apparently undeterred by having been accepted for admission and awarded a scholarship by Princeton College). Although she returned several times to break into their home and rob piggy banks, her parents didn't see her again for a decade, after she had married Tommy Hueng. Christine Hull credits Hueng with saving Lynda's life by helping her along the path to getting clean and sober. She and he moved to Arkansas when he found employment there, and she studied for and received her G.E.D. and then her B.A. (summa cum laude) at the University of Arkansas. By the time she earned her M.A. in 1985 from Johns Hopkins (also summa cum laude), she and Hueng had divorced and she had married David Wojahn.

Although Lynda had, according to Wojahn in his afterword to the *Collected Poems,* a fairly "typical suburban childhood," he also mentions in a 2009 interview that her family was "very dysfunctional during her childhood, for a number of reasons." Mark Doty's account (in *Heaven's Coast*) of his friendship with Lynda, which lists things they had in common, suggests that perhaps alcohol or drug abuse or addiction was a part of that dysfunction: "We both came from households racked with alcohol or chemicals" (p. 97). Apparently the dysfunction/addiction was successfully addressed; as Wojahn says, "later on they grew vastly more stable." After the years "of being incommunicado with them… she reconnected with them, and had an especially close relationship with them in the last decade of her life," including a visit with them to their ancestral country, Poland, which she wrote about in her poem "Street of Crocodiles."

According to Wojahn (interview), she spent the first several years after running away from home "largely in Boston; these years are recalled fairly explicitly in the poetry, and involved drug use and prostitution. At the age of twenty-one she married Tommy Hueng, a Chinese immigrant from Shanghai, and lived with him in various Chinatowns in the United States and Canada for the next several years. They divorced sometime around 1979, around the same time that she became drug- and alcohol-free and began to practice a twelve-step program." While she lived in Arkansas, Hull worked variously as a counselor, as a sociological worker for the state, and as a member of a panel on drug abuse appointed by then-governor Bill Clinton. Wojahn believes that she "brought the sense of civic and ethical responsibility that these positions taught her to her writing and poetry as well." He and Hull met at the University of Arkansas in 1982 and were married in 1984 in Provincetown, Massachusetts. Hull went on to earn an M.F.A. from Indiana University in 1989, and she taught at a number of universities including Indiana, Johns Hopkins, DePaul, and Brandeis. She taught longest in the M.F.A. in Creative Writing Program at Vermont College (now Vermont College of Fine Arts), where she worked from 1987 until 1994. During their marriage they lived in Provincetown, Bloomington (Indiana), Madrid, London, and Chicago.

As a teacher, Hull was by all accounts rigorous and demanding of her students, as much from her own example as a poet as from criticisms she offered, and generous and affectionate far beyond the norm in teacher-student relationships. One of Hull's former students, the poet Susan Aizenberg, wrote (in "A Woman of Genius") that "it's true we adored her—once a group of us, women poets, joked with her that we would get leather jackets studded with 'Lynda's Girls' on the back." Lynda's love of teaching, her compassion, empathy, and love for her students, and her thoughtful gestures all helped to inspire this sort of gratitude and devotion, but so, just as importantly, did her respect and encouragement—and her inspiring example. Aizenberg alludes to that as well in her essay: "A consummate artist, she was also an astute and rigorous critic, as unflinching in her critical assessment of one's work as she was unstinting with her praise. She paid attention, treating one's work with a respect that made one feel less a student and more a poet."

According to Mark Doty (*Heaven's Coast*), Lynda Hull spent the last year and a half of her life battling to recover from an auto accident in Chicago wherein she was hit head-on by a taxi, and the bones in both of her feet were crushed. She spent months in physical therapy and appears to have spent the rest of her life attempting to regain lasting sobriety, after becoming addicted to the painkillers she was given after the accident. It seems a terrible irony that she died just before her remarkable third book (a finalist for the National Book Critics Circle Award) was published, in the midst of her struggle to recover from one car crash, only to die in another, on March 29, 1994, at the age of thirty-nine, in a single-car accident in Massachusetts.

LITERARY AND BIOGRAPHICAL INFLUENCES

Poets who knew Lynda Hull agree that Hart Crane's poetry had more influence on hers than that of any other poet, though her literary models and muses were many because she was so well read and such a serious student of poetry. The poet Betsy Sholl, who was a student of Hull's before becoming a friend and colleague teaching in the Vermont College M.F.A. in Creative Writing Program, acknowledges in her interview that "She was a longtime reader of Hart Crane, and I'm sure her love of diction, of unique words, of specific and surprising adjective/noun combinations, vivid verbs comes in part from Crane. Also, her attraction to a density of language, and to rich and complex syntax." The poet Tony Whedon, a longtime friend of Wojahn and Hull, notes in his 2009 interview that "Hart Crane provided Lynda a prosody. Through Crane she connected rhetorically with the Elizabethans—Kit Marlowe in particular. She plays, parodistically, with Elizabethan pentameter, juxtaposing it with spondaic street-talk—a demotic influence that is overlooked in discussions of her work."

Sholl also mentions Elizabeth Bishop and Robert Lowell as important influences for Hull, and from among her contemporaries and friends, Denis Johnson, Mark Doty (her closest literary friend), and most significantly, her husband, David Wojahn. Sholl rightly indicates Hull and Doty's shared meditative narrative lyric mode, and their shared "use of anaphora, periodic sentences, complex sentences with a series of phrases, appositives." Doty himself mentions (*Heaven's Coast*), in discussing his and Hull's shared appreciation of Hart Crane, Constantine Cavafy, Billie Holiday, Chet Baker, Joseph Cornell, and film noir, that they both loved "art marked by the transubstantiation of pain into style. Art full of anguish and pleasure in the racked beauty of the world, the kind of alloy she loved, and understood: the sort of thing we make when we're true to the world's comminglings of gorgeousness and terror," which is an apt description of both his (certainly of the poems in *My Alexandria* and *Atlantis*) and Hull's poetry.

In discussing other influences, Sholl says that Hull "found in Denis Johnson a fellow traveler who also was able to use complex diction, a mix of high rhetoric and colloquial language, in depicting worlds for which low diction would normally be considered appropriate. Johnson's capacity for compassion, his social and spiritual vision, were also crucial to her." The Romantics, especially John Keats, Percy Bysshe Shelley, and William Wordsworth, were important influences

for her, as were Emily Dickinson and a number of late-nineteenth and twentieth-century poets in translation: Anna Akhmatova, Cesare Pavese, César Vallejo, and Czeslaw Milosz (Wojahn interview).

Originally Wojahn's student at the University of Arkansas, Little Rock, Hull must have been influenced by his teaching and no doubt benefited from his ongoing support and poetic acuity throughout their marriage: "She acquired with David Wojahn, besides a husband, a library, a partner with highly developed poetic taste and skill. I know they exchanged work, and am sure she benefited in many ways from his excellent eye and ability to read and encourage" (Sholl interview). Whedon points to what he calls a "decade-long dialogue" between Hull and Wojahn about "memory narrative" (Wojahn's term), which fuses memoir with the historical and metaphysical, an approach that even a casual reading of Hull's work suggests she mastered. David Jauss, with whom Hull also studied (he was her first poetry teacher) at UA, wrote that he could "think of no one who would have been better suited to developing her particular gifts.... Under his guidance, Lynda began to write the first poems she found worthy of publishing" ("To Become Music or Break"). He also, in his interview, says that Wojahn "had an extraordinary influence on the development of her poetry, first as her teacher at UALR and later as her husband and colleague at Vermont College. He introduced her to many poets, both in print and in person, and he had the wisdom and generosity of spirit not to impose his own aesthetics on her but instead encouraged her to continue developing her own."

Jauss himself was an important influence for Hull, having introduced her (as far as he knows) to Hart Crane's work. Although, in his usual modest and generous fashion, Jauss does not take much credit for his influence, it is clear in reading his descriptions of Hull's evolution as a poet under his care that she went from being a highly intimidated, underconfident, but talented beginning poet to one who had begun, by the time she studied with other poets, to have some confidence in her art—and unswerving dedication to it.

Wojahn states in his interview that Hull considered Jauss her "best and most inspiring teacher." Jauss also mentions nonliterary influences on Hull's work: "I believe her poetry, her sense of fashion (vintage black dresses, shawls, cloches, etc.), and her sensibility in general were strongly influenced by '40s and '50s film noir and jazz. She was also profoundly affected by the poverty, alcoholism, and heroin addiction she experienced in Chinatowns in Boston, New York, San Francisco, and elsewhere during her marriage to Tommy Hueng, an illegal Chinese alien" (Jauss interview). Indeed, all three of Hull's collections are rife with these influences.

GHOST MONEY

Hull's first collection of poems, *Ghost Money,* published when she was thirty-two, is possessed of an already sure sense of craft, poetic style, and voice—reminiscent of Hart Crane, but perhaps preceding her knowledge of his work (see Jauss's surmise on this in "To Become Music or Break"). Her voice was and is, however, very much her own, influenced by her own sense of drama and trauma—and of the romantic and joyful, as well as of danger and mortality. In Hull's work, the tragic and the beautiful are ever-present, and often one.

The first poem in *Ghost Money,* "Tide of Voices" (*Collected,* pp. 7–8), illustrates this throughout, with Hull's exquisite use of language describing tragic subject matter geographically close at hand in her own life (suicides in the Hudson river, the pollution of the river, and the fragility of the speaker's romantic relationship), and in the ending lines—which also suggest Hart Crane's suicide at sea and the influence of his "singing" on Hull's work (her poem title is taken from the first line of Crane's poem "The Harbor Dawn"):

a tide of voices. And this is how the dead
Rise to us, transformed: wet and singing,
The tide of voices pearling in our hands.

The prologue poem to *Ghost Money,* "Spell for the Manufacture & Use of a Magic Carpet" (pp.

3–4), must be given its due for its prominent placement, which suggests, as does the text, that it functioned in some way as an *ars poetica* for Hull, for whom writing poetry seemed to be a kind of magic spell for making beauty out of pain and suffering, out of our mutual dooms— and as an invitation to the reader to do the same, to rise above a gritty (or worse, perhaps to her, merely ordinary) existence.

After its transformative power, much of the magic of poetry for Hull was in its singing—its music—and thus music was a primary concern throughout her poetic career. Jazz and jazz heroes are frequent subjects in her work, but more importantly, the music of the poems she crafted received her unstinting and inspired attention. Her music owes its genius to the masterful use not just of particular poetic tools but to the way she combined and varied her uses of repetition (vowels, consonants, words, phrases, parallelism, lists), use of polysyllabic words and the possessive, the technique of turning nouns and other forms of speech into verbs, and the use of varied, unusual, and elastic syntax, including the syntax of delay. This device, wherein the action, discovery, or wit comes at the end of a string of dependent clauses, is also a tool for heightening dramatic tension and is employed for dual purpose in Hull's work.

Another reason perhaps that music figured so prominently in Hull's poetry was her acute awareness of the world's music, not just in poetry but in daily sounds heard by her as music. "Insect Life in Florida" (pp. 9–10) describes the noise of insects as music from the first line and continues the musical allusions throughout. The poet is marked indelibly as a child by the world's music, doomed or blessed—or both—to hear music where many do not, every beautiful and tragic musical permutation in a world where no love, even familial love, is safe, and no beauty unmarked by threat.

The poet uses syntactical delay for both the music (and pace and flow) and for building narrative tension here, as we are pulled relentlessly along by the dependent clauses. If the syntax were reversed, if the last shocking phrase had come nearer the beginning of the sentence, the tension would have been dissipated and the revelatory power of the phrase greatly diminished. The same kind of tension and discovery is delivered by similar use of syntax in the fifth stanza in a similar recognition of the threats inherent in love and in beauty much as Wallace Stevens recognized them in his poem "Sunday Morning" in his famed statement "Death is the mother of beauty."

Hull's poem also contains references to magic, in the poet's early recognition of the world, especially of music, and words, as having magical power, and in the evocation of items commonly employed in performing spells such as candles, here the citronella candles that keep away the mosquitoes but also play with the light and cause her father's face to float. Music and magic recur throughout Hull's three books, and we will return to both.

Breaking is another recurring subject and theme, and another example of the tragedy of beauty or beauty of tragedy in all three of her books—another way in which loss/death is always threatening but also beckoning, with its mystery, its unknowable possibilities. David Jauss titled his essay remembering Hull ("To Become Music or Break") after a seminal phrase, "she would become music / or break," taken from her poem "Autumn, Mist" (pp. 30–32). These words confirm this obsession in her work, in a passage where the poet identifies strongly with a random—and fragile—stranger observed:

And, perhaps, the body
really is a gift, this small beating
in my ribs a reasoned rhythm. Once, a woman
at the museum reminded me of a harp. Her supple
  spine
defined a frame. She was so tense, I could see wires
as if at any moment she would become music
or break.

Breakage, in "Maquillage" (pp. 20–21), brings illumination: "You're the empty room / morning pours into through a torn shade." In the book's first poem, "Tide of Voices" (pp. 7–8), to break is to surrender to beauty, "a break and fall into the glamour / attending each kind of surrender." And finally, near this poem's end, the river may

or may not "be cleaned of its tender and broken histories— / a tide of voices"; it is "how the dead / rise to us, transformed: wet and singing." Breakage, in *Ghost Money,* allows, creates, and substitutes itself for beauty, and in the frequent use of the words "fragile" and "frail" and in imagery invoking fragility, the threat and beauty of breakage beckons.

Hull's life mirrored her art in a story Jauss tells ("To Become Music or Break") about her driving "through a thunderstorm without turning on her wipers because the patterns the streetlights and stars created on her rain-streaked windshield reminded her of Monet's water lilies. As a result, she drove into a parked car and suffered cuts and bruises on her head." This determined, sometimes heedless, pursuit of beauty directed her poetic efforts as well; as Jauss suggests, "Lynda was nothing if not willing to suffer to achieve the vision she pursued, to risk breaking in order to become music" (p. 13).

In his essay, Jauss lists some of the words that "became magic words" for her, ones she appropriated as her own as her poetic career advanced: *tide, voices, fog, steam, adrift, window, sill,* and later, *nocturne, departure, travel, chiaroscuro, dangerous, indigo, trains* and *blue, lacquered, dust, sifts, hollows, grace, hunger, laced, diesel, rooms, tides* and *violet.* Intriguingly, her use of *violet* often occurs in the context of imagery that might seem to describe traditional depictions of the crown chakra as a kind of violet halo, crown, or aura, and typically described as the chakra that corresponds with the death of the body, with wisdom, spirituality, oneness, harmony, surrender, understanding, karma, and other spiritual and mindful associations.

The first such imagery is in an early *Ghost Money* poem, "The Fitting" (pp. 11–12):

> I touched my hair,
> the same soft hair
> that aureoled her face.
> A bright drop welled
> on my finger, and everywhere,
> the scent of violets, steam.

The implied halo here isn't violet-colored, but the suggestion remains in the use of the word and is elaborated on as we progress through the book in "Jackson Hotel" (pp. 22–23) Love and beauty and harm continue to be inextricably linked in this and other poems. Do they seek healing of the crown chakra energy?—Or to transcend the painful pairing of love or beauty and harm, to transcend the paradox? Or to accept a perceived truth? Regardless of whether Hull had knowledge of the chakras, that painful pairing is one of the most obsessive themes in all three of Hull's books and is perhaps her most memorable, if not her greatest, strength as a poet—beauty that sears the psyche.

Another recurring trope in Hull's work is the deliberate use of imagery commonly used in film noir: dark shadows contrasting with light, light shining through venetian blinds, mist, steam, fog, smoke, trains, urban settings, lonely streets, and hotel rooms. Her work shares film noir's focus on troubled and desperate characters and situations, on fragile but tough, sexy, glamorous women and shadowy, dangerous men, and on melodrama and thrill-seeking. Beyond any personal identification or affection Hull may have felt for the genre (she refers directly to such films in her poems) or the characters and lives depicted in such dramas, she was, according to Laurence Goldstein in his essay "'Coruscating Glamour': Lynda Hull and the Movies," acutely conscious of belonging to a generation of film watchers who had helped to create an ongoing cultural shift in seeing their own lives as films and themselves as characters acting scenes in those films. Goldstein quotes Hull from her unpublished lecture on movies and poetry: "The movies have thoroughly saturated the culture, have changed the way we perceive experience." She praises cinematic techniques as a model for poetry for "the fluid shifts between exteriors and interiors" and "continually changing perspectives on passing objects, as if perceived from continually shifting orientations."

The ability to see characters and situations from different points of view is important to any writer, but Hull extends that notion further, seeming to identify so strongly with the characters in her poems that in particular poems and overall in the books, the poet or poet-as-persona becomes

conflated with the many descriptions of physically small, fragile, and troubled women (an apt description of Hull), and the self is multiple or fragmented. In "Jackson Hotel" (pp. 22–23), the speaker is one of those troubled women alone in a hotel room yet she also identifies strongly with a neighboring hotel guest.

Here are two women, each alone in a hotel room, the speaker (presumably drunk), and the other woman high on Methedrine, and the speaker is afraid. The poem ends with the erasure of the other woman (so indistinguishable from the speaker), performed by the speaker and followed by compassionate gesture seemingly meant to comfort both women.

"Chinese New Year" (pp. 43–44) is an important poem in the book (and no doubt to Hull, who spent years living in various Chinatowns), not least because the volume's title, *Ghost Money*, is taken from the final sentence of the poem. It is also another poem where the speaker's identity is elusive, impermanent, insubstantial, and conflated with others', in this case with ghosts, as she watches people celebrating the new year exchanging "ghost money," a Chinese tradition of appeasing and providing for the dead in their afterlife, performed at funerals and holidays by burning imitation money. The speaker watches, seemingly from a window.

She is living a life so alien to her identity as she once knew it that she feels a ghost of herself, watching herself live an alien life, touching the railing in the room where she lives with her Chinese husband, where beauty and harm, and perhaps too much self-knowledge, threaten her as she stands in the light entering the room from a nearby neon sign.

In one sense, her life seems to be going on without her, and in another, her life consists of waiting for some sort of answer, solution, or comfort from her husband, whose arrival she awaits. The insubstantiality or ghostliness of the speaker's self is a recurring theme, appearing again in the next poem, "Arias, 1971" (pp. 45–46), where her identity is conflated with her Chinese neighbor's: "The train rocked and windows gave our faces back // ghost twins, sisters from some other life." In the early poem

"The Fitting" (pp. 11–12), the speaker is "thin as glass," having actually become a window herself; glass with the power to view both the external and internal.

The imagery and symbolism of windows in all three of her books is so obsessive as to be central to her work. Any art is about perception to some degree, but it is a strong theme for Hull, as is the sense of identification/alienation and inclusion/exclusion. Depending on which side of the glass we are on, windows either keep out or cage—as well as allowing vision, illuminating, mirroring, framing, and substituting for movie screens. The window is, in that last passage, both movie screen and cage, where the speaker watches the film noir scene character through a window, then edits the "movie" with her own breath, and finally, reaches through the screen to make contact, ending her isolation/alienation.

In "The Fitting," the speaker, as a child, is brought to watch her mother's dress fitting, which she does, "until / my head ached / and felt thin as glass," and she leans her cheek against the window, "elbow / pushed among violets / and cactus" (beauty and harm again). Unable to bear the reality inside, she watches the "movie" outside, until she pricks her finger on the cactus. She doesn't cry out or speak, but her mother steps toward her,

> changing the air.
> In the dimness,
> I touched my hair,
> the same soft hair
> that aureoled her face.
> A bright drop welled
> On my finger, and everywhere,
> The scent of violets, steam.

We don't know if her mother coincidentally finished the fitting at the exact right moment or saw her daughter prick her finger or responded intuitively to her unspoken cry, but she, with her love, "changes the air," presumably comforting the speaker, who is suddenly present again in the moment, back in her real life, surrounded by warmth and beauty and feeling a strong sense of identity with her mother—yet also bleeding. Love and loss, beauty and danger, inextricably intertwined.

LYNDA HULL

STAR LEDGER

Hull's second collection, *Star Ledger* (named after the Newark newspaper), takes everything up a notch: her already considerable skills as a poet improve; the language (in consistently longer-lined poems), now describing the increasingly gritty and dangerous, is even more beautiful and lush to the extent that it begins to feel almost baroque in its excess—and that excess is also a theme, a desire, and a philosophy.

While the book title refers to the newspaper, it also, with the first, and title, poem (*Collected,* pp. 69–71) refers to the movie stars featured in the newspaper and to the album or "ledger" of stars the speaker as a child accounts beautiful and glamorous. We are back in the movies again, back to the blurring of reality and stage (oddly, anticipating "reality TV"), where the speaker plans to "dress for the sun's total eclipse" while pasting movie star photos in her album. We also return immediately to the pairing of love or beauty and danger: as her grandmother brushes her hair, she sees "Above the corset her back was soft, black moles / she called her 'melanomas' dusted across / powdery skin like a night sky, inside out." The potentially deadly moles become a starry sky, but reversed: the stars become black holes that might presumably disappear her grandmother into the void, and their city, Newark, "will collapse to burn like another dying star" (a reference to the infamous 1967 Newark riots).

While the poems that dealt with autobiographical material in *Ghost Money* often dealt with childhood, and began to deal with the life Hull lived after running away from home, those harrowing years are a primary focus of the autobiographical poems in *Star Ledger,* a kind of film noir poetry on speed. The girl who loved its stars went on to live a life that so closely resembled film noir, at least as described in her poetry, that the two are at times indistinguishable, as in "The Real Movie, with Stars" (pp. 81–83), wherein the poet is conscious of acting—or living—a role, and has an audience even if it is composed of other "actors" in the "movie."

Early in the poem, accosted by a begging stranger in evening clothes on the boardwalk of an Atlantic beach, the speaker describes herself as the stranger in the scene. Another man in the balcony of a theater is weeping—and suddenly we seem to be in Los Angeles, in the speaker's past, except she wasn't herself. Yet another man is playing with her hair perhaps because she looks like an actress from a B-movie suddenly being described—and just as suddenly, we are back on the Atlantic coast where we began, a technique taken from film called "jump-cutting."

It is a fractured, disorienting technique well suited to a fracturing or multiplying of the lyric "I" in the poem, and to the poem/life as film. It is also suited to the subject (here, we jump to an abstract scene). Then we're back in Los Angeles again, and the man is kissing her. What belongs to the speaker is a moment's pleasure, or the fulfillment of one desire whose pleasure is already dissolving into the next desire—as if the lip of a waterfall, which is the exact beginning of the waterfall, could somehow keep the water from falling, as if the rim of an eyelid could dam tears. Either way, what belongs to her is endless desire or hunger as long as she is alive to feel it.

Hull returns again, overtly, to Hart Crane's influence in the title of "Love Song During Riot with Many Voices," her poem about the Newark riots, and in "Adagio," which seems to be part of her imagined poetic duet (or ongoing dialogue) with Crane—just as "Tide of Voices," whose setting is dusk, and whose title is the first line from Crane's "The Harbor Dawn," seems to have been a deliberate inversion of his poem (see Jauss's essay, "To Become Music or Break"). Although "Adagio" (pp. 86–87) is written in the third person, it seems fair to assume that the third person in this case is a masked first person, given Hull's history of addiction to alcohol and drugs (and her love for Crane's work, shared by the woman described in the poem), and given how the poet continually identifies with the women she writes about. The details of drug use in "Adagio" seem to be one of Hull's direct poetic references to her own history of addiction.

The descriptions of addiction are interwoven with descriptions of the woman drifting in an imaginary boat, identifying her with Crane's addiction (to alcohol) and known fondness for sailors (he was homosexual), and with his final

act, his suicide by drowning, having leapt from a boat into the ocean. The woman described sounds a lot like Hull.

The idea of spending life lavishly extends in Hull's work so far beyond a description of Crane or his poetry as to have become a seeming *ars poetica*—or *ars vita*—for Hull, who dedicated herself to writing lavishly beautiful poems about harrowing subjects. The woman in the poem rejects Crane's fate—and the room housing her addiction yet the poem ends with her injecting heroin into herself and a lavish description of her high that follows, mirroring Hull's own struggles with addiction and sobriety.

In "Magical Thinking" (pp. 111–112), Hull returns to several poetic obsessions: magic, music/breaking, windows, alienation/erasure, and illusion/transformation. The speaker (presumably the poet) returns to her old neighborhood to find it more desolate and damaged than it had been, and the magic references herein seem to be mainly ironic. The speaker's thinking in the poem is also magical in painfully ironic ways. This is combined with her recurring imagery of music/breaking but less glamorously imagined, more painful and real than previously in her work.

The poem moves to a description of the view out the window, and then she disappears. Her identity has been erased, and she has been not just transformed or reduced to her dresses thrown from the window but exploded—and the breaking did not, after all, cause her to become music. Rather, she is aware now of seeing the world as through rose-colored glasses, the speaker becoming aware of errors in her magical thinking. The final lines, musically beautiful though they are, are about as bald and unadorned as Hull ever gets, a rare glimpse of a less gorgeous pain and suffering, a refusal perhaps to glamorize this particular pain.

By contrast, in "Cubism, Barcelona" (pp. 117–120), ostensibly about Picasso's early work, Hull apparently touches upon the dissolution of her first marriage (to Hueng), "another rift / between us, this commerce of silences and mysteries / called marriage," which, even while it is in progress, she is consciously turning into art, comparing her writing process to Picasso's

painting process: "I can fill in the blank space of this room // between you and me, between the raucous promenade, / with all the rooms and galleries I've known, now so wantonly / painting themselves across this room." The emotional void is filled or transformed to art in a search for meaning, truth, and self-knowledge: "the dark abundant hair a woman / I could have been is brushing ... some drag diva strung out on something I can't name, something / kicking like this vicious twin inside who longs to walk / where guidebooks say not to, who longs to follow beyond all / common sense, that childhood love of terror propelling us." Whether it is thrill-seeking for its own sake or a desire to escape from mundane or gritty miseries is not clear, as we flash back from Barcelona to a hardscrabble life stateside: "Boston's damp cold / and we're stuffing rags again in broken windows, that condemned // brownstone.... Simply trying like always / to con our way to some new dimension. And weren't we glamorous?" Here, Hull appears to poke dark fun at both her and her husband's false perceptions about their chosen lifestyle, but also about her own impulse as a poet to glamorize the unglamorous—while at the same time demonstrating Picasso's adage that "Art is a lie that makes us realize the truth."

"Lost Fugue for Chet" (pp. 133–135) is much more than a simple homage to a beloved jazz musician; it considers his heroin addiction (one she experienced herself), his thrill-seeking, his flirtation with death (and actual death), and his dedication to his art, all of which she seems to have shared to some degree, at least as she describes her life in her poetry. Baker's face is marked and worn and Amsterdam, where he performed his final gig and where he died, is a place where beauty coexists with the urban detritus of drugs and junkies. The last phrase is an ironic reference to another kind of "music" both of them heard.

Hull makes the dark suggestion to lose onself in this environment and asks a terrifying question, intended it seems for both of them, since she uses second person address. Yet it is Baker who finally does not step back from the brink in falling to his death. In these final lines, Hull

refers to both his literal impact on the street and his last high. As in "Adagio," the poet refuses the same death as her hero, leaving and locking the room and losing the key in the earlier poem, and returning to an earlier time in this one.

That stepping back is followed by a poem titled "Vita Brevis" (pp. 136–138), referring to Hippocrates' famous aphorism "Art is long, life is short, opportunity fleeting, experiment dangerous, judgment difficult." Also set in Holland, it describes the painting of another artist, Johannes Vermeer, who died young. Artists (including musicians) and friends dying young (often as a result of addictions) is a recurring subject in Hull's work, and the next poem, "Hospice" (pp. 139–142) deals with the dying of a childhood friend, seemingly from drug-related complications (probably AIDS contracted from sharing needles, since "the orderlies were afraid to / touch [her]"), describing her "face with its hollows against hospital linen." "Newark's empty asylum wings opened again this year / for the terminal cases," the poet relates. "Each day another / strung-out welfare mother, the street-corner romeos / we used to think so glamorous, all jacked-up / on two-buck shots."

Her friend, Loretta, taught her to "find the good vein / in the blue and yellow hours of our sixteenth year.... buoyed by whatever would lift us above the smoldering / asphalt ... we must have felt beyond all damage." Clearly the poet at this point has experienced enough damage to have lost her youthful sense of invincibility, remembering as she does how many times she watched Loretta "rise again, and again from the dead," from the near death of drug overdoses, which makes the speaker wish for "the cancellation of that hungering that turns us / toward the mortal arms of lovers or highways / or whatever form of forgetfulness we choose." Her friend's fate haunts and threatens her: "Loretta, this evening washes / over my shoulders, this provisional reprieve. // I've been telling myself your story for months." But she ends the poem with gratitude, and though the final stanza refers to "a girl" lighting a cigarette in a doorway, this is one of those favorite female character/authorial self conflations Hull so often employs: "Listen, how all

along the avenue trees / are shaken with rumor of this strange good fortune"—her own fortune, we assume, in having escaped her friend's fate.

THE ONLY WORLD

Hull had written the poems for her third (and posthumous) book, *The Only World,* before she died, but it fell to her widower, David Wojahn (see his foreword to the book), to arrange the poems and choose a book title based on their recent discussions. Where *Star Ledger* took everything up a notch—the language (in consistently longer-lined poems) delving into the increasingly gritty and dangerous, the description so beautiful and lush that it began to feel almost baroque in its excess—*The Only World* represented a truly awe-inspiring leap in her mastery of her poetic skills and of her poetic obsessions, including excess.

The book opens with "Chiffon" (*Collected,* pp. 151–153), a poem as much about perception as anything, but a perception not merely aesthetic, despite the intense, lavish artistry of the description. It is about a spiritual perception of the world's present beauty, about the grace of having been spared to see it, and the gratitude felt by the speaker for the privilege. There is gratitude in every baroque phrase or line of her descriptions; her love of excess has become an excess of love, an embrace of all her life has been and is. There is gratitude in every lavish adjective, an insistence on seeing completely, and perhaps at last the beginning of an acceptance of the beauty/breaking conundrum. The beauty amongst ruin is a shock, but it is lovingly, musically described, as is ruin itself. A survivor's gratitude (as opposed to guilt) is also evident in the poem. Though we end with harm at beauty's and the speaker's center there is an acceptance in that imperative, made more to the self than to the reader. Yes, the heart is dark and pained but it is also beautiful, worthy of loving attention.

"Ornithology" (pp. 158–160), which describes her visit with a friend to Charlie Parker's grave in Kansas City and is titled after his famous jazz piece punning on his nickname, "Bird," has been much written about, thanks in part to the

Brilliant Corners: A Journal of Jazz & Literature issue that featured three of Hull's jazz poems and essay responses to them by David Wojahn, Mark Doty, David Jauss, and Yusef Komunyakaa. Jauss's essay "Ways of Breaking: Lynda Hull's 'Ornithology'" points out that she pushes her breaking theme to new heights in the poem and describes it as an *ars poetica,* "through her exploration, and illustration, of various 'ways of breaking.' By the end of the poem, the word 'break' has become a complex pun, one far more serious than that of Parker's title: it refers to Bird's solo break, to his breaking of the conventions of musical time, to line breaks ('Take a phrase, then / fracture it'), to the way the past breaks into the present, and ultimately, to emotional heartbreak and, even, breakdown." So much of Hull's poetry relies on her inhabiting, claiming, embracing—and transforming—her suffering, that it is hard not to see beauty-equals-breaking as an *ars poetica* for her, as it seems to have been for Parker; she ends the poem quoting his words, *"If you don't live it, it won't come out your horn."*

Hull inhabits her subjects and characters in "Ornithology" as she does in so many of her poems, here fusing descriptions of her life and Parker's life and art. She mirrors his music with her poetic techniques, breaking her usual long lines into fragments, and fragmenting her identity, as she combines two of her favorite tropes: "The alto's / liquid geometry weaves *a way of thinking,* / a way of breaking / synchronistic / through time / so the girl / on the corner / has the bones of my face." Again Hull returns to identifying with lone, often frail-seeming women, in this case so strongly that the girl "has the bones of [her] face," and the speaker has to break, to fracture her thinking or fragment herself to do it. The two women become one, as the girl "has the bones of my face, / the old photos, beneath the Kansas City hat, // black fedora lifting hair off my neck." The photos are, presumably, of Hull's youthful self, from her actual trip to the city to see Parker's grave, so that the description begins with shared bone structure with a girl in the present on a Chicago street corner, moves to a merging of the two in the old photos, and ends

with the reference to her own body and her mental return to the past—to her history of addiction and adventure, to her *ars vita,* shared with Parker (who shared similar addictions to heroin and alcohol), to the idea of a life lived as fully and courageously as possible, regardless of suffering, because to reject it is to reject experience, knowledge, truth, and beauty. In a sense, to reject suffering is to reject life itself, at least as life is described in Hull's poems—but then, who among us expects to live an entire life without suffering, without loss?

Magic returns in this last book, most notably in "Amulets" (pp. 164–167). Where the magic references in "Magical Thinking" are ironic or cynical in comparison to "Spell for the Manufacture and Use of a Magic Carpet," the desire for magic in "Amulets" is the darkest and least hopeful of all. Here, magic is desired not to protect the speaker from abuse or betrayal but to protect a friend from death by AIDS, "The latest t-cell count report crumpled / in her pocket." The speaker needs "some amulet, / those charms we made as girls of locks / scissored from each other's hair / because mere faith did not seem harbor enough / in a world of brute possibility." The speaker is seeking an amulet to protect her friend from the magical fates, ready with their scissors to cut her life's thread, "phantoms a child might magically / appease." "How is a spell woven … ?" she finally asks, seeking "charms meant to cheat fate, to stay the journeyer / a little while longer, who'll never pass this way again." In the end, the best magic she can muster is, as always, the magic of her art, which immortalizes her friend and her suffering in this poem, and in the seminal "Suite for Emily," surely one of the best poems of Hull's generation.

At sixteen pages, "Suite for Emily" (pp. 177–192), is Hull's "Howl," the cry for a lost generation. It is her longest, most epic poem and certainly among her best, with its flawless music, stunning description, and harrowing narrative. Beautiful and dangerous from the first four lines the twinning and artistry never falters. The poem begins with windows, which have meant and shown and given so much in Hull's poetry but now give away nothing except beauty, and of

course harm, meaning: everything. The poem itself functions as a kind of many-paned window: mirror and film noir, prayer, spell, incantation, elegy, and homage to that other Emily—Emily Dickinson, quoting as it does from several of her poems.

Prayer, or faith, is no help at the poem's beginning but neither is magic. Nor is that old crutch, drugs, of any assistance out in the cold. Her friend Emily is incarcerated, having lost her child. The speaker remembers times they shared, when drug use seemed like a good idea, lamenting that, after all, they were not immune—the word used as the darkest of ironies, since Emily is dying from Acquired Immune Deficiency Syndrome.

The book title is taken from a phrase in this poem, from a passage describing either a return to the past (Emily's or the speaker's or both) or an imagined hellish fate where either or both get back into drug addiction and prostitution. Though the world consumes, the speaker acknowledges that the life lived is a result of choices, and takes responsibility for hers—grateful, as in earlier poems, for her transcendence of her damaging past and embracing her suffering, but also accepting responsibility for creating a heaven on earth instead of a hell. Though her friend Emily is dying of AIDS in prison, Hull is at this point in her life a successful poet and professor, living in Chicago with her poet-professor husband. She escaped the hell she had created for herself, aware of how things could have turned out. Indeed, how they did turn out for Emily.

Hull chose to leave that underworld, to get clean and sober and educated. The final section of "Suite for Emily," titled "A Style of Prayer," begins: "There is a prayer that goes Lord I am powerless / over these carnivorous streets, the fabulous / breakage," a reference to the first step of the Alcoholics Anonymous twelve steps, "We admitted we were powerless over alcohol." The speaker is increasingly conscious of having made and continuing to make choices ("There is a prayer that goes Lord, // we are responsible"), to choose a lifestyle, of having the freedom and responsibility to create either a heaven or hell while the underworld beckons or threatens, not

just from outside, but from inside ("Parallel worlds, worlds within worlds—chutes//& trapdoors in the mind"). The speaker accepts responsibility for creating her life and world, and accepts that regardless of whether we each create a heaven or hell on earth for ourselves, we face the same fate in the end: death. The speaker worries that perhaps "prayer's merely a style of waiting" for the inevitable, and can only hope that there is an afterlife or experience of becoming one with the world after we die, a hope that "Death is the mother of beauty," and that Emily will become "that warm music glazing the panes, / each fugitive moment the heaven we choose to make."

"Fortunate Traveler" (pp. 219–222) is the penultimate poem in the book. The prominent placement of that poem, so near to Hull's last words to her readers, emphasizes her gratitude for the grace that allowed her to make healthier life choices, to both embrace and transcend her past. The poem is another that refers directly to film noir, and another that merges a film's narrative, in this case, *The Misfits* (a deliberately ironic choice), with description of the speaker's and her friends' pasts. The poem also returns to description of the speaker as ghostly, "my reflection rippled, // insubstantial," but broadens that to include others. "Everyone I talk to these days // is both here and not here," says the speaker, seeming to refer to the present but also referring to the ghosts she speaks to and sees in her visits to her past, "the group of friends I had when I was young." It is clear that the speaker is the "fortunate traveler" of the poem's title: "Of all that group, I alone / am left" to enjoy films and travel, to "taste the foreign coffee, sweet / and thick." She also, finally, distances herself from her past: "Of all that group I'd meet when I was young … / I can't recall what we spoke of—it meant so much."

The final poem, "The Window" (pp. 223–226), feels like a perfect way to end the book because it returns to most of Hull's obsessions, including windows, which are so emblematic in her work. It also creates an interesting paradox, coming directly after "Fortunate Traveler," in which the speaker seems finally to distance

herself from her past; in "The Window," the speaker is inescapably drawn not only to returning to her past but perhaps to staying there, suggested by her use of the word "stop." The poem also returns to a room that sounds eerily like the one in "Adagio," where the speaker knows she will leave the room of self-harm and never enter it again.

The speaker is remembering living in a squalid-sounding room with someone, perhaps referring to Hull's first husband, Tommy Hueng, since the room is in "Chinatown." The poem moves from first-person singular to plural to a second-person address, shifting between these points of view, and ending with the second-person address. The "I" is once again insubstantial, fractured and multiple, past and present. The speaker remembers making love as a confirmation of existence and identity, yet that act or memory of it is also no more. Hull also returns to breakage/fragmentation in the poem. It references numerous broken or dilapidated items but it is not just the surroundings that are broken or fragmented, it is the speaker, and it is a beautiful breakage.

The self contains infinite possibilities, including the ability to live multiple lives at once, as the poet creates multiple selves in her poems, and the speaker in the present remembers the past. The beauty in breaking, of the self's fragmenting and multiplying, reaches a crescendo in this poem. Yet the speaker appears to hesitate in considering the vertigo of surrendering, which is reminiscent of the scene described in "Lost Fugue for Chet," his "accidental" fall from the window to the street. The speaker's accompanying memory of heroin addiction also recalls that poem, yet the drug also engenders the beautiful multiplication of self. It suggests an ongoing struggle with her relationship to drug use: it too is a kind of beautiful breaking or ruin.

The poem approaches its end with the speaker as a wraith moving through the remembered rooms behind the window being gazed at in the present. It is unclear whether the speaker at the end is speaking as the wraith moving through the past or the woman gazing at the window in the present—or both at once—but the poem ends

with Hull's familiar twinning of beauty and harm, love and danger, lines that are shiver-inducing for both their artistry and implication. Placed as they are at the end of Hull's last book, they are in effect her last words to her readers.

In choosing "The Window" as the final poem, Wojahn chose not just a stunning end to *The Only World* but a perfect bookend (intentional or not) to the first poem in her first book, "Spell for the Manufacture & Use of a Magic Carpet," a bookend that becomes clear in reading the three books together in Hull's *Collected Poems. The Only World* and the *Collected* both end with Hull's *ars poetica,* braving danger and embracing suffering for the sake of art, beauty, truth, love, and light.

CONCLUSION

Hull's life and art mirrored each other in so many ways it can be difficult to discern where one ended and the other began: her poetry was highly autobiographical, but it also contained multiple selves and conflations of the self with other, similar-sounding personae. And Hull in her life (and in her poems) was a great lover of artifice, well known for her beautiful attire, so lavish as to exceed style and become costume, dressing as she did in vintage clothing and jewelry, performing versus merely reading her poetry, conscious of living a film-noir-like existence. As Mark Doty wrote, "She was a lover of appearances, of performance, of bravura, of failed but honorable gestures toward beauty," yet "[b]eneath her achieved surface, Lynda's vulnerability was always visible; this is what made her such a wonderful teacher, and such a wonderful friend. It made her emphatic, grounded, real" (*Heaven's Coast*). It is also a part of her genius as a poet, the genesis of the aforementioned beauty that sears the psyche—of her embrace of breaking as a necessary part of creating beauty. Sadly, she did both in the end, dying young and tragically, yet leaving a music behind that continues to sing beautifully, and harrowingly, to new generations of readers.

Selected Bibliography

WORKS OF LYNDA HULL

POETRY COLLECTIONS

Ghost Money. Amherst: University of Massachusetts Press, 1986.

Star Ledger. Iowa City: University of Iowa Press, 1991.

The Only World. New York: HarperCollins, 1995.

Collected Poems. St. Paul, Minn.: Graywolf Press, 2006.

RECORDING

Lynda Hull reading "The Window." *Blackbird: An Online Journal of Literature and the Arts* 7, no. 1 [spring 2008] (http://www.blackbird.vcu.edu/v7n1/nonfiction/hull_l/video.htm).

CRITICAL AND BIOGRAPHICAL STUDIES

Aizenberg, Susan. "A Woman of Genius." *Blackbird: An Online Journal of Literature and the Arts* 7, no. 1 [spring 2008] (http://www.blackbird.vcu.edu/v7n1/nonfiction/aizenberg_s/woman_genius.htm).

Alexander, Elizabeth. "Red-Headed Blueswoman." *Blackbird: An Online Journal of Literature and the Arts* 7, no. 1 [spring 2008] (http://www.blackbird.vcu.edu/v7n1/nonfiction/alexander_e/hull.htm).

Doty, Mark. *Heaven's Coast: A Memoir.* New York: HarperCollins, 1996.

———. "Extraordinary Ruins: Lynda Hull's 'Lost Fugue for Chet.'" *Brilliant Corners: A Journal of Jazz & Literature* 7, no. 2: 56–59 (summer 2003).

———. "Lynda Hull's 'Ornithology.'" *Blackbird: An Online Journal of Literature and the Arts* 7, no. 1 [spring 2008] (http://www.blackbird.vcu.edu/v7n1/nonfiction/doty_m/ornithologyhull.htm).

Goldstein, Laurence. "'Coruscating Glamour': Lynda Hull and the Movies." *Iowa Review* 29, no. 1 [spring 1999] (http://www.uiowa.edu/~iareview/reviews/laurence_goldstein.htm).

Jauss, David. "To Become Music or Break: Remembering Lynda Hull." *Crazyhorse* 55: 74–95 (1999).

———. "Ways of Breaking: Lynda Hull's 'Ornithology.'" *Brilliant Corners: A Journal of Jazz & Literature* 7, no. 2: 60–63 (summer 2003).

Komunyakaa, Yusef. "Pneumatic Grace: Lynda Hull and Hollywood Jazz." *Brilliant Corners: A Journal of Jazz & Literature* 7, no. 2: 52–55 (summer 2003).

Shaughnessy, Brenda. "The Poetry of Danger." *Blackbird: An Online Journal of Literature and the Arts* 7, no. 1 [spring 2008] (http://www.blackbird.vcu.edu/v7n1/nonfiction/shaughnessy_b/danger.htm).

Wojahn, David. "'If You Don't Live It': Lynda Hull and Jazz." *Brilliant Corners: A Journal of Jazz & Literature* 7, no. 2: 48–51 (summer 2003).

———. "Being Shades Ourselves." *Blackbird: An Online Journal of Literature and the Arts* 7, no. 1 [spring 2008] (http://www.blackbird.vcu.edu/v7n1/nonfiction/wojahn_d/shades.htm).

———. "A Tribute to the Poetry of Lynda Hull": Panel Introduction. AWP Conference Panel, January 31, 2008. *Blackbird: An Online Journal of Literature and the Arts* 7, no. 1 [spring 2008] (http://www.blackbird.vcu.edu/v7n1/nonfiction/wojahn_d/intro.htm).

INTERVIEWS

Hull, Christine. Notes from a telephone interview by April Ossmann: Questions About Lynda Hull. Unpublished; created November 19, 2009.

Jauss, David. Interview by April Ossmann: Questions About Lynda Hull. Unpublished; created August 2009.

Sholl, Betsy. Interview by April Ossmann: Questions About Lynda Hull. Unpublished; created August 2009.

Singer, Sean. Interview by April Ossmann: Questions About Lynda Hull. Unpublished; created August 2009.

Whedon, Tony. Interview by April Ossmann: Questions About Lynda Hull. Unpublished; created August 2009.

Wojahn, David. Interview by April Ossmann: Questions About Lynda Hull. Unpublished; created September 2009.

———. "How Do You Bottle Lightning?: Anna Journey Sits Down with David Wojahn." *Gulf Coast: A Journal of Literature and Fine Arts* 22, no. 1 [winter–spring 2010] (http://www.gulfcoastmag.org/index.php?n=2&s=934).

OTHER WORKS

Aizenberg, Susan. *Muse.* Carbondale: Crab Orchard Review / Southern Illinois University Press, 2002.

Crane, Hart. *The Complete Poems and Selected Letters and Prose of Hart Crane.* Garden City, N.Y.: Anchor Books / Doubleday, 1966.

DAVID HENRY HWANG

(1957—)

L. Bailey McDaniel

DAVID HENRY HWANG is an American playwright who has enjoyed frequent critical and commercial success and is best known for his multi-award-winning and often-anthologized play, *M. Butterfly* (1988). Although much of his work engages topics specific to Asian American identity, Hwang (pronounced "wong") is also generally considered one of the most prominent American playwrights working today. In addition to his work in the theater, Hwang has amassed significant professional experience as a musician, songwriter, operatic and musical theater librettist, stage director, teacher, and screenwriter.

BIOGRAPHY

David Henry Hwang was born into a first-generation Chinese immigrant family on August 11, 1957, in Los Angeles, California, and grew up in the San Gabriel Valley. His father, Henry Yuan, was a banker, and his mother, Dorothy Yu, (maiden name Huang), was a professor of piano. Hwang's parents assumed their son would end up in law school as he began his four years of undergraduate study in English at Stanford University in 1975. Hwang saw his first professionally staged drama during his freshman year at Stanford, and he began writing plays within that same year. Before he graduated from Stanford in 1979, however, Hwang experienced early and easy success with his first play, *FOB*, which was staged originally in a campus dormitory. Following *FOB*'s warm and supportive reception from investing individuals within and outside of professional theater, not to mention audiences, Hwang changed his academic plans. Aspirations for a professional life in the theater had permanently replaced his earlier goal of law school by the time he graduated with a bachelor of arts degree in 1979.

Shortly after graduating, and after a brief stint as a high school teacher, Hwang headed to the East Coast, where thanks to *FOB*'s momentum as well as his quickly established connection with impresario Joseph, he met with success relatively quickly. In 1980 he was accepted to the prestigious graduate program at the Yale School of Drama, but Hwang left Yale before finishing his master's degree, and by 1981 he was working professionally in New York City theater.

In 1985, five years after his first play *FOB* won, among other accolades, the Obie Award (for off-Broadway theater, presented by the New York weekly *Village Voice*) for Best New American Play of the 1980–1981 season, Hwang married the artist Ophelia Y. M. Chong on September 21. The two divorced in October 1989. Hwang married Kathryn Layng, an actress, on December 17, 1993. Among other projects, Layng played the character of Jane in the original cast of Hwang's semiautobiographical satire, *Yellow Face* (2007). David Henry Hwang and Kathryn Layng live in New York City with their children, Noah David and Eva Veanne.

Hwang has amassed a diverse and large body of work throughout the arts, with an impressive expertise that exceeds the profession of playwriting. As a kind of real life imitating the typically overly hyphenated American arts, however, Hwang is still often thought of and written about primarily, if not exclusively, as an *Asian* artist. This "one note" characterization of Hwang and his work continues into the twenty-first century despite his creation of, among other texts, a television program on international politics, a science fiction libretto, screenplays adapted from modern British fiction, and theatrical works that do not feature Asian characters.

Since 1980, Hwang has received numerous grants and awards, many for his theater work as well as for his activism as an Asian American and an artist. Among some of the more significant are awards from the National Endowment for the Arts, the Guggenheim Foundation, the Rockefeller Foundation, the New York State Council on the Arts, and the Pew Charitable Trusts. Hwang is the first Asian American to win the Tony Award for Best Play. In 1998, East West Players, the longest-standing Asian American theater company in the United States, named its primary stage the David Henry Hwang Theatre. Located in the historic Little Tokyo district of Los Angeles, this 240-seat venue operates at an Actors Equity Association contract level and plays to over ten thousand audience members annually (including free and discounted admission to low-income patrons and deaf audiences attending American Sign Language–interpreted productions).

Hwang is a member of the Writers Guild of America and has served on the executive board of directors of the PEN American Center (1990–1991). He is also a member of the American Civil Liberties Union, serves on the board of the Dramatists Guild, and is a member of the oldest American honor society, Phi Beta Kappa.

CAREER OVERVIEW

As Hwang completed his coursework at Stanford for a major in English, his plans for a career in law waned and eventually disappeared as he became increasingly engaged in theater in California. When asked about his initial plans for law school and his eventual move toward a career in the arts, Hwang told the interviewer Jean Ross in *Contemporary Authors*, "I think law is often the default-option for kids who are fairly bright and verbal but don't exactly know what they want to do. I think it was more a question of going to Stanford to figure out what I wanted to do, and I thought, if nothing else, I could always go to law school." After graduating with a bachelor of arts degree, Hwang briefly taught high school writing and English in Menlo Park, California, at Menlo-Atherton High School. Within one year, however,

he left his home state of California for the East Coast in order to pursue professional theater in earnest. This move was made easier by the fact that Hwang had been admitted to the extremely competitive Yale University School of Drama's MFA program, which he began in 1980, studying, among other subjects, theater history. That same year, when he was only twenty-one years old, his first play, *FOB*, was performed at New Haven's O'Neill Theater Center as part of the National Playwrights Conference, a well-known conference that often features works from noteworthy up-and-coming playwrights and that frequently serves as a springboard for professional productions in neighboring New York City. After one year at Yale, before completing his degree, Hwang left the MFA program to work in New York City.

During this early stage of his professional development, Hwang also studied playwriting at some length with the actor and playwright Sam Shepard and the playwright Maria Irene Fornés; Fornés was also an early playwriting mentor to several other American playwrights of color. Hwang specifically credits Shepard as an early literary inspiration, a particularly "American" playwright he sought to emulate, because of Shepard's tendency "to create a sort of American mythology" (Ross). In Shepard's case, Hwang points out, "It's the cowboy mythology, but nonetheless, it's something that is larger than simply our present-day, fast-food existence." The earlier political awareness Hwang began cultivating in California found a productive venue in theater's ability to create mythologies, American or otherwise. Hwang explained to Ross that a newly discovered power, particularly as a playwright, to create a past for himself—"going into Chinese history and Chinese-American history ... the combination of wanting to delve into those things for artistic reasons and being exposed to an active third-world-consciousness movement"—was a powerful source of motivation as he moved to playwriting as a profession (Ross). Hwang credits his 1978 attendance of the Padua Playwrights Workshop, where he studied under Shepard and Fornés, as a period that "taught me to write from my unconscious" as well as from a

burgeoning awareness of "Asian Pacific American stories and issues"—all of which led to "both a desire to know more about my heritage, and involvement with budding APA (Asian Pacific American) cultural organizations (such as San Francisco's Asian American Theatre Company)" (Ross). In 1980, while a student in Shepard's playwriting workshop, Hwang's burgeoning and complementary interests in his "Chineseness" and in playwriting dovetailed powerfully under Shepard's tutelage. Indeed, Hwang's *Family Devotions* (1981), which began originally as Hwang's attempt to retell Shepard's Obie Award– and Pulitzer Prize–winning play *Buried Child* (1978), is dedicated in part to Shepard.

Hwang's first professional play, *FOB*, was originally produced at Stanford University's Okada House dormitory during his last year as an undergraduate student. This early play mirrored the content and style that much of Hwang's early work would continue to investigate: the changing, often conflicting identities of Chinese Americans specifically and Asian Americans more generally as they attempt to negotiate two worlds, an older and more traditional world defined by recent immigrants and filial pressures versus a more Americanized, modern one that frequently stands in direct contrast to the former.

While he was still in California, part of Hwang's early interest in drama was sparked as a result of his exposure to live theater at the prestigious American Conservatory in San Francisco. The American Conservatory Theater, or ACT, is one of a small handful of critically established, long-standing, and profitable American repertory theater companies. While few in number, American repertory theaters such as ACT, the Goodman Theatre in Chicago, the Mark Taper Forum in Los Angeles, and the Guthrie Theater in Minneapolis have been and are crucial to the survival of drama created by artists in the United States, particularly since the United States provides comparably sparse financial support for the dramatic arts compared to government support found in Europe and Australia. (Without the valuable exceptions provided by American repertory companies, New York City would continue to be the only source for new American drama.) Indeed, as one of the more important American playwrights working in modern drama, Hwang (and his early inspiration from exposure to the American Conservatory Theater) exists as powerful evidence for the need for new, professional theater outside the confines of New York City.

Hwang's associations with live theater outside of the more insular and cost-prohibitive venues of New York City can also be seen in his repeated work with the Humana Festival at the Actors Theatre of Louisville, Kentucky. The Actors Theatre began in 1964 and in 1979 began hosting the Humana Festival of New American Plays, an annual event that has launched the careers of many significant U.S. playwrights, including Tony Kushner, Beth Henley, Donald Margulies, and Marsha Norman.

Hwang's first professionally produced play was a more fully developed version of the dorm production of *FOB* (an abbreviation indicating recent immigrants who are "fresh off the boat"), and it marked the first of a long list of the playwright's critically and commercially successful stage ventures. It is a testament to Hwang's considerable talents early on that his first play—that is, a play that was written by an English major and staged for a dormitory audience—went on to win several notable awards in professional theater within a short time, including the 1980–1981 Obie. After a brief workshop at the National Playwrights Conference, the fully developed play had premiered in 1980 at the Joseph Papp Public Theater in New York City, a theatrical institution that is considered the mecca of off-Broadway American drama and is named for the man who, in part, created the genre of "off-Broadway" drama in the United States.

Started in 1954 as the Shakespeare Workshop, the Public continues to be one of the most highly regarded institutions supporting and producing American drama, particularly in its direct support of plays that represent diverse voices and experiences. Before his death in 1991, Joseph Papp worked with Hwang closely on four additional productions, including Hwang's full-length play *The Dance and the Railroad* (1981) and *Family Devotions* (1981), both of which,

along with *FOB*, are described by Hwang as his "trilogy of Chinese America."

The earlier plays that comprise Hwang's trilogy are considered by many critics as among his best; readers and audiences are exposed to characters who struggle to define their "American-ness" within landscapes that are sometimes heartbreaking (as in the case of *The Dance and the Railroad*) and sometimes comic (as in *Family Devotions*). Produced originally as a component of a New Federal Theater grant in 1981, *The Dance and the Railroad* premiered July 16, 1981, off-Broadway with John Lone and Tzi Ma in the cast (and Lone also serving as director), both of whom would continue to work with Hwang through subsequent decades. In addition to being a finalist for the Pulitzer Prize for Drama, the first of three times Hwang was so nominated, *Railroad* was also nominated for a Drama Desk Award.

Set in the 1800s, *The Dance and the Railroad* explores the life of two Chinese immigrant men who work as laborers on the transcontinental railroad. As the characters attempt to reconcile their past (and past identities) with their corresponding present, not to mention the psychological disconnect that exists between both past and present, they must also face less-than-certain futures in a new country that does not always welcome them with open arms. Set in the nineteenth century, this play asks audiences to consider the conflation of Chinese and American identities and the many parallels the play contains for present-day Chinese American immigrants. The lines (and identity issues) within the play and the real world are blurred in the casting (Lone and Ma are both Chinese American artists) and even the characters' names (named John Lone and Tzi Ma), but also in the dramatic form itself, as Hwang makes use of a blend of both Eastern and Western theatrical traditions, particularly in his use of nonrealistic (Chinese opera–influenced) performance modes. Asked about his actors' actual involvement in the creation or shaping of *Railroad's* plot and characterizations, Hwang explained to Jean Ross,

One of the great things about working on *The Dance and the Railroad* was that it was very much a collaborative process. While I actually wrote all the words, nonetheless I think that John and Tzi and I created a community way of working. They had a lot of input into their characters and in expressing things that they felt.... The production and the text were quite seamlessly linked simply because we had been working so collaboratively.

(*Contemporary Authors*)

The final play within Hwang's trilogy, *Family Devotions,* is a more comic read of these same identity issues, in this case focusing on a Chinese American family in the twentieth century who, unlike those in the earlier play, enjoy a degree of economic privilege. This play also plays with form, but from a more contemporary lens, in this case staging the drama through the point of view of a mainstream television sitcom. With the use of characters such as a visiting Communist uncle from China and a young Chinese American man trying to reconcile the ideologies of his heritage against American materialism and Christianity, this final play of the trilogy continues to ask audiences and readers to define for themselves not only what they consider "American" but also who gets a voice in constructing one's identity.

Following the three plays of the trilogy, and still at the Public, Hwang's final play to be produced with Papp was *Sound and Beauty* in 1983. Set in Japan, *Sound and Beauty* consists of two one-act plays: *The House of Sleeping Beauties,* a theatrical adaptation of Yasunari Kawabata's novella of the same title, and *The Sound of a Voice*, a Japanese folktale-inspired ghost story that Hwang and his frequent collaborator Philip Glass later adapted into an opera. At around the same time as *Sound and Beauty*, Hwang also worked on teleplays (television scripts), such as the Pat Morita and Cloris Leachman television film *Blind Alleys*, which he wrote with Frederic Kimball.

In 1986, Hwang's next play, *Rich Relations*, was his first to feature non-Asian characters. Premiering at New York's *Second Stage Theatre*, *Rich Relations* marked another first for Hwang: his first critical failure. Characterized by the theater critic Frank Rich as "tired," this play was not specifically about Asian Americans, but it did

conspicuously include several other elements found in much of Hwang's earlier works: identity crises and a family at odds. American materialism, existential angst produced by vacuous wealth, and evangelical Christianity also came under Hwang's dramatic microscope in this play that the critic Jeremy Gerard also found lacking. Calling the drama a "spiritual farce" that missed its mark, Gerard echoed many critics when he faulted Hwang for invoking what was beginning to be a repeated theme in his plays, namely a family dealing with interpersonal tensions over identity issues and generational conflicts.

In 1988, Hwang gave audiences the play that would permanently place him in the annals of great American drama. As Hwang writes in the published version of the play, *M. Butterfly* was inspired in part by the true story of Bernard Boursicot, a French diplomat who was convicted on charges of espionage as a result of his long-term love affair with a Chinese opera singer named Shi Pei Pu. Despite the affair lasting for many years and having been consummated on more than one occasion, Boursicot maintained that he was completely ignorant of his lover's identity as a Chinese government spy as well as a biological man. Among the numerous awards *M. Butterfly* garnered Hwang, the play also made him the first Asian American to win the Tony Award for Best Play.

Amazingly, *M. Butterfly* was not the only work Hwang offered audiences in 1988. Working in collaboration with the scene designer Jerome Sirlin and the composer Philip Glass, Hwang contributed the text for *1000 Airplanes on the Roof,* an ambitious multimedia project that incorporated Hwang's script as a kind of narrative framework alongside music provided by Glass and a set designed by Sirlin. Conceived originally and directed by Glass (with whom Hwang collaborated often thereafter), *1000 Airplanes on the Roof* revolves around a character who believes she may have been kidnapped by aliens visiting earth. Hwang's protagonist is understandably conflicted about her need to talk about her experience versus her awareness that she will likely be ridiculed or not believed if she does reveal herself. Faced with the difficult choice between derision and insanity, Hwang's protagonist must negotiate authentic expression against a need to fit in. While Sirlin's work was praised by most critics, Hwang's narrative was described in less than positive terms.

Following *M. Butterfly's* explosive success, Hwang's career did not slow down in terms of critical accolades or financial success. In 1992 the Humana Festival staged Hwang's play *Bondage*, a full-length play in which a masked female dominatrix and her long-standing male submissive, also masked, psychologically and philosophically engage each other on issues of race and identity without revealing their own ethnicity. Hwang staged new work at the festival again in 1996 with his play *Trying to Find Chinatown* and then *Merchandising* in 1999.

Hwang also contributed significantly to the film world beginning in the 1990s. He wrote the screenplay for the John Madden–directed film *Golden Gate* (starring Matt Dillon and Joan Chen), which was released in the United States in 1994. Hwang's early draft of a screenplay adaptation of A. S. Byatt's 1990 Man Booker Prize–winning novel, *Possession,* was also well received. (This screenplay was for a version of the film that was originally to be directed by Sydney Pollack; however, the project eventually was assumed by the director and playwright Neil LaBute. The version ultimately released in 2002 departed significantly both from the novel and from Hwang's script.)

Hwang's 1996 play *Golden Child* debuted at the South Coast Repertory in Costa Mesa, California, in 1996. Only six years following the success of *M. Butterfly, Golden Child* went on to become another success commercially and critically. Before eventually landing on Broadway at the Longacre Theater on April 2, 1998, the play began off-Broadway at Hwang's old home, the Public Theater, and was directed by James Lapine. Following success at the Public, during which it won Hwang another Obie Award for playwriting, as well as a performance Obie Award for one of its actors, Tsai Chin, the play moved to productions in California and Singapore before its Broadway debut, still directed by Lapine, in 1998. The Broadway version earned Hwang his

second Tony nomination for best play, which he lost that year to Yasmina Reza's play *Art*. (*Golden Child* also earned Tony nominations for best actress in a featured role (Julyana Soelistyo) and costume designer (Martin Pakledinaz).)

Not long after *Golden Child*'s success, Hwang accepted an offer from Robert Falls to help the director collaborate with Linda Woolverton on the book for the upcoming rock musical *Aida*. Based on the Giuseppe Verdi opera of the same title, *Aida's* music was written by the rock icon Elton John with lyrics composed by the musical theater legend Tim Rice. From its March 23, 2000, opening on Broadway at the Palace Theatre to its close on September 4, 2004 (a total of 1,852 performances), *Aida* drew huge crowds and eventually also spurred a national tour and several international productions.

Hwang next assumed the responsibility for a major rewrite of one of Broadway's sacred cows, the Richard Rodgers and Oscar Hammerstein musical *Flower Drum Song*. This beloved text from musical theater was extremely successful in the 1950s and early 1960s but, as the original text stood, presented many problematic characters and plot points in a post–civil rights era America, particularly in its representation of ethnic minority characters. Hwang's "reimagining" of the musical is, like Rodgers and Hammerstein's 1958 version, adapted from an original text, C. Y. Lee's 1957 novel, *The Flower Drum Song*. Hwang's version also comes with the blessing (and legal permission) of the Rogers and Hammerstein Organization and met with some critical success. Still broadly exploring the culture clashes experienced by Chinese and Chinese American characters living in San Francisco, and still retaining all of the original characters' names, Hwang's *Flower Drum Song* alters (and sensitizes) the plot and the characterizations so that the musical's Asian characters read more as human beings and less as caricatures.

This postwar musical is fitting subject matter for Hwang, not the least of which for its ground-breaking casting history. In its 1958 premiere at the St. James Theatre in New York, *Flower Drum Song* was the first American musical to have a predominantly Asian cast, although the two leads were played by non-Asian performers, with the African American actress Juanita Hill in the role of Arabella Hong and the Caucasian actor Larry Blyden in the role of Sammy Fong. Hwang's re-imagined version is the first Broadway musical to have ethnically Asian actors in all major roles (and this is including the significant, also-Hwang-connected case of *Miss Saigon*, in which the white Welsh actor Jonathan Pryce was cast as an Asian character). Directed by Gene Kelly, the 1958 *Flower Drum Song* was lighter in tone compared to Lee's novel, but it remained faithful to the major plot points of a shy young mail-order bride, Mei Lei, who immigrates illegally to San Francisco with her father. Although she is already promised in marriage to the assimilated club owner Sammy Fong, Sammy's love for the showgirl Linda Yow complicates things.

While some critics took issue with Hwang for changing (in any way) what many considered a "classic," a large number of critics found more to like about the new incarnation. Winning Hwang and his libretto his third Tony nomination, the Robert Longbottom–directed musical also earned Tony Award nominations for best book and for choreography, and it toured throughout the United States after its New York production closed. Coinciding with Asian Pacific Heritage Month, the musical premiered again in August 2010. The production was directed and choreographed by Baayork Lee, who directed an enormously successful Broadway revival of *A Chorus Line* in 2006.

Hwang's early failure with a 1993 play titled *Face Value* (which closed during previews) was eventually turned into the subject matter of a 2007 drama that many critics praised as his strongest work since *M. Butterfly*: *Yellow Face*, a full-length Obie Award–winning and Pulitzer-nominated play that features a character named David Henry Hwang as he deals with the failure of his "play" *Face Value*.

MAJOR PLAYS: ANALYSIS IN DETAIL

FOB

FOB reflects a growing interest for Hwang throughout his young adulthood and especially

during his four years at Stanford. In the latter part of the 1960s and the 1970s, California witnessed the emergence of a handful of political consciousness movements whose visibility and power increased steadily. Looking to the results garnered by the black civil rights movement of the American South and later the Black Power movement, other ethnic minorities, particularly where Hwang was located, in California, attempted to organize and demand equal rights. Most notably the Chicano civil rights movement (sometimes referred to as El Movimiento) and the Yellow Power movement (also called the Asian Power movement) amplified their efforts and voices, working toward greater civil rights and increased political representation for their respective populations. As early as 1969, the third world student strikes took place at San Francisco State University as well as at the Berkeley campus of the University of California. Growing up in California during this time, Hwang experienced the encouragement if not pressure to become increasingly politically aware of his status as an ethnic minority. His first play, *FOB*, staged while he was still an undergraduate English major, is a direct outgrowth of this increasing political consciousness.

FOB details the experiences of Steve, a young male protagonist who is forced to negotiate a kind of border culture, a world that is neither completely part of one world nor another. (This border culture is revisited with regularity in much of Hwang's oeuvre, as the playwright continues to offer audiences both comedies and dramas that feature characters attempting to straddle identities based in American-ness as well as Chinese-ness.) Played originally off-Broadway by the actor John Lone (a frequent collaborator with Hwang on- as well as offstage), Steve is a young immigrant who is "fresh off the boat" and finds a less-than-peaceful existence alongside a fellow Chinese American, Dale. Dale is a second-generation Chinese American, referred to as an "ABC" (American-born Chinese). He and Steve both have issues getting white America to deal with them as equals, but as an "FOB" and an "ABC" they also face the equally challenging task of finding common ground among each

other. Steve's more Westernized, less-than-tolerant ABC acquaintances force him to figure out how he feels about his ethnicity and what, if any, his position is as an Asian man and an immigrant living in a world that is not originally "home." A factor that further complicates Steve's journey and personal crises is that one of the characters forcing him to evaluate his own self-concept is a woman. Played originally in the Joseph Papp production by Ginny Yang, the character of Grace provides dramatic foil to Steve's ethnically inspired angst by adding gender to the categories of identity with which the major characters wrestle. Indeed, attempting to accommodate more than one "tradition," Grace becomes a motivation behind as well as a symptom of Steve's increasingly conflicted identity crises, particularly as he wrestles with notions of "American" masculinity, "Chinese" masculinity, the advantages and liabilities involved in the process of assimilation, and what it does (and does not) mean to transform one's self from FOB to ABC.

The culture clashes and inter- and intrapersonal conflicts explored in *FOB* and many of Hwang's plays reflect what Hwang was seeing and experiencing offstage. As a result of the Asian Power movement and an increased political consciousness experienced by Hwang along with many ethnic minorities in the United States throughout the 1970s, Hwang incorporates real-world exchanges and conflicts between cultural nationalism and assimilation. Hwang also adds to this conflict the typical real-world circumstances of age or generational differences, including parent-child-oriented conflicts. In his book *Japanese Americans: The Formation and Transformations of an Ethnic Group*, Paul Spickard explains a large component of this generational conflict, which is relevant to Asian immigrants in general:

There were two elements to the ideology that propelled the Asian power movement: cultural nationalism and pan-Asian ethnicity.... Most [first-generation immigrants] had subscribed to some version of the American melting pot myth—that people would come to America from all over the earth ... and benignly be transformed into a new people, unhyphenated Americans. Those [second-generation immigrants] who were active in the Asian power

movement radically rejected this assimilationist ... vision and called for enduring ethnic subcultures, with a reapportionment of power away from White America and to the subcultures.

(p. 162)

Without a doubt, much of Hwang's work, particularly his earlier plays such as those in his trilogy, are a direct comment on this generational and political conflict, which finds no easy result or compromise.

Dovetailing "Eastern" and "Western" form as well as content in powerful and dramatically effective ways on stage, *FOB* also blends American and Chinese forms of live performance. While most of the play, particularly the first act, is laid out in a straightforward and Western theatrical format, *FOB*'s second act involves several (explicitly non-Western) Chinese theatrical techniques as well as nods to and invocations of figures from Chinese mythology.

Premiering professionally at the Joseph Papp Public Theater (Martinson Hall), *FOB* was directed by Mako Iwamatsu. The play opened on June 8, 1980, and was staged for forty-two performances, closing July 13, 1980. Among the play's awards and recognitions (including the Obie for best new American play) was an Obie for best performance earned by John Lone for his portrayal of Steve. In 2005, a revival of the play was staged in San Francisco by the Asian American Theater Company at the Magic Theatre. The revival was directed by Mitzie Abe and ran from March 24 through April 10.

M. BUTTERFLY

As is typical for many New York–bound productions, *M. Butterfly* began early run-throughs out of town; it was staged originally in Washington, D.C. After developing outside of New York, *M. Butterfly* moved to Broadway, where it was immediately commercially successful. Although the play was also quite successful in terms of its critical reception, a few theater critics found problems with it, specifically in issues surrounding the believability of the some of the characterizations and individual plot twists. These disap-

proving voices were in the minority, however. In general, the play received a warm reception from critics as well as award committees. Some of the more prominent of the play's many awards, nominations, and recognitions include a Pulitzer Prize nomination, a Tony Award for Best Play, the Outer Critics Circle Award for Best Play, and a Drama Desk Award for Outstanding Play. For his portrayal of the opera singer Song Liling, the actor B. D. Wong received the Drama Desk Award for Outstanding Featured Actor in a Play as well as the Tony Award for Best Performance by a Featured Actor in a Play. For his directing, John Dexter received the Drama Desk Award for Outstanding Director as well as a Tony Award.

Among other nominations and recognitions associated with the play, Eiko Ishioka received Drama Desk Award nominations for outstanding set design and outstanding costume design. For his portrayal of Gallimard, the actor John Lithgow received a Drama Desk Award nomination for outstanding actor in a play as well as a Tony nomination for best actor in a play. In his role as Song, B. D. Wong won in the category of best debut performance from the Outer Critics Circle Awards. The playwriting award for the Outer Critics Circle, the John Gassner Playwriting Award, also went to Hwang for his text.

Although the play is inspired in large part by the real-life activities of Shi Pei Pu and Bernard Boursicot in the mid-twentieth century, Giacomo Puccini's 1904 opera *Madama Butterfly* is also source material for Hwang's play. Indeed, mention of Puccini's opera, its characters, and even its themes are often self-consciously and self-referentially mentioned throughout the play, in both plot and dialogue. This is especially true of the way that the opera's racial and gender politics become engaged (and deconstructed) powerfully in Hwang's text.

Puccini's *Madama Butterfly* remains one of the composer's best-known works; it is listed as the most performed opera in the United States by *Opera America* in its list of North America's top twenty most frequently performed operas (followed by Puccini's *La bohème*). Told in three acts, the opera is heavily inspired by the John Luther Long short story of the same title. This

1898 short story was later adapted into a hugely successful stage production by the American theatrical impresario David Belasco and, according to some literary and theater historians, can also be traced to a parallel narrative that transpired in real life, around the 1890s in Nagasaki, Japan. During the summer of 1900 the Belasco musical stage version was seen by Puccini in a London theater, and four years later, Puccini staged the first of five different incarnations of his opera. As was the case with Long's short story, Belasco's stage version was hugely popular and generated significant revenue, in large part because of a (white) public's fascination with what it considered "the exotic" East.

Evidenced powerfully in examples such as John Thompson's hugely successful *Illustrations of China and Its People* (1873), the London International Exhibition of 1862, any number of Victorian novels, or even W. S. Gilbert and Arthur Sullivan's comic opera *The Mikado* (1885), the West's obsession with an exoticized Asian culture that was often constructed as "barbaric" or uncivilized manifested in a predictable pattern: white, Western individuals are represented as the "norm" (or the character with whom the reader or audience identifies) who must deal with an exoticized, often eroticized, "other" from the East. This preoccupation on the part of the West with all things Asian, and a corresponding "imagined account" of what the East actually comprises (from the point of view of the West), is more than just an interesting piece of history behind *Madama Butterfly's* commercial success as a short story, musical, and eventual opera. The ability and enthusiasm of one, more politically powerful group (the West) to "imagine" and exoticize the identity of a less politically powerful group (the East) is a major theme within Hwang's play.

Hwang's play casts the (supposed) Asian "Butterfly" character as Chinese, whereas Puccini's opera features a Japanese female protagonist, Cio-Cio San, whose beauty is only exceeded by her delicate nature. The vulnerable and submissive Butterfly falls deeply in love with a white military figure, the Western soldier-savior figure who often comes to the feminized Easterner's rescue, the brave, handsome Pinkerton. As the prototypical Western "hero" who saves the Eastern flower, Puccini's Pinkerton has an ironic counterpart in Hwang's Gallimard, the latter a character who self-consciously refers to himself as "Pinkerton" several times throughout Hwang's play.

The stereotype of the delicate and exotic Asian female "butterfly" is reductive and dehumanizing not just for her unbelievable vulnerability, nor for her exoticized and essentialized sexuality (the latter also shared with another stereotype of Asian femininity, the "dragon lady" construct); this caricature is also typically represented as passive to the point of an almost cartoonish submissiveness, as Puccini's opera powerfully attests. In the opera, Cio-Cio San learns of her previously rejecting lover's return to Japan, but this time he has returned with his white wife, and worse, he plans to take away with him the child Cio-Cio San has born, a child she gave birth to alone and to whom she painfully says good-bye. Then the hurt, shamed, isolated, and thoroughly rejected Cio-Cio San, in pseudo-heroic self-sacrifice, takes her own life in the opera's conclusion—a dramatic climax described problematically by critics and audiences, including (repeatedly) Hwang's Gallimard, as "beautiful."

A major tool Hwang employs in his rejection of the reductive, cartoonishly submissive Butterfly identity is with the play's white male lead. Hwang's Gallimard self-consciously (in his own words, in lines delivered early in the play) stands in for Puccini's Pinkerton; he makes repeated and adoring references to the original opera; and he makes no secret as to how "beautiful" he considers the opera's final depiction of Cio-Cio San's suicide, which was motivated out of shame, rejection, and passive worship for her "white savior" Pinkerton. Furthermore, it is Hwang's quasi-female lead, the biologically male Song, who fluctuates in her/his political alliance, villain/martyr status, and of course gender, all while he occupies the role of a kind of Pinkerton himself. Literally, figuratively, often metatheatrically, Song underscores the "role" of woman, Asian woman, and even mother and spy as s/he (often

consciously) performs a fluid and unstable gender identity. Flipping, or perhaps deconstructing, Puccini's original male and female leads, Hwang's Song, as well as his Gallimard, illustrate the artificial and constructed nature of identity, particularly when such constructs are conflated with specific notions of ethnicity.

While audiences watch Song betray, manipulate, and debatably fall for Gallimard, the biological gender of the character (male) is always known. Song's biological gender keeps the character from falling into any reductive "dragon lady" construct (as the audience is always reminded of the culturally specific nature and "performance" of gender identity itself), but it also serves to underscore the ridiculousness behind Gallimard's Western fetishization of his "Asian Butterfly."

As is the case with the David Cronenberg film adaptation of Hwang's play, Hwang's staged version ends by invoking that which deems the opera's "tragic" description, the successful, shame-motivated suicide of its woman-done-wrong: Cio-Cio San in her icon-generating performance as a paradigmatic "Asian Butterfly." In Hwang's final act, audiences see a broken character commit suicide, but for Hwang, unlike Puccini, it is a convicted, jailed, and (with plenty of pseudo-geisha, Asian-inspired white makeup) cosmetically made-up Gallimard. In Hwang's text, then, it is a white, Western "hero" whom the spectator perceives as a passive, indeed stereotypically submissive and feminized, Asian-inspired character who "performs" sacrifice-rich love for a new type of "audience" in his French prison. Gallimard, self-consciously performing the (still artificial and reductive) stereotypical Butterfly role, commits seppuku, the same honor-infused suicide via disembowelment that Puccini's Cio-Cio San commits after *her* shame and rejection at the hands of her own more powerful, less interested, masculine lover. (In Hwang's version, Gallimard performs his ritual-informed (literal) suicide as Song coolly watches from afar, smoking a cigarette, without expression.)

The real-life inspiration behind *M. Butterfly*'s stage life deserves attention for reasons beyond mere curiosity or an interesting footnote: a kind of real life imitating culturally specific stereotypes can be found in much of the chaos experienced by the play's real-life inspirations, Shi Pei Pu and Bernard Boursicot. When Shi first met Boursicot, the former was employed as a soprano for the Beijing Opera. In addition to performing, however, Shi also worked as a Chinese language tutor for the families of Western diplomats living in China. As a result of Shi's association with various French diplomats, he met Boursicot at a holiday party in 1964, when the twenty-year-old Boursicot was working as a clerk for the French Embassy in Beijing. Although their relationship began as a platonic friendship, it eventually grew into a consummated romance. During their long romance, Boursicot later testified, Shi kept his biological gender as a man hidden from his French lover. Boursicot claimed that his inexperience with women was a major reason why Shi's true gender identity was never discovered by him throughout his relationship with the Chinese man. But it was another of Boursicot's statements made in an attempt to explain his decades-long ignorance of Shi's maleness that caught David Henry Hwang's eye. In his supplementary notes to the published version of the play, Hwang writes that during a dinner conversation in 1986 a friend asked him if he had read about a real-life French diplomat who had reportedly had a long-term relationship with a Chinese actress and was now in legal trouble with France because the Chinese lover had turned out to be a spy as well as a biological man. This story, of course, was about Boursicot and Shi. Hwang considered the diplomat's claim of his lover's modesty (to account for the fact that "she" had never been without clothes in his presence), and created a play that pointed directly at what literary critics understand as the practice of "orientalism," In Hwang's rendering of the relationship between the unlikely pair, he explored the stereotype of the submissive Asian woman, a caricature that Boursicot embraced, and that Shi, as a spy, exploited. It was this perception of the East and of Asian women in particular—from the point of view of the white, male, Westerner—that touched on a larger theme with which Hwang was familiar

and that much of his *M. Butterfly* would explore. Hwang explains that this real-life situation, and in particular, Boursicot's printed response, generated the idea for his play.

Hwang knew more than a little about the cultural stereotype of the Asian woman as a submissive "butterfly." It is this stereotype (a reductive concept upon which so much of Puccini's opera relies) that Hwang's play turns on its head. In the play, unlike the opera, the white Western male ends up in the role of the passive lotus flower, the butterfly. And while the Asian counterpart in the "romance" does end up performing a kind of femme fatale role to the duped and ultimately victimized white male, s/he (Song Liling) never completely approaches the "dragon lady" stereotype, because the reader and audience are always aware that Song is a male, further underscoring the performative nature of gender and ethnic identity.

In other words, Hwang's play attempts, among other objectives, to look at and deconstruct the shared resonances of the real-world spy case involving Boursicot and Shi and the early twentieth-century opera by Puccini. Although the former is an actual event that transpired in the courts and international newspapers and the latter is a fictional opera, they are both "texts" that, as Hwang demonstrates in his drama, rely on and engage preconceived notions of how one group of people, the West, imagines or "constructs" the identity of another group of people, in this case the East.

The play thus addresses (although it never explicitly names) the phenomenon of "orientalism," a term that had been coined by the literary critic and political activist Edward Said in 1979 to convey how the West, largely through centuries of fiction, visual art, and historical accounts, constructed and continues to construct what it (largely imagined and) thought of as "the East"; put another way, the notion of orientalism asserts that in order to better define and understand itself, the West can be seen to have spent a good deal of time and energy, through the creation of various "texts," in "inventing" an identity of "the other" (the East).

As might be imagined, the "invention" of the identity belonging to the "other" (the East), as Said and others argue, often manifests into an identity that benefits, often dramatically, the identity of the West: that is, a passive, submissive, or needy and feminized East exists alongside a stronger, more independent, masculinized West. The (imagined) weakness of one helps define the strength of the other. As Hwang himself explains in *M. Butterfly's* afterword, in the representations of literary, popular, film, and generally Western culture, "'good' Asian women are those who serve the White protagonist in his battle against her own people, often sleeping with him in the process. Stallone's *Rambo II*, Cimino's *Year of the Dragon*, Clavell's *Shogun*, Van Lustbader's *The Ninja* are all familiar examples . . . good natives serve Whites, bad natives rebel." While this is, as Hwang and others argue, a fairly paradigmatic mindset within colonialism, if one goes a step further it can also be deduced, he says, that since the colonized-oppressed "are submissive and obedient, [then] good natives of both sexes necessarily take on 'feminine' characteristics in a colonial world. Gunga Din's unfailing devotion to his British master, for instance, is not so far removed from Butterfly's slavish faith in Pinkerton,"

In this sense also the real-life scenario of Boursicot and Shi shares significant resonance with the narratives of orientalism that Hwang's play is attempting to deconstruct. Continuing his work with the French Embassy, Boursicot eventually left China but maintained his relationship with Shi Pei Pu, even during separations that sometimes lasted years. Indeed, lending some credibility to Boursicot's claims that he actually did not know that Shi was a man, at one point Boursicot learned of a "son," Shi Du Du (whom Boursicot called "Bertrand"), whom he was led to believe that he and Shi had conceived and who had been born during one of Boursicot's absences from China. In truth the infant was of Muslim Uighur descent and had been sold as a baby by his birth mother as she attempted to survive and feed her other children.

By the end of the 1960s, when Boursicot was again with Shi in China (and as the situation is

also represented in the play via Gallimard and Song), Boursicot began sharing with Shi government documents obtained from his work with the French Embassy. Although the relationship had been going on for years, during the time in which Boursicot believed he had produced a child with Shi, the Chinese government became aware of the relationship; Boursicot believed that his covert delivery of classified documents, which Shi forwarded to Chinese government agents, would help protect the mother of his "child." Nearly ten years later, while stationed in Mongolia, Boursicot was still working clandestinely for the Chinese government. In his role as a French diplomat, Boursicot decided to return to France in the face of increasing stress from his illegal activities. Although he was living with a male lover in Paris, Boursicot managed to have Shi and their "child" move to France with diplomatic visas in 1982. At around this same time, Shi's relationship with Boursicot was receiving increased attention from the French government and by 1983, both Shi and Boursicot were arrested.

Boursicot claimed that he did not learn of Shi's true gender identity until the actual trial. Shi explained that the pair engaged in intercourse only rarely and that when they did, they proceeded quickly and with the lights off, Shi also claimed that Boursicot had no idea of his lover's true gender until both had been charged for their crimes and that, while Shi never explicitly claimed a male or female gender to his lover, he also never corrected any incorrect assumptions. "I never told Bernard I was a woman," Shi told Joyce Wadler of the *New York Times*. "I only let it be understood that I could be a woman" (C13).

In 1986, three years after their arrest, Shi and Boursicot were found guilty by a French court and each received six-year prison sentences. After serving only eleven months, Shi Pei Pu was pardoned by the French president François Mitterrand. After his release from prison in 1987, Shi lived out the rest of his life in Paris, where, among other jobs, he sang in minor operas, capitalizing on his fame from the notoriety he shared with Boursicot. Boursicot also received a pardon and served only four months of his

sentence. Throughout the years following their trial and conviction, Boursicot and Shi maintained sporadic contact with each other. In 2009, while the sixty-four-year-old Boursicot was recovering from a stroke and living in a French nursing home, Shi died in Paris at the age of seventy on June 30, survived by one son and three grandchildren.

Premiering on Broadway at the Eugene O'Neill Theater on March 20, 1988, *M. Butterfly* ran for 777 performances and earned Hwang his second nomination for the Pulitzer Prize for drama, following his 1981 nomination for *The Dance and the Railroad*. After the departure of Lithgow as Gallimard, *M. Butterfly* continued to present stage luminaries in the part of the French diplomat, including Anthony Hopkins, Tony Randall, John Rubenstein, and David Dukes.

One of *M. Butterfly*'s original stage producers, David Geffen—who along with Steven Spielberg and Jeffrey Katzenberg comprise the film company DreamWorks SKG—played a leading role in getting the film version of Hwang's masterpiece produced and eventually released by Warner Brothers pictures in 1993. David Cronenberg directed the film, with a screenplay written by Hwang. The roles made famous on stage by the actors B. D. Wong and John Lithgow were played on screen by Hwang's frequent and longtime collaborator on and off the stage, John Lone, and Jeremy Irons.

YELLOW FACE

The tumultuous, not necessarily voluntary, role Hwang occupies as a one of the few voices of color in the canon of American drama is a position with which he has not always been comfortable, and it serves as the inspiration for his 2007 play, the full-length satire *Yellow Face*. In addition to being significantly informed by the early and wide-ranging failure of Hwang's 1993 play *Face Value*, the hugely successful *Yellow Face* takes as its inspiration: (1) the complicated position occupied by American theater practitioners who are also ethnic minorities; (2) the intricate maneuvers one must engage in while trying to balance identity politics, commercial interests,

and legitimate artistic expression; and (3) the always complex issues behind the practice known as "color-blind" casting.

In 2007 *Yellow Face* premiered in Los Angeles at the Mark Taper Forum and in New York at the Joseph Papp Public Theater. Blending (autobiographical) fact with fiction to great effect, the play garnered Hwang his third Obie Award for playwriting as well as his third nomination for a Pulitzer. *Yellow Face* presents audiences with a protagonist named DHH (David Henry Hwang) who is staging a play titled *Face Value*.

Hwang told *L.A. Stage*'s Sylvie Drake, "Some of the stuff in the play is true and some of it isn't and I hope it's hard to tell the difference" (p. 17). His desire is likely fulfilled, and without much difficulty. For example, the 1993 failed Hwang play *Face Value* (which closed during previews, before its official opening night scheduled for New York's Cort Theater) features prominently in the plot of *Yellow Face*, but the 2007 play also comments, often and directly, on the practice of casting white actors in "yellowface"—that is, in makeup to play Asian roles (which is where the 2007 play gets its title)—a practice on which Hwang has publicly commented. The now-frowned-upon (and considered offensive) practice of casting a play or film in "yellowface" (similar to a white actor performing in "blackface") was a major topic running through Hwang's (real play) *Face Value*.

Some history to bear in mind: Hwang's Broadway musical *Miss Saigon* became the tenth-longest-running Broadway musical in American history, achieving near record-breaking commercial success. This Claude-Michel Schönberg and Alain Boublil blockbuster also went on to tour internationally to equally strong numbers for years. But significantly, *Miss Saigon* has a spotted history in terms of its racial politics. When the play made its initial move from London to New York's Broadway Theater in 1991, a good deal of debate surrounded the decision of producers to cast the white European actor Jonathan Pryce as one of the lead roles, that of a Eurasian male. Further adding to the controversy of the casting of Pryce, *Miss Saigon* (like *M. Butterfly*) is also partially inspired by Puccini's *Madama Butterfly*, and it therefore raised associations with that opera's racial insensitivity, in its portrayal of the overtly passive, stereotypically submissive Asian "butterfly" characters who live at the mercy of a white, Western "hero." Although the decision to have a white actor don makeup to make him look Asian for the musical had numerous precedents in the history of American theater, film, and television (and was a practice that was ongoing, despite the political accomplishments made by ethnic minorities through the consciousness-raising years throughout the 1970s), many theater practitioners as well as activists voiced objection to the casting of Pryce. Eminent among these voices was that of David Henry Hwang, the first Asian American playwright to have won a Tony Award for Best Play.

Unlike the similarly offensive practice of "blackface"—which was universally considered outdated and in bad taste going as far back as Al Jolson's 1927 turn at "Mammy" in *The Jazz Singer*—the practice of "yellowface" casting still had more than a few noteworthy examples to which critics could sadly point. For example, consider Marlon Brando's performance as Sakini in *The Teahouse of the August Moon* (1956), Mickey Rooney's infamously offensive turn as Mr. Yunioshi in *Breakfast at Tiffany's* (1961), Peter Sellers' 1976 Charlie Chan–inspired portrayal of the character Sidney Wang in *Murder by Death*, or even the 1999 comedy *Galaxy Quest* featuring the Wisconsin-born Lebanese American actor Tony Shaloub playing the double roles of Fred Kwan and Tech Sergeant Chen.

In the Jerry Zaks–directed play *Yellow Face,* the (fictional) character named DHH (for David Henry Hwang) casts a white male actor to play the male Asian lead in his upcoming (fictional) play *Face Value,* without knowledge of the white actor's actual ethnicity. *Yellow Face* is a comedy and accordingly, audiences watch the "character" of DHH try and eventually fail to convince several people that his white actor is a Jew from Siberia who has "some" Asian ethnicity in his background. As the character DHH begins to realize that his (white) lead indeed is not Asian in any way, his play (the fictional *Face Value)* is

already nearly two million dollars in the red. As DHH attempts to hide, dissemble, and basically cover his tracks in the casting debacle, the white actor that DHH cast in *Face Value* performs the role of an Asian man in his (fictional) life and begins working as an activist for Asian rights, essentially becoming what DHH angrily calls an "ethnic tourist."

More than just a farce on the politics and practice of yellowface casting and an exploration of a playwright navigating the slippery waters of identity politics, *Yellow Face* brilliantly incorporates less farce-worthy themes such as father-son relationships and racial profiling, most obviously in the relationship between the main character DHH and his father, who like Hwang's own father is a banker and (only in the play) becomes the target of a criminal investigation at the hands of a character named Senator Fred Thompson (who is, himself, based on the real-life U.S. senator Fred Thompson, who starred on the American television program *Law and Order*, a spin-off of which, *Law and Order: SVU*, also stars the frequent Hwang collaborator and real-life star of the actual 1993 play *Face Value*, the actor B. D. Wong). The *Yellow Face* character of Senator Fred Thompson accuses Hwang's successful immigrant banker father of illegally influencing American politics through the latter's dealings with the Chinese and his secret funneling of money. Without much intellectual traveling, *Yellow Face*'s audience sees the connections between the investigations of Hwang's banker father in the play and the real-world investigations of the Los Alamos Laboratory scientist Wen Ho Lee, the Taiwanese American very publicly indicted for and eventually cleared of charges surrounding the criminal dissemination of US state secrets to the People's Republic of China.

In addition to garnering the 2008 Obie Award for Hwang for playwriting, *Yellow Face* earned the actor Francis Jue an Obie Award for his performance of HYH (Hwang's father). For his performance as DHH, the actor Hoon Lee received the 2008 Theater World Award. Originally premiering in 2007 in Los Angeles at the Mark Taper Forum, *Yellow Face* eventually moved to Hwang's old home, the Public Theater in New York, where it ran from December 10, 2007, until January 13, 2008.

Selected Bibliography

WORKS OF DAVID HENRY HWANG

PLAYS

Broken Promises: Four Plays. New York: Avon, 1983. (Includes *The Dance and the Railroad*, *FOB*, *Family Devotions*, and *Sound and Beauty*.)

The House of Sleeping Beauties. New York: Dramatists Play Service, 1983.

M. Butterfly. New York: Plume, 1993; actor's edition, New York: Dramatists Play Service, 1998.

Trying to Find Chinatown and *Bondage*. New York: Dramatists Play Service, 1993.

Golden Child. New York: Dramatists Play Service, 1998.

Rich Relations. New York: Playscripts, Inc., 2006.

Peer Gynt. With Stephan Muller. New York: Playscripts, Inc., 2006.

Yellow Face. New York: Theater Communications Group, 2009; actor's edition, New York: Dramatists Play Service, 2009.

TELEPLAYS

Blind Alleys. With Frederic Kimball. Metromedia, September 4, 1985.

The Lost Empire. NBC, March 11, 2001.

SCREENPLAYS

M. Butterfly. Directed by David Cronenberg. Warner Brothers, 1993.

Golden Gate. American Playhouse, 1994.

MUSICAL THEATER AND OPERA

1000 Airplanes on the Roof. U.S. premiere September 1988 at the American Music Theater Festival, Philadelphia. Layton, Utah: Peregrine Smith Books, 1989.

Elaborate Lives: The Legend of Aida. Book written with Linda Woolverton and Robert Falls. Premiered at the Alliance Theatre, Atlanta, Ga., 1998. Broadway premiere, as *Elton John and Tim Rice's Aida*, Palace Theatre, 2000. (Adapted from the Giuseppe Verdi opera *Aida*, with music by Elton John and lyrics by Tim Rice.)

Flower Drum Song. Broadway premiere, Virginia Theatre, 2002. New York: Theater Communications Group, 2003.

(Adaptation of the 1958 musical by Rodgers and Hammerstein.)

The Fly. U.S. premiere, Los Angeles, 2008. (With music by Howard Shore. Libretto adapted from the 1957 short story of the same title by George Langelaan.)

BIOGRAPHICAL AND CRITICAL STUDIES

Drake, Sylvie. "David Henry Hwang: A Mellow Second Act." *L.A. Stage*, no. 37:17–19.

Groos, Arthur. "Lieutenant F. B. Pinkerton: Problems in the Genesis and Performance of *Madama Butterfly*." In *The Puccini Companion*. Edited by William Weaver and Simonetta Puccini. New York: Norton, 1994. Pp. 154–201.

Hernandez, Ernio. "Long Runs on Broadway." *Playbill.com* (http://www.playbill.com/celebritybuzz/article/75222. html), February 17, 2009.

Jenkins, Chadwick. "The Original Story: John Luther Long and David Belasco." *New York City Opera Project* (http://www.col umbia.edu/itc/music/NYCO/butterfly /luther. html).

Oliver, Edith. "Poor Butterfly." *The New Yorker*. April 4, 1988. 72.

"OPERA America." *Cornerstones*. http://web.archive.org/web/20080803023151/www.operaamerica.org/Content/Audiences/Programs/Cornerstones/operalist.html#traviata.

Rich, Frank. "*M. Butterfly*, a Story Of a Strange Love, Conflict and Betrayal." *The New York Times*. on the Web. March 21, 1988. http://theater.nytimes.com/mem/theater/treview.html?res=940defde143ef932a15750c0a96e948260 May 10, 2010.

Ross, Jean. "David Henry Hwang." Author interview in *Contemporary Authors Vol. 132*. Detroit: Gale, April, 1991.

Shapiro, T. Rees. "Shi Pei Pu Dies at 70; Chinese Opera Singer Inspired *M. Butterfly*." *Los Angeles Times* (http://articles.latimes.com/2009/jul/06/local/me-shi-pei-pu6), July 6, 2009.

Spickard, Paul. *Japanese Americans: The Formation and Transformations of an Ethnic Group*. New Brunswick, N.J.: Rutgers University Press, 2009.

Wadler, Joyce. "The True Story of *M. Butterfly*: The Spy Who Fell in Love with a Shadow." *New York Times Magazine*, 15 August 1993. (http://www nytimes.com /1993/08/15/magazine/the-true-story-of-m-butterfly-the-spy-who-fell-=/5in-love-with-a-shadow.html?pagewanted =12&pagewanted=print).

C. L. R. JAMES

(1901—1989)

Stephen Soitos

CYRIL LIONEL ROBERT (C. L. R.) James is one of the truly remarkable figures of the twentieth century, whose life spanned continents and categories in a virtually unprecedented way. Born to a former slave family on the remote Caribbean island of Trinidad, James stunned three continents with his erudition, political activism, and literary accomplishments. He has been described as the prophet and intellectual father of West Indian and African independence. His books *The Case for West-Indian Self-Government* (1933) and *Nkrumah and the Ghana Revolution* (1977) were important assessments of revolutionary politics. James was the author of historical studies including his most famous work, *The Black Jacobins* (1938), about the first successful slave revolt in the New World (Haiti, 1791–1803). His early short stories and novel *Minty Alley* (1936) were groundbreaking naturalist treatments of slum barrack life in Port of Spain, Trinidad. As a co-founder of the literary group the Beacon he helped develop the cultural self-identity of Trinidad. He wrote a play based on *The Black Jacobins* that featured the controversial African American singer and actor Paul Robeson. His many political works on socialist working-class and black consciousness are considered visionary in scope. He was a noted journalist who published many articles on his lifelong appreciation of the game of cricket. James was also a literary critic and supporter of popular culture studies and black studies before the concepts were adopted by university scholars. His *Mariners, Renegades, and Castaways* (1953) offered an original interpretation of Melville's *Moby Dick*. And in *Beyond a Boundary* (1963) he wrote an unusual assessment of his life in Trinidad. James worked as a teacher, speaker, and political activist in Trinidad, England, and the United States. He was an early Pan-Africanist and a seminal figure in black

politics. He delivered lectures and speeches to a wide variety of populations and creeds. During the 1970s he taught and lectured extensively in the United States at Howard University, Northwestern, Harvard, Yale, and Princeton. He received honorary doctorates from universities in the West Indies, England, and the United States. During his last years in London he was visited by many writers and leaders of independence movements who reflected his influence in all areas of the world. He was the rare combination of artist, politician, and historian who throughout his long life always worked for the betterment of humankind.

EARLY LIFE: TRINIDAD

C. L. R. James was born on January 4, 1901, in the village of Caroni, Trinidad, the eldest of three children. His father Robert Alexander and his mother Ida Elizabeth (Bessie) James were active citizens of their community and urged their children to pursue education to better their society. His father was the head of a teacher's training school and his mother was a self-educated woman who introduced him to books at an early age. Both of James's grandfathers had immigrated to Trinidad from Barbados in the 1800s. James's paternal grandfather worked as a pan boiler on a sugar estate. The James family came from the Tunapuna-Tacarigua-Arouca area, one of the most culturally complex areas of nineteenth-century Trinidad.

Trinidad is an island republic of the West Indies, lying off the coast of Venezuela in the Caribbean Sea. It is a small island, about fifty miles long and thirty miles wide and contains the smaller northern island of Tobago. When Christopher Columbus visited Trinidad in 1498 during

his third voyage, the island was inhabited by the Arawak Indians. The Arawaks were destroyed during Spain's three-hundred-year rule. In 1797 British forces conquered Trinidad and introduced African slaves to the island workforce. Thereafter, a slave-based plantation economy centering on exported sugar, coffee, and rum was the norm until slavery was abolished in 1833. Freed slaves bargained with their former masters for better wages and resources. These early acts of collective bargaining resulted in improved conditions that attracted immigrants from Barbados, the Caribbean island of James's ancestors. The area of Tunapuna had the highest percentage of Africans of any of Trinidad's communities. Consequently, James's background was a combination of African and West Indian cultural practices.

A national cultural identity developed among Trinidad's population as the masses took the annual Carnival celebration from the British. Carnival became a forum for popular culture, political commentary, and satire. The government attempted to end the Carnival, resulting in the Canboulay riots (1881), the Hosea riots (1884) and the Port of Spain rebellion (1900). The Carnival parade featured the verbal dexterity of the calypso singers, wild dancing and drumming, stick fighters and *jamettes* (emancipated women of the streets), and parodies of official life by troupes portraying iconic characters such as the bombastic Midnight Robber. James was a great admirer of Trinidad's musical artists and political rebels. He was one of the first to write an essay defending calypso and the famous island singer Mighty Sparrow.

James's early youth was influenced by his parents' move to a house located next to a cricket field, and he spent his formative years watching and playing cricket in his own backyard. From 1910 to 1918 he attended Queen's Royal College, a colonial secondary school for boys. He was active in sports, theater, and politics during his years as a scholarship student in English classical literature and French. He studied Maxwell Philip (1829–1888), the first black solicitor general and creative writer of Trinidad. Philip's history novel *Emmanuel Appadocca; or, A Blighted Life* (1854) was written in the aftermath of the U.S. Fugitive Slave Law (1851) and urged African Americans to reject slavery. James was also influenced by A. R. F. Webber's *Those That Be in Bondage* (1915), a novel that included one of the earliest appearances of the Trickster—a folklore figure based on traditional African tales. Webber, an early socialist, proclaimed the rights of the working people of the Caribbean and urged a pan-Caribbean federation.

In the 1920s James worked as teacher at Queen's Royal College. He was also an amateur theatrical producer, avid cricket player, and reporter. James began writing fiction in the 1920s as part of the literary group that shared its name with the magazine it published, the *Beacon,* a group that also included Alfred Mendes, Albert Gomes, and Ralph de Boissière. These writers were considered to be the originators of a new movement advancing indigenous creative efforts, especially literary arts.

James's first literary success came in 1927 with the publication of "La Divina Pastora" in the British *Saturday Review.* Its protagonist is Anita, a woman who picks coca ten hours a day for thirty cents a day and who visits a south Trinidad pilgrim site to enlist the help of the saint in her quest for marriage. James was also published in other magazines, including the first issue of *Trinidad* in 1929, which contained his controversial story "Triumph," the earliest depiction of "barrack yard," or slum life, in Port of Spain. The barracks were long buildings surrounding a yard in which local workers, servants, and prostitutes lived in a communal setting that often led to conflict. Sexual freedom as well as violence and a reliance on tough survival skills were part of everyday living. This was a way of life, often with obeah or voodoo religious overtones, that ran counter to gentrified British colonial rules and behavior. Charges of obscenity were brought against James's work because his frank depiction offended the ruling British class. Undeterred, in the *Beacon* in 1931 he published "Revolution" and "The Star That Would Not Shine," two stories that brought attention to an emerging discontent among blacks and Creoles. These early works were in the social realist vein

and brought a new vision to West Indian fiction, which had formerly used British language and sentiments in depicting island life. James and other *Beacon* writers were related in some ways to the Harlem Renaissance writers of the 1920s and 1930s who wrote of the streets and jazz clubs and used local slang. There were many critics, middle-class religious blacks among them, who thought this real and raw material denigrated the black race as a whole.

In the late 1920s James wrote *Minty Alley,* his first and only novel, which did not see print until it was published in England in 1936. The novel is set in the barracks yards of Port of Spain and was one of the first Caribbean novels to deal with the class and religious differences within the black community itself. While educated blacks like James were often excluded from the society of black workers, the novel, featuring a young bookstore clerk protagonist named Haynes who moves to the barrack yard, shows how this gap between classes can be bridged. By living in the alley near the harbor, Haynes is drawn into the life of the working poor and finds their values very attractive. He is introduced to sex by the passionate young Maisie, who lives in the room across from him. Haynes immerses himself in the vernacular of the barrack yard and finds the folk elements and African retentions of that life rewarding and meaningful.

In politics at this time James supported Arthur Andrew Cipriani. a populist politician who challenged the crown colony system of government. Cipriani was elected president of the Trinidad Workingmen's Association (TWA), which agitated for universal suffrage, free education, and better working conditions. James wrote a biography of Cipriani in late 1920s. This was the first of other books on prominent Pan-African figures that James was to write during his career, including Toussaint l'Ouverture of Haiti and Kwame Nkrumah of Ghana. *The Life of Captain Cipriani: An Account of British Government in the West Indies* (1932) was both an attack on colonial rule and a study of racial tensions and divisions within Trinidad's society. In 1937–1938 labor riots in Trinidad reached a violent stage involving working-class blacks against white

rulers. James's book was in some accounts said to have influenced the widespread dissension.

Cipriani, as leader of the Trinidad Labor Party, incited workers to strike for higher wages and better living conditions. The results were not immediately forthcoming, but over time social progress did occur. James was no longer in Trinidad when universal suffrage became law in 1945, followed by limited self-government in 1956 and independence in 1962.

ENGLAND

In 1932 James traveled to England to try and become a full-time writer. His short two-year marriage to a woman of Spanish heritage had ended in Trinidad, and James found job opportunities (owing to the color barrier) lacking on the island. He first lived in Nelson, Lancashire, near Manchester in the north of Britain. His good friend, the famous cricketer Learie Constantine, put him up and introduced him to friends. In 1933 James spoke on a BBC program commemorating the centenary of the abolition of slavery in the British colonies. James declared that West Indians were ready for self-determination. Protests were lodged at the radio station, and James's name circulated in local political circles as a radical to watch closely. He also published *The Case for West-Indian Self-Government* (1933), an abridged version of his *Captain Cipriani,* which outlined conditions in Trinidad concerning population, social divisions, and inherent racism as well as attacking colonial government in subversive and satirical tones. James was swept up in the political turmoil of prewar Europe as he continued his radical political education. Nelson was an industrial town of forty thousand with a core of militant socialist mill workers so strong that it was called "little Moscow." James met trade unionists and members of the Independent Labour Party (ILP). He read Leon Trotsky's *A History of the Russian Revolution* and Karl Marx's *Das Kapital* among other important communist texts.

In its focus on class, race, and social conflict as the defining elements of history, Marxist

thought held a powerful fascination for James, not only because of his natural disposition toward improving the conditions of working-class blacks in his native West Indies but because of the theoretical light it cast on the nature and evolution of European and American colonialism as a whole. At a time when self-determination movements for former colonies were beginning to hold the promise for revolutionary change, James felt the need to school himself in the Russian Revolution and the principles of international socialist and communist theory.

JAMES'S THEORETICAL BASE: COMMUNISM, SOCIALISM, AND THE RUSSIAN REVOLUTION

The Russian Revolution of 1917 remains without doubt one of the most important events of modern history. It was central to the shaping of twentieth-century world history, and its legacy continues to be influential to the present. In retrospect, it is difficult to imagine the power and fascination that the first successful socialist revolution had for the intellectuals of the post–World War I era. Although the revolution occurred when James was a youth living in Trinidad, its influence had spread to the Caribbean by the time James was entering his maturity. Furthermore, independence movements in the Caribbean and Africa were equally entangled in socialist theory as well as indigenous populist rhetoric.

Such was the case with the large populist and worker's political movement engendered by Cipriani, which James had been enamored enough with to write and publish his first political work. Although this work is unsophisticated and, one might say, an unsocialized anticolonialist and antielitist argument, it is packed with fervor, outrage, and revolutionary tendencies. What it lacked was the armature of a consistent left politic. With his adoption of socialist principles based on the Bolshevik model of communism, James found his theoretical base. He would move on in his pursuit of political understanding over the years until it can be said that his lasting fame can be attributed to his social activism combined with his theoretical expertise in socialist and communist analysis.

James was a methodical and intense worker, and his study of the Russian Revolution growing out of his work with the Lancashire socialists was to be a pervasive influence. Socialist theory was James's mainstay for the rest of his long life. And only with an understanding of socialism and communism can we hope to appreciate James's full significance. Along with his intellectual hunger, James also yearned for a practical application of his ideas. Before he moved to England he had little contact with radical political organizations and activists. His time there opened up a new world of social politics and launched his eminent career as a political speaker, activist, organizer, and writer.

He started his study with the German political theorist Karl Marx (1818–1883) the most influential figure in communist thought in the nineteenth century. As coauthor, with Friedrich Engels, of *The Communist Manifesto* (1848) and later as author of *Das Kapital* (1860), Marx was an important early influence on radical figures of the Russian Revolution such as Vladimir Lenin and Leon Trotsky. *The Communist Manifesto* contains a summary of Marx's whole social philosophy. It was written to serve as the platform of the Communist League, a nascent political organization with which Marx and Engels were involved. The *Manifesto* was published at a moment most favorable to its effectiveness, on the eve of the February (1848) revolution in France, during which socialism first showed its power. Marx and Engels wrote the *Manifesto* in an attempt to clarify the working conditions of the growing industrial proletariat. Later, Marx would become one of the leaders of the London-based International Working Men's Association, which influenced the writing of his magnum opus *Das Kapital.*

The Communist Manifesto posited that all history had hitherto been a history of class struggles and asserted that the forthcoming victory of the proletariat would put an end to class society forever. Marx and Engels defined communists as the most advanced and resolute section of the working-class parties of every country in that they were in the vanguard of social change. The *Manifesto* set forth ten immediate

measures as first steps toward communism, ranging from progressive income tax to abolition of inheritances to free education for all children. It closed with the words that inspired future millions and were the catalyst for many revolutions in various countries throughout the twentieth century: "The Proletarians (wage workers) have nothing to lose but their chains. They have a world to win. Working men of all countries unite!"

James then tackled Marx's masterpiece, *Das Kapital,* published in three massive volumes and sometimes called the "bible of the working class." Using the organizing concept he called "historical materialism," Marx argued that the social relations of humans are based on the evolution of capitalist productions that are independent of their personal will. Thus each stage of material production corresponds to a definite stage of development of social relations. The real foundation of the structure of society is based on the legal and political structures associated with material production. In this way the mode of production in material terms determines the general character of the social, political, and intellectual processes of life. It is not the consciousness of human beings that determines their social level but rather their social condition that determines their consciousness.

This was supplemented by the socialist argument that private property was responsible for oppression, poverty, war, and many other problems, and that only a socialist reconstruction of the economy could solve social problems. Dispossessing the privileged classes was seen as an essential part of improving government and people's lives. Raised to the level of historical law, these tenets of grievance and redress lie at the very foundation of "dialectical materialism," or Marx's vehement argument with the suffering of the working class under rule of a capitalist society.

The Russian Revolution of 1917 would bring the first major test of these ideas. The revolution was, first of all, a political revolution that overthrew the monarchy of Tsar Nicholas II and made the construction of a new government system a central problem. In the beginning of the twentieth century, Russia was the last major power of Europe in which the monarch was an autocrat with unlimited power and unrestricted by laws or institutions. In his empire the populace was made up of subjects, not citizens. The Russian Revolution was also a profound social realignment that reached back to the early 1800s for its genesis. The social history of this revolution stresses the importance of popular activism and of social and economic issues in shaping the course and outcome of a country's history.

Russia was a vast country of six time zones and incredible diversity, with over a hundred different national and ethnic minorities. It was a varied kingdom of huge provinces, vast wilderness, and packed urbanized zones of various languages, religions, and populations. It was an empire of huge wealth and tremendous poverty ruled by the Romanovs for more than three hundred years. For most of its existence Russia had been a country of agricultural estates owned by princes who ran them with the slave labor of the peasants (serfs). Under this feudal arrangement the serfs (in some ways) shared the same degrading and physically draining existence suffered by New World African slaves brought to work the plantations of the Caribbean and southern United States.

The emancipation of the serfs occurred in 1861, two years before the emancipation of the slaves in United States in 1863. But as with the Reconstruction period in United States (1863–1900), there were many unanswered problems concerning serfs now free but unemployed and the system of renting and working land for the owners of the estates. The former serfs and peasant workers influenced major revolts against the Russian monarchy in 1881 and 1905. The population of Russia more than doubled between 1860 and 1914. The famine of 1890–1891 alone killed four hundred thousand people, and many peasants and immigrants fled to the cities to work in the growing industrial sector.

A series of peasant revolts spread to the cities where "worker collectives" in the industrial areas united around a growing communist movement organized by intellectuals, dissatisfied workers, and students. The working class and laboring

industrial class organized strikes to fight for an eight-hour workday, sick leave, and healthier living and working conditions. Political radicalization resulted because the regime mostly denied the workers' rights to organize and pursue economic interests legally. Workers then became linked with the revolutionary parties who were concentrated in St. Petersburg and Moscow. Marxism provided an explanation of why factories had emerged according to capitalist principles, what the workers' conditions were, and how to change those conditions.

The situation in Russia at that time, with unrest and ferment at all levels, spawned a professional class of revolutionaries. Vladimir Lenin, Leon Trotsky, and Joseph Stalin, all of whom emerged as leaders of the Bolshevik Party that came to power in 1917, were full-time revolutionaries who spent their entire lives writing political tracts, agitating, and in some cases using terrorist tactics to gain what they wanted.

The intricacies of the Russian Revolution and its concomitant factions, purges, civil wars, and steady evolution into a totalitarian state were matters that James studied closely. In particular he studied the roots of the socialist movement to learn how to apply its lessons to his own activism for social change and how to organize workers into party politics.

The most important early revolutionary movement in Russia was populism, which grew out of the conditions of the mid-nineteenth century and called for the overthrow of the autocracy and a social revolution that would distribute land to the peasants. The populists' problem was how to find a way to mobilize and organize the scattered peasant masses to make it a revolution. This led some revolutionaries known as Narodnaya Volya (The People's Will) to turn to terrorism. In 1881 they assassinated Tsar Alexander II, and the growing movement riddled the country with an underground network of radicals threatening the state. Vladimir Lenin's older brother Alexander was tried as a revolutionary terrorist at this time and was hung. Many other radical revolutionaries were imprisoned or sent into exile, as was Lenin himself in 1905

after the suppression of an unsuccessful socialist revolt in St. Petersburg.

After 1880 a rethinking of revolutionary tactics created a more unified socialist movement that focused on the new industrial working class as well as peasants. In March 1898 the first meeting was held in Minsk of the Russian Social Democratic Worker's Party (eventually to become the Communist Party). Only ten delegates were present (chief among them Vladimir Lenin), but the foundation was laid for a Russian working-class movement to form a social order in which there would be no place for the exploitation of man by man.

In the winter of 1901–1902 Lenin wrote a pamphlet that sketched out the revolutionary principles he was to employ sixteen years later. In *What Is To Be Done?* Lenin hammered his philosophy into shape. It combines the ideas of Marx with those of Sergey Nechayev and Dimitri Pisarev, two early anarchists from the terrorist period. But Marx's earliest and strongest thesis—that "the emancipation of the working class is the work of the working class itself"—is conveniently ignored, while the concept of a small, highly trained group of intellectuals acting as "the vanguard of the revolution" is maintained. In order for a "dictatorship of the proletariat" to come into existence, there must be a core of professional revolutionaries leading the way. Lenin advocates a dogmatic ruling party elite. As it turned out, Lenin's elite evolved into a powerful, secret, and centralized organization that controlled society from the top. This was to prove to be a deadly script for the Russian people. But Lenin goes even further, insisting that his brand of socialism would become a worldwide phenomenon leading to international communism.

It never occurred to Lenin until too late that this vanguard of the proletariat would inevitably destroy the initiative of the proletariat and act as an unlimited autocracy itself. Lenin proceeded to create a party emphasizing a higher degree of centralization and discipline and that exalted the importance of leadership and distrusted initiative from below.

The continuing economic and social strife leading up to World War I only helped Lenin's

cause. There were seventeen thousand peasant revolts between 1910 and 1914. During the same period a new spurt of industrial growth began, leading to a competing and ill-paid industrial workforce. In 1912 striking gold miners at the Lena works were massacred. A much more assertive strike and labor protest movement emerged, which led to a great strike in July 1914 that was both violent and widespread.

The war and its defeats and lack of food encouraged waves of strikes in 1915–1916 that energized the socialist parties to capitalize on popular discontent and try to promote, even lead, any revolution that might be developing. By late 1916 worker soviets (councils) had grown into a significant presence.

Competing socialist parties issued an increasing number of manifestos, leaflets, and other anti-regime propaganda. The series of strikes in January–February 1917 leading up to the revolution were a combination of unplanned actions sparked by worker grievance and demonstrations planned ahead by the socialists.

Through January and February the combination of hunger, intense cold, military defeats by the Germans, and governmental chaos fueled the growing Bolshevik (majority) movement in St. Petersburg (Petrograd). On February 23 a crowd of women workers celebrating international women's day inspired thousands of women to leave the breadlines and join the strikers from the Putilov arms works, taking to the streets with banners reading "Down with the autocracy." As the protest grew into a citywide general strike, Tsar Nicolas II, soon to be deposed and assassinated with his whole family, ordered troops to fire on the huge crowds, but most of the troops, many of them peasants or workers themselves, refused. This anger and confusion culminated in the soldiers' revolt on February 27, when the army refused to continue fighting and began to desert.

In April, the city of St. Petersburg was in turmoil on the day Lenin arrived to clamoring crowds from his exile in Switzerland. In speeches and in the pages of *Pravda,* he immediately put forth his blueprint for the coming new world order, known as the April Theses. In these theses

Lenin laid out ideas for the nationalization of banks and industries, confiscation of all landed estates, and redistribution of land into collectives. He outlined the end of the state and the destruction and abolition of the army, the courts, and the police. Most importantly he championed a republic of soviets including agricultural laborers, peasants, and soldiers' deputies. He insisted on one state bank under control of soviets. He announced a program deliberately calculated to antagonize—and indeed, destroy—all the other revolutionary parties and to channel the revolution into the path he had ordained for it. Of all the documents written in the twentieth century perhaps none other had such a pervasive effect on the lives of the people living on this planet.

One huge flaw in this program was that Lenin interpreted the revolutionary struggle in terms of government by the soviets without in any way showing how that government would operate. The original meaning of "soviet" power implied a government that would use state power in the interests of worker and peasant councils to solve their problems. But for Lenin it was enough to abolish the state without defining its replacement except in the most general terms. And it was only a step from this to the "dictatorship of the proletariat" represented by the dictatorship of one man.

Lenin originally expected that with the triumph of the proletariat, the state that Marx defined as the organ of class rule would "wither away" because class conflicts would come to an end. Instead, Communist Party rule in the Soviet Union resulted in the vastly increased power of the state apparatus. Nor could Lenin have foreseen the stroke he would suffer in late 1922 and death in 1924, resulting in a power struggle in which the authoritarian Joseph Stalin, not the more democratically inclined Leon Trotsky, would eventually emerge the winner. By the time James came to embrace Marxism, Stalin was well on his way to cementing his murderous, totalitarian rule, while Leon Trotsky, in exile in Mexico, continued to direct an anti-Stalinist communist movement abroad. The rift among intellectuals between those who continued to support Stalin's Soviet Union and those who, like James, sup-

ported Trotsky, would significantly shape James's theoretical approach to Marxism and his life as an activist.

LONDON AND PAN-AFRICANISM

In 1934, James, who was working as a cricket reporter for the *Manchester Guardian,* left northern England and moved to London, a center of international communist thought but also of the increasingly visible Pan-African movement. In 1936, Italian troops under the fascist dictator Benito Mussolini invaded Ethiopia, and James's response was the essay *Abyssinia and the Imperialists* (1936), a radical statement on independence movements in Africa. James developed this theme with the noted Africanist George Padmore in the International African Service Bureau (IASB), an anticolonialist organization dedicated to Pan-African thought.

Briefly defined, Pan-Africanism is a concept of unity expressing the common attributes of all black peoples, whether from Africa or as part of the diaspora (spread) of Africans through slavery and immigration. Interestingly, it was first expressed as a theory in the late 1800s by a lawyer from Trinidad named Henry Sylvester Williams. Common themes included the unjust nature of slavery and oppression and the need for an independent black leadership. Pan-Africanism explored the dynamic connections between different aspects of the black diaspora. It also established the presence of Africa at the center of the emerging postwar order. The movement stressed that colonial peoples could be a decisive force in the shaping of modern society. Henry Williams brought together thirty West Indians, African Americans, and Africans in London in 1900 for the first of six Pan-African congresses. One of the delegates, the prominent African American sociologist W. E. B. Du Bois, organized three further conferences in the coming decades. Initially the rhetoric of Pan-Africanism was less militant than Marcus Garvey's "back-to-Africa" movement. In 1945 George and Dorothy Padmore organized the fifth Pan-African congress, which came out strongly for a unity movement between African and Caribbean peoples to end colonial rule. The sixth Pan-African congress, partially organized by James, was held in Africa in 1974 and was even more radical. Other important Pan-African texts were George Padmore's *How Britain Rules Africa* (1936), Eric Williams' *The Negro in the Caribbean* (1942), and Jomo Kenyatta's *Kenya, the Land of Conflict* (1945).

THE BLACK JACOBINS

During the years 1936–1938 James visited Paris to do research on the first successful black slave revolt, which occurred on the Caribbean island of Santo Domingo in 1791. James was intrigued by the Haitian revolution for a number of reasons, including the proximity of the island to Trinidad and the influence of Haiti throughout the Caribbean basin. James's primary thesis is that the Haitian revolt, led by Toussaint L'Ouverture, a former slave, was inspired by a link to the Jacobinism (radical republicanism) of the 1789 French Revolution. This connection between an enslaved French colony and the call for liberation in the French Revolution inspired James to see continuity in modern socialist revolts as well as freedom movements for black people. James was impressed by the popular uprising in Haiti, which organized and designed a new society based on improved legal codes, a black militia and government, fair and just labor practices, and a utopian vision that led to a declaration of a free state on January 1, 1804. The book *The Black Jacobins* (1938) is perhaps James's most famous work. It is one of the first historical studies combining black diaspora history with revolutionary politics while praising the collective mobilization of slaves. James also makes a connection between the central African people from which slaves first came, as well as a history of the Atlantic slave trade. The work dovetailed with James's interest in socialism and full independence for all colonial nations and linked revolutionary politics in Europe to the colonies. James showed how slavery in Santo Domingo had been abolished by the direct action of a united people. James was convinced that this successful revolt eventually brought the end of slavery in the Brit-

ish colonies in 1833. *The Black Jacobins* contains deeply felt and historically accurate sentiments against slavery and racism. By analyzing the black revolution in Santo Domingo through the perspective of the French Revolution James puts the Caribbean firmly on the world stage. The book has proven to be a thrilling inspiration to oppressed people in struggle everywhere, and some critics claim that James became the founding father of African emancipation with the publication of this classic volume. James also wrote a play called *Toussaint L'Ouverture* around these same themes. Paul Robeson, a noted communist and African American singer, played the revolutionary leader. The play had considerable impact in left-wing circles.

MELDING TWO MOVEMENTS: TROTSKYISM AND PAN-AFRICANISM

Throughout his time in England, James's work in Pan-Africanism influenced his thinking about communism and vice versa. In 1937 James defined his position in the international communist movement with *World Revolution,* which advocated opposition to Stalin's repression of Russian citizens and his betrayal of fundamental revolutionary principles. One of the firm tenets of the Russian Revolution and communism was that the revolution was a central part of a broader, sweeping world revolution. James and many others outside of Russia were attracted by this idea and became active socialists in an attempt to achieve this goal. James would spend the rest of his life writing, speaking, and advocating communist and socialist principles. He became better known as a political speaker of amazing clarity and fervor than as a writer. But during these years he also struggled with the legacy of the Russian Communist movement and its evolution into rigid totalitarianism.

James's form of socialism relied more on Marx's original intent of a revolution amongst the lower classes in which they would achieve autonomy and dignity as the masters of their own fate. In particular, James did not support Communist expansion under the terms dictated by Lenin and Stalin. This was one of the factors that led him to embrace the Trotsky faction of socialism.

Leon Trotsky (1879–1940) was by no means an uncontroversial figure. He was a leader in Russia's Revolution in 1917 and later commissar of foreign affairs and of war in the first Communist government. He functioned as the military leader of the Communists during the brutal three-year civil war and was known for his ruthless suppression of dissent among the populists.

In the beginning of the revolution Trotsky was a major figure second in power only to Lenin, and his program differed from the dictator's in fundamental ways. In intellectual power and administrative effectiveness he was Lenin's superior. After the triumph of Communist forces and the end of the Russian civil war in 1920, Trotsky turned his attention to the economic reconstruction of Russia. He allowed for relaxation of stringent centralization and lured "market forces" back into the nationalized system. When Lenin was stricken with a stroke in May 1922, the question of succession to leadership was left in the air. Trotsky was assumed to be logical heir, but jealousy among his colleagues on the politburo prompted them to combine against him. A troika of Joseph Stalin, Grigory Zinovyev, and Lev Kamenev took over at Lenin's death. (The latter two would be executed in 1936 as part of Stalin's "Great Purge.")

Trotsky rebelled against party doctrine and the Central Committee, stressing the violation of democracy in the party and the failure to develop adequate economic planning. Trotsky condemned Stalin's concessions to bourgeois elements and denounced Stalin's theory of socialism in one country as a pretext for abandoning world revolution. In October 1926 Trotsky was expelled from the politburo and dropped from the Central Committee. And then he was expelled from the party and exiled from the country. In 1933 he gave up hope of reforming the Communist Party and called on his followers to establish their own revolutionary party. This movement, whose English and American branches were the Socialist Workers Party, was the party that James joined and worked with for most of his life.

James embraced Trotsky's theory of "permanent revolution," which held that historically an economic system was a world system rather than a national one. Thus for the Russian Revolution to be permanently successful it would have to depend on revolutions in other countries, particularly in western Europe. Trotsky's theory also emphasized the hegemony of the working class over the revolutionary class because of their strategic position in industry and other advance sectors of the economy. He attacked Soviet bureaucracy and the support of the dictatorship of one man. He called for more democracy within the party and more dependence on the rank-and-file workers and more freedom of independent thought.

UNITED STATES

James was invited to United States in 1938 to make a series of political addresses on the feverish prewar situation in Europe and to contribute to the work of the Trotsky movement. He expected to stay a year but quickly developed high hopes for social change in the United States and ended up staying eighteen years. Beginning in November 1938 he went on an extensive speaking tour, traveling to Philadelphia, Boston, Cleveland, Detroit, Minneapolis, Denver, San Francisco, and Los Angeles. At a meeting in Los Angeles he met Constance Webb, a young American actress, poet, and emerging political figure. They began a relationship in 1939 that lasted a decade and resulted in James's second marriage, his first and only child, and his eventual second divorce. Some of their personal difficulties can be attributed to harassment by the FBI and the social problems afflicting an interracial couple.

Although James was immediately struck upon his arrival in New York with the relative lack of organized protest by American blacks, he was also a historian of black nationalist movements in the United States such as the African Blood Brotherhood, which was formed by radical black veterans of World War I and was a fierce defendant of black citizens' rights. A race riot in Tulsa, Oklahoma, in 1920 saw African Blood Brotherhood members fighting the police and white racists in the streets. James also praised Marcus Garvey's Universal Negro Improvement Association, a Pan-African organization which, by the mid-1920s, had one thousand branches on five continents. With this history in mind, James argued for the establishment of black organizations dedicated to the civil rights, suffrage, and sweeping integration of all public institutions.

In pursuit of these goals, James elected to work with the Trotskyist Socialist Workers Party in large part because Trotsky advocated strong recruitment of African Americans into the party. As an activist James was a tireless supporter of black inclusion in workers' unions and socialist study groups in the United States. Indeed, it might be said that his life was dedicated to the continued enfranchisement of black peoples in all countries, and, in the United States as elsewhere, he became famous for his speeches in which he addressed large crowds of workers both black and white for hours without looking at any notes.

Soon, however, James began to see a severe curtailment of funding and recruitment of black workers by the Socialist Workers Party. In April 1939 James traveled to Coyoacan, Mexico, to meet with Trotsky and argue for more resources and attention for African American socialists and emerging black nationalists. After his return to New York, James broke with Trotsky over the issue of black nationalism in the socialist camp, and for a time he left the party. However, James would remain a fervent socialist advocate.

James had returned from Mexico by bus through the southern United States, which had given him firsthand experience of segregation. Neither in Europe nor in the Caribbean had he witnessed the kind of discrimination against blacks he found there. The segregation and poor social conditions for blacks in America infuriated James, and he turned to activism on a local level in New York City. During 1940 he was a contributor on the black question to the *Socialist Appeal* and *Labor Action,* two radical papers. He played a significant role in protests against World War II, which he saw as a conflict among fascist and imperialist powers whose exploitation of populations worldwide would only continue without

worker insurrection. After the Soviet invasion of Finland in 1939 and the signing in 1940 of the Hitler-Stalin pact, James was quick to divorce himself from any association with international communism. Also in 1940, James's U.S. visa expired and he went underground, assuming the political alias "J. R. Johnson."

This temporarily put an end to his public speaking career, but he continued to write, and it was under the name of Johnson that he penned an admiring review of Richard Wright's *Native Son* (1940). James, however, added a cautionary note about Wright's Communist Party sympathies and advocated disengagement from the party for the sake of Wright's talents. James and Constance Webb were friends of Richard Wright, who was perhaps the most influential African American writer of the first half of the century. (Constance Webb later wrote an uneven biography of Wright.)

In 1941 James spent five months in Missouri engaged in strike support work for oppressed sharecroppers. His pamphlet *Down with Starvation Wages in Southeast Missouri* was an influential text for social activism. The strikers won their demands. This success increased James's activity with African American politics and culture. In his regular column, "The Negro Fight," published in the Workers Party *New International* (1940–1947), he covered a wide range of topics concerning race relations.

During the war, factional disputes intensified among American socialist leaders. (Trotsky had been assassinated by an agent of Stalin's secret police in 1940.) These splits continued after the war. James's response was to join forces with Raya Dunayevskaya, a Russian-born intellectual who had been a translator and personal secretary to Trotsky, and together they formed a theoretical component of the Socialist Workers Party pseudonymously called the Johnson-Forest Tendency. Their radical newspaper *Correspondence* analyzed Marxist theory and practice in terms of black nationalism. James's pamphlet *Dialectical Materialism and the Fate of Humanity* (1947) and book *Notes on Dialectics* (1948) defined degrees of integration and segregation within American society and how it related to socialist

theory. The Johnson-Forest Tendency favored a more humanist approach to socialism, trying to incorporate Enlightenment ideas as well as early Marxist theories of democratic and communal socialist politics. In 1947 James's socialist convention statement "The Revolutionary Answer to the Negro Problem in the USA" was an important document of the American Far Left. In it, James argued for the specificity and specialness of black culture in United States. He believed that African Americans had great influence on the development of American culture and working-class solidarity. And, much as James Baldwin would argue later, James was convinced that white and black were integral parts of one nation which could not progress without the combined efforts of both peoples. Their ideas would influence New Left politics in the sixties.

For all his well-founded critiques of the racial situation in America, James found the nation fascinating. His *American Civilization* (written 1950, published 1993) posited the thesis that America's contribution to world civilization was centered on individual rights and that American culture was a unique blend of diverse elements. The first half of the book was a critical reading of Walt Whitman and Herman Melville. In the second half he dealt with the popular arts, including soap operas, Hollywood films, and detective novels, and how they helped define the national character. To James there was no separation between high and low art. James anticipated a utopian future in which art, life, and politics formed a relationship for the good of all.

In the spring of 1952 James was arrested by U.S. immigration authorities for passport violation. He was confined on Ellis Island and faced deportation. His arrest came at the height of the cold war between United States and the Soviet Union and was part of a wider crackdown on illegal aliens identified with radical causes. The book *Mariners, Renegades, and Castaways* (1953) was completed during the author's confinement on Ellis Island and was intended to support his case for U.S. citizenship. James applies a socialist reading to the ship's cast of characters and sees the exploitation of the sailors and crew

in Ahab's pursuit of the white whale a symbol of American materialism.

LONDON AND RETURN TO TRINIDAD

James was deported to England in the fall of 1953. His second marriage had failed, and after James returned to London he was joined by Selma Weinstein, a woman he had met and worked with in New York City. She became his third wife in 1956. Selma James was interested in feminist study and political activism around women's issues, and she cowrote the popular pamphlet *A Woman's Place* (1952). James and Selma worked together for over a decade, but their marriage proved difficult for both of them, and they would part in the 1960s. Among other works during this period, James delivered a noteworthy paper entitled "Popular Art and the Cultural Tradition" at a forum on mass culture sponsored by the Congress of Cultural Freedom held in Paris in March 1954. The paper praised the work of the filmmakers D. W. Griffith, Charlie Chaplin, and Sergei Eisenstein, whom he saw as philosophers presenting issues on the relationship between the individual and society, and made other interesting points about the capacity of the individual artist in creating works of art for mass consumption. In 1957 James was honored by a visit from Dr. Martin Luther King and Coretta Scott King, during which they discussed James's possible return to United States to work in the civil rights movement.

Instead, however, James returned to Trinidad in 1958 after an absence of twenty-six years. He accepted an invitation to speak at the opening ceremonies of the Trinidad Parliament. James was encouraged to remain on his home island. His former student and friend Eric Williams now led the People's National Movement (PNM). Williams was the first leader of an independent, nationalist Trinidad movement. Under his auspices James became the secretary of the West Indian Federal Labour Party, which allied progressive nationalist organizations in the Caribbean. He also offered James the editorship of the *Nation,* the PNM's newspaper. James realized that independence for Trinidad and other islands was imminent and it was time for the Caribbean to create a new society by forming a West Indies federation. In a series of articles and speeches James argued that federation was the best possible approach for a unified and powerful black presence in upcoming global affairs. The years between 1958 and 1962 saw constant debate among West Indian writers, including George Lamming, V. S. Naipaul, Wilson Harris, and James, over ways to advance the movement of West Indian cultural identity.

The so-called Chaguarama Affair ended James's involvement in island politics for a period of time. Chaguarama was a district in northwest Trinidad that had been used by the U.S. military as a naval base during World War II and was continuing to be accessed and controlled by U.S. military personnel. James strongly supported the base's removal, as did a large percentage of the population. A 1960 demonstration called the March in the Rain, intended to bring the United States to the bargaining table, was the high point of militant Trinidad nationalism. When Trinidad President Eric Williams sat down with the United States and ended up keeping the base in operation, James considered it a personal blow and in October 1960 divorced himself from Williams' political party. James's political career was over, and he quietly left the country in 1962 to return to Britain, just days before Trinidad and Tobago's full independence was officially declared and celebrated.

BEYOND A BOUNDARY

In England James resided with his nephew Darcus Howe, an editor of the British black documentary television series *Bandung File.* They lived in Brixton, a district of London known for its Caribbean and African culture. James continued to be a significant force in political and literary circles. With his past and the Caribbean on his mind, James published one of his most idiosyncratic books, the semiautobiographical *Beyond a Boundary* (1963).

Most of the book had been written in the 1950s, but James's return to Trinidad had sparked the final revision of this classic of Caribbean

literature. Not strictly a memoir or an autobiography, it is more a rumination about Trinidad's culture, using cricket as an organizing metaphor and literary conceit. The book is a wide-ranging political and philosophical analysis that connects cricket with artistic and social practices. He argues for the centrality of major sporting figures such as W. G. Grace, the most famous and successful cricket player in Trinidad, in the cultural development of the West Indies. A key formative influence on James was his maternal grandfather, Josh Rudder, the first black railroad engine driver on the Trinidad government railway.

The author's youth, cricket, art, and politics are interconnected. Cricket and literature represented two paths away from his modest island upbringing, and they both reinforced his sense of discipline, fair play, and reward for hard work. But James is also critical of Britain's influence on the island because it inflicted an impossible ideal on the native Trinidad population by enforcing British cultural hegemony. The noted feminist and African American studies scholar Hazel Carby called *Beyond a Boundary* "one of the most outstanding works of cultural studies ever produced" (p. 51).

In spring 1965 James again returned to Trinidad. But the island was experiencing serious labor strife, and Eric Williams, fearing that James might exacerbate the situation, had James placed under house arrest. He was released after about six weeks, and by summer he was back in the thick of Trinidadian politics, cofounding the Workers and Farmers Party and its newspaper *We the People*.

FROM THE 1960S: ACTIVISM AND HONORS

As the 1960s progressed, James was much in demand as a speaker and spent a good deal of his time traveling in Africa, Europe, the Caribbean, and (after regaining his right to enter the country) the United States, giving lectures and attending conferences on topics ranging from politics and history to literature and cricket. In Africa he visited Ghana and Nigeria in 1967 and Tanzania and Uganda the following year. His visits were part of a growing Pan-African movement across the African diaspora during this period, and he directed much of his intellectual energy to addressing the problems faced by newly independent nations in the wake of colonialism, including the issue of developing a specifically African form of socialism.

James's book *The Gathering Forces* (1963) combined history, culture, and politics in a way that appealed to the New Left of the 1960s. James began to be more widely read on college campuses during this period, especially as the black studies movement began to take hold. Between 1968 and 1975 James held several teaching posts and lectured at universities including Howard, Yale, Harvard, and Princeton. In significant ways, policies that he had spent his whole life advocating were now coming to fruition. In 1968 James was invited take part in an academic conference in Havana, Cuba. Although James was never particularly close to Fidel Castro, he did believe that Castro's Caribbean revolution was more than simply a retread of Soviet-style communism. However, the Caribbean leader with whom he felt the most kinship was Walter Rodney of the Working People's Alliance (WPA) of Guyana. Rodney had returned to Guyana in 1974 after spending years educating himself in England and Africa. His revolutionary party was formed in 1975 and achieved some success before Rodney was threatened by rival political camps; he was assassinated in 1980.

James helped issue the call for a sixth Pan-African congress in 1974 in Tanzania. Among the organizers were the African Americans H. Rap Brown and Shirley Graham Du Bois. Its main theme called for the liberation of South Africa. At the last minute James canceled his trip because of perceived dissension in the ranks and called for a boycott. The congress went on but proved to be a failure owing to infighting between different nationalist and socialist agendas.

In 1977 he published *Nkrumah and the Ghana Revolution*. Much of the book had been written in 1960, after Kwame Nkrumah had invited him to participate in independence celebrations in Ghana (formerly the Gold Coast). Nkrumah had become president of the new

republic of Ghana in 1957 on a program of socialist principles. Although James had known Nkrumah since 1943, when Nkrumah was a student in the United States, in this book James did not hide his disappointment with his leadership and criticized Nkrumah for failing to complete the African nation's revolution.

During the 1970s and 1980s James had many visitors to his flat in Brixton. He stressed the fundamentals of his politics to a younger generation, imparting a belief in the creative power of the masses and the importance of social organizations and an understanding of history.

Anna Grimshaw, later to be an editor of James's work, spent six years as his personal assistant. Grimshaw was trained as an anthropologist at Cambridge University. She was instrumental in helping James write one of his most widely circulated essays, "Three Black Women Writers" (1981), on Toni Morrison, Alice Walker, and Ntozake Shange. Maya Angelou and Amiri Baraka made visits to see him, and he was a strong supporter of Poland's Solidarity movement in 1980–1981. He was awarded honorary Doctor of Letters degrees by England's University of Hull (1983) and University of Kent (1984). A television program called *Talking History* filmed a one-hour conversation between James and the historian Edward Thompson in 1983. The book *Cricket,* edited by Anna Grimshaw and published in 1986, collected a half-century's worth of writings. Allison & Busby published three volumes of selected writings: *The Future in the Present* (1977), *Spheres of Existence* (1980), and *At the Rendezvous of Victory* (1984). In 1988 James was awarded the Trinity Cross, Trinidad and Tobago's highest national honor, at a ceremony in London attended by the prime minister of Trinidad. For reasons of health, James withdrew from public speaking in early 1984. He continued to see many people in his home. Paul Buhle's biography *The Artist as Revolutionary* was published in 1988 in London, and James was present for the book launch. It was his last public appearance. James was eighty-eight when he died on May 31, 1989. He was buried in his native Trinidad.

Selected Bibliography

WORKS OF C. L. R. JAMES

NOVEL AND SHORT STORIES

"La Divina Pastora." *Saturday Review* (London), October 15, 1927. Reprinted in *Best Short Stories*. Edited by E. J. O'Brien. London, 1928. Also in *Stories from the Caribbean*. Edited by Andrew Salkey. London: Elek Books, 1965.

"Triumph." *Trinidad* 1, no. 1, Christmas 1929. Reprinted in *Island Voices*. New York: Liveright, York, 1930. Also in *Stories from the Caribbean*. Edited by Andrew Salkey. London: Elek Books, 1965.

Minty Alley. London: Secker & Warburg, 1936. Reprint, with an introduction by Kenneth Ramchand, Jackson: University Press of Mississippi, 1997.

NONFICTION BOOKS AND ESSAYS

The Life of Captain Cipriani: An Account of British Government in the West Indies. Nelson, Lancashire: Couton, 1932. Extracted version, *The Case for West-Indian Self-Government,* London: L. & V. Woolf, 1933.

World Revolution, 1917–1936: The Rise and Fall of the Communist International. London: Secker & Warburg, 1937. Westport, Conn.: Hyperion Press, 1973.

The Black Jacobins: Toussaint L'Ouverture and the San Domingo Revolution. London: Secker & Warburg, 1938. Rev. ed., London: Allison & Busby, 1980.

A History of Negro Revolt. London: Fact Monograph, 1938. London: Race Today Publications, 1988.

"Notes on American Civilization," 1950. Published as *American Civilization*. Edited by Anna Grimshaw and Keith Hart. Oxford: Blackwell, 1993.

Mariners, Renegades, and Castaways: The Story of Herman Melville and the World We Live In. New York, privately published, 1953. London: Allison & Busby, 1985.

Party Politics in the West Indies, Port of Spain: Vedic, 1962.

Beyond a Boundary. London: Stanley Paul/Hutchinson, 1963. New York: Pantheon, 1984.

The Future in the Present: Selected Writings. London: Allison & Busby, 1977.

Nkrumah and the Ghana Revolution. London: Allison & Busby, 1977.

Spheres of Existence. Selected Writings. London: Allison & Busby, 1980.

"C. L. R. James at Black Ink: A Talk on Toni Morrison, Alice Walker, and Ntozake Shange." In *Cultural Correspondence*, winter 1983, pp. 22–25. Reprinted in *At the Rendezvous of Victory: Selected Writings*. London: Allison & Busby, 1984.

At the Rendezvous of Victory: Selected Writings. London: Allison & Busby, 1984.

Cricket. Edited by Anna Grimshaw. London: Allison & Busby, 1986.

Additional collections of C. L. R. James materials can be found at the C. L. R. James Institute, New York City. James Collection: Library of West Indies in St. Augustine, Trinidad. The Archives of Labor and Urban Affairs at Wayne State University in Detroit, Michigan.

CRITICAL AND BIOGRAPHICAL STUDIES

Buhle, Paul, ed. *C. L. R. James: His Life and Work.* London: Allison & Busby, 1986.

Buhle, Paul. *C. L. R. James: The Artist as Revolutionary.* London: Verso, 1988.

Buhle, Paul, and Paget Henry. *C. L. R. James's Caribbean.* Durham, N.C.: Duke University Press, 1992.

Carby, Hazel. "Proletarian or Revolutionary Literature: C.L.R James and the Politics of Trinidadian Renaissance." *South Atlantic Quarterly* 87: 51 (winter 1988).

Grimshaw, Anna, ed. *The C. L. R. James Reader.* Oxford: Blackwell, 1992.

King, Nicole. *C. L. R. James and Creolization: Circles of Influence.* Jackson: University Press of Mississippi, 2001.

Lamming, George. *Kas-Kas: Interviews with Three Caribbean Writers in Texas.* Edited by Ian Munro and Reinhard Sander. Austin: University of Texas. African/Afro-American Research Institute, 1972.

Nordquist, Joan. *C. L. R. James: A Bibliography.* Santa Cruz, Calif.: Reference and Research Service, 2001.

Oxaal, Ivar. *Black Intellectuals and Dilemmas of Race & Class in Trinidad.* Cambridge, Mass.: Schenkman, 1982.

Rosengarten, Frank. *Urbane Revolutionary: C. L. R. James and the Struggle for a New Society.* Jackson: University Press of Mississippi, 2008.

Worcester, Kent. *C.L.R James: A Political Biography.* Albany: State University of New York Press, 1996.

JHUMPA LAHIRI

(1967—)

Patricia J. Ferreira

WITHIN JUST TEN years following her literary debut, Jhumpa Lahiri published three international best sellers and garnered many of the top honors accorded a writer: the O. Henry Award (1999), the PEN/Hemingway Award (1999), a Pulitzer Prize (2000), an American Academy of Arts and Letters Addison Metcalf Award (2000), a Guggenheim Fellowship (2002), and the Frank O'Connor International Short Story Award (2008). Two of her works were selected for *The Best American Short Stories* (1999, 2002), and in 2010 she was named to President Barack Obama's Committee on the Arts and Humanities.

The daughter of Bengali Indian nationals who immigrated to London, where she was born, and then to the United States when she was three, Lahiri takes the reader inside the intricacies of newly arrived Americans of Indian descent who simultaneously strive to maintain their indigenous customs as well as undertake, most times painfully, the demands of settling and establishing family in their adopted country. Although writing that concerns itself with race, ethnicity, and culture constitutes a significant portion of the American canon, in Lahiri's work the line between old world and new is far more tenuous because it is so thoroughly set in the late-twentieth and early twenty-first centuries, when technology enables continued and sustained contact between the newly arrived and those they left behind.

As Lahiri's fiction has achieved an international readership, it also has spurred a significant amount of critical writing on her work, especially for an author who could still be categorized as "emerging." Certainly much of this writing focuses on her work's preoccupation with cultural identity, but it is largely in keeping with the "transnational" lens she uses rather than one that locates her on any exclusive side of a border. Likewise, the syllabi of college courses that make use of her fiction, when looked at in total, are also representative of Lahiri's international markings. She can just as easily be found on the reading lists of comparative literature courses as on those restricted to American literature or, more specifically, fiction by Asian American women. Moreover, because two of her books consist of short stories, which have been responsible for most of her acclaim, she also merits attention in more genre-specific studies.

INTERPRETATION AND DISLOCATION

With the publication of the short story collection *Interpreter of Maladies* (1999), for which she won the Pulitzer Prize, Lahiri explained in a number of interviews the origins of the title. She described meeting a friend with whom she had lost touch and asking about his job. He worked for a doctor, translating the Russian of immigrant patients into English when they gave details of their ailments. Intrigued, the phrase "interpreter of maladies" came to Lahiri immediately after the get-together, and she jotted it down for future use in her fiction. Though it would take her four years to write the corresponding story, a central concept of much of her writing, well beyond the title piece, involves the way a narrator articulates symptoms of conflict that build as the plot unfolds. It is tempting to promote Lahiri herself as some behind-the-scenes agent in charge of clarifying how particular circumstances are problematic. Indeed, given her authorial role, there is some truth to that supposition, and in many of the interviews where she details how she arrived at the title of her first collection, Lahiri does accede to such a claim, though

demurely. The real quality of her writing, however, is her capacity to follow the classic tenet "Show, don't tell." As a result, Lahiri deftly passes a responsibility to her reader to infer meaning from particular characters' actions and, mostly, from their inner sentiments, subtly requiring a hands-on engagement to accomplish understanding. Little is articulated outright. Instead, her stories revolve around what is not said yet nonetheless known by the reader.

Additional characteristics span Lahiri's work. She continually peppers her fiction with the distinctive characteristics of her parents' native Bengali traditions. Although Lahiri's characters often struggle with their own uptake of such customs, especially when they, like her, are second-generation Americans, her work has enabled her, in some measure, to keep them in practice, if only vicariously. Likewise, often the conflicts that arise in her fiction have their origins in Lahiri's own life. Whether in *Interpreter of Maladies* or her novel, *The Namesake* (2003), or her second short-story collection, *Unaccustomed Earth* (2008), there are characters who are culturally dislocated, the result of emigrating from India, usually Calcutta, to the United States, inhabiting mostly Cambridge, Massachusetts, or Boston's suburbs. As previously suggested, the route, to a degree, follows her own biography. Her father Amar K. Lahiri and mother Tapati Lahiri grew up in Calcutta but left India, for London, where Jhumpa Lahiri was born on July 11, 1967. They then moved to Cambridge for a brief stint before eventually settling in South Kingston, Rhode Island. Moreover, she spent a considerable amount of time in Boston, first as a graduate student at Boston University and subsequently as a creative writing instructor. Landmarks, place names, and long-established cultural institutions such as Central Square, Memorial Drive, the Charles River, Massachusetts Avenue, Massachusetts General Hospital, the *Boston Globe,* Filene's department store, Harvard, and MIT all feature in her work. More importantly, the demands and strains of assimilation and integration that were an obvious part of her childhood play a central role in her fiction. Lahiri has explained that as a child of immigrants she was privy to the way her parents oscillated between two worlds, which in turn produced in her a sense that she was not completely part of either. The inability to explain one world to the other provoked in Lahiri a keen understanding of the limitations of communication, and because of such insight, it makes sense that her characters often function in a reality where certain knowledge is made known only to the reader, rather than to each other, and through the circuitous route of storytelling.

THE ADJUSTMENT OF WOMEN

Women in particular bear the brunt of adjustment that comes with such dramatic resettlement when countries such as India and the United States are so different from one another. Not only must women navigate the intricacies of their new surroundings in a vastly different climate and social register, but they must do so alone. As with immigrants before them, the impetus for relocation is work. However, it is their husbands who have been invited to the United States, usually by a university, to take up professorships, scholarly fellowships, or other professional appointments. These are not the settlers of yore who contended with the limitations and humiliations of arduous menial labor. Lahiri's male immigrants are mostly highly educated, and their work routines among Americans challenge them in ways that are less visible than the stresses of their wives, who lead solitary lives in the home, forced to venture into the new world without family and friends. Moreover, because their marriages are often arranged, women's partnerships with their husbands have yet to take hold, making their transitions doubly tenuous. Such circumstances, however, as integral as they are to much of Lahiri's fiction, are largely the backdrop for the more profound aspect of her writing, which relies upon allusions to and ruminations about inner tumult or underlying complications within a given character—complications to which the reader is delicately charged with becoming attuned as the story moves forward. With brilliant dexterity, Lahiri instills in the reader a sense of investment in the plot line that is much like the involvement of a

diagnostician, who learns from particular details how and why certain circumstances present a dilemma.

The story "Mrs. Sen's," in *Interpreter of Maladies,* illustrates the narrative technique. The young protagonist, Eliot, is an eleven-year-old boy who needs someone to care for him when he arrives home from school. Eventually Mrs. Sen is hired; however, Eliot must take the school bus to her home because she does not drive. Although this would seem a minor detail, the reader is cued into Eliot's past experiences with babysitters— one a vegetarian college student who refused to cook meat and another who was fired because she sipped whiskey while on the job. As a result, Eliot's mother's apprehension about Mrs. Sen based on her incapacity to drive is given credence, and the reader wonders what role it will play, especially because Eliot's mother works fifty miles away while his father, last they knew, lives "two thousand miles west" (p. 113). The description of the Sens' home only adds to the reader's initial worry that something is not quite right. It is an apartment owned by the university that hired Mr. Sen as a math professor and is located on the "fringes of the campus" (p. 112). The lobby is tiled in "unattractive squares of tan," and the word "frozen" is used to describe the inside, where the carpet, lampshades, television, and telephone are all covered to protect soiling. In a way, Mrs. Sen herself knows the context within which she lives is out of kilter, but her only rationale, which is never declared outright, is that her life will never be ideal because she is not living in India.

As the story progresses, the reader sees that Eliot becomes an avenue by which Mrs. Sen can travel back home as she recounts to him her way of life there. Although the Sens' living environment is not what it could be, it fades from importance as the relationship between Mrs. Sen and Eliot comes more into focus. While she prepares dinner, cutting up a myriad of vegetables, she wields a unique knife and explains how, back home, to prepare for celebrations her mother would call neighborhood women together and, with similar knives, they would gather on the rooftop, cutting enough vegetables for the oc-

casion while they gossiped and laughed. The "chatter," Mrs. Sen laments, made it hard to sleep at night. Conversely, "in this place where Mr. Sen has brought [her]" it is difficult to sleep because of the quiet (p. 115). Bowls and colanders that eventually brim with chopped vegetables line the countertop, but the reader connects them to Mrs. Sen's isolation: the bounty of squash, cabbage, and cauliflower will feed only her and her husband. She asks Eliot whether anyone in this neighborhood would come even if she were to "scream" at the top of her lungs. Her question is raised as he is confined to the couch because Mrs. Sen seems to fret that he will be harmed if he gets too close to the knife. Eliot, though, is not fazed. Instead, he is intrigued by her stories as well as concerned for her well-being and replies, "Maybe." Mrs. Sen, however, again expresses her longing for India, explaining that because there were no telephones back home, if one's voice was raised in either sorrow or joy a whole neighborhood and "half of another" would respond (p. 116).

Despite the pain Mrs. Sen's homesickness causes her, the reader also notices that it provides a sense of commonality between her and Eliot. Because he is the only child of a single mother, abandoned by his father, Eliot too spends quite a bit of time alone. In fact, when Mrs. Sen extols the sense of community surrounding her family in India and the reader witnesses her regrets about her seclusion in the United States, Eliot immediately considers, to himself, circumstances that illustrate how his home, just five miles from the Sens', also lacks personal intimacy. He and his mother rent a beach house which during the winter months is cold and barren. A young couple lives next door; however, when they have a Labor Day party, Eliot and his mother are not invited. Since it is one of her "rare" days off, it would seem an opportunity for them to do something special, but she spends the day doing laundry, balancing her checkbook, and vacuuming the inside of her car. Such details explain why, though never directly articulated, Eliot would feel a kinship with Mrs. Sen. When his mother first hires her, Eliot is happy to make the bus journey. For him, her home is literally warmer

than his own. She also seems eager to see him and greets him with sandwiches, peeled oranges, or peanuts. Such attentiveness contrasts with the uninspired care Eliot receives from his mother, who normally orders take-out pizza for dinner. Instead of eating it together, she goes outside on the deck for a cigarette, leaving Eliot alone "to wrap up the leftovers" (p. 118).

The intimacy between Mrs. Sen and Eliot, even though they are from different cultures, is echoed in another story in *Interpreter of Maladies,* "The Third and Final Continent," where the Indian male narrator and his elderly American landlady, Mrs. Croft, form a similar bond. Although the two stories have vastly different conclusions, for each pair, their relationship to each other becomes, for a time, more significant than the ones that should customarily hold such attachment. Mrs. Sen shares more with Eliot than she does with her husband. Likewise, Eliot's connection to Mrs. Sen is more rewarding than the one with his mother. In "The Third and Final Continent," the narrator and Mrs. Croft develop more of an understanding with one another than he with his newly married wife and she with her sixty-eight-year-old daughter. While some of Lahiri's characters remain estranged from one another, the ability of other characters to form bonds occurs in part because they possess an ability to move past cultural boundaries as well as any additional impediments that life presents. Eliot's open-mindedness is exhibited as Mrs. Sen applies vermilion to the part in her hair and explains to him that it is an Indian custom that signifies she is married. Without an intonation of judgment, he likens it to a wedding ring. "Exactly," she responds. "Only with no fear of losing it in the dishwasher" (p. 117). He more than obliges another Indian custom requiring him to take off his shoes in the entryway before walking into the house proper. The narrator of "The Third and Final Continent" will do the same before he enters the room he temporarily rents from Mrs. Croft, even though it is not expected.

However, unlike Eliot, who, as a child, seems quickly to become enmeshed in Indian ways with an air of curious nonchalance, the narrator of "The Third and Final Continent" is an adult, and

as such is initially more challenged by Mrs. Croft's brusque New England peculiarities. His skepticism in the end does not prove to be of any consequence; however, the difference in age between him and Eliot does explain why the child is initially more predisposed to Mrs. Sen, whereas in the "Third and Final Continent," the narrator hesitates. He describes Mrs. Croft's voice as "bold and clamorous" (p. 176), which sharply contrasts with his own manner, describing himself as "soft-spoken by nature" (p. 180). Their differences are even further pronounced as he automatically refers to her as "madame" with unwavering, polite deference while she calls him "boy," more often than not, and usually speaks in clipped sentences. Though the narrator is taken aback by her sharpness, he does not demur, especially when he learns that she is over a hundred years old. In "Mrs. Sen's," Eliot's awareness of the differences between him and the title character are greeted with a similar respect, but he has little control over any of the complexities that arise from Mrs. Sen's loneliness because he is a minor and is supposed to follow an adult's lead. In contrast, in the "Third and Final Continent," the narrator's choice to indulge Mrs. Croft suggests behavior that is more compelling because he could move out—as, her daughter one day confirms, many before him have done. It seems even Americans are daunted by Mrs. Croft's demeanor.

"The Third and Final Continent" takes place in 1969, soon after astronauts landed on the moon, and Mrs. Croft creates an idiosyncratic ritual regarding it when the narrator comes home from his job as a librarian at MIT. She asks him to sit next to her on a piano bench as she recounts how an American flag now flies on the moon. "Isn't that splendid?" she asks the narrator. When he simply responds, "Yes, madame," she commands that he instead say "splendid!" He conceals his initial annoyance, and soon concedes to her demands, thinking "it was a small enough thing to ask" (pp. 182–183). Each evening, as she repeats the request and the narrator agrees, they become more and more accustomed to one another and Mrs. Croft eventually falls asleep, leaving the narrator free to retreat to his room.

Just as Eliot and Mrs. Sen provide one another with welcome companionship, the narrator's and Mrs. Croft's mutual regard for decorum enables an unspoken fondness to develop between them. Even her daughter confides to the narrator that he is the first boarder she has ever called a "gentleman" (p. 185).

The narrator is especially taken with Mrs. Croft's ability to adapt. He learns that after her husband died she supported herself and her family by teaching piano at her home for forty years, which also explains the significance of the bench she sits on throughout the day. Moreover, that she rents rooms in her home to those affiliated with Harvard or MIT is evidence that, despite her elderly peccadilloes, she possesses an ability to adjust. This character trait is in sharp contrast to the narrator's own mother, back in Calcutta, who, upon his father's death, sank into a depression from which she was unable to recover despite support from her family and treatment at a variety of psychiatric clinics. Likewise, the reader surmises that many of Mrs. Sen's struggles arise from her incapacity, for whatever reason, to begin a new life in the United States. In contrast, the flexible nature of Mrs. Croft, though sometimes concealed by her briskness, enables the narrator to develop an affinity for her as well as insight into the traits that promise success in his new surroundings. Making his way around Cambridge, not to mention around the nuances of Mrs. Croft's personality, he demonstrates that he has the capacity to transform strangeness into the familiar, even faced with so formidable a challenge as finding comfort in the domain of an eccentric hundred-and-three-year-old woman. He follows her almost Victorian rules of the house, which include locking the door when he enters, cleaning his own sheets and towels, and not entertaining women in his room, even though he himself is not attracted to the thought, asserting, "I am a married man, madame" (p. 181).

As the story unfolds, the narrator's role as Mrs. Croft's tenant, just like Eliot's role as Mrs. Sen's charge, is overtaken by the characters' genuine regard for one another. In "The Third and Final Continent" the narrator admits that he is in "awe of how many years [Mrs. Croft] had

spent on this earth" (p. 189). Before going to sleep he checks to make sure she is either sitting upright on the piano bench or has made it safely to her bedroom. Despite his growing relationship with her, by the end of six weeks his transition to the United States takes a new turn when he is notified that a passport and green card have been secured for his wife, Mala. As a result, he must find more spacious living arrangements than his single room at Mrs. Croft's. The narrator recognizes the incongruity of leaving the ease of his routine to take up his life with Mala, especially because their arranged introduction and subsequent marriage, combined with the circumstances surrounding the couple's immigration to the United States that required he leave first, means that he has come to know his landlady better than he knows his wife. Soon after he receives the notice of Mala's impending arrival, however, he accepts his responsibility to help his wife adjust to her new surroundings, despite any initial inhibitions.

His sense of duty to Mala, though they are so unfamiliar with one another, materializes on his way to work one morning. As he walks down Massachusetts Avenue, he observes an Indian woman across the street, pushing a baby in a stroller while the free end of her sari, unbeknownst to her, drags on the ground. Suddenly a passing dog begins to bark and jumps at it, taking the end of the sari between its teeth. The "American" owner of the dog scolds it and apologizes; however, the Indian woman is obviously shaken and her child is crying. Though the scene is conspicuously laden with the hostility immigrants have historically confronted in the United States, it is also significant because it causes the narrator to realize that when Mala arrives he will need to "welcome her and protect her" (p. 190), orienting her to her new surroundings. As they take up their lives as husband and wife, the narrator, however, readily admits that becoming a couple did not happen automatically.

The reader is continually made aware that adjustment requires effort and is not simply the result of being willing to change. The narrator expresses to himself unease about eating and

sleeping together as well as having an extra key cut to their apartment, and he "reluctantly" gives her money that she uses to buy accoutrements that will make her chores easier and their apartment homier: a potato peeler and a tablecloth. Additionally, though Mala serves him familiar dishes, she also reminds him of Indian ways, such as eating with the hands, that he seems uncomfortable about exercising in the United States. In the midst of their awkwardness with one another, he proposes going for a walk, yet becomes chagrined as she seems to ready herself too formally, especially given the casualness of dress in the United States. She puts on a new sari and marks her body with the traditional Hindu symbols of a married woman, imprinting a red *bindi* on her forehead and tinting her feet with red dye. As they stroll along Massachusetts Avenue, they eventually arrive at Mrs. Croft's street and ring the bell at her house. The narrator is surprised that door is answered by her daughter, who informs him that Mrs. Croft has broken her hip and is lying on the couch in the parlor.

Even though it has been several weeks since the narrator moved out, he and Mrs. Croft revert to their usual ways; she perfunctorily calls him "boy" while he addresses her as "madame." When she explains that she called the police when she fell even though it was the middle of the night, without hesitation he replies, "Splendid!" This causes Mala to laugh with a voice "full of kindness" and her eyes "bright with amusement" (p. 195). Suddenly Mrs. Croft realizes her presence and asks the narrator, "Who is she, boy?" He responds, "She is my wife, madame." Recognizing that Mala is sitting on the piano bench, Mrs. Croft asks if she plays. When Mala says, "No, madame," the old woman, in her usual abrupt way, commands her to "stand up!" Aware that Mala is startled by Mrs. Croft's brash manner, the narrator feels sympathy and remembers his own moments of difficulty in a new culture. He once again appreciates that Mala "had traveled far from home, not knowing where she was going, or what she would find, for no reason other than to be [his] wife." Simultaneously, he watches Mrs. Croft "scrutinizing Mala from top to toe with what seemed to be placid disdain."

Doubting that the old woman has ever seen someone in a sari, wearing stacks of bracelets and a "painted dot" on her forehead, he wonders what she will object to. Yet in a moment that surely demonstrates Lahiri's certainty about the difficulty of communicating, especially when the players are from different parts of the world, Mrs. Croft declares in "equal measures of disbelief and delight … 'She is a perfect lady!'" The narrator, realizing his misinterpretation, exchanges what seems to be a knowing look with Mala, and this instant is marked as the time when the "distance" between the two "began to lessen" (p. 196).

In "The Third and Final Continent," Lahiri presents an affirming resolution to the quagmire of cultural dislocation, a resolution made possible by the ability to change exhibited by Mrs. Croft and the narrator as well as by his recognition and appreciation of Mala's needs as she navigates the new terrain made necessary by their marriage. In "Mrs. Sen's," however, the title character evinces no capacity to adjust, and this deficiency becomes compounded by Eliot's limited ability to help her, given his age. Her alienation and isolation, though tempered by her caretaking of Eliot and his compassion for her, ultimately ends in disaster. Additionally, the adults in the story, namely Eliot's mother and Mr. Sen, fail to assist Mrs. Sen with her transition to the United States. Whenever Eliot's mother picks him up, she refuses to take off her shoes as she enters the house and even fends off Mrs. Sen's attempts at conventional courtesies, snubbing the after-work refreshments she is offered, privately confessing to Eliot that she does not like them, and making only marginal efforts to engage in conversation. Mr. Sen is little better. Although he initially indulges his wife, his attentions are clearly focused on his life at the university.

At the very start of the story, it becomes apparent that Mr. Sen believes if Mrs. Sen learns to drive, her life will improve. Yet she remains unconvinced, declaring to Eliot one day that driving will still not make it possible for her to travel the ten thousand miles to Calcutta. She waits for Eliot to get dropped off from school before she

begins her reluctant attempts to practice. As he sits beside her in the passenger seat, he takes on the role of a surrogate instructor for Mr. Sen, who is at work. Every moment is plagued with awkwardness. Even the "roar of the ignition" (p. 119) frightens Mrs. Sen. As she backs out of the parking space, inch by inch, to circle the apartment complex, Eliot realizes she has not the slightest instinct for driving. She becomes distracted by the radio, frequently takes her eyes off the road, or beeps at objects too far in the distance for her to worry about hitting. Eliot tries to teach her the rules of the road, explaining she cannot turn onto a main thoroughfare unless no one is coming; however, she argues that oncoming traffic should yield to her. Eventually, when she risks taking Eliot to a distant fish store, she turns too soon. The driver of a car, approaching in the opposite lane, swerves to avoid hitting them head-on but leans on the horn, startling Mrs. Sen, who in turn crashes into a telephone pole.

Mr. Sen is contacted by the police and taken to the scene by a colleague. After filling out accident forms, he manages to drive everyone home, since the car suffered only a dented fender, but he also must tell Eliot's mother what happened, especially because the policeman at the scene had told him that Eliot had been very lucky to escape without injury. As expected, Mrs. Sen's after-school caretaking of Eliot ends. Instead, he will look after himself at his own house. On the first day of the new situation, his mother calls to make sure he is okay. Though he responds that he is fine, the reader is less convinced, aware that his only company is the "gray waves receding from the shore" (p. 135) of their beach rental. One wonders if he peers out across the ocean, thinking of Mrs. Sen and her longing for the familiarity of her Indian homeland. Unlike "The Third and Final Continent," "Mrs. Sen's" ends in misery, with both Mr. Sen and Eliot's mother refusing their loved ones' need for more companionship.

In Lahiri's second short-story collection, *Unaccustomed Earth,* the piece "Hell-Heaven" also takes up the theme of isolation, this time in the life of a newly immigrated woman whose husband is hired as a microbiologist at Massachusetts General Hospital. Elements of the plot bear resemblance to its predecessors in *Interpreter of Maladies* in that the main character, like Mrs. Sen, at first lives a solitary life, made somewhat less lonely because she has a child. As the story progresses, however, the likeness with "Mrs. Sen" diminishes. Adaptation to her new surroundings is inevitable, a tacit expectation because of her husband's employment. Moreover, her assimilation, like Mala's in "The Third and Final Continent," is successful because she has help; however, this similarity too, like the one with Mrs. Sen, lessens because the character who assists her ultimately complicates the action. As a result, her acclimatization is hard won and occurs almost backhandedly. Though it is no less rewarding, assimilation happens because of her unintended tenacity.

That the main character survives, despite the emotional odds against her, is in keeping with the general premise of *Unaccustomed Earth.* Prefaced by an epigraph taken from Nathaniel Hawthorne's "The Custom-House," the collection works off of his assertion that "human nature will not flourish" if it keeps inhabiting "the same worn-out soil." The passage implies that growth only occurs amid new circumstances and surroundings. Thus Lahiri promotes change, yet she is surely not glib. As in "Hell-Heaven," the means by which most of her characters profit is their contention with daunting circumstances. Whereas many of the stories in *Interpreter of Maladies* revolve around the deciphering of problems, in *Unaccustomed Earth* difficulties are still clarified but resolution is also brought to bear, rendered with Lahiri's characteristic obliqueness.

"Hell-Heaven" revolves around Aparna, who follows her husband, Shyamal, to the United States for job-related reasons. They have a young daughter, Usha, and it is the grown Usha who narrates this retrospective story about her mother, one whose details she only fully learned as an adult.

Although raising a young child gives Aparna a certain purpose, references to the differences between her and Shyamal imply his deficiencies

in fulfilling her ultimate needs for true camaraderie. Aparna grew up in a sophisticated neighborhood in Calcutta, while Shyamal comes from a rural suburb, twenty miles outside the city, where women still adhere to the custom of covering their heads with the ends of their saris and the homes lack indoor toilets as well as more refined comforts. Whereas Aparna craves the familiar society of her urban upbringing, Shyamal loves "silence and solitude" (p. 65). The reader is told he married Aparna only to appease his parents, who were disheartened by his decision to move to the United States. Rather than involving himself in the intricacies of a relationship, however, he forsakes family life for his job, "his research," from which neither his wife nor daughter can distract him. One day, by accident, while Aparna is playing with Usha in the environs surrounding Harvard Square, she meets up with a fellow Bengali, Pranab Chakraborty, who happens to be from the same neighborhood in North Calcutta. Not only do he and Aparna know the same landmarks back home, they share a similar social standing and indulge in a mutual "love of music, film, leftist politics, poetry" (p. 64). Immediately Pranab is brought back to the apartment and Aparna introduces him to Shyamal. Without hesitation, he becomes a member of the family. He refers to Shyamal as he would an older brother and calls Aparna the polite Bengali "Boudi," a term reserved for a sister-in-law. In turn, Usha learns to call him "Pranab Kaku" as if he were her uncle.

Given Shyamal's shortcomings as a husband, Pranab becomes the perfect companion for Aparna. In addition to their shared background and similar interests, he also experiences the same estrangement felt by many of the women who inhabit Lahiri's stories, including Aparna, when he first arrives in the United States. His landing at Logan Airport to begin graduate school as an engineering student at MIT was in the midst of a snowstorm. As if the climate was not foreign enough, his living arrangements made life even stranger, renting an attic room from a divorced woman with two small children whom he only heard cry. When Pranab, therefore, meets Aparna and she welcomes him into the family's apartment, he is able to speak Bengali, eat the food he is accustomed to, and make their place his home away from home. In turn, his affability, which contrasts with Shyamal's remoteness, enables him to become Aparna's soul mate, their friendship facilitating not only a sense of the life they left behind in Calcutta but also compensating for the insufficiencies both endure, she with Shyamal and Pranab because he is alone, the two in a strange country. When they meet, their lives take a beneficial turn. Whereas Shyamal devotes all his energy to work in the chemistry lab at the hospital, Pranab regularly skips classes to take Aparna and Usha on outings. In fact, when he eventually buys a car, a blue Volkswagen Beetle, the threesome goes on extended trips to the White Mountains of New Hampshire or the beach at Walden Pond, taking picnics, swimming, and hiking in the woods. On such occasions, strangers would assume that Pranab and Aparna were husband and wife and Usha was their child.

The couple's relationship poses not even a hint of difficulty for Shyamal because of his disposition. In fact, he views Aparna and Pranab's friendship with welcome relief since it absolves him from the guilt he feels for marrying her without truly becoming vested in their union. Pranab also exhibits the expected deference to Shyamal and does so with sincerity, as if he truly were his older brother. The plot line, however, is fueled by the fact that Aparna, in her yearning for intimacy, unwittingly falls in love with Pranab. Because her cultural upbringing precludes such feelings, her stirrings must remain indirect, and as a result they play into Lahiri's dominant storytelling hallmark of showing what cannot be said. Their involvement with one another appears harmless, but Aparna clearly operates in an undercurrent of infatuation, planning meals for Pranab in advance, making the apartment more hospitable for him, and wearing her best saris when he visits.

In light of her efforts it might seem a double standard not to assign equal blame to Aparna and Pranab for the consequences that unfold. Aparna, however, cannot be faulted. Pranab's attention, in the face of her husband's disregard, is the reason she so fully falls in love. Yet Pranab proceeds

without fully appreciating Aparna's situation or true feelings and remains oblivious to the potential dangers of what is literally characterized as his "woo[ing]" (p. 67). Remember too that he derives considerable pleasure from Aparna's attention. As a result, his contentment seems the only explanation for his unwise, unyielding devotion to her. He ultimately cannot marry her; however, there is a sense that he conveniently ignores the eventual harm that will arise from his dealings with her, at least until he finds a suitable replacement. Through the building conflict, Lahiri remarkably illustrates the instances that occur throughout life, in all kinds of situations, where communication fails. Pranab and Aparna are from the same world, but despite having so much to talk about, they cannot truly explain themselves to each other.

ADULTERY

Adultery is a preoccupation of Lahiri's work, and given the crucial role that secrecy plays in infidelity, it provides a reasonable plot line from which to explore the idea of the incommunicable in life. In *Interpreter of Maladies,* the title story and "Sexy" both revolve around the theme. In *Unaccustomed Earth,* in addition to the nuanced take on unfaithfulness illustrated in "Hell-Heaven," the stories "A Choice of Accommodations" and "Nobody's Business" as well as the novella "Hema and Kaushik" all explore it in varying degrees, demonstrating the array of circumstances that prevent her characters from achieving relationships in fully realized ways, largely because they cannot or do not say what they feel to one another. For instance, in "Nobody's Business," the plot revolves around Sang and her inability to confront her lover, Farouk, who is two-timing her. "Sexy," in turn, provides a useful comparison to "Hell-Heaven," especially when arguing that Pranab's lack of sensitivity to Aparna's real feelings is ultimately self-serving.

To be sure, "Sexy" takes up adultery in more typical ways than "Hell-Heaven." Dev, one of the main characters, meets and engages Miranda at the cosmetics counter in Filene's while his wife is out of the country. The only facet that provides distinction to the story's projection of their affair is their differing cultural backgrounds, Dev being from India and Miranda from the Midwest. Otherwise the plot is conventional, depicting a man who is clearly only interested in the sexual gratifications of the relationship instead of the ways it could offer long-term commitment. In "Hell-Heaven," by contrast, the characters and all of their attending details make the relationship between Pranab and Aparna more convoluted, and indeed in a literal sense their relationship does not constitute infidelity at all. Despite the significant differences between the two stories, however, "Sexy" does explain how Pranab's attention to Aparna in "Hell-Heaven," like that of Dev to Miranda, is more at fault.

Miranda's circumstances, like Aparna's, make her vulnerable to the attentions of an attractive man, at least initially. Her job is at a public radio station, raising money by phone, and having recently moved to Boston from Michigan, she has no circle of friends other than Laxmi, a woman she works with who is already married. As with Pranab and Aparna, when Dev initiates conversation with Miranda as they leave the department store, she is predisposed to his flirtation. At first she rationalizes her involvement with him as acceptable because his wife is away. Likewise, Aparna fools herself into believing she has no sustaining interest in Pranab by engaging him in conversations about other women who could potentially be his wife. As "Sexy" proceeds, however, Miranda, like Aparna with Pranab, becomes more and more smitten with Dev.

While his wife is in India they spend nearly every night together, though Dev must leave her apartment early in the morning so that he will be home for phone calls from abroad. He and Miranda have only two weeks before his wife returns, so they go on a whirlwind of dates: out to dinner, the movies, museum exhibitions, symphony concerts, and an especially significant afternoon in the Mapparium at the Christian Science center. When Dev's wife returns, however, his outings with Miranda, like Pranab's with Aparna, dramatically cease, and he only visits her for a few hours each Sunday for sex, telling

his wife he is going running along the Charles. That he lies to his wife is bad enough; however, his sense of entitlement when he shows up at Miranda's with nothing to offer other than desire makes him the worst possible cad. After their lovemaking, to add insult to injury, he falls asleep. Except for sex, nothing, not even worthwhile conversation, occurs. All of Miranda's solitary ruminations about the possibility of she and Dev having more than a classic extramarital affair begin to recede. He clearly has only one intention.

Ironically, the entire time that Miranda and Dev have been secretly seeing one another, Laxmi, Miranda's work colleague, has been involved, though indirectly, in parallel circumstances. Her cousin's marriage is on the verge of breaking up, the victim of infidelity. As a result, Laxmi, in the cubicle next to Miranda's, spends a good deal of time on the phone dealing with her cousin's heartbreak. Miranda is forced to listen to the conversations, given the proximity of their workstations. In the process, she learns that Laxmi's cousin and her son, Rohin, are both casualties of her husband's desertion for a younger woman. Eventually her cousin visits Laxmi in Boston and Miranda is asked to babysit Rohin, which, when combined with the phone conversations, gives her a painfully unvarnished portrait of the destruction that can result from betrayal. That Miranda's comprehension in part comes through someone else's situation is another instance in which Lahiri fuels the plot line indirectly rather than through outright communication. Miranda's awareness, via Rohin, proves to be the trigger that causes her to end her relationship with Dev.

In "Hell-Heaven," Pranab, unlike Miranda, makes no connection to the injury his attentions will ultimately cause Aparna. In fact, Lahiri's explorations of adultery, more often than not, reveal that it is the result, in varying degrees, of male characters who are self-absorbed and selfish. The story "Interpreter of Maladies" and part of her novel, *The Namesake,* are the only instances where women initiate infidelity. In both cases, however, their betrayal is largely instigated by their husbands' preoccupation with their own

interests, which in turn makes their wives' lives more confining. Though Pranab has no official hold over Aparna, she eventually appreciates the limitations of their relationship. Yet because the two have never truly been conjoined, the subterranean nature of their "affair" will also cause its finish to be equally inconspicuous—another instance in which Lahiri only intimates to the reader the complications.

The ending between Aparna and Pranab begins when he meets a fellow student, Deborah, who attends Radcliffe. She accompanies him on his regular visits to Aparna and Shyamal's apartment, and as Pranab introduces her to Bengali customs and the Bengali community, he and Deborah become more and more demonstrative, sometimes embarrassingly so, given the cultural decorum of modesty in relation to the way courtship is carried out. In many of Lahiri's pieces, it is explained that a couple, even when married, seldom refers to a spouse by first name, signifying the sacredness of intimacy. In contrast, as Pranab and Deborah's relationship unfolds so visibly in front of Aparna, her dreams, though never openly acted upon, painfully evaporate, becoming, instead, delusions. When they continue to go on excursions in the car, now as a foursome instead of a threesome, Aparna, tellingly, sits in the backseat with Usha. Though Pranab continues to involve Aparna in his life, it largely takes the form of seeking her approval for his relationship with Deborah and, eventually, her blessing of their impending marriage. He even asks Aparna and Shyamal to write to his parents, endorsing Deborah as his future wife, mindful that their sanction could help smooth any objections, especially given her nationality. Although Aparna never reveals her true feelings openly to Pranab, one day, when alone, she smashes the teacup he uses as an ashtray in their house, cutting her hand when it shatters.

After their wedding, Pranab and Deborah settle into a typical American marriage, having children and moving to the Boston suburbs. In the ensuing years their ties to the Bengali community wane, and Aparna, Shyamal, and Usha see them only infrequently, even though they too eventually move to the suburbs. Although for a

significant amount of time Aparna casts aspersions on the ways Deborah has corrupted Pranab's life, stripping him of his culture, eventually her enmity subsides, if for no other reason than the reality that their separate lives overtakes their former friendship. Usha's growing integration into American life becomes the focal point. Despite the new direction, however, at times when her daughter does something or desires something that Aparna disapproves of, she references Deborah to illustrate the corrupting influence of the United States.

Not unlike Mrs. Sen, who felt so isolated living in an apartment on the fringes of campus, Aparna complains about her life in the suburbs without a job, family network, or friendships. In loneliness she harkens back to the fleeting fulfillment she once derived from her sightseeing excursions with Pranab when they first immigrated. In turn, Shyamal, with a directness uncharacteristic of Lahiri, responds to her objections by saying she can return to Calcutta if she desires, "making it clear that their separation would not affect him one way or the other" (p. 76). In time, however, especially as her daughter leaves adolescence for adulthood, even these demonstrations of Aparna's heartbreak end. Moreover, her relationship with Shyamal strengthens. "A warmth" develops between them "that had not been there before, a quiet teasing, a solidarity, a concern when one of them fell ill" (p. 81).

Although Aparna's more contented relationship with Shyamal would seem to bring the narrative to a close on a note of reconciliation, the story's real conclusion contains an unexpected twist, reverting back to Pranab and a more realized version of the penchant for self-centeredness he had demonstrated from the start. Though he and Deborah have been married for twenty-three years, they divorce when Pranab takes up with a married Bengali woman, "destroying two families in the process" (p. 81). That Deborah suffers a fate similar to Aparna's was, in some measure, foretold when he abruptly "left" Aparna for Deborah. And there have been additional clues to his impetuousness. Pranab's efforts to sustain relationships, even those that would seem central,

have always been marginal. The very construction of the story speaks to Pranab's impulsive nature. As soon as the reader is told that he was the "one totally unanticipated pleasure in [Aparna's] life" (p. 67), the very next paragraph describes his meeting Deborah. The way that one woman follows another dramatically suggests he merely replaced one with the other, especially given that his "affair" with Aparna could never really be consummated. Additionally, when his parents refuse to give their blessing to his marriage to Deborah, he simply shrugs it off. The reader wonders what really matters to Pranab. In these glimpses of his character, he seems to satisfy only moments of desire and then moves on. Deborah confides to Aparna that she begged Pranab to keep in contact with the Bengali community he was part of when he first came to the United States. She also tried to get him to reestablish himself in his parents' graces. To both, however, he "resisted" (p. 82).

In Deborah's own heartbreak, Aparna becomes her confidante, yet as significant as their interaction is in revealing Pranab's shortcomings, it also bespeaks the way Aparna's and Deborah's cultural differences ultimately prevent them from truly connecting. As Deborah recounts the unraveling of her relationship with Pranab, Aparna does seem to acknowledge how inaccurate she was in casting Deborah as the reason for Pranab's abandonment. Yet it is mostly a one-way conversation, with Deborah confessing more about her sense of things than Aparna ever does. Deborah asks Aparna outright if she blames her "for taking [Pranab] away" (p. 82). Aparna, however, cannot bring herself to be truthful with Deborah. Instead, she lies and says that she never "blamed" her for anything when in reality a great deal of the balance of Aparna's life has been spent reeling from Pranab's abandonment and holding Deborah responsible, especially because she is an American. Although she is talking about her own relationship with Pranab, Deborah alludes to the way a cultural divide prevents people from knowing one another. She tells Aparna of her jealousy caused by her belief that she could never really know Pranab, "understand" him, in a

way that Aparna could because the two were both from Calcutta.

By the end of the story Aparna does reveal to her daughter the degree to which Pranab hurt her, and of course it is Usha, as the first-person narrator of the story, who in turn reveals it to the reader. With Lahiri, information is seldom directly expressed, and her choice about who transmits the story suggests the importance of cultural, and perhaps familial, alliance with regard to telling and knowing. As signified by Aparna's and Pranab's destructive inability to communicate, however, Lahiri also implies that such commonalities do not always enable the capacity to explain and to understand. In this instance, Usha confirms that only after she told of her own heartbreaking experience with a man she intended to marry did her mother follow suit and confess her real feelings for Pranab. It is these particular circumstances, rather than cultural and/or familial association, that seemed more important to Aparna and functioned as the reason for speaking to Usha. In so doing, the reader also learns of the profound state of agony she was in when Pranab married Deborah. After the wedding, Aparna actually intended to immolate herself. One day she pinned the layers of her sari with countless safety pins so it could not be removed when it caught flame after dousing herself with lighter fluid. In the end, however, she was unable to light the match. Aparna achieves resolution with Shyamal, Deborah, and, mostly, Usha, but only through circumstances that intensely challenge her ideals and force her to inhabit "unaccustomed earth."

THE IMPACT ON CHILDREN

That Usha is the narrator of her mother's experience in "Hell-Heaven" explains the importance Lahiri places on recounting the ways children are impacted by their parents' immigration. She has often expressed that, for her own parents, leaving India prompted a powerful sense of loss and alienation that was palpable throughout her childhood as they resettled in the United States. "Only Goodness" and the title story of *Unaccustomed Earth* revolve around the children of immigrants

and the stresses they contend with to at once acknowledge their ancestral heritage and establish lives of their own, independent of their cultural background.

Her novel, *The Namesake,* also explores this theme. As in many of Lahiri's stories, it begins with a couple, Ashima and Ashoke, who have immigrated to the United States because Ashoke is completing his doctoral work at MIT. They are among the couples in Lahiri's fiction whose marriage is a shared union, so their immigration has the promise of success. Despite Ashima's initial homesickness, the birth of their first child further ameliorates any melancholy. She and Ashoke intend to use a combination of family tradition and Bengali ritual to name him. After a series of mishaps, however, that include the death of Ashima's grandmother back home as well as the bureaucratic needs of the hospital, they convolutedly resort to calling him "Gogol" because this was the author Ashoke was reading when he was in a train wreck that nearly killed him as an adolescent in India.

Eventually Ashoke and Ashima formally name their son "Nikhil," reserving "Gogol" as a pet name to be used only by the family. Confusion ensues, however, once the child starts attending school because "Nikhil" is not the name he knows to answer to. Lahiri has recounted how similar circumstances prevailed in her own life, when, as a child, she became known by her pet name, "Jhumpa," rather than her "good names," Nilanjana Sudeshna, because her teachers found it easier to pronounce. In *The Namesake,* eventually "Gogol" is settled on for public and private use; however, his name will continually cause anxiety and ultimately signifies his struggle to find his own way, oscillating between obliging his parents' Indian heritage and responding to his own motivations linked to his birth and upbringing in the United States. As a result, throughout the novel, he constantly changes his name, at one point legally, to "Nikhil" and allows his friends to use various abbreviated forms of it, such as "Nick." Yet he also still responds to "Gogol," especially because it is what his family calls him.

In addition to the ways "Gogol" and "Nikhil" serve as indicators of the main character's duel-

ing nationalities, relationships with women become markers in the story that define the various stages of his life. Prior to his maturation, however, the novel illustrates Gogol's coming-of-age, wherein the standard awkwardness of adolescence is complicated by his embarrassment about his family's Indian heritage, which he comes to shun outright. Once he becomes an undergraduate at Yale, however, women become the means through which he attempts to define his identity. As in Lahiri's short stories, such relationships also prove to be the mechanism through which the author can demonstrate the limitations of communication. Moreover, because the women that Gogol becomes involved with are not first-generation Americans, they are much more independent, with careers and aspirations that are not linked to their husbands' destinies. As such they inhabit a vastly different world than the one Gogol is accustomed to with Ashima and Ashoke.

The first of any consequence is Ruth, whom Gogol meets while in college in New Haven, and his relationship with her signifies an initial break from his parents. To a degree, even before he meets Ruth, the independence afforded him by life away at school enables him to assert a new identity. He introduces himself as Nikhil and believes that the use of his "public" name makes it "easier to ignore his parents, to tune out their concerns and pleas" (p. 105). As a result, when he starts dating Ruth despite his parents' objections, he further claims his own individuality. He also eventually decides to major in architecture instead of engineering, as his father wished, staking out his own destiny even further. How Gogol thinks of himself, however, becomes too wrapped up in Ruth. Though he rightly protests his parents' objections to her, which are founded on her being an American, he becomes obsessed with her and is unable to handle her choice to study abroad in England for a semester. While Ruth fully undertakes her own ambitions, Gogol seems rudderless, and eventually their romance ends, in large part because he is too empty.

With graduation, Gogol continues his quest for independence, moving to New York. There he meets Maxine Ratliff, and she becomes the next avenue by which he can further ingratiate himself into American society. As their love affair becomes more serious, they tacitly move in with her well-heeled parents, who make Gogol's life incredibly comfortable, introducing him to the bourgeois interests of "foodie" culture and refined living. In a way, the Ratliffs become Gogol's surrogate parents and, with an almost Svengali-like power, enable his American identity to thoroughly take hold. Any time the Ratliffs acknowledge Gogol's ethnic background or any other intrinsic detail, he responds, but simultaneously analyzes the conversations to himself, assessing the tenor of how they unfold. The Ratliffs' interest, though, is mostly passing. They are clearly more interested in their own world, and Gogol, like Maxine, follows along. Gogol unwittingly panders to them while he all but abandons Ashima and Ashoke back in Massachusetts, not to mention their Indian ways.

With the sudden death of his father, however, Gogol gets jolted back home, with all of its attendant customs and outlooks. Before long his relationship to Maxine no longer feels right, and he breaks up with her. Ironically, parallel to Gogol's return, Ashima, conversely, begins venturing out more into American society. She takes a part-time job in the local library and makes friends with her American coworkers. Still, she also reintroduces Gogol to Moushumi, the daughter of some old Bengali friends, whom he had known as a child. Because Gogol and Moushumi subsequently marry, Ashima has functioned in the traditional capacity despite her increasingly independent behavior. But even though Gogol and Moushumi are Indian, have a quasi-arranged beginning and a wedding that takes up many of the customs of their heritage, within a year their relationship begins to disintegrate. Similar backgrounds never amount to certainty in relations between Lahiri's characters. Moushumi rejects a fellowship to study in Paris because of Gogol and begins to resent him. Eventually she has an affair with an old high school friend, causing her and Gogol to divorce. The novel ends with Gogol returning to Boston to attend a holiday party his mother is hosting before she moves back to Calcutta. Given

what he has been through with Moushumi in the past year, Gogol is glad to be home. As he roams the rooms where he grew up, he finds the book by Nikolai Gogol for whom he is named that belonged to his father. As he sits down to read, he is once again beginning his life, though this time alone and at a much more measured pace, rid of much of the confusion that has plagued him to this point.

Lahiri's conclusion to *The Namesake* bespeaks the direction much of her fiction has taken since the publication of *Interpreter of Maladies*. Whereas many of her initial pieces in that collection dissolve into loss in varying degrees, as she has progressed her work often concludes with characters in a more affirming mode. Like *The Namesake,* the stories that make up *Unaccustomed Earth* are mostly concerned with characters taking up the various conflicts presented by the intricacies of their lives, and by the end they have achieved a degree of contentment. To be sure, there are pieces, namely "Only Goodness" and the novella "Hema and Kaushik," whose endings are more tentative. On balance, however, the majority of work in *Unaccustomed Earth* lives up to its epigraph, which promotes the idea of unfamiliar territory as a crucible of personal growth. Even women, who are consistently subjugated in Lahiri's work, mostly by cultural restrictions, become more realized. In the title story, Ruma learns that her father has truly started a new life after the death of his wife. With this knowledge she is more prepared to begin her own with her American husband and their children. In "Hell-Heaven," as previously examined, Aparna's daughter, Usha, develops a greater regard for her mother's acculturation, especially given the terms upon which it was founded. Her acknowledgment grants her mother's experiences a certain credence and in turn suggests that it will function as a benchmark for her own self-realization. Usha also recognizes that Aparna too is more satisfied. In almost every story, resolution comes when characters achieve an understanding that tempers the difficulties they initially confronted. Seasoned by struggle, they seem ready to begin anew.

Selected Bibliography

WORKS OF JHUMPA LAHIRI

SHORT STORIES
Interpreter of Maladies. Boston: Houghton Mifflin, 1999.
Unaccustomed Earth. New York: Knopf, 2008.

NOVEL
The Namesake. Boston: Houghton Mifflin, 2003.

CRITICAL STUDIES AND INTERVIEWS

Bahri, Deepika. "The Namesake." *Film Quarterly* 61, no. 1: 10–15 (2007).

Bolonik, Kera. "Migration, Assimilation, and Inebriation: Jhumpa Lahiri Talks with Bookforum." *BookForum: The Review for Art, Fiction, & Culture* 15, no. 1: 34–35 (2008).

Brada-Williams, Noelle. "Reading Jhumpa Lahiri's *Interpreter of Maladies* as a Short Story Cycle." *MELUS* 29, nos. 3–4: 451–464 (fall–winter 2004).

Caesar, Judith. "Beyond Cultural Identity in Jhumpa Lahiri's 'When Mr. Pirzada Came to Dine.'" *North Dakota Quarterly* 70, no. 1: 82–91 (winter 2003).

———. "American Spaces in the Fiction of Jhumpa Lahiri." *English Studies in Canada* 31, no. 1: 50–68 (March 2005).

———. "Gogol's Namesake: Identity and Relationships in Jhumpa Lahiri's *The Namesake*." *Atenea* 27, no. 1: 103–119 (June 2007).

Chakrabarti, Basudeb, and Angana Chakrabarti. "Context: A Comparative Study of Jhumpa Lahiri's 'A Temporary Matter' and Shubodh Ghosh's 'Jatugriha.'" *Journal of Indian Writing in English* 30, no. 1: 23–29 (2002).

Chetty, Raj. "The Indian on the Bookshelf: Placing Jhumpa Lahiri in Contemporary American Literature." In *South Asia and Its Others: Reading the "Exotic."* Edited by V. G. Julie Rajan and Atreyee Phukan. Newcastle upon Tyne, England: Cambridge Scholars, 2009. Pp. 55–77.

Chowdhury, Enakshi. "Facing the Millennium." In *Indian Response to American Literature*. Edited by T. S. Anand. New Delhi, India; Creative; 2003. Pp. 126–132.

Cox, Michael W. "Interpreters of Cultural Difference: The Use of Children in Jhumpa Lahiri's Short Fiction." *South Asian Review* 24, no. 2: 120–132 (2003).

Daiya, Kavita. "Provincializing America: Engaging Postcolonial Critique and Asian American Studies in a Transnational Mode." *South Asian Review* 26, no. 2: 265 (2005).

———. *Violent Belongings: Partition, Gender, and National Culture in Postcolonial India*. Philadelphia: Temple University Press, 2008.

Dubey, Ashutosh. "Immigrant Experience in Jhumpa Lahiri's *Interpreter of Maladies.*" *Journal of Indian Writing in English* 30, no. 2: 22–26 (2002).

Field, Robin E. "Writing the Second Generation: Negotiating Cultural Borderlands in Jhumpa Lahiri's *Interpreter of Maladies* and *The Namesake.*" *South Asian Review* 25, no. 2: 165–177 (2004).

Fitz, Brewster E. "Bibi's Babel: Treating Jhumpa Lahiri's 'The Treatment of Bibi Haldar' as the Malady of Interpreters." *South Asian Review* 26, no. 2: 116–131, 305 (2005).

Flaherty, Kate. "Jhumpa Lahiri's *The Namesake.*" *Philament* 5 (http://www.arts.usyd.edu.au/publications/philament/issue5_Commentary_Flaherty.htm), 2005.

Friedman, Natalie. "From Hybrids to Tourists: Children of Immigrants in Jhumpa Lahiri's *The Namesake.*" *Critique* 50, no. 1: 111–124 (fall 2008).

Ganapathy-Doré, Geetha. "The Narrator as a Global Soul in Jumpha Lahiri's *Interpreter of Maladies.*" In *The Global and the Particular in the English-Speaking World.* Edited by Jean-Pierre Durix. Dijon, France: Editions Universitaires de Dijon, 2002. Pp. 53–65.

Goldblatt, Patricia. "School Is Still the Place: Stories of Immigration and Education." *MultiCultural Review* 13, no. 1: 49–54 (2004).

Harte, Leah. "The Borderlands of Identity and a B-Side to the Self: Jhumpa Lahiri's 'When Mr. Pirzada Came to Dine,' 'The Third and Final Continent,' and 'Unaccustomed Earth.'" In *Passages: Movements and Moments in Text and Theory.* Edited by Maeve Tynan, Maria Beville, and Marita Ryan. Newcastle upon Tyne, England: Cambridge Scholars, 2009. Pp. 63–75.

Heinze, Ruediger. "A Diasporic Overcoat? Naming and Affection in Jhumpa Lahiri's *The Namesake.*" *Journal of Postcolonial Writing* 43, no. 2: 191–202 (2007).

James, Nick. "Out of Gogol's Overcoat." *Sight and Sound* 17, no. 4: 12 (2007).

Karim, Rezaul. "Jhumpa Lahiri." In *Dictionary of Literary Biography, Vol. 323: South Asian Writers in English.* Edited by Fakrul Alam. Detroit: Gale, 2006. Pp. 205–210.

Karttunen, Laura. "A Sociostylistic Perspective on Negatives and the Disnarrated: Lahiri, Roy, Rushdie." *Partial Answers: Journal of Literature and the History of Ideas* 6, no. 2: 419–441 (2008).

Kluwick, Ursula. "Postcolonial Literatures on a Global Market: Packaging the 'Mysterious East' for Western Consumption." In *Translation of Cultures.* Edited by Petra Rüdiger and Konrad Gross. Amsterdam: Rodopi, 2009. Pp. 75–92.

Kral, Françoise. "Shaky Ground and New Territorialities in *Brick Lane* by Monica Ali and *The Namesake* by Jhumpa Lahiri." *Journal of Postcolonial Writing* 43, no. 1: 65–76 (2007).

Kuortti, Joel. "Problematic Hybrid Identity in the Diasporic Writings of Jhumpa Lahiri." In *Reconstructing Hybridity: Post-Colonial Studies in Transition.* Edited by Joel Kuortti and Jopi Nyman. Amsterdam: Rodopi, 2007. Pp. 205–219.

Kung, Shao-ming. "'I Translate, Therefore I Am': Names and Cultural Translation in Jhumpa Lahiri's *The Namesake.*" *Tamkang Review: A Quarterly of Literary and Cultural Studies* 40, no. 1: 119–140 (2009).

McCarron, Bill. "The Color Blue in Jhumpa Lahiri's 'This Blessed House.'" *Notes on Contemporary Literature* 34, no. 1: 4–5 (2004).

Mitra, Madhuparna. "Border Crossings in Lahiri's 'A Real Durwan.'" *Explicator* 65, no. 4: 242–245 (2007).

Munos, Delphine. "*The Namesake* by Jhumpa Lahiri: The Accident of Inheritance." *Commonwealth Essays and Studies* 30, no. 2: 106–117 (2008).

Prusse, Michael C. "Towards a Cosmopolitan Readership: New Literatures in English in the Classroom." *Transcultural English Studies: Theories, Fictions, Realities.* Edited by Frank Schulze-Engler and Sissy Helff. Amsterdam: Rodopi, 2009. Pp. 373–391.

Rajan, Gita. "Ethical Responsibility in Intersubjective Spaces: Reading Jhumpa Lahiri's 'Interpreter of Maladies' and 'A Temporary Matter.'" In *Transnational Asian American Literature: Sites and Transits.* Edited by Shirley Geok-lin Lim, John Blair Gamber, Stephen Hong Sohn, and Gina Valentino. Philadelphia: Temple University Press, 2006. Pp. 123–141.

———. "Poignant Pleasures: Feminist Ethics as Aesthetics in Jhumpa Lahiri and Anita Rao Badami." In *Literary Gestures: The Aesthetic in Asian American Writing.* Edited by Rocío G. Davis and Sue-Im Lee. Philadelphia: Temple University Press, 2006. Pp. 104–120.

Shankar, Lavina Dhingra. "Not Too Spicy: Exotic Mistresses of Cultural Translation in the Fiction of Chitra Divakaruni and Jhumpa Lahiri." In *Other Tongues: Rethinking the Language Debates in India.* Edited by Nalini Iyer and Bonnie Zare. Amsterdam: Rodopi, 2009. Pp. 23–52.

Shariff, Farha. "Straddling the Cultural Divide: Second-Generation South Asian Identity and *The Namesake.*" *Changing English* 15, no. 4: 457–466 (December 2008).

Tettenborn, Eva. "Jhumpa Lahiri's *Interpreter of Maladies*: Colonial Fantasies in 'Sexy.'" *Notes on Contemporary Literature* 32, no. 4: 11–12 (2002).

Trivedi, Harish. "Anglophone Transnation, Postcolonial Translation: The Book and the Film as Namesakes." In *Semiotic Encounters: Text, Image, and Trans-Nation.* Edited by Sarah Säckel, Walter Göbel, and Noha Hamdy. Amsterdam: Rodopi, 2009. Pp. 31–49.

Williams, Laura Anh. "Foodways and Subjectivity in Jhumpa Lahiri's *Interpreter of Maladies.*" *MELUS* 32, no. 4: 69–79 (winter 2007).

Zare, Bonnie. "Evolving Masculinities in Recent Stories by South Asian American Women." *Journal of Commonwealth Literature* 42, no. 3: 99–111 (September 2007).

SAM PICKERING

(1941—)

John Gatta

ALTHOUGH SAM PICKERING is a prolific author with publications in a broad array of subgenres and venues, he remains best known for writing his own inimitable style of creative nonfiction. Possessing a peculiar blend of gifts as humorist, raconteur, and provocateur, Pickering has become a leading figure in latter-day attempts to revive the once-popular literary form of the familiar essay. Pickering's joyously free-flowing, slightly zany but rarely acerbic wit is a hallmark of his compositional style. So is his playful blend of factual report and self-mythologizing fancy. Deliberately obscuring the divide between autobiographical narrative and fiction, his essays wander unpredictably from straightforward description of Pickering's "doings" in the here and now into hilariously fabricated anecdotes, highly embellished recollections of Pickering ancestors or relatives or other eccentric characters, and imaginary conversations between Pickering's persona and a foil friend named "Josh." The author gleefully mixes references to actual places—for example, sites near his home in northeast Connecticut—with tales of fictive or partly invented settlements in the South. What this blending amounts to is an endlessly regenerative formula of creativity that Pickering has sustained, with noteworthy variations, across the thirty-year span of his writing career.

A Pickering essay typically includes at least some passages of forthright description, in which the author details his reaction to ordinary creatures and events he encounters in the course of his fairly ordinary, middle-class life as a middle-aged English professor. The common experiences he shares include reading, child rearing, shopping, gardening, workplace and student-teacher interactions, domestic chores, rituals of bereavement, and wanderings across local woods and fields. Much of what he describes comes directly from what he sees and does each day. As in real life, Pickering's implied author continually runs road races, grades student papers, performs self-ridiculing pranks, investigates mosses and box turtles, indulges in banter with friends or repartee with his wife, and frets about his children. Yet the author invents more than a few of the outlandish episodes he narrates. He also scripts or substantially embellishes reports of the letters he receives from strangers.

In any event, what seems most distinctive about Pickering's essays is the artistry with which they draw readers toward an uncommon appreciation of commonplace things. Paradoxically, this artistry supports the impression of an unplanned, impulsive sequence of narration. The essays seem to have no organizational logic, to follow an order determined purely by forces of nature, unfolding along the random course of Pickering's own outdoor wanderings. At first, those accustomed to the urbane irony and stylishness associated with *New Yorker*–style journalism might suspect that the homespun manner of Pickering's essays betrays naïveté. Such is not the case. This author is actually learned, even bookish in sensibility, though scornful of pedantry. True, Pickering has insisted from the first that he embraces "simplicity" of life and expression, rejecting postmodern narrative techniques and complex sentence structures in favor of directness. "I have only one style," he concedes in the essay "Composing a Life", "the solid, economical, fifty-thousand mile warranteed reliable style of the short declarative sentence" (*A Continuing Education* p. 159).

Better acquaintance with the essays nonetheless reveals their considerable subtlety and craft. Their pacing, voicing of dialogue, word choices,

and smoothly spun transitions from one topic to another—all of this contributes to the shaping of a literary personality unlike any other in contemporary American letters. As Jay Parini remarks in his foreword to *The Best of Pickering* (p. v. 2004), Pickering "remains sui generis" in the character of his expression, though his work "stands firmly in the line" of classic American essayists stretching "from Thoreau and Emerson through Mark Twain, E. B. White, Robert Benchley, John McPhee, Scott Russell Sanders, Barry Lopez, and others." Moreover, the "simplicity" Pickering expounds is more complex than it first sounds, insofar as it reflects—as it does in other contexts for Henry Thoreau or, for that matter, George Herbert—not simplemindedness but the elusive project of coming to know and to accept one's place in the world. For Pickering, the project of finding that place begins, quite literally, with a resolve to learn the names of plants growing in his backyard.

What else is implied by the "familiar" aspect of Pickering's essays? The term suggests, among other things, that their mood is relatively informal, thereby conveying to readers the sense of an author's personal presence. For Pickering the familiar essay is often familial as well. Figures who play prominent roles throughout the essays include Pickering's wife, Vicki, whose character often projects an irreverent skepticism toward the author and his antics; his three children, Edward, Eliza, and Francis; and his household pets.

Another distinctive element of familiarity in Pickering's writing concerns the relation he aims to develop with his readers. Pickering claims in a piece titled "Man of Letters" that, toward the start of his essayistic career, the *New Yorker* rejected a piece he had hoped to publish with a note calling the submission "A bit too familiar" (p. 2). One more tall tale? Perhaps. Yet Pickering's gesture of confiding such unflattering information to his readers, even in jest, serves the rhetorical end of solidifying his connection with them. Thus, the amiable self-mockery so often displayed by Pickering's persona renders these essays all the more "familiar" in the sense of accessible, congenial, and open to readerly sympathy. The author's accounts of unsolicited

mail he receives from readers reflect this same disposition to establish a dialogical relation with his audience. Pickering aims, in his familiar essays, to preserve a conversational sort of congeniality, so that he is perceived to speak *with* his readers rather than simply *to* them.

Beneath the tide of cheerful exuberance that sweeps the reader along through much of Pickering's work, an undercurrent of sorrow can also be felt in these essays. One even senses, at times, the author's determination to resist a temperamental inclination toward melancholy. Even in his earlier writing, he laments in passing some of the indignities that accompany aging, the inevitable reminders of mortality, and experiences of disappointment or failure. Unashamed to call himself a "sentimentalist," Pickering writes most often in a major key yet is occasionally willing to expose heartfelt grief, as when describing the deaths of his father, his mother, and his beloved dog George. He sometimes satirizes but can also feel disheartened by land developers, polluters, bureaucrats, and mean-spirited people in general.

It is reasonable, though, to regard his prevailing vision of things as comic, rather than satiric or elegiac. What surfaces above all in Pickering's writing is a sense of spirited thankfulness for life's variability, humorous incongruities, and ordinary satisfactions. He did have a brief encounter with fame, when he learned that a screenplay writer had taken him as the model for Robin Williams' character of an inspiring teacher in the 1989 film *Dead Poets Society*. But he prefers to center his imagination on experiences drawn from a quiet, unglamorous life planted solidly on home ground.

Thus far, Pickering's large corpus of published work includes fifteen volumes of familiar essays. Because many of these essays contain noteworthy descriptions of outdoor phenomena, Pickering's work also deserves to be known within the ever-expanding sphere of American nature writing. He has written, in addition to scores of reviews and articles and separately published essays, three books of travel writing and three books of critical scholarship. Most

recently, he has composed a book of memoirs focused on his early life.

BACKGROUND

Samuel Francis Pickering, Jr., was born on September 30, 1941, in Nashville, Tennessee, to a father of the same name and Katherine Winston Ratcliffe. He was an only child. His father worked in the personnel department of the Traveler's Insurance Company, and his mother was a homemaker. His paternal grandfather, yet another Sam Pickering, was born in Carthage, Tennessee, a town not far from Nashville that the future writer visited fairly often as a child and later came to recreate in his own essayistic fables.

In his adulthood, the writer also became increasingly curious about his ancestry as he found occasion to sort through memorabilia and letters from the past, discovering such material to be a catalyst for his creative imagination. He came to understand early on that among his forebears in the Pickering and Ratcliffe lines, were combatants representing both sides of the Civil War. A great-great-grandfather, William B. Pickering, had served as a Union captain in the Ohio Volunteer Infantry, and later as chief clerk of the Tennessee House of Representatives. His Ratcliffe ancestors had lived in Virginia since the eighteenth century; and Pickering spent childhood summers wandering through fields and woods, capturing lizards and turtles, at his maternal grandfather's farm in Hanover, Virginia, just north of Richmond. While in college, he served as a summer camp counselor in Maine.

For his secondary education, Pickering attended Montgomery Bell Academy, a preparatory school for boys in Nashville, where he signed up for numerous extracurricular activities, longed to become accepted as an athlete, and would later return to teach. His father urged him to remain in the South for his college education, proposing that he major in English by way of preparing for a career in business.

So after a brief stint at Vanderbilt, his father's alma mater, Pickering completed his undergraduate studies in 1963 as an English major at the University of the South, otherwise known as Sewanee, situated on a forested plateau in rural Tennessee. Known for its colorful literary personalities and traditions and, at the time, its respect for regional culture, Sewanee contributed to Pickering's emerging sense of himself as a southern man of letters. There he studied so diligently that his classmates dubbed him "the machine." Still, in the early 1960s, the college was a small, all-male conclave of around six hundred students with conservative traits that occasionally ran counter to Pickering's high-spirited disposition. Pickering retains an association with Sewanee by frequently contributing his writing to the *Sewanee Review,* whose editor George Core is a close friend. The name of a group called the "Dead Plants Society," associated with the university's herbarium, is another reminder of Pickering's continuing legacy in this college town.

After leaving Sewanee and beginning post-graduate studies at Cambridge University, he taught for just one year at Montgomery Bell Academy in Nashville. That year would later prove to be significant, though, because one of his M.B.A. students, Tom Schulman, ended up writing the film screenplay for *Dead Poets Society.* And after that year, 1965–1966, Pickering never again took up residence in the South. He would live in New England mostly, and for shorter periods in England, Scotland, Syria, Jordan, and Australia. But while he never found another occasion to stay long in Tennessee, the experience of having spent his formative years there, along with summers in Virginia, permanently shaped his identity as a writer cognizant of his southern roots and appreciative of its folkways, yet critical of its racial history and "lost cause" mythology. He entertained no real regrets about making his home in the North yet found it gratifying to be named a member of the Fellowship of Southern Writers in 2005. If to grow up as an American is, as Henry James put it, a "complex fate," it is perhaps still more complicated to have grown up as a white southerner during the last years of segregation, and to be burdened accordingly with decidedly ambivalent feelings about one's regional heritage.

After taking an M.A. at St. Catherine's College, Cambridge, Pickering moved to Princeton University to further his doctoral studies in eighteenth- and nineteenth-century English literature. He came to develop particular scholarly interests in fiction of this period written for children, and in the ideas and patterns of moral instruction this writing embodied. Later on, as coeditor of the journal *Children's Literature,* he helped to make the study of children's books more acceptable as a subject worthy of literary and cultural criticism. His second wife, Vicki Johnson, grew up in Princeton. Her father, E. D. H. Johnson, was a noted scholar of Victorian literature who had also served as chair of Princeton's English department and as one of Pickering's grad school instructors.

In 1970, with his Ph.D. completed, Pickering moved to Hanover, New Hampshire, to become an assistant professor of English at Dartmouth College. After the University of Connecticut showed eagerness to offer him a faculty appointment in 1978, he moved to Storrs and has remained there ever since, in a home situated directly adjacent to the campus. At Connecticut he soon became known as an energetic and heartily gregarious instructor, a professor much in demand for his course offerings in children's literature, the short story (otherwise dubbed by him "teensy tales"), creative writing, and nature writing.

In 1973, while he was still teaching at Dartmouth, Pickering ventured to publish the first of his familiar essays, called "Letter from a London Attic," in the *Dartmouth College Library Bulletin.* It is fitting that this first essay should have been inspired by his love of libraries and reading, considering that Pickering's zeal to unearth striking passages from offbeat, obscure old books has continued to feed his writing ever since. For the next four or five years he turned out new essays only sporadically. He continued to regard composition in this genre as something of a diversion from the scholarly research and writing that he took to be his main professional commitment in addition to teaching. Soon after moving to Connecticut, though, he began writing familiar essays more frequently. By the late 1970s he was composing and sending them out in a steady stream, year after year, until both he and his reading audience came to recognize them as a distinctive subgenre, a mode of expression central to his vocation as a writer. By 1985, with the publication of his first essay collection, *A Continuing Education,* he had discovered grounds for confidence that other such books would follow.

All of these familiar essay volumes have thus far been issued by university presses. Though Pickering has sometimes regretted not pursuing what might have been a more profitable mode of disseminating his work through trade publishers, he likes the freedom that university presses allow him to serve as his own agent. He has also seemed content, for the most part, to address the loyal but restricted audience that university press outlets have provided for his work. For a time, after the film *Dead Poets Society* appeared in 1989, Pickering received a surge of popular attention with the disclosure that his onetime student Tom Schulman had modeled his portrayal of the film's lead character on this teacher whose unconventional style of instruction had impressed him. Although the major boost in book sales from such publicity was temporary, Pickering continued to be identified with the film character and still receives numerous speaking invitations as a consequence. For good or ill, his reputation endures as the living prose writer who inspired *Dead Poets.*

Fortunately, though, he is known for other things as well. At least part of his literary reputation derives from the notable proportion of his essays devoted to nature writing. Pickering has often taught courses in American nature writing and has been praised for the vivid word sketches of bogs, plants, wild and domestic animals, and other facts of nature that appear throughout his familiar essays. Favoring portrayals of a lightly settled middle landscape, with its fields and woodlands open to interaction between nonhumans and rambling observers like himself, he rarely tries to chronicle ventures into primitive wilderness terrain. Instead of praising the grandeur of mountain or desert scenes, he usually

prefers to notice the modest life forms that flourish in local landscapes.

In any case, a strong sense of place characterizes most of Pickering's work. Though he has traveled widely, five particular regions dominate his imagination. These essential territories include his adopted home ground of northeastern Connecticut, which is also the home base for his writing life; the farm in Nova Scotia, owned by his wife's family, where he has for many years retreated during summer months; middle Tennessee, the territory of his childhood memory and college experience; the United Kingdom, where he studied as a young adult and resided later in life as a research fellow in Edinburgh; and Australia, the site of two sabbatical expeditions and the subject of two books. Within this geographic pentangle, Connecticut and Nova Scotia figure most prominently. These places have long provided something of a center of gravity for Pickering's life and writing. It makes sense, therefore, to read his accounts of sojourning elsewhere as counterpoints to these fixed points of imagination, since Pickering has particularly endeavored to become a writer who knows where he belongs.

In later volumes of familiar essays, certain shifts in Pickering's subject matter and tone begin to reflect inevitable changes in his life—as his children have left home, for example, or as he has aged and approaches his retirement from full-time teaching. His *Letters to a Teacher,* published in 2004, marks a new genre of writing for Pickering, since this work falls somewhere between the rambling, idiosyncratic style of his familiar essays and more focused commentary on the teacher's vocation. It is also the only volume that Pickering has published thus far with a trade press. He has given no sign, however, of slowing the pace with which he continues to turn out new essays, books, and critical reviews.

REINVENTING THE FAMILIAR ESSAY

Just as Pickering's essays abound in humorously recounted, serendipitous discoveries, so also it was through a kind of serendipity that Pickering found his vocation as a familiar essayist. After he tried publishing one personally voiced essay in the *Dartmouth College Library Bulletin,* he found it so satisfying to learn that readers of the piece had been moved to send him letters in response that he was encouraged to write more such essays. He knew that scholarly publication rarely offered this sort of satisfaction. A few years later, his essays had begun to appear in a number of academic and popular periodicals, and word of his exceptional writing style began to spread. At that point Charles Backis, then an editor with the University Press of New England, approached him to propose that he consider publishing a bound collection of his essays. The result was *A Continuing Education* (1985). Though Pickering was already in his mid-forties by the time this volume appeared, it set the pattern for many of his books to follow.

The volume's introductory piece, "Man of Letters," amounts to a fairly enduring statement of the literary identity this author would maintain for decades. Pickering tells of abandoning his ambition to be recognized as a famous scholar at the Modern Language Association's convention, declaring it "better to write familiar essays and remain unknown" (p. 3). He confides to readers that he would rather stay close to his home in Connecticut than gain celebrity elsewhere, that he likes to read children's books and to write about turtles. Within the book's first few pages, he establishes for his audience much of what he will want them to know about his immediate family and his familial-ancestral ties to sites he would continue to write about in Virginia, Nova Scotia, and Tennessee. He also stakes out the modest boundaries of his subject matter in a manner remarkably consistent with his practice in later volumes:

> I write about the little things of life like starlings and dandelions and picking up sticks. I do so because the little things are about all most people have. None of my friends live romantic lives vibrant with excitement; instead they jog through the quiet byways of ordinary existence with its leaves and laundry, unread newspapers, diapers and Matchbox cars, and Masterpiece Theater on Sunday night. I also write about small things because they bring me letters. I live in a rambling, old-fashioned house;

since I will never earn enough from my essays to redecorate it, I have let it decorate me.

(p. 4)

Sandwiched between Pickering's accounts of such homely matters, two essays in this volume describe his experiences as Fulbright lecturer in Syria and Jordan. Even these essays, however, focus not on large-scale political issues in the Middle East but on quirky, humorously memorable incidents involving his relation to students he encountered while teaching abroad.

Writing about his reading is another familiar topic in Pickering's essays that finds representation in *A Continuing Education*. Essays such as "The Books I Left Behind" and "Reading at Forty" sound a theme he will develop extensively in later writing. Like most other academicians, Pickering owns many books. But in "The Books I Left Behind" he explains the grounds for selecting the more than six hundred volumes he decided not to take with him when he moved from New Hampshire to Connecticut. The list included not only how-to manuals and etiquette books but volumes of literary criticism and even many classic works of history and literature. What are we to make of this English professor's shameless disclosure that, among the books he left behind, were volumes by the likes of Shakespeare and William Faulkner, Herman Melville, Nathaniel Hawthorne, and the Russian novelists—along with the *Iliad* and the *Odyssey*? Can he be serious about preferring cheery, "warm books," any books he had autographed himself, and children's books to classics like *Moby-Dick*?

Clearly Pickering's irreverent remarks about the canonical classics are not inspired by a zeal to fulfill ideals of political correctness. It is evident too that his dismissive assessment of "great books" is laced with tongue-in-cheek humor. Pickering enjoys the chance to scandalize over-solemn academics, just as he enjoyed reporting, in his second book of familiar essays, that his ribald writing had shocked relatives back in Tennessee. Moreover, he could well afford on moving day to "leave behind" heavy books of classic literature that he had already read, marked, and inwardly digested years ago.

But beneath all the fun, his book-purging essays also convey a characteristically American approach to reading and learning that enlarges upon views presented by nineteenth-century writers such as Ralph Waldo Emerson, Thoreau, and Twain. In "The American Scholar," for example, Emerson argues that instead of idolizing great books, one should read them creatively, as sources of personal inspiration. Books should not simply be revered, or passively emulated, but used to stir original thought and action. Such is likewise the spirit of Pickering's reasoning as he identifies the reading he now elects to pursue. As one who enjoys wandering across fields and noticing flowers, he will hold on to his volume of William Wordsworth; and he'll retain a copy of Lord Byron because he recalls his father's reading to him from *Childe Harold* when he was young. He preserves most of his children's books as well since they conjure for him, as he approaches middle age, a pleasing refuge from cynicism and "a world of transformations" ("The Books I Left Behind" p. 103). And because he believes in letting "reading rise out of living" ("Reading at Forty" p. 123) he wants to read about the Civil War not by consulting respected historical tomes but by pulling from his barn in Nova Scotia faded issues of the *Yarmouth Herald* dating from 1862 and 1863.

That Pickering takes writing seriously, albeit according to his own manner of jest, is a point reinforced by this first volume's concluding essay, "Composing a Life." There is, he insists, a correlation between the care with which he composes sentences—the style of his writing—and the "familiar, relaxed style" (p. 162) he aims to cultivate in his life. In composing his life, he strives to maintain an aesthetic of simplicity mirrored in his prose. Yet Pickering reminds his readers that finding the right words, and a way of life styled to fit his words, remains an ongoing project of discovery—or, in effect, "a continuing education."

In *The Right Distance,* Pickering's second book of familiar essays, he continues to address the challenge of aligning his craft as a writer with his personal experience. The title essay underscores the author's perennial need to

reconcile his sense of life in the here and now with shades of memory from his personal and ancestral past. This project of "getting the right distance on things" (p. 11) can never quite succeed, but it offers a tension between memory and immediacy that is often comic yet sometimes poignant.

The Right Distance expands upon Pickering's saga of family antecedents in Virginia and Tennessee. The author begins this recollection of family ties by mentioning his mother's humorous dismissal of his essays as "bullshit" rather than "literature"; he introduces along the way more family stories, both real and reimagined, and citations of letters written by Pickerings from the Civil War era; and he features, toward the close, a moving account of how he discovered further grounds of sympathy and identification with his father in "Son and Father." In this collection, as in several subsequent books, Pickering tags each essay with an exceedingly simple title.

Among these unadorned tags are invitations to read of "Particulars," "Foolishness," "Pictures," "Moving On," and "Country Life." One technique Pickering advances here to explore such topics is to wander freely around some sort of framing aphoristic statement—in the case of the essay "Too Late," for example, Pickering's rhapsodic storytelling ends up both lamenting and celebrating the general proposition that "Messages are forever reaching me too late" (p. 32). And like Flannery O'Connor, he shows a special talent for exploiting and exploding clichés. Thus, he begins "Country Life" by shattering sentimental tropes, declaring that "Good country people scare the hell out of me" (p. 146). In "Moving On" he combines reminders of the inevitable transience of things—a prominent theme throughout Pickering's writing—with the admission that he often simply refuses to accept change. So having reached the age when he usually wants "things to remain as they are" and finds "climbing out of the past" to be "almost impossible," he will keep patronizing Albert, the unfashionable, 1950s-style barber, when he needs his hair cut. Despite "the evanescence of everything," we need "the comforting illusion" that life is not moving so swiftly toward extinction as

we fear (pp. 16, 158, 162). In "Pictures," one of this collection's strongest essays, Pickering succeeds in dramatizing both the beauty and the sadness of perusing old photographs. The gentle humor characteristic of *The Right Distance* often exposes an element of compassion—as in the tale of a college janitor's generous solicitude for Sam's clothing, or in the "foolishness" with which Pickering insists on saving from destruction insects that find their way into his home.

As its title suggests, *May Days* (1988) ranks among Pickering's most light-hearted essay collections. Its balmy atmosphere gives little hint of that melancholy or undercurrent of loss found in his other books. Describing himself as "a summer person" ("Summering," p. 171). Pickering basks in the recollection of carefree days spent rambling outdoors across fields and beaches in Nova Scotia. His indoor exploration shows him rummaging through an old trunk at the farm in Beaver River, dreamily recounting stories of an earlier life recorded by his wife's grandmother. In this collection he recalls tales of his schooldays, offers droll anecdotes about his life as a professor, and reports the escapades he enjoyed while a student at St. Catherine's College, Cambridge.

Interspersed with these rollicking narratives about his own experience are yarns about Carthage characters such as Doctor Sollows, Sodus Rutledge, and the Reverend Harbottle. Amidst all this play, the book's opening essay, "Outside In," manifests Pickering's growing inclination to "become a naturalist, or if not a real naturalist, at least a nature writer" (p. 2). Inspired in part by reading an old botany book, the author says he developed a particular interest in studying wildflowers. *May Days* demonstrates the fruit of this attentiveness in several passages of lyrical grace, as when he describes "wild roses, tumbling and spilling over each other like fragrant potpourri" (p. 3); or orange hawkweed, "a slender flower six to twenty inches high with a small dandelionlike blossom, orange and red like the last moments of the evening sun, below the horizon but burning vivid against the clouds" (p. 174). Such botanical observations, vividly and knowledgeably rendered but with some

impressionistic coloring, would become a more characteristic feature of Pickering's writing in future essays.

CONFRONTING CELEBRITY: IN THE COMPANY OF DEAD POETS

In "Celebrity," which appears as the closing essay in *Still Life* (1990), Pickering confronts the inevitable recasting of his image that followed his marketing as "the real-life hero of *Dead Poets Society*." Pickering expresses mixed feelings about his newfound celebrity. Both in *Still Life* and in subsequent volumes, particularly *Let it Ride,* he expresses by turns embarrassment, annoyance, amusement, and pleasure over his flirtation with fame. His response to this turn of events, as with most other occurrences in his life, is to make full use of it as matter for his essays—and as further cause for mirth and ironic musing. Nor is he above admitting that, by accepting new invitations for speaking engagements, he can happily supplement his income; and that he can sometimes welcome the renewed attention publicity offers for his writing. Above all, though, he insists that he is "still" the same unassuming, home-centered chronicler of ordinary life that he had been before *Dead Poets,* an identity he means to retain.

For that matter, by virtue of the subtle changes that Pickering rings on the notion of "still" life in one essay after another, this volume as a whole ranks among his finest. The selections offered in *The Best of Pickering* (2004) draw more plentifully from *Still Life* than from any other volume. A masterful example of its artistry can be found in the book's title essay. This richly evocative piece opens with a description of a painting hung in his parents' dining room, takes the reader through a kaleidoscope of familial recollections and observations including an account of his mother's recent death, and concludes with a dreamlike fantasy of "Sammy's" postmortem reunion with her. All in all, the essay confirms the value of a quietly centered, "still" rather than glamorously active life as the seed ground for creative imagination. It is more subdued or even sober than most Pickering essays, acknowledging as it does that "cold tug of mortality" (p. 16) the author elsewhere in the volume says he feels as he holds his young children. Nonetheless, the title essay ends up supporting a characteristically optimistic hope that "despite the grave there is still life" (p. 104).

Another compelling essay in this volume, "Canned Stuff," expounds on the beauty of spontaneity, immediacy, and originality. In its embrace of common life, epitomized by the greenery cultivated in Pickering's backyard, and its scorn for derivative thought and behavior, "Canned Stuff" expresses sentiments that are in the American grain. To this extent it echoes Emerson's insistence on enjoying an "original relation to the universe"—except that Pickering's brief for this case is considerably more playful and exuberant. Like his rustic invented character Billie Dinwidder, Pickering rejects prepackaged commodities, preferring instead "things fresh, brown dirt clinging to roots and dew, even a white worm or two, on leaves" (p. 14).

Through its description of plantings and plant lore, its survey of soils and insects, *Still Life* extends the range of nature writing presented in earlier volumes. This dimension of the author's concern is particularly evident in "Bogs," "September," and "Near Spring." In "Bogs," for example, Pickering offers an appreciative testimony to the beauty of wetlands he has slogged through in Nova Scotia and Connecticut. In the course of these explorations, he rhapsodizes on the marvels of lichens, ferns, shrubs, algae, and fungi. He crawls on his hands and knees, entranced by water-soaked mosses, so that "squeezing them like sponges I wrung out great droplets" (p. 126). Such experience, like the moist earth he traverses, is regenerative. In neoromantic fashion, he avows that "alone in the woods I was wonderfully content," to the point where he "forgot the irritations which made me petty and sometimes cruel, and after two hours of studying spiders or lying on the ground looking at moss, I returned home, happy and refreshed, and a better member of the family" (p. 128).

In the opening essay of *Let it Ride* (1991), Pickering comments further on his relation to the Robin Williams film character, here mocking the

suggestion that he might himself embrace that "carpe diem" or "seize the day" philosophy attributed to his counterpart in *Dead Poets Society*. "I am too old to live anywhere near the fullest," he insists, "and if I tried to seize but an hour, I would be swept away by a cardiovascular storm ..." (p. 2). To be sure, Pickering's aging persona by now shows little inclination toward the sort of athletically vigorous, lusty hedonism commonly associated with the "carpe diem" motto of youth.

Still, Pickering demonstrates anew in this volume such relish for tales of comic absurdity, such zeal to register in writing the common details he witnesses—both outdoors and in—through the course of each day, that it is fair to see him committed indeed to making the most of life in the face of death. In this quieter sense, what "carpe diem" seems to mean for Pickering is appreciating how, for example, on a given day, hemlocks drape the Fenton River beside the Nipmuck Trail; it means spotting groundhogs on Horsebarn Hill, or enjoying what it feels like to brush his hands across some of the large oaks in Storrs. During his walks, which he says "often seem sweet hours of prayer" (p. 118), he delights in pausing to recognize the distinct beauty of sensitive ferns, shady bracken, New York and interrupted ferns, Christmas ferns or polypody, or the spores of cinnamon ferns. He revels as well in the chance to read old graveyard inscriptions, or to chortle at the notices and warnings he finds posted on the office doors of his professorial colleagues, having noticed that "Generally speaking, English teachers seem to be against racism, capitalism, nuclear war, and being male" (p. 30).

And if the joyous aspect of carpe diem is inevitably defined and qualified by an awareness of impending death, this poignant aspect of seizing the day likewise finds expression in *Let It Ride*. Recounting how he came to terms with the then-recent death of his father, Pickering explains in this volume how the event marked a turning point in his life. He testifies to feeling, after thus losing his last living parent, new distance from his childhood experiences and familial origins in Tennessee, deepened attachment to his home in Connecticut, and fresh willingness to call himself a writer. Nonetheless, *Let It Ride* continues, more

than ever, to interlard Pickering's localized personal narrative with fictive, whimsical anecdotes about Tennessee characters from Carthage, including Googoo Hooberry or the Reverend Slubey Garts with his Tabernacle of Love. For the first time, too, *Let It Ride* ventures to name as "Josh" the author's invention of a mordant, quizzical, and sometimes cynical friend who will appear in subsequent volumes as well. But even when derisive, this "joshing" character figures as more of an entertaining than a genuinely scornful voice.

TRAVELS DOWN UNDER

Pickering's two books of first-person narrative about sabbatical years he spent in Australia fall within the broad generic category of travel literature. They describe the author's orchestration of a short-term migration to a distant continent as well as the travels he undertakes within its western territories. As such, these books are chronologically ordered and conspicuously unified in a way that the familiar essay volumes are not. Not surprisingly, though, *Walkabout Year: Twelve Months in Australia* (1995) and *Waltzing the Magpies: A Year in Australia* (2004) also display traits readers had already come to recognize in the familiar essayist. Pickering's peculiar flourishes of self-mockery, delight in absurdity, and attentiveness to quotidian detail all figure abundantly in these books, as do occasional side trips from Perth back to Pickering's favored land of fancy in Carthage, Tennessee.

Much of America's best-known travel literature features protagonists who are solitary-minded adventurers. In the spirit of William Bartram, Thoreau, Melville, Richard Henry Dana, John Muir, or Edward Abbey, these masculinist adventurers typically describe excursions into wilderness territory—remote western terrain of the United States, for example, or voyages to distant exotic lands. By contrast, Pickering's Australia travel writings highlight the familial, shared rather than individualistic, and social character of his adventures abroad. The author relates not so much the perils of his travels within

Australia as his entrepreneurial efforts to fund them through commercial bartering and speaking engagements.

In *Walkabout Year,* Pickering relates the partly accidental circumstances that first led him to select Australia—and, in turn, Perth, capital of Western Australia—as his sabbatical destination. Declining to offer any definitive assessment of the Australian character, he also admits to maintaining his middle-class lifestyle in this unthreatening, English-speaking land. Aside from a solo speaking tour in New Zealand and Papua New Guinea, he shares most of the year's travel experiences with his family members. With little difficulty, his wife and two children settle into new, workable patterns of schooling and domestic life. Still, the Australia captured in Pickering's writing is often colorful, if not exotic. At times, in the lush beauty of its birds and vegetative life, it offers delectable images of Paradise: "In February, Perth was still a garden, if not quite Eden.... From mottlecah, blossoms hung like pink grapefruit. On Burdett's banksia flowers resembled chunks of vanilla ice cream dipped in orange sherbet. Showy banksia was lemony, and southern plains banksia, yellow" (p. 142). And of course the presence of distinctive creatures—including kangaroos, wallabies, and lethal spiders—adds further coloring to the Pickering family's discovery of a vast new world. Much of Pickering's walkabout year involves close-to-home wanderings in the vicinity of urban Perth, though this account of settled observations is interrupted now and then by more adventurous travels, including a twelve-day family expedition through wild territory in the Kimberley region.

The product of a subsequent sabbatical year's residence, seven years after the first, *Waltzing the Magpies* shows the author returning to Perth and the University of Western Australia but settling in a different neighborhood. The family circumstances of his visit have also changed. With one of his sons now away and studying elsewhere, and Vicki gone part of the time, his approach to daily living must shift accordingly. Among the episodes highlighted in *Waltzing the Magpies* are a weeklong, horse-mounted trip in Alpine National Park in Victoria, otherwise known as the Australian Alps, and an eight-day camping exploration of Kakadu National Park. For Pickering this last trip, taken with benefit of an unusually capable guide, offered a look at creatures he had never seen before, including "chestnut-quilled rock pigeons and a red-browed pardalote; and in water, grunters, gudgeons, and archer fish" (p. 244). As one might expect, Pickering in this volume calls attention to the calls of magpies. Beach scenes and odors become memorable as well—in Alpine National Park, for example, how "the medicinal fragrances of penny royal, mint bush, and eucalyptus drifted through the thick air almost as if sprayed from atomizers" (pp. 143–144). Later on, at a stop during his long trip home to Connecticut, Pickering describes the marvels of gazing on undersea creatures while swimming near a coral reef in Fiji.

ALONE IN EDINBURGH

Unlike the family man whose travels inspired books about Australia, the travel narrator of *Edinburgh Days; or, Doing What I Want to Do* (2007) is a lone ranger. Except for a vacation interlude when his daughter comes to visit, Pickering lives in quiet solitude during the four-and-a-half months of his appointment in 2004 as fellow at Edinburgh's Institute for Advanced Studies in the Humanities. Most of the trekking related in this travel book takes place within the bounds of Scotland's capital city. Undecided about whether he is more "tourist" or "sojourner," Pickering not only adopts a semi-hermetic regime of domestic life but also agrees to attach himself, in the manner of a medieval solitary, to that rock-faced metropolis within which his roaming is confined. No wonder he dubs himself, as the title of one essay suggests, an "Anchorite."

Though attached to Edinburgh, Pickering prowls freely and widely within its fabled precincts. This "urban spelunker" (p. 109) writes about his close inspection of the city's numerous monuments, castles, churches, theaters, art galleries, botanical gardens, and shops. He visits the Edinburgh Zoo, the National Gallery, and other museums. Pausing at one site to admire a fifteenth-century painting of Madonna and Child,

adorned with brightness and greenery, he also expresses his distaste for the military apparatus he finds exhibited elsewhere. Toward the end of his stay, he takes part in the Great Caledonian Run, a ten-kilometer road race. And he occasionally attends boxing and soccer matches, as well as theatrical and ballet productions. For the most part, though, he is content simply to observe—to participate imaginatively and hypothetically, rather than actively, in the scenes presented before him.

Thus Pickering browses continually through Edinburgh's retail outlets—in candy stores, antique shops, bookstores, clock shops, and curio shops—more often than he buys. He becomes the consummate window shopper, the writer-as-hypothetical-consumer. Even in museums, he enjoys imagining which display items he would possess if he could. "Actually," he confesses, "my mind is a curio shop" (p. 31).

This sense of the writer as a detached onlooker is conveyed with peculiar force in the essay "Invisible." Particularly toward the start of his residence in Edinburgh, Pickering finds himself observing others, without his speaking or otherwise interacting with them at all: "I am simply an aging stranger in a big city, a faceless gray shadow passing along the sidewalk, the invisible man whose animal spirits time has reduced to dregs" (p. 5). Yet he comes to enjoy the privilege of wandering the streets incognito, like a god. Pickering as "invisible man" recalls not so much a character from the fiction of H. G. Wells or Ralph Ellison as he does the narrative persona of Nathaniel Hawthorne. For in nonfictional pieces such as "Sights from a Steeple," "Sunday at Home," and "Night Sketches: Beneath an Umbrella," Hawthorne exposed the ironic circumstance of the writer-as-observer who must inevitably become invisible and separated—in one way or another—from his human subjects, must objectify them, to serve the ends of his own literary compositions. Such interplay between the writer's subjective impressions and external observations of the world is explored with rare sensitivity in "Invisible," one of Pickering's finest essays.

The overall mood of *Edinburgh Days* is more gently reflective, less flamboyant, than that of other Pickering volumes. Among the many Edinburgh sites described in this book, none figure more prominently than gardens and graveyards. This preoccupation with graveyards is not, for Pickering, a function of morbidity. Indeed he regards burial grounds, together with their stone inscriptions that he studies assiduously, as "calming, happy places." ("Tourist," p. 50). Nonetheless, a visit with his daughter to one lush garden provokes bittersweet feelings of elation tinged with intimations of mortality: "I lingered over plants, not wanting to move on because I knew I would not see them again. Eliza was young and didn't ponder limitations. Before her the future stretched endlessly blooming..." ("Out," p. 140).

LETTERS FROM A TEACHER'S TEACHER

Thus far the only Pickering volume to be issued by a trade publisher rather than a university press, *Letters to a Teacher* (2004) draws on material related to pedagogy that had been included in previous volumes of familiar essays. But it is decidedly different from those books in its epistolary format, its audience, and its aims. Organized in the form of ten letters to "Dear Teacher," the book addresses classroom instructors at all levels, particularly those who are relatively new to the profession and thus prone to feel disheartened or diffident about mentoring. Much of the presentation is lighthearted, freewheeling, interspersed with anecdotes derived from the author's experiences teaching in diverse settings.

Pickering avoids offering his readers systematic instructions about how to teach. Those seeking a how-to-do-it instructor's manual for pedagogy must look elsewhere. Just as education itself remains for Pickering a mysterious, largely ungovernable and unpredictable process, so also he regards teaching as "both art and gift" rather than anything approaching an exact science. He scorns belief in the myth of aspiring to become a great, charismatically inspired teacher, arguing that instructors should instead aim simply to "be competent and kind" (p. 26). But *Letters to a*

Teacher does voice many authorial opinions—on matters ranging from terms of address for the teacher (best to avoid too much familiarity), what the teacher should consider wearing, or what curricular requirements an institution should maintain (few if any, in his estimation), to ways of dealing with troubled students and complaints about grading. It also describes, and plentifully illustrates, qualities that Pickering identifies with good teachers. Such qualities include adaptability, a willingness to think well of people, the ability to stir curiosity, and a commitment to teaching students—rather than any particular, narrowly defined subject matter. Pickering, for his part, expresses a cheerful readiness to meddle in his students' lives. What he presents as his sphere of instruction extends well beyond literary training, as he shows no hesitation about exhorting students in his class to wear bicycle helmets and to quit smoking and jaywalking.

LATER MUSINGS ON THE GIFT OF LIFE

By the time Pickering published *Trespassing* in 1994, he had become so prolific a writer that he would continue to issue a new collection of familiar essays practically every year thereafter. So ample is this production in later stages of Pickering's career that it becomes necessary here to offer only a few brief remarks about the eight volumes of this sort that have appeared since 1994, with mention of just one or two representative essays collected in each.

The "trespassing" described in the volume of that title does not turn out to be radically transgressive. True, Pickering insists in the title essay that he will continue to wander beyond closed gates into properties he does not own. True, he had once been willing to stand on top of his desk to teach; he still indulges in some odd campus pranks with firecrackers; and he reports flirting with civil disobedience when he pulls up stakes planted in woods and farmlands by university developers hoping to build an industrial park. But most of the volume's essays describe behavior that scarcely qualifies as outlaw conduct. Such decidedly unthreatening activities include sorting through mail, noticing buds on trees, play-

ing a cameo role in a production of *The Magic Flute,* serving on a local school board, or cleaning out a campus study space to be relinquished for another occupant. In fact, the author admits that a Vermont hippie he knew in his youth declined to date him because she feared he was too conventional. So what "trespassing" mostly means for Pickering throughout this volume is commitment to the sort of free-spirited wandering, beyond the boundaries of what mass culture approves or expect, that promises to reveal the "magic" inherent in ordinary life. The opening essays on "Magic" and "Belonging" thus complement later pieces such as "Outrageous" and "Trespassing."

The central image in *The Blue Caterpillar* (1997), highlighted in the volume's title essay, reflects a convergence of references to wooly nature, a literary text, and the author's domestic experience. Having agreed to participate in his daughter's ballet school performance of *Alice's Adventures in Wonderland,* Pickering tells of his assuming a new stage role as the blue caterpillar. He acts the part by reading selections from Lewis Carroll's book, sitting on an orange mushroom stool while garbed in an outlandish and colorful costume. His daughter Eliza is the Queen of Hearts. "I was excited," he writes. "Never had I been in a ballet. Fifty-two years is a long time to be a chrysalis, and I was eager to split the pupal shell, pump up my wings, and flutter through an auditorium" (p. 46). This playful allusion to metamorphosis becomes part of a subtle, evocative pattern of reference sustained throughout the title essay, as well as through the volume as a whole. Several versions of transformation figure in this pattern. The authorial adult becomes once more an innocent child, the professor turns play actor, a human turns momentarily into an insect animal, and Carroll's nineteenth-century text is reborn dramatically in present-day America. Elsewhere in the volume, Pickering finds himself momentarily transformed into a fly fisherman, at a reunion in Pennsylvania of old friends. And time itself inevitably exposes our lives to metamorphosis, whether or not we will it to be so. Toward the volume's close, an essay titled "There Have Been Changes" expounds on this

theme with a characteristic blend of wit and discernment.

A large share of *Living to Prowl* (1997) tells of the frustrations and occasional joys Pickering encounters while trying to arrange care for his aged Uncle Coleman in Houston, following the death of Coleman's wife. The volume's two opening essays are devoted to the topic, as is its closing account of life in Coleman's nursing home. Complementing this portrait of a dutiful nephew and his stationary uncle, though, the volume also exposes Pickering's freewheeling spirit. Just as wild animals must often prowl for food to live, so also Pickering "lives to prowl," as his grandmother in a letter once described his younger self. Convinced that "life ought to be a ramble in which distraction provided the stuff of joy" ("Wood Thrush," p. 164), this untamed Pickering refuses to be governed by predefined goals or an overzealous work ethic. So he includes essays here in praise of "Indolence" and "Wideness." His writing too reflects the wandering ways of a prowler: "My days resemble paragraphs without topic sentences. Beginnings and endings are arbitrary, and thoughts dangle like participial phrases" ("Indolence," p. 72). And like Thoreau and Aldo Leopold, two classic American authors whom Pickering has often taught, he writes in several essays of how nature inspires him—even in relatively settled landscapes, such as those surrounding him in northeastern Connecticut—with its inexhaustible wildness, its springtime excess of energy.

Both the giftedness of life and the omnipresence of mortality are prominent themes in essays appearing in Pickering's next five volumes. In the title essay of *Deprived of Unhappiness* (1998), Pickering admits that his life story lacks the sort of dramatic reversals or triumph over adversity that make for inspirational autobiography. But he is content, in ways the essay whimsically demonstrates, to forget worrying about whether he is happy. As he claims in another essay, paraphrasing Water Rat in *The Wind in the Willows,* he finds that at his stage of life, instead of nurturing grand ambitions, "nothing seems half so much worth doing as messing about" ("Messing About," p. 46). Occasioned by

Pickering's attending a Festival of Southern Autobiography in Arkansas, "An Orgy of Southernness" is an essay notable for articulating the author's relation to his southern roots. Is there anything like a distinctively southern sensibility? If so, for Pickering that disposition has something to do with the flavor of southern storytelling, with the ways that narratives are allied with communal associations. Though he feels "freer" in New England than in the South, he finds that in the land of his origin offhand remarks are more readily perceived to be part of narratives and "communal play." One thing southerners do well, he suggests, is tell stories. The essay reinforces this point by spinning its own tall tale about bizarre happenings in a motel swimming pool. Incorporated here as well is a touching story of Pickering's chance encounter, years later, of a woman he had loved from afar during his first freshman year of college.

"The Traveled World," collected in *A Little Fling* (1999), images a number of simple satisfactions, gratefully received—watching a Memorial Day parade with one's children for example, or savoring an ice cream cone at Dairy Queen. The essay's course winds, in its irregular itinerary, from Hanover, New Hampshire, through a parade route in Mansfield, Connecticut, and down to Tennessee. After delivering an address at Montgomery Bell Academy in Nashville, Pickering makes a side trip that reacquaints him with Sewanee. This essay is memorable for its account of botanical features observed on the Cumberland Plateau and for Pickering's disclosure of how he tried to talk to his dead parents when he visited their graves in Carthage.

Consistent with Pickering's style, the title of *The Last Book* (2001) must be read as teasingly ironic. Pickering knows, as the volume's closing essay confirms, that he intends to write more books—and he concedes, in self-deprecating fashion, that the thoughts informing his essays have changed little over the years. So this volume is his "last" only insofar as it is his most recent. Content to acknowledge that many "years in Storrs have worn grooves in my behavior," he will continue to seek fresh encounters with the world on familiar ground, as he wanders "field

and hill, the land a magical canopic jar, gold and vital, circling the bowl, a cartouche carved by seasons" ("The Lost Book" p. 184)

In "Road Warrior," the author does wander farther afield, as he describes one of his book tours through sites in Tennessee, Georgia, and North Carolina. Yet the trip is scarcely presented as a glamorous, triumphant opening toward literary fame. Instead, in characteristically self-diminishing fashion, Pickering's road narrative features minor mishaps, tongue-in-cheek reports of quirky personalities encountered along the way, and a business accounting of his profits and losses. By such accounting, the author claims that his trip earned him a net profit of $35.31. For Pickering, as for Thoreau, the perennial humor of tallying such particularities also complements his urge to remain rooted in factual realities. His essay on "Familiar Things" fits readily into this pattern. But the more fanciful side of Pickering's disposition likewise receives ample play in *The Last Book,* in essays such as "Lies and Consequences" or "Split Infinitive." "Split Infinitive" describes the publicity notice that followed Pickering's response to an inquiry about whether he, in accord with the new edition of the *Oxford American Desk Dictionary,* accepted the split infinitive as proper English usage. Perhaps surprisingly, Pickering's offhand remark to the reporter that "I do not dine with those who split infinitives" (p. 13) ended up provoking a flood of further media reactions and misunderstandings—all of which seem to delight the author. Thus "Split Infinitive" becomes a masterfully comic exposition on the theme of how public media reactions can be strangely entangled with, or contradict, impressions of a private self.

"Musings on the Gift of Life," the subtitle of *Indian Summer* (2005) captures the main sense not only of this volume but of Pickering's overall approach to writing. Among the simple gifts of life this book muses upon are the author's experiences of raking leaves, attending a rabbit show, clearing trash from a hiking trail, and, as always, fanciful visits to survey the doings of plain folks in Carthage. "Toolless" amounts to a witty, metaphorically elaborated musing on what it means for Pickering to have shunned the use of all hand tools other than hammer and screwdriver. Declining to view either the world or his own way of life as polished, neatly ordered, Pickering welcomes disorder as blessed. "My pages are outbuildings cluttered with dusty tales," he admits; but though "my paragraphs masquerade as ramshackle, they are more tightly constructed than meets the galloping mind" (pp. 104, 105). All in all, gratitude for the gift of life is tempered, in *Indian Summer,* by recognition of ills such as the author's swollen ankle, worries and disappointment about his two sons, the melancholic isolation described in "Alone," or the diminished expectations of vigor voiced in "Maintenance."

Throughout *Autumn Spring* (2007), further reminders of the author's bodily ills are outshone by occasions of grace and mirth. As though zealous to outrun death, Pickering writes about continuing to run road races despite his advancing age and the weight of diverse infirmities. He writes of undergoing knee surgery, of accidentally eating his own teeth, and of having polyps scooped from his innards. He grieves at the loss of those he has known and loved, and finds even the long-standing pleasure of sauntering through scenes in the natural world limited by adult awareness of that world's fragility. He climbs with a friend, in the footsteps of Emerson and Thoreau, to the summit of Mt. Monadnock in New Hampshire; and later that summer, while sitting quietly on a grassy bluff in Nova Scotia, he wonders if he had somehow missed his life.

Still, the volume as a whole conveys the sense of an autumnal mellowness. *Autumn Spring* is far from doleful. Happiness, as the author now conceives it, is not an aspiration, an ideal to be pursued, but a matter of accepting one's place in the world as it is. So one can and should decide to accept "the happenstance nature of life" (Introduction, p. xvi). This autumnal stoicism is a note sounded from the volume's opening sentence, where Pickering cites Robert Louis Stevenson to the effect that "There is no duty we so much underrate as the duty of being happy" (p. xi). So the author now accepts with equanimity—even relish—the fact that he may strike others as slightly mad. Appreciative of Bertie Wooster, a cheerfully zany character in P. G.

Wodehouse's fiction, he accepts the blessed absurdity of finding himself labeled a "mad humanist" and gleefully sticks a bumper sticker on his lawnmower. He tells once more of visiting his fanciful town of Carthage, enjoying the chance to report on the crazy deeds of characters such as Biblical, his wife named Good Counsel, and sons Much and Little.

An especially moving essay relates in loving detail the decline and death of George, an arthritic dachshund who had won a special place in Pickering's affections during the author's middle years. Although this account is alive with sentiment, unfolding a tale with which most readers can identify, it manages to surpass sentimentality. It achieves this artful exposure of emotion partly through its touches of physical realism—its attentiveness, for example, to precisely how George's limbs had been arranged for burial—and partly through the author's willingness to voice skepticism about how he responded at the time to George's demise. Finally, though, the mood of this essay is not so much melancholic as it is thoughtfully elegiac. Despite his grief, the author records with satisfaction that he had at least taken care of his "pal" for fourteen years, and had dug him "a humdinger of a grave" (p. 57). Returning to gaze on the site of his pal's remains in Nova Scotia, he finds that "The moss on George's grave remains wondrously green" (p. 57).

If this volume suggests that for Pickering, as for Robert Frost, "fall" says much about the author's sensibility, as well as about his current phase of life, the other crucial season of his soul is spring. True, this book avoids most conventional figures of springtime rebirth. But it brings vividly to mind the perennial psychological import of this season for those in northern climes, insofar as "Spring ... momentarily strips veneer from thought and restores the quick to sight, so patching the flakes and the cracked that from a distance the world seems fresh" ("Mad," p. 2). Echoing many of Pickering's earlier writings, it concludes with a litany of praise for ordinary matters, homage to the god of small things. "The small patches on which we ... stand," he insists, "are indeed the closest we come to holy ground"

(Afterword, p. 141). And it is possible to see the closing pages of *Autumn Spring* encapsulating the larger meaning of Pickering's familiar essays, all of which attest in one way or another to this author's conviction that "When people raise their expectations above the ordinary and neglect the little world about them, they miss the big things of life" (p. 141).

CONCLUSION

Given Pickering's prolific output, with scores of familiar essays published to date, one might fairly ask how, or how much longer, this author can conceive enough variation on the theme of a saunterer's musings to sustain new productions. There is, after all, no conspicuous ordering or sequence of development across Pickering's work as a whole. Nor does any one text of his stand out as central or definitive. Yet this ceaselessly flowing, open-ended character of the corpus seems for Pickering, as for Walt Whitman in *Leaves of Grass,* expressive of a sensibility that is perpetually on the move. No single book of his can sum up his sense of things. Pickering has more than once cited Michel de Montaigne, one of his literary models, to the effect that "essayists depict passing"—that is, ceaseless process, rather than progress toward some end point of artistic completion. Such is Pickering's approach to the creation of familiar writings that are, as the French derivation of "essay" suggests, repeated attempts—never fully achieved—to record someone's personal impressions of the world he inhabits.

Though ultimately unique in its identity, Pickering's creative personality draws upon both cultivated, verbally polished European traditions of essay composition—shaped by figures such as Montaigne and William Hazlitt—and wilder American strains reminiscent of Twain, backwoods southern humor, and the tall tale. But must one see the genial, slow-paced wanderings of Pickering's essayistic persona as outdated, outpaced by the rush of words and images confronting us in this frenetic age of multitasking and instant communication? Not at all, if the need of today's readers for reflective leisure is taken

into account. In a culture possessed by personal ambition and electronic abstractions, the opposing worth of Pickering's rambling and jests becomes, arguably, all the greater. Confident that "for the person who looks carefully life is miraculous" ("Mad," p. 4), Pickering wants above all to urge readers toward adopting a more measured pace in their life-journeying, by virtue of which they are able to see that nothing in their ordinary world is unworthy of notice. As he declares in *Autumn Spring,*

> My days are all small. I try to make them memorable or at least slow their slipping from mind by writing essays. And sappy as it sounds, I hope that my writing slows readers so that they, too, will pause, examine their lives, and find days wonderful, if not unforgettable.

(p. 140)

Selected Bibliography

WORKS OF SAM PICKERING

COLLECTIONS OF FAMILIAR ESSAYS

A Continuing Education. Hanover, N.H.: University Press of New England, 1985.

The Right Distance. Athens: University of Georgia Press, 1987.

May Days. Iowa City: University of Iowa Press, 1988.

Still Life. Hanover, N.H.: University Press of New England, 1990.

Let It Ride. Columbia: University of Missouri Press, 1991.

Trespassing. Hanover, N.H.: University Press of New England, 1994.

The Blue Caterpillar. Gainesville: University Press of Florida, 1997.

Living to Prowl. Athens: University of Georgia Press, 1997.

Deprived of Unhappiness. Athens: Ohio University Press, 1998.

A Little Fling. Knoxville: University of Tennessee Press, 1999.

The Last Book. Knoxville: University of Tennessee Press, 2001.

The Best of Pickering. Ann Arbor: University of Michigan Press, 2004.

Indian Summer: Musings on the Gift of Life. Columbia: University of Missouri Press, 2005.

Autumn Spring. Knoxville: University of Tennessee Press, 2007.

TRAVEL AND OTHER BOOKS

Walkabout Year: Twelve Months in Australia. Columbia: University of Missouri Press, 1995.

Waltzing the Magpies: A Year in Australia. Ann Arbor: University of Michigan Press, 2004.

Letters to a Teacher. New York: Atlantic Monthly Press, 2004.

Edinburgh Days; or, Doing What I Want to Do. Columbia: University of South Carolina Press, 2007.

A Comfortable Bay: A Memoir. Macon, GA: Mercer University Press, 2010.

CRITICAL BOOKS

The Moral Tradition in English Fiction, 1785–1850. Hanover, N.H.: University Press of New England, 1976.

John Locke and Children's Books in Eighteenth-Century England. Knoxville: University of Tennessee Press, 1981.

Moral Instruction and Fiction for Children, 1749–1820. Athens: University of Georgia Press, 1993.

SELECTED ESSAYS

"Letter from a London Attic." *Dartmouth College Library Bulletin* 14: 29–33 (1973).

"Taking the Night Plane to Tulsa." *New England Review* 1: 433–439 (1979). Reprinted in *Best of New England Review,* winter 1993, pp. 286–290.

"The Sage's Progress (Pomposity in Academia)." *National Review* 31: 1236 (September 28, 1979).

"The Starling." *New York Times* (Connecticut Weekly), March 1, 1981.

"American Beauty." *New York Times* (Connecticut Weekly), May 30, 1982. Condensed in *Reader's Digest,* May 1986, pp. 31–32.

"How to Grow Wise Studying Box Turtles." *Yankee Magazine,* May 1983, pp. 86-87. Condensed in *Reader's Digest,* September 1983, pp. 99–103.

"Reading at Forty." *Sewanee Review* 92: 78–90 (1984).

"Running to Lose." *Yankee Magazine,* September 1984, pp. 136–140, 222–223.

"Pictures." *Southern Review* 22: 532–545 (1986). Reprinted in *Best American Essays.* Edited by Gay Talese. Boston: Houghton Mifflin, 1987. Pp. 181–196.

"Son and Father." *Virginia Quarterly Review* 62: 706–724 (1986). Excerpted in *Reader's Digest,* March 1989, p. 92. Reprinted in *The Norton Book of American Autobiography.* Edited by Jay Parini. New York: Norton, 1999. Pp. 526–540. Again reprinted in *Our Fathers: Reflections by Sons.* Edited by Steven L. Shepherd. Boston: Beacon, 2001. Pp. 92–114.

"Lessons and Carols at Sewanee." *Southern Accents* 14: 64–69 (December–January 1991). Excerpted in *Anglican Digest* 6: 19–11 (1992).

"Real." In *Home Ground: Southern Autobiography*. Edited by J. Bill Berry. Columbia: University of Missouri Press, 1991. Pp. 148–160.

"George." *Southwest Review* 90: 251–270 (spring 2005). Reprinted in *Dachsmania,* autumn 2006, pp. 3–15. Again reprinted in *Best American Essays 2006*. Edited by Lauren Slater. Boston: Houghton Mifflin, 2006.

"Invisible." *Sewanee Review* 113: 566–580 (fall 2005).

"Shadows." *Harvard Review* 31: 18–23 (December 2006).

CRITICAL STUDIES AND REVIEWS

Albin, C. D. "Indian Summer: Musings on the Gift of Life." *Harvard Review* 29: 241–242 (December 2005). (Review.)

Atkins, C. Douglas. "Envisioning the Stranger's Heart." *College English* 56: 629–641 (October 1994).

Braun, Janice. "The Blue Caterpillar and Other Essays." *Library Journal,* March 15, 1997, p. 64. (Review.)

Core, George. "Procrustes' Bed: Review of *The Art of Teaching* and *Letters to a Teacher.*" *Sewanee Review* 113: xxii–xxvi (winter 2005).

Gundy, Jeff. "A Little Fling and Other Essays." *Georgia Review* 54: 559 (fall 2000). (Review.)

Harvey, Steven. "The Blue Caterpillar and Other Essays." *Georgia Review* 51: 793-794 (winter 1997). (Review.)

Hoy, Pat C. "The Art of Remembering." *Sewanee Review* 96: 688–695 (fall 1998).

Kingstone, Lisa. "Loving Life and Teaching It." *Publishers Weekly,* May 24, 2004, pp. 39–40.

Minken, Judy. "Trespassing." *Library Journal,* May 1, 1994, p. 104. (Review.)

Pitts, Greenfield. "Mr. Keating from 'Dead Poets Society': From Reel to Real." *Education Digest* 56: 3–4 (December 1990).

Ryden, Kent C. *Mapping the Invisible Landscape: Folklore, Writing, and the Sense of Place.* Iowa City: University of Iowa Press, 1993. Pp. 219–220.

Smith, Louise Z. "Prosaic Rhetoric in Still-Life Paintings and Personal Essays." *Mosaic* 31: 125–142 (1998).

INTERVIEWS

Frantz, Janie. "On Writing." *Critique Magazine* (http://www.critiquemagazine.com/article/pickering.html).

Spinner, Jenny. "Interview with Sam Pickering." *Fourth Genre: Explorations in Nonfiction* 5: 192–207 (spring 2003).

MARILYNNE ROBINSON

(1943—)

Joseph Dewey

THAT MARILYNNE ROBINSON has a favorite psalm is sufficient to make uneasy most hip readers of post-postmodern American fiction. That Psalm 8 effusively celebrates God's living, loving presence ("O Lord, how majestic is your name in all the earth") and unironically affirms our joyful dependence on the vast reach of God's intention; that Robinson herself preaches on occasion; that she is not only an accomplished novelist but one of the most provocative Protestant theological writers since Karl Barth; that she credits a treatise by the Puritan firebrand Jonathan Edwards with igniting her narrative imagination (specifically a footnote in his *Great Christian Doctrine of Original Sin* that sees God's continuing energy as the inexhaustible momentum that sustains the material world)—all this leads us to suspect that hers is agenda fiction, medieval temple rhetoric. How are we to handle fictions in which characters make their way to joy in the harrowing environment of the late twentieth century, which here drops its convincing pretense of routine horror and tedious banality to reveal itself for what it has been since Genesis: creation. After all, in the two millennia since the apostles stared dumbfounded as Christ vanished into the chalk-white vacancy over Bethany, Christians themselves have engaged their deity only in an elaborate hide-and-seek. God speaks in silences or in codes they cannot break; confirmation must be found in doubt, power in helplessness, presence in absence. Stranded inconveniently between Incarnation and Parousia, Christians affirm a God they know only through endlessly replaying rehearsed rituals within the cool sanitized spaces of churches. What Christians know of joy is how to live without it.

In Robinson's fictions, however, we are gifted with the revelation that the apparent dramas of loving and dying are absurd inconsequentialities—save that the entire sorry enterprise has been commissioned by an embracing energy that bends our every turn into wonder. We elect, Robinson argues, to live unconvinced by the implication of graspable joy, we embrace drab, we choose to see death as graceless and premature. Robinson convinces us not that joy matters—that is the especial benediction of the narrow audience of those who affirm, with Robinson, the reward of blessed assurance—but rather that our inability to access joy matters, that joy is a right we have relinquished too easily. Robinson passionately engages a congregation-culture that moves with stony somnambulistic steps unaware of the elegant wonder of the Christian immediate. Yet, unlike so much religious fiction, her narratives never sound tinny or smug, with doctrine masquerading as plot, saints pretending to be characters, and lessons dressed up as themes. With the care and patience of a theological thinker, Robinson in three landmark works of fiction subtly crafts a cohesive argument that, taken as whole, encourages rather than demands the magisterial declaration of Christian assent: the unironic Amen.

LIFE

Marilynne Summers was born November 26, 1943, in the crossroads town of Sandpoint in the panhandle of rural northern Idaho. Because her father, John J. Summers, harvested timber for lumber companies, the family often relocated to towns along the border of Idaho and Washington to follow the jobs. But Marilynne grew up principally in the small village of Coolin on the southern shore of Priest Lake about fifty miles north of Sandpoint. Her family was Presbyterian

but without the intense commitment that would mark Marilynne's later spiritual evolution; religion was more an "inherited intuition than an actual fact" (*Paris Review,* p. 3). Perhaps because of the family's peripatetic life, Marilynne found friendships difficult and took comfort in books— her only sibling, an older brother, David, to whom she was very close, assured her early on that she would be a great poet. Given the father's inevitable absences, Robinson has described her childhood home as matriarchal (itself unusual in that rugged western culture); her mother, Ellen, read to Marilynne as a child, thus tying storytelling early to the intimacy of voice.

Marilynne herself became an ambitious reader—she tackled *Moby-Dick* at age nine. But it was in high school, in the district school in Coeur d'Alene, that Robinson first tried writing. Initially she was inspired by her introduction in Latin class to Roman writers of antiquity, particularly Cicero, Horace, and Virgil, whose florescent rhetoric, carefully terraced sentences, and exquisitely elevated diction opened her young eyes (and ears) to the rich possibilities of language in an era, the early 1960s, when the lean colloquial style of Hemingwayesque writing was the rage. After graduating high school in 1962, Robinson headed to Brown University in distant Rhode Island to join her brother, who was finishing an art history degree. Robinson majored in nineteenth-century American literature—Herman Melville, Henry David Thoreau, Ralph Waldo Emerson, and supremely Emily Dickinson—whose works, unlike much of the arch-experimental literature of her era, grappled with cosmic questions, questions about the nature of reality itself and how human perception struggled to understand such vast mystery. And far more important for Robinson, it was a body of literature informed by the energy, structures, and rhetoric of Protestant Christianity. She found particular encouragement in creative writing classes conducted by the novelist John Hawkes, who found in Robinson's studied style and confident use of language a distinct, even promising voice.

After completing her B.A. degree in 1966, Robinson returned to the Pacific Northwest, enrolling in the graduate program in English at the University of Washington. She married and had two children, both sons—dedicated to that responsibility, she would not complete her dissertation until 1977. Her doctorate, a reenvisioning of Shakespeare's *Henry VI, Part 2,* broke new ground with an analytic approach fixed not on the play's political themes but rather on its subtle play of language, its dense layers of metaphor and allusion, and supremely its sonic accomplishment. It was as she was toiling through the dissertation that a committee professor, impressed by Robinson's own lyrical prose, so strikingly different from thick academic writing, asked whether she had ever attempted fiction. In a way she had—when she tired of the rigid discipline of dissertation writing, she would playfully tease out extended metaphors, bundles of which she had kept. But she had nothing to share. Days later, anxious, overwhelmed, she fell asleep in the university library and promptly "witnessed" a catastrophic train wreck. She rendered that vivid dream into a short prose piece and shared that with the adviser.

Upon graduation, Robinson went to northwestern France, where she taught for a year at the Université de Haute Bretagne in Rennes. By this time she had gathered a significant collection of her quirky metaphors. Convinced of the worth of the train wreck scene, in less than a year and a half she developed it all into what would become the manuscript of *Housekeeping.* Drawing on her childhood in the forbidding lake country of northern Idaho, she fashioned an unconventional coming-of-age story about the relationship between a socially awkward teenage girl and the eccentric, free-spirited aunt who raises her and her sister after their mother commits suicide. Robinson was convinced that few publishers would be interested in the manuscript, with its carefully wrought Ciceronian flourishes and its gloomy ambience (indeed, the ending left open the possibility that its first-person narrator might actually be speaking from the grave). To her surprise, the first agent to review the manuscript eagerly agreed to represent it. Then, in quick succession, Farrar, Straus and Giroux agreed to publish it. Robinson was stunned. When the book appeared in late 1980, it generated immediate

praise for its rhapsodic prose as well as for its exploration of empowered women. The book received the PEN/Ernest Hemingway Foundation Award for Best First Novel and the Rosenthal Award from the American Academy and Institute of Arts and Letters, and it was short-listed for the Pulitzer Prize. More to the point, it was among the best-selling novels of the year—it would later be adapted (if hugely simplified) into a modestly successful 1987 film by the respected director Bill Forsyth.

Hailed by the literati as a rising talent, Robinson, however, turned to teaching, specifically working with young writers—accepting prestigious appointments at Washington University (1983), the University of Kent in England (1983–1984), the Fine Arts Center in Provincetown, Massachusetts (1985), Amherst College (1985–1986), the University of Massachusetts (1987), and the University of Alabama (1988). In 1989 she divorced and was granted custody of her sons. To shoulder the responsibilities of family and home, ready now for roots, she accepted an appointment to the University of Iowa's Writers' Workshop program in late 1990. It was in Iowa City that Robinson would find her home—delighting not only in the environment of challenge that had long defined the university's storied fiction-writing program but as well responding to the rich history of Iowa itself, specifically its place in the abolitionist movement and its complex religious culture.

Although *Housekeeping* proved a stimulating text for critical explications, generating scores of published readings, Robinson herself published no new fiction. During her stay at the University of Kent, however, she became passionately involved with the implications of environmental mismanagement surrounding the Sellafield nuclear reprocessing plant on the coast of the Irish Sea. Researching a piece for *Harper's* in 1985, Robinson found that millions of gallons of radioactive waste were being pumped daily into the Irish Sea and had been for more than thirty years. Her outrage over the large-scale contamination and British indifference to it became a book-length polemic, *Mother Country: Britain, the Welfare State and Nuclear Pollution* (1989).

Robinson indicted an array of British government agencies, the utility managers of Sellafield (British Nuclear Fuels), media watchdogs (whom she dismissed as lax), and even environmental protection groups (in fact, Greenpeace would sue her for libel). To make her case, Robinson put the Sellafield contamination scandal within a broader historic context of British indifference to the underprivileged, whose health was being jeopardized by the large-scale dumping at Sellafield. Although a finalist for the National Book Award's nonfiction prize and considered now a landmark cri de coeur in the nascent Green movement, *Mother Country* at the time brought Robinson much criticism—over her nonscientific background and her research derived largely from newspapers and magazines, her evident bias against the nuclear industry, her insistence on seeing the treatment of the poor in America as far superior to that of Britain, and her invective against the British government as mercenary and impersonal.

In addition to completing *Mother Country*, Robinson published a series of lengthy (and eloquent) essays that explored her own religious sensibility and her profound unease over the contemporary estrangement from the consolations of the Christian vision, most notably essays that indicted the thinness of post-Enlightenment discourse with its emphasis on individual survival and competition. She reinvigorated traditional figures of Christian Protestantism thinned into stereotypes by the secular imagination (refurbishing the popular image of John Calvin as dour and intolerant, for instance, and first-generation American Puritans as joyless untutored busybodies). She reinvestigated books of the Bible. She challenged the sway of science and capitalism over religion. The essays were confrontational and contrarian, building their bracing arguments with the careful use of primary texts, some of which Robinson rescued from obscurity, all sustained by her imposing, vibrant intellectualism (Robinson relished the joy of research and the discovery of forgotten texts and maintained a voracious curiosity about history, economics, politics, education, and sociology). Those essays

were gathered in *The Death of Adam: Essays on Modern Thought* (1998).

But she published no fiction. In 1985, when Robinson was teaching in Provincetown, Massachusetts, she was unexpectedly marooned alone at a bed-and-breakfast waiting for her sons to join her for the Christmas holidays. During that stay, all alone, listening to the ocean's unforgiving winter roar and bathed in what she described as "Emily Dickinson" sunlight (*Paris Review,* p. 4), she first heard a powerful voice, a voice of religious conviction; it was, she sensed almost instinctively, a dying minister whose faith was tempered by a fierce love of the busy beauty of this world. Working on and off for nearly two decades, writing it like a nineteenth-century serial novel in bursts of thirty pages, Robinson would give that voice a narrative, completing her second novel, *Gilead,* in 2004.

Published to glowing praise for its stately prose and its tonic celebration of nature, of family, of love written as a letter from a dying father, a Congregationalist pastor in a small Iowa town in the mid-1950s, to a young son he will never see grow up, *Gilead* was a surprise best seller and earned Robinson the Pulitzer Prize in Fiction. Robinson followed *Gilead* four years later with *Home,* a book that retold the same events in *Gilead* save from a perspective of a far different family, one cut by strife and grudges. The relative speed with which Robinson completed this novel suggests the two books are companion pieces: indeed, one affirms the reach of the horizontal vision; the other celebrates the vertical arc of the Christian vision. Critical reception was again laudatory—the novel garnered Robinson the prestigious Orange Prize for Fiction in mid-2009, awarded annually by a phalanx of British publishers and critics to the best work of fiction by a woman in any country. The committee cited *Home* not only for its luminous prose but for its confident sense of Christian hope and expectation.

With three books in nearly a quarter century, it is tempting, perhaps inevitable, to see them as a cooperative trilogy, the three main characters—Ruth Stone, John Ames, and Glory Boughton—an expression of a single temperament, an interrogation of our position in a post-postmodern Chris-

tian universe. In Ruth, the liberated storyteller, Robinson begins (inevitably as she was herself a fledgling writer and an inveterate reader) by testing the reach of the imagination; then with the large-hearted and courageously moral Reverend Ames, Robinson moves to the emotional mayhem of the heart and confirms the value and worth of a world whose every moment is shot through with the wonder of its creator; and in the unprepossessing Glory Boughton, Robinson, herself approaching seventy, celebrates at last the conviction and strength of the soul and the certainty of the reach of grace, the reward of glory. It is to trace that narrative-pilgrimage—from transformation to transfiguration to transcendence—that we now turn.

HOUSEKEEPING: *NARRATIVE OF TRANSFORMATION*

In her earliest memory, Ruth Stone, the narrator of *Housekeeping,* recalls as a youngster happily hiding beneath her grandmother's ironing board while her grandmother finished the laundry; the parlor curtains, starched, white, and fragrant, draped over the board made for Ruth a cloister, a shelter—a protective retreat compromised only by glimpses of the unalterable real, in this case her grandmother's wrinkled ankles and her clunky black shoes. It is a telling moment—Ruth caught up within the fetching lure of her imagination, joyfully abandoning anchorage in drab reality.

Stubborn fact and fetching fiction.

Not surprisingly, the story the adult Ruth spins—the text of *Housekeeping*—is similarly contested. Consider the opening paragraphs. Ruth's matter-of-fact recitation of her family genealogy seamlessly morphs into an account of her grandfather's death in a spectacular train accident years before Ruth was born, an accident that baffled explanation then because there were no witnesses. And yet we are given a riveting account of that moonlight night when the doomed train slipped off its tracks and hurtled soundlessly into the icy black river. Enthralled by the verbal suction of Ruth's narration, by its immediacy, its detailing, we readily accept the

account. Yet we are actually buying into a fanciful embroidery, a counterfeit history, Ruth's invention. Throughout *Housekeeping,* Ruth explores the reach of her imagination, her novel defiantly centripetal, a study in how those sensitive few, traumatized by the hard play of accident, the hammer-blow intrusion of mortality, and the abundant disappointments of ordinary life find the solace of a full-throttle imagination, constructing refuges that offer the design that the everyday so evidently lacks, indeed makes so devastatingly ironic. *Housekeeping* is thus a narrative that interrogates its own premise, that in fact delights in foregrounding its manufacture. Recall the novel's inception: a graduate student in literature, word-fed and book-fat, falling into a charmed sleep amid the dusty shelves of a university library.

Ruth is a writer. She is less a character, more a deliberate written act (we are never given any physical description and her conversations are occasional and spare—she is inarticulate to the point of rudeness). Ruth is not heard, we don't listen to her—we read her. Unlike first-person coming-of-age narrators from Huck Finn to Holden Caulfield whose narrations strive for colloquial intimacy, Ruth is a writer, not a talker. Her opening line—"My name is Ruth"—suggests her deliberate literariness. Commentators on the novel have teased echoes of *Huckleberry Finn, David Copperfield, The Catcher in the Rye,* the Old Testament book of Ruth, *Walden,* and above all *Moby-Dick.* It is pointless to settle on one— rather Ruth comes to us from the first as a written thing, an intertextual event, a literary (and highly literate) echo. Her high-caloric language, her lush vocabulary, her cantilevered sentence structures, her compulsive indulgence of figurative language, her stunningly broad range of allusions—in short, the overarching presence of her prose line—defines her. During a spring flood, for instance, she recalls how "downstairs the flood bumped and fumbled like a blind man in a strange house, but outside it hissed and trickled, like the pressure of water against your eardrums, and like the sounds you hear in the moment before you faint" (pp. 65–66)—it is a flood, yes, of metaphors, to the point of parody, that abandons as irrelevant the authentic experience

itself. Ruth's life, harrowing and disturbing, is transformed by the alchemic energy of her imagination into a self-sufficient, self-justifying prose that glitters, distracts, delights. As she acknowledges, "I was always reminded of pictures, images, in places where images never were, in marble, in the blue net of veins at my wrists, in the pearled walls of seashells" (p. 90).

Hers is prose, voluptuous and indulgent, that demands to be savored. Events occur, of course, but in a gauzy, impressionistic ambience rich with freighted archetypal images (bridges, water, rain, birds, fire, darkness, forbidding woods). Ruth herself prefers the soft light of evening and the forgiving shadows of moonlight to the bald scalp of sunlight. Appropriate to a storyteller, she regularly fancies herself invisible and periodically communes with ghosts. She indulges in vivid dreams. And when she does recall events, she does not recollect (her text resists the raw confessional directness of flashbacks); rather, Ruth embroiders. She invades characters' psychologies, she invents entire scenes she did not witness, she imbeds fabricated stories, she imagines her way into alternative histories, poetic transcriptions of fabulous worlds of "what ifs" and "must haves" and "seems" that freely, joyfully refute the heavy claustrophobic impress of reality with an excessive brio that belies the disturbing tragedies of the experiences she relates. In the ghostly moonlight of a quarry, for instance, Ruth conjures the soaring stony walls of an ancient civilization. When, as part of her aunt's unconventional parenting style, she is left alone in the ruins of a lakeside cottage (she is to learn independence), Ruth imagines perished settlers and even excavates into the rotten floorboards to help rescue children she imagines trapped below. Typical of lonely children (and for that matter overtired graduate students in literature programs), Ruth taps the consolation of the imagination; she does not confront her memories so much as re-enchant their unyielding facticity into suggestive nuance.

Of course, Ruth's story would certainly have sustained a traditional flashback. She and her younger sister, Lucille, growing up in the town of Fingerbone in backwoods northern Idaho, have

lived with their grandmother since their mother drove a car off a cliff into a nearby lake (the father had abandoned the family years earlier). Ruth's family is haunted by the death years earlier of Ruth's grandfather, killed one winter night while working on a train that plunged into the forbidding waters of the same lake into which Ruth's mother would later drive her car. After five years of caring for the two young girls, the grandmother dies unexpectedly in her sleep. Two hapless great aunts try their hands at raising the young girls, followed by the arrival of an aunt, Sylvie, who, if a bit eccentric (despite being married, she has lived most of her adult life happily homeless) undertakes the responsibility of caring for the orphan girls. The aunt's unorthodox parenting techniques alienate Ruth's conventionally minded sister (who eventually goes to live with her home economics teacher). But Sylvie intrigues Ruth. Although the aunt is given to long walks in the middle of the night and to staring off in empty rooms, Ruth is drawn to her carefree joie de vivre. When confronted by the possibility of legal action to place Ruth in foster care, Sylvie and Ruth head out of town on foot (after trying unsuccessfully to burn down the house), certain that a treacherous night walk across the railroad bridge leading out of town would convince the locals that they had in fact died. The narrative is being written some seven years later, Ruth now in her early twenties.

Suicide, catastrophic accidents, shattered families, eccentric relatives with intriguing touches of madness, profound betrayals, the cutting intrusion of violent death, the grinding disappointment of dreary domesticity, the fathomless ache of abandonment, dramatic showdowns with entrenched authority figures, a high-risk flight into freedom—Ruth's story would certainly have made a conventionally enthralling narrative given its rich tangle of tragedies, its psychological intricacies, its trove of suggestive symbols, and its extravagance of latent epiphanies (in fact, that is largely the 1987 film). Yet in the hands of Ruth, the integrity of realism itself is interrogated into a supple irony. In this, as Thomas Gardner has argued, Ruth's narrative is dominated by the fragile resilience and transformative energy of

Emily Dickinson (Ruth recites "I Heard a Fly Buzz" in school). Dickinson, in her most wounded moments, celebrates the capacity of the imagination to console her, how the imagination, with its apparently narrow hands, nevertheless encompasses the wide spread of entire interior universes of its own fashioning. Ruth at every turn celebrates the imagined, not the real (when Ruth and Sylvie try unsuccessfully to burn down her house, Ruth uses as first kindling stacks of nonfiction—almanacs, Sears catalogs, newspapers, National Geographic magazines, even telephone books). Wounded by loss and abandonment, Ruth has been deprived of the horizon, denied the expectations typical of adolescents (confronted by the principal concerned over the drift of Ruth's schooling, Ruth cannot think of anything that matters to her); unavailable to perspective, she is sustained by her own imagination.

Such interior life is not for everyone. Ruth, as narrative authority, offers in her sister Lucille a necessary counterargument, a striking alternative. Lucille is fiercely (and unimaginatively) bound to the immediate—she frets about school (she is appalled when she is accused, wrongly, of cheating); with robotic precision, she plays compositions (never her own) on the parlor piano; if her sister treasures moonlight and shadows, Lucille is given to flipping on harsh overhead lights; she cut dresses from patterns; she tends her cat with careful routine; she collects postage stamps; she wants to know specifics about her dead mother, unlike Ruth who conjures the mother in dreams and invented scenarios. With ruthless dedication to routine, Lucille follows a regimen of self-improvement that includes styling her hair after ads in magazines, doing her nails, losing weight, touching her toes every morning, and always abiding by (literally) a list of etiquette rules she compiles from (nonfiction) self-help books; she dreams, yes, but of setting up a conventional household in faraway Boston. Lucille lacks imagination. Unsure what pinking shears are, Lucille consults the family's ancient dictionary and there finds dried flowers her grandfather had evidently placed in the book decades earlier; unmoved, Lucille unthinkingly

crushes them into dusty powder, at which a stunned Ruth, immediately engaged of course by the talismanic quality of the dead flowers, angrily slaps her.

With Ruth, then, we are less in the uneasy hands of a wounded woman-child now making her way through life after a traumatic childhood and more in the safe keep of a gifted storyteller, a confident embroiderer (we recall her grandfather, who, before heading west, had been a promising artist who painted extravagant flourishes on dreary household furniture, cherubs and turbaned horsemen, that even after coats of paint were applied over the years, would resurface, insisting on their own integrity, their own resilience). Like the Monopoly game that Sylvie and the girls play on the second floor of their house during the fiercest night of the spring flood that devastates the town and even floods the ground floor of their home, Ruth's narrative is a precious and entirely symbolic environment, a contentment of design, a privileged place apart. Imagination becomes the vested energy of extravagant truancy (after Sylvie's arrival, Ruth takes to playing hooky, missing nearly half the school year). Ruth transforms her memories, shoddy and sorry, into exquisitely rendered images freighted with the feel of importance; marvelously ambiguous scenes; supple prose; and supremely the gorgeous sheen of figurative language. "All this is fact," she complains. "Fact explains nothing" (p. 217). Like that long-ago refuge beneath the ironing board, her narrative, another protective space she inhabits, is at once fragile and resilient.

In this, the reader is actually empowered to participate in an imaginative interaction, to take Ruth's freighted images and the plethora of complex psychologies and ambiguous actions and to construct explications that are themselves exertions of our imagination. Like a schoolroom round of "Row, Row, Row Your Boat" in staggered simultaneity, we keep the round going by adding our voice, our reading; we venture into the symbolic environment of Ruth's story—made-up people doing made-up things in a made-up place—and extract from that artfully constructed chaos the satisfying argument of a consistent reading, our own under-the-ironing-board shelter of order and design. Not surprisingly, *Housekeeping* has generated readings that collide in giddy contradiction—this is a Thelma-and-Louise *ur*-feminist text that celebrates the bonding between two empowered women while marginalizing the place of men, indeed banishing them entirely (Anne-Marie Mallon; Maureen Ryan); this is a coming-of-age text in which an inventive child full of sorrow, like Huck Finn and Holden Caulfield, must find a way ultimately to the freedom of identity apart from the tender shackles of conventionality (Martha Ravits; Maggie Galehouse); this is an arch-tragedy that explores, as every tragedy since Aeschylus, the matrix of a doomed family and the effects of violent death and madness (Christine Caver; Katy Ryan); this is an edgy postmodern deconstruction of the American home that sees such a traditional nurturing space as a cage and that celebrates the exhilarating freedom of life on the unmarked road (Jacqui Smyth; William Burke). We relish this imaginative play of textual engagement that transforms the materials of Ruth's text into a richness of themes and symbols. The elusive text refuses to confirm any single reading, each "definitive" take presuming later amendment, an unscripted choreography of readings sustained now across more than thirty years.

This celebration of the imagination is clearest in the novel's closing, when the vulnerable outcast Ruth at last spreads wide her narrow hands and transforms into a storyteller. Bold, grasping, at once solitary and privileged, she spins an extravagance of endings for her narrative, upending any expectations of reassuring tidiness, indeed invalidating our conservative need to know what is "real." She imagines multiple ways her story might end. "For need," as she confesses, "can blossom into all the compensations it requires. To crave and to have are as like as a thing and its shadow" (p. 152). We thus depart Ruth engaged not so much by as within her imaginative energy—like that child long ago contentedly tending her castle keep draped by fragrant curtains. Ruth departs her story (appropriately) a homeless drifter who exists only within the stories she tells—she admits how she

gets temporary work in truck stops and there listens to strangers tell stories, always partial, always open-ended; she is thus a connoisseur of narrating itself rather than narrative. She closes imagining a reunion with her sister, imagining Lucille's conventional Boston home—we leave her there, in effect under the ironing board, her lyrical fictions the house she keeps, a much fairer house than prose.

But something disturbs. Inevitably, for a writer whose vision is so rigorously engaged by the trajectory of the Christian sensibility, this essentially centripetal vision must collapse of its own irony. Robinson understands that the constructions of the imagination cannot sustain: we recall Ruth's attempts to fashion a snowwoman and the heartbreaking meltdown of each version, form unable to sustain the grand design of its own brave conception. Thus, taken (as it inevitably must be) with Robinson's later narratives, *Housekeeping* emerges as a cautionary tale; later arguments will make ironic the serious busyness of Ruth's imagination. Retreat is elegant surrender; the material world, for Robinson the very manifestation into form of the divine energy of God's creation, must be engaged. It is a measure of the distance between her character and Robinson, a practicing Congregationalist lay preacher, that in Ruth's account of Christ's passion, the resurrection itself becomes a convincing fantasy constructed by apostles who felt so keenly the loss of Christ that they gratefully imagined him returned. Transformation is clearly not enough. It is time, Robinson will argue, to emerge from under the ironing board.

GILEAD: *NARRATIVE OF TRANSFIGURATION*

If Ruth Stone's earliest memory, that safe retreat beneath her grandmother's ironing board, is revealing, surely Reverend John Ames's earliest memory is similarly telling: as a boy on his Iowa farm, he baptized a litter of dusty, scraggly barn kittens in the creek, his way of making sacramental what so amazed him, the warm feel of each kitten's brow, that mysterious surge of life itself. If Ruth's relish of her protective cloister sets in motion her evolution into a storyteller, surely

John Ames's eccentric baptism foretells his own long career in the ministry, tending to the immediate world with love and care. If *Housekeeping* is defiantly centripetal, *Gilead* is radiantly centrifugal. Unlike Ruth, who writes without the presumption of an audience—indeed we eavesdrop on her embroidered fictions, steal into her hermetically sealed fiction-world, crowd with her under her ironing board—John Ames uses language to reach outward. He has been a Congregationalist minister for more than a half century. In that time he has gathered boxes of his sermons, written word for word (he estimates they are the equivalent of 250 books)—language that creates, literally, a community, a congregation (a sermon, he says, is one side of a "passionate conversation" [p. 45]).

Gilead is itself an epistolary novel; Ames writes a sumptuous two-hundred-plus-page letter to his seven-year-old son. At seventy-six, Ames knows he is dying—he has angina pectoris and every morning could be his last. He is determined to leave behind a testimonial—as much fatherly wisdom as family history—for a son he will never watch grow up. In this bittersweet endeavor, Ames confronts (and interprets) the vexing and imperfect world of love and death that Ruth in her fabulations so deftly abandons. His is a narrative very much about family, friendships, betrayals and disappointments, jealousies and grudges, and the steady drag of death. And it is as well informed by Ames's historic perspective, which ranges from the Civil War to the racial tensions in the segregated South of his own era, the mid-1950s. It is, in short, a narrative engaged in the immediate. In the intimate persuasion of second-person (inevitably felt by the reader), Ames seeks to give his young son the wisdom to embrace this world. His narrative elegantly celebrates an immersion in the immediate with an intimacy of detail that Ruth, with all her elaborate metaphors and sly allusions, never provokes. As Ames admits, "This is an interesting planet. It deserves all the attention you can give it" (p. 28). It is tempting, of course, to import biography—after all, during Robinson's nearly twenty-year hiatus from fiction writing, she committed her considerable energies to the

world that so commands Ames's attention: she discovered the joys of teaching; she raised two sons; she became embroiled in the Sellafield catastrophe; she became passionately engaged in the liturgical life of her church. She had in short evolved from being a graduate student, that fledgling writer so fascinated by the coaxing pull of the imagination, the sturdy structures of narrative, and the stunning impress of language.

Unlike Ruth, Ames has a horizontal sensibility, justified by an unshakeable piety. Ames is certain that the material universe, a manifestation of a benevolent creative energy, shimmers with an illuminating grace most do not begin to suspect (he writes often of the intoxicating strangeness of ordinary light—sunlight, moonlight, starlight). "Each morning I'm like Adam waking up in Eden, amazed at the cleverness of my hands and at the brilliance pouring into my mind through my eyes" (pp. 66–67). Ruth, of course, never taps that exaltation. Death imminent, Ames lingers over ordinary moments that casually scalp his senses—the scent of honeysuckle, his cat asleep in his lap, waltz music on the parlor radio, the shimmer of a lawn sprinkler, the sound of trees at night, the taste of syrupy pancakes or peanut butter and apple butter on raisin bread, his son's tousled hair in the morning. "I have lived my life on the prairie and a line of oak trees can still astonish me" (p. 57). Indeed, when, at twelve, he accompanies his father to Kansas to visit the grave of his grandfather, at the tearful moment when his father prays over the grave of a father from whom he had been profoundly estranged, a young and very distracted Ames finds his eyes wandering skyward to take in the "wonderful light" (p. 14) of the luscious summer full moon that, to his eye, is as sumptuous and as generous as the sun itself.

If the lonely autonomy of Emily Dickinson sustains *Housekeeping, Gilead* is animated by the radiant wonder of Thoreau, Emerson, and Walt Whitman, a gravitas at once solemn and giddy, a vision not of transformation but rather of transfiguration, a redemptive vision in which the organic universe itself, rightly regarded, is shot through with the glint of grace itself. Laura E. Tanner argues that it is exactly the hard press of

mortality that makes Ames's horizontal sensibility so deeply, so keenly persuasive. Clearly Ames brings to his keen alertness to the absolute pleasures of the world all around him his studied Christianity—withdraw the elegant hand of the creator and Ames's lyrical celebrations of pancakes and sunlight are a gaudy, empty hedonism, the contented atheism of his brother, Edward, a philosophy professor at the University of Kansas. As he closes his letter to his son, Ames rhapsodizes on the beauty of the earth, an ember that the Lord breathes into radiance, "more beauty than our eyes can bear" (p. 246). He perceives his approaching burial into the heart of the prairie as a "last wild gesture of love" (p. 247). Like Whitman at his brashest, Ames cannot live indifferently in the physical world, cannot inhabit the present complacently; perception stuns. Like Whitman, Ames is part mystic, part pagan, part Christian, part naturalist. As he listens one night to a Cubs game on his radio (he loves baseball), Ames has an epiphanic moment in which he realizes with stunning simplicity that the full moon, "icy white in a blue sky" (p. 45), and the Earth were at that very moment spinning in a stunning planetary choreography. Ames later recalls going with his father to a burned church to help the devastated parishioners and how, even as the distraught congregation prepared to raze the blackened walls of their beloved church, the father had salvaged biscuits from the smoldering ruins and had fed the ashy bread to Ames—there amid the ashes, amid the unpromising stuff of the immediate, we find what sustains.

But immersion in the sensory is not sufficient to the reach of Ames's vision (nor Robinson's). The human enterprise, the daily engagement with other people, is part of the horizontal vision that Reverend Ames explores. Unlike Ruth, Ames grants integrity to the imperfect, inelegant constructions of family and friendships (the narrative is rife with references to both the Civil War and to the epical Hatfield and McCoy feud). But Ames refuses to yield to the centripetal logic of Ruth. Rather than withdraw from sorrow, Ames cannot abide even the idea that once he attains his eternity his earthly grief must be forgotten. "And I can't believe that, when we

have all been changed and put on incorruptibility, we will forget our fantastic condition of mortality and impermanence ... that meant the whole world to us" (p. 57). If *Housekeeping* explores the first-person singular, the narrow joy that a writer feels in manipulating the cutting disappointments and brutal traumas of experience into the delightful design of sentences and the seductive symmetry of plot, *Gilead* extols the first-person plural, the seeking of community, the complicated dynamics of family and friendship. Here bindings that are so absolutely sundered in *Housekeeping* maintain their suasion; families struggle against the pressure to give way to estrangement; no one concedes to the dark logic of suicide. Indeed the premise behind the entire narrative is to bridge that most absolute sundering that overwhelms Ruth: a dead parent and a surviving child.

Ames's recollections reveal the heartbreaking realities, the joys and the tragedies inevitable when we engage one with the other. Ames's first wife, Louisa, died shortly after giving birth to their daughter, who died soon after. Ames remarried, years later, to a woman nearly thirty years his junior, Lila. Their child, the son to whom he writes his letter, fulfills Ames's deepest prayers—the old man delights in the child. It is bittersweet, of course; Ames writes as a way to say goodbye to a son who will remember little of him. Such endearing love is further countered by the narrative Ames tells of his own father and his long estrangement from Ames's grandfather, both ministers, over the appropriate mission of a preacher. As a child growing up in Maine, the grandfather had had a powerful vision of Christ in chains, manacles cutting both wrists, that had inspired him to a life of uncompromising activism. He had become a charismatic abolitionist (he had headed to Kansas to help John Brown carry out raids on Southern sympathizers and later served as a chaplain in the Union Army, losing one eye); returning to his ministry, in incendiary sermons (like a man "everlastingly struck by lightning" [p. 49]), he had incited his congregation to embrace the Union cause. When Ames's father returns from service in World War I, however, he seeks the contemplative quiet of a

Quaker meetinghouse near Gilead, unable to face his own half-filled church, its congregation reduced to orphans and widows. Ames's father becomes a pacifist and dismisses the grandfather's ministry as showy and wrongheaded and the vision of the manacled Jesus as improbable. When the grandfather, now past eighty, comes to Gilead to attend one of the father's services, he walks out minutes into the sermon, disturbed by the lack of conviction. Without vision, he says in a note he leaves, the people perish. Father and son never speak again.

That difficult father-son chasm, resolved only in the father's pilgrimage to Kansas to find the grandfather's forgotten grave long after his death, is paralleled by the narrative Ames relates of his longtime friend and neighbor, the Reverend Robert Boughton, and his ne'er-do-well son Jack. Twenty years earlier, after a troubling adolescence of mischief that had steadily escalated into reckless criminal behavior, Jack had bolted Gilead after getting a young girl from a poor family outside of town pregnant. The daughter born of that union died at the age of three from neglect, specifically a perfectly treatable foot infection. For twenty years Jack had not returned to Gilead, had not inquired about his child, had not even returned for his own mother's funeral. Jack's unexpected return to Gilead centers much of Ames's narrative present. Ames knows nothing of the intervening years—yet he must contend with the resurgence of his dislike of Jack. Jack's father is Ames's oldest friend; indeed Ames was the boy's godfather, the boy had been named after him. Yet for years young Jack had tormented Ames out of a sly and lonely meanness—nuisance pranks like coating his porch with molasses to attract swarms of ants, setting fire to his mailbox, hurling rocks through his study windows, stealing his reading glasses, and even stealing a framed photo of Ames's dead wife. To Ames, young Jack appeared to be a striking exception to his belief in the essential goodness of God's creations—uncomplicated by a moral sense, destined to be estranged from God, from family, from others.

As such, Jack is for the dying Ames his last and greatest trial. Ames cannot forgive how

lightly Jack squandered the miracle of his own child, how he had abandoned his unborn daughter. When Jack now visits Ames, they engage in a contentious debate over the Christian doctrine of predestination: Jack cynically argues that some people are born deficient, that character improvement cannot be squared with an omnipotent God who, apparently for his own amusement, fashions some creatures unavailable to grace, "intentionally and irretrievably consigned to perdition" (p. 150). With grinning skepticism and cagey Mephistophelean charm, Jack tempts Ames to concede that the drama of salvation cannot be squared with the logic of predestination—frustrated, Ames can say only that God's ways are beyond our understanding. But that doctrinal dispute pales next to Ames's growing jealousy, his certainty that the much-younger and fetchingly charismatic Jack intends to move in on Lila and in turn become the stepfather of his son, a calamitous possibility in Ames's eyes. He watches with growing alarm as Jack and his son bond: they talk in his yard, take looping walks, play catch. While he watches his wife and the grinning Jack sitting next to each other in church like a couple, he goes off-text (a radical departure for him) and delivers a caustic impromptu sermon on Old Testament offspring victimized by cruel parents who rejected them, a message not too subtly directed against the errant Jack and his abandonment of his daughter. Jack brings out the worst in Ames. Ames cannot contain his jealousy, his paranoia, his suspicions. His graceful movement toward a Christian death falters. Desperate, he admits, "I don't want to be old. And I certainly don't want to be dead" (p. 141).

But in Ames's closing days, he realizes the wrongheadedness of his envy of the young man, and it is this movement toward compassion, this vision of transfiguration, that marks Ames as a heroic presence in this centrifugal narrative. As Jack prepares once again to leave Gilead, he admits to Ames why he returned in the first place, confesses what he cannot bring himself to tell his own father: that he has maintained an eight-year relationship with a black woman, Della, a schoolteacher he met in St. Louis; that they have a child, a son; and that her family long objected

to the relationship. (Although such relationships were still illegal in most states, Della's father, himself a minister, objected more to Jack's atheism.) Jack tells Ames how they had attempted to set up house in St. Louis but had run afoul of antimiscegenation laws and that, since then, Della and their child had relocated to Memphis—he had written to her often but had received no reply. Jack's trip to Gilead, he admits to a stunned Ames, had been to test the possibility of bringing his family there. That conversation, however, ends disastrously—Jack says he has come to Ames because, as a man in a scandalous marriage himself (Ames is nearly thirty years older than Lila), he might sympathize. The remark cuts Ames. When Jack admits he fears telling his father about the child, Ames returns fire: he devastates Jack by remarking how much the father had taken to the daughter Jack had abandoned. Ames then refuses any support in Jack's endeavor to bring his family to Gilead.

But Ames is tormented. Two days later, Ames sees Jack, carrying a battered suitcase, headed for the bus station. Jack tells Ames that he has decided to leave Gilead without telling his father about his wife and child, indeed without even saying goodbye even though he is sure that his father's death is imminent, and he asks Ames to say goodbye for him. The goodbye between Ames and Jack is at once heartbreaking and inspiring—ready now to embrace the largest implications of the horizontal experience, ready at last for compassion, Ames sets aside his pettiness and evidences genuine sympathy. He gives Jack money for the trip to Memphis, but far more significantly, he offers him a pastoral blessing, asks the Lord to grant the troubled man-child some measure of peace. When Ames then visits Boughton, he finds his ailing friend sound asleep. To wake the old man with news of such dimension would be to grieve beyond consolation a dying friend. Ames deftly manages to keep his word to Jack and still not upset the father. He whispers in his ear, "I blessed that boy of yours for you. I still feel the weight of his brow on my hand.... I love him as much as you meant me to. So certain of your prayers are finally answered, old fellow. And mine too, mine too" (p. 244).

Thus, Ames puts the finishing touches on his last and greatest sermon, the narrative of his own long road to peace with the reach of the heart, offered to his own son as a testimony of the enduring power and promise of the real world. It is not merely the syrupy taste of flapjacks or the careless play of morning light on laundry drying on the line—it is the heartbreaking work of embracing others. Ames now readies for death. His long letter to his son closes with a rhapsody on the prairie's stunning wonder, and then, with elegant simplicity, Ames exits his letter. "I'll pray," he writes, "and then I'll sleep" (p. 247). Unlike Ruth's narrative, which resists endings and implodes into a rich embarrassment of storylines, a freewheeling, giddy open-endedness, Ames's letter delights in its own austere ending, a mighty peroration to the beauty of the world and then a settling into tranquil death.

HOME: NARRATIVE OF TRANSCENDENCE

Like Ruth Stone, like John Ames, Glory Boughton can be defined by her earliest recollection—at four, she wept for three days over the death of a dog. A dog on a radio show.

Too young to understand the pretense of the staged production, Glory takes it very much to her tender heart; she is devastated by the impress of death visited so casually, so completely on a helpless animal. Glory is capable, even at four, of the empathy and compassion Ames counsels his son to embrace, but it is extended with a largesse that at once inspires and, as is the case with every heroic Christian in this post-postmodern era, borders on parody (the "dog" is, after all, just a sound effect). In this, Glory offers a perception far different from that of Ames—or Ruth. Glory is the character toward which Robinson had been journeying since *Housekeeping*. Although Robinson, nearing seventy, is clearly a writer very much at her peak, *Home* could serve as a fitting capstone. Ruth celebrated how we invent splendid aesthetic artifacts, weave dense and gorgeous sentences and spin enthralling stories; John Ames reminded us to risk the emotional mayhem of the heart and to open our senses to the onrush of the immediate—but Glory

Boughton reveals the difficult responsibilities of joyful sacrifice and promiscuous compassion that are the core of the Christian vision. After all, even as Reverend Ames brings his epistle to its all too fitting close, we suspect a rigged game as the good pastor, just shy of his own death, embraces his bitterest enemy. Robinson, herself a seasoned preacher, surely understood how a contemporary reader might be wary. How better to confront her age of stubborn cynicism than to return to the very same events that Reverend Ames chronicles, revisit the very events that step by step cleared the way for his transfigurative moment—but this time reveal how, with stunning indifference to the significance of their actions, Christians refuse the argument of their own wisdom literature. Robinson returns to Gilead, returns to the Ames-Boughton narrative, returns to the very weeks covered in *Gilead*—but shifts her attention to the Boughton house, where the template of the prodigal son parable ultimately founders, where the heart ends bitter, frustrated, denied.

Rather than despair over how resolutely Christians refuse to act Christianly, however, even as the Boughton father and son collapse into pettiness and misunderstanding, Robinson introduces her most complex character to date, the spinster Glory Boughton. Amid the noisy dramatics and distracting busyness as the unforgiving father and the black-sheep son move to stalemate, Glory introduces in unassuming counterargument a Christian sensibility, rare but nevertheless holding firm in the fragile close of Christianity's second millennium. That Glory refuses to become parody to us, that she maintains both the integrity of her humanity and the implications of her Christianity, makes her Robinson's most intriguing—and least accessible—character. Indeed for the first time, Robinson uses third-person narration—unlike Ruth, unlike John Ames, we are never given the intimacy implicit in first-person narrations. Rather we must approach Glory from a distance. But unlike those cartoon cutouts in traditional parables whose moral heroics are so improbable that we easily dismiss the lessons they teach, Glory struggles, she stumbles, she despairs, she

agonizes, she sins, she aspires; in short, she leaves us no reason not to follow her example. She is not merely a Christian, she is Christian.

Alone of her eight siblings, it is the youngest, Glory, who returns to Gilead to tend the aging father, a crabby Lear-like intemperate who never acknowledges the enormity of the sacrifice of the only child who loves him. Glory welcomes Jack, the brother she barely knows, the cynic who derides her Christian sensibility; Glory caters to him (she cooks great heaping breakfasts, she cuts his hair and shaves him to encourage his rehabilitation efforts, she pulls a painful splinter from his hand, she tidies his room), she frets over his melancholia and (despite her own disastrous five-year engagement) counsels him with generous compassion as he gradually confides in her about Della and his son. And when in despair over his estrangement from his family, when he goes on a drunken bender out in the barn, Glory searches out the disheveled Jack, passed out on the front seat of the DeSoto that he keeps in the barn, and cleans him up so that their father will never suspect the dark truth about the son upon whom he dotes. Her own lacerated heart struggling against the easy concession to bitterness and self-pity—her life has been a crushing cycle of expectation and disappointment—Glory affirms what neither Ruth nor John Ames can, a transcendent vision larger than the self, a vision vertical rather than horizontal. In Gilead, Glory is at home, yes, but not home. She is the Christian pilgrim making her way to promised glory, the greater home, and she has far to go (when the family plays Monopoly, she always selects the shoe).

In revisiting the storyline of *Gilead, Home* begins shortly before Jack Boughton returns. We first meet the Boughtons, father and daughter. Reverend Robert Boughton, a Presbyterian minister and longtime friend (and theological debater) of John Ames, is slipping into his dotage and feeling the cold approach of death. And Glory, nearly forty, has returned home after thirteen years teaching English in Minneapolis, in part to recover from a catastrophic engagement (the man turned out to be married). She has assumed the thankless work of caring for the

mercurial father. Father and daughter together await Jack's return after more than twenty years. Glory is anxious—she was only sixteen when her wastrel brother left town, abandoning the responsibilities for the impoverished girl who carried his child. When Jack finally arrives, he is days late and predictably hungover. It is the growing tension, the strained politeness, the simmering grudges between father and son that command the narrative center. Jack struggles to conform to the expectations of his presumed reclamation as prodigal son (ironically, Jack throws himself into rehabbing the family's ancient DeSoto—Robinson reminding us how that rehab is far easier than Jack's). The very awkwardness of the effort is underscored by the secondhand suit Jack wears—it smells of the gasoline he uses in an effort to dry clean it.

Of course, we want Jack redeemed—we recognize the template. Like Esau, like Joseph, like the Prodigal Son, the wayward Jack attempts to find his way to forgiveness, to reconcile with a dying, if irascible, father. Now at midlife, Jack wrestles with existential questions of his life's direction and of his estrangement from God; he struggles with guilt over abandoning his child. He tells Glory how he had spiraled into alcohol abuse and had spent time in jail for theft. We want—even expect—the largesse of forgiveness, the prodigal to be reclaimed, the family unsundered if for no other reason than the father, a minister nearing his own death, imperils his soul should he die with such resentments unreconciled; after all, as he tells Teddy, Jack's brother, a successful chiropractor who visits during Jack's stay, family is all about kindness, acceptance, and support. Despite Reverend Boughton's teary welcome of Jack, however, the father cannot find his way to acceptance, much less forgiveness. Reverend Boughton cannot get past his son's precipitous fall from promise, his long years on skid row, and, most problematic, his decades-long estrangement from his faith, his complex struggle with doubt. Jack tries to placate the father. He favors the old man with hymn requests at the parlor piano. He attends church services. When he does succumb to his alcoholism and drinks himself into a stupor in the barn, he is

careful before he gets too intoxicated to stuff rolled socks into the DeSoto's exhaust pipe, disabling the car and preventing the possibility that he might hurt someone by driving recklessly. But encouraged by Teddy to let the father die happy by lying to him and saying he has returned to his faith, Jack cannot. His honesty infuriates the father; Jack, he rages, has brought only grief and sorrow to him.

But the schism between father and son is more troubling than discontent over the past. Unaware of Jack's common-law marriage to an African American woman and Jack's biracial son (Boughton's grandson) now living in Memphis, unaware that Jack has returned to Gilead to see whether he might bring his family there to live, the Reverend Boughton, an Eisenhower conservative, reveals a disturbing bigotry as he watches on his tiny black-and-white Philco news coverage of the violence in southern schools over desegregation. Boughton arrogantly dismisses the discrimination under which blacks have suffered, certain that "they" will first have to improve themselves if they want to be accepted. Rioting, he insists, simply provokes additional violence. Certain of the hypocrisy of his father's unexamined racism, Jack never tells his father about his family. Rather, he decides to leave just as his siblings gather to be with the father when he dies. When Jack goes to say goodbye to the father, when he extends his hand, the old man refuses the gesture, cradles his hand in his own lap. "Tired of it," he snaps, and turns away (p. 317). The prodigal son parable skewed, Jack, suitcase in hand, returns to exile.

Amid the failings of the intractable father and errant son and their determined resistance to the argument of the Christianity they so rigorously (and ironically) debate, Glory Boughton with unassuming modesty embodies that transcendent vision. Faith is part of what she is—she wanted to be a minister, an opportunity denied women at the time; now, she offers grace before meals; she prays, supplicant-like, on her knees; she reads the Bible daily on the sun porch just to feel the "thrilling quiet" (p. 118) of such immediacy, the uncluttered contact of sponsorship. Engaged for five years to a cad who was already

married, who borrowed money from her, and who even visited Gilead with her twice as her fiancé, Glory has not soured into ugly bitterness—without rancor, she recalls tossing one by one his 452 love letters into the sewer in Minneapolis. Rather, with stoic calm, she sees the powerful lure of love and its illusions. Just days after he returns, when Jack plays on the family's piano "Smoke Gets in Your Eyes," Glory disparages the song, its lyrics reminding her how willfully blind are those who fall under the spell of love. Approaching forty, she accepts she will never have a husband, a baby, a home—"Ah, well," she says (p. 102). She prays not for God's help but for the strength to fulfill her lot. Her patience with her father as he edges toward death, the grind of commonplace sacrifice that would easily oppress other women of her age, her promise, her education (a master's in literature) exemplifies a complicated selflessness. She accepts that once the father is dead, she will become the kindly spinster aunt maintaining the family home for holiday visits from brothers and sisters blessed with their children and then grandchildren. Without complaint, she is imprisoned by her father and brother's rancorous civil war (she is reading MacKinlay Kantor's best seller *Andersonville,* an account of the horrific conditions in the infamous Confederate prisoner of war camp). When Jack, the glib atheist, and the Reverend Boughton, the eloquent hypocrite, dissect Christian tenets with fervor, Glory cannot tolerate the heated exchange. Five minutes into their arguments over the predestination, Glory excuses herself, heads to the parlor, and turns on the radio (a classical music station plays the *William Tell Overture,* recalling yet another father/son showdown). Glory admits that, although a palpable reality for her, the soul defies attempts to explicate it into clarity.

Rather Glory embodies the complicated Christian protocol of the Golden Rule. She is the peacemaker, so generously gifted with compassion that she is much derided for her tears that spill with generous ease. We learn that years earlier, after Jack had abandoned the woman who was carrying his child, it was Glory who reached out to the poor family after the child was born.

Glory had even invited the mother and her baby to the house to pick apples and bake a pie, to feel part of the family. The outreach does not work—the baby gets fussy and Glory cannot quiet her, kisses her only to have the baby reject her. But Glory never abandons her faith in reconciliation. It is Glory who masterminds the reconciliation between her father and Reverend Ames when they feud over Ames's sermon directed specifically at Jack. It is Glory who advises a depressed Jack to circumvent Della's family entirely (he is sure they intercept his letters and return them unopened to him) and send a letter through a friend of hers in Memphis (the plan works—although Della and her son show up in Gilead just two days after a despairing Jack had departed). And after the prodigal son parable so clumsily deconstructs into irony, we are given in rich counterplay Glory's closing vision, a magnificent exertion of her quiet Christian conviction: a radiant vision of a future moment when Jack's grown son will return to Gilead, a homecoming that would manifest the steady work of God amid the tangled miseries of people's lives. For Glory, that moment would be the summa of her Christian faith, the moment her "entire life ha[d] come down to" (p. 325). Glory's Christian strength resists the catastrophic surrender to pessimism. We close with her moving, unironic testimony, "The Lord is wonderful" (p. 325). That unassuming turn upward is at once companion, counterpoint, and corrective to Robinson's earlier works in which Ruth Stone and John Ames had, from her overarching Christian vision, played themselves into dead ends.

Where does that leave Robinson's hip post-postmodern reader? Uneasy over the implications of joyful dependency explicit in the Christian protocol; estranged from a creator God after three centuries of watching his magnificent cosmos methodically measured out into something called a universe; uncomfortable, given our intransigent egoism, with the humbling implications of judgment at the heart of the drama of salvation, readers want to find Glory, her joy, and that closing transcendent affirmation ironic. But in this shadowy world of moral cowardice, lapsed virtue, and easy hypocrisy, Glory emerges as an entirely convincing exemplum of what Christianity might produce. It is Glory's perception—and Robinson's wisdom—that sorrow and guilt are themselves acts of revelation, that the act of sin and the burden of suffering are ultimately the same. In the end, Glory finds her way to Christian transcendence, a compassion that might stand as Robinson's unifying theme. In a novel so centered on the yearning for home, the need for the stability and comfort of family and roots, the sanctuary of the familiar, Glory, in the end, knows that home is not for here. Such riches await once this plane of experience has been transcended. "[God] lets us wander so we will know what it means to come home" (p. 102).

CONCLUSION

When, shortly after he arrives, Jack Boughton returns to the farmhouse from a long walk carrying a bundle of rare (and delectable) tiny morel mushrooms, Glory begs to know where he had found such treasures. Initially he teases her and refuses to say. Shortly before he departs, however, he presents her a carefully labeled map drawn meticulously to scale and marked with a bold X and the word "morels" showing where in the woods the mushrooms could be found. But Glory notices that, despite the map's detailing, Jack had neglected to indicate exactly which woods these were, making the map useless. Treasure, as she learns again and again, is not for here, not for now. With an inscrutable smile, before turning her attention to the chicken and dumplings she is preparing for dinner, Glory promises that she will frame the pretty map, content with its tantalizing promise of riches, at peace with anticipation and existence on the keen edge of expectation, the life, in short, of the pilgrim Christian. Jack responds, "You're a good soul, Glory" (p. 270), confirming what we had already suspected—from the centripetal vision of *Housekeeping* to the centrifugal energy of *Gilead*, inward to outward, it is Glory's upward vision that gives Robinson's work, like the classic expressions of the Christian temperament since Dante, its hard shine, its radiant energy, and its deepest consolation.

Selected Bibliography

WORKS OF MARILYNNE ROBINSON

NOVELS

Housekeeping. New York: Farrar, Straus and Giroux, 1980. (Page numbers in the text refer to the 1981 paperback edition published by Farrar, Straus and Giroux.)

Gilead. New York: Farrar, Straus and Giroux 2004.

Home. New York: Farrar, Straus and Giroux, 2008. (Page numbers in the text refer to the 2009 paperback edition published by Farrar, Straus and Giroux.)

NONFICTION

Mother Country: Britain, the Nuclear State and Nuclear Pollution. New York: Farrar, Straus and Giroux, 1989.

The Death of Adam: Essays on Modern Thought. Boston: Houghton Mifflin, 1998.

CRITICAL STUDIES AND INTERVIEWS

"The Art of Fiction Number 198: An Interview with Marilynne Robinson." *Paris Review* 186 (fall 2008). Available online (http://www.theparisreview.org/viewmedia.php/prmMID/5863).

Burke, William M. "Border Crossings in Marilynne Robinson's *Housekeeping*." *Modern Fiction Studies* 37, no. 4: 716–724 (1991).

Caver, Christine. "Nothing Left to Lose: *Housekeeping*'s Strange Freedoms." *American Literature* 68, no. 1: 111–137 (1996).

Galehouse, Maggie. "Their Own Private Idaho: Transience in Marilynne Robinson's *Housekeeping*." *Contemporary Literature* 41, no. 1: 117–137 (2000).

Gardner, Thomas. "Enlarging Loneliness: Marilynne Robinson's *Housekeeping* as a Reading of Emily Dickinson." *Emily Dickinson Journal* 10, no. 1: 9–33 (2001).

Mallon, Anne-Marie. "Sojourning Women: Homelessness and Transcendence in *Housekeeping*." *Critique* 30, no. 2: 95–105 (1989).

Ravits, Martha. "Extending the American Range: Marilynne Robinson's *Housekeeping*." *American Literature* 61, no. 4: 644–666 (1989).

Ryan, Katy. "Horizons of Grace: Marilynne Robinson and Simone Weil." *Philosophy and Literature* 29, no. 2: 349–364 (2005).

Ryan, Maureen. "Marilynne Robinson's *Housekeeping*: The Subversive Narrative and the New American Eve." *South Atlantic Review* 56, no. 1 (1991): 79–86.

Smyth, Jacqui. "Sheltered Vagrancy in Marilynne Robinson's *Housekeeping*." *Critique* 40, no. 3: 281–291 (1999).

Tanner, Laura E. "'Looking Back from the Grave': Sensory Perception and the Anticipation of Absence in Marilynne Robinson's *Gilead*." *Contemporary Literature* 48, no. 2: 227–252 (2007).

GILBERT SORRENTINO

(1929—2006)

John Domini

EVEN IN HIS posthumous work, Gilbert Sorrentino went his own way. The author died on May 18, 2006, and *The Abyss of Human Illusion* appeared almost four years later, capping his output at twenty novels. The math is complicated, however, because right through the final drafts of *Abyss,* Sorrentino went on rejiggering what constitutes a novel. Thus his 2010 title isn't some hash of materials left behind, like the posthumous work of Ernest Hemingway. *Abyss* opens with a "Note" by the author's son Chris, himself a novelist (*Sound on Sound,* 1995; *Trance,* 2005), in which he admits to minor emendations—but insists that the work was finished, its final adjustments made by hand. This argument is then borne out by the text, which everywhere bears the mark of a born iconoclast.

Abyss is a novel without narrative, fifty prose shards designated by Roman numerals and lacking in consistent characters or sequences of events. Form rather than content generates momentum. Each section is a bit longer than the previous (an organizing principle undetectable in the pieces that had appeared three years earlier, in the magazine *Golden Handcuffs*). *Abyss* begins in flash-fiction and ends in three- or four-page summaries of a relationship, if not an entire life. Indeed the latter selections, in a conventional novel, might serve as digressions establishing background. The material is rooted in ordinary experience, mostly New York City experience, as lived in the middle twentieth century. The book begins: "Mundane things, pitiful in their mundane assertiveness" (p. 1) and such stuff pervades even the dream passages. Those occur at intervals regular enough to suggest some mathematical principle at work, a structure that recalls the later Italo Calvino, but *Abyss* has none of the fantasy that enlivens *If on a Winter's Night a Traveler.*

Sorrentino's novel does include a closing "commentary," a playful device it would seem, assigning a few notes to each entry or chapter. But the few lines of "commentary" always underscore the fiction's basis in the real. Typical is the gloss on "highball": "In this instance, Canada Dry ginger ale and Seagram's 7 blended whiskey. The term 'highball' is no longer in general use" (p. 131).

The note's dry irony may fetch a smile, like much of the commentary, but it also names names. It chills the glow of nostalgia and reveals the abyss of human illusion. Several of the novel's longer entries sketch a life story that arrives at a happy ending, success of some kind, but the happiness always rings hollow. Accomplishment proves empty even in the creative arena. In two chapters *Abyss* considers artists of genuine gifts, but each suffers an awareness of fraudulence, the sinkhole of the title. This "abyss," though, is a literary reference. It is a line from Henry James, cited in the epigraph. Such light-fingered pilfering of other texts, such as a poem by Arthur Rimbaud, occurs elsewhere as well. In short, the novel makes a fitting last effort for this author: learned and alert to form, yet also joshing, yet also melancholy.

There is not a bad sentence to be found, either. *Abyss* dances Astaire-like through diverse points of view and rhetoric high and low: "He was no better, no cleverer, no more insightful than any shuffling old bastard in the street, absurdly bundled against the slightest breeze" (p. 7). Then too, this final quintessence sets its most moving anecdotes in Sorrentino's imaginative homeland. The players may move up in the world, they may transfer to Manhattan, but in their hearts they never get out of hard-knocks

Brooklyn. Sorrentino knew those hard knocks, and his brutal honesty is a form of empathy.

Then again, the kitchen-sink stuff is couched within a metafiction—given the commentary, the formal rigor—and so even Sorrentino's realism makes a jarring break from literary convention. The man dedicated his career to such breakage, really. In some cases he attacked head-on: no other serious writer generated such creative energy out of savaging the publishing industry. As early as 1971, referring to mid-Manhattan's powers-that-be in *Imaginative Qualities of Actual Things,* he sneered, "You could die laughing" (p. 75), and he went on dying for another thirty-five years. Nor was he reluctant to bite the other hand that fed him. He taught nearly twenty years at Stanford, but that institution is savaged by name, more than once, in *Lunar Follies* (2005). In the earlier *Blue Pastoral* (1983), the chapter "The Gala Cocktail Party" skewers phoniness in the academy gleefully. And was honored for it; the piece earned a place in that year's Pushcart Prize anthology.

This was just one of many honors over a career that spanned a half-century, because for all his contrariness this writer was far more than a curmudgeon. He won two fellowships each from the Guggenheim Foundation and the National Endowment for the Arts, as well as a Lannan Lifetime Achievement Award in 2005. He earned the praise of celebrated peers, poets such as Denise Levertov and Robert Creeley and novelists such as Philip Roth and Don DeLillo (for Sorrentino, as for almost no one else, the latter two were willing to commit blurbs). Besides, why should cutting remarks about the country's arbiters of taste stand in the way of mainstream success? Readers will see the same knives flashing in Kurt Vonnegut or T. C. Boyle. Neither of them, however, had this author's ferocious commitment to innovation.

In a 1970 essay-review on William Carlos Williams—his enduring inspiration—Sorrentino insists, "America eats her artists alive" (*Something Said,* p. 20). The culture, that is, celebrates creative spirits who produce "trash" (p. 27). In 1981, again considering Williams for the *New York Times Book Review,* he elaborated: "Writing

is almost always most admired when it is decorously resting.... the more comatose, the more static a mirror image of 'reality' the better" (*Something Said,* p. 41). So the great majority of his countrymen "employ language and techniques inadequate" (p. 41) to the times, creating drama via hand-me-down emotional signals, interactions across "a sea of manners" (p. 27). In John Updike, to name one of his bêtes noires, catharsis was nothing but a papier-maché of chewed-up and regurgitated convention. Trash.

Such defiance of cultural norms finds its most direct expression, naturally, in the essays and reviews of *Something Said,* first published in 1984, expanded and reissued in 2001. Getting beyond the sham that passes for represented reality also animates his dozen books of poetry, the best perhaps *Corrosive Sublimate* (1971), extensively featured in both volumes of his *Selected Poems* (1981, 2004). Sorrentino's last years also saw publication of a story collection, *The Moon in Its Flight* (2004). Ultimately, though, his reputation must rest on the book-length fiction, "novels" for lack of a better word. This essay will concentrate on those, and on the questions they raise about the form. The novel after all is usually a vehicle for drama, for the development of character and catharsis. Yet Sorrentino combined a radical's sensibility with a fondness for an often retrograde form. Then what does he supply by way of catharsis? Does he have an alternative?

Restless an artist as he was, with a range as broad as that of any American contemporary, this author nonetheless understood that work made of language can't help but engage the passions. In his praise for the poetry of Williams, he never neglects the emotional content, the "savagery, ... harshness," and "open wounds" (*Something Said,* p. 13). And when he writes about book-length prose, Sorrentino never suggests the reading experience depends entirely on formal qualities. His rave review for William Gaddis' *JR* bears a title that is all about the passions: "Lost Lives" (p. 180). This author's complaint about the common run of contemporary novels doesn't lie with their emotional content per se but with what he perceived as an emotional charade, as dated as

the Gibson girls that decorate a creaky carnival ride (to borrow a pertinent metaphor from John Barth's story "Lost in the Funhouse"). So the question remains: What does he offer instead?

"GENETIC CODING," THE AUTODIDACT, AND THE POETRY

Gilbert Sorrentino was born April 27, 1929, in Brooklyn. He had an Irish mother, née Anne Marie Davis, and his father, August (employed in the Brooklyn Navy Yard and elsewhere), was the son of immigrants from Sicily and Naples. A single essay in *Something Said*, "Genetic Coding," makes mention of the parents, but the piece does without autobiography. "Coding" looks instead at its author's aesthetics and argues that both sides of his ethnic makeup prize "the brilliance of formal invention" as an antidote to "the essential idiocy of living" (p. 264).

So too Sorrentino's interviews are devoid of childhood reminiscence. What he reveals about early experience is refracted through the prism of fiction, which returns often to his home borough and the years between the Depression and the Korean War. Examples begin with *Steelwork* in 1970 and continue through *Abyss of Human Illusion,* and these novels do sometimes involve children. Like all the other characters, the kids tend to suffer. A novel from 1995, *Red the Fiend,* presents a harrowing portrayal of child abuse. Still, the author never gave any indication of having suffered such horrors himself, and eventually he raised three healthy children. It seems safe to infer an unexceptional factory-class upbringing— with little or no literary training.

Sorrentino discovered his calling shortly after high school. According to a friend of those years, the inspiration came from reading: while working as a clerk, young Gil first encountered Walt Whitman. After that came a couple of stints at Brooklyn College, to either side of a two-year stretch in the army (at the height of the Korean conflict, 1951–1953, though he never went overseas). In the classroom his primary interest was the English Renaissance, and the language of Christopher Marlowe and Andrew Marvell turns up in the novels. These studies also took

him to French, Latin, and Greek. Still, Sorrentino never earned a degree. He is best appreciated as an autodidact who served the rare apprenticeship available in 1950s New York, amid "an incredible artistic ferment" (to quote David Andrews' Sorrentino essay in the *Review of Contemporary Fiction,* 2001). The young author was a jazz buff and a regular at the Cedar Tavern, the bar frequented by Jackson Pollock and the abstract expressionists. Literary connections included Williams himself and the other significant early influence, Robert Creeley, founder of the "Black Mountain school" of poetry.

Sorrentino reconnected as well with a childhood friend, a figure with whom he is still identified, Hubert Selby, Jr. In 1956, while still at college, these two founded *Neon,* a shoestring publication that nonetheless offered a forum for everything from early episodes of Selby's *Last Exit to Brooklyn* (the novel appeared in 1964) to the Black Mountain poets. *Neon* folded in 1960 and Sorrentino moved on to edit *Kulchur,* a more established avant-garde journal. The work put him in touch with LeRoi Jones (Amiri Baraka) and John Ashbery.

Inspiring as it might be to rub so many artists' shoulders, Sorrentino nonetheless needed paying work as well. Not long after his 1953 discharge from the army, he married Elsene Wiessner, and the couple soon had two children. Their son Jesse arrived in July 1954, and a daughter, Delia, was born in April 1957 (she would die relatively young, in 2003). The young father made do with more clerk-level jobs, in insurance and shipping. He found a more fitting appointment only in 1965, when he began a four-year stint as an editor with Grove Press. The financial anxiety, combined with the need to write, couldn't have been easy. In 1960 Sorrentino brought out his first book of poetry, *The Darkness Surrounding Us.* In the dedication he professed his love: "THIS BOOK FOR ELSENE." But he had underwritten publication himself, and the marriage dissolved that same year.

The following year, 1961, he set up housekeeping with Victoria Ortiz, born Vivian Ortiz, herself previously married. The relationship

proved congenial and lasted till the author's death. Still, the mother's name on the May 1963 birth certificate of their son Christopher (the eventual novelist) is from the woman's earlier marriage: Vivian Bradt (per e-mail from Christopher Sorrentino). The father's bohemian inclinations carried over into his personal life; he and Victoria didn't marry until May 1968.

By then she too had a book dedicated to her. This was Sorrentino's first novel, *The Sky Changes,* which in 1966 actually brought in a publisher's advance of $750. Not that his parlous finances improved. *Sky Changes* earned nothing more for decades, and well into his forties, this author was more a poet than novelist.

Darkness included a number of pieces that had appeared in the *Nation,* and the magazine ran a respectful if mixed review from Denise Levertov. LeRoi Jones requested the subsequent collection, *Black and White* (1964), for his own Totem Press, and Jones helped get the book a decent showing around New York. Next, Levertov picked up *The Perfect Fiction* (1968) for her poetry series at Norton, a commercial house. And while *Corrosive Sublimate* (1971) brought Sorrentino back to a smaller press, this was the highly esteemed Black Sparrow. The collection won a celebratory review in *Parnassus,* where James Guimond praised the work's urbanity and intensity.

The decade that followed saw two more collections, *White Sail* in 1977 and *The Orangery* in 1978, as well as a brief translation from the Latin. *Selected Poems, 1958–1980,* on Black Sparrow, included thirty-five new pieces, post-1978. Sorrentino himself, according to his later editor John O'Brien, claimed he had hit a creative peak with *The Orangery* (a remark cited in William McPheron's *Descriptive Bibliography*). The title alludes to the Paris structure that now houses Monet's *Water Lilies,* formerly a Bourbon playground, and the formal principle is likewise playful; each poem mentions the fruit, its name famously impossible to rhyme. Yet the orchard is haunted by decay and mortality. The first piece ends with the death of the poet's mother, "ice-gray in Jersey City" (*Selected,* p. 183), and the last considers old photos fading to "twilight" and

"smoke." Its key line might be a tolling bell: "Nothing is the thing that rhymes with orange" (p. 222).

Darkness, starting with Sorrentino's debut title, pervades the work in this genre. In the *New York Times Book Review,* Hugh Seidman declared the 1981 *Selected Poems* "important and unique," in large part because of its encompassing gloom. He appreciated the work from before *Orangery* especially, and quoted an entire piece from *Corrosive Sublimate,* "Anatomy." The opening stanza:

Certain portions of the heart
die, and are dead. They are
dead.

(*Selected,* p. 150)

J. D. O'Hara, in the *Nation,* instead found the later poems more rewarding, and chafed against the "persistent" concern with death. O'Hara did acknowledge the writer's formal control. He noted how *Perfect Fiction* adheres rigorously, throughout a cycle of fifty-two pieces, to three-line stanzas (the form favored by Williams). But O'Hara found only the recent poems "pleasant reading"; for him the earlier books felt unrelentingly "sour and irritable."

Which could be their strength, of course. Charles Baudelaire is often a reference in the *Selected Poems,* and he too was a lifelong connoisseur of rot. So too, the Latin translation Sorrentino published in 1977 is from Sulpicia, the lone woman of Augustan Rome whose poetry survives, and she implies she would prefer death to her loveless existence. Sorrentino knows his poetic tradition, energized by "the essential idiocy of living." *White Sail,* for him, is an ironic signifier for a gravestone. In a powerful sequence from *Corrosive Sublimate,* first he mourns a couple of dead friends, in a piece with a punning title—"Morning Roundup," ostensibly about the news—and then he moves on, in "Rose Room," to a general elegy: any "quality of American light / that is not bitter // is departed" (p. 113).

Sorrentino's poetry doesn't always achieve such power, but he mined enough out of its bitter vein to make one wonder at the critical neglect. Even the long posthumous article on the Poetry

Foundation Web site has a single paragraph about the poetry, and hardly anyone noticed when a second selection appeared in 2004 (on a still smaller press). Yet while this shelf of the author's work deserves further investigation, there can be no denying that he himself lost interest. The 2004 *New and Selected Poems, 1958–1998,* lists no stand-alone titles after *The Orangery.* The miscellany from the end of the 1981 volume is reprinted as it first appeared, and after that comes another, just thirty-seven newer poems. A number function primarily as satire: on the literary life, or on foibles of San Francisco culture.

MIDLIFE TRANSITION: FIRST NOVELS AND FIRST CREATIVE PEAK

The Bay area and its milieu was much on the author's mind after 1981. That year, at the age of fifty-two, Sorrentino at last landed a permanent professor position, in creative writing at Stanford University. A long way from his old stomping grounds, the new situation left him with an ambivalence that doesn't just come out in the poetry. In an interview on National Public Radio, the author revealed that he first learned to drive in California, where he had no other option. Still, he taught at Stanford for seventeen years, and though he returned to Brooklyn in 2000, his Stanford colleagues remember him as "funny, and sweet-natured" (Palmer). His students included the future Pulitzer Prize winner Jeffrey Eugenides, and he devised a popular course in generative devices for the novel—alternative means of creating structure and momentum.

Teaching was hardly new to Sorrentino by the time he reached Stanford. The author continued to snipe at the academic establishment in both his criticism (for instance a *New York Times* review of Paul Mariani's Williams biography, in 1981) and his fiction (*Blue Pastoral,* with its "Gala Cocktail Party," appeared shortly after he moved to the Bay Area). Nonetheless, he couldn't ignore the advantages of teaching. By the later 1960s, working as an editor at Grove, he must have realized his own work had little commercial potential. During those same years, 1965–1969, he wrote on nights and weekends, and he must

have noticed the toll this took on his family. Some of those nights and weekends, he and Victoria had all three children at home. So Sorrentino began to take on short-term academic positions, not just in New York (at Columbia) but also at the Aspen writers workshops in Colorado. In 1971 he began ten years of visiting appointments, none beyond commuting distance: first Sarah Lawrence, then the New School, then the University of Scranton. By the time he reached Stanford, in the fall of 1982, Sorrentino had come to terms with the compromises of a teacher's life.

The transition from shipping clerk to tenured faculty may have taken a decade and a half, yet its disruptions made little dent in his productivity. Before the move west Sorrentino published most of his poetry and a half-dozen novels. These include a couple of contenders for his greatest book-length fiction, and there were a few short stories as well. Most notable are "The Moon in Its Flight" in *New American Review* (1971) and "Decades" in *Esquire* (1977; selected for *Best American Short Stories,* 1978).

What's more, between the late 1960s and early 1980s Sorrentino finished the majority of the essays and reviews in *Something Said.* Both editions of the text begin with an essay published in 1981, "The Act of Creation and Its Artifact." As much a meditation as an essay, this appeared in the *Review of Contemporary Fiction,* where John O'Brien was editor; highly erudite, with reference to everyone from St. Thomas Aquinas to Sorrentino's fellow poetic iconoclast Jack Spicer, "Act of Creation" nonetheless argues for what is beyond book learning. Rather, the essay insists on art's "mystery and secret" (p. 12). Indeed, its author's own accomplishments, as he endured one jarring transition after another, embodies the mystery of artistic production.

That mystery is lessened, a bit, when one considers the other assistance Sorrentino received. In 1973 he was awarded the first of his fellowships from the Guggenheim Foundation (the second would come in 1987), and the following year his first from the National Endowment (Peede). An annus mirabilis was 1975, when he won a Creative Artists Service Award, a grant from the Ariadne Foundation, and a Fels Award.

The money involved varied; only the Guggenheim offered enough to support a family for long. Still, the recognition and reward must have meant a lot—especially because his midlife transitions included a shift from poetry to the novel.

The Sky Changes (1966) carried epigraphs from two of his poetic forebears: Williams, to be sure, and also Hart Crane. As for Robert Creeley, he committed a blurb, and Sorrentino's apprenticeship in poetry was especially evident in the style. This owed something to Creeley's "open formalism" in that it eschewed the loaded rhetoric of the modernists, the weight of significance that the previous literary generation could give every detail. *Sky Changes* feels looser than that, throwing in sensory data for its own sake. Occasional sentences compile the run-on catalogs of the Beats, but neither individual episodes nor the story as a whole feels shapeless.

The novel takes us through a recognizable crisis, a divorce story. A troubled couple attempts to flee their breakup by taking a cross-country jaunt, on the cheap, with their two children. The chapters have place names, from Brooklyn to San Francisco, but their length is irregular and their sequence anachronistic. Each, however, gets across a shudder of pain; each drives another nail into the coffin of the relationship.

Still, the couple's dissolution is a forgone conclusion and delivers less impact than the prose. This mattered so much to Sorrentino that, almost as soon as the book saw print, he began expressing misgivings about certain passages. Never mind that the novel's few reviews, for instance from Gwendolyn Brooks in *Bookweek,* all praised the style. Sorrentino brought up his dissatisfaction even in his fiction; the 1971 novel *Imaginative Qualities of Actual Things* mentions "a failure of tone in *The Sky Changes*" (p. 78). The corrections he wanted had to wait twenty years, but this later edition is still available (on Dalkey Archive, the press of Sorrentino's great champion John O'Brien). Even a brief sample conveys the style's flexibility, coarse yet subtle, extending deep sympathy yet casting a cold eye:

> They had another drink, and C told him how happy he was that his wife and P had finally decided to make it together, because he was good for the kids,

and the husband agreed. So they lied warmly to each other and their friendship resumed where insanity and despair had cut it off.

> (p. 50)

Such a sample also demonstrates how *Changes* does without full names or direct quotation, and how it toys with authorial intrusion. This on top of its cavalier attitude toward unities of time and place! Yet in 1970 and 1971 the author distanced himself further from the Aristotelian rules of drama, with *Steelwork* and *Imaginative Qualities of Actual Things*. These establish the mode at which he excelled, the community portrait. Portraits of misery, to be sure, all about "the idiocy of living," both books nonetheless deftly fillet out any trace of bathos. They are too funny for that, and too frank. Also helping defeat sentimentality is the disrupted chronology, which goes further than in *Sky Changes* because both the subsequent novels look over a greater time period and both lack a central narrative. Rather they achieve the equilibrium of a great bebop workout, in which every fresh racket loops back eventually to the head. Not for nothing does *Steelwork* begin with the Charlie Parker rave-up, "KoKo," its "great blasts of foreign air" (p. 3) disrupting the afternoon of two young men in Brooklyn, 1945.

Brooklyn: the borough became Sorrentino's turf with the 1970 novel. The dedication is to a childhood friend and the material must include touches of autobiography. Someone named Gibby figures in several of the brief chapters, and a friend describes him as "a young man of great promise who reads many books" (p. 168). Gibby would be a stand-in for Gil in another sort of novel, in for instance the Brooklyn of Daniel Fuchs, where a narrative follows a central character through events in sequence. But here one entry is dated 1939, the next 1950, the next 1946, and no character emerges as the protagonist. The more fitting model than bildungsroman might be some immigrant soap opera, the stuff of Henry Roth. Earlier New York novelists like Fuchs and Roth, in any case, present a tenement hardscrabble that informs Sorrentino's vision. In *Steelwork,* to pull yourself up by your bootstraps only exposes you to worse punishment.

Physical punishment, more often than not: the author was never more violent. In later books, episodes of fights and torture tend to the surreal; while *Red the Fiend* shares the setting of the earlier book (indeed, Red and his malevolent Grandma may turn up in *Steelwork*), the abuse goes to impossible extremes. But for the 1970 novel the closest model seems to be *Last Exit to Brooklyn,* notorious for its harsh realism. In *Last Exit* too, every bruise is slow to fade. Likewise, for both Sorrentino and his old friend, dialog demands close mimesis; the talk rambles, profusely obscene and viciously ill-informed (especially about sex). The difference between the books has to do with structure, far freer in *Steelwork.*

The most thoughtful review of the novel, Shaun O'Connell's in the *Nation,* noted both the similarity to *Last Exit* and the "quite original method of narration." That method, according to O'Connell, suited Sorrentino's vision of "American civilization as a terminal ward." Overall, the reviewer judged the work "artful ... and striking"—yet failed to mention the specific impact of World War II. Sorrentino's microcosm of America, indeed, could be criticized for how oppressively it demonstrates the damage done by the war and war profiteering. One former infantryman, Monte, carries a plate in his head and has lately "been fuckin up a lotta bars" (p. 65). Despite his disability, though, Monte's the one who makes the connection between destruction abroad and at home. On yet another trip to the psych ward, Monte grasps how his neighborhood has changed: "Where the hell are all the lots ... ? Member all the fuckin *lots* when we were kids?" A moment later, he murmurs: "They give us some royal fuckin" (pp. 65–66). In the chapters set in the 1950s, the Red Terror seems a hysterical reaction to the same tragedy.

"Tragedy," however, won't sit well with *Imaginative Qualities of Actual Things.* Nor bildungsroman, because while a character or two may come of age, soon enough they revert to childishness. And as for immigrants, the people in Sorrentino's second group portrait are all young New Yorkers of the sixties; they view anyone from the old country as largely incomprehensible and figures of fun. *Imaginative Qualities* doesn't even have much truck with Brooklyn. It crosses the river to join the Manhattan art world—or rather the world that wishes it were. Nearly everyone is on a tight budget and proves to be a fraud.

Antecedents for *Sky Changes* and *Steelwork* are fairly easy to discern, but in his third novel this author establishes a model of his own. Of course pretensions to culture, like those of Sorrentino's sad-sack bohemians, have often been targets of satire. Reading *Imaginative Qualities* can call to mind, in particular, Marcel Proust's "little clan" of poseurs, grappling for position at Mme. Verdurin's. Like Proust too, Sorrentino has a central consciousness. An unnamed narrator spins one loose-limbed anecdote after another, spilling the dirt on people who might be loosely characterized as "friends." But unlike the narrator of *A La Recherche du temps perdu,* the author of *Imaginative Qualities* never gets caught up personally, nor assumes a rarified sensibility. Sorrentino's novel remains fundamentally something else again.

Imaginative Qualities has just eight chapters, each concentrating on another man or woman of the group. Even before these folks begin to stab one another in the back, both author and reader fully comprehend what a bunch of losers they are working with. Yet the opening at once raises social critique to a more challenging level:

> What if this young woman, who writes such bad poems, ... should stretch her remarkably long and well-made legs out before you, so that her skirt slips up to the tops of her stockings? It is an old story. Then she asks what you think of the trash you have just read—her latest effort.
>
> (p. 3)

An old story, yes, an exchange of sexual favors for career advancement. Yet this fable has a subtler moral as well, in that *both* figures are implicated. The bad poet with the good legs is as deluded as the critic or editor about to jettison his standards; she believes in her trash. So the author extends understanding even when the subject is this pretty dud, Sheila Henry. The promiscuous Sheila deserves her chapter title, "Lady the Brach," yet by its end her vacancy

invites pity more than contempt: "She was waiting for life to give her something, this was intolerable. Take me to the zoo. Fly me to the moon" (p. 22).

So *Imaginative Qualities* proves sui generis in yet another way, combining character assassination with wincing empathy. The paradox is rooted in the form. Because the chapters run as long as any in Sorrentino's oeuvre, there is room for a degree of identification rare for him. The openness to detail for its own sake, that inheritance from Williams and the Beats, here develops into an openness about personality—without, importantly, any sacrifice of blistering candor. The author requires only a single paragraph from an old letter to demonstrate that one of the group, the painter, engraver, and short-story writer Guy Lewis, has genuine talent. Yet Guy's chapter suffers no sentimental allegiance to the artist figure. Rather it reveals him to be a tormented closet homosexual, hence a clumsy and destructive lover, and besides that lacking the spine to stand up to the gatekeepers of artistic success. It is in this section, too, that Sorrentino's excoriation of American publishing first reaches full throat. His sardonic handling of Guy's failed efforts in fiction (tearing into "the myth that editors are somehow on a par with the writers," p. 76) amounts to the opening salvo in a barrage that lasted the rest of his career.

The sneering has a purpose beyond simple elitism. After all, it is only via the text itself—the imaginative quality given these actual things—that the author can transcend his flawed circle. The novel has touches of *Steelwork*'s streetwise poetics but goes far further in its ventriloquism. Sentences wiggle in and out of journalese, advertising, ethnic slurs, whiskey blather, and the sweet nothings of loveless sex. The patchwork in the later text tends to be more colorful, the combinations more gleeful, a difference implied in the titles. For *Imaginative Qualities,* Sorrentino uses a phrase from Williams' *Kora in Hell* (1920), and he repeatedly references the New Jersey poet's famed passage "it is only in isolate flecks that / something / is given off" (from "To Elsie," 1923, in Williams, p. 217). Indeed, those lines might speak for everything Sorrentino

wrote, though he would touch his old mentor for a title only once more, in his penultimate work, *A Strange Commonplace.*

These citations and others can be easy to track down. Many of the novels provide all you need in the epigraphs. What matters more is that the intertextuality (some of it far subtler) helps defines this author as postmodern, as an innovator. Beyond that, the echoes of Williams throughout *Imaginative Qualities* raise the question of emotional content: whether Sorrentino's postmodernism has room for finding what hurts and sharing it. "To Elsie" is among other things a miracle of empathy. The poet gives expression to a reality far more brutish than his own.

Sorrentino's assemblages from 1970 and 1971, at the least, strive for the same degree of caring. They forge a connection to their battered creatures, all the more rueful when it fetches a startled laugh. One might even say the novels move us to pity and terror, though their people possess nothing Aristotle would call tragic stature. A signal case from *Imaginative Qualities* occurs in the chapter on Bunny. This is another woman figure, assessed without pretension yet with great sensitivity. Bunny has no artistic aspirations, she is just a pretty hanger-on, briefly and disastrously married to Guy:

> It would've been better had I simply not got involved with Bunny, she's hopeless. I'll bet you a dollar that she gets a job in a publishing house assisting a hip young editor.... She's one of those bright, lovely, intelligent people who should never have been born. We'll finish with her postmarital career by putting her in a Connecticut motel one December afternoon, with a gang of young, creative professionals, half-drunk. She's in the middle of a laugh, those perfect white teeth. They're all watching the Giant game. Bunny, who is now called Jo, suddenly recalls Guy's absolute contempt for football: "For morons who like pain." She looks around at her friends and hands her empty glass, smiling, to her escort. Her heart a chunk of burning metal. She will marry this man.
>
> (pp. 104–105)

The scene, in narrative terms, comes out of nowhere and goes nowhere. We never again encounter these young creative morons. Yet within the fiction's abstract expressionist whole,

the moment's a climax, its agony piercing. And within the career of the author, the work of this period presents a creative peak.

HÔTEL, STEW, ABERRATION: *BRUSHES WITH FAME AND CONVENTION*

The accomplishment didn't alter Sorrentino's outsider status, but it didn't go unnoticed either. *Imaginative Qualities* earned the author his first notice in the *New York Times*. In mid-1972 appeared an unsigned review, admiring in some respects, and the following year Wilfrid Sheed, discussing a number of recent titles, called the book "a fine novel." More significantly, Sorrentino's adversarial stance toward the prevailing culture drew intense attention from like-minded critics. In 1973 Jerome Klinkowitz placed a substantive overview of the fiction in the *Village Voice,* an essay later worked into his *Literary Disruptions* (1975) and *Structuring the Void* (1992). In 1974 the New York quarterly *Vort* ran an entire issue on Sorrentino, and this included John O'Brien's first long appreciation. At the start of the following decade, O'Brien initiated the *Review of Contemporary Fiction* in similar fashion, with an issue dedicated to Sorrentino. In spring 2003, the *Review* focused exclusively on *Imaginative Qualities.*

The essays in the latter issue tend to emphasize what is experimental about the novel, its postmodern earmarks. Indeed, none of the fifteen book-length fictions published after 1971 much resemble what E. M. Forster was talking about in *Aspects of the Novel* (1927). Yet like-thinking contemporaries also have problems with Sorrentino's oeuvre. There is little agreement regarding his greatest work. His best-known is another matter, an obvious pick: *Mulligan Stew,* published in 1979.

The *Stew* was Sorrentino's longest stand-alone work at nearly 450 pages. Before it appeared, however, he brought out a slender complement to the beefy fiction on the way, namely *Splendide-Hôtel* (1973). Pamphlet-sized, this was an alphabet text. The first brief entry scats an improvisation on "A," the second on "B," and so forth. "J," for instance, begins "J is a

hook" (p. 27), then goes into a memory of fishing in a New Jersey vacation spot (anticipating *Aberration of Starlight,* 1980), and then meditates on the fishing lure, the potency of its metal and color, in contrast to the flaccidity of most literary representations. The last point recalls Williams, "no ideas but in things" (from "Paterson," 1927 in Williams, p. 264), and it's hardly the only such case in *Hôtel.* Brief as the book is, it's rife with references to Sorrentino's old mentor—and even more to Rimbaud. The locale of the title is taken from Rimbaud's *Illuminations* (1886), the first prose poem, and *Hôtel* reflects throughout on Rimbaud's sonnet assigning colors to the vowels (in *Une Saison en Enfer,* 1873).

Such an ultra-literary scrapbook might seem like impossible reading. Yet *Hôtel* proves a satisfying zany artifact, constructed of words and yet "indecipherable, untranslatable!" (p. 10). Among its inspired entries is the box score under "K," in which an unnamed pitcher strikes out, or "Ks," such figures as Che Guevara and Richard Nixon. Art shuts down politics. So outlandish an exercise naturally found a small publisher and narrow readership. But for those readers, reviewing the book in places like the *Voice* and *Vort,* the *Hôtel* was cause for celebration.

Nonetheless, Sorrentino's work made little headway in mainstream publishing. *Mulligan Stew* presents the foremost case in point, rejected nearly thirty times. In the end, though, this sorry history helped the novel achieve notoriety. It finally found a home at Grove, where Sorrentino still had friends on staff, and these editors wanted to preface the text with the rejections received elsewhere. Sorrentino agreed on the condition that he could select the letters and brush them up a bit. The result was a dozen vicious parodies, with names changed—and reviewers, just as Grove had hoped, couldn't resist. Michael Dirda, in the *Washington Post,* praised the *Stew* as "utterly dazzling," and in the *New York Times,* John Leonard, the most prominent critic of the day, pronounced it "hilarious" and "full of rage." Leonard particularly savored the attack on the "the New York publishing community." Even naysayers gave the book extensive coverage.

Thus three decades after publication, in Sorrentino's surprisingly brusque *Times* obituary, *Mulligan Stew* was the only title mentioned. It is also the lone novel of his that Frederick Karl examined, free of deadline pressure, in his critical omnibus *American Fictions 1940–1980*. Karl tempered his praise, but not when it came to the madcap lists. He understood the usefulness of this device, first indulged in *Steelwork* but here exploited to the hilt: now enumerating the clutter of an old barn, now the inventory of mail-order sexual aids.

Lists provide a safety valve, when someone who is not much for narrative means to tell a story. The *Stew* presents a classic metamorphosis, in which the novelist Tony Lamont declines into madness while his characters attain freedom and power. An ordinary Big Book would shape the reversal around mounting tensions and confrontations, but ordinary won't do for "lonely, lonely, lonely Lamont" (p. 400), as defiantly avant-garde as his creator. For serious novelists, Lamont presents an all-too-familiar nightmare: "mad as a hatter in his ... loneliness and *failure!*" (p. 354). He invents a murder mystery, but his characters seem the better detectives; he courts estranged family and old friends, plus academics and editors, but suffers every kind of snub. Yet these agonies are embodied, by and large, in lengthy parodies that include many a demented list. A *lot* of the comedy has to do with sex, most spectacularly the overheated and execrable poems of Lorna Flambeaux. Her inventories of positions and body parts, in *The Sweat of Love,* allow Sorrentino to set loose his own far greater rhetorical skills. They allow for verbal performances that take the place of action and climax. *Mulligan Stew* closes with just such a flourish, a six-page list, all gifts to people never mentioned previously: "to Helena Walsh, the goatish glance of the cockeyed lecher; to Twisty Abe DeHarvarde, shimmering hose of glittering glows ..." (p. 444).

Astonishing lists, tokens perhaps for Lamont's departure, and Frederick Karl grasped their dramatic purpose. But Karl found other elements of the novel disappointing, indeed "unimaginative" (Karl, p. 555). Lamont's situation never sustains any possibility for better, as you might expect when so pessimistic an author spends so long with one character, and Karl found this an ineffective platform for all the "fraternity-house male-female antics" (p. 555). Misgivings such as these, from the present perspective, seem right. *Mulligan Stew* seems a lesser accomplishment, despite how it benefited from an aggressive publisher. To return to the bebop metaphor, it delivers splashy solos around a feeble riff. The novel hasn't enjoyed the later attention given *Imaginative Qualities,* and its weakness stands out in comparison to the grim little masterpiece that followed.

Aberration of Starlight appeared just a year after *Mulligan Stew*—this author was never one to rest on his laurels. What first strikes one about the novel isn't that it appeared on a commercial press, Random House, with a squib from Philip Roth, or that it made the short list for the PEN/Faulkner Award. Rather what you notice is its anomalous material, straightforward realism.

The prose is flexible as ever, but within careful restraints. The present action occupies a single weekend in New Jersey, and the voices, both interior and spoken, are those of a few Brooklyn wage slaves at a cheap New Jersey resort. It's the end of summer 1939, and a Holocaust looms for these people as well, though here there is nothing like the violence of *Steelwork. Aberration* generates suspense via a literary experiment. Its devastation coheres as we work through four successive points of view, in an order that has the inevitability of aging: first a boy, then his divorced mother, her Saturday-night seducer, and last the boy's embittered grandfather. The structure allows room for another brief spate of pornography, but here the fantasy feels apropos. It occurs in the head of the Saturday-night Lothario, the salesman Tom, also recently divorced and lonely. As for the actual sex, that may be the most fully rendered in Sorrentino's oeuvre—though since it too is viewed from Tom's perspective, it is limited and deluded:

Then she took her hands off him and looked away as he cleaned himself.... She was covering herself up too, smoothing her dress down, and buttoning up. "I love you," he whispered, and they kissed again, chastely, but she was trembling.... Give her a

chance, kid, plenty of time. Am I complaining? He wasn't complaining, hell no. A hand job from a doll who's almost a nun on the first date? Tom had no beef, kiddo.

(p. 146)

The sparse elements of *Aberration* achieve exquisite balance, revealing an essential fragility. That balance might be called classic, and the novel won critical approval even in a bastion of conservative aesthetics like the *Atlantic Monthly*. Then too, an innovative postmodernist like Guy Davenport found much to praise, in a review for the *New York Times*: "Mr. Sorrentino's imagination is rich and fine.... a triumph."

THE EIGHTIES AND NINETIES: RADICAL AT FULL LENGTH

A triumph, perhaps, but short lived—none of the later novels basked in such widespread applause. For that matter, the excitement over *Aberration* must have felt hollow to its author, since at the time he had another manuscript, finished earlier, fruitlessly making the rounds. This was *Crystal Vision*, which at last landed on a San Francisco–based press, North Point, the same year (1981) as Sorrentino found the job at nearby Stanford. North Point would remain his publisher for a half-decade, by which time Dalkey Archive was beginning to bring out new editions of the earlier work. A regular university paycheck coincided with more regular publishing support, and during the same period Sorrentino's youngest child, Chris, began life on his own. In short, the writer enjoyed stability and freedom such as he had never known. His response was a sustained and radical rejection of storytelling norms.

This repudiation of norms wouldn't have seemed so abrupt had *Crystal Vision* appeared before *Aberration* in compositional sequence. The 1981 novel is another experiment, seventy-eight brief chapters in which men with comic names (the Arab, Professor Kooba) gather and share some story, comic but of little point, and largely unrelated to the tales that come before or after. Rather, each chapter has some subtle connection with a card of the Tarot (the traditional deck has seventy-eight). Only the setting feels

familiar, the Brooklyn stoops and stores; these voluble slackers could be the gang of *Steelwork*, though not so bruised and bruising. Indeed, among the many challenges set by *Crystal Vision* (far less widely reviewed than either *Aberration* or *Mulligan Stew*) is the way its pleasures depend on knowledge of the earlier novel and its milieu. This reiteration of what went before became a hallmark of the next three or four book-length texts.

These first years in the Bay Area also saw the initial publication of *Something Said*, the selected essays and reviews. The 1984 compilation, as noted earlier, puts forward a revisionist literary history; it tears down honored figures such as Updike and esteems the little known, such as the poet Jack Spicer and the novelist Edward Dahlberg. In so doing, *Something Said* amounts to the author's *ars poetica*, his statement of principles. This element asserts itself more strongly in the 2001 expanded edition, which pairs the visionary first essay, "The Act of Creation ... ," with a bookend closer, "Writing and Writers: *Disjecta Membra*." The latter offers an assortment of insights and rants, a rough distillation of the sensibility. But in either version *Something Said* presents compelling evidence of its author's erudition, integrity, and perspicuity. The original received long and complimentary write-ups in prominent places that, more often than not, ignored Sorrentino's novels of the same period. The most impressive review may have come from the noted scholar and critic Hugh Kenner, in the *Washington Post;* Kenner deemed *Something Said* "a releasing of formidable energy and light."

The man behind that "energy and light," however, remained first and foremost a creative artist. His latest projects entailed, among other things, reconfiguring what he had imagined previously. So *Blue Pastoral*, in 1983, recast the breakup journey of *Sky Changes* as nutty pastiche. John Domini, in an otherwise approving piece for the *Boston Phoenix*, wondered whether a text of such length could succeed despite the absence of "emotional satisfactions." The question hangs over all the fictions that occupied Sorrentino during his years out in the Bay Area. Not only are

they stories without story, never arriving at a climax, but they also eschew character tension or other gateways to mimetic connection. Granted, this author had always flirted with artistic extremes. But with his work of the 1980s Sorrentino subverted the expectations for fiction more thoroughly than any American of his stature. Robert Coover, to name one fellow iconoclast, was more respectful about narrative; Kathy Acker, to name another, was more direct about social critique. Sorrentino plays in a more freewheeling league. By 1997 the late philosopher-critic Louis Mackey—himself a boundary-blurring figure, with cameos in two Richard Linklater movies—claimed that this author had brought off "the ultimate postmodern novel" (p. 18).

In *Fact, Fiction, and Representation: Four Novels by Gilbert Sorrentino*, Mackey provides an exegesis of *Crystal Vision* and the subsequent threesome *Odd Number* (1985), *Rose Theatre* (1987), and *Misterioso* (1989). Sorrentino regarded the latter as a trilogy, and in 1997 he oversaw the repackaging of the three novels together, under the title *Pack of Lies*. This publication was with the not-for-profit Dalkey Archive Press, which now keeps most of his titles in print. After *Odd Number,* North Point gave up on the author, and since the stalwart John O'Brien had now established Dalkey, Sorrentino began to rely more on publishing his works there. Not that his wandering was over. Later titles appeared on Fromm International, Green Integer, and Coffee House.

The press doesn't much matter, though, when one turns to *Odd Number, Rose Theater,* and *Misterioso.* Whatever edition one looks at, it swiftly becomes obvious that many generations will pass before literary evolution produces a more bizarre adaptation. All three scatter shards of a murder mystery, hinting that they might come together, but none deliver a solution. The victim seems to be Sheila Henry from *Imaginative Qualities,* promiscuous as ever, and the various loser detectives recall Tony Lamont. Both earlier novels, indeed, supply a number of characters—if you could call them that—and situations. As ever, the prose takes nifty turns.

Sentences swagger with panache, in a breathtaking variety of formats and tones; it is impossible to isolate any one defining quotation. Any number of passages set you chuckling, and comedy is no small part of the trilogy's raison d'être. This is Mackey's assertion, in *Fact, Fiction, and Representation*: that the books exemplify "the compassionate comedy of the fictional text" (p. 4). Mackey notes the problem of Sorrentino's downbeat vision, a constraint whenever he worked in a realistic mode, and argues that the alternative in *Pack of Lies* amounts to the author's "ultimate triumph" (p. 67). As the individual titles appeared, too, they enjoyed occasional good notices, for instance from Donna Seaman of *Booklist.*

But the trilogy enacts a comedy without humanity. The sexual hijinks have a sterile affect, involving names rather than people. Even the figures that aren't recycled from earlier books pair up with familiar sordidness, and before long there is little glee in discovering another twosome and threesome in flagrante delicto, less still in another snarling evisceration of big publishing. Nothing, however, burdens texts of this length so much as the absence of some developing coherence. Even an acolyte like Mackey admits that *Misterioso,* the longest of the three by far, "appears to be utterly shapeless" (p. 59). After that, to his credit, the critic divines an organizing principle. He tracks down an obscure seventeenth-century catalog of demons, alluded to in the novel, and reveals how the devils' names and those of the characters have been worked into a double-alphabet, proceeding in X shape, one backwards and the other forwards. A thing of rare device, *Misterioso,* but nothing remotely so inviting as the eponymous tune by Thelonious Monk.

The baroque idiosyncrasy of these texts wasn't the last such gesture of this period. In 1991 came a fiction that seems strange even for Sorrentino. *Under the Shadow* presents discrete vignettes, often static, with a few recurring images (a snowman, a woman at a window) but otherwise no discernible system, not even one borrowed from the alphabet or a card deck—there are fifty-nine entries total. The "shadow" of

the title may be that of reality, under which ordinary fiction reposes but from which artifacts like Sorrentino's seek to escape. Then in 1995, with *Red the Fiend,* the author returned to the reality of mid-century Brooklyn, but with a portrait of such unrelenting viciousness as to seem no story at all. The title character grows from child to teenager, in the process inheriting the sick ways of his tormentor grandma. The novel could be called a case study of the domestic-abuse cycle, except the case is so exaggerated. No child could survive what Red goes through, and Sorrentino wondered, in a 2001 interview, why readers had not noticed that this novel too was a work of imagination, deliberate in its hellish redundancy. Yet reviews of both early nineties works tend to recognize their literary artistry, even when they express uncertainty about readership.

THE OLD NEIGHBORHOOD, THE NEW POWER: THE FINAL NOVELS

Louis Mackey makes a cogent argument on behalf of *Pack of Lies.* A later set of novels, however, may offer the more rewarding distillation of what this author was about. These are the three that preceded the posthumous *Abyss of Human Illusion: Little Casino* in 2002, *Lunar Follies* in 2005, and *A Strange Commonplace* early in 2006. Each seems a legitimate candidate for that hard-to-determine honor, the Best of Sorrentino. *Little Casino* is the only one that Mackey saw, before his death in 2004, and it returned Sorrentino to the PEN/Faulkner short list. Yet *Follies* and *Commonplace* also make a terrific initial impression. The posthumous novel is a bit weaker overall, but it shares in what distinguishes the previous three. *Abyss* too reasserts the place of emotional content, even in constructs that have no truck with convention.

It is difficult not to associate this renewal of humanity—engaging sympathies beyond the narrow range of *Red the Fiend*—with the return to Brooklyn. At Stanford, Sorrentino's last classes were done with in 1999, and in the months that followed he and Victoria left the West. Newspaper accounts of the next few years describe the author enjoying his former neighborhoods, for instance walking his dog, and the first book following the move ventures remarkably close to nostalgia.

Nostalgia of an unlikely kind, to be sure: *Gold Fools* (2001) is a parody, wreaking comic havoc on the boys' adventure novels that young readers used to devour. In *Misterioso,* such stuff turned up in one of the aborted story lines, and *Gold Fools* flogs its joke an awfully long time, over 350 pages. Staying with the material, however, allows for something like discovery and confrontation. Not that the novel isn't a burlesque, written entirely in interrogatives, tossing in assorted scraps of linguistic deadwood. Still, if *Red the Fiend* embraced cruelty, *Gold Fools* indulged a certain fondness.

The three novels that came next (each considerably shorter than *Fools*) brought that fondness back home, while sacrificing none of this author's prickliness or intensity. In a formal sense too, *Casino, Follies,* and *Commonplace* achieve rare equilibrium. Each modulates skillfully from one perspective or format to another, so that no single narrative ever emerges, but none tumble into the excesses of *Mulligan Stew* or *Pack of Lies.* Sorrentino is done with sex-capades, but his new surrogates for action and plot remain sophisticated, though apprehensible. The texts provide the sense of perceiving and completing a whole, a central pleasure of the medium, but via alternative developmental devices like the recurrent suicide fantasies in *Strange Commonplace.* Above all, they offer a sorrow anyone can recognize, the sorrow of feelings never expressed. In all three books, ill-will and discouragement accumulate till they quash the life force. Thus four decades into his vocation, this tireless innovator ventured into the passions as yet another territory of the new.

In that territory, Sorrentino remains a cleansing agent. He strips away the veil of politesse in his drive to get at the impulses his people deny. Still, in so doing he awards value to the identification with another's suffering; he affirms that identification as a purpose for art made of words. In *Abyss,* an old writer finds he can't quit, despite his sober awareness that his work "proved nothing, changed nothing, and spoke to about as many

people as one could fit into a small movie theater" (p. 96). He continues "to blunder... until finally, perhaps, he would get said what could never be said" (p. 110).

Now, this interpretation runs an obvious risk. It is a sentimental interpretation, insisting that the novels of 2002, 2005, and 2006 are worthy because they open a window on the soul. The very idea! Whenever Sorrentino encountered such a cliché, he lashed out wickedly. So the hypothesis needs to be tested, in particular against the 2005 book *Lunar Follies*. If this author recommitted to something like "humanity" in these texts, then where do we find it in the *Follies*? As the title implies, the book is out there. Plot, protagonists, chronology are nowhere to be found.

Casino and *Commonplace* at least revisit the broken families of mid-century New York. These meager lives undergo biopsies, none more than a few pages, all exposing some abnegation at once painful and familiar. No character turns up more than once, and while *Little Casino* makes mention of a figure or two from previous novels, they play no larger a part than anyone else. *Casino* also features a commentary after every entry, like *Abyss*, but in the earlier novel these authorial intrusions are more acid. They burn away illusion. *Strange Commonplace* does without such an agitator, but it shares other elements with *Casino*, one being Brooklyn, of course, and besides that, both novels run to fifty-two chapters.

The number raises two obvious associations, a deck of cards and the weeks of the year. These concepts must be central to how the two texts hold together, yet few reviews mentioned the figure and none investigated its purpose. Trey Strecker, in *American Book Review*, issued a ringing endorsement for *Little Casino*—yet he ignored the question of structure. Even at the end of Sorrentino's career, even among apparent supporters, he suffered from refusal to grapple with his aesthetic. That aesthetic found its most succinct expression in 1983, in an interview with Charles Trueheart of *Publishers Weekly:* "Form not only determines content, but form *invents* content."

Regarding form in *Little Casino,* then, the number that "invents" this text has to do with the

passage of the year. *Casino* toys with chronology more than does *Commonplace*. In *Little Casino* the population grows steadily older, yet the entry titled "The Christmas Tree" appears next to "4th of July," and both fall at the center of a text that begins and ends in midsummer. Midsummer of course makes one think of dangerous dreaming, and so the novel undermines, first to last, standard notions of growth or maturation. As for *A Strange Commonplace,* that's a round of cards. It's divided into two sections of twenty-six, in which chapter titles recur but their order changes. Among those titles, one tips the hand: "Pair of Deuces." No high-rollers here, clearly, and the first occurrence of those lowly deuces prompts the first reverie of suicide. So too, *Commonplace* refers throughout to apparel and cosmetics, more glossy surfaces, face cards played against our inevitable fall. Published a few months before the author's death, the novel makes a lovely valediction.

All of which is to reiterate that it has humanity and passion—as does *Little Casino,* with its coming-of-age element and its receptiveness to the turning seasons. But the text between those two, *Lunar Follies,* hardly has people in it at all.

Lunar Follies collects trash, of the kind its author spent a lifetime contending against. "Folly" here refers to the detritus of the art world, as Sorrentino dreams up catalog copy for exhibits beneath contempt, as well as numbskull reviews, vicious gossip, and so on. There is also an academic deconstruction, hopelessly clotted. Stranger still, each chapter or whatever it might be called is titled with the name of some lunar landmark, some fifty-three mountains and seas, arranged alphabetically. Nonetheless, this mooncalf wears a leer we know well. From the first page, "it's on to the snow-chains story; the heat-wave story; the story of the tough coach and his swell young protégé; the killer-hurricane (with puppy) story ..." (p. 14). It's on, that is, to brief but scorching rounds of parody, the context always easy to grasp. In this opening instance the butt of the joke is narrative itself, story, and that is a pertinent target, certainly. But the particular art form matters less than the degradation it suffers, in one piece of *poshlost* after another, where

the wit swiftly clusters and explodes. As Sorrentino's moon illuminates his detested "sea of manners," that is, the game invites participation. The book is densely intertextual, as one might expect, indeed it refers to work in all media, but a reader by no means needs to catch all the isolate flecks in order to appreciate the fun.

The participatory quality of *Lunar Follies* appealed to many reviewers; John Leonard, then writing for *Harper's,* applauded the novel in one of his last published reviews. Yet the novel's openness makes us aware, as well, of the pain that underlies the comedy. Consider, for instance, the list of personalities in an exhibit of photographs. The chapter has an Italian name, "Fra Mauro" (the moon highlands where Apollo 14 landed), and the exhibit is titled "Our Neighbors, the Italians":

> Familiar Carmine, who cursed out a Puerto Rican mother, hey, why not, they breed like animals....
>
> Benign Giannino, who once read a book for fun....
>
> Garish Richie, who has a mouth he shoulda gone to law school.
>
> Exuberant Frankie Hips, who don't mind moolanyans if they mind their fuckin' business.
>
> (pp. 52–53)

No-nonsense Gil Sorrentino, who worked a dig at ethnic solidarity into nearly every one of books. Wisecracking Sorrentino, whose wit provides his best, last defense against such stunted lives. The list makes us laugh, but it is a chilling sketch nonetheless, full of ignorance, violence, and machismo at its worst.

Yet it's not the rhetoric of *Lunar Follies* but rather the structure that best demonstrates how the writer developed new apparatus for catharsis, or at least apparatus that have rarely been used so well. Nearly all the book's longest sections are those named after the wide-open spaces known as the moon's seas. These of course start with the letter *S,* and so the novel reaches a kind of climax, with its late entries among the most complex. Among the least comical, too. The first, "Sea of Clouds," touches on "regrets" and

"gravestones" before concluding "Don't see nothin' too goddamn funny *here*" (pp. 110–111). "Sea of Moisture" depicts the melancholy encounters between Texas GIs and Mexican whores. A number of "Sea" pieces cast shadows of mortality over the project they are concerned with, and so create, of all things, an epiphany. A pang. They dramatize how paltry would be the gain—a few bucks or a few strokes—from even the oiliest con. They assert, with Flaubert, that of all lies, art is the least untrue.

To argue that Gilbert Sorrentino's work was ultimately about what's *true* might seem a dubious exercise. Anyone can see that he never wrote a word that pandered to the marketplace, neither in poetry nor in prose. Besides that, to this author the *t*-word was a signifier long perverted by abuse. His own writing, the novels especially, was intended as an escape from that abuse, enlarging the field of discourse, putting a healthy distance between his texts and routine constructions. To his way of thinking, only by dint of such far-ranging exploration could the art form locate that ground where once again truth could be itself, free of decay, vulnerable and volatile. The results of his search most likely will never have mass appeal. Those books that work best, however, will feel like a homecoming to any sympathetic reader; they will arrive finally at a place of power and durability, all the more so for the odyssey they require and the monsters they reveal.

Selected Bibliography

WORKS OF GILBERT SORRENTINO

FICTION

The Sky Changes. New York: Hill & Wang, 1966. Rev. ed., Normal, Ill.: Dalkey Archive Press, 1998.

Steelwork. New York: Pantheon, 1970. Normal, Ill.: Dalkey Archive Press, 1992.

Imaginative Qualities of Actual Things. New York: Pantheon, 1971. Normal, Ill.: Dalkey Archive Press, 2007.

Splendide-Hôtel. New York: New Directions, 1973. Normal, Ill.: Dalkey Archive Press, 1984.

Mulligan Stew. New York: Grove Press, 1979. Normal, Ill.: Dalkey Archive Press, 1996.

Aberration of Starlight. New York: Random House, 1980. Normal, Ill.: Dalkey Archive Press, 2005.

Crystal Vision. San Francisco: North Point Press, 1981. Normal, Ill.: Dalkey Archive Press, 1999.

Blue Pastoral. San Francisco: North Point Press, 1983. Normal, Ill.: Dalkey Archive Press, 2000.

Odd Number. San Francisco: North Point Press, 1985.

Rose Theatre. Normal, Ill.: Dalkey Archive Press, 1987.

Misterioso. Normal, Ill.: Dalkey Archive Press, 1989, 2001.

Under the Shadow. Normal, Ill.: Dalkey Archive Press, 1991.

Red the Fiend. New York: Fromm International, 1995. Normal, Ill.: Dalkey Archive Press, 2006.

Pack of Lies: A Trilogy. Normal, Ill.: Dalkey Archive Press, 1997. (Contains *Odd Number, Rose Theatre,* and *Misterioso.*)

Gold Fools. Los Angeles: Green Integer Press, 2001.

Little Casino. Minneapolis, Minn.: Coffee House Press, 2002.

The Moon in Its Flight. Minneapolis, Minn.: Coffee House Press, 2004. (Short stories.)

Lunar Follies. Minneapolis, Minn.: Coffee House Press, 2005.

A Strange Commonplace. Minneapolis, Minn.: Coffee House Press, 2006.

The Abyss of Human Illusion. Minneapolis, Minn.: Coffee House Press, 2010.

POETRY

The Darkness Surrounds Us. Highlands, N.C.: Jargon Society, 1960.

Black and White. New York: Totem Press, 1964.

The Perfect Fiction. New York: Norton, 1968.

Corrosive Sublimate. Santa Barbara, Calif.: Black Sparrow Press, 1971.

White Sail. Santa Barbara, Calif.: Black Sparrow Press, 1977.

The Orangery. Santa Barbara, Calif.: Black Sparrow Press, 1978.

Selected Poems, 1958–1980. Santa Barbara, Calif.: Black Sparrow Press, 1981.

New and Selected Poems, 1958–1998. Los Angeles: Green Integer Press, 2004.

OTHER WORKS

Elegiacs of Sulpicia. Mt. Horeb, Wis.: Perishable Press, 1977. (Translation from the Latin.)

Something Said. San Francisco: North Point Press, 1984. Expanded ed., Normal, Ill.: Dalkey Archive Press, 2001. (Essays.)

CRITICISM, INTERVIEWS, AND REVIEWS

The items cited below are available in libraries and on the major research databases. Stanford University keeps most of Sorrentino's papers, including manuscripts and literary correspondence.

Alpert, Barry, ed. *Vort* 2, no. 3 (fall 1974). Special issue on Gilbert Sorrentino. Essays by John O'Brien, Stephen Emerson, Robert Caserio, others.

Andrews, David. "Gilbert Sorrentino." *Review of Contemporary Fiction* 21, no. 3: 7–59 (fall 2001).

———. "The Art Is the Act of Smashing the Mirror: A Conversation with Gilbert Sorrentino." *Review of Contemporary Fiction* 21, no. 3: 60–68 (fall 2001).

Barone, Dennis. "An Interview with Gilbert Sorrentino." *Partisan Review* 48, no. 2: 236–246 (1981).

Davenport, Guy. "In Late Eclectic Modern." *New York Times Book Review,* Aug. 10, 1980, p. 15. (Review of *Aberration of Starlight.*)

Dirda, Michael. "The Far Side of Parodies." *Washington Post Book World,* June 17, 1979, pp. 1, 6. (Review of *Mulligan Stew.*)

Domini, John. "Blue Without Blues: Gilbert Sorrentino and the Subversion of the Novel." *Boston Phoenix,* July 5, 1983, sec. 3, pp. 3–6. (Review of *Blue Pastoral* and others.)

———. "Catharsis in Bebop." *Believer* 8, no. 1: 37–42 (January 2010). (Essay on entire career.)

Karl, Frederick Robert. *American Fictions, 1940–1980: A Comprehensive History and Critical Evaluation.* New York: Harper & Row, 1983.

Kenner, Hugh. "Gilbert Sorrentino: A Critical Mass." *Washington Post Book World,* February 10, 1985, pp. 3, 7. (Review of *Something Said.*)

Klinkowitz, Jerome. Review-essay on *Imaginative Qualities* and others. *Village Voice,* November 22, 1973, pp. 27–28.

———. *Literary Disruptions: The Making of a Post-Contemporary American Fiction.* Urbana: University of Illinois Press, 1980.

Leonard, John. "Mulligan Stew." *New York Times,* May 24, 1979, p. C21.

Mackey, Lewis. *Fact, Fiction, and Representation: Four Novels by Gilbert Sorrentino.* Columbia, S.C.: Camden House, 1997.

McPheron, William. *Gilbert Sorrentino: A Descriptive Bibliography.* Normal, Ill.: Dalkey Archive Press, 1991.

O'Brien, John, ed. *Review of Contemporary Fiction* 23, no. 1 (spring 2003). Five essays on *Imaginative Qualities of Actual Things,* by David Andrews, Tyrus Miller, Stacey Olster, Joseph Tabbi, Kevin Boon, plus bibliography.

O'Connell, Shaun. "Just What Grows in Brooklyn." *Nation* 212, June 21, 1971, pp. 790–792. (Review of *Steelwork.*)

O'Hara, J. D. "Coteries and Poetries." *Nation* 234, January 2, 1982, pp. 20–21. (Review of *Selected Poems.*)

Palmer, Barbara. "Professor Gilbert Sorrentino, leading avant-garde novelist, dead at 77." *Stanford News Service,* May 31, 2006. Available online (http://news.stanford.edu/pr/2006/pr-sorrentino-053106.html).

Peede, Jon. E-mail to John Domini. November 18, 2009.

Seidman, Hugh. "Poems and Excitement." *New York Times Book Review,* November 8, 1981, pp. 13, 32, 34–35. (Review of *Selected Poems.*)

Sorrentino, Christopher. E-mail to John Domini. October 14, 2009.

Trueheart, Charles. "PW Interviews Gilbert Sorrentino." May 27, 1983, pp. 70–71.

Williams, William Carlos. *The Collected Poems of William Carlos Williams.* Vol. 1, *1909–1939.* Edited by A. Walton Litz and Christopher MacGowan. New York: New Directions, 1991.

Natasha Trethewey

(1966—)

Joan Wylie Hall

THE PULITZER PRIZE–WINNING author Natasha Trethewey has written poetry about forgotten people, from early twentieth-century prostitutes and domestic workers to black Civil War soldiers and mixed-blood people in colonial Mexico. "I think I'm always asking myself a historical question," she told Sarah Dorn of the *Oklahoma Daily*, "because of my obsession with historical memory and erasure." Intrigued by intersections of public and private history, Trethewey finds subjects both in the communal past and in her own family. Many of the characters in her poems are of mixed race, like Trethewey herself; and many of the poems in her first and third volumes, *Domestic Work* (2000) and *Native Guard* (2006), confront her personal experience of marginalization. In *Bellocq's Ophelia* (2002), her second collection, she approaches issues of race, gender, and class through the persona of a New Orleans sex worker. Trethewey's poems and interviews cite many literary, photographic, artistic, and musical figures—among them Nina Simone, Toni Morrison, Richard Hugo, Susan Sontag, Langston Hughes, Winslow Homer, Rita Dove, and Seamus Heaney. Landscapes and people of the American South recur throughout her work: in her elegies for her mother, her laments on Hurricane Katrina, and her tributes to slaves and sharecroppers.

Trethewey in an interview with Robin Wright Gunn has said that she has a commitment to the education of underrepresented groups, especially in view of "the difficult history of blacks in America in education." Like her father, Eric Trethewey, she has given readings and workshops in the schools, in prisons, and in other public settings. Her poetry is often technically complex, yet she considers accessibility of ideas a virtue rather than a liability. She cites Robert Pinsky's "Favorite Poem" website, Ted Kooser's "American Life in Poetry" newspaper columns, and similar projects as evidence, she told Gunn, that "the future of poetry is bright."

BIOGRAPHY

Natasha Trethewey was born on April 26, 1966, in Gulfport, Mississippi, the daughter of the poet Eric Trethewey and Gwendolyn Ann Turnbough Trethewey, a social worker. She told Ray Suarez of the PBS *NewsHour* that the date of her birth was "exactly 100 years to the day that Mississippi celebrated the first Confederate Memorial Day." Trethewey's first name was inspired by that of the beautiful Natasha Rostov in Leo Tolstoy's *War and Peace*, a novel her father was reading before she was born. Her African American mother and her white Canadian father met as students at Kentucky State College, a historically black liberal arts school where Eric Trethewey, an amateur boxer, won a track scholarship. As Trethewey portrays them in the poem "Early Evening, Frankfort, Kentucky" (collected in *Domestic Work*), the couple were "full of laughter," the air around them "heady and sweet as Kentucky bourbon" (p. 27). Because interracial marriage was illegal in Mississippi, her mother's home state, the couple married in 1965 in Cincinnati, Ohio.

The family spent about a year in Canada, where her father was an officer in the Canadian Navy, but they relocated to the U.S. Gulf Coast. Eric Trethewey earned a master's degree in English at the University of New Orleans and began doctoral work at Tulane University, commuting from a New Orleans apartment to spend weekends in Gulfport with his wife and daughter. In the poem "Mythmaker," Trethewey describes

her young father—"squint-eyed / from books and lamplight"—telling bedtime stories about gods and goddesses (*Domestic Work.* p. 31). She told the interviewer Pearl McHaney that she had a "letter writing relationship" with her paternal grandmother and that, when she visited her Canadian family as an adult, "We felt that we knew each other" (p. 105). Yet, "in many ways they were the periphery, the part of a photograph that from a particular angle you won't get to see," she elaborated in conversation with Jill Petty (p. 369). Growing up in Gulfport, Trethewey was close to her maternal grandmother, Leretta Dixon Turnbough, and to her great-aunt Sugar, whom she considers her "muse" (Petty, p. 367). She memorializes these Mississippi elders in *Domestic Work*, particularly in the second section of the book, which describes black women's labors as domestic workers, beauticians, and factory employees.

Several pieces in *Domestic Work* and *Native Guard* reflect on Trethewey's experiences as a child who was "high-yellow, red-boned / in a black place" ("White Lies," *Domestic Work,* p. 37). "White Lies" recalls her occasional attempts to pass as white in grade school; ironically, her mother punishes her by washing out her mouth with Ivory soap. In "Flounder," Aunt Sugar tells Natasha to wear a hat when they go fishing since *"You 'bout as white as your dad, / and you gone stay like that"* (*Domestic Work,* p. 35). Sugar explains that their catch is a flounder because it has a black side and a white side; but "flounder" also means "struggle," and the flip-flopping fish of the poem "switch[es] sides with every jump" (*Domestic Work,* p. 36). Discussing this poem with Jonathan Fink, Trethewey said she couldn't have invented a better image "to represent my own tension as a mixed-race person." Her aunt, she adds, was "trying to help me understand" in her "subtle ways" (p. 21).

In the *Native Guard* poem "Blond," Trethewey wryly speculates that her parents' recessive genes could have endowed her with spirited blond hair; and she remembers the year her Christmas gifts included a tall blond ballerina doll, a blond wig, and a pink tutu. Dancing about she becomes the child she might have been. Tre-

thewey hints at her parents' reaction by comparing her father to Joseph, father of baby Jesus, beholding the unexpected birth.

In the late 1960s, when Trethewey was a few years old, the Ku Klux Klan burned a cross, "trussed like a Christmas tree" ("Incident," *Native Guard,* p. 41), in front of their house. Although the action might have been directed at an activist black church across the street rather than her biracial household, the effect on the child was lasting. "We tell the story every year" is both the first and final line of the poem (p. 41), which compares the gowned white men to a gathering of angels who leave the scene quietly while the family watches behind drawn shades. The "trembling" wicks of the hurricane lamps that her parents light in their darkened home contrast with the startling flames of the Klan's cross; the image also suggests a parallel between the natural disaster of coastal hurricanes and the tragedy of racial hatred.

Trethewey's parents divorced when she was six. Trethewey moved to Atlanta with her mother, who enrolled in a graduate program in social work; she spent summers on the Gulf Coast, splitting the time between her grandmother in Gulfport and her father in New Orleans. She told Emory University's Eric Rangus that the excellent food in New Orleans restaurants and the stimulating conversations afterward with her father's friends convinced her that "this is the life I want to have—reading, writing and thinking all day, and talking with interesting people." In a 2008 essay for the *Antioch Review*, Eric Trethewey characterizes the divorce as amicable and confesses that he had lacked the maturity to commit himself fully to marriage and fatherhood. He says, "Most of my energies were going into working long hours just to survive, to doing domestic chores—such as painting the house, mowing the yard—and into reading, writing, and, in general, pursuing the literary life that might someday bring success" (p. 684). The father and daughter have frequently shared the platform for poetry readings. "He has been proud of me from day one," Trethewey told the Savannah journalist Robin Wright Gunn. "It didn't take the Pulitzer to make him proud of me."

Trethewey began composing verse at an early age. In an interview with Deborah Solomon of the *New York Times*, she said that her father suggested she write poems when she was bored on long car trips. In third grade at an all-black school, she wrote poems about Martin Luther King, Jr., George Washington, and other historic figures. Her teacher bound the pages, and the Venetian Hills Elementary librarian placed the volume in the library. A couple of years later, Trethewey read *The Diary of Anne Frank*, a volume that appeared on her *Newsweek* list of "My Five Most Important Books" in 2007. In an interview with Jonathan Fink of the University of West Florida journal *Panhandler*, Trethewey said Anne Frank "articulated something that I felt I had begun to understand as a child growing up in the deep south between Mississippi and Georgia. Her experience spoke to me and I think it was reading that that I first felt what it means to have empathy for someone else who is different yet very much the same" (p. 20). At Redan High School in Stone Mountain, Georgia, Trethewey wrote fiction and edited the school newspaper.

Her parents maintained a friendly relationship, even after her mother remarried; but Eric Trethewey says he did not realize that the second husband was increasingly abusive. Natasha's stepfather drove her around Atlanta when she was young and threatened to drop her off at a mental institution; for years, her mother was the victim of the man's physical abuse. Her mother filed for divorce when Trethewey was a high school senior, and her stepfather spent a year in prison for abducting her mother at gunpoint. In 1985, when Trethewey was a freshman at the University of Georgia in Athens, and her brother Joe was ten, their mother was shot to death by the boy's father. Trethewey told the *Emory Magazine* writer Mary J. Loftus that she "turned to poetry" to "try to grapple with that huge loss" and to "try to make sense of the world and me in it." She told Loftus that some of her early efforts at poetry writing were embarrassing: "I actually wrote a poem that had a line in it about sinking into an ocean of despair, with the word 'sinking' going diagonally down the page." With self-deprecating humor, Trethewey added that her

father and her stepmother, the poet Katherine Soniat, "ripped that poem to shreds. I ran upstairs sobbing, vowing never to write another poem."

As Trethewey remarks in her *Virginia Quarterly Review* essay "Congregation," her brother moved to their grandmother Turnbough's house in Mississippi after their mother's death and became a statistic, "one of the many African-American children living with a grandparent." In 1989, Trethewey completed her bachelor's degree in English at the University of Georgia, where she was a varsity cheerleader. After working for a year and a half as a food stamp caseworker in Augusta, Georgia, she earned an MA in English and creative writing at Hollins, a private liberal arts college in Roanoke, Virginia, whose award-winning graduates include such writers as Annie Dillard, Lee Smith, Madison Smartt Bell, and Kiran Desai. Trethewey's teachers at Hollins included her father and her stepmother. She says Eric Trethewey was "literally my first professor in a creative writing classroom, beyond what you learn from a parent who's a writer" (Gunn).

Dedicated to Eric Trethewey and Soniat, her unpublished thesis, "Working Roots: A Collection of Poetry and Prose," opens with an epigraph from the African American author James Baldwin. The final thesis selection, a poem titled "Warming," is dedicated to Trethewey's mother. Anticipating such *Native Guard* elegies as "Graveyard Blues" and "Myth," the poem portrays her mother's burial site as muddy, cold, yet spiritually important. An early version of "Flounder" appears in the thesis, along with other poems about childhood, memory, and passing for white that look ahead to both the *Domestic Work* and *Native Guard* collections. The serious sort of wordplay in the titles "Flounder" and "Working Roots" remains a significant feature of Trethewey's writing. Another powerful example in the thesis is the "Crossing Over" section, whose poems refer to racial passing, death, thresholds, and sleep, together with the physical crossing of roads and streets. Years later, Trethewey introduced the first section of *Native Guard* poems with an epigraph from "Going over Jordan," a traditional spiritual about "crossing over."

Some of the "Working Roots" poetry, such as the nightmarish "Baptism," speaks more directly about her mother's violent death than any of Trethewey's published work. Both the language and the situations of several thesis pieces are rougher and more raw than those usually associated with her poetry. Her experience as a caseworker, her own working roots, was a probable influence on three stories—"When It's Clear and Hot," "QUILLA," and "Mary"—as well as the poem "The Welfare Worker, Disenchanted, Contemplates Friday Afternoon." Although a large portion of the thesis is fiction, Trethewey focused on poetry during her subsequent MFA studies at the University of Massachusetts at Amherst. There, her professors included the PEN/ Faulkner Award–winner John Wideman.

In Massachusetts, Trethewey joined the Dark Room, a Boston collective of young African American writers—among them, Sharan Strange, Cornelius Eady, and Thomas Sayers Ellis—with whom she "felt safe to try new things because I [knew I'd] get a close and careful reading, an honest response" (Petty, p. 375). She had begun to publish poetry at Hollins; and a year before she graduated from the University of Massachusetts MFA program for poets and writers, four of her poems were collected in anthologies. "Flounder" and "White Lies" appeared in *Two Worlds Walking: A Mixed-Blood Anthology*, edited by Diane Glancy and C. W. Truesdale (New Rivers Press, 1994), while "Drapery Factory, Gulfport, Mississippi, 1956" and "Naola Beauty Academy, New Orleans, 1943" were selected for *On the Verge: Emerging Poets*, edited by Thomas Sayers Ellis and Joseph Lease for New Cambridge Press (1994). Before the publication of Trethewey's *Domestic Work*, additional poems were anthologized in books as diverse as *Spirit and Flame: An Anthology of African American Poetry*, edited by Keith Gilyard (Syracuse University Press, 1997); *Boomer Girls: Poems by Women of the Baby Boom Generation*, edited by Pamela Gemin and Paula Sergi (University of Iowa Press, 1999); and *The Best American Poetry 2000*, edited by Rita Dove and David Lehman for Scribner Books (2000).

Dove, the United States poet laureate and consultant to the Library of Congress from 1993 to 1995, selected Trethewey in 1999 as winner of the inaugural Cave Canem Poetry Prize, the first of her many national honors. A first-book award for outstanding African American writers, the Cave Canem recognition entails not only a cash prize and guaranteed publication but also a public reading in New York cosponsored by the Academy of American Poets. In 2001, *Domestic Work* won the Lillian Smith Book Award, established by the Southern Regional Council in honor of Smith's outspoken rejection of segregation and other forms of social injustice. The *Domestic Work* manuscript incorporated several poems from Trethewey's MFA thesis and was published in 2000 by Graywolf, a press whose poetry list includes Tess Gallagher, William Stafford, Elizabeth Alexander, Carl Phillips, and other highly regarded authors. Just two years later, Graywolf published *Bellocq's Ophelia*, a very different poetic venture.

Like *Domestic Work*, *Bellocq's Ophelia* won a Mississippi Institute of Arts and Letters poetry award; but Trethewey's biracial Ophelia is a fictional creation whose life in a Storyville brothel in early twentieth-century New Orleans is far removed from the world of *Domestic Work*. Moreover, the newer book develops a more cohesive narrative, and free verse and unrhymed sonnets are prominent, in contrast to the more varied verse forms of *Domestic Work*. The inspiration for Trethewey's title character was a group of E. J. Bellocq's photographs of unnamed prostitutes, pictures she discovered in a graduate course titled Materials for the Study of American Culture. Debora Rindge and Anna Leahy call attention to the "complex intertexuality of this ekphrastic art in which two artists' imaginations—Bellocq's and Trethewey's—are at play" (p. 304). Trethewey has cited Ruth Whitman's verse narrative in *Tamsen Donner: A Woman's Journey* (1977), a fictionalized account of the doomed travels of the Donner Party, as another influence on her second book. Several of Trethewey's Ophelia poems appeared first in anthologies and in such well-known journals as *Callaloo, New England Review, Shenandoah*, and the *Southern*

Review. While teaching as an assistant professor at Auburn University in Alabama, she won a Bunting Fellowship to spend a year at the Radcliffe Institute for Advanced Study at Harvard University so she could complete the manuscript in 2000–2001. Her extensive research, which was also supported by the National Endowment for the Arts, involved trips to New Orleans archives.

Trethewey joined the faculty of Emory University in Atlanta as assistant professor in 2001. On sabbatical, she served as the Lehman Brady Joint Chair Professor of Documentary and American Studies at Duke University and the University of North Carolina at Chapel Hill during the 2005–2006 school year. In the aftermath of Hurricane Katrina, her grandmother Turnbough temporarily moved from Gulfport to join Trethewey in Durham, North Carolina. The storm's massive devastation became a subject of Trethewey's poetry, essays, lectures, and interviews with survivors. Some of her conversations with Gulf Coast residents, photographed by Joshua Cogan, appear on the *YouTube* website as segments of *In Verse*, a multimedia documentary project that combines photos, poems, and audio footage. Trethewey's essay "Congregation" and a series of poems from this project appeared in the fall 2009 issue of *Virginia Quarterly Review*, accompanied by Cogan's photography. Some of the pictures are portraits of her brother, who worked for months clearing the beach and watching the Gulf waters for storm wreckage, including human remains. As a keynote speaker at the September 2009 Berry College Southern Women Writers Conference in Rome, Georgia, Trethewey read "Watcher," one of the *In Verse* poems, in moving tribute to her brother, who attended the program.

In support of her Pulitzer Prize–winning third collection, Trethewey received grants from the Guggenheim Foundation and the Rockefeller Foundation Bellagio Study and Conference Center. The book also won the 2008 Mississippi Governor's Award for Excellence in the Arts in Poetry. Published by Houghton Mifflin, *Native Guard* extends further back in southern history than Trethewey's previous volumes. The title sequence of unrhymed sonnets is narrated by an African American soldier from Louisiana who serves with a Union regiment at Ship Island, Mississippi, during the Civil War. The book also reprises Trethewey's family story, especially her mother's death. Several poems in the final section of *Native Guard* address Trethewey's complicated relationship with the South. In the concluding poem, titled simply "South," she contrasts monuments of the Confederacy with the unacknowledged suffering of generations of African Americans, recalling the illegality of her own parents' marriage in Mississippi.

Trethewey is currently a professor of English at Emory, where she holds the Phillis Wheatley Distinguished Chair in Poetry. She lives in Decatur, Georgia, with her husband, Brett Gadsden, a historian who teaches in the African American Studies department at Emory. In 2008, the Georgia Commission on Women named her the Georgia Woman of the Year; she was also honored at Georgia's Men Stopping Violence annual awards dinner. Trethewey attended the inauguration of President Barack Obama in January 2009, and she told National Public Radio's *Fresh Air* host Terry Gross, "As a poet, I am always concerned about history and bearing witness to history. But so often, it's through the research that I do, the reading. And this is an amazing opportunity to be there in the flesh to bear witness to a historical moment." In April 2009, Trethewey was inducted into the Fellowship of Southern Writers in Chattanooga, Tennessee, along with Rita Dove, Will D. Campbell, Edward P. Jones, and other new members. The following month, she visited Korea as a guest cultural speaker at the invitation of the American Embassy. Trethewey spent the fall semester at Yale University as the Beinecke Library's 2009 James Weldon Johnson Fellow in African American Studies.

During her 2009–2010 sabbatical from Emory, Trethewey continued to give readings on many campuses and was a featured guest at literary conferences and book festivals. In January 2010, she joined a rare gathering of poets laureate, Pulitzer poets, and other award-winning writers at the Key West Literary Seminar to honor Richard Wilbur by celebrating sixty years of

American poetry. She was on the spring program at New York's 92nd Street Y, a legendary venue for poetry readings. Trethewey was working on two books in 2010. Her first nonfiction volume, *Beyond Katrina: A Meditation on the Mississippi Gulf Coast*, expands her lectures from the University of Virginia's 2007 Page-Barbour Lecture Series. Her fourth poetry collection, which Trethewey says will be titled *Thrall*, was inspired by paintings of eighteenth-century Mexicans of mixed race. Trethewey's research for this exploration of a deeper South includes elements that are new to her poems—not only the codified artwork but also colonial maps, captivity narratives, and botany books. Once again, however, she gives voice to forgotten people, writing their histories in vivid lines.

DOMESTIC WORK

Domestic Work, Trethewey's first poetry collection, underscores her realization that personal and public histories are often intertwined. The poet's mother, grandmother, and great-aunt are central figures in *Domestic Work*; but Trethewey also portrays laboring African Americans whom she knows only through their century-old photographs. In the first of the volume's four divisions, she brackets private material (a poem about Son Dixon, her great-uncle) with more public matters (poems based on Clifton Johnson's photographic portraits of black workers from 1901 and 1902). When Trethewey was an MFA student, one of her poetry teachers, Margaret Gibson, made her aware of the relationship between the family poems she was then writing and an exhibit of Johnson's photos they viewed together at a University of Massachusetts gallery. "Until that moment," says Trethewey in an interview with Jonathan Fink, "I hadn't thought that, as I was writing my grandmother's story, that I was writing a larger narrative of a people, that her story (that seemed so personal and so family) was also a story that spoke to the larger condition of people in the Jim Crow south" (p. 22).

The poem "History Lesson" illustrates this insight especially well by juxtaposing two family photographs taken at the shore. First, Trethewey describes a 1970 picture of herself at four in a "bright" flowered bikini, taken by her grandmother on a "wide strip of Mississippi beach" (*Domestic Work,* p. 45). She contrasts this snapshot with a photo of her grandmother, taken forty years earlier on "a narrow plot / of sand marked *colored*" (p. 45); in her youth, the grandmother wears a flowered "cotton meal-sack dress," a detail that evokes the grueling sharecropper economy of the past. Born in 1916, Leretta Dixon Turnbough would have been fourteen as the country entered the Depression era. While the narrowness of the segregated space in the older picture hints at the restrictions limiting earlier generations of black southerners, the picture of young Natasha was made two years after the beach was integrated in 1968. The contrast indicates at least a small degree of progress for black southerners during the Civil Rights era. The grandmother posed in 1930 in a handmade dress of cheap material, inappropriate garb for swimming; but her bikini-clad granddaughter is ready to test the waters. In "Domestic Work, 1937" and other poems, Trethewey imagines both her grandmother's physical labors and her dreams of escape when she was in her twenties; but, because the protagonist is not always identified, the poetry represents the lives of many black southern women. Trethewey told the interviewer Jill Petty that the "she" of the *Domestic Work* poems is "filled with all sorts of characteristics that are my own," but this character inhabits "a different time" and undergoes "different experiences" (p. 373).

Watching for good-luck signs, longing to see new sights, a young woman in "Signs, Oakvale, Mississippi, 1941" reviews the promises made to her by the man who is driving her northward on Highway 49. Trethewey reminded Petty that this is "*the* Highway 49 of all the blues songs" (p. 368). With its story of cotton fields, a road trip, and threatened heartache, the poem could be a blues narrative; but Trethewey shapes it as a sonnet, unexpectedly using Shakespeare's genre to portray her humble characters. The driver in Trethewey's lyrics promises his companion "new dresses, a house where she'd be / queen"

(*Domestic Work,* p. 16). Unfortunately, he has a gap between his teeth ("*cause for alarm?*"); and, on the journey away from home, the only other signs the woman notices are equally bad: "cotton and road signs—*stop* or *slow*" (p. 16).

In her introduction to *Domestic Work*, the former poet laureate Rita Dove admires the "steely grace" with which Trethewey "tells the hard facts of lives pursued on the margins, lived out under oppression and scripted oblivion, with fear and a tremulous hope" (p. xii). Trethewey's grandmother smiles in "History Lesson," even though she is relegated to a small strip of sand at a far edge of the South. Throughout the collection, Trethewey's characters remain hopeful in a number of ways, despite the "hard facts" of their lives. Women who could be her grandmother, her great-aunt, her mother, and their peers rejoice in good omens; they also sing, dance, style their hair, decorate their homes, gather fruit, go fishing, and—in the poem "Housekeeping"—watch all day "for the mail, some news from a distant place" (p. 52). Chilled colas and a "dripping green" melon are Sunday treats in the poem "Secular": "parlor music" and "blues parlando" play on a "brand new graphanola" down the street (p. 15). The "she" in this same scene steps out in lipstick, nylon stockings, and a fragrant pomade:

Dixie Peach in her hair,
greased forehead shining
like gospel, like gold.

Many lines in "Secular" are fewer than seven syllables, as if to emphasize the brief span of the day of rest. In these precious segments, each small luxury glows, and hair grease is transformed to gold.

Women are more in evidence than men in *Domestic Work*, both at work and at leisure; but Trethewey's uncle Son Dixon establishes a hopeful note near the start of the book. Manning his cash register, and with more money in his pocket, he stands at the center of the action in his "New Orleans tailored suits" in the poem "At the Owl Club, North Gulfport, Mississippi, 1950" (p. 4). Kelly Ellis praises Trethewey's "eye for the fine threads woven into ordinary lives" (Ellis 52), a metaphor that is actualized in Son Dixon's fine

apparel. The mirrors of his bar reflect the crowd of workers from the city's dangerous docks as they gather in the "colored man's club" on payday (*Domestic Work,* p. 4). Mirrors, windows, lenses, and reflections appear in many contexts in Trethewey's books, beginning with the Romare Bearden cover art for *Domestic Work*; at her uncle's bar, mirrors double the energy in a room where there is "nothing idle" (p. 4). The patrons' "lace-up boots say *shipyard.* / Dirt-caked trousers, *yard work.*" Rough though it is, such employment is hard to find; nevertheless, these men hold "Regal Quarts in hand" (p. 5). Their beers, like Son Dixon's suits, come from New Orleans, a more cosmopolitan, more accepting society than Mississippi was for black males in 1950. At the same time, the word "Regal" dignifies the Owl Club scene, much as the dream of becoming queen in a home of her own—instead of domestic help in a white woman's house—lifts a young woman's spirit in "Signs, Oakvale, Mississippi, 1941."

Trethewey told Jill Petty that she read Rita Dove's Pulitzer Prize–winning *Thomas and Beulah* (1986) "upside down and back and forth" when she was "trying to write the poems about my grandmother's life and trying to get away from being the first-person narrator in all my poems" (p. 368). Like Trethewey, Dove merges personal narratives with public ones: her grandparents Thomas and Beulah shared the experience of thousands of African Americans who hopefully made the Great Migration from South to North. Trethewey learned from Dove's poetry that "there are moments in any story that can make up the whole world of a poem" (Petty, p. 368). Thus, the *Domestic Work* poet expresses the mixture of pain and beauty in her mother's life by means of a hair straightening ritual in "Hot Combs"; and her aunt's harvest of green figs in "Gathering" sums up Trethewey's early instructions in patient waiting.

Trethewey also admires Sharon Olds's poetry because "she can attach meaning to the smallest details in a photograph, and I think for any poet that's a wonderful thing" (Petty, p. 369). Like Olds, Trethewey finds significance in the photograph's most prosaic scenes. "Gesture of a

Woman-in-Process," the title of the opening poem in *Domestic Work*, interprets the blurred motion of a working woman's hands and apron as a deliberate sign of resistance. Discussing the 1902 photo with the *Callaloo* editor Charles Rowell, Trethewey explains: "It suggested to me something about the way people will not simply be confined to the frames into which we might put them, historically or in memory, and that indeed her gesture of continual movement enables her to resist being trapped in that particular historical framework" (p. 1024).

Trethewey's analysis of this "very domestic kind of photograph" (Rowell, p. 1024), reveals the multiplicity of meanings she attaches to "domestic work," a term that can include her own poetic labors as well as the pictured woman's struggles with her laundry, her garden, and her photographer. But Trethewey told Rowell that her poems also explore a deeper sense of domestic work as "the everyday work that we do as human beings to live with or without people that we've lost, the work of memory and forgetting, and of self-discovery—not simply the work of earning a living and managing our households, but that larger, daily, domestic work that all of us do" (pp. 1026–1027). The woman photographed a century ago by Clifton Johnson has much in common with the Dixons and Turnboughs of Gulfport, Mississippi. That woman's blurred gesture, says Trethewey, "keeps moving on into our contemporary days, and suggests something to us about the continual process of her life, of history, and of the creation and revision of cultural memory" (Rowell, p. 1024).

Most of the *Domestic Work* poems were first published in literary journals and anthologies, but they are not randomly arranged in the collection. Trethewey told Rowell that the book "moves from historical figures in photographs—people I don't know—to the life of my maternal grandmother within a particular historical moment, to an exploration of the immediate family history, as in the poem 'Early Evening, Frankfort, Kentucky,' to poems like 'Carpenter Bee' and 'Limen,' which end the collection with the speaker reflecting on the nature of personal memory" (p. 1027). Adopting a photographic metaphor, Trethewey compares this movement to a lens whose aperture progressively narrows. The four-part movement roughly corresponds to the four divisions of *Domestic Work*. And the concluding poem, "Limen"—as Trethewey explains to Rowell—circles back to "Gesture of a Woman-in-Process" by portraying women engaged in the domestic work of laundry. In both poems, memory and imagination allow the speaker to bridge a distance "across time and space," effecting a liminal or threshold experience (p. 1027).

In "the cluttered house of memory," the speaker of the haunting "Limen" can "almost see my mother's face" (*Domestic Work*, p. 58). Similarly, a beloved mother is the goal of memory's difficult search in many other pieces from the last two sections of *Domestic Work*. The autobiographical element is unmistakable to readers familiar with the tragedy of Trethewey's mother's violent death after a long period of physical abuse by Trethewey's stepfather. Anticipating the elegiac lyrics of *Native Guard*, poems like "Cameo" and "Family Portrait" summon up the mother's presence. With a title that evokes royal profiles, semiprecious materials, and family heirlooms, "Cameo" recollects a cameo scene from childhood mornings. A girl watches her mother apply makeup at the vanity mirror, "the warm scent of her body filling the tiny room" (*Domestic Work*, p. 28), but metaphors of a mastectomy and a severed head add a dark tenor to this memory. And, although the mother's cameo is on a velvet ribbon, it presses "hard enough to bruise" (p. 28). Ominous, too, is "Family Portrait," which remembers "our only portrait," photographed by a legless man who "scratch[es] air" for his phantom limbs, "as—years later—I'd itch for what's not there" (p. 30). The psychological itch is not only for a mother lost to death but for a family lost to divorce. Written in the present tense and the first person, this poem portrays the mother in ongoing action, cheerfully cleaning house with her daughter before the photo session: "She hums / Motown, doles out chores" (p. 30). Trethewey refers twice to "Mama" and twice, more remotely, to "my father" (never Papa); they pose for their picture with "me / in between" (p. 30). Trethewey told Jill Petty that

men "do make their presence known in my work, often by their absences," and that the absence is often "the reason for the photographs" (p. 369).

By picturing herself "in between," the speaker implies the opposing pull of her parents on her emotions, but the position also states her situation as a biracial child. In the third section of *Domestic Work*, the poems "Flounder" and "White Lies" are followed by two other meditations on the inner struggles of mixed-race children. Moreover, the speaker of "Microscope" and "Saturday Matinee" remembers herself at an in-between age. As an enthusiastic sixth grader, she is excited about science class until she comes upon a disturbing entry on "*Races of Man*" when she is looking for "*Rays of Light*" in the *World Book Encyclopedia 1966*, "bought for the year / I was born" (*Domestic Work*, p. 38). Because Trethewey herself was born in 1966, she could be relating a personal encounter with racial stereotyping. The biracial speaker of "Microscope" fits none of the categories defined in the family encyclopedia: "*Caucasoid, Negroid, Mongoloid*" (p. 38). Mathematical calculations of body parts, from skull to tibia, turn people into equations: "Hair texture, eye shape, color. Each image / a template for measure, mismeasure" (p. 38). And, under the lens of the teacher's microscope, the girl's "straight and shiny" hair sample "lose[s] its luster" (pp. 38, 39).

The 1959 film *Imitation of Life* provides an escapist fantasy in the poem "Saturday Matinee." Blocking out the sound of her stepfather's loud voice, her mother's whisper, and "the dull smack" in the next room, the young speaker is dazzled by "rays of light, a sparkling world" at the start of the televised movie about "a mixed girl … someone like me" (*Domestic Work*. pp. 41, 40). Repeated from the preceding poem, the phrase "rays of light" illuminates these episodes of childhood suffering. Like the celluloid girl, the speaker wants her mother to be the golden Lana Turner character, not "the run-down mama, her blues—" (p. 40). In the larger context of her first book, however, Trethewey embraces these blues, echoing the genre's narratives and rhythms. Rita Dove praises the many forms Trethewey's lyrics take: "From sonnets and traditional ballads to free verses shot through with the syncopated attitude of blues, the poems in *Domestic Work* sing with a muscular luminosity" (*Domestic Work*, p. xii).

BELLOCQ'S OPHELIA

While blues and Motown are familiar rhythms in *Domestic Work*, a jazz piano supplies the background beat for *Bellocq's Ophelia*, Trethewey's second poetry volume and a 2003 Notable Book of the American Library Association. Set in the Storyville red-light district of New Orleans between 1910 and 1912, the story describes a young woman who leaves a life of rural poverty in Mississippi to find a "modest position" in the city ("Letter Home," *Bellocq's Ophelia*, p. 7). Instead, she catches the eye of "Countess P—," the madam of an elegant brothel that features beautiful women of mixed race for a white clientele. Trethewey's prefatory note explains that Ophelia is the poet's "*imagined name*" for the prostitute in some of E. J. Bellocq's famous Storyville photographs. A "*very white-skinned black woman—mulatto, quadroon, or octoroon*" (*Bellocq's Ophelia*, p. 6), she is pictured on the cover of *Bellocq's Ophelia* in white furs and white beaded gown. Most Storyville prostitutes were white, and Trethewey observes that the few houses staffed by African American women included the Basin Street mansion of Willie Piazza and "*Lula White's Mahogany Hall, which, according to the* Blue Book, *was known as the 'Octoroon Club'*" (*Bellocq's Ophelia*, p. 6).

Trethewey's research in New Orleans archives is evident in the authenticity of historic details in *Bellocq's Ophelia*. The combination of jazz and Storyville was a vibrant component of the city's culture at the start of the twentieth century. In the first of her fourteen free-verse "Letters from Storyville," Ophelia describes "the 'professor' working the piano / into a frenzy" each night in Countess P—'s parlor (*Bellocq's Ophelia*, p. 12). Jelly Roll Morton and other solo pianists in the city's brothels were typically called "professor" by respectful young women like Ophelia. Among the lavish reception rooms in Willie Piazza's house was the "Mirrored Parlor";

and Countess P—boasts to her "girls" that everything is multiplied in her own "mirrored parlor," where "one glass of champagne is twenty. You'll see / yourself a hundred times" (*Bellocq's Ophelia*, p. 11). The surreal duplication has a freak-show element, as does Ophelia's reference to "the lewd sights of Emma Johnson's circus" (*Bellocq's Ophelia*, p. 40) in one of the more boisterous brothels. Johnson, a particularly notorious madam, arranged sex shows in her "House of All Nations." Ophelia also alludes to Storyville's "blue books," or guides for visitors, quoting a profile that Countess P—writes for "the book" (*Bellocq's Ophelia*, p. 40). Violet, as the madam renames Ophelia, is a "*fair-skinned beauty*" who recites poetry and "*performs her tableau vivant, becomes / a living statue, an object of art*" (p. 40). Violet, Ophelia explains in another poem, is "a common name here in Storyville"; in the 1978 film *Pretty Baby*, Brooke Shields plays an adolescent named Violet, born in a Storyville brothel and, like Trethewey's Ophelia, an intriguing subject for Bellocq. Ophelia, however, is marketed as "the *African Violet*," with the allure of a "wild continent hidden beneath / my white skin" (p. 13).

The national fashion for tableaux vivants was not limited to Storyville; but these "living pictures" or frozen scenes are powerful metaphors for the carefully displayed women of the district's houses. Like expensive paintings on the walls, the prostitutes become cold objects of strangers' scrutiny. Although some public tableaux of the Victorian era represented religious scenes, others meticulously imitated paintings; and the late-nineteenth-century popularity of the nude tableau vivant probably influenced Storyville entertainments. Countess P—commands Ophelia to practice "strange postures" until the call of "*Tableau vivant*" frees her to move again (*Bellocq's Ophelia*, p. 13). Ophelia says "visitors from the North" make an especially "great fuss" about the Countess's octoroons (p. 26), because the women's very existence constitutes a show: "customers fill our parlors / to see the spectacle: black women / with white skin" (p. 26). In another poem, Ophelia admits she is distressed that she has a talent "for this work—spectacle

and fetish— / a pale odalisque" (p. 20). Instructed by the madam to please the customer always, Ophelia understands that exercises in movement and stillness make her body a highly desirable commodity. The "musical undulation of my hips, my grace" will assure gentlemen that she can "pose still as a statue for hours, / a glass or a pair of boots propped upon my back" (p. 14).

The grotesque image of boots resting for hours on a woman's back—as if she is a floor— is a shocking reminder that Storyville's prostitutes remain vulnerable to a partner's most perverse desires. Even though Ophelia writes home to assure her friend and former teacher Constance that she is well paid and content with her labors, both her letters and her private journal—the forms these poems take—also record doubts and confusion. Some encounters at the brothel awaken nightmarish scenes from Ophelia's past, when she worked in Mississippi's cotton fields and was sexually threatened by at least two white males. Confronted with brothel clients "whose desires I cannot commit / to paper," Ophelia remembers a day at the farm store, when a "sneering" man "pinch[ed] / the tiny buds of my new breasts" (*Bellocq's Ophelia*, p. 18). In another letter to Constance, she describes her fear when she was unable to answer a Storyville client's surprising question: "*What do* you *want?*" (*Bellocq's Ophelia*, p. 23). She felt cornered, as she feels in a recurring dream about a man who apparently raped her in a tobacco barn back home. In the nightmare, the white man "wears a carnival mask, / and I am the grinning *nigger* / on whose tongue he places a shiny coin" (*Bellocq's Ophelia*, p. 23). Consistent with many other references to money and commodification in *Bellocq's Ophelia*, the racist image describes a Jim Crow–era mechanical toy bank; the figure's tongue moves to receive and deposit coins in a cartoonish African American head. In light of Trethewey's narrative, the tongue also indicates a phallic threat against Ophelia, whose subconscious forces her to connect her current business with her past victimization.

One of Ophelia's worst fears is the possibility that her father might present himself as her client. In the first diary sonnet, we learn that this

white man was responsible for naming her Ophelia. But in the journal entry labeled "Father," Ophelia acknowledges that she knows very little about him; she does recall that, when she was a child, "I feared his visits, though he would bring gifts" (*Bellocq's Ophelia*, p. 38). Her dealings with men at the brothel have obvious parallels with this paternal relationship. In "exchange" for her father's gifts, Ophelia writes, she had to "present fingernails / and ears, open my mouth to show the teeth" (p. 38). While treating her like a prized horse (the gifts include apples), or possibly a prized slave, he also expects his daughter to amuse him intellectually. In a low voice, Ophelia would "recite my lessons" (p. 38); now, she recites poetry for brothel visitors. If her childhood grammar and punctuation were careless—confusing "*lay* for *lie*," for example—her father "would stop me there" (p. 38). Trethewey's choice of mistaken verbs is hardly accidental; Ophelia dreads the day a man, "both customer and father" (p. 38), might come to Storyville to lie with her.

Fortunately, Papá Bellocq, as Ophelia calls him, arrives instead; and he lies neither to her nor with her. In the diary entry "Bellocq," the photographer comes to her room, proposing to "take me / as I would arrange myself" (p. 39), either dressed in full finery or nude. Placing "take me" at the end of a line, Trethewey briefly allows the reader to assume Bellocq is just another customer, perhaps one with a camera fetish since he carries one on his back. Ophelia tries to guess which poses he might prefer; "shy / at first," she becomes "bolder," even though she somewhat cynically remarks that "this photograph *we* make / will bear the stamp of his name, not mine" (p. 39). She is right; it takes Trethewey to recover Ophelia's voice and her name. In the study *Ordering the Façade: Photography and Contemporary Southern Women's Writing*, Katherine Henninger argues that "in addition to a disarmingly candid approach, Bellocq's Storyville portraits reflect a long tradition of sexual exploitation of light-skinned 'black' women in the South that in New Orleans became a cultural institution" (p. 44).

Nevertheless, the collaboration between Bellocq and Trethewey's Ophelia has a happy ending of an unconventional sort. The prostitute becomes not only the photographer's model but his assistant as well. In Bellocq's time, he was known for his commercial photographs, and Ophelia accompanies him to a New Orleans shipyard, where she sharpens her eye for lines and angles. Studying the camera's reflection of light and dark, she discovers she is "drawn to what shines": "iridescent" fish scales, gilded words on a shop window, bottles struck by sunlight, and—most tellingly—flesh that "glow[s] / as if the soul's been caught / shimmering just beneath the skin" (*Bellocq's Ophelia*, p. 27). As Henninger remarks, "Ophelia learns to seize creative initiative" (p. 172). In both her final message to Constance and her last diary entry, she declares that she has left Countess P—'s house and is traveling to the American west by train. On a postcard dated March 1912, Ophelia tells her friend she is aware of spring's advent "as I've never been"; like trees "budding, green sheaths splitting," she breaks forth into new life (*Bellocq's Ophelia*, p. 33). Her final journal entry, also from March 1912, is headed "(Self) Portrait." At the end of her story, Ophelia is no longer viewed through a male lens. In an interview with David Haney, Trethewey emphasizes that "Ophelia has been victimized" but she still "is an agent, and she is making choices to get to where she wants to go" (p. 25).

The book's final poem, the retrospective "Vignette," envisions Ophelia at the close of a modeling session with Bellocq: "stepping out / of the frame, wide-eyed, into her life" (*Bellocq's Ophelia*, p. 48). Full of conjectures, the unidentified speaker describes the cover photo of *Bellocq's Ophelia* and imagines Ophelia's past labors in Storyville: "the weight of a body pressing her down," her breath "shallow," and her back "straining the stays of a bustier" (*Bellocq's Ophelia*, p. 47). The reviewer Adrian Oktenberg links the gradual metamorphosis recorded in Ophelia's letters and journal to her purchase of a camera: "So equipped, she literally begins to see for herself, to shape her own world" (p. 21). And, in contrast to Bellocq's bulky equipment and fragile photographic plates, Ophelia's small and sturdy Kodak is a light burden to carry—much

lighter than the burdens of the brothel. "Vignette" closes the frame that opens with the title poem, "Bellocq's Ophelia"; each focuses on a different photographic portrait. The opening poem compares John Everett Millais's painting of Shakespeare's tragic Ophelia, floating lifeless on a pond, to Bellocq's pose of a cold and naked Ophelia, prone on a divan. At the end of the poem, however, the lips of the Storyville woman are "poised to open, to speak" (*Bellocq's Ophelia*, p. 3). "Instead of insanity and death," says Annette Debo, "Trethewey's Ophelia is given a voice with which to recount lost American history" (p. 202).

Trethewey told Charles Rowell that "Bellocq's Ophelia," "Vignette," and "Photograph of a Bawd Drinking Raleigh Rye" (situated between Ophelia's letters and her diary entries) introduce "the voice of the viewer, who is looking at the photographs, that voice which is closest to the poet's" (Rowell, p. 1029). Trethewey has also commented on her identification with Ophelia. "I was searching for a persona through whom I might investigate aspects of my own mixed-race experience growing up in the Deep South," she told Rowell; but the fictionalized character "became her own self as well—which is what I enjoyed so much about writing *Bellocq's Ophelia*" (p. 1027). The biracial speaker's childhood yearning to pass as white in *Domestic Work* is closer to Trethewey's own experience; but there is a parallel in Ophelia's desperate hope that light skin will enhance her employment opportunities in New Orleans. With her "plain English," "lace gloves," and industrious attitude, she "walk[s] these streets / a white woman, or so I think, until I catch the eyes / of some stranger upon me" (*Bellocq's Ophelia*, p. 7), Ophelia writes in "Letter Home." Under even this casual glance, she feels her mask slip and lowers her eyes, "a *negress* again" (*Bellocq's Ophelia*, p. 7). Working at Countess P—'s house, she encounters men who obsessively "look for evidence" of the octoroons' ancestry: "telltale / half-moons in our fingernails, / a bluish tint beneath the skin" (*Bellocq's Ophelia*, p. 26). One hot-breathed customer with a monocle is so persistent that Ophelia turns away from her reflection, "small

and distorted—in his lens" (p. 26). Bellocq's lens, in contrast, helps her to become, as Trethewey says, "her own self."

NATIVE GUARD

Ophelia's temptation to forget her Mississippi past is as strong as her temptation to pass as a white woman in New Orleans. Although her days in Constance's schoolroom were joyful, her mind often fills with scenes of her father's rejection, her mother's desperate poverty, lynchings, and her own grueling work in the cotton fields near Oakvale, a setting also in Trethewey's *Domestic Work*. Ophelia tells her former teacher: "I want freedom from memory. / I could then be somebody else, born again, / free in the white space of forgetting" (*Bellocq's Ophelia*, p. 24). Several months later, however, she realizes that she must accept all of the past if she wants to retain any part of it: "hold each moment / up to the light like a photograph" (*Bellocq's Ophelia*, p. 29). Later still, she learns that pictures can tell dangerous "half-truths"; yet the camera's power is great: it "fastens us to our pasts" (p. 30). She wants to make a photograph of Constance "to accompany what is left in my head" (p. 30). Embedded in Trethewey's Pulitzer Prize–winning third volume, *Native Guard*, is another historical narrative by an African American who makes the conscious decision not to forget. A former slave, the speaker was "delivered into a new life" (*Native Guard*, p. 26) when he became a Civil War soldier in the Native Guard. The term "native guard" accrued a much broader meaning, however, as Trethewey developed her manuscript from this core; the resulting collection comprises her most direct critique of historical amnesia and her most complex art.

In a 2002 interview with Eric Rangus, Trethewey said she was working on a book about black soldiers from Louisiana who guarded Confederate captives of the Union Army on Ship Island off the Mississippi Gulf Coast. The prisoners' surviving letters made her realize "that there is something about the nature of authority in recording and documenting stories, especially when you have the power to write something

down." In 2008, a year after winning the Pulitzer, Trethewey told Wendy Anderson that the book changed as she saw connections between the Civil War material and the personal poems she was writing during the same period "about me and my place in the South" as a biracial person. She thought about "what gets left out of history and who's responsible for remembering, recording, those things that are left out—the native duty of many of us" (Anderson). Trethewey understood that she was as much a native guard as the soldier who narrates the title sequence.

Trethewey's final design for the book also included a series of poems on her mother's death and burial; she began writing the elegies as she approached her own fortieth birthday, twenty years after her mother died at that age in 1985. Living again in the Atlanta area, where her mother was killed, Trethewey was finally able to express her deep grief in work that satisfied her aesthetic demands as a poet. In a substantial interview with Georgia State University's Pearl McHaney, Trethewey traces the complicated process by which she learned that the poems about soldiers belonged with her mother's elegies: "Like them, she had no marker" (p. 101).

The comment was literally true. Her mother's grave lacked a headstone because Trethewey did not want her stepfather's last name to appear on the monument. Interviewed by NPR's Terry Gross after winning the Pulitzer, Trethewey said she eventually realized that the stone could bear her mother's birth name instead. This insight also led her to change the wording of the dedication to *Native Guard*. In place of the first edition's "For my mother, in memory," the reissued volume with accompanying CD reads: "For my mother, Gwendolyn Ann Turnbough, in memory." Years after her mother's death, Trethewey and her grandmother Turnbough first learned about the black Civil War soldiers from a friendly white stranger in a Gulfport beach restaurant. Even though Trethewey's family had taken the ferry to nearby Ship Island for Fourth of July picnics when she was a girl, they saw no sign of an African American presence at the Union fort. Her penultimate poem, "Elegy for the Native Guards," recalls a plaque donated by the Daughters of the Confederacy, which prominently portrayed the Confederate soldiers but the former slaves and free men of color who guarded the prisoners were not even mentioned by park rangers. The grave markers of Native Guardsmen who died on the island were washed away in Gulf storms, leaving their burial places unmarked like her mother's. *Native Guard* eulogizes Gwendolyn Turnbough and these nineteenth-century warriors, along with others whose lives are not recorded in standard histories or commemorated with bronze tablets. Her book, Trethewey told the interviewer Sally Hicks, is "a kind of lyrical marker."

Charles Wright compares memory to a cemetery in the epigraph to *Native Guard*, and Trethewey speaks of the entombed landscape of history in her prefatory poem, "Theories of Time and Space" (*Native Guard*, p. 1). Her elegiac enterprise answers the plea of her Native Guardsman in his final sonnet: "Truth be told" (p. 30). Trethewey told Jonathan Fink: "I absolutely see my role as a poet in some way is to try to recollect the collective and historical memory of a people through the very individual people because I have always been deeply concerned with erasure: those things that are left out of the larger story" (p. 24). The contraband journal in which the Guardsman narrator leaves his record is a layered text, like the Civil War diary pictured on the cover of *Native Guard*. Writing sideways over a white man's existing script, the black soldier sees "his story intersecting with my own" on each page (*Native Guard*. p. 26). Together, their accounts relate a fuller history of the South.

Like *Domestic Work* and *Bellocq's Ophelia*, Trethewey's third volume is carefully organized. In her 2004 interview with Charles Rowell, two years before the publication of *Native Guard*, she anticipated a three-part structure: "document, monument, and testament" (p. 1033). Subsequently, she rearranged the first two sections to give premiere place to her monument for her mother in "Graveyard Blues," "What the Body Can Say," "After Your Death," "Myth," and related elegies. Most of the documentary material appears in part 2—not only the soldier's "Native Guard" sequence but also "Pilgrimage" and "Scenes from a Documentary History of Missis-

sippi," inspired by four photographs from the first half of the twentieth century. Most of Trethewey's notes at the back of the volume clarify allusions and bibliographical resources for the poems in this section.

The poetry of "testament" in part 3, as Trethewey explains to Rowell, involves "other aspects of Mississippi history—some that intersect with the lives of people in my family" (p. 1033). Part 3 is especially pertinent to her remark to McHaney that "throughout the collection I am trying to assert the part of my work which is Southern" (p. 115). With poems like "Southern History," "Southern Gothic," and "South," and allusions to William Faulkner, Robert Penn Warren, and Allen Tate, Trethewey presents herself as both insider and outsider. The epigraph to the testimonial poems cites the Civil War poet Walt Whitman, Trethewey's kindred spirit in many ways:

O magnet-South! O glistening perfumed South! my
  South!
O quick mettle, rich blood, impulse and love! good
  and evil!
O all dear to me!

(*Native Guard*, p. 33)

Asked about stylistic technique in *Native Guard*, Trethewey emphasizes "the formal issue of repetition," explaining to her Emory colleague Bill Chace: "Since the book is about things that have been forgotten, repetition seemed to be the right method to follow. I wanted to inscribe, or reinscribe, the past as it is reborn organically." The palindrome "Myth," with its metaphor of Orpheus and Eurydice's underworld journey, is a tour de force of reinscription. Trethewey told Jonathan Fink that, as she worked on the poem, she became aware that a line referencing abandonment was not the closing statement on her mother's death. Rather, it was the "hinge" to a second stanza that would be a "mirror image" to the preceding verses (Fink, p. 23). "Myth" became a two-part poem about loss that reads backward and forward, doubling the loss. Trethewey believes a variety of influences could have been at work, including her memory of Shahid Ali, a University of Massachusetts poetry

professor who told students to listen for weaknesses by reading poems backward. Commenting on "Myth," "Genus Narcissus," and "Graveyard Blues," Trethewey told the poet and interviewer Remica L. Bingham that she had to use "formal constraints" in writing these poems, or "the pages would be dripping wet, soaked with my tears when a reader picked them up" (pp. 12–13).

The sonnet corona or crown form of the "Native Guard" narrative is another remarkable vehicle of expression. Linking the ten poems that comprise his dated diary entries, the soldier narrator repeats the last line of each sonnet as the first line of the next, with minor variations. In her analysis of *Native Guard*, Giorgia De Cenzo remarks that this process creates relationships across the gaps between entries; thus, says De Cenzo, Trethewey shapes a "discourse" in which "pauses and silences become important and part of the text itself" (p. 112). The closing words of the tenth entry, the imperative "Truth be told" (*Native Guard* 30), direct the reader back to the first line of the whole sequence: "Truth be told, I do not want to forget / anything of my former life" (*Native Guard,* p. 25). Among the soldier's memories are the whippings that left a "history ... inscribed upon my back" (p. 25); but he also describes a more recent and kinder master, a biracial Creole who taught him to read and write, skills that some of the captives lack. The interrelationship of lines in the sonnet corona corresponds to the unique interaction of narrator and Confederates.

Despite the white men's distrust, the Native Guard serves as their scribe, writing letters home for prisoners: "I listen, put down in ink what I know / they labor to say between silences" (p. 27). Trethewey told Bingham that the soldiers' diaries and letters she read at the Library of Congress displayed a poetic formality, and she speculates that an educated slave like her narrator might well have had an "interior life" with a "core of dignity and intelligence and seriousness of thought" (Bingham, p. 14). For these reasons, Trethewey does not express his thoughts in dialect. She compares the Guardsman to the great orator and former slave Frederick Douglass, whose words form the epigraph to these sonnets:

"If this war is to be forgotten, I ask in the name of all things sacred what shall men remember?" (*Native Guard*, p. 25). In recording the disdain with which the Native Guard regiments are treated on Ship Island, both by their Confederate prisoners and their white Yankee colleagues, the narrator inscribes an unfamiliar history that must not be forgotten.

In part 3 of *Native Guard*, two sonnets reinscribe the Guardsman's poetic form and his theme. A memory from a high school history course shows just how falsely the Civil War has been represented in academic texts and the popular media. Trethewey's "Southern History," probably an autobiographical poem, opens with a teacher's uncritical reading from the textbook. His students do not question his assertion that life under a slave master was preferable, a fact that a classroom screening of *Gone with the Wind* seems to verify. In the closing couplet of this Shakespearean sonnet, the narrator indicates her complicity in her instructor's falsehood. The stereotypical image of a slave in the film only reinforces the lie.

In the unrhymed sonnet "Pastoral," however, the narrator speaks out as a biracial poet claiming her place in the South. A comic dream about a photo session with the Fugitive Poets turns nightmarish. It features Robert Penn Warren whose action is a witty allusion to the 1930 Agrarian manifesto *I'll Take My Stand*, a work that has been read as a defense of both the Lost Cause and the South's rural heritage. As the camera flashes in "Pastoral," the narrator suddenly finds herself in blackface, but she holds her ground, informing her fellow poets that her father is white. The poem closes by reinscribing one of the most famous sentences in southern literature. The Fugitive Poets turn Quentin Compson's defense of the South in William Faulkner's 1936 novel *Absalom, Absalom!* into a question for the poet-narrator.

Trethewey told Pearl McHaney that, throughout *Native Guard*, "I am very much asking, after Eric Foner's *Who Owns History?*, 'Who owns southern history or southern poetry?' History belongs to all of us and our one charge is to present it well with all the complexity and humanity that peoples' lives deserve and that art requires" (p. 115). Trethewey discusses such issues with several poets in videotaped interviews for the online journal *Southern Spaces*. Male and female, black and white, the authors in these dialogues are expanding the canon of southern literature through their explorations of southern history. One interviewee, the African American writer Elizabeth Alexander, read the inaugural poem for Barack Obama. Another, the Caucasian Alabama poet Jake Adam York, is publishing a series of poetry volumes on the civil rights martyrs. Trethewey's own current poems about the mixed-race people of colonial Mexico are a contribution to the "new southern studies," which emphasizes a South that is both regional and global. Her continuing fascination with "hybridity"—in people, plants, and even language—will be evident in her forthcoming poetry collection, which Trethewey has said will be titled *Thrall*. With a focus on the colonized body, these poems examine the intersection of personal history, public history, and art.

Selected Bibliography

WORKS OF NATASHA TRETHEWEY

POETRY COLLECTIONS
Domestic Work. Saint Paul, Minn.: Graywolf, 2000.
Bellocq's Ophelia. Saint Paul, Minn.: Graywolf, 2002.
Native Guard. Boston: Houghton Mifflin, 2006.

UNCOLLECTED WORK
"From *Taxonomy*: De Español y de Negra Produce Mulato." *New England Review* 27, no. 2:6–7 (2006).
"Taxonomy: De Español y de India Produce Mestizo." *Ploughshares* 32, no. 1:180–181 (spring 2006).
"On Captivity." *Five Points* 11, no. 3:116–117 (2007).
"From *Taxonomy*: 3. De Español y Mestiza Produce Castiza, 4. The Book of Castas." *Gulf Coast* 20, no. 1:94–97 (winter–spring 2008).
"Liturgy." *Virginia Quarterly Review* 84, no. 3:27 (summer 2008).
"Vespertina Cognitio." *Waccamaw* (http://www.waccamawjournal.com/pages.html?x=162), no. 2 (fall 2008).

"Believer." *Virginia Quarterly Review* 85, no. 4:151 (fall 2009).

"Benediction." *Virginia Quarterly Review* 85, no. 4:160 (fall 2009).

"Elegy." *New England Review* 30, no. 4:6–7 (2009).

"Exegesis." *Virginia Quarterly Review* 85, no. 4:154 (fall 2009).

"Kin." *Virginia Quarterly Review* 85, no. 4:153 (fall 2009).

"Knowledge." *New England Review* 30, no. 4:8–9 (2009).

"Prodigal I." *Virginia Quarterly Review* 85, no. 4:156 (fall 2009).

"Prodigal II." *Virginia Quarterly Review* 85, no. 4:158 (fall 2009).

"Tower." *Virginia Quarterly Review* 85, no. 4:147 (fall 2009).

"Watcher." *Virginia Quarterly Review* 85, no. 4:148 (fall 2009).

"Witness." *Virginia Quarterly Review* 85, no. 4:145 (fall 2009).

Essays

"A Profile of Cornelius Eady." *Ploughshares* 28, no. 1:193–197 (spring 2002).

"On Whitman, Civil War Memory, and My South." *Virginia Quarterly Review* 8, no. 2:50–65 (spring 2005).

"On Close Reading: Yusef Komunyakaa's 'White Lady.'" *Callaloo* 28, no. 3:775–779 (summer 2005).

"The Gulf: A Meditation on the Mississippi Coast after Katrina." *Virginia Quarterly Review* 84, no. 3:4–27 (summer 2008). (The epilogue to this illustrated essay is Trethewey's post-Katrina poem "Liturgy.")

"Congregation." *Virginia Quarterly Review* 85, no. 4:140–143 (fall 2009).

Video Interviews

"Interview with Natasha Trethewey: Jake Adam York, University of Colorado, Denver." *Southern Spaces* (http://www.southernspaces.org/contents/2008/york/1b.htm), Poets in Place Series, June 19, 2008.

"Shadows Along the Waccamaw: Dan Albergotti, Coastal Carolina University." *Southern Spaces* (http://www.southernspaces.org/contents/2008/albergotti/1b.htm), Poets in Place Series, November 24, 2008.

"An Absence I Know I Won't Reclaim: Rodney Jones, Southern Illinois University: Audio Interview with Natasha Trethewey." *Southern Spaces* (http://www.southernspaces.org/contents/2009/jones/1a.htm), Poets in Place Series, January 22, 2009.

"The Morning with Many Tongues: Sean Hill, Stanford University: Interview with Natasha Trethewey." *Southern Spaces* (http://www.southernspaces.org/contents/2009/hill/1b.htm), Poets in Place Series, February 27, 2009.

"Watching the Surface for a Sign: Patrick Phillips, Drew University: Interview with Natasha Trethewey." *Southern Spaces* (http://www.southernspaces.org/contents/2009/phillips/1b.htm), Poets in Place Series, April 14, 2009.

"Natasha Trethewey Interviews Jericho Brown: Jericho Brown, University of San Diego." *Southern Spaces* (http://www.southernspaces.org/contents/2009/brown/1a.html), Poets in Place Series, September 28, 2009.

"Natasha Trethewey Interviews Elizabeth Alexander: Elizabeth Alexander, Yale University." *Southern Spaces* (http://www.southernspaces.org/contents/2009/alexander/1a.html), December 10, 2009.

Other Work

"Working Roots: A Collection of Poetry and Prose." Master's thesis, Hollins College, 1991.

Best New Poets 2007: 50 Poems from Emerging Writers. Charlottesville: University of Virginia Press, 2007. (Edited volume.)

CRITICAL AND BIOGRAPHICAL STUDIES

Debo, Annette. "Ophelia Speaks: Resurrecting Still Lives in Natasha Trethewey's *Bellocq's Ophelia*." *African American Review* 42, no. 2:201–214 (summer 2008).

De Cenzo, Giorgia. "Natasha Trethewey: The Native Guard of Southern History." *Annali di Ca' Foscari* 46, no. 1:101–126 (2007).

Dove, Rita. Introduction. *Domestic Work*, by Natasha Trethewey. Saint Paul, Minn.: Graywolf, 2000. Pp. xi–xii.

Hall, Joan Wylie. "'I shirk not': Domestic Labor, Sex Work, and Warfare in the Poetry of Natasha Trethewey." *Mississippi Quarterly* 62, no. 2:265–280 (spring 2009).

Henninger, Katherine. *Ordering the Façade: Photography and Contemporary Southern Women's Writing.* Chapel Hill: University of North Carolina Press, 2007.

Rindge, Debora, and Anna Leahy. "'Become What You Must': Trethewey's Poems and Bellocq's Photographs." *English Language Notes* 44, no. 2:291–305 (fall–winter 2006).

Trethewey, Eric. "Connections and Correspondences." *Antioch Review* 66, no. 4:682–694 (fall 2008). (An account of the murder of his former wife, Natasha Trethewey's mother.)

Wilson, Charles Reagan. "Natasha Trethewey." In *Literature.* Edited by M. Thomas Inge. *The New Encyclopedia of Southern Literature,* vol. 9. Chapel Hill: University of North Carolina Press, 2008. Pp. 449–450.

Wilson, Mindy. "Natasha Trethewey (b. 1966)." *New Georgia Encyclopedia* (http://www.georgiaencyclopedia.org/nge/Article.jsp?id=h-3697).

Book Reviews

Campo, Rafael. Review of *Domestic Work* and *Bellocq's Ophelia*; and *The Paintings of Our Lives* and *Days of*

Wonder, by Grace Schulman. *Prairie Schooner* 77, no. 4:181–85 (2003).

Ellis, Kelly. Review of *Domestic Work*. *Black Issues Book Review*, November–December 2000, p. 52.

Gilewicz, Nicholas. Review of *Native Guard*. *Bookslut* (http://www.bookslut.com), April 2006.

Hogue, Cynthia. "Poets Without Borders." *Women's Review of Books*, May 2001, pp. 15–16. (Review of *Pity the Bathtub Its Forced Embrace of the Human Form*, by Matthea Harvey, and *Domestic Work*.)

Oktenberg, Adrian. "New Blues, Old Photos." *Women's Review of Books*, October 2003, pp. 20–21. (Review of *Outlandish Blues*, by Honorée Fanonne Jeffers, and *Bellocq's Ophelia*.)

Pope, Jacquelyn. Review of *Domestic Work*. *Callaloo* 25, no. 2:695–697 (spring 2002).

Wellington, Darryl Lorenzo. "My Bondage, My Freedom." *Washington Post Book World*, April 16, 2006, p. BW4. (Review of *Native Guard*.)

Young, Kevin. Review of *Domestic Work*. *Ploughshares* 26, no. 4:205–207 (winter 2000).

INTERVIEWS

Anderson, Wendy. "An Interview with Natasha Trethewey." *Bookslut* (http://www.bookslut.com/features/2008_02_012353.php), February 2008.

Bingham, Remica L. "Interview with Natasha Trethewey." *PMS poemmemoirstory*, no. 8:1–20 (2008).

Brown, Jeffrey. "Pulitzer Prize Winner Trethewey Discusses Poetry Collection." PBS Online *NewsHour* (http://www.pbs.org/newshour/bb/entertainment/jan-june07/trethewey_04-25.html), April 25, 2007. (Transcript.)

Browning, Maria. "Making a Necessity of Memory." *Chapter 16: A Community of Tennessee Writers, Readers, and Passersby* (http://www.chapter16.org/content/making-necessity-memory), October 28, 2009.

Chace, Bill. "Letting Her 'Guard' Down." *EmoryWire* (http://www.alumni.emory.edu/news/emorywirearticles/archives/October2007/mainlist_article7.html), October 2007.

DeVries, Lisa. "Because of Blood: Natasha Tretheway's [sic] Historical Memory—Interview." *Common Reader* (Eastern Carolina University) 26, no. 6 (http://www.ecu.edu/english/tcr/26-6/trethwayinterview.html), May 2008.

Dorn, Sarah. "Pulitzer-Winning Poet on How to Tell the Stories." *Oklahoma Daily* (http://hubdev.ou.edu/news/2009/feb/23/pulitzer-winning-poet-how-tell-stories/), February 23, 2009.

Elam, Angela. "Natasha Trethewey Interview." *New Letters on the Air*. KCUR-FM/NPR, Kansas City, Mo., April 13, 2008.

Fink, Jonathan. "Natasha Trethewey Interview." *Panhandler*, no. 2:19–25 (2008).

Fox, Alan. "Conversation Between Natasha Trethewey and Alan Fox in New York City, January 31st, 2008." *Rattle: Poetry for the 21st Century* 14, no. 2:179–190 (winter 2008).

Gross, Terry. "Interview: Natasha Trethewey, Winner of the Pulitzer Prize for Poetry, on Her Book *Native Guard*, Growing up Biracial in Mississippi and Georgia, and Her Mother's Murder." *NPR: Fresh Air* (http://www.npr.org/templates/story/story.php?storyId=12003278), July 16, 2007.

———. "Natasha Trethewey: If My Mom Could See Us Now." *NPR: Fresh Air* (http://www.npr.org/templates/story/story.php?storyId=99474984), January 20, 2009.

Gunn, Robin Wright. "Books: When the Historical Is Personal." *Connect Savannah* (http://www.connectsavannah.com/news/archive/6976/), March 18, 2008.

Haney, David P. *Cold Mountain Review* 33, no. 1:19–34 (fall 2004).

Hicks, Sally. "Lyrical Markers." *Duke University News and Communications* (www.dukenews.duke.edu/2006/02/trethewey_tmad.html), February 28, 2006.

Kaplan, Sara. "Interview: Natasha Trethewey on Facts, Photographs, and Loss." *Fugue*, no. 32:66–74 (winter–spring 2007).

Loftus, Mary J. "A Working-Class Dreamscape." *Emory Magazine* (http://www.emory.edu/EMORY_MAGAZINE/winter2002/precis_five.html), winter 2002.

McHaney, Pearl. "An Interview with Natasha Trethewey." *Five Points* 11, no. 3:96–115 (2007).

Pettus, Emily Wagster. "Through a Poet's Eyes: History Gets a Second Look." *Clarion-Ledger* (Jackson, Miss.), January 28, 2008, pp. 4B, 7B.

Petty, Jill. "An Interview with Natasha Trethewey." *Callaloo* 19, no. 2:364–375 (1996).

Pfefferle, W. T. "Natasha Trethewey—Decatur, Georgia." *Poets on Place: Tales and Interviews from the Road*. Logan: Utah State University Press, 2005. Pp. 163–165.

Rangus, Eric. "Trethewey's Ophelia." *Emory Report* (http://www.emory.edu/EMORY_REPORT/erarchive/2002/October/erOct.7/10_07_02profile.html), October 7, 2002.

Rowell, Charles Henry. "Inscriptive Restorations: An Interview with Natasha Trethewey." *Callaloo* 27, no. 4:1022–34 (2004).

Solomon, Deborah. "Native Daughter: Questions for Natasha Trethewey." *New York Times* (http://www.nytimes.com/2007/05/13/magazine/13wwln-Q4-t.html), May 13, 2007.

Stasio, Frank. *The State of Things*, WUNC 91.5FM, May 1, 2006. (Radio interview.)

Suarez, Ray. "Poet Visits Hurricane-Ravaged Birthplace." *NewsHour Poetry Series* (http://www.pbs.org/newshour/bb/entertainment/jan-june06/misspoet_05-12.html), May 12, 2006. (Transcript of radio interview.)

Ira Wolfert

(1908—1997)

Joseph G. Ramsey

AN IMPORTANT WRITER of the 1940s, Ira Wolfert today appears to be a largely forgotten figure. The author of several ambitious novels, including the complex and critically acclaimed *Tucker's People* (1943), Wolfert has been often overlooked, in part because this major work of radical fiction, his major achievement, emerged not in but *after* the "red decade" of the 1930s, the period most often associated with literary radicalism. He has, in a sense, fallen between the cracks of twentieth-century U.S. literary historiography. An American-born antifascist who won the Pulitzer Prize for his journalism covering U.S. military operations during World War II, Wolfert made a major contribution to the American radical novel, became a target for anticommunist political repression, and yet, at the height of McCarthyism, managed to settle into a long-term position writing for the notoriously conservative *Reader's Digest*. As even this brief glimpse suggests, Wolfert's career complicates common understandings of mid-twentieth-century U.S. literary radicalism. Yet his seemingly exceptional trajectory, which may account for his marginalization, makes Ira Wolfert a compelling figure for reconsideration. Thankfully, such a rediscovery has been made possible by the 1997 republication of his major work as a part of the Radical Novel Reconsidered series, published by the University of Illinois Press and edited by Alan Wald. The rerelease of the 1948 film noir classic *Force of Evil* (directed by Abraham Polonsky and based on *Tucker's People*) in a critical edition in 1996 promises to further spur long-deserved interest in this "lost" radical writer.

A peculiar and innovative fusion of hard-boiled fiction, proletarian social realism, and modernist metafiction, Wolfert's oeuvre is remarkable for the way it traces the complex interrelations of social forces and individual lives, revealing the "personal" to be social and political in startling and original ways. Through short stories, reportage, essays, and novels, Wolfert traced the contradictory functioning of American individualism in an increasingly postindividualistic world, exploring characters that are caught up in forces—whether military, economic, or political—that they can scarcely understand, let alone escape or adequately confront. To borrow Wolfert's own words, from his 1943 novel *Tucker's People*, his work presents us with "people cutting the world to measure where they can and cutting themselves to measure where they have to, and of the two, world and people, rolling through the universe embraced in battle and altered by battle" (p. 3). Although these words were written during World War II, and although he won major accolades as a war correspondent, Wolfert was primarily concerned with the "battle" that characterized modern-day "peacetime," which he saw as brutally shaped by widespread economic insecurity, cutthroat competition, and an increasingly permeable, even meaningless, line between "legitimate" business and "criminal" enterprise. Delving beneath the surface of this everyday "battle," his fiction explores the way that often suppressed sociopsychological prehistories and internalized class struggles established the basis for what appear later to be unavoidable moments of crisis. Similarly, his journalistic writings are remarkable for the way they focus not only on "news events" but also on the social and psychological effects—and the historical causes—hidden by such official "news" frames. It is high past time to give Wolfert the serious attention he deserves.

IRA WOLFERT

EARLY YEARS

Ira Wolfert was born on November 1, 1908, in New York City, in the neighborhood of 119th Street and Fifth Avenue in Manhattan, to struggling lower-middle-class Jewish immigrant parents originally from Latvia. Raised in an essentially secular household in Brooklyn, Ira went to public schools, attending Hebrew school only briefly before his bar mitzvah (at the insistence of his grandfather). His father, Moses Wolfert, struggled as a small businessman in various fields, from ladies' garments to real estate, assisted by his mother, Sophie (whose family name was Seidl). His parents showed little to no interest in Jewish folk culture or their European heritage. Indeed, like many American Jewish writers on the left during this period, later in life Ira Wolfert would seldom if ever depict, let alone emphasize, the Jewishness of his multiethnic characters, even as he made antifascism and anti-Nazism a key feature of this work.

Wolfert was encouraged to pursue a career in journalism by his positive early experiences working in the editorial office of the *Brooklyn American*, a Hearst-owned paper, where, at the age of fourteen, he took his first job more out of boredom than poverty. Following this, in 1926 Wolfert entered Columbia University's School of Journalism. While in college, he worked in the city's public transportation system driving electric streetcars—a job in which he took considerable pride. Later, after being fired and blacklisted from railway work (for running his trolley car too fast to make up for a late shift start), he worked as a taxicab driver.

In 1928, at the age of nineteen, Wolfert married Helen Herschdorfer. The two remained together until Helen's death in 1985. Helen was from a more scholarly Jewish family, and she was an accomplished poet. Wolfert later spoke of the important role she had played as the main audience for his writing; she often gave him detailed feedback on his work. Moses Wolfert disapproved of Helen, however, and so the marriage created a major rift in the family; the father further resented Ira Wolfert's choice not to join him in the family business. The result of this double conflict was that Ira did not see nor speak to his father for more than five years, a personal trauma that appears to have left a strong mark on several of Wolfert's later works. Indeed, there are striking correspondences between Wolfert's biography and his later literary production, in particular to the story of Frederick Bauer in *Tucker's People*, a character whose rift with his father leaves him psychologically damaged and socially insecure.

As a young reader, Wolfert was more inclined toward history than toward literature, but, as he later recalled, his biggest conscious literary influences were Ernest Hemingway and F. Scott Fitzgerald. One can see parallels between the themes of these better-known authors and Wolfert's work, which often deals with the Hemingwayesque problem of would-be "tough" men caught in a world that threatens them, physically and psychologically, as well as with the classically Fitzgeraldian conundrum of the loneliness and emptiness that plagues even those who succeed in accumulating financial riches.

Newly married and working full-time, Ira Wolfert struggled to find time to read the books for his college courses, often doing his homework in his cab while waiting for fares. It was, as he later put it in a 1993 interview with Alan Filreis and Alan Wald, "one helluva grind" (p. 3). No doubt informed by these early experiences, the conflict between the struggle to survive within a "business society" and the desire to pursue one's higher calling became a prominent and recurring theme in Wolfert's later writings. Such struggles grew still more apparent after Wolfert graduated in 1930.

INTELLECTUAL AND POLITICAL DEVELOPMENT

Like many of his generation, Wolfert was not only personally affected but politically radicalized by the economic conditions of the Great Depression. Wolfert later recalled that he, like many U.S. writers, artists, and intellectuals during this period, had "felt the Communists had the right answer" as early as 1929, the year of the stock market crash (Filreis Interview p. 4). What exactly he meant by this statement is somewhat

difficult to discern. Though Wolfert claimed later to have found some of the Communist Party members he encountered personally to be "too bossy," and he had no love for the Communists in the USSR, no doubt Wolfert was inspired, like many other anxious intellectuals of the 1930s, by the Communist-led protests for unemployment relief and against evictions. It also seems likely that the party's antifascist agitation in the early 1930s would have drawn his approval. Such approval would have been mutual. After he published a story in *Harper's* magazine titled "In Right" in September 1936, a tale that focused sympathetic if indirect attention on "red"-led union efforts, Wolfert was personally invited to join the party. He declined. He did, however, attend classes at the Communist-led Workers School (later the Jefferson School), as he wanted to read and to study the work of Karl Marx. Wolfert continued to work with individual Communists and other progressives on a series of projects after the war. According to the House Un-American Activities Committee and FBI files, Wolfert was reported to have been a member of as many as five to ten "Communist front" organizations, though he often denied being a "political" person at all.

While there is no explicit referencing of Marx in Wolfert's literary oeuvre, it is not difficult to discern the traces of this early intellectual encounter. Very much in line with a certain Marxian tradition, Wolfert's work traces the dialectical relationship between material and historical conditions, on the one hand, and individual ideologies and attitudes, on the other, examining the relationship between economic structures and modes of individual as well as collective consciousness and behavior.

Wolfert was further politicized by witnessing firsthand the rise of fascism in Europe, and especially the emergence of Nazism in Germany. Working in the Berlin office of the *New York Post*, he had the opportunity not only to follow events in Germany but to visit that nation with Helen, in 1931, in the midst of the Nazis' rise to power. He returned convinced that "the Germans were insane" (Filreis Interview p. 5). Wolfert's comment was not meant to dismiss Nazism as an es-

sentially foreign development, an enigma defying intellectual explanation—quite to the contrary, he took the task of explaining this kind of collective "insanity" very seriously. Indeed, tracing the social, economic, and historical causes of such self-destructive social regression at the heart of "modern civilization" would become a—if not *the*—central focus of his writing throughout the 1940s. In this way, Wolfert obliquely weighed in on a crucial debate about the nature of German fascism.

Departing from those in the United States who sought to locate the roots of fascism in some particular feature of German national character or culture, Wolfert emphasized that a universal dynamic was at work in "Hitlerism," yet he resisted the idea that the seeds of fascism were to be best located in "human nature." Rather, he maintained that the roots of fascism were being sown wherever the "business world," as he called it, organized people at the top of society into cartels and monopolies while rendering "little people" at the bottom so economically insecure that they become inclined to seek out demagogic, imaginary ("insane") solutions to their real economic and social anxieties. A sad corollary to his theory, of course, was that the very monopoly business interests that were, in his view, largely responsible for rendering the "little guy" so insecure and isolated in daily life were often the same ones that then provided the comforting demagogues who, like Adolf Hitler or Benito Mussolini, assisted the "little guy" down the road to self-delusion and self-destruction. In essence (most clearly in *Tucker's People*), Wolfert interpreted fascism as the natural and even inevitable product of the perverse human "ripening" that was being cultivated by what he referred to as modern "business society." But this ripening was best understood as a social and a historical process, an expression of the modern world's "business game."

Such a comprehensive, economically based theory of fascism led Wolfert not only to oppose fascist regimes and aggression abroad but to seek out, expose, and oppose what he saw as the "ripening" of fascism at home as well. It was in this spirit that Wolfert publicly defended the right

of American workers in defense plants to strike for improved wages and working conditions, even at the height of an ostensibly antifascist war effort that depended on the workers' continued production. Articulating a position that arguably put him to the left of the Communist Party of the United States at the time—the CPUSA, along with most U.S. labor unions, had a signed a wartime "no strike" pledge—Wolfert argued in the *Nation* magazine in January 1943 ("Talk on Guadalcanal") that workers' struggles on the home front were just as much a part of the battle against fascism as was the military campaign against Hitler and the Japanese emperor Hirohito. This article touched a nerve, provoking a prompt and harsh response on the editorial page of the *New York Times* ("Unity in War Aims," January 25, 1943). Implicitly, Wolfert questioned whether the "Good War" would in fact truly be antifascist at all, when so few of the soldiers that it mobilized had any idea what fascism was or why it was bad in the first place. Writing from the Pacific war front and basing his claims on conversations with U.S. troops in the field, Wolfert lamented what he saw as the dearth of developed antifascist or properly democratic consciousness or program in the military. He observed that most soldiers in this allegedly antifascist war had little political grasp of what the war was (supposed to be) about; many conceived of it merely as an act of brutal self-defense against "Japs" or "Huns." He wrote of GIs who were more concerned with major-league baseball scores than with the fate of Stalingrad. Far from blaming the troops for such gaps in consciousness, Wolfert framed this depressing deficiency as signaling a monumental failure on the part of intellectuals, artists, and culture bearers in American society. In Wolfert's view, these cultural leaders—at least to that point—had not been able to put antifascist ideas into forms that the American masses could take up as their own. The goal, as yet unachieved in Wolfert's view, was to integrate antifascism into the very practices of everyday life, at home and abroad. His article was both a reality check for "popular front" antifascists about the world the war was in fact making (and not making) and a challenge to

progressive public intellectuals to do better. In retrospect, this article remains a prescient take on the political situation the war would create, a situation that would see many American progressive and radical antifascists quickly labeled, marginalized, and repressed as enemies of the state: almost overnight in the postwar years, outspoken antifascists like Wolfert found that the very institutions they had sought alliance with now saw them as "un-American."

EARLY SHORT FICTION

Wolfert's early works of fiction already demonstrate what became a lifelong concern with the negative social and psychological effects of economic insecurity. His 1936 story "In Right," for example, which apparently won him that early invitation to join the CPUSA, tells the story of an unemployed worker who, to feed his family, reluctantly takes a job as a hired strikebreaker. He later kills a striking steelworker on a picket line, in part because he is so overwhelmed by his emotions (including shame) upon being ordered to attack people whom he sees as basically no different from himself. Ironically, as he shoves the strikers back from the gate, prompting calls of "Murderer!" from the crowd, he lashes out and becomes what they accuse him of being, what he had promised himself he would never become. Later, inside the factory walls, he becomes guilt-stricken and disgusted with himself, even as he realizes that, not only will management protect their own, but that his murderous actions have got him "in right" with the boss. The employer has need of a man who is willing and able to do such dirty work, someone who is bound to obedience by his own murderous transgression. (The story bears remarkable similarities—often word for word—to a key chapter of Wolfert's later *Tucker's People,* to be discussed below.)

In the way its central character is made to become a reluctant and ambivalent agent of the employers, "In Right" resembles other texts by Depression-era writers including Nelson Algren (*Somebody in Boots,* 1938), William Attaway (*Blood on the Forge,* 1941), and Paul William

IRA WOLFERT

Ryan (better known as "Mike Quin"), each of whom depict similarly unemployed workers lurching toward becoming hirelings for employers or for fascism, out of a mixture of psychological and economic anxieties. One further element that Wolfert adds to the mix is his narrator-protagonist's longing to please his worried wife by securing a steady job. He is depicted as literally lashing out at hungry mothers and their children on the line in order to procure some semblance of elusive domestic peace for himself and his own family-to-be. The fact that such a pessimistic story of working-class fratricide and betrayal attracted the positive attention of the Communist Party serves as a reminder that the proletarian literary movement in the United States was rather more complex in how it represented actual workers of the day than persistent stereotypes suggest. Like Wolfert, many radical writers of the 1930s and later made a central concern of their work the fact that economic desperation—as well as psychological strain—among the unemployed could lead them to serve, and even to identify with (what these radical writers saw as) those workers' class enemies. Contrary to vulgar doctrines of "workerism," an oppressed or exploited class position was no guarantee of progressive political identification or affiliation; far from it.

Wolfert's awareness of this possibility of workers being pit against one another may have been fueled in part by his own personal experiences as a cab driver, where, as a new employee, he felt he was used as a "stooge of the bosses" (as he reports in his 1993 interview with Filreis and Wald, p. 5). After being coaxed by his employer to bring in more fare money than his veteran coworkers, Wolfert was accused by fellow workers of making them look bad and of giving the employer an argument for speeding the rest of them up. The ensuing altercation resulted in Wolfert quitting the job. His innocent individual efforts had been used against his fellow workers, who had then turned against him.

Developing the motif of the isolated individual beyond the realm of labor struggle, several of Wolfert's early short stories appear to be influenced by the "hard-boiled" school of fiction.

For the most part, these tales feature alienated, at-risk male characters caught in situations beyond the law, up against forces beyond their control. The tough circumstances Wolfert's characters face, however, are often quite clearly social in origin, suggesting Wolfert's early interest in using stories of criminality and violence not only to voice existential anxiety but also to present legible social critique. These characters face not only the shotgun blasts of an inexplicable lunatic lone gunman (in "Off the Highway," 1938) and the unpredictable violence of tramps, prostitutes, boozers, and bouncers (in "In the Black Morning," 1939), but also unemployment, homelessness, and even raw hunger, as well as police persecution or prosecution for "vagrancy" (in "The Way the Luck Runs," 1938).

One early story in particular suggests a major theme that would characterize Wolfert's mature work: the collision of economic trauma and masculine individualism. This story, "Finally Harriet," dramatizes the suicidal tendency of the wage-earning "lower middle" classes to cling to ideas, perspectives, and values that are no longer applicable to their increasingly precarious social position. Appearing in *Harper's* magazine in October 1938, "Finally Harriet" focuses on three characters: Tom, Dick, and Harriet. Clearly Wolfert here is playing off the colloquial expression "Tom, Dick, and Harry," to suggest the typicality or allegorical nature of his characters and the drama they play out; it is as if this tale could be about any "Tom, Dick, and Harriet." The plot is fairly simple and straightforward, though interrupted and enriched by flashbacks and stream-of-consciousness narration. It is, in essence, the story of a death (whether a murder or a suicide is left to the reader's judgment).

It is 1938, well into the Depression. A married couple, Tom and Harriet, are sitting on the beach, when they are approached by the story's third character—appropriately named Dick—who is a former business associate of Tom. Dick and Harriet almost immediately fall into flirting with one another, while Tom is distant and lost in thought. As it turns out, he is contemplating suicide. Tom, we learn, has recently—in fact just the day before—been laid off from his job (not

the first time, this has happened to him in recent years). Confronted with the possibility of yet another period of long-term unemployment, Tom anticipates losing everything that he has, including Harriet, whom he has yet to tell about his most recent firing.

While Dick flirts with Harriet right in front of him, Tom suddenly and without a word heads out into the water. Eventually, Harriet notices his absence and expresses concern at how far from shore he is. Chiefly to impress her, Dick dives into the water after Tom. Without much trouble, he reaches Tom, only to find him pathetically taking on water through the mouth. Tom is reluctant to be helped, but Dick pulls him onto a nearby raft. At this point, waving back and forth to Harriet on the shore, Tom decides that he wants to live after all. After a period of rest, the two men head in, Dick helping Tom along, until, near shore, Tom asks Dick to go on alone, as he does not want Harriet to see him depending on another man. Dick quickly obliges. Thus left to swim in by himself, Tom returns again to depressive thoughts, now with the added recognition that Harriet—whom he has just identified as his one reason to continue living—was flirting with Dick back on the beach. The prospect of losing her once again—after just having "found" her—is too much for him and quickly saps his already wounded will to live. Meanwhile, Dick swims in ahead and returns to Harriet, who is impressed with his heroic physical performance. Alone together, the two look raptly into each other's eyes, anticipating more to come—when suddenly Harriet again remembers Tom and finds that she cannot see him anywhere. He has gone under. Deeply gazing into her eyes, Dick seems to have forgotten all about Tom already.

Wolfert complicates and enriches what might seem a fairly straightforward—and melodramatic—story of a tragic love triangle by using flashbacks to explore the contradictory economic class standpoint of its main character. Tom, we learn, is a former manager, who used to have secretaries and employees under him and who still thinks of himself as a "business man." Despite having been laid off on more than one occasion—and having long been stripped of his managerial authority—he identifies not as a worker but rather with his employer. Tom is—or thinks that he is—a member of middle-class America, and an unsentimental one at that. Devoid of liberal illusions about the place of benevolence in a profit-driven enterprise, he knows the way things are. And yet he can find no solace in the recognition that what is happening to him is nothing personal or that it is happening to many others around him at the same time. Wolfert suggests, without stating it outright, that Tom's lack of any sense of community or solidarity renders him particularly vulnerable to psychological and economic depression.

Exploring this problematic middle-class nostalgia further, Wolfert' Tom reminisces about a lost world, in which he enjoyed professional status and power. That old world was one in which the prospects of retirement and security seemed clear and solid to Tom. At this point his thoughts run to cynicism, and he paints his employers as being something like cannibalistic torturers. He considers his notice of termination a "death sentence." Collecting his (one week's) severance pay from the office cashier, Tom thinks silently that suicide would be preferable to sharing the news of his dismissal with Harriet. As is often the case in Wolfert's work, the masculine reluctance to confess fears and failures compounds a character's psychological despair, hastening a spiral to self-destruction. Tom's anger and his militant resentment at his own victimization is not in itself adequate to mounting any sort of meaningful or effective resistance; he does not force his superiors to confront his anger at being fired, but rather keeps all these feelings to himself.

Also worth noting here is the way that Wolfert probes beneath the surface of putatively "innocent," "benevolent," or "good" actions to reveal hidden motive causes that are not at all "nice." Thus, Dick's (ultimately unsuccessful) "rescue" of Tom is cast as little more than a performance of physicality and "heroism" meant for Harriet's eyes. His act of helping Tom is in fact a coded act of aggression. To Dick, Tom is nothing but a cipher, a means to an end, an obstacle that suddenly can be turned into a

springboard toward his true goal. As Michael Szaylay has argued, one can discern in Wolfert's work, here and especially in *Tucker's People,* an implicit call for something like Social Security, in the broadest sense. For in light of the reluctance of society to help the truly needy, who but the state could fill the gap? Indeed, the closest that Wolfert came in his last interview to giving a definition of his personal "communism" was an insistence that individuals needed to form a strong community to protect themselves from "the bosses" and the cold, callous business world (Filreis Interview p. 15). Tom in this story serves as a case in point.

WAR REPORTAGE

While trying his hand at fiction periodically throughout the 1930s, Wolfert worked full-time as a journalist for the North American Newspaper Alliance, briefly covering the theater beat around Broadway and occasionally writing sports and celebrity news. He made his name for himself, however, covering the American military forces in the Pacific, particularly in the Solomon Islands. His journalism from this period is represented in three critically acclaimed books: *Battle for the Solomons* (1943), which collects articles that won a Pulitzer Prize for international reporting; *Torpedo 8: The Story of Swede Larsen's Bomber Squadron* (1943); and *American Guerrilla in the Philippines* (1945), which was a Book of the Month Club selection.

Wolfert's reportage on the war brought him critical acclaim. The *New York Times,* for instance, reported that on the force and unflinching honesty of his war writing, Wolfert, unlike many war reporters "can look ... his soldier friends in the eye" (Duffus). In particular the *Times* reviewer appreciated the way in which Wolfert brought out the similarities between wartime and peace-time struggles; in his work, the soldiers "don't look like actors being brave; they look mostly like fellows working." Indeed, the stark contrast between Hollywood depictions of war heroes and the actuality of combat was a theme of Wolfert's own reportage.

Wolfert's critical questioning of the actual, as opposed to imagined, political meaning of the war effort, however, prompted a much sterner editorial reply from the *New York Times,* which likened Wolfert's support of the workers' right to strike, even in the war industries, to that of the French popular front. The latter, according to the *Times* editors, had led to the French "collapse" in the face of the Nazi invasion. Wolfert responded to this attack two days later with a letter of his own ("Mr. Wolfert States Position"). Pointing out that the *Times* had misquoted and misleadingly contextualized material from his article, Wolfert not only took issue with the paper's blaming the popular front for the collapse in France but also insisted that the sense of cynicism which he had identified among the marines on Guadalcanal was not his own personal opinion, as the *Times* had suggested, but rather that it reflected the actual sentiments of the rank and file. It was in defense of the soldiers' morale that Wolfert defended strikes and worker rights on the home front. He saw workers' struggles for economic and social security as a key bulwark against the kind of widespread fear and psychological neurosis that, in *Tucker's People,* he would show to be paving the way for fascism and warmongering.

THE MAKING OF TUCKER'S PEOPLE: FROM FACT TO FICTION

Arguably, Wolfert's real masterpiece would not focus on the war but on the battles on the home front (though Alan Filreis is correct to highlight the war's influence on this novel, too). Back in the United States, before the outbreak of war, in 1938, Wolfert had been assigned to cover the criminal trial of James "Jimmy" Hines. Hines was accused of protecting an illegal $20 million lottery, run out of Harlem, a numbers racket run by the notorious gangster Dutch Schultz. Through covering this case, Wolfert developed a strong dislike for the prosecuting attorney, Thomas Dewey, and conversely a strong affection for the accused Hines, who was well-known as one of the few pro–New Deal politicians still working in Tammany Hall. Dewey, on the other hand, was an ambitious gangbusting New York district attorney, who would go on to become governor of New York in 1942 and later head two unsuccess-

ful Republican bids for president: one in 1944, against Franklin Delano Roosevelt, and another (more infamously) in 1948, where he was upset by Harry Truman. Throughout the entire 1930s, Dewey had been gaining national recognition as a leading prosecutor of urban organized crime; his name had become synonymous with "crime fighting" and taking down "gangsters." (There was even a commercial radio program named after him.) Commentators on the Hines trial at the time rightly saw it as a highly politicized affair. Wolfert did as well, though in a deeper sense of the word "political"; he saw the defendants in the trial as principally pawns in a top-down bureaucratic and political scheme that had little to do with justice or the protecting the public good and that, furthermore, could be seen as a microcosm for power dynamics at work in the broader society.

For quite some time, Angus Cameron, Wolfert's longtime friend and editor at Little Brown and Company, had been encouraging Ira to try his hand at a novel. Upon witnessing the spectacle of the Hines trial, Wolfert decided to give it a go, and he set out to write a very different sort of "gangster story" than the mass media and newspapers of the time preferred to tell. Writing the lengthy book while continuing to work as a journalist and war correspondent, Wolfert based several of the characters and events in *Tucker's People* (1943) on real figures and events he encountered during the Hines trial. As Alan Filreis notes in his introduction to the 1997 edition of the book, several key moments in the novel, including the way that the gangster Ben Tucker rises to monopoly control over the New York lotteries, were "written straight out of the trial— from testimony about 'Black Wednesday,' November 23, 1931." As Filreis explains, this had been "a day of integration and consolidation for the corporate bosses, when the favorite holiday combination 5-2-7, actually won (in a fix). The fixed big win drove out of business many of Harlem's smaller 'bankers,' who were suddenly unable to pay the many who hit the lucky number, at which point precisely Hines' (and Tucker's) people bought out the bigger independents" (Filreis, p. xix).

While witnessing and discussing the trial, Wolfert became most interested in the stories of those "little guys" who were working not against but *inside* Hines (Tucker's) organizations. Indeed, even the few police officers who are depicted in any detail in *Tucker's People*, such as the lonely Officer Egan, are shown to be alienated "little guys" struggling to survive and to understand the machinations of callous, impersonal bureaucratic organizations that seek to use them as pawns for ends that are not at all their own.

Against the grain of sensationalist crime reportage and heroic police drama, *Tucker's People* presents us with a complex portrait of how the pressures and dictates of business determine the lives of individuals living within and beyond the law alike. The basic plot of the book involves two estranged brothers, Joe and Leo Minch, who are thrown back together again late in life by the business schemes and growing corporate structures of the gangster Ben Tucker. Raised in poverty, the Minch brothers' "love had no chance to grow straight" (p. 24), Wolfert writes. The scarcity and insecurity of their lives pit them against each other, as well as against the world around them. Eventually both brothers, independently, are able to climb out of poverty and into some sort of business enterprise. Yet even where they seem to have acquired a certain success, that position remains a costly and an insecure one. As Wolfert puts it, Leo's thoughts

> ran, nagged, tickled and prickled on Leo's mind like bugs on a ball … There was nothing secure about betting on a market like this, but he had to do it to stay in business and he did it unhappily and fearfully, fear unbalancing his judgment, until a steeply falling market caught him with his shelves loaded and, before the market could recover, his creditors ganged up on him for their money and put him out of business.
>
> (p. 9)

Moving on from the wool business to selling butter and eggs door to door, what success Leo is able to achieve feels to him like he is "a mouse eating when the cat is away" (p. 10). Leo moves out of sales and into renting real estate,

> But, however he tried to hide, the world in which he lived hunted him down. Whatever barricade he

tried to erect for himself, the world tore it down and got at him....

Money was not enough to keep his feeling of insecurity under control.... His mind needed money to breathe, exactly as his lungs needed air. But money itself was insecure. He required "position," too, a commendable piece of society, one in which he need not feel vulnerable to his enemies.

(p. 11)

Ironically, Leo's long estranged brother, Joe, shows up offering what appears to be a sort of stabilizing "position," namely a place within Ben Tucker's rising "policy" (lottery) syndicate. A street-smart tough who as a youth had once decided to "live like a bum" (p. 37), Joe is shown to have been hardened and dangerously wizened by his experiences in World War I:

He had joined the army to join the human race. He had taken a gun in his hand and had gone to the killing so that people would look at him as if he were a human being. But it hadn't worked out, because as soon as the killing had stopped and he had dropped his gun, he had seen people thinking of him once more as a dangerous animal who needed feeding.

(p. 46)

Left to fend for himself, Joe Minch turns to becoming a bookie, later becoming one of Tucker's managers.

Wolfert emphasizes economic factors in a way that complicates easy morality; he suggests that social and financial pressures determine whether one has the practical privilege of "being good" in the first place. Both Minch brothers are depicted as characters who are trying to salvage some sort of "goodness" out of the scramble and anarchy of business. But as often as not the forces of business are shown to make either a monstrosity or a mockery of these moral personal impulses. So for instance, when Joe, who has become one of "Tucker's people," is placed in the awkward position of having to convince— and if not convince, then force—his older brother to join the lottery combination that Tucker and his lawyer and associate, Henry Wheelock, are devising, or else be crushed and thrown to the wayside like the rest of the small operators in the

area, Joe tells himself (and Leo) that he is doing a "good" thing, making up for his past wrongs against his brother. Similarly Leo, though he knows on some level that he is in fact being *forced* into this combination against his will, eventually assents to the idea, by telling himself that it is at least a way in which he can guarantee the continued job security of his collection of employees. Needless to say, the planned merger and acquisition does not work out as smoothly as Joe or Tucker plan. (For one thing, Leo finds himself in the position of having to force his own staff not to leave their positions, regardless of their wishes to do so, for fear of bringing Tucker's wrath down on all of them. This then creates a psychological crisis for at least one of the employees, Frederick Bauer, discussed more below.) The police for their part merely exacerbate the situation, adding yet another layer of fear and insecurity for those involved by carrying out raids on the policy offices, not in pursuit of justice or the public good, but in order to forward the careers of distant politicians.

The intricate details of the unfolding plot are in some ways less important to grasping this highly discursive novel than is the thematic and psychologically nuanced development of its major social theme, as it unfolds through the exploration of characters, major and minor. As Angus Cameron wrote in the foreword to the 1997 edition of the novel, the "Balzacian" book's "social import lay hidden in the play of deeply revealed characters" (p. xxii). The remarkable thing about the novel is that these characters are so richly individuated and yet so fundamentally similar and interconnected by what they are up *against*. As Alan Filreis writes in the novel's introduction,

Readers of *Tucker's People*, perhaps expecting that the Minch brothers would draw off the greatest share of the novel's energy for examining such a personal crisis, discover that nearly all of Tucker's many people face something of the same crisis. It is in seeing the Minches' dilemma written across the lives of all the people in the novel that enables its critique of the social organization to be so devastating.

(p. xvi)

The novel is as textured and rich in as it is united in its fundamental theme, and overarching thesis: that the "normal" functioning of "business society" stunts the healthy growth of individuals in such a way as to lay the foundation for a kind of fascism. Along these lines, *Tucker's People* argues implicitly first that big "business society" organizationally lays the grid for fascism through its entrenching of increasingly monopolistic, top-down command-structures and second, more subtly, but just as insidiously, that—from top to bottom—the "ordinary" functioning of capitalism psychologically *prepares* people (even and perhaps especially the "little people") *for* fascism, through the widespread insecurity, alienation, anxiety, and fear it sows. This fear in turn drives *individuals* to seek ultimate psychological security and safety in the guise of unquestionable authority. Both of these business-centered social forces are then exacerbated by a third force: the entire business system's tendency toward crisis. It is at such moments of crisis, Wolfert suggests, both through the novel's plot and through more overtly narrative digressions, that people, already "ripened" by the "normal" functioning of business society, are shaken loose from the tree of reason by the anarchic winds of change. Wolfert was drawn again and again in his longer fiction to the concept of crucial moments, turning points, and crises as concentrating and determining the arcs of entire lives. He would later describe his war novel *An Act of Love* (1948) as an elaborate attempt to explain the prehistory of one single moment of time, one "act of love" and self-sacrifice in the middle of combat. Examining several of such crisis moments in *Tucker's People* helps to illuminate how Wolfert worked out his concept of the dialectical unfolding of human social development (or "ripening") through individual characters.

EXCAVATING MOMENTS OF "PERSONAL" CRISIS

Among the most moving and memorable moments in *Tucker's People* are the depictions of the "little people" whose lives we encounter on the margins of this gangster narrative. These minor characters are often able to mount a certain resistance, however futile, to the corporate-crime syndicates that otherwise dominate the social landscape. Arguably, the most significant and resistant of these minor figures is Roger Wheelock. We encounter Roger in a crucial back-story chapter titled "An American Hero's Son." The father of Henry Wheelock—Ben Tucker's lawyer and partner—Roger Wheelock is a midwestern small businessman (a hotel owner-manager) who struggles—and ultimately fails—to keep from losing his hotel to the bank after the lumber corporations finish clear-cutting the trees in his town. Wheelock's father "knew the end" of his business was coming "the minute the big lumber companies started working on the forests" (p. 153). For Roger Wheelock,

> the rock began to sink and he had to fight to hold the rock up. It was a hopeless fight. He was a man holding up something that was holding up him. The old man must have known it would be hopeless and must have known it was hopeless, but he kept right on with it. It was heroic. It was a life to which music should be played.
>
> (p. 153)

Roger Wheelock represents a poignant portrait of the stubborn small businessman within an increasingly corporate, industrial capitalism. His holding out against encroaching corporations reflects what Filreis has called a "basic American resistance to business" (p. xxxiv). However, the fact that Roger Wheelock continues in his isolated resistance even when he and others know that it is "hopeless" implies that he is engaged not only in going beyond individualist economic rationality but also in a practical futility. Roger's stubborn individualism is shown by Wolfert to be simultaneously a principle of resistance and *part of the problem* that perpetuates his own victimization. It represents an inability on his part—and by extension on his town's part—to forge a new kind of resistance appropriate to the social and economic encroachments of modern corporate capital. Roger Wheelock's "heroism," then, appears to be as much a problem as it is a solution. (Indeed, his very family name, Wheelock, calls to mind a well-intentioned but dangerously ineffective attempt to "put the brakes" on a movement that he cannot control.) That Roger's tragedy has been

read as "heroism" (as it has been by Filreis and no doubt by others) only further compounds its problematic nature. Such an episode highlights Wolfert's deeply ambivalent relationship to an American individualism that he nonetheless saw as one of the few available models for resisting the encroachment of "business society."

In fact, it is only from a distance, in his recollections from New York City, that Henry Wheelock—the son of the "American hero"—is able to view this attempt at resistance by his father as "heroic." "Up close," he observes, once he returns to the town,

> it didn't seem heroic. It seemed crippled and full of hate and stupid. It was a sucker town. The people's energy seemed to be for hating and hurting each other. They spent all their time gouging dimes out of their neighbors. They lived like animals in a slaughterhouse—fighting, fornicating, tearing at each other for a place to stay, forgetful of what had happened to them, knowing only what they were doing.
>
> (pp. 156–157)

In his 1993 interview with Filreis and Wald, Wolfert expressed that he had intended to present the savvy Henry Wheelock as a largely sympathetic character, suggesting that Henry's extensive social views—including his criticisms of his father and his hometown—warrant serious consideration. Thus when from the midst of doing Tucker's business in New York, Wheelock thinks back on his hometown, it is not only to contrast his sordid present "success" working for Tucker with the backdrop of his father's "heroism" but also to reflect on the shortcomings of that small-town individual "heroism" itself. He remembers how at home, "If you stood on a hill and looked down,

> the stumps stretched away like gravestones ... in a forgotten graveyard. The big lumber people moved in and then moved on and the only place they ever stayed put was on the society pages of the newspapers or in "Who's Who in America." They were loved and admired and envied by everybody except the people they left behind in assassinated towns. These people hated them, but what was their hate? They were just bums. They were alone. They had been made to feel alone by what business had done to them. They did not join each other to fight

business. They abandoned themselves to their feeling of loneliness and fought each other instead.

> (pp. 181–182)

And indeed, Roger Wheelock, in his single-minded, even suicidal "resistance," is shown to be pulling all the other members of the Wheelock family into the vortex of the failing hotel. Henry Wheelock is the only son, who—as Wolfert himself had done years before—ultimately refuses to devote his life (and death) to carrying on the (sinking) family business.

As here voiced by the junior Wheelock, what keeps the assassinated small-town folk from a more authentic opposition is that, first, they act as if they have forgotten what happened to them, repressing the historical cause for the hardship and the murder that had determined their lives, and that, second, they do not "join each other to fight business." The small-town folks' failure to remember and to unite around the source of their collective suffering thus still haunts the town and—despite his business success—the "successful" and cynical son who has left it.

Later in the novel, as Ben Tucker's plans are coming apart in the face of unexpected rivalries and betrayals, Henry Wheelock, alone among Wolfert's characters, refers to himself cynically as having "communistic" ideas. Of these we get a small taste, when Henry nonchalantly tells Joe Minch, who has been sent into a guilt-ridden crisis after a rival gangster kills his brother Leo as a way to wage war on Tucker's syndicate, "That's the profit system. Dog eat dog. Your loss is my profit. That's the way the world is. What do you want to do, change the world?" (p. 304). That it is only the lonely sellout intellectual Wheelock who articulates this situation—and he is drunk at the time—indicates the bleakness of Wolfert's radical vision. As Diana Trilling pointed out sharply, contrasting the book against what she considered—somewhat uncharitably—to be the typical radical novel of the period, *Tucker's People* "cuts through the whole bleary notion that all you have to do is drop the 'Communist Manifesto' in the social slot machine and out will come a society of smiling Workers and Peasants" (p. 45). In the world of *Tucker's People* even that radical consciousness that does emerge is com-

promised or constrained by the social position of its appearance.

If there is hope in the world of this novel, then, Wolfert suggests that it is to be approached through the act of *remembering*, by unearthing the complex, oft-repressed history of how individuals have been made and unmade by the impersonal forces of business society. Arguably, Wolfert's own project in *Tucker's People* is to draw out these forgotten, repressed memories and buried struggles, so as to expose for the reader prehistories that suggest possible alternative roads not taken, for individuals and by extension for the societies that have shaped them.

As if to dramatize this repression of history itself, the novel's structure again and again intersperses the "present" internal monologues and current actions of its characters with prehistories (or psychological archaeologies) relayed through a more omniscient narrator, deploying a sort of free indirect discourse. Perhaps the most remarkable such historical interruption in the story casts light on the origins of the gang boss Ben Tucker himself (while also giving yet another meaning to the section title "An American Hero's Son"). Unlike most of the major characters, Ben Tucker's family background and childhood experiences never appear in the text. Instead, Wolfert presents us with the moment of his "birth" as a corporate gangster. "Tucker was not made in one day either," Wolfert writes, again exemplifying his interest in moments of life crisis and determination. "Yet there was a single day when something happened to Tucker that made him decide what to do with himself ... that day he learned what to do to make a place for himself where he could fit, and he didn't fool around any more" (p. 157). On this day of decision Tucker finds himself effectively "fathered" as a gangster by Newell Smith, an industrial mill owner, who is faced with a popularly supported labor strike sometime in the 1920s. Smith attempts to win the help of the National Guard to break the strike, through denouncing the strikers in the press as "red," "atheistic," "anarchist-socialists" and "bomb-throwing foreign agitators" (pp. 157–158). From here on Tucker's origin story is drawn almost word for word from Wolfert's 1936 story

"In Right." Calling on the National Guard to clean up the "foreign" radicals, Newell Smith and his Company in effect *pose* as "American heroes," standing up for the principles of private property, religion, labor "peace," and the right of replacement workers to take others' jobs without being intimidated by "bomb-throwers" (p. 158). (Ironically, however, as Wolfert notes, "The Company was a foreign agitator itself because the mill was only one of its branches and its main office was in New York, but it was throwing whatever it could find" (p. 158).) When his "American" propaganda fails to convince local politicians to unleash the Guard, Smith enlists professional strikebreakers, headed by a veteran officer of the U.S. invasion of Cuba, including the novice Ben Tucker. In short, Ben Tucker gets his start as an agent of labor repression. He will later, we learn, continue his rise to wealth and power as a corrupt union boss, where various men of industry will lace his pockets in exchange for keeping the "Reds" and "real organizers" out of the union leadership. Though this formative aspect of Tucker's gangsterism was completely excised from the later film version of the novel, *Force of Evil* (1948), the fact remains that Tucker is "fathered" by a union-busting big businessman. This "forties" gangster novel can then be in a sense read as the sequel to the "thirties" story of the suppressed strike, developing in more depth a theme that had been hinted at in such influential works of hard-boiled crime fiction as Dashiell Hammett's *Red Harvest* (1929).

Adding one more layer of complexity and irony, Wolfert suggests that it is Ben Tucker's desire to be a "hard man" in his wife Edna's eyes, that motivates his decision to "make a place for himself" even if it is by turning against his fellow workers. Yet Tucker's idea that Edna desires a "hard man," in this sense, is shown to be tragically mistaken; in fact the narrative reveals that Tucker's social "hardness" hurts and alienates Edna.

After killing a man in the ensuing riot, along the lines already sketched out in "In Right," Tucker quickly finds that he is "in right" with Smith for his head-cracking. He then escorts the owner into his limousine and watches it as it

leaves the plant. The following text from the novel is a noteworthy addition by Wolfert to the 1936 version of the story; the car moves:

> past the troops and past four pickets and past sullen men standing silently in small bunches. Tucker didn't pay attention to the people. He saw only the car. There weren't any people left for Tucker on earth anymore—only himself and human beings he could use or ignore or must fight. Business and its law of self-defense had taught him that.
>
> (p. 169)

Unlike the 1936 story, which ends with the (nameless) killer-narrator stuck in his own guilt, the novel version suggests that through his violent transgression of his own initial instincts of class solidarity, his attack on those who seemed "just like him," the killer Ben Tucker cuts himself off from acknowledging the humanity of others forever. His feeling of "guilt" is left behind as well. Ostensibly transcendent codes of morality and human recognition, which frame the 1936 story, are shown to be themselves subject to the economic power of business. Class affiliation here trumps the experience of morality. Furthermore, this episode adds considerable irony to the very title of the novel, *Tucker's People*; for after this point, we are to understand, through Tucker's eyes, there are no longer "people" at all.

What makes *Tucker's People* such a dark and pessimistic book, however, is that even the "little people" are afflicted by a similar sense of alienation. Consider Frederick Bauer, whom Filreis deems "unforgettably resistant" (p. xix). Bauer's resistance is similarly self-destructive, eventually bringing down crisis not only upon himself but also on Leo Minch, Joe Minch, Henry Wheelock, and even Ben Tucker himself. An accountant who works under Leo, under the bossy "new management" of Joe Minch and Ben Tucker, Bauer buckles under the pressure of knowing that he *must* now continue working for the good of the corporation—or *else*! As his neurotic, paranoid, suicidal spiral begins, the narrative highlights Bauer's failure to see himself and others in a social and historical context: "To see into this blankness [of Bauer's loneliness and hopelessness], it is necessary to understand Bauer far better than he understood himself" (p. 313).

Grasping for a solution to his personal crisis, Bauer goes to visit his father, a railway worker. After a halting, bitter conversation, Bauer "thought of how empty the old man's life was, but didn't wonder what had emptied it" (p. 330). This empty life, however, the narrator explains, though yet another economic-psychological history, has been directly caused by the railway company that has exploited his father's labor. Even though he was a "loyal" employee who refused to leave work during the big railroad strike, the elder Bauer has nothing to show for it but a one-room apartment with no furniture and a pension that is so small it forces him back to outdoor work in winter. Filling the painful pauses in the father-son conversation, Wolfert writes, "The old man had railroaded almost all the waking hours of his adult life. The company had shut him out from everything else in the world, even his family. Now that he had time for his family and the world, he was too gone in age to rouse himself to absorb anything new" (p. 328). Yet, rather than developing a sense of solidarity or even sympathy with his father, whose own insecurity and poverty have been created by forces quite similar to those that are shaking his own existence to its core, Bauer ends up feeling more cut off from him than ever. He zones in on his father's neglectful, domineering parenting for making him into such an insecure man. He ends the conversation wishing for his "empty" rheumatic father a quick death, leading him then to contemplate his own. Again, for Wolfert, the prospect of community—albeit a community of loss, vulnerability, and unspoken desperation—is derailed by an individualistic dwelling on "personal" victimization.

After this encounter with his father, as Bauer prepares for his final descent, Wolfert draws out the historical significance of this seemingly insignificant moment:

> The weight of history that a man carries on his shoulders as he goes about his daily life is not a small weight, although Bauer was among the great majority in never being aware of it. He never thought of himself and of each other man on earth as living all day in the stream of history. To him, history was not what was happening to all people but something in school books. Historical events

were made by "big shots" who got their names in the papers and lived in government buildings or tried to live there. While they were alive, they were boss and people paid attention to what they said. After they died, statues were made of them.

(pp. 368–369)

The text continues, drawing specific connections between Bauer's "personal" desperation and the rise of fascism abroad:

> It was now Tuesday night of the second week in December, 1934, and an incident that will never be recorded in written history had occurred in the small life of a little man. The little man had a heritage of insecurity that had begun from the day of his birth to make him into a certain kind of infant. He was born into a world given over to business played with profit as the goal and man staking his life on reaching it. There was no security in that for him ... [He] could see no way out of insecurity except death ...

(p. 369)

Out of this terrifying insecurity, Bauer eventually puts his blind faith in Wally, a diseased-looking upstart from a rival gang-corporation, who asks Bauer—in exchange for a new job—to set up a meeting between his boss (Ficco) and Leo Minch. (This "meeting" is in fact a setup for the shooting of Leo.) This sudden naive belief in Wally is a novelistic parallel to the growth of fascism across the world. Its rhetoric rising to a climax, the text continues:

> Now, you may ask, what have these rather shabby confusions in a little man's inconsequential life to do with so great a thing as history?

> Well, the time was 1934. Already a nation of Germans, ripened by history, as the little man had been, and then flung into economic crisis, as the little man had been, had invented enemies, as he had, and stirred hatreds and nursed and fueled and fanned fear and had allowed itself to turn to a leader, a gross, gruesome, diseased-seeming man—all as the little man had. The German's leader was one of them. He had the will to death in him and he knew the way to it. He knew how to delude himself into gratifying the will to death. The leader meant Germany's death, but he promised Germany a better life. Being put into power he did not change. He invented more enemies for his nation and stirred more hatreds and nursed and fueled and fanned more fears....

This thing called the Nazi idea, the promise of wholesale death, crept across the earth. It was a climax to the modern world and its business game.... All of Tucker's people, and, of course, Tucker himself, were climax men of the modern world.

(pp. 371–372)

In such passages Wolfert's reworking of the gangster-crime story into a forum for antifascism, implicit throughout, is rendered explicit indeed.

In attending so closely to the stories of the forgotten "little guys" and in dwelling on the historical significance of their experiences, it is clear that Wolfert sought to set off his novel from typical Hollywood gangster and crime drama, with its neat beginnings and pat happy endings. As he writes in the first sentence of the book: "This story has no beginning and, as you will discover if you read to the last page, no real ending either" (p. 3). This opening is then mirrored by the final section of the text, an epilogue in which Wolfert repeats that "there is no proper ending to this story."

> An ending requires a conclusion or a resolution. Leo and Bauer were dead, but their lives had not been concluded or resolved by death, merely interrupted....

> The state sought to contrive a conclusion for the story, but it could not. How could it, where the bulk of its energies were devoted to perpetuating itself and, for that, it needs must conceal from itself and its citizens what its way of life was doing.

(p. 495)

As he continues, "Yet, the state staged a great trial and conducted an expensive, patient and talented search for the 'truth' and this was the 'truth' with which it emerged—that ... Wheelock [and others] ... belonged in jail for contriving and operating a lottery" (p. 495). Set against the richness and complexity of the historical, social, and individual "truth" that overflows this novel's nearly five hundred pages, these closing lines offer a literary indictment of the superficiality and the self-serving nature of prevailing "law and order" discourse, whether in fiction, in mass cultural "whodunits?" or in the actual courtrooms. Certainly the bitter reverberations of Wolfert's

own experiences covering the Hines trial are nowhere more apparent.

Tucker's People was greeted with glowing reviews, despite the terrible difficulty its author and editor had encountered in getting it published. The *New York Times* dubbed the novel "an important book," praising its "blowtorch intensity" (Collins). The Book-of-the-Month Club likened the novel to the greatest works of Theodore Dreiser. Diana Trilling writing in the *Nation* deemed the novel "the most serious and in some ways the most talented novel" of the year, a "truly radical book."

Before this critical success, however, the work had been repeatedly rejected—by at least twenty-six publishers. In most cases the official reason for rejection was that novel was merely another "gangster novel," a form that some saw as played out by the 1940s; but the antibusiness politics of the book seems a likely factor as well. That the book saw print at all appears to have been in large part thanks to the near-heroic efforts of Angus Cameron, who, after his own firm rejected the book against his wishes, continued to support Wolfert's project independently. (Cameron later resigned from Little, Brown over the company's refusal to publish Howard Fast's famous slave-revolt novel, *Spartacus,* in 1950.) After twenty-six rejections, it took yet another editor, Albert Erskine, going to bat for Wolfert to get his novel published. And even then, apparently for political reasons, *Tucker's People* was not promoted or distributed to the extent that it probably deserved. As Wolfert puts it, despite their editors' admiration for the book, the Book-of-the-Month Club removed it from its final list because the novel "attacked American business," a particular offense at a time of patriotic war—even if that the war was also ostensibly against fascism.

In the increasingly conservative and anticommunist climate of the cold war, during which Wolfert would be red-baited, slandered, and

targeted by congressional committees, *Tucker's People* eventually fell out of print. Initially, however, the book sold rather well, going through three print runs and even being reissued in 1950, as a pulp paperback retitled *The Underworld,* with a cover and jacket blurb that played up the exotic "gangster" aspects of the book.

Tucker's People was also admired in Hollywood, by Abraham Polonsky, the Communist screenwriter and director who was himself later blacklisted, but who—before then—worked with Wolfert to adapt the novel for the screen. Directed by Polonksy, and released on Christmas Day, 1948, the film *Force of Evil* featured the acclaimed actor John Garfield in the leading role (as Joe Morse, not Minch), as well as Thomas Gomez (as Leo). Relatively underappreciated in its own day, *Force of Evil* has more recently received praise both for the gritty urban lyricism of its dialogue and for its striking, impressionistic visual shots, which use shadows to emphasize the overwhelming presence of the urban business environment on characters struggling to survive. While the union-busting backstory of Ben Tucker is excised, as are the psychological histories of its various characters, the film does stay true to Wolfert's vision of calling into question the line between "criminal" and "legitimate" business enterprise, and it remains a powerful indictment of the personal impacts of big business on the lives of everyday people. Though Wolfert himself later seemed indifferent to the film, in 1994 *Force of Evil* was chosen by the Library of Congress for preservation in the National Film Registry and has received praise as a classic, perhaps most notably from the director Martin Scorcese.

AN ACT OF LOVE

Like *Tucker's People*, Wolfert's next novel, *An Act of Love* (1948), had its inception in actual events, specifically the brutal wounding of a U.S. soldier, which Wolfert witnessed on a Pacific island in July 1943. This young man had the top of his head shot away by machine-gun fire, at the very start of a battle. As Wolfert later described in a 1993 interview with Alan Filreis and Alan

Wald, "The man wouldn't die. This skirmish, a simple one, took place in a true bottom of the world: jungle, and under the jungle, swamp. And all the enemies of man were assembled there—natural, political and human. And they had done their absolute worst to this one human being. I know then I had to make a search—to find out what remains hidden in man that allows him to survive all the hostilities in the modern world."

The novel upon which Wolfert then launched was an attempt to reveal the meaning of this act of struggle against death, not just for the injured man himself but also as it appeared through the eyes of an outside observer, for whom this act took on special, indeed life-changing significance. The plot focused on Lieutenant Harry Brunner, the sole survivor of a sunken American battle cruiser, who is washed ashore on an unspecified South Pacific island. Nursed back to life by the natives, he takes refuge at the home of an American planter who never evacuated the island and yet who has not yet been driven out by the Japanese occupiers. Predictably, Brunner proceeds to fall in love with the planter's daughter, Julia. He is kept back from expressing his affection for her, however, by some suppressed neurotic anxiety. More than the effect of war trauma, Harry's alienation is depicted as the expression of competing instincts imbued in him by modern civilization. After six months, the American military invades to retake the island, at which point Brunner witnesses the "act of love," an act of self-sacrifice by the aforementioned American marine. So moved is he by the marine's action that he loses his neurotic fear and plunges into heroic action in the battle against the Japanese. Brunner emerges from the fray able to express his long-frustrated and suppressed love for Julia. Though it deploys a plot infused by Hollywood-type romantic melodrama, *An Act of Love* can be read as Wolfert's attempt to extract some sort of redemptive human meaning from the massive military sacrifices and human suffering that he saw unfolding before him, a massive slog that, left to its own devices, seemed unlikely to bring about the democratic and peaceful world order that progressives like him had hoped for.

Though the book sold well, *An Act of Love* was criticized in several quarters for being too full of needless detail and too overly psychoanalytic in emphasis, a criticism that prompted Wolfert to defend himself more than once by stating bluntly that he had "never even read Freud." Nonetheless, in describing the writer's task, Wolfert etched an image not far from Freud's figures for the layered archeology of the unconscious: "The writer," he wrote, "must search beneath this world, deeply beneath it (man has in this sense, a depth existence equivalent to an iceberg) for the true meanings of his every-day, common gestures, statements and acts." Marc Brandel, reviewing the book for the *New York Times*, devised a somewhat harsher "theory" for explaining the searching nature of Wolfert's prose. As he put it, the fiction manuscripts of newspaper man like Wolfert "are frequently less an attempt to write serious fiction than a passionate rebellion against newspaper work. Every rule of good writing, conciseness, simplicity, clarity, which the reporter has to obey on the job, he tends to break with his fictional work with the happy abandon of a drunk swinging an axe against Carrie Nation's front door" (p. 10).

Despite occasional defensiveness, Wolfert took criticisms of the book to heart, and he set out on the unusual task of totally rewriting this novel from cover to cover. The new version of the novel was published in 1954 as *An Act of Love: A Completely Retold Version of the Novel*. In keeping with his interest in delving into past histories to explain present circumstances, Wolfert revised the book so that chapter 1 of the old version was not reached until chapter 26 in the new. Frustrated not only by the criticism of the first version but by the praise of it, Wolfert commented that "the trouble was that everybody seemed to relish the action of the story, but too few could believe in the reality of the one dimension that gave the story its reality." Reviewing for the *New York Times Book Review*, the Marxist literary critic Granville Hicks praised the new work, asserting, "What most needs to be said ... is that *An Act of Love*, which was always worth reading, is now more than ever" (p. 4).

As for role models in the genre of the "war novel," Wolfert identified John Dos Passos' *Three Soldiers* (1921), Ernest Hemingway's *A Farewell to Arms* (1929), E. E. Cummings' *The Enormous Room* (1922), and Stephen Crane's *The Red Badge of Courage* (1895) as books that delved deeply into the consciousness and the subconscious lives of their characters. Crane, in particular, was singled out for Wolfert's praise (in an interview with Harvey Breit) for how he "tried to see the world of war as a dramatization of the conflicts that exist in normal life. And that is why he could write so truly about war without having seen it." Wolfert clearly aspired to do something similar in his own war writing. Such views led him to write a largely critical, if appreciative, review of Norman Mailer's war novel *The Naked and the Dead* in 1948.

AFTER THE WAR: A DIFFERENT KIND OF POLITICS AND ECONOMICS

Though he would later paint himself as a nonpolitical person, Wolfert took an active, if defensive, role in politics during and after World War II, working with a writers' group organized around Jack Goodman to support those who came under McCarthy-era anticommunist attacks, including the Hollywood Ten. He further met regularly with several publicly known Communists and other radicals, including W. E. B. Du Bois, Howard Fast, Shirley Graham, Louis Untermeyer, and F. O. Matthiessen. Despite these affiliations and his pronounced radical tendencies, however, Wolfert would later himself deny that he even voted for the Progressive presidential candidate Henry Wallace in 1948, voting instead for Harry Truman. Wolfert's politics at this point, then, may be characterized as anti-anti-Communist (rather than pro-Communist). For instance, while he did give a speech at the Communist Party–organized Scientific and Cultural Conference for World Peace, held at the Waldorf-Astoria hotel in New York City in 1949, it was a speech expressing his opposition to anti-Communist passport restrictions.

Later, watching the New Left movements of the 1960s emerge, Wolfert kept his distance, despite sharing their anti–Vietnam War sentiments. As he saw it, the student movement seemed to him to "reject responsibility," whereas he saw that one could only grow by accepting it. Further, Wolfert saw the movement as somewhat "anti-economic," no doubt a major problem in the eyes of a writer who had devoted so much attention to the influence of economic forces in everyday life.

Though Wolfert persisted in the belief that it was his best work, his third and final published novel, *Married Men*, was met with harsh reviews and nonexistent sales in 1954. A sprawling 1,007 pages, representing the labor of the better part of a decade, the work was once again based on actual events and people whom Wolfert had encountered, namely a war veteran and his wealthy industrialist father. Once again his work dealt with familiar themes, including the conflict between economic and human aspirations, expressing a continued fascination with depth psychology and the hidden drives and desires of individuals caught up in business society. However, unlike *Tuckers' People* and *An Act of Love*, *Married Men* left him $30,000 in debt.

Having long quit journalism after the war, Wolfert had been virtually without income for ten years. It was in this pressing economic context that he was persuaded to accept an offer from David Wallace to work for *Readers Digest* in 1954, and he stayed at the magazine for almost two decades, until his retirement in 1973. Though he was baited as "Communist" at the time of his hiring, Wolfert weathered the attacks, on the strength of his journalism and his personal connections with his immediate supervisor. As he put it later in his almost consciously "apolitical" way: "What does it matter if I am a communist. You read the article." No doubt it did not hurt, however, that he had become somewhat distanced from his formerly radical associates by this point. He later admitted to Alan Filreis and Alan Wald (in 1993) that his writings for the *Digest* were routinely vetted by his editors, but he seems to have accepted such scrutiny as the price of a steady paycheck. He distanced himself from the often extremely conservative (and anti-

Communist) editorial content of the magazine by noting simply that "that's their business."

In his later writings, Wolfert took a decidedly more optimistic tone toward modern capitalism than in his earlier works. Furthermore, his writing for the magazine was so popular that the *Digest* decided to bring his pieces out as a book collection in 1960, under the title *An Epidemic of Genius*. This book offered an in-depth, often celebratory discussion of the social changes made possible by mid-twentieth-century American technological breakthroughs. Late in life, Wolfert's lifelong focus on the impact of economics had taken a surprising affirmative tone.

Nonetheless, on the side, Wolfert continued to work on a lengthy autobiographical novel that expressed a continuing pessimistic ambivalence about the impact of modern economic conditions on human lives. He worked on this still-unpublished manuscript for "more than 20 years, seven days per week," he told Filreis and Wald, but he had apparently given up on the project by the time of the interview in 1993, after his longtime advocate and advisor Angus Cameron showed a lack of interest in the novel; his approach in this work remained premised on the notion that, as he put it to Filreis and Wald, "Every life no matter how long and complicated it may be consists of a single moment when a man finds out who he is, once and for all, who he is" (p. 27). Further, his main theme remained, as he put it in his final interview, the conflict between "earning a living and suffering to earn a living, and enjoying" life. It seems likely that without his longtime editor's support, and without the reading presence of his wife, Helen, Wolfert had difficulty bringing this final literary vision to fruition. As he put it simply, "a writer needs an audience."

Sadly, Wolfert passed away just as he was about to regain one. He died in 1997, at the age of eighty-nine, in Margaretville, New York. (He was survived by two children, Ruth and Michael, the latter of whom was at that time a working novelist.) His death came just before the republication of his masterwork, *Tucker's People*, by the University of Illinois Press (though he knew of the republication plans). The book was reissued, with a foreword by Angus Cameron and an introduction by Alan Filreis, as part of the Radical Novel Reconsidered series, edited by Alan Wald. Among the many subjects of this (since discontinued) radical literary recovery project, Wolfert is especially deserving of reconsideration today. Perhaps in this moment, when once old-fashioned discussions of the intersection between psychological and economic crises seem once again vital and necessary, he may once again find the readership that he deserves.

Selected Bibliography

WORKS OF IRA WOLFERT

BOOK-LENGTH WORKS

Battle for the Solomons. Boston: Houghton Mifflin, 1943.

Torpedo 8: The Story of Swede Larsen's Bomber Squadron, Boston: Houghton Mifflin, 1943.

Tucker's People. New York: L. B. Fischer, 1943. Reprint, Urbana: University of Illinois Press, 1997. (Part of the Radical Novel Reconsidered series; page numbers in the text refer to the 2007 edition).

American Guerrilla in the Philippines. New York: Simon and Schuster, 1945.

An Act of Love. New York: Simon and Schuster, 1948.

The Underworld. New York: Bantam Books, 1950. (Pulp paperback edition of *Tucker's People*.)

Married Men. New York: Simon and Schuster, 1953.

An Act of Love: A Completely Retold Version of the Novel. New York: Simon and Schuster, 1954.

An Epidemic of Genius. New York: Simon and Schuster, 1960.

SHORT FICTION AND ARTICLES

"In Right." *Harper's Magazine,* September 1936, pp. 378–385.

"Off the Highway." *Esquire,* October, 1937.

"Finally Harriet." *Harper's Magazine,* October 1938, pp. 528–537.

"The Way the Luck Runs." *Harper's Magazine,* November 1938, pp. 637–645.

"In the Black Morning." *American Mercury,* August 1939, pp. 451–458.

"Song Hits, and Misses." *New York Times,* January 19, 1941, p. 11.

"Talk on Guadalcanal." *Nation*, January 23, 1943, pp. 117–119.

"Mr. Wolfert States Position; Upholds His Report of Conditions as He Found Them on Guadalcanal." *New York Times*, January 27, 1943, p. 20. (Response to "Unity in War Aims," *New York Times*, January 25, 1943.)

"Winners." *Collier's*, July 10, 1943, p. 13.

"Spearhead." *Collier's,* January 6, 1945, pp. 16, 24.

"What Do You Know About La-Haye-du-Puits?" *Saturday Review of Literature*, April 14, 1945, pp. 9–10, 12, 71.

"That's How It Is, Brother." *Collier's*, September 22, 1945, p. 14.

"War Novelist." *Nation*, June 26, 1948, pp. 22–33. (Review of Norman Mailer's *The Naked and the Dead*).

CRITICAL AND BIOGRAPHICAL STUDIES

Brandel, Marc. "Catharthis of Fear." *New York Times Book Review*, January 9, 1949, p. 10. (Review of an *Act of Love*.)

Breit, Harvey. "An Interview with Ira Wolfert." *New York Times Book Review,* February 6, 1949, p. 16.

Collins, Thomas Lyle. "New York Underworld." *New York Times*. April 25, 1943.

Denning, Michael. *The Cultural Front: The Laboring of American Culture in the Twentieth Century*. New York: Verso, 1997.

Duffus, R. L. "He Brings a Message from the Men at the Front." *New York Times Book Review,* January 17, 1943, p. 3.

Filreis, Alan. "More Political than Criminal." Introduction to *Tucker's People*. Urbana: University of Illinois Press, 1997.

Filreis, Alan, and Alan Wald. Interview with Ira Wolfert. Lake Hill, N.Y. June 21, 1993. (transcript provided by Alan Filreis).

Foley, Barbara. *Radical Representations: Politics and Form in U.S. Proletarian Fiction, 1929–1941*. Durham, N.C., and London: Duke University Press, 1993.

Hicks, Granville. "A Story Retold." *New York Times Book Review*, May 30, 1954, p. 4.

Mandel, Ernest. *Delightful Murder: A Social History of the Crime Story*. Minneapolis: University of Minnesota Press, 1968.

Rideout, Walter. *The Radical Novel in the United States, 1900–1954*. New York: Columbia University Press, 1956.

Szaylay, Michael. *New Deal Modernism: American Literature and the Invention of the Welfare State*. Durham, N.C.: Duke University Press, 2000.

Trilling, Diana. "Fiction in Review." *Nation,* June 26, 1943, pp. 899–900.

"Unity in War Aims." *New York Times,* January 25, 1943, p. 12.

Wald, Alan. *Trinity of Passion: The Literary Left and the Antifascist Crusade*. Chapel Hill: University of North Carolina Press, 2007.

Wald, Alan. "The Urban Landscape of Marxist Noir." Interview by Graham Barnfield for *Crime Time* (http://www.crimetime.co.uk/features/marxistnoir.php).

Cumulative Index

Arabic numbers printed in bold-face type refer to extended treatment of a subject.

A

"A" (Zukofsky), **Supp. III Part 2:** 611, 612, 614, 617, 619, 620, 621, 622, 623, 624, 626, 627, 628, 629, 630, 631; **Supp. IV Part 1:** 154; **Supp. XVI:** 287, *287*

Aal, Katharyn, **Supp. IV Part 1:** 332

Aaron, Daniel, **IV:** 429; **Supp. I Part 2:** 647, 650

Aaron's Rod (Lawrence), **Supp. I Part 1:** 255

Abacus (Karr), **Supp. XI: 240–242,** 248, 254

Abádi-Nagy, Zoltán, **Supp. IV Part 1:** 280, 289, 291

"Abandoned Farmhouse" (Kooser), **Supp. XIX:** 117, 119

"Abandoned House, The" (L. Michaels), **Supp. XVI:** 214

"Abandoned Newborn, The" (Olds), **Supp. X:** 207

"Abandoned Stone Schoolhouse in the Nebraska Sandhills, An" (Kooser), **Supp. XIX:** 124–125

"Abba Jacob" (Nelson), **Supp. XVIII:** 177

Abbey, Edward, **Supp. VIII:** 42; **Supp. X:** 24, 29, 30, 31, 36; **Supp. XIII: 1–18; Supp. XIV:** 179

Abbey's Road (Abbey), **Supp. XIII:** 12

Abbott, Carl, **Supp. XVIII:** 142

Abbott, Edith, **Supp. I Part 1:** 5

Abbott, George, **Supp. IV Part 2:** 585

Abbott, Grace, **Supp. I Part 1:** 5

Abbott, Jack Henry, **Retro. Supp. II:** 210

Abbott, Jacob, **Supp. I Part 1:** 38, 39

Abbott, Lyman, **III:** 293

Abbott, Sean, **Retro. Supp. II:** 213

ABC of Color, An: Selections from Over a Half Century of Writings (Du Bois), **Supp. II Part 1:** 186

ABC of Reading (Pound), **III:** 468, 474–475

"Abdication, An" (Merrill), **Supp. III Part 1:** 326

'Abdu'l-Bahá, **Supp. XX:**117, 122

Abel, Lionel, **Supp. XIII:** 98

Abel, Sam, **Supp. XIII:** 199

Abelard, Peter, **I:** 14, 22

Abeles, Sigmund, **Supp. VIII:** 272

Abercrombie, Lascelles, **III:** 471; **Retro. Supp. I:** 127, 128

Abernathy, Milton, **Supp. III Part 2:** 616

Abernon, Edgar Vincent, Viscount d', **Supp. XVI:** 191

Aberration of Starlight (Sorrentino), **Supp. XXI:** 234–235

Abhau, Anna. *See* Mencken, Mrs. August (Anna Abhau)

"Abide with Me" (Hoffman), **Supp. XVIII:** 86

"Ability" (Emerson), **II:** 6

Abingdon, Alexander, **Supp. XVI:** 99

Abish, Walter, **Supp. V:** 44

"Abishag" (Glück), **Supp. V:** 82

"Abnegation, The" (Bronk), **Supp. XXI:** 32

"Abortion, The" (Sexton), **Supp. II Part 2:** 682

"Abortions" (Dixon), **Supp. XII:** 153

"About C. D. Wright" (Colburn), **Supp. XV:** 341

"About Effie" (Findley), **Supp. XX:**50

"About Hospitality" (Jewett), **Retro. Supp. II:** 131

"About Kathryn" (Dubus), **Supp. VII:** 91

"About Language" (Wrigley), **Supp. XVIII:** 300–301

"About Looking Alone at a Place: Arles" (M. F. K. Fisher), **Supp. XVII:** 89, 91

About the House (Auden), **Supp. II Part 1:** 24

About Town: "The New Yorker" and the World It Made (Yagoda), **Supp. VIII:** 151

"Above Pate Valley" (Snyder), **Supp. VIII:** 293

Above the River (Wright), **Supp. III Part 2:** 589, 606

"Abraham" (Schwartz), **Supp. II Part 2:** 663

Abraham, Nelson Algren. *See* Algren, Nelson

Abraham, Pearl, **Supp. XVII:** 49; **Supp. XX:**177

"Abraham Davenport" (Whittier), **Supp. I Part 2:** 699

"Abraham Lincoln" (Emerson), **II:** 13

Abraham Lincoln: The Prairie Years (Sandburg), **III:** 580, 587–589, 590

Abraham Lincoln: The Prairie Years and the War Years (Sandburg), **III:** 588, 590

Abraham Lincoln: The War Years (Sandburg), **III:** 588, 589–590; **Supp. XVII:** 105

"Abraham Lincoln Walks at Midnight" (Lindsay), **Supp. I Part 2:** 390–391

"Abram Morrison" (Whittier), **Supp. I Part 2:** 699

Abramovich, Alex, **Supp. X:** 302, 309

Abrams, M. H., **Supp. XVI:** 19

Abridgment of Universal Geography, An: Together with Sketches of History (Rowson), **Supp. XV:** 243

"Absalom" (Rukeyser), **Supp. VI:** 278–279

Absalom, Absalom! (Faulkner), **II:** 64, 65–67, 72, 223; **IV:** 207; **Retro. Supp. I:** 75, 81, 82, 84, 85, 86, 87, 88, 89, 90, 92, 382; **Supp. V:** 261; **Supp. X:** 51; **Supp. XIV:** 12–13

"Absence of Mercy" (Stone), **Supp. V:** 295

"Absentee, The" (Levertov), **Supp. III Part 1:** 284

Absentee Ownership (Veblen), **Supp. I Part 2:** 642

"Absent-Minded Bartender" (X. J. Kennedy), **Supp. XV:** 159

"Absent Thee from Felicity Awhile" (Wylie), **Supp. I Part 2:** 727, 729

"Absolution" (Fitzgerald), **Retro. Supp. I:** 108

"Absolution" (Sobin), **Supp. XVI:** 289

"Abuelita's Ache" (Mora), **Supp. XIII:** 218

Abysmal Brute, The (London), **II:** 467

Abyssinia and the Imperialists (C. L. R. James), **Supp. XXI:** 166

Abyss of Human Illusion, The (Sorrentino), **Supp. XXI:** 225, 227, 237–238

"Academic Story, An" (Simpson), **Supp. IX:** 279–280

"Academic Zoo, The: Theory—in Practice" (Epstein), **Supp. XIV:** 107–108, 109

"A Capella" (Wrigley), **Supp. XVIII:** 300

"Accident" (Minot), **Supp. VI: 208–209**

"Accident, The" (Southern), **Supp. XI:** 295

"Accident, The" (Strand), **Supp. IV Part 2:** 624

Accident/A Day's News (Wolf), **Supp. IV Part 1:** 310

Accidental Tourist, The (Tyler), **Supp. IV Part 2:** 657, 668–669; **Supp. V:** 227

Accordion Crimes (Proulx), **Supp. VII:** 259–261

"Accountability" (Dunbar), **Supp. II Part 1:** 197, 204

"Account of the Method of Drawing Birds" (Audubon), **Supp. XVI:** 12

"Accusation, The" (Wright), **Supp. III Part 2:** 595

"Accusation of the Inward Man, The" (Taylor), **IV:** 156
"Accusing Message from Dead Father" (Karr), **Supp. XI:** 244
Ace, Goodman, **Supp. IV Part 2:** 574
Achievement in American Poetry (Bogan), **Supp. III Part 1:** 63–64
Acker, Kathy, **Supp. XII:1–20; Supp. XXI:** 236
Ackerley, J. R., **Supp. XX:**237
Ackerman, Diane, **Supp. XIII:** 154
"Acknowledgment" (Lanier), **Supp. I Part 1:** 364
Ackroyd, Peter, **Supp. V:** 233; **Supp. XVII:** 180
"Acquaintance in the Heavens, An" (Dillard), **Supp. VI:** 34
"Acquainted with the Night" (Frost), **II:** 155; **Retro. Supp. I:** 137; **Supp. XXI:** 26
Across Spoon River (Masters), **Supp. I Part 2:** 455, 457, 459, 460, 466, 474–475, 476
Across the Layers: Poems Old and New (Goldbarth), **Supp. XII:** 181, **187–189**
Across the River and into the Trees (Hemingway), **I:** 491; **II:** 255–256, 261; **Retro. Supp. I:** 172, **184–185;** **Supp. XIX:** 248
"Actfive" (MacLeish), **III:** 18–19, 22
Actfive and Other Poems (MacLeish), **III:** 3, 17–19, 21
Action (Shepard), **Supp. III Part 2:** 446
Active Anthology (Pound), **Supp. III Part 2:** 617
Active Service (Crane), **I:** 409
"Act of Creation and Its Artifact, The" (Sorrentino), **Supp. XXI:** 229, 235
Act of Love, An (Wolfert), **Supp. XXI:** 270, **275–277**
Act of Love, An: A Completely Retold Version of the Novel (Wolfert), **Supp. XXI:** 276
Acton, Patricia Nassif, **Supp. X:** 233
Acts of Faith (Caputo), **Supp. XIX:** **29–30**
"Acts of the Apostles, The" (Bronk), **Supp. XXI:** 28
Actual, The (Bellow), **Retro. Supp. II:** 33
"Actual Experience, Preferred Narratives" (Julier), **Supp. IV Part 1:** 211
Acuff, Roy, **Supp. V:** 335
Ada (Nabokov), **Retro. Supp. I:** 265, 266, 270, 276–277, 278, 279
"Ada" (Stein), **IV:** 43
"Adagia" (Stevens), **IV:** 78, 80, 88, 92
"Adagio" (Hull), **Supp. XXI:** 136–137
"Adam" (Hecht), **Supp. X:** 62
"Adam" (W. C. Williams), **Retro. Supp. I:** 422, 423
"Adam and Eve" (Eugene), **Supp. X:** 204
"Adam and Eve" (Shapiro), **Supp. II Part 2:** 708, 712
"Adamantine Practice of Poetry, The" (Wright), **Supp. XV:** 341–342, 343–344
Adam Bede (G. Eliot), **II:** 181
Adamé, Leonard, **Supp. XIII:** 316

Adam & Eve & the City (W. C. Williams), **Retro. Supp. I:** 423
"Adamic Purity as Double Agent" (Whalen-Bridge), **Retro. Supp. II:** 211–212
"Adams" (Saunders), **Supp. XIX:** 232
Adams, Althea. *See* Thurber, Mrs. James (Althea Adams)
Adams, Annie. *See* Fields, Annie Adams
Adams, Brooks, **Supp. I Part 2:** 484
Adams, Charles, **Supp. I Part 2:** 644
Adams, Charles Francis, **I:** 1, 4; **Supp. I Part 2:** 484
Adams, Franklin P., **Supp. I Part 2:** 653; **Supp. IX:** 190; **Supp. XV:** 294, 297
Adams, Henry, **I:** **1–24,** 111, 243, 258; **II:** 278, 542; **III:** 396, 504; **IV:** 191, 349; **Retro. Supp. I:** 53, 59; **Retro. Supp. II:** 207; **Supp. I Part 1:** 299–300, 301, 314; **Supp. I Part 2:** 417, 492, 543, 644; **Supp. II Part 1:** 93–94, 105; **Supp. III Part 2:** 613; **Supp. IV Part 1:** 31, 208
Adams, Mrs. Henry (Marian Hooper), **I:** 1, 5, 10, 17–18
Adams, Henry B., **Supp. I Part 1:** 369
Adams, James Truslow, **Supp. I Part 2:** 481, 484, 486
Adams, J. Donald, **IV:** 438
Adams, John, **I:** 1; **II:** 103, 301; **III:** 17, 473; **Supp. I Part 2:** 483, 506, 507, 509, 510, 511, 517, 518, 520, 524
Adams, John Luther, **Supp. XII:** 209
Adams, John Quincy, **I:** 1, 3, 16–17; **Supp. I Part 2:** 685, 686
Adams, Léonie, **Supp. I Part 2:** 707; **Supp. V:** 79; **Supp. IX:** 229; **Supp. XVII:** 75
Adams, Luella, **Supp. I Part 2:** 652
Adams, Noah, **Supp. XVII:** 218
Adams, Phoebe, **Supp. IV Part 1:** 203; **Supp. VIII:** 124
Adams, Samuel, **Supp. I Part 2:** 516, 525
Adams, Timothy Dow, **Supp. XVI:** 67, 69
Ada; or Ardor (Nabokov), **III:** 247
"Ad Castitatem" (Bogan), **Supp. III Part 1:** 50
Adcock, Betty, **Supp. XVIII:** 181–182, 182
Addams, Jane, **Supp. I Part 1:** **1–26; Supp. XI:** 200, 202
Addams, John Huy, **Supp. I Part 1:** 2
"Addendum" (Wright), **Supp. V:** 339
Addiego, John, **Supp. XII:** 182
Adding Machine, The (Rice), **I:** 479
Adding Machine, The: Selected Essays (Burroughs), **Supp. III Part 1:** 93, 97
Addison, Joseph, **I:** 8, 105, 106–107, 108, 114, 131, 300, 304; **III:** 430
"Addressed to a Political Shrimp, or, Fly upon the Wheel" (Freneau), **Supp. II Part 1:** 267
"Address to My Soul" (Wylie), **Supp. I Part 2:** 729
"Address to the Deist, An" (Wheatley), **Supp. XX:**287
"Address to the Devil" (Jarman), **Supp. XVII:** 114

Address to the Government of the United States on the Cession of Louisiana to the French, An (Brown), **Supp. I Part 1:** 146
"Address to the Scholars of New England" (Ransom), **III:** 491
"Address with Exclamation Points, A" (Simic), **Supp. VIII:** 283
"Adjutant Bird, The" (Banks), **Supp. V:** 5
Adkins, Nelson F., **II:** 20
Adler, Alfred, **I:** 248
Adler, Betty, **III:** 103
Adler, George J., **III:** 81
Adler, Renata, **Supp. X:** 171
Admiral of the Ocean Sea: A Life of Christopher Columbus (Morison), **Supp. I Part 2:** 486–488
"Admirals" (Chabon), **Supp. XI:** 72
"Admonition, An" (Brodsky), **Supp. VIII:** 33
"Adolescence" (Bidart), **Supp. XV:** 32
"Adolescence" (Dove), **Supp. IV Part 1:** 245
"Adolescence" (Olds), **Supp. X:** 211
"Adolescence II" (Dove), **Supp. IV Part 1:** 242, 244–245
Adolescent's Christmas, An: 1944 (C. Bly), **Supp. XVI:** 31–32
"Adolf Eichmann" (Carruth), **Supp. XVI:** 47
"Adonais" (Shelley), **II:** 516, 540
Adorno, Theodor, **Supp. I Part 2:** 645, 650; **Supp. IV Part 1:** 301
"Adrienne Rich: The Poetics of Change" (Gelpi), **Supp. I Part 2:** 554
"Adultery" (Banks), **Supp. V:** 15
"Adultery" (Dubus), **Supp. VII:** 85
Adultery and Other Choices (Dubus), **Supp. VII:** 83–85
Adulthood Rites (O. Butler), **Supp. XIII:** 63, **64–65**
Adult Life of Toulouse Lautrec by Henri Toulouse Lautrec, The (Acker), **Supp. XII:** 5, 6, **8–9**
Adventure (London), **II:** 466
Adventures in Ancient Egypt (Goldbarth), **Supp. XII:** 191
Adventures in Value (Cummings), **I:** 430
"Adventures of a Book Reviewer" (Cowley), **Supp. II Part 1:** 137, 142
Adventures of Augie March, The (Bellow), **I:** 144, 147, 149, 150, 151, 152–153, 154, 155, 157, 158–159, 164; **Retro. Supp. II:** 19, 20, **22–23,** 24, 30; **Supp. VIII:** 234, 236–237
Adventures of a Young Man (Dos Passos), **I:** 488, 489, 492
Adventures of Captain Bonneville (Irving), **II:** 312
Adventures of Harry Franco, The: A Tale of the Great Panic (Briggs), **Supp. XVIII:** 1, 2, 5–8
Adventures of Harry Richmond, The (Meredith), **Supp. XX:**234
Adventures of Huckleberry Finn, The (Twain), **I:** 307, 506; **II:** 26, 72, 262, 266–268, 290, 418, 430; **III:** 101, 112–113, 357, 554, 558, 577; **IV:** 198, 201–204, 207; **Retro. Supp. I:** 188;

Retro. Supp. II: 121; **Supp. I Part 1:** 247; **Supp. IV Part 1:** 247, 257; **Supp. IV Part 2:** 502; **Supp. V:** 131; **Supp. VIII:** 198; **Supp. X:** 230; **Supp. XII:** 16; **Supp. XVI:** 222; **Supp. XX:**171

Adventures of Jimmy (Broughton), **Supp. XV:** 146

Adventures of Roderick Random, The (Smollett), **I:** 134

Adventures of the Letter I (Simpson), **Supp. IX:** 266, **273–274**

Adventures of Tom Sawyer, The (Twain), **II:** 26; **III:** 223, 572, 577; **IV:** 199–200, 203, 204; **Supp. I Part 2:** 456, 470; **Supp. XVI:** 66

Adventures While Preaching the Gospel of Beauty (Lindsay), **Supp. I Part 2:** 374, 376, 381, 382–384, 389, 399

Adventures with Ed (Loeffler), **Supp. XIII:** 1

Advertisements for Myself (Mailer), **III:** 27, 35–38, 41–42, 45, 46; **Retro. Supp. II:** 196, 199, 200, 202, 203, 212; **Supp. IV Part 1:** 90, 284; **Supp. XIV:** 157

"Advertisements for Myself on the Way Out" (Mailer), **III:** 37

"Advice to a Prophet" (Wilbur), **Supp. III Part 2:** 555–557

Advice to a Prophet and Other Poems (Wilbur), **Supp. III Part 2:** 554–558

"Advice to a Raven in Russia" (Barlow), **Supp. II Part 1:** 65, 74, 80, 83

"Advice to Players" (Bidart), **Supp. XV:** 35

Advice to the Lovelorn (film), **Retro. Supp. II:** 328

Advice to the Privileged Orders, Part I (Barlow), **Supp. II Part 1:** 80

"Aeneas and Dido" (Brodsky), **Supp. VIII:** 24–25

"Aeneas at Washington" (Tate), **IV:** 129

Aeneid (Virgil), **I:** 396; **II:** 542; **III:** 124; **Supp. XV:** 23

Aeneus Tacticus, **I:** 136

Aerial View (Barabtarlo), **Retro. Supp. I:** 278

"Aeria the Evanescent" (Sobin), **Supp. XVI:** 292

Aeschylus, **I:** 274, 433; **III:** 398; **IV:** 358, 368, 370; **Retro. Supp. I:** 65; **Supp. I Part 2:** 458, 494

Aesop, **I:** 387; **II:** 154, 169, 302; **III:** 587

Aesthetic (Croce), **III:** 610

"Aesthetics" (Mumford), **Supp. II Part 2:** 476

"Aesthetics of Silence, The" (Sontag), **Supp. III Part 2:** 459

"Aesthetics of the Shah" (Olds), **Supp. X:** 205

"Affair at Coulter's Notch, The" (Bierce), **I:** 202

Affaire de viol, Une (C. Himes). *See Case of Rape, A* (C. Himes)

"Affair of Outposts, An" (Bierce), **I:** 202

Affliction (Banks), **Supp. V:** 15, 16

Affluent Society, The (Galbraith), **Supp. I Part 2:** 648

Afghanistan Picture Show, An: or, How I Saved the World (Vollmann), **Supp. XVII:** 226, **228–229,** 233

"Aficionados, The" (Carver), **Supp. III Part 1:** 137

"Afloat" (Beattie), **Supp. V:** 29

Afloat and Ashore (Cooper), **I:** 351, 355

"Afoot" (P. N. Warren as Kilina), **Supp. XX:**261–262

Africa, Its Geography, People, and Products (Du Bois), **Supp. II Part 1:** 179

Africa, Its Place in Modern History (Du Bois), **Supp. II Part 1:** 179

"Africa, to My Mother" (D. Diop), **Supp. IV Part 1:** 16

Africana (H. L. Gates, ed.), **Supp. XX:**99

African American Century, The : How Black Americans Have Shaped Our Country (H. L. Gates), **Supp. XX:**102

African American Lives (television production), **Supp. XX:**99

African American Lives 2 (television production), **Supp. XX:**99

African American National Biography (H. L. Gates, ed.), **Supp. XX:**99

African American Writers (Smith, ed.), **Supp. XIII:** 115, 127

"African Book" (Hemingway), **II:** 259

"African Chief, The" (Bryant), **Supp. I Part 1:** 168

"African Fragment" (Brooks), **Supp. III Part 1:** 85

African Queen, The (film), **Supp. XI:** 17

"African Roots of War, The" (Du Bois), **Supp. I Part 1:** 174

African Silences (Matthiessen), **Supp. V:** 203

African Treasury, An (Hughes, ed.), **Supp. I Part 1:** 344

"Afrika Revolution" (Baraka), **Supp. II Part 1:** 53

"AFRO-AMERICAN LYRIC" (Baraka), **Supp. II Part 1:** 59

After (Bukiet), **Supp. XVII:** 43, **44–45**

After All: Last Poems (Matthews), **Supp. IX:** 155, **167–169**

After and Before the Lightning (Ortiz), **Supp. IV Part 2:** 513

"After a Party" (Salinas), **Supp. XIII:** 327

"After Apple-Picking" (Frost), **Retro. Supp. I:** 126, 128

"After Arguing against the Contention That Art Must Come from Discontent" (Stafford), **Supp. XI:** 327

After Confession: Poetry as Autobiography (Harris), **Supp. XIV:** 269

After Confession: Poetry as Autobiography (K. Sontag and D. Graham), **Supp. XV:** 104

"After Cowboy Chicken Came to Town" (Jin), **Supp. XVIII:** 97–98

"After Disappointment" (Jarman), **Supp. XVII:** 118–119

After Experience (Snodgrass), **Supp. VI:** 314–316, 317

"After great pain, a formal feeling comes" (Dickinson), **Retro. Supp. I:** 37

"After Hearing a Waltz by Bartók" (Lowell), **II:** 522

After Henry (Didion), **Supp. IV Part 1:** 195, 196, 199, 207, 208, 211

"After Henry" (Didion), **Supp. IV Part 1:** 211

"After Holbein" (Wharton), **IV:** 325; **Retro. Supp. I:** 382

After Ikkyu and Other Poems (Harrison), **Supp. VIII:** 42

"After-Image" (Bierds), **Supp. XVII:** 31–32

"After-Image" (Caldwell), **I:** 309

After-Images: Autobiographical Sketches (Snodgrass), **Supp. VI:** 314, **319–323,** 324, 326–327

After I's (Zukofsky), **Supp. III Part 2:** 628, 629

Afterlife (Monette), **Supp. X:** 153

Afterlife (Updike), **Retro. Supp. I:** 322

Afterlife, The (Levis), **Supp. XI:** 259, **260–264**

"After Magritte" (McClatchy), **Supp. XII:** 264

"After Making Love" (Dunn), **Supp. XI:** 153

Aftermath (Longfellow), **II:** 490

"Aftermath" (Longfellow), **II:** 498

After New Formalism (A. Finch, ed.), **Supp. XVII:** 74

"Afternoon" (Ellison), **Supp. II Part 1:** 238

"Afternoon at MacDowell" (Kenyon), **Supp. VII:** 159

"Afternoon Miracle, An" (O. Henry), **Supp. II Part 1:** 390

Afternoon of a Faun (Hearon), **Supp. VIII: 63–64**

Afternoon of an Author: A Selection of Uncollected Stories and Essays (Fitzgerald), **II:** 94

"Afternoon of a Playwright" (Thurber), **Supp. I Part 2:** 620

Afternoon of the Unreal (Salinas), **Supp. XIII:** 311, **316–318**

"Afternoon with the Old Man, An" (Dubus), **Supp. VII:** 84

"After Punishment Was Done with Me" (Olds), **Supp. X:** 213

"After Reading *Barely and Widely,*" (Zukofsky), **Supp. III Part 2:** 625, 631

"After Reading 'In the Clearing' for the Author, Robert Frost" (Corso), **Supp. XII:** 130

"After Reading *Mickey in the Night Kitchen* for the Third Time before Bed" (Dove), **Supp. IV Part 1:** 249

"After Reading Tu Fu, I Go Outside to the Dwarf Orchard" (Wright), **Supp. V:** 343

"After Reading Wang Wei, I Go Outside to the Full Moon" (Wright), **Supp. V:** 343

After Shocks, Near Escapes (Dobyns), **Supp. XIII: 80–82**

"After Song, An" (W. C. Williams), **Retro. Supp. I:** 413

After Strange Gods (T. S. Eliot), **I:** 588

After Such Knowledge: Memory, History, and the Legacy of the Holocaust (E. Hoffman), **Supp. XVI:** 152–153, **158–161**

"After the Alphabets" (Merwin), **Supp. III Part 1:** 356

"After the Argument" (Dunn), **Supp. XI:** 149

"After the Baptism" (C. Bly), **Supp. XVI:** 40

"After the Burial" (Lowell), **Supp. I Part 2:** 409

"After the Curfew" (Holmes), **Supp. I Part 1:** 308

"After the Death of John Brown" (Thoreau), **IV:** 185

"After the Denim" (Carver), **Supp. III Part 1:** 144

"After the Dentist" (Swenson), **Supp. IV Part 2:** 645

After the Fall (A. Miller), **III:** 148, 149, 156, 161, 162, 163–165, 166

"After the Fire" (Merrill), **Supp. III Part 1:** 328

"After the Flood" (Sanders), **Supp. XVI:** 274–275

After the Fox (film), **Supp. IV Part 2:** 575

After the Genteel Tradition (Cowley), **Supp. II Part 1:** 143

"After the Heart's Interrogation" (Komunyakaa), **Supp. XIII:** 120

After the Lost Generation: A Critical Study of the Writers of Two Wars (Aldridge), **Supp. IV Part 2:** 680; **Supp. XIX:** 250

"After the Night Office—Gethsemani Abbey" (Merton), **Supp. VIII:** 195–196

After the Others (Weigl), **Supp. XIX:** 282, 283–284

"After the Persian" (Bogan), **Supp. III Part 1:** 64

After the Plague (Boyle), **Supp. XX:**20

"After the Plague" (Boyle), **Supp. XX:**20

"After the Pleasure Party" (Melville), **III:** 93

"After the Rain" (Halliday), **Supp. XIX:** 91

"After the Resolution" (Dunn), **Supp. XI:** 151

After the Stroke (Sarton), **Supp. VIII:** 264

"After the Surprising Conversions" (Lowell), **I:** 544, 545; **II:** 550; **Retro. Supp. II:** 187

"After 37 Years My Mother Apologizes for My Childhood" (Olds), **Supp. X:** 208

After This (McDermott), **Supp. XVIII:** 155, **166–167**

Afterthoughts (L. P. Smith), **Supp. XIV:** 339, 345

"Afterthoughts on the Rosenbergs" (Fiedler), **Supp. XIII:** 99

"After Twenty Years" (Rich), **Supp. I Part 2:** 559–560

"Afterwake, The" (Rich), **Supp. I Part 2:** 553

"Afterward" (Wharton), **Retro. Supp. I:** 372

"After Working Long" (Kenyon), **Supp. VII:** 170

"After Yitzl" (Goldbarth), **Supp. XII:** 186

"After You, My Dear Alphonse" (Jackson), **Supp. IX:** 119

"After Your Death" (Trethewey), **Supp. XXI:** 255

"After Your Nap" (B. Kelly), **Supp. XVII:** 124

"Again" (Dixon), **Supp. XII:** 157

"Again, Kapowsin" (Hugo), **Supp. VI:** 141

"Again Just Now" (Budbill), **Supp. XIX:** 11

"Against" (Goldbarth), **Supp. XII:** 193

"Against Decoration" (Karr), **Supp. XI:** 248

"Against Epiphanies" (C. Baxter), **Supp. XVII:** 20

Against Interpretation (Sontag), **Supp. III Part 2:** 451, 455; **Supp. XIV:** 15

"Against Interpretation" (Sontag), **Supp. III Part 2:** 456–458, 463

"Against Modernity" (Ozick), **Supp. V:** 272

"Against Nature" (Karr), **Supp. XI:** 243

Against Nature (Updike), **Retro. Supp. I:** 323

Against Our Vanishing: Winter Conversations with Allen Grossman on the Theory and Practice of Poetry (Halliday), **Supp. XIX: 82–84,** 88

"Against Realism" (Halliday), **Supp. XIX:** 93

Against the Cold (Bynner), **Supp. XV:** 51

"Against the Crusades" (Stern), **Supp. IX:** 300

Against the Current: As I Remember F. Scott Fitzgerald (Kroll Ring), **Supp. IX:** 63

Agamben, Giorgio, **Supp. XVI:** 289

Agapida, Fray Antonio (pseudonym). *See* Irving, Washington

"Agassiz" (Lowell), **Supp. I Part 2:** 414, 416

Agassiz, Louis, **II:** 343; **Supp. I Part 1:** 312; **Supp. IX:** 180

Âge cassant, L' (Char; Sobin, trans.), **Supp. XVI:** 282

"Aged Wino's Counsel to a Young Man on the Brink of Marriage, The" (X. J. Kennedy), **Supp. XV:** 156

Agee, Emma, **I:** 26

Agee, James, **I: 25–47,** 293; **IV:** 215; **Supp. IX:** 109; **Supp. XIV:** 92; **Supp. XV:** 143

"Agent, The" (Wilbur), **Supp. III Part 2:** 557–561

Age of Anxiety, The (Auden), **Supp. II Part 1:** 2, 19, 21

"Age of Conformity, The" (Howe), **Supp. VI:** 117

Age of Grief, The: A Novella and Stories (Smiley), **Supp. VI:** 292, **299–301**

Age of Innocence, The (Wharton), **IV:** 320–322, 327–328; **Retro. Supp. I:** 372, 374, **380–381; Supp. IV Part 1:** 23

Age of Longing, The (Koestler), **I:** 258

Age of Reason, The (Paine), **Supp. I Part 2:** 503, 515–517, 520

"Age of Strolling, The" (Stern), **Supp. IX:** 297

"Ages, The" (Bryant), **Supp. I Part 1:** 152, 155, 166, 167

"Ages of the Women, The" (Gibran), **Supp. XX:**115

"Aggrandizement, The" (Bronk), **Supp. XXI:** 32

"Aging" (Jarrell), **II:** 388

Aging and Gender in Literature (George), **Supp. IV Part 2:** 450

"Agio Neró" (Mora), **Supp. XIII:** 224

"Agitato ma non Troppo" (Ransom), **III:** 493

"Agnes of Iowa" (Moore), **Supp. X:** 165, 178

Agnes of Sorrento (Stowe), **Supp. I Part 2:** 592, 595–596

Agnon, S. Y., **Supp. V:** 266

"Agosta the Winged Man and Rasha the Black Dove" (Dove), **Supp. IV Part 1:** 246–247

Agrarian Justice (Paine), **Supp. I Part 2:** 517–518

"Agricultural Show, The" (McKay), **Supp. X:** 139

Agrippa: A Book of the Dead (W. Gibson), **Supp. XVI:** 125

Agua de dos ríos/Water from Two Rivers (Espaillat), **Supp. XXI:** 104, 112–113

Agua Fresca: An Anthology of Raza Poetry (Rodríguez, ed.), **Supp. IV Part 2:** 540

Agua Santa/Holy Water (Mora), **Supp. XIII: 222–225**

Agüero Sisters, The (García), **Supp. XI: 185–190**

Aguiar, Sarah Appleton, **Supp. XIII:** 30

Ah, Wilderness! (O'Neill), **III:** 400–401; **Supp. IV Part 2:** 587

Ah, Wilderness!: The Frontier in American Literature (Humphrey), **Supp. IX:** 104

Ahearn, Barry, **Retro. Supp. I:** 415

Ahearn, Frederick L., Jr., **Supp. XI:** 184

Ahearn, Kerry, **Supp. IV Part 2:** 604

Ahmed Arabi Pasha, **I:** 453

Ahnebrink, Lars, **III:** 328

Ahrens, Sylvia, **Supp. XX:**162

Ah Sin (Harte), **Supp. II Part 1:** 354–355

"Ah! Sun-flower" (Blake), **III:** 19

Aida (rock musical), **Supp. XXI:** 148

AIDS and Its Metaphors (Sontag), **Supp. III Part 2:** 452, 466–468

Aids to Reflection (Coleridge), **II:** 10

Aiieeeee! An Anthology of Asian-American Writers (The Combined Asian Resources Project), **Supp. X:** 292

Aiken, Conrad, **I: 48–70,** 190, 211, 243; **II:** 55, 530, 542; **III:** 458, 460; **Retro. Supp. I:** 55, 56, 57, 58, 60, 62; **Supp. X:** 50, 115; **Supp. XV:** 144, 297, 298, 302, 306, 309; **Supp. XVII:** 135

"Aimless Love" (Collins), **Supp. XXI:** 61

"Aim Was Song, The" (Frost), **Retro. Supp. I:** 133
Ainger, Arthur Campbell, **Supp. XX:**230
Ainsworth, Linda, **Supp. IV Part 1:** 274
Ainsworth, William, **III:** 423
Air-Conditioned Nightmare, The (H. Miller), **III:** 186
Airing Dirty Laundry (Reed), **Supp. X:** 241
"Airmail from Mother" (Kooser), **Supp. XIX:** 120
"Air Plant, The" (Crane), **I:** 401
Air Raid: A Verse Play for Radio (MacLeish), **III:** 21
"Airs above the Ground" (Sarton), **Supp. VIII:** 261
Air Tight: A Novel of Red Russia. See We the Living (Rand)
Air Up There, The (film, Glaser), **Supp. XVII:** 9
"Airwaves" (Mason), **Supp. VIII:** 146
Airways, Inc. (Dos Passos), **I:** 482
"A is for Dining Alone" (M. F. K. Fisher), **Supp. XVII:** 86
Aitken, Robert, **Supp. I Part 2:** 504
Aizenberg, Susan, **Supp. XXI:** 131
Akhmadulina, Bella, **Supp. III Part 1:** 268
Akhmatova, Anna, **Supp. III Part 1:** 268, 269; **Supp. VIII:** 20, 21, 25, 27, 30; **Supp. XXI:** 132
Akhmatova Translations, The (Kenyon), **Supp. VII:** 160
"Akhnilo" (Salter), **Supp. IX:** 260
Akins, Zoë, **Supp. XVI:** 187
Aksenev, Vasily P., **Retro. Supp. I:** 278
"Al Aaraaf" (Poe), **III:** 426–427
Al Aaraaf, Tamerlane, and Minor Poems (Poe), **III:** 410
"Alain Locke and Cultural Pluralism" (Kallen), **Supp. XIV:** 197
"Alain Locke: Bahá'í Philosopher" (Buck), **Supp. XIV:** 199
Alain Locke: Faith and Philosophy (Buck), **Supp. XIV:** 200
Alarçon, **Supp. XVII:** 74
Alarcón, Justo, **Supp. IV Part 2:** 538, 539, 540
À la Recherche du Temps Perdu (Proust), **IV:** 428
"Alarm" (X. J. Kennedy), **Supp. XV:** 163
"Alastor" (Shelley), **Supp. I Part 2:** 728
"Alatus" (Wilbur), **Supp. III Part 2:** 563
"Alba" (Creeley), **Supp. IV Part 1:** 150
Alba, Richard D., **Supp. XX:**43
Albee, Edward, **I:** 71–96, 113; **II:** 558, 591; **III:** 281, 387; **IV:** 4, 230; **Retro. Supp. II:** 104; **Supp. VIII:** 331; **Supp. XIII:** 196, 197
Albers, Joseph, **Supp. IV Part 2:** 621
Alberti, Rafael, **Supp. XV:** 75
Albright, Margery, **Supp. I Part 2:** 613
"Album, The" (Morris), **III:** 220
Alcestiad, The (Wilder), **IV:** 357, 374
"Alchemist, The" (Bogan), **Supp. III Part 1:** 50
"Alchemist in the City, The" (Hopkins), **Supp. IV Part 2:** 639
Alchymist's Journal, The (Connell), **Supp. XIV:** 80

"Alcmena" (Winters), **Supp. II Part 2:** 801
Alcott, Abba. *See* Alcott, Mrs. Amos Bronson (Abigail May)
Alcott, Amos Bronson, **II:** 7, 225; **IV:** 172, 173, 184; **Retro. Supp. I:** 217; **Supp. I Part 1:** 28, 29–32, 35, 39, 41, 45; **Supp. II Part 1:** 290; **Supp. XVI:** 84, 89
Alcott, Mrs. Amos Bronson (Abigail May), **IV:** 184; **Supp. I Part 1:** 29, 30, 31, 32, 35
Alcott, Anna. *See* Pratt, Anna
Alcott, Louisa May, **IV:** 172; **Supp. I Part 1: 28–46; Supp. IX:** 128; **Supp. XV:** 338; **Supp. XVI:** 84
Alcott, May, **Supp. I Part 1:** 41
Alcuin: A Dialogue (Brown), **Supp. I Part 1:** 126–127, 133
Alden, Hortense. *See* Farrell, Mrs. James T. (Hortense Alden)
Alden, John, **I:** 471; **II:** 502–503
"Alder Fork, The" (Leopold), **Supp. XIV:** 186
Aldington, Perdita, **Supp. I Part 1:** 258
Aldington, Richard, **II:** 517; **III:** 458, 459, 465, 472; **Retro. Supp. I:** 63, 127; **Supp. I Part 1:** 257–262, 270
Aldington, Mrs. Richard. *See* Doolittle, Hilda
Aldo Leopold: His Life and Work (Meine), **Supp. XIV:** 179
"Aldo Leopold's Intellectual Heritage" (Nash), **Supp. XIV:** 191–192
Aldon, Raymond, **Supp. XV:** 297
Aldrich, Thomas Bailey, **II:** 400; **Supp. II Part 1:** 192; **Supp. XIV:** 45; **Supp. XVIII:** 4
Aldrich, Tom, **Supp. I Part 2:** 415
Aldridge, John W., **Supp. I Part 1:** 196; **Supp. IV Part 1:** 286; **Supp. IV Part 2:** 680, 681; **Supp. VIII:** 189; **Supp. XI:** 228; **Supp. XIX:** 250
Aleck Maury Sportsman (Gordon), **II:** 197, 200, 203–204
Alegría, Claribel, **Supp. IV Part 1:** 208
Aleichem, Sholom, **IV:** 3, 10; **Supp. IV Part 2:** 585
"Alert Lovers, Hidden Sides, and Ice Travelers: Notes on Poetic Form and Energy" (Dunn), **Supp. XI:** 153
"Alesă Debeljak" (Simic), **Supp. VIII:** 279
"Alex" (Oliver), **Supp. VII:** 232
Alexander, Doris, **Supp. XVII:** 99
Alexander, Elizabeth, **Supp. XVIII:** 171, 185, 186; **Supp. XXI:** 246, 257
Alexander, George, **II:** 331
Alexander, Michael, **Retro. Supp. I:** 293
"Alexander Crummell Dead" (Dunbar), **Supp. II Part 1:** 207, 208–209
Alexander's Bridge (Cather), **I:** 313, 314, 316–317, 326; **Retro. Supp. I:** 1, 6, 7, 8
Alexander the Great, **IV:** 322
"Alexandra" (Cather), **Retro. Supp. I:** 7, 9, 17
Alexandrov, V. E., **Retro. Supp. I:** 270
Alexie, Sherman, **Supp. XVIII:** 58

Algonquin Round Table, **Supp. IX:** 190, 191, 197
Algren, Nelson, **I:** 211; **Supp. V:** 4; **Supp. IX: 1–18; Supp. XII:** 126; **Supp. XIII:** 173; **Supp. XIV:** 3; **Supp. XVII:** 161; **Supp. XXI:** 264
Alhambra, The (Irving), **II:** 310–311
Ali, Agha Shahid, **Supp. XVII:** 74
Alias Grace (Atwood), **Supp. XIII:** 20, 31–32
Alice (film; Allen), **Supp. XV:** 2, 11
"Alice Doane's Appeal" (Hawthorne), **II:** 227
"Alice Drops Her Cigarette on the Floor ... " (Findley), **Supp. XX:**50–51
Alice in Wonderland (Carroll), **Supp. I Part 2:** 622
Alice's Adventures in Wonderland (Carroll), **Supp. XVI:** 261
"Alicia and I Talking on Edna's Steps" (Cisneros), **Supp. VII:** 64
"Alicia Who Sees Mice" (Cisneros), **Supp. VII:** 60
Alien 3 (screenplay, W. Gibson), **Supp. XVI:** 120, 124
"Ali in Havana" (Talese), **Supp. XVII:** 207, 208
Alison, Archibald, **Supp. I Part 1:** 151, 159
Alison's House (Glaspell), **Supp. III Part 1:** 182, 188, 189
Alive (screenplay, Shanley), **Supp. XIV:** 316
Alive and Writing: Interviews with American Authors of the 1980s (McCaffery and Gregory), **Supp. X:** 260
"Alki Beach" (Hugo), **Supp. VI:** 135
Alla Breve Loving (Wright), **Supp. XV:** 339, 340
"Alla Breve Loving" (Wright), **Supp. XV:** 340
"All Around the Town" (Benét), **Supp. XI:** 48, 58
All at Sea (Lardner), **II:** 427
"All Boy" (Rawlings), **Supp. X:** 222
Allegiances (Stafford), **Supp. XI:** 322–323, 329
"Allegory of the Cave" (Dunn), **Supp. XI:** 150
"Allegory Unlimited" (Cassill), **Supp. XIX:** 266
Allegro, Johnny (film, Tetzloff), **Supp. XVII:** 62
"Allegro, L' " (Milton), **Supp. XIV:** 8
Allen, Brooke, **Supp. VIII:** 153
Allen, Dick, **Supp. IX:** 279
Allen, Donald, **Supp. VIII:** 291; **Supp. XIII:** 112
Allen, Frank, **Supp. XI:** 126; **Supp. XII:** 186
Allen, Frederick Lewis, **Supp. I Part 2:** 655
Allen, Gay Wilson, **IV:** 352; **Supp. I Part 2:** 418
Allen, Paula Gunn. *See* Gunn Allen, Paula
Allen, Robert Moore, **Supp. XX:**164
Allen, Walter, **I:** 505; **III:** 352; **Supp. IV Part 2:** 685; **Supp. IX:** 231

Allen, Woody, **Supp. I Part 2:** 607, 623; **Supp. IV Part 1:** 205; **Supp. X:** 164; **Supp. XI:** 307; **Supp. XV:** 1–18; **Supp. XVII:** 48

"Aller et Retour" (Barnes), Supp. III Part 1: 36

Aller Retour New York (H. Miller), **III:** 178, 182, 183

Allessandrini, Goffredo, **Supp. IV Part 2:** 520

Alleys of Eden, The (R. O. Butler), **Supp. XII:** 62, **62–64**, 68

All God's Children Need Traveling Shoes (Angelou), **Supp. IV Part 1:** 2, 9–10, 12–13, 17

All God's Chillun Got Wings (O'Neill), **III:** 387, 391, 393–394

All Gone (Dixon), **Supp. XII:** 148, 149

"All Hallows" (Glück), **Supp. V:** 82

"All I Can Remember" (Jackson), **Supp. IX:** 115

"Alligators, The" (Updike), **IV:** 219

Allingham, John Till, **Supp. XV:** 243

All in the Family (Boyce), **Supp. XXI:** 8

"ALL IN THE STREET" (Baraka), **Supp. II Part 1:** 53

Allison, Dorothy, **Supp. XVIII:** 195

"All I Want" (Tapahonso), **Supp. IV Part 2:** 508

"All Little Colored Children Should Play the Harmonica" (Patchett), **Supp. XII:** 309

"All Mountains" (Doolittle), **Supp. I Part 1:** 271

All My Friends Are Going to Be Strangers (McMurtry), **Supp. V:** 224, 228, 229

All My Pretty Ones (Sexton), **Supp. II Part 2:** 678, 679–683

"All My Pretty Ones" (Sexton), **Supp. II Part 2:** 681–682

"All My Sad Captains" (Jewett), **Retro. Supp. II:** 134

All My Sons (A. Miller), **III:** 148, 149, 150, 151–153, 154, 155, 156, 158, 159, 160, 164, 166

All New People (Lamott), **Supp. XX:**135–136

"All Night, All Night" (Schwartz), **Supp. II Part 2:** 665

All Night Long (Caldwell), **I:** 297

"All-Night Melodies" (Nelson), **Supp. XVIII:** 185

All of What We Loved (Bronk), **Supp. XXI:** 32

"All Our Lost Children: Trauma and Testimony in the Performance of Childhood" (Pace), **Supp. XI:** 245

All Our Yesterdays (Parker), **Supp. XIX: 187–188**

"All Out" (Hecht), **Supp. X:** 72

All Over (Albee), **I:** 91–94

"Allowance" (Minot), **Supp. VI:** 206, 207–208

"Alloy" (Rukeyser), **Supp. VI:** 279

"All Parrots Speak" (Bowles), **Supp. IV Part 1:** 89

Allport, Gordon, **II:** 363–364

All Quiet on the Western Front (Remarque), **Supp. IV Part 1:** 380, 381

"ALL REACTION IS DOOMED-!-!-!" (Baraka), **Supp. II Part 1:** 59

"All Revelation" (Frost), **II:** 160–162

All Shot Up (C. Himes), **Supp. XVI:** 143, 144

"All Souls" (Gioia), **Supp. XV:** 117

"All Souls" (Wharton), **IV:** 315–316; **Retro. Supp. I:** 382

"All Souls' Night" (Yeats), **Supp. X:** 69

All Souls' Rising (Bell), **Supp. X:** 12, **13–16**, 17

"All-Star Literary Vaudeville" (Wilson), **IV:** 434–435

Allston, Washington, **II:** 298

All Stories Are True (Wideman), **Supp. X:** 320

"All That Is" (Wilbur), **Supp. III Part 2:** 563

All That Was Possible (Sturgis), **Supp. XX:**227, 232, **235–237**

"All the Bearded Irises of Life: Confessions of a Homospiritual" (Walker), **Supp. III Part 2:** 527

"All the Beautiful Are Blameless" (Wright), **Supp. III Part 2:** 597

ALL: The Collected Poems, 1956–1964 (Zukofsky), **Supp. III Part 2:** 630

ALL: The Collected Short Poems, 1923–1958 (Zukofsky), **Supp. III Part 2:** 629

All the Conspirators (Isherwood), **Supp. XIV:** 156, 159, 160

All the Dark and Beautiful Warriors (Hansberry), **Supp. IV Part 1:** 360, 374

All the Days and Nights: The Collected Stories (Maxwell), **Supp. VIII:** 151, 158, 169

"All the Dead Dears" (Plath), **Retro. Supp. II:** 246; **Supp. I Part 2:** 537

All the Good People I've Left Behind (Oates), **Supp. II Part 2:** 510, 522, 523

"All the Hippos Were Boiled in Their Tanks" (Burroughs and Kerouac), **Supp. III Part 1:** 94

All the King's Men (Warren), **I:** 489; **IV:** 243, 248–249, 252; **Supp. V:** 261; **Supp. VIII:** 126; **Supp. X:** 1; **Supp. XVIII:** 77, 79

All the Little Live Things (Stegner), **Supp. IV Part 2:** 599, 604, 605, 606, 609–610, 611, 613

All the Pretty Horses (film), **Supp. VIII:** 175

All the Pretty Horses (McCarthy), **Supp. VIII:** 175, **182–183**, 188

All the Sad Young Men (Fitzgerald), **II:** 94; **Retro. Supp. I:** 108

"All the Time in the World" (Dubus), **Supp. VII:** 91

"All the Way to Flagstaff, Arizona" (Bausch), **Supp. VII:** 47, 49

"All This and More" (Karr), **Supp. XI:** 243

All Tomorrow's Parties (W. Gibson), **Supp. XVI:** 119, 121, 123, 124, **130**

"All Too Real" (Vendler), **Supp. V:** 189

All Trivia: Triva, More Trivia, Afterthoughts, Last Words (L. P. Smith), **Supp. XIV:** 339

All-True Travels and Adventures of Lidie Newton (Smiley), **Supp. VI:** 292, **305–307**

All We Need of Hell (Crews), **Supp. XI: 114**

Almack, Edward, **Supp. IV Part 2:** 435

al-Maghut, Muhammad, **Supp. XIII:** 278

"Almanac" (Swenson), **Supp. IV Part 2:** 641

Almanac of the Dead (Silko), **Supp. IV Part 2:** 558–559, 560, 561, 570–571

Almon, Bert, **Supp. IX:** 93

"Almost" (Untermeyer), **Supp. XV:** 304

Almost Revolution, The (Priaulx and Ungar), **Supp. XI:** 228

Alnilam (Dickey), **Supp. IV Part 1:** 176, 186, 188–189

"Alone" (Caputo), **Supp. XIX:** 29

"Alone" (Levine), **Supp. V:** 184, 185, 186

"Alone" (Pickering), **Supp. XXI:** 204

"Alone" (Poe), **Retro. Supp. II:** 266

"Alone" (Singer), **IV:** 15

"Alone" (Winters), **Supp. II Part 2:** 786, 811

"Alone and Lonely" (Budbill), **Supp. XIX:** 10

Aloneness (Brooks), **Supp. III Part 1:** 85, 86

Alone with America (Corso), **Supp. XII:** 131

Alone with America (Howard), **Supp. IX:** 326

"Along America's Edges" (Sobin), **Supp. XVI:** 288

"Along the Color Line" (Du Bois), **Supp. II Part 1:** 173

Along the Illinois (Masters), **Supp. I Part 2:** 472

Alouette, L' (Anouilh), **Supp. I Part 1:** 286–288

"Alphabet" (Nye), **Supp. XIII:** 283

Alphabet, An (Doty), **Supp. XI:** 120

Alphabet for Gourmets, An (M. F. K. Fisher), **Supp. XVII:** 86, 87, 92

Alphabet of Grace, The (Buechner), **Supp. XII:** 52

"Alphabet of My Dead, An" (Pinsky), **Supp. VI:** 235, 250

"Alphabet of Subjects, An" (Zukofsky), **Supp. III Part 2:** 624

"Alpine Christ, The" (Jeffers), **Supp. II Part 2:** 415, 419

Alpine Christ and Other Poems, The (Jeffers), **Supp. II Part 2:** 419

"Alpine Idyll, An" (Hemingway), **II:** 249; **Retro. Supp. I:** 176

Al Que Quiere! (W. C. Williams), **Retro. Supp. I:** 414, 416, **417,** 428

Alraune (Ewers; Endore, trans.), **Supp. XVII:** 54

Alsop, Joseph, **II:** 579

"Altar, The" (Herbert), **Supp. IV Part 2:** 646

"Altar, The" (MacLeish), **III:** 4

"Altar Boy" (Fante), **Supp. XI:** 160, 164

"Altar of the Dead, The" (James), **Retro. Supp. I:** 229

"Altars in the Street, The" (Levertov), **Supp. III Part 1:** 280

Alter, Robert, **Supp. XII:** 167

Altgeld, John Peter, **Supp. I Part 2:** 382, 455

Althea (Masters), **Supp. I Part 2:** 455, 459

Altick, Richard, **Supp. I Part 2:** 423

Altieri, Charles, **Supp. VIII:** 297, 303

Altman, Robert, **Supp. IX:** 143

"Alto" (C. Frost), **Supp. XV:** 101

"Altra Ego" (Brodsky), **Supp. VIII:** 31–32

A Lume Spento (Pound), **Retro. Supp. I:** 283, 285

"Aluminum House" (F. Barthelme), **Supp. XI:** 26

Alvares, Mosseh, **Supp. V:** 11

Alvarez, A., **Supp. I Part 2:** 526, 527; **Supp. II Part 1:** 99; **Supp. IX:** 248

Alvarez, Julia, **Supp. VII:** 1–21; **Supp. XI:** 177; **Supp. XVII:** 71, 112

"Always a Rose" (L.-Y. Lee), **Supp. XV:** 215, 216

"Always in Good Humor" (Adams), **Supp. XV:** 294

Always Outnumbered, Always Outgunned (Mosley), **Supp. XIII:** 242

"Always the Stories" (Ortiz), **Supp. IV Part 2:** 499, 500, 502, 504, 512

Always the Young Strangers (Sandburg), **III:** 577–578, 579

Always Young and Fair (Richter), **Supp. XVIII: 215–216**

Amadeus (Shaffer), **Supp. XIV:** 330

"Amahl and the Night Visitors: A Guide to the Tenor of Love" (Moore), **Supp. X:** 167

"Am and Am Not" (Olds), **Supp. X:** 212

"Amanita, The" (Francis), **Supp. IX:** 81

Amaranth (Robinson), **III:** 509, 510, 512, 513, 522, 523

"Amateurs, The" (Swados), **Supp. XIX:** 256

Amazing Adele, The (Barillet and Grédy; Loos, trans.), **Supp. XVI:** 194

Amazing Adventures of Kavalier and Clay, The (Chabon), **Supp. XI:** 68, 76, **77–80**

Amazing Adventures of the Escapist, The (Chabon, ed.), **Supp. XIX:** 174

Amazing Science Fiction Stories, **Supp. XVI:** 121

Amazons: An Intimate Memoir by the First Woman to Play in the National Hockey League (DeLillo), **Supp. VI:** 2

Ambassador of Peace, An (Abernon), **Supp. XVI:** 191

Ambassadors, The (H. James), **II:** 320, 333–334, 600; **III:** 517; **IV:** 322; **Retro. Supp. I:** 215, 218, 219, 220, 221, **232–233**

Ambelain, Robert, **Supp. I Part 1:** 260, 273, 274

"Ambition Bird, The" (Sexton), **Supp. II Part 2:** 693

Ambition: The Secret Passion (Epstein), **Supp. XIV:** 113–114

Ambler, Eric, **III:** 57

Ambrose Holt and Family (Glaspell), **Supp. III Part 1:** 175, 181, 184, 187, 188

"Ambrose Seyffert" (Masters), **Supp. I Part 2:** 464

"Ambush" (Komunyakaa), **Supp. XIII:** 122

Amen Corner, The (Baldwin), **Retro. Supp. II:** 5, 7; **Supp. I Part 1:** 48, 51, 54, 55, 56

America (Benét), **Supp. XI:** 46, 47, 51

"America" (Ginsberg), **Supp. II Part 1:** 58–59, 317

"America" (song), **IV:** 410

"America, America!" (poem) (Schwartz), **Supp. II Part 2:** 665

"America, Commerce, and Freedom" (Rowson and Reinagle), **Supp. XV:** 240

"America, Seen Through Photographs, Darkly" (Sontag), **Supp. III Part 2:** 464

"America! America!" (story) (Schwartz), **Supp. II Part 2:** 640, 658–659, 660

America and Americans (Steinbeck), **IV:** 52

"America and the Vidal Chronicles" (Pease), **Supp. IV Part 2:** 687

America as a Civilization (Lerner), **III:** 60

America Behind the Color Line (H. L. Gates), **Supp. XX:** 102, 105

America Beyond the Color Line (television program), **Supp. XX:** 99

America Hispana: A Portrait and a Prospect (W. Frank), **Supp. XX:** 76

"America Independent" (Freneau), **Supp. II Part 1:** 261

America Is Worth Saving (Dreiser), **Retro. Supp. II:** 96

American, The (James), **I:** 226; **II:** 326–327, 328, 331, 334; **IV:** 318; **Retro. Supp. I:** 220, **221,** 228, 376, 381

Americana (DeLillo), **Supp. VI:** 2, **3,** 5, 6, 8, 13, 14

American Adam, The (R. W. B. Lewis), **II:** 457–458; **Supp. XIII:** 93

American Almanac (Leeds), **II:** 110

American Anthem (Doctorow and Suares), **Supp. IV Part 1:** 234

"American Apocalypse" (Gunn Allen), **Supp. IV Part 1:** 325

American Aristocracy (film), **Supp. XVI:** 185–186

American Blood, (Nichols), **Supp. XIII:** 268

American Blues (T. Williams), **IV:** 381, 383

American Buffalo (Mamet), **Supp. XIV:** 239, 241, 242, 244–245, 246, 254, 255

American Caravan: A Yearbook of American Literature (Mumford, ed.), **Supp. II Part 2:** 482

American Cause, The (MacLeish), **III:** 3

American Childhood, An (Dillard), **Supp. VI: 19–21,** 23, 24, 25, 26, 30, 31

"American Childhood in the Dominican Republic, An" (Alvarez), **Supp. VII:** 2, 5

American Child Supreme, An: The Education of a Liberation Ecologist (Nichols), **Supp. XIII:** 256, 257, 258, 264, 265, 266, 267, 268, 269

American Civilization (C. L. R. James), **Supp. XXI:** 169

American Claimant, The (Twain), **IV:** 194, 198–199

American Crisis I (Paine), **Supp. I Part 2:** 508

American Crisis II (Paine), **Supp. I Part 2:** 508

American Crisis XIII (Paine), **Supp. I Part 2:** 509

"American Critic, The" (J. Spingarn), **I:** 266

American Culture, Canons, and the Case of Elizabeth Stoddard (Smith and Weinauer), **Supp. XV:** 270

American Daughter, An (Wasserstein), **Supp. XV: 330–332,** 333

American Democrat, The (Cooper), **I:** 343, 346, 347, 353

American Desert (Everett), **Supp. XVIII: 62–63**

American Diary (Webb), **Supp. I Part 1:** 5

American Drama since World War II (Weales), **IV:** 385

American Dream, An (Mailer), **III:** 27, 33–34, 35, 39, 41, 43, 44; **Retro. Supp. II:** 203, **204–205**

American Dream, The (Albee), **I:** 74–76, 77, 89, 94

"American Dreams" (Simpson), **Supp. IX:** 274

American Earth (Caldwell), **I:** 290, 308

"American Emperors" (Poirier), **Supp. IV Part 2:** 690

American Exodus, An (Lange and Taylor), **I:** 293

American Experience, The (Parkes), **Supp. I Part 2:** 617–618

American Express (Corso), **Supp. XII:** 129

"American Express" (Salter), **Supp. IX:** 260–261

"American Fear of Literature, The" (Lewis), **II:** 451

American Female Patriotism (S. Warner as Wetherell), **Supp. XVIII: 260–261,** 262**,** 263

American Fictions (Hardwick), **Supp. X:** 171

American Fictions, 1940–1980 (Karl), **Supp. IV Part 1:** 384; **Supp. XXI:** 234

"American Financier, The" (Dreiser), **II:** 428

American Folkways (book series), **I:** 290

American Guerilla in the Philippines (Wolfert), **Supp. XXI:** 267

American Heroine: The Life and Legend of Jane Addams (A. F. Davis), **Supp. I Part 1:** 1

American Historical Novel, The (Leisy), **Supp. II Part 1:** 125

"American Horse" (Erdrich), **Supp. IV Part 1:** 333

American Humor: A Study of the National Character (Rourke), **IV:** 339, 352; **Supp. XIX:** 147

American Hunger (Wright), **Supp. IV Part 1:** 11

American Indian Anthology, An (Tvedten, ed.), **Supp. IV Part 2:** 505

"American Indian Women: At the Center of Indigenous Resistance in Contemporary North America" (Jaimes and Halsey), **Supp. IV Part 1:** 331

"American in England, An" (Wylie), **Supp. I Part 2:** 707

American Jitters, The: A Year of the Slump (Wilson), **IV:** 427, 428

American Journal (Hayden), **Supp. II Part 1:** 367

American Journey: The Times of Robert F. Kennedy (Plimpton, ed.), **Supp. XVI:** 245

"American Land Ethic, An" (Momaday), **Supp. IV Part 2:** 488

American Landscape, The, **Supp. I Part 1:** 157

American Language, The (Mencken), **II:** 289, 430; **III:** 100, 104, 105, 108, 111, 119–120

American Language, The: Supplement One (Mencken), **III:** 111

American Language, The: Supplement Two (Mencken), **III:** 111

"American Letter" (MacLeish), **III:** 13

"American Liberty" (Freneau), **Supp. II Part 1:** 257

"American Life in Poetry" (column, Kooser), **Supp. XIX:** 116, 127

American Literary History (Harrison), **Supp. VIII:** 37

American Mercury, **Supp. XI:** 163, 164

American Mind, The (Commager), **Supp. I Part 2:** 650

American Moderns: Bohemian New York and the Creation of a New Century (Stansell), **Supp. XVII:** 106

American Moderns: From Rebellion to Conformity (Geismar), **Supp. IX:** 15; **Supp. XI:** 223

"American Names" (Benét), **Supp. XI:** 47

American Nature Writers (Elder, ed.), **Supp. IX:** 25

American Nature Writers (Winter), **Supp. X:** 104

American Negro, The (W. H. Thomas), **Supp. II Part 1:** 168

American Notebooks, The (Hawthorne), **II:** 226

American Novel Since World War II, The (Klein, ed.), **Supp. XI:** 233

Americano, The (film), **Supp. XVI:** 185

"American Original, An: Learning from a Literary Master" (Wilkinson), **Supp. VIII:** 164, 165, 168

American Ornithology (Wilson), **Supp. XVI:** 4, 6

American Pastoral (P. Roth), **Retro. Supp. II:** 279, 289, **292–293;** **Supp. XI:** 68

American Places (Porter, Stegner and Stegner), **Supp. IV Part 2:** 599

"American Poet" (Shapiro), **Supp. II Part 2:** 701

"American Poetry" (Simpson), **Supp. IX:** 272

American Poetry, 1922: A Miscellany (Untermeyer, ed.), **Supp. XV:** 306

"American Poetry and American Life" (Pinsky), **Supp. VI:** 239–240

American Poetry from the Beginning to Whitman (Untermeyer, ed.), **Supp. XV:** 310

American Poetry since 1900 (Untermeyer, ed.), **Supp. XV:** 306

American Poetry since 1945: A Critical Survey (Stepanchev), **Supp. XI:** 312

American Poetry since 1960 (Mesic), **Supp. IV Part 1:** 175

American Poets since World War II Dictionary of Literary Biography (Gwynn, ed.), **Supp. XV:** 343

American Primer, An (Boorstin), **I:** 253

American Primer, An (Whitman), **IV:** 348

"American Primitive" (W. J. Smith), **Supp. XIII:** 333

American Primitive: Poems (Oliver), **Supp. VII:** 234–237, 238

American Procession, An: The Major American Writers from 1830–1930—the Crucial Century (Kazin), **Supp. VIII:** **105–106,** 108

"American Prose Writers" articles (Briggs), **Supp. XVIII:** 11

American Radio Company, The (radio show, Keillor), **Supp. XVI:** 176–177

"American Realist Playwrights, The" (McCarthy), **II:** 562

American Register, or General Repository of History, Politics, and Science, The (Brown, ed.), **Supp. I Part 1:** 146

American Renaissance (Matthiessen), **I:** 259–260; **III:** 310; **Supp. XIII:** 93

"American Rendezvous, An" (Beauvoir), **Supp. IX:** 4

American Scene, The (James), **II:** 336; **III:** 460; **Retro. Supp. I:** 232, 235

American Scenes (Kozlenko, ed.), **IV:** 378

"American Scholar, The" (Emerson), **I:** 239; **II:** 8, 12–13; **Retro. Supp. I:** 62, 74–75, 149, 298; **Retro. Supp. II:** 155; **Supp. I Part 2:** 420; **Supp. IX:** 227, 271; **Supp. XIV:** 104

"American Scholar, The" (Pickering), **Supp. XXI:** 196

Americans in England; or, Lessons for Daughters (Rowson), **Supp. XV:** 240

"American Soldier, The" (Freneau), **Supp. II Part 1:** 269

American Songbag, The (Sandburg), **III:** 583

"American Student in Paris, An" (Farrell), **II:** 45

"American Sublime, The" (Stevens), **IV:** 74

"American Tar, The; or, The Press Gang Defeated" (Rowson and Taylor), **Supp. XV:** 238

"American Temperament, The" (Locke), **Supp. XIV:** 211

American Tragedy, An (Dreiser), **I:** 497, 498, 499, 501, 502, 503, 511–515, 517, 518, 519; **III:** 251; **IV:** 35, 484; **Retro. Supp. II:** 93, 95, **104–108;** **Supp. XVII:** 155

"American Triptych" (Kenyon), **Supp. VII:** 165

"American Use for German Ideals" (Bourne), **I:** 228

American Village, The (Freneau), **Supp. II Part 1:** 256, 257

"American Village, The" (Freneau), **Supp. II Part 1:** 256

America's Coming-of-Age (Brooks), **I:** 228, 230, 240, 245, 258; **IV:** 427

America's Humor: From Poor Richard to Doonesbury (Blair and Hill), **Retro. Supp. II:** 286

"America's Part in World Peace" (Locke), **Supp. XIV:** 208

America's Rome (Vance), **Supp. IV Part 2:** 684

America: The Story of a Free People (Commager and Nevins), **I:** 253

America Was Promises (MacLeish), **III:** 16, 17

"Amerika" (Snyder), **Supp. VIII:** 301

Ames, Christopher, **Supp. XVIII:** 242–243

Ames, Fisher, **Supp. I Part 2:** 486

Ames, Lois, **Supp. I Part 2:** 541, 547

Ames, William, **IV:** 158

Ames Stewart, Beatrice, **Supp. IX:** 200

Amichai, Yehuda, **Supp. XI:** 267

Amidon, Stephen, **Supp. XI:** 333

Amiel, Henri F., **I:** 241, 243, 250

Amis, Kingsley, **IV:** 430; **Supp. IV Part 2:** 688; **Supp. VIII:** 167; **Supp. XIII:** 93; **Supp. XV:** 117

Amis, Martin, **Retro. Supp. I:** 278

"Amity Hills" (Skloot), **Supp. XX:** 204

Ammons, A. R., **Supp. III Part 2:** 541; **Supp. VII: 23–38;** **Supp. IX:** 41, 42, 46; **Supp. XII:** 121; **Supp. XV:** 115; **Supp. XVII:** 242; **Supp. XIX:** 83

Ammons, Elizabeth, **Retro. Supp. I:** 364, 369; **Retro. Supp. II:** 140

Amnesia Moon (Lethem), **Supp. XVIII:** 136, **138–139**

"Among Children" (Levine), **Supp. V:** 192

Among Friends (M. F. K. Fisher), **Supp. XVII:** 89, 90–91, 92

Among My Books (Lowell), **Supp. I Part 2:** 407

"Among School Children" (Yeats), **III:** 249; **Supp. IX:** 52; **Supp. XIV:** 8

"Among the Hills" (Whittier), **Supp. I Part 2:** 703

Among the Isles of Shoals (Thaxter), **Supp. XIII:** 152

"Among Those Present" (Benét), **Supp. XI:** 53

"Amoral Moralist" (White), **Supp. I Part 2:** 648

Amory, Cleveland, **Supp. I Part 1:** 316

Amory, Fred, **Supp. III Part 1:** 2

Amos (biblical book), **II:** 166

Amos and Andy (television program), **Supp. XX:**103

Amran, David, **Supp. XIV:** 150

"Am Strand von Tanger" (Salter), **Supp. IX:** 257

"AMTRAK" (Baraka), **Supp. II Part 1:** 60

"Amulet, The" (Antin), **Supp. XX:**10

"Amulets" (Hull), **Supp. XXI:** 139

Amy and Isabelle (Strout), **Supp. X:** 86

"Amy Lowell of Brookline, Mass." (Scott), **II:** 512

Amy Lowell: Portrait of the Poet in Her Time (Gregory), **II:** 512

"Amy Wentworth" (Whittier), **Supp. I Part 2:** 694, 696

Anabase (Perse), **III:** 12

"Anabasis (I)" (Merwin), **Supp. III Part 1:** 342, 346

"Anabasis (II)" (Merwin), **Supp. III Part 1:** 342, 346

Anagrams: A Novel (Moore), **Supp. X:** 163, 164, 167, **169–171,** 172

Analects (Confucius), **Supp. IV Part 1:** 14

Analects, The (Pound, trans.), **III:** 472

Analogy (J. Butler), **II:** 8

"Analysis of a Theme" (Stevens), **IV:** 81

Anarchiad, The, A Poem on the Restoration of Chaos and Substantial Night, in Twenty Four Books (Barlow), **Supp. II Part 1:** 70

Anarchist Woman, An (Hapgood), **Supp. XVII:** 102–103; **Supp. XXI:** 5

Anatomy Lesson, and Other Stories, The (Connell), **Supp. XIV:** 84, 87, 89

"Anatomy Lesson, The" (Connell), **Supp. XIV:** 84, 86, 87

Anatomy Lesson, The (P. Roth), **Retro. Supp. II:** 286, 290; **Supp. III Part 2:** 422–423, 425

"Anatomy Lesson of Dr. Nicholaas Tulp, Amsterdam, 1632, The" (Bierds), **Supp. XVII:** 27–28

Anatomy of Criticism (Frye), **Supp. XIII:** 19; **Supp. XIV:** 15

Anatomy of Melancholy (Burton), **III:** 78; **Supp. XVII:** 229

Anatomy of Nonsense, The (Winters), **Supp. II Part 2:** 811, 812

Anaya, Rudolfo A., **Supp. IV Part 2:** 502; **Supp. XIII:** 213, 220; **Supp. XIX:** 97

"Ancestor" (A. Finch), **Supp. XVII:** 72

Ancestors (Maxwell), **Supp. VIII:** 152, 168

"Ancestors, The" (Tate), **IV:** 128

Ancestral Voice: Conversations with N. Scott Momaday (Woodard), **Supp. IV Part 2:** 484, 485, 486, 489, 493

"Anchorage" (Harjo), **Supp. XII:** 220–221

Ancient Child, The: A Novel (Momaday), **Supp. IV Part 2:** 488, 489–491, 492, 493

"Ancient Egypt/Fannie Goldbarth" (Goldbarth), **Supp. XII:** 191–192

Ancient Evenings (Mailer), **Retro. Supp. II:** 206, 210, 213

Ancient Law, The (Glasgow), **II:** 179–180, 192

Ancient Musics (Goldbarth), **Supp. XII:** 191–192

"Ancient Semitic Rituals for the Dead" (Goldbarth), **Supp. XII:** 191–192

"Ancient World, The" (Doty), **Supp. XI:** 122

& (And) (Cummings), **I:** 429, 431, 432, 437, 445, 446, 448

Andersen, Hans Christian, **I:** 441; **Supp. I Part 2:** 622

Andersen, Hendrik Christian, **Supp. XX:**232

Anderson, Charles R., **Supp. I Part 1:** 356, 360, 368, 371, 372

Anderson, Frances, **I:** 231

Anderson, Guy, **Supp. X:** 264, 265

Anderson, Henry J., **Supp. I Part 1:** 156

Anderson, Irwin M., **I:** 98–99

Anderson, Mrs. Irwin M., **I:** 98–99

Anderson, Jon, **Supp. V:** 338

Anderson, Judith, **III:** 399

Anderson, Karl, **I:** 99, 103

Anderson, Lorraine, **Supp. XVIII:** 189

Anderson, Margaret, **I:** 103; **III:** 471

Anderson, Margaret Bartlett, **III:** 171

Anderson, Mary Jane. *See* Lanier, Mrs. Robert Sampson (Mary Jane Anderson)

Anderson, Maxwell, **III:** 159

Anderson, Quentin, **Retro. Supp. I:** 392

Anderson, Robert, **Supp. I Part 1:** 277; **Supp. V:** 108

Anderson, Sally, **Supp. XIII:** 95

Anderson, Sherwood, **I:** **97–120,** 211, 374, 375, 384, 405, 423, 445, 480, 487, 495, 506, 518; **II:** 27, 38, 44, 55, 56, 68, 250–251, 263, 271, 289, 451, 456–457; **III:** 220, 224, 382–383, 453, 483, 545, 576, 579; **IV:** 27, 40, 46, 190, 207, 433, 451, 482; **Retro. Supp. I:** 79, 80, 177; **Supp. I Part 2:** 378, 430, 459, 472, 613; **Supp. IV Part 2:** 502; **Supp. V:** 12, 250; **Supp. VIII:** 39, 152; **Supp. IX:** 14, 309; **Supp. XI:** 159, 164; **Supp. XII:** 343; **Supp. XV:** 298; **Supp. XVI:** 17, 20; **Supp. XVII:** 105; **Supp. XX:**69, 75

Anderson, Mrs. Sherwood (Tennessee Mitchell), **I:** 100; **Supp. I Part 2:** 459, 460

Anderson, T. J., **Supp. XIII:** 132

Anderson, Wendy, **Supp. XXI:** 255

Anderssen, A., **III:** 252

"And Hickman Arrives" (Ellison), **Retro. Supp. II:** 118, 126; **Supp. II Part 1:** 248

And in the Hanging Gardens (Aiken), **I:** 63

"And It Came to Pass" (Wright), **Supp. XV:** 348

And I Worked at the Writer's Trade (Cowley), **Supp. II Part 1:** 137, 139, 141, 143, 147, 148

"...And Ladies of the Club" (J. W. Miller), **Supp. XX:**161

And Live Apart (Peacock), **Supp. XIX: 196–197**

Andorra (Cameron), **Supp. XII:** 79, 81, **88–91**

"—and Other Poets" (column; Untermeyer), **Supp. XV:** 294

"—and Other Poets" (Untermeyer), Supp. XV: 297

Andral, Gabriel, **Supp. I Part 1:** 302

Andre, Michael, **Supp. XII:** 117–118, 129, 132, 133–134

Andre's Mother (McNally), **Supp. XIII:** 206

Andress, Ursula, **Supp. XI:** 307

"Andrew Jackson" (Masters), **Supp. I Part 2:** 472

Andrews, Bruce, **Supp. IV Part 2:** 426

Andrews, Peter, **Supp. XX:**87

Andrews, Roy Chapman, **Supp. X:** 172

Andrews, Tom, **Supp. XI:** 317

Andrews, Wayne, **IV:** 310

Andrews, William L., **Supp. IV Part 1:** 13; **Supp. XIX:** 72; **Supp. XX:**105

Andreyev, Leonid Nikolaevich, **I:** 53; **II:** 425

Andria (Terence), **IV:** 363

"Andromache" (Dubus), **Supp. VII:** 84

"And Summer Will Not Come Again" (Plath), **Retro. Supp. II:** 242

"And That Night Clifford Died" (Levine), **Supp. V:** 195

And the Band Played On (Shilts), **Supp. X:** 145

"And the Moon Be Still as Bright" (Bradbury), **Supp. IV Part 1:** 106

"And the Sea Shall Give up Its Dead" (Wilder), **IV:** 358

And Things That Go Bump in the Night (McNally), **Supp. XIII: 196–197,** 205, 208

And to Think That I Saw It on Mulberry Street (Geisel), **Supp. XVI:** 100, 101, 104

"And *Ut Pictura Poesis* Is Her Name" (Ashbery), **Supp. III Part 1:** 19

And We Are Millions (Ryan), **Supp. XVIII:** 225

"Anecdote and Storyteller" (Howe), **Supp. VI:** 127

"Anecdote of the Jar" (Stevens), **IV:** 83–84

"Anemone" (Rukeyser), **Supp. VI:** 281, 285

"Angel, The" (Buck), **Supp. II Part 1:** 127

"Angel and Unicorn and Butterfly" (Everwine), **Supp. XV:** 76

Angela's Ashes (McCourt), **Supp. XII: 271–279,** 283, 285

"Angel at the Grave, The" (Wharton), **IV:** 310; **Retro. Supp. I:** 365

"Angel Butcher" (Levine), **Supp. V:** 181

Angel City (Shepard), **Supp. III Part 2:** 432, 445

"Angel Is My Watermark!, The" (H. Miller), **III:** 180

Angell, Carol, **Supp. I Part 2:** 655

Angell, Katharine Sergeant. *See* White, Katharine

Angell, Roger, **Supp. I Part 2:** 655; **Supp. V:** 22; **Supp. VIII:** 139

Angel Landing (Hoffman), **Supp. X: 82–83**

"Angel Levine" (Malamud), **Supp. I Part 2:** 431, 432, 433–434, 437

Angel of Bethesda, The (Mather), **Supp. II Part 2:** 464

"Angel of the Bridge, The" (Cheever), **Supp. I Part 1:** 186–187

"Angel of the Odd, The" (Poe), **III:** 425

Angelo Herndon Jones (Hughes), **Retro. Supp. I:** 203

"Angel on the Porch, An" (Wolfe), **IV:** 451

Angelou, Maya, **Supp. IV Part 1: 1–19; Supp. XI:** 20, 245; **Supp. XIII:** 185; **Supp. XVI:** 259; **Supp. XXI:** 172

"Angel Poem, The" (Stern), **Supp. IX:** 292

Angels and Earthly Creatures (Wylie), **Supp. I Part 2:** 709, 713, 724–730

Angels Flight (Connelly), **Supp. XXI:** 72, **72–73,** 75, 80

Angels in America: A Gay Fantasia on National Themes (Kushner), **Supp. IX:** 131, 134, **141–146**

"Angels of the Love Affair" (Sexton), **Supp. II Part 2:** 692

"Angel Surrounded by Paysans" (Stevens), **IV:** 93

Angel That Troubled the Waters, The (Wilder), **IV:** 356, 357–358

"Anger" (Creeley), **Supp. IV Part 1:** 150–152

Anger (Sarton), **Supp. VIII: 256**

"Anger against Children" (R. Bly), **Supp. IV Part 1:** 73

Angle of Ascent (Hayden), **Supp. II Part 1:** 363, 367, 370

"Angle of Geese" (Momaday), **Supp. IV Part 2:** 485

Angle of Geese and Other Poems (Momaday), **Supp. IV Part 2:** 487, 491

Angle of Repose (Stegner), **Supp. IV Part 2:** 599, 605, 606, 610–611

"*Angle of Repose* and the Writings of Mary Hallock Foote: A Source Study" (Williams-Walsh), **Supp. IV Part 2:** 611

Anglo-Saxon Century, The (Dos Passos), **I:** 474–475, 483

Angoff, Charles, **III:** 107

"Angola Question Mark" (Hughes), **Supp. I Part 1:** 344

Angry Hills, The (Uris), **Supp. XX:**246, **250**

Angry Wife, The (Sedges), **Supp. II Part 1:** 125

"Angry Women Are Building: Issues and Struggles Facing American Indian Women Today" (Gunn Allen), **Supp. IV Part 1:** 324

"Animal, Vegetable, and Mineral" (Bogan), **Supp. III Part 1:** 66

"Animal Acts" (Simic), **Supp. VIII:** 278

Animal and Vegetable Physiology Considered with Reference to Natural Theology (Roget), **Supp. I Part 1:** 312

"Animal Bodies: Corporeality, Class, and Subject Formation in *The Wide, Wide World*" (Mason), **Supp. XVIII:** 263

Animal Dreams (Kingsolver), **Supp. VII:** 199, 204–207

Animal Magnetism (Prose), **Supp. XVI:** 251, 260

"Animals, The" (Merwin), **Supp. III Part 1:** 348

"Animals Are Passing from Our Lives" (Levine), **Supp. V:** 181, 182

Animals in That Country, The (Atwood), **Supp. XIII:** 20, 33

Animals of the Soul: Sacred Animals of the Oglala Sioux (Brown), **Supp. IV Part 2:** 487

"Animals You Eat, The" (X. J. Kennedy), **Supp. XV:** 169

"Animula" (Eliot), **Retro. Supp. I:** 64

Anita Loos Rediscovered (M. A. Loos), **Supp. XVI:** 196

Ankor Wat (Ginsberg), **Supp. II Part 1:** 323

"Annabelle" (Komunyakaa), **Supp. XIII:** 117

"Annabel Lee" (Poe), **Retro. Supp. I:** 273; **Retro. Supp. II:** 266

Anna Christie (O'Neill), **III:** 386, 389, 390

"Anna Grasa" (Weigl), **Supp. XIX:** 278

"Anna in Mourning" (Weigl), **Supp. XIX:** 288

Anna Karenina (Tolstoy), **I:** 10; **II:** 290; **Retro. Supp. I:** 225; **Supp. V:** 323

"*Anna Karenina*" (Trilling), *Supp. III Part 2:* 508

Annan, Noel, **Supp. XX:**240

"Anna's Grace" (Weigl), **Supp. XIX:** 282–283

"Anna Who Was Mad" (Sexton), **Supp. II Part 2:** 692

"Ann Burlak" (Rukeyser), **Supp. VI:** 280

"Anne" (Oliver), **Supp. VII:** 232

"Anne" (R. H. Davis), **Supp. XVI:** 91, 92

"Anne at the Symphony" (Shields), **Supp. VII:** 310

"Anne Bradstreet's Poetic Voices" (Requa), **Supp. I Part 1:** 107

Anne of Geierstein: or, The Maiden of the Mist (Scott), **Supp. XX:**234

Anne Sexton: The Artist and Her Critics (McClatchy), **Supp. XII:** 253

"Ann from the Street" (Dixon), **Supp. XII:** 146–147

"Ann Garner" (Agee), **I:** 27

"Anniad, The" (Brooks), **Supp. III Part 1:** 77, 78

Annie (musical), **Supp. IV Part 2:** 577

Annie Allen (Brooks), **Supp. III Part 1:** 76–79

Annie Dillard Reader, The (Dillard), **Supp. VI:** 23

Annie Hall (film; Allen), **Supp. IV Part 1:** 205; **Supp. XV:** 1, 2, 4, 5, **6–7,** 14

Annie John (Kincaid), **Supp. VII:** 184–186, 193

Annie Kilburn, a Novel (Howells), **II:** 275, 286, 287

"Annihilation" (X. J. Kennedy), **Supp. XV:** 168

"Annihilation of Matter, The" (Bronk), **Supp. XXI:** 30

Anniversary (Shields), **Supp. VII:** 320, 322, 323, 324

"Annunciation" (Nelson), **Supp. XVIII:** 174

"Annunciation, The" (Le Sueur), **Supp. V:** 130

Ann Vickers (Lewis), **II:** 453

"A No-Account Creole, A" (Chopin), **Retro. Supp. II:** 64

"Anodyne" (Komunyakaa), **Supp. XIII:** 130

Another America/Otra America (Kingsolver), **Supp. VII:** 207–209

"Another Animal" (Swenson), **Supp. IV Part 2:** 639

Another Animal: Poems (Swenson), **Supp. IV Part 2:** 639–641, 649

Another Antigone (Gurney), **Supp. V:** 97, 98, 100, 101, 102, 105

"Another August" (Merrill), **Supp. III Part 1:** 326

"Another Beer" (Matthews), **Supp. IX:** 158

Another Country (Baldwin), **Retro. Supp. II: 9–11,** 14; **Supp. I Part 1:** 51, 52, 56–58, 63, 67, 337; **Supp. II Part 1:** 40; **Supp. VIII:** 349

"Another Language" (Jong), **Supp. V:** 131

Another Mother Tongue: Gay Words, Gay Worlds (Grahn), **Supp. IV Part 1:** 330

"Another Night in the Ruins" (Kinnell), **Supp. III Part 1:** 239, 251

"Another Night with Snow" (W. V. Davis), **Supp. XXI:** 90, 91

"Another Old Woman" (W. C. Williams), **Retro. Supp. I:** 423

Another Part of the Forest (Hellman), **Supp. I Part 1:** 282–283, 297

Another Republic: 17 European and South American Writers (Strand, trans.), **Supp. IV Part 2:** 630

Another Roadside Attraction (Robbins), **Supp. X:** 259, 261, 262, 263, 264, 265–266, **267–269,** 274, 275, 277, 284

Another Side of Bob Dylan (album, Dylan), **Supp. XVIII:** 25

"Another Spring Uncovered" (Swenson), **Supp. IV Part 2:** 644

Another Thin Man (film), **Supp. IV Part 1:** 355

Another Time (Auden), **Supp. II Part 1:** 15

Another Turn of the Crank (Berry), **Supp. X:** 25, 35

"Another upon the Same" (Taylor), **IV:** 161

"Another Voice" (Wilbur), **Supp. III Part 2:** 557

"Another Wife" (Anderson), **I:** 114

"Another Winter Night" (Budbill), **Supp. XIX:** 10

Another Woman (film; Allen), **Supp. XV:** 11

Another You (Beattie), **Supp. V:** 29, 31, 33–34

Anouilh, Jean, **Supp. I Part 1:** 286–288, 297

Ansa, Tina McElroy, **Supp. XVIII:** 195

Ansky, S., **IV:** 6

Ansky, Shloime, **Supp. IX:** 131, 138

"Answer, The" (Jeffers), **Supp. III Part 2:** 423

Answered Prayers: The Unfinished Novel (Capote), **Supp. III Part 1:** 113, 125, 131–132; **Supp. XVI:** 245

"Answering the Deer: Genocide and Continuance in the Poetry of American Indian Women" (Gunn Allen), **Supp. IV Part 1:** 322, 325

"Answer of Minerva, The: Pacifism and Resistance in Simone Weil" (Merton), **Supp. VIII:** 204

Antaeus (Wolfe), **IV:** 461

"Ante-Bellum Sermon, An" (Dunbar), **Supp. II Part 1:** 203–204

Antheil, George, **III:** 471, 472; **IV:** 404

Anthem (Rand), **Supp. IV Part 2:** 523

Anthology of Holocaust Literature (Glatstein, Knox, and Margoshes, eds.), **Supp. X:** 70

Anthology of Twentieth-Century Brazilian Poetry, An (Bishop and Brasil, eds.), **Retro. Supp. II:** 50; **Supp. I Part 1:** 94

Anthon, Kate, **I:** 452

Anthony, Andrew, **Supp. XVI:** 235, 245, 246

Anthony, Saint, **III:** 395

Anthony, Susan B., **Supp. XI:** 200

"Anthropologist as Hero, The" (Sontag), **Supp. III Part 2:** 451

"Anthropology of Water, The" (Carson), **Supp. XII: 102–103**

Anthropos: The Future of Art (Cummings), **I:** 430

Antichrist (Nietzsche), **III:** 176

"Anti-Father" (Dove), **Supp. IV Part 1:** 246

"Anti-Feminist Woman, The" (Rich), **Supp. I Part 2:** 550

Antigone (Sophocles), **Supp. I Part 1:** 284; **Supp. X:** 249

Antin, David, **Supp. VIII:** 292; **Supp. XII:** 2, 8

Antin, Mary, **Supp. IX:** 227; **Supp. XVI:** 148, 149; **Supp. XX:1–16**

Anti-Oedipus: Capitalism and Schizophrenia (Deleuze and Guattari), **Supp. XII:** 4

Antiphon, The (Barnes), **Supp. III Part 1:** 43–44

"Antiquities" (Mather), **Supp. II Part 2:** 452

"Antiquity of Freedom, The" (Bryant), **Supp. I Part 1:** 168

"Antislavery Tocsin, An" (Douglass), **Supp. III Part 1:** 171

Antoine, Andre, **III:** 387

Antonioni, Michelangelo, **Supp. IV Part 1:** 46, 47, 48

Antony and Cleopatra (Shakespeare), **I:** 285

"Antony on Behalf of the Play" (Burke), **I:** 284

"An trentiesme de mon Eage, L'" (MacLeish), **III:** 9

Antrim, Donald, **Supp. XX:**90

"Ants" (R. Bly), **Supp. IV Part 1:** 71

Anxiety of Influence, The (Bloom), **Supp. XIII:** 46

"Any City" (Untermeyer), **Supp. XV:** 296

"Any Object" (Swenson), **Supp. IV Part 2:** 640

"Any Porch" (Parker), **Supp. IX:** 194

Anything Else (film; Allen), **Supp. XV:** 2, 11

"Anywhere Out of This World" (Baudelaire), **II:** 552

Any Woman Can't (Wasserstein), **Supp. XV:** 322

Any Woman's Blues (Jong), **Supp. V:** 115, 123, 126

Anzaldúa, Gloria, **Supp. IV Part 1:** 330; **Supp. XIII:** 223

"Aphorisms on Society" (Stevens), **Retro. Supp. I:** 303

"Apiary IX" (C. Frost), **Supp. XV:** 106

"Apisculptures" (Bierds), **Supp. XVII:** 29

Apollinaire, Guillaume, **I:** 432; **II:** 529; **III:** 196; **IV:** 80; **Retro. Supp. II:** 326; **Supp. XV:** 182

Apologies to the Iroquois (Wilson), **IV:** 429

"Apology" (C. Frost), **Supp. XV:** 103

"Apology, An" (Malamud), **Supp. I Part 2:** 435, 437

"Apology for Bad Dreams" (Jeffers), **Supp. II Part 2:** 427, 438; **Supp. XVII:** 112

"Apology for Crudity, An" (Anderson), **I:** 109

Apology for Poetry (Sidney), **Supp. II Part 1:** 105

"Apostle of the Tules, An" (Harte), **Supp. II Part 1:** 356

"Apostrophe to a Dead Friend" (Kumin), **Supp. IV Part 2:** 442, 451, 452

"Apostrophe to a Pram Rider" (White), **Supp. I Part 2:** 678

"Apostrophe to Man (on reflecting that the world is ready to go to war again)" (Millay), **III:** 127

"Apostrophe to Vincentine, The" (Stevens), **IV:** 90

"Apotheosis" (Kingsolver), **Supp. VII:** 208

"Apotheosis of Martin Luther King, The" (Hardwick), **Supp. III Part 1:** 203–204

Appalachia (Wright), **Supp. V:** 333, 345

Appalachia Inside Out (Miller, Higgs, and Manning, eds.), **Supp. XX:**166

"Appalachian Book of the Dead III" (Wright), **Supp. V:** 345

"Appalachian Education: A Critique and Suggestions for Reform" (J. W. Miller), **Supp. XX:**165

"Appalachian Literature: At Home in This World" (J. W. Miller), **Supp. XX:**165

"Appalachian Values/American Values" (J. W. Miller), **Supp. XX:**165

Appaloosa (Parker), **Supp. XIX:** 187

"Appeal to H. G. Wells" (Sturgis), **Supp. XX:**233, 240

"Appeal to Progressives, An" (Wilson), **IV:** 429

Appeal to Reason (Paine), **I:** 490

Appeal to the World, An (Du Bois), **Supp. II Part 1:** 184

Appearance and Reality (Bradley), **I:** 572

"Appendix to 'The Anniad' " (Brooks), **Supp. III Part 1:** 77

Apple, Max, **Supp. VIII:** 14; **Supp. XVII: 1–11,** 49–50

Apple, Sam, **Supp. XVII:** 8

"Apple, The" (Kinnell), **Supp. III Part 1:** 250

Applebaum, Anne, **Supp. XVI:** 153

Applebome, Peter, **Supp. XXI:** 38

Applegarth, Mabel, **II:** 465, 478

"Apple of Discord, The" (Humphrey), **Supp. IX:** 109

"Apple Peeler" (Francis), **Supp. IX:** 82

"Apple Rind" (C. Frost), **Supp. XV:** 102

"Apples, The" (Di Piero), **Supp. XIX:** 46

Appleseed, Johnny (pseudonym). *See* Chapman, John (Johnny Appleseed)

Apple That Astonished Paris, The (Collins), **Supp. XXI:** 53, 57

Appleton, Nathan, **II:** 488

Appleton, Thomas Gold, **Supp. I Part 1:** 306; **Supp. I Part 2:** 415

"Apple Tree, The" (McCarriston), **Supp. XIV:** 263, 268

"Applicant, The" (Plath), **Retro. Supp. II:** 252; **Supp. I Part 2:** 535, 544, 545

"Application, The" (Neugeboren), **Supp. XVI:** 219, 220, 225

"Applications of the Doctrine" (Hass), **Supp. VI: 100–101**

Appointment, The (film), **Supp. IX:** 253

Appointment in Samarra (O'Hara), **III:** 361, 363–364, 365–367, 371, 374, 375, 383

Appreciation of Sarah Orne Jewett (Cary), **Retro. Supp. II:** 132

"Approaches, The" (Merwin), **Supp. III Part 1:** 350

"Approaching Artaud" (Sontag), **Supp. III Part 2:** 470–471

"Approaching Prayer" (Dickey), **Supp. IV Part 1:** 175

Approach to Literature, An: A Collection of Prose and Verse with Analyses and Discussions (Brooks, Warren, and Purser), **Su pp. XIV:**4

"Approach to Thebes, The" (Kunitz), **Supp. III Part 1:** 265–267

Approach to Vedanta, An (Isherwood), **Supp. XIV:** 157, 163, 164

"Appropriation of Cultures, The" (Everett), **Supp. XVIII:** 66

Approximately Paradise (Skloot), **Supp. XX:**196, 202, **203–204**

"Après-midi d'un faune, L' " (Mallarmé), **III:** 8

"April" (Bierds), **Supp. XVII:** 29

"April" (W. C. Williams), **Retro. Supp. I:** 422

"April" (Winters), **Supp. II Part 2:** 788

April, Steve. *See* Lacy, Ed

April Galleons (Ashbery), **Supp. III Part 1:** 26

"April Galleons" (Ashbery), **Supp. III Part 1:** 26

April Hopes (Howells), **II:** 285, 289

"April Lovers" (Ransom), **III:** 489–490

"April Showers" (Wharton), **Retro. Supp. I:** 361

"April Today Main Street" (Olson), **Supp. II Part 2:** 581

April Twilights (Cather), **I:** 313; **Retro. Supp. I:** 5

"Apt Pupil" (King), **Supp. V:** 152

Arabian Nights, **I:** 204; **II:** 8; **Supp. I Part 2:** 584, 599; **Supp. IV Part 1:** 1

"Arabic Coffee" (Nye), **Supp. XIII:** 276

"Araby" (Joyce), **I:** 174; **Supp. VIII:** 15

Aragon, Louis, **I:** 429; **III:** 471; **Retro. Supp. II:** 85, 321

Arana-Ward, Marie, **Supp. VIII:** 84

Ararat (Glück), **Supp. V:** 79, 86–87

Arbre du voyageur, L' (W. J. Smith; Haussmann, trans.), **Supp. XIII:** 347

Arbus, Diane, **Supp. XII:** 188

Arbuthnott, John (pseudonym). *See* Henry, O.

"Arc, The" (Bidart), **Supp. XV:** 25–26, 27

Archaeologist of Morning (Olson), **Supp. II Part 2:** 557

Archaeology of the Circle: New and Selected Poems (Weigl), **Supp. XIX:** 282

"Archaic Maker, The" (Merwin), **Supp. III Part 1:** 357

"Archaic Torso of Apollo" (Rilke), **Supp. XV:** 148

"Archaischer Torso Apollos" (Rilke), **Supp. XVII:** 244

"Archbishop, The" (Gioia), **Supp. XV:** 126, 127

Archer (television show), **Supp. IV Part 2:** 474

Archer, William, **IV:** 131; **Retro. Supp. I:** 228

Archer at Large (Macdonald), **Supp. IV Part 2:** 473

Archer in Hollywood (Macdonald), **Supp. IV Part 2:** 474

"Archetype and Signature: The Relationship of Poet and Poem" (Fiedler), **Supp. XIII:** 101

"Archibald Higbie" (Masters), **Supp. I Part 2:** 461

"Architect, The" (Bourne), **I:** 223

Architect, The (Briggs and Ranlett), **Supp. XVIII:** 3

Arctic Dreams (Lopez), **Supp. V:** 211

Arctic Refuge: A Circle of Testimony (Haines), **Supp. XII:** 205

"Arcturus" (Connell), **Supp. XIV:** 88

À rebours (Huysmans), **Supp. XX:** 239

Arendt, Hannah, **II:** 544; **Retro. Supp. I:** 87; **Retro. Supp. II:** 28, 117; **Supp. I Part 2:** 570; **Supp. IV Part 1:** 386; **Supp. VIII:** 98, 99, 100, 243; **Supp. XII:** 166–167

Arensberg, Walter, **IV:** 408; **Retro. Supp. I:** 416

Aren't You Happy for Me? (Bausch), **Supp. VII:** 42, 51, 54

Areopagitica (Milton), **Supp. I Part 2:** 422

"Are You a Doctor?" (Carver), **Supp. III Part 1:** 139–141

"Are You Mr. William Stafford? (Stafford), **Supp. XI:** 317

Argall: The True Story of Pocahontas and Captain John Smith (Vollmann), **Supp. XVII:** 225, 226, 231, 232, 233

"Argonauts of 49, California's Golden Age" (Harte), **Supp. II Part 1:** 353, 355

"Arguments of Everlasting" (B. Kelly), **Supp. XVII:** 129

"Arguments with the Gestapo Continued: II" (Wright), **Supp. XV:** 344

"Arguments with the Gestapo Continued: Literary Resistance" (Wright), **Supp. XV:** 344

Ari (musical, Uris), **Supp. XX:** 247

Aria da Capo (Millay), **III:** 137–138

Ariadne's Thread: A Collection of Contemporary Women's Journals (Lifshin, ed.), **Supp. XVI:** 37–38

"Arias, 1971" (Hull), **Supp. XXI:** 135

Ariel (Plath), **Retro. Supp. II:** 250–255; **Supp. I Part 2:** 526, 539, 541; **Supp. V:** 79; **Supp. XXI:** 58

"Ariel" (Plath), **Supp. I Part 2:** 542, 546

"Ariel Poems" (Eliot), **I:** 579

Ariosto, Ludovico, **Supp. XV:** 175

"Ariosto: Critical Notice of His Life and Genius" (Hunt), **Supp. XV:** 175

Arise, Arise (Zukofsky), **Supp. III Part 2:** 619, 629

Aristides. *See* Epstein, Joseph

"Aristocracy" (Emerson), **II:** 6

Aristocracy and Justice (More), **I:** 223

Aristocrat, The (Richter), **Supp. XVIII:** 220

Aristophanes, **I:** 436; **II:** 577; **Supp. I Part 2:** 406

Aristotle, **I:** 58, 265, 280, 527; **II:** 9, 12, 198, 536; **III:** 20, 115, 145, 157, 362, 422, 423; **IV:** 10, 18, 74–75, 89; **Supp. I Part 1:** 104, 296; **Supp. I Part 2:** 423; **Supp. IV Part 1:** 391; **Supp. IV Part 2:** 526, 530; **Supp. X:** 78; **Supp. XI:** 249; **Supp. XII:** 106; **Supp. XIV:** 242–243

Aristotle Contemplating the Bust of Homer (Rembrandt), **Supp. IV Part 1:** 390, 391

"Arkansas Traveller" (Wright), **Supp. V:** 334

"Arm, The" (X. J. Kennedy), **Supp. XV:** 169

"Armadillo, The" (Bishop), **Supp. I Part 1:** 93

Armadillo in the Grass (Hearon), **Supp. VIII:** 58–59

"Armageddon" (Ransom), **III:** 489, 492

Armageddon (Uris), **Supp. XX:** 243, 247, 248, **252–253**

Armah, Aiy Kwei, **Supp. IV Part 1:** 373

Armies of the Night, The (Mailer), **III:** 39–40, 41, 42, 44, 45, 46; **Retro. Supp. II:** 205, 206–207, 208; **Supp. IV Part 1:** 207; **Supp. XIV:** 49, 162

"Arm in Arm" (Simpson), **Supp. IX:** 267–268

Arminius, Jacobus, **I:** 557

Armitage, Shelley, **Supp. IV Part 2:** 439

Arm of Flesh, The (Salter), **Supp. IX:** 251

"Armor" (Dickey), **Supp. IV Part 1:** 179

Armored Attack (film), **Supp. I Part 1:** 281

Arms, George W., **Supp. I Part 2:** 416–417

Armstrong, George, **Supp. I Part 2:** 386

Armstrong, Louis, **Retro. Supp. II:** 114

"'Arm the Paper Arm': Kenneth Koch's Postmodern Comedy" (Chinitz), **Supp. XV:** 180, 185

"Army" (Corso), **Supp. XII:** 117, 127

Army Brat (W. J. Smith), **Supp. XIII:** 331, 347

Arna Bontemps Langston Hughes: Letters 1925–1967 (Nichols), **Retro. Supp. I:** 194

Arner, Robert D., **Retro. Supp. II:** 62

"Arnie" (Budbill), **Supp. XIX:** 6

Arnold, Edwin T., **Supp. VIII:** 189

Arnold, George W., **Supp. I Part 2:** 411

Arnold, Marilyn, **Supp. IV Part 1:** 220

Arnold, Matthew, **I:** 222, 228, 275; **II:** 20, 110, 338, 541; **III:** 604; **IV:** 349; **Retro. Supp. I:** 56, 325; **Supp. I Part 2:** 416, 417, 419, 529, 552, 602; **Supp. IX:** 298; **Supp. XIV:** 11, 335; **Supp. XIX:** 41; **Supp. XXI:** 90

Arnold, Thurman, **Supp. I Part 2:** 645

Aronson, Steven M. L., **Supp. V:** 4

Around about America (Caldwell), **I:** 290

"Arrangement in Black and White" (Parker), **Supp. IX:** 198

"Arrival at Santos" (Bishop), **Retro. Supp. II:** 46; **Supp. IX:** 45–46

"Arrival of the Bee Box, The" (Plath), **Retro. Supp. II:** 255

Arrivistes, The: Poem 1940–1949 (Simpson), **Supp. IX:** 265, **267–268**

Arrogance (J. Scott), **Supp. XVII:** **186–188**, 189, **191**, **192**, 194

"Arrow" (Dove), **Supp. IV Part 1:** 250

Arrowsmith (Lewis), **I:** 362; **II:** 445–446, 449

"Arsenal at Springfield, The" (Longfellow), **Retro. Supp. II:** 168

"Arson at Midnight" (Nelson), **Supp. XVIII:** 186

"Arson Plus" (Hammett), **Supp. IV Part 1:** 343; **Supp. XXI:** 68

"Ars Poetica" (Dove), **Supp. IV Part 1:** 250

"Ars Poetica" (Dunn), **Supp. XI:** 154

"Ars Poetica" (MacLeish), **III:** 9–10

"Ars Poetica" (X. J. Kennedy), **Supp. XV:** 154

Ars Poetica: A Found Poem (Kumin), **Supp. IV Part 2:** 455

"Ars Poetica; or, Who Lives in the Ivory Tower" (McGrath), **Supp. X:** 117

"Ars Poetica: Some Recent Criticism" (Wright), **Supp. III Part 2:** 603
"Art" (Emerson), **II:** 13
Art (Reza), **Supp. XXI:** 148
"Art and Neurosis" (Trilling), **Supp. III Part 2:** 502
Art and Technics (Mumford), **Supp. II Part 2:** 483
Art & Ardor: Essays (Ozick), **Supp. V:** 258, 272
Art as Experience (Dewey), **I:** 266
Art by Subtraction (Reid), **IV:** 41
Art de toucher le clavecin, L' (Couperin), **III:** 464
Artemis to Actaeon and Other Verse (Wharton), **Retro. Supp. I:** 372
Arte of English Poesie (Puttenham), **Supp. I Part 1:** 113
Arthur, Anthony, **Supp. IV Part 2:** 606
Arthur Mervyn; or, Memoirs of the Year 1793 (Brown), **Supp. I Part 1:** 137–140, 144
"Article of Faith" (Sobin), **Supp. XVI:** 291
Articles of Light & Elation (Sobin), **Supp. XVI:** 291
Articulation of Sound Forms in Time (Howe), **Supp. IV Part 2:** 419, 431–433
"Artificer" (X. J. Kennedy), **Supp. XV:** 160
"Artificial Nigger, The" (O'Connor), **III:** 343, 351, 356, 358; **Retro. Supp. II:** 229, 232
Artist, The: A Drama without Words (Mencken), **III:** 104
Artist as Revolutionary, The (Buhle), **Supp. XXI:** 172
"Artist of the Beautiful, The" (Hawthorne), **Retro. Supp. I:** 149
Artistry of Grief (Torsney), **Retro. Supp. I:** 224
"Artists' and Models' Ball, The" (Brooks), **Supp. III Part 1:** 72
Art of Detective Fiction, The (Swales), **Supp. XIX:** 183
"Art of Disappearing, The" (Nye), **Supp. XIII:** 287
Art of Drowning, The (Collins), **Supp. XXI:** 54, 60, 64
Art of Eating, The (M. F. K. Fisher), **Supp. XVII:** 87, 90, 91
Art of Fiction, The (Gardner), **Supp. VI:** 73
"Art of Fiction, The" (H. James), **Retro. Supp. I:** 226; **Retro. Supp. II:** 223
Art of Hunger, The (Auster), **Supp. XII:** 22
"Art of Keeping Your Mouth Shut, The" (Heller), **Supp. IV Part 1:** 383
"Art of Literature and Commonsense, The" (Nabokov), **Retro. Supp. I:** 271
Art of Living and Other Stories, The (Gardner), **Supp. VI:** 72
Art of Love, The (Koch), **Supp. XV:** 182
"Art of Love, The" (Koch), **Supp. XV:** 182
Art of Poetry, The (Koch), **Supp. XV:** 175–176, 178, 188

"Art of Poetry, The" (Koch), **Supp. XV:** 182
"Art of Poetry, The" (McClatchy), **Supp. XII:** 262
"Art of Romare Bearden, The" (Ellison), **Retro. Supp. II:** 123
"Art of Storytelling, The" (Simpson), **Supp. IX:** 277
Art of Sylvia Plath, The (Newman), **Supp. I Part 2:** 527
Art of the Moving Picture, The (Lindsay), **Supp. I Part 2:** 376, 391–392, 394; **Supp. XVI:** 185
Art of the Novel (H. James), **Retro. Supp. I:** 227
"Art of Theodore Dreiser, The" (Bourne), **I:** 235
Art of the Personal Essay, The (Lopate, comp.), **Supp. XIII:** 280–281; **Supp. XVI:** 266
Art of the Self, The: Essays a Propos "Steps" (Kosinski), **Supp. VII:** 222
Arts and Sciences (Goldbarth), **Supp. XII: 184–186**
Arts and Sciences: A Seventies Seduction (Mallon), **Supp. XIX:** 132, 135
"Art's Bread and Butter" (Benét), **Retro. Supp. I:** 108
Arvin, Newton, **I:** 259; **II:** 508; **Retro. Supp. I:** 19, 137
Asali, Muna, **Supp. XIII:** 121, 126
Asbury, Herbert, **Supp. IV Part 1:** 353
Ascent of F6, The (Auden), **Supp. II Part 1:** 11, 13
Ascent to Truth, The (Merton), **Supp. VIII:** 208
Asch, Nathan, **Supp. XV:** 133, 134
Asch, Sholem, **IV:** 1, 9, 11, 14; **Retro. Supp. II:** 299
Ascherson, Neal, **Supp. XII:** 167
Ascher-Walsh, Rebecca, **Supp. XIX:** 54
"As Close as Breathing" (Jarman), **Supp. XVII:** 120
As David Danced (Bronk), **Supp. XXI:** 24
"As David Danced" (Bronk), **Supp. XXI:** 26
As Does New Hampshire and Other Poems (Sarton), **Supp. VIII:** 259
"As Evening Lays Dying" (Salinas), **Supp. XIII:** 319
"As Flowers Are" (Kunitz), **Supp. III Part 1:** 265
"Ash" (Sobin), **Supp. XVI:** 284–285
Ashbery, John, **Retro. Supp. I:** 313; **Supp. I Part 1:** 96; **Supp. III Part 1:** 1–29; **Supp. III Part 2:** 541; **Supp. IV Part 2:** 620; **Supp. VIII:** 272; **Supp. IX:** 52; **Supp. XI:** 139; **Supp. XIII:** 85; **Supp. XV:** 176, 177, 178, 188, 250; **Supp. XIX:** 40, 83; **Supp. XXI:** 227
"Ashes" (Lamott), **Supp. XX:** 141
"Ashes" (Levine), **Supp. V:** 188
"Ashes of the Beacon" (Bierce), **I:** 209
Ashes: Poems Old and New (Levine), **Supp. V:** 178, 188–189
Ashford, Margaret Mary (Daisy), **II:** 426
"Ash Wednesday" (Garrett), **Supp. VII:** 109–110

"Ash Wednesday" (Merton), **Supp. VIII:** 199
Ash Wednesday (T. S. Eliot), **I:** 570, 574–575, 578–579, 580, 582, 584, 585; **Retro. Supp. I:** 64
"Ash Wednesday" (T. S. Eliot), **Supp. IV Part 2:** 436
Asian American Authors (Hsu and Palubinskas, eds.), **Supp. X:** 292
Asian American Heritage: An Anthology of Prose and Poetry (Wand), **Supp. X:** 292
Asian Figures (Mervin), **Supp. III Part 1:** 341
Asian Journal of Thomas Merton, The (Merton), **Supp. VIII:** 196, 206, 208
"Asian Peace Offers Rejected without Publication" (R. Bly), **Supp. IV Part 1:** 61
"Asides on the Oboe" (Stevens), **Retro. Supp. I:** 305
"As I Ebb'd with the Ocean of Life" (Whitman), **IV:** 342, 345–346; **Retro. Supp. I:** 404, 405
As I Lay Dying (Faulkner), **II:** 60–61, 69, 73, 74; **IV:** 100; **Retro. Supp. I:** 75, 82, 84, 85, 86, 88, 89, 91, 92; **Supp. IV Part 1:** 47; **Supp. VIII:** 37, 178; **Supp. IX:** 99, 103, 251; **Supp. XIV:** 24
"As I Lay with My Head in Your Lap, Camerado" (Whitman), **IV:** 347
Asimov, Isaac, **Supp. IV Part 1:** 116; **Supp. XVI:** 122
Asinof, Eliot, **II:** 424
As I Remember It (PBS documentary), **Supp. XVIII:** 277
Asirvatham, Sandy, **Supp. XVI:** 249
"As Is the Daughter, So Is Her Mother" (Patchett), **Supp. XII:** 310
"As It Was in the Beginning" (Benét), **Supp. XI:** 56
"As I Walked Out One Evening" (Auden), **Supp. II Part 1:** 13; **Supp. XV:** 126; **Supp. XX:** 138
"As I Went Down by Havre de Grace" (Wylie), **Supp. I Part 2:** 723
Ask a Policeman (Hinojosa), **Supp. XIX:** 110–111
"Ask Me" (Stafford), **Supp. XI:** 326–327
Ask Me Tomorrow (Cozzens), **I:** 365–367, 379
Ask the Dust (Fante), **Supp. XI:** 159, 160, 166, **167–169**, 172, 173, 174
"Ask the Optimist!" (Saunders), **Supp. XIX:** 235
Ask Your Mama (Hughes), **Supp. I Part 1:** 339, 341–342
Ask Your Mama: 12 Moods for Jazz (Hughes), **Retro. Supp. I:** 210, 211
As Little Children (R. P. Smith), **Supp. XIV:** 333
"As One Put Drunk into the Packet Boat" (Ashbery), **Supp. III Part 1:** 18
"Asparagus" (Nelson), **Supp. XVIII:** 178
"Aspects of Robinson" (Kees), **Supp. XV:** 134
Aspects of the Novel (Forster), **Retro. Supp. I:** 232; **Supp. VIII:** 155; **Supp. XXI:** 233

"Aspen and the Stream, The" (Wilbur), **Supp. III Part 2:** 555, 556

Aspern Papers, The (James), **Supp. V:** 101, 102

"Aspern Papers, The" (James), **Retro. Supp. I:** 219, 227, 228

Asphalt Georgics (Carruth), **Supp. XVI:** 54

Asphalt Jungle (film, Huston), **Supp. XIII:** 174

"Asphodel" (Welty), **IV:** 265, 271

"Asphodel, That Greeny Flower" (W. C. Williams), **Retro. Supp. I:** 429

"Aspic and Buttermilk" (Olds), **Supp. X:** 213

Asquith, Herbert Henry, **Retro. Supp. I:** 59

"Ass" (Cisneros), **Supp. VII:** 67

Assante, Armand, **Supp. VIII:** 74

Assassin, The: A Play in Three Acts (Shaw), **Supp. XIX:** 248

Assassins, The (Oates), **Supp. II Part 2:** 512, 517–519

"Assault" (Millay), **III:** 130–131

"Assemblage of Husbands and Wives, An" (Lewis), **II:** 455–456

Assembly (O'Hara), **III:** 361

As She Climbed Across the Table (Lethem), **Supp. XVIII:** 140–141, 148

Assignment, Wildlife (LaBastille), **Supp. X:** 99, 104

"Assimiliation in Recent American Jewish Autobiographies" (Krupnick), **Supp. XVI:** 153

Assistant, The (Malamud), **Supp. I Part 2:** 427, 428, 429, 431, 435, 441–445, 451; **Supp. XVI:** 220

Assommoir, L' (Zola), **II:** 291; **III:** 318

Assorted Prose (Updike), **IV:** 215–216, 218; **Retro. Supp. I:** 317, 319, 327

Astaire, Adele, **Supp. XVI:** 187

As They Were (M. F. K. Fisher), **Supp. XVII:** 88, 89, 91

Astor, Mary, **Supp. IV Part 1:** 356; **Supp. XII:** 173

Astoria, or, Anecdotes of an Enterprise beyond the Rocky Mountains (Irving), **II:** 312

"Astounding News by Electric Express via Norfolk! The Atlantic Crossed in Three Days Signal Triumph of Mr. Monck's Flying-Machine . . ." (Poe), **III:** 413, 420

Astraea (Holmes), **III:** 82

Astro, Richard, **Supp. I Part 2:** 429, 445

"Astrological Fricassee" (H. Miller), **III:** 187

Astrophil and Stella (Sidney), **Supp. XIV:** 128

"As Weary Pilgrim" (Bradstreet), **Supp. I Part 1:** 103, 109, 122

As We Know (Ashbery), **Supp. III Part 1:** 9, 21–25

"As We Know" (Ashbery), **Supp. III Part 1:** 21–22

Aswell, Edward C., **IV:** 458, 459, 461

"Asylum, The" (Carruth), **Supp. XVI:** 48–49

"As You Like It" (Chopin), **Supp. I Part 1:** 217

As You Like It (Shakespeare), **Supp. I Part 1:** 308

"At a Bar in Charlotte Amalie" (Updike), **IV:** 214

"At a Lecture" (Brodsky), **Supp. VIII:** 33

"At a March against the Vietnam War" (R. Bly), **Supp. IV Part 1:** 61

"At a Reading" (McClatchy), **Supp. XII:** 256–257

"Atavism of John Tom Little Bear, The" (O. Henry), **Supp. II Part 1:** 410

"At Chênière Caminada" (Chopin), **Supp. I Part 1:** 220

"At Chinese Checkers" (Berryman), **I:** 182

Atchity, Kenneth John, **Supp. XI:** 227

"At Death's Window" (Lamott), **Supp. XX:** 144

At Eighty-Two (Sarton), **Supp. VIII:** 264

"At Every Gas Station There Are Mechanics" (Dunn), **Supp. XI:** 144

At Fault (Chopin), **Retro. Supp. II:** 57, 60, 62–63; **Supp. I Part 1:** 207, 209–211, 220

"At Fifty" (Bronk), **Supp. XXI:** 31

At Heaven's Gate (Warren), **IV:** 243, 247–248, 251

Atheism Refuted: in a Discourse to Prove the Existence of God (Paine), **Supp. I Part 2:** 517

"Athénaïse" (Chopin), **Retro. Supp. II:** 66, 67; **Supp. I Part 1:** 219–220

Atherton, Gertrude, **I:** 199, 207–208

Athey, Jean L., **Supp. XI:** 184

At Home: Essays, 1982–1988 (Vidal), **Supp. IV Part 2:** 682, 687, 688

"At Home With" (column; Leland), **Supp. XV:** 69

"At Kino Viejo, Mexico" (Ríos), **Supp. IV Part 2:** 541

Atkinson, Brooks, **IV:** 288; **Supp. IV Part 2:** 683; **Supp. XIX:** 244

Atlantis (Doty), **Supp. XI:** 121, 126–129

"Atlantis" (Doty), **Supp. XI:** 127–128

Atlas, James, **Supp. V:** 233; **Supp. XV:** 25

Atlas, The (Vollmann), **Supp. XVII:** 226, 227

Atlas Shrugged (Rand), **Supp. IV Part 2:** 517, 521, 523, 524–526, 528, 531

At Liberty (T. Williams), **IV:** 378

"At Melville's Tomb" (H. Crane), **I:** 393; **Retro. Supp. II:** 76, 78, 80, 82

"At Mother Teresa's" (Nye), **Supp. XIII:** 276

"At Nightfall" (Kooser), **Supp. XIX:** 122–123

At Night the Salmon Move (Carver), **Supp. III Part 1:** 142

"At North Farm" (Ashbery), **Supp. III Part 1:** 1–2

At Paradise Gate (Smiley), **Supp. VI:** 292, 293–294

"At Paso Rojo" (Bowles), **Supp. IV Part 1:** 87

At Play in the Fields of the Lord (Matthiessen), **Supp. V:** 199, 202, 204–206, 212

"At Play in the Paradise of Bombs" (Sanders), **Supp. XVI:** 272–273, 274, 277

"At Pleasure By" (Pinsky), **Supp. VI:** 245

At Risk (Hoffman), **Supp. X:** 87

"At Sea" (Hemingway), **II:** 258

"At Shaft 11" (Dunbar), **Supp. II Part 1:** 212

"At Slim's River" (Haines), **Supp. XII:** 208–209

"At St. Croix" (Dubus), **Supp. VII:** 83, 87

At Sundown (Whittier), **Supp. I Part 2:** 704

"At Sunset" (Simic), **Supp. VIII:** 282

Attaway, William, **Supp. XXI:** 264

Attebery, Brian, **Supp. IV Part 1:** 101

Attendant, The (Bronk), **Supp. XXI:** 24

"Attendant, The" (Bronk), **Supp. XXI:** 26

"At That Time, or The History of a Joke" (Paley), **Supp. VI:** 229–230

At the Back of the North Wind (Macdonald), **Supp. XIII:** 75

"At the Birth of an Age" (Jeffers), **Supp. II Part 2:** 432

"At the Bomb Testing Site" (Stafford), **Supp. XI:** 317–318, 321, 323

At the Bottom of the River (Kincaid), **Supp. VII:** 182–184, 185

"At the 'Cadian Ball" (Chopin), **Retro. Supp. II:** 64, 65, 68

"At the Cancer Clinic" (Kooser), **Supp. XIX:** 127

"At the Chelton-Pulver Game" (Auchincloss), **Supp. IV Part 1:** 27

"At the Drugstore" (Taylor), **Supp. V:** 323

At the Edge of the Body (Jong), **Supp. V:** 115, 130

At the End of the Open Road (Simpson), **Supp. IX:** 265, 269, 271–273, 277

At the End of This Summer: Poems 1948–1954, **Supp. XII:** 211

"At the End of War" (Eberhart), **I:** 522–523

"At the Executed Murderer's Grave" (Wright), **Supp. III Part 2:** 595, 597

"At the Fishhouses" (Bishop), **Retro. Supp. II:** 45; **Supp. I Part 1:** 90, 92

At the Gates of the Animal Kingdom (Hempel), **Supp. XXI:** 115, 122–124

"At the Grave of My Guardian Angel: St. Louis Cemetery, New Orleans" (Levis), **Supp. XI:** 268–269

"At the Gym" (Doty), **Supp. XI:** 135

"At the Indian Store" (McCarriston), **Supp. XIV:** 271

"At the Lake" (Oliver), **Supp. VII:** 244

"At the Landing" (Welty), **IV:** 265–266; **Retro. Supp. I:** 348

"At the Last" (Bynner), **Supp. XV:** 44

"At the Last Rites for Two Hot Rodders" (X. J. Kennedy), **Supp. XV:** 166

"At the Owl Club, North Gulfport, Mississippi, 1950" (Trethewey), **Supp. XXI:** 249

"At the Premiere" (Keillor), **Supp. XVI:** 167

At the Rendezvous of Victory (C. L. R. James), **Supp. XXI:** 172

At the Root of Stars (Barnes), **Supp. III Part 1:** 34

"At the Slackening of the Tide" (Wright), **Supp. III Part 2:** 597

"At the Tomb of Walt Whitman" (Kunitz), **Supp. III Part 1:** 262

"At the Tourist Centre in Boston" (Atwood), **Supp. XIII:** 33

"At the Town Dump" (Kenyon), **Supp. VII:** 167

"At the Worcester Museum" (Pinsky), **Supp. VI:** 251

"Atticus Finch and the Mad Dog: Harper Lee's *To Kill a Mockingbird*" (Jones), **Supp. VIII:** 128

"Atticus Finch—Right and Wrong" (Freedman), **Supp. VIII:** 127–128

"Attic Which Is Desire, The" (W. C. Williams), **Retro. Supp. I:** 422

"At Tikal" (Bronk), **Supp. XXI: 28–29**

"At Times in Flight: A Parable" (H. Roth), **Supp. IX:** 234

Attitudes toward History (Burke), **I:** 274

Atwan, Robert, **Supp. XVI:** 273, 277

At Weddings and Wakes (McDermott), **Supp. XVIII:** 155, **160–162,** 166

"At White River" (Haines), **Supp. XII:** 208–209

Atwood, Margaret, **Supp. IV Part 1:** 252; **Supp. V:** 119; **Supp. XI:** 317; **Supp. XIII: 19–39,** 291, 306; **Supp. XXI:** 39, 42

"Atwood's Gorgon Touch" (Davey), **Supp. XIII:** 33

"Aubade" (McCarriston), **Supp. XIV:** 271

"Aubade: November" (McCarriston), **Supp. XIV:** 261–262

"Aubade of an Early Homo Sapiens" (C. Frost), **Supp. XV:** 97–98

"Aubade: Opal and Silver" (Doty), **Supp. XI:** 129

"Au Bal Musette" (Van Vechten), **Supp. II Part 2:** 735

Auchincloss, Hugh D., **Supp. IV Part 2:** 679

Auchincloss, Louis, **I:** 375; **III:** 66; **Retro. Supp. I:** 370, 373; **Supp. IV Part 1: 21–38**

"Auction" (Simic), **Supp. VIII:** 278

"Auction, The" (Crane), **I:** 411

"Auction Model 1934" (Z. Fitzgerald), **Supp. IX:** 61

Auden, W. H., **I:** 71, 381, 539; **II:** 367, 368, 371, 376, 586; **III:** 17, 134, 269, 271, 292, 476–477, 504, 527, 530, 542, 615; **IV:** 136, 138, 240, 430; **Retro. Supp. I:** 430; **Retro. Supp. II:** 183, 242, 244, 323; **Supp. I Part 1:** 270; **Supp. I Part 2:** 552, 610; **Supp. II Part 1: 1–28; Supp. III Part 1:** 2, 3, 14, 26, 60, 61, 64, 341; **Supp. III Part 2:** 591, 595; **Supp. IV Part 1:** 79, 84, 136, 225, 302, 313; **Supp. IV Part 2:** 440, 465; **Supp. V:** 337; **Supp. VIII:** 19, 21, 22, 23, 30, 32, 155, 190; **Supp. IX:** 94, 287, 288; **Supp. X:** 35, 57, 59, 115–116, 117, 118–119; **Supp.**

XI: 243, 244; **Supp. XII:** 253, 264–265, 266, 269–270; **Supp. XIV:** 156, 158, 160, 162, 163; **Supp. XV:** 74, 117–118, 139, 144, 186; **Supp. XIX:** 147, 151; **Supp. XX:** 138; **Supp. XXI:** 60, 98

"Auden's OED" (McClatchy), **Supp. XII:** 264–265

"Audition" (Alvarez), **Supp. VII:** 10

Audubon, John James, **III:** 210; **IV:** 265; **Supp. IX:** 171; **Supp. XVI: 1–14**

Audubon, John Woodhouse, **Supp. XVI:** 10

Audubon, Maria Rebecca, **Supp. XVI:** 11

Audubon, Victor Gifford, **Supp. XVI:** 10

Audubon and His Journals (M. Audubon, ed.), **Supp. XVI:** 11, 12

Audubon Reader, The: The Best Writings of John James Audubon (Sanders, ed.), **Supp. XVI:** 269

Auer, Jane. *See* Bowles, Jane

Auerbach, Eric, **III:** 453

Auerbach, Nina, **Supp. I Part 1:** 40

"August" (Oliver), **Supp. VII:** 235

"August" (Rich), **Supp. I Part 2:** 564

"August 1968" (Auden), **Supp. II Part 1:** 25

"August Darks, The" (Clampitt), **Supp. IX:** 43, **50–51,** 52

Augustine, Saint, **I:** 279, 290; **II:** 537; **III:** 259, 270, 292, 300; **IV:** 69, 126; **Retro. Supp. I:** 247; **Supp. VIII:** 203; **Supp. XI:** 245; **Supp. XIII:** 89; **Supp. XXI:** 83

August Snow (Price), **Supp. VI:** 264

"Au Jardin" (Pound), **III:** 465–466

Aunt Carmen's Book of Practical Saints (Mora), **Supp. XIII: 227–229**

"Aunt Cynthy Dallett" (Jewett), **II:** 393

"Aunt Gladys" (Karr), **Supp. XI:** 241

"Aunt Granny Lith" (Offutt), **Supp. XIX:** 165, 166

"Aunties, The" (Lamott), **Supp. XX:** 141

"Aunt Imogen" (Robinson), **III:** 521

"Aunt Jemima of the Ocean Waves" (Hayden), **Supp. II Part 1:** 368, 379

"Aunt Jennifer's Tigers" (Rich), **Supp. XV:** 252

Aunt Jo's Scrapbooks (Alcott), **Supp. I Part 1:** 43

"Aunt Mary" (Oliver), **Supp. VII:** 232

"Aunt Mary" (Stowe), **Supp. I Part 2:** 587

"Aunt Moon's Young Man" (Hogan), **Supp. IV Part 1:** 400

"Aunt Rectita's Good Friday" (X. J. Kennedy), **Supp. XV:** 166

"Aunt Sarah" (Lowell), **II:** 554

"Aunt Sue's Stories" (Hughes), **Retro. Supp. I:** 197, 199

"Aunt Violet's Canadian Honeymoon/ 1932" (Shields), **Supp. VII:** 311

"Aunt Violet's Things" (Shields), **Supp. VII:** 311–312

"Aurelia: Moon Jellies" (Mora), **Supp. XIII:** 224

"Aurelio" (Di Piero), **Supp. XIX:** 38

Aurora 7 (Mallon), **Supp. XIX:** 132, **135–136**

Aurora Leigh (E. Browning), **Retro. Supp. I:** 33; **Supp. XI:** 197

Aurora Means Dawn (Sanders), **Supp. XVI:** 268

Auroras of Autumn, The (Stevens), **Retro. Supp. I:** 297, 300, **309–312**

"Auroras of Autumn, The" (Stevens), **Retro. Supp. I:** 311, 312; **Supp. III Part 1:** 12

Auschwitz: the Nazis and the "Final Solution" (television documentary), **Supp. XVII:** 40

Auslander, Joseph, **Supp. XIV:** 120

"Auspex" (Frost), **Retro. Supp. I:** 122

"Auspex" (Lowell), **Supp. I Part 2:** 424

Austen, Jane, **I:** 130, 339, 375, 378; **II:** 272, 278, 287, 568–569, 577; **IV:** 8; **Retro. Supp. I:** 354; **Supp. I Part 1:** 267; **Supp. I Part 2:** 656, 715; **Supp. IV Part 1:** 300; **Supp. VIII:** 125, 167; **Supp. IX:** 128; **Supp. XII:** 310; **Supp. XV:** 338; **Supp. XX:** 108

Auster, Paul, **Supp. XII: 21–39; Supp. XIV:** 292; **Supp. XXI:** 20

Austerities (Simic), **Supp. VIII: 276–278,** 283

"Austerities" (Simic), **Supp. VIII:** 277

Austin, Mary Hunter, **Retro. Supp. I:** 7; **Supp. IV Part 2:** 503; **Supp. X:** 29; **Supp. XIII:** 154

"Authentic Unconscious, The" (Trilling), **Supp. III Part 2:** 512

Author and Agent: Eudora Welty and Diarmuid Russell (Kreyling), **Retro. Supp. I:** 342, 345, 347, 349–350

"Author at Sixty, The" (Wilson), **IV:** 426

"Author of 'Beltraffio,' The" (James), **Retro. Supp. I:** 227

"Author's Explanation, The" (Larsen), **Supp. XVIII:** 131

"Author's House" (Fitzgerald), **Retro. Supp. I:** 98

"Author's Reflections, An: Willie Loman, Walter Younger, and He Who Must Live" (Hansberry), **Supp. IV Part 1:** 370

"Author to Her Book, The" (Bradstreet), **Supp. I Part 1:** 119; **Supp. V:** 117–118; **Supp. XV:** 125–126

"Autobiographical Note" (H. Miller), **III:** 174–175

"Autobiographical Notes" (Baldwin), **Supp. I Part 1:** 54

"Autobiographical Notes" (Holmes), **Supp. I Part 1:** 301

"Autobiographic Chapter, An" (Bourne), **I:** 236

Autobiography (Franklin), **II:** 102, 103, 108, 121–122, 302

Autobiography (James), **I:** 462

"Autobiography" (MacLeish), **III:** 20

Autobiography (Van Buren), **III:** 473

Autobiography (W. C. Williams), **Supp. I Part 1:** 254

Autobiography (Zukofsky), **Supp. III Part 2:** 627

"Autobiography in the Shape of a Book Review" (Bynner), **Supp. XV:** 40

"Autobiography of a Confluence, The" (Gunn Allen), **Supp. IV Part 1:** 321

Autobiography of Alice B. Toklas, The (Stein), **IV:** 26, 30, 35, 43; **Supp. IV Part 1:** 11, 81

Autobiography of an Ex-Colored Man, The (Johnson), **Supp. II Part 1:** 33, 194; **Supp. XVIII:** 127

Autobiography of a Schizophrenic Girl (Renée), **Supp. XVI:** 64, 66

Autobiography of a Thief, The (Hapgood), **Supp. XVII:** 96, 101–102

Autobiography of Benjamin Franklin (Franklin), **Supp. I Part 1:** 5

Autobiography of LeRoi Jones, The (Baraka), **Retro. Supp. I:** 411

Autobiography of Malcolm X (Little), **Supp. I Part 1:** 66; **Supp. X:** 27; **Supp. XIII:** 264

Autobiography of Mark Twain, The (Twain), **IV:** 209

Autobiography of My Mother, The (Kincaid), **Supp. VII:** 182, 188–190, 191, 192, 193

Autobiography of Red: A Novel in Verse (Carson), **Supp. XII:** 97, **106–110**

Autobiography of Upton Sinclair, The (Sinclair), **Supp. V:** 276, 282

Autobiography of W. E. B. Du Bois, The (Du Bois), **Supp. II Part 1:** 159, 186

Autobiography of William Carlos Williams, The (W. C. Williams), **Retro. Supp. I:** 51, 428

Autocrat of the Breakfast-Table, The (Holmes), **Supp. I Part 1:** 306–307

"Automatic Gate, The" (Southern), **Supp. XI:** 294

"Automotive Passacaglia" (H. Miller), **III:** 186

"Autopsy Room, The" (Carver), **Supp. III Part 1:** 137

"Auto Wreck" (Shapiro), **Supp. II Part 2:** 706

"Autre Temps" (Wharton), **IV:** 320, 324

"Autumn, Mist" (Hull), **Supp. XXI:** 133

"Autumn Afternoon" (Farrell), **II:** 45

"Autumnal" (Eberhart), **I:** 540–541

"Autumn Begins in Martins Ferry, Ohio" (Wright), **Supp. III Part 2:** 599

"Autumn Courtship, An" (Caldwell), **I:** 309

"Autumn Equinox" (Skloot), **Supp. XX:**202

Autumn Garden, The (Hellman), **Supp. I Part 1:** 285–286, 290

"Autumn Garden, The: Mechanics and Dialectics" (Felheim), **Supp. I Part 1:** 297

"Autumn Holiday, An" (Jewett), **II:** 391; **Retro. Supp. II:** 140–141

"Autumn Musings" (Harte), **Supp. II Part 1:** 336

Autumn Spring (Pickering), **Supp. XXI:** 204–205, 206

"Autumn Within" (Longfellow), **II:** 499

"Autumn Woods" (Bryant), **Supp. I Part 1:** 164

"Au Vieux Jardin" (Aldington), **Supp. I Part 1:** 257

"Aux Imagistes" (W. C. Williams), **Supp. I Part 1:** 266

Avakian, Aram, **Supp. XI:** 294, 295, 309

"*Ave Atque Vale*" (Bynner), *Supp. XV:* 49

Avedon, Richard, **Supp. I Part 1:** 58; **Supp. V:** 194; **Supp. X:** 15

Aveling, Edward, **Supp. XVI:** 85

"Avenue" (Pinsky), **Supp. VI:** 248

Avenue Bearing the Initial of Christ into the New World: Poems 1946–1964 (Kinnell), **Supp. III Part 1:** 235, 239–241

"Avenue of the Americas" (Simic), **Supp. VIII:** 278

"Average Torture" (Karr), **Supp. XI:** 243

Avery, George C., **Supp. XX:**84

Avery, John, **Supp. I Part 1:** 153

"Avey" (Toomer), **Supp. IX:** 317

Avon's Harvest (Robinson), **III:** 510

Awake and Sing! (Odets), **Supp. II Part 2:** 530, 531, 536–538, 550; **Supp. IV Part 2:** 587

Awakening, The (Chopin), **Retro. Supp. I:** 10; **Retro. Supp. II:** 57, 59, 60, 67, **68–71,** 73; **Supp. I Part 1:** 200, 201, 202, 211, 220–225; **Supp. V:** 304; **Supp. VIII:** 198; **Supp. XII:** 170

Awakening Land, The (Richter), **Supp. XVIII:** 207, 215

Awful Rowing Toward God, The (Sexton), **Supp. II Part 2:** 694–696

Awiakta, Marilou, **Supp. IV Part 1:** 319, 335

Awkward Age, The (James), **II:** 332; **Retro. Supp. I:** 229, **230–231**

Axe Handles (Snyder), **Supp. VIII: 303–305**

Axel's Castle: A Study in the Imaginative Literature of 1870 to 1930 (Wilson), **I:** 185; **II:** 577; **IV:** 428, 431, 438, 439, 443; **Supp. VIII:** 101

"Ax-Helve, The" (Frost), **Retro. Supp. I:** 133

Azikewe, Nnamdi, **Supp. IV Part 1:** 361

"Aztec Angel" (Salinas), **Supp. XIII:** 314

Aztec Treasure House, The: New and Selected Essays (Connell), **Supp. XIV:** 80, 97

B

Babbitt (Lewis), **II:** 442, 443–445, 446, 447, 449; **III:** 63–64, 394; **IV:** 326

Babbitt, Irving, **I:** 247; **II:** 456; **III:** 315, 461, 613; **IV:** 439; **Retro. Supp. I:** 55; **Supp. I Part 2:** 423

Babcock, Elisha, **Supp. II Part 1:** 69

Babel, Isaac, **IV:** 1; **Supp. IX:** 260; **Supp. XII:** 308–309; **Supp. XVII:** 41

Babel, Isaak, **Supp. XIV:** 83, 84

Babel to Byzantium (Dickey), **Supp. IV Part 1:** 177, 185

Babeuf, François, **Supp. I Part 2:** 518

"Babies, The" (Strand), **Supp. IV Part 2:** 625

Babouk (Endore), **Supp. XVII: 56–57, 61,** 64

Baby, Come on Inside (Wagoner), **Supp. IX:** 335

"Baby, The" (Barthelme), **Supp. IV Part 1:** 49

Baby Doll (T. Williams), **IV:** 383, 386, 387, 389, 395

"Baby Face" (Sandburg), **III:** 584

"Babylon Revisited" (Fitzgerald), **II:** 95; **Retro. Supp. I:** 109

"Baby or the Botticelli, The" (Gass), **Supp. VI:** 92

"Baby Pictures of Famous Dictators" (Simic), **Supp. VIII:** 276

"Baby's Breath" (Bambara), **Supp. XI:** 15, 16

"Babysitter, The" (Coover), **Supp. V:** 43–44

"Baby Villon" (Levine), **Supp. V:** 182

Bacall, Lauren, **Supp. IV Part 1:** 130

"Baccalaureate" (MacLeish), **III:** 4

Bacchae, The (Euripides), **Supp. VIII:** 182

Bach, Johann Sebastian, **Supp. I Part 1:** 363; **Supp. III Part 2:** 611, 612, 619

Bachardy, Don, **Supp. XIV:** 166, 170, 172, 173

Bache, Richard, **Supp. I Part 2:** 504

Bachelard, Gaston, **Supp. XIII:** 225; **Supp. XVI:** 292

"Bachelor Girl, The" (Boyce), **Supp. XXI:** 3

Bachelor Girls (Wasserstein), **Supp. XV:** **327–328,** 332

Bachman, John, **Supp. XVI:** 10, 11

Bachmann, Ingeborg, **Supp. IV Part 1:** 310; **Supp. VIII:** 272

Bachofen, J. J., **Supp. I Part 2:** 560, 567

Back Bog Beast Bait (Shepard), **Supp. III Part 2:** 437, 438

Backbone (C. Bly), **Supp. XVI: 34–36,** 37, 40, 41

Back Country, The (Snyder), **Supp. VIII: 296–299**

"Back from the Argentine" (Leopold), **Supp. XIV:** 186

"Background with Revolutionaries" (MacLeish), **III:** 14–15

"Back in the Saddle Again" (Swados), **Supp. XIX:** 259

Back in the World (Wolff), **Supp. VII:** 344, 345

Backis, Charles, **Supp. XXI:** 195

"Backlash Blues, The" (Hughes), **Supp. I Part 1:** 343

"Backlash of Kindness, A" (Nye), **Supp. XIII:** 285, 286

"Backslider, The" (R. Fisher), **Supp. XIX:** 70, 71

"Back Street Guy" (Halliday), **Supp. XIX:** 88

Back to China (Fiedler), **Supp. XIII: 102–103**

Back to Methuselah (Shaw), **IV:** 64

"Backwacking: A Plea to the Senator" (Ellison), **Retro. Supp. II:** 126; **Supp. II Part 1:** 248

Backward Glance, A (Wharton), **Retro. Supp. I:** 360, 363, 366, 378, 380, 382; **Supp. XX:**229

"Backward Glance o'er Travel'd Roads, A" (Whitman), **IV:** 348

Bacon, Francis, **II:** 1, 8, 11, 15–16, 111; **III:** 284; **Retro. Supp. I:** 247; **Supp. I Part 1:** 310; **Supp. I Part 2:** 388; **Supp. IX:** 104; **Supp. XIV:** 22, 210

Bacon, Helen, **Supp. X:** 57

Bacon, Leonard, **II:** 530

Bacon, Roger, **IV:** 69
"Bacterial War, The" (Nemerov), **III:** 272
Bad and the Beautiful, The (film), **Supp. XVIII:** 250
Bad Boy Brawly Brown (Mosley), **Supp. XIII:** 237, 239, 240–241
Bad Boys (Cisneros), **Supp. VII:** 58
"Bad Dream" (Taylor), **Supp. V:** 320
Badè, William Frederic, **Supp. IX:** 178
"Bad Fisherman, The" (Wagoner), **Supp. IX:** 328
Bad for Each Other (film), **Supp. XIII:** 174
"Badger" (Clare), **II:** 387
Badger, A. G., **Supp. I Part 1:** 356
Bad Government and Silly Literature (C. Bly), **Supp. XVI:** 37, 38, 40
Badlands (film; Malick), **Supp. XV:** 351
"Bad Lay" (McCarriston), **Supp. XIV:** 267
Badley, Linda, **Supp. V:** 148
Bad Man, A (Elkin), **Supp. VI: 47**
Bad Man Ballad (Sanders), **Supp. XVI:** 268
Bad Man Blues: A Portable George Garrett (Garrett), **Supp. VII:** 111
"Bad Music, The" (Jarrell), **II:** 369
"Bad People" (Halliday), **Supp. XIX:** 90, 91
"Bad Summer on K2, A" (Krakauer and Child), **Supp. XVIII:** 107, 108
"Bad Woman, A" (Fante), **Supp. XI:** 165
Baeck, Leo, **Supp. V:** 260
Baecker, Diann L., **Supp. VIII:** 128
Baer, William, **Supp. XIII:** 112, 118, 129
Baez, Joan, **Supp. IV Part 1:** 200; **Supp. VIII:** 200, 202; **Supp. XVIII:** 24, 25–26, 27
Bag of Bones (King), **Supp. V:** 139, 148, 151
"Bagpipe Music" (MacNeice), **Supp. X:** 117
"Bahá'í Faith: Only Church in World That Does Not Discriminate" (Locke), **Supp. XIV:** 200
Bahá'u'lláh, **Supp. XX:**117, 121, 122
"Bahá'u'lláh in the Garden of Ridwan" (Hayden), **Supp. II Part 1:** 370, 378
Bahr, David, **Supp. XV:** 66
"Bailbondsman, The" (Elkin), **Supp. VI:** 49, **50,** 58
Bailey, Gamaliel, **Supp. I Part 2:** 587, 590
Bailey, Peter, **Supp. XVI:** 69
Bailey, William, **Supp. IV Part 2:** 631, 634
Bailey's Café (Naylor), **Supp. VIII: 226–228**
Bailyn, Bernard, **Supp. I Part 2:** 484, 506
Bair, Deirdre, **Supp. X:** 181, 186, 187, 188, 192, 194, 195, 196, 197
Baird, Linnett, **Supp. XII:** 299
Baird, Peggy, **I:** 385, 401
Bakan, David, **I:** 59
Baker, Carlos, **II:** 259
Baker, Chet, **Supp. XXI:** 131
Baker, David, **Supp. IX:** 298; **Supp. XI:** 121, 142, 153; **Supp. XII:** 175, 191–192; **Supp. XIX:** 115

Baker, George Pierce, **III:** 387; **IV:** 453, 455
Baker, Gladys, **Supp. XIV:** 121
Baker, Houston A., Jr., **Retro. Supp. II:** 121; **Supp. IV Part 1:** 365; **Supp. X:** 324
Baker, Katherine, **Supp. XX:**69
Baker, Kevin, **Supp. XIV:** 96
Baker, Mabel, **Supp. XVIII:** 259, 263, 266–267, 269
Baker, Nicholson, **Supp. XIII: 41–57**
Baker, Robert, **Supp. XVI:** 288, 290
Bakerman, Jane S., **Supp. IV Part 2:** 468
Bakhtin, Mikhail, **Retro. Supp. II:** 273; **Supp. IV Part 1:** 301; **Supp. X:** 120, 239
Bakst, Léon, **Supp. IX:** 66
Bakunin, Mikhail Aleksandrovich, **IV:** 429
Balaban, John, **Supp. XIX:** 281
Balakian, Jan, **Supp. XV:** 327
"Balance" (Bierds), **Supp. XVII:** 31
"Balance" (Nelson), **Supp. XVIII:** 174–175
Balbo, Ned, **Supp. XVII:** 120; **Supp. XIX:** 161
Balbuena, Bernado de, **Supp. V:** 11
Balch, Emily Greene, **Supp. I Part 1:** 25
Balcony, The (Genet), **I:** 84
Bald Soprano, The (Ionesco), **I:** 74
Baldwin, David, **Supp. I Part 1:** 47, 48, 49, 50, 51, 54, 65, 66
Baldwin, James, **Retro. Supp. II: 1–17; Supp. I Part 1: 47–71,** 337, 341; **Supp. II Part 1:** 40; **Supp. III Part 1:** 125; **Supp. IV Part 1:** 1, 10, 11, 163, 369; **Supp. V:** 201; **Supp. VIII:** 88, 198, 235, 349; **Supp. X:** 136, 324; **Supp. XI:** 288, 294; **Supp. XIII:** 46, 111, 181, 186, 294; **Supp. XIV:** 54, 71, 73, 306; **Supp. XVI:** 135, 141, 143; **Supp. XVIII:** 25; **Supp. XX:**147; **Supp. XXI:** 245
Baldwin, Samuel, **Supp. I Part 1:** 48
Balitas, Vincent D., **Supp. XVI:** 222
Balkian, Nona, **Supp. XI:** 230
Balkun, Mary McAleer, **Supp. XX:**281
Ball, Gordon, **Supp. XIV:** 148
Ball, John, **Supp. XV:** 202
"Ballad: Between the Box Cars" (Warren), **IV:** 245
"Ballade" (MacLeish), **III:** 4
"Ballade at Thirty-Five" (Parker), **Supp. IX:** 192
"Ballade for the Duke of Orléans" (Wilbur), **Supp. III Part 2:** 556
"Ballade of Broken Flutes, The" (Robinson), **III:** 505
"Ballade of Meaty Inversions" (White), **Supp. I Part 2:** 676
"Ballad of a Thin Man" (song, Dylan), **Supp. XVIII:** 30, 31
"Ballad of Aunt Geneva, The" (Nelson), **Supp. XVIII:** 175
"Ballad of Billie Potts, The" (Warren), **IV:** 241–242, 243, 253
"Ballad of Carmilhan, The" (Longfellow), **II:** 505
"ballad of chocolate Mabbie, the" (Brooks), **Supp. IV Part 1:** 15

"Ballad of Dead Ladies, The" (Villon), **Retro. Supp. I:** 286
Ballad of Dingus Magee, The (Markson), **Supp. XVII:** 139, 141
"Ballad of East and West, The" (Kipling), **Supp. IX:** 246; **Supp. XX:**23
"Ballad of Jesse Neighbours, The" (Humphrey), **Supp. IX:** 100
"Ballad of Jesus of Nazareth, A" (Masters), **Supp. I Part 2:** 459
"Ballad of John Cable and Three Gentlemen" (Merwin), **Supp. III Part 1:** 342
"Ballad of Larry and Club" (Jarman), **Supp. XVII:** 115
"Ballad of Nat Turner, The" (Hayden), **Supp. II Part 1:** 378
"Ballad of Pearl May Lee, The" (Brooks), **Supp. III Part 1:** 74, 75
Ballad of Remembrance, A (Hayden), **Supp. II Part 1:** 367
"Ballad of Remembrance, A" (Hayden), **Supp. II Part 1:** 368, 372, 373
"Ballad of Ruby, The" (Sarton), **Supp. VIII:** 259–260
"Ballad of San Isidro, The" (Espaillat), **Supp. XXI:** 108
"Ballad of Sue Ellen Westerfield, The" (Hayden), **Supp. II Part 1:** 364
Ballad of the Brown Girl, The (Cullen), **Supp. IV Part 1:** 167, 168, 169–170, 173
"Ballad of the Brown Girl, The" (Cullen), **Supp. IV Part 1:** 168
"Ballad of the Children of the Czar, The" (Schwartz), **Supp. II Part 2:** 649
"Ballad of the Girl Whose Name Is Mud" (Hughes), **Retro. Supp. I:** 205
"Ballad of the Goodly Fere", **III:** 458
"Ballad of the Harp-Weaver" (Millay), **III:** 135
"Ballad of the Sad Cafe, The" (McCullers), **II:** 586, 587, 588, 592, 595, 596–600, 604, 605, 606
"Ballad of the Sixties" (Sarton), **Supp. VIII:** 259
"Ballad of Trees and the Master, A" (Lanier), **Supp. I Part 1:** 370
"Ballad of William Sycamore, The" (Benét), **Supp. XI:** 44, 47
Ballads and Other Poems (Longfellow), **II:** 489; **III:** 412, 422; **Retro. Supp. II:** 157, 168
Ballads for Sale (Lowell), **II:** 527
"Ballads of Lenin" (Hughes), **Supp. I Part 1:** 331
Ballantyne, Sheila, **Supp. V:** 70
Ballard, J. G., **Supp. XVI:** 123, 124; **Supp. XVIII:** 136
Ballard, Josephine. *See* McMurtry, Josephine
"Ballena" (Mora), **Supp. XIII:** 224
"Ballet in Numbers for Mary Ellen, A" (Karr), **Supp. XI:** 241
"Ballet of a Buffoon, The" (Sexton), **Supp. II Part 2:** 693
"Ballet of the Fifth Year, The" (Schwartz), **Supp. II Part 2:** 650
Ball Four (Bouton), **Supp. XX:**274
"Ball Game, The" (Creeley), **Supp. IV Part 1:** 140

Ballistics (Collins), **Supp. XXI:** 57, 65
"Ballistics" (Collins), **Supp. XXI:** 65
"Balloon Hoax, The" (Poe), **III:** 413, 420
"Balm of Recognition, The: Rectifying Wrongs through Generations" (E. Hoffman, lecture), **Supp. XVI:** 155
Balo (Toomer), **Supp. III Part 2:** 484
Balsan, Consuelo, **IV:** 313–314
Balthus, **Supp. IV Part 2:** 623
Balthus Poems, The (Dobyns), **Supp. XIII:** 87
Baltimore, Lord, **I:** 132
Balzac, Honoré de, **I:** 103, 123, 339, 376, 474, 485, 499, 509, 518; **II:** 307, 322, 324, 328, 336, 337; **III:** 61, 174, 184, 320, 382; **IV:** 192; **Retro. Supp. I:** 91, 217, 218, 235; **Retro. Supp. II:** 93; **Supp. I Part 2:** 647; **Supp. XVI:** 72
Bambara, Toni Cade, **Supp. XI:** 1–23
Banana Bottom (McKay), **Supp. X:** 132, **139–140**
Bananas (film; Allen), **Supp. XV:** 3, 4
Bancal, Jean, **Supp. I Part 2:** 514
Bancroft, George, **I:** 544; **Supp. I Part 2:** 479
Band, Millen, **Supp. XVIII:** 238
Bandaged Nude, The (Ryan as Finnegan), **Supp. XVIII:** 233, **235–236**
Bandbox (Mallon), **Supp. XIX:** 132, 143
Band of Angels (Warren), **IV:** 245, 254–255
Bandung Files (television series), **Supp. XXI:** 170
Bang the Drum Slowly (Harris), **II:** 424–425
Banjo: A Story without a Plot (McKay), **Supp. X:** 132, **138–139**
"Banjo Song, A" (Dunbar), **Supp. II Part 1:** 197
Bankhead, Tallulah, **IV:** 357; **Supp. IV Part 2:** 574
"Banking Potatoes" (Komunyakaa), **Supp. XIII:** 126
"Bank of England Restriction, The" (Adams), **I:** 4
Banks, Joanne Trautmann, **Supp. XIII:** 297
Banks, Russell, **Supp. V:** 1–19, 227; **Supp. IX:** 153; **Supp. X:** 85; **Supp. XI:** 178; **Supp. XII:** 295, 309, 343; **Supp. XX:**90
"Banned Poem" (Nye), **Supp. XIII:** 282
Bannon, Barbara, **Supp. XI:** 228
"Banyan" (Swenson), **Supp. IV Part 2:** 651, 652
"Baptism" (Olsen). *See* "O Yes" (Olsen)
"Baptism" (Trethewey), **Supp. XXI:** 246
Baptism, The (Baraka), **Supp. II Part 1:** 40, 41–42, 43
Baptism of Desire (Erdrich), **Supp. IV Part 1:** 259
Barabtarlo, Gennady, **Retro. Supp. I:** 278
Baraka, Imamu Amiri (LeRoi Jones), **Retro. Supp. I:** 411; **Retro. Supp. II:** 280; **Supp. I Part 1:** 63; **Supp. II Part 1:** 29–63, 247, 250; **Supp. III Part 1:** 83; **Supp. IV Part 1:** 169, 244, 369; **Supp. VIII:** 295, 329, 330,

332; **Supp. X:** 324, 328; **Supp. XIII:** 94; **Supp. XIV:** 125, 144; **Supp. XXI:** 172, 227, 228
"Bar at the Andover Inn, The" (Matthews), **Supp. IX:** 168
"Barbados" (Marshall), **Supp. XI:** 281
"Barbara Frietchie" (Whittier), **Supp. I Part 2:** 695–696
Barbarella (film), **Supp. XI:** 293, **307–308**
"Barbarian Status of Women, The" (Veblen), **Supp. I Part 2:** 636–637
Barbarous Coast, The (Macdonald), **Supp. IV Part 2:** 472, 474
Barbary Shore (Mailer), **III:** 27, 28, 30–31, 33, 35, 36, 40, 44; **Retro. Supp. II:** 199–200, 207; **Supp. XIV:** 162
Barber, David, **Supp. IV Part 2:** 550; **Supp. XII:** 188–189
Barber, Rowland, **Supp. IV Part 2:** 581
Barber, Samuel, **Supp. IV Part 1:** 84
"Barber's Unhappiness, The" (Saunders), **Supp. XIX:** 229
"Barclay of Ury" (Whittier), **Supp. I Part 2:** 693
Barcott, Bruce, **Supp. XVII:** 32
Bard of Savagery, The: Thorstein Veblen and Modern Social Theory (Diggins), **Supp. I Part 2:** 650
"Barefoot Boy, The" (Whittier), **Supp. I Part 2:** 691, 699–700
Barefoot in the Park (Simon), **Supp. IV Part 2:** 575, 578–579, 586, 590
Bare Hills, The (Winters), **Supp. II Part 2:** 786, 788
"Bare Hills, The" (Winters), **Supp. II Part 2:** 790
Barely and Widely (Zukofsky), **Supp. III Part 2:** 627, 628, 635
Barenblat, Rachel, **Supp. XIII:** 274
Barfield, Owen, **III:** 274, 279
"Bargain Lost, The" (Poe), **III:** 411
Barillas, William, **Supp. XIV:** 177
Barillet, Pierre, **Supp. XVI:** 194
Barker, Arthur, **Supp. XIII:** 167
Barker, Clive, **Supp. V:** 142
Barking Dog (Budbill), **Supp. XIX:** 1, 5
"Barking Man" (Bell), **Supp. X:** 9
Barking Man and Other Stories (Bell), **Supp. X:** 9
Barksdale, Richard, **Retro. Supp. I:** 202, 205; **Supp. I Part 1:** 341, 346
Barlow, Joel, **Supp. I Part 1:** 124; **Supp. I Part 2:** 511, 515, 521; **Supp. II Part 1:** 65–86, 268
Barlow, Judith, **Supp. XXI:** 6
Barlow, Ruth Baldwin (Mrs. Joel Barlow), **Supp. II Part 1:** 69
"B.A.R. Man, The" (Yates), **Supp. XI:** 341
Barnaby Rudge (Dickens), **III:** 421
Barnard, Frederick, **Supp. I Part 2:** 684
Barnard, Rita, **Retro. Supp. II:** 324
Barn Blind (Smiley), **Supp. VI:** 292–293
"Barn Burning" (Faulkner), **II:** 72, 73; **Supp. IV Part 2:** 682; **Supp. XX:**174
Barnes, Djuna, **Supp. III Part 1:** 31–46; **Supp. IV Part 1:** 79, 80; **Supp. XVI:** 282
Barnes, Kim, **Supp. XVIII:** 293

Barnett, Claudia, **Supp. XV:** 323, 330, 334
Barnett, Samuel, **Supp. I Part 1:** 2
"Barn Owl" (Kooser), **Supp. XIX:** 123
Barnstone, Tony, **Supp. XIII:** 115, 126
Barnstone, Willis, **Supp. I Part 2:** 458
Barnum, P. T., **Supp. I Part 2:** 703
Baroja, Pío, **I:** 478
Baron, Zach, **Supp. XVIII:** 150
"Baroque Comment" (Bogan), **Supp. III Part 1:** 56, 58
"Baroque Sunburst, A" (Clampitt), **Supp. IX:** 49
"Baroque Wall-Fountain in the Villa Sciarra, A" (Wilbur), **Supp. III Part 2:** 553
Barr, Robert, **I:** 409, 424
Barracks Thief, The (Wolff), **Supp. VII:** 344–345
"Barred Owl" (Offutt), **Supp. XIX:** 170
Barren Ground (Glasgow), **II:** 174, 175, 178, 179, 184–185, 186, 187, 188, 189, 191, 192, 193, 194; **Supp. X:** 228
Barrés, Auguste M., **I:** 228
Barresi, Dorothy, **Supp. XV:** 100, 102
Barrett, Amy, **Supp. XVIII:** 136
Barrett, E. B., **Supp. XV:** 309
Barrett, Elizabeth, **Supp. IV Part 2:** 430
Barrett, George, **Supp. IX:** 250
Barrett, Ralph, **Supp. I Part 2:** 462
Barrie, J. M., **Supp. XX:**234
Barrier, Rober G., **Supp. XXI:** 48–49
Barrier of a Common Language: An American Looks at Contemporary British Poetry (Gioia), **Supp. XV:** 112, **116–117**
"Barroco: An Essay" (Sobin), **Supp. XVI:** 291
Barron, Jonathan, **Supp. IX:** 299
Barrow, John, **II:** 18
Barrus, Clara, **I:** 220
Barry, Iris, **Supp. XIII:** 170
Barry, Philip, **Retro. Supp. I:** 104; **Supp. IV Part 1:** 83; **Supp. V:** 95
Barstow, Elizabeth Drew. *See* Stoddard, Elizabeth
Bartas, Seigneur du, **IV:** 157
Barth, John, **I:** 121–143; **Supp. I Part 1:** 100; **Supp. III Part 1:** 217; **Supp. IV Part 1:** 48, 379; **Supp. V:** 39, 40; **Supp. IX:** 208; **Supp. X:** 263, 301, 302, 307; **Supp. XI:** 309; **Supp. XII:** 29, 289, 316; **Supp. XIII:** 41, 101, 104; **Supp. XVII:** 183; **Supp. XVIII:** 136, 140, 141; **Supp. XX:**21
Barth, Karl, **III:** 40, 258, 291, 303, 309; **IV:** 225; **Retro. Supp. I:** 325, 326, 327
Barth, Robert C., **Supp. XV:** 169
Barthé, Richmond, **Retro. Supp. II:** 115
Barthelme, Donald, **Supp. IV Part 1:** 39–58, 227; **Supp. V:** 2, 39, 44; **Supp. VIII:** 75, 138; **Supp. X:** 263; **Supp. XI:** 25; **Supp. XII:** 29; **Supp. XIII:** 41, 46; **Supp. XVI:** 206; **Supp. XIX:** 235
Barthelme, Frederick, **Supp. XI:** 25–41; **Supp. XXI:** 38
Barthelme, Peter, **Supp. XI:** 25
Barthelme, Steven, **Supp. XI:** 25, 27, 37

Barthes, Roland, **Supp. IV Part 1:** 39, 119, 126; **Supp. XIII:** 83; **Supp. XVI:** 285, 294; **Supp. XVII:** 244

Bartholomew and the Oobleck (Geisel), **Supp. XVI:** 104

"Bar Time" (B. Collins), **Supp. XVII:** 245

"Bartleby, the Scrivener; A Story of Wall-Street" (Melville), **III:** 88–89; **Retro. Supp. I:** 255

Bartleby in Manhattan and Other Essays (Hardwick), **Supp. III Part 1:** 204, 210

"Bartleby the Scrivener" (Melville), **Supp. XVIII:** 4

Bartlet, Phebe, **I:** 562

Bartlett, Lee, **Supp. VIII:** 291

Bartlett, Mary Dougherty, **Supp. IV Part 1:** 335

Barton, Bruce, **III:** 14; **Retro. Supp. I:** 179

Barton, Priscilla. *See* Morison, Mrs. Samuel Eliot (Priscilla Barton)

Barton, Ralph, **Supp. XVI:** 195

Barton, Rev. William E., **Retro. Supp. I:** 179

Bartov, Omer, **Supp. XVI:** 153–154

Bartram, John, **Supp. I Part 1:** 244

Bartram, William, **II:** 313; **Supp. IX:** 171; **Supp. X:** 223

Barzun, Jacques, **Supp. XIV:** 54

"Basement" (Bambara), **Supp. XI:** 5

Basement Tapes, The (album, Dylan), **Supp. XVIII:** 27, 30, 32

"Base of All Metaphysics, The" (Whitman), **IV:** 348

"Base Stealer, The" (Francis), **Supp. IX:** 82

Bashevis, Isaac. *See* Singer, Isaac Bashevis

Bashir, Antonious, **Supp. XX:** 116, 120

Basil Stories, The (Fitzgerald), **Retro. Supp. I:** 109

Basin and Range (McPhee), **Supp. III Part 1:** 309

"Basin of Eggs, A" (Swenson), **Supp. IV Part 2:** 645

"Basket, The" (Lowell), **II:** 522

"Basketball and Beefeaters" (McPhee), **Supp. III Part 1:** 296

"Basketball and Poetry: The Two Richies" (Dunn), **Supp. XI:** 140

"Basketball Player" (L. Michaels), **Supp. XVI:** 209

Baskin, Leonard, **Supp. X:** 58, 71; **Supp. XV:** 348

Bass, Rick, **Supp. XIV:** 227; **Supp. XVI:** 15–29; **Supp. XXI:** 40, 45

Basso, Hamilton, **Retro. Supp. I:** 80

Bastard, The (Caldwell), **I:** 291, 292, 308

"Bastille Day" (Lamott), **Supp. XX:** 143

"Bat, The" (Kenyon), **Supp. VII:** 168

Bataille, Georges, **Supp. VIII:** 4; **Supp. XII:** 1

"Batard" (London), **II:** 468–469

Batchelor, John Calvin, **Supp. XIX:** 142

Bate, W. J., **II:** 531

Bates, Arlo, **Retro. Supp. I:** 35

Bates, Blanche, **Supp. XVI:** 182

Bates, Kathy, **Supp. XIII:** 207

Bates, Lee, **Retro. Supp. II:** 46

Bates, Milton J., **Supp. XII:** 62

Bates, Sylvia Chatfield, **II:** 586

Bateson, Gregory, **Supp. XV:** 146

"Bath, The" (Carver), **Supp. III Part 1:** 144, 145

"Bath, The" (Snyder), **Supp. VIII:** 302

Bathwater Wine (Coleman), **Supp. XI:** 83, 90, **91**

"Batter my heart, three person'd God" (Donne), **Supp. I Part 2:** 726; **Supp. XVII:** 119

"Battle, The" (Simpson), **Supp. IX:** 268–269

Battle Cry (film), **Supp. XX:** 246

Battle Cry (Uris), **Supp. XX:** 243, 246, **248–250,** 255, 256

Battlefield Where the Moon Says I Love You, The (Stanford), **Supp. XV:** 345

Battle for the Solomons (Wolfert), **Supp. XXI:** 267

Battle-Ground, The (Glasgow), **II:** 175, 176, 177, 178, 193

"Battle Hymn of the Republic" (Sandburg), **III:** 585

"Battle Hymn of the Republic, The" (Howe), **III:** 505

"Battle Hymn of the Republic, The" (Updike), **Retro. Supp. I:** 324

Battle of Angels (T. Williams), **IV:** 380, 381, 383, 385, 386, 387

"Battle of Lovell's Pond, The" (Longfellow), **II:** 493

Battle of the Atlantic, The (Morison), **Supp. I Part 2:** 490

"Battle of the Baltic, The" (Campbell), **Supp. I Part 1:** 309

"Battle of the Bunker, The" (Snodgrass), **Supp. VI:** 319–320

"***Battle of the Century!!!, The***" (Goldbarth), **Supp. XII:** 193

Battle-Pieces and Aspects of the War (Melville), **II:** 538–539; **III:** 92; **IV:** 350; **Retro. Supp. I:** 257

"Battler, The" (Hemingway), **II:** 248; **Retro. Supp. I:** 175

"Baubles after Bombs" (Peacock), **Supp. XIX:** 200

"Baudelaire" (Schwartz), **Supp. II Part 2:** 663

Baudelaire, Charles, **I:** 58, 63, 384, 389, 420, 569; **II:** 543, 544–545, 552; **III:** 137, 141–142, 143, 409, 417, 418, 421, 428, 448, 466, 474; **IV:** 74, 79, 80, 87, 211, 286; **Retro. Supp. I:** 56, 90; **Retro. Supp. II:** 261, 262, 322, 326; **Supp. I Part 1:** 271; **Supp. III Part 1:** 4, 6, 105; **Supp. XIII:** 77, 284; **Supp. XV:** 165; **Supp. XXI:** 228

Baudrillard, Jean, **Supp. IV Part 1:** 45

Bauer, Dale, **Retro. Supp. I:** 381

Bauer, Douglas, **Supp. XII:** 290

Baum, L. Frank, **Supp. I Part 2:** 621; **Supp. IV Part 1:** 101, 113; **Supp. XII:** 42

Baumann, Walter, **III:** 478

Bausch, Richard, **Supp. VII: 39–56; Supp. XVII:** 21

Bawer, Bruce, **Supp. VIII:** 153; **Supp. IX:** 135; **Supp. X:** 187

Baxter, Charles, **Supp. XII:** 22; **Supp. XIV:** 89, 92; **Supp. XVII: 13–24**

Baxter, John, **Supp. XI:** 302

Baxter, Richard, **III:** 199; **IV:** 151, 153; **Supp. I Part 2:** 683

"Baxter's Procrustes" (Chesnutt), **Supp. XIV:** 76

"Bay City Blues" (Chandler), **Supp. IV Part 1:** 129

Baylies, William, **Supp. I Part 1:** 153

Baym, Nina, **Supp. IV Part 2:** 463; **Supp. X:** 229; **Supp. XVI:** 92; **Supp. XVIII:** 258, 259

"Bayou" (Di Piero), **Supp. XIX:** 37

Bayou Folk (Chopin), **Retro. Supp. II: 64–65,** 73; **Supp. I Part 1:** 200, 216, 218

Baziotes, William, **Supp. XV:** 144

Beach, Anna Hampstead, **Supp. XVII:** 75

Beach, Joseph Warren, **I:** 309, 500; **II:** 27; **III:** 319

Beach, Sylvia, **IV:** 404; **Retro. Supp. I:** 109, 422

"Beach Women, The" (Pinsky), **Supp. VI:** 241

"Beaded Pear, The" (Simpson), **Supp. IX:** 276

Beagle, Peter, **Supp. X:** 24

Beam, Jeffrey, **Supp. XII:** 98

Beaman, E. O., **Supp. IV Part 2:** 604

Bean, Michael, **Supp. V:** 203

Bean, Robert Bennett, **Supp. II Part 1:** 170

Bean Eaters, The (Brooks), **Supp. III Part 1:** 79–81

Be Angry at the Sun (Jeffers), **Supp. II Part 2:** 434

"Beanstalk Country, The" (T. Williams), **IV:** 383

Bean Trees, The (Kingsolver), **Supp. VII:** 197, 199–201, 202, 207, 209

"Bear" (Hogan), **Supp. IV Part 1:** 412

Bear, The (Faulkner), **Supp. VIII:** 184

"Bear, The" (Faulkner), **II:** 71–72, 73, 228; **IV:** 203; **Supp. IV Part 2:** 434; **Supp. IX:** 95; **Supp. X:** 30; **Supp. XIV:** 32; **Supp. XXI:** 37

"Bear, The" (Kinnell), **Supp. III Part 1:** 244

"Bear, The" (Momaday), **Supp. IV Part 2:** 480, 487

Bear and His Daughter: Stories (Stone), **Supp. V:** 295, 308

Beard, Charles, **I:** 214; **IV:** 429; **Supp. I Part 2:** 481, 490, 492, 632, 640, 643, 647

Beard, James, **I:** 341; **Supp. XVII:** 89, 90

Beard, Mary, **Supp. I Part 2:** 481

"Bearded Oaks" (Warren), **IV:** 240

Bearden, Romare, **Retro. Supp. I:** 209; **Supp. VIII:** 337, 342; **Supp. XXI:** 249

"Beard of Bees, A" (X. J. Kennedy), **Supp. XV:** 171

Beardon, Romare, **Supp. XV:** 144

"Beards, The" (Lethem), **Supp. XVIII:** 148

Beardsley, Aubrey, **II:** 56; **IV:** 77

Beaser, Robert, **Supp. XV:** 259

"Beast" (Swenson), **Supp. IV Part 2:** 639

"Beast & Burden, The: Seven Improvisations" (Komunyakaa), **Supp. XIII:** 120, 121

Beast God Forgot to Invent, The (Harrison), **Supp. VIII:** 37, 46, **51–52**

Beast in Me, The (Thurber), **Supp. I Part 2:** 615

"Beast in the Jungle, The" (James), **I:** 570; **II:** 335; **Retro. Supp. I:** 235; **Supp. V:** 103–104

Beast in View (Rukeyser), **Supp. VI:** 272, 273, 279, 280

Beasts of Bethlehem, The (X. J. Kennedy), **Supp. XV:** 163

"Beat! Beat! Drums!" (Whitman), **III:** 585

Beat Down to Your Soul: What Was the Beat Generation? (Charters, ed.), **Supp. XIV:** 152

"Beatific Effigies" (Bronk), **Supp. XXI:** 31

Beaton, Cecil, **Supp. XVI:** 191

"Beatrice Palmato" (Wharton), **Retro. Supp. I:** 379

Beats, The (Krim, ed.), **Supp. XV:** 338

Beattie, Ann, **Supp. V:** 21–37; **Supp. XI:** 26; **Supp. XII:** 80, 139, 294; **Supp. XXI:** 118

Beattie, L. Elisabeth, **Supp. XX:**164, 165

Beatty, General Sam, **I:** 193

Beaty, Jerome, **Supp. IV Part 1:** 331

"Beau Monde of Mrs. Bridge, The" (Connell), **Supp. XIV:** 88, 89

Beaumont, Francis, **Supp. I Part 2:** 422

"Beauties of Santa Cruz, The" (Freneau), **Supp. II Part 1:** 260

Beautiful and Damned, The (Fitzgerald), **II:** 88, 89–91, 93, 263; **Retro. Supp. I:** **103–105,** 105, 106, 110; **Supp. IX:** 56, 57

Beautiful Changes, The (Wilbur), **Supp. III Part 2:** 544–550

"Beautiful Changes, The" (Wilbur), **Supp. III Part 2:** 549, 550

"Beautiful Child, A" (Capote), **Supp. III Part 1:** 113, 125

"Beautiful & Cruel" (Cisneros), **Supp. VII:** 63, 67

"Beautiful Wall, Machu Picchu, The" (Bronk), **Supp. XXI:** 31, 32

"Beautiful Woman Who Sings, The" (Gunn Allen), **Supp. IV Part 1:** 326

"Beauty" (Emerson), **II:** 2, 5

"Beauty" (Sanders), **Supp. XVI:** 277

"Beauty" (Wylie), **Supp. I Part 2:** 710

"Beauty and the Beast" (Dove), **Supp. IV Part 1:** 245

"Beauty and the Beast" (fairy tale), **IV:** 266; **Supp. X:** 88

"Beauty and the Shoe Sluts" (Karr), **Supp. XI:** 250

Beauty of the Husband, The: A Fictional Essay in Twenty-Nine Tangos (Carson), **Supp. XII:** 113–114

Beauty Queen, The (P. N. Warren), **Supp. XX:268–269**

Beauty's Punishment (Rice), **Supp. VII:** 301

Beauty's Release: The Continued Erotic Adventures of Sleeping Beauty (Rice), **Supp. VII:** 301

Beauvoir, Simone de, **IV:** 477; **Supp. I Part 1:** 51; **Supp. III Part 1:** 200–201, 208; **Supp. IV Part 1:** 360; **Supp. IX:** 4

"Be Careful" (Zach; Everwine, trans.), **Supp. XV:** 86

Be Careful How You Live (Lacy), **Supp. XV:** 203–204

"Because I could not stop for Death—" (Dickinson), **Retro. Supp. I:** **38–40,** 41, 43, 44

"Because It Happened" (Goldbarth), **Supp. XII:** 192

"Because of Libraries We Can Say These Things" (Nye), **Supp. XIII:** 283

"Because You Mentioned the Spiritual Life" (Dunn), **Supp. XI:** 154

Bech: A Book (Updike), **IV:** 214; **Retro. Supp. I:** 329, 335

Beck, Dave, **I:** 493

Beck, Jack, **Supp. IV Part 2:** 560

Beck, Nicholas, **Supp. XVIII:** 252

Becker, Carl, **Supp. I Part 2:** 492, 493

Becker, Paula. *See* Modersohn, Mrs. Otto (Paula Becker)

Beckett, Samuel, **I:** 71, 91, 142, 298, 461; **III:** 387; **IV:** 95; **Retro. Supp. I:** 206; **Supp. IV Part 1:** 297, 368–369; **Supp. IV Part 2:** 424; **Supp. V:** 23, 53; **Supp. XI:** 104; **Supp. XII:** 21, 150–151; **Supp. XIII:** 74; **Supp. XIV:** 239; **Supp. XVII:** 185; **Supp. XX:**17; **Supp. XXI:** 18

Beckett, Tom, **Supp. IV Part 2:** 419

Beckford, William, **I:** 204

Beckonings (Brooks), **Supp. III Part 1:** 85

"Becky" (Toomer), **Supp. III Part 2:** 481, 483; **Supp. IX:** 312

Becky and Her Friends (Hinojosa), **Supp. XIX: 108–109**

Becoming a Man: Half a Life Story (Monette), **Supp. X:** 146, 147, 149, 151, 152, **155–157**

"Becoming a Meadow" (Doty), **Supp. XI:** 124–125

"Becoming and Breaking: Poet and Poem" (Ríos), **Supp. IV Part 2:** 539

Becoming Canonical in American Poetry (Morris), **Retro. Supp. I:** 40

Becoming Light: New and Selected Poems (Jong), **Supp. V:** 115

Bécquer, Gustavo Adolfo, **Supp. XIII:** 312

"Bed, The" (Dixon), **Supp. XII:** 154

Beddoes, Thomas Lovell, **III:** 469; **Retro. Supp. I:** 285

Bedichek, Roy, **Supp. V:** 225

Bedient, Calvin, **Supp. IX:** 298; **Supp. XII:** 98

"Bed in the Sky, The" (Snyder), **Supp. VIII:** 300

Bednarik, Joseph, **Supp. VIII:** 39

"Bedrock" (Proulx), **Supp. VII:** 253

"Bee, The" (Lanier), **Supp. I Part 1:** 364

Beecher, Catharine, **Supp. I Part 2:** 581, 582–583, 584, 586, 588, 589, 591, 599; **Supp. X:** 103; **Supp. XI:** 193

Beecher, Charles, **Supp. I Part 2:** 588, 589

Beecher, Edward, **Supp. I Part 2:** 581, 582, 583, 584, 588, 591

Beecher, Harriet. *See* Stowe, Harriet Beecher

Beecher, Henry Ward, **II:** 275; **Supp. I Part 2:** 581; **Supp. XI:** 193; **Supp. XVIII:** 4

Beecher, Lyman, **Supp. I Part 2:** 580–581, 582, 583, 587, 588, 599; **Supp. XI:** 193

Beecher, Mrs. Lyman (Roxanna Foote), **Supp. I Part 2:** 580–581, 582, 588, 599

Beeching, Jack, **Supp. X:** 114, 117, 118, 123, 125, 126

"Beehive" (Toomer), **Supp. IX:** 317

"Bee Hunt, The" (Irving), **II:** 313

"Beekeeper's Daughter, The" (Plath), **Retro. Supp. II:** 246–247

"Bee Meeting, The" (Plath), **Retro. Supp. II:** 254–255

Bee Poems (Plath), **Retro. Supp. II:** 254–255

Beer, John, **Supp. XVII:** 239

Beer, Thomas, **I:** 405

Beerbohm, Max, **III:** 472; **IV:** 436; **Supp. I Part 2:** 714

"Beer Bottle" (Kooser), **Supp. XIX:** 117

"Beer in the Sergeant Major's Hat, or The Sun Also Sneezes" (Chandler), **Supp. IV Part 1:** 121

Beers, Henry A., **Supp. XX:**68

"Bees Bees Bees" (J. Scott), **Supp. XVII:** 188, 190

Beethoven, Ludwig van, **II:** 536; **III:** 118; **IV:** 274, 358; **Supp. I Part 1:** 363; **Supp. VIII:** 103

Beet Queen, The (Erdrich), **Supp. IV Part 1:** 259, 260, 264–265, 266, 273, 274, 275

Befo' de War: Echoes in Negro Dialect (Gordon), **Supp. II Part 1:** 201

"Before" (Goldbarth), **Supp. XII:** 175

"Before" (Snyder), **Supp. VIII:** 301

Before Adam (London), **II:** 466

Before Disaster (Winters), **Supp. II Part 2:** 786, 800

"Before Disaster" (Winters), **Supp. II Part 2:** 801, 815

"Before I Knocked" (D. Thomas), **III:** 534

Beforelife, The (F. Wright), **Supp. XVII:** 240, 245–246

"Before March" (MacLeish), **III:** 15

Before My Life Began (Neugeboren), **Supp. XVI: 224–225**

"Before the Altar" (Lowell), **II:** 516

"Before the Birth of one of her children" (Bradstreet), **Supp. I Part 1:** 118

"Before the Sky Darkens" (Dunn), **Supp. XI:** 155

"Begat" (Sexton), **Supp. II Part 2: 693**

Beggarman, Thief (Shaw), **Supp. XIX:** 251–252

Beggar on Horseback (Kaufman and Connelly), **III:** 394
"Beggar Said So, The" (Singer), **IV:** 12
Beggars in the House of Plenty (Shanley), **Supp. XIV:** 316, **327–328**
Beggar's Opera, The (Gay), **Supp. I Part 2:** 523
Begiebing, Robert, **Retro. Supp. II:** 210
Begin Again (Paley), **Supp. VI:** 221
"Beginning and the End, The" (Jeffers), **Supp. II Part 2:** 420–421, 424
"Beginning of Decadence, The" (Jeffers), **Supp. II Part 2:** 420
"Beginning of Enthusiasm, The" (Salinas), **Supp. XIII:** 327–328
Beginning of Wisdom, The (Benét), **I:** 358; **Supp. XI:** 44
Be Glad You're Neurotic (Bisch), **Supp. I Part 2:** 608
"Begotten of the Spleen" (Simic), **Supp. VIII:** 277
"Behaving Like a Jew" (Stern), **Supp. IX:** 290–291, 294
"Behavior" (Emerson), **II:** 2, 4
Behavior of Titans, The (Merton), **Supp. VIII:** 201
Behind a Mask (Alcott), **Supp. I Part 1:** 36–37, 43–44
"Behind a Wall" (Lowell), **II:** 516
Behind the Movie Camera (radio show), **Supp. XV:** 147
"Behold the Key" (Malamud), **Supp. I Part 2:** 437
Behrendt, Stephen, **Supp. X:** 204
Behrman, S. N., **Supp. V:** 95
Beidler, Peter G., **Supp. IV Part 2:** 557
Beidler, Philip D., **Supp. XII:** 69
Beige Dolorosa (Harrison), **Supp. VIII:** 40, 51
Beiles, Sinclair, **Supp. XII:** 129
Beiliss, Mendel, **Supp. I Part 2:** 427, 446, 447, 448
"Being a Constellation" (A. Finch), **Supp. XVII:** 72
"Being a Lutheran Boy-God in Minnesota" (R. Bly), **Supp. IV Part 1:** 59, 67
Being and Race (Johnson), **Supp. VI:** 193, 199
Being and Time (Heidegger), **Supp. VIII:** 9
Being Busted (Fiedler), **Supp. XIII:** 95, 102, 104
Being John Malkovich (Kaufman), **Supp. XV:** 16
Being Perfect (Quindlen), **Supp. XVII:** 167, 179
Being There (Kosinski), **Supp. VII:** 215, 216, 222–223
Beiswanger, George, **Retro. Supp. II:** 220
Belasco, David, **Supp. XVI:** 182; **Supp. XXI:** 151
Bel Canto (Patchett), **Supp. XII:** 307, 310, **320–322**
Belchamber (Sturgis), **Supp. XX:**227, 233, **238–240**
"Beleaguered City, The" (Longfellow), **II:** 498

Belfry of Bruges, The, and Other Poems (Longfellow), **II:** 489; **Retro. Supp. II:** 157, 168
"Belief" (Levine), **Supp. V:** 186, 190
"Belief in the Self Abandoned, The" (Bronk), **Supp. XXI:** 30
"Beliefs of Writers, The" (Doctorow), **Supp. IV Part 1:** 235–236
Believeniks! (Lethem and Sorrentino), **Supp. XVIII:** 148–149
Believers (C. Baxter), **Supp. XVII:** 20–21, 22
"Believers" (C. Baxter), **Supp. XVII:** 21
"Believers, The/Los Creyentes" (Kingsolver), **Supp. VII:** 208
Belinda (Rice), **Supp. VII:** 301–302
"Belinda's Petition" (Dove), **Supp. IV Part 1:** 245
"Belita" (Ríos), **Supp. IV Part 2:** 541
Belitt, Ben, **Supp. XII:** 260
Bell, Archibald, **Supp. XX:**284, 285
Bell, Clive, **IV:** 87
Bell, Daniel, **Supp. I Part 2:** 648
Bell, George Kennedy Allen, **Retro. Supp. I:** 65
Bell, Madison Smartt, **Supp. X:** 1–20; **Supp. XVII:** 236; **Supp. XIX:** 58–59, 60–61; **Supp. XXI:** 48
Bell, Marvin, **Supp. V:** 337, 339; **Supp. IX:** 152; **Supp. XI:** 316
Bell, Michael, **Retro. Supp. II:** 139
Bell, Pearl, **Supp. XI:** 233
Bell, Quentin, **Supp. I Part 2:** 636
Bell, Whitfield J., Jr., **II:** 123
Bellafante, Gina, **Supp. VIII:** 85
Bellamy, Edward, **II:** 276; **Supp. I Part 2:** 641; **Supp. XI:** 200, 203
Bellarosa Connection, The (Bellow), **Retro. Supp. II:** 31, 32
"Belle Dollinger" (Masters), **Supp. I Part 2:** 463
Belleforest, François de, **IV:** 370
"Belle Zoraïde, La" (Chopin), **Supp. I Part 1:** 215–216
Bell Jar, The (Plath), **Retro. Supp. II:** 242, **249–250; Supp. I Part 2:** 526, 527, 529, 531–536, 539, 540, 541, 542, 544
Belloc, Hilary, **III:** 176; **IV:** 432
"Bellocq" (Trethewey), **Supp. XXI:** 253
Bellocq, E. J., **Supp. XXI:** 246, 251
Bellocq's Ophelia (Trethewey), **Supp. XXI:** 243, 246, **251–254**
"Bellocq's Ophelia" (Trethewey), **Supp. XXI:** 254
Bellow, Saul, **I:** 113, 138–139, **144–166,** 375, 517; **II:** 579; **III:** 40; **IV:** 3, 19, 217, 340; **Retro. Supp. II: 19–36,** 118, 279, 307, 324; **Supp. I Part 2:** 428, 451; **Supp. II Part 1:** 109; **Supp. IV Part 1:** 30; **Supp. V:** 258; **Supp. VIII:** 98, 176, 234, 236–237, 245; **Supp. IX:** 212, 227; **Supp. XI:** 64, 233; **Supp. XII:** 159, 165, 170, 310; **Supp. XIII:** 106; **Supp. XV:** 143; **Supp. XVI:** 208; **Supp. XVIII:** 90; **Supp. XIX:** 157, 158, 261; **Supp. XX:**244
Bellows, George, **Supp. XV:** 295

"Bells, The" (Poe), **III:** 593; **Retro. Supp. II:** 266; **Supp. I Part 2:** 388
"Bells, The" (Sexton), **Supp. II Part 2:** 673
"Bells for John Whiteside's Daughter" (Ransom), **III:** 490
"Bells of Lynn, The" (Longfellow), **II:** 498
"Bells of San Blas, The" (Longfellow), **II:** 490–491, 493, 498
"Bell Tower, The" (Melville), **III:** 91
"Belly, The" (Dobyns), **Supp. XIII:** 87
"Belonging" (Pickering), **Supp. XXI:** 202
"Belonging Kind, The" (W. Gibson and J. Shirley), **Supp. XVI:** 123
Beloved (Morrison), **Supp. III Part 1:** 364, 372–379; **Supp. IV Part 1:** 13–14; **Supp. V:** 259; **Supp. VIII:** 343; **Supp. XIII:** 60
Beloved, The (Gibran), **Supp. XX:**125
"Beloved, The" (Halliday), **Supp. XIX:** 92
Beloved Lady: A History of Jane Addams' Ideas on Reform and Peace (Farrell), **Supp. I Part 1:** 24
Beloved Stranger, The (Bynner), **Supp. XV:** 44, 50
Bemorse, John, **Supp. XX:**62
Benchley, Robert, **I:** 48, 482; **II:** 435; **III:** 53; **Supp. IX:** 190, 195, 204
Benda, W. T., **Retro. Supp. I:** 13
Bending of a Twig, The (Coke), **Supp. XX:**235
Bend Sinister (Nabokov), **III:** 253–254; **Retro. Supp. I:** 265, 266, 270
"Beneath the Sidewalk" (Dunn), **Supp. XI:** 145
"Beneath the Smooth Skin of America" (Sanders), **Supp. XVI:** 275
Benedict, Elizabeth, **Supp. XVIII:** 289
Benedict, Ruth, **Supp. IX:** 229
Benefactor, The (Sontag), **Supp. III Part 2:** 451, 455, 468, 469
"Benefit Performance" (Malamud), **Supp. I Part 2:** 431
Benét, Laura, **Supp. XI:** 44
Benét, Rosemary, **Supp. XI:** 44, 51
Benét, Stephen Vincent, **I:** 358; **II:** 177; **III:** 22; **IV:** 129; **Supp. XI: 43–61**
Benét, William Rose, **II:** 530; **Retro. Supp. I:** 108; **Supp. I Part 2:** 709; **Supp. XI:** 43, 44; **Supp. XIV:** 119, 122, 129
Ben Franklin's Wit and Wisdom (Franklin), **II:** 111
Ben-Gurion, David, **Supp. XX:**243
Ben-Hur (film), **Supp. IV Part 2:** 683
Benigna Machiavelli (Gilman), **Supp. XI:** 201, 208
Benitez, R. Michael, **Retro. Supp. II:** 264
Benito Cereno (Lowell), **II:** 546; **Retro. Supp. II:** 181
"Benito Cereno" (Melville), **III:** 91; **Retro. Supp. I:** 255; **Retro. Supp. II:** 188; **Supp. XVII:** 185
Benito's Dream Bottle (Nye), **Supp. XIII:** 278

"Bênitou's Slave, The" (Chopin), **Retro. Supp. II:** 64
Benjamin, Walter, **Supp. IX:** 133; **Supp. XVI:** 290, 291
Benjamin Franklin (Van Doren), **Supp. I Part 2:** 486
"Benjamin Pantier" (Masters), **Supp. I Part 2:** 461
Bennett, Anne Virginia, **II:** 184
Bennett, Arnold, **I:** 103; **II:** 337; **Supp. XVI:** 190
Bennett, Elizabeth, **Supp. VIII:** 58
Bennett, Patrick, **Supp. V:** 225
Bennett, Paula, **Retro. Supp. I:** 29, 33, 42; **Supp. XX:** 286
Bennett, William, **Supp. VIII:** 245
Benson, A. C., **Supp. XX:** 238
Benson, Arthur, **Supp. XX:** 233
Benson, E. F., **Supp. XX:** 229
Benson, Heidi, **Supp. XVIII:** 136
Benson, Jackson J., **Supp. IV Part 2:** 613
Benson, Martin, **Supp. XVIII:** 38
Benstock, Shari, **Retro. Supp. I:** 361, 368, 371, 382; **Supp. XX:** 240
Bentham, Jeremy, **I:** 279; **Supp. I Part 2:** 635
Bentley, Anna, **Supp. XXI:** 5
Bentley, Arthur, **Supp. XXI:** 4, 5
Bentley, Eric R., **IV:** 396
Bentley, Nelson, **Supp. IX:** 324
Bentley, Richard, **III:** 79, 86
Benton, Robert, **Supp. IV Part 1:** 236
"Bent Tones" (Wright), **Supp. XV:** 346
Benveniste, Emile, **Supp. XVI:** 292
Benzel, Jan, **Supp. XVI:** 112
Beowulf, **Supp. II Part 1:** 6; **Supp. XVII:** 70, 73
Beran, Carol, **Supp. XIII:** 25
"Berck-Plage" (Plath), **Retro. Supp. II:** 253–254
Bercovitch, Sacvan, **Retro. Supp. I:** 408; **Retro. Supp. II:** 325, 330; **Supp. I Part 1:** 99; **Supp. I Part 2:** 659
Berdyaev, Nikolai, **I:** 494; **III:** 292
"Bereaved Apartments" (Kingsolver), **Supp. VII:** 203
"Bereavement in their death to feel" (Dickinson), **Retro. Supp. I:** 43, 44
"Berenice" (Poe), **III:** 415, 416, 425; **Retro. Supp. II:** 270
Bérénice (Racine), **II:** 573
Berenson, Bernard, **Retro. Supp. I:** 381; **Supp. IV Part 1:** 314; **Supp. XIV:** 335, 336, 337; **Supp. XVII:** 99; **Supp. XXI:** 5
Berenson, Mary Smith, **Supp. XXI:** 4, 5, 6
Berg, James, **Supp. XIV:** 157, 159
Berg, Stephen, **Supp. IV Part 1:** 60
Berger, Alan, **Supp. XVII:** 39
Berger, Charles, **Retro. Supp. I:** 311
Berger, John, **Supp. XVI:** 284
Berger, Roger, **Supp. XIII:** 237
Berger, Thomas, **III:** 258; **Supp. XII:** 171
Bergman, Ingmar, **I:** 291; **Supp. XV:** 7, 8, 12

Bergson, Henri, **I:** 224; **II:** 163, 165, 166, 359; **III:** 8, 9, 488, 619; **IV:** 86, 122, 466, 467; **Retro. Supp. I:** 55, 57, 80; **Supp. IV Part 1:** 42
Berkeley, Anthony, **Supp. IV Part 1:** 341
Berkeley, George, **II:** 10, 349, 357, 480, 554
Berkman, Leonard, **Supp. XV:** 321
Berkowitz, Gerald, **Supp. IV Part 2:** 590
Berlin Alexanderplatz (Döblin), **Supp. XV:** 137
Berlin Stories (Isherwood), **Supp. IV Part 1:** 82; **Supp. XIV:** 155, 156, 161, 162, 164, 165
Berlioz, Hector, **Supp. XV:** 33
Berlyne, Daniel E., **Supp. I Part 2:** 672
Berman, Alexander, **Supp. XVII:** 103
Bernard Clare (Farrell), **II:** 38, 39
Bernard of Clairvaux, Saint, **I:** 22; **II:** 538
Bernays, Thekla, **Retro. Supp. II:** 65
Berne, Suzanne, **Supp. XII:** 320
Berne, Victoria (pseudonym). *See* Fisher, M. F. K.
Berneis, Peter, **IV:** 383
Bernhard, Brendan, **Supp. XIV:** 163
Bernhard, Thomas, **Supp. XX:** 91
Bernhardt, Sarah, **I:** 484; **Retro. Supp. I:** 377
Bernice (Glaspell), **Supp. III Part 1:** 179
"Bernice Bobs Her Hair" (Fitzgerald), **II:** 88; **Retro. Supp. I:** 103
Bernstein, Aline, **IV:** 455, 456
Bernstein, Andrea, **Supp. IX:** 146
Bernstein, Charles, **Supp. IV Part 2:** 421, 426
Bernstein, Elizabeth, **Supp. XII:** 318
Bernstein, Leonard, **I:** 28; **Supp. I Part 1:** 288, 289; **Supp. IV Part 1:** 83, 84
Bernstein, Melvin, **Supp. XIV:** 41, 46
Bernstein, Michael André, **Retro. Supp. I:** 427
Bernstein, Richard, **Supp. IX:** 253, 262; **Supp. XII:** 113; **Supp. XIV:** 33
Berrett, Jesse, **Supp. XIII:** 241, 242
Berrigan, Ted, **Supp. XIV:** 150
Berroa y Canelo, Quiterio, **Supp. XXI:** 104
"Berry" (Hughes), **Supp. I Part 1:** 329, 330
Berry, Faith, **Retro. Supp. I:** 194, 201
Berry, Walter, **IV:** 313–314, 326
Berry, Wendell, **Supp. VIII:** 304; **Supp. X: 21–39; Supp. XII:** 202; **Supp. XIII:** 1–2; **Supp. XIV:** 179; **Supp. XVI:** 39, 56; **Supp. XVIII:** 192; **Supp. XXI:** 90
"Berry Feast, A" (Snyder), **Supp. VIII:** 289, 297
Berryman, John, **I: 167–189,** 405, 441–442, 521; **II:** 554; **III:** 273; **IV:** 138, 430; **Retro. Supp. I:** 430; **Retro. Supp. II:** 175, 178; **Supp. I Part 1:** 109; **Supp. III Part 2:** 541, 561, 595, 596, 603; **Supp. IV Part 2:** 620, 639; **Supp. V:** 179–180, 337; **Supp. IX:** 152; **Supp. XI:** 240; **Supp. XV:** 93; **Supp. XVII:** 111
Berryman, Mrs. John, **I:** 168–169

Berryman's Sonnets (Berryman), **I:** 168, 175–178
"Berry Territory" (Snyder), **Supp. VIII:** 304
Berthoff, Warner, **Supp. I Part 1:** 133
Bertolucci, Bernardo, **Supp. IV Part 1:** 94
"Bertrand Hume" (Masters), **Supp. I Part 2:** 463–464
"Best, the Most, The" (Carruth), **Supp. XVI:** 59
Best American Essays 1987, The (G. Talese and R. Atwan, eds.), **Supp. XVI:** 273
Best American Essays 1988, The (Dillard, ed.), **Supp. VIII:** 272
Best American Essays 1989, The (Wolff, ed.), **Supp. XVII:** 208
Best American Essays 1993, The (J. Epstein, ed.), **Supp. XVI:** 275
Best American Essays 1997, The (Frazier, ed.), **Supp. VIII:** 272; **Supp. XVII:** 207
Best American Essays 1999, The (E. Hoagland and R. Atwan, eds.), **Supp. XVI:** 277
Best American Essays for College Students, The (R. Atwan, ed.), **Supp. XVI:** 273
Best American New Voices 2001 (C. Baxter, ed.), **Supp. XVII:** 22
Best American Poetry, The: 1988 (Ashbery, ed.), **Supp. III Part 1:** 26
Best American Poetry 2000, The (Dove and Lehman, eds.), **Supp. XXI:** 246
Best American Poetry 2006, The (Collins, ed.), **Supp. XXI:** 54
Best American Short Stories, **I:** 174; **II:** 587; **III:** 443; **Supp. IV Part 1:** 102, 315; **Supp. IX:** 114; **Supp. X:** 301
Best American Short Stories, 1915–1050, The, **Supp. IX:** 4
Best American Short Stories 1965, The (Foley, ed.), **Supp. XVI:** 225
Best American Short Stories 1982, The (Gardner, ed.), **Supp. XVII:** 16
Best American Short Stories 1983, The (A. Tyler, ed.), **Supp. XVI:** 37
Best American Short Stories 1986, The (Carver, ed.), **Supp. XVII:** 17
Best American Short Stories 1988, The (Helprin, ed.), **Supp. XVI:** 16
Best American Short Stories 1989, The (Atwood, ed.), **Supp. XVII:** 18; **Supp. XXI:** 39, 42
Best American Short Stories 1991, The (Adams and Kenison, eds.), **Supp. XVI:** 256
Best American Short Stories 2001, The (Kenison and Kingsover, eds.), **Supp. XVI:** 24
Best American Short Stories of 1942, The, **Supp. V:** 316
Best American Short Stories of 1944, The, **Supp. IX:** 119
Best American Short Stories of the Century (Updike, ed.), **Supp. X:** 163
Best American Short Stories of the Eighties, The (Ravenal, ed.), **Supp. IV Part 1:** 93

Best American Sports Writing of the Century, The (Halberstam, ed.), **Supp. XVII:** 204

"Best China Saucer, The" (Jewett), **Retro. Supp. II:** 145–146

Bester, Alfred, **Supp. XVI:** 123

Best Hour of the Night, The (Simpson), **Supp. IX: 277–279**

Bestiaire, Le (Apollinaire), **IV:** 80

Bestiary, A (Wilbur), **Supp. III Part 2:** 552

"Bestiary for the Fingers of My Right Hand" (Simic), **Supp. VIII:** 274, 275

Best Man, The: A Play About Politics (Vidal), **Supp. IV Part 2:** 683

"Best of Everything, The" (Yates), **Supp. XI:** 341

Best of Pickering, The (Pickering), **Supp. XXI:** 192, 198

Best of Plimpton (Plimpton), **Supp. XVI:** 238, 239, 240

Best Short Plays, The (Mayorga), **IV:** 381

Best Short Stories, The (O'Brien, ed.), **I:** 289

Best Short Stories by Negro Writers, The (Hughes, ed.), **Supp. I Part 1:** 345

Best Short Stories of 1926, The (O'Brien, ed.), **Supp. XVIII:** 279

Best Short Stories of 1934 (O'Brien, ed.), **Supp. XVIII:** 227

Best Short Stories of 1938 (O'Brien, ed.), **Supp. XIX:** 256; **Supp. XX:**34

Best That Ever Did It, The (Lacy), **Supp. XV:** 201–202

Best Times, The: An Informal Memoir (Dos Passos), **I:** 475, 482

Best Words, Best Order: Essays on Poetry (Dobyns), **Supp. XIII:** 74, **76–78,** 87

Best Years of Our Lives, The (film; Wyler), **Supp. XV:** 195

"BETANCOURT" (Baraka), **Supp. II Part 1:** 33, 34

Bête humaine, La (Zola), **III:** 316, 318

"Bethe" (Hellman), **Supp. I Part 1:** 293

Bethea, David, **Supp. VIII:** 27

Bethel Merriday (Lewis), **II:** 455

Bethke, Bruce, **Supp. XVI:** 121

Bethlehem in Broad Daylight (Doty), **Supp. XI:** 121, **122–123**

Bethune, Mary McLeod, **Retro. Supp. I:** 197; **Supp. I Part 1:** 333

Bethurum, Dorothy, **IV:** 121

"Betrayal" (Lanier), **Supp. I Part 1:** 364

"Betrothed" (Bogan), **Supp. III Part 1:** 49–51

Bettelheim, Bruno, **Supp. I Part 2:** 622; **Supp. X:** 77, 84; **Supp. XIV:** 126; **Supp. XVI:** 33

Better Days (Price), **Supp. VI:** 264

Better Sort, The (James), **II:** 335

"Better Things in Life, The" (Loos), **Supp. XVI:** 194

Betty Leicester (Jewett), **II:** 406

Betty Leicester's Christmas (Jewett), **II:** 406; **Retro. Supp. II:** 145

Between Angels (Dunn), **Supp. XI: 149–159**

"Between Angels" (Dunn), **Supp. XI:** 150

Between Fantoine and Agapa (Pinget), **Supp. V:** 39

"Between Memory and History: A Writer's Voice" (Kreisler), **Supp. XVI:** 155

Between Silences: A Voice from China (Jin), **Supp. XVIII:** 91, 92, 93

"Between the Porch and the Altar" (Lowell), **II:** 540–541

"Between the World and Me" (Wright), **Supp. II Part 1:** 228

Between Time and Timbuktu (Vonnegut), **Supp. II Part 2:** 753, 759

Beuka, Robert A., **Supp. XIX:** 263; **Supp. XXI:** 47

"Be Very Afraid—Of Loss of Liberty at Home" (P. N. Warren), **Supp. XX:**272–273

Bevis, Howard L., **Supp. I Part 2:** 611

Bevis, John, **Supp. I Part 2:** 503

"Bewitched" (Wharton), **IV:** 316

Bewley, Marius, **I:** 336

Beyle, Marie Henri. *See* Stendhal

Beyond (Goldbarth), **Supp. XII:** 192

Beyond a Boundary (C. L. R. James), **Supp. XXI:** 159, 170–171

Beyond Black Bear Lake (LaBastille), **Supp. X:** 95, **99–102,** 108

"Beyond Charles River to the Acheron" (Lowell), **II:** 541

Beyond Criticism (Shapiro), **Supp. II Part 2:** 703, 711

Beyond Culture (Trilling), **Supp. III Part 2:** 508–512

Beyond Desire (Anderson), **I:** 111

Beyond Document: The Art of Nonfiction Film (Warren, ed.), **Supp. IV Part 2:** 434

Beyond Good and Evil (Nietzsche), **Supp. IV Part 2:** 519

"Beyond Harm" (Olds), **Supp. X:** 210

Beyond Katrina: A Meditation on the Mississippi Gulf Coast (Trethewey), **Supp. XXI:** 248

"Beyond My Solitude" (Gibran), **Supp. XX:**119

"Beyond the Alps" (Lowell), **II:** 547, 550

"Beyond the Bayou" (Chopin), **Supp. I Part 1:** 215

Beyond the Boom: New Voices on American Life, Culture and Politics (Teachout), **Supp. XIX:** 137

Beyond the Horizon (O'Neill), **III:** 389; **Supp. XXI:** 13

Beyond the Hundredth Meridian: John Wesley Powell and the Second Opening of the West (Stegner), **Supp. IV Part 2:** 599, 603–604, 611

"Beyond the Kittery Bridge" (Hatlen), **Supp. V:** 138

Beyond the Law (film) (Mailer), **Retro. Supp. II:** 205

"Beyond the Sea (at the sanatorium)" (Salinas), **Supp. XIII:** 325

Beyond the Wall: Essays from the Outside (Abbey), **Supp. XIII:** 13

Beyond the Writers' Workshop: New Ways to Write Creative Nonfiction (C. Bly), **Supp. XVI:** 41

Beyond Tragedy (Niebuhr), **III:** 300–303

Bezner, Kevin, **Supp. XII:** 202

B. F.'s Daughter (Marquand), **III:** 59, 65, 68, 69

Bhagavad Gita, **III:** 566; **IV:** 183

"Biafra: A People Betrayed" (Vonnegut), **Supp. II Part 2:** 760

Bianchi, Martha Dickinson, **I:** 470; **Retro. Supp. I:** 35, 37, 38

Bible, **I:** 191, 280, 414, 421, 490, 506; **II:** 6, 12, 15, 17, 108, 231, 237, 238, 252, 267, 302; **III:** 28, 199, 308–309, 341, 343, 350, 356, 402, 492, 519, 565, 577; **IV:** 11, 13, 42, 57, 60, 67, 152, 153, 154, 155, 164, 165, 296, 337, 341, 367, 369, 370, 371, 438; **Retro. Supp. I:** 91; **Supp. I Part 1:** 4, 6, 63, 101, 104, 105, 113, 193, 369; **Supp. I Part 2:** 388, 433, 494, 515, 516, 517, 583, 584, 587, 589, 653, 689, 690, 691; **Supp. IV Part 1:** 284; **Supp. VIII:** 20; **Supp. IX:** 246; **Supp. XIV:** 225. *See also* names of biblical books; New Testament; Old Testament

Biblia Americana (Mather), **Supp. II Part 2:** 442

Biblical Dialogues between a Father and His Family (Rowson), **Supp. XV:** 245–246

"Bibliography of the King's Book, A, or, Eikon Basilike" (Howe), **Supp. IV Part 2:** 435

Bibliography of the King's Book, A; or, Eikon Basilike (Almack), **Supp. IV Part 2:** 435

Bickel, Freddy. *See* March, Fredric

Bidart, Frank, **Retro. Supp. II:** 48, 50, 52, 182, 183, 184; **Supp. XV: 19–37; Supp. XVIII:** 91,92; **Supp. XIX:** 82

Bid Me to Live (Doolittle), **Supp. I Part 1:** 258, 260, 268, 269, 270

"Bien Pretty" (Cisneros), **Supp. VII:** 70

"Bienvenidos" (Mora), **Supp. XIII:** 220

Bierce, Albert, **I:** 191, 209

Bierce, Ambrose, **I: 190–213,** 419; **II:** 74, 264, 271; **IV:** 350; **Retro. Supp. II:** 72

Bierce, Mrs. Ambrose, **I:** 194–195, 199

Bierce, Day, **I:** 195, 199

Bierce, Helen, **I:** 210

Bierce, Leigh, **I:** 195, 198, 208

Bierce, General Lucius Verus, **I:** 191

Bierce, Marcus, **I:** 190, 191

Bierce, Mrs. Marcus, **I:** 190, 191

Bierds, Linda, **Supp. XVII: 25–37**

Biffle, Kent, **Supp. V:** 225

"Bi-Focal" (Stafford), **Supp. XI:** 318, 321

Bigamist's Daughter, A (McDermott), **Supp. XVIII:** 155, **156–158,** 160, 166

Big as Life (Doctorow), **Supp. IV Part 1:** 231, 234

Big Bad Love (film, Howard), **Supp. XXI:** 39

Big Bad Love (L. Brown), **Supp. XXI:** 40, 42, **44–45**

"Big Bite" (Mailer), **Retro. Supp. II:** 204

"Big Blonde" (Parker), **Supp. IX:** 189, 192, 193, 195, 196, 203

Big Bozo, The (Glaspell), **Supp. III Part 1:** 182

Bigelow, Gordon, **Supp. X:** 222, 227, 229

Bigelow, Jacob, **Supp. I Part 1:** 302

Bigelow Papers, Second Series, The (Lowell), **Supp. I Part 2:** 406, 415–416

Bigelow Papers, The (Lowell), **Supp. I Part 2:** 406, 407, 408, 410, 411–412, 415, 417, 424

Big Fix, The (Lacy), **Supp. XV:** 204–205

Bigfoot Dreams (Prose), **Supp. XVI:** 253–254

Big Funk, The: A Casual Play (Shanley), **Supp. XIV:** 316, **327**

"Big Game" (Boyle), **Supp. XX:** 20

Big Game, The (film), **Supp. XIX:** 244

Big Gold Dream, The (C. Himes), **Supp. XVI:** 143, 144

"Bight, The" (Bishop), **Retro. Supp. II:** 38, 45

Big Hunger: Stories 1932–1959 (Fante), **Supp. XI:** 160

Big Knife, The (Odets), **Supp. II Part 2:** 546, 547, 548

Big Knockover, The (Hammett), **Supp. I Part 1:** 292; **Supp. IV Part 1:** 344, 345, 356

Big Laugh, The (O'Hara), **III:** 362, 373–375

Big Man (Neugeboren), **Supp. XVI:** 219, **220,** 221, 225

Big Money, The (Dos Passos), **I:** 482, 483, 486–487, 489; **Supp. I Part 2:** 646, 647

Big Picture (Everett), **Supp. XVIII:** 54, 66

"Big Picture" (Everett), **Supp. XVIII:** 66

"Big Picture" (Halliday), **Supp. XIX:** 93

"Big Rock Candy Figgy Pudding Pitfall, The" (Didion), **Supp. IV Part 1:** 195

Big Rock Candy Mountain, The (Stegner), **Supp. IV Part 2:** 596, 597, 598, 599, 600, 603, 604, 605, 606–607, 608, 610–611

Bigsby, C. W. E. (Christopher), **Supp. IX:** 137, 140; **Supp. XV:** 332

Big Sea, The (Hughes), **Retro. Supp. I:** 195, 197, 199, 201, 204; **Supp. I Part 1:** 322, 332, 333; **Supp. II Part 1:** 233–234; **Supp. XIX:** 77

Big Sky, The (Mora), **Supp. XIII:** 221

Big Sleep, The (Chandler), **Supp. IV Part 1:** 122–125, 127, 128, 134

Big Sleep, The (film), **Supp. IV Part 1:** 130; **Supp. XVIII:** 148

Big Strike, The (Ryan as Quin), **Supp. XVIII:** 226, **232–233**

Big Sur (Kerouac), **Supp. III Part 1:** 230

Big Sur and the Oranges of Hieronymous Bosch (H. Miller), **III:** 189–190

Big Town, The (Lardner), **II:** 426, 429

"Big Two-Hearted River" (Hemingway), **II:** 249; **Retro. Supp. I:** 170–171; **Supp. IX:** 106; **Supp. XIV:** 227, 235

"Big Wind" (Roethke), **III:** 531

"Big Winner Rises Late, The" (Dunn), **Supp. XI:** 146

"Bilingual/*Bilingüe*" (essay; Espaillat), *Supp. XXI:* 103

"Bilingual/*Bilingüe*" (poem; Espaillat), *Supp. XXI:* 104

"Bilingual Christmas" (Mora), **Supp. XIII:** 216–217

"Bilingual Sestina" (Alvarez), **Supp. VII:** 10

"Bill" (Winters), **Supp. II Part 2:** 792

"Bill, The" (Malamud), **Supp. I Part 2:** 427, 430, 434

"Billie Holiday" (Carruth), **Supp. XVI:** 50

Billings, Gladys. *See* Brooks, Mrs. Van Wyck

Billings, Josh, **Supp. XVIII:** 1, 4

Bill of Rites, a Bill of Wrongs, a Bill of Goods, A (Morris), **III:** 237

"Bill's Beans" (Nye), **Supp. XIII:** 283

"Billy" (Gordon), **Supp. IV Part 1:** 306

"Billy" (McCarriston), **Supp. XIV:** 265

Billy Bathgate (Doctorow), **Supp. IV Part 1:** 217, 219, 222, 224, 227, 229–231, 231, 232, 233, 238

Billy Bathgate (film), **Supp. IV Part 1:** 236

Billy Budd, Sailor (Melville), **III:** 40, 93–95; **IV:** 105; **Retro. Supp. I:** 249, **258–260**

Billy Collins Live: A Performance at the Peter Norton Symphony Space April 20, 2005 (CD, Collins), **Supp. XXI:** 51

"Billy Gardner's Ground Out" (Skloot), **Supp. XX:** 205, 207

Billy Phelan's Greatest Game (W. Kennedy), **Supp. VII:** 131, 132, 134, 135, 142–147, 149, 151, 153, 155

Billy Ray's Farm: Essays from a Place Called Tula (L. Brown), **Supp. XXI:** 48, 49

Billy's Boy (P. N. Warren), **Supp. XX:** 261, **265–267**

Billy the Kid, **Supp. IV Part 2:** 489, 490, 492

Biloxi Blues (Simon), **Supp. IV Part 2:** 576, 577, 584, 586–587, 590

"Bimini" (Hemingway), **II:** 258

Bingham, Anne, **Supp. XV:** 239

Bingham, Millicent Todd, **I:** 470; **Retro. Supp. I:** 36

Bingham, Remica L., **Supp. XXI:** 256

Bingo Palace, The (Erdrich), **Supp. IV Part 1:** 259, 260, 261, 263–264, 265, 266–267, 268–269, 270, 271–273, 274, 275

"Binsey Poplars" (Hopkins), **Supp. I Part 1:** 94; **Supp. IV Part 2:** 639

Binswanger, Ludwig, **Supp. XV:** 26

Biographia Literaria (Coleridge), **II:** 10; **Retro. Supp. I:** 308

"Biography" (Francis), **Supp. IX:** 77

"Biography" (Pinsky), **Supp. VI:** 235, 236, 239, 241, **243,** 249, 250

Biography and Poetical Remains of the Late Margaret Miller Davidson (Irving), **II:** 314

"Biography in the First Person" (Dunn), **Supp. XI:** 144

"Biography of an Armenian Schoolgirl" (Nye), **Supp. XIII:** 275, 280

"Biography of a Story" (Jackson), **Supp. IX:** 113

Biondi, Joann, **Supp. XI:** 103

"Biopoetics Sketch for *Greenfield Review*" (Harjo), **Supp. XII:** 216

"Birchbrook Mill" (Whittier), **Supp. I Part 2:** 699

"Birches" (Frost), **II:** 154; **Retro. Supp. I:** 132; **Supp. XIII:** 147

Bird, Alan, **Supp. I Part 1:** 260

Bird, Gloria, **Supp. XII:** 216

Bird, Isabella, **Supp. X:** 103

Bird, Robert M., **III:** 423

"Bird, The" (Simpson), **Supp. IX:** 269–270

"Bird, the Bird, the Bird, The" (Creeley), **Supp. IV Part 1:** 149

"Bird Banding with the Biologists" (Ray), **Supp. XVIII:** 194

Bird by Bird: Some Instructions on Writing and Life (Lamott), **Supp. XX:** 132, **137–138**

"Bird came down the Walk, A" (Dickinson), **Retro. Supp. I:** 37

"Bird Frau, The" (Dove), **Supp. IV Part 1:** 245

"Bird in Hand" (screen story) (West and Ingster), **Retro. Supp. II:** 330

Bird Kingdom of the Mayas (LaBastille), **Supp. X:** 96

Birds and Beasts (W. J. Smith), **Supp. XIII:** 346

"Birds for Christmas, The" (Richard), **Supp. XIX:** 221

Bird's Nest, The (Jackson), **Supp. IX:** **124–125**

Birds of America (McCarthy), **II:** 579–583; **Supp. X:** 177

Birds of America (Moore), **Supp. X:** 163, 165, 167, 168, 171, **177–179**

Birds of America, The (Audubon), **Supp. XVI:** **5–6,** 7, 9, 10, 12, 13

"Birds of Killingsworth, The" (Longfellow), **Retro. Supp. II:** 164

Birds of North America (Audubon Society), **Supp. X:** 177

"Birds of Vietnam, The" (Carruth), **Supp. XVI:** 55

"Bird-Witted" (Moore), **III:** 214

Birkelo, Cheryl, **Supp. XX:** 220–221

Birkerts, Sven, **Supp. IV Part 2:** 650; **Supp. V:** 212; **Supp. VIII:** 85; **Supp. X:** 311; **Supp. XX:** 92

Birkhead, L. M., **III:** 116

"Birmingham Sunday" (Hughes), **Supp. I Part 1:** 343

Birnbaum, Henry, **Supp. XII:** 128

Birnbaum, Robert, **Supp. X:** 13; **Supp. XVI:** 75

Birney, James G., **Supp. I Part 2:** 587, 588

Birstein, Ann, **Supp. VIII:** 100

"Birthday, A" (Untermeyer), **Supp. XV:** 296

Birthday Basket for Tía, A (Mora), **Supp. XIII:** 221

"Birthday Cake" (Carruth), **Supp. XVI:** 59

"Birthday Cake for Lionel, A" (Wylie), **Supp. I Part 2:** 721

"Birthday Girl: 1950" (McCarriston), **Supp. XIV:** 261

"Birthday of Mrs. Pineda, The" (Ríos), **Supp. IV Part 2:** 542, 546

"Birthday Poem, A" (Hecht), **Supp. X:** 64

"Birthday Present, A" (Plath), **Supp. I Part 2:** 531

"Birthmark, The" (Ellison), **Retro. Supp. II:** 116; **Supp. II Part 1:** 237–238

"Birth-mark, The" (Hawthorne), **Retro. Supp. I:** 152

Birth-mark, The: Unsettling the Wilderness in American Literary History (Howe), **Supp. IV Part 2:** 422, 431, 434

Birth of a Nation, The (film), **Supp. I Part 1:** 66

Birth of a World: Bolívar in Terms of His Peoples (W. Frank), **Supp. XX:** 80

Birth of the Poet, The (Gordon), **Supp. XII:** 7

Birth of Tragedy, The (Nietzsche), **Supp. IV Part 1:** 105, 110; **Supp. IV Part 2:** 519; **Supp. VIII:** 182

"Birth of Venus, The" (Botticelli), **IV:** 410

"Birth of Venus, The" (Rukeyser), **Supp. VI:** 281

"Birthplace Revisited" (Corso), **Supp. XII:** 123

"Birthright" (McKay), **Supp. X:** 136

Bisch, Louis E., **Supp. I Part 2:** 608

Bisco, John, **Supp. XVIII:** 11

"B is for Bachelors" (M. F. K. Fisher), **Supp. XVII:** 86

Bishop, Elizabeth, **Retro. Supp. I:** 140, 296, 303; **Retro. Supp. II:** 37–56, 175, 178, 189, 233, 234, 235; **Supp. I Part 1:** 72–97, 239, 320, 326; **Supp. III Part 1:** 6, 7, 10, 18, 64, 239, 320, 326; **Supp. III Part 2:** 541, 561; **Supp. IV Part 1:** 249, 257; **Supp. IV Part 2:** 439, 626, 639, 641, 644, 647, 651, 653; **Supp. V:** 337; **Supp. IX:** 40, 41, 45, 47, 48; **Supp. X:** 58; **Supp. XI:** 123, 136; **Supp. XIII:** 115, 348; **Supp. XV:** 20–21, 100, 101, 112, 119, 249, 251; **Supp. XVII:** 36, 76; **Supp. XXI:** 58, 84, 131

Bishop, James, Jr., **Supp. XIII:** 1, 5, 6, 7, 9, 11, 15

Bishop, John Peale, **I:** 432, 440; **II:** 81, 85, 86–87, 91, 209; **IV:** 35, 140, 427; **Retro. Supp. I:** 109; **Supp. I Part 2:** 709

Bishop, John W., **Supp. I Part 1:** 83

Bishop, Judith, **Supp. XVI:** 295

Bishop, Morris, **Supp. I Part 2:** 676

Bishop, William Thomas, **Supp. I Part 1:** 83

"Bishop Orders His Tomb at St. Praxed's Church, The" (R. Browning), **Supp. XV:** 127

"Bishop's Beggar, The" (Benét), **Supp. XI:** 56

"Bismarck" (Chapman), **Supp. XIV:** 52, 53

Bismark, Otto von, **Supp. I Part 2:** 643

"Bistro Styx, The" (Dove), **Supp. IV Part 1:** 250–251

Bitov, Andrei, **Retro. Supp. I:** 278

Bits of Gossip (R. H. Davis), **Supp. XVI:** 82–83, 84, 85, 89

"Bitter Drink, The" (Dos Passos), **Supp. I Part 2:** 647

"Bitter Farce, A" (Schwartz), **Supp. II Part 2:** 640, 657–658

"Bitter Pills for the Dark Ladies" (Jong), **Supp. V:** 118

Bitterroot (Burke), **Supp. XIV:** 34, 35

"Bittersweet Nightshade" (Skloot), **Supp. XX:** 202

Bitter Victory (Hardy; Kinnell, trans.), **Supp. III Part 1:** 235

Bittner, William, **Supp. XX:** 74, **Supp. XX:** 77, 76, 78, 80

Bitzer, G. W. "Billy", **Supp. XVI:** 183

Bixby, Horace, **IV:** 194

Bjerre, Thomas Aervold, **Supp. XXI:** 41, 47

Bjorkman, Frances Maule, **Supp. V:** 285

Bjorkman, Stig, **Supp. XV:** 6

Björnson, Björnstjerne, **II:** 275

Black, Cheryl, **Supp. XXI:** 6

Black 100, The (Salley), **Supp. XIV:** 195

Blackamerican Literature, 1760-Present (R. Miller), **Supp. X:** 324

Black American Literature Forum, **Supp. XI:** 86, 92, 93

Black and Blue (Quindlen), **Supp. XVII:** 166, **176–178**

"Black and Tan" (Bell), **Supp. X:** 9

Black and White (Sorrentino), **Supp. XXI:** 228

Black Armour (Wylie), **Supp. I Part 2:** 708, 709, 712–714, 729

"Black Art" (Baraka), **Supp. II Part 1:** 49, 50–51, 59, 60

"Black Art, The" (Sexton), **Supp. II Part 2:** 682

"Black Ball, The" (Ellison), **Retro. Supp. II:** 124

Black Bart and the Sacred Hills (Wilson), **Supp. VIII:** 330, 331

Black Beetles in Amber (Bierce), **I:** 204, 209

"Blackberries" (Komunyakaa), **Supp. XIII:** 126

"Blackberry Eating" (Kinnell), **Supp. III Part 1:** 250

"Blackberrying" (D. West), **Supp. XVIII:** 283

Blackberry Winter (Warren), **IV:** 243, 251, 252

Black Betty (Mosley), **Supp. XIII:** 237, **Supp. XIII:** 240, 243

"Black Birch in Winter, A" (Wilbur), **Supp. III Part 2:** 561

Black Boy (Wright), **IV:** 477, 478, 479, 480–482, 488, 489, 494; **Retro. Supp. II:** 117; **Supp. II Part 1:** 235–236; **Supp. IV Part 1:** 11; **Supp. XVIII:** 286

"Black Boys and Native Sons" (Howe), **Retro. Supp. II:** 112

Blackburn, Alex, **Supp. XIII:** 112

Blackburn, William, **IV:** 100

"Black Buttercups" (Clampitt), **Supp. IX:** 42

Black Cargo, The (Marquand), **III:** 55, 60

Black Cargoes: A History of the Atlantic Slave Trade (Cowley), **Supp. II Part 1:** 140

"Black Cat, The" (Poe), **III:** 413, 414, 415; **Retro. Supp. II:** 264, 267, 269, 270

Black Cherry Blues (Burke), **Supp. XIV:** 30

"Black Christ, The" (Cullen), **Supp. IV Part 1:** 170, 171–172

Black Christ and Other Poems, The (Cullen), **Supp. IV Part 1:** 166, 170

"Black Clay Fish from Oaxaca, A" (Bronk), **Supp. XXI:** 31

"Black Cottage, The" (Frost), **Retro. Supp. I:** 128

"BLACK DADA NIHILISMUS" (Baraka), **Supp. II Part 1:** 39, 41

"Black Death" (Hurston), **Supp. VI:** 153

Black Dog, Red Dog (Dobyns), **Supp. XIII:** 87, **88–89**

"Black Dog, Red Dog" (Dobyns), **Supp. XIII:** 89

"Black Earth" (Moore), **III:** 197, 212

Black Echo, The (Connelly), **Supp. XXI:** 67, 68, 75, 80

Black Fire (Jones and Neal, eds.), **Supp. X:** 324, 328

Black Fire: An Anthology of Afro American Writing (Baraka, ed.), **Supp. II Part 1:** 53

Black Flame, The (Du Bois), **Supp. II Part 1:** 159, 185–186

Black Folk, Then and Now: An Essay in the History and Sociology of the Negro Race (Du Bois), **Supp. II Part 1:** 159, 178, 183, 185

"Black Fox, The" (Whittier), **Supp. I Part 2:** 692

Black Freckles (Levis), **Supp. XI:** 257, 271

"Black Gang", **IV:** 406, 407

Black Genius (Mosley, ed.), **Supp. XIII:** 246

"Black Hood, The" (Francis), **Supp. IX:** 83, 91

Black House, The (Theroux), **Supp. VIII:** 319

Black Humor (Johnson), **Supp. VI:** 187, 199

Black Ice, The (Connelly), **Supp. XXI:** 70, 75

Black Image in the White Mind, The (Fredrickson), **Supp. I Part 2:** 589

"Black Is My Favorite Color" (Malamud), **Supp. I Part 2:** 437

Black Jacobins, The (C. L. R. James), **Supp. XXI:** 159, 166–167

"Black Jewel, The" (Merwin), **Supp. III Part 1:** 355

Black Lamb and Grey Falcon (R. West), **Supp. XVI:** 152

"Blacklegs" (B. Kelly), **Supp. XVII:** 131

Black Light (Kinnell), **Supp. III Part 1:** 235, 243

"Blacklist and the Cold War, The" (Kramer), **Supp. I Part 1:** 295

Black Literature in America (Baker), **Supp. X:** 324

Black Magic, A Pictorial History of the Negro in American Entertainment (Hughes), **Supp. I Part 1:** 345

Black Magic: Collected Poetry 1961–1967 (Baraka), **Supp. II Part 1:** 45, 49–50

"Blackmailers Don't Shoot" (Chandler), **Supp. IV Part 1:** 121–122

Black Manhattan (Johnson), **Supp. IV Part 1:** 169

Black Mass, A (Baraka), **Supp. II Part 1:** 46, 48–49, 56, 57

"Black Mesa, The" (Merrill), **Supp. III Part 1:** 328

Black Metropolis (Cayton and Drake), **IV:** 475, 486, 488

Black Misery (Hughes), **Supp. I Part 1:** 336

Blackmur, Helen Dickson (Mrs. R. P. Blackmur), **Supp. II Part 1:** 90

Blackmur, Richard P., **I:** 50, 63, 67, 280, 282, 386, 455, 472; **II:** 320, 537; **III:** 194, 208, 462, 478, 497; **Supp. II Part 1:** 87–112, 136; **Supp. II Part 2:** 543, 643; **Supp. XII:** 45

Black Music (Baraka), **Supp. II Part 1:** 47, 51

Black Nativity (Hughes), **Retro. Supp. I:** 196

Black No More (Schuyler), **Supp. XVI:** 142; **Supp. XIX:** 73

Black on Black: "Baby Sister" and Selected Writings (C. Himes), **Supp. XVI:** 145

"Blackout" (Hay), **Supp. XIV:** 121

"Black Panther" (Hughes), **Retro. Supp. I:** 211

"Black Petal" (L.-Y. Lee), **Supp. XV:** 224–225

Black Power (Wright), **IV:** 478, 488, 494

"Black Rainbow, A: Modern Afro-American Poetry" (Dove and Waniek), **Supp. IV Part 1:** 244

Black Reconstruction (Du Bois), **Supp. II Part 1:** 159, 162, 171, 182

Black Riders and Other Lines, The (Crane), **I:** 406, 419

Black Riviera, The (Jarman), **Supp. XVII:** 109, 110, **115–116**

"Black Rook in Rainy Weather" (Plath), **Supp. I Part 2:** 543, 544

Blacks (Brooks), **Supp. III Part 1:** 69, 72, 86, 87

Blacks, The (Genet), **Supp. IV Part 1:** 8

Black Skin, White Masks (Fanon), **Retro. Supp. II:** 118

Black Sleuth, The (J. Bruce), **Supp. XVI:** 143

Black Spear, The (Hayden), **Supp. II Part 1:** 375

Black Spring (H. Miller), **III:** 170, 175, 178, 180–182, 183, 184; **Supp. X:** 187

"Black Stone Lying on a White Stone" (Vallejo), **Supp. XIII:** 324

Black Sun (Abbey), **Supp. XIII:** 4, **8–9,** 17

"Black Swan" (B. Kelly), **Supp. XVII:** 130–131

"Black Swan, The" (Jarrell), **II:** 382

Black Swan, The (Merrill), **Supp. III Part 1:** 319, 320

"Black Tambourine" (Crane), **I:** 387–388; **II:** 371

"Black Tuesday" (Swenson), **Supp. IV Part 2:** 646

Black Voices (Chapman), **IV:** 485

"Blackwater Mountain" (Wright), **Supp. V:** 335, 340

"Black Wedding, The" (Singer), **IV:** 12–13

Blackwell, Alice Stone, **Supp. XI:** 195, 197

Blackwell, Elizabeth, **Retro. Supp. II:** 146

Black Woman, The (Bambara, ed.), **Supp. XI:** 1

"Black Workers" (Hughes), **Retro. Supp. I:** 202

"Black Writer and the Southern Experience, The" (Walker), **Supp. III Part 2:** 521

Black Zodiac (Wright), **Supp. V:** 333, 344, 345

Blade Runner (film), **Supp. XI:** 84

Blades, John, **Supp. XX:**87

"Blades of Steel" (R. Fisher), **Supp. XIX:** 72

Blaine, Anita McCormick, **Supp. I Part 1:** 5

Blaine, Nell, **Supp. XV:** 179

Blair, Hugh, **II:** 8, 17; **Supp. I Part 2:** 422

Blair, Robert, **Supp. I Part 1:** 150

Blair, Walter, **II:** 20; **Retro. Supp. II:** 286

Blaisdell, Gus, **Supp. XIV:** 87

Blake, Casey Nelson, **Supp. XX:**69, 70, 78

Blake, William, **I:** 381, 383, 389, 390, 398, 447, 476, 525, 526, 533; **II:** 321; **III:** 5, 19, 22, 195, 196, 197, 205, 485, 528, 540, 544–545, 567, 572; **IV:** 129; **Retro. Supp. II:** 76, 300; **Supp. I Part 1:** 80; **Supp. I Part 2:** 385, 514, 517, 539, 552, 708; **Supp. V:** 208, 257, 258; **Supp. VIII:** 26, 99, 103; **Supp. X:** 120; **Supp. XII:** 45; **Supp. XIV:** 344; **Supp. XVI:** 282; **Supp. XVII:** 119; **Supp. XX:**115, 116

Blakely, Barbara, **Supp. XIII:** 32

Blanc, Marie Thérèse, **Retro. Supp. II:** 135

Blanc-Bentzon, Mme. Thérèse, **II:** 405

Blanchard, Paula, **Retro. Supp. II:** 131, 133–134, 135

Blanche, Jacques-Émile, **Supp. XX:**232

Blanchot, Maurice, **Supp. XVI:** 288

Blancs, Les (Hansberry), **Supp. IV Part 1:** 359, 364, 365, 369, 372–374

Blancs, Les: The Collected Last Plays of Lorraine Hansberry (Nemiroff, ed.), **Supp. IV Part 1:** 365, 368, 374

"'Blandula, Tenulla, Vagula'" (Pound), **III:** 463; **Supp. V:** 336, 337, 345

Blankenship, Tom, **IV:** 193

"Blank Paper" (Peacock), **Supp. XIX:** 198–199

Blanshard, Rufus A., **I:** 67

Blassingame, John, **Supp. XX:**106

Blauvelt, William Satake, **Supp. V:** 171, 173

Blavatsky, Elena Petrovna, **III:** 176

"Blazing in Gold and Quenching in Purple" (Dickinson), **Retro. Supp. I:** 30

Bleak House (Dickens), **II:** 291; **Supp. IV Part 1:** 293

Blechman, Burt, **Supp. I Part 1:** 290

"Bleeder" (Dobyns), **Supp. XIII:** 88

"Bleeding" (Swenson), **Supp. IV Part 2:** 646–647

"Blessed Is the Man" (Moore), **III:** 215

"Blessed Man of Boston, My Grandmother's Thimble, and Fanning Island, The" (Updike), **IV:** 219

"Blessing, A" (Wright), **Supp. III Part 2:** 600, 606

Blessing on the Moon, A (Skibell), **Supp. XVII:** 48

Blessings (Quindlen), **Supp. XVII:** 167, **178–179**

"Blessing the Animals" (Komunyakaa), **Supp. XIII:** 129–130

"Blessing the Children" (Hogan), **Supp. IV Part 1:** 401

Bless Me, Ultima (Anya), **Supp. XIII:** 220

Blew, Mary Clearman, **Supp. XIV:** 227

Bligh, S. M., **I:** 226

Blind Alleys (film), **Supp. XXI:** 146

Blind Assassin, The (Atwood), **Supp. XIII:** 20, **32**

Blind Bow-Boy, The (Van Vechten), **Supp. II Part 2:** 737, 740–742

"Blind Date" (Halliday), **Supp. XIX:** 85

Blind Date (Kosinski), **Supp. VII:** 215, 224–225

"Blinded by the Light" (Boyle), **Supp. XX:**20

Blind Lion, The (Gunn Allen), **Supp. IV Part 1:** 324

"Blind Man's Holiday" (O. Henry), **Supp. II Part 1:** 401

Blind Man with a Pistol (C. Himes), **Supp. XVI:** 143, 144

Blindness and Insight (de Man), **Retro. Supp. I:** 67

"Blind Poet, The: Sidney Lanier" (Warren), **Supp. I Part 1:** 371, 373

"Blind Tom" (R. H. Davis), **Supp. XVI:** 89, 90

Blithedale Romance, The (Hawthorne), **II:** 225, 231, 239, 241–242, 271, 282, 290; **IV:** 194; **Retro. Supp. I:** 63, 149, 152, 156–157, **162–163; Supp. I Part 2:** 579; **Supp. II Part 1:** 280; **Supp. VIII:** 153, 201

Blitzstein, Marc, **Supp. I Part 1:** 277

Blix (Norris), **III:** 314, 322, 327, 328, 333

Blixen, Karen Denisen Baroness. *See* Dinesen, Isak

"Blizzard in Cambridge" (Lowell), **II:** 554

Blizzard Voices, The (Kooser), **Supp. XIX: 123**

Bloch, Ernest, **Supp. XX:75**

Block, Lawrence, **Supp. XXI: 67**

Blok, Aleksandr Aleksandrovich, **IV: 443**

"Blond" (Trethewey), **Supp. XXI: 244**

Blonde Bait (Lacy), **Supp. XV: 204**

Blonde on Blonde (album, Dylan), **Supp. XVIII: 20, 27, 30**

Blondin, Antoine, **Supp. XVI: 230**

"Blood" (Hoffman), **Supp. XVIII: 86**

"Blood" (Singer), **IV: 15, 19**

Blood, Tin, Straw (Olds), **Supp. X: 212–215**

Blood and Guile (Hoffman), **Supp. XVIII: 83–84**

Blood and Guts in High School (Acker), **Supp. XII: 5, 6, 11–12**

"Blood Bay, The" (Proulx), **Supp. VII: 262–263**

"Blood-Burning Moon" (Toomer), **Supp. III Part 2: 483; Supp. IX: 314–315**

"Bloodchild" (O. Butler), **Supp. XIII: 61, 69–70**

Bloodchild and Other Stories (O. Butler), **Supp. XIII: 69**

"Blood Donor" (Hay), **Supp. XIV: 121**

Blood for a Stranger (Jarrell), **II: 367, 368–369, 370–371, 375, 377**

Blood Issue (Crews), **Supp. XI: 103**

Bloodlines (Wright), **Supp. V: 332, 335, 340**

Blood Meridian; or, The Evening Redness in the West (McCarthy), **Supp. VIII: 175, 177, 180–182, 188, 190**

Blood of My Blood (Gambino), **Supp. XX:35**

"Blood of the Conquistadores, The" (Alvarez), **Supp. VII: 7**

"Blood of the Lamb, The" (hymn), **Supp. I Part 2: 385**

Blood of the Martyr (Crane), **I: 422**

"Blood of the Martyrs, The" (Benét), **Supp. XI: 56, 58**

Blood of the Prophets, The (Masters), **Supp. I Part 2: 458, 459, 461**

Blood on the Forge (Attaway), **Supp. II Part 1: 234–235**

Blood on the Tracks (album, Dylan), **Supp. XVIII: 20, 27, 30**

"Blood Relatives" (Apple), **Supp. XVII: 6**

"Blood Returns, The" (Kingsolver), **Supp. VII: 209**

"Bloodshed" (C. Ozick), **Supp. XVII: 43**

Bloodshed and Three Novellas (Ozick), **Supp. V: 259–260, 261, 266–268**

"Blood Stains" (Francis), **Supp. IX: 86**

Blood Work (Connelly), **Supp. XXI: 72**

Blood Work (film, Eastwood), **Supp. XXI: 74**

Bloody Crossroads, The: Where Literature and Politics Meet (Podhoretz), **Supp. VIII: 241–242**

Bloom, Alice, **Supp. IV Part 1: 308**

Bloom, Allan, **Retro. Supp. II: 19, 30, 31, 33–34**

Bloom, Claire, **Retro. Supp. II: 281; Supp. IX: 125**

Bloom, Harold, **Retro. Supp. I: 67, 193, 299; Retro. Supp. II: 81, 210, 262; Supp. IV Part 2: 620, 689; Supp. V: 178, 272; Supp. VIII: 180; Supp. IX: 146, 259; Supp. XII: 261; Supp. XIII: 46, 47; Supp. XIV: 14; Supp. XV: 134; Supp. XVII: 70, 141**

Bloom, Larry, **Supp. XIII: 133**

Bloom, Leopold, **I: 27, 150; III: 10**

Bloom, Lynn Z., **Supp. IV Part 1: 6**

Bloomfield, Leonard, **I: 64**

Bloomingdale Papers, The (Carruth), **Supp. XVI: 48–50**

"Blossom and Fruit" (Benét), **Supp. XI: 52–53**

Blotner, Joseph, **Retro. Supp. I: 88**

Blouin, Lenora, **Supp. VIII: 266**

"Blowin' in the Wind" (song, Dylan), **Supp. XVIII: 24, 25, 26, 29**

Blue Angel (Prose), **Supp. XVI: 249, 259–260**

Blue Angel, The (film), **Supp. XVIII: 243**

"Blue Battalions, The" (Crane), **I: 419–420**

"Bluebeard" (Barthelme), **Supp. IV Part 1: 47**

"Bluebeard" (Millay), **III: 130**

"Blueberries" (Frost), **Retro. Supp. I: 121, 128**

Blue Calhoun (Price), **Supp. VI: 265–266**

Blue Caterpillar, The (Pickering), **Supp. XXI: 202–203**

Blue City (Macdonald, as Millar), **Supp. IV Part 2: 466–467**

Blue Devils of Nada, The: A Contemporary American Approach to Aesthetics (Murray), **Supp. XIX: 159–160**

Blue Estuaries, The: Poems, 1923–1968 (Bogan), **Supp. III Part 1: 48, 57, 66**

Blue Hammer, The (Macdonald), **Supp. IV Part 2: 462**

"Blue Hotel, The" (Crane), **I: 34, 415–416, 423**

"Blue Hour, The" (Komunyakaa), **Supp. XIII: 130**

Blue in the Face (Auster), **Supp. XII: 21**

Blue Jay's Dance, The: A Birth Year (Erdrich), **Supp. IV Part 1: 259–260, 265, 270, 272**

"Blue Juniata" (Cowley), **Supp. II Part 1: 144**

Blue Juniata: Collected Poems (Cowley), **Supp. II Part 1: 140**

"Blue Lick" (Offutt), **Supp. XIX: 164, 165**

Blue Light (Mosley), **Supp. XIII: 245–247, 248, 249**

"Blue Light Lounge Sutra for the Performance Poets at Harold Park Hotel" (Komunyakaa), **Supp. XIII: 125**

"Blue Meridian" (Toomer), **Supp. III Part 2: 476, 487; Supp. IX: 320**

"Blue Moles" (Plath), **Supp. I Part 2: 539**

Blue Mountain Ballads (music) (Bowles), **Supp. IV Part 1: 84**

Blue Movie (Southern), **Supp. XI: 309**

"Blue Notes" (Matthews), **Supp. IX: 169**

Blue Pastoral (Sorrentino), **Supp. XXI: 226, 235–236**

Blue Pastures (Oliver), **Supp. VII: 229–230, 245**

"Blueprint for Negro Writing" (Wright), **Supp. XVIII: 282–283**

"Blueprints" (Kingsolver), **Supp. VII: 203**

Blue Religion, The (Connelly, ed.), **Supp. XXI: 74–75, 79**

Blue Rhine, Black Forest (Untermeyer), **Supp. XV: 310**

"Blue Ribbon at Amesbury, A" (Frost), **Retro. Supp. I: 138**

"Blues Ain't No Mockin Bird" (Bambara), **Supp. XI: 3**

"Blues and the Fable in the Flesh, The" (lecture, Murray), **Supp. XIX: 153**

"Blues Chant Hoodoo Rival" (Komunyakaa), **Supp. XIII: 117, 118**

Blue Screen (Parker), **Supp. XIX: 186**

"Blues for Another Time" (Dunn), **Supp. XI: 148**

"Blues for Jimmy" (McGrath), **Supp. X: 116**

"Blues for John Coltraine, Dead at 41" (Matthews), **Supp. IX: 157**

Blues for Mister Charlie (Baldwin), **Retro. Supp. II: 8; Supp. I Part 1: 48, 61–62, 63**

"Blues for Warren" (McGrath), **Supp. X: 116**

Blue Shoe (Lamott), **Supp. XX:138–140**

Blues If You Want (Matthews), **Supp. IX: 155, 163–165**

"Blues I'm Playing, The" (Hughes), **Retro. Supp. I: 204; Supp. XIX: 75**

"Blue Sky, The" (Snyder), **Supp. VIII: 306**

"Blues on a Box" (Hughes), **Retro. Supp. I: 208**

"Blues People" (Ellison), **Retro. Supp. II: 124**

Blues People: Negro Music in White America (Baraka), **Retro. Supp. II: 124; Supp. II Part 1: 30, 31, 33–35, 37, 41, 42, 53**

"Blue Spruces in Pairs, a Bird Bath Between": (Bronk), **Supp. XXI: 30**

Bluest Eye, The (Morrison), **Supp. III Part 1: 362, 363–367, 379; Supp. IV Part 1: 2, 253; Supp. VIII: 213, 214, 227; Supp. XI: 4, 91**

Bluestone, George, **Supp. IX: 7, 15**

Blue Swallows, The (Nemerov), **III: 269, 270, 271, 274–275, 278, 284, 286–288**

"Blue Tattoo" (Nelson and Espeland), **Supp. XVIII: 181**

Blue Voyage (Aiken), **I: 53, 56**

Blum, Gustav, **Supp. XV: 194**

Blum, Morgan, **I: 169**

Blum, W. C (pseudonym). *See* Watson, James Sibley, Jr.

Blumenthal, Nathaniel. *See* Branden, Nathaniel

Blumenthal, Sidney, **Supp. VIII: 241**

Blunden, Edmund, **Supp. XIX: 133**

Blunt, Wilfrid Scawen, **III: 459**

Bly, Carol, **Supp. XVI: 31–43**

Bly, Robert, **I:** 291; **Supp. III Part 2:** 599; **Supp. IV Part 1: 59–77,** 177; **Supp. IV Part 2:** 623; **Supp. V:** 332; **Supp. VIII:** 279; **Supp. IX:** 152, 155, 265, 271, 290; **Supp. X:** 127; **Supp. XI:** 142; **Supp. XIII:** 284; **Supp. XV:** 74, 176; **Supp. XVI:** 32, 36, 39, 177, 212, 230; **Supp. XVII:** 243, 244; **Supp. XXI:** 83, 84–86, 87, 91, 93, 94, 95

"B Negative" (X. J. Kennedy), **Supp. XV: 156–157**

"Boarder, The" (Simpson), **Supp. IX:** 269

Boarding House Blues (Farrell), **II:** 30, 43, 45

Boas, Franz, **I:** 214; **Supp. I Part 2:** 641; **Supp. VIII:** 295; **Supp. IX:** 329; **Supp. XIV:** 199, 209, 210

"Boat, The" (Oliver), **Supp. VII:** 247

"Boat, The" (Sexton), **Supp. II Part 2:** 692

Boating Party, The (Renoir), **Supp. XII:** 188

Boat of Quiet Hours, The (Kenyon), **Supp. VII:** 167–169, 171

"Boat of Quiet Hours, The" (Kenyon), **Supp. VII:** 168

"Bob and Spike" (Wolfe), **Supp. III Part 2:** 580

"Bobby Shafter's Gone to Sea" (Swados), **Supp. XIX:** 267

"Bob Dylan's 115th Dream" (song, Dylan), **Supp. XVIII:** 25

Bobrowski, Johannes, **Supp. XV:** 78

Bob the Gambler (F. Barthelme), **Supp. XI:** 30, 31, 32, 34–35, 36–37

Boccaccio, Giovanni, **III:** 283, 411; **IV:** 230

Bocock, Maclin, **Supp. X:** 79

Bodelson, Anders, **Supp. XVI:** 33

Bodenheim, Maxwell, **II:** 42, 530; **Retro. Supp. I:** 417; **Supp. I Part 1:** 257

"Bodies" (Oates), **Supp. II Part 2:** 520

"Bodies and Souls: The Haitian Revolution and Madison Smartt Bell's *All Souls' Rising*" (Trouillot), **Supp. X:** 14

Bodies of Work: Essays (Acker), **Supp. XII:** 7

Bodily Harm (Atwood), **Supp. XIII: 25–27**

Bodley Head Jack London (London), **II:** 483

Body (Crews), **Supp. XI: 108–109**

"Body, The" (Heldreth), **Supp. V:** 151

Body and Soul (Conroy), **Supp. XVI:** 63, **72–74,** 77

"Body and Soul: A Meditation" (Kumin), **Supp. IV Part 2:** 442, 452

Body and Soul: Essays on Poetry (Jarman), **Supp. XVII:** 110, **111–112**

"Body and Soul: Parts of a Life" (Jarman), **Supp. XVII:** 112, 113

Body and the Song, The (Bishop), **Retro. Supp. II:** 40

"Body Bright" (Sanders), **Supp. XVI:** 276

Body of Martin Aquilera, The (Everett), **Supp. XVIII:** 57

Body of Poetry, The: Essays on Women, Form, and the Poetic Self (A. Finch), **Supp. XVII:** 69–70, **77–78**

Body of This Death: Poems (Bogan), **Supp. III Part 1:** 47, 49–52, 58

Body of Waking (Rukeyser), **Supp. VI:** 274, 281

"Body of Waking" (Rukeyser), **Supp. VI:** 279

"Body on Fire, the Soul in Flight, The" (Jarman), **Supp. XVII:** 111, 112

Body Rags (Kinnell), **Supp. III Part 1:** 235, 236, 243–245, 250, 253, 254

"Body's Curse, The" (Dobyns), **Supp. XIII:** 87

"Body's Weight" (Espaillat), **Supp. XXI:** 111

"Body's Weight, The" (Dobyns), **Supp. XIII:** 89

Body Traffic (Dobyns), **Supp. XIII:** 87, 89

"'Body with the Lamp Lit Inside, The'" (Mills), **Supp. IV Part 1:** 64

Boehm, David, **Supp. XVII:** 58

Boehme, Jakob, **I:** 10

Bogan, Louise, **I:** 169, 185; **Retro. Supp. I:** 36; **Supp. I Part 2:** 707, 726; **Supp. III Part 1: 47–68; Supp. VIII:** 171, 265; **Supp. IX:** 229; **Supp. X:** 58, 102; **Supp. XIII:** 347; **Supp. XIV:** 129; **Supp. XVII:** 75

Bogan, Major Benjamin Lewis, **IV:** 120

Bogart, Humphrey, **Supp. I Part 2:** 623; **Supp. IV Part 1:** 130, 356

Bogdanovich, Peter, **Supp. V:** 226

Bogey Man, The (Plimpton), **Supp. XVI:** 241

Boggs, Francis W., **Supp. XVI:** 182

"Bogs" (Pickering), **Supp. XXI:** 198

"Bohemian, The" (Hapgood), **Supp. XVII:** 103

"Bohemian, The" (Harte), **Supp. II Part 1:** 339

"Bohemian Girl, The" (Cather), **Retro. Supp. I:** 7

"Bohemian Hymn, The" (Emerson), **II:** 19

"Bohemians" (Saunders), **Supp. XIX:** 234

"Boids and Beasties" (Geisel), **Supp. XVI:** 100

Boissevain, Eugen, **III:** 124

Boissière, Ralph de, **Supp. XXI:** 160

Boit, Edward, **Retro. Supp. I:** 366

Bojorquez, Jennifer, **Supp. XII:** 318

Boker, George, **Supp. XV:** 269

"Bold Words at the Bridge" (Jewett), **II:** 394

Boleslavsky, Richard, **Supp. XIV:** 240, 243

Boleyn, Anne, **Supp. I Part 2:** 461

Bolick, Katie, **Supp. XVI:** 167

Bolivar, Simon, **Supp. I Part 1:** 283, 284, 285

Bolonik, Kera, **Supp. XVIII:** 60

Bolton, Guy, **Supp. I Part 1:** 281

Bolts of Melody: New Poems of Emily Dickinson (Todd and Bingham, eds.), **I:** 470; **Retro. Supp. I:** 36

"Bomb" (Corso), **Supp. XII:** 117, 124, 125–126, 127

Bombeck, Erma, **Supp. XVII:** 168

Bombs Away (Steinbeck), **IV:** 51–52

"Bona and Paul" (Toomer), **Supp. IX:** 307, 318–319

Bonaparte, Marie, **III:** 418; **Retro. Supp. II:** 264, 266

"Bon-Bon" (Poe), **III:** 425

Bond, The (Boyce), **Supp. XXI:** 5, **11–12**

Bond, The (N. Boyce), **Supp. XVII:** 99, 100

Bondage (Hwang), **Supp. XXI:** 147

Bondsman, The (Massinger), **Supp. XV:** 238

Bondwoman's Narrative, by Hannah Crafts, a Fugitive Slave, Recently Escaped from North Carolina, The, **Supp. XX:** 105

Bone, Robert, **Supp. IX:** 318–319; **Supp. XI:** 283; **Supp. XVIII:** 285

Bone by Bone (Matthiessen), **Supp. V:** 199, 212, 213, 214

"Bone Deposit" (Ray), **Supp. XVIII:** 194

Boners (Abingdon). *See Schoolboy Howlers* (Abingdon)

"Bones" (Goldbarth), **Supp. XII: 173–174**

"Bones and Jewels" (Monette), **Supp. X:** 159

"Bones and Shells" (Sanders), **Supp. XVI:** 271–272

"Bones of a House" (Cowley). *See* "Blue Juniata"

Bones on Black Spruce Mountain, The (Budbill), **Supp. XIX: 11–12**

Bonetti, Kay, **Supp. VIII:** 47, 152, 159, 160, 165, 168, 170, 223; **Supp. XII:** 61; **Supp. XIV:** 232, 234; **Supp. XXI:** 36

Bonfire of the Vanities, The (Wolfe), **Supp. III Part 2:** 584–586

Bonheur, Rosa, **Supp. XV:** 276

Bonhoeffer, Dietrich, **Supp. VIII:** 198

Boni, Charles, **Supp. XIV:** 288

Boni and Liveright, **Retro. Supp. I:** 59, 80, 178

Bonicelli, Vittorio, **Supp. XI:** 307

Bonifacius (Mather), **Supp. II Part 2:** 461, 464

Bonnefoy, Yves, **Supp. III Part 1:** 235, 243

Bonner, Robert, **Retro. Supp. I:** 246

Bonneville, Mme. Marguerite, **Supp. I Part 2:** 520, 521

Bonneville, Nicolas de, **Supp. I Part 2:** 511, 518, 519

Bonney, William. *See* Billy the Kid

Bontemps, Arna, **Retro. Supp. I:** 194, 196, 203; **Supp. I Part 1:** 325; **Supp. IV Part 1:** 170; **Supp. IX:** 306, 309; **Supp. XVIII:** 282

Book, A (Barnes), **Supp. III Part 1:** 36, 39, 44

Book about Myself, A (Dreiser), **I:** 515; **Retro. Supp. II:** 104

"Book as a Container of Consciousness, The" (Gass), **Supp. VI:** 92

Booker, Keith, **Supp. XV:** 197

"Bookies, Beware!" (Heller), **Supp. IV Part 1:** 383

"Book Notes and News" (column, Boyce), **Supp. XXI:** 2

Book of American Negro Poetry, The (Johnson), **Supp. IV Part 1:** 165, 166

Book of Americans, A (Benét), **Supp. XI:** 46, 47, 51

Book of Beb, The (Buechner), **Supp. XII:** 53

Book of Breeething, The (Burroughs), **Supp. III Part 1:** 97, 103

Book of Burlesques, A (Mencken), **III:** 104

Book of Common Prayer, A (Didion), **Supp. IV Part 1:** 196, 198, 203–205, 207, 208

Book of Daniel, The (Doctorow), **Supp. IV Part 1:** 218, 219, 220–222, 227, 231, 237–238, 238; **Supp. V:** 45

Book of Dreams (Kerouac), **Supp. III Part 1:** 225

"Book of Ephraim, The" (Merrill), **Supp. III Part 1:** 330–334

Book of Folly, The (Sexton), **Supp. II Part 2:** 691, 692–694

Book of Gods and Devils, The (Simic), **Supp. VIII:** 281

Book of Guys, The (Keillor), **Supp. XVI:** 177

"Book of Hours of Sister Clotilde, The" (Lowell), **II:** 522

Book of Jamaica, The (Banks), **Supp. V:** 11, 12, 16

"Book of Life" (Bidart), **Supp. XV:** 23

Book of Living Verse, The; English and American Poetry from the Thirteenth Century to the Present Day (Untermeyer, ed.), **Supp. XV:** 310

Book of Love, A (Vildrac; Bynner, trans.), **Supp. XV:** 50

Book of Lyrics (Bynner), **Supp. XV:** 51

Book of Medicines, The (Hogan), **Supp. IV Part 1:** 397, 410, 411–414

"Book of Medicines, The" (Hogan), **Supp. IV Part 1:** 412, 413

"Book of Memory, The" (Auster), **Supp. XII:** 21–22

Book of My Nights (L.-Y. Lee), **Supp. XV:** 215, **223–226**

Book of Negro Folklore, The (Hughes, ed.), **Supp. I Part 1:** 345

Book of Nightmares, The (Kinnell), **Supp. III Part 1:** 235, 236, 243, 244, 246–254

Book of One's Own, A: People and Their Diaries (Mallon), **Supp. XIX:** 134

Book of Prefaces, A (Mencken), **III:** 99–100, 105

Book of Repulsive Women, The (Barnes), **Supp. III Part 1:** 33

Book of Roses, The (Parkman), **Supp. II Part 2:** 597, 598

Book of the Body, The (Bidart), **Supp. XV:** 21, **25–27**

"Book of the Dead, The" (Rukeyser), **Supp. VI:** 272, 278, 279; **Supp. XV:** 349

"Book of the Grotesque, The" (Anderson), **I:** 106

Book of the Homeless, The (Wharton), **Retro. Supp. I:** 377

Book of the Hopi (Waters), **Supp. X:** 124

Book of Tobit (Bible), **Supp. XII:** 54

Book of Verses, A (Masters), **Supp. I Part 2:** 458

Book of Yaak, The (Bass), **Supp. XVI:** **18–19**

"Book of Yolek, The" (Hecht), **Supp. X:** 69, **70–71**

"Books" (Collins), **Supp. XXI:** 55

"Books Considered" (Bloom), **Supp. I Part 1:** 96

"Books I Left Behind, The" (Pickering), **Supp. XXI:** 196

Books in My Life, The (H. Miller), **II:** 176, 189

"Books/P,L,E, The" (Goldbarth), **Supp. XII:** 190

Bookviews, **Supp. XI:** 216

"Book World Live", **Supp. XVIII:** 143–144

"Boolean Algebra: $X^{2=X}$" (Bronk), **Supp. XXI:** 30

"Boom" (Nemerov), **III:** 278

Boom! (T. Williams), **IV:** 383

Boomer Girls: Poems by Women of the Baby Boom Generation (Gemin and Sergi, eds.), **Supp. XXI:** 246

Boom Town (Wolfe), **IV:** 456

"Boom Town" (Wolfe), **IV:** 469

Boone, Daniel, **II:** 207; **III:** 444; **IV:** 192, 193

Boorstin, Daniel, **I:** 253

Booth, Charles, **Supp. I Part 1:** 13

Booth, John Wilkes, **III:** 588

Booth, Philip, **I:** 522; **Supp. IX:** 269; **Supp. XI:** 141; **Supp. XIII:** 277; **Supp. XV:** 92

Booth, General William, **Supp. I Part 2:** 384, 386

Borah, William, **III:** 475

Borden, Lizzie, **II:** 5

Borderlands/La Frontera: The New Mestiza (Anzaldúa), **Supp. XIII:** 223

Border Matters (Saldívar), **Supp. XIX:** 112–113

Borders (Mora), **Supp. XIII:** 213, **215–217**

Border Trilogy (McCarthy), **Supp. VIII:** 175, 182

"Border View, Hot Springs, Texas" (W. V. Davis), **Supp. XXI:** 95

Borel, Pétrus, **III:** 320

Borges, Jorge Luis, **I:** 123, 135, 138, 140, 142; **Supp. III Part 2:** 560; **Supp. IV Part 2:** 623, 626, 630; **Supp. V:** 238; **Supp. VIII:** 15, 348, 349; **Supp. XII:** 21, 147; **Supp. XV:** 34; **Supp. XVI:** 201, 206; **Supp. XVII:** 47; **Supp. XIX:** 131

"Borges and I" (Bidart), **Supp. XV:** 34, 35

"Borinken Blues" (Komunyakaa), **Supp. XIII:** 117

"Born, The" (Lamott), **Supp. XX:** 143–144

"Born a Square: The Westerner's Dilemma" (Stegner), **Supp. IV Part 2:** 595; **Supp. V:** 224

"Born Bad" (Cisneros), **Supp. VII:** 62

Born on the Fourth of July (Kovic), **Supp. XIX:** 17

"Borough of Cemeteries" (Shaw), **Supp. XIX:** 246

Borrowed Time: An AIDS Memoir (Monette), **Supp. X:** 145, 146, 147, 152, 154, 155

"Bosque del Apache Wildlife Refuge" (Mora), **Supp. XIII:** 218

Boss Dog, The: A Story of Provence (M. F. K. Fisher), **Supp. XVII:** 91

"Boston" (Hardwick), **Supp. III Part 1:** 201

Boston (Sinclair), **Supp. V:** 282, 288–289

Boston, B. H., **Supp. XIII:** 312

Boston Adventure (Stafford), **Retro. Supp. II:** 177, 178

"Boston Common" (Berryman), **I:** 172

"Boston Hymn" (Emerson), **II:** 13, 19

Bostonians, The (H. James), **I:** 9; **II:** 282; **IV:** 202; **Retro. Supp. I:** 216, 225

Boston Marriage (Mamet), **Supp. XIV:** 247

"Boston Nativity, The" (Lowell), **II:** 538

Boswell, James, **IV:** 431; **Supp. I Part 2:** 656

Boswell: A Modern Comedy (Elkin), **Supp. VI:** 42, **44–45**, 57

Bosworth, Patricia, **Supp. IV Part 2:** 573, 591

"Bothersome Sex and O'Brien, The" (Ryan as Quin), **Supp. XVIII:** 238

Botticelli (McNally), **Supp. XIII:** 197

Botticelli, Sandro, **IV:** 410; **Retro. Supp. I:** 422

"Botticellian Trees, The" (W. C. Williams), **Retro. Supp. I:** 422

"Bottle of Milk for Mother, A" (Algren), **Supp. IX:** 3

"Bottle of Perrier, A" (Wharton), **IV:** 316

"Bottles" (Kenyon), **Supp. VII:** 171

"Bottom Line, The" (Elkin), **Supp. VI:** 52, **53**

Bottom: On Shakespeare (Zukofsky), **Supp. III Part 2:** 622, 624, 625, 626, 627, 629

Boublil, Alain, **Supp. XXI:** 155

Boucher, Anthony, **Supp. IV Part 2:** 473; **Supp. XV:** 203, 205

Boughton, Henrietta Breckenridge. *See* Young, Barbara

Boukreev, Anatoli, **Supp. XVIII:** 112

Boulanger, Nadia, **Supp. IV Part 1:** 81

"Boulot and Boulette" (Chopin), **Supp. I Part 1:** 211

Boulton, Agnes, **III:** 403

Bound East for Cardiff (O'Neill), **III:** 388

Bound for Glory (Guthrie), **Supp. XVIII:** 23

"Bounty" (Saunders), **Supp. XIX:** 226, 227

"Bouquet, The" (Stevens), **IV:** 90

"Bouquet of Roses in Sunlight" (Stevens), **IV:** 93

Bourdin, Henri L., **Supp. I Part 1:** 251

Bourgeois Poet, The (Shapiro), **Supp. II Part 2:** 701, 703, 704, 713, 714–716

Bourget, James, **IV:** 319

Bourget, Paul, **II:** 325, 338; **IV:** 311, 315; **Retro. Supp. I:** 224, 359, 373; **Supp. XX:**232

Bourjaily, Vance, **III:** 43; **Supp. IX:** 260

Bourke-White, Margaret, **I:** 290, 293, 295, 297

Bourne, Charles Rogers, **I:** 215

Bourne, Mrs. Charles Rogers, **I:** 215

Bourne, Randolph, **I:** 214–238, 243, 245, 246–247, 251, 259; **Supp. I Part 2:** 524; **Supp. XV:** 141, 298, 301

Boursicot, Bernard, **Supp. XXI:** 152, 153, 154

Bouton, Jim "Bulldog", **Supp. XX:**274

Bowden, Charles, **Supp. XIII:** 17

Bowditch, Nathaniel, **Supp. I Part 2:** 482

Bowen, Barbara, **Supp. IX:** 311

Bowen, Elizabeth, **Retro. Supp. I:** 351; **Supp. IV Part 1:** 299; **Supp. VIII:** 65, 165, 251, 265; **Supp. IX:** 128

Bowen, Francis, **Supp. I Part 2:** 413

Bowen, Henry, **Supp. XVIII:** 4

Bowen, Louise de Koven, **Supp. I Part 1:** 5

Bowen, Michael, **Supp. VIII:** 73

Bowers, John, **Supp. XI:** 217–218

"Bowlers Anonymous" (Dobyns), **Supp. XIII:** 86

Bowles, Emily, **Supp. XVIII:** 200, 202

Bowles, Jane (Jane Auer), **II:** 586; **Supp. IV Part 1:** 89, 92

Bowles, Paul, **I:** 211; **II:** 586; **Supp. II Part 1:** 17; **Supp. IV Part 1:** 79–99

Bowles, Samuel, **I:** 454, 457; **Retro. Supp. I:** 30, 32, 33

"Bowl of Blood, The" (Jeffers), **Supp. II Part 2:** 434

"Bowls" (Moore), **III:** 196

Bowman, James, **I:** 193

"Bows to Drouth" (Snyder), **Supp. VIII:** 303

Box, Edgar (pseudonym). *See* Vidal, Gore

Box and Quotations from Chairman Mao Tse-tung (Albee), **I:** 89–91, 94

Boxer and the Spy, The (Parker), **Supp. XIX:** 190

Box Garden, The (Shields), **Supp. VII:** 314–315, 320

"Box of Pastels, A" (Kooser), **Supp. XIX:** 128

"Box Seat" (Toomer), **Supp. III Part 2:** 484; **Supp. IX:** 316, 318

Boy, A (Ashbery), **Supp. III Part 1:** 5

"Boy and Dog" (L. Brown), **Supp. XXI:** 38, 42, **43–44**

Boyce, Horace, **II:** 136

Boyce, Neith, **Supp. XVII:** 96, 97, 98–99, 100, 106; **Supp. XXI:** 1–16

Boyd, Brian, **Retro. Supp. I:** 270, 275

Boyd, Janet L., **Supp. X:** 229

Boyd, Nancy (pseudonym). *See* Millay, Edna St. Vincent

Boyd, Thomas, **I:** 99; **IV:** 427

Boyesen, H. H., **II:** 289

"Boyhood" (Collins), **Supp. XXI:** 64

"Boyhood" (Farrell), **II:** 28

"Boy in France, A" (Salinger), **III:** 552–553

Boy in the Water (Dobyns), **Supp. XIII:** 75, **84**

Boyle, Kay, **IV:** 404

Boyle, T. Coraghessan, **Supp. VIII:** 1–17; **Supp. XX:**17–32; **Supp. XXI:** 226

Boyle, Thomas John. *See* Boyle, T. C.

Boynton, H. W., **Supp. IX:** 7

Boynton, Percy Holmes, **Supp. I Part 2:** 415

Boynton, Robert, **Supp. XVII:** 209; **Supp. XVIII:** 105, 107, 116

"Boy on a Train" (Ellison), **Retro. Supp. II:** 124

"Boy Riding Forward Backward" (Francis), **Supp. IX:** 82

"Boys and Girls" (Cisneros), **Supp. VII:** 59–60

Boy's Froissart, The (Lanier), **Supp. I Part 1:** 361

Boy's King Arthur, The (Lanier), **Supp. I Part 1:** 361

Boy's Mabinogion, The (Lanier), **Supp. I Part 1:** 361

"Boys of '29, The" (Holmes), **Supp. I Part 1:** 308

Boys of '76, The (Coffin), **III:** 577

Boy's Percy, The (Lanier), **Supp. I Part 1:** 361

Boy's Town (Howells), **I:** 418

Boy's Will, A (Frost), **II:** 152, 153, 155–156, 159, 164, 166; **Retro. Supp. I:** 124, 127, 128, 131; **Retro. Supp. II:** 168

"Boy Up a Tree" (Hoffman), **Supp. XVIII:** 86

"Boy Who Wrestled with Angels, The" (Hoffman), **Supp. X:** 90

"Boy with One Shoe, The" (Jewett), **Retro. Supp. II:** 132

"Brace, The" (Bausch), **Supp. VII:** 48

Bracebridge Hall, or, The Humorists (Irving), **I:** 339, 341; **II:** 308–309, 313

Bracher, Frederick, **I:** 378, 380; **Supp. I Part 1:** 185

Brackenridge, Hugh Henry, **Supp. I Part 1:** 124, 127, 145; **Supp. II Part 1:** 65

Brackett, Leigh, **Supp. IV Part 1:** 130

Bradbury, John M., **I:** 288–289; **IV:** 130, 135

Bradbury, Malcolm, **Supp. VIII:** 124; **Supp. XVIII:** 140

Bradbury, Ray, **Supp. I Part 2:** 621–622; **Supp. IV Part 1:** 101–118; **Supp. XVI:** 122; **Supp. XVII:** 41

"Brad Carrigan, American" (Saunders), **Supp. XIX:** 233

Braddon, Mary E., **Supp. I Part 1:** 35, 36

Bradfield, Scott, **Supp. VIII:** 88

Bradford, Gamaliel, **I:** 248, 250

Bradford, Roark, **Retro. Supp. I:** 80

Bradford, William, **Retro. Supp. II:** 161, 162; **Supp. I Part 1:** 110, 112; **Supp. I Part 2:** 486, 494

Bradlee, Ben, **Supp. V:** 201

Bradley, Bill, **Supp. VIII:** 47

Bradley, F. H., **Retro. Supp. I:** 57, 58

Bradley, Francis Herbert, **I:** 59, 567–568, 572, 573

Bradshaw, Barbara, **Supp. XIII:** 313

Bradstreet, Anne, **I:** 178–179, 180, 181, 182, 184; **III:** 505; **Retro. Supp. I:** 40; **Supp. I Part 1:** 98–123, 300; **Supp. I Part 2:** 484, 485, 496, 546, 705; **Supp. V:** 113, 117–118; **Supp. XIII:** 152; **Supp. XIV:** 128; **Supp. XVIII:** 304

Bradstreet, Elizabeth, **Supp. I Part 1:** 108, 122

Bradstreet, Simon, **I:** 178; **Supp. I Part 1:** 103, 110, 116

Bradstreet, Mrs. Simon. *See* Bradstreet, Anne

Brady, Alice, **III:** 399

Brady, Matthew, **Supp. XVIII:** 4

Bragdon, Claude, **Supp. XX:**117

"Bragdowdy and the Busybody, The" (Thurber), **Supp. I Part 2:** 617

Bragg, Rick, **Supp. XVIII:** 195

"Brahma" (Emerson), **II:** 19, 20

Brahms, Johannes, **III:** 118, 448

"Brahms in Delirium" (Skloot), **Supp. XX:**203

Braided Creek (Kooser and Harrison), **Supp. XIX:** 126

"Braiding" (L.-Y. Lee), **Supp. XV:** 214

"Brain and the Mind, The" (James), **II:** 346

Brainard, Joe, **Supp. XV:** 33

"Brain Damage" (Barthelme), **Supp. IV Part 1:** 44

"Braindead Megaphone, The" (Saunders), **Supp. XIX:** 235

Braindead Megaphone, The: Essays (Saunders), **Supp. XIX:** 234–236

"Brain Scan" (Skloot), **Supp. XX:**200

"Brain to the Heart, The" (Komunyakaa), **Supp. XIII:** 120

Braithwaite, William Stanley, **Retro. Supp. I:** 131; **Supp. IX:** 309; **Supp. XV:** 296–297, 301–302, 305, 306

Brakhage, Stan, **Supp. XII:** 2

Braly, Malcolm, **Supp. XVIII:** 147

"Bramble, The" (Wrigley), **Supp. XVIII:** 301

Brame, Gloria, **Supp. XV:** 113

Bramer, Monte, **Supp. X:** 152

Branch Will Not Break, The (Wright), **Supp. III Part 2:** 596, 598–601; **Supp. IV Part 1:** 60; **Supp. IX:** 159

Brancusi, Constantin, **III:** 201; **Retro. Supp. I:** 292

Brande, Dorothea, **Supp. I Part 2:** 608

Brandel, Marc, **Supp. XXI:** 276

Branden, Nathaniel, **Supp. IV Part 2:** 526, 528

"Brand-Name Blues" (Kaufmann), **Supp. XI:** 39

Brand New Life, A (Farrell), **II:** 46, 48

Brando, Marlon, **II:** 588; **Supp. IV Part 2:** 560; **Supp. XVIII:** 251

Brandon, Henry, **Supp. I Part 2:** 604, 612, 618

Brandt, Alice, **Supp. I Part 1:** 92

Brandt, Carl, **Supp. XI:** 45

Brant, Sebastian, **III:** 447, 448

Braque, Georges, **III:** 197; **Supp. IX:** 66

Brashford, Jake, **Supp. X:** 252

Brasil, Emanuel, **Supp. I Part 1:** 94

"Brasília" (Plath), **Supp. I Part 2:** 544, 545

"Brass Buttons" (McCoy), **Supp. XIII:** 161

"Brass Candlestick, The" (Francis), **Supp. IX:** 89

Brass Check, The (Sinclair), **Supp. V:** 276, 281, 282, 284–285

"Brass Ring, The" (Carver), **Supp. III Part 1:** 137

"Brass Spittoons" (Hughes), **Supp. I Part 1:** 326–327

Brass Verdict, The (Connelly), **Supp. XXI: 78–79**

Brats (X. J. Kennedy), **Supp. XV:** 163

Brautigan, Richard, **III:** 174; **Supp. VIII:** 42, 43; **Supp. XII:** 139; **Supp. XVI:** 172; **Supp. XXI:** 53

Brave Cowboy, The (Abbey), **Supp. XIII:** 4–5

Brave Men (Pyle), **Supp. XVII:** 61

Brave New World (Huxley), **II:** 454; **Supp. XIII:** 29; **Supp. XVIII:** 137

"Brave New World" (MacLeish), **III:** 18

Bravery of Earth, A (Eberhart), **I:** 522, 524, 525, 526, 530

"Brave Tailors of Maida, The" (Talese), **Supp. XVII:** 208

"Brave Words for a Startling Occasion" (Ellison), **Retro. Supp. II:** 118

Braving the Elements (Merrill), **Supp. III Part 1:** 320, 323, 325–327, 329

Bravo, The (Cooper), **I:** 345–346, 348

"Bravura" (Francis), **Supp. IX:** 90

Brawley, Benjamin, **Supp. I Part 1:** 327, 332

Brawl in a Tavern, A (Shaw), **Supp. XIX:** 241

Brawne, Fanny, **I:** 284; **II:** 531

Braxton, Joanne, **Supp. IV Part 1:** 12, 15

Brazil (Bishop), **Retro. Supp. II:** 45; **Supp. I Part 1:** 92

"Brazil" (Marshall), **Supp. XI:** 281

Brazil (Updike), **Retro. Supp. I:** 329, 330, 334

"Brazil, January 1, 1502" (Bishop), **Retro. Supp. II:** 47

Braziller, George, **Supp. X:** 24

Brazzi, Rossano, **Supp. IV Part 2:** 520

"Bread" (Dickey), **Supp. IV Part 1:** 182

"Bread" (Olds), **Supp. X:** 206

"Bread Alone" (Wylie), **Supp. I Part 2:** 727

Bread in the Wilderness (Merton), **Supp. VIII:** 197, 208

"Bread of Desire, The" (Nelson), **Supp. XVIII:** 177

Bread of Idleness, The (Masters), **Supp. I Part 2:** 460

"Bread of This World, The" (McGrath), **Supp. X:** 119, 127

Bread of Time, The (Levine), **Supp. V:** 180

Bread without Sugar (Stern), **Supp. IX: 297–298**

"Break, The" (Sexton), **Supp. II Part 2:** 689

Breakfast at Tiffany's (Capote), **Supp. III Part 1:** 113, 117, 119–121, 124, 126

Breakfast of Champions (Vonnegut), **Supp. II Part 2:** 755, 759, 769, 770, 777–778

Breaking and a Death, A (Kees), **Supp. XV:** 145

Breaking and Entering (X. J. Kennedy), **Supp. XV:** 153, **160–162**

Breaking Hard Ground (D. Hunter), **Supp. XVI:** 38

Breaking Ice (McMillan, ed.), **Supp. XIII:** 182–183

Breaking Open (Rukeyser), **Supp. VI:** 274, 281

"Breaking Open" (Rukeyser), **Supp. VI:** 286

Breaking Ranks: A Political Memoir (Podhoretz), **Supp. VIII: 239–241,** 245

"Breaking the Code of Silence: Ideology and Women's Confessional Poetry" (Harris), **Supp. XIV:** 269

"Breaking Up of the Winships, The" (Thurber), **Supp. I Part 2:** 616

Breast, The (P. Roth), **Retro. Supp. II:** 287–288; **Supp. III Part 2:** 416, 418

"Breast, The" (Sexton), **Supp. II Part 2:** 687

"Breasts" (Simic), **Supp. VIII:** 275

"Breath" (Espaillat), **Supp. XXI:** 109

"Breath" (Levine), **Supp. V:** 185

Breathe No More, My Lady (Lacy), **Supp. XV:** 203

Breathing Lessons (Tyler), **Supp. IV Part 2:** 669–670

Breathing the Water (Levertov), **Supp. III Part 1:** 274, 283, 284

"Breath of Life, The" (C. Baxter), **Supp. XVII:** 23

Breath's Burials (Sobin), **Supp. XVI: 288–289**

Breaux, Zelia, **Retro. Supp. II:** 114

Brecht, Bertolt, **I:** 60, 301; **III:** 161, 162; **IV:** 394; **Supp. I Part 1:** 292; **Supp. II Part 1:** 10, 26, 56; **Supp. IV Part 1:** 359; **Supp. IX:** 131, 133, 140; **Supp. X:** 112; **Supp. XIII:** 206, 286; **Supp. XIV:** 162; **Supp. XVIII:** 33

Breen, Joseph I., **IV:** 390

Breines, Ron, **Supp. XVIII:** 97

Breit, Harvey, **I:** 433; **III:** 575; **Retro. Supp. II:** 230; **Supp. XVIII:** 254; **Supp. XXI:** 277

Bremer, Fredrika, **Supp. I Part 1:** 407

Brendan: A Novel (Buechner), **Supp. XII:** 53

Brennan, Matthew C., **Supp. XV:** 113, 125; **Supp. XIX:** 121

Brent, Linda, **Supp. IV Part 1:** 12, 13

Brentano, Franz, **II:** 350; **Supp. XIV:** 198, 199

Brer Rabbit (tales), **Supp. IV Part 1:** 11, 13; **Supp. XIV:** 88

Breslin, James E. B., **Retro. Supp. I:** 430

Breslin, John B., **Supp. IV Part 1:** 308

Breslin, Paul, **Supp. VIII:** 283

Bresson, Robert, **Supp. IV Part 1:** 156

"Bresson's Movies" (Creeley), **Supp. IV Part 1:** 156–157

Breton, André, **III:** 425; **Supp. XIII:** 114; **Supp. XVII:** 244

Brett, George, **II:** 466; **Supp. V:** 286

Brett, Reginald Baliol, **Supp. XX:**230

Brevoort, Henry, **II:** 298

Brew, Kwesi, **Supp. IV Part 1:** 10, 16

Brewer, Gaylord, **Supp. XV:** 330

"Brewing of Soma, The" (Whittier), **Supp. I Part 2:** 704

Brewsie and Willie (Stein), **IV:** 27

Brewster, Martha, **Supp. I Part 1:** 114

"Brewsterville Croesus, A" (Briggs), **Supp. XVIII:** 16

Brewsterville letters (Briggs), **Supp. XVIII:** 1, 5, **15–16**

"Brian Age 7" (Doty), **Supp. XI:** 136

Briand, Paul, **Supp. XVIII:** 155

"Briar Patch, The" (Warren), **IV:** 237

Briar Rose (Coover), **Supp. V:** 52

"Briar Rose (Sleeping Beauty)" (Sexton), **Supp. II Part 2:** 690

Brice, Fanny, **II:** 427

"Brick, The" (Nye), **Supp. XIII:** 276

"Bricklayer in the Snow" (Fante), **Supp. XI:** 164–165

"Brick Layer's Lunch Hour, The" (Ginsberg), **Supp. II Part 1:** 318

Brickman, Marshall, **Supp. XV:** 5

"Bricks, The" (Hogan), **Supp. IV Part 1:** 413

"Bridal Ballad, The" (Poe), **III:** 428

"Bridal Bed, The" (Gibran), **Supp. XX:**124

Bridal Dinner, The (Gurney), **Supp. V:** 109, 110

"Bride Comes to Yellow Sky, The" (Crane), **I:** 34, 415, 416, 423

Bridegroom, The (Jin), **Supp. XVIII: 97–98**

"Bridegroom, The" (Jin), **Supp. XVIII:** 98

Bridegroom Cometh, The (W. Frank), **Supp. XX:**77

"Bride in the 30's, A" (Auden), **Supp. II Part 1:** 9

Bride of Lammermoor (Scott), **II:** 291

Bride of Samoa (film), **Supp. IV Part 1:** 82

"Bride of the Innisfallen, The" (Welty), **IV:** 278–279; **Retro. Supp. I:** 353

Bride of the Innisfallen, The, and Other Stories (Welty), **IV:** 261, 275–279; **Retro. Supp. I:** 352–353, 355

Brides of the South Wind: Poems 1917–1922 (Jeffers), **Supp. II Part 2:** 419

Bridge, Horatio, **II:** 226

"BRIDGE, THE" (Baraka), **Supp. II Part 1:** 32, 36

Bridge, The (H. Crane), **I:** 62, 109, 266, 385, 386, 387, 395–399, 400, 402; **IV:** 123, 341, 418, 419, 420; **Retro. Supp. I:** 427; **Retro. Supp. II:** 76, 77, 81, 83, **84–87**; **Supp. V:** 342; **Supp. IX:** 306

Bridge, The (Talese), **Supp. XVII:** 202, 203, 208

Bridge at Remagen, The (film), **Supp. XI:** 343

"Bridge Burners, The" (Van Vechten), **Supp. II Part 2:** 733

Bridgehead: The Drama of Israel (W. Frank), **Supp. XX:**80

Bridge of San Luis Rey, The (Wilder), **I:** 360; **IV:** 356, 357, 360–363, 365, 366

Bridge of Years, The (Sarton), **Supp. VIII:** 253

"Bridges" (Kingsolver), **Supp. VII:** 208

Bridges, Harry, **I:** 493; **Supp. XVIII:** 238; **Supp. XIX:** 264

Bridges, Lloyd, **Supp. XV:** 202

Bridges, Robert, **II:** 537; **III:** 527; **Supp. I Part 2:** 721; **Supp. II Part 1:** 21; **Supp. XIV:** 336, 341, 342, 343

"Bridging" (Apple), **Supp. XVII:** 5

Bridgman, P. W., **I:** 278

"Bridle, The" (Carver), **Supp. III Part 1:** 138

"Brief and Blameless Outline of the Ontogeny of Crow, A" (Wright), **Supp. XV:** 347

Brief and Frightening Reign of Phil, The (Saunders), **Supp. XIX:** 230–231, 233

"Brief Début of Tildy, The" (O. Henry), **Supp. II Part 1:** 408

"Brief Encounters on the Inland Waterway" (Vonnegut), **Supp. II Part 2:** 760

Briefings (Ammons), **Supp. VII:** 29

Brief Interviews with Hideous Men (Wallace), **Supp. X: 308–310**

"Brief Interviews with Hideous Men" (Wallace), **Supp. X:** 309

"Briefly It Enters, and Briefly Speaks" (Kenyon), **Supp. VII:** 174

"Brief Study of the British, A" (Saunders), **Supp. XIX:** 235

Brier, His Book (J. W. Miller), **Supp. XX:**165, 168, **170**

"Brier Grows Wild, The" (J. W. Miller), **Supp. XX:**170

"Brier Losing Touch with His Traditions, The" (J. W. Miller), **Supp. XX:**165, 169

Brier Poems, The (J. W. Miller), **Supp. XX:**168

"Brier Sermon, The—You Must Be Born Again" (J. W. Miller), **Supp. XX:**165, 169–170

Briffault, Robert, **Supp. I Part 2:** 560, 567

"Brigade de Cuisine" (McPhee), **Supp. III Part 1:** 307–308

Brigadier and the Golf Widow, The (Cheever), **Supp. I Part 1:** 184–185, 192

Briggs, Charles Frederick, **Supp. I Part 2:** 411; **Supp. XVIII: 1–18**

brigham, besmilr, **Supp. XV:** 349

"Bright and Morning Star" (Wright), **IV:** 488

Bright Book of Life: American Novelists and Storytellers from Hemingway to Mailer (Kazin), **Supp. VIII:** 102, 104

Bright Center of Heaven (Maxwell), **Supp. VIII: 153–155,** 164

"Brightness from the North" (B. Kelly), **Supp. XVII:** 131

Brighton Beach Memoirs (Simon), **Supp. IV Part 2:** 576, 577, 584, 586–587, 590

Bright Procession (Sedges), **Supp. II Part 1:** 125

Bright Room Called Day, A (Kushner), **Supp. IX:** 133, **138–141,** 142

Brillat-Savarin, Jean Anthelme, **Supp. XVII:** 82, 86, 87

"Brilliance" (Doty), **Supp. XI:** 124, 128

"Brilliant Leaves" (Gordon), **II:** 199

"Brilliant Sad Sun" (W. C. Williams), **Retro. Supp. I:** 422

"Bringing Back the Trumpeter Swan" (Kumin), **Supp. IV Part 2:** 454

Bringing It All Back Home (album, Dylan), **Supp. XVIII:** 20, 25, 26, 30

Bringing It All Back Home (McNally), **Supp. XIII:** 197–198

Bringing the Devil to His Knees (C. Baxter), **Supp. XVII:** 22

"Bringing the Strange Home" (Dunn), **Supp. XI:** 141

"Bring the Day!" (Roethke), **III:** 536

Brinkley, Douglas, **Supp. XIII:** 9

Brinkmeyer, Robert H., Jr., **Supp. XI:** 38

Brinnin, John Malcolm, **IV:** 26, 27, 28, 42, 46; **Supp. XV:** 139

Brissot, Jacques Pierre, **Supp. I Part 2:** 511

"Britain's Negro Problem in Sierra Leone" (Du Bois), **Supp. I Part 1:** 176

"British Guiana" (Marshall), **Supp. XI:** 281–282

"British Poets, The" (Holmes), **Supp. I Part 1:** 306

"British Prison Ship, The" (Freneau), **Supp. II Part 1:** 261

Brittan, Gordon G., Jr., **Supp. XIV:** 234

Britten, Benjamin, **II:** 586; **Supp. II Part 1:** 17; **Supp. IV Part 1:** 84

Broadwater, Bowden, **II:** 562

Broadway, Broadway (McNally). *See It's Only a Play* (McNally)

Broadway, J. William, **Supp. V:** 316

Broadway Bound (Simon), **Supp. IV Part 2:** 576, 577, 584, 586–587, 590

Broadway Danny Rose (film; Allen), **Supp. XV:** 9

"Broadway Sights" (Whitman), **IV:** 350

Broccoli, Albert R. "Cubby", **Supp. XI:** 307

Bröck, Sabine, **Supp. XI:** 275, 277, 278

Brodhead, Richard, **Retro. Supp. II:** 139; **Supp. XIV:** 61

Brodkey, Harold, **Supp. VIII:** 151; **Supp. X:** 160

Brodskii, Iosif Alexsandrovich. *See* Brodsky, Joseph

Brodsky, Joseph, **Supp. VIII: 19–35; Supp. X:** 65, 73; **Supp. XV:** 134, 135, 256

Brody, Alter, **Supp. XV:** 302, 307

Brodyar, Anatole, **Supp. XIV:** 106

Brokeback Mountain (film), **Supp. XX:**273

"Brokeback Mountain" (Proulx), **Supp. VII:** 264–265

"Broken Balance, The" (Jeffers), **Supp. II Part 2:** 426

"Broken Field Running" (Bambara), **Supp. XI:** 10, 11

Broken Frieze, The (Everwine), **Supp. XV:** 74, 75, 89

Broken Ground, The (Berry), **Supp. X:** 30

"Broken Home, The" (Merrill), **Supp. III Part 1:** 319, 325

"Broken Oar, The" (Longfellow), **Retro. Supp. II:** 169

"Broken Promise" (MacLeish), **III:** 15

Broken Span, The (W. C. Williams), **IV:** 419; **Retro. Supp. I:** 424

"Broken Tower, The" (H. Crane), **I:** 385, 386, 400, 401–402; **Retro. Supp. II:** 89, 90

Broken Vessels (Dubus), **Supp. VII:** 90–91; **Supp. XI:** 347

"Broken Vessels" (Dubus), **Supp. VII:** 90

Broken Wings, The (al-Ajni&hudot;a al-Mutakassirah) (Gibran), **Supp. XX:**115, 124, 125

"Broker" (H. Roth), **Supp. IX:** 234

Bromfield, Louis, **IV:** 380

"Brompton Cocktail" (Mamet), **Supp. XIV:** 252

Bromwich, David, **Retro. Supp. I:** 305; **Supp. XII:** 162

"Broncho That Would Not Be Broken, The" (Lindsay), **Supp. I Part 2:** 383

Bronk, William, **Supp. XV:** 115; **Supp. XXI: 17–34**

Brontë, Anne, **Supp. IV Part 2:** 430

Brontë, Branwell, **I:** 462

Brontë, Charlotte, **I:** 458; **II:** 175; **Supp. IV Part 2:** 430; **Supp. IX:** 128; **Supp. XII:** 104, 303; **Supp. XV:** 338; **Supp. XVI:** 158; **Supp. XX:**108

Brontë, Emily, **I:** 458; **Retro. Supp. I:** 43; **Supp. IV Part 2:** 430; **Supp. IX:** 128; **Supp. X:** 78, 89; **Supp. XV:** 338

"Bronze" (Francis), **Supp. IX:** 76

"Bronze" (Merrill), **Supp. III Part 1:** 336

Bronze Booklets on the History, Problems, and Cultural Contributions of the Negro series, **Supp. XIV:** 202

"Bronze Buckaroo, The" (Baraka), **Supp. II Part 1:** 49

"Bronze Horses, The" (Lowell), **II:** 524

"Bronze Tablets" (Lowell), **II:** 523

Bronzeville Boys and Girls (Brooks), **Supp. III Part 1:** 79

"Bronzeville Mother Loiters in Mississippi, A. Meanwhile, a Mississippi Mother Burns Bacon" (Brooks), **Supp. III Part 1:** 80

"Brooch, The" (Singer), **IV:** 20

Brook, Peter, **Retro. Supp. II:** 182

Brooke, Rupert, **II:** 82; **III:** 3

Brook Evans (Glaspell), **Supp. III Part 1:** 182–185

"Brooking Likeness" (Glück), **Supp. V:** 85

"Brooklyn" (Marshall), **Supp. XI:** 281, 282

"Brooklyn" (Shaw), **Supp. XIX:** 239, 240

Brooks, Albert (Al Pew), **Supp. XXI:** 22

Brooks, Cleanth, **I:** 280, 282; **III:** 517; **IV:** 236, 279; **Retro. Supp. I:** 40, 41, 90; **Retro. Supp. II:** 235; **Supp. I Part 2:** 423; **Supp. III Part 2:** 542;

Supp. V: 316; Supp. IX: 153, 155; Supp. X: 115, 123; Supp. XIV: 1–20; Supp. XIX: 246

Brooks, David, Supp. IV Part 2: 623, 626, 630; Supp. VIII: 232

Brooks, Gwendolyn, Retro. Supp. I: 208; Supp. III Part 1: 69–90; Supp. IV Part 1: 2, 15, 244, 251, 257; Supp. XI: 1, 278; Supp. XIII: 111, 112, 296; Supp. XIV: 73; Supp. XVIII: 175, 181, 185; Supp. XXI: 230

Brooks, Mel, Supp. IV Part 1: 390; Supp. IV Part 2: 591

Brooks, Paul, Supp. IX: 26, 31, 32

Brooks, Phillips, II: 542; Retro. Supp. II: 134; Supp. XIII: 142

Brooks, Van Wyck, I: 106, 117, 215, 222, 228, 230, 231, 233, 236, 239–263, 266, 480; II: 30, 271, 285, 309, 337, 482; III: 394, 606; IV: 171, 312, 427, 433; Retro. Supp. II: 46, 137; Supp. I Part 2: 423, 424, 650; Supp. II Part 1: 137; Supp. VIII: 98, 101; Supp. XIV: 11; Supp. XV: 298, 301; Supp. XX:68

Brooks, Mrs. Van Wyck (Eleanor Kenyon Stimson), I: 240, 245, 250, 252

Brooks, Mrs. Van Wyck (Gladys Billings), I: 258

Broom of the System, The (Wallace), Supp. X: 301, 302–305, 310

"Brooms" (Simic), Supp. VIII: 275

Brosi, George, Supp. XX:166

Brosnan, Jim, II: 424–425; Supp. XX:195

Brother Carl (Sontag), Supp. III Part 2: 452

"Brother Death" (Anderson), I: 114

Brother Fire (Di Piero), Supp. XIX: 35, 38, 45–47

Brotherhood of the Grape, The (Fante), Supp. XI: 160, 171–172

Brother in Elysium, The: Ideas of Friendship and Society in the United States (Bronk), Supp. XXI: 21, 22, 25, 31

"Brothers" (Anderson), I: 114

Brothers, The (F. Barthelme), Supp. XI: 25, 28, 29, 30, 32–33

Brothers and Keepers (Wideman), Supp. X: 320, 321–322, 323, 325–327, 328, 329–330, 331, 332

Brothers Ashkenazi, The (Singer), IV: 2

Brothers Karamazov, The (Dostoevsky), II: 60; III: 146, 150, 283; Supp. IX: 102, 106; Supp. XI: 172; Supp. XII: 322

Brothers of No Kin (Richter), Supp. XVIII: 209

"Brothers of No Kin" (Richter), Supp. XVIII: 208

Brother to Dragons: A Tale in Verse and Voices (Warren), IV: 243–244, 245, 246, 251, 252, 254, 257

Broughton, James, Supp. XV: 146

Broughton, Rhoda, II: 174; IV: 309, 310; Supp. XX:232

Broun, Heywood, I: 478; II: 417; IV: 432; Supp. IX: 190

Broussais, François, Supp. I Part 1: 302

Browder, Earl, I: 515; Supp. XX:76, 77

Brower, David, Supp. X: 29

Brower, Reuben, Supp. XV: 20

Brown, Alice, II: 523; Retro. Supp. II: 136

Brown, Andrew, Supp. XVI: 150

Brown, Ashley, Retro. Supp. II: 48; Supp. I Part 1: 79, 80, 82, 84, 92

Brown, Charles Brockden, I: 54, 211, 335; II: 74, 267, 298; III: 415; Supp. I Part 1: 124–149; Supp. II Part 1: 65, 292

Brown, Mrs. Charles Brockden (Elizabeth Linn), Supp. I Part 1: 145, 146

Brown, Clifford, Supp. V: 195

Brown, Deborah, Supp. XVII: 75

Brown, Dee, Supp. IV Part 2: 504

Brown, Elijah, Supp. I Part 1: 125

Brown, George Douglas, III: 473

Brown, Harry, Supp. IV Part 2: 560

Brown, Harvey, Supp. XIV: 148

Brown, Himan, Supp. XIX: 241, 242

Brown, H. Rap, Supp. XXI: 171

Brown, John, II: 13; IV: 125, 126, 172, 237, 249, 254; Supp. I Part 1: 345; Supp. VIII: 204

Brown, Joseph Epes, Supp. IV Part 2: 487

Brown, Larry, Supp. XVIII: 195; Supp. XXI: 35–50

Brown, Leonard, Supp. IX: 117

Brown, Mary Armitt, Supp. I Part 1: 125

Brown, Percy, II: 20

Brown, Robert E., Supp. X: 12

Brown, Scott, Supp. XI: 178

Brown, Slater, IV: 123; Retro. Supp. II: 79

Brown, Solyman, Supp. I Part 1: 156

Brown, Sterling, Retro. Supp. I: 198; Supp. IV Part 1: 169; Supp. XIV: 202

Brown, Tina, Supp. XVI: 176–177

Brown, Wesley, Supp. V: 6

Brown Decades, The (Mumford), Supp. II Part 2: 475, 478, 491–492

Brown Dog (Harrison), Supp. VIII: 51

Brown Dog of the Yaak: Essays on Art and Activism (Bass), Supp. XVI: 22

"Brown Dwarf of Rügen, The" (Whittier), Supp. I Part 2: 696

Browne, Charles Farrar, II: 289; IV: 193, 196; Supp. XVIII: 1, 4

Browne, Roscoe Lee, Supp. VIII: 345

Browne, Thomas, II: 15–16, 304; III: 77, 78, 198, 487; IV: 147; Supp. IX: 136; Supp. XII: 45; Supp. XVI: 292

Browne, William, Supp. I Part 1: 98

Brownell, W. C., II: 14

Brownell, William Crary, Retro. Supp. I: 365, 366

Browner, Stephanie P., Supp. XVIII: 17

Brown Girl, Brownstones (Marshall), Supp. XI: 275, 276, 278–280, 282

Brownies' Book, The (Hughes), Supp. I Part 1: 321

Browning, Elizabeth Barrett, I: 458, 459; Retro. Supp. I: 33, 43; Supp. XVIII: 175–176; Supp. XX:108

Browning, Oscar, Supp. XX:231

Browning, Robert, I: 50, 66, 103, 458, 460, 468; II: 338, 478, 522; III: 5, 8,

467, 469, 484, 511, 521, 524, 606, 609; IV: 135, 245, 366, 416; Retro. Supp. I: 43, 55, 217; Retro. Supp. II: 188, 190; Supp. I Part 1: 2, 6, 79, 311; Supp. I Part 2: 416, 468, 622; Supp. III Part 1: 5, 6; Supp. IV Part 2: 430; Supp. X: 65; Supp. XV: 92, 250, 275

Brownmiller, Susan, Supp. X: 252

"Brown River, Smile" (Toomer), Supp. IV Part 1: 16

Brownstone Eclogues and Other Poems (Aiken), I: 65, 67

Brown: The Last Discovery of America (Rodriguez), Supp. XIV: 297, 298, 300, 305–309, 310, 311–312

Broyard, Anatole, Supp. IV Part 1: 39; Supp. VIII: 140; Supp. X: 186; Supp. XI: 348; Supp. XVI: 213

Broyles, Yolanda Julia, Supp. XIX: 112

Bruccoli, Matthew, Retro. Supp. I: 98, 102, 105, 114, 115, 359; Supp. IV Part 2: 468, 470

Bruce, John Edward, Supp. XVI: 143

Bruce, Lenny, Supp. VIII: 198

Bruce, Virginia, Supp. XII: 173

Bruce-Novoa, Juan, Supp. VIII: 73, 74

Bruchac, Joseph, Supp. IV Part 1: 261, 319, 320, 321, 322, 323, 325, 328, 398, 399, 403, 408, 414; Supp. IV Part 2: 502, 506

Brueghel, Pieter, I: 174; Supp. I Part 2: 475

Brueghel, Pieter, the Elder, Retro. Supp. I: 430

Bruell, Edwin, Supp. VIII: 126

Brugh, Spangler Arlington. See Taylor, Robert

"Bruja: Witch" (Mora), Supp. XIII: 214, 220, 221, Supp. XIII: 222

Brulé, Claude, Supp. XI: 307

Brumer, Andy, Supp. XIII: 88

Brummels, J. V., Supp. XIX: 119

Brunner, Emil, III: 291, 303

"Brush Fire" (J. Wright), Supp. XVII: 241

Brustein, Robert, Supp. VIII: 331

Brutus, IV: 373, 374; Supp. I Part 2: 471

"Brutus and Antony" (Masters), Supp. I Part 2: 472

"Bryan, Bryan, Bryan, Bryan" (Lindsay), Supp. I Part 2: 394, 395, 398

Bryan, George, Retro. Supp. II: 76

Bryan, Sharon, Supp. IX: 154

Bryan, William Jennings, I: 483; IV: 124; Supp. I Part 2: 385, 395–396, 455, 456

Bryant, Austin, Supp. I Part 1: 152, 153

Bryant, Frances, Supp. I Part 1: 153

Bryant, Louise, Supp. X: 136

Bryant, Peter, Supp. I Part 1: 150, 151, 152, 153. See also George, Peter

Bryant, William Cullen, I: 335, 458; II: 311; III: 81; IV: 309; Retro. Supp. I: 217; Retro. Supp. II: 155; Supp. I Part 1: 150–173, 312, 362; Supp. I Part 2: 413, 416, 420; Supp. IV Part 1: 165; Supp. XIII: 145; Supp. XIX: 4

Bryant, Mrs. William Cullen (Frances Fairchild), **Supp. I Part 1:** 153, 169

Bryer, Jackson R., **Supp. IV Part 2:** 575, 583, 585, 586, 589, 591; **Supp. XIII:** 200, **Supp. XIII:** 205

Bryher, Jackson R. (pseudonym). *See* Ellerman, Winifred

"Bubbs Creek Haircut" (Snyder), **Supp. VIII:** 306

Buber, Martin, **II:** 228; **III:** 45, 308, 528; **IV:** 11; **Supp. I Part 1:** 83, 88; **Supp. XVI:** 291

Buccaneers, The (Wharton), **IV:** 327; **Retro. Supp. I:** 382

Buchanan Dying (Updike), **Retro. Supp. I:** 331, 335

Buchbinder, David, **Supp. XIII:** 32

Buchwald, Art, **Supp. XII:** 124–125; **Supp. XVI:** 110–111

Buchwald, Emilie, **Supp. XVI:** 35, 36

Buck, Dudley, **Supp. I Part 1:** 362

Buck, Gene, **II:** 427

Buck, Pearl S., **Supp. II Part 1:** 113–134; **Supp. XIV:** 274

Buckdancer's Choice (Dickey), **Supp. IV Part 1:** 176, 177, 178, 180

"Buckdancer's Choice" (Dickey), **Supp. IV Part 1:** 191

Bucke, Richard Maurice, **Retro. Supp. I:** 407

"Buck Fever" (Humphrey), **Supp. IX:** 109

"Buck in the Snow, The" (Millay), **III:** 135

Buckley, Christopher, **Supp. IX:** 169; **Supp. XI:** 257, 329; **Supp. XV:** 76–77, 86

Buckley, James, Jr., **Supp. XVII:** 220

Buckminster, Joseph, **Supp. II Part 1:** 66–67, 69

Bucknell, Katherine, **Supp. XIV:** 170

Bucolics (Auden), **Supp. II Part 1:** 21, 24

Budbill, David, **Supp. XIX:** 1–16

Budd, Louis J., **IV:** 210

Buddha, **I:** 136; **II:** 1; **III:** 173, 179, 239, 567; **Supp. I Part 1:** 363; **Supp. I Part 2:** 397

"Buddha Boy" (Saunders), **Supp. XIX:** 235

"Buddha's Last Instruction, The" (Oliver), **Supp. VII:** 239

Budding Prospects (Boyle), **Supp. VIII:** 8–9; **Supp. XX:27–28**

Buechner, Frederick, **III:** 310; **Supp. XII:** 41–59

Buell, Lawrence, **Supp. V:** 209; **Supp. IX:** 29; **Supp. XV:** 269, 282

"Buffalo" (Peacock), **Supp. XIX:** 198

"Buffalo, The" (Moore), **III:** 215

"Buffalo Bill". *See* Cody, William

Buffalo Girls (screenplay) (McMurtry), **Supp. V:** 232

Buffalo Girls (McMurtry), **Supp. V:** 229

Buffett, Jimmy, **Supp. VIII:** 42

Buffon, Comte de, **II:** 101

Buford, Fanny McConnell, **Retro. Supp. II:** 117

Bugeja, Michael, **Supp. X:** 201

Bugged for Murder (Lacy), **Supp. XV:** 205

"Buglesong" (Stegner), **Supp. IV Part 2:** 606

Buhle, Paul, **Supp. XXI:** 172

"Buick" (Shapiro), **Supp. II Part 2:** 705

"Builders" (Yates), **Supp. XI:** 342–343

Builders, The (Glasgow), **II:** 183–184, 193

"Builders, The" (Hay), **Supp. XIV:** 125

Builders in Sand (W. Frank), **Supp. XX:68**

Builders of the Bay Colony (Morison), **Supp. I Part 2:** 484–485

"Builders of the Bridge, The" (Mumford), **Supp. II Part 2:** 475

"Building" (Snyder), **Supp. VIII:** 305

"Building, Dwelling, Thinking" (Heidegger), **Retro. Supp. II:** 87

Building a Character (Stanislavsky), **Supp. XIV:** 243

" 'Building' Larry Brown(s) at Algonquin Books of Chapel Hill" (Perry), **Supp. XXI:** 42

"Building of the Ship, The" (Longfellow), **II:** 498; **Retro. Supp. II:** 159, 167, 168

"Build Soil" (Frost), **Retro. Supp. I:** 138, 139

"Build Soil" (Snyder), **Supp. VIII:** 304

Build-Up, The (W. C. Williams), **Retro. Supp. I:** 423

Bukiet, Melvin Jules, **Supp. XVII:** 39–51

Bukowski, Charles, **Supp. III Part 1:** 147; **Supp. XI:** 159, 161, 172, 173; **Supp. XVII:** 245

Bulgakov, Mikhail, **Supp. XIV:** 97

"Bulgarian Poetess, The" (Updike), **IV:** 215, 227; **Retro. Supp. I:** 329

Bull, Ole, **II:** 504

"Bulldozer, The" (Francis), **Supp. IX:** 87

"Bullet in the Brain" (Wolff), **Supp. VII:** 342–343

Bullet Park (Cheever), **Supp. I Part 1:** 185, 187–193, 194, 195

Bullets over Broadway (film; Allen), **Supp. XV:** 12, 12–13

Bullfight, The (Mailer), **Retro. Supp. II:** 205

Bullins, Ed, **Supp. II Part 1:** 34, 42

Bullock, Sandra, **Supp. X:** 80

"Bull-Roarer, The" (Stern), **Supp. IX:** 297

"Bully, The" (Dubus), **Supp. VII:** 84

"Bulsh" (X. J. Kennedy), **Supp. XV:** 161

Bultmann, Rudolf, **III:** 309

Bulwark, The (Dreiser), **I:** 497, 506, 516–517; **Retro. Supp. II:** 95, 96, 105, 108

Bulwer-Lytton, Edward George, **IV:** 350

"Bums in the Attic" (Cisneros), **Supp. VII:** 62

Bunche, Ralph, **Supp. I Part 1:** 343; **Supp. XIV:** 202

"Bunchgrass Edge of the World, The" (Proulx), **Supp. VII:** 263

Bunge, Nancy, **Supp. XVII:** 218

"Bunner Sisters, The" (Wharton), **IV:** 317

Bunting, Basil, **Retro. Supp. I:** 422; **Supp. III Part 2:** 616, 620, 624; **Supp. XIV:** 286

Buñuel, Luis, **III:** 184; **Retro. Supp. II:** 337

Bunyan, John, **I:** 445; **II:** 15, 104, 228; **IV:** 80, 84, 156, 437; **Supp. I Part 1:** 32

Burana, Lily, **Supp. XI:** 253

Burbank, Luther, **I:** 483

Burbank, Rex, **IV:** 363

Burch, Michael, **Supp. XXI:** 99

Burchfield, Alice, **Supp. I Part 2:** 652, 660

Burden of Proof, The (Turow), **Supp. XVII:** 216–217, 218

Burden of Southern History, The (Woodward), **Retro. Supp. I:** 75

Burdens of Formality, The (Lea, ed.), **Supp. X:** 58

Burger, Gottfried August, **II:** 306

Burgess, Anthony, **Supp. IV Part 1:** 227; **Supp. IV Part 2:** 685; **Supp. V:** 128

Burgh, James, **Supp. I Part 2:** 522

"Burglar of Babylon, The" (Bishop), **Retro. Supp. II:** 47; **Supp. I Part 1:** 93

Burgum, E. B., **IV:** 469, 470

Burham, Philip, **Supp. XX:44**

Buried Child (Shepard), **Supp. III Part 2:** 433, 447, 448; **Supp. XIV:** 327

"Buried Lake, The" (Tate), **IV:** 136

Burke, Edmund, **I:** 9; **III:** 310; **Supp. I Part 2:** 496, 511, 512, 513, 523; **Supp. II Part 1:** 80; **Supp. XVII:** 236

Burke, James Lee, **Supp. XIV:** 21–38; **Supp. XXI:** 67, 72, 80

Burke, Kenneth, **I:** 264–287, 291; **III:** 497, 499, 546; **IV:** 123, 408; **Retro. Supp. I:** 297; **Retro. Supp. II:** 117, 120; **Supp. I Part 2:** 630; **Supp. II Part 1:** 136; **Supp. VIII:** 105; **Supp. IX:** 229; **Supp. XIV:** 3; **Supp. XXI:** 89

Burke, William, **Supp. XXI:** 215

Burley, Justin, **Supp. XVI:** 158

"Burly Fading One, The" (Hayden), **Supp. II Part 1:** 366

"Burned" (Levine), **Supp. V:** 186, 192

"Burned Diary, The" (Olds), **Supp. X:** 215

Burnett, Allison, **Supp. XVII:** 22

Burnett, David, **Supp. XI:** 299

Burnett, Frances Hodgson, **Supp. I Part 1:** 44

Burnett, Whit, **III:** 551; **Supp. XI:** 294

Burney, Fanny, **Supp. XV:** 232; **Supp. XX:108**

Burnham, James, **Supp. I Part 2:** 648

Burnham, John Chynoweth, **I:** 59

"Burning, The" (Welty), **IV:** 277–278; **Retro. Supp. I:** 353

Burning Angel (Burke), **Supp. XIV:** 30, 32

Burning Bright (Steinbeck), **IV:** 51, 61–62

Burning Bush (Untermeyer), **Supp. XV:** 309

"Burning Bush" (Untermeyer), **Supp. XV:** 309

Burning Bush, The (H. and G. Herczeg), **Supp. XVII:** 62

Burning Chrome (W. Gibson), **Supp. XVI:** 118, 122, **128**

"Burning Chrome" (W. Gibson), **Supp. XVI:** 117, 120, 123, 124, 128

Burning City (Benét), **Supp. XI:** 46, 58

Burning Daylight (London), **II:** 474, 481

Burning Down the House: Essays on Fiction (C. Baxter), **Supp. XVII:** 13, 20, 21

Burning House, The (Beattie), **Supp. V:** 29

"Burning Ladder, The" (Gioia), **Supp. XV:** 118

Burning Mystery of Anna in 1951, The (Koch), **Supp. XV:** 182–183

"Burning of Paper Instead of Children, The" (Rich), **Supp. I Part 2:** 558

"Burning Shit at An Khe" (Weigl), **Supp. XIX:** 279–280

Burning the Days (Salter), **Supp. XIX:** 252

Burning the Days: Recollections (Salter), **Supp. IX:** 245, 246, 248, 260, **261–262**

"Burning the Small Dead" (Snyder), **Supp. VIII:** 298

"Burning Tobacco Beds" (J. W. Miller), **Supp. XX:**167

Burns, Carol, **Supp. XVIII:** 162

Burns, David, **III:** 165–166

Burns, Ken, **Supp. XIV:** 14

Burns, Michael, **Supp. XV:** 339

Burns, Robert, **II:** 150, 306; **III:** 592; **IV:** 453; **Supp. I Part 1:** 158; **Supp. I Part 2:** 410, 455, 683, 685, 691, 692; **Supp. IX:** 173; **Supp. XII:** 171; **Supp. XIII:** 3; **Supp. XVIII:** 82

Burns, Stephen J., **Supp. XX:**85

Burnshaw, Stanley, **Retro. Supp. I:** 298, 303; **Supp. III Part 2:** 615

"Burn the Cities" (West), **Retro. Supp. II:** 338

Burnt Norton (T. S. Eliot), **I:** 575, 580–581, 582, 584, 585; **III:** 10

"Burnt Norton" (T. S. Eliot), **Retro. Supp. I:** 66; **Supp. XV:** 216

Burnt-Out Case, A (Greene), **Supp. VIII:** 4

"Burnt-out Spa, The" (Plath), **Retro. Supp. II:** 246

Burn Witch Burn (A. Merritt), **Supp. XVII:** 58

Burr, Aaron, **I:** 7, 549, 550; **II:** 300; **IV:** 264; **Supp. I Part 2:** 461, 483

Burr: A Novel (Vidal), **Supp. IV Part 2:** 677, 682, 684, 685, 687, 688, 689, 691

Burr Oaks (Eberhart), **I:** 533, 535

Burroughs, Edgar Rice, **Supp. IV Part 1:** 101

Burroughs, John, **I:** 220, 236, 506; **IV:** 346; **Supp. IX:** 171

Burroughs, William S., **III:** 45, 174, 258; **Supp. II Part 1:** 320, 328; **Supp. III Part 1: 91–110**, 217, 226; **Supp. IV Part 1:** 79, 87, 90; **Supp. XI:** 297, 308; **Supp. XII:** 1, 3, 118, 121, 124, 129, 131, 136; **Supp. XIV:** 137, 140–141, 143–144, 150; **Supp. XVI:** 123, 135; **Supp. XVII:** 225; **Supp. XVIII:** 137

Burrow, Trigant, **Supp. II Part 1:** 6

Burrows, Ken, **Supp. V:** 115

Burson, Claudia, **Supp. XV:** 343

Burstein, Janet, **Supp. XVII:** 41, 44, 48

"Bursts of Light" (Bronk), **Supp. XXI:** 33

Burt, Stephen, **Supp. XV:** 341, 342, 345, 347, 351; **Supp. XVII:** 18, 246

Burt, Steve, **Supp. V:** 83

Burtis, Thomson, **Supp. XIII:** 163

Burton, Robert, **II:** 535; **III:** 77, 78; **Supp. I Part 1:** 349

Burton, Sue D., **Supp. XIX:** 90

Burton, William Evans, **III:** 412

"Burying Ground by the Ties" (MacLeish), **III:** 14

Bury My Heart at Wounded Knee (Brown), **Supp. IV Part 2:** 504

Bury the Dead (Shaw), **IV:** 381; **Supp. XIX: 242–244**, 249, 252

"Bus Along St. Clair: December, A" (Atwood), **Supp. XIII:** 33

Busch, Frederick, **Supp. X:** 78; **Supp. XII:** 343; **Supp. XVII:** 175

Bush, Barney, **Supp. XII:** 218, 222

Bush, Douglas, **Supp. I Part 1:** 268; **Supp. XIV:** 10

"Busher Comes Back, The" (Lardner), **II:** 422

"Busher's Letters Home, A" (Lardner), **II:** 418–419, 421

Bushrui, Suheil, **Supp. XX:**113, 117, 120, 122, 126–127

"Business and Poetry" (Gioia), **Supp. XV:** 113, 115

"Business Deal" (West), **IV:** 287

"Business Man, A" (Jewett), **Retro. Supp. II:** 132

Business of Memory, The: The Art of Remembering in an Age of Forgetting (C. Baxter, ed.), **Supp. XVII:** 21

"Business Trip" (Hoffman), **Supp. XVIII:** 86

Buss, Helen M., **Supp. IV Part 1:** 12

Butcher, Margaret Just, **Supp. XIV:** 203

"Butcher, The" (Southern), **Supp. XI:** 294

"Butcher Shop" (Simic), **Supp. VIII:** 273

But Gentlemen Marry Brunettes (Loos), **Supp. XVI:** 190–191

Butler, Benjamin, **I:** 457

Butler, Dorothy. *See* Farrell, Mrs. James T. (Dorothy Butler)

Butler, Elizabeth, **Supp. I Part 1:** 260

Butler, Ethel, **Supp. XIV:** 125

Butler, Hugo, **Supp. XVII:** 63

Butler, James D., **Supp. IX:** 175

Butler, Joseph, **II:** 8, 9

Butler, Judith, **Supp. XII:** 6

Butler, Maud. *See* Falkner, Mrs. Murray C. (Maud Butler)

Butler, Nicholas Murray, **I:** 223; **Supp. I Part 1:** 23; **Supp. III Part 2:** 499

Butler, Octavia, **Supp. XIII: 59–72**

Butler, Robert Olen, **Supp. XII: 61–78**, 319

Butler, Samuel, **II:** 82, 86; **IV:** 121, 440; **Supp. VIII:** 171

Butler-Evans, Elliot, **Retro. Supp. II:** 121

"But Only Mine" (Wright), **Supp. III Part 2:** 595

Butscher, Edward, **Supp. I Part 2:** 526

Butter Battle Book, The (Geisel), **Supp. XVI:** 110

"Buttercups" (Lowell), **Retro. Supp. II:** 187

Butterfield, R. W., **I:** 386

Butterfield, Stephen, **Supp. IV Part 1:** 3, 11

Butterfield 8 (O'Hara), **III:** 361

"Butterflies Under Persimmon" (Jarman), **Supp. XVII:** 120

Butterfly (Harvey), **Supp. XIII:** 184

"Butterfly, The" (Brodksy), **Supp. VIII:** 26

"Butterfly and the Traffic Light, The" (Ozick), **Supp. V:** 263, 265

Butterfly Plague, The (Findley), **Supp. XX:**50, **52,** 53

Butterfly Stories (Vollmann), **Supp. XVII:** 226

"Butterfly-toed Shoes" (Komunyakaa), **Supp. XIII:** 126

Butter Hill and Other Poems (Francis), **Supp. IX:** 88, 89

Buttons, Red, **Supp. IV Part 2:** 574

Buttrick, George, **III:** 301; **Supp. XII:** 47–48

"But What Is the Reader to Make of This?" (Ashbery), **Supp. III Part 1:** 25

Butz, Earl, **Supp. X:** 35

"Buz" (Alcott), **Supp. I Part 1:** 43

Buzinski, Jim, **Supp. XX:**273

Byatt, A. S., **Supp. XXI:** 147

By Avon River (Doolittle), **Supp. I Part 1:** 272

"By Blue Ontario's Shore" (Whitman), **Retro. Supp. I:** 399, 400

"By Disposition of Angels" (Moore), **III:** 214

"By Earth" (Olds), **Supp. X:** 214

"By Fire" (Olds), **Supp. X:** 214

Bygones (Untermeyer), **Supp. XV:** 304, **308–309,** 312, 313

By Land, By Sea (Hoffman), **Supp. XVIII:** 86

By Land and by Sea (Morison), **Supp. I Part 2:** 492

Byles, Mather, **Supp. XX:**279, 282

By-Line: Ernest Hemingway (Hemingway), **II:** 257–258

By Love Possessed (Cozens), **I:** 358, 365, 372–374, 375, 376, 377, 378, 379

"By Morning" (Swenson), **Supp. IV Part 2:** 642

"By Night" (Francis), **Supp. IX:** 76

Bynner, Witter, **II:** 513, 527; **Supp. XIII:** 347; **Supp. XV: 39–54**

Byrd, William, **Supp. IV Part 2:** 425; **Supp. XXI:** 35

Byrne, Donn, **IV:** 67

Byron, George Gordon, Lord, **I:** 343, 568, 577; **II:** 135, 193, 296, 301, 303, 310, 315, 331, 566; **III:** 82, 137, 170, 409, 410, 412, 469; **IV:** 245, 435; **Supp. I**

Part 1: 150, 312, 349; **Supp. I Part 2:** 580, 591, 683, 685, 719; **Supp. XIII:** 139; **Supp. XVI:** 188, 203, 206, 210

"Byron's Cain" (L. Michaels), **Supp. XVI:** 203

"Bystanders" (Matthews), **Supp. IX:** 160

By the Bias of Sound (Sobin), **Supp. XVI:** 281

By the North Gate (Oates), **Supp. II Part 2:** 504

"By the People" (Stratton-Porter), **Supp. XX:**221

"By the Waters of Babylon" (Benét), **Supp. XI:** 56, 58

By the Waters of Manhattan (Reznikoff), **Supp. XIV:** 288, 293, 294

By the Waters of Manhattan: An Annual (Reznikoff), **Supp. XIV:** 277, 280, 289

By the Waters of Manhattan: Selected Verse (Reznikoff), **Supp. XIV:** 281, 291

By the Well of Living and Seeing and the Fifth Book of the Maccabees (Reznikoff), **Supp. XIV:** 281

By the Well of Living and Seeing: New and Selected Poems 1918–1973 (Reznikoff), **Supp. XIV:** 281, 287–288, 295

By Way of Orbit (O'Neill), **III:** 405

C

"C 33" (H. Crane), **I:** 384; **Retro. Supp. II:** 76

Cabala, The (Wilder), **IV:** 356, 358–360, 369, 374

Cabaret (film), **Supp. XIV:** 155, 162

Cabaret (play), **Supp. XIV:** 162; **Supp. XVII:** 45

Cabbages and Kings (O. Henry), **Supp. II Part 1:** 394, 409

Cabell, James Branch, **II:** 42; **III:** 394; **IV:** 67, 359, 360; **Retro. Supp. I:** 80; **Supp. I Part 2:** 613, 714, 718, 721; **Supp. X:** 223

"Cabin, The" (Carver), **Supp. III Part 1:** 137, 146

Cabin, The: Reminiscence and Diversions (Mamet), **Supp. XIV:** 240

Cabinet of Dr. Caligari, The (film), **Retro. Supp. I:** 268

Cable, George Washington, **II:** 289; **Retro. Supp. II:** 65; **Supp. I Part 1:** 200; **Supp. II Part 1:** 198; **Supp. XIV:** 63

Cables to the Ace; or, Familiar Liturgies of Misunderstanding (Merton), **Supp. VIII:** 208

Cabot, James, **II:** 14; **IV:** 173

Cabot, John, **Supp. I Part 2:** 496, 497

Cachoeira Tales and Other Poems, The (Nelson), **Supp. XVIII: 178–179**

"Cachoiera Tales, The" (Nelson), **Supp. XVIII:** 179

Cactus Flower (Barillet and Grédy), **Supp. XVI:** 194

"Caddy's Diary, A" (Lardner), **II:** 421–422

"Cadence" (Dubus), **Supp. VII:** 84–85

Cadieux, Isabelle, **Supp. XIII:** 127

"Cadillac Flambé" (Ellison), **Retro. Supp. II:** 119, 126; **Supp. II Part 1:** 248

Cadillac Jack (McMurtry), **Supp. V:** 225

Cadillac Jukebox (Burke), **Supp. XIV:** 32

Cadle, Dean, **Supp. I Part 2:** 429

Cady, Edwin H., **II:** 272

"Caedmon" (Garrett), **Supp. VII:** 96–97

Caesar, Julius, **II:** 12, 502, 561–562; **IV:** 372, 373

Caesar, Sid, **Supp. IV Part 2:** 574, 591

"Cafeteria, The" (Singer), **Retro. Supp. II:** 316

Cage, John, **Supp. IV Part 1:** 84; **Supp. V:** 337, 341

"Cage and the Prairie: Two Notes on Symbolism, The" (Bewley), **Supp. I Part 1:** 251

Cage of Age, The (Bronk), **Supp. XXI:** 32

Cage of Spines, A (Swenson), **Supp. IV Part 2:** 641–642, 647

Cagney, James, **Supp. IV Part 1:** 236; **Supp. XIII:** 174

Cagney, William, **Supp. XIII:** 174

Cahalan, James, **Supp. XIII:** 1, 2, 3, 4, 12

Cahan, Abraham, **Supp. IX:** 227; **Supp. XIII:** 106; **Supp. XXI:** 3, 14

Cahill, Tim, **Supp. XIII:** 13

Cain, James M., **III:** 99; **Supp. IV Part 1:** 130; **Supp. XI:** 160; **Supp. XIII:** 159, 165

Cain, Kathleen Shine, **Supp. XX:**247, 248

Caird, G. B., **Supp. XXI:** 91–92

Cairns, Huntington, **III:** 103, 108, 114, 119

Cairo! Shanghai! Bombay! (Williams and Shapiro), **IV:** 380

Cake (Bynner), **Supp. XV:** 50

Cakes and Ale (Maugham), **III:** 64

Calabria, Frank, **Supp. XIII:** 164

Calamity Jane (Martha Jane Canary), **Supp. V:** 229–230; **Supp. X:** 103

"Calamus" (Whitman), **IV:** 342–343; **Retro. Supp. I:** 52, 403, 404, 407

Calasso, Roberto, **Supp. IV Part 1:** 301

Calderón, Hector, **Supp. IV Part 2:** 544

Caldwell, Christopher, **Supp. IV Part 1:** 211

Caldwell, Erskine, **I:** 97, 211, **288–311**; **IV:** 286; **Supp. IV Part 2:** 601; **Supp. XXI:** 35

Caldwell, Mrs. Erskine (Helen Lannegan), **I:** 289

Caldwell, Mrs. Erskine (Margaret Bourke-White), **I:** 290, 293–295, 297

Caldwell, Mrs. Erskine (Virginia Fletcher), **I:** 290

Caldwell, Reverend Ira Sylvester, **I:** 289, 305

Caldwell, Zoe, **Supp. XIII:** 207

Caleb Williams (Godwin), **III:** 415

"Calendar" (Creeley), **Supp. IV Part 1:** 158

Calendar of Saints for Unbelievers, A (Wescott), **Supp. XIV:** 342

Calendars (A. Finch), **Supp. XVII: 76–77**

Calhoun, John C., **I:** 8; **III:** 309

"Caliban in the Coal Mines" (Untermeyer), **Supp. XV:** 296

"California" (Carruth), **Supp. XVI:** 56

"California" (Didion), **Supp. IV Part 1:** 195

"California, This Is Minnesota Speaking" (Dunn), **Supp. XI:** 146

California and Oregon Trail, The (Parkman), **Supp. I Part 2:** 486

"California Hills in August" (Gioia), **Supp. XV:** 118–119

Californians (Jeffers), **Supp. II Part 2:** 415, 418, 420

"California Oaks, The" (Winters), **Supp. II Part 2:** 798

"California Plush" (Bidart), **Supp. XV:** 23

"California Republic" (Didion), **Supp. IV Part 1:** 205

"California Requiem, A" (Gioia), **Supp. XV:** 126

California Suite (film), **Supp. IV Part 2:** 589

California Suite (Simon), **Supp. IV Part 2:** 581, 582

"Caligula" (Lowell), **II:** 554

Callahan, John F., **Retro. Supp. II:** 119, 126, 127

"Call at Corazón" (Bowles), **Supp. IV Part 1:** 82, 87

Calle, Sophia, **Supp. XII:** 22

"Called Back" (Kazin), **Supp. VIII:** 104

Calley, Captain William, **II:** 579

Calley, John, **Supp. XI:** 305

Callicott, J. Baird, **Supp. XIV:** 184

Calligrammes (Apollinaire), **I:** 432

"Calling Jesus" (Toomer), **Supp. III Part 2:** 484

Calling Myself Home (Hogan), **Supp. IV Part 1:** 397, 399, 400, 401, 413

Call It Experience (Caldwell), **I:** 290–291, 297

"Call It Fear" (Harjo), **Supp. XII:** 220

Call It Sleep (H. Roth), **Supp. VIII:** 233; **Supp. IX:** 227, 228, **229–231**; **Supp. XIII:** 106

"Call Letters: Mrs. V. B." (Angelou), **Supp. IV Part 1:** 15

Call Me Ishmael (Olson), **Supp. II Part 2:** 556; **Supp. XXI:** 21

Call Me Shakespeare (Endore), **Supp. XVII:** 65

Call of the Gospel, The (Mather), **Supp. II Part 2:** 448

Call of the Wild, The (London), **II:** 466, 470–471, 472, 481

"Call of the Wild, The" (Snyder), **Supp. VIII:** 301

"Calloway's Code" (O. Henry), **Supp. II Part 1:** 404

"Call to Arms" (Mumford), **Supp. II Part 2:** 479

Call to Arms, The (film), **Retro. Supp. I:** 325

Calmer, Ned, **Supp. XI:** 219

Calvert, George H., **Supp. I Part 1:** 361

Calverton, V. F., **Supp. VIII:** 96

Calvin, John, **II:** 342; **IV:** 160, 490
Calvino, Italo, **Supp. IV Part 2:** 623, 678; **Supp. XIX:** 34; **Supp. XXI:** 225
Cambridge Companion to Native American Literature, The (Porter and Roemer, eds.), **Supp. XX:**270
Cambridge Edition of the Works of F. Scott Fitzgerald, The (Bruccoli, ed.), **Retro. Supp. I:** 115
Cambridge Film Handbook for *On the Waterfront* (Rapf), **Supp. XVIII:** 251
"Cambridge Thirty Years Ago" (Lowell), **Supp. I Part 2:** 419
Cambridge University Press, **Retro. Supp. I:** 115
"Camellia Sabina" (Moore), **III:** 208, 215
"Cameo" (Trethewey), **Supp. XXI:** 250
"Cameo Appearance" (Simic), **Supp. VIII:** 283
"Camera Notes" (column, Stratton-Porter), **Supp. XX:**217
Camera Obscura (Nabokov), **III:** 255
Cameron, Angus, **Supp. XXI:** 268, 269, 275, 278
Cameron, Elizabeth, **I:** 10, 17
Cameron, Kenneth W., **II:** 16
Cameron, Peter, **Supp. XII: 79–95**
Cameron, Sharon, **Retro. Supp. I:** 43; **Retro. Supp. II:** 40
Camerson, Don, **I:** 10, 17
Camino, Léon Felipe, **Retro. Supp. II:** 89
Camino Real (T. Williams), **IV:** 382, 385, 386, 387, 388, 391, 392, 395, 398
Camões, Luiz Vaz de, **II:** 133; **Supp. I Part 1:** 94
"Camouflaging the Chimera" (Komunyakaa), **Supp. XIII: 122–123**
Camp, James, **Supp. XV:** 165
Camp, Walter, **II:** 423
Campana, Dino, **Supp. V:** 337
Campbell, Alan, **Supp. IV Part 1:** 353; **Supp. IX:** 196, 198, 201
Campbell, Alexander, **Supp. I Part 2:** 381, 395
Campbell, Donna, **Retro. Supp. II:** 139
Campbell, Helen, **Supp. XI:** 200, 206
Campbell, James, **Supp. XII:** 127
Campbell, James Edwin, **Supp. II Part 1:** 202
Campbell, Joanna (pseudonym). *See* Bly, Carol
Campbell, Joseph, **I:** 135; **IV:** 369, 370; **Supp. IX:** 245
Campbell, Lewis, **III:** 476
Campbell, Thomas, **II:** 8, 303, 314; **III:** 410; **Supp. I Part 1:** 309, 310
Campbell, Virginia, **Supp. XIII:** 114
Campbell, Will D., **Supp. XXI:** 247
Campbell (Hale), Janet, **Supp. IV Part 2:** 503
"Campers Leaving: Summer 1981" (Kenyon), **Supp. VII:** 169
"Camp Evergreen" (Kenyon), **Supp. VII:** 168
"Camping in Madera Canyon" (Swenson), **Supp. IV Part 2:** 649
Campion, Thomas, **I:** 439; **Supp. VIII:** 272
Campo, Rafael, **Supp. XVII:** 112

Camus, Albert, **I:** 53, 61, 292, 294, 494; **II:** 57, 244; **III:** 292, 306, 453; **IV:** 6, 211, 236, 442, 487; **Retro. Supp. I:** 73; **Retro. Supp. II:** 20; **Supp. I Part 2:** 621; **Supp. VIII:** 11, 195, 241; **Supp. XI:** 96; **Supp. XIII:** 74, 165, 233, 247; **Supp. XVII:** 137
Camuto, Christopher, **Supp. V:** 212–213
"Canada" (Di Piero), **Supp. XIX:** 39
Canada Fragrant with Resin, **Supp. XVI:** 149
Canadé, Eugene, **Supp. XXI:** 22, 23
"Canadian Mosaic, The" (Beran), **Supp. XIII:** 25
"Canadians and Pottawatomies" (Sandburg), **III:** 592–593
"Can a Good Wife Be a Good Sport?" (T. Williams), **IV:** 380
"Canal, The: A Poem on the Application of Physical Science to Political Economy" (Barlow), **Supp. II Part 1:** 73
Canary, Martha Jane. *See* Calamity Jane (Martha Jane Canary)
"Canary for One, A" (Hemingway), **Retro. Supp. I:** 170, 189
Canary in a Cat House (Vonnegut), **Supp. II Part 2:** 758
"Canary in a Bloom" (Dove), **Supp. IV Part 1:** 248
Canby, Henry Seidel, **IV:** 65, 363
"Cancer" (McClatchy), **Supp. XII:** 266
"Cancer Match, The" (Dickey), **Supp. IV Part 1:** 182
"Canción y Glosa" (Merwin), **Supp. III Part 1:** 342
Candide (Hellman), **I:** 28; **Supp. I Part 1:** 288–289, 292
Candide (Voltaire), **Supp. I Part 1:** 288–289; **Supp. XI:** 297; **Supp. XVI:** 189
Candide (Voltaire; Wilbur, trans.), **Supp. III Part 2:** 560
"Candle Hat" (Collins), **Supp. XXI:** 60
Candle in the Cabin, The (Lindsay), **Supp. I Part 2:** 398, 400
"Candles" (Plath), **Retro. Supp. II:** 248, 257
Candles in Babylon (Levertov), **Supp. III Part 1:** 283
Candles in the Sun (T. Williams), **IV:** 381
Candles of Your Eyes, The (Purdy), **Supp. VII:** 278
Candy (Southern), **Supp. XI:** 297, **298–299,** 305
"Candy-Man Beechum" (Caldwell), **I:** 309
Cane (Toomer), **Supp. III Part 2:** 475, 481–486, 488; **Supp. IV Part 1:** 164, 168; **Supp. IX:** 305, 306, 307, **308–320; Supp. XIX:** 73; **Supp. XX:**73
"Cane in the Corridor, The" (Thurber), **Supp. I Part 2:** 616
Canfield, Cass, **Supp. I Part 2:** 668
Canfield, Dorothy, **Retro. Supp. I:** 4, 11, 14, 18; **Supp. XX:**39. *See also* Fisher, Dorothy Canfield
Can Grande's Castle (Lowell), **II:** 518, 524
"Canicula di Anna" (Carson), **Supp. XII: 101–102**

"Canis Major" (Frost), **Retro. Supp. I:** 137
"Canned Stuff" (Pickering), **Supp. XXI:** 198
Cannery Row (Steinbeck), **IV:** 50, 51, 64–65, 66, 68
Cannibal Galaxy, The (Ozick), **Supp. V:** 270
Cannibals and Christians (Mailer), **III:** 38–39, 40, 42; **Retro. Supp. II:** 203, 204, 205
Canning, George, **I:** 7, 8
Canning, Richard, **Supp. X:** 147
Cannon, Jimmy, **II:** 424
Cannon, Steve, **Retro. Supp. II:** 111
Cannon between My Knees, A (Gunn Allen), **Supp. IV Part 1:** 324
Canolle, Jean, **Supp. XVI:** 194
"Canonization, The" (Donne), **Supp. XIV:** 8
"Can Poetry Matter?" (Gioia), **Supp. XV:** 113, 114
Can Poetry Matter?: Essays on Poetry and American Culture (Gioia), **Supp. XV:** 112, **113–115**
"Canso" (Merwin), **Supp. III Part 1:** 344
Can Such Things Be? (Bierce), **I:** 203, 204, 205, 209
Canterbury Tales (Chaucer), **II:** 504; **III:** 411; **IV:** 65
Canterbury Tales, The (Chaucer), **Supp. XIX:** 4
"Canticle of Her Coming and Going" (Espaillat), **Supp. XXI:** 106
"Canto Amor" (Berryman), **I:** 173
Canto I (Pound), **III:** 469, 470; **Retro. Supp. I:** 286
Canto II (Pound), **III:** 470
Canto III (Pound), **III:** 470
Canto IV (Pound), **III:** 470
Canto VIII (Pound), **III:** 472
Canto IX (Pound), **III:** 472
Canto X (Pound), **III:** 472
Canto XIII (Pound), **III:** 472
Canto XXXIX (Pound), **III:** 468
Canto LXV (Pound), **Retro. Supp. I:** 292
Canto LXXXI (Pound), **III:** 459; **Retro. Supp. I:** 293
Cantor, Lois, **Supp. IV Part 1:** 285
Cantos (Pound), **I:** 482; **III:** 13–14, 17, 457, 462, 463, 466, 467, 469–470, 472–473, 474, 475, 476, 492; **Retro. Supp. I:** 284, 292, **292–293,** 293, 427; **Supp. I Part 1:** 272; **Supp. II Part 1:** 5; **Supp. II Part 2:** 420, 557, 564, 644; **Supp. IV Part 1:** 153; **Supp. V:** 343, 345; **Supp. VIII:** 305; **Supp. XIV:** 55, 96; **Supp. XV:** 349
"Cantus Planis" (Pound), **III:** 466
Cantwell, Robert, **Retro. Supp. I:** 85; **Supp. VIII:** 96; **Supp. XIII:** 292
"Can You Carry Me" (O'Hara), **III:** 369
Can You See Me Yet? (Findley), **Supp. XX:**52–53
Canzoneri, Robert, **IV:** 114, 116
Canzoni (Pound), **Retro. Supp. I:** 286, 288, 413
"Cap" (Shaw), **Supp. IV Part 1:** 345
"Cape Breton" (Bishop), **Supp. I Part 1:** 92; **Supp. IX:** 45

Cape Cod (Thoreau), **II:** 540
"Cape Cod, Rome, and Jerusalem" (Chapman), **Supp. XIV:** 55
Capitalism: The Unknown Ideal (Rand), **Supp. IV Part 2:** 518, 527, 531, 532
Caponi, Gena Dagel, **Supp. IV Part 1:** 95
Capote, Truman, **Supp. I Part 1:** 291, 292; **Supp. III Part 1:** 111–133; **Supp. III Part 2:** 574; **Supp. IV Part 1:** 198, 220; **Supp. VIII:** 105; **Supp. XII:** 43, 249; **Supp. XV:** 146; **Supp. XVI:** 245–246; **Supp. XVII:** 236
Capouya, Emile, **Supp. I Part 1:** 50
Cappetti, Carla, **Supp. IX:** 4, 8
Capra, Frank, **Supp. XVI:** 102
Capra, Fritjof, **Supp. X:** 261
Capron, Marion, **Supp. IX:** 193
"Capsule History of Conservation, A" (Stegner), **Supp. IV Part 2:** 600
"Captain Carpenter" (Ransom), **III:** 491
Captain Craig (Robinson), **III:** 508, 523; **Supp. II Part 1:** 192
"Captain Jim's Friend" (Harte), **Supp. II Part 1:** 337
"Captain Jones's Invitation" (Freneau), **Supp. II Part 1:** 261
"Captain's Son, The" (Taylor), **Supp. V:** 314, 325, 327
"Captain's Wife, The" (Salter), **Supp. IX:** 261
"Capt Christopher Levett (of York)" (Olson), **Supp. II Part 2:** 576, 577
Captive Israel (Reznikoff), **Supp. XIV:** 283
"Captivity and Restoration of Mrs. Mary Rowlandson, The" (Howe), **Supp. IV Part 2:** 419, 431, 434
"Captivity of the Fly" (MacLeish), **III:** 19
"Captured Goddess, The" (Lowell), **II:** 520
Caputi, Jane, **Supp. IV Part 1:** 334, 335
Caputo, Philip, **Supp. XI:** 234; **Supp. XIX:** 17–31
Capuzzo, Michael, **Supp. XIII:** 254
Car (Crews), **Supp. XI:** 110–111
Carabi, Angels, **Supp. VIII:** 223; **Supp. XII:** 215
"Caramels" (Zinberg), **Supp. XV:** 195
"Caravaggio: Swirl & Vortex" (Levis), **Supp. XI:** 258, 269
Caravan (Bynner), **Supp. XV:** 50
Carby, Hazel B., **Supp. IV Part 1:** 13; **Supp. XXI:** 171
"Carcassonne" (Faulkner), **Retro. Supp. I:** 81
Card, Antha E., **Supp. I Part 2:** 496
Cárdenas, Lupe, **Supp. IV Part 2:** 538, 539, 540
Cardinale, Anthony, **Supp. XVII:** 239
Cardinale, Ernesto, **Supp. XII:** 225
"Cardinal Ideograms" (Swenson), **Supp. IV Part 2:** 645
"Cards" (Beattie), **Supp. V:** 31
"Career Woman" (Hay), **Supp. XIV:** 131
Carefree (film, Sandrich), **Supp. XVII:** 59
"Careful" (Carver), **Supp. III Part 1:** 138

Careful and Strict Enquiry into the Modern Prevailing Notions of That Freedom of Will, Which Is Supposed to be Essential to Moral Agency, Vertue and Vice, Reward and Punishment, Praise and Blame, A (Edwards), **I:** 549, 557, 558, 562
Carel: A Poem and Pilgrimage in the Holy Land (Melville), **III:** 92–93
Careless Love and Its Apostrophes (Bronk), **Supp. XXI:** 32
"Carentan O Carentan" (Simpson), **Supp. IX:** 267
Carew, Thomas, **IV:** 453
Carey, Gary, **Supp. XVI:** 186
Carey, Mathew, **Supp. XV:** 238
"Car Games" (Conroy), **Supp. XVI:** 72
Cargill, Oscar, **Supp. II Part 1:** 117
Caribbean as Columbus Saw It (Morison and Obregon), **Supp. I Part 2:** 488
"Caribou Kitchen" (A. Finch), **Supp. XVII:** 76–77
Caribou Rising: Defending the Porcupine Herd, Gwich-'in Culture, and the Arctic National Wildlife Refuge (Bass), **Supp. XVI:** 27–28, 28
Carl, K. A., **III:** 475
Carleton, George W., **Supp. XVIII:** 4
Carlin, George, **Supp. XXI:** 51
Carlin, Terry, **Supp. XXI:** 4, 5, 14
Carlisle, Harry, **Supp. XVIII:** 223, 233
Carl Krinken: His Christmas Stocking (S. and A. Warner), **Supp. XVIII:** 264
"Carlos Who Died, and Left Only This, The" (Ríos), **Supp. IV Part 2:** 547
Carlotta (empress of Mexico), **Supp. I Part 2:** 457
Carl Sandburg (Golden), **III:** 579
Carlson, Susan L., **Supp. XV:** 323
Carlyle, Thomas, **I:** 103, 279; **II:** 5, 7, 11, 15–16, 17, 20, 145, 315; **III:** 82, 84, 85, 87; **IV:** 169, 182, 338, 350; **Retro. Supp. I:** 360, 408; **Supp. I Part 1:** 2, 349; **Supp. I Part 2:** 410, 422, 482, 485, 552
"Carma" (Toomer), **Supp. III Part 2:** 481–483; **Supp. IX:** 312–313
"Carmen de Boheme" (Crane), **I:** 384
Carmen Jones (film), **Supp. I Part 1:** 66
Carmina Burana (Orff), **Supp. X:** 63
Carnegie, Andrew, **I:** 483; **IV:** 192; **Supp. I Part 2:** 639, 644; **Supp. V:** 285
Carnegie, Dale, **Supp. I Part 2:** 608
"Carnegie Hall: Rescued" (Moore), **III:** 215
Carne-Ross, D. S., **Supp. I Part 1:** 268, 269
Carnes, Mark C., **Supp. X:** 14
"Carnets" poems (Sobin), **Supp. XVI:** 286–287
Carnovsky, Morris, **III:** 154
"Carol for Carolyn, A" (A. Finch), **Supp. XVII:** 74, 75
Caroling Dusk: An Anthology of Verse by Negro Poets (Cullen), **Supp. IV Part 1:** 166, 169
"Carol of Occupations" (Whitman), **I:** 486
"Carolyn Kizer and the Chain of Women" (A. Finch), **Supp. XVII:** 74–75

Carolyn Kizer: Perspectives on Her Life and Work (A. Finch), **Supp. XVII:** 74–75
"Carpe Diem" (Frost), **Supp. XII:** 303
"Carpe Noctem, if You Can" (Thurber), **Supp. I Part 2:** 620
Carpenter, Dan, **Supp. V:** 250
Carpenter, David, **Supp. VIII:** 297
Carpenter, Edward, **Supp. XX:** 230
Carpenter, Frederic I., **II:** 20
"Carpenter Bee" (Trethewey), **Supp. XXI:** 250
Carpentered Hen and Other Tame Creatures, The (Updike), **IV:** 214; **Retro. Supp. I:** 320
Carpenter's Gothic (Gaddis), **Supp. IV Part 1:** 288, 289–291, 293, 294
Carr, Dennis W., **Supp. IV Part 2:** 560
Carr, Elias, **Supp. XIV:** 57
Carr, Rosemary. *See* Benét, Rosemary
Carrall, Aaron, **Supp. IV Part 2:** 499
Carrel, Alexis, **IV:** 240
"Carrell/Klee/and Cosmos's Groom" (Goldbarth), **Supp. XII:** 183
"Carriage from Sweden, A" (Moore), **III:** 212
Carrie (King), **Supp. V:** 137
Carried Away (Harrison), **Supp. VIII:** 39
Carrier of Ladders (Merwin), **Supp. III Part 1:** 339, 346, 350–352, 356, 357
"Carriers of the Dream Wheel" (Momaday), **Supp. IV Part 2:** 481
Carriers of the Dream Wheel: Contemporary Native American Poetry (Niatum, ed.), **Supp. IV Part 2:** 484, 505
Carrington, Carroll, **I:** 199
"Carrion Spring" (Stegner), **Supp. IV Part 2:** 604
Carroll, Charles, **Supp. I Part 2:** 525
Carroll, Lewis, **I:** 432; **II:** 431; **III:** 181; **Supp. I Part 1:** 44; **Supp. I Part 2:** 622, 656; **Supp. XVI:** 103
"Carrots, Noses, Snow, Rose, Roses" (Gass), **Supp. VI:** 87
Carrouges, Michel, **Supp. IV Part 1:** 104
"Carrousel, The" (Rilke), **III:** 558
Carruth, Hayden, **Supp. IV Part 1:** 66; **Supp. VIII:** 39; **Supp. IX:** 291; **Supp. XIII:** 112; **Supp. XIV:** 273–274; **Supp. XVI:** 45–61; **Supp. XIX:** 1; **Supp. XXI:** 31
Carruth, Joe-Anne McLaughlin, **Supp. XVI:** 47
"Carry" (Hogan), **Supp. IV Part 1:** 412
"Carrying On" (Dunn), **Supp. XI:** 145
Cars of Cuba (García), **Supp. XI:** 190
Carson, Anne, **Supp. XII:** 97–116; **Supp. XV:** 252
Carson, Johnny, **Supp. IV Part 2:** 526
Carson, Rachel, **Supp. V:** 202; **Supp. IX:** 19–36; **Supp. X:** 99; **Supp. XVI:** 36
Carson, Tom, **Supp. XI:** 227
Cart, Michael, **Supp. X:** 12
Carter, Elliott, **Supp. III Part 1:** 21
Carter, Hodding, **Supp. XIV:** 2
Carter, Jared, **Supp. XVII:** 110
Carter, Jimmy, **Supp. I Part 2:** 638; **Supp. XIV:** 107
Carter, Marcia, **Supp. V:** 223
Carter, Mary, **Supp. IV Part 2:** 444

Carter, Paul, **Supp. XX:**77, 78
Carter, Peter, **Supp. XVIII:** 267
Carter, Stephen, **Supp. XI:** 220
Cartesian Sonata and Other Novellas (Gass), **Supp. VI: 92–93**
Cartier, Jacques, **Supp. I Part 2:** 496, 497
Cartier-Bresson, Henri, **Supp. VIII:** 98
"Cartographies of Silence" (Rich), **Supp. I Part 2:** 571–572
"Cartography" (Espaillat), **Supp. XXI:** 107
Cartwright, Louis, **Supp. XIV:** 147, 149, 151
Carver, Raymond, **Supp. III Part 1: 135–151; Supp. IV Part 1:** 342; **Supp. V:** 22, 23, 220, 326; **Supp. VIII:** 15; **Supp. X:** 85, 167; **Supp. XI:** 26, 65, 116, 153; **Supp. XII:** 79, 139, 289, 294; **Supp. XIX:** 209; **Supp. XXI:** 36, 115, 116, 118, 119
Carver: A Life in Poems (Nelson), **Supp. XVIII:** 171, 172, **181–182,** 183
Cary, Alice, **Retro. Supp. II:** 145; **Supp. XV:** 273
Cary, Phoebe, **Supp. XV:** 273
Cary, Richard, **Retro. Supp. II:** 132, 137
"Casabianca" (Bishop), **Retro. Supp. II:** 42; **Supp. I Part 1:** 86
Casablanca (film), **Supp. VIII:** 61; **Supp. XV:** 14
Casanova: His Known and Unknown Life (Endore), **Supp. XVII:** 54
"Casa solariega, La" ("The Family Mansion") (Espaillat), **Supp. XXI:** 107
"Case Against Mist, The" (Halliday), **Supp. XIX:** 91
Case for West-Indian Self-Government, The (C. L. R. James), **Supp. XXI:** 159, 161
Case of Rape, A (C. Himes), **Supp. XVI:** 143
Case of the Crushed Petunias, The (T. Williams), **IV:** 381
Case of the Officers of Excise (Paine), **Supp. I Part 2:** 503–504
Casey, John, **Supp. X:** 164
Cash, Arthur, **Supp. IV Part 1:** 299
Cashman, Nellie, **Supp. X:** 103
Casiero, Robert, **Supp. XIV:** 167
Casino Royale (film), **Supp. XI: 306–307**
Caskey, William, **Supp. XIV:** 166
"Cask of Amontillado, The" (Poe), **II:** 475; **III:** 413; **Retro. Supp. II:** 268, 269, 270, 273
Caso, Frank, **Supp. XVIII:** 95
Caspary, Vera, **Supp. XIX:** 78
Casper, Robert N., **Supp. XV:** 339, 347
Casper and His Friends (S. and A. Warner), **Supp. XVIII:** 264
Cassada (Salter), **Supp. IX: 251–252**
Cassady, Carolyn, **Supp. XIV:** 150
Cassady, Neal, **Supp. II Part 1:** 309, 311; **Supp. XIV:** 137, 144
"Cassandra Southwick" (Whittier), **Supp. I Part 2:** 693
Cassell, Verlin, **Supp. XI:** 315

Cassill, Ronald Verlin, **Supp. V:** 323; **Supp. XVIII:** 72; **Supp. XIX:** 266
Cassirer, Ernst, **I:** 265; **IV:** 87, 89
Cass Timberlane (Lewis), **II:** 455–456
Cast a Cold Eye (McCarthy), **II:** 566
Castaway (Cozzens), **I:** 363, 370, 374, 375, 379
"Caste in America" (Du Bois), **Supp. II Part 1:** 169
Castiglione, Baldassare, **I:** 279; **III:** 282
"Castilian" (Wylie), **Supp. I Part 2:** 714
Castillo, Ana, **Supp. XI:** 177
"Castle in Lynn, A" (McCarriston), **Supp. XIV:** 265, 268
"Castles and Distances" (Wilbur), **Supp. III Part 2:** 550
Castle Sinister (Marquand), **III:** 58
Cast of Thousands (Loos), **Supp. XVI:** 192, 193, 195
Castro, Fidel, **II:** 261, 434; **Supp. XX:**80
Cast the First Stone (C. Himes), **Supp. XVI:** 135, 137–138
"Casual Incident, A" (Hemingway), **II:** 44
"Casualty Report" (Halliday), **Supp. XIX:** 85
"Cat, The" (Matthews), **Supp. IX: 157–158**
Cat, You Better Come Home (Keillor), **Supp. XVI:** 177
"Catbird Seat, The" (Thurber), **Supp. I Part 2:** 623
"Catch" (Francis), **Supp. IX:** 82
Catch-22 (Heller), **III:** 558; **Supp. IV Part 1:** 379, 380, 381–382, 383, 384–386, 387, 390, 391, 392, 393, 394; **Supp. V:** 244, 248; **Supp. XII:** 167–168
Catcher in the Rye, The (Salinger), **I:** 493; **III:** 551, 552, 553–558, 567, 571; **Retro. Supp. I:** 102; **Retro. Supp. II:** 222, 249; **Supp. I Part 2:** 535; **Supp. V:** 119; **Supp. VIII:** 242; **Supp. XI:** 65; **Supp. XVII:** 2
"Catching Frogs" (Kenyon), **Supp. VII:** 170
Catching the Mermother (A. Finch), **Supp. XVII:** 72
catechism of d neoamerican hoodoo church (Reed), **Supp. X:** 240, 241
Catered Affair, The (film), **Supp. IV Part 2:** 683
"Cathay" (Goldbarth), **Supp. XII:** 185, 186
Cathay (Pound), **II:** 527; **Retro. Supp. I:** 289
Cathedral (Carver), **Supp. III Part 1:** 144–146; **Supp. XII:** 139
"Cathedral" (Carver), **Supp. III Part 1:** 144–145
Cathedral, The (Lowell), **Supp. I Part 2:** 407, 416–417
Cather, Willa, **I:** 312–334, 405; **II:** 51, 96, 177, 404, 412; **III:** 453; **IV:** 190; **Retro. Supp. I: 1–23,** 355, 382; **Retro. Supp. II:** 71, 136; **Supp. I Part 2:** 609, 719; **Supp. IV Part 1:** 31; **Supp. VIII:** 101, 102, 263; **Supp.**

X: 103; **Supp. XIII:** 253; **Supp. XIV:** 112; **Supp. XV:** 40, 51; **Supp. XVI:** 226; **Supp. XVIII:** 207; **Supp. XIX:** 131
Catherine, Saint, **II:** 211
Catherine II, **Supp. I Part 2:** 433
Catholic Art and Culture (Watkin), **Retro. Supp. II:** 187
"Catholic Novelist in the Protestant South, The" (O'Connor), **Retro. Supp. II:** 223, 224
"Cathy Queen of Cats" (Cisneros), **Supp. VII:** 59
Cat Inside, The (Burroughs), **Supp. III Part 1:** 105
Cat in the Hat, The (Geisel), **Supp. XVI:** 106–107, 112
Cat in the Hat Come Back, The (Geisel), **Supp. XVI:** 107
"Cat in the Hat for President, The" (Coover), **Supp. V:** 44, 46–47
Cat in The Hat Songbook, The (Geisel), **Supp. XVI:** 104
Cato, **II:** 114, 117
Cat on a Hot Tin Roof (T. Williams), **II:** 190; **IV:** 380, 382, 383, 386, 387, 389, 390, 391, 394, 395, 397–398
"Cat People: What Dr. Seuss Really Taught Us" (Menand), **Supp. XVI:** 106
Cat's Cradle (Vonnegut), **Supp. II Part 2:** 758, 759, 767–768, 770, 771, 772; **Supp. V:** 1
Cat's Eye (Atwood), **Supp. XIII: 29–30**
Catskill Eagle, A (Parker), **Supp. XIX:** 185
"Cat's Meow, A" (Brodsky), **Supp. VIII:** 31
Cat's Quizzer, The (Geisel), **Supp. XVI:** 111
"Catterskill Falls" (Bryant), **Supp. I Part 1:** 160
"Cattle Car Complex" (T. Rosenbaum), **Supp. XVII:** 48
Catullus, **Supp. XII:** 2, 13, **112; Supp. XV:** 23, 27, 35, 36
Catullus, Gaius Valerius, **I:** 381; **Supp. I Part 1:** 261; **Supp. I Part 2:** 728
Catullus (Gai Catulli Veronensis Liber) (Zukofsky), **Supp. III Part 2:** 625, 627, 628, 629
"Catullus: *Carmina*" (Carson), **Supp. XII: 112**
"*Catullus: Excrucior*" (Bidart), **Supp. XV:** 32, 35
"Cat Walked Through the Casserole, The" (Nelson and Espeland), **Supp. XVIII: 181**
Cat Walked Through the Casserole and Other Poems for Children (Nelson and Espeland), **Supp. XVIII:** 181
"Cat Who Aspired to Higher Things, The" (X. J. Kennedy), **Supp. XV:** 163
"Caucasian Storms Harlem, The" (R. Fisher), **Supp. XIX:** 78
Caudwell, Christopher, **Supp. X:** 112
"Caul, The" (Banks), **Supp. V:** 10–11
Cause for Wonder (Morris), **III:** 232–233
"Causerie" (Tate), **IV:** 129

Causes and Consequences (Chapman), **Supp. XIV:** 41, 49, 51

"Causes of American Discontents before 1768, The" (Franklin), **II:** 120

Causley, Charles, **Supp. XV:** 117

Cavafy, Constantine P., **Supp. IX:** 275; **Supp. XI:** 119, 123; **Supp. XXI:** 131

Cavalcade of America, The (radio program), **III:** 146

Cavalcanti (Pound, opera), **Retro. Supp. I:** 287

Cavalcanti, Guido, **I:** 579; **III:** 467; **Supp. III Part 2:** 620, 621, 622, 623

Cavalieri, Grace, **Supp. IV Part 2:** 630, 631

"Cavalry Crossing the Ford" (Whitman), **IV:** 347

"Cave, The" (Bass), **Supp. XVI:** 23

Cave, The (Warren), **IV:** 255–256

Cavell, Stanley, **Retro. Supp. I:** 306–307, 309

Cavender's House (Robinson), **III:** 510

Caver, Christine, **Supp. XXI:** 215

"Caviar" (Boyle), **Supp. XX:**19

Caviare at the Funeral (Simpson), **Supp. IX:** 266, **276–277**

"Cawdor" (Jeffers), **Supp. II Part 2:** 431

Caxton, William, **III:** 486

Cayton, Horace, **IV:** 475, 488

Cazamian, Louis, **II:** 529

Celan, Paul, **Supp. X:** 149; **Supp. XII:** 21, 110–111; **Supp. XVI:** 284–285, 288; **Supp. XVII:** 241

"Celebrated Jumping Frog of Calaveras County, The" (Twain), **IV:** 196

Celebrated Jumping Frog of Calaveras County, The, and Other Sketches (Twain), **IV:** 197

Celebration (Crews), **Supp. XI:** 103, **108**

Celebration (Swados), **Supp. XIX: 269–270**

Celebration at Dark (W. J. Smith), **Supp. XIII:** 332

"Celebration for June 24th" (McGrath), **Supp. X:** 116

Celebration of the Sound Through (Sobin), **Supp. XVI:** 284–285

Celebrations after the Death of John Brennan (X. J. Kennedy), **Supp. XV:** 165

Celebrity (film; Allen), **Supp. XV:** 11

"Celebrity" (Pickering), **Supp. XXI:** 198

"Celery" (Stein), **IV:** 43

"Celestial Games" (Conroy), **Supp. XVI:** 72

"Celestial Globe" (Nemerov), **III:** 288

Celestial Navigation (Tyler), **Supp. IV Part 2:** 662–663, 671

"Celestial Railroad, The" (Hawthorne), **Retro. Supp. I:** 152; **Supp. I Part 1:** 188

Celibate Season, A (Shields), **Supp. VII:** 323, 324

Cellini (Shanley), **Supp. XIV:** 316, **329–330**

"Cemetery at Academy, California" (Levine), **Supp. V:** 182

Cemetery Nights (Dobyns), **Supp. XIII:** 85, 87, 89

"Censors As Critics: *To Kill a Mockingbird* As a Case Study" (May), **Supp. VIII:** 126

"Census-Taker, The" (Frost), **Retro. Supp. I:** 129

"Centaur, The" (Swenson), **Supp. IV Part 2:** 641

Centaur, The (Updike), **IV:** 214, 216, 217, 218, 219–221, 222; **Retro. Supp. I:** 318, 322, 324, 331, 336

"Centennial Meditation of Columbia, The" (Lanier), **Supp. I Part 1:** 362

Centeno, Agusto, **IV:** 375

"Centipede" (Dove), **Supp. IV Part 1:** 246

"Central Man, The" (Bloom), **Supp. IV Part 2:** 689

"Central Park" (Lowell), **II:** 552

Central Park (Wasserstein and Drattel), **Supp. XV:** 333

Central Park West (Allen), **Supp. XV:** 13

Century of Dishonor, A (Jackson), **Retro. Supp. I:** 31

"Cerebral Snapshot, The" (Theroux), **Supp. VIII:** 313

"Ceremonies" (Rukeyser), **Supp. VI:** 279

Ceremony (Silko), **Supp. IV Part 1:** 274, 333; **Supp. IV Part 2:** 557–558, 558–559, 559, 561–566, 570; **Supp. XVIII:** 59

Ceremony (Wilbur), **Supp. III Part 2:** 550–551

"Ceremony, The" (Harjo), **Supp. XII:** 230

"Ceremony, The—Anatomy of a Massacre" (E. Hoffman, play), **Supp. XVI:** 160

Ceremony in Lone Tree (Morris), **III:** 229–230, 232, 238, 558

Ceremony of Brotherhood, A (Anaya and Ortiz, eds.), **Supp. IV Part 2:** 502

Cerf, Bennett, **III:** 405; **IV:** 288; **Retro. Supp. II:** 330; **Supp. XIII:** 172; **Supp. XIX:** 244

"Certain Attention to the World, A" (Haines), **Supp. XII:** 201

"Certain Beasts, Like Cats" (Bronk), **Supp. XXI:** 30

Certain Distance, A (Francis), **Supp. IX:** 85

"Certain Music, A" (Rukeyser), **Supp. VI:** 273

Certain Noble Plays of Japan (Pound), **III:** 458

Certain People (Wharton), **Retro. Supp. I:** 382

"Certain Poets" (MacLeish), **III:** 4

"Certain Testimony" (Bausch), **Supp. VII:** 48

Certificate, The (Singer), **IV:** 1; **Retro. Supp. II:** 314–315

"Cerulean" (Everett), **Supp. XVIII:** 66

Cervantes, Lorna Dee, **Supp. IV Part 2:** 545

Cervantes, Miguel de, **I:** 130, 134; **II:** 8, 272, 273, 276, 289, 302, 310, 315; **III:** 113, 614; **IV:** 367; **Retro. Supp. I:** 91; **Supp. I Part 2:** 406; **Supp. V:** 277; **Supp. XIII:** 17

Césaire, Aimé, **Supp. X:** 132, 139; **Supp. XIII:** 114

"Cesarean" (Kenyon), **Supp. VII:** 173

Cézanne, Paul, **II:** 576; **III:** 210; **IV:** 26, 31, 407; **Supp. V:** 333, 341–342; **Supp. XIX:** 36

Chabon, Michael, **Supp. XI: 63–81;** **Supp. XVI:** 259; **Supp. XIX:** 135, 138, 174, 223; **Supp. XX:**177

Chaboseau, Jean, **Supp. I Part 1:** 260

Chace, Bill, **Supp. XXI:** 256

Chaikin, Joseph, **Supp. III Part 2:** 433, 436–437

"Chain, The" (Kumin), **Supp. IV Part 2:** 452

Chainbearer, The (Cooper), **I:** 351, 352–353

"Chain of Love, A" (Price), **Supp. VI: 258–259,** 260

Chain Saw Dance, The (Budbill), **Supp. XIX: 5–6**

Chains of Dew (Glaspell), **Supp. III Part 1:** 181

Chalk Face (W. Frank), **Supp. XX:73–74**

Challacombe, Robert Hamilton, **III:** 176

Challenge (Untermeyer), **Supp. XV:** 296, 303

"Challenge" (Untermeyer), **Supp. XV:** 296

Chalmers, George, **Supp. I Part 2:** 514, 521

"Chambered Nautilus, The" (Holmes), **Supp. I Part 1:** 254, 307, 312–313, 314

Chamberlain, John, **Supp. I Part 2:** 647; **Supp. IV Part 2:** 525

Chamberlain, Neville, **II:** 589; **Supp. I Part 2:** 664

Chamber Music (Joyce), **III:** 16

Chambers, Richard, **Supp. III Part 2:** 610, 611, 612

Chambers, Whittaker, **Supp. III Part 2:** 610; **Supp. IV Part 2:** 526; **Supp. XV:** 143

Chameleon (C. Baxter), **Supp. XVII:** 14–15

"Champ, The" (Zinberg), **Supp. XV:** 193

"Champagne Regions" (Ríos), **Supp. IV Part 2:** 553

"Champion" (Lardner), **II:** 420–421, 428, 430

Champion, Laurie, **Supp. VIII:** 128

Champollion-Figeac, Jean Jacques, **IV:** 426

"Chance" (Doolittle), **Supp. I Part 1:** 271

Chance, Frank, **II:** 418

Chance Acquaintance, A (Howells), **II:** 278

"Chance Encounter, A" (Swados), **Supp. XIX:** 261, 262

"Chanclas" (Cisneros), **Supp. VII:** 61

Chandler, Raymond, **Supp. III Part 1:** 91; **Supp. IV Part 1: 119–138,** 341, 344, 345; **Supp. IV Part 2:** 461, 464, 469, 470, 471, 472, 473; **Supp. XI:** 160, 228; **Supp. XII:** 307; **Supp. XIII:** 159, 233; **Supp. XIV:** 21; **Supp.**

XV: 119; **Supp. XVI:** 122; **Supp. XVII:** 137; **Supp. XVIII:** 136,137, 137–138; **Supp. XIX:** 178, 189; **Supp. XXI:** 67

Chaney, "Professor" W. H., **II:** 463–464

Chang, Leslie C., **Supp. IV Part 1:** 72

"Change, The: Kyoto-Tokyo Express" (Ginsberg), **Supp. II Part 1:** 313, 329

Changed Man, A (Prose), **Supp. XVI:** 261–262

"Changeling" (Espaillat), **Supp. XXI:** 100

Changeling (Middleton), **Retro. Supp. I:** 62

"Changeling, The" (Lowell), **Supp. I Part 2:** 409

"Changeling, The" (Whittier), **Supp. I Part 2:** 697

Change of World, A (Rich), **Supp. I Part 2:** 551, 552

"Changes of Mind" (Baker), **Supp. XIII:** 52

"Change the Joke and Slip the Yoke" (Ellison), **Retro. Supp. II:** 118

Changing Light at Sandover, The (Merrill), **Supp. III Part 1:** 318, 319, 323, 327, 332, 335–336; **Supp. XII:** 269–270; **Supp. XV:** 264

"Changing Same, The" (Baraka), **Supp. II Part 1:** 47, 51, 53

Changing the Bully Who Rules the World: Reading and Thinking about Ethics (C. Bly), **Supp. XVI:** 32, **39–40,** 41

Chanler, Mrs. Winthrop, **I:** 22; **IV:** 325

Channing, Carol, **IV:** 357

Channing, Edward, **Supp. I Part 2:** 479–480

Channing, Edward Tyrrel, **Supp. I Part 1:** 155; **Supp. I Part 2:** 422

Channing, William Ellery, **I:** 336; **II:** 224, 495; **IV:** 172, 173, 176, 177; **Retro. Supp. I:** 54; **Supp. I Part 1:** 103; **Supp. I Part 2:** 589

Channing, William Henry, **IV:** 178; **Supp. II Part 1:** 280, 285

Chanson de Roland, La, **I:** 13

"Chanson un Peu Naïve" (Bogan), **Supp. III Part 1:** 50–51

"Chanteuse" (Doty), **Supp. XI:** 119

"Chant for May Day" (Hughes), **Supp. I Part 1:** 331

Chants (Mora), **Supp. XIII: 214–215**

Chaos (Dove), **Supp. IV Part 1:** 243

"Chaperone, The" (Van Vechten), **Supp. II Part 2:** 728

Chaplin, Charles Spencer "Charlie", **I:** 27, 32, 43, 386, 447; **III:** 403; **Supp. I Part 2:** 607; **Supp. IV Part 1:** 146; **Supp. IV Part 2:** 574; **Supp. XX:**75; **Supp. XXI:** 170

"Chaplinesque" (H. Crane), **Retro. Supp. II:** 79

"Chapman" (Rukeyser), **Supp. VI:** 273

Chapman, Abraham, **IV:** 485

Chapman, George, **Supp. I Part 2:** 422

Chapman, John (Johnny Appleseed), **Supp. I Part 2:** 397

Chapman, John Jay, **IV:** 436; **Supp. XIV: 39–56**

Chapman, Stephen, **Supp. XIII:** 12

Chappell, Fred, **Supp. IV Part 1:** 69; **Supp. XI:** 317; **Supp. XVIII:** 87

Chapters in a Mythology: The Poetry of Sylvia Plath (Kroll), **Supp. I Part 2:** 541–543

Chapters on Erie (Adams and Adams), **Supp. I Part 2:** 644

Chapter Two (Simon), **Supp. IV Part 2:** 575, 586

"Chapter VI" (Hemingway), **II:** 252

Char, René, **Supp. XVI:** 282; **Supp. XVII:** 244

"Character" (Emerson), **II:** 6

"Character of Presidents, The" (Doctorow), **Supp. IV Part 1:** 224

"Character of Socrates, The" (Emerson), **II:** 8–9

Character of the Poet, The (Simpson), **Supp. IX:** 273, 275, 278

"Characters in Fiction" (McCarthy), **II:** 562

"Charades" (Moore), **Supp. X:** 178

"Charge It" (Fante), **Supp. XI:** 164–165

"Charity" (Peacock), **Supp. XIX:** 221–222

Charity (Richard), **Supp. XIX: 220–222**

Charlatan, The (Singer), **IV:** 1

"Charles" (Jackson), **Supp. IX:** 125

Charles, Larry, **Supp. XVIII:** 21

"Charles Baxter, August Kleinzahler, Adrienne Rich: Contemporary Stevensians and the Problem of 'Other Lives' " (S. Burt), **Supp. XVII:** 18–19

Charles Goodnight: Cowman and Plainsman (Haley), **Supp. V:** 226

Charles Simic: Essays on the Poetry (Weigl), **Supp. VIII:** 269

Charles the Bold, Duke of Burgundy, **III:** 487

Charleville, Victoria Verdon, **Supp. I Part 1:** 200–201, 205, 206, 210

Charley's Aunt (B. Thomas), **II:** 138

Charlie Chan Is Dead: An Anthology of Contemporary Asian American Fiction (Hagedorn), **Supp. X:** 292

"Charlie Christian Story, The" (Ellison), **Retro. Supp. II:** 121

"Charlie Howard's Descent" (Doty), **Supp. XI:** 122

Charlotte: A Tale of Truth (Rowson), **Supp. I Part 1:** 128; **Supp. XV: 234–235,** 238. *See also Charlotte Temple* (Rowson)

Charlotte's Daughter; or, The Three Orphans (Rowson), **Supp. XV: 246**

Charlotte's Web (White), **Supp. I Part 2:** 655, 656, 658, 667, 670

Charlotte Temple (Rowson), **Supp. XV:** 229, **238–239.** *See also Charlotte: A Tale of Truth* (Rowson)

Charm, The (Creeley), **Supp. IV Part 1:** 139, 141, 144, 149–150

Charmed Life, A (McCarthy), **II:** 571–574

Charming Billy (McDermott), **Supp. XVIII:** 155, **162–164,** 166

Charms for the Easy Life (Gibbons), **Supp. X:** 45, **47–48**

Charnel Rose, The (Aiken), **I:** 50, 57, 62

Charon's Cosmology (Simic), **Supp. VIII: 276–278**

Charterhouse, The (Percy), **Supp. III Part 1:** 388

Chart for Rough Water (W. Frank), **Supp. XX:**78

Charvat, William, **II:** 244

Charyn, Jerome, **Supp. XVII:** 5

Chase, Mary Ellen, **Retro. Supp. II:** 243, 245

Chase, Richard, **IV:** 202, 443; **Retro. Supp. I:** 40, 395

Chase, Salmon P., **Supp. I Part 2:** 584

Chase, Stuart, **Supp. I Part 2:** 609

Chase, The (Foote), **Supp. I Part 1:** 281

Chasing the Dime (Connelly), **Supp. XXI: 74**

"Chaste Land, The" (Tate), **IV:** 122

Château, The (Maxwell), **Supp. VIII:** 152, 160, **165–167,** 168, 169

Chatham, Russell, **Supp. VIII:** 40

"Chattanooga Nights" (L. Brown), **Supp. XXI:** 39

Chatterdon, The Black Death, and Meriwether Lewis (Reznikoff), **Supp. XIV:** 288

Chatterton, Thomas, **Supp. I Part 1:** 349; **Supp. I Part 2:** 410, 716

Chatterton, Wayne, **Supp. IX:** 2, 4, 11–12

Chatwin, Bruce, **Supp. VIII:** 322

Chaucer, Geoffrey, **I:** 131; **II:** 11, 504, 516, 542, 543; **III:** 283, 411, 473, 492, 521; **Retro. Supp. I:** 135, 426; **Supp. I Part 1:** 356, 363; **Supp. I Part 2:** 422, 617; **Supp. V:** 259; **Supp. XII:** 197; **Supp. XVII:** 70; **Supp. XIX:** 4

Chauncy, Charles, **I:** 546–547; **IV:** 147

Chavez, César, **Supp. V:** 199

Chávez, Denise, **Supp. IV Part 2:** 544; **Supp. XI:** 316

Chavez, Lydia, **Supp. VIII:** 75

Chavkin, Allan, **Supp. IV Part 1:** 259

Chavkin, Nancy Feyl, **Supp. IV Part 1:** 259

Chawla, Louise, **Supp. XXI:** 24

Chayefsky, Paddy, **Supp. XI:** 306

Cheang, Shu Lea, **Supp. XI:** 20

"Cheat Takes Over" (Leopold), **Supp. XIV:** 189

"Cheers" (Carver), **Supp. III Part 1:** 138

Cheetham, James, **Supp. I Part 2:** 521

Cheever, Benjamin Hale, **Supp. I Part 1:** 175

Cheever, David W., **Supp. I Part 1:** 304

Cheever, Ezekiel, **Supp. I Part 1:** 174, 193

Cheever, Federico, **Supp. I Part 1:** 175

Cheever, Fred, **Supp. I Part 1:** 174

Cheever, Frederick L., **Supp. I Part 1:** 174

Cheever, John, **Retro. Supp. I:** 116, 333, 335; **Supp. I Part 1: 174–199; Supp. V:** 23, 95; **Supp. VIII:** 151; **Supp. IX:** 114, 208; **Supp. XI:** 65, 66, 99; **Supp. XII:** 140; **Supp. XIV:** 93; **Supp. XV:** 119, 142

Cheever, Mrs. John (Mary Winternitz), **Supp. I Part 1:** 175

Cheever, Mary Liley, **Supp. I Part 1:** 174

Cheever, Susan. *See* Cowley, Susan Cheever (Susan Cheever)

Cheever Evening, A (Gurney), **Supp. V:** 95

Chekhov, Anton, **I:** 52, 90; **II:** 27, 38, 44, 49, 198, 542; **III:** 362, 467; **IV:** 17, 53, 359, 446; **Retro. Supp. I:** 5, 355; **Retro. Supp. II:** 299; **Supp. I Part 1:** 196; **Supp. II Part 1:** 6; **Supp. IV Part 2:** 585; **Supp. V:** 265; **Supp. VIII:** 153, 332; **Supp. IX:** 260, 265, 274; **Supp. XI:** 66; **Supp. XII:** 94, 307; **Supp. XIII:** 79; **Supp. XIV:** 87, 242; **Supp. XV:** 320, 329; **Supp. XVIII:** 102; **Supp. XIX:** 172, 241

"Chekhov's Sense of Writing as Seen Through His Letters" (Dobyns), **Supp. XIII:** 77–78

"Chemin de Fer" (Bishop), **Retro. Supp. II:** 41; **Supp. I Part 1:** 80, 85, 86

Cheney, Brainard, **Retro. Supp. II:** 229

Chenzira, Ayoka, **Supp. XI:** 19

Chéri (Colette; stage adaptation, Loos), **Supp. XVI:** 194

Cherkovski, Neeli, **Supp. XII:** 118, 132, 134

Chernyshevski, Nikolai, **III:** 261, 262, 263; **Retro. Supp. I:** 269

Cherokee Lottery, The: A Sequence of Poems (W. J. Smith), **Supp. XIII:** 340–344

Cherry (Karr), **Supp. XI:** 239, **251–254**

"Cherrylog Road" (Dickey), **Supp. XVIII:** 191

Cherry Orchard, The (Chekhov), **IV:** 359, 426; **Supp. VIII:** 153

Cheslock, Louis, **III:** 99, 118, 119

Chesnutt, Charles Waddell, **Supp. II Part 1:** 174, 193, 211; **Supp. IV Part 1:** 257; **Supp. XIV:** **57–78**

"Chess House, The" (Dixon), **Supp. XII:** 139

Chessman, Caryl, **Supp. I Part 2:** 446

Chester, Alfred, **Retro. Supp. II:** 111, 112; **Supp. X:** 192

Chesterfield, Lord, **II:** 36

Chesterton, Gilbert Keith, **I:** 226; **IV:** 432

Cheuse, Alan, **Supp. IV Part 2:** 570

Chevigny, Bell Gale, **Supp. XI:** 283

"Chicago" (Sandburg), **III:** 581, 592, 596; **Supp. III Part 1:** 71

Chicago (Shepard), **Supp. III Part 2:** 439

Chicago: City on the Make (Algren), **Supp. IX:** 1, 3

"*Chicago Defender* Sends a Man to Little Rock, The" (Brooks), **Supp. III Part 1:** 80–81

"Chicago Hamlet, A" (Anderson), **I:** 112

Chicago Loop (Theroux), **Supp. VIII:** 324

"Chicago Picasso, The" (Brooks), **Supp. III Part 1:** 70–71, 84

Chicago Poems (Sandburg), **III:** 579, 581–583, 586

"Chicano/Borderlands Literature and Poetry" (Ríos), **Supp. IV Part 2:** 537, 538, 542, 545

Chick, Nancy, **Supp. IV Part 1:** 1

"Chickamauga" (Bierce), **I:** 201

"Chickamauga" (Wolfe), **IV:** 460

Chickamauga (Wright), **Supp. V:** 333, 343–344

"Chickamauga" (Wright), **Supp. V:** 334

"Chicken Market" (Skloot), **Supp. XX:** 198, 200

"Chiefly about War Matters" (Hawthorne), **II:** 227; **Retro. Supp. I:** 165

"Chiffon" (Hull), **Supp. XXI:** 138

"Child" (Plath), **Supp. I Part 2:** 544

Child, Greg, **Supp. XVIII:** 107

Child, Julia, **Supp. XVII:** 89, 90

Child, Lydia Maria, **Supp. XIII:** 141; **Supp. XVIII:** 11

"Child, The" (Ríos), **Supp. IV Part 2:** 543

"Child by Tiger, The" (Wolfe), **IV:** 451

"Childhood" (Wright), **Supp. V:** 341

Childhood, A: The Biography of a Place (Crews), **Supp. XI:** 102–103, 245

"Childhood, When You Are in It . . ." (Kenyon), **Supp. VII:** 160, 170

"Childhood Sketch" (Wright), **Supp. III Part 2:** 589

"Child Is Born, A" (Benét), **Supp. XI:** 46

"Child Is the Meaning of This Life, The" (Schwartz), **Supp. II Part 2:** 659–660

"Childlessness" (Merrill), **Supp. III Part 1:** 323

"Childless Woman" (Plath), **Supp. I Part 2:** 544

Child-Life (Whittier and Larcom, eds.), **Supp. XIII:** 142

Child-Life in Prose (Whittier and Larcom, eds.), **Supp. XIII:** 142

Childlike Life of the Black Tarantula, The (Acker), **Supp. XII:** 4, 6, **7–8**

"Child Margaret" (Sandburg), **III:** 584

"Child of Courts, The" (Jarrell), **II:** 378, 379, 381

Child of God (McCarthy), **Supp. VIII:** **177–178**

Child of My Heart (McDermott), **Supp. XVIII:** 155, **164–166**

"CHILD OF THE THIRTIES" (Baraka), **Supp. II Part 1:** 60

"Child on Top of a Greenhouse" (Roethke), **III:** 531

Children (Gurney), **Supp. V:** 95, 96

"Children" (Stowe), **Supp. I Part 2:** 587

"Children, The" (Jarman), **Supp. XVII:** 116

Children, The (Wharton), **IV:** 321, 326; **Retro. Supp. I:** 381

"Children, the Sandbar, That Summer" (Rukeyser), **Supp. VI:** 274

Children and Others (Cozzens), **I:** 374

Children Is All (Purdy), **Supp. VII:** 277, 278, 282

"Children of Adam" (Whitman), **IV:** 342; **Retro. Supp. I:** 403, 405

Children of Job, The: American Second-Generation Witnesses to the Holocaust (A. Berger), **Supp. XVII:** 39

Children of Light (Stone), **Supp. V:** 304–306

Children of Light and the Children of Darkness, The (Niebuhr), **III:** 292, 306, 310

Children of the Frost (London), **II:** 469, 483

Children of the Holocaust (H. Epstein), **Supp. XVII:** 48

"Children of the Lord's Supper, The" (Tegnér), **Retro. Supp. II:** 155, 157

Children of the Market Place (Masters), **Supp. I Part 2:** 471

"Children on Their Birthdays" (Capote), **Supp. III Part 1:** 114, 115

"Children Selecting Books in a Library" (Jarrell), **II:** 371

Children's Hour, The (Hellman), **Supp. I Part 1:** 276–277, 281, 286, 297

"Children's Rhymes" (Hughes), **Supp. I Part 1:** 340

Childress, Mark, **Supp. X:** 89

Child's Garden of Verses, A (Stevenson), **Supp. IV Part 1:** 298, 314; **Supp. XIII:** 75

"Child's Nature, A" (Jin), **Supp. XVIII:** 93

"Child's Reminiscence, A" (Whitman), **IV:** 344

Childwold (Oates), **Supp. II Part 2:** 519–520

Chill, The (Macdonald), **Supp. IV Part 2:** 473

Chills and Fever (Ransom), **III:** 490, 491–492, 493

Chilly Scenes of Winter (Beattie), **Supp. V:** 21, 22, 23, 24, 26, 27

Chime of Words, A: The Letters of Logan Pearsall Smith (Tribble, ed.), **Supp. XIV:** 348–349

Chimera (C. Frost), **Supp. XV:** 94, 95, 100

"Chimes for Yahya" (Merrill), **Supp. III Part 1:** 329

Chin, Frank, **Supp. V:** 164, 172

Chin, Mei, **Supp. XVIII:** 95

"China" (Johnson), **Supp. VI:** **193–194**

Chinaberry Tree, The (Fauset), **Supp. XIX:** 73

"Chinaman's Hat" (Kingston), **Supp. V:** 169

China Men (Kingston), **Supp. V:** 157, 158, 159, 160, 161, 164–169; **Supp. X:** 292; **Supp. XV:** 220

"China Poet, The" (Sturgis), **Supp. XX:** 233, 240

China Trace (Wright), **Supp. V:** 332, 340, 341, 342

"Chinese Apples" (Di Piero), **Supp. XIX:** 40

Chinese Apples: New and Selected Poems (Di Piero), **Supp. XIX:** 33, 36, 37, 38, 39, 40, 44, 45, 46, 47–48

Chinese Classics (Legge), **III:** 472

Chinese Materia Medica (P. Smith), **III:** 572

"Chinese New Year" (Hull), **Supp. XXI:** 135

"Chinese Nightingale, The" (Lindsay), **Supp. I Part 2:** 392–393, 394

Chinese Nightingale and Other Poems, The (Lindsay), **Supp. I Part 2:** 392

Chinese Siamese Cat, The (Tan), **Supp. X:** 289
Chinese Translations, The (Bynner), **Supp. XV:** 47, 52
Chinitz, David, **Supp. XV:** 180, 185
"Chinoiseries" (Lowell), **II:** 524–525
Chip (Untermeyer), **Supp. XV:** 310
Chirico, Giorgio de, **Supp. III Part 1:** 14
Chirico, Miriam M., **Supp. XV:** 323
"Chiron" (Winters), **Supp. II Part 2:** 801
"Chitlins at the Waldorf" (Crouch), **Supp. XIX:** 158
"Chloroform Jags" (J. Scott), **Supp. XVII:** 189
Chodorov, Jerome, **IV:** 274
"Choice, The" (Karr), **Supp. XI:** 251
"Choice of Accommodations, A" (Lahiri), **Supp. XXI:** 183
"Choice of Profession, A" (Malamud), **Supp. I Part 2:** 437
Choice of Wars, A (Shaw), **Supp. XIX:** 245
Chomei, Kamo No, **IV:** 170, 171, 184
Chomsky, Noam, **Supp. IV Part 2:** 679
Choosing not Choosing (Cameron), **Retro. Supp. I:** 43
Chopin, Felix, **Supp. I Part 1:** 202
Chopin, Frédéric, **Supp. I Part 1:** 363
Chopin, Jean, **Supp. I Part 1:** 206
Chopin, Kate, **II:** 276; **Retro. Supp. I:** 10, 215; **Retro. Supp. II:** 57–74; **Supp. I Part 1:** 200–226; **Supp. V:** 304; **Supp. X:** 227; **Supp. XVIII:** 194
"Choral: The Pink Church" (W. C. Williams), **Retro. Supp. I:** 428
"Chord" (Merwin), **Supp. III Part 1:** 356
"Chords and Dischords" (column; Untermeyer), **Supp. XV:** 294
Choruses from Iphigenia in Aulis (Doolittle, trans.), **Supp. I Part 1:** 257, 268, 269
"Chosen Blindness" (Karr), **Supp. XI:** 251
Chosen Country (Dos Passos), **I:** 475, 490–491
Chosen Place, The Timeless People, The (Marshall), **Supp. XI:** 275, 276, 282–284
Chosŏn (Lowell), **II:** 513
Choukri, Mohamed, **Supp. IV Part 1:** 92
Chovteau, Mane Thérèse, **Supp. I Part 1:** 205
"ChrisEaster" (Peacock), **Supp. XIX:** 198, 199
Chrisman, Robert, **Supp. IV Part 1:** 1
Christabel (Coleridge), **Supp. IV Part 2:** 465
"Christ for Sale" (Lowell), **II:** 538
Christian, Graham, **Supp. XII:** 193
Christian Dictionary, A (Wilson), **IV:** 153
"Christian in World Crisis, The" (Merton), **Supp. VIII:** 203
Christianity and Power Politics (Niebuhr), **III:** 292, 303
"Christianity and the Survival of Creation" (Berry), **Supp. X:** 30
"Christian Minister, The" (Emerson), **II:** 10
Christian Philosopher, The (Mather), **Supp. II Part 2:** 463–464

Christian Realism and Practical Problems (Niebuhr), **III:** 292, 308
"Christian Roommates, The" (Updike), **IV:** 226–227; **Retro. Supp. I:** 319, 323
Christiansen, Carrie, **I:** 210
Christian's Secret of a Happy Life, The (H. W. Smith), **Supp. XIV:** 333–334
Christie, Agatha, **Supp. IV Part 1:** 341; **Supp. IV Part 2:** 469
Christ in Concrete (di Donato), **Supp. XX:**33, **34–40**, 42, 43, 46
"Christ in Concrete" (di Donato), **Supp. XX:**34
Christine (King), **Supp. V:** 139, 148
"Christ Light, The" (Chopin), **Retro. Supp. II:** 61
"Christmas" (Saunders), **Supp. XIX:** 232
"Christmas, or the Good Fairy" (Stowe), **Supp. I Part 2:** 586
"Christmas 1944" (Levertov), **Supp. III Part 1:** 274
"Christmas Banquet, The" (Hawthorne), **II:** 227
Christmas Card, A (Theroux), **Supp. VIII:** 322
Christmas Carol, A (Dickens), **Retro. Supp. I:** 196; **Supp. I Part 2:** 409–410; **Supp. X:** 252, 253
"Christmas Eve at Johnson's Drugs N Goods" (Bambara), **Supp. XI:** 11–12
"Christmas Eve in the Time of War: A Capitalist Meditates by a Civil War Monument" (Lowell), **II:** 538
"Christmas Eve under Hooker's Statue" (Lowell), **II:** 539–540
"Christmas Gift" (Warren), **IV:** 252–253
"Christmas Greeting, A" (Wright), **Supp. III Part 2:** 601
"Christmas Hymn, A" (Wilbur), **Supp. III Part 2:** 557
Christmas Memory, A (Capote), **Supp. III Part 1:** 118, 119, 129
"Christmass Poem" (West), **Retro. Supp. II:** 338
Christmas Story (Mencken), **III:** 111
"Christmas to Me" (Lee), **Supp. VIII:** 113
Christographia (Taylor), **IV:** 164–165
"Christ on the Cross/Nuestro Señor Crucificado" (Mora), **Supp. XIII:** 229
Christopher, Mary (pseudonym). *See* West, Dorothy
Christopher and His Kind: 1929–1939 (Isherwood), **Supp. XIV:** 157, 163, 164, 171
"Christopher Cat" (Cullen), **Supp. IV Part 1:** 173
Christopher Columbus, Mariner (Morison), **Supp. I Part 2:** 488
Christopher Isherwood: A Critical Biography (Finney), **Supp. XIV:** 158
Christophersen, Bill, **Supp. IX:** 159, 167; **Supp. XI:** 155; **Supp. XIII:** 87; **Supp. XXI:** 103
"Christ's Passion" (Karr), **Supp. XI:** 251
Christus: A Mystery (Longfellow), **II:** 490, 493, 495, 505–507; **Retro. Supp. II:** 161, 165, 166

Chroma (F. Barthelme), **Supp. XI:** 30, 33, 34
"Chroma" (F. Barthelme), **Supp. XI:** 31
"Chronicle of Race Relations, A" (Du Bois), **Supp. II Part 1:** 182
Chronicle of the Conquest of Granada (Irving), **II:** 310
Chronicles: Volume One (Dylan), **Supp. XVIII:** 20, 21, 23, 24, 28, **32–33**
"Chronologues" (Goldbarth), **Supp. XII:** 183, 184
"Chrysanthemums, The" (Steinbeck), **IV:** 53
"Chrysaor" (Longfellow), **II:** 498
Chu, Louis, **Supp. X:** 291
Chuang, Hua, **Supp. X:** 291
Chuang-Tzu, **Supp. VIII:** 206
"Chunk of Amethyst, A" (R. Bly), **Supp. IV Part 1:** 72
Church, Margaret, **IV:** 466
"Church and the Fiction Writer, The" (O'Connor), **Retro. Supp. II:** 223, 233; **Supp. XVIII:** 161
"Church Going" (Larkin), **Supp. XXI:** 93
"Churchgoing" (Nelson), **Supp. XVIII:** 173
Churchill, Charles, **Supp. XV:** 232
Churchill, Winston, **I:** 9, 490; **Supp. I Part 2:** 491
Church of Dead Girls, The (Dobyns), **Supp. XIII:** 75, **83–84**
"Church of Omnivorous Light, The" (Wrigley), **Supp. XVIII:** 306–307
"Church Porch, The" (Herbert), **IV:** 153
Church Psalmody, Selected from Dr. Watts and Other Authors (Mason and Greene, ed.), **I:** 458
Ciannic, Saint, **II:** 215
Ciano, Edda, **IV:** 249
Ciardi, John, **I:** 169, 179, 535; **III:** 268; **Supp. IV Part 1:** 243; **Supp. IV Part 2:** 639; **Supp. IX:** 269, 324; **Supp. XII:** 119
Cicada (Haines), **Supp. XII:** 206–207
"Cicadas" (Wilbur), **Supp. III Part 2:** 549
Cicero, **I:** 279; **II:** 8, 14–15; **III:** 23; **Supp. I Part 2:** 405
Cider House Rules, The (Irving), **Supp. VI:** 164, **173–175**
"Cigales" (Wilbur), **Supp. III Part 2:** 549
"Cigarette" (L. Michaels), **Supp. XVI:** 214
Cimarron, Rose (Burke), **Supp. XIV:** 22, 35
"Cimetière Marin, Le" (Valéry), **IV:** 91–92
Cimino, Michael, **Supp. X:** 126
Cincinnati Kid, The (film), **Supp. XI:** 306
"Cinderella" (Jarrell), **II:** 386
"Cinderella" (Perrault), **IV:** 266, 267
"Cinderella" (Sexton), **Supp. II Part 2:** 691
"Cinema, The" (Salter), **Supp. IX:** 257
Cinema of Tony Richardson, The: Essays and Interviews (Phillips), **Supp. XI:** 306
Cinthio, **IV:** 370

Ciolkowski, Laura, **Supp. XVI:** 24
CIOPW (Cummings), **I:** 429
"Circe" (Welty), **Retro. Supp. I:** 353
Circle Game, The (Atwood), **Supp. XIII:** 20, 33
"Circle in the Fire, A" (O'Connor), **III:** 344–345, 349–350, 351, 353, 354; **Retro. Supp. II:** 229, 232
"Circle of Breath" (Stafford), **Supp. XI:** 318, 322
Circle of Hanh, The (Weigl), **Supp. XIX:** 273, 275, 282, **284–286**
"Circles" (Emerson), **I:** 455, 460
"Circles" (Lowell), **II:** 554
"Circus, The" (Porter), **III:** 443, 445
"Circus Animals' Desertion" (Yeats), **I:** 389
"Circus in the Attic" (Warren), **IV:** 253
Circus in the Attic, The (Warren), **IV:** 243, 251–253
"Circus in Three Rings" (Plath), **Retro. Supp. II:** 243; **Supp. I Part 2:** 536
Circus of Needs, A (Dunn), **Supp. XI:** **147–148**
"Cirque d'Hiver" (Bishop), **Supp. I Part 1:** 85
Cisneros, Sandra, **Supp. IV Part 2:** 544; **Supp. VII:** **57–73; Supp. XI:** 177; **Supp. XVII:** 71
Cities of the Interior (Nin), **Supp. X:** 182
Cities of the Plain (McCarthy), **Supp. VIII:** 175, **186–187**
Cities of the Red Night (Burroughs), **Supp. III Part 1:** 106
"Citizen Cain" (Baraka), **Supp. II Part 1:** 49
Citizen Kane (film), **Retro. Supp. I:** 115; **Supp. V:** 251; **Supp. XI:** 169
"Citizen of the World" (Goldsmith), **II:** 299
"City" (Francis), **Supp. IX:** 87
City and the Pillar, The (Vidal), **Supp. IV Part 2:** 677, 680–681; **Supp. XIV:** 170
"*City and the Pillar, The,* as Gay Fiction" (Summers), **Supp. IV Part 2:** 680–681
"City Articles" series (Briggs), **Supp. XVIII:** 12
City Block (W. Frank), **Supp. XX:** 71, 72, 76
City Boy (L. Michaels), **Supp. XVI:** 212
"City Boy" (L. Michaels), **Supp. XVI:** 203–204
City Dog (Di Piero), **Supp. XIX:** 33–34, 35, 38, 46, 48
"City Dog" (Di Piero), **Supp. XIX:** 47
City in History, The (Mumford), **Supp. II Part 2:** 495
"City in the Sea, The" (Poe), **III:** 411; **Retro. Supp. II:** 274
City in Which I Love You, The (L.-Y. Lee), **Supp. XV:** 212, **215–220**
"City in Which I Love You, The" (L.-Y. Lee), **Supp. XV:** 215, **217–218**
City Life (Barthelme), **Supp. IV Part 1:** 44, 47
City of Bones (Connelly), **Supp. XXI:** **74–75,** 77

"City of Change, A" (Bynner), **Supp. XV:** 45
City of Glass (Auster), **Supp. XII:** 22, **24–26**
City of God, The (St. Augustine), **IV:** 126
"City of Refuge, The" (R. Fisher), **Supp. XIX:** 65, 66, **67–68**
City of Refuge, The: The Collected Stories of Rudolph Fisher (McCluskey, ed.), **Supp. XIX:** 68–69
City of the Living and Other Stories, The (Stegner), **Supp. IV Part 2:** 599, 609, 613
City of Words: American Fiction 1950-1970 (T. Tanner), **Supp. XVI:** 69
City of Your Final Destination, The (Cameron), **Supp. XII:** 79, 82, **91–94**
"City on a Hill" (Lowell), **II:** 552
"City Person Encountering Nature, A" (Kingston), **Supp. V:** 170
"City Planners, The" (Atwood), **Supp. XIII:** 33
City Without Men (film), **Supp. XVIII:** 247
City Without Walls (Auden), **Supp. II Part 1:** 24
Civil Disobedience (Thoreau), **IV:** 185; **Supp. I Part 2:** 507
Civilization in the United States (Stearns), **I:** 245
"Civil Rights" (Lanier), **Supp. I Part 1:** 357
CivilWarLand in Bad Decline (Saunders), **Supp. XIX:** **224–227**
"CivilWarLand in Bad Decline" (Saunders), **Supp. XIX:** 224–225, 227
Civitatis Anthology of African American Slave Narratives, The (H. L. Gates and Andrews, eds.), **Supp. XX:** 105
Cixous, Hélène, **Supp. X:** 102; **Supp. XIII:** 297; **Supp. XV:** 347
Claiborne, Craig, **Supp. XVII:** 89
Claiborne, William, **I:** 132
Claiming of Sleeping Beauty, The (Rice), **Supp. VII:** 301
Clampitt, Amy, **Supp. IX:** **37–54; Supp. X:** 120; **Supp. XI:** 249; **Supp. XV:** 251, 256
Clancy's Wake, At (Crane), **I:** 422
"Clandeboye" (Leopold), **Supp. XIV:** 189
Clara Howard; or, The Enthusiasm of Love (Brown), **Supp. I Part 1:** 145
Clara's Ole Man (Bullins), **Supp. II Part 1:** 42
Clare, John, **II:** 387; **III:** 528; **Supp. XVI:** 295
Clarel: A Poem and Pilgrimage in the Holy Land (Melville), **Retro. Supp. I:** 257
Clarissa (Richardson), **II:** 111; **Supp. I Part 2:** 714; **Supp. V:** 127; **Supp. XV:** 231; **Supp. XX:** 236
Clark, Alex, **Supp. XII:** 307
Clark, Charles, **I:** 470
Clark, Eleanor. *See* Warren, Mrs. Robert Penn (Eleanor Clark)
Clark, Francis Edward, **II:** 9
Clark, Geoffrey, **Supp. XI:** 342

Clark, Harry Hayden, **Supp. I Part 2:** 423
Clark, John Bates, **Supp. I Part 2:** 633
Clark, Kenneth, **Supp. XIV:** 342, 348; **Supp. XIX:** 151
Clark, Lewis Gaylord, **Supp. XVIII:** 4, 7, 8
Clark, Shirley, **Supp. XXI:** 22
Clark, Thomas, **Supp. III Part 2:** 629; **Supp. IV Part 1:** 140, 145, 147
Clark, Walter, **Supp. XI:** 315
Clark, William, **III:** 14; **IV:** 179, 283
Clark, Willis Gaylord, **Supp. I Part 2:** 684
Clarke, James Freeman, **Supp. II Part 1:** 280
Clarke, John, **Supp. IV Part 1:** 8
Clarke, John J., **III:** 356
Clarke, Samuel, **II:** 108
Clark Lectures, **Retro. Supp. I:** 65
Claros varones de Belken (Hinojosa). *See Fair Gentlemen of Belken County* (Hinojosa)
Clash by Night (Odets), **Supp. II Part 2:** 531, 538, 544–546, 550, 551
Classical Tradition, The (Highet), **Supp. I Part 1:** 268
Classic Ballroom Dances (Simic), **Supp. VIII:** 271, **276–278,** 283
Classics and Commercials: A Literary Chronicle of the Forties (Wilson), **IV:** 433
"CLASS STRUGGLE" (Baraka), **Supp. III Part 1:** 55
"Claude Glass, The: 1890" (Bierds), **Supp. XVII:** 27
Claudel, Paul, **I:** 60
Claudelle Inglish (Caldwell), **I:** 304
Clavel, Marcel, **I:** 343
"CLAY" (Baraka), **Supp. II Part 1:** 54
Clay, Henry, **I:** 8; **Supp. I Part 2:** 684, 686
Clay's Ark (O. Butler), **Supp. XIII:** 63
Clayton, John J., **Supp. IV Part 1:** 238
"Clean, Well Lighted Place, A" (Hemingway), **Retro. Supp. I:** 181
"Clear, with Light Variable Winds" (Lowell), **II:** 522
"Clear Days" (White), **Supp. I Part 2:** 664, 665
Clearing (Berry), **Supp. X:** 22
"Clearing, A" (Simpson), **Supp. IX:** 280
"Clearing, The" (Kenyon), **Supp. VII:** 174
"Clearing the Title" (Merrill), **Supp. III Part 1:** 336
"Clearing Up the Question of Stesichoros' Blinding by Helen" (Carson), **Supp. XII:** 107–108
"Clear Morning" (Glück), **Supp. V:** 88
"Clearness" (Wilbur), **Supp. III Part 2:** 544, 550
"Clear Night" (Wright), **Supp. V:** 341
Clear Pictures: First Loves, First Guides (Price), **Supp. VI:** 253, 254, 255, 256, 265
Clear Springs (Mason), **Supp. VIII:** 134–136, 137–138, 139, 147
Cleary, Rebecca Lauck, **Supp. XVIII:** 195

Cleaver, Eldridge, **Retro. Supp. II:** 12; **Supp. IV Part 1:** 206; **Supp. X:** 249

"Cleaving, The" (L.-Y. Lee), **Supp. XV:** 215, **218–220**

Cleland, John, **Supp. V:** 48, 127

Clemenceau, Georges, **I:** 490

"Clemency" (Wrigley), **Supp. XVIII:** 307–308

Clemens, Jane, **I:** 247

Clemens, Orion, **IV:** 193, 195

Clemens, Samuel Langhorne. *See* Twain, Mark

Clemens, Mrs. Samuel Langhorne (Olivia Langdon), **I:** 197, 208, 247; **Supp. I Part 2:** 457

Clemens, Susie, **IV:** 208

Clementine Recognitions (novel), **Supp. IV Part 1:** 280

Clements, Colin Campbell, **Supp. XVI:** 190

Clemons, Walter, **Supp. IV Part 1:** 305, 307

Cleopatra, **III:** 44; **IV:** 373; **Supp. I Part 1:** 114

"Clepsydra" (Ashbery), **Supp. III Part 1:** 10–15

"Clerks, The" (Robinson), **III:** 517–518

"Cleveland" (Halliday), **Supp. XIX:** 90

Cleveland, Carol, **Supp. IX:** 120, 125

Cleveland, Ceil, **Supp. V:** 222

Cleveland, Grover, **II:** 126, 128, 129, 130, 137, 138; **Supp. I Part 2:** 486

"Clever Magician Carrying My Heart, A" (Salinas), **Supp. XIII:** 323

"Cliff, The" (C. Baxter), **Supp. XVII:** 16–17

Clifford, Craig, **Supp. IX:** 99

Clift, Montgomery, **III:** 161

Clifton, Lucille, **Supp. XVIII:** 177

Climate of Monastic Prayer, The (Merton), **Supp. VIII:** 205, 207

Climb, The (Boukreev), **Supp. XVIII:** 112

"Climber, The" (Mason), **Supp. VIII:** 140–141

Climbing High: A Woman's Account of Surviving the Everest Tragedy (Gammelgaard), **Supp. XVIII:** 112

"Climbing the Tower" (Crews), **Supp. XI:** 102

Clinton, De Witt, **I:** 338

"Clipped Wings" (H. Miller), **III:** 176–177

Clippinger, David, **Supp. XXI:** 24

Clive, Robert, **Supp. I Part 2:** 505

Clock Winder, The (Tyler), **Supp. IV Part 2:** 661–662, 670

Clock Without Hands (McCullers), **II:** 587–588, 604–606

Clockwork Orange, A (Burgess), **Supp. XIII:** 29

Clorindy (Cook), **Supp. II Part 1:** 199

"Close, The" (Jarman), **Supp. XVII:** 113

"Close Calls" (Wolff), **Supp. VII:** 332–333

"Closed Book, A" (Mosley), **Supp. XIII:** 237

Close Range: Wyoming Stories (Proulx), **Supp. VII:** 261–265

Closers, The (Connelly), **Supp. XXI:** **76–77**

Closest Possible Union, The (J. Scott), **Supp. XVII: 185–186,** 188, 191

Close the Book (Glaspell), **Supp. III Part 1:** 179

"Close the Book" (Lowell), **II:** 554

Close to Shore: A True Story of Terror in an Age of Innocence (Capuzzo), **Supp. XIII:** 254

Closet Writing & Gay Reading: The Case of Melville's Pierre (Creech), **Retro. Supp. I:** 254

Closing Circle, The (Commoner), **Supp. XIII:** 264

Closing of the American Mind, The (Bloom), **Retro. Supp. II:** 19, 30, 31

"Closing of the Rodeo, The" (W. J. Smith), **Supp. XIII:** 332

Closing Time (Heller), **Supp. IV Part 1:** 382, 386, 391–394

Closset, Marie, **Supp. VIII:** 251, 265

"Cloud, The" (Shelley), **Supp. I Part 2:** 720

"Cloud and Fame" (Berryman), **I:** 173

Cloud Forest, The: A Chronicle of the South American Wilderness (Matthiessen), **Supp. V:** 202, 204

"Cloud on the Way, The" (Bryant), **Supp. I Part 1:** 171

"Cloud River" (Wright), **Supp. V:** 341

"Clouds" (Levine), **Supp. V:** 184

Cloudsplitter (Banks), **Supp. V:** 16

"Clover" (Lanier), **Supp. I Part 1:** 362–364

Clover and Other Poems (Lanier), **Supp. I Part 1:** 362

"Clown" (Corso), **Supp. XII:** 127

Clown in the Belfry, The: Writings on Faith and Fiction (Buechner), **Supp. XII:** 53

Cluck, Julia, **Supp. I Part 2:** 728

Clum, John M., **Supp. XIII: 200,** 201, 209

Cluny, Hugo, **IV:** 290

Clurman, Harold, **I:** 93; **IV:** 381, 385

Clytus, Radiclani, **Supp. XIII:** 128, **Supp. XIII:** 129, 132

"C.O." (Wrigley), **Supp. XVIII:** 298

"Coal: Beginning and End" (Winters), **Supp. II Part 2:** 791

Coale, Howard, **Supp. XIII:** 15

"Coals" (Hoffman), **Supp. XVIII:** 86

"Coast, The" (column), **Supp. IV Part 1:** 198

"Coast Guard's Cottage, The" (Wylie), **Supp. I Part 2:** 723

Coast of Trees, A (Ammons), **Supp. VII:** 24, 34

"Coast-Range Christ, The" (Jeffers), **Supp. II Part 2:** 414, 419

"Coast-Road, The" (Jeffers), **Supp. II Part 2:** 425

"Coat, The" (Everwine), **Supp. XV:** 80

Coates, Joseph, **Supp. VIII:** 80

Coates, Robert, **I:** 54; **IV:** 298

"Coatlicue's Rules: Advice from an Aztec Goddess" (Mora), **Supp. XIII:** 223

"Coats" (Kenyon), **Supp. VII:** 172

Cobb, Lee J., **III:** 153

Cobb, Ty, **III:** 227, 229

Cobbett, William, **Supp. I Part 2:** 517; **Supp. XV:** 237

"Cobbler Keezar's Vision" (Whittier), **Supp. I Part 2:** 699

"Cobweb, The" (Carver), **Supp. III Part 1:** 148

Cobwebs From an Empty Skull (Bierce), **I:** 195

Coccimiglio, Vic, **Supp. XIII:** 114

"Cock-a-Doodle-Doo!" (Melville), **III:** 89

"Cockayne" (Emerson), **II:** 6

"Cock-Crow" (Gordon), **II:** 219

Cock Pit (Cozzens), **I:** 359, 378, 379

Cockpit (Kosinski), **Supp. XII:** 21

Cockpit: A Novel (Kosinski), **Supp. VII:** 215, 223–224, 225

"Cock Robin Takes Refuge in the Storm House" (Snodgrass), **Supp. VI:** 319

Cocktail Hour, The (Gurney), **Supp. V:** 95, 96, 100, 101, 103, 105, 108

Cocktail Hour and Two Other Plays: Another Antigone and *The Perfect Party* (Gurney), **Supp. V:** 100

Cocktail Party, The (Eliot), **I:** 571, 582–583; **III:** 21; **Retro. Supp. I:** 65; **Supp. V:** 101, 103

Cocteau, Jean, **III:** 471; **Retro. Supp. I:** 82, 378; **Supp. IV Part 1:** 82; **Supp. XVI:** 135; **Supp. XX:236**

"Coda: Wilderness Letter" (Stegner), **Supp. IV Part 2:** 595

"Code, The" (Frost), **Retro. Supp. I:** 121, 128

Codman, Florence, **Supp. II Part 1:** 92, 93

Codman, Ogden, Jr., **Retro. Supp. I:** 362, 363

Cody, William ("Buffalo Bill"), **I:** 440; **III:** 584; **Supp. V:** 230

Coffey, Michael, **Supp. V:** 243; **Supp. XV:** 65; **Supp. XX:88**

Coffey, Warren, **III:** 358

Coffin, Charles, **III:** 577

Cogan, David J., **Supp. IV Part 1:** 362

Cogan, Joshua, **Supp. XXI:** 247

Coghill, Nevill, **Supp. II Part 1:** 4; **Supp. XIV:** 13

Cohan, George M., **II:** 427; **III:** 401

Cohen, Edward M., **Supp. XVI:** 212

Cohen, Esther, **Supp. XV:** 323

Cohen, Hettie, **Supp. II Part 1:** 30

Cohen, Marty, **Supp. X:** 112

Cohen, Norman J., **Supp. IX:** 132, 143

Cohen, Rosetta, **Supp. XV:** 257

Cohen, Sarah Blacher, **Supp. V:** 273

Cohen, Victor, **Supp. XVIII:** 235, 236

"Coherent Decentering: Towards a New Model of the Poetic Self" (A. Finch), **Supp. XVII:** 76

"Coin" (Goldbarth), **Supp. XII:** 187

Coindreau, Maurice, **III:** 339

Coiner, Constance, **Supp. XIII:** 297, 302

Coit, Lille Hitchcock, **Supp. X:** 103

"Coitus" (Pound), **III:** 466

Coke, Desmond, **Supp. XX:235**

Colburn, Nadia Herman, **Supp. XV:** 339, 341, 347

"Cold, The" (Kenyon), **Supp. VII:** 164

"Cold, The" (Winters), **Supp. II Part 2:** 790–791, 809, 811

"Cold-blooded Creatures" (Wylie), **Supp. I Part 2:** 729

Colden, Cadwallader, **Supp. I Part 1:** 250

"Colder the Air, The" (Bishop), **Supp. I Part 1:** 86

Cold Feet (Harrison), **Supp. VIII:** 39

Cold Frame (C. Frost), **Supp. XV:** 93, 96

Cold Ground Was My Bed Last Night (Garrett), **Supp. VII:** 98

"Cold Ground Was My Bed Last Night" (Garrett), **Supp. VII:** 100

"Cold Night, The" (W. C. Williams), **Retro. Supp. I:** 418

"Cold Plunge into Skin Diving, A" (Knowles), **Supp. XII:** 241

Cold Spring, A (Bishop), **Retro. Supp. II:** 45

Cold Springs Harbor (Yates), **Supp. XI:** 348

Cold War American Poetry, **Supp. V:** 182

Cold War and the Income Tax, The (Wilson), **IV:** 430

Cole, Bruce, **Supp. XX:** 106

Cole, Goody, **Supp. I Part 2:** 696–697

Cole, Lester, **Retro. Supp. II:** 329

Cole, Nat King, **Retro. Supp. I:** 334; **Supp. X:** 255

Cole, Thomas, **Supp. I Part 1:** 156, 158, 171

Cole, William, **Supp. XIX:** 120

"Coleman" (Karr), **Supp. XI:** 244

Coleman, Wanda, **Supp. XI: 83–98**

Coleridge, Samuel Taylor, **I:** 283, 284, 447, 522; **II:** 7, 10, 11, 19, 71, 169, 273, 301, 502, 516, 549; **III:** 77, 83–84, 424, 461, 488, 523; **IV:** 74, 173, 250, 349, 453; **Retro. Supp. I:** 65, 308; **Supp. I Part 1:** 31, 311, 349; **Supp. I Part 2:** 376, 393, 422; **Supp. IV Part 2:** 422, 465; **Supp. V:** 258; **Supp. IX:** 38, 50; **Supp. XIII:** 139; **Supp. XIV:** 21–22; **Supp. XV:** 250; **Supp. XXI:** 52, 55

Coles, Katharine, **Supp. IV Part 2:** 630

Colette, Sidonie-Gabrielle, **Supp. VIII:** 40, 171; **Supp. XVI:** 193–194

"Coliseum, The" (Poe), **III:** 411

Collage of Dreams (Spencer), **Supp. X:** 196

"Collapse of Tomorrow, The" (Mumford), **Supp. II Part 2:** 482

"Collected by a Valetudinarian" (E. Stoddard), **Supp. XV:** 286–287

Collected Earlier Poems (Hecht), **Supp. X:** 58, 59

Collected Earlier Poems (W. C. Williams), **Retro. Supp. I:** 414, 428

Collected Earlier Poems 1940–1960 (Levertov), **Supp. III Part 1:** 273, 275

Collected Essays (Tate), **IV:** 133–134

Collected Essays of Ralph Ellison, The (Ellison), **Retro. Supp. II:** 119

Collected Essays of Robert Creeley, The (Creeley), **Supp. IV Part 1:** 153, 154

Collected Later Poems (W. C. Williams), **Retro. Supp. I:** 428

Collected Plays (A. Miller), **III:** 158

Collected Plays, 1974–1983 (Gurney), **Supp. V:** 99

Collected Poems (Aiken), **I:** 50

Collected Poems (Burke), **I:** 269

Collected Poems (Cummings), **I:** 430, 439, 441

Collected Poems (Doolittle), **Supp. I Part 1:** 264–267, 269

Collected Poems (Frost), **Retro. Supp. I:** 136

Collected Poems (Hull), **Supp. XXI:** 141

Collected Poems (Kees; Justice, ed.), **Supp. XV:** 134

Collected Poems (Lindsay), **Supp. I Part 2:** 380, 387, 392, 396–397, 400

Collected Poems (Lowell), **Supp. XV:** 20

Collected Poems (Markson), **Supp. XVII:** 143

Collected Poems (Moore), **III:** 194, 215

Collected Poems (Price), **Supp. VI:** 267

Collected Poems (Simpson), **Supp. IX:** 279

Collected Poems (W. C. Williams), **IV:** 415; **Retro. Supp. I:** 430

Collected Poems (Winters), **Supp. II Part 2:** 791, 810

Collected Poems (Wright), **Supp. III Part 2:** 602

Collected Poems (Yeats), **Supp. XV:** 152

Collected Poems, 1923–1953 (Bogan), **Supp. III Part 1:** 64

Collected Poems, 1936–1976 (Francis), **Supp. IX:** 77, 80, **87**

Collected Poems, The (Stevens), **III:** 273; **IV:** 75, 76, 87, 93; **Retro. Supp. I:** 296, 309

Collected Poems 1909–1935 (Eliot), **I:** 580; **Retro. Supp. I:** 66

Collected Poems 1909–1962 (Eliot), **I:** 583

Collected Poems 1917–1952 (MacLeish), **III:** 3, 4, 19

Collected Poems 1921–1931 (W. C. Williams), **Retro. Supp. I:** 422; **Supp. XIV:** 285

Collected Poems 1930–1960 (Eberhart), **I:** 522, 525–526, 540, 541

Collected Poems: 1939–1989 (W. J. Smith), **Supp. XIII:** 332, 340, 343, 345

Collected Poems: 1940–1978 (Shapiro), **Supp. II Part 2:** 703, 717

Collected Poems: 1951–1971 (Ammons), **Supp. VII:** 24, 26–29, 32, 33

Collected Poems: 1956–1976 (Wagoner), **Supp. IX:** 323, **328–329**

Collected Poems of Amy Clampitt, The (Clampitt), **Supp. IX:** 37, 44, 53

Collected Poems of George Garrett (Garrett), **Supp. VII:** 109

Collected Poems of Hart Crane, The (Crane), **I:** 399–402

Collected Poems of James Agee, The (Fitzgerald, ed.), **I:** 27–28

Collected Poems of James T. Farrell, The (Farrell), **II:** 45

Collected Poems of Langston Hughes, The (Rampersad and Roessel, ed.), **Retro. Supp. I:** 194, 196, 212

Collected Poems of Muriel Rukeyser, The (Rukeyser), **Supp. VI:** 274

Collected Poems of Thomas Merton, The, **Supp. VIII:** 207, 208

Collected Poetry (Auden), **Supp. II Part 1:** 18

Collected Prose (Wright), **Supp. III Part 2:** 596

Collected Prose, The (Bishop), **Retro. Supp. II:** 51

Collected Recordings (W. C. Williams), **Retro. Supp. I:** 431

Collected Shorter Poems, 1946-1991 (Carruth), **Supp. XVI:** 47

Collected Short Stories, The (Wharton), **Retro. Supp. I:** 362, 363, 366

Collected Sonnets (Millay), **III:** 136–137

Collected Stories, 1939–1976 (Bowles), **Supp. IV Part 1:** 92

Collected Stories, The (Paley), **Supp. VI:** 218

Collected Stories, The (Price), **Supp. VI:** 266

Collected Stories, The (Theroux), **Supp. VIII:** 318

Collected Stories, The (Wharton), **Retro. Supp. I:** 361

Collected Stories of Amy Hempel, The (Hempel), **Supp. XXI:** 115, 117

Collected Stories of Eudora Welty, The (Welty), **Retro. Supp. I:** 355

Collected Stories of Isaac Bashevis Singer (Singer), **Retro. Supp. II: 307–308**

Collected Stories of Katherine Anne Porter (Porter), **III:** 454

Collected Stories of Peter Taylor (Taylor), **Supp. V:** 314, 320, 323–324, 325, 326

Collected Stories of Richard Yates, The, **Supp. XI:** 349

Collected Stories of Wallace Stegner (Stegner), **Supp. IV Part 2:** 599, 605

Collected Stories of William Faulkner (Faulkner), **II:** 72; **Retro. Supp. I:** 75

Collected Stories of William Humphrey, The (Humphrey), **Supp. IX:** 106

Collected Works (Bierce), **I:** 204, 208–210

Collected Works of Buck Rogers in the 25th Century, The (Bradbury), **Supp. IV Part 1:** 101

Collected Writings, The (Z. Fitzgerald; Bruccoli, ed.), **Supp. IX:** 65, 68

Collecting the Animals (Everwine), **Supp. XV:** 73, 75, **78–81**, 85, 88

Collection of Epigrams, **II:** 111

Collection of Poems, on American Affairs, and a Variety of Other Subjects . . . (Freneau), **Supp. II Part 1:** 274

Collection of Select Aphorisms and Maxims (Palmer), **II:** 111

"Collectors" (Carver), **Supp. III Part 1:** 141–142

Collette, **Supp. XVII:** 86

Collier, John, **Supp. XXI:** 8

Collier, Lucy Wood, **Supp. XXI:** 8

Collier, Michael, **Supp. XVII:** 23, 110

Collingwood, R. G., **I:** 278

Collins, Billy, **Supp. XI:** 143; **Supp. XIV:** 123; **Supp. XVII:** 245; **Supp. XXI: 51–66**

Collins, Doug, **Supp. V:** 5
Collins, Eddie, **II:** 416
Collins, Richard, **Supp. XI:** 171
Collins, Ronald, **Supp. XXI:** 24
Collins, Wilkie, **Supp. I Part 1:** 35, 36; **Supp. IV Part 1:** 341; **Supp. XX:**236
Collins, William, **Supp. I Part 2:** 714
Collinson, Peter , **II:** 114
Collinson, Peter (pseudonym). *See* Hammett, Dashiell
Colloff, Pamela, **Supp. XIII:** 281
Colloque Sentimental (ballet), **Supp. IV Part 1:** 83
"Colloquy" (Kees), **Supp. XV:** 133
"Colloquy in Black Rock" (Lowell), **II:** 535; **Retro. Supp. II:** 178
"Colloquy of Monos and Una, The" (Poe), **III:** 412
"Colloquy on a Bed" (Bronk), **Supp. XXI:** 31
Colonel's Dream, The (Chesnutt), **Supp. XIV:** 63, 75–76
Colônia, Regina, **Retro. Supp. II:** 53
Color (Cullen), **Supp. IV Part 1:** 164, 166, 167, 168
"Colorado" (Beattie), **Supp. V:** 27
Color and Democracy: Colonies and Peace (Du Bois), **Supp. II Part 1:** 184, 185
Color Curtain, The (Wright), **IV:** 478, 488
"Colored Americans" (Dunbar), **Supp. II Part 1:** 197
Colored People (H. L. Gates), **Supp. XX:**101, 103, 104–105, 109, 111
"Color Line, The" (Douglass), **Supp. III Part 1:** 163–165
Color Line, The (W. B. Smith), **Supp. II Part 1:** 168
Color of a Great City, The (Dreiser), **Retro. Supp. II:** 104
Color of Darkness (Purdy), **Supp. VII:** 271
Color Purple, The (Walker), **Supp. III Part 2:** 517, 518, 520, 525–529, 532–537; **Supp. VIII:** 141; **Supp. X:** 252, 330; **Supp. XX:**107
Color Schemes (Cheang; film), **Supp. XI:** 20
"Colors of Night, The" (Momaday), **Supp. IV Part 2:** 490
"Colors without Objects" (Swenson), **Supp. IV Part 2:** 645
"Color: The Unfinished Business of Democracy" (Locke), **Supp. XIV:** 202, 207
Colossus, The (Plath), **Retro. Supp. II:** 245–247; **Supp. I Part 2:** 529, 531, 536, 538, 540; **Supp. V:** 79; **Supp. XI:** 317
"Colossus, The" (Plath), **Retro. Supp. II:** 250
Colossus of Maroussi, The (H. Miller), **III:** 178, 185–186
"Colt, The" (Stegner), **Supp. IV Part 2:** 600
Coltelli, Laura, **Supp. IV Part 1:** 323, 330, 335, 409; **Supp. IV Part 2:** 493, 497, 559

Colter: The True Story of the Best Dog I Ever Had (Bass), **Supp. XVI:** 23
Coltrane, John, **Supp. VIII:** 197
Colum, Mary, **I:** 246, 252, 256; **Supp. I Part 2:** 708, 709
Columbiad, The (Barlow), **Supp. II Part 1:** 67, 72, 73, 74, 75–77, 79
Columbia History of the American Novel, **Supp. XV:** 270
Columbia Literary History of the United States, **Supp. XV:** 270
"Columbian Ode" (Dunbar), **Supp. II Part 1:** 199
"Columbia U Poesy Reading—1975" (Corso), **Supp. XII:** 134
Columbus, Christopher, **I:** 253; **II:** 6, 310; **III:** 8; **Supp. I Part 2:** 397, 479, 480, 483, 486–488, 491, 495, 497, 498
"Columbus to Ferdinand" (Freneau), **Supp. II Part 1:** 255
Comanche Moon (McMurtry), **Supp. V:** 232
"Come, Break With Time" (Bogan), **Supp. III Part 1:** 52
Come Along with Me (Jackson), **Supp. IX:** 117, 118, 122
Come Back, Charleston Blue (film), **Supp. XVI:** 144
Comeback, The (Gurney), **Supp. V:** 97
"Come Back to the Raft Ag'in, Huck Honey!" (Fiedler), **Supp. XIII:** 93, **96–97,** 101
Come Blow Your Horn (Simon), **Supp. IV Part 2:** 574, 575, 577, 578, 586, 587, 591
"Come Dance with Me in Ireland" (Jackson), **Supp. IX:** 119
"Comedian as the Letter C, The" (Stevens), **IV:** 84–85, 88; **Retro. Supp. I:** 297, 301, 302
"Comedy Cop" (Farrell), **II:** 45
Comedy of a Country House (J. Sturgis), **Supp. XX:**238
"Comedy's Greatest Era" (Agee), **I:** 31
"Come In" (Frost), **Retro. Supp. I:** 139
"Come On, Baby" (Zinberg), **Supp. XV:** 195
"Come on Back" (Gardner), **Supp. VI:** 73
"Come Out into the Sun" (Francis), **Supp. IX:** 82
Come Out into the Sun: Poems New and Selected (Francis), **Supp. IX: 82–83**
"Come out the Wilderness" (Baldwin), **Supp. I Part 1:** 63
Comer, Anjanette, **Supp. XI:** 305
Comer, Cornelia, **I:** 214
"Come Shining: The Spiritual South" (exhibition; Luster), **Supp. XV:** 350
Come with Me: Poems for a Journey (Nye), **Supp. XIII:** 279
"Comforts of Home, The" (O'Connor), **III:** 349, 351, 355; **Retro. Supp. II:** 237
Comic Artist, The (Glaspell and Matson), **Supp. III Part 1:** 182
"Comic Imagination of the Young Dickens, The" (Wright), **Supp. III Part 2:** 591

"Comic Textures and Female Communities 1937 and 1977: Clare Boothe and Wendy Wasserstein" (Carlson), **Supp. XV:** 323
Comic Tragedies (Alcott), **Supp. I Part 1:** 33
"Coming Close" (Levine), **Supp. V:** 192
Coming Forth by Day of Osiris Jones, The (Aiken), **I:** 59
"Coming Home" (Gordon), **Supp. IV Part 1:** 309
"Coming Home to Vermont" (McCarriston), **Supp. XIV:** 269
"Coming in From the Cold" (Walker), **Supp. III Part 2:** 526
Coming into Eighty (Sarton), **Supp. VIII:** 262
"Coming into Eighty" (Sarton), **Supp. VIII:** 262
Coming into the Country (McPhee), **Supp. III Part 1:** 298, 301–306, 309, 310
Coming Into Writing (Cixous), **Supp. X:** 102
Coming of Age in Mississippi (Moody), **Supp. IV Part 1:** 11
Comings Back (Goldbarth), **Supp. XII:** 180
"Coming to Canada--Age Twenty Two" (Shields), **Supp. VII:** 311
Coming to Canada: Poems (Shields), **Supp. VII:** 311–312
"Coming to the Morning" (Merwin), **Supp. III Part 1:** 356
"Coming to This" (Strand), **Supp. IV Part 2:** 627
Comiskey, Charles, **II:** 422
Commager, Henry Steele, **I:** 253; **Supp. I Part 1:** 372; **Supp. I Part 2:** 484, 647, 650
Command the Morning (Buck), **Supp. II Part 1:** 125
"CommComm" (Saunders), **Supp. XIX:** 234
"Commencement Address, A" (Brodsky), **Supp. VIII:** 31
"Commencement Day Address, The" (Schwartz), **Supp. II Part 2:** 660
Commentaries (Caesar), **II:** 502, 561
"Commentary" (Auden), **Supp. II Part 1:** 13
"Comment on Curb" (Hughes), **Supp. I Part 1:** 340
"Comments/Questions" (Nelson), **Supp. XVIII:** 172
"Commerce" (Nye), **Supp. XIII:** 281
Commins, Saxe, **Retro. Supp. I:** 73; **Retro. Supp. II:** 337
Commodity of Dreams & Other Stories, A (Nemerov), **III:** 268–269, 285
Common Carnage (Dobyns), **Supp. XIII:** 87
"Common Ground, A" (Levertov), **Supp. III Part 1:** 277
"Common Life, The" (Auden), **Supp. IV Part 1:** 302, 313
"Common Meter" (R. Fisher), **Supp. XIX:** 71
Common Room, A: Essays 1954–1987 (Price), **Supp. VI:** 264–265, 267

Commons, John, **Supp. I Part 2:** 645

Common Sense (Paine), **II:** 117; **Supp. I Part 1:** 231; **Supp. I Part 2:** 505, 506–508, 509, 513, 516, 517, 521

"Communication" (Dobyns), **Supp. XIII:** 91

"Communion" (Dubus), **Supp. VII:** 91

Communion (Mora), **Supp. XIII:** 217–219

Communist Manifesto, The (Marx and Engels), **II:** 463; **Supp. XXI:** 162, 162–163

"Community Life" (Moore), **Supp. X:** 178

"Community of Glaciers, The" (Bass), **Supp. XVI:** 23

Comnes, Gregory, **Supp. IV Part 1:** 283, 284, 291

"Companions, The" (Nemerov), **III:** 269, 278, 287

Company of Poets, A (Simpson), **Supp. IX:** 265, 275

Company of Women, The (Gordon), **Supp. IV Part 1:** 302–304, 304, 306, 313

Company She Keeps, The (McCarthy), **II:** 562, 563–566

"Comparisons of Wonder" (Jarman), **Supp. XVII:** 114

Compass Flower, The (Merwin), **Supp. III Part 1:** 353, 357

"Compassionate Friendship" (Doolittle), **Supp. I Part 1:** 257, 258, 259, 260, 271

"Compatibility" (C. Frost), **Supp. XV:** 103

"Compendium" (Dove), **Supp. IV Part 1:** 248

"Complaint" (W. C. Williams), **Retro. Supp. I:** 418

"Complete Birth of the Cool, The" (Wright), **Supp. XV:** 343, 344

Complete Collected Poems of William Carlos Williams, 1906–1938, The (W. C. Williams), **Retro. Supp. I:** 424

"Complete Destruction" (W. C. Williams), **IV:** 413

"Complete Life of John Hopkins, The" (O. Henry), **Supp. II Part 1:** 405

Complete Poems (Frost), **II:** 155, 164

Complete Poems (Reznikoff), **Supp. XIV:** 281

Complete Poems (Sandburg), **III:** 590–592, 594, 596

Complete Poems, The (Bishop), **Retro. Supp. II:** 49; **Supp. I Part 1:** 72, 82, 94

Complete Poems, The (Bradbury), **Supp. IV Part 1:** 105

Complete Poems, The: 1927–1979 (Bishop), **Retro. Supp. II:** 51

Complete Poems of Emily Dickinson, The (Bianchi and Hampson, eds.), **Retro. Supp. I:** 35

Complete Poems of Emily Dickinson, The (Johnson, ed.), **I:** 470

Complete Poems of Frederick Goddard Tuckerman, The (Momaday), **Supp. IV Part 2:** 480

Complete Poems of Hart Crane, **Retro. Supp. II:** 81

Complete Poems to Solve, The (Swenson), **Supp. IV Part 2:** 652

Complete Poetical Works (Hulme), **III:** 464

Complete Poetical Works (Longfellow), **Retro. Supp. II:** 154

Complete Poetical Works (Lowell), **II:** 512, 516–517

Complete Poetical Works of Amy Lowell, The, **Supp. XV:** 295–296

Complete Stories (O'Connor), **Supp. X:** 1

Complete Tragedies, The: Euripedes II, **Supp. XV:** 50

"Complete with Starry Night and Bourbon Shots" (Goldbarth), **Supp. XII:** 192–193

Complete Works of Kate Chopin, The (Seyersted, ed.), **Supp. I Part 1:** 212, 225

Complete Works of the Gawain-Poet (Gardner), **Supp. VI:** 64, 65

"Complex Histories, Contested Memories: Some Reflections on Remembering Difficult Pasts" (E. Hoffman, lecture), **Supp. XVI:** 155

"Complicated Thoughts About a Small Son" (White), **Supp. I Part 2:** 678

"Compliments of the Season" (O. Henry), **Supp. II Part 1:** 392, 399

"Compline" (Auden), **Supp. II Part 1:** 23

"Composing a Life" (Pickering), **Supp. XXI:** 191, 196

Composition as Explanation (Stein), **IV:** 32, 33, 38

"Composition as Explanation" (Stein), **IV:** 27, 28

"Compounding of Consciousness" (James), **II:** 358–359

Comprehensive Bibliography (Hanneman), **II:** 259

Compton-Burnett, Ivy, **I:** 93; **II:** 580

"Comrade Laski, C.P.U.S.A. \[M.L.\]" (Didion), **Supp. IV Part 1:** 200

Comstock, Anthony, **Retro. Supp. II:** 95

Comus (Milton), **II:** 12; **Supp. I Part 2:** 622

Conan Doyle, Arthur. *See* Doyle, Arthur Conan

Conceptions of Reality in Modern American Poetry (Dembo), **Supp. I Part 1:** 272

"Concept of Character in Fiction, The" (Gass), **Supp. VI:** 85, **86**

Concept of Dread, The (Kierkegaard), **III:** 305

Concerning Children (Gilman), **Supp. XI:** 206

"Concerning Mold upon the Skin, Etc." (J. Scott), **Supp. XVII:** 188

"Concerning Necessity" (Carruth), **Supp. XVI:** 57

"Concerning Some Recent Criticism of His Work" (Doty), **Supp. XI:** 131

Concerning the End for Which God Created the World (Edwards), **I:** 549, 557, 559

Concerto for Two Pianos, Winds, and Percussion (Bowles), **Supp. IV Part 1:** 83

Conchologist's First Book, The (Poe), **III:** 412

Conclusive Evidence (Nabokov), **III:** 247–250, 252

"Concord Hymn" (Emerson), **II:** 19

Concrete Blonde, The (Connelly), **Supp. XXI:** **70–71,** 78, 80

"Concrete Universal, The: Observations on the Understanding of Poetry" (Ransom), **III:** 480

Concurring Beasts (Dobyns), **Supp. XIII:** 76

Condensed Novels and Other Papers (Harte), **Supp. II Part 1:** 342

"Condition, The" (Karmi; Everwine, trans.), **Supp. XV:** 78

Condition of Man, The (Mumford), **Supp. II Part 2:** 483, 484, 486, 495–496, 498

"Condolence" (Parker), **Supp. IX:** 191

"Condominium, The" (Elkin), **Supp. VI:** 49, **50–51,** 55, 56

Condon, Charles R., **Supp. XIII:** 163

Condor and the Cows, The: A South American Travel Diary (Isherwood and Caskey), **Supp. XIV:** 166

"Condor and the Guests, The" (Connell), **Supp. XIV:** 86

Condorcet, Marquis de, **Supp. I Part 2:** 511

Conduct of Life, The (Emerson), **II:** 1–5, 8

Conduct of Life, The (Mumford), **Supp. II Part 2:** 485, 496–497

"Conductor of Nothing, The" (Levine), **Supp. V:** 189

Coney Island of the Mind, A (Ferlinghetti), **Supp. XIX:** 4; **Supp. XXI:** 53

"Conference Male, The" (Mora), **Supp. XIII:** 218

"Confession" (Peacock), **Supp. XIX:** 206

"Confessional" (Bidart), **Supp. XV:** 29–30, 31

"Confessional Poem" (Nelson), **Supp. XVIII:** 174

Confession de Claude, La (Zola), **I:** 411

"Confession of a House-Breaker, The" (Jewett), **Retro. Supp. II:** 146–147

Confession of Jereboam O. Beauchamp, The (pamphlet), **IV:** 253

Confessions (Augustine), **I:** 279; **Supp. XVI:** 288

Confessions (Rousseau), **I:** 226

Confessions of a Barbarian: Selections from the Journals of Edward Abbey, 1951–1989 (Abbey; Petersen, ed.), **Supp. XIII:** 2, 4

"Confessions of a Latina Author" (Mora), **Supp. XIII:** 221

"Confessions of a Wannabe Negro" (McKnight), **Supp. XX:** 152–153, 158

Confessions of Nat Turner, The (Styron), **IV:** 98, 99, 105, 113–117; **Supp. X:** 16, 250

Confetti (Mora), **Supp. XIII:** 221

Confidence (James), **II:** 327, 328

Confidence-Man, The (Melville), **III:** 91; **Retro. Supp. I:** 255–256, 257; **Retro. Supp. II:** 121; **Supp. XIV:** 49

Confidence Man, The (Van Vechten), **Supp. II Part 2:** 737

Confidential Clerk, The (Eliot), **I:** 570, 571–572, 583, 584; **Retro. Supp. I:** 65

Confident Years, 1885–1915, The (Brooks), **I:** 257, 259; **Supp. I Part 2:** 650

"Configurations" (Ammons), **Supp. VII:** 28

Confronting the Horror: The Novels of Nelson Algren (Giles), **Supp. IX:** 11, 15

Confucius, **II:** 1; **III:** 456, 475; **Supp. IV Part 1:** 14

Confusion (Cozzens), **I:** 358, 359, 377, 378

"Confusion of Planes We Must Wander in Sleep, The" (Weigl), **Supp. XIX:** 283

Congo (film), **Supp. IV Part 1:** 83

Congo (screenplay, Shanley), **Supp. XIV:** 316

"Congo, The" (Lindsay), **Supp. I Part 2:** 388–389, 392, 395

Congo and Other Poems, The (Lindsay), **Supp. I Part 2:** 379, 382, 389, 390, 391

"Congregation" (Trethewey), **Supp. XXI:** 245, 247

"Congress of the Insomniacs, The" (Simic), **Supp. VIII:** 281–282

Congreve, William, **III:** 195; **Supp. V:** 101; **Supp. XVIII:** 12

Coningsby (Disraeli), **II:** 127

"Conjectural Reading" (Bronk), **Supp. XXI:** 31

Conjectures of a Guilty Bystander (Merton), **Supp. VIII:** 197, 206, 207

Conjugal Bliss: A Comedy of Marital Arts (Nichols), **Supp. XIII:** 269

"Conjugation of the Paramecium, The" (Rukeyser), **Supp. VI:** 271

Conjugations and Reiterations (Murray), **Supp. XIX:** 161

"Conjuration" (Wilbur), **Supp. III Part 2:** 551

Conjure (recording), **Supp. X:** 241

Conjure (Reed), **Supp. X:** 240, 242

Conjure-Man Dies, The: A Mystery Tale of Dark Harlem (R. Fisher), **Supp. XVI:** 143; **Supp. XIX:** 65, 71, **77–78**

Conjure Woman, The (Chesnutt), **Supp. II Part 1:** 193; **Supp. XIV:** 57, **58–61,** 62, 63

Conklin, Grof, **Supp. I Part 2:** 672

Conkling, Hilda, **II:** 530

Conkling, Roscoe, **III:** 506

Conley, Robert J., **Supp. V:** 232

Conley, Susan, **Supp. XIII:** 111, 112

Connaroe, Joel, **Supp. IV Part 2:** 690

"Connecticut Lad, A" (White), **Supp. I Part 2:** 677

"Connecticut Valley" (Cowley), **Supp. II Part 1:** 141–142

Connecticut Yankee in King Arthur's Court, A (Twain), **I:** 209; **II:** 276; **IV:** 205

Connell, Evan S., **Supp. XIV: 79–100**

Connell, Norreys (pseudonym). *See* O'Riordan, Conal Holmes O'Connell

Connelly, Marc, **III:** 394; **Supp. I Part 2:** 679; **Supp. IX:** 190

Connelly, Michael, **Supp. XXI: 67–82**

Connery, Thomas B., **Supp. XVII:** 106

Connoisseur, The (Connell), **Supp. XIV:** 87

"Connoisseur of Chaos" (Stevens), **IV:** 89; **Retro. Supp. I:** 306

Connolly, Cyril, **Supp. XIV:** 158, 343, 348

Connors, Elizabeth. *See* Lindsay, Mrs. Vachel (Elizabeth Connors)

Conover, Roger, **Supp. I Part 1:** 95

Conquering Horse (Manfred), **Supp. X:** 126

"Conqueror Worm, The" (Poe), **Retro. Supp. II:** 261

Conquest of Canaan (Dwight), **Supp. I Part 1:** 124

Conquistador (MacLeish), **III:** 2, 3, 13–14, 15

Conrad, Alfred, **Retro. Supp. II:** 245

Conrad, Alfred H., **Supp. I Part 2:** 552

Conrad, David, **Supp. I Part 2:** 552

Conrad, Jacob, **Supp. I Part 2:** 552

Conrad, Joseph, **I:** 123, 343, 394, 405, 409, 415, 421, 485, 506, 575–576, 578; **II:** 58, 73, 74, 91, 92, 144, 263, 320, 338, 595; **III:** 28, 102, 106, 328, 464, 467, 491, 512; **IV:** 476; **Retro. Supp. I:** 80, 91, 106, 108, 231, 274, 377; **Retro. Supp. II:** 222; **Supp. I Part 1:** 292; **Supp. I Part 2:** 621, 622; **Supp. IV Part 1:** 197, 341; **Supp. IV Part 2:** 680; **Supp. V:** 249, 251, 262, 298, 307, 311; **Supp. VIII:** 4, 310; **Supp. XIV:** 112; **Supp. XVI:** 158, 212; **Supp. XVIII:** 98, 102; **Supp. XIX:** 27; **Supp. XX:**195

Conrad, Paul, **Supp. I Part 2:** 552

Conrad, Peter, **Supp. IV Part 2:** 688

"Conrad Aiken: From Savannah to Emerson" (Cowley), **Supp. II Part 1:** 43

Conrad Richter's Ohio Trilogy (Edwards), **Supp. XVIII:** 220

Conroy, Frank, **Supp. VIII:** 145; **Supp. XI:** 245; **Supp. XVI: 63–78**

Conroy, Pat, **Supp. XVIII:** 193

Cons, Scams, and Grifts (Gores), **Supp. XXI:** 70

Conscience with the Power and Cases thereof (Ames), **IV:** 158

"Conscientious Objector, The" (Shapiro), **Supp. II Part 2:** 710

"Consciousness and Dining" (Harrison), **Supp. VIII:** 46

"Conscription Camp" (Shapiro), **Supp. II Part 2:** 705

"Consejos de Nuestra Señora de Guadalupe: Counsel from the Brown Virgin" (Mora), **Supp. XIII:** 224

"Conservation Esthetic" (Leopold), **Supp. XIV:** 179, 181, 186, 189–190

"Conserving Natural and Cultural Diversity: The Prose and Poetry of Pat Mora" (Murphy), **Supp. XIII:** 214

Considerable Town, A (M. F. K. Fisher), **Supp. XVII:** 90

"Considerations by the Way" (Emerson), **II:** 2, 5

Consider the Oyster (M. F. K. Fisher), **Supp. XVII:** 84, 87

Considine, Bob, **II:** 424

"Consolation" (Bausch), **Supp. VII:** 48

"Consolations" (Stafford), **Supp. XI:** 329

"Conspiracy of History, The: E. L. Doctorow's *The Book of Daniel*" (Levine), **Supp. IV Part 1:** 221

Conspiracy of Kings, The (Barlow), **Supp. II Part 1:** 80

Conspiracy of Pontiac, The (Parkman), **Supp. II Part 2:** 590, 595, 596, 599–600

Constab Ballads (McKay), **Supp. X:** 131, 133

Constance (Kenyon), **Supp. VII:** 170–172

Constancy (Boyce), **Supp. XVII:** 100; **Supp. XXI:** 6, 7, 12

"Constellation Orion, The" (Kooser), **Supp. XIX:** 120

Construction of Boston, The (Koch), **Supp. XV:** 187

"Constructive Work" (Du Bois), **Supp. II Part 1:** 172

"Consumer's Report" (X. J. Kennedy), **Supp. XV:** 161–162

"Consumption" (Bryant), **Supp. I Part 1:** 169–170

"Contagiousness of Puerperal Fever, The" (Holmes), **Supp. I Part 1:** 303–304

"Contemplation in a World of Action" (Merton), **Supp. VIII:** 204

"Contemplation of Poussin" (Sarton), **Supp. VIII:** 261

"Contemplations" (Bradstreet), **Supp. I Part 1:** 112, 113, 119–122

Contemporaries (Kazin), **Supp. VIII:** 102, **103–104**

Contemporary American Playwrights (Bigsby), **Supp. XV:** 332

Contemporary American Poetry (Poulin, ed.), **Supp. IX:** 272; **Supp. XI:** 259

Contending Forces (Hopkins), **Supp. XVIII:** 284

"Contentment" (Holmes), **Supp. I Part 1:** 307

"Contents" (Halliday), **Supp. XIX:** 92

"Contest, The" (Paley), **Supp. VI:** 223, 230, 231

"Contest for Aaron Gold, The" (P. Roth), **Supp. III Part 2:** 403

Continental Drift (Banks), **Supp. V:** 13–14, 16, 227

Continental Op, The (Hammett), **Supp. IV Part 1:** 344

Continuing Education, A (Pickering), **Supp. XXI:** 194, 195–196

Continuity of American Poetry, The (Pearce), **Supp. I Part 1:** 111; **Supp. I Part 2:** 475

Continuous Harmony, A: Essays Cultural and Agricultural (Berry), **Supp. X:** 33

Continuous Life, The (Strand), **Supp. IV Part 2:** 630, 631–633

Contoski, Victor, **Supp. XII:** 181

"Contract" (Lardner), **II:** 432

"Contraption, The" (Swenson), **Supp. IV Part 2:** 643

"Contrariness of the Mad Farmer, The" (Berry), **Supp. X:** 35

"Contrition" (Dubus), **Supp. VII:** 84

"Control Burn" (Snyder), **Supp. VIII:** 301

"Control Is the Mainspring" (Komunyakaa), **Supp. XIII:** 122, 124

"Controlling the 'Sloppiness of Things' in Frank Conroy's *Stop-Time*" (Strychacz), **Supp. XVI:** 69–70

Control of Nature, The (McPhee), **Supp. III Part 1:** 310–313

"Conventional Wisdom, The" (Elkin), **Supp. VI:** 52–53

"Convergence" (Ammons), **Supp. VII:** 28

"Convergence of the Twain, The" (Hardy), **Supp. VIII:** 31, 32

Conversation (Aiken), **I:** 54

Conversation at Midnight (Millay), **III:** 138

"Conversation of Eiros and Charmion, The" (Poe), **III:** 412

"Conversation on Conversation" (Stowe), **Supp. I Part 2:** 587

"Conversations in Moscow" (Levertov), **Supp. III Part 1:** 282

Conversations on Some of the Old Poets (Lowell), **Supp. I Part 2:** 405

Conversations with Albert Murray (Maguire, ed.), **Supp. XIX:** 160–161

Conversations with Byron (Blessington), **Retro. Supp. II:** 58

Conversations with Eudora Welty (Prenshaw, ed.), **Retro. Supp. I:** 339, 340, 341, 342, 343, 352, 354

"Conversations with Helmholtz" (Allen), **Supp. XV:** 15

Conversations with Ishmael Reed (Dick and Singh, eds.), **Supp. X:** 244

Conversations with James Baldwin (Standley and Pratt, eds.), **Retro. Supp. II:** 6

Conversations with Richard Wilbur (Wilbur), **Supp. III Part 2:** 542–543

"Conversation with My Father, A" (Paley), **Supp. VI:** 220

"Conversion of the Jews, The" (P. Roth), **Retro. Supp. II:** 281; **Supp. III Part 2:** 404, 406

Convict, The: Stories (Burke), **Supp. XIV:** 25

"Convicta et Combusta" (J. Scott), **Supp. XVII:** 189

"Convoy" (Weigl), **Supp. XIX:** 278

Conway, Jill, **Supp. I Part 1:** 19

Coode, John, **I:** 132

Cook, Bruce, **Supp. XII:** 130, 131, 133–134

Cook, Captain James, **I:** 2

Cook, Eleanor, **Retro. Supp. I:** 311

Cook, Elisha, **Supp. IV Part 1:** 356

Cook, Elizabeth Christine, **II:** 106

Cook, George Cram "Jig", **Supp. XXI:** 5, 6

Cook, Mercer, **Supp. IV Part 1:** 368

Cooke, Alistair, **III:** 113, 119, 120

Cooke, Delmar G., **II:** 271

Cooke, Grace MacGowan, **Supp. V:** 285

Cooke, Philip Pendleton, **III:** 420

Cooke, Rose Terry, **II:** 401; **Retro. Supp. II:** 51, 136, 138; **Supp. XIII:** 152

"Cookie" (Taylor), **Supp. V:** 320

"Cookies, The" (Nye), **Supp. XIII:** 281

Cooking of Provincial France, The (M. F. K. Fisher), **Supp. XVII:** 89

Cook-Lynn, Elizabeth, **Supp. IV Part 1:** 325

Coolbrith, Ina, **I:** 193, 196

"Coole Park" (Yeats), **Supp. VIII:** 155, 159

"Coole Park and Ballylee" (Yeats), **Supp. VIII:** 156

Cooley, John, **Supp. V:** 214

Cooley, Peter, **Supp. XIII:** 76

Coolidge, Calvin, **I:** 498; **II:** 95; **Supp. I Part 2:** 647

Cooling Time: An American Poetry Vigil (Wright), **Supp. XV:** 353

"Cool Million, A" (screen story) (West and Ingster), **Retro. Supp. II:** 330

Cool Million, A (West), **III:** 425; **IV:** 287, 288, 297–299, 300; **Retro. Supp. II:** 321, 322–323, 328, **335–337**

"Cool Tombs" (Sandburg), **III:** 554

Coon, Ross, **IV:** 196

Cooney, Seamus, **Supp. XIV:** 289

"Coon Hunt" (White), **Supp. I Part 2:** 669

Co-op (Sinclair), **Supp. V:** 290

Cooper, Bernard, **Supp. XI:** 129

Cooper, Frederic Taber, **Supp. XX:**219–220

Cooper, Gary, **Supp. IV Part 2:** 524

Cooper, James Fenimore, **I:** 211, 257, **335–357; II:** 74, 277, 295–296, 302, 306, 309, 313, 314; **III:** 51; **IV:** 205, 333; **Retro. Supp. I:** 246; **Retro. Supp. II:** 160; **Supp. I Part 1:** 141, 155, 156, 158, 171, 372; **Supp. I Part 2:** 413, 495, 579, 585, 652, 660; **Supp. IV Part 1:** 80; **Supp. IV Part 2:** 463, 469; **Supp. V:** 209–210; **Supp. VIII:** 189; **Supp. XIV:** 227; **Supp. XVIII:** 4

Cooper, Mrs. James Fenimore (Susan A. De Lancey), **I:** 338, 351, 354

Cooper, Jane, **Supp. XV:** 259

Cooper, Rand Richards, **Supp. XVI:** 74

Cooper, Susan Fenimore, **I:** 337, 354

Cooper, William, **I:** 337–338, 351

Cooper, Mrs. William, **I:** 337

Coover, Robert, **Supp. IV Part 1:** 388; **Supp. V: 39–55; Supp. XII:** 152; **Supp. XIV:** 96; **Supp. XVII:** 6; **Supp. XXI:** 236

Copacetic (Komunyakaa), **Supp. XIII: 116–118,** 126

Cope, Wendy, **Supp. XV:** 117

Copland, Aaron, **II:** 586; **Supp. I Part 1:** 281; **Supp. III Part 2:** 619; **Supp. IV Part 1:** 79, 80–81, 84

Coplas de Don Jorge Manrique (Longfellow, trans.), **II:** 488, 492

Coppée, François Edouard Joachim, **II:** 325

Copperhead, The (Frederic), **II:** 134–135

Copperhead Cane (J. W. Miller), **Supp. XX:**163, 164, **166–167**

Copper Sun (Cullen), **Supp. IV Part 1:** 167, 168

Coppola, Francis Ford, **Supp. XI:** 171, 172; **Supp. XII:** 75

Coprolites (Goldbarth), **Supp. XII: 177–178,** 180, 183

Coral and Captive Israel (Reznikoff), **Supp. XIV:** 288

"Coral Ring, The" (Stowe), **Supp. I Part 2:** 586

"Cora Unashamed" (Hughes), **Supp. I Part 1:** 329, 330

"Corazón del Corrido" (Mora), **Supp. XIII:** 225

Corban Ephphata (Li Lin Lee), **Supp. XV:** 225

Corbett, Gentlemen Jim, **II:** 416

Corbett, William, **Supp. XI:** 248; **Supp. XVI:** 286, 295

Corbière, Jean Antoine, **II:** 354–355, 528

Cordiall Water, A: A garland of Odd & Old Receipts to Assuage the Ills of Man and Beast (M. F. Fisher), **Supp. XVII:** 88, 90

Cording, Robert, **Supp. IX:** 328; **Supp. XII:** 184

Core, George, **Supp. XVIII:** 86; **Supp. XXI:** 193

Corelli, Marie, **III:** 579

Corey, Lewis, **Supp. I Part 2:** 645

"Corinna's Going a-Maying" (Herrick), **Supp. XIV:** 8, 9

"Coriolan" (Eliot), **I:** 580

"Coriolanus and His Mother" (Schwartz), **Supp. II Part 2:** 643, 644–645

"Corkscrew" (Hammett), **Supp. IV Part 1:** 345, 347

Corkum, Gerald, **I:** 37

Corky's Brother (Neugeboren), **Supp. XVI:** 225

"Corky's Brother" (Neugeboren), **Supp. XVI:** 225

Corliss, Richard, **Supp. VIII:** 73

Corman, Cid, **Supp. III Part 2:** 624, 625, 626, 627, 628; **Supp. IV Part 1:** 144; **Supp. VIII:** 292; **Supp. XV:** 74, 153; **Supp. XXI:** 23, 27

"Corn" (Lanier), **Supp. I Part 1:** 352, 353, 354, 356–361, 364, 366

Corn, Alfred, **Supp. IX:** 156; **Supp. XV:** 250

Corneille, Pierre, **Supp. I Part 2:** 716; **Supp. IX:** 131

Cornell, Esther, **I:** 231

Cornell, Joseph, **Supp. XXI:** 131

Cornell, Katherine, **IV:** 356

Cornell, Valerie, **Supp. XX:**94–95

"Corners" (Dunn), **Supp. XI:** 148

Cornhuskers (Sandburg), **III:** 583–585

"Corn-Planting, The" (Anderson), **I:** 114

Cornucopia: New and Selected Poems, 1975–2002 (Peacock), **Supp. XIX: 203–204**

"Coroner's Report" (Wrigley), **Supp. XVIII:** 295

"Corporal of Artillery" (Dubus), **Supp. VII:** 84, 85

"Corpse Plant, The" (Rich), **Supp. I Part 2:** 555

Corpus Christi (McNally), **Supp. XIII:** 205–206, 209

Corradi, Juan, **Supp. IV Part 1:** 208

Corrections, The (Franzen), **Supp. XIX:** 54; **Supp. XX:**83, 84, 85, 90, 91, **91–93,** 95

"Correspondences" (Baudelaire), **I:** 63

"Corrido de Gregorio Cortez" (Mora), **Supp. XIII:** 225

"Corrigenda" (Komunyakaa), **Supp. XIII:** 115, 116

Corrosive Sublimate (Sorrentino), **Supp. XXI:** 226, 228

Corruption City (McCoy), **Supp. XIII:** 175

Corso, Gregory, **Supp. II Part 1:** 30; **Supp. IV Part 1:** 90; **Supp. XII:** 117–138; **Supp. XIV:** 150; **Supp. XVI:** 135; **Supp. XXI:** 53

Corsons Inlet (Ammons), **Supp. VII:** 25–26, 28–29, 36

"Corsons Inlet" (Ammons), **Supp. VII:** 25–26

Cortázar, Julio, **Retro. Supp. I:** 278

"Cortège for Rosenbloom" (Stevens), **IV:** 81

Cortez, Hernando, **III:** 2

" 'Coruscating Glamour': Lynda Hull and the Movies" (Goldstein), **Supp. XXI:** 134

Cory, William Johnson, **Supp. XX:**230, 231

Coser, Lewis, **Supp. I Part 2:** 650

Cosgrave, Patrick, **Retro. Supp. II:** 185

Cosmic Optimism: A Study of the Interpretation of Evolution by American Poets from Emerson to Robinson (Conner), **Supp. I Part 1:** 73

Cosmological Eye, The (H. Miller), **III:** 174, 184

"Cosmological Eye, The" (H. Miller), **III:** 183

"Cosmos" (Beattie), **Supp. V:** 35

"Cost, The" (Hecht), **Supp. X:** 62–63

Costello, Bonnie, **Retro. Supp. II:** 40

Costner, Kevin, **Supp. VIII:** 45

"Cost of Living, The" (Malamud), **Supp. I Part 2:** 429, 437

"Costume as Metaphor" (Bronk), **Supp. XXI:** 26

Cott, Jonathan, **Supp. XVI:** 104, 106

"Cottagers' Corner" column (D. West), **Supp. XVIII:** 286

"Cottage Street, 1953" (Wilbur), **Supp. III Part 2:** 543, 561

"Cottagette, The" (Gilman), **Supp. XI:** 207

Cotten, Joseph, **Supp. IV Part 2:** 524

Cotter, James Finn, **Supp. X:** 202

Cotton, John, **Supp. I Part 1:** 98, 101, 110, 111, 116

Cotton, Joseph, **Supp. XII:** 160

Cotton, Seaborn, **Supp. I Part 1:** 101

"Cotton Club Classics" (Halliday), **Supp. XIX:** 92, 93

Cotton Comes to Harlem (C. Himes), **Supp. XVI:** 143, 144

Cotton Comes to Harlem (film, O. Davis), **Supp. XVI:** 144

"Cotton Song" (Toomer), **Supp. IX:** 312

Couch, W. T., **Supp. X:** 46

Coughlin, Ruth Pollack, **Supp. VIII:** 45

Coulette, Henri, **Supp. V:** 180; **Supp. XIII:** 312; **Supp. XV:** 74, 75

Coultrap-McQuin, Susan, **Supp. XVI:** 85, 92

"Council of State, A" (Dunbar), **Supp. II Part 1:** 211, 213

"Count Dracula" (Allen), **Supp. XV:** 15

"Countee Cullen at 'The Heights' " (Tuttleton), **Supp. IV Part 1:** 166

Counterfeiters, The (Gide), **Supp. IV Part 1:** 80; **Supp. IV Part 2:** 681

"Countering" (Ammons), **Supp. VII:** 28

Counterlife, The (P. Roth), **Retro. Supp. II:** 279, 280, 291; **Supp. III Part 2:** 424–426

Counter-Statement (Burke), **I:** 270–272; **IV:** 431

"Countess, The" (Whittier), **Supp. I Part 2:** 691, 694

Count Frontenac and New France Under Louis XIV (Parkman), **Supp. II Part 2:** 607, 609–610

"Counting Small-Boned Bodies" (R. Bly), **Supp. IV Part 1:** 62

"Counting the Children" (Gioia), **Supp. XV:** 122–123

"Counting the Mad" (Justice), **Supp. VII:** 117

Count of Monte Cristo, The (Dumas), **III:** 386, 396; **Supp. XVII:** 64, 216

"Countries We Live In, The" (Zach; Everwine, trans.), **Supp. XV:** 87

"Country Boy in Boston, The" (Howells), **II:** 255

Country By-Ways (Jewett), **II:** 402

Country Doctor, A (Jewett), **II:** 391, 392, 396, 404–405; **Retro. Supp. II:** 131, 141, 146

"Country Full of Swedes" (Caldwell), **I:** 297, 309

Country Girl, The (Odets), **Supp. II Part 2:** 546, 547, 548–549

"Country House" (Kumin), **Supp. IV Part 2:** 446

"Country Husband, The" (Cheever), **Supp. I Part 1:** 184, 189

"Country Life" (Pickering), **Supp. XXI:** 197

"Country Marriage" (C. Frost), **Supp. XV:** 99

Countrymen of Bones (R. O. Butler), **Supp. XII:** 62, **65–66**

"Country Mouse, The" (Bishop), **Retro. Supp. II:** 37, 38, 51

Country Music: Selected Early Poems (Wright), **Supp. V:** 332, 335, 338, 342

Country of a Thousand Years of Peace, The (Merrill), **Supp. III Part 1:** 321, 322, 331

"Country of Elusion, The" (O. Henry), **Supp. II Part 1:** 407

Country Of Language, The (Sanders), **Supp. XVI:** 277

Country of Marriage, The (Berry), **Supp. X:** 33

Country of Strangers, A (Richter), **Supp. XVIII:** 217

Country of Survivors (Di Piero), **Supp. XIX:** 36

Country of the Pointed Firs, The (Jewett), **II:** 392, 399, 405, 409–411; **Retro. Supp. I:** 6; **Retro. Supp. II:** 134, 136, 139, 140, 141, 145, 146, 147; **Supp. VIII:** 126; **Supp. XIII:** 152

"Country Printer, The" (Freneau), **Supp. II Part 1:** 269

"Country Wife, The" (Gioia), **Supp. XV:** 120

Count Your Bullets (film), **Supp. XVII:** 141

Count Zero (W. Gibson), **Supp. XVI:** 19, **126–127,** 129

Coup, The (Updike), **Retro. Supp. I:** 331, 334, 335

"Coup de Grâce, The" (Bierce), **I:** 202

Couperin, François, **III:** 464

"Couple, The" (Olds), **Supp. X:** 206

"Couple of Hamburgers, A" (Thurber), **Supp. I Part 2:** 616

"Couple of Nuts, A" (Z. Fitzgerald), **Supp. IX:** 58, 71, 72

"Couples" (Halliday), **Supp. XIX:** 89

Couples (Updike), **IV:** 214, 215, 216, 217, 227, 229–230; **Retro. Supp. I:** 320, 327, 330; **Supp. XII:** 296

Cournos, John, **III:** 465; **Supp. I Part 1:** 258

"Course in Creative Writing, A" (Stafford), **Supp. XI:** 327

"Course of a Particular, The" (Stevens), **Retro. Supp. I:** 312

"Coursier de Jeanne d'Arc, Le" (McCarriston), **Supp. XIV:** 267–268

Courtier, The (Castiglione), **III:** 282

" 'Courtin,' The" (Lowell), **Supp. I Part 2:** 415

"Courting of Sister Wisby, The" (Jewett), **Retro. Supp. II:** 134, 135, 146

"Courting the Famous Figures at the Grotto of Improbable Thought" (B. Kelly), **Supp. XVII:** 127–128

"Courtship" (Dove), **Supp. IV Part 1:** 248

"Courtship, Diligence" (Dove), **Supp. IV Part 1:** 248

Courtship of Miles Standish, The (Longfellow), **II:** 489, 502–503; **Retro. Supp. II:** 155, **161–162,** 163, 166, 168

"Cousin Aubrey" (Taylor), **Supp. V:** 328

Cousine Bette (Balzac), **Retro. Supp. II:** 98

Couturier, Maurice, **Supp. IV Part 1:** 44

Covarrubias, Miguel, **Supp. XVI:** 187

"Covered Bridges" (Kingsolver), **Supp. VII:** 203

"Cover Photograph" (Nelson), **Supp. XVIII:** 173

"Cover Stories" (Skloot), **Supp. XX:**195, 207

"Cover Versions" (Halliday), **Supp. XIX:** 84

Cowan, Lester, **III:** 148

Cowan, Louise, **IV:** 120, 125

Coward, Noel, **Retro. Supp. I:** 65; **Supp. I Part 1:** 332; **Supp. V:** 101; **Supp. XV:** 329

"Cowardice" (Theroux), **Supp. VIII:** 313

Cowboy Mouth (Shepard), **Supp. III Part 2:** 441–442

"Cowboys" (Salter). *See* "Dirt" (Salter)

Cowboys (Shepard), **Supp. III Part 2:** 432

Cowboys #2 (Shepard), **Supp. III Part 2:** 437, 438

Cowell, Henry, **Supp. IV Part 1:** 80, 82

Cowen, Philip, **Supp. XX:**2

Cowen, Wilson Walker, **Supp. IV Part 2:** 435

Cowie, Alexander, **IV:** 70

"Cow in Apple Time, The" (Frost), **II:** 154; **Retro. Supp. I:** 131

Cowl, Jane, **IV:** 357

Cowley, Abraham, **III:** 508; **IV:** 158; **Supp. I Part 1:** 357

Cowley, Malcolm, **I:** 246, 253, 254, 255, 256, 257, 283, 385; **II:** 26, 57, 94, 456; **III:** 606; **IV:** 123; **Retro. Supp. I:** 73, 91, 97; **Retro. Supp. II:** 77, 83, 89, 221, 330; **Supp. I Part 1:** 174; **Supp. I Part 2:** 609, 610, 620, 647, 654, 678; **Supp. II Part 1:** 103, 135–156; **Supp. VIII:** 96; **Supp. XV:** 142; **Supp. XX:**76

Cowley, Marguerite Frances Baird (Mrs. Malcolm Cowley), **Supp. I Part 2:** 615; **Supp. II Part 1:** 138, 139

Cowley, Muriel Maurer (Mrs. Malcolm Cowley), **Supp. II Part 1:** 139

Cowley, Susan Cheever (Susan Cheever), **Supp. I Part 1:** 175; **Supp. IX:** 133

Cowper, William, **II:** 17, 304; **III:** 508, 511; **Supp. I Part 1:** 150, 151, 152; **Supp. I Part 2:** 539

"Cow Wandering in the Bare Field, The" (Jarrell), **II:** 371, 388

Cox, Martha Heasley, **Supp. IX:** 2, 4, 11–12

Cox, Sidney, **Retro. Supp. I:** 131; **Supp. XXI:** 19, 21

Cox, Stephen, **Supp. IV Part 2:** 523, 524

Cox, Steve, **Supp. XIX:** 116, 128

Coxey, Jacob, **II:** 464

"Coxon Fund, The" (James), **Retro. Supp. I:** 228

"Coy Mistress" (A. Finch), **Supp. XVII:** 72

Coyne, Patricia, **Supp. V:** 123

"Coyote Ortiz: *Canis latrans latrans* in the Poetry of Simon Ortiz" (P. C. Smith), **Supp. IV Part 2:** 509

Coyote's Daylight Trip (Gunn Allen), **Supp. IV Part 1:** 320, 324

Coyote Was Here (Ortiz), **Supp. IV Part 2:** 499

Cozzens, James Gould, **I:** 358–380; **II:** 459

Crabbe, George, **II:** 304; **III:** 469, 508, 511, 521

"Crab-Boil" (Dove), **Supp. IV Part 1:** 249

"Cracked Looking-Glass, The" (Porter), **III:** 434, 435, 446

"Cracker Chidlings" (Rawlings), **Supp. X:** 224, 228

Cracks (Purdy), **Supp. VII:** 277–278

Crack-Up, The (Fitzgerald), **II:** 80; **III:** 35, 45; **Retro. Supp. I:** 113, 115; **Supp. V:** 276; **Supp. IX:** 61

"Crack-Up, The" (Fitzgerald), **I:** 509; **Retro. Supp. I:** 113, 114

"Crack-up of American Optimism, The: Vachel Lindsay, the Dante of the Fundamentalists" (Viereck), **Supp. I Part 2:** 403

Cradle Will Rock, The (Blitzstein), **Supp. I Part 1:** 277, 278

Craft of Fiction, The (Lubbock), **I:** 504; **Supp. VIII:** 165

Craft of Peter Taylor, The (McAlexander, ed.), **Supp. V:** 314

Craig, Gordon, **III:** 394; **Supp. XXI:** 6

Crain, Jane Larkin, **Supp. V:** 123; **Supp. XII:** 167, 168

Crais, Robert, **Supp. XXI:** 70

Cram, Ralph Adams, **I:** 19

Cramer, Steven, **Supp. XI:** 139; **Supp. XV:** 26

Crandall, Reuben, **Supp. I Part 2:** 686

Crane, Agnes, **I:** 406

Crane, Edmund, **I:** 407

Crane, Hart, **I:** 61, 62, 97, 109, 116, 266, 381–404; **II:** 133, 215, 306, 368, 371, 536, 542; **III:** 260, 276, 453, 485, 521; **IV:** 122, 123–124, 127, 128, 129, 135, 139, 140, 141, 341, 380, 418, 419; **Retro. Supp. I:** 427; **Retro. Supp. II:** 75–91; **Supp. I Part 1:** 86; **Supp. II Part 1:** 89, 152; **Supp. III Part 1:** 20, 63, 350; **Supp. V:** 342; **Supp. VIII:** 39; **Supp. IX:** 38, 229, 320; **Supp. X:** 115, 116, 120; **Supp. XI:** 123, 131; **Supp. XII:** 198; **Supp. XV:** 138; **Supp. XIX:** 35; **Supp. XX:**80; **Supp. XXI:** 131, 132, 136, 230

Crane, Jonathan, Jr., **I:** 407

Crane, Jonathan Townley, **I:** 406

Crane, Mrs. Jonathan Townley, **I:** 406

Crane, Luther, **I:** 406

Crane, Milton, **Supp. XV:** 144

Crane, Nellie, **I:** 407

Crane, R. S., **Supp. I Part 2:** 423

Crane, Stephen, **I:** 34, 169–170, 201, 207, 211, 405–427, 477, 506, 519; **II:** 58, 144, 198, 262, 263, 264, 276, 289, 290, 291; **III:** 314, 317, 334, 335, 454, 505, 585; **IV:** 207, 208, 256, 350, 475; **Retro. Supp. I:** 231, 325; **Retro. Supp. II:** 97, 123; **Supp. I Part 1:** 314; **Supp. III Part 2:** 412; **Supp. IV Part 1:** 350, 380; **Supp. IV Part 2:** 680, 689, 692; **Supp. VIII:** 98, 105; **Supp. IX:** 1, 14; **Supp. X:** 223; **Supp. XI:** 95; **Supp. XII:** 50; **Supp. XIV:** 21, 50, 51, 227; **Supp. XVII:** 71, 228; **Supp. XVIII:** 74, 75

Crane, William, **I:** 407

Cranford (Gaskell), **Supp. IX:** 79

Crashaw, William, **IV:** 145, 150, 151, 165

"Crash Report" (McGrath), **Supp. X:** 116

Crater, The (Cooper), **I:** 354, 355

Cratylus (Plato), **II:** 10

"Craven Street Gazette" (Franklin), **II:** 119

"Crawdad, The" (F. Wright), **Supp. XVII:** 244

Crawdad Creek (Sanders), **Supp. XVI:** 269

Crawford, Brad, **Supp. XI:** 133

Crawford, Eva, **I:** 199

Crawford, F. Marion, **III:** 320

Crawford, Joan, **Supp. I Part 1:** 67

Crawford, Kathleen, **I:** 289

"Crayon House" (Rukeyser), **Supp. VI:** 273

Crayon Miscellany, The (Irving), **II:** 312–313

Crazed, The (Jin), **Supp. XVIII:** 99–100

"Crazy about her Shrimp" (Simic), **Supp. VIII:** 282

"Crazy Cock" (H. Miller), **III:** 177

Crazy Gypsy (Salinas), **Supp. XIII:** 311, 313–315, 316

"Crazy Gypsy" (Salinas), **Supp. XIII:** 313–314

Crazy Horse, **Supp. IV Part 2:** 488, 489

Crazy Horse (McMurtry), **Supp. V:** 233

Crazy Horse in Stillness (Heyen), **Supp. XIII:** 344

"Crazy in the Stir" (C. Himes), **Supp. XVI:** 137

Crazy Kill, The (C. Himes), **Supp. XVI:** 143

Creating a Role (Stanislavsky), **Supp. XIV:** 243

"Creation, According to Coyote, The" (Ortiz), **Supp. IV Part 2:** 505

Creation: A Novel (Vidal), **Supp. IV Part 2:** 677, 685, 688

"Creation of Anguish" (Nemerov), **III:** 269

"Creation Story" (Gunn Allen), **Supp. IV Part 1:** 325

"Creative and Cultural Lag" (Ellison), **Retro. Supp. II:** 116; **Supp. II Part 1:** 229; **Supp. XVIII:** 283

Creative Criticism (Spingarn), **I:** 266

"Creative Democracy" (Locke), **Supp. XIV:** 208

Creative Present, The (Balkian and Simmons, eds.), **Supp. XI:** 230

Creatures in an Alphabet (illus. Barnes), **Supp. III Part 1:** 43

"Credences of Summer" (Stevens), **IV:** 93–94

"Credentials" (Halliday), **Supp. XIX:** 90

"Credo" (Bynner), **Supp. XV:** 50

"Credo" (Du Bois), **Supp. II Part 1:** 169

"Credo" (Jeffers), **Supp. II Part 2:** 424

"Credos and Curios" (Thurber), **Supp. I Part 2:** 606, 613

Creech, James, **Retro. Supp. I:** 254

"Creed for Americans, A" (Benét), **Supp. XI:** 52

"Creed of a Beggar, The" (Lindsay), **Supp. I Part 2:** 379

Creegan, Andy, **Supp. XIX:** 205

Creekmore, Hubert, **II:** 586

Creeley, Robert, **Retro. Supp. I:** 411; **Supp. II Part 1:** 30; **Supp. III Part 1:** 2; **Supp. III Part 2:** 622, 626, 629; **Supp. IV Part 1:** **139–161,** 322, 325; **Supp. XI:** 317; **Supp. XIII:** 104, 112; **Supp. XIV:** 150; **Supp. XVI:** 283; **Supp. XXI:** 23, 27, 227, 230

Creelman, James Ashmore, **Supp. XVI:** 186–187

"Cremona Violin, The" (Lowell), **II:** 523

"Crêpe de Chine" (Doty), **Supp. XI:** 128

"Cressy" (Harte), **Supp. II Part 1:** 354, 356

"Cretan Woman, The" (Jeffers), **Supp. II Part 2:** 435

Crèvecoeur, Michel-Guillaume Jean de, **I:** 229; **Supp. I Part 1:** **227–252**

Crèvecoeur's Eighteenth-Century Travels in Pennsylvania and New York (Adams), **Supp. I Part 1:** 251

Crevel, René, **Supp. XIV:** 343

Crewe-Jones, Florence, **Supp. XVII:** 58

Crewe Train (Macaulay), **Supp. XII:** 88

Crews, Harry, **Supp. X:** 11, 12; **Supp. XI:** **99–117,** 245; **Supp. XVIII:** 195; **Supp. XXI:** 35, 38, 40, 44

Crichton, Michael, **Supp. XIV:** 316

Crick, Philip, **Supp. XVI:** 289

Cricket (C. L. R. James; Grimshaw, ed.), **Supp. XXI:** 172

"Crickets" (R. O. Butler), **Supp. XII:** 71

Criers and Kibitzers, Kibitzers and Criers (Elkin), **Supp. VI:** **45–46,** 57

Crime and Punishment (Dostoevsky), **II:** 60, 130; **IV:** 484; **Supp. IV Part 2:** 525; **Supp. VIII:** 282; **Supp. XII:** 281; **Supp. XVII:** 155; **Supp. XVIII:** 278; **Supp. XIX:** 276

Crime at Scottsboro, The (Endore), **Supp. XVII:** 59

Crime Beat (Connelly), **Supp. XXI:** 67, 79

Crimes and Misdemeanors (film; Allen), **Supp. XV:** 1, 2, **11,** 12

Crisis papers (Paine), **Supp. I Part 2:** 508–509, 510

"Criteria of Negro Art" (Du Bois), **Supp. II Part 1:** 181; **Supp. XIX:** 66–67

"Critiad, The" (Winters), **Supp. II Part 2:** 794, 799

Critical Anthology A (Untermeyer), **Supp. XV:** 310

Critical Essays on Charlotte Perkins Gilman (Karpinski, ed.), **Supp. XI:** 201

Critical Essays on Peter Taylor (McAlexander), **Supp. V:** 319, 320, 323–324

Critical Essays on Robert Bly (W. V. Davis), **Supp. IV Part 1:** 64, 69

Critical Essays on Wallace Stegner (Arthur), **Supp. IV Part 2:** 606

Critical Fable, A (Lowell), **II:** 511–512, 527, 529–530

Critical Guide to Leaves of Grass, A (J. Miller), **IV:** 352

Critical Response to Joan Didion, The (Felton), **Supp. IV Part 1:** 210

Critical Temper of Alain Locke, The: A Selection of His Essays on Art and Culture (Stewart, ed.), **Supp. XIV:** 196, **210–211,** 213

"Critic as Artist, The" (Wilde), **Supp. X:** 189

Criticism and Fiction (Howells), **II:** 288

Criticism and Ideology (Eagleton), **Retro. Supp. I:** 67

Criticism in the Borderlands (Calderón and Saldívar, eds.), **Supp. IV Part 2:** 544

"Critics, The" (Jong), **Supp. V:** 119

"Critics and Connoisseurs" (Moore), **III:** 209

Critic's Notebook, A (Howe), **Supp. VI:** 126–128

"Critic's Task, The" (Kazin), **Supp. VIII:** 103

"Critic Who Does Not Exist, The" (Wilson), **IV:** 431

"Critique de la Vie Quotidienne" (Barthelme), **Supp. IV Part 1:** 50

Critique of Pure Reason (Kant), **Supp. XVI:** 184

Croce, Benedetto, **I:** 58, 255, 265, 273, 281; **III:** 610

Crockett, Davy, **II:** 307; **III:** 227; **IV:** 266; **Supp. I Part 2:** 411

Crofter and the Laird, The (McPhee), **Supp. III Part 1:** 301–302, 307

Croly, Herbert, **I:** 229, 231, 235; **IV:** 436

Cromwell, Oliver, **IV:** 145, 146, 156; **Supp. I Part 1:** 111

Cronenberg, David, **Supp. XXI:** 152, 154

Cronin, A. J., **Supp. XVII:** 59

Cronin, Dr. Archibald, **III:** 578

Cronin, Justin, **Supp. X:** 10

Crooke, Dr. Helkiah, **Supp. I Part 1:** 98, 104

Crooked Little Heart (Lamott), **Supp. XX:**138

Crooks, Alan, **Supp. V:** 226

Crooks, Robert, **Supp. XIII:** 237

"Crop, The" (O'Connor), **Retro. Supp. II:** 223–225

Crosby, Caresse, **I:** 385; **III:** 473; **Retro. Supp. II:** 85; **Supp. XII:** 198

Crosby, Harry, **I:** 385; **Retro. Supp. II:** 85

"Cross" (Hughes), **Supp. I Part 1:** 325; **Supp. XVIII:** 124

Crossan, John Dominic, **Supp. V:** 251

"Cross Country Snow" (Hemingway), **II:** 249

Cross Creek (Rawlings), **Supp. X:** 223, 226, 228, **231–232,** 233, 234, 235

Cross Creek Cookery (Rawlings), **Supp. X:** 233

Crossing, The (McCarthy), **Supp. VIII:** 175, **184–186**

"Crossing, The" (Swenson), **Supp. IV Part 2:** 644

"Crossing Brooklyn Ferry" (Whitman), **IV:** 333, 340, 341; **Retro. Supp. I:** 389, 396, 397, 400–401

"Crossing into Poland" (Babel), **Supp. XIV:** 84

Crossings (Chuang), **Supp. X:** 291

"Crossings" (Hogan), **Supp. IV Part 1:** 412

Crossing the Water (Plath), **Retro. Supp. II:** 248; **Supp. I Part 2:** 526, 538

Crossing to Safety (Stegner), **Supp. IV Part 2:** 599, 606, 612, 613–614

"Cross of Snow, The" (Longfellow), **II:** 490; **Retro. Supp. II:** 169–170

"Crossover" (O. Butler), **Supp. XIII:** 61

"Cross-Roads, The" (Lowell), **II:** 523

"Crossroads of the World Etc." (Merwin), **Supp. III Part 1:** 347, 348

Cross-Section (Seaver), **IV:** 485

Cross the Border, Close the Gap (Fiedler), **Supp. XIII:** 104

Cross Ties (X. J. Kennedy), **Supp. XV:** 165, **166–167**

"Cross Ties" (X. J. Kennedy), **Supp. XV:** 158

Crouch, Stanley, **Supp. XIX:** 158

"Croup" (Karr), **Supp. XI:** 243

Crouse, Russel, **III:** 284

"Crow" (Hogan), **Supp. IV Part 1:** 405

Crow (Hughes), **Supp. XV:** 347, 348

"Crow, The" (Creeley), **Supp. IV Part 1:** 148–149

Crow and the Heart,The (Carruth), **Supp. XVI:** 47–48

"Crowded Street, The" (Bryant), **Supp. I Part 1:** 168

Crowder, A. B., **Supp. XI:** 107

"Crow Jane" (Baraka), **Supp. II Part 1:** 38

Crowninshield, Frank, **III:** 123; **Supp. IX:** 201

Crown of Columbus (Erdrich and Dorris), **Supp. IV Part 1:** 260

"Crows, The" (Bogan), **Supp. III Part 1:** 50, 51

Crucial Instances (Wharton), **Retro. Supp. I:** 365, 367

Crucible, The (A. Miller), **III:** 147, 148, 155, 156–158, 159, 166; **Supp. XIII:** 206

"Crucified" (Gibran), **Supp. XX:**119

"Crucifix in the Filing Cabinet" (Shapiro), **Supp. II Part 2:** 712

"Crude Foyer" (Stevens), **Retro. Supp. I:** 310

"Cruel and Barbarous Treatment" (McCarthy), **II:** 562, 563

"Cruel Mother, The" (B. Kelly), **Supp. XVII:** 126

Cruise of the Dazzler, The (London), **II:** 465

Cruise of the Snark, The (London), **II:** 476–477

"Cruising with the Beach Boys" (Gioia), **Supp. XV:** 118

" 'Crumbling Idols' by Hamlin Garland" (Chopin), **Supp. I Part 1:** 217

"Crusade of the Excelsior, The" (Harte), **Supp. II Part 1:** 336, 354

"Crusoe in England" (Bishop), **Retro. Supp. II:** 50; **Supp. I Part 1:** 93, 95, 96; **Supp. III Part 1:** 10, 18

Cruz-Hacker, Alba, **Supp. XXI:** 107

Cry, the Beloved Country (Paton), **Supp. VIII:** 126

Cryer, Dan, **Supp. VIII:** 86, 88; **Supp. XII:** 164

Crying of Lot 49, The (Pynchon), **Supp. II Part 2:** 618, 619, 621, 630–633

"Crying Sisters, The" (Rand), **Supp. IV Part 2:** 524

"Crying Wolf" (C. Frost), **Supp. XV:** 101

"Cry of the Graves, The" (Gibran), **Supp. XX:** 124

Cryptogram, The (Mamet), **Supp. XIV:** 240, 247, 255

"Crystal, The" (Aiken), **I:** 60

"Crystal, The" (Lanier), **Supp. I Part 1:** 364, 370

"Crystal Cage, The" (Kunitz), **Supp. III Part 1:** 258

Crystal Vision (Sorrentino), **Supp. XXI:** 235, 236

"Crytal" (Sobin), **Supp. XVI:** 283

Cry to Heaven (Rice), **Supp. VII:** 300–301

"Cuba" (Hemingway), **II:** 258

"Cuba Libre" (Baraka), **Supp. II Part 1:** 33

Cuba: Prophetic Island (W. Frank), **Supp. XX:** 80, 81

"Cubism, Barcelona" (Hull), **Supp. XXI:** 137

Cudjoe, Selwyn, **Supp. IV Part 1:** 6

"Cudjo's Own Story of the Last American Slaver" (Hurston), **Supp. VI:** 153

Cudlipp, Thelma, **I:** 501

Cudworth, Ralph, **II:** 9, 10

"Cuentista" (Mora), **Supp. XIII:** 224

"Cuento de agua santa, Un" (Mora), **Supp. XIII:** 224

Cujo (King), **Supp. V:** 138–139, 143, 149, 152

Cukor, George, **Supp. XVI:** 192

Cullen, Countee, **Retro. Supp. I:** 207; **Retro. Supp. II:** 114; **Supp. I Part 1:** 49, 325; **Supp. III Part 1:** 73, 75, 76; **Supp. IV Part 1:** 163–174; **Supp. IX:** 306, 309; **Supp. X:** 136, 140; **Supp. XIII:** 186; **Supp. XVIII:** 122, 131, 185, 279, 280, 282, 284; **Supp. XIX:** 78

"Cultivation of Christmas Trees, The" (Eliot), **I:** 579

"Cult of Personality in American Letters, The" (Swados), **Supp. XIX:** 265

"Cult of the Best, The" (Arnold), **I:** 223

"Cultural Exchange" (Hughes), **Supp. I Part 1:** 341

"Cultural Pluralism: A New Americanism" (Locke), **Supp. XIV:** 195

"Cultural Relativism and Ideological Peace" (Locke), **Supp. XIV:** 202, 212

"Culture" (Emerson), **III:** 2, 4

"Culture, Self, and Style" (Gass), **Supp. VI:** 88

"Culture and Religion" (Olds), **Supp. X:** 214

Culture of Cities, The (Mumford), **Supp. II Part 2:** 492, 494–495

Cummings, E. E., **I:** 44, 48, 64, 105, 176, **428–450,** 475, 477, 482, 526; **III:** 20, 196, 476; **IV:** 384, 402, 415, 427, 433; **Retro. Supp. II:** 178, 328; **Supp. I**

Part 2: 622, 678; **Supp. III Part 1:** 73; **Supp. IV Part 2:** 637, 641; **Supp. IX:** 20; **Supp. XV:** 312, 338

Cummings, Robert, **Supp. IV Part 2:** 524

Cummins, James, **Supp. XVII:** 74

Cunard, Lady, **III:** 459

Cunningham, J. V., **Supp. XV:** 169

Cunningham, Merce, **Supp. IV Part 1:** 83; **Supp. XV:** 187

Cunningham, Michael, **Supp. XII:** 80; **Supp. XV:** 55–71

Cup of Gold (Steinbeck), **IV:** 51, 53, 61–64, 67

"Cupola, The" (Bogan), **Supp. III Part 1:** 53

"Curandera" (Mora), **Supp. XIII:** 214, 222

Curé de Tours, Le (Balzac), **I:** 509

Cure for Dreams, A: A Novel (Gibbons), **Supp. X:** 45–47, 48, 50

Curie, Marie, **IV:** 420, 421; **Supp. I Part 2:** 569

Curie, Pierre, **IV:** 420

Curiosa Americana (Mather), **Supp. II Part 2:** 463

Curiosities (Matthews), **Supp. IX:** 151, 152

"Curious Case of Sidd Finch, The" (Plimpton), **Supp. XVI:** 244

"Curious Shifts of the Poor" (Dreiser), **Retro. Supp. II:** 97

"Current" (Espaillat), **Supp. XXI:** 106

"Currents and Counter-Currents in Medical Science" (Holmes), **Supp. I Part 1:** 305

"Curried Cow" (Bierce), **I:** 200

Curry, Professor W. C., **IV:** 122

Curse of the Jade Scorpion, The (film; Allen), **Supp. XV:** 11

Curse of the Starving Class (Shepard), **Supp. III Part 2:** 433, 447–448

Curse of the Werewolf, The (film), **Supp. XVII:** 56

"Curse on a Thief, A" (X. J. Kennedy), **Supp. XV:** 171

"Curtain, The" (Chandler), **Supp. IV Part 1:** 122

Curtain Calls: British and American Women and the Theater, 1660–1820 (Saar), **Supp. XV:** 237

Curtain of Green, A (Welty), **IV:** 261–264, 268, 283

"Curtain of Green, A" (Welty), **IV:** 263–264

Curtain of Green and Other Stories, A (Welty), **Retro. Supp. I:** 343, 344, 345, 346, 347, 355

Curtain of Trees (opera), **Supp. IV Part 2:** 552

"Curtain Raiser, A" (Stein), **IV:** 43, 44

"Curtains" (Cisneros), **Supp. VII:** 66

Curtin, John, **Supp. IX:** 184

Curtis, George William, **Supp. I Part 1:** 307; **Supp. XVIII:** 3, 14

Curve (Goldbarth), **Supp. XII:** 181

Curve of Binding Energy, The (McPhee), **Supp. III Part 1:** 301

Curzon, Mary, **III:** 52

Cushing, Caleb, **Supp. I Part 2:** 684, 686

Cushman, Howard, **Supp. I Part 2:** 652

Cushman, Stephen, **Retro. Supp. I:** 430

"Custard Heart, The" (Parker), **Supp. IX:** 201

Custer, General George, **I:** 489, 491

Custer Died for Your Sins (Deloria), **Supp. IV Part 1:** 323; **Supp. IV Part 2:** 504

"Custom House, The" (Hawthorne), **II:** 223; **Retro. Supp. I:** 147–148, 157; **Supp. XXI:** 181

Custom of the Country, The (Wharton), **IV:** 318; **Retro. Supp. I:** 374, **375–376**

"Cut" (Plath), **Retro. Supp. II:** 253

"Cut-Glass Bowl, The" (Fitzgerald), **II:** 88

Cutting, Bronson, **III:** 600

Cutting Lisa (Everett), **Supp. XVIII: 56**

"Cuttings, *later*" (Roethke), **III:** 532

"Cyberpunk" (Bethke), **Supp. XVI:** 121

Cyberspace trilogy (W. Gibson). *See* Sprawl trilogy (W. Gibson)

"Cycles, The" (Pinsky), **Supp. VI:** 250–252

Cynic's Word Book, The (Bierce), **I:** 197, 205, 208, 209, 210

Cynthia Ozick (Lowin), **Supp. V:** 273

Cynthia Ozick's Comic Art (Cohen), **Supp. V:** 273

Cynthia Ozick's Fiction (Kauvar), **Supp. V:** 273

D

Da Capo: Best Music Writing 2002 (Lethem, ed.), **Supp. XVIII:** 148

Dacey, Philip, **Supp. IV Part 1:** 70

Dacier, André, **II:** 10

"Dad" (Cullen), **Supp. IV Part 1:** 167

"Daddy" (Plath), **Retro. Supp. II:** 250–251; **Supp. I Part 2:** 529, 542, 545, 546; **Supp. II Part 2:** 688

Daddy's Little Boy (Collins), **Supp. XXI:** 54

"Daemon, The" (Bogan), **Supp. III Part 1:** 58, 61

"Daemon Lover, The" (Jackson), **Supp. IX:** 116–117

"Daffodils" (Nelson and Espeland), **Supp. XVIII:** 181

"Daffodils" (Wordsworth), **Supp. XIII:** 284

"Daffy Duck in Hollywood" (Ashbery), **Supp. III Part 1:** 18

D'Agata, John, **Supp. XII:** 97, 98

Dago Red (Fante), **Supp. XI:** 160, 169

Dahl, Roald, **Supp. IX:** 114

Dahlberg, Edward, **I:** 231; **Retro. Supp. I:** 426; **Supp. III Part 2:** 624; **Supp. XIV:** 148; **Supp. XVIII:** 148

Dahlberg, R'lene, **Supp. XIV:** 148

Daiches, David, **Retro. Supp. II:** 243; **Supp. I Part 2:** 536

Daily Horoscope (Gioia), **Supp. XV:** 112, **118–121,** 126

"Daily Horoscope" (Gioia), **Supp. XV:** 119

Daily Modernism (Podnieks), **Supp. X:** 189

Dain Curse, The (Hammett), **Supp. IV Part 1:** 348

"Daisies" (Glück), **Supp. V:** 88

"Daisy" (Oates), **Supp. II Part 2:** 523

Daisy (S. and A. Warner), **Supp. XVIII:** 268

Daisy-Head Mayzie (Geisel), **Supp. XVI:** 112

Daisy Miller (H. James), **Retro. Supp. I:** 216, 220, 222, 223, 228, 231; **Supp. XVIII:** 165

"Daisy Miller" (H. James), **II:** 325, 326, 327, 329; **IV:** 316

Dale, Charlie, **Supp. IV Part 2:** 584

Dali, Salvador, **II:** 586; **Supp. IV Part 1:** 83; **Supp. XIII:** 317

Dalibard, Thomas-François, **II:** 117

"Dallas-Fort Worth: Redband and Mistletoe" (Clampitt), **Supp. IX:** 45

"Dalliance of Eagles, The" (Whitman), **IV:** 348

Dalva (Harrison), **Supp. VIII:** 37, 45, 46, **48–49**

Daly, Carroll John, **Supp. IV Part 1:** 343, 345

Daly, John, **II:** 25, 26

Daly, Julia Brown, **II:** 25, 26

"Dalyrimple Goes Wrong" (Fitzgerald), **II:** 88

"Dam, The" (Rukeyser), **Supp. VI:** 283

Damas, Leon, **Supp. X:** 139

Damascus Gate (Stone), **Supp. V:** 308–311

Damballah (Wideman), **Supp. X:** 319, 320, 321, 322, 323, 326, 327, 331, 333–334

Dameshek, Brandon, **Supp. XIX:** 273, 277, 287

Damnation of Theron Ware, The (Frederic), **II:** 140–143, 144, 146, 147; **Retro. Supp. I:** 325

Damned If I Do (Everett), **Supp. XVIII:** 66

"Damned Thing, The" (Bierce), **I:** 206

Damon, Matt, **Supp. VIII:** 175

Damon, S. Foster, **I:** 26; **II:** 512, 514, 515

"Damon and Vandalia" (Dove), **Supp. IV Part 1:** 252

Dana, H. W. L., **I:** 225

Dana, Richard Henry, **I:** 339, 351; **Supp. I Part 1:** 103, 154, 155; **Supp. I Part 2:** 414, 420

Dana, Richard Henry, Jr., **III:** 81; **Supp. XX:**227

Dana, Robert, **Supp. V:** 178, 180

"Dana Gioia and Fine Press Printing" (Peich), **Supp. XV:** 117

"Dance, The" (Crane), **I:** 109

"Dance, The" (Roethke), **III:** 541

"Dance, The" (W. C. Williams), **Supp. XVII:** 113

Dance and the Railroad, The (Hwang), **Supp. XXI:** 145, 146

Dance of Death, The (Auden), **Supp. II Part 1:** 10

Dance of Death, The (Bierce and Harcourt), **I:** 196

Dance of Life, The (Ellis), **Supp. XX:**117

Dance of the Sleepwalkers (Calabria), **Supp. XIII:** 164

"Dance of the Solids, The" (Updike), **Retro. Supp. I:** 323

"Dancer" (Hoffman), **Supp. XVIII:** 86

"Dancer, The" (Swados), **Supp. XIX:** 261, 263–264

"Dancers Work by Forgetting" (Espaillat), **Supp. XXI:** 102

Dances with Wolves (film), **Supp. X:** 124

Dance to the Music of Time, A (Powell), **Supp. XVIII:** 146

Dancing After Hours (Dubus), **Supp. VII:** 91

Dancing Bears, The (Merwin), **Supp. III Part 1:** 343–344

Dancing on the Stones (Nichols), **Supp. XIII:** 256, 257, 259, 267, 269

"Dancing the Jig" (Sexton), **Supp. II Part 2:** 692

Dandelion Wine (Bradbury), **Supp. IV Part 1:** 101, 109–110

Dandurand, Karen, **Retro. Supp. I:** 30

"Dandy Frightening the Squatters, The" (Twain), **IV:** 193–194

Dangel, Mary Jo, **Supp. XVIII:** 156

Dangerous Crossroads (film), **Supp. XIII:** 163

Dangerous Moonlight (Purdy), **Supp. VII:** 278

"Dangerous Road Before Martin Luther King" (Baldwin), **Supp. I Part 1:** 52

"Dangerous Summer, The" (Hemingway), **II:** 261

Dangerous Thoughts (Ryan as Quin), **Supp. XVIII:** 226

"Dangers of Authorship, The" (Blackmur), **Supp. II Part 1:** 147

Dangling Man (Bellow), **I:** 144, 145, 147, 148, 150–151, 153–154, 158, 160, 161, 162, 163; **Retro. Supp. II:** 19, 20–21, 22, 23; **Supp. VIII:** 234; **Supp. XIX:** 157

Daniel (biblical book), **Supp. I Part 1:** 105

Daniel (film), **Supp. IV Part 1:** 236

Daniel, Arnaut, **III:** 467

Daniel, Robert W., **III:** 76

Daniel, Samuel, **Supp. I Part 1:** 369

Daniel Deronda (G. Eliot), **I:** 458

Daniels, Kate, **Supp. XVII:** 112

Danielson, Linda, **Supp. IV Part 2:** 569

D'Annunzio, Gabriele, **II:** 515

Danny and the Deep Blue Sea: An Apache Dance (Shanley), **Supp. XIV:** 315, **318–319**, 320, 321, 323, 324

Danny O'Neill pentalogy (Farrell), **II:** 35–41

Danse Macabre (King), **Supp. IV Part 1:** 102; **Supp. V:** 144

"Danse Russe" (W. C. Williams), **IV:** 412–413

"Dans le Restaurant" (Eliot), **I:** 554, 578

Dans l'ombre des cathédrales (Ambelain), **Supp. I Part 1:** 273

Dante Alighieri, **I:** 103, 136, 138, 250, 384, 433, 445; **II:** 8, 274, 278, 289, 490, 492, 493, 494, 495, 504, 508, 524, 552; **III:** 13, 77, 124, 182, 259, 278, 448, 453, 467, 533, 607, 609, 610–612, 613; **IV:** 50, 134, 137, 138, 139, 247, 437, 438; **Retro. Supp. I:** 62, 63, 64, 66, 360; **Retro. Supp. II:** 330; **Supp. I Part 1:** 256, 363; **Supp. I Part 2:** 422, 454; **Supp. III Part 2:** 611, 618, 621; **Supp. IV Part 2:** 634; **Supp. V:** 277, 283, 331, 338, 345; **Supp. VIII:** 27, 219–221; **Supp. X:** 120, 121, 125; **Supp. XII:** 98; **Supp. XV:** 254; **Supp. XVII:** 227, 241

Danvis Tales: Selected Stories (Robinson; Budbill, ed.), **Supp. XIX:** 6

Danziger, Adolphe, **I:** 199–200

Dar (Nabokov), **III:** 246, 255

D'Arcy, Randall, **Supp. XVII:** 76

Dardis, Tom, **Supp. XVIII:** 249

"Dare's Gift" (Glasgow), **II:** 190

Dark Angel, The (Bolton), **Supp. I Part 1:** 281

"Dark Angel Travels With Us to Canada and Blesses Our Vacation, The" (Dunn), **Supp. XI:** 146

Dark Carnival (Bradbury), **Supp. IV Part 1:** 102

Darker (Strand), **Supp. IV Part 2:** 619, 626–628

Darker Face of the Earth, The (Dove), **Supp. IV Part 1:** 255–257

Dark Green, Bright Red (Vidal), **Supp. IV Part 2:** 677

Dark Half, The (King), **Supp. V:** 141

Dark Harbor: A Poem (Strand), **Supp. IV Part 2:** 633–634

"Dark Hills, The" (Robinson), **III:** 523

Dark Horses (X. J. Kennedy), **Supp. XV:** **167–170**

Dark Hours, The (W. V. Davis), **Supp. XXI:** **91–92,** 93

Dark Laughter (Anderson), **I:** 111, 116; **II:** 250–251

"Darkling Alphabet, A" (Snodgrass), **Supp. VI:** 323

Darkling Child (Merwin and Milroy), **Supp. III Part 1:** 346

"Darkling Summer, Ominous Dusk, Rumorous Rain" (Schwartz), **Supp. II Part 2:** 661

"Darkling Thrush" (Hardy), **Supp. IX:** 40

"Dark Men, The" (Dubus), **Supp. VII:** 86

Dark Mirrors (Sobin), **Supp. XVI:** 295

Dark Mother, The (W. Frank), **Supp. XX:**70–71

Dark Mountains, The (Hoffman), **Supp. XVIII:**76–77

Darkness and the Light, The (Hecht), **Supp. X:** 58

Darkness More Than Night, A (Connelly), **Supp. XXI:** 73–74, 80

"Darkness on the Edge of Town" (O'Brien), **Supp. V:** 246

Darkness Surrounding Us, The (Sorrentino), **Supp. XXI:** 227, 228

Darkness under the Trees/Walking behind the Spanish (Salinas), **Supp. XIII:** 311, **319–324**

"Dark Night" (St. John of the Cross), **Supp. XV:** 30

Dark Night of the Soul, The (St. John of the Cross), **I:** 1, 585

"Dark Ones" (Dickey), **Supp. IV Part 1:** 182

Dark Princess: A Romance (Du Bois), **Supp. II Part 1:** 179, 181–182

Dark Room, The (T. Williams), **IV:** 381

Dark Sacred Night (CD), **Supp. XXI:** 75

Dark Shadows (television show), **Supp. XIX:** 57

"Dark Summer" (Bogan), **Supp. III Part 1:** 51, 53

Dark Summer: Poems (Bogan), **Supp. III Part 1:** 52–53, 57

"Dark Tower, The" (column), **Supp. IV Part 1:** 168, 170

Dark Tower, The: The Gunslinger (King), **Supp. V:** 152

Dark Tower IV, The: Wizard and Glass (King), **Supp. V:** 139

Dark Tunnel, The (Macdonald as Millar), **Supp. IV Part 2:** 465, 466

"Dark TV Screen" (Simic), **Supp. VIII:** 282

"Dark Voyage, The" (McLay), **Supp. XIII:** 21

"Dark Walk, The" (Taylor), **Supp. V:** 320–321, 322, 326

Darkwater: Voices from Within the Veil (Du Bois), **Supp. II Part 1:** 178, 180, 183

Dark Waves and Light Matter (Goldbarth), **Supp. XII:** 176, 193

Dark World (Carruth), **Supp. XVI:** 55

"Darling" (Nye), **Supp. XIII:** 283–284

"Darling, The" (Chekhov), **Supp. IX:** 202

Darling-Darling (Barillet and Grédy; Loos, trans.), **Supp. XVI:** 194

Darnell, Linda, **Supp. XII:** 173

Darragh, Tina, **Supp. IV Part 2:** 427

Darreu, Robert Donaldson, **Supp. II Part 1:** 89, 98, 102

Darrow, Clarence, **Supp. I Part 1:** 5; **Supp. I Part 2:** 455

Dartmouth, Earl of, **Supp. XX:**284

Darwin, Charles, **I:** 457; **II:** 323, 462, 481; **III:** 226, 231; **IV:** 69, 304; **Retro. Supp. I:** 254; **Retro. Supp. II:** 60, 65; **Supp. I Part 1:** 368; **Supp. IX:** 180; **Supp. XI:** 203; **Supp. XVI:** 13; **Supp. XX:**18

"Darwin in 1881" (Schnackenberg), **Supp. XV:** 253, 254, 258

Daryush, Elizabeth, **Supp. V:** 180

Dasburg, Andrew, **Supp. XXI:** 6

Dash, Julie, **Supp. XI:** 17, 18, 20

Dashell, Alfred, **Supp. X:** 224

"DAS KAPITAL" (Baraka), **Supp. II Part 1:** 55

Datlow, Ellen, **Supp. XVI:** 123

"Datum Centurio" (Wallace), **Supp. X:** 309

Daudet, Alphonse, **II:** 325, 338

"Daughter" (Caldwell), **I:** 309

"Daughter in the House" (X. J. Kennedy), **Supp. XV:** 160

Daughter of Earth (Smedly), **Supp. XIII:** 295

Daughter of the Land, A (Stratton-Porter), **Supp. XX:**222

Daughter of the Snows, A (London), **II:** 465, 469–470

"Daughters" (Anderson), **I:** 114

Daughters (Marshall), **Supp. XI:** 275, 276, 277, **286–288,** 289, 290

"Daughters, 1900" (Nelson), **Supp. XVIII:** 175

Daughters, I Love You (Hogan), **Supp. IV Part 1:** 397, 399, 401

"Daughters of Invention" (Alvarez), **Supp. VII:** 9

Daughters of the Dust (Dash; film), **Supp. XI:** 17, 18; **Supp. XX:**154

Daumier, Honoré, **IV:** 412

Dave, R. A., **Supp. VIII:** 126

Davenport, Abraham, **Supp. I Part 2:** 699

Davenport, Gary, **Supp. IX:** 98

Davenport, Guy, **Supp. XIV:** 96; **Supp. XXI:** 235

Davenport, Herbert J., **Supp. I Part 2:** 642

Davenport, James, **I:** 546

Daves, E. G., **Supp. I Part 1:** 369

Davey, Frank, **Supp. XIII:** 33

"David" (Garrett), **Supp. VII:** 109–110

"David" (Gordon), **Supp. IV Part 1:** 298–299

David, Gray, **Supp. XX:**260

"David and Agnes, a Romance" (Keillor), **Supp. XVI:** 175

David Blaize (Benson), **Supp. XX:**234

David Copperfield (Dickens), **I:** 458; **II:** 290; **Retro. Supp. I:** 33; **Supp. XVI:** 65, 72; **Supp. XX:**234

"David Crockett's Other Life" (Nye), **Supp. XIII:** 282

Davideis (Cowley), **IV:** 158

David Harum (Westcott), **I:** 216

"David Lynch Keeps His Head" (Wallace), **Supp. X:** 314

David Show, The (Gurney), **Supp. V:** 97

Davidson, Cathy, **Supp. XV:** 238

Davidson, Donald, **I:** 294; **III:** 495, 496; **IV:** 121, 122, 124, 125, 236; **Supp. II Part 1:** 139; **Supp. XIV:** 2; **Supp. XX:**164

Davidson, Jo, **Supp. XXI:** 7

Davidson, John, **Retro. Supp. I:** 55

Davidson, Michael, **Supp. VIII:** 290, 293, 294, 302–303

Davidson, Sara, **Supp. IV Part 1:** 196, 198, 203

Davidson, Sue, **Supp. XIX:** 260

Davidsz de Heem, Jan, **Supp. XI:** 133

Davie, Donald, **III:** 478; **Supp. IV Part 2:** 474; **Supp. V:** 331; **Supp. X:** 55, 59; **Supp. XVII:** 111, 112, 121

Davies, Arthur, **III:** 273

Davies, Sir John, **III:** 541

Davies, Marion, **Supp. XVI:** 186

Da Vinci, Leonardo, **I:** 274; **II:** 536; **III:** 210

Davis, Allen F., **Supp. I Part 1:** 1, 7

Davis, Allison, **Supp. I Part 1:** 327

Davis, Angela, **Supp. I Part 1:** 66; **Supp. X:** 249

Davis, Arthur B., **Supp. XVIII:** 119

Davis, Bette, **I:** 78; **Supp. I Part 1:** 67

Davis, Bill, **Supp. XIII:** 267

Davis, Christina, **Supp. XV:** 264

Davis, Cynthia, **Supp. XVIII:** 281, 286

Davis, Donald, **Supp. XIII:** 93

Davis, Elizabeth Gould, **Supp. I Part 2:** 567

Davis, George, **II:** 586

Davis, Glover, **Supp. V:** 180, 182, 186

Davis, Jefferson, **II:** 206; **IV:** 122, 125, 126

Davis, Jordan, **Supp. XV:** 178, 181, 186, 188

Davis, Katie, **Supp. VIII:** 83

Davis, L. J., **Supp. XI:** 234

Davis, Lydia, **Supp. XII:** 24; **Supp. XVII:** 21

Davis, Marcia, **Supp. XVIII:** 91, 100

Davis, Mary H., **Supp. XVIII:** 77

Davis, Miles, **Supp. XV:** 346

Davis, Ossie, Jr., **Supp. IV Part 1:** 362; **Supp. XVI:** 144

Davis, Rebecca Harding, **Supp. I Part 1:** 45; **Supp. XIII:** 292, 295, 305; **Supp. XVI: 79–96**

Davis, Richard Harding, **III:** 328; **Supp. II Part 1:** 393; **Supp. XVI:** 85

Davis, Robert Gorham, **II:** 51; **IV:** 108

Davis, Stuart, **IV:** 409; **Supp. XV:** 295; **Supp. XXI:** 6

Davis, Thadious, **Supp. XVIII:** 120, 121, 123, 127, 129

Davis, Thulani, **Supp. XI:** 179; **Supp. XIII:** 233, 234, 239

Davis, William Virgil, **Supp. IV Part 1:** 63, 64, 68, 69, 70; **Supp. XXI: 83–96**

Davison, Peter, **Supp. XXI:** 91

Davy's Lake (M. Finch), **Supp. XVII:** 69

Dawn (Dreiser), **I:** 498, 499, 503, 509, 515, 519

Dawn (O. Butler), **Supp. XIII:** 63, **64**

"Dawnbreaker" (Hayden), **Supp. II Part 1:** 370

Dawn in Russia (W. Frank), **Supp. XX:**76

Dawn Patrol, The (film), **Supp. XIV:** 81

"Dawn Patrol: A Review of the Literature of the Negro for 1948" (Locke), **Supp. XIV:** 211

Dawson, Edward, **IV:** 151

Dawson, Emma, **I:** 199

Dawson, Ruth, **Supp. XI:** 120

Day, Dorothy, **II:** 215; **Supp. I Part 2:** 524; **Supp. X:** 142

Day, Fred Holland, **Supp. XX:**114, 115

Day, Georgiana, **Supp. I Part 2:** 585

Day, Richard, **Supp. XVIII:** 251

Dayan, Joan, **Retro. Supp. II:** 270

Day Book, A (Creeley), **Supp. IV Part 1:** 155

"Daybreak" (Kinnell), **Supp. III Part 1:** 250

"Daybreak Blues" (Kees), **Supp. XV:** 133

"Daybreak in Alabama" (Hughes), **Retro. Supp. I:** 211; **Supp. I Part 1:** 344

Day by Day (Lowell), **Retro. Supp. II:** 184, 186, 191

"Day-Care Field Trip: Aquarium" (Karr), **Supp. XI:** 243

"Day-Dream, A" (Bryant), **Supp. I Part 1:** 160

"Day-Dream of a Grocer, The" (Twain), **Supp. XVIII:** 9

"Day for Poetry and Song, A" (Douglass), **Supp. III Part 1:** 172
"Day Lady Died, The" (O'Hara), **Supp. XIX:** 85
Day Late and a Dollar Short, A (McMillan), **Supp. XIII:** 184, **Supp. XIII:** 185, **191–192**
"Day longs for the evening, The" (Levertov), **Supp. III Part 1:** 274
Daynard, Jodi, **Supp. XVIII:** 97
Day of a Stranger (Merton), **Supp. VIII:** 203
"Day of Days, A" (James), **II:** 322
Day of Doom (Wigglesworth), **IV:** 147, 155, 156
Day of the Body (C. Frost), **Supp. XV:** 93, **98–100,** 106
Day of the Locust, The (West), **I:** 298; **IV:** 288, 299–306; **Retro. Supp. II:** 321, 323, 324, 329, **337–338; Supp. II Part 2:** 626; **Supp. XI:** 296; **Supp. XII:** 173; **Supp. XIII:** 170; **Supp. XIV:** 328; **Supp. XVIII:** 246
"Day on the Big Branch, A" (Nemerov), **III:** 275–276
"Day on the Connecticut River, A" (Merrill), **Supp. III Part 1:** 336
Day Room, The (DeLillo), **Supp. VI:** 4
"Days" (Emerson), **II:** 19, 20
"Days and Nights" (Koch), **Supp. XV:** 179, 180
"Days and Nights: A Journal" (Price), **Supp. VI:** 265
Days Before, The (Porter), **III:** 433, 453
Days in the Yellow Leaf (Hoffman), **Supp. XVIII:** 75
"Days of 1935" (Merrill), **Supp. III Part 1:** 325, 328
"Days of 1941 and '44" (Merrill), **Supp. III Part 1:** 336
"Days of 1964" (Merrill), **Supp. III Part 1:** 328, 352
"Days of 1971" (Merrill), **Supp. III Part 1:** 328
"Days of 1981" (Doty), **Supp. XI:** 123
"Days of Awe: The Birth of Lucy Jane" (Wasserstein), **Supp. XV:** 332
"Days of Edward Hopper" (Haines), **Supp. XII:** 210
"Days of Heaven" (Bass), **Supp. XVI:** 20
Days of Obligation: An Argument with My Mexican Father (Rodriguez), **Supp. XIV:** 298, 300, **302–305,** 307, 310
Days of Our Lives (soap opera), **Supp. XI:** 83
Days of Our Lives Lie in Fragments: New and Old Poems (Garrett), **Supp. VII:** 109–110, 111
Days of the Phoenix (Brooks), **I:** 266
Days of Wine and Roses (J. P. Miller), **Supp. XIII:** 262
Days: Tangier Journal, 1987–1989 (Bowles), **Supp. IV Part 1:** 94
Days to Come (Hellman), **Supp. I Part 1:** 276, 277–278
Days without End (O'Neill), **III:** 385, 391, 397

"Day's Work, A" (Capote), **Supp. III Part 1:** 120
"Day's Work, A" (Porter), **III:** 443, 446
"Day the Presidential Candidate Came to Ciudad Tamaulipas, The" (Caldwell), **I:** 309
"Day the Singer Fell, The" (Swados), **Supp. XIX:** 258
Day the World ended, The (Coover), **Supp. V:** 1
"Day with Conrad Green, A" (Lardner), **II:** 428–429, 430
"Deacon's Masterpiece, The" (Holmes), **Supp. I Part 1:** 302, 307
"Dead, The" (Collins), **Supp. XXI:** 64
"Dead, The" (Joyce), **I:** 285; **III:** 343
Dead and the Living, The (Olds), **Supp. X:** 201, **204–206,** 207
"Dead Body, The" (Olds), **Supp. X:** 210
"Dead by the Side of the Road, The" (Snyder), **Supp. VIII:** 301
"Dead Doe" (B. Kelly), **Supp. XVII:** 128–129
Dead End (Kingsley), **Supp. I Part 1:** 277, 281
Dead Father, The (Barthelme), **Supp. IV Part 1:** 43, 47, 50–51
"Dead Fiddler, The" (Singer), **IV:** 20
Dead Fingers Talk (Burroughs), **Supp. III Part 1:** 103
"Dead Hand" series (Sinclair), **Supp. V:** 276, 277, 281
"Dead Languages, The" (Humphrey), **Supp. IX:** 109
Dead Lecturer, The (Baraka), **Supp. II Part 1:** 31, 33, 35–37, 49
Deadline at Dawn (Odets), **Supp. II Part 2:** 546
"Dead-Lock and Its Key, A" (E. Stoddard), **Supp. XV:** 286
"Dead Loon, The" (Bynner), **Supp. XV:** **44–45**
Deadly Affair, A (Lacy), **Supp. XV:** 205–206
Deadly is the Female (film), **Supp. XVII:** 62
Dead Man's Walk (McMurtry), **Supp. V:** 231, 232
Dead Man's Walk (screenplay; McMurtry and Ossana), **Supp. V:** 231
Dead Man Walking (opera libretto, McNally), **Supp. XIII:** 207
Dead Poets Society (film), **Supp. XXI:** 192, 193, 194, 199
"Dead Reckoning" (Jarman), **Supp. XVII:** 113
"Dead Soldier's Talk, The" (Jin), **Supp. XVIII:** 92
Dead Souls (Gogol), **I:** 296
"Dead Souls on Campus" (Kosinski), **Supp. VII:** 222
"Dead Wingman, The" (Jarrell), **II:** 374
"Dead Yellow Women" (Hammett), **Supp. IV Part 1:** 345
Dead Zone, The (King), **Supp. V:** 139, 143, 144, 148, 152
Dean, James, **I:** 493
Dean, Man Mountain, **II:** 589
Deane, Silas, **Supp. I Part 2:** 509, 524

"Dean of Men" (Taylor), **Supp. V:** 314, 323
Dean's December, The (Bellow), **Retro. Supp. II:** 30–31
"Dear Adolph" (Benét), **Supp. XI:** 46
"Dear America" (Ortiz), **Supp. IV Part 2:** 503
"Dearest M—" (Carruth), **Supp. XVI:** 59
"Dear Judas" (Jeffers), **Supp. II Part 2:** 431–432, 433
Dear Juliette (Sarton), **Supp. VIII:** 265
Dear Lovely Death (Hughes), **Retro. Supp. I:** 203; **Supp. I Part 1:** 328
Dear Rafe (Hinojosa), **Supp. XIX:** 98, **105–106**
"Dear Villon" (Corso), **Supp. XII:** 135
"Dear World" (Gunn Allen), **Supp. IV Part 1:** 321
Deasy, Philip, **Supp. XX:** 42
Death (Allen), **Supp. XV:** 3
"Death" (Corso), **Supp. XII:** 127
"Death" (Lowell), **II:** 536
"Death" (Mailer), **III:** 38
"Death" (W. C. Williams), **Retro. Supp. I:** 422
"Death" (West), **IV:** 286
"Death and Absence" (Glück), **Supp. V:** 82
Death and Birth of David Markand, The (W. Frank), **Supp. XX:** 76–77
Death and Taxes (Parker), **Supp. IX:** 192
"Death and the Child" (Crane), **I:** 414
"Death as a Society Lady" (Hecht), **Supp. X:** 71–72
Death before Bedtime (Vidal as Box), **Supp. IV Part 2:** 682
"Death Be Not Proud" (Donne), **Supp. XVI:** 158
"Death by Water" (Eliot), **I:** 395, 578
Death Comes for the Archbishop (Cather), **I:** 314, 327, 328–330; **Retro. Supp. I:** 16–18, 21; **Supp. XIII:** 253
Death in Paradise (Parker), **Supp. XIX:** 186
Death in the Afternoon (Hemingway), **II:** 253; **IV:** 35; **Retro. Supp. I:** 182; **Supp. VIII:** 182; **Supp. XVI:** 205; **Supp. XIX:** 246; **Supp. XX:** 76
"Death in the Country, A" (Benét), **Supp. XI:** 53–54
Death in the Family, A (Agee), **I:** 25, 29, 42, 45
Death in the Fifth Position (Vidal as Box), **Supp. IV Part 2:** 682
"Death in the Woods" (Anderson), **I:** 114, 115
Death in the Woods and Other Stories (Anderson), **I:** 112, 114, 115
Death in Venice (Mann), **III:** 231; **Supp. IV Part 1:** 392; **Supp. V:** 51
"Death in Viet Nam" (Salinas), **Supp. XIII:** 315
"Death in Winter" (C. Frost), **Supp. XV:** 98
Death Is a Lonely Business (Bradbury), **Supp. IV Part 1:** 102, 103, 111–112, 115
"Death Is Not the End" (Wallace), **Supp. X:** 309

Death Is the Place (Bronk), **Supp. XXI:** 32

Death Kit (Sontag), **Supp. III Part 2:** 451, 468–469

Death Likes It Hot (Vidal as Box), **Supp. IV Part 2:** 682

"*Death*/Muerta" (Mora), **Supp. XIII:** 228

Death Notebooks, The (Sexton), **Supp. II Part 2:** 691, 694, 695

Death of Adam, The: Essays on Modern Thought (Robinson), **Supp. XXI:** 212

"Death of a Jazz Musician" (W. J. Smith), **Supp. XIII:** 334

Death of a Kinsman, The (Taylor), **Supp. V:** 324, 326

"Death of an Old Seaman" (Hughes), **Retro. Supp. I:** 199

"Death of a Pig" (White), **Supp. I Part 2:** 665–668

Death of a Salesman (A. Miller), **I:** 81; **III:** 148, 149, 150, 153–154, 156, 157, 158, 159, 160, 163, 164, 166; **IV:** 389; **Supp. IV Part 1:** 359; **Supp. XIV:** 102, 239, 254, 255; **Supp. XV:** 205; **Supp. XX:** 27

"Death of a Soldier, The" (Stevens), **Retro. Supp. I:** 299, 312. *see also* "Lettres d'un Soldat" (Stevens)

"Death of a Soldier, The" (Wilson), **IV:** 427, 445

"Death of a Toad" (Wilbur), **Supp. III Part 2:** 550

"Death of a Traveling Salesman" (Welty), **IV:** 261; **Retro. Supp. I:** 344

"Death of a Young Son by Drowning" (Atwood), **Supp. XIII:** 33

Death of Bessie Smith, The (Albee), **I:** 76–77, 92

Death of Billy the Kid, The (Vidal), **Supp. IV Part 2:** 683

Death of Cock Robin, The (Snodgrass), **Supp. VI:** 315, **317–319,** 324

Death of Dreams, A (Hoffman), **Supp. XVIII:** 79

"Death of General Wolfe, The" (Paine), **Supp. I Part 2:** 504

"Death of Halpin Frayser, The" (Bierce), **I:** 205

"Death of Justina, The" (Cheever), **Supp. I Part 1:** 184–185

Death of Life, The (Barnes), **Supp. III Part 1:** 34

Death of Malcolm X, The (Baraka), **Supp. II Part 1:** 47

"Death of Marilyn Monroe, The" (Olds), **Supp. X:** 205

"Death of Me, The" (Malamud), **Supp. I Part 2:** 437

"Death of Slavery, The" (Bryant), **Supp. I Part 1:** 168–169

"Death of St. Narcissus, The" (Eliot), **Retro. Supp. I:** 291

"Death of the Ball Turret Gunner, The" (Jarrell), **II:** 369–370, 372, 374, 375, 376, 378

"Death of the Fathers, The" (Sexton), **Supp. II Part 2:** 692

"Death of the Flowers, The" (Bryant), **Supp. I Part 1:** 170

Death of the Fox (Garrett), **Supp. VII:** 99, 101–104, 108

"Death of the Hat, The" (Collins), **Supp. XXI:** 59

"Death of the Hired Man, The" (Frost), **III:** 523; **Retro. Supp. I:** 121, 128; **Supp. IX:** 261

Death of the Kapowsin Tavern (Hugo), **Supp. VI:** 133–135

"Death of the Kapowsin Tavern" (Hugo), **Supp. VI:** 137, 141

"Death of the Lyric, The: The Achievement of Louis Simpson" (Jarman and McDowell), **Supp. IX:** 266, 270, 276

"Death of Venus, The" (Creeley), **Supp. IV Part 1:** 143, 144–145

"Death on All Fronts" (Ginsberg), **Supp. II Part 1:** 326

"Deaths" (Dunn), **Supp. XI:** 147

"Death Sauntering About" (Hecht), **Supp. X:** 72

Deaths for the Ladies (and Other Disasters) (Mailer), **Retro. Supp. II:** 203

Death's Jest-Book (Beddoes), **Retro. Supp. I:** 285

Death Song (McGrath), **Supp. X:** 127

"Death the Carnival Barker" (Hecht), **Supp. X:** 72

"Death the Film Director" (Hecht), **Supp. X:** 72

"Death the Judge" (Hecht), **Supp. X:** 72

"Death the Mexican Revolutionary" (Hecht), **Supp. X:** 72

"Death the Oxford Don" (Hecht), **Supp. X:** 72

"Death the Painter" (Hecht), **Supp. X:** 72

Death the Proud Brother (Wolfe), **IV:** 456

"Death to Van Gogh's Ear!" (Ginsberg), **Supp. II Part 1:** 320, 322, 323

"Death Warmed Over!" (Bradbury), **Supp. IV Part 1:** 104–105, 112

Débâcle, La (Zola), **III:** 316

"Debate with the Rabbi" (Nemerov), **III:** 272

Debeljak, Aleš, **Supp. VIII:** 272

De Bellis, Jack, **Supp. I Part 1:** 366, 368, 372

Debo, Annette, **Supp. XXI:** 254

DeBoer-Langworthy, Carol, **Supp. XVII:** 98, 99, 100

De Bosis, Lauro, **IV:** 372

"Debriefing" (Sontag), **Supp. III Part 2:** 468–470

Debs, Eugene, **I:** 483, 493; **III:** 580, 581; **Supp. I Part 2:** 524; **Supp. IX:** 1, 15

Debt to Pleasure, The (Lanchester), **Retro. Supp. I:** 278

Debussy, Claude, **Retro. Supp. II:** 266; **Supp. XIII:** 44

"Decades" (Sorrentino), **Supp. XXI:** 229

Decameron (Boccaccio), **III:** 283, 411; **Supp. IX:** 215

"Deceased" (Hughes), **Retro. Supp. I:** 208

"December" (Oliver), **Supp. VII:** 245

"December 1, 1994" (Stern), **Supp. IX:** 299

December 7 (film, Ford), **Supp. XVIII:** 247

"December 24" (Di Piero), **Supp. XIX:** 39

"December 28: Returning to Chicago" (Di Piero), **Supp. XIX:** 39

"December Dawn" (Skloot), **Supp. XX:** 202

"December Eclogue" (Winters), **Supp. II Part 2:** 794

De Cenzo, Giorgia, **Supp. XXI:** 256

Deception (P. Roth), **Retro. Supp. II:** 291; **Supp. III Part 2:** 426–427

"Deceptions" (Dobyns), **Supp. XIII:** 77

De Chiara, Ann. *See* Malamud, Mrs. Bernard (Ann de Chiara)

De Chirico, Giorgio, **Supp. XIII:** 317

"Decided Loss, A" (Poe), **II:** 411

"Decisions to Disappear" (Dunn), **Supp. XI:** 144

"Decisive Moment, The" (Auster), **Supp. XIV:** 292

Decker, James A., **Supp. III Part 2:** 621

Declaration of Gentlemen and Merchants and Inhabitants of Boston, and the Country Adjacent, A (Mather), **Supp. II Part 2:** 450

"Declaration of Paris, The" (Adams), **I:** 4

Declaration of the Rights of Man and the Citizen, **Supp. I Part 2:** 513, 519

Declaration of Universal Peace and Liberty (Paine), **Supp. I Part 2:** 512

Declension in the Village of Chung Luong (Weigl), **Supp. XIX:** 287, 288

Decline and Fall (Waugh), **Supp. I Part 2:** 607; **Supp. XV:** 142

Decline and Fall of the English System of Finance, The (Paine), **Supp. I Part 2:** 518

Decline and Fall of the Roman Empire, The (Gibbons), **Supp. III Part 2:** 629

"Decline of Book Reviewing, The" (Hardwick), **Supp. III Part 1:** 201–202

Decline of the West, The (Spengler), **I:** 270; **IV:** 125

Deconstructing Harry (film; Allen), **Supp. XV:** 12, **13**

"Décor" (X. J. Kennedy), **Supp. XV:** 171

"Decoration Day" (Jewett), **II:** 412; **Retro. Supp. II:** 138

Decoration of Houses, The (Wharton and Codman), **IV:** 308; **Retro. Supp. I:** 362, 363–364, 366

"Decoy" (Ashbery), **Supp. III Part 1:** 13–14

Decter, Midge, **Supp. XX:** 248

Dedalus, Stephen, **Supp. XIX:** 47

"De Daumier-Smith's Blue Period" (Salinger), **III:** 560–561

"Dedication" (Nelson), **Supp. XVIII:** 173, 180

"Dedication and Household Map" (Erdrich), **Supp. IV Part 1:** 272

"Dedication Day" (Agee), **I:** 34

"Dedication for a Book" (Hay), **Supp. XIV:** 125

"Dedication for a Book of Criticism" (Winters), **Supp. II Part 2:** 801

"Dedication in Postscript, A" (Winters), **Supp. II Part 2:** 801

Dedications and Other Darkhorses (Komunyakaa), **Supp. XIII:** 112, **113–114**

"Dedication to Hunger" (Glück), **Supp. V:** 83

"Dedication to My Wife, A" (Eliot), **I:** 583

Dee, Ruby, **Supp. IV Part 1:** 362

Deeds of Utmost Kindness (Gander), **Supp. XV:** 340

"Deep Breath at Dawn, A" (Hecht), **Supp. X:** 58

Deeper into Movies: The Essential Kael Collection from '69 to '72 (Kael), **Supp. IX:** 253

"Deeper Wisdom, The" (Hay), **Supp. XIV:** 129

Deep Green Sea (R. O. Butler), **Supp. XII:** 62, **74**

Deephaven (Jewett), **II:** 398–399, 400, 401, 410, 411; **Retro. Supp. II:** 133, 134, 135, 136, 137, 138, 140, 141, 143, 144

"Deep Sight and Rescue Missions" (Bambara), **Supp. XI:** 18–19

Deep Sightings and Rescue Missions: Fiction, Essays, and Conversations (Bambara), **Supp. XI:** 1, 3, **14–20**

Deep Sleep, The (Morris), **III:** 224–225

Deep South (Caldwell), **I:** 305, 309, 310

Deepstep Come Shining (Wright), **Supp. XV:** 337, 341, 344, **349–350**, 351, 353

"Deep Water" (Marquand), **III:** 56

"Deep Woods" (Nemerov), **III:** 272–273, 275

"Deer at Providencia, The" (Dillard), **Supp. VI:** 28, 32

"Deer Dancer" (Harjo), **Supp. XII:** 224–225

"Deer Ghost" (Harjo), **Supp. XII:** 225

Deer Park, The (Mailer), **I:** 292; **III:** 27, 31–33, 35–36, 37, 39, 40, 42, 43, 44; **Retro. Supp. II: 200–202**, 205, 207, 211

Deer Park, The: A Play (Mailer), **Retro. Supp. II:** 205

Deer Pasture, The (Bass), **Supp. XVI:** 15, 16, 23

Deerslayer, The (Cooper), **I:** 341, 349, 350, 355; **Supp. I Part 1:** 251

"Defence of Poesie, The" (Bronk), **Supp. XXI:** 32

"Defence of Poesy, The" (Sidney), **Supp. V:** 250

"Defence of Poetry" (Longfellow), **II:** 493–494

"Defender of the Faith" (P. Roth), **Retro. Supp. II:** 281; **Supp. III Part 2:** 404, 407, 420

"Defending *The Searchers* (Scenes in the Life of an Obsession)" (Lethem), *Supp. XVIII:* 136,141

"Defenestration in Prague" (Matthews), **Supp. IX:** 168

Defenestration of Prague (Howe), **Supp. IV Part 2:** 419, 426, 429–430

Defense, The (Nabokov), **III:** 251–252; **Retro. Supp. I:** 266, 268, **270–272**

"Defense of Poetry" (Francis), **Supp. IX:** 83–84

Defiant Ones, The (film), **Supp. I Part 1:** 67

"Defining the Age" (W. V. Davis), **Supp. IV Part 1:** 64

"Definition" (Ammons), **Supp. VII:** 28

Defoe, Daniel, **I:** 204; **II:** 104, 105, 159, 304–305; **III:** 113, 423; **IV:** 180; **Supp. I Part 2:** 523; **Supp. V:** 127

De Forest, John William, **II:** 275, 280, 288, 289; **IV:** 350

DeFrees, Madeline, **Supp. XVIII:** 293

Degas, Brian, **Supp. XI:** 307

Degler, Carl, **Supp. I Part 2:** 496

"Degrees of Fidelity" (Dunn), **Supp. XI:** 148, 156

Deguy, Michel, **Supp. XV:** 178

De Haven, Tom, **Supp. XI:** 39; **Supp. XII:** 338–339

Deitch, Joseph, **Supp. VIII:** 125

"Dejection" (Coleridge), **II:** 97

DeJong, Constance, **Supp. XII:** 4

DeJong, David Cornel, **I:** 35

Dekker,Thomas, **Supp. XVII:** 232

de Kooning, Willem, **Supp. XII:** 198; **Supp. XV:** 177, 178

Delacroix, Henri, **I:** 227

De La Mare, Walter, **III:** 429; **Supp. II Part 1:** 4; **Supp. XVII:** 69

Delamotte, Eugenia C., **Supp. XI:** 279

De Lancey, James, **I:** 338

De Lancey, Mrs. James (Anne Heathcote), **I:** 338

De Lancey, Susan A. *See* Cooper, Mrs. James Fenimore

De Lancey, William Heathcote, **I:** 338, 353

Delano, Amasa, **III:** 90

Delattre, Roland A., **I:** 558

De Laurentiis, Dino, **Supp. XI:** 170, 307

De la Valdéne, Guy, **Supp. VIII:** 40, 42

Del Cabral, Manuel, **Supp. XXI:** 104

DelCorso's Gallery (Caputo), **Supp. XIX:** 22–23

De l'éducation d'un homme sauvage (Itard), **Supp. I Part 2:** 564

"Delft" (Goldbarth), **Supp. XII:** 189

Delft: An Essay-Poem (Goldbarth), **Supp. XII:** 187

Delicate Balance, A (Albee), **I:** 86–89, 91, 93, 94

Delicate Balance, The (Hay), **Supp. XIV:** 121, 122, 124, 129, 133–134

"Delicate Balance, The" (Hay), **Supp. XIV:** 122

"Delicate Prey, The" (Bowles), **Supp. IV Part 1:** 86

Delicate Prey and Other Stories, The (Bowles), **Supp. IV Part 1:** 86–87

Délie (Scève), **Supp. III Part 1:** 11

Delights & Shadows (Kooser), **Supp. XIX:** 115, 116, 117, 121, **127–128**

DeLillo, Don, **Retro. Supp. I:** 278; **Retro. Supp. II:** 279; **Supp. VI: 1–18**; **Supp. IX:** 212; **Supp. XI:** 68; **Supp. XII:** 21, 152; **Supp. XVII:** 183; **Supp. XVIII:** 136, 140; **Supp. XIX:** 54; **Supp. XX:**83, 87, 91

DeLisle, Anne, **Supp. VIII:** 175

Deliverance (Dickey), **Supp. IV Part 1:** 176, 186–188, 190; **Supp. X:** 30; **Supp. XX:**173–174

Deliverance, The (Glasgow), **II:** 175, 176, 177–178, 181

"Delivering" (Dubus), **Supp. VII:** 87

Dell, Floyd, **I:** 103, 105; **Supp. I Part 2:** 379; **Supp. XV:** 295; **Supp. XVII:** 96; **Supp. XXI:** 6

Della Francesca, Piero, **Supp. XV:** 262

"Della Primavera Trasportata al Morale" (W. C. Williams), **Retro. Supp. I:** 419, 422

DeLoria, Philip J., **Supp. XIV:** 306

Deloria, Vine, Jr., **Supp. IV Part 1:** 323; **Supp. IV Part 2:** 504

"Delta Autumn" (Faulkner), **II:** 71

"Delta Factor, The" (Percy), **Supp. III Part 1:** 386

Delta of Venus: Erotica (Nin), **Supp. X:** 192, 195

Delta Wedding (Welty), **IV:** 261, 268–271, 273, 281; **Retro. Supp. I:** 349–350, 351

Delusions (Berryman), **I:** 170

De Man, Paul, **Retro. Supp. I:** 67; **Supp. XVII:** 70

DeMarinis, Rick, **Supp. XIV:** 22

DeMars, James, **Supp. IV Part 2:** 552

Dembo, L. S., **I:** 386, 391, 396, 397, 398, 402; **III:** 478; **Supp. I Part 1:** 272; **Supp. XIV:** 277, 282, 288, 290

"Dementia Translucida" (Bierds), **Supp. XVII:** 33

Demetrakopoulous, Stephanie A., **Supp. IV Part 1:** 12

DeMille, Cecil B., **Supp. IV Part 2:** 520; **Supp. XV:** 42

Demme, Jonathan, **Supp. V:** 14

Democracy (Adams), **I:** 9–10, 20; **Supp. IV Part 1:** 208; **Supp. XIX:** 139

Democracy (Didion), **Supp. IV Part 1:** 198, 208–210

"Democracy" (Lowell), **Supp. I Part 2:** 419

Democracy and Education (Dewey), **I:** 232

Democracy and Other Addresses (Lowell), **Supp. I Part 2:** 407

Democracy and Social Ethics (Addams), **Supp. I Part 1:** 8–11

Democracy in America (Tocqueville), **Retro. Supp. I:** 235; **Supp. XIV:** 306

Democratic Vistas (Whitman), **IV:** 333, 336, 348–349, 351, 469; **Retro. Supp. I:** 408; **Supp. I Part 2:** 456

Democritus, **I:** 480–481; **II:** 157; **III:** 606; **Retro. Supp. I:** 247

"Demon Lover, The" (Rich), **Supp. I Part 2:** 556

"Demonstrators, The" (Welty), **IV:** 280; **Retro. Supp. I:** 355

DeMott, Benjamin, **Supp. IV Part 1:** 35; **Supp. V:** 123; **Supp. XIII:** 95; **Supp. XIV: 106**

DeMott, Robert, **Supp. VIII:** 40, 41

Demuth, Charles, **IV:** 404; **Retro. Supp. I:** 412, 430; **Supp. XXI:** 6

"Demystified Zone" (Paley), **Supp. VI:** 227

Denmark Vesey (opera) (Bowles), **Supp. IV Part 1:** 83

Denney, Joseph Villiers, **Supp. I Part 2:** 605

Denney, Reuel, **Supp. XII:** 121; **Supp. XXI:** 19

Dennie, Joseph, **II:** 298; **Supp. I Part 1:** 125

Denniston, Dorothy Hamer, **Supp. XI:** 276, 277

"Den of Lions" (Plath), **Retro. Supp. II:** 242

"Dental Assistant, The" (Simpson), **Supp. IX:** 280

Den Uyl, Douglas, **Supp. IV Part 2:** 528, 530

"Deodand, The" (Hecht), **Supp. X:** 65

"Departing" (Cameron), **Supp. XII:** 81

"Departure" (Glück), **Supp. V:** 89

"Departure" (Plath), **Supp. I Part 2:** 537

"Departure, The" (Freneau), **Supp. II Part 1:** 264

"Departure from Hydra, The" (Koch), **Supp. XV:** 180–181

Departures (Justice), **Supp. VII:** 124–127

Departures and Arrivals (Shields), **Supp. VII:** 320, 322

"Depressed by a Book of Bad Poetry, I Walk Toward an Unused Pasture and Invite the Insects to Join Me" (Wright), **Supp. III Part 2:** 600

"Depressed Person, The" (Wallace), **Supp. X:** 309

"Depression Days" (Mora), **Supp. XIII:** 224–225

"Deprived of Unhappiness" (Pickering), **Supp. XXI:** 203

De Puy, John, **Supp. XIII:** 12

D'Erasmo, Stacey, **Supp. IX:** 121

Derby, J. C., **Supp. XVIII:** 4

De Reilhe, Catherine, **Supp. I Part 1:** 202

De Rerum Natura (Lucretius), **II:** 162

"De Rerum Virtute" (Jeffers), **Supp. II Part 2:** 424

De Rioja, Francisco, **Supp. I Part 1:** 166

"Derivative Sport in Tornado Alley" (Wallace), **Supp. X:** 314

Derleth, August, **Supp. I Part 2:** 465, 472

Deronda, Daniel, **II:** 179

Derricotte, Toi, **Supp. XVIII:** 177

Derrida, Jacques, **Supp. IV Part 1:** 45; **Supp. XV:** 215, 224; **Supp. XVI:** 285, 288

Deruddere, Dominique, **Supp. XI:** 173

Der Wilde Jäger (Bürger), **II:** 306

Derzhavin, Gavrila Romanovich, **Supp. VIII:** 27

Desai, Anita, **Supp. XVI:** 156, 157, 158

De Santis, Christopher, **Retro. Supp. I:** 194

Descartes, René, **I:** 255; **III:** 618–619; **IV:** 133

Descendents, The (Glasgow), **II:** 173, 174–175, 176

Descending Figure (Glück), **Supp. V:** 83–84

"Descending Theology: Christ Human" (Karr), **Supp. XI:** 251

"Descending Theology: The Garden" (Karr), **Supp. XI:** 251

"Descent, The" (W. C. Williams), **Retro. Supp. I:** 428, 429

"Descent from the Cross" (Eliot), **Retro. Supp. I:** 57, 58

"Descent in the Maelström, A" (Poe), **Retro. Supp. II:** 274

"Descent into Proselito" (Knowles), **Supp. XII:** 237

"Descent into the Maelström, A" (Poe), **III:** 411, 414, 416, 424

Descent of Man (Boyle), **Supp. VIII:** 1, 12–13; **Supp. XX:**17, **18**, 20

"Descent of Man" (Boyle), **Supp. VIII:** 14; **Supp. XX:**18

Descent of Man, The (Darwin), **Supp. XIV:** 192

Descent of Man, The (Wharton), **IV:** 311; **Retro. Supp. I:** 367

Descent of Man and Other Stories, The (Wharton), **Retro. Supp. I:** 367

Descent of Winter, The (W. C. Williams), **Retro. Supp. I:** 419, 428

De Schloezer, Doris, **III:** 474

"Describers" (Halliday), **Supp. XIX:** 85

"Description" (Doty), **Supp. XI:** 126

"Description of the great Bones dug up at Clavarack on the Banks of Hudsons River A.D. 1705, The" (Taylor), **IV:** 163, 164

"Description without Place" (Stevens), **Retro. Supp. I:** 422

"Desert" (Hughes), **Retro. Supp. I:** 207

"Deserted Cabin" (Haines), **Supp. XII:** 203

Deserted Village, The (Goldsmith), **II:** 304

Desert Is My Mother, The/El desierto es mi madre (Mora), **Supp. XIII:** 214, 221

Desert Music, The (W. C. Williams), **IV:** 422; **Retro. Supp. I:** 428, 429

"Desert Music, The" (W. C. Williams), **Retro. Supp. I:** 428, 429

"Desert Places" (Frost), **II:** 159; **Retro. Supp. I:** 121, 123, 129, 138, 299; **Supp. XIV:** 229

Desert Rose, The (McMurtry), **Supp. V:** 225, 231

Desert Solitaire (Abbey), **Supp. X:** 30; **Supp. XIII:** 7–8, 12; **Supp. XIV:** 177, 179

"Design" (Frost), **II:** 158, 163; **Retro. Supp. I:** 121, 126, 138, 139; **Supp. IX:** 81; **Supp. XVII:** 132; **Supp. XVIII:** 298

"Designated National Park, A" (Ortiz), **Supp. IV Part 2:** 509

"Designs on a Point of View" (Everwine), **Supp. XV:** 76

Des Imagistes (Pound), **II:** 513; **Supp. I Part 1:** 257, 261, 262

Desire (album, Dylan), **Supp. XVIII:** 28

"Desire" (Beattie), **Supp. V:** 29

Desire (Bidart), **Supp. XV:** **32–34,** 35

"Desire" (Everwine), **Supp. XV:** 85

"Desire and Denial" (Bronk), **Supp. XXI:** 26

"Désirée's Baby" (Chopin), **Retro. Supp. II:** 64, 65; **Supp. I Part 1:** 213–215

Desire under the Elms (O'Neill), **III:** 387, 390

"Desolate Field, The" (W. C. Williams), **Retro. Supp. I:** 418

"Desolation, A" (Ginsberg), **Supp. II Part 1:** 313

Desolation Angels (Kerouac), **Supp. III Part 1:** 218, 225, 230

"Desolation Is a Delicate Thing" (Wylie), **Supp. I Part 2:** 729

"Desolation Row" (song, Dylan), **Supp. XVIII:** 30

Despair (Nabokov), **Retro. Supp. I:** 270, 274

Desperate Characters (Fox), **Supp. XX:**91

"Despisals" (Rukeyser), **Supp. VI:** 282

Des Pres, Terrence, **Supp. X:** 113, 120, 124

"Destiny and the Lieutenant" (McCoy), **Supp. XIII:** 171

"Destruction of Kreshev, The" (Singer), **IV:** 13; **Retro. Supp. II:** 307

Destruction of the European Jews, The (Hilberg), **Supp. V:** 267

"Destruction of the Goetheanum, The" (Salter), **Supp. IX:** 257

"Destruction of the Long Branch, The" (Pinsky), **Supp. VI:** 239, 240, 243–244, 245, 247, 250

Destructive Element, The (Spender), **Retro. Supp. I:** 216

"Detail & Parody for the poem 'Paterson' " (W. C. Williams), **Retro. Supp. I:** 424

Detmold, John, **Supp. I Part 2:** 670

Detour at Night (Endore), **Supp. XVII:** 64

Deuce, The (R. O. Butler), **Supp. XII:** 62, **69–70,** 72

Deus Lo Volt! (Connell), **Supp. XIV:** 80, 81, 95

Deuteronomy (biblical book), **II:** 166

Deutsch, Andre, **Supp. XI:** 297, 301

Deutsch, Babette, **Supp. I Part 1:** 328, 341; **Supp. XV:** 305

Deutsch, Michel, **Supp. IV Part 1:** 104

"Devaluation Blues: Ruminations on Black Families in Crisis" (Coleman), **Supp. XI:** 87

Devane, William, **Supp. XI:** 234

"Development of the Literary West" (Chopin), **Retro. Supp. II:** 72

"Development of the Modern English Novel, The" (Lanier), **Supp. I Part 1:** 370–371

DeVeriante (Herbert of Cherbury), **II:** 108

"Devil and Daniel Webster, The" (Benét), **III:** 22; **Supp. XI:** 45–46, 47, 50–51, 52

Devil and Daniel Webster and Other Writings, The (Benét), **Supp. XI:** 48

"Devil and Tom Walker, The" (Irving), **II:** 309–310

Devil At Large, The: Erica Jong on Henry Miller (Jong), **Supp. V:** 115, 131
Devil-Doll, The (film, Browning), **Supp. XVII:** 58–59
Devil Finds Work, The (Baldwin), **Retro. Supp. II:** 14; **Supp. I Part 1:** 48, 52, 66–67
Devil in a Blue Dress (Mosley), **Supp. XIII:** 237, 239
"Devil in Manuscript, The" (Hawthorne), **II:** 226; **Retro. Supp. I:** 150–151
Devil in Paradise, A (H. Miller), **III:** 190
"Devil in the Belfry, The" (Poe), **III:** 425; **Retro. Supp. II:** 273
"Devil Is a Busy Man, The" (Wallace), **Supp. X:** 309
Devil's Dictionary, The (Bierce), **I:** 196, 197, 205, 208, 209, 210
Devil's Stocking, The (Algren), **Supp. IX:** 5, 16
"Devil's Thumb, The" (Krakauer), **Supp. XVIII:** 107
Devil's Tour, The (Karr), **Supp. XI:** 240, **242–244**
Devil Tree, The (Kosinski), **Supp. VII:** 215, 222, 223
"Devising" (Ammons), **Supp. VII:** 28
Devlin, Paul, **Supp. XIX:** 159
De Voto, Bernard, **I:** 247, 248; **II:** 446; **Supp. IV Part 2:** 599, 601
"Devout Meditation in Memory of Adolph Eichmann, A" (Merton), **Supp. VIII:** 198, 203
De Vries, Peter, **Supp. I Part 2:** 604
Dewberry, Elizabeth, **Supp. XII:** 62, 72
Dewey, John, **I:** 214, 224, 228, 232, 233, 266, 267; **II:** 20, 27, 34, 229, 361; **III:** 112, 294–295, 296, 303, 309–310, 599, 605; **IV:** 27, 429; **Supp. I Part 1:** 3, 5, 7, 10, 11, 12, 24; **Supp. I Part 2:** 493, 641, 647, 677; **Supp. V:** 290; **Supp. IX:** 179; **Supp. XIV:** 3; **Supp. XV:** 41
Dewey, Joseph, **Supp. IX:** 210
Dewey, Thomas, **IV:** 161
Dewey Defeats Truman (Mallon), **Supp. XIX:** 132, 137, **138**
Dexter, Peter, **Supp. XIV:** 221
De Young, Charles, **I:** 194
Dhairyam, Sagari, **Supp. IV Part 1:** 329, 330
Dharma Bums, The (Kerouac), **Supp. III Part 1:** 230, 231; **Supp. VIII:** 289, 305
"D. H. Lawrence" (Bynner), **Supp. XV:** 46
D. H. Lawrence: An Unprofessional Study (Nin), **Supp. X:** 182–183
D. H. Lawrence: The World of the Major Novels (Sanders), **Supp. XVI:** 267
D'Houdetot, Madame, **Supp. I Part 1:** 250
"Diabetes" (Dickey), **Supp. IV Part 1:** 182
Diaghilev, Sergei, **Supp. I Part 1:** 257
Dial (publication), **I:** 58, 109, 115, 116, 215, 231, 233, 245, 261, 384, 429; **II:** 8, 430; **III:** 194, 470, 471, 485; **IV:** 122, 171, 427; **Retro. Supp. I:** 58; **Retro. Supp. II:** 78; **Supp. I Part 2:**

642, 643, 647; **Supp. II Part 1:** 168, 279, 291; **Supp. II Part 2:** 474; **Supp. III Part 2:** 611
"Dialectical Materialism" (Weigl), **Supp. XIX:** 281
Dialectical Materialism and the Fate of Humanity (C. L. R. James), **Supp. XXI:** 169
"Dialectics of Love, The" (McGrath), **Supp. X:** 116
"Dialogue" (Rich), **Supp. I Part 2:** 560
Dialogue, A (Baldwin and Giovanni), **Supp. I Part 1:** 66
"Dialogue Between Franklin and the Gout" (Franklin), **II:** 121
"Dialogue Between General Wolfe and General Gage in a Wood near Boston, A" (Paine), **Supp. I Part 2:** 504
"Dialogue between Old England and New" (Bradstreet), **Supp. I Part 1:** 105–106, 110–111, 116
"Dialogue between the Writer and a Maypole Dresser, A" (Taylor), **IV:** 155
Dialogues (Bush, ed.), **III:** 4
Dialogues in Limbo (Santayana), **III:** 606
"Dialogue: William Harvey; Joan of Arc" (Goldbarth), **Supp. XII:** 178
Dialogue with a Dead Man (J. W. Miller), **Supp. XX:** 163, 164, **167**
"Diamond as Big as the Ritz, The" (Fitzgerald), **II:** 88–89
Diamond Cutters and Other Poems, The (Rich), **Supp. I Part 2:** 551, 552, 553
"Diamond Guitar, A" (Capote), **Supp. III Part 1:** 124
"Diana and Persis" (Alcott), **Supp. I Part 1:** 32, 41
"Diaper Brigade, The" (Ryan as Quin), **Supp. XVIII:** 230
Diaries of Charlotte Perkins Gilman (Knight, ed.), **Supp. XI:** 201
"Diary–1903" (Boyce), **Supp. XXI:** 8
Diary of a Chambermaid, The (film; Renoir), **Supp. XVI:** 193
Diary of Anaïs Nin, The (1931–1974), **Supp. X:** 181, 185–189, 191, 192, 193, 195
Diary of Anne Frank, The, **Supp. XXI:** 245
Diary of a Rapist, The: A Novel (Connell), **Supp. XIV:** 80, 82, 94
Diary of a Yuppie (Auchincloss), **Supp. IV Part 1:** 31, 32–33
Diary of "Helena Morley", The (Bishop, trans.), **Retro. Supp. II:** 45, 51; **Supp. I Part 1:** 92
Díaz del Castillo, Bernál, **III:** 13, 14
Dick, Philip K., **Supp. XVI:** 123; **Supp. XVIII:** 136, 137, 138, 139, 142
Dickens, Charles, **I:** 152, 198, 505; **II:** 98, 179, 186, 192, 271, 273–274, 288, 290, 297, 301, 307, 316, 322, 559, 561, 563, 577, 582; **III:** 146, 247, 325, 368, 411, 421, 426, 572, 577, 613–614, 616; **IV:** 21, 192, 194, 211, 429; **Retro. Supp. I:** 33, 91, 218; **Retro. Supp. II:** 204; **Supp. I Part 1:** 13, 34, 35, 36, 41, 49; **Supp. I Part 2:** 409, 523, 579, 590, 622, 675; **Supp. IV Part 1:** 293, 300, 341; **Supp. IV**

Part 2: 464; **Supp. VIII:** 180; **Supp. IX:** 246; **Supp. XI:** 277; **Supp. XII:** 335, 337; **Supp. XIII:** 233; **Supp. XV:** 62; **Supp. XVI:** 63, 65–66, 72–73, 202; **Supp. XVIII:** 7, 136, 146; **Supp. XX:** 21, 87, 195
Dickey, James, **I:** 29, 535; **III:** 268; **Retro. Supp. II:** 233; **Supp. III Part 1:** 354; **Supp. III Part 2:** 541, 597; **Supp. IV Part 1: 175–194; Supp. V:** 333; **Supp. X:** 30; **Supp. XI:** 312, 317; **Supp. XV:** 115, 348; **Supp. XVIII:** 191, 299; **Supp. XIX:** 282; **Supp. XXI:** 35
Dick Gibson Show, The (Elkin), **Supp. VI:** 42, **48–49**
Dickie, Margaret, **Retro. Supp. II:** 53, 84
Dickinson, Donald, **Retro. Supp. I:** 206, 212
Dickinson, Edward, **I:** 451–452, 453
Dickinson, Mrs. Edward, **I:** 451, 453
Dickinson, Emily, **I:** 384, 419, 433, **451–473; II:** 272, 276, 277, 530; **III:** 19, 194, 196, 214, 493, 505, 508, 556, 572, 576; **IV:** 134, 135, 331, 444; **Retro. Supp. I: 25–50; Retro. Supp. II:** 39, 40, 43, 45, 50, 76, 134, 155, 170; **Supp. I Part 1:** 29, 79, 188, 372; **Supp. I Part 2:** 375, 546, 609, 682, 691; **Supp. II Part 1:** 4; **Supp. III Part 1:** 63; **Supp. III Part 2:** 600, 622; **Supp. IV Part 1:** 31, 257; **Supp. IV Part 2:** 434, 637, 641, 643; **Supp. V:** 79, 140, 332, 335; **Supp. VIII:** 95, 104, 106, 108, 198, 205, 272; **Supp. IX:** 37, 38, 53, 87, 90; **Supp. XII:** 226; **Supp. XIII:** 153, 339; **Supp. XIV:** 45, 127–128, 133, 261, 284; **Supp. XV:** 287, 303, 309; **Supp. XVI:** 288; **Supp. XVII:** 71, 73, 74, 75, 132; **Supp. XVIII:** 301; **Supp. XIX:** 86; **Supp. XX:** 106, 108; **Supp. XXI:** 52, 61, 64, 132, 214
Dickinson, Gilbert, **I:** 469
Dickinson, Goldsworthy Lowes, **Supp. XIV:** 336
Dickinson, Lavinia Norcross, **I:** 451, 453, 462, 470
Dickinson, Mrs. William A. (Susan Gilbert), **I:** 452, 453, 456, 469, 470
Dickinson, William Austin, **I:** 451, 453, 469
Dickinson and the Strategies of Reticence (Dobson), **Retro. Supp. I:** 29, 42
Dickson, Helen. *See* Blackmur, Helen Dickson
Dickstein, Morris, **Supp. XIII:** 106
"Dick Whittington and His Cat", **Supp. I Part 2:** 656
"DICTATORSHIP OF THE PROLETARIAT, THE" (Baraka), **Supp. II Part 1:** 54
Dictionary of Literary Biography (Barron and Meyer, eds.), **Supp. XVIII:** 173; **Supp. XIX:** 195
Dictionary of Literary Biography (Gwynn, ed.), **Supp. XVIII:** 173; **Supp. XIX:** 121

Dictionary of Literary Biography (Kibler, ed.), **Supp. IX:** 94, 109; **Supp. XI:** 297

Dictionary of Literary Biography (Knight, ed.), **Supp. XIV:** 144

Dictionary of Literary Biography (Sicher, ed.), **Supp. XVII:** 41

Dictionary of Modern English Usage, A (Fowler), **Supp. I Part 2:** 660

"Dictum: For a Masque of Deluge" (Merwin), **Supp. III Part 1:** 342–343

"Didactic Poem" (Levertov), **Supp. III Part 1:** 280

Diderot, Denis, **II:** 535; **IV:** 440; **Supp. XVI:** 293; **Supp. XVII:** 145

Did I Ever Tell You How Lucky You Are? (Geisel), **Supp. XVI:** 109

Didion, Joan, **Retro. Supp. I:** 116; **Retro. Supp. II:** 209; **Supp. I Part 1:** 196, 197; **Supp. III Part 1:** 302; **Supp. IV Part 1: 195–216; Supp. XI:** 221; **Supp. XII:** 307

Dido, **I:** 81

Di Donato, Peter, **Supp. XX:** 34

Di Donato, Pietro, **Supp. XX:33–47**

"Did You Ever Dream Lucky?" (Ellison), **Supp. II Part 1:** 246

"Die-Hard, The" (Benét), **Supp. XI:** 54–55, 56

Diehl, Digby, **Supp. IV Part 1:** 204

Dien Cai Dau (Komunyakaa), **Supp. XIII:** 121, **122–124,** 125, 131, 132

Dies, Martin, **Supp. XVIII:** 229

"Dies Irae" (Lowell), **II:** 553

Die Zeit Ohne Beispiel, (Goebbels), **III:** 560

Difference Engine, The (W. Gibson and B. Sterling), **Supp. XVI:** 121, 124, **128–129**

Different Drummer, A (Larkin; film), **Supp. XI:** 20

Different Fleshes (Goldbarth), **Supp. XII:** 181–182, 188

Different Hours (Dunn), **Supp. XI:** 139, 142, 143, 155

Different Seasons (King), **Supp. V:** 148, 152

Different Ways to Pray (Nye), **Supp. XIII:** 274, 275, 277, 285, 287

"Different Ways to Pray" (Nye), **Supp. XIII:** 275

"Difficulties of a Statesman" (Eliot), **I:** 580

"Difficulties of Modernism and the Modernism of Difficulty" (Poirier), **Supp. II Part 1:** 136

Diff'rent (O'Neill), **III:** 389

DiGaetani, John L., **Supp. XIII:** 200

"Digging" (Sanders), **Supp. XVI:** 272

"Digging in the Garden of Age I Uncover a Live Root" (Swenson), **Supp. IV Part 2:** 649

Diggins, John P., **Supp. I Part 2:** 650

"Dignity of Life, The" (C. Bly), **Supp. XVI:** 34, 36–37

Digregorio, Charles, **Supp. XI:** 326

"Dilemma" (Budbill), **Supp. XIX:** 2

"Dilemma of Determinism, The" (James), **II:** 347–348, 352

"Dilemma of the Negro Writer, The" (speech, C. Himes), **Supp. XVI:** 140

"Dilettante, The" (Wharton), **IV:** 311, 313

"Dilettante, The: A Modern Type" (Dunbar), **Supp. II Part 1:** 199

Dillard, Annie, **Supp. VI: 19–39; Supp. VIII:** 272; **Supp. X:** 31; **Supp. XIII:** 154

Dillard, R. H. W., **Supp. XII:** 16

Dillman, Bradford, **III:** 403; **Supp. XII:** 241

Dillon, Brian, **Supp. X:** 209

Dillon, George, **III:** 141; **Supp. III Part 2:** 621

Dillon, Millicent, **Supp. IV Part 1:** 95

Dilsaver, Paul, **Supp. XIII:** 112

Dilthey, Wilhelm, **I:** 58

Dime-Store Alchemy: The Art of Joseph Cornell, **Supp. VIII:** 272

"Diminuendo" (Dunn), **Supp. XI:** 152–153

"Dimout in Harlem" (Hughes), **Supp. I Part 1:** 333

"Dinah's Lament" (Nelson), **Supp. XVIII:** 183

Dinesen, Isak, **IV:** 279; **Supp. VIII:** 171; **Supp. XVI:** 250

Dining Room, The (Gurney), **Supp. V:** 105–106

"Dinner at ------, A" (O. Henry), **Supp. II Part 1:** 402

"Dinner at Sir Nigel's" (Bowles), **Supp. IV Part 1:** 94

Dinner at the Homesick Restaurant (Tyler), **Supp. IV Part 2:** 657, 667–668

"Dinner at Uncle Borris's" (Simic), **Supp. VIII:** 272

Dinner Bridge (Lardner), **II:** 435

Dinosaur Tales (Bradbury), **Supp. IV Part 1:** 103

"Diogenes Invents a Game" (Karr), **Supp. XI:** 240–241

"Diogenes Tries to Forget" (Karr), **Supp. XI:** 241

Diomede, Matthew, **Supp. XX:** 46

Dionysis in Doubt (Robinson), **III:** 510

Diop, Birago, **Supp. IV Part 1:** 16

Diop, David, **Supp. IV Part 1:** 16

Di Piero, W. S., **Supp. XVII:** 241; **Supp. XIX: 33–48**

Di Prima, Diane, **Supp. III Part 1:** 30; **Supp. XIV:** 125, 144, 148, 150

Dirda, Michael, **Supp. XXI:** 233

Direction of Poetry, The: An Anthology of Rhymed and Metered Verse Written in the English Language since 1975 (Richman, ed.), **Supp. XV:** 250, 251

Direction of Poetry, The: Rhymed and Metered Verse Written in the English Language since 1975 (Richman), **Supp. XI:** 249

"Directive" (Bishop), **Retro. Supp. II:** 42

"Directive" (Frost), **III:** 287; **Retro. Supp. I:** 140; **Supp. VIII:** 32, 33

"Dire Cure" (Matthews), **Supp. IX:** 168

"Dirge" (Dunbar), **Supp. II Part 1:** 199

"Dirge without Music" (Millay), **III:** 126

"Dirt" (Salter), **Supp. IX:** 257, 260, 261

"Dirt and Desire: Essay on the Phenomenology of Female Pollution in Antiquity" (Carson), **Supp. XII: 111**

Dirty Dingus Magee (film), **Supp. XVII:** 139

"Dirty English Potatoes" (X. J. Kennedy), **Supp. XV:** 165

"Dirty Memories" (Olds), **Supp. X:** 211

Dirty Story (Shanley), **Supp. XIV:** 316, 331

"Dirty Word, The" (Shapiro), **Supp. II Part 2:** 710

Dirty Work (L. Brown), **Supp. XXI:** 37, 39, 40, 42, **45**

Disappearance of the Jews, The (Mamet), **Supp. XIV:** 249–250, 250–251, 252, 254

Disappearances (Auster), **Supp. XII:** 23

"Disappearances" (Hogan), **Supp. IV Part 1:** 401

"Disappeared, The " (C. Baxter), **Supp. XVII:** 19

Disappearing Acts (McMillan), **Supp. XIII:** 182, 183, **188–189,** 192

Disappearing Ink: Poetry at the End of Print Culture (Gioia), **Supp. XV:** 112

"Disappointment, The" (Creeley), **Supp. IV Part 1:** 143

"Disappointment and Desire" (R. Bly), **Supp. IV Part 1:** 71

Disappointment Artist, The (Lethem), **Supp. XVIII:** 135, 141, **148**

"Discards" (Baker), **Supp. XIII:** 53, 55–56

Discerning the Signs of the Times (Niebuhr), **III:** 300–301, 307–308

Disch, Thomas M., **Supp. XIX:** 1

"Disciple of Bacon, The" (Epstein), **Supp. XII:** 163–164

"Discipline" (L. Brown), **Supp. XXI:** 44

Discomfort, Zone, The: A Personal History (Franzen), **Supp. XX:** 83, 84, 95, **95**

"Discordants" (Aiken), **I:** 65

Discourse on Method (Descartes), **I:** 255

"Discourtesies" (Kirsch), **Supp. XV:** 341

"Discovering Theme and Structure in the Novel" (Schuster), **Supp. VIII:** 126

"Discovery" (Freneau), **Supp. II Part 1:** 258

"Discovery of the Madeiras, The" (Frost), **Retro. Supp. I:** 139

"Discovery of What It Means to Be an American, The" (Baldwin), **Supp. I Part 1:** 54–55

Discovery! The Search for Arabian Oil (Stegner), **Supp. IV Part 2:** 599

"Discrete Series" (Zukofsky), **Supp. III Part 2:** 616

"Discretions of Alcibiades" (Pinsky), **Supp. VI:** 241

"Disease, The" (Rukeyser), **Supp. VI:** 279

Disenchanted, The (play, Schulberg and Breit), **Supp. XVIII:** 254

Disenchanted, The (Schulberg), **II:** 98; **Retro. Supp. I:** 113; **Supp. XVIII: 247–250,** 253

Disenchantments: An Anthology of Modern Fairy Tale Poetry (Mieder), **Supp. XIV:** 126

"Dish of Green Pears, A" (Ríos), **Supp. IV Part 2:** 552

"Disillusion and Dogma" (Untermeyer), **Supp. XV:** 306

Dismantling the Silence (Simic), **Supp. VIII:** 273–274, 275, 276

Disney, Walt, **III:** 275, 426

"Disney of My Mind" (Chabon), **Supp. XI:** 63

Dispatches (Herr), **Supp. XI:** 245; **Supp. XIX:** 17

"Displaced Person, The" (O'Connor), **III:** 343–344, 350, 352, 356; **Retro. Supp. II:** 229, 232, 236

"Disposal" (Snodgrass), **Supp. VI:** 314

Dispossessed, The (Berryman), **I:** 170, 172, 173, 174, 175, 176, 178

"Disquieting Muses, The" (Plath), **Supp. I Part 2:** 538

Disraeli, Benjamin, **II:** 127

Dissent (Didion), **Supp. IV Part 1:** 208

"Dissent in Ashcroft's America" (P. N. Warren), **Supp. XX:**273

"Dissenting Opinion on Kafka, A" (Wilson), **IV:** 437–438

Dissent in Three American Wars (Morison, Merk, and Freidel), **Supp. I Part 2:** 495

Dissertation on Liberty and Necessity, Pleasure and Pain, A (Franklin), **II:** 108

Dissertations on Government; the Affairs of the Bank: and Paper Money (Paine), **Supp. I Part 2:** 510

"Distance" (Carver), **Supp. III Part 1:** 146

"Distance" (Everwine), **Supp. XV:** 85

"Distance" (Paley), **Supp. VI:** 222

"Distance, The" (Karr), **Supp. XI:** 241

"Distance from the Sea, A" (Kees), **Supp. XV:** 147

"Distance Nowhere" (Hughes), **Retro. Supp. I:** 207

"Distance Up Close, The" (Peacock), **Supp. XIX:** 196–197, 198

"Distant Episode, A" (Bowles), **Supp. IV Part 1:** 84–85, 86, 90

Distant Episode, A: The Selected Stories (Bowles), **Supp. IV Part 1:** 79

Distinguished Guest, The (Miller), **Supp. XII:** 299–301

Distortions (Beattie), **Supp. V:** 21, 23, 24, 25, 27

"Distrest Shepherdess, The" (Freneau), **Supp. II Part 1:** 258

District of Columbia (Dos Passos), **I:** 478, 489–490, 492

Disturber of the Peace (Manchester), **III:** 103

Disturbing the Peace (Yates), **Supp. XI:** 345, 346

"Diver, The" (Hayden), **Supp. II Part 1:** 368, 372, 373

"Divided Life of Jean Toomer, The" (Toomer), **Supp. III Part 2:** 488

Divided Self, The (Laing), **Supp. XX:**95

Divina Commedia (Longfellow, trans.), **II:** 490, 492, 493

"Divina Pastora, La" (C. L. R. James), **Supp. XXI:** 160

"Divine, The" (Di Piero), **Supp. XIX:** 41

"Divine Collaborator" (Simic), **Supp. VIII:** 282

Divine Comedies (Merrill), **Supp. III Part 1:** 324, 329–332

Divine Comedy (Dante), **I:** 137, 265, 400, 446; **II:** 215, 335, 490, 492, 493; **III:** 13, 448, 453; **Supp. V:** 283, 331, 338, 345; **Supp. X:** 253; **Supp. XIV:** 6; **Supp. XIX:** 36, 39

"Divine Image, The" (Blake), **Supp. V:** 257

Divine Pilgrim, The (Aiken), **I:** 50, 55

Divine Tragedy, The (Longfellow), **II:** 490, 500, 505, 506, 507; **Retro. Supp. II:** 165, 166

Divine Weekes and Workes (Sylvester, trans.), **Supp. I Part 1:** 104

Divine Weeks (Du Bartas), **IV:** 157–158

Diving into the Wreck: Poems 1971–1972 (Rich), **Supp. I Part 2:** 550, 559–565, 569; **Supp. XV:** 252

"Diving Past African Violets" (A. Finch), **Supp. XVII:** 72

Diving Rock on the Hudson, A (H. Roth), **Supp. IX:** 236, **237–238**

"Divinity in Its Fraying Fact, A" (Levis), **Supp. XI:** 271

"Divinity School Address" (Emerson), **II:** 12–13

"Divisions upon a Ground" (Hecht), **Supp. X:** 58

"Divorce" (Karr), **Supp. XI:** 244

"Divorced Fathers and Pizza Crusts" (Halliday), **Supp. XIX:** 93

Divorced in America: Marriage in an Age of Possibility (Epstein), **Supp. XIV:** 113

"Divorce Dream" (Halliday), **Supp. XIX:** 90

Dix, Douglas Shields, **Supp. XII:** 14

Dixie City Jam (Burke), **Supp. XIV:** 32

Dixon, Ivan, **Supp. IV Part 1:** 362

Dixon, Stephen, **Supp. XII:** **139–158**

Dixon, Terrell F., **Supp. XVI:** 21

Dixon, Thomas, Jr., **Supp. II Part 1:** 169, 171, 177

Djinn (Robbe-Grillet), **Supp. V:** 48

D'Lugoff, Burt, **Supp. IV Part 1:** 362, 370

Dmytryk, Edward, **Supp. XX:**41

Do, Lord, Remember Me (Garrett), **Supp. VII:** 98–100, 110

"Doaksology, The" (Wolfe), **IV:** 459

Do Androids Dream of Electric Sheep? (Dick), **Supp. XVIII:** 137

Dobie, J. Frank, **Supp. V:** 225; **Supp. XIII:** 227

Döblin, Alfred, **Supp. XV:** 137

Dobriansky, Lev, **Supp. I Part 2:** 648, 650

Dobrin, Sidney I., **Supp. XVIII:** 192, 195

Dobson, Joanne, **Retro. Supp. I:** 29, 31, 42; **Supp. XVIII:** 259

Dobyns, Stephen, **Supp. XIII:** **73–92**

"Docking at Palermo" (Hugo), **Supp. VI:** 137–138

"Dock Rats" (Moore), **III:** 213

"Dock-Witch, The" (Ozick), **Supp. V:** 262, 264

"Doc Mellhorn and the Pearly Gates" (Benét), **Supp. XI:** 55

"Doctor, The" (Dubus), **Supp. VII:** 80–81

"Doctor and the Doctor's Wife, The" (Hemingway), **II:** 248; **Retro. Supp. I:** 174, 175

Doctor Breen's Practice, a Novel (Howells), **I:** 282

Doctor Faustus (Mann), **III:** 283

Doctor Jazz (Carruth), **Supp. XVI:** 47, 59

"Doctor Jekyll" (Sontag), **Supp. III Part 2:** 469

"Doctor Leavis and the Moral Tradition" (Trilling), **Supp. III Part 2:** 512–513

Doctor Martino and Other Stories (Faulkner), **II:** 72; **Retro. Supp. I:** 84

"Doctor of the Heart, The" (Sexton), **Supp. II Part 2:** 692

Doctorow, E. L., **Retro. Supp. I:** 97; **Supp. III Part 2:** 590, 591; **Supp. IV Part 1: 217–240; Supp. V:** 45; **Supp. XVI:** 73; **Supp. XVII:** 183; **Supp. XX:**84, 90; **Supp. XXI:** 18–19

Doctor Sax (Kerouac), **Supp. III Part 1:** 220–222, 224–227

Doctor Sleep (Bell), **Supp. X: 9–11**

"Doctors' Row" (Aiken), **I:** 67

Doctor's Son and Other Stories, The (O'Hara), **III:** 361

Doctor Stories, The (W. C. Williams), **Retro. Supp. I:** 424

"Doctor's Wife, The" (Ozick), **Supp. V:** 262, 265

Doctor Zhivago (Pasternak), **IV:** 434, 438, 443

"Documentary" (Simic), **Supp. VIII:** 282

Dodd, Elizabeth, **Supp. V:** 77

Dodd, Wayne, **Supp. IV Part 2:** 625

Dodge, Mabel, **Supp. XX:**69; **Supp. XXI:** 5, 6, 8, 12. *See also* Luhan, Mabel Dodge

Dodson, Owen, **Supp. I Part 1:** 54

Dodsworth (Lewis), **II:** 442, 449–450, 453, 456

Doenitz, Karl, **Supp. I Part 2:** 491

Does Civilization Need Religion? (Niebuhr), **III:** 293–294

"Does 'Consciousness' Exist?" (James), **II:** 356

"Does Education Pay?" (Du Bois), **Supp. II Part 1:** 159

"Dog" (B. Kelly), **Supp. XVII:** 126

Dog (Shepard), **Supp. III Part 2:** 434

"Dog Act, The" (Komunyakaa), **Supp. XIII:** 114–115

"Dog and the Playlet, The" (O. Henry), **Supp. II Part 1:** 399

Dog Beneath the Skin, The (Auden), **Supp. II Part 1:** 10

"Dog Creek Mainline" (Wright), **Supp. V:** 340

"Dogfight" (W. Gibson and Swanwick), **Supp. XVI:** 128

Dog in the Manger, The (Vega; Merwin, trans.), **Supp. III Part 1:** 341, 347

Dog of the Marriage, The (Hempel), **Supp. XXI:** 115, 116, 117, 118, **126–127**

Dogs Bark, but the Caravan Rolls On (Conroy), **Supp. XVI:** 63, 70, 74, .**75–76**

Dogs Bark, The: Public People and Private Places (Capote), **Supp. III Part 1:** 120, 132

"Dog's Eye" (J. W. Miller), **Supp. XX:** 167

Dog Soldiers (Stone), **Supp. V:** 298, 299–301

Dog Star, The (Di Piero), **Supp. XIX:** 38, **40–41,** 43

"Dog Stories" (Prose), **Supp. XVI:** 256

Dog & the Fever, The (Quevedo), **Retro. Supp. I:** 423

"Dogtown Letters, The" (Jarman and R. McDowell), **Supp. XVII:** 111

"Dogwood, The" (Levertov), **Supp. III Part 1:** 276

"Dogwood Tree, The: A Boyhood" (Updike), **IV:** 218; **Retro. Supp. I:** 318, 319

Doig, Ivan, **Supp. XIV:** 227

"Doing Battle with the Wolf" (Coleman), **Supp. XI:** 87–88

Doing Literary Business: American Women Writers in the Nineteenth Century (Coultrap-McQuin), **Supp. XVI:** 85

Doings and Undoings (Podhoretz), **Supp. VIII:** 236–237

"Do-It-Yourself" (C. Baxter), **Supp. XVII:** 14–15

Dolan, Jill, **Supp. XV:** 327

Dolben, Digby Mackworth, **Supp. XX:** 230

"Dolce Far' Niente" (Humphrey), **Supp. IX:** 106

Dolci, Carlo, **III:** 474–475

Dollars and Cents (A. Warner), **Supp. XVIII:** 264

"Dollhouse, The" (Haines), **Supp. XII:** 204

Dollmaker's Ghost, The (Levis), **Supp. XI:** 259, 260, **264–268**

Doll's House, A (Ibsen), **III:** 523; **IV:** 357; **Supp. XVI:** 182

Dolmetsch, Arnold, **III:** 464

Dolores Claiborne (King), **Supp. V:** 138, 141, 147, 148, 149–150, 152

"Dolph Heyliger" (Irving), **II:** 309

Dolphin, The (Lowell), **Retro. Supp. II:** 183, 186, 188, **190–191; Supp. XII:** 253–254

"Dolphins" (Francis), **Supp. IX:** 83

Dome of Many-Coloured Class, A (Lowell), **II:** 515, 516–517

Domesday Book (Masters), **Supp. I Part 2:** 465, 466–469, 471, 473, 476

"Domestic Economy" (Gilman), **Supp. XI:** 206

"Domestic Manners" (Hardwick), **Supp. III Part 1:** 211

Domestic Work (Trethewey), **Supp. XXI:** 243, 244, **248–251,** 254

"Domestic Work, 1937" (Trethewey), **Supp. XXI:** 248

"Dominant White, The" (McKay), **Supp. X:** 134

Dominguez, Robert, **Supp. VIII:** 83

Domini, John, **Supp. XIX:** 45; **Supp. XXI:** 235

Dominique, Jean. *See* Closset, Marie

Donahoe, Edward, **Supp. XVIII:** 132

Donahue, Phil, **Supp. IV Part 2:** 526; **Supp. X:** 311

Doña Perfecta (Galdós), **II:** 290

Dong, Stella, **Supp. XVI:** 222

Don Juan (Byron), **Supp. XV:** 259

"DON JUAN IN HELL" (Baraka), **Supp. II Part 1:** 33

Donkey of God, The (Untermeyer), **Supp. XV:** 310

"Donna mi Prega" (Cavalcanti), **Supp. III Part 2:** 620, 621, 622

Donn-Byrne, Brian Oswald. *See* Byrne, Donn

Donne, John, **I:** 358–359, 384, 389, 522, 586; **II:** 254; **III:** 493; **IV:** 83, 88, 135, 141, 144, 145, 151, 156, 165, 331, 333; **Retro. Supp. II:** 76; **Supp. I Part 1:** 80, 364, 367; **Supp. I Part 2:** 421, 424, 467, 725, 726; **Supp. III Part 2:** 614, 619; **Supp. VIII:** 26, 33, 164; **Supp. IX:** 44; **Supp. XII:** 45, 159; **Supp. XIII:** 94, 130; **Supp. XIV:** 122; **Supp. XV:** 92, 251; **Supp. XVI:** 158, 204; **Supp. XVIII:** 35, 39, 50–51, 307

Donne's Sermons: Selected Passages (L. P. Smith, ed.), **Supp. XIV:** 342

Donoghue, Denis, **I:** 537; **Supp. IV Part 1:** 39; **Supp. VIII:** 105, 189

Donohue, H. E. F., **Supp. IX:** 2, 3, 15, 16

"Do Not Weep Maiden, For War Is Kind" (Crane), **Supp. XVIII:** 75

Donovan, Josephine, **Retro. Supp. II:** 138, 139, 147

Don Quixote (Cervantes), **I:** 134; **II:** 291, 434; **III:** 113, 614; **Supp. I Part 2:** 422; **Supp. IX:** 94

Don Quixote: Which Was a Dream (Acker), **Supp. XII:** 5, **12–14**

Don't Ask (Levine), **Supp. V:** 178

Don't Ask Questions (Marquand), **III:** 58

Don't Bet on the Prince: Contemporary Feminist Fairy Tales in North America and England (Zipes), **Supp. XIV:** 126

Don't Drink the Water (Allen), **Supp. XV:** 3, **14**

Don't Look Back (film, Pennebaker), **Supp. XVIII:** 19

"Don't Shoot the Warthog" (Corso), **Supp. XII:** 123

"Don't Tell Mother" (Wasserstein), **Supp. XV:** 319

"Don't Think Twice, It's All Right" (song, Dylan), **Supp. XVIII:** 24

Don't Worry About the Kids (Neugeboren), **Supp. XVI:** 226

"Don't Worry About the Kids" (Neugeboren), **Supp. XVI:** 226

Don't You Want to Be Free? (Hughes), **Retro. Supp. I:** 203; **Supp. I Part 1:** 339

"Doodler, The" (Merrill), **Supp. III Part 1:** 321

Doolan, Moira, **Retro. Supp. II:** 247

Doolittle, Hilda (H. D.), **II:** 517, 520–521; **III:** 194, 195–196, 457, 465; **IV:** 404, 406; **Retro. Supp. I:** 288, 412, 413, 414, 415, 417; **Supp. I Part 1:** **253–275; Supp. I Part 2:** 707; **Supp. III Part 1:** 48; **Supp. III Part 2:** 610; **Supp. IV Part 1:** 257; **Supp. V:** 79; **Supp. XV:** 43, 249, 301, 302; **Supp. XVII:** 77

Doolittle, Thomas, **IV:** 150

"Doomed by Our Blood to Care" (Orfalea), **Supp. XIII:** 278

"Doomsday" (Plath), **Retro. Supp. II:** 242

Doomsters, The (Macdonald), **Supp. IV Part 2:** 462, 463, 472, 473

"Door, The" (Creeley), **Supp. IV Part 1:** 145, 146, 156–157

"Door, The" (White), **Supp. I Part 2:** 651, 675–676

"Door in the Dark, The" (Frost), **II:** 156

Door in the Hive, A (Levertov), **Supp. III Part 1:** 283, 284

"Door of the Trap, The" (Anderson), **I:** 112

Doors (Hoffman), **Supp. XVIII:** 86–87

"Doors" (Hoffman), **Supp. XVIII:** 86–87

"Doors, Doors, Doors" (Sexton), **Supp. II Part 2:** 681

Doors, The, **Supp. X:** 186

"Doorways into the Depths" (Sanders), **Supp. XVI:** 272

Doreski, William, **Retro. Supp. II:** 185

Dorfman, Ariel, **Supp. IX:** 131, 138

Dorfman, Joseph, **Supp. I Part 2:** 631, 647, 650

Dorman, Jen, **Supp. XI:** 240

Dorn, Edward, **Supp. IV Part 1:** 154

Dorn, Sarah, **Supp. XXI:** 243

"Dorothea Dix, Samaritan" (J. Scott), **Supp. XVII:** 189

Dorr, Julia, **Supp. XV:** 286

Dorris, Michael, **Supp. IV Part 1:** 260, 272

Dos Passos, John, **I:** 99, 288, 374, 379, **474–496,** 517, 519; **II:** 74, 77, 89, 98; **III:** 2, 28, 29, 70, 172, 382–383; **IV:** 340, 427, 433; **Retro. Supp. I:** 105, 113, 187; **Retro. Supp. II:** 95, 196; **Supp. I Part 2:** 646; **Supp. III Part 1:** 104, 105; **Supp. V:** 277; **Supp. VIII:** 101, 105; **Supp. XIV:** 24; **Supp. XV:** 135, 137, 182; **Supp. XVII:** 105, 107; **Supp. XXI:** 8

"Dos Passos: Poet Against the World" (Cowley), **Supp. II Part 1:** 143, 145

Dostoevsky, Fyodor, **I:** 53, 103, 211, 468; **II:** 60, 130, 275, 320, 587; **III:** 37, 61, 155, 174, 176, 188, 189, 267, 272, 283, 286, 354, 357, 358, 359, 467, 571, 572; **IV:** 1, 7, 8, 17, 21, 50, 59, 106, 110, 128, 134, 285, 289, 476, 485, 491; **Retro. Supp. II:** 20, 204, 299; **Supp. I Part 1:** 49; **Supp. I Part**

2: 445, 466; **Supp. IV Part 2:** 519, 525; **Supp. VIII:** 175; **Supp. X:** 4–5; **Supp. XI:** 161; **Supp. XII:** 322; **Supp. XVI:** 63; **Supp. XVII:** 225; **Supp. XVIII:** 278, 280; **Supp. XX:**45

Doty, Mark, **Supp. IX:** 42, 300; **Supp. XI:** 119–138; **Supp. XXI:** 129, 130, 131, 139, 141

Doty, M. R. *See* Dawson, Ruth; Doty, Mark

Double, The (Dostoevsky), **Supp. IX:** 105

"Double, The" (Levis), **Supp. XI:** 260, **261–263**

Double, The (Rank), **Supp. IX:** 105

Double Agent, The (Blackmur), **Supp. II Part 1:** 90, 108, 146

Double Axe, The (Jeffers), **Supp. II Part 2:** 416, 434

"Double Blind" (Skloot), **Supp. XX:**194, 208

Doubleday, Frank, **I:** 500, 502, 515, 517; **III:** 327

Doubleday, Mrs. Frank, **I:** 500

Double Deuce (Parker), **Supp. XIX:** 183

Double Down (F. and S. Barthelme), **Supp. XI:** 27, 34, 35, 36–38

Double Dream of Spring, The (Ashbery), **Supp. III Part 1:** 11–13

Double Fold: Libraries and the Assault on Paper (Baker), **Supp. XIII:** 52, 56

Double Game (Calle), **Supp. XII:** 22

"Double Gap, The" (Auchincloss), **Supp. IV Part 1:** 33

"Double-Headed Snake of Newbury, The" (Whittier), **Supp. I Part 2:** 698

Double Honeymoon (Connell), **Supp. XIV:** 80, 87

Double Image, The (Levertov), **Supp. III Part 1:** 274, 276

"Double Image, The" (Sexton), **Supp. II Part 2:** 671, 677–678

Double Indemnity (film), **Supp. IV Part 1:** 130

"Double Limbo" (Komunyakaa), **Supp. XIII:** 132

Double Man, The (Auden), **Supp. III Part 1:** 16; **Supp. X:** 118

"Double Ode" (Rukeyser), **Supp. VI:** 282–283, 286

Double Persephone (Atwood), **Supp. XIII:** 19

Double Play (Parker), **Supp. XIX: 189–190**

Doubles in Literary Psychology (Tymms), **Supp. IX:** 105

Double Vision: American Thoughts Abroad (Knowles), **Supp. XII:** 249

"Doubt on the Great Divide" (Stafford), **Supp. XI:** 322

Dougherty, Steve, **Supp. X:** 262

Douglas, Aaron, **Supp. I Part 1:** 326

Douglas, Alfred, **Supp. X:** 151

Douglas, Ann, **Supp. XII:** 136; **Supp. XVIII:** 258; **Supp. XX:**69

Douglas, Claire, **III:** 552

Douglas, Ellen, **Supp. XXI:** 38

Douglas, George (pseudonym). *See* Brown, George Douglas

Douglas, Kirk, **Supp. XIII:** 5–6

Douglas, Lloyd, **IV:** 434

Douglas, Marjory Stoneman, **Supp. XVIII:** 195

Douglas, Melvyn, **Supp. V:** 223

Douglas, Michael, **Supp. XI:** 67

Douglas, Paul, **III:** 294

Douglas, Stephen A., **III:** 577, 588–589; **Supp. I Part 2:** 456, 471

Douglas, William O., **III:** 581

Douglass, Frederick, **Supp. I Part 1:** 51, 345; **Supp. I Part 2:** 591; **Supp. II Part 1:** 157, 195, 196, 292, 378; **Supp. III Part 1:** 153–174; **Supp. IV Part 1:** 1, 2, 13, 15, 256; **Supp. VIII:** 202; **Supp. XVIII:** 16; **Supp. XX:**109, 281

Douglass Pilot, The (Baldwin, ed.), **Supp. I Part 1:** 49

Dove, Belle, **I:** 451

Dove, Rita, **Supp. IV Part 1: 241–258; Supp. XVII:** 71, 110; **Supp. XVIII:** 172, 174; **Supp. XXI:** 243, 246, 247, 249, 251

"Dover Beach" (Arnold), **Retro. Supp. I:** 325; **Supp. XIX:** 41

Dow, Lorenzo, **IV:** 265

Dowd, Douglas, **Supp. I Part 2:** 645, 650

"Do We Understand Each Other?" (Ginsberg), **Supp. II Part 1:** 311

Dowie, William, **Supp. V:** 199

Do with Me What You Will (Oates), **Supp. II Part 2:** 506, 515–517

Dowling, Eddie, **IV:** 394

Down and Out (Shanley), **Supp. XIV:** 317

"Down at City Hall" (Didion), **Supp. IV Part 1:** 211

"Down at the Cross" (Baldwin), **Retro. Supp. II:** 1, 2, 7, 12, 13, 15; **Supp. I Part 1:** 60, 61

"Down at the Dinghy" (Salinger), **III:** 559, 563

"Down by the Station, Early in the Morning" (Ashbery), **Supp. III Part 1:** 25

Downey, Sharon D., **Supp. XX:**244

Downhill Racer (film), **Supp. IX:** 253

"Down Home" (J. W. Miller), **Supp. XX:**169

"Down in Alabam" (Bierce), **I:** 193

Downing, Ben, **Supp. XII:** 175, 189, 190–191

Downing, Major Jack (pseudonym). *See* Smith, Seba

Down in My Heart (Stafford), **Supp. XI:** 313, 315

Down Mailer's Way (Solotaroff), **Retro. Supp. II:** 203

"Down the Highway" (song, Dylan), **Supp. XVIII:** 24

Down the Rabbit Hole: Adventures and Misadventures in the Realm of Children's Literature (Lanes), **Supp. XVI:** 104

Down There on a Visit (Isherwood), **Supp. XIV:** 159, 161, 164, **168–169**, 170, 171

Down the River (Abbey), **Supp. XIII:** 12–13

"Down the River with Henry Thoreau" (Abbey), **Supp. XIII:** 12–13

Down These Mean Streets (P. Thomas), **Supp. XIII:** 264

Down the Starry River (Purdy), **Supp. VII:** 278

Down to the River: Portraits of Iowa Musicians (Dyas), **Supp. XIX:** 174

"Downtrodden Mary's Failed Campaign of Terror" (Saunders), **Supp. XIX:** 226

"Downward Path to Wisdom, The" (Porter), **III:** 442, 443, 446

"Down Where I Am" (Hughes), **Supp. I Part 1:** 344

Down with Starvation Wages in Southeast Missouri (C. L. R. James), **Supp. XXI:** 169

"Dowsing for Joy" (Skloot), **Supp. XX:**203

Dowson, Ernest C., **I:** 384

Doyle, Arthur Conan, **Retro. Supp. I:** 270; **Supp. IV Part 1:** 128, 341; **Supp. IV Part 2:** 464, 469; **Supp. XI:** 63

Doyle, C. W., **I:** 199

"Draba" (Leopold), **Supp. XIV:** 186

Drabble, Margaret, **Supp. IV Part 1:** 297, 299, 305

Drabelle, Dennis, **Supp. XIII:** 13

Drach, Ivan, **Supp. III Part 1:** 268

Dracula (film), **Supp. IV Part 1:** 104; **Supp. XVII:** 57

"Draft Horse, The" (Frost), **Retro. Supp. I:** 141

"Draft Lyrics for *Candide*" (Agee), **I:** 28

Draft of XVI Cantos, A (Pound), **III:** 472; **Retro. Supp. I:** 292

Draft of XXX Cantos, A (Pound), **III:** 196; **Retro. Supp. I:** 292

Drafts &Fragments (Pound), **Retro. Supp. I:** 293

Dragon Country (T. Williams), **IV:** 383

Dragon Seed (Buck), **Supp. II Part 1:** 124

Dragon's Teeth (Sinclair), **Supp. V:** 290

Drake, Benjamin, **Supp. I Part 2:** 584

Drake, Daniel, **Supp. I Part 2:** 584

Drake, Sir Francis, **Supp. I Part 2:** 497

Drake, Robert, **Supp. XX:**274

Drake, St. Clair, **IV:** 475

Drake, Sylvia, **Supp. XXI:** 155

Drake, William, **Supp. XV:** 295

Dramatic Duologues (Masters), **Supp. I Part 2:** 461

"Drapery Factory, Gulfport. Mississippi, 1956" (Trethewey), **Supp. XXI:** 246

Drattel, Deborah, **Supp. XV:** 333

Drat These Brats (X. J. Kennedy), **Supp. XV:** 163

"Draught" (Cowley), **Supp. II Part 1:** 141, 142

Drayton, Michael, **IV:** 135; **Retro. Supp. II:** 76

"Dr. Bergen's Belief" (Schwartz), **Supp. II Part 2:** 650

Dr. Bloodmoney (Dick), **Supp. XVIII:** 138

"Dreadful Has Already Happened, The" (Strand), **Supp. IV Part 2:** 627

"Dream, A" (Ginsberg), **Supp. II Part 1:** 312

"Dream, A" (Tate), **IV:** 129

"Dream, The" (Hayden), **Supp. II Part 1:** 368, 377

Dream at the End of the World, The: Paul Bowles and the Literary Renegades in Tangier (Green), **Supp. IV Part 1:** 95

"Dream Avenue" (Simic), **Supp. VIII:** 282

"Dream Boogie" (Hughes), **Retro. Supp. I:** 208; **Supp. I Part 1:** 339–340

"Dreambook Bestiary" (Komunyakaa), **Supp. XIII:** 120

Dreamer (Johnson), **Supp. VI:** 186, **196–199**

dreamer examines his pillow, the (Shanley), **Supp. XIV:** 315, **327**

"Dreamer in a Dead Language" (Paley), **Supp. VI:** 217

Dreaming in Cuban (García), **Supp. XI:** 178, **179–185,** 190

"Dreaming of Hair" (L.-Y. Lee), **Supp. XV:** 214

"Dreaming the Breasts" (Sexton), **Supp. II Part 2:** 692

"Dreaming Water" (Espaillat), **Supp. XXI:** 102

"Dream Interpreted, The" (Paine), **Supp. I Part 2:** 505

Dream Jumbo (Longo), **Supp. XVI:** 124

Dream Keeper, The (Hughes), **Supp. I Part 1:** 328, 332, 333, 334

Dream Keeper and Other Poems, The (Hughes), **Retro. Supp. I:** 201, 202

Dreamland (Baker), **Supp. XIV:** 96

"Dream-Land" (Poe), **Retro. Supp. II:** 274

Dream Life of Balso Snell, The (West), **IV:** 286, 287, 288–290, 291, 297; **Retro. Supp. II:** 321, 322, 327, 328, **330–332**

Dream of a Common Language, The: Poems, 1974–1977 (Rich), **Supp. I Part 2:** 551, 554, 569–576

Dream of Arcadia: American Writers and Artists in Italy (Brooks), **I:** 254

Dream of Governors, A (Simpson), **Supp. IX:** 265, **269–270**

"Dream of Italy, A" (Masters), **Supp. I Part 2:** 458

"Dream of Mourning, The" (Glück), **Supp. V:** 84

"Dream of the Blacksmith's Room, A" (R. Bly), **Supp. IV Part 1:** 73

"Dream of the Cardboard Lover" (Haines), **Supp. XII:** 204

Dream of the Golden Mountains, The (Cowley), **Supp. II Part 1:** 139, 141, 142, 144

"Dream Pang, A" (Frost), **II:** 153

"Dreams About Clothes" (Merrill), **Supp. III Part 1:** 328–329

Dreams from Bunker Hill (Fante), **Supp. XI:** 160, 166, **172–173**

"Dreams of Adulthood" (Ashbery), **Supp. III Part 1:** 26

"Dreams of Glory on the Mound" (Plimpton), **Supp. XVI:** 238–239

"Dreams of Math" (Kenyon), **Supp. VII:** 160–161

"Dreams of the Animals" (Atwood), **Supp. XIII:** 33

"Dream Variations" (Hughes), **Retro. Supp. I:** 198; **Supp. I Part 1:** 323

"Dream Vision" (Olsen), **Supp. XIII:** 295–296

Dream Work (Oliver), **Supp. VII:** 234–235, 236–238, 240

Dred: A Tale of the Great Dismal Swamp (Stowe), **Supp. I Part 2:** 592

Dreiser, Theodore, **I:** 59, 97, 109, 116, 355, 374, 375, 475, 482, **497–520;** **II:** 26, 27, 29, 34, 38, 44, 74, 89, 93, 180, 276, 283, 428, 444, 451, 456–457, 467–468; **III:** 40, 103, 106, 251, 314, 319, 327, 335, 453, 576, 582; **IV:** 29, 35, 40, 135, 208, 237, 475, 482, 484; **Retro. Supp. I:** 325, 376; **Retro. Supp. II: 93–110,** 114, 322; **Supp. I Part 1:** 320; **Supp. I Part 2:** 461, 468; **Supp. III Part 2:** 412; **Supp. IV Part 1:** 31, 236, 350; **Supp. IV Part 2:** 689; **Supp. V:** 113, 120; **Supp. VIII:** 98, 101, 102; **Supp. IX:** 1, 14, 15, 308; **Supp. XI:** 207; **Supp. XIV:** 111; **Supp. XVII:** 95, 96–97, 105, 155; **Supp. XVIII:** 1, 6, 76, 226; **Supp. XXI:** 275

"Drenched in Light" (Hurston), **Supp. VI:** 150–151

Dresser, Paul, **Retro. Supp. II:** 94, 103

Dress Gray (teleplay), **Supp. IV Part 2:** 683

Dress Gray (Truscott), **Supp. IV Part 2:** 683

"Dressing for Dinner" (Ríos), **Supp. IV Part 2:** 548

Dressing Up for the Carnival (Shields), **Supp. VII:** 328

"Dress Rehearsal" (Skloot), **Supp. XX:** 204

Drew, Bettina, **Supp. IX:** 2, 4

Drew, Elizabeth, **Retro. Supp. II:** 242, 243

Drexler, Eric, **Supp. XVI:** 121

Dreyfus, Alfred, **Supp. I Part 2:** 446

"Dr. Hanray's Second Chance" (Richter), **Supp. XVIII:** 218

Drift and Mastery (Lippmann), **I:** 222–223

"Driftwood" (C. Frost), **Supp. XV:** 106–107

"Drinker, The" (Lowell), **II:** 535, 550

"Drinking Cold Water" (Everwine), **Supp. XV:** 80–81

"Drinking from a Helmet" (Dickey), **Supp. IV Part 1:** 180

Drinking Gourd, The (Hansberry), **Supp. IV Part 1:** 359, 365–367, 374

Drinks before Dinner (Doctorow), **Supp. IV Part 1:** 231, 234–235

Driscoll, David, **Supp. XIX:** 241, 242

Drive, He Said (Larner), **Supp. XVI:** 220

"Drive Home, The" (Banks), **Supp. V:** 7

"Driver" (Merrill), **Supp. III Part 1:** 331

"Driving Alone in Winter" (W. V. Davis), **Supp. XXI:** 89, 90, 94

"Driving Through Minnesota During the Hanoi Bombings" (R. Bly), **Supp. IV Part 1:** 61; **Supp. XVII:** 243

"Driving through Oregon" (Haines), **Supp. XII:** 207

"Driving toward the Lac Qui Parle River" (R. Bly), **Supp. IV Part 1:** 61

"Dr. Jack-o'-Lantern" (Yates), **Supp. XI:** 340–341

Dr. Jekyll and Mr. Hyde (film), **Supp. XVII:** 57

"Drone" (Coleman), **Supp. XI:** 85–86

Drop City (Boyle), **Supp. XX:30–31**

"Drowned Man, The: Death between Two Rivers" (McGrath), **Supp. X:** 116

"Drowning" (Boyle), **Supp. XX:18**

"Drowning 1954" (Keillor), **Supp. XVI:** 172

Drowning Pool, The (film), **Supp. IV Part 2:** 474

Drowning Pool, The (Macdonald), **Supp. IV Part 2:** 470, 471

Drowning Season, The (Hoffman), **Supp. X:** 82

Drowning with Others (Dickey), **Supp. IV Part 1:** 176, 178, 179

"Drowsy Day, A" (Dunbar), **Supp. II Part 1:** 198

Dr. Seuss. *See* Geisel, Theodor Seuss (Dr. Seuss)

Dr. Seuss and Mr. Geisel (J. and N. Morgan), **Supp. XVI:** 103

Dr. Seuss Goes to War: The World War II Editorial Cartoons of Theodor Seuss Geisel (Minear), **Supp. XVI:** 101

Dr. Seuss's ABC (Geisel), **Supp. XVI:** 99

Dr. Strangelove; or, How I Learned to Stop Worrying and Love the Bomb (film), **Supp. XI:** 293, **301–305**

Drugiye Berega (Nabokov), **III:** 247–250, 252

"Drug Shop, The, or Endymion in Edmonstoun" (Benét), **Supp. XI:** 43

"Drug Store" (Shapiro), **Supp. II Part 2:** 705

"Drugstore in Winter, A" (Ozick), **Supp. V:** 272

Drukman, Steven, **Supp. XIII:** 195, 197, 202

"Drum" (Hogan), **Supp. IV Part 1:** 413

"Drum, The" (Alvarez), **Supp. VII:** 7

"Drumlin Woodchuck, A" (Frost), **II:** 159–160; **Retro. Supp. I:** 138

Drummond, William, **Supp. I Part 1:** 369

Drummond de Andrade, Carlos, **Supp. IV Part 2:** 626, 629, 630

Drum-Taps (Whitman), **IV:** 346, 347, 444; **Retro. Supp. I:** 406

"Drunken Fisherman, The" (Lowell), **II:** 534, 550

"Drunken Sisters, The" (Wilder), **IV:** 374

Drunk in the Furnace, The (Merwin), **Supp. III Part 1:** 345–346

"Drunk in the Furnace, The" (Merwin), **Supp. III Part 1:** 346

Druten, John van, **Supp. XIV:** 162

"Dr. Williams' Position" (Pound), **Supp. XVII:** 226–227

Dryden, John, **II:** 111, 542, 556; **III:** 15; **IV:** 145; **Retro. Supp. I:** 56; **Supp. I**

Part 1: 150; **Supp. I Part 2:** 422; **Supp. IX:** 68; **Supp. XIV:** 5; **Supp. XV:** 258; **Supp. XX:**280

Drye, Captain Frank, **Retro. Supp. II:** 115

Dry Salvages, The (Eliot), **I:** 581

"Dry Salvages, The" (Eliot), **Retro. Supp. I:** 66

"Dry September" (Faulkner), **II:** 72, 73

Dry Sun, Dry Wind (Wagoner), **Supp. IX:** 323, 324

D'Souza, Dinesh, **Supp. X:** 255

"Dual" (Goldbarth), **Supp. XII:** 188

"Dual Curriculum" (Ozick), **Supp. V:** 270

"Dualism" (Reed), **Supp. X:** 242

Duane's Depressed (McMurtry), **Supp. V:** 233

Du Bartas, Guillaume, **Supp. I Part 1:** 98, 104, 111, 118, 119

Duberman, Martin, **Supp. I Part 2:** 408, 409

"Dubin's Lives" (Malamud), **Supp. I Part 2:** 451

Dubious Honors (M. F. K. Fisher), **Supp. XVII:** 91

"Dubliners" (J. Joyce), **Supp. XVI:** 41

Dubliners (Joyce), **I:** 130, 480; **III:** 471; **Supp. VIII:** 146

Dublin's Lives (Malamud), **Supp. XIX:** 142

Du Bois, Nina Gomer (Mrs. W. E. B. Du Bois), **Supp. II P art 1:** 158; **Supp. XIV:** 200

Du Bois, Shirley Graham, **Supp. II Part 1:** 186; **Supp. XXI:** 171. *See also* Graham, Shirley

Du Bois, W. E. B., **I:** 260; **Supp. I Part 1:** 5, 345; **Supp. II Part 1:** 33, 56, 61, **157–189,** 195; **Supp. IV Part 1:** 9, 164, 170, 362; **Supp. X:** 133, 134, 137, 139, 242; **Supp. XIII:** 185, **Supp. XIII:** 186, 233, 238, 243, 244, 247; **Supp. XIV:** 54, 69, 72, 201, 202; **Supp. XVI:** 135; **Supp. XVIII:** 119, 122, 126, 130; **Supp. XIX:** 67, 69, 77; **Supp. XX:**102, 105, 106; **Supp. XXI:** 166, 277

Dubreuil, Jean, **Supp. IV Part 2:** 425

Dubus, Andre, **Supp. VII: 75–93; Supp. XI:** 347,**Supp. XI:** 349; **Supp. XIV:** 21

Duchamp, Marcel, **IV:** 408; **Retro. Supp. I:** 416, 417, 418, 430; **Supp. IV Part 2:** 423, 424; **Supp. XII:** 124; **Supp. XV:** 157

"Duchess at Prayer, The" (Wharton), **Retro. Supp. I:** 365

Duchess of Malfi, The (Webster), **IV:** 131

Duck Soup (film), **Supp. IV Part 1:** 384

Duck Variations, The (Mamet), **Supp. XIV:** 239, 240, 249

Dudley, Anne. *See* Bradstreet, Anne

Dudley, Joseph, **III:** 52

Dudley, Thomas, **III:** 52; **Supp. I Part 1:** 98, 99, 110, 116

"Duet, With Muffled Brake Drums" (Updike), **Retro. Supp. I:** 319

Duet for Cannibals (Sontag), **Supp. III Part 2:** 452, 456

Duffey, Bernard, **Supp. I Part 2:** 458, 471

Duffield, Pitts, **Supp. XXI:** 3

Duffus, R. L., **Supp. I Part 2:** 650

Duffy, Martha, **Supp. IV Part 1:** 207; **Supp. XX:**244

Duffy, William, **Supp. XVI:** 32

Du Fu (Tu Fu), **Supp. XV:** 217

Dufy, Raoul, **I:** 115; **IV:** 80

Dugan, Alan, **Supp. XIII:** 76

Dugan, James, **Supp. XV:** 197

Duhamel, Marcel, **Supp. XVI:** 135, 143

Dujardin, Edouard, **I:** 53

"Duke de l'Omelette, The" (Poe), **III:** 411, 425

"Duke in His Domain, The" (Capote), **Supp. III Part 1:** 113, 126

Duke of Deception, The (G. Wolff), **Supp. II Part 1:** 97; **Supp. XI:** 246

"Duke's Child, The" (Maxwell), **Supp. VIII:** 172

"Dulce et Decorum Est" (Owen), **Supp. XVIII:** 92

"Dulham Ladies, The" (Jewett), **II:** 407, 408; **Retro. Supp. II:** 143

Duluth (Vidal), **Supp. IV Part 2:** 677, 685, 689, 691–692

Dumas, Alexandre, **III:** 386; **Supp. XVII:** 64

"Dumb Oax, The" (Lewis), **Retro. Supp. I:** 170

"Dummy, The" (Sontag), **Supp. III Part 2:** 469

"Dump Ground, The" (Stegner), **Supp. IV Part 2:** 601

Dunant, Sarah, **Supp. XIX:** 186

Dunayevskaya, Raya, **Supp. XXI:** 169

Dunbar, Alice Moore (Mrs. Paul Laurence Dunbar), **Supp. II Part 1:** 195, 200, 217

Dunbar, Paul Laurence, **Supp. I Part 1:** 320; **Supp. II Part 1:** 174, **191–219; Supp. III Part 1:** 73; **Supp. IV Part 1:** 15, 165, 170; **Supp. X:** 136; **Supp. XI:** 277; **Supp. XIII:** 111

Duncan, Harry, **Supp. XV:** 75

Duncan, Isadora, **I:** 483; **Supp. XV:** 42, 50

Duncan, Robert, **Retro. Supp. II:** 49; **Supp. III Part 2:** 625, 626, 630, 631; **Supp. VIII:** 304; **Supp. XVI:** 282–283

Dunciad, The (Pope), **I:** 204

Dunford, Judith, **Supp. VIII:** 107

Dunlap, William, **Supp. I Part 1:** 126, 130, 137, 141, 145

Dunn, Stephen, **Supp. XI: 139–158; Supp. XIX:** 85

Dunne, Finley Peter, **II:** 432

Dunne, John Gregory, **Supp. IV Part 1:** 197, 198, 201, 203, 207

"Dunnet Shepherdess, A" (Jewett), **II:** 392–393; **Retro. Supp. II:** 139

Dunning, Stephen, **Supp. XIV:** 126

Dunning, William Archibald, **Supp. II Part 1:** 170; **Supp. XIV:** 48

Dunnock, Mildred, **III:** 153

Dunster, Henry, **Supp. I Part 2:** 485

"Duo Tried Killing Man with Bacon" (Goldbarth), **Supp. XII:** 176

Dupee, F. W., **I:** 254; **II:** 548; **Supp. VIII:** 231; **Supp. IX:** 93, 96

DuPlessis, Rachel Blau, **Supp. IV Part 2:** 421, 426, 432; **Supp. XVI:** 284

Duplicate Keys (Smiley), **Supp. VI:** 292, **294–296**

Duplications, The (Koch), **Supp. XV:** 181, 183, 186

Durable Fire, A (Sarton), **Supp. VIII:** 260

Durand, Asher, B., **Supp. I Part 1:** 156, 157

Durand, Régis, **Supp. IV Part 1:** 44

"Durango Suite" (Gunn Allen), **Supp. IV Part 1:** 326

"Durations" (Matthews), **Supp. IX:** 152–153, 154

Dürer, Albrecht, **III:** 212; **Supp. XII:** 44

Durham, David Anthony, **Supp. XVIII:** 100

"During Fever" (Lowell), **II:** 547

Durkheim, Émile, **I:** 227; **Retro. Supp. I:** 55, 57; **Supp. I Part 2:** 637, 638

Durrell, Lawrence, **III:** 184, 190; **IV:** 430; **Supp. X:** 108, 187; **Supp. XVI:** 294

Dürrenmatt, Friedrich, **Supp. IV Part 2:** 683

Duse, Eleonora, **II:** 515, 528

Dusk and Other Stories (Salter), **Supp. IX: 260–261**

Dusk of Dawn: An Essay Toward an Autobiography of a Race Concept (Du Bois), **Supp. II Part 1:** 159, 183, 186

"Dust" (R. Fisher), **Supp. XIX:** 71

"Dusting" (Alvarez), **Supp. VII:** 4

"Dusting" (Dove), **Supp. IV Part 1:** 247, 248

"Dusting" (Schnackenberg), **Supp. XV:** 256

"Dust of Snow" (Frost), **II:** 154

Dust Tracks on a Road (Hurston), **Supp. IV Part 1:** 5, 11; **Supp. VI:** 149, 151, 158–159

"Dusty Braces" (Snyder), **Supp. VIII:** 302

Dutchman (Baraka), **Supp. II Part 1:** 38, 40, 42–44, 54, 55

"Dutch Nick Massacre, The" (Twain), **IV:** 195

"Dutch Picture, A" (Longfellow), **Retro. Supp. II:** 171

Dutton, Charles S., **Supp. VIII:** 332, 342

Dutton, Clarence Earl, **Supp. IV Part 2:** 598

Duvall, Robert, **Supp. V:** 227

"Duwamish" (Hugo), **Supp. VI:** 136

"Duwamish, Skagit, Hoh" (Hugo), **Supp. VI:** 136–137

"Duwamish No. 2" (Hugo), **Supp. VI:** 137

Duyckinck, Evert, **III:** 77, 81, 83, 85; **Retro. Supp. I:** 155, 247, 248; **Supp. I Part 1:** 122, 317

Duyckinck, George, **Supp. I Part 1:** 122

"Dvonya" (Simpson), **Supp. IX:** 274

Dwellings: A Spiritual History of the Living World (Hogan), **Supp. IV Part 1:** 397, 410, 415–416, 417

Dwight, Sereno E., **I:** 547

Dwight, Timothy, **Supp. I Part 1:** 124; **Supp. I Part 2:** 516, 580; **Supp. II Part 1:** 65, 69

Dworkin, Andrea, **Supp. XII:** 6

Dwyer, Jim, **Supp. XVI:** 16, 19

Dyas, Sandra, **Supp. XIX:** 174

Dybbuk, A, or Between Two Worlds: Dramatic Legend in Four Acts (Kushner), **Supp. IX:** 138

Dybbuk, The (Ansky), **IV:** 6

Dyer, Geoff, **Supp. X:** 169

Dyer, Joyce, **Supp. XX:** 166

Dyer, R. C., **Supp. XIII:** 162

Dying Animal, The (P. Roth), **Retro. Supp. II:** 288

"Dying Elm, The" (Freneau), **Supp. II Part 1:** 258

"Dying Indian, The" (Freneau), **Supp. II Part 1:** 262

"Dying Man, The" (Roethke), **III:** 540, 542, 543–545

Dykeman, Wilma, **Supp. XX:** 163

Dylan, Bob, **Supp. VIII:** 202; **Supp. XIII:** 114, 119; **Supp. XV:** 349, 350; **Supp. XVIII:** 19–34

Dylan's Visions of Sin (Ricks), **Supp. XVIII:** 20

"Dynamics of Heroic Action, The" (lecture, Murray), **Supp. XIX:** 153

Dynamo (O'Neill), **III:** 396

"Dynasties" (Gibran), **Supp. XX:** 118

"Dysfunctional Narratives: Or, 'Mistakes Were Made' " (C. Baxter), **Supp. XVII:** 20

"Dysfunctional Nation" (Karr), **Supp. XI:** 245

Dyson, A. E., **Retro. Supp. II:** 247

Dyson, Freeman, **Supp. XVII:** 42

E

"Each and All" (Emerson), **II:** 19

Each in His Season (Snodgrass), **Supp. VI:** 324, 327

"Each Like a Leaf" (Swenson), **Supp. IV Part 2:** 644

Eads, Martha Greene, **Supp. XVIII:** 49

Eady, Cornelius, **Supp. XXI:** 246

Eager, Allen, **Supp. XI:** 294

"Eagle, The" (Tate), **IV:** 128

"Eagle and the Mole, The" (Wylie), **Supp. I Part 2:** 710, 711, 713, 714, 729

"Eagle and the Skylark, The" (Gibran), **Supp. XX:** 124

Eagle as Wide as the World, The (X. J. Kennedy), **Supp. XV:** 162, 164

"Eagle Poem" (Harjo), **Supp. XII:** 224, 226

"Eagles" (Dickey), **Supp. IV Part 1:** 186

Eagle's Mile, The (Dickey), **Supp. IV Part 1:** 178, 185–186

"Eagle That Is Forgotten, The" (Lindsay), **Supp. I Part 2:** 382, 387

Eagleton, Terry, **Retro. Supp. I:** 67

Eakin, Paul John, **Supp. VIII:** 167, 168; **Supp. XIII:** 225; **Supp. XVI:** 70

Eakins, Thomas, **Supp. XIV:** 338

Eames, Emma, **Supp. XX:** 232, 240

Eames, Roscoe, **II:** 476

"Earl: My Life with a Louse" (Keillor), **Supp. XVI:** 176

"Earl Painter" (Banks), **Supp. V:** 14–15

"Early Adventures of Ralph Ringwood, The" (Irving), **II:** 314

Early Americana (Richter), **Supp. XVIII:** 208, 210, 211, 220

Early Autumn (Parker), **Supp. XIX:** 184–185

Early Ayn Rand, The: A Selection of Her Unpublished Fiction (Rand), **Supp. IV Part 2:** 520

Early Dark (Price), **Supp. VI:** 262

Early Diary of Anaïs Nin, The, **Supp. X:** 184, 192

Early Elkin (Elkin), **Supp. VI:** 42–43, 45

"Early Evenin' Blues" (Hughes), **Retro. Supp. I:** 205

"Early Evening, Frankfort, Kentucky" (Trethewey), **Supp. XXI:** 243, 250

"Early History of a Seamstress" (Reznikoff), **Supp. XIV:** 277, 289

Early History of a Sewing-Machine Operator (Reznikoff), **Supp. XIV:** 289

"Early History of a Sewing-Machine Operator" (Reznikoff), **Supp. XIV:** 277

"Early History of a Writer" (Reznikoff), **Supp. XIV:** 278, 290

"Early in the Morning" (L.-Y. Lee), **Supp. XV:** 214

Early Lectures of Ralph Waldo Emerson, The (Emerson), **II:** 11

Early Light (Di Piero), **Supp. XIX:** 38, 38–40

Early Lives of Melville, The (Sealts), **Retro. Supp. I:** 257

"Early Marriage" (Richter), **Supp. XVIII:** 209

Early Martyr and Other Poems, An (W. C. Williams), **Retro. Supp. I:** 423

"Early Morning: Cape Cod" (Swenson), **Supp. IV Part 2:** 641

"Early Spring between Madison and Bellingham" (R. Bly), **Supp. IV Part 1:** 71

Earnhardt, Dale, **Supp. XII:** 310

Earnshaw, Doris, **Supp. IV Part 1:** 310

"Earth" (Bryant), **Supp. I Part 1:** 157, 164, 167

"Earth, The" (Sexton), **Supp. II Part 2:** 696

Earth Abides (Stewart), **Supp. XVIII:** 138

"Earth and Fire" (Berry), **Supp. X:** 27

Earth as Air, The: An Ars Poetica (Sobin), **Supp. XVI:** 285–286

"Earth Being" (Toomer), **Supp. IX:** 320

Earth Gods, The (Gibran), **Supp. XX:** 116, **123**

"Earthly Care a Heavenly Discipline" (Stowe), **Supp. I Part 2:** 586

"Earthly City of the Jews, The" (Kazin), **Retro. Supp. II:** 286

Earthly Meditations (Wrigley), **Supp. XVIII:** 304–305

"Earthly Meditations" (Wrigley), **Supp. XVIII:** 304–306

Earthly Possessions (Tyler), **Supp. IV Part 2:** 665–666, 671

Earth Power Coming (Ortiz, ed.), **Supp. IV Part 2:** 502

"Earth's Holocaust" (Hawthorne), **II:** 226, 231, 232, 242; **III:** 82; **Retro. Supp. I:** 152

Earth Without You, The (F. Wright), **Supp. XVII:** 243

East Coker (Eliot), **I:** 580, 581, 582, 585, 587

"East Coker" (Eliot), **Retro. Supp. I:** 66; **Supp. VIII:** 195, 196

"Easter" (Toomer), **Supp. III Part 2:** 486

"Easter, an Ode" (Lowell), **II:** 536

"Easter 1916" (Yeats), **Supp. XXI:** 61

"Easter Morning" (Ammons), **Supp. VII:** 34

"Easter Morning" (Clampitt), **Supp. IX:** 45

"Easter Ode, An" (Dunbar), **Supp. II Part 1:** 196

Easter Parade, The (Yates), **Supp. XI:** 346, 349

"Easter Sermon, 1866" (Nelson), **Supp. XVIII:** 177

"Easter Service" (Di Piero), **Supp. XIX:** 39–40

"Easter Sunday: Recollection" (Gunn Allen), **Supp. IV Part 1:** 322

"Easter Wings" (Herbert), **Supp. IV Part 2:** 646

"East European Cooking" (Simic), **Supp. VIII:** 277

East Is East (Boyle), **Supp. VIII:** 1–3; **Supp. XX:** 23–24, 25, 28

Eastlake, William, **Supp. XIII:** 12

East Lynne (Wood), **Supp. I Part 1:** 35, 36; **Supp. I Part 2:** 459, 462; **Supp. XVI:** 182

Eastman, Elaine Goodale, **Supp. X:** 103

Eastman, Max, **Supp. III Part 2:** 620; **Supp. X:** 131, 134, 135, 137; **Supp. XV:** 295; **Supp. XVI:** 185; **Supp. XVII:** 96; **Supp. XXI:** 6

East of Eden (Steinbeck), **IV:** 51, 56–57, 59

"East of the Sun and West of the Moon" (Merwin), **Supp. III Part 1:** 344

Easton, Alison, **Retro. Supp. II:** 143, 144, 145

Easton, Bret Ellis, **Supp. XI:** 65

Easton, Nina J., **Supp. XIX:** 137

Easton, Robert, **Supp. IV Part 2:** 461, 474

East Wind (Lowell), **II:** 527

East Wind: West Wind (Buck), **Supp. II Part 1:** 114–115

Easy Rawlins mysteries, **Supp. XIII:** 236, **237–241,** 242

Easy Rider (film), **Supp. XI:** 293, **308,** 309

Eat a Bowl of Tea (Chu), **Supp. X:** 291

"Eating " (Bass), **Supp. XVI:** 23–24

"Eating Alone" (L.-Y. Lee), **Supp. XV:** 214

Eating Naked (Dobyns), **Supp. XIII:** 78–79

"Eating Out" (L. Michaels), **Supp. XVI:** 209

"Eating Poetry" (Strand), **Supp. IV Part 2:** 626

"Eating the Whole" (C. Frost), **Supp. XV:** 101

"Eating Together" (L.-Y. Lee), **Supp. XV:** 214

"Eating with My Fingers" (C. Frost), **Supp. XV:** 97

Eaton, Edith, **Supp. X:** 291

Eaton, Peggy, **Supp. I Part 2:** 461

Eaton, Winnifred, **Supp. X:** 291

"Eatonville Anthology, The" (Hurston), **Supp. VI:** 152

Eat the Document (film, Pennebaker), **Supp. XVIII:** 19, 26, 27, 28

"Ebb and Flow, The" (Taylor), **IV:** 161

"Ebenezer Marsh, 1725" (Schnackenberg), **Supp. XV:** 256

Eben Holden (Bacheller), **I:** 216

Eberhardt, Isabelle, **Supp. IV Part 1:** 92

Eberhart, Mrs., **I:** 521–522, 530

Eberhart, Richard, **I: 521–543; II:** 535–536; **III:** 527; **IV:** 416; **Retro. Supp. II:** 176, 178; **Supp. I Part 1:** 83; **Supp. XII:** 119

Eble, Kenneth E., **Supp. I Part 1:** 201

Eccentricities of a Nightingale (T. Williams), **IV:** 382, 385, 397, 398

Ecclesiastica Historia Integram Ecclesiae (Taylor), **IV:** 163

"Echart" (Sobin), **Supp. XVI:** 289

"Echo, The" (Bowles), **Supp. IV Part 1:** 84, 86, 87

Echoes inside the Labyrinth (McGrath), **Supp. X:** 127

Echo Park (Connelly), **Supp. XXI: 77–78**

Eckehart, Meister, **Supp. XV:** 225

Eckhart, Maria, **Supp. V:** 212

Eclipse (Hogan), **Supp. IV Part 1:** 397, 400, 402

Eclipse, a Nightmare (Montalembert), **Supp. XV:** 349

Eclogues (Virgil), **Supp. VIII:** 31

"Ecologue" (Ginsberg), **Supp. II Part 1:** 326

"Ecologues of These States 1969–1971" (Ginsberg), **Supp. II Part 1:** 325

Ecology of a Cracker Childhood (Ray), **Supp. XVIII:** 189, 191, 192, 193, **195–199**, 201, 202, 204

"Economics of Negro Emancipation in the United States, The" (Du Bois), **Supp. II Part 1:** 174

"Economics of the Cracker Landscape: Poverty as an Environmental Issue in Larry Brown's *Joe*" (Watson), *Supp. XXI:* 46

"Economic Theory of Women's Dress, The" (Veblen), **Supp. I Part 2:** 636

Economy of the Unlost: Reading Simonides of Keos with Paul Celan (Carson), **Supp. XII:** 110–111

Ecotactics: The Sierra Club Handbook for Environmental Activists (Mitchell and Stallings, eds.), **Supp. IV Part 2:** 488

"Ecstasy" (Bierds), **Supp. XVII:** 34

"Ecstasy" (Olds), **Supp. X:** 206

"Ecstasy of Influence, The" (Lethem), **Supp. XVIII:** 150

"Ecstatic" (Komunyakaa), **Supp. XIII:** 131

Edda, **Supp. X:** 114

Eddy, Mary Baker, **I:** 583; **III:** 506

Edel, Leon, **I:** 20; **II:** 338–339; **Retro. Supp. I:** 218, 224, 231

Edelberg, Cynthia, **Supp. IV Part 1:** 155

"Eden and My Generation" (Levis), **Supp. XI:** 270

Edenbaum, Robert, **Supp. IV Part 1:** 352

Eden Tree (Bynner), **Supp. XV:** 42, 51

Edenville Owls (Parker), **Supp. XIX:** 190

Eder, Richard, **Supp. XII:** 189; **Supp. XV:** 62, 187, 259, 261

Edgar Huntly; or, Memoirs of a Sleep-Walker (Brown), **Supp. I Part 1:** 140–144, 145

"Edge" (Plath), **Retro. Supp. II:** 256; **Supp. I Part 2:** 527, 547

Edge, Mary E., **II:** 316

"Edge of Possibility, The: Susan Warner and the World of Sunday School Fiction" (S. Gates), **Supp. XVIII:** 267

"Edge of the Great Rift, The" (Theroux), **Supp. VIII:** 325

Edge of the Sea, The (Carson), **Supp. IX:** 19, **25–31,** 32

Edgers, Geoff, **Supp. XV:** 113

Edgeworth, Maria, **II:** 8; **Supp. XV:** 231; **Supp. XX:**108

Edible Woman, The (Atwood), **Supp. XIII:** 19, 20, **20–21**

"Edict by the King of Prussia, An" (Franklin), **II:** 120

Edie: An American Biography (Stein), **Supp. XVI:** 245

Edinburgh Days: or, Doing What I Want to Do (Pickering), **Supp. XXI:** 200–201

Edison, Thomas A., **I:** 483; **Supp. I Part 2:** 392

Edith Wharton (Joslin), **Retro. Supp. I:** 376

Edith Wharton: A Biography (Lewis), **Retro. Supp. I:** 362

Edith Wharton: A Woman in Her Time (Auchincloss), **Retro. Supp. I:** 370

Edith Wharton: Matters of Mind and Spirit (Singley), **Retro. Supp. I:** 373

Edith Wharton's Argument with America (Ammons), **Retro. Supp. I:** 364

Edith Wharton's Brave New Politics (Bauer), **Retro. Supp. I:** 381

Edith Wharton's Letters from the Underworld (Waid), **Retro. Supp. I:** 360

Edith Wharton: Traveller in the Land of Letters (Goodwyn), **Retro. Supp. I:** 370

"Editing and Glosses" (Reznikoff), **Supp. XIV:** 283

Editing of Emily Dickinson, The (Franklin), **Retro. Supp. I:** 41

"Editor and the Schoolma'am, The" (Frederic), **II:** 130

"Editor's Easy Chair" (Howells), **II:** 276

"Editor's Study, The" (Howells), **II:** 275, 276, 285

"Editor Whedon" (Masters), **Supp. I Part 2:** 463

Edlin, Mari, **Supp. X:** 266

Edman, Irwin, **III:** 605

Edmond (Mamet), **Supp. XIV:** 241, 248, 249, 250

Edmundson, Mark, **Retro. Supp. II:** 262

Edsel (Shapiro), **Supp. II Part 2:** 703, 704, 717–719

Edson, Margaret, **Supp. XVIII: 35–52**

Edson, Russell, **Supp. VIII:** 279

"Educated American Woman, An" (Cheever), **Supp. I Part 1:** 194

"Education, An" (Ozick), **Supp. V:** 267

Education and Living (Bourne), **I:** 252

"Education by Poetry" (Frost), **Supp. XV:** 215

"Education of a Storyteller, The" (Bambara), **Supp. XI:** 20

Education of Black People, The (Du Bois), **Supp. II Part 1:** 186

Education of Harriet Hatfield, The (Sarton), **Supp. VIII: 257–258**

Education of Henry Adams, The (Adams), **I:** 1, 5, 6, 11, 14, 15–18, 19, 20–21, 111; **II:** 276; **III:** 504; **Retro. Supp. I:** 53, 59; **Supp. IX:** 19; **Supp. XIV:** 299

Education of H*y*m*a*n K*a*p*l*a*n, The (Rosten), **Supp. XVII:** 9

"Education of Mingo, The" (Johnson), **Supp. VI:** 193, 194

"Education of Norman Podhoretz, The" (Goldberg), **Supp. VIII:** 238

Education of Oscar Fairfax, The (Auchincloss), **Supp. IV Part 1:** 25, 36

"Education of the Poet" (Glück), **Supp. V:** 78, 80

Education sentimentale (Flaubert), **III:** 315

"Education the Imagination" (Koch), **Supp. XV:** 175–176, 177

Edwards, Clifford, **Supp. XVIII:** 220

Edwards, Eli. *See* McKay, Claude

Edwards, Esther, **I:** 545

Edwards, John, **I:** 478

Edwards, Jonathan, **I: 544–566; II:** 432; **Retro. Supp. II:** 187; **Supp. I Part 1:** 301, 302; **Supp. I Part 2:** 552, 594, 700; **Supp. IV Part 2:** 430; **Supp. VIII:** 205

Edwards, Sarah, **I:** 545

Edwards, Thomas, **Supp. XV:** 20

Edwards, Thomas R., **Supp. XVI:** 207

Edwards, Timothy, **I:** 545

Edwards-Yearwood, Grace, **Supp. VIII:** 81

"Edwin Arlington Robinson" (Cowley), **Supp. II Part 1:** 144

Edwin Arlington Robinson (Winters), **Supp. II Part 2:** 812

Edwin Booth (play), **Supp. IV Part 1:** 89

E. E. Cummings (Marks), **I:** 438

E. E. Cummings: A Miscellany (Cummings), **I:** 429, 441

E. E. Cummings: A Miscellany, Revised (Cummings), **I:** 429

"Effects of Analogy" (Stevens), **Retro. Supp. I:** 297

Effluences from the Sacred Caves; More Selected Essays and Reviews (Carruth), **Supp. XVI:** 46

"Effort at Speech between Two People" (Rukeyser), **Supp. VI:** 276, 284

"Efforts of Affection" (Moore), **III:** 214

"Efforts of Affection: A Memoir of Marianne Moore" (Bishop), **Retro. Supp. II:** 52

Egan, Jennifer, **Supp. XIX: 49–63**

Egan, Leona, **Supp. XXI:** 6

"Egg, The" (Anderson), **I:** 113, 114

"Egg, The" (Snyder), **Supp. VIII:** 302

Eggleston, George Cary, **Supp. XVIII:** 15

"Eggplant Epithalamion, The" (Jong), **Supp. V:** 119

"Eggs" (Olds), **Supp. X:** 206

"Eggshell" (Stern), **Supp. IX:** 299

Egoist, The (Meredith), **II:** 186

Egorova, Lubov, **Supp. IX:** 58

"Egotism, or the Bosom Sergent" (Hawthorne), **II:** 227, 239

"Egyptian Pulled Glass Bottle in the Shape of a Fish, An" (Moore), **III:** 195, 213

Ehrenfels, Christian von, **Supp. XIV:** 198

Ehrenpreis, Irvin, **Supp. XII:** 128

Ehrenreich, Barbara, **Supp. XVII:** 210

Ehrhart, W. D., **Supp. XIX:** 281

Ehrlich, Gretel, **Supp. XIV:** 227; **Supp. XVIII:** 189

Eichmann, Adolf, **Supp. XII:** 166

Eichmann in Jerusalem (Arendt), **Retro. Supp. II:** 28; **Supp. VIII:** 243; **Supp. XII:** 166

"Eichmann in New York: The New York Intellectuals and the Hannah Arendt Controversy" (Rabinbach), **Supp. XII:** 166

"Eidolon" (Warren), **IV:** 239

"Eiger Dreams" (Krakauer), **Supp. XVIII:** 107

Eiger Dreams: Ventures Among Men and Mountains (Krakauer), **Supp. XVIII:** 105, 106, 107

Eight Cousins (Alcott), **Supp. I Part 1:** 29, 38, 42, 43

18 Poems from the Quechua (Strand, trans.), **Supp. IV Part 2:** 630

"18 West 11th Street" (Merrill), **Supp. III Part 1:** 323, 328

1876: A Novel (Vidal), **Supp. IV Part 2:** 677, 684, 688, 689, 691, 692; **Supp. XIX:** 141

"18,000 CDs" (Halliday), **Supp. XIX:** 92

"Eighth Air Force" (Jarrell), **II:** 373–374, 377

Eight Harvard Poets, **I:** 429, 475

"Eighth Avenue Incident" (Halliday), **Supp. XIX:** 89–90

"Eighth Day, The" (Apple), **Supp. XVII:** 6, 50

"Eighth Ditch, The" (Baraka), **Supp. II Part 1:** 40

"'80s Pastoral: Frederick Barthelme's *Moon Deluxe* Ten Years On" (Peters), **Supp. XI:** 39

Eight Men (Wright), **IV:** 478, 488, 494

80 Flowers (Zukofsky), **Supp. III Part 2:** 631

Eikon Basilike, The, **Supp. IV Part 2:** 435

Eileen (Masters), **Supp. I Part 2:** 460

Eimi (Cummings), **I:** 429, 433, 434, 439–440

"Einstein" (MacLeish), **III:** 5, 8, 10–11, 18–19

Einstein, Albert, **I:** 493; **III:** 8, 10, 21, 161; **IV:** 69, 375, 410, 411, 421; **Retro. Supp. I:** 63; **Supp. I Part 2:** 609, 643; **Supp. III Part 2:** 621; **Supp. V:** 290; **Supp. XII:** 45

Eiseley, Loren, **III:** 227–228

Eisenhower, Dwight D., **I:** 136, 376; **II:** 548; **III:** 215; **IV:** 75; **Supp. I Part 1:** 291; **Supp. III Part 2:** 624; **Supp. V:** 45

Eisenstadt, Jill, **Supp. XVIII:** 135

Eisenstein, Sergei, **I:** 481; **Supp. XXI:** 170

Eisinger, Chester E., **I:** 302; **II:** 604; **Supp. IX:** 15

Eisner, Douglas, **Supp. X:** 155

Elam, Angela, **Supp. XI:** 290

El Bernardo (Balbuena), **Supp. V:** 11

Elbert, Sarah, **Supp. I Part 1:** 34, 41

Elder, Donald, **II:** 417, 426, 435, 437; **Supp. XV:** 137

Elder, John, **Supp. IX:** 25

Elder, Lonne, III, **Supp. IV Part 1:** 362

Elder, Richard, **Supp. XII:** 172

"Elder Sister, The" (Olds), **Supp. X:** 205–206

Elder Statesman, The (Eliot), **I:** 572, 573, 583; **Retro. Supp. I:** 53, 65

E. L. Doctorow (Harter and Thompson), **Supp. IV Part 1:** 217

Eldredge, Kay, **Supp. IX:** 254, 259

Eldridge, Florence, **III:** 154, 403; **IV:** 357

Eleanor of Aquitaine, **III:** 470

Eleanor of Guienne, **I:** 14

"Elect, The" (Taylor), **Supp. V:** 323

"Elections, Nicaragua, 1984" (Kingsolver), **Supp. VII:** 208

Elective Affinities (Goethe; Bogan and Mayer, trans.), **Supp. III Part 1:** 63

Electra (Euripides), **III:** 398

Electra (Sophocles), **III:** 398; **IV:** 370; **Supp. IX:** 102

"Electra on Azalea Path" (Plath), **Supp. I Part 2:** 538

"Electrical Storm" (Bishop), **Supp. I Part 1:** 93

"Electrical Storm" (Hayden), **Supp. II Part 1:** 370

"Electric Arrows" (Proulx), **Supp. VII:** 256

"Electricity Saviour" (Olds), **Supp. X:** 215

Electric Kool-Aid Acid Test, The (Wolfe), **Supp. III Part 2:** 575–577, 582–584; **Supp. XI:** 239

Electric Lady, The (film), **Supp. XI:** 309

Elegant Extracts (Knox), **II:** 8

"Elegant Tom Dillar" (Briggs), **Supp. XVIII:** 17

Elegiac Feelings American (Corso), **Supp. XII: 131–134**

"Elegiac Fragments" (Everwine), **Supp. XV:** 89

Elegies (Rukeyser), **Supp. VI:** 273

"Elegies" (Rukeyser), **Supp. VI:** 272

"Elegies for Paradise Valley" (Hayden), **Supp. II Part 1:** 363

"Elegy" (Bidart), **Supp. XV:** 25, 29

Elegy (Levis), **Supp. XI:** 257, 259, 261, **271–272**

"Elegy" (Merwin), **Supp. III Part 1:** 351

"Elegy" (Stafford), **Supp. XI:** 322

"Elegy" (Tate), **IV:** 128

"Elegy, for the U.S.N. Dirigible, Macon, An" (Winters), **Supp. II Part 2:** 810

"Elegy Ending in the Sound of a Skipping Rope" (Levis), **Supp. XI:** 271–272

"Elegy for 41 Whales Beached in Florence, Oregon, June 1979" (Bierds), **Supp. XVII:** 27

"Elegy for D. H. Lawrence, An" (W. C. Williams), **Retro. Supp. I:** 421

"Elegy for My Father" (Strand), **Supp. IV Part 2:** 628

"Elegy for My Mother" (Wagoner), **Supp. IX:** 330

"Elegy for Redondo Beach" (Jarman), **Supp. XVII:** 112, 113

Elegy for September, An (Nichols), **Supp. XIII:** 268

"Elegy for Thelonious" (Komunyakaa), **Supp. XIII:** 118

"Elegy for the Native Guards" (Trethewey), **Supp. XXI:** 255

"Elegy for the U.S.N. Dirigible, Macon, A" (Winters), **Supp. II Part 2:** 810

"Elegy of Last Resort" (Nemerov), **III:** 271

"Elegy with a Thimbleful of Water in the Cage" (Levis), **Supp. XI:** 272

Elegy Written in a Country Churchyard (Gray), **I:** 68

"Elegy Written in a Country Churchyard" (Gray), **Supp. XIV:** 8

"Elementary Scene, The" (Jarrell), **II:** 387, 388, 389

"Elements" (M. Frank), **Supp. X:** 213

Elements of Style, The (Strunk), **Supp. I Part 2:** 670

"Elenita, Cards, Palm, Water" (Cisneros), **Supp. VII:** 64

"Eleonora" (Poe), **III:** 412

Eleothriambos (Lee), **IV:** 158

"Elephants" (Moore), **III:** 203

"Elephant's Dance, The" (D. West), **Supp. XVIII:** 281

"Elevator, The" (Dixon), **Supp. XII:** 154

"Elevator Boy" (Hughes), **Retro. Supp. I:** 200; **Supp. I Part 1:** 326

"Eleven" (Cisneros), **Supp. VII:** 69

Eleven Essays in the European Novel (Blackmur), **Supp. II Part 1:** 91, 111

Eleven Kinds of Loneliness (Yates), **Supp. XI: 340–343,** 349

Eleven Poems on the Same Theme (Warren), **IV:** 239–241

"Eleven Times a Poem" (Corso), **Supp. XII:** 132, 133

El Greco (Doménikos Theotokópoulos), **I:** 387; **III:** 212

El-Hage, George N., **Supp. XX:** 116

"El-Hajj Malik El-Shabazz" (Hayden), **Supp. II Part 1:** 379

"Eli, the Fanatic" (P. Roth), **Supp. III Part 2:** 407–408

Eliade, Mircea, **Supp. XVI:** 292

Eliot, Charles William, **I:** 5; **II:** 345; **Retro. Supp. I:** 55; **Supp. I Part 2:** 479; **Supp. IX:** 94

Eliot, George, **I:** 375, 458, 459, 461, 467; **II:** 179, 181, 191–192, 275, 319, 324, 338, 577; **IV:** 311, 322; **Retro. Supp. I:** 218, 220, 225; **Supp. I Part 1:** 370; **Supp. I Part 2:** 559, 579; **Supp. IV Part 1:** 31, 297; **Supp. IV Part 2:** 677; **Supp. V:** 258; **Supp. IX:** 38, 43, 51; **Supp. XI:** 68; **Supp. XII:** 335; **Supp. XIV:** 344; **Supp. XX:**108

Eliot, T. S., **I:** 48, 49, 52, 59, 60, 64, 66, 68, 105, 107, 215–216, 236, 243, 256, 259, 261, 266, 384, 386, 395, 396, 399, 403, 430, 433, 441, 446, 475, 478, 479, 482, 521, 522, 527, **567–591; II:** 65, 96, 158, 168, 316, 371, 376, 386, 529, 530, 532, 537, 542, 545; **III:** 1, 4, 5, 6, 7–8, 9, 10, 11, 14, 17, 20, 21, 23, 26, 34, 174, 194, 195–196, 205–206, 220, 236, 239, 269, 270–271, 277–278, 301, 409, 428, 435, 436, 453, 456–457, 459–460, 461–462, 464, 466, 471, 476, 478, 485, 488, 492, 493, 498, 504, 509, 511, 517, 524, 527, 539, 572, 575, 586, 591, 594, 600, 613; **IV:** 27, 74, 82, 83, 95, 122, 123, 127, 129, 134, 138, 140, 141, 191, 201, 237, 331, 379, 402, 403, 418, 419, 420, 430, 431, 439, 442, 491; **Retro. Supp. I:** **51–71**, 74, 80, 89, 91, 171, 198, 210, 283, 289, 290, 292, 296, 298, 299, 311, 324, 359, 411, 413, 414, 416, 417, 420, 428; **Retro. Supp. II:** 79, 178, 189, 262, 326; **Supp. I Part 1:** 257, 264, 268, 270, 274, 299; **Supp. I Part 2:** 387, 423, 455, 536, 554, 624, 659, 721; **Supp. II Part 1:** 1, 4, 8, 20, 30, 91, 98, 103, 136, 314; **Supp. III Part 1:** 9, 10, 26, 31, 37, 41, 43, 44, 48, 62–64, 73, 91, 99–100, 105–106, 273; **Supp. III Part 2:** 541, 611, 612, 617, 624; **Supp. IV Part 1:** 40, 47, 284, 380, 404; **Supp. IV Part 2:** 436; **Supp. V:** 79, 97, 101, 338, 343, 344; **Supp. VIII:** 19, 21, 93, 102, 105, 182, 195, 205, 290, 292; **Supp. IX:** 158–159, 229; **Supp. X:** 59, 115, 119, 124, 187, 324; **Supp. XI:** 242; **Supp. XII:** 45, 159, 198, 308; **Supp. XIII:** 77, 104, 115, 332, 341–342, 344, 346; **Supp. XIV:** 5, 13, 107, 287, 290, 306, 347; **Supp. XV:** 20, 51, 139, 177, 181, 186, 216, 218, 250, 251, 258, 298, 302, 303, 306, 307; **Supp. XVI:** 158–159, 204, 207, 282; **Supp. XVII:** 36, 71, 75, 111, 240; **Supp. XVIII:** 136; **Supp. XIX:** 12; **Supp. XX:**86, 108, 199

Eliot's Early Years (Gordon), **Retro. Supp. I:** 55

"Elizabeth" (Longfellow), **I:** 502

"Elizabeth, 1905" (Schnackenberg), **Supp. XV:** 253, 256

Elizabeth Appleton (O'Hara), **III:** 362, 364, 375–377

"Elizabeth Bishop (1911–1979)" (Merrill), **Retro. Supp. II:** 53

"Elizabeth Bishop in Brazil" (Brown), **Supp. I Part 1:** 96

"Elizabeth Bishop's *North & South*" (Lowell), *Retro. Supp. II:* 40–41

"Elizabeth Gone" (Sexton), **Supp. II Part 2:** 674, 681

Elizabeth Rex (Findley), **Supp. XX:62–63**

Elizabeth Stoddard and the Boundaries of Bourgeois Culture (Mahoney), **Supp. XV:** 270

Elk Heads on the Wall (Ríos), **Supp. IV Part 2:** 540

Elkin, Stanley, **Supp. VI: 41–59**

"Elk Song" (Hogan), **Supp. IV Part 1:** 406

Ella in Bloom (Hearon), **Supp. VIII: 70–71**

Elledge, Jim, **Supp. XIII:** 88

Ellen Foster: A Novel (Gibbons), **Supp. X:** 41, **42–44**, 46, 47, 49, 50

Ellen Montgomery's Bookshelf (S. and A. Warner), **Supp. XVIII:** 264

Ellen Rogers (Farrell), **II:** 42–43

"Ellen's Dream" (Gioia), **Supp. XV:** 128

"Ellen West" (Bidart), **Supp. XV: 26–27**

Eller, Ernest, **Supp. I Part 2:** 497

Ellerman, Winifred, **Supp. I Part 1:** 258–259. *See also* McAlmon, Mrs. Robert (Winifred Ellerman)

"*El libro de la sexualidad*" (Simic), *Supp. VIII:* 283

Ellington, Duke, **Retro. Supp. II:** 115; **Supp. IV Part 1:** 360; **Supp. IX:** 164

Elliot, Charles, **Supp. V:** 161

Elliot, George P., **Supp. XV:** 92

Elliott, George B., **III:** 478

Ellipse, The: Selected Poems of Leonardo Sinisgalli (Di Piero, trans.), **Supp. XIX:** 34

"Ellipsis" (C. Frost), **Supp. XV:** 107

Ellis, Albert, **Supp. IV Part 2:** 527

Ellis, Anne, **Supp. XVI:** 38

Ellis, Bret Easton, **Supp. XII:** 81; **Supp. XVIII:** 135

Ellis, Brett Easton, **Supp. X:** 7

Ellis, Charles, **Supp. I Part 1:** 99

Ellis, Havelock, **II:** 276; **Supp. XX:**117, 235

Ellis, John Harvard, **Supp. I Part 1:** 103

Ellis, Katherine, **IV:** 114

Ellis, Kelly, **Supp. XXI:** 249

Ellis, Thomas Sayers, **Supp. XXI:** 246

Ellison, Harlan, **Supp. XIII:** 61

Ellison, Ralph, **IV:** 250, 493; **Retro. Supp. II:** 3, **111–130; Supp. II Part 1:** 33, **221–252; Supp. IV, Part 1:** 374; **Supp. VIII:** 105, 245; **Supp. IX:** 114, 316; **Supp. X:** 324; **Supp. XI:** 18, 92, 275; **Supp. XIII:** 186, 233, 305; **Supp. XIV:** 306; **Supp. XV:** 194; **Supp. XVI:** 135, 139; **Supp. XVIII:** 59, 61, 62, 277, 283; **Supp. XIX:** 148, 149, 155

Ellmann, Maud, **Supp. IV Part 1:** 302

Ellmann, Richard, **Supp. VIII:** 105; **Supp. XV:** 74

Ellroy, James, **Supp. XIV:** 26; **Supp. XXI:** 71

Elman, Richard, **Supp. V:** 40

"Elmer" (Faulkner), **Retro. Supp. I:** 79, 80

Elmer Gantry (Lewis), **I:** 26, 364; **II:** 447–449, 450, 455

Elmer the Great (Lardner), **II:** 427

"Elms" (Glück), **Supp. V:** 85

"Elms Dying, The—And My Friend, Lew Stillwell, Dead" (Bronk), **Supp. XXI:** 31

Eloges (Perse), **Supp. XIII:** 344

"Eloquence of Grief, An" (Crane), **I:** 411

"El Río Grande" (Mora), **Supp. XIII:** 224

"*El* Round up" (Alvarez), **Supp. VII:** 11

"El Salvador: Requiem and Invocation" (Levertov), **Supp. III Part 1:** 284

Elsasser, Henry, **I:** 226

"Elsa Wertman" (Masters), **Supp. I Part 2:** 462–463

Elsie John and Joey Martinez: Two Stories (Huncke), **Supp. XIV:** 148

Elsie Venner (Holmes), **Supp. I Part 1:** 243, 315–316

Elton, Charles, **Supp. XIV:** 192

Éluard, Paul, **III:** 528; **Supp. IV Part 1:** 80; **Supp. XVII:** 244

Elvins, Kells, **Supp. III Part 1:** 93, 101

Ely, Richard T., **Supp. I Part 1:** 5; **Supp. I Part 2:** 640, 645

"Emancipation. A Life Fable" (Chopin), **Retro. Supp. II:** 59; **Supp. I Part 1:** 207–208

"Emancipation in the British West Indies" (Emerson), **II:** 13

"Emancipation Proclamation, The" (Emerson), **II:** 13

Emanuel, James, **Supp. I Part 1:** 346

Embargo, The (Bryant), **Supp. I Part 1:** 152–153

Embarrassments (James), **Retro. Supp. I:** 229

Embezzler, The (Auchincloss), **Supp. IV Part 1:** 24, 30–31

"Embroidery, The" (C. Frost), **Supp. XV:** 97

"Emerald" (Doty), **Supp. XI:** 131

"Emerald, The" (Merrill), **Supp. III Part 1:** 328

Emerald City (Egan), **Supp. XIX:** 49, **52–53**

"Emerald City" (Egan), **Supp. XIX:** 52

"Emergence of Flight from Aristotle's Mud, The" (Goldbarth), **Supp. XII:** 190

"Emergency Haying" (Carruth), **Supp. XVI:** 55

"Emergency Room" (Mora), **Supp. XIII:** 218

"Emerging Voices: The Teaching of Writing" (Mora), **Supp. XIII:** 220

Emerson, and Other Essays (Chapman), **Supp. XIV:** 41–44

Emerson, Ellen, **Supp. I Part 1:** 33

Emerson, John, **Supp. XVI:** 185, 186, 190, 192

Emerson, Ralph Waldo, **I:** 98, 217, 220, 222, 224, 228, 239, 246, 251, 252, 253, 257, 260, 261, 283, 386, 397, 402, 424, 433, 444, 447, 455, 458, 460–461, 463, 464, 485, 561; **II: 1–24,**

49, 92, 127–128, 169, 170, 226, 233, 237, 273–274, 275, 278, 289, 295, 301, 313, 315, 336, 338, 344, 402, 491, 503; **III:** 53, 82, 171, 174, 260, 277, 409, 424, 428, 453, 454, 507, 576–577, 606, 614; **IV:** 60, 167, 169, 170, 171, 172, 173–174, 176, 178, 183, 186, 187, 192, 201, 202, 211, 335, 338, 340, 342, 350; **Retro. Supp. I:** 34, 53, 54, 57, 62, 74–75, 76, 125, 148–149, 152–153, 159, 217, 250, 298, 392, 400, 403; **Retro. Supp. II:** 96, 113, 135, 142, 155, 207, 262; **Supp. I Part 1:** 2, 28–29, 31, 33, 188, 299, 308–309, 317, 358, 365, 366, 368; **Supp. I Part 2:** 374, 383, 393, 407, 413, 416, 420, 422, 474, 482, 580, 582, 602, 659, 679; **Supp. II Part 1:** 280, 288; **Supp. III Part 1:** 387; **Supp. IV Part 2:** 439, 597, 619; **Supp. V:** 118; **Supp. VIII:** 42, 105, 106, 108, 198, 201, 204, 205, 292; **Supp. IX:** 38, 90, 175, 176, 181; **Supp. X:** 42, 45, 121, 223; **Supp. XI:** 203; **Supp. XIII:** 141, 145, 233, 246, **Supp. XIII:** 247; **Supp. XIV:** 41–44, 46, 54, 104, 177; **Supp. XV:** 219, 224; **Supp. XVI:** 84; **Supp. XVII:** 42, 236; **Supp. XX:** 115, 116; **Supp. XXI:** 217

"Emerson and the Essay" (Gass), **Supp. VI:** 88

"Emerson the Lecturer" (Lowell), **Supp. I Part 2:** 420, 422

Emerson-Thoreau Award, **Retro. Supp. I:** 67

Emery, Clark, **III:** 478

E. M. Forster (Trilling), **Supp. III Part 2:** 496, 501, 504

"Emigre in Autumn, An" (Gioia), **Supp. XV:** 120

"Emily Dickinson and Class" (Erkkila), **Retro. Supp. I:** 42–43

Emily Dickinson Editorial Collective, **Retro. Supp. I:** 47

Emily Dickinson in Southern California (X. J. Kennedy), **Supp. XV: 164–165**

"Emily Dickinson's Defunct" (Nelson), **Supp. XVIII:** 173

Emily Dickinson: Woman Poet (Bennett), **Retro. Supp. I:** 42

Eminent Victorians (Strachey), **Supp. I Part 2:** 485

Emma (Austen), **Supp. XVIII:** 149

"Emma and Eginhard" (Longfellow), **III:** 505

"Emma Enters a Sentence of Elizabeth Bishop's" (Gass), **Supp. VI:** 93

Emmanuel Appodocca: or, A Blighted Life (Philip), **Supp. XXI:** 160

"Emmaus" (Di Piero), **Supp. XIX:** 42, 43

Emperor Jones, The (O'Neill), **II:** 278; **III:** 391, 392

Emperor of Haiti (Hughes), **Supp. I Part 1:** 339

"Emperor of Ice Cream, The" (Stevens), **IV:** 76, 80–81

"Emperors" (Dunn), **Supp. XI:** 155

"Emperor's New Clothes, The" (Anderson), **I:** 441

"Empire" (Ford), **Supp. V:** 69

Empire: A Novel (Vidal), **Supp. IV Part 2:** 677, 684, 686, 690; **Supp. XIX:** 132

"Empire Builders" (MacLeish), **III:** 14

Empire Falls (Russo), **Supp. XII: 339–343**

Empire of Summer, The (Doty), **Supp. XI:** 120

Empire of the Senseless (Acker), **Supp. XII:** 5, **6,** 14–16

"Empires" (Simic), **Supp. VIII:** 282

"Emporium" (Shapiro), **Supp. II Part 2:** 705

Empress of the Splendid Season (Hijuelos), **Supp. VIII:** 86–89

Empson, William, **I:** 522, 533; **II:** 536; **III:** 286, 497, 498, 499; **IV:** 136, 431; **Retro. Supp. I:** 263; **Retro. Supp. II:** 253; **Supp. XVI:** 190

Empty Hands, The (Bronk), **Supp. XXI:** 31

"Empty Hills, The" (Winters), **Supp. II Part 2:** 792, 793, 796

Empty Mirror, Early Poems (Ginsberg), **Supp. II Part 1:** 308, 311, 313–314, 319, 329

"Empty Room" (Hughes), **Supp. I Part 1:** 337

"Empty Threat, An" (Frost), **II:** 159

Emshwiller, Ed, **Supp. XVIII:** 145

"Encantadas, The" (Melville), **III:** 89; **Supp. XVIII:** 4

Enchanter, The (Nabokov), **Retro. Supp. I:** 266

"Enclosed Dreams, Highways and Labyrinths: Jonathan Lethem's *Amnesia Moon*" (Rossi), *Supp. XVIII:* 139

"Encomium Twenty Years Later" (Tate), **I:** 381

"Encounter" (Espaillat), **Supp. XXI:** 107

"Encounter, The" (Pound), **III:** 466

Encounter in April (Sarton), **Supp. VIII:** 259

"Encounter in April" (Sarton), **Supp. VIII:** 259

"Encountering the Sublime" (McClatchy), **Supp. XII:** 261

"Encounter on the Seine: Black Meets Brown" (Baldwin), **Retro. Supp. II:** 2

Encounters with Chinese Writers (Dillard), **Supp. VI:** 19, 23, 31

Encounters with the Archdruid (McPhee), **Supp. III Part 1:** 292–294, 301; **Supp. X:** 30

Encyclopedia of Scotland, The (A. Finch), **Supp. XVII: 70–71**

Encyclopedia of World Biography, The, **Supp. XXI:** 74

"End, The" (Olds), **Supp. X:** 205

"Endangered Species" (Mora), **Supp. XIII:** 219–220

Endecott and the Red Cross (Lowell), **II:** 545

Endgame (Beckett), **Supp. XIII:** 196

"Endgame" (Tan), **Supp. X:** 290

"Endicott and the Red Cross" (Hawthorne), **Retro. Supp. II:** 181, 187–188

"End of Books, The" (Coover), **Supp. V:** 53

End of Dreams, The (Skloot), **Supp. XX:** 196, **202–203**

End of Education, The (Postman), **Supp. XI:** 275

"End of FIRPO in the World, The" (Saunders), **Supp. XIX:** 229

"End of Season" (Warren), **IV:** 239–240

"End of Something, The" (Hemingway), **II:** 248

End of the Affair, The (Greene), **Supp. XI:** 99

End of the Age of Innocence, The (Price), **Retro. Supp. I:** 377

"End of the Line, The" (Jarrell), **III:** 527

"End of the Rainbow, The" (Jarrell), **II:** 386

End of the Road (film), **Supp. XI:** 309

End of the Road, The (Barth), **I:** 121, 122, 126–131; **Supp. XI:** 309; **Supp. XVIII:** 140, 141

"End of the World, The" (Gioia), **Supp. XV:** 126

"End of the World, The" (MacLeish), **III:** 8

Endor (Nemerov), **III:** 269, 270, 279

Endore, Guy, **Supp. XVII: 53–67**

"Ends" (Dixon), **Supp. XII:** 153

End to Innocence, An: Essays on Culture and Politics (Fiedler), **Supp. XIII: 98–99**

Endure: The Diaries of Charles Walter Stetson (Stetson), **Supp. XI:** 196

"Enduring Chill, The" (O'Connor), **III:** 349, 351, 357; **Retro. Supp. II:** 236

Enduring Vision of Norman Mailer, The (Leeds), **Retro. Supp. II:** 204

Endymion (Keats), **IV:** 405; **Retro. Supp. I:** 412

End Zone (DeLillo), **Supp. VI:** 2, 3, 4, 10, 11, 12

Enemies (Boyce and Hapgood), **Supp. XVII:** 100; **Supp. XXI:** 7, 13

Enemies: A Love Story (Singer), **IV:** 1; **Retro. Supp. II: 310–311**

Enemy, The: Time (T. Williams), **IV:** 391

Enemy of the People, An (adapt. Miller), **III:** 154–156

"Energy Vampire" (Ginsberg), **Supp. II Part 1:** 326

"Enforcement of the Slave Trade Laws, The" (Du Bois), **Supp. II Part 1:** 161

"Engaging the Past" (Bell), **Supp. X:** 17

Engel, Bernard F., **II:** 532

Engels, Friedrich, **IV:** 429, 443–444; **Supp. I Part 1:** 13; **Supp. XXI:** 162

Engineer of Beasts, The (Sanders), **Supp. XVI:** 270

Engineer of Moonlight (DeLillo), **Supp. VI:** 4

Engineers and the Price System, The (Veblen), **I:** 475–476; **Supp. I Part 2:** 638, 642, 648

Engines of Creation: the Coming Era of Nanotechnology (Drexler), **Supp. XVI:** 121

"England" (Moore), **III:** 203, 207, 214

Englander, Nathan, **Supp. XX:** 177, 179

Engle, Paul, **III:** 542; **Retro. Supp. II:** 220, 221; **Supp. V:** 337; **Supp. XI:** 315; **Supp. XIII:** 76; **Supp. XVIII:** 72

English, Zoë, **Supp. XVI:** 293

English Elegy, The: Studies in the Genre from Spenser to Yeats (Sacks), **Supp. IV Part 2:** 450

English Hours (James), **II:** 337; **Retro. Supp. I:** 235

English Language, The (L. P. Smith), **Supp. XIV:** 341

English-Latin Gradus or Verse Dictionary, An (Ainger), **Supp. XX:** 230

Englishmen of Letters (James), **II:** 327

English Notebooks, The (Hawthorne), **II:** 226, 227–228

English Novel, The (Lanier), **Supp. I Part 1:** 371

English Poets, The: Lessing, Rousseau (Lowell), **Supp. I Part 2:** 407

English Prosody and Modern Poetry (Shapiro), **Supp. II Part 2:** 710

English Traits (Emerson), **II:** 1, 5, 6–7, 8

"English Writers on America" (Irving), **II:** 308

Engstrand, Stuart, **Supp. I Part 1:** 51

"Enigma Variations" (Nelson), **Supp. XVIII:** 177

"Enoch and the Gorilla" (O'Connor), **Retro. Supp. II:** 225

Enormous Changes at the Last Minute (Paley), **Supp. VI:** 218

"Enormous Changes at the Last Minute" (Paley), **Supp. VI:** 226, 232

"Enormous Radio, The" (Cheever), **Supp. I Part 1:** 175–177, 195

Enormous Radio and Other Stories, The (Cheever), **Supp. I Part 1:** 175–177

Enormous Room, The (Cummings), **I:** 429, 434, 440, 445, 477; **Supp. XXI:** 277

"Enough for a Lifetime" (Buck), **Supp. II Part 1:** 127

Enough Rope (Parker), **Supp. IX:** 189, 192

Enquiry Concerning Political Justice (Godwin), **Supp. I Part 1:** 126, 146

Entered From the Sun (Garrett), **Supp. VII:** 105–106, 107–109

"Entering the Kingdom" (Oliver), **Supp. VII:** 234

Entertaining Strangers (Gurney), **Supp. V:** 98, 99

Enter without Desire (Lacy), **Supp. XV:** 201

Entrance: Four Chicano Poets, **Supp. XIII:** 316

Entrance to Porlock, The (Buechner), **Supp. XII:** 52

Entries (Berry), **Supp. X:** 23

"Entropy" (Pynchon), **Supp. II Part 2:** 619, 621

Entry in an Unknown Hand (F. Wright), **Supp. XVII:** 240, 244, 245

Environmental Imagination, The (Buell), **Supp. V:** 209; **Supp. IX:** 29

"Envoy" (Collins), **Supp. XXI:** 57

"Envoys, The" (Merrill), **Supp. III Part 1:** 326

"Envy; or, Yiddish in America" (Ozick), **Supp. V:** 263, 265–266

"Eolian Harp, The" (Coleridge), **I:** 284

"Eototo" (Sobin), **Supp. XVI:** 283–284

"Ephemera, The" (Franklin), **II:** 121

Ephesians (biblical book), **Supp. I Part 1:** 117

Epictetus, **III:** 566

"Epicurean, The" (Auchincloss), **Supp. IV Part 1:** 25

Epicurus, **I:** 59

Epidemic of Genius, An (Wolfert), **Supp. XXI:** 278

"Epigram" (Lowell), **II:** 550

"Epilogue" (Lowell), **Retro. Supp. II:** 191

"Epimanes" (Poe), **III:** 411

"Epimetheus" (Longfellow), **II:** 494

"Epiphany" (X. J. Kennedy), **Supp. XV:** 166, 167

"Epipsychidion" (Shelley), **Supp. I Part 2:** 718

Episode in Palmetto (Caldwell), **I:** 297, 307

"Epistle" (L.-Y. Lee), **Supp. XV:** 212

Epistle to a Godson (Auden), **Supp. II Part 1:** 24

"Epistle to Be Left in the Earth" (MacLeish), **III:** 13

"Epistle to George William Curtis" (Lowell), **Supp. I Part 2:** 416

"Epistle to Léon-Paul Fargue" (MacLeish), **III:** 15

"Epitaph Ending in And, The" (Stafford), **Supp. XI:** 321–322

Epitaph for a Dead Beat (Markson), **Supp. XVII: 136–138,** 141; 139

Epitaph for a Desert Anarchist (Bishop), **Supp. XIII:** 1

Epitaph for a Tramp (Markson), **Supp. XVII:** 136, 137, 139 142

"Epitaph for Fire and Flower" (Plath), **Supp. I Part 2:** 537

"Epitaph for the Race of Man" (Millay), **III:** 127–128

"Epithalamium" (Auden), **Supp. II Part 1:** 15

"Epstein" (P. Roth), **Retro. Supp. II:** 281; **Supp. III Part 2:** 404, 406–407, 412, 422

Epstein, Barbara, **Supp. XIX:** 268

Epstein, Helen, **Supp. XVII:** 47

Epstein, Jason, **Supp. VIII:** 233

Epstein, Joseph, **Supp. IV Part 2:** 692; **Supp. VIII:** 236, 238; **Supp. XIV: 101–117; Supp. XVI:** 230, 275

Epstein, Leslie, **Supp. XII: 159–174; Supp. XVIII:** 92, 99

Epstein, Philip, **Supp. XII:** 159

"Equal in Paris" (Baldwin), **Retro. Supp. II:** 3; **Supp. I Part 1:** 52

"Equals" (Untermeyer), **Supp. XV:** 304

Equation for Evil (Caputo), **Supp. XIX:** 25–26

"Equations of the Light" (Gioia), **Supp. XV:** 125

"Equilibrists, The" (Ransom), **III:** 490, 494

"Equipment for Pennies" (H. Roth), **Supp. IX:** 233

Erasmus, Desiderius, **Supp. XV:** 258

Erasure (Everett), **Supp. XVIII:** 54, 60, **61–62**

"Erat Hora" (Pound), **III:** 463; **Retro. Supp. I:** 413

Erdrich, Louise, **Supp. IV Part 1: 259–278,** 333, 404; **Supp. X:** 290; **Supp. XVIII:** 189

"Erectus" (Karr), **Supp. XI:** 243

"Ere Sleep Comes Down to Soothe the Weary Eyes" (Dunbar), **Supp. II Part 1:** 199, 207–208

"Ergo Non Sum. Est." (Bronk), **Supp. XXI:** 31

Erikson, Erik, **I:** 58, 214, 218

Erisman, Fred, **Supp. VIII:** 126

Erkkila, Betsy, **Retro. Supp. I:** 42; **Supp. XX:** 281, 287–288

Ernest, John, **Supp. XXI:** 24

"Ernest: or Parent for a Day" (Bourne), **I:** 232

Ernst, Max, **Retro. Supp. II:** 321

"Eros" (Komunyakaa), **Supp. XIII:** 130

"Eros and Anteros" (E. Stoddard), **Supp. XV:** 283

Eros and Civilization (Marcuse), **Supp. XII:** 2

"Eros at Temple Stream" (Levertov), **Supp. III Part 1:** 278–279

Eros the Bittersweet (Carson), **Supp. XII:** 97, **98–99**

"Eros Turannos" (Robinson), **III:** 510, 512, 513–516, 517, 518

"Eroticism in Women" (Nin), **Supp. X:** 195

"Errand" (Carver), **Supp. III Part 1:** 149

Erskine, Albert, **IV:** 261; **Retro. Supp. II:** 117

Erskine, John, **I:** 223; **Supp. X:** 183; **Supp. XIV:** 120

Erstein, Hap, **Supp. IV Part 2:** 589, 590

"Escape" (MacLeish), **III:** 4

Escape Artist, The (Wagoner), **Supp. IX:** 324, **334–335**

Escher, M. C., **Supp. XII:** 26; **Supp. XVI:** 102

"Escudilla" (Leopold), **Supp. XIV:** 188

Eshleman, Clayton, **Supp. XVI:** 284

"Eskimo Love" (Apple), **Supp. XVII:** 5

Espaillat, Rhina P., **Supp. XXI: 97–114**

Espeland, Pamela, **Supp. XVIII:** 180, 181

Espen, Hal, **Supp. X:** 15

Espey, John, **III:** 463, 468, 478

Esposito, Michael, **Supp. XX:** 34, 40

Esposito, Scott, **Supp. XVII:** 234

Essais (Renouvier), **II:** 344–345

Essay Concerning Human Understanding, An (Locke), **I:** 554; **II:** 8, 348–349

Essay on American Poetry (Brown), **Supp. I Part 1:** 156

"Essay on Aristocracy" (Paine), **Supp. I Part 2:** 515

"Essay on Friendship, An" (McClatchy), **Supp. XII:** 258–259

"Essay on Love" (Carruth), **Supp. XVI:** 56

Essay on Man (Pope), **II:** 111; **Supp. I Part 2:** 516

"Essay on Marriage" (Carruth), **Supp. XVI:** 48

Essay on Our Changing Order (Veblen), **Supp. I Part 2:** 629, 642

"Essay on Poetics" (Ammons), **Supp. VII:** 29–31

Essay on Projects (Defoe), **II:** 104

"Essay on Psychiatrists" (Pinsky), **Supp. VI:** 237, 238, 241, 242, 249, 250

Essay on Rime (Shapiro), **I:** 430; **Supp. II Part 2:** 702, 703, 708–711

"Essay on Sanity" (Dunn), **Supp. XI:** 147

"Essay on the Character of Robespierre" (Paine), **Supp. I Part 2:** 515

Essay on the Chinese Written Character (Fenollosa), **III:** 474

"Essay on What I Think About Most" (Carson), **Supp. XII: 111–112**

Essays (Emerson), **II:** 1, 7, 8, 12–13, 15, 21

Essays, Speeches, and Public Letters by William Faulkner (Meriweather, ed.), **Retro. Supp. I:** 77

Essays in Anglo-Saxon Law (Adams), **I:** 5

Essays in London (James), **II:** 336

Essays in Radical Empiricism (James), **II:** 355, 356–357

Essays on Norman Mailer (Lucid), **Retro. Supp. II:** 195

Essays on the Nature and Principles of Taste (Alison), **Supp. I Part 1:** 151

Essays to Do Good (Mather), **II:** 104; **Supp. II Part 2:** 461, 467

"Essay: The Love of Old Houses" (Doty), **Supp. XI:** 136

"Essay Toward a Point of View, An" (Brooks), **I:** 244

"Essence, Absence, and Sobin's *Venus Blue*" (English), **Supp. XVI:** 293

Essential Haiku, The (Hass), **Supp. VI:** 102

Essential Keats (Levine, ed.), **Supp. V:** 179

"Essential Oils—are wrung" (Dickinson), **I:** 471; **Retro. Supp. I:** 43, 46

"Essentials" (Toomer), **Supp. III Part 2:** 486

Essentials: A Philosophy of Life in Three Hundred Definitions and Aphorisms (Toomer), **Supp. III Part 2:** 486

Essentials: Definitions and Aphorisms (Toomer), **Supp. IX:** 320

"Essentials of Spontaneous Prose" (Kerouac), **Supp. III Part 1:** 227–228

Estampas del valle y otras obras (Hinojosa). *See Valley, The* (Hinojosa)

"Estate Sale" (Nye), **Supp. XIII:** 283

Estess, Sybil, **Supp. IV Part 2:** 449, 452

Esther (Adams), **I:** 9–10, 20

"Esther" (Toomer), **Supp. IX:** 313–314

"Esther Kahn" (Symons), **Supp. XX:** 239

"Esthétique du Mal" (Stevens), **IV:** 79; **Retro. Supp. I:** 300, 311, 312

"Estoy-eh-muut and the Kunideeyahs (Arrowboy and the Destroyers)" (film), **Supp. IV Part 2:** 560

Estrada, Genaro, **Retro. Supp. II:** 89

Estray, The (Longfellow, ed.), **Retro. Supp. II:** 155

Esty, William, **III:** 358

"Etching, An" (Masters), **Supp. I Part 2:** 458

"Eternal Goodness, The" (Whittier), **Supp. I Part 2:** 704

Eternal Spring, The (Boyce), **Supp. XVII:** 100; **Supp. XXI:** 4, 5, 11

"Eternity, An" (W. C. Williams), **Retro. Supp. I:** 423

"Eternity Is Now" (Roethke), **III:** 544–545

"Ethan Brand" (Hawthorne), **II:** 227

Ethan Frome (Wharton), **IV:** 316–317, 327; **Retro. Supp. I:** 372–373; **Supp. IX:** 108; **Supp. XVIII:** 216

Ethics (Spinoza), **IV:** 12; **Retro. Supp. II:** 300

"Ethics of Culture, The" (Locke), **Supp. XIV:** 211

"Ethnics of Frank Costello, The" (Talese), **Supp. XVII:** 202

"Etude" (Kooser), **Supp. XIX:** 115

Etulain, Richard, **Supp. IV Part 2:** 597, 601, 604, 606, 607, 608, 610, 611

"Etymology" (Nelson), **Supp. XVIII:** 185

Euclid, **III:** 6, 620

"Euclid Alone Has Looked on Beauty Bare" (Millay), **III:** 133

"Euclidean Spaces: Linear Time" (Bronk), **Supp. XXI:** 31

Eugene, Frank, **Supp. X:** 204

Eugene Onegin (Pushkin), **III:** 246, 263

Eugene Onegin (Pushkin; Nabokov, trans.), **Retro. Supp. I:** 266, 267, 272

Eugenides, Jeffrey, **Supp. XIX:** 138; **Supp. XXI:** 229

Eugénie, Empress, **IV:** 309

Eugénie Grandet (Balzac), **II:** 328

"Eugénie Grandet" (Barthelme), **Supp. IV Part 1:** 47

"Eulogy for Richard Hugo (1923–1982)" (Wagoner), **Supp. IX:** 330–331

"Eulogy on the Flapper" (Z. Fitzgerald), **Supp. IX:** 71

Eumenides (Aeschylus), **Retro. Supp. I:** 65

"E Unibus Pluram: Television and U.S. Fiction" (Wallace), **Supp. X:** 315–316

"Euphemisms" (Matthews), **Supp. IX: 167–168**

Eureka (Poe), **III:** 409, 424, 428–429

Eurekas (Goldbarth), **Supp. XII:** 181

Euripides, **I:** 325; **II:** 8, 282, 543; **III:** 22, 145, 398; **IV:** 370; **Supp. I Part 1:** 268, 269, 270; **Supp. I Part 2:** 482; **Supp. V:** 277

"Euripides and Professor Murray" (Eliot), **Supp. I Part 1:** 268

"Euripides—A Playwright" (West), **IV:** 286; **Retro. Supp. II:** 326

"Europe" (Ashbery), **Supp. III Part 1:** 7–10, 13, 18

European Discovery of America, The: The Northern Voyages (Morison), **Supp. I Part 2:** 496–497

European Discovery of America, The: The Southern Voyages (Morison), **Supp. I Part 2:** 497

Europeans, The (H. James), **I:** 452; **II:** 327, 328; **Retro. Supp. I:** 216, 220

Europe Central (Vollmann), **Supp. XVII:** 225, 226, 227, 229, 231, **233–235,** 236

"Europe! Europe!" (Ginsberg), **Supp. II Part 1:** 320, 322

Europe of Trusts, The: Selected Poems (Howe), **Supp. IV Part 2:** 420, 422, 426

Europe without Baedeker (Wilson), **IV:** 429

Eurydice in the Underworld (Acker), **Supp. XII:** 7

Eustace, Saint, **II:** 215

Eustace Chisholm and the Works (Purdy), **Supp. VII:** 273–274, 279–280

"Euthanasia" (Tate), **IV:** 122

"Evaluation" (Bronk), **Supp. XXI:** 32

Eva-Mary (McCarriston), **Supp. XIV:** 259, 260, **263–268**

"Evangeline" (Dixon), **Supp. XII:** 153

Evangeline (Longfellow), **II:** 489, 501–502; **Retro. Supp. II:** 155, **156–159,** 162, 164; **Supp. I Part 2:** 586

Evanier, David, **Supp. XVI:** 212

Evans, Alice, **Supp. XVII:** 71, 72

Evans, Mary Ann. *See* Eliot, George

Evans, Oliver, **Supp. IV Part 1:** 85, 91

Evans, Sandy, **Supp. XIII:** 129

Evans, Walker, **I:** 36, 38, 293; **Retro. Supp. II:** 85

Eve (A. Finch), **Supp. XVII: 72–74**

"Eve" (W. C. Williams), **Retro. Supp. I:** 423

Even Cowgirls Get the Blues (Robbins), **Supp. X:** 259, 260, 261, 262–263, 264, 266, **269–271,** 272, 274, 277, 284; **Supp. XIII:** 11

"Evening" (Carver), **Supp. III Part 1:** 148

Evening (Minot), **Supp. VI:** 204–205, 208, **213–215**

"Evening at a Country Inn" (Kenyon), **Supp. VII:** 167

"Evening in Advent, An" (W. V. Davis), **Supp. XXI:** 92

"Evening in a Sugar Orchard" (Frost), **Retro. Supp. I:** 133

"Evening in Nuevo Leon, An" (Caldwell), **I:** 309

"Evening in the Sanitarium" (Bogan), **Supp. III Part 1:** 61

Evening Light, The (Skloot), **Supp. XX:** 196, **201–202**

"Evening of the 4th of July, The" (Kees), **Supp. XV:** 140, 142

"Evening on the Cote d'Azur" (Yates), **Supp. XI:** 349

Evening Performance, An: New and Selected Short Stories (Garrett), **Supp. VII:** 109

"Evenings at Home" (Hardwick), **Supp. III Part 1:** 195–196

"Evening's at Seven, The" (Thurber), **Supp. I Part 2:** 616

"Evening Star" (Bogan), **Supp. III Part 1:** 56

Evening Star, The (McMurtry), **Supp. V:** 230

Evening Star, The (screenplay, McMurtry), **Supp. V:** 232

"Evening Sun" (Kenyon), **Supp. VII:** 168

Evening Sun Turned Crimson, The (Huncke), **Supp. XIV:** 140, 149–150

"Evening Sun Turned Crimson, The" (Huncke), **Supp. XIV:** 137–138, 139

"Evening Wind, The" (Bryant), **Supp. I Part 1:** 164

"Evening without Angels" (Stevens), **Retro. Supp. I:** 302

Evening with Richard Nixon, An (Vidal), **Supp. IV Part 2:** 683

"Even Sea, The" (Swenson), **Supp. IV Part 2:** 641

Even Stephen (Perelman and West), **Retro. Supp. II:** 328

"Event, An" (Wilbur), **Supp. III Part 2:** 547, 554

"Event, The" (Dove), **Supp. IV Part 1:** 242, 247–248

"Eventide" (Brooks), **Supp. III Part 1:** 73

"Eventide" (Purdy), **Supp. VII:** 270

"Event Itself, The" (Carruth), **Supp. XVI:** 47

Eve of Saint Agnes, The (Keats), **II:** 82, 531

"Eve of St. Agnes, The" (Clampitt), **Supp. IX:** 40

"Ever a Bridegroom: Reflections on the Failure of Texas Literature" (McMurtry), **Supp. V:** 225

Everett, Alexander Hill, **Supp. I Part 1:** 152

Everett, Percival, **Supp. XVIII:** 53–67

Everlasting Story of Nory, The (Baker), **Supp. XIII:** 52, **Supp. XIII:** 53–55

"Everly Brothers, The" (Skloot), **Supp. XX:**199

Ever-Present Past, The (Hamilton), **Supp. XVI:** 196

Evers, Medgar, **IV:** 280; **Retro. Supp. II:** 13; **Supp. I Part 1:** 52, 65

Everwine, Peter, **Supp. V:** 180; **Supp. XIII:** 312; **Supp. XV:** 73–90

"Everybody's Protest Novel" (Baldwin), **Retro. Supp. II:** 4; **Supp. I Part 1:** 50, 51

"Everybody's Reading Li Po' Silk-screened on a Purple T-Shirt" (Komunyakaa), **Supp. XIII:** 120

Everybody's Story: Writing by Older Minnesotans (C. Bly, ed.), **Supp. XVI:** 38

"Everybody Was Very Nice" (Benét), **Supp. XI:** 53

"Every-Day Girl, A" (Jewett), **Retro. Supp. II:** 132

"Everyday Use" (Walker), **Supp. III Part 2:** 534

"Every-Day Work" (Jewett), **Retro. Supp. II:** 132

Everyone Says I Love You (film; Allen), **Supp. XV:** 11

Every Pleasure (Goldbarth), **Supp. XII:** 181

Every Soul Is a Circus (Lindsay), **Supp. I Part 2:** 384, 394, 399

"Everything Is a Human Being" (Walker), **Supp. III Part 2:** 527

Everything Is Illuminated (Foer), **Supp. XII:** 169

"Everything Stuck to Him" (Carver), **Supp. III Part 1:** 143

Everything That Moves (Schulberg), **Supp. XVIII:** 254

Everything That Rises Must Converge (O'Connor), **III:** 339, 348–349, 350–351; **Retro. Supp. II:** 235, 236–237

"Everything That Rises Must Converge" (O'Connor), **III:** 349, 352, 357; **Retro. Supp. II:** 236

Everything You Always Wanted to Know about Sex (film; Allen), **Supp. XV:** 4–5, 13

Eve's Diary (Twain), **IV:** 208–209

"Eve Speaks" (Untermeyer), **Supp. XV:** 300

"Eve the Fox" (Gunn Allen), **Supp. IV Part 1:** 331

"Evidence" (Harjo), **Supp. XII:** 219

Evidence of the Senses, The (Kelley), **Supp. IV Part 2:** 529

Evidence of Things Not Seen, The (Baldwin), **Retro. Supp. II:** 15

"Evil Seekers, The" (Sexton), **Supp. II Part 2:** 696

"Evolution" (Swenson), **Supp. IV Part 2:** 639

Evolving the Idol: The Poetry of Gustaf Sobin (Crick), **Supp. XVI:** 289

Ewing, Jon, **Supp. X:** 253

Ewings, The (O'Hara), **III:** 383

"Examination at the Womb Door" (Hughes), **Supp. XV:** 347

"Examination of the Hero in a Time of War" (Stevens), **Retro. Supp. I:** 305–306, 308

"Excavation of Troy" (MacLeish), **III:** 18

Excellent Becomes the Permanent, The (Addams), **Supp. I Part 1:** 25

"Excelsior" (Longfellow), **Retro. Supp. II:** 169

"Excerpts from Swan Lake" (Cameron), **Supp. XII:** 80, **84**

"Excerpts from the Epistemology Workshops" (Rand), **Supp. IV Part 2:** 529

"Excess of Charity" (Wylie), **Supp. I Part 2:** 720

"Exchange, The" (Swenson), **Supp. IV Part 2:** 644

"Excitement, The " (Jarman), **Supp. XVII:** 120–121

"Exclusive" (Olds), **Supp. X:** 206

"Excrement Poem, The" (Kumin), **Supp. IV Part 2:** 448

"Excursion" (Garrett), **Supp. VII:** 100

Excursions (Thoreau), **IV:** 188

"Excursion to Canada, An" (Thoreau), **Supp. XVIII:** 4

"Excursus of Reassurance in Begonia Time, An" (Carruth), **Supp. XVI:** 58

Executioner (Weigl), **Supp. XIX:** 277

Executioner's Song, The (Mailer), **Retro. Supp. II:** 108, 209

Exekiel, **Supp. XXI:** 91

"Exercise and Abstinence" (Swados), **Supp. XIX:** 265

Exercises in History, Chronology, and Biography, in Question and Answer (Rowson), **Supp. XV:** 245

Ex-Friends: Falling Out with Allen Ginsberg, Lionel and Diana Trilling, Lillian Hellman, Hannah Arendt, and Norman Mailer (Podhoretz), **Supp. VIII:** 239, **242–244**

"Exhausted Bug, The" (R. Bly), **Supp. IV Part 1:** 73

"Exhortation" (Bogan), **Supp. III Part 1:** 58

"Exhortation" (McKay), **Supp. X:** 135

"Exile" (Gass), **Supp. VI:** 92

"Exile" (Oates), **Supp. II Part 2:** 523

Exile, The (Buck), **Supp. II Part 1:** 119, 131

"Exiles, The" (Bradbury), **Supp. IV Part 1:** 113

"Exiles, The" (Whittier), **Supp. I Part 2:** 692–693

Exiles and Fabrications (Scott), **II:** 512

Exile's Daughter, The (Spencer), **Supp. II Part 1:** 121

"Exile's Departure, The" (Whittier), **Supp. I Part 2:** 683

Exiles from Paradise: Zelda and Scott Fitzgerald (Mayfield), **Supp. IX:** 65

"Exile's Letter" (Karr), **Supp. XI:** 241

Exile's Return (Cowley), **Supp. III Part 1:** 136, 138, 140, 141, 144, 147, 148

"Exile's Return, The" (Lowell), **II:** 539; **Retro. Supp. II:** 187

Exiles: Three Short Novels (Caputo), **Supp. XIX:** 25, **26–27**

"Existences" (Stafford), **Supp. XI:** 324

Existentialism from Dostoevsky to Sartre (W. Kaufmann), **Supp. XVII:** 137

Exit into History (Hoffman), **Supp. XVI:** 148, 150, **151–153**

Exit to Eden (Rampling), **Supp. VII:** 301–302

Exley, Frederick, **Supp. XVII:** 135

Exley, Frederick, **Supp. XVI:** 69

Exodus (biblical book), **IV:** 300

Exodus (film), **Supp. XX:**246

Exodus (Uris), **Supp. IV Part 1:** 379; **Supp. XX:**243–244, 244, 245, 247, 248, **250–251**, 257

Exodus Revisited (Uris), **Supp. XX:**247

"Exorcism" (Snodgrass), **Supp. VI:** 314

"Exorcism, An" (Malamud), **Supp. I Part 2:** 435

Exorcist, The (film), **Supp. I Part 1:** 66

"Expanses" (Dickey), **Supp. IV Part 1:** 186

"Ex Parte" (Lardner), **II:** 432

"Expatiation on the Combining of Weathers at Thirty-seventh and Indiana Where the Southern More or Less Crosses th e Dog, The" (Carruth), **Supp. XVI:**51–52

"Expectant Father Compares His Wife to a Rabbit, An" (White), **Supp. I Part 2:** 678

"Expedition to the Pole, An" (Dillard), **Supp. VI:** 32, 34

"Expelled" (Cheever), **Supp. I Part 1:** 174, 186

Expense of Greatness, The (Blackmur), **Supp. II Part 1:** 90, 107

Expense of Vision, The (Holland), **Retro. Supp. I:** 216

"Expensive Gifts" (Miller), **Supp. XII:** 294

"Expensive Moment, The" (Paley), **Supp. VI:** 222, **227–228,** 230

Expensive People (Oates), **Supp. II Part 2:** 509, 510–511

"Experience" (Emerson), **Supp. XIV:** 42

"Experience and Fiction" (Jackson), **Supp. IX:** 121

"Experience and the Objects of Knowledge in the Philosophy of F. H. Bradley" (Eliot), **I:** 572; **Retro. Supp. I:** 59

Experience of Literature, The (Trilling), **Supp. III Part 2:** 493

"Experiences and Principles of an Historian" (Morison), **Supp. I Part 2:** 492

Experimental Death Unit # 1 (Baraka), **Supp. II Part 1:** 46

"Experimental Life, The" (Bourne), **I:** 217, 220

"Experiment in Misery, An" (S. Crane), **I:** 411; **Retro. Supp. II:** 97

Experiments and Observations on Electricity (Franklin), **II:** 102, 114–115

"Expiation" (Hoffman), **Supp. XVIII:** 86

"Expiation" (Wharton), **Retro. Supp. I:** 367

"Explaining Evil" (Gordon), **Supp. IV Part 1:** 310

"Explaining Ted Kooser" (Gioia), **Supp. XIX:** 121

"Explanation" (Stevens), **IV:** 79

Explanation of America, An (Pinsky), **Supp. VI:** 237, **241–243**

Exploding Gravy (X. J. Kennedy), **Supp. XV:** 163

"Exploit" (Wharton), **IV:** 324

"Exploration in the Great Tuolumne Cañon" (Muir), **Supp. IX:** 181

"Explorer, The" (Brooks), **Supp. III Part 1:** 79–80

"Exploring the Magalloway" (Parkman), **Supp. II Part 2:** 591

Expositor's Bible, The (G. A. Smith), **III:** 199

Expressions of Sea Level (Ammons), **Supp. VII:** 24, 28, 36

Extract from Captain Stormfeld's Visit to Heaven (Twain), **IV:** 209–210

Extracts from Adam's Diary (Twain), **IV:** 208–209

"Exulting, The" (Roethke), **III:** 544

"Eye, The" (Bowles), **Supp. IV Part 1:** 93

Eye, The (Nabokov), **III:** 251

Eye-Beaters, Blood, Victory, Madness, Buckhead and Mercy, The (Dickey), **Supp. IV Part 1:** 178, 182–183

"Eye for an Eye, An" (Humphrey), **Supp. IX:** 108

"Eye in the Rock, The" (Haines), **Supp. XII:** 208, 209

Eye in the Sky (Dick), **Supp. XVIII:** 138

"Eye-Mote, The" (Plath), **Retro. Supp. II:** 246, 247

"Eye of Paris, The" (H. Miller), **III:** 183–184

Eye of the Poet, The: Six Views of the Art and Craft of Poetry (Citino, ed.), **Supp. XIII:** 115; **Supp. XXI:** 54

"Eye of the Rock, The" (Haines), **Supp. XII:** 208

"Eye of the Story, The" (Porter), **IV:** 279

Eye of the Story, The: Selected Essays and Reviews (Welty), **Retro. Supp. I:** 339, 342, 344, 345, 346, 351, 354, 355, 356

"Eyes, The" (Wharton), **IV:** 315

"Eyes like They Say the Devil Has" (Ríos), **Supp. IV Part 2:** 543, 544

Eyes of the Dragon, The (King), **Supp. V:** 139, 152

Eyes of the Heart: A Memoir of the Lost and Found (Buechner), **Supp. XII:** 53

"Eyes of Zapata" (Cisneros), **Supp. VII:** 70

"Eyes to See" (Cozzens), **I:** 374

Eye-to-Eye (Nye), **Supp. XIII:** 274

Eysturoy, Annie O., **Supp. IV Part 1:** 321, 322, 323, 328

Ezekiel (biblical book), **II:** 541

"Ezekiel" (R. Fisher), **Supp. XIX:** 71

Ezekiel, Mordecai, **Supp. I Part 2:** 645

"Ezekiel Learns" (R. Fisher), **Supp. XIX:** 71

"Ezra Pound" (Bynner), **Supp. XV:** 49

"Ezra Pound: His Cantos" (Zukofsky), **Supp. III Part 2:** 612, 619, 622

Ezra Pound's Mauberley (Espey), **III:** 463

"Ezra Pound's Very Useful Labors" (Schwartz), **Supp. II Part 2:** 644

F

Faas, Ekbert, **Supp. VIII:** 292

"Fabbri Tape, The" (Auchincloss), **Supp. IV Part 1:** 21–22

Faber, Geoffrey, **Retro. Supp. I:** 63

Faber Book of Movie Verse, The (French and Wlaschin, eds.), **Supp. XVI:** 294

"Fable" (Merwin), **Supp. III Part 1:** 343

"Fable" (Wylie), **Supp. I Part 2:** 714

Fable, A (Faulkner), **II:** 55, 73; **Retro. Supp. I:** 74

"Fable, A" (Glück), **Supp. V:** 86

"Fable, The" (Winters), **Supp. II Part 2:** 792, 793, 796

Fable for Critics, A (Lowell), **Supp. I Part 2:** 406, 407–408, 409, 412–413, 416, 420, 422

"Fable for Critics, A" (Lowell), **Supp. XVIII:** 3, 8

"Fable of the War, A" (Nemerov), **III:** 272

Fables (Gay), **II:** 111

Fables and Distances: New and Selected Essays (Haines), **Supp. XII:** 197, 199, 207–208, 211

Fables for Our Time (Thurber), **Supp. I Part 2:** 610

Fables of Identity: Studies in Poetic Mythology (Frye), **Supp. X:** 80

Fables of La Fontaine, The (Moore), **III:** 194, 215

"Fables of Representation: Poetry of the New York School" (Hoover), **Supp. XV:** 179

"Fables of the Fallen Guy" (Rosaldo), **Supp. IV Part 2:** 544

"Fables of the Moscow Subway" (Nemerov), **III:** 271

Fabulators, The (Scholes), **Supp. V:** 40

Fabulous Small Jews (Epstein), **Supp. XIV:** 112

Face against the Glass, The (Francis), **Supp. IX:** 80–81

Face in the Crowd, A (film, Kazan), **Supp. XVIII:** 252–253

Face of Time, The (Farrell), **II:** 28, 34, 35, 39

Faces of Jesus, The (Buechner), **Supp. XII:** 53

Face to the Wind (film), **Supp. XVII:** 141

Face Value (Hwang), **Supp. XXI:** 148, 154, 155

Fachinger, Petra, **Supp. XVI:** 153

"Facing It" (Komunyakaa), **Supp. XIII:** 117, 124, 125

Facing Shadows (Jin), **Supp. XVIII:** 92, 93

Facing the Music (L. Brown), **Supp. XXI:** 39, 42, **42–44**

"Facing the Music" (L. Brown), **Supp. XXI:** **38–39,** 41, 42, 43

"*Facing the Music:* What's Wrong with All Those Happy Endings" (Neal), **Supp. XXI:** 41

"Facing West from California's Shores" (Jeffers), **Supp. II Part 2:** 437–438

Fact, Fiction, and Representation: Four Novels by Gilbert Sorrentino (Mackey), **Supp. XXI:** 236

"Fact in Fiction, The" (McCarthy), **II:** 562

"Fact of Blackness, The" (Fanon), **Supp. XX:**152

"Facts" (Franzen), **Supp. XX:**85

"Facts" (Levine), **Supp. V:** 193

"Facts" (Oliver), **Supp. VII:** 231–232

"Facts" (Snyder), **Supp. VIII:** 301

"Facts, The" (Lardner), **II:** 431

Facts, The: A Novelist's Autobiography (P. Roth), **Retro. Supp. II:** 280, 291; **Supp. III Part 2:** 401, 405, 417, 426

"Facts and Traditions Respecting the Existence of Indigenous Intermittent Fever in New England" (Holmes), **Supp. I Part 1:** 303

"Facts in the Case of M. Valdemar, The" (Poe), **III:** 416

Faderman, Lillian, **Retro. Supp. II:** 135; **Supp. XIII:** 313

Fadiman, Clifton, **II:** 430, 431, 443, 591–592; **Supp. IX:** 8; **Supp. XVI:** 100, 106; **Supp. XVII:** 87, 90

Fading, My Parmacheene Belle (J. Scott), **Supp. XVII:** **184–185,** 188

"Fado" (McClatchy), **Supp. XII:** 265–266

Faerie Queene, The (Spenser), **III:** 487; **IV:** 253; **Supp. XIV:** 6; **Supp. XV:** 181

Faery, Rebecca Blevins, **Retro. Supp. I:** 374

Fagan, Kathy, **Supp. V:** 180; **Supp. XV:** 73

Fagan, Louise, **Supp. XIX:** 204, 205

Fahrenheit 451 (Bradbury), **Supp. IV Part 1:** 101, 102, 104, 107–109, 110, 113; **Supp. XIII:** 29

"Failure" (Gioia), **Supp. XV:** 125

"Failure" (Zach; Everwine, trans.), **Supp. XV:** 86

"Failure of David Barry, The" (Jewett), **Retro. Supp. II:** 132

Fainlight, Ruth, **Supp. XV:** 261, 264

Faint Perfume (Gale), **Supp. I Part 2:** 613

Fair, Bryan K., **Supp. VIII:** 128

Fairbanks, Douglas, **Supp. XVI:** 185, 186

Fairchild, Frances. *See* Bryant, Mrs. William Cullen (Frances Fairchild)

Fairchild, Hoxie, **Supp. XIV:** 120

Fairfield, Flora (pseudonym). *See* Alcott, Louisa May

Fair Gentlemen of Belken County (Hinojosa), **Supp. XIX:** 105

Fairly Conventional Woman, A (Shields), **Supp. VII:** 312, 316, 318

"Fairly Sad Tale, A" (Parker), **Supp. IX:** 192

Fair Warning (R. O. Butler), **Supp. XII:** 62, **75–76**

Faith (Goldbarth), **Supp. XII:** 181, **182–183**

Faith and History (Niebuhr), **III:** 308

Faith and the Good Thing (Johnson), **Supp. VI:** 187, **188–190,** 191, 193, 194, 196

Faith for Living (Mumford), **Supp. II Part 2:** 479–480

Faithful Narrative of the Surprising Works of God in the Conversion of Many Hundred Souls in Northampton, and the Neighboring Towns and Villages of New-Hampshire in New-England, A (Edwards), **I:** 545, 562

"Faith Healer" (Komunyakaa), **Supp. XIII:** 117

"Faith in a Tree" (Paley), **Supp. VI:** 217–218, 224, 230

"Faith in Search of Understanding" (Updike), **Retro. Supp. I:** 327

"Faith of an Historian" (Morison), **Supp. I Part 2:** 492

"Faith of Fishermen, The" (J. W. Miller), **Supp. XX:** 170

Faker's Dozen, A (Bukiet), **Supp. XVII:** 47

Falcoff, Mark, **Supp. VIII:** 88

Falcon (Hammett), **Supp. IV Part 1:** 351

Falconer (Cheever), **Supp. I Part 1:** 176, 193–195, 196

Falconer, A. F., **Supp. XIV:** 2

"Falcon of Ser Federigo, The" (Longfellow), **II:** 505

Falk, Peter, **Supp. XI:** 174

Falkner, Dean, **II:** 55

Falkner, John, **II:** 55

Falkner, Murray, **II:** 55

Falkner, Murray C., **II:** 55

Falkner, Mrs. Murray C. (Maud Butler), **II:** 55

Falkner, William C., **II:** 55

"Fall" (Francis), **Supp. IX:** 76

"Fall, The" (Bass), **Supp. XVI:** 25

"Fall 1961" (Lowell), **II:** 550

"Fallen Western Star: The Decline of San Francisco as a Literary Region" (Gioia), **Supp. XV:** 112, **115–116**

"Fallen Western Star" Wars, The: A Debate about Literary California (Foley, ed.), **Supp. XV:** 112, 116

"Fall in Corrales" (Wilbur), **Supp. III Part 2:** 556

Falling (Dickey), **Supp. IV Part 1:** 178, 181–182

"Falling" (Dickey), **Supp. IV Part 1:** 182

"Falling Asleep over the Aeneid" (Lowell), **II:** 542; **Retro. Supp. II:** 188

Falling in Place (Beattie), **Supp. V:** 28–29

"Falling into Holes in Our Sentences" (R. Bly), **Supp. IV Part 1:** 71

"Fall Journey" (Stafford), **Supp. XI:** 322

Fall of America, The: 1965–1971 (Ginsberg), **Supp. II Part 1:** 323, 325, 327; **Supp. XV:** 264

Fall of Eve, The (Loos), **Supp. XVI:** 187

Fall of the City, The: A Verse Play for Radio (MacLeish), **III:** 20

"Fall of the House of Usher, The" (Poe), **III:** 412, 414, 415, 419; **Retro. Supp. II:** 270

Fall of the Magicians, The (Kees), **Supp. XV:** 144

Fallows, James, **Supp. VIII:** 241

Fall Quarter (Kees), **Supp. XV:** 141

Fall & Rise (Dixon), **Supp. XII:** 147–148, 148, 153, 157

Falls, Robert, **Supp. XXI:** 148

"Falls, The" (Olds), **Supp. X:** 215

"Falls, The" (Saunders), **Supp. XIX:** 229

"Falls Fight, The" (Howe), **Supp. IV Part 2:** 431–432

Falon, Janet Ruth, **Supp. IV Part 2:** 422

False Coin (Swados), **Supp. XIX:** **260–261,** 263

"False Dawn" (Wharton), **Retro. Supp. I:** 381

"False Documents" (Doctorow), **Supp. IV Part 1:** 220, 236

"False Leads" (Komunyakaa), **Supp. XIII:** 116

Falwell, Jerry, **Supp. XX:** 273

Fame and Obscurity: Portraits by Gay Talese (Talese), **Supp. XVII:** 202, 203, 204

Fame & Folly: Essays (Ozick), **Supp. V:** 272

"Familiar Epistle to a Friend, A" (Lowell), **Supp. I Part 2:** 416

Familiar Territory: Observations on American Life (Epstein), **Supp. XIV:** 106

"Familiar Things" (Pickering), **Supp. XXI:** 204

"Family" (Sanders), **Supp. XVI:** 276

"Family" (Wilson), **IV:** 426

Family, Kinship, and Sympathy in Nineteenth-Century America (Weinstein), **Supp. XVIII:** 261

"Family Affair, A" (Chopin), **Retro. Supp. II:** 71

"Family and Socialism, The" (Ryan as Quin), **Supp. XVIII:** 238

Family Arsenal, The (Theroux), **Supp. VIII:** 322

Family Chronicle: An Odyssey from Russia to America (Reznikoff), **Supp. XIV:** 277, 288, 289

Family Devotions (Hwang), **Supp. XXI:** 145, 146

"Family History" (Mora), **Supp. XIII:** 217

"Family History, A" (R. H. Davis), **Supp. XVI:** 82

Family Honor (Parker), **Supp. XIX:** 186

Family Life (Banks), **Supp. V:** 7

"Family Matters" (Alvarez), **Supp. VII:** 10

Family Moskat, The (Singer), **IV:** 1, 17, 20, 46; **Retro. Supp. II:** 304

"Family of Little Feet, The" (Cisneros), **Supp. VII:** 61

Family Party, A (O'Hara), **III:** 362

Family Pictures (Brooks), **Supp. III Part 1:** 69, 85, 86

Family Pictures (Miller), **Supp. XII:** 291, **295–297,** 299

"Family Portrait" (Trethewey), **Supp. XXI:** 250

"Family Reunion" (J. W. Miller), **Supp. XX:** 167

"Family Reunion" (X. J. Kennedy), **Supp. XV:** 169

Family Reunion, The (Eliot), **I:** 570–571, 572, 581, 584, 588; **Retro. Supp. I:** 62, 65

"Family Secrets" (Kingsolver), **Supp. VII:** 208

"Family Sideshow, The" (Karr), **Supp. XI:** 245

"Family Story, The" (Skloot), **Supp. XX:** 195

"Family Ties" (Mora), **Supp. XIII:** 215

"Family Tree" (Komunyakaa), **Supp. XIII:** 117–118, 126

"Family Wasserstein, The" (Hoban), **Supp. XV:** 319, 325

Famous American Negroes (Hughes), **Supp. I Part 1:** 345

"Famous Gilson Bequest, The" (Bierce), **I:** 204

Famous Last Words (Findley), **Supp. XX:** 49, **55–56**

Famous Negro Music Makers (Hughes), **Supp. I Part 1:** 345

"Famous New York Trials" (Ellison), **Supp. II Part 1:** 230

Fanatics, The (Dunbar), **Supp. II Part 1:** 213–214

Fancher, Edwin, **Retro. Supp. II:** 202

Fancher, Lou, **Supp. XVI:** 177

"Fancy and Imagination" (Poe), **III:** 421

Fancy Dancer, The (P. N. Warren), **Supp. XX:** 267–268

"Fancy Flights" (Beattie), **Supp. V:** 25

"Fancy's Show Box" (Hawthorne), **II:** 238

"Fancy Woman, The" (Taylor), **Supp. V:** 316–317, 319, 323

"Fang" (Goldbarth), **Supp. XII:** 190

Fanny: Being the True History of the Adventures of Fanny Hackabout-Jones (Jong), **Supp. V:** 115, 127

Fanny Hill (Cleland), **Supp. V:** 48, 127

Fan of Swords, The (al-Maghut), **Supp. XIII:** 278

Fanon, Frantz, **Retro. Supp. II:** 118; **Supp. X:** 131, 141; **Supp. XX:** 152

Fanshawe (Hawthorne), **II:** 223–224; **Retro. Supp. I:** 149, 151

Fan's Notes, A (Exley), **Supp. XVI:** 69

"Fantasia on 'The Nut-Brown Maid' " (Ashbery), **Supp. III Part 1:** 19

"Fantasia on the Relations between Poetry and Photography" (Strand), **Supp. IV Part 2:** 631

"Fantastic Fables" (Bierce), **I:** 209

Fante, John, **Supp. XI: 159–176**

Faraday, Michael, **I:** 480–481

Far and Away (Jarman), **Supp. XVII:** 110, 115

"Far and Away" (Jarman), **Supp. XVII:** 115

"Farewell" (Emerson), **II:** 13

"Farewell" (Ryan as Quin), **Supp. XVIII:** 229

Farewell, My Lovely (Chandler), **Supp. IV Part 1:** 122, 125–126, 127, 128, 130

"Farewell, My Lovely!" (White), **Supp. I Part 2:** 661–663, 665

Farewell, The (Gibran), **Supp. XX:** 121

"Farewell Performance" (Merrill), **Supp. III Part 1:** 336–337

Farewell-Sermon Preached at the First Precinct in Northampton, after the People's Publick Rejection of their Minister, A (Edwards), **I:** 548, 562

"Farewell Sweet Dust" (Wylie), **Supp. I Part 2:** 727–728

"Farewell to America, A" (Wheatley), **Supp. XX:** 283

Farewell to Arms, A (Hemingway), **I:** 212, 421, 476, 477; **II:** 68–69, 248–249, 252–253, 254, 255, 262, 265; **Retro. Supp. I:** 171, 178, **180–182,** 187, 189; **Retro. Supp. II:** 108; **Supp. IV Part 1:** 380–381, 381; **Supp. VIII:** 179; **Supp. XII:** 241–242; **Supp. XXI:** 277

"Farewell to Miles" (Berryman), **I:** 173

"Farewell to My Union Brothers" (Ryan as Quin), **Supp. XVIII:** 238

Farewell to Reform (Chamberlain), **Supp. I Part 2:** 647

Farewell to Sport (Gallico), **Supp. XVI:** 238

"Farewell to the Middle Class" (Updike), **Retro. Supp. I:** 321

Far Field, The (Roethke), **III:** 528, 529, 539, 545, 547–548

"Far Field, The" (Roethke), **III:** 537, 540

Far-Flung (Cameron), **Supp. XII:** 81

Far from the Madding Crowd (Hardy), **II:** 291

Faríd, 'Umar ibn al-, **Supp. XX:** 117

Faris, Athénaíse Charleville, **Supp. I Part 1:** 204

Farley, Abbie, **I:** 458

Farley, Harriet, **Supp. XIII:** 140

"Farm, The" (Creeley), **Supp. IV Part 1:** 155

Farmer (Harrison), **Supp. VIII:** 39, **44–45**

Farmer, Frances, **Supp. XV:** 196–197

Farmer, Richard, **Supp. XIV:** 2

"Farmer and the Fox, The" (Leopold), **Supp. XIV:** 188

"Farmers' Daughters, The" (W. C. Williams), **Retro. Supp. I:** 423

Farmers Hotel, The (O'Hara), **III:** 361

"Farmer's Sorrow, A" (Jewett), **Retro. Supp. II:** 132

"Farmer's Wife, The" (Sexton), **Supp. II Part 2:** 676

"Farm Garden" (Nelson), **Supp. XVIII:** 186

"Farm Implements and Rutabagas in a Landscape" (Ashbery), **Supp. III Part 1:** 13

Farming: A Hand Book (Berry), **Supp. X:** 31, 35

"Farmlights in Iowa" (Kooser), **Supp. XIX:** 120

"Farm on the Great Plains, The" (Stafford), **Supp. XI:** 322

Farnol, Jeffrey, **Supp. I Part 2:** 653

Far North (Shepard), **Supp. III Part 2:** 433, 435

"Far Northern Birch, The" (Francis), **Supp. IX:** 90

Farnsworth, Elizabeth, **Supp. XI:** 139

"Farrago" (Kees), **Supp. XV:** 145

Farrand, Max, **II:** 122

Farrar, Geraldine, **Retro. Supp. I:** 10

Farrar, John, **II:** 191; **Supp. XI:** 47

Farrell, Barry, **Supp. XIV:** 142

Farrell, James Francis, **II:** 25, 26

Farrell, James T., **I:** 97, 288, 475, 508, 517, 519; **II: 25–53,** 416, 424; **III:** 28, 114, 116, 118, 119, 317, 382; **IV:** 211, 286; **Retro. Supp. II:** 196, 327; **Supp. I Part 2:** 679; **Supp. VIII:** 96, 97; **Supp. XIV:** 3; **Supp. XV:** 141

Farrell, Mrs. James T. (Dorothy Butler), **II:** 26

Farrell, Mrs. James T. (Hortense Alden), **II:** 26, 27, 45, 48

Farrell, John, **II:** 26

Farrell, John C., **Supp. I Part 1:** 24

Farrell, Kate, **Supp. XV:** 187–188, **Supp. XV:** 190

Farrell, Kevin, **II:** 26

Farrell, Mary, **II:** 25

"Far Rockaway" (Schwartz), **Supp. II Part 2:** 649

Farrow, Mia, **Supp. XV:** 8, 10

Far Side of the Dollar, The (Macdonald), **Supp. IV Part 2:** 473

Farther Off from Heaven (Humphrey), **Supp. IX:** 93, 96, 101, **103–104,** 105, 109

Far Tortuga (Matthiessen), **Supp. V:** 201, 206–207

"Fascinating Fascism" (Sontag), **Supp. III Part 2:** 465

"Fascination of Cities, The" (Hughes), **Supp. I Part 1:** 325

Fashion, Power, Guilt and the Charity of Families (Shields), **Supp. VII:** 323

Fasman, Jonathan, **Supp. V:** 253

Fast, Howard, **Supp. I Part 1:** 295; **Supp. XXI:** 277

Fast, Jonathan, **Supp. V:** 115

Fast and Loose (Wharton), **Retro. Supp. I:** 361

"Faster than Light" (Nelson), **Supp. XVIII:** 178–179

"Fastest Runner on Sixty-first Street, The" (Farrell), **II:** 45

"Fat" (Carver), **Supp. III Part 1:** 141

Fatal Interview (Millay), **III:** 128–129, 130

"Fatality" (Bausch), **Supp. VII:** 54

Fatal Lady (film), **Supp. XIII:** 166

"Fate" (Emerson), **II:** 2–3, 4, 16; **Supp. XIV:** 42

"Fate" (Koch), **Supp. XV:** 183

"Fate" (Mailer), **Retro. Supp. II:** 207

"Fate of Pleasure, The" (Trilling), **Supp. III Part 2:** 510

Fate of the Jury, The (Masters), **Supp. I Part 2:** 466, 468, 469

"Fat Girl, The" (Dubus), **Supp. VII:** 84, 85

"Father" (Kooser), **Supp. XIX:** 117, 127

"Father" (Levine), **Supp. V:** 188

"Father" (Sanders), **Supp. XVI:** 277

"Father" (Trethewey), **Supp. XXI:** 253

"Father" (Walker), **Supp. III Part 2:** 522

"Father, The" (Carver), **Supp. III Part 1:** 137, 140

Father, The (Olds), **Supp. X: 209–211**

"Father Abraham" (Faulkner), **Retro. Supp. I:** 81, 82

Fatheralong: A Meditation on Fathers and Sons, Race and Society (Wideman), **Supp. X:** 320, 332–333, 334, 335

"Father and Daughter" (Eberhart), **I:** 539

Father and Glorious Descendant (Lowe), **Supp. X:** 291

"Father and Son" (Eberhart), **I:** 539

Father and Son (Farrell), **II:** 34, 35, 290, 291

Father and Son (Gosse), **Supp. VIII:** 157

"Father and Son" (Hughes), **Retro. Supp. I:** 204; **Supp. I Part 1:** 329, 339

"Father and Son" (Kunitz), **Supp. III Part 1:** 262

Father and Son (L. Brown), **Supp. XXI:** 36, 40, 41, **46–47**

"Father and Son" (Schwartz), **Supp. II Part 2:** 650

Father Bombo's Pilgrimage to Mecca (Freneau), **Supp. II Part 1:** 254

"Father Fitzgerald" (Nelson and Espeland), **Supp. XVIII:** 181

"Father Guzman" (Stern), **Supp. IX: 293,** 296

"Father out Walking on the Lawn, A" (Dove), **Supp. IV Part 1:** 246

"Fathers" (Creeley), **Supp. IV Part 1:** 157–158

Fathers, The (Tate), **IV:** 120, 127, 130, 131–133, 134, 141; **Supp. X:** 52

Fathers and Crows (Vollmann), **Supp. XVII:** 226, 231–232

"Fathers and Sons" (Hemingway), **II:** 249, 265–266; **Retro. Supp. I:** 175
"Father's Body, The" (Dickey), **Supp. IV Part 1:** 176
"Father's Day" (Connelly), **Supp. XXI:** 79–80
"Father's Story, A" (Dubus), **Supp. VII:** 88
"Father's Voice" (Stafford), **Supp. XI:** 322
"Fat Lady, The" (Carruth), **Supp. XVI:** 48
"Fat Man, Floating" (Dunn), **Supp. XI:** 144
Faulkner, Barry, **Supp. XV:** 41
Faulkner, William, **I:** 54, 97, 99, 105, 106, 115, 117, 118, 123, 190, 204–205, 211, 288, 289, 291, 292, 297, 305, 324, 374, 378, 423, 480, 517; **II:** 28, 51, **54–76,** 131, 174, 194, 217, 223, 228, 230, 259, 301, 306, 431, 458–459, 542, 594, 606; **III:** 45, 70, 108, 164, 218, 220, 222, 236–237, 244, 292, 334, 350, 382, 418, 453, 454, 482, 483; **IV:** 2, 4, 33, 49, 97, 98, 100, 101, 120, 131, 203, 207, 211, 217, 237, 257, 260, 261, 279, 280, 352, 461, 463; **Retro. Supp. I:** 73–95, 215, 339, 347, 356, 379, 382; **Retro. Supp. II:** 19, 221, 326; **Supp. I Part 1:** 196, 197, 242, 372; **Supp. I Part 2:** 450, 621; **Supp. III Part 1:** 384–385, 396; **Supp. IV Part 1:** 47, 130, 257, 342; **Supp. IV Part 2:** 434, 463, 468, 502, 677, 682; **Supp. V:** 58, 59, 138, 210, 226, 237, 261, 262, 334–336; **Supp. VIII:** 37, 39, 40, 104, 105, 108, 175, 176, 180, 181, 183, 184, 188, 189, 215; **Supp. IX:** 20, 95; **Supp. X:** 44, 228; **Supp. XI:** 92, 247; **Supp. XII:** 16, 289, 310, 313; **Supp. XIII:** 100, 169; **Supp. XIV:** 1, 12–13, 21, 24, 93, 306; **Supp. XV:** 92, 135, 338; **Supp. XVI:** 148, 189; **Supp. XVII:** 225; **Supp. XVIII:** 76, 84, 90, 148, 249; **Supp. XIX:** 97, 154, 166; **Supp. XX:** 137, 162, 185, 195; **Supp. XXI:** 36, 38, 256
Faulkner: A Collection of Critical Essays (Warren), **Retro. Supp. I:** 73
Faulkner at Nagano (Jelliffe, ed.), **I:** 289; **II:** 63, 65
Faulkner-Cowley File, The: Letters and Memories 1944–1962 (Cowley, ed.), **Retro. Supp. I:** 73, 92; **Supp. II Part 1:** 140, 141
"Faun" (Plath), **Supp. I Part 2:** 537
"Fauna" (Jeffers), **Supp. II Part 2:** 415
Fauset, Arthur Huff, **Supp. XVIII:** 126
Fauset, Jessie, **Supp. I Part 1:** 321, 325; **Supp. IV Part 1:** 164
Fauset, Jessie Redmon, **Supp. XVIII:** 122,127; **Supp. XIX:** 69, 78
Faust (Goethe), **I:** 396; **II:** 489; **III:** 395; **Supp. II Part 1:** 16; **Supp. IX:** 141
Faust, Beatrix Hapgood, **Supp. XXI:** 8
Faust, Clarence H., **II:** 20
Faute de l'Abbé Mouret, La (Zola), **III:** 322

Favor Island (Merwin), **Supp. III Part 1:** 346, 347
"Favor of Love, A" (Peacock), **Supp. XIX:** 203
"Favrile" (Doty), **Supp. XI:** 131
"Fawn, with a Bit of Green" (Swados), **Supp. XIX:** 258
Fay (L. Brown), **Supp. XXI:** 40, 41, 47
Fay, Bernard, **IV:** 41
"Fear, The" (Frost), **Retro. Supp. I:** 128
Fear and Trembling (Kierkegaard), **Supp. XX:** 132
"Fear & Fame" (Levine), **Supp. V:** 192
Fearful Child, The (C. Frost), **Supp. XV:** 96, 97, 106
"Fearful Child, The" (C. Frost), **Supp. XV:** 96
Fearing, Kenneth, **Supp. XV:** 138
"Fearless" (Mosley), **Supp. XIII:** 241
Fearless Jones (Mosley), **Supp. XIII:** 241–242
"Fear of Concrete" (Halliday), **Supp. XIX:** 91
Fear of Fifty: A Midlife Memoir (Jong), **Supp. V:** 114, 115, 116, 131
Fear of Flying (Jong), **Supp. V:** 113, 115, 116, 119–123, 124, 129
"Feast, The" (Kinnell), **Supp. III Part 1:** 239, 250
Feast of All Saints, The (Rice), **Supp. VII:** 299–301
Feast of Love, The (C. Baxter), **Supp. XVII:** 13, 21–22
Feast of Love, The (film, R. Benton), **Supp. XVII:** 22
Feast of Snakes, A (Crews), **Supp. XI:** 102, 107–108; **Supp. XXI:** 40
"Feast of Stephen, The" (Hecht), **Supp. X:** 63–64
"Featherbed for Critics, A" (Blackmur), **Supp. II Part 1:** 93, 151
Feather Crowns (Mason), **Supp. VIII:** 146–147
"Feathers" (Carver), **Supp. III Part 1:** 145
Feathers (Van Vechten), **Supp. II Part 2:** 736, 749
"Feathers, The" (Hogan), **Supp. IV Part 1:** 416
"February" (Ellison), **Supp. II Part 1:** 229
"February 14th" (Levine), **Supp. V:** 194
February in Sydney (Komunyakaa), **Supp. XIII:** 124–125, 129
"February in Sydney" (Komunyakaa), **Supp. XIII:** 125
"February: Thinking of Flowers" (Kenyon), **Supp. VII:** 171
"Feces" (McClatchy), **Supp. XII:** 266, 267–268
Fechner, Gustav, **II:** 344, 355, 358, 359, 363
Feder, Lillian, **IV:** 136; **Supp. XVI:** 49, 50
Federal Arts Project, **Supp. III Part 2:** 618
Federigo, or, The Power of Love (Nemerov), **III:** 268, 276, 282, 283–284, 285
"Fedge, The" (Halliday), **Supp. XIX:** 93

"Fedora" (Chopin), **Supp. I Part 1:** 220
Fedorko, Kathy A., **Retro. Supp. I:** 361, 374
"Feeling and Precision" (Moore), **III:** 206
Feeling Italian: The Art of Ethnicity in America (Ferraro), **Supp. XX:** 43
"Feeling of Effort, The" (James), **II:** 349
Feeling Very Strange: The Slipstream Anthology (Kelly and Kessel, eds.), **Supp. XIX:** 231
"Feel Like a Bird" (Swenson), **Supp. IV Part 2:** 639
"Feel Me" (Swenson), **Supp. IV Part 2:** 647
Feeney, Mary, **Supp. IX:** 152, 154
Feinsilver, Pamela, **Supp. XX:** 135
Feinstein, Herbert, **Supp. XIX:** 260
Feinstein, Sascha, **Supp. XIII:** 125
Feldman, Charles K., **Supp. XI:** 307
Fellini, Federico, **Supp. XII:** 172; **Supp. XV:** 8
"Fellini the Cat" (Peacock), **Supp. XIX:** 206
"Fellow Citizens" (Sandburg), **III:** 553
Fellows, John, **Supp. I Part 2:** 520
Fellow Travelers (Mallon), **Supp. XIX:** 132, 143–144
"Felo de Se" (Wylie), **Supp. I Part 2:** 727, 729
Felton, Sharon, **Supp. IV Part 1:** 210
"Female Author" (Plath), **Retro. Supp. II:** 243
"Female Frailty" (Freneau), **Supp. II Part 1:** 258
"Female Laughter and Comic Possibilities: *Uncommon Women and Others*" (Chirico), **Supp. XV:** 323
Female Patriot, The; or, Nature's Rights (Rowson), **Supp. XV:** 237–238
Female Prose Writers of America (Hart), **Supp. XVIII:** 257, 264
"Female Voice in *To Kill a Mockingbird,* The: Narrative Strategies in Film and Novel" (Shakelford), **Supp. VIII:** 129
"Feminine Landscape of Leslie Marmon Silko's *Ceremony,* The" (Gunn Allen), **Supp. IV Part 1:** 324
Feminism and the Politics of Literary Reputation: The Example of Erica Jong (Templin), **Supp. V:** 116
"Feminismo" (Robbins), **Supp. X:** 272
"Feminist Criticism in the Wilderness" (Showalter), **Supp. X:** 97
Feminization of American Culture, The (Douglas), **Supp. XVIII:** 258
"Fence, The" (Oliver), **Supp. VII:** 232
"Fence Posts" (Snyder), **Supp. VIII:** 304
Fences (Wilson), **Supp. VIII:** 329, 330, 331, 334–337, 350
Fenick, Elizabeth, **Retro. Supp. II:** 221
"Fenimore Cooper's Literary Offenses" (Twain), **IV:** 204–205
Fennell, Frank L., **Supp. XVII:** 177–178
Fenollosa, Ernest, **III:** 458, 465, 466, 474, 475, 477; **Retro. Supp. I:** 289; **Supp. IV Part 1:** 154
Fenollosa, Mrs. Ernest, **III:** 458
"Fenstad's Mother" (C. Baxter), **Supp. XVII:** 18
Fenton, Charles, **Supp. XI:** 43

Fenton, James, **Supp. XV:** 117
Ferdinand: Including "It Was" (Zukofsky), *Supp. III Part 2:* 630
"Fergus" (Bourne), **I:** 229
Ferguson, James, **Supp. I Part 2:** 503
Ferguson, Otis, **Supp. IX:** 7
Ferguson, William, **Supp. XII:** 189
Ferguson Affair, The (Macdonald), **Supp. IV Part 2:** 473
Fergusson, Francis, **I:** 265, 440; **Supp. XV:** 20
Ferlinghetti, Lawrence, **Supp. IV Part 1:** 90; **Supp. VIII:** 290, 292; **Supp. XII:** 121, 125; **Supp. XIII:** 275; **Supp. XIX:** 4; **Supp. XXI:** 53
Fermata, The (Baker), **Supp. XIII: 49–52, 54**
"Fern" (Toomer), **Supp. III Part 2:** 481; **Supp. IX:** 313
Fern, Fanny, **Retro. Supp. I:** 246; **Supp. V:** 122
Fernández, Enrique, **Supp. VIII:** 73
Fernandez, Ramon, **Retro. Supp. I:** 302, 303; **Supp. XVI:** 214
"Fern-Beds in Hampshire Country" (Wilbur), **Supp. III Part 2:** 558
"Fern Hill" (D. Thomas), **IV:** 93; **Supp. XX:**204
"Fern-Life" (Larcom), **Supp. XIII:** 143
Ferragammo, Salvatore, **Supp. XVI:** 192
Ferraro, Thomas J., **Supp. XX:**34, 43
Ferreo, Guglielmo, **Supp. I Part 2:** 481
Ferris, Anthony, **Supp. XX:**124
Fessenden, Thomas Green, **II:** 300
Fessier, Michael, **Supp. XIII:** 164
"Festival Aspect, The" (Olson), **Supp. II Part 2:** 585
"Festival of Regrets, The" (Wasserstein), **Supp. XV:** 333
Fetching the Dead (Sanders), **Supp. XVI:** 269
Fêtes galantes (Verlaine), **IV:** 79
"Fetish" (McClatchy), **Supp. XII:** 256
Fetterley, Judith, **Retro. Supp. II:** 139
"Feud" (Zinberg), **Supp. XV:** 195
"Fever" (Carver), **Supp. III Part 1:** 145
"Fever 103°" (Plath), **Supp. I Part 2:** 541
Fever Pitch (Hornby), **Supp. XII:** 286
Fever: Twelve Stories (Wideman), **Supp. X:** 320
"Few Don'ts by an Imagiste, A" (Pound), **III:** 465; **Retro. Supp. I:** 288; **Supp. I Part 1:** 261–262
"Few Stray Comments on the Cultivation of the Lyric, A" (Sobin), **Supp. XVI:** 285
"Few Words of Introduction, A" (McNally), **Supp. XIII:** 198–199
Fiamengo, Janice, **Supp. XIII:** 35
Fiber (Bass), **Supp. XVI:** 22
"Fiber: A Post-Pastoral Georgic" (Gifford), **Supp. XVI:** 22
Ficke, Arthur Davison, **Supp. XIII:** 347; **Supp. XV:** 40, 42, 43, 46, 48, 49
"Fiction" (Stafford), **Supp. XI:** 327
"Fiction: A Lens on Life" (Stegner), **Supp. IV Part 2:** 595, 596, 600
Fictional World of William Hoffman, The (Frank, ed.), **Supp. XVIII:** 74, 79, 80, 87

Fiction and the Figures of Life (Gass), **Supp. VI:** 85
Fiction of Joseph Heller, The (Seed), **Supp. IV Part 1:** 391
Fiction of Paule Marshall, The (Denniston), **Supp. XI:** 276
Fiction of the Forties (Eisinger), **I:** 302; **II:** 604
Fictions in Autobiography: Studies in the Art of Self-Invention (Eakin), **Supp. XVI:** 70
"Fiction Writer and His Country, The" (O'Connor), **III:** 342; **Retro. Supp. II:** 223, 225; **Supp. II Part 1:** 148
Fiddler's Trance, The (Skloot), **Supp. XX:**196, 202
Fidelity (Glaspell), **Supp. III Part 1:** 177
Fiedler, Leslie A., **II:** 27; **III:** 218; **Retro. Supp. I:** 280, 324; **Supp. II Part 1:** 87; **Supp. IV Part 1:** 42, 86; **Supp. IX:** 3, 227; **Supp. X:** 80; **Supp. XIII:** 93–110; **Supp. XIV:** 11; **Supp. XVIII:** 146; **Supp. XIX:** 251
Fiedler on the Roof: Essays on Literature and Jewish Identity (Fiedler), **Supp. XIII:** 106–107
"Fie! Fie! Fi-Fi!" (Fitzgerald), **Retro. Supp. I:** 100
Field, Eugene, **Supp. II Part 1:** 197
Field, John, **IV:** 179
"Field Events" (Bass), **Supp. XVI:** 19
"Field Full of Black Cats, A" (C. Frost), **Supp. XV:** 101
Field Guide, (Hass), **Supp. VI:** 97–98, **99–101,** 102, 103, 106
Field Guide to Contemporary Poetry and Poetics (Friebert and Young, eds.), **Supp. XI:** 270
"Field Guide to the Western Birds" (Stegner), **Supp. IV Part 2:** 609
Fielding, Henry, **I:** 134; **II:** 302, 304–305; **III:** 61; **Supp. I Part 2:** 421, 422, 656; **Supp. IV Part 2:** 688; **Supp. V:** 127; **Supp. IX:** 128; **Supp. XI:** 277; **Supp. XVIII:** 2, 7
Fielding, Richard, **Supp. XV:** 232
"Field-larks and Blackbirds" (Lanier), **Supp. I Part 1:** 355
Field of Honor (Hay), **Supp. XIV:** 120–121, 125, 130
"Field of Honor" (Hay), **Supp. XIV:** 120–121, 129–130
Field of Vision, The (Morris), **III:** 226–228, 229, 232, 233, 238
"Field Report" (Corso), **Supp. XII:** 124, **136**
"Fields" (Wright), **Supp. XV:** 342
Fields, Annie Adams, **II:** 401, 402, 403–404, 406, 412; **IV:** 177; **Retro. Supp. II:** 134, 135, 142; **Supp. I Part 1:** 317; **Supp. XVI:** 84, 88
Fields, James T., **II:** 274, 279, 402–403; **Retro. Supp. II:** 135; **Supp. I Part 1:** 317; **Supp. XIII:** 150; **Supp. XVI:** 84, 88
Fields, Mrs. James T., **Supp. XIV:** 44, 46. *See* Fields, Annie Adams
Fields, Joseph, **IV:** 274
Fields, The (Richter), **Supp. XVIII: 213– 214,** 220

Fields, W. C., **II:** 427; **IV:** 335
"Fields at Dusk, The" (Salter), **Supp. IX:** 260
Fields of Praise, The (Nelson), **Supp. XVIII:** 171, 173, **177–178**
Fields of Wonder (Hughes), **Retro. Supp. I:** 206, 207; **Supp. I Part 1:** 333–334
Fierce Invalids Home from Hot Climates (Robbins), **Supp. X:** 267, 276–277, **282–285**
Fiery Chariot, The (Hurston), **Supp. VI:** 155–156
15 Poems (Banks), **Supp. V:** 5
"Fifteenth Farewell" (Bogan), **Supp. III Part 1:** 51, 58
"Fifth Avenue, Uptown" (Baldwin), **Supp. I Part 1:** 52
"Fifth Avenue—Spring Afternoon" (Untermeyer), **Supp. XV:** 296
Fifth Book of Peace, The (Kingston), **Supp. V:** 173
Fifth Chinese Daughter (Wong), **Supp. X:** 291
Fifth Column, The (Hemingway), **II:** 254, 258; **Retro. Supp. I:** 184
"Fifth Column of the Fencerow" (Leopold), **Supp. XIV:** 185
Fifth Decad of Cantos, The (Pound), **Retro. Supp. I:** 292
"Fifth Movement: *Autobiography*" (Zukofsky), **Supp. III Part 2:** 611
Fifth Sunday (Dove), **Supp. IV Part 1:** 251, 252–253
"Fifth Sunday" (Dove), **Supp. IV Part 1:** 252
50 Poems (Cummings), **I:** 430, 440, 442–443, 444–445, 446
Fifty Best American Short Stories (O'Brien), **III:** 56
"Fifty Dollars" (Elkin), **Supp. VI: 43–44**
"55 Miles to the Gas Pump" (Proulx), **Supp. VII:** 264
55 Poems (Zukofsky), **Supp. III Part 2:** 611, 621
"Fifty Grand" (Hemingway), **II:** 250, 424; **Retro. Supp. I:** 177
"Fifty Suggestions" (Poe), **Retro. Supp. II:** 266
"52 Oswald Street" (Kinnell), **Supp. III Part 1:** 251
Fifty Years Among Authors, Editors, and Publishers (Derby), **Supp. XVIII:** 4
"Fifty Years Among the Black Folk" (Du Bois), **Supp. II Part 1:** 169
"Fifty Years of American Poetry" (Jarrell), **Retro. Supp. I:** 52
Fig Connection, The (Franzen and Siebert), **Supp. XX:**84
Fight, The (Mailer), **Retro. Supp. II:** 207, 208
Fight Back: For the Sake of the People, For the Sake of the Land (Ortiz), **Supp. IV Part 2:** 497, 498, 499, 503, 510–512, 514
"Fighters, The" (Zinberg), **Supp. XV:** 193
Fight for Freedom (Hughes), **Supp. I Part 1:** 345
Fighting Angel (Buck), **Supp. II Part 1:** 119, 131

Fighting France; From Dunkerque to Belfort (Wharton), **Retro. Supp. I:** 377, 378

Fightin': New and Collected Stories (Ortiz), **Supp. IV Part 2:** 513

"Figlia che Piange, La" (Eliot), **I:** 570, 584; **III:** 9

Figliola, Samantha, **Supp. V:** 143

"Figure a Poem Makes, The" (Frost), **Retro. Supp. I:** 139

"Figured Wheel, The" (Pinsky), **Supp. VI:** 243, 244, 245, 246

Figured Wheel, The: New and Collected Poems (Pinsky), **Supp. VI:** 247–248

"Figure in the Carpet, The" (James), **Retro. Supp. I:** 228, 229

"Figure in the Doorway, The" (Frost), **Retro. Supp. I:** 138

Figure of Fulfillment, The (Lerperger; Miller, trans.), **Supp. XX:**165, 167–168

Figures from the Double World (McGrath), **Supp. X:** 118–119

Figures in Black: Words, Signs, and the "Racial" Self (H. L. Gates), **Supp. XX:**99, 100, 106, 107

"Figures in the Clock, The" (McCarthy), **II:** 561–562

Figures Made Visible in the Sadness of Time (Everwine), **Supp. XV:** 75, 88

Figures of Time (Hayden), **Supp. II Part 1:** 367

"Filling Out a Blank" (Wagoner), **Supp. IX:** 324

Fillmore, Millard, **III:** 101

Film Flam: Essays on Hollywood (McMurtry), **Supp. V:** 228

Films of Ayn Rand, The (Cox), **Supp. IV Part 2:** 524

Filo, John, **Supp. XII:** 211

Filreis, Alan, **Supp. XXI:** 262, 267, 268, 269, 271, 273, 275, 277, 278

Filson, John, **Retro. Supp. I:** 421

Final Beast, The (Buechner), **Supp. XII:** 49–51

"Finale" (Longfellow), **II:** 505, 506–507

"Final Fear" (Hughes), **Supp. I Part 1:** 338

Final Harvest: Emily Dickinson's Poems (Johnson, ed.), **I:** 470, 471

"Finally Harriet" (Wolfert), **Supp. XXI:** 265–267

Final Payments (Gordon), **Supp. IV Part 1:** 297, 299, 300–302, 304, 306, 314

"Final Report, A" (Maxwell), **Supp. VIII:** 169

"Final Soliloquy of the Interior Paramour" (Stevens), **Retro. Supp. I:** 312

Final Solution, The (Reitlinger), **Supp. XII:** 161

Financier, The (Dreiser), **I:** 497, 501, 507, 509; **Retro. Supp. II:** 94, 101–102, 105; **Supp. XVIII:** 246

Finch, Annie, **Supp. XVII: 69–79**

Finch, Henry Leroy, **Supp. XVII:** 69

Finch, Margaret Rockwell, **Supp. XVII:** 69

Finch, Robert, **Supp. XIV:** 186–187

Find a Victim (Macdonald), **Supp. IV Part 2:** 467, 472, 473

Fin de Chéri, La (Colette; stage adaptation, Loos), **Supp. XVI:** 194

Finder, Henry, **Supp. XX:**90

"Fin de Saison Palm Beach" (White), **Supp. I Part 2:** 673

"Finding a Bible in an Abandoned Cabin" (Wrigley), **Supp. XVIII: 293–294,** 296, 297, 300, 301, 303

Finding a Form (Gass), **Supp. VI:** 91–92, 93

Finding a Girl in America (Dubus), **Supp. VII:** 85–88

"Finding a Girl in America" (Dubus), **Supp. VII:** 87

"Finding Beads" (Hogan), **Supp. IV Part 1:** 400

Finding Losses (Bronk), **Supp. XXI:** 31, 32

"Finding of Zach, The" (Dunbar), **Supp. II Part 1:** 212

Findings and Keepings: Analects for an Autobiography (Mumford), **Supp. II Part 2:** 483

Finding the Center: Narrative Poetry of the Zuni Indians (Tedlock), **Supp. IV Part 2:** 509

Finding the Islands (Merwin), **Supp. III Part 1:** 353, 357

"Finding the Place: A Migrant Childhood" (Stegner), **Supp. IV Part 2:** 597

Findley, Timothy, **Supp. XX:**49–65

"Find the Woman" (Macdonald, as Millar), **Supp. IV Part 2:** 466

Fine, David, **Supp. XI:** 160

Fine, Richard, **Supp. XVIII:** 248

Fine Clothes to the Jew (Hughes), **Retro. Supp. I:** 200, 201, 203, 205; **Supp. I Part 1:** 326–328

"Fine Old Firm, A" (Jackson), **Supp. IX:** 120

Fine Preserving (Plagemann), **Supp. XVII:** 91

Fine Preserving: M. F. K. Fisher's Annotated Edition of Catherine Plagemann's Cookbook (Plagemann; M. F. K. Fisher, ed.), **Supp. XVII:** 91

Finer Grain, The (James), **II:** 335

Fine Writing (L. P. Smith), **Supp. XIV:** 347

"Finis" (X. J. Kennedy), **Supp. XV:** 169

"Finished Basement" (Di Piero), **Supp. XIX:** 47

Finished Man, The (Garrett), **Supp. VII:** 96, 97–98

Fink, Jonathan, **Supp. XXI:** 244, 245, 248, 255, 256

Fink, Mike, **IV:** 266

Finkelstein, Norman, **Supp. XXI:** 24, 33

Finkle, David, **Supp. XXI:** 47

Finley, John H., **II:** 418

Finn, David, **Supp. VIII:** 106–107

Finnegan, Robert (pseudonym). *See* Ryan, Paul William

Finnegans Wake (Joyce), **III:** 7, 12, 14, 261; **IV:** 182, 369–370, 418, 421; **Supp. I Part 2:** 620; **Supp. II Part 1:** 2; **Supp. XIII:** 191; **Supp. XVIII:** 32

Finney, Brian, **Supp. XIV:** 158, 160, 161, 165, 166, 167, 169

"Finnish Rhapsody" (Ashbery), **Supp. III Part 1:** 26

Finster, Howard, **Supp. XV:** 349

Firbank, Ronald, **IV:** 77, 436

"Fire" (Hughes), **Supp. I Part 1:** 327

"Fire and Cloud" (Wright), **IV:** 488

"Fire and Ice" (Frost), **II:** 154; **Retro. Supp. I:** 133; **Supp. XIX:** 122

Fire and Ice (Stegner), **Supp. IV Part 2:** 598, 607–608

"Fire and the Cloud, The" (Hurston), **Supp. VI:** 158

"Fire and the Hearth, The" (Faulkner), **II:** 71

Firebird (Doty), **Supp. XI:** 119–120, 121, **132–133,** 134

"Firebombing, The" (Dickey), **Supp. IV Part 1:** 180–181, 187, 189–190

"Fireborn Are at Home in Fire, The" (Sandburg), **III:** 591

"Fire by Night" (R. Fisher), **Supp. XIX:** 70–71

"Fire Chaconne" (Francis), **Supp. IX:** 87

Firecrackers (Van Vechten), **Supp. II Part 2:** 740, 742–744, 749

Fire: From "A Journal of Love," the Unexpurgated Diary of Anaïs Nin, 1934–1937, **Supp. X:** 184, 185, 189, 194, 195

"Fireman, The " (Bass), **Supp. XVI:** 24

Fireman's Wife and Other Stories, The (Bausch), **Supp. VII:** 48, 54

Fire Next Time, The (Baldwin), **Retro. Supp. II:** 5, 8, 9; **Supp. I Part 1:** 48, 49, 52, 60–61

"Fire Next Time, The" (Baldwin). *See* "Down at the Cross" (Baldwin)

"Fire of Driftwood, The" (Longfellow), **II:** 499; **Retro. Supp. II:** 159, 168

"Fire of Life" (McCullers), **II:** 585

Fire on the Mountain (Abbey), **Supp. XIII:** 6

"Fire Poem" (Merrill), **Supp. III Part 1:** 321

"Fires" (Bass), **Supp. XVI:** 20

"Fires" (Carver), **Supp. III Part 1:** 136–139, 147

Fire Screen, The (Merrill), **Supp. III Part 1:** 319, 325–329

"Fire Season" (Didion), **Supp. IV Part 1:** 199

"Fire Sequence" (Winters), **Supp. II Part 2:** 791, 796, 800

Fire Sermon (Morris), **III:** 238–239

"Fire Sermon, The" (Eliot), **Retro. Supp. I:** 60–61

Fires: Essays, Poems, Stories (Carver), **Supp. III Part 1:** 136, 140, 142, 146–147

Fireside Travels (Lowell), **Supp. I Part 2:** 407, 419–420

Firestarter (King), **Supp. V:** 140, 141, 144; **Supp. IX:** 114

"fire the bastards" (Green), **Supp. IV Part 1:** 285

"Fire-Truck, A" (Wilbur), **Supp. III Part 2:** 556

"Fireweed" (Clampitt), **Supp. IX: 44–45**

"Firewood" (Banks), **Supp. V:** 15

"Fireworks" (Ford), **Supp. V:** 69

"Fireworks" (Shapiro), **Supp. II Part 2:** 707

Fireworks: A History and Celebration (Plimpton), **Supp. XVI:** 245

Fir-Flower Tablets (Lowell), **II:** 512, 526–527

Firger, Jessica, **Supp. XIX:** 51, 58, 59, 62

Firkins, Oscar W., **II:** 271; **Supp. XV:** 297, 309

"Firmament, The" (Bryant), **Supp. I Part 1:** 162

Firmat, Gustavo Pérez, **Supp. VIII:** 76, 77, 79; **Supp. XI:** 184

"First American, The" (Toomer), **Supp. III Part 2:** 480, 487

"First Birth" (Olds), **Supp. X:** 212

First Book of Africa, The (Hughes), **Supp. I Part 1:** 344–345

First Book of Jazz, The (Hughes), **Supp. I Part 1:** 345

First Book of Negroes, The (Hughes), **Supp. I Part 1:** 345

First Book of Rhythms, The (Hughes), **Supp. I Part 1:** 345

First Book of the West Indies, The (Hughes), **Supp. I Part 1:** 345

Firstborn (Glück), **Supp. V:** 80, 81, 82, 84

"Firstborn" (Wright), **Supp. V:** 340

"First Chaldaic Oracle" (Carson), **Supp. XII:** 111

"First Communion" (Fante), **Supp. XI:** 160

"First Confession" (X. J. Kennedy), **Supp. XV: 154–155**

"First Day of School, The" (Gibbons), **Supp. X:** 41, 42

"First Death in Nova Scotia" (Bishop), **Supp. I Part 1:** 73

"First Formal" (Olds), **Supp. X:** 212

First Four Books of Poems, The (Glück), **Supp. V:** 81, 83

"First Grade" (Stafford), **Supp. XI:** 328

First Hand (Bierds), **Supp. XVII:** 32, 34–36

"First Hawaiian Bank" (Nye), **Supp. XIII:** 278

"First Heat" (Taylor), **Supp. V:** 323

First Hour, The (Di Piero), **Supp. XIX:** 36–37, 40

"First Hour of the Night, The" (Bidart), **Supp. XV: 30–32**

"First Hunters and the Last, The" (Sobin), **Supp. XVI:** 292

"First Job, The" (Cisneros), **Supp. VII:** 62

"1st Letter on Georges" (Olson), **Supp. II Part 2:** 578

First Light (C. Baxter), **Supp. XVII: 15, 17–18,** 19, 22

First Light (Preston), **Supp. XVII:** 18

First Light (Wagoner), **Supp. IX:** 330

"First Love" (Welty), **IV:** 264; **Retro. Supp. I:** 347

First Love: A Lyric Sequence (Untermeyer), **Supp. XV:** 295

First Man, The (O'Neill), **III:** 390

First Manifesto (McGrath), **Supp. X:** 115

"First Meditation" (Roethke), **III:** 545–546

"First Noni Daylight, The" (Harjo), **Supp. XII:** 219

"First Passover" (Longfellow), **II:** 500–501

"First Person Female" (Harrison), **Supp. VIII:** 40, 41, 48

"First Place, The" (Wagoner), **Supp. IX:** 328

First Poems (Buechner), **Supp. XII:** 45

First Poems (Merrill), **Supp. III Part 1:** 318–321, 323

First Poems 1946–1954 (Kinnell), **Supp. III Part 1:** 235, 238–239

"First Praise" (W. C. Williams), **Retro. Supp. I:** 413

First Principles (Spencer), **Supp. I Part 1:** 368

"First Reader" (Collins), **Supp. XXI:** 55–56

"First Ride and First Walk" (Goldbarth), **Supp. XII:** 182–183

"First Seven Years, The" (Malamud), **Supp. I Part 2:** 431

"First Sex" (Olds), **Supp. X:** 208

"First Snow in Alsace" (Wilbur), **Supp. III Part 2:** 545, 546, 559

"First Song" (Kinnell), **Supp. III Part 1:** 239

"First Spade in the West, The" (Fiedler), **Supp. XIII:** 103

"First Steps" (McClatchy), **Supp. XII:** 256

First There Is the Need (Reznikoff), **Supp. XIV:** 291

"First Things First" (Auden), **Supp. II Part 1:** 13

"First Thought, Best Thought" (Ginsberg), **Supp. II Part 1:** 327

"First Time I Saw Paris, The" (Fante), **Supp. XI:** 174

"First Travels of Max" (Ransom), **III:** 490–491

"First Tycoon of Teen, The" (Wolfe), **Supp. III Part 2:** 572

"First Views of the Enemy" (Oates), **Supp. II Part 2:** 508

"First Wife, The" (Buck), **Supp. II Part 1:** 127

First Words before Spring (Untermeyer), **Supp. XV:** 310

"First World War" (White), **Supp. I Part 2:** 665

"Fish" (F. Barthelme), **Supp. XI:** 26

"Fish" (Levis), **Supp. XI:** 259–260

Fish, Stanley, **Supp. IV Part 1:** 48; **Supp. XIV:** 14, 15

"Fish, The" (Bishop), **Supp. XV:** 100, 102

"Fish, The" (Moore), **III:** 195, 197, 209, 211, 213–214; **Supp. XXI:** 26

"Fish, The" (Oliver), **Supp. VII:** 236

"Fish, The/Lago Chapala" (Everwine), **Supp. XV:** 82–83

"Fish and Shadow" (Pound), **III:** 466

"Fishboy" (Richard), **Supp. XIX:** 212–213

Fishboy: A Ghost's Story (Richard), **Supp. XIX:** 209, **213–220,** 221

Fishburne, Laurence, **Supp. VIII:** 345

"Fish Cannery" (Fante), **Supp. XI:** 167

Fisher, Alexander Metcalf, **Supp. I Part 2:** 582

Fisher, Alfred, **Retro. Supp. II:** 243

Fisher, Craig, **Supp. V:** 125

Fisher, Dorothy Canfield, **Retro. Supp. I:** 21, 133; **Supp. II Part 1:** 117. *See also* Canfield, Dorothy

Fisher, Mary, **Supp. I Part 2:** 455

Fisher, M. F. K., **Supp. XVII: 81–93**

Fisher, Phillip, **Retro. Supp. I:** 39

Fisher, Rudolph, **Retro. Supp. II:** 200; **Supp. I Part 1:** 325; **Supp. X:** 139; **Supp. XVI:** 143; **Supp. XIX: 65–80**

Fisher, Vardis, **Supp. IV Part 2:** 598

Fisher King, The (Marshall), **Supp. XI:** 275–276, **288–290**

"Fisherman, The" (Merwin), **Supp. II Part 1:** 346

"Fisherman and His Wife, The" (Welty), **IV:** 266

"Fisherman from Chihuahua, The" (Connell), **Supp. XIV:** 86

"Fishing" (Harjo), **Supp. XII:** 227–228

"Fish in the Stone, The" (Dove), **Supp. IV Part 1:** 245, 257

"Fish in the unruffled lakes" (Auden), **Supp. II Part 1:** 8–9

"Fish R Us" (Doty), **Supp. XI:** 135

Fisk, James, **I:** 4, 474

Fiske, John, **Supp. I Part 1:** 314; **Supp. I Part 2:** 493

"Fit Against the Country, A" (Wright), **Supp. III Part 2:** 591–592, 601

Fitch, Clyde, **Supp. IV Part 2:** 573

Fitch, Elizabeth. *See* Taylor, Mrs. Edward (Elizabeth Fitch)

Fitch, James, **IV:** 147

Fitch, Noël Riley, **Supp. X:** 186, 187

"Fitting, The" (Hull), **Supp. XXI:** 134, 135

Fitts, Dudley, **I:** 169, 173; **Supp. I Part 1:** 342, 345; **Supp. XIII:** 346

FitzGerald, Edward, **Supp. I Part 2:** 416; **Supp. III Part 2:** 610

Fitzgerald, Ella, **Supp. XIII:** 132

Fitzgerald, F. Scott, **I:** 107, 117, 118, 123, 188, 221, 288, 289, 358, 367, 374–375, 382, 423, 476, 482, 487, 495, 509, 511; **II: 77–100,** 257, 263, 272, 283, 415, 416, 417–418, 420, 425, 427, 430, 431, 432, 433, 434, 436, 437, 450, 458–459, 482, 560; **III:** 2, 26, 35, 36, 37, 40, 44, 45, 69, 106, 244, 284, 334, 350–351, 453, 454, 471, 551, 552, 572; **IV:** 27, 49, 97, 101, 126, 140, 191, 222, 223, 287, 297, 427, 471; **Retro. Supp. I:** 1, 74, **97–120,** 178, 180, 186, 215, 359, 381; **Retro. Supp. II:** 257, 321, 326, 328; **Supp. I Part 1:** 196, 197; **Supp. I Part 2:** 622; **Supp. III Part 2:** 409, 411, 585; **Supp. IV Part 1:** 123, 197, 200, 203, 341; **Supp. IV Part 2:** 463, 468, 607, 689; **Supp. V:** 23, 95, 226, 251, 262, 276, 313; **Supp. VIII:** 101, 103, 106, 137; **Supp. IX:** 15, 20, 55, 57–63, 199; **Supp. X:** 225; **Supp. XI:** 65, 221, 334; **Supp. XII:** 42, 173, 295;

Supp. XIII: 170, 263; Supp. XV: 135; Supp. XVI: 64, 75, 191, 192, 294; Supp. XVIII: 148, 246, 248, 251, 254; Supp. XX:74; Supp. XXI: 262

Fitzgerald, Robert, I: 27–28; III: 338, 348; Retro. Supp. II: 179, 221, 222, 223, 228, 229; Supp. IV Part 2: 631; Supp. XV: 112, 249

Fitzgerald, Zelda (Zelda Sayre), I: 482; II: 77, 79, 82–85, 88, 90–91, 93, 95; Supp. IV Part 1: 310; Supp. IX: 55–73; Supp. X: 172. See also Sayre, Zelda

"Fitzgerald's Tragic Sense" (Schorer), Retro. Supp. I: 115

"Fitzgerald: The Romance of Money" (Cowley), Supp. II Part 1: 143

5 Detroits (Levine), Supp. V: 178

Five Came Back (West), IV: 287

Five Corners (screenplay, Shanley), Supp. XIV: 316

"Five-Dollar Bill, The" (D. West as Mary Christopher), Supp. XVIII: 282

"Five Dollar Guy, The" (W. C. Williams), Retro. Supp. I: 423

Five Easy Pieces (film), Supp. V: 26

"Five Elephants" (Dove), Supp. IV Part 1: 244–245

"Five Fucks" (Lethem), Supp. XVIII: 139

Five Groups of Verse (Reznikoff), Supp. XIV: 279, 282

Five Hundred Hats of Bartholomew Cubbins, The (Geisel), Supp. XVI: 100

Five Hundred Scorpions (Hearon), Supp. VIII: 57, 65, 66

Five Indiscretions (Ríos), Supp. IV Part 2: 545–547

Five Men and Pompey (Benét), Supp. XI: 43, 44

Five Plays (Hughes), Retro. Supp. I: 197, 209

"Five Psalms" (Jarman), Supp. XVII: 120

Five Temperaments (Kalstone), Retro. Supp. II: 40

5,000 Fingers of Dr. T, The (film), Supp. XVI: 103

Five Young American Poets, I: 170; II: 367

Fixer, The (Malamud), Supp. I Part 2: 428, 435, 445, 446–448, 450, 451

Fjellestad, Danuta Zadworna, Supp. XVI: 150

Flaccus, Kimball, Retro. Supp. I: 136

Flacius, Matthias, IV: 163

"Flagellant's Song" (X. J. Kennedy), Supp. XV: 165

Flag for Sunrise, A (Stone), Supp. V: 301–304

Flag of Childhood, The: Poems from the Middle East (Nye, ed.), Supp. XIII: 280

"Flag of Summer" (Swenson), Supp. IV Part 2: 645

Flagons and Apples (Jeffers), Supp. II Part 2: 413, 414, 417–418

Flags in the Dust (Faulkner), Retro. Supp. I: 81, 82, 83, 86, 88

Flamel, Nicolas, Supp. XII: 178

Flaming Corsage, The (W. Kennedy), Supp. VII: 133, 153–156

Flammarion, Camille, Supp. I Part 1: 260

Flanagan, John T., Supp. I Part 2: 464, 465, 468

Flanner, Janet, Supp. XVI: 195

"Flannery O'Connor: Poet to the Outcast" (Sister Rose Alice), III: 348

Flappers and Philosophers (Fitzgerald), II: 88; Retro. Supp. I: 103; Supp. IX: 56

Flash and Filigree (Southern), Supp. XI: 295, 296–297

"Flashcards" (Dove), Supp. IV Part 1: 250

Flash Fiction: Seventy-two Very Short Stories (J. Thomas, ed.), Supp. XVI: 268

"Flash in the Pan" (Shaw), Supp. XIX: 245

Flatt, Lester, Supp. V: 335

Flaubert, Gustave, I: 66, 123, 130, 272, 312, 314, 315, 477, 504, 506, 513, 514; II: 182, 185, 194, 198–199, 205, 209, 230, 289, 311, 316, 319, 325, 337, 392, 401, 577, 594; III: 196, 207, 251, 315, 461, 467, 511, 564; IV: 4, 29, 31, 37, 40, 134, 285, 428; Retro. Supp. I: 5, 215, 218, 222, 225, 235, 287; Supp. III Part 2: 411, 412; Supp. XI: 334; Supp. XIV: 87, 336

"Flavia and Her Artists" (Cather), Retro. Supp. I: 5

Flavoring of New England, The (Brooks), I: 253, 256

Flavor of Man, The (Toomer), Supp. III Part 2: 487

"Flaw, The" (Peacock), Supp. XIX: 206

Flaxman, Josiah, Supp. I Part 2: 716

"Flea, The" (Donne), Supp. XVIII: 307

"Flèche d'Or" (Merrill), Supp. III Part 1: 328

Flecker, James Elroy, Supp. I Part 1: 257

"Flee on Your Donkey" (Sexton), Supp. II Part 2: 683, 685

Fleming, Ian, Supp. XI: 307; Supp. XX:195

Fleming, Rene, Supp. XII: 321

Fleming, Robert E., Supp. XVII: 155

Flesch, Rudolf, Supp. XVI: 105, 106

Flesh and Blood (Cunningham), Supp. XV: 63–65

Flesh and Blood (play; Cunnigham and Gaitens), Supp. XV: 65

"Fleshbody" (Ammons), Supp. VII: 27

Fletcher, H. D., II: 517, 529

Fletcher, John, Supp. IV Part 2: 621

Fletcher, John Gould, I: 243; II: 517, 529; III: 458; Supp. I Part 1: 263; Supp. I Part 2: 422; Supp. XV: 298, 302, 306, 307, 308

Fletcher, Phineas, Supp. I Part 1: 369

Fletcher, Virginia. See Caldwell, Mrs. Erskine (Virginia Fletcher)

Fleurs du mal, Les (Baudelaire; Millay and Dillon, trans.), III: 141–142

"Flight" (Bierds), Supp. XVII: 36

"Flight" (Updike), IV: 218, 222, 224; Retro. Supp. I: 318

Flight (White), Supp. XVIII: 127

"Flight, The" (Haines), Supp. XII: 204–205

"Flight, The" (Roethke), III: 537–538

Flight among the Tombs (Hecht), Supp. X: 58, 71–74

"Flight for Freedom" (McCoy), Supp. XIII: 170

"Flight from Byzantium" (Brodsky), Supp. VIII: 30–31

"Flight of Besey Lane, The" (Jewett), Retro. Supp. II: 139

Flight of the Rocket, The (Fitzgerald), II: 89

Flights of the Harvest-Mare (Bierds), Supp. XVII: 26–27

Flight to Canada (Reed), Supp. X: 240, 249–252

Flinn, Mary, Supp. XVII: 110

Flint, F. S., II: 517; III: 459, 464, 465; Retro. Supp. I: 127; Supp. I Part 1: 261, 262

Flint, R. W., Supp. XVI: 47, 49, 57

"Flitting Flies" (X. J. Kennedy), Supp. XV: 166, 167

Flivver King, The (Sinclair), Supp. V: 290

Floating House, The (Sanders), Supp. XVI: 269

Floating Light Bulb, The (Allen), Supp. XV: 2, 3, 13

Floating Opera, The (Barth), I: 121, 122–126, 127, 129, 130, 131

"Floating Poem, Unnumbered, The" (Rich), Supp. I Part 2: 572–573

"Floating Trees" (Wright), Supp. XV: 348

Flood (Matthews), Supp. IX: 154, 160–161

Flood (Warren), IV: 252, 256–257

"Flood of Years, The" (Bryant), Supp. I Part 1: 159, 170, 171; Supp. I Part 2: 416

"Floor and the Ceiling, The" (W. J. Smith), Supp. XIII: 345, 346

"Floor Plans" (Komunyakaa), Supp. XIII: 114

"Floral Conversation" (Peacock), Supp. XIX: 200

"Floral Decorations for Bananas" (Stevens), IV: 8

Florida (Acker), Supp. XII: 5

"Florida" (Bishop), Retro. Supp. II: 43

"Florida Road Workers" (Hughes), Retro. Supp. I: 203

"Florida Sunday, A" (Lanier), Supp. I Part 1: 364, 366

"Flossie Cabanis" (Masters), Supp. I Part 2: 461–462

"Flounder" (Trethewey), Supp. XXI: 244, 245, 246, 251

Flow Chart (Ashbery), Supp. VIII: 275

"Flowchart" (Ashbery), Supp. III Part 1: 26

Flower, Fruit, and Thorn Pieces (Richter), Supp. XVI: 182

Flower-de-Luce (Longfellow), II: 490

Flower Drum Song (Rodgers and Hammerstein), **Supp. XXI:** 148
Flower Drum Song, The (Lee), **Supp. XXI:** 148
Flower Fables (Alcott), **Supp. I Part 1:** 33
"Flower-Fed Buffaloes, The" (Lindsay), **Supp. I Part 2:** 398
"Flower Garden" (Jackson), **Supp. IX:** 119
"Flower-gathering" (Frost), **II:** 153
Flower Herding on Mount Monadnock (Kinnell), **Supp. III Part 1:** 235, 239, 241–244
"Flower Herding on Mount Monadnock" (Kinnell), **Supp. III Part 1:** 242
"Flowering Death" (Ashbery), **Supp. III Part 1:** 22
"Flowering Dream, The" (McCullers), **II:** 591
"Flowering Judas" (Porter), **III:** 434, 435–436, 438, 441, 445, 446, 450–451
Flowering Judas and Other Stories (Porter), **III:** 433, 434
Flowering of New England, The (Brooks), **IV:** 171–172; **Supp. VIII:** 101
Flowering of the Rod (Doolittle), **Supp. I Part 1:** 272
Flowering Peach, The (Odets), **Supp. II Part 2:** 533, 547, 549–550
"Flowering Plum" (Glück), **Supp. V:** 82
"Flowers for Marjorie" (Welty), **IV:** 262
"Flowers of the Fallow" (Larcom), **Supp. XIII:** 143, 145–146
"Flowers Well if anybody" (Dickinson), **Retro. Supp. I:** 30
"Fluff and Mr. Ripley" (D. West), **Supp. XVIII:** 284
"Fly, The" (Kinnell), **Supp. III Part 1:** 249
"Fly, The" (Shapiro), **Supp. II Part 2:** 705
"Fly, The" (Simic), **Supp. VIII:** 278
Flye, Father James Harold, **I:** 25, 26, 35–36, 37, 42, 46; **IV:** 215
"Fly in Buttermilk, A" (Baldwin), **Retro. Supp. II:** 8
Flying at Night: Poems 1965–1985 (Kooser), **Supp. XIX:** 128
"Flying High" (Levertov), **Supp. III Part 1:** 284
"Flying Home" (Ellison), **Retro. Supp. II:** 117, **125–126; Supp. II Part 1:** 235, 238–239
"Flying Home" (Kinnell), **Supp. III Part 1:** 250
"Flying Home" and Other Stories (Ellison), **Retro. Supp. II:** 119, 124
"Flying Home from Utah" (Swenson), **Supp. IV Part 2:** 645
"Flying over Clouds" (Gioia), **Supp. XV:** 118
"Flying to Hanoi" (Rukeyser), **Supp. VI:** 279
Flynn, Elizabeth Gurley, **Supp. XVIII:** 225
Flynn, Richard, **Supp. XVII:** 115; **Supp. XVIII:** 183
Fly-Truffler, The (Sobin), **Supp. XVI: 294–295,** 296

Foata, Anne, **Supp. XI:** 104
FOB (Hwang), **Supp. XXI:** 143, 144, 145, 146, **148–150**
Focillon, Henri, **IV:** 90
Focus (A. Miller), **III:** 150–151, 156
Foer, Jonathan Safran, **Supp. XII:** 169; **Supp. XX:** 177
Foerster, Norman, **I:** 222; **Supp. I Part 2:** 423, 424; **Supp. IV Part 2:** 598
"Fog" (Sandburg), **III:** 586
"Fog Galleon" (Komunyakaa), **Supp. XIII:** 127
"Foggy and dripping" (Kooser), **Supp. XIX:** 125
"Foggy Lane, The" (Simpson), **Supp. IX:** 274
"Fog Man, The" (Boyle), **Supp. XX:** 20
Folded Leaf, The (Maxwell), **Supp. III Part 1:** 62; **Supp. VIII: 159–162**
Folding Star, The (Hollinghurst), **Supp. XIII:** 52
Foley, Jack, **Supp. X:** 125; **Supp. XV:** 112, 116; **Supp. XVII:** 77
Foley, Martha, **II:** 587; **Supp. XVI:** 225
Folk-Lore in the Old Testament (Frazer), **Supp. XX:** 116–117
Folks from Dixie (Dunbar), **Supp. II Part 1:** 211–212
Folkways (Sumner), **III:** 102
Follain, Jean, **Supp. IX:** 152, 154
Follett, Wilson, **I:** 405; **Supp. XIII:** 173
Follower of Dusk (Salinas), **Supp. XIII:** 326
"Following the Bones" (W. V. Davis), **Supp. XXI:** 96
Following the Equator (Twain), **II:** 434; **IV:** 208
Follow Me Home (Hoffman), **Supp. XVIII:** 86
Folly (Minot), **Supp. VI:** 205, 208, **210–213**
Folly of Others, The (Boyce), **Supp. XVII:** 100; **Supp. XXI:** 10
Folsom, Charles, **Supp. I Part 1:** 156
Folsom, Ed, **Retro. Supp. I:** 392
Folson, Marcia McClintock, **Retro. Supp. II:** 139
Fonda, Henry, **Supp. I Part 1:** 67; **Supp. IV Part 1:** 236
Fonda, Jane, **III:** 284; **Supp. XI:** 307
Fonda, Peter, **Supp. VIII:** 42; **Supp. XI:** 293, 308
"Fondled Memories" (Molesworth), **Supp. XIX:** 121–122
"Fond Memories of a Black Childhood" (D. West), **Supp. XVIII:** 289
Foner, Eric, **Supp. I Part 2:** 523
Fong and the Indians (Theroux), **Supp. VIII:** 314, 315, **316–317**
Fontanne, Lynn, **III:** 397
Food and Drink (Untermeyer), **Supp. XV:** 310
Fool for Love (Shepard), **Supp. III Part 2:** 433, 447, 448
"Foolishness" (Pickering), **Supp. XXI:** 197
Fools (Simon), **Supp. IV Part 2:** 584–585
Fool's Progress, The: An Honest Novel (Abbey), **Supp. XIII:** 4, **13–15**

Foot Book, The (Geisel), **Supp. XVI:** 108
Foote, Horton, **Supp. I Part 1:** 281; **Supp. VIII:** 128, 129
Foote, Mary Hallock, **Retro. Supp. II:** 72; **Supp. IV Part 2:** 611
Foote, Roxanna. *See* Beecher, Mrs. Lyman (Roxanna Foote)
Foote, Samuel, **Supp. I Part 2:** 584
Foote, Stephanie, **Retro. Supp. II:** 139
"Foot Fault" (pseudonym). *See* Thurber, James
Footing on This Earth, A (Hay), **Supp. XIV:** 125, 126, 130
"Footing up a Total" (Lowell), **II:** 528
"Footnote to Howl" (Ginsberg), **Supp. II Part 1:** 316–317
"Footnote to Weather Forecasts, A" (Brodsky), **Supp. VIII:** 32
Footprints (Hearon), **Supp. VIII: 69–70**
Footprints (Levertov), **Supp. III Part 1:** 272, 281
"Footsteps of Angels" (Longfellow), **II:** 496
"For A, at Fourteen" (Weigl), **Supp. XIX:** 287
For a Bitter Season: New and Selected Poems (Garrett), **Supp. VII:** 99–100
"For a Dead Kitten" (Hay), **Supp. XIV:** 119–120
"For a Dead Lady" (Robinson), **III:** 508, 513, 517
"For a Ghost Who Once Placed Bets in the Park" (Levis), **Supp. XI:** 265
"For a Lamb" (Eberhart), **I:** 523, 530, 531
"For All" (Snyder), **Supp. VIII:** 304
"For All Tuesday Travelers" (Cisneros), **Supp. VII:** 67–68
"For a Lost Child" (Stafford), **Supp. XI:** 329
"For a Marriage" (Bogan), **Supp. III Part 1:** 52
"For an Emigrant" (Jarrell), **II:** 371
"For Anna Akmatova" (Lowell), **II:** 544
"For Anna Mae Pictou Aquash, Whose Spirit Is Present Here and in the Dappled Stars" (Harjo), **Supp. XII:** 225
"For Anne, at a Little Distance" (Haines), **Supp. XII:** 207
"For Annie" (Poe), **III:** 427; **Retro. Supp. II:** 263
"For an Old Friend Encountered Unexpectedly" (Espaillat), **Supp. XXI:** 111–112
"For a Southern Man" (Cisneros), **Supp. VII:** 67
"For Bailey" (Angelou), **Supp. IV Part 1:** 15
Forbes, Malcolm, **Supp. IV Part 1:** 94
"Forbidden, The" (Glück), **Supp. XIV:** 269
"For Bill Nestrick (1940–96)" (Bidart), **Supp. XV:** 35
For Bread Alone (Choukri), **Supp. IV Part 1:** 92
"Force" (Di Piero), **Supp. XIX:** 35–36, 42, 44
Force of Desire, The (Bronk), **Supp. XXI:** 31, 32

Force of Evil (film, Polonsky), **Supp. XXI:** 261, 272, 275

Force of Spirit, The (Sanders), **Supp. XVI:** 277–278

Forché, Carolyn, **Supp. IV Part 1:** 208; **Supp. XIX:** 193

Ford, Arthur, **Supp. IV Part 1:** 140

Ford, Ford Madox, **I:** 288, 405, 409, 417, 421, 423; **II:** 58, 144, 198, 257, 263, 265, 517, 536; **III:** 458, 464–465, 470–471, 472, 476; **IV:** 27, 126, 261; **Retro. Supp. I:** 127, 177, 178, 186, 231, 286–287, 418; **Supp. II Part 1:** 107; **Supp. III Part 2:** 617; **Supp. VIII:** 107; **Supp. XIV:** 3

Ford, Harrison, **Supp. VIII:** 323

Ford, Harry, **Supp. V:** 179; **Supp. XIII:** 76

Ford, Henry, **I:** 295, 480–481; **III:** 292, 293; **Supp. I Part 1:** 21; **Supp. I Part 2:** 644; **Supp. III Part 2:** 612, 613; **Supp. IV Part 1:** 223; **Supp. V:** 290

Ford, John, **Supp. I Part 2:** 422; **Supp. III Part 2:** 619; **Supp. XVIII:** 247

Ford, Mary K., **Supp. XX:** 239

Ford, Richard, **Supp. IV Part 1:** 342; **Supp. V:** 22, **57–75**

Ford, Webster (pseudonym). *See* Masters, Edgar Lee

"Fording and Dread" (Harrison), **Supp. VIII:** 41

"Ford Madox Ford" (Lowell), **II:** 547; **Retro. Supp. II:** 188

"For Dudley" (Wilbur), **Supp. III Part 2:** 558

Fordyce, David, **II:** 113

Foregone Conclusion, A (Howells), **II:** 278–279, 282

"Foreign Affairs" (Kunitz), **Supp. III Part 1:** 265

"Foreigner, A" (Bynner), **Supp. XV:** 46

"Foreigner, The" (Jewett), **II:** 409–410; **Retro. Supp. II:** 133, 142

"Foreigners" (Jarman), **Supp. XVII:** 113

"Foreign Language, The" (Franzen), **Supp. XX:** 84

"Foreign Shores" (Salter), **Supp. IX:** 260

Forensic and the Navigators (Shepard), **Supp. III Part 2:** 439

Forerunner, The (Boyce), **Supp. XXI:** 2, 4, **10–11**

Forerunner, The: His Parables and Poems (Gibran), **Supp. XX:** 115, **118–119,** 119

Foreseeable Future, The (Price), **Supp. VI:** 265

Foreseeable Futures (Matthews), **Supp. IX:** 155, **163,** 169

"For Esmé with Love and Squalor" (Salinger), **III:** 560

"Forest" (Simic), **Supp. VIII:** 273

Forest, Jean-Claude, **Supp. XI:** 307

Forester's Letters (Paine), **Supp. I Part 2:** 508

"Forest Hymn, A" (Bryant), **Supp. I Part 1:** 156, 162, 163, 164, 165, 170

"Forest in the Seeds, The" (Kingsolver), **Supp. VII:** 203

Forest of the South, The (Gordon), **II:** 197

"Forest of the South, The" (Gordon), **II:** 199, 201

Forest without Leaves (Adams and Haines), **Supp. XII:** 209

"Forever, Said the Duck" (Lethem), **Supp. XVIII:** 139

"Forever and the Earth" (Bradbury), **Supp. IV Part 1:** 102

"Forever in That Year" (Carruth), **Supp. XVI:** 51

"Forever Young" (Jarman and R. McDowell), **Supp. XVII:** 111

"For Fathers of Girls" (Dunn), **Supp. XI:** 146

"For/From Lew" (Snyder), **Supp. VIII:** 303

"For Garrison Keillor, Fantasy Is a Lot More Fun then Reality" (Letofsky), **Supp. XVI:** 167

"For George Santayana" (Lowell), **II:** 547

"Forgetfulness" (Collins), **Supp. XXI:** 58

"Forgiveness" (Peacock), **Supp. XIX:** 200

Forgotten Helper, The: A Story for Children (Moore), **Supp. X:** 175

"Forgotten in an Old Notebook" (F. Wright), **Supp. XVII:** 244

Forgotten Village, The (Steinbeck), **IV:** 51

"For Grizzel McNaught (1709–1792)" (A. Finch), **Supp. XVII:** 72

Forgue, Guy J., **III:** 118, 119

For Her Dark Skin (Everett), **Supp. XVIII:** 56, 60

"FOR HETTIE" (Baraka), **Supp. II Part 1:** 32

"FOR HETTIE IN HER FIFTH MONTH" (Baraka), **Supp. II Part 1:** 32, 38

"For Homer" (Corso), **Supp. XII:** 135

"For I'm the Boy" (Barthelme), **Supp. IV Part 1:** 47

"For Jeff" (Kooser), **Supp. XIX:** 125

"For Jessica, My Daughter" (Strand), **Supp. IV Part 2:** 629

"For John, Who Begs Me not to Enquire Further" (Sexton), **Supp. II Part 2:** 676

"For Johnny Pole on the Forgotten Beach" (Sexton), **Supp. II Part 2:** 675

"For Joy to Leave Upon" (Ortiz), **Supp. IV Part 2:** 508

"Fork" (Simic), **Supp. VIII:** 275

"For Karl Shapiro, Having Gone Back to the Sonnet" (Kooser), **Supp. XIX:** 118

For Lancelot Andrewes (Eliot), **Retro. Supp. I:** 64

For Lizzie and Harriet (Lowell), **Retro. Supp. II:** 183, 186, 190

"Forlorn Hope of Sidney Lanier, The" (Leary), **Supp. I Part 1:** 373

For Love (Creeley), **Supp. IV Part 1:** 139, 140, 142–145, 147–149, 150, 154

"For Love" (Creeley), **Supp. IV Part 1:** 145

For Love (Miller), **Supp. XII:** **297–299,** 299

For Love of Imabelle (C. Himes), **Supp. XVI:** 135, 143, 144

"Formal Elegy" (Berryman), **I:** 170

Formal Feeling Comes, A (A. Finch, ed.), **Supp. XVII:** 71–72

"Formalist Criticism: Its Principles and Limits" (Burke), **I:** 282

Forman, Milos, **Supp. IV Part 1:** 236

"Form and Function of the Novel, The" (Goldbarth), **Supp. XII:** 183

"For Marse Chouchoute" (Chopin), **Retro. Supp. II:** 60

"For Mary Ann Youngren" (Bidart), **Supp. XV:** 29

"Format and Form" (A. Rich), **Supp. XVII:** 74

"Formation of a Separatist, I" (Howe), **Supp. IV Part 2:** 427

"Form Is Emptiness" (Baraka), **Supp. II Part 1:** 51

"For Mr. Death Who Stands with His Door Open" (Sexton), **Supp. II Part 2:** 695

Forms of Discovery (Winters), **Supp. II Part 2:** 812, 813

Forms of Fiction, The (Gardner and Dunlap), **Supp. VI:** 64

"For My Children" (Karr), **Supp. XI:** 254

"For My Daughter" (Kees), **Supp. XV:** 141, 147

"For My Daughter" (Olds), **Supp. X:** 206

"For My Former Wife, Watching TV, in the Past" (Kooser), **Supp. XIX:** 120

"For My Lover, Returning to His Wife" (Sexton), **Supp. II Part 2:** 688

Fornés, Maria Irene, **Supp. XXI:** 144

"For Night to Come" (Stern), **Supp. IX:** 292

"For Once, Then, Something" (Frost), **II:** 156–157; **Retro. Supp. I:** 126, 133, 134

"For Peg: A Remnant of Song Still Distantly Sounding" (Carruth), **Supp. XVI:** 54

"For Pot-Boiling" (Hay), **Supp. XIV:** 128

"For Radicals" (Bourne), **I:** 221

"For Rainer Gerhardt" (Creeley), **Supp. IV Part 1:** 142–143, 147

Forrestal, James, **I:** 491; **Supp. I Part 2:** 489

Forrester, Fanny, **Supp. XVIII:** 13

"For Richard After All" (Kingsolver), **Supp. VII:** 208

"For Sacco and Vanzetti" (Kingsolver), **Supp. VII:** 208

"Forsaken Merman" (Arnold), **Supp. I Part 2:** 529

"For S.F.S. 1875–1962" (J. W. Miller), **Supp. XX:** 166

For Spacious Skies (Buck), **Supp. II Part 1:** 131

Forster, E. M., **I:** 292; **IV:** 201; **Retro. Supp. I:** 59, 232; **Supp. III Part 2:** 503; **Supp. V:** 258; **Supp. VIII:** 155, 171; **Supp. IX:** 128; **Supp. XII:** 79, 81; **Supp. XIV:** 159, 160, 163; **Supp. XV:** 62; **Supp. XVI:** 236; **Supp. XVIII:** 143; **Supp. XX:** 229, 235, 239, 240; **Supp. XXI:** 233

Forster, John, **II:** 315

Fort, Paul, **II:** 518, 528, 529; **Retro. Supp. I:** 55

"For the Ahkoond" (Bierce), **I:** 209

For the Body (Nelson), **Supp. XVIII:** 173

For the Century's End: Poems 1990–1999 (Haines), **Supp. XII:** 211–213

"For the Dedication of the New City Library, Boston" (Holmes), **Supp. I Part 1:** 308

"For the Fallen" (Levine), **Supp. V:** 188

For the Health of the Land: Previously Unpublished Essays and Other Writings (Leopold), **Supp. XIV:** 183

"For the Lady in the Black Raincoat Who Slept Through an Entire Poetry Reading" (Espaillat), **Supp. XXI:** 108

"For the Last Wolverine" (Dickey), **Supp. IV Part 1:** 182

"For the Lovers of the Absolute" (Simic), **Supp. VIII:** 278–279

"For the Man Cutting the Grass" (Oliver), **Supp. VII:** 235

"For the Marriage of Faustus and Helen" (H. Crane), **I:** 395–396, 399, 402; **Retro. Supp. II:** 78–79, 82

"For the Meeting of the National Sanitary Association, 1860" (Holmes), **Supp. I Part 1:** 307

For the New Intellectual (Rand), **Supp. IV Part 2:** 521, 526–527, 527, 532

"For the New Railway Station in Rome" (Wilbur), **Supp. III Part 2:** 554

"For the Night" (Kenyon), **Supp. VII:** 163

"For Theodore Roethke: 1908–1963" (Lowell), **II:** 554

"For the Poem *Patterson*" (W. C. Williams), **Retro. Supp. I:** 424

"For the Poets of Chile" (Levine), **Supp. V:** 188

"FOR THE REVOLUTIONARY OUTBURST BY BLACK PEOPLE" (Baraka), **Supp. II Part 1:** 55

"For the Sleepless" (Dunn), **Supp. XI:** 145

For the Time Being (Auden), **Supp. II Part 1:** 2, 17, 18

For the Time Being (Dillard), **Supp. VI:** 23, 27, 29, 32, **34–35**

"For the Twentieth Century" (Bidart), **Supp. XV:** 35

For the Union Dead (Lowell), **II:** 543, 550–551, 554, 555; **Retro. Supp. II:** 181, 182, 186, 189; **Supp. X:** 53

"For the Union Dead" (Lowell), **II:** 551; **Retro. Supp. II:** 189

"For the Walking Dead" (Komunyakaa), **Supp. XIII:** 121

"For the West" (Snyder), **Supp. VIII:** 299

"For the Word Is Flesh" (Kunitz), **Supp. III Part 1:** 262–264

"Fortress, The" (Glück), **Supp. V:** 82

"Fortress, The" (Sexton), **Supp. II Part 2:** 682

Fortress of Solitude, The (Lethem), **Supp. XVIII:** 135, 136, **145–148,** 150

"Fort Robinson" (Kooser), **Supp. XIX:** 120

"Fortunate Traveler" (Hull), **Supp. XXI:** 140

Fortune, T. Thomas, **Supp. II Part 1:** 159

Fortune's Bones: The Manumission Requiem (Nelson), **Supp. XVIII:** 171, 172–173, 182–183

Fortune's Daughter (Hoffman), **Supp. X:** 77, 85

"Fortune Spill, The" (Nelson), **Supp. XVIII:** 175

45 Mercy Street (Sexton), **Supp. II Part 2:** 694, 695, 697

Forty Poems Touching on Recent American History (Bly, ed.), **Supp. IV Part 1:** 61

42nd Parallel, The (Dos Passos), **I:** 482, 484–485

Forty Stories (Barthelme), **Supp. IV Part 1:** 47, 49, 53, 54

For Whom the Bell Tolls (Hemingway), **II:** 249, 254–255, 261; **III:** 18, 363; **Retro. Supp. I:** 115, 176–177, 178, **184,** 187; **Supp. XVII:** 229

Foscolo, Ugo, **II:** 543

Foss, Sam Walter, **Supp. II Part 1:** 197

"Fossils, The" (Kinnell), **Supp. III Part 1:** 244

Foster, Edward, **Supp. IV Part 2:** 431, 434; **Supp. XVI:** 281, 293; **Supp. XXI:** 33

Foster, Edward Halsey, **Supp. XII:** 120, 129, 130, 135; **Supp. XVIII:** 265, 268

Foster, Emily, **II:** 309

Foster, Frances Smith, **Supp. XX:**287

Foster, Hannah, **Supp. XV:** 234

Foster, John Wilson, **Supp. XIII:** 32–33

Foster, Phil, **Supp. IV Part 2:** 574

Foster, Richard, **Supp. XV:** 269

Foster, Stephen, **Supp. I Part 1:** 100–101; **Supp. I Part 2:** 699

Foucault, Michel, **Supp. VIII:** 5; **Supp. XII:** 98; **Supp. XV:** 344; **Supp. XVI:** 285

"Founder, The" (Stern), **Supp. IX:** 297

Founding of Harvard College, The (Morison), **Supp. I Part 2:** 485

"Fountain, The" (Bryant), **Supp. I Part 1:** 157, 165, 166, 168

Fountain, The (O'Neill), **III:** 391

Fountain and Other Poems, The (Bryant), **Supp. I Part 1:** 157

Fountainhead, The (film), **Supp. IV Part 2:** 524

Fountainhead, The (Rand), **Supp. IV Part 2:** 517, 521–523, 525, 531

Fountainhead, The: A Fiftieth Anniversary Celebration (Cox), **Supp. IV Part 2:** 523

"Fountain Piece" (Swenson), **Supp. IV Part 2:** 641

4-H Club (Shepard), **Supp. III Part 2:** 439

"Four Ages of Man, The" (Bradstreet), **Supp. I Part 1:** 111, 115

Four American Indian Literary Masters (Velie), **Supp. IV Part 2:** 486

"Four Beasts in One; the Homo Cameleopard" (Poe), **III:** 425

Four Black Revolutionary Plays (Baraka), **Supp. II Part 1:** 45; **Supp. VIII:** 330

"Four Brothers" (Di Piero), **Supp. XIX:** 37

"Four Brothers, The" (Sandburg), **III:** 585

Four Dogs and a Bone and the Wild Goose (Shanley), **Supp. XIV:** 316, **328–329**

"Four Evangelists, The" (Komunyakaa), **Supp. XIII:** 131

"Four for Sir John Davies" (Roethke), **III:** 540, 541

"Four Girls, The" (Alvarez), **Supp. VII:** 7

"Four Horse Songs" (Harjo), **Supp. XII:** 220

"400-Meter Free Style" (Kumin), **Supp. IV Part 2:** 442

"400-Pound CEO, The" (Saunders), **Supp. XIX:** 225

Fourier, Charles, **II:** 342

"Four in a Family" (Rukeyser), **Supp. VI:** 272

Four in Hand: A Quartet of Novels (Warner), **Supp. VIII:** 164

"Four Lakes' Days" (Eberhart), **I:** 525

"Four Mad Studies" (Di Piero), **Supp. XIX:** 37

"Four Meetings" (James), **II:** 327

Four Million, The (O. Henry), **Supp. II Part 1:** 394, 408

"Four Monarchyes" (Bradstreet), **Supp. I Part 1:** 105, 106, 116

"Four Mountain Wolves" (Silko), **Supp. IV Part 2:** 561

Four of a Kind (Marquand), **III:** 54, 55

"Four of the Horsemen (Hypertense and Stroke, Coronary Occlusion and Cerebral Insult)" (Karr), **Supp. XI:** 250

"Four Poems" (Bishop), **Supp. I Part 1:** 92

"Four Preludes on Playthings of the Wind" (Sandburg), **III:** 586

Four Quartets (T. S. Eliot), **I:** 570, 576, 580–582, 585, 587; **II:** 537; **III:** 539; **Retro. Supp. I:** 66, 67; **Supp. II Part 1:** 1; **Supp. IV Part 1:** 284; **Supp. V:** 343, 344; **Supp. VIII:** 182, 195; **Supp. XIII:** 344; **Supp. XIV:** 167; **Supp. XV:** 216, 260, 266

Four Saints in Three Acts (Stein), **IV:** 30, 31, 33, 43, 44–45

"Four Seasons" (Bradstreet), **Supp. I Part 1:** 112–113

Four Seasons of Success, The (Schulberg), **Supp. XVIII:** 254

"Four Sides of One Story" (Updike), **Retro. Supp. I:** 328

"Four Skinny Trees" (Cisneros), **Supp. VII:** 64

"14: In A Dark Wood: Wood Thrushes" (Oliver), **Supp. VII:** 244

"14 Men Stage Head Winter 1624/ 25" (Olson), **Supp. II Part 2:** 574

14 Stories (Dixon), **Supp. XII:** 141, **145–147**

Fourteen Hundred Thousand (Shepard), **Supp. III Part 2:** 439

Fourteen Sisters of Emilio Montez O'Brien, The (Hijuelos), **Supp. VIII:** **82–85**

Fourteen Stories (Buck), **Supp. II Part 1:** 126

"Fourteenth Ward, The" (H. Miller), **III:** 175

Fourth Book of Peace, The (Kingston), **Supp. V:** 173

"Fourth Down" (Marquand), **III:** 56

Fourth Group of Verse, A (Reznikoff), **Supp. XIV:** 282, 284

"Fourth of July in Maine" (Lowell), **II:** 535, 552–553

Fourth Wall, The (Gurney), **Supp. V:** 109–110

Fowler, Douglas, **Supp. IV Part 1:** 226, 227

Fowler, Gene, **Supp. VIII:** 290

Fowler, Henry Watson, **Supp. I Part 2:** 660

Fowler, Singrid, **Supp. VIII:** 249, 258

Fowler, Virginia C., **Supp. VIII:** 224

Fox, Alan, **Supp. XIII:** 120

Fox, Dixon Ryan, **I:** 337

Fox, Joe, **Supp. IX:** 259, 261

Fox, John, **Supp. XIII:** 166

Fox, Linda C., **Supp. XIII:** 217–218

Fox, Paula, **Supp. XX:**91

Fox, Ruth, **Supp. I Part 2:** 619

"Fox, The" (Levine), **Supp. V:** 181, 189

Fox-Genovese, Elizabeth, **Supp. IV Part 1:** 286

Fox in Socks (Geisel), **Supp. XVI:** 108, 112

"Fox Night" (Jarman), **Supp. XVII:** 120

Fox of Peapack, The (White), **Supp. I Part 2:** 676, 677–678

"Fox of Peapack, The" (White), **Supp. I Part 2:** 677

"Fox Point Health Clinic, 1974" (Halliday), **Supp. XIX:** 89, 93

Foye, Raymond, **Supp. XIV:** 150

Fradkin, Lori, **Supp. XIX:** 52

Fraenkel, Michael, **III:** 178, 183

"Fragging" (Komunyakaa), **Supp. XIII:** 123

Fragile Beauty, A: John Nichols' Milagro Country: Text and Photographs from His Life and Work (Nichols), **Supp. XIII:** 268

"Fragility" (Shields), **Supp. VII:** 318

"Fragment" (Ashbery), **Supp. III Part 1:** 11, 13, 14, 19, 20

"Fragment" (Lowell), **II:** 516

"Fragment" (Ortiz), **Supp. IV Part 2:** 507

"Fragment of a Meditation" (Tate), **IV:** 129

"Fragment of an Agon" (Eliot), **I:** 579–580

"Fragment of a Prologue" (Eliot), **I:** 579–580

"Fragment of New York, 1929" (Eberhart), **I:** 536–537

"Fragments" (Emerson), **II:** 19

"Fragments for Fall" (Salinas), **Supp. XIII:** 320–321

"Fragments of a Hologram Rose" (W. Gibson), **Supp. XVI:** 122, 123, 128

"Fragments of a Liquidation" (Howe), **Supp. IV Part 2:** 426

Fragonard, Jean Honoré, **III:** 275; **IV:** 79

Fraiman, Susan, **Supp. IV Part 1:** 324

"Frame for Poetry, A" (W. J. Smith), **Supp. XIII:** 333

France, Anatole, **IV:** 444; **Supp. I Part 2:** 631; **Supp. XIV:** 79

France and England in North America (Parkman), **Supp. II Part 2:** 596, 600–605, 607, 613–614

Franchere, Hoyt C., **II:** 131

Franchiser, The (Elkin), **Supp. VI:** 51–52, 58

Franciosi, Robert, **Supp. XIV:** 283

Francis, Lee, **Supp. IV Part 2:** 499

Francis, Richard, **Supp. XV:** 121

Francis, Robert, **Supp. IX:** 75–92

Francis of Assisi, Saint, **III:** 543; **IV:** 69, 375, 410; **Supp. I Part 2:** 394, 397, 441, 442, 443

Franco, Francisco, **II:** 261

Franco, Harry (pseudonym). *See* Briggs, Charles Frederick

Franconia (Fraser), **Retro. Supp. I:** 136

"Franconia" tales (Abbott), **Supp. I Part 1:** 38

Frank, Anne, **Supp. X:** 149; **Supp. XVII:** 39

Frank, Frederick S., **Retro. Supp. II:** 273

Frank, James M., **Supp. XIV:** 1

Frank, Jerome, **Supp. I Part 2:** 645

Frank, Joseph, **II:** 587

Frank, Mary, **Supp. X:** 213

Frank, Robert, **Supp. XI:** 295; **Supp. XII:** 127; **Supp. XIV:** 150

Frank, Waldo, **I:** 106, 109, 117, 229, 236, 245, 259, 400; **Retro. Supp. II:** 77, 79, 83; **Supp. IX:** 308, 309, 311, 320; **Supp. XV:** 298; **Supp. XX:**67–82

Frank, W. L., Jr., **Supp. XVIII:** 77

Frankel, Charles, **III:** 291

Frankel, Haskel, **Supp. I Part 2:** 448

Frankenberg, Lloyd, **I:** 436, 437, 445, 446; **III:** 194

Frankenheimer, John, **Supp. XI:** 343

Frankenstein (film), **Supp. IV Part 1:** 104; **Supp. XVII:** 57

Frankenstein (Gardner), **Supp. VI:** 72

Frankenstein (Shelley), **Supp. XII:** 79

Frankfurter, Felix, **I:** 489

"Frankie" (Keillor), **Supp. XVI:** 167

Frankie and Johnny (film), **Supp. XIII:** 206

Frankie and Johnny in the Clair de Lune (McNally), **Supp. XIII: 200,** 201

Franklin, Benjamin, **II:** 6, 8, 92, **101–125,** 127, 295, 296, 302, 306; **III:** 74, 90; **IV:** 73, 193; **Supp. I Part 1:** 306; **Supp. I Part 2:** 411, 503, 504, 506, 507, 510, 516, 518, 522, 524, 579, 639; **Supp. VIII:** 202, 205; **Supp. XIII:** 150; **Supp. XIV:** 306; **Supp. XVIII:** 12; **Supp. XX:**284

Franklin, Cynthia, **Supp. IV Part 1:** 332

Franklin, Ruth, **Supp. XVI:** 160

Franklin, R. W., **Retro. Supp. I:** 29, 41, 43, 47

Franklin, Sarah, **II:** 122

Franklin, Temple, **II:** 122

Franklin, William, **II:** 122; **Supp. I Part 2:** 504

Franklin Evans (Whitman), **Retro. Supp. I:** 393

"Frank O'Connor and *The New Yorker*" (Maxwell), **Supp. VIII:** 172

Franks, Lucinda, **Supp. XIII:** 12

"Frank Sinatra Has a Cold" (Talese), **Supp. XVII:** 203

"Frank Stanford of the Mulberry Family: An Arkansas Epilogue" (Wright), **Supp. XV:** 339–340

"Franny" (Salinger), **III:** 564, 565–566

Franny and Zooey (Salinger), **III:** 552, 564–567; **IV:** 216; **Supp. XIII:** 263

Franzen, Jonathan, **Retro. Supp. II:** 279; **Supp. XIX:** 54; **Supp. XX:**83–97

Fraser, G. S., **Supp. XII:** 128; **Supp. XIV:** 162

Fraser, Joe, **III:** 46

Fraser, Marjorie Frost, **Retro. Supp. I:** 136

Frayn, Michael, **Supp. IV Part 2:** 582

Frazee, E. S., **Supp. I Part 2:** 381

Frazee, Esther Catherine. *See* Lindsay, Mrs. Vachel Thomas (Esther Catherine Frazee)

Frazer, Sir James G., **I:** 135; **II:** 204; **III:** 6–7; **IV:** 70; **Retro. Supp. I:** 80; **Supp. I Part 1:** 18; **Supp. I Part 2:** 541; **Supp. XX:**117

Frazier, Ian, **Supp. VIII:** 272

Frazier, Kathleen, **Supp. XXI:** 22

"Freak Show, The" (Sexton), **Supp. II Part 2:** 695

Freaks: Myths and Images of the Secret Self (Fiedler), **Supp. XIII:** 106, 107

Freckles (film), **Supp. XX:**223

Freckles (Stratton-Porter), **Supp. XX:**211, 218–219, 222

Freddy's Book (Gardner), **Supp. VI: 72**

Frederic, Harold, **I:** 409; **II: 126–149,** 175, 276, 289; **Retro. Supp. I:** 325

"Frederick Douglass" (Dunbar), **Supp. II Part 1:** 197, 199

"Frederick Douglass" (Hayden), **Supp. II Part 1:** 363

Frederick the Great, **II:** 103; **Supp. I Part 2:** 433

Fredrickson, George M., **Supp. I Part 2:** 589

"Free" (O'Hara), **III:** 369

Free, and Other Stories (Dreiser), **Retro. Supp. II:** 104

Free Agents (Apple), **Supp. XVII:** 5–6

Free Air (Lewis), **II:** 441

Freedman, Monroe H., **Supp. VIII:** 127

Freedman, Richard, **Supp. V:** 244

"Freedom" (Larsen), **Supp. XVIII:** 124

"Freedom" (White), **Supp. I Part 2:** 659

"Freedom, New Hampshire" (Kinnell), **Supp. III Part 1:** 238, 239, 251

"Freedom and Discipline" (Carruth), **Supp. XVI:** 50

Freedom Business, The (Nelson), **Supp. XVIII: 186**

Freedom Is the Right to Choose: An Inquiry into the Battle for the American Future (MacLeish), **III:** 3

"Freedom's a Hard-Bought Thing" (Benét), **Supp. XI:** 47, 48

"Freedom's Plow" (Hughes), **Supp. I Part 1:** 346

"Free Fantasia: Tiger Flowers" (Hayden), **Supp. II Part 1:** 363, 366

Freeing of the Dust, The (Levertov), **Supp. III Part 1:** 281–282

"Free Lance, The" (Mencken), **III:** 104, 105

Free-Lance Pallbearers, The (Reed), **Supp. X:** 240, **242–243,** 244

Free Life, A (Jin), **Supp. XVIII: 101– 102**

Freeloaders, The (Lacy), **Supp. XV:** 204

"Free Man" (Hughes), **Supp. I Part 1:** 333

Freeman, Chris, **Supp. XIV:** 157, 159

Freeman, Douglas Southall, **Supp. I Part 2:** 486, 493

Freeman, John, **Supp. XVIII:** 90

Freeman, Joseph, **II:** 26; **Supp. I Part 2:** 610

Freeman, Mary E. Wilkins, **II:** 401; **Retro. Supp. II:** 51, 136, 138; **Supp. IX:** 79

Freeman, Morgan, **Supp. XII:** 317

Freeman, Suzanne, **Supp. X:** 83

Free Man, The (Richter), **Supp. XVIII:** 215

"Free Man's Worship, A" (Russell), **Supp. I Part 2:** 522

Freewheelin' Bob Dylan, The (album, Dylan), **Supp. XVIII:** 20, 24, 29

Freilicher, Jane, **Supp. XV:** 178

Freinman, Dorothy, **Supp. IX:** 94

Frémont, John Charles, **Supp. I Part 2:** 486

Fremont-Smith, Eliot, **Supp. XIII:** 263

Fremstad, Olive, **I:** 319; **Retro. Supp. I:** 10

French, Warren, **Supp. XII:** 118–119

French Chef, The (television program), **Supp. XVII:** 89

French Connection, The (film), **Supp. V:** 226

French Leave (X. J. Kennedy), **Supp. XV:** 165

French Poets and Novelists (James), **II:** 336; **Retro. Supp. I:** 220

"French Scarecrow, The" (Maxwell), **Supp. VIII:** 169, 170

French Ways and Their Meaning (Wharton), **IV:** 319; **Retro. Supp. I:** 378

Freneau, Eleanor Forman (Mrs. Philip Freneau), **Supp. II Part 1:** 266

Freneau, Philip M., **I:** 335; **II:** 295; **Supp. I Part 1:** 124, 125, 127, 145; **Supp. II Part 1:** 65, **253–277**

Frenzy (Everett), **Supp. XVIII: 59–60**

Frescoes for Mr. Rockefeller's City (MacLeish), **III:** 14–15

"Fresh Air" (Koch), **Supp. XV:** 181, 185

Fresh Air Fiend: Travel Writings, 1985– 2000 (Theroux), **Supp. VIII:** 325

Fresh Brats (X. J. Kennedy), **Supp. XV:** 163

"Freshman" (Sanders), **Supp. XVI:** 277

Freud, Sigmund, **I:** 55, 58, 59, 66, 67, 135, 241, 242, 244, 247, 248, 283; **II:** 27, 370, 546–547; **III:** 134, 390, 400, 418, 488; **IV:** 7, 70, 138, 295; **Retro. Supp. I:** 80, 176, 253; **Retro. Supp.**

II: 104; **Supp. I Part 1:** 13, 43, 253, 254, 259, 260, 265, 270, 315; **Supp. I Part 2:** 493, 527, 616, 643, 647, 649; **Supp. IV Part 2:** 450; **Supp. VIII:** 103, 196; **Supp. IX:** 102, 155, 161, 308; **Supp. X:** 193, 194; **Supp. XII:** 14–15; **Supp. XIII:** 75; **Supp. XIV:** 83; **Supp. XV:** 219; **Supp. XVI:** 157– 158, 161, 292

"Freud and Literature" (Trilling), **Supp. III Part 2:** 502–503

Freudian Psychology and Veblen's Social Theory, The (Schneider), **Supp. I Part 2:** 650

Freudian Wish and Its Place in Ethics, The (Holt), **I:** 59

"Freud's Room" (Ozick), **Supp. V:** 268

Freud: The Mind of the Moralist (Sontag and Rieff), **Supp. III Part 2:** 455

"Freud: Within and Beyond Culture" (Trilling), **Supp. III Part 2:** 508

Frey, Hillary, **Supp. XIX:** 55

"Friday Morning Trial of Mrs. Solano, The" (Ríos), **Supp. IV Part 2:** 538, 548

Friebert, Stuart, **Supp. XIX:** 276

Frieburger, William, **Supp. XIII:** 239

Friede, Donald, **Supp. XVII:** 85, 86, 87, 90

Friedenberg, Edgar Z., **Supp. VIII:** 240

Friedman, Bruce Jay, **I:** 161; **Supp. IV Part 1:** 379

Friedman, Lawrence S., **Supp. V:** 273

Friedman, Milton, **Supp. I Part 2:** 648

Friedman, Norman, **I:** 431–432, 435, 439

Friedman, Stan, **Supp. XII:** 186

Friedmann, Georges, **Supp. I Part 2:** 645

"Fried Sausage" (Simic), **Supp. VIII:** 270

Friend, Julius, **Retro. Supp. I:** 80

Friend, The (Coleridge), **II:** 10

"Friend Husband's Latest" (Sayre), **Retro. Supp. I:** 104

"Friendly Debate between a Conformist and a Non-Conformist, A" (Wild), **IV:** 155

"Friendly Neighbor" (Keillor), **Supp. XVI:** 172

Friend of the Earth, A (Boyle), **Supp. VIII:** 12, 16; **Supp. XX:29–30**

"Friend of the Fourth Decade, The" (Merrill), **Supp. III Part 1:** 327

"Friends" (Beattie), **Supp. V:** 23, 27

"Friends" (Paley), **Supp. VI:** 219, 226

"Friends" (Sexton), **Supp. II Part 2:** 693

Friend's Delight, The (Bierce), **I:** 195

"Friends from Philadelphia" (Updike), **Retro. Supp. I:** 319

"Friendship" (Emerson), **Supp. II Part 1:** 290

Friends: More Will and Magna Stories (Dixon), **Supp. XII:** 148, 149

"Friends of Heraclitus, The" (Simic), **Supp. VIII:** 284

"Friends of Kafka, The" (Singer), **Retro. Supp. II:** 308

"Friends of the Family, The" (McCarthy), **II:** 566

"Friend to Alexander, A" (Thurber), **Supp. I Part 2:** 616

"Frigate Pelican, The" (Moore), **III:** 208, 210–211, 215

"Frill, The" (Buck), **Supp. XIV:** 274

"Fringe, The" (Bass), **Supp. XVI:** 19

Frobenius, Leo, **III:** 475; **Supp. III Part 2:** 620

Froebel, Friedrich, **Supp. XIV:** 52–53

Frog (Dixon), **Supp. XII:** 151

"Frog Dances" (Dixon), **Supp. XII:** 151

"Frog Pond, The" (Kinnell), **Supp. III Part 1:** 254

"Frogs" (Nelson), **Supp. XVIII:** 176

"Frog Takes a Swim" (Dixon), **Supp. XII:** 152

Frohock, W. M., **I:** 34, 42

Frolic of His Own, A (Gaddis), **Supp. IV Part 1:** 279, 291, 292–294; **Supp. XX:91**

"From a Mournful Village" (Jewett), **Retro. Supp. II:** 146

"From an Alabama Farm" (Nelson), **Supp. XVIII:** 182

"From an Old House in America" (Rich), **Supp. I Part 2:** 551, 565–567

From Another World (Untermeyer), **Supp. XV:** 293, 303, 310–311, 313

"From a Roadside Motel" (F. Wright), **Supp. XVII:** 245

"From a Survivor" (Rich), **Supp. I Part 2:** 563

From A to Z (musical review; Allen), **Supp. XV:** 3, 13

From a Writer's Notebook (Brooks), **I:** 254

From Bauhaus to Our House (Wolfe), **Supp. III Part 2:** 580, 581, 584

From Bondage (H. Roth), **Supp. IX:** 236, **238–240**

"From *Chants* to *Borders* to *Communion*" (Fox), **Supp. XIII:** 217, 217–218

"From Chicago" (Anderson), **I:** 108–109

From Death to Morning (Wolfe), **IV:** 450, 456, 458

"From Dick to Lethem: The Dickian Legacy, Postmodernism, and Avant-Pop in Jonathan Lethem's *Amnesia Moon*" (Rossi), **Supp. XVIII:** 137, 138–139

"From Discord, a Wife Makes a Nice New Life—Too Nice" (Linfield), **Supp. XVII:** 177

From Down to the Village (Budbill), **Supp. XIX: 6–7**

"From Feathers to Iron" (Kunitz), **Supp. III Part 1:** 261

"From Fifth Avenue Up" (Barnes), **Supp. III Part 1:** 33, 44

"From Gorbunov and Gorchakov" (Brodsky), **Supp. VIII:** 26

"From Grand Canyon to Burbank" (H. Miller), **III:** 186

"From Hell to Breakfast", **Supp. IX:** 326–327

From Here to Eternity (film), **Supp. XI:** 221

From Here to Eternity (Jones), **I:** 477; **Supp. XI:** 215, 216, 217, 218, **219– 221,** 223, 224, 226, 229, 230, 231, 232, 234; **Supp. XIX:** 248; **Supp. XX:248**

From Here to Eternity (miniseries), **Supp. XI:** 234

From Jordan's Delight (Blackmur), **Supp. II Part 1:** 91

"From Lumaghi Mine" (Wrigley), **Supp. XVIII:** 295

Fromm, Erich, **I:** 58; **Supp. VIII:** 196

From Morn to Midnight (Kaiser), **I:** 479

"From Native Son to Invisible Man" (Locke), **Supp. IX:** 306

"From Pico, the Women: A Life" (Creeley), **Supp. IV Part 1:** 149

From Plotzk to Boston (Antin), **Supp. XX:** 2

From Ritual to Romance (Weston), **II:** 540; **III:** 12; **Supp. I Part 2:** 439

From Room to Room (Kenyon), **Supp. VII:** 163–165, 166, 167

"From Room to Room" (Kenyon), **Supp. VII:** 159, 163–165

From Sand Creek: Rising in this Heart Which Is Our America (Ortiz), **Supp. IV Part 2:** 512–513

"From Sea Cliff, March" (Swenson), **Supp. IV Part 2:** 649

From Stone Orchard: A Collection of Memories (Findley), **Supp. XX:** 57

"From the Antigone" (Yeats), **III:** 459

From the Ashes: Voices of Watts (Schulberg, ed.), **Supp. XVIII:** 254

From the Barrio: A Chicano Anthology (Salinas and Faderman, eds.), **Supp. XIII:** 313

From the Briarpatch File: On Context, Procedure, and American Identity (Murray), **Supp. XIX:** 161

"From the Childhood of Jesus" (Pinsky), **Supp. VI:** 244–245, 247

"From the Corpse Woodpiles, From the Ashes" (Hayden), **Supp. II Part 1:** 370

"From the Country to the City" (Bishop), **Supp. I Part 1:** 85, 86

"From the Cupola" (Merrill), **Supp. III Part 1:** 324–325, 331

"From the Dark Side of the Earth" (Oates), **Supp. II Part 2:** 510

"From the Diary of a New York Lady" (Parker), **Supp. IX:** 201

"From the Diary of One Not Born" (Singer), **IV:** 9

"From the East, Light" (Carver), **Supp. III Part 1:** 138

From the First Nine: Poems 1946–1976 (Merrill), **Supp. III Part 1:** 336

"From the Flats" (Lanier), **Supp. I Part 1:** 364

From the Flower Courtyard (Everwine), **Supp. XV:** 75

From the Heart of Europe (Matthiessen), **III:** 310

From the Meadow: Selected and New Poems (Everwine), **Supp. XV:** 75, 88–89

"From the Memoirs of a Private Detective" (Hammett), **Supp. IV Part 1:** 343

"From the Nursery" (Kenyon), **Supp. VII:** 171

"From the Poets in the Kitchen" (Marshall), **Supp. XI:** 277

From the Terrace (O'Hara), **III:** 362

"From the Thirties: Tillie Olsen and the Radical Tradition" (Rosenfelt), **Supp. XIII:** 296, 304

"From Trollope's Journal" (Bishop), **Retro. Supp. II:** 47

"Front, A" (Jarrell), **II:** 374

Front, The (film), **Supp. I Part 1:** 295

"Front and the Back Parts of the House, The" (Maxwell), **Supp. VIII:** 169

Frontier Eden (Bigelow), **Supp. X:** 227

"Frontiers of Culture" (Locke), **Supp. XIV:** 213

"Front Lines" (Snyder), **Supp. VIII:** 301

Front Runner, The (P. N. Warren), **Supp. XX:** 259, 262–264

Frost, A. B., **Retro. Supp. II:** 72

Frost, Carol, **Supp. XV:** 91–109

Frost, Isabelle Moodie, **II:** 150, 151

Frost, Jeanie, **II:** 151

Frost, Richard, **Supp. XV:** 92

Frost, Robert, **I:** 26, 27, 60, 63, 64, 171, 229, 303, 326, 418; **II:** 55, 58, **150–172,** 276, 289, 388, 391, 471, 523, 527, 529, 535; **III:** 5, 23, 67, 269, 271, 272, 275, 287, 453, 510, 523, 536, 575, 581, 591; **IV:** 140, 190, 415; **Retro. Supp. I:** 67, **121–144,** 276, 287, 292, 298, 299, 311, 413; **Retro. Supp. II:** 40, 47, 50, 146, 178, 181; **Supp. I Part 1:** 80, 242, 263, 264; **Supp. I Part 2:** 387, 461, 699; **Supp. II Part 1:** 4, 19, 26, 103; **Supp. III Part 1:** 63, 74–75, 239, 253; **Supp. III Part 2:** 546, 592, 593; **Supp. IV Part 1:** 15; **Supp. IV Part 2:** 439, 445, 447, 448, 599, 601; **Supp. VIII:** 20, 30, 32, 98, 100, 104, 259, 292; **Supp. IX:** 41, 42, 75, 76, 80, 87, 90, 266, 308; **Supp. X:** 64, 65, 66, 74, 120, 172; **Supp. XI:** 43, 123, 150, 153, 312; **Supp. XII:** 130, 241, 303, 307; **Supp. XIII:** 143, 147, 334–335; **Supp. XIV:** 42, 122, 222, 229; **Supp. XV:** 21, 51, 65, 96, 212, 215, 250, 256, 293, 296, 299, 301, 302, 306, 348; **Supp. XVII:** 36, 110, 115–116; **Supp. XVIII:** 298, 300; **Supp. XIX:** 1, 123; **Supp. XX:** 69, 199; **Supp. XXI:** 19, 28, 51, 99, 104, 107, 205

Frost, William Prescott, **II:** 150–151

"Frost: A Dissenting Opinion" (Cowley), **Supp. II Part 1:** 143

Frost: A Time to Talk (Francis), **Supp. IX:** 76, **85–86**

"Frost at Midnight" (Coleridge), **Supp. X:** 71

"Frost Flowers" (Kenyon), **Supp. VII:** 168

"Frost: He Is Sometimes a Poet and Sometimes a Stump-Speaker" (Newsweek), **Retro. Supp. I:** 137

Frothingham, Nathaniel, **I:** 3

Frothingham, Octavius B., **IV:** 173

"Frozen City, The" (Nemerov), **III:** 270

"Frozen Fields, The" (Bowles), **Supp. IV Part 1:** 80

"Fruit Garden Path, The" (Lowell), **II:** 516

"Fruit of the Flower" (Cullen), **Supp. IV Part 1:** 167

Fruit of the Tree, The (Wharton), **IV:** 314–315; **Retro. Supp. I:** 367, **370–371,** 373

"Fruit of Travel Long Ago" (Melville), **III:** 93

Fruits and Vegetables (Jong), **Supp. V:** 113, 115, 117, 118, 119

"Fruits of the Sea, The" (Di Piero), **Supp. XIX:** 47

Frumkes, Lewis Burke, **Supp. XII:** 335–336

Fry, Christopher, **Supp. I Part 1:** 270

Fry, Roger, **Supp. XIV:** 336

Fry, Stephen M., **Supp. XIX:** 159

Frye, Joanne, **Supp. XIII:** 292, 296, 298, 302

Frye, Northrop, **Supp. I Part 2:** 530; **Supp. II Part 1:** 101; **Supp. X:** 80; **Supp. XIII:** 19; **Supp. XIV:** 11, 15; **Supp. XVI:** 149, 156; **Supp. XX:** 50

Fryer, Judith, **Retro. Supp. I:** 379

F. Scott Fitzgerald: A Critical Portrait (Piper), **Supp. IX:** 65

"F. S. F., 1896–1996, R.I.P." (Doctorow), **Retro. Supp. I:** 97

Fuchs, Daniel, **Supp. XIII:** 106

Fuchs, Miriam, **Supp. IV Part 1:** 284

Fuehrer Bunker, The (Snodgrass), **Supp. VI:** 314, 315–317, 319–321

Fuel (Nye), **Supp. XIII:** 277, **282–284**

"Fuel" (Nye), **Supp. XIII:** 283

Fuertes, Gloria, **Supp. V:** 178

Fugard, Athol, **Supp. VIII:** 330; **Supp. XIII:** 205

Fugitive Group, The (Cowan), **IV:** 120

Fugitive Kind, The (T. Williams), **IV:** 381, 383

Fugitives, The (group), **IV:** 122, 124, 125, 131, 237, 238

Fugitives, The: A Critical Account (Bradbury), **IV:** 130

"Fugitive Slave Law, The" (Emerson), **II:** 13

Fugitive's Return (Glaspell), **Supp. III Part 1:** 182–184

Fuller, B. A. G., **III:** 605

Fuller, Hiram, **Supp. XVIII:** 12, 14

Fuller, Jesse "Lonecat", **Supp. XV:** 147

Fuller, Margaret, **I:** 261; **II:** 7, 276; **IV:** 172; **Retro. Supp. I:** 155–156, 163; **Retro. Supp. II:** 46; **Supp. I Part 2:** 524; **Supp. II Part 1:** 279–306; **Supp. IX:** 37; **Supp. XVIII:** 3, 11, 12, 16

Fuller, Thomas, **II:** 111, 112

Fullerton, Morton, **Supp. XX:** 231

Fullerton Street (Wilson), **Supp. VIII:** 331

"Full Fathom Five" (Plath), **Supp. I Part 2:** 538

Full Measure: Modern Short Stories on Aging (D. Sennett, ed.), **Supp. XVI:** 37

Full Monty, The (musical, McNally), **Supp. XIII:** 207

"Full Moon" (Hayden), **Supp. II Part 1:** 370

Full Moon and Other Plays (Price), **Supp. VI:** 266

"Full Moon and You're Not Here" (Cisneros), **Supp. VII:** 71–72

"Full Moon: New Guinea" (Shapiro), **Supp. II Part 2:** 707

"Fullness of Life, The" (Wharton), **Retro. Supp. I:** 363

Full of Life (Fante), **Supp. XI:** 160

Full of Life (film), **Supp. XI:** 170

Full of Lust and Good Usage (Dunn), **Supp. XI: 145–147**

"Full Summer" (Olds), **Supp. X:** 212

Fulton, Robert, **Supp. I Part 2:** 519; **Supp. II Part 1:** 73

"Functional Poem" (Halliday), **Supp. XIX:** 85

Function of Criticism, The (Winters), **Supp. II Part 2:** 812, 813

"Fundamentalism" (Tate), **IV:** 125

"Fundamental Project of Technology, The" (Kinnell), **Supp. III Part 1:** 253

"Funeral of Bobò, The" (Brodsky), **Supp. VIII:** 27, 28

"Funnel" (Sexton), **Supp. II Part 2:** 675

"Furious Seasons, The" (Carver), **Supp. III Part 1:** 137

Furious Seasons and Other Stories (Carver), **Supp. III Part 1:** 142, 143, 146

"Furious Versions" (L.-Y. Lee), **Supp. XV: 215–217**, 218, 220

"Furnished Room, The" (Hayden), **Supp. II Part 1:** 386–387, 394, 397, 399, 406, 408

"Furor Scribendi" (O. Butler), **Supp. XIII:** 70

Furors Die (Hoffman), **Supp. XVIII: 80–81**

Fur Person, The (Sarton), **Supp. VIII: 264–265**

Further Adventures with You (Wright), **Supp. XV:** 339, 342, **343–345**

Further Fables for Our Time (Thurber), **Supp. I Part 2:** 612

"Further in Summer than the Birds" (Dickinson), **I:** 471

Further Poems of Emily Dickinson (Bianchi and Hampson, ed.), **Retro. Supp. I:** 35

Further Range, A (Frost), **II:** 155; **Retro. Supp. I:** 132, 136, 137, 138, 139

"Fury, The (Skloot), **Supp. XX:**197

"Fury of Aerial Bombardment, The" (Eberhart), **I:** 535–536

"Fury of Flowers and Worms, The" (Sexton), **Supp. II Part 2:** 694

"Fury of Rain Storms, The" (Sexton), **Supp. II Part 2:** 695

Fury of the Jungle (film), **Supp. XIII:** 163

Fussell, Paul, **Supp. V:** 241

"Future, if Any, of Comedy, The" (Thurber), **Supp. I Part 2:** 620

Future in the Present, The (C. L. R. James), **Supp. XXI:** 172

Future is Ours, Comrade, The: Conversations with the Russians (Kosinski), **Supp. VII:** 215

Futureland: Nine Stories of an Imminent World (Mosley), **Supp. XIII: 247–249**

"Future Life, The" (Bryant), **Supp. I Part 1:** 170

Future of Southern Letters, The (J. W. Miller), **Supp. XX:**161

Future of the Race, The (H. L. Gates), **Supp. XX:**101, 104, 111

Future Punishment of the Wicked, The (Edwards), **I:** 546

G

"Gabriel" (Rich), **Supp. I Part 2:** 557

Gabriel, Ralph H., **Supp. I Part 1:** 251

Gabriel, Trip, **Supp. V:** 212

Gabriel Conroy (Harte), **Supp. II Part 1:** 354

"Gabriel's Truth" (Kenyon), **Supp. VII:** 166

Gaddis, William, **Supp. IV Part 1: 279–296; Supp. IV Part 2:** 484; **Supp. V:** 52; **Supp. IX:** 208; **Supp. X:** 301, 302; **Supp. XX:**83, 91; **Supp. XXI:** 226

Gadiot, Pud, **Supp. XI:** 295

Gain (Powers), **Supp. IX:** 212, **220–221**

Gaines, Ernest J., **Supp. X:** 24, 250

Gaines, James R., **Supp. IX:** 190

Gainor, J. Ellen, **Supp. XXI:** 6

Gaitens, Peter, **Supp. XV:** 65

Galamain, Ivan, **Supp. III Part 2:** 624

Galassi, Jonathan, **Supp. XVIII:** 92; **Supp. XIX:** 34

Galatea 2.2 (Powers), **Supp. IX:** 212, **219–220**

"Galatea Encore" (Brodsky), **Supp. VIII:** 31

Galbraith, John Kenneth, **Supp. I Part 2:** 645, 650

Galdós, Benito Pérez. *See* Pérez Galdós, Benito

Gale, Zona, **Supp. I Part 2:** 613; **Supp. VIII:** 155

Galehouse, Maggie, **Supp. XXI:** 215

"Gale in April" (Jeffers), **Supp. II Part 2:** 423

Galignani, Giovanni Antonio, **II:** 315

Galileo Galilei, **I:** 480–481; **Supp. XII:** 180; **Supp. XIII:** 75

Gallagher, Tess, **Supp. XVI:** 36; **Supp. XVII:** 110; **Supp. XXI:** 246

Gallant, Mavis, **Supp. VIII:** 151

Gallatin, Albert, **I:** 5

"Gallery" (Goldbarth), **Supp. XII:** 188

"Gallery of Real Creatures, A" (Thurber), **Supp. I Part 2:** 619

Gallico, Paul, **Supp. XVI:** 238

Gallows Songs (Snodgrass), **Supp. VI:** 317

Gallup, Donald, **III:** 404, 478

Galsworthy, John, **III:** 70, 153, 382

Galton Case, The (Macdonald), **Supp. IV Part 2:** 463, 473, 474

Galvin, Frances, **Supp. XXI:** 5

"Gal Young 'Un" (Rawlings), **Supp. X:** 228

Gambino, Richard, **Supp. XX:**35

"Gambler, the Nun, and the Radio, The" (Hemingway), **II:** 250

"Gambler's Wife, The" (Dunbar), **Supp. II Part 1:** 196

Gambone, Philip, **Supp. XII:** 81

"Gambrel Roof, A" (Larcom), **Supp. XIII:** 144

"Game at Salzburg, A" (Jarrell), **II:** 384, 389

Game Management (Leopold), **Supp. XIV:** 182

"Game of Catch, A" (Wilbur), **Supp. III Part 2:** 552

Game Players of Titan, The (Dick), **Supp. XVIII:** 138

"Games in Frank Conroy's *Stop-Time*" (T. Adams), **Supp. XVI:** 67

"Games Two" (Wilbur), **Supp. III Part 2:** 550

Gammelgaard, Lene, **Supp. XVIII:** 112

"Gamut, The" (Angelou), **Supp. IV Part 1:** 15

Gander, Forrest, **Supp. XV:** 339, 340, 342

Gandhi, Indira, **Supp. X:** 108

Gandhi, Mahatma, **III:** 179, 296–297; **IV:** 170, 185, 367; **Supp. VIII:** 203, 204; **Supp. X:** 27

Gandhi on Non-Violence (Merton, ed.), **Supp. VIII:** 204–205

Gang of Five: Leaders at the Center of the Conservative Crusade (Easton), **Supp. XIX:** 137

"Gang of Mirrors, The" (Simic), **Supp. VIII:** 283

Gansevoort, Guert, **III:** 94

Gansevoort, Peter, **III:** 92

"Gap" (Bierds), **Supp. XVII:** 35–36

Garabedian, Michael, **Supp. XIII:** 115

Garbage (Ammons), **Supp. VII:** 24, 35–36

Garbage (Dixon), **Supp. XII:** 147, 148

Garbage Man, The (Dos Passos), **I:** 478, 479, 481, 493

Garber, Frederick, **Supp. IX:** 294–295

Garbo, Greta, **Supp. I Part 2:** 616

García, Cristina, **Supp. VIII:** 74; **Supp. XI: 177–192**

García Lorca, Federico. *See* Lorca, Federico García

"García Lorca: A Photograph of the Granada Cemetery, 1966" (Levis), **Supp. XI:** 264

García Márquez, Gabriel, **Supp. V:** 244; **Supp. VIII:** 81, 82, 84, 85; **Supp. XII:** 147, 310, 316, 322; **Supp. XIII:** 226; **Supp. XVII:** 45

Gardaphe, Fred, **Supp. XX:**38, 41

"Garden" (Marvell), **IV:** 161; **Supp. XVI:** 204

"Garden, The" (Glück), **Supp. V:** 83

"Garden, The" (Strand), **Supp. IV Part 2:** 629

"Garden Among Tombs" (B. Kelly), **Supp. XVII:** 126

"Garden by Moonlight, The" (Lowell), **II:** 524

"Gardener Delivers a Fawn, The" (C. Frost), **Supp. XV:** 99

Gardener's Son, The (McCarthy), **Supp. VIII:** 187

Garden God, The: A Tale of Two Boys (Reid), **Supp. XX:**235

"Gardenias" (Doty), **Supp. XI:** 122

"Gardenias" (Monette), **Supp. X:** 159

"Garden Lodge, The" (Cather), **I:** 316, 317

Garden of Adonis, The (Gordon), **II:** 196, 204–205, 209

Garden of Earthly Delights, A (Oates), **Supp. II Part 2:** 504, 507–509

"Garden of Eden" (Hemingway), **II:** 259

Garden of Eden, The (Hemingway), **Retro. Supp. I:** 186, **187–188**

"Garden of Flesh, Garden of Stone" (B. Kelly), **Supp. XVII:** 128

"Garden of the Moon, The" (Doty), **Supp. XI:** 122

Garden of the Prophet, The (Gibran), **Supp. XX:**119, 122

"Garden of the Trumpet Tree, The" (B. Kelly), **Supp. XVII:** 131

"Gardens, The" (Oliver), **Supp. VII:** 236

"Gardens of Mont-Saint-Michel, The" (Maxwell), **Supp. VIII:** 169

"Gardens of the Villa D'Este, The" (Hecht), **Supp. X:** 59

"Gardens of Zuñi, The" (Merwin), **Supp. III Part 1:** 351

Gardiner, Judith Kegan, **Supp. IV Part 1:** 205

Gardner, Erle Stanley, **Supp. IV Part 1:** 121, 345

Gardner, Isabella, **IV:** 127

Gardner, John, **Supp. I Part 1:** 193, 195, 196; **Supp. III Part 1:** 136, 142, 146; **Supp. VI:** **61–76**

Gardner, Thomas, **Supp. XXI:** 214

Gardons, S. S. *See* Snodgrass, W. D.

"Gare de Lyon" (M. F. K. Fisher), **Supp. XVII:** 91

Garfield, John, **Supp. XII:** 160

Garibaldi, Giuseppe, **I:** 4; **II:** 284

Garibay, Angel M., **Supp. XV:** 77

Garland, Hamlin, **I:** 407; **II:** 276, 289; **III:** 576; **Retro. Supp. I:** 133; **Retro. Supp. II:** 72; **Supp. I Part 1:** 217; **Supp. IV Part 2:** 502; **Supp. XVIII:** 6

Garland Companion, The (Zverev), **Retro. Supp. I:** 278

"Garments" (Gibran), **Supp. XX:**124

Garments the Living Wear (Purdy), **Supp. VII:** 278–279, 280–281

Garner, Dwight, **Supp. X:** 202; **Supp. XVIII:** 89

Garnett, Edward, **I:** 405, 409, 417; **III:** 27

Garrett, George P., **Supp. I Part 1:** 196; **Supp. VII:** **95–113; Supp. X:** 3, 7; **Supp. XI:** 218; **Supp. XVIII:** 74, 75

Garrigue, Jean, **Supp. XII:** 260

Garrison, Deborah, **Supp. IX:** 299

Garrison, Fielding, **III:** 105

Garrison, William Lloyd, **Supp. I Part 2:** 524, 588, 683, 685, 686, 687; **Supp. XIV:** 54

"Garrison of Cape Ann, The" (Whittier), **Supp. I Part 2:** 691, 694

Garry Moore Show (television show), **Supp. IV Part 2:** 575

"Garter Motif" (White), **Supp. I Part 2:** 673

Gartner, Zsuzsi, **Supp. X:** 276

Garvey, Marcus, **Supp. III Part 1:** 175, 180; **Supp. IV Part 1:** 168; **Supp. X:** 135, 136; **Supp. XXI:** 166, 168

Gas (Kaiser), **I:** 479

Gas-House McGinty (Farrell), **II:** 41–42

Gaskell, Elizabeth, A., **Supp. I Part 2:** 580

Gasoline (Corso), **Supp. XII:** 118, **121–123,** 134

Gass, William H., **Supp. V:** 44, 52, 238; **Supp. VI: 77–96; Supp. IX:** 208; **Supp. XII:** 152; **Supp. XIV:** 305; **Supp. XVII:** 183

Gassner, John, **IV:** 381; **Supp. I Part 1:** 284, 292

"Gas Stations" (Apple), **Supp. XVII:** 4

Gastronomical Me, The (M. F. K. Fisher), **Supp. XVII:** 84, 85, 87, 91, 92

Gates, David, **Supp. V:** 24; **Supp. XIII:** 93; **Supp. XVI:** 73, 74; **Supp. XX:**92

Gates, Elmer, **I:** 515–516

Gates, Henry Louis, Jr., **Retro. Supp. I:** 194, 195, 203; **Supp. X:** 242, 243, 245, 247; **Supp. XVIII:** 287; **Supp. XIX:** 147, 149; **Supp. XX:99–112,** 279, 286

Gates, Lewis E., **III:** 315, 330

Gates, Sondra Smith, **Supp. XVIII:** 267, 269

Gates, The (Rukeyser), **Supp. VI:** 271, 274, 281

"Gates, The" (Rukeyser), **Supp. VI:** 286

Gates, Tudor, **Supp. XI:** 307

Gates of Ivory, the Gates of Horn, The (McGrath), **Supp. X:** 118

Gates of Wrath, The; Rhymed Poems (Ginsberg), **Supp. II Part 1:** 311, 319

"Gathering" (Trethewey), **Supp. XXI:** 249

Gathering Forces, The (C. L. R. James), **Supp. XXI:** 171

"Gathering of Dissidents, A" (Applebaum), **Supp. XVI:** 153

Gathering of Fugitives, A (Trilling), **Supp. III Part 2:** 506, 512

Gathering of Zion, The: The Story of the Mormon Trail (Stegner), **Supp. IV Part 2:** 599, 602–603

Gather Together in My Name (Angelou), **Supp. IV Part 1:** 2, 3, 4–6, 11

Gathorne-Hardy, Robert, **Supp. XIV:** 344, 347, 348, 349

Gaudier-Brzeska, Henri, **III:** 459, 464, 465, 477

Gaughran, Richard, **Supp. XXI:** 47–48

Gauguin, Paul, **I:** 34; **IV:** 290; **Supp. IV Part 1:** 81; **Supp. XII:** 128

"Gauguin in Oregon" (Skloot), **Supp. XX:**203

"Gauley Bridge" (Rukeyser), **Supp. VI:** 278

Gauss, Christian, **II:** 82; **IV:** 427, 439–440, 444

Gauthier, Jacquie, **Supp. XIX:** 204

Gautier, Théophile, **II:** 543; **III:** 466, 467; **Supp. I Part 1:** 277

Gay, John, **II:** 111; **Supp. I Part 2:** 523; **Supp. XIV:** 337

Gay, Peter, **I:** 560

Gay, Sydney Howard, **Supp. I Part 1:** 158; **Supp. XVIII:** 3

Gay, Walter, **IV:** 317

Gayatri Prayer, The, **III:** 572

Gay Canon, The (Drake), **Supp. XX:**274

"Gay Chaps at the Bar" (Brooks), **Supp. III Part 1:** 74, 75

" 'Gay Culture': Still of the Wild Frontier" (P. N. Warren), **Supp. XX:**272

Gaylord, Winfield R., **III:** 579–580

Gay Talese Reader, The: Portraits & Encounters (Talese), **Supp. XVII:** 202, 208

"Gazebo" (Carver), **Supp. III Part 1:** 138, 144, 145

Gazer's Spirit, The (Hollander), **Supp. XIX:** 121

Gazer Within, The, and Other Essays by Larry Levis, **Supp. XI:** 270

Gazzara, Ben, **Supp. VIII:** 319

Gazzo, Michael V., **III:** 155

"Geese Gone Beyond" (Snyder), **Supp. VIII:** 304

Geffen, David, **Supp. XXI:** 154

"Gegenwart" (Goethe), **Supp. II Part 1:** 26

Geisel, Theodor Seuss (Dr. Seuss), **Supp. X:** 56; **Supp. XVI: 97–115**

Geismar, Maxwell, **II:** 178, 431; **III:** 71; **Supp. IX:** 15; **Supp. XI:** 223

Gelb, Arthur, **IV:** 380; **Supp. XXI:** 12

Gelb, Barbara, **Supp. XXI:** 12

Gelbart, Larry, **Supp. IV Part 2:** 591

Gelder, Robert Van, **Supp. XIII:** 166

Gelfant, Blanche H., **II:** 27, 41; **Supp. XVII:** 161

Gelfman, Jean, **Supp. X:** 3

Gellhorn, Martha. *See* Hemingway, Mrs. Ernest (Martha Gellhorn)

Gelpi, Albert, **Supp. I Part 2:** 552, 554, 560

Gelpi, Barbara, **Supp. I Part 2:** 560

Gemin, Pamela, **Supp. XXI:** 246

Gemini: an extended autobiographical statement on my first twenty-five years of being a black poet (Giovanni), **Supp. IV Part 1:** 11

"Gen" (Snyder), **Supp. VIII:** 302

"Gender Norms" (Radinovsky), **Supp. XV:** 285

"Gender of Sound, The" (Carson), **Supp. XII: 106**

"Genealogy" (Komunyakaa), **Supp. XIII:** 129

"General Aims and Theories" (Crane), **I:** 389

General Died at Dawn, The (Odets), **Supp. II Part 2:** 546

"General Gage's Confession" (Freneau), **Supp. II Part 1:** 257

"General Gage's Soliloquy" (Freneau), **Supp. II Part 1:** 257

General History of the Robberies and Murders of the Most Notorious Pyrates from Their First Rise and Settlement in the Island of New Providence to the Present Year, A (Johnson), **Supp. V:** 128

"General William Booth Enters into Heaven" (Lindsay), **Supp. I Part 2:** 374, 382, 384, 385–388, 389, 392, 399

General William Booth Enters into Heaven and Other Poems (Lindsay), **Supp. I Part 2:** 379, 381, 382, 387–388, 391

"Generation of the Dispossessed" (P. N. Warren), **Supp. XX:**272

"Generations of Men, The" (Frost), **Retro. Supp. I:** 128; **Supp. XIII:** 147

Generous Man, A (Price), **Supp. VI:** 259, 260, 261

Genesis (biblical book), **I:** 279; **II:** 540; **Retro. Supp. I:** 250, 256; **Supp. XII:** 54

"Genesis" (Stegner), **Supp. IV Part 2:** 604

Genesis: Book One (Schwartz), **Supp. II Part 2:** 640, 651–655

Gene Stratton-Porter (Richards), **Supp. XX:**217–218

Gene Stratton-Porter, Naturalist and Novelist (Long), **Supp. XX:**212

"Gene Stratton-Porter: Women's Advocate" (Obuchowski), **Supp. XX:**222

Genet, Jean, **I:** 71, 82, 83, 84; **Supp. IV Part 1:** 8; **Supp. XI:** 308; **Supp. XII:** 1; **Supp. XIII:** 74; **Supp. XVII:** 95

"Genetic Coding" (Sorrentino), **Supp. XXI:** 227

"Genetic Expedition" (Dove), **Supp. IV Part 1:** 249, 257

"Genetics of Justice" (Alvarez), **Supp. VII:** 19

"Genial Host, The" (McCarthy), **II:** 564

"Genie in the Bottle, The" (Wilbur), **Supp. III Part 2:** 542

"Genius, The" (MacLeish), **III:** 19

Genius and Lust: A Journey through the Major Writings of Henry Miller (Mailer), **Retro. Supp. II:** 208

"Genius Child" (Hughes), **Retro. Supp. I:** 203

"Genius of Bob Dylan, The" (Lethem), **Supp. XVIII:** 146

"Genius," The (Dreiser), **I:** 497, 501, 509–511, 519; **Retro. Supp. II:** 94–95, **102–103,** 104, 105

"Genteel Tradition in American Philosophy, The" (Santayana), **I:** 222

"Gentle Communion" (Mora), **Supp. XIII:** 218–219

Gentle Crafter, The (O. Henry), **Supp. II Part 1:** 410

"Gentle Lena, The" (Stein), **IV:** 37, 40

Gentleman Caller, The (T. Williams), **IV:** 383

"Gentleman from Cracow, The" (Singer), **IV:** 9

"Gentleman of Bayou Têche, A" (Chopin), **Supp. I Part 1:** 211–212

"Gentleman of Shalott, The" (Bishop), **Supp. I Part 1:** 85, 86

Gentleman's Agreement (Hobson), **III:** 151

"Gentleman's Agreement" (Richard), **Supp. XIX:** 220–221

Gentlemen Prefer Blondes (Loos; musical adaptation), **Supp. XVI:** 193

Gentlemen Prefer Blondes: The Illuminating Diary of a Professional Lady (Loos), **Supp. XVI:** 181, 183, 186, **188–189**

Gentlemen Prefer "Books" (J. Yeats), **Supp. XVI:** 190

Gentle People, The: A Brooklyn Fable (Shaw), **Supp. XIX:** 244–245, 249

Gentry, Marshall Bruce, **Supp. IV Part 1:** 236

"Genuine Man, The" (Emerson), **II:** 10

"Genus Narcissus" (Trethewey), **Supp. XXI:** 256

Geo-Bestiary (Harrison), **Supp. VIII:** 53

"Geode" (Frost), **II:** 161

Geographical History of America, The (Stein), **IV:** 31, 45; **Supp. XVIII:** 148

Geography and Plays (Stein), **IV:** 29–30, 32, 43, 44

Geography III (Bishop), **Retro. Supp. II:** 50; **Supp. I Part 1:** 72, 73, 76, 82, 93, 94, 95

Geography of a Horse Dreamer (Shepard), **Supp. III Part 2:** 432

Geography of Home, The: California's Poetry of Place (Bluckey and Young, eds.), **Supp. XIII:** 313

Geography of Lograire, The (Merton), **Supp. VIII:** 208

Geography of the Heart (Johnson), **Supp. XI:** 129

"Geometric Poem, The" (Corso), **Supp. XII:** 132, 133–134

George, Diana Hume, **Supp. IV Part 2:** 447, 449, 450

George, Henry, **II:** 276; **Supp. I Part 2:** 518

George, Jan, **Supp. IV Part 1:** 268

George, Lynell, **Supp. XIII:** 234–235, 237, 249

George, Peter, **Supp. XI:** 302, 303, 304

George and the Dragon (Shanley), **Supp. XIV:** 315

George Bernard Shaw: His Plays (Mencken), **III:** 102

George Mills (Elkin), **Supp. VI: 53–54**

George Palmer Putnam: Representative American Publisher (Greenspan), **Supp. XVIII:** 257

"George Robinson: Blues" (Rukeyser), **Supp. VI:** 279

George's Mother (Crane), **I:** 408

"George Thurston" (Bierce), **I:** 202

George Washington Crossing the Delaware (Koch), **Supp. XV:** 186

Georgia Boy (Caldwell), **I:** 288, 305–306, 308, 309, 310

"Georgia Dusk" (Toomer), **Supp. IX:** 309

"Georgia: Invisible Empire State" (Du Bois), **Supp. II Part 1:** 179

"Georgia Night" (Toomer), **Supp. III Part 2:** 481

Georgia Scenes (Longstreet), **II:** 70, 313; **Supp. I Part 1:** 352

Georgics (Virgil), **Retro. Supp. I:** 135; **Supp. XVI:** 22

Georgoudaki, Ekaterini, **Supp. IV Part 1:** 12

Gerald McBoing-Boing (film), **Supp. XVI:** 102

"Geraldo No Last Name" (Cisneros), **Supp. VII:** 60–61

Gerald's Game (King), **Supp. V:** 141, 148–150, 151, 152

Gerald's Party (Coover), **Supp. V:** 49–50, 51, 52

Gérando, Joseph Marie de, **II:** 10

"Geranium" (O'Connor), **Retro. Supp. II:** 221, 236

Gerard, Jeremy, **Supp. XXI:** 147

Gerber, Dan, **Supp. VIII:** 39

Gerhardt, Rainer, **Supp. IV Part 1:** 142

"German Girls! The German Girls!, The" (MacLeish), **III:** 16

"German Refugee, The" (Malamud), **Supp. I Part 2:** 436, 437

"Germany's Reichswehr" (Agee), **I:** 35

Germinal (Zola), **III:** 318, 322

Gernsback, Hugo, **Supp. IV Part 1:** 101

"Gernsback Continuum, The" (W. Gibson), **Supp. XVI:** 123, 128

"Gerontion" (Eliot), **I:** 569, 574, 577, 578, 585, 588; **III:** 9, 435, 436; **Retro. Supp. I:** 290; **Supp. XV:** 341; **Supp. XVI:** 158–159

Gerry, Elbridge, **Supp. I Part 2:** 486

"Gerry's Jazz" (Komunyakaa), **Supp. XIII:** 125

Gershwin, Ira, **Supp. I Part 1:** 281

"Gert" (Monette), **Supp. X:** 158

Gertrude of Stony Island Avenue (Purdy), **Supp. VII:** 281–282

Gertrude Stein (Sprigge), **IV:** 31

Gertrude Stein: A Biography of Her Work (Sutherland), **IV:** 38

"Gertrude Stein and the Geography of the Sentence" (Gass), **Supp. VI:** 87

Gesell, Silvio, **III:** 473

"Gestalt at Sixty" (Sarton), **Supp. VIII:** 260

"Gesture of a Woman-in-Process" (Trethewey), **Supp. XXI:** 249–250

"Gesture toward an Unfound Renaissance, A" (Stafford), **Supp. XI:** 323

"Get It Again" (Halliday), **Supp. XIX:** 85

Getlin, Josh, **Supp. V:** 22; **Supp. VIII:** 75, 76, 78, 79

"Getting Along" (Larcom), **Supp. XIII:** 144

"Getting Along with Nature" (Berry), **Supp. X:** 31–32

"Getting Away from Already Pretty Much Being Away from It All" (Wallace), **Supp. X:** 314–315

"Getting Born" (Shields), **Supp. VII:** 311

Getting Even (Allen), **Supp. XV:** 3, 14, 15

"Getting Lucky" (L. Michaels), **Supp. XVI:** 205, 209

"Getting Out of Jail on Monday" (Wagoner), **Supp. IX:** 327

"Getting There" (Plath), **Supp. I Part 2:** 539, 542

"Getting to the Poem" (Corso), **Supp. XII:** 135

Getty, J. Paul, **Supp. X:** 108

Getty, Norris, **Supp. XV:** 136–137, 138, 139, 142, 143, 145, 146

Gettysburg, Manila, Acoma (Masters), **Supp. I Part 2:** 471
"Gettysburg: July 1, 1863" (Kenyon), **Supp. VII:** 172
Ghachem, Malick, **Supp. X:** 17
Ghazálí, al-, **Supp. XX:** 117
"Ghazals: Homage to Ghalib" (Rich), **Supp. I Part 2:** 557
Ghost, The (Crane), **I:** 409, 421
"Ghost, The" (Peacock), **Supp. XIX:** 199
"Ghost Cat" (Peacock), **Supp. XIX:** 206
"Ghost Chant, et alii" (Komunyakaa), **Supp. XIII:** 114
Ghost in the Music, A (Nichols), **Supp. XIII:** 267
"Ghostlier Demarcations, Keener Sounds" (Vendler), **Supp. I Part 2:** 565
"Ghostly Father, I Confess" (McCarthy), **II:** 565–566
Ghostly Lover, The (Hardwick), **Supp. III Part 1:** 194–196, 208, 209
Ghost Money (Hull), **Supp. XXI:** 129, **132–135,** 136
Ghost of Meter, The (A. Finch), **Supp. XVII:** 71, 73
"Ghost of the Buffaloes, The" (Lindsay), **Supp. I Part 2:** 393
Ghost of Tradition, The (Walzer), **Supp. XVIII:** 174
Ghosts (Auster), **Supp. XII:** 22, 24, **26–27**
Ghosts (Ibsen), **III:** 152
Ghosts (Wharton), **IV:** 316, 327
Ghosts of Tsavo: Stalking the Mystery Lions of East Africa (Caputo), **Supp. XIX:** 28
Ghost Town (Coover), **Supp. V:** 52–53
Ghost Trio, The (Bierds), **Supp. XVII:** 29, **30**
Ghost Writer, The (P. Roth), **Retro. Supp. II:** 22, 290, 291; **Supp. III Part 2:** 420–421; **Supp. XVII:** 43
Giachetti, Fosco, **Supp. IV Part 2:** 520
"Giacometti" (Wilbur), **Supp. III Part 2:** 551
Giacometti, Alberto, **Supp. VIII:** 168, 169
Giacomo, Padre, **II:** 278–279
Giant's House, The: A Romance (McCracken), **Supp. X:** 86
"Giant Snail" (Bishop), **Retro. Supp. II:** 49
Giant Weapon, The (Winters), **Supp. II Part 2:** 810
"Giant Woman, The" (Oates), **Supp. II Part 2:** 523
Gibbon, Edward, **I:** 4, 378; **IV:** 126; **Supp. I Part 2:** 503; **Supp. III Part 2:** 629; **Supp. XIII:** 75; **Supp. XIV:** 97
Gibbons, James, **Supp. XVII:** 228
Gibbons, Kaye, **Supp. X: 41–54; Supp. XII:** 311
Gibbons, Reginald, **Supp. X:** 113, 124, 127; **Supp. XV:** 105; **Supp. XIX:** 40, 41–42, 281
Gibbons, Richard, **Supp. I Part 1:** 107
"Gibbs" (Rukeyser), **Supp. VI:** 273
Gibbs, Barbara, **Supp. IV Part 2:** 644

Gibbs, Wolcott, **Supp. I Part 2:** 604, 618; **Supp. VIII:** 151
Gibran, Kahlil, **Supp. XX:** 69, **113–129**
"GIBSON" (Baraka), **Supp. II Part 1:** 54
Gibson, Charles Dana, **Supp. X:** 184
Gibson, Graeme, **Supp. XIII:** 20
Gibson, Wilfrid W., **Retro. Supp. I:** 128
Gibson, William, **Supp. XVI:** 117–133
Giddins, Gary, **Supp. XIII:** 245
Gide, André, **I:** 271, 290; **II:** 581; **III:** 210; **IV:** 53, 289; **Supp. I Part 1:** 51; **Supp. IV Part 1:** 80, 284, 347; **Supp. IV Part 2:** 681, 682; **Supp. VIII:** 40; **Supp. X:** 187; **Supp. XIV:** 24, 348; **Supp. XVII:** 242
Gideon Planish (Lewis), **II:** 455
Gielgud, John, **I:** 82; **Supp. XI:** 305
Gierow, Dr. Karl Ragnar, **III:** 404
Gifford, Bill, **Supp. XI:** 38
Gifford, Terry, **Supp. XVI:** 22
"Gift, The" (Creeley), **Supp. IV Part 1:** 153
"Gift, The" (Doolittle), **Supp. I Part 1:** 267
Gift, The (Hyde), **Supp. XVIII:** 150
"Gift, The" (Jarman), **Supp. XVII:** 116
"Gift, The" (L.-Y. Lee), **Supp. XV:** 213, 214
Gift, The (Nabokov), **III:** 246, 255, 261–263; **Retro. Supp. I:** 264, 266, **268–270,** 273, 274–275, 278
"Gift from the City, A" (Updike), **Retro. Supp. I:** 320
"Gift of God, The" (Robinson), **III:** 512, 517, 518–521, 524
Gift of the Black Folk, The: The Negroes in the Making of America (Du Bois), **Supp. II Part 1:** 179
"Gift of the Magi, The" (O. Henry), **Supp. II Part 1:** 394, 406, 408
"Gift of the *Osuo*, The" (Johnson), **Supp. VI:** 194
"Gift of the Prodigal, The" (Taylor), **Supp. V:** 314, 326
"Gift Outright, The" (Frost), **II:** 152; **Supp. IV Part 1:** 15
Gigi (Colette; stage adaptation, Loos), **Supp. XVI:** 193
"Gigolo" (Plath), **Retro. Supp. II:** 257
"G.I. Graves in Tuscany" (Hugo), **Supp. VI:** 138
"Gila Bend" (Dickey), **Supp. IV Part 1:** 185–186
Gilbert, Jack, **Supp. IX:** 287
Gilbert, Peter, **Supp. IX:** 291, 300
Gilbert, Roger, **Supp. XI:** 124
Gilbert, Sandra M., **Retro. Supp. I:** 42; **Retro. Supp. II:** 324; **Supp. IX:** 66; **Supp. XV:** 270
Gilbert, Susan. *See* Dickinson, Mrs. William A.
Gilbert and Sullivan, **Supp. IV Part 1:** 389
"Gilbert Stuart Portrait of Washington, The" (Kooser), **Supp. XIX:** 124
Gil Blas (Le Sage), **II:** 290
Gilded Age, The (Twain), **III:** 504; **IV:** 198

Gilded Lapse of Time, A (Schnackenberg), **Supp. XV:** 258, **260–263**
"Gilded Lapse of Time, A" (Schnackenberg), **Supp. XV:** 257
"Gilded Six-Bits, The" (Hurston), **Supp. VI:** 154–155
Gilder, R. W., **Retro. Supp. II:** 66; **Supp. I Part 2:** 418
Gildersleeve, Basil, **Supp. I Part 1:** 369
Gilead (Robinson), **Supp. XXI:** 212, **216–220,** 223
Giles, H. A., **Retro. Supp. I:** 289
Giles, James R., **Supp. IX:** 11, 15; **Supp. XI:** 219, 223–224, 228, 234
"Giles Corey of the Salem Farms" (Longfellow), **II:** 505, 506; **Retro. Supp. II:** 166, 167
Giles Goat-Boy (Barth), **I:** 121, 122–123, 129, 130, 134, 135–138; **Supp. V:** 39
Gill, Brendan, **Supp. I Part 2:** 659, 660
Gillespie, Nick, **Supp. XIV:** 298, 311
Gillette, Chester, **I:** 512
Gilligan, Carol, **Supp. XIII:** 216
Gillis, Jim, **IV:** 196
Gillis, Steve, **IV:** 195
Gilman, Charlotte Perkins, **Supp. I Part 2:** 637; **Supp. V:** 121, 284, 285; **Supp. XI: 193–211; Supp. XIII:** 295, 306; **Supp. XVI:** 84
Gilman, Daniel Coit, **Supp. I Part 1:** 361, 368, 370
Gilman, Richard, **IV:** 115; **Supp. IV Part 2:** 577; **Supp. XIII:** 100; **Supp. XIX:** 251
Gilmore, Eddy, **Supp. I Part 2:** 618
Gilmore, Lyman, **Supp. XXI:** 20, 22, 24
Gilmore, Mikal, **Supp. XVI:** 123, 124
Gilpin, Charles, **III:** 392
Gilpin, Dewitt, **Supp. XV:** 197
Gilpin, Laura, **Retro. Supp. I:** 7
Gilpin, Sam, **Supp. V:** 213
Gilpin, William, **Supp. IV Part 2:** 603
"Gil's Furniture Bought & Sold" (Cisneros), **Supp. VII:** 61–62, 64
Gilyard, Keith, **Supp. XXI:** 246
"Gimcrackery" articles (Briggs), **Supp. XVIII:** 8–9
"Gimpel the Fool" (Singer), **IV:** 14; **Retro. Supp. II:** 22, 307
Gimpel the Fool and Other Stories (Singer), **IV:** 1, 7–9, 10, 12
"Gin" (Levine), **Supp. V:** 193
"Gingerbread House, The" (Coover), **Supp. V:** 42–43
Gingerbread Lady, The (Simon), **Supp. IV Part 2:** 580, 583–584, 588
Gingerich, Willard, **Supp. IV Part 2:** 510
Gingertown (McKay), **Supp. X:** 132, 139
Gingold, Hermione, **Supp. XV:** 13
Gingrich, Arnold, **Retro. Supp. I:** 113; **Supp. XVII:** 88; **Supp. XX:** 34
Ginna, Robert, **Supp. IX:** 259
Ginsberg, Allen, **I:** 183; **Retro. Supp. I:** 411, 426, 427; **Retro. Supp. II:** 280; **Supp. II Part 1:** 30, 32, 58, **307–333; Supp. III Part 1:** 2, 91, 96, 98, 100, 222, 226; **Supp. III Part 2:** 541, 627; **Supp. IV Part 1:** 79, 90, 322; **Supp. IV Part 2:** 502; **Supp. V:** 168, 336; **Supp. VIII:** 239, 242–243, 289; **Supp.**

IX: 299; **Supp. X:** 120, 204; **Supp. XI:** 135, 297; **Supp. XII:** 118–119, 121–122, 124, 126, 130–131, 136, 182; **Supp. XIV:** 15, 53, 54, 125, 137, 141, 142, 143–144, 148, 150, 269, 280, 283; **Supp. XV:** 134, 177, 263; **Supp. XVI:** 123, 135; **Supp. XVII:** 138, 243; **Supp. XVIII:** 20, 27, 29, 30; **Supp. XXI:** 53

Gioia, Dana, **Supp. IX:** 279; **Supp. XII:** 209; **Supp. XIII:** 337; **Supp. XV:** **111–131**, 251; **Supp. XVII:** 69, 72, 112; **Supp. XIX:** 117, 144; **Supp. XXI:** 99

Giono, Jean, **Supp. XVI:** 135

Giotto di Bondone, **Supp. I Part 2:** 438; **Supp. XI:** 126

Giovani, Regula, **Supp. XV:** 270

Giovanni, Nikki, **Supp. I Part 1:** 66; **Supp. II Part 1:** 54; **Supp. IV Part 1:** 11; **Supp. VIII:** 214

Giovanni's Room (Baldwin), **Retro. Supp. II:** 5, 6, **6–7,** 8, 10; **Supp. I Part 1:** 51, 52, 55–56, 57, 60, 63, 67; **Supp. III Part 1:** 125

Giovannitti, Arturo, **I:** 476; **Supp. XV:** 299, 301, 302, 307

"Giraffe" (Swenson), **Supp. IV Part 2:** 651

Giraldi, Giovanni Battista. *See* Cinthio

"Girl" (Kincaid), **Supp. VII:** 182–183

"Girl, The" (Olds), **Supp. X:** 207

"Girl Friend Poems" (Wright), **Supp. XV:** 349

"Girl from Lynn Bathes Horse!!" (McCarriston), **Supp. XIV:** 266

"Girl from Red Lion, P.A., A" (Mencken), **III:** 111

Girl in Glass, The: Love Poems (W. J. Smith), **Supp. XIII:** 335

Girl in Landscape (Lethem), **Supp. XVIII:** 136, **141–143**

"Girl in the Grave, The" (McCoy), **Supp. XIII:** 170

Girl Like I, A (Loos), **Supp. XVI:** 181, 183, 184, 187, 194, 196

"Girl of the Golden West" (Didion), **Supp. IV Part 1:** 195, 208, 211

Girl of the Golden West, The (Puccini), **III:** 139

Girl of the Limberlost (film), **Supp. XX:**223

Girl of the Limberlost (Stratton-Porter), **Supp. XX:**211, 221–222

"Girl on a Scaffold" (C. Frost), **Supp. XV:** 98

"Girl on the Baggage Truck, The" (O'Hara), **III:** 371–372

Girls at Play (Theroux), **Supp. VIII:** 314, 315, 316, **317**

"Girls at the Sphinx, The" (Farrell), **II:** 45

"Girls in Their Summer Dresses, The" (Shaw), **Supp. XIX:** 246

Girl Sleuth, The: A Feminist Guide (Mason), **Supp. VIII:** 133, 135, **139,** 142

"Girl's Story, A" (Bambara), **Supp. XI:** 10–11

"Girl the Prince Liked, The" (Z. Fitzgerald), **Supp. IX:** 71

Girl Who Loved Tom Gordon, The (King), **Supp. V:** 138, 152

Girl with Curious Hair (Wallace), **Supp. X:** 301, **305–308**

"Girl with Curious Hair" (Wallace), **Supp. X:** 306

"Girl with Silver Eyes, The" (Hammett), **Supp. IV Part 1:** 344, 345

"Girl with Talent, The" (Z. Fitzgerald), **Supp. IX:** 71

Girodias, Maurice, **III:** 171; **Supp. XI:** 297

Giroux, Robert, **Retro. Supp. II:** 177, 229, 235; **Supp. IV Part 1:** 280; **Supp. VIII:** 195; **Supp. XV:** 146

Gish, Dorothy, **Retro. Supp. I:** 103

Gish, Lillian, **Supp. XVI:** 184

Gissing, George, **II:** 138, 144

Gittings, Robert, **II:** 531

"Given" (C. Frost), **Supp. XV:** 96

"Give Us Back Our Country" (Masters), **Supp. I Part 2:** 472

Give Us This Day (film, Dmytryk), **Supp. XX:**40–41

"Give Way, Ye Gates" (Roethke), **III:** 536

"Give Your Heart to the Hawks" (Jeffers), **Supp. II Part 2:** 433

"Giving Blood" (Updike), **IV:** 226; **Retro. Supp. I:** 332

Giving Good Weight (McPhee), **Supp. III Part 1:** 307

"Giving in to You" (X. J. Kennedy), **Supp. XV:** 160

"Giving Myself Up" (Strand), **Supp. IV Part 2:** 627

G. K. the DJ (Keillor), **Supp. XVI:** 171

Glackens, William, **Retro. Supp. II:** 103

Gladden, Washington, **III:** 293; **Supp. I Part 1:** 5

Gladstone, William Ewart, **Supp. I Part 2:** 419

"Gladys Poem, The" (Alvarez), **Supp. VII:** 10

"Glance at German 'Kultur,' A" (Bourne), **I:** 228

Glance Away, A (Wideman), **Supp. X:** 320

"Glance from the Bridge, A" (Wilbur), **Supp. III Part 2:** 551

"Glance in the Mirror, A" (Swados), **Supp. XIX:** 261–262

Glance toward Shakespeare, A (Chapman), **Supp. XIV:** 44

Glancy, Diane, **Supp. XXI:** 246

Glanville-Hicks, Peggy, **Supp. IV Part 1:** 84

Glare (Ammons), **Supp. VII:** 35–36

Glasgow, Cary, **II:** 173, 182

Glasgow, Ellen, **II:** **173–195;** **IV:** 328; **Supp. X:** 228, 234

Glasmon, Kubec, **Supp. XIII:** 166

Glaspell, Susan, **Supp. III Part 1:** 175–191; **Supp. X:** 46; **Supp. XVII:** 99; **Supp. XXI:** 5

"Glass" (Francis), **Supp. IX:** 80

Glass, Irony, and God (Carson), **Supp. XII:** 97, **104–106**

Glass, Philip, **Supp. XXI:** 146, 147

"Glass Ark, The" (Komunyakaa), **Supp. XIII:** 129

Glass Bees, The (Jünger; Bogan and Mayer, trans.), **Supp. III Part 1:** 63

"Glass Blower of Venice" (Malamud), **Supp. I Part 2:** 450

"Glass Essay, The" (Carson), **Supp. XII:** **104–105**

"Glass Face in the Rain, A: New Poems" (Stafford), **Supp. XI:** **327–328**

Glass Key, The (Hammett), **Supp. IV Part 1:** 351–353

"Glass Meadows" (Bausch), **Supp. VII:** 53–54

Glass Menagerie, The (T. Williams), **I:** 81; **IV:** 378, 379, 380, 382, 383, 385, 386, 387, 388, 389, 390, 391, 392, 393–394, 395, 398; **Supp. IV Part 1:** 84

"Glass Mountain, The" (Barthelme), **Supp. IV Part 1:** 47

"Glass Tent, The" (Everwine), **Supp. XV:** 76

Glatstein, Jacob, **Supp. X:** 70

Glazer, Nathan, **Supp. VIII:** 93, 243

"Gleaners, The" (Merwin), **Supp. III Part 1:** 346

Gleanings in Europe (Cooper), **I:** 346

Gleason, Ralph J., **Supp. IX:** 16

Glenday, Michael, **Retro. Supp. II:** 210

Glengarry Glen Ross (film), **Supp. XIV:** 242

Glengarry Glen Ross (Mamet), **Supp. XIV:** 239, 240, 242, 245, 246, 250, 254, 255

Glimcher, Arne, **Supp. VIII:** 73

"Glimpses" (Jones), **Supp. XI:** 218

Glimpses of the Moon, The (Wharton), **II:** 189–190; **IV:** 322–323; **Retro. Supp. I:** 381

"Glimpses of Vietnamese Life" (Levertov), **Supp. III Part 1:** 282

Glisson, J. T., **Supp. X:** 234

Gloria Mundi (Frederic), **II:** 144–145

Gloria Naylor (Fowler), **Supp. VIII:** 224

"Glorious Fourth, The" (Ryan as Quin), **Supp. XVIII:** 229

Glorious Ones, The (Prose), **Supp. XVI:** 251

Glory of Hera, The (Gordon), **II:** 196–197, 198, 199, 217–220

Glory of the Conquered, The (Glaspell), **Supp. III Part 1:** 176

Glossary of Literary Terms (Abrams), **Supp. XVI:** 19

Glotfelty, Cheryll, **Supp. IX:** 25

Glover, Joyce Lee, **Supp. XIX:** 112

Glow, The (Wrigley), **Supp. XVIII:** 295

"Glow, The" (Wrigley), **Supp. XVIII:** 296–297, 307

Gluck, Christoph Willibald, **II:** 210, 211

Glück, Louise, **Supp. V:** **77–94;** **Supp. VIII:** 272; **Supp. X:** 209; **Supp. XIV:** 269; **Supp. XV:** 19, 252; **Supp. XVII:** 241

"Glutton, The" (Shapiro), **Supp. II Part 2:** 705

"Glutton for Punishment, A" (Yates), **Supp. XI:** 341

Glyph (Everett), **Supp. XVIII:** **60–61**

Gnädiges Fräulein, The (T. Williams), **IV:** 382, 395, 398

Gnomes and Occasions (Nemerov), **III:** 269

Gnomologia (Fuller), **II:** 111

"Gnothis Seauton" (Emerson), **II:** 11, 18–19

Go (Holmes), **Supp. XIV:** 144

"Go Ahead; Goodbye; Good Luck; and Watch Out" (Bronk), **Supp. XXI:** 31

"Goal of Intellectual Men, The" (Eberhart), **I:** 529–530

Go-Between, The (Hartley), **Supp. I Part 1:** 293

Gobineau, Joseph Arthur de, **Supp. XIV:** 209

God (Allen), **Supp. XV:** 3

God and the American Writer (Kazin), **Supp. VIII:** 108–109

Godard, Jean-Luc, **Supp. I Part 2:** 558

Godbey (Masters), **Supp. I Part 2:** 472

God Bless You, Mr. Rosewater (Vonnegut), **Supp. II Part 2:** 758, 767, 768–769, 771, 772

Goddess Abides, The (Buck), **Supp. II Part 1:** 129, 131–132

Gödel, Kurt, **Supp. IV Part 1:** 43

Godfather (Puzo), **Supp. IV Part 1:** 390

Godfires (Hoffman), **Supp. XVIII:** 81–82

God in Ruins, A (Uris), **Supp. XX:**247, **256**

"God in the Doorway" (Dillard), **Supp. VI:** 28

"God is a distant-stately Lover" (Dickinson), **I:** 471

Godkin, E. L., **II:** 274

God Knows (Heller), **Supp. IV Part 1:** 386, 388–389

God Made Alaska for the Indians (Reed), **Supp. X:** 241

God of His Fathers, The (London), **II:** 469

God of Vengeance (Asch), **IV:** 11

Go Down, Moses (Faulkner), **Retro. Supp. I:** 75, 82, 85, 86, 88, 89, 90, 92; **Supp. XVIII:** 203

"Go Down, Moses" (Faulkner), **II:** 71–72

Go Down, Moses (Hayden), **Supp. II Part 1:** 365

Go Down, Moses and Other Stories (Faulkner), **II:** 71; **Supp. X:** 52

"Go Down Death A Funeral Sermon" (Johnson), **Supp. IV Part 1:** 7

"God Rest Ye Merry, Gentlemen" (Hemingway), **IV:** 122

Godric (Buechner), **Supp. XII:** 53

Gods, The (Goldbarth), **Supp. XII:** 189, 190

Gods Arrive, The (Wharton), **IV:** 326–327; **Retro. Supp. I:** 382

God Save the Child (Parker), **Supp. XIX:** 183–184

"God Save the Rights of Man" (Freneau), **Supp. II Part 1:** 268

"Gods|Children" (Swenson), **Supp. IV Part 2:** 645

"God's Christ Theory" (Carson), **Supp. XII: 106**

God's Country (Everett), **Supp. XVIII: 57–58**, 64, 65

God's Country and My People (Morris), **III:** 238

Gods Determinations touching his Elect: and the Elects Combat in their Conversion, and Coming up to God in Christ together with the Comfortable Effects thereof (Taylor), **IV:** 155–160, 165

God-Seeker, The (Lewis), **II:** 456

God's Favorite (Simon), **Supp. IV Part 2:** 575, 586, 588, 590

"God's Fool" (Gibran), **Supp. XX:**118

God's Little Acre (Caldwell), **I:** 288, 289, 290, 297, 298–302, 305–306, 309, 310

God's Man: A Novel in Wood Cuts (Ward), **I:** 31

Gods of Winter, The (Gioia), **Supp. XV:** 112, **121–125**

"Gods of Winter, The" (Gioia), **Supp. XV:** 117

"God's Peace in November" (Jeffers), **Supp. II Part 2:** 420

God's Silence (F. Wright), **Supp. XVII:** 240, 246–247

"God Stiff" (Carson), **Supp. XII: 106**

God's Trombones (Johnson), **Supp. II Part 1:** 201

"God's Youth" (Untermeyer), **Supp. XV:** 296

"God the Father and the Empty House" (McCarriston), **Supp. XIV:** 273

Godwin, William, **II:** 304; **III:** 415; **Supp. I Part 1:** 126, 146; **Supp. I Part 2:** 512, 513–514, 522, 709, 719

God without Thunder (Ransom), **III:** 495–496, 499

Godwulf Manuscript, The (Parker), **Supp. XIX: 178–182**

Goebbels, Josef, **III:** 560

Goebel, Irma, **Supp. X:** 95

Goen, C. C., **I:** 560

Goethe, Johann Wolfgang von, **I:** 181, 396, 587–588; **II:** 5, 6, 320, 344, 488, 489, 492, 502, 556; **III:** 395, 453, 607, 612, 616; **IV:** 50, 64, 173, 326; **Retro. Supp. I:** 360; **Retro. Supp. II:** 94; **Supp. I Part 2:** 423, 457; **Supp. II Part 1:** 26; **Supp. III Part 1:** 63; **Supp. IX:** 131, 308; **Supp. X:** 60; **Supp. XI:** 169; **Supp. XVIII:** 278; **Supp. XX:**84

Go for the Body (Lacy), **Supp. XV:** 201, 204

Gogan, Robert, **Supp. XXI:** 24

Gogol, Nikolai, **I:** 296; **IV:** 1, 4; **Retro. Supp. I:** 266, 269; **Supp. VIII:** 14; **Supp. XVII:** 45; **Supp. XVIII:** 102

Goia, Dana, **Supp. XIX:** 121

"Going, Going, Gone" (Skloot), **Supp. XX:**207

Going, William T., **Supp. VIII:** 126

Going After Cacciato (O'Brien), **Supp. V:** 237, 238, 239, 244–246, 248, 249

Going All the Way (Wakefield), **Supp. VIII:** 43

"Going Critical" (Bambara), **Supp. XI:** 14

Going Down (Markson), **Supp. XVII:** 136, 138, **139–140**, 141, 142–143, 144, 145

Going for the Rain (Ortiz), **Supp. IV Part 2:** 499, 505–508, 509, 514

"Going Home by Last Night" (Kinnell), **Supp. III Part 1:** 244

"Going Home in America" (Hardwick), **Supp. III Part 1:** 205

"Going North" (Salinas), **Supp. XIII:** 316

Going Places (L. Michaels), **Supp. XVI:** 201, **203–206**

"Going Places" (L. Michaels), **Supp. XVI:** 203

"Going South" (J. W. Miller), **Supp. XX:**169

Going South (Lardner and Buck), **II:** 427

Going To and Fro and Walking Up and Down (Reznikoff), **Supp. XIV:** 280, 282, 284, 285

Going to Meet the Man (Baldwin), **Supp. I Part 1:** 60, 62–63; **Supp. XX:**147

"Going to Meet the Man" (Baldwin), **Retro. Supp. II:** 8, 9; **Supp. I Part 1:** 62–63

"Going to Naples" (Welty), **IV:** 278; **Retro. Supp. I:** 352, 353

"Going to Shrewsbury" (Jewett), **II:** 393

"Going to the Bakery" (Bishop), **Supp. I Part 1:** 93

Going-to-the-Stars (Lindsay), **Supp. I Part 2:** 398

Going-to-the-Sun (Lindsay), **Supp. I Part 2:** 397–398

Going to the Territory (Ellison), **Retro. Supp. II:** 119, 123–124

"Going towards Pojoaque, A December Full Moon/72" (Harjo), **Supp. XII:** 218

"Going Under" (Dubus), **Supp. VII:** 83

"Gold" (Francis), **Supp. IX:** 82

Gold (O'Neill), **III:** 391

Gold, Michael, **II:** 26; **IV:** 363, 364, 365; **Retro. Supp. II:** 323; **Supp. I Part 1:** 331; **Supp. I Part 2:** 609; **Supp. XIV:** 288

Goldbarth, Albert, **Supp. XII: 175–195**

Goldbarth's Book of Occult Phenomena (Goldbarth), **Supp. XII:** 181

Goldberg, S. L., **Supp. VIII:** 238

"Gold Bug, The" (Poe), **III:** 410, 413, 419, 420

Gold Bug Variations, The (Powers), **Supp. IX:** 210, 212, **216–217,** 219

Gold Cell, The (Olds), **Supp. X: 206–209**

Gold Diggers, The (Monette), **Supp. X:** 153

Golde, Miss (Mencken's Secretary), **III:** 104, 107

Golden, Harry, **III:** 579, 581; **Supp. VIII:** 244

Golden, Mike, **Supp. XI:** 294, 295, 297, 299, 303

Golden Age, The (Gurney), **Supp. V:** 101–103

Golden Apples (Rawlings), **Supp. X: 228–229,** 230, 234

Golden Apples, The (Welty), **IV:** 261, 271–274, 281, 293; **Retro. Supp. I:** 341, 342, 343, **350–351,** 352, 355

Golden Apples of the Sun, The (Bradbury), **Supp. IV Part 1:** 102, 103

Golden Book of Springfield, The (Lindsay), **Supp. I Part 2:** 376, 379, 395, 396

Golden Bough, The (Frazer), **II:** 204, 549; **III:** 6–7; **Supp. I Part 1:** 18; **Supp. IX:** 123; **Supp. X:** 124

Golden Bowl, The (James), **II:** 320, 333, 335; **Retro. Supp. I:** 215, 216, 218–219, 232, **234–235,** 374

Golden Boy (Odets), **Supp. II Part 2:** 538, 539, 540–541, 546, 551

Golden Calves, The (Auchincloss), **Supp. IV Part 1:** 35

Golden Child (Hwang), **Supp. XXI:** 147–148

Golden Day, The (Mumford), **Supp. II Part 2:** 471, 475, 477, 483, 484, 488–489, 493

Golden Fleece, The (Gurney), **Supp. V:** 97

Golden Gate (film, Madden), **Supp. XXI:** 147

Golden Gate, The (Seth), **Supp. XVII:** 117

Golden Grove, The: Selected Passages from the Sermons and Writings of Jeremy Taylor (L. P. Smith), **Supp. XIV:** 345

"Golden Heifer, The" (Wylie), **Supp. I Part 2:** 707

"Golden Honeymoon, The" (Lardner), **II:** 429–430, 431

Golden Journey, The (W. J. Smith and Bogan, comps.), **Supp. XIII:** 347

Golden Ladder series (S. and A. Warner), **Supp. XVIII:** 267

"Golden Lads" (Marquand), **III:** 56

Golden Legend, The (Longfellow), **II:** 489, 490, 495, 505, 506, 507; **Retro. Supp. II:** 159, 165, 166

Golden Mean and Other Poems, The (Tate and Wills), **IV:** 122

"Golden Retrievals" (Doty), **Supp. XI:** 132

Golden Shakespeare, The: An Anthology (L. P. Smith), **Supp. XIV:** 349

Goldensohn, Lorrie, **Retro. Supp. II:** 51

Golden State (Bidart), **Supp. XV:** 21, **23–25**

"Golden State" (Bidart), **Supp. XV:** 23, 24, 25

Golden States (Cunningham), **Supp. XV:** 55, **56–59,** 63

Golden Treasury of Best Songs and Lyrical Poems in the English Language (Palgrave), **Retro. Supp. I:** 124

Golden Treasury of the Best Songs and Lyrical Poems in the English Language (Palgrave), **Supp. XIV:** 340

Golden Whales of California and Other Rhymes in the American Language, The (Lindsay), **Supp. I Part 2:** 394–395, 396

"Goldfish Bowl, The" (Francis), **Supp. IX:** 78

Gold Fools (Sorrentino), **Supp. XXI:** 237

Goldin Boys, The (Epstein), **Supp. XIV:** 112

Golding, Arthur, **III:** 467, 468

Golding, William, **Supp. IV Part 1:** 297

Goldini, Carlo, **II:** 274

Goldkorn Tales (Epstein), **Supp. XII:** **163–164**

Goldman, Albert, **Supp. XI:** 299

Goldman, Arnold, **Supp. XXI:** 13

Goldman, Emma, **III:** 176, 177; **Supp. I Part 2:** 524; **Supp. XVII:** 96, 103, 104

Goldman, William, **Supp. IV Part 2:** 474

"Gold Mountain Stories" project (Kingston), **Supp. V:** 164

Gold of Chickaree, The (S. and A. Warner), **Supp. XVIII:** 267, 268, 269

Goldring, Douglas, **III:** 458

Goldsmith, Oliver, **II:** 273, 282, 299, 304, 308, 314, 315, 514; **Retro. Supp. I:** 335; **Supp. I Part 1:** 310; **Supp. I Part 2:** 503, 714, 716; **Supp. XVIII:** 12

Gold Standard and the Logic of Naturalism, The (W. B. Michaels), **Retro. Supp. I:** 369

Goldstein, Laurence, **Supp. XXI:** 134

Goldstein, Rebecca, **Supp. XVII:** 44

Goldwater, Barry, **I:** 376; **III:** 38

Goldwyn, Samuel, **Retro. Supp. II:** 199; **Supp. I Part 1:** 281

Golem, The (Leivick), **IV:** 6

"Goliardic Song" (Hecht), **Supp. X:** 63

"Go Like This" (Moore), **Supp. X:** 165

Goll, Ivan, **Supp. III Part 1:** 235, 243–244; **Supp. III Part 2:** 621

Gomes, Albert, **Supp. XXI:** 160

Goncharova, Natalya, **Supp. IX:** 66

Goncourt, Edmond de, **II:** 325, 328; **III:** 315, 317–318, 321; **Retro. Supp. I:** 226

Goncourt, Jules de, **II:** 328; **III:** 315, 317–318, 321

Gone Fishin' (Mosley), **Supp. XIII:** **235–236,** 240

"Gone to War" (E. Stoddard), **Supp. XV:** 282

"Gone West" (Rodriguez), **Supp. XIV:** 308

Gone with the Wind (film), **Retro. Supp. I:** 113

Gone with the Wind (Mitchell), **II:** 177; **Retro. Supp. I:** 340; **Supp. XX:** 243

Gongora y Argote, Luis de, **II:** 552

Gonzalez, David, **Supp. VIII:** 85

González, Jovita, **Supp. XIX:** 99

Gooch, Brad, **Supp. XII:** 121

Good, George, **Supp. XI:** 306

"Good, the Plaid, and the Ugly, The" (Wasserstein), **Supp. XV:** 327

"Good and Not So Good, The" (Dunn), **Supp. XI:** 141

"Good Anna, The" (Stein), **IV:** 37, 40, 43

Good As Gold (Heller), **Supp. IV Part 1:** 386, 388, 394

Good as I Been to You (album, Dylan), **Supp. XVIII:** 28

Good Boys and Dead Girls and Other Essays (Gordon), **Supp. IV Part 1:** 309–310

Good Brother, The (Offutt), **Supp. XIX:** 163, **168–169**

"Good-by and Keep Cold" (Frost), **Retro. Supp. I:** 135

"Good-bye" (Emerson), **II:** 19

"Goodbye, Christ" (Hughes), **Retro. Supp. I:** 202, 203

Goodbye, Columbus (P. Roth), **Retro. Supp. II:** 280, 281, 290; **Supp. III Part 2:** 403–406; **Supp. XIV:** 112; **Supp. XX:** 177

"Goodbye, Columbus" (P. Roth), **Supp. III Part 2:** 401, 404, 408–409, 411

Goodbye, Columbus and Five Short Stories (P. Roth), **Retro. Supp. II:** 279

"Goodbye, Goldeneye" (Swenson), **Supp. IV Part 2:** 651

"Goodbye, Mr. Chipstein" (Epstein), **Supp. XIV:** 103, 108

"Goodbye, My Brother" (Cheever), **Supp. I Part 1:** 175, 177, 193

"Goodbye and Good Luck" (Paley), **Supp. VI:** 219, 223

Goodbye Girl, The (film), **Supp. IV Part 2:** 589

Goodbye Girl, The (musical), **Supp. IV Part 2:** 576, 588

Goodbye Girl, The (Simon), **Supp. IV Part 2:** 575

Goodbye Look, The (Macdonald), **Supp. IV Part 2:** 473, 474

"Good-Bye My Fancy" (Whitman), **IV:** 348

"Goodbye to All That" (Didion), **Supp. IV Part 1:** 197

Goodbye to All That (Graves), **I:** 477

Goodbye to Berlin (Isherwood), **Supp. XIV:** 159, 161, 162, 169

"Good-Bye to the Mezzogiorno" (Auden), **Supp. II Part 1:** 19

"Goodbye to the Poetry of Calcium" (Wright), **Supp. III Part 2:** 599

"Good Company" (Matthews), **Supp. IX:** 160

"Good Country People" (O'Connor), **III:** 343, 350, 351, 352, 358; **Retro. Supp. II:** 229, 232

Good Day to Die, A (Harrison), **Supp. VIII:** **42–44,** 45, 47

Good Doctor, The (Simon), **Supp. IV Part 2:** 575, 585

Good Earth, The (Buck), **Supp. I Part 1:** 49; **Supp. II Part 1:** 115–175, 118, 125, 132

Good European, The (Blackmur), **Supp. II Part 1:** 91

Good Evening Mr. & Mrs. America, and All the Ships at Sea (Bausch), **Supp. VII:** 41, 47, 52

"Good Friday" (Jarman), **Supp. XVII:** 116

"Good Girl" (Peacock), **Supp. XIX:** 199

Good Gray Poet, The (O'Connor), **Retro. Supp. I:** 407

Good Health and How We Won It (Sinclair), **Supp. V:** 285–286

Good Hearts (Price), **Supp. VI:** 259, 265

"Good Job Gone, A" (Hughes), **Retro. Supp. I:** 204

Good Journey, A (Ortiz), **Supp. IV Part 2:** 497, 499, 503, 505, 509–510, 514

Good Luck in Cracked Italian (Hugo), **Supp. VI:** 133, 137–138

Goodman, Allegra, **Supp. XII:** 159; **Supp. XVI:** 205; **Supp. XX:**177

Goodman, Ellen, **Supp. XVI:** 103

Goodman, Jack, **Supp. XXI:** 277

Goodman, Jenny, **Supp. XV:** 343, 344

Goodman, Paul, **I:** 218, 261; **III:** 39; **Supp. I Part 2:** 524; **Supp. VIII:** 239–240

Goodman, Philip, **III:** 105, 108

Goodman, Walter, **Supp. IV Part 2:** 532

Good Man Is Hard to Find, A (O'Connor), **III:** 339, 343–345

"Good Man Is Hard to Find, A" (O'Connor), **III:** 339, 344, 353; **Retro. Supp. II:** 230–231

Good Man Is Hard to Find and Other Stories, A (O'Connor), **Retro. Supp. II:** 229, **230–232**

Good Morning, America (Sandburg), **III:** 592–593

"Good Morning, Major" (Marquand), **III:** 56

Good Morning, Midnight (Rhys), **Supp. III Part 1:** 43

"Good Morning, Revolution" (Hughes), **Retro. Supp. I:** 201, 203

Good Morning Blues: The Autobiography of Count Basie (Murray), **Supp. XIX:** 159

Good Morning Revolution: Uncollected Writings of Social Protest (Hughes), **Retro. Supp. I:** 194, 201, 202, 209

Good Mother, The (Miller), **Supp. XII:** 289, **290–294**, 299, 301

Good News (Abbey), **Supp. XIII:** **11–12**

"Good News from New-England" (Johnson), **Supp. I Part 1:** 115

Good News of Death and Other Poems (Simpson), **Supp. IX:** 265, **268–269**

"Goodnight, Saigon" (lecture, Caputo), **Supp. XIX:** 17, 30

Good Night, Willie Lee, I'll See You in the Morning (Walker), **Supp. III Part 2:** 520, 531

"Good Oak" (Leopold), **Supp. XIV:** 185, 187, 191

"Good Old Times, The: New York Fifty Years Ago" (Briggs), **Supp. XVIII:** 15

"Good Pine, A" (Offutt), **Supp. XIX:** 174

Goodrich, Samuel G., **Supp. I Part 1:** 38

Good Scent from a Strange Mountain, A (R. O. Butler), **Supp. XII:** 62, **70–72**

Good School, A (Yates), **Supp. XI:** 334, **346–347**, 348, 349

"*Good Shepherdess, The*/La Buena Pastora" (Mora), **Supp. XIII:** 228–229

Good Will (Smiley), **Supp. VI:** 292, **299–300**

Goodwin, K. L., **III:** 478

Goodwin, Stephen, **Supp. V:** 314, 316, 322, 323, 325

"Good Word for Winter, A" (Lowell), **Supp. I Part 2:** 420

Goodwyn, Janet, **Retro. Supp. I:** 370

"Goophered Grapevine, The" (Chesnutt), **Supp. XIV:** 57, **58–61**

"Goose Fish, The" (Nemerov), **III:** 272, 284

"Goose Pond" (Kunitz), **Supp. III Part 1:** 262

Goose-Step, The (Sinclair), **Supp. V:** 276

Gordimer, Nadine, **Supp. XV:** 251

Gordon, Ambrose, **Supp. XV:** 144

Gordon, A. R., **III:** 199

Gordon, Caroline, **II:** **196–222**, 536, 537; **III:** 454, 482; **IV:** 123, 126–127, 139, 282; **Retro. Supp. II:** 177, 222, 229, 233, 235; **Supp. II Part 1:** 139

Gordon, Charles G., **I:** 454

Gordon, Don, **Supp. X:** 119

Gordon, Eugene, **Supp. II Part 1:** 170; **Supp. XVIII:** 280

Gordon, Fran, **Supp. XIII:** 111

Gordon, James Morris, **II:** 197

Gordon, Lois, **Supp. IV Part 1:** 48; **Supp. V:** 46

Gordon, Lyndall, **Retro. Supp. I:** 55

Gordon, Mary, **Supp. IV Part 1:** **297–317**

Gordon, Neil, **Supp. XVI:** 156

Gordon, Peter, **Supp. XII:** 3–4, 4–5, 8

Gordon, Ruth, **IV:** 357; **Supp. XX:**50

Gore, Thomas Pryor, **Supp. IV Part 2:** 679

Gores, Joe, **Supp. XXI:** 70

Gorey, Edward, **IV:** 430, 436

Gorilla, My Love (Bambara), **Supp. XI:** 1, **2–7**

"Gorilla, My Love" (Bambara), **Supp. XI:** 2, 3–4

Gorki, Maxim, **I:** 478; **II:** 49; **III:** 402; **IV:** 299; **Supp. I Part 1:** 5, 51; **Supp. XIX:** 241

Gorney, Cynthia, **Supp. XVI:** 112

Gorra, Michael, **Supp. V:** 71

Goslings, The (Sinclair), **Supp. V:** 276, 281

Go South to Sorrow (Rowan), **Supp. XIV:** 306

Gospel According to Joe, The (Gurney), **Supp. V:** 99

"Gospel According to Saint Mark, The" (Gordon), **Supp. IV Part 1:** 310

Gospel according to the Son (Mailer), **Retro. Supp. II:** 213

"Gospel for the Twentieth Century, The" (Locke), **Supp. XIV:** 206

"Gospel of Beauty, The" (Lindsay), **Supp. I Part 2:** 380, 382, 384, 385, 391, 396

Gospels, The (di Donato), **Supp. XX:**45–46

Gospel Singer, The (Crews), **Supp. XI:** 102, **109**

Gosse, Edmund, **II:** 538; **IV:** 350; **Supp. VIII:** 157

"Gossip" (Conroy), **Supp. XVI:** 71–72

Gossips, Gorgons, and Crones: The Fates of the Earth (Caputi), **Supp. IV Part 1:** 335

Go Tell It on the Mountain (Baldwin), **Retro. Supp. II:** 1, 2, 3, **4–5**, 7, 14; **Supp. I Part 1:** 48, 49, 50, 51, 52, 53–54, 55, 56, 57, 59, 61, 63, 64, 67; **Supp. II Part 1:** 170

Gotera, Vince, **Supp. XIII:** 115, 116, 119, 121, 127

Gothic Revival, The: An Essay on the History of Taste (Clark), **Supp. XIV:** 348

Gothic Writers (Thomson, Voller, and Frank, eds.), **Retro. Supp. II:** 273

"Go to the Devil and Shake Yourself" (song), **Supp. I Part 2:** 580

"Go to the Shine That's on a Tree" (Eberhart), **I:** 523

Go to the Widow-Maker (Jones), **Supp. XI:** 214, **225–226**, 227, 229, 233

"Gots Is What You Got" (Di Piero), **Supp. XIX:** 35, 36, 38, 41, 42, 45–46

Gottfried, Alex, **Supp. XIX:** 260

Gottfried, Martin, **Supp. IV Part 2:** 584

Gotthelf, Allan, **Supp. IV Part 2:** 528

Gottlieb, Adolph, **Supp. XV:** 144

Gottlieb, Edward, **Supp. XX:**250

Gottlieb, Morton, **Supp. XVI:** 196

Gottlieb, Robert, **Supp. IV Part 2:** 474

Gottschalk and the Grande Tarantelle (Brooks), **Supp. III Part 1:** 86

"Gottschalk and the Grande Tarantelle" (Brooks), **Supp. III Part 1:** 86–87

Gould (Dixon), **Supp. XII:** 152, **153**

Gould, Edward Sherman, **I:** 346

Gould, Janice, **Supp. IV Part 1:** 322, 327; **Supp. XII:** 229

Gould, Jay, **I:** 4

Gould, Joe, **Supp. XV:** 143

Gourd Dancer, The (Momaday), **Supp. IV Part 2:** 481, 487, 491, 493

Gourmont, Remy de, **I:** 270, 272; **II:** 528, 529; **III:** 457, 467–468, 477; **Retro. Supp. I:** 55

Gouverneurs de la Rosée (Roumain), **Supp. IV Part 1:** 360, 367

Government Girl (film, Nichols), **Supp. XVIII:** 247

"Governors of Wyoming, The" (Proulx), **Supp. VII:** 264

Goyen, William, **Supp. V:** 220

Grabhorn, Janet, **Supp. XV:** 142

"Grace" (Budbill), **Supp. XIX:** 2

"Grace" (Dubus), **Supp. VII:** 91

"Grace" (Harjo), **Supp. XII:** 224

Grace Notes (Dove), **Supp. IV Part 1:** 248–250, 252

Grace (Eventually): Thoughts on Faith (Lamott), **Supp. XX:**143–145

Grade, Chaim, **Supp. XVII:** 41

"Graduation" (Dubus), **Supp. VII:** 84

Grady, Henry W., **Supp. I Part 1:** 370

Graeber, Laurel, **Supp. V:** 15

Graham, Billy, **I:** 308

Graham, David, **Supp. XV:** 104; **Supp. XIX:** 81

Graham, Don, **Supp. XI:** 252, 254

Graham, Jorie, **Supp. IX:** 38, 52; **Supp. X:** 73; **Supp. XII:** 209; **Supp. XIII:** 85; **Supp. XVII:** 110, 111, 133, 240, 241, 242

Graham, Martha, **Supp. XI:** 152

Graham, Maryemma, **Retro. Supp. I:** 201, 204

Graham, Nan, **Supp. XII:** 272

Graham, Sheilah, **II:** 94; **Retro. Supp. I:** 97, 113–114, 115; **Supp. IX:** 63

Graham, Shirley, **Supp. I Part 1:** 51; **Supp. XXI:** 277. *See also* Du Bois, Shirley Graham

Graham, Stephen, **Supp. I Part 2:** 397

Graham, Tom (pseudonym). *See* Lewis, Sinclair

Grahn, Judy, **Supp. IV Part 1:** 325, 330

"Grain Field" (Crapsey), **Supp. XVII:** 77

Grainger, Percy, **Supp. I Part 2:** 386

Grain of Mustard Seed, A (Sarton), **Supp. VIII:** 259–260, 263

Gramar (Lowth), **II:** 8

Grammar of Motives, A (Burke), **I:** 272, 275, 276–278, 283, 284

Gramsci, Antonio, **Supp. XX:** 35–36

Granados, Gabriel Bernal, **Supp. XV:** 350

Granath, Jack, **Supp. XVIII:** 93

Granberry, Edwin, **I:** 288

Grand Canyon, Inc. (Everett), **Supp. XVIII:** 66

Grand Design, The (Dos Passos), **I:** 489–490

"Grande Malade, The" (Barnes), **Supp. III Part 1:** 36

"Grandfather" (Dunn), **Supp. XI:** 147

"Grandfather and Grandson" (Singer), **Retro. Supp. II:** 307

Grandfathers, The (Richter), **Supp. XVIII:** 219–220

"Grandfather's Blessing" (Alvarez), **Supp. VII:** 2

"Grand Forks" (Bierds), **Supp. XVII:** 34

"Grand Forks" (Simpson), **Supp. IX:** 280–281

"Grand Inquisitor" (Dostoevsky), **IV:** 106

Grandissimes (Cable), **II:** 291

"Grand-Master Nabokov" (Updike), **Retro. Supp. I:** 317

"Grand Miracle, The" (Karr), **Supp. XI:** 251

"Grandmother" (Gunn Allen), **Supp. IV Part 1:** 320, 325

"Grandmother in Heaven" (Levine), **Supp. V:** 186

"Grandmother of the Sun: Ritual Gynocracy in Native America" (Gunn Allen), **Supp. IV Part 1:** 328

Grandmothers of the Light: A Medicine Woman's Sourcebook (Gunn Allen, ed.), **Supp. IV Part 1:** 332, 333–334

"Grandmother Songs, The" (Hogan), **Supp. IV Part 1:** 413

"Grandpa and the Statue" (A. Miller), **III:** 147

"Grandparents" (Lowell), **II:** 550

"Grandsire Bells, The" (Bierds), **Supp. XVII:** 28–29

"Grandstand Complex, The" (McCoy), **Supp. XIII:** 166

Grange, Red, **II:** 416

Granger's Index to Poetry (anthology), **Retro. Supp. I:** 37, 39

Grant, Gavin, **Supp. XIX:** 175

Grant, Lee, **Supp. XIII:** 295

Grant, Madison, **Supp. II Part 1:** 170

Grant, Richard, **Supp. X:** 282

Grant, Ulysses S., **I:** 4, 15; **II:** 542; **III:** 506, 584; **IV:** 348, 446; **Supp. I Part 2:** 418

Grantwood, **Retro. Supp. I:** 416, 417

"Grapes, The" (Hecht), **Supp. X:** 65–66

"Grape Sherbet" (Dove), **Supp. IV Part 1:** 246

Grapes of Wrath, The (Steinbeck), **I:** 301; **III:** 589; **IV:** 51, 53–55, 59, 63, 65, 67, 68, 69; **Supp. V:** 290; **Supp. XI:** 169; **Supp. XIV:** 181; **Supp. XV:** 351; **Supp. XX:** 28

"Grapevine, The" (Ashbery), **Supp. III Part 1:** 4

"Grass" (Sandburg), **III:** 584

Grass, Günter, **Supp. VIII:** 40

Grass County (Kooser), **Supp. XIX:** 119

"Grasse: The Olive Trees" (Wilbur), **Supp. III Part 2:** 550

Grass Harp, The (Capote), **Supp. III Part 1:** 114–117, 123

Grass Still Grows, The (A. Miller), **III:** 146

Gratitude to Old Teachers (R. Bly), **Supp. IV Part 1:** 73

Graupner, Gottlieb, **Supp. XV:** 240, 244

"Grave, A" (Moore), **III:** 195, 202, 208, 213

Grave, The (Blair), **Supp. I Part 1:** 150

"Grave, The" (Porter), **III:** 433, 443, 445–446

"Grave, The" (Winters), **Supp. II Part 2:** 795, 796

"Graven Image" (O'Hara), **III:** 320

Grave of the Right Hand, The (Wright), **Supp. V:** 332, 338, 339

"Grave Piece" (Eberhart), **I:** 533

Graves, Billy, **Supp. I Part 2:** 607

Graves, John, **Supp. V:** 220

Graves, Morris, **Supp. X:** 264

Graves, Peter, **Supp. IV Part 2:** 474

Graves, Rean, **Supp. I Part 1:** 326

Graves, Robert, **I:** 437, 477, 523; **Supp. I Part 2:** 541; **Supp. IV Part 1:** 280, 348; **Supp. IV Part 2:** 685

"Graveyard Blues" (Trethewey), **Supp. XXI:** 245, 255, 256

Graveyard for Lunatics, A (Bradbury), **Supp. IV Part 1:** 102, 114–116

Gravity's Rainbow (Pynchon), **Supp. II Part 2:** 617, 618–619, 621–625, 627, 630, 633–636; **Supp. IV Part 1:** 279; **Supp. V:** 44; **Supp. XIV:** 49; **Supp. XVII:** 236

Gray, Cecil, **Supp. I Part 1:** 258

Gray, Francine Du Plessix, **Supp. V:** 169

Gray, James, **III:** 207; **Supp. I Part 2:** 410

Gray, Jeffrey, **Supp. XV:** 27

Gray, Paul, **Supp. IV Part 1:** 305; **Supp. IV Part 2:** 639; **Supp. XVI:** 74; **Supp. XVIII:** 94

Gray, Thomas, **I:** 68; **Supp. I Part 1:** 150; **Supp. I Part 2:** 422, 716

Gray, Thomas A., **Supp. I Part 2:** 710

"Gray Heron, The" (Kinnell), **Supp. III Part 1:** 250

"Gray Mills of Farley, The" (Jewett), **Retro. Supp. II:** 132, 144

"Gray Poem" (Everwine), **Supp. XV:** 81

Grayson, Charles, **Supp. XIII:** 171

"Gray Squirrel" (Francis), **Supp. IX:** 90

"Gray Wolf's H 'ant, The" (Chesnutt), **Supp. XIV:** 60

Grealy, Lucy, **Supp. XII:** 310

Greasy Lake (Boyle), **Supp. VIII:** 14–15

"Greasy Lake" (Boyle), **Supp. VIII:** 15; **Supp. XX:** 18–19

Greasy Lake & Other Stories (Boyle), **Supp. XX:** 17, 18–19

"Great Adventure of Max Breuck, The" (Lowell), **II:** 522

Great American Novel, The (P. Roth), **Retro. Supp. II:** 283, 288–289; **Supp. III Part 2:** 414–416

Great American Short Novels (Phillips, ed.), **Supp. VIII:** 156

Great Battles of the World (Crane), **I:** 415

"Great Carousel, The" (Untermeyer), **Supp. XV:** 296

Great Christian Doctrine of Original Sin Defended, The . . . (Edwards), **I:** 549, 557, 559

Great Circle (Aiken), **I:** 53, 55, 57

"Great Class-Reunion Bazaar, The" (Theroux), **Supp. VIII:** 312

Great Day, The (Hurston), **Supp. VI:** 154

Great Days (Barthelme), **Supp. IV Part 1:** 39

Great Days, The (Dos Passos), **I:** 491

Great Digest (Pound, trans.), **III:** 472

"Great Divider, The" (Saunders), **Supp. XIX:** 235

"Great Elegy for John Donne" (Brodsky), **Supp. VIII:** 21, 23

"Greater Good, A" (Di Piero), **Supp. XIX:** 39

Greater Inclination, The (Wharton), **Retro. Supp. I:** 363, 364–365, 366

Greater Sea, The (Gibran), **Supp. XX:** 118

"Greater Self, The" (Gibran), **Supp. XX:** 118

"Greater Torment, The" (Blackmur), **Supp. II Part 1:** 92

Greatest Hits 1969–1996 (Salinas), **Supp. XIII:** 311

"Greatest Thing in the World, The" (Mailer), **Retro. Supp. II:** 196

Great Expectations (Acker), **Supp. XII:** 5, 9–11

Great Expectations (Dickens), **III:** 247; **Supp. I Part 1:** 35; **Supp. XVI:** 73; **Supp. XVIII:** 146

"Great Expectations, No Satisfaction" (D. Gates), **Supp. XVI:** 73

"Great Figure, The" (W. C. Williams), **IV:** 414

"Great Fillmore Street Buffalo Drive, The" (Momaday), **Supp. IV Part 2:** 493

Great Gatsby, The (Fitzgerald) (Modern Library), **Retro. Supp. I:** 113

Great Gatsby, The (Fitzgerald), **I:** 107, 375, 514; **II:** 77, 79, 83, 84, 85, 87, 91–93, 94, 96, 98; **III:** 244, 260, 372, 572; **IV:** 124, 297; **Retro. Supp. I:** 98, 105, **105–108**, 110, 114, 115, 335, 359; **Retro. Supp. II:** 107, 201; **II Part 2:** 626; **Supp. III Part 2:** 585; **Supp. IV Part 2:** 468, 475; **Supp. IX:** 57, 58; **Supp. X:** 175; **Supp. XI:** 65, 69, 334; **Supp. XVI:** 64, 75; **Supp. XVIII:** 76, 148, 165; **Supp. XX:** 59, 60, 61, 72

Great God Brown, The (O'Neill), **III:** 165, 391, 394–395

Great Goodness of Life: A Coon Show (Baraka), **Supp. II Part 1:** 47

Great Inclination, The (Wharton), **IV:** 310

"Great Infirmities" (Simic), **Supp. VIII:** 277

Great Jones Street (DeLillo), **Supp. VI:** 2, 3, 8–9, 11, 12

"Great Lawsuit, The: Man *versus* Men: Woman *versus* Women" (Fuller), **Retro. Supp. I:** 156; **Supp. II Part 1:** 292

"Great Men and Their Environment" (James), **II:** 347

"Great Mississippi Bubble, The" (Irving), **II:** 314

Great Railway Bazaar, The: By Train through Asia (Theroux), **Supp. VIII:** 318, 319, **320–321,** 322

"Great Scott" (Conroy), **Supp. XVI:** 75, 77

"Great Sleigh-Ride of Brewsterville, The" (Briggs), **Supp. XVIII:** 16

Great Stories of Suspense (Millar, ed.), **Supp. IV Part 2:** 474

Great Topics of the World (Goldbarth), **Supp. XII:** 187, 189, 191

Great Valley, The (Masters), **Supp. I Part 2:** 465

Great World and Timothy Colt, The (Auchincloss), **Supp. IV Part 1:** 25, 31, 32

Grédy, Jean-Pierre, **Supp. XVI:** 194

"Greek Boy, The" (Bryant), **Supp. I Part 1:** 168

Greek Mind/Jewish Soul: The Conflicted Art of Cynthia Ozick (Strandberg), **Supp. V:** 273

"Greek Partisan, The" (Bryant), **Supp. I Part 1:** 168

"Greeks, The" (McCarriston), **Supp. XIV:** 271

"Greeks, the Chines, or Say the Mayans, The" (Bronk), **Supp. XXI:** 31

Greeley, Horace, **II:** 7; **IV:** 197, 286–287

Green, Ashbel, **Supp. IV Part 2:** 474

Green, Henry, **IV:** 279; **Retro. Supp. I:** 354; **Supp. III Part 1:** 3; **Supp. XI:** 294–295, 296, 297; **Supp. XII:** 315

Green, Jack, **Supp. IV Part 1:** 284–285

Green, Martin, **Supp. I Part 1:** 299

Green, Michelle, **Supp. IV Part 1:** 95

Green, Rose Basile, **Supp. XX:** 33, 41

"Green Automobile, The" (Ginsberg), **Supp. II Part 1:** 322

Greenberg, Clement, **Supp. XV:** 141, 143, 144, 145

Greenberg, Eliezer, **Supp. I Part 2:** 432

Greenberg, Jonathan, **Supp. XII:** 285

Greenberg, Samuel, **I:** 393

Green Bough, A (Faulkner), **Retro. Supp. I:** 84

"Green Canoe" (Halliday), **Supp. XIX:** 88

Green Centuries (Gordon), **II:** 196, 197–207, 209

"Green Crab's Shell, A" (Doty), **Supp. XI:** 126

"Green Door, The" (O. Henry), **Supp. II Part 1:** 395

Greene, A. C., **Supp. V:** 223, 225

Greene, Graham, **I:** 480; **II:** 62, 320; **III:** 57, 556; **Retro. Supp. I:** 215; **Supp. I Part 1:** 280; **Supp. IV Part 1:** 341; **Supp. V:** 298; **Supp. IX:** 261; **Supp. XI:** 99,**Supp. XI:** 104; **Supp. XIII:** 233; **Supp. XVIII:** 79; **Supp. XIX:** 29–30

Greene, Helga, **Supp. IV Part 1:** 134, 135

Greene, J. Lee, **Retro. Supp. II:** 121

Greene, Nathanael, **Supp. I Part 2:** 508

Greene, Richard Tobias, **III:** 76

Greene, Robert, **Supp. XVII:** 232

Green Eggs and Ham (Geisel), **Supp. XVI:** 108, 109

"Greene-ing of the Portables, The" (Cowley), **Supp. II Part 1:** 140

"Greenest Continent, The" (Stevens), **Retro. Supp. I:** 304

Greenfeld, Josh, **III:** 364

Greenfield, Josh, **Supp. XIX:** 269

"Green Hell" (Boyle), **Supp. XX:** 18

Green Hills of Africa (Hemingway), **II:** 253; **Retro. Supp. I:** 182, 186

Greening of America, The (C. Reich), **Supp. XVII:** 3

"Green Lagoons, The" (Leopold), **Supp. XIV:** 188

"Green Lampshade" (Simic), **Supp. VIII:** 283

Greenlanders, The (Smiley), **Supp. VI:** 292, **296–298,** 299, 305, 307

Greenlaw, Edwin A., **IV:** 453

"Greenleaf" (O'Connor), **III:** 350, 351; **Retro. Supp. II:** 233, 237

Greenman, Walter F., **I:** 217, 222

Green Memories (Mumford), **Supp. II Part 2:** 474, 475, 479, 480–481

"Green Pasture, The" (Leopold), **Supp. XIV:** 184

Green Pastures, The (Connelly), **Supp. II Part 1:** 223

"Green Red Brown and White" (Swenson), **Supp. IV Part 2:** 639

"Green River" (Bryant), **Supp. I Part 1:** 155, 164

Green Shadows, White Whale (Bradbury), **Supp. IV Part 1:** 102, 103, 116

"Green Shirt, The" (Olds), **Supp. X:** 209

"Greensleeves" (Jarman), **Supp. XVII:** 113

Greenslet, Ferris, **I:** 19; **Retro. Supp. I:** 9, 10, 11, 13; **Retro. Supp. II:** 41

Greenspan, Alan, **Supp. IV Part 2:** 526

Greenspan, Ezra, **Supp. XVIII:** 257

Greenstreet, Sydney, **Supp. IV Part 1:** 356

"Green Thought, A" (L. Michaels), **Supp. XVI:** 204

"Green-Thumb Boy" (Nelson), **Supp. XVIII:** 182

Greenwald, Ted, **Supp. IV Part 2:** 423

Green Wall, The (Wright), **Supp. III Part 2:** 591, 593, 595

Green Wave, The (Rukeyser), **Supp. VI:** 273, 280

"Green Ways" (Kunitz), **Supp. III Part 1:** 265

Green with Beasts (Merwin), **Supp. III Part 1:** 340, 344–346

Greenwood, Grace, **Supp. XIII:** 141

"Greeting Card Verse" (Peacock), **Supp. XIX:** 200

Gregerson, Linda, **Supp. IV Part 2:** 651; **Supp. X:** 204–205; **Supp. XI:** 142

"Gregorio Valdes" (Bishop), **Retro. Supp. II:** 51

Gregory, Alyse, **I:** 221, 226, 227, 231

Gregory, Horace, **II:** 512; **Supp. III Part 2:** 614, 615; **Supp. IX:** 229; **Supp. XV:** 143

Gregory, Lady Isabella Augusta, **III:** 458

Gregory, Sinda, **Supp. X:** 260, 268

Grendel (Gardner), **Supp. VI:** 63, **67,** 68, 74

Grenstone Poems (Bynner), **Supp. XV:** 44

"Gretel in Darkness" (Glück), **Supp. V:** 82

Gretta (Caldwell), **I:** 301, 302

Greuze, Jean Baptiste, **Supp. I Part 2:** 714

Grey, Zane, **Supp. XIII:** 5

"Grief Has Stamped" (Pedersen; Nelson, trans.), **Supp. XVIII:** 180

Grieg, Michael, **Supp. XV:** 133, 148

Griffin, Bartholomew, **Supp. I Part 1:** 369

Griffin, John Howard, **Supp. VIII:** 208; **Supp. XXI:** 74

Griffin, Merv, **Supp. IV Part 2:** 526

Griffith, Albert J., **Supp. V:** 325

Griffith, D. W., **I:** 31, 481–482; **Retro. Supp. I:** 103, 325; **Supp. XI:** 45; **Supp. XVI:** 183, 184; **Supp. XXI:** 170

Griffith, Paul, **Supp. XVIII:** 173, 175

Griffiths, Clyde, **I:** 511

Grile, Dod (pseudonym). *See* Bierce, Ambrose

Grimm, Herman, **II:** 17

Grimm brothers, **II:** 378; **III:** 101, 491, 492; **IV:** 266; **Supp. I Part 2:** 596, 622; **Supp. X:** 78, 84, 86

Grimshaw, Anna, **Supp. XXI:** 172

Grinnell, George Bird, **Supp. XVI:** 13

Gris, Juan, **I:** 442; **Retro. Supp. I:** 430

Griswold, Rufus Wilmot, **III:** 409, 429; **Retro. Supp. II:** 261, 262; **Supp. XV:** 277, 278; **Supp. XVI:** 8, 10–11

Grogg, Sam, Jr., **Supp. IV Part 2:** 468, 471

Gromer, Crystal, **Supp. XII:** 297

Gronlund, Laurence, **II:** 276

Grooms, Red, **Supp. XV:** 178

"Groping for Trouts" (Gass), **Supp. VI:** 87

Grosholz, Emily, **Supp. XII:** 185; **Supp. XIX:** 37–38, 278

Gross, Robert A., **Supp. XIX:** 151

Gross, Terry, **Supp. XVI:** 167; **Supp. XXI:** 247, 255

"Grosse Fuge" (Doty), Supp. XI: 126–127

Grossman, Allen, **Retro. Supp. II:** 83; **Supp. XVIII:** 91; **Supp. XIX:** 82, 86, 94

Grosz, George, **III:** 172; **IV:** 438; **Retro. Supp. II:** 321; **Supp. X:** 137

"Grotesque in Modern Fiction, The" (E. Hoffman, Ph.D. dissertation), **Supp. XVI:** 147

"Groundhog, The" (Eberhart), **I:** 523, 530–532, 533

"Ground on Which I Stand, The" (Wilson), **Supp. VIII:** 331

"Ground Swell" (Jarman), **Supp. XVII:** 118

Group, The (McCarthy), **II:** 570, 574–578

"Group of Two, A" (Jarrell), **II:** 368

Group Therapy (Hearon), **Supp. VIII: 64–65**

"Grove" (Goldbarth), **Supp. XII:** 176

Groves of Academe, The (McCarthy), **II:** 568–571

Growing into Love (X. J. Kennedy), **Supp. XV:** 153, **158–160**

Growing Pains (J. S. Untermeyer), **Supp. XV:** 303

"Growing Season, The" (Caldwell), **I:** 309

Growing Up Gay: A Literary Anthology (Singer, ed.), **Supp. IV Part 1:** 330

"Growing Up Good in Maycomb" (Shaffer), **Supp. VIII:** 128

"Grown-Up" (Jewett), **Retro. Supp. II:** 134

"Growth" (Lowell), **II:** 554

"Growth and Decay in Recent Verse" (Untermeyer), **Supp. XV:** 299

Growth of the American Republic, The (Morison and Commager), **Supp. I Part 2:** 484

"Growtown Buggle, The" (Jewett), **Retro. Supp. II:** 132

Gruenberg, Louis, **III:** 392

Grumbach, Doris, **II:** 560

"Gryphon" (C. Baxter), **Supp. XVII:** 14, 17

"Guacamaja" (Leopold), **Supp. XIV:** 188–189

Guardian Angel, The (Holmes), **Supp. I Part 1:** 315–316

"Guardian of the Law" (R. Fisher), **Supp. XIX:** 71

Guard of Honor (Cozzens), **I:** 370–372, 375, 376–377, 378, 379

Guardsman, The (Molnar), **Supp. XVI:** 187

Guare, John, **Supp. XIII:** 196, 207

Gubar, Susan, **Retro. Supp. I:** 42; **Retro. Supp. II:** 324; **Supp. IX:** 66; **Supp. XV:** 270

Guerard, Albert, Jr., **Supp. X:** 79; **Supp. XIII:** 172

Guérin, Maurice de, **I:** 241

"Guerrilla Handbook, A" (Baraka), **Supp. II Part 1:** 36

Guess and Spell Coloring Book, The (Swenson), **Supp. IV Part 2:** 648

Guess Who's Coming to Dinner (film), **Supp. I Part 1:** 67

Guest, Judith, **Supp. XVI:** 36

Guest, Val, **Supp. XI:** 307

Guest Book (Bynner), **Supp. XV:** 51

"Guests of Mrs. Timms, The" (Jewett), **II:** 408; **Retro. Supp. II:** 135

Guevara, Martha, **Supp. VIII:** 74

Guevara, Fray Miguel de, **Supp. XXI:** 104

"Guevara . . .Guevara" (Salinas), **Supp. XIII:** 312–313, 315

Guided Tours of Hell (Prose), **Supp. XVI:** 257, 261

"Guided Tours of Hell" (Prose), **Supp. XVI:** 257

Guide for the Perplexed (Maimonides), **Supp. XVII:** 46

Guide in the Wilderness, A (Cooper), **I:** 337

"Guidelines" (Espaillat), **Supp. XXI:** 99

"Guide to Dungeness Spit, A" (Wagoner), **Supp. IX:** 325–326, 329

Guide to Ezra Pound's Selected Cantos' (Kearns), *Retro. Supp. I:* 292

Guide to Kulchur (Pound), **III:** 475

Guide to the Ruins (Nemerov), **III:** 269, 270–271, 272

Guillén, Nicolás, **Retro. Supp. I:** 202; **Supp. I Part 1:** 345

Guillevic, Eugene, **Supp. III Part 1:** 283

"Guilt, The" (Peacock), **Supp. XIX:** 200

"Guilty Man, The" (Kunitz), **Supp. II Part 1:** 263

Guilty of Everything: The Autobiography of Herbert Huncke (Huncke), **Supp. XIV:** 138, 140, 141, 150

Guilty Pleasures (Barthelme), **Supp. IV Part 1:** 44, 45, 53

Guimond, James, **Supp. XXI:** 228

Guinness, Alec, **Retro. Supp. I:** 65; **Supp. XX:** 50

Gulag Archipelago, The (Solzhenitsyn), **Supp. XVII:** 229

"Gulf, The" (Dunn), **Supp. XI:** 149

Gulistan (Saadi), **II:** 19

Gullible's Travels (Lardner), **II:** 426, 427

Gulliver, Adelaide Cromwell, **Supp. XVIII:** 286

"Gulliver Found" (Bronk), **Supp. XXI:** 33

Gulliver's Travels (Swift), **I:** 209, 348, 366; **II:** 301; **Supp. I Part 2:** 656; **Supp. XI:** 209; **Supp. XVI:** 110

"Gulls" (Hayden), **Supp. II Part 1:** 367

"Gulls, The" (Nemerov), **III:** 272

"Gulls on Dumps" (Di Piero), **Supp. XIX:** 41

"Gun, The" (Dobyns), **Supp. XIII:** 88

Gun, with Occasional Music (Lethem), **Supp. XVIII: 137–138**

Günderode: A Translation from the German (Fuller), **Supp. II Part 1:** 293

Gundy, Jeff, **Supp. XI:** 315; **Supp. XVI:** 46, 265, 275

Gunfight at the O.K. Corral (film), **Supp. XX:** 246

Gunman's Rhapsody (Parker), **Supp. XIX:** 187

Gunn, Robin Wright, **Supp. XXI:** 243, 244

Gunn, Thom, **Supp. IX:** 269

Gunn, Thomas, **Supp. V:** 178

Gunn Allen, Paula, **Supp. IV Part 1: 319–340,** 404; **Supp. IV Part 2:** 499, 502, 557, 568; **Supp. XII:** 218

"Gunnar's Sword" (C. Bly), **Supp. XVI:** 34, 35, 37, 42

"Guns as Keys; and the Great Gate Swings" (Lowell), **II:** 524

Gurdjieff, Georges, **Supp. V:** 199; **Supp. IX:** 320

Gurganus, Allan, **Supp. XII:** 308–309, 310

Gurko, Leo, **III:** 62

Gurney, A. R., **Supp. V: 95–112;** **Supp. IX:** 261

Gurney, Mary (Molly) Goodyear, **Supp. V:** 95

Gussow, Mel, **Supp. IX:** 93; **Supp. XII:** 325, 328, 341

Gustavus Vassa, the African (Vassa), **Supp. IV Part 1:** 11

Gusto, Thy Name Was Mrs. Hopkins: A Prose Rhapsody (Francis), **Supp. IX:** 89

Gute Mensch von Sezuan, Der (Brecht), **Supp. IX:** 138

Gutenberg, Johann, **Supp. I Part 2:** 392

Guthrie, A. B., **Supp. X:** 103

Guthrie, Woody, **Supp. XVIII:** 23

Gutman, Herbert, **Supp. I Part 1:** 47

Guttenplan, D. D., **Supp. XI:** 38

"Gutting of Couffignal, The" (Hammett), **Supp. IV Part 1:** 345

Guy Domville (James), **II:** 331; **Retro. Supp. I:** 228

"Gwendolyn" (Bishop), **Retro. Supp. II:** 51

Gwynn, R. S., **Supp. XVIII:** 184

Gypsy Ballads (Hughes, trans.), **Supp. I Part 1:** 345

Gypsy's Curse, The (Crews), **Supp. XI: 110**

"Gyroscope, The" (Rukeyser), **Supp. VI:** 271

Gysin, Brion, **Supp. XII:** 129

H

Haardt, Sara. *See* Mencken, Mrs. H. L. (Sara Haardt)

Habakkuk (biblical book), **III:** 200, 347

Habibi (Nye), **Supp. XIII:** 273, **279**

"Habit" (James), **II:** 351

Habitations of the Word (Gass), **Supp. VI:** 88

"Hack, The" (Swados), **Supp. XIX:** 267

Hacker, Marilyn, **Supp. XV:** 250; **Supp. XVII:** 71, 76, 112; **Supp. XVIII:** 177, 178

Hackett, David, **Supp. XII:** 236

Hadda, Janet, **Retro. Supp. II:** 317

Haddád, 'Abd al-Masíh, **Supp. XX:** 116

Haeckel, Ernst Heinrich, **II:** 480

Haegert, John, **Supp. XVI:** 69

Hafif, Marcia, **Supp. IV Part 2:** 423

Hagar's Daughter (P. Hopkins), **Supp. XVI:** 143

Hagedorn, Jessica, **Supp. X:** 292

Hagen, Beulah, **Supp. I Part 2:** 679

Hager, Kelly, **Supp. XVIII:** 183

Haggard, Rider, **III:** 189

Hagoromo (play), **III:** 466

Hagstrum, Jean, **Supp. XV:** 74
"Hail Mary" (Fante), **Supp. XI:** 160, 164
Haines, George, IV, **I:** 444
Haines, John, **Supp. XII: 197–214**
"Hair" (Corso), **Supp. XII:** 117, 126, 127
"Hair, The" (Carver), **Supp. III Part 1:** 137
"Haircut" (Lardner), **II:** 430, 436
"Hair Dressing" (Untermeyer), **Supp. XV:** 304, 305
Hairpiece: A Film for Nappy-Headed People (Chenzira; film), **Supp. XI:** 19–20
"Hairs" (Cisneros), **Supp. VII:** 59
Hairs/Pelitos (Cisneros), **Supp. VII:** 58
Hairy Ape, The (O'Neill), **III:** 391, 392, 393
"Haïta the Shepherd" (Bierce), **I:** 203
Haj, The (Uris), **Supp. XX:**244, 245, 247, **255–256**
Haldeman, Anna, **Supp. I Part 1:** 2
Hale, Edward Everett, **Supp. I Part 2:** 584; **Supp. XI:** 193, 200
Hale, John Parker, **Supp. I Part 2:** 685
Hale, Nancy, **Supp. VIII:** 151, 171
Haley, Alex, **Supp. I Part 1:** 47, 66
Haley, J. Evetts, **Supp. V:** 226
"Half a Century Gone" (Lowell), **II:** 554
Half-a-Hundred: Tales by Great American Writers (Grayson, ed.), **Supp. XIII:** 171
Half Asleep in Frog Pajamas (Robbins), **Supp. X:** 259, **279–282**
Half Breed, The (film), **Supp. XVI:** 185
Half-Century of Conflict, A (Parkman), **Supp. II Part 2:** 600, 607, 610
"Half Deity" (Moore), **III:** 210, 214, 215
"Half Hour of August" (Ríos), **Supp. IV Part 2:** 552
Half-Lives (Jong), **Supp. V:** 115, 119
Half Moon Street: Two Short Novels (Theroux), **Supp. VIII:** 322, 323
Half of Paradise (Burke), **Supp. XIV:** 22, 24
Half-Past Nation Time (Johnson), **Supp. VI:** 187
"Half-Skinned Steer, The" (Proulx), **Supp. VII:** 261–262
"Half Sonnets" (Jarman), **Supp. XVII:** 115
Half Sun Half Sleep (Swenson), **Supp. IV Part 2:** 645–646
Halfway (Kumin), **Supp. IV Part 2:** 441–442
"Halfway" (Rich), **Supp. I Part 2:** 553
Halfway Home (Monette), **Supp. X:** 154
Halfway to Silence (Sarton), **Supp. VIII:** 261
Half You Don't Know, The: Selected Stories (Cameron), **Supp. XII:** 79, 80, 81
Haliburton, Thomas Chandler, **II:** 301; **IV:** 193; **Supp. I Part 2:** 411
Halifax, Lord, **II:** 111
Hall, Daniel, **Supp. XII:** 258
Hall, Donald, **I:** 567; **III:** 194; **Supp. IV Part 1:** 63, 72; **Supp. IV Part 2:** 621; **Supp. IX:** 269; **Supp. XIV:** 82, 126; **Supp. XV:** 21, 153, 176; **Supp. XVI:** 39, 230, 235; **Supp. XX:**194; **Supp. XXI:** 86

Hall, James, **II:** 313; **Supp. I Part 2:** 584, 585
Hall, James Baker, **Supp. X:** 24
Hall, Timothy L., **Supp. VIII:** 127, 128
Halleck, Fitz-Greene, **Supp. I Part 1:** 156, 158
"Hallelujah: A Sestina" (Francis), **Supp. IX:** 82
"Hallelujah on the Bum" (Abbey), **Supp. XIII:** 2
"Haller's Second Home" (Maxwell), **Supp. VIII:** 169
Halliday, Mark, **Supp. XV:** 19, 20, 21, 23, 25, 27, 30; **Supp. XIX: 81–95**
Hallock, Rev. Moses, **Supp. I Part 1:** 153
Hall of Mirrors, A (Stone), **Supp. V:** 295, 296–299, 300, 301
"Hallowe'en" (Huncke), **Supp. XIV:** 145
"Halloween Party, The" (Chabon), **Supp. XI:** 72
Halloween Tree, The (Bradbury), **Supp. IV Part 1:** 102, 112–113
"Halls, The" (Halliday), **Supp. XIX:** 90
Hallwas, John E., **Supp. I Part 2:** 454
Halpern, Daniel, **Supp. IV Part 1:** 94–95, 95
Halsey, Theresa, **Supp. IV Part 1:** 330, 331
"Halt in the Desert, A" (Brodsky), **Supp. VIII:** 24
"Halves" (Dunn), **Supp. XI:** 149
Hamburg, Victoria, **Supp. XVI:** 126
Hamerik, Asger, **Supp. I Part 1:** 356
Hamill, Pete, **Supp. XX:**244, 255
Hamill, Sam, **Supp. X:** 112, 125, 126, 127
Hamilton, Alexander, **I:** 485; **Supp. I Part 2:** 456, 483, 509
Hamilton, Alice, **Supp. I Part 1:** 5
Hamilton, David, **Supp. IX:** 296
Hamilton, Edith, **Supp. XVI:** 196
Hamilton, Lady Emma, **II:** 524
Hamilton, Hamish, **Supp. I Part 2:** 617
Hamilton, Walton, **Supp. I Part 2:** 632
Hamilton Stark (Banks), **Supp. V:** 8, 9–10, 11
"Hamlen Brook" (Wilbur), **Supp. III Part 2:** 564
"Hamlet" (Laforgue), **I:** 573; **III:** 11
Hamlet (Miller and Fraenkel), **III:** 178, 183
Hamlet (Shakespeare), **I:** 53, 183, 205, 377, 586–587; **II:** 158, 531; **III:** 7, 11, 12, 183; **IV:** 116, 131, 227; **Supp. I Part 1:** 369; **Supp. I Part 2:** 422, 457, 471; **Supp. IV Part 2:** 612; **Supp. IX:** 14
Hamlet, The (Faulkner), **II:** 69–71, 73, 74; **IV:** 131; **Retro. Supp. I:** 82, 91, 92; **Supp. VIII:** 178; **Supp. IX:** 103; **Supp. XI:** 247
"Hamlet and His Problems" (Eliot), **I:** 586–587
Hamlet of A. MacLeish, The (MacLeish), **III:** 11–12, 14, 15, 18
Hamlin, Eva, **Retro. Supp. II:** 115
"Hammer" (Bidart), **Supp. XV:** 35
Hammer, Adam, **Supp. XIII:** 112

Hammer, Langdon, **Retro. Supp. II:** 45, 53; **Supp. X:** 65
"Hammer Man, The" (Bambara), **Supp. XI:** 4–5
Hammett, Dashiell, **IV:** 286; **Retro. Supp. II:** 327; **Supp. I Part 1:** 286, 289, 291, 292, 293, 294, 295; **Supp. III Part 1:** 91; **Supp. IV Part 1:** 120, 121, **341–357; Supp. IV Part 2:** 461, 464, 468, 469, 472, 473; **Supp. IX:** 200; **Supp. XI:** 228; **Supp. XIII:** 159; **Supp. XIV:** 21; **Supp. XVII:** 137; **Supp. XIX:** 178; **Supp. XXI:** 68
Hammond, John, **Supp. XVIII:** 24
Hammond, Karla, **Supp. IV Part 2:** 439, 442, 448, 637, 640, 644, 648
Hampl, Patricia, **Supp. IX:** 291; **Supp. XI:** 126; **Supp. XVII:** 21
Hampson, Alfred Leete, **Retro. Supp. I:** 35–36, 38
"Hamrick's Polar Bear" (Caldwell), **I:** 309–310
Hamsun, Knut, **Supp. VIII:** 40; **Supp. XI:** 161, 167; **Supp. XII:** 21, 128
Hancock, John, **Supp. I Part 2:** 524; **Supp. XX:**282
Hancock, Wade, **Supp. XVI:** 34
Handbook of North American Indians (Sando), **Supp. IV Part 2:** 510
Handcarved Coffins: A Nonfiction Account of an American Crime (Capote), **Supp. III Part 1:** 131
Handel, Georg Friedrich, **III:** 210; **IV:** 369
"Handfasting" (Wright), **Supp. XV:** 343
"Handfuls" (Sandburg), **III:** 584
"Handle with Care" (Fitzgerald), **Retro. Supp. I:** 114
Handley, William R., **Supp. XVIII:** 58
Handmaid's Tale, The (Atwood), **Supp. XIII:** 19, 20, **27–29**
"Hand of Casino, 1954, A" (Skloot), **Supp. XX:**194, 202
"Hand of Emmagene, The" (Taylor), **Supp. V:** 314, 325–326
Hand of the Potter, The: A Tragedy in Four Acts (Dreiser), **Retro. Supp. II:** 104; **Supp. XVII:** 96
"Hands" (Anderson), **I:** 106, 107
"Hands" (Mora), **Supp. XIII:** 215
Hands of Orlac, The (M. Renard; Crewe-Jones, trans.), **Supp. XVII:** 58
Hand to Mouth (Auster), **Supp. XII:** 21
"Hand to Mouth" (Auster), **Supp. XII:** 31
Handy, Lowney, **Supp. XI:** 217, 220, 221, 225
Handy, W. C., **Supp. VIII:** 337
Handy Guide for Beggars, A (Lindsay), **Supp. I Part 2:** 376–378, 380, 382, 399
Haney, David, **Supp. XXI:** 253
"Hanging Burley" (J. W. Miller), **Supp. XX:**167
Hanging Garden, The (Wagoner), **Supp. IX: 338–339**
"Hanging Gardens of Tyburn, The" (Hecht), **Supp. X:** 58

"Hanging of the Crane, The" (Longfellow), **Retro. Supp. II:** 169, 171

Hanging On (Conroy), **Supp. XVI:** 69

"Hanging Pictures in Nanny's Room" (Kenyon), **Supp. VII:** 164

"Hanging the Wash" (Alvarez), **Supp. VII:** 4

"Hangman, The" (Sexton), **Supp. II Part 2:** 680, 691

Hangover Mass (X. J. Kennedy), **Supp. XV:** 165

Hangsaman (Jackson), **Supp. IX:** 116, 123, **124**

Hanh, Thich Nhat, **Supp. V:** 199

Hanks, Lucy, **III:** 587

Hanks, Nancy. *See* Lincoln, Mrs. Thomas (Nancy Hanks)

Hanley, Lynne T., **Supp. IV Part 1:** 208

"Hanlon Mountain in Mist" (J. W. Miller), **Supp. XX:**164, 166–167

Hanna, Mark, **Supp. I Part 2:** 395

Hannah, Barry, **Supp. X:** 285; **Supp. XIX:** 209; **Supp. XXI:** 38, 118

Hannah and Her Sisters (film; Allen), **Supp. XV:** 9, **10–11**

"Hannah Armstrong" (Masters), **Supp. I Part 2:** 461

"Hannah Binding Shoes" (Larcom), **Supp. XIII:** 141, 143

"Hannah Byde" (D. West), **Supp. XVIII:** 280

Hannah's House (Hearon), **Supp. VIII:** 58, **60–61**

Hanneman, Audre, **II:** 259

Hannibal Lecter, My Father (Acker), **Supp. XII:** 6

Hanoi (McCarthy), **II:** 579

"Hanoi Drifting, January 2003" (Weigl), **Supp. XIX:** 288

Hansberry, Lorraine, **Supp. IV Part 1: 359–377; Supp. VIII:** 329

Hanscom, Leslie, **Supp. XI:** 229

"Hansel and Gretel" (Prose), **Supp. XVI:** 256, 258

Hansen, Erik, **Supp. V:** 241

Hansen, Harry, **IV:** 366

Han-shan, **Supp. VIII:** 292

Hanson, Curtis, **Supp. XI:** 67

Han Suyin, **Supp. X:** 291

Hanzlicek, C. G., **Supp. XV:** 73

Hapgood, Charles H., II, **Supp. XXI:** 6

Hapgood, Hutchins, **Supp. XVII: 95–108; Supp. XXI:** 1, 3, 9, 10

Hapgood, Norman, **Supp. XXI:** 2

Hapgoods, The: Three Earnest Brothers (Marcaccio), **Supp. XVII:** 106

"Happenings: An Art of Radical Juxtaposition" (Sontag), **Supp. III Part 2:** 456

"Happenstance" (Komunyakaa), **Supp. XIII:** 130

Happenstance (Shields), **Supp. VII:** 315–318, 320, 323, 324, 326

Happersberger, Lucien, **Supp. I Part 1:** 51

"Happiest I've Been, The" (Updike), **IV:** 219

Happily Ever After (Quindlen), **Supp. XVII:** 167

"Happiness" (Oliver), **Supp. VII:** 236

"Happiness" (Sandburg), **III:** 582–583

Happiness of Getting It Down Right, The (Steinman, ed.), **Supp. VIII:** 172

"Happiness of the Garden Variety" (Richard), **Supp. XIX:** 212

"Happy Birthday" (Bambara), **Supp. XI:** 4

Happy Birthday (Loos), **Supp. XVI:** 193

Happy Birthday, Wanda June (Vonnegut), **Supp. II Part 2:** 759, 776–777

Happy Birthday of Death, The (Corso), **Supp. XII: 127–129**

Happy Childhood, A (Matthews), **Supp. IX:** 155, 160, **161–163**

Happy Days (Beckett), **Retro. Supp. I:** 206

Happy Days, 1880–1892 (Mencken), **III:** 100, 111, 120

"Happy End" (Simic), **Supp. VIII:** 276–277

"Happy Failure, The" (Melville), **III:** 90

Happy Families Are All Alike (Taylor), **Supp. V:** 322–323, 325

Happy Isles of Oceania, The: Paddling the Pacific (Theroux), **Supp. VIII:** 324

"Happy Journey to Trenton and Camden, The" (Wilder), **IV:** 366

"Happy Man, The" (Lethem), **Supp. XVIII:** 139

"Happy Marriage, The" (MacLeish), **III:** 15–16

Happy Marriage and Other Poems, The (MacLeish), **III:** 4

Happy to Be Here (Keillor), **Supp. XVI:** 165, 171

"Happy To Be Here" (Keillor), **Supp. XVI:** 168

"Hapworth 16, 1924" (Salinger), **III:** 552, 571–572

"Harbor Dawn, The" (H. Crane), **Supp. XXI:** 132, 136

"Harbor Lights" (Doty), **Supp. XI:** 122

Harcourt, Alfred, **II:** 191, 451–452; **III:** 587; **Retro. Supp. I:** 131; **Supp. XV:** 308

Harcourt, Lewis, **Supp. XX:**232–233

Harcourt, T. A., **I:** 196

Hard Candy, a Book of Stories (T. Williams), **IV:** 383

"Hardcastle Crags" (Plath), **Supp. I Part 2:** 537

"Hard Daddy" (Hughes), **Retro. Supp. I:** 200

"Hardened Criminals, The" (Lethem), **Supp. XVIII:** 139

Harder They Fall, The (Schulberg), **Supp. XV:** 194, 201

Hard Facts (Baraka), **Supp. II Part 1:** 54, 55, 58

Hard Freight (Wright), **Supp. V:** 332, 339–340

Hard Hours, The (Hecht), **Supp. X:** 57, **59–62,** 63, 64

Hardie, Kier, **Supp. I Part 1:** 5

Harding, Walter, **IV:** 177, 178

Harding, Warren G., **I:** 486; **II:** 253, 433; **Supp. I Part 1:** 24

"Hard Kind of Courage, The" (Baldwin), **Supp. I Part 1:** 52

Hard Laughter (Lamott), **Supp. XX:132–133**

Hard Maple (S. and A. Warner), **Supp. XVIII:** 264

"Hard Rain's A-Gonna Fall, A" (song, Dylan), **Supp. XVIII:** 26, 29

"Hard Time Keeping Up, A" (Ellison), **Retro. Supp. II:** 124

Hard Times (Dickens), **Supp. I Part 2:** 675

"Hard Times in Elfland, The" (Lanier), **Supp. I Part 1:** 365

"Hard Traveling: *Fay's* Deep South Landscape of Violence" (Beuka), **Supp. XXI:** 47

Hardwick, Elizabeth, **II:** 543, 554, 566; **Retro. Supp. II:** 179, 180, 183, 184, 190, 221, 228–229, 245; **Supp. I Part 1:** 196; **Supp. III Part 1: 193–215; Supp. IV Part 1:** 299; **Supp. V,** 319; **Supp. X,** 171; **Supp. XII:** 209; **Supp. XIV:** 89

"Hard Work 1956" (Dunn), **Supp. XI:** 147

Hardy, Barbara, **Supp. I Part 2:** 527

Hardy, Oliver, **Supp. I Part 2:** 607; **Supp. IV Part 2:** 574

Hardy, René, **Supp. III Part 1:** 235

Hardy, Thomas, **I:** 59, 103, 292, 317, 377; **II:** 181, 184–185, 186, 191–192, 271, 275, 372, 523, 542; **III:** 32, 453, 485, 508, 524; **IV:** 83, 135, 136; **Retro. Supp. I:** 141, 377–378; **Supp. I Part 1:** 217; **Supp. I Part 2:** 429, 512; **Supp. II Part 1:** 4, 26; **Supp. VIII:** 32; **Supp. IX:** 40, 78, 85, 108, 211; **Supp. X:** 228; **Supp. XI:** 311; **Supp. XIII:** 294, **Supp. XIII:** 130; **Supp. XIV:** 24; **Supp. XV:** 170; **Supp. XVIII:** 74; **Supp. XIX:** 86, 87; **Supp. XX:**195; **Supp. XXI:** 109

Hardy and the Poetry of Truth-Seeking (Halliday), **Supp. XIX:** 82

Harjo, Joy, **Supp. IV Part 1:** 325, 404; **Supp. IV Part 2:** 499, 507; **Supp. XII: 215–234; Supp. XVIII:** 189

Harlan's Race (P. N. Warren), **Supp. XX:264–265**

"Harlem" (Hughes), **Retro. Supp. I:** 194, 204; **Supp. I Part 1:** 340; **Supp. VIII:** 213

Harlem, Mecca of the New Negro (Locke), **Supp. XIV:** 201

"Harlem Dancer, The" (McKay), **Supp. X:** 134

Harlem Gallery (Tolson), **Retro. Supp. I:** 208, 209, 210

Harlem Glory: A Fragment of Aframerican Life (McKay), **Supp. X:** 132, **141–142**

Harlem: Negro Metropolis (McKay), **Supp. X:** 132, 141, 142

"Harlem Runs Wild" (McKay), **Supp. X:** 140

Harlem Shadows (McKay), **Supp. X:** 131–132, 136

Harlem Underground (Lacy), **Supp. XV:** 206

"Harlequin of Dreams, The" (Lanier), **Supp. I Part 1:** 365

Harlot's Ghost (Mailer), **Retro. Supp. II:** 211–212

Harlow, Jean, **IV:** 256; **Retro. Supp. I:** 110

"Harm" (C. Frost), **Supp. XV:** 101

Harmon, William, **Retro. Supp. I:** 37; **Supp. XI:** 248

"Harmonic" (F. Barthelme), **Supp. XI:** 26

Harmonium (Stevens), **III:** 196; **IV:** 76, 77, 78, 82, 87, 89, 92; **Retro. Supp. I:** 296, 297, 299, **300–302,** 301, 302

"Harmony of the Gospels" (Taylor), **IV:** 149

Harmony of the World (C. Baxter), **Supp. XVII:** 16–17

"Harmony of the World" (C. Baxter), **Supp. XVII:** 16

Harnett, Vincent, **Supp. XV:** 198

"Harp, The" (Weigl), **Supp. XIX:** 278

Harper (film), **Supp. IV Part 2:** 473

Harper, Donna, **Retro. Supp. I:** 194, 195, 209

Harper, Frances E. Watkins, **Supp. II Part 1:** 201–202; **Supp. XVIII:** 284

Harper, Gordon Lloyd, **Retro. Supp. II:** 23

Harper, Michael, **Supp. XV:** 74

Harper, Michael S., **Retro. Supp. II:** 116, 123

Harper, William Rainey, **Supp. I Part 2:** 631

Harper's Anthology of 20th Century Native American Poetry (Niatum, ed.), **Supp. IV Part 1:** 331

"Harriet" (Lowell), **II:** 554

Harrigan, Edward, **II:** 276; **III:** 14

Harrington, Michael, **I:** 306

Harrington, Ollie, **Supp. XVI:** 142–143

Harris, Celia, **Retro. Supp. I:** 9

Harris, George, **II:** 70

Harris, Joel Chandler, **III:** 338; **Supp. I Part 1:** 352; **Supp. II Part 1:** 192, 201; **Supp. XIV:** 61; **Supp. XX:**103

Harris, Judith, **Supp. XIV:** 269

Harris, Julie, **II:** 587, 601; **Supp. IX:** 125

Harris, Leonard, **Supp. XIV:** 196, 211–212

Harris, MacDonald, **Supp. XI:** 65

Harris, Marie, **Supp. IX:** 153

Harris, Peter, **Supp. X:** 206, 207

Harris, Susan K., **Supp. XV:** 269

Harris, Thomas, **Supp. XIV:** 26; **Supp. XXI:** 67, 78

Harris, Victoria Frenkel, **Supp. IV Part 1:** 68, 69

Harris, Wilson, **Supp. XXI:** 170

Harrison, Colin, **Supp. XIV:** 26

Harrison, Hazel, **Retro. Supp. II:** 115

Harrison, Jim, **Supp. VIII: 37–56; Supp. XIX:** 125, 126

Harrison, Kathryn, **Supp. X:** 191

Harrison, Ken, **Supp. IX:** 101

Harrison, Oliver (pseudonym). *See* Smith, Harrison

Harry: A Portrait (Boyce), **Supp. XVII:** 104; **Supp. XXI:** 7, 13–14

Harryhausen, Ray, **Supp. IV Part 1:** 115

Harryman, Carla, **Supp. XV:** 344

"Harry of Nothingham" (Hugo), **Supp. VI:** 146–147

"Harry's Death" (Carver), **Supp. III Part 1:** 146

"Harsh Judgment, The" (Kunitz), **Supp. III Part 1:** 264

Hart, Albert Bushnell, **Supp. I Part 2:** 479, 480, 481

Hart, Bernard, **I:** 241, 242, 248–250, 256

Hart, Henry, **Retro. Supp. II:** 187; **Supp. XIV:** 97

Hart, James D., **Supp. XVIII:** 257

Hart, John Seely, **Supp. XVIII:** 257, 258, 264

Hart, Lorenz, **III:** 361

Hart, Moss, **Supp. IV Part 2:** 574; **Supp. XV:** 329

Hart, Pearl, **Supp. X:** 103

"Hart Crane" (Tate), **I:** 381

"Hart Crane and Poetry: A Consideration of Crane's Intense Poetics with Reference to 'The Return' " (Grossman), **Retro. Supp. II:** 83

Harte, Anna Griswold, **Supp. II Part 1:** 341

Harte, Bret, **I:** 193, 195, 203; **II:** 289; **IV:** 196; **Retro. Supp. II:** 72; **Supp. II Part 1: 335–359,** 399; **Supp. XV:** 115

Harte, Walter Blackburn, **I:** 199

Harter, Carol C., **Supp. IV Part 1:** 217

Hartley, David, **III:** 77

Hartley, Lois, **Supp. I Part 2:** 459, 464–465

Hartley, L. P., **Supp. I Part 1:** 293

Hartley, Marsden, **IV:** 409, 413; **Retro. Supp. I:** 430; **Supp. X:** 137; **Supp. XV:** 298

Hartman, Geoffrey, **Supp. IV Part 1:** 119; **Supp. XII:** 130, 253

Hartman, Saidiya, **Supp. XX:**154

Harum, David, **II:** 102

"Harvard" (Lowell), **II:** 554

Harvard College in the Seventeenth Century (Morison), **Supp. I Part 2:** 485

"Harvest, The" (Hempel), **Supp. XXI:** 115, **122–123**

Harvester, The (Stratton-Porter), **Supp. XX:**211, 212, 218, 221

"*Harvester, The:* The Natural Bounty of Gene Stratton-Porter" (Birkelo), **Supp. XX:**220–221

"Harvesters of Night and Water" (Hogan), **Supp. IV Part 1:** 412

"Harvest Song" (Toomer), **Supp. III Part 2:** 483

Harvill Book of 20th Century Poetry in English, **Supp. X:** 55

"Harv Is Plowing Now" (Updike), **Retro. Supp. I:** 318

Haselden, Elizabeth Lee, **Supp. VIII:** 125

Haskell, Mary, **Supp. XX:**115, 117

Hass, Robert, **Supp. VI: 97–111; Supp. VIII:** 24, 28; **Supp. XI:** 142, 270; **Supp. XIV:** 83, 84; **Supp. XXI:** 60

Hassam, Childe, **Retro. Supp. II:** 136

Hassan, Ihab, **IV:** 99–100, 115; **Supp. XI:** 221

Hasse, Henry, **Supp. IV Part 1:** 102

Hasty-Pudding, The (Barlow), **Supp. II Part 1:** 74, 77–80

Hate That Hate Produced, The (CBS documentary), **Supp. XX:**102

Hatful of Rain, A (Gazzo), **III:** 155

Hatlen, Burton, **Supp. V:** 138, 139–140; **Supp. XXI:** 24

"Hattie Bloom" (Oliver), **Supp. VII:** 232

Haunch, Paunch, and Jowl (Ornitz), **Supp. IX:** 227

"Haunted Landscape" (Ashbery), **Supp. III Part 1:** 22

Haunted Merchant, The (Briggs), **Supp. XVIII:** 2, 8

"Haunted Mind" (Simic), **Supp. VIII:** 282

"Haunted Mind, The" (Hawthorne), **II:** 230–231

"Haunted Oak, The" (Dunbar), **Supp. II Part 1:** 207, 208

"Haunted Palace, The" (Poe), **III:** 421

"Haunted Valley, The" (Bierce), **I:** 200

Haunting, The (film), **Supp. IX:** 125

Haunting of Hill House, The (Jackson), **Supp. IX:** 117, 121, 126

Hauptmann, Gerhart, **III:** 472

Haussmann, Sonja, **Supp. XIII:** 331, **Supp. XIII:** 347

"Havanna vanities come to dust in Miami" (Didion), **Supp. IV Part 1:** 210

Havel, Hippolyte, **Supp. XXI:** 4, 6

Haven, Cynthia, **Supp. XV:** 252, 264

Haven's End (Marquand), **III:** 55, 56, 63, 68

"Have You Ever Faked an Orgasm" (Peacock), **Supp. XIX:** 199

"Have You Ever Tried to Enter the Long Black Branches" (Oliver), **Supp. VII:** 247

"Having Been Interstellar" (Ammons), **Supp. VII:** 25

"Having It Out With Melancholy" (Kenyon), **Supp. VII:** 171

"Having Lost My Sons, I Confront the Wreckage of the Moon: Christmas, 1960" (Wright), **Supp. III Part 2:** 600

"Having Snow" (Schwartz), **Supp. II Part 2:** 652

Hawai'i One Summer (Kingston), **Supp. V:** 157, 160, 166, 169–170

"Hawk, The" (Francis), **Supp. IX:** 81

Hawke, David Freeman, **Supp. I Part 2:** 511, 516

Hawkes, John, **I:** 113; **Retro. Supp. II:** 234; **Supp. III Part 1:** 2; **Supp. V:** 40; **Supp. IX:** 212; **Supp. XVII:** 183; **Supp. XXI:** 210

Hawkins, Gary, **Supp. XXI:** 35, 39

Hawkins, William, **II:** 587

Hawk in the Rain, The (Hughes), **Retro. Supp. II:** 244; **Supp. I Part 2:** 537, 540

Hawk Is Dying, The (Crews), **Supp. XI:** 111

Hawk Moon (Shepard), **Supp. III Part 2:** 445

Hawks, Howard, **Supp. IV Part 1:** 130; **Supp. XVIII:** 148

"Hawk's Cry in Autumn, The" (Brodsky), **Supp. VIII:** 29

"Hawk's Shadow" (Glück), **Supp. V:** 85

Hawk's Well, The (Yeats), **III:** 459–460

Hawley, Adelaide, **Supp. XIV:** 207

Hawley, Joseph, **I:** 546

Hawthorne (James), **II:** 372–378; **Retro. Supp. I:** 220, **223–224**

"Hawthorne" (Longfellow), **Retro. Supp. II:** 169

"Hawthorne" (Lowell), **II:** 550

Hawthorne, Julian, **II:** 225; **Supp. I Part 1:** 38; **Supp. XV:** 274

Hawthorne, Nathaniel, **I:** 106, 204, 211, 340, 355, 363, 384, 413, 458, 561–562; **II:** 7, 8, 40, 60, 63, 74, 89, 127–128, 138, 142, 198, **223–246,** 255, 259, 264, 267, 272, 274, 277, 281, 282, 295, 307, 309, 311, 313, 322, 324, 326, 402, 408, 446, 501, 545; **III:** 51, 81–82, 83, 84, 85, 87, 88, 91, 92, 113, 316, 359, 412, 415, 421, 438, 453, 454, 507, 565, 572; **IV:** 2, 4, 167, 172, 179, 194, 333, 345, 453; **Retro. Supp. I:** 1, 53, 59, 62, 63, 91, **145–167,** 215, 218, 220, 223, 248–249, 252, 257, 258, 330, 331, 365; **Retro. Supp. II:** 136, 142, 153, 156–157, 158, 159, 187, 221; **Supp. I Part 1:** 38, 188, 197, 317, 372; **Supp. I Part 2:** 420, 421, 545, 579, 580, 582, 587, 595, 596; **Supp. III Part 2:** 501; **Supp. IV Part 1:** 80, 127, 297; **Supp. IV Part 2:** 463, 596; **Supp. V:** 152; **Supp. VIII:** 103, 105, 108, 153, 201; **Supp. IX:** 114; **Supp. X:** 78; **Supp. XI:** 51, 78; **Supp. XII:** 26; **Supp. XIII:** 102; **Supp. XIV:** 48; **Supp. XV:** 269, 272, 282; **Supp. XVI:** 83, 84, 157; **Supp. XVII:** 42; **Supp. XVIII:** 258, 260; **Supp. XXI:** 201

Hawthorne, Mrs. Nathaniel (Sophia Peabody), **II:** 224, 244; **III:** 75, 86

Hawthorne, Rose, **II:** 225

Hawthorne, Una, **II:** 225

"Hawthorne and His Mosses" (Melville), **Retro. Supp. I:** 254; **Supp. XIV:** 48

"Hawthorne Aspect \[of Henry James\], The" (Eliot), **Retro. Supp. I:** 63

"Hawthorne in Solitude" (Cowley), **Supp. II Part 1:** 143

Hay, John, **I:** 1, 10, 12, 14–15; **Supp. I Part 1:** 352

Hay, Mrs. John, **I:** 14

Hay, Sara Henderson, **Supp. XIV: 119–135**

Hayakawa, S. I., **I:** 448; **Supp. I Part 1:** 315; **Supp. XV:** 176

Hayden, Robert, **Supp. II Part 1: 361–383; Supp. IV Part 1:** 169; **Supp. XIII:** 115, 127; **Supp. XIV:** 119, 123

Hayden, Sterling, **Supp. XI:** 304

Haydn, Hiram, **IV:** 100, 358

Hayduke Lives! (Abbey), **Supp. XIII:** 16

Hayek, Friedrich A. von, **Supp. IV Part 2:** 524

Hayes, Helen, **Supp. XVI:** 193, 195

Hayes, Ira, **Supp. IV Part 1:** 326

Hayes, Richard, **Supp. V:** 320

Hayes, Rutherford B., **Supp. I Part 2:** 419

Haygood, Wil, **Supp. VIII:** 79

Hayne, Paul Hamilton, **Supp. I Part 1:** 352, 354, 355, 360, 372

Haynes, Todd, **Supp. XVIII:** 23

Haynes-Smith, William, **Supp. XX:**231, 232, 233

Hayward, Florence, **Retro. Supp. II:** 65

Hayward, John, **Retro. Supp. I:** 67

Hayward, Leland, **Supp. XIX:** 250

Haywood, "Big" Bill, **I:** 483; **Supp. V:** 286

Hazard, Grace, **II:** 530

Hazard of Fortunes, A (Howells), **Retro. Supp. II:** 288

Hazard of New Fortunes, A (Howells), **II:** 275, 276, 286–297, 290

Hazel, Robert, **Supp. VIII:** 137, 138

Hazen, General W. B., **I:** 192, 193

Hazlitt, Henry, **Supp. IV Part 2:** 524

Hazlitt, William, **I:** 58, 378; **II:** 315; **Supp. XXI:** 205

Hazmat (McClatchy), **Supp. XII: 265–270**

Hazo, Samuel, **I:** 386; **Supp. XIV:** 123, 124

Hazzard, Shirley, **Supp. VIII:** 151

H.D. *See* Doolittle, Hilda

"He" (Porter), **III:** 434, 435

"Head and Shoulders" (Fitzgerald), **Retro. Supp. I:** 101

Headhunter (Findley), **Supp. XX:57–59,** 60, 61

"Head-Hunter, The" (O. Henry), **Supp. II Part 1:** 403

"Headless Hawk, The" (Capote), **Supp. III Part 1:** 124

Headlines (T. Williams), **IV:** 381

Headlong Hall (Peacock), **Supp. I Part 1:** 307

Headmaster, The (McPhee), **Supp. III Part 1:** 291, 294, 298

"Head of Joaquín Murrieta, The" (Rodriguez), **Supp. XIV:** 303

Headsman, The (Cooper), **I:** 345–346

Heads of Grain (al-Sanábil) (Gibran), **Supp. XX:**124

"Headwaters" (Momaday), **Supp. IV Part 2:** 486

"Head Wound" (Halliday), **Supp. XIX:** 92

Healy, Eloise Klein, **Supp. XI:** 121, 124, 126, 127, 129, 137

Healy, Tim, **II:** 129, 137

Heaney, Sally, **Supp. XVII:** 241

Heaney, Seamus, **Retro. Supp. II:** 245; **Supp. IX:** 41, 42; **Supp. X:** 67, 122; **Supp. XI:** 249; **Supp. XV:** 256; **Supp. XXI:** 54, 243

"Heard through the Walls of the Race-track Glen Motel" (X. J. Kennedy), **Supp. XV:** 170

Hearn, Lafcadio, **I:** 211; **II:** 311

Hearon, Shelby, **Supp. VIII: 57–72**

Hearst, Patty, **Supp. IV Part 1:** 195

Hearst, William Randolph, **I:** 198, 207, 208; **IV:** 298

Heart and Perimeter (Bierds), **Supp. XVII: 28–29**

"Heart and the Lyre, The" (Bogan), **Supp. III Part 1:** 65

"Heartbeat" (Harjo), **Supp. XII:** 221–222

Heartbreak Kid, The (film), **Supp. IV Part 2:** 575, 589

Heart for the Gods of Mexico, A (Aiken), **I:** 54

"Hear the Nightingale Sing" (Gordon), **II:** 200

Hear the Wind Blow (Sanders), **Supp. XVI:** 268

Heart is a Lonely Hunter, The (McCullers), **II:** 586, 588–593, 604, 605

Heart of a Woman, The (Angelou), **Supp. IV Part 1:** 2, 5, 7–9, 9, 14, 17

Heart of Darkness (Conrad), **Retro. Supp. II:** 292; **Supp. V:** 249, 311; **Supp. VIII:** 4, 316; **Supp. XIX:** 28; **Supp. XX:**18, 57–58

"Heart of Darkness" (Conrad), **I:** 575, 578; **II:** 595; **Supp. XVI:** 212

Heart of Darkness (Didion), **Supp. IV Part 1:** 207

Heart of Happy Hollow, The (Dunbar), **Supp. II Part 1:** 214

Heart of Knowledge, The: American Indians on the Bomb (Gunn Allen and Caputi, eds.), **Supp. IV Part 1:** 334–335

"Heart of Knowledge, The: Nuclear Themes in Native American Thought and Literature" (Caputi), **Supp. IV Part 1:** 335

"Heart of the Park, The " (O'Connor), **Retro. Supp. II:** 225

Heart of the West (O. Henry), **Supp. II Part 1:** 410

"Hearts, The" (Pinsky), **Supp. VI:** 245–247, 248

"'Hearts and Flowers' " (MacLeish), **III:** 8

"Hearts and Heads" (Ransom), **Supp. I Part 1:** 373

"Heart's Graveyard Shift, The" (Komunyakaa), **Supp. XIII:** 120

Heart-Shape in the Dust (Hayden), **Supp. II Part 1:** 365, 366

Heart's Needle (Snodgrass), **I:** 400

"Heart's Needle" (Snodgrass), **Supp. VI: 311–313,** 320

"Hearts of Oak" (Rowson), **Supp. XV:** 243

"Heart Songs" (Proulx), **Supp. VII:** 254

Heart Songs and Other Stories (Proulx), **Supp. VII:** 252–256, 261

Heart to Artemis, The (Bryher), **Supp. I Part 1:** 259

Heartwood (Burke), **Supp. XIV:** 35

Heath, Shirley, **Supp. XX:**90

Heath Anthology of American Literature, The, **Supp. IX:** 4; **Supp. XV:** 270, 313

Heathcote, Anne. *See* De Lancey, Mrs. James

"Heathen Chinee, The" (Harte), **Supp. II Part 1:** 350–351, 352

Heathen Days, 1890–1936 (Mencken), **III:** 100, 111

Heath-Stubbs, John, **Supp. XV:** 153

Heat's On, The (C. Himes), **Supp. XVI:** 143, 144

"Heaven" (Dunn), **Supp. XI:** 154

"Heaven" (Levine), **Supp. V:** 182

"Heaven" (Patchett), **Supp. XII:** 309

Heaven and Earth: A Cosmology (Goldbarth), **Supp. XII:** 187

"Heaven and Earth in Jest" (Dillard), **Supp. VI:** 24, 28

"Heaven as Anus" (Kumin), **Supp. IV Part 2:** 448

Heavenly Conversation, The (Mather), **Supp. II Part 2:** 460

"Heavenly Feast, The" (Schnackenberg), **Supp. XV:** 257, 259

Heavens (Untermeyer), **Supp. XV:** 306

Heavens and Earth (Benét), **Supp. XI:** 44

Heaven's Coast (Doty), **Supp. XI:** 119, 121, **129–130,** 134

Heaven's Prisoners (Burke), **Supp. XIV:** 23, 29

"Heavy Angel, The" (Everwine), **Supp. XV:** 80

"Heavy Bear Who Goes with Me, The" (Schwartz), **Supp. II Part 2:** 646

"Heavy Trash" (Halliday), **Supp. XIX:** 92, 93

"He Came Also Still" (Zukofsky), **Supp. III Part 2:** 612

Hecht, Anthony, **IV:** 138; **Supp. III Part 2:** 541, 561; **Supp. X: 55–75; Supp. XII:** 269–270; **Supp. XV:** 251, 256

Hecht, Ben, **I:** 103; **II:** 42; **Supp. I Part 2:** 646; **Supp. XI:** 307; **Supp. XIII:** 106

Hecht, S. Theodore, **Supp. III Part 2:** 614

Heckewelder, John, **II:** 503

"Hedge Island" (Lowell), **II:** 524

Hedges, William I., **II:** 311–312

"He 'Digesteth Harde Yron' " (Moore), **Supp. IV Part 2:** 454

Hedin, Robert, **Supp. XII:** 200, 202

Hedylus (Doolittle), **Supp. I Part 1:** 259, 270

"Heel & Toe To the End" (W. C. Williams), **Retro. Supp. I:** 430

Heffernan, Michael, **Supp. XII:** 177

"HEGEL" (Baraka), **Supp. II Part 1:** 53

Hegel, Georg Wilhelm Friedrich, **I:** 265; **II:** 358; **III:** 262, 308–309, 480, 481, 487, 607; **IV:** 86, 333, 453; **Supp. I Part 2:** 633, 635, 640, 645; **Supp. XVI:** 289

"Hegemony of Race, The" (Du Bois), **Supp. II Part 1:** 181

Hegger, Grace Livingston. *See* Lewis, Mrs. Sinclair (Grace Livingston Hegger)

"He Had Spent His Youth Dreaming" (Dobyns), **Supp. XIII:** 90

Heidegger, Martin, **II:** 362, 363; **III:** 292; **IV:** 491; **Retro. Supp. II:** 87; **Supp. V:** 267; **Supp. VIII:** 9; **Supp. XVI:** 283, 288

Heidenmauer, The (Cooper), **I:** 345–346

Heidi Chronicles, The (Wasserstein), **Supp. IV Part 1:** 309; **Supp. XV:** 319, **325–327**

"Height of the Ridiculous, The" (Holmes), **Supp. I Part 1:** 302

Heilbroner, Robert, **Supp. I Part 2:** 644, 648, 650

Heilbrun, Carolyn G., **Supp. IX:** 66; **Supp. XI:** 208; **Supp. XIV:** 161, 163; **Supp. XX:** 108

Heilman, Robert Bechtold, **Supp. XIV:** 11, 12

Heilpern, John, **Supp. XIV:** 242

Heim, Michael, **Supp. V:** 209

Heine, Heinrich, **II:** 272, 273, 277, 281, 282, 387, 544; **IV:** 5; **Supp. XV:** 293, 299; **Supp. XVI:** 188

Heineman, Frank, **Supp. III Part 2:** 619

Heinlein, Robert, **Supp. IV Part 1:** 102; **Supp. XVI:** 122; **Supp. XVIII:** 149

Heinz, Helen. *See* Tate, Mrs. Allen (Helen Heinz)

Heiress, The (film), **Retro. Supp. I:** 222

"Heirs" (Nye), **Supp. XIII:** 284

"He Is Not Worth the Trouble" (Rowson), **Supp. XV:** 240

"He Knew" (C. Himes), **Supp. XVI:** 137

"Helas" (Creeley), **Supp. IV Part 1:** 150, 158

Helburn, Theresa, **IV:** 381

Heldreth, Leonard, **Supp. V:** 151

"Helen" (Lowell), **II:** 544

"Helen, Thy Beauty Is to Me" (Fante), **Supp. XI:** 169

"Helen: A Courtship" (Faulkner), **Retro. Supp. I:** 81

"Helen I Love You" (Farrell), **II:** 28, 45

Helen in Egypt (Doolittle), **Supp. I Part 1:** 260, 272, 273, 274; **Supp. XV:** 264

Helen Keller: Sketch for a Portrait (Brooks), **I:** 254

"Helen of Tyre" (Longfellow), **II:** 496

Heliodora (Doolittle), **Supp. I Part 1:** 266

"He Lives On the Landing" (Espaillat), **Supp. XXI:** 108

"Helix" (Sobin), **Supp. XVI:** 283

Hellbox (O'Hara), **III:** 361

Heller, Joseph, **III:** 2, 258; **IV:** 98; **Retro. Supp. II:** 324; **Supp. I Part 1:** 196; **Supp. IV Part 1:** 379–396; **Supp. V:** 244; **Supp. VIII:** 245; **Supp. XI:** 307; **Supp. XII:** 167–168; **Supp. XV:** 322; **Supp. XVII:** 139

"Hell-Heaven" (Lahiri), **Supp. XXI: 181–183,** 183, 184–186, 188

Hellman, Lillian, **I:** 28; **III:** 28; **Supp. I Part 1: 276–298; Supp. IV Part 1:** 1, 12, 83, 353, 355, 356; **Supp. VIII:** 243; **Supp. IX:** 196, 198, 200–201, 204

Hellmann, Lillian, **Retro. Supp. II:** 327

Hello (Creeley), **Supp. IV Part 1:** 155, 157

"Hello, Hello Henry" (Kumin), **Supp. IV Part 2:** 446

"Hello, Stranger" (Capote), **Supp. III Part 1:** 120

Hello Dolly! (musical play), **IV:** 357

Hellyer, John, **Supp. I Part 2:** 468

Helm, Bob, **Supp. XV:** 147

Helm, Levon, **Supp. XVIII:** 26

Helmets (Dickey), **Supp. IV Part 1:** 175, 178, 180

"Helmsman, The" (Doolittle), **Supp. I Part 1:** 266

"Help" (Barth), **I:** 139

"Help Her to Believe" (Olsen). *See* "I Stand There Ironing" (Olsen)

Helprin, Mark, **Supp. XIX:** 142

"Helsinki Window" (Creeley), **Supp. IV Part 1:** 158

"Hema and Kaushik" (Lahiri), **Supp. XXI:** 183, 188

Hemenway, Robert E., **Supp. IV Part 1:** 6

Hemingway, Dr. Clarence Edwards, **II:** 248, 259

Hemingway, Ernest, **I:** 28, 64, 97, 99, 105, 107, 117, 150, 162, 190, 211, 221, 288, 289, 295, 367, 374, 378, 421, 423, 445, 476, 477, 478, 482, 484–485, 487, 488, 489, 491, 495, 504, 517; **II:** 27, 44, 51, 58, 68–69, 78, 90, 97, 127, 206, **247–270,** 289, 424, 431, 456, 457, 458–459, 482, 560, 600; **III:** 2, 18, 20, 35, 36, 37, 40, 61, 108, 220, 334, 363, 364, 382, 453, 454, 471–472, 476, 551, 575, 576, 584; **IV:** 27, 28, 33, 34, 35, 42, 49, 97, 108, 122, 126, 138, 190, 191, 201, 216, 217, 257, 297, 363, 404, 427, 433, 451; **Retro. Supp. I:** 74, 98, 108, 111, 112, 113, 115, **169–191,** 215, 292, 359, 418; **Retro. Supp. II:** 19, 24, 30, 68, 115, 123; **Supp. I Part 2:** 621, 658, 678; **Supp. II Part 1:** 221; **Supp. III Part 1:** 146; **Supp. III Part 2:** 617; **Supp. IV Part 1:** 48, 102, 123, 197, 236, 342, 343, 344, 348, 350, 352, 380–381, 383; **Supp. IV Part 2:** 463, 468, 502, 607, 679, 680, 681, 689, 692; **Supp. V:** 237, 240, 244, 250, 336; **Supp. VIII:** 40, 101, 105, 179, 182, 183, 188, 189, 196; **Supp. IX:** 16, 57, 58, 94, 106, 260, 262; **Supp. X:** 137, 167, 223, 225; **Supp. XI:** 214, 221; **Supp. XIII:** 96, 255, 270; **Supp. XIV:** 24, 83; **Supp. XV:** 69, 135; **Supp. XVI:** 203, 205–206, 208, 210, 233, 236–237, 281–282; **Supp. XVII:** 4, 105, 107, 137, 228, 229; **Supp. XVIII:** 74, 90, 102; **Supp. XIX:** 131, 154, 157, 246; **Supp. XX:** 45, 74, 76; **Supp. XXI:** 7, 8, 36, 262

Hemingway, Mrs. Ernest (Hadley Richardson), **II:** 257, 260, 263

Hemingway, Mrs. Ernest (Martha Gellhorn), **II:** 260

Hemingway, Mrs. Ernest (Mary Welsh), **II:** 257, 260

Hemingway, Mrs. Ernest (Pauline Pfeiffer), **II:** 260

"Hemingway in Paris" (Cowley), **Supp. II Part 1:** 144

"Hemingway Story, A" (Dubus), **Supp. VII:** 91

"Hemingway: The Old Lion" (Cowley), **Supp. II Part 1:** 143

"Hemp, The" (Benét), **Supp. XI:** 44

Hempel, Amy, **Supp. XIX:** 209; **Supp. XXI:** 115–128

"Henchman, The" (Whittier), **Supp. I Part 2:** 696

Henderson, Alice Corbin, **Supp. I Part 2:** 387; **Supp. XV:** 302–303

Henderson, Darwin L., **Supp. XIII:** 213, 221–222

Henderson, Jane, **Supp. VIII:** 87; **Supp. XX:** 84

Henderson, Katherine, **Supp. IV Part 1:** 203, 207

Henderson, Linda. *See* Hogan, Linda

Henderson, Robert W., **Supp. VIII:** 124

Henderson, Stephen, **Supp. IV Part 1:** 365

Henderson, the Rain King (Bellow), **I:** 144, 147, 148, 152, 153, 154, 155, 158, 160, 161, 162–163; **Retro. Supp. II:** 19, **24–25,** 30

"Hen Flower, The" (Kinnell), **Supp. III Part 1:** 247–248

Henie, Sonja, **Supp. XII:** 165

Henle, James, **II:** 26, 30, 38, 41; **Supp. IX:** 2

Henley, Beth, **Supp. XXI:** 145

Hennesy, Dale, **Supp. XV:** 5

Henninger, Katherine, **Supp. XXI:** 253

Henri, Robert, **IV:** 411; **Supp. I Part 2:** 376

Henry, Arthur, **I:** 515; **Retro. Supp. II:** 97

Henry, DeWitt, **Supp. XI:** 342

Henry, O., **I:** 201; **III:** 5; **Supp. I Part 2:** 390, 462; **Supp. II Part 1: 385–412; Supp. XV:** 40

Henry, Robert, **Retro. Supp. II:** 103

Henry, William A., III, **Supp. IV Part 2:** 574

Henry and Clara (Mallon), **Supp. XIX:** 132, **136–137,** 139, 141

Henry and June (film), **Supp. X:** 186

Henry and June: From the Unexpurgated Diary of Anaïs Nin, **Supp. X:** 184, 185, 187, 194

Henry Holt and Company, **Retro. Supp. I:** 121, 131, 133, 136

Henry IV (Shakespeare), **III:** 166; **Supp. VIII:** 164

"Henry James, Jr." (Howells), **II:** 289; **Retro. Supp. I:** 220

"Henry James and the Art of Teaching" (Rowe), **Retro. Supp. I:** 216

"Henry Manley, Living Alone, Keeps Time" (Kumin), **Supp. IV Part 2:** 451

"Henry Manley Looks Back" (Kumin), **Supp. IV Part 2:** 451

"Henry Manley" poems (Kumin), **Supp. IV Part 2:** 446

Henry Miller Reader, The (Durrell, ed.), **III:** 175, 190

"Henry's Confession" (Berryman), **I:** 186

Henry VIII (Shakespeare), **Supp. IX:** 235

Henslee, **Supp. IV Part 1:** 217

Henson, Josiah, **Supp. I Part 2:** 589

Hentoff, Margot, **Supp. IV Part 1:** 205

Hentz, Caroline Lee, **Supp. I Part 2:** 584

Henze, Hans Werner, **Supp. II Part 1:** 24

"He of the Assembly" (Bowles), **Supp. IV Part 1:** 90

Hepburn, Katharine, **Supp. IX:** 189; **Supp. XI:** 17

Heraclitus, **II:** 1, 163; **IV:** 86

Herakles: A Play in Verse (MacLeish), **III:** 21, 22

Herald of the Autochthonic Spirit (Corso), **Supp. XII:** 134–136

He Ran All the Way (film), **Supp. XVII:** 63

Herberg, Will, **III:** 291

Herbert, Edward, **II:** 11

Herbert, Francis (pseudonym). *See* Bryant, William Cullen

Herbert, George, **II:** 12; **IV:** 141, 145, 146, 151, 153, 156, 165; **Retro. Supp. II:** 40; **Supp. I Part 1:** 80, 107, 108, 122; **Supp. IV Part 2:** 646; **Supp. XV:** 92, 212, 251; **Supp. XXI:** 109

Herbert, Zbigniew, **Supp. VIII:** 20

Herbert Huncke Reader, The (Schafer, ed.), **Supp. XIV:** 137, 138, 139, 140, 145, 147, 150, 151–152

Herbert of Cherbury, Lord, **II:** 108

"Herbert White" (Bidart), **Supp. XV:** 24, 27

Herbst, Josephine, **Retro. Supp. II:** 325, 328; **Supp. XIII:** 295

"Her Choice" (Larcom), **Supp. XIII:** 144

"Her Dead Brother" (Lowell), **Retro. Supp. II:** 188

"Her Dream Is of the Sea" (Ríos), **Supp. IV Part 2:** 546

"Here" (Kenyon), **Supp. VII:** 164

Here and Beyond (Wharton), **Retro. Supp. I:** 382

Here and Now (Levertov), **Supp. III Part 1:** 275, 276

"Here and There" (Wallace), **Supp. X:** 305–306

Here Comes the Mystery Man (Sanders), **Supp. XVI:** 269

Heredia, Juanita, **Supp. XI:** 185, 190

Heredity and Variation (Lock), **Retro. Supp. I:** 375

Heredity: A Psychological Study of Its Phenomena, Laws, Causes, and Consequences (Ribot), **Supp. XX:** 238

"Here Inside My Forehead" (Rasmussen; Nelson and Espeland, trans.), **Supp. XVIII:** 180

Here is Your War (Pyle), **Supp. XVII:** 61

Here Let Us Feast (M. F. K. Fisher), **Supp. XVII:** 86, 87

Here Lies (Parker), **Supp. IX:** 192

Here on Earth (Hoffman), **Supp. X:** 77, 89

Heresy and the Ideal: On Contemporary Poetry (Baker), **Supp. XI:** 142

"Here to Learn" (Bowles), **Supp. IV Part 1:** 93

"Here to Yonder" (Hughes), **Retro. Supp. I:** 205

"Her Father's Letters" (Milburn), **Supp. XI:** 242

"Her Favorite Story" (Richard), **Supp. XIX:** 211, 212

Herford, Reverend Brooke, **I:** 471

"Her Game" (Skloot), **Supp. XX:** 196, 202

Hergesheimer, Joseph, **Supp. I Part 2:** 620; **Supp. XVI:** 187

"Heritage" (Cullen), **Supp. IV Part 1:** 164–165, 168, 170, 171

"Heritage" (Hogan), **Supp. IV Part 1:** 413

"Her Kind" (Sexton), **Supp. II Part 2:** 687

Herland (Gilman), **Supp. XI:** 208–209

Herman, Florence. *See* Williams, Mrs. William Carlos (Florence Herman)

Herman, Jan, **Supp. XIV:** 150–151

Herman, William (pseudonym). *See* Bierce, Ambrose

"Her Management" (Swenson), **Supp. IV Part 2:** 642

"Herman Melville" (Auden), **Supp. II Part 1:** 14

Herman Melville (Mumford), **Supp. II Part 2:** 471, 476, 489–491

"Hermes of the Ways" (Doolittle), **Supp. I Part 1:** 266

"Hermes: Port Authority: His Song" (Di Piero), **Supp. XIX:** 47

Hermetic Definition (Doolittle), **Supp. I Part 1:** 271, 272, 273, 274

"Hermitage, The" (Haines), **Supp. XII:** 205–206

Hermit and the Wild Woman, The (Wharton), **IV:** 315; **Retro. Supp. I:** 371

"Hermit and the Wild Woman, The" (Wharton), **Retro. Supp. I:** 372

"Hermit Meets the Skunk, The" (Kumin), **Supp. IV Part 2:** 447

Hermit of 69th Street, The: The Working Papers or Norbert Kosky (Kosinski), **Supp. VII:** 215, 216, 223, 226–227

"Hermit of Saba, The" (Freneau), **Supp. II Part 1:** 259

"Hermit Picks Berries, The" (Kumin), **Supp. IV Part 2:** 447

Hermit's Story, The (Bass), **Supp. XVI:** 23–24

"Hermit Thrush, A" (Clampitt), **Supp. IX:** 40

Hernández, Miguel, **Supp. V:** 194; **Supp. XIII:** 315, 323; **Supp. XXI:** 104

Herne, James A., **II:** 276; **Supp. II Part 1:** 198

Hernton, Calvin, **Supp. X:** 240

"Hero, The" (Moore), **III:** 200, 211, 212

Hero, The: A Study in Tradition, Myth, and Drama (Raglan), **I:** 135; **Supp. XIX:** 147

Hero and the Blues, The (Murray), **Supp. XIX:** 153, 154

Hérodiade (Mallarmé), **I:** 66

Herodotus, **Supp. I Part 2:** 405

Heroes, The (Ashbery), **Supp. III Part 1:** 3

Hero in America, The (Van Doren), **II:** 103

"Heroines of Nature: Four Women Respond to the American Landscape" (Norwood), **Supp. IX:** 24

"Heron, The" (Roethke), **III:** 540–541

"Her One Bad Eye" (Karr), **Supp. XI:** 244

"Her Own People" (Warren), **IV:** 253

Her Place in These Designs (Espaillat), **Supp. XXI:** 99, 104

"Her Quaint Honour" (Gordon), **II:** 196, 199, 200

Herr, Michael, **Supp. XI:** 245; **Supp. XIX:** 17

Herreshoff, David, **Supp. XIX:** 265

Herrick, Robert, **II:** 11, 18, 444; **III:** 463, 592; **IV:** 453; **Retro. Supp. I:** 319; **Retro. Supp. II:** 101; **Supp. I Part 2:** 646; **Supp. XIII:** 334; **Supp. XIV:** 8, 9; **Supp. XV:** 155; **Supp. XXI:** 14

Herrmann, John, **Retro. Supp. II:** 328

Herron, George, **Supp. I Part 1:** 7

"Hers" (column, Prose), **Supp. XVI:** 254

Herschdorfer, Helen, **Supp. XXI:** 262

Herschel, Sir John, **Supp. I Part 1:** 314

"Her Sense of Timing" (Elkin), **Supp. VI:** 56, 58

Hersey, John, **IV:** 4; **Supp. I Part 1:** 196; **Supp. XVI:** 105–106; **Supp. XX:**251

"Her Sweet turn to leave the Homestead" (Dickinson), **Retro. Supp. I:** 44

Herzog (Bellow), **I:** 144, 147, 149, 150, 152, 153, 154, 155, 156, 157, 158, 159–160; **Retro. Supp. II:** 19, **26–27; Supp. IV Part 1:** 30; **Supp. XIX:** 157

Heschel, Abraham, **Supp. XXI:** 110, 112

Hesford, Walter A., **Supp. XV:** 215, 217, 218

"He/She" (Dunn), **Supp. XI:** 149

"Hesitation Blues" (Hughes), **Retro. Supp. I:** 211

He Sleeps (McKnight), **Supp. XX:**151, **152–155,** 158

"He Sleeps" (McKnight), **Supp. XX:**152, 155

Hesse, Hermann, **Supp. V:** 208

Hester, Carolyn, **Supp. XVIII:** 24

"Hetch Hetchy Valley" (Muir), **Supp. IX:** 185

He Who Gets Slapped (Andreyev), **II:** 425

"He Who Spits at the Sky" (Stegner), **Supp. IV Part 2:** 605

"He Will Not Leave a Note" (Ríos), **Supp. IV Part 2:** 548

Hewitt, James, **Supp. XV:** 240

Hewlett, Maurice, **I:** 359

Heyen, William, **Supp. XIII:** 285, 344; **Supp. XV:** 212

"Hey! Hey!" (Hughes), **Supp. I Part 1:** 327–328

Hey Rub-a-Dub-Dub (Dreiser), **I:** 515; **II:** 26; **Retro. Supp. II:** 104, 105, 108

"Hey Sailor, What Ship?" (Olsen), **Supp. XIII:** 293, 294, 298, **299**

Heyward, DuBose, **Supp. XVIII:** 281; **Supp. XIX:** 78

Hiawatha (Longfellow), **Supp. I Part 1:** 79; **Supp. III Part 2:** 609, 610; **Supp. XXI:** 53

"Hibernaculum" (Ammons), **Supp. VII:** 26–27

Hichborn, Philip, **Supp. I Part 2:** 707, 708

Hichborn, Mrs. Philip. *See* Wylie, Elinor

"Hic Jacet" (W. C. Williams), **Retro. Supp. I:** 414

Hickok, Guy, **Supp. XXI:** 7

Hickok, James Butler ("Wild Bill"), **Supp. V:** 229, 230

Hicks, Granville, **I:** 254, 259, 374; **II:** 26; **III:** 342, 355, 452; **Supp. I Part 1:** 361; **Supp. I Part 2:** 609; **Supp. IV Part 1:** 22; **Supp. IV Part 2:** 526; **Supp. VIII:** 96, 124; **Supp. XII:** 250; **Supp. XIII:** 263; **Supp. XXI:** 276

Hicks, Sally, **Supp. XXI:** 255

Hicok, Bethany, **Retro. Supp. II:** 39

"Hidden" (Nye), **Supp. XIII:** 283

"Hidden Gardens" (Capote), **Supp. III Part 1:** 125

Hidden Law, The (Hecht), **Supp. X:** 58

"Hidden Name and Complex Fate" (Ellison), **Supp. II Part 1:** 245

Hidden Wound, The (Berry), **Supp. X:** 23, 25, 26–27, 29, 34, 35

"Hide-and-Seek" (Francis), **Supp. IX:** 81

"Hiding" (Minot), **Supp. VI:** 203, 206

Hiding Place (Wideman), **Supp. X:** 320, 321, 327, 329, 331–332, 333

"Hidin' Out in Honky Heaven: On Race Relations in Vermont" (Budbill), **Supp. XIX:** 5

Hienger, Jorg, **Supp. IV Part 1:** 106

Higgins, George, **Supp. IV Part 1:** 356

Higginson, Thomas Wentworth, **I:** 451–452, 453, 454, 456, 458, 459, 463, 464, 465, 470; **Retro. Supp. I:** 26, 31, 33, 35, 39, 40; **Supp. I Part 1:** 307, 371; **Supp. IV Part 2:** 430

Higgs, Robert, **Supp. XX:**166

"High Bridge above the Tagus River at Toledo, The" (W. C. Williams), **Retro. Supp. I:** 429

"High Dive: A Variant" (Kumin), **Supp. IV Part 2:** 442

"High Diver" (Francis), **Supp. IX:** 82

"Higher Keys, The" (Merrill), **Supp. III Part 1:** 335–336

Higher Learning in America, The (Veblen), **Supp. I Part 2:** 630, 631, 641, 642

Highet, Gilbert, **Supp. I Part 1:** 268

High Noon (film), **Supp. V:** 46

"High on Sadness" (Komunyakaa), **Supp. XIII:** 114

"High School Senior" (Olds), **Supp. X:** 212

Highsmith, Patricia, **Supp. IV Part 1:** 79, 94, 132

"High Tide" (Marquand), **III:** 56

High Tide in Tucson: Essays from Now or Never (Kingsolver), **Supp. VII:** 198, 201, 209

"High-Toned Old Christian Woman, A" (Stevens), **Retro. Supp. I:** 301

"Highway, The" (Merwin), **Supp. III Part 1:** 346

Highway 61 Revisited (album, Dylan), **Supp. XVIII:** 20, 27, 30, 32

"Highway 61 Revisited" (song, Dylan), **Supp. XVIII:** 30

"Highway 99E from Chico" (Carver), **Supp. III Part 1:** 136

"Highway Apple Trees" (Espaillat), **Supp. XXI: 100–102**

High Window, The (Chandler), **Supp. IV Part 1:** 127–129, 130, 131

"High Yaller" (R. Fisher), **Supp. XIX:** 72

Hijuelos, Oscar, **Supp. IV Part 1:** 54; **Supp. VIII: 73–91**

Hike and the Aeroplane (Lewis), **II:** 440–441

Hilberg, Raul, **Supp. V:** 267

Hildebrand, Al, **III:** 118

Hiler, Hilaire, **Retro. Supp. II:** 327; **Supp. III Part 2:** 617

"Hill, A" (Hecht), **Supp. X:** 59–60, 63

Hill, Abram, **Supp. XV:** 194

Hill, Anita, **Supp. XX:**110

Hill, Hamlin, **Retro. Supp. II:** 286

Hill, James J., **Supp. I Part 2:** 644

Hill, Joe, **I:** 493; **Supp. XVIII:** 224

Hill, Lee, **Supp. XI:** 293, 294, 297, 299, 301, 305, 307

Hill, Patti, **I:** 289

Hill, Peggy, **Supp. XIII:** 163

"Hill, The" (Strand), **Supp. IV Part 2:** 627

"Hill, The" (Toomer), **Supp. III Part 2:** 486

Hill, Vernon, **Supp. I Part 2:** 397

"Hillcrest" (Robinson), **III:** 504

Hill-Lubin, Mildred A., **Supp. IV Part 1:** 13

Hillman, Sidney, **Supp. I Part 1:** 5

Hillringhouse, Mark, **Supp. IX:** 286, 288, 299

Hills Beyond, The (Wolfe), **IV:** 450, 451, 460, 461

"Hills Beyond, The" (Wolfe), **IV:** 460

Hillside and Seaside in Poetry (Larcom, ed.), **Supp. XIII:** 142

"Hillside Thaw, A" (Frost), **Retro. Supp. I:** 133

"Hills Like White Elephants" (Hemingway), **Retro. Supp. I:** 170

Hills of the Shatemuc, The (S. Warner), **Supp. XVIII:** 266

"Hill-Top View, A" (Jeffers), **Supp. II Part 2:** 417

"Hill Wife, The" (Frost), **II:** 154; **Retro. Supp. I:** 131

Hillyer, Catherine, **Supp. XV:** 244

Hillyer, Robert, **I:** 475; **Supp. IX:** 75; **Supp. XIV:** 11

Hilton, James, **Supp. XIII:** 166

"Hiltons' Holiday, The" (Jewett), **II:** 391; **Retro. Supp. II:** 134

Him (Cummings), **I:** 429, 434–435

Himes, Chester Bomar, **Retro. Supp. II:** 117; **Supp. I Part 1:** 51, 325; **Supp. XIII:** 233; **Supp. XVI: 135–146**

Himes, Norman, **Supp. V:** 128

"Him on a Bicycle" (Weigl), **Supp. XIX:** 276

"Him with His Foot in His Mouth" (Bellow), **Retro. Supp. II:** 34

Him with His Foot in His Mouth and Other Stories (Bellow), **Retro. Supp. II:** 31

Hinchman, Sandra K., **Supp. IV Part 1:** 210

Hindemith, Paul, **IV:** 357; **Supp. IV Part 1:** 81

Hindsell, Oliver, **Supp. XIII:** 162

Hindus, Milton, **Supp. XIV:** 288, 291, 292, 293

Hines, Suzanne, **Supp. XIV:** 151

Hinge Picture (Howe), **Supp. IV Part 2:** 423–424

Hinojosa, Rolando, **Supp. XIX:** 97–114

"Hinterlands" (W. Gibson), **Supp. XVI:** 123, 128

"Hippies: Slouching towards Bethlehem" (Didion), **Supp. IV Part 1:** 200

Hippolytus (Euripides), **II:** 543; **Supp. I Part 1:** 270

Hippolytus Temporizes (Doolittle), **Supp. I Part 1:** 270

"Hips" (Cisneros), **Supp. VII:** 61, 62

"Hipster's Hipster" (Ginsberg), **Supp. XIV:** 141

Hirsch, Edward D., **Supp. V:** 177; **Supp. IX:** 262; **Supp. XIV:** 15; **Supp. XV:** 78, 225; **Supp. XVII:** 23; **Supp. XIX:** 202

Hirsch, Sidney, **Supp. XIV:** 1. *See* Mttron-Hirsch, Sidney

Hirschfeld, Jane, **Supp. XVII:** 241

Hirschorn, Clive, **Supp. IV Part 2:** 577, 579

Hirson, Roger, **Supp. XI:** 343

"His Bride of the Tomb" (Dunbar), **Supp. II Part 1:** 196

"His Chest of Drawers" (Anderson), **I:** 113, 114

"His Father's Whistle" (Wrigley), **Supp. XVIII:** 299

His First, Best Country (J. W. Miller), **Supp. XX:** 163, 166, 172–175

"His Last Day" (C. Himes), **Supp. XVI:** 137

"His Lover" (Dubus), **Supp. VII:** 86

"His Music" (Dunn), **Supp. XI:** 149

"His Own Key" (Ríos), **Supp. IV Part 2:** 543

His Picture in the Papers (film; Emerson), **Supp. XVI:** 185

His Religion and Hers (Gilman), **Supp. XI:** 209

Hiss, Alger, **Supp. XV:** 143

"Hiss, Chambers, and the Age of Innocence" (Fiedler), **Supp. XIII:** 99

"His Shield" (Moore), **III:** 211

"His Story" (Cisneros), **Supp. VII:** 67

His Thought Made Pockets & the Plane Buckt (Berryman), **I:** 170

"His Three Women" (Gioia), **Supp. XV:** 119–120

Histoire comparée des systèmes de philosophie (Gérando), **II:** 10

Historical and Moral View of the Origin and Progress of the French Revolution (Wollstonecraft), **Supp. I Part 1:** 126

"Historical Conceptualization" (Huizinga), **I:** 255

Historical Evidence and the Reading of Seventeenth-Century Poetry (Brooks), **Supp. XIV:** 11

"Historical Interpretation of Literature, The" (Wilson), **IV:** 431, 433, 445

Historical Jesus, The: The Life of a Mediterranean Jewish Peasant (Crossan), **Supp. V:** 251

"Historical Value of Crèvecoeur's *Voyage . . .*," (Adams), *Supp. I Part 1:* 251

"History" (Emerson), **II:** 13, 15

"History" (Hughes), **Supp. I Part 1:** 344

History (Lowell), **Retro. Supp. II:** 183, 190

"History" (Simic), **Supp. VIII:** 279

"History, Myth, and the Western Writer" (Stegner), **Supp. IV Part 2:** 596, 601

"History among the Rocks" (Warren), **IV:** 252

History as a Literary Art (Morison), **Supp. I Part 2:** 493

"History as Fate in E. L. Doctorow's Tale of a Western Town" (Arnold), **Supp. IV Part 1:** 220

"History Is the Memory of Time" (Olson), **Supp. II Part 2:** 574

"History Lesson" (Trethewey), **Supp. XXI:** 248, 249

"History Lessons" (Komunyakaa), **Supp. XIII:** 126

History Man, The (Bradbury), **Supp. XVIII:** 140

"History of a Literary Movement" (Nemerov), **III:** 270

"History of a Literary Radical, The" (Bourne), **I:** 215, 235, 236

History of a Radical: Essays by Randolph Bourne (Brooks), **I:** 245

"History of Buttons, The" (Goldbarth), **Supp. XII:** 187

History of English Literature (Taine), **III:** 323

History of English Prosody (Saintsbury), **Supp. XV:** 181

History of Fortus, The (Emerson), **II:** 8

History of Henry Esmond, The (Thackeray), **II:** 91, 130

History of Modern Poetry, A (Perkins), **Supp. I Part 2:** 475; **Supp. XV:** 185

History of My Heart (Pinsky), **Supp. VI:** 243, 244, 245

History of New York, from the Beginning of the World to the End of the Dutch Dynasty, A (Irving), **II:** 300–303, 304, 310

History of Pendennis, The (Thackeray), **II:** 291

"History of Red, The" (Hogan), **Supp. IV Part 1:** 411

"History of Rodney, The" (Bass), **Supp. XVI:** 20

History of Roxbury Town (Ellis), **Supp. I Part 1:** 99

History of Southern Literature, The (Rubin), **Supp. XX:** 161

History of the African-American People (Proposed) by Strom Thurmond, The (Everett and Kincaid), **Supp. XVIII:** 62, **63–64**

History of the Conquest of Mexico (Prescott), **Retro. Supp. I:** 123

History of the Conquest of Peru (Morison, ed.), **Supp. I Part 2:** 494

History of the Dividing Line betwixt Virginia and North Carolina (Byrd), **Supp. IV Part 2:** 425

History of the Life and Voyages of Christopher Columbus, A (Irving), **II:** 310, 314

History of the Navy of the United States of America (Cooper), **I:** 347

History of the Rise and Fall of the Slave-power in America (Wilson), **Supp. XIV:** 48, 49

History of the Russian Revolution, A (Trotsky), **Supp. XXI:** 161

History of the United States of America during the Administrations of Thomas Jefferson and James Madison (Adams), **I:** 6–9, 10, 20, 21

History of the Work of Redemption, A (Edwards), **I:** 560

History of United States Naval Operations in World War II (Morison), **Supp. I Part 2:** 490–492

History of Womankind in Western Europe, The, **Supp. XI:** 197

"History Teacher, The" (Collins), **Supp. XXI:** 57

"History Through a Beard" (Morison), **Supp. I Part 2:** 490

His Toy, His Dream, His Rest (Berryman), **I:** 169, 170, 183, 184–186

"His Words" (Roethke), **III:** 544

Hitchcock, Ada. *See* MacLeish, Mrs. Archibald (Ada Hitchcock)

Hitchcock, Alfred, **IV:** 357; **Supp. IV Part 1:** 132; **Supp. VIII:** 177; **Supp. XX:** 253

Hitchcock, George, **Supp. X:** 127; **Supp. XVII:** 110

"Hitch Haiku" (Snyder), **Supp. VIII:** 297

"Hitch-Hikers, The" (Welty), **IV:** 262

"Hitchhiking Is Illegal in Nevada" (Lethem), **Supp. XVIII:** 136

Hitchins, Christopher, **Supp. VIII:** 241

Hitler, Adolf, **I:** 261, 290, 492; **II:** 146, 454, 561, 565, 592; **III:** 2, 3, 110, 115, 140, 156, 246, 298, 446; **IV:** 5, 17, 18, 298, 372; **Supp. I Part 2:** 431, 436, 446, 664; **Supp. V:** 290

Hitler, Wendy, **III:** 404

Hitler Lives ? (film), **Supp. XVI:** 102

Hix, H. L., **Supp. XV:** 114

H. L. Mencken, a Portrait from Memory (Angoff), **III:** 107

"H. L. Mencken Meets a Poet in the West Side Y.M.C.A." (White), **Supp. I Part 2:** 677

H. L. Mencken: The American Scene (Cairns), **III:** 119

H. M. Pulham, Esquire (Marquand), **II:** 482–483; **III:** 58, 59, 65, 68–69

Hnizdovsky, Jacques, **Supp. XIII:** 346

"Hoadley's Test Case in Indiana" (Neugeboren), **Supp. XVI:** 219

Hoagland, Edward, **Supp. XIV:** 80; **Supp. XVI:** 277

Hoagland, Tony, **Supp. XIX:** 81, 89

"Hoarder, The" (Sexton), **Supp. II Part 2:** 692

"Hoarfrost" (C. Baxter), **Supp. XVII:** 15

Hoban, Phoebe, **Supp. XV:** 319, 325

Hobb, Gormley, **I:** 203
Hobbes, Thomas, **I:** 277; **II:** 9, 10, 540; **III:** 306; **IV:** 88; **Supp. XII:** 33; **Supp. XIV:** 5, 7
Hobson, Geary, **Supp. IV Part 1:** 321; **Supp. IV Part 2:** 502
Hobson, J. A., **I:** 232
Hobson, John A., **Supp. I Part 2:** 650
Hobson, Laura Z., **III:** 151
Hocking, Agnes, **Supp. VIII:** 251
Hocking, William Ernest, **III:** 303
Hodges, Campbell B., **Supp. XIV:** 8
Hodgson, Captain Joseph, **III:** 328
Hoffa, Jimmy, **I:** 493
Hoffenberg, Mason, **Supp. XI:** 294, 297, 299, 305
Hoffer, Eric, **Supp. VIII:** 188; **Supp. XIX:** 264
Hoffman, Abbie, **Supp. XIV:** 150
Hoffman, Alice, **Supp. X: 77–94; Supp. XIII:** 13
Hoffman, Allen, **Supp. XVII:** 42, 44
Hoffman, Daniel, **Retro. Supp. II:** 265
Hoffman, Daniel G., **I:** 405; **II:** 307; **Supp. XI:** 152
Hoffman, Dustin, **Supp. IV Part 1:** 236
Hoffman, E. T. A., **Supp. XVI:** 157
Hoffman, Eva, **Supp. XVI: 147–164**
Hoffman, Frederick J., **I:** 60, 67; **II:** 443; **IV:** 113
Hoffman, Josiah Ogden, **II:** 297, 300
Hoffman, Matilda, **II:** 300, 314
Hoffman, Paul, **Supp. XV:** 141–142
Hoffman, Roy, **Supp. XX:**177
Hoffman, Todd, **Supp. XVIII:** 101
Hoffman, William, **Supp. XVIII: 69–88**
Hoffman, William M., **Supp. X:** 153
Hoffmann, E. T. A., **III:** 415
Hofmann, Hans, **Supp. XV:** 144
Hofmeister, Tim, **Supp. XIX:** 115
Ho for a Hat (W. J. Smith), **Supp. XIII:** 346
Hofstadter, Richard, **Supp. VIII:** 98, 99, 108
Hogan, Linda, **Supp. IV Part 1:** 324, 325, **397–418; Supp. XVIII:** 189
Hogan, Randolph, **Supp. XVI:** 252–253
Hogan, Ron, **Supp. XVIII:** 138, 139
Hogarth, William, **Supp. XII:** 44
Hogg, James, **I:** 53; **Supp. I Part 1:** 349; **Supp. IX:** 275
Hoggart, Richard, **Supp. XIV:** 299
"Hog-Nosed Snake, The" (Kooser), **Supp. XIX:** 128
Hohne, Karen, **Supp. V:** 147
Hojoki (Chomei), **IV:** 170
Holbrook, David, **Supp. I Part 2:** 526–527, 546
Holcroft, Thomas, **Supp. I Part 2:** 514
Holden, Jonathan, **Supp. XI:** 143
Holden, Raymond, **Supp. XIV:** 121–122
Holden, William, **Supp. XI:** 307
Hölderlin, Friedrich, **Supp. XVI:** 48
"Holding On" (Levine), **Supp. V:** 184
Holding the Line: Women in the Great Arizona Mine Strike of 1983 (Kingsolver), **Supp. VII:** 197, 201–202, 204
"Holding the Mirror Up to Nature" (Nemerov), **III:** 275, 276

"Hold Me" (Levine), **Supp. V:** 186
Hold the Press (film), **Supp. XIII:** 163
Hold with the Hares (Zinberg), **Supp. XV:** 197–198,**Supp. XV:** 203
"Hole in the Floor, A" (Wilbur), **Supp. III Part 2:** 556–557
Holiday (Barry), **Retro. Supp. I:** 104
"Holiday" (Porter), **III:** 454
Holiday (W. Frank), **Supp. XX:72–73**
Holiday, Billie, **Supp. I Part 1:** 80; **Supp. IV Part 1:** 2, 7; **Supp. XIX:** 147
Holinshed, Raphael, **IV:** 370
Holladay, Polly, **Supp. XXI:** 6
Holland, Josiah, **Supp. I Part 2:** 420
Holland, Laurence Bedwell, **Retro. Supp. I:** 216
Holland, Theodore, **I:** 453
Holland, Mrs. Theodore, **I:** 453, 455, 465
Holland, William, **IV:** 381
Hollander, John, **Supp. III Part 2:** 541; **Supp. IV Part 2:** 642; **Supp. IX:** 50, 153, 155; **Supp. XII:** 254, 255, 260; **Supp. XV:** 256; **Supp. XVII:** 112; **Supp. XIX:** 121
Holley, Marietta, **Supp. XIII:** 152
Holliday, Billie, **Supp. XXI:** 131
Hollinghurst, Alan, **Supp. XIII:** 52
Hollins Critic (Nelson), **Supp. XIX:** 3
Hollis, Thomas Brand, **Supp. I Part 2:** 514
Hollow Men, The (T. S. Eliot), **I:** 574, 575, 578–579, 580, 585; **III:** 586; **Retro. Supp. I:** 63, 64
"Hollow Tree, A" (R. Bly), **Supp. IV Part 1:** 64, 66
Hollyberrys at the Shore, The, **Supp. X:** 42
"Hollywood!" (Vidal), **Supp. IV Part 2:** 688
Hollywood: American Movie-City (Rand, unauthorized), **Supp. IV Part 2:** 519
Hollywood: A Novel of America in the 1920s (Vidal), **Supp. IV Part 2:** 677, 684, 686, 688, 690, 691
Hollywood Ending (film; Allen), **Supp. XV:** 11
Hollywood on Trial (film), **Supp. I Part 1:** 295
Holmes, Abiel, **Supp. I Part 1:** 300, 301, 302, 310
Holmes, Mrs. Abiel (Sarah Wendell), **Supp. I Part 1:** 300
Holmes, John, **I:** 169; **Supp. II Part 1:** 87; **Supp. IV Part 2:** 440–441; **Supp. XIV:** 119
Holmes, John Clellon, **Supp. XII:** 118; **Supp. XIV:** 144, 150
Holmes, Martha Stoddard, **Supp. XX:**205, 207
Holmes, Oliver Wendell, **I:** 487; **II:** 225, 273–274, 402, 403; **III:** 81–82, 590, 591–592; **IV:** 429, 436; **Retro. Supp. II:** 155; **Supp. I Part 1:** 103, 243, 254, **299–319; Supp. I Part 2:** 405, 414, 415, 420, 593, 704, 705; **Supp. XI:** 194
Holmes, Oliver Wendell, Jr., **I:** 3, 19; **Supp. IV Part 2:** 422
Holmes, Mrs. Oliver Wendell (Amelia Jackson), **Supp. I Part 1:** 303

Holmes, Steven J., **Supp. IX:** 172, 177
Holmes, Ted, **Supp. V:** 180
Holmes, William Henry, **Supp. IV Part 2:** 603–604
Holocaust (Reznikoff), **Supp. XIV:** 281, **291–293**
Holocaust in American Life, The (Novick), **Supp. XVI:** 154
Holt, Edwin E., **I:** 59
Holt, Felix, **II:** 179
Holt, Henry, **II:** 348; **III:** 587
Holt, Patricia, **Supp. XIV:** 89
Holtby, Winifred, **Supp. I Part 2:** 720
Holy Ghostly, The (Shepard), **Supp. III Part 2:** 437–438, 447
"Holy Innocents, The" (Lowell), **II:** 539
Holy Sonnets (Donne), **IV:** 145; **Supp. I Part 1:** 367; **Supp. III Part 2:** 619; **Supp. XIII:** 130–131; **Supp. XVIII:** 50–51
"Holy Terror, A" (Bierce), **I:** 203
"Holy Terror, The" (Maxwell), **Supp. VIII:** 169
Holy the Firm (Dillard), **Supp. VI:** 23, **29**, 30, 31, 32
Holy War, The (Bunyan), **IV:** 156
"Homage to Arthur Rimbaud" (Wright), **Supp. V:** 339
Homage to Baudelaire (Duncan, ed.), **Supp. XV:** 75
Homage to Catalonia (Orwell), **Supp. XVII:** 229
"Homage to Che Guevara" (Banks), **Supp. V:** 5
Homage to Clio (Auden), **Supp. II Part 1:** 24
"Homage to Elizabeth Bishop" (Ivask, ed.), **Supp. I Part 1:** 96
"Homage to Ezra Pound" (Wright), **Supp. V:** 339
Homage to Frank O'Hara (Ashbery), **Supp. III Part 1:** 2–3
"Homage to Franz Joseph Haydn" (Hecht), **Supp. X:** 69
"Homage to Hemingway" (Bishop), **IV:** 35
Homage to Mistress Bradstreet (Berryman), **I:** 168, 169, 170–171, 172, 174, 175, 178–183, 184, 186
"Homage to Paul Cézanne" (Wright), **Supp. V:** 341–342
Homage to Sextus Propertius (Pound), **Retro. Supp. I:** 290
"Homage to Sextus Propertius" (Pound), **III:** 462, 476; **Supp. III Part 2:** 622
"Homage to Shakespeare" (Cheever), **Supp. I Part 1:** 180
"Homage to the Empress of the Blues" (Hayden), **Supp. II Part 1:** 379
"Homage to the Memory of Wallace Stevens" (Justice), **Supp. VII:** 126
Homage to Theodore Dreiser (Warren), **I:** 517
Homans, Margaret, **Supp. X:** 229
"Home" (Hughes), **Supp. I Part 1:** 329, 330
"Home" (Mora), **Supp. XIII:** 217
Home (Robinson), **Supp. XXI:** 212, **220–223**
Home (Updike), **Retro. Supp. I:** 320

"Home" (Weigl), **Supp. XIX:** 287

"Home, Home on the Strange" (J. D. Reed), **Supp. XVI:** 174

"Home, Sweet Home" (Fante), **Supp. XI:** 164, 165

Home, The (Gilman), **Supp. XI: 206–207**

"Home, The" (Jarman), **Supp. XVII:** 116

"Home Address" (Bronk), **Supp. XXI:** 27

"Home after Three Months Away" (Lowell), **II:** 547

Home and Colonial Library (Murray), **Retro. Supp. I:** 246

"Home and the Open Road: The Nonfiction of Larry Brown" (Barrier), **Supp. XXI:** 48–49

Home as Found (Cooper), **I:** 348, 349, 350, 351

Home at the End of the World, A (Cunningham), **Supp. XV:** 59–62, 63

"Home Away from Home, A" (Humphrey), **Supp. IX:** 101

Home Book of Shakespeare Quotations (Stevenson), **Supp. XIV:** 120

"Home Burial" (Frost), **Retro. Supp. I:** 124, 125, 128, **129–130; Supp. VIII:** 31; **Supp. XV:** 159; **Supp. XIX:** 9

Homecoming (Alvarez), **Supp. VII:** 1, 3–5, 9

"Homecoming" (Carruth), **Supp. XVI:** 55

"Homecoming" (McGrath), **Supp. X:** 116

"Homecoming, The" (Gioia), **Supp. XV:** 123, 124

Homecoming, The (Wilson), **Supp. VIII:** 330

Homecoming Game, The (Nemerov), **III:** 268, 282, 284–285

"Home during a Tropical Snowstorm I Feed My Father Lunch" (Karr), **Supp. XI:** 241–242, 248

Home Economics (Berry), **Supp. X:** 28, 31–32, 35, 36, 37

"Home Economics for Halfbacks" (Skloot), **Supp. XX:**195, 207

Home from the Hill (film), **Supp. IX:** 95

Home from the Hill (Humphrey), **Supp. IX:** 93, 95, **96–98,** 104, 106, 109

"Home Grown" (Vital), **Supp. XVI:** 160

"Homeland" (Merwin), **Supp. III Part 1:** 351

Homeland and Other Stories (Kingsolver), **Supp. VII:** 199, 202–204, 207

Home on the Range (Baraka), **Supp. II Part 1:** 47

Home Place, The (Morris), **III:** 221, 222, 232

Homeplace, The (Nelson), **Supp. XVIII: 174–175**

Homer, **I:** 312, 433; **II:** 6, 8, 133, 302, 543, 544, 552; **III:** 14, 21, 278, 453, 457, 473, 567; **IV:** 54, 371; **Retro. Supp. I:** 59; **Supp. I Part 1:** 158, 283; **Supp. I Part 2:** 494; **Supp. X:** 36, 120, 122; **Supp. XIV:** 21; **Supp. XVII:** 70, 227

Homer, Louise, **Retro. Supp. I:** 10

Homer, Winslow, **Supp. XXI:** 243

"Home Range" (Leopold), **Supp. XIV:** 184, 185

"Home Repairs" (Skloot), **Supp. XX:**204

"Homesick Blues" (Hughes), **Supp. I Part 1:** 327

Home: Social Essays (Baraka), **Supp. II Part 1:** 45, 61

"Homesteading on the Extraterrestrial Frontier" (Abbott), **Supp. XVIII:** 142

Home to Harlem (McKay), **Supp. X:** 132, 137–138, **138–139; Supp. XVIII:** 127

Homeward Bound (Cooper), **I:** 348

"Homeward Star, The" (Palmer), **Supp. XV:** 81–82

Homewood trilogy (Wideman), **Supp. X:** 319

"Homework" (Cameron), **Supp. XII:** 80, **83,** 84

"Homily" (Tate), **IV:** 121–122

Homing with the Birds (Stratton-Porter), **Supp. XX:**212, 216, 222

"Homme Moyen Sensuel, L' " (Pound), **III:** 462

Homme révolté, L' (Camus), **III:** 306

"Homoeopathy and Its Kindred Delusions" (Holmes), **Supp. I Part 1:** 303–304, 305

Homo Ludens (Huizinga), **II:** 416–417, 425

"Homosexual Villain, The" (Mailer), **III:** 36

"Homo Will Not Inherit" (Doty), **Supp. XI:** 128

Homunculus, The: A Novel in One Chapter (McKnight), **Supp. XX:**152

Hone and Strong Diaries of Old Manhattan, The (Auchincloss, ed.), **Supp. IV Part 1:** 23

"Honey" (Beattie), **Supp. V:** 33

"Honey" (Wright), **Supp. III Part 2:** 589

"Honey, We'll Be Brave" (Farrell), **II:** 45

Honey and Salt (Sandburg), **III:** 594–596

"Honey and Salt" (Sandburg), **III:** 594

"Honey Babe" (Hughes), **Supp. I Part 1:** 334

"Honey Tree, The" (Oliver), **Supp. VII:** 236

Hong, Maxine. *See* Kingston, Maxine Hong

Hongo, Garrett, **Supp. X:** 292; **Supp. XIII:** 114; **Supp. XVII:** 112

"Honkytonk" (Shapiro), **Supp. II Part 2:** 705

"Honky Tonk in Cleveland, Ohio" (Sandburg), **III:** 585

Honorable Men (Auchincloss), **Supp. IV Part 1:** 23

Honor Thy Father (Talese), **Supp. XVII:** 204–205, 210

Hood, Tom, **I:** 195

"Hoodoo in America" (Hurston), **Supp. VI:** 153–154

"Hook" (Wright), **Supp. III Part 2:** 604

Hook, Sidney, **I:** 265; **Supp. IV Part 2:** 527; **Supp. VIII:** 96, 100; **Supp. XIV:** 3

Hooker, Adelaide. *See* Marquand, Mrs. John P. (Adelaide Hooker)

Hooker, Isabella Beecher, **Supp. XI:** 193

Hooker, Samuel, **IV:** 162, 165

Hooker, Thomas, **II:** 15–16; **IV:** 162

Hooper, Marian. *See* Adams, Mrs. Henry (Marian Hooper)

Hoosier Holiday, A (Dreiser), **Retro. Supp. II:** 104

Hoover, Herbert, **Supp. I Part 2:** 638

Hoover, J. Edgar, **Supp. XIII:** 170

Hoover, Paul, **Supp. XV:** 179

"Hope" (Jarrell), **II:** 389

"Hope" (Matthews), **Supp. IX:** 163

Hope, A. D., **Supp. XIII:** 347

Hope, Lynn, **Supp. II Part 1:** 38

"Hope Atherton's Wanderings" (Howe), **Supp. IV Part 2:** 432

Hope of Heaven (O'Hara), **III:** 361

"Hopes Rise" (Boyle), **Supp. XX:**20

"Hop-Frog" (Poe), **Retro. Supp. II:** 264, 268, 269

Hopkin, Pauline, **Supp. XVI:** 143

Hopkins, Anne Yale, **Supp. I Part 1:** 100, 102, 113

Hopkins, Gerard Manley, **I:** 171, 179, 397, 401, 522, 525, 533; **II:** 537; **III:** 197, 209, 523; **IV:** 129, 135, 141, 421; **Retro. Supp. II:** 40; **Supp. I Part 1:** 79, 81, 94; **Supp. III Part 2:** 551; **Supp. IV Part 1:** 178; **Supp. IV Part 2:** 637, 638, 639, 641, 643; **Supp. V:** 337; **Supp. IX:** 39, 42; **Supp. X:** 61, 115; **Supp. XIII:** 294; **Supp. XIV:** 83; **Supp. XV:** 250, 347; **Supp. XVI:** 282; **Supp. XVII:** 241; **Supp. XVIII:** 78, 79; **Supp. XX:**230

Hopkins, Gerard Walter Sturgis, **Supp. XX:**229, 233, 240

Hopkins, L. A., **I:** 502

Hopkins, Lemuel, **Supp. II Part 1:** 70

Hopkins, Miriam, **IV:** 381; **Supp. I Part 1:** 281

Hopkins, Pauline, **Supp. XVIII:** 284

Hopkins, Samuel, **I:** 547, 549

Hopkins, Vivian, **II:** 20

Hopkinson, Francis, **Supp. I Part 2:** 504

Hopper (Strand), **Supp. IV Part 2:** 632

Hopper, Dennis, **Supp. XI:** 293, 308

Hopper, Edward, **IV:** 411, 413; **Supp. IV Part 2:** 619, 623, 631, 634; **Supp. XIX:** 117

Hopwood, Avery, **Supp. IV Part 2:** 573

Horace, **II:** 8, 154, 169, 543, 552, 568; **III:** 15; **IV:** 89; **Supp. I Part 2:** 423; **Supp. IX:** 152; **Supp. X:** 65; **Supp. XII:** 258, 260, 262

Horae Canonicae (Auden), **Supp. II Part 1:** 21

"Horatian Ode" (Marvell), **IV:** 135

"Horatian Ode upon Cromwell's Return from Ireland" (Marvell), **Supp. XIV:** 10

Horgan, Paul, **Supp. XV:** 46, 49, 52

Horkheimer, Max, **Supp. I Part 2:** 645; **Supp. IV Part 1:** 301

Horn, Dara, **Supp. XVII:** 50; **Supp. XX:**177

Horn, Mother, **Supp. I Part 1:** 49, 54

Hornby, Nick, **Supp. XII:** 286

Horn of Africa (Caputo), **Supp. XIX:** 21–23

"Horn of Plenty" (Hughes), **Retro. Supp. I:** 210; **Supp. I Part 1:** 342
Horovitz, Israel, **Supp. XV:** 321
Horowitz, James. *See* Salter, James
Horowitz, Mark, **Supp. V:** 219, 231
"Horrible" (Halliday), **Supp. XIX:** 91
"Horse, The" (Levine), **Supp. V:** 182
"Horse, The" (Wright), **Supp. III Part 2:** 592, 601
Horse Eats Hay (play), **Supp. IV Part 1:** 82
Horse Feathers (film), **Supp. IV Part 1:** 384
"Horseflies" (Wrigley), **Supp. XVIII:** 307
Horse Has Six Legs, The (Simic), **Supp. VIII:** 272
"Horselaugh on Dibber Lannon" (Fante), **Supp. XI:** 164
Horseman, Pass By (McMurtry), **Supp. V:** 220–221, 224
"Horses" (Doty), **Supp. XI:** 122
Horses and Men (Anderson), **I:** 112–113, 114
"Horses and Men in Rain" (Sandburg), **III:** 584
"Horse Show, The" (W. C. Williams), **Retro. Supp. I:** 423
Horses Make a Landscape More Beautiful (Walker), **Supp. III Part 2:** 521, 533
"Horse Thief" (Caldwell), **I:** 310
"Horseweed" (Offutt), **Supp. XIX:** 166, 167
Horse With a Green Vinyl Mane (P. N. Warren), **Supp. XX:**261
"Horsie" (Parker), **Supp. IX:** 193
Horton, Philip, **I:** 383, 386, 387, 393, 441; **Supp. XV:** 138
Horton Hatches the Egg (Geisel), **Supp. XVI:** 100, 112
Horton Hears a Who! (Geisel), **Supp. XVI:** 102
Horwitz, Tony, **Supp. XVIII:** 195–196
Hosea (biblical book), **II:** 166
Hospers, John, **Supp. IV Part 2:** 528
"Hospice" (Hull), **Supp. XXI:** 138
Hospital, Janette Turner, **Supp. IV Part 1:** 311–302
Hospital Sketches (Alcott), **Supp. I Part 1:** 34, 35
Hostages to Fortune (Humphrey), **Supp. IX:** 96, **104–106,** 109
"Hot Combs" (Trethewey), **Supp. XXI:** 249
"Hot Dog" (Stern), **Supp. IX: 298–299**
"Hotel Bar" (McClatchy), **Supp. XII:** 269
Hotel Dwellers, The (Lacy), **Supp. XV:** 205
Hotel Insomnia (Simic), **Supp. VIII:** 280, **281–282**
Hotel Lambosa and Other Stories (Koch), **Supp. XV:** 186
Hotel New Hampshire, The (Irving), **Supp. VI:** 163, 164, **172–173,** 177, 179; **Supp. XIX:** 164
"Hot-Foot Hannibal" (Chesnutt), **Supp. XIV:** 60

"Hot Night on Water Street" (Simpson), **Supp. IX:** 269, 270
"Hot Time, A" (Gunn Allen), **Supp. IV Part 1:** 333
Houdini, Harry, **IV:** 437
"Hound of Heaven" (Thompson), **Retro. Supp. I:** 55
"Hourglass, The" (Kees), **Supp. XV:** 147
"Hour in Chartres, An" (Bourne), **I:** 228
Hours, The (Cunningham), **Supp. XII:** 80; **Supp. XV: 65–68**
"Hours before Eternity" (Caldwell), **I:** 291
House, Bridge, Fountain, Gate (Kumin), **Supp. IV Part 2:** 448, 449, 451, 454
House, Edward, **Supp. I Part 2:** 643
"House, The" (Merrill), **Supp. III Part 1:** 323
House at Pooh Corner, The (Milne), **Supp. IX:** 189
House Behind the Cedars, The (Chesnutt), **Supp. XIV: 69–71**
Houseboat Days (Ashbery), **Supp. III Part 1:** 18–20
Housebreaker of Shady Hill and Other Stories, The (Cheever), **Supp. I Part 1:** 184
"House by the Sea, The" (E. Stoddard), **Supp. XV:** 277
House by the Sea, The (Sarton), **Supp. VIII:** 264
House Divided, A (Buck), **Supp. II Part 1:** 118
"House Divided, The/La Casa Divida" (Kingsolver), **Supp. VII:** 207
"House Guest" (Bishop), **Retro. Supp. II:** 49; **Supp. I Part 1:** 93
Household Saints (film), **Supp. XVI:** 256
Household Saints (Prose), **Supp. XVI:** 252–253, 254, 261
"House in Athens, The" (Merrill), **Supp. III Part 1:** 323
House in the Uplands, A (Caldwell), **I:** 297, 301, 306
"House in Turk Street, The" (Hammett), **Supp. IV Part 1:** 344
"House in Winter, The" (Sarton), **Supp. VIII:** 259
"Housekeeping" (Alvarez), **Supp. VII:** 3–5, 10
Housekeeping (Robinson), **Supp. XXI:** 210–211, **212–216,** 218, 223
"Housekeeping" (Trethewey), **Supp. XXI:** 249
"Housekeeping for Men" (Bourne), **I:** 231
House Made of Dawn (Momaday), **Supp. IV Part 1:** 274, 323, 326; **Supp. IV Part 2:** 479, 480, 481–484, 485, 486, 504, 562
Houseman, John, **Supp. IV Part 1:** 173
House of Dust, The: A Symphony (Aiken), **I:** 50
House of Earth trilogy (Buck), **Supp. II Part 1:** 118, 123
House of Five Talents, The (Auchincloss), **Supp. IV Part 1:** 21, 25–27
"House of Flowers" (Capote), **Supp. III Part 1:** 123

House of Games (Mamet), **Supp. XIV:** 243
House of Houses (Mora), **Supp. XIII:** 213, 215, 218, 219, 223–224, **225–227,** 228, 229
House of Incest (Nin), **Supp. III Part 1:** 43; **Supp. X:** 187, 190, 193
House of Life, The: Rachel Carson at Work (Brooks), **Supp. IX:** 26
House of Light (Oliver), **Supp. VII:** 238–240
House of Mirth, The (Wharton), **II:** 180, 193; **IV:** 311–313, 314, 316, 318, 323, 327; **Retro. Supp. I:** 360, 366, 367, **367–370,** 373, 380; **Supp. XX:**239, 240
"House of Mist, The" (Rand), **Supp. IV Part 2:** 524
"House of My Own, A" (Cisneros), **Supp. VII:** 64
"House of Night, The" (Freneau), **Supp. II Part 1:** 259, 260
"House of Representatives and Me, The" (Conroy), **Supp. XVI:** 75
House of Sleeping Beauties, The (Hwang), **Supp. XXI:** 146
House of the Far and Lost, The (Wolfe), **IV:** 456
"House of the Injured, The" (Haines), **Supp. XII:** 203
"House of the One Father" (Antin), **Supp. XX:**3, 13
House of the Prophet, The (Auchincloss), **Supp. IV Part 1:** 31
House of the Seven Gables (Hawthorne), **I:** 106; **II:** 60, 224, 225, 231, 237, 239, 240–241, 243, 244; **Retro. Supp. I:** 63, 149, **160–162,** 163, 164; **Supp. I Part 2:** 579
House of the Solitary Maggot, The (Purdy), **Supp. VII:** 274–275
"House on 15th S.W., The" (Hugo), **Supp. VI:** 140
"House on Main Street, The" (B. Kelly), **Supp. XVII:** 127
House on Mango Street, The (Cisneros), **Supp. VII:** 58, 59–64, 65, 66, 67, 68, 72
"House on Mango Street, The" (Cisneros), **Supp. VII:** 59
House on Marshland, The (Glück), **Supp. V:** 81–83, 84
"House on Moscow Street, The" (Nelson), **Supp. XVIII:** 174
"House on the Heights, A" (Capote), **Supp. III Part 1:** 120
"House on the Hill, The" (Robinson), **III:** 505, 524
"House Raising" (Offutt), **Supp. XIX:** 166
"Houses" (Hogan), **Supp. IV Part 1:** 402
"Houses, The" (Merwin), **Supp. III Part 1:** 354
"Houses of the Spirit" (Karr), **Supp. XI:** 250
"House Sparrows" (Hecht), **Supp. X:** 68
"House That Doesn't House, The" (Bronk), **Supp. XXI:** 34
House That Tai Maing Built, The (Lee), **Supp. X:** 291

"House Unroofed by the Gale" (Tu Fu), **II:** 526

"House Where Mark Twain Was Born, The" (Masters), **Supp. I Part 2:** 472

"Housewife" (Hempel), **Supp. XXI:** 124

"Housewife" (Sexton), **Supp. II Part 2:** 682

Housman, A. E., **III:** 15, 136, 606; **Supp. II Part 1:** 4; **Supp. IV Part 1:** 165; **Supp. XV:** 40–41

Houston Trilogy (McMurtry), **Supp. V:** 223–225

How" (Ginsberg), **Supp. XIV:** 142, 143

"How" (Moore), **Supp. X:** 167

"How About This?" (Carver), **Supp. III Part 1:** 141

"How America Came to the Mountains" (J. W. Miller), **Supp. XX:**169

"How Annandale Went Out" (Robinson), **III:** 513

Howard, Arliss, **Supp. XXI:** 39

Howard, Ben, **Supp. XVI:** 54

Howard, Gerald, **Supp. XII:** 21

Howard, Jane, **Retro. Supp. I:** 334

Howard, June, **Retro. Supp. II:** 139

Howard, Leon, **Supp. I Part 2:** 408, 422, 423

Howard, Maureen, **Supp. XII:** 285; **Supp. XVII:** 183

Howard, Richard, **Retro. Supp. II:** 43; **Supp. IV Part 2:** 624, 626, 640; **Supp. VIII:** 273; **Supp. IX:** 324, 326; **Supp. X:** 152; **Supp. XI:** 317; **Supp. XII:** 254; **Supp. XIII:** 76; **Supp. XV:** 23, 24

Howard, Vilma, **Retro. Supp. II:** 111, 112

Howards, J. Z., **Supp. VIII:** 178

Howards End (Forster), **Supp. XII:** 87

Howarth, Cora, **I:** 408, 409

Howbah Indians (Ortiz), **Supp. IV Part 2:** 513

"How Black Sees Green and Red" (McKay), **Supp. X:** 136

How Britain Rules Africa (Padmore), **Supp. XXI:** 166

"How David Did Not Care" (R. Bly), **Supp. IV Part 1:** 73

"How Did I Love Him?" (Nelson), **Supp. XVIII:** 176

"How Do I Love Thee?" (Browning), **Supp. XVIII:** 176

Howe, Darcus, **Supp. XXI:** 170

Howe, E.W., **I:** 106

Howe, Florence, **Supp. XIII:** 295, 306

Howe, Harriet, **Supp. XI:** 200, 201

Howe, Irving, **IV:** 10; **Retro. Supp. I:** 369; **Retro. Supp. II:** 112, 286; **Supp. I Part 2:** 432; **Supp. II Part 1:** 99; **Supp. VI:** 113–129; **Supp. VIII:** 93, 232; **Supp. IX:** 227; **Supp. X:** 203, 245; **Supp. XII:** 160; **Supp. XIII:** 98; **Supp. XIV:** 103–104, 104; **Supp. XVII:** 50; **Supp. XIX:** 257, 265

Howe, James Wong, **Supp. I Part 1:** 281; **Supp. V:** 223

Howe, Julia Ward, **III:** 505; **Retro. Supp. II:** 135

Howe, M. A. DeWolfe, **I:** 258; **II:** 406; **Supp. XIV:** 54

Howe, Mary Manning, **Supp. IV Part 2:** 422

Howe, Samuel, **Supp. I Part 1:** 153

Howe, Susan, **Retro. Supp. I:** 33, 43; **Supp. IV Part 2: 419–438; Supp. XVI:** 284

Howell, Chris, **Supp. XIII:** 112

Howell, James, **II:** 111

Howells, Margaret, **II:** 271

Howells, William C., **II:** 273

Howells, William Dean, **I:** 109, 192, 204, 210, 211, 254, 355, 407, 411, 418, 459, 469; **II:** 127–128, 130, 131, 136, 137, 138, 140, **271–294,** 322, 331–332, 338, 397–398, 400, 415, 444, 451, 556; **III:** 51, 118, 314, 327–328, 461, 576, 607; **IV:** 192, 202, 342, 349; **Retro. Supp. I:** 220, 334, 362, 378; **Retro. Supp. II:** 93, 101, 135, 288; **Supp. I Part 1:** 306, 318, 357, 360, 368; **Supp. I Part 2:** 414, 420, 645–646; **Supp. II Part 1:** 198, 352; **Supp. IV Part 2:** 678; **Supp. VIII:** 98, 101, 102; **Supp. XI:** 198, 200; **Supp. XIV:** 45–46; **Supp. XV:** 269, 274, 285, 287; **Supp. XVIII:** 6

Howells, Mrs. William Dean (Elinor Mead), **II:** 273

Howells, Winifred, **II:** 271

"Howells as Anti-Novelist" (Updike), **Retro. Supp. I:** 334

Howells: His Life and World (Brooks), **I:** 254

Hower, Edward, **Supp. XII:** 330, 343

Howes, Barbara, **Supp. XIII:** 331

How Good Is David Mamet, Anyway? (Heilpern), **Supp. XIV:** 242

"How I Became a Shadow" (Purdy), **Supp. VII:** 269

"How I Came to Vedanta" (Isherwood), **Supp. XIV:** 164

"How I Come to You" (Peacock), **Supp. XIX:** 198

"How I Learned to Sweep" (Alvarez), **Supp. VII:** 4

"How I Spent My Forties" (Wasserstein), **Supp. XV:** 325, 330, 332

"How It Began" (Stafford), **Supp. XI:** 327

"How It Feels to Be Colored Me" (Hurston), **Supp. VI:** 152

"How It Is" (Budbill), **Supp. XIX:** 10

"How It Is" (Everwine), **Supp. XV:** 79, 86

"How I Told My Child About Race" (Brooks), **Supp. III Part 1:** 78

"How I Went to the Mines" (Harte), **Supp. II Part 1:** 336

"How I Write" (Franzen), **Supp. XX:**84

"How I Write" (Welty), **IV:** 279, 280

"How I Wrote *The Promised Land*" (Antin), **Supp. XX:**3

"How Jonah Did Not Care" (R. Bly), **Supp. IV Part 1:** 73

Howl (Ginsberg), **Retro. Supp. I:** 426; **Supp. III Part 1:** 92; **Supp. IV Part 1:** 90; **Supp. V:** 336; **Supp. VIII:** 290; **Supp. XIV:** 15, 126, 157; **Supp. XVIII:** 20, 29

"How Laddie and the Princess Spelled Down at the Christmas Bee" (Stratton-Porter), **Supp. XX:**216

Howl and Other Poems (Ginsberg), **Supp. II Part 1:** 308, 317–318, 319; **Supp. X:** 123

Howlett, William, **Retro. Supp. I:** 17

Howl: Original Draft Facsimile, Transcript and Variant Versions (Gimsberg), **Supp. XIV:** 142

"How Many Midnights" (Bowles), **Supp. IV Part 1:** 86–87

"How Many Nights" (Kinnell), **Supp. III Part 1:** 245–246

How Much? (Blechman), **Supp. I Part 1:** 290

"How Much Are You Worth" (Salinas), **Supp. XIII:** 325–326

"How Much Earth" (Levine), **Supp. V:** 184

How Much Earth: The Fresno Poets (Buckley, Oliveira, and Williams, eds.), **Supp. XIII:** 313

"How Not to Forget" (Bartov), **Supp. XVI:** 153–154

"How Poetry Comes to Me" (Corso), **Supp. XII:** 122

"How Poetry Comes to Me" (Snyder), **Supp. VIII:** 305

How Reading Changed My Life (Quindlen), **Supp. XVII:** 167, 179–180

"How She Came By Her Name: An Interview with Louis Massiah" (Bambara), **Supp. XI:** 20

"How Soon Hath Time" (Ransom), **IV:** 123

How Stella Got Her Groove Back (McMillan), **Supp. XIII:** 185, **190–191**

How the Alligator Missed Breakfast (Kinney), **Supp. III Part 1:** 235, 253

"How the Devil Came Down Division Street" (Algren), **Supp. IX:** 3

How the García Girls Lost Their Accents (Alvarez), **Supp. VII:** 3, 5–9, 11, 15, 17, 18

How the Grinch Stole Christmas! (Geisel), **Supp. XVI:** 102

How the Other Half Lives (Riis), **I:** 293

"How the Saint Did Not Care" (R. Bly), **Supp. IV Part 1:** 73

"How the Women Went from Dover" (Whittier), **Supp. I Part 2:** 694, 696, 697

"How To" (Carruth), **Supp. XVI:** 51

How To Be Alone: Essays (Franzen), **Supp. XX:**83, 90, **93–94**

"How to Be an Other Woman" (Moore), **Supp. X:** 165, 167, 168

"How to Become a Writer" (Moore), **Supp. X:** 167, 168

"How to Be Happy: Another Memo to Myself" (Dunn), **Supp. XI:** 145

How To Cook a Wolf (M. F. K. Fisher), **Supp. XVII:** 84–85, 87

How to Develop Your Personality (Shellow), **Supp. I Part 2:** 608

How to Know God: The Yoga Aphorisms of Patanjali (Isherwood and Prabhavananda)), **Supp. XIV:** 164

"How To Like It" (Dobyns), **Supp. XIII:** 85–86

"How to Live on $36,000 a Year" (Fitzgerald), **Retro. Supp. I:** 105

"How to Live. What to Do" (Stevens), **Retro. Supp. I:** 302

"How Tom is Doin' " (Kees), **Supp. XV:** 143

How to Read (Pound), **Supp. VIII:** 291

How to Read a Novel (Gordon), **II:** 198

How to Read a Poem and Fall in Love with Poetry (Hirsch), **Supp. XIX:** 202

How to Read a Poem . . . and Start a Poetry Circle (Peacock), **Supp. XIX:** 194, 202–203, 205

How to Save Your Own Life (Jong), **Supp. V:** 115, 123–125, 130

"How to Study Poetry" (Pound), **III:** 474

"How to Talk to Your Mother" (Moore), **Supp. X:** 167, 172

How to Win Friends and Influence People (Carnegie), **Supp. I Part 2:** 608

How to Worry Successfully (Seabury), **Supp. I Part 2:** 608

How to Write (Stein), **IV:** 32, 34, 35

"How to Write a Blackwood Article" (Poe), **III:** 425; **Retro. Supp. II:** 273

"How to Write a Memoir Like This" (Oates), **Supp. III Part 2:** 509

"How to Write Like Somebody Else" (Roethke), **III:** 540

How to Write Short Stories (Lardner), **II:** 430, 431

"How Vincentine Did Not Care" (R. Bly), **Supp. IV Part 1:** 73

How We Became Human: New and Selected Poems (Harjo), **Supp. XII:** 230–232

"How We Danced" (Sexton), **Supp. II Part 2:** 692

How We Got Insipid (Lethem), **Supp. XVIII:** 149

"How We Got in Town and Out Again" (Lethem), **Supp. XVIII:** 149

"How You Sound??" (Baraka), **Supp. II Part 1:** 30

Hoy, Philip, **Supp. X:** 56, 58

Hoyer, Linda Grace (pseudonym). *See* Updike, Mrs. Wesley

Hoyt, Constance, **Supp. I Part 2:** 707

Hoyt, Elinor Morton. *See* Wylie, Elinor

Hoyt, Henry (father), **Supp. I Part 2:** 707

Hoyt, Henry (son), **Supp. I Part 2:** 708

Hoyt, Henry Martyn, **Supp. I Part 2:** 707

Hsu, Kai-yu, **Supp. X:** 292

Hsu, Ruth Y., **Supp. XV:** 212

Hubba City (Reed), **Supp. X:** 241

Hubbard, Elbert, **I:** 98, 383

Hubbell, Jay B., **Supp. I Part 1:** 372

"Hubbub, The" (Ammons), **Supp. VII:** 35

Huber, François, **II:** 6

Huckins, Olga, **Supp. IX:** 32

Huckleberry Finn (Twain). *See Adventures of Huckleberry Finn, The* (Twain)

Hud (film), **Supp. V:** 223, 226

Hudgins, Andrew, **Supp. X:** 206; **Supp. XVII:** 111, 112; **Supp. XVIII:** 176

Hudson, Henry, **I:** 230

"Hudsonian Curlew, The" (Snyder), **Supp. VIII:** 302

Hudson River Bracketed (Wharton), **IV:** 326–327; **Retro. Supp. I:** 382

Huebsch, B. W., **III:** 110

Hueffer, Ford Madox, **Supp. I Part 1:** 257, 262. *See also* Ford, Ford Madox

Huene-Greenberg, Dorothee von, **Supp. XX:**46

Huff (television series), **Supp. XIX:** 222

Hug Dancing (Hearon), **Supp. VIII:** 67–68

Huge Season, The (Morris), **III:** 225–226, 227, 230, 232, 233, 238

Hugging the Jukebox (Nye), **Supp. XIII:** 275–276, 277

"Hugging the Jukebox" (Nye), **Supp. XIII:** 276

Hughes, Brigid, **Supp. XVI:** 247

Hughes, Carolyn, **Supp. XII:** 272, 285

Hughes, Frieda, **Supp. I Part 2:** 540, 541

Hughes, Glenn, **Supp. I Part 1:** 255

Hughes, H. Stuart, **Supp. VIII:** 240

Hughes, James Nathaniel, **Supp. I Part 1:** 321, 332

Hughes, Ken, **Supp. XI:** 307

Hughes, Langston, **Retro. Supp. I:** 193–214; **Retro. Supp. II:** 114, 115, 117, 120; **Supp. I Part 1:** 320–348; **Supp. II Part 1:** 31, 33, 61, 170, 173, 181, 227, 228, 233, 361; **Supp. III Part 1:** 72–77; **Supp. IV Part 1:** 15, 16, 164, 168, 169, 173, 243, 368; **Supp. VIII:** 213; **Supp. IX:** 306, 316; **Supp. X:** 131, 136, 139, 324; **Supp. XI:** 1; **Supp. XIII:** 75, 111, 132, 233; **Supp. XVI:** 135, 138; **Supp. XVIII:** 90, 277, 279, 280, 281, 282; **Supp. XIX:** 72, 75, 77; **Supp. XXI:** 243

Hughes, Nicholas, **Supp. I Part 2:** 541

Hughes, Robert, **Supp. X:** 73

Hughes, Ted, **IV:** 3; **Retro. Supp. II:** 244, 245, 247, 257; **Supp. I Part 2:** 536, 537, 538, 539, 540, 541; **Supp. XV:** 117, 347, 348

Hughes, Thomas, **Supp. I Part 2:** 406

"Hugh Harper" (Bowles), **Supp. IV Part 1:** 94

Hughie (O'Neill), **III:** 385, 401, 405

Hugh Selwyn Mauberley (Pound), **I:** 66, 476; **III:** 9, 462–463, 465, 468; **Retro. Supp. I:** 289–290, 291, 299; **Supp. XIV:** 272

Hugo, Richard, **Supp. VI:** 131–148; **Supp. IX:** 296, 323, 324, 330; **Supp. XI:** 315, 317; **Supp. XII:** 178; **Supp. XIII:** 112, 113, 133; **Supp. XVIII:** 293, 299; **Supp. XXI:** 243

Hugo, Victor, **II:** 290, 490, 543; **Supp. IV Part 2:** 518; **Supp. IX:** 308

Hui-neng, **III:** 567

Huis Clos (Sartre), **Supp. IV Part 1:** 84

Huizinga, Johan, **I:** 225; **II:** 416–417, 418, 425

Hulbert, Ann, **Supp. XI:** 38–39

Hull, Lynda, **Supp. XI:** 131; **Supp. XXI:** 129–142

Hulme, Thomas E., **I:** 68, 69, 475; **III:** 196, 209, 463–464, 465; **IV:** 122; **Supp. I Part 1:** 261, 262; **Supp. XV:** 43

Human, All Too Human (Nietzsche), **Supp. X:** 48

"Human Culture" (Emerson), **II:** 11–12

Human Factor, The (Greene), **Supp. V:** 298

"Human Figures" (Doty), **Supp. XI:** 123–124

"Human Fly, The" (Boyle), **Supp. XX:**19

"Human Geography" (Jarman), **Supp. XVII:** 116

"Human Immortality" (James), **II:** 353–354

"Human Life" (Emerson), **II:** 11–12

"Human Pig" (Jin), **Supp. XVIII:** 99

Human Rights, Human Wrongs: The Oxford Amnesty Lectures, 2001, **Supp. XVI:** 155

Human Stain, The (P. Roth), **Retro. Supp. II:** 279, 289, 294–295

"Human Things" (Nemerov), **III:** 279

Human Universe (Olson), **Supp. II Part 2:** 571

"Human Universe" (Olson), **Supp. II Part 2:** 565, 567

Human Vibration (Richter), **Supp. XVIII:** 209

Human Wishes (Hass), **Supp. VI:** 105–106, 107

Human Work (Gilman), **Supp. XI:** 206

Humbert, Humbert, **Supp. X:** 283

Humble Inquiry into the Rules of the Word of God, An, Concerning the Qualifications Requisite to a Complete Standing and Full Communion in the Visible Christian Church (Edwards), **I:** 548

Humboldt, Alexander von, **III:** 428

Humboldt's Gift (Bellow), **Retro. Supp. II:** 19, 28–29, 34; **Supp. XIII:** 320

Hume, David, **I:** 125; **II:** 349, 357, 480; **III:** 618

Humes, Harold, **Supp. V:** 201; **Supp. XIV:** 82

Humes, Harry, **Supp. XIX:** 281

Humes, H. L. "Doc", **Supp. XI:** 294

"Humility" (Hoffman), **Supp. XVIII:** 86

Hummer, T. R., **Supp. XIX:** 278; **Supp. XXI:** 91

"Hummingbirds, The" (Welty), **IV:** 273

Humphrey, William, **Supp. IX:** 93–112; **Supp. XV:** 353

Humphreys, Christmas, **Supp. V:** 267

Humphreys, David, **Supp. II Part 1:** 65, 69, 70, 268

Humphreys, Josephine, **Supp. XII:** 311

Humphries, Rolfe, **III:** 124; **Retro. Supp. I:** 137

Hunchback of Notre Dame, The (film), **Supp. IV Part 1:** 101

Hunches in Bunches (Geisel), **Supp. XVI:** 111

Huncke, Herbert, **Supp. XII:** 118; **Supp. XIV:** 137–153

Huncke's Journal (Huncke), **Supp. XIV:** 139, 144, 145, 146

Hundred Camels in the Courtyard, A (Bowles), **Supp. IV Part 1:** 90

"Hundred Collars, A" (Frost), **Retro. Supp. I:** 128; **Supp. XIII:** 147

Hundred Secret Senses, The (Tan), **Supp. X:** 289, 293, 295, 297, 298, 299

Hundreds of Hens and Other Poems for Children by Halfdan Rasmussen (Nelson and Espeland, trans.), **Supp. XVIII:** 180

Hundred White Daffodils, A: Essays, Interviews, Newspaper Columns, and One Poem (Kenyon), **Supp. VII:** 160–162, 165, 166, 167, 174

Huneker, James, **III:** 102

Hunger (Hamsun), **Supp. XI:** 167

"Hunger" (Hogan), **Supp. IV Part 1:** 411

"Hunger . . ." (Rich), **Supp. I Part 2:** 571

"Hungerfield" (Jeffers), **Supp. II Part 2:** 416–417, 436

Hungerfield and Other Poems (Jeffers), **Supp. II Part 2:** 422

Hunger of Memory: The Education of Richard Rodriguez (Rodriguez), **Supp. XIV:** 297, 298, **298–302,** 310

Hungry Ghosts, The (Oates), **Supp. II Part 2:** 504, 510

Hungry Hearts (Prose), **Supp. XVI:** 253

Hunnewell, Susannah, **Supp. VIII:** 83

Hunt, Harriot K., **Retro. Supp. II:** 146

Hunt, Leigh, **II:** 515–516; **Supp. XV:** 175

Hunt, Richard Morris, **IV:** 312

Hunt, Robert, **Supp. XV:** 42, 49, 52

Hunt, William, **II:** 343

"Hunter" (Bierds), **Supp. XVII:** 30

Hunter, Dianna, **Supp. XVI:** 38

Hunter, Dr. Joseph, **II:** 217

Hunter, J. Paul, **Supp. IV Part 1:** 332

Hunter, Kim, **Supp. I Part 1:** 286

"Hunter of Doves" (Herbst), **Retro. Supp. II:** 325

"Hunter of the West, The" (Bryant), **Supp. I Part 1:** 155

Hunters, The (film), **Supp. IX:** 250

Hunters, The (Salter), **Supp. IX:** 246, **249–250**

Hunters and Gatherers (Prose), **Supp. XVI:** 257

"Hunters in the Snow" (Brueghel), **I:** 174; **Retro. Supp. I:** 430

"Hunters in the Snow" (Wolff), **Supp. VII:** 339–340

"Hunter's Moon—Eating the Bear" (Oliver), **Supp. VII:** 234

"Hunter's Vision, The" (Bryant), **Supp. I Part 1:** 160

Hunting for Hope: A Father's Journey (Sanders), **Supp. XVI:** 276–277, 278

"Hunting Is Not Those Heads on the Wall" (Baraka), **Supp. II Part 1:** 45

Huntington, Collis P., **I:** 198, 207

"Hunt in the Black Forest, The" (Jarrell), **II:** 379–380

Huntley, Jobe, **Supp. I Part 1:** 339

"Hurrah, Hurrah" (Nelson), **Supp. XVIII:** 175

Hurray Home (Wideman), **Supp. X:** 320

Hurricane (radio play, Boyce), **Supp. XXI:** 13

"Hurricane, The" (Crane), **I:** 401

"Hurricane, The" (Freneau), **Supp. II Part 1:** 262

"Hurry Kane" (Lardner), **II:** 425, 426, 427

"Hurry up Please It's Time" (Sexton), **Supp. II Part 2:** 694, 695

Hurst, Fannie, **Supp. XVIII:** 278, 279

Hurston, Zora Neale, **Retro. Supp. I:** 194, 198, 200, 201, 203; **Supp. I Part 1:** 325, 326, 332; **Supp. II Part 1:** 33; **Supp. IV Part 1:** 5, 11, 12, 164, 257; **Supp. VI:** 149–161; **Supp. VIII:** 214; **Supp. X:** 131, 139, 232, 242; **Supp. XI:** 85; **Supp. XIII:** 185, 233, 236, 295, 306; **Supp. XVIII:** 122, 279, 280, 282; **Supp. XIX:** 72, 75; **Supp. XX:** 107

Hurt, John, **Supp. XIII:** 132

Husbands and Wives (film; Allen), **Supp. XV:** 12

"Husband's Song, The" (Di Piero), **Supp. XIX:** 39

Husband's Story, The (Shields), **Supp. VII:** 316. *See also* "Happenstance" (Shields)

Husserl, Edmund, **II:** 362, 363; **IV:** 491; **Supp. IV Part 1:** 42, 43

Hussey, Jo Ella, **Supp. XII:** 201

Hustler, The (film), **Supp. XI:** 306

Huston, John, **I:** 30, 31, 33, 35; **II:** 588; **III:** 161; **Supp. IV Part 1:** 102, 116, 355; **Supp. XI:** 307; **Supp. XIII:** 174

"Huswifery" (Taylor), **IV:** 161; **Supp. I Part 2:** 386

"Hut, The" (Sobin), **Supp. XVI:** 284–285

Hutchens, John K., **Supp. IX:** 276

Hutcheson, Francis, **I:** 559

Hutchins, Patricia, **III:** 478

Hutchinson, Abigail, **I:** 562

Hutchinson, Anne, **Supp. I Part 1:** 100, 101, 113; **Supp. IV Part 2:** 434; **Supp. VIII:** 202, 205

Hutchinson, George, **Supp. XVIII:** 119–120, 121, 132

Hutchinson, Thomas, **Supp. XX:** 282

Hutton, James, **Supp. IX:** 180

Huwayyik, Yusuf, **Supp. XX:** 115

Huxley, Aldous, **II:** 454; **III:** 281, 428, 429–430; **IV:** 77, 435; **Supp. I Part 2:** 714; **Supp. XIV:** 3, 164; **Supp. XVI:** 189, 192; **Supp. XVIII:** 137

Huxley, Julian, **Supp. VIII:** 251; **Supp. X:** 108

Huxley, Juliette, **Supp. VIII:** 251, 265

Huxley, Thomas, **III:** 102, 108, 113, 281; **Retro. Supp. II:** 60, 65, 93

Huxley, Thomas Henry, **Supp. I Part 1:** 368

Huysmans, Joris Karl (Charles Marie Georges), **I:** 66; **III:** 315; **IV:** 286; **Retro. Supp. II:** 326; **Supp. XX:** 239

"Hwame, Koshkalaka, and the Rest: Lesbians in American Indian Cultures" (Gunn Allen), **Supp. IV Part 1:** 330

Hwang, David Henry, **Supp. X:** 292; **Supp. XXI:** 143–157

"Hyacinth Drift" (Rawlings), **Supp. X:** 226–227

Hyde, Lewis, **Supp. XVIII:** 150

"Hydrangeas" (C. Frost), **Supp. XV:** 106

"Hydras, The" (Merwin), **Supp. III Part 1:** 349

Hydriotaphia, The; or, Death of Dr. Browne: An Epic Farce about Death and Primitive Capital Accumulation (Kushner), **Supp. IX:** 133, **136–138**

"Hydriotaphia; or, Urne-Buriall" (Browne), **Supp. IX:** 136–137

Hyman, Stanley Edgar, **I:** 129, 264, 363, 377, 379; **Retro. Supp. II:** 118; **Supp. IX:** 113, 114, 117, 118, 121, 122, 128

Hymen (Doolittle), **Supp. I Part 1:** 266

"Hymie's Bull" (Ellison), **Retro. Supp. II:** 124; **Supp. II Part 1:** 229

"Hymn Books" (Emerson), **II:** 10

"HYMN FOR LANIE POO" (Baraka), **Supp. II Part 1:** 31, 37

"Hymn from a Watermelon Pavilion" (Stevens), **IV:** 81

"Hymn of the Sea, A" (Bryant), **Supp. I Part 1:** 157, 163, 165

"Hymns of the Marshes" (Lanier), **Supp. I Part 1:** 364

"Hymn to Death" (Bryant), **Supp. I Part 1:** 169, 170

"Hymn to Earth" (Wylie), **Supp. I Part 2:** 727–729

"Hymn to the Night" (Longfellow), **Supp. I Part 2:** 409

Hynes, Jennifer, **Supp. XV:** 207

Hynes, Samuel, **Supp. XIV:** 159

Hyperion (Longfellow), **II:** 488, 489, 491–492, 496; **Retro. Supp. II:** 58, 155–156

"Hypocrite Auteur" (MacLeish), **III:** 19

"Hypocrite Swift" (Bogan), **Supp. III Part 1:** 55

"Hysteria" (Eliot), **I:** 570

I

I (Dixon), **Supp. XII:** 141, 155, **156–157**

I, etcetera (Sontag), **Supp. III Part 2:** 451–452, 469

I, Governor of California and How I Ended Poverty (Sinclair), **Supp. V:** 289

I, the Jury (Spillane), **Supp. XVIII:** 236

"I, Too" (Hughes), **Retro. Supp. I:** 193, 199; **Supp. I Part 1:** 320

I Accuse! (film), **Supp. IV Part 2:** 683

"I Almost Remember" (Angelou), **Supp. IV Part 1:** 15

"'I Always Wanted You to Admire My Fasting'; or, Looking at Kafka"(P. Roth), **Retro. Supp. II:** 282

I am a Camera (Druten), **Supp. XIV:** 162

"I am a cowboy in the boat of Ra" (Reed), **Supp. X:** 242

"I Am a Dangerous Woman" (Harjo), **Supp. XII:** 216, 219

"I Am Alive" (Momaday), **Supp. IV Part 2:** 489

I Am a Sonnet (Goldbarth), **Supp. XII:** 181

"I Am a Writer of Truth" (Fante), **Supp. XI:** 167

"If We Had Known" (Francis), **Supp. IX:** 78

"If We Must Die" (McKay), **Supp. IV Part 1:** 3; **Supp. X:** 132, 134

"If We Take All Gold" (Bogan), **Supp. III Part 1:** 52

If You Call This a Cry Song (Carruth), **Supp. XVI:** 56

If You Want to Write (Ueland), **Supp. XVII:** 13

I Gaspiri (Lardner), **II:** 435

"I Gather the Limbs of Osiris" (Pound), **Retro. Supp. I:** 287

I Get on the Bus (McKnight), **Supp. XX:**148–150, 152

"I Give You Back" (Harjo), **Supp. XII:** 223

Ignatius of Loyola, **IV:** 151; **Supp. XI:** 162

Ignatow, David, **Supp. XIII:** 275

"Ignis Fatuus" (Tate), **IV:** 128

"Ignorant Lust after Knowledge, The" (Bronk), **Supp. XXI:** 31

"I Go Back to May 1937" (Olds), **Supp. X:** 207

I Go Dreaming Serenades (Salinas), **Supp. XIII:** 316

I Got the Blues (Odets), **Supp. II Part 2:** 530

Iguana Killer, The (Ríos), **Supp. IV Part 2:** 542–544

"I Had Eight Birds Hatcht in One Nest" (Bradstreet), **Supp. I Part 1:** 102, 115, 117, 119

"I had no time to Hate" (Dickinson), **Retro. Supp. I:** 44–45, 46

I Had Trouble in Getting to Solla Sollew (Geisel), **Supp. XVI:** 108, 109

"I Have a Rendezvous with Life" (Cullen), **Supp. IV Part 1:** 168

"I Have Increased Power" (Ginsberg), **Supp. II Part 1:** 313

"I Have Seen Black Hands" (Wright), **Supp. II Part 1:** 228

"I Hear an Army" (Joyce), **Supp. I Part 1:** 262

"I heard a Fly buzz when I died" (Dickinson), **Retro. Supp. I:** 38

"I Heard Immanuel Singing" (Lindsay), **Supp. I Part 2:** 379

I Heard It Through the Grapevine (Turner), **Supp. XX:**110

"I Hear It Was Charged against Me" (Whitman), **IV:** 343

"I Held a Shelley Manuscript" (Corso), **Supp. XII:** 128

"I Held His Name" (Ríos), **Supp. IV Part 2:** 547

"Ike and Nina" (Boyle), **Supp. XX:**19

I Knew a Phoenix (Sarton), **Supp. VIII:** 249, 251–252

"I Know a Man" (Creeley), **Supp. IV Part 1:** 147–148, 149

I Know Some Things: Stories about Childhood by Contemporary Writers (Moore, ed.), **Supp. X:** 175

"I Know Why the Caged Bird Cannot Read" (Prose), **Supp. XVI:** 259

I Know Why the Caged Bird Sings (Angelou), **Supp. IV Part 1:** 2–4, 5, 7, 11, 12, 13, 14, 15, 17; **Supp. XVI:** 259

"Ikon: The Harrowing of Hell" (Levertov), **Supp. III Part 1:** 284

Ile (O'Neill), **III:** 388

"I Led Three Lives" (television program), **Supp. XX:**195

"I Let Him Take Me" (Cisneros), **Supp. VII:** 71

Iliad (Bryant, trans.), **Supp. I Part 1:** 158

Iliad (Homer), **II:** 470; **Supp. IV Part 2:** 631; **Supp. IX:** 211; **Supp. X:** 114; **Supp. XVII:** 117; **Supp. XXI:** 36

Iliad (Pope, trans.), **Supp. I Part 1:** 152

"I like to see it lap the Miles" (Dickinson), **Retro. Supp. I:** 37

"I Live Up Here" (Merwin), **Supp. III Part 1:** 349

"I'll Be Doing More of Same" (Franzen), **Supp. XX:**89

"Illegal Alien" (Mora), **Supp. XIII:** 215

"Illegal Days, The" (Paley), **Supp. VI:** 222

"Illegibility" (F. Wright), **Supp. XVII:** 244

Illig, Joyce, **Retro. Supp. II:** 20

"Illinois" (Masters), **Supp. I Part 2:** 458

"Illinois Bus Ride" (Leopold), **Supp. XIV:** 189

Illinois Poems (Masters), **Supp. I Part 2:** 472

"Illinois Village, The" (Lindsay), **Supp. I Part 2:** 381

"Ill-Lit" (F. Wright), **Supp. XVII:** 245

Ill-Lit: Selected & New Poems (F. Wright), **Supp. XVII:** 245

Illness as Metaphor (Sontag), **Supp. III Part 2:** 452, 461, 466

I'll Take My Stand ("Twelve Southerners"), **II:** 196; **III:** 496; **IV:** 125, 237; **Supp. X:** 25, 52–53; **Supp. XIV:** 3

"I'll Take You to Tennessee" (Connell), **Supp. XIV:** 82

Illumination (Frederic), **II:** 141

Illumination Night (Hoffman), **Supp. X:** 85, **86,** 88, 89

Illuminations (Rimbaud), **Supp. XXI:** 233

Illusion comique, L' (Corneille), Supp. IX: 138

"Illusion of Eternity, The" (Eberhart), **I:** 541

"Illusion of Fiction in Frank Conroy's *Stop-Time,* The" (R. Ramsey), **Supp. XVI:** 69

Illusions (Dash; film), **Supp. XI:** 20

"Illusions" (Emerson), **II:** 2, 5, 14, 16

Illustrated Man, The (Bradbury), **Supp. IV Part 1:** 102, 103, 113

Illustrations of China and Its People (Thompson), **Supp. XXI:** 151

Illustrations of Political Economy (Martineau), **Supp. II Part 1:** 288

"I Look at My Hand" (Swenson), **Supp. IV Part 2:** 638, 647

I Love Gootie: My Grandmother's Story (Apple), **Supp. XVII:** 9–10

I Love Myself When I Am Laughing . . . : A Zora Neale Hurston Reader (Walker), **Supp. III Part 2:** 531, 532

"I'm a Fool" (Anderson), **I:** 113, 114, 116; **Supp. I Part 2:** 430

Image and Idea (Rahv), **Supp. II Part 1:** 146

Image and the Law, The (Nemerov), **III:** 268, 269–271, 272

"Image in the Mirror, The" (Swados), **Supp. XIX:** 265

"Images" (Hass), **Supp. VI:** 103

"Images and 'Images' " (Simic), **Supp. VIII:** 274

"Images for Godard" (Rich), **Supp. I Part 2:** 558

"Images of Walt Whitman" (Fiedler), **IV:** 352

"Imaginary Dialogue, An" (Espaillat), **Supp. XXI:** 103

"Imaginary Friendships of Tom McGrath, The" (Cohen), **Supp. X:** 112

"Imaginary Iceberg, The" (Bishop), **Retro. Supp. II:** 42; **Supp. I Part 1:** 86, 88

"Imaginary Jew, The" (Berryman), **I:** 174–175

Imaginary Letters (Pound), **III:** 473–474

Imaginary Paintings (C. Baxter), **Supp. XVII:** 18–19

"Imaginary Prisons" (Schnackenberg), **Supp. XV:** 257, 258

Imagination and Fancy; or, Selections from the English Poets, illustrative of those first requisites of their art; with markings of the best passages, critical notices of the writers, and an essay in answer to the question'What is Poetry?' (Hunt), II: 515–516

"Imagination as Value" (Stevens), **Retro. Supp. I:** 298

"Imagination of Disaster, The" (Gordon), **Supp. IV Part 1:** 306

Imaginative Qualities of Actual Things (Sorrentino), **Supp. XXI:** 226, 230, 231–232, 234

"Imagine a Day at the End of Your Life" (Beattie), **Supp. V:** 33

Imagined London: A Tour of the World's Greatest Fictional City (Quindlen), **Supp. XVII:** 167, 180

"Imagine Kissing Pete" (O'Hara), **III:** 372; **Supp. VIII:** 156

Imaging Robert: My Brother, Madness, and Survival (Neugeboren), **Supp. XVI:** 225, **226–229**

"Imagining How It Would Be to Be Dead" (Eberhart), **I:** 533

Imagining Los Angeles: A City in Fiction (Fine), **Supp. XI:** 160

"Imagining Their Own Hymns" (B. Kelly), **Supp. XVII:** 126–127

"Imagining the Midwest" (Sanders), **Supp. XVI:** 275–276

Imagining the Worst: Stephen King and the Representations of Women (Lant and Thompson), **Supp. V:** 141

"Imagisme" (Pound), **Retro. Supp. I:** 288

Imagistes, Des: An Anthology of the Imagists (Pound, ed.), **III:** 465, 471; **Retro. Supp. I:** 288

Imago (O. Butler), **Supp. XIII:** 63, **65–66**

"Imago" (Stevens), **IV:** 74, 89

Imagoes (Coleman), **Supp. XI:** 89–90

I Married a Communist (P. Roth), **Retro. Supp. II:** 289, 293–294

I Married an Angel (film), **Supp. XVI:** 193

"I May, I Might, I Must" (Moore), **III:** 215

"I'm Crazy" (Salinger), **III:** 553

"I'm Here" (Roethke), **III:** 547

Imitations (Lowell), **II:** 543, 544–545, 550, 555; **Retro. Supp. II:** 181, 187

"Imitations of Drowning" (Sexton), **Supp. II Part 2:** 684, 686

"Immaculate Man" (Gordon), **Supp. IV Part 1:** 311

"Immanence of Dostoevsky, The" (Bourne), **I:** 235

"Immigrants" (Mora), **Supp. XIII:** 216

Immigrant Saint: The Life of Mother Cabrini (di Donato), **Supp. XX:44**

"Immigrant Story, The" (Paley), **Supp. VI:** 230

Immobile Wind, The (Winters), **Supp. II Part 2:** 786

"Immobile Wind, The" (Winters), **Supp. II Part 2:** 788, 811

"Immolatus" (Komunyakaa), **Supp. XIII:** 126

"Immoral Proposition, The" (Creeley), **Supp. IV Part 1:** 144

"Immortal Autumn" (MacLeish), **III:** 13

"Immortality Ode" (Nemerov), **III:** 87

Immortality Ode (Wordsworth), **II:** 17; **Supp. I Part 2:** 673

"Immortal Woman, The" (Tate), **IV:** 130, 131, 137

"I'm Not Ready to Die Yet" (Harjo), **Supp. XII:** 231

I'm Not There (film, Haynes), **Supp. XVIII:** 23

"I'm on My Way" (Salinas), **Supp. XIII:** 320

"Impasse" (Hughes), **Supp. I Part 1:** 343

Imperative Duty, An, a Novel (Howells), **II:** 286

Imperial Eyes: Travel Writing and Transculturation (Pratt), **Retro. Supp. II:** 48

Imperial Germany and the Industrial Revolution (Veblen), **Supp. I Part 2:** 642, 643

Imperial Way, The: By Rail from Peshawar to Chittagong (Theroux), **Supp. VIII:** 323

"Implosions" (Rich), **Supp. I Part 2:** 556

"Imp of the Perverse, The" (Poe), **III:** 414–415; **Retro. Supp. II:** 267

Impolite Interviews, **Supp. XI:** 293

"Importance of Artists' Biographies, The" (Goldbarth), **Supp. XII:** 183, 184, 191

Importance of Being Earnest, The (Wilde), **Supp. XIV:** 324, 339

"Important Houses, The" (Gordon), **Supp. IV Part 1:** 315

"Impossible Indispensability of the Ars Poetica, The" (Carruth), **Supp. XVI:** 57

"Impossible to Tell" (Pinsky), **Supp. VI:** 247, 248

"Imposter, The" (West), **Retro. Supp. II:** 322, 327

"Impressionism and Symbolism in *Heart of Darkness*" (Watt), **Supp. VIII:** 4

"Impressions of a European Tour" (Bourne), **I:** 225

"Impressions of a Plumber" (H. Roth), **Supp. IX:** 228, 234

"Impressions of Europe, 1913–1914" (Bourne), **I:** 225

"I'm Walking behind the Spanish" (Salinas), **Supp. XIII:** 323–324

"I/Myself" (Shields), **Supp. VII:** 311

"In Absence" (Lanier), **Supp. I Part 1:** 364

"In Absentia" (Bowles), **Supp. IV Part 1:** 94

"In a Cab" (Untermeyer), **Supp. XV:** 296

"In a Country Cemetery" (Kooser), **Supp. XIX:** 120

Inada, Lawson Fusao, **Supp. V:** 180

"In a Dark Room, Furniture" (Nye), **Supp. XIII:** 274

"In a Dark Time" (Roethke), **III:** 539, 547, 548

"In a Disused Graveyard" (Frost), **Retro. Supp. I:** 126, 133

In a Dusty Light (Haines), **Supp. XII:** 207

"In a Garden" (Lowell), **II:** 513

"In a Hard Intellectual Light" (Eberhart), **I:** 523

"In a Hollow of the Hills" (Harte), **Supp. II Part 1:** 354

In America (Sontag), **Supp. XIV:** 95–96

"In Amicitia" (Ransom), **IV:** 141

In a Narrow Grave: Essays on Texas (McMurtry), **Supp. V:** 220, 223

"Inanna" (A. Finch), **Supp. XVII:** 72

"In Another Country" (Hemingway), **I:** 484–485; **II:** 249

In April Once (Percy), **Retro. Supp. I:** 341

"In a Prominent Bar in Secaucus One Day" (X. J. Kennedy), **Supp. XV:** 154, 155–156

In A Shallow Grave (Purdy), **Supp. VII:** 272

"In a Station of the Metro" (Pound), **Retro. Supp. I:** 288; **Supp. I Part 1:** 265; **Supp. XIV:** 284–285

"In a Strange Town" (Anderson), **I:** 114, 115

"In Athens Once" (Rodriguez), **Supp. XIV:** 303

"In a Tub" (Hempel), **Supp. XXI:** 119

In Battle for Peace: The Story of My 83rd Birthday (Du Bois), **Supp. II Part 1:** 185

In Bed One Night & Other Brief Encounters (Coover), **Supp. V:** 49, 50

"In Bertram's Garden" (Justice), **Supp. VII:** 117

"In Blackwater Woods" (Oliver), **Supp. VII:** 244, 246

In Black & Whitey (Lacy), **Supp. XV:** 206–207

"In Broad Daylight" (Jin), **Supp. XVIII:** 94

In Broken Country (Wagoner), **Supp. IX:** 330

"In California" (Simpson), **Supp. IX:** 271

"In Camp" (Stafford), **Supp. XI:** 329

"Incant against Suicide" (Karr), **Supp. XI:** 249

"In Celebration of My Uterus" (Sexton), **Supp. II Part 2:** 689

"Incendiary, The" (Rowson), **Supp. XV:** 234

"In Certain Places and Certain Times There Can Be More of You" (Dunn), **Supp. XI:** 144

Incest: From "A Journal of Love," the Unexpurgated Diary of Anaïs Nin, 1932–1934 (Nin), **Supp. X:** 182, 184, 185, 187, 191

"In Chandler Country" (Gioia), **Supp. XV:** 119

Inchbald, Elizabeth, **II:** 8

"In Cheever Country" (Gioia), **Supp. XV:** 119

Inchiquin, the Jesuit's Letters (Ingersoll), **I:** 344

"Incident" (Cullen), **Supp. IV Part 1:** 165, 166

Incidental Numbers (Wylie), **Supp. I Part 2:** 708

Incidentals (Sandburg), **III:** 579

Incident at Vichy (A. Miller), **III:** 165, 166

Incidents in the Life of a Slave Girl (Brent), **Supp. IV Part 1:** 13

Incidents in the Life of a Slavegirl (Jacobs), **Supp. XVI:** 85

"Incipience" (Rich), **Supp. I Part 2:** 559

"In Clare" (McCarriston), **Supp. XIV:** 270–271

Including Horace (Untermeyer), **Supp. XV:** 301, 303–304

In Cold Blood: A True Account of a Multiple Murder and Its Consequences (Capote), **Retro. Supp. II:** 107–108; **Supp. I Part 1:** 292; **Supp. III Part 1:** 111, 117, 119, 122, 123, 125–131; **Supp. III Part 2:** 574; **Supp. IV Part 1:** 220; **Supp. XIV:** 162

In Cold Hell, in Thicket (Olson), **Supp. II Part 2:** 571

"In Cold Hell, in Thicket" (Olson), **Supp. II Part 2:** 558, 563–564, 566, 572, 580

"Incomparable Light, The" (Eberhart), **I:** 541

Incorporative Consciousness of Robert Bly, The (Harris), **Supp. IV Part 1:** 68

In Country (Mason), **Supp. VIII:** 133, **142–143,** 146

"In Country of Conscience" (J. W. Miller), **Supp. XX:165**

"Incredible Survival of Coyote, The" (Snyder), **Supp. VIII:** 297

"Increment" (Ammons), **Supp. VII:** 28

In Defense of Ignorance (Shapiro), **Supp. II Part 2:** 703, 704, 713–714

In Defense of Reason (Winters), **Supp. I Part 1:** 268

In Defense of Women (Mencken), **III:** 109

Independence Day (film), **Supp. X:** 80

Independence Day (Ford), **Supp. V:** 57, 62–63, 67–68

"Independent Candidate, The, a Story of Today" (Howells), **II:** 277

"Indestructible Mr. Gore, The" (Vidal), **Supp. IV Part 2:** 679

Index of American Design, **Supp. III Part 2:** 618

"India" (Rodriguez), **Supp. XIV:** 302

"Indian at the Burial-Place of His Fathers, An" (Bryant), **Supp. I Part 1:** 155–156, 167–168

"Indian Burying Ground, The" (Freneau), **Supp. II Part 1:** 264, 266

"Indian Camp" (Hemingway), **II:** 247–248, 263; **Retro. Supp. I:** 174–175, 176, 177, 181; **Supp. XVI:** 208

Indian Country (Caputo), **Supp. XIX:** 22–25

Indian Country (Matthiessen), **Supp. V:** 211

"Indian Country" (McCarriston), **Supp. XIV:** 271

"Indian Country" (Simpson), **Supp. IX:** 274

Indian Earth (Bynner), **Supp. XV:** 46

"Indian Girls" (McCarriston), **Supp. XIV:** 272–273

"Indian Manifesto" (Deloria), **Supp. IV Part 1:** 323

"Indian Names" (Sigourney), **Retro. Supp. II:** 47

"Indian Student, The" (Freneau), **Supp. II Part 1:** 264

"Indian Student, The" (Simpson), **Supp. IX:** 280

Indian Summer (Howells), **II:** 275, 279–281, 282

Indian Summer (Knowles), **Supp. XII:** 249, 250

Indian Summer: Musings on the Gift of Life (Pickering), **Supp. XXI:** 204

"Indian Uprising, The" (Barthelme), **Supp. IV Part 1:** 44

Indifferent Children, The (Auchincloss), **Supp. IV Part 1:** 25

Indirections (Cox), **Supp. XXI:** 21

Indiscretions (Pound), **Retro. Supp. I:** 284

"Indispensability of the Eyes, The" (Olds), **Supp. X:** 202

"In Distrust of Merits" (Moore), **III:** 201, 214

"Individual and the State, The" (Emerson), **II:** 10

Individualism, Old and New (Dewey), **Supp. I Part 2:** 677

"Indolence" (Pickering), **Supp. XXI:** 203

In Dreams Begin Responsibilities (Schwartz), **Supp. II Part 2:** 642, 645–650

"In Dreams Begin Responsibilities" (Schwartz), **Supp. II Part 2:** 641, 649, 654

In Dubious Battle (Steinbeck), **IV:** 51, 55–56, 59, 63

"In Durance" (Pound), **Retro. Supp. I:** 285

"Industry of Hard Kissing, The" (Ríos), **Supp. IV Part 2:** 547

"In Duty Bound" (Gilman), **Supp. XI:** 196–197

"I Need, I Need" (Roethke), **III:** 535–536

"I Need Help" (Stern), **Supp. IX:** 290

"Inés in the Kitchen" (García), **Supp. XI:** 190

"I never saw a Moor" (Dickinson), **Retro. Supp. I:** 37

I Never Told Anybody: Teaching Poetry Writing in a Nursing Home (Koch), **Supp. XV:** 190

"I Never Will Be Married, I'd Rather Be Excus'd" (Rowson), **Supp. XV:** 240

Inevitable Exiles (Kielsky), **Supp. V:** 273

"Inevitable Trial, The" (Holmes), **Supp. I Part 1:** 318

"Inexhaustible Hat, The" (Wagoner), **Supp. IX:** 327

"In Extremis" (Berry), **Supp. X:** 23

"Infancy" (Wilder), **IV:** 375

"Infant Boy at Midcentury" (Warren), **IV:** 244–245, 252

Infante, Guillermo Cabrera, **Retro. Supp. I:** 278

"Infant Sea Turtles" (F. Wright), **Supp. XVII:** 245

Infants of the Spring (Thurman), **Supp. XVIII:** 281; **Supp. XIX:** 73

Inferno (Dante), **IV:** 139; **Supp. V:** 338; **Supp. VIII:** 219–221

Inferno of Dante, The (Pinsky), **Supp. VI:** 235, 248

"Infidelity" (Komunyakaa), **Supp. XIII:** 130

Infidels (album, Dylan), **Supp. XVIII:** 28

"Infiltration of the Universe" (MacLeish), **III:** 19

Infinite Jest: A Novel (Wallace), **Supp. X:** 301, **310–314; Supp. XX:**91

"Infinite Reason, The" (MacLeish), **III:** 19

"Infirmity" (Lowell), **II:** 554

"Infirmity" (Roethke), **III:** 548

In Five Years Time (Haines), **Supp. XII:** 206

"In Flower" (Snodgrass), **Supp. VI:** 325

"Influence of Landscape upon the Poet, The" (Eliot), **Retro. Supp. I:** 67

"In Football Season" (Updike), **IV:** 219

Informer, The (film), **Supp. III Part 2:** 619

Ingersoll, Charles J., **I:** 344

Ingersoll, Robert Green, **Supp. II Part 1:** 198

Ingraham, Lloyd, **Supp. XVI:** 184

Ingster, Boris, **Retro. Supp. II:** 330

Inhabitants, The (Morris), **III:** 221–222

"Inheritance and Invention in Li-Young Lee's Poetry" (Xiaojing), **Supp. XV:** 214

"Inheritance of Tools, The" (Sanders), **Supp. XVI:** 273

Inheritors (Glaspell), **Supp. III Part 1:** 175, 179–181, 186, 189

"In Honor of David Anderson Brooks, My Father" (Brooks), **Supp. III Part 1:** 79

"Inhumanist, The" (Jeffers), **Supp. II Part 2:** 423, 426

"In Illo Tempore" (Karr), **Supp. XI:** 242

"In Interims: Outlyer" (Harrison), **Supp. VIII:** 38

"Initial" (F. Wright), **Supp. XVII:** 243

"Injudicious Gardening" (Moore), **III:** 198

"Injustice" (Paley), **Supp. VI:** 220

Injustice Collectors, The (Auchincloss), **Supp. IV Part 1:** 25

Ink, Blood, Semen (Goldbarth), **Supp. XII:** 181, 183

Ink Truck, The (W. Kennedy), **Supp. VII:** 132, 133–138, 140, 141, 149, 152

In Life Sentences: Literary Essays (Epstein), **Supp. XIV:** 112

"In Limbo" (Wilbur), **Supp. III Part 2:** 544, 561

In Limestone Country (Sanders), **Supp. XVI:** 272

In Love and Trouble: Stories of Black Women (Walker), **Supp. III Part 2:** 520, 521, 530, 531, 532

In Mad Love and War (Harjo), **Supp. XII: 224–226**

"In Memoriam" (Emerson), **II:** 13

"In Memoriam" (Hay), **Supp. XIV:** 122, 127

"In Memoriam" (Tennyson), **Retro. Supp. I:** 325; **Supp. I Part 2:** 416

In Memoriam: 1933 (Reznikoff), **Supp. XIV:** 280, 285

In Memoriam to Identity (Acker), **Supp. XII:** 5, **16–18**

"In Memory of Arthur Winslow" (Lowell), **II:** 541, 547, 550; **Retro. Supp. II:** 187

"In Memory of Congresswoman Barbara Jordan" (Pinsky), **Supp. VI:** 250

"In Memory of Joe Brainard" (Bidart), **Supp. XV:** 33

"In Memory of My Feelings" (O'Hara), **Supp. XV:** 215–216

"In Memory of W. B. Yeats" (Auden), **Supp. VIII:** 19, 30; **Supp. XI:** 243, 244; **Supp. XIX:** 85

"In Memory of W. H. Auden" (Stern), **Supp. IX:** 288

"In Mercy on Broadway" (Doty), **Supp. XI:** 132

In Morocco (Wharton), **Retro. Supp. I:** 380; **Supp. IV Part 1:** 81

Inmost Leaf, The: A Selection of Essays (Kazin), **Supp. VIII:** 102, 103

In Motley (Bierce), **I:** 209

In My Father's Court (Singer), **IV:** 16–17; **Retro. Supp. II: 301–302**

"In My Life" (Dubus), **Supp. VII:** 81

"In Navaho Country" (Bronk), **Supp. XXI:** 30

Inner Circle, The (Boyle), **Supp. XX:**24, **26**

Inner Landscape (Sarton), **Supp. VIII:** 259

Inner Room, The (Merrill), **Supp. III Part 1:** 336

"In Nine Sleep Valley" (Merrill), **Supp. III Part 1:** 328

Innocents, The: A Story for Lovers (Lewis), **II:** 441

Innocents Abroad, The; or, The New Pilgrim's Progress (Twain), **II:** 275, 434; **IV:** 191, 196, 197–198

Innocents at Cedro, The: A Memoir of Thorstein Veblen and Some Others (Duffus), **Supp. I Part 2:** 650

"In Off the Cliffs of Moher" (McCarriston), **Supp. XIV:** 270

In Old Plantation Days (Dunbar), **Supp. II Part 1:** 214

In Ole Virginia (Page), **Supp. II Part 1:** 201

In Orbit (Morris), **III:** 236

In Other Words (Swenson), **Supp. IV Part 2:** 650–652

In Other Words: Literature by Latinas of the United States (Fernandez, ed.), **Supp. XXI:** 104

In Our Terribleness (Some elements and meaning in black style) (Baraka), **Supp. II Part 1:** 52, 53

In Our Time (Hemingway), **I:** 117; **II:** 68, 247, 252, 263; **IV:** 42; **Retro. Supp. I:** 170, 173, 174, 178, 180; **Supp. IX:** 106

"In Our Time" (Wolfe), **Supp. III Part 2:** 584

"Inpatient" (Kenyon), **Supp. VII:** 169

In Persuasion Nation (Saunders), **Supp. XIX:** 231–234

"In Persuasion Nation" (Saunders), **Supp. XIX:** 233–234

In Pharaoh's Army: Memories of the Lost War (Wolff), **Supp. VII:** 331–334, 335, 338

"In Plaster" (Plath), **Supp. I Part 2:** 540

"In Prague, in Montmartre" (Bierds), **Supp. XVII:** 27

"In Praise of Johnny Appleseed" (Lindsay), **Supp. I Part 2:** 397

"In Praise of Limestone" (Auden), **Supp. II Part 1:** 20–21; **Supp. VIII:** 23

In Pursuit of a Vanishing Star (Sobin), **Supp. XVI:** 294

In Quest of the Ordinary (Cavell), **Retro. Supp. I:** 307

Inquiry into the Moral and Religious Character of the American Government, An (H. Warner), **Supp. XVIII:** 259

Inquiry into the Nature of Peace, An (Veblen), **Supp. I Part 2:** 642

Inquisitor, The (Rowson), **Supp. XV:** 232, 238

In Radical Pursuit (Snodgrass), **Supp. VI:** 312, 316, 318

In Reckless Ecstasy (Sandburg), **III:** 579

In Recognition of William Gaddis (Kuehl and Moore), **Supp. IV Part 1:** 279

"In Retirement" (Malamud), **Supp. I Part 2:** 437

"In Retrospect" (Angelou), **Supp. IV Part 1:** 15

"In Right" (Wolfert), **Supp. XXI:** 263, 264, 272

"Inroads of Time, The" (D. West), **Supp. XVIII:** 286–287

In Russia (A. Miller), **III:** 165

"In Sabine" (Chopin), **Supp. I Part 1:** 213

"In School-Days" (Whittier), **Supp. I Part 2:** 699–700

"Inscription for the Entrance to a Wood" (Bryant), **Supp. I Part 1:** 154, 155, 161–162

Inscriptions, 1944–1956 (Reznikoff), **Supp. XIV:** 281

In Search of Bisco (Caldwell), **I:** 296

In Search of Nella Larsen: A Biography of the Color Line (Hutchinson), **Supp. XVIII:** 120

"In Search of Our Mothers' Gardens" (Walker), **Supp. III Part 2:** 520–532, 524, 525, 527, 529, 532–533, 535, 536; **Supp. IX:** 306; **Supp. XVIII:** 200, 283

"In Search of Thomas Merton" (Griffin), **Supp. VIII:** 208

"In Search of Yage" (Burroughs), **Supp. III Part 1:** 98

"Insect Life in Florida" (Hull), **Supp. XXI:** 133

"Insertion of Self into a Space of Borderless Possibilities, The" (Fjellestad), **Supp. XVI:** 150

"In Shadow" (Crane), **I:** 386

"In Sickness and in Health" (Auden), **Supp. II Part 1:** 15

"In Sickness and in Health" (Humphrey), **Supp. IX:** 94

Inside His Mind (A. Miller), **III:** 154

Inside Memory (Findley), **Supp. XX:** 51, 63

"Inside Norman Mailer" (Apple), **Supp. XVII:** 3, 4

"Insider Baseball" (Didion), **Supp. IV Part 1:** 211

Inside Sports magazine, **Supp. V:** 58, 61

"Insipid Profession of Jonathan Horneboom, The" (Lethem), **Supp. XVIII:** 149

"In So Many Dark Rooms" (Hogan), **Supp. IV Part 1:** 400

"Insomnia" (Bishop), **Supp. I Part 1:** 92

"Insomniac" (Plath), **Supp. I Part 2:** 539

"In Spain, Throwing Carnations" (P. N. Warren), **Supp. XX:** 272

"Inspiration for Greatness" (Caldwell), **I:** 291

"Instability of Race Types, The" (Boas), **Supp. XIV:** 209

"Installation #6" (Beattie), **Supp. V:** 33

Instinct of Workmanship and the State of the Industrial Arts, The (Veblen), **Supp. I Part 2:** 642

Instincts of the Herd in Peace and War, The (Trotter), **I:** 249

Institute (Calvin), **IV:** 158, 160

"Instruction Manual, The" (Ashbery), **Supp. III Part 1:** 6–7, 10, 12

"Instructions for the Afternoon" (Gioia), **Supp. XV:** 120

"Instruction to Myself" (Brooks), **Supp. III Part 1:** 87

Instrument, The (O'Hara), **III:** 362, 364

"In Such Times, Ties Must Bind" (Nye), **Supp. XIII:** 286

"Insurance and Social Change" (Stevens), **Retro. Supp. I:** 297

Insurgent Mexico (Reed), **I:** 476

In Suspect Terrain (McPhee), **Supp. III Part 1:** 309, 310

"In Tall Grass" (Sandburg), **III:** 585

"Integer Vitae" (Horace), **Supp. XV:** 304

Intellectual History, An (Senghor), **Supp. X:** 139

"Intellectual Pre-Eminence of Jews in Modern Europe, The" (Veblen), **Supp. I Part 2:** 643–644

Intellectual Things (Kunitz), **Supp. III Part 1:** 260, 262–264

Intellectual versus the City, The (White), **I:** 258

"In Temporary Pain" (Bynner), **Supp. XV:** 41–42

Intentions (Wilde), **Retro. Supp. I:** 56

"Interest in Life, An" (Paley), **Supp. VI:** 222, 224–225

Interest of Great Britain Considered, with Regard to Her Colonies and the Acquisition of Canada and Guadeloupe, The (Franklin), **II:** 119

Interior Landscapes (Vizenor), **Supp. IV Part 1:** 262

Interiors (film; Allen), **Supp. IV Part 1:** 205; **Supp. XV:** 1, 7, 10

Interlocking Lives (Koch), **Supp. XV:** 185

"Interlude" (A. Lowell), **Retro. Supp. II:** 46

Interlunar (Atwood), **Supp. XIII:** 35

"Intermezzo" (Schnackenberg), **Supp. XV:** 254

"In Terms of the Toenail: Fiction and the Figures of Life" (Gass), **Supp. VI:** 85

"International Episode, An" (James), **II:** 327

International Workers Order, **Retro. Supp. I:** 202

Interpretation of Christian Ethics, An (Niebuhr), **III:** 298–300, 301, 302

"Interpretation of Dreams, The" (Matthews), **Supp. IX:** 162–163

Interpretation of Music of the XVIIth and XVIIIth Centuries, The (Dolmetsch), **III:** 464

Interpretations and Forecasts: 1922–1972 (Mumford), **Supp. II Part 2:** 481

Interpretations of Poetry and Religion (Santayana), **III:** 611

Interpreter of Maladies (Lahiri), **Supp. XXI:** 175–176, **177–180**, 183

"Interpreter of Maladies" (Lahiri), **Supp. XXI:** 183, 184

Interpreters and Interpretations (Van Vechten), **Supp. II Part 2:** 729, 733–734

"Interrogate the Stones" (MacLeish), **III:** 9

Interrogations at Noon (Gioia), **Supp. XV:** 112, **125–127**, 128, 129

"Interrupted Conversation, An" (Van Vechten), **Supp. II Part 2:** 735

"Interrupted Elegy" (Peacock), **Supp. XIX:** 200

Intersect: Poems (Shields), **Supp. VII:** 310–311

Intersexes, The (Prime-Stevenson as Mayne), **Supp. XX:**235

Interstate (Dixon), **Supp. XII:** 140, 152–153, 153, 156

"Interview" (Hay), **Supp. XIV:** 132

"Interview, The" (Thurber), **Supp. I Part 2:** 616

"Interview With a Lemming" (Thurber), **Supp. I Part 2:** 603

"Interview with Peter Everwine, An" (Veinberg and Buckley), **Supp. XV:** 76–77

"Interview with the Crab" (Lethem), **Supp. XVIII:** 148

Interview with the Vampire (Rice), **Supp. VII:** 287, 288–291, 297–298, 303

"Interview with the Vampire" (Rice), **Supp. VII:** 288

Interzone (Burroughs), **Supp. IV Part 1:** 90

"In the Absence of Bliss" (Kumin), **Supp. IV Part 2:** 453

"In the Afternoon" (Dunn), **Supp. XI:** 146

"In the Alley" (Elkin), **Supp. VI: 46–47**

In the American Grain (W. C. Williams), **Retro. Supp. I:** 420–421

In the American Jungle (W. Frank), **Supp. XX:**76

In the American Tree (Silliman), **Supp. IV Part 2:** 426

In the Bank of Beautiful Sins (Wrigley), **Supp. XVIII: 300–302**

In the Bar of a Tokyo Hotel (T. Williams), **IV:** 382, 386, 387, 391, 393

In the Beauty of the Lilies (Updike), **Retro. Supp. I:** 322, 325, 326, 327, 333

"In the Beeyard" (Bierds), **Supp. XVII:** 29

"In the Beginning" (Quindlen), **Supp. XVII:** 166

"In the Beginning . . ." (Simic), **Supp. VIII:** 270, 271

In the Belly of the Beast: Letters from Prison (Abbott), **Retro. Supp. II:** 210

"In the Black Morning" (Wolfert), **Supp. XXI:** 265

"In the Black Museum" (Nemerov), **III:** 275

"In the Bodies of Words" (Swenson), **Supp. IV Part 2:** 651

"In the Cage" (Gass), **Supp. VI:** 85

In the Cage (James), **Retro. Supp. I:** 229

"In the Cage" (James), **II:** 332; **Retro. Supp. I:** 231

"In the Cage" (Lowell), **Retro. Supp. II:** 187

"In the Cave at Lone Tree Meadow" (Haines), **Supp. XII:** 212

"In the Cemetery Where Al Jolson Is Buried" (Hempel), **Supp. XXI:** 115, **121–122**

"In the City Ringed with Giants" (Kingsolver), **Supp. VII:** 209

"In the Clearing" (Brodsky), **Supp. VIII:** 32

In the Clearing (Frost), **II:** 153, 155, 164; **Retro. Supp. I:** 121, 122, 141

"In the Closet of the Soul" (Walker), **Supp. III Part 2:** 526

"In the Cold Air Register" (W. V. Davis), **Supp. XXI:** 94

"In the Confidence of a Story-Writer" (Chopin), **Retro. Supp. II:** 66–67; **Supp. I Part 1:** 217

In the Country of Last Things (Auster), **Supp. XII:** 23, **29–30,** 31, 32

"In the Courtyard of the Isleta Missions" (R. Bly), **Supp. IV Part 1:** 71

"In the Dark" (Levine), **Supp. V:** 194

"In the Dark New England Days" (Jewett), **Retro. Supp. II:** 139

"In the Days of Prismatic Colour" (Moore), **III:** 205, 213

In the Days of the Comet (Wells), **Supp. XX:**233, 240

In the Electric Mist with Confederate Dead (Burke), **Supp. XIV:** 30, 31–32

"In the Field" (Wilbur), **Supp. III Part 2:** 558

"In the First Stanza" (C. Kizer), **Supp. XVII:** 75

"In the Fleeting Hand of Time" (Corso), **Supp. XII:** 122–123

"In the Footsteps of Gutenberg" (Mencken), **III:** 101

"In the Forest" (Simpson), **Supp. IX:** 270

"In the Forest of the Laughing Elephant" (Caputo), **Supp. XIX:** 27

"In the Forties" (Lowell), **II:** 554

In the Garden of the North American Martyrs (Wolff), **Supp. VII:** 341–342

In the Garret (Van Vechten), **Supp. II Part 2:** 735

"In the Grove: The Poet at Ten" (Kenyon), **Supp. VII:** 160

"In the Hall of Mirrors" (Merrill), **Supp. III Part 1:** 322

In the Harbor (Longfellow), **II:** 491

In the Heart of the Heart of the Country (Gass), **Supp. VI: 82–83,** 84, 85, 93

In the Heat of the Night (Ball), **Supp. XV:** 202

In the Heat of the Night (film), **Supp. I Part 1:** 67

In the Hollow of His Hand (Purdy), **Supp. VII:** 278–280

In the House of Light (Everwine, trans.), **Supp. XV:** 73, 75, **76–78,** 82

In the Lake of the Woods (O'Brien), **Supp. V:** 240, 243, 250–252

In the Land of the White Death: A Epic Story of Survival in the Siberian Arctic (Albanov), **Supp. XVIII:** 114

"In the Last Days" (Everwine), **Supp. XV:** 88, 89

In the Loyal Mountains (Bass), **Supp. XVI: 19–20**

"In the Loyal Mountains" (Bass), **Supp. XVI:** 20

In the Mecca (Brooks), **Supp. III Part 1:** 74

"In the Mecca" (Brooks), **Supp. III Part 1:** 70, 83–84

In the Midst of Life (Bierce), **I:** 200–203, 204, 206, 208, 212

"In the Miro District" (Taylor), **Supp. V:** 323

In the Miro District and Other Stories (Taylor), **Supp. V:** 325–326

In the Money (W. C. Williams), **Retro. Supp. I:** 423

"In the Motel" (X. J. Kennedy), **Supp. XV:** 163

"In the Naked Bed, in Plato's Cave" (Schwartz), **Supp. II Part 2:** 646–649

In the Name of the Neither (Sobin), **Supp. XVI:** 291

"In the Night" (Kincaid), **Supp. VII:** 183

In the Night Season: A Novel (Bausch), **Supp. VII:** 52–53

"In the Old Neighborhood" (Dove), **Supp. IV Part 1:** 241, 257

"In the Old World" (Oates), **Supp. II Part 2:** 503, 504

"In the Park" (Huncke), **Supp. XIV:** 139

"In the Pit" (Proulx), **Supp. VII:** 255, 261

In the Pond (Jin), **Supp. XVIII: 95–96**

In the Presence of the Sun (Momaday), **Supp. IV Part 2:** 489, 490, 491–493, 493

"In the Quiet Night" (Li Po), **Supp. XV:** 47

"In the Realm of the Fisher King" (Didion), **Supp. IV Part 1:** 211

"In the Red Room" (Bowles), **Supp. IV Part 1:** 93

"In the Region of Ice" (Oates), **Supp. II Part 2:** 520

In the Room We Share (Simpson), **Supp. IX:** 279

"In These Dissenting Times" (Walker), **Supp. III Part 2:** 522

"In the Shadow of Gabriel, A.D.1550" (Frederic), **II:** 139

In the Shadow of Memory (Skloot), **Supp. XX:**193, 196, 205, **205–206**

"In the Shadow of Memory" (Skloot), **Supp. XX:**206

In the Shadow of the Morning: Essays on Wild Lands, Wild Waters, and a Few Untamed People (Caputo), **Supp. XIX:** 28–29

In the Spirit of Crazy Horse (Matthiessen), **Supp. V:** 211

"In the Subway" (Untermeyer), **Supp. XV:** 296

In the Summer House (Jane Bowles), **Supp. IV Part 1:** 83, 89

In the Tennessee Country (Taylor), **Supp. V:** 328

"In the Thick of Darkness" (Salinas), **Supp. XIII:** 325

"In the Time of the Blossoms" (Mervin), **Supp. III Part 1:** 352

In the Time of the Butterflies (Alvarez), **Supp. VII:** 1, 12–15, 18

"In the Tube" (Jarman), **Supp. XVII:** 121

"In the Tunnel Bone of Cambridge" (Corso), **Supp. XII:** 120–121

"In the Upper Pastures" (Kumin), **Supp. IV Part 2:** 453

In the Valley (Frederic), **II:** 133–134, 136, 137

"In the Village" (Bishop), **Retro. Supp. II:** 38; **Supp. I Part 1:** 73, 74–75, 76, 77, 78, 88

"In the Waiting Room" (Bishop), **Retro. Supp. II:** 50; **Supp. I Part 1:** 81, 94, 95; **Supp. IV Part 1:** 249

"In the Ward: The Sacred Wood" (Jarrell), **II:** 376, 377

In the Western Night: Collected Poems 1965–90 (Bidart), **Supp. XV:** 19, **30–32**

"In the White Night" (Beattie), **Supp. V:** 30–31

"In the Wind My Rescue Is" (Ammons), **Supp. VII:** 25

"In the Winter Dark" (Peacock), **Supp. XIX:** 206

In the Winter of Cities (T. Williams), **IV:** 383

"In the X-Ray of the Sarcophagus of Tapero" (Goldbarth), **Supp. XII:** 191

"In the Yard" (Swenson), **Supp. IV Part 2:** 647

In the Zone (O'Neill), **III:** 388

In This, Our Life (film), **Supp. I Part 1:** 67

"In This Country, but in Another Language, My Aunt Refuses to Marry the Men Everyone Wants Her To" (Paley), **Supp. VI:** 225

"In This Dream" (J. W. Miller), **Supp. XX:**170

In This Hung-up Age (Corso), **Supp. XII:** **119–120,** 129

In This Our Life (Glasgow), **II:** 175, 178, 189

In This Our World (Gilman), **Supp. XI:** 196, 200, 202

"In Those Days" (Jarrell), **II:** 387–388

"Intimately Connected to the Zeitgeist" (Franzen), **Supp. XX:**94

"In Time of War" (Auden), **Supp. II Part 1:** 8, 13

"Into Egypt" (Benét), **Supp. XI:** 56, 57–58

Intolerance (film; Griffith), **Supp. XVI:** 184

"Into My Own" (Frost), **II:** 153; **Retro. Supp. I:** 127

"Into Night" (McKnight), **Supp. XX:**151–152

"Into the Night Life . . ." (H. Miller), **III:** 180, 184

"Into the Nowhere" (Rawlings), **Supp. X:** 220

Into the Stone (Dickey), **Supp. IV Part 1:** 178

"Into the Stone" (Dickey), **Supp. IV Part 1:** 179

Into the Stone and Other Poems (Dickey), **Supp. IV Part 1:** 176

Into the Wild (Krakauer), **Supp. XVIII:** 106, **107–108,** 116, 117

Into Thin Air: A Personal Account of the Mount Everest Disaster (Krakauer), **Supp. XVII:** 210; **Supp. XVIII:** 105, **109–113,** 117

In Touch: The Letters of Paul Bowles (J. Miller, ed.), **Supp. IV Part 1:** 95

"Intoxicated, The" (Jackson), **Supp. IX:** 116

"Intrigue" (Crane), **I:** 419

"Introducing the Fathers" (Kumin), **Supp. IV Part 2:** 452

Introductio ad Prudentiam (Fuller), **II:** 111

"Introduction to a Haggadah" (Paley), **Supp. VI:** 219

Introduction to Objectivist Epistemology (Rand), **Supp. IV Part 2:** 527, 528–529

Introduction to Objectivist Epistemology 2nd ed. (Rand), **Supp. IV Part 2:** 529

"Introduction to Poetry" (Collins), **Supp. XXI:** 57

Introduction to Poetry, An (Gioia and X. J. Kennedy), **Supp. XV:** 113, 153

"Introduction to Some Poems, An" (Stafford), **Supp. XI:** 311, 324

Introduction to the Geography of Iowa, The (Doty), **Supp. XI:** 120

"Introduction to the Hoh" (Hugo), **Supp. VI:** 136–137

"Introduction to *The New Writing in the USA*" (Creeley), **Supp. IV Part 1:** 153–154

"Introduction to William Blake, An" (Kazin), **Supp. VIII:** 103

Introitus (Longfellow), **II:** 505, 506–507

"Intruder, The" (Dubus), **Supp. VII:** 76–78, 91

Intruder, The (Maeterlinck), **I:** 91

Intruder in the Dust (Faulkner), **II:** 71, 72; **Supp. XVI:** 148

"Invaders, The" (Haines), **Supp. XII:** 205

Invaders, The (W. Frank), **Supp. XX:79–80**

Invasion of Privacy: The Cross Creek Trial of Marjorie Kinnan Rawlings (Acton), **Supp. X:** 233

Inventing Memory: A Novel of Mothers and Daughters (Jong), **Supp. V:** 115, 129

Inventing the Abbotts (Miller), **Supp. XII:** **294–295**

"Invention of God in a Mouthful of Milk, The" (Karr), **Supp. XI:** 250

Invention of Solitude, The (Auster), **Supp. XII:** 21–22

Inventions of the March Hare (Eliot), **Retro. Supp. I:** 55–56, 58

"Inventions of the March Hare" (Eliot), **Retro. Supp. I:** 55

"Inventory" (Parker), **Supp. IX:** 192

"Inverted Forest, The" (Salinger), **III:** 552, 572

"Investigation" (Ryan as Quin), **Supp. XVIII:** 227–228

"Investigations of a Dog" (Kafka), **IV:** 438

"Investiture, The" (Banks), **Supp. V:** 7

"Investiture at Cecconi's" (Merrill), **Supp. III Part 1:** 336

"Invisible" (Pickering), **Supp. XXI:** 201

Invisible Circus, The (Egan), **Supp. XIX:** 49, **50–52**

Invisible Company, The (Sanders), **Supp. XVI:** 270–271

Invisible Man (Ellison), **IV:** 493; **Retro. Supp. II:** 3, 12, 111, 112, 113, 117, 119, **120–123,** 125; **Supp. II Part 1:** 40, 170, 221, 224, 226, 227, 230, 231–232, 235, 236, 241–245; **Supp. IX:** 306; **Supp. X:** 242; **Supp. XI:** 18, 92; **Supp. XVIII:** 59; **Supp. XIX:** 154, 155

Invisible: Poems (Nye), **Supp. XIII:** 277

Invisible Spectator, An (Sawyer-Lauçanno), **Supp. IV Part 1:** 95

Invisible Swords (Farrell), **II:** 27, 46, 48–49

Invisible Worm, The (Millar), **Supp. IV Part 2:** 465

Invitation to a Beheading (Nabokov), **III:** 252–253, 254, 257–258; **Retro. Supp. I:** 265, 270, 273

"Invitation to the Country, An" (Bryant), **Supp. I Part 1:** 160

"Invocation" (McKay), **Supp. X:** 134

"Invocation" (Untermeyer), **Supp. XV:** 296

"Invocation to Kali" (Sarton), **Supp. VIII:** 260

"Invocation to the Social Muse" (MacLeish), **III:** 15

"In Weather" (Hass), **Supp. VI:** **102–103**

"In Your Fugitive Dream" (Hugo), **Supp. VI:** 143

"In Your Good Dream" (Hugo), **Supp. VI:** 143–144

"Iola, Kansas" (Clampitt), **Supp. IX:** **45–46**

Iola Leroy (Harper), **Supp. XVIII:** 284

Ion (Doolittle, trans.), **Supp. I Part 1:** 269, 274

Ion (Plato), **I:** 523

"Ione" (Dunbar), **Supp. II Part 1:** 199

Ionesco, Eugène, **I:** 71, 74, 75, 84, 295; **II:** 435; **Supp. VIII:** 201; **Supp. XIX:** 131

Ionica (Cory), **Supp. XX:**230

Ionica II (Cory), **Supp. XX:**230

"I Only Am Escaped Alone to Tell Thee" (Nemerov), **III:** 272, 273–274

"I Opened All the Portals Wide" (Chopin), **Retro. Supp. II:** 71

I Ought to Be in Pictures (Simon), **Supp. IV Part 2:** 584

Iphigenia in Tauris (Euripedes), **Supp. XV:** 42, 50

I Promessi Sposi (Manzoni), **II:** 291

"I Put My Hand on My Son's Head" (Kooser), **Supp. XIX:** 120

Iram, Dhāt al-'Imād (Gibran), **Supp. XX:**116

"Iraq Drifting, July 2003" (Weigl), **Supp. XIX:** 288

"Irascibles, The" (Kees), **Supp. XV:** 145–146

Ireland: A Terrible Beauty (Uris), **Supp. XX:**244, 245–246, 246, 254

"I Remember" (Sexton), **Supp. II Part 2:** 680

"Irenicon" (Shapiro), **Supp. II Part 2:** 704

Irigaray, Luce, **Supp. XII:** 6

Iris (Jarman), **Supp. XVII:** 110, **116–117**

"Iris by Night" (Frost), **Retro. Supp. I:** 132

"Irises" (L.-Y. Lee), **Supp. XV:** 214–215

Irish in America, The (Coffey, ed.), **Supp. XIX:** 133

Irish Stories of Sarah Orne Jewett, The (Jewett), **Retro. Supp. II:** 142

Irish Triangle, An (Barnes), **Supp. III Part 1:** 34

"Iron Characters, The" (Nemerov), **III:** 279, 282

"Iron Hans" (Sexton), **Supp. II Part 2:** 691

Iron Heel, The (London), **II:** 466, 480

Iron John: A Book about Men (R. Bly), **Supp. IV Part 1:** 59, 67; **Supp. XVI:** 177

"Iron Table, The" (Jane Bowles), **Supp. IV Part 1:** 82–83

"Iron Throat, The" (Olsen), **Supp. XIII:** 292, 297, 299

Ironweed (W. Kennedy), **Supp. VII:** 132, 133, 134, 135, 142, 144, 145–147, 148, 150, 153

"Irony as Art: The Short Fiction of William Humphrey" (Tebeaux), **Supp. IX:** 109

"Irony Is Not Enough: Essay on My Life as Catherine Deneuve" (Carson), **Supp. XII: 112–113**

Irony of American History, The (Niebuhr), **III:** 292, 306–307, 308

"Irrational Element in Poetry, The" (Stevens), **Retro. Supp. I:** 298, 301

"Irrevocable Diameter, An" (Paley), **Supp. VI:** 231–232

Irvine, Lorna, **Supp. XIII:** 26

Irving, Ebenezer, **II:** 296

Irving, Sir Henry, **IV:** 350

Irving, John, **Supp. VI: 163–183; Supp. X:** 77, 85

Irving, John Treat, **II:** 296

Irving, Peter, **II:** 296, 297, 298, 299, 300, 303

Irving, Washington, **I:** 211, 335, 336, 339, 343; **II: 295–318,** 488, 495; **III:** 113; **IV:** 309; **Retro. Supp. I:** 246; **Supp. I Part 1:** 155, 157, 158, 317; **Supp. I Part 2:** 377, 487, 585; **Supp. II Part 1:** 335; **Supp. IV Part 1:** 380; **Supp. XVIII:** 12

Irving, William, **II:** 296

Irving, William, Jr., **II:** 296, 297, 298, 299, 303

Irwin, Mark, **Supp. XII:** 21, 22, 24, 29

Irwin, Robert, **Supp. XX:** 120

Irwin, William Henry, **Supp. II Part 1:** 192

Is 5 (Cummings), **I:** 429, 430, 434, 435, 440, 445, 446, 447

"Isaac and Abraham" (Brodsky), **Supp. VIII:** 21

"Isaac and Archibald" (Robinson), **III:** 511, 521, 523

Isaacs, Neil D., **Supp. XIX:** 255

"Isabelle" (Saunders), **Supp. XIX:** 225

"Isabel Sparrow" (Oliver), **Supp. VII:** 232

Isaiah (biblical book), **Supp. I Part 1:** 236; **Supp. I Part 2:** 516; **Supp. XXI:** 107

"Isaiah Beethoven" (Masters), **Supp. I Part 2:** 461

"I Saw in Louisiana a Live-Oak Growing" (Whitman), **I:** 220

"I Shall Be Released" (Dylan), **Supp. XV:** 349

I Shall Spit on Your Graves (film), **Supp. I Part 1:** 67

Isháq, Adib, **Supp. XX:** 117

Isherwood, Christopher, **II:** 586; **Supp. II Part 1:** 10, 11, 13; **Supp. IV Part 1:** 79, 82, 102; **Supp. XI:** 305; **Supp. XIV: 155–175; Supp. XVI:** 194

Isherwood Century, The (Berg and Freeman), **Supp. XIV:** 157, 159

Isherwood's Fiction (Schwerdt), **Supp. XIV:** 155

Ishiguro, Kazuo, **Supp. VIII:** 15

Ishi Means Man (Merton), **Supp. VIII:** 208

"Ishmael's Dream" (Stern), **Supp. IX:** 287

I Should Have Stayed Home (McCoy), **Supp. XIII:** 167, **168–170,** 171

"I Should Worry" (Kees), **Supp. XV:** 140

"I Sigh in the Afternoon" (Salinas), **Supp. XIII:** 318

"I Sing the Body Electric" (Whitman), **Retro. Supp. I:** 394, 395

"Isis: Dorothy Eady, 1924" (Doty), **Supp. XI:** 122

"Is It O.K. to Be a Luddite?" (Pynchon), **Supp. XVI:** 128

"Is It True?" (Hughes), **Supp. I Part 1:** 342

I: Six Nonlectures (Cummings), **I:** 430, 433, 434

"Island" (Hughes), **Supp. I Part 1:** 340

Island Garden, An (Thaxter), **Retro. Supp. II:** 136; **Supp. XIII:** 152

Island Holiday, An (Henry), **I:** 515

Island in the Atlantic (W. Frank), **Supp. XX:** 79

"Island of the Fay, The" (Poe), **III:** 412, 417

"Islands, The" (Hayden), **Supp. II Part 1:** 373

"Island Sheaf, An" (Doty), **Supp. XI:** 136

Islands in the Stream (Hemingway), **II:** 258; **Retro. Supp. I:** 186

Isn't It Romantic (Wasserstein), **Supp. XV: 323–325,** 327

Is Objectivism a Religion? (Ellis), **Supp. IV Part 2:** 527

"Isolation of Modern Poetry, The" (Schwartz), **Supp. II Part 2:** 644

"Israel" (Reznikoff), **Supp. XIV:** 283

Israel Potter, or Fifty Years of Exile (Melville), **III:** 90; **Supp. XVIII:** 4

"Israfel" (Poe), **III:** 411

Is Sex Necessary? (Thurber and White), **Supp. I Part 2:** 607, 612, 614, 653

"Issues, The" (Olds), **Supp. X:** 205

"Istanbul" (Collins), **Supp. XXI:** 60

"I Stand Here Ironing" (Olsen), **Supp. XIII:** 292, 294, 296, 298, 300, 305

I Stole a Million (West), **IV:** 287

"Is Verse a Dying Technique?" (Wilson), **IV:** 431

It (Creeley), **Supp. IV Part 1:** 157, 158

IT (King), **Supp. V:** 139, 140, 141, 146–147, 151, 152

"It" (Olds), **Supp. X:** 208

Italian American Reconciliation: A Folktale (Shanley), **Supp. XIV:** 315, **324–326,** 328, 330

Italian Backgrounds (Wharton), **Retro. Supp. I:** 370

Italian Hours (James), **I:** 12; **II:** 337; **Retro. Supp. I:** 235

Italian Journeys (Howells), **II:** 274

"Italian Morning" (Bogan), **Supp. III Part 1:** 58

Italian Villas and Their Gardens (Wharton), **IV:** 308; **Retro. Supp. I:** 361, 367

Italie, Hillel, **Supp. XV:** 128

It All Adds Up: From the Dim Past to the Uncertain Future (Bellow), **Retro. Supp. II:** 32

"It Always Breaks Out" (Ellison), **Retro. Supp. II:** 126; **Supp. II Part 1:** 248

Itard, Jean-Marc Gaspard, **Supp. I Part 2:** 564

"I taste a liquor never brewed" (Dickinson), **Retro. Supp. I:** 30, 37

It Came from Outer Space (film), **Supp. IV Part 1:** 102

It Can't Happen Here (Lewis), **II:** 454

"It Don't Mean a Thing If It Ain't Got That Swing" (Matthews), **Supp. IX: 164–165**

I Tell You Now (Ortiz), **Supp. IV Part 2:** 500

"Ithaca" (Glück), **Supp. V:** 89

It Happened One Night (Capra), **Supp. XV:** 197

It Has Come to Pass (Farrell), **II:** 26

"I think to live May be a Bliss" (Dickinson), **Retro. Supp. I:** 44

"I Thought It Was Harry" (Bronk), **Supp. XXI:** 31

I Thought of Daisy (Wilson), **IV:** 428, 434, 435

"Itinerary of an Obsession" (Kumin), **Supp. IV Part 2:** 450

"It Is a Strange Country" (Ellison), **Supp. II Part 1:** 238

"It Is Dangerous to Read Newspapers" (Atwood), **Supp. XIII:** 33

"It Must Be Abstract" (Stevens), **IV:** 95; **Retro. Supp. I:** 307

"It Must Change" (Stevens), **Retro. Supp. I:** 300, 307, 308

"It Must Give Pleasure" (Stevens), **Retro. Supp. I:** 307, 308, 309

"'It Out-Herods Herod. Pray You, Avoid It'" (Hecht), **Supp. X:** 62, 64

"It's All Over Now, Baby Blue" (song, Dylan), **Supp. XVIII:** 30

It's Loaded, Mr. Bauer (Marquand), **III:** 59

It's Nation Time (Baraka), **Supp. II Part 1:** 52, 53

"It's Nation Time" (Baraka), **Supp. II Part 1**: 53

It's Only a Play (McNally), **Supp. XIII**: 198

It Was (Zukofsky), **Supp. III Part 2**: 630

It Was the Nightingale (Ford), **III**: 470–471

"It Was When" (Snyder), **Supp. VIII**: 300

Ivanhoe (Scott), **I**: 216; **Supp. I Part 2**: 410

Ivens, Bryna, **Supp. XV**: 311, 312

Ivens, Joris, **I**: 488; **Retro. Supp. I**: 184

"Iverson Boy, The" (Simpson), **Supp. IX**: 280

"Ives" (Rukeyser), **Supp. VI**: 273, 283

Ives, George H., **Supp. I Part 1**: 153

Ivory Grin, The (Macdonald), **Supp. IV Part 2**: 471, 472

"Ivory Novel, The" (Halliday), **Supp. XIX**: 90

Ivory Tower, The (James), **II**: 337–338

"Ivory Tower, The: Louis Untermeyer as Critic" (Aiken), **Supp. XV**: 298

Ivry, Sara, **Supp. XX:**179

"Ivy Winding" (Ammons), **Supp. VII**: 33

Iwamatsu, Mako, **Supp. XXI**: 150

"I Wandered Lonely as a Cloud" (Wordsworth), **Retro. Supp. I**: 121–122; **Supp. X**: 73; **Supp. XIV**: 184

"I want, I want" (Plath), **Retro. Supp. II**: 246

"I Wanted to Be There When My Father Died" (Olds), **Supp. X**: 210

"I Want to Be a Father Like the Men" (Cisneros), **Supp. VII**: 71

"I Want to Be Miss America" (Alvarez), **Supp. VII**: 18

"I Want to Know Why" (Anderson), **I**: 114, 115, 116; **II**: 263

"I Want You Women Up North To Know" (Olsen), **Supp. XIII**: 292, 297

"I Was Born in Lucerne" (Levine), **Supp. V**: 181, 189

"I Was Really Very Hungry" (M. F. K. Fisher), **Supp. XVII**: 91

"I Went into the Maverick Bar" (Snyder), **Supp. VIII**: 301

"I Will Lie Down" (Swenson), **Supp. IV Part 2**: 640

I Will Say Beauty (C. Frost), **Supp. XV**: 96, **105–107**

I Wonder As I Wander (Hughes), **Retro. Supp. I**: 196, 203; **Supp. I Part 1**: 329, 332–333

I Would Have Saved Them If I Could (L. Michaels), **Supp. XVI**: 203, 205, **206–210**

"Iyani: It goes this Way" (Gunn Allen), **Supp. IV Part 1**: 321

"I years had been from home" (Dickinson), **I**: 471

Iyer, Pico, **Supp. V**: 215

Izzo, David Garrett, **Supp. XIV**: 155, 156, 159, 160, 161, 163, 169, 171

J

Jab (Halliday), **Supp. XIX**: **91–94**

"Jachid and Jechidah" (Singer), **IV**: 15

Jack and Jill (Alcott), **Supp. I Part 1**: 42

"Jack and the Beanstalk" (Hay), **Supp. XIV**: 124

"Jack in the Pot" (D. West), **Supp. XVIII**: 283

Jack Kelso (Masters), **Supp. I Part 2**: 456, 471–472

Jacklight (Erdrich), **Supp. IV Part 1**: 259, 270

Jack London, Hemingway, and the Constitution (Doctorow), **Supp. IV Part 1**: 220, 222, 224, 232, 235

Jackman, Harold, **Supp. XVIII**: 131

Jackpot (Caldwell), **I**: 304

"Jack Schmidt, Arts Administrator" (Keillor), **Supp. XVI**: 171

"Jack Schmidt on the Burning Sands" (Keillor), **Supp. XVI**: 171

Jackson, Amelia. *See* Holmes, Mrs. Oliver Wendell (Amelia Jackson)

Jackson, Andrew, **I**: 7, 20; **III**: 473; **IV**: 192, 248, 298, 334, 348; **Supp. I Part 2**: 456, 461, 473, 474, 493, 695

Jackson, Blyden, **Supp. I Part 1**: 337

Jackson, Charles, **Supp. I Part 1**: 303

Jackson, George, **Supp. I Part 1**: 66

Jackson, Helen Hunt, **I**: 459, 470; **Retro. Supp. I**: 26, 27, 30–31, 32, 33

Jackson, James, **Supp. I Part 1**: 302, 303

Jackson, J. O., **III**: 213

Jackson, Joe, **Supp. I Part 2**: 441

Jackson, Katherine Gauss, **Supp. VIII**: 124

Jackson, Lawrence, **Retro. Supp. II**: 113, 115

Jackson, Melanie, **Supp. X**: 166

Jackson, Michael, **Supp. VIII**: 146

Jackson, Richard, **II**: 119; **Supp. IX**: 165

Jackson, Shelley, **Supp. XVIII**: 136

Jackson, Shirley, **Supp. IX**: **113–130**

Jackson, Thomas J. ("Stonewall"), **IV**: 125, 126

"Jackson Hotel" (Hull), **Supp. XXI**: 134, 135

"Jackson Square" (Levertov), **Supp. III Part 1**: 276

Jackstraws (Simic), **Supp. VIII**: 280, 282–283

"Jackstraws" (Simic), **Supp. VIII**: **283**

Jack Tier (Cooper), **I**: 354, 355

"Jacob" (Garrett), **Supp. VII**: 109–110

"Jacob" (Schwartz), **Supp. II Part 2**: 663

Jacob, Max, **Supp. XV**: 178, 182

"Jacob and the Indians" (Benét), **Supp. XI**: 47–48

Jacobs, Catherine Haydon, **Supp. XXI**: 98

Jacobs, Harriet, **Supp. XVI**: 85

Jacobs, Jill Suzanne, **Supp. XX:**178, 186

Jacobs, Rita D., **Supp. XII**: 339

Jacobsen, Josephine, **Supp. XIII**: 346; **Supp. XIV**: 260

"Jacob's Ladder" (Rawlings), **Supp. X**: 224, 228

Jacob's Ladder, The (Levertov), **Supp. III Part 1**: 272, 276–278, 281

"Jacob's Ladder, The" (Levertov), **Supp. III Part 1**: 278

Jacobson, Dale, **Supp. X**: 112

Jacobson, Kristin, **Supp. XVIII**: 113

Jacobson, Leslie, **Supp. XV**: 323

Jacoby, Russell, **Supp. IV Part 2**: 692

"Jacquerie, The" (Lanier), **Supp. I Part 1**: 355, 356, 360, 364, 370

Jacques le fataliste (D. Diderot), **Supp. XVII**: 145

Jade Mountain, The: A Chinese Anthology, Being Three Hundred Poems of the T'ang Dynasty (Bynner, trans.), **II**: 527; **Supp. XV**: 46, 47, 48

Jafsie and John Henry: Essays on Hollywood, Bad Boys, and Six Hours of Perfect Poker (Mamet), **Supp. XIV**: 252

Jaguar Totem (LaBastille), **Supp. X**: 99, 106, **107–109**

Jailbird (Vonnegut), **Supp. II Part 2**: 760, 779–780

Jaimes, M. Annette, **Supp. IV Part 1**: 330, 331

Jain, Manju, **Retro. Supp. I**: 53, 58

Jake's Women (Simon), **Supp. IV Part 2**: 576, 588

"Jakie's Mother" (Fante), **Supp. XI**: 164

Jakobson, Roman, **Supp. IV Part 1**: 155

"Jamaica Kincaid's New York" (Kincaid), **Supp. VII**: 181

James, Alice, **I**: 454; **Retro. Supp. I**: 228, 235

James, A. Lloyd, **Supp. XIV**: 343

James, Caryn, **Supp. X**: 302, 303

James, C. L. R. (Cyril Lionel Robert), **Supp. XXI**: **159–173**

James, Etta, **Supp. X**: 242

James, Henry, **I**: 4, 5, 9, 10, 12, 15, 16, 20, 52, 93, 109, 211, 226, 228, 244, 246, 251, 255, 258, 259, 336, 363, 374, 375, 379, 384, 409, 429, 436, 439, 452, 454, 459, 461–462, 463, 464, 485, 500, 504, 513, 514, 517–518, 571; **II**: 38, 58, 60, 73, 74, 95, 138, 140, 144, 147, 196, 198, 199, 228, 230, 234, 243, 259, 267, 271, 272, 275, 276, 278, 281, 282, 283, 284, 285, 286, 287, 288, 290, 306, 309, 316, **319–341**, 398, 404, 410, 415, 427, 444, 542, 544, 547–548, 556, 600; **III**: 44, 51, 136, 194–195, 199, 206, 208, 218, 228–229, 237, 281, 319, 325, 326, 334, 409, 453, 454, 457, 460, 461, 464, 511, 522, 576, 607; **IV**: 8, 27, 34, 37, 40, 53, 58, 73, 74, 134, 168, 172, 182, 198, 202, 285, 308, 309, 310, 311, 314, 316, 317, 318, 319, 321, 322, 323, 324, 328, 347, 352, 359, 433, 439, 476; **Retro. Supp. I**: 1, 8, 53, 56, 59, 108, 112, **215–242,** 272, 283, 284, 362, 366, 367, 368, 371, 373, 374, 375, 376, 377, 378, 379; **Retro. Supp. II**: 93, 135, 136, 203, 223; **Supp. I Part 1**: 35, 38, 43; **Supp. I Part 2**: 414, 454, 608, 609, 612–613, 618, 620, 646; **Supp. II Part 1**: 94–95; **Supp. III Part 1**: 14, 200; **Supp. III Part 2**: 410, 412; **Supp. IV Part 1**: 31, 35, 80, 127, 197, 349, 353; **Supp. IV Part 2**: 613, 677, 678, 682, 689, 693; **Supp. V**: 97, 101, 103, 258, 261,

263, 313; **Supp. VIII:** 98, 102, 156, 166, 168; **Supp. IX:** 121; **Supp. XI:** 153; **Supp. XIII:** 102; **Supp. XIV:** 40, 110, 112, 335, 336, 348, 349; **Supp. XV:** 41; **Supp. XVII:** 5, 47; **Supp. XVIII:** 160, 258; **Supp. XX:** 227, 228, 232, 233, 238, 240; **Supp. XXI:** 225
James, Henry (father), **II:** 7, 275, 321, 337, 342–344, 364; **IV:** 174; **Supp. I Part 1:** 300
James, Henry (nephew), **II:** 360
James, Horace, **Supp. XIV:** 57
James, P. D., **Supp. XIX:** 131
James, William, **I:** 104, 220, 224, 227, 228, 255, 454; **II:** 20, 27, 165, 166, 276, 321, 337, **342–366,** 411; **III:** 303, 309, 509, 599, 600, 605, 606, 612; **IV:** 26, 27, 28–29, 31, 32, 34, 36, 37, 43, 46, 291, 486; **Retro. Supp. I:** 57, 216, 227, 228, 235, 295, 300, 306; **Supp. I Part 1:** 3, 7, 11, 20; **Supp. XIV:** 40, 50, 197, 199, 212, 335; **Supp. XVII:** 97
James, William (grandfather), **II:** 342
James Baldwin: The Legacy (Troupe, ed.), **Retro. Supp. II:** 15
James Baldwin—The Price of the Ticket (film), **Retro. Supp. II:** 2
James Dickey and the Politics of Canon (Suarez), **Supp. IV Part 1:** 175
"James Dickey on Yeats: An Interview" (Dickey), **Supp. IV Part 1:** 177
James Hogg: A Critical Study (Simpson), **Supp. IX:** 269, 276
"James Is a Girl" (Egan), **Supp. XIX:** 61
James Jones: A Friendship (Morris), **Supp. XI:** 234
James Jones: An American Literary Orientalist Master (Carter), **Supp. XI:** 220
"James Jones and Jack Kerouac: Novelists of Disjunction" (Stevenson), **Supp. XI:** 230
James Jones: Reveille to Taps (television documentary), **Supp. XI:** 234
Jameson, F. R., **Supp. IV Part 1:** 119
Jameson, Sir Leander Starr, **III:** 327
James Shore's Daughter (Benét), **Supp. XI:** 48
"James Thurber" (Pollard), **Supp. I Part 2:** 468
"James Whitcomb Riley (From a Westerner's Point of View)" (Dunbar), **Supp. II Part 1:** 198
Jammes, Francis, **II:** 528; **Retro. Supp. I:** 55
"Jan, the Son of Thomas" (Sandburg), **III:** 593–594
Jan. 31 (Goldbarth), **Supp. XII:** 177, **178–179,** 180
Janeczko, Paul, **Supp. XIII:** 280
Jane Eyre (Brontë), **Supp. XVI:** 158
Janet, Pierre, **I:** 248, 249, 252; **Retro. Supp. I:** 55, 57
Jane Talbot: A Novel (Brown), **Supp. I Part 1:** 145–146
"Janet Waking" (Ransom), **III:** 490, 491
"Janice" (Jackson), **Supp. IX:** 117
Janowitz, Tama, **Supp. X:** 7
Jantz, Harold S., **Supp. I Part 1:** 112

"January" (Barthelme), **Supp. IV Part 1:** 54
"January" (W. V. Davis), **Supp. XXI:** 89, 90
January Man, The (screenplay, Shanley), **Supp. XIV:** 316
"January Thaw" (Leopold), **Supp. XIV:** 183–184
"Janus" (Beattie), **Supp. V:** 31
Janzen, Jean, **Supp. V:** 180
"Japan" (Collins), **Supp. XXI:** 56
Japanese Americans: The Formation and Transformations of an Ethnic Group (Spickard), **Supp. XXI:** 149
"Japanese Beetles" (X. J. Kennedy), **Supp. XV:** 161, 165
Japanese by Spring (Reed), **Supp. X:** 241, **253–255**
Japanese Cooking: A Simple Art (Tsuji), **Supp. XVII:** 90
"Japan's Young Dreams" (Geisel), **Supp. XVI:** 102
Jara, Victor, **Supp. IV Part 2:** 549
Jarman, Mark, **Supp. IV Part 1:** 68; **Supp. IX:** 266, 270, 276; **Supp. XII:** 209; **Supp. XV:** 251; **Supp. XVIII:** 178
Jarmon, Mark, **Supp. XVII: 109–122**
Jarrell, Randall, **I:** 167, 169, 173, 180; **II: 367–390,** 539–540; **III:** 134, 194, 213, 268, 527; **IV:** 352, 411, 422; **Retro. Supp. I:** 52, 121, 135, 140; **Retro. Supp. II:** 44, 177, 178, 182; **Supp. I Part 1:** 89; **Supp. I Part 2:** 552; **Supp. II Part 1:** 109, 135; **Supp. III Part 1:** 64; **Supp. III Part 2:** 541, 550; **Supp. IV Part 2:** 440; **Supp. V:** 315, 318, 323; **Supp. VIII:** 31, 100, 271; **Supp. IX:** 94, 268; **Supp. XI:** 311, 315; **Supp. XII:** 121, 260, 297; **Supp. XV:** 93, 153; **Supp. XVII:** 111
Jarrell, Mrs. Randall (Mary von Schrader), **II:** 368, 385
Jarry, Alfred, **Retro. Supp. II:** 326; **Supp. XV:** 177–178, 182, 188
Jarvis, John Wesley, **Supp. I Part 2:** 501, 520
Jaskoski, Helen, **Supp. IV Part 1:** 325
"Jasmine" (Komunyakaa), **Supp. XIII:** 132
"Jason" (Hecht), **Supp. X:** 62
"Jason" (MacLeish), **III:** 4
Jason and Medeia (Gardner), **Supp. VI:** 63, **68–69**
Jaspers, Karl, **III:** 292; **IV:** 491
Jauss, David, **Supp. XXI:** 129, 132, 133, 134, 139
Jay, William, **I:** 338
Jayber Crow (Berry), **Supp. X:** 28, 34
"Jaz Fantasia" (Sandburg), **III:** 585
"Jazz Age Clerk, A" (Farrell), **II:** 45
Jazz Country: Ralph Ellison in America (Porter), **Retro. Supp. II:** 127
"Jazzonia" (Hughes), **Supp. I Part 1:** 324
Jazz Poetry Anthology, The (Komunyakaa and Feinstein, eds.), **Supp. XIII:** 125
"Jazztet Muted" (Hughes), **Supp. I Part 1:** 342

J. B.: A Play in Verse (MacLeish), **II:** 163, 228; **III:** 3, 21–22, 23; **Supp. IV Part 2:** 586
"Jealous" (Ford), **Supp. V:** 71
Jealousies, The: A Faery Tale, by Lucy Vaughan Lloyd of China Walk, Lambeth (Keats), **Supp. XII:** 113
Jean-Christophe (Rolland), **Supp. XX:** 70
"Jean Harlow's Wedding Night" (Wasserstein), **Supp. XV:** 328
Jean Huguenot (Benét), **Supp. XI:** 44
"Jeff Briggs's Love Story" (Harte), **Supp. II Part 1:** 355
Jeffers, Robinson, **I:** 66; **III:** 134; **Retro. Supp. I:** 202; **Supp. II Part 2: 413–440;** **Supp. VIII:** 33, 292; **Supp. IX:** 77; **Supp. X:** 112; **Supp. XI:** 312; **Supp. XV:** 113, 114, 115; **Supp. XVII:** 111, 112, 117; **Supp. XXI:** 87
Jeffers, Una Call Kuster (Mrs. Robinson Jeffers), **Supp. II Part 2:** 414
Jefferson, Blind Lemon, **Supp. VIII:** 349
Jefferson, Margo, **Supp. XX:** 87
Jefferson, Thomas, **I:** 1, 2, 5, 6–8, 14, 485; **II:** 5, 6, 34, 217, 300, 301, 437; **III:** 3, 17, 18, 294–295, 306, 310, 473, 608; **IV:** 133, 243, 249, 334, 348; **Supp. I Part 1:** 146, 152, 153, 229, 230, 234, 235; **Supp. I Part 2:** 389, 399, 456, 474, 475, 482, 507, 509, 510, 511, 516, 518–519, 520, 522; **Supp. X:** 26; **Supp. XIV:** 191; **Supp. XX:** 285
Jefferson and/or Mussolini (Pound), **Retro. Supp. I:** 292
"Jefferson Davis as a Representative American" (Du Bois), **Supp. II Part 1:** 161
J-E-L-L-O (Baraka), **Supp. II Part 1:** 47
"Jelly-Bean, The" (Fitzgerald), **II:** 88
"Jellyfish, A" (Moore), **III:** 215
Jemie, Onwuchekwa, **Supp. I Part 1:** 343
Jenkins, J. L., **I:** 456
Jenkins, Joe, **Supp. XX:** 117, 120, 122
Jenkins, Kathleen, **III:** 403
Jenkins, Susan, **IV:** 123
Jenks, Deneen, **Supp. IV Part 2:** 550, 554
Jenks, Tom, **Supp. XIX:** 51
Jennie Gerhardt (Dreiser), **I:** 497, 499, 500, 501, 504–505, 506, 507, 519; **Retro. Supp. II:** 94, **99–101**
"Jennie M'Grew" (Masters), **Supp. I Part 2:** 468
Jennifer Lorn (Wylie), **Supp. I Part 2:** 709, 714–717, 718, 721, 724
Jennison, Peter S., **Supp. XIX:** 268
"Jenny Garrow's Lover" (Jewett), **II:** 397
"Jerboa, The" (Moore), **III:** 203, 207, 209, 211–212
Jeremiah, **Supp. X:** 35
Jeremy's Version (Purdy), **Supp. VII:** 274
"Jericho" (Lowell), **II:** 536
"Jerry's Garage" (Budbill), **Supp. XIX:** 7
"Jersey City Gendarmerie, Je T'aime" (Lardner), **II:** 433
Jersey Rain (Pinsky), **Supp. VI:** 235, **247–250**
"Jerusalem" (Nye), **Supp. XIII:** 287

Jerusalem: Song of Songs (Uris), **Supp. XX**:244–245, 246, 255
Jerusalem the Golden (Reznikoff), **Supp. XIV**: 280, 285, 286
Jessup, Richard, **Supp. XI**: 306
"Je Suis Perdu" (Taylor), *Supp. V*: 314, 321–322
Jesuits in North America in the Seventeenth Century, The (Parkman), **Supp. II Part 2**: 597, 603–605
Jesus, **I**: 27, 34, 68, 89, 136, 552, 560; **II**: 1, 16, 197, 198, 214, 215, 216, 218, 219, 239, 373, 377, 379, 537, 538, 539, 549, 569, 585, 591, 592; **III**: 39, 173, 179, 270, 291, 296–297, 300, 303, 305, 307, 311, 339, 340, 341, 342, 344, 345, 346, 347, 348, 352, 353, 354, 355, 436, 451, 489, 534, 564, 566, 567, 582; **IV**: 51, 69, 86, 107, 109, 117, 137, 138, 141, 144, 147, 149, 150, 151, 152, 155, 156, 157, 158, 159, 163, 164, 232, 241, 289, 293, 294, 296, 331, 364, 392, 396, 418, 430; **Supp. I Part 1**: 2, 54, 104, 107, 108, 109, 121, 267, 371; **Supp. I Part 2**: 379, 386, 458, 515, 580, 582, 583, 587, 588, 683; **Supp. V**: 280
Jesus, the Son of Man (Gibran), **Supp. XX**:115–116, 117, **122–123**
"Jesus Asleep" (Sexton), **Supp. II Part 2**: 693
"Jesus of Nazareth, Then and Now" (Price), **Supp. VI**: 268
"Jesus Papers, The" (Sexton), **Supp. II Part 2**: 693
"Jesus Raises Up the Harlot" (Sexton), **Supp. II Part 2**: 693
Jetée, La (film), **Supp. IV Part 2**: 436
"Jeune Parque, La" (Valéry), **IV**: 92
"Jew as Writer/The Writer as Jew, The: Reflections on Literature and Identity" (Apple), **Supp. XVII**: 1, 9
"Jewbird, The" (Malamud), **Supp. I Part 2**: 435
"Jewboy, The" (P. Roth), **Supp. III Part 2**: 412
Jewett, Caroline, **II**: 396
Jewett, Katharine, **Retro. Supp. II**: 46
Jewett, Mary, **II**: 396, 403
Jewett, Rutger, **Retro. Supp. I**: 381
Jewett, Sarah Orne, **I**: 313; **II**: **391–414**; **Retro. Supp. I**: 6, 7, 19; **Retro. Supp. II**: 51, 52, **131–151**, 156; **Supp. I Part 2**: 495; **Supp. VIII**: 126; **Supp. IX**: 79; **Supp. XIII**: 153
Jewett, Theodore Furber, **II**: 395
Jewett, Dr. Theodore Herman, **II**: 396–397, 402
"Jew for Export, The" (Mamet), **Supp. XIV**: 251–252
Jew in Our Day, The (W. Frank), **Supp. XX**:79
Jew in the American Novel, The (Fiedler), **Supp. XIII**: 106
"Jewish Graveyards, Italy" (Levine), **Supp. V**: 190
"Jewish Hunter, The" (Moore), **Supp. X**: 163, 165, **174**

Jewison, Norman, **Supp. XI**: 306; **Supp. XIV**: 316
Jews of Shklov (Schneour), **IV**: 11
Jews without Money (Gold), **Supp. XIV**: 288–289
JFK (film), **Supp. XIV**: 48
Jig of Forslin, The: A Symphony (Aiken), **I**: 50, 51, 57, 62, 66
"Jig Tune: Not for Love" (McGrath), **Supp. X**: 116
"Jihad" (McClatchy), **Supp. XII**: 266
"Jilting of Granny Weatherall, The" (Porter), **III**: 434, 435, 438
Jim Crow's Last Stand (Hughes), **Retro. Supp. I**: 205
Jiménez, Juan Ramón, **Supp. XIII**: 315, 323
Jimmie Higgins (Sinclair), **Supp. V**: 288
"Jimmy Harlow" (X. J. Kennedy), **Supp. XV**: 170
Jimmy's Blues (Baldwin), **Retro. Supp. II**: 8, 9, 15
Jim's Book: A Collection of Poems and Short Stories (Merrill), **Supp. III Part 1**: 319
Jin, Ha, **Supp. XVIII**: **89–104**
Jitney (Wilson), **Supp. VIII**: 330, 331, 351
Jitterbug Perfume (Robbins), **Supp. X**: 273, **274–276**, 279
Joachim, Harold, **Retro. Supp. I**: 58
Joan, Pope, **IV**: 165
Joanna and Ulysses (Sarton), **Supp. VIII**: **254–255**
Joan of Arc, **IV**: 241; **Supp. I Part 1**: 286–288; **Supp. I Part 2**: 469
Joans, Ted, **Supp. IV Part 1**: 169
Job (biblical book), **II**: 165, 166–167, 168; **III**: 21, 199, 512; **IV**: 13, 158; **Supp. I Part 1**: 125
Job, The (Burroughs and Odier), **Supp. III Part 1**: 97, 103
Job, The: An American Novel (Lewis), **II**: 441
"Job History" (Proulx), **Supp. VII**: 262
Jobim, Antonio Carlos, **Supp. IV Part 2**: 549
Jobim, Antônio Carlos, **Supp. XXI**: 100
"Job of the Plains, A" (Humphrey), **Supp. IX**: 101
"Jody Rolled the Bones" (Yates), **Supp. XI**: 335, 341
"Joe" (Alvarez), **Supp. VII**: 7–8
Joe (Brown), **Supp. XVIII**: 195
Joe (L. Brown), **Supp. XXI**: 41, **45–46**, 47
"Joe, the Vanishing American" (Swados), **Supp. XIX**: 258–259
Joe Hill: A Biographical Novel (Stegner), **Supp. IV Part 2**: 599
Joe Jones (Lamott), **Supp. XX**:134–135
"Joe Louis: The King as a Middle-Aged Man" (Talese), **Supp. XVII**: 202
"Joe's Jitters" (Bronk), **Supp. XXI**: 27
Joe Turner's Come and Gone (Wilson), **Supp. VIII**: 334, **337–342**, 345
Joe versus the Volcano (screenplay, Shanley), **Supp. XIV**: 316
"Joey Martiney" (Huncke), **Supp. XIV**: 149

Johannes in Eremo (Mather), **Supp. II Part 2**: 453
John XXIII, Pope, **Supp. I Part 2**: 492
John (biblical book), **I**: 68; **Supp. XV**: 222, 224
"John" (Shields), **Supp. VII**: 310–311
John, Elton, **Supp. XXI**: 148
"John, John Chinaman" (Buck), **Supp. II Part 1**: 128
John Addington Symonds: A Biographical Study (Brooks), **I**: 240, 241
John-a Dreams: A Tale (J. Sturgis), **Supp. XX**:233
"John Archer's Nose" (R. Fisher), **Supp. XIX**: 71–72, 78
John Barleycorn (London), **II**: 467, 481
John Brown (Du Bois), **Supp. II Part 1**: 171–172
"John Brown" (Emerson), **II**: 13
"John Brown" (Lindsay), **Supp. I Part 2**: 393
John Brown's Body (Benét), **II**: 177; **Supp. XI**: 45, 46, 47, **56–57**
John Brown: The Making of a Martyr (Warren), **IV**: 236
John Bull in America; or, The New Munchausen (Paulding), **I**: 344
"John Burke" (Olson), **Supp. II Part 2**: 579, 580
"John Burns of Gettysburg" (Harte), **Supp. II Part 1**: 343
"John Carter" (Agee), **I**: 27
"John Coltrane: Where Does Art Come From?" (Baraka), **Supp. II Part 1**: 60
John Deth: A Metaphysical Legend and Other Poems (Aiken), **I**: 61
"John Endicott" (Longfellow), **II**: 505, 506; **Retro. Supp. II**: 165–166, 167
"John Evereldown" (Robinson), **III**: 524
John Fante Reader, The (Cooper, ed.), **Supp. XI**: 174
John Fante: Selected Letters, 1932–1981 (Cooney, ed.), **Supp. XI**: 170
"John Gardner: The Writer As Teacher" (Carver), **Supp. III Part 1**: 136, 146–147
John Gaunt (R. H. Davis), **Supp. XVI**: 89
John Jay Chapman and His Letters (Howe), **Supp. XIV**: 54
John Keats (Lowell), **II**: 530–531
"John Kinsella's Lament for Mrs. Mary Moore" (Yeats), **Supp. XVII**: 144
"John Lamar" (R. H. Davis), **Supp. XVI**: 89–90
John Lane, **Retro. Supp. I**: 59
"John L. Sullivan" (Lindsay), **Supp. I Part 2**: 394, 395
"John Marr" (Melville), **III**: 93
John Marr and Other Sailors (Melville), **III**: 93; **Retro. Supp. I**: 257
John Muir: A Reading Bibliography (Kimes and Kimes), **Supp. IX**: 178
Johnny Appleseed and Other Poems (Lindsay), **Supp. I Part 2**: 397
"Johnny Bear" (Steinbeck), **IV**: 67
Johnny Got His Gun (Trumbo), **Supp. XXI**: 45
"Johnny Mnemonic" (W. Gibson), **Supp. XVI**: 122, 123–125, 128, 131

"Johnny Panic and the Bible of Dreams" (Plath), **Retro. Supp. II:** 245

"Johnny Ray" (Ríos), **Supp. IV Part 2:** 543

Johnny Tremain (Forbes), **Supp. XIX:** 235

John of the Cross (Saint), **I:** 585; **Supp. IV Part 1:** 284; **Supp. XV:** 223; **Supp. XVII:** 112

John Paul Jones: A Sailor's Biography (Morison), **Supp. I Part 2:** 494–495

"John Redding Goes to Sea" (Hurston), **Supp. VI:** 150

Johns, George Sibley, **Retro. Supp. II:** 65

Johns, Orrick, **Retro. Supp. II:** 71

John Sloan: A Painter's Life (Brooks), **I:** 254

"John Smith Liberator" (Bierce), **I:** 209

Johnson, Alexandra, **Supp. X:** 86

Johnson, Alvin, **I:** 236; **Supp. XV:** 304

Johnson, Ben, **Retro. Supp. I:** 56

Johnson, Buffie, **Supp. IV Part 1:** 94

Johnson, Charles, **Supp. I Part 1:** 325; **Supp. V:** 128; **Supp. VI: 185–201; Supp. X:** 239; **Supp. XIII:** 182; **Supp. XIX:** 160

Johnson, Charles S., **Supp. IX:** 309

Johnson, Claudia Durst, **Supp. VIII:** 126–127

Johnson, Clifton, **Supp. XXI:** 248, 250

Johnson, Denis, **Supp. XXI:** 118, 131

Johnson, Dennis, **Supp. XIX:** 209

Johnson, Diane, **Supp. XIII:** 127

Johnson, Dianne, **Retro. Supp. I:** 196

Johnson, Eastman, **IV:** 321

Johnson, Edward, **IV:** 157; **Supp. I Part 1:** 110, 115

Johnson, Fenton, **Supp. XI:** 129

Johnson, Georgia Douglas, **Supp. IV Part 1:** 164

Johnson, Helene, **Supp. XVIII:** 282

Johnson, James Weldon, **Retro. Supp. II:** 114; **Supp. I Part 1:** 324, 325; **Supp. II Part 1:** 33, 194, 200, 202–203, 206–207; **Supp. III Part 1:** 73; **Supp. IV Part 1:** 7, 11, 15, 16, 164, 165, 166, 169; **Supp. X:** 42, 136, **246; Supp. XVIII:** 122, 127, 282; **Supp. XIX:** 73

Johnson, Joyce, **Supp. XIV:** 150

Johnson, Kent, **Supp. XV:** 347

Johnson, Lady Bird, **Supp. IV Part 1:** 22

Johnson, Lyndon B., **I:** 254; **II:** 553, 582; **Retro. Supp. II:** 27

Johnson, Marguerite. *See* Angelou, Maya

Johnson, Maurice, **Supp. XV:** 136, 137, 138

Johnson, Michael K., **Supp. XVIII:** 59, 64

Johnson, Mordecai, **Supp. XIV:** 202

Johnson, Nunnally, **Supp. IV Part 1:** 355

Johnson, Pamela Hansford, **IV:** 469

Johnson, Rafer, **Supp. I Part 1:** 271

Johnson, Reed, **Supp. IV Part 2:** 589

Johnson, Richard, **Supp. XIII:** 132

Johnson, Robert, **Supp. IV Part 1:** 146; **Supp. VIII:** 15, 134

Johnson, Robert K., **Supp. IV Part 2:** 573, 584

Johnson, Robert Underwood, **Supp. IX:** 182, 184, 185

Johnson, Samuel, **II:** 295; **III:** 491, 503; **IV:** 452; **Retro. Supp. I:** 56, 65; **Supp. I Part 1:** 33; **Supp. I Part 2:** 422, 498, 503, 523, 656; **Supp. IV Part 1:** 34, 124; **Supp. XI:** 209; **Supp. XII:** 159; **Supp. XIII:** 55, 347; **Supp. XVI:** 204; **Supp. XVII:** 1

Johnson, Sarah Anne, **Supp. XVIII:** 145; **Supp. XIX:** 49, 50, 52, 54, 55, 56, 58, 59, 60, 61

Johnson, Steve, **Supp. XVI:** 177

Johnson, Thomas H., **I:** 470–471; **IV:** 144, 158; **Retro. Supp. I:** 26, 28, 36, 39, 40, 41, 43

Johnson, Walter, **II:** 422

Johnson, Willard "Spud", **Supp. XV:** 42, 46

"Johnson Girls, The" (Bambara), **Supp. XI:** 7

Johnsrud, Harold, **II:** 562

Johnston, Basil, **Supp. IV Part 1:** 269

Johnston, Mary, **II:** 194

Johnston, Robert M., **Supp. I Part 1:** 369

"John Sutter" (Winters), **Supp. II Part 2:** 810

John's Wife (Coover), **Supp. V:** 51–52

John the Baptist, **I:** 389; **II:** 537, 591

John Wesley Harding (album, Dylan), **Supp. XVIII:** 27

Jolas, Eugène, **Retro. Supp. II:** 85, 328; **Supp. IV Part 1:** 80

Jolie Blon's Bounce (Burke), **Supp. XIV:** 26, 33–34

Jolly (Mamet), **Supp. XIV:** 240, 254

"Jolly Corner, The" (James), **I:** 571; **Retro. Supp. I:** 235

"Jon" (Saunders), **Supp. XIX:** 232, 234

"Jonah" (Lowell), **II:** 536

Jonah's Gourd Vine (Hurston), **Supp. VI:** 149, 155

"Jonathan Edwards" (Holmes), **Supp. I Part 1:** 302, 315

"Jonathan Edwards in Western Massachusetts" (Lowell), **II:** 550

Jonathan Franzen at the End of Postmodernism (Burns), **Supp. XX:** 85

Jonathan Troy (Abbey), **Supp. XIII:** 4, 13

Jones, Anne, **Supp. X:** 8

Jones, Carolyn M., **Supp. VIII:** 128; **Supp. XIX:** 160

Jones, Chuck, **Supp. XVI:** 102

Jones, David, **Supp. XVII:** 241

Jones, Derek Anson, **Supp. XVIII:** 38, 39

Jones, Edith Newbold. *See* Wharton, Edith

Jones, Edward P., **Supp. XXI:** 247

Jones, E. Stanley, **III:** 297

Jones, Everett LeRoi. *See* Baraka, Imamu Amiri

Jones, George Frederic, **IV:** 309

Jones, Grover, **Supp. XIII:** 166

Jones, Harry, **Supp. I Part 1:** 337

Jones, Howard Mumford, **I:** 353; **Supp. IV Part 2:** 606; **Supp. XIV:** 11

Jones, James, **III:** 40; **IV:** 98; **Supp. XI: 213–237; Supp. XIX:** 248, 252; **Supp. XX:**248

Jones, James Earl, **Supp. VIII:** 334; **Supp. XI:** 309

Jones, Jennifer, **Supp. IV Part 2:** 524

Jones, John Paul, **II:** 405–406; **Supp. I Part 2:** 479, 480, 494–495

Jones, Kirkland C., **Supp. XVIII:** 173, 174, 175

Jones, LeRoi. *See* Baraka, Imamu Amiri

Jones, Louis B., **Supp. XVI:** 41

Jones, Loyal, **Supp. XX:**170

Jones, Lucretia Stevens Rhinelander, **IV:** 309

Jones, Madison, **Retro. Supp. II:** 235; **Supp. X:** 1

Jones, Major (pseudonym). *See* Thompson, William T.

Jones, Malcolm, **Supp. V:** 219; **Supp. XX:**93, 138

Jones, Mildred, **Supp. XVIII:** 281

Jones, Robert Edmond, **III:** 387, 391, 394, 399; **Supp. XXI:** 6, 12

Jones, Sharon L., **Supp. XVIII:** 280, 285, 286

Jones, Tommy Lee, **Supp. V:** 227

"Jones's Private Argyment" (Lanier), **Supp. I Part 1:** 352

"Jones's *The Thin Red Line:* The End of Innocence" (Michel-Michot), **Supp. XI:** 224–225

Jong, Allan, **Supp. V:** 115

Jong, Erica, **Supp. V: 113–135**

Jong-Fast, Molly Miranda, **Supp. V:** 115

Jonson, Ben, **I:** 58, 358; **II:** 11, 16, 17, 18, 436, 556; **III:** 3, 463, 575–576; **IV:** 395, 453; **Retro. Supp. II:** 76; **Supp. I Part 2:** 423; **Supp. IV Part 2:** 585; **Supp. XX:**197

Jonsson, Thorsten, **Retro. Supp. I:** 73

Joplin, Janis, **Supp. IV Part 1:** 206; **Supp. XI:** 239

Joplin, Scott, **Supp. IV Part 1:** 223

Jordan, A. Van, **Supp. XVIII:** 172

Jordan, Barbara, **Supp. VIII:** 63; **Supp. XI:** 249

Jordan, David, **Supp. XIX:** 141

Jordan, June, **Supp. XII:** 217

Jordan, Marie, **Supp. XV:** 224

Jo's Boys (Alcott), **Supp. I Part 1:** 32, 35, 40–41, 42

Joseph Heller (Ruderman), **Supp. IV Part 1:** 380

"Josephine Has Her Day" (Thurber), **Supp. I Part 2:** 606

Josephine Stories, The (Fitzgerald), **Retro. Supp. I:** 109

"Joseph Martinez" (Huncke), **Supp. XIV:** 149

"Joseph Pockets" (Stern), **Supp. IX:** 292

Josephson, Matthew, **I:** 259

"José's Country" (Winters), **Supp. II Part 2:** 789, 790

Joshua (biblical book), **Supp. I Part 2:** 515

Joslin, Katherine, **Retro. Supp. I:** 376

Journal (Emerson), **Supp. I Part 1:** 309

"Journal" (L. Michaels), **Supp. XVI:** 213

Journal (Thoreau), **IV:** 175

Journal (Woolman), **Supp. VIII:** 202

"Journal for My Daughter" (Kunitz), **Supp. III Part 1:** 268

"Journal of an Airman" (Auden), **Supp. XIX:** 151

Journal of Arthur Stirling, The (Sinclair), **Supp. V:** 280

"Journal of a Solitary Man, The" (Hawthorne), **II:** 226

Journal of a Solitude (Sarton), **Supp. VIII:** 256, 262–263

Journal of My Other Self (Rilke), **Retro. Supp. II:** 20

Journal of the Fictive Life (Nemerov), **III:** 267, 268, 269, 272, 273, 274, 280–281, 284–285, 286, 287

Journal of the Plague Year, A (Defoe), **III:** 423

"Journal of the Year of the Ox, A" (Wright), **Supp. V:** 343

Journals (Thoreau), **Supp. I Part 1:** 299

Journals and Other Documents on the Life and Voyages of Christopher Columbus (Morison, ed.), **Supp. I Part 2:** 494

Journals of Ralph Waldo Emerson, The (Emerson), **II:** 8, 17, 21

Journals of Susanna Moodie, The: Poems (Atwood), **Supp. XIII:** 33

"Journey, A" (Wharton), **Retro. Supp. I:** 364

"Journey, The" (Winters), **Supp. II Part 2:** 795

"Journey, The" (Wright), **Supp. III Part 2:** 605–606

"Journey, the Arrival and the Dream, The" (Gioia), **Supp. XV:** 120

"Journey, The: For Jane at Thirteen" (Kumin), **Supp. IV Part 2:** 442

Journey and Other Poems, The (Winters), **Supp. II Part 2:** 786, 794, 795, 796, 799, 800, 801

Journey Around My Room: The Autobiography of Louise Bogan—A Mosaic (Bogan), **Supp. III Part 1:** 47, 48, 52, 53

Journey Down, The (Bernstein), **IV:** 455

Journey Home, The (Abbey), **Supp. XIII:** 2, 12

Journeyman (Caldwell), **I:** 297, 302–304, 307, 309

Journeyman: Travels of a Writer (Findley), **Supp. XX:** 50

Journey of Tai-me, The (Momaday), **Supp. IV Part 2:** 485

"Journey of the Magi" (Eliot), **Retro. Supp. I:** 64

Journey to a War (Auden and Isherwood), **Supp. II Part 1:** 13; **Supp. XIV:** 156, 158, 162

Journey to Love (W. C. Williams), **IV:** 422; **Retro. Supp. I:** 429

Journey to My Father; Isaac Bashevis Singer (Zamir), **Retro. Supp. II:** 317

"Journey to Nine Miles" (Walker), **Supp. III Part 2:** 527

"Journey to the Interior" (W. J. Smith), **Supp. XIII:** 339, 340

Journey with Genius: Recollections and Reflections Concerning the D. H. Lawrences (Bynner), **Supp. XV:** 46

Jowett, Benjamin, **Supp. XIV:** 335

"Joy" (Moore), **Supp. X:** 174

"Joy" (Singer), **IV:** 9; **Retro. Supp. II:** 307

Joyce, Cynthia, **Supp. X:** 194, 195, 196

Joyce, James, **I:** 53, 105, 108, 130, 174, 256, 285, 377, 395, 475–476, 478, 480, 483, 576; **II:** 27, 42, 58, 73, 74, 198, 209, 264, 320, 569; **III:** 7, 16, 26–27, 45, 174, 181, 184, 261, 273, 277, 343, 396, 398, 465, 471, 474; **IV:** 32, 73, 85, 95, 103, 171, 182, 211, 286, 370, 412, 418, 419, 428, 434, 456; **Retro. Supp. I:** 59, 63, 75, 80, 89, 91, 108, 109, 127, 287, 290, 292, 334, 335, 420; **Retro. Supp. II:** 221, 326; **Supp. I Part 1:** 257, 262, 270; **Supp. I Part 2:** 437, 546, 613, 620; **Supp. II Part 1:** 136; **Supp. III Part 1:** 35, 36, 65, 225, 229; **Supp. III Part 2:** 611, 617, 618; **Supp. IV Part 1:** 40, 47, 80, 227, 300, 310; **Supp. IV Part 2:** 424, 677; **Supp. V:** 261, 331; **Supp. VIII:** 14, 40, 103; **Supp. IX:** 211, 229, 235, 308; **Supp. X:** 115, 137, 194, 324; **Supp. XI:** 66; **Supp. XII:** 139, 151, 165, 191, 289; **Supp. XIV:** 83; **Supp. XVI:** 41, 189, 282; **Supp. XVII:** 44; **Supp. XIX:** 151, 172; **Supp. XXI:** 7

Joy Comes in the Morning (J. Rosen), **Supp. XVII:** 50

Joy Luck Club, The (Tan), **Supp. X:** 289, 291, 293, 294, 296, 297, 298, 299

"Joy of Sales Resistance, The" (Berry), **Supp. X:** 36

J R (Gaddis), **Supp. IV Part 1:** 279, 280, 285–289, 291, 294; **Supp. IV Part 2:** 484; **Supp. XXI:** 226

Juana Inés de la Cruz, Sor, **Supp. XXI:** 94, 104

Juan de la Cruz (John of the Cross), **Supp. XXI:** 99, 104

"Juan's Song" (Bogan), **Supp. III Part 1:** 50

Jubilate Agno (Smart), **Supp. IV Part 2:** 626

Judah, Hettie, **Supp. XIII:** 246

Judah the Pious (Prose), **Supp. XVI:** 249, 250, 262

"Judas Maccabaeus" (Longfellow), **II:** 506; **Retro. Supp. II:** 165, 167

Judd, Sylvester, **II:** 290; **Supp. I Part 2:** 420

Judd Rankin's Daughter (Glaspell), **Supp. III Part 1:** 186–188

Jude the Obscure (Hardy), **Supp. I Part 1:** 217

Judevine (Budbill), **Supp. XIX:** 4, 8–9, 12

Judevine: A Play in Three Acts/Two Acts (Budbill), **Supp. XIX:** 12–13

"Judgement Day" (O'Connor), **III:** 349, 350; **Retro. Supp. II:** 236

Judgment Day (Farrell), **II:** 29, 31, 32, 34, 39

"Judgment of Paris, The" (Merwin), **Supp. III Part 1:** 350

Judgment of Paris, The (Vidal), **Supp. IV Part 2:** 680, 682

"Judgment of the Sage, The" (Crane), **I:** 420

Judith (Farrell), **II:** 46, 48

"Judith" (Garrett), **Supp. VII:** 109–110

"Juggernaut" (Bass), **Supp. XVI:** 16–17

"Jug of Sirup, A" (Bierce), **I:** 206

"Jugurtha" (Longfellow), **II:** 499

"Juice or Gravy" (P. Roth), **Retro. Supp. II:** 279

"Juke Box Love Song" (Hughes), **Retro. Supp. I:** 209

"Julia" (Hellman), **Supp. I Part 1:** 280, 293

"Julia Miller" (Masters), **Supp. I Part 2:** 461

Julian (Vidal), **Supp. IV Part 2:** 677, 684–685, 685, 689

Julian the Apostate, **Retro. Supp. I:** 247

"Julian Vreden" (Bowles), **Supp. IV Part 1:** 94

Julie and Romeo (Ray), **Supp. XII:** 308, 310

Julien, Isaac, **Supp. XI:** 19

Julie; ou, La nouvelle Héloïse (Rousseau), **Supp. XVI:** 184

Julier, Laura, **Supp. IV Part 1:** 211

Julip (Harrison), **Supp. VIII:** 51

Julius Caesar (Shakespeare), **I:** 284

"July Midnight" (Lowell), **II:** 521

Jumel, Madame, **Supp. I Part 2:** 461

Jumping Out of Bed (R. Bly), **Supp. IV Part 1:** 71

"Jump-Up Day" (Kingsolver), **Supp. VII:** 203

"Junctions" (Lamott), **Supp. XX:** 143

"June 1940" (Kees), **Supp. XV:** 141

"June Light" (Wilbur), **Supp. III Part 2:** 545

June Moon (Lardner and Kaufman), **II:** 427

"June Recital" (Welty), **IV:** 272–273

Juneteenth (Ellison), **Retro. Supp. II:** 119, 124, **126–128**

"Juneteenth" (Ellison), **Retro. Supp. II:** 119, 126; **Supp. II Part 1:** 248

"June the Third" (Gander), **Supp. XV:** 340

Jung, Carl, **I:** 58, 135, 241, 248, 252, 402; **III:** 400, 534, 543; **Supp. I Part 2:** 439; **Supp. IV Part 1:** 68, 69; **Supp. VIII:** 45; **Supp. X:** 193; **Supp. XV:** 214; **Supp. XX:** 63, 117

Junger, Ernst, **Supp. III Part 1:** 63

Jungle, The (Sinclair), **III:** 580; **Supp. V:** 281–284, 285, 289

Jungle Lovers (Theroux), **Supp. VIII:** 314, 315, 316, **317**

"Junior Addict" (Hughes), **Supp. I Part 1:** 343

"Juniper" (Francis), **Supp. IX:** 79

"Junk" (Wilbur), **Supp. III Part 2:** 556

Junker, Howard, **Supp. XV:** 116

Junkie: Confessions of an Unredeemed Drug Addict (Burroughs), **Supp. III Part 1:** 92, 94–96, 101

Junky (Burroughs), **Supp. XIV:** 143

Juno and the Paycock (O'Casey), **Supp. IV Part 1:** 361

"Jupiter Doke, Brigadier General" (Bierce), **I:** 204

Jupiter Laughs (A. Cronin), **Supp. XVII:** 59

Jurgen (Cabell), **III:** 394; **IV:** 286; **Retro. Supp. I:** 80; **Supp. I Part 2:** 718

Jury of Her Peers, A: American Women Writers from Anne Bradstreet to Annie Proulx (Showalter), **Supp. XX:**274

Jusserand, Jules, **II:** 338

Just above My Head (Baldwin), **Retro. Supp. II:** 14–15

"Just a Little One" (Parker), **Supp. IX:** 191

Just and the Unjust, The (Cozzens), **I:** 367–370, 372, 375, 377, 378, 379

Just an Ordinary Day (Jackson), **Supp. IX:** 120

Just Before Dark: Collected Nonfiction (Harrison), **Supp. VIII:** 41, 45, 46, 53

"Just Before the War with the Eskimos" (Salinger), **III:** 559

"Just Boys" (Farrell), **II:** 45

"Just for the Thrill: An Essay on the Difference Between Women and Men" (Carson), **Supp. XII: 103–104**

"Justice" (Hughes), **Supp. I Part 1:** 331

"Justice, A" (Faulkner), **Retro. Supp. I:** 83

Justice, Donald, **Retro. Supp. I:** 313; **Supp. III Part 2:** 541; **Supp. V:** 180, 337, 338, 341; **Supp. VII: 115–130;** **Supp. XI:** 141, 315; **Supp. XIII:** 76, 312; **Supp. XV:** 74, 93, 118, 119, 134; **Supp. XVII:** 110, 120, 246; **Supp. XX:**199

Justice and Expediency (Whitter), **Supp. I Part 2:** 686

"Justice Denied in Massachusetts" (Millay), **III:** 140

Justice for Salcido (Endore), **Supp. XVII:** 63

Justice of Gold in the Damnation of Sinners, The (Edwards), **I:** 559

"Justice to Feminism" (Ozick), **Supp. V:** 272

"Just Like a Woman" (Dylan), **Supp. XV:** 350

"Just Like Job" (Angelou), **Supp. IV Part 1:** 15

"Just One of the Boys" (Swados), **Supp. XIX:** 259

Just Whistle: A Valentine (Wright), **Supp. XV: 346–348**

Just Wild About Harry (H. Miller), **III:** 190

Juvenal, **II:** 8, 169, 552

K

"K, The" (Olson), **Supp. II Part 2:** 558, 563, 569

Kabir, **Supp. IV Part 1:** 74

"Kabnis" (Toomer), **Supp. III Part 2:** 481, 484; **Supp. IX:** 309, 310, **319–320**

Kachel, Elsie. *See* Stevens, Mrs. Wallace (Elsie Kachel)

"Kaddish" (Ginsberg), **Supp. II Part 1:** 319, 327

Kaddish and Other Poems, 1958–1960 (Ginsberg), **Supp. II Part 1:** 309, 319–320; **Supp. XIV:** 269

Kael, Pauline, **Supp. IX:** 253; **Supp. XV:** 147, 148

Kafka, Franz, **II:** 244, 565, 569; **III:** 51, 253, 418, 566, 572; **IV:** 2, 113, 218, 437–439, 442; **Retro. Supp. II:** 20, 221, 282; **Supp. I Part 1:** 197; **Supp. III Part 1:** 105; **Supp. III Part 2:** 413; **Supp. IV Part 1:** 379; **Supp. IV Part 2:** 623; **Supp. VIII:** 14, 15, 103; **Supp. XII:** 21, 37, 98, 168; **Supp. XIII:** 305; **Supp. XVI:** 17, 201, 206, 209; **Supp. XVII:** 244; **Supp. XX:**18, 21, 85, 87

Kafka Americana (Lethem and Scholtz), **Supp. XVIII:** 144–145

Kaganoff, Penny, **Supp. XI:** 122

Kagan's Superfecta (A. Hoffman), **Supp. XVII:** 42

Kahane, Jack, **III:** 171, 178

Kahn, Otto, **I:** 385; **IV:** 123; **Retro. Supp. II:** 81, 84, 85; **Supp. XX:**75

Kahn, R. T., **Supp. XI:** 216

"Kai, Today" (Snyder), **Supp. VIII:** 300

Kaiser, Georg, **I:** 479

Kaiser, Henry, **Supp. I Part 2:** 644

Kakutani, Michiko, **Supp. IV Part 1:** 196, 201, 205, 211, 212; **Supp. V:** 63; **Supp. VIII:** 81, 84, 86, 88, 141; **Supp. X:** 171, 301, 302, 310, 314; **Supp. XI:** 38, 179; **Supp. XII:** 165, 171, 172, 299; **Supp. XVI:** 71; **Supp. XVII:** 6; **Supp. XIX:** 142; **Supp. XX:**92, 94

Kalem, T. E., **Supp. IV Part 2:** 585

Kalevala (Finnish epic), **II:** 503, 504; **Retro. Supp. II:** 155

Kalevala (Lönnrot), **Retro. Supp. II:** 159, 160

Kalfus, Ken, **Supp. XVII:** 50

Kalki: A Novel (Vidal), **Supp. IV Part 2:** 677, 682, 685, 691, 692

Kallan, Richard A., **Supp. XX:**244

Kallen, Horace, **I:** 229; **Supp. I Part 2:** 643; **Supp. XIV:** 195, 197, 198

Kallman, Chester, **II:** 586; **Supp. II Part 1:** 15, 17, 24, 26

"Kallundborg Church" (Whittier), **Supp. I Part 2:** 696

Kalstone, David, **Retro. Supp. II:** 40

Kamel, Rose, **Supp. XIII:** 306

Kamenev, Lev, **Supp. XXI:** 167

Kamera Obskura (Nabokov), **III:** 255

Kamhi, Michelle Moarder, **Supp. IV Part 2:** 529, 530

Kaminsky, Wally, **Supp. XVIII:** 72

Kamp, David, **Supp. XVIII:** 150

Kandy-Kolored Tangerine-Flake Streamline Baby, The (Wolfe), **Supp. III Part 2:** 569, 573–576, 580, 581

Kane, Julie, **Supp. XVII:** 78

Kane, Lesley, **Supp. XIV:** 250

Kanellos, Nicolás, **Supp. VIII:** 82; **Supp. XIII:** 213

Kanin, Garson, **Supp. IV Part 2:** 574

"Kansas City Coyote" (Harjo), **Supp. XII:** 219, 222

"Kansas Emigrants, The" (Whittier), **Supp. I Part 2:** 687

Kant, Immanuel, **I:** 61, 277, 278; **II:** 10–11, 362, 480, 580–581, 582, 583; **III:** 300, 480, 481, 488, 612; **IV:** 90; **Supp. I Part 2:** 640; **Supp. IV Part 2:** 527; **Supp. XIV:** 198, 199; **Supp. XVI:** 184

Kanter, Hal, **IV:** 383

Kapital, Das (Marx), **III:** 580; **Supp. XXI:** 161, 162, 163

Kaplan, Abraham, **I:** 277

Kaplan, Justin, **I:** 247–248; **Retro. Supp. I:** 392

Kaplan, Mary Jo, **Supp. XIX:** 266

Kaplan, Steven, **Supp. V:** 238, 241, 243, 248

Karate Is a Thing of the Spirit (Crews), **Supp. XI: 112–113**

Karbo, Karen, **Supp. X:** 259, 262

"Karintha" (Toomer), **Supp. IX:** 311

Karl, Frederick R., **Supp. IV Part 1:** 384; **Supp. XXI:** 234

"Karloff and the Rock" (Di Piero), **Supp. XIX:** 44

Karl Shapiro's America (film), **Supp. II Part 2:** 703

Karmi, T., **Supp. XV:** 78, 88

Karr, Mary, **Supp. XI: 239–256; Supp. XIII:** 285; **Supp. XV:** 223; **Supp. XVI:** 63, 70, 77; **Supp. XVII:** 242

Kasabian, Linda, **Supp. IV Part 1:** 206

Kasper, Catherine, **Supp. XVI:** 294–295

Kate Chopin (Toth), **Retro. Supp. II:** 71

Kate Chopin: A Critical Biography (Seyersted), **Retro. Supp. II:** 65; **Supp. I Part 1:** 225

Kate Chopin and Edith Wharton: An Annotated Bibliographical Guide to Secondary Sources (Springer), **Supp. I Part 1:** 225

Kate Chopin and Her Creole Stories (Rankin), **Retro. Supp. II:** 57; **Supp. I Part 1:** 200, 225

"Kate Chopin's *The Awakening* in the Perspective of Her Literary Career" (Arms), **Supp. I Part 1:** 225

Kate Vaiden (Price), **Supp. VI:** 264, 265

"Käthe Kollwitz" (Rukeyser), **Supp. VI:** 283, 284

Katherine and Jean (Rice), **Supp. VII:** 288

"Kathleen" (Whittier), **Supp. I Part 2:** 693

Kathleen and Frank: The Autobiography of a Family (Isherwood), **Supp. XIV:** 158, 171

Kathy Goes to Haiti (Acker), **Supp. XII:** 5

Katz, Alex, **Supp. XV:** 185

Katz, Jonathan, **Supp. XII:** 179

Katz, Steve, **Supp. V:** 44

Katz, Steven T., **Supp. XVI:** 154

Katzenberg, Jffrey, **Supp. XXI:** 154

Kauffman, Carol, **Supp. XI:** 295

Kauffmann, Stanley, **III:** 452; **Supp. I Part 2:** 391; **Supp. XVI:** 74

Kaufman, Boris, **Supp. XVIII:** 251

Kaufman, Charlie, **Supp. XV:** 16

Kaufman, George S., **II:** 427, 435, 437; **III:** 62, 71–72, 394; **Retro. Supp. II:** 327; **Supp. IV Part 2:** 574; **Supp. IX:** 190; **Supp. XV:** 329

Kaufmann, James, **Supp. XI:** 39

Kaufmann, Walter, **Supp. XVII:** 137

Kauvar, Elaine M., **Supp. V:** 273

Kavanaugh (Longfellow), **I:** 458; **II:** 489, 491; **Retro. Supp. II:** 156; **Supp. I Part 2:** 420

Kaveney, Roz, **Supp. XI:** 39

Kawabata, Yasunari, **Supp. XV:** 186; **Supp. XXI:** 146

Kaye-Smith, Sheila, **Supp. XVIII:** 130–131

Kazan, Elia, **III:** 153, 163; **IV:** 383; **Supp. I Part 1:** 66, 295; **Supp. XVI:** 193; **Supp. XVIII:** 250–251, 252

Kazin, Alfred, **I:** 248, 417, 419, 517; **II:** 177, 459; **IV:** 236; **Retro. Supp. II:** 206, 243, 246, 286; **Supp. I Part 1:** 195, 196, 294, 295, 296; **Supp. I Part 2:** 536, 631, 647, 650, 678, 679, 719; **Supp. II Part 1:** 143; **Supp. IV Part 1:** 200, 382; **Supp. V:** 122; **Supp. VIII:** 93–111; **Supp. IX:** 3, 227; **Supp. XIII:** 98, 106; **Supp. XIV:** 11; **Supp. XV:** 142

Keach, Stacey, **Supp. XI:** 309

Kean, Danuta, **Supp. XXI:** 80

Keane, Sarah, **Supp. I Part 1:** 100

Kearns, Cleo McNelly, **Retro. Supp. I:** 57

Kearns, George, **Retro. Supp. I:** 292

Keating, AnnLouise, **Supp. IV Part 1:** 330

Keaton, Buster, **I:** 31; **Supp. I Part 2:** 607; **Supp. IV Part 2:** 574

Keaton, Diane, **Supp. XV:** 5

Keats, John, **I:** 34, 103, 284, 314, 317–318, 385, 401, 448; **II:** 82, 88, 97, 214, 368, 512, 516, 530–531, 540, 593; **III:** 4, 10, 45, 122, 133–134, 179, 214, 237, 272, 275, 469, 485, 523; **IV:** 360, 405, 416; **Retro. Supp. I:** 91, 301, 313, 360, 395, 412; **Supp. I Part 1:** 82, 183, 266, 267, 312, 349, 362, 363, 365; **Supp. I Part 2:** 410, 422, 424, 539, 552, 675, 719, 720; **Supp. III Part 1:** 73; **Supp. IV Part 1:** 123, 168, 325; **Supp. IV Part 2:** 455; **Supp. VIII:** 41, 273; **Supp. IX:** 38, 39, 45; **Supp. XI:** 43, 320; **Supp. XII:** 9, 113, 255; **Supp. XIII:** 131, 281; **Supp. XIV:** 274; **Supp. XV:** 92; **Supp. XVII:** 76, 112; **Supp. XIX:** 33, 276; **Supp. XX:**115, 116; **Supp. XXI:** 131

Keats, John (other), **Supp. IX:** 190, 195, 200

"Keela, the Outcast Indian Maiden" (Welty), **IV:** 263

Keeley, Mary Paxton, **Supp. XV:** 136

"Keen Scalpel on Racial Ills" (Bruell), **Supp. VIII:** 126

Keep, The (Egan), **Supp. XIX:** 49, **56–61**

"Keep A-Inchin' Along" (Van Vechten), **Supp. III Part 2:** 744

Keeping (Goldbarth), **Supp. XII:** 179–180, 180

"Keeping Informed in D.C." (Nemerov), **III:** 287

Keeping Slug Woman Alive: A Holistic Approach to American Indian Texts (Sarris), **Supp. IV Part 1:** 329

"'Keeping Their World Large' " (Moore), **III:** 201–202

Keeping the Night (Everwine), **Supp. XV:** 75, **81–85,** 86

"Keeping Things Whole" (Strand), **Supp. IV Part 2:** 624

Keep It Simple: A Defense of the Earth (Nichols), **Supp. XIII:** 268

Kees, Weldon, **Supp. X:** 118; **Supp. XII:** 198; **Supp. XV:** 113, 114, 115, **133–149**

Keillor, Garrison, **Supp. XII:** 343; **Supp. XIII:** 274; **Supp. XVI:** **165–179;** **Supp. XXI:** 53, 62

Keillor, Gary Edward. *See* Keiller, Garrison

Keith, Brian, **Supp. IV Part 2:** 474

Keith, Minor C., **I:** 483

Kelleghan, Fiona, **Supp. XVIII:** 136, 139, 140

Keller, A. G., **III:** 108

Keller, Christopher J., **Supp. XVIII:** 192, 195

Keller, Helen, **I:** 254, 258

Keller, Lynn, **Supp. IV Part 2:** 423; **Supp. V:** 78, 80

Kelley, David, **Supp. IV Part 2:** 528, 529

Kelley, Florence, **Supp. I Part 1:** 5, 7

Kelley, Mary, **Supp. XVIII:** 257, 260

Kelley, Robin, **Supp. XVIII:** 231

Kellogg, Reverend Edwin H., **III:** 200

Kellogg, Paul U., **Supp. I Part 1:** 5, 7, 12

Kelly, **II:** 464

Kelly, Brigit Pegeen, **Supp. XVII:** 123–134

Kelly, Emmett, **Supp. XI:** 99, 106

Kelly, Gene, **Supp. XXI:** 148

Kelly, James Patrick, **Supp. XVIII:** 145; **Supp. XIX:** 231

Kelly, Walt, **Supp. XI:** 105

Kelly, William, **Supp. XV:** 75, 88

Kelsh, Nick, **Supp. XVII:** 167, 179

Kemble, Fanny, **Retro. Supp. I:** 228

Kemble, Gouverneur, **II:** 298

Kemble, Peter, **II:** 298

Kempton, Murray, **Supp. VIII:** 104

Kempton-Wace Letters, The (London and Strunsky), **II:** 465

Kennan, George F., **Supp. VIII:** 241

Kennedy, Albert J., **Supp. I Part 1:** 19

Kennedy, Arthur, **III:** 153

Kennedy, Burt, **Supp. IV Part 1:** 236

Kennedy, Jeffery, **Supp. XXI:** 6

Kennedy, J. Gerald, **Retro. Supp. II:** 271

Kennedy, John F., **I:** 136, 170; **II:** 49, 152–153; **III:** 38, 41, 42, 234, 411, 415, 581; **IV:** 229; **Supp. I Part 1:** 291; **Supp. I Part 2:** 496; **Supp. VIII:** 98, 104, 203; **Supp. XII:** 132

Kennedy, Mrs. John F., **I:** 136

Kennedy, John Pendleton, **II:** 313

Kennedy, Robert, **Supp. V:** 291

Kennedy, Robert F., **I:** 294; **Supp. I Part 1:** 52; **Supp. XI:** 343

Kennedy, Sarah, **Supp. XVIII:** 293, 299, 301

Kennedy, William, **Supp. VII:** **131–157;** **Supp. XVII:** 135; **Supp. XIX:** 141; **Supp. XX:**90

Kennedy, X. J., **Supp. V:** 178, 182; **Supp. XV:** 113, **151–173**

Kenner, Hugh, **III:** 475, 478; **IV:** 412; **Supp. I Part 1:** 255; **Supp. IV Part 2:** 474; **Supp. XV:** 147; **Supp. XXI:** 235

"Kenneth Koch's 'Serious Moment' " (Spurr), **Supp. XV:** 183

Kenneth Millar/Ross Macdonald: A Checklist (Bruccoli), **Supp. IV Part 2:** 464, 469, 471

Kenney, Michael, **Supp. XIX:** 51, 52–53

Kenney, Susan, **Supp. XVIII:** 288, 289

Kenny, Maurice, **Supp. IV Part 2:** 502

Kent, George, **Supp. IV Part 1:** 11

Kent, Rockwell, **Supp. XV:** 41

Kenton, Edna, **Supp. XXI:** 6

Kenton, Maxwell. *See* Burnett, David; Hoffenberg, Mason; Southern, Terry

"Kent State, May 1970" (Haines), **Supp. XII:** 211

Kentucky Straight (Offutt), **Supp. XIX:** **163–167,** 171, 172

Kenya, the Land of Conflict (Kenyatta), **Supp. XXI:** 166

Kenyatta, Jomo, **Supp. X:** 135; **Supp. XXI:** 166

Kenyon, Jane, **Supp. VII:** **159–177;** **Supp. VIII:** 272

Keogh, Tom, **Supp. XVI:** 230

Kepler, Johannes, **III:** 484; **IV:** 18

Keplinger, David, **Supp. V:** 273

Keppel, Frederick P., **I:** 214

"Kéramos" (Longfellow), **II:** 494; **Retro. Supp. II:** 167, 169

Kéramos and Other Poems (Longfellow), **II:** 490

Kercheval, Jesse Lee, **Supp. XIX:** 51

Kerim, Ussin, **Supp. IX:** 152

Kermode, Frank, **IV:** 133; **Retro. Supp. I:** 301

Kern, Jerome, **II:** 427

Kerouac, Jack, **III:** 174; **Retro. Supp. I:** 102; **Supp. II Part 1:** 31, 307, 309, 318, 328; **Supp. III Part 1:** 91–94, 96, 100, **217–234;** **Supp. IV Part 1:** 90, 146; **Supp. V:** 336; **Supp. VIII:** 42, 138, 289, 305; **Supp. IX:** 246; **Supp. XII:** 118, 121, 122, 123, 126, 131, 132; **Supp. XIII:** 275, 284; **Supp. XIV:** 137, 138, 141, 142, 143–144; **Supp. XV:** 134, 221; **Supp. XVI:** 123; **Supp. XVII:** 135, 138; **Supp. XX:**17

Kerr, Deborah, **Supp. XI:** 307

Kerr, Orpheus C. (pseudonym). *See* Newell, Henry

Kerr, Walter, **Supp. IV Part 2:** 575, 579

Kerridge, Richard, **Supp. XVI:** 26

Kesey, Ken, **III:** 558; **Supp. III Part 1:** 217; **Supp. V:** 220, 295; **Supp. X:** 24, 265; **Supp. XI:** 104

Kessel, John, **Supp. XVIII:** 145; **Supp. XIX:** 231

Kessler, Milton, **Supp. XIX:** 195

Kesten, Stephen, **Supp. XI:** 309

Ketchum, Liza, **Supp. XIX:** 266
Ketchup (Shanley), **Supp. XIV:** 315
Kevane, Bridget, **Supp. XI:** 185, 190
"Key, The" (Welty), **IV:** 262
"Keys" (Nye), **Supp. XIII:** 281
"Key to the Highway" (Halliday), **Supp. XIX:** 84
Key to Uncle Tom's Cabin, A (Stowe), **Supp. I Part 2:** 580
Key West (H. Crane), **Retro. Supp. II:** 84
"Key West" (H. Crane), **I:** 400
Key West: An Island Sheaf (Crane), **I:** 385, 399–402
"Khalil the Heretic" (Gibran), **Supp. XX:**124
Khrushchev, Nikita, **I:** 136
Kiang Kang-hu, **Supp. XV:** 45, 47
Kick for a Bite, A (Cobbett), **Supp. XV:** 237
"Kicking the Candles Out" (Jarman), **Supp. XVII:** 113
Kid, The (Aiken), **I:** 61
Kid, The (Chaplin), **I:** 386
Kidder, Tracy, **Supp. III Part 1:** 302; **Supp. XVIII:** 106, 114
Kidman, Nicole, **Supp. X:** 80
"Kidnapping in the Family, A" (Fante), **Supp. XI:** 164
"Kid's Guide to Divorce, The" (Moore), **Supp. X:** 167, 172
Kidwell, Clara Sue, **Supp. IV Part 1:** 333
Kielsky, Vera Emuma, **Supp. V:** 273
Kiely, Brendan, **Supp. XVII:** 75
Kieran, John, **II:** 417
Kierkegaard, Søren Aabye, **II:** 229; **III:** 292, 305, 309, 572; **IV:** 438, 491; **Retro. Supp. I:** 326; **Retro. Supp. II:** 222; **Supp. V:** 9; **Supp. VIII:** 7–8; **Supp. XX:**132
Kiernan, Robert F., **Supp. IV Part 2:** 684
Kieseritsky, L., **III:** 252
Kilgo, Jim, **Supp. XVIII:** 192
"Kilim" (McClatchy), **Supp. XII:** 258
Kilina, Patricia (pseudonym). *See* Warren, Patricia Nell
"Killed at Resaca" (Bierce), **I:** 202
"Killed at the Ford" (Longfellow), **Retro. Supp. II:** 170–171
Killens, John Oliver, **Supp. IV Part 1:** 8, 369
"Killer in the Rain" (Chandler), **Supp. IV Part 1:** 122
"Killers, The" (Hemingway), **II:** 249; **Retro. Supp. I:** 188, 189
Killing Mister Watson (Matthiessen), **Supp. V:** 212, 214
"Killing of a State Cop, The" (Ortiz), **Supp. IV Part 2:** 499
Killing of Sister George, The (Marcus), **Supp. I Part 1:** 277
"Killings" (Dubus), **Supp. VII:** 85–86
"Killing the Ghost of Ripton" (Carruth), **Supp. XIX:** 1
"Killing the Plants" (Kenyon), **Supp. VII:** 167, 168
Kilmer, Joyce, **Supp. I Part 2:** 387; **Supp. XV:** 294
Kilpatrick, James K., **Supp. X:** 145

Kilvert, Francis, **Supp. VIII:** 172
Kim (Kipling), **Supp. X:** 230
Kim, Alfred, **Supp. XI:** 140
Kim, Sharon, **Supp. XVIII:** 267
Kimball, Frederic, **Supp. XXI:** 146
Kimball, J. Golden, **Supp. IV Part 2:** 602
Kimbrough, Mary Craig. *See* Sinclair, Mary Craig (Mary Craig Kimbrough)
Kimes, Maymie B., **Supp. IX:** 178
Kimes, William F., **Supp. IX:** 178
Kimmelman, Bert, **Supp. XXI:** 24
"Kin" (Welty), **IV:** 277; **Retro. Supp. I:** 353
Kinard, Agnes Dodds, **Supp. XIV:** 122, 123, 127
Kincaid, Jamaica, **Supp. VII: 179–196**
Kincaid, James, **Supp. XVIII:** 62, 63
"Kindness" (Dunn), **Supp. XI:** 149, 150
"Kindness" (Nye), **Supp. XIII:** 285
"Kindness" (Plath), **Retro. Supp. II:** 256
Kind of Light that Shines on Texas, The (McKnight), **Supp. XX:151–152**
"Kind of Light that Shines on Texas, The" (McKnight), **Supp. XX:151**
Kind of Order, A Kind of Folly, A: Essays and Conversations (Kunitz), **Supp. III Part 1:** 262, 268
Kindred (O. Butler), **Supp. XIII: 59–60,** 69
"Kind Sir: These Woods" (Sexton), **Supp. II Part 2:** 673
Kinds of Love (Sarton), **Supp. VIII: 253–254,** 256
Kinfolk (Buck), **Supp. II Part 1:** 126
King, Alexander, **IV:** 287
King, Carole, **Supp. XII:** 308
King, Clarence, **I:** 1
King, Ernest, **Supp. I Part 2:** 491
King, Fisher, **II:** 425
King, Francis, **Supp. XIV:** 155, 156, 166, 169
King, Grace, **Retro. Supp. II:** 136
King, Martin Luther, Jr., **Retro. Supp. II:** 12, 13; **Supp. XVIII:** 24; **Supp. XX:281**
King, Michael, **Supp. XII:** 182
King, Queen, Knave (Nabokov), **III:** 251; **Retro. Supp. I:** 270
King, Starr, **Supp. II Part 1:** 341, 342
King, Stephen, **Supp. IV Part 1:** 102, 104; **Supp. IV Part 2:** 467; **Supp. V: 137–155; Supp. IX:** 114; **Supp. XIII:** 53
King, Tabitha (Mrs. Stephen King), **Supp. V:** 137
King, The (Barthelme), **Supp. IV Part 1:** 47, 52
"King, The" (Gibran), **Supp. XX:123–124**
King Coffin (Aiken), **I:** 53–54, 57
"King David" (Benét), **Supp. XI:** 44
"King David" (Reznikoff), **Supp. XIV:** 283
Kingdom and the Power, The (Talese), **Supp. XVII:** 202, 203, 204, 210
Kingdom by the Sea, The: A Journey around Great Britain (Theroux), **Supp. VIII:** 323

Kingdom of Earth (T. Williams), **IV:** 382, 386, 387, 388, 391, 393, 398
"Kingdom of Earth, The" (T. Williams), **IV:** 384
Kingfisher, The (Clampitt), **Supp. IX:** 38
"Kingfishers, The" (Olson), **Supp. II Part 2:** 557, 558–563, 582
King Jasper (Robinson), **III:** 523
King Kong (film), **Supp. IV Part 1:** 104; **Supp. XVII:** 58
King Lear (Shakespeare), **I:** 538; **II:** 540, 551; **Retro. Supp. I:** 248; **Supp. IV Part 1:** 31, 36; **Supp. IX:** 14; **Supp. XI:** 172; **Supp. XV:** 349
King Leopold's Soliloquy (Twain), **IV:** 208
King My Father's Wreck, The (Simpson), **Supp. IX:** 266, 267, 270, 275, 276
King of Babylon Shall Not Come Against You, The (Garrett), **Supp. VII:** 110–111; **Supp. X:** 3
"King of Beasts" (P. N. Warren), **Supp. XX:272**
"King of Folly Island, The" (Jewett), **II:** 394; **Retro. Supp. II:** 132, 133
King of Kings (film), **Supp. IV Part 2:** 520
King of Paris (Endore), **Supp. XVII:** 64
"King of the Bingo Game" (Ellison), **Retro. Supp. II:** 117, 125; **Supp. II Part 1:** 235, 238, 240–241
"King of the Cats, The" (Benét), **Supp. XI:** 49–50
"King of the Clock Tower" (Yeats), **III:** 473
"King of the Desert, The" (O'Hara), **III:** 369
King of the Fields, The (Singer), **Retro. Supp. II:** 317
King of the Jews (Epstein), **Supp. XII:** 161, **166–170,** 172
King of the Mountain (Garrett), **Supp. VII:** 96, 97
"King of the River" (Kunitz), **Supp. III Part 1:** 263, 267–268
"King of the Sea" (Marquand), **III:** 60
"King over the Water" (Blackmur), **Supp. II Part 1:** 107
"King Pandar" (Blackmur), **Supp. II Part 1:** 92, 102
"King Pest" (Poe), **Retro. Supp. II:** 273
Kingsblood Royal (Lewis), **II:** 456
Kingsbury, John, **Supp. I Part 1:** 8
"King's Daughters, Home for Unwed Mothers, 1948" (Stanford), **Supp. XV:** 345
King's Henchman, The (Millay), **III:** 138–139
Kingsley, Sidney, **Supp. I Part 1:** 277, 281
King's Mare, The (Canolle; Loos, trans.), **Supp. XVI:** 194
"King's Missive, The" (Whittier), **Supp. I Part 2:** 694
Kingsolver, Barbara, **Supp. VII: 197–214; Supp. XIII:** 16; **Supp. XVIII:** 189
King's Stilts, The (Geisel), **Supp. XVI:** 100, 104
Kingston, Earll, **Supp. V:** 160

Kingston, Maxine Hong, **Supp. IV Part 1:** 1, 12; **Supp. V: 157–175,** 250; **Supp. X:** 291–292; **Supp. XI:** 18, 245; **Supp. XV:** 220, 223

"King Volmer and Elsie" (Whittier), **Supp. I Part 2:** 696

Kinmont, Alexander, **Supp. I Part 2:** 588–589

Kinnaird, John, **Retro. Supp. I:** 399

Kinnell, Galway, **Supp. III Part 1: 235–256; Supp. III Part 2:** 541; **Supp. IV Part 2:** 623; **Supp. V:** 332; **Supp. VIII:** 39; **Supp. XI:** 139; **Supp. XII:** 241; **Supp. XV:** 212; **Supp. XVI:** 53

Kinsella, Thomas, **Supp. XX:**195–196, 197, 207

Kinsey, Alfred, **IV:** 230; **Supp. XIV:** 140

Kinzie, Mary, **Supp. XII:** 181

"Kipling" (Trilling), **Supp. III Part 2:** 495

Kipling, Rudyard, **I:** 421, 587–588; **II:** 271, 338, 404, 439; **III:** 55, 328, 508, 511, 521, 524, 579; **IV:** 429; **Supp. IV Part 2:** 603; **Supp. X:** 255; **Supp. XX:**23

Kirby, David, **Supp. XIII:** 89; **Supp. XIX:** 81

Kirkland, Caroline, **Supp. XVIII:** 258

Kirkland, David, **Supp. XVI:** 186

Kirkland, Jack, **I:** 297

Kirkpatrick, Jeane, **Supp. VIII:** 241

Kirkus, Virginia, **Supp. XV:** 198

Kirkwood, Cynthia A., **Supp. XI:** 177, 178, 179

Kirp, David L., **Supp. XI:** 129

Kirsch, Adam, **Supp. XV:** 251, 260, 264, 266, 341, 347, 350–351

Kirstein, Lincoln, **Supp. II Part 1:** 90, 97; **Supp. IV Part 1:** 82, 83

"Kiss, The" (Di Piero), **Supp. XIX:** 45, 47

Kiss, The (Harrison), **Supp. X:** 191

"Kiss, The" (Sexton), **Supp. II Part 2:** 687

"Kiss Away" (C. Baxter), **Supp. XVII:** 20

Kissel, Howard, **Supp. IV Part 2:** 580

Kiss Hollywood Good-by (Loos), **Supp. XVI:** 190, 195

Kissinger, Henry, **Supp. IV Part 1:** 388; **Supp. XII:** 9, 14

Kiss of the Spider Woman, the Musical (McNally), **Supp. XIII:** 207, **Supp. XIII:** 208

Kiss Tomorrow Good-bye (McCoy), **Supp. XIII:** 170, **172–173,** 174

"Kit and Caboodle" (Komunyakaa), **Supp. XIII:** 115

Kit Brandon: A Portrait (Anderson), **I:** 111

Kitchen, Judith, **Supp. IV Part 1:** 242, 245, 252; **Supp. IX:** 163; **Supp. XI:** 312, 313, 315, 317, 319, 320, 326, 329; **Supp. XV:** 215, 219

"Kitchenette" (Brooks), **Retro. Supp. I:** 208

Kitchen God's Wife, The (Tan), **Supp. X:** 289, 292, 293, 294–295, 296–297, 298–299

"Kitchen Terrarium: 1983" (McCarriston), **Supp. XIV:** 270

Kit O'Brien (Masters), **Supp. I Part 2:** 471

Kittel, Frederick August. *See* Wilson, August

Kittredge, Charmian. *See* London, Mrs. Jack (Charmian Kittredge)

Kittredge, William, **Supp. VIII:** 39; **Supp. XI:** 316; **Supp. XII:** 209; **Supp. XIII:** 16

"Kitty Hawk" (Frost), **II:** 164; **Retro. Supp. I:** 124, 141

Kizer, Carolyn, **Supp. XVII:** 71, 72, 73, 74

Klaidman, Stephen, **Supp. XIX:** 269

Klail City (Hinojosa), **Supp. XIX: 97, 101–103**

Klail City Death Trip (Hinojosa). *See Ask a Policeman* (Hinojosa); *Becky and Her Friends* (Hinojosa); *Dear Rafe* (Hinojosa); *Fair Gentlemen of Belken County* (Hinojosa); *Klail City* (Hinojosa); *Korean Love Songs from Klail City Death Trip* (Hinojosa); *Partners in Crime: A Rafe Buenrostro Mystery* (Hinojosa); *Rites and Witnesses: A Comedy* (Hinojosa); *Useless Servants, The* (Hinojosa); *Valley, The* (Hinojosa)

Klein, Joe, **Supp. XII:** 67–68

Klein, Marcus, **Supp. I Part 2:** 432; **Supp. XI:** 233

Kleist, Heinrich von, **Supp. IV Part 1:** 224

Kline, Franz, **Supp. XII:** 198

Kline, George, **Supp. VIII:** 22, 28

Klinghoffer, David, **Supp. XVI:** 74

Klinkowitz, Jerome, **Supp. IV Part 1:** 40; **Supp. X:** 263; **Supp. XI:** 347; **Supp. XXI:** 233

Kloefkorn, Bill, **Supp. XIX:** 119

Knapp, Adeline, **Supp. XI:** 200

Knapp, Friedrich, **III:** 100

Knapp, Samuel, **I:** 336

Knapp, Samuel Lorenzo, **Supp. XV:** 246

"Kneeling Down to Look into a Culvert" (R. Bly), **Supp. XXI:** 88

Kneel to the Rising Sun (Caldwell), **I:** 304, 309

"Knees/Dura-Europos" (Goldbarth), **Supp. XII:** 185

"Knife" (Simic), **Supp. VIII:** 275

Knight, Arthur, **Supp. XIV:** 144

Knight, Etheridge, **Supp. XI:** 239

"Knight in Disguise, The" (Lindsay), **Supp. I Part 2:** 390

Knightly Quest, The (T. Williams), **IV:** 383

Knight's Gambit (Faulkner), **II:** 72

Knish, Anne. *See* Ficke, Arthur Davison

"Knit One, Purl Two" (K. Snodgrass), **Supp. XVI:** 42

"Knock" (Dickey), **Supp. IV Part 1:** 182

Knocked Out Loaded (album, Dylan), **Supp. XVIII:** 28

"Knocking Around" (Ashbery), **Supp. III Part 1:** 22

"Knocking on Heaven's Door" (Lamott), **Supp. XX:**140–141

"Knocking on Three, Winston" (Epstein), **Supp. XIV:** 109

Knock on Any Door (film, Ray), **Supp. XVII:** 150

Knock on Any Door (W. Motley), **Supp. XVII: 150–155,** 159, 160; 158

Knockout Artist, The (Crews), **Supp. XI: 113–114**

Knoll, Robert E., **Supp. XV:** 118

Knopf, Alfred A., **III:** 99, 105, 106, 107; **Retro. Supp. I:** 13, 19, 317; **Supp. I Part 1:** 324, 325, 327; **Supp. IV Part 1:** 125, 354; **Supp. XIII:** 172

Knopf, Blanche, **Supp. I Part 1:** 324, 325, 327, 328, 332, 341; **Supp. IV Part 1:** 128, 346, 348; **Supp. XIII:** 169

"Knot, The" (Rich), **Supp. I Part 2:** 555

Knotts, Kristina, **Supp. XIII:** 238

"Knowing, The" (Olds), **Supp. X:** 215

"Knowledge Forwards and Backwards" (Stern), **Supp. IX:** 296

"Knowledge of Plates" (Bronk), **Supp. XXI:** 33

Knowles, John, **Supp. IV Part 2:** 679; **Supp. XII: 235–250; Supp. XX:**84

Knox, Frank, **Supp. I Part 2:** 488, 489

Knox, Israel, **Supp. X:** 70

Knox, Vicesimus, **II:** 8

Knoxville: Summer of 1915 (Agee), **I:** 42–46

Knudson, R. Rozanne, **Supp. IV Part 2:** 648

Kober, Arthur, **Supp. I Part 1:** 292

Koch, Frederick, **IV:** 453

Koch, John, **Supp. VIII:** 88

Koch, Kenneth, **Supp. XV: 175–192; Supp. XIX:** 81

Koch, Vivienne, **III:** 194; **IV:** 136, 140; **Retro. Supp. I:** 428, 430

"Kochinnenako in Academe: Three Approaches to Interpreting a Keres Indian Tale" (Gunn Allen), **Supp. IV Part 1:** 329

"Kodachromes of the Island" (Hayden), **Supp. II Part 1:** 367, 380

Koestler, Arthur, **I:** 258; **Supp. I Part 2:** 671

Kokkinen, Eila, **Supp. XIV:** 146, 148

Kolba, Ellen D., **Supp. XVIII:** 257

Kolbenheyer, Dr. Frederick, **Supp. I Part 1:** 207

Kolodny, Annette, **Supp. X:** 97, 103, 229

"Komodo" (C. Frost), **Supp. XV:** 95

Komunyakaa, Yusef, **Supp. XIII: 111–136; Supp. XXI:** 129, 139

Konigsberg, Allan Stewart. *See* Allen, Woody

Kon-Tiki (Heyerdahl), **II:** 477

Koopman, Harry Lyman, **Retro. Supp. I:** 40

Ko; or, A Season on Earth (Koch), **Supp. XV:** 175, 180, 181, 183, 186

Kooser, Ted, **Supp. XV:** 113, 115; **Supp. XIX: 115–130; Supp. XXI:** 243

Kootz, Samuel, **Supp. XV:** 144

Kora and Ka (Doolittle), **Supp. I Part 1:** 270

Kora in Hell (W. C. Williams), **Retro. Supp. I:** 416, **417–418,** 419, 430, 431; **Supp. XXI:** 232
Korb, Rena, **Supp. XI:** 2
Korczak, Janosz, **Supp. X:** 70
Korean Love Songs from Klail City Death Trip (Hinojosa), **Supp. XIX:** 98, **103–104**
Kornblatt, Joyce Reiser, **Supp. XV:** 62
Kornfield, Jack, **Supp. XX:** 142
Korrektur (Bernhard), **Supp. XX:** 91
Kort, Amy, **Supp. XIII:** 148
Korwin, Yala, **Supp. XXI:** 99
Kosinski, Jerzy, **Supp. VII: 215–228; Supp. XII:** 21
"Kostas Tympakianakis" (Merrill), **Supp. III Part 1:** 326
Koteliansky, S. S., **Supp. VIII:** 251, 265
Kovic, Ron, **Supp. XIX:** 17
Kowloon Tong (Theroux), **Supp. VIII:** 325
Kozlenko, William, **IV:** 378, 381
Krabbenhoft, Ken, **Supp. XVII:** 112
Kraft, James, **Supp. XV:** 40, 41, 42, 43, 52
Krakauer, Jon, **Supp. XVII:** 210; **Supp. XVIII: 105–118**
Kramer, Dale, **Supp. I Part 2:** 669
Kramer, Hilton, **III:** 537; **Supp. I Part 1:** 295, 296; **Supp. VIII:** 239; **Supp. XV:** 113; **Supp. XIX:** 269
Kramer, Lawrence, **Supp. IV Part 1:** 61, 65, 66; **Supp. IX:** 291
Kramer, Peter D., **Supp. XVI:** 229
Kramer, Stanley, **II:** 421, 587
Krapp's Last Tape (Beckett), **I:** 71; **III:** 387; **Retro. Supp. I:** 206
Krassner, Paul, **Supp. IV Part 1:** 385; **Supp. XI:** 293
Kraus, Karl, **Supp. XX:** 84
Krauth, Leland, **Supp. XVIII:** 58
Kreisler, Harry, **Supp. XVI:** 155
Kreitman, Esther, **IV:** 2
"Kremlin of Smoke" (Schnackenberg), **Supp. XV:** 257–258
Kreymborg, Alfred, **II:** 530; **III:** 465; **IV:** 76; **Retro. Supp. I:** 417; **Supp. XV:** 301, 306
Krim, Seymour, **Supp. XV:** 338; **Supp. XVI:** 217; **Supp. XVIII:** 285
Krisak, Len, **Supp. XXI:** 99, 104
Kristeva, Julia, **Supp. XII:** 6
Kristofferson, Kris, **Supp. XIII:** 119
Kristol, Irving, **Supp. VIII:** 93, 244; **Supp. XIII:** 98
Krivak, Andrew, **Supp. XVII:** 242
Kroll, Jack, **Supp. IV Part 2:** 590
Kroll, Judith, **Supp. I Part 2:** 541–543, 544, 546
Kroll Ring, Frances. *See* Ring, Frances Kroll
Krondorfer, Björn, **Supp. XVI:** 160
Krook, Dorothea, **Retro. Supp. II:** 243
Kropotkin, Peter, **I:** 493; **Supp. I Part 1:** 5; **Supp. IV Part 2:** 521
Kruif, Paul de, **II:** 446
Krupat, Arnold, **Supp. IV Part 2:** 500
Krupnick, Mark, **Supp. XVI:** 153
Krutch, Joseph Wood, **II:** 459; **III:** 425; **IV:** 70, 175

Kublai Khan, **III:** 395
"Kubla Khan" (Coleridge), **Supp. XIII:** 131, 283
Kubrick, Stanley, **Supp. IV Part 1:** 392; **Supp. XI:** 293, **Supp. XI:** 301, 302–303
"Kubuku Rides (This Is It) " (L. Brown), **Supp. XXI:** 39, 42–43
Kuehl, John, **Supp. IV Part 1:** 279, 284, 285, 287
Kuehl, Linda, **Supp. IV Part 1:** 199
"Kugelmass Episode, The" (Allen), **Supp. XV:** 15, 16
Kukachin, Princess, **III:** 395
"Ku Klux" (Hughes), **Retro. Supp. I:** 205
Kulshrestha, Chirantan, **Retro. Supp. II:** 21
Kumin, Maxine, **Supp. IV Part 2: 439–457; Supp. XIII:** 294; **Supp. XVII:** 71, 75–76; **Supp. XX:** 164
Kundera, Milan, **Supp. VIII:** 241
Kunerth, Jeff, **Supp. XXI:** 47
Kunitz, Stanley, **I:** 179, 180, 181, 182, 521; **II:** 545; **Supp. III Part 1: 257–270; Supp. V:** 79; **Supp. XI:** 259; **Supp. XIII:** 341
Kuo, Helena, **Supp. X:** 291
Kuropatkin, General Aleksei Nikolaevich, **III:** 247–248
Kurth, Peter, **Supp. XVIII:** 145
Kurzy of the Sea (Barnes), **Supp. III Part 1:** 34
Kushner, Tony, **Supp. IX: 131–149; Supp. XX:** 177; **Supp. XXI:** 145
Kussy, Bella, **IV:** 468
Kuttner, Henry, **Supp. IV Part 1:** 102
Kuzma, Greg, **Supp. XV:** 118

L
LaBastille, Anne, **Supp. X: 95–110**
"Labor's Cultural Degradation" (Swados), **Supp. XIX:** 264–265
"Labours of Hercules, The" (Moore), **III:** 201
La Bruyère, Jean de, **I:** 58
La Bufera e Altro (Montale), **Supp. V:** 337
LaBute, Neil, **Supp. XXI:** 147
Labyrinth of Love (Untermeyer), **Supp. XV:** 312
Labyrinth of Solitude, The (Paz), **Supp. XIII:** 223
Lacan, Jacques, **Supp. IV Part 1:** 45; **Supp. VIII:** 5; **Supp. XII:** 98
La Casa en Mango Street (Cisneros), **Supp. VII:** 58–59
Lachaise, Gaston, **I:** 434
"Lackawanna" (Merwin), **Supp. III Part 1:** 350
Lackawanna Elegy (Goll; Kinnell, trans.), **Supp. III Part 1:** 235, 243–244
Laclède, Pierre, **Supp. I Part 1:** 205
"Lacquer Prints" (Lowell), **II:** 524–525
Lacy, Ed, **Supp. XV: 193–210**
Ladder, The (Rasmussen; Nelson, trans.), **Supp. XVIII:** 180–181
Ladder of Years (Tyler), **Supp. IV Part 2:** 657, 671–672
Ladders to Fire (Nin), **Supp. X:** 185

Laddie (Stratton-Porter), **Supp. XX:** 211, 213
"Laddie, the Princess and the Pie" (Stratton-Porter), **Supp. XX:** 216
"Ladies" (Coleman), **Supp. XI:** 93
Ladies Almanack (Barnes), **Supp. III Part 1:** 37–39, 42
Ladies Auxiliary, The (Mirvis), **Supp. XX:** 177, **179–185**
"Ladies in Spring" (Welty), **IV:** 276–277; **Retro. Supp. I:** 353
Lady, The (Richter), **Supp. XVIII: 211–212,** 220
Lady Audley's Secret (Braddon), **Supp. I Part 1:** 35, 36
"Lady Barberina" (James), **Retro. Supp. I:** 227
"Lady Bates" (Jarrell), **II:** 380–381
Lady Chatterley's Lover (Lawrence), **III:** 170; **IV:** 434; **Supp. XVI:** 267
Lady from Louisiana (film, Vorhaus), **Supp. XVII:** 59
"Lady from Redhorse, A" (Bierce), **I:** 203
Lady in Kicking Horse Reservoir, The (Hugo), **Supp. VI:** 134, **138–139**
Lady in the Lake, The (Chandler), **Supp. IV Part 1:** 127, 129–130
"Lady in the Lake, The" (Chandler), **Supp. IV Part 1:** 129
Lady in the Lake, The (film), **Supp. IV Part 1:** 130
"Lady in the Pink Mustang, The" (Erdrich), **Supp. IV Part 1:** 270
"Lady Is Civilized, The" (Taylor), **Supp. V:** 315
Lady Is Cold, The (White), **Supp. I Part 2:** 653
"Lady Lazarus" (Plath), **Retro. Supp. II:** 250, 251, 255; **Supp. I Part 2:** 529, 535, 542, 545
Lady of Aroostook, The (Howells), **II:** 280
"Lady of Bayou St. John, A" (Chopin), **Retro. Supp. II:** 58
"Lady of the Lake, The" (Malamud), **Supp. I Part 2:** 437
Lady Oracle (Atwood), **Supp. XIII:** 21, **23–24**
Lady Sings the Blues (film), **Supp. I Part 1:** 67
"Lady's Maid's Tale, The" (Wharton), **IV:** 316
"Lady Wentworth" (Longfellow), **II:** 505
"Lady with a Lamp" (Parker), **Supp. IX:** 193
"Lady with the Heron, The" (Merwin), **Supp. III Part 1:** 343
La Farge, John, **I:** 1, 2, 20; **II:** 322, 338; **Retro. Supp. I:** 217
La Farge, Oliver, **Supp. IV Part 2:** 503
Lafayette, Marquis de, **I:** 344, 345; **II:** 405–406; **Supp. I Part 2:** 510, 511, 683
"La Figlia che Piange" (Eliot), **Retro. Supp. I:** 63
La Follette, Robert, **I:** 483, 485, 492; **III:** 580
La Fontaine, Jean de, **II:** 154; **III:** 194; **IV:** 80

Laforgue, Jules, **I:** 386, 569, 570, 572–573, 575, 576; **II:** 528; **III:** 8, 11, 466; **IV:** 37, 79, 80, 122; **Retro. Supp. I:** 55, 56; **Supp. XIII:** 332, 335, 346; **Supp. XV:** 165

La Gallienne, Eva, **Supp. VIII:** 251

"Lager Beer" (Dunbar), **Supp. II Part 1:** 193

"La Gringuita: On Losing a Native Language" (Alvarez), **Supp. VII:** 18

Laguna Woman (Silko), **Supp. IV Part 2:** 557, 560–561

Lahiri, Jhumpa, **Supp. XXI: 175–189**

Lahr, John, **Supp. XXI:** 18

Laing, R. D., **Supp. I Part 2:** 527; **Supp. XX:**94

La kabbale pratique (Ambelain), **Supp. I Part 1:** 273

"Lake, The" (Bradbury), **Supp. IV Part 1:** 101

Lake, The (play), **Supp. IX:** 189

Lakeboat (Mamet), **Supp. XIV:** 240–241

"Lake Chelan" (Stafford), **Supp. XI:** 321

Lake Effect Country (Ammons), **Supp. VII:** 34, 35

"Lake Isle of Innisfree, The" (Yeats), **Retro. Supp. I:** 413; **Supp. XIX:** 92

"Lake Return" (Wright), **Supp. XV:** 345

Lake Wobegon Days (Keillor), **Supp. XVI:** 165, 166, **173–174**

Lake Wobegon Summer 1956 (Keillor), **Supp. XVI:** 178

Lalic, Ivan V., **Supp. VIII:** 272

Lamantia, Philip, **Supp. VIII:** 289

Lamb, Brian, **Supp. XIX:** 156; **Supp. XX:**101

Lamb, Charles, **III:** 111, 207; **Supp. VIII:** 125

Lamb, Wendy, **Supp. IV Part 2:** 658

Lambardi, Marilyn May, **Retro. Supp. II:** 45–46

"Lame Feet of Salvation, The" (W. V. Davis), **Supp. XXI:** 87–88

"Lament" (Wilbur), **Supp. III Part 2:** 550

"Lamentations" (Glück), **Supp. V:** 83, 84

"Lament for Dark Peoples" (Hughes), **Retro. Supp. I:** 199

"Lament for Saul and Jonathan" (Bradstreet), **Supp. I Part 1:** 111

"Lament-Heaven" (Doty), **Supp. XI:** 125

"Lament of a New England Mother, The" (Eberhart), **I:** 539

Laments for the Living (Parker), **Supp. IX:** 192

"Lame Shall Enter First, The" (O'Connor), **III:** 348, 351, 352, 355, 356–357, 358; **Retro. Supp. II:** 237

Lamia (Keats), **II:** 512; **III:** 523

Lamming, George, **Supp. XXI:** 170

Lamott, Anne, **Supp. XX:131–146**

La Motte-Fouqué, Friedrich Heinrich Karl, **III:** 77, 78

L'Amour, Louis, **Supp. XIII:** 5

Lamp for Nightfall, A (Caldwell), **I:** 297

Lamplit Answer, The (Schnackenberg), **Supp. XV:** 251, 254, **256–260**

"Lance" (Nabokov), **Retro. Supp. I:** 266

Lancelot (Percy), **Supp. III Part 1:** 384, 395–396

Lancelot (Robinson), **III:** 513, 522

Lanchester, John, **Retro. Supp. I:** 278

"Land" (Emerson), **II:** 6

"Land Aesthetic, The" (Callicott), **Supp. XIV:** 184

"Land and Language" (J. W. Miller), **Supp. XX:**170

Landau, Deborah, **Supp. XI:** 122, 123

"Land beyond the Blow, The" (Bierce), **I:** 209

"Land Ethic, The" (Leopold), **Supp. XIV:** 179, 180, 183, 191, 192

Landfall (Wagoner), **Supp. IX:** 330

"Landing in Luck" (Faulkner), **Retro. Supp. I:** 85

"Landing on the Moon" (Swenson), **Supp. IV Part 2:** 643

"Landings" (Hoffman), **Supp. XVIII:** 86

"Landing Under Water, I See Roots" (A. Finch), **Supp. XVII:** 76

Landlord at Lion's Head, The (Howells), **II:** 276, 287–288

Landmarks of Healing: A Study of House Made of Dawn (Scarberry-García), **Supp. IV Part 2:** 486

Land of Little Rain, The (Dillard), **Supp. VI:** 27–28

Land of the Free U.S.A. (MacLeish), **I:** 293; **III:** 16–17

Land of Unlikeness (Lowell), **II:** 537–538, 539, 547; **Retro. Supp. II:** 177, 178, **184–185**

Landor, Walter Savage, **III:** 15, 469; **Supp. I Part 2:** 422

"Landscape" (Sarton), **Supp. VIII:** 259

"Landscape #11" (Halliday), **Supp. XIX:** 93

Landscape and Journey (W. V. Davis), **Supp. XXI:** 83, 88, 90, **92–93**, 95

"Landscape as a Nude" (MacLeish), **III:** 14

Landscape at the End of the Century (Dunn), **Supp. XI:** 139, 143, **150–151**

"Landscape Chamber, The" (Jewett), **II:** 408–409

"Landscape for the Disappeared" (Komunyakaa), **Supp. XIII:** 120, 126

Landscape in American Poetry (Larcom), **Supp. XIII:** 142

"Landscape Painter, A" (James), **II:** 322; **Retro. Supp. I:** 219

"Landscape Symbolism in Kate Chopin's *At Fault*" (Arner), **Retro. Supp. II:** 62

"Landscape: The Eastern Shore" (Barth), **I:** 122

"Landscape with Boat" (Stevens), **Retro. Supp. I:** 306

"Landscape with the Fall of Icarus" (Brueghel), **Retro. Supp. I:** 430

Land's End: A Walk through Provincetown (Cunningham), **Supp. XV:** 69

Land That Drank the Rain, The (Hoffman), **Supp. XVIII:** 76, 80, 81, 82

"Land Where There Is No Death, The" (Benét), **Supp. XI:** 56

Lane, Ann, **Supp. XI:** 195, 208

Lane, Cornelia. *See* Anderson, Mrs. Sherwood

Lane, Homer, **Supp. II Part 1:** 6; **Supp. XIV:** 160

Lane, Nathan, **Supp. XIII:** 207

Lane, Rose Wilder, **Supp. IV Part 2:** 524

Lanes, Selma G., **Supp. XVI:** 104, 107

Lang, Andrew, **Retro. Supp. I:** 127

Lang, Violet, **Supp. XII:** 119

Langdon, Olivia. *See* Clemens, Mrs. Samuel Langhorne (Olivia Langdon)

Lange, Carl Georg, **II:** 350

Lange, Dorothea, **I:** 293; **Supp. XIV:** 181

Langland, Joseph, **III:** 542

Langston Hughes, American Poet (Walker), **Supp. III Part 2:** 530–531

Langston Hughes and the "Chicago Defender": Essays on Race, Politics, and Culture (De Santis, ed.), **Retro. Supp. I:** 194

Langston Hughes: Modern Critical Views (Bloom, ed.), **Retro. Supp. I:** 193

Langston Hughes Reader, The (Hughes), **Retro. Supp. I:** 202; **Supp. I Part 1:** 345

Langston Hughes: The Poet and His Critics (Barksdale), **Retro. Supp. I:** 202

"Language, Visualization and the Inner Library" (Shepard), **Supp. III Part 2:** 436, 438, 449

Language and Imagery of the Bible, The (Caird), **Supp. XXI:** 91–92

"Language and the Writer" (Bambara), **Supp. XI:** 18

Language As Gesture (Blackmur), **Supp. II Part 1:** 108

Language as Symbolic Action (Burke), **I:** 275, 282, 285

Language Book, The (Andrews and Bernstein), **Supp. IV Part 2:** 426

Language in Thought and Action (Hayakawa), **I:** 448

"Language of Being and Dying, The" (Gass), **Supp. VI:** 91

"Language of Home, The" (Wideman), **Supp. X:** 320, 323–324

Language of Life, The (Moyers, television series), **Supp. XIII:** 274, 276

Language of the American South, The (Brooks), **Supp. XIV:** 14

"Language of the Brag, The" (Olds), **Supp. X:** 204

"Language We Know, The" (Ortiz), **Supp. IV Part 2:** 500

Lanier, Clifford, **Supp. I Part 1:** 349, 350, 353, 355, 356, 371

Lanier, James F. D., **Supp. I Part 1:** 350

Lanier, Lyle H., **Supp. X:** 25

Lanier, Robert Sampson, **Supp. I Part 1:** 349, 351, 355, 356, 361

Lanier, Mrs. Robert Sampson (Mary Jane Anderson), **Supp. I Part 1:** 349

Lanier, Sidney, **IV:** 444; **Supp. I Part 1:** **349–373**; **Supp. I Part 2:** 416; **Supp. IV Part 1:** 165

Lanier, Mrs. Sidney (Mary Day), **Supp. I Part 1:** 351, 355, 357, 361, 362, 364, 370, 371

"Lanier as Poet" (Parks), **Supp. I Part 1:** 373

"Lanier's Reading" (P. Graham), **Supp. I Part 1:** 373

"Lanier's Use of Science for Poetic Imagery" (Beaver), **Supp. I Part 1:** 373

Lannegan, Helen. *See* Caldwell, Mrs. Erskine

Lannin, Paul, **II:** 427

Lanny Budd novels (Sinclair), **Supp. V:** 290

Lant, Kathleen Margaret, **Supp. V:** 141

Lanthenas, François, **Supp. I Part 2:** 515

"Lanyard, The" (Collins), **Supp. XXI:** 56, **62–64**

Laotzu, **III:** 173, 189, 567; **Supp. XV:** 39, 46, 48

Lapine, James, **Supp. XXI:** 147–148

"Lapis Lazuli" (Yeats), **I:** 532; **III:** 40

Laplace, Pierre Simon de, **III:** 428

Lapouge, M. G., **Supp. I Part 2:** 633

Lappa, Katherine, **Supp. XV:** 176

Lapsing to Grace (Espaillat), **Supp. XXI:** 99, 100

Lapsley, Gaillard, **Supp. XX:**231

Laqueur, Thomas, **Supp. XVI:** 154

Larbaud, Valery, **IV:** 404; **Supp. XIII:** 332; **Supp. XIV:** 338

Larcom, Lucy, **Retro. Supp. II:** 145; **Supp. XIII: 137–157**

Larcom's Poetical Works (Larcom), **Supp. XIII:** 142

Lardner, John, **II:** 437

Lardner, Ring, **I:** 487; **II:** 44, 91, 259, 263, **415–438; III:** 566, 572; **IV:** 433; **Retro. Supp. I:** 105; **Retro. Supp. II:** 222; **Supp. I Part 2:** 609; **Supp. IX:** 200; **Supp. XVI:** 189

Lardner, Ring, Jr., **Supp. XI:** 306

"Lardner, Shakespeare and Chekhov" (Matthews), **II:** 430

"Large Bad Picture" (Bishop), **Retro. Supp. II:** 43; **Supp. I Part 1:** 73, 80–82, 85, 86, 89, 90

"Large Coffee" (Lardner), **II:** 437

Large Glass, or The Bride Stripped Bare by Her Bachelors, Even (Duchamp), **Supp. IV Part 2:** 423, 424

Largo (Handel), **IV:** 369

Lark, The (Hellman), **Supp. I Part 1:** 286–288, 297

Larkin, Philip, **Supp. I Part 2:** 536; **Supp. XI:** 243, 249; **Supp. XIII:** 76, 85; **Supp. XV:** 117, 251; **Supp. XVII:** 110; **Supp. XVIII:** 173; **Supp. XX:**199; **Supp. XXI:** 84, 93

Larkin, Sharon Alile, **Supp. XI:** 20

Larmore, Phoebe, **Supp. X:** 266

Larner, Jeremy, **Supp. XVI:** 220

La Rochefoucauld, François de, **I:** 279; **II:** 111; **Supp. XIV:** 130

"La Rose des Vents" (Wilbur), **Supp. III Part 2:** 550

"Larry Brown's *Dirty Work:* A Study of Man's Responsibility for Suffering" (Prevost), **Supp. XXI:** 45

Larry's Party (Shields), **Supp. VII:** 324, 326–327

Larsen, Nella, **Supp. I Part 1:** 325, 326; **Supp. IV Part 1:** 164; **Supp. XVIII:** 119–134

Larson, Charles, **Supp. IV Part 1:** 331

Larson, Clinton, **Supp. XI:** 328

Larson, Kelli, **Supp. XVIII:** 131

LaRue, Dorie, **Supp. XXI:** 43

"Larval Stage of a Bookworm" (Mencken), **III:** 101

La Salle and the Discovery of the Great West (Parkman), **Supp. II Part 2:** 595, 598, 605–607; **Supp. XVIII:** 114

Lasch, Christopher, **I:** 259

Lasher (Rice), **Supp. VII:** 299–300

Lask, Thomas, **III:** 576; **Supp. XVI:** 250

Laski, Harold, **Supp. I Part 2:** 632, 643

Lassalle, Ferdinand, **IV:** 429

Lasser, Louise, **Supp. XV:** 4

"Last Acts" (Olds), **Supp. X:** 210

Last Adam, The (Cozzens), **I:** 362–363, 364, 368, 375, 377, 378, 379

Last Analysis, The (Bellow), **I:** 152, 160, 161; **Retro. Supp. II:** 26

Last and Lost Poems of Delmore Schwartz (Phillips, ed.), **Supp. II Part 2:** 661, 665

Last Avant-Garde, The: The Making of the New York School of Poets (Lehman), **Supp. XV:** 178–179, 187

Last Beautiful Days of Autumn, The (Nichols), **Supp. XIII:** 254, 255, 267, 269

Last Blue (Stern), **Supp. IX: 299–300**

Last Book, The (Pickering), **Supp. XXI:** 203–204

Last Carousel, The (Algren), **Supp. IX:** 16

Last Centennial, The (P. N. Warren as Kilina), **Supp. XX:**261–262

"Last Child" (X. J. Kennedy), **Supp. XV:** 162, 165

Last Coyote, The (Connelly), **Supp. XXI:** 71

"Last Day in the Field, The" (Gordon), **II:** 200

"Last Day of the Last Furlough" (Salinger), **III:** 552–553

"Last Days of Alice" (Tate), **IV:** 129

"Last Days of August, The" (Nye), **Supp. XIII:** 284

"Last Days of John Brown, The" (Thoreau), **IV:** 185

Last Days of Louisiana Red, The (Reed), **Supp. X:** 240, **248–249**

Last Decade, The (Trilling), **Supp. III Part 2:** 493, 499

"Last Demon, The" (Singer), **IV:** 15, 21

Last Detective, The (Crais), **Supp. XXI:** 70

Last Exit to Brooklyn (Selby), **Supp. III Part 1:** 125; **Supp. XXI:** 227, 231

Last Flower, The (Thurber), **Supp. I Part 2:** 610

"Last Frontier" (McCarriston), **Supp. XIV:** 272

Last Gentleman, The (Percy), **Supp. III Part 1:** 383–388, 392–393

"Last Good Country, The" (Hemingway), **II:** 258–259

Last Good Time, The (Bausch), **Supp. VII:** 45–46

"Last Hiding Places of Snow, The" (Kinnell), **Supp. III Part 1:** 252

"Last Hours, The" (Dunn), **Supp. XI:** 141

Last House: Reflections, Dreams, and Observations, 1943–1991 (M. F. K. Fisher), **Supp. XVII:** 92

Last Husband and Other Stories, The (Humphrey), **Supp. IX:** 94

Last Jew in America, The (Fiedler), **Supp. XIII:** 103

"Last Jew in America, The" (Fiedler), **Supp. XIII:** 103

Last Laugh, Mr. Moto (Marquand), **III:** 57

"Last Leaf, The" (Holmes), **Supp. I Part 1:** 302, 309

"Last Leaf, The" (Porter), **III:** 444

"Last Lie, The" (Weigl), **Supp. XIX:** 279

"Last Look at the Lilacs" (Stevens), **IV:** 74

Last Man, The (Kees), **Supp. XV:** 142, 143, 145

"Last May" (Dixon), **Supp. XII: 143**

"Last Mermother, The" (A. Finch), **Supp. XVII:** 72

"Last Mohican, The" (Malamud), **Supp. I Part 2:** 437–438, 450, 451

"Lastness" (Kinnell), **Supp. III Part 1:** 248–249

"Last Night" (Olds), **Supp. X:** 212

"Last Night at Tía's" (Alvarez), **Supp. VII:** 5

Last Night of Summer, The (Caldwell), **I:** 292–293

Last of Mr. Norris, The (Isherwood), **Supp. XIV:** 161

"Last of the Brooding Miserables, The" (Karr), **Supp. XI:** 250

"Last of the Caddoes, The" (Humphrey), **Supp. IX:** 101

Last of the Crazy People, The (Findley), **Supp. XX:**51–52

"Last of the Gold Star Mothers, The" (C. Bly), **Supp. XVI:** 34, 35, 36

"Last of the Legions, The" (Benét), **Supp. XI:** 56, 57

Last of the Mohicans, The (Cooper), **I:** 341, 342, 349

Last of the Red Hot Lovers (Simon), **Supp. IV Part 2:** 575, 583, 589

"Last of the Valerii, The" (James), **II:** 327; **Retro. Supp. I:** 218

"Last One, The" (Merwin), **Supp. III Part 1:** 355

Last Picture Show, The (film), **Supp. V:** 223, 226

Last Picture Show, The (McMurtry), **Supp. V:** 220, 222–223, 233

Last Place on Earth, The: Scott and Amundsen's Race to the South Pole (Huntford), **Supp. XVIII:** 114

Last Puritan, The (Santayana), **III:** 64, 600, 604, 607, 612, 615–617

"Last Ride Together, The" (Browning), **I:** 468

"Last River, The" (Kinnell), **Supp. III Part 1:** 236

Last Song, The (Harjo), **Supp. XII:** 218

"Last Song for the Mend-It Shop" (Nye), **Supp. XIII:** 283

"Last Tango in Fresno" (Salinas), **Supp. XIII:** 318

Last Tycoon, The: An Unfinished Novel (Fitzgerald), **II**: 84, 98; **Retro. Supp. I**: 109, 114, **114–115**; **Retro. Supp. II**: 337; **Supp. IV Part 1**: 203; **Supp. IX**: 63; **Supp. XII**: 173; **Supp. XIII**: 170; **Supp. XVIII**: 248, 250

"Last WASP in the World, The" (Fiedler), **Supp. XIII**: 103

"Last Watch, The" (Gibran), **Supp. XX**: 119

Last Watch of the Night: Essays Too Personal and Otherwise (Monette), **Supp. X**: 147, 148, 153, **157–159**

"Last Word, The" (column, Quindlen), **Supp. XVII**: 165, 167, 170

Last Word, The: Letters between Marcia Nardi and William Carlos Williams (O'Neil, ed.), **Retro. Supp. I**: 427

"Last Words" (Levine), **Supp. V**: 190

"Last Words" (Olds), **Supp. X**: 210

Last Worthless Evening, The (Dubus), **Supp. VII**: 87–88

"Las Vegas (What?) Las Vegas (Can't Hear You! Too Noisy) Las Vegas!!!!" (Wolfe), **Supp. III Part 2**: 572

"Late" (Bogan), **Supp. III Part 1**: 53

"Late Air" (Bishop), **Supp. I Part 1**: 89

"Late Autumn" (Sarton), **Supp. VIII**: 261

"Late Bronze, Early Iron: A Journey Book" (Sobin), **Supp. XVI**: 290

Late Child, The (McMurtry), **Supp. V**: 231

"Late Conversation" (Doty), **Supp. XI**: 122

"Late Elegy for John Berryman, A" (W. V. Davis), **Supp. XXI**: 91

"Late Encounter with the Enemy, A" (O'Connor), **III**: 345; **Retro. Supp. II**: 232

Late Fire, Late Snow (Francis), **Supp. IX**: **89–90**

Late George Apley, The (Marquand), **II**: 482–483; **III**: 50, 51, 52, 56–57, 58, 62–64, 65, 66

Late George Apley, The (Marquand and Kaufman), **III**: 62

"Late Hour" (Everwine), **Supp. XV**: 85

Late Hour, The (Strand), **Supp. IV Part 2**: 620, 629–630

"Lately, at Night" (Kumin), **Supp. IV Part 2**: 442

"Late Moon" (Levine), **Supp. V**: 186

"Late Night Ode" (McClatchy), **Supp. XII**: 262–263

Later (Creeley), **Supp. IV Part 1**: 153, 156, 157

Later Life (Gurney), **Supp. V**: 103, 105

La Terre (Zola), **III**: 316, 322

Later the Same Day (Paley), **Supp. VI**: 218

"Late September in Nebraska" (Kooser), **Supp. XIX**: 120

Late Settings (Merrill), **Supp. III Part 1**: 336

"Late Sidney Lanier, The" (Stedman), **Supp. I Part 1**: 373

"Late Snow & Lumber Strike of the Summer of Fifty-Four, The" (Snyder), **Supp. VIII**: 294

"Late Start, A" (L. Brown), **Supp. XXI**: 40–41

"Latest Freed Man, The" (Stevens), **Retro. Supp. I**: 306

"Latest Injury, The" (Olds), **Supp. X**: 209

Latest Literary Essays and Addresses (Lowell), **Supp. I Part 2**: 407

"Late Subterfuge" (Warren), **IV**: 257

"Late Summer Lilies" (Weigl), **Supp. XIX**: 288

"Late Supper, A" (Jewett), **Retro. Supp. II**: 137

"Late Victorians" (Rodriguez), **Supp. XIV**: 303–304

"Late Walk, A" (Frost), **II**: 153; **Retro. Supp. I**: 127

Latham, Edyth, **I**: 289

Lathrop, George Parsons, **Supp. I Part 1**: 365

Lathrop, H. B., **Supp. III Part 2**: 612

Lathrop, Julia, **Supp. I Part 1**: 5

Latière de Trianon, La (Wekerlin), **II**: 515

"La Tigresse" (Van Vechten), **Supp. II Part 2**: 735, 738

Latimer, Hugh, **II**: 15

Latimer, Margery, **Supp. IX**: 320

La Traviata (Verdi), **III**: 139

"Latter-Day Warnings" (Holmes), **Supp. I Part 1**: 307

La Turista (Shepard), **Supp. III Part 2**: 440

Lauber, John, **Supp. XIII**: 21

Laud, Archbishop, **II**: 158

"Lauds" (Auden), **Supp. II Part 1**: 23

"Laughing Man, The" (Salinger), **III**: 559

Laughing to Keep From Crying (Hughes), **Supp. I Part 1**: 329–330

"Laughing with One Eye" (Schnackenberg), **Supp. XV**: 253

Laughlin, James, **III**: 171; **Retro. Supp. I**: 423, 424, 428, 430, 431; **Supp. VIII**: 195; **Supp. XV**: 140; **Supp. XVI**: 284; **Supp. XXI**: 29

Laughlin, Jay, **Supp. II Part 1**: 94

Laughlin, J. Laurence, **Supp. I Part 2**: 641

Laughter in the Dark (Nabokov), **III**: 255–258; **Retro. Supp. I**: 270

Laughter on the 23rd Floor (Simon), **Supp. IV Part 2**: 575, 576, 588, 591–592

"Launcelot" (Lewis), **II**: 439–440

"Laura Dailey's Story" (Bogan), **Supp. III Part 1**: 52

Laurel, Stan, **Supp. I Part 2**: 607; **Supp. IV Part 2**: 574

Laurel and Hardy Go to Heaven (Auster), **Supp. XII**: 21

Laurence, Alexander, **Supp. XVIII**: 138

Laurence, Dan H., **II**: 338–339

Laurens, John, **Supp. I Part 2**: 509

Lauter, Paul, **Supp. XV**: 313

Lautréamont, Comte de, **III**: 174

Lavender Locker Room, The (P. N. Warren), **Supp. XX**: 261, **273–274**

Law, John, **Supp. XI**: 307

Law and Order (television), **Supp. XVII**: 153

Law and the Testimony, The (S. and A. Warner), **Supp. XVIII**: 264

Lawd Today (Wright), **IV**: 478, 492

Law for the Lion, A (Auchincloss), **Supp. IV Part 1**: 25

"Law Lane" (Jewett), **II**: 407

"Lawns of June, The" (Peacock), **Supp. XIX**: 196

"Law of Nature and the Dream of Man, The: Ruminations of the Art of Fiction" (Stegner), **Supp. IV Part 2**: 604

Lawrence, D. H., **I**: 291, 336, 377, 522, 523; **II**: 78, 84, 98, 102, 264, 517, 523, 532, 594, 595; **III**: 27, 33, 40, 44, 46, 172, 173, 174, 178, 184, 229, 261, 423, 429, 458, 546–547; **IV**: 138, 339, 342, 351, 380; **Retro. Supp. I**: 7, 18, 203, 204, 421; **Retro. Supp. II**: 68; **Supp. I Part 1**: 227, 230, 243, 255, 257, 258, 263, 329; **Supp. I Part 2**: 546, 613, 728; **Supp. II Part 1**: 1, 9, 20, 89; **Supp. IV Part 1**: 81; **Supp. VIII**: 237; **Supp. X**: 137, 193, 194; **Supp. XII**: 172; **Supp. XIV**: 310; **Supp. XV**: 45, 46, 158, 254; **Supp. XVI**: 267; **Supp. XX**: 69

Lawrence, Frieda, **Supp. XV**: 46

Lawrence, Rhoda, **Supp. I Part 1**: 45

Lawrence, Seymour, **Supp. IX**: 107; **Supp. XI**: 335, 346, 348

Lawrence, T. E., **Supp. XIV**: 159

Lawrence of Arabia (Aldington), **Supp. I Part 1**: 259

Lawrence of Arabia (film), **Supp. I Part 1**: 67

Laws (Plato), **Supp. IV Part 1**: 391

Laws of Ice, The (Price), **Supp. VI**: 264

Laws of Our Fathers, The (Turow), **Supp. XVII**: **218–219**

Lawson, John Howard, **I**: 479, 482

Lawton Girl, The (Frederic), **II**: 132–133, 144

Layachi, Larbi (Driss ben Hamed Charhadi), **Supp. IV Part 1**: 92, 93

Layard, John, **Supp. XIV**: 160

Lay Down My Sword and Shield (Burke), **Supp. XIV**: 22, 25, 34

"Layers, The" (Kunitz), **Supp. III Part 1**: 260, 266–267

"Layers, The: Some Notes on 'The Abduction' " (Kunitz), **Supp. III Part 1**: 266

"Lay-mans Lamentation, The" (Taylor), **IV**: 162–163

Lay of the Land, The: Metaphor as Experience and History in American Life and Letters (Kolodny), **Supp. X**: 97

"Layover" (Hass), **Supp. VI**: 109

"Lay Preacher" (Dennie), **Supp. I Part 1**: 125

Layton, Irving, **Supp. XII**: 121

Lazar, Irving "Swifty", **Supp. XIX**: 250

Lazarillo de Tormes (Mendoza), **III**: 182

Lazar Malkin Enters Heaven (S. Stern), **Supp. XVII**: 42; **Supp. XX**: 178

Lazarus Laughed (O'Neill), **III**: 391, 395–396

Lazer, Hank, **Supp. IX**: 265

Lea, Luke, **IV**: 248

Leachman, Cloris, **Supp. XXI:** 146

Leacock, Stephen, **Supp. IV Part 2:** 464

"LEADBELLY GIVES AN AUTO-GRAPH" (Baraka), **Supp. II Part 1:** 49

Leaflets: Poems, 1965–1968 (Rich), **Supp. I Part 2:** 551, 556–557

"League of American Writers, The: Communist Organizational Activity among American Writers 1929–1942" (Wolfe), **Supp. III Part 2:** 568

League of Brightened Philistines and Other Papers, The (Farrell), **II:** 49

Leahy, Anna, **Supp. XXI:** 246

"Leakage" (Skloot), **Supp. XX:**202

Leal, Luis, **Supp. XIX:** 98, 112

"Leaning" (Webb), **Supp. XX:**56

Leaning Forward (Paley), **Supp. VI:** 221

"Leaning Tower, The" (Porter), **III:** 442, 443, 446–447

Leaning Tower and Other Stories, The (Porter), **III:** 433, 442, 443–447

"Leap, The" (Dickey), **Supp. IV Part 1:** 182

"Leaping Up into Political Poetry" (R. Bly), **Supp. IV Part 1:** 61, 63

Leap Year (Cameron), **Supp. XII:** 79–80, 81, **85–86,** 88

Lear, Edward, **III:** 428, 536; **Supp. XVI:** 103

Lear, Linda, **Supp. IX:** 19, 22, 25, 26

Learned Ladies, The (Molière; Wilbur, trans.), **Supp. III Part 2:** 560

"Learning a Dead Language" (Merwin), **Supp. III Part 1:** 345

Learning a Trade: A Craftsman's Notebooks, 1955–1997 (Price), **Supp. VI:** 254, 255, 267

"Learning Bones" (Espaillat), **Supp. XXI:** 107

Learning to Love: Exploring Solitude and Freedom (Merton), **Supp. VIII:** 200

"Learning to Read" (Harper), **Supp. II Part 1:** 201–202

"Learning to Speak" (Everwine), **Supp. XV:** 79

Learning Tree, The (Park), **Supp. XIX:** 154

Leary, Lewis, **III:** 478

Leary, Paris, **Supp. IV Part 1:** 176

Leary, Timothy, **Supp. X:** 265; **Supp. XIV:** 150

Lease, Joseph, **Supp. XXI:** 246

Least Heat Moon, William, **Supp. V:** 169

Leather-Stocking Tales, The (Cooper), **I:** 335

Leatherwood God, The (Howells), **II:** 276, 277, 288

Leave It to Beaver (television show), **Supp. XX:**103

"Leaves" (Updike), **Retro. Supp. I:** 323, 329, 335

Leaves and Ashes (Haines), **Supp. XII:** 206

Leaves from the Notebook of a Tamed Cynic (Niebuhr), **III:** 293

Leaves of Grass (1856) (Whitman), **Retro. Supp. I:** 399–402

Leaves of Grass (1860) (Whitman), **Retro. Supp. I:** 402–405

Leaves of Grass (Whitman), **II:** 8; **IV:** 331, 332, 333, 334, 335, 336, 340, 341–342, 348, 350, 405, 464; **Retro. Supp. I:** 387, 388, 389, 390, **392–395,** 406, 407, 408; **Retro. Supp. II:** 93; **Supp. I Part 1:** 365; **Supp. I Part 2:** 416, 579; **Supp. III Part 1:** 156; **Supp. V:** 170; **Supp. VIII:** 275; **Supp. IX:** 265; **Supp. X:** 120; **Supp. XIV:** 334; **Supp. XV:** 218; **Supp. XVIII:** 4; **Supp. XIX:** 276; **Supp. XXI:** 205

"Leaves of Grass" (Whitman), **IV:** 463

Leaves of the Tree, The (Masters), **Supp. I Part 2:** 460

"Leaving" (Hogan), **Supp. IV Part 1:** 400

"Leaving" (Wilbur), **Supp. III Part 2:** 563

"Leaving, The" (B. Kelly), **Supp. XVII:** 127, 132

Leaving a Doll's House: A Memoir (C. Bloom), **Retro. Supp. II:** 281

Leaving Another Kingdom: Selected Poems (Stern), **Supp. IX:** 296

"Leaving Bartram's Garden in Southwest Philadelphia" (Di Piero), **Supp. XIX:** 46

"Leaving Brooklyn" (Neugeboren), **Supp. XVI:** 226

Leaving Cheyenne (McMurtry), **Supp. V:** 220, 221–222, 224, 229

Leaving Home (Keillor), **Supp. XVI:** 175

"Leaving One, The" (Offutt), **Supp. XIX:** 165–166

"Leaving the Island" (Olds), **Supp. X:** 214

"Leaving the Yellow House" (Bellow), **Retro. Supp. II:** 27, 32

"Leaving Town" (Kenyon), **Supp. VII:** 163

Leavis, F. R., **I:** 522; **III:** 462–463, 475, 478; **Retro. Supp. I:** 67; **Retro. Supp. II:** 243; **Supp. I Part 2:** 536; **Supp. VIII:** 234, 236, 245

Leavis, Queenie, **Supp. XX:**232

"Leavis-Snow Controversy, The" (Trilling), **Supp. III Part 2:** 512

Leavitt, Caroline, **Supp. XX:**186

Leavitt, David, **Supp. VIII:** 88

Le Braz, Anatole, **Supp. XIII:** 253

Le Carre, John, **Supp. XX:**195

Lecker, Robert, **Supp. XIII:** 21

LeClair, Thomas, **Supp. IV Part 1:** 286

LeClair, Tom, **Supp. V:** 53; **Supp. XII:** 152; **Supp. XX:**93

Le Conte, Joseph, **II:** 479; **III:** 227–228

"Lecture, The" (Singer), **IV:** 21

"LECTURE PAST DEAD CATS" (Baraka), **Supp. II Part 1:** 52

Lectures in America (Stein), **IV:** 27, 32, 33, 35, 36, 41, 42

"Lectures on Poetry" (Bryant), **Supp. I Part 1:** 159, 161

Lectures on Rhetoric (Blair), **II:** 8

"Leda and the Swan" (Yeats), **III:** 347; **Supp. IX:** 52

Ledger (Fitzgerald), **Retro. Supp. I:** 109, 110

Lee (Masters), **Supp. I Part 2:** 471

Lee, Baayork, **Supp. XXI:** 148

Lee, C. Y., **Supp. XXI:** 148

Lee, Don, **Supp. XII:** 295; **Supp. XVII:** 13, 14, 15, 16

Lee, Don L. *See* Madhubuti, Haki R.

Lee, Gypsy Rose, **II:** 586; **III:** 161; **Supp. IV Part 1:** 84

Lee, Harper, **Supp. VIII: 113–131**

Lee, Harriett, **Supp. XV:** 230

Lee, James Kyun-Jin, **Supp. XV:** 213

Lee, James W., **Supp. IX:** 94, 97, 109

Lee, James Ward, **Supp. VIII:** 57

Lee, Li Lin, **Supp. XV:** 211, 212

Lee, Li-Young, **Supp. XV: 211–228; Supp. XVII:** 241

Lee, Richard E., **Supp. XIX:** 226, 227

Lee, Robert E., **II:** 150, 206; **IV:** 126; **Supp. I Part 2:** 471, 486

Lee, Samuel, **IV:** 158

Lee, Spike, **Retro. Supp. II:** 12; **Supp. XI:** 19; **Supp. XIII:** 179, 186; **Supp. XVI:** 144; **Supp. XX:**110

Lee, Virginia Chin-lan, **Supp. X:** 291

Leeds, Barry, **Retro. Supp. II:** 204

Leeds, Daniel, **II:** 110

Leeds, Titan, **II:** 110, 111

Leeming, David, **Retro. Supp. II:** 4, 10

"Lees of Happiness, The" (Fitzgerald), **II:** 88

"Le Filme" (Weigl), **Supp. XIX:** 288

Left Out in the Rain: New Poems 1947–1985 (Snyder), **Supp. VIII:** 305

"Legacy" (Dunn), **Supp. XI:** 148

"Legacy" (Komunyakaa), **Supp. XIII:** 132

"Legacy" (W. V. Davis), **Supp. XXI:** 93–94

"Legacy of Aldo Leopold, The" (Stegner), **Supp. XIV:** 193

Legacy of Fear, A (Farrell), **II:** 39

"Legacy of the Ancestral Arts, The" (Locke), **Supp. XIV:** 201

Legacy of the Civil War, The: Meditations on the Centennial (Warren), **IV:** 236

"Legal Alien" (Mora), **Supp. XIII:** 215

"Legal Tender Act, The" (Adams), **I:** 5

Légende de la mort, La (Le Braz), **Supp. XIII:** 253

"Legend of Duluoz, The" (Kerouac), **Supp. III Part 1:** 218, 226, 227, 229

"Legend of Lillian Hellman, The" (Kazin), **Supp. I Part 1:** 297

"Legend of Monte del Diablo, The" (Harte), **Supp. II Part 1:** 339

"Legend of Paper Plates, The" (Haines), **Supp. XII:** 204

"Legend of Sammtstadt, A" (Harte), **Supp. II Part 1:** 355

"Legend of Sleepy Hollow, The" (Irving), **II:** 306–308

Legends (Lowell), **II:** 525–526

Legends and Dreams (P. N. Warren), **Supp. XX:**261

Legends of New England (Whittier), **Supp. I Part 2:** 684, 692

Legends of the Fall (Harrison), **Supp. VIII:** 38, 39, **45–46,** 48

Legends of the West (Hall), **II:** 313

Léger, Fernand, **Retro. Supp. I:** 292

Legge, James, **III:** 472

Leggett, William, **Supp. I Part 1:** 157

"Legion, The" (Karr), **Supp. XI:** 243

"Legs" (Halliday), **Supp. XIX:** 90

Legs (W. Kennedy), **Supp. VII:** 133, 134, 138–142, 143, 151

Le Guin, Ursula K., **Supp. IV Part 1:** 333

Lehan, Richard, **Retro. Supp. II:** 104

Lehman, David, **Supp. IX:** 161; **Supp. XIII:** 130; **Supp. XV:** 178–179, 180, 187, 190; **Supp. XXI:** 246

Lehmann, John, **Retro. Supp. II:** 243; **Supp. XIV:** 158, 159

Lehmann, Paul, **III:** 311

Lehmann-Haupt, Christopher, **Retro. Supp. II:** 291; **Supp. IV Part 1:** 205, 209, 306; **Supp. IX:** 95, 103; **Supp. XVI:** 73, 210, 294, 295

Lehrer, Jim, **Supp. XVIII:** 39

Leiber, Fritz, **Supp. XVI:** 123

Leibling, A. J., **Supp. XIV:** 112

Leibniz, Gottfried Wilhelm von, **II:** 103; **III:** 428

Leibowitz, Herbert A., **I:** 386; **Supp. XV:** 78

Leich, Roland, **Supp. XIV:** 123

Leichum, Laura, **Supp. XIX:** 197

Leighton, Betty, **Supp. XXI:** 42

Leithauser, Brad, **Retro. Supp. I:** 133; **Supp. XV:** 250; **Supp. XVII:** 112

Leitz, Robert, **Supp. XIV:** 62

Leivick, H., **IV:** 6

Lekachman, Robert, **Supp. I Part 2:** 648

Leland, Charles, **Supp. II Part 1:** 193

Leland, Charles Godfrey, **I:** 257

Leland, John, **Supp. XV:** 69; **Supp. XIX:** 157

Lem, Stanislaw, **Supp. IV Part 1:** 103

"Le marais du cygne" (Whittier), **Supp. I Part 2:** 687

Lemay, Harding, **Supp. VIII:** 125; **Supp. IX:** 98

Lemercier, Eugène, **Retro. Supp. I:** 299

"Lemorne *versus* Huell" (E. Stoddard), **Supp. XV:** 270, 273, 283

Le Morte D'Arthur Notes (Gardner), **Supp. VI:** 65, 66

Lenin, V. I., **I:** 366, 439, 440; **III:** 14–15, 262, 475; **IV:** 429, 436, 443–444; **Supp. I Part 2:** 647; **Supp. XXI:** 164

"Lenore" (Poe), **III:** 411

"Lenox Avenue: Midnight" (Hughes), **Retro. Supp. I:** 198

"Lens of Poetry, The" (Bronk). *See Attendant, The* (Bronk)

Leonard, Elmore, **Supp. IV Part 1:** 356; **Supp. X:** 5; **Supp. XIV:** 26

Leonard, John, **Supp. IV Part 1:** 24; **Supp. IV Part 2:** 474; **Supp. V:** 164, 223–224; **Supp. XI:** 13; **Supp. XVIII:** 147, 148; **Supp. XIX:** 269; **Supp. XXI:** 233, 239

Leonardo da Vinci, **Supp. XII:** 44

León-Portilla, Miguel, **Supp. XV:** 77

Leontiev, Constantine, **Supp. XIV:** 98

Leopard, The (Lampedusa), **Supp. XII:** 13–14

Leopardi, Giacomo, **II:** 543; **Supp. XIX:** 33, 43

"Leopard Man's Story, The" (London), **II:** 475

Leopard's Mouth Is Dry and Cold Inside, The (Levis), **Supp. XI:** 258

Leopold, Aldo, **Supp. V:** 202; **Supp. X:** 108; **Supp. XIV: 177–194; Supp. XXI:** 203

"Leper's Bell, the" (Komunyakaa), **Supp. XIII:** 118

Lerman, Leo, **Supp. X:** 188; **Supp. XVI:** 194

Lerner, Max, **III:** 60; **Supp. I Part 2:** 629, 630, 631, 647, 650, 654

Lerperger, Emil, **Supp. XX:** 165, 167

"Lesbos" (Plath), **Retro. Supp. II:** 254

Lesesne, Teri, **Supp. XIII:** 277

LeSieg, Theo (pseudonym). *See* Geisel, Theodor Seuss (Dr. Seuss)

Leskov, Nikolai, **IV:** 299

Leslie, Alfred, **Supp. XII:** 127

"Less and Less Human, O Savage Spirit" (W. Stevens), **Supp. XVI:** 64

Lesser, Wendy, **Supp. IV Part 2:** 453; **Supp. XII:** 297; **Supp. XVI:** 201

Lessing, Gotthold, **Supp. I Part 2:** 422

"Lesson, The" (Bambara), **Supp. XI:** 5–6

"Lesson, The" (Dunbar), **Supp. II Part 1:** 199

"Lesson, The" (Olsen), **Supp. XIII:** 297

"Lesson for the Ill Clothed and Ill Fed, A" (Ryan as Quin), **Supp. XVIII:** 230–231

Lesson of the Master, The (James), **Supp. XVIII:** 248

"Lesson of the Master, The" (James), **Retro. Supp. I:** 227

Lesson of the Masters: An Anthology of the Novel from Cervantes to Hemingway (Cowley-Hugo, ed.), **Supp. II Part 1:** 140

"Lesson on Concealment, A" (Brown), **Supp. I Part 1:** 133

"Lessons" (Epstein), **Supp. XII:** 163

"Lessons of the Body" (Simpson), **Supp. IX:** 267

Less than One (Brodsky), **Supp. VIII:** 22, 29–31

Lester, Jerry, **Supp. IV Part 2:** 574

Lester, Ketty, **Supp. XV:** 133, 147

Le Style Apollinaire (Zukofsky), **Supp. III Part 2:** 616

Le Sueur, Meridel, **Supp. V:** 113, 130; **Supp. XII:** 217

"Let America Be America Again" (Hughes), **Retro. Supp. I:** 202; **Supp. I Part 1:** 331

Let Evening Come (Kenyon), **Supp. VII:** 160, 169–171

Lethem, Jonathan, **Supp. IX:** 122; **Supp. XVIII: 135–153**

Let It Come Down (Bowles), **Supp. IV Part 1:** 87

Let It Ride (Pickering), **Supp. XXI:** 198–199

"Let Me Be" (Levine), **Supp. V:** 181, 189

"Let Me Begin Again" (Levine), **Supp. V:** 181, 189

"Let No Charitable Hope" (Wylie), **Supp. I Part 2:** 713–714, 729

Let No Man Write My Epitaph (film, Leacock), **Supp. XVII:** 150, 158

Let No Man Write My Epitaph (W. Motley), **Supp. XVII:** 150, **158–160**

Let Noon Be Fair (W. Motley), **Supp. XVII: 161**

Letofsky, Irv, **Supp. XVI:** 167

"Let one Eye his watches keep/While the Other Eye doth sleep" (Fletcher), **Supp. IV Part 2:** 621

Let's Balance the Books (radio show; Untermeyer), **Supp. XV:** 311

"Letter . . ." (Whittier), **Supp. I Part 2:** 687

"Letter, A" (Bogan), **Supp. III Part 1:** 54

"Letter, May 2, 1959" (Olson), **Supp. II Part 2:** 579, 580

"Letter, Much Too Late" (Stegner), **Supp. IV Part 2:** 613

"Letter, The" (Gioia), **Supp. XV:** 120

"Letter, The" (Malamud), **Supp. I Part 2:** 435–436

"Letter about Money, Love, or Other Comfort, If Any, The" (Warren), **IV:** 245

Letter Addressed to the People of Piedmont, on the Advantages of the French Revolution, and the Necessity of Adopting Its Principles in Italy, A (Barlow), **Supp. II Part 1:** 80, 81

"Letter for Marion, A" (McGrath), **Supp. X:** 116

"Letter from Aldermaston" (Merwin), **Supp. III Part 1:** 347

"Letter from a London Attic" (Pickering), **Supp. XXI:** 194

"Letter from a Region in My Mind" (Baldwin). *See* "Down at the Cross"

"Letter from Aunt Belle, A" (Kooser), **Supp. XIX:** 117

Letter from Li Po, A (Aiken), **I:** 68

"Letter from 'Manhattan' " (Didion), **Supp. IV Part 1:** 205

"Letter from the Country" (column, C. Bly), **Supp. XVI:** 33

Letter from the End of the Twentieth Century (Harjo), **Supp. XII:** 223

"Letter from the End of the Twentieth Century" (Harjo), **Supp. XII:** 227

"Letter Home" (Trethewey), **Supp. XXI:** 254

"Letter on Céline" (Kerouac), **Supp. III Part 1:** 232

Letters (Cato), **II:** 114

Letters (Landor), **Supp. I Part 2:** 422

Letters (White), **Supp. I Part 2:** 651, 653, 675, 680

Letters (Wolfe), **IV:** 462

"Letters, The" (Swados), **Supp. XIX:** 261, 262

Letters and Leadership (Brooks), **I:** 228, 240, 245, 246

"Letters for the Dead" (Levine), **Supp. V:** 186

Letters from an American Farmer (Crèvecoeur), **Supp. I Part 1:** 227–251

Letters from Maine (Sarton), **Supp. VIII: 261**

"Letters from Maine" (Sarton), **Supp. VIII:** 261

"Letters from My Father" (R. O. Butler), **Supp. XII:** 71

Letters from the Country (C. Bly), **Supp. XVI:** 33–34, 35, 37

Letters from the Earth (Twain), **IV:** 209

Letters from the East (Bryant), **Supp. I Part 1:** 158

"Letters from the Ming Dynasty" (Brodsky), **Supp. VIII:** 28

Letters of a Traveller (Bryant), **Supp. I Part 1:** 158

Letters of a Traveller, Second Series (Bryant), **Supp. I Part 1:** 158

Letters of Emily Dickinson, The (Johnson and Ward, eds.), **I:** 470; **Retro. Supp. I:** 28

Letters of William James (Henry James, ed.), **II:** 362

Letters on Various Interesting and Important Subjects . . . (Freneau), **Supp. II Part 1:** 272

Letters to a Niece (Adams), **I:** 22

Letters to a Teacher (Pickering), **Supp. XXI:** 195, 201–202

Letters to a Young Poet (Rilke), **Supp. XIII:** 74; **Supp. XV:** 93

"Letters to Dead Imagists" (Sandburg), **I:** 421

"Letters Written on a Ferry While Crossing Long Island Sound" (Sexton), **Supp. II Part 2:** 683

"Letter to Abbé Raynal" (Paine), **Supp. I Part 2:** 510

Letter to a Man in the Fire: Does God Exist or Does He Care? (Price), **Supp. VI:** 267–268

"Letter to American Teachers of History, A" (Adams), **I:** 19

Letter to an Imaginary Friend (McGrath), **Supp. X:** 111, 112–113, 116, **119–125**

"Letter to a Reader" (Sanders), **Supp. XVI:** 266, 267, 268, 269, 275

"Letter to a Young Author" (P. N. Warren), **Supp. XX:** 272

"Letter to a Young Contributor" (Higginson), **Retro. Supp. I:** 31

"Letter to a Young Writer" (Price), **Supp. VI:** 267

"Letter to Bell from Missoula" (Hugo), **Supp. VI:** 142–143

"Letter to E. Franklin Frazier" (Baraka), **Supp. II Part 1:** 49

"Letter to Elaine Feinstein" (Olson), **Supp. II Part 2:** 561

"Letter to Freddy" (music) (Bowles), **Supp. IV Part 1:** 82

"Letter to Garber from Skye" (Hugo), **Supp. VI:** 146

"Letter to George Washington" (Paine), **Supp. I Part 2:** 517

"Letter to His Brother" (Berryman), **I:** 172, 173

Letter to His Countrymen, A (Cooper), **I:** 346, 347, 349

"Letter to Kizer from Seattle" (Hugo), **Supp. VI:** 142

Letter to Lord Byron (Auden), **Supp. II Part 1:** 11

"Letter to Lord Byron" (Mumford), **Supp. II Part 2:** 494

"Letter to Matthews from Barton Street Flats" (Hugo), **Supp. VI:** 133

"Letter to Minnesota" (Dunn), **Supp. XI:** 146

"Letter to Mr." (Poe), **III:** 411

"Letter Too Late to Vallejo" (Salinas), **Supp. XIII:** 313, 324

"Letter to Sister Madeline from Iowa City" (Hugo), **Supp. VI:** 142–143

"Letter to Soto" (Salinas), **Supp. XIII:** 325

"Letter to the Lady of the House" (Bausch), **Supp. VII:** 48

"Letter to the Rising Generation, A" (Comer), **I:** 214

"Letter to Walt Whitman" (Doty), **Supp. XI:** 135–136

"Letter to Wendell Berry, A" (Stegner), **Supp. IV Part 2:** 600

"Letter Writer, The" (Singer), **IV:** 20–21

"Let the Air Circulate" (Clampitt), **Supp. IX:** 45

"Letting Down of the Hair, The" (Sexton), **Supp. II Part 2:** 692

Letting Go (P. Roth), **Retro. Supp. II:** 282, 283; **Supp. III Part 2:** 403, 404, 409–412

"Letting the Puma Go" (Dunn), **Supp. XI:** 149

"Lettres d'un Soldat" (Stevens), **Retro. Supp. I:** 299

Let Us Go into the Starry Night (Shanley), **Supp. XIV:** 317

Let Us Highly Resolve (Stratton-Porter), **Supp. XX:** 223

Let Us Now Praise Famous Men (Agee and Evans), **I:** 25, 27, 35, 36–39, 42, 45, 293

Let Your Mind Alone! (Thurber), **Supp. I Part 2:** 608

Leutze, Emanuel, **Supp. X:** 307

Levels of the Game (McPhee), **Supp. III Part 1:** 292, 294, 301

Levertov, Denise, **Retro. Supp. I:** 411; **Supp. III Part 1: 271–287; Supp. III Part 2:** 541; **Supp. IV Part 1:** 325; **Supp. VIII:** 38, 39; **Supp. XVI:** 39, 40; **Supp. XIX:** 282; **Supp. XXI:** 228

Levi, Primo, **Supp. X:** 149; **Supp. XVII:** 48

Leviathan (Auster), **Supp. XII:** 27, **33–34**

"Leviathan" (Lowell), **II:** 537, 538

"Leviathan" (Merwin), **Supp. III Part 1:** 345

Levin, Harry, **Supp. I Part 2:** 647

Levin, Jennifer, **Supp. X:** 305

Levin, Meyer, **Supp. XX:** 34

Lévinas, Emmanuel, **Supp. XVI:** 290, 291

Levine, Ellen, **Supp. V:** 4; **Supp. XI:** 178

Levine, Paul, **Supp. IV Part 1:** 221, 224

Levine, Philip, **Supp. III Part 2:** 541; **Supp. V: 177–197**, 337; **Supp. IX:** 293; **Supp. XI:** 123, 257, 259, 267, 271, 315; **Supp. XIII:** 312; **Supp. XV:** 73, 74, 212; **Supp. XIX:** 45

Levine, Rosalind, **Supp. XII:** 123

Levine, Sherry, **Supp. XII:** 4

Lewis, Larry, **Supp. V:** 180; **Supp. IX:** 299; **Supp. XI: 257–274; Supp. XIII:** 312; **Supp. XV:** 73; **Supp. XVII:** 110

Lévi-Strauss, Claude, **Supp. I Part 2:** 636; **Supp. IV Part 1:** 45; **Supp. IV Part 2:** 490; **Supp. XVIII:** 190

Levitation: Five Fictions (Ozick), **Supp. V:** 268–270

"Levitation with Baby" (Nelson), **Supp. XVIII:** 173

Levitt, Saul, **Supp. XV:** 197

Levy, Alan, **Supp. IV Part 2:** 574, 589

Levy, G. Rachel, **Supp. I Part 2:** 567

Lévy-Bruhl, Lucien, **Retro. Supp. I:** 57

Levy Mayer and the New Industrial Era (Masters), **Supp. I Part 2:** 473

Lewes, George Henry, **II:** 569

Lewin, Albert, **Supp. XIV:** 279, 293

Lewis, C. Day, **III:** 527

Lewis, Dr. Claude, **II:** 442

Lewis, David Levering, **Supp. XVIII:** 127; **Supp. XIX:** 74, 75

Lewis, Edith, **I:** 313; **Retro. Supp. I:** 19, 21, 22

Lewis, Edwin, J., **II:** 439, 442

Lewis, Jerry, **Supp. IV Part 2:** 575; **Supp. X:** 172

Lewis, John L., **I:** 493

Lewis, Lilburn, **IV:** 243

Lewis, Lorene, **Supp. IV Part 2:** 596, 597

Lewis, Lucy, **IV:** 243

Lewis, Maggie, **Supp. V:** 23

Lewis, Meriwether, **II:** 217; **III:** 14; **IV:** 179, 243, 283

Lewis, Merrill, **Supp. IV Part 2:** 596, 597

Lewis, Michael, **II:** 451, 452; **Supp. XVII:** 210

Lewis, Robert Q., **Supp. IV Part 2:** 574

Lewis, R. W. B., **I:** 386, 561; **II:** 457–458; **Retro. Supp. I:** 362, 367; **Supp. I Part 1:** 233; **Supp. XIII:** 93

Lewis, Sinclair, **I:** 116, 212, 348, 355, 362, 374, 378, 487, 495; **II:** 27, 34, 74, 79, 271, 277, 306, **439–461**, 474; **III:** 28, 40, 51, 60, 61, 63–64, 66, 70, 71, 106, 394, 462, 572, 606; **IV:** 53, 326, 366, 455, 468, 475, 482; **Retro. Supp. I:** 332; **Retro. Supp. II:** 95, 108, 197, 322; **Supp. I Part 2:** 378, 613, 709; **Supp. IV Part 2:** 678; **Supp. V:** 278; **Supp. IX:** 308; **Supp. X:** 137; **Supp. XVII:** 41; **Supp. XVIII:** 278

Lewis, Mrs. Sinclair (Dorothy Thompson), **II:** 449–450, 451, 453

Lewis, Mrs. Sinclair (Grace Livingston Hegger), **II:** 441

Lewis, Wyndham, **III:** 458, 462, 465, 470; **Retro. Supp. I:** 59, 170, 292; **Supp. III Part 2:** 617

Lexicon Tetraglotton (Howell), **II:** 111

"Lexington Avenue Musedog" (Peacock), **Supp. XIX:** 204

"Leyenda" (Mora), **Supp. XIII:** 214

Leyner, Mark, **Supp. XIX:** 223

Leyte (Morison), **Supp. I Part 2:** 491

"Liar, The" (Baraka), **Supp. II Part 1:** 36

"Liars, The" (Sandburg), **III:** 586
Liars' Club, The: A Memoir (Karr), **Supp. XI:** 239, 240, 241, 242, **244–248,** 252, 254; **Supp. XVI:** 70
Liar's Dice (C. Frost), **Supp. XV:** 93, 96
"Liar's Dice" (C. Frost), **Supp. XV:** 94, 107
Liars in Love (Yates), **Supp. XI:** 348, 349
Libation Bearers, The (Aeschylus), **III:** 398; **Supp. IX:** 103
Li Bay. *See* Li Po
Libby, Anthony, **Supp. XIII:** 87
Libera, Padre, **II:** 278
Liberal Imagination, The (Trilling), **III:** 308; **Retro. Supp. I:** 97, 216; **Supp. II Part 1:** 146; **Supp. III Part 2:** 495, 498, 501–504
Liberation (J. Scott), **Supp. XVII:** 192, **194–196**
"Liberation" (Winters), **Supp. II Part 2:** 791
Liber Brunenesis (yearbook), **IV:** 286
Liberties, The (Howe), **Supp. IV Part 2:** 426–428, 430, 432
Liberties of America, The (H. Warner), **Supp. XVIII:** 259
Liberty Jones (play), **Supp. IV Part 1:** 83
"Liberty Tree" (Paine), **Supp. I Part 2:** 505
Libra (DeLillo), **Supp. VI:** 2, **4, 5,** 6, **7,** 9, 10, 12, 13, 14, 16
Library for Juana, A (Mora), **Supp. XIII:** 218
Library of America, **Retro. Supp. I:** 2
"Library of Babel, The" (J. Borges), **Supp. XVII:** 47
"Library of Law, A" (MacLeish), **III:** 4
"Library of Moloch, The" (Bukiet), **Supp. XVII:** 47, 49
"Librettos for Eros" (Gander), **Supp. XV:** 340
Lice, The (Merwin), **Supp. III Part 1:** 339, 341–342, 346, 348, 349, 355
Lichtenberg, Georg Christoph, **Supp. XIV:** 339
Lichtenstein, Roy, **Supp. I Part 2:** 665; **Supp. XV:** 186
"Liddy's Orange" (Olds), **Supp. X:** 209
"Lie, The" (Antin), **Supp. XX:** 7, 9–10
Lieberman, Laurence, **Supp. XI:** 323–324
Liebestod (Wagner), **I:** 284, 395
Liebling, A. J., **IV:** 290; **Supp. VIII:** 151; **Supp. XVI:** 167
Lie Down in Darkness (Styron), **IV:** 98, 99, 100–104, 105, 111; **Supp. XI:** 343
Lie of the Mind, A (Shepard), **Supp. III Part 2:** 433, 435, 441, 447–449
"Lies" (Haines), **Supp. XII:** 204
Lies (Hoffman), **Supp. XVIII: 78–79**
"Lies and Consequences" (Pickering), **Supp. XXI:** 204
Lies Like Truth (Clurman), **IV:** 385
Lieutenant, The (Dubus), **Supp. VII:** 78
"Life" (Wharton), **Retro. Supp. I:** 372
Life along the Passaic River (W. C. Williams), **Retro. Supp. I:** 423

Life Among the Savages (Jackson), **Supp. IX:** 115, **125**
"Life and Death Kisses, The" (Grossman), **Supp. XIX:** 87
Life and Gabriella (Glasgow), **II:** 175, 176, 182–183, 184, 189
"Life and I" (Wharton), **Retro. Supp. I:** 360, 361, 362
"Life and Letters" (Epstein), **Supp. XIV:** 104–105
Life and Letters of Harrison Gray Otis, Federalist, 1765–1848, The (Morison), **Supp. I Part 2:** 480–481
Life and Letters of Sir Henry Wotton (L. P. Smith), **Supp. XIV:** 340–341
Life and Times of Frederick Douglass, Written by Himself, The (Douglass), **Supp. III Part 1:** 155, 159–163
Life and Writings of Horace McCoy, The (Wolfson), **Supp. XIII:** 172, 174
"Life as a Visionary Spirit" (Eberhart), **I:** 540, 541
"Life at Angelo's, A" (Benét), **Supp. XI:** 53
Life at Happy Knoll (Marquand), **III:** 50, 61
Life Before Man (Atwood), **Supp. XIII: 24–25**
"Life Cycle of Common Man" (Nemerov), **III:** 278
"Lifecycle Stairmaster" (Karr), **Supp. XI:** 250
Life Estates (Hearon), **Supp. VIII: 68–69**
Life for Life's Sake (Aldington), **Supp. I Part 1:** 256
Life Full of Holes, A (Layachi), **Supp. IV Part 1:** 92
"Lifeguard" (Updike), **IV:** 226; **Retro. Supp. I:** 325
"Lifeguard, The" (Dickey), **Supp. IV Part 1:** 179–180
"Life in the 30s" (column, Quindlen), **Supp. XVII:** 165, 167–169
Life in the Clearings (Shields), **Supp. VII:** 313
"Life in the Country: A City Friend Asks, 'Is It Boring?' " (Paley), **Supp. VI:** 231
Life in the Forest (Levertov), **Supp. III Part 1:** 282–283
Life in the Iron Mills (R. H. Davis), **Supp. XIII:** 292, 295, 299, 305; **Supp. XVI:** 79–82, 85–88, 91
Life in the Iron Mills and Other Stories (T. Olson, ed.), **Supp. XVI:** 83
Life in the Theatre, A (Mamet), **Supp. XIV:** 241, 255
Life Is a Miracle: An Essay Against Modern Superstition (Berry), **Supp. X:** 35
"Life Is Fine" (Hughes), **Supp. I Part 1:** 334, 338
"Life Is Motion" (Stevens), **IV:** 74
Life & Letters of Gene Stratton-Porter (Meehan), **Supp. XX:** 213
Life of Albert Gallatin, The (Adams), **I:** 6, 14
Life of an Ordinary Woman, The: Anne Ellis (A. Ellis), **Supp. XVI:** 38

Life of Captain Cipriani, The: An Account of British Government in the West Indies (C. L. R. James), **Supp. XXI:** 161
Life of Dryden (Johnson), **Retro. Supp. II:** 223
Life of Emily Dickinson, The (Sewall), **Retro. Supp. I:** 25
Life of Forms, The (Focillon), **IV:** 90
Life of Franklin Pierce (Hawthorne), **Retro. Supp. I:** 163
Life of George Cabot Lodge, The (Adams), **I:** 21
Life of George Washington (Irving), **II:** 314, 315–316
Life of Henry James (Edel), **Retro. Supp. I:** 224
"Life of Irony, The" (Bourne), **I:** 219
Life of Jesus (Renan), **Supp. XX:** 122
"Life of Lincoln West, The" (Brooks), **Supp. III Part 1:** 86
Life of Mary, The (Rilke; F. Wright, trans.), **Supp. XVII:** 244
Life of Michelangelo (Grimm), **II:** 17
"Life of Nancy, The" (Jewett), **Retro. Supp. II:** 133, 144
Life of Oliver Goldsmith, The, with Selections from His Writings (Irving), **II:** 315
Life of Phips (Mather), **Supp. II Part 2:** 451, 452, 459
Life of Poetry, The (Rukeyser), **Supp. VI:** 271, 273, 275–276, 282, 283, 286
Life of Samuel Johnson (Boswell), **Supp. I Part 2:** 656
Life of Savage (Johnson), **Supp. I Part 2:** 523
Life of the Drama, The (Bentley), **IV:** 396
"Life of the Mind, The" (Kees), **Supp. XV:** 140
Life of the Right Reverend Joseph P. Machebeuf, The (Howlett), **Retro. Supp. I:** 17
Life of Thomas Paine, author of Rights of Men, With a Defence of his Writings (Chalmers), **Supp. I Part 2:** 514
Life of Thomas Paine, The (Cobbett), **Supp. I Part 2:** 517
"Life of Towne, The" (Carson), **Supp. XII: 102**
"Life on Beekman Place, A" (Naylor), **Supp. VIII:** 214
"Life on the Black List" (Endore), **Supp. XVII:** 63
Life on the Hyphen: The Cuban-American Way (Firmat), **Supp. VIII:** 76; **Supp. XI:** 184
Life on the Mississippi (Twain), **I:** 209; **IV:** 198, 199; **Supp. I Part 2:** 440
"Life on the Rocks: The Galápagos" (Dillard), **Supp. VI:** 32
"Life Stories, East and West" (E. Hoffman), **Supp. XVI:** 157
Life Story (Baker), **II:** 259
Life Studies (Lowell), **I:** 400; **II:** 384, 386, 543, 546–550, 551, 555; **Retro. Supp. II:** 180, 185, 186, 188, 189, 191; **Supp. I Part 2:** 543; **Supp. XI:** 240, 244, 250, 317; **Supp. XII:** 255; **Supp. XIV:** 15; **Supp. XV:** 252

"Life Studies" (Lowell), **Retro. Supp. II:** 188

"Life Styles in the Golden Land" (Didion), **Supp. IV Part 1:** 200

Life Supports: New and Collected Poems (Bronk), **Supp. XXI:** 19, 31, 32

"Life That Is, The" (Bryant), **Supp. I Part 1:** 169

"Life Work" (Stafford), **Supp. XI:** 329–330

"Life You Save May Be Your Own, The" (O'Connor), **III:** 344, 350, 354; **Retro. Supp. II:** 229, 230, 233

Lifshin, Lyn, **Supp. XVI:** 37

"Lifting, The" (Olds), **Supp. X:** 210

"Ligeia" (Poe), **III:** 412, 414; **Retro. Supp. II:** 261, 270, 271, 275

Liggett, Walter W., **Supp. XIII:** 168

Light, James F., **IV:** 290; **Retro. Supp. II:** 325

Light, Kate, **Supp. XVII:** 109

Light and Dark (Bronk), **Supp. XXI:** 27–29, 31

"Light and the Sufferer" (Lethem), **Supp. XVIII:** 139–140

Light around the Body, The (R. Bly), **Supp. IV Part 1:** 61–62, 62; **Supp. XVII:** 243; **Supp. XXI:** 84–85

"Light Comes Brighter, The" (Roethke), **III:** 529–530

"Light from Above" (Eberhart), **I:** 541

Light in August (Faulkner), **II:** 63–64, 65, 74; **IV:** 207; **Retro. Supp. I:** 82, 84, 85, 86, 89, 92; **Supp. XIV:** 12

Light in the Forest, The (Richter), **Supp. XVIII:** 216–217

Light in the Morning (Baker), **Supp. XVIII:** 263, 269

"Light Man, A" (James), **II:** 322; **Retro. Supp. I:** 219

"Lightning" (Barthelme), **Supp. IV Part 1:** 53

"Lightning" (Bynner), **Supp. XV:** 44

"Lightning" (Oliver), **Supp. VII:** 235

"Lightning, The" (Swenson), **Supp. IV Part 2:** 645

"Lightning Flash, The" (Gibran), **Supp. XX:** 123

"Lightning Rod Man, The" (Melville), **III:** 90; **Supp. XVIII:** 4

"Light of the World, The" (Hemingway), **II:** 249

"Lights in the Windows" (Nye), **Supp. XIII:** 280

Light Verse and Satires (Bynner), **Supp. XV:** 52

Light Years (Salter), **Supp. IX:** 257–259

"LIKE, THIS IS WHAT I MEANT!" (Baraka), **Supp. II Part 1:** 59

"Like All the Other Nations" (Paley), **Supp. VI:** 220

"Like a Rolling Stone" (song, Dylan), **Supp. XVIII:** 20, 30

"Like Decorations in a Nigger Cemetery" (Stevens), **IV:** 74, 79; **Retro. Supp. I:** 305

Like Ghosts of Eagles (Francis), **Supp. IX:** 86

"Like Life" (Moore), **Supp. X:** 163, 165, **172–173**

Like Life: Stories (Moore), **Supp. X:** 163, **171–175**, 177, 178

"Like Talk" (Mills), **Supp. XI:** 311

"Like the New Moon I Will Live My Life" (R. Bly), **Supp. IV Part 1:** 71

Li'l Abner (Capp), **IV:** 198

"Lilacs" (Lowell), **II:** 527

"Lilacs, The" (Wilbur), **Supp. III Part 2:** 557–558

"Lilacs for Ginsberg" (Stern), **Supp. IX:** 299

Liliom (Molnar), **Supp. XVI:** 187

Lilith's Brood (O. Butler), **Supp. XIII:** 63

Lillabulero Press, **Supp. V:** 4, 5

Lillian Hellman (Adler), **Supp. I Part 1:** 297

Lillian Hellman (Falk), **Supp. I Part 1:** 297

Lillian Hellman: Playwright (Moody), **Supp. I Part 1:** 280

Lillo, George, **II:** 111, 112

"Lily Daw and the Three Ladies" (Welty), **IV:** 262

Lima, Agnes de, **I:** 231, 232

"Limbo: Altered States" (Karr), **Supp. XI:** 249–250

"Limen" (Trethewey), **Supp. XXI:** 250

Lime Orchard Woman, The (Ríos), **Supp. IV Part 2:** 538, 547–550, 553

"Lime Orchard Woman, The" (Ríos), **Supp. IV Part 2:** 548

Limitations (Turow), **Supp. XVII:** **222–223**

"Limits" (Emerson), **II:** 19

Lincoln, Abraham, **I:** 1, 4, 30; **II:** 8, 13, 135, 273, 555, 576; **III:** 576, 577, 580, 584, 587–590, 591; **IV:** 192, 195, 298, 347, 350, 444; **Supp. I Part 1:** 2, 8, 26, 309, 321; **Supp. I Part 2:** 379, 380, 382, 385, 390, 397, 399, 418, 424, 454, 456, 471, 472, 473, 474, 483, 579, 687; **Supp. VIII:** 108; **Supp. IX:** 15; **Supp. XIV:** 73

Lincoln, Kenneth, **Supp. IV Part 1:** 329; **Supp. IV Part 2:** 507

Lincoln, Thomas, **III:** 587

Lincoln, Mrs. Thomas (Nancy Hanks), **III:** 587

Lincoln: A Novel (Vidal), **Supp. IV Part 2:** 677, 684, 685, 688, 689–690, 691, 692

Lincoln Lawyer, The (Connelly), **Supp. XXI:** **77**, 78

Lincoln on Race and Slavery (H. L. Gates), **Supp. XX:** 108–109

"Lincoln Relics, The" (Kunitz), **Supp. III Part 1:** 269

Lincoln: The Man (Masters), **Supp. I Part 2:** 471, 473–474

Lindbergh, Charles A., **I:** 482

"Linden Branch, The" (MacLeish), **III:** 19, 20

Linden Hills (Naylor), **Supp. VIII:** 214, 218, **219–223**

Linderman, Lawrence, **Supp. IV Part 2:** 579, 583, 585, 589

Lindner, April, **Supp. XV:** 111, 119

Lindsay, Howard, **III:** 284

Lindsay, John, **Supp. I Part 2:** 374

Lindsay, Olive, **Supp. I Part 2:** 374, 375, 392

Lindsay, Vachel, **I:** 384; **II:** 263, 276, 530; **III:** 5, 505; **Retro. Supp. I:** 133; **Supp. I Part 1:** 324; **Supp. I Part 2:** **374–403,** 454, 473, 474; **Supp. III Part 1:** 63, 71; **Supp. XV:** 293, 297, 299, 301, 306; **Supp. XVI:** 184–185

Lindsay, Mrs. Vachel (Elizabeth Connors), **Supp. I Part 2:** 398, 399, 473

Lindsay, Vachel Thomas, **Supp. I Part 2:** 374, 375

Lindsay, Mrs. Vachel Thomas (Esther Catherine Frazee), **Supp. I Part 2:** 374, 375, 384–385, 398

Lindsey, David, **Supp. XIV:** 26

"Line, The" (Olds), **Supp. X:** 206

Lineage of Ragpickers, Songpluckers, Elegiasts, and Jewelers, A (Goldbarth), **Supp. XII:** 191

"Line of Least Resistance, The" (Wharton), **Retro. Supp. I:** 366

Line Out for a Walk, A: Familiar Essays (Epstein), **Supp. XIV:** **107**

"Liner Notes for the Poetically Unhep" (Hughes), **Retro. Supp. I:** 210

"Lines After Rereading T. S. Eliot" (Wright), **Supp. V:** 343

"Lines Composed a Few Miles Above Tintern Abbey" (Wordsworth), **Supp. III Part 1:** 12

"Lines Composed Over Three Thousand Miles from Tintern Abbey" (Collins), **Supp. XXI:** 57–58

"Lines for an Interment" (MacLeish), **III:** 15

"Lines for My Father" (Cullen), **Supp. IV Part 1:** 167

"Lines from Israel" (Lowell), **II:** 554

"Lines from Pietro Longhi" (Sobin), **Supp. XVI:** 289

"Lines on Revisiting the Country" (Bryant), **Supp. I Part 1:** 164

"Lines Suggested by a Tennessee Song" (Agee), **I:** 28

"Line-Storm Song, A" (Frost), **Retro. Supp. I:** 127

"Lines Written at Port Royal" (Freneau), **Supp. II Part 1:** 264

"Lines Written in an Asylum" (Carruth), **Supp. XVI:** 48

"Lines Written in Manassas", **Supp. XV:** 99–100

Lineup, The (Connelly), **Supp. XXI:** 67, 68–69

"Line Written in the Dark Illegible Next Day" (F. Wright), **Supp. XVII:** 242

Linfield, Susie, **Supp. XVII:** 169, 177

Lingeman, Richard, **Supp. X:** 82

Linn, Elizabeth. *See* Brown, Mrs. Charles Brockden (Elizabeth Linn)

Linn, John Blair, **Supp. I Part 1:** 145

Linnaeus, Carolus, **II:** 6; **Supp. I Part 1:** 245

"Linnets" (Levis), **Supp. XI:** 260, 261

"Linoleum Roses" (Cisneros), **Supp. VII:** 63, 66

Linotte: 1914–1920 (Nin), **Supp. X:** 193, 196, 197

Linschoten, Hans, **II:** 362, 363, 364
"Lion" (B. Kelly), **Supp. XVII:** 133
"Lion and Honeycomb" (Nemerov), **III:** 275, 278, 280
Lion and the Archer, The (Hayden), **Supp. II Part 1:** 366, 367
Lion and the Honeycomb, The (Blackmur), **Supp. II Part 1:** 91
Lion Country (Buechner), **Supp. XII:** 52, 53
Lionel Lincoln (Cooper), **I:** 339, 342
"Lion for Real, The" (Ginsberg), **Supp. II Part 1:** 320
Lionhearted, The: A Story about the Jews of Medieval England (Reznikoff), **Supp. XIV:** 280, 289
Lion in the Garden (Meriweather and Millgate), **Retro. Supp. I:** 91
"Lionizing" (Poe), **III:** 411, 425
"Lions, Harts, and Leaping Does" (Powers), **III:** 356
Lions and Shadows: An Education in the Twenties (Isherwood), **Supp. XIV:** 158, 159, 160, 162
"Lions in Sweden" (Stevens), **IV:** 79–80
Lipman, William R., **Supp. XIII:** 170
Li Po, **Supp. XI:** 241; **Supp. XII:** 218; **Supp. XV:** 47, 217
Lippmann, Walter, **I:** 48, 222–223, 225; **III:** 291, 600; **IV:** 429; **Supp. I Part 2:** 609, 643; **Supp. VIII:** 104
Lips Together, Teeth Apart (McNally), **Supp. XIII: 201–202,** 208, 209
Lipsyte, Robert, **Supp. XVI:** 220
Lipton, James, **Supp. IV Part 2:** 576, 577, 579, 583, 586, 588
Lipton, Lawrence, **Supp. IX:** 3
Lisbon Traviata, The (McNally), **Supp. XIII:** 198, **199–200,** 201, 204, 208
Lish, Gordon, **Supp. XIX:** 209; **Supp. XXI:** 115, 121
Lisicky, Paul, **Supp. XI:** 120, 131, 135
Lisk, Thomas, **Supp. XXI:** 24
"Lisp, The" (Olds), **Supp. X:** 211
Listen, Ruben Fontanez (Neugeboren), **Supp. XVI: 220–221**
"Listeners, The" (de la Mare), **Supp. XVII:** 69
"Listeners and Readers: The Unforgetting of Vachel Lindsay" (Trombly), **Supp. I Part 2:** 403
"Listening" (J. W. Miller), **Supp. XX:** 167
"Listening" (Paley), **Supp. VI:** 218, 231, 232
"Listening" (Stafford), **Supp. XI:** 321, 322
Listening to Prozac (P. Kramer), **Supp. XVI:** 229
"Listening to the Desert" (Henderson), **Supp. XIII:** 221–222
"Listening to the Mockingbird" (Woodard), **Supp. VIII:** 128
Listening to Your Life: Daily Meditations with Frederick Buechner (Buechner), **Supp. XII:** 53
Listen to the Desert/Oye al desierto (Mora), **Supp. XIII:** 221
"Listen to the People" (Benét), **Supp. XI:** 51–52
Liston, Sonny, **III:** 38, 42

Li T'ai-po, **II:** 526
"Litany" (Ashbery), **Supp. III Part 1:** 21–22, 25, 26
"Litany" (Collins), **Supp. XXI:** 56–57
"Litany" (Sandburg), **III:** 593
"Litany, The" (Gioia), **Supp. XV:** 125, 126
"Litany for Dictatorships" (Benét), **Supp. XI:** 46, 58
"Litany for Survival, A" (Lorde), **Supp. XII:** 220
"Litany of the Dark People, The" (Cullen), **Supp. IV Part 1:** 170, 171
"Litany of the Heroes" (Lindsay), **Supp. I Part 2:** 397
"Litany of Washington Street, The" (Lindsay), **Supp. I Part 2:** 376, 398–399
Literary Anthropology (Trumpener and Nyce), **Retro. Supp. I:** 380
Literary Art and Activism of Rick Bass, The (Weltzien), **Supp. XVI:** 20–21
"Literary Blacks and Jews" (Ozick), **Supp. V:** 272
"Literary Career of Elizabeth Barstow Stoddard, The" (Matlack), **Supp. XV:** 269
Literary Criticism: A Short History (Brooks and Wimsatt), **Supp. XIV:** 12
"Literary Criticism of Georg Lukács, The" (Sontag), **Supp. III Part 2:** 453
Literary Disruptions (Klinkowitz), **Supp. XXI:** 233
Literary Essays of Thomas Merton, The, **Supp. VIII:** 207
"Literary Folk As They Came and Went with Ourselves" (E. Stoddard), **Supp. XV:** 274
Literary Friends and Acquaintance (Howells), **Supp. I Part 1:** 318; **Supp. XV:** 287
"Literary Heritage of Tennyson, The" (Locke), **Supp. XIV:** 197
Literary History of the United States (Spiller et al., ed.), **Supp. I Part 1:** 104; **Supp. II Part 1:** 95
"Literary Importation" (Freneau), **Supp. II Part 1:** 264
"Literary Life of America, The" (Brooks), **I:** 245
Literary Outlaw: The Life and Times of William S. Burroughs (Morgan), **Supp. XIV:** 141
Literary Situation, The (Cowley), **Supp. II Part 1:** 135, 140, 144, 146, 147, 148
"Literary Worker's Polonius, The" (Wilson), **IV:** 431, 432
"Literature" (Emerson), **II:** 6
Literature (X. J. Kennedy), **Supp. XV:** 153
Literature and American Life (Boynton), **Supp. I Part 2:** 415
Literature and Life (Howells), **Supp. XIV:** 45–46
Literature and Morality (Farrell), **II:** 49
"Literature and Place: Varieties of Regional Experience" (Erisman), **Supp. VIII:** 126

"Literature as a Symptom" (Warren), **IV:** 237
"Literature in Low Life" (Hapgood), **Supp. XVII:** 103
"Literature of Exhaustion, The" (Barth), **Supp. IV Part 1:** 48
"Lithuanian Nocturne" (Brodsky), **Supp. VIII:** 29
"Lit Instructor" (Stafford), **Supp. XI:** 321
Littauer, Kenneth, **Retro. Supp. I:** 114
Little Acts of Kindness (Budbill), **Supp. XIX:** 3, **14–15**
"Little Bernhardt" (Shaw), **Supp. XIX:** 246
Little Big Man (Berger), **Supp. XII:** 171
Little Big Man (film), **Supp. X:** 124
Littlebird, Harold, **Supp. IV Part 2:** 499
Littlebird, Larry, **Supp. IV Part 2:** 499, 505
Little Birds: Erotica (Nin), **Supp. X:** 192, 195
"Little Brown Baby" (Dunbar), **Supp. II Part 1:** 206
"Little Brown Jug" (Baraka), **Supp. II Part 1:** 51
Little Casino (Sorrentino), **Supp. XXI:** 237, 238
"Little Clown, My Heart" (Cisneros), **Supp. VII:** 71
"Little Cosmic Dust Poem" (Haines), **Supp. XII:** 209–210
"Little Country Girl, A" (Chopin), **Retro. Supp. II:** 71
"Little Curtis" (Parker), **Supp. IX:** 193
Little Disturbances of Man, The (Paley), **Supp. VI:** 218
"Little Dog" (Hughes), **Supp. I Part 1:** 329
Little Dorrit (Dickens), **Supp. I Part 1:** 35
"Little Edward" (Stowe), **Supp. I Part 2:** 587
"Little Elegy" (X. J. Kennedy), **Supp. XV:** 155
Little Essays Drawn from the Writings of George Santayana (L. P. Smith), **Supp. XIV:** 342
"Little Expressionless Animals" (Wallace), **Supp. X:** 305
"Little Fable" (Hay), **Supp. XIV:** 131
Littlefield, Catherine, **Supp. IX:** 58
Little Fling, A (Pickering), **Supp. XXI:** 203
Little Foxes, The (Hellman), **Supp. I Part 1:** 276, 278–279, 281, 283, 297
"Little Fred, the Canal Boy" (Stowe), **Supp. I Part 2:** 587
"Little French Mary" (Jewett), **II:** 400
Little Friend, Little Friend (Jarrell), **II:** 367, 372, 375–376
"Little Gidding" (Eliot), **I:** 582, 588; **II:** 539; **Retro. Supp. I:** 66
"Little Girl, My Stringbean, My Lovely Woman" (Sexton), **Supp. II Part 2:** 686
"Little Girl, The" (Paley), **Supp. VI:** 222, **228–229**
"Little Girl Tells a Story to a Lady, A" (Barnes), **Supp. III Part 1:** 36

"Little Goose Girl, The" (Grimm), **IV:** 266

Little Ham (Hughes), **Retro. Supp. I:** 203; **Supp. I Part 1:** 328, 339

Little King, The (Bynner), **Supp. XV:** 42, 50

Little Lady of the Big House, The (London), **II:** 481–482

Little Liar, The (film; Ingraham), **Supp. XVI:** 184–185

"Little Lion Face" (Swenson), **Supp. IV Part 2:** 651

"Little Lobelia's Song" (Bogan), **Supp. III Part 1:** 66

"Little Local Color, A" (Henry), **Supp. II Part 1:** 399

Little Lord Fauntleroy (Burnett), **Retro. Supp. I:** 188; **Supp. XVI:** 182

"Little Lyric" (Hughes), **Supp. I Part 1:** 334

Little Man, Little Man (Baldwin), **Supp. I Part 1:** 67

"Little Man at Chehaw Station, The" (Ellison), **Retro. Supp. II:** 123

Little Me (musical), **Supp. IV Part 2:** 575

Little Men (Alcott), **Supp. I Part 1:** 32, 39, 40

"Little Morning Music, A" (Schwartz), **Supp. II Part 2:** 662–663

Little Ocean (Shepard), **Supp. III Part 2:** 447

"Little Old Girl, A" (Larcom), **Supp. XIII:** 144

"Little Old Spy" (Hughes), **Supp. I Part 1:** 329

Little Orphan Annie (film), **Supp. XVIII:** 244

"Little Owl Who Lives in the Orchard" (Oliver), **Supp. VII:** 239

"Little Peasant, The" (Sexton), **Supp. II Part 2:** 690

"Little Rapids, The" (Swenson), **Supp. IV Part 2:** 645

Little Red Song Book (Hill), **Supp. XVIII:** 224

Little Regiment and Other Episodes of the American Civil War, The (Crane), **I:** 408

Little River: New and Selected Poems (McCarriston), **Supp. XIV: 269–272**

"Little Road not made of Man , A" (Dickinson), **Retro. Supp. I:** 44

Little Sister, The (Chandler), **Supp. IV Part 1:** 122, 130, 131–132

"Little Sleep's-Head Sprouting Hair in the Moonlight" (Kinnell), **Supp. III Part 1:** 247

"Little Snow White" (Grimm), **IV:** 266

Little Star (Halliday), **Supp. XIX:** 82, **84–85,** 87

"Little Star" (Halliday), **Supp. XIX:** 83, 84, 93

"Little Testament of Bernard Martin, Aet. 30" (Mumford), **Supp. II Part 2:** 472, 473, 474

"Little Things" (Olds), **Supp. X:** 208

Little Tour in France (James), **II:** 337

Little Women (Alcott), **Supp. I Part 1:** 28, 29, 32, 35, 37, 38, 39–40, 41, 43, 44; **Supp. IX:** 128

Little Yellow Dog, A (Mosley), **Supp. XIII:** 237, 241

"Liturgy and Spiritual Personalism" (Merton), **Supp. VIII:** 199

Litz, A. Walton, **Retro. Supp. I:** 306

"Liu Ch'e" (Pound), **III:** 466

"Live" (Sexton), **Supp. II Part 2:** 684, 686

Live from Baghdad (screenplay, Shanley), **Supp. XIV:** 316

Live from Golgotha (Vidal), **Supp. IV Part 2:** 677, 682, 691, 692

Live Now and Pay Later (Garrett), **Supp. VII:** 111

"Live-Oak with Moss" (Whitman), **Retro. Supp. I:** 403

Live or Die (Sexton), **Supp. II Part 2:** 670, 683–687

Liveright, Horace, **Retro. Supp. I:** 80, 81, 83; **Supp. I Part 2:** 464; **Supp. XX:** 71, 75

Lives (Plutarch), **II:** 5, 104

Lives of a Cell, The (L. Thomas), **Retro. Supp. I:** 322, 323

Lives of Distinguished American Naval Officers (Cooper), **I:** 347

"Lives of Gulls and Children, The" (Nemerov), **III:** 271, 272

Lives of the Animals (Wrigley), **Supp. XVIII: 306–308**

Lives of the Artists (Vasari), **Supp. I Part 2:** 450

"Lives of the Bohemians" (Lethem), **Supp. XVIII:** 135

Lives of the Muses, The: Nine Women and the Artists They Inspired (Prose), **Supp. XVI:** 250, 260

Lives of the Poets (Doctorow), **Supp. IV Part 1:** 234

"Lives of the Poets" (Doctorow), **Supp. IV Part 1:** 234

"Lives of the—Wha'?, The" (Goldbarth), **Supp. XII:** 191

"Living" (Wright), **Supp. XV:** 345

Living, The (Dillard), **Supp. VI:** 23

"Living at Home" (Gordon), **Supp. IV Part 1:** 311

Living by Fiction (Dillard), **Supp. VI:** 23, 31, **32,** 33

Living by the Word (Walker), **Supp. III Part 2:** 521, 522, 526, 527, 535

Living End, The (Elkin), **Supp. VI: 54,** 58

Living Instead (Bronk), **Supp. XXI:** 32

"Living in the Flatlands" (Carruth), **Supp. XVI:** 54

Living Is Easy, The (D. West), **Supp. XVIII:** 277, 280, **284–286,** 287

"Living Like Weasels" (Dillard), **Supp. VI:** 26, 33

Living Novel, The (Hicks), **III:** 342

Living of Charlotte Perkins Gilman, The (Gilman), **Supp. XI:** 193, 209

Living off the Country: Essays on Poetry and Place (Haines), **Supp. XII:** 199, 203, 207

"Living on a Giant" (X. J. Kennedy), **Supp. XV:** 163

Living Out Loud (Quindlen), **Supp. XVII:** 166, **167–169**

Living Reed, The (Buck), **Supp. II Part 1:** 129–130

Livingston, Myra Cohn, **Supp. XV:** 153, 162

Living Theater, **Retro. Supp. I:** 424

"Living There" (Dickey), **Supp. IV Part 1:** 182–183

Living the Spirit: A Gay American Indian Anthology (Roscoe, ed.), **Supp. IV Part 1:** 330

Living to Prowl (Pickering), **Supp. XXI:** 203

"Living with a Peacock" (O'Connor), **III:** 350

"Livvie" (Welty), **IV:** 265; **Retro. Supp. I:** 348–349

"Livvie Is Back" (Welty), **Retro. Supp. I:** 351

Livy, **II:** 8

Lizzie (film), **Supp. IX:** 125

"Llantos de La Llorona: Warnings from the Wailer" (Mora), **Supp. XIII:** 217, 224

"L'Lapse" (Barthelme), **Supp. IV Part 1:** 45–47, 48

Llosa, Mario Vargas, **Supp. XIX:** 131

Lloyd, Henry Demarest, **Supp. I Part 1:** 5

Lloyd George, Harold, **I:** 490

"LMFBR" (Snyder), **Supp. VIII:** 302

"Loaded Inflections" (Halliday), **Supp. XIX:** 90, 91

"Loam" (Sandburg), **III:** 584–585

"Loan, The" (Malamud), **Supp. I Part 2:** 427, 428, 431, 437

Loberer, Eric, **Supp. XV:** 339

"Local" (McCarriston), **Supp. XIV:** 270

Local Color (Capote), **Supp. III Part 1:** 120

"Local Color" (London), **II:** 475

"Local Family Keeps Son Happy" (Keillor), **Supp. XVI:** 168, 169

Local Girls (Hoffman), **Supp. X:** 77, **90–91,** 92

"Local Girls" (Hoffman), **Supp. X:** 90

Local Habitation & A Name, A (Kooser), **Supp. XIX:** 116, 118, **119–120**

Local Men (Whitehead), **Supp. XV:** 339

Local Time (Dunn), **Supp. XI:** 143, **148–149**

Local Wonders: Seasons in the Bohemian Alps (Kooser), **Supp. XIX:** 115, **126**

"Location" (Halliday), **Supp. XIX:** 87

Lock, Helen, **Supp. XIII:** 233, 237–238

Lock, Robert H., **IV:** 319; **Retro. Supp. I:** 375

Locke, Alain, **Retro. Supp. II:** 115; **Supp. I Part 1:** 323, 325, 341; **Supp. II Part 1:** 53, 176, 182, 228, 247; **Supp. IV Part 1:** 170; **Supp. IX:** 306, 309; **Supp. X:** 134, 137, 139; **Supp. XIV: 195–219; Supp. XVIII:** 122; **Supp. XIX:** 69, 75

Locke, Duane, **Supp. IX:** 273

Locke, John, **I:** 554–555, 557; **II:** 15–16, 113–114, 348–349, 480; **III:** 294–295; **IV:** 149; **Supp. I Part 1:** 130, 229, 230; **Supp. I Part 2:** 523

Locke, Sondra, **II:** 588

"Locked House, A" (Snodgrass), **Supp. VI:** 323

Locked Room, The (Auster), **Supp. XII:** 22, 24, **27–28**

Locket, The (Masters), **Supp. I Part 2:** 460

Lockridge, Ross, Jr., **Supp. XIX:** 263

"Locksley Hall" (Tennyson), **Supp. IX:** 19

Lockwood Concern, The (O'Hara), **III:** 362, 364, 377–382

"Locus" (Ammons), **Supp. VII:** 28

"Locus" (Hayden), **Supp. II Part 1:** 361–362, 381

"Locusts, the Plaza, the Room, The" (Kees), **Supp. XV:** 141

Loden, Barbara, **III:** 163

Lodge, Henry Cabot, **I:** 11–12, 21

Lodge, Mrs. Henry Cabot, **I:** 11–12, 19

Lodge, Thomas, **IV:** 370

Loeb, Gerald, **Supp. IV Part 2:** 523

Loeb, Jacques, **I:** 513; **Retro. Supp. II:** 104; **Supp. I Part 2:** 641

Loeffler, Jack, **Supp. XIII:** 1, 3, 12, 14, 16

Loftus, Mary J., **Supp. XXI:** 245

Lofty Dogmas (A. Finch, M. Kumin and D. Brown, eds.), **Supp. XVII:** 75–76

"Log" (Merrlll), **Supp. III Part 1:** 328

Logan, Rayford W., **Supp. II Part 1:** 171, 194; **Supp. XIV:** 73

Logan, William, **Supp. X:** 201, 213; **Supp. XI:** 131, 132; **Supp. XII:** 98, 107, 113, 184; **Supp. XV:** 212, 226, 251, 257, 260–261, 262, **Supp. XV:** 263, 266

Log Book of "The Loved One," The, **Supp. XI:** 306

Logenbach, James, **Supp. XVII:** 183

"Logging and Pimping and 'Your Pal, Jim' " (Maclean), **Supp. XIV:** 229

Logue, Christopher, **Supp. XIV:** 82

Lohengrin (Wagner), **I:** 216

Lohrfinck, Rosalind, **III:** 107, 117

Lolita (Nabokov), **III:** 246, 247, 255, 258–261; **Retro. Supp. I:** 263, 264, 265, 266, 269, 270, **272–274,** 275; **Supp. V:** 127, 252; **Supp. VIII:** 133; **Supp. XVI:** 294

"Lolita" (Parker), **Supp. IX:** 193

Lolly Dinks' Doings (E. Stoddard), **Supp. XV:** 273, **Supp. XV:** 286

Lombardi, Marilyn May, **Retro. Supp. II:** 40

London, Eliza, **II:** 465

London, Jack, **I:** 209; **II:** 264, 440, 444, 451, **462–485; III:** 314, 580; **Supp. IV Part 1:** 236; **Supp. V:** 281; **Supp. IX:** 1, 14; **Supp. XIII:** 312; **Supp. XIV:** 227; **Supp. XV:** 115; **Supp. XVI:** 181; **Supp. XVIII:** 90

London, Mrs. Jack (Bessie Maddern), **II:** 465, 466, 473, 478

London, Mrs. Jack (Charmian Kittredge), **II:** 466, 468, 473, 476, 478, 481

London, John, **II:** 464, 465

London, Scott, **Supp. XIV:** 301, 307, 311

London Embassy, The (Theroux), **Supp. VIII:** 323

London Fields (Amis), **Retro. Supp. I:** 278

"London Letter" (column; Eliot), **Supp. XV:** 306

London Magazine (Plath), **Supp. I Part 2:** 541

London Snow: A Christmas Story (Theroux), **Supp. VIII:** 322

London Suite (Simon), **Supp. IV Part 2:** 576, 581, 582, 588

London: The Biography (Ackroyd), **Supp. XVII:** 180

Loneliness of the Long Distance Runner, The (Sillitoe), **Supp. XX:**195

Lonely Are the Brave (film), **Supp. XIII:** 6

"Lonely Coast, A" (Proulx), **Supp. VII:** 264

Lonely Crusade (C. Himes), **Supp. XVI:** 135, 139–140

Lonely for the Future (Farrell), **II:** 46, 47

"Lonely Gay Teen Seeking Same" (Egan), **Supp. XIX:** 61

Lonely Impulse of Delight, A (Shanley), **Supp. XIV:** 317–318

"Lonely Street, The" (W. C. Williams), **IV:** 413

"Lonely Worker, A" (Jewett), **Retro. Supp. II:** 132

Lonergan, Wayne, **Supp. I Part 1:** 51

Lonesome Dove (McMurtry), **Supp. V:** 226–228, 231, 232, 233

Lonesome Traveler (Kerouac), **Supp. III Part 1:** 219, 225

"Lonesome Whistle Blowing" (Skow), **Supp. XVI:** 174

"Lone Striker, A" (Frost), **Retro. Supp. I:** 136, 137

Long, Ada, **Supp. V:** 178

Long, Haniel, **Supp. XV:** 46, 49

Long, Huey, **I:** 489; **II:** 454; **IV:** 249; **Supp. IV Part 2:** 679; **Supp. XIV:** 14

Long, John Luther, **Supp. XXI:** 150

Long, Judith Reick, **Supp. XX:**212, 215, 217, 223

Long, Ray, **II:** 430; **III:** 54

Long after Midnight (Bradbury), **Supp. IV Part 1:** 102

Long Ago in France: The Years in Dijon (M. F. K. Fisher), **Supp. XVII:** 91

Long and Happy Life, A (Price), **Supp. VI:** 258, **259–260,** 262, 264, 265

Long Approach, The (Kumin), **Supp. IV Part 2:** 452–453, 453

Longbottom, Robert, **Supp. XXI:** 148

Long Christmas Dinner, The (Wilder), **IV:** 357, 365; **Supp. V:** 105

Long Christmas Dinner and Other Plays (Wilder), **IV:** 365–366

Long Day's Dying, A (Buechner), **Supp. XII: 45–47**

Long Day's Journey into Night (O'Neill), **III:** 385, 401, 403–404; **Supp. IV Part 1:** 359; **Supp. XIV:** 327; **Supp. XXI:** 13

Long Desire, A (Connell), **Supp. XIV:** 79, 80, 97

"Long Distance" (Stafford), **Supp. XI:** 329

"Long-Distance Runner, The" (Paley), **Supp. VI:** 221–222, 228, 230

Long Dream, The (Wright), **IV:** 478, 488, 494

"Long Embrace, The" (Levine), **Supp. V:** 187

"Long Enough" (Rukeyser), **Supp. VI:** 274

"Longest Night of My Life, The " (Nichols), **Supp. XIII:** 269

Longfellow, Henry Wadsworth, **I:** 458, 471; **II:** 274, 277, 295–296, 310, 313, 402, **486–510; III:** 269, 412, 421, 422, 577; **IV:** 309, 371; **Retro. Supp. I:** 54, 123, 150, 155, 362; **Retro. Supp. II: 153–174; Supp. I Part 1:** 158, 299, 306, 317, 362, 368; **Supp. I Part 2:** 405, 406, 408, 409, 414, 416, 420, 586, 587, 602, 699, 704; **Supp. II Part 1:** 291, 353; **Supp. III Part 2:** 609; **Supp. IV Part 1:** 165; **Supp. IV Part 2:** 503; **Supp. XII:** 260; **Supp. XIII:** 141; **Supp. XIV:** 120; **Supp. XVIII:** 4; **Supp. XXI:** 51

"Long Feud" (Untermeyer), **Supp. XV:** 309

Long Feud: Selected Poems (Untermeyer), **Supp. XV:** 312

"Long Fourth, A" (Taylor), **Supp. V:** 313

Long Fourth and Other Stories, A (Taylor), **Supp. V:** 318–319

Long Gay Book, A (Stein), **IV:** 42

Long Goodbye, The (Chandler), **Supp. IV Part 1:** 120, 122, 132–134, 135

Long Goodbye, The (T. Williams), **IV:** 381

"Long Hair" (Snyder), **Supp. VIII:** 300

Longing for Home, The: Recollections and Reflections (Buechner), **Supp. XII:** 53

Longinus, Dionysius Cassius, **I:** 279

"Long-Legged House, The" (Berry), **Supp. X:** 21, 24–25, 27, 31

Long Live Man (Corso), **Supp. XII:** 129–130, 132

Long Love, The (Sedges), **Supp. II Part 1:** 125

Long Made Short (Dixon), **Supp. XII:** 152

Long March, The (Styron), **IV:** 97, 99, 104–107, 111, 113, 117

"Long Night, The" (Bambara), **Supp. XI:** 9

"Long Novel, A" (Ashbery), **Supp. III Part 1:** 6

Longo, Robert, **Supp. XVI:** 124

Long Patrol, The (Mailer), **III:** 46

"Long Point Light" (Doty), **Supp. XI:** 127

Long Road of Woman's Memory, The (Addams), **Supp. I Part 1:** 17–18

"Long Run, The" (Wharton), **IV:** 314

Long Season, The (Brosnan), **II:** 424, 425; **Supp. XX:**195

"Long Shadow of Lincoln, The: A Litany" (Sandburg), **III:** 591, 593

Longshot O'Leary (McGrath), **Supp. X:** 117

"Long Shower, The" (Francis), **Supp. IX:** 90

"Long Stemmed Roses" (Jarman), **Supp. XVII:** 115

Longstreet, Augustus B., **II:** 70, 313; **Supp. I Part 1:** 352.; **Supp. V:** 44; **Supp. X:** 227

"Long Summer" (Lowell), **II:** 553–554

"Long Term" (Dunn), **Supp. XI:** 149

Longtime Companion (film), **Supp. X:** 146, 152

Long Valley, The (Steinbeck), **IV:** 51

Long Voyage Home, The (O'Neill), **III:** 388

"Long Wail, A" (Crews), **Supp. XI:** 101

"Long Walk, The" (Bogan), **Supp. III Part 1:** 61

Long Walks and Intimate Talks (Paley), **Supp. VI:** 221

Long Way from Home, A (McKay), **Supp. X:** 132, 140

Lönnrot, Elias, **Retro. Supp. II:** 159

Looby, Christopher, **Supp. XIII:** 96

Look, Stranger! (Auden), **Supp. II Part 1:** 11

"Look, The" (Olds), **Supp. X:** 210

Look at Me (Egan), **Supp. XIX:** 49, **53–56**, 60, 61

Look at the Harlequins (Nabokov), **Retro. Supp. I:** 266, 270

"Look for My White Self" (Ammons), **Supp. VII:** 25

Look Homeward, Angel (Wolfe), **II:** 457; **IV:** 450, 452, 453, 454, 455–456, 461, 462, 463, 464, 468, 471; **Supp. XI:** 216

"Looking" (Sanders), **Supp. XVI:** 277

"Looking a Mad Dog Dead in the Eyes" (Komunyakaa), **Supp. XIII:** 114

"Looking at Each Other" (Rukeyser), **Supp. VI:** 280, 285–286

"Looking at Kafka" (P. Roth), **Supp. III Part 2:** 402

"Looking at Women" (Sanders), **Supp. XVI:** 274

"Looking Back" (Harjo), **Supp. XII:** 218

"Looking Back" (Merwin), **Supp. III Part 1:** 352

"Looking Back at Girlhood" (Jewett), **Retro. Supp. II:** 131, 133

Looking Backward (Bellamy), **II:** 276; **Supp. I Part 2:** 641; **Supp. XI:** 200

"Looking for a Ship" (McPhee), **Supp. III Part 1:** 312–313

"Looking for Dragon Smoke" (R. Bly), **Supp. IV Part 1:** 60

Looking for Holes in the Ceiling (Dunn), **Supp. XI:** 139, **143–145**

Looking for Langston (Julien; film), **Supp. XI:** 19, 20

Looking for Lincoln (television production), **Supp. XX:**99

Looking for Luck (Kumin), **Supp. IV Part 2:** 453, 454–455

"Looking for Mr. Green" (Bellow), **Retro. Supp. II:** 27

"Looking for the Buckhead Boys" (Dickey), **Supp. IV Part 1:** 182, 183

"Looking Forward to Age" (Harrison), **Supp. VIII:** 49

"Looking from Inside My Body" (R. Bly), **Supp. IV Part 1:** 71

"Looking Glass, The" (Wharton), **Retro. Supp. I:** 382

"Lookout's Journal" (Snyder), **Supp. VIII:** 291

"Looks Like They'll Never Learn" (McCoy), **Supp. XIII:** 166

"Look to the Woods" (P. N. Warren), **Supp. XX:**272

"Look to Thy Heart . . ." (Hay), **Supp. XIV:** 130

Loon, Hendrik Willem van, **Supp. XVI:** 185

Loon Lake (Doctorow), **Supp. IV Part 1:** 219, 222, 224–227, 230, 231, 232, 233

"Loon Point" (O'Brien), **Supp. V:** 237

Loos, Adolf, **Supp. XVI:** 187

Loos, Anita, **Supp. XVI: 181–199**

Loos, Mary Anita, **Supp. XVI:** 196

Loose Canons (H. L. Gates), **Supp. XX:**101, 108, **109–110**, 111

Loosestrife (Dunn), **Supp. XI: 152–154**

"Loosestrife" (Dunn), **Supp. XI:** 154

"Loose Woman" (X. J. Kennedy), **Supp. XV:** 159

Loose Woman: Poems (Cisneros), **Supp. VII:** 58, 71–72

Lopate, Edward, **Supp. XVI:** 266

Lopate, Philip, **Supp. XII:** 184; **Supp. XIII:** 280–281; **Supp. XVI:** 230

Lopatnikoff, Nikolai, **Supp. XIV:** 123

Lopez, Barry, **Supp. IV Part 1:** 416; **Supp. V:** 211; **Supp. X:** 29, 31; **Supp. XIII:** 16; **Supp. XIV:** 227

Lopez, Rafael, **Supp. IV Part 2:** 602

Lorax, The (Geisel), **Supp. XVI:** 109–110

Lorca, Federico García, **IV:** 380; **Supp. I Part 1:** 345; **Supp. IV Part 1:** 83; **Supp. VIII:** 38, 39; **Supp. XIII:** 315, 323, 324; **Supp. XV:** 186; **Supp. XXI:** 100

Lord, Judge Otis P., **I:** 454, 457, 458, 470

Lorde, Audre, **Supp. I Part 2:** 550, 571; **Supp. IV Part 1:** 325; **Supp. XI:** 20; **Supp. XII:** 217, 220; **Supp. XIII:** 295; **Supp. XVII:** 71

Lord Jim (Conrad), **I:** 422; **II:** 26; **Retro. Supp. II:** 292; **Supp. I Part 2:** 623; **Supp. IV Part 2:** 680; **Supp. V:** 251

"Lord of Hosts" (Pinsky), **Supp. VI:** 244

Lord of the Flies (W. Golding), **Supp. XVI:** 65

Lord of the Rings (Tolkien), **Supp. V:** 140

Lords of Misrule, The (X. J. Kennedy), **Supp. XV:** 154, **170–171**

Lords of the Housetops (Van Vechten), **Supp. II Part 2:** 736

Lord's Prayer, **I:** 579

Lord Timothy Dexter of Newburyport, Mass. (Marquand), **III:** 55

Lord Weary's Castle (Lowell), **II:** 538, 542–551; **Retro. Supp. II:** 178, **186–187**, 188; **Supp. XV:** 252

"Lorelei" (Plath), **Retro. Supp. II:** 246; **Supp. I Part 2:** 538

"Lorenzo" (Bynner), **Supp. XV:** 46, 50

Lorimer, George Horace, **II:** 430; **Retro. Supp. I:** 101, 113

Lorre, Peter, **Supp. IV Part 1:** 356

"Los Alamos" (Momaday), **Supp. IV Part 2:** 482

Los Amigos de Becky (Hinojosa). *See Becky and Her Friends* (Hinojosa)

"Los Angeles, 1980" (Gunn Allen), **Supp. IV Part 1:** 325

"Los Angeles Days" (Didion), **Supp. IV Part 1:** 211

"Loser, The" (Talese), **Supp. XVII:** 202, 208

Loser and Still Champion: Muhammad Ali (Schulberg), **Supp. XVIII:** 254

Losey, Joseph, **IV:** 383

Lose Your Mother: A Journey Along the Atlantic Slave Route (Hartman), **Supp. XX:**154

"Losing a Language" (Merwin), **Supp. III Part 1:** 356

Losing Battles (Welty), **IV:** 261, 281–282; **Retro. Supp. I:** 341, 352, **353–354**

"Losing the Marbles" (Merrill), **Supp. III Part 1:** 337

"Losing Track of Language" (Clampitt), **Supp. IX:** 38, 40

Losses (Jarrell), **II:** 367, 372, 373–375, 376, 377, 380–381

"Losses" (Jarrell), **II:** 375–376

Lossky, N. O., **Supp. IV Part 2:** 519

"Loss of Breath" (Poe), **III:** 425–426

"Loss of My Arms and Legs, The" (Kingsolver), **Supp. VII:** 208

"Loss of the Creature, The" (Percy), **Supp. III Part 1:** 387

"Lost" (Wagoner), **Supp. IX:** 328

"Lost, The/Los Perdidos" (Kingsolver), **Supp. VII:** 208

"Lost and Found" (Levine), **Supp. V:** 188

"Lost and Found" (Nelson), **Supp. XVIII:** 176

"Lost Bodies" (Wright), **Supp. V:** 342

"Lost Boy, The" (Wolfe), **IV:** 451, 460, 466–467

"Lost Decade, The" (Fitzgerald), **II:** 98

"Lost Fugue for Chet" (Hull), **Supp. XXI:** 137–138, 141

Lost Galleon and Other Tales, The (Harte), **Supp. II Part 1:** 344

Lost Get-Back Boogie, The (Burke), **Supp. XIV:** 22, 25

"Lost Girls, The" (Hogan), **Supp. IV Part 1:** 406–407

Lost Grizzlies, The: A Search for Survivors in the Wilderness of Colorado (Bass), **Supp. XVI:** 25, 26

Lost Highway (film), **Supp. X:** 314

Lost Illusions (Balzac), **I:** 500

"Lost in Nostalgia: The Autobiographies of Eva Hoffman and Richard Rodriguez" (Fachinger), **Supp. XVI:** 153

Lost in the Bonewheel Factory (Komunyakaa), **Supp. XIII: 114–115**, 116

Lost in the Cosmos: The Last Self-Help Book (Percy), **Supp. III Part 1:** 397

Lost in the Funhouse (Barth), **I:** 122, 135, 139; **Supp. X:** 307

"Lost in the Whichy Thicket" (Wolfe), **Supp. III Part 2:** 573, 574

Lost in Translation (E. Hoffman), **Supp. XVI:** 147, **148–151,** 153, 154, 159

"Lost in Translation" (Hass), **Supp. VIII:** 28

"Lost in Translation" (Merrill), **Supp. III Part 1:** 324, 329–330

Lost in Yonkers (film), **Supp. IV Part 2:** 588

Lost in Yonkers (Simon), **Supp. IV Part 2:** 576, 577, 584, 587–588, 590–591

"Lost Jerusalem" (Untermeyer), **Supp. XV:** 307

Lost Lady, A (Cather), **I:** 323–325, 327; **Retro. Supp. I: 15–16,** 20, 21, 382

Lost Light (Connelly), **Supp. XXI:** 72, **75–76**

"Lost Lives" (Sorrentino), **Supp. XXI:** 226

"Lost Lover, A" (Jewett), **II:** 400–401, 402; **Retro. Supp. II:** 137

"Lost Loves" (Kinnell), **Supp. III Part 1:** 237, 245

Lost Man's River (Matthiessen), **Supp. V:** 212, 213, 214, 215

"Lost on September Trail, 1967" (Ríos), **Supp. IV Part 2:** 540

Lost Puritan (Mariani), **Retro. Supp. II:** 189

Lost Roads Project, The: A Walk-In Book of Arkansas (exhibition; Wright and Luster), **Supp. XV:** 337, 348

"Lost Sailor, The" (Freneau), **Supp. II Part 1:** 264

Lost Son, The (Roethke), **III:** 529, 530–532, 533

"Lost Son, The" (Roethke), **III:** 536, 537–539, 542

"Lost Sons" (Salter), **Supp. IX:** 260

Lost Souls (Singer). *See* Meshugah (Singer)

Lost Weekend, The (Jackson), **Supp. XIII:** 262

"Lost World, A" (Ashbery), **Supp. III Part 1:** 9

"Lost World, The" (Chabon), **Supp. XI:** 72–73

Lost World, The (Jarrell), **II:** 367, 368, 371, 379–380, 386, 387

"Lost World, The" cycle (Chabon), **Supp. XI: 71–73**

"Lost World of Richard Yates, The: How the Great Writer of the Age of Anxiety Disappeared from Print" (O'Nan), **Supp. XI:** 348

"Lost Young Intellectual, The" (Howe), **Supp. VI:** 113, **115–116**

Lost Zoo, The: (A Rhyme for the Young, But Not Too Young) (Cullen), **Supp. IV Part 1:** 173

Loti, Pierre, **II:** 311, 325; **Supp. IV Part 1:** 81

"Lot of People Bathing in a Stream, A" (Stevens), **IV:** 93

Lotringer, Sylvère, **Supp. XII:** 4

"Lot's Wife" (Nemerov), **III:** 270

"Lottery, The" (Jackson), **Supp. IX:** 113, 114, 118, 120, **122–123**

Lottery, The; or, The Adventures of James Harris (Jackson), **Supp. IX:** 113, 115, 116, 124, 125

Lotze, Hermann, **III:** 600

Loud and Clear (Quindlen), **Supp. XVII:** 167, **170–172**

Louganis, Greg, **Supp. XX:**264

"Louie, His Cousin & His Other Cousin" (Cisneros), **Supp. VII:** 60

Louis, Joe, **II:** 589; **Supp. IV Part 1:** 360

Louis, Pierre Charles Alexandre, **Supp. I Part 1:** 302, 303

"Louisa, Please Come Home" (Jackson), **Supp. IX:** 122

Louis Lambert (Balzac), **I:** 499

"Louis Simpson and Walt Whitman: Destroying the Teacher" (Lazer), **Supp. IX:** 265

"Louis Zukofsky: *All: The Collected Short Poems, 1923–1958*" (Creeley), **Supp. IV Part 1:** 154

"Lounge" (Francis), **Supp. IX:** 83

Lounsberry, Barbara, **Supp. XVII:** 208

Lounsbury, Thomas R., **I:** 335

Louter, Jan, **Supp. XI:** 173

"Love" (Collins), **Supp. XXI:** 61

"Love," (Gibran), **Supp. XX:**119

"Love" (Olson), **Supp. II Part 2:** 571

"Love" (Paley), **Supp. VI:** 219, 222, 230

Love, Deborah, **Supp. V:** 208, 210

Love Alone: 18 Elegies for Rog (Monette), **Supp. X:** 146, 154

Love Always (Beattie), **Supp. V:** 29, 30, 35

Love among the Cannibals (Morris), **III:** 228, 230–231

"Love Among the Ruins" (Mosley), **Supp. XIII:** 247

Love and Death (film; Allen), **Supp. XV:** 2, **5–6,** 7, 11

Love and Death in the American Novel (Fiedler), **Supp. XIII:** 93, 96, **99–101,** 104

Love and Exile (Singer), **Retro. Supp. II: 302–304,** 315

Love and Fame (Berryman), **I:** 170

Love and Friendship (Bloom), **Retro. Supp. II:** 31, 33–34

Love and Glory (Parker), **Supp. XIX:** 189

"Love and How to Cure It" (Wilder), **IV:** 365

Love and Scorn: New and Selected Poems (C. Frost), **Supp. XV:** 95, 96, 100, 103–105, 106

Love and Theft (album, Dylan), **Supp. XVIII:** 28, 31

"Love and the Hate, The" (Jeffers), **Supp. II Part 2:** 434–435

Love and Will (Dixon), **Supp. XII:** 148, 149

Love and Work (Price), **Supp. VI:** 261

"Love as a Great Power" (Bronk), **Supp. XXI:** 31

"Love Calls Us to the Things of This World" (Wilbur), **Supp. III Part 2:** 544, 552–553

Love Course, The (Gurney), **Supp. V:** 98

Loved One, The (film), **Supp. XI: 305–306,** 307

Loved One, The (Waugh), **Supp. XI:** 305

Love Expert, The (film; Kirkland), **Supp. XVI:** 186

Love Feast (Buechner), **Supp. XII:** 52

Love for Love (Congreve), **Supp. XVIII:** 12

"Love Fossil" (Olds), **Supp. X:** 203

Love in Buffalo (Gurney), **Supp. V:** 96

"Love—In Other Words" (Lee), **Supp. VIII:** 113

"Love in the Air" (Jin), **Supp. XVIII:** 93–94

"Love in the Morning" (Dubus), **Supp. VII:** 91

Love in the Ruins: The Adventures of a Bad Catholic at a Time near the End of the World (Percy), **Supp. III Part 1:** 385, 387, 393–394, 397–398

Love in the Western World (de Rougemont), **Retro. Supp. I:** 328

"Love Is a Deep and a Dark and a Lonely" (Sandburg), **III:** 595

Lovejoy, Elijah P., **Supp. I Part 2:** 588

Lovejoy, Owen R., **Supp. I Part 1:** 8

Lovejoy, Thomas, **Supp. X:** 108

Lovelace, Richard, **II:** 590

"Love Letter (Schnackenberg), **Supp. XV:** 258–259

Love Letters (film), **Supp. IV Part 2:** 524

Love Letters (Gurney), **Supp. V:** 105, 108–109

Love Letters, The (Massie), **Supp. IV Part 2:** 524

Love Letters and Two Other Plays: The Golden Age and *What I Did Last Summer* (Gurney), **Supp. V:** 100

"Love Lies Sleeping" (Bishop), **Retro. Supp. II:** 42

Love Life (Mason), **Supp. VIII:** 145–146

"Love Life" (Mason), **Supp. VIII: 145–146**

Lovell, Julia, **Supp. XVIII:** 101

Lovely Lady, The (Lawrence), **Retro. Supp. I:** 203

"Lovely Lady, The" (Lawrence), **Supp. I Part 1:** 329

Love Me (Keillor), **Supp. XVI:** 178

Love Medicine (expanded version) (Erdrich), **Supp. IV Part 1:** 263, 273, 274, 275

Love Medicine (Erdrich), **Supp. IV Part 1:** 259, 260, 261, 263, 265, 266, 267–268, 270, 271, 274–275; **Supp. X:** 290

"Love Minus Zero/No Limit" (song, Dylan), **Supp. XVIII:** 31

"Love Nest, The" (Lardner), **II:** 427, 429

Love Nest, The, and Other Stories (Lardner), **II:** 430–431, 436

Lovenheim, Barbara, **Supp. X:** 169

"Love of Annunziata, The" (di Donato), **Supp. XX:**40

"Love of Elsie Barton: A Chronicle, The" (Warren), **IV:** 253

Love of Landry, The (Dunbar), **Supp. II Part 1:** 212

"Love of Morning, The" (Levertov), **Supp. III Part 1:** 284

Love of the Last Tycoon, The: A Western.
  See Last Tycoon, The
"Love on the Bon Dieu" (Chopin), **Supp.**
  I Part 1: 213
Love Poems (Sexton), **Supp. II Part 2:**
  687–689
Love Poems of May Swenson, The
  (Swenson), **Supp. IV Part 2:** 652, 653
"Love Poet" (Agee), **I:** 28
"Lover" (Hoffman), **Supp. XVIII:** 87
"Love Ritual" (Mora), **Supp. XIII:** 215
Loveroot (Jong), **Supp. V:** 115, 130
"Lovers, The" (Berryman), **I:** 174
"Lovers, The" (Buck), **Supp. II Part 1:**
  128
"Lover's Garden, A" (Ginsberg), **Supp.**
  II Part 1: 311
"Lovers of the Poor, The" (Brooks),
  Supp. III Part 1: 81, 85
Lovers Should Marry (Martin), **Supp. IV**
  Part 1: 351
"Lover's Song" (Yeats), **Supp. I Part 1:**
  80
"Love Rushes By" (Salinas), **Supp. XIII:**
  326–327
"Love's Ghost" (Nelson), **Supp. XVIII:**
  176
Lovesick (Stern), **Supp. IX: 295–296**
Love's Labour's Lost (Shakespeare), **III:**
  263
Love's Old Sweet Song (Saroyan), **Supp.**
  IV Part 1: 83
"Love Song During Riot with Many
  Voices" (Hull), **Supp. XXI:** 136
"Love Song of J. Alfred Prufrock, The"
  (T. S. Eliot), **I:** 52, 66, 569–570; **III:**
  460; **Retro. Supp. I:** 55, 56, 57, 60;
  Supp. II Part 1: 5; **Supp. XIII:** 346;
  Supp. XVI: 150
"Love Song of St. Sebastian" (Eliot),
  Retro. Supp. I: 57
Love's Pilgrimage (Sinclair), **Supp. V:**
  286
"Love the Wild Swan" (Jeffers), **Supp.**
  VIII: 33
Love to Mamá: A Tribute to Mothers
  (Mora, ed.), **Supp. XIII:** 221
Lovett, Robert Morss, **II:** 43
"Love-Unknown" (Herbert), **Supp. I Part**
  1: 80
Love! Valor! Compassion! (film), **Supp.**
  XIII: 206
Love! Valour! Compassion! (McNally),
  Supp. XIII: 199, **203–204,** 208, 209
"Love *versus* Law" (Stowe), **Supp. I**
  Part 2: 585–586
"Love Wall" (Peacock), **Supp. XIX:** 200
Love with a Few Hairs (Mrabet), **Supp.**
  IV Part 1: 92
Loving a Woman in Two Worlds (R. Bly),
  Supp. IV Part 1: 66, 67, 68–69, 71,
  72
"Loving on Borrowed Time" (J. W.
  Miller), **Supp. XX:**164
"Loving Shepherdess, The" (Jeffers),
  Supp. II Part 2: 432
"Loving the Killer" (Sexton), **Supp. II**
  Part 2: 688
Lovin' Molly (film), **Supp. V:** 223, 226
Lowe, John, **Supp. XIII:** 238

Lowe, Pardee, **Supp. X:** 291
Lowell, Abbott Lawrence, **I:** 487; **II:** 513;
  Supp. I Part 2: 483
Lowell, Amy, **I:** 231, 384, 405, 475, 487;
  II: 174, **511–533,** 534; **III:** 465, 581,
  586; **Retro. Supp. I:** 131, 133, 288;
  Retro. Supp. II: 46, 175; **Supp. I**
  Part 1: 257–259, 261–263, 265, 266;
  Supp. I Part 2: 465, 466, 707, 714,
  729; **Supp. XIV:** 128; **Supp. XV:** 43,
  293, 295, 297, 298, 299, 300, 301,
  303, 306; **Supp. XX:**69
Lowell, Blanche, **Supp. I Part 2:** 409
Lowell, Harriet, **II:** 553, 554
Lowell, James Russell, **I:** 216, 458; **II:**
  273, 274, 289, 302, 320, 402, 529,
  530, 532, 534, 551; **III:** 409; **IV:** 129,
  171, 175, 180, 182–183, 186; **Retro.**
  Supp. I: 228; **Retro. Supp. II:** 155,
  175, 326; **Supp. I Part 1:** 168, 299,
  300, 303, 306, 311, 312, 317, 318,
  362; **Supp. I Part 2: 404–426; Supp.**
  II Part 1: 197, 291, 352; **Supp. XV:**
  278, 279; **Supp. XVI:** 84; **Supp.**
  XVIII: 2–3, 4, 8, 12
Lowell, Mrs. James Russell (Maria
  White), **Supp. I Part 2:** 405, 406, 414,
  424
Lowell, Percival, **II:** 513, 525, 534
Lowell, Robert, **I:** 172, 381, 382, 400,
  442, 521, 544–545, 550; **II:** 371, 376,
  377, 384, 386–387, 532, **534–557; III:**
  39, 44, 142, 508, 527, 528–529, 606;
  IV: 120, 138, 402, 430; **Retro. Supp.**
  I: 67, 140, 411; **Retro. Supp. II:** 27,
  40, 44, 46, 48, 50, **175–193,** 221, 228–
  229, 235, 245; **Supp. I Part 1:** 89;
  Supp. I Part 2: 538, 543, 554; **Supp.**
  III Part 1: 6, 64, 84, 138, 147, 193,
  194, 197–202, 205–208; **Supp. III**
  Part 2: 541, 543, 555, 561, 599; **Supp.**
  IV Part 2: 439, 620, 637; **Supp. V:**
  81, 179, 180, 315–316, 337, 344;
  Supp. VIII: 27, 100, 271; **Supp. IX:**
  325; **Supp. X:** 53, 58; **Supp. XI:** 146,
  240, 244, 250, 317; **Supp. XII:** 253–
  254, 255; **Supp. XIII:** 76; **Supp. XIV:**
  15, 126, 269; **Supp. XV:** 20, 22, 93,
  184, 249, 251, 253, 340; **Supp. XVII:**
  239; **Supp. XIX:** 197; **Supp. XX:**199,
  203; **Supp. XXI:** 131
Lowell, Rose, **Supp. I Part 2:** 409
"Lowell in the Classroom" (Vendler),
  Retro. Supp. II: 191
Lowenthal, Michael, **Supp. XII:** 82
Lower Depths, The (Gorki), **III:** 402
"Lower the Standard" (Shapiro), **Supp.**
  II Part 2: 715
Lowes, John Livingston, **II:** 512, 516,
  532; **IV:** 453, 455
Lowin, Joseph, **Supp. V:** 273
"Low-Lands" (Pynchon), **Supp. II Part**
  2: 620, 624
Lowle, Percival, **Supp. I Part 2:** 404
Lownsbrough, John, **Supp. IV Part 1:**
  209, 211
Lowry, Beverly, **Supp. XXI:** 48
Lowry, Malcolm, **Supp. XVII:** 135, 136
Lowth, Richard, **II:** 8
Loy, Mina, **III:** 194

Loy, Myrna, **Supp. IV Part 1:** 355
"Loyal Woman's No, A" (Larcom), **Supp.**
  XIII: 142, 143–144
"Luani of the Jungle" (Hughes), **Supp. I**
  Part 1: 328
Lubbock, Percy, **I:** 504; **II:** 337; **IV:** 308,
  314, 319, 322; **Retro. Supp. I:** 366,
  367, 373; **Supp. VIII:** 165; **Supp.**
  XX:231
Lubin, Isidor, **Supp. I Part 2:** 632
Lubow, Arthur, **Supp. VIII:** 310
Lucas, Victoria (pseudonym). *See* Plath,
  Sylvia
Luce, Dianne C., **Supp. VIII:** 189
Lucid, Robert F., **Retro. Supp. II:** 195,
  204
"Lucid Eye in Silver Town, The"
  (Updike), **IV:** 218
"Lucid Walking" (A. Finch), **Supp.**
  XVII: 72
"Lucinda Matlock" (Masters), **Supp. I**
  Part 2: 461, 465
"Luck" (Dunn), **Supp. XI:** 149
Luck of Barry Lyndon, The (Thackeray),
  II: 290
"Luck of Roaring Camp, The" (Harte),
  Supp. II Part 1: 335, 344, 345–347
"Luck of the Bogans, The" (Jewett),
  Retro. Supp. II: 142
Lucky Life (Stern), **Supp. IX: 290–291**
"Lucky Lucy's Daily Dream Book" (Di
  Piero), **Supp. XIX:** 38–39
Lucretius, **I:** 59; **II:** 162, 163; **III:** 600,
  610–611, 612; **Supp. I Part 1:** 363
Lucy (Kincaid), **Supp. VII:** 180, 185,
  186, 187–188, 194
Lucy, Saint, **II:** 211
Lucy Crown (Shaw), **Supp. XIX:** 251
Lucy Gayheart (Cather), **I:** 331; **Retro.**
  Supp. I: 19
"Lucy Tavish's Journey" (E. Stoddard),
  Supp. XV: 286
Lucy Temple (Rowson). *See Charlotte's*
  Daughter; or, The Three Orphans
Ludlow, Andrea, **Supp. XVIII:** 90
Ludvigson, Susan, **Supp. IV Part 2:** 442,
  446, 447, 448, 451
Lueders, Edward, **Supp. XVI:** 265
"Luggage" (Bidart), **Supp. XV:** 35
Luhan, Mabel Dodge, **Retro. Supp. I:** 7;
  Supp. XV: 46, 50. *See also* Dodge,
  Mabel
Lu Ji, **Supp. VIII:** 303
Luke (biblical book), **III:** 606
"Luke Havergal" (E. A. Robinson), **Supp.**
  XVII: 69
"Luke Havergal" (Robinson), **III:** 524
Lukeman, Gary, **Supp. XV:** 221
Luks, George, **IV:** 411; **Retro. Supp. II:**
  103
"Lullaby" (Auden), **Supp. II Part 1:** 9
"Lullaby" (Bishop), **Supp. I Part 1:** 85
"Lullaby" (Everwine), **Supp. XV:** 89
"Lullaby" (Silko), **Supp. IV Part 2:** 560,
  568–569
"Lullaby for Amy" (Jarman), **Supp.**
  XVII: 113, 121
"Lullaby of Cape Cod" (Brodsky), **Supp.**
  VIII: 27–28
Lullaby Raft (Nye), **Supp. XIII:** 278

Lullaby Raft (Nye, album), **Supp. XIII:** 274

Lullaby: The Comforting of Cock Robin (Snodgrass), **Supp. VI:** 324

"Lulls" (Walker), **Supp. III Part 2:** 525

"Lulu" (Wedekind), **Supp. XII:** 14

Lulu on the Bridge (film), **Supp. XII:** 21

Lulu's Library (Alcott), **Supp. I Part 1:** 43

"Lumber" (Baker), **Supp. XIII:** 55, 56

"Lumens, The" (Olds), **Supp. X:** 209

Lume Spento, A (Pound), **III:** 470

Lumet, Sidney, **Supp. IV Part 1:** 236; **Supp. IX:** 253

Luminous Debris: Reflecting on Vestige in Provence and Languedoc (Sobin), **Supp. XVI:** 291–293, 293–294

"Lumumba's Grave" (Hughes), **Supp. I Part 1:** 344

"Luna, Luna" (Mora), **Supp. XIII:** 217

Lunar Follies (Sorrentino), **Supp. XXI:** 226, 237, 238, 238–239

Lunsford, Bascom Lamar, **Supp. XX:** 163

Lupercal (Hughes), **Retro. Supp. II:** 245; **Supp. I Part 2:** 540

Lupton, Mary Jane, **Supp. IV Part 1:** 7

Luria, Isaac, **IV:** 7

Lurie, Alison, **Supp. X:** 166; **Supp. XVI:** 103, 111–112

Lust and Other Stories (Minot), **Supp. VI:** 205

Luster, Deborah, **Supp. XV:** 337, **Supp. XV:** 353, 348, 349, 350

Lustgarten, Edith, **III:** 107

Lustra (Pound), **Retro. Supp. I:** 289, 290

Luther, Martin, **II:** 11–12, 506; **III:** 306, 607; **IV:** 490

"Luther on Sweet Auburn" (Bambara), **Supp. XI:** 16–17

Lux, Thomas, **Supp. XI:** 270; **Supp. XIX:** 276

Luxury Girl, The (McCoy), **Supp. XIII:** 163

Lyall, Sarah, **Supp. XIII:** 247

Lycidas (Milton), **II:** 540; **IV:** 347; **Retro. Supp. I:** 60; **Retro. Supp. II:** 186; **Supp. I Part 1:** 370; **Supp. IX:** 41

Lycographia (Paullini), **Supp. XVII:** 55

"Lydia and Marian" (Rowson), **Supp. XV:** 234

Lydon, Susan, **Supp. XII:** 170

Lyell, Charles, **Supp. IX:** 180

Lyell, Frank H., **Supp. VIII:** 125

Lyford, Harry, **Supp. I Part 2:** 679

"Lying" (Wilbur), **Supp. III Part 2:** 547, 562

"Lying and Looking" (Swenson), **Supp. IV Part 2:** 652

"Lying in a Hammock at William Duffy's Farm in Pine Island, Minnesota" (Wright), **Supp. III Part 2:** 589, 599, 600

"Lying in the Pollen and Water" (C. Frost), **Supp. XV:** 96

Lying Ladies, The (Ryan as Finnegan), **Supp. XVIII:** 233–235, 237

Lyles, Lois F., **Supp. XI:** 7, 8

Lyly, John, **III:** 536; **Supp. I Part 1:** 369

Lynch, Anne, **Supp. XV:** 273

Lynch, Doris, **Supp. XVI:** 294

Lynchburg (Gander), **Supp. XV:** 340

"Lynched Man, The" (Karr), **Supp. XI:** 241

Lynchers, The (Wideman), **Supp. X:** 320

"Lynching, The" (McKay), **Supp. I Part 1:** 63

"Lynching of Jube Benson, The" (Dunbar), **Supp. II Part 1:** 214

"Lynching Song" (Hughes), **Supp. I Part 1:** 331

Lynd, Staughton, **Supp. VIII:** 240

Lynda Hull: Collected Poems (Hull), **Supp. XXI:** 129

Lynn, Kenneth, **Supp. XIII:** 96–97

Lynn, Kenneth S., **Supp. XIV:** 103

Lynn, Vera, **Supp. XI:** 304

Lyon, George Ella, **Supp. XX:** 161–162

Lyon, Kate, **I:** 409; **II:** 138, 143, 144

Lyon, Thomas, **Supp. IX:** 175

"Lyonnesse" (Plath), **Supp. I Part 2:** 541

Lyons, Bonnie, **Supp. V:** 58; **Supp. VIII:** 138

Lyotard, Jean-François, **Supp. IV Part 1:** 54

Lyrical Ballads (Wordsworth), **III:** 583; **IV:** 120; **Supp. IX:** 274; **Supp. XI:** 243; **Supp. XV:** 21; **Supp. XIX:** 1

Lyrics of Love and Laughter (Dunbar), **Supp. II Part 1:** 207

Lyrics of Lowly Life (Dunbar), **Supp. II Part 1:** 197, 199, 200, 207

Lyrics of the Hearthside (Dunbar), **Supp. II Part 1:** 206

Lytal, Tammy, **Supp. XI:** 102

Lytle, Andrew, **IV:** 125; **Retro. Supp. II:** 220, 221, 235; **Supp. II Part 1:** 139; **Supp. X:** 1, 25; **Supp. XI:** 101

Lyttelton, Alfred, **Supp. XX:** 230

Lytton of Knebworth. *See* Bulwer-Lytton, Edward George

M

Mabie, Hamilton W., **Supp. XVIII:** 257

McAlexander, Hubert H., **Supp. V:** 314, 319, 320, 323

McAlmon, Robert, **IV:** 404; **Retro. Supp. I:** 418, 419, 420; **Retro. Supp. II:** 328; **Supp. I Part 1:** 259; **Supp. III Part 2:** 614

McAlmon, Mrs. Robert (Winifred Ellerman), **III:** 194. *See also* Ellerman, Winifred

McAninch, Jerry, **Supp. XI:** 297, 298

Macaulay, Catherine, **Supp. I Part 2:** 522

Macaulay, Rose, **Supp. XII:** 88; **Supp. XIV:** 348

Macaulay, Thomas, **II:** 15–16; **III:** 113, 591–592

Macauley, Robie, **Retro. Supp. II:** 228; **Supp. X:** 56

Macbeth (Shakespeare), **I:** 271; **IV:** 227; **Retro. Supp. I:** 131; **Supp. I Part 1:** 67; **Supp. I Part 2:** 457; **Supp. IV Part 1:** 87; **Supp. XIV:** 8

Macbeth (silent film), **Supp. XVI:** 184

MacBeth, George, **Retro. Supp. II:** 250

McCafferty, Larry, **Supp. XVII:** 227

McCaffery, Larry, **Supp. IV Part 1:** 217, 227, 234; **Supp. V:** 53, 238; **Supp. VIII:** 13, 14; **Supp. X:** 260, 268, 301, 303, 307; **Supp. XVI:** 117

McCann, Jannet, **Supp. XXI:** 92

McCarriston, Linda, **Supp. X:** 204; **Supp. XIV:** 259–275

McCarthy, Charles Joseph, Jr. *See* McCarthy, Cormac

McCarthy, Cormac, **Supp. VIII:** 175–192; **Supp. XII:** 310; **Supp. XVII:** 185; **Supp. XXI:** 38, 40

McCarthy, Eugene, **Retro. Supp. II:** 182

McCarthy, Joseph, **I:** 31, 492; **II:** 562, 568; **Supp. I Part 1:** 294, 295; **Supp. I Part 2:** 444, 611, 612, 620; **Supp. XV:** 198, 311–312

McCarthy, Mary, **II:** 558–584; **Supp. I Part 1:** 84; **Supp. IV Part 1:** 209, 297, 310; **Supp. VIII:** 96, 99, 100; **Supp. X:** 177; **Supp. XI:** 246; **Supp. XIV:** 3; **Supp. XV:** 142; **Supp. XVI:** 64, 70; **Supp. XVII:** 43

McCay, Maura, **Supp. XII:** 271, 276

McClanahan, Ed, **Supp. X:** 24

McClanahan, Thomas, **Supp. XII:** 125–126

McClatchy, J. D., **Supp. XII:** 253–270; **Supp. XV:** 185, 257, 258

McClellan, John L., **I:** 493

McClung, Isabelle, **Retro. Supp. I:** 5

McClure, John, **Retro. Supp. I:** 80

McClure, Michael, **Supp. II Part 1:** 32; **Supp. VIII:** 289; **Supp. XVI:** 283

McClure, S. S., **I:** 313; **II:** 465; **III:** 327; **Retro. Supp. I:** 5, 6, 9; **Supp. XV:** 40

McCluskey, John, Jr., **Supp. XIX:** 65, 68, 71, 72, 78

McCombs, Judith, **Supp. XIII:** 33

McConagha, Alan, **Supp. XVI:** 166

McConnell, Frank, **Supp. X:** 260, 274

McCorkle, Jill, **Supp. X:** 6; **Supp. XVIII:** 195

McCourt, Frank, **Supp. XII:** 271–287

McCoy, Horace, **Supp. XIII:** 159–177

McCracken, Elizabeth, **Supp. X:** 86; **Supp. XII:** 310, 315–316, 321

McCrae, Fiona, **Supp. XVIII:** 60, 62

McCullers, Carson, **I:** 113, 190, 211; **II:** 585–608; **IV:** 282, 384, 385, 386; **Retro. Supp. II:** 324; **Supp. II Part 1:** 17; **Supp. IV Part 1:** 31, 84; **Supp. IV Part 2:** 502; **Supp. VIII:** 124; **Supp. XII:** 309; **Supp. XIV:** 120; **Supp. XV:** 338

McCullers, Reeves, **III:** 585, 586, 587

McDavid, Raven I., **III:** 120; **Supp. XIV:** 14

McDermott, Alice, **Supp. XII:** 311; **Supp. XVIII:** 155–169

McDermott, John J., **II:** 364

MacDiarmid, Hugh, **Supp. X:** 112

Macdonald, C. G., **Supp. XVII:** 73–74

Macdonald, Dwight, **I:** 233, 372, 379; **III:** 39; **Supp. V:** 265; **Supp. XIV:** 340; **Supp. XV:** 140

McDonald, E. J., **Supp. I Part 2:** 670

Macdonald, George, **Supp. XIII:** 75

MacDonald, Jeanette, **II:** 589

Macdonald, Ross, **Supp. IV Part 1:** 116, 136; **Supp. IV Part 2: 459–477; Supp. XIII:** 233; **Supp. XVIII:** 137,136; **Supp. XXI:** 67
MacDonald, Ruth K., **Supp. XVI:** 102
McDonnell, Thomas P., **Supp. XX:**45
MacDougall, Ruth Doan, **Supp. XV:** 58; **Supp. XVI:** 174
MacDowell, Edward, **I:** 228; **III:** 504, 508, 524
McDowell, Frederick P. W., **II:** 194
McDowell, Mary, **Supp. I Part 1:** 5
McDowell, Robert, **Supp. IX:** 266, 270, 276, 279
MacDowell, Robert, **Supp. XI:** 249
McDowell, Robert, **Supp. XVII:** 109, 110, 111
McDowell. Deborah, **Supp. XVIII:** 125, 129
McElderry, Margaret K., **Supp. XV:** 162
McElligot's Pool (Geisel), **Supp. XVI:** 104
McElrath, Joseph, **Supp. XIV:** 62
McElroy, Joseph, **Supp. IV Part 1:** 279, 285
McEuen, Kathryn, **II:** 20
McEwen, Arthur, **I:** 206
McFarland, Ron, **Supp. IX:** 323, 327, 328, 333
McGann, Jerome, **Retro. Supp. I:** 47
McGill, Meredith, **Supp. XVIII:** 17
McGillis, Ian, **Supp. XVIII:** 150
MacGillivray, William, **Supp. XVI:** 8
McGinity, Keren, **Supp. XX:**9
McGovern, Edythe M., **Supp. IV Part 2:** 573, 582, 585
McGovern, George, **III:** 46
MacGowan, Christopher, **Retro. Supp. I:** 430
MacGowan, Kenneth, **III:** 387, 391
McGrath, Douglas, **Supp. XV:** 12
McGrath, Joseph, **Supp. XI:** 307, 309
McGrath, Patrick, **Supp. IX:** 113
McGrath, Thomas, **Supp. X: 111–130**
"McGrath on McGrath" (McGrath), **Supp. X:** 119, 120
McGuane, Thomas, **Supp. V:** 53, 220; **Supp. VIII:** 39, 40, 42, 43
MacGuffin, The (Elkin), **Supp. VI: 55–56**
McGuiness, Daniel, **Supp. XV:** 261
Machado y Ruiz, Antonio, **Supp. XIII:** 315, 323
Machan, Tibor, **Supp. IV Part 2:** 528
McHaney, Pearl, **Supp. XXI:** 244, 255, 256, 257
McHaney, Thomas, **Supp. XVIII:** 199,203
Machen, Arthur, **IV:** 286
Machiavelli, Niccolò, **I:** 485; **Supp. XIX:** 34
"Machine-Gun, The" (Jarrell), **II:** 371
"Machine Song" (Anderson), **I:** 114
McHugh, Heather, **Supp. XIX:** 84
McHugh, Vincent, **Supp. XV:** 147
McInerney, Jay, **Supp. X:** 7, 166; **Supp. XI:** 65; **Supp. XII:** 81; **Supp. XVIII:** 148
"Mac in Love" (Dixon), **Supp. XII: 142**
McIntire, Holly, **Supp. V:** 338
McIntosh, Maria, **Retro. Supp. I:** 246

Mack, Maynard, **Supp. XIV:** 12
Mackail, John William, **Supp. I Part 1:** 268; **Supp. I Part 2:** 461
McKay, Claude, **Supp. I Part 1:** 63; **Supp. III Part 1:** 75, 76; **Supp. IV Part 1:** 3, 79, 164; **Supp. IX:** 306; **Supp. X: 131–144; Supp. XI:** 91; **Supp. XVII:** 74; **Supp. XVIII:** 122, 127, 280, 282; **Supp. XIX:** 73; **Supp. XX:**69
McKay, Donald, **Supp. I Part 2:** 482
McKay, Nellie Y., **Supp. XX:**105
McKee, Elizabeth, **Retro. Supp. II:** 221, 222
McKee, Ellen, **Retro. Supp. II:** 67
McKenney, Eileen, **IV:** 288; **Retro. Supp. II:** 321, 330
McKenney, Ruth, **IV:** 288; **Retro. Supp. II:** 321; **Supp. XVIII:** 238
MacKenzie, Agnes, **I:** 199
Mackenzie, Captain Alexander, **III:** 94
Mackenzie, Compton, **II:** 82; **Retro. Supp. I:** 100, 102
McKenzie, Geraldine, **Supp. XII:** 107
MacKenzie, Margaret, **I:** 199
Mackey, Louis, **Supp. XXI:** 236, 237
McKibben, Bill, **Supp. XVIII:** 192
McKinley, William, **I:** 474; **III:** 506; **Supp. I Part 2:** 395–396, 707
MacKinnon, Catharine, **Supp. XII:** 6
McKnight, Reginald, **Supp. XX:**147–159
MacLachlan, Suzanne L., **Supp. XII:** 300,**Supp. XII:** 299
McLaverty, Michael, **Supp. X:** 67
McLay, Catherine, **Supp. XIII:** 21
Maclean, Alasdair, **Supp. V:** 244
McLean, Carolyn (pseudonym). *See* Bly, Carol
Maclean, Norman, **Supp. XIV: 221–237; Supp. XVI:** 98
MacLeish, Archibald, **I:** 283, 293, 429; **II:** 165, 228; **III: 1–25,** 427; **Supp. I Part 1:** 261; **Supp. I Part 2:** 654; **Supp. IV Part 1:** 359; **Supp. IV Part 2:** 586; **Supp. X:** 120; **Supp. XIV:** 11
MacLeish, Mrs. Archibald (Ada Hitchcock), **III:** 1
MacLeish, Kenneth, **III:** 1
McLennan, Gordon Lawson, **Supp. IX:** 89
McLeod, A. W., **Supp. I Part 1:** 257
McLuhan, Marshall, **Supp. IV Part 2:** 474
McLure, Michael, **Supp. XIV:** 150
Macmahon, Arthur, **I:** 226
McMahon, Helen, **Supp. IV Part 2:** 579
McMichael, George, **Supp. VIII:** 124
McMichael, Morton, **Supp. I Part 2:** 707
McMichaels, James, **Supp. XIII:** 114
McMillan, James B., **Supp. VIII:** 124
McMillan, Terry, **Supp. XIII: 179–193**
McMullan, Jim, **Supp. XIV:** 124
McMurtry, Josephine, **Supp. V:** 220
McMurtry, Larry, **Supp. V: 219–235; Supp. X:** 24; **Supp. XI:** 172
McNally, Terrence, **Supp. XIII: 195–211**
McNally, T. M., **Supp. XX:**92
McNamer, Deirdre, **Supp. XI:** 190
McNeese, Gretchen, **Supp. V:** 123

MacNeice, Louis, **II:** 586; **III:** 527; **Supp. II Part 1:** 17, 24; **Supp. IV Part 2:** 440; **Supp. X:** 116; **Supp. XIII:** 347
McNeil, Claudia, **Supp. IV Part 1:** 360, 362
M-a-c-n-o-l-i-a (Jordan), **Supp. XVIII:** 172
McPhee, John, **Supp. III Part 1: 289–316; Supp. X:** 29, 30; **Supp. XVIII:** 106–107, 114
MacPherson, Aimee Semple, **Supp. V:** 278
McPherson, Dolly, **Supp. IV Part 1:** 2, 3, 4, 6, 8, 11, 12
McPherson, James Allen, **Retro. Supp. II:** 126
Macpherson, Jay, **Supp. XIII:** 19
MacPherson, Kenneth, **Supp. I Part 1:** 259
McPhillips, Robert, **Supp. XV:** 119, 250, 251, 252, 264, 266
McQuade, Molly, **Supp. VIII:** 277, 281; **Supp. IX:** 151, 163; **Supp. XX:**90
McQueen, Steve, **Supp. XI:** 306
Macrae, John, **I:** 252–253
McRobbie, Angela, **Supp. IV Part 2:** 691
MacShane, Frank, **Supp. IV Part 2:** 557; **Supp. XI:** 214, 216
"MacSwiggen" (Freneau), **Supp. II Part 1:** 259
McTaggart, John, **I:** 59
McTeague (Norris), **III:** 314, 315, 316–320, 322, 325, 327–328, 330, 331, 333, 335; **Retro. Supp. II:** 96; **Supp. IX:** 332
McWilliams, Carey, **Supp. XI:** 169
Madama Butterfly (opera, Puccini), **III:** 139; **Supp. XXI:** 150, 155
"Madam and the Minister" (Hughes), **Supp. I Part 1:** 335
"Madam and the Wrong Visitor" (Hughes), **Supp. I Part 1:** 335
"Madame and Ahmad" (Bowles), **Supp. IV Part 1:** 93
"Madame Bai and the Taking of Stone Mountain" (Bambara), **Supp. XI:** 14–15
Madame Bovary (Flaubert), **II:** 185; **Retro. Supp. I:** 225; **Retro. Supp. II:** 70; **Supp. XI:** 334; **Supp. XX:**58
"Madame Célestin's Divorce" (Chopin), **Supp. I Part 1:** 213
Madame Curie (film), **Retro. Supp. I:** 113
"Madame de Mauves" (James), **II:** 327; **Retro. Supp. I:** 218, 220
Madame de Treymes (Wharton), **IV:** 314, 323; **Retro. Supp. I:** 376
"Madame Rose Hanie" (Gibran), **Supp. XX:**124
"Madam's Calling Cards" (Hughes), **Retro. Supp. I:** 206
Madden, David, **Supp. IV Part 1:** 285
Maddern, Bessie. *See* London, Mrs. Jack (Bessie Maddern)
Mad Dog Black Lady (Coleman), **Supp. XI: 85–89,** 90
Mad Dog Blues (Shepard), **Supp. III Part 2:** 437, 438, 441

Maddox, Lucy, **Supp. IV Part 1:** 323, 325

Mad Ducks and Bears: Football Revisited (Plimpton), **Supp. XVI:** 243

Mademoiselle Coeur-Brisé (Sibon, trans.), **IV:** 288

Mademoiselle de Maupin (Gautier), **Supp. I Part 1:** 277

"Mad Farmer, Flying the Flag of Rough Branch, Secedes from the Union, The" (Berry), **Supp. X:** 35

"Mad Farmer Manifesto, The: The First Amendment" (Berry), **Supp. X:** 35

"Mad Farmer's Love Song, The" (Berry), **Supp. X:** 35

Madheart (Baraka), **Supp. II Part 1:** 47

Madhouse, The (Farrell), **II:** 41

Madhubuti, Haki R. (Don L. Lee), **Supp. II Part 1:** 34, 247; **Supp. IV Part 1:** 244

Madison, Dolley, **II:** 303

Madison, James, **I:** 1, 2, 6–9; **II:** 301; **Supp. I Part 2:** 509, 524

"Madison Smartt Bell: *The Year of Silence*" (Garrett), **Supp. X:** 7

Mad Love (film, Freund), **Supp. XVII:** 58

"Madman, A" (Updike), **Retro. Supp. I:** 320

Madman, The: His Parables and Poems (Gibran), **Supp. XX:**115, **118,** 125

"Madman's Song" (Wylie), **Supp. I Part 2:** 711, 729

Madonick, Michael, **Supp. XVII:** 123

"Madonna" (Lowell), **II:** 535–536

"Madonna of the Evening Flowers" (Lowell), **II:** 524

"Madonna of the Future, The" (James), **Retro. Supp. I:** 219

"Mad Song" (Gioia), **Supp. XV:** 128

Madwoman in the Attic, The (Gilbert and Gubar), **Retro. Supp. I:** 42; **Supp. IX:** 66

"Maelzel's Chess-Player" (Poe), **III:** 419, 420

"Maestria" (Nemerov), **III:** 275, 278–279

Maeterlinck, Maurice, **I:** 91, 220; **Supp. XX:**115, 116

"Magazine-Writing Peter Snook" (Poe), **III:** 421

Magdeburg Centuries (Flacius), **IV:** 163

Magellan, Ferdinand, **Supp. I Part 2:** 497

Maggie: A Girl of the Streets (S. Crane), **I:** 407, 408, 410–411, 416; **IV:** 208; **Retro. Supp. II:** 97, 107; **Supp. XVII:** 228

Maggie Cassidy (Kerouac), **Supp. III Part 1:** 220–221, 225, 227, 229, 232

"Maggie of the Green Bottles" (Bambara), **Supp. XI:** 2–3

"Maggie's Farm" (song, Dylan), **Supp. XVIII:** 25, 26

"Magi" (Plath), **Supp. I Part 2:** 544–545

"Magi, The" (Garrett), **Supp. VII:** 97

"Magic" (Pickering), **Supp. XXI:** 202

"Magic" (Porter), **III:** 434, 435

"Magical Thinking" (Hull), **Supp. XXI:** 137, 139

Magic Barrel, The (Malamud), **Supp. I Part 2:** 427, 428, 430–434

"Magic Barrel, The" (Malamud), **Supp. I Part 2:** 427, 428, 431, 432–433

Magic Christian, The (film), **Supp. XI:** 309

Magic Christian, The (Southern), **Supp. XI:** 297, **299–301,** 309

Magic City (Komunyakaa), **Supp. XIII:** **125–127,** 128, 131

"Magic Flute, The" (Epstein), **Supp. XII:** 165

Magic Flute, The (Mozart), **III:** 164

Magician of Lublin, The (Singer), **IV:** 6, 9–10; **Retro. Supp. II: 308–309**

Magician's Assistant, The (Patchett), **Supp. XII:** 307, 310, **317–320,** 322

"Magician's Wife, The" (Gordon), **Supp. IV Part 1:** 306

Magic Journey, The (Nichols), **Supp. XIII:** 266–267

Magic Keys, The (Murray), **Supp. XIX: 157–158**

Magic Kingdom, The (Elkin), **Supp. VI:** 42, **54–55,** 56, 58

"Magic Mirror, The: A Study of the Double in Two of Doestoevsky's Novels" (Plath), **Supp. I Part 2:** 536

Magic Mountain, The (Mann), **III:** 281–282; **Supp. IV Part 2:** 522; **Supp. XII:** 321; **Supp. XVII:** 137

Magic Tower, The (Willams), **IV:** 380

Magnaghi, Ambrogio, **Supp. XVI:** 286

Magnalia Christi Americana (Mather), **II:** 302; **Supp. I Part 1:** 102; **Supp. I Part 2:** 584; **Supp. II Part 2:** 441, 442, 452–455, 460, 467, 468; **Supp. IV Part 2:** 434

Magnificat (Nelson), **Supp. XVIII: 176–177**

"Magnificent Little Gift" (Salinas), **Supp. XIII:** 318

"Magnifying Mirror" (Karr), **Supp. XI:** 240

Magpie, The (Baldwin, ed.), **Supp. I Part 1:** 49

Magpie's Shadow, The (Winters), **Supp. II Part 2:** 786, 788

"Magpie's Song" (Snyder), **Supp. VIII:** 302

Magritte, René, **Supp. IV Part 2:** 623

Maguire, Roberta S., **Supp. XIX:** 160–161

Magus, The (Fowles), **Supp. XIX:** 58

Mahan, Albert Thayer, **Supp. I Part 2:** 491

Mahan, David C., **Supp. XXI:** 86

"Mahatma Joe" (Bass), **Supp. XVI:** 19

"Mahogany Tree, The" (M. F. K. Fisher), **Supp. XVII:** 88

Mahomet and His Successors (Irving), **II:** 314

Mahoney, Jeremiah, **IV:** 285

Mahoney, Lynn, **Supp. XV:** 270

"Maiden in a Tower" (Stegner), **Supp. IV Part 2:** 613

"Maiden Without Hands" (Sexton), **Supp. II Part 2:** 691

"Maid of St. Philippe, The" (Chopin), **Retro. Supp. II:** 63

"Maid's Shoes, The" (Malamud), **Supp. I Part 2:** 437

Mailer, Fanny, **III:** 28

Mailer, Isaac, **III:** 28

Mailer, Norman, **I:** 261, 292, 477; **III: 26–49,** 174; **IV:** 98, 216; **Retro. Supp. II:** 182, **195–217,** 279; **Supp. I Part 1:** 291, 294; **Supp. III Part 1:** 302; **Supp. IV Part 1:** 90, 198, 207, 236, 284, 381; **Supp. IV Part 2:** 689; **Supp. VIII:** 236; **Supp. XI:** 104, 218, 222, 229; **Supp. XIV:** 49, 53, 54, 111, 162; **Supp. XVII:** 225, 228, 236; **Supp. XVIII:** 19–20; **Supp. XX:**90

"Maimed Man, The" (Tate), **IV:** 136

Maimonides, Moses, **Supp. XVII:** 46–47

Main Currents in American Thought: The Colonial Mind, 1625–1800 (Parrington), **I:** 517; **Supp. I Part 2:** 484

"Maine Roustabout, A" (Eberhart), **I:** 539

"Maine Speech" (White), **Supp. I Part 2:** 669–670

Maine Woods, The (Thoreau), **IV:** 188

Mains d'Orlac, Les (M. Renard), **Supp. XVII:** 58

Main Street (Lewis), **I:** 362; **II:** 271, 440, 441–442, 447, 449, 453; **III:** 394; **Supp. XIX:** 142

"Maintenance" (Pickering), **Supp. XXI:** 204

Maitland, Margaret Todd, **Supp. XVI:** 292

Majdoubeh, Ahmad, **Supp. XX:**116

"Majorat, Das" (Hoffman), **III:** 415

Major Barbara (Shaw), **III:** 69

"Major Chord, The" (Bourne), **I:** 221

Majors and Minors (Dunbar), **Supp. II Part 1:** 197, 198

"Major's Tale, The" (Bierce), **I:** 205

Make Believe (J. Scott), **Supp. XVII: 191–192,** 193, 194, 195

Make-Believe Town: Essays and Remembrances (Mamet), **Supp. XIV:** 240, 251

Make It New (Pound), **III:** 470

Makers and Finders (Brooks), **I:** 253, 254, 255, 257, 258

Makers of the Modern World (Untermeyer), **Supp. XV:** 312

"Making a Change" (Gilman), **Supp. XI:** 207

"Making a Living" (Sexton), **Supp. II Part 2:** 695

"Making Changes" (L. Michaels), **Supp. XVI:** 204

"Making Do" (Hogan), **Supp. IV Part 1:** 406

Making Face, Making Soul: Haciendo Caras, Creative and Critical Perspectives by Feminists of Color (Anzaldúa, ed.), **Supp. IV Part 1:** 330

Making It (Podhoretz), **Supp. VIII:** 231, 232, 233, **237–238,** 239, 244

"Making Light of Auntie" (X. J. Kennedy), **Supp. XV:** 163

"Making of a Marginal Farm, The" (Berry), **Supp. X:** 22

Making of Americans, The (Stein), **IV:** 35, 37, 40–42, 45, 46; **Supp. III Part 1:** 37

"Making of Ashenden, The" (Elkin), **Supp. VI:** 49, 50

"Making of a Soldier USA, The" (Simpson), **Supp. IX:** 270

"Making of Garrison Keillor, The" (McConagha), **Supp. XVI:** 166"

"Making of Paths, The" (Stegner), **Supp. IV Part 2:** 614

"Making of Poems, The" (W. J. Smith), **Supp. XIII:** 348

Making of the Modern Mind (Randall), **III:** 605

Making the Light Come: The Poetry of Gerald Stern (Somerville), **Supp. IX:** 296–297

"Making Up Stories" (Didion), **Supp. IV Part 1:** 196, 203, 205

Making Your Own Days: The Pleasures of Reading and Writing Poetry (Koch), **Supp. XV:** 188

Maladies de la volonté, Les (Ribot), **Supp. XX:**238

Malady of the Ideal, The: Oberman, Maurice de Guérin, and Amiel (Brooks), **I:** 240, 241, 242

Malamud, Bernard, **I:** 144, 375; **II:** 424, 425; **III:** 40, 272; **IV:** 216; **Retro. Supp. II:** 22, 279, 281; **Supp. I Part 2: 427–453; Supp. IV Part 1:** 297, 382; **Supp. V:** 257, 266; **Supp. IX:** 114, 227; **Supp. XIII:** 106, 264, 265, 294; **Supp. XVI:** 220

Malamud, Mrs. Bernard (Ann de Chiara), **Supp. I Part 2:** 451

Malanga, Gerard, **Supp. III Part 2:** 629

Malaquais, Jean, **Retro. Supp. II:** 199

Malatesta, Sigismondo de, **III:** 472, 473

Malcolm (Purdy), **Supp. VII:** 270–273, 277

"Malcolm Cowley and the American Writer" (Simpson), **Supp. II Part 1:** 147

Malcolm Lowry's "Volcano": Myth Symbol Meaning (Markson), **Supp. XVII:** 142, 144

"MALCOLM REMEMBERED (FEB. 77)" (Baraka), **Supp. II Part 1:** 60

Malcolm X, **Retro. Supp. II:** 12, 13; **Supp. I Part 1:** 52, 63, 65, 66; **Supp. IV Part 1:** 2, 10; **Supp. VIII:** 330, 345; **Supp. X:** 240; **Supp. XIV:** 306

Malcolm X (film), **Retro. Supp. II:** 12

"Maldrove" (Jeffers), **Supp. II Part 2:** 418

Male, Roy, **II:** 239

Male Animal, The (Thurber), **Supp. I Part 2:** 605, 606, 610–611

"Malediction upon Myself" (Wylie), **Supp. I Part 2:** 722

Malefactors, The (Gordon), **II:** 186, 199, 213–216; **IV:** 139

"Malest Cornifici Tuo Catullo" (Ginsberg), **Supp. II Part 1:** 315

Malick, Terrence, **Supp. XI:** 234; **Supp. XV:** 351

Malin, Irving, **I:** 147; **Supp. XVI:** 71–72

"Malinche's Tips: Pique from Mexico's Mother" (Mora), **Supp. XIII:** 223

"Malinke's Atonement" (Antin), **Supp. XX:**10

"Mallard" (C. Frost), **Supp. XV:** 98, 99

Mallarmé, Stéphane, **I:** 66, 569; **II:** 529, 543; **III:** 8, 409, 428; **IV:** 80, 86; **Retro. Supp. I:** 56; **Supp. I Part 1:** 261; **Supp. II Part 1:** 1; **Supp. III Part 1:** 319–320; **Supp. III Part 2:** 630; **Supp. XIII:** 114; **Supp. XV:** 158; **Supp. XVI:** 282, 285

Mallia, Joseph, **Supp. XII:** 26, 29, 37

Mallon, Anne-Marie, **Supp. XXI:** 215

Mallon, Thomas, **Supp. IV Part 1:** 200, 209; **Supp. XIX: 131–145**

Maloff, Saul, **Supp. VIII:** 238

Malory, Thomas, **II:** 302; **III:** 486; **IV:** 50, 61; **Supp. IV Part 1:** 47

"Mal Paso Bridge" (Jeffers), **Supp. II Part 2:** 415, 420

Malraux, André, **I:** 33–34, 127, 509; **II:** 57, 376; **III:** 35, 310; **IV:** 236, 247, 434; **Retro. Supp. I:** 73; **Retro. Supp. II:** 115–116, 119; **Supp. II Part 1:** 221, 232; **Supp. XIX:** 157

Maltese Falcon, The (film), **Supp. IV Part 1:** 342, 353, 355

Maltese Falcon, The (Hammett), **IV:** 286; **Supp. IV Part 1:** 345, 348–351

Mama (McMillan), **Supp. XIII:** 182, **187–188**

"Mama and Daughter" (Hughes), **Supp. I Part 1:** 334

Mama Day (Naylor), **Supp. VIII: 223–226,** 230

"Mama I Remember" (Nelson), **Supp. XVIII:** 173

Mama Poc: An Ecologist's Account of the Extinction of a Species (LaBastille), **Supp. X:** 99, **104–105,** 106

Mama's Bank Account (K. Forbes), **Supp. XVII:** 9

Mama's Promises (Nelson), **Supp. XVIII: 173–174**

"Mama Still Loves You" (Naylor), **Supp. VIII:** 214

Mambo Hips and Make Believe (Coleman), **Supp. XI: 94–96**

Mambo Kings, The (film), **Supp. VIII:** 73, 74

Mambo Kings Play Songs of Love, The (Hijuelos), **Supp. VIII:** 73–74, **79–82**

"Ma'me Pélagie" (Chopin), **Retro. Supp. II:** 64

Mamet, David, **Supp. XIV: 239–258,** 315

"Mamie" (Sandburg), **III:** 582

Mammedaty, Novarro Scott. *See* Momaday, N. Scott

"Mammon and the Archer" (O. Henry), **Supp. II Part 1:** 394, 408

Mammonart (Sinclair), **Supp. V:** 276–277

"Mammy" (D. West), **Supp. XVIII:** 283

"Mamouche" (Chopin), **Retro. Supp. II:** 66

Mamoulian, Rouben, **Supp. XVIII:** 281

"Man" (Corso), **Supp. XII:** 130

"Man" (Herbert), **II:** 12

"Man Against the Sky, The" (Robinson), **III:** 509, 523

"Man and a Woman Sit Near Each Other, A" (R. Bly), **Supp. IV Part 1:** 71

Man and Boy (Morris), **III:** 223, 224, 225

"Man and the Snake, The" (Bierce), **I:** 203

"Man and Woman" (Caldwell), **I:** 310

Manassas (Sinclair), **Supp. V:** 280, 281, 285

"Man Bring This Up Road" (T. Williams), **IV:** 383–384

"Man Carrying Thing" (Stevens), **IV:** 90

Manchester, William, **III:** 103

"Man Child, The" (Baldwin), **Supp. I Part 1:** 63

Man Could Stand Up, A (Ford), **I:** 423

"Mandarin's Jade" (Chandler), **Supp. IV Part 1:** 125

Mandel, Charlotte, **Supp. XVI:** 57

Mandelbaum, Maurice, **I:** 61

Mandelstam, Osip, **Retro. Supp. I:** 278; **Supp. III Part 1:** 268; **Supp. VIII:** 21, 22, 23, 27; **Supp. XIII:** 77; **Supp. XV:** 254, 261, 263

"Mandelstam: The Poem as Event" (Dobyns), **Supp. XIII:** 78

"Mandolin" (Dove), **Supp. IV Part 1:** 247

"Mandoline" (Verlaine), **IV:** 79

"Man Eating" (Kenyon), **Supp. VII:** 173

"Manet in Late Summer" (Skloot), **Supp. XX:**201

"Man Feeding Pigeons" (Clampitt), **Supp. IX: 49–50,** 52

Manfred, Frederick, **Supp. X:** 126

Man From Limbo, The (Endore), **Supp. XVII:** 55

"Mango Says Goodbye Sometimes" (Cisneros), **Supp. VII:** 64

Manhattan (film; Allen), **Supp. IV Part 1:** 205; **Supp. XV:** 5, **7–8,** 13

"Manhattan Dawn" (Justice), **Supp. VII:** 117

"Manhattan: Luminism" (Doty), **Supp. XI:** 135

Manhattan Murder Mystery (film; Allen), **Supp. XV:** 5, 11

Manhattan Transfer (Dos Passos), **I:** 26, 475, 478, 479, 480, 481, 482–484, 487; **II:** 286; **Supp. I Part 1:** 57

"Mania" (Lowell), **II:** 554

"Manic in the Moon, The" (Thurber), **Supp. I Part 2:** 620

Manifest; and Furthermore (Bronk), **Supp. XXI:** 32

"Manifesto: A Press Release from PRKA" (Saunders), **Supp. XIX:** 235

Manikin, The (J. Scott), **Supp. XVII: 189–191,** 192, **194**

"Man in Black" (Plath), **Supp. I Part 2:** 538

Man in Prehistory (Chard), **Supp. XII:** 177–178

Man in the Black Coat Turns, The (R. Bly), **Supp. IV Part 1:** 66–68, 71, 73

"Man in the Brooks Brothers Shirt, The" (McCarthy), **II:** 563–564

"Man in the Drawer, The" (Malamud), **Supp. I Part 2:** 437

Man in the Flying Lawn Chair and Other Excursions and Observations, The (Plimpton), **Supp. XVI:** 234

Man in the Gray Flannel Suit, The (Wilson), **Supp. IV Part 1:** 387

Man in the High Castle, The (Dick), **Supp. XVIII:** 138

Man in the Middle, The (Wagoner), **Supp. IX:** 324, **332–333**

"Man in the Rain, The" (Ryan as Quin), **Supp. XVIII:** 226

"Man in the Toolhouse, The" (Swados), **Supp. XIX:** 263

Mankiewicz, Herman, **Supp. XVI:** 189

Mankiewicz, Joseph, **Retro. Supp. I:** 113

Mankowitz, Wolf, **Supp. XI:** 307

"Man Made of Words, The" (Momaday), **Supp. IV Part 2:** 481, 484–485, 486, 487, 488

Man-Made World, The (Gilman), **Supp. XI:** 207

"Man-Moth, The" (Bishop), **Retro. Supp. II:** 42; **Supp. I Part 1:** 85–87, 88

Mann, Charles, **Retro. Supp. II:** 40

Mann, Erika, **Supp. II Part 1:** 11

Mann, Seymour (Samuel Weisman), **Supp. V:** 113

Mann, Thomas, **I:** 271, 490; **II:** 42, 539; **III:** 231, 281–282, 283; **IV:** 70, 73, 85; **Supp. IV Part 1:** 392; **Supp. IV Part 2:** 522; **Supp. V:** 51; **Supp. IX:** 21; **Supp. XI:** 275; **Supp. XII:** 173, 310, 321; **Supp. XIV:** 87; **Supp. XVII:** 137; **Supp. XIX:** 147, 151, 157; **Supp. XX:**85

Mannequins' Demise: A Play in Eight Scenes (Budbill), **Supp. XIX: 12**

Mannerhouse (Wolfe), **IV:** 460

Manner Music, The (Reznikoff), **Supp. XIV: 293–295**

"Manners" (Bishop), **Supp. I Part 1:** 73

"Manners" (Emerson), **II:** 4, 6

"Manners, Morals, and the Novel" (Trilling), **Supp. III Part 2:** 502, 503

Mannheim, Karl, **I:** 279; **Supp. I Part 2:** 644

Manning, Ambrose, **Supp. XX:**166

Manning, Frederic, **III:** 459

Manning, Robert, **Supp. IX:** 236

Mannix, Daniel P., **Supp. II Part 1:** 140

Man Nobody Knows, The (B. Barton), **Retro. Supp. I:** 179

Mano, D. Keith, **Supp. XVI:** 250

Mano, Guy Levis, **Supp. XVI:** 282

"Man of Indeterminate Age on a Subway Grate, A" (DI Piero), **Supp. XIX:** 47

"Man of Letters" (Pickering), **Supp. XXI:** 192, 195–196

"Man of Letters as a Man of Business, The" (Howells), **Supp. XIV:** 45–46

"Man of No Account, The" (Harte), **Supp. II Part 1:** 339

"Man of the Crowd, The" (Poe), **III:** 412, 417; **Retro. Supp. I:** 154

Man on Spikes (Asinof), **II:** 424

Man on Stage (Dixon), **Supp. XII:** 141, **154–155**

"Man on the Dump, The" (Stevens), **IV:** 74; **Retro. Supp. I:** 306

"Man on the Train, The" (Percy), **Supp. III Part 1:** 387

Manor, The (Singer), **IV:** 6, 17–19

Manrique, Jorge, **Retro. Supp. II:** 154

Mansart Builds a School (Du Bois), **Supp. II Part 1:** 185–186

Man's Fate (Malraux), **I:** 127; **Retro. Supp. I:** 121

"Man's Fate A Film Treatment of the Malraux Novel" (Agee), **I:** 33–34

Mansfield, June, **Supp. X:** 183, 194

Mansfield, Katherine, **III:** 362, 453

Mansfield, Stephanie, **Supp. IV Part 1:** 227

Man's Hope (Malraux), **IV:** 247

Mansion, The (Faulkner), **II:** 73; **Retro. Supp. I:** 74, 82

Man's Nature and His Communities (Niebuhr), **III:** 308

Manson, Charles, **Supp. IV Part 1:** 205

"Man Splitting Wood in the Daybreak, The" (Kinnell), **Supp. III Part 1:** 254

"Man's Pride" (Jeffers), **Supp. II Part 2:** 417

"Man's Story, The" (Anderson), **I:** 114

Man's Woman, A (Norris), **III:** 314, 322, 328, 329, 330, 332, 333

Man That Corrupted Hadleyburg, The (Twain), **I:** 204; **IV:** 208

"Man That Was Used Up, The" (Poe), **III:** 412, 425

"Mantis" (Zukofsky), **Supp. III Part 2:** 617

"'Mantis': An Interpretation" (Zukofsky), **Supp. III Part 2:** 617–618

Man to Send Rain Clouds, The (Rosen, ed.), **Supp. IV Part 2:** 499, 505, 513

"Man to Send Rain Clouds, The" (Silko), **Supp. IV Part 2:** 559

Mantrap (Lewis), **II:** 447

Manuductio Ad Ministerium (Mather), **Supp. II Part 2:** 465–467

"Manuelzinho" (Bishop), **Retro. Supp. II:** 47–48

Manuscript Books of Emily Dickinson, The (Franklin, ed.), **Retro. Supp. I:** 29, 41

"Man Waiting for It to Stop, A" (Dunn), **Supp. XI:** 144

"Man Who Became a Woman, The" (Anderson), **I:** 114

"Man Who Carries the Desert Around Inside Himself, The: For Wally" (Komunyakaa), **Supp. XIII:** 125

"Man Who Closed Shop, The" (Dunn), **Supp. XI:** 149

Man Who Gave Up His Name, The (Harrison), **Supp. VIII:** 45, 52

Man Who Had All the Luck, The (A. Miller), **III:** 148, 149, 164, 166

"Man Who Knew Belle Star, The" (Bausch), **Supp. VII:** 46

"Man Who Knew Coolidge, The" (Lewis), **II:** 449

Man Who Knew Coolidge, The: Being the Soul of Lowell Schmaltz, Constructive and Nordic Citizen (Lewis), **II:** 450

Man Who Lived Underground, The (Wright), **Supp. II Part 1:** 40

"Man Who Lived Underground, The" (Wright), **IV:** 479, 485–487, 492; **Retro. Supp. II:** 121

"Man Who Made Me Love Him, The" (Weigl), **Supp. XIX:** 278

"Man Who Makes Brooms, The" (Nye), **Supp. XIII:** 276

"Man Who Studied Yoga, The" (Mailer), **III:** 35–36; **Retro. Supp. II:** 200

"Man Who Wanted to Win, The" (McCoy), **Supp. XIII:** 161

Man Who Was There, The (Morris), **III:** 220–221

"Man Who Writes Ants, The" (Merwin), **Supp. III Part 1:** 348

"Man with a Family" (Humphrey), **Supp. IX:** 94

Man without a Country, The (Hale), **I:** 488

"Man with the Blue Guitar, The" (Stevens), **I:** 266; **IV:** 85–87; **Retro. Supp. I: 303–305,** 306, 307, 309

Man with the Blue Guitar and Other Poems, The (Stevens), **IV:** 76; **Retro. Supp. I:** 303, 422

Man with the Golden Arm, The (Algren), **Supp. V:** 4; **Supp. IX:** 1, 3, **9–11,** 14, 15

Man with the Golden Arm, The (film), **Supp. IX:** 3

"Man with the Golden Beef, The" (Podhoretz), **Supp. IX:** 3

"Man with the Hoe, The" (Markham), **Supp. XV:** 115

Many a Monster (Ryan as Finnegan), **Supp. XVIII:** 233, **236–238**

Manyan Letters (Olson), **Supp. II Part 2:** 571

Many Circles (Goldbarth), **Supp. XII:** 193

"Many Handles" (Sandburg), **III:** 594

"Many Happy Returns" (Auden), **Supp. II Part 1:** 15

Many Loves (W. C. Williams), **Retro. Supp. I:** 424

"Many Mansions" (H. Roth), **Supp. IX:** 233, 234

Many Marriages (Anderson), **I:** 104, 111, 113

"Many of Our Waters: Variations on a Poem by a Black Child" (Wright), **Supp. III Part 2:** 602

"Many Swans" (Lowell), **II:** 526

"Many Thousands Gone" (Baldwin), **Retro. Supp. II:** 4; **Supp. I Part 1:** 51

"Many Wagons Ago" (Ashbery), **Supp. III Part 1:** 22

Many-Windowed House, A (Cowley), **Supp. II Part 1:** 141, 143

"Many-Windowed House, A" (Cowley), **Supp. II Part 1:** 137

Mao II (DeLillo), **Supp. VI:** 2, 4, **5,** 6, **7,** 8, 9, 14, 16

"Map, The" (Bishop), **Retro. Supp. II:** 41; **Supp. I Part 1:** 72, 82, 85–88, 93

"Map, The" (Strand), **Supp. IV Part 2:** 623–624

"Maple Leaf, The" (Joplin), **Supp. IV Part 1:** 223

"Maple Tree, The" (D. West), **Supp. XVIII:** 284

Map of Another Town: A Memoir of Provence (M. F. K. Fisher), **Supp. XVII:** 88, 89, 92

"Map of Montana in Italy, A" (Hugo), **Supp. VI:** 139

Mapp and Lucia (Benson), **Supp. XX:** 229

"Maps" (Hass), **Supp. VI:** 103–104

Mapson, Jo-Ann, **Supp. IV Part 2:** 440, 454

Map to the Next World, A: Poems and Tales (Harjo), **Supp. XII: 228–230**

"Maquillage" (Hull), **Supp. XXI:** 133

"Mara" (Jeffers), **Supp. II Part 2:** 434

Ma Rainey's Black Bottom (Wilson), **Supp. VIII:** 331, **332–334,** 346, 349, 350

Marat, Jean Paul, **IV:** 117; **Supp. I Part 2:** 514, 515, 521

"Marathon" (Glück), **Supp. V:** 85

Marble Faun, The (Faulkner), **II:** 55, 56; **Retro. Supp. I:** 79

Marble Faun, The; or, The Romance of Monte Beni (Hawthorne), **II:** 225, 239, 242–243, 290, 324; **IV:** 167; **Retro. Supp. I:** 63, 149, 163, **164–165; Supp. I Part 1:** 38; **Supp. I Part 2:** 421, 596; **Supp. XIII:** 102

Marbles (Brodsky), **Supp. VIII:** 26–27

Marcaccio, Michael, **Supp. XVII:** 97, 106

"March" (W. C. Williams), **Retro. Supp. I:** 418

March, Alan, **Supp. XVI:** 242

March, Fredric, **III:** 154, 403; **IV:** 357; **Supp. X:** 220

"March, March on Down the Field" (Shaw), **Supp. XIX:** 246

Marchalonis, Shirley, **Supp. XIII:** 138, 140, 141, 143, 147–148

"Marché aux Oiseaux" (Wilbur), **Supp. III Part 2:** 550

"Märchen, The" (Jarrell), **II:** 378–379

March Hares (Frederic), **II:** 143–144

Marching Men (Anderson), **I:** 99, 101, 103–105, 111

"Marching Music" (Simic), **Supp. VIII:** 281

"Marcia" (R. H. Davis), **Supp. XVI:** 91–92

Marcks, Greg, **Supp. XVIII:** 150

Marco Millions (O'Neill), **III:** 391, 395

Marcosson, Isaac, **III:** 322

Marcus, Greil, **Supp. XVIII:** 30, 53

Marcus, Steven, **Retro. Supp. II:** 196, 200

Marcus Aurelius, **II:** 1; **III:** 566; **Supp. XVIII:** 304

Marcuse, Herbert, **Supp. I Part 2:** 645; **Supp. VIII:** 196; **Supp. XII:** 2

Mardi and a Voyage Thither (Melville), **I:** 384; **II:** 281; **III:** 77–79, 84, 87, 89; **Retro. Supp. I:** 247, 254, 256

Margaret (Judd), **II:** 290

"Margaret Fuller, 1847" (Clampitt), **Supp. IX:** 43

"Marginalia" (Wilbur), **Supp. III Part 2:** 544

Margin of Hope, A: An Intellectual Autobiography (Howe), **Supp. VI:** 113–114, 117, 125, 128

"Margins of Maycomb, The: A Rereading of *To Kill a Mockingbird*" (Phelps), **Supp. VIII:** 128

Margoshes, Samuel, **Supp. X:** 70

"Margrave" (Jeffers), **Supp. II Part 2:** 426

Margret Howth (R. H. Davis), **Supp. XVI:** 81, 83, 84, **88–89**

Margret Howth: A Story of Today (J. Yellin, ed.), **Supp. XVI:** 88

Margulies, Donald, **Supp. XXI:** 145

"Maria Concepción" (Porter), **III:** 434–435, 451

Mariani, Paul L., **Retro. Supp. I:** 412, 419; **Retro. Supp. II:** 189

Marianne Moore Reader, (Moore), **III:** 199

Marie Antoinette (film), **Retro. Supp. I:** 113

Marie Laveau (Prose), **Supp. XVI:** 251

Mariella Gable, Sister, **III:** 339, 355

"Marijuana and a Pistol" (C. Himes), **Supp. XVI:** 137

"Marijuana Notation" (Ginsberg), **Supp. II Part 1:** 313

Maril, Herman, **Supp. XXI:** 22, 23

Marilyn: A Biography (Mailer), **Retro. Supp. II:** 208

"Marin" (Cisneros), **Supp. VII:** 60, 61

Marin, Jay, **Retro. Supp. II:** 325

"Marina" (Eliot), **I:** 584, 585; **Retro. Supp. I:** 64

Mariners, Renegades, and Castaways (C. L. R. James), **Supp. XXI:** 159, 169–170

"Marine Surface, Low Overcast" (Clampitt), **Supp. IX: 47–48**

Marinetti, Tommaso, **Retro. Supp. I:** 59

Marionettes, The (Faulkner), **Retro. Supp. I:** 79

Maritain, Jacques, **I:** 402

Maritime Compact (Paine), **Supp. I Part 2:** 519

Maritime History of Massachusetts, 1783–1860, The (Morison), **Supp. I Part 2:** 481–483

Marjolin, Jean-Nicolas, **Supp. I Part 1:** 302

Marjorie Kinnan Rawlings: Sojourner at Cross Creek (Silverthorne), **Supp. X:** 220, 234

"Mark, The" (Bogan), **Supp. III Part 1:** 52

Marker, Chris, **Supp. IV Part 2:** 434, 436

"Market" (Hayden), **Supp. II Part 1:** 368, 369

Marketplace, The (Frederic), **II:** 145–146

Markham, Edwin, **I:** 199, 207; **Supp. XV:** 115

Markings (Hammarskjold), **Supp. II Part 1:** 26

Mark of the Vampire (film, Browning), **Supp. XVII:** 58

Markopoulos, Gregory, **Supp. XII:** 2

Markowick-Olczakowa, Hanna, **Supp. X:** 70

Marks, Alison, **Supp. I Part 2:** 660

Marks, Barry A., **I:** 435, 438, 442, 446

Markson, David, **Supp. XVII: 135–147**

Mark Twain in Eruption (Twain), **IV:** 209

Mark Twain's America (De Voto), **I:** 248

Mark Twain's Autobiography (Twain), **IV:** 209

Marley, Bob, **Supp. IX:** 152

Marlowe, Christopher, **I:** 68, 368, 384; **II:** 590; **III:** 259, 491; **Retro. Supp. I:** 127; **Retro. Supp. II:** 76; **Supp. I Part 2:** 422; **Supp. XXI:** 227

"Marlowe Takes on the Syndicate" (Chandler), **Supp. IV Part 1:** 135

Marne, The (Wharton), **IV:** 319, 320; **Retro. Supp. I:** 378

Marquand, John, **Supp. XI:** 301

Marquand, Mrs. John P. (Adelaide Hooker), **III:** 57, 61

Marquand, Mrs. John P. (Christina Sedgwick), **III:** 54, 57

Marquand, J. P., **I:** 362, 375; **II:** 459, 482–483; **III: 50–73,** 383; **Supp. I Part 1:** 196; **Supp. IV Part 1:** 31; **Supp. V:** 95

Marquand, Philip, **III:** 52

Marquis, Don, **Supp. I Part 2:** 668

Marrásh, Francis al-, **Supp. XX:** 117

"Marriage" (Corso), **Supp. XII:** 117, 124, **127–128**

Marriage (Moore), **III:** 194

"Marriage" (Moore), **III:** 198–199, 213

"Marriage, A" (Untermeyer), **Supp. XV:** 305

Marriage A-la-Mode (Dryden), **Supp. IX:** 68

Marriage and Other Science Fiction (Goldbarth), **Supp. XII:** 189, 190

"Marriage in the Sixties, A" (Rich), **Supp. I Part 2:** 554

"Marriage of Heaven and Hell, The" (Blake), **III:** 544–545; **Supp. VIII:** 99

"Marriage of Phaedra, The" (Cather), **Retro. Supp. I:** 5

Married Men (Wolfert), **Supp. XXI:** 277

Marrow of Tradition, The (Chesnutt), **Supp. XIV:** 63, **71–75,** 76

Marryat, Captain Frederick, **III:** 423

"Marrying Absurd" (Didion), **Supp. IV Part 1:** 200

"Marrying Iseult?" (Updike), **Retro. Supp. I:** 329

Marrying Man (Simon), **Supp. IV Part 2:** 588

"Marrying the Hangman" (Atwood), **Supp. XIII:** 34

Marry Me: A Romance (Updike), **Retro. Supp. I:** 329, 330, 332

"Mars and Hymen" (Freneau), **Supp. II Part 1:** 258

Marsden, Dora, **III:** 471; **Retro. Supp. I:** 416

Marsena (Frederic), **II:** 135, 136–137

Marsh, Edward, **Supp. I Part 1:** 257, 263

Marsh, Frederick T., **Supp. XX:** 39, 46

Marsh, Fred T., **Supp. IX:** 232

Marsh, John R., **Supp. XIX:** 187

Marsh, Mae, **Supp. I Part 2:** 391

Marshall, George, **III:** 3

Marshall, John, **Supp. I Part 2:** 455; **Supp. XVI:** 117; **Supp. XIX:** 62

Marshall, Paule, **Supp. IV Part 1:** 8, 14, 369; **Supp. XI:** 18, **275–292; Supp. XIII:** 295; **Supp. XX:**154

Marshall, Tod, **Supp. XV:** 224; **Supp. XVII:** 25, 26, 29, 32

"Marshall Carpenter" (Masters), **Supp. I Part 2:** 463

"Marshes of Glynn, The" (Lanier), **Supp. I Part 1:** 364, 365–368, 370, 373

"'Marshes of Glynn, The': A Study in Symbolic Obscurity" (Ross), **Supp. I Part 1:** 373

Marsh Island, A (Jewett), **II:** 405; **Retro. Supp. II:** 134

"Marshland Elegy" (Leopold), **Supp. XIV:** 187, 189

"Mars Is Heaven!" (Bradbury), **Supp. IV Part 1:** 103, 106

Mars-Jones, Adam, **Supp. XXI:** 116

Marsman, Henrik, **Supp. IV Part 1:** 183

Marston, Ed, **Supp. IV Part 2:** 492

Marta y Maria (Valdes), **II:** 290

"Martha's Lady" (Jewett), **Retro. Supp. II:** 140, 143

Marthe, Saint, **II:** 213

Martial, **II:** 1, 169; **Supp. IX:** 152

Martian Chronicles, The (Bradbury), **Supp. IV Part 1:** 102, 103, 106–107

Martian Time-Slip (Dick), **Supp. XVIII:** 142

Martin, Benjamin, **Supp. I Part 2:** 503

Martin, Charles, **Supp. XVII:** 112

Martin, Dick, **Supp. XII:** 44

Martin, Jay, **I:** 55, 58, 60, 61, 67; **III:** 307; **Retro. Supp. II:** 326, 327, 329; **Supp. XI:** 162

Martin, John, **Supp. XI:** 172

Martin, Judith, **Supp. V:** 128

Martin, Nell, **Supp. IV Part 1:** 351, 353

Martin, Reginald, **Supp. X:** 247, 249

Martin, Robert, **Supp. XX:**165

Martin, Stephen-Paul, **Supp. IV Part 2:** 430

Martin, Tom, **Supp. X:** 79

Martin du Gard, Roger, **Supp. I Part 1:** 51

Martineau, Harriet, **Supp. II Part 1:** 282, 288, 294; **Supp. XVIII:** 7

Martin Eden (London), **II:** 466, 477–481

Martinelli, Sheri, **Supp. IV Part 1:** 280

Martínez, Guillermo, **Supp. XIII:** 313

Martini, Adrienne, **Supp. XVIII:** 35

Mart'nez, Rafael, **Retro. Supp. I:** 423

Martone, John, **Supp. V:** 179

Marty (Chayefsky), **Supp. XV:** 205

"Martyr, The" (Porter), **III:** 454

Martz, Louis L., **IV:** 151, 156, 165; **Supp. I Part 1:** 107; **Supp. XIV:** 12; **Supp. XXI:** 85

Marvell, Andrew, **IV:** 135, 151, 156, 161, 253; **Retro. Supp. I:** 62, 127; **Retro. Supp. II:** 186, 189; **Supp. I Part 1:** 80; **Supp. XII:** 159; **Supp. XIV:** 10; **Supp. XVI:** 204; **Supp. XXI:** 227

"Marvella, for Borrowing" (Ríos), **Supp. IV Part 2:** 551

"Marvelous Sauce, The", **Supp. XVII:** 189

Marvels and Masterpieces (al-Badá'i' wa'l-Tará'if) (Gibran), **Supp. XX:**116, 124

Marx, Eleanor, **Supp. XVI:** 85

Marx, Karl, **I:** 60, 267, 279, 283, 588; **II:** 376, 462, 463, 483, 577; **IV:** 429, 436, 443–444, 469; **Retro. Supp. I:** 254; **Supp. I Part 2:** 518, 628, 632, 633, 634, 635, 639, 643, 645, 646; **Supp. III Part 2:** 619; **Supp. IV Part 1:** 355; **Supp. VIII:** 196; **Supp. IX:** 133; **Supp. X:** 119, 134; **Supp. XIII:** 75; **Supp. XXI:** 162, 263

Marx, Leo, **Supp. I Part 1:** 233

"Marxism and Monastic Perpectives" (Merton), **Supp. VIII:** 196

Mary (Nabokov), **Retro. Supp. I:** 267–268, 270, 277

"Mary" (Trethewey), **Supp. XXI:** 246

"Mary Karr, Mary Karr, Mary Karr, Mary Karr" (Harmon), **Supp. XI:** 248

Maryles, Daisy, **Supp. XII:** 271

Mary Magdalene, **I:** 303

Mary; or, The Test of Honour (Rowson), **Supp. XV:** **233,** 236

"Mary O'Reilly" (Anderson), **II:** 44

"Mary Osaka , I Love You" (Fante), **Supp. XI:** 169

"Mary Snorak the Cook, Skermo the Gardener, and Jack the Parts Man Provide Dinner for a Wandering Stranger" (Grossman), **Supp. XIX:** 87

"Mary's Song" (Plath), **Supp. I Part 2:** 541

"Mary Winslow" (Lowell), **Retro. Supp. II:** 187

Marzynski, Marian, **Supp. XVI:** 153

Masefield, John, **II:** 552; **III:** 523

Masked and Anonymous (film, Dylan and Charles), **Supp. XVIII:** 21, 28

Mask for Janus, A (Merwin), **Supp. III Part 1:** 339, 341, 342

Maslin, Janet, **Supp. XVI:** 213; **Supp. XXI:** 79

Maslow, Abraham, **Supp. I Part 2:** 540

Mason, Bobbie Ann, **Supp. VIII:** **133–149; Supp. XI:** 26; **Supp. XII:** 294, 298, 311; **Supp. XX:**162

Mason, Charlotte, **Supp. XIV:** 201

Mason, David, **Supp. V:** 344; **Supp. XV:** 116, 251; **Supp. XVII:** 109, 110, 112, 121; **Supp. XVIII:** 182, 183

Mason, Jennifer, **Supp. XVIII:** 263

Mason, Lowell, **I:** 458

Mason, Marsha, **Supp. IV Part 2:** 575, 586

Mason, Otis Tufton, **Supp. I Part 1:** 18

Mason, Walt, **Supp. XV:** 298

Mason & Dixon (Pynchon), **Supp. XVII:** 232

"Mason Jars by the Window" (Ríos), **Supp. IV Part 2:** 548

Masque of Mercy, A (Frost), **II:** 155, 165, 167–168; **Retro. Supp. I:** 131, 140

"Masque of Mummers, The" (MacLeish), **III:** 18

"Masque of Pandora, The" (Longfellow), **Retro. Supp. II:** 167

Masque of Pandora, The, and Other Poems (Longfellow), **II:** 490, 494, 506; **Retro. Supp. II:** 169

Masque of Poets, A (Lathrop, ed.), **Retro. Supp. I:** 31; **Supp. I Part 1:** 365, 368

Masque of Reason, A (Frost), **II:** 155, 162, 165–167; **Retro. Supp. I:** 131, 140; **Retro. Supp. II:** 42

"Masque of the Red Death, The" (Poe), **III:** 412, 419, 424; **Retro. Supp. II:** 262, 268–269

"Masquerade" (Banks), **Supp. V:** 7

Massachusetts, Its Historians and Its History (Adams), **Supp. I Part 2:** 484

"Massachusetts 1932" (Bowles), **Supp. IV Part 1:** 94

"Massachusetts to Virginia" (Whittier), **Supp. I Part 2:** 688–689

"Massacre and the Mastermind, The" (Bausch), **Supp. VII:** 49

"Massacre at Scio, The" (Bryant), **Supp. I Part 1:** 168

"Massacre of the Innocents, The" (Simic), **Supp. VIII:** 282

Masses and Man (Toller), **I:** 479

"Masseur de Ma Soeur, Le" (Hecht), **Supp. X:** 58

Massey, Raymond, **Supp. IV Part 2:** 524

"Mass Eye and Ear: The Ward" (Karr), **Supp. XI:** 244

"Mass for the Day of St. Thomas Didymus" (Levertov), **Supp. III Part 1:** 283

Massie, Chris, **Supp. IV Part 2:** 524

Massing, Michael, **Supp. IV Part 1:** 208

Massinger, Philip, **Supp. I Part 2:** 422; **Supp. XV:** 238

Master Builder, The (Ibsen), **Supp. IV Part 2:** 522

Master Class (McNally), **Supp. XIII:** **204–205,** 208

"Masterful" (Matthews), **Supp. IX:** **161–162**

Mastering the Art of French Cooking (Child), **Supp. XVII:** 89

"Master Misery" (Capote), **Supp. III Part 1:** 117

Master of Dreams: A Memoir of Isaac Bashevis Singer (Telushkin), **Retro. Supp. II:** 317

"Master of Secret Revenges, The" (Gass), **Supp. VI:** 93

Master of the Crossroads (Bell), **Supp. X:** **16–17**

"'Masterpiece of Filth, A': Portrait of Knoxville Forgets to Be Fair" (Howards), **Supp. VIII:** 178

Masterpieces of American Fiction, **Supp. XI:** 198

"Master Player, The" (Dunbar), **Supp. II Part 1:** 200

Masters, Edgar Lee, **I:** 106, 384, 475, 480, 518; **II:** 276, 529; **III:** 505, 576, 579; **IV:** 352; **Retro. Supp. I:** 131; **Supp. I Part 2:** 378, 386, 387, **454–478; Supp. III Part 1:** 63, 71, 73, 75; **Supp. IV Part 2:** 502; **Supp. IX:** 308; **Supp. XIV:** 282–283; **Supp. XV:** 256, 293, 297, 301, 306

Masters, Hardin W., **Supp. I Part 2:** 468

Masters, Hilary, **Supp. IX:** 96

Masters of Sociological Thought (Coser), **Supp. I Part 2:** 650

Masters of the Dew (Roumain), **Supp. IV Part 1:** 367

"Masters of War" (song, Dylan), **Supp. XVIII:** 24

"Master's Pieces, The" (H. L. Gates), **Supp. XX:**109

Matchmaker, The (Wilder), **IV:** 357, 369, 370, 374; **Supp. XX:**50

Mate of the Daylight, The, and Friends Ashore (Jewett), **II:** 404; **Retro. Supp. II:** 146–147

Materassi, Mario, **Supp. IX:** 233

Mather, Cotton, **II:** 10, 104, 302, 506, 536; **III:** 442; **IV:** 144, 152–153, 157; **Supp. I Part 1:** 102, 117, 174, 271; **Supp. I Part 2:** 584, 599, 698; **Supp. II Part 2: 441–470; Supp. IV Part 2:** 430, 434

Mather, Increase, **II:** 10; **IV:** 147, 157; **Supp. I Part 1:** 100

Mathews, Cornelius, **III:** 81; **Supp. I Part 1:** 317

Mathews, Shailer, **III:** 293

"Matinees" (Merrill), **Supp. III Part 1:** 319, 327

"Matins" (C. Frost), **Supp. XV:** 105

"Matins" (Glück), **Supp. V:** 88

"Matins" (Nelson), **Supp. XVIII:** 177

Matisse, Henri, **III:** 180; **IV:** 90, 407; **Supp. I Part 2:** 619; **Supp. VIII:** 168; **Supp. IX:** 66; **Supp. X:** 73, 74

"Matisse: Blue Interior with Two Girls–1947" (Hecht), **Supp. X: 73–74**

"Matisse: The Red Studio" (Snodgrass), **Supp. VI:** 316–317

Matlack, James, **Supp. XV:** 269, 271, 286

Matlock, Lucinda, **Supp. I Part 2:** 462

Matos, Juan, **Supp. XXI:** 104

Matrimaniac, The (film), **Supp. XVI:** 185, 186

Matrix Trilogy, The (film), **Supp. XVI:** 271

Matson, Harold, **Supp. XIII:** 164, 166, 167, 169, 172

Matson, Peter, **Supp. IV Part 1:** 299

Matson, Suzanne, **Supp. VIII:** 281

Matters of Fact and Fiction: Essays 1973–1976 (Vidal), **Supp. IV Part 2:** 687

Matthew (biblical book), **IV:** 164; **Supp. XV:** 222

Matthew Arnold (Trilling), **Supp. III Part 2:** 500–501

Matthews, Jackson, **Supp. XVI:** 282

Matthews, T. S., **II:** 430; **Supp. XV:** 142

Matthews, William, **Supp. V:** 4, 5; **Supp. IX: 151–170; Supp. XIII:** 112; **Supp. XXI:** 87

Matthiessen, F. O., **I:** 254, 259–260, 517; **II:** 41, 554; **III:** 310, 453; **IV:** 181; **Retro. Supp. I:** 40, 217; **Retro. Supp. II:** 137; **Supp. IV Part 2:** 422; **Supp. XIII:** 93; **Supp. XIV:** 3; **Supp. XXI:** 277

Matthiessen, Peter, **Supp. V: 199–217,** 332; **Supp. XI:** 231, 294; **Supp. XIV:** 82; **Supp. XVI:** 230; **Supp. XIX:** 268

Mattingly, Garrett, **Supp. IV Part 2:** 601

Mattu, Ravi, **Supp. XVI:** 124

"Maud Island" (Caldwell), **I:** 310

Maud Martha (Brooks), **Supp. III Part 1:** 74, 78–79, 87; **Supp. XI:** 278

"Maud Muller" (Whittier), **Supp. I Part 2:** 698

Maugham, W. Somerset, **III:** 57, 64; **Supp. IV Part 1:** 209; **Supp. X:** 58; **Supp. XIV:** 161

Maule's Curse: Seven Studies in the History of American Obscurantism (Winters), **Supp. II Part 2:** 807–808, 812

"Mau-mauing the Flak Catchers" (Wolfe), **Supp. III Part 2:** 577

Maupassant, Guy de, **I:** 309, 421; **II:** 191–192, 291, 325, 591; **IV:** 17; **Retro. Supp. II:** 65, 66, 67, 299; **Supp. I Part 1:** 207, 217, 223, 320; **Supp. XIV:** 336

"Maurice Barrès and the Youth of France" (Bourne), **I:** 228

Maurier, George du, **II:** 338

Maurras, Charles, **Retro. Supp. I:** 55

Maus II: And Here My Troubles Began (A. Speigelman), **Supp. XVII:** 48

Mauve Gloves & Madmen, Clutter & Vine (Wolfe), **Supp. III Part 2:** 581

Maverick, Augustus, **Supp. XVIII:** 4

Maverick in Mauve (Auchincloss), **Supp. IV Part 1:** 26

"Mavericks, The" (play) (Auchincloss), **Supp. IV Part 1:** 34

"Mavericks, The" (story) (Auchincloss), **Supp. IV Part 1:** 32

"Max" (H. Miller), **III:** 183

Max, D. T., **Supp. XXI:** 117

Max and the White Phagocytes (H. Miller), **III:** 178, 183–184

Maximilian (emperor of Mexico), **Supp. I Part 2:** 457–458

Maximilian: A Play in Five Acts (Masters), **Supp. I Part 2:** 456, 457–458

"Maximus, to Gloucester" (Olson), **Supp. II Part 2:** 574

"Maximus, to himself" (Olson), **Supp. II Part 2:** 565, 566, 567, 569, 570, 572

Maximus Poems, The (Olson), **Retro. Supp. I:** 209; **Supp. II Part 2:** 555, 556, 563, 564–580, 584; **Supp. VIII:** 305; **Supp. XV:** 170, 264, 349; **Supp. XVI:** 287

Maximus Poems 1–10, The (Olson), **Supp. II Part 2:** 571

Maximus Poems IV, V, VI (Olson), **Supp. II Part 2:** 555, 580, 582–584

Maximus Poems Volume Three, The (Olson), **Supp. II Part 2:** 555, 582, 584–585

"Maximus to Gloucester, Letter 19 (A Pastoral Letter)" (Olson), **Supp. II Part 2:** 567

"Maximus to Gloucester, Sunday July 19" (Olson), **Supp. II Part 2:** 580

"Maximus to himself June 1964" (Olson), **Supp. II Part 2:** 584

Maxwell, Glyn, **Supp. XV:** 252, 253, 260, 261, 263, 264

Maxwell, William, **Supp. I Part 1:** 175; **Supp. III Part 1:** 62; **Supp. VIII:** 151–174; **Supp. XVII:** 23

May, Abigail (Abba). *See* Alcott, Mrs. Amos Bronson (Abigail May)

May, Jill, **Supp. VIII:** 126

"May 24, 1980" (Brodsky), **Supp. VIII:** 28

"May 1968" (Olds), **Supp. X:** 211–212

"Mayan Glyphs Unread, The" (Bronk), **Supp. XXI:** 31

"Mayan Warning" (Mora), **Supp. XIII:** 214

Maybe (Hellman), **Supp. IV Part 1:** 12

"Maybe" (Oliver), **Supp. VII:** 239

"Maybe, Someday" (Ritsos), **Supp. XIII:** 78

May Blossom (Belasco), **Supp. XVI:** 182

"Mayday" (Faulkner), **Retro. Supp. I:** 80

"May Day" (Fitzgerald), **II:** 88–89; **Retro. Supp. I:** 103

"May Day Dancing, The" (Nemerov), **III:** 275

May Days (Pickering), **Supp. XXI:** 197–198

"May Day Sermon to the Women of Gilmer County, Georgia, by a Woman Preacher Leaving the Baptist Church" (Dickey), **Supp. IV Part 1:** 182

Mayer, Elizabeth, **Supp. II Part 1:** 16; **Supp. III Part 1:** 63

Mayer, John, **Retro. Supp. I:** 58

Mayer, Louis B., **Supp. XII:** 160; **Supp. XVIII:** 250

Mayes, Wendell, **Supp. IX:** 250

Mayfield, Sara, **Supp. IX:** 65

Mayflower, The (Stowe), **Supp. I Part 2:** 585, 586

Mayle, Peter, **Supp. XVI:** 295

Maynard, Joyce, **Supp. V:** 23

Maynard, Tony, **Supp. I Part 1:** 65

Mayne, Xavier. *See* Prime-Stevenson, Edward Irenaeus

Mayo, Robert, **III:** 478

Mayorga, Margaret, **IV:** 381

"Maypole of Merrymount, The" (Hawthorne), **II:** 229

"May Queen" (Di Piero), **Supp. XIX:** 41

May Sarton: Selected Letters 1916–1954, **Supp. VIII:** 265

"May Sun Sheds an Amber Light, The" (Bryant), **Supp. I Part 1:** 170

"May Swenson: The Art of Perceiving" (Stanford), **Supp. IV Part 2:** 637

"Maze" (Eberhart), **I:** 523, 525–526, 527

Mazel (R. Goldstein), **Supp. XVII:** 44

Mazur, Gail, **Supp. XVIII:** 92

Mazurkiewicz, Margaret, **Supp. XI:** 2

Mazzini, Giuseppe, **Supp. I Part 1:** 2, 8; **Supp. II Part 1:** 299

M. Butterfly (Hwang), **Supp. X:** 292; **Supp. XXI:** 143, 147, **150–154**

Mc. Names starting with Mc are alphabetized as if spelled Mac.

"M. Degas Teaches Art & Science at Durfee Intermediate School, Detroit, 1942" (Levine), **Supp. V:** 181, 193

"Me, Boy Scout" (Lardner), **II:** 433

Me, Vashya! (T. Williams), **IV:** 381

Mead, Elinor. *See* Howells, Mrs. William Dean (Elinor Mead)

Mead, George Herbert, **II:** 27, 34; **Supp. I Part 1:** 5; **Supp. I Part 2:** 641

Mead, Margaret, **Supp. I Part 1:** 49, 52, 66; **Supp. IX:** 229

Mead, Taylor, **Supp. XV:** 187

Meade, Frank, **Retro. Supp. II:** 114

Meade, Marion, **Supp. IX:** 191, 193, 194, 195

Meadow, Lynne, **Supp. XIII:** 198

"Meadow House" (Carruth), **Supp. XVI:** 48

Meadowlands (Glück), **Supp. V:** 88–90

"Mean, Mrs." (Gass), **Supp. VI:** 83

"Me and the Mule" (Hughes), **Supp. I Part 1:** 334

"Meaningless Institution, A" (Ginsberg), **Supp. II Part 1:** 313

"Meaning of a Literary Idea, The" (Trilling), **Supp. III Part 2:** 498

"Meaning of Birds, The" (C. Smith), **Supp. X:** 177

"Meaning of Death, The, An After Dinner Speech" (Tate), **IV:** 128, 129

"Meaning of Life, The" (Tate), **IV:** 137

"Meaning of Simplicity, The" (Ritsos), **Supp. XIII:** 78

Means of Escape (Caputo), **Supp. XIX:** 18, 21, 25

Mean Spirit (Hogan), **Supp. IV Part 1:** 397, 404, 407–410, 415, 416–417

Meantime, The (Bronk), **Supp. XXI:** 31

Mearns, Hughes, **III:** 220

"Measure" (Hass), **Supp. VI: 99–100,** 101

"Measuring My Blood" (Vizenor), **Supp. IV Part 1:** 262

Meatyard, Gene, **Supp. X:** 30

Me: By Jimmy (Big Boy) Valente (Keillor), **Supp. XVI:** 177

Mechan, Dennis B., **Supp. XVI:** 267–268

Mechanic, The (Bynner and DeMille), **Supp. XV:** 42, 50

"Mechanism" (Ammons), **Supp. VII:** 28

"Mechanism in Thought and Morals" (Holmes), **Supp. I Part 1:** 314

Mecom, Mrs. Jane, **II:** 122

"Meddlesome Jack" (Caldwell), **I:** 309

Medea (Jeffers), **Supp. II Part 2:** 435

Medea and Some Poems, The (Cullen), **Supp. IV Part 1:** 169, 173

"Me Decade and the Third Great Awakening, The" (Wolfe), **Supp. III Part 2:** 581

"Médecin Malgré Lui, Le" (W. C. Williams), **IV:** 407–408

"Medfield" (Bryant), **Supp. I Part 1:** 157

Medical History of Contraception, A (Himes), **Supp. V:** 128

"Medicine Song" (Gunn Allen), **Supp. IV Part 1:** 326

Médicis, Marie de, **II:** 548

Medina (McCarthy), **II:** 579

"Meditation, A" (Eberhart), **I:** 533–535

"Meditation 1.6" (Taylor), **IV:** 165

"Meditation 1.20" (Taylor), **IV:** 165

"Meditation 2.68A" (Taylor), **IV:** 165

"Meditation 2.102" (Taylor), **IV:** 150

"Meditation 2.112" (Taylor), **IV:** 165

"Meditation 20" (Taylor), **IV:** 154–155

"Meditation 40" (Second Series) (Taylor), **IV:** 147

"Meditation at Lagunitas" (Hass), **Supp. VI:** 104–105; **Supp. XXI:** 60

"Meditation at Oyster River" (Roethke), **III:** 537, 549

Meditations (Descartes), **III:** 618

Meditations (Marcus Aurelius), **Supp. XVIII:** 304

"Meditations for a Savage Child" (Rich), **Supp. I Part 2:** 564–565

Meditations from a Movable Chair (Dubus), **Supp. VII:** 91

"Meditations in a Swine Yard" (Komunyakaa), **Supp. XIII:** 131

"Meditations of an Old Woman" (Roethke), **III:** 529, 540, 542, 543, 545–547, 548

Meditations on the Insatiable Soul (R. Bly), **Supp. IV Part 1:** 72–73

Meditative Poems, The (Martz), **IV:** 151

"Mediterranean, The" (Tate), **IV:** 129

"Medium of Fiction, The" (Gass), **Supp. VI:** 85–86

"Medley" (Bambara), **Supp. XI:** 9

"Medusa" (Bogan), **Supp. III Part 1:** 50, 51

Meehan, Jeannette Porter, **Supp. XX:** 213, 214, 217, 220, 224

Meehan, Thomas, **Supp. IV Part 2:** 577–578, 586, 590

Meek, Martha, **Supp. IV Part 2:** 439, 440, 441, 442, 445, 447, 448

Meeker, Richard K., **II:** 190

Meese, Elizabeth, **Supp. XIII:** 297

"Meeting" (J. W. Miller), **Supp. XX:** 167

"Meeting, The" (F. Wright), **Supp. XVII:** 245

"Meeting and Greeting Area, The" (Cameron), **Supp. XII: 84–85**

Meeting by the River, A (Isherwood), **Supp. XIV:** 164, **170–171,** 172

"Meeting-House Hill" (Lowell), **II:** 522, 527

"Meeting in the Kitchen, The" (Schnackenberg), **Supp. XV:** 256

"Meeting South, A" (Anderson), **I:** 115

"Meeting the Mountains" (Snyder), **Supp. VIII:** 300

Meeting Trees (Sanders), **Supp. XVI:** 269

Meet Me at the Morgue (Macdonald), **Supp. IV Part 2:** 472

Mehta, Sonny, **Supp. XI:** 178

Mehta, Ved, **Supp. XX:** 87

Meine, Curt, **Supp. XIV:** 179

Meiners, R. K., **IV:** 136, 137, 138, 140

Meinong, Alexius, **Supp. XIV:** 198, 199

Meisner, Sanford, **Supp. XIV:** 240, 242

Meister, Charles W., **II:** 112

Mejia, Jaime, **Supp. XIX:** 97

"Melancholia" (Dunbar), **Supp. II Part 1:** 194

Melancholy Baby (Parker), **Supp. XIX:** 186

"Melanctha" (Stein), **IV:** 30, 34, 35, 37, 38–40, 45

"Melancthon" (Moore), **III:** 212, 215

Melbourne House (S. and A. Warner), **Supp. XVIII:** 268

Meliboeus Hipponax (Lowell). *See Bigelow Papers, The* (Lowell)

Melinda and Melinda (Allen), **Supp. XV:** 16

Mellaart, James, **Supp. I Part 2:** 567

Mellard, James, **Supp. IV Part 1:** 387

Mellon, Andrew, **III:** 14

Mellor, W. M., **Supp. XX:** 56

Melnick, Jeffrey, **Supp. X:** 252

Melnyczuk, Askold, **Supp. IV Part 1:** 70

Melodrama Play (Shepard), **Supp. III Part 2:** 440–441, 443, 445

Melodramatists, The (Nemerov), **III:** 268, 281–283, 284

Melopoeia (Espaillat and Tavano), **Supp. XXI:** 99–100

Melting-Pot, The (Zangwill), **I:** 229

"Melungeons" (Offutt), **Supp. XIX:** 171

Melville, Allan, **III:** 74, 77

Melville, Gansevoort, **III:** 76

Melville, Herman, **I:** 104, 106, 211, 288, 340, 343, 348, 354, 355, 561–562; **II:** 27, 74, 224–225, 228, 230, 232, 236, 255, 259, 271, 272, 277, 281, 295, 307, 311, 319, 320, 321, 418, 477, 497, 539–540, 545; **III:** 29, 45, 70, **74–98,** 359, 438, 453, 454, 507, 562–563, 572, 576; **IV:** 57, 105, 194, 199, 202, 250, 309, 333, 345, 350, 380, 444, 453; **Retro. Supp. I:** 54, 91, 160, 215, 220, **243–262; Retro. Supp. II:** 76; **Supp. I Part 1:** 147, 238, 242, 249, 309, 317, 372; **Supp. I Part 2:** 383, 495, 579, 580, 582, 602; **Supp. IV Part 2:** 463, 613; **Supp. V:** 279, 281, 298, 308; **Supp. VIII:** 48, 103, 104, 105, 106, 108, 156, 175, 181, 188; **Supp. XI:** 83; **Supp. XII:** 282; **Supp. XIII:** 294, 305; **Supp. XIV:** 48, 227; **Supp. XV:** 287; **Supp. XVII:** 42, 185; **Supp. XVIII:** 1, 4, 6, 7, 9; **Supp. XXI:** 169

Melville, Mrs. Herman (Elizabeth Shaw), **III:** 77, 91, 92

Melville, Maria Gansevoort, **III:** 74, 77, 85

Melville, Thomas, **III:** 77, 79, 92; **Supp. I Part 1:** 309

Melville, Whyte, **IV:** 309

Melville Goodwin, USA (Marquand), **III:** 60, 65–66

Melville's Marginalia (Cowen), **Supp. IV Part 2:** 435

"Melville's Marginalia" (Howe), **Supp. IV Part 2:** 435

Member of the Wedding, The (McCullers), **II:** 587, 592, 600–604, 605, 606; **Supp. VIII:** 124

"Meme Ortiz" (Cisneros), **Supp. VII:** 60

Memnon (song cycle) (Bowles), **Supp. IV Part 1:** 82

Memnoch the Devil (Rice), **Supp. VII:** 289, 290, 294, 296–299

"Memoir" (Hempel), **Supp. XXI:** 118

"Memoir" (Untermeyer), **II:** 516–517

"Memoir, A" (Koch), **Supp. XV:** 184

"Memoirist's Apology, A" (Karr), **Supp. XI:** 245, 246

Memoir of Mary Ann, A (O'Connor), **III:** 357

Memoir of Thomas McGrath, A (Beeching), **Supp. X:** 114, 118

Memoirs (W. Frank), **Supp. XX:**67, 69, 70, 81

Memoirs of Arii Taimai (Adams), **I:** 2–3

"Memoirs of Carwin, the Biloquist" (Brown), **Supp. I Part 1:** 132

Memoirs of Hecate County (Wilson), **IV:** 429

Memoirs of Margaret Fuller Ossoli (Fuller), **Supp. II Part 1:** 280, 283, 285

"Memoirs of Stephen Calvert" (Brown), **Supp. I Part 1:** 133, 144

Memorabilia (Xenophon), **II:** 105

Memorable Providences (Mather), **Supp. II Part 2:** 458

Memorial, The: Portrait of a Family (Isherwood), **Supp. XIV:** 156, 159, 160–161

"Memorial Day" (Cameron), **Supp. XII:** 80, **82–83**

"Memorial for the City" (Auden), **Supp. II Part 1:** 20

"Memorial Rain" (MacLeish), **III:** 15

"Memorial to Ed Bland" (Brooks), **Supp. III Part 1:** 77

"Memorial Tribute" (Wilbur), **Supp. IV Part 2:** 642

"Memories" (Whittier), **Supp. I Part 2:** 699

Memories of a Catholic Girlhood (McCarthy), **II:** 560–561, 566; **Supp. XI:** 246; **Supp. XVI:** 64, 70

"Memories of East Texas" (Karr), **Supp. XI:** 239

"Memories of Uncle Neddy" (Bishop), **Retro. Supp. II:** 38; **Supp. I Part 1:** 73, 93

"Memories of West Street and Lepke" (Lowell), **II:** 550

"Memory" (Epstein), **Supp. XII:** 163

"Memory" (Everwine), **Supp. XV:** 82

"Memory, A" (Welty), **IV:** 261–262; **Retro. Supp. I:** 344–345

"Memory, The" (Gioia), **Supp. XV:** 119

Memory and Enthusiasm: Essays, 1975– 1985 (Di Piero), **Supp. XIX:** 34, 41, 42

Memory Gardens (Creeley), **Supp. IV Part 1:** 141, 157

"Memory Harbor" (Skloot), **Supp. XX:**201

Memory of Murder, A (Bradbury), **Supp. IV Part 1:** 103

Memory of Old Jack, The (Berry), **Supp. X:** 34

Memory of Two Mondays, A (A. Miller), **III:** 153, 156, 158–159, 160, 166

"Memo to Non-White Peoples" (Hughes), **Retro. Supp. I:** 209

Men, Women and Ghosts (Lowell), **II:** 523–524

Menaker, Charlotte, **Supp. XIX:** 266

Menaker, Daniel, **Supp. VIII:** 151

Menand, Louis, **Supp. XIV:** 40, 197; **Supp. XVI:** 106, 107

Men and Angels (Gordon), **Supp. IV Part 1:** 304–305, 306, 308

Men and Brethen (Cozzens), **I:** 363–365, 368, 375, 378, 379

Men and Cartoons (Lethem), **Supp. XVIII:** 145, **148**

"Men and Women" (R. Bly), **Supp. IV Part 1:** 72

"Men at Forty" (Justice), **Supp. VII:** 126–127

Mencius (Meng-tzu), **IV:** 183

Mencken, August, **III:** 100, 108

Mencken, August, Jr., **III:** 99, 109, 118– 119

Mencken, Mrs. August (Anna Abhau), **III:** 100, 109

Mencken, Burkhardt, **III:** 100, 108

Mencken, Charles, **III:** 99

Mencken, Gertrude, **III:** 99

Mencken, H. L., **I:** 199, 210, 212, 235, 245, 261, 405, 514, 515, 517; **II:** 25, 27, 42, 89, 90, 91, 271, 289, 430, 443, 449; **III:** **99–121,** 394, 482; **IV:** 76, 432, 440, 475, 482; **Retro. Supp. I:** 1, 101; **Retro. Supp. II:** 97, 98, 102, 265; **Supp. I Part 2:** 484, 629–630, 631, 647, 651, 653, 659, 673; **Supp. II Part 1:** 136; **Supp. IV Part 1:** 201, 314, 343; **Supp. IV Part 2:** 521, 692, 693; **Supp. XI:** 163–164, 166; **Supp. XIII:** 161; **Supp. XIV:** 111; **Supp. XV:** 297, 301, 303; **Supp. XVI:** 187– 188, 189; **Supp. XVIII:** 106

Mencken, Mrs. H. L. (Sara Haardt), **III:** 109, 111

"Men Deified Because of Their Cruelty" (Simic), **Supp. VIII:** 282

Mendelbaum, Paul, **Supp. V:** 159

Mendele, **IV:** 3, 10

Mendelief, Dmitri Ivanovich, **IV:** 421

Mendelsohn, Daniel, **Supp. X:** 153, 154; **Supp. XV:** 257, 258, 261, 266

Mendes, Alfred, **Supp. XXI:** 160

"Mending Wall" (Frost), **II:** 153–154; **Retro. Supp. I:** 128, 130; **Supp. X:** 64

Men from the Boys, The (Lacy), **Supp. XV:** 202, 205

Men in the Off Hours (Carson), **Supp. XII:** **111–113**

"Men in the Storm, The" (Crane), **I:** 411

"Men Loved Wholly Beyond Wisdom" (Bogan), **Supp. III Part 1:** 50

"Men Made Out of Words" (Stevens), **IV:** 88

Men Must Act (Mumford), **Supp. II Part 2:** 479

Mennes, John, **II:** 111

Mennoti, Gian Carlo, **Supp. IV Part 1:** 84

Men of Brewster Place, The (Naylor), **Supp. VIII:** 213, **228–230**

"Men of Color, to Arms!" (Douglass), **Supp. III Part 1:** 171

Men of Good Hope: A Story of American Progressives (Aaron), **Supp. I Part 2:** 650

Mens' Club, The (film), **Supp. XVI:** 212– 213

Men's Club, The (L. Michaels), **Supp. XVI:** 206, **210–212**

"Menstruation at Forty" (Sexton), **Supp. II Part 2:** 686

"Mental Hospital Garden, The" (W. C. Williams), **Retro. Supp. I:** 428

Mental Radio (Sinclair), **Supp. V:** 289

Mentoria; or, The Young Lady's Friend (Rowson), **Supp. XV:** **233–234,** 238

"Men We Carry in Our Minds, The" (Sanders), **Supp. XVI:** 273

Men Who Made the Nation, The (Dos Passos), **I:** 485

Men Without Women (Hemingway), **II:** 249; **Retro. Supp. I:** 170, 176; **Supp. IX:** 202

"Merced" (Rich), **Supp. I Part 2:** 563

"Mercedes" (E. Stoddard), **Supp. XV:** 278

"Mercedes Hospital" (Bishop), **Retro. Supp. II:** 51

"Mercenary, A" (Ozick), **Supp. V:** 267

Merchandising (Hwang), **Supp. XXI:** 147

Merchant of Venice, The (Shakespeare), **IV:** 227; **Supp. XIV:** 325

Mercury Theatre, **Retro. Supp. I:** 65

Mercy, Pity, Peace, and Love (Ozick), **Supp. V:** 257, 258

Mercy, The (Levine), **Supp. V:** 194–195

Mercy of a Rude Stream (H. Roth), **Supp. IX:** 231, 234, **235–242**

Mercy Philbrick's Choice (Jackson), **Retro. Supp. I:** 26, 27, 33

Mercy Street (Sexton), **Supp. II Part 2:** 683, 689

Meredith, George, **II:** 175, 186; **Supp. IV Part 1:** 300

Meredith, Mary. *See* Webb, Mary

Meredith, William, **II:** 545; **Retro. Supp. II:** 181

"Merely by Wilderness" (Peacock), **Supp. XIX:** 199

"Merely to Know" (Rich), **Supp. I Part 2:** 554

"Mère Pochette" (Jewett), **II:** 400

"Merger II, The" (Auchincloss), **Supp. IV Part 1:** 34

"Mericans" (Cisneros), **Supp. VII:** 69

"Merida, 1969" (Matthews), **Supp. IX:** 151

"Meridian" (Clampitt), **Supp. IX:** **48–49**

Meridian (Walker), **Supp. III Part 2:** 520, 524, 527, 528, 531–537

Mérimée, Prosper, **II:** 322

Meriwether, James B., **Retro Supp. I:** 77, 91

"Meriwether Connection, The" (Cowley), **Supp. II Part 1:** 142

Merker, Kim K., **Supp. XI:** 261; **Supp. XV:** 75, 77

"Merlin" (Emerson), **II:** 19, 20

Merlin (Robinson), **III:** 522

"Merlin Enthralled" (Wilbur), **Supp. III Part 2:** 544, 554

"Mermother" (A. Finch), **Supp. XVII:** 72

Merril, Judith, **Supp. XVI:** 123

Merrill, Christopher, **Supp. XI:** 329

Merrill, James, **Retro. Supp. I:** 296; **Retro. Supp. II:** 53; **Supp. III Part 1:** 317–338; **Supp. III Part 2:** 541, 561; **Supp. IX:** 40, 42, 48, 52; **Supp. X:** 73; **Supp. XI:** 123, 131, 249; **Supp. XII:** 44, 254, 255, 256, 261–262, 269–270; **Supp. XIII:** 76, 85; **Supp. XV:** 249, 250, 253; **Supp. XVII:** 123

Merrill, Mark (pseudonym). *See* Markson, David

Merrill, Robert, **Retro. Supp. II:** 201

Merrill, Ronald, **Supp. IV Part 2:** 521

Merritt, Abraham, **Supp. XVII:** 58

Merritt, Theresa, **Supp. VIII:** 332

"Merry-Go-Round" (Hughes), **Retro. Supp. I:** 194, 205; **Supp. I Part 1:** 333

Merry-Go-Round, The (Van Vechten), **Supp. II Part 2:** 734, 735

Merry Month of May, The (Jones), **Supp. XI:** 227–228

Merry Widow, The (Lehar), **III:** 183

Merton, Thomas, **III:** 357; **Supp. VIII:** 193–212

Merwin, W. S., **Supp. III Part 1:** 339–360; **Supp. III Part 2:** 541; **Supp. IV Part 2:** 620, 623, 626; **Supp. V:** 332; **Supp. IX:** 152, 155, 290; **Supp. XIII:** 274, 277; **Supp. XV:** 222, 342; **Supp. XIX:** 82; **Supp. XXI:** 95

Meryman, Richard, **Supp. IV Part 2:** 579, 583

Meshugah (Singer), **Retro. Supp. II:** 315–316

Mesic, Michael, **Supp. IV Part 1:** 175

Mesic, Penelope, **Supp. X:** 15

Message in the Bottle, The (Percy), **Supp. III Part 1:** 387–388, 393, 397

"Message in the Bottle, The" (Percy), **Supp. III Part 1:** 388

"Message of Flowers and Fire and Flowers, The" (Brooks), **Supp. III Part 1:** 69

Messengers Will Come No More, The (Fiedler), **Supp. XIII:** 103

Messerli, Douglas, **Supp. XVI:** 293

Messiah (Vidal), **Supp. IV Part 2:** 677, 680, 681–682, 685, 691, 692

"Messiah, The" (Wasserstein), **Supp. XV:** 328

Messiah of Stockholm, The (Ozick), **Supp. V:** 270–271; **Supp. XVII:** 42

Messud, Claire, **Supp. XVIII:** 98

Metamorphic Tradition in Modern Poetry (Quinn), **IV:** 421

Metamorphoses (Ovid), **II:** 542–543; **III:** 467, 468; **Supp. XV:** 33; **Supp. XVI:** 20; **Supp. XX:** 280

Metamorphoses (Pound, trans.), **III:** 468–469

Metamorphosis (Kafka), **Supp. XXI:** 89

Metamorphosis, The (Kafka), **IV:** 438; **Retro. Supp. II:** 287–288; **Supp. VIII:** 3

"Metamorphosis and Survival" (Woodcock), **Supp. XIII:** 33

"Metaphor as Mistake" (Percy), **Supp. III Part 1:** 387–388

Metaphor & Memory: Essays (Ozick), **Supp. V:** 272

Metaphor of Trees and Last Poems (Bronk), **Supp. XXI:** 32

"Metaphors of a Magnifico" (Stevens), **IV:** 92

Metaphysical Club, The (Menand), **Supp. XIV:** 40, 197

"Metaphysical Poets, The" (Eliot), **I:** 527, 586

"Metaphysics" (Ginsberg), **Supp. II Part 1:** 313

Metcalf, Paul, **Supp. XIV:** 96

"Meteor, The" (Bradbury), **Supp. IV Part 1:** 102

Methinks the Lady...(Endore), **Supp. XVII:** 61–62

"Metonymy as an Approach to the Real World" (Bronk), **Supp. XXI:** 30

Metress, Christopher P., **Supp. V:** 314

Metrical History of Christianity, The (Taylor), **IV:** 163

Metropolis, The (Sinclair), **Supp. V:** 285

"Metterling Lists, The" (Allen), **Supp. XV:** 15

"Metzengerstein" (Poe), **III:** 411, 417

Mew, Charlotte, **Retro. Supp. II:** 247

Mewshaw, Michael, **Supp. V:** 57; **Supp. X:** 82

"Mexican Hands" (Ryan as Quin), **Supp. XVIII:** 227

"Mexico" (Lowell), **II:** 553, 554

"Mexico, Age Four" (Salinas), **Supp. XIII:** 315

Mexico City Blues (Kerouac), **Supp. III Part 1:** 225, 229

"Mexico Is a Foreign Country: Five Studies in Naturalism" (Warren), **IV:** 241, 252

"Mexico's Children" (Rodriguez), **Supp. XIV:** 302

Meyer, Carolyn, **Supp. XIX:** 194–195, 197

Meyer, Donald B., **III:** 298

Meyer, Ellen Hope, **Supp. V:** 123

Meyer, Robert, **Supp. XXI:** 23

Meyers, Jeffrey, **Retro. Supp. I:** 124, 138; **Retro. Supp. II:** 191

Meynell, Alice, **Supp. I Part 1:** 220

Mezey, Robert, **Supp. IV Part 1:** 60; **Supp. V:** 180; **Supp. XIII:** 312; **Supp. XV:** 74

Mezzanine, The (Baker), **Supp. XIII:** 41–43, 44, 45, 48, 55

"Mezzo Cammin" (Longfellow), **II:** 490

"Mi Abuelo" (Ríos), **Supp. IV Part 2:** 541

Miami (Didion), **Supp. IV Part 1:** 199, 210

Miami and the Siege of Chicago (Mailer), **Retro. Supp. II:** 206

"Michael" (Wordsworth), **III:** 523

Michael, Magali Cornier, **Supp. XIII:** 32

"Michael Angelo: A Fragment" (Longfellow), **II:** 490, 494, 495, 506; **Retro. Supp. II:** 167

"Michael Egerton" (Price), **Supp. VI:** 257–258, 260

Michael Kohlhaas (Kleist), **Supp. IV Part 1:** 224

Michael O'Halloran (Stratton-Porter), **Supp. XX:** 222

Michaels, Leonard, **Supp. XVI:** 201–215

Michaels, Walter Benn, **Retro. Supp. I:** 115, 369, 379

Michael Scarlett (Cozens), **I:** 358–359, 378

"Michael's Veterans Remember" (Espaillat), **Supp. XXI:** 110

Michaux, Henri, **Supp. XVI:** 288

Michelangelo, **I:** 18; **II:** 11–12; **III:** 124; **Supp. I Part 1:** 363; **Supp. XVII:** 112

Michel-Michot, Paulette, **Supp. XI:** 224–225

Michelson, Albert, **IV:** 27

Mickelsson's Ghosts (Gardner), **Supp. VI:** 63, 73–74

Mickiewicz, Adam, **Supp. II Part 1:** 299

"Microscope" (Trethewey), **Supp. XXI:** 251

Midair (Conroy), **Supp. XVI:** 63, 71–72

"Mid-Air" (Conroy), **Supp. XVI:** 69, 71

Mid-American Chants (Anderson), **I:** 109, 114

"Midas" (Winters), **Supp. II Part 2:** 801

"Mid-August at Sourdough Mountain Lookout" (Snyder), **Supp. VIII:** 292–293

Midcentury (Dos Passos), **I:** 474, 475, 478, 490, 492–494; **Supp. I Part 2:** 646

Mid-Century American Poets, **III:** 532

"Mid-Day" (Doolittle), **Supp. I Part 1:** 266–267

"Middle Age" (Lowell), **II:** 550

"Middleaged Man, The" (Simpson), **Supp. IX:** 274–275

Middle Ages, The (Gurney), **Supp. V:** 96, 105, 108

Middlebrook, Diane Wood, **Supp. IV Part 2:** 444, 451

"Middle Daughter, The" (Kingsolver), **Supp. VII:** 209

Middlemarch (G. Eliot), **I:** 457, 459; **II:** 290, 291; **Retro. Supp. I:** 225; **Supp. I Part 1:** 174; **Supp. IX:** 43; **Supp. XI:** 68; **Supp. XII:** 335

Middle of My Tether, The: Familiar Essays (Epstein), **Supp. XIV:** 106–107

"Middle of Nowhere, The" (Wagoner), **Supp. IX:** 327–328

Middle of the Journey, The (Trilling), **Supp. III Part 2:** 495, 504–506

"Middle of the Way" (Kinnell), **Supp. III Part 1:** 242

"Middle Passage" (Hayden), **Supp. II Part 1:** 363, 375–376

Middle Passage (Johnson), **Supp. VI:** 194–196, 198, 199; **Supp. XIII:** 182

"Middle Toe of the Right Foot, The" (Bierce), **I:** 203

Middleton, Thomas, **Retro. Supp. I:** 62

Middle Years, The (James), **II:** 337–338; **Retro. Supp. I:** 235

"Middle Years, The" (James), **Retro. Supp. I:** 228, 272

"Midnight" (Dunn), **Supp. XI:** 147

"Midnight Consultations, The" (Freneau), **Supp. II Part 1:** 257

Midnight Cry, A (Mather), **Supp. II Part 2:** 460

"Midnight Gladness" (Levertov), **Supp. III Part 1:** 284–285

"Midnight Magic" (Mason), **Supp. VIII:** 146

Midnight Magic: Selected Stories of Bobbie Ann Mason (Mason), **Supp. VIII:** 148

Midnight Mass (Bowles), **Supp. IV Part 1:** 93

"Midnight Postscript" (F. Wright), **Supp. XVII:** 245, 246

"Midnight Show" (Shapiro), **Supp. II Part 2:** 705

"Midpoint" (Updike), **Retro. Supp. I:** 321, 323, 327, 330, 335

Midpoint and Other Poems (Updike), **IV:** 214

"Midrash on Happiness" (Paley), **Supp. VI:** 217

"Midsummer" (Bronk), **Supp. XXI:** 30

"Midsummer in the Blueberry Barrens" (Clampitt), **Supp. IX:** 40–41

"Midsummer Letter" (Carruth), **Supp. XVI:** 47

Midsummer Night's Dream, A (Shakespeare), **Supp. I Part 1:** 369–370; **Supp. X:** 69

Midsummer Night's Sex Comedy, A (film; Allen), **Supp. XV:** 8

"Midwest" (Stafford), **Supp. XI:** 317

"Midwest Poetics" (C. Baxter), **Supp. XVII:** 18

Mieder, Wolfgang, **Supp. XIV:** 126

Mies van der Rohe, Ludwig, **Supp. IV Part 1:** 40

Mighty Aphrodite (film; Allen), **Supp. XV:** 11

"Mighty Fortress, A" (Leopold), **Supp. XIV:** 185

"Mighty Lord, The (Rowson), **Supp. XV:** 243

"Migration, The" (Tate), **IV:** 130

Mihailovitch, Bata, **Supp. VIII:** 272

Mikado, The (Gilbert and Sullivan), **Supp. XXI:** 151

Miklitsch, Robert, **Supp. IV Part 2:** 628, 629

Mila 18 (Uris), **Supp. IV Part 1:** 379; **Supp. XX:** 244, 247, 248, **251–252,** 253

Milagro Beanfield War, The (film), **Supp. XIII:** 267

Milagro Beanfield War, The (Nichols), **Supp. XIII:** 253, **265–266**

Milburn, Michael, **Supp. XI:** 239, 242

Milch, David, **Supp. XI:** 348

Mild Day, The (Bronk), **Supp. XXI:** 32

Miles, Barry, **Supp. XII:** 123

Miles, Jack, **Supp. VIII:** 86

Miles, Josephine, **Supp. XIII:** 275

Miles, Julie, **I:** 199

Miles, Kitty, **I:** 199

"Miles of Night, The" (Halliday), **Supp. XIX:** 91

Milestone, Lewis, **Supp. I Part 1:** 281

Miles Wallingford (Cooper). *See Afloat and Ashore* (Cooper)

Milford, Kate, **Supp. XVIII:** 150

Milford, Nancy, **II:** 83; **Supp. IX:** 60

Milhaud, Darius, **Supp. IV Part 1:** 81

Miligate, Michael, **IV:** 123, 130, 132

"Militant Nudes" (Hardwick), **Supp. III Part 1:** 210–211

Milk (film), **Supp. XX:** 269

"Milk Bottles" (Anderson), **I:** 114

"Milk Prose" (Weigl), **Supp. XIX:** 278

Milk Train Doesn't Stop Here Anymore, The (T. Williams), **IV:** 382, 383, 384, 386, 390, 391, 392, 393, 394, 395, 398

Mill, James, **II:** 357

Mill, John Stuart, **III:** 294–295; **Supp. XI:** 196; **Supp. XIV:** 22

Millar, Kenneth. *See* Macdonald, Ross

Millar, Margaret (Margaret Sturm), **Supp. IV Part 2:** 464, 465

Millay, Cora, **III:** 123, 133–134, 135–136

Millay, Edna St. Vincent, **I:** 482; **II:** 530; **III: 122–144; IV:** 433, 436; **Retro. Supp. II:** 48; **Supp. I Part 2:** 707, 714, 726; **Supp. IV Part 1:** 168; **Supp. IV Part 2:** 607; **Supp. V:** 113; **Supp. IX:** 20; **Supp. XIV:** 120, 121, 122, 127; **Supp. XV:** 42, 46, 51, 250, 293, 307; **Supp. XVII:** 69, 75, 96

Millennium Approaches (Kushner), **Supp. IX:** 141, 142, 145

Miller, Arthur, **I:** 81, 94; **III: 145–169; Supp. IV Part 1:** 359; **Supp. IV Part 2:** 574; **Supp. VIII:** 334; **Supp. XIII:** 127; **Supp. XIV:** 102, 239; **Supp. XVI:** 194

Miller, Mrs. Arthur (Ingeborg Morath), **III:** 162–163

Miller, Mrs. Arthur (Marilyn Monroe), **III:** 161, 162–163

Miller, Mrs. Arthur (Mary Grace Slattery), **III:** 146, 161

Miller, Brown, **Supp. IV Part 1:** 67

Miller, Carol, **Supp. IV Part 1:** 400, 405, 409, 410, 411

Miller, Henry, **I:** 97, 157; **III:** 40, **170–192; IV:** 138; **Retro. Supp. II:** 327; **Supp. I Part 2:** 546; **Supp. V:** 119, 131; **Supp. X:** 183, 185, 187, 194, 195; **Supp. XIII:** 1, 17

Miller, Henry (actor), **Supp. XVI:** 182

Miller, Herman, **Supp. I Part 2:** 614, 617

Miller, James E., Jr., **IV:** 352

Miller, Jeffrey, **Supp. IV Part 1:** 95

Miller, J. Hillis, **Supp. IV Part 1:** 387

Miller, Jim Wayne, **Supp. XX: 161–176**

Miller, Joaquin, **I:** 193, 195, 459; **Supp. II Part 1:** 351

Miller, John Duncan, **Supp. I Part 2:** 604

Miller, Jonathan, **Retro. Supp. II:** 181

Miller, Laura, **Supp. XIII:** 48; **Supp. XIX:** 53, 54, 56

Miller, Marilyn, **Supp. XVI:** 187

Miller, Matt, **Supp. XV:** 211

Miller, Matthew, **Supp. XVI:** 47, 51

Miller, Orilla, **Supp. I Part 1:** 48

Miller, Perry, **I:** 546, 547, 549, 550, 560; **IV:** 186; **Supp. I Part 1:** 31, 104; **Supp. I Part 2:** 484; **Supp. IV Part 2:** 422; **Supp. VIII:** 101

Miller, R. Baxter, **Retro. Supp. I:** 195, 207

Miller, Robert Ellis, **II:** 588

Miller, Ruth, **Supp. X:** 324

Miller, Stuart, **Supp. XVI:** 242

Miller, Sue, **Supp. X:** 77, 85; **Supp. XI:** 190; **Supp. XII: 289–305**

Miller of Old Church, The (Glasgow), **II:** 175, 181

"Miller's Tale" (Chaucer), **III:** 283

Miller Williams and the Poetry of the Particular (Burns), **Supp. XV:** 339

Millett, Kate, **Supp. X:** 193, 196

Millgate, Michael, **Retro. Supp. I:** 91

Mill Hand's Lunch Bucket (Bearden), **Supp. VIII:** 337

Millier, Brett C., **Retro. Supp. II:** 39

Milligan, Bryce, **Supp. XIII:** 274, 275, 277

Millions of Strange Shadows (Hecht), **Supp. X:** 57, **62–65**

"Million Young Workmen, 1915, A" (Sandburg), **III:** 585

Millroy the Magician (Theroux), **Supp. VIII:** 325

Mills, Alice, **Supp. XIII:** 233

Mills, Benjamin Fay, **III:** 176

Mills, C. Wright, **Supp. I Part 2:** 648, 650

Mills, Florence, **Supp. I Part 1:** 322

Mills, Ralph J., Jr., **III:** 530; **Supp. IV Part 1:** 64; **Supp. XI:** 311

Mills, Tedi López, **Supp. XVI:** 281

Mills of the Kavanaughs, The (Lowell), **II:** 542–543, 546, 550; **III:** 508; **Retro. Supp. II:** 178, 179, 188

"Mills of the Kavanaughs, The" (Lowell), **II:** 542–543

Milne, A. A., **Supp. IX:** 189

Milne, A. J. M., **I:** 278

Milosz, Czeslaw, **Supp. III Part 2:** 630; **Supp. VIII:** 20, 22; **Supp. XI:** 267, 312; **Supp. XVII:** 241; **Supp. XX:** 165; **Supp. XXI:** 132

Miltner, Robert, **Supp. XI:** 142

Milton, Edith, **Supp. VIII:** 79; **Supp. X:** 82

Milton, John, **I:** 6, 138, 273, 587–588; **II:** 11, 15, 113, 130, 411, 540, 542; **III:** 40, 124, 201, 225, 274, 468, 471, 486, 487, 503, 511; **IV:** 50, 82, 126, 137, 155, 157, 241, 279, 347, 422, 461, 494; **Retro. Supp. I:** 60, 67, 127, 360; **Retro. Supp. II:** 161, 295; **Supp. I Part 1:** 124, 150, 370; **Supp. I Part 2:** 412, 422, 491, 501, 522, 622, 722, 724; **Supp. IV Part 2:** 430, 634; **Supp. VIII:** 294; **Supp. X:** 22, 23, 36; **Supp. XII:** 180; **Supp. XIV:** 5, 7; **Supp. XX:** 108

Milton, John R., **Supp. IV Part 2:** 503

Milton and His Modern Critics (L. P. Smith), **Supp. XIV:** 347

"Milton by Firelight" (Snyder), **Supp. II Part 1:** 314; **Supp. VIII:** 294

"Miltonic Sonnet, A" (Wilbur), **Supp. III Part 2:** 558

Mimesis (Auerbach), **III:** 453

"Mimnermos and the Motions of Hedonism" (Carson), **Supp. XII: 99–100**

"Mimnermos Interviews, The" (Carson), **Supp. XII: 100–101**

Mims, Edwin, **Supp. I Part 1:** 362, 364, 365, 371

"Mind" (Wilbur), **Supp. III Part 2:** 554

"Mind, The" (Kinnell), **Supp. III Part 1:** 245

Mind Breaths: Poems 1972–1977 (Ginsberg), **Supp. II Part 1:** 326

Mindfield: New and Selected Poems (Corso), **Supp. XII: 136**

"Mind in the Modern World" (Trilling), **Supp. III Part 2:** 512

"Mind Is Shapely, Art Is Shapely" (Ginsberg), **Supp. II Part 1:** 327

Mindlin, Henrique, **Supp. I Part 1:** 92

Mind of My Mind (O. Butler), **Supp. XIII:** 62, 63

Mind of Primitive Man, The (Boas), **Supp. XIV:** 209

Mind-Reader, The (Wilbur), **Supp. III Part 2:** 560–562

"Mind-Reader, The" (Wilbur), **Supp. III Part 2:** 561–562

"Mind's Landscape on an Early Winter Day, The" (Bronk), **Supp. XXI:** 28

Mindwheel (Pinsky), **Supp. VI:** 235

Minear, Richard H., **Supp. XVI:** 101, 102

"Mined Country" (Wilbur), **Supp. III Part 2:** 546–548

"Minefields" (Espaillat), **Supp. XXI:** 106

"Mine Own John Berryman" (Levine), **Supp. V:** 179–180

Miner, Bob, **Supp. V:** 23

Miner, Earl, **III:** 466, 479

Miner, Madonne, **Supp. XIII:** 29

"Minerva Writes Poems" (Cisneros), **Supp. VII:** 63–64, 66

Mingus, Charles, **Supp. IX:** 152

"Mingus in Diaspora" (Matthews), **Supp. IX:** 166

"Mingus in Shadow" (Matthews), **Supp. IX:** 168–169

Ming Yellow (Marquand), **III:** 56

"Minimal, The" (Roethke), **III:** 531–532

Minimus Poems, The (X. J. Kennedy), **Supp. XV:** 169–170

"Mini-novela: *Rosa y sus espinas*" (Mora), *Supp. XIII:* 218

"Minions of Midas, The" (London), **II:** 474–475

Minister's Charge, The, or The Apprenticeship of Lemuel Barber (Howells), **II:** 285–286, 287

Minister's Wooing, The (Stowe), **II:** 541

"Minister's Wooing, The" (Stowe), **Supp. I Part 2:** 592–595

"Ministration of Our Departed Friends, The" (Stowe), **Supp. I Part 2:** 586–587

"Minneapolis Poem, The" (Wright), **Supp. III Part 2:** 601–602

Minnesota Grain Show, The (radio, Keillor), **Supp. XVI:** 170

"Minnesota Transcendentalist" (Peseroff), **Supp. IV Part 1:** 71

Minnie, Temple, **II:** 344

Minority Report: H. L. Mencken's Notebooks (Mencken), **III:** 112

Minor Pleasures of Life, The (Macaulay), **Supp. XIV:** 348

"Minor Poems" (Eliot), **I:** 579

"Minor Poet" (Hay), **Supp. XIV:** 127

"Minor Topics" (Howells), **II:** 274

Minot, Susan, **Supp. VI: 203–215**

"Minotaur Loves His Labyrinth, The" (Simic), **Supp. VIII:** 270, 279, 281

"Minstrel Man" (Hughes), **Supp. I Part 1:** 325

Mint (Nye), **Supp. XIII:** 277

"Minting Time" (Sarton), **Supp. VIII:** 259

Mint Snowball (Nye), **Supp. XIII:** 277–278, **284–285**

"Mint Snowball" (Nye), **Supp. XIII:** 278, 284

"Mint Snowball II" (Nye), **Supp. XIII:** 284, 285

Minty Alley (C. L. R. James), **Supp. XXI:** 159, 161

Mintzlaff, Dorothy, **Supp. XV:** 153

Minus, Marian, **Supp. XVIII:** 282

Minutes to Go (Corso, Gysin, Beiles and Burroughs), **Supp. XII:** 129

Mi querido Rafa (Hinojosa). *See Dear Rafe* (Hinojosa)

Mirabell: Books of Number (Merrill), **Supp. III Part 1:** 332–334

"Miracle" (Carver), **Supp. III Part 1:** 139–140

Miracle at Verdun (Chlumberg), **Supp. XIX:** 242

"Miracle for Breakfast, A" (Bishop), **Retro. Supp. II:** 43

Miracle of Catfish, A (L. Brown), **Supp. XXI:** 39–40, 47, **48**

"Miracle of Lava Canyon, The" (Henry), **Supp. II Part 1:** 389, 390

Miracle of Mindfulness, The: A Manual on Meditation (Thich Nhat Hanh), **Supp. V:** 199–200

Mirage (Masters), **Supp. I Part 2:** 459, 470, 471

"Mirages, The" (Hayden), **Supp. II Part 1:** 373

"Miranda" (Buck), **Supp. II Part 1:** 128

Miranda, Carmen, **Supp. XII:** 165

Miranda, Francisco de, **Supp. I Part 2:** 522

"Miranda Over the Valley" (Dubus), **Supp. VII:** 81–83

"Miriam" (Capote), **Supp. III Part 1:** 117, 120, 122

"Miriam" (Whittier), **Supp. I Part 2:** 691, 703

"Miriam Tazewell" (Ransom), **Supp. X:** 58

"Mirror" (Merrill), **Supp. III Part 1:** 322

"Mirror" (Plath), **Retro. Supp. II:** 248–249, 257

"Mirror, The" (Glück), **Supp. V:** 83

"Mirroring Evil: Nazi Images/Recent Art" (Epstein), **Supp. XII:** 166

Mirrors (Creeley), **Supp. IV Part 1:** 156

Mirrors and Windows (Nemerov), **III:** 269, 275–277

"Mirrors of Chartres Street" (Faulkner), **II:** 56

Mirsky, Norman, **Supp. XX:** 244

Mirvis, Tova, **Supp. XX: 177–191**

Misanthrope, The (Molière; Wilbur, trans.), **Supp. III Part 2:** 552, 560

Miscellaneous Poems (Rowson), **Supp. XV:** 243

Miscellaneous Works of Mr. Philip Freneau, Containing His Essays and Additional Poems (Freneau), **Supp. II Part 1:** 263, 264, 266

Miscellany of American Poetry, A (Untermeyer, ed.), **Supp. XV:** 305, 310

Misérables, Les (Hugo), **II:** 179; **Supp. I Part 1:** 280

Misery (King), **Supp. V:** 140, 141, 142, 147–148, 151, 152

Mises, Ludwig von, **Supp. IV Part 2:** 524

Misfits, The (A. Miller), **III:** 147, 149, 156, 161–162, 163

"Misogamist, The" (Dubus), **Supp. VII:** 86–87

Misread City, The: New Literary Los Angeles (Gioia and Timberg, eds.), **Supp. XV:** 116

Misrepresentations Corrected, and Truth Vindicated, in a Reply to the Rev. Mr. Solomon Williams's Book (Edwards), **I:** 549

Miss Crandall's School for Young Ladies & Little Misses of Color (Nelson and Alexander), **Supp. XVIII:** 171, 175, 181, **185–186**

"Miss Cynthie" (R. Fisher), **Supp. XIX:** 65, 69

Miss Doll, Go Home (Markson), **Supp. XVII:** 138

"Miss Ella" (Z. Fitzgerald), **Supp. IX:** 57, 59, **71–72**

"Miss Emily and the Bibliographer" (Tate), **Supp. II Part 1:** 103

"Miss Furr and Miss Skeene" (Stein), **IV:** 29–30

"Missing Child" (Simic), **Supp. VIII:** 282

"Missing in Action" (Komunyakaa), **Supp. XIII:** 123, 124

Missing/Kissing: Missing Marisa, Kissing Christine (Shanley), **Supp. XIV:** 316

Missing Link (X. J. Kennedy), **Supp. XV:** 165

"Missing Poem, The" (Halliday), **Supp. XIX:** 93–94

"Mission of Jane, The" (Wharton), **Retro. Supp. I:** 367

"Missions, The" (Rodriguez), **Supp. XIV:** 303

Mission to Moscow (film), **Supp. I Part 1:** 281

"Mississippi" (Bass), **Supp. XVI:** 17

"Mississippi" (Faulkner), **Retro. Supp. I:** 77

"Mississippi" (Simpson), **Supp. IX:** 271

"Miss Kate in H-1" (Twain), **IV:** 193

Miss Leonora When Last Seen (Taylor), **Supp. V:** 323

Miss Lonelyhearts (West), **I:** 107; **II:** 436; **III:** 357; **IV:** 287, 288, 290–297, 300, 301, 305, 306; **Retro. Supp. II:** 321, 322, 325, 328, **332–335**

Miss Mamma Aimee (Caldwell), **I:** 308, 309, 310

"Miss Mary Pask" (Wharton), **IV:** 316; **Retro. Supp. I:** 382

"Miss McEnders" (Chopin), **Retro. Supp. II:** 67

"Missoula Softball Tournament" (Hugo), **Supp. VI:** 132

Miss Ravenel's Conversion from Secession to Loyalty (De Forest), **IV:** 350

Miss Saigon (musical), **Supp. XXI:** 155

"Miss Tempy's Watchers" (Jewett), **II:** 401; **Retro. Supp. II:** 139

"Miss Terriberry to Wed in Suburbs" (Updike), **Retro. Supp. I:** 335

"Miss Urquhart's Tiara" (Jarman), **Supp. XVII:** 116

"Mist, The" (King), **Supp. V:** 144

"Mistaken Charity, A" (Freeman), **Retro. Supp. II:** 138

"Mister Brother" (Cunningham), **Supp. XV:** 68

Misterioso (Sorrentino), **Supp. XXI:** 236, 237

"Mister Toussan" (Ellison), **Retro. Supp. II:** 124–125; **Supp. II Part 1:** 238

"Mistress of Sydenham Plantation, The" (Jewett), **Retro. Supp. II:** 141

Mitcham, Matthew, **Supp. XX:**264

Mitchell, Burroughs, **Supp. XI:** 218, 222, 227

Mitchell, Margaret, **II:** 177; **Supp. XX:**243

Mitchell, Roger, **Supp. IV Part 1:** 70; **Supp. XV:** 213, 215

Mitchell, Dr. S. Weir, **IV:** 310

Mitchell, Tennessee. *See* Anderson, Mrs. Sherwood (Tennessee Mitchell)

Mitchell, Verner, **Supp. XVIII:** 281, 286

Mitchell, Wesley C., **Supp. I Part 2:** 632, 643

Mitch Miller (Masters), **Supp. I Part 2:** 456, 466, 469–471, 474, 475, 476

Mitchum, Robert, **Supp. IX:** 95, 250

Mitgang, Herbert, **Supp. IV Part 1:** 220, 226, 307; **Supp. VIII:** 124; **Supp. XIX:** 251; **Supp. XX:**243

Mitla Pass (Uris), **Supp. XX:**244, 247, 248, **256**

Mixed Company: Collected Short Stories (Shaw), **Supp. XIX:** 251

"Mixed Sequence" (Roethke), **III:** 547

Miyazawa Kenji, **Supp. VIII:** 292

Mizener, Arthur, **II:** 77, 81, 84, 94; **IV:** 132; **Supp. XVIII:** 249

Mizner, Addison, **Supp. XVI:** 191

Mizner, Wilson, **Supp. XVI:** 191, 195

Mladenoff, Nancy, **Supp. X:** 176

"M'liss: An Idyl of Red Mountain" (Harte), **Supp. II Part 1:** 339

"Mnemonic Devices" (Goldbarth), **Supp. XII:** 183

"Mobile in Back of the Smithsonian, The" (Swenson), **Supp. IV Part 2:** 646

Mobilio, Albert, **Supp. VIII:** 3; **Supp. XVIII:** 144; **Supp. XIX:** 45

Moby Dick (film), **Supp. IV Part 1:** 102, 116

Moby Dick; or, The Whale (Melville), **I:** 106, 354; **II:** 33, 224–225, 236, 539–540; **III:** 28–29, 74, 75, 77, 81, 82, 83–86, 87, 89, 90, 91, 93, 94, 95, 359, 453, 556; **IV:** 57, 199, 201, 202;

Retro. Supp. I: 160, 220, 243, 244, 248, **249–253,** 254, 256, 257, 335; **Retro. Supp. II:** 121, 186, 275; **Supp. I Part 1:** 249; **Supp. I Part 2:** 579; **Supp. IV Part 2:** 613; **Supp. V:** 281; **Supp. VIII:** 106, 188, 198; **Supp. XXI:** 159

Mock, John, **Supp. XIII:** 174

"Mocking-Bird, The" (Bierce), **I:** 202

"Mock Orange" (Glück), **Supp. V:** 84–85

Modarressi, Mitra, **Supp. IV Part 2:** 657

Models of Misrepresentation: On the Fiction of E. L. Doctorow (Morris), **Supp. IV Part 1:** 231

Model World and Other Stories, A (Chabon), **Supp. XI:** 66

Modern American and British Poetry (Untermeyer, ed.), **Supp. XV:** 306

Modern American Poetry (Untermeyer, ed.), **Supp. XV:** 293, 303, 306, 312

Modern American Verse (Untermeyer, ed.), **Supp. XV:** 301

Modern Brazilian Architecture (Bishop, trans.), **Supp. I Part 1:** 92

Modern British Poetry (Untermeyer, ed.), **Supp. XV:** 305, 308, 312

Modern Fiction Studies, **Supp. V:** 238

Modern Fiction Studies (Haegert), **Supp. XVI:** 69

Modern Instance a Novel, A (Howells), **II:** 275, 279, 282–283, 285

Modern Library, The, **Retro. Supp. I:** 112, 113

Modern Mephistopheles, A (Alcott), **Supp. I Part 1:** 37–38

Modern Poetic Sequence, The (Rosenthal), **Supp. V:** 333

"Modern Poetry" (Crane), **I:** 390

Modern Poetry and the Tradition (Brooks), **Supp. XIV:** 5–7

"Modern Race Creeds and Their Fallacies" (Locke), **Supp. XIV:** 210

Modern Rhetoric, with Readings (Brooks and Warren), **Supp. XIV:** 11

"Modern Sorcery" (Simic), **Supp. VIII:** 283

Modern Times (album, Dylan), **Supp. XVIII:** 28, 31, 33

"Modern Times" (Zukofsky), **Supp. III Part 2:** 624

Modern Writer, The (Anderson), **I:** 117

Modersohn, Otto, **Supp. I Part 2:** 573

Modersohn, Mrs. Otto (Paula Becker), **Supp. I Part 2:** 573–574

"Modes of Being" (Levertov), **Supp. III Part 1:** 282

Modest Enquiry into the Nature and Necessity of a Paper-Currency, A (Franklin), **II:** 108–109

"Modest Proposal, A" (Swift), **I:** 295; **Retro. Supp. II:** 287

"Modest Proposal with Feline Feeling, A" (Neugeboren), **Supp. XVI:** 219

"Modest Self-Tribute, A" (Wilson), **IV:** 431, 432

Moeller, Philip, **III:** 398, 399

"Moench von Berchtesgaden, Der" (Voss), **I:** 199–200

Moers, Ellen, **Retro. Supp. II:** 99

Moe's Villa and Other Stories (Purdy), **Supp. VII:** 270, 280

Moffat, Juan, **Supp. XX:**52

Mogen, David, **Supp. IV Part 1:** 106

Mohammed, **I:** 480; **II:** 1

Mohawk (Russo), **Supp. XII: 326–328**

Moir, William Wilmerding, **Supp. V:** 279

Moldaw, Carol, **Supp. XV:** 264; **Supp. XVII:** 127, 130

"Moles" (Oliver), **Supp. VII:** 235

Molesworth, Charles, **Supp. IV Part 1:** 39; **Supp. VIII:** 292, 306; **Supp. XIX:** 121–122

Molière (Jean-Baptiste Poquelin), **III:** 113; **Supp. I Part 2:** 406; **Supp. III Part 2:** 552, 560; **Supp. IV Part 2:** 585; **Supp. V:** 101

"Molino Rojo, El" (Ríos), **Supp. IV Part 2:** 544

Moll Flanders (Defoe), **Supp. V:** 127; **Supp. XIII:** 43

"Molloch in State Street" (Whittier), **Supp. I Part 2:** 687

"Moll Pitcher" (Whittier), **Supp. I Part 2:** 684

"Molly Brant, Iroquois Matron" (Gunn Allen), **Supp. IV Part 1:** 331

Molnar, Ferenc, **Supp. XVI:** 187

"Moloch" (H. Miller), **III:** 177

Momaday, N. Scott, **Supp. IV Part 1:** 274, 323, 324, 404; **Supp. IV Part 2: 479–496,** 504, 557, 562; **Supp. XII:** 209; **Supp. XVIII:** 58

" 'Momentary Stay against Confusion,' A: Frank Conroy's *Stop-Time*" (T. Adams), **Supp. XVI:** 69

Moment of Untruth (Lacy), **Supp. XV:** 206, 207

Moments of the Italian Summer (Wright), **Supp. III Part 2:** 602

Moment to Moment: Poems of a Mountain Recluse (Budbill), **Supp. XIX:** 2, 7, **9–10**

"Momus" (Robinson), **III:** 508

Monaghan, Charles, **Supp. XIX:** 155

Monaghan, Pat, **Supp. XI:** 121

Monaghan, Patricia, **Supp. XVII:** 76, 123, 127, 129

Mona Lisa Overdrive (W. Gibson), **Supp. XVI:** 119, 120, **127–128**

"Mon Ami" (Bourne), **I:** 227

Monet, Claude, **Retro. Supp. I:** 378

"Monet's 'Waterlilies' " (Hayden), **Supp. II Part 1:** 361–362

Monette, Paul, **Supp. X: 145–161**

Money (Amis), **Retro. Supp. I:** 278

"Money" (Matthews), **Supp. IX:** 166

"Money" (Nemerov), **III:** 287

Money, Money, Money (Wagoner), **Supp. IX:** 324, **333–334**

Moneyball: The Art of Winning an Unfair Game (M. Lewis), **Supp. XVII:** 210

Moneychangers, The (Sinclair), **Supp. V:** 285

Money Writes! (Sinclair), **Supp. V:** 277

Monica, Saint, **IV:** 140

Monikins, The (Cooper), **I:** 348, 354

Monk, Thelonious, **Supp. XVIII:** 62

Monk and the Hangman's Daughter, The (Bierce), **I:** 199–200, 209

"Monkey" (Weigl), **Supp. XIX:** 278

"Monkey Garden, The" (Cisneros), **Supp. VII:** 63

"Monkey Puzzle, The" (Moore), **III:** 194, 207, 211

Monkeys (Minot), **Supp. VI:** 203–205, **206–210**

"Monkeys, The" (Moore), **III:** 201, 202

Monkey Wars, The (Weigl), **Supp. XIX:** 276, 278–280

Monkey Wrench Gang, The (Abbey), **Supp. VIII:** 42; **Supp. XIII: 9–11,** 16

"Monk of Casal-Maggiore, The" (Longfellow), **II:** 505

"Monocle de Mon Oncle, Le" (Stevens), **IV:** 78, 84; **Retro. Supp. I:** 301; **Supp. III Part 1:** 20; **Supp. X:** 58

"Monolog from a Mattress" (Untermeyer), **Supp. XV:** 307

Monro, Harold, **III:** 465; **Retro. Supp. I:** 127; **Supp. XV:** 296

Monroe, Harriet, **I:** 235, 384, 390, 393; **III:** 458, 581, 586; **IV:** 74; **Retro. Supp. I:** 58, 131; **Retro. Supp. II:** 82, 83; **Supp. I Part 1:** 256, 257, 258, 262, 263, 267; **Supp. I Part 2:** 374, 387, 388, 464, 610, 611, 613, 614, 615, 616; **Supp. XIV:** 286; **Supp. XV:** 43, 299, 302

Monroe, James, **Supp. I Part 2:** 515, 517

Monroe, Lucy, **Retro. Supp. II:** 70

Monroe, Marilyn, **III:** 161, 162–163

Monroe's Embassy; or, the Conduct of the Government in Relation to Our Claims to the Navigation of the Mississippi (Brown), **Supp. I Part 1:** 146

"Monsoon Season" (Komunyakaa), **Supp. XIII:** 122

Monsour, Leslie, **Supp. XV:** 125

"Monster, The" (Crane), **I:** 418

Monster, The, and Other Stories (Crane), **I:** 409

Montage of a Dream Deferred (Hughes), **Retro. Supp. I:** 194, **208–209; Supp. I Part 1:** 333, 339–341

Montagu, Ashley, **Supp. I Part 1:** 314

"Montaigne" (Emerson), **II:** 6

Montaigne, Michel de, **II:** 1, 5, 6, 8, 14–15, 16, 535; **III:** 600; **Retro. Supp. I:** 247; **Supp. XIV:** 105; **Supp. XXI:** 111, 205

Montale, Eugenio, **Supp. III Part 1:** 320; **Supp. V:** 337–338; **Supp. VIII:** 30; **Supp. XV:** 112

Montalembert, Hughes de, **Supp. XV:** 349

"Montana Memory" (Maclean), **Supp. XIV:** 221

"Montana; or the End of Jean-Jacques Rousseau" (Fiedler), **Supp. XIII: 97–98**

"Montana Ranch Abandoned" (Hugo), **Supp. VI:** 139

"Mont Blanc" (Shelley), **Supp. IX:** 52

Montcalm, Louis Joseph de, **Supp. I Part 2:** 498

Montcalm and Wolfe (Parkman), **Supp. II Part 2:** 596, 609, 610, 611–613

Montemarano, Nicholas, **Supp. XVI:** 227

Montgomery, Benilde, **Supp. XIII:** 202

Montgomery, Robert, **Supp. I Part 2:** 611; **Supp. IV Part 1:** 130

Month of Sundays, A (Updike), **Retro. Supp. I:** 325, 327, 329, 330, 331, 333, 335

Monti, Luigi, **II:** 504

Montoya, José, **Supp. IV Part 2:** 545

"Montrachet-le-Jardin" (Stevens), **IV:** 82

Mont-Saint-Michel and Chartres (Adams), **I:** 1, 9, 12–14, 18, 19, 21; **Supp. I Part 2:** 417

Montserrat (Hellman), **Supp. I Part 1:** 283–285

Montserrat (Robles), **Supp. I Part 1:** 283–285

"Monument, The" (Bishop), **Supp. I Part 1:** 89

Monument, The (Strand), **Supp. IV Part 2:** 629, 630

"Monument in Utopia, A" (Schnackenberg), **Supp. XV:** 261, 263

"Monument Mountain" (Bryant), **Supp. I Part 1:** 156, 162

"Monument to After-Thought Unveiled, A" (Frost), **Retro. Supp. I:** 124

Moo (Smiley), **Supp. VI:** 292, **303–305**

Moods (Alcott), **Supp. I Part 1:** 33, 34–35, 43

Moody, Anne, **Supp. IV Part 1:** 11

Moody, Richard, **Supp. I Part 1:** 280

Moody, Rick, **Supp. XXI:** 117

Moody, William Vaughn, **III:** 507; **IV:** 26

Moody, Mrs. William Vaughn, **I:** 384; **Supp. I Part 2:** 394

"Moon" (A. Finch), **Supp. XVII:** 77

Moon, Henry Lee, **Supp. XVIII:** 281, 285

"Moon and the Night and the Men, The" (Berryman), **I:** 172

"Moon Deluxe" (F. Barthelme), **Supp. XI:** 26, 27, 33, 36

Mooney, Tom, **I:** 505

"Moon-Face" (London), **II:** 475

Moon-Face and Other Stories (London), **II:** 483

"Moon Flock" (Dickey), **Supp. IV Part 1:** 186

Moon for the Misbegotten, A (O'Neill), **III:** 385, 401, 403, 404

Moon in a Mason Jar (Wrigley), **Supp. XVIII: 295–298**

Moon in Its Flight, The (Sorrentino), **Supp. XXI:** 226

"Moon in Its Flight, The" (Sorrentino), **Supp. XXI:** 229

Moon Is a Gong, The (Dos Passos). *See Garbage Man, The* (Dos Passos)

Moon Is Down, The (Steinbeck), **IV:** 51

Moon Lady, The (Tan), **Supp. X:** 289

"Moonlight Alert" (Winters), **Supp. II Part 2:** 801, 811, 815

"Moonlight: Chickens on a Road" (Wrigley), **Supp. XVIII:** 295–296, 297

"Moonlit Night" (Reznikoff), **Supp. XIV:** 285–286

Moon of the Caribbees, The (O'Neill), **III:** 388

Moon Palace (Auster), **Supp. XII:** 22, 27, **30–32**

"Moonshine" (Komunyakaa), **Supp. XIII:** 127, 128

"Moon Solo" (Laforgue), **Supp. XIII:** 346

Moonstone, The (Collins), **Supp. XX:**236

Moonstruck (screenplay, Shanley), **Supp. XIV:** 315, 316, **321–324**

"Moon upon her fluent Route, The" (Dickinson), **I:** 471

Moony's Kid Don't Cry (T. Williams), **IV:** 381

Moore, Arthur, **Supp. I Part 1:** 49

Moore, Deborah Dash, **Supp. XX:**246

Moore, George, **I:** 103

Moore, Hannah, **Supp. XV:** 231

Moore, John Milton, **III:** 193

Moore, Lorrie, **Supp. VIII:** 145; **Supp. X: 163–180**

Moore, Marianne, **I:** 58, 285, 401, 428; **III: 193–217,** 514, 592–593; **IV:** 74, 75, 76, 91, 402; **Retro. Supp. I:** 416, 417; **Retro. Supp. II:** 39, 44, 48, 50, 82, 178, 179, 243, 244; **Supp. I Part 1:** 84, 89, 255, 257; **Supp. I Part 2:** 707; **Supp. II Part 1:** 21; **Supp. III Part 1:** 58, 60, 63; **Supp. III Part 2:** 612, 626, 627; **Supp. IV Part 1:** 242, 246, 257; **Supp. IV Part 2:** 454, 640, 641; **Supp. XIV:** 124, 130; **Supp. XV:** 306, 307; **Supp. XVII:** 131; **Supp. XXI:** 98

Moore, Marie Lorena. *See* Moore, Lorrie

Moore, Mary Tyler, **Supp. V:** 107

Moore, Mary Warner, **III:** 193

Moore, Dr. Merrill, **III:** 506

Moore, Steven, **Supp. IV Part 1:** 279, 283, 284, 285, 287; **Supp. XII:** 151; **Supp. XVII:** 230, 231, 232

Moore, Sturge, **III:** 459

Moore, Thomas, **II:** 296, 299, 303; **Supp. IX:** 104; **Supp. X:** 114

Moore, Virginia, **Supp. XV:** 308

Moorehead, Caroline, **Supp. XIV:** 337

Moorepack, Howard, **Supp. XV:** 199

"Moorings" (Hoffman), **Supp. XVIII:** 87

Moos, Malcolm, **III:** 116, 119

"Moose, The" (Bishop), **Retro. Supp. II:** 50; **Supp. I Part 1:** 73, 93, 94, 95; **Supp. IX:** 45, 46

"Moose Wallow, The" (Hayden), **Supp. II Part 1:** 367

"Moquihuitzin's Answer" (Everwine), **Supp. XV:** 78

Mora, Pat, **Supp. XIII: 213–232**

"Moral Bully, The" (Holmes), **Supp. I Part 1:** 302

"Moral Character, the Practice of Law, and Legal Education" (Hall), **Supp. VIII:** 127

"Moral Equivalent for Military Service, A" (Bourne), **I:** 230

"Moral Equivalent of War, The" (James), **II:** 361; **Supp. I Part 1:** 20

"Moral Imperatives for World Order" (Locke), **Supp. XIV:** 207, 213

Moralités Légendaires (Laforgue), **I:** 573

"Morality and Mercy in Vienna" (Pynchon), **Supp. II Part 2:** 620, 624

"Morality of Indian Hating, The" (Momaday), **Supp. IV Part 2:** 484

"Morality of Poetry, The" (Wright), **Supp. III Part 2:** 596–597, 599

Moral Man and Immoral Society (Niebuhr), **III:** 292, 295–297

"Morals Is Her Middle Name" (Hughes), **Supp. I Part 1:** 338

"Morals of Chess, The" (Franklin), **II:** 121

"Moral Substitute for War, A" (Addams), **Supp. I Part 1:** 20

"Moral Theology of Atticus Finch, The" (Shaffer), **Supp. VIII:** 127

"Moral Thought, A" (Freneau), **Supp. II Part 1:** 262

Moran, Thomas, **Supp. IV Part 2:** 603–604

Moran of the Lady Letty (Norris), **II:** 264; **III:** 314, 322, 327, 328, 329, 330, 331, 332, 333

Morath, Ingeborg. *See* Miller, Mrs. Arthur (Ingeborg Morath)

Moravec, Paul, **Supp. XIX:** 123

Moravia, Alberto, **I:** 301

Moré, Gonzalo, **Supp. X:** 185

More, Henry, **I:** 132

More, Paul Elmer, **I:** 223–224, 247; **Supp. I Part 2:** 423

Moreau, Gustave, **I:** 66

"More Blues and the Abstract Truth" (Wright), **Supp. XV:** 345

More Boners (Abingdon), **Supp. XVI:** 99

More Conversations with Eudora Welty (Prenshaw, ed.), **Retro. Supp. I:** 340, 341, 342, 343, 344, 352, 353, 354

More Dangerous Thoughts (Ryan as Quin), **Supp. XVIII:** 226, **229–230,** 231, 238

More Die of Heartbreak (Bellow), **Retro. Supp. II:** 31, 33, 34

"More Girl Than Boy" (Komunyakaa), **Supp. XIII:** 117

"More Light! More Light! (Hecht), **Supp. X:** 60

"Morella" (Poe), **III:** 412; **Retro. Supp. II:** 270

"More Love in the Western World" (Updike), **Retro. Supp. I:** 327–328, 329

"Morels" (W. J. Smith), **Supp. XIII: 336–339**

Moreno, Gary, **Supp. XV:** 5

"More Observations Now" (Conroy), **Supp. XVI:** 75

"More of a Corpse Than a Woman" (Rukeyser), **Supp. VI:** 280

"More Pleasant Adventures" (Ashbery), **Supp. III Part 1:** 1

More Poems to Solve (Swenson), **Supp. IV Part 2:** 640, 642, 648

More Stately Mansions (O'Neill), **III:** 385, 401, 404–405

"More Than Human" (Chabon), **Supp. XI:** 71–72

More Things Change The More They Stay the Same, The (J. W. Miller), **Supp. XX:**164

More Triva (L. P. Smith), **Supp. XIV:** 339

Morgan, Edmund S., **IV:** 149; **Supp. I Part 1:** 101, 102; **Supp. I Part 2:** 484

Morgan, Edwin, **Supp. IV Part 2:** 688

Morgan, Emanuel. *See* Bynner, Witter

Morgan, Henry, **II:** 432; **IV:** 63

Morgan, Jack, **Retro. Supp. II:** 142

Morgan, J. P., **I:** 494; **III:** 14, 15

Morgan, Judith, **Supp. XVI:** 103

Morgan, Neil, **Supp. XVI:** 103

Morgan, Robert, **Supp. V:** 5; **Supp. XX:**161, 162

Morgan, Robin, **Supp. I Part 2:** 569

Morgan, Ted, **Supp. XIV:** 141

Morgan's Passing (Tyler), **Supp. IV Part 2:** 666–667, 668, 669

Morgenstern, Dan, **Supp. XIX:** 159

Morgenthau, Hans, **III:** 291, 309

Morgesons, The (E. Stoddard), **Supp. XV:** 270, 273, 274, 278, **279–282,** 283

Morgesons and Other Writings, Published and Unpublished, The (Buell and Zagarell), **Supp. XV:** 269

Moricand, Conrad, **III:** 190

Morison, Samuel Eliot, **Supp. I Part 2: 479–500**

Morison, Mrs. Samuel Eliot (Elizabeth Shaw Greene), **Supp. I Part 2:** 483

Morison, Mrs. Samuel Eliot (Priscilla Barton), **Supp. I Part 2:** 493, 496, 497

Morita, Pat, **Supp. XXI:** 146

"Morituri Salutamus" (Longfellow), **II:** 499, 500; **Retro. Supp. II:** 169; **Supp. I Part 2:** 416

"Moriturus" (Millay), **III:** 126, 131–132

Morley, Christopher, **III:** 481, 483, 484; **Supp. I Part 2:** 653; **Supp. IX:** 124

Morley, Edward, **IV:** 27

Morley, Lord John, **I:** 7

Mormon Country (Stegner), **Supp. IV Part 2:** 598, 601–602

"Morning, The" (Updike), **Retro. Supp. I:** 329

"Morning after My Death, The" (Levis), **Supp. XI:** 260, 263–264

"Morning Arrives" (F. Wright), **Supp. XVII:** 244

Morning Face (Stratton-Porter), **Supp. XX:**223

Morning for Flamingos, A (Burke), **Supp. XIV:** 30, 31, 32

"Morning Glory" (Merrill), **Supp. III Part 1:** 337

Morning Glory, The (R. Bly), **Supp. IV Part 1:** 63–65, 66, 71

"Morning Imagination of Russia, A" (W. C. Williams), **Retro. Supp. I:** 428

Morning in Antibes (Knowles), **Supp. XII:** 249

Morning in the Burned House (Atwood), **Supp. XIII:** 20, 35

Morning Is Near Us, The (Glaspell), **Supp. III Part 1:** 184–185

Morning Noon and Night (Cozzens), **I:** 374, 375, 376, 377, 379, 380

"Morning of the Day They Did It, The" (White), **Supp. I Part 2:** 663

"Morning Prayers" (Harjo), **Supp. XII:** 231

"Morning Roll Call" (Anderson), **I:** 116

"Morning Roudup" (Sorrentino), **Supp. XXI:** 228

"Morning Shadows" (Skloot), **Supp. XX:**199

"Mornings in a New House" (Merrill), **Supp. III Part 1:** 327

Mornings Like This (Dillard), **Supp. VI:** 23, 34

"Morning Song" (Plath), **Retro. Supp. II:** 252

Morning Watch, The (Agee), **I:** 25, 39–42

"Morning with Broken Window" (Hogan), **Supp. IV Part 1:** 405

Morrell, Ottoline, **Retro. Supp. I:** 60

Morris, Bernard E., **Supp. XV:** 154, 169

Morris, Christopher D., **Supp. IV Part 1:** 231, 236

Morris, George Sylvester, **Supp. I Part 2:** 640

Morris, Gouverneur, **Supp. I Part 2:** 512, 517, 518

Morris, Lloyd, **III:** 458

Morris, Robert, **Supp. I Part 2:** 510

Morris, Timothy, **Retro. Supp. I:** 40

Morris, William, **II:** 323, 338, 523; **IV:** 349; **Supp. I Part 1:** 260, 356; **Supp. XI:** 202

Morris, Willie, **Supp. XI:** 216, 231, 234; **Supp. XIX:** 151, 252

Morris, Wright, **I:** 305; **III: 218–243,** 558, 572; **IV:** 211

Morrison, Charles Clayton, **III:** 297

Morrison, Jim, **Supp. IV Part 1:** 206

Morrison, Toni, **Retro. Supp. II:** 15, 118; **Supp. III Part 1: 361–381; Supp. IV Part 1:** 2, 13, 14, 250, 253, 257; **Supp. V:** 169, 259; **Supp. VIII:** 213, 214; **Supp. X:** 85, 239, 250, 325; **Supp. XI:** 4, 14, 20, 91; **Supp. XII:** 289, 310; **Supp. XIII:** 60, 185; **Supp. XVI:** 143; **Supp. XVII:** 183; **Supp. XX:**108; **Supp. XXI:** 172, 243

"Morro Bay" (Jeffers), **Supp. II Part 2:** 422

Morrow, W. C., **I:** 199

Morse, Jedidiah, **Supp. XV:** 243

Morse, Robert, **Supp. XI:** 305

Morse, Samuel F. B., **Supp. I Part 1:** 156

Morse, Samuel French, **Supp. XXI:** 17, 19, 23, 27

Mortal Acts, Mortal Words (Kinnell), **Supp. III Part 1:** 235, 236, 237, 249–254

Mortal Antipathy, A (Holmes), **Supp. I Part 1:** 315–316

"Mortal Enemies" (Humphrey), **Supp. IX:** 109

"Mortal Eternal" (Olds), **Supp. X:** 214

Mortal No, The (Hoffman), **IV:** 113

Mortal Stakes (Parker), **Supp. XIX:** 183–184

Morte D'Arthur, Le (Malory), **Supp. IV Part 1:** 47

Mortmere Stories, The (Isherwood and Upward), **Supp. XIV:** 159

Morton, David, **Supp. IX:** 76

Morton, Jelly Roll, **Supp. X:** 242

"Mosaic of the Nativity: Serbia, Winter 1993" (Kenyon), **Supp. VII:** 173

Mosby's Memoirs and Other Stories (Bellow), **Retro. Supp. II:** 27

"Moscow, Idaho" (Offutt), **Supp. XIX:** 170

Moscow under Fire (Caldwell), **I:** 296

Moser, Barry, **Supp. XIV:** 223

Moses (Untermeyer), **Supp. XV: 309**

Moses, Man of the Mountain (Hurston), **Supp. VI:** 149, 158, 160

"Moses on Sinai" (Untermeyer), **Supp. XV:** 300

Moskowitz, Alfred, **Supp. XXI:** 98, 106

Mosle, Sara, **Supp. XI:** 254

Mosley, Walter, **Supp. XIII: 233–252; Supp. XVI:** 143

Mosquito Coast, The (film), **Supp. VIII:** 323

Mosquito Coast, The (Theroux), **Supp. VIII:** 321, **322–323**

Mosquitos (Faulkner), **II:** 56; **Retro. Supp. I:** 79, 81

Moss, Howard, **III:** 452; **Supp. IV Part 2:** 642; **Supp. IX:** 39; **Supp. XIII:** 114; **Supp. XV:** 143, 152

Moss, Stanley, **Supp. XI:** 321

Moss, Thylias, **Supp. XI:** 248

Mosses from an Old Manse (Hawthorne), **I:** 562; **II:** 224; **III:** 82, 83; **Retro. Supp. I:** 157, 248

"Moss of His Skin" (Sexton), **Supp. II Part 2:** 676

Most, Doug, **Supp. XVIII:** 101

"Most Extraordinary Case, A" (James), **II:** 322; **Retro. Supp. I:** 218

"Most Girl Part of You, The" (Hempel), **Supp. XXI:** 116

Most Likely to Succeed (Dos Passos), **I:** 491

"Most of It, The" (Frost), **Retro. Supp. I:** 121, 125, 129, 139; **Supp. XVIII:** 300

"Most Popular Novels in America, The" (Mabie), **Supp. XVIII:** 257

Motel Chronicles (Shepard), **Supp. III Part 2:** 445

"Mother" (Kooser), **Supp. XIX:** 117, 126, 127

"Mother" (Paley), **Supp. VI: 222–223**

"Mother" (Snyder), **Supp. VIII:** 298

Mother (Whistler), **IV:** 369

Mother, The (Buck), **Supp. II Part 1:** 118–119

"Mother and Jack and the Rain" (Sexton), **Supp. II Part 2:** 686

"Mother and Son" (Tate), **IV:** 128, 137–138

Mother Country: Britain, the Welfare State and Nuclear Pollution (Robinson), **Supp. XXI:** 211

Mother Courage and Her Children (Brecht), **III:** 160; **Supp. IX:** 140; **Supp. XII:** 249

"Mother Earth: Her Whales" (Snyder), **Supp. VIII:** 302

"Motherhood" (Swenson), **Supp. IV Part 2:** 645

Mother Hubbard (Reed), **Supp. X:** 241

Motherless in Brooklyn (Lethem), **Supp. XVIII:** 135, **143–144**

Mother Love (Dove), **Supp. IV Part 1:** 250–251, 254

"Mother Marie Therese" (Lowell), **Retro. Supp. II:** 188

Mother Night (Vonnegut), **Supp. II Part 2:** 757, 758, 767, 770, 771

"Mother Rosarine" (Kumin), **Supp. IV Part 2:** 442

"Mothers and Daughters in the Fiction of the New Republic" (Davidson), **Supp. XV:** 238

Mother's Recompense, The (Wharton), **IV:** 321, 324; **Retro. Supp. I:** 382

"Mother's Tale, A" (Agee), **I:** 29–30

"Mother's Things" (Creeley), **Supp. IV Part 1:** 141

"Mother's Voice" (Creeley), **Supp. IV Part 1:** 156

Mother to Daughter, Daughter to Mother (Olsen, ed.), **Supp. XIII:** 295

"Mother Tongue" (Simic), **Supp. VIII:** 283

"Mother to Son" (Hughes), **Retro. Supp. I:** 199, 203; **Supp. I Part 1:** 321–322, 323

Motherwell, Robert, **Supp. XV:** 145; **Supp. XXI:** 125

"Mother Writes to the Murderer, The: A Letter" (Nye), **Supp. XIII:** 276

Moths of the Limberlost (Stratton-Porter), **Supp. XX:**218

"Motion, The" (Olson), **Supp. II Part 2:** 571

Motion of History, The (Baraka), **Supp. II Part 1:** 55, 56

"Motive for Metaphor, The" (Stevens), **IV:** 89; **Retro. Supp. I:** 310

Motiveless Malignity (Auchincloss), **Supp. IV Part 1:** 31

Motley, John Lothrop, **Supp. I Part 1:** 299; **Supp. I Part 2:** 479; **Supp. XX:**228, 231

Motley, Willard, **Supp. XVII: 149–163**

"Motor Car, The" (White), **Supp. I Part 2:** 661

Motor-Flight Through France (Wharton), **I:** 12; **Retro. Supp. I:** 372

Mott, Michael, **Supp. VIII:** 204, 208

Mottetti: Poems of Love: The Motets of Eugenio Montale (Montale; Gioia, trans.), **Supp. XV:** 112, **127–128**

Mouawad, Nelly, **Supp. XX:**126

"Mountain, The" (Frost), **Retro. Supp. I:** 121

"Mountain Hermitage, The: Pages from a Japanese Notebook" (Passin), **Supp. XIII:** 337

Mountain Interval (Frost), **II:** 154; **Retro. Supp. I:** 131, 132, 133

"Mountain Lion" (Hogan), **Supp. IV Part 1:** 412

"Mountain Music" essays (Sanders), **Supp. XVI:** 276–277

Mountain on the Desert, The (Richter), **Supp. XVIII:** 216, 219

Mountainous Journey, A (Tuqan), **Supp. XIII:** 278

Mountains, The (Wolfe), **IV:** 461

Mountains and Rivers without End (Snyder), **Supp. VIII:** 295, **305–306**

"Mountains grow unnoticed, The" (Dickinson), **Retro. Supp. I:** 46

Mountains Have Come Closer, The (J. W. Miller), **Supp. XX:**165, 168, **169–170**

Mountains of California, The (Muir), **Supp. IX:** 183

"Mountain Whippoorwill, The" (Benét), **Supp. XI:** 44–45, 46, 47

"Mount-Joy: or Some Passages Out of the Life of a Castle-Builder" (Irving), **II:** 314

"Mount Venus" (Wright), **Supp. XV:** 346

"Mourners" (Kooser), **Supp. XIX:** 127

"Mourners, The" (Malamud), **Supp. I Part 2:** 431, 435, 436–437

Mourners Below (Purdy), **Supp. VII:** 274, 280

"Mourning and Melancholia" (Freud), **Supp. IV Part 2:** 450; **Supp. XVI:** 161

Mourning Becomes Electra (O'Neill), **III:** 391, 394, 398–400

"Mourning Doves" (Pedersen; Nelson, trans.), **Supp. XVIII:** 180

"Mourning Poem for the Queen of Sunday" (Hayden), **Supp. II Part 1:** 379–380

"Mouse Elegy" (Olds), **Supp. X:** 209

Mouse Is Born, A (Loos), **Supp. XVI:** 193

"Mouse Roulette Wheel, The" (C. Bly), **Supp. XVI:** 34

Moustapha's Eclipse (McKnight), **Supp. XX:**147, 150

"Mouth of Brass" (Humphrey), **Supp. IX:** 101

Moveable Feast, A (Hemingway), **II:** 257; **Retro. Supp. I:** 108, 171, **186–187**

Movement, The: Documentary of a Struggle for Equality (Student Nonviolent Coordinating Committee), **Supp. IV Part 1:** 369

"Move over Macho, Here Comes Feminismo" (Robbins), **Supp. X:** 272

Movers and Shakers (Sochen), **Supp. XXI:** 1

"Move to California, The" (Stafford), **Supp. XI:** 318, 321

"Movie" (Shapiro), **Supp. II Part 2:** 707

Movie at the End of the World, The (McGrath), **Supp. X:** 127

Moviegoer, The (Percy), **Supp. III Part 1:** 383–385, 387, 389–392, 394, 397

"Movie Magazine, The: A Low 'Slick' " (Percy), **Supp. III Part 1:** 385

Movies (Dixon), **Supp. XII:** 147

Movies About the Movies (Ames), **Supp. XVIII:** 242–243

"Moving Around" (Matthews), **Supp. IX:** 155

"Moving Finger, The" (Wharton), **Retro. Supp. I:** 365

"Moving Inward at Last" (Bly), **Supp. XXI:** 84–85

Moving On (McMurtry), **Supp. V:** 223–224

"Moving On" (Pickering), **Supp. XXI:** 197

Moving Pictures: Memoirs of a Hollywood Prince (Schulberg), **Supp. XVIII:** 242, 243, 254

Moving Target, The (Macdonald), **Supp. IV Part 2:** 462, 463, 467, 470, 471, 473, 474

Moving Target, The (Merwin), **Supp. III Part 1:** 346, 347–348, 352, 357

"Mowbray Family, The" (Farrell and Alden), **II:** 45

"Mowing" (Frost), **II:** 169–170; **Retro. Supp. I:** 127, 128

"Moxan's Master" (Bierce), **I:** 206

Moxley, Jennifer, **Supp. XVII:** 70

Moyers, Bill, **Supp. IV Part 1:** 267; **Supp. VIII:** 331; **Supp. XI:** 126, 132; **Supp. XII:** 217; **Supp. XIII:** 274, 276; **Supp. XV:** 212

Moynihan, Daniel Patrick, **Retro. Supp. II:** 123; **Supp. VIII:** 241; **Supp. XIX:** 150–151

"Mozart" (C. Frost), **Supp. XV:** 94

Mozart, Wolfgang Amadeus, **I:** 479, 588; **IV:** 74, 358; **Supp. IV Part 1:** 284

"Mozart and the Gray Steward" (Wilder), **IV:** 358

Mrabet, Mohammed, **Supp. IV Part 1:** 92, 93

Mr. and Mrs. Baby and Other Stories (Strand), **Supp. IV Part 2:** 631

"Mr. and Mrs. Fix-It" (Lardner), **II:** 431

Mr. Arcularis (Aiken), **I:** 54, 56

"Mr. Big" (Allen), **Supp. XV:** 15

Mr. Bridge (Connell), **Supp. XIV:** 80, 82, 93

Mr. Brown Can Moo! Can You? (Geisel), **Supp. XVI:** 104

"Mr. Bruce" (Jewett), **II:** 397; **Retro. Supp. II:** 134, 143

"Mr. Burnshaw and the Statue" (Stevens), **Retro. Supp. I:** 298, 303

"Mr. Carson Death on His Nights Out" (McGrath), **Supp. X:** 118

Mr. Clemens and Mark Twain (Kaplan), **I:** 247–248

"Mr. Coffee and Mr. Fixit" (Carver), **Supp. III Part 1:** 145

"Mr. Cornelius Johnson, Office-Seeker" (Dunbar), **Supp. II Part 1:** 211, 213

"Mr. Costyve Duditch" (Toomer), **Supp. III Part 2:** 486

"Mr. Dajani, Calling from Jericho" (Nye), **Supp. XIII:** 286–287

"Mr. Edwards and the Spider" (Lowell), **I:** 544; **II:** 550; **Retro. Supp. II:** 187

Mr. Field's Daughter (Bausch), **Supp. VII:** 47–48, 51–52

"Mr. Flood's Party" (Robinson), **III:** 512

"Mr. Forster's Pageant" (Maxwell), **Supp. VIII:** 172

"Mr. Frost's Chickens" (Oliver), **Supp. VII:** 232–233

Mr. Hodge and Mr. Hazard (Wylie), **Supp. I Part 2:** 708, 709, 714, 721–724

"Mr. Hueffer and the Prose Tradition" (Pound), **III:** 465

Mr. Ives' Christmas (Hijuelos), **Supp. VIII:** 85–86

"Mr. Longfellow and His Boy" (Sandburg), **III:** 591

"Mr. Luna and History" (Ríos), **Supp. IV Part 2:** 551

"Mr. Mitochondria" (Stollman), **Supp. XVII:** 50

Mr. Moto Is So Sorry (Marquand), **III:** 57, 58

Mr. Norris Changes Trains (Isherwood), **Supp. XIV:** 161

"Mr. Preble Gets Rid of His Wife" (Thurber), **Supp. I Part 2:** 615

"Mr. Rolfe" (Wilson), **IV:** 436

Mr. Rutherford's Children (S. and A. Warner), **Supp. XVIII:** 264

"Mrs. Adis" (Kaye-Smith), **Supp. XVIII:** 130–131

Mrs. Albert Grundy: Observations in Philistia (Frederic), **II:** 138–139

Mr. Sammler's Planet (Bellow), **I:** 144, 147, 150, 151, 152, 158; **Retro. Supp. II:** 19, 28, 30

"Mrs. Bilingsby's Wine" (Taylor), **Supp. V:** 323

Mrs. Bridge: A Novel (Connell), **Supp. XIV:** 79, 80, 81, 82, **89–94,** 95

"Mrs. Cassidy's Last Year" (Gordon), **Supp. IV Part 1:** 306

Mrs. Dalloway (Woolf), **Supp. IV Part 1:** 299; **Supp. VIII:** 5; **Supp. XV:** 55, 65–66

"Mr. Shelley Speaking" (Wylie), **Supp. I Part 2:** 719

"Mrs. Jellison" (Hay), **Supp. XIV:** 123

"Mrs. Krikorian" (Olds), **Supp. X:** 211

"Mrs. Maecenas" (Burke), **I:** 271

"Mrs. Mandrill" (Nemerov), **III:** 278

"Mrs. Manstey's View" (Wharton), **Retro. Supp. I:** 362, 363

"Mrs. Mobry's Reason" (Chopin), **Retro. Supp. II:** 61

Mr. Spaceman (R. O. Butler), **Supp. XII:** 62, **74–75**

Mrs. Reynolds (Stein), **IV:** 43

"Mrs. Sen's" (Lahiri), **Supp. XXI: 177–178,** 180–181

Mrs. Stevens Hears the Mermaids Singing (Sarton), **Supp. VIII:** 252–253, **256–257**

Mrs. Ted Bliss (Elkin), **Supp. VI: 56,** 58

"Mrs. Turner Cutting the Grass" (Shields), **Supp. VII:** 319–320

"Mrs. Walpurga" (Rukeyser), **Supp. VI:** 273

"Mr. Thompson's Prodigal" (Harte), **Supp. II Part 1:** 354

Mr. Vertigo (Auster), **Supp. XII: 34–35,** 36

"Mr. Vonnegut in Sumatra" (Saunders), **Supp. XIX:** 235

"Mr. Whittier" (Scott), **Supp. I Part 2:** 705

Mr. Wilson's War (Dos Passos), **I:** 485

"MS. Found in a Bottle" (Poe), **III:** 411, 416; **Retro. Supp. II:** 274

"Ms. Lot" (Rukeyser), **Supp. VI:** 281

Ms. Magazine, **Supp. V:** 259

Mttron-Hirsch, Sidney, **III:** 484–485

"Muchas Gracias Por Todo" (Nye), **Supp. XIII:** 282–283

"Much Madness is divinest Sense" (Dickinson), **Retro. Supp. I:** 37–38

"Muck-A-Muck" (Harte), **Supp. II Part 1:** 342

"Mud Below, The" (Proulx), **Supp. VII:** 262

Mudge, Alden, **Supp. XIV:** 35

Mudrick, Marvin, **Retro. Supp. II:** 289

"Mud Season" (Kenyon), **Supp. VII:** 167–168

Mueller, Lisel, **Supp. I Part 1:** 83, 88; **Supp. XIV:** 268

Muggli, Mark, **Supp. IV Part 1:** 207

Muhammad, Elijah, **Supp. I Part 1:** 60

Muir, Edwin, **I:** 527; **II:** 368; **III:** 20

Muir, John, **Supp. VIII:** 296; **Supp. IX:** 33, **171–188;** **Supp. X:** 29; **Supp. XIV:** 177, 178, 181

Muirhead, Deborah, **Supp. XVIII:** 186

Mujica, Barbara, **Supp. VIII:** 89

Mulas, Franco, **Supp. XX:** 38

Mulatto (Hughes), **Retro. Supp. I:** 197, 203; **Supp. I Part 1:** 328, 339

Mulching of America, The (Crews), **Supp. XI:** 107

Muldoon, William, **I:** 500–501

Mule Bone (Hughes and Hurston), **Retro. Supp. I:** 194, 203; **Supp. VI:** 154

Mules and Men (Hurston), **Supp. VI:** 149, 153, 154, 160

Mulford, Prentice, **I:** 193

Mulligan, Robert, **Supp. VIII:** 128, 129

Mulligan Stew (Sorrentino), **Supp. XII:** 139; **Supp. XXI:** 233

Mullins, Eustace, **III:** 479

Mullins, Priscilla, **II:** 502–503

"Multiplication of Wool, The" (Sanders), **Supp. XVI:** 268

Multitudes, Multitudes (Clampitt), **Supp. IX:** 39

Mumbo Jumbo (Reed), **Supp. X:** 240, 242, **245–248,** 251

Mumford, Lewis, **I:** 245, 250, 251, 252, 259, 261; **II:** 271, 473–474; **Supp. I Part 2:** 632, 638; **Supp. II Part 2:** **471–501**

Mumford, Sophia Wittenberg (Mrs. Lewis Mumford), **Supp. II Part 2:** 474, 475

"Mummers, The" (Di Piero), **Supp. XIX:** 44

Mummy, The (film), **Supp. IV Part 1:** 104; **Supp. XVII:** 57

Mundo y Palabra (Espaillat), **Supp. XXI:** 104

"Mundus et Infans" (Auden), **Supp. II Part 1:** 15

"Munich, 1938" (Lowell), **II:** 554

"Munich Mannequins, The" (Plath), **Retro. Supp. II:** 256

"Municipal Report, A" (Henry), **Supp. II Part 1:** 406–407

Munro, Alice, **Supp. IX:** 212; **Supp. X:** 290; **Supp. XII:** 289–290, 310

Munsey, Frank, **I:** 501

Munson, Gorham, **I:** 252, 388, 432; **Retro. Supp. II:** 77, 78, 79, 82, 83; **Supp. I Part 2:** 454; **Supp. XX:** 70, 74

Münsterberg, Hugo, **Supp. XIV:** 197

Murakami, Haruki, **Supp. XVI:** 124

"Murano" (Doty), **Supp. XI:** 131

Murasaki, Lady, **II:** 577

Muratori, Fred, **Supp. XVI:** 281

Muray, Nicholas, **Supp. I Part 2:** 708

Murder, My Sweet (film), **Supp. IV Part 1:** 130

"Murderer Guest, The" (Gordon), **Supp. IV Part 1:** 306

"Murderers" (L. Michaels), **Supp. XVI:** 207–208

Murder in Mount Holly (Theroux), **Supp. VIII:** 315–316

Murder in the Cathedral (T. S. Eliot), **I:** 571, 573, 580, 581; **II:** 20; **Retro. Supp. I:** 65; **Retro. Supp. II:** 222

Murder of Lidice, The (Millay), **III:** 140

"Murders in the Rue Morgue, The" (Poe), **III:** 412, 416, 419–420; **Retro. Supp. II:** 271, 272; **Supp. XIX:** 77

Murdoch, Iris, **Supp. VIII:** 167; **Supp. XVIII:** 136,149

Murnau, F. W., **Supp. XV:** 128

Murphy, Brenda, **Supp. XXI:** 6

Murphy, Jacqueline Shea, **Retro. Supp. II:** 143

Murphy, Patrick, **Supp. XIII:** 214

Murphy, Richard, **Retro. Supp. II:** 250

Murray, Albert, **Retro. Supp. II:** 119, 120; **Supp. XIX:** 147–162

Murray, Bill, **Supp. XXI:** 51

Murray, Edward, **I:** 229

Murray, G. E., **Supp. X:** 201; **Supp. XI:** 143, 155

Murray, Gilbert, **III:** 468–469

Murray, Jan, **Supp. IV Part 2:** 574

Murray, John, **II:** 304; **III:** 76, 79; **Retro. Supp. I:** 246

Murray, Judith Sargent, **Supp. XV:** 236–237

Murray, Les, **Supp. XIX:** 131

Murray, Margaret A., **Supp. V:** 128

Murrell, John A., **IV:** 265

Mursell, James L., **Supp. I Part 2:** 608

"Muse" (Ammons), **Supp. VII:** 29

"Muse, Postmodern and Homeless, The" (Ozick), **Supp. V:** 272

"Musée des Beaux Arts" (Auden), **Retro. Supp. I:** 430; **Supp. II Part 1:** 14

"Musée des Beaux Arts Revisited" (Collins), **Supp. XXI:** 60

"Muse of Aboutness, The" (Baker), **Supp. XVI:** 288

Muses Are Heard, The (Capote), **Supp. III Part 1:** 126

"Muses of Terrence McNally, The" (Zinman), **Supp. XIII:** 207–208

"Muse's Tragedy, The" (Wharton), **Retro. Supp. I:** 364

Museum (Dove), **Supp. IV Part 1:** 245–247, 248

"Museum" (Hass), **Supp. VI:** 107

Museums and Women (Updike), **Retro. Supp. I:** 321

"Museum Vase" (Francis), **Supp. IX:** 83

"Mushrooms" (Plath), **Retro. Supp. II:** 246; **Supp. I Part 2:** 539

"Music" (Oliver), **Supp. VII:** 236

Music (al-Músíqá) (Gibran), **Supp. XX:** 115, 124

Music After the Great War (Van Vechten), **Supp. II Part 2:** 732

Music and Bad Manners (Van Vechten), **Supp. II Part 2:** 733

Music Appreciation (Skloot), **Supp. XX:** 196, 197–201

"Music for a Farce" (Bowles), **Supp. IV Part 1:** 83

Music for Chameleons (Capote), **Supp. III Part 1:** 120, 125–127, 131, 132

"Music for Museums?" (Van Vechten), **Supp. II Part 2:** 732

"Music for the Movies" (Van Vechten), **Supp. II Part 2:** 733

"Music from Spain" (Welty), **IV:** 272

Music Like Dirt (Bidart), **Supp. XV:** 35

"Music Like Dirt" (Bidart), **Supp. XV:** 35

Music of Chance, The (Auster), **Supp. XII:** 21, 23, 32–33

"Music of My Own Kind Too, The" (Budbill), **Supp. XIX:** 10

"Music of Prose, The" (Gass), **Supp. VI:** 92

Music of Spain, The (Van Vechten), **Supp. II Part 2:** 734, 735

"Music of the Spheres" (Epstein), **Supp. XII:** 165

"Music School" (B. Kelly), **Supp. XVII:** 124

Music School, The (Updike), **IV:** 214, 215, 219, 226, 227; **Retro. Supp. I:** 320, 328, 329, 330

"Music School, The" (Updike), **Retro. Supp. I:** 326, 329, 335

"Music Swims Back to Me" (Sexton), **Supp. II Part 2:** 673

Muske, Carol, **Supp. IV Part 2:** 453–454

"Mussel Hunter at Rock Harbor" (Plath), **Supp. I Part 2:** 529, 537

Musset, Alfred de, **I:** 474; **II:** 543

Mussolini, Benito, **III:** 115, 473, 608; **IV:** 372, 373; **Supp. I Part 1:** 281, 282; **Supp. I Part 2:** 618; **Supp. V:** 290; **Supp. XVI:** 191

"Mustafa Ferrari" (X. J. Kennedy), **Supp. XV:** 170–171

Mustich, James, **Supp. XXI:** 52

"Must the Novelist Crusade?" (Welty), **IV:** 280

"Mutability of Literature, The" (Irving), **II:** 308

"Mutation of the Spirit" (Corso), **Supp. XII:** 132, 133

Mute, The (McCullers), **II:** 586

Mutilated, The (T. Williams), **IV:** 382, 386, 393

Mutiny of the Elsinore, The (London), **II:** 467

"Muttsy" (Hurston), **Supp. XVIII:** 279

Muyumba, Walton, **Supp. XIX:** 158

"My Adventures as a Social Poet" (Hughes), **Retro. Supp. I:** 194, 207

"My Alba" (Ginsberg), **Supp. II Part 1:** 320, 321

My Alexandria (Doty), **Supp. XI:** 119, 120, 121, 123–125, 130

"My Amendment" (Saunders), **Supp. XIX:** 232

My Ántonia (Cather), **I:** 321–322; **Retro. Supp. I:** 1, 3, 4, 11–13, 14, 17, 18, 22; **Supp. IV Part 2:** 608; **Supp. XVI:** 226

"My Appearance" (Wallace), **Supp. X:** 306–307

My Argument with the Gestapo: A Macaronic Journal (Merton), **Supp. VIII:** 207; **Supp. XV:** 344

"My Arkansas" (Angelou), **Supp. IV Part 1:** 15

"My Aunt" (Holmes), **Supp. I Part 1:** 302, 310

"My Beginnings" (Simpson), **Supp. IX:** 273

"My Bird Problem" (Franzen), **Supp. XX:** 94

My Bondage and My Freedom (Douglass), **Supp. III Part 1:** 155, 173

My Brother (Kincaid), **Supp. VII:** 191–193

"My Brother Paul" (Dreiser), **Retro. Supp. II:** 94

"My Brothers the Silent" (Merwin), **Supp. III Part 1:** 349–350

"My Brother's Work" (Dunn), **Supp. XI:** 147

"My Brother Takes a Hammer to the Mirror" (F. Wright), **Supp. XVII:** 244

"My Butterfly" (Frost), **II:** 151; **Retro. Supp. I:** 124

"My Children, and a Prayer for Us" (Ortiz), **Supp. IV Part 2:** 507

"My College Sex Group" (Peacock), **Supp. XIX:** 199

"My Coney Island Uncle" (Swados), **Supp. XIX:** 267–268

"My Confession" (McCarthy), **II:** 562

"My Confessional Sestina" (Gioia), **Supp. XV:** 123

My Country and My People (Yutang), **Supp. X:** 291

"My Country 'Tis of Thee" (Reznikoff), **Supp. III Part 2:** 616

"My Daughter Considers Her Body" (Skloot), **Supp. XX:** 197–198, 200

My Days of Anger (Farrell), **II:** 34, 35–36, 43

"My Dear Niece" (Boyce), **Supp. XXI:** 10

"My Dear Republican Mother" (C. Bly), **Supp. XVI:** 31–32

My Death My Life by Pier Paolo Pasolini (Acker), **Supp. XII:** 7

My Dog Stupid (Fante), **Supp. XI:** 160, 170–171

My Dog Tulip (Ackerley), **Supp. XX:** 237

My Emily Dickinson (Howe), **Retro. Supp. I:** 33, 43; **Supp. IV Part 2:** 430–431

"My English" (Alvarez), **Supp. VII:** 2

Myers, Linda A., **Supp. IV Part 1:** 10

"My Extended Family" (Theroux), **Supp. VIII:** 311

"My Father" (Budbill), **Supp. XIX:** 5

"My Father" (L. Michaels), **Supp. XVI:** 214

"My Father" (Sterne), **IV:** 466

"My Father at Eighty-Five" (R. Bly), **Supp. IV Part 1:** 73

"My Father Is a Simple Man" (Salinas), **Supp. XIII:** 324

"My Father Is with Me" (Budbill), **Supp. XIX:** 15

"My Father: October 1942" (Stafford), **Supp. XI:** 323

My Father Photographed with Friends (Bronk), **Supp. XXI:** 26–27,**Supp. XXI:** 31

"My Father Photographed with Friends" (Bronk), **Supp. XXI:** 23, 27

"My Fathers Came From Kentucky" (Lindsay), **Supp. I Part 2:** 395

"My Father's Friends" (Maxwell), **Supp. VIII:** 171

"My Father's Ghost" (Wagoner), **Supp. IX:** 330

"My Father's God" (Fante), **Supp. XI:** 160, 174

"My Father's House" (L.-Y. Lee), **Supp. XV:** 225

"My Father's Love Letters" (Komunyakaa), **Supp. XIII:** 127

"My Father Speaks to me from the Dead" (Olds), **Supp. X:** 210

"My Father's Telescope" (Dove), **Supp. IV Part 1:** 246, 248

"My Father with Cigarette Twelve Years Before the Nazis Could Break His Heart" (Levine), **Supp. V:** 194

"My Favorite Murder" (Bierce), **I:** 205

My Favorite Plant: Writers and Gardeners on the Plants They Love (Kincaid), **Supp. VII:** 193–194

"My Fifty-Plus Years Celebrate Spring" (Salinas), **Supp. XIII:** 327

"My First Book" (Harte), **Supp. II Part 1:** 343

My First Summer in the Sierra (Muir), **Supp. IX:** 172, 173, **178–181**, 183, 185; **Supp. XIV:** 177

"My Flamboyant Grandson" (Saunders), **Supp. XIX:** 231–232

"My Fountain Pen" (McClatchy), **Supp. XII:** 254, 260

My Friend, Henry Miller (Perlès), **III:** 189

My Friend, Julia Lathrop (Addams), **Supp. I Part 1:** 25

"My Friend, Walt Whitman" (Oliver), **Supp. VII:** 245

"My Garden Acquaintance" (Lowell), **Supp. I Part 2:** 420

My Garden \[Book\]: (Kincaid), **Supp. VII:** 193–194

"My Good-bye" (Weigl), **Supp. XIX:** 288

"My Grandfather" (Lowell), **II:** 554

"My Grandmother's Love Letters" (H. Crane), **Retro. Supp. II:** 78

"My Grandson, Home at Last" (Angelou), **Supp. IV Part 1:** 13

My Green Hills of Jamaica (McKay), **Supp. X:** 132, 142

My Guru and His Disciple (Isherwood), **Supp. XIV:** 157, 164, 172

"My Heart" (Collins), **Supp. XXI:** 58

My Heart's in the Highlands (Saroyan), **Supp. IV Part 1:** 83

"My High School Reunion" (Kingston), **Supp. V:** 169

"My House New-Painted" (Bronk), **Supp. XXI:** 30

"My Ideal Home" (Stratton-Porter), **Supp. XX:** 222

"My Indigo" (L.-Y. Lee), **Supp. XV:** 214

"My Kinsman, Major Molineux" (Hawthorne), **II:** 228, 229, 237–239, 243; **Retro. Supp. I:** 153–154, 158, 160, 161; **Retro. Supp. II:** 181, 187; **Supp. XVI:** 157

My Kinsman, Major Molineux (Lowell), **II:** 545–546

"My Last Afternoon with Uncle Devereux Winslow" (Lowell), **II:** 547–548; **Retro. Supp. II:** 189

"My Last Drive" (Hardy), **Supp. VIII:** 32

"My Last Duchess" (Browning), **Supp. XV:** 121

"My Life" (Strand), **Supp. IV Part 2:** 627

My Life, Starring Dara Falcon (Beattie), **Supp. V:** 31, 34–35

My Life a Loaded Gun: Dickinson, Plath, Rich, and Female Creativity (Bennett), **Retro. Supp. I:** 29

My Life and Hard Times (Thurber), **Supp. I Part 2:** 607, 609

My Life as a Man (P. Roth), **Retro. Supp. II:** 281, 286, 289; **Supp. III Part 2:** 401, 404, 405, 417–418

"My Life as a P.I.G., or the True Adventures of Smokey the Cop" (Abbey), **Supp. XIII:** 3

"My life closed twice before its close" (Dickinson), **Retro. Supp. I:** 38

"My Life had stood a Loaded Gun" (Dickinson), **Retro. Supp. I:** 42, 43, 45, 46; **Supp. IV Part 2:** 430

My Life of Absurdity (C. Himes), **Supp. XVI:** 145

"My Life with Medicine" (Nye), **Supp. XIII:** 282

"My Life with *Playboy*" (Plimpton), **Supp. XVI:** 246

"My Life with R. H. Macy" (Jackson), **Supp. IX:** 118

"My Little Utopia" (Simic), **Supp. VIII:** 283

My Lives and How I Lost Them (Cullen), **Supp. IV Part 1:** 173

"My Lord Bag of Rice" (C. Bly), **Supp. XVI:** 40

My Lord Bag of Rice: New and Selected Stories (C. Bly), **Supp. XVI:** 41

"My Lost City" (Fitzgerald), **Retro. Supp. I:** 102

"My Lost Youth" (Longfellow), **II:** 487, 499; **Retro. Supp. II:** 168

My Love Affair with America: The Cautionary Tale of a Cheerful Conservative (Podhoretz), **Supp. VIII:** 232, 233, 237, **244–246**

"My Lover Has Dirty Fingernails" (Updike), **Retro. Supp. I:** 332, 333

"My Lucy Friend Who Smells Like Corn" (Cisneros), **Supp. VII:** 68–69

"My Mammogram" (McClatchy), **Supp. XII:** 263–264

"My Man Bovanne" (Bambara), **Supp. XI:** 2

"My Mariner" (Larcom), **Supp. XIII:** 147

My Mark Twain (Howells), **II:** 276

"My Metamorphosis" (Harte), **Supp. II Part 1:** 339

"My Moby Dick" (Humphrey), **Supp. IX:** 95

"My Monkey" (Nelson), **Supp. XVIII:** 178

"My Moral Life" (Halliday), **Supp. XIX:** 89

My Mortal Enemy (Cather), **I:** 327–328; **Retro. Supp. I:** 16–17; **Supp. I Part 2:** 719

My Mother, My Father and Me (Hellman), **Supp. I Part 1:** 290–291

"My Mother and My Sisters" (Ortiz), **Supp. IV Part 2:** 499

My Mother: Demonology (Acker), **Supp. XII:** 6

"My Mother Is Speaking from the Desert" (Gordon), **Supp. IV Part 1:** 309, 314

"My Mother's Goofy Song" (Fante), **Supp. XI:** 164

"My Mother's Memoirs, My Father's Lie, and Other True Stories" (Banks), **Supp. V:** 15

"My Mother's Nipples" (Hass), **Supp. VI:** 109

"My Mother's Story" (Kunitz), **Supp. III Part 1:** 259

"My Mother Then and Now" (Wasserstein), **Supp. XV:** 327

"My Mother with Purse the Summer They Murdered the Spanish Poet" (Levine), **Supp. V:** 194

My Movie Business: A Memoir (Irving), **Supp. VI:** 164

"My Name" (Cisneros), **Supp. VII:** 60

"My Negro Problem—And Ours" (Podhoretz), **Supp. VIII: 234–236**

"My New Diet" (Karr), **Supp. XI:** 241

"My Number" (Collins), **Supp. XXI:** 64

"My Old Man" (Hemingway), **II:** 263

My Other Life (Theroux), **Supp. VIII:** 310, 324

"My Own Story" (E. Stoddard), **Supp. XV:** 273, 279, 283

My Own True Name: New and Selected Poems for Young Adults, 1984–1999 (Mora), **Supp. XIII:** 222

"My Parents Have Come Home Laughing" (Jarman), **Supp. XVII:** 113

"My Passion for Ferries" (Whitman), **IV:** 350

"My People" (Hughes), **Retro. Supp. I:** 197; **Supp. I Part 1:** 321–322, 323

"My Philosophy" (Allen), **Supp. XV:** 15

"My Playmate" (Whittier), **Supp. I Part 2:** 699–700

"My Priests" (Monette), **Supp. X:** 159

Myra Breckinridge (Vidal), **Supp. IV Part 2:** 677, 685–686, 689, 691

"My Raptor" (A. Finch), **Supp. XVII:** 72

"My Recollections of S. B. Fairchild" (Jackson), **Supp. IX:** 118–119

"My Religion" (Carson), **Supp. XII:** 105–106

"My Road to Hell Was Paved" (Patchett), **Supp. XII:** 310–311

Myron (Vidal), **Supp. IV Part 2:** 677, 685, 686, 691

"My Roomy" (Lardner), **II:** 420, 421, 428, 430

"My Sad Self" (Ginsberg), **Supp. II Part 1:** 320

My Secret History (Theroux), **Supp. VIII:** 310, 324

"Myself" (Audubon), **Supp. XVI:** 1–2, 5, 12

"My Shoes" (Simic), **Supp. VIII:** 275

"My Side of the Matter" (Capote), **Supp. III Part 1:** 114, 115

My Silk Purse and Yours: The Publishing Scene and American Literary Art (Garrett), **Supp. VII:** 111; **Supp. X:** 7

My Sister Eileen (McKenney), **IV:** 288; **Retro. Supp. II:** 321

My Sister's Hand in Mine: The Collected Works of Jane Bowles, **Supp. IV Part 1:** 82–83

"My Son" (Strand), **Supp. IV Part 2:** 629

My Son, John (film), **Supp. I Part 1:** 67

"My Son, the Murderer" (Malamud), **Supp. I Part 2:** 437

"My Son the Man" (Olds), **Supp. X:** 212

"My Speech to the Graduates" (Allen), **Supp. XV:** 16

"Mysteries of Caesar, The" (Hecht), **Supp. X:** 73

"Mysteries of Eleusis, The" (Hardwick), **Supp. III Part 1:** 195

Mysteries of Pittsburgh, The (Chabon), **Supp. XI:** 65, 68, **69–71**; **Supp. XIX:** 135

"Mysterious Case of R, The" (Conroy), **Supp. XVI:** 72

Mysterious Stranger, The (Twain), **IV:** 190–191, 210

Mystery, A (Shields). *See Swann* (Shields)

"Mystery, The" (Dunbar), **Supp. II Part 1:** 199, 210

"Mystery, The" (Glück), **Supp. V:** 91

Mystery and Manners (O'Connor), **Retro. Supp. II:** 230

"'Mystery Boy' Looks for Kin in Nashville" (Hayden), **Supp. II Part 1:** 366, 372

"Mystery of Coincidence, The" (Conroy), **Supp. XVI:** 74

"Mystery of Heroism, A" (Crane), **I:** 414

"Mystery of Marie Rogêt, The" (Poe), **III:** 413, 419; **Retro. Supp. II:** 271

"Mystic" (Plath), **Retro. Supp. II:** 257; **Supp. I Part 2:** 539, 541

"Mystical Poet, A" (Bogan), **Retro. Supp. I:** 36

"Mystic of Sex, The—A First Look at D. H. Lawrence" (Nin), **Supp. X:** 188

"Mystic Vision in 'The Marshes of Glynn'" (Warfel), **Supp. I Part 1:** 366, 373

"Mystification" (Poe), **III:** 425

"My Strange New Poetry" (Halliday), **Supp. XIX:** 88, 94

My Study Windows (Lowell), **Supp. I Part 2:** 407

"My Teacher" (Conroy), **Supp. XVI:** 75

"Myth" (Rukeyser), **Supp. VI:** 281–282

"Myth" (Trethewey), **Supp. XXI:** 245, 255, 256

"Mythmaker" (Trethewey), **Supp. XXI:** 243

Myth of Sisyphus, The (Camus), **I:** 294; **Supp. XIII:** 165

"Myth of the Happy Worker, The" (Swados), **Supp. XIX:** 265

"Myth of the Isolated Artist, The" (Oates), **Supp. II Part 2:** 520

Myth of the Machine, The (Mumford), **Supp. II Part 2:** 476, 478, 482, 483, 493, 497

"Myth of the Powerful Worker, The" (Swados), **Supp. XIX:** 265

Mythology and the Romantic Tradition in English Poetry (Bush), **Supp. I Part 1:** 268

Myths and Texts (Snyder), **Supp. VIII:** 295–296

"Myths of Bears, The" (Bass), **Supp. XVI:** 19, 20

"My *Tocaya*" (Cisneros), **Supp. VII:** 69

My Uncle Dudley (Morris), **I:** 305; **III:** 219–220

"My Uncle's Favorite Coffee Shop" (Nye), **Supp. XIII:** 283

"My Weariness of Epic Proportions" (Simic), **Supp. VIII:** 276

My Wicked Wicked Ways (Cisneros), **Supp. VII:** 58, 64–68, 71

"My Wicked Wicked Ways" (Cisneros), **Supp. VII:** 58, 64–66

"My Word-house" (Mora), **Supp. XIII:** 219, 225

My Works and Days (Mumford), **Supp. II Part 2:** 475, 477, 481

"My World and My Critics" (Stratton-Porter), **Supp. XX:** 220

My World and Welcome to It (Thurber), **Supp. I Part 2:** 610

N

Nabokov, Peter, **Supp. IV Part 2:** 490

Nabokov, Véra, **Retro. Supp. I:** 266, 270

Nabokov, Vladimir, **I:** 135; **III:** 244–266, 283, 286; **Retro. Supp. I:** 263–281, 317, 335; **Supp. I Part 1:** 196; **Supp. II Part 1:** 2; **Supp. IV Part 1:** 135; **Supp. V:** 127, 237, 251, 252, 253; **Supp. VIII:** 105, 133, 138; **Supp. IX:** 152, 212, 261; **Supp. X:** 283; **Supp. XI:** 66; **Supp. XII:** 310; **Supp. XIII:** 46, 52; **Supp. XVI:** 148, 294; **Supp. XVIII:** 98, 102

Nabokov's Dozen (Nabokov), **Retro. Supp. I:** 266

Nabokov's Garden: A Guide to Ada (Mason), **Supp. VIII:** 138

Naca, Kristin, **Supp. XIII:** 133

Nadeau, Robert, **Supp. X:** 261, 270

Nadel, Alan, **Supp. IV Part 1:** 209

Naimy, Mikhail, **Supp. XX:** 116, 119, 120

Naipaul, V. S., **Supp. IV Part 1:** 297; **Supp. VIII:** 314; **Supp. X:** 131; **Supp. XIV:** 111; **Supp. XX:** 87; **Supp. XXI:** 170

Naison, Mark, **Supp. XVIII:** 231

Naked and the Dead, The (Mailer), **I:** 477; **III:** 26, 27, 28–30, 31, 33, 35, 36, 44; **Retro. Supp. II:** 197–199; **Supp. IV Part 1:** 381; **Supp. XI:** 218; **Supp. XIX:** 248; **Supp. XX:** 248; **Supp. XXI:** 277

Naked Author (di Donato), **Supp. XX:** 45

Naked Babies (Quindlen and Kelsh), **Supp. XVII:** 167, 179

Naked in Garden Hills (Crews), **Supp. XI:** 102, **110**

Naked Lunch (Burroughs), **Supp. III Part 1:** 92–95, 97–105; **Supp. IV Part 1:** 90

"Naked Nude" (Malamud), **Supp. I Part 2:** 450

Naked Poetry (Berg and Mezey, eds.), **Supp. IV Part 1:** 60

Naked Poetry (Levine), **Supp. V:** 180

Naked Revenge (film), **Supp. XVII:** 141

Namedropping: Mostly Literary Memoirs (Coover), **Supp. V:** 40

"Name in the Papers" (Hughes), **Supp. I Part 1:** 330

Name Is Archer, The (Macdonald, under Millar), **Supp. IV Part 2:** 466

"Name Is Burroughs, The" (Burroughs), **Supp. III Part 1:** 93

Name Is Fogarty, The: Private Papers on Public Matters (Farrell), **II:** 49

"Names" (Carruth), **Supp. XVI:** 54, 56

"Names, The" (Collins), **Supp. XXI:** 54, 61–62

Names, The (DeLillo), **Supp. VI:** 3, 10, 13, 14

Names, The (Momaday), **Supp. IV Part 2:** 479, 480, 483, 486, 487, 488, 489

Namesake, The (Lahiri), **Supp. XXI:** 176, 184, **186–188**

Names and Faces of Heroes, The (Price), **Supp. VI:** 258, 260

Names of the Lost, The (Levine), **Supp. V:** 177–178, 179, 187–188

"Naming for Love" (Carruth), **Supp. XVI:** 48

"Naming Myself" (Kingsolver), **Supp. VII:** 208

"Naming of Names, The" (Sanders), **Supp. XVI:** 268

Naming of the Beasts, The (Stern). *See Rejoicings: Selected Poems, 1966–1972* (Stern)

Naming the Unseen (Ray), **Supp. XVIII:** 192, **193–195**

"Naming the Unseen" (Ray), **Supp. XVIII:** 203

Nana (Zola), **III:** 321

"Nancy Culpepper" (Mason), **Supp. VIII:** 141

Nancy Drew stories, **Supp. VIII:** 133, 135, 137, 142

"Nancy Knapp" (Masters), **Supp. I Part 2:** 461

"Naola Beauty Academy, New Orleans, 1943" (Trethewey), **Supp. XXI:** 246

"Naomi Shihab Nye: U.S. Mideast-History a Harbinger of 9-11?" (Nye), **Supp. XIII:** 286

"Naomi Trimmer" (X. J. Kennedy), **Supp. XV:** 170

"Nap, The" (Banks), **Supp. V:** 7

"Napoleon" (Emerson), **II:** 6

Napoleon I, **I:** 6, 7, 8, 474; **II:** 5, 309, 315, 321, 523; **Supp. I Part 1:** 153; **Supp. I Part 2:** 518, 519

Napolitano, Louise, **Supp. XX:** 35, 45, 46–47

Narcissa and Other Fables (Auchincloss), **Supp. IV Part 1:** 21, 34

"Narcissus as Narcissus" (Tate), **IV:** 124

"Narcissus Leaves the Pool" (Epstein), **Supp. XIV:** 110

Narcissus Leaves the Pool: Familiar Essays (Epstein), **Supp. XIV:** 110

Nardal, Paulette, **Supp. X:** 139

Nardi, Marcia, **Retro. Supp. I:** 426, 427

"Narragansett Boulevard" (Halliday), **Supp. XIX:** 91

Narration (Stein), **IV:** 27, 30, 32, 33, 36

Narrative of a Four Months' Residence among the Natives of a Valley of the Marquesas Islands (Melville), **III:** 76

Narrative of Arthur Gordon Pym, The (Poe), **III:** 412, 416; **Retro. Supp. II:** 265, 273–275; **Supp. XI:** 293

Narrative of the Life of Frederick Douglass, an American Slave, Written by Himself (Douglass), **Supp. III Part 1:** 154–159, 162, 165; **Supp. IV Part 1:** 13; **Supp. VIII:** 202

"Narrativity Scenes" (Wright), **Supp. XV:** 345

Narrenschiff, Das (Brant), **III:** 447

"Narrow Fellow in the Grass, A" (Dickinson), **Retro. Supp. I:** 30, 37

Narrow Heart, A: Portrait of a Woman (Gordon), **II:** 197, 217

Narrow Rooms (Purdy), **Supp. VII:** 274

Narrows, The (Connelly), **Supp. XXI:** 71, **76**

Nasby, Petroleum, **Supp. XVIII:** 1

Nash, Ogden, **Supp. XXI:** 51

Nash, Roderick, **Supp. IX:** 185; **Supp. XIV:** 191–192

Nash, Susan Smith, **Supp. XVI:** 274

Nash, Thomas, **Supp. III Part 1:** 387–388

Nashe, Thomas, **I:** 358; **Supp. XVII:** 232

Nashville (film), **Supp. IX:** 143

"Nashville Gone to Ashes" (Hempel), **Supp. XXI:** 115, 118, **120–121**

Nashville Skyline (album, Dylan), **Supp. XVIII:** 27

Nason, Elias, **Supp. XV:** 242

Nasser, Gamal Abdel, **IV:** 490

Natalie Mann (Toomer), **Supp. III Part 2:** 484–486

Nathan, George Jean, **II:** 91; **III:** 103, 104, 106, 107; **IV:** 432; **Supp. IV Part 1:** 343; **Supp. IX:** 56–57; **Supp. XIII:** 161

"Nathanael West" (Herbst), **Retro. Supp. II:** 325

Nathanael West: The Art of His Life (Martin), **Retro. Supp. II:** 325

Nathan Coulter (Berry), **Supp. X:** 24, 33

National Dream, The: Building the Impossible Railway (Findley and Whitehead), **Supp. XX:** 51

"Nationalist, The" (Anderson), **I:** 115

"Nation Is Like Ourselves, The" (Baraka), **Supp. II Part 1:** 53

"Native, The" (Olds), **Supp. X:** 215

"Native American Attitudes to the Environment" (Momaday), **Supp. IV Part 2:** 481, 491

Native American Renaissance (Lincoln), **Supp. IV Part 2:** 507

Native American Testimony (Nabokov, ed.), **Supp. IV Part 2:** 490

"Native Blessing" (Ray), **Supp. XVIII:** 202

Native Guard (Trethewey), **Supp. XXI:** 243, 244, 247, **254–257**

"Native Guard" (Trethewey), **Supp. XXI:** 256

"Native Hill, A" (Berry), **Supp. X:** 21

Native in a Strange Land: Trials & Tremors (Coleman), **Supp. XI: 84–85,** 87

Native of Winby and Other Tales, A (Jewett), **II:** 396; **Retro. Supp. II:** 138

Native Son (Wright), **IV:** 476, 477, 478, 479, 481, 482–484, 485, 487, 488, 491, 495; **Retro. Supp. II:** 107, 116; **Supp. I Part 1:** 51, 64, 67, 337; **Supp. II Part 1:** 170, 235–236; **Supp. IX:** 306; **Supp. XIV:** 73; **Supp. XVII:** 155; **Supp. XVIII:** 283, 286; **Supp. XXI:** 169

"Native Trees" (Merwin), **Supp. III Part 1:** 355

Natorp, Paul, **Supp. XIV:** 198

Natural, The (Malamud), **II:** 424, 425; **Retro. Supp. II:** 288; **Supp. I Part 2:** 438–441, 443

"*Natural, The*: Malamud's World Ceres" (Wasserman), **Supp. I Part 2:** 439

"Natural History" (Olds), **Supp. X:** 210

"Natural History Note" (Hay), **Supp. XIV:** 124, 130

"Natural History of Some Poems, A" (Harrison), **Supp. VIII:** 53

"Natural History of the Dead" (Hemingway), **II:** 206; **Retro. Supp. I:** 176

"Naturally Superior School, A" (Knowles), **Supp. XII:** 235, 240–241

"Natural Method of Mental Philosophy" (Emerson), **II:** 14

"Natural Resources" (Rich), **Supp. I Part 2:** 575

Natural Selection (F. Barthelme), **Supp. XI:** 2, 28, 32, 33

Nature (Emerson), **I:** 463; **II:** 1, 8, 12, 16; **IV:** 171, 172–173

"Nature" (Emerson), **Retro. Supp. I:** 250; **Supp. I Part 2:** 383; **Supp. III Part 1:** 387; **Supp. IX:** 178

"Nature, Inc." (Lewis), **II:** 441

Nature and Destiny of Man, The (Niebuhr), **III:** 292, 303–306, 310

"Nature and Life" (Emerson), **II:** 19

"Nature and Nurture: When It Comes to Twins, Sometimes It's Hard to Tell the Two Apart" (Bausch), **Supp. VII:** 40

"Nature-Metaphors" (Lanier), **Supp. I Part 1:** 352

Nature Morte (Brodsky), **Supp. VIII:** 25

Nature of Evil, The (James), **II:** 343

Nature of Peace, The (Veblen), **Supp. I Part 2:** 642

Nature of Things, The (television show), **Supp. XX:** 51

Nature of True Virtue, The (Edwards), **I:** 549, 557–558, 559

Nature: Poems Old and New (Swenson), **Supp. IV Part 2:** 652

Nature's Economy: A History of Ecological Ideas (Worster), **Supp. IX:** 19

Naumburg, Margaret, **Supp. XX:** 68, 74–75

Nausea (Sartre), **Supp. VIII:** 7

"Navajo Blanket, A" (Swenson), **Supp. IV Part 2:** 649

Navarette, Don Martín de, **II:** 310

Navarro, Ramon, **Supp. IV Part 1:** 206

Navigator, The (film), **I:** 31

Navratilova, Martina, **Supp. XX:** 264

Naylor, Gloria, **Supp. VIII: 213–230; Supp. XX:** 108

Naylor, Paul Kenneth, **Supp. IV Part 2:** 420

Nazimova, **III:** 399

Neal, Darlin', **Supp. XXI:** 41

Neal, Larry, **Retro. Supp. II:** 112, 128; **Supp. X:** 324, 328

Neal, Lawrence P., **Supp. II Part 1:** 53

Neal, Patricia, **Supp. I Part 1:** 286; **Supp. IV Part 2:** 524; **Supp. V:** 223

Neale, Walter, **I:** 192, 208

"Near Damascus" (Di Piero), **Supp. XIX:** 43

Nearer the Moon: From "A Journal of Love," the Unexpurgated Diary of Anaïs Nin, 1937–1939, **Supp. X:** 184, 185

Near-Johannesburg Boy and Other Poems, The (Brooks), **Supp. III Part 1:** 86

Near Klamath (Carver), **Supp. III Part 1:** 137

"Near Perigord" (Pound), **Retro. Supp. I:** 289, 290

"Near Spring" (Pickering), **Supp. XXI:** 198

Near the Ocean (Lowell), **II:** 543, 550, 551–553, 554, 555; **Retro. Supp. II:** 182, 186, 189–190

"Near View of the High Sierra, A" (Muir), **Supp. IX:** 183

Nebeker, Helen, **Supp. IX:** 122

"Nebraska Blizzard" (F. Wright), **Supp. XVII:** 247

Necessary Angel, The (Stevens), **IV:** 76, 79, 89, 90

Necessities of Life: Poems, 1962–1965 (Rich), **Supp. I Part 2:** 553, 555

Nechayev, Sergey, **Supp. XXI:** 164

"Necrological" (Ransom), **III:** 486–489, 490, 492

Ned Christie's War (Conley), **Supp. V:** 232

"Need for a Cultural Base to Civil Rites & Bpower Mooments, The" (Baraka), **Supp. II Part 1:** 48

"Need for Christian Preaching, The" (Buechner), **Supp. XII:** 49

Needful Things (King), **Supp. V:** 139, 146

"Needle" (Simic), **Supp. VIII:** 275

"Needle Trade" (Reznikoff), **Supp. XIV:** 277, 289

"Need of Being Versed in Country Things, The" (Frost), **II:** 154; **Retro. Supp. I:** 133, 135

Neel, Philippe, **Supp. XIV:** 338

Neelakantappa, Tara, **Supp. XV:** 104–105

Neeley, Barbara, **Supp. XVI:** 143

"Negative Capability" (Komunyakaa), **Supp. XIII:** 131

Negligible Tales (Bierce), **I:** 209

"Negotiating the Darkness, Fortified by Poets' Strength" (Karr), **Supp. XI:** 254; **Supp. XIII:** 285

Negotiating with the Dead (Atwood), **Supp. XIII:** 20, 35

Negritude movement, **Supp. X:** 131, 139

"Negro" (Hughes), **Supp. I Part 1:** 321–322

Negro, The (Du Bois), **Supp. II Part 1:** 178, 179, 185

Negro, The: The Southerner's Problem (Page), **Supp. II Part 1:** 168

Negro and His Music, The (Locke), **Supp. XIV:** 202

"Negro Artisan, The" (Du Bois), **Supp. II Part 1:** 166

"Negro Artist and the Racial Mountain, The" (Hughes), **Retro. Supp. I:** 200, 207; **Supp. I Part 1:** 323, 325; **Supp. IV Part 1:** 169

Negro Art: Past and Present (Locke), **Supp. XIV:** 202

"Negro Assays the Negro Mood, A" (Baldwin), **Supp. I Part 1:** 52

"Negro Citizen, The" (Du Bois), **Supp. II Part 1:** 179

"Negro Dancers" (Hughes), **Retro. Supp. I:** 199; **Supp. I Part 1:** 324

Negroes in America, The (McKay), **Supp. X:** 132, 136

"Negroes of Farmville, Virginia, The: A Social Study" (Du Bois), **Supp. II Part 1:** 166

Negro Family, The: The Case for National Action (Moynihan), **Retro. Supp. II:** 123

"Negro Farmer, The" (Du Bois), **Supp. II Part 1:** 167

"Negro Fight, The" (column, C. L. R. James), **Supp. XXI:** 169

"Negro Ghetto" (Hughes), **Supp. I Part 1:** 331

Negro in America, The (Locke), **Supp. XIV:** 208

Negro in American Civilization, The (Du Bois), **Supp. II Part 1:** 179

Negro in American Culture, The (Locke and Butcher), **Supp. XIV:** 202–203

Negro in Art, The: A Pictorial Record of the Negro Artist and of the Negro Theme in Art (Locke), **Supp. XIV:** 202

"Negro in Large Cities, The" (Du Bois), **Supp. II Part 1:** 169

"Negro in Literature and Art, The" (Du Bois), **Supp. II Part 1:** 174

Negro in New York, The (Ellison), **Supp. II Part 1:** 230

"Negro in the Black Belt, The: Some Social Sketches" (Du Bois), **Supp. II Part 1:** 166

Negro in the Caribbean, The (Williams), **Supp. XXI:** 166

"Negro in the Three Americas, The" (Locke), **Supp. XIV:** 211

"Negro in the Well, The" (Caldwell), **I:** 309

"Negro Love Song, A" (Dunbar), **Supp. II Part 1:** 204

"Negro Martyrs Are Needed" (C. Himes), **Supp. XVI:** 138

Negro Mother, The (Hughes), **Supp. I Part 1:** 328

Negro Mother and Other Dramatic Recitations, The (Hughes), **Retro. Supp. I:** 203

Negro Novel in America, The (Bone), **Supp. IX:** 318–319; **Supp. XVIII:** 285

Negro Publication Society of America, **Retro. Supp. I:** 205

"Negro Renaissance, The: Jean Toomer and the Harlem of the 1920s" (Bontemps), **Supp. IX:** 306

"Negro Schoolmaster in the New South, A" (Du Bois), **Supp. II Part 1:** 168

"Negro's Contribution to American Culture, The" (Locke), **Supp. XIV:** 210, 211

"Negro Sermon, A: Simon Legree" (Lindsay), **Supp. I Part 2:** 393

"Negro Sings of Rivers, The" (Hughes), **Supp. IV Part 1:** 16

"Negro Speaks of Rivers, The" (Hughes), **Retro. Supp. I:** 199; **Supp. I Part 1:** 321

"Negro Spirituals, The (Locke), **Supp. XIV:** 201

"Negro Takes Stock, The" (Du Bois), **Supp. II Part 1:** 180

"Negro Theatre, The" (Van Vechten), **Supp. II Part 2:** 735

"Negro Voter Sizes Up Taft, A" (Hurston), **Supp. VI:** 160

"Negro Writer and His Roots, The: Toward a New Romanticism" (Hansberry), **Supp. IV Part 1:** 364

"Negro Youth Speaks" (Locke), **Supp. XIV:** 201

"Nehemias Americanus" (Mather), **Supp. II Part 2:** 453

Nehru, Jawaharlal, **IV:** 490

"Neighbor" (Hugo), **Supp. VI:** 135–136

"Neighbors" (Carver), **Supp. III Part 1:** 135, 139, 141; **Supp. XI:** 153

"Neighbors" (Hogan), **Supp. IV Part 1:** 405

"Neighbors, The" (Hay), **Supp. XIV:** 126

"Neighbour Rosicky" (Cather), **I:** 331–332

Neil Simon (Johnson), **Supp. IV Part 2:** 573

"Neil Simon's Jewish-Style Comedies" (Walden), **Supp. IV Part 2:** 584, 591

"Neil Simon: Toward Act III?" (Walden), **Supp. IV Part 2:** 591

Neilson, Heather, **Supp. IV Part 2:** 681

Neiman, Gilbert, **Supp. XV:** 140

"Neither Out Far Nor In Deep" (Frost), **I:** 303; **Retro. Supp. I:** 121, 138

"Nellie Clark" (Masters), **Supp. I Part 2:** 461

Nelson, Alice Dunbar, **Supp. XVII:** 75

Nelson, Cary, **Supp. XVIII:** 226, 227, 230, 231

Nelson, Ernest, **I:** 388

Nelson, Howard, **Supp. IV Part 1:** 66, 68; **Supp. XIX:** 3; **Supp. XXI:** 95

Nelson, Lord Horatio, **II:** 524

Nelson, Lynn (pseudonym). *See* Nelson, Marilyn

Nelson, Marilyn, **Supp. XVII:** 74, 112; **Supp. XVIII:** 171–188

Nelson, Shirley, **Supp. XII:** 293

Nelson, Steve, **Supp. XVIII:** 226

Nelson Algren (Cox and Chatterton), **Supp. IX:** 11–12

Nelson Algren: A Life on the Wild Side (Drew), **Supp. IX:** 2

Nemerov, David, **II:** 268

Nemerov, Howard, **III:** 267–289; **IV:** 137, 140; **Supp. III Part 2:** 541; **Supp. IV Part 2:** 455, 650; **Supp. IX:** 114

Nemiroff, Robert Barron, **Supp. IV Part 1:** 360, 361, 365, 369, 370, 374

Neoconservative Criticism: Norman Podhoretz, Kenneth S. Lynn, and Joseph Epstein (Winchell), **Supp. VIII:** 241; **Supp. XIV:** 103

"Neo-Formalism: A Dangerous Nostalgia" (Sadoff), **Supp. XXI:** 100

"Neo-Hoodoo Manifesto, The" (Reed), **Supp. X:** 242

Neon Rain, The (Burke), **Supp. XIV:** 22, 24, 26–27, 28–29, 30

Neon Vernacular (Komunyakaa), **Supp. XIII:** 121, 127–128, 131

Neon Wilderness, The (Algren), **Supp. IX:** 3, 4

Neo-Slave Narratives (Rushdy), **Supp. X:** 250

Nepantla: Essays from the Land in the Middle (Mora), **Supp. XIII:** 213, 219–221, 227

Nephew, The (Purdy), **Supp. VII:** 271, 273, 282

"Nereids of Seriphos, The" (Clampitt), **Supp. IX:** 41

Nericcio, William, **Supp. XIV:** 304–305

Neruda, Pablo, **Supp. I Part 1:** 89; **Supp. IV Part 2:** 537; **Supp. V:** 332; **Supp. VIII:** 272, 274; **Supp. IX:** 157, 271; **Supp. X:** 112; **Supp. XI:** 191; **Supp. XII:** 217; **Supp. XIII:** 114, 315, 323; **Supp. XXI:** 61, 100

Nesbit, Edith, **Supp. VIII:** 171

Nesbitt, Robin, **Supp. VIII:** 89

Nessmuk (George Washington Sears), **Supp. XIX:** 10

Nesting Ground, The (Wagoner), **Supp. IX:** 324, 325–326

Nest of Ninnies, A (Ashbery and Schuyler), **Supp. III Part 1:** 3; **Supp. XV:** 178

Nets to Catch the Wind (Wylie), **Supp. I Part 2:** 709, 710–712, 714

Nettleton, Asahel, **I:** 458

"Net to Snare the Moonlight, A" (Lindsay), **Supp. I Part 2:** 387

Neubauer, Carol E., **Supp. IV Part 1:** 9

Neugeboren, Jacob Mordecai. *See* Neugeboren, Jay

Neugeboren, Jay, **Supp. XVI: 217–231**

Neugroschel, Joachim, **Supp. IX:** 138

Neuhaus, Richard John, **Supp. VIII:** 245; **Supp. XIX:** 144

Neumann, Erich, **Supp. I Part 2:** 567; **Supp. IV Part 1:** 68, 69

Neuromancer (W. Gibson), **Supp. XII:** 15; **Supp. XVI:** 117, 119–120, 122, 124, **125–126**, 127, 129, 131

Neurotica: Jewish Writers on Sex (Bukiet, ed.), **Supp. XVII:** 48

"Neurotic America and the Sex Impulse" (Dreiser), **Retro. Supp. II:** 105

Neutra, Richard, **Supp. XVI:** 192

"Never Bet the Devil Your Head" (Poe), **III:** 425; **Retro. Supp. II:** 273

Never Come Morning (Algren), **Supp. IX:** 3, **7–9**

Never in a Hurry: Essays on People and Places (Nye), **Supp. XIII:** 273, **280– 282,** 286

"Never Marry a Mexican" (Cisneros), **Supp. VII:** 70

"Never Room with a Couple" (Hughes), **Supp. I Part 1:** 330

"Nevertheless" (Moore), **III:** 214

Nevins, Allan, **I:** 253; **Supp. I Part 2:** 486, 493

"Nevsky Prospekt" (Olds), **Supp. X:** 205

New Adam, The (Untermeyer), **Supp. XV:** 304, 305

New Addresses (Koch), **Supp. XV:** 177, 184

"New Age of the Rhetoricians, The" (Cowley), **Supp. II Part 1:** 135

New American Cyclopedia, **Supp. XVIII:** 4

New American Literature, The (Pattee), **II:** 456

New American Novel of Manners, The (Klinkowitz), **Supp. XI:** 347

"New American Ode, The" (Wright), **Supp. XV:** 346

New American Poetry, 1945–1960 (Allen, ed.), **Supp. XIII:** 112

New American Poetry, The (Allen, ed.), **Supp. VIII:** 291, 292

"New American Writer, A" (W. C. Williams), **Retro. Supp. II:** 335

New and Collected Poems (Reed), **Supp. X:** 241

New and Collected Poems (Wilbur), **Supp. III Part 2:** 562–564

New and Selected Poems (Nemerov), **III:** 269, 275, 277–279

New and Selected Poems (Oliver), **Supp. VII:** 240–241, 245

New and Selected Poems (W. J. Smith), **Supp. XIII:** 332

New and Selected Poems (Wagoner), **Supp. IX: 326–327**

New and Selected Poems, 1958–1998 (Sorrentino), **Supp. XXI:** 229

New and Selected Poems: 1974–1994 (Dunn), **Supp. XI: 151–152**

New and Selected Things Taking Place (Swenson), **Supp. IV Part 2:** 648– 650, 651

"New Art Gallery Society, The" (Wolfe), **Supp. III Part 2:** 580

Newberger, Julee, **Supp. XVIII:** 168

"New Capitalist Tool, The" (Wasserstein), **Supp. XV:** 328

Newcomb, Ralph, **Supp. XIII:** 12

Newcomb, Robert, **II:** 111

New Conscience and an Ancient Evil, A (Addams), **Supp. I Part 1:** 14–15, 16

"New Conservatism in American Poetry, The" (Wakoski), **Supp. XVII:** 112

"New Conservatives, The: Intellectuals in Retreat" (Epstein), **Supp. XIV:** 103

New Criticism, The (Ransom), **III:** 497– 498, 499, 501

"New Day, A" (Levine), **Supp. V:** 182

Newdick, Robert Spangler, **Retro. Supp. I:** 138

Newdick's Season of Frost (Newdick), **Retro. Supp. I:** 138

New Dictionary of Quotations, A (Mencken), **III:** 111

New Directions Anthology in Prose and Poetry (Laughlin, ed.), **Supp. XVI:** 284

"New Directions in Poetry" (D. Locke), **Supp. IX:** 273

"New Dog, The: Variations on a Text by Jules Laforgue" (C. Frost), **Supp. XV:** 98

Newell, Henry, **IV:** 193

"New England" (Lowell), **II:** 536

"New England" (Robinson), **III:** 510, 524

"New England Bachelor, A" (Eberhart), **I:** 539

"New Englander, The" (Anderson), **I:** 114

New England Girlhood, A (Larcom), **Supp. XIII:** 137, 142, 143, 144, **147– 154**

New England: Indian Summer (Brooks), **I:** 253, 256

New England Local Color Literature (Donovan), **Retro. Supp. II:** 138

"New England Sabbath-Day Chace, The" (Freneau), **Supp. II Part 1:** 273

New-England Tale, A (Sedgwick), **I:** 341

New England Tragedies, The (Longfellow), **II:** 490, 505, 506; **Retro. Supp. II:** 165, 167

New Era in American Poetry, The (Untermeyer, ed.), **Supp. XV:** 301, 303, 306

Newer Ideals of Peace (Addams), **Supp. I Part 1:** 11–12, 15, 16–17, 19, 20–21

"New Experience in Millinery, A" (Stratton-Porter), **Supp. XX:**216

New Feminist Criticism, The: Essays on Women, Literature, and Theory (Showalter), **Supp. X:** 97

"New Folsom Prison" (Matthews), **Supp. IX:** 165

New Formalism, The: A Critical Introduction (McPhillips), **Supp. XV:** 250, 251, 252, 264

Newfound (J. W. Miller), **Supp. XX:**163, 166, **170–172**

New Found Land: Fourteen Poems (MacLeish), **III:** 12–13

"New Hampshire, February" (Eberhart), **I:** 536

New Hampshire: A Poem with Notes and Grace Notes (Frost), **II:** 154–155; **Retro. Supp. I:** 132, 133, 135

New Hard-Boiled Writers (Panek), **Supp. XIV:** 27

"New Home" (Richter), **Supp. XVIII:** 209

New Industrial State, The (Galbraith), **Supp. I Part 2:** 648

"New Journalism, The" (Wolfe), **Supp. III Part 2:** 571

New Journalism, The (Wolfe and Johnson, eds.), **Supp. III Part 2:** 570, 579–581, 583, 586

New Left, The: The Anti-Industrial Revolution (Rand), **Supp. IV Part 2:** 527

"New Letters from Thomas Jefferson" (Stafford), **Supp. XI:** 324

New Letters on the Air: Contemporary Writers on Radio, **Supp. X:** 165, 169, 173

"New Life" (Glück), **Supp. V:** 90

New Life, A (Malamud), **Supp. I Part 2:** 429–466

"New Life, The" (Bynner), **Supp. XV:** 44

"New Life at Kyerefaso" (Sutherland), **Supp. IV Part 1:** 9

"New Light on Veblen" (Dorfman), **Supp. I Part 2:** 650

Newman, Charles, **Supp. I Part 2:** 527, 546–548

Newman, Edwin, **Supp. IV Part 2:** 526

Newman, Judie, **Supp. IV Part 1:** 304, 305

Newman, Paul, **Supp. IV Part 2:** 473, 474

New Man, The (Merton), **Supp. VIII:** 208

"New Mecca, The" (Saunders), **Supp. XIX:** 235, 236

"New Medea, The" (Howells), **II:** 282

New Mexico trilogy (Nichols), **Supp. XIII:** 269

New Morning (album, Dylan), **Supp. XVIII:** 27, 33

"New Mother" (Olds), **Supp. X:** 206

"New Mothers, The" (Shields), **Supp. VII:** 310

New Music (Price), **Supp. VI:** 264, 265

"New Mutants, The" (Fiedler), **Supp. XIII:** 104

"New Name for Some Old Ways of Thinking, A" (James), **II:** 353

New Native American Novel, The: Works in Progress (Bartlett), **Supp. IV Part 1:** 335

"New Natural History, A" (Thurber), **Supp. I Part 2:** 619

New Negro, The (Locke), **Supp. XIX:** 69

"New Negro, The" (Locke), **Supp. XIV:** 201

New Negro, The (Locke, ed.), **Supp. II Part 1:** 176; **Supp. IX:** 309; **Supp. X:** 137

New Negro, The: An Interpretation (Locke, ed.), **Retro. Supp. I:** 199; **Supp. IV Part 1:** 170; **Supp. XIV:** 195, 201–202

New Negro for a New Century, A (Washington, Wood, and Williams), **Supp. XIV:** 201

New New Journalism, The (R. Boynton), **Supp. XVII:** 209

"New Nomads, The" (E. Hoffman), **Supp. XVI:** 161

"New Orleans" (Carruth), **Supp. XVI:** 50

New Orleans Sketches (Faulkner), **Retro. Supp. I:** 80

New Path to the Waterfall, A (Carver), **Supp. III Part 1:** 138–140, 147, 149

"New Poem, The" (Wright), **Supp. V:** 339, 340

"New Poems" (MacLeish), **III:** 19

"New Poems" (Oliver), **Supp. VII:** 240

New Poems 1960 (Bynner), **Supp. XV:** 51

New Poems: 1980–88 (Haines), **Supp. XII: 209–210**

New Poetry, The (Monroe and Henderson, eds.), **Supp. I Part 2:** 387

"New Poetry Handbook, The" (Strand), **Supp. IV Part 2:** 626

New Poetry of Mexico (Strand, trans.), **Supp. IV Part 2:** 630

New Poets of England and America (Hall, Pack, and Simpson, eds.), **Supp. IV Part 2:** 621

"Newport of Anchuria" (Henry), **Supp. II Part 1:** 409

New Princeton Encyclopedia of Poetry and Poetics (Preminger and Brogan, eds.), **Supp. XV:** 250

"*New Republic* Moves Uptown, The" (Cowley), **Supp. II Part 1:** 142

"New Rose Hotel" (W. Gibson), **Supp. XVI:** 120, 122, 124

"News, The" (McClatchy), **Supp. XII:** 269

"New Season" (Levine), **Supp. V:** 188

New Seeds of Contemplation (Merton), **Supp. VIII:** 200, 208

News from the Glacier: Selected Poems 1960–1980 (Haines), **Supp. XII:** 207, 208–209

"News Item" (Parker), **Supp. IX:** 190

New Song, A (Hughes), **Retro. Supp. I:** 202; **Supp. I Part 1:** 328, 331–332

"New South, The" (Lanier), **Supp. I Part 1:** 352, 354, 370

New Southern Girl, The: Female Adolescence in the Works of 12 Women Authors (Town), **Supp. XVIII:** 195

Newspaper Days, 1899–1906 (Mencken), **III:** 100, 102, 120

"New Spirit, The" (Ashbery), **Supp. III Part 1:** 14, 15

New Spoon River, The (Masters), **Supp. I Part 2:** 461–465, 473

New Star Chamber and Other Essays, The (Masters), **Supp. I Part 2:** 455–456, 459

New Tales of the Vampires (Rice), **Supp. VII:** 290

New Testament, **I:** 303, 457, 458; **II:** 167; **III:** 305; **IV:** 114, 134, 152; **Retro. Supp. I:** 58, 140, 360; **Supp. I Part 1:** 104, 106; **Supp. I Part 2:** 516; **Supp. XVII:** 155. *See also* names of New Testament books

New Testament, A (Anderson), **I:** 101, 114

"New Theory of Thorstein Veblen, A" (Galbraith), **Supp. I Part 2:** 650

Newton, Benjamin Franklin, **I:** 454

Newton, Huey P., **Supp. I Part 1:** 66; **Supp. IV Part 1:** 206

Newton, Isaac, **I:** 132, 557; **II:** 6, 103, 348–349; **III:** 428; **IV:** 18, 149

Newton, Sarah Emily, **Supp. XV:** 234

"New-Wave Format, A" (Mason), **Supp. VIII:** 141, 143, 147

New West of Edward Abbey, The (Ronald), **Supp. XIII:** 4

"New Wife" (Halliday), **Supp. XIX:** 89

New Wolves, The: The Return of the Mexican Wolf to the American Southwest (Bass), **Supp. XVI:** 26–27

New Woman's Survival Sourcebook, The (Rennie and Grimstead, eds.), **Supp. I Part 2:** 569

New World, The (Bronk), **Supp. XXI:** 25–26, 31

New World, The (Bynner), **Supp. XV:** 41, 42

New World, The: Tales (Banks), **Supp. V:** 8, 9, 10

New World Naked, A (Mariani), **Retro. Supp. I:** 419

New Worlds of Literature (Beaty and Hunter, eds.), **Supp. IV Part 1:** 331

New World Writing (Updike), **IV:** 217

New Year Letter (Auden), **Supp. II Part 1:** 14, 16

"New Year's Day" (Wharton), **Retro. Supp. I:** 381

"New Year's Eve" (Schwartz), **Supp. II Part 2:** 640, 656–657

New Year's Eve/1929 (Farrell), **II:** 43

"New Year's Eve 1968" (Lowell), **II:** 554

New Year's Eve: A Play (W. Frank), **Supp. XX:** 75

"New Year's Gift, The" (Stowe), **Supp. I Part 2:** 587

"New Year Two Thousand, The" (Weigl), **Supp. XIX:** 287–288

"New York" (Capote), **Supp. III Part 1:** 122

"New York" (Moore), **III:** 196, 198, 202, 206

"New York 1965" (Bowles), **Supp. IV Part 1:** 94

New York: A Serendipiter's Journey (Talese), **Supp. XVII:** 202, 203

"New York Breeze" (Halliday), **Supp. XIX:** 85

New York City Arts Project, **Supp. III Part 2:** 618

"New York City in 1979"(Acker), **Supp. XII:** 5

New York Edition, **Retro. Supp. I:** 235

"New York Edition" (James), **II:** 336, 337

"New York Gold Conspiracy, The" (Adams), **I:** 4

New York Hat, The (film; Griffith), **Supp. XVI:** 183

New York Intellectuals, **Supp. VIII:** 93

"New York Intellectuals, The" (Howe), **Supp. VI:** 120

"New York Is a City of Things Unnoticed" (Talese), **Supp. XVII:** 202, 209

New York Jew (Kazin), **Supp. VIII:** 95, **97–100**

"New York Theater: Isn't It Romantic" (Wasserstein), **Supp. XV:** 320

New York Trilogy, The (Auster), **Supp. XII:** 21, **24–28**

Next (McNally), **Supp. XIII:** 197

"Next in Line, The" (Bradbury), **Supp. IV Part 1:** 102

Next Room of the Dream, The (Nemerov), **III:** 269, 275, 278, 279–280, 284

"Next Time I Crossed the Line into Oklahoma, The" (Wright), **Supp. XV:** 345

Next-to-Last Things: New Poems and Essays (Kunitz), **Supp. III Part 1:** 257–259, 261, 262, 265, 266, 268

"'Next to Reading Matter'" (Henry), **Supp. II Part 1:** 399

Nexus (H. Miller), **III:** 170, 187, 188, 189

Niatum, Duane, **Supp. IV Part 1:** 331; **Supp. IV Part 2:** 505

Nice and Noir (Schwartz), **Supp. XIV:** 23

"Nice Girl" (Nelson), **Supp. XVIII:** 178

Nice Jewish Boy, The (P. Roth), **Supp. III Part 2:** 412

Nicholas II, Tsar, **Supp. I Part 2:** 447

"Nicholas in the Park" (Halliday), **Supp. XIX:** 88

Nicholls, Peter, **Supp. XIX:** 232

Nichols, Charles, **Retro. Supp. I:** 194

Nichols, Dudley, **Supp. XVIII:** 247

Nichols, John Treadwell, **Supp. XIII: 253–272**

Nichols, Luther, **Supp. X:** 265

Nichols, Mike, **Supp. IV Part 1:** 234; **Supp. IV Part 2:** 577

Nicholson, Colin, **Supp. VIII:** 129

Nicholson, Harold, **Supp. XIV:** 163

Nicholson, Jack, **Supp. V:** 26; **Supp. VIII:** 45; **Supp. XI:** 308

Nicholson, John, **Supp. XVI:** 293

Nick Adams Stories, The (Hemingway), **II:** 258; **Retro. Supp. I:** 174

"Nick and the Candlestick" (Plath), **Supp. I Part 2:** 544

Nickel and Dimed: On (Not) Getting By in America (Ehrenreich), **Supp. XVII:** 210

Nickel Mountain: A Pastoral Novel (Gardner), **Supp. VI:** 63, 64, 68, **69**

"Nicodemus" (Keillor), **Supp. XVI:** 167

Nicoll, Allardyce, **III:** 400

Nicoloff, Philip, **II:** 7

Niebuhr, Gustav, **III:** 292

Niebuhr, H. Richard, **I:** 494

Niebuhr, Lydia, **III:** 292

Niebuhr, Reinhold, **III: 290–313; Supp. I Part 2:** 654; **Supp. XX:**79

Niedecker, Lorine, **Supp. III Part 2:** 616, 623; **Supp. XIV:** 287

Nielsen, Ed, **Supp. IX:** 254

Nielson, Dorothy, **Supp. I Part 2:** 659

Nietzsche, Friedrich Wilhelm, **I:** 227, 283, 383, 389, 396, 397, 402, 509; **II:** 7, 20, 27, 42, 90, 145, 262, 462, 463, 577, 583, 585; **III:** 102–103, 113, 156, 176; **IV:** 286, 491; **Supp. I Part 1:** 254, 299, 320; **Supp. I Part 2:** 646; **Supp. IV Part 1:** 104, 105–106, 107, 110, 284; **Supp. IV Part 2:** 519; **Supp. V:** 277, 280; **Supp. VIII:** 11, 181, 189; **Supp. X:** 48; **Supp. XII:** 98; **Supp. XIV:** 339; **Supp. XX:**117

Nieves, Felipe, **Supp. XVIII:** 90

Niflis, N. Michael, **Supp. IV Part 1:** 175

Nigger Heaven (Van Vechten), **Supp. II Part 2:** 739, 744–746; **Supp. XVIII:** 123, 127; **Supp. XIX:** 76

"Nigger Jeff" (Dreiser), **Retro. Supp. II:** 97

Nigger of the "Narcissus," The (Conrad), **II:** 91; **Retro. Supp. I:** 106; **Supp. XVIII:** 224

"NIGGY THE HO" (Baraka), **Supp. II Part 1:** 54

"Night, Death, Mississippi" (Hayden), **Supp. II Part 1:** 369

'Night, Mother (Norman), **Supp. VIII:** 141

"Night above the Avenue" (Merwin), **Supp. III Part 1:** 355

"Night among the Horses, A" (Barnes), **Supp. III Part 1:** 33–34, 39, 44

"Night and the Madman" (Gibran), **Supp. XX:**118

Night at the Movies, A, or, You Must Remember This: Fictions (Coover), **Supp. V:** 50–51

"Night at the Opera, A" (Matthews), **Supp. IX:** 167

"Night before the Sentence Is Carried Out, The" (Wright), **Supp. XV:** 341

"Nightbird" (Komunyakaa), **Supp. XIII:** 132

Night-Blooming Cereus, The (Hayden), **Supp. II Part 1:** 367, 373

"Night-Blooming Cereus, The" (Hayden), **Supp. II Part 1:** 367

Night-Born, The (London), **II:** 467

"Nightbreak" (Rich), **Supp. I Part 2:** 556

"Nightclub" (Collins), **Supp. XXI:** 60

Night Dance (Price), **Supp. VI:** 264

"Night Dances, The" (Plath), **Supp. I Part 2:** 544

"Night Dream, The" (MacLeish), **III:** 15

"Night Ferry" (Doty), **Supp. XI:** 124

"Nightfishing" (Schnackenberg), **Supp. XV:** 254

"Night I Met Little Floyd, The" (Wright), **Supp. XV:** 345–346

Night in Acadie, A (Chopin), **Retro. Supp. II:** 66–67, 73; **Supp. I Part 1:** 200, 219, 220, 224

"Night in Acadie, A" (Chopin), **Retro. Supp. II:** 66

"Night in June, A" (W. C. Williams), **Retro. Supp. I:** 424

"Night in New Arabia, A" (Henry), **Supp. II Part 1:** 402

Night in Question, The: Stories (Wolff), **Supp. VII:** 342–344

"Night Journey" (Roethke), **Supp. III Part 1:** 260

"Night Letter to the Reader" (Collins), **Supp. XXI:** 55

Night Light (Justice), **Supp. VII:** 126–127

"Nightmare" (Kumin), **Supp. IV Part 2:** 442

Nightmare Factory, The (Kumin), **Supp. IV Part 2:** 444–447, 451

"Nightmare Factory, The" (Kumin), **Supp. IV Part 2:** 445, 453

Nightmare on Main Street (Poe), **Retro. Supp. II:** 262

"Nightmare" poems (Benét), **Supp. XI:** 46, 58

"Night Mirror" (L.-Y. Lee), **Supp. XV:** 225

Night Music (Odets), **Supp. II Part 2:** 541, 543, 544

"Night of First Snow" (R. Bly), **Supp. IV Part 1:** 71

Night of January 16th (Rand), **Supp. IV Part 2:** 527

Night of the Iguana, The (T. Williams), **IV:** 382, 383, 384, 385, 386, 387, 388, 391, 392, 393, 394, 395, 397, 398

"Night of the Iguana, The" (T. Williams), **IV:** 384

"Night of the Living Beanfield: How an Unsuccessful Cult Novel Became an Unsuccessful Cult Film in Only Fourteen Years, Eleven Nervous Breakdowns, and $20 Million" (Nichols), **Supp. XIII:** 267

Night Passage (Parker), **Supp. XIX:** 185–186

Night Rider (Warren), **IV:** 243, 246–247

Nights (Doolittle), **Supp. I Part 1:** 270, 271

Nights and Days (Merrill), **Supp. III Part 1:** 319, 320, 322–325

"Nights and Days" (Rich), **Supp. I Part 2:** 574

"Night's for Cryin,' The" (C. Himes), **Supp. XVI:** 137

"Night Shift" (Plath), **Supp. I Part 2:** 538

Night-Side (Oates), **Supp. II Part 2:** 522

"Night-Side" (Oates), **Supp. II Part 2:** 523

Night-Side, The (Skloot), **Supp. XX:**193, 196, 205, 208

Nights in the Gardens of Brooklyn (Swados), **Supp. XIX:** 261–264

"Nights in the Gardens of Brooklyn" (Swados), **Supp. XIX:** 261

"Night Sketches: Beneath an Umbrella" (Hawthorne), **II:** 235–237, 238, 239, 242; **Supp. XXI:** 201

"Night Sport" (Hoffman), **Supp. XVIII:** 86, 87

"Night-Sweat" (Lowell), **II:** 554

"Night-Talk" (Ellison), **Retro. Supp. II:** 126; **Supp. II Part 1:** 248

Night Thoughts (Young), **III:** 415

Night Traveler, The (Oliver), **Supp. VII:** 233

"Night Watch" (Gioia), **Supp. XV:** 117

"Night Watch, The" (Wright), **Supp. V:** 339

"Night We All Had Grippe, The" (Jackson), **Supp. IX:** 118

Nightwood (Barnes), **Supp. III Part 1:** 31, 32, 35–37, 39–43

Night World and the Word Night, The (F. Wright), **Supp. XVII:** 240, 244–245

"Nihilist as Hero, The" (Lowell), **II:** 554; **Retro. Supp. II:** 190

Nijinsky, Vaslav, **Supp. XV:** 28–29

Nikolai Gogol (Nabokov), **Retro. Supp. I:** 266

Niles, Thomas, **Retro. Supp. I:** 35

Niles, Thomas, Jr., **Supp. I Part 1:** 39

Nilsson, Christine, **Supp. I Part 1:** 355

Nilsson, Harry, **Supp. XI:** 309

Nilsson, Jenny Lind, **Supp. XVI:** 177

Nimitz, Chester, **Supp. I Part 2:** 491

"Nimram" (Gardner), **Supp. VI:** 73

Nims, John Frederick, **III:** 527; **Supp. XVII:** 112

Nin, Anaïs, **III:** 182, 184, 190; **Supp. III Part 1:** 43; **Supp. IV Part 2:** 680; **Supp. X: 181–200; Supp. XIX:** 134

"9" (Oliver), **Supp. VII:** 244

"9 Failures of the Imagination" (Lethem), **Supp. XVIII:** 148

"Nine-Ball" (Offutt), **Supp. XIX:** 166, 167

Nine Dragons (Connelly), **Supp. XXI:** 74, **79–80**

"Nine from Eight" (Lanier), **Supp. I Part 1:** 352–354

Nine Headed Dragon River: Zen Journals 1969–1982 (Matthiessen), **Supp. V:** 199

Nine Horses (Collins), **Supp. XXI:** 55, 60, 61, 62, 65

"Nine Horses" (Collins), **Supp. XXI:** 61

Ninemile Wolves,The (Bass), **Supp. XVI:** 24–25, 26

"Nine Nectarines" (Moore), **III:** 203, 209, 215

Nine Plays (Reznikoff), **Supp. XIV:** 288

"Nine Poems for the Unborn Child" (Rukeyser), **Supp. VI:** 280–281, 284

Nine Stories (Nabokov), **Retro. Supp. I:** 266

Nine Stories (Salinger), **III:** 552, 558–564

"19 Hadley Street" (Schnackenberg), **Supp. XV:** 253

19 Necromancers from Now (Reed), **Supp. X:** 240

19 Varieties of Gazelle (Nye), **Supp. XIII:** 275, **286–288**

"19 Varieties of Gazelle" (Nye), **Supp. XIII:** 286

1984 (Orwell), **Supp. XIII:** 29; **Supp. XVIII:** 137, 138

"1940" (Stafford), **Supp. XI:** 328–329

"1945–1985: Poem for the Anniversary" (Oliver), **Supp. VII:** 237

1919 (Dos Passos), **I:** 482, 485–486, 487, 489, 490, 492
"1975" (Wright), **Supp. V:** 341
"1910" (Mora), **Supp. XIII:** 215
"1938" (Komunyakaa), **Supp. XIII:** 114
"1939" (Taylor), **Supp. V:** 316
1933 (Levine), **Supp. V:** 185–187
"1933" (Levine), **Supp. V:** 188
"Nineteenth New York, The" (Doctorow), **Supp. IV Part 1:** 232
"1929" (Auden), **Supp. II Part 1:** 6
"1926" (Kees), **Supp. XV:** 135
"93990" (Saunders), **Supp. XIX:** 233
"90 North" (Jarrell), **II:** 370, 371
90 Trees (Zukofsky), **Supp. III Part 2:** 631
95 Poems (Cummings), **I:** 430, 433, 435, 439, 446, 447
"91 Revere Street" (Lowell), **II:** 547; **Retro. Supp. II:** 188; **Supp. XI:** 240
Ninety Percent of Everything (Lethem, Kelly and Kessel), **Supp. XVIII:** 145
"92 Days" (L. Brown), **Supp. XXI:** 44–45
"Nine Years Later" (Brodsky), **Supp. VIII:** 32
"Nirvana" (Lanier), **Supp. I Part 1:** 352
Nirvana Blues, The (Nichols), **Supp. XIII:** 266, 267
Nishikigi (play), **III:** 466
Niven, David, **Supp. XI:** 307
Nixon (film), **Supp. XIV:** 48
Nixon, Richard M., **I:** 376; **III:** 38, 46; **Supp. I Part 1:** 294, 295; **Supp. V:** 45, 46, 51; **Supp. XII:** 14; **Supp. XIV:** 306
"NJ Transit" (Komunyakaa), **Supp. XIII:** 132
Nketia, J. H., **Supp. IV Part 1:** 10
Nketsia, Nana, **Supp. IV Part 1:** 2, 10
Nkize, Julius, **Supp. IV Part 1:** 361
Nkrumah, Kwame, **I:** 490, 494; **Supp. IV Part 1:** 361; **Supp. X:** 135
Nkrumah and the Ghana Revolution (C. L. R. James), **Supp. XXI:** 159, 171–172
Noailles, Anna de, **IV:** 328
Noa Noa (Gauguin), **I:** 34
Nobel Lecture (Singer), **Retro. Supp. II:** 300
"No Better Than a 'Withered Daffodil' " (Moore), **III:** 216
Noble, David W., **Supp. I Part 2:** 650
Noble, Marianne, **Supp. XVIII:** 267
"Noble Rider and the Sound of Words, The" (Stevens), **Retro. Supp. I:** 299
Noble Savage, The (Coover), **Supp. V:** 40
"No Bobolink reverse His Singing" (Dickinson), **Retro. Supp. I:** 45
Nobodaddy (MacLeish), **III:** 5–6, 8, 10, 11, 18, 19, 20
"Nobodaddy" (W. Blake), **Supp. XVII:** 245
"Nobody in Hollywood" (Bausch), **Supp. VII:** 54
Nobody Knows My Name (Baldwin), **Supp. XIII:** 111

"Nobody Knows My Name" (Baldwin), **Retro. Supp. II:** 8; **Supp. I Part 1:** 52
Nobody Knows My Name: More Notes of a Native Son (Baldwin), **Retro. Supp. II:** 6, 8; **Supp. I Part 1:** 47, 52, 55
"Nobody knows this little Rose" (Dickinson), **Retro. Supp. I:** 30
"Nobody Said Anything" (Carver), **Supp. III Part 1:** 141
"Nobody's Business" (Lahiri), **Supp. XXI:** 183
Nobody's Fool (Russo), **Supp. XII:** 326, **331–335**, 340
"No Change of Place" (Auden), **Supp. II Part 1:** 5
"Noche Triste, La" (Frost), **Retro. Supp. I:** 123
Nock, Albert Jay, **I:** 245; **Supp. IV Part 2:** 521, 524
"No Coward Soul Is Mine" (Brontë), **I:** 458
"No Crime in the Mountains" (Chandler), **Supp. IV Part 1:** 129
"Nocturne" (Komunyakaa), **Supp. XIII:** 126
"Nocturne" (MacLeish), **III:** 8
"Nocturne in a Deserted Brickyard" (Sandburg), **III:** 586
Nocturne of Remembered Spring (Aiken), **I:** 50
No Direction Home (documentary film, Scorsese), **Supp. XVIII:** 22, 23, 29
No Direction Home (Shelton), **Supp. XVIII:** 21
No Door (Wolfe), **IV:** 451–452, 456
"No Door" (Wolfe), **IV:** 456
"No Epitaph" (Carson), **Supp. XII:** 111
No Exit (Sartre), **I:** 82, 130; **Supp. XIV:** 320
No Exit (Sartre; Bowles, trans.), **Supp. IV Part 1:** 84
No Gifts from Chance (Benstock), **Retro. Supp. I:** 361
"No-Good Blues" (Komunyakaa), **Supp. XIII:** 130
No Hero (Marquand), **III:** 57
No Heroes: A Memoir of Coming Home (Offutt), **Supp. XIX:** 163, **172–174**, 175
No! In Thunder (Fiedler), **Supp. XIII:** 101
"Noiseless Patient Spider" (Whitman), **III:** 555; **IV:** 348; **Supp. IV Part 1:** 325
Noises Off (Frayn), **Supp. IV Part 2:** 582
Noi vivi. See We the Living (film)
"No Jury Would Convict" (Shaw), **Supp. XIX:** 245
"No Lamp Has Ever Shown Us Where to Look" (MacLeish), **III:** 9
Nolan, Sidney, **Retro. Supp. II:** 189
No Laughing Matter (Heller and Vogel), **Supp. IV Part 1:** 384, 389
No Love Lost, a Romance of Travel (Howells), **II:** 277
No Man Is an Island (Merton), **Supp. VIII:** 207
No Mother to Guide Her (Loos), **Supp. XVI:** 194

No Name in the Street (Baldwin), **Retro. Supp. II:** 13, 14; **Supp. I Part 1:** 47, 48, 52, 65–66, 67
No Nature: New and Selected Poems (Snyder), **Supp. VIII: 305**
Nonconformist's Memorial, The (Howe), **Supp. IV Part 2:** 434, 435–436
Nonconformity (Algren), **Supp. IX:** 15
None but the Lonely Heart (film), **Supp. II Part 2:** 546
Nones (Auden), **Supp. II Part 1:** 21
"Nones" (Auden), **Supp. II Part 1:** 22–23
None Shall Look Back (Gordon), **II:** 205–207, 208
"No No, Bad Daddy" (Nelson), **Supp. XVIII:** 177, 178
"Non-Tenured" (Halliday), **Supp. XIX:** 90, 91
Nonverbal Communication: Notes on the Visual Perception of Human Relations (Kees and Ruesch), **Supp. XV:** 147
"Noon" (Bryant), **Supp. I Part 1:** 157
"No One Remembers" (Levine), **Supp. V:** 187
"Noon Walk on the Asylum Lawn" (Sexton), **Supp. II Part 2:** 673
"Noon Wine" (Porter), **III:** 436, 437–438, 442, 446
"No Pain Whatsoever" (Yates), **Supp. XI:** 341
"No Place for You, My Love" (Welty), **IV:** 278, 279; **Retro. Supp. I:** 353
No Plays of Japan, The (Waley), **III:** 466
No Pockets in a Shroud (McCoy), **Supp. XIII: 166–168**, 171, 172, 173, 174
"No Poem So Fine" (Francis), **Supp. IX:** 83
Norcross, Frances, **I:** 456, 462
Norcross, Louise, **I:** 456, 462
Nordfeldt, B. J. O., **Supp. XXI:** 6
Nordfeldt, Margaret, **Supp. XXI:** 6
Nordyke, Lewis, **Supp. XIII:** 5
No Relief (Dixon), **Supp. XII:** 139, **142–143**
No Resting Place (Humphrey), **Supp. IX:** 94, **106–108**
Norfolk Poems, The (Carruth), **Supp. XVI:** 47, 48
Norma (Bellini), **IV:** 309
Norma Ashe (Glaspell), **Supp. III Part 1:** 175, 186–187
"Normal Motor Adjustments" (Stein and Solomons), **IV:** 26
Norman, Charles, **III:** 479
Norman, Gurney, **Supp. X:** 24
Norman, Jessye, **Supp. XX:**110
Norman, Marsha, **Supp. VIII:** 141; **Supp. XXI:** 145
Norman Mailer (Poirier), **Retro. Supp. II:** 207–208
Norman Mailer: Modern Critical Views (Bloom), **Retro. Supp. II:** 205
Norman Mailer Revisited (Merrill), **Retro. Supp. II:** 201
Norna; or, The Witch's Curse (Alcott), **Supp. I Part 1:** 33
Norris, Charles, **III:** 320; **Retro. Supp. I:** 100; **Supp. XVIII:** 226

Norris, Frank, **I:** 211, 355, 500, 506, 517, 518, 519; **II:** 89, 264, 276, 289, 307; **III:** 227, **314–336,** 596; **IV:** 29; **Retro. Supp. I:** 100, 325; **Retro. Supp. II:** 96, 101; **Supp. III Part 2:** 412; **Supp. VIII:** 101, 102; **Supp. IX:** 14, 15; **Supp. XV:** 115

"North" (Budbill), **Supp. XIX:** 7–8

"North" (Hugo), **Supp. VI:** 135

North, Milou (pseudonym), **Supp. IV Part 1:** 260. *See also* Dorris, Michael; Erdrich, Louise

North, Sir Thomas, **IV:** 370

"North American Sequence" (Roethke), **I:** 171–172, 183; **III:** 529, 545, 547, 548

"North Beach" (Snyder), **Supp. VIII:** 289

"North Country Sketches" (McClatchy), **Supp. XII:** 256

"Northeast Playground" (Paley), **Supp. VI:** 226–227, 229

Northern Lights (O'Brien), **Supp. V:** 237, 239, 241–244, 250

"Northern Motive" (Levine), **Supp. V:** 195

Northfield Poems (Ammons), **Supp. VII:** 29

"Northhanger Ridge" (Wright), **Supp. V:** 335, 340

"North Haven" (Bishop), **Retro. Supp. II:** 50

"North Labrador" (Crane), **I:** 386

North of Boston (Frost), **II:** 152, 153–154, 527; **Retro. Supp. I:** 121, 125, 127, **128–130,** 131; **Supp. I Part 1:** 263; **Supp. XIII:** 146

North of Jamaica (Simpson), **Supp. IV Part 2:** 448; **Supp. IX:** 275, 276

North of the Danube (Caldwell), **I:** 288, 290, 293, 294, 309, 310

Northrup, Cyrus, **Supp. I Part 1:** 350

North Sea (Jarman), **Supp. XVII:** 110, 113

"North Sea Undertaker's Complaint, The" (Lowell), **II:** 550

North & South (Bishop), **Retro. Supp. II:** 41–43; **Supp. I Part 1:** 72, 84, 85, 89

North Star, The (Hellman), **Supp. I Part 1:** 281

Northup, Solomon, **Supp. XIV:** 32

"North Winter" (Carruth), **Supp. XVI:** 53

Norton, Charles Eliot, **I:** 223, 568; **II:** 279, 322–323, 338; **Retro. Supp. I:** 371; **Retro. Supp. II:** 135; **Supp. I Part 1:** 103; **Supp. I Part 2:** 406, 479

Norton, Jody, **Supp. VIII:** 297

Norton, John, **Supp. I Part 1:** 99, 110, 112, 114

Norton Anthology of African American Literature, The, **Supp. X:** 325

Norton Anthology of African American Literature, The (H. L. Gates and McKay, eds.), **Supp. XX:**105

Norton Anthology of American Literature, **Supp. X:** 325; **Supp. XV:** 270

Norton Anthology of Literature by Women (Gilbert and Gubar, eds.), **Supp. XV:** 270

Norton Anthology of Modern Poetry, The, **Supp. XI:** 259; **Supp. XV:** 258

Norton Anthology of Poetry, The, **Supp. XVIII:** 20

Norton Anthology of Short Fiction, The, **Supp. IX:** 4

Norton Book of Personal Essays, The, **Supp. XIV:** 105

Norton Lectures, **Retro. Supp. I:** 65

Norwood, Vera, **Supp. IX:** 24

No Safe Harbour (Porter), **III:** 447

Nosferatu: An Opera Libretto (Gioia), **Supp. XV:** 112, **128**

"Nosferatu's Serenade" (Gioia), **Supp. XV:** 128

No Siege Is Absolute (Char; version of F. Wright), **Supp. XVII:** 244

"No Snake" (A. Finch), **Supp. XVII:** 72

"No Speak English" (Cisneros), **Supp. VII:** 63

"Nostalgia" (Collins), **Supp. XXI:** 57

"Nostalgia" (Saunders), **Supp. XIX:** 235

Nostalgia for 70 (J. W. Miller), **Supp. XX:**165

"Nostalgia of the Lakefronts" (Justice), **Supp. VII:** 118, 119, 120

"Nostalgic Mood" (Farrell), **II:** 45

No Star Is Lost (Farrell), **II:** 34, 35, 44

Nostrandt, Jeanne, **Supp. XVIII:** 80–81

Nostromo (Conrad), **II:** 600; **IV:** 245

"Nosty Fright, A" (Swenson), **Supp. IV Part 2:** 651

Not about Nightingales (T. Williams), **IV:** 381

"Not a Womb in the House" (Quindlen), **Supp. XVII:** 166, 171

Not Coming to Be Barked At (Kooser), **Supp. XIX:** 116, **120**

Not Dancing (Dunn), **Supp. XI:** 143, **148**

"Note about *Iconographs,* A" (Swenson), **Supp. IV Part 2:** 646

Notebook (Lowell), **Retro. Supp. II:** 186, 190; **Supp. V:** 343

Notebook 1967–68 (Lowell), **II:** 553–555; **Retro. Supp. II:** 182, 186, 190

Notebook of Malte Laurids Brigge, The (Rilke), **III:** 571

Notebooks (Fitzgerald), **Retro. Supp. I:** 110

"Note on Abraham Lincoln" (Vidal), **Supp. IV Part 2:** 688

"Note on Commercial Theatre" (Hughes), **Retro. Supp. I:** 207

"Note on Ezra Pound, A" (Eliot), **Retro. Supp. I:** 290

"Note on Lanier's Music, A" (P. Graham), **Supp. I Part 1:** 373

Note on Literary Criticism, A (Farrell), **II:** 26, 49

"Note on Poetry, A" (Doolittle), **Supp. I Part 1:** 254, 267–268

"Note on Realism, A" (Anderson), **I:** 110

"Note on the Limits of 'History' and the Limits of 'Criticism,' A" (Brooks), **Supp. XIV:** 11

"Note on the Poetry of Love, A" (Untermeyer), **Supp. XV:** 304

"Note on the Truth of the Tales, A" (Vollmann), **Supp. XVII:** 230

"Notes" (Dove), **Supp. IV Part 1:** 246

"Notes for a Moving Picture: The House" (Agee), **I:** 33, 34

"Notes for an Autobiography" (Van Vechten), **Supp. II Part 2:** 749

"Notes for a Novel About the End of the World" (Percy), **Supp. III Part 1:** 393

"Notes for a Preface" (Sandburg), **III:** 591, 596–597

"NOTES FOR A SPEECH" (Baraka), **Supp. II Part 1:** 33

Notes for the Green Box (Duchamp), **Supp. IV Part 2:** 423

Notes from a Bottle Found on the Beach at Carmel (Connell), **Supp. XIV:** 80, 87, 96, 97

Notes from a Sea Diary: Hemingway All the Way (Algren), **Supp. IX:** 16

"Notes from the Childhood and Girlhood" (Brooks), **Supp. III Part 1:** 77

"Notes from the River" (Stern), **Supp. IX:** 285, 287, 294, 295

Notes from Underground (Dostoevsky), **III:** 571; **IV:** 485; **Retro. Supp. II:** 121

"Notes of a Faculty Wife" (Jackson), **Supp. IX:** 126

"Notes of a Native Daughter" (Didion), **Supp. IV Part 1:** 196, 197, 200, 201

Notes of a Native Son (Baldwin), **Retro. Supp. II:** 1, 2, 3, 5, 6; **Supp. I Part 1:** 50, 52, 54; **Supp. IV Part 1:** 163

"Notes of a Native Son" (Baldwin), **Supp. I Part 1:** 50, 54

Notes of a Son and Brother (James), **II:** 337; **Retro. Supp. I:** 235

"Notes on a Departure" (Trilling), **Supp. III Part 2:** 498

"Notes on Babbitt and More" (Wilson), **IV:** 435

"Notes on 'Camp' " (Sontag), **Supp. III Part 2:** 455–456

"Notes on Camp" (Sontag), **Supp. XIV:** 167

Notes on Democracy (Mencken), **III:** 104, 107–108, 109, 116, 119

Notes on Dialectics (C. L. R. James), **Supp. XXI:** 169

"Notes on Free Verse" (Dobyns), **Supp. XIII:** 77

"Notes on 'Layover' " (Hass), **Supp. VI:** 109

"Notes on Memory and Enthusiasm" (Di Piero), **Supp. XIX:** 42

Notes on Novelists (James), **II:** 336, 337; **Retro. Supp. I:** 235

"Notes on Nukes, Nookie, and Neo-Romanticism" (Robbins), **Supp. X:** 272

"Notes on Poetry" (Eberhart), **I:** 524, 527–528, 529

"Notes on the Craft of Poetry" (Strand), **Supp. IV Part 2:** 626

"Notes on the Decline of Outrage" (Dickey), **Supp. IV Part 1:** 181

"Notes on the New Formalism" (Gioia), **Supp. XV:** 113, 114–115

"Notes on the Novel-as-Autobiography" (P. Bailey), **Supp. XVI:** 69

Notes on the State of Virginia (1781–1782) (Jefferson), **Supp. XIV:** 191

"Notes to Be Left in a Cornerstone" (Benét), **Supp. XI:** 46, 58

"Notes toward a Supreme Fiction" (Stevens), **IV:** 87–89; **Retro. Supp. I:** 300, 306, **306–309,** 311; **Supp. I Part 1:** 80

"Notes towards a Poem That Can Never Be Written" (Atwood), **Supp. XIII:** 34–35

"Not Exactly for Talia" (Halliday), **Supp. XIX:** 94

No Thanks (Cummings), **I:** 430, 431, 432, 436, 437, 441, 443, 446

Not Heaven: A Novel in the Form of Prelude, Variations, and Theme (W. Frank), **Supp. XX:** 80

"Nothing" (C. Frost), **Supp. XV:** 94

"Nothing Big" (Komunyakaa), **Supp. XIII:** 121

Nothing for Tigers (Carruth), **Supp. XVI:** 47, 48, 50

"Nothing Gold Can Stay" (Frost), **Retro. Supp. I:** 133

"Nothing in Heaven Functions as It Ought" (X. J. Kennedy), **Supp. XV:** 158–159

Nothing Makes You Free: Writings by Descendants of Jewish Holocaust Survivors (Bukiet, ed.), **Supp. XVII: 39–40,** 48–49

"Nothing Missing" (O'Hara), **III:** 369

Nothing Personal (Baldwin), **Supp. I Part 1:** 58, 60

Nothing Sacred (film), **Supp. XVIII:** 243

"Nothing Song, The" (Snodgrass), **Supp. VI:** 326

"Nothing Stays Put" (Clampitt), **Supp. IX:** 42

"Nothing Will Yield" (Nemerov), **III:** 279

No Third Path (Kosinski), **Supp. VII:** 215

"Not Ideas About the Thing but the Thing Itself" (Stevens), **IV:** 87

"No Time" (Collins), **Supp. XXI:** 61

Notions of the Americans: Picked up by a Travelling Bachelor (Cooper), **I:** 343–345, 346

"Not-Knowing" (Barthelme), **Supp. IV Part 1:** 48

"Not Leaving the House" (Snyder), **Supp. VIII:** 300

"'Not Marble nor the Gilded Monument'" (MacLeish), **III:** 12

"Not My Bones" (Nelson), **Supp. XVIII:** 183

Not Now But Now (M. F. K. Fisher), **Supp. XVII:** 86, 90

"Not Quite Social" (Frost), **II:** 156

"Not Sappho, Sacco" (Rukeyser), **Supp. VI:** 277

"Not Sixteen" (Anderson), **I:** 114

"Not Slightly" (Stein), **IV:** 44

Not So Deep as a Well (Parker), **Supp. IX:** 192

"Not Somewhere Else, but Here" (Rich), **Supp. I Part 2:** 552, 573

Not-So-Simple Neil Simon (McGovern), **Supp. IV Part 2:** 573

Not So Simple: The "Simple" Stories by Langston Hughes (Harper), **Retro. Supp. I:** 194, 209

"Not the Point" (Cameron), **Supp. XII:** 83

"Not They Who Soar" (Dunbar), **Supp. II Part 1:** 199

Not This Pig (Levine), **Supp. V:** 178, 181, 182–183

"Not to Be Satan nor to Deal with Him" (Bronk), **Supp. XXI:** 32

Not to Eat; Not for Love (Weller), **III:** 322

Not Wanted on the Voyage (Findley), **Supp. XX:** 50, **56–57,** 59

Not Without Laughter (Hughes), **Retro. Supp. I:** 197, 198, 201; **Supp. I Part 1:** 328, 332; **Supp. XIX:** 73, 154

Nouvelle Héloïse, La (Rousseau), **Supp. XV:** 232

Nova Express (Burroughs), **Supp. III Part 1:** 93, 103, 104; **Supp. XVIII:** 137

Novel, The (Bulwer), **Retro. Supp. II:** 58

"Novel as a Function of American Democracy, The" (Ellison), **Retro. Supp. II:** 124

"Novel Démeublé, The" (Cather), **Retro. Supp. I:** 15

Novel History: Historians and Novelists Confront America's Past (and Each Other) (Carnes), **Supp. X:** 14

"Novelists of 2007" (Halliday), **Supp. XIX:** 90

Novella (Goethe; Bogan and Mayer, trans.), **Supp. III Part 1:** 63

Novellas and Other Writings (Wharton), **Retro. Supp. I:** 360

"Novel of the Thirties, A" (Trilling), **Supp. III Part 2:** 499

Novels and Other Writings (Bercovitch), **Retro. Supp. II:** 325

Novels and Tales of Henry James, The (James), **Retro. Supp. I:** 232

"Novel-Writing and Novel-Reading" (Howells), **II:** 276, 290

"November" (Larcom), **Supp. XIII:** 143

"November Cotton Flower" (Toomer), **Supp. IX:** 312

November Twenty Six Nineteen Sixty Three (Berry), **Supp. X:** 24

"Novices" (Moore), **III:** 200–201, 202, 213

Novick, Peter, **Supp. XVI:** 154–155

"Novogodnee" ("New Year's Greetings") (Tsvetayeva), **Supp. VIII:** 30

"Novotny's Pain" (P. Roth), **Supp. III Part 2:** 403

"No Voyage" (Oliver), **Supp. VII:** 231

No Voyage and Other Poems (Oliver), **Supp. VII:** 230–231, 232

Now and Another Time (Hearon), **Supp. VIII:** 58, **61–62**

Now and Then (Buechner), **Supp. XII:** 49, 53

"Now and Then, America" (Mora), **Supp. XIII:** 217

"Nowhere" (J. Scott), **Supp. XVII:** 189

Nowhere Is a Place: Travels in Patagonia (Theroux and Chatwin), **Supp. VIII:** 322

"Now I Am Married" (Gordon), **Supp. IV Part 1:** 299

"Now I Lay Me" (Hemingway), **II:** 249; **Retro. Supp. I:** 175

"Now I Lay Me" (Olds), **Supp. X:** 208

"Now Is the Air Made of Chiming Balls" (Eberhart), **I:** 523

"No Word" (Kunitz), **Supp. III Part 1:** 263

"No Worst" (Nelson), **Supp. XVIII:** 177, 178

Now Sheba Sings the Song (Angelou), **Supp. IV Part 1:** 16

"Now That We Live" (Kenyon), **Supp. VII:** 165

"Now the Servant's Name Was Malchus" (Wilder), **IV:** 358

"Now We Know" (O'Hara), **III:** 368–369

NOW with Bill Moyers (television), **Supp. XIII:** 286

Noyes, Alfred, **IV:** 434

Nuamah, Grace, **Supp. IV Part 1:** 10

"Nuances of a Theme by Williams" (Stevens), **Retro. Supp. I:** 422

Nuclear Age, The (O'Brien), **Supp. V:** 238, 243, 244, 246–248, 249, 251

"Nuclear Arms and Morality" (Sanders), **Supp. XVI:** 266

"Nude at a Dressing Table" (Peacock), **Supp. XIX:** 204

Nude Croquet (Fiedler), **Supp. XIII:** 103

"Nude Descendig a Staircase" (X. J. Kennedy), **Supp. XV:** 168

"Nude Descending a Staircase" (Duchamp), **IV:** 408; **Retro. Supp. I:** 416

Nude Descending a Staircase (X. J. Kennedy), **Supp. XV:** 153, **154–157**

Nugent, Bruce, **Retro. Supp. I:** 200

Nugent, Elliot, **Supp. I Part 2:** 606, 611, 613

Nuggets and Dust (Bierce), **I:** 195

"Nullipara" (Olds), **Supp. X:** 209

Number One (Dos Passos), **I:** 489

"Numbers" (Skloot), **Supp. XX:** 196, 207

"Numbers, Letters" (Baraka), **Supp. II Part 1:** 50

Nunc Dimittis (Brodsky), **Supp. VIII:** 25–26, 28

"Nun No More, A" (Fante), **Supp. XI:** 160

"Nun's Priest's Tale" (Chaucer), **III:** 492

Nunzio, Nanzia, **IV:** 89

Nuptial Flight, The (Masters), **Supp. I Part 2:** 460, 471

"Nuptials" (Tate), **IV:** 122

"Nurse Whitman" (Olds), **Supp. X:** 203

Nurture (Kumin), **Supp. IV Part 2:** 453–454, 455

Nussbaum, Emily, **Supp. XI:** 143

Nussbaum, Felicity A., **Supp. X:** 189

Nutcracker, The (Tchaikovsky), **Retro. Supp. I:** 196

"Nux Postcoenatica" (Holmes), **Supp. I Part 1:** 303

Nyce, James M., **Retro. Supp. I:** 380

Nye, Naomi Shihab, **Supp. XI:** 316; **Supp. XIII: 273–290**
Nyerere, Julius, **Supp. X:** 135
"Nympholepsy" (Faulkner), **Retro. Supp. I:** 81
Nymphs of the Valley ('Ará'is al-Murúj) (Gibran), **Supp. XX:**115, 124, 125

O

"Ö" (Dove), **Supp. IV Part 1:** 245
Oak and Ivy (Dunbar), **Supp. II Part 1:** 98
"Oak Bluffs" column (D. West), **Supp. XVIII:** 286
Oak Openings, The (Cooper), **I:** 354, 355
Oandasan, Bill, **Supp. IV Part 2:** 499
Oasis, The (McCarthy), **II:** 566–568
Oates, Joyce Carol, **Supp. II Part 2: 503–527; Supp. IV Part 1:** 205; **Supp. IV Part 2:** 447, 689; **Supp. V:** 323; **Supp. XI:** 239; **Supp. XII:** 343; **Supp. XIII:** 306; **Supp. XIV:** 26, 109
"Oath, The" (Tate), **IV:** 127
Obbligati (Hecht), **Supp. X:** 57
Ober, Harold, **Retro. Supp. I:** 101, 103, 105, 110, 113
Oberndorf, Clarence P., **Supp. I Part 1:** 315
Obey, André, **IV:** 356, 375
"Obit" (Lowell), **II:** 554
"Obituaries" (Collins), **Supp. XXI:** 65
"Objective Value of a Social Settlement, The" (Addams), **Supp. I Part 1:** 4
"Objective Woman, The" (Jong), **Supp. V:** 119
Objectivist Anthology, An, **Supp. XIV:** 287
"Objectivist Ethics, The" (Rand), **Supp. IV Part 2:** 530–532
"Objectivists" Anthology, An (Zukofsky), **Supp. III Part 2:** 613, 615
Object Lessons (Quindlen), **Supp. XVII: 173–174**
"Objects" (Wilbur), **Supp. III Part 2:** 545–547
Oblique Prayers (Levertov), **Supp. III Part 1:** 283
"Oblivion" (Justice), **Supp. VII:** 121
Oblivion Seekers, The (Eberhardt), **Supp. IV Part 1:** 92
"Oblong Box, The" (Poe), **III:** 416
Obregon, Maurice, **Supp. I Part 2:** 488
O'Briant, Don, **Supp. X:** 8
O'Brien, Edward, **Supp. XV:** 140
O'Brien, Edward J., **I:** 289; **III:** 56; **Supp. XVIII:** 227; **Supp. XIX:** 256; **Supp. XX:**34
O'Brien, Edwin, **Supp. XVIII:** 208
O'Brien, Fitzjames, **I:** 211
O'Brien, Geoffrey, **Supp. IV Part 2:** 471, 473
O'Brien, Joe, **Supp. XXI:** 5, 6
O'Brien, John, **Supp. V:** 48, 49; **Supp. X:** 239, 244; **Supp. XXI:** 228, 229, 233
O'Brien, Tim, **Supp. V: 237–255; Supp. XI:** 234; **Supp. XVII:** 14; **Supp. XXI:** 122
"Obscene Poem, An" (Creeley), **Supp. IV Part 1:** 150

Obscure Destinies (Cather), **I:** 331–332; **Retro. Supp. I:** 19
"Observation Relative to the Intentions of the Original Founders of the Academy in Philadelphia" (Franklin), **II:** 114
"Observations" (Dillard), **Supp. VI:** 34
Observations (Moore), **III:** 194, 195–196, 197, 199, 203, 205, 215
"Observations Now" (Conroy), **Supp. XVI:** 75
Observations: Photographs by Richard Avedon: Comments by Truman Capote, **Supp. III Part 1:** 125–126
Obuchowski, Mary DeJong, **Supp. XX:**222
O Canada: An American's Notes on Canadian Culture (Wilson), **IV:** 429–430
"O Carib Isle!" (Crane), **I:** 400–401
O'Casey, Sean, **III:** 145; **Supp. IV Part 1:** 359, 361, 364
"Occidentals" (Ford), **Supp. V:** 71–72
Occom, Samuel, **Supp. XX:**288
"Occultation of Orion, The" (Longfellow), **Retro. Supp. II:** 168
"Occurrence at Owl Creek Bridge, An" (Bierce), **I:** 200–201; **II:** 264
"Ocean 1212-W" (Plath), **Supp. I Part 2:** 528
"Ocean of Words" (Jin), **Supp. XVIII:** 94
Ocean of Words: Army Stories (Jin), **Supp. XVIII:** 89, 92, **93–94**
O'Connell, Nicholas, **Supp. IX:** 323, 325, 334
O'Connell, Shaun, **Supp. XXI:** 231
O'Connor, Edward F., Jr., **III:** 337
O'Connor, Flannery, **I:** 113, 190, 211, 298; **II:** 606; **III: 337–360; IV:** 4, 217, 282; **Retro. Supp. II:** 179, **219–239,** 272, 324; **Supp. I Part 1:** 290; **Supp. III Part 1:** 146; **Supp. V:** 59, 337; **Supp. VIII:** 13, 14, 158; **Supp. X:** 1, 26, 69, 228, 290; **Supp. XI:** 104; **Supp. XIII:** 294; **Supp. XIV:** 93; **Supp. XV:** 338; **Supp. XVI:** 219; **Supp. XVII:** 43, 114; **Supp. XVIII:** 156, 161, 194; **Supp. XIX:** 166, 209, 223; **Supp. XXI:** 197
O'Connor, Frank, **III:** 158; **Retro. Supp. II:** 242; **Supp. I Part 2:** 531; **Supp. VIII:** 151, 157, 165, 167, 171; **Supp. XV:** 74
O'Connor, Richard, **II:** 467
O'Connor, T. P., **II:** 129
O'Connor, William, **IV:** 346; **Retro. Supp. I:** 392, 407
O'Connor, William Van, **III:** 479; **Supp. I Part 1:** 195
"Octascope" (Beattie), **Supp. V:** 27, 28
"Octaves" (Robinson), **Supp. III Part 2:** 593
"Octet" (Wallace), **Supp. X:** 309
October (Isherwood), **Supp. XIV:** 157, 164
"October" (Oliver), **Supp. VII:** 241
"October" (Swenson), **Supp. IV Part 2:** 649
"October, 1866" (Bryant), **Supp. I Part 1:** 169

"October 1913" (McCarriston), **Supp. XIV:** 266
"October and November" (Lowell), **II:** 554
"October in the Railroad Earth" (Kerouac), **Supp. III Part 1:** 225, 227, 229
October Light (Gardner), **Supp. VI:** 63, **69–71,** 72
"October Maples, Portland" (Wilbur), **Supp. III Part 2:** 556
"October: With Rain" (W. V. Davis), **Supp. XXI:** 94
"Octopus, An" (Moore), **III:** 202, 207–208, 214
"Octopus, The" (Merrill), **Supp. III Part 1:** 321
Octopus, The (Norris), **I:** 518; **III:** 314, 316, 322–326, 327, 331–333, 334, 335
"O Daedalus, Fly Away Home" (Hayden), **Supp. II Part 1:** 377–378
"OD and Hepatitis Railroad or Bust, The" (Boyle), **Supp. VIII:** 1
Odd Couple, The (1985 version, Simon), **Supp. IV Part 2:** 580
Odd Couple, The (film), **Supp. IV Part 2:** 589
Odd Couple, The (Simon), **Supp. IV Part 2:** 575, 579–580, 585, 586; **Supp. XVII:** 8
Odd Jobs (Updike), **Retro. Supp. I:** 334
Odd Mercy (Stern), **Supp. IX: 298–299**
Odd Number (Sorrentino), **Supp. XXI:** 236
"Odds, The" (Hecht), **Supp. X:** 64–65
"Odds, The" (Salinas), **Supp. XIII:** 321
"Ode" (Emerson), **II:** 13
"Ode" (Sobin), **Supp. XVI:** 284–285
"Ode" (X. J. Kennedy), **Supp. XV:** 160
"Ode (Intimations of Immortality)" (Matthews), **Supp. IX:** 162
"Ode for Memorial Day" (Dunbar), **Supp. II Part 1:** 199
"Ode for the American Dead in Asia" (McGrath), **Supp. X:** 119
"Ode: For the Budding of Islands" (Sobin), **Supp. XVI:** 287
"Ode Inscribed to W. H. Channing" (Emerson), **Supp. XIV:** 46
"Ode: Intimations of Immortality" (Wordsworth), **Supp. I Part 2:** 729; **Supp. III Part 1:** 12; **Supp. XIV:** 8
Odell, Margaretta Matilda, **Supp. XX:**278, 284, 288
"Ode: My 24th Year" (Ginsberg), **Supp. II Part 1:** 312
"Ode on a Grecian Urn" (Keats), **I:** 284; **III:** 472; **Supp. XII:** 113; **Supp. XIV:** 8, 9–10; **Supp. XV:** 100; **Supp. XXI:** 64
"Ode on Human Destinies" (Jeffers), **Supp. II Part 2:** 419
"Ode on Indolence" (Keats), **Supp. XII:** 113
"Ode on Melancholy" (Keats), **Retro. Supp. I:** 301
Ode Recited at the Harvard Commemoration (Lowell), **Supp. I Part 2:** 416–418, 424

"Ode Recited at the Harvard Commemoration" (Lowell), **II:** 551
"Ode Secrète" (Valéry), **III:** 609
"Odes of Estrangement" (Sobin), **Supp. XVI:** 289
"Odes to Natural Processes" (Updike), **Retro. Supp. I:** 323
"Ode: The Capris" (Halliday), **Supp. XIX:** 88
"Ode to a Nightingale" (Keats), **II:** 368; **Retro. Supp. II:** 261; **Supp. IX:** 52
"Ode to Autumn" (Masters), **Supp. I Part 2:** 458
"Ode to Cervantes" (Salinas), **Supp. XIII:** 324
"Ode to Coit Tower" (Corso), **Supp. XII:** 122
"Ode to Ethiopia" (Dunbar), **Supp. II Part 1:** 199, 207, 208, 209
"Ode to Fear" (Tate), **IV:** 128
Ode to Harvard and Other Poems, An (Bynner), **Supp. XV:** 41, 44
"Ode to Meaning" (Pinsky), **Supp. VI:** 249–250, 251
"Ode to Night" (Masters), **Supp. I Part 2:** 458
"Ode to Our Young Pro-Consuls of the Air" (Tate), **IV:** 135
"Ode to the Austrian Socialists" (Benét), **Supp. XI:** 46, 58
"Ode to the Confederate Dead" (Tate), **II:** 551; **IV:** 124, 133, 137; **Supp. X:** 52
"Ode to the Johns Hopkins University" (Lanier), **Supp. I Part 1:** 370
"Ode to the Maggot" (Komunyakaa), **Supp. XIII:** 130
"Ode to the Mexican Experience" (Salinas), **Supp. XIII:** 316–317
"Ode to the Virginian Voyage" (Drayton), **IV:** 135
"Ode to the West Wind" (Shelley), **Retro. Supp. I:** 308; **Supp. I Part 2:** 728; **Supp. IX:** 52; **Supp. XII:** 117; **Supp. XIV:** 271–272; **Supp. XV:** 221
"Ode to Walt Whitman" (Benét), **Supp. XI:** 52
Odets, Clifford, **Supp. I Part 1:** 277, 295; **Supp. I Part 2:** 679; **Supp. II Part 2:** 529–554; **Supp. IV Part 2:** 587; **Supp. V:** 109; **Supp. VIII:** 96; **Supp. XVIII:** 238; **Supp. XX:** 34
Odier, Daniel, **Supp. III Part 1:** 97
"Odi et Amo" (Catullus), **Supp. XV:** 27, 32, 35
O'Donnell, George Marion, **II:** 67
O'Donnell, Mary King, **Supp. XVIII:** 232
O'Donnell, Thomas F., **II:** 131
"Odor of Verbena" (Faulkner), **II:** 66
O'Doul, Lefty, **II:** 425
"Odysseus to Telemachus" (Brodsky), **Supp. VIII:** 25
Odyssey (Bryant, trans.), **Supp. I Part 1:** 158
Odyssey (Homer), **III:** 14, 470; **Retro. Supp. I:** 286, 290; **Retro. Supp. II:** 121; **Supp. I Part 1:** 185; **Supp. IV**

Part 2: 631; **Supp. IX:** 211; **Supp. X:** 114; **Supp. XIV:** 191; **Supp. XVII:** 117; **Supp. XXI:** 36
"Odyssey of a Wop, The" (Fante), **Supp. XI:** 164, 165
Oedipus Rex (Sophocles), **I:** 137; **III:** 145, 151, 152, 332; **Supp. I Part 2:** 428
Oedipus Tyrannus (Sophocles), **II:** 203; **Supp. XV:** 265
Oehlschlaeger, Fritz, **Supp. IX:** 123
"Of Alexander Crummell" (Du Bois), **Supp. II Part 1:** 170
O'Faoláin, Seán, **Supp. II Part 1:** 101
Of a World That Is No More (Singer), **IV:** 16
"Of Booker T. Washington and Others" (Du Bois), **Supp. II Part 1:** 168
"Of Bright & Blue Birds & the Gala Sun" (Stevens), **IV:** 93
"Of Christian Heroism" (Ozick), **Supp. V:** 272
"Of Dying Beauty" (Zukofsky), **Supp. III Part 2:** 610
"Of Epiphanies and Poets" (Phillips), **Supp. XX:** 221
"Of 'Father and Son'" (Kunitz), **Supp. III Part 1:** 262
Offenbach, Jacques, **II:** 427
"Offering for Mr. Bluehart, An" (Wright), **Supp. III Part 2:** 596, 601
"Offerings" (Mason), **Supp. VIII:** 141
"Offertory" (Hempel), **Supp. XXI:** 126–127
Official Entry Blank (Kooser), **Supp. XIX:** 116, 117–118
"Official Entry Form" (Kooser), **Supp. XIX:** 117
"Official Piety" (Whittier), **Supp. I Part 2:** 687
"Offloading for Mrs. Schwartz" (Saunders), **Supp. XIX:** 225–226
"Of Freemasons, Kings, and Constitutions" (P. N. Warren), **Supp. XX:** 273
"Off-Shore Pirates, The" (Fitzgerald), **II:** 88
Off the Beaten Path (Proulx), **Supp. VII:** 261
Off the Beaten Path: Stories of Place, **Supp. XVI:** 22
"Off the Cuff" (Simpson), **Supp. IX:** 278
"Off the Highway" (Wolfert), **Supp. XXI:** 265
Off the Map (Levine), **Supp. V:** 178
Offut, Chris, **Supp. XIX:** 163–176
O'Flaherty, George, **Supp. I Part 1:** 202, 205–206
O'Flaherty, Kate. *See* Chopin, Kate
O'Flaherty, Thomas, **Supp. I Part 1:** 202, 203–204, 205
O'Flaherty, Thomas, Jr., **Supp. I Part 1:** 202
"Of Maids and Other Muses" (Alvarez), **Supp. VII:** 11
"Of Margaret" (Ransom), **III:** 491
Of Mice and Men (Steinbeck), **IV:** 51, 57–58
"Of Modern Poetry" (Stevens), **IV:** 92
Of Plymouth Plantation (Bradford), **Retro. Supp. II:** 161, 162

Of Plymouth Plantation (Morison, ed.), **Supp. I Part 2:** 494
"Ofrenda for Lobo" (Mora), **Supp. XIII:** 224
"Often" (Kenyon), **Supp. VII:** 171
"Often, in Dreams, He Moved through a City" (Dobyns), **Supp. XIII:** 90
"Of the Coming of John" (Du Bois), **Supp. II Part 1:** 170
"Of the Culture of White Folk" (Du Bois), **Supp. II Part 1:** 175
Of the Farm (Updike), **IV:** 214, 217, 223–225, 233; **Retro. Supp. I:** 318, 329, 332
"Of the Four-Winged Cherubim as Signature" (Sobin), **Supp. XVI:** 287
"Of 'The Frill'" (McCarriston), **Supp. XIV:** 274
"Of the Passing of the First-Born" (Du Bois), **Supp. II Part 1:** 170
"Of the Sorrow Songs" (Du Bois), **Supp. II Part 1:** 170
"Of the Wings of Atlanta" (Du Bois), **Supp. II Part 1:** 170
Of This Time, Of This Place (Trilling), **Supp. III Part 2:** 498, 504
Of Time and the River (Wolfe), **IV:** 450, 451, 452, 455, 456, 457, 458, 459, 462, 464–465, 467, 468, 469
Of Woman Born: Motherhood as Experience and Institution (Rich), **Supp. I Part 2:** 554, 567–569
Of Women and Their Elegance (Mailer), **Retro. Supp. II:** 209
Ogden, Archie, **Supp. XIII:** 174
Ogden, Henry, **II:** 298
Ogden, Uzal, **Supp. I Part 2:** 516
"Oh, Atonement" (Weigl), **Supp. XIX:** 287
"Oh, Fairest of the Rural Maids" (Bryant), **Supp. I Part 1:** 169
"Oh, Immobility, Death's Vast Associate" (Dobyns), **Supp. XIII:** 89
"Oh, Joseph, I'm So Tired" (Yates), **Supp. XI:** 348
Oh, the Places You'll Go! (Geisel), **Supp. XVI:** 111
Oh, the Thinks You can Think! (Geisel), **Supp. XVI:** 111
"O'Halloran's Luck" (Benét), **Supp. XI:** 47
O'Hara, Frank, **Supp. XII:** 121; **Supp. XV:** 93, 176, 177, 178, 179–180, 182, 186, 187, 215–216; **Supp. XIX:** 81, 85
O'Hara, J. D., **Supp. IV Part 1:** 43; **Supp. V:** 22; **Supp. XVI:** 221; **Supp. XXI:** 228
O'Hara, John, **I:** 375, 495; **II:** 444, 459; **III:** 66, 361–384; **IV:** 59; **Retro. Supp. I:** 99, 112; **Supp. I Part 1:** 196; **Supp. II Part 1:** 109; **Supp. IV Part 1:** 31, 383; **Supp. IV Part 2:** 678; **Supp. V:** 95; **Supp. VIII:** 151, 156; **Supp. IX:** 208; **Supp. XIX:** 209
O'Hara's Choice (Uris), **Supp. XX:** 247, 256–257
O'Hehir, Andrew, **Supp. XII:** 280
O. Henry Biography (C. A. Smith), **Supp. II Part 1:** 395

"Ohio Pagan, An" (Anderson), **I:** 112, 113

Ohio trilogy (Richter), **Supp. XVIII:** 212–215

Oh Mercy (album, Dylan), **Supp. XVIII:** 28, 33

Oh Say Can You Say? (Geisel), **Supp. XVI:** 111

Oil! (Sinclair), **Supp. V:** 276, 277–279, 282, 288, 289

Oil Notes (Bass), **Supp. XVI:** 17

"Oil Painting of the Artist as the Artist" (MacLeish), **III:** 14

O'Keeffe, Georgia, **Supp. IX:** 62, 66; **Supp. XX:**75

"Oklahoma" (Levis), **Supp. XI:** 267

Oktenberg, Adrian, **Supp. XVII:** 76; **Supp. XXI:** 253

"Old, Old, Old, Old Andrew Jackson" (Lindsay), **Supp. I Part 2:** 398

"Old Amusement Park, An" (Moore), **III:** 216

"Old Angel Midnight" (Kerouac), **Supp. III Part 1:** 229–230

"Old Apple Dealer, The" (Hawthorne), **II:** 227, 233–235, 237, 238

"Old Apple-Tree, The" (Dunbar), **Supp. II Part 1:** 198

"Old Army Game, The" (Garrett), **Supp. VII:** 100–101

"Old Aunt Peggy" (Chopin), **Retro. Supp. II:** 64

"Old Barn at the Bottom of the Fogs, The" (Frost), **Retro. Supp. I:** 138

Old Beauty and Others, The (Cather), **I:** 331

Old Bruin: Commodore Matthew C. Perry, 1794–1858 (Morison), **Supp. I Part 2:** 494–495

"Old Cracked Tune, An" (Kunitz), **Supp. III Part 1:** 264

Old Curiosity Shop, The (Dickens), **I:** 458; **Supp. I Part 2:** 409

Oldest Killed Lake in North America, The (Carruth), **Supp. XVI:** 51

"Oldest Man, The" (M. F. K. Fisher), **Supp. XVII:** 91

"Old Farmer, The" (Jeffers), **Supp. II Part 2:** 418

Old-Fashioned Girl, An (Alcott), **Supp. I Part 1:** 29, 41, 42

"Old Father Morris" (Stowe), **Supp. I Part 2:** 586

"Old Flame, The" (Lowell), **II:** 550

"Old Florist" (Roethke), **III:** 531

"Old Folsom Prison" (Matthews), **Supp. IX:** 165

Old Forest, The (Taylor), **Supp. V:** 320, 321, 326, 327

"Old Forest, The" (Taylor), **Supp. V:** 313, 321, 323, 326

Old Forest and Other Stories (Taylor), **Supp. V:** 326

Old Friends and New (Jewett), **II:** 402; **Retro. Supp. II:** 137, 140

Old Glory, The (Lowell), **II:** 543, 545–546, 555; **Retro. Supp. II:** 188

Old Helmet, The (S. and A. Warner), **Supp. XVIII:** 267

"Old Homestead, The" (Dunbar), **Supp. II Part 1:** 198

"Old House" (Espaillat), **Supp. XXI:** 112, 113

"Old Iron" (Nye), **Supp. XIII:** 276

"Old Ironsides" (Holmes), **Supp. I Part 1:** 302

"Old Lady We Saw, An" (Shields), **Supp. VII:** 310–311

"Old Love" (Singer), **Retro. Supp. II:** 307

"Old McGrath Place, The" (McGrath), **Supp. X:** 114

"Old Maid, The" (Wharton), **Retro. Supp. I:** 381, 382

"Old Man" (Faulkner), **II:** 68, 69

Old Man and the Sea, The (Hemingway), **II:** 250, 256–257, 258, 265; **III:** 40; **Retro. Supp. I:** 180, **185,** 186

"Old Man Drunk" (Wright), **Supp. III Part 2:** 595

"Old Man Feeding Hens" (Francis), **Supp. IX:** 78

"Old Man on the Hospital Porch" (Ríos), **Supp. IV Part 2:** 546–547

Old Man Rubbing His Eyes (R. Bly), **Supp. IV Part 1:** 65

"Old Manse, The" (Hawthorne), **II:** 224

"Old Man's Winter Night, An" (Frost), **Retro. Supp. I:** 126, 131

Old Man Who Love Cheese, The (Keillor), **Supp. XVI:** 177

"Old Man with a Dog" (Wright), **Supp. XV:** 346

Old Marriage and New (Kooser), **Supp. XIX: 120–121**

"Old Meeting House, The" (Stowe), **Supp. I Part 2:** 586

"Old Memory, An" (Dunbar), **Supp. II Part 1:** 198

"Old Men, Old Horses" (P. N. Warren as Kilina), **Supp. XX:**262

"Old Men, The" (McCarthy), **II:** 566

"Old Men Pitching Horseshoes" (X. J. Kennedy), **Supp. XV:** 166

Old Money (Wasserstein), **Supp. XV: 333–334**

"Old Morgue, The" (Prose), **Supp. XVI:** 250

Old Morning Program, The (radio show, Keillor). See *Prairie Home Companion, A* (radio show, Keillor)

"Old Mortality" (Porter), **III:** 436, 438–441, 442, 445, 446

"Old Mrs. Harris" (Cather), **I:** 332; **Retro. Supp. I:** 19

Old Neighborhood, The (Mamet), **Supp. XIV:** 240, 241, 242, 249–250, 251, 252, 254

Old New York (Wharton), **IV:** 322; **Retro. Supp. I:** 381

"Ol' Doc Hyar" (Campbell), **Supp. II Part 1:** 202

"Old of the Moon" (Offutt), **Supp. XIX:** 165, 166

Old One-Two, The (Gurney), **Supp. V:** 98

"Old Order, The" (Porter), **III:** 443, 444–445, 451

"Old Osawatomie" (Sandburg), **III:** 584

Old Patagonia Express, The: By Train through the Americas (Theroux), **Supp. VIII:** 322

"Old People, The" (Faulkner), **II:** 71–72

"Old Photograph, An" (Kooser), **Supp. XIX:** 121

"Old Poet Moves to a New Apartment 14 Times, The" (Zukofsky), **Supp. III Part 2:** 628

Old Possum's Book of Practical Cats (T. S. Eliot), **Supp. XIII:** 228, 344

"Old Red" (Gordon), **II:** 199, 200, 203

Old Red and Other Stories (Gordon), **II:** 157

Old Régime in Canada, The (Parkman), **Supp. II Part 2:** 600, 607, 608–609, 612

Old Religion, The (Mamet), **Supp. XIV:** 253

Olds, Sharon, **Supp. X: 201–217; Supp. XI:** 139, 142, 244; **Supp. XII:** 229; **Supp. XIV:** 265; **Supp. XVII:** 114, 240; **Supp. XXI:** 249

"Old Saws" (Garrett), **Supp. VII:** 96–97

"Old Stories" (Skloot), **Supp. XX:**200

Old Testament, **I:** 109, 181, 300, 328, 401, 410, 419, 431, 457, 458; **II:** 166, 167, 219; **III:** 270, 272, 348, 390, 396; **IV:** 41, 114, 152, 309; **Retro. Supp. I:** 122, 140, 249, 311, 360; **Retro. Supp. II:** 299; **Supp. I Part 1:** 60, 104, 106, 151; **Supp. I Part 2:** 427, 515, 516; **Supp. IX:** 14. *See also* names of Old Testament books

"Old Things, The" (James), **Retro. Supp. I:** 229

"Old Times on the Mississippi" (Twain), **IV:** 199

Oldtown Folks (Stowe), **Supp. I Part 2:** 587, 596–598

"Old Town of Berwick, The" (Jewett), **Retro. Supp. II:** 132

"Old Trails" (Robinson), **III:** 513, 517

"Old Tyrannies" (Bourne), **I:** 233

"Old West" (Bausch), **Supp. VII:** 48

"Old Whorehouse, An" (Oliver), **Supp. VII:** 235

"Old Woman" (Pinsky), **Supp. VI:** 238

"Old Woman of Beare, The" (X. J. Kennedy), **Supp. XV:** 156

"Old Word, The" (Simic), **Supp. VIII:** 282

"Old-World Landowners" (Gogol), **Supp. XV:** 262

Oldys, Francis. *See* Chalmers, George

Oleanna (Mamet), **Supp. XIV:** 239, 241, 245, 248, 250

Olendorf, Donna, **Supp. IV Part 1:** 196

"Olga Poems, The" (Levertov), **Supp. III Part 1:** 279–281

"Olive Groves of Thasos, The" (Clampitt), **Supp. IX:** 51–52

Oliver, Bill, **Supp. VIII:** 138

Oliver, Mary, **Supp. VII: 229–248; Supp. X:** 31; **Supp. XVI:** 39; **Supp. XVII:** 111, 240

Oliver, Sydney, **I:** 409

Oliver Goldsmith: A Biography (Irving), **II:** 315

Oliver Twist (Dickens), **I**: 354; **Supp. IV Part 2**: 464
"Olivia" (Salinas), **Supp. XIII**: 316
"Olivier Bergmann" (Halliday), **Supp. XIX**: 93–94
Olivieri, David (pseudonym), **Retro. Supp. I**: 361. *See also* Wharton, Edith
Ollive, Samuel, **Supp. I Part 2**: 503
Olmsted, Frederick Law, **Supp. I Part 1**: 355
Olor de la memoria, El/The Scent of Memory (Espaillat), **Supp. XXI**: 104
Olsen, Lance, **Supp. IV Part 1**: 54; **Supp. IV Part 2**: 623
Olsen, Tillie, **Supp. V**: 114, 220; **Supp. XIII**: 291–309; **Supp. XVI**: 83, 90
Olshan, Joseph, **Supp. XIX**: 52
Olson, Charles, **Retro. Supp. I**: 209; **Supp. II Part 1**: 30, 328; **Supp. II Part 2**: 555–587; **Supp. III Part 1**: 9, 271; **Supp. III Part 2**: 542, 624; **Supp. IV Part 1**: 139, 144, 146, 153, 154, 322; **Supp. IV Part 2**: 420, 421, 423, 426; **Supp. VIII**: 290, 291; **Supp. XII**: 2, 198; **Supp. XIII**: 104; **Supp. XIV**: 96; **Supp. XV**: 177; **Supp. XXI**: 19, 21, 23
Olson, Clarence, **Supp. XX**:84, 85, 86
Olson, Ray, **Supp. XVII**: 111, 112, 119
"Ol' Tunes, The" (Dunbar), **Supp. II Part 1**: 197
"O Lull Me, Lull Me" (Roethke), **III**: 536–537
Omar Khayyam, **Supp. I Part 1**: 363
O'Meally, Robert, **Retro. Supp. II**: 112
Omega the Unknown (comic book series), **Supp. XVIII**: 149
"Omen" (Komunyakaa), **Supp. XIII**: 126, 127
Omensetter's Luck (Gass), **Supp. VI**: 80–82, 87
Omeros (Walcott), **Supp. XV**: 264
"Ominous Baby, An" (Crane), **I**: 411
Ommateum, with Doxology (Ammons), **Supp. VII**: 24–26, 27, 28, 36
Omni-Americans, The: New Perspectives on Black Experience and American Culture (Murray), **Supp. XIX**: 147, 149–151, 154
"Omnibus Jaunts and Drivers" (Whitman), **IV**: 350
Omoo: A Narrative of Adventures in the South Seas (Melville), **III**: 76–77, 79, 84; **Retro. Supp. I**: 247
O My Land, My Friends (H. Crane), **Retro. Supp. II**: 76
"On Abrigador Hill" (Nelson), **Supp. XVIII**: 183
"On a Certain Condescension in Foreigners" (Lowell), **Supp. I Part 2**: 419
"On a Certain Engagement South of Seoul" (Carruth), **Supp. XVI**: 47
"On a Child Who Lived One Minute" (X. J. Kennedy), **Supp. XV**: 152, 155
"On Acquiring Riches" (Banks), **Supp. V**: 5
On a Darkling Plain (Stegner), **Supp. IV Part 2**: 598, 607
On a Fire on the Moon (Mailer), **Retro. Supp. II**: 206

"On a Hill Far Away" (Dillard), **Supp. VI**: 28
"On a Honey Bee, Drinking from a Glass and Drowned Therein" (Freneau), **Supp. II Part 1**: 273
"On a Monument to a Pigeon" (Leopold), **Supp. XIV**: 187–188
"On a Mountainside" (Wagoner), **Supp. IX**: 332
O'Nan, Stewart, **Supp. XI**: 348
"On an Old Photograph of My Son" (Carver), **Supp. III Part 1**: 140
"Onan's Soliloquy" (X. J. Kennedy), **Supp. XV**: 165
"On a Proposed Trip South" (W. C. Williams), **Retro. Supp. I**: 413
Onassis, Jacqueline Kennedy, **Supp. XVIII**: 287
"On a Tree Fallen across the Road" (Frost), **Retro. Supp. I**: 134
"On a View of Pasadena from the Hills" (Winters), **Supp. II Part 2**: 795, 796–799, 814
"On a Visit to a Halfway House after a Long Absence" (Salinas), **Supp. XIII**: 325
"On a Windy Night" (Dixon), **Supp. XII**: 155
On Becoming a Novelist (Gardner), **Supp. VI**: 64
"On Being an American" (Toomer), **Supp. III Part 2**: 479
"On Being Asked to Write a Poem against the War in Vietnam" (Carruth), **Supp. XVI**: 55–56
"On Being a Woman" (Parker), **Supp. IX**: 201
On Being Blue (Gass), **Supp. VI**: 77, 78, 86, 94; **Supp. XIV**: 305
"On Being Brought from Africa to America" (Wheatley), **Supp. XX**:280–281, 286–287
"On Being Too Inhibited" (Hay), **Supp. XIV**: 130
"On Being Unable to Read" (Cornell), **Supp. XX**:94–95
On Beyond Zebra! (Geisel), **Supp. XVI**: 105
"On Burroughs' Work" (Ginsberg), **Supp. II Part 1**: 320
Once (Walker), **Supp. III Part 2**: 519, 522, 530
Once at Antietam (Gaddis), **Supp. IV Part 1**: 285
"Once by the Pacific" (Frost), **II**: 155; **Retro. Supp. I**: 122, 137
"Once More, the Round" (Roethke), **III**: 529
Once More around the Block: Familiar Essays (Epstein), **Supp. XIV**: 107
"Once More to the Lake" (White), **Supp. I Part 2**: 658, 668, 673–675
"On Certain Political Measures Proposed to Their Consideration" (Barlow), **Supp. II Part 1**: 82
"Once There Was Light" (Kenyon), **Supp. VII**: 171–172
"On *Credo Ut Intelligam*" (Bronk), **Supp. XXI**: 31
Ondaatje, Michael, **Supp. IV Part 1**: 252

"On Dining Alone" (M. F. K. Fisher), **Supp. XVII**: 83
On Distant Ground (R. O. Butler), **Supp. XII**: 62, 66–68, 69, 74
"On Divers Geometries" (Bronk), **Supp. XXI**: 31
"One, The" (Weigl), **Supp. XIX**: 282–283
"1 January 1965" (Brodsky), **Supp. VIII**: 23–24
O'Neale, Sondra, **Supp. IV Part 1**: 2
"One A.M. with Voices" (X. J. Kennedy), **Supp. XV**: 157
"One Arm" (T. Williams), **IV**: 383
One Arm, and Other Stories (T. Williams), **IV**: 383
"One Art" (Bell), **Supp. X**: 2
One Art (Bishop), **Retro. Supp. II**: 51
"One Art" (Bishop), **Retro. Supp. II**: 50; **Supp. I Part 1**: 72, 73, 82, 93, 94–95, 96; **Supp. XV**: 126; **Supp. XXI**: 58
"One Art: The Poetry of Elizabeth Bishop, 1971–1976" (Schwartz), **Supp. I Part 1**: 81
One Big Self: Prisoners of Louisiana (Wright and Luster), **Supp. XV**: 337, 344, 350, 351–353
"One Blessing had I than the rest" (Dickinson), **Retro. Supp. I**: 45
"One Body" (Hass), **Supp. VI**: 106
One Boy's Boston, 1887–1901 (Morison), **Supp. I Part 2**: 494
"One Coat of Paint" (Ashbery), **Supp. III Part 1**: 26
"One Dash-Horses" (Crane), **I**: 416
One Day (Morris), **III**: 233–236
One Day, When I Was Lost (Baldwin), **Retro. Supp. II**: 13; **Supp. I Part 1**: 48, 66, 67
"One Dead Friend" (Kumin), **Supp. IV Part 2**: 441
One Fish Two Fish Red Fish Blue Fish (Geisel), **Supp. XVI**: 108
One Flew Over the Cuckoo's Nest (Kesey), **III**: 558
"One for the Road" (Swados), **Supp. XIX**: 259
One for the Rose (Levine), **Supp. V**: 178, 179, 181, 187, 189–191
"One for the Rose" (Levine), **Supp. V**: 181, 190
"One Friday Morning" (Hughes), **Supp. I Part 1**: 330
"One Holy Night" (Cisneros), **Supp. VII**: 69–70
"One Home" (Stafford), **Supp. XI**: 321
100 Faces of Death, The, Part IV (Boyle), **Supp. VIII**: 16
100 Great Poets of the English Language (Gioia, ed.), **Supp. XXI**: 99
$106,000 Blood Money (Hammett), **Supp. IV Part 1**: 345
"$106,000 Blood Money" (Hammett), **Supp. IV Part 1**: 345, 346
One Hundred Days in Europe (Holmes), **Supp. I Part 1**: 317
180 More: Extraordinary Poems for Every Day (Collins, ed.), **Supp. XXI**: 54

158-Pound Marriage, The (Irving), **Supp. VI:** 163, 164, **167–170**

O'Neil, Elizabeth Murrie, **Retro. Supp. I:** 427

O'Neill, Brendan, **Supp. XII:** 286

O'Neill, Eugene, **I:** 66, 71, 81, 94, 393, 445; **II:** 278, 391, 427, 585; **III:** 151, 165, **385–408; IV:** 61, 383; **Retro. Supp. II:** 82, 104; **Supp. III Part 1:** 177–180, 189; **Supp. IV Part 1:** 359; **Supp. IV Part 2:** 587, 607; **Supp. V:** 277; **Supp. VIII:** 332, 334; **Supp. XIV:** 239, 320, 328; **Supp. XVI:** 193; **Supp. XVII:** 96, 99–100, 103, 105, 107; **Supp. XX:**69; **Supp. XXI:** 6, 13

"One Is a Wanderer" (Thurber), **Supp. I Part 2:** 616

One Is the Sun (P. N. Warren), **Supp. XX:269–270**

One L (Turow), **Supp. XVII: 214,** 215, 217

"One Last Look at the Adige: Verona in the Rain" (Wright), **Supp. III Part 2:** 603

One Life (Rukeyser), **Supp. VI:** 273, 281, 283

One Life at a Time, Please (Abbey), **Supp. XIII:** 13

One Man in His Time (Glasgow), **II:** 178, 184

"One Man's Fortunes" (Dunbar), **Supp. II Part 1:** 211, 212–213

One Man's Initiation (Dos Passos), **I:** 476–477, 479, 488

One Man's Meat (White), **Supp. I Part 2:** 654, 669, 676

"One Man's Meat" (White), **Supp. I Part 2:** 655

"One Moment on Top of the Earth" (Nye), **Supp. XIII:** 282

One More July: A Football Dialogue with Bill Curry (Plimpton), **Supp. XVI:** 243

"One More Song" (Lindsay), **Supp. I Part 2:** 400–401

"One More Thing" (Carver), **Supp. III Part 1:** 138, 144

"One More Time" (Gordon), **II:** 200

One Nation (Stegner), **Supp. IV Part 2:** 599, 608

"One-Night Homecoming" (X. J. Kennedy), **Supp. XV:** 167

"ONE NIGHT STAND" (Baraka), **Supp. II Part 1:** 32

"One of Our Conquerors" (Bourne), **I:** 223

One of Ours (Cather), **I:** 322–323; **Retro. Supp. I:** 1, 3, **13–15,** 20

"One of the Missing" (Bierce), **I:** 201–202

"One of the Rooming Houses of Heaven" (Doty), **Supp. XI:** 131

"One of the Smallest" (Stern), **Supp. IX:** 299–300

"One of Us" (Fante), **Supp. XI:** 165

"One Out of Twelve: Writers Who Are Women in Our Century" (Olsen), **Supp. XIII:** 294

"One Part Humor, 2 Parts Whining" (Kakutani), **Supp. XI:** 38

"One Person" (Wylie), **Supp. I Part 2:** 709, 724–727

"One Sister have I in our house" (Dickinson), **Retro. Supp. I:** 34

"One Song, The" (Strand), **Supp. IV Part 2:** 619

"One Summer in Spain" (Coover), **Supp. V:** 40

One That Got Away, The (Everett), **Supp. XVIII:** 54

1000 Airplanes on the Roof (Glass, Hwang, and Sirlin), **Supp. XXI:** 147

One Thousand Avant-Garde Plays (Koch), **Supp. XV:** 187

"One Thousandth, The" (Weigl), **Supp. XIX:** 288

One Time, One Place: Mississippi in the Depression, a Snapshot Album (Welty), **Retro. Supp. I:** 339, 343, 344

1 x 1 (One Times One) (Cummings), **I:** 430, 436, 438–439, 441, 446, 447, 448

"One Touch of Nature" (McCarthy), **II:** 580

One Train (Koch), **Supp. XV:** 177, 184

"One Trip Abroad" (Fitzgerald), **II:** 95

One True Thing (film), **Supp. XVII:** 176

One True Thing (Quindlen), **Supp. XVII:** 166, **174–176**

"One Way" (Creeley), **Supp. IV Part 1:** 150–151

One Way or Another (Cameron), **Supp. XII:** 81

One-Way Ticket (Hughes), **Retro. Supp. I:** 206, 207, 208; **Supp. I Part 1:** 333–334

One Way to Heaven (Cullen), **Supp. IV Part 1:** 170, 172

One Way to Reconstruct the Scene (W. V. Davis), **Supp. XXI:** 83, **88–91**

"One Way to Reconstruct the Scene" (W. V. Davis), **Supp. XXI: 88–89,** 90, 91, 92, 93

One Way to Spell Man (Stegner), **Supp. IV Part 2:** 595, 598, 601, 609

"One Way to Spell Man" (Stegner), **Supp. IV Part 2:** 601

One Whose Eyes Open When You Close Your Eyes, The (F. Wright), **Supp. XVII:** 240, 243

"One Who Skins Cats, The" (Gunn Allen), **Supp. IV Part 1:** 331

"One Who Went Forth to Feel Fear" (Grimms), **Supp. X:** 86

"One Winter I Devise a Plan of My Own" (Ríos), **Supp. IV Part 2:** 549

One Winter Night in August (X. J. Kennedy), **Supp. XV:** 154, 162

One World at a Time (Kooser), **Supp. XIX:** 116, **122–123**

One Writer's Beginnings (Welty), **Retro. Supp. I:** 339, 340, 341, 343, 344, 355–356

"One Year" (Olds), **Supp. X:** 210

On Fire (L. Brown), **Supp. XXI:** 41, **48–49**

"On First Looking Into Chapman's Homer" (Keats), **Supp. XXI:** 64

"On First Looking Out through Juan de la Cosa's Eyes" (Olson), **Supp. II Part 2:** 565, 566, 570, 579

"On First Opening *The Lyric Year*" (W. C. Williams), **Retro. Supp. I:** 414

"On Freedom's Ground" (Wilbur), **Supp. III Part 2:** 562

On Glory's Course (Purdy), **Supp. VII:** 275–276, 279, 280

On Grief and Reason (Brodsky), **Supp. VIII: 31–32**

"On Hearing a Symphony of Beethoven" (Millay), **III:** 132–133

"On Hearing the Airlines Will Use a Psychological Profile to Catch Potential Skyjackers" (Dunn), **Supp. XI:** 144–145

On Human Finery (Bell), **Supp. I Part 2:** 636

"On *Imagerie:* Esther Williams, 1944" (Sobin), **Supp. XVI:** 294

"On Imagination" (Wheatley), **Supp. XX:281**

"On Imminence: An Essay" (Sobin), **Supp. XVI:** 291

On Liberty (Mill), **Supp. XI:** 196

"On Looking Alone at a Place" (M. F. K. Fisher), **Supp. XVII:** 91

"On Looking at a Copy of Alice Meynell's Poems, Given Me, Years Ago, by a Friend" (Lowell), **II:** 527–528

"On Lookout Mountain" (Hayden), **Supp. II Part 1:** 380

Only a Few of Us Left (Marquand), **III:** 55

"Only Animal, The" (F. Wright), **Supp. XVII:** 245

"Only a Pawn in Their Game" (song, Dylan), **Supp. XVIII:** 24

"Only Bar in Dixon, The" (Hugo), **Supp. VI:** 140, 141

Only Dangerous Thing, The (Di Piero), **Supp. XIX: 37–38**

Only Dark Spot in the Sky, The (Dove), **Supp. IV Part 1:** 244

"Only Good Indian, The" (Humphrey), **Supp. IX:** 101

"Only Goodness" (Lahiri), **Supp. XXI:** 186, 188

Only in America (Golden), **Supp. VIII:** 244

"Only in the Dream" (Eberhart), **I:** 523

"Only Path to Tomorrow, The" (Rand), **Supp. IV Part 2:** 524

"Only Rose, The" (Jewett), **II:** 408

"Only Son of the Doctor, The" (Gordon), **Supp. IV Part 1:** 305, 306

"Only the Cat Escapes", **Supp. XII:** 150–151

"Only the Dead Know Brooklyn" (Wolfe), **IV:** 451

Only When I Laugh (Simon), **Supp. IV Part 2:** 575

Only World, The (Hull), **Supp. XXI:** 129, **138–141**

"On Messrs. Hussey and Coffin" (Wheatley), **Supp. XX:280**

On Moral Fiction (Gardner), **Supp. VI:** 61, **71,** 72, 73

"On Morality" (Didion), **Supp. IV Part 1:** 196

"On Mt. Philo in November" (Di Piero), **Supp. XIX:** 37, 39

"On My Own" (Levine), **Supp. V:** 181, 189–190

"On My Own Work" (Wilbur), **Supp. III Part 2:** 541–542

On Native Grounds: An Interpretation of Modern American Prose Literature (Kazin), **I:** 517; **Supp. I Part 2:** 650; **Supp. VIII:** 93, 96–97, 98, **100–102**

"On Not Being a Dove" (Updike), **Retro. Supp. I:** 323

"On Open Form" (Merwin), **Supp. III Part 1:** 347–348, 353

On Photography (Sontag), **Supp. III Part 2:** 451, 458, 462–465

"On Political Poetry" (R. Bly), **Supp. IV Part 1:** 61

On Politics: A Carnival of Buncombe (Moos, ed.), **III:** 116

"On Pretentiousness" (Kushner), **Supp. IX:** 131–132

"On Quitting a Little College" (Stafford), **Supp. XI:** 321

"On Reading Eckerman's Conversations with Goethe" (Masters), **Supp. I Part 2:** 458

On Reading Shakespeare (L. P. Smith), **Supp. XIV:** 345–346

"On Reading to Oneself" (Gass), **Supp. VI:** 88, 89

"On Recollection" (Wheatley), **Supp. XX:** 287

On Revolution (Arendt), **Retro. Supp. I:** 87

"On Seeing Larry Rivers' *Washington Crossing the Delaware* at the Museum of Modern Art" (O'Hara), **Supp. XV:** 186

"On Seeing Red" (Walker), **Supp. III Part 2:** 527

"On Social Plays" (A. Miller), **III:** 147, 148, 159

"On Steinbeck's Story 'Flight' " (Stegner), **Supp. IV Part 2:** 596

"On Style" (Sontag), **Supp. III Part 2:** 456–459, 465–466

"On Suicide" (Hay), **Supp. XIV:** 130, 132

"On Teaching the Young Laurel to Shoot" (Bynner), **Supp. XV:** 50

"On the Antler" (Proulx), **Supp. VII:** 252–253

"On the Avenue" (Espaillat), **Supp. XXI:** 112

"On the Banks of the Wabash" (Paul Dresser), **Retro. Supp. II:** 94

"On the Beach, at Night" (Whitman), **IV:** 348

"On the Bosom of This Grave and Wasted Land I Will Lay My Head" (Ray), **Supp. XVIII:** 189

On the Boundary (Tillich), **Retro. Supp. I:** 326

"On the Building of Springfield" (Lindsay), **Supp. I Part 2:** 381

"On the Coast of Maine" (Hayden), **Supp. II Part 1:** 381

On the Contrary: Articles of Belief (McCarthy), **II:** 559, 562

"On the Death of a Friend's Child" (Lowell), **Supp. I Part 2:** 409

"On the Death of Cardinal Tisserant" (Bronk), **Supp. XXI:** 32

"On the Death of General Wooster" (Wheatley), **Supp. XX:** 287

"On the Death of Rev. Mr. George Whitefield—1770" (Wheatley), **Supp. XX:** 280, **Supp. XX:** 282–283

"On the Death of Senator Thomas J. Walsh" (Winters), **Supp. II Part 2:** 802, 806

"On the Death of Yeats" (Bogan), **Supp. III Part 1:** 59

"On the Death of Zhukov" (Brodsky), **Supp. VIII:** 27

"On the Disadvantages of Central Heating" (Clampitt), **Supp. IX:** 41, 47, 52

On the Drumhead: A Selection from the Writing of Mike Quin (Carlisle, ed.), **Supp. XVIII:** 223, 226

"On the Edge" (Levine), **Supp. V:** 181–182

On the Edge and Over (Levine), **Supp. V:** 178, 180–182, 186

On the Edge of the Great Rift: Three Novels of Africa (Theroux), **Supp. VIII:** 316

"On the Eve of the Feast of the Immaculate Conception, 1942" (Lowell), **II:** 538; **Retro. Supp. II:** 185

"On the Eyes of an SS Officer" (Wilbur), **Supp. III Part 2:** 548

"On the Failure of Meaning in the Absence of Objective Analogs" (Bronk), **Supp. XXI:** 31

"On the Fall of General Earl Cornwallis" (Freneau), **Supp. II Part 1:** 261

"On the Folly of Writing Poetry" (Freneau), **Supp. II Part 1:** 263

On the Frontier (Auden and Isherwood), **Supp. II Part 1:** 13; **Supp. XIV:** 163

On the Great Atlantic Rainway: Selected Poems, 1950–1988 (Koch), **Supp. XV:** 177

"On the History of Poetry" (Halliday), **Supp. XIX:** 88, 89

"On the Hysterical Playground" (Watman), **Supp. XX:** 93

"On the Island" (Stern), **Supp. IX:** 290

"On the Late Eclipse" (Bryant), **Supp. I Part 1:** 152

On the Laws of the Poetic Art (Hecht), **Supp. X:** 58

On the Line (Swados), **Supp. XIX:** **258–260**

"On the Line" (Swados), **Supp. XIX:** 259

"On the Marginal Way" (Wilbur), **Supp. III Part 2:** 558, 559

On the Mesa (Nichols), **Supp. XIII:** 268

"On the Moon and Matriarchal Consciousness" (Neumann), **Supp. IV Part 1:** 68

"On the Morning after the Sixties" (Didion), **Supp. IV Part 1:** 205, 206

On the Motion and Immobility of Douve (Bonnefoy; Kinnell, trans.), **Supp. III Part 1:** 235

"On the Murder of Lieutenant José del Castillo by the Falangist Bravo Martinez, July 12, 1936" (Levine), **Supp. V:** 187

"On the Night of a Friend's Wedding" (Robinson), **III:** 524

"On the Occasion of a Poem: Richard Hugo" (Wright), **Supp. III Part 2:** 596

On the Occasion of My Last Afternoon (Gibbons), **Supp. X:** 46, **50–53**

On the Origin of Species (Darwin), **Supp. XIV:** 192

"On the Parapet" (Tanner), **Retro. Supp. II:** 205

"On the Platform" (Nemerov), **III:** 287

On the Poetry of Philip Levine: Stranger to Nothing (Levis), **Supp. XI:** 257

"On the Pottlecombe Cornice" (Sturgis), **Supp. XX:** 233, 240

"On the Powers of the Human Understanding" (Freneau), **Supp. II Part 1:** 274

On the Prejudices, Predilections, and Firm Beliefs of William Faulkner (Brooks), **Supp. XIV:** 13

"On the Pulse of Morning" (Angelou), **Supp. IV Part 1:** 15–17

"On the Railway Platform" (Jarrell), **II:** 370

"On the Rainy River" (O'Brien), **Supp. V:** 250

On the Rebound: A Story and Nine Poems (Purdy), **Supp. VII:** 276–277

"On the Religion of Nature" (Freneau), **Supp. II Part 1:** 275

"On the River" (Dunbar), **Supp. II Part 1:** 193

"On the River" (Levine), **Supp. V:** 193

On the River Styx and Other Stories (Matthiessen), **Supp. V:** 212

On the Road (Kerouac), **Retro. Supp. I:** 102; **Supp. III Part 1:** 92, 218, 222–224, 226, 230–231; **Supp. V:** 336; **Supp. X:** 269; **Supp. XIII:** 275; **Supp. XIV:** 138, 150; **Supp. XV:** 221; **Supp. XVIII:** 20, 138; **Supp. XXI:** 53

"On the Road Home" (Stevens), **Retro. Supp. I:** 306

On the Road with the Archangel (Buechner), **Supp. XII:** 54

"On the Rope" (Richard), **Supp. XIX:** 211–212

On These I Stand: An Anthology of the Best Poems of Countee Cullen (Cullen), **Supp. IV Part 1:** 173

"On the Skeleton of a Hound" (Wright), **Supp. III Part 2:** 593

"On the Street" (Peacock), **Supp. XIX:** 199

"On the Street: Monument" (Gunn Allen), **Supp. IV Part 1:** 326

"On the Subway" (Olds), **Supp. X:** 207

"On the System of Policy Hitherto Pursued by Their Government" (Barlow), **Supp. II Part 1:** 82

"On the Teaching of Modern Literature" (Trilling), **Supp. III Part 2:** 509–510

"On the Uniformity and Perfection of Nature" (Freneau), **Supp. II Part 1:** 275

"On the Universality and Other Attributes of the God of Nature" (Freneau), **Supp. II Part 1:** 275

"On the Use of Trisyllabic Feet in Iambic Verse" (Bryant), **Supp. I Part 1:** 156

On the Verge: Emerging Poets (Ellis and Lease, eds.), **Supp. XXI:** 246

On the Waterfront (film, Kazan), **Supp. XVIII:** 250–251, 252, 253

On the Way toward a Phenomenological Psychology: The Psychology of William James (Linschoten), **II:** 362

"On the Way to Work" (Dunn), **Supp. XI:** 149–150

"On the Wide Heath" (Millay), **III:** 130

"On the Writing of Novels" (Buck), **Supp. II Part 1:** 121

On the Yard (Braly), **Supp. XVIII:** 147

On This Island (Auden), **Supp. II Part 1:** 11

"On Time" (O'Hara), **III:** 369–370

"Ontological Episode of the Asylum" (Carruth), **Supp. XVI:** 48, 50

"Ontology of the Sentence, The" (Gass), **Supp. VI:** 77

"On Top" (Leopold), **Supp. XIV:** 188

"On Top" (Snyder), **Supp. VIII:** 304

"On Translating Akhmatova" (Kunitz), **Supp. III Part 1:** 268

"On Turning Ten" (Collins), **Supp. XXI:** 64

"On Waking to Old Debts" (Keillor), **Supp. XVI:** 167

On William Stafford: The Worth of Local Things (Andrews, ed.), **Supp. XI:** 311, 312, 317, 321, 324, 326

"On Writing" (Carver), **Supp. III Part 1:** 142–143

"On Writing" (Nin), **Supp. X:** 182

Opatoshu, Joseph, **IV:** 9

"Open Boat, The" (Crane), **I:** 408, 415, 416–417, 423; **Retro. Supp. I:** 325; **Supp. XIV:** 51

Open Boat and Other Stories (Crane), **I:** 408

Open Door, The (Skloot), **Supp. XX:** 194, 196, **208**

Open Heart: A Patient's Story of Life-Saving Medicine and Life-Giving Friendship (Neugeboren), **Supp. XVI:** 217, **229–230**

Open House (Roethke), **III:** 529–530, 540

"Open House" (Roethke), **III:** 529

"Opening, An" (Swenson), **Supp. IV Part 2:** 639

Opening of the Field, The (Duncan), **Supp. III Part 2:** 625

Opening the Hand (Merwin), **Supp. III Part 1:** 341, 353, 355

"Open Letter" (Roethke), **III:** 532, 534

"Open Letter to Surrealists Everywhere, An" (H. Miller), **III:** 184

Open Meeting, The (Gurney), **Supp. V:** 98

Open Net (Plimpton), **Supp. XVI:** 241

"Open Road, The" (Dreiser), **II:** 44

Open Sea, The (Masters), **Supp. I Part 2:** 471

Open Season: Sporting Adventures (Humphrey), **Supp. IX:** 95

"Open Secret" (Nelson), **Supp. XVIII:** 185

"Open the Gates" (Kunitz), **Supp. III Part 1:** 264–265, 267

"Opera Company, The" (Merrill), **Supp. III Part 1:** 326

Operating Instructions: A Journal of My Son's First Year (Lamott), **Supp. XX:136–137,** 142

"Operation, The" (Sanders), **Supp. XVI:** 266

"Operation, The" (Sexton), **Supp. II Part 2:** 675, 679

Operation Shylock: A Confession (P. Roth), **Retro. Supp. II:** 279, 280, 291

Operation Sidewinder (Shepard), **Supp. III Part 2:** 434–435, 439, 446–447

Operations in North African Waters (Morison), **Supp. I Part 2:** 490

Operation Wandering Soul (Powers), **Supp. IX:** 212, **217–219**

Opffer, Emil, **Retro. Supp. II:** 80

"Opinion" (Du Bois), **Supp. II Part 1:** 173

Opinionator, The (Bierce), **I:** 209

Opinions of Oliver Allston (Brooks), **I:** 254, 255, 256

O Pioneers! (Cather), **I:** 314, 317–319, 320; **Retro. Supp. I:** 1, 5, 6, **7–9,** 10, 13, 20; **Retro. Supp. II:** 136

Oppen, George, **IV:** 415; **Supp. III Part 2:** 614, 615, 616, 626, 628; **Supp. XIV:** 285, 286, 287; **Supp. XVI:** 282, 283; **Supp. XVII:** 243; **Supp. XXI:** 19, **Supp. XXI:** 29, 23

Oppenheim, James, **I:** 106, 109, 239, 245; **Supp. XV:** 294, 296, 298, 299, 301, 302, 307, 313; **Supp. XX:68**

Oppenheimer, J. Robert, **I:** 137, 492

Oppenheimer, Judy, **Supp. IX:** 115, 116, 118, 120, 126

"Opportunity for American Fiction, An" (Howells), **Supp. I Part 2:** 645–646

Opposing Self, The (Trilling), **Supp. III Part 2:** 506–507

"Opposition" (Lanier), **Supp. I Part 1:** 368, 373

Oprah's Roots: An African American Lives Special (television production), **Supp. XX:99**

Opticks: A Poem in Seven Sections (Goldbarth), **Supp. XII:** 177, **178**

Optimist's Daughter, The (Welty), **IV:** 261, 280; **Retro. Supp. I:** 339, 355

"Optimist's Daughter, The" (Welty), **IV:** 280–281

Options (O. Henry), **Supp. II Part 1:** 410

Opus Posthumous (Stevens), **IV:** 76, 78

Opus Posthumous (W. Stevens), **Supp. XVII:** 241

Oracle at Stoneleigh Court, The (Taylor), **Supp. V:** 328

Orage, Alfred, **III:** 473

Orange, Max (pseudonym). *See* Heller, Joseph

Orange Fish, The (Shields), **Supp. VII:** 318, 320, 323, 328

Orangery, The (Sorrentino), **Supp. XXI:** 228

Oranges (McPhee), **Supp. III Part 1:** 298–299, 301, 309

"Oranging of America, The" (Apple), **Supp. XVII:** 3–4, 6

Oranging of America and Other Short Stories, The (Apple), **Supp. XVII:** 1–2, **3–4,** 7, 8

Oration Delivered at Washington, July Fourth, 1809 (Barlow), **Supp. II Part 1:** 80, 83

Orations and Addresses (Bryant), **Supp. I Part 1:** 158

Orators, The (Auden), **Supp. II Part 1:** 6, 7, 11, 18–19

Orb Weaver, The (Francis), **Supp. IX:** **81–82**

"Orchard" (Doolittle), **Supp. I Part 1:** 263–264, 265, 266

"Orchard" (Eberhart), **I:** 539

Orchard, The (B. Kelly), **Supp. XVII:** 123, 127, **130–133**

"Orchard, The" (B. Kelly), **Supp. XVII:** 133

Orchard Keeper, The (McCarthy), **Supp. VIII:** 175–176

Orchestra (Davies), **III:** 541

"Orchids" (Roethke), **III:** 530–531

"Or Consider Prometheus" (Clampitt), **Supp. IX:** 44

Ordeal of Mansart, The (Du Bois), **Supp. II Part 1:** 185–186

Ordeal of Mark Twain, The (Brooks), **I:** 240, 247, 248; **II:** 482

Ordering the Façade: Photography and Contemporary Southern Women's Writing (Henninger), **Supp. XXI:** 253

"Order of Insects" (Gass), **Supp. VI:** 83

Order Out of Chaos (McPherson), **Supp. IV Part 1:** 2, 12

"Ordinary Afternoon in Charlottesville, An" (Wright), **Supp. V:** 344

"Ordinary Days" (Dunn), **Supp. XI:** 151

"Ordinary Evening in New Haven, An" (Stevens), **IV:** 91–92; **Retro. Supp. I:** 297, 300, 311, 312

Ordinary Heroes (Turow), **Supp. XVII:** **221–222,** 223

Ordinary Love (Smiley), **Supp. VI:** 292, **299–300**

Ordinary Love; and Good Will: Two Novellas (Smiley), **Supp. VI:** 292, **299–300**

Ordinary Miracles (Jong), **Supp. V:** 115, 130–131

"Ordinary Time: Virginia Woolf and Thucydides on War" (Carson), **Supp. XII:** 111

"Ordinary Women, The" (Stevens), **IV:** 81

Ordways, The (Humphrey), **Supp. IX:** 95, **98–100,** 109; **Supp. XV:** 353

"Oread" (Doolittle), **II:** 520–521; **Supp. I Part 1:** 265–266

Oregon Message, An (Stafford), **Supp. XI:** **328–329**

Oregon Trail, The (Parkman), **II:** 312; **Supp. II Part 2:** 592, 595–596, 598, 606

Oresteia (Aeschylus), **Supp. IX:** 103

"Orestes at Tauris" (Jarrell), **II:** 376, 377

Orfalea, Gregory, **Supp. XIII:** 278

Orfeo ed Euridice (Gluck), **II:** 210, 211

Orff, Carl, **Supp. X:** 63

"Organizer's Wife, The" (Bambara), **Supp. XI:** 8–9

"Organmeister: Hasse After Marien-kirche" (Bierds), **Supp. XVII:** 34

"Orgy" (Rukeyser), **Supp. VI:** 280

Orgy, The (Rukeyser), **Supp. VI:** 274, 283

"Orgy of Southerness, An" (Pickering), **Supp. XXI:** 203

"Orientation of Hope, The" (Locke), **Supp. XIV:** 212–213

Orient Express (Dos Passos), **I:** 480

"Orient Express, The" (Jarrell), **II:** 382, 383–384

Origen, Adamantius, **IV:** 153

"Origin" (Harjo), **Supp. XII:** 219

Original Child Bomb: Points for Meditation to Be Scratched on the Walls of a Cave (Merton), **Supp. VIII:** 203

Original Essays on the Poetry of Anne Sexton (George), **Supp. IV Part 2:** 450

"Original Follies Girl, The" (Z. Fitzgerald), **Supp. IX:** 71

Original Light (Goldbarth), **Supp. XII:** 181, **183–184,** 188

Original Love (Peacock), **Supp. XIX:** **199–201,** 206

Original of Laura, The (Nabokov), **Retro. Supp. I:** 266

"Original Sin" (Jeffers), **Supp. II Part 2:** 426

"Original Sin" (Warren), **IV:** 245

"Origin of Extermination in the Imagination, The" (Gass), **Supp. VI:** 89

Origin of Species, The (Darwin), **II:** 173, 462; **Supp. XVI:** 13

Origin of the Brunists, The (Coover), **Supp. V:** 39, 41, 52

"Origins and History of Consciousness" (Rich), **Supp. I Part 2:** 570

"Origins of a Nonfiction Writer" (Talese), **Supp. XVII:** 208

"Origins of a Poem" (Levertov), **Supp. III Part 1:** 273

"Origins of the Beat Generation, The" (Kerouac), **Supp. III Part 1:** 231

Origo, Iris, **IV:** 328

"O'Riley's Late-Bloomed Little Son" (X. J. Kennedy), **Supp. XV:** 159

"Orion" (Rich), **Supp. I Part 2:** 557

O'Riordan, Conal Holmes O'Connell, **III:** 465

Orlacs Hände (film, Weine), **Supp. XVII:** 58

Orlando (V. Woolf), **Supp. XVII:** 86

Orlando (Woolf), **Supp. I Part 2:** 718; **Supp. VIII:** 263; **Supp. XII:** 9

Orlando Furioso (Ariosto), **Supp. XV:** 175

Orlovsky, Peter, **Supp. XII:** 121, 126; **Supp. XIV:** 150; **Supp. XVIII:** 27

Ormonde, Czenzi, **Supp. IV Part 1:** 132

Ormond; or, The Secret Witness (Brown), **Supp. I Part 1:** 133–137

Ornament and Crime (Loos), **Supp. XVI:** 187

Orne, Sarah. *See* Jewett, Sarah Orne

Ornithological Biography; or, An Account of the Habits of the Birds of the United States of America, and Interspersed with Delin eations of American Scenery and Manners (Audubon), **Supp. XVI:** 13

Ornithological Biography; or, An Account of the Habits of the Birds of the United States of America, and Interspersed with Delineations of American Scenery and Manners (Audubon), **7–10**

"Ornithology" (Hull), **Supp. XXI:** 138–139

Ornitz, Samuel, **Supp. IX:** 227; **Supp. XIII:** 166

Ornstein, Leo, **Supp. XX:**75

Orphan Angel, The (Wylie), **Supp. I Part 2:** 707, 709, 714, 717, 719–721, 722, 724

Orphan's Tale, An (Neugeboren), **Supp. XVI:** 222, 223

Orpheus (Rukeyser), **Supp. VI:** 273

"Orpheus" (Winters), **Supp. II Part 2:** 801

"Orpheus, Eurydice, Hermes" (Rilke), **Supp. VIII:** 31, 32

"Orpheus (1)" (Atwood), **Supp. XIII:** 35

"Orpheus (2)" (Atwood), **Supp. XIII:** 35

"Orpheus Alone" (Strand), **Supp. IV Part 2:** 632

Orpheus Descending (T. Williams), **IV:** 380, 381, 382, 385, 386, 387, 389, 391–392, 395, 396, 398

Orr, David, **Supp. XXI:** 62

Orr, Peter, **Supp. I Part 2:** 538, 540, 543

Orse, Brian, **Supp. XX:**264

Ortega y Gasset, José, **I:** 218, 222; **Supp. IV Part 2:** 521

Ortiz, Simon J., **Supp. IV Part 1:** 319, 404; **Supp. IV Part 2: 497–515,** 557; **Supp. XII:** 217, 218

"Ortlieb's Uptown Taproom" (Di Piero), **Supp. XIX:** 46, 47

O'Ruddy, The (Crane), **I:** 409, 424

Orwell, George, **I:** 489; **II:** 454, 580; **Supp. I Part 2:** 523, 620; **Supp. II Part 1:** 143; **Supp. IV Part 1:** 236; **Supp. V:** 250; **Supp. VIII:** 241; **Supp. XIV:** 112, 158; **Supp. XVII:** 228, 229; **Supp. XVIII:** 137, 138; **Supp. XX:**86

Osborn, Dwight, **III:** 218–219, 223

"Osborn Look, The" (Morris), **III:** 221

Osgood, Frances, **Supp. XVII:** 75

Osgood, J. R., **II:** 283

O'Shea, Kitty, **II:** 137

O'Shea, Milo, **Supp. XI:** 308

"Oshkikwe's Baby" (traditional Chippewa story), **Supp. IV Part 1:** 333

Oshogay, Delia, **Supp. IV Part 1:** 333

Ossana, Diana, **Supp. V:** 230–231, 232

Ossian, **Supp. I Part 2:** 491

Ossip, Kathleen, **Supp. X:** 201

"Osso Bucco" (Collins), **Supp. XXI:** 60

Ostanovka v Pustyne (A halt in the wilderness) (Brodsky), **Supp. VIII:** 21

Oster, Judith, **Supp. XVI:** 151

Ostriker, Alicia, **Supp. I Part 2:** 540; **Supp. IV Part 2:** 439, 447, 449; **Supp. X:** 207, 208; **Supp. XI:** 143; **Supp. XV:** 251

Ostrom, Hans, **Retro. Supp. I:** 195

Oswald, Lee Harvey, **III:** 234, 235

Oswald II (DeLillo), **Supp. VI:** 16

Oswald's Tale (Mailer), **Retro. Supp. II:** 212–213

O Taste and See (Levertov), **Supp. III Part 1:** 278–279, 281

Othello (Shakespeare), **I:** 284–285

"Other, The" (Sexton), **Supp. II Part 2:** 692

Other America, The (Harrington), **I:** 306

"Other American Renaissance, The" (Tompkins), **Supp. XVIII:** 258

Other Destinies: Understanding the American Indian Novel (Owens), **Supp. IV Part 1:** 404

"Other Frost, The" (Jarrell), **Retro. Supp. I:** 121

Other Gods: An American Legend (Buck), **Supp. II Part 1:** 123, 130–131

Other House, The (James), **Retro. Supp. I:** 229

"Other League of Nations, The" (Ríos), **Supp. IV Part 2:** 552

"Other Margaret, The" (Trilling), **Supp. III Part 2:** 504–505

"Other Miller, The" (Wolff), **Supp. VII:** 343–344

"Other Mothers" (Paley), **Supp. VI:** 225

"Other Night at Columbia, The" (Trilling), **Supp. XII:** 126

"Other Robert Frost, The" (Jarrell), **Retro. Supp. I:** 135

Others (Shields), **Supp. VII:** 310

Other Side, The (Gordon), **Supp. IV Part 1:** 299, 306, 307–309, 310–311

Other Side, The/El Otro Lado (Alvarez), **Supp. VII:** 9–12

Other Side of the River, The (Wright), **Supp. V:** 332–333, 342

"Other Side of the River, The" (Wright), **Supp. V:** 335

"Other Tradition, The" (Ashbery), **Supp. III Part 1:** 15, 18

"Other Two, The" (Wharton), **Retro. Supp. I:** 367

Other Voices, Other Rooms (Capote), **Supp. III Part 1:** 113–118, 121, 123–124

"Other Wanderer, The" (Gibran), **Supp. XX:**124

"Other War, The" (Cowley), **Supp. II Part 1:** 144

"Otherwise" (Kenyon), **Supp. VII:** 172, 174

Otherwise: New and Selected Poems (Kenyon), **Supp. VII:** 167, 172–174

Otherwise Than Being; or, Beyond Essence (Lévinas), **Supp. XVI:** 290, 291

"Other Woman, The" (Anderson), **I:** 114

"Other World, The" (Wrigley), **Supp. XVIII:** 307

Otho the Great: A Tragedy in Five Acts (Keats), **Supp. XII:** 113

Otis, Harrison Gray, **Supp. I Part 2:** 479–481, 483, 486, 488

Otis, James, **III:** 577; **Supp. I Part 2:** 486; **Supp. XV:** 229

O to Be a Dragon (Moore), **III:** 215

Otto, Rudolf, **Supp. XVII:** 243

"Ouija" (McClatchy), **Supp. XII:** 269–270

Oupensky, Peter, **Supp. XIV:** 188

Our America (Michaels), **Retro. Supp. I:** 379

Our America (W. Frank), **I:** 229; **Supp. IX:** 308; **Supp. XX:**69–70, 75

"Our Assistant's Column" (Twain), **IV:** 193

"Our Bourgeois Literature" (Sinclair), **Supp. V:** 281

Our Brains and What Ails Them (Gilman), **Supp. XI:** 207

Our Century (Wilder), **IV:** 374

"Our Christmas Party" (E. Stoddard), **Supp. XV:** 273, 278

Our Country (Strong), **Supp. XIV:** 64

"Our Countrymen in Chains!" (Whittier), **Supp. I Part 2:** 688

"Our Cultural Humility" (Bourne), **I:** 223, 228

Our Depleted Society (Seymour), **Supp. XIII:** 264

"Our Dust" (Wright), **Supp. XV:** 345, 346

"Our Father Who Drowns the Birds" (Kingsolver), **Supp. VII:** 208–209

"Our First House" (Kingston), **Supp. V:** 169

Our Gang (P. Roth), **Retro. Supp. II:** 287; **Supp. III Part 2:** 414; **Supp. IV Part 1:** 388

"Our Good Day" (Cisneros), **Supp. VII:** 60

Our Ground Time Here Will Be Brief (Kumin), **Supp. IV Part 2:** 450–452

Our House in the Last World (Hijuelos), **Supp. VIII:** 73, **76–79,** 87, 88

"Our Lady" (A. Finch), **Supp. XVII:** 77

"*Our Lady of the Annunciation*/Nuestra Señora de Anunciación" (Mora), **Supp. XIII:** 217, 224, 228

"Our Lady of Troy" (MacLeish), **III:** 3, 20

"Our Limitations" (Holmes), **Supp. I Part 1:** 314

"Our Martyred Soldiers" (Dunbar), **Supp. II Part 1:** 193

"Our Master" (Whittier), **Supp. I Part 2:** 704

"Our Mother Pocahontas" (Lindsay), **Supp. I Part 2:** 393

Our Mr. Wrenn: The Romantic Adventures of a Gentle Man (Lewis), **II:** 441

Our National Parks (Muir), **Supp. IX:** 181, 184

Our New York: A Personal Vision in Words and Photographs (Kazin), **Supp. VIII: 106–107**

Our Nig (Wilson), **Supp. XX:**105

"Our Old Aunt Who Is Now in a Retirement Home" (Shields), **Supp. VII:** 310

Our Old Home: A Series of English Sketches (Hawthorne), **II:** 225; **Retro. Supp. I:** 163

"Our Own Movie Queen" (Z. Fitzgerald), **Supp. IX:** 71

"Our River Now" (L.-Y. Lee), **Supp. XV:** 224, 225

Our Selves (Bronk), **Supp. XXI:** 32

Ourselves to Know (O'Hara), **III:** 362, 365

"Our Story Begins" (Wolff), **Supp. VII:** 345

"Our Sweating Selves" (Di Piero), **Supp. XIX:** 36

Our Town (Wilder), **IV:** 357, 364, 365, 366, 368–369

"Our Unplanned Cities" (Bourne), **I:** 229, 230

Our Wonder World, **Retro. Supp. I:** 341

Ouspensky, P. D., **I:** 383; **Supp. XX:**116

"Out" (Harjo), **Supp. XII:** 219

"'Out, Out' " (Frost), **Retro. Supp. I:** 131

"Outcast" (McKay), **Supp. X:** 135

"Outcasts of Poker Flats, The" (Harte), **Supp. II Part 1:** 345, 347–348

Outcroppings (Harte), **Supp. II Part 1:** 343

Out Cry (T. Williams), **IV:** 383, 393

Outcry, The (James), **Retro. Supp. I:** 235

"Outdoor Shower" (Olds), **Supp. X:** 214

Outerbridge Reach (Stone), **Supp. V:** 306–308

Outer Dark (McCarthy), **Supp. VIII: 176–177**

Outermost Dream, The: Essays and Reviews (Maxwell), **Supp. VIII: 171–172**

"Outing, The" (Baldwin), **Supp. I Part 1:** 63

"Out Like a Lamb" (Dubus), **Supp. VII:** 91

"Outline of an Autobiography" (Toomer), **Supp. III Part 2:** 478

Outlyer and Ghazals (Harrison), **Supp. VIII:** 41

"Out of Business" (Mora), **Supp. XIII:** 217

Out of Eden: Essays on Modern Art (Di Piero), **Supp. XIX:** 41, 42

"Out of My Deeper Heart" (Gibran), **Supp. XX:**118

Out of My League (Plimpton), **Supp. XVI:** 233, 239

"Out of Nowhere into Nothing" (Anderson), **I:** 113

"Out of Season" (Hemingway), **II:** 263

"Out of the Cradle Endlessly Rocking" (Whitman), **IV:** 342, 343–345, 346, 351; **Retro. Supp. I:** 404, 406

"Out of the Deeps" (E. Stoddard), **Supp. XV:** 286

"Out of the Hospital and Under the Bar" (Ellison), **Retro. Supp. II:** 118–119; **Supp. II Part 1:** 246

"Out of the Rainbow End" (Sandburg), **III:** 594–595

"Out of the Sea, Early" (Swenson), **Supp. IV Part 2:** 645

"Out of the Snow" (Dubus), **Supp. VII:** 91

Out of the Stars (Purdy), **Supp. VII:** 281–282

"Out of the Woods" (Offutt), **Supp. XIX:** 169–170

Out of the Woods: Stories (Offutt), **Supp. XIX:** 163, 167, **169–172,** 175

"Outrageous" (Pickering), **Supp. XXI:** 202

Outre-Mer: A Pilgrimage beyond the Sea (Longfellow), **II:** 313, 491; **Retro. Supp. II:** 155, 165

"Outside" (Stafford), **Supp. XI:** 318

Outside, The (Glaspell), **Supp. III Part 1:** 179, 187

"Outside In" (Pickering), **Supp. XXI:** 197

Outsider, The (Wright), **IV:** 478, 481, 488, 491–494, 495

Outside World, The (Mirvis), **Supp. XX:**177, 178, **185–190**

Out Went the Candle (Swados), **Supp. XIX: 257**

Out West (Shanley), **Supp. XIV:** 317

"Out with the Old" (Yates), **Supp. XI:** 342

"Ouzo for Robin" (Merrill), **Supp. III Part 1:** 326

"Oval Portrait, The" (Poe), **III:** 412, 415; **Retro. Supp. II:** 270

"Oven Bird, The" (Frost), **Retro. Supp. I:** 131; **Supp. XI:** 153; **Supp. XIX:** 15

"Over 2,000 Illustrations and a Complete Concordance" (Bishop), **Retro. Supp. II:** 45; **Supp. I Part 1:** 90–91

"Over by the River" (Maxwell), **Supp. VIII:** 169, 170

"Overgrown Pasture, The" (Lowell), **II:** 523

"Overheard through the Walls of the Invisible City" (Bidart), **Supp. XV:** 32

"Over Kansas" (Ginsberg), **Supp. II Part 1:** 320

Overland to the Islands (Levertov), **Supp. III Part 1:** 275, 276

Overlook, The (Connelly), **Supp. XXI: 78**

"Overlooking Lake Champlain" (Di Piero), **Supp. XIX:** 47

"Overnight Pass" (X. J. Kennedy), **Supp. XV:** 168

Overreachers, The (Talese), **Supp. XVII:** 202

"Over-Soul, The" (Emerson), **II:** 7

Over the Blue Mountain (Richter), **Supp. XVIII:** 220

"Over the Hill" (Dubus), **Supp. VII:** 76, 79–80

Overtime (Gurney), **Supp. V:** 104

"Overwhelming Question, An" (Taylor), **Supp. V:** 323

Ovid, **I:** 62; **II:** 542–543; **III:** 457, 467, 468, 470; **Retro. Supp. I:** 63; **Supp. IV Part 2:** 634; **Supp. XII:** 264

"Ovid in Exile" (Di Piero), **Supp. XIX:** 44

"Ovid's Farewell" (McClatchy), **Supp. XII:** 257–258
Owen, David, **II:** 34
Owen, Maureen, **Supp. IV Part 2:** 423
Owen, Wilfred, **II:** 367, 372; **III:** 524; **Supp. X:** 146; **Supp. XVII:** 245; **Supp. XVIII:** 92; **Supp. XIX:** 17
Owens, Hamilton, **III:** 99, 109
Owens, Louis, **Supp. IV Part 1:** 404
"O Where Are You Going?" (Auden), **Supp. X:** 116
"Owl, The" (Wrigley), **Supp. XVIII:** 297–298, 301
Owl in the Attic, The (Thurber), **Supp. I Part 2:** 614
Owl in the Mask of the Dreamer, The: Collected Poems (Haines), **Supp. XII:** 211
"Owl in the Sarcophagus, The" (Stevens), **Retro. Supp. I:** 300
Owl's Clover (Stevens), **Retro. Supp. I:** 298, **303–304**
"Owl's Clover" (Stevens), **IV:** 75
Owl's Insomnia, Poems by Rafael Alberti, The (Strand, trans.), **Supp. IV Part 2:** 630
Owlstone Crown, The (X. J. Kennedy), **Supp. XV:** 162, **164**
"Owl Who Was God, The" (Thurber), **Supp. I Part 2:** 610
Owning Jolene (Hearon), **Supp. VIII:** **66–67**
"Owning the Masters" (Nelson), **Supp. XVIII:** 171
Oxford Anthology of American Literature, The, **III:** 197; **Supp. I Part 1:** 254
Oxford Book of American Verse (Matthiessen, ed.), **Retro. Supp. I:** 40
Oxford Book of Children's Verse in America, The (Hall, ed.), **Supp. XIV:** 126
Oxford Companion to Twentieth-Century Poetry (Hamilton, ed.), **Supp. XVII:** 243
Oxford History of the American People, The (Morison), **Supp. I Part 2:** 495–496
Oxford History of the United States, 1783–1917, The (Morison), **Supp. I Part 2:** 483–484
"Oxford Town" (song, Dylan), **Supp. XVIII:** 24
Oxherding Tale (Johnson), **Supp. VI:** **190–192**, 193, 194, 196
Oxley, William, **Supp. XV:** 125
"O Yes" (Olsen), **Supp. XIII:** 294, 298, **299–300**, 301
"O Youth and Beauty!" (Cheever), **Retro. Supp. I:** 335
"Oysters" (Sexton), **Supp. II Part 2:** 692
"Ozark Odes" (Wright), **Supp. XV:** 346
Ozick, Cynthia, **Supp. V:** **257–274;** **Supp. VIII:** 141; **Supp. X:** 192; **Supp. XVII:** 42, 43, 49, 50
O-Zone (Theroux), **Supp. VIII:** 323–324

P
Pace, Patricia, **Supp. XI:** 245
Pacernik, Gary, **Supp. IX:** 287, 291

"Pacific Distances" (Didion), **Supp. IV Part 1:** 211
"Pacific Village" (M. F. K. Fisher), **Supp. XVII:** 83
Pack, Robert, **Supp. IV Part 2:** 621
"Packed Dirt, Churchgoing, a Dying Cat, a Traded Cat" (Updike), **IV:** 219
"Packing Mother's Things" (C. Frost), **Supp. XV:** 97
Pack of Lies (Sorrentino), **Supp. XXI:** 236, 237
Paddock, Joe, **Supp. XVI:** 36
Paddock, Nancy, **Supp. XVI:** 36
Padel, Ruth, **Supp. XII:** 107
Padgett, Ron, **Supp. XV:** 190
Padmore, Dorothy, **Supp. XXI:** 166
Padmore, George, **Supp. XXI:** 166
"Paesano with a Trowel" *(Time)*, **Supp. XX:**46
Pafko at the Wall (DeLillo), **Supp. VI:** 4
"Paganini and the Powers of Darkness" (Skloot), **Supp. XX:**201
"Pagan Prayer" (Cullen), **Supp. IV Part 1:** 170
"Pagan Rabbi, The" (Ozick), **Supp. V:** 262, 264, 265; **Supp. XVII:** 43
Pagan Rabbi and Other Stories, The (Ozick), **Supp. V:** 260, 261, 263–265
Pagan Spain (Wright), **IV:** 478, 488, 495
Page, Geraldine, **Supp. XV:** 7
Page, Kirby, **III:** 297
Page, Thomas Nelson, **II:** 174, 176, 194; **Supp. XIV:** 61
Page, Walter Hines, **II:** 174, 175; **Supp. I Part 1:** 370
Page, William, **Supp. XVIII:** 2, 11
"Pages from Cold Point" (Bowles), **Supp. IV Part 1:** 85, 86, 87
Paid on Both Sides: A Charade (Auden), **Supp. II Part 1:** 6, 18–19
Paige, Satchel, **Supp. I Part 1:** 234
Paige, T. D. D., **III:** 475
"Pail, The" (R. Bly), **Supp. XXI:** 85
Pain, Joseph, **Supp. I Part 2:** 502
Paine, Albert Bigelow, **I:** 249
Paine, Thomas, **I:** 490; **II:** 117, 302; **III:** 17, 148, 219; **Retro. Supp. I:** 390; **Supp. I Part 1:** 231; **Supp. I Part 2:** **501–525;** **Supp. XI:** 55
"Pain has an Element of Blank" (Dickinson), **Retro. Supp. I:** 44
"Painstaking Historian, The" (Skloot), **Supp. XX:**205–206
"Paint and Powder" (Z. Fitzgerald), **Supp. IX:** 71
Painted Bird, The (Kosinski), **Supp. VII:** 215–217, 219–221, 222, 227
Painted Desert (F. Barthelme), **Supp. XI:** 28–29, 32
Painted Dresses (Hearon), **Supp. VIII:** 63
"Painted Head" (Ransom), **III:** 491, 494; **Supp. II Part 1:** 103, 314
Painted Word, The (Wolfe), **Supp. III Part 2:** 580–581, 584; **Supp. XV:** 143
"Painter, The" (Ashbery), **Supp. III Part 1:** 5–6, 13
Painter Dreaming in the Scholar's House, The (Nemerov), **III:** 269
"Painters" (Rukeyser), **Supp. VI:** 281

"Painting a Mountain Stream" (Nemerov), **III:** 275
"Pair a Spurs" (Proulx), **Supp. VII:** 263–264
"Pair of Bright Blue Eyes, A" (Taylor), **Supp. V:** 321
"Pajamas" (Olds), **Supp. X:** 206
Pakula, Alan, **Supp. XIII:** 264
Palace at 4 A.M. (Giacometti), **Supp. VIII:** 169
Palahniuk, Chuck, **Supp. XXI:** 116
"Palantine, The" (Whittier), **Supp. I Part 2:** 694, 696
Palatella, John, **Retro. Supp. II:** 48
Pale Fire (Nabokov), **III:** 244, 246, 252, 263–265; **Retro. Supp. I:** 264, 265, 266, 270, 271, 272, 276, 278, 335; **Supp. V:** 251, 253
"Pale Horse, Pale Rider" (Porter), **III:** 436, 437, 441–442, 445, 446, 449
Pale Horse, Pale Rider: Three Short Novels (Porter), **III:** 433, 436–442; **Supp. VIII:** 157
"Pale Pink Roast, The" (Paley), **Supp. VI:** 217
"Pale Rider" (B. Kelly), **Supp. XVII:** 132–133
Paley, Grace, **Supp. VI:** **217–233;** **Supp. IX:** 212; **Supp. X:** 79, 164; **Supp. XII:** 309; **Supp. XXI:** 118
Paley, William, **II:** 9
Palgrave, Francis Turner, **Retro. Supp. I:** 124; **Supp. XIV:** 340
Palgrave's Golden Treasury (Palgrave), **IV:** 405
Palimpsest (Doolittle), **Supp. I Part 1:** 259, 268, 269, 270–271
Palimpsest (Vidal), **Supp. X:** 186
"Palingenesis" (Longfellow), **II:** 498
Pal Joey (O'Hara), **III:** 361, 367–368
"Pal Joey" stories (O'Hara), **III:** 361
Pallbearers Envying the One Who Rides (Dobyns), **Supp. XIII:** 89
"Palm, The" (Merwin), **Supp. III Part 1:** 355
Palmer, Charles, **II:** 111
Palmer, Elihu, **Supp. I Part 2:** 520
Palmer, George Herbert, **Supp. XIV:** 197
Palmer, Michael, **Supp. IV Part 2:** 421; **Supp. XVI:** 284; **Supp. XVII:** 240
Palmer, Samuel, **Supp. XV:** 81
Palmerston, Lord, **I:** 15
Palm-of-the-Hand-Stories (Kawabata), **Supp. XV:** 186
"Palm Wine" (McKnight), **Supp. XX:**155
"Palo Alto: The Marshes" (Hass), **Supp. VI:** 100
Palpable God, A: Thirty Stories Translated from the Bible with an Essay on the Origins and Life of Narrative (Price), **Supp. VI:** 262, 267
Palubinskas, Helen, **Supp. X:** 292
Pamela (Richardson), **Supp. V:** 127; **Supp. XX:**236
Pamela's First Musical (Wasserstein), **Supp. XV:** 333
Panache de bouquets (Komunyakaa; Cadieux, trans.), **Supp. XIII:** 127
Pan-African movement, **Supp. II Part 1:** 172, 175

Pandaemonium (Epstein), **Supp. XII:** 161, **172–173**

"Pandora" (Adams), **I:** 5

Pandora: New Tales of Vampires (Rice), **Supp. VII:** 295

Panek, LeRoy, **Supp. XIV:** 27

"Pangolin, The" (Moore), **III:** 210

Panic: A Play in Verse (MacLeish), **III:** 2, 20

Panic in Needle Park (film), **Supp. IV Part 1:** 198

Pankey, Eric, **Supp. XIX:** 44

Pantagruel (Rabelais), **II:** 112

"Pantaloon in Black" (Faulkner), **II:** 71

Panther and the Lash, The (Hughes), **Retro. Supp. I:** 204, 211; **Supp. I Part 1:** 342–344, 345–346

"Panthers, The" (Southern), **Supp. XI:** 295

"Panties and the Buddha" (Peacock), **Supp. XIX:** 199

"Pan *versus* Moses" (Ozick), **Supp. V:** 262

"Paolo Castelnuovo" (Everwine), **Supp. XV:** 83–84

"Papa and Mama Dance, The" (Sexton), **Supp. II Part 2:** 688

"Papa Who Wakes Up Tired in the Dark" (Cisneros), **Supp. VII:** 62

Pape, Greg, **Supp. V:** 180; **Supp. XIII:** 312; **Supp. XV:** 73

Paper Doll (Parker), **Supp. XIX:** 184

"Paper Dolls Cut Out of a Newspaper" (Simic), **Supp. VIII:** 282

"Paper House, The" (Mailer), **III:** 42–43

Paper Lion (film, March), **Supp. XVI:** 242

Paper Lion: Confessions of a Last-String Quarterback (Plimpton), **Supp. XVI:** **242–243**

Papernick, Jon, **Supp. XVII:** 50

Papers on Literature and Art (Fuller), **Supp. II Part 1:** 292, 299

Papini, Giovanni, **Supp. XVI:** 195

Papp, Joseph, **Supp. IV Part 1:** 234; **Supp. XXI:** 145

"Paprika Johnson" (Barnes), **Supp. III Part 1:** 33

"Par" (Bausch), **Supp. VII:** 54

"Parable in the Later Novels of Henry James" (Ozick), **Supp. V:** 257

"Parable of the Gift" (Glück), **Supp. V:** 89

"Parable of the Hostages" (Glück), **Supp. V:** 89

"Parable of the King" (Glück), **Supp. V:** 89

Parable of the Sower (O. Butler), **Supp. XIII:** **66–67,** 69

Parable of the Talents (O. Butler), **Supp. XIII:** 61,**Supp. XIII:** 66, **67–69**

"Parable of the Trellis" (Glück), **Supp. V:** 89

Parachutes & Kisses (Jong), **Supp. V:** 115, 123, 125–126, 129

"Paradelle for Susan" (Collins), **Supp. XXI:** 58

"Parade of Painters" (Swenson), **Supp. IV Part 2:** 645

"Paradigm, The" (Tate), **IV:** 128

Paradise (Barthelme), **Supp. IV Part 1:** 52

"Paradise" (Caputo), **Supp. XIX:** 26–27

"Paradise" (Doty), **Supp. XI:** 123

Paradise, Piece by Piece (Peacock), **Supp. XIX:** 193, 194–195, 195–196, **201–202**

Paradise Lost (Milton), **I:** 137; **II:** 168, 549; **IV:** 126; **Supp. XII:** 173, 297; **Supp. XV:** 181; **Supp. XX:**280

Paradise Lost (Odets), **Supp. II Part 2:** 530, 531, 538–539, 550

"Paradise of Bachelors and the Tartarus of Maids, The" (Melville), **III:** 91

Paradise of Bombs, The (Sanders), **Supp. XVI:** 265, 272–273

Paradise Poems (Stern), **Supp. IX:** **293– 294,** 295

Paradiso (Dante), **Supp. IX:** 50

"Paradoxes and Oxymorons" (Ashbery), **Supp. III Part 1:** 23–24

Paradox of Progressive Thought, The (Noble), **Supp. I Part 2:** 650

Paragon, The (Knowles), **Supp. XII:** 249

"Paragraphs" (Carruth), **Supp. XVI:** 52–53

"Parameters" (Dunn), **Supp. XI:** 154

"Para Mi Tataranieto El Astropionero" (Espaillat), **Supp. XXI:** 104

"Paraphrase" (Crane), **I:** 391–392, 393

"Pardon, The" (Wilbur), **Supp. III Part 2:** 544, 550

Paredes, Américo, **Supp. XIII:** 225; **Supp. XIX:** 97, 98, 100

Paredes, Raymund A., **Supp. XIII:** 320, 321

"Parentage" (Stafford), **Supp. XI:** 321, 322

Parentheses: An Autobiographical Journey (Neugeboren), **Supp. XVI:** 217, 218, 219, 221, 226

"Parents" (F. Barthelme), **Supp. XI:** 34

"Parents Taking Shape" (Karr), **Supp. XI:** 243

"Parents' Weekend: Camp Kenwood" (Kenyon), **Supp. VII:** 169

Pareto, Vilfredo, **II:** 577

Paretsky, Sara, **Supp. IV Part 2:** 462; **Supp. XIV:** 26

Parini, Jay, **Supp. X:** 17; **Supp. XIX:** 120, 129; **Supp. XX:**243; **Supp. XXI:** 192

"Paris" (Collins), **Supp. XXI:** 60

"Paris" (Stern), **Supp. IX:** 300

"Paris, 7 A.M." (Bishop), **Retro. Supp. II:** 41, 42; **Supp. I Part 1:** 85, 89

Paris, Bob, **Supp. XX:**264

Paris, Paris (Shaw), **Supp. XIX:** 240

Paris France (Stein), **IV:** 45

Park, Robert, **IV:** 475

"Park Bench" (Hughes), **Supp. I Part 1:** 331–332

Park City (Beattie), **Supp. V:** 24, 35–36

"Park City" (Beattie), **Supp. V:** 35

Parker, Charlie, **Supp. I Part 1:** 59; **Supp. X:** 240, 242, 246; **Supp. XIII:** 129

Parker, Dorothy, **Retro. Supp. II:** 327; **Supp. IV Part 1:** 353; **Supp. IX:** 62, 114, **189–206; Supp. X:** 164; **Supp. XI:** 28; **Supp. XVIII:** 242, 246, 252

Parker, Emily, **Supp. XVIII:** 102

Parker, Idella, **Supp. X:** 232, 234–235

Parker, Joan, **Supp. XIX:** 187

Parker, Muriel, **Supp. IX:** 232

Parker, Patricia, **Supp. XV:** 242

Parker, Robert B., **Supp. IV Part 1:** 135, 136; **Supp. XIX:** **177–192**

Parker, Theodore, **Supp. I Part 1:** 38; **Supp. I Part 2:** 518

Parker, Thomas, **Supp. I Part 1:** 102

"Parker's Back" (O'Connor), **III:** 348, 352, 358

"Parkersburg" (Halliday), **Supp. XIX:** 92

Parkes, Henry Bamford, **Supp. I Part 2:** 617

Park-Fuller, Linda, **Supp. XIII:** 297

Parkman, Francis, **II:** 278, 310, 312; **IV:** 179, 309; **Supp. I Part 2:** 420, 479, 481–482, 486, 487, 493, 498; **Supp. II Part 2:** **589–616**

Parkman Reader, The (Morison, ed.), **Supp. I Part 2:** 494

Parks, Gordon, Sr., **Supp. XI:** 17

Parks, Larry, **Supp. I Part 1:** 295

Parks, Rosa, **Supp. I Part 1:** 342

"Park Street Cemetery, The" (Lowell), **II:** 537, 538

Par le Détroit (cantata) (Bowles), **Supp. IV Part 1:** 82

Parliament of Fowls, The (Chaucer), **III:** 492

Parmenides (Plato), **II:** 10

Parnassus (Emerson), **II:** 8, 18

Parnell, Charles Stewart, **II:** 129, 137

Parole (film), **Supp. XIII:** 166

Parole Fixer (film), **Supp. XIII:** 170

Parrington, Vernon Louis, **I:** 254, 517, 561; **III:** 335, 606; **IV:** 173; **Supp. I Part 2:** 484, 640

Parrish, Dillwyn, **Supp. XVII:** 83–84, 90

Parrish, Robert, **Supp. XI:** 307

"Parrot, The" (Merrill), **Supp. III Part 1:** 320

"Parsley" (Dove), **Supp. IV Part 1:** 245, 246

Parson, Annie, **Supp. I Part 2:** 655

Parsons, Elsie Clews, **I:** 231, 235

Parsons, Ian, **Supp. IX:** 95

Parsons, Louella, **Supp. XII:** 173

Parsons, Talcott, **Supp. I Part 2:** 648

Parsons, Theophilus, **II:** 396, 504; **Retro. Supp. II:** 134; **Supp. I Part 1:** 155

"Parthian Shot, The" (Hammett), **Supp. IV Part 1:** 343

Partial Glossary, A (Bronk), **Supp. XXI:** 26

Partial Payments: Essays on Writers and Their Lives (Epstein), **Supp. XIV:** 111

Partial Portraits (James), **II:** 336

"Partial Relief" (Halliday), **Supp. XIX:** 91

Partial Truth (Nelson), **Supp. XVIII:** **175–176,** 178

"Particulars" (Pickering), **Supp. XXI:** 197

Parties (Van Vechten), **Supp. II Part 2:** 739, 747–749

"Parting" (Kunitz), **Supp. III Part 1:** 263

"Parting Gift" (Wylie), **Supp. I Part 2:** 714

"Parting Glass, The" (Freneau), **Supp. II Part 1:** 273

"Partings" (Hogan), **Supp. IV Part 1:** 413

Partington, Blanche, **I:** 199

Partisans (Matthiessen), **Supp. V:** 201

"Partner, The" (Roethke), **III:** 541–542

Partners, The (Auchincloss), **Supp. IV Part 1:** 31, 34

Partners in Crime: A Rafe Buenrostro Mystery (Hinojosa), **Supp. XIX: 107–108**

"Part of a Letter" (Wilbur), **Supp. III Part 2:** 551

Part of Speech, A (Brodsky), **Supp. VIII:** 22

"Part of the Bee's Body Embedded in the Flesh, The" (C. Frost), **Supp. XV:** 105, 107

"Part of the Story" (Dobyns), **Supp. XIII:** 79

Parton, Sara, **Retro. Supp. I:** 246

Partridge, Jeffrey F., **Supp. XV:** 219

Partridge, John, **II:** 110, 111

"Parts of a Journal" (Gordon), **Supp. IV Part 1:** 310

Parts of a World (Stevens), **Retro. Supp. I: 305–306,** 307, 309, 313

"Party, The" (Dunbar), **Supp. II Part 1:** 198, 205–206

"Party, The" (Taylor), **Supp. V:** 315

Party at Jack's, The (Wolfe), **IV:** 451–452, 469

"Party Down at the Square, A" (Ellison), **Retro. Supp. II:** 124

Party of Five (television series), **Supp. XIX:** 222

Pascal, Blaise, **II:** 8, 159; **III:** 292, 301, 304, 428; **Retro. Supp. I:** 326, 330

"Paskudnyak" (Pilcer), **Supp. XVII:** 50

"Pass, The" (Neugeboren), **Supp. XVI:** 225

"Passage" (Crane), **I:** 391

"Passage in the Life of Mr. John Oakhurst, A" (Harte), **Supp. II Part 1:** 353–354

"Passages" (Duncan), **Supp. XVI:** 287

"Passages from a Relinquished Work" (Hawthorne), **Retro. Supp. I:** 150

Passages toward the Dark (McGrath), **Supp. X:** 126, 127

"Passage to India" (Whitman), **IV:** 348

Passage to India, A (Forster), **II:** 600; **Supp. XVIII:** 143

Passaro, Vince, **Supp. X:** 167, 302, 309, 310

"Passenger Pigeons" (Jeffers), **Supp. II Part 2:** 437

Passin, Herbert, **Supp. XIII:** 337

Passing (Larsen), **Supp. XVIII:** 119, 123, **127–130**

"Passing Beauty" (C. Frost), **Supp. XV:** 97

"Passing of Grandison, The" (Chesnutt), **Supp. XIV:** 62, **66–69**

"Passing of Sister Barsett, The" (Jewett), **Retro. Supp. II:** 138–139, 143

"Passing Show, The" (Bierce), **I:** 208

"Passing Through" (Kunitz), **Supp. III Part 1:** 265

"Passion, The" (Barnes), **Supp. III Part 1:** 36

"Passion, The" (Merwin), **Supp. III Part 1:** 343

Passionate, Accurate Story, The: Making Your Heart's Truth into Literature (C. Bly), **Supp. XVI: 41–42**

Passionate Pilgrim, A (James), **II:** 324; **Retro. Supp. I:** 219

"Passionate Pilgrim, A" (James), **II:** 322, 323–324; **Retro. Supp. I:** 218

Passion Play (Kosinski), **Supp. VII:** 215, 225–226

Passions of Uxport, The (Kumin), **Supp. IV Part 2:** 444

"Passive Resistance" (McKay), **Supp. X:** 133

Passport to the War (Kunitz), **Supp. III Part 1:** 261–264

Passwords (Stafford), **Supp. XI: 329–330**

"Past, The" (Bryant), **Supp. I Part 1:** 157, 170

Past, The (Kinnell), **Supp. III Part 1:** 235, 253–254

"Past, The" (Kinnell), **Supp. III Part 1:** 254

Past and Present (Carlyle), **Supp. I Part 2:** 410

Pasternak, Boris, **II:** 544

"Pastiches et Pistaches" (Van Vechten), **Supp. II Part 2:** 732

"Past Is the Present, The" (Moore), **III:** 199–200

"Pastoral" (Carver), **Supp. III Part 1:** 137, 146

"Pastoral" (Dove), **Supp. IV Part 1:** 249

"Pastoral" (Trethewey), **Supp. XXI:** 257

"Pastoral Hat, A" (Stevens), **IV:** 91

Pastoralia (Saunders), **Supp. XIX: 227–229**

"Pastoralia" (Saunders), **Supp. XIX:** 227, 229

"Pastor Dowe at Tacaté" (Bowles), **Supp. IV Part 1:** 87

Pastorela (ballet) (Kirstein), **Supp. IV Part 1:** 83

Pastorius, Francis Daniel, **Supp. I Part 2:** 700

"Pasture Poems" (Kumin), **Supp. IV Part 2:** 446

Pastures of Heaven, The (Steinbeck), **IV:** 51

Patch, Jerry, **Supp. XVIII:** 38

Patchen, Kenneth, **Supp. III Part 2:** 625

Patchett, Ann, **Supp. XII: 307–324**

Patchwork Planet (Lethem), **Supp. XVIII:** 150

Pater, Walter, **I:** 51, 272, 476; **II:** 27, 338; **III:** 604; **IV:** 74; **Retro. Supp. I:** 56, 79; **Retro. Supp. II:** 326; **Supp. I Part 2:** 552; **Supp. IX:** 66

Paterna (Mather), **Supp. II Part 2:** 451

"Paterson" (Ginsberg), **Supp. II Part 1:** 314–315, 321, 329

Paterson (W. C. Williams), **I:** 62, 446; **IV:** 418–423; **Retro. Supp. I:** 209, 284, 413, 419, 421, **424–428,** 428, 429, 430; **Retro. Supp. II:** 321, 328; **Supp. II Part 2:** 557, 564, 625; **Supp. VIII:** 275, 305; **Supp. XIV:** 96; **Supp. XV:** 264, 349

Paterson, Book Five (W. C. Williams), **IV:** 422–423

Paterson, Book One (W. C. Williams), **IV:** 421–422

Paterson, Isabel, **Supp. IV Part 2:** 524

Paterson, Part Three (W. C. Williams), **IV:** 420–421

Pat Garrett and Billy the Kid (film, Peckinpah), **Supp. XVIII:** 27

"Path, The" (Bryant), **Supp. I Part 1:** 169

Pathfinder, The (Cooper), **I:** 349, 350, 355

Pat Hobby Stories, The (Fitzgerald), **Retro. Supp. I:** 114

"Pathos of Low Life, The" (Hapgood), **Supp. XVII:** 103

"Patience of a Saint, The" (Humphrey), **Supp. IX:** 106

Patient 002 (Skloot), **Supp. XX:** 194, 208

Patinkin, Mandy, **Supp. IV Part 1:** 236

Paton, Alan, **Supp. VIII:** 126

Patria Mia (Pound), **III:** 460–461; **Retro. Supp. I:** 284

"Patria Mia" (Pound), **Retro. Supp. I:** 284

"Patriarch, The" (Alvares), **Supp. V:** 11

"Patrick Kavanagh at First Light" (Skloot), **Supp. XX:** 204

Patrimony: A True Story (P. Roth), **Retro. Supp. II:** 279, 280, 291; **Supp. III Part 2:** 427

Patriot, The (Buck), **Supp. II Part 1:** 122–123

Patriot, The (Connell), **Supp. XIV:** 94–95

Patriotic Gore: Studies in the Literature of the American Civil War (Wilson), **III:** 588; **IV:** 430, 438, 443, 445–445, 446; **Supp. VIII:** 100

"Patriotic Thing, The" (Ryan as Quin), **Supp. XVIII:** 229

"Patriots, The/Los Patriotas" (Kingsolver), **Supp. VII:** 209

Patron Saint of Liars, The (Patchett), **Supp. XII:** 307, 310, **311–314,** 317

Pattee, Fred L., **II:** 456

Patten, Gilbert, **II:** 423

Patten, Simon, **Supp. I Part 2:** 640

Patternmaster (O. Butler), **Supp. XIII:** 61, 62, 63

Patternmaster Series (O. Butler), **Supp. XIII: 62–63**

Pattern Recognition (W. Gibson), **Supp. XVI:** 124, **130–131**

"Patterns" (Lowell), **II:** 524

Patterson, Floyd, **III:** 38

Patterson, William M., **Supp. I Part 1:** 265

Patton, General George, **III:** 575; **Supp. I Part 2:** 664

"Patty-Cake, Patty-Cake...A Memoir" (Apple), **Supp. XVII:** 7

Paul, Saint, **I:** 365; **II:** 15, 494; **IV:** 122, 154, 164, 335; **Retro. Supp. I:** 247; **Supp. I Part 1:** 188

Paul, Sherman, **I:** 244; **IV:** 179

"Paula Becker to Clara Westhoff" (Rich), **Supp. I Part 2:** 573–574

"Paula Gunn Allen" (Ruppert), **Supp. IV Part 1:** 321

Paul Bowles: Romantic Savage (Caponi), **Supp. IV Part 1:** 95

Paulding, James Kirke, **I:** 344; **II:** 298, 299, 303; **Supp. I Part 1:** 157

Pauley, Jane, **Supp. XXI:** 39

Paul Jones (Hapgood), **Supp. XVII:** 100–101

Paul Marchand, F.M.C. (Chesnutt), **Supp. XIV:** 76

"Paul Monette: The Brink of Summer's End" (film), **Supp. X:** 152

"Paul Revere" (Longfellow), **II:** 489, 501

"Paul Revere's Ride" (Longfellow), **Retro. Supp. II:** 163

"Paul's Case" (Cather), **I:** 314–315; **Retro. Supp. I:** 3, 5

Paulsen, Friedrich, **III:** 600

"Pauper Witch of Grafton, The" (Frost), **Retro. Supp. II:** 42

"Pause by the Water, A" (Merwin), **Supp. III Part 1:** 354

"Pavane for the Nursery, A" (W. J. Smith), **Supp. XIII:** 335

"Pavement, The" (Olson), **Supp. II Part 2:** 571

Pavese, Cesare, **Supp. XXI:** 132

Pavilion of Women (Buck), **Supp. II Part 1:** 125–126

"Pawnbroker, The" (Kumin), **Supp. IV Part 2:** 442, 443–444, 451

Pawnbroker, The (Wallant), **Supp. XVI:** 220

"Paying Dues" (Bass), **Supp. XVI:** 16

Payne, Daniel, **Supp. V:** 202

Payne, John Howard, **II:** 309

Paz, Octavio, **Supp. III Part 2:** 630; **Supp. VIII:** 272; **Supp. XI:** 191; **Supp. XIII:** 223

P. D. Kimerakov (Epstein), **Supp. XII:** 160, **162**

Peabody, Elizabeth, **Retro. Supp. I:** 155–156, 225

Peabody, Francis G., **III:** 293; **Supp. I Part 1:** 5

Peabody, Josephine Preston, **III:** 507; **Supp. XX:**115

Peaceable Kingdom, The (Prose), **Supp. XVI:** 256–257

Peace and Bread in Time of War (Addams), **Supp. I Part 1:** 21, 22–23

"Peace Between Black and White in the United States" (Locke), **Supp. XIV:** 205

Peace Breaks Out (Knowles), **Supp. XII:** 249

"Peace March, The" (Simpson), **Supp. IX:** 279

"Peace of Cities, The" (Wilbur), **Supp. III Part 2:** 545

"Peace of Mind" (Boyle), **Supp. XX:**19

"Peaches—Six in a Tin Box, Sarajevo" (Cisneros), **Supp. VII:** 67

Peacock, Doug, **Supp. VIII:** 38; **Supp. XIII:** 12

Peacock, Gibson, **Supp. I Part 1:** 360

Peacock, Molly, **Supp. XVII:** 74; **Supp. XIX: 193–207**

"Peacock, The" (Merrill), **Supp. III Part 1:** 320

Peacock, Thomas Love, **Supp. I Part 1:** 307; **Supp. VIII:** 125

"Peacock Room, The" (Hayden), **Supp. II Part 1:** 374–375

"Peacocks of Avignon, The" (Swados), **Supp. XIX:** 263

Pearce, Richard, **Supp. IX:** 254

Pearce, Roy Harvey, **II:** 244; **Supp. I Part 1:** 111, 114; **Supp. I Part 2:** 475

"Pearl" (Kooser), **Supp. XIX:** 127–128

Pearl, The (Steinbeck), **IV:** 51, 62–63

Pearlman, Daniel, **III:** 479

Pearlman, Mickey, **Supp. XIII:** 293, 306

Pearl of Orr's Island, The (Stowe), **Supp. I Part 2:** 592–593, 595

"Pearls" (A. Finch), **Supp. XVII:** 72

Pears, Peter, **II:** 586; **Supp. IV Part 1:** 84

Pearson, Drew, **Supp. XIV:** 126

Pearson, Norman Holmes, **Supp. I Part 1:** 259, 260, 273

"Pear Tree" (C. Frost), **Supp. XV:** 105

"Peasants' Way O' Thinkin' " (McKay), **Supp. X:** 133

Pease, Donald E., **Supp. IV Part 2:** 687

Peck, Gregory, **Supp. VIII:** 128, 129; **Supp. XVI:** 160, 173

Peckinpah, Sam, **Supp. XI:** 306; **Supp. XVIII:** 27

"Peck of Gold, A" (Frost), **II:** 155

Peculiar Treasures: A Biblical Who's Who (Buechner), **Supp. XII:** 53

"Pedal Point" (Francis), **Supp. IX:** 87

Pedersen, Inge, **Supp. XVIII:** 179

"Pedersen Kid, The" (Gass), **Supp. VI:** 83

"Pedigree, The" (Creeley), **Supp. IV Part 1:** 150

Peebles, Melvin Van, **Supp. XI:** 17; **Supp. XVI:** 144

"Peed Onk" (Moore). *See* "People Like That Are the Only People Here: Canonical Babbling in Peed Onk" (Moore)

"Peeler, The" (O'Connor), **Retro. Supp. II:** 225

Peich, Michael, **Supp. XV:** 113, 117

Peikoff, Leonard, **Supp. IV Part 2:** 520, 526, 529

Peirce, Charles Sanders, **II:** 20, 352–353; **III:** 599; **Supp. I Part 2:** 640; **Supp. III Part 2:** 626

Pelagius, **III:** 295

"Pelican, The" (Merrill), **Supp. III Part 1:** 320

"Pelican, The" (Wharton), **IV:** 310; **Retro. Supp. I:** 364

Pellacchia, Michael, **Supp. XIII:** 16

Pelley, Denise, **Supp. XIX:** 205

Peltier, Leonard, **Supp. V:** 212

"Pen and Paper and a Breath of Air" (Oliver), **Supp. VII:** 245

Pence, Amy, **Supp. XV:** 211, 223

"Pencil, The" (Chandler), **Supp. IV Part 1:** 135

Pencillings by the Way (Willis), **II:** 313; **Supp. XVIII:** 12

"Pencils" (Sandburg), **III:** 592

Pendleton, Devon, **Supp. XVIII:** 151

"Pendulum" (Bradbury and Hasse), **Supp. IV Part 1:** 102

"Penelope's Song" (Glück), **Supp. V:** 89

Penhally (Gordon), **II:** 197, 199, 201–203, 204

"Penis" (McClatchy), **Supp. XII:** 266–267

Penitent, The (di Donato), **Supp. XX:**44, **45**

Penitent, The (Singer), **Retro. Supp. II:** **309–310,** 313

Penn, Robert, **I:** 489

Penn, Sean, **Supp. XI:** 107

Penn, Thomas, **II:** 118

Penn, William, **Supp. I Part 2:** 683

Penna, Sandro, **Supp. XIX:** 34

Pennebaker, D. A., **Supp. XVIII:** 19, 26

"Pennsylvania Pilgrim, The" (Whittier), **Supp. I Part 2:** 700

"Pennsylvania Planter, The" (Freneau), **Supp. II Part 1:** 268

Penny, Rob, **Supp. VIII:** 330

"Penny, The" (D. West), **Supp. XVIII:** 283–284

Penrod (Tarkington), **III:** 223

"Penseroso, Il" (Milton), **Supp. XIV:** 8

Pensieri (Leopardi; Di Piero, trans.), **Supp. XIX:** 34

Pentagon of Power, The (Mumford), **Supp. II Part 2:** 498

Pentimento (Hellman), **Supp. I Part 1:** 280, 292–294, 296; **Supp. IV Part 1:** 12; **Supp. VIII:** 243

"Peonies at Dusk" (Kenyon), **Supp. VII:** 171

People, The (Glaspell), **Supp. III Part 1:** 179

People, Yes, The (Sandburg), **III:** 575, 589, 590, 591

"PEOPLE BURNING, THE" (Baraka), **Supp. II Part 1:** 49

"People in Hell Just Want a Drink of Water" (Proulx), **Supp. VII:** 263

"People Like That Are the Only People Here: Canonical Babbling in Peed Onk" (Moore), **Supp. X:** 168, **178–179**

People Live Here: Selected Poems 1949–1983 (Simpson), **Supp. IX:** 269, 277

"People Next Door, The" (Simpson), **Supp. IX:** 279

People of the Abyss, The (London), **II:** 465–466

"People on the Roller Coaster, The" (Hardwick), **Supp. III Part 1:** 196

People Shall Continue, The (Ortiz), **Supp. IV Part 2:** 510

"People's Surroundings" (Moore), **III:** 201, 202, 203

"People v. Abe Lathan, Colored, The" (Caldwell), **I:** 309

"Peppermint Lounge Revisited, The" (Wolfe), **Supp. III Part 2:** 571

Pepys, Samuel, **Supp. I Part 2:** 653

"Perchance to Dream" (Franzen), **Supp. XX:** 90, 93

Perchance to Dream: Robert B. Parker's Sequel to Raymond Chandler's "Big Sleep" (Parker), *Supp. XIX:* 189

"Perch'io non spero di tornar giammai" (Cavalcanti), **Supp. III Part 2:** 623

Percy, Thomas, **Supp. XIV:** 2

Percy, Walker, **Supp. III Part 1: 383–400; Supp. IV Part 1:** 297; **Supp. V:** 334; **Supp. X:** 42; **Supp. XIV:** 21; **Supp. XIX:** 209

Percy, William, **Supp. V:** 334

Percy, William Alexander, **Retro. Supp. I:** 341

Peregrin, Tony, **Supp. XV:** 69

"Peregrine" (Wylie), **Supp. I Part 2:** 712–713, 714

Perelman, Bob, **Supp. XII:** 23

Perelman, S. J., **IV:** 286; **Retro. Supp. I:** 342; **Retro. Supp. II:** 321, 322, 325, 326, 327, 336; **Supp. IV Part 1:** 353; **Supp. XI:** 66

Perestroika (Kushner), **Supp. IX:** 141, 142, 145

Péret, Benjamin, **Supp. VIII:** 272

Peretz, Isaac Loeb, **IV:** 1, 3; **Retro. Supp. II:** 299

Pérez Galdós, Benito, **II:** 275

Perfect Analysis Given by a Parrot, A (T. Williams), **IV:** 395

"Perfect Couple, The" (Nelson), **Supp. XVIII:** 173

"Perfect Day for Bananafish, A" (Salinger), **III:** 563–564, 571

Perfect Fiction, The (Sorrentino), **Supp. XXI:** 228

Perfect Ganesh, A (McNally), **Supp. XIII: 202–203,** 208, 209

"Perfect Gerbil, The: Reading Barthelme's 'The School' " (Saunders), **Supp. XIX:** 235

"Perfect Knight, The" (Chandler), **Supp. IV Part 1:** 120

Perfect Party, The (Gurney), **Supp. V:** 100, 105, 106–107

"Perfect Things" (F. Barthelme), **Supp. XI:** 30, 33–34

"Performance, The" (Dickey), **Supp. IV Part 1:** 178–179, 181

"Perfume" (Mora), **Supp. XIII:** 218

"Perhaps the World Ends Here" (Harjo), **Supp. XII:** 228, 231

Perhaps Women (Anderson), **I:** 114

Pericles (Shakespeare), **I:** 585; **Supp. III Part 2:** 624, 627, 629

"Period Metaphor" (Bronk), **Supp. XXI:** 33

Period of Adjustment (T. Williams), **IV:** 382, 386, 387, 388, 389, 390, 392, 393, 394, 397

"Period Pieces from the Mid-Thirties" (Agee), **I:** 28

"Periphery" (Ammons), **Supp. VII:** 28

Perkins, David, **Supp. I Part 2:** 459, 475; **Supp. XV:** 185

Perkins, Maxwell, **I:** 252, 289, 290; **II:** 87, 93, 95, 252; **IV:** 452, 455, 457, 458, 461, 462, 463, 469; **Retro. Supp. I:** 101, 105, 108, 109, 110, 113, 114,

178; **Supp. IX:** 57, 58, 60, 232; **Supp. X:** 219, 224, 225, 229, 230, 233; **Supp. XI:** 218, 227

Perlès, Alfred, **III:** 177, 183, 187, 189

Perloff, Marjorie, **Supp. I Part 2:** 539, 542; **Supp. IV Part 1:** 68; **Supp. IV Part 2:** 420, 424, 432

Permanence and Change (Burke), **I:** 274

Permanent Errors (Price), **Supp. VI:** 261

"Permanent Traits of the English National Genius" (Emerson), **II:** 18

Permit Me Voyage (Agee), **I:** 25, 27

"Perosa Canavese" (Everwine), **Supp. XV:** 84

Perrault, Charles, **IV:** 266; **Supp. I Part 2:** 622

Perrin, Noel, **Supp. XVI:** 34

Perrins, Carol. *See* Frost, Carol

Perry, Anne, **Supp. V:** 335

Perry, Bliss, **I:** 243

Perry, Donna, **Supp. IV Part 1:** 322, 327, 335

Perry, Edgar A., **III:** 410

Perry, Keith Ronald, **Supp. XXI:** 42

Perry, Lincoln, **Supp. V:** 24, 33

Perry, Matthew C., **Supp. I Part 2:** 494–495

Perry, Patsy Brewington, **Supp. I Part 1:** 66

Perry, Phyllis Alesia, **Supp. XVIII:** 96

Perry, Ralph Barton, **I:** 224; **II:** 356, 362, 364; **Supp. XIV:** 197

Perry, Dr. William, **II:** 395, 396

Perse, St.-John, **III:** 12, 13, 14, 17; **Supp. III Part 1:** 14; **Supp. IV Part 1:** 82; **Supp. XIII:** 344; **Supp. XV:** 178

"Persephone in Hell" (Dove), **Supp. IV Part 1:** 250, 251

"Persimmons" (L.-Y. Lee), **Supp. XV:** 211, 213

"Persistence of Desire, The" (Updike), **IV:** 222–223, 228

"Persistence of Poetry, The" (Bynner), **Supp. XV:** 49

"Persistences" (Hecht), **Supp. X: 68–69**

Person, Place, and Thing (Shapiro), **Supp. II Part 2:** 702, 705

Personae of Ezra Pound (Pound), **III:** 458

Personae: The Collected Poems (Pound), **Retro. Supp. I:** 285, 286; **Supp. I Part 1:** 255; **Supp. XVII:** 32

"Personal" (Stern), **Supp. IX:** 299

"Personal and Occasional Pieces" (Welty), **Retro. Supp. I:** 355

"Personal and the Individual, The" (L. Michaels), **Supp. XVI:** 201

Personal Injuries (Turow), **Supp. XVII: 219–220,** 221, 223

"Personalities" (column, Briggs), **Supp. XVIII:** 15

Personal Narrative (Edwards), **I:** 545, 552, 553, 561, 562; **Supp. I Part 2:** 700

Personal Recollection of Joan of Arc (Twain), **IV:** 208

"Personals" (Didion), **Supp. IV Part 1:** 200

"Personism" (O'Hara), **Supp. XV:** 181

Persons and Places (Santayana), **III:** 615

Persons in Hiding (film), **Supp. XIII:** 170

Persons in Hiding (Hoover), **Supp. XIII:** 170

Person Sitting in Darkness, A (Twain), **IV:** 208

"Perspective" (Francis), **Supp. IX:** 78

"Perspective: Anniversary D-Day" (Karr), **Supp. XI:** 241

Perspectives by Incongruity (Burke), **I:** 284–285

"Perspectives: Is It Out of Control?" (Gleason), **Supp. IX:** 16

Perspectives on Cormac McCarthy (Arnold and Luce, eds.), **Supp. VIII:** 189

Persse, Dudley Jocelyn, **Supp. XX:** 232

Pertes et Fracas (McCoy), **Supp. XIII:** 175

"Peruvian Child" (Mora), **Supp. XIII:** 218

Peseroff, Joyce, **Supp. IV Part 1:** 71

"Pestilence" (Nelson), **Supp. XVIII:** 186

"Peter" (Cather), **Retro. Supp. I:** 4

"Peter" (Moore), **III:** 210, 212

Peter, Saint, **III:** 341, 346; **IV:** 86, 294

Peterkin, Julia, **Supp. I Part 1:** 328

"Peter Klaus" (German tale), **II:** 306

Peter Pan (Barrie), **Supp. XV:** 319

"Peter Parley" works (Goodrich), **Supp. I Part 1:** 38

"Peter Pendulum" (Poe), **III:** 425

"Peter Quince at the Clavier" (Stevens), **IV:** 81, 82

Peter Rabbit tales, **Retro. Supp. I:** 335

Peters, Cora, **Supp. I Part 2:** 468

Peters, Jacqueline, **Supp. XII:** 225

Peters, Margot, **Supp. VIII:** 252

Peters, Robert, **Supp. XIII:** 114

Peters, S. H. (pseudonym). *See* Henry, O.

Peters, Timothy, **Supp. XI:** 39

"Peter's Avocado" (Rodriguez), **Supp. XIV:** 308–309

Petersen, David, **Supp. XIII:** 2

Petersen, Donald, **Supp. V:** 180; **Supp. XV:** 74, 92

Peterson, Dorothy, **Supp. XVIII:** 131, 132

Peterson, Houston, **I:** 60

Peterson, Roger Tory, **Supp. V:** 202

Peterson, Virgilia, **Supp. IV Part 1:** 30

Peter Whiffle: His Life and Works (Van Vechten), **Supp. II Part 2:** 728–729, 731, 735, 738–741, 749

"Petey and Yotsee and Mario" (H. Roth), **Supp. IX:** 234

"Petition, A" (Winters), **Supp. II Part 2:** 785

"'Pet Negro' System, The" (Hurston), **Supp. VI:** 159

"Petra and Its Surroundings" (Frost), **Retro. Supp. I:** 124

Petrarch, **I:** 176; **II:** 590; **III:** 4

"Petrarch, Shakespeare, and the Blues" (C. Frost), **Supp. XV:** 92, 104, 105

"Petrified Man" (Welty), **IV:** 262; **Retro. Supp. I:** 345, 351

"Petrified Man, The" (Twain), **IV:** 195

"Petrified Woman, The" (Gordon), **II:** 199

Petronius, **III:** 174, 179

Petry, Ann, **Supp. VIII:** 214; **Supp. XI:** 6, 85; **Supp. XVIII:** 286

Pet Sematary (King), **Supp. V:** 138, 143, 152

Pettengill, Richard, **Supp. VIII:** 341, 345, 348

Pettingell, Phoebe, **Supp. XV:** 251, 256–257, 262

Pettis, Joyce, **Supp. XI:** 276, 277, 278, 281

Petty, Jill, **Supp. XXI:** 244, 248, 249, 250

Pfaelzer, Jean, **Supp. XVI:** 88, 90

Pfaff, Timothy, **Supp. V:** 166

Pfeil, Fred, **Supp. XIV:** 36

Pfister, Karin, **IV:** 467, 475

Phaedo (Plato), **II:** 10

Phaedra (Lowell and Barzun, trans.), **II:** 543–544

"Phantasia for Elvira Shatayev" (Rich), **Supp. I Part 2:** 570

Phantasms of War (Lowell), **II:** 512

"Phantom of the Movie Palace, The" (Coover), **Supp. V:** 50–51

Phantom Ship, The (Marryat), **Supp. XVII:** 55

"Pharaoh, The" (Kenyon), **Supp. VII:** 172

Pharr, Mary, **Supp. V:** 147

"Phases" (E. Stoddard), **Supp. XV:** 273

"Phases" (Stevens), **Retro. Supp. I:** 299

Phases of an Inferior Planet (Glasgow), **II:** 174–175

"Pheasant, The" (Carver), **Supp. III Part 1:** 146

Pheloung, Grant, **Supp. XI:** 39

Phelps, Elizabeth Stuart, **Retro. Supp. II:** 146; **Supp. XIII:** 141; **Supp. XVI:** 80

Phelps, Teresa Godwin, **Supp. VIII:** 128

Phelps, William Lyon "Billy", **Supp. XX:** 68, 75, 220

"Phenomena and Laws of Race Contacts, The" (Locke), **Supp. XIV:** 210

"Phenomenology of Anger, The" (Rich), **Supp. I Part 2:** 562–563, 571

Phenomenology of Moral Experience, The (Mandelbaum), **I:** 61

"Phenomenology of *On Moral Fiction*" (Johnson), **Supp. VI:** 188

Phidias, **Supp. I Part 2:** 482

Philadelphia Fire (Wideman), **Supp. X:** 320, 334

Philadelphia Negro, The (Du Bois), **Supp. II Part 1:** 158, 163–164, 166

Philbrick, Thomas, **I:** 343

"Phil in the Marketplace" (Lethem), **Supp. XVIII:** 148

Philip, Jim, **Supp. XII:** 136

Philip, Maxwell, **Supp. XXI:** 160

Philip, Prince, **Supp. X:** 108

"Philip of Pokanoket" (Irving), **II:** 303

Philippians (biblical book), **IV:** 154

"Philippine Conquest, The" (Masters), **Supp. I Part 2:** 456

"Philip Roth Reconsidered" (Howe), **Retro. Supp. II:** 286

"Philistinism and the Negro Writer" (Baraka), **Supp. II Part 1:** 39, 44

Phillips, Adam, **Supp. XII:** 97–98

Phillips, Anne K., **Supp. XX:** 221

Phillips, Carl, **Supp. XXI:** 246

Phillips, David Graham, **II:** 444; **Retro. Supp. II:** 101

Phillips, Gene D., **Supp. XI:** 306

Phillips, Jayne Anne, **Supp. XIV:** 21

Phillips, J. O. C., **Supp. I Part 1:** 19

Phillips, Robert, **Supp. XIII:** 335, 344

Phillips, Wendell, **Supp. I Part 1:** 103; **Supp. I Part 2:** 524

Phillips, Willard, **Supp. I Part 1:** 154, 155

Phillips, William, **Supp. VIII:** 156

Phillips, William L., **I:** 106

"Philly Babylon" (Di Piero), **Supp. XIX:** 46

"Philosopher, The" (Farrell), **II:** 45

Philosopher of the Forest (pseudonym). *See* Freneau, Philip

Philosophes classiques, Les (Taine), **III:** 323

"Philosophical Cobbler, The" (Sanders), **Supp. XVI:** 268

"Philosophical Concepts and Practical Results" (James), **II:** 352

"Philosophical Investigation of Metaphor, A" (Gass), **Supp. VI:** 79

Philosophical Transactions (Watson), **II:** 114

"Philosophy, Or Something Like That" (P. Roth), **Supp. III Part 2:** 403

"Philosophy and Its Critics" (James), **II:** 360

"Philosophy and the Form of Fiction" (Gass), **Supp. VI:** 85

"Philosophy for People" (Emerson), **II:** 14

"Philosophy in Warm Weather" (Kenyon), **Supp. VII:** 168

"Philosophy Lesson" (Levine), **Supp. V:** 195

Philosophy of Alain Locke, The: Harlem Renaissance and Beyond (Harris, ed.), **Supp. XIV:** 196, 211–212

"Philosophy of Composition, The" (Poe), **III:** 416, 421; **Retro. Supp. II:** 266, 267, 271

Philosophy of Friedrich Nietzsche, The (Mencken), **III:** 102–103

"Philosophy of Handicap, A" (Bourne), **I:** 216, 218

"Philosophy of History" (Emerson), **II:** 11–12

Philosophy of Literary Form, The (Burke), **I:** 275, 281, 283, 291

Philosophy of the Human Mind, The (Stewart), **II:** 8

Philosophy: Who Needs It (Rand), **Supp. IV Part 2:** 517, 518, 527, 533

Philoxenes, **Supp. VIII:** 201

"Phineas" (Knowles), **Supp. XII:** 238–240

Phineas: Six Stories (Knowles), **Supp. XII:** 249

"Phocion" (Lowell), **II:** 536

Phoenix and the Turtle, The (Shakespeare), **I:** 284

"Phoenix Lyrics" (Schwartz), **Supp. II Part 2:** 665

"Phone Booths, The" (Jarman), **Supp. XVII:** 112–113

"Phony War Films" (Jones), **Supp. XI:** 217, 232

"Photograph: Migrant Worker, Parlier, California, 1967" (Levis), **Supp. XI:** 272

"Photograph of a Bawd Drinking Raleigh Rye" (Trethewey), **Supp. XXI:** 254

"Photograph of a Child on a Vermont Hillside" (Kenyon), **Supp. VII:** 168

"Photograph of My Mother as a Young Girl" (Gioia), **Supp. XV:** 119

"Photograph of the Girl" (Olds), **Supp. X:** 205

"Photograph of the Unmade Bed" (Rich), **Supp. I Part 2:** 558

Photographs (Welty), **Retro. Supp. I:** 343

"Photographs, The" (Barthelme), **Supp. IV Part 1:** 53

"Photography" (Levine), **Supp. V:** 194

Phyrrho, **Retro. Supp. I:** 247

"Physical Universe" (Simpson), **Supp. IX:** 278

"Physicist We Know, A" (Shields), **Supp. VII:** 310

"Physics and Cosmology in the Fiction of Tom Robbins" (Nadeau), **Supp. X:** 270

Physiologie du goût (Brillat-Savarin), **Supp. XVII:** 82, 86

Physiology of Taste, The; or, Meditations on Transcendent Gastronomy (Brillat-Savarin; M. F. K. Fisher, trans.), **Supp. XVII:** 86, 87, 91

"Physiology of Versification, The: Harmonies of Organic and Animal Life" (Holmes), **Supp. I Part 1:** 311

Physique de l'Amour (Gourmont), **III:** 467–468

Piaf, Edith, **Supp. IV Part 2:** 549

Piaget, Jean, **Supp. XIII:** 75

"Piano" (Lawrence), **Supp. XV:** 254

"Piano Fingers" (Mason), **Supp. VIII:** 146

Piano Lesson, The (Bearden), **Supp. VIII:** 342

Piano Lesson, The (Wilson), **Supp. VIII:** 342–345

Piano Man's Daughter, The (Findley), **Supp. XX:** 59–61

Piatt, James, **Supp. I Part 2:** 420

Piatt, John J., **II:** 273

Piazza, Ben, **Supp. XIII:** 163

Piazza, Paul, **Supp. XIV:** 157, 160, 171

"Piazza de Spagna, Early Morning" (Wilbur), **Supp. III Part 2:** 553

Piazza Tales (Melville), **III:** 91

Picabia, Francis, **Retro. Supp. I:** 416; **Retro. Supp. II:** 331

Picasso (Stein), **IV:** 28, 32, 45

Picasso, Pablo, **I:** 429, 432, 440, 442, 445; **II:** 602; **III:** 197, 201, 470; **IV:** 26, 31, 32, 46, 87, 407, 436; **Retro. Supp. I:** 55, 63; **Supp. IV Part 1:** 81; **Supp. IX:** 66

Piccione, Anthony, **Supp. XV:** 212

"Piccola Comedia" (Wilbur), **Supp. III Part 2:** 561

Pickard, Samuel T., **Supp. I Part 2:** 682
Picked-Up Pieces (Updike), **Retro. Supp. I:** 320, 322, 323, 335
Picker, Lauren, **Supp. VIII:** 78, 83
Picker, Tobias, **Supp. XII:** 253
Pickering, Sam, **Supp. XXI: 191–207**
Pickford, Mary, **Retro. Supp. I:** 325; **Supp. I Part 2:** 391
"Picking and Choosing" (Moore), **III:** 205
"Picnic" (Peacock), **Supp. XIX:** 206
Picnic, Lightning (Collins), **Supp. XXI:** 54, 60
"Picnic, Lightning" (Collins), **Supp. XXI:** 64–65
Picnic Cantata (music) (Bowles), **Supp. IV Part 1:** 89
"Picnic Remembered" (Warren), **IV:** 240
Pictorial History of the Negro in America, A (Hughes), **Supp. I Part 1:** 345
"Picture, The" (Olson), **Supp. II Part 2:** 574
Picture Bride (Son), **Supp. X:** 292
"Picture I Want, The" (Olds), **Supp. X:** 209
Picture of Dorian Gray, The (Wilde), **Supp. IX:** 105
"Picture of Little J. A. in a Prospect of Flowers, A" (Ashbery), **Supp. III Part 1:** 3
Picture Palace (Theroux), **Supp. VIII:** 322
"Pictures" (Pickering), **Supp. XXI:** 197
"Pictures at an Extermination" (Epstein), **Supp. XII:** 161
"Pictures from an Expedition" (Duffy), **Supp. IV Part 1:** 207
Pictures from an Institution (Jarrell), **II:** 367, 385
Pictures from Brueghel (W. C. Williams), **Retro. Supp. I:** 429–431
"Pictures from Brueghel" (W. C. Williams), **Retro. Supp. I:** 419
"Pictures of Columbus, the Genoese, The" (Freneau), **Supp. II Part 1:** 258
Pictures of Fidelman: An Exhibition (Malamud), **Supp. I Part 2:** 450–451
"Pictures of the Artist" (Malamud), **Supp. I Part 2:** 450
Pictures of the Floating World (Lowell), **II:** 521, 524–525
Pictures of Travel (Heine), **II:** 281
Picturesque America; or, the Land We Live In (Bryant, ed.), **Supp. I Part 1:** 158
"Picturesque Ghetto, The" (Hapgood), **Supp. XVII:** 101
"Picturesque: San Cristóbal de las Casas" (Mora), **Supp. XIII:** 218
Picture This (Heller), **Supp. IV Part 1:** 386, 388, 390–391
Picturing Will (Beattie), **Supp. V:** 29, 31–32, 34
"Pie" (X. J. Kennedy), **Supp. XV:** 170
"Piece, A" (Creeley), **Supp. IV Part 1:** 155, 156
"Piece of Moon, A" (Hogan), **Supp. IV Part 1:** 407
Piece of My Heart, A (Ford), **Supp. V:** 57, 58–61, 62

Piece of My Mind, A: Reflections at Sixty (Wilson), **IV:** 426, 430, 438, 441
"Piece of News, A" (Welty), **IV:** 263; **Retro. Supp. I:** 345, 346
Pieces (Creeley), **Supp. IV Part 1:** 155
Pieces and Pontifications (Mailer), **Retro. Supp. II:** 209–210
Pieces of the Frame (McPhee), **Supp. III Part 1:** 293
Pierce, Franklin, **II:** 225, 226, 227; **III:** 88; **Retro. Supp. I:** 150, 163, 164, 165
Pierce, Frederick, **Retro. Supp. I:** 136
Piercy, Josephine K., **Supp. I Part 1:** 103
"Pierian Handsprings" (column, Untermeyer), **Supp. XV:** 294
Pierpont, Claudia Roth, **Supp. X:** 192, 193, 196
Pierre et Jean (Maupassant), **I:** 421
Pierre: or The Ambiguities (Melville), **III:** 86–88, 89; **IV:** 194; **Retro. Supp. I:** 249, 253–254, 256; **Supp. I Part 2:** 579
Pierrepont, Sarah. *See* Edwards, Sarah
Pierrot qui pleure et Pierrot qui rit (Rostand), **II:** 515
Pig Cookies (Ríos), **Supp. IV Part 2:** 537, 550, 552–554
Pigeon Feathers (Updike), **IV:** 214, 218, 219, 221–223, 226
"Pigeon Feathers" (Updike), **Retro. Supp. I:** 318, 322, 323
"Pigeons" (Rilke), **II:** 544
"Pigeons, The" (Espaillat), **Supp. XXI:** 98
"Pigeon Woman" (Swenson), **Supp. IV Part 2:** 644
Pigs in Heaven (Kingsolver), **Supp. VII:** 197, 199, 209–210
Pike County Ballads, The (Hay), **Supp. I Part 1:** 352
Piket, Vincent, **Supp. IV Part 1:** 24
Pilar San-Mallafre, Maria del, **Supp. V:** 40
Pilcer, Sonya, **Supp. XVII:** 50
Pilgrim (Findley), **Supp. XX:61–62**
"Pilgrim" (Freneau), **Supp. I Part 1:** 125
"Pilgrimage" (Ray), **Supp. XVIII:** 193
"Pilgrimage" (Sontag), **Supp. III Part 2:** 454–455
"Pilgrimage" (Trethewey), **Supp. XXI:** 255
"Pilgrimage, The" (Maxwell), **Supp. VIII:** 169, 171
Pilgrimage of Festus, The (Aiken), **I:** 50, 55, 57
Pilgrimage of Henry James, The (Brooks), **I:** 240, 248, 250; **IV:** 433
Pilgrim at Tinker Creek (Dillard), **Supp. VI:** 22, **23–26,** 28, 29, **30–31,** 34; **Supp. XVIII:** 189
"Pilgrim Makers" (Lowell), **II:** 541
Pilgrim's Harbor (Skloot), **Supp. XX:196, 207**
Pilgrim's Progress (Bunyan), **I:** 92; **II:** 15, 168, 572; **Supp. I Part 1:** 32, 38; **Supp. I Part 2:** 599
Pili's Wall (Levine), **Supp. V:** 178, 183–184

"Pillar of Fire" (Bradbury), **Supp. IV Part 1:** 113–114
Pillars of Hercules, The: A Grand Tour of the Mediterranean (Theroux), **Supp. VIII:** 325
"Pillow" (L.-Y. Lee), **Supp. XV:** 224
Pilot, The (Cooper), **I:** 335, 337, 339, 342–343, 350
"Pilot from the Carrier, A" (Jarrell), **II:** 374
"Pilots, Man Your Planes" (Jarrell), **II:** 374–375
"Pilots, The" (Levertov), **Supp. III Part 1:** 282
"Pimp's Revenge, A" (Malamud), **Supp. I Part 2:** 435, 450, 451
Pinball (Kosinski), **Supp. VII:** 215, 226
Pinchot, Gifford, **Supp. IX:** 184; **Supp. XIV:** 178
Pindar, **I:** 381; **II:** 543; **III:** 610
"Pine" (Dickey), **Supp. IV Part 1:** 183
Pine Barrens, The (McPhee), **Supp. III Part 1:** 298–301, 309
"Pineys, The" (Stern), **Supp. IX:** 288, 296
Pinget, Robert, **Supp. V:** 39
Pinhook: Finding Wholeness in a Fragmented Land (Ray), **Supp. XVIII:** 189, 192, 202–204
"Pink Dog" (Bishop), **Retro. Supp. II:** 48
Pinker, James B., **I:** 409; **Retro. Supp. I:** 231
Pinkerton, Jan, **Supp. V:** 323–324
"Pink Moon—The Pond" (Oliver), **Supp. VII:** 234
Pinktoes (C. Himes), **Supp. XVI: 142**
Pinocchio in Venice (Coover), **Supp. V:** 40, 51
Pinsker, Sanford, **Retro. Supp. II:** 23; **Supp. V:** 272; **Supp. IX:** 293, 327; **Supp. XI:** 251, 254, 317
Pinsky, Robert, **Retro. Supp. II:** 50; **Supp. VI: 235–251; Supp. IX:** 155, 158; **Supp. XIII:** 277, 285; **Supp. XXI:** 243
Pinter, Harold, **I:** 71; **Supp. XIII:** 20, 196; **Supp. XIV:** 239; **Supp. XVI:** 207
Pinto, Ferdinand Mendes (pseudonym). *See* Briggs, Charles Frederick
Pinto and Sons (Epstein), **Supp. XII:** 170, **171–172**
Pinto letters (Briggs), **Supp. XVIII:** 3, **12–13**
"Pinup" (Collins), **Supp. XXI:** 59
Pioneers, The (Cooper), **I:** 336, 337, 339, 340–341, 342, 348; **II:** 313
Pioneers of France in the New World (Parkman), **Supp. II Part 2:** 599, 602
"Pioneers! O Pioneers!" (Whitman), **Retro. Supp. I:** 8
"Pioneer's Vision, The" (Larcom), **Supp. XIII:** 140
Pious and Secular America (Niebuhr), **III:** 308
Pipe Night (O'Hara), **III:** 361, 368
Piper, Dan, **Supp. IX:** 65

Pipers at the Gates of Dawn: The Wisdom of Children's Literature (Cott), **Supp. XVI:** 104

"Piper's Rocks" (Olson), **Supp. IV Part 1:** 153

"Pipistrelles" (B. Kelly), **Supp. XVII:** 129–130

Pipkin, Charles W., **Supp. XIV:** 3

Pippa Passes (Browning), **IV:** 128

Piquion, René, **Supp. I Part 1:** 346

Pirandello, Luigi, **Supp. IV Part 2:** 576, 588

Piranesi, Giovanni Battista, **Supp. XV:** 258

Pirate, The (Robbins), **Supp. XII:** 6

Pirate, The (Scott), **I:** 339

Pirates of Penzance, The (Gilbert and Sullivan), **IV:** 386

Pisan Cantos, The (Pound), **III:** 476; **Retro. Supp. I:** 140, 283, 285, 293; **Supp. III Part 1:** 63; **Supp. V:** 331, 337; **Supp. XIV:** 11; **Supp. XV:** 351

Pisarev, Dimitri, **Supp. XXI:** 164

Piscator, Erwin, **IV:** 394

Pissarro, Camille, **I:** 478

"Pissing off the Back of the Boat into the Nevernais Canal" (Matthews), **Supp. IX:** 160–161

Pistol, The (Jones), **Supp. XI:** 219, **223–224,** 227, 234

Pit, The (Norris), **III:** 314, 322, 326–327, 333, 334

"Pit, The" (Roethke), **III:** 538

"Pit and the Pendulum, The" (Poe), **III:** 413, 416; **Retro. Supp. II:** 264, 269–270, 273

"Pitcher" (Francis), **Supp. IX:** 82

"Pitcher, The" (Dubus), **Supp. VII:** 87

Pitchford, Nicola, **Supp. XII:** 13

"Pits, The" (D. Graham), **Supp. XI:** 252, 254

Pitt, William, **Supp. I Part 2:** 510, 518

"Pittsburgh" (Carruth), **Supp. XVI:** 58

"Pity Me" (Wylie), **Supp. I Part 2:** 729

Pity the Monsters (Williamson), **Retro. Supp. II:** 185

Pius II, Pope, **III:** 472

Pius IX, Pope, **II:** 79

"Piute Creek" (Snyder), **Supp. VIII:** 293

Pixley, Frank, **I:** 196

Pizer, Donald, **III:** 321; **Retro. Supp. II:** 100, 199

"Place" (Hoffman), **Supp. XVIII:** 86

"Place at the Outskirts" (Simic), **Supp. VIII:** 282

Place Called Estherville, A (Caldwell), **I:** 297, 307

Place Called Freedom, A (Sanders), **Supp. XVI:** 269

Place for My Head, A (Hoffman), **Supp. XVIII:** 76

"Place in Fiction" (Welty), **IV:** 260, 279

Place of Dead Roads, The (Burroughs), **Supp. III Part 1:** 196

Place of Love, The (Shapiro), **Supp. II Part 2:** 702, 706

"Place of Poetry, The" (Stevens), **Retro. Supp. I:** 304

Place of Science in Modern Civilization and Other Essays, The (Veblen), **Supp. I Part 2:** 629, 642

"Place of Trumpets, The" (B. Kelly), **Supp. XVII:** 127

Place on Earth, A (Berry), **Supp. X:** 33–34, 36

Places Left Unfinished at the Time of Creation (Santos), **Supp. XIII:** 274

"Places to Look for Your Mind" (Moore), **Supp. X:** 174–175

"Place They'd Never Seen, A: The Theater" (Wasserstein), **Supp. XV:** 332

"Place to Live, A" (Levertov), **Supp. III Part 1:** 281

"Place to Stand, A" (Price), **Supp. VI:** 258

Place to Stand, A (Wagoner), **Supp. IX:** 324

"Place (Any Place) to Transcend All Places, A" (W. C. Williams), **Retro. Supp. I:** 422

Placi, Carlo, **IV:** 328

Plagemann, Catherine, **Supp. XVII:** 91

"Plagiarist, The" (Singer), **IV:** 19

Plague of Dreamers, A (Stern), **Supp. XX:** 178

Plainest Narrative, The (Bronk), **Supp. XXI:** 31

"Plain Language from Truthful James" (Harte). See "Heathen Chinee, The"

"Plain Sense of Things, The" (Stevens), **Retro. Supp. I:** 298, 299, 307, 312

"Plain Song" (Carruth), **Supp. XVI:** 54

Plain Song (Harrison), **Supp. VIII:** **38–39**

"Plain Song" (Kooser), **Supp. XIX:** 120

"Plain Song for Comadre, A" (Wilbur), **Supp. III Part 2:** 554

"Plain Talk". See *Common Sense* (Paine)

Plaint of a Rose, The (Sandburg), **III:** 579

Plain Truth: Or, Serious Considerations on the Present State of the City of Philadelphia, and Province of Pennsylvania (Franklin), **II:** 117–119

Plainwater: Essays and Poetry (Carson), **Supp. XII:** 97, **99–104**

Plan B (C. Himes), **Supp. XVI:** 143, 144

Plan B: Further Thoughts on Faith (Lamott), **Supp. XX:** **142–143**

"Planchette" (London), **II:** 475–476

"Planetarium" (Rich), **Supp. I Part 2:** 557

Planet News: 1961–1967 (Ginsberg), **Supp. II Part 1:** 321

Planet Waves (album, Dylan), **Supp. XVIII:** 27

"Plantation a beginning, a" (Olson), **Supp. II Part 2:** 573

Plant Dreaming Deep (Sarton), **Supp. VIII:** 250, 263

Plante, David, **Supp. IV Part 1:** 310

Planting a Sequoia (Gioia), **Supp. XV:** 117

"Planting a Sequoia" (Gioia), **Supp. XV:** 111, 112, 117, **121–122**

"Plants Fed On By Fawns" (B. Kelly), **Supp. XVII:** 133

Plarr, Victor, **III:** 459, 477

Plath, James, **Retro. Supp. I:** 334

Plath, Sylvia, **Retro. Supp. II:** 181, **241–260; Supp. I Part 2: 526–549,** 554, 571; **Supp. III Part 2:** 543, 561; **Supp. IV Part 2:** 439; **Supp. V:** 79, 81, 113, 117, 118, 119, 344; **Supp. X:** 201, 202, **203,** 215; **Supp. XI:** 146, 240, 241, 317; **Supp. XII:** 217, 308; **Supp. XIII:** 35, 76, 312; **Supp. XIV:** 269; **Supp. XV:** 123, 148, 184, 252, 253, 340; **Supp. XVII:** 239; **Supp. XXI:** 58

Plath, Warren, **Supp. I Part 2:** 528

Plato, **I:** 224, 279, 383, 389, 485, 523; **II:** 5, 8, 10, 15, 233, 346, 391–392, 591; **III:** 115, 480, 600, 606, 609, 619–620; **IV:** 74, 140, 333, 363, 364; **Retro. Supp. I:** 247; **Retro. Supp. II:** 31; **Supp. I Part 2:** 595, 631; **Supp. IV Part 1:** 391; **Supp. IV Part 2:** 526; **Supp. X:** 78

"Plato" (Emerson), **II:** 6

"Platonic Relationship, A" (Beattie), **Supp. V:** 22

Platonic Scripts (Justice), **Supp. VII:** 115

Platonov, Dmitri, **Supp. VIII:** 30

Platt, Anthony M., **Supp. I Part 1:** 13–14

Platte River (Bass), **Supp. XVI:** 19

"Platte River" (Bass), **Supp. XVI:** 20

Plausible Prejudices: Essays on American Writing (Epstein), **Supp. XIV:** 111

Plautus, Titus Maccius, **IV:** 155; **Supp. III Part 2:** 630

Play and Other Stories, The (Dixon), **Supp. XII:** 148, 149

Playback (script) (Chandler), **Supp. IV Part 1:** 131

Playback (Chandler), **Supp. IV Part 1:** 134–135; **Supp. XVIII:** 138

"Play Ball!" (Francis), **Supp. IX:** 89

Playboy of the Western World, The (Synge), **Supp. III Part 1:** 34

Play Days (Jewett), **Retro. Supp. II:** 135

Play Days: A Book of Stories for Children (Jewett), **II:** 401–402

Player Piano (Vonnegut), **Supp. II Part 2:** 756, 757, 760–765

Players (DeLillo), **Supp. VI:** 3, 6, 8, 14

"Players, The" (W. J. Smith), **Supp. XIII:** 340, 343

"Playground, The" (Bradbury), **Supp. IV Part 1:** 104

Playing at Stillness (Espaillat), **Supp. XXI:** 112

Playing in the Dark (Morrison), **Retro. Supp. II:** 118; **Supp. XIII:** 185–186

"Playing the Bawd at Twenty" (Skloot), **Supp. XX:** 204–205

Play in Poetry (Untermeyer), **Supp. XV:** 310

"Playin with Punjab" (Bambara), **Supp. XI:** 6

Play It Again Sam (Allen), **Supp. XV:** 2, 3, 14

Play It as It Lays (Didion), **Supp. IV Part 1:** 198, 201–203, 203, 211

Play It as It Lays (film), **Supp. IV Part 1:** 198

"Plays and Operas Too" (Whitman), **IV:** 350

Plays of Negro Life: A Source-Book of Native American Drama (Locke and Gregory), **Supp. XIV:** 202

Plays: Winesburg and Others (Anderson), **I:** 113

"Playthings" (Komunyakaa), **Supp. XIII:** 126

"Playtime: Danish Fun" (Larsen), **Supp. XVIII:** 120, 122–123

"Playtime: Three Scandinavian Stories" (Larsen), **Supp. XVIII:** 122–123

Playwright's Voice, The (Savran), **Supp. XIII:** 209; **Supp. XV:** 321

Plaza Suite (Simon), **Supp. IV Part 2:** 575, 581–582, 583, 589

Pleading Guilty (Turow), **Supp. XVII:** 218, 219

"Plea for Captain Brown, A" (Thoreau), **IV:** 185

"Please" (Komunyakaa), **Supp. XIII:** 122

"Please Don't Kill Anything" (A. Miller), **III:** 161

"Please Don't Take My Sunshine Away" (Conroy), **Supp. XVI:** 69

Pleasure Dome (Frankenberg), **I:** 436

Pleasure Dome (Komunyakaa), **Supp. XIII:** 113, 121, **131–133**

Pleasure of Hope, The (Emerson), **II:** 8

"Pleasure of Ruins, The" (McClatchy), **Supp. XII:** 256

"Pleasures of Formal Poetry, The" (Bogan), **Supp. III Part 1:** 51

"Pleasures of Peace, The" (Koch), **Supp. XV:** 180

"Plea to the Protestant Churches, A" (Brooks), **Supp. XIV:** 4

Plimpton, George, **Supp. IV Part 1:** 386; **Supp. V:** 201; **Supp. VIII:** 82, 157; **Supp. IX:** 256; **Supp. XI:** 294; **Supp. XIV:** 82; **Supp. XVI: 233–248**

Pliny the Elder, **Supp. XVI:** 292

Pliny the Younger, **II:** 113

"Ploesti Isn't Long Island" (Zinberg), **Supp. XV:** 195

"Plot against the Giant, The" (Stevens), **IV:** 81

Plotinus, **Supp. XV:** 33; **Supp. XVI:** 291

Plough and the Stars, The (O'Casey), **III:** 159

"Ploughing on Sunday" (Stevens), **IV:** 74

Plowing the Dark (Powers), **Supp. IX:** 212–213, **221–224**

Plum Bun (Fauset), **Supp. XVIII:** 127; **Supp. XIX:** 73

Plumed Serpent, The (Lawrence), **Supp. XV:** 46

"Plumet Basilisk, The" (Moore), **III:** 203, 208, 215

Plumly, Stanley, **Supp. IV Part 2:** 625

Plummer, Amanda, **Supp. IV Part 1:** 236

Plunder (serial movie), **Supp. IV Part 2:** 464

Plunket, Robert, **Supp. XV:** 68

"Plunkville Patriot" (O'Henry), **Supp. II Part 1:** 389

"Pluralism and Ideological Peace" (Locke), **Supp. XIV:** 202, 212

"Pluralism and Intellectual Democracy" (Locke), **Supp. XIV:** 202, 208, 212

Pluralistic Universe, A (James), **II:** 342, 348, 357–358

Plutarch, **II:** 5, 8, 16, 555; **Retro. Supp. I:** 360; **Supp. XVI:** 292

Plymell, Charles, **Supp. XIV:** 149

Plymell, Pam, **Supp. XIV:** 149

Pnin (Nabokov), **III:** 246; **Retro. Supp. I:** 263, 265, 266, 275, 335

"Po' Boy Blues" (Hughes), **Supp. I Part 1:** 327

Pocahontas, **I:** 4; **II:** 296; **III:** 584

"Pocahontas to Her English Husband, John Rolfe" (Gunn Allen), **Supp. IV Part 1:** 331

"Pocketbook and Sauerkraut" (Di Piero), **Supp. XIX:** 35, 36, 41, 42, 45

"Pocket Poem" (Kooser), **Supp. XIX:** 128

Podhoretz, Norman, **IV:** 441; **Retro. Supp. II:** 323; **Supp. IV Part 1:** 382; **Supp. VIII:** 93, **231–247; Supp. IX:** 3; **Supp. XIV:** 103

Podnieks, Elizabeth, **Supp. X:** 189, 190, 191, 192

"Pod of the Milkweed" (Frost), **Retro. Supp. I:** 141

Poe, Edgar Allan, **I:** 48, 53, 103, 190, 194, 200, 210, 211, 261, 340, 459; **II:** 74, 77, 194, 255, 273, 295, 308, 311, 313, 421, 475, 482, 530, 595; **III:** 259, **409–432,** 485, 507, 593; **IV:** 123, 129, 133, 141, 187, 261, 345, 350, 432, 438, 439, 453; **Retro. Supp. I:** 41, 273, 365, 421; **Retro. Supp. II:** 102, 104, 160, 164, 220, **261–277,** 322; **Supp. I Part 1:** 36, 309; **Supp. I Part 2:** 376, 384, 385, 388, 393, 405, 413, 421, 474, 682; **Supp. II Part 1:** 385, 410; **Supp. III Part 2:** 544, 549–550; **Supp. IV Part 1:** 80, 81, 101, 128, 341, 349; **Supp. IV Part 2:** 464, 469; **Supp. VIII:** 105; **Supp. IX:** 115; **Supp. X:** 42, 78; **Supp. XI:** 85, 293; **Supp. XIII:** 100, 111; **Supp. XVI:** 294; **Supp. XVIII:** 3, 11; **Supp. XX:**74

Poe, Edgar Allen, **Supp. XV:** 275; **Supp. XXI:** 51

Poe Abroad: Influence, Reputation, Affinities (Vines), **Retro. Supp. II:** 261

"Poem" (Bishop), **Retro. Supp. II:** 40; **Supp. I Part 1:** 73, 76–79, 82, 95

"Poem" (Harrison), **Supp. VIII:** 38

"Poem" (Justice), **Supp. VII:** 125

"Poem" (Kunitz), **Supp. III Part 1:** 263

"Poem" (O'Hara), **Supp. XIX:** 85

"Poem" (Wright), **Supp. III Part 2:** 590

"Poem About George Doty in the Death House, A" (Wright), **Supp. III Part 2:** 594–595, 597–598

"Poem about People" (Pinsky), **Supp. VI: 240–241,** 244, 248

"Poem as Mask, The" (Rukeyser), **Supp. VI:** 281, 285

"Poem Beginning 'The' " (Zukofsky), **Supp. III Part 2:** 610, 611, 614

"Poem Catching Up with an Idea" (Carruth), **Supp. XVI:** 56

"POEM FOR ANNA RUSS AND FANNY JONES, A" (Baraka), **Supp. II Part 1:** 58

"Poem for Black Hearts, A" (Baraka), **Supp. II Part 1:** 50

"POEM FOR DEEP THINKERS, A" (Baraka), **Supp. II Part 1:** 55

"Poem for D. H. Lawrence" (Creeley), **Supp. IV Part 1:** 141

"Poem for Dorothy, A" (Merwin), **Supp. III Part 1:** 342

"Poem for Hemingway and W. C. Williams" (Carver), **Supp. III Part 1:** 147

"Poem for my Son" (Kumin), **Supp. IV Part 2:** 442

"Poem for People Who Are Understandably Too Busy to Read Poetry" (Dunn), **Supp. XI:** 147

"Poem for Someone Killed in Spain, A" (Jarrell), **II:** 371

"Poem for the Blue Heron, A" (Oliver), **Supp. VII:** 235–236

"Poem for Two Voices" (Everwine), **Supp. XV:** 89

"Poem For Willie Best, A" (Baraka), **Supp. II Part 1:** 36

"Poem in Prose" (Bogan), **Supp. III Part 1:** 58

"Poem in Which I Refuse Contemplation" (Dove), **Supp. IV Part 1:** 249

"Poem Is a Walk, A" (Ammons), **Supp. VII:** 36

"Poem Like a Grenade, A" (Haines), **Supp. XII:** 204

"Poem of Flight, The" (Levine), **Supp. V:** 189

"Poem of Liberation, The" (Stern), **Supp. IX:** 292

Poem of the Cid (Merwin, trans.), **Supp. III Part 1:** 347

"Poem of the Forgotten" (Haines), **Supp. XII:** 202–203

"Poem on the Memorable Victory Obtained by the Gallant Captain Paul Jones" (Freneau), **Supp. II Part 1:** 261

"Poem out of Childhood" (Rukeyser), **Supp. VI:** 272, 277

"Poem Read at the Dinner Given to the Author by the Medical Profession" (Holmes), **Supp. I Part 1:** 310–311

Poems (Auden), **Supp. II Part 1:** 6

Poems (Berryman), **I:** 170

Poems (Bryant), **II:** 311; **Supp. I Part 1:** 155, 157

Poems (Cummings), **I:** 430, 447

Poems (E. Stoddard), **Supp. XV:** 274

Poems (Eliot), **I:** 580, 588; **IV:** 122; **Retro. Supp. I:** 59, 291

Poems (Emerson), **II:** 7, 8, 12–13, 17

Poems (Holmes), **Supp. I Part 1:** 303

Poems (Koch), **Supp. XV:** 179

Poems (Lowell), **Supp. I Part 2:** 405

Poems (Moore), **III:** 194, 205, 215

Poems (Poe), **III:** 411

Poems (Reznikoff), **Supp. XIV:** 282, 283, 284, 285

Poems (Tate), **IV:** 121

Poems (W. C. Williams), **Retro. Supp. I:** 412–413, 416, 424

Poems (W. J. Smith), **Supp. XIII:** 332

Poems (Winters), **Supp. II Part 2:** 809, 810

Poems (Wordsworth), **I:** 468

Poems, 1909–1925 (Eliot), **Retro. Supp. I:** 64

Poems, 1924–1933 (MacLeish), **III:** 7, 15

Poems, 1943–1956 (Wilbur), **Supp. III Part 2:** 554

Poems, The (Freneau), **Supp. II Part 1:** 263

Poems 1918–1975 : The Complete Poems of Charles Reznikoff (Cooney, ed.), **Supp. XIV:** 289

Poems 1940–1953 (Shapiro), **Supp. II Part 2:** 703, 711

Poems 1947–1954 (Kees), **Supp. XV:** 147

Poems: 1947–1957 (W. J. Smith), **Supp. XIII:** 333

Poems 1957–1967 (Dickey), **Supp. IV Part 1:** 178, 181

Poems about God (Ransom), **III:** 484, 486, 491; **IV:** 121

"Poems about Painting" (Snodgrass), **Supp. VI:** 316

Poems and Essays (Ransom), **III:** 486, 490, 492

Poems and New Poems (Bogan), **Supp. III Part 1:** 60–62

"Poems and Places" (Haines), **Supp. XII:** 203

Poems and Poetry of Europe, The (Longfellow, ed.), **Retro. Supp. II:** 155

Poems by Emily Dickinson (Todd and Higginson, eds.), **I:** 469, 470; **Retro. Supp. I:** 35, 39

Poems by Emily Dickinson, Second Series (Todd and Higginson, eds.), **I:** 454; **Retro. Supp. I:** 35

Poems by Emily Dickinson, The (Bianchi and Hampson, eds.), **Retro. Supp. I:** 35

Poems by Emily Dickinson, Third Series (Todd, ed.), **Retro. Supp. I:** 35

Poems by James Russell Lowell, Second Series (Lowell), **Supp. I Part 2:** 406, 409

Poems by Sidney Lanier, (Lanier), **Supp. I Part 1:** 364

Poems from Black Africa (Hughes, ed.), **Supp. I Part 1:** 344

"Poems I Have Lost, The" (Ortiz), **Supp. IV Part 2:** 507

Poems: North & South–A Cold Spring, (Bishop), **Supp. I Part 1:** 83, 89

Poems of a Jew (Shapiro), **Supp. II Part 2:** 703, 712–713

"Poems of a Mountain Recluse" (Budbill), **Supp. XIX:** 9, 10

Poems of Anna Akhmatova, The (Kunitz and Hayward, trans.), **Supp. III Part 1:** 269

Poems of Emily Dickinson, The (Bianchi and Hampson, eds.), **Retro. Supp. I:** 35

Poems of Emily Dickinson, The (Johnson, ed.), **I:** 470

Poems of François Villon (Kinnell, trans.), **Supp. III Part 1:** 235, 243, 249

"Poems of Our Climate, The" (Stevens), **Retro. Supp. I:** 313

Poems of Philip Freneau, Written Chiefly during the Late War (Freneau), **Supp. II Part 1:** 261

Poems of Places (Longfellow, ed.), **II:** 490; **Retro. Supp. II:** 155; **Supp. I Part 1:** 368

Poems of Stanley Kunitz, The (Kunitz), **Supp. III Part 1:** 258, 263, 264, 266, 268

"Poems of These States" (Ginsberg), **Supp. II Part 1:** 323, 325

Poems of Two Friends (Howells and Piatt), **II:** 273, 277

"POEM SOME PEOPLE WILL HAVE TO UNDERSTAND, A" (Baraka), **Supp. II Part 1:** 49

Poems on Slavery (Longfellow), **II:** 489; **Retro. Supp. II:** 157, 168; **Supp. I Part 2:** 406

Poems on Various Subjects (Rowson), **Supp. XV:** 232

Poems on Various Subjects, Religious and Moral (Wheatley), **Supp. XX:**277, 282, 284, 285, 289

Poem Spoken at the Public Commencement at Yale College, in New Haven; September 1, 1781, A (Barlow), **Supp. II Part 1:** 67–68, 74, 75

Poems to Solve (Swenson), **Supp. IV Part 2:** 642

Poems Written and Published during the American Revolutionary War (Freneau), **Supp. II Part 1:** 273, 274

Poems Written between the Years 1768 and 1794 (Freneau), **Supp. II Part 1:** 269

"Poem That Took the Place of a Mountain" (Olson), **Supp. II Part 2:** 582

"Poem to My First Lover" (Olds), **Supp. X:** 206

"Poem to the Reader" (Olds), **Supp. X:** 213

"Poem with No Ending, A" (Levine), **Supp. V:** 186, 190

"Poem You Asked For, The" (Levis), **Supp. XI:** 259–260

Poe Poe Poe Poe Poe Poe Poe (Hoffman), **Retro. Supp. II:** 265

Poesía Náhuatl, **Supp. XV:** 77

Poésies 1917–1920 (Cocteau), **Retro. Supp. I:** 82

"Poesis: A Conceit" (Sobin), **Supp. XVI:** 288

Poet, The (Connelly), **Supp. XXI: 71,** 78

"Poet, The" (Dunbar), **Supp. II Part 1:** 207, 209–210

"Poet, The" (Emerson), **II:** 13, 19, 20, 170

"Poet, The" (Ortiz), **Supp. IV Part 2:** 505

"Poet and His Book, The" (Millay), **III:** 126, 138

"Poet and His Public, The" (Jarrell), **Supp. I Part 1:** 96

"Poet and His Song, The" (Dunbar), **Supp. II Part 1:** 199

"Poet and the Person, The" (Kinard), **Supp. XIV:** 127

"Poet and the Queen, The" (Shaw), **Supp. XIX:** 241

"Poet and the World, The" (Cowley), **Supp. II Part 1:** 145

"Poet as Anti-Specialist, The" (Swenson), **Supp. IV Part 2:** 638, 643

"Poet as *Curandera*" (Mora), **Supp. XIII:** 214, 220

"Poet as Hero, The: Keats in His Letters" (Trilling), **Supp. III Part 2:** 506–507

"Poet as Religious Moralist, The" (Larson), **Supp. XI:** 328

"Poet at Seven, The" (Rimbaud), **II:** 545

Poet at the Breakfast-Table, The (Holmes), **Supp. I Part 1:** 313–314

"Poète contumace, Le" (Corbiere), **II:** 384–385

"Poet for President, A" (Mora), **Supp. XIII:** 220–221

Poetic Achievement of Ezra Pound, The (Alexander), **Retro. Supp. I:** 293

Poetic Diction: A Study in Meaning (Barfield), **III:** 274, 279

"Poetic Principle, The" (Poe), **III:** 421, 426; **Retro. Supp. II:** 266

"Poetics" (Ammons), **Supp. VII:** 29–30

Poetics (Aristotle), **III:** 422; **Supp. XI:** 249; **Supp. XIII:** 75; **Supp. XIV:** 243; **Supp. XV:** 265

Poetics of Space, The (Bachelard), **Supp. XIII:** 225; **Supp. XVI:** 292

"Poetics of the Periphery: Literary Experimentalism in Kathy Acker's *In Memoriam to Identity*" (Acker), **Supp. XII:** 17

"Poetics of the Physical World, The" (Kinnell), **Supp. III Part 1:** 239

"Poetics of Tourette Syndrome, The: Language, Neurobiology, and Poetry" (Schleifer), **Supp. XVIII:** 144

Poet in the World, The (Levertov), **Supp. III Part 1:** 271, 273, 278, 282

"Poet or the Growth of a Lit'ry Figure" (White), **Supp. I Part 2:** 676

Poetry (Barber), **Supp. IV Part 2:** 550

"Poetry" (Moore), **III:** 204–205, 215

"Poetry" (Nye), **Supp. XIII:** 282

"Poetry" (Wrigley), **Supp. XVIII:** 301–302

"Poetry, Community and Climax" (Snyder), **Supp. VIII:** 290

"Poetry, Pleasure, and the Hedonist Reader" (Collins), **Supp. XXI:** 54

"Poetry: A Metrical Essay" (Holmes), **Supp. I Part 1:** 310

"Poetry and Belief in Thomas Hardy" (Schwartz), **Supp. II Part 2:** 666

Poetry and Criticism (Nemerov, ed.), **III:** 269

"Poetry and Drama" (Eliot), **I:** 588

Poetry and Fiction: Essays (Nemerov), **III:** 269, 281

"Poetry and Place" (Berry), **Supp. X:** 22, 28, 31, 32

Poetry and Poets (Lowell), **II:** 512

"Poetry and Religion" (Jarman), **Supp. XVII:** 111

Poetry and the Age (Jarrell), **IV:** 352; **Retro. Supp. I:** 121; **Supp. II Part 1:** 135

"Poetry and the Primitive: Notes on Poetry as an Ecological Survival Technique" (Snyder), **Supp. VIII:** 291, 292, 299, 300

"Poetry and the Public World" (MacLeish), **III:** 11

Poetry and the World (Pinsky), **Supp. VI:** 236, 239, 244, 247

Poetry and Truth (Olson), **Supp. II Part 2:** 583

"Poetry As a Way of Life" (Bishop interview), **Retro. Supp. II:** 53

"Poetry as Survival" (Harrison), **Supp. VIII:** 45

"Poetry Failure" (Halliday), **Supp. XIX:** 92

Poetry for Students (Taibl), **Supp. XV:** 255

"Poetry for the Advanced" (Baraka), **Supp. II Part 1:** 58

"Poetry Friendship on Earth" (Halliday), **Supp. XIX:** 90, 91

Poetry Handbook, A (Oliver), **Supp. VII:** 229, 245

Poetry Home Repair Manual, The (Kooser), **Supp. XIX:** 116, 128

Poetry in Motion: 100 Poems from the Subways and Buses (Peacock, ed.), **Supp. XIX:** 195

"Poetry of Barbarism, The" (Santayana), **IV:** 353

Poetry of Chaucer, The (Gardner), **Supp. VI:** 63

Poetry of Meditation, The (Martz), **IV:** 151; **Supp. I Part 1:** 107

Poetry of Mourning: The Modern Elegy from Hardy to Heaney (Ramazani), **Supp. IV Part 2:** 450

Poetry of Stephen Crane, The (Hoffman), **I:** 405

Poetry of the Negro 1746–1949, The (Hughes, ed.), **Supp. I Part 1:** 345

Poetry 180: A Turning Back to Poetry (Collins, ed.), **Supp. XXI:** 54

Poetry Reading against the Vietnam War, A (Bly and Ray, eds.), **Supp. IV Part 1:** 61, 63

"Poetry Workshop, The" (column, Kumin), **Supp. XX:**164

"Poetry Wreck, The" (Shapiro), **Supp. II Part 2:** 717

Poetry Wreck, The: Selected Essays (Shapiro), **Supp. II Part 2:** 703, 704, 717

"Poets" (X. J. Kennedy), **Supp. XV:** 158

Poet's Alphabet, A: Reflections on the Literary Art and Vocation (Bogan), **Supp. III Part 1:** 55, 64

Poets and Poetry of America (Griswold), **Supp. XV:** 277

Poet's Choice (Engle and Langland, eds.), **III:** 277, 542

"Poet's Husband Engages in Gourmet Cooking, The" (Espaillat), **Supp. XXI:** 99

Poets of the Old Testament, The (Gordon), **III:** 199

Poets of Today (Wheelock, ed.), **Supp. IV Part 2:** 639

Poets on Poetry (Nemerov, ed.), **III:** 269

"Poet's Tact, and a Necessary Tactlessness, The" (C. Frost), **Supp. XV:** 94–95

"Poet's View, A" (Levertov), **Supp. III Part 1:** 284

"Poet's Voice, The" (Oliver), **Supp. VII:** 245

"Poet Turns on Himself, The" (Dickey), **Supp. IV Part 1:** 177, 181, 185

Poganuc People (Stowe), **Supp. I Part 2:** 581, 596, 599–600

Pogo (comic strip), **Supp. XI:** 105

Pohrt, Tom, **Supp. XIX:** 123

Poincaré, Raymond, **IV:** 320

"Point, The" (Hayden), **Supp. II Part 1:** 373

"Point at Issue!, A" (Chopin), **Retro. Supp. II:** 61; **Supp. I Part 1:** 208

"Point of Age, A" (Berryman), **I:** 173

Point of No Return (Marquand), **III:** 56, 59–60, 65, 67, 69

Point Reyes Poems (R. Bly), **Supp. IV Part 1:** 71

"Points" (Hoffman), **Supp. XVIII:** 86

Points for a Compass Rose (Connell), **Supp. XIV:** 79, 80, 96

"Point Shirley" (Plath), **Supp. I Part 2:** 529, 538

Points in Time (Bowles), **Supp. IV Part 1:** 93

"Points West" (column), **Supp. IV Part 1:** 198

Poirier, Richard, **I:** 136, 239; **III:** 34; **Retro. Supp. I:** 134; **Retro. Supp. II:** 207–208; **Supp. I Part 2:** 660, 665; **Supp. IV Part 2:** 690

Poison Pen (Garrett), **Supp. VII:** 111

Poisonwood Bible, The (Kingsolver), **Supp. VII:** 197–198, 202, 210–213

Poitier, Sidney, **Supp. IV Part 1:** 360, 362

Pokerface (Collins), **Supp. XXI:** 53

"Polack Reverie" (Halliday), **Supp. XIX:** 88

Polanco, Richard, **Supp. XX:**260

"Polar Bear" (Heller), **Supp. IV Part 1:** 383

"Polar Seas and Sir John Franklin, The" (Briggs), **Supp. XVIII:** 14

Pole, Rupert, **Supp. X:** 185

"Pole Star" (MacLeish), **III:** 16

Po Li, **Supp. I Part 1:** 262

Police (Baraka), **Supp. II Part 1:** 47

"Police" (Corso), **Supp. XII:** 117, 127

"Police Court Saturday Morning" (X. J. Kennedy), **Supp. XV:** 170

"Police Dreams" (Bausch), **Supp. VII:** 47

Politian (Poe), **III:** 412

"Political and Practical Conceptions of Race, The" (Locke), **Supp. XIV:** 209–210

Political Essays (Lowell), **Supp. I Part 2:** 407

Political Fable, A (Coover), **Supp. V:** 44, 46, 47, 49, 51

"Political Fables" (Mather), **Supp. II Part 2:** 450

"Political Interests" (Stevens), **Retro. Supp. I:** 295

"Political Litany, A" (Freneau), **Supp. II Part 1:** 257

"Political Migrations: A Family Story" (Mallon), **Supp. XIX:** 141–142

"Political Pastoral" (Frost), **Retro. Supp. I:** 139

"Political Poem" (Baraka), **Supp. II Part 1:** 36

Politics (Acker), **Supp. XII:** 3, 4

Politics (Macdonald), **I:** 233–234

"Politics" (Paley), **Supp. VI:** 217

"Politics, Structure, and Poetic Development" (McCombs), **Supp. XIII:** 33

"Politics and the English Language" (Orwell), **Retro. Supp. II:** 287; **Supp. I Part 2:** 620

Politics and the Novel (Howe), **Supp. VI:** 113

"Politics and the Personal Lyric in the Poetry of Joy Harjo and C. D. Wright" (Goodman), **Supp. XV:** 344

"Politics of Ethnic Authorship, The: Li-Young Lee, Emerson, and Whitman at the Banquet Table" (Partridge), **Supp. XV:** 219

"Politics of Silence, The" (Monette), **Supp. X:** 148

Polito, Robert, **Supp. XVIII:** 33

Politt, Katha, **Supp. XII:** 159

Polk, James, **Supp. XIII:** 20

Polk, James K., **I:** 17; **II:** 433–434

Pollack, Sydney, **Supp. XIII:** 159

"Pollen" (Nye), **Supp. XIII:** 284

Pollitt, Katha, **Supp. X:** 186, 191, 193; **Supp. XVI:** 39

Pollock, Jackson, **IV:** 411, 420; **Supp. XV:** 145, 177, 178; **Supp. XIX:** 33

"Polly" (Chopin), **Retro. Supp. II:** 72

Polo, Marco, **III:** 395

Polonsky, Abraham, **Supp. XXI:** 261, 275

Polybius, **Supp. I Part 2:** 491

"Polydore" (Chopin), **Retro. Supp. II:** 66

"Pomegranate" (Glück), **Supp. V:** 82

"Pomegranate Seed" (Wharton), **IV:** 316; **Retro. Supp. I:** 382

Ponce de Leon, Luis, **III:** 391

"Pond, The" (Nemerov), **III:** 272

"Pond at Dusk, The" (Kenyon), **Supp. VII:** 168

Ponder Heart, The (Welty), **IV:** 261, 274–275, 281; **Retro. Supp. I:** 351–352

"Ponderosa Pine" (Huncke), **Supp. XIV:** 146

Ponsot, Margaret, **Supp. XVII:** 241

"Pony" (Sanders), **Supp. XVI:** 277

Poodle Springs (Parker and Chandler), **Supp. IV Part 1:** 135; **Supp. XIX:** 189

Poodle Springs Story, The (Chandler), **Supp. IV Part 1:** 135

"Pool, The" (Doolittle), **Supp. I Part 1:**
264–265
Poole, Ernest, **II:** 444
"Pool Lights" (F. Barthelme), **Supp. XI:**
25, 26–27, 36
"Pool Room in the Lions Club" (Merwin),
Supp. III Part 1: 346
"Poolside" (Skloot), **Supp. XX:**202–203
"Poor Black Fellow" (Hughes), **Retro.
Supp. I:** 204
"Poor Bustard, The" (Corso), **Supp. XII:**
134
"Poor but Happy" (Mamet), **Supp. XIV:**
252, 253
Poore, Charles, **III:** 364; **Supp. XIX:**
257, 264; **Supp. XX:**38
Poor Fool (Caldwell), **I:** 291, 292, 308
Poorhouse Fair, The (Updike), **IV:** 214,
228–229, 232; **Retro. Supp. I:** 317,
320
"Poor Joanna" (Jewett), **II:** 394
"Poor Man's Pudding and Rich Man's
Crumbs" (Melville), **III:** 89–90
"Poor Richard" (James), **II:** 322
Poor Richard's Almanac (undated)
(Franklin), **II:** 112
Poor Richard's Almanac for 1733
(Franklin), **II:** 108, 110
Poor Richard's Almanac for 1739
(Franklin), **II:** 112
Poor Richard's Almanac for 1758
(Franklin), **II:** 101
Poor White (Anderson), **I:** 110–111
"Poor Working Girl" (Z. Fitzgerald),
Supp. IX: 71
Popa, Vasko, **Supp. VIII:** 272
Pope, Alexander, **I:** 198, 204; **II:** 17, 114;
III: 263, 267, 288, 517; **IV:** 145;
Retro. Supp. I: 335; **Supp. I Part 1:**
150, 152, 310; **Supp. I Part 2:** 407,
422, 516, 714; **Supp. II Part 1:** 70,
71; **Supp. X:** 32, 36; **Supp. XII:** 260;
Supp. XV: 258; **Supp. XX:**280
Pope-Hennessy, James, **Supp. XIV:** 348
"Pope's Penis, The" (Olds), **Supp. X:** 207
"Poplar, Sycamore" (Wilbur), **Supp. III
Part 2:** 549
Popo and Fifina (Hughes and Bontemps),
Retro. Supp. I: 203
"Poppies" (Oliver), **Supp. VII:** 240
"Poppies in July" (Plath), **Supp. I Part
2:** 544
"Poppies in October" (Plath), **Supp. I
Part 2:** 544
"Poppycock" (Francis), **Supp. IX:** 87
"Poppy Seed" (Lowell), **II:** 523
"Popular Art and the Cultural Tradition"
(C. L. R. James), **Supp. XXI:** 170
*Popular Book, The: A History of
America's Literary Taste* (Hart), **Supp.
XVIII:** 257, 258
Popular Culture (Goldbarth), **Supp. XII:**
186
Popular History of the United States
(Gay), **Supp. I Part 1:** 158
"Popular Songs" (Ashbery), **Supp. III
Part 1:** 6
"Populist Manifesto" (Ferlinghetti),
Supp. VIII: 290
"Porcelain Bowl" (Glück), **Supp. V:** 83

Porcher, Frances, **Retro. Supp. II:** 71
Porco, Mike, **Supp. XVIII:** 24
"Porcupine, The" (Kinnell), **Supp. III
Part 1:** 244
Porcupine's Kiss, The (Dobyns), **Supp.
XIII: 89–90**
"Por esas coases que pasan" (Hinojosa),
Supp. XIX: 101
Porgy and Bess (film), **Supp. I Part 1:**
66
Porgy and Bess (play), **Supp. IV Part 1:**
6
"Porn Bought my Football" (Offutt),
Supp. XIX: 163
"Porphyria's Lover" (Browning), **II:** 522
Portable Beat Reader, The (Charters, ed.),
Supp. XIV: 152
Portable Blake, The (Kazin, ed.), **Supp.
VIII:** 103
Portable Faulkner, The (Cowley, ed.), **II:**
57, 59; **Retro. Supp. I:** 73
Portable Paul and Jane Bowles, The
(Dillon), **Supp. IV Part 1:** 95
Portable Veblen, The (Veblen), **Supp. I
Part 2:** 630, 650
"Porte-Cochere" (Taylor), **Supp. V:** 320
"Porter" (Hughes), **Supp. I Part 1:** 327
"Porter" (Nelson), **Supp. XVIII:** 175
Porter, Bern, **III:** 171
Porter, Cole, **Supp. IX:** 189
Porter, Eliot, **Supp. IV Part 2:** 599
Porter, Fairfield, **Supp. XV:** 178
Porter, Herman W., **Supp. I Part 1:** 49
Porter, Horace, **Retro. Supp. II:** 4, 127
Porter, Jacob, **Supp. I Part 1:** 153
Porter, Katherine Anne, **I:** 97, 385; **II:**
194, 606; **III: 433–455,** 482; **IV:** 26,
138, 246, 261, 279, 280, 282; **Retro.
Supp. I:** 354; **Retro. Supp. II:** 233,
235; **Supp. IV Part 1:** 31, 310; **Supp.
V:** 225; **Supp. VIII:** 156, 157; **Supp.
IX:** 93, 94, 95, 98, 128; **Supp. X:** 50;
Supp. XIII: 294; **Supp. XIV:** 3;
Supp. XV: 338
Porter, Noah, **Supp. I Part 2:** 640
Porter, William Sydney. *See* Henry, O.
Porteus, Beilby, **Supp. I Part 1:** 150
"Portland Going Out, The" (Merwin),
Supp. III Part 1: 345
Portnoy's Complaint (P. Roth), **Retro.
Supp. II: 282–286,** 291; **Supp. III
Part 2:** 401, 404, 405, 407, 412–414,
426; **Supp. V:** 119, 122; **Supp. XI:**
140; **Supp. XVII:** 8, 43; **Supp.
XX:**177
Port of Saints (Burroughs), **Supp. III
Part 1:** 106
"Portrait" (Dixon), **Supp. XII:** 154
"Portrait, A" (Parker), **Supp. IX:** 192–
193
"Portrait, The" (Kunitz), **Supp. III Part
1:** 263
"Portrait, The" (Wharton), **Retro. Supp.
I:** 364
"Portrait d'une Femme" (Pound), **Retro.
Supp. I:** 288
Portrait in Brownstone (Auchincloss),
Supp. IV Part 1: 21, 23, 27, 31
"Portrait in Georgia" (Toomer), **Supp.
IX:** 314

"Portrait in Greys, A" (W. C. Williams),
Retro. Supp. I: 416
"Portrait of a Girl in Glass" (T. Williams),
IV: 383
"Portrait of a Jewelry Drummer"
(Untermeyer), **Supp. XV:** 299–300
"Portrait of a Lady" (Eliot), **I:** 569, 570,
571, 584; **III:** 4; **Retro. Supp. I:** 55,
56, 62
Portrait of a Lady, The (James), **I:** 10,
258, 461–462, 464; **II:** 323, 325, 327,
328–329, 334; **Retro. Supp. I:** 215,
216, 217, 219, 220, 223, **224–225,**
232, 233, 381
"Portrait of an Artist" (P. Roth), **Supp.
III Part 2:** 412
Portrait of an Eye: Three Novels (Acker),
Supp. XII: 6, **7–9**
"Portrait of an Invisible Man" (Auster),
Supp. XII: 21
"Portrait of a Supreme Court Judge"
(Untermeyer), **Supp. XV:** 299
Portrait of Bascom Hawkes, A (Wolfe),
IV: 451–452, 456
Portrait of Edith Wharton (Lubbock),
Retro. Supp. I: 366
*Portrait of Logan Pearsall Smith, Drawn
from His Letters and Diaries, A*
(Russell, ed.), **Supp. XIV:** 349
Portrait of Picasso as a Young Man
(Mailer), **Retro. Supp. II:** 213
"Portrait of the Artist as an Old Man, A"
(Humphrey), **Supp. IX:** 109
Portrait of the Artist as a Young Man, A
(Joyce), **I:** 475–476; **III:** 471, 561;
Retro. Supp. I: 127; **Retro. Supp. II:**
4, 331; **Supp. IX:** 236; **Supp. XIII:**
53, 95
"Portrait of the Artist with Hart Crane"
(Wright), **Supp. V:** 342
"Portrait of the Intellectual as a Yale
Man" (McCarthy), **II:** 563, 564–565
"Portrait of the Reader with a Bowl of
Cereal, A" (Collins), **Supp. XXI:** 55
"Portrait of the Self . . . , A" (Sobin),
Supp. XVI: 288
Portraits and Elegies (Schnackenberg),
Supp. XV: 249, **253–256**
"Portraits of Grief" *(New York Times),*
Supp. XIX: 142
"Port Town" (Hughes), **Retro. Supp. I:**
199
*Portuguese Voyages to America in the
Fifteenth Century* (Morison), **Supp. I
Part 2:** 488
"Po' Sandy" (Chesnutt), **Supp. XIV:** 60
Poseidon Adventure, The (film), **Supp.
XII:** 321
Poseidon Adventure, The (Gallico), **Supp.
XVI:** 238
"Poseidon and Company" (Carver), **Supp.
III Part 1:** 137
"Positive Obsession" (O. Butler), **Supp.
XIII:** 70
Poss, Stanley, **Supp. XIV:** 166
Possession (Byatt), **Supp. XXI:** 147
"Possessions" (H. Crane), **I:** 392–393;
Retro. Supp. II: 78
Possible World, A (Koch), **Supp. XV:** 184
Postal Inspector (film), **Supp. XIII:** 166

Postcards (Proulx), **Supp. VII:** 249, 256–258, 262

"Postcard to Send to Sumer, A" (Bronk), **Supp. XXI:** 31

"Postcolonial Tale, A" (Harjo), **Supp. XII:** 227

"Posthumous Letter to Gilbert White" (Auden), **Supp. II Part 1:** 26

"Post-Larkin Triste" (Karr), **Supp. XI:** 242–243

Postlethwaite, Diana, **Supp. XII:** 317–318; **Supp. XVI:** 176

"Postlude" (W. C. Williams), **Retro. Supp. I:** 415

Postman, Neil, **Supp. XI:** 275

Postman Always Rings Twice, The (Cain), **Supp. XIII:** 165–166

Postman Always Rings Twice, The (film), **Supp. XIV:** 241

"Postmaster and the Clerk, The" (Budbill), **Supp. XIX:** 9

"Postmortem Guide, A" (Dunn), **Supp. XI:** 155

Postrel, Virginia, **Supp. XIV:** 298, 311

"Postscript" (Du Bois), **Supp. II Part 1:** 173

"Postscript" (Nye), **Supp. XIII:** 287

"Potato" (Wilbur), **Supp. III Part 2:** 545

"Potatoes' Dance, The" (Lindsay), **Supp. I Part 2:** 394

Pot of Earth, The (MacLeish), **III:** 5, 6–8, 10, 12, 18

"Pot Roast" (Strand), **Supp. IV Part 2:** 629

Potshot (Parker), **Supp. XIX:** 185

Pot Shots at Poetry (Francis), **Supp. IX:** 83–84

Potter, Beatrix, **Supp. I Part 2:** 656; **Supp. XVI:** 100

Potter, Stephen, **IV:** 430

Potter's House, The (Stegner), **Supp. IV Part 2:** 598, 606

Poulenc, Francis, **Supp. IV Part 1:** 81

Poulin, Al, Jr., **Supp. IX:** 272; **Supp. XI:** 259

Pound, Ezra, **I:** 49, 58, 60, 66, 68, 69, 105, 236, 243, 256, 384, 403, 428, 429, 475, 476, 482, 487, 521, 578; **II:** 26, 55, 168, 263, 316, 371, 376, 513, 517, 520, 526, 528, 529, 530; **III:** 2, 5, 8, 9, 13–14, 17, 174, 194, 196, 278, 430, 453, **456–479,** 492, 504, 511, 523, 524, 527, 575–576, 586, 590; **IV:** 27, 28, 407, 415, 416, 433, 446; **Retro. Supp. I:** 51, 52, 55, 58, 59, 63, 82, 89, 127, 140, 171, 177, 178, 198, 216, **283–294,** 298, 299, 359, 411, 412, 413, 414, 417, 418, 419, 420, 423, 426, 427, 430, 431; **Retro. Supp. II:** 178, 183, 189, 326; **Supp. I Part 1:** 253, 255–258, 261–268, 272, 274; **Supp. I Part 2:** 387, 721; **Supp. II Part 1:** 1, 8, 20, 30, 91, 136; **Supp. III Part 1:** 48, 63, 64, 73, 105, 146, 225, 271; **Supp. III Part 2:** 542, **609–617,** 619, 620, 622, 625, 626, 628, 631; **Supp. IV Part 1:** 153, 314; **Supp. V:** 331, 338, 340, 343, 345; **Supp. VIII:** 39, 105, 195, 205, 271, 290, 291, 292, 303; **Supp. IX:** 291;

Supp. X: 24, 36, 112, 120, 122; **Supp. XII:** 97; **Supp. XIV:** 11, 55, 83, 272, 284, 286, 287, 347; **Supp. XV:** 20, 42, 43, 51, 93, 161, 181, 297, 298, 299, 301, 302, 306; **Supp. XVI:** 47, 282; **Supp. XVII:** 111, 226–227; **Supp. XIX:** 42; **Supp. XXI:** 33

Pound, Louise, **Retro. Supp. I:** 4; **Supp. XV:** 137

Pound, T. S., **I:** 428

"Pound Reweighed" (Cowley), **Supp. II Part 1:** 143

Powell, Anthony, **Supp. XVIII:** 136, 146; **Supp. XIX:** 131

Powell, Betty, **Retro. Supp. II:** 140

Powell, Dawn, **Supp. IV Part 2:** 678, 682; **Supp. XIX:** 143

Powell, Dick, **Supp. IX:** 250

Powell, John Wesley, **Supp. IV Part 2:** 598, 604, 611

Powell, Lawrence Clark, **III:** 189

Powell, William, **Supp. IV Part 1:** 355

"Power" (Corso), **Supp. XII:** 117, 126, 127, **128**

"Power" (Emerson), **II:** 2, 3

"Power" (Rich), **Supp. I Part 2:** 569

"Power and Light" (Dickey), **Supp. IV Part 1:** 182

Power and the Glory, The (Greene), **III:** 556

"Powerhouse" (Welty), **Retro. Supp. I:** 343, 346

"Power Never Dominion" (Rukeyser), **Supp. VI:** 281

"Power of Fancy, The" (Freneau), **Supp. II Part 1:** 255

Power of Myth, The (Campbell), **Supp. IX:** 245

"Power of Prayer, The" (Lanier), **Supp. I Part 1:** 357

"Power of Stories, The" (Sanders), **Supp. XVI:** 278

"Power of Suggestion" (Auchincloss), **Supp. IV Part 1:** 33

Power of Sympathy, The (Brown), **Supp. II Part 1:** 74

Power Politics (Atwood), **Supp. XIII:** 20, 33–34, 35

Powers, J. F., **Supp. V:** 319; **Supp. XVII:** 43

Powers, Kim, **Supp. VIII:** 329, 340

Powers, Richard, **Supp. IX: 207–225;** **Supp. XVII:** 183; **Supp. XX:** 93

Powers of Attorney (Auchincloss), **Supp. IV Part 1:** 31, 32, 33

"Powers of Darkness" (Wharton), **Retro. Supp. I:** 379

Powys, John Cowper, **Supp. I Part 2:** 454, 476; **Supp. IX:** 135

Poynton, Jerome, **Supp. XIV:** 147, 150

Practical Agitation (Chapman), **Supp. XIV:** 41

Practical Criticism: A Study of Literary Judgment (Richards), **Supp. XIV:** 3, 16

Practical Magic (film), **Supp. X:** 80

Practical Magic (Hoffman), **Supp. X:** 78, 82, **88–89**

"Practical Methods of Meditation, The" (Dawson), **IV:** 151

Practical Navigator, The (Bowditch), **Supp. I Part 2:** 482

Practice of Perspective, The (Dubreuil), **Supp. IV Part 2:** 425

Practice of Reading, The (Donoghue), **Supp. VIII:** 189

Pragmatism: A New Name for Some Old Ways of Thinking (James), **II:** 352

"Pragmatism's Conception of Truth" (James), **Supp. XIV:** 40

Prague Orgy, The (P. Roth), **Retro. Supp. II:** 280

"Praire, The" (Clampitt), **Supp. IX:** 42

"Prairie" (Sandburg), **III:** 583, 584

Prairie, The (Cooper), **I:** 339, 342

"Prairie Birthday" (Leopold), **Supp. XIV:** 185

Prairie Home Companion, A (Keillor, radio program), **Supp. XIII:** 274; **Supp. XVI:** 169–171, 173–178

Prairie Home Morning Show, A (Keillor, radio program), **Supp. XVI:** 171

"Prairie Life, A Citizen Speaks" (Dunn), **Supp. XI:** 145

"Prairies, The" (Bryant), **Supp. I Part 1:** 157, 162, 163, 166

Praise (Hass), **Supp. VI:** 104–105, 106

"Praise for an Urn" (Crane), **I:** 388

"Praise for Sick Women" (Snyder), **Supp. VIII:** 294

"Praise in Summer" (Wilbur), **Supp. III Part 2:** 546–548, 560, 562

"Praise of a Palmtree" (Levertov), **Supp. III Part 1:** 284

"Praise of the Committee" (Rukeyser), **Supp. VI:** 278

"Praises, The" (Goldbarth), **Supp. XII:** 185

"Praises, The" (Olson), **Supp. II Part 2:** 558, 560, 563, 564

Praises and Dispraises (Des Pres), **Supp. X:** 120

Praisesong for the Widow (Marshall), **Supp. IV Part 1:** 14; **Supp. XI:** 18, 276, 278, **284–286,** 287; **Supp. XX:** 154

"Praise to the End!" (Roethke), **III:** 529, 532, 539

Prajadhipok, King of Siam, **I:** 522

Prater Violet (Isherwood), **Supp. XIV: 164–166,** 169–170, 171

Pratt, Anna (Anna Alcott), **Supp. I Part 1:** 33

Pratt, Louis H., **Retro. Supp. II:** 6

Pratt, Mary Louise, **Retro. Supp. II:** 48

Pratt, Parley, **Supp. IV Part 2:** 603

"Prattler" (newspaper column), **I:** 207

"Prattler, The" (Bierce), **I:** 196

"Prayer" (Gioia), **Supp. XV:** 117

"Prayer" (Olds), **Supp. X:** 204

"Prayer" (Peacock), **Supp. XIX:** 198, 199, 200

"Prayer" (Toomer), **Supp. IX:** 318

"Prayer, A" (Kushner), **Supp. IX: 134**

"Prayer for Columbus" (Whitman), **IV:** 348

"Prayer for My Daughter" (Yeats), **II:** 598

"Prayer for My Grandfather to Our Lady, A" (Lowell), **II:** 541–542

"Prayer for my Son" (C. Frost), **Supp. XV:** 98–99

"Prayer for Our Daughters" (Jarman), **Supp. XVII:** 120

Prayer for Owen Meany, A (Irving), **Supp. VI:** 164, 165, 166, **175–176**

"PRAYER FOR SAVING" (Baraka), **Supp. II Part 1:** 52–53

"Prayer in Spring, A" (Frost), **II:** 153, 164

"Prayer Meeting" (Di Piero), **Supp. XIX:** 46, 47

"Prayer on All Saint's Day" (Cowley), **Supp. II Part 1:** 138, 153

Prayers for Dark People (Du Bois), **Supp. II Part 1:** 186

"Prayer to Hermes" (Creeley), **Supp. IV Part 1:** 156, 157

"Prayer to Masks" (Senghor), **Supp. IV Part 1:** 16

"Prayer to the Child of Prague" (Salinas), **Supp. XIII:** 327

"Prayer to the Good Poet" (Wright), **Supp. III Part 2:** 603

"Prayer to the Pacific" (Silko), **Supp. IV Part 2:** 560

"Pray without Ceasing" (Emerson), **II:** 9–10

Praz, Mario, **IV:** 430

"Preacher, The" (Whittier), **Supp. I Part 2:** 698–699

Preacher and the Slave, The (Stegner), **Supp. IV Part 2:** 599, 608, 609

Precaution (Cooper), **I:** 337, 339

"Preconceptions of Economic Science, The" (Veblen), **Supp. I Part 2:** 634

Predecessors, Et Cetera (Clampitt), **Supp. IX:** 37

"Predicament, A" (Poe), **Retro. Supp. II:** 273

Predilections (Moore), **III:** 194

Prefaces and Prejudices (Mencken), **III:** 99, 104, 106, 119

Preface to a Twenty Volume Suicide Note. . . . (Baraka), **Supp. II Part 1:** 31, 33–34, 51, 61

"Preference" (Wylie), **Supp. I Part 2:** 713

"Prejudice against the Past, The" (Moore), **IV:** 91

Prejudices (Mencken), **Supp. I Part 2:** 630

Prejudices: A Selection (Farrell, ed.), **III:** 116

Prejudices: First Series (Mencken), **III:** 105

"Preliminary Remarks on the Poetry in the First Person" (Wright), **Supp. XV:** 339

Prelude, A: Landscapes, Characters and Conversations from the Earlier Years of My Life (Wilson), **IV:** 426, 427, 430, 434, 445

Prelude, The (Wordsworth), **III:** 528; **IV:** 331, 343; **Supp. I Part 2:** 416, 676; **Supp. XI:** 248

Prelude and Liebestod (McNally), **Supp. XIII:** 201

"Preludes" (Eliot), **I:** 573, 576, 577; **Retro. Supp. I:** 55; **Supp. IV Part 2:** 436

Preludes for Memnon (Aiken), **I:** 59, 65

Preludes from Memnon (Aiken), **Supp. X:** 50

"Prelude to an Evening" (Ransom), **III:** 491, 492–493

Prelude to Darkness (Salinas), **Supp. XIII:** 311, **318–319,** 320

"Prelude to the Present" (Mumford), **Supp. II Part 2:** 471

"Premature Burial, The" (Poe), **III:** 415, 416, 418; **Retro. Supp. II:** 270

Preminger, Otto, **Supp. IX:** 3, 9; **Supp. XX:**246–247

"Premonition" (Hay), **Supp. XIV:** 122

"Premonitions of the Bread Line" (Komunyakaa), **Supp. XIII:** 114, 115

Prenshaw, Peggy Whitman, **Supp. X:** 229

"Preparations" (Silko), **Supp. IV Part 2:** 560

Preparatory Meditations (Taylor), **IV:** 145, 148, 149, 150, 152, 153, 154–155, 164, 165

"Prepare" (Carruth), **Supp. XVI:** 59

Prepositions: The Collected Critical Essays of Louis Zukofsky (Zukofsky), **Supp. III Part 2:** 630

Prescott, Anne, **Supp. IV Part 1:** 299

Prescott, Orville, **Supp. IV Part 2:** 680; **Supp. XI:** 340

Prescott, Peter, **Supp. X:** 83

Prescott, Peter S., **Supp. XVI:** 212

Prescott, William, **Retro. Supp. I:** 123

Prescott, William Hickling, **II:** 9, 310, 313–314; **IV:** 309; **Supp. I Part 2:** 414, 479, 493, 494

"Prescription of Painful Ends" (Jeffers), **Supp. II Part 2:** 424

"Presence, The" (Gordon), **II:** 199, 200

"Presence, The" (Kumin), **Supp. IV Part 2:** 445, 455

Presence and Desire: Essays on Gender, Sexuality, Performance (Dolan), **Supp. XV:** 327

"Presence of Others, The" (Kenyon), **Supp. VII:** 164

Presences (Taylor), **Supp. V:** 325

"Present Age, The" (Emerson), **II:** 11–12

Present Danger, The: Do We Have the Will to Reverse the Decline of American Power? (Podhoretz), **Supp. VIII:** 241

"Present for the Boy, A" (Swados), **Supp. XIX:** 259

Present for Young Ladies, A (Rowson), **Supp. XV:** 245

"Present Hour" (Sandburg), **III:** 593–594

Present Philosophical Tendencies (Perry), **I:** 224

"Present State of Ethical Philosophy, The" (Emerson), **II:** 9

"Present State of Poetry, The" (Schwartz), **Supp. II Part 2:** 666

"Preservation of Innocence" (Baldwin), **Supp. I Part 1:** 51

"Preserving Wildness" (Berry), **Supp. X:** 28, 29, 32

"President and Other Intellectuals, The" (Kazin), **Supp. VIII:** 104

Presidential Papers, The (Mailer), **III:** 35, 37–38, 42, 45; **Retro. Supp. II:** 203, 204, 206

"Presidents" (Merwin), **Supp. III Part 1:** 351

Presnell, Robert, Sr., **Supp. XIII:** 166

Pressley, Nelson, **Supp. XVIII:** 37–38

"PRES SPOKE IN A LANGUAGE" (Baraka), **Supp. II Part 1:** 60

Presumed Innocent (Turow), **Supp. XVII:** 214–216, 223; 217

"Pretext, The" (Wharton), **Retro. Supp. I:** 371

Pretty Baby (film), **Supp. XXI:** 252

Pretty Boy Floyd (McMurtry), **Supp. V:** 231

"Pretty Girl, The" (Dubus), **Supp. VII:** 87–88

"Pretty Mouth and Green My Eyes" (Salinger), **III:** 560

"Previous Condition" (Baldwin), **Supp. I Part 1:** 51, 55, 63

"Previous Tenant, The" (Simpson), **Supp. IX:** 278–279

Prevost, Verbie Lovorn, **Supp. XXI:** 45

Priaulx, Allan, **Supp. XI:** 228

Price, Alan, **Retro. Supp. I:** 377

Price, Reynolds, **Supp. VI:** 253–270; **Supp. IX:** 256, 257

Price, Richard, **II:** 9; **Supp. I Part 2:** 522; **Supp. XX:**85

Price, The (A. Miller), **III:** 165–166

"Price Is Right, The" (Skloot), **Supp. XX:**198–199

"Price of the Harness, The" (Crane), **I:** 414

Pricksongs & Descants; Fictions (Coover), **Supp. V:** 39, 42, 43, 49, 50

"Pride" (Hughes), **Supp. I Part 1:** 331

Pride and Prejudice (Austen), **II:** 290

Prideaux, Tom, **Supp. IV Part 2:** 574, 590

"Priesthood, The" (Winters), **Supp. II Part 2:** 786

Priestly, Joseph, **Supp. I Part 2:** 522

Primary Colors, The (A. Theroux), **Supp. VIII:** 312

"Primary Ground, A" (Rich), **Supp. I Part 2:** 563

"Prime" (Auden), **Supp. II Part 1:** 22

"Primer Class" (Bishop), **Retro. Supp. II:** 38, 51

Primer for Blacks (Brooks), **Supp. III Part 1:** 85

"Primer for the Nuclear Age" (Dove), **Supp. IV Part 1:** 246

Primer mensaje a la América Hispana (W. Frank), **Supp. XX:**76

Primer of Ignorance, A (Blackmur), **Supp. II Part 1:** 91

Prime-Stevenson, Edward Irenaeus, **Supp. XX:**235

Primitive, The (C. Himes), **Supp. XVI:** 139, **141–142**

"Primitive Black Man, The" (Du Bois), **Supp. II Part 1:** 176

"Primitive Like an Orb, A" (Stevens), **IV:** 89; **Retro. Supp. I:** 309

Primitive People (Prose), **Supp. XVI:** 255, 256, 257

"Primitive Singing" (Lindsay), **Supp. I Part 2:** 389–390

Primitivism and Decadence (Winters), **Supp. II Part 2:** 786, 803–807, 812

Primrose, Archibald Philip, **Supp. XX:**230

Prince, Richard, **Supp. XII:** 4

"Prince, The" (Jarrell), **II:** 379

"Prince, The" (Winters), **Supp. II Part 2:** 802

Prince and the Pauper, The (Twain), **IV:** 200–201, 206

Prince Hagen (Sinclair), **Supp. V:** 280

Prince of a Fellow, A (Hearon), **Supp. VIII:** 58, **62–63**

Princess, The (Tennyson), **Supp. I Part 2:** 410

Princess and the Goblins, The (Macdonald), **Supp. XIII:** 75

Princess Casamassima, The (James), **II:** 276, 291; **IV:** 202; **Retro. Supp. I:** 216, 221, 222, 225, **226–227**

"Princess Casamassima, The" (Trilling), **Supp. III Part 2:** 502, 503

Princess of Arcady, A (Henry), **Retro. Supp. II:** 97

"Principles" (Du Bois), **Supp. II Part 1:** 172

Principles of Literary Criticism (Richards), **I:** 274; **Supp. I Part 1:** 264; **Supp. XIV:** 3

Principles of Psychology, The (James), **II:** 321, 350–352, 353, 354, 357, 362, 363–364; **IV:** 28, 29, 32, 37

Principles of Psychology, The (W. James), **Supp. XVII:** 97

Principles of Zoölogy (Agassiz), **Supp. I Part 1:** 312

Prior, Sir James, **II:** 315

Prior, Matthew, **II:** 111; **III:** 521

"Prison, The" (Malamud), **Supp. I Part 2:** 431, 437

"Prisoned Love" (Boyce), **Supp. XXI:** 9

"Prisoner of Ours, The" (Weigl), **Supp. XIX:** 288

Prisoner of Second Avenue, The (Simon), **Supp. IV Part 2:** 583, 584

Prisoner of Sex, The (Mailer), **III:** 46; **Retro. Supp. II:** 206

Prisoner of Zenda, The (film), **Supp. I Part 2:** 615

Prisoner's Dilemma (Powers), **Supp. IX:** 212, **214–216**, 221

Prison Memoirs of an Anarchist (A. Berkman), **Supp. XVII:** 103–104

Pritchard, William, **Supp. XVI:** 71

Pritchard, William H., **Retro. Supp. I:** 131, 141; **Supp. IV Part 1:** 285; **Supp. IV Part 2:** 642; **Supp. XI:** 326

Pritchett, V. S., **II:** 587; **Supp. II Part 1:** 143; **Supp. VIII:** 171; **Supp. XIII:** 168

"Privatation and Publication" (Cowley), **Supp. II Part 1:** 149

Private Contentment (Price), **Supp. VI:** 263

"Private History of a Campaign That Failed" (Twain), **IV:** 195

Private I, The: Privacy in a Public World (Peacock, ed.), **Supp. XIX:** 193, 203

Private Life of Axie Reed, The (Knowles), **Supp. XII:** 249

"Private Man Confronts His Vulgarities at Dawn, A" (Dunn), **Supp. XI:** 146

Private Memoirs and Confessions of a Justified Sinner, The (Hogg), **Supp. IX:** 276

"Private Property and the Common Wealth" (Berry), **Supp. X:** 25

Private Snafu series (Geisel), **Supp. XVI:** 102

"Private Theatricals" (Howells), **II:** 280

Private Women, Public Stage: Literary Domesticity in Nineteenth-Century America (Kelley), **Supp. XVIII:** 257

Privilege, The (Kumin), **Supp. IV Part 2:** 442–444, 451

Prize Stories 1918 : The O. Henry Awards, **Supp. XVI:** 16

"Probe" (Ryan as Quin), **Supp. XVIII:** 229

"Probing the Dark" (Komunyakaa), **Supp. XIII:** 131

"Problem from Milton, A" (Wilbur), **Supp. III Part 2:** 550

"Problem of Anxiety, The" (Koch), **Supp. XV:** 183

"Problem of Being, The" (James), **II:** 360

Problem of Classification in the Theory of Value, The (Locke), **Supp. XIV:** 199

"Problem of Housing the Negro, The" (Du Bois), **Supp. II Part 1:** 168

"Problem of the Religious Novel, The" (Isherwood), **Supp. XIV:** 172

Problems and Other Stories (Updike), **Retro. Supp. I:** 322, 329

"Problem Solving" (Goldbarth), **Supp. XII:** 185

Procedures for Underground (Atwood), **Supp. XIII:** 33

"Procedures for Underground" (Atwood), **Supp. XIII:** 33

Procession, The (al-Mawákib) (Gibran), **Supp. XX:**116, 124

Processional (Lawson), **I:** 479

"Procession at Candlemas, A" (Clampitt), **Supp. IX:** 41

"Proclamation" (Saunders), **Supp. XIX:** 235

Proclus, **Retro. Supp. I:** 247

"Prodigal" (Ammons), **Supp. VII:** 29

"Prodigal" (Hoffman), **Supp. XVIII:** 86

"Prodigal, The" (Bishop), **Supp. I Part 1:** 90, 92

Prodigal Parents, The (Lewis), **II:** 454–455

"Prodigy" (Simic), **Supp. VIII:** 278

Producers, The (film, M. Brooks), **Supp. XVII:** 45

"Proem" (Crane), **I:** 397

"Proem, The: By the Carpenter" (O. Henry), **Supp. II Part 1:** 409

"Professions for Women" (Woolf), **Supp. XIII:** 305

"Professor" (Hughes), **Supp. I Part 1:** 330

"Professor, The" (Bourne), **I:** 223

Professor at the Breakfast Table, The (Holmes), **Supp. I Part 1:** 313, 316

"Professor Clark's Economics" (Veblen), **Supp. I Part 2:** 634

Professor of Desire, The (P. Roth), **Retro. Supp. II:** 288; **Supp. III Part 2:** 403, 418–420

Professor's House, The (Cather), **I:** 325–336; **Retro. Supp. I:** 16

"Professor Veblen" (Mencken), **Supp. I Part 2:** 630

Proffer, Carl R., **Supp. VIII:** 22

Profile Makers, The (Bierds), **Supp. XVII:** 29, **30–32**, 33

"Profile of the Tenderloin Street Prostitute, A" (Vollmann), **Supp. XVII:** 230

Profits of Religion, The (Sinclair), **Supp. V:** 276

"Prognosis" (Warren), **IV:** 245

"Progress" (F. Wright), **Supp. XVII:** 247

"Progress Report" (Simic), **Supp. VIII:** 278

"Project for a Trip to China" (Sontag), **Supp. II Part 2:** 454, 469

"Project for *The Ambassadors*" (James), **Retro. Supp. I:** 229

"Projection" (Nemerov), **III:** 275

"Projective Verse" (Olson), **Supp. III Part 1:** 30; **Supp. III Part 2:** 555, 556, 557, 624; **Supp. IV Part 1:** 139, 153; **Supp. VIII:** 290

"Projector, The" (Baker), **Supp. XIII:** 53, 55

Prokofiev, Sergey Sergeyevich, **Supp. IV Part 1:** 81

"Prolegomena, Section 1" (Pound), **Supp. III Part 2:** 615–616

"Prolegomena, Section 2" (Pound), **Supp. III Part 2:** 616

"Prolegomenon to a Biography of Mailer" (Lucid), **Retro. Supp. II:** 195

Proletarian Literature in the United States (Hicks), **Supp. I Part 2:** **609–610**

"Prologue" (MacLeish), **III:** 8, 14

"Prologue to a Life" (D. West), **Supp. XVIII:** 280

"Prologue to Our Time" (Mumford), **Supp. III Part 2:** 473

"Prometheus" (Longfellow), **II:** 494

Prometheus Bound (Lowell), **II:** 543, 544, 545, 555

Promise, The (Buck), **Supp. II Part 1:** 124

"Promise, The" (Olds), **Supp. X:** 213

"Promise and Fulfillment" (D. West), **Supp. XVIII:** 278

Promised Land (Parker), **Supp. XIX:** 183, 184, 190

Promised Land, The (M. Antin), **Supp. IX:** 227; **Supp. XVI:** 148, 149; **Supp. XX:**1, 2, 3, **4–9**, 11

Promised Land, The (Porter), **III:** 447

"Promised Land, The" (R. Fisher), **Supp. XIX:** 72

Promised Lands (Sontag), **Supp. III Part 2:** 452

Promise of American Life, The (Croly), **I:** 229

"Promise of Blue Horses, The" (Harjo), **Supp. XII:** 228

Promise of Rest, The (Price), **Supp. VI:** 262, 266

Promises (Warren), **Supp. XIV:** 15

Promises, Promises (musical), **Supp. IV Part 2:** 575

Promises: Poems 1954–1956 (Warren), **IV:** 244–245, 249, 252

"Promise This When You Be Dying" (Dickinson), **Retro. Supp. I:** 44, 46

Proof, The (Winters), **Supp. II Part 2:** 786, 791, 792–794

Proofs and Theories: Essays on Poetry (Glück), **Supp. V:** 77, 79, 92; **Supp. XIV:** 269

"Propaganda of History, The" (Du Bois), **Supp. II Part 1:** 182

Propertius, Sextus, **III:** 467; **Retro. Supp. II:** 187; **Supp. XII:** 2

Property Of: A Novel (Hoffman), **Supp. X:** 77, 79, 80–82

"Property of Loss" (W. V. Davis), **Supp. XXI:** 95

"Prophecy of Samuel Sewall, The" (Whittier), **Supp. I Part 2:** 699

Prophet, The (Gibran), **Supp. XX:**113, 115, 119–121, 126

"Prophet and the Child, The" (Gibran), **Supp. XX:**123

Propheteers, The (Apple), **Supp. XVII:** 6–7

"Prophetic Pictures, The" (Hawthorne), **II:** 227

"Proportion" (Lowell), **II:** 525

"Proposal" (Carver), **Supp. III Part 1:** 149

Proposals Relating to the Education of Youth in Pensilvania (Franklin), **II:** 113

"Proposed New Version of the Bible" (Franklin), **II:** 110

Prose, Francine, **Supp. XII:** 333; **Supp. XVI:** 249–264; **Supp. XIX:** 209

"Prose for Departure" (Merrill), **Supp. III Part 1:** 336

Prose Pieces (Bynner), **Supp. XV:** 52

"Prose Poem as an Evolving Form, The" (R. Bly), **Supp. IV Part 1:** 64

"Proserpina and the Devil" (Wilder), **IV:** 358

"Prosody" (Espaillat), **Supp. XXI:** 102

"Prosody" (Shapiro), **Supp. II Part 2:** 710

Prospect before Us, The (Dos Passos), **I:** 491

"Prospective Immigrants Please Note" (Rich), **Supp. I Part 2:** 555

Prospect of Peace, The (Barlow), **Supp. II Part 1:** 67, 68, 75

Prospects of Literature, The (L. P. Smith), **Supp. XIV:** 343

Prospects on the Rubicon (Paine), **Supp. I Part 2:** 510–511

Prospectus of a National Institution, to Be Established in the United States (Barlow), **Supp. II Part 1:** 80, 82

Prospice (Browning), **IV:** 366

"Protestant Easter" (Sexton), **Supp. II Part 2:** 684

"Prothalamion" (Schwartz), **Supp. II Part 2:** 649, 652

"Prothalamion" (Spenser), **Retro. Supp. I:** 62

Proud, Robert, **Supp. I Part 1:** 125

"Proud Farmer, The" (Lindsay), **Supp. I Part 2:** 381

Proud Flesh (Humphrey), **Supp. IX:** 94, 95, 96, 102–103, 104, 105, 109

"Proud Flesh" (Warren), **IV:** 243

Proud Lady (Boyce), **Supp. XXI:** 7, 12

"Proud Lady" (Wylie), **Supp. I Part 2:** 711–712

Proulx, Annie, **Supp. VII: 249–267**

Proust, Marcel, **I:** 89, 319, 327, 377, 461; **II:** 377, 514, 606; **III:** 174, 181, 184, 244–245, 259, 471; **IV:** 32, 201, 237, 301, 312, 328, 359, 428, 431, 434, 439, 443, 466, 467; **Retro. Supp. I:** 75, 89, 169, 335; **Supp. III Part 1:** 10, 12, 14, 15; **Supp. IV Part 2:** 600; **Supp. VIII:** 103; **Supp. IX:** 211; **Supp. X:** 193, 194; **Supp. XII:** 289; **Supp. XIV:** 24, 83, 95; **Supp. XVI:** 295; **Supp. XXI:** 231

Proverbs, **Supp. X:** 45

"Proverbs" (Jarman), **Supp. XVII:** 118

"Providence" (Komunyakaa), **Supp. XIII:** 132

"Provident Woman, A" (Boyce), **Supp. XXI:** 10

"Provincetown Postcards" (F. Wright), **Supp. XVII:** 244

"Provincia deserta" (Pound), **Retro. Supp. I:** 289

"Provisional Remarks on Being / A Poet / of Arkansas" (Wright), **Supp. XV:** 337

Pruette, Lorine, **Supp. IV Part 2:** 522

Prufrock and Other Observations (Eliot), **I:** 569–570, 571, 573, 574, 576–577, 583, 584, 585; **Retro. Supp. I:** 59, 62

"Prufrock's Perivigilium" (T. S. Eliot), **Retro. Supp. I:** 57

Pryor, Richard, **Supp. XIII:** 343

Pryse, Marjorie, **Retro. Supp. II:** 139, 146

"Psalm" (Ginsberg), **Supp. II Part 1:** 312

"Psalm" (Simic), **Supp. VIII:** 282

"Psalm and Lament" (Justice), **Supp. VII:** 116, 117–118, 120–122, 124

"Psalm for Pinhook" (Ray), **Supp. XVIII:** 202

"Psalm of Life, A" (Longfellow), **II:** 489, 496; **Retro. Supp. II:** 164, 168, 169; **Supp. I Part 2:** 409

"Psalm of the West" (Lanier), **Supp. I Part 1:** 362, 364

"Psalm: Our Fathers" (Merwin), **Supp. III Part 1:** 350

Psalms (biblical book), **I:** 83; **II:** 168, 232; **Retro. Supp. I:** 62; **Supp. I Part 1:** 125

Psalms, Hymns, and Spiritual Songs of the Rev. Isaac Watts, The (Worcester, ed.), **I:** 458

Psychiatric Novels of Oliver Wendell Holmes, The (Oberndorf), **Supp. I Part 1:** 315

"Psychology and Form" (Burke), **I:** 270

Psychology: Briefer Course (James), **II:** 351–352

Psychology of Art (Malraux), **IV:** 434

Psychology of Insanity, The (Hart), **I:** 241–242, 248–250

Psychopathia Sexualis (Shanley), **Supp. XIV:** 316, 329

Psychophysiks (Fechner), **II:** 358

"Pu-239" (Kalfus), **Supp. XVII:** 50

"Publication is the Auction" (Dickinson), **Retro. Supp. I:** 31

"Public Bath, The" (Snyder), **Supp. VIII:** 298

Public Burning, The (Coover), **Supp. IV Part 1:** 388; **Supp. V:** 44, 45, 46–47, 48, 51, 52; **Supp. XVII:** 6

"Public Burning of Julius and Ethel Rosenberg, The: An Historical Romance" (Coover), **Supp. V:** 44

"Public Figure" (Hay), **Supp. XIV:** 124

"Public Garden, The" (Lowell), **II:** 550

Public Good (Paine), **Supp. I Part 2:** 509–510

Public Poetry of Robert Lowell, The (Cosgrave), **Retro. Supp. II:** 185

"Public & Private" (column, Quindlen), **Supp. XVII:** 165, 167, 169–170

Public Speech: Poems (MacLeish), **III:** 15–16

Public Spirit (Savage), **II:** 111

Puccini, Giacomo, **Supp. XXI:** 150, 151

"Puck" (Monette), **Supp. X:** 157–158

Pudd'nhead Wilson (Twain), **I:** 197

"Pudd'nhead Wilson's Calendar" (Twain), **I:** 197

"Pueblo Revolt, The" (Sando), **Supp. IV Part 2:** 510

Puella (Dickey), **Supp. IV Part 1:** 178, 185

Pulitzer, Alfred, **Retro. Supp. I:** 257

Pull Down Vanity (Fiedler), **Supp. XIII:** 103

Pullman, George, **Supp. I Part 1:** 9

"Pullman Car Hiawatha" (Wilder), **IV:** 365–366

Pull My Daisy (film), **Supp. XII:** 126–127

"Pulp Cutters' Nativity, A" (Budbill), **Supp. XIX:** 9

"Pulpit and the Pew, The" (Holmes), **Supp. I Part 1:** 302

"Pulse-Beats and Pen-Strokes" (Sandburg), **III:** 579

"Pump, The" (Humphrey), **Supp. IX:** 101

Pump House Gang, The (Wolfe), **Supp. III Part 2:** 575, 578, 580, 581

Punch, Brothers, Punch and Other Sketches (Twain), **IV:** 200

Punch: The Immortal Liar, Documents in His History (Aiken), **I:** 57, 61

Punishment Without Vengeance (Vega; Merwin, trans.), **Supp. III Part 1:** 341, 347

"Pupil" (F. Barthelme), **Supp. XI:** 26

"Pupil, The" (H. James), **Supp. XX:**233

"Pupil, The" (James), **II:** 331; **Retro. Supp. I:** 217, 219, 228

"Purchase" (Banks), **Supp. V:** 6

"Purchase of Some Golf Clubs, A" (O'Hara), **III:** 369

"Purdah" (Plath), **Supp. I Part 2:** 602
Purdy, Charles, **Supp. VIII:** 330
Purdy, James, **Supp. VII: 269–285**
Purdy, Theodore, **Supp. VIII:** 153
Pure (C. Frost), **Supp. XV:** 93, **101–102,** 104, 106
"Pure" (C. Frost), **Supp. XV:** 101–102
"Pure and the Good, The: On Baseball and Backpaking" (Maclean), **Supp. XIV:** 222
"Pure Good of Theory, The" (Stevens), **Retro. Supp. I:** 310
Purgatorio (Dante), **III:** 182
"Purim Parade" (Espaillat), **Supp. XXI:** 108
Puritan Family (Morgan), **Supp. I Part 1:** 101
"Puritanical Pleasures" (Hardwick), **Supp. III Part 1:** 213–214
Puritan Origins of the American Self, The (Bercovitch), **Supp. I Part 1:** 99
Puritan Pronaos, The: Studies in the Intellectual Life of New England in the Seventeenth Century (Morison), **Supp. I Part 2:** 485
"Puritan Realism: *The Wide, Wide World* and *Robinson Crusoe*" (Kim), **Supp. XVIII:** 267
Puritans, The (P. Miller), **Supp. VIII:** 101
"Puritan's Ballad, The" (Wylie), **Supp. I Part 2:** 723
"Purloined Letter, The" (Poe), **Retro. Supp. II:** 271, 272
Purple Cane Road (Burke), **Supp. XIV:** 32, 33
Purple Decades, The (Wolfe), **Supp. III Part 2:** 584
"Purple Hat, The" (Welty), **IV:** 264
Purple Rose of Cairo, The (film; Allen), **Supp. XV:** 1, **9–10,** 12, 14
Purser, John T., **Supp. XIV:** 4
"Pursuit of Happiness" (Simpson), **Supp. IX:** 279
"Pursuit of Happiness, The" (Ashbery), **Supp. III Part 1:** 23
Pursuit of the Prodigal, The (Auchincloss), **Supp. IV Part 1:** 25
Pushcart at the Curb, A (Dos Passos), **I:** 478, 479
"Pushcart Man" (Hughes), **Supp. I Part 1:** 330
Pushcart Prize, XIII, The (Ford), **Supp. V:** 58
Pushcart Prize VII, The (Hendeson, ed.), **Supp. XVII:** 16
Pushcart Prize XIV, The (Henderson, ed.), **Supp. XVII:** 18
Pushcart Prize XX, The (Henderson, ed.), **Supp. XVII:** 20
"Pushing 100" (Mora), **Supp. XIII:** 215
Pushkin, Aleksander, **III:** 246, 261, 262; **Retro. Supp. I:** 266, 269; **Supp. XVI:** 188
Pussy, King of the Pirates (Acker), **Supp. XII:** 6–7
"Pussycat and the Expert Plumber Who Was a Man, The" (A. Miller), **III:** 146–147
Pussycat Fever (Acker), **Supp. XII:** 6

Putnam, George Haven, **Supp. XVIII:** 257, 260
Putnam, George P., **II:** 314; **Supp. XVIII:** 3–4, 14, 260
Putnam, Phelps, **I:** 288
Putnam, Samuel, **II:** 26; **III:** 479; **Supp. III Part 2:** 615
"Put Off the Wedding Five Times and Nobody Comes to It" (Sandburg), **III:** 586–587
Puttenham, George, **Supp. I Part 1:** 113
Puttermesser Papers, The (Ozick), **Supp. V:** 269
"Putting a Burden Down" (Peacock), **Supp. XIX:** 199
"Putting on *Visit to a Small Planet*" (Vidal), **Supp. IV Part 2:** 683
Put Yourself in My Shoes (Carver), **Supp. III Part 1:** 139
"Put Yourself in My Shoes" (Carver), **Supp. III Part 1:** 139, 141
Putzi, Jennifer, **Supp. XV:** 284
Puzo, Mario, **Supp. IV Part 1:** 390
"Puzzle of Modern Society, The" (Kazin), **Supp. VIII:** 103
Pygmalion (Shaw), **Supp. XII:** 14
Pyle, Ernie, **III:** 148; **Supp. V:** 240; **Supp. XVII:** 61
Pylon (Faulkner), **II:** 64–65, 73; **Retro. Supp. I:** 84, 85
Pynchon, Thomas, **III:** 258; **Retro. Supp. I:** 278; **Retro. Supp. II:** 279, 324; **Supp. II Part 2:** 557, **617–638; Supp. III Part 1:** 217; **Supp. IV Part 1:** 53, 279; **Supp. IV Part 2:** 570; **Supp. V:** 40, 44, 52; **Supp. VIII:** 14; **Supp. IX:** 207, 208, 212; **Supp. X:** 260, 301, 302; **Supp. XI:** 103; **Supp. XII:** 289; **Supp. XIV:** 49, 53, 54, 96; **Supp. XVI:** 123, 128; **Supp. XVII:** 183, 225, 232, 236; **Supp. XIX:** 223, **Supp. XX:** 21, 83, 87
Pyne, John, **Supp. XXI:** 7
Pyne, Mary, **Supp. XXI:** 7
Pyrah, Gill, **Supp. V:** 126
"Pyramid Club, The" (Doctorow), **Supp. IV Part 1:** 234
"Pyrography" (Ashbery), **Supp. III Part 1:** 18
Pythagoras, **I:** 332
Pythagorean Silence (Howe), **Supp. IV Part 2:** 426, 428–429

Q
QBVII (television movie), **Supp. XX:** 247
QBVII (Uris), **Supp. XX:** 244, 247, 248, 251, **253–254**
"Qebehseneuf" (Goldbarth), **Supp. XII:** 186
"Quadroons, The" (Child), **Supp. XVIII:** 124
"Quai d'Orléans" (Bishop), **Supp. I Part 1:** 89
"Quail for Mr. Forester" (Humphrey), **Supp. IX:** 94
"Quail in Autumn" (W. J. Smith), **Supp. XIII:** 334–335, 339
"Quaker Graveyard in Nantucket, The" (Lowell), **II:** 54, 550; **Retro. Supp. II:** 178, 186–187

"Quake Theory" (Olds), **Supp. X:** 203
Qualey, Carlton C., **Supp. I Part 2:** 650
Quality of Hurt, The (C. Himes), **Supp. XVI:** 137, 145
"Quality of Wine" (Carruth), **Supp. XVI:** 59
"Quality Time" (Kingsolver), **Supp. VII:** 203
"Quandary" (F. Wright), **Supp. XVII:** 244
Quang-Ngau-chè, **III:** 473
Quarles, Francis, **I:** 178, 179
Quarry, The (Chesnutt), **Supp. XIV:** 76
"Quarry, The" (Nemerov), **III:** 272
Quarry, The: New Poems (Eberhart), **I:** 532, 539
Quartermain, Peter, **Supp. IV Part 2:** 423, 434
"Quaternions, The" (Bradstreet), **Supp. I Part 1:** 104–106, 114, 122
"Quatrains for Ishi" (Komunyakaa), **Supp. XIII:** 129
Queechy (S. Warner as Wetherell), **Supp. XVIII:** 257, **264–266**
"Queen Elizabeth and the Blind Girl or Music for the Dead Children" (B. Kelly), **Supp. XVII:** 124, 125
"Queen of the Blues" (Brooks), **Supp. III Part 1:** 75
Queen of the Damned, The (Rice), **Supp. VII:** 290, 292–293, 297, 299
Queen of the Mob (film), **Supp. XIII:** 170
"Queens of France" (Wilder), **IV:** 365
"Queen's Twin, The" (Jewett), **Retro. Supp. II:** 138
Queen's Twin, The, and Other Stories (Jewett), **Retro. Supp. II:** 140
Queen Victoria (Strachey), **Supp. I Part 2:** 485, 494; **Supp. XIV:** 342
Queer (Burroughs), **Supp. III Part 1:** 93–102
"Queer Beer" (Hansberry), **Supp. IV Part 1:** 374
"Quelques considérations sur la méthode subjective" (James), **II:** 345–346
"Quest, The" (Gibran), **Supp. XX:** 124
"Question" (Swenson), **Supp. IV Part 2:** 640
"Question and Answer" (Hughes), **Retro. Supp. I:** 211
"Questioning Faces" (Frost), **Retro. Supp. I:** 141
"Question Mark in the Circle, The" (Stegner), **Supp. IV Part 2:** 597
"Questionnaire, The" (Snodgrass), **Supp. VI:** 318
"Question of Fidelity, A" (Beauvoir), **Supp. IX:** 4
"Question of Loneliness, A" (Swados), **Supp. XIX:** 262
"Question of Our Speech, The" (Ozick), **Supp. V:** 272
"Question of Simone de Beauvoir, The" (Algren), **Supp. IX:** 4
Questions About Angels (Collins), **Supp. XXI:** 54, 58, 59, 60, 64
Questions for Ecclesiastes (Jarman), **Supp. XVII:** 109, 110, **118–119**

"Questions of Geography" (Hollander), **Supp. I Part 1:** 96

Questions of Travel (Bishop), **Retro. Supp. II: 46–48; Supp. I Part 1:** 72, 83, 92, 94

"Questions of Travel" (Bishop), **Retro. Supp. II:** 47

"Questions to Tourists Stopped by a Pineapple Field" (Merwin), **Supp. III Part 1:** 355

"Questions without Answers" (T. Williams), **IV:** 384

"Quest of the Purple-Fringed, The" (Frost), **Retro. Supp. I:** 139

Quest of the Silver Fleece, The (Du Bois), **Supp. II Part 1:** 176–178

Quevedo y Villegas, Francisco Gómez, **Retro. Supp. I:** 423

Quickly: A Column for Slow Readers (Mailer), **Retro. Supp. II:** 202

Quicksand (Larsen), **Supp. XVIII:** 119, 121, 122, **124–127**

Quicksand and Passing (Larsen; McDowell, ed.), **Supp. XVIII:** 125

"Quies," (Pound), **Retro. Supp. I:** 413

Quiet American, The (Greene), **Supp. XIX:** 29

"Quiet and clear" (Kooser), **Supp. XIX:** 125

Quiet City (Shaw), **Supp. XIX:** 244

Quiet Days in Clichy (H. Miller), **III:** 170, 178, 183–184, 187

"Quiet Desperation" (Simpson), **Supp. IX:** 277–278

"Quiet Light, A" (Skloot), **Supp. XX:** 203

"Quiet of the Mind" (Nye), **Supp. XIII:** 284

"QUILLA" (Trethewey), **Supp. XXI:** 246

"Quilting" (D. West), **Supp. XVIII:** 283

Quin, Mike (pseudonym). *See* Ryan, Paul William

Quincy, Edmund, **Supp. XVIII:** 4

Quindlen, Anna, **Supp. XVI:** 108; **Supp. XVII: 165–181**

Quinlan, Kathleen, **Supp. X:** 80

Quinn, Anthony, **Supp. XXI:** 46

Quinn, John, **III:** 471

Quinn, Paul, **Supp. V:** 71

Quinn, Sister M. Bernetta, **III:** 479; **IV:** 421

Quinn, Vincent, **I:** 386, 401, 402; **Supp. I Part 1:** 270

"Quinnapoxet" (Kunitz), **Supp. III Part 1:** 263

Quinn's Book (W. Kennedy), **Supp. VII:** 133, 148–150, 153

Quintero, José, **III:** 403

Quintilian, **IV:** 123

Quinzaine for This Yule, A (Pound), **Retro. Supp. I:** 285

Quite Contrary: The Mary and Newt Story (Dixon), **Supp. XII: 144,** 153

Quod Erat Demonstrandum (Stein), **IV:** 34

Quo Vadis? (Sienkiewicz), **Supp. IV Part 2:** 518; **Supp. XVI:** 182

R

Raab, Max, **Supp. XI:** 309

"Rabbi, The" (Hayden), **Supp. II Part 1:** 363, 369

Rabbit, Run (Updike), **IV:** 214, 223, 230–234; **Retro. Supp. I:** 320, 325, 326, 327, 331, 333, 335; **Supp. XI:** 140; **Supp. XII:** 298; **Supp. XVI:** 220

"Rabbit, The" (Barnes), **Supp. III Part 1:** 34

Rabbit at Rest (Updike), **Retro. Supp. I:** 334

Rabbit Factory, The (L. Brown), **Supp. XXI:** 40, **47–48**

"*Rabbit Factory, The:* Escaping the Isolation of the Cage" (Gaughran), **Supp. XXI:** 47–48

Rabbit Is Rich (Updike), **Retro. Supp. I:** 334

Rabbit novels (Updike), **Supp. V:** 269

Rabbit Redux (Updike), **IV:** 214; **Retro. Supp. I:** 332, 333

Rabbit's Umbrella, The (Plimpton), **Supp. XVI:** 244

"Rabbits Who Caused All the Trouble, The" (Thurber), **Supp. I Part 2:** 610

Rabelais, and His World (Bakhtin), **Retro. Supp. II:** 273

Rabelais, François, **I:** 130; **II:** 111, 112, 302, 535; **III:** 77, 78, 174, 182; **IV:** 68; **Supp. I Part 2:** 461

Rabelais and His World (Bakhtin), **Supp. X:** 120

Rabinbach, Anson, **Supp. XII:** 166

Rabinowitz, Paula, **Supp. V:** 161

"Race" (Emerson), **II:** 6

"Race Contacts and Inter-Racial Relations" (Locke), **Supp. XIV:** 211

"Race Contacts and Inter-Racial Relations: A Study in the Theory and Practice of Race" (lectures, Locke), **Supp. XIV:** 199, 209

Race Contacts and Interracial Relations: Lectures on the Theory and Practice of Race (Locke, Stewart, ed.), **Supp. XIV:** 196, **209–210**

"'RACE LINE' IS A PRODUCT OF CAPITALISM, THE" (Baraka), **Supp. II Part 1:** 61

"Race of Life, The" (Thurber), **Supp. I Part 2:** 614

"Race Problems and Modern Society" (Toomer), **Supp. III Part 2:** 486

Race Questions, Provincialism, and Other American Problems (Royce), **Supp. XIV:** 199

"Race Riot, Tulsa, 1921" (Olds), **Supp. X:** 205

Race Rock (Matthiessen), **Supp. V:** 201

"Races, The" (Lowell), **II:** 554

"Rachel" (D. West), **Supp. XVIII:** 289

Rachel Carson: Witness for Nature (Lear), **Supp. IX:** 19

Rachel River (film, Smolan), **Supp. XVI:** 36

"Racial Progress and Race Adjustment" (Locke), **Supp. XIV:** 210

Racine, Jean Baptiste, **II:** 543, 573; **III:** 145, 151, 152, 160; **IV:** 317, 368, 370; **Supp. I Part 2:** 716

Radcliffe, Ann, **Supp. XX:** 108

"Radical" (Moore), **III:** 211

"Radical Chic" (Wolfe), **Supp. III Part 2:** 577–578, 584, 585

Radical Chic & Mau-mauing the Flak Catchers (Wolfe), **Supp. III Part 2:** 577–578

Radical Empiricism of William James, The (Wild), **II:** 362, 363–364

Radicalism in America, The (Lasch), **I:** 259

"Radical Jewish Humanism: The Vision of E. L. Doctorow" (Clayton), **Supp. IV Part 1:** 238

"Radically Condensed History of Postindustrial Life, A" (Wallace), **Supp. X:** 309

Radical's America, A (Swados), **Supp. XIX: 264–265**

Radinovsky, Lisa, **Supp. XV:** 284, 285

"Radio" (O'Hara), **III:** 369

Radio Days (film; Allen), **Supp. XV:** 9

"Radio Pope" (Goldbarth), **Supp. XII:** 188, 192

Raditzer (Matthiessen), **Supp. V:** 201

Radkin, Paul, **Supp. I Part 2:** 539

"Rafaela Who Drinks Coconut & Papaya Juice on Tuesdays" (Cisneros), **Supp. VII:** 63

Rafelson, Bob, **Supp. XIV:** 241

Raffalovich, Marc-André, **Supp. XIV:** 335

Rafferty, Terence, **Supp. XX:** 87, 92

"Raft, The" (Lindsay), **Supp. I Part 2:** 393

Rag and Bone Shop of the Heart, The: Poems for Men (Bly, Hillman, and Meade, eds.), **Supp. IV Part 1:** 67

Rage in Harlem (C. Himes). *See For Love of Imabelle* (C. Himes)

Rage to Live, A (O'Hara), **III:** 361

Raglan, Lord, **I:** 135

Rago, Henry, **Supp. III Part 2:** 624, 628, 629

Ragtime (Doctorow), **Retro. Supp. II:** 108; **Supp. IV Part 1:** 217, 222–224, 231, 232, 233, 234, 237, 238; **Supp. V:** 45

"Ragtime" (Doctorow), **Supp. IV Part 1:** 234

Ragtime (film), **Supp. IV Part 1:** 236

Ragtime (musical, McNally), **Supp. XIII:** 207

Rahab (W. Frank), **Supp. XX:** 71–72, 76

Rahaim, Liz, **Supp. XVII:** 2

Rahv, Philip, **Retro. Supp. I:** 112; **Supp. II Part 1:** 136; **Supp. VIII:** 96; **Supp. IX:** 8; **Supp. XIV:** 3; **Supp. XV:** 140

"Raid" (Hughes), **Retro. Supp. I:** 208

Raids on the Unspeakable (Merton), **Supp. VIII:** 201, 208

Rail, DeWayne, **Supp. XIII:** 312

"Rain and the Rhinoceros" (Merton), **Supp. VIII:** 201

Rainbow, The (Lawrence), **III:** 27

"Rainbows" (Marquand), **III:** 56

Rainbow Stories, The (Vollmann), **Supp. XVII:** 226, 227, 230, 231, 233

Rainbow Tulip, The (Mora), **Supp. XIII:** 221

"Rain Country" (Haines), **Supp. XII:** 210

"Rain-Dream, A" (Bryant), **Supp. I Part 1:** 164

Raine, Kathleen, **I:** 522, 527

"Rain Falling Now, The" (Dunn), **Supp. XI:** 147

"Rain in the Heart" (Taylor), **Supp. V:** 317, 319

Rain in the Trees, The (Merwin), **Supp. III Part 1:** 340, 342, 345, 349, 354–356

"Rainmaker, The" (Humphrey), **Supp. IX:** 101

Raintree County (Lockridge), **Supp. XIX:** 263

Rainwater, Catherine, **Supp. V:** 272

"Rainy Day" (Longfellow), **II:** 498

"Rainy Day, The" (Buck), **Supp. II Part 1:** 127

"Rainy Mountain Cemetery" (Momaday), **Supp. IV Part 2:** 486

Rainy Mountain Christmas Doll (painting) (Momaday), **Supp. IV Part 2:** 493

"Rainy Season: Sub-Tropics" (Bishop), **Supp. I Part 1:** 93

"Rainy Sunday" (Espaillat), **Supp. XXI:** 106

"Raise High the Roof Beam, Carpenters" (Salinger), **III:** 567–569, 571

Raise High the Roof Beam, Carpenters; and Seymour: An Introduction (Salinger), **III:** 552, 567–571, 572

Raise Race Rays Raze: Essays Since 1965 (Baraka), **Supp. II Part 1:** 47, 52, 55

Raisin (musical), **Supp. IV Part 1:** 374

Raising Demons (Jackson), **Supp. IX:** 125–126

Raisin in the Sun, A (unproduced screenplay) (Hansberry), **Supp. IV Part 1:** 360

Raisin in the Sun, A (film: Columbia Pictures), **Supp. IV Part 1:** 360, 367

Raisin in the Sun, A (Hansberry), **Supp. IV Part 1:** 359, 360, 361, 362–364; **Supp. VIII:** 343

Raisin in the Sun, A (television film: American Playhouse), **Supp. IV Part 1:** 367, 374

Rajan, R., **I:** 390

"Rake, The" (Mamet), **Supp. XIV:** 240

Rake's Progress, The (opera), **Supp. II Part 1:** 24

Rakosi, Carl, **Supp. III Part 2:** 614, 615, 616, 617, 618, 621, 629; **Supp. XIV:** 286, 287

Ralegh, Sir Walter, **Supp. I Part 1:** 98

Raleigh, John Henry, **IV:** 366

Ralph, Brett, **Supp. XVII:** 245

Ramakrishna, Sri, **III:** 567

Ramakrishna and His Disciples (Isherwood), **Supp. XIV:** 164

Ramazani, Jahan, **Supp. IV Part 2:** 450

"Ramble of Aphasia, A" (O. Henry), **Supp. II Part 1:** 410

Ramey, Phillip, **Supp. IV Part 1:** 94

Rampersad, Arnold, **Retro. Supp. I:** 196, 200, 201, 204; **Supp. IV Part 1:** 244, 250

Rampling, Anne, **Supp. VII:** 201. *See also* Rice, Anne

Rampling, Charlotte, **Supp. IX:** 253

Ramsey, Priscilla R., **Supp. IV Part 1:** 15

Ramsey, Roger, **Supp. XVI:** 69

Ramsey, William, **Supp. XVIII:** 66

Ramus, Petrus, **Supp. I Part 1:** 104

Rand, Ayn, **Supp. I Part 1:** 294; **Supp. IV Part 2:** 517–535

Randall, Jarrell, 1914–1965 (Lowell, Taylor, and Warren, eds.), **II:** 368, 385

Randall, John H., **III:** 605

Randolph, John, **I:** 5–6

"Range-Finding" (Frost), **Retro. Supp. I:** 131

Range of the Possible (T. Marshall), **Supp. XVII:** 36

Rangoon (F. Barthelme), **Supp. XI:** 25

Rangus, Eric, **Supp. XXI:** 244, 254

Rank, Otto, **I:** 135; **Supp. IX:** 105; **Supp. X:** 183, 185, 193

Ranke, Leopold von, **Supp. I Part 2:** 492

Rankin, Daniel, **Retro. Supp. II:** 57, 72; **Supp. I Part 1:** 200, 203, 225

Rankin, Tom, **Supp. XXI:** 36

Rankine, Annette, **Supp. XX:** 69

Ranlett, William H., **Supp. XVIII:** 3

Ransohoff, Martin, **Supp. XI:** 305, 306

Ransom, John Crowe, **I:** 265, 301; **II:** 34, 367, 385, 389, 536–537, 542; **III:** 454, **480–502,** 549; **IV:** 121, 122, 123, 124, 125, 127, 134, 140, 141, 236, 237, 433; **Retro. Supp. I:** 90; **Retro. Supp. II:** 176, 177, 178, 183, 220, 228, 246; **Supp. I Part 1:** 80, 361; **Supp. I Part 2:** 423; **Supp. II Part 1:** 90, 91, 136, 137, 139, 318; **Supp. II Part 2:** 639; **Supp. III Part 1:** 318; **Supp. III Part 2:** 542, 591; **Supp. IV Part 1:** 217; **Supp. V:** 315, 331, 337; **Supp. X:** 25, 56, 58; **Supp. XIV:** 1; **Supp. XIX:** 123

"Rape" (Coleman), **Supp. XI:** 89–90

"Rape, The" (Baraka), **Supp. II Part 1:** 40

Rape of Bunny Stuntz, The (Gurney), **Supp. V:** 109

"Rape of Philomel, The" (Shapiro), **Supp. II Part 2:** 720

"Rape of the Lock, The" (Pope), **Supp. XIV:** 8

Rapf, Joanna, **Supp. XVIII:** 251

Raphael, **I:** 15; **III:** 505, 521, 524; **Supp. I Part 1:** 363

"Rapist" (Dunn), **Supp. XI:** 144

Rap on Race, A (Baldwin and Mead), **Supp. I Part 1:** 66

"Rappaccini's Daughter" (Hawthorne), **II:** 229

"Rapture of the Deep" (Hempel), **Supp. XXI:** 123

"Rapunzel" (Sexton), **Supp. II Part 2:** 691

Rare & Endangered Species: A Novella & Short Stories (Bausch), **Supp. VII:** 51, 54

"Raree Show" (MacLeish), **III:** 9

Rascoe, Burton, **III:** 106, 115

Raskin, Jonah, **Supp. XV:** 116

"Raskolnikov" (Simic), **Supp. VIII:** 282

Rasmussen, Douglas, **Supp. IV Part 2:** 528, 530

Rasmussen, Halfdan, **Supp. XVIII:** 180

Rasselas (Johnson), **Supp. XI:** 209

Rathmann, Andrew, **Supp. XV:** 34

"Rat in the Engine" (Espaillat), **Supp. XXI:** 106

"Ration" (Baraka), **Supp. II Part 1:** 50

"Rationale of Verse, The" (Poe), **III:** 427–428; **Retro. Supp. II:** 266

Ratner, Rochelle, **Supp. XV:** 105

Ratner's Star (DeLillo), **Supp. VI:** 1, 2, 3, 4, 10, 12, 14; **Supp. XVIII:** 140

"Rat of Faith, The" (Levine), **Supp. V:** 192

Rattigan, Terence, **III:** 152

Raugh, Joseph, **Supp. I Part 1:** 286

Rauh, Ida, **Supp. XXI:** 6

Rauschenberg, Robert, **Supp. XV:** 187

Rauschenbusch, Walter, **III:** 293; **Supp. I Part 1:** 7

Ravelstein (Bellow), **Retro. Supp. II:** 19, **33–34**

Raven, Simon, **Supp. XII:** 241

Raven, The (film, Friedlander), **Supp. XVII:** 58

"Raven, The" (Poe), **III:** 413, 421–422, 426; **Retro. Supp. II:** 265, 266–267; **Supp. XVII:** 58

Raven, The, and Other Poems (Poe), **III:** 413

Ravenal, Shannon, **Supp. IV Part 1:** 93

"Raven Days, The" (Lanier), **Supp. I Part 1:** 351

Ravenel, Shannon, **Supp. XXI:** 39

Ravenna, Michael. *See* Welty, Eudora

"Ravens at Deer Creek" (Wrigley), **Supp. XVIII:** 299–300, 306

Raven's Road (Gunn Allen), **Supp. IV Part 1:** 330, 335

Raver, Anne, **Supp. XVIII:** 191

"Ravine, The" (Carruth), **Supp. XVI:** 53

Ravits, Martha, **Supp. XXI:** 215

Raw Heaven (Peacock), **Supp. XIX:** 196–197

Rawlings, Marjorie Kinnan, **Supp. X:** 219–237; **Supp. XVIII:** 194–195

Rawlins, C. L., **Supp. XVII:** 72, 73

Ray, David, **Supp. IV Part 1:** 61

Ray, Janisse, **Supp. XVIII:** 189–206

Ray, Jeanne Wilkinson, **Supp. XII:** 308, 310

Ray, John, **II:** 111, 112

Ray, Man, **IV:** 404; **Retro. Supp. I:** 416; **Supp. XII:** 124

Ray, Nicholas, **Supp. XVIII:** 253

Ray Bradbury Theatre, The (television show), **Supp. IV Part 1:** 103

Raymond, Henry J., **Supp. XVIII:** 4

"Raymond and Ann" (Budbill), **Supp. XIX:** 9

"Razor's Edge, The" (Wasserstein), **Supp. XV:** 328

Reactionary Essays on Poetry and Ideas (Tate), **Supp. II Part 1:** 106, 146

Read, Deborah, **II:** 122

Read, Forrest, **III:** 478

Read, Herbert, **I:** 523; **II:** 372–373, 377–378; **Retro. Supp. I:** 54; **Supp. III Part 1:** 273; **Supp. III Part 2:** 624, 626

Read, William A., **Supp. XIV:** 4

Reade, Charles, **Supp. I Part 2:** 580

Reader, Constant. *See* Parker, Dorothy

Reader, Dennis J., **Supp. I Part 2:** 454

"Reader, The" (F. Wright), **Supp. XVII:** 246

Reader's Block (Markson), **Supp. XVII: 143–145,** 146

Reader's Encyclopedia, The: An Encyclopedia of World Literature and the Arts (W. Benét), **Supp. XI:** 44

Reader's Guide to William Gaddis's The Recognitions, A (Moore), **Supp. IV Part 1:** 283

Reader's Map of Arkansas (Wright), **Supp. XV:** 348

"Reader's Tale, A" (Doty), **Supp. XI:** 119, 120, 128, 129

"Reading" (Auden), **Supp. VIII:** 155

"Reading, The" (Di Piero), **Supp. XIX:** 41

"Reading, Writing, Region" (J. W. Miller), **Supp. XX:** 165

"Reading an Anthology of Chinese Poems of the Sung Dynasty, I Pause to Admire the Length and Clarity of Their Titles" (Collins), **Supp. XXI:** 56

"Reading at Forty" (Pickering), **Supp. XXI:** 196

"Reading Group Guide", **Supp. XI:** 244–245

"Reading Lao Tzu Again in the New Year" (Wright), **Supp. V:** 343

"Reading Late of the Death of Keats" (Kenyon), **Supp. VII:** 169

"Reading Myself" (Lowell), **II:** 555

Reading Myself and Others (P. Roth), **Retro. Supp. II:** 282; **Supp. V:** 45

"Reading *Ode to the West Wind* 25 Years Later" (McCarriston), **Supp. XIV:** 271–272

"Reading of the Psalm, The" (Francis), **Supp. IX:** 79

"Reading Ovid" (Di Piero), **Supp. XIX:** 44

"Reading Philosophy at Night" (Simic), **Supp. VIII:** 272

Reading Rilke: Reflections on the Problems of Translation (Gass), **Supp. VI:** 92, **93–94**

"Reading Rorty and Paul Celan One Morning in Early June" (Wright), **Supp. V:** 343

"Reading Sarcophagi: An Essay" (Sobin), **Supp. XVI:** 290

"Readings of History" (Rich), **Supp. I Part 2:** 554

"Reading the Signs, Empowering the Eye" (Bambara), **Supp. XI:** 17–18

Reading the Spirit (Eberhart), **I:** 525, 527, 530

Ready, Richard M., **Supp. XIX:** 154

"Ready Or Not" (Baraka), **Supp. II Part 1:** 50

Reagan, Ronald, **Supp. IV Part 1:** 224–225

"Real Bowery, The" (Hapgood), **Supp. XVII:** 103

"Real Class" (Vidal), **Supp. IV Part 1:** 35

Real Cool Killers, The (C. Himes), **Supp. XVI:** 143

Real Dope, The (Lardner), **II:** 422–423

"Real Estate" (Moore), **Supp. X:** 178

"Real Gone Guy, A" (McGrath), **Supp. X:** 117

"Real Horatio Alger Story, The" (Cowley), **Supp. II Part 1:** 143

"Realities" (MacLeish), **III:** 4

"Reality in America" (Trilling), **Supp. III Part 2:** 495, 502

"Reality! Reality! What Is It?" (Eberhart), **I:** 536

Reality Sandwiches, 1953–60 (Ginsberg), **Supp. II Part 1:** 315, 320

"Reality U.S.A." (Halliday), **Supp. XIX:** 89

Real Life of Sebastian Knight, The (Nabokov), **III:** 246; **Retro. Supp. I:** 266, 269, 270, 274

"Really Good Jazz Piano, A" (Yates), **Supp. XI:** 342

"Real Movie, with Stars, The" (Hull), **Supp. XXI:** 136

Real Presence: A Novel (Bausch), **Supp. VII:** 42–43, 50

"Real Revolution Is Love, The" (Harjo), **Supp. XII:** 224, 225–226

"Real Surrounding, The: On Canaletto's Venice" (Bronk), **Supp. XXI:** 32

"Real Thing, The" (H. James), **Retro. Supp. I:** 228; **Retro. Supp. II:** 223

"Real Two-Party System" (Vidal), **Supp. IV Part 2:** 679

Real West Marginal Way, The (Hugo), **Supp. VI:** 132, 134; **Supp. XVIII:** 299

"Real World around Us, The" (Carson), **Supp. IX:** 21

Reaper Essays, The (Jarman and McDowell), **Supp. IX:** 270; **Supp. XVII:** 110–111

"*Reaper* Interviews Jean Doh and Sean Dough, The" (Jarman and McDowell), **Supp. XVII:** 110

"Reapers" (Toomer), **Supp. III Part 2:** 481; **Supp. IX:** 312

"Reason and Race: A Review of the Literature of the Negro for 1946" (Locke), **Supp. XIV:** 206

"Reason for Moving, A" (Strand), **Supp. IV Part 2:** 624

"Reason for Stories, The: Toward a Moral Fiction" (Stone), **Supp. V:** 298, 300

Reasons for Moving (Strand), **Supp. IV Part 2:** 624–626, 626

"Reasons for Music" (MacLeish), **III:** 19

"Reasons of the Body" (Sanders), **Supp. XVI:** 274

Reasons to Live (Hempel), **Supp. XXI:** 115, 117, 118, **119–122**

Rebecca (du Maurier), **Supp. XIX:** 57–58

Rebecca, or, The Fille de Chambre (Rowson), **Supp. XV:** 229, **235–236,** 238

Rebecca Harding Davis Reader, A (Pfaelzer, ed.), **Supp. XVI:** 88, 90

Rebel Angels: Twenty-five Poets of the New Formalism (Jarman and Mason, eds.), **Supp. XV:** 251; **Supp. XVII:** 109, 110, 112, 121

"Rebellion" (Lowell), **Retro. Supp. II:** 187

Rebel Powers (Bausch), **Supp. VII:** 41, 45–46, 49–51

Rebel without a Cause (film), **Supp. XII:** 9

"Rebirth" (McKnight), **Supp. XX:** 147, 157

"Rebirth of God and the Death of Man, The " (Fiedler), **Supp. XIII:** 108

Rebolledo, Tey Diana, **Supp. XIII:** 214

Recapitulation (Stegner), **Supp. IV Part 2:** 598, 600, 612–613

"Recapitulation, The" (Eberhart), **I:** 522

"Recapitulations" (Shapiro), **Supp. II Part 2:** 701, 702, 708, 710–711

"Receding Horizons" (Lethem and Scholtz), **Supp. XVIII:** 145

"Recencies in Poetry" (Zukofsky), **Supp. III Part 2:** 615

Recent Killing, A (Baraka), **Supp. II Part 1:** 55

"Recent Negro Fiction" (Ellison), **Supp. II Part 1:** 233, 235

"Recessional" (A. Finch), **Supp. XVII:** 70–71

"Recital, The" (Ashbery), **Supp. III Part 1:** 14

"Recitative" (H. Crane), **I:** 390; **Retro. Supp. II:** 78

Reckless Eyeballing (Reed), **Supp. X:** 241

Recognitions, The (Gaddis), **Supp. IV Part 1:** 279, 280–285, 286, 287, 288, 289, 291, 292, 294; **Supp. XX:** 91

"Recollection and Perhaps a Tribute, A" (Espaillat), **Supp. XXI:** 103–104

Recollections (R. H. Stoddard), **Supp. XV:** 271

Recollections of Logan Pearsall Smith: The Story of a Friendship (Gathorne-Hardy), **Supp. XIV:** 344

"Reconciliation" (Whitman), **IV:** 347

"Reconstructed but Unregenerate" (Ransom), **III:** 496

"Reconstruction and Its Benefits" (Du Bois), **Supp. II Part 1:** 171

Recovering (Sarton), **Supp. VIII:** 264

Recovering the U.S. Hispanic Literary Heritage (Paredes), **Supp. XIII:** 320

"Recovery" (Dove), **Supp. IV Part 1:** 248

Rector of Justin, The (Auchincloss), **Supp. IV Part 1:** 21, 23, 27–30, 36

"Recurrent Dream" (Nelson), **Supp. XVIII:** 176

"RED AUTUMN" (Baraka), **Supp. II Part 1:** 55

Red Badge of Courage, The (S. Crane), **I:** 201, 207, 212, 405, 406, 407, 408, 412–416, 419, 421, 422, 423, 477, 506; **II:** 264; **III:** 317; **IV:** 350; **Retro.**

Supp. II: 108; **Supp. IV Part 1:** 380; **Supp. XIV:** 51; **Supp. XVII:** 228; **Supp. XVIII:** 75; **Supp. XXI:** 277

"Redbirds" (C. Frost), **Supp. XV:** 99

"Red Bow, The" (Saunders), **Supp. XIX:** 232–233, 234

"Redbreast in Tampa" (Lanier), **Supp. I Part 1:** 364

"Red Brocade" (Nye), **Supp. XIII:** 288

Redburn: His First Voyage (Melville), **III:** 79–80, 84; **Retro. Supp. I:** 245, 247–248, 249; **Supp. XVIII:** 6

"Red Carpet for Shelley, A" (Wylie), **Supp. I Part 2:** 724

Red Channels (Harnett), **Supp. XV:** 198

"Red Clowns" (Cisneros), **Supp. VII:** 63

Red Coal, The (Stern), **Supp. IX:** 291–**292**

Red Coat, The (Shanley), **Supp. XIV:** 316–317

"Red Cords" (Lamott), **Supp. XX:** 142

"Red Cross" (Hughes), **Retro. Supp. I:** 205

Red Cross (Shepard), **Supp. III Part 2:** 440, 446

Red Death, A (Mosley), **Supp. XIII:** 237, 239, 240

"Red Deer" (C. Frost), **Supp. XV:** 101

Redding, Josephine, **Supp. XXI:** 2

Redding, Saunders, **Supp. I Part 1:** 332, 333

Reddings, J. Saunders, **Supp. IV Part 1:** 164

Red Dust (Levine), **Supp. V:** 178, 183–184, 188

"Red Dust" (Levine), **Supp. V:** 184

"Redemption" (Gardner), **Supp. VI:** 72

Redemption (Uris), **Supp. XX:** 244, 246, 247, 248, 254, **255**

"Redeployment" (Nemerov), **III:** 267, 272

Redfield, Robert, **IV:** 475

Redford, Robert, **Supp. IX:** 253, 259; **Supp. XIII:** 267; **Supp. XIV:** 223

Redgrave, Lynn, **Supp. V:** 107

Red Harvest (Hammett), **Supp. IV Part 1:** 346–348, 348; **Supp. IV Part 2:** 468; **Supp. XXI:** 272

Red-Headed Woman (film), **Retro. Supp. I:** 110; **Supp. XVI:** 191

"Red Horse Wind over Albuquerque" (Harjo), **Supp. XII:** 219

Red Hot Vacuum, The (Solotaroff), **Retro. Supp. II:** 281

Rediscovery of America, The (W. Frank), **Supp. XX:** 75

Rediscovery of Man, The (W. Frank), **Supp. XX:** 67–68, 80

"Red Leaves" (Faulkner), **II:** 72

"Red Meat: What Difference Did Stesichoros Make?" (Carson), **Supp. XII:** 107

"Red Pawn" (Rand), **Supp. IV Part 2:** 520

Red Pony, The (Steinbeck), **IV:** 50, 51, 58, 70

Redrawing the Boundaries (Fisher), **Retro. Supp. I:** 39

Red Robins, The (Koch), **Supp. XV:** 185–186, 187

Red Roses for Bronze (Doolittle), **Supp. I Part 1:** 253, 268, 271

Red Rover, The (Cooper), **I:** 342–343, 355

"Red Silk Stockings" (Hughes), **Retro. Supp. I:** 200

Redskins, The (Cooper), **I:** 351, 353

"Red Star, Winter Orbit" (W. Gibson and B. Sterling), **Supp. XVI:** 123

Red Suitcase (Nye), **Supp. XIII:** 277, 278, 287

Red the Fiend (Sorrentino), **Supp. XXI:** 227, 231, 237

Red Wallflower, A (S. Warner), **Supp. XVIII:** 260

"Red Wheelbarrow, The" (W. C. Williams), **IV:** 411–412; **Retro. Supp. I:** 419, 430

"Red Wind" (Chandler), **Supp. IV Part 1:** 122

"Red Wing Church, The" (Kooser), **Supp. XIX:** 119

"Redwings" (Wright), **Supp. III Part 2:** 603

Reed, Edward Bliss, **Supp. XV:** 297, 298, 300

Reed, Ishmael, **Retro. Supp. II:** 111, 324–325; **Supp. II Part 1:** 34; **Supp. X:** 239–**257**, 331; **Supp. XIII:** 181, 182; **Supp. XVI:** 143; **Supp. XX:** 107

Reed, J. D., **Supp. XVI:** 174

Reed, John, **I:** 48, 476, 483; **Supp. X:** 136; **Supp. XV:** 295, 299; **Supp. XVII:** 96, 99, 100; **Supp. XVIII:** 225; **Supp. XXI:** 6, 12

Reed, Lou, **Retro. Supp. II:** 266

"Reedbeds of the Hackensack, The" (Clampitt), **Supp. IX:** 41

"Reed of Pan, A" (McCullers), **II:** 585

Reedy, Billy, **Retro. Supp. II:** 65, 67, 71, 73

Reedy, William Marion, **Supp. I Part 2:** 456, 461, 465

Reef, The (Wharton), **IV:** 317–318, 322; **Retro. Supp. I:** 372, **373–374**

Reena and Other Stories (Marshall), **Supp. XI:** 275, 277, 278

"Reese in Evening Shadow" (Skloot), **Supp. XX:** 204

Reeve, F. D., **Supp. XV:** 344, 349

Reeve's Tale (Chaucer), **I:** 131

"Reflection from Anita Loos" (Empson), **Supp. XVI:** 190

"Reflections" (Carruth), **Supp. XVI:** 54

"Reflections" (Komunyakaa), **Supp. XIII:** 117

Reflections at Fifty and Other Essays (Farrell), **II:** 49

"Reflections by a Fire" (Sarton), **Supp. VIII:** 259

Reflections in a Golden Eye (McCullers), **II:** 586, 588, 593–596, 604; **IV:** 384, 396

Reflections of a Jacobite (Auchincloss), **Supp. IV Part 1:** 31

Reflections on a Gift of Watermelon Pickle (Dunning), **Supp. XIV:** 126

Reflections on Poetry and Poetics (Nemerov), **III:** 269

"Reflections on the Constitution of Nature" (Freneau), **Supp. II Part 1:** 274

"Reflections on the Death of the Reader" (Morris), **III:** 237

Reflections on the End of an Era (Niebuhr), **III:** 297–298

"Reflections on the Life and Death of Lord Clive" (Paine), **Supp. I Part 2:** 505

Reflections on the Revolution in France (Burke), **Supp. I Part 2:** 511, 512

Reflections: Thinking Part I (Arendt), **Supp. I Part 2:** 570

"Reflex Action and Theism" (James), **II:** 345, 363

"Refrains/Remains/Reminders" (Goldbarth), **Supp. XII:** 180–181, 181

"Refuge" (Kingsolver), **Supp. VII:** 208

"Refuge, A" (Goldbarth), **Supp. XII:** 190

Refugee Children: Theory, Research, and Services (Ahearn and Athey, eds.), **Supp. XI:** 184

"Refugees, The" (Jarrell), **II:** 371

"Refusal" (C. Frost), **Supp. XV:** 102

"Refusal to Publish Fifth Book" (Halliday), **Supp. XIX:** 94

Regarding Wave (Snyder), **Supp. VIII:** 299–**300**

Regina (Epstein), **Supp. XII:** 170–**171**

"Regional Literature of the South" (Rawlings), **Supp. X:** 228

"Regional Writer, The" (O'Connor), **Retro. Supp. II:** 223, 225

Régnier, Henri de, **II:** 528–529

Regulators, The (King), **Supp. V:** 141

Rehder, Robert, **Supp. IV Part 1:** 69

Rehearsing Absence (Espaillat), **Supp. XXI:** 99

Reich, Tova, **Supp. XVI:** 158

Reichel, Hans, **III:** 183

Reichl, Ruth, **Supp. X:** 79, 85

Reid, B. L., **II:** 41, 47

Reid, Forrest, **Supp. XX:** 235

Reid, Thomas, **II:** 9; **Supp. I Part 1:** 151

Reign of Snakes (Wrigley), **Supp. XVIII:** 293, **302–306**

"Reign of Snakes" (Wrigley), **Supp. XVIII:** 302–304

Reign of Wonder, The (Tanner), **I:** 260

Rein, Yevgeny, **Supp. VIII:** 22

Reinagle, Alexander, **Supp. XV:** 238, 240

"Reincarnation" (Dickey), **Supp. IV Part 1:** 181–182

Reine des pommes, La (C. Himes). *See For Love of Imabelle* (C. Himes)

Reiner, Carl, **Supp. IV Part 2:** 591

Reinfeld, Linda, **Supp. IV Part 2:** 421

Reinhardt, Max, **Supp. XV:** 307

Reinventing the Enemy's Language: Contemporary Native Women's Writing of North America (Bird and Harjo, eds.), **Supp. XII:** 216, 217

Reisman, Jerry, **Supp. III Part 2:** 618

Reiter, Amy, **Supp. XIX:** 54, 56

Reitlinger, Gerald, **Supp. XII:** 161

Reivers, The: A Reminiscence (Faulkner), **I:** 305; **II:** 57, 73; **Retro. Supp. I:** 74, 82, 91

"Rejoicings" (Stern), **Supp. IX:** 289–290

Rejoicings: Selected Poems, 1966–1972 (Stern), **Supp. IX: 289–290**
Relation of My Imprisonment, The (Banks), **Supp. V:** 8, 12–13
"Relations between Poetry and Painting, The" (Stevens), **Retro. Supp. I:** 312
Relations of the Alabama-Georgia Dialect to the Provincial Dialects of Great Britain, The (Brooks), **Supp. XIV:** 3
Relative Stranger, A (C. Baxter), **Supp. XVII:** 19, 22
"Relativity of Beauty, The" (Rawlings), **Supp. X:** 226
Relearning the Alphabet (Levertov), **Supp. III Part 1:** 280, 281
"Release" (C. Baxter), **Supp. XVII:** 15
"Release, The" (MacLeish), **III:** 16
Reles, Abe ("Kid Twist"), **Supp. IV Part 1:** 382
"Relevance of an Impossible Ethical Ideal, The" (Niebuhr), **III:** 298
"Religion" (Dunbar), **Supp. II Part 1:** 199
"Religion" (Emerson), **II:** 6
Religion of Nature Delineated, The (Wollaston), **II:** 108
"Religious Instruction" (Peacock), **Supp. XIX:** 200, 201
Religious Rebel, A: The Letters of "H. W. S." (Mrs. Pearsall Smith) (L. P. Smith), **Supp. XIV:** 349
"Reluctance" (Frost), **II:** 153
Reluctantly: Autobiographical Essays (Carruth), **Supp. XVI:** 45–46, 50
Remains (Snodgrass), **Supp. VI:** 311, **313–314**
"Remains, The" (Strand), **Supp. IV Part 2:** 627
"Remarks on Color" (Wright), **Supp. XV:** 346
"Remarks on Spencer's *Definition of Mind as Correspondence*" (James), **II:** 345
Remarque, Erich Maria, **Retro. Supp. I:** 113; **Supp. IV Part 1:** 380
Rembrandt, **II:** 536; **IV:** 310; **Supp. IV Part 1:** 390, 391
"Rembrandt, The" (Wharton), **IV:** 310
"Rembrandt's Hat" (Malamud), **Supp. I Part 2:** 435, 437
Rembrandt Takes a Walk (Strand), **Supp. IV Part 2:** 631
"Rembrandt to Rembrandt" (Robinson), **III:** 521–522
Remembered Earth, The: An Anthology of Contemporary Native American Literature (Hobson, ed.), **Supp. IV Part 1:** 321
Remembered Yesterdays (Johnson), **Supp. IX:** 184
"Remembering" (Angelou), **Supp. IV Part 1:** 15
"Remembering Allen Tate" (Cowley), **Supp. II Part 1:** 153
"Remembering Barthes" (Sontag), **Supp. III Part 2:** 451, 471
"Remembering Guston" (Kunitz), **Supp. III Part 1:** 257
"Remembering James Laughlin" (Karr), **Supp. XI:** 242

Remembering Laughter (Stegner), **Supp. IV Part 2:** 598, 606, 607, 608, 611, 614
"Remembering Lobo" (Mora), **Supp. XIII:** 220, 227
"Remembering My Father" (Berry), **Supp. X:** 23
"Remembering My Parents Remembering the Books They Read" (Espaillat), **Supp. XXI:** 107
"Remembering that Island" (McGrath), **Supp. X:** 116
"Remembering the Children of Auschwitz" (McGrath), **Supp. X:** 127
"Remembering the Lost World" (Jarrell), **II:** 388
"Remembering the Sixties" (Simpson), **Supp. IX:** 279
Remember Me to Tom (T. Williams), **IV:** 379–380
"Remember the Moon Survives" (Kingsolver), **Supp. VII:** 209
Remember to Remember (H. Miller), **III:** 186
"Remembrance, A" (Gioia), **Supp. XV:** 112
Remembrance of Things Past (Proust), **Supp. IV Part 2:** 600; **Supp. XII:** 9; **Supp. XIII:** 44
Remembrance Rock (Sandburg), **III:** 590
Reminiscence, A (Ashbery), **Supp. III Part 1:** 2
Remnick, David, **Supp. XVI:** 246
"Remora" (Merrill), **Supp. III Part 1:** 326
"Removal" (White), **Supp. I Part 2:** 664–665
"Removal, The" (Merwin), **Supp. III Part 1:** 350, 351
"Removal Service Request" (Halliday), **Supp. XIX:** 90
Removed from Time (Matthews and Feeney), **Supp. IX:** 154
Remsen, Ira, **Supp. I Part 1:** 369
"Rémy de Gourmont, A Distinction" (Pound), **III:** 467
Renaissance (Carruth), **Supp. XVI:** 56
Renaissance in the South (Bradbury), **I:** 288–289
Renaldo and Clara (film, Dylan and Shepard), **Supp. XVIII:** 21, 28, 31
"Renaming the Kings" (Levine), **Supp. V:** 184
Renan, Ernest, **Supp. XX:** 122
Renan, Joseph Ernest, **II:** 86; **IV:** 440, 444
Renard, Jules, **IV:** 79
"Renascence" (Millay), **III:** 123, 125–126, 128; **Supp. XV:** 42
Renault, Mary, **Supp. IV Part 2:** 685
"Rendezvous, The" (Kumin), **Supp. IV Part 2:** 455
René, Norman, **Supp. X:** 146, 152
Renée (anonymous author), **Supp. XVI:** 64, 66
"Renegade, The" (Jackson), **Supp. IX:** 120
Renewal of Life series (Mumford), **Supp. II Part 2:** 476, 479, 481, 482, 485, 495, 497

Renoir, Jean, **Supp. XII:** 259
Renouvrier, Charles, **II:** 344–345, 346
"Renunciation" (Banks), **Supp. V:** 10
Renza, Louis A., **Retro. Supp. II:** 142
"Repair" (Peacock), **Supp. XIX:** 204
"Repeating Dream" (Gander), **Supp. XV:** 340
Repent in Haste (Marquand), **III:** 59
Reperusals and Re-Collections (L. P. Smith), **Supp. XIV:** 346–347
"Repetitive Heart, The: Eleven Poems in Imitation of the Fugue Form" (Schwartz), **Supp. II Part 2:** 645–646
"Replacing Regionalism" (Murphy), **Retro. Supp. II:** 143
Replansky, Naomi, **Supp. X:** 119
"Reply to Mr. Wordsworth" (MacLeish), **III:** 19
"Report, A" (Jin), **Supp. XVIII:** 93
"Report from a Forest Logged by the Weyhaeuser Company" (Wagoner), **Supp. IX:** 328
"Report from North Vietnam" (Paley), **Supp. VI:** 227
Report from Part One (Brooks), **Supp. III Part 1:** 70, 72, 80, 82–85
Report from Part Two (Brooks), **Supp. III Part 1:** 87
Report on a Game Survey of the North Central States (Leopold), **Supp. XIV:** 182
"Report on the Barnhouse Effect" (Vonnegut), **Supp. II Part 2:** 756
"Report to an Academy, A" (Kafka), **Supp. XX:** 18
"Report to Crazy Horse" (Stafford), **Supp. XI: 324–325**
"Repose of Rivers" (H. Crane), **I:** 393; **Retro. Supp. II:** 78, 81
"Repossession of a Heritage, The" (Zagarell), **Supp. XV:** 270, 281
"Representation and the War for Reality" (Gass), **Supp. VI:** 88
Representative Men (Emerson), **II:** 1, 5–6, 8
"Representing Far Places" (Stafford), **Supp. XI:** 321
Repression and Recovery (Nelson), **Supp. XVIII:** 226
"REPRISE OF ONE OF A. G.'S BEST POEMS" (Baraka), **Supp. II Part 1:** 59
"Reproducing Ourselves Is All Very Well" (E. Hoffman), **Supp. XVI:** 155
Republic (Plato), **I:** 485
"Republican Manifesto, A" (Paine), **Supp. I Part 2:** 511
Republic of Love, The (Shields), **Supp. VII:** 323–324, 326, 327
"Requa" (Olsen), **Supp. XIII:** 294, **302–303,** 304
Requa, Kenneth A., **Supp. I Part 1:** 107
"Requa I" (Olsen). *See* "Requa" (Olsen)
"Request for Offering" (Eberhart), **I:** 526
"Requiem" (Akhmatova), **Supp. VIII:** 20
"Requiem" (LaBastille), **Supp. X:** 105
Requiem for a Nun (Faulkner), **II:** 57, 72–73
Requiem for Harlem (H. Roth), **Supp. IX:** 235, 236, **240–242**

"Rescue, The" (Updike), **IV:** 214
Rescued Year, The (Stafford), **Supp. XI: 321–322**
"Rescued Year, The" (Stafford), **Supp. XI:** 322, 323
"Rescue with Yul Brynner" (Moore), **III:** 215
"Resemblance" (Bishop), **Supp. I Part 1:** 86
"Resemblance between a Violin Case and a Coffin, A" (T. Williams), **IV:** 378–379
"Reservations" (Taylor), **Supp. V:** 323
"Reserved Memorials" (Mather), **Supp. II Part 2:** 446, 449
"Resignación" (Espaillat), **Supp. XXI:** 104
"Resistance to Civil Government" (Thoreau), **Supp. X:** 27, 28
Resist Much, Obey Little (Berry), **Supp. XIII:** 2
Resolution (Parker), **Supp. XIX:** 187
"Resolution and Independence" (Wordsworth), **Supp. XV:** 346
Resources of Hope (R. Williams), **Supp. IX:** 146
"Respectable Place, A" (O'Hara), **III:** 369
"Respectable Woman, A" (Chopin), **Retro. Supp. II:** 66
"Respite" (Pedersen; Nelson, trans.), **Supp. XVIII:** 180
Responses (Wilbur), **Supp. III Part 2:** 541
"Response to a Rumor that the Oldest Whorehouse in Wheeling, West Virginia, Has Been Condemned" (Wright), **Supp. III Part 2:** 602
Restif de La Bretonne, Nicolas, **III:** 175
"Rest of Life, The" (Gordon), **Supp. IV Part 1:** 311
Rest of Life, The: Three Novellas (Gordon), **Supp. IV Part 1:** 310–312
Rest of the Way, The (McClatchy), **Supp. XII:** 255, **258–259**
Restoration comedy, **Supp. I Part 2:** 617
Restorers, The (Di Piero), **Supp. XIX:** 42–43, 44
"Restorers, The" (Di Piero), **Supp. XIX:** 43
"Restraint" (F. Barthelme), **Supp. XI:** 26
"Result" (Emerson), **II:** 6
"Résumé" (Parker), **Supp. IX:** 189
Resurrection (Della Francesca), **Supp. XV:** 262
"Resurrection" (Harjo), **Supp. XII:** 224
"Resurrection" (Jin), **Supp. XVIII:** 94–95
Resurrection, The (Gardner), **Supp. VI:** 61, 63, **64–65**, 68, 69, 73, 74
"Retort" (Hay), **Supp. XIV:** 133
Retour amont (Char; Sobin, trans.), **Supp. XVI:** 282
Retrieval System, The (Kumin), **Supp. IV Part 2:** 449, 451, 452
"Retrievers in Translation" (Doty), **Supp. XI:** 132
"Retroduction to American History" (Tate), **IV:** 129
"Retrospects and Prospects" (Lanier), **Supp. I Part 1:** 352

"Return" (Corso), **Supp. XII:** 135
"Return" (Creeley), **Supp. IV Part 1:** 141, 145
"Return" (MacLeish), **III:** 12
"Return, The" (Bidart), **Supp. XV:** 32–33
"Return, The" (Pound), **Retro. Supp. I:** 288
"Return, The" (Ray), **Supp. XVIII:** 194
"Return, The" (Roethke), **III:** 533
"Return, The: Orihuela, 1965" (Levine), **Supp. V:** 194
"Return: An Elegy, The" (Warren), **IV:** 239
"Return: Buffalo" (Hogan), **Supp. IV Part 1:** 411
"Returning" (Komunyakaa), **Supp. XIII:** 122
"Returning a Lost Child" (Glück), **Supp. V:** 81
"Returning from the Enemy" (Harjo), **Supp. XII:** 229–230
"Returning the Borrowed Road" (Komunyakaa), **Supp. XIII:** 113, 133
"Return of Alcibiade, The" (Chopin), **Retro. Supp. II:** 58, 64
Return of Ansel Gibbs, The (Buechner), **III:** 310; **Supp. XII:** 48
"Return of Eros to Academe, The" (Bukiet), **Supp. XVII:** 47
"Return of Spring" (Winters), **Supp. II Part 2:** 791
Return of the Native, The (Hardy), **II:** 184–185, 186
Return of the Vanishing American, The (Fiedler), **Supp. XIII:** 103
Return to a Place Lit by a Glass of Milk (Simic), **Supp. VIII:** 274, 276, 283
"Return to Lavinia" (Caldwell), **I:** 310
"Return to Thin Air: The Everest Disaster Ten Years Later" *(Outside)*, **Supp. XVIII:** 113
Reuben (Wideman), **Supp. X:** 320
Reuben and Rachel; or, Tales of Old Times (Rowson), **Supp. XV: 240–241**
Reunion (Mamet), **Supp. XIV:** 240, 247, 254
"Reunion in Brooklyn" (H. Miller), **III:** 175, 184
Reuther brothers, **I:** 493
"Reveille" (Kingsolver), **Supp. VII:** 208
"Reveille" (Untermeyer), **Supp. XV:** 300
"Reveille, The" (Harte), **Supp. II Part 1:** 342–343
Revelation (biblical book), **II:** 541; **IV:** 104, 153, 154; **Supp. I Part 1:** 105, 273
"Revelation" (O'Connor), **III:** 349, 353–354; **Retro. Supp. II:** 237
"Revelation" (Warren), **III:** 490
Revenge (Harrison), **Supp. VIII:** 39, 45
"Revenge of Hamish, The" (Lanier), **Supp. I Part 1:** 365
"Revenge of Hannah Kemhuff, The" (Walker), **Supp. III Part 2:** 521
"Revenge of Rain-in-the-Face, The" (Longfellow), **Retro. Supp. II:** 170
Reverberator, The (James), **Retro. Supp. I:** 227
"Reverdure" (Berry), **Supp. X:** 22
Reverdy, Pierre, **Supp. XV:** 178, 182

"Reverend Father Gilhooley" (Farrell), **II:** 45
Reverse Transcription (Kushner), **Supp. IX:** 138
Reversible Errors (Turow), **Supp. XVII: 220–221**
"Rev. Freemont Deadman" (Masters), **Supp. I Part 2:** 463
Reviewer's ABC, A (Aiken), **I:** 58
Review of Contemporary Fiction, 1990 (Tabbi, ed.), **Supp. XVII:** 143
"Revolt, against the Crepuscular Spirit in Modern Poetry" (Pound), **Retro. Supp. I:** 286
"Revolution" (C. L. R. James), **Supp. XXI:** 160
"Revolutionary Answer to the Negro Problem in the USA, The" (statement, C. L. R. James), **Supp. XXI:** 169
Revolutionary Petunias (Walker), **Supp. III Part 2:** 520, 522, 530
Revolutionary Road (Yates), **Supp. XI:** 334, **335–340**
"Revolutionary Symbolism in America" (Burke), **I:** 272
"Revolutionary Theatre, The" (Baraka), **Supp. II Part 1:** 42
Revolution in Taste, A: Studies of Dylan Thomas, Allen Ginsberg, Sylvia Plath, and Robert Lowell (Simpson), **Supp. IX:** 276
"Revolution in the Revolution in the Revolution" (Snyder), **Supp. VIII:** 300
Revon, Marcel, **II:** 525
"Rewaking, The" (W. C. Williams), **Retro. Supp. I:** 430
"Rewrite" (Dunn), **Supp. XI:** 147
Rexroth, Kenneth, **II:** 526; **Supp. II Part 1:** 307; **Supp. II Part 2:** 436; **Supp. III Part 2:** 625, 626; **Supp. IV Part 1:** 145–146; **Supp. VIII:** 289; **Supp. XIII:** 75; **Supp. XIV:** 287; **Supp. XV:** 140, 141, 146
Reynolds, Ann (pseudonym). *See* Bly, Carol
Reynolds, Clay, **Supp. XI:** 254
Reynolds, David, **Supp. XV:** 269
Reynolds, Sir Joshua, **Supp. I Part 2:** 716
Reynolds, Quentin, **IV:** 286
Reza, Yasmina, **Supp. XXI:** 148
Reznikoff, Charles, **IV:** 415; **Retro. Supp. I:** 422; **Supp. III Part 2:** 615, 616, 617, 628; **Supp. XIV: 277–296**
"Rhapsodist, The" (Brown), **Supp. I Part 1:** 125–126
"Rhapsody on a Windy Night" (Eliot), **Retro. Supp. I:** 55
Rhetoric of Motives, A (Burke), **I:** 272, 275, 278, 279
Rhetoric of Religion, The (Burke), **I:** 275, 279
"Rhobert" (Toomer), **Supp. IX:** 316–317
"Rhode Show" (Mallon), **Supp. XIX:** 137–138
"Rhododendrons" (Levis), **Supp. XI:** 260, 263
Rhubarb Show, The (radio, Keillor), **Supp. XVI:** 178

"Rhyme of Sir Christopher, The" (Longfellow), **II:** 501
Rhymes to Be Traded for Bread (Lindsay), **Supp. I Part 2:** 380, 381–382
Rhys, Ernest, **III:** 458
Rhys, Jean, **Supp. III Part 1:** 42, 43; **Supp. XVIII:** 131
"Rhythm & Blues" (Baraka), **Supp. II Part 1:** 37–38
Rhythms (Reznikoff), **Supp. XIV:** 279, 282, 283
Rhythms II (Reznikoff), **Supp. XIV:** 282, 283, 284
Ribalow, Harold, **Supp. IX:** 236
Ribbentrop, Joachim von, **IV:** 249
Ribicoff, Abraham, **Supp. IX:** 33
Ribot, Théodule Armand, **Supp. XX:**238
Ricardo, David, **Supp. I Part 2:** 628, 634
Rice, Allen Thorndike, **Retro. Supp. I:** 362
Rice, Anne, **Supp. VII: 287–306**
Rice, Elmer, **I:** 479; **III:** 145, 160–161
Rice, Mrs. Grantland, **II:** 435
Rice, Philip Blair, **IV:** 141
Rice, Stan, **Supp. XII:** 2
Rice, Tim, **Supp. XXI:** 148
Rice, Tom, **Supp. XIV:** 125
Rich, Adrienne, **Retro. Supp. I:** 8, 36, 42, 47, 404; **Retro. Supp. II:** 43, 191, 245; **Supp. I Part 2:** 546–547, **550–578; Supp. III Part 1:** 84, 354; **Supp. III Part 2:** 541, 599; **Supp. IV Part 1:** 257, 325; **Supp. V:** 82; **Supp. VIII:** 272; **Supp. XII:** 217, 229, 255; **Supp. XIII:** 294; **Supp. XIV:** 126, 129; **Supp. XV:** 176, 252; **Supp. XVII:** 32, 74; **Supp. XIX:** 83, 193
Rich, Arnold, **Supp. I Part 2:** 552
Rich, Frank, **Supp. IV Part 2:** 585, 586; **Supp. V:** 106; **Supp. XXI:** 146
Richard, Mark, **Supp. XIX: 209–222**
Richard Cory (Gurney), **Supp. V:** 99–100, 105
"Richard Hunt's 'Arachne' " (Hayden), **Supp. II Part 1:** 374
Richard II (Shakespeare), **Supp. XVII:** 244
Richard III (Shakespeare), **Supp. I Part 2:** 422
Richards, Bertrand F., **Supp. XX:**217–218
Richards, David, **Supp. IV Part 2:** 576
Richards, Grant, **I:** 515
Richards, I. A., **I:** 26, 273–274, 279, 522; **III:** 498; **IV:** 92; **Supp. I Part 1:** 264, 265; **Supp. I Part 2:** 647
Richards, Ivor Armonstrong, **Supp. XIV:** 2–3, 16
Richards, Laura E., **II:** 396; **III:** 505–506, 507
Richards, Leonard, **Supp. XIV:** 48
Richards, Lloyd, **Supp. IV Part 1:** 362; **Supp. VIII:** 331
Richards, Rosalind, **III:** 506
Richards, Tad, **Supp. XVII:** 77
Richardson, Alan, **III:** 295
Richardson, Charles, **Supp. XVIII:** 14, 15
Richardson, Dorothy, **I:** 53; **II:** 320; **Supp. III Part 1:** 65

Richardson, Helen Patges, **Retro. Supp. II:** 95
Richardson, Henry Hobson, **I:** 3, 10
Richardson, Maurice, **Supp. XII:** 241
Richardson, Samuel, **I:** 134; **II:** 104, 111, 322; **Supp. V:** 127; **Supp. IX:** 128; **Supp. XV:** 232; **Supp. XX:**236
Richardson, Tony, **Supp. XI:** 305, 306
"Richard Wright and Recent Negro Fiction" (Ellison), **Retro. Supp. II:** 116
"Richard Wright's Blues" (Ellison), **Retro. Supp. II:** 117, 124
"Richard Yates: A Requiem" (Lawrence), **Supp. XI:** 335
"Rich Boy, The" (Fitzgerald), **II:** 94; **Retro. Supp. I:** 98, 108
Richer, the Poorer, The: Sketches and Reminiscences (D. West), **Supp. XVIII:** 277, 289
"Riches" (Bausch), **Supp. VII:** 54
Richler, Mordecai, **Supp. XI:** 294, 297
Rich Man, Poor Man (miniseries), **Supp. XIX:** 252
Rich Man, Poor Man (Shaw), **Supp. XIX:** 251–252
Richman, Robert, **Supp. XI:** 249; **Supp. XV:** 120–121, 251
Richmond (Masters), **Supp. I Part 2:** 471
Richmond, M. A., **Supp. XX:**277, 279, 282, 286, 289, 290
Rich Relations (Hwang), **Supp. XXI:** 146–147
Richter, Conrad, **Supp. X:** 103; **Supp. XVIII: 207–222**
Richter, Jean Paul, **II:** 489, 492; **Supp. XVI:** 182
Rick Bass (Weltzien), **Supp. XVI:** 20
Rickman, Clio, **Supp. I Part 2:** 519
Ricks, Christopher, **Retro. Supp. I:** 56; **Supp. XVIII:** 20, 30, 32
Riddel, Joseph N., **IV:** 95
"Riddle, The" (Hay), **Supp. XIV:** 130
"Ride in an Omnibus, A" (Briggs), **Supp. XVIII:** 9, 16
"Riders to the Blood-Red Wrath" (Brooks), **Supp. III Part 1:** 82–83
Riders to the Sea (Synge), **III:** 157
Ridge, Lola, **Supp. IX:** 308; **Supp. XV:** 307
Riding, Alan, **Supp. XVI:** 294
Riding, Laura, **I:** 437
"Riding Out at Evening" (McCarriston), **Supp. XIV:** 262–263
Riding the Iron Rooster: By Train through China (Theroux), **Supp. VIII:** 324
Riesenberg, Felix, **I:** 360, 361
Riesman, David, **Supp. I Part 2:** 649, 650
"Rif, to Music, The" (Bowles), **Supp. IV Part 1:** 89
Riffs & Reciprocities (Dunn), **Supp. XI: 154–155**
Rifles, The (Vollmann), **Supp. XVII:** 226, 233
Riggs, Marlon, **Supp. XI:** 19
Right Distance, The (Pickering), **Supp. XXI:** 196–197
Right Madness on Skye, The (Hugo), **Supp. VI:** 145–147

Rights of Man (Paine), **Supp. I Part 2:** 508, 511, 512–514, 516, 519, 523
"Rights of Woman" (Rowson), **Supp. XV:** 243
"Rights of Women, The" (Brown). *See Alcuin: A Dialogue* (Brown)
Right Stuff, The (Wolfe), **Supp. III Part 2:** 581–584
Right Thoughts in Sad Hours (Mather), **IV:** 144
Rigney, Barbara Hill, **Supp. VIII:** 215
"Rigorists" (Moore), **III:** 198
Rihani, Ameen, **Supp. XX:**115
Riis, Jacob A., **I:** 293; **Supp. I Part 1:** 13; **Supp. XVII:** 101, 106
Riley, James Whitcomb, **I:** 205; **Supp. II Part 1:** 192, 193, 196, 197
Rilke, Rainer Maria, **I:** 445, 523; **II:** 367, 381, 382–383, 389, 543, 544; **III:** 552, 558, 563, 571, 572; **IV:** 380, 443; **Retro. Supp. II:** 20, 187; **Supp. I Part 1:** 264; **Supp. I Part 2:** 573; **Supp. III Part 1:** 239, 242, 246, 283, 319–320; **Supp. IV Part 1:** 284; **Supp. V:** 208, 343; **Supp. VIII:** 30, 40; **Supp. X:** 164; **Supp. XI:** 126; **Supp. XIII:** 74, 88; **Supp. XV:** 93, 212, 222,**Supp. XV:** 223, 225; **Supp. XVI:** 292; **Supp. XVII:** 244
Rilke on Love and Other Difficulties (Rilke), **Supp. X:** 164
"Rilke's Growth as a Poet" (Dobyns), **Supp. XIII:** 77
"Rimbaud" (Kerouac), **Supp. III Part 1:** 232
Rimbaud, Arthur, **I:** 381, 383, 389, 391, 526; **II:** 528, 543, 545; **III:** 23, 174, 189; **IV:** 286, 380, 443; **Retro. Supp. I:** 56; **Retro. Supp. II:** 187, 326; **Supp. III Part 1:** 14, 195; **Supp. IV Part 2:** 624; **Supp. VIII:** 39, 40; **Supp. XII:** 1, 16, 128, 255; **Supp. XIII:** 284; **Supp. XIV:** 338; **Supp. XVIII:** 23, 33; **Supp. XXI:** 225, 233
Rindge, Debora, **Supp. XXI:** 246
Rinehart, Stanley, **III:** 36
Ring, Frances Kroll, **Supp. IX:** 63, 64
Ring and the Book, The (Browning), **Supp. I Part 2:** 416, 468
Ring cycle (Wagner), **Supp. IV Part 1:** 392
Ringe, Donald, **I:** 339, 343; **Retro. Supp. II:** 270
"Ringing" (Bierds), **Supp. XVII:** 28
"Ringing the Bells" (Sexton), **Supp. II Part 2:** 672, 687
Ringle, Ken, **Supp. X:** 15
Ring of Heaven: Poems (Hongo), **Supp. X:** 292
Rink, The (musical, McNally), **Supp. XIII:** 207
Rio Lobo (film), **Supp. XVI:** 246
Ríos, Alberto Alvaro, **Supp. IV Part 2:** **537–556**
"Riot" (Brooks), **Supp. III Part 1:** 71, 84–85
Ripley, Ezra, **II:** 8; **IV:** 172
Rip-off Red, Girl Detective (Acker), **Supp. XII:** 3–4

Ripostes (Pound), **Retro. Supp. I:** 287–288, 413

Ripostes of Ezra Pound, The, Whereunto Are Appended the Complete Poetical Works of T. E. Hulme, with Prefatory Note (Pound), **III:** 458, 464, 465

Riprap (Snyder), **Supp. VIII: 292–294,** 295

"Riprap" (Snyder), **Supp. VIII:** 293–294

"Rip Van Winkle" (Irving), **II:** 304–306; **Supp. I Part 1:** 185

Rischin, Moses, **Supp. XVII:** 101, 103, 106

Risco-Lozado, Eliezar, **Supp. XIII:** 313

Rise and Shine (Quindlen), **Supp. XVII:** 179

Rise of David Levinsky, The (Cahan), **Supp. IX:** 227; **Supp. XIII:** 106

Rise of Silas Lapham, The (Howells), **II:** 275, 279, 283–285; **IV:** 202; **Retro. Supp. II:** 93, 101

"Rise of the Middle Class" (Banks), **Supp. V:** 10

Rising and Falling (Matthews), **Supp. IX:** 154, **160**

"Rising Daughter, The" (Olds), **Supp. X:** 204

Rising from the Plains (McPhee), **Supp. III Part 1:** 309–310

Rising Glory of America, The (Brackenridge and Freneau), **Supp. I Part 1:** 124; **Supp. II Part 1:** 67, 253, 256, 263

"Rising of the Storm, The" (Dunbar), **Supp. II Part 1:** 199

Rising Sun in the Pacific, The (Morison), **Supp. I Part 2:** 490

Rising Up and Rising Down (Vollmann), **Supp. XVII:** 225, 226, **229–230,** 232, 233, 235–236

Risk Pool, The (Russo), **Supp. XII: 328–331**

Ristovic, Aleksandar, **Supp. VIII:** 272

"Rita Dove: Identity Markers" (Vendler), **Supp. IV Part 1:** 247, 257

Ritchey, John, **Supp. XIV:** 122

Ritchie, Anne Thackeray, **Supp. XX:**231, 233

"Rite of Passage" (Olds), **Supp. X:** 206

"Rites and Ceremonies" (Hecht), **Supp. X:** 61

Rites and Witnesses: A Comedy (Hinojosa), **Supp. XIX: 106–107**

"Rites of Spring, The" (Morris), **III:** 223

Ritivoi, Andreea Deciu, **Supp. XVI:** 148

Ritschl, Albrecht, **III:** 309, 604

Ritsos, Yannis, **Supp. X:** 112

"Ritsos and the Metaphysical Moment" (Dobyns), **Supp. XIII:** 78

Rittenhouse, David, **Supp. I Part 2:** 507

Rittenhouse, Jessie, **Supp. XV:** 295

"Ritual, The" (Jarman), **Supp. XVII:** 114

"Ritual and Renewal: Keres Traditions in the Short Fiction of Leslie Silko" (Ruoff), **Supp. IV Part 2:** 559

Ritz, The (film), **Supp. XIII:** 206

Ritz, The (McNally), **Supp. XIII:** 198

"Rival, The" (Plath), **Retro. Supp. II:** 254

Riven Rock (Boyle), **Supp. VIII:** 5–6; **Supp. XX:25–26**

"River" (Ammons), **Supp. VII:** 28

"River, The" (O'Connor), **III:** 344, 352, 353, 354, 356; **Retro. Supp. II:** 229, 231–232

Rivera, Tomás, **Supp. XIII:** 216, 221; **Supp. XIX:** 97, 102

Riverbed (Wagoner), **Supp. IX: 327–328**

"River Driftwood" (Jewett), **Retro. Supp. II:** 132, 133, 147

"River Jordan, The" (DeLillo), **Supp. VI:** 3, 4

River King, The (Hoffman), **Supp. X:** 78, 85, 90, **91–92**

"River Merchant's Wife: A Letter, The" (Pound), **III:** 463

"River Now, The" (Hugo), **Supp. VI:** 144

"River of Rivers in Connecticut, The" (Stevens), **Retro. Supp. I:** 313

River of the Mother of God and Other Essays by Aldo Leopold, The (Leopold), **Supp. XIV:** 180

"River Profile" (Auden), **Supp. II Part 1:** 26

"River Road" (Kunitz), **Supp. III Part 1:** 260

"River Runs Through It, A" (Maclean), **Supp. XIV:** 222–223, **223–229,** 233, 234, 235; **Supp. XVI:** 98

River Runs Through It and Other Stories, A (Maclean), **Supp. XIV:** 221, 223

Rivers, Larry, **Supp. III Part 1:** 3; **Supp. XV:** 177, 178, 186

Rivers and Mountains (Ashbery), **Supp. III Part 1:** 10, 26

Riverside Drive (Simpson), **Supp. IX: 275–276**

Riverside Poetry (Auden, Moore, and Shapiro, eds.), **Supp. XXI:** 98

Rivers to the Sea (Teasdale), **Supp. XV:** 295

River Styx, Ohio, and Other Poems, The (Oliver), **Supp. VII:** 231, 232

"River That Is East, The" (Kinnell), **Supp. III Part 1:** 241–242

"River Towns" (Masters), **Supp. I Part 2:** 473

Rives, Amélie, **II:** 194

Rivière, Jacques, **Retro. Supp. I:** 63

"Rivington's Last Will and Testament" (Freneau), **Supp. II Part 1:** 261

"Rivulet, The" (Bryant), **Supp. I Part 1:** 155, 162

Rix, Alice, **I:** 199

RL's Dream (Mosley), **Supp. XIII:** 234, **244–245,** 249

Roach, Max, **Supp. X:** 239

"Road, Roadsides, and the Disparate Frames of a Sequence" (Sobin), **Supp. XVI:** 288

Road Between, The (Farrell), **II:** 29, 38, 39–40

"Road Between Here and There, The" (Kinnell), **Supp. III Part 1:** 254

"Road Home, The" (Hammett), **Supp. IV Part 1:** 343

Road Home, The (Harrison), **Supp. VIII:** 37, 45, 48, **49–50,** 53

Roadless Yaak, The: Reflections and Observations about One of Our Last Great Wild Places (Bass, ed.), **Supp. XVI:** 23

"Road Not Taken, The" (R. Frost), **II:** 154; **Retro. Supp. I:** 131; **Supp. XI:** 150; **Supp. XV:** 127

"Roadside Flowers" (Collins), **Supp. XXI:** 61

Roadside Poems for Summer Travellers (Larcom, ed.), **Supp. XIII:** 142

"Roadside Resurrection, A" (L. Brown), **Supp. XXI:** 40, 42

Roads of Destiny (O. Henry), **Supp. II Part 1:** 410

Road through the Wall, The (Jackson), **Supp. IX:** 115, 118, 120, 123–124

"Road to Avignon, The" (Lowell), **II:** 516

"Road to Hell, The" (Fante), **Supp. XI:** 160

Road to Los Angeles, The (Fante), **Supp. XI:** 160, 166, 167, **168,** 172

Road to Many a Wonder, The (Wagoner), **Supp. IX:** 327, **336**

Road to the Temple, The (Glaspell), **Supp. III Part 1:** 175, 182, 186; **Supp. XXI:** 6

Road to Wellville, The (Boyle), **Supp. VIII:** 6–8; **Supp. XX:24–25,** 26, 28

Road to Xanadu, The (Lowes), **IV:** 453

"Road Warrior" (Pickering), **Supp. XXI:** 204

"Roan Stallion" (Jeffers), **Supp. II Part 2:** 428–429

"Roast-beef" (Stein), **IV:** 43

Roast Leviatham (Untermeyer), **Supp. XV:** 307

"Roast Possum" (Dove), **Supp. IV Part 1:** 247, 248

Robards, Jason, Jr., **III:** 163, 403

Robb, Christina, **Supp. XV:** 251

Robbe-Grillet, Alain, **I:** 123; **IV:** 95; **Supp. IV Part 1:** 42; **Supp. V:** 47, 48

Robber Bride, The (Atwood), **Supp. XIII: 30–31**

Robber Bridegroom, The (Welty), **IV:** 261, 266–268, 271, 274; **Retro. Supp. I:** 347

Robbins, Harold, **Supp. XII:** 6

Robbins, Henry, **Supp. IV Part 1:** 198, 201, 210, 211

Robbins, Katherine Robinson, **Supp. X:** 264

Robbins, Thomas, **Supp. XV:** 271

Robbins, Tom, **Supp. IV Part 1:** 227; **Supp. VIII:** 14; **Supp. X: 259–288;** **Supp. XIII:** 11

"Robe, The" (Douglas), **IV:** 434

Robert Bly (Sugg), **Supp. IV Part 1:** 68

"Robert Bly" (W. V. Davis), **Supp. IV Part 1:** 70

"Robert Bly and the Trouble with America" (Mitchell), **Supp. IV Part 1:** 70

Robert Bly: An Introduction to the Poetry (Nelson), **Supp. IV Part 1:** 66

Robert Bly: The Poet and His Critics (W. V. Davis), **Supp. IV Part 1:** 63; **Supp. XXI:** 84, **85–86,** 87, 95

Robert Coover: The Universal Fiction-making Process (Gordon), **Supp. V:** 46

Robert Creeley (Ford), **Supp. IV Part 1:** 140

Robert Creeley and the Genius of the American Common Place (Clark), **Supp. IV Part 1:** 140

Robert Creeley's Poetry: A Critical Introduction (Edelberg), **Supp. IV Part 1:** 155

Robert Frost (Meyers), **Retro. Supp. I:** 138

Robert Lowell (Meyers), **Retro. Supp. II:** 191

Robert Lowell and the Sublime (Hart), **Retro. Supp. II:** 187

Robert Lowell's Shifting Colors (Doreski), **Retro. Supp. II:** 185

Robert Lowell: The First Twenty years (Staples), **Retro. Supp. II:** 187

Roberts, Carol, **Supp. XX:**53

Roberts, David, **Supp. XVIII:** 106

Roberts, Diane, **Supp. X:** 15

Roberts, J. M., **IV:** 454

Roberts, Leo, **II:** 449

Roberts, Margaret, **II:** 449; **IV:** 453, 454

Roberts, Matthew, **Retro. Supp. II:** 324

Roberts, Meade, **IV:** 383

Roberts, Michael, **I:** 527, 536

Roberts, Richard, **III:** 297

Roberts, Victoria, **Supp. XIX:** 205

Roberts, Wally, **Supp. XI:** 119, 120, 126

Roberts, William, **Supp. XI:** 343

Roberts Brothers, **Retro. Supp. I:** 31, 35

Robertson, David, **Supp. VIII:** 305

Robertson, D. B., **III:** 311

Robertson, Nan, **Supp. IV Part 1:** 300

Robertson, William, **II:** 8

Robert the Devil (Merwin, trans.), **Supp. III Part 1:** 341, 346

Robeson, Paul, **III:** 392; **Supp. IV Part 1:** 360, 361; **Supp. X:** 137; **Supp. XIX:** 66; **Supp. XXI:** 167

Robeson, Susan L., **Supp. XVIII:** 268

Robespierre, Maximilien, **Supp. I Part 2:** 514, 515, 517

"Robinson" (Kees), **Supp. XV:** 143–144

Robinson, Christopher L., **Supp. XII:** 13, 14

Robinson, Dean, **III:** 506

Robinson, Edward, **III:** 505

Robinson, Edward G., **Supp. XI:** 306

Robinson, Edwin Arlington, **I:** 480; **II:** 388, 391, 529, 542; **III:** 5, **503–526,** 576; **Supp. I Part 2:** 699; **Supp. II Part 1:** 191; **Supp. III Part 1:** 63, 75; **Supp. III Part 2:** 592, 593; **Supp. IX:** 77, 266, 276, 308; **Supp. XV:** 256, 299, 300, 301, 306; **Supp. XVII:** 69; **Supp. XIX:** 123

Robinson, Forrest G., **Supp. IV Part 2:** 597, 601, 604

Robinson, Herman, **III:** 506–507

Robinson, H. M., **IV:** 369, 370

Robinson, Jackie, **Supp. I Part 1:** 338

Robinson, James Harvey, **I:** 214; **Supp. I Part 2:** 492

Robinson, James K., **Supp. IX:** 328

Robinson, Margaret G., **Supp. IV Part 2:** 597, 601, 604

Robinson, Marilynne, **Supp. XXI:** 209–224

Robinson, Mary, **Supp. XI:** 26

Robinson, Rowland E., **Supp. XIX:** 6

Robinson, Sugar Ray, **Supp. IV Part 1:** 167

Robinson, Ted, **Supp. XIII:** 166

Robinson Crusoe (Defoe), **II:** 159; **III:** 113, 423; **IV:** 369; **Retro. Supp. II:** 274; **Supp. I Part 2:** 714; **Supp. IV Part 2:** 502

Robison, Mary, **Supp. V:** 22; **Supp. XXI:** 115, 116, 118

Roblès, Emmanuel, **Supp. I Part 1:** 283

"Robstown" (Salinas), **Supp. XIII:** 315

Rochefort, Christina, **Supp. XVI:** 143

Rochefoucauld, Louis Alexandre, **Supp. I Part 2:** 510

"Rock" (Nye), **Supp. XIII:** 287

Rock (Wagoner), **Supp. IX:** 324, **334,** 335

Rock, Catherine, **Supp. XII:** 17

Rock, The (Eliot), **Retro. Supp. I:** 65

Rock, The (Stevens), **Retro. Supp. I:** 309, 312

"Rock, The" (Stevens), **Retro. Supp. I:** 312

Rockaway (Shanley), **Supp. XIV:** 315

"Rock Climbers, The" (Francis), **Supp. IX:** 82

Rock-Drill (Pound), **Retro. Supp. I:** 293

Rockefeller, John D., **I:** 273; **III:** 580; **Supp. I Part 2:** 486; **Supp. V:** 286

Rockefeller, Nelson, **III:** 14, 15

Rockets and Rodeos and Other American Spectacles (Mallon), **Supp. XIX:** 137

Rocket to the Moon (Odets), **Supp. II Part 2:** 541–543, 544

Rock Garden, The (Shepard), **Supp. III Part 2:** 432, 447

"Rocking Horse Winner, The" (Lawrence), **Supp. I Part 1:** 329

Rocking the Boat (Vidal), **Supp. IV Part 2:** 683

"Rockpile, The" (Baldwin), **Supp. I Part 1:** 63

Rock Springs (Ford), **Supp. V:** 57, 58–59, 68–69

Rocky Mountains, The: or, Scenes, Incidents, and Adventures in the Far West; Digested from the Journal of Captain E. L. E Bonneville, of the Army of the United States, and Illustrated from Various Other Sources (Irving), **II:** 312

Rodden, John, **Supp. XVI:** 63, 69, 72

Roderick, David, **Supp. XV:** 223

Roderick Hudson (James), **II:** 284, 290, 324, 326, 328; **Retro. Supp. I:** 219, **220–221,** 221, 226; **Supp. IX:** 142

Rodgers, Richard, **III:** 361

Rodgers, Ronald, **Supp. IV Part 2:** 503

Rodker, John, **III:** 470

Rodman, Selden, **Supp. I Part 1:** 83; **Supp. X:** 115

Rodney, Walter, **Supp. XXI:** 171

"Rodrigo Returns to the Land and Linen Celebrates" (Cisneros), **Supp. VII:** 68

Rodriguez, Randy A., **Supp. XIV:** 312

Rodriguez, Richard, **Supp. XIV:** 297–313

Roethke, Charles, **III:** 531

Roethke, Theodore, **I:** 167, 171–172, 183, 254, 285, 521; **III:** 273, **527–550;** **IV:** 138, 402; **Retro. Supp. II:** 178, 181, 246; **Supp. I Part 2:** 539; **Supp. III Part 1:** 47, 54, 56, 239, 253, 260–261, 350; **Supp. IV Part 2:** 626; **Supp. IX:** 323; **Supp. XV:** 140, 145, 212; **Supp. XVIII:** 90; **Supp. XX:**199

"Roger Malvin's Burial" (Hawthorne), **II:** 243; **Retro. Supp. I:** 153

Rogers, Michael, **Supp. X:** 265, 266

Rogers, Pattiann, **Supp. XVIII:** 189

Rogers, Samuel, **II:** 303; **Supp. I Part 1:** 157

Rogers, Will, **I:** 261; **IV:** 388

Roger's Version (Updike), **Retro. Supp. I:** 325, 327, 330

Roget, Peter Mark, **Supp. I Part 1:** 312

"Rogue River Jet-Board Trip, Gold Beach, Oregon, July 4, 1977" (Carver), **Supp. III Part 1:** 140

"Rogue's Gallery" (McCarthy), **II:** 563

Rohr, Richard, **Supp. XX:**143

Roland de La Platière, Jean Marie, **II:** 554

Rolando Hinojosa and the American Dream (Glover), **Supp. XIX:** 112

Rolando Hinojosa: A Reader's Guide (Zilles), **Supp. XIX:** 112

Rolando Hinojosa Reader, The (Saldívar, ed.), **Supp. XIX:** 112

Rôle du Nègre dans la culture des Amériques, La (Locke), **Supp. XIV:** 202

"Role of a Lifetime, The" (Skloot), **Supp. XX:**203

"Role of Society in the Artist, The" (Ammons), **Supp. VII:** 34

Rolfe, Alfred, **IV:** 427

Rolfe, Frederick, **Supp. XX:**235

"Roll, Jordan, Roll" (spiritual), **Supp. IV Part 1:** 16

Rolland, Romain, **Supp. XX:**70

"Roll Call" (Hoffman), **Supp. XVIII:** 86

"Roll Call" (Komunyakaa), **Supp. XIII:** 123

Rolle, Esther, **Supp. IV Part 1:** 367

Rollin, Charles, **II:** 113

Rolling Stones (O. Henry), **Supp. II Part 1:** 410

Rolling Thunder Logbook (Shepard), **Supp. III Part 2:** 433

Rolling Thunder Logbook, The (Shepard), **Supp. XVIII:** 31

"Rolling Up" (Simpson), **Supp. IX:** 265, 274, 280

Rollins, Howard E., Jr., **Supp. IV Part 1:** 236

Rollins, Hyder E., **Supp. IV Part 1:** 168

Rollins, Sonny, **Supp. V:** 195

"Rollo" tales (Abbott), **Supp. I Part 1:** 38

"Roma I" (Wright), **Supp. V:** 338

"Roma II" (Wright), **Supp. V:** 338

Romains, Jules, **I:** 227

Román, David, **Supp. XIII:** 208

Romance, A (Weigl), **Supp. XIX: 277–278**

"Romance, A" (Weigl), **Supp. XIX:** 278

"Romance and a Reading List" (Fitzgerald), **Retro. Supp. I:** 101

Romance of a Plain Man, The (Glasgow), **II:** 175, 180–181

"Romance of Certain Old Clothes, The" (James), **II:** 322; **Retro. Supp. I:** 218

"Roman Elegies" (Brodsky), **Supp. VIII:** 29

"Roman Fever" (Wharton), **Retro. Supp. I:** 382

"Roman Fountain" (Bogan), **Supp. III Part 1:** 56

"*Romanitas* of Gore Vidal, The" (Tatum), **Supp. IV Part 2:** 684

Romaniuk, Zbigniew, **Supp. XVI:** 154

Romano, John, **Supp. XV:** 253

"Roman Sarcophagus, A" (Lowell), **II:** 544

Roman Spring of Mrs. Stone, The (T. Williams), **IV:** 383, 385

"Romantic, The" (Bogan), **Supp. III Part 1:** 50

Romantic Comedians, The (Glasgow), **II:** 175, 186, 190, 194

Romantic Egoists, The (Auchincloss), **Supp. IV Part 1:** 25

Romantic Egotist, The (Fitzgerald), **II:** 82

"Romantic Egotist, The" (Fitzgerald), **Retro. Supp. I:** 100

"Romanticism and Classicism" (Hulme), **III:** 196

"Romanticism Comes Home" (Shapiro), **Supp. II Part 2:** 713

Romantic Manifesto, The: A Philosophy of Literature (Rand), **Supp. IV Part 2:** 521, 523, 527, 529–530

"Romantic Regionalism of Harper Lee, The" (Erisman), **Supp. VIII:** 126

"Rome" (W. C. Williams), **Retro. Supp. I:** 420

Rome Brothers, **Retro. Supp. I:** 393

Romeo and Juliet (Shakespeare), **Supp. V:** 252; **Supp. VIII:** 223

Romola (G. Eliot), **II:** 291; **IV:** 311

Romulus: A New Comedy (Vidal), **Supp. IV Part 2:** 683

Romulus der Grosse (Dürrenmatt), **Supp. IV Part 2:** 683

Ronald, Ann, **Supp. XIII:** 4, 5, 6, 7, 9, 11

"Rondel for a September Day" (White), **Supp. I Part 2:** 676

"Ron Narrative Reconstructions, The" (Coleman), **Supp. XI:** 83

Ronsard, Pierre de, **Supp. X:** 65; **Supp. XV:** 165

Rood, John, **IV:** 261

"Roof, the Steeple, and the People, The" (Ellison), **Retro. Supp. II:** 118, 126; **Supp. II Part 1:** 248

"Room" (Levertov), **Supp. III Part 1:** 282

Roomates (film, P. Yates), **Supp. XVII:** 8, 9

Roomates: My Grandfather's Story (Apple), **Supp. XVII:** 2, **7–9**

"Room at the Heart of Things, A" (Merrill), **Supp. III Part 1:** 337

Room Called Remember, A: Uncollected Pieces (Buechner), **Supp. XII:** 53

"Roomful of Hovings, A" (McPhee), **Supp. III Part 1:** 291, 294

Room of One's Own, A (Woolf), **Supp. V:** 127; **Supp. IX:** 19; **Supp. XIII:** 305

Room Rented by a Single Woman (Wright), **Supp. XV:** 340–341

"Rooms" (Collins), **Supp. XXI:** 61

Room Temperature (Baker), **Supp. XIII:** 41, **43–45,** 48, 50

Room to Swing (Lacy), **Supp. XV:** 202, 203, 205, 207

"Room Upstairs, The" (Gioia), **Supp. XV:** 120–121, 124

Roosevelt, Eleanor, **IV:** 371; **Supp. IV Part 2:** 679

Roosevelt, Franklin, **Supp. V:** 290

Roosevelt, Franklin Delano, **I:** 482, 485, 490; **II:** 553, 575; **III:** 2, 18, 69, 110, 297, 321, 376, 476, 580, 581; **Supp. I Part 2:** 488, 489, 490, 491, 645, 654, 655

Roosevelt, Kermit, **III:** 508

Roosevelt, Theodore, **I:** 14, 62; **II:** 130; **III:** 508; **IV:** 321; **Retro. Supp. I:** 377; **Supp. I Part 1:** 1, 21; **Supp. I Part 2:** 455, 456, 502, 707; **Supp. V:** 280, 282; **Supp. IX:** 184; **Supp. XIX:** 29; **Supp. XX:**221

Roosevelt After Inauguration And Other Atrocities (Burroughs), **Supp. III Part 1:** 98

"Roosevelt Chair, The" (Skloot), **Supp. XX:**205

"Roosters" (Bishop), **Retro. Supp. II:** 39, 43, 250; **Supp. I Part 1:** 89

Root, Abiah, **I:** 456

Root, Elihu, **Supp. IV Part 1:** 33

Root, Simeon, **I:** 548

Root, Timothy, **I:** 548

Rootabaga Stories (Sandburg), **III:** 583, 587

"Rootedness: The Ancestor as Foundation" (Morrison), **Supp. III Part 1:** 361

"Roots" (Halliday), **Supp. XIX:** 88

Roots in the Soil (film), **Supp. IV Part 1:** 83

"Rope" (Porter), **III:** 451

Rope, The (O'Neill), **III:** 388

Ropemakers of Plymouth, The (Morison), **Supp. I Part 2:** 494

"Ropes" (Nye), **Supp. XIII:** 276

"Rope's End, The" (Nemerov), **III:** 282

Roquelaure, A. N., **Supp. VII:** 301. *See also* Rice, Anne

Rorem, Ned, **Supp. IV Part 1:** 79, 84

Rorschach Test (F. Wright), **Supp. XVII:** 240, 245

"Rosa" (Ozick), **Supp. V:** 271

Rosa, Rodrigo Rey, **Supp. IV Part 1:** 92

Rosaldo, Renato, **Supp. IV Part 2:** 544

"Rosalia" (Simic), **Supp. VIII:** 278

Roscoe, Will, **Supp. IV Part 1:** 330

"Roscoe in Hell" (McKnight), **Supp. XX:**151

"Rose" (Dubus), **Supp. VII:** 88

Rose (L.-Y. Lee), **Supp. XV:** 211, **212–215,** 218

Rose, Alice, Sister, **III:** 348

Rose, Charlie, **Supp. XIX:** 26, 30

Rose, Mickey, **Supp. XV:** 3

Rose, Philip, **Supp. IV Part 1:** 362

"Rose, The" (Roethke), **III:** 537

"Rose, The" (W. C. Williams), **Retro. Supp. I:** 419

Rose, Where Did You Get That Red?: Teaching Great Poetry to Children (Koch), **Supp. XV:** 189

"Rose for Emily, A" (Faulkner), **II:** 72; **Supp. IX:** 96; **Supp. XX:**179

Rose-Hued Cities (P. N. Warren), **Supp. XX:**261

Rose in Bloom (Alcott), **Supp. I Part 1:** 42

"Rose-Johnny" (Kingsolver), **Supp. VII:** 203

Rose Madder (King), **Supp. V:** 141, 148, 150, 152

"Rose-Morals" (Lanier), **Supp. I Part 1:** 364

Rosen, Jonathan, **Supp. XVII:** 50; **Supp. XX:**179

Rosen, Kenneth, **Supp. IV Part 2:** 499, 505, 513

Rosen, Norma, **Supp. XVII:** 49, 50

Rosenbaum, Alissa Zinovievna. *See* Rand, Ayn

Rosenbaum, Thane, **Supp. XVII:** 48

Rosenberg, Bernard, **Supp. I Part 2:** 650

Rosenberg, Harold, **Supp. XV:** 143; **Supp. XIX:** 159

Rosenberg, Julia, **Supp. XVIII:** 136

Rosenberg, Julius and Ethel, **Supp. I Part 1:** 295; **Supp. I Part 2:** 532; **Supp. V:** 45

Rosenberg, Liz, **Supp. XV:** 251

Rosenbloom, Joel, **Supp. IV Part 2:** 527

Rosenfeld, Alvin H., **Supp. I Part 1:** 120

Rosenfeld, Isaac, **Supp. XII:** 160

Rosenfeld, Paul, **I:** 116, 117, 231, 245

Rosenfelt, Deborah, **Supp. XIII:** 296, 304

Rosenfield, Isaac, **IV:** 3

Rosengarten, Theodore, **Supp. XVIII:** 183

Rosenthal, Ira, **Supp. XIV:** 146–147

Rosenthal, Lois, **Supp. VIII:** 258

Rosenthal, M. L., **II:** 550; **III:** 276, 479; **Supp. V:** 333

Rosenthal, Peggy, **Supp. XVII:** 119

"Rose Pogonias" (Frost), **Retro. Supp. I:** 127

"Rose Red and Snow White" (Grimms), **Supp. X:** 82

"Rose Room" (Sorrentino), **Supp. XXI:** 228

"Roses" (Conroy), **Supp. XVI:** 72

"Roses" (Dove), **Supp. IV Part 1:** 246

"Roses and Skulls" (Goldbarth), **Supp. XII:** 192

"Roses for Lubbock" (Nye), **Supp. XIII:** 281

"Roses Only" (Moore), **III:** 195, 198, 200, 202, 215

Rose Tattoo, The (T. Williams), **IV:** 382, 383, 387, 388, 389, 392–393, 394, 397, 398

Rose Theatre (Sorrentino), **Supp. XXI:** 236

"Rosewood, Ohio" (Matthews), **Supp. IX:** 160

Rosie (Lamott), **Supp. XX:133–134**

Rosinante to the Road Again (Dos Passos), **I:** 478

Roskies, David, **Supp. XVII:** 39, 44, 49–50

Roskolenko, Harry, **Supp. XV:** 179

Rosmersholm (Ibsen), **III:** 152

Rosmond, Babette, **II:** 432

Ross, Eleanor. *See* Taylor, Eleanor Ross

Ross, Harold, **Supp. I Part 1:** 174; **Supp. I Part 2:** 607, 617, 653, 654, 655, 660; **Supp. VIII:** 151, 170; **Supp. IX:** 190

Ross, Herbert, **Supp. XV:** 2

Ross, Jean, **Supp. XXI:** 144, 146

Ross, John F., **II:** 110

Ross, Lillilan, **Retro. Supp. II:** 198

Ross, Mitchell S., **Supp. IV Part 2:** 692; **Supp. X:** 260

Rossen, Robert, **Supp. XI:** 306

Rosset, Barney, **III:** 171

Rossetti, Christina, **Supp. XIV:** 128

Rossetti, Dante Gabriel, **I:** 433; **II:** 323; **Retro. Supp. I:** 128, 286; **Supp. I Part 2:** 552

Rossetti, William Michael, **Retro. Supp. I:** 407

Rossi, Umberto, **Supp. XVIII:** 137, 138–139

Rossini, Clare, **Supp. XVII:** 111

Rosskam, Edwin, **IV:** 477

Ross Macdonald (Bruccoli), **Supp. IV Part 2:** 468, 470

Rostand, Edmond, **II:** 515; **Supp. IV Part 2:** 518

Rosten, Leo, **Supp. XVII:** 9

Rosy Crucifixion, The (H. Miller), **III:** 170, 187, 188–189, 190

Rote Walker, The (Jarman), **Supp. XVII:** 110**, 113–115**

Roth, Henry, **Supp. IV Part 1:** 314; **Supp. VIII:** 233; **Supp. IX: 227–243; Supp. XIII:** 106

Roth, Philip, **I:** 144, 161; **II:** 591; **Retro. Supp. II:** 22, **279–297; Supp. I Part 1:** 186, 192; **Supp. I Part 2:** 431, 441, 443; **Supp. II Part 1:** 99; **Supp. III Part 2: 401–429; Supp. IV Part 1:** 236, 379, 388; **Supp. V:** 45, 119, 122, 257, 258; **Supp. VIII:** 88, 236, 245; **Supp. IX:** 227; **Supp. XI:** 64, 68, 99, 140; **Supp. XII:** 190, 310; **Supp. XIV:** 79, 93, 111, 112; **Supp. XVI:** 206; **Supp. XVII:** 43, 48, 183; **Supp. XVIII:** 89; **Supp. XXI:** 234

Roth, Rita, **Supp. XVI:** 112

Roth, William, **Supp. XV:** 142

Rothenberg, Jerome, **Supp. VIII:** 292; **Supp. XII:** 3

Rothermere, Lady Mary, **Retro. Supp. I:** 63

Rothko, Mark, **Supp. XV:** 144

Rothstein, Mervyn, **Supp. VIII:** 142

"Rouge High" (Hughes), **Supp. I Part 1:** 330

Rougemont, Denis de, **II:** 586; **IV:** 216; **Retro. Supp. I:** 328, 329, 330, 331

Rough Edges (Skloot), **Supp. XX:196**

Roughing It (Twain), **II:** 312; **IV:** 195, 197, 198

Roughing It in the Bush (Shields), **Supp. VII:** 313

"Rough Outline" (Simic), **Supp. VIII:** 276

Rough South of Larry Brown, The (film, Hawkins), **Supp. XXI:** 39

Rougon-Macquart, Les (Zola), **II:** 175–176

Roumain, Jacques, **Retro. Supp. I:** 202; **Supp. IV Part 1:** 360, 367

"Round, The" (Kunitz), **Supp. III Part 1:** 268

"Round Trip" (Dunn), **Supp. XI:** 148–149

Round Up (Lardner), **II:** 426, 430, 431

Rourke, Constance, **I:** 258; **IV:** 339, 352

Rourke, Milton, **Retro. Supp. II:** 89

Rousseau, Jean-Jacques, **I:** 226; **II:** 8, 343; **III:** 170, 178, 259; **IV:** 80, 173, 440; **Supp. I Part 1:** 126; **Supp. I Part 2:** 637, 659; **Supp. IV Part 1:** 171; **Supp. XI:** 245; **Supp. XVI:** 292; **Supp. XXI:** 83

Roussel, Raymond, **Supp. III Part 1:** 6, 7, 10, 15, 16, 21; **Supp. XV:** 182

"Route 302" (Halliday), **Supp. XIX:** 93

"Routes" (Everwine), **Supp. XV:** 82

"Route Six" (Kunitz), **Supp. III Part 1:** 258

Route Two (Erdrich and Dorris), **Supp. IV Part 1:** 260

"Routine Things Around the House, The" (Dunn), **Supp. XI:** 148

Rover Boys (Winfield), **III:** 146

Rovit, Earl, **IV:** 102

Rowan, Carl T., **Supp. XIV:** 306

Rowe, Anne E., **Supp. X:** 223

Rowe, John Carlos, **Retro. Supp. I:** 216

Rowell, Charles, **Supp. XXI:** 250, 254, 255

"Rowing" (Sexton), **Supp. II Part 2:** 696

"Rowing Endeth, The" (Sexton), **Supp. II Part 2:** 696

Rowlandson, Mary, **Supp. IV Part 2:** 430, 431

"Rows of Cold Trees, The" (Winters), **Supp. II Part 2:** 790–791, 800

Rowson, Susanna, **Supp. I Part 1:** 128; **Supp. XV: 229–248**

Roxanna Slade (Price), **Supp. VI:** 267

Roxie Hart (Watkins), **Supp. XVI:** 188

Royal Family, The (Vollmann), **Supp. XVII:** 226, 230, 233

"Royal Palm" (Crane), **I:** 401

Royce, Josiah, **I:** 443; **III:** 303, 600; **IV:** 26; **Retro. Supp. I:** 57; **Supp. XIV:** 197, 199; **Supp. XVII:** 97

"Roy McInnes" (Budbill), **Supp. XIX:** 6–7

Royster, Sarah Elmira, **III:** 410, 429

Royte, Elizabeth, **Supp. XV:** 59

Rózewicz, Tadeusz, **Supp. X:** 60

R. S. Thomas: Poetry and Theology (W. V. Davis), **Supp. XXI:** 86–87

Ruas, Charles, **Supp. IV Part 1:** 383

Rubáiyát (Khayyám), **I:** 568

Rubáiyát of Omar Khayyam (Fitzgerald), **Supp. I Part 2:** 416; **Supp. III Part 2:** 610; **Supp. XV:** 156

"Rubber Life" (Prose), **Supp. XVI:** 256

Rub from Snub, A (Swanwick), **Supp. XV:** 237

Rubin, Louis, **Supp. I Part 2:** 672, 673, 679; **Supp. X:** 42

Rubin, Louis D., Jr., **IV:** 116, 462–463

Rubin, Stan, **Supp. XIV:** 307, 310

Rubin, Stan Sanvel, **Supp. IV Part 1:** 242, 245, 252

Rubins, Josh, **Supp. XX:89**

"Ruby Brown" (Hughes), **Supp. I Part 1:** 327

"Ruby Daggett" (Eberhart), **I:** 539

Rucker, Rudy, **Supp. X:** 302

Rudd, Hughes, **Supp. XII:** 141

"Rude Awakening, A" (Chopin), **Retro. Supp. II:** 64

Rudens (Plautus), **Supp. III Part 2:** 630

Ruderman, Judith, **Supp. IV Part 1:** 380

Rudge, Olga, **Supp. V:** 338

Rudikoff, Sonya, **Supp. XIV:** 113

Rueckert, William, **I:** 264

Ruesch, Jurgen, **Supp. XV:** 147

Rugby Chapel (Arnold), **Supp. I Part 2:** 416

"Rugby Road" (Garrett), **Supp. VII:** 100

Ruining the New Road (Matthews), **Supp. IX:** 154, **155–157**

"Ruins of Italica, The" (Bryant, trans.), **Supp. I Part 1:** 166

Rukeyser, Muriel, **Retro. Supp. II:** 48; **Supp. VI: 271–289; Supp. XV:** 349; **Supp. XVII:** 74

"Rule of Phase Applied to History, The" (Adams), **I:** 19

Rule of the Bone (Banks), **Supp. V:** 16

"Rules by Which a Great Empire May Be Reduced to a Small One" (Franklin), **II:** 120

Rules For the Dance: A Handbook for Reading and Writing Metrical Verse (Oliver), **Supp. VII:** 229, 247

Rules of the Game, The (film), **Supp. XII:** 259

Rulfo, Juan, **Supp. IV Part 2:** 549

Rumba (film, Gering), **Supp. XVII:** 57

Rumbaut, Rubén, **Supp. XI:** 184

Rümelin-Oesterlen, Natalie, **Supp. XX:235**

Rumens, Carol, **Supp. XI:** 14; **Supp. XVI:** 212

Rumi, **Supp. XX:117**

"Rumination of Rivers, The" (Bronk), **Supp. XXI:** 32

Rumkowski, Chaim, **Supp. XII:** 168

Rummel, Mary Kay, **Supp. XIII:** 280

"Rumor and a Ladder" (Bowles), **Supp. IV Part 1:** 93

Rumor of War, A (Caputo), **Supp. XIX: 17–21,** 25, 30

Rumors (Simon), **Supp. IV Part 2:** 582–583, 591

Rumpelstiltskin (Gardner), **Supp. VI:** 72

"Rumpelstiltskin" (Grimm), **IV:** 266

"Rumpelstiltskin" (Sexton), **Supp. II Part 2:** 690

"Runagate Runagate" (Hayden), **Supp. II Part 1:** 377

"Runes" (Nemerov), **III:** 267, 277–278

Run Man Run (C. Himes), **Supp. XVI:** 142, 143

"Runner, The" (Grossman), **Supp. XIX:** 83

"Running" (Wilbur), **Supp. III Part 2:** 558–559

Running Dog (DeLillo), **Supp. VI:** 3, 6, 8, 14

"Running in Church" (A. Finch), **Supp. XVII:** 72

"Running the Table" Conroy), **Supp. XVI:** 75

"Run of Bad Luck, A" (Proulx), **Supp. VII:** 253–254

Run of Jacks, A (Hugo), **Supp. VI:** 131, 133, 134, 135, 136

Run River (Didion), **Supp. IV Part 1:** 197, 199–200, 201

Ruoff, A. LaVonne Brown, **Supp. IV Part 1:** 324, 327; **Supp. IV Part 2:** 559

Rupert, Jim, **Supp. XII:** 215

Ruppert, James, **Supp. IV Part 1:** 321

Rural Hours (Cooper), **Supp. XIII:** 152

"Rural Route" (Wright), **Supp. V:** 340

"Rural South, The" (Du Bois), **Supp. II Part 1:** 174

Rush, Benjamin, **Supp. I Part 2:** 505, 507

Rushdie, Salman, **Supp. IV Part 1:** 234, 297

Rushdy, Ashraf, **Supp. X:** 250

Rushing, Jimmy, **Retro. Supp. II:** 113

Rusk, Dean, **II:** 579

Ruskin, John, **II:** 323, 338; **IV:** 349; **Retro. Supp. I:** 56, 360; **Supp. I Part 1:** 2, 10, 87, 349; **Supp. I Part 2:** 410

Rusnak, Karl, **Supp. XVIII:** 149

Russell, Ada Dwyer, **II:** 513, 527

Russell, Bertrand, **II:** 27; **III:** 605, 606; **Retro. Supp. I:** 57, 58, 59, 60; **Supp. I Part 2:** 522; **Supp. V:** 290; **Supp. XII:** 45; **Supp. XIV:** 337

Russell, Diarmuid, **Retro. Supp. I:** 342, 345, 346–347, 349–350

Russell, George, **Retro. Supp. I:** 342

Russell, Herb, **Supp. I Part 2:** 465–466

Russell, John, **Supp. XIV:** 344, 347, 348

Russell, Peter, **III:** 479

Russell, Richard, **Supp. XI:** 102

Russell, Robert, **Supp. XX:**195

Russell, Sue, **Supp. IV Part 2:** 653

Russert, Margaret, **Supp. XVIII:** 62

Russert, Tim, **Supp. XII:** 272

Russia at War (Caldwell), **I:** 296

Russian Journal, A (Steinbeck), **IV:** 52, 63

Russo, Richard, **Supp. XI:** 349; **Supp. XII: 325–344**

"Rusty Autumn" (Swenson), **Supp. IV Part 2:** 640

Rutabaga-Roo: I've Got a Song and It's for You (Nye, album), **Supp. XIII:** 274

Ruth (biblical book), **Supp. I Part 2:** 516

Ruth, George Herman ("Babe"), **II:** 423; **Supp. I Part 2:** 438, 440

Ruth Hall (Fern), **Supp. V:** 122

Rutledge, Ann, **III:** 588; **Supp. I Part 2:** 471

Ruwe, Donelle R., **Supp. XII:** 215

Ryan, Katy, **Supp. XXI:** 215

Ryan, Kay, **Supp. XXI:** 20

Ryan, Maureen, **Supp. XXI:** 215

Ryan, Paul William, **Supp. XVIII: 223–239**

Ryan, Paul William (Mike Quin), **Supp. XXI:** 264–265

Ryder (Barnes), **Supp. III Part 1:** 31, 36–38, 42, 43

"Ryder" (Rukeyser), **Supp. VI:** 273, 283

Ryle, Herbert Edward, **Supp. XX:**230

Rymer, Thomas, **IV:** 122

"Ryōkan Says" (Budbill), **Supp. XIX:** 11

S

S. (Updike), **Retro. Supp. I:** 330, 331, 332, 333

S-1 (Baraka), **Supp. II Part 1:** 55, 57

Saadi, **II:** 19

Saar, Doreen Alvarez, **Supp. XV:** 237

"Sabbath, The" (Stowe), **Supp. I Part 2:** 587

"Sabbath Mom" (White), **Supp. I Part 2:** 671–672

Sabbaths (Berry), **Supp. X:** 31

Sabbath's Theater (P. Roth), **Retro. Supp. II:** 279, 288

"Sabbioneta to Parma" (Di Piero), **Supp. XIX:** 36–37

Sabines, Jaime, **Supp. V:** 178

"Sabotage" (Baraka), **Supp. II Part 1:** 49, 53

"Saboteur" (Jin), **Supp. XVIII:** 97

Sacco, Nicola, **I:** 482, 486, 490, 494; **II:** 38–39, 426; **III:** 139–140; **Supp. I Part 2:** 446; **Supp. V:** 288–289; **Supp. IX:** 199

Sachs, Hanns, **Supp. I Part 1:** 259; **Supp. X:** 186

Sack Full of Old Quarrels, A (Weigl), **Supp. XIX:** 277

"Sacks" (Carver), **Supp. III Part 1:** 143–144

Sacks, Oliver, **Supp. XVIII:** 143

Sacks, Peter, **Supp. IV Part 2:** 450

Sackville-West, Vita, **Supp. VIII:** 263

"Sacrament of Divorce, The" (Patchett), **Supp. XII:** 309

"Sacraments" (Dubus), **Supp. VII:** 91

Sacred and Profane Memories (Van Vechten), **Supp. II Part 2:** 735, 749

"Sacred Chant for the Return of Black Spirit and Power" (Baraka), **Supp. II Part 1:** 51

"Sacred Factory, The" (Toomer), **Supp. IX:** 320

Sacred Fount, The (James), **II:** 332–333; **Retro. Supp. I:** 219, 228, 232

"Sacred Heart" (Egan), **Supp. XIX:** 52

"Sacred Hoop, The: A Contemporary Perspective" (Gunn Allen), **Supp. IV Part 1:** 324

Sacred Hoop, The: Recovering the Feminine in American Indian Traditions (Gunn Allen), **Supp. IV Part 1:** 319, 320, 322, 324, 325, 328–330, 331, 333, 334

Sacred Journey, The (Buechner), **Supp. XII:** 42, 53

"Sacred Thing, The" (Ryan as Quin), **Supp. XVIII:** 227

Sacred Wood, The (Eliot), **IV:** 431; **Retro. Supp. I:** 59, 60; **Supp. I Part 1:** 268; **Supp. II Part 1:** 136, 146

Sacrifice, The (Bidart), **Supp. XV:** 22, **27–30,** 35

"Sacrifice, The" (Bidart), **Supp. XV:** 29

"Sacrifice, The" (Oates), **Supp. II Part 2:** 523

Sacrilege of Alan Kent, The (Caldwell), **I:** 291–292

"Sad Brazil" (Hardwick), **Supp. III Part 1:** 210

"Sad Dust Glories" (Ginsberg), **Supp. II Part 1:** 376

Sad Dust Glories: Poems Written Work Summer in Sierra Woods (Ginsberg), **Supp. II Part 1:** 326

Sade, Marquis de, **III:** 259; **IV:** 437, 442; **Supp. XII:** 1, 14–15

Sad Flower in the Sand, A (film), **Supp. XI:** 173

Sad Heart at the Supermarket, A (Jarrell), **II:** 386

"Sadie" (Matthiessen), **Supp. V:** 201

"Sadie and Maud" (Brooks), **Supp. XVIII:** 175

Sadness and Happiness (Pinsky), **Supp. VI:** 235, **237–241**

"Sadness of Brothers, The" (Kinnell), **Supp. III Part 1:** 237, 251

"Sadness of Days, The" (Salinas), **Supp. XIII:** 325

Sadness of Days, The: Selected and New Poems (Salinas), **Supp. XIII:** 311, **324–326**

"Sadness of Lemons, The" (Levine), **Supp. V:** 184

Sadoff, Ira, **Supp. XVII:** 241; **Supp. XXI:** 100

"Sad Rite" (Karr), **Supp. XI:** 243

"Sad Strains of a Gay Waltz" (Stevens), **Retro. Supp. I:** 302

"Safe" (Gordon), **Supp. IV Part 1:** 299, 306

"Safe in their Alabaster Chambers" (Dickinson), **Retro. Supp. I:** 30

Safer, Morley, **Supp. XIX:** 25

"Safe Subjects" (Komunyakaa), **Supp. XIII:** 118

"Safeway" (F. Barthelme), **Supp. XI:** 26, 27, 36

Saffin, John, **Supp. I Part 1:** 115

Saffy, Edna, **Supp. X:** 227

"Saga of an American Ranch" (P. N. Warren), **Supp. XX:**261

"Saga of Arturo Bandini" (Fante), **Supp. XI:** 159, **166–169**

"Saga of King Olaf, The" (Longfellow), **II:** 489, 505; **Retro. Supp. II:** 154, 155, 164

"Sage of Stupidity and Wonder, The" (Goldbarth), **Supp. XII:** 191

Sahl, Mort, **II:** 435–436

"Said" (Dixon), **Supp. XII:** 149–150

Said, Edward, **Supp. XXI:** 153

"Sailing after Lunch" (Stevens), **IV:** 73

Sailing Alone Around the Room: New and Selected Poems (Collins), **Supp. XXI:** 54, 56, 62

"Sailing Home from Rapallo" (Lowell), **Retro. Supp. II:** 189

Sailing through China (Theroux), **Supp. VIII:** 323

"Sailing to Byzantium" (Yeats), **III:** 263; **Supp. VIII:** 30; **Supp. X:** 74; **Supp. XI:** 281

"Sail Made of Rags, The" (Nye), **Supp. XIII:** 277

"Sailor off the Bremen" (Shaw), **Supp. XIX:** 247

"Sailors Lost at Sea" (Shields), **Supp. VII:** 318

"*St Anne*/Santa Ana" (Mora), **Supp. XIII:** 229

"*Saint Anthony of Padua*/San Antonio de Padua" (Mora), **Supp. XIII:** 228

"St. Augustine and the Bullfights" (Porter), **III:** 454

Sainte-Beuve, Charles Augustin, **IV:** 432

St. Elmo (Wilson), **Retro. Supp. I:** 351–352

"Saint Emmanuel the Good, Martyr" (Unamuno; Everwine, trans.), **Supp. XV:** 79

Sainte Vierge, La (Picabia), **Retro. Supp. II:** 331

Saint-Exupéry, Antoine de, **Supp. IX:** 247

"St. Francis Einstein of the Daffodils" (W. C. Williams), **IV:** 409–411

Saint-Gaudens, Augustus, **I:** 18, 228; **II:** 551

Saint-Gaudens, Homer, **Supp. XV:** 41

"St. George, the Dragon, and the Virgin" (R. Bly), **Supp. IV Part 1:** 73

St. George and the Godfather (Mailer), **III:** 46; **Retro. Supp. II:** 206, 208

Saint Jack (Theroux), **Supp. VIII:** 319

St. John, David, **Supp. V:** 180; **Supp. XI:** 270, 272; **Supp. XIII:** 312

St. John, Edward B., **Supp. IV Part 2:** 490

St. John, James Hector. *See* Crèvecoeur, Michel-Guillaume Jean de

"Saint John and the Back-Ache" (Stevens), **Retro. Supp. I:** 310

Saint Judas (Wright), **Supp. III Part 2:** 595–599

"Saint Judas" (Wright), **Supp. III Part 2:** 598–599

St. Louis Woman (Bontemps and Cullen), **Supp. IV Part 1:** 170

St. Mawr (Lawrence), **II:** 595

Saint Maybe (Tyler), **Supp. IV Part 2:** 670–671

"Saint Nicholas" (Moore), **III:** 215

St. Petersburg (Biely), **Supp. XII:** 13

Saint-Phalle, Niki de, **Supp. XV:** 187

"St. Roach" (Rukeyser), **Supp. VI:** 286

"Saint Robert" (Dacey), **Supp. IV Part 1:** 70

Saintsbury, George, **IV:** 440; **Supp. XV:** 181

Saints' Everlasting Rest, The (Baxter), **III:** 199; **IV:** 151, 153

Saint-Simon, Claude Henri, **Supp. I Part 2:** 648

"St. Thomas Aquinas" (Simic), **Supp. VIII:** 281

Saks, Gene, **Supp. IV Part 2:** 577, 588

Salamun, Tomaz, **Supp. VIII:** 272

Salazar, Dixie, **Supp. V:** 180; **Supp. XV:** 73

Saldívar, José David, **Supp. IV Part 2:** 544, 545; **Supp. XIX:** 110, 112–113

Sale, Richard, **Supp. IV Part 1:** 379

Sale, Roger, **Supp. V:** 244

Saleh, Dennis, **Supp. V:** 182, 186

"Salem" (Lowell), **II:** 550

Salemi, Joseph, **Supp. IV Part 1:** 284

Salem's Lot (King), **Supp. V:** 139, 144, 146, 151

"Sale of the Hessians, The" (Franklin), **II:** 120

Salinas, Luis Omar, **Supp. IV Part 2:** 545; **Supp. V:** 180; **Supp. XIII:** 311–330; **Supp. XV:** 73

"Salinas Is on His Way" (Salinas), **Supp. XIII:** 317

"Salinas Sends Messengers to the Stars" (Salinas), **Supp. XIII:** 317

"Salinas Summering at the Caspian and Thinking of Hamlet" (Salinas), **Supp. XIII:** 320

"Salinas Wakes Early and Goes to the Park to Lecture Sparrows" (Salinas), **Supp. XIII:** 320

Salinger, Doris, **III:** 551

Salinger, J. D., **II:** 255; **III:** 551–574; **IV:** 190, 216, 217; **Retro. Supp. I:** 102, 116, 335; **Supp. IV Part 2:** 502; **Supp. V:** 23, 119; **Supp. VIII:** 151; **Supp. XI:** 2, 66; **Supp. XIV:** 93

Salisbury, Harrison, **Supp. I Part 2:** 664

Salle, David, **Supp. XII:** 4

Salley, Columbus, **Supp. XIV:** 195

"Sally" (Cisneros), **Supp. VII:** 63

"Sally's Choice" (E. Stoddard), **Supp. XV:** 282

Salmagundi; or, The Whim-Whams and Opinions of Launcelot Langstaff Esq., and Others (Irving), **II:** 299, 300, 304

Salmon, Edward G., **Supp. XVIII:** 258

Salome (Strauss), **IV:** 316

Salon (online magazine), **Supp. VIII:** 310; **Supp. X:** 202

Salt Eaters, The (Bambara), **Supp. XI:** 1, 12–14

Salt Ecstasies, The (White), **Supp. XI:** 123

Salter, James, **Supp. IX:** 245–263; **Supp. XVI:** 237, 247; **Supp. XIX:** 252

Salter, Mary Jo, **Supp. IV Part 2:** 653; **Supp. IX:** 37, 292; **Supp. XV:** 251, 253; **Supp. XVII:** 112

Salt Garden, The (Nemerov), **III:** 269, 272–275, 277

"Salt Garden, The" (Nemerov), **III:** 267–268

Salting the Ocean (Nye, ed.), **Supp. XIII:** 280

Salt Lesson, The (C. Frost), **Supp. XV:** 92, 96

"Salt Lesson, The" (C. Frost), **Supp. XV:** 99

"Salts and Oils" (Levine), **Supp. V:** 190

Salt to the Devil (film, Dmytryk), **Supp. XX:** 41

Saltzman, Arthur, **Supp. XIII:** 48

Saltzman, Harry, **Supp. XI:** 307

"Salut au Monde!" (Whitman), **Retro. Supp. I:** 387, 396, 400

"Salute" (MacLeish), **III:** 13

Salute (Shaw), **Supp. XIX:** 244

"Salute to Mister Yates, A" (Dubus), **Supp. XI:** 347, 349

Salvador (Didion), **Supp. IV Part 1:** 198, 207–208, 210

"Salvage" (Clampitt), **Supp. IX:** 41

Salvos: An Informal Book About Books and Plays (W. Frank), **Supp. XX:** 75

Samain, Albert, **II:** 528

Same Door, The (Updike), **IV:** 214, 219, 226; **Retro. Supp. I:** 320

"Same in Blues" (Hughes), **Retro. Supp. I:** 208

Same River Twice, The (Offutt), **Supp. XIX:** 163, 164, 167–168, 175

"Samhain" (A. Finch), **Supp. XVII:** 72

Sam Lawson's Oldtown Fireside Stories (Stowe), **Supp. I Part 2:** 587, 596, 598–599

"Sa'm Pèdi" (Bell), **Supp. X:** 17

"Sampler, A" (MacLeish), **III:** 4

Sampoli, Maria, **Supp. V:** 338

Sampson, Edward, **Supp. I Part 2:** 664, 673

Sampson, Martin, **Supp. I Part 2:** 652

"Sam's Dad" (Lamott), **Supp. XX:** 142–143

Sam's Legacy (Neugeboren), **Supp. XVI:** 221, 222

Samson Agonistes (Milton), **III:** 274

"Samson and Delilah" (Masters), **Supp. I Part 2:** 459

Samuel de Champlain: Father of New France (Morison), **Supp. I Part 2:** 496–497

Samuels, Charles Thomas, **Retro. Supp. I:** 334

"Samuel Sewall" (Hecht), **Supp. X:** 58

"Samwheel" (Lamott), **Supp. XX:** 144–145

Sanborn, Franklin B., **IV:** 171, 172, 178

Sanborn, Kate, **Supp. XIII:** 152

Sanborn, Sara, **Supp. XIV:** 113

Sanchez, Carol Anne, **Supp. IV Part 1:** 335

Sanchez, Carol Lee, **Supp. IV Part 2:** 499, 557

Sanchez, Sonia, **Supp. II Part 1:** 34

Sánchez Beras, César, **Supp. XXI:** 100, 104

Sanctified Church, The (Hurston), **Supp. VI:** 150

"Sanction of the Victims, The" (Rand), **Supp. IV Part 2:** 528

Sanctuary (Faulkner), **II:** 57, 61–63, 72, 73, 74, 174; **Retro. Supp. I:** 73, 84, 86–87, 87; **Supp. I Part 2:** 614; **Supp. XII:** 16

"Sanctuary" (Larsen), **Supp. XVIII:** 119, 130–131

Sanctuary (Wharton), **IV:** 311

"Sanctuary" (Wylie), **Supp. I Part 2:** 711

"Sanctuary, The" (Nemerov), **III:** 272, 274

Sanctuary V (Schulberg), **Supp. XVIII:** 254

"Sanctus" (Nelson), **Supp. XVIII:** 183

Sand, George, **II:** 322; **Retro. Supp. I:** 235, 372; **Supp. XV:** 275

"Sandalphon" (Longfellow), **II:** 498

Sand and Foam: A Book of Aphorisms (Gibran), **Supp. XX:**115, **121–122**

Sandbox, The (Albee), **I:** 74–75, 89

Sandburg, Carl, **I:** 103, 109, 384, 421; **II:** 529; **III:** 3, 20, **575–598; Retro. Supp. I:** 133, 194; **Supp. I Part 1:** 257, 320; **Supp. I Part 2:** 387, 389, 454, 461, 653; **Supp. III Part 1:** 63, 71, 73, 75; **Supp. IV Part 1:** 169; **Supp. IV Part 2:** 502; **Supp. IX:** 1, 15, 308; **Supp. XIII:** 274, 277; **Supp. XV:** 293, 299, 300, 301, 302, 306

Sandburg, Mrs. Carl (Lillian Steichen), **III:** 580

Sandburg, Helga, **III:** 583

Sandburg, Janet, **III:** 583, 584

Sandburg, Margaret, **III:** 583, 584

Sand County Almanac and Sketches Here and There, A (Leopold), **Supp. XIV:** 177, 178, **182–192**

"Sand Dabs" (Oliver), **Supp. VII:** 245

"Sand Dunes" (Frost), **Retro. Supp. I:** 137; **Retro. Supp. II:** 41

Sander, August, **Supp. IX:** 211

Sanders, Mark, **Supp. XIX:** 119, 121

Sanders, Scott Russell, **Supp. XVI: 265–280**

"Sandman, The" (Barthelme), **Supp. IV Part 1:** 47

Sandman's Dust (Bukiet), **Supp. XVII:** 40, 41

Sando, Joe S., **Supp. IV Part 2:** 510

Sandoe, James, **Supp. IV Part 1:** 131; **Supp. IV Part 2:** 470

Sandoz, Mari, **Supp. XV:** 141

Sandperl, Ira, **Supp. VIII:** 200

"Sand-Quarry and Moving Figures" (Rukeyser), **Supp. VI:** 271, 278

Sand Rivers (Matthiessen), **Supp. V:** 203

"Sand Roses, The" (Hogan), **Supp. IV Part 1:** 401

Sands, Diana, **Supp. IV Part 1:** 362

Sands, Robert, **Supp. I Part 1:** 156, 157

"Sands at Seventy" (Whitman), **IV:** 348

"Sandstone Farmhouse, A" (Updike), **Retro. Supp. I:** 318

Sandy Bottom Orchestra,The (Keillor and Nilsson), **Supp. XVI:** 177

Sanford, John, **IV:** 286, 287

San Francisco (film), **Supp. XVI:** 181, 192

"San Francisco" (Hempel), **Supp. XXI:** 118

"San Francisco Blues" (Kerouac), **Supp. III Part 1:** 225

Sangamon County Peace Advocate, The (Lindsay), **Supp. I Part 2:** 379

Sanger, Margaret, **Supp. I Part 1:** 19; **Supp. XXI:** 6

Sankofa (film), **Supp. XX:**154

Sansom, William, **IV:** 279

Sans Soleil (film), **Supp. IV Part 2:** 436

"Santa" (Sexton), **Supp. II Part 2:** 693

Santa Claus: A Morality (Cummings), **I:** 430, 441

"Santa Fé Trail, The" (Lindsay), **Supp. I Part 2:** 389

"Santa Lucia" (Hass), **Supp. VI:** 105–106

"Santa Lucia II" (Hass), **Supp. VI:** 105–106

Santayana, George, **I:** 222, 224, 236, 243, 253, 460; **II:** 20, 542; **III:** 64, **599–622; IV:** 26, 339, 351, 353, 441; **Retro. Supp. I:** 55, 57, 67, 295; **Retro. Supp. II:** 179; **Supp. I Part 2:** 428; **Supp. II Part 1:** 107; **Supp. X:** 58; **Supp. XIV:** 199, 335, 340, 342; **Supp. XVI:** 189; **Supp. XVII:** 97, 106; **Supp. XX:**228, 229, 231

Santiago, Esmeralda, **Supp. XI:** 177

"Santorini: Stopping the Leak" (Merrill), **Supp. III Part 1:** 336

Santos, John Phillip, **Supp. XIII:** 274

Santos, Sherod, **Supp. VIII:** 270

Sapir, Edward, **Supp. VIII:** 295; **Supp. XVI:** 283

"Sapphics for Patience" (A. Finch), **Supp. XVII:** 72

Sapphira and the Slave Girl (Cather), **I:** 331; **Retro. Supp. I:** 2, **19–20**

Sappho, **II:** 544; **III:** 142; **Supp. I Part 1:** 261, 269; **Supp. I Part 2:** 458; **Supp. XII:** 98, 99; **Supp. XVII:** 74

"Sappho" (Wright), **Supp. III Part 2:** 595, 604

"Sara" (song, Dylan), **Supp. XVIII:** 28

"Sarah" (Schwartz), **Supp. II Part 2:** 663

Sarah; or, The Exemplary Wife (Rowson), **Supp. XV:** 242

"Saratoga" mysteries (Dobyns), **Supp. XIII:** 79–80

Sargent, John Singer, **II:** 337, 338; **Supp. XX:**231

Sarlós, Robert K., **Supp. XXI:** 7, 12, 13

Saroyan, Aram, **Supp. XV:** 182

Saroyan, William, **III:** 146–147; **IV:** 393; **Supp. I Part 2:** 679; **Supp. IV Part 1:** 83; **Supp. IV Part 2:** 502; **Supp. XIII:** 280

Sarris, Greg, **Supp. IV Part 1:** 329, 330

Sarton, George, **Supp. VIII:** 249

Sarton, May, **Supp. III Part 1:** 62, 63; **Supp. VIII: 249–268; Supp. XIII:** 296; **Supp. XVII:** 71

Sartoris (Faulkner), **II:** 55, 56–57, 58, 62; **Retro. Supp. I:** 77, 81, 82, 83, 88

Sartor Resartus (Carlyle), **II:** 26; **III:** 82

Sartre, Jean-Paul, **I:** 82, 494; **II:** 57, 244; **III:** 51, 204, 292, 453, 619; **IV:** 6, 223, 236, 477, 487, 493; **Retro. Supp. I:** 73; **Supp. I Part 1:** 51; **Supp. IV**

Part 1: 42, 84; **Supp. VIII:** 11; **Supp. IX:** 4; **Supp. XIII:** 74, 171; **Supp. XIV:** 24; **Supp. XVII:** 137

Sassone, Ralph, **Supp. X:** 171

Sassoon, Siegfried, **II:** 367; **Supp. XV:** 308; **Supp. XIX:** 18

Satan in Goray (Singer), **IV:** 1, 6–7, 12; **Retro. Supp. II:** 303, **304–305**

Satan Says (Olds), **Supp. X:** 201, 202, **202–204,** 215

"Satan Says" (Olds), **Supp. X:** 202; **Supp. XVII:** 114

Satanstoe (Cooper), **I:** 351–352, 355

"Sather Gate Illumination" (Ginsberg), **Supp. II Part 1:** 329

"Satire as a Way of Seeing" (Dos Passos), **III:** 172

Satires of Persius, The (Merwin, trans.), **Supp. III Part 1:** 347

Satirical Rogue on Poetry, The (Francis). *See Pot Shots at Poetry* (Francis)

Satori in Paris (Kerouac), **Supp. III Part 1:** 231

"Saturday" (Salinas), **Supp. XIII:** 315

"Saturday Matinee" (Trethewey), **Supp. XXI:** 251

Saturday Night at the War (Shanley), **Supp. XIV:** 315

"Saturday Rain" (Kees), **Supp. XV:** 136

"Saturday Route, The" (Wolfe), **Supp. III Part 2:** 580

Satyagraha (Gandhi), **IV:** 185

"Satyr's Heart, The" (B. Kelly), **Supp. XVII:** 132

Saul and Patsy (C. Baxter), **Supp. XVII:** 22–23

"Saul and Patsy" (C. Baxter), **Supp. XVII:** 17

"Saul and Patsy Are Getting Comfortable in Michigan" (C. Baxter), **Supp. XVII:** 22

"Saul and Patsy Are in Labor" (C. Baxter), **Supp. XVII:** 20, 22

"Saul and Patsy Are Pregnant" (C. Baxter), **Supp. XVII:** 22

Saunders, George, **Supp. XIX: 223–237**

Saunders, Richard, **II:** 110

Savage, Augusta, **Retro. Supp. II:** 115

Savage, James, **II:** 111

Savage Holiday (Wright), **IV:** 478, 488

Savage in Limbo: A Concert Play (Shanley), **Supp. XIV:** 315, **319–321,** 323, 324

Savage Love (Shepard and Chaikin), **Supp. III Part 2:** 433

Savage Place, A (Parker), **Supp. XIX:** 185

Savage Wilds (Reed), **Supp. X:** 241

Save Me, Joe Louis (Bell), **Supp. X:** 7, 10, **11–12**

Save Me the Waltz (Z. Fitzgerald), **II:** 95; **Retro. Supp. I:** 110; **Supp. IX:** 58, 59, 65, **66–68**

Savers, Michael, **Supp. XI:** 307

Saving Lives (Goldbarth), **Supp. XII:** 192

Saving Private Ryan (film), **Supp. V:** 249; **Supp. XI:** 234

Savings (Hogan), **Supp. IV Part 1:** 397, 404, 405, 406, 410

Savo, Jimmy, **I:** 440

Savran, David, **Supp. IX:** 145; **Supp. XIII:** 209; **Supp. XV:** 321
"Sawdust" (Offutt), **Supp. XIX:** 164
Sawyer-Lauçanno, Christopher, **Supp. IV Part 1:** 95
Saxon, Lyle, **Retro. Supp. I:** 80
"Saxophone" (Di Piero), **Supp. XIX:** 38
"Sax's and Selves" (Halliday), **Supp. XIX:** 88
"Say All" (Ray), **Supp. XVIII:** 193
Say and Seal (S. and A. Warner), **Supp. XVIII:** 258, 266
Saye and Sele, Lord, **Supp. I Part 1:** 98
Sayer, Mandy, **Supp. XIII:** 118
Sayers, Dorothy, **Supp. IV Part 1:** 341; **Supp. IV Part 2:** 464
Sayers, Valerie, **Supp. XI:** 253; **Supp. XVIII:** 99
"Say Good-bye" (Weigl), **Supp. XIX:** 288
"Sayings/For Luck" (Goldbarth), **Supp. XII:** 176
"Saying What Needs To Be Said" (Skloot), **Supp. XX:**201
Say! Is This the U.S.A.? (Caldwell), **I:** 293, 294–295, 304, 309, 310
Saylor, Bruce, **Supp. XII:** 253
Sayre, Joel, **Supp. XIII:** 166
Sayre, Nora, **Supp. XII:** 119
Sayre, Zelda, **Retro. Supp. I:** 101, 102–103, 104, 105, 108, 109, 110, 113, 114. *See also* Fitzgerald, Zelda (Zelda Sayre)
"Say Yes" (Wolff), **Supp. VII:** 344
"Say You Love Me" (Peacock), **Supp. XIX:** 198
"Scale" (Halliday), **Supp. XIX:** 92
"Scales of the Eyes, The" (Nemerov), **III:** 272, 273, 277
Scalpel (McCoy), **Supp. XIII: 174–175**
Scalpel (screen treatment, McCoy), **Supp. XIII:** 174
Scandalabra (Zelda Fitzgerald), **Supp. IX:** 60, 61, 65, 67, **68–70**
"Scandal Detectives, The" (Fitzgerald), **II:** 80–81; **Retro. Supp. I:** 99
Scarberry-García, Susan, **Supp. IV Part 2:** 486
Scarborough, Dorothy, **Supp. XVIII:** 279–280
Scarecrow, The (Connelly), **Supp. XXI:** 71, 74, 78, **79**
"Scarecrow, The" (Farrell), **II:** 45
"Scarf, A" (Shields), **Supp. VII:** 328
Scarlet Letter, The (Hawthorne), **II:** 63, 223, 224, 231, 233, 239–240, 241, 243, 244, 255, 264, 286, 290, 291, 550; **Retro. Supp. I:** 63, 145, 147, 152, **157–159,** 160, 163, 165, 220, 248, 330, 335; **Retro. Supp. II:** 100; **Supp. I Part 1:** 38; **Supp. II Part 1:** 386; **Supp. VIII:** 108, 198; **Supp. XII:** 11; **Supp. XVII:** 143; **Supp. XX:**178, 183
"Scarlet Letter Aleph, The" (Mirvis), **Supp. XX:**183
Scarlet Plague, The (London), **II:** 467
Scar Lover (Crews), **Supp. XI:** 103, 107, **114–115**

"Scarred Girl, The" (Dickey), **Supp. IV Part 1:** 180
Scates, Maxine, **Supp. XIV:** 264, 265, 274
"Scenario" (H. Miller), **III:** 184
"Scene" (Howells), **II:** 274
"Scene in Jerusalem, A" (Stowe), **Supp. I Part 2:** 587
"Scenes" (Shields), **Supp. VII:** 318
Scènes d'Anabase (chamber music) (Bowles), **Supp. IV Part 1:** 82
"Scenes from a Documentary History of Mississippi" (Trethewey), **Supp. XXI:** 255–256
Scenes from American Life (Gurney), **Supp. V:** 95, 96, 105, 108
Scenes from Another Life (McClatchy), **Supp. XII: 255–256**
"Scenes from Childhood" (W. V. Davis), **Supp. XXI:** 95
"Scenes of Childhood" (Merrill), **Supp. III Part 1:** 322, 323, 327
"Scented Herbage of My Breast" (Whitman), **IV:** 342–343
"Scent of a Woman's Ink" (Prose), **Supp. XVI:** 259
"Scent of Unbought Flowers, The" (Ríos), **Supp. IV Part 2:** 547
Scepticisms (Aiken), **I:** 58
Scève, Maurice, **Supp. III Part 1:** 11
Schad, Christian, **Supp. IV Part 1:** 247
Schafer, Benjamin G., **Supp. XIV:** 144
Schafer, William, **Supp. XIX:** 164, 172
Schaller, George, **Supp. V:** 208, 210–211
Schapiro, Meyer, **II:** 30
Scharmann, Hermann Balthazar, **Supp. XII:** 41
Schary, Dore, **Supp. IV Part 1:** 365; **Supp. XIII:** 163
Schatz, Tom, **Supp. XVIII:** 242
Schaumbergh, Count de, **II:** 120
Scheele, Roy, **Supp. XVI:** 54; **Supp. XXI:** 103
Scheffauer, G. H., **I:** 199
"Scheherazade" (Ashbery), **Supp. III Part 1:** 18
Scheick, William, **Supp. V:** 272
Schelberg, Budd, **Supp. XVIII: 241–256**
Scheler, Max, **I:** 58
Schelling, Friedrich, **Supp. I Part 2:** 422
Schenck, Joseph, **Supp. XVI:** 186
Schenk, Margaret, **I:** 199
Scheponik, Peter, **Supp. X:** 210
Scherer, Loline, **Supp. XIII:** 161
Schevill, James, **I:** 116
Schickel, Richard, **Supp. XV:** 1
Schilder, Paul, **Supp. I Part 2:** 622
Schiller, Andrew, **II:** 20
Schiller, Frederick, **Supp. V:** 290
Schiller, Johann Christoph Friedrich von, **I:** 224; **Supp. IV Part 2:** 519; **Supp. XVI:** 292
Schiller, Lawrence, **Retro. Supp. II:** 208, 212, 214
Schimmel, Harold, **Supp. V:** 336
"Schizoid Nature of the Implied Author in Twentieth-Century American Ethnic Novels, The" (Nelson), **Supp. XVIII:** 172

Schlegel, Augustus Wilhelm, **III:** 422, 424
Schlegell, David von, **Supp. IV Part 2:** 423
Schleiermacher, Friedrich, **III:** 290–291, 309
Schleifer, Ronald, **Supp. XVIII:** 144
Schlepping Through the Alps (S. Apple), **Supp. XVII:** 8
Schlesinger, Arthur, Jr., **III:** 291, 297–298, 309
Schmidt, Jon Zlotnik, **Supp. IV Part 1:** 2
Schmidt, Kaspar. *See* Stirner, Max
Schmidt, Michael, **Supp. X:** 55
Schmitt, Carl, **I:** 386–387
Schmitz, Neil, **Supp. X:** 243
Schnackenberg, Gjertrud, **Supp. XV: 249–268**
Schneider, Alan, **I:** 87
Schneider, Louis, **Supp. I Part 2:** 650
Schneider, Romy, **Supp. IV Part 2:** 549
Schneider, Steven, **Supp. IX:** 271, 274
Schnellock, Emil, **III:** 177
Schneour, Zalman, **IV:** 11
"Schnetzer Day" (Halliday), **Supp. XIX:** 93
Schnitzler, Arthur, **Supp. XV:** 307; **Supp. XVI:** 187
Schoerke, Meg, **Supp. XVII:** 110
"Scholar Gypsy, The" (Arnold), **II:** 541
"Scholastic and Bedside Teaching" (Holmes), **Supp. I Part 1:** 305
Schöler, Bo, **Supp. IV Part 1:** 399, 400, 403, 407, 409; **Supp. IV Part 2:** 499
Scholes, Robert, **Supp. V:** 40, 42
Scholtz, Carter, **Supp. XVIII:** 144
Schomburg, Arthur, **Supp. X:** 134
Schomburg Library of Nineteenth-Century Black Women Writers (H. L. Gates, ed.), **Supp. XX:**105
Schönberg, Claude-Michel, **Supp. XXI:** 155
Schoolboy Howlers (Abingdon), **Supp. XVI:** 99
Schoolcraft, Henry Rowe, **II:** 503; **Retro. Supp. II:** 160
"School Daze" (Bambara), **Supp. XI:** 19
School Daze (film), **Supp. XI:** 19, 20
"Schoolhouse" (Levis), **Supp. XI:** 258
"School of Giorgione, The" (Pater), **I:** 51
"School Play, The" (Merrill), **Supp. III Part 1:** 336
"Schooner Fairchild's Class" (Benét), **Supp. XI:** 55
Schopenhauer, Arthur, **III:** 600, 604; **IV:** 7; **Retro. Supp. I:** 256; **Retro. Supp. II:** 94; **Supp. I Part 1:** 320; **Supp. I Part 2:** 457; **Supp. X:** 187; **Supp. XVI:** 184
Schorer, Mark, **II:** 28; **III:** 71; **Retro. Supp. I:** 115; **Supp. IV Part 1:** 197, 203, 211; **Supp. XVI:** 206
Schott, Webster, **Supp. IX:** 257
Schotts, Jeffrey, **Supp. XII:** 193
Schrader, Mary von. *See* Jarrell, Mrs. Randall (Mary von Schrader)
Schreiber, Jan, **Supp. XXI:** 105, 111
Schreiner, Olive, **I:** 419; **Supp. XI:** 203
Schroeder, Eric James, **Supp. V:** 238, 244

Schubert, Bernard L., **Supp. XVII:** 58
Schubert, Franz Peter, **Supp. I Part 1:** 363
Schubnell, Matthias, **Supp. IV Part 2:** 486
Schulberg, Budd, **II:** 98; **Retro. Supp. I:** 113; **Supp. XIII:** 170; **Supp. XV:** 194
Schulberg, Stuart, **Supp. XVIII:** 254
Schulman, Tom, **Supp. XXI:** 193, 194
Schulz, Bruno, **Supp. IV Part 2:** 623; **Supp. XVII:** 41
Schuman, William, **Supp. XII:** 253
Schumann, Dr. Alanson Tucker, **III:** 505
Schuster, Edgar H., **Supp. VIII:** 126
Schuyler, George S., **III:** 110; **Supp. XVI:** 142; **Supp. XIX:** 78
Schuyler, James, **Supp. XV:** 177, 178
Schuyler, William, **Supp. I Part 1:** 211
"Schuylkill, The" (Halliday), **Supp. XIX:** 92
Schwartz, Delmore, **I:** 67, 168, 188, 288; **IV:** 128, 129, 437; **Retro. Supp. II:** 29, 178; **Supp. II Part 1:** 102, 109; **Supp. II Part 2: 639–668; Supp. VIII:** 98; **Supp. IX:** 299; **Supp. XIII:** 320; **Supp. XIV:** 3; **Supp. XV:** 184; **Supp. XIX:** 257
Schwartz, Leonard, **Supp. XVI:** 289
Schwartz, Lloyd, **Supp. I Part 1:** 81
Schwartz, Marilyn, **Supp. XII:** 126, 128, 130, 132
Schwartz, Richard B., **Supp. XIV:** 23, 27
Schwarz, A. B. Christa, **Supp. XIX:** 77, 79
Schweitzer, Albert, **Supp. IV Part 1:** 373
Schweitzer, Harold, **Supp. X:** 210
Schwerdt, Lisa M., **Supp. XIV:** 155, 171
Schwitters, Kurt, **III:** 197; **Retro. Supp. II:** 322, 331, 336; **Supp. IV Part 1:** 79
"Science" (Jeffers), **Supp. II Part 2:** 426
Science and Health with Key to the Scriptures (Eddy), **I:** 383
"Science Favorable to Virtue" (Freneau), **Supp. II Part 1:** 274
Science of English Verse, The (Lanier), **Supp. I Part 1:** 368, 369
"Science of the Night, The" (Kunitz), **Supp. III Part 1:** 258, 265
"Sci-Fi Floater Genius" (Halliday), **Supp. XIX:** 91
Sciolino, Martina, **Supp. XII:** 9
"Scissors" (C. Baxter), **Supp. XVII:** 19
Scofield, Sandra, **Supp. XXI:** 119
Scooter tetralogy (Murray). *See Magic Keys, The* (Murray); *Seven League Boots, The* (Murray); *Spyglass Tree, The* (Murray); *Train Whistle Guitar* (Murray)
Scopes, John T., **III:** 105, 495
"Scorched Face, The" (Hammett), **Supp. IV Part 1:** 344
"Scorn" (C. Frost), **Supp. XV:** 105
"Scorpion, The" (Bowles), **Supp. IV Part 1:** 84, 86
Scorsese, Martin, **Supp. IV Part 1:** 356; **Supp. XVIII:** 22
Scott, Anne Firor, **Supp. I Part 1:** 19
Scott, A. O., **Supp. X:** 301, 302; **Supp. XII:** 343

Scott, Evelyn, **Retro. Supp. I:** 73
Scott, George C., **III:** 165–166; **Supp. XI:** 304
Scott, George Lewis, **Supp. I Part 2:** 503, 504
Scott, Herbert, **Supp. V:** 180
Scott, Howard, **Supp. I Part 2:** 645
Scott, Joanna, **Supp. XVII: 183–197**
Scott, Lizabeth, **Supp. IV Part 2:** 524
Scott, Lynn Orilla, **Retro. Supp. II:** 12
Scott, Mark, **Retro. Supp. I:** 127
Scott, Nathan A., Jr., **II:** 27
Scott, Paul, **Supp. IV Part 2:** 690
Scott, Ridley, **Supp. XIII:** 268
Scott, Walter, **Supp. XVI:** 7, 13
Scott, Sir Walter, **I:** 204, 339, 341, 343, 354; **II:** 8, 17, 18, 217, 296, 301, 303, 304, 308; **III:** 415, 482; **IV:** 204, 453; **Retro. Supp. I:** 99; **Supp. I Part 2:** 579, 580, 685, 692; **Supp. IV Part 2:** 690; **Supp. IX:** 175; **Supp. X:** 51, 114
Scott, Winfield Townley, **II:** 512; **Supp. I Part 2:** 705; **Supp. XV:** 51
Scottsboro boys, **I:** 505; **Supp. I Part 1:** 330
Scottsboro Limited (Hughes), **Retro. Supp. I:** 203; **Supp. I Part 1:** 328, 330–331, 332
Scoundrel Time (Hellman), **Supp. I Part 1:** 294–297; **Supp. IV Part 1:** 12; **Supp. VIII:** 243
Scrambled Eggs Super! (Geisel), **Supp. XVI:** 105
Scrambled Eggs & Whiskey: Poems, 1991–1995 (Carruth), **Supp. XVI:** 47
Scratch (MacLeish), **III:** 22–23
"Scratch Music" (Wright), **Supp. XV:** 343
"Scream, The" (Lowell), **II:** 550
"Screamer, The" (Coleman), **Supp. XI: 92–93**
"Screamers, The" (Baraka), **Supp. II Part 1:** 38
"Screen Guide for Americans" (Rand), **Supp. IV Part 2:** 524
"Screeno" (Schwartz), **Supp. II Part 2:** 660
Screens, The (Genet), **Supp. XII:** 12
Scribblers on the Roof: Contemporary American Jewish Fiction (Bukiet and Roskies, eds.), **Supp. XVII:** 39, 49–50
Scripts for the Pageant (Merrill), **Supp. III Part 1:** 332, 333, 335
Scrolls from the Dead Sea, The (Wilson), **IV:** 429
Scruggs, Earl, **Supp. V:** 335
Scudder, Horace Elisha, **II:** 400, 401; **Retro. Supp. II:** 67; **Supp. I Part 1:** 220; **Supp. I Part 2:** 410, 414
Scully, James, **Supp. XII:** 131
"Sculpting the Whistle" (Ríos), **Supp. IV Part 2:** 549
"Sculptor" (Plath), **Supp. I Part 2:** 538
"Sculptor's Funeral, The" (Cather), **I:** 315–316; **Retro. Supp. I:** 5, 6; **Supp. XV:** 40
Scum (Singer), **Retro. Supp. II:** 316–317
Scupoli, Lorenzo, **IV:** 156
"Scythe Song" (Lang), **Retro. Supp. I:** 128

Sea and the Mirror, The: A Commentary on Shakespeare's "The Tempest" (Auden), *Supp. II Part 1:* 2, 18
Sea around Us, The (Carson), **Supp. IX:** 19, **23–25**
Sea around Us, The (film), **Supp. IX:** 25
Sea Birds Are Still Alive, The (Bambara), **Supp. XI:** 1, 4, **7–12**
"Sea Birds Are Still Alive, The" (Bambara), **Supp. XI:** 8
"Sea-Blue and Blood-Red" (Lowell), **II:** 524
Seabrook, John, **Supp. VIII:** 157
"Sea Burial from the Cruiser Reve" (Eberhart), **I:** 532–533
Seabury, David, **Supp. I Part 2:** 608
"Sea Calm" (Hughes), **Retro. Supp. I:** 199
"Sea Chanty" (Corso), **Supp. XII:** 118
"Sea Dream, A" (Whitter), **Supp. I Part 2:** 699
"Seafarer, The" (Pound, trans.), **Retro. Supp. I:** 287
Seagall, Harry, **Supp. XIII:** 166
Sea Garden (Doolittle), **Supp. I Part 1:** 257, 259, 266, 269, 272
Seager, Allan, **IV:** 305
"Seagulls and Children" (C. Frost), **Supp. XV:** 95
Sea Lady, The (Boyce), **Supp. XXI:** 8, 13
"Sea Lily" (Doolittle), **Supp. I Part 1:** 266
Sea Lions, The (Cooper), **I:** 354, 355
Sealts, Merton M., Jr., **Retro. Supp. I:** 257
Seaman, Donna, **Supp. VIII:** 86; **Supp. X:** 1, 4, 12, 16, 213; **Supp. XV:** 65; **Supp. XVIII:** 102; **Supp. XIX:** 53, 55, 57, 58, 59, 60, 61; **Supp. XXI:** 236
"Séance, The" (Singer), **IV:** 20
Séance and Other Stories, The (Singer), **IV:** 19–21
"Sea Oak" (Saunders), **Supp. XIX:** 228, 229, 231
Sea of Cortez (Steinbeck), **IV:** 52, 54, 62, 69
Sea of Grass, The (film), **Supp. XVIII:** 211
Sea of Grass, The (Richter), **Supp. XVIII: 210–211**, 215–216, 217, 220
"Sea Pieces" (Melville), **III:** 93
Searchers, The (film, Ford), **Supp. XVIII:** 57, 58, 135–136, 141
Searches and Seizures (Elkin), **Supp. VI:** 49
"Search for Southern Identity, The" (Woodward), **Retro. Supp. I:** 75
Search for the King, A: A Twelfth-Century Legend (Vidal), **Supp. IV Part 2:** 681
Searching for Caleb (Tyler), **Supp. IV Part 2:** 663–665, 671
"Searching for Poetry: Real *vs.* Fake" (B. Miller), **Supp. IV Part 1:** 67
Searching for Survivors (Banks), **Supp. V:** 7
"Searching for Survivors (I)" (Banks), **Supp. V:** 8

"Searching for Survivors (II)" (Banks), **Supp. V:** 7, 8

Searching for the Ox (Simpson), **Supp. IX:** 266, **274–275**

"Searching for the Ox" (Simpson), **Supp. IX:** 275, 280

"Searching in the Britannia Tavern" (Wagoner), **Supp. IX:** 327

Searching Wing, The, (Hellman), **Supp. I Part 1:** 277, 278, 281–282, 283, 292, 297

Search-Light. *See* Frank, Waldo

"Search Party, The" (Matthews), **Supp. IX: 156**

Searle, Ronald, **Supp. I Part 2:** 604, 605

Sea Road to the Indies (Hart), **Supp. XIV:** 97

"Seascape" (Bishop), **Retro. Supp. II:** 42–43

"Sea's Green Sameness, The" (Updike), **IV:** 217

Seaside and the Fireside, The (Longfellow), **II:** 489; **Retro. Supp. II:** 159, 168

Season in Hell, A (Rimbaud), **III:** 189

Seasons, The (Thomson), **II:** 304; **Supp. I Part 1:** 151

Seasons' Difference, The (Buechner), **Supp. XII:** 47

Seasons of Celebration (Merton), **Supp. VIII:** 199, 208

Seasons of the Heart: In Quest of Faith (Kinard, comp.), **Supp. XIV:** 127

"Seasons of the Soul" (Tate), **IV:** 136–140

Seasons on Earth (Koch), **Supp. XV: 183–184**

"Sea Surface Full of Clouds" (Stevens), **IV:** 82

"Sea Tides" (Hoffman), **Supp. XVIII:** 87

"Sea Treader" (Hoffman), **Supp. XVIII:** 87

"Sea Unicorns and Land Unicorns" (Moore), **III:** 202–203

Seaver, Richard, **Supp. XI:** 301

"Seaweed" (Longfellow), **II:** 498

Sea-Wolf, The (London), **II:** 264, 466, 472–473

Sebald, W. G., **Supp. XIV:** 96; **Supp. XXI:** 92

Seckler, David, **Supp. I Part 2:** 650

"2nd Air Force" (Jarrell), **II:** 375

Second American Revolution and Other Essays (1976–1982), The (Vidal), **Supp. IV Part 2:** 679, 687, 688

Secondary Colors, The (A. Theroux), **Supp. VIII:** 312

Second Blush, The (Peacock), **Supp. XIX:** 197, **205–206**

Second Chance (Auchincloss), **Supp. IV Part 1:** 33

"Second Chances" (Hugo), **Supp. VI:** 144, 145

Second Coming, The (Percy), **Supp. III Part 1:** 383, 384, 387, 388, 396–397

"Second Coming, The" (Yeats), **III:** 294; **Retro. Supp. I:** 290, 311; **Supp. VIII:** 24; **Supp. XVI:** 159; **Supp. XIX:** 85

Second Decade, The. See Stephen King, The Second Decade: "Danse Macabre" to "The Dark Half" (Magistrale)

Second Dune, The (Hearon), **Supp. VIII:** 58, **59–60**

Second Flowering, A: Works and Days of the Lost Generation (Cowley), **Retro. Supp. II:** 77; **Supp. II Part 1:** 135, 141, 143, 144, 147, 149

Second Growth (Stegner), **Supp. IV Part 2:** 599, 608

"Second Hour of the Night, The" (Bidart), **Supp. XV:** 32, **33–34**

Second Marriage (F. Barthelme), **Supp. XI:** 32, 33

"Second Marriage" (McCarriston), **Supp. XIV:** 262

"Second Mortgage" (Shaw), **Supp. XIX:** 245–246

Second Nature (Hoffman), **Supp. X:** 88, 89

Seconds, The (Bierds), **Supp. XVII: 33–34**

Second Set, The (Komunyakaa and Feinstein, eds.), **Supp. XIII:** 125

Second Sex, The (Beauvoir), **Supp. IV Part 1:** 360

Second Stone, The (Fiedler), **Supp. XIII:** 102

"Second Swimming, The" (Boyle), **Supp. VIII:** 13, 14

Second Tree from the Corner (White), **Supp. I Part 2:** 654

"Second Tree from the Corner" (White), **Supp. I Part 2:** 651

Second Twenty Years at Hull-House, The: September 1909 to September 1929, with a Record of a Growing World Consciousness (Addams), **Supp. I Part 1:** 24–25

Second Voyage of Columbus, The (Morison), **Supp. I Part 2:** 488

Second Words (Atwood), **Supp. XIII:** 35

Second World, The (Blackmur), **Supp. II Part 1:** 91

Secret, The (E. Hoffman), **Supp. XVI:** 151, **155–158**, 161

"Secret, The" (Levine), **Supp. V:** 195

Secret Agent, The (Conrad), **Supp. IV Part 1:** 341

Secret Agent X-9 (Hammett), **Supp. IV Part 1:** 355

"Secret Courts of Men's Hearts, The: Code and Law in Harper Lee's *To Kill a Mockingbird*" (Johnson), **Supp. VIII:** 126

"Secret Dog, The" (Cameron), **Supp. XII: 83–84**

Secret Garden, The (Burnett), **Supp. I Part 1:** 44

"Secret Garden, The" (Hoffman), **Supp. XVIII:** 86

"Secret Gladness, A" (C. Frost), **Supp. XV:** 91

Secret Historie (J. Smith), **I:** 131

Secret History of the Dividing Line (Howe), **Supp. IV Part 2:** 424, 425–426

"Secret Integration, The" (Pynchon), **Supp. II Part 2:** 624

"Secret Life of Musical Instruments, The" (Wright), **Supp. XV:** 343

"Secret Life of Walter Mitty, The" (Thurber), **Supp. I Part 2:** 623; **Supp. XVI:** 233

"Secret Lion, The" (Ríos), **Supp. IV Part 2:** 543, 544

"Secret Ocean, The" (Jarman), **Supp. XVII:** 120

Secret of Poetry, The: Essays (Jarman), **Supp. XVII:** 110, 111, 120

"Secret of the Russian Ballet, The" (Van Vechten), **Supp. II Part 2:** 732

"Secret Prune" (Ríos), **Supp. IV Part 2:** 549

Secret River, The (Rawlings), **Supp. X:** 233

Secrets and Surprises (Beattie), **Supp. V:** 23, 27, 29

Secrets from the Center of the World (Harjo), **Supp. XII: 223–224**

"Secret Sharer, The" (Conrad), **Supp. IX:** 105

"Secret Sharer, The" (J. Conrad), **Supp. XVI:** 158

"Secret Society, A" (Nemerov), **III:** 282

Secrets of the Heart (Gibran), **Supp. XX:** 116

Secrets of the Universe: Scenes from the Journey Home (Sanders), **Supp. XVI:** 273–274

"Secular" (Trethewey), **Supp. XXI:** 249

Secular Journal of Thomas Merton, The, **Supp. VIII:** 206

"Security" (Stafford), **Supp. XI:** 329

Sedges, John (pseudonym). *See* Buck, Pearl S.

Sedgwick, Catherine Maria, **I:** 341; **Supp. I Part 1:** 155, 157

Sedgwick, Christina. *See* Marquand, Mrs. John P. (Christina Sedgwick)

Sedgwick, Ellery, **I:** 217, 229, 231; **III:** 54–55

Sedgwick, Eve, **Supp. XX:** 267

Sedgwick, Henry, **Supp. I Part 1:** 156

Sedgwick, Robert, **Supp. I Part 1:** 156

Sedore, Timothy, **Supp. XIV:** 312

"Seduction and Betrayal" (Hardwick), **Supp. III Part 1:** 207

Seduction and Betrayal: Women and Literature (Hardwick), **Supp. III Part 1:** 194, 204, 206–208, 212, 213; **Supp. XIV:** 89

Seed, David, **Supp. IV Part 1:** 391

"Seed Eaters, The" (Francis), **Supp. IX:** 82

"Seed Leaves" (Wilbur), **Supp. III Part 2:** 558

"Seeds" (Anderson), **I:** 106, 114

Seeds of Contemplation (Merton), **Supp. VIII:** 199, 200, 207, 208

Seeds of Destruction (Merton), **Supp. VIII:** 202, 203, 204, 208

"Seeing Red" (column, Ryan as Quin), **Supp. XVIII:** 226

"See(k)ing the Self: Mirrors and Mirroring in Bicultural Texts" (Oster), **Supp. XVI:** 151

Seeing through the Sun (Hogan), **Supp. IV Part 1:** 397, 400, 401–402, 402, 413

"See in the Midst of Fair Leaves" (Moore), **III:** 215

"Seekers, The" (McGrath), **Supp. X:** 117

"Seeking a Vision of Truth, Guided by a Higher Power" (Burke), **Supp. XIV:** 21, 23

"Seele im Raum" (Jarrell), **II:** 382–383

"Seele im Raum" (Rilke), **II:** 382–383

"See Naples and Die" (Hecht), **Supp. X:** 69, 70

"Seen from the 'L' " (Barnes), **Supp. III Part 1:** 33

"See the Moon?" (Barthelme), **Supp. IV Part 1:** 42, 49–50, 50

Segal, D. (pseudonym). *See* Singer, Isaac Bashevis

Segal, George, **Supp. XI:** 343

Segal, Lore, **Supp. XVI:** 203

Segregation: The Inner Conflict in the South (Warren), **IV:** 237, 238, 246, 252

"*Se:* Hegel's Absolute and Heidegger's *Ereignis*" (Agamben), **Supp. XVI:** 289

Seidel, Frederick, **I:** 185

Seidman, Hugh, **Supp. XXI:** 228

Seize the Day (Bellow), **I:** 144, 147, 148, 150, 151, 152, 153, 155, 158, 162; **Retro. Supp. II:** 19, 23–24, 27, 32, 34; **Supp. I Part 2:** 428

Selby, Hubert, **Supp. III Part 1:** 125

Selby, Hubert, Jr., **Supp. XXI:** 227

Selby, John, **Retro. Supp. II:** 221, 222

Selden, John, **Supp. XIV:** 344

Seldes, Gilbert, **II:** 437, 445; **Retro. Supp. I:** 108

Selected Criticism: Prose, Poetry (Bogan), **Supp. III Part 1:** 64

Selected Essays (Eliot), **I:** 572

Selected Essays and Reviews (Carruth), **Supp. XVI:** 46

Selected Journals and Other Writings (Audubon), **Supp. XVI:** 10, 12, 13

Selected Letters (Bynner), **Supp. XV:** 52

Selected Letters (W. C. Williams), **Retro. Supp. I:** 430

Selected Letters, 1940–1956 (Kerouac), **Supp. XIV:** 137, 144

Selected Letters of Robert Frost (Thompson, ed.), **Retro. Supp. I:** 125

Selected Levis, The (Levis), **Supp. XI:** 257, 272

Selected Poems (Aiken), **I:** 69

Selected Poems (Ashbery), **Supp. III Part 1:** 25–26

Selected Poems (Brodsky), **Supp. VIII:** 22

Selected Poems (Brooks), **Supp. III Part 1:** 82–83

Selected Poems (Bynner), **Supp. XV:** 51, 52

Selected Poems (Corso), **Supp. XII:** 129

Selected Poems (Dove), **Supp. IV Part 1:** 241, 243, 250

Selected Poems (Frost), **Retro. Supp. I:** 133, 136

Selected Poems (Guillevic; Levertov, trans.), **Supp. III Part 1:** 283

Selected Poems (Hayden), **Supp. II Part 1:** 363, 364, 367

Selected Poems (Hughes), **Retro. Supp. I:** 202; **Supp. I Part 1:** 341, 345, 346

Selected Poems (Hugo), **Supp. VI:** 143

Selected Poems (Jarrell), **II:** 367, 370, 371, 374, 377, 379, 380, 381, 382, 384

Selected Poems (Justice), **Supp. VII:** 115

Selected Poems (Kinnell), **Supp. III Part 1:** 235, 253

Selected Poems (Levine, 1984), **Supp. V:** 178, 179

Selected Poems (Lowell), **II:** 512, 516; **Retro. Supp. II:** 184, 186, 188, 190

Selected Poems (Merton), **Supp. VIII:** 207, 208

Selected Poems (Moore), **III:** 193, 194, 205–206, 208, 215

Selected Poems (Pound), **Retro. Supp. I:** 289, 291

Selected Poems (R. Bly), **Supp. IV Part 1:** 60, 62, 65, 66, 68, 69–71

Selected Poems (Ransom), **III:** 490, 492

Selected Poems (Reznikoff), **Supp. XIV:** 288

Selected Poems (Rukeyser), **Supp. VI:** 274

Selected Poems (Sexton), **Supp. IV Part 2:** 449

Selected Poems (Sorrentino), **Supp. XXI:** 226

Selected Poems (Strand), **Supp. IV Part 2:** 630

Selected Poems, 1923–1943 (Warren), **IV:** 241–242, 243

Selected Poems, 1928–1958 (Kunitz), **Supp. III Part 1:** 261, 263–265

Selected Poems, 1938–1988 (McGrath), **Supp. X:** 127

Selected Poems, 1958–1980 (Sorrentino), **Supp. XXI:** 228

Selected Poems, 1963–1983 (Simic), **Supp. VIII:** 275

Selected Poems 1936–1965 (Eberhart), **I:** 541

Selected Poems: 1957–1987 (Snodgrass), **Supp. VI:** 314–315, 323, 324

Selected Poems 1965–1975 (Atwood), **Supp. XIII: 32–34**

Selected Poems: 1975–2005 (Skloot), **Supp. XX:** 196

Selected Poems II: Poems Selected and New, 1976–1986 (Atwood), **Supp. XIII:** 20, **34–35**

Selected Poems of Ezra Pound (Pound), **Supp. V:** 336

Selected Poems of Gabriela Mistral (Hughes, trans.), **Supp. I Part 1:** 345

Selected Poetry of Amiri Baraka/LeRoi Jones (Baraka), **Supp. II Part 1:** 58

Selected Poetry of Hayden Carruth, The (Carruth), **Supp. XVI:** 53

Selected Stories (Dubus), **Supp. VII:** 88–89

Selected Stories of Richard Bausch, The (Bausch), **Supp. VII:** 42

Selected Translations (Snodgrass), **Supp. VI:** 318, 324, **325–326**

Selected Verse of Margaret Haskins Durber, The (Keillor), **Supp. XVI:** 171

Selected Witter Bynner, The, **Supp. XV:** 52

Selected Works of Djuna Barnes, The (Barnes), **Supp. III Part 1:** 44

Selected Writings 1950–1990 (Howe), **Supp. VI:** 116–117, 118, 120

Selected Writings of John Jay Chapman, The (Barzun), **Supp. XIV:** 54

Select Epigrams from the Greek Anthology (Mackail), **Supp. I Part 2:** 461

"Selecting a Reader" (Kooser), **Supp. XIX:** 119–120

"Selene Afterwards" (MacLeish), **III:** 8

"Self" (James), **II:** 351

Self and the Dramas of History, The (Niebuhr), **III:** 308

Self-Consciousness (Updike), **Retro. Supp. I:** 318, 319, 320, 322, 323, 324

"Self-Exposed, The" (X. J. Kennedy), **Supp. XV:** 159

Self-Help: Stories (Moore), **Supp. X:** 163, 166, **167–169,** 174, 175

"Self-Importance" (Halliday), **Supp. XIX:** 90

Self-Interviews (Dickey), **Supp. IV Part 1:** 179

"Self-Made Man, A" (Crane), **I:** 420

"Self Pity" (C. Frost), **Supp. XV:** 93, 94, 101, 102, 104

Self Portrait (album, Dylan), **Supp. XVIII:** 27

"Self-Portrait" (Creeley), **Supp. IV Part 1:** 156

"Self-Portrait" (Mumford), **Supp. II Part 2:** 471

"(Self) Portrait" (Trethewey), **Supp. XXI:** 253

"Self-Portrait" (Wylie), **Supp. I Part 2:** 729

"Self Portrait at Fifty-three" (Weigl), **Supp. XIX:** 288

Self-Portrait: Ceaselessly into the Past (Millar, ed. Sipper), **Supp. IV Part 2:** 464, 469, 472, 475

"Self-Portrait in a Convex Mirror" (Ashbery), **Supp. III Part 1:** 5, 7, 9, 16–19, 22, 24, 26

"Self-Portrait with 1911 NY Yankees Cap" (Skloot), **Supp. XX:** 202

"Self-Reliance" (Emerson), **II:** 7, 15, 17; **Retro. Supp. I:** 159; **Retro. Supp. II:** 155; **Supp. X:** 42, 45

Selfwolf (Halliday), **Supp. XIX:** 81, **89–91,** 93

Sélincourt, Ernest de, **Supp. I Part 2:** 676

Selinger, Eric, **Supp. XVI:** 47

Selinger, Eric Murphy, **Supp. XI:** 248

Sell, Henry, **Supp. XVI:** 188

Sellers, Isaiah, **IV:** 194–195

Sellers, Peter, **Supp. XI:** 301, 304, 306, 307, 309

Sellers, William, **IV:** 208

Seltzer, Mark, **Retro. Supp. I:** 227

Selznick, David O., **Retro. Supp. I:** 105, 113; **Supp. IV Part 1:** 353; **Supp. XVIII:** 242

Semi, Allen (pseudonym). *See* Larsen, Nella

"Semi-Lunatics of Kilmuir, The" (Hugo), **Supp. VI:** 145

"Semiotics/The Doctor's Doll" (Goldbarth), **Supp. XII:** 183–184

Semmelweiss, Ignaz, **Supp. I Part 1:** 304

Senancour, Étienne Divert de, **I:** 241

Sendak, Maurice, **Supp. IX:** 207, 208, 213, 214; **Supp. XVI:** 110

Seneca, **II:** 14–15; **III:** 77

Senghor, Leopold Sédar, **Supp. IV Part 1:** 16; **Supp. X:** 132, 139

Senier, Siobhan, **Supp. IV Part 1:** 330

"Senility" (Anderson), **I:** 114

"Senior Partner's Ethics, The" (Auchincloss), **Supp. IV Part 1:** 33

Senlin: A Biography (Aiken), **I:** 48, 49, 50, 52, 56, 57, 64

Sennett, Dorothy, **Supp. XVI:** 43

Sennett, Mack, **III:** 442

"Señora X No More" (Mora), **Supp. XIII:** 218

"Señor Ong and Señor Ha" (Bowles), **Supp. IV Part 1:** 87

Sensational Designs: The Cultural Work of American Fiction, 1790–1860 (Tompkins), **Supp. XVIII:** 258–259

Sense of Beauty, The (Santayana), **III:** 600

Sense of Life in the Modern Novel, The (Mizener), **IV:** 132

"Sense of Shelter, A" (Updike), **Retro. Supp. I:** 318

"Sense of the Meeting, The" (Conroy), **Supp. XVI:** 72

Sense of the Past, The (James), **II:** 337–338

"Sense of the Past, The" (Trilling), **Supp. III Part 2:** 503

"Sense of the Present, The" (Hardwick), **Supp. III Part 1:** 210

"Sense of the Sleight-of-Hand Man, The" (Stevens), **IV:** 93

"Sense of Where You Are, A" (McPhee), **Supp. III Part 1:** 291, 296–298

"Sensibility! O La!" (Roethke), **III:** 536

"Sensible Emptiness, A" (Kramer), **Supp. IV Part 1:** 61, 66

"Sensuality Plunging Barefoot Into Thorns" (Cisneros), **Supp. VII:** 68

"Sentence" (Barthelme), **Supp. IV Part 1:** 47

Sent for You Yesterday (Wideman), **Supp. X:** 320, 321

"Sentimental Education, A" (Banks), **Supp. V:** 10

"Sentimental Journey" (Oates), **Supp. II Part 2:** 522, 523

"Sentimental Journey, A" (Anderson), **I:** 114

Sentimental Journey, A (Sterne), **Supp. I Part 2:** 714

"Sentimental Journeys" (Didion), **Supp. IV Part 1:** 211

Sentimental Journey through France and Italy, A (Sterne), **Supp. XV:** 232

"Sentiment of Rationality, The" (James), **II:** 346–347

"Separated Father" (Halliday), **Supp. XIX:** 92, 93

Separate Flights (Dubus), **Supp. VII:** 78–83

"Separate Flights" (Dubus), **Supp. VII:** 83

Separate Peace, A (Knowles), **Supp. IV Part 2:** 679; **Supp. XII: 241–249**

Separate Way (Reznikoff), **Supp. XIV:** 280

"Separating" (Updike), **Retro. Supp. I:** 321

"Separation, The" (Kunitz), **Supp. III Part 1:** 263

"Sepia High Stepper" (Hayden), **Supp. II Part 1:** 379

September (film; Allen), **Supp. XV:** 11

"September" (Komunyakaa), **Supp. XIII:** 130

"September" (Pickering), **Supp. XXI:** 198

"September 1, 1939" (Auden), **Supp. II Part 1:** 13; **Supp. IV Part 1:** 225; **Supp. VIII:** 30, 32; **Supp. XV:** 117–118

September 11, 2001: American Writers Respond (Heyen), **Supp. XIII:** 285

September Song (Humphrey), **Supp. IX:** 101, 102, **108–109**

"September Twelfth, 2001" (X. J. Kennedy), **Supp. XV:** 171

"Sept Vieillards, Les" (Millay, trans.), **III:** 142

Sequel to Drum-Taps (Whitman), **Retro. Supp. I:** 406

"Sequence, Sometimes Metaphysical" (Roethke), **III:** 547, 548

Sequence of Seven Plays with a Drawing by Ron Slaughter, A (Nemerov), **III:** 269

Sequoya, Jana, **Supp. IV Part 1:** 334

Seraglio, The (Merrill), **Supp. III Part 1:** 331

Seraphita (Balzac), **I:** 499

Seraph on the Suwanee (Hurston), **Supp. VI:** 149, 159–160

Serenissima: A Novel of Venice (Jong). *See Shylock's Daughter: A Novel of Love in Venice (Serenissima)* (Jong)

Sergeant, Elizabeth Shepley, **I:** 231, 236, 312, 319, 323, 328

Sergeant Bilko (television show), **Supp. IV Part 2:** 575

Sergi, Paula, **Supp. XXI:** 246

"Serious Talk, A" (Carver), **Supp. III Part 1:** 138, 144

Serly, Tibor, **Supp. III Part 2:** 617, 619

"Sermon by Doctor Pep" (Bellow), **I:** 151

Sermones (Horace), **II:** 154

"Sermon for Our Maturity" (Baraka), **Supp. II Part 1:** 53

"Sermon in the Cotton Field" (Nelson), **Supp. XVIII:** 177

Sermons and Soda Water (O'Hara), **III:** 362, 364, 371–373, 382

"Sermons on the Warpland" (Brooks), **Supp. III Part 1:** 84

"Serpent in the Wilderness, The" (Masters), **Supp. I Part 2:** 458

Servant of the Bones (Rice), **Supp. VII:** 298, 302

"Servant to Servants, A" (Frost), **Retro. Supp. I:** 125, 128; **Supp. X:** 66

Serve It Forth (M. F. K. Fisher), **Supp. XVII:** 83, 86, 87, 89, 92

Service, Robert, **Supp. XXI:** 51

Seshachari, Neila, **Supp. V:** 22

"Session, The" (Adams), **I:** 5

"Sestina" (Bishop), **Supp. I Part 1:** 73, 88

Set-angya, **Supp. IV Part 2:** 493

Seth, Vikram, **Supp. XVII:** 117

Seth's Brother's Wife (Frederic), **II:** 131–132, 137, 144

Set This House on Fire (Styron), **IV:** 98, 99, 105, 107–113, 114, 115, 117

Setting Free the Bears (Irving), **Supp. VI:** 163, **166–167,** 169–170

Setting the Tone (Rorem), **Supp. IV Part 1:** 79

Settle, Mary Lee, **Supp. IX:** 96

Settlement Horizon, The: A National Estimate (Woods and Kennedy), **Supp. I Part 1:** 19

"Settling the Colonel's Hash" (McCarthy), **II:** 559, 562

Setzer, Helen, **Supp. IV Part 1:** 217

"Seurat's Sunday Afternoon along the Seine" (Schwartz), **Supp. II Part 2:** 663–665

7 Years from Somehwere (Levine), **Supp. V:** 178, 181, 188–189

Seven against Thebes (Aeschylus; Bacon and Hecht, trans.), **Supp. X:** 57

Seven Ages of Man, The (Wilder), **IV:** 357, 374–375

Seven Deadly Sins, The (Wilder), **IV:** 357, 374–375

Seven Descents of Myrtle, The (T. Williams), **IV:** 382

"Seven Fat Brides, The" (P. Abraham), **Supp. XVII:** 50

Seven Guitars (Wilson), **Supp. VIII:** 331, **348–351**

Seven Lady Godivas, The (Geisel), **Supp. XVI:** 100, 103

Seven League Boots, The (Murray), **Supp. XIX: 156–157**

Seven-League Crutches, The (Jarrell), **II:** 367, 372, 381, 382, 383–384, 389

Seven Mountains of Thomas Merton, The (Mott), **Supp. VIII:** 208

Seven-Ounce Man, The (Harrison), **Supp. VIII:** 51

"Seven Places of the Mind" (Didion), **Supp. IV Part 1:** 200, 210

Seven Plays (Shepard), **Supp. III Part 2:** 434

"Seven Selves, The" (Gibran), **Supp. XX:** 118

"Seven Stanzas at Easter" (Updike), **IV:** 215

Seven Storey Mountain, The (Merton), **Supp. VIII:** 193, 195, 198, 200, 207, 208

Seventh Heaven (Hoffman), **Supp. X:** 87, 89

"Seventh of March" (Webster), **Supp. I Part 2:** 687

"7000 Romaine, Los Angeles 38" (Didion), **Supp. IV Part 1:** 200
"Seventh Street" (Toomer), **Supp. IX:** 316
Seven Types of Ambiguity (Empson), **II:** 536; **IV:** 431
77 Dream Songs (Berryman), **I:** 168, 169, 170, 171, 174, 175, 183–188
73 Poems (Cummings), **I:** 430, 431, 446, 447, 448
Seven Valleys and the Four Valleys, The (Bahá'u'lláh), **Supp. XX:** 121
Sevier, Jack, **IV:** 378
Sévigné, Madame de, **IV:** 361
Sewall, Richard, **Retro. Supp. I:** 25
Sewall, Samuel, **IV:** 145, 146, 147, 149, 154, 164; **Supp. I Part 1:** 100, 110
Sewell, Elizabeth, **Supp. XIII:** 344
"Sex" (Carruth), **Supp. XVI:** 58
Sex, Economy, Freedom and Community (Berry), **Supp. X:** 30, 36
"Sex Camp" (Mamet), **Supp. XIV:** 240
Sex Castle, The (Lacy), **Supp. XV:** 206
Sex & Character (Weininger), **Retro. Supp. I:** 416
"Sext" (Auden), **Supp. II Part 1:** 22
Sexton, Anne, **Retro. Supp. II:** 245; **Supp. I Part 2:** 538, 543, 546; **Supp. II Part 2: 669–700; Supp. III Part 2:** 599; **Supp. IV Part 1:** 245; **Supp. IV Part 2:** 439, 440–441, 442, 444, 447, 449, 451, 620; **Supp. V:** 113, 118, 124; **Supp. X:** 201, 202, 213; **Supp. XI:** 146, 240, 317; **Supp. XII:** 217, 253, 254, 256, 260, 261; **Supp. XIII:** 35, 76, 294, 312; **Supp. XIV:** 125, 126, 132, 269; **Supp. XV:** 123, 252, 340; **Supp. XVII:** 239; **Supp. XIX:** 82, 203; **Supp. XX:** 199
Sexual Behavior in the American Male (Kinsey), **Supp. XIII:** 96–97
Sexual Perversity in Chicago (Mamet), **Supp. XIV:** 239, 240, 246–247, 249
"Sexual Revolution, The" (Dunn), **Supp. XI:** 142
Sexus (H. Miller), **III:** 170, 171, 184, 187, 188
"Sex Without Love" (Olds), **Supp. X:** 206
"Sexy" (Lahiri), **Supp. XXI:** 183–184
Seyersted, Per E., **Retro. Supp. II:** 65; **Supp. I Part 1:** 201, 204, 211, 216, 225; **Supp. IV Part 2:** 558
Seyfried, Robin, **Supp. IX:** 324
Seymour, Miranda, **Supp. VIII:** 167
"Seymour: An Introduction" (Salinger), **III:** 569–571, 572
"Shack" (L. Brown), **Supp. XXI:** 49
Shacochis, Bob, **Supp. VIII:** 80
"Shadow" (Creeley), **Supp. IV Part 1:** 158
"Shadow, The" (Lowell), **II:** 522
Shadow and Act (Ellison), **Retro. Supp. II:** 119; **Supp. II Part 1:** 245–246
"Shadow and Shade" (Tate), **IV:** 128
"Shadow and the Flesh, The" (London), **II:** 475
"Shadow A Parable" (Poe), **III:** 417–418
Shadow Country (Gunn Allen), **Supp. IV Part 1:** 322, 324, 325–326

Shadow Man, The (Gordon), **Supp. IV Part 1:** 297, 298, 299, 312–314, 315
Shadow of a Dream, The, a Story (Howells), **II:** 285, 286, 290
"Shadow of the Crime, The: A Word from the Author" (Mailer), **Retro. Supp. II:** 214
Shadow on the Dial, The (Bierce), **I:** 208, 209
"Shadow Passing" (Merwin), **Supp. III Part 1:** 355
Shadowplay (C. Baxter), **Supp. XVII:** 15, 19–20
Shadows (Gardner), **Supp. VI:** 74
Shadows and Fog (film; Allen), **Supp. XV:** 11
Shadows Burning (Di Piero), **Supp. XIX:** 42, 43–44
Shadows by the Hudson (Singer), **IV:** 1
Shadows of Africa (Matthiessen), **Supp. V:** 203
Shadows on the Hudson (Singer), **Retro. Supp. II:** 311–313
Shadows on the Rock (Cather), **I:** 314, 330–331, 332; **Retro. Supp. I:** 18
Shadow Train (Ashbery), **Supp. III Part 1:** 23–24, 26
"Shad-Time" (Wilbur), **Supp. III Part 2:** 563
Shaffer, Thomas L., **Supp. VIII:** 127, 128
Shaft (Parks; film), **Supp. XI:** 17
Shaftesbury, Earl of, **I:** 559
Shahid, Irfan, **Supp. XX:** 113, 127
Shahn, Ben, **Supp. X:** 24
Shakedown for Murder (Lacy), **Supp. XV:** 203
Shakelford, Dean, **Supp. VIII:** 129
Shaker, Why Don't You Sing? (Angelou), **Supp. IV Part 1:** 16
Shakespear, Mrs. Olivia, **III:** 457; **Supp. I Part 1:** 257
"Shakespeare" (Emerson), **II:** 6
Shakespeare, William, **I:** 103, 271, 272, 284–285, 358, 378, 433, 441, 458, 461, 573, 585, 586; **II:** 5, 8, 11, 18, 72, 273, 297, 302, 309, 320, 411, 494, 577, 590; **III:** 3, 11, 12, 82, 83, 91, 124, 130, 134, 145, 153, 159, 183, 210, 263, 286, 468, 473, 492, 503, 511, 567, 575–576, 577, 610, 612, 613, 615; **IV:** 11, 50, 66, 127, 132, 156, 309, 313, 362, 368, 370, 373, 453; **Retro. Supp. I:** 43, 64, 91, 248; **Retro. Supp. II:** 114, 299; **Supp. I Part 1:** 79, 150, 262, 310, 356, 363, 365, 368, 369, 370; **Supp. I Part 2:** 397, 421, 422, 470, 494, 622, 716, 720; **Supp. II Part 2:** 624, 626; **Supp. IV Part 1:** 31, 83, 87, 243; **Supp. IV Part 2:** 430, 463, 519, 688; **Supp. V:** 252, 280, 303; **Supp. VIII:** 160, 164; **Supp. IX:** 14, 133; **Supp. X:** 42, 62, 65, 78; **Supp. XII:** 54–57, 277, 281; **Supp. XIII:** 111, 115, 233; **Supp. XIV:** 97, 120, 225, 245, 306; **Supp. XV:** 92; **Supp. XVIII:** 278
Shakespeare and His Forerunners (Lanier), **Supp. I Part 1:** 369

Shakespeare in Harlem (Hughes), **Retro. Supp. I:** 194, 202, 205, 206, 207, 208; **Supp. I Part 1:** 333, 334, 345
Shalit, Gene, **Supp. VIII:** 73
Shalit, Wendy, **Supp. XX:** 179, 182, 186
Shall We Gather at the River (Wright), **Supp. III Part 2:** 601–602; **Supp. XVII:** 241
"Shame" (Oates), **Supp. II Part 2:** 520
"Shame" (Wilbur), **Supp. III Part 2:** 556
"Shame and Forgetting in the Information Age" (C. Baxter), **Supp. XVII:** 21
"Shameful Affair, A" (Chopin), **Retro. Supp. II:** 61
Shamela (Fielding), **Supp. V:** 127
"Shampoo, The" (Bishop), **Retro. Supp. II:** 46; **Supp. I Part 1:** 92
Shange, Ntozake, **Supp. VIII:** 214; **Supp. XVII:** 70; **Supp. XVIII:** 172; **Supp. XXI:** 172
Shank, Randy, **Supp. X:** 252
Shankaracharya, **III:** 567
Shanley, John Patrick, **Supp. XIV: 315–332**
Shannon, Sandra, **Supp. VIII:** 333, 348
"Shape of Flesh and Bone, The" (MacLeish), **III:** 18–19
Shape of Me and Other Stuff, The (Geisel), **Supp. XVI:** 111
Shape of the Journey, The (Harrison), **Supp. VIII:** 53
Shapes of Clay (Bierce), **I:** 208, 209
Shaping Joy, A: Studies in the Writer's Craft (Brooks), **Supp. XIV:** 13
Shapiro, Charles, **Supp. XIX:** 257, 259–260
Shapiro, David, **Supp. XII:** 175, 185
Shapiro, Dorothy, **IV:** 380
Shapiro, Karl, **I:** 430, 521; **II:** 350; **III:** 527; **Supp. II Part 2: 701–724; Supp. III Part 2:** 623; **Supp. IV Part 2:** 645; **Supp. X:** 116; **Supp. XI:** 315; **Supp. XIX:** 117, 118, 119; **Supp. XXI:** 98
Shapiro, Laura, **Supp. IX:** 120; **Supp. XX:** 87, 89
Sharif, Omar, **Supp. IX:** 253
"Shark Meat" (Snyder), **Supp. VIII:** 300
Shatayev, Elvira, **Supp. I Part 2:** 570
Shaviro, Steven, **Supp. VIII:** 189
Shaw, Colonel Robert Gould, **II:** 551
Shaw, Elizabeth. See Melville, Mrs. Herman (Elizabeth Shaw)
Shaw, George Bernard, **I:** 226; **II:** 82, 271, 276, 581; **III:** 69, 102, 113, 145, 155, 161, 162, 163, 373, 409; **IV:** 27, 64, 397, 432, 440; **Retro. Supp. I:** 100, 228; **Supp. IV Part 1:** 36; **Supp. IV Part 2:** 585, 683; **Supp. V:** 243–244, 290; **Supp. IX:** 68, 308; **Supp. XI:** 202; **Supp. XII:** 94; **Supp. XIV:** 343; **Supp. XVII:** 100
Shaw, Irwin, **IV:** 381; **Supp. IV Part 1:** 383; **Supp. IX:** 251; **Supp. XI:** 221, 229, 231; **Supp. XIX: 239–254**
Shaw, Joseph Thompson ("Cap"), **Supp. IV Part 1:** 121, 345, 351; **Supp. XIII:** 161
Shaw, Judge Lemuel, **III:** 77, 88, 91

Shaw, Peter, **Supp. XVI:** 70
Shaw, Sarah Bryant, **Supp. I Part 1:** 169
Shaw, Wilbur, Jr., **Supp. XIII:** 162
Shawl, The (Mamet), **Supp. XIV:** 245
Shawl, The (Ozick), **Supp. V:** 257, 260, 271
"Shawl, The" (Ozick), **Supp. V:** 271–272
Shawl and Prarie du Chien, The: Two Plays (Mamet), **Supp. XIV:** 243–244
Shawn, William, **Supp. VIII:** 151, 170
"Shawshank Redemption, The" (King), **Supp. V:** 148
She (Haggard), **III:** 189
Sheaffer, Louis, **Supp. XXI:** 6
Shearer, Flora, **I:** 199
"Sheaves, The" (Robinson), **III:** 510, 524
"She Came and Went" (Lowell), **Supp. I Part 2:** 409
"She-Devil" (Nelson), **Supp. XVIII:** 178
She-Devil Circus (Nelson), **Supp. XVIII:** 176, **178**
Sheed, Wilfrid, **IV:** 230; **Supp. XI:** 233; **Supp. XXI:** 233
Sheeler, Charles, **IV:** 409; **Retro. Supp. I:** 430
"Sheep Child" (B. Kelly), **Supp. XVII:** 131–132
"Sheep Child, The" (Dickey), **Supp. XVII:** 131–132
Sheeper (Rosenthal), **Supp. XIV:** 147
Sheffer, Jonathan, **Supp. IV Part 1:** 95
She Had Some Horses (Harjo), **Supp. XII: 220–223,** 231
"She Had Some Horses" (Harjo), **Supp. XII:** 215, 222
"Shell, The" (Humphrey), **Supp. IX:** 94
Shelley, Mary, **Supp. XX:**108
Shelley, Percy Bysshe, **I:** 18, 68, 381, 476, 522, 577; **II:** 331, 516, 535, 540; **III:** 412, 426, 469; **IV:** 139; **Retro. Supp. I:** 308, 360; **Supp. I Part 1:** 79, 311, 349; **Supp. I Part 2:** 709, 718, 719, 720, 721, 722, 724, 728; **Supp. IV Part 1:** 235; **Supp. V:** 258, 280; **Supp. IX:** 51; **Supp. XII:** 117, 132, 136–137, 263; **Supp. XIV:** 271–272; **Supp. XV:** 92, 175, 182; **Supp. XX:**115; **Supp. XXI:** 131
Shellow, Sadie Myers, **Supp. I Part 2:** 608
"Shelter" (C. Baxter), **Supp. XVII:** 19
"Shelter" (Doty), **Supp. XI:** 132
Sheltered Life, The (Glasgow), **II:** 174, 175, 179, 186, 187–188
Sheltering Sky, The (Bowles), **Supp. IV Part 1:** 82, 84, 85–86, 87
Sheltering Sky, The (film), **Supp. IV Part 1:** 94, 95
Shelton, Frank, **Supp. IV Part 2:** 658
Shelton, Richard, **Supp. XI:** 133; **Supp. XIII:** 7
Shelton, Robert, **Supp. XVIII:** 20, 21, 22, 23, 24, 25, 26
Shelton, Mrs. Sarah. *See* Royster, Sarah Elmira
Shenandoah (Schwartz), **Supp. II Part 2:** 640, 651–652
"Shenandoah" (Shapiro), **Supp. II Part 2:** 704
Shepard, Alice, **IV:** 287

Shepard, Harvey, **Supp. XVII:** 240
Shepard, Jim, **Supp. XXI:** 115
Shepard, Odell, **II:** 508; **Supp. I Part 2:** 418
Shepard, Sam, **Supp. III Part 2: 431–450; Supp. XVIII:** 21, 28, 31; **Supp. XXI:** 144, 145
Shepard, Thomas, **I:** 554; **IV:** 158
"Shepherd of Resumed Desire, The" (Wright), **Supp. XV:** 349
Sheppard Lee (Bird), **III:** 423
"She Remembers the Future" (Harjo), **Supp. XII:** 222
Sheridan, Richard Brinsley, **Retro. Supp. I:** 127
Sherlock, William, **IV:** 152
Sherman, Sarah Way, **Retro. Supp. II:** 145
Sherman, Stuart Pratt, **I:** 222, 246–247; **Supp. I Part 2:** 423
Sherman, Susan, **Supp. VIII:** 265
Sherman, Tom, **IV:** 446
Sherman, William T., **IV:** 445, 446
Sherwood, Robert, **II:** 435; **Supp. IX:** 190
Sherwood Anderson & Other Famous Creoles (Faulkner), **I:** 117; **II:** 56
Sherwood Anderson Reader, The (Anderson), **I:** 114, 116
Sherwood Anderson's Memoirs (Anderson), **I:** 98, 101, 102, 103, 108, 112, 116
Sherwood Anderson's Notebook (Anderson), **I:** 108, 115, 117
She Stoops to Conquer (Goldsmith), **II:** 514
Shestov, Lev, **Supp. VIII:** 20, 24
Shetley, Vernon, **Supp. IX:** 292; **Supp. XI:** 123
"She Wept, She Railed" (Kunitz), **Supp. III Part 1:** 265
"Shiddah and Kuziba" (Singer), **IV:** 13, 15
Shidyak, Paris al-, **Supp. XX:**117
Shield of Achilles, The (Auden), **Supp. II Part 1:** 21
"Shield of Achilles, The" (Auden), **Supp. II Part 1:** 21, 25
Shields, Carol, **Supp. VII: 307–330**
Shields, John C., **Supp. XX:**279, 280, 281, 286
Shifting Landscape: A Composite, 1925–1987 (H. Roth), **Supp. IX: 233–235**
Shifts of Being (Eberhart), **I:** 525
Shigematsu, Soiko, **Supp. III Part 1:** 353
Shihab, Aziz, **Supp. XIII:** 273
Shih-hsiang Chen, **Supp. VIII:** 303
Shiksa Goddess; or, How I Spent My Forties (Wasserstein), **Supp. XV:** 319, 320, 325, 332, 333
"Shiloh" (Mason), **Supp. VIII:** 140
Shiloh and Other Stories (Mason), **Supp. VIII:** 133, **139–141,** 143, 145
Shilts, Randy, **Supp. X:** 145
Shimmering Verge, The (one-woman show, Peacock), **Supp. XIX:** 194, **204–205**
Shining, The (King), **Supp. V:** 139, 140, 141, 143–144, 146, 149, 151, 152

"Shining Ones, The" (P. N. Warren), **Supp. XX:**272
Shining Victory (film, Rapper), **Supp. XVII:** 60
Shinn, Everett, **Retro. Supp. II:** 103
Shi Pei Pu, **Supp. XXI:** 152, 153, 154
"Ship of Death" (Lawrence), **Supp. I Part 2:** 728
Ship of Fools (Porter), **III:** 433, 447, 453, 454; **IV:** 138
Shipping News, The (Proulx), **Supp. VII:** 249, 258–259
"Ships" (O. Henry), **Supp. II Part 1:** 409
Ships Going into the Blue: Essays and Notes on Poetry (Simpson), **Supp. IX:** 275
Ship to America, A (Singer), **IV:** 1
"Shipwreck, The" (Merwin), **Supp. III Part 1:** 346
Shirley, John, **Supp. XVI:** 123, 128
"Shirt" (Pinsky), **Supp. VI: 236–237,** 239, 240, 241, 245, 247
"Shirt Poem, The" (Stern), **Supp. IX:** 292
"Shirts of a Single Color" (Ryan), **Supp. XVIII:** 227
"Shiva and Parvati Hiding in the Rain" (Pinsky), **Supp. VI:** 244
Shively, Charley, **Retro. Supp. I:** 391; **Supp. XII:** 181, 182
Shnayerson, Michael, **Supp. XIX:** 248
Shock of Recognition, The (Wilson), **II:** 530
Shock of the New, The (Hughes), **Supp. X:** 73
Shoe Bird, The (Welty), **IV:** 261; **Retro. Supp. I:** 353
Shoemaker of Dreams (Ferragammo), **Supp. XVI:** 192
"Shoes" (O. Henry), **Supp. II Part 1:** 409
"Shoes of Wandering, The" (Kinnell), **Supp. III Part 1:** 248
Sholl, Betsy, **Supp. XXI:** 129, 131
"Shooters, Inc." (Didion), **Supp. IV Part 1:** 207, 211
"Shooting, The" (Dubus), **Supp. VII:** 84, 85
"Shooting Niagara; and After?" (Carlyle), **Retro. Supp. I:** 408
"Shooting Script" (Rich), **Supp. I Part 2:** 558; **Supp. IV Part 1:** 257
Shooting Star, A (Stegner), **Supp. IV Part 2:** 599, 608–609
"Shooting the Works" (Di Piero), **Supp. XIX:** 41–42
Shooting the Works: On Poetry and Pictures (Di Piero), **Supp. XIX: 41–42**
"Shooting Whales" (Strand), **Supp. IV Part 2:** 630
"Shopgirls" (F. Barthelme), **Supp. XI:** 26, 27, 33, 36
"Shopping with Bob Berwick" (Halliday), **Supp. XIX:** 88
Shop Talk (P. Roth), **Retro. Supp. II:** 282
Shoptaw, John, **Supp. IV Part 1:** 247
Shore Acres (Herne), **Supp. II Part 1:** 198
Shorebirds of North America, The (Matthiessen), **Supp. V:** 204
"Shore House, The" (Jewett), **II:** 397

Shore Leave (Wakeman), **Supp. IX:** 247
"Shoreline Horses" (Ríos), **Supp. IV Part 2:** 553
"Shoreline Life" (Skloot), **Supp. XX:**201
Shores of Light, The: A Literary Chronicle of the Twenties and Thirties (Wilson), **IV:** 432, 433
Shorey, Paul, **III:** 606
Short Cuts (film), **Supp. IX:** 143
"Short End, The" (Hecht), **Supp. X:** 65
"Shorter View, The" (X. J. Kennedy), **Supp. XV:** 160, 168
Short Fiction of Norman Mailer, The (Mailer), **Retro. Supp. II:** 205
Short Friday and Other Stories (Singer), **IV:** 14–16
Short Guide to a Happy Life, A (Quindlen), **Supp. XVII:** 167, 179
"Short Happy Life of Francis Macomber, The" (Hemingway), **II:** 250, 263–264; **Retro. Supp. I:** 182; **Supp. IV Part 1:** 48; **Supp. IX:** 106
Short Night, The (Turner), **Supp. XV:** 201
Short Novels of Thomas Wolfe, The (Wolfe), **IV:** 456
Short Poems (Berryman), **I:** 170
"SHORT SPEECH TO MY FRIENDS" (Baraka), **Supp. II Part 1:** 35
Short Stories (Rawlings), **Supp. X:** 224
Short Stories: Five Decades (Shaw), **Supp. XIX:** 252–253
"Short Story, The" (Welty), **IV:** 279
Short Story Masterpieces, **Supp. IX:** 4
Short Studies of American Authors (Higginson), **I:** 455
"Short-timer's Calendar" (Komunyakaa), **Supp. XIII:** 125
Shosha (Singer), **Retro. Supp. II:** 313–314
Shostakovich, Dimitri, **IV:** 75; **Supp. VIII:** 21
Shot of Love (album, Dylan), **Supp. XVIII:** 28
"Shots" (Ozick), **Supp. V:** 268
Shotts, Jeffrey, **Supp. XV:** 103, 104
"Should Wizard Hit Mommy?" (Updike), **IV:** 221, 222, 224; **Retro. Supp. I:** 335
Shoup, Barbara, **Supp. XV:** 55, 59, 62, 69
"Shoveling Snow with Buddha" (Collins), **Supp. XXI:** 60
"Shovel Man, The" (Sandburg), **III:** 553
Showalter, Elaine, **Retro. Supp. I:** 368; **Supp. IV Part 2:** 440, 441, 444; **Supp. X:** 97; **Supp. XVI:** 80, 92; **Supp. XX:**274
"Shower of Gold" (Welty), **IV:** 271–272
"Shrike and the Chipmunks, The" (Thurber), **Supp. I Part 2:** 617
Shrimp Girl (Hogarth), **Supp. XII:** 44
"Shrine and the Burning Wheel, The" (Jarman), **Supp. XVII:** 116
"Shrine with Flowers" (Di Piero), **Supp. XIX:** 43, 44
"Shriveled Meditation" (X. J. Kennedy), **Supp. XV:** 170
Shropshire Lad, A (Housman), **Supp. XV:** 41

"Shrouded Stranger, The" (Ginsberg), **Supp. II Part 1:** 312
"Shroud of Color, The" (Cullen), **Supp. IV Part 1:** 166, 168, 170, 171
Shtetl (film; Marzynski), **Supp. XVI:** 153
Shtetl: The Life and Death of a Small Town and the World of Polish Jews (E. Hoffman), **Supp. XVI:** 152, **153–155**
Shuffle (L. Michaels), **Supp. XVI:** 202, 203, 213
Shuffle Along (musical), **Supp. I Part 1:** 322; **Supp. X:** 136
Shultz, George, **Supp. IV Part 1:** 234
Shurr, William, **Retro. Supp. I:** 43
Shuster, Joel, **Supp. XI:** 67
Shusterman, Richard, **Retro. Supp. I:** 53
"Shut a Final Door" (Capote), **Supp. III Part 1:** 117, 120, 124
Shut Up, He Explained (Lardner), **II:** 432
Shylock's Daughter: A Novel of Love in Venice (Serenissima) (Jong), **Supp. V:** 115, 127, 128–129
"Siasconset: How It Arose and What It Is" (Briggs), **Supp. XVIII:** 9
Siberian Village, The (Dove), **Supp. IV Part 1:** 255, 256
Sibley, Mulford Q., **Supp. I Part 2:** 524
"Sibling Mysteries" (Rich), **Supp. I Part 2:** 574
Siblings (Quindlen and Kelsh), **Supp. XVII:** 167, 179
Sibon, Marcelle, **IV:** 288
"Sicilian Emigrant's Song" (W. C. Williams), **Retro. Supp. I:** 413
Sicilian Miniatures (Sobin), **Supp. XVI:** 288
"Sick Wife, The" (Kenyon), **Supp. VII:** 173, 174
"'Sic transit gloria mundi' " (Dickinson), **Retro. Supp. I:** 30
Sid Caesar Show (television show), **Supp. IV Part 2:** 575
Siddons, Sarah, **II:** 298
Side Effects (Allen), **Supp. XV:** 3, 14, **15–16**
Side of Paradise, This (Fitgerald), **Supp. IX:** 56
Sidnee Poet Heroical, The (Baraka), **Supp. II Part 1:** 55
Sidney, Algernon, **II:** 114
Sidney, Mary, **Supp. I Part 1:** 98
Sidney, Philip, **II:** 470; **Supp. I Part 1:** 98, 111, 117–118, 122; **Supp. I Part 2:** 658; **Supp. II Part 1:** 104–105; **Supp. V:** 250; **Supp. XII:** 264; **Supp. XIV:** 128
Sidney, Sylvia, **Supp. I Part 1:** 67
Sidney Lanier: A Bibliographical and Critical Study (Starke), **Supp. I Part 1:** 371
Sidney Lanier: A Biographical and Critical Study (Starke), **Supp. I Part 1:** 371
Siebert, Kathy, **Supp. XX:**84
Siege (Shaw), **Supp. XIX:** 244
Siegel, Barry, **Supp. XIV:** 82
Siegel, Catherine, **Supp. XII:** 126
Siegel, Jerry, **Supp. XI:** 67

"Siege of London, The" (James), **Retro. Supp. I:** 227
Siegle, Robert, **Supp. XII:** 8
Sienkiewicz, Henryk, **Supp. IV Part 2:** 518; **Supp. XVI:** 182
"Sierra Kid" (Levine), **Supp. V:** 180–181
Sigal, Clancy, **Supp. XXI:** 44
Sigg, Eric, **Retro. Supp. I:** 53
"Sight" (Merwin), **Supp. III Part 1:** 356
Sighted Singer, The (Halliday), **Supp. XIX:** 82, **86–87**
"Sight in Camp in the Daybreak Gray and Dim, A" (Whitman), **II:** 373
Sights and Spectacles (McCarthy), **II:** 562
"Sights from a Steeple" (Hawthorne), **Retro. Supp. I:** 62; **Supp. XXI:** 201
Sights Unseen (Gibbons), **Supp. X:** **49–50**
"Signals" (Carver), **Supp. III Part 1:** 143
"Signature for Tempo" (MacLeish), **III:** 8–9
"Signed Confession of Crimes against the State" (Merton), **Supp. VIII:** 201
Signifying Monkey, The (H. L. Gates), **Supp. X:** 243
Signifying Monkey, The (Hughes), **Retro. Supp. I:** 195
Signifying Monkey, The: A Theory of Afro-American Literary Criticism (H. L. Gates), **Supp. XX:**99, 106–107
"Signing, The" (Dixon), **Supp. XII:** 146
Sign in Sidney Brustein's Window, The (Hansberry), **Supp. IV Part 1:** 359, 365, 369, 370–372
Sign of Jonas, The (Merton), **Supp. VIII:** 194–195, 195, 197, 200, 206, 207
"Sign of Saturn, The" (Olds), **Supp. X:** 206
"Signs, Oakvale, Mississippi, 1941" (Trethewey), **Supp. XXI:** 248–249
Signs and Wonders (Bukiet), **Supp. XVII:** **45–46**
Sigourney, Lydia, **Supp. I Part 2:** 684
Sikora, Malgorzata, **Retro. Supp. II:** 324
Silas Marner (G. Eliot), **II:** 26
Silberg, Richard, **Supp. XV:** 116
"Silence" (Moore), **III:** 212
"Silence" (Poe), **III:** 416
"Silence" (Sanders), **Supp. XVI:** 278
"Silence, A" (Clampitt), **Supp. IX:** 53
"Silence—A Fable" (Poe), **III:** 416
Silence and Metaphor (Bronk), **Supp. XXI:** 31, 32
"Silence Before Harvest, The" (Merwin), **Supp. III Part 1:** 352
Silence Dogood Papers, The (Franklin), **II:** 106–107
Silence in the Snowy Fields (R. Bly), **Supp. IV Part 1:** 60–61, 62, 63, 65, 66, 72; **Supp. XXI:** 84, 85
Silence of History, The (Farrell), **II:** 46–47
Silence of the Lambs, The (T. Harris), **Supp. XXI:** 78
Silence Opens, A (Clampitt), **Supp. IX:** 53
Silences (Olsen), **Supp. XIII:** 293, 294, 295, 296, **304–306**

"Silences: When Writers Don't Write" (Olsen), **Supp. XIII:** 294

Silencing the Past: Power and the Production of History (Trouillot), **Supp. X:** 14

"Silent in America" (Levine), **Supp. V:** 183

Silent Life, The (Merton), **Supp. VIII:** 208

Silent Partner, The (Odets), **Supp. II Part 2:** 539

"Silent Poem" (Francis), **Supp. IX:** 86

"Silent Season of a Hero, The" (Talese), **Supp. XVII:** 203–204

"Silent Slain, The" (MacLeish), **III:** 9

"Silent Snow, Secret Snow" (Aiken), **I:** 52

Silent Spring (Carson), **Supp. V:** 202; **Supp. IX:** 19, 24, **31–34; Supp. XIV:** 177; **Supp. XVI:** 36; **Supp. XVIII:** 189

Silhouettes of American Life (R. H. Davis), **Supp. XVI:** 85

"Silken Tent, The" (Frost), **Retro. Supp. I:** 138–139; **Supp. IV Part 2:** 448

Silko, Leslie Marmon, **Supp. IV Part 1:** 274, 319, 325, 333–334, 335, 404; **Supp. IV Part 2:** 499, 505, **557–572; Supp. V:** 169; **Supp. XI:** 18; **Supp. XII:** 217; **Supp. XVIII:** 58

Silliman, Ron, **Supp. IV Part 2:** 426; **Supp. XV:** 344; **Supp. XVII:** 70, 77

Silliman's Blog (R. Silliman), **Supp. XVII:** 70

Silman, Roberta, **Supp. X:** 6

Silverblatt, Michael, **Supp. XV:** 224

"Silver Crown, The" (Malamud), **Supp. I Part 2:** 434–435, 437; **Supp. V:** 266

"Silver Dish, The" (Bellow), **Retro. Supp. II:** 30

"Silver Filigree" (Wylie), **Supp. I Part 2:** 707

"Silver Lake" (B. Kelly), **Supp. XVII:** 130

Silvers, Phil, **Supp. IV Part 2:** 574

Silverthorne, Elizabeth, **Supp. X:** 220, 221, 222, 226, 234

"Silver To Have and to Hurl" (Didion), **Supp. IV Part 1:** 197

Simic, Charles, **Supp. V:** 5, 332; **Supp. VIII:** 39, **269–287; Supp. XI:** 317; **Supp. XV:** 179, 185; **Supp. XIX:** 277, 282

"Similar Cases" (Gilman), **Supp. XI:** 200, 202

Similitudes, from the Ocean and Prairie (Larcom), **Supp. XIII:** 141

Simmel, Georg, **Supp. I Part 2:** 644; **Supp. XVII:** 98

Simmons, Charles, **Supp. XI:** 230

Simmons, Maggie, **Retro. Supp. II:** 21

Simms, Michael, **Supp. XII:** 184

Simms, William Gilmore, **I:** 211

Simon, John, **Supp. IV Part 2:** 691

Simon, Neil, **Supp. IV Part 2: 573–594; Supp. XVII:** 8

Simone, Nina, **Supp. XXI:** 243

"Simon Gerty" (Wylie), **Supp. I Part 2:** 713

Simonides, **Supp. XII:** 110–111

"Simon Ortiz" (Gingerich), **Supp. IV Part 2:** 510

Simon Ortiz (Wiget), **Supp. IV Part 2:** 509

Simonson, Lee, **III:** 396; **Supp. XXI:** 6

"Simple" (Peacock), **Supp. XIX:** 200

"Simple Art of Murder, The" (Chandler), **Supp. IV Part 1:** 121, 341

"Simple Autumnal" (Bogan), **Supp. III Part 1:** 52–53

Simple Heart (Flaubert), **I:** 504

Simple Honorable Man, A (Richter), **Supp. XVIII:** 208, 218, **219,** 220

"Simple Purchase, A" (Peacock), **Supp. XIX:** 199

Simple Speaks his Mind (Hughes), **Retro. Supp. I:** 209; **Supp. I Part 1:** 337

Simple Stakes a Claim (Hughes), **Retro. Supp. I:** 209; **Supp. I Part 1:** 337

Simple's Uncle Sam (Hughes), **Retro. Supp. I:** 209; **Supp. I Part 1:** 337

Simple Takes a Wife (Hughes), **Retro. Supp. I:** 209; **Supp. I Part 1:** 337

Simple Truth, The (Hardwick), **Supp. III Part 1:** 199, 200, 208

Simple Truth, The (Levine), **Supp. V:** 178, 179, 193–194

"Simple Widsom, The" (Skloot), **Supp. XX:**207

"Simplicity" (Sanders), **Supp. XVI:** 276

Simply Heavenly (Hughes), **Retro. Supp. I:** 209; **Supp. I Part 1:** 338, 339

Simpson, Louis, **Supp. III Part 2:** 541; **Supp. IV Part 2:** 448, 621; **Supp. VIII:** 39, 279; **Supp. IX: 265–283,** 290; **Supp. XI:** 317; **Supp. XII:** 130; **Supp. XIII:** 337

Simpson, Mona, **Supp. XVI:** 206

"Sin" (C. Frost), **Supp. XV:** 96

Sinatra, Frank, **Supp. IX:** 3; **Supp. X:** 119; **Supp. XI:** 213

Sincere Convert, The (Shepard), **IV:** 158

Sincerely, Willis Wayde (Marquand), **III:** 61, 63, 66, 67–68, 69

Sincerity (Rowson), **Supp. XV:** 242

Sincerity and Authenticity (Trilling), **Supp. III Part 2:** 510–512

"Sincerity and Objectification: With Special Reference to the Work of Charles Reznikoff" (Zukofsky), **Supp. XIV:** 286

Sinclair, Mary Craig (Mary Craig Kimbrough), **Supp. V:** 275, 286, 287

Sinclair, Upton, **II:** 34, 440, 444, 451; **III:** 580; **Retro. Supp. II:** 95; **Supp. V: 275–293; Supp. VIII:** 11

Sinclair Lewis: An American Life (Schorer), **II:** 459

"Singapore" (Oliver), **Supp. VII:** 239, 240

Singer, Bennett L., **Supp. IV Part 1:** 330

Singer, Beth, **Supp. XIV:** 203

Singer, Isaac Bashevis, **I:** 144; **IV: 1–24; Retro. Supp. II:** 22, **299–320; Supp. IX:** 114; **Supp. XVIII:** 215, 220; **Supp. XXI:** 106

Singer, Israel Joshua, **IV:** 2, 16, 17; **Retro. Supp. II:** 302; **Supp. XVII:** 41

Singer, Joshua, **IV:** 4

Singer, Rabbi Pinchos Menachem, **IV:** 16

Singin' and Swingin' and Gettin' Merry Like Christmas (Angelou), **Supp. IV Part 1:** 2, 5, 6–7, 9, 13, 14

"Singing & Doubling Together" (Ammons), **Supp. VII:** 34–35

Singing Jailbirds (Sinclair), **Supp. V:** 277

"Singing the Black Mother" (Lupton), **Supp. IV Part 1:** 7

Single Hound, The (Sarton), **Supp. VIII:** 251, 265

Single Hound, The: Poems of a Lifetime (Dickinson; Bianchi, ed.), **Retro. Supp. I:** 35

Single Man, A (Isherwood), **Supp. XIV:** 157, 164, **169–170,** 171

"Single Sonnet" (Bogan), **Supp. III Part 1:** 56–58

Singley, Carol, **Retro. Supp. I:** 373

Singular Family, A: Rosacoke and Her Kin (Price), **Supp. VI: 258–259,** 260

"Singular First Person, The" (Sanders), **Supp. XVI:** 274

Singularities (Howe), **Supp. IV Part 2:** 431

Sin in Their Blood (Lacy), **Supp. XV:** 200

"Sinister Adolescents, The" (Dos Passos), **I:** 493

Sinister Street (Mackenzie), **II:** 82

Sinking of Clay City, The (Wrigley), **Supp. XVIII: 294–295**

Sinners in the Hands of an Angry God (Edwards), **I:** 546, 552–553, 559, 562

Sinning with Annie, and Other Stories (Theroux), **Supp. VIII:** 318

"Sins of Kalamazoo, The" (Sandburg), **III:** 586

Sintram and His Companions (La Motte-Fouqué), **III:** 78

"Siope" (Poe), **III:** 411

"Sipapu: A Cultural Perspective" (Gunn Allen), **Supp. IV Part 1:** 323

Sipchen, Bob, **Supp. X:** 145

Sipper, Ralph B., **Supp. IV Part 2:** 475

"Sire" (Cisneros), **Supp. VII:** 62–63, 64

"Siren and Signal" (Zukofsky), **Supp. III Part 2:** 611, 612

Sirens of Titan, The (Vonnegut), **Supp. II Part 2:** 757, 758, 760, 765–767

"Sir Galahad" (Tennyson), **Supp. I Part 2:** 410

Sirin, V. (pseudonym), **Retro. Supp. I:** 266. *See also* Nabokov, Vladimir

Sirlin, Jerome, **Supp. XXI:** 147

Sir Vadia's Shadow: A Friendship across Five Continents (Theroux), **Supp. VIII:** 309, 314, 321, 325

"Sis" (F. Barthelme), **Supp. XI:** 26

"S is for Sad" (M. F. K. Fisher), **Supp. XVII:** 86

Sisley, Alfred, **I:** 478

Sissman, L. E., **Supp. X:** 69

"Sister" (Hughes), **Retro. Supp. I:** 208

"Sister" (Lamott), **Supp. XX:**142

Sister Age (M. F. K. Fisher), **Supp. XVII:** 88, 91

Sister Carrie (Dreiser), **I:** 482, 497, 499, 500, 501–502, 503–504, 505, 506,

515, 519; **III:** 327; **IV:** 208; **Retro. Supp. I:** 376; **Retro. Supp. II:** 93, **96–99; Supp. XVIII:** 76, 243
"Sister of the Minotaur" (Stevens), **IV:** 89; **Supp. IX:** 332
"Sisters" (Nelson), **Supp. XVIII:** 176
"Sisters, The" (Whittier), **Supp. I Part 2:** 696
Sister's Choice (Showalter), **Retro. Supp. I:** 368
Sisters of the Earth: Women's Prose and Poetry About Nature (Anderson, ed.), **Supp. XVIII:** 189
Sisters Rosensweig, The (Wasserstein), **Supp. XV:** 320, **328–330**
"Sisyphus" (Kumin), **Supp. IV Part 2:** 443, 444, 451
"Sitalkas" (Doolittle), **Supp. I Part 1:** 266
Sitney, P. Adams, **Supp. XII:** 2
Sitting Bull, **Supp. IV Part 2:** 492
"Sitting in a Rocking Chair Going Blind" (Komunyakaa), **Supp. XIII:** 114
Sitting In: Selected Writings on Jazz, Blues, and Related Topics (Carruth), **Supp. XVI:** 46
"Sitting Up Late with My Father, 1977" (F. Wright), **Supp. XVII:** 247
Sitti's Secrets (Nye), **Supp. XIII:** 278
Situation Normal (A. Miller), **III:** 148, 149, 156, 164
Situation of Poetry, The: Contemporary Poetry and Its Traditions (Pinsky), **Supp. VI: 237–238,** 239, 241, 242
Sitwell, Edith, **IV:** 77; **Supp. I Part 1:** 271
"Six Brothers" (Cisneros), **Supp. VII:** 67
Six Characters in Search of an Author (Pirandello), **Supp. IV Part 2:** 576
"Six Days: Some Rememberings" (Paley), **Supp. VI:** 226
"65290" (Leopold), **Supp. XIV:** 184–185
Six French Poets (Lowell), **II:** 528–529
"Six in All" (Bierds), **Supp. XVII:** 31
"Six Persons" (Baraka), **Supp. II Part 1:** 53
Six Sections from Mountains and Rivers without End (Snyder), **Supp. VIII:** 305
"Sixteen Months" (Sandburg), **III:** 584
1601, or Conversation as It Was by the Fireside in the Time of the Tudors (Twain), **IV:** 201
"Sixth-Month Song in the Foothills" (Snyder), **Supp. VIII:** 297
Sixties, The (magazine) (R. Bly), **Supp. IV Part 1:** 60; **Supp. IX:** 271
"Sixty" (Dunn), **Supp. XI:** 155
"Sixty Acres" (Carver), **Supp. III Part 1:** 141
"64 Elmgrove" (Halliday), **Supp. XIX:** 88
"69 Hidebound Opinions, Propositions, and Several Asides from a Manila Folder concerning the Stuff of Poetry" (Wright), **Supp. XV:** 344–345
Sixty Stories (Barthelme), **Supp. IV Part 1:** 41, 42, 44, 47, 49, 50
63: Dream Palace (Purdy), **Supp. VII:** 270–271

"Six Variations" (Levertov), **Supp. III Part 1:** 277–278
"Six-Year-Old Boy" (Olds), **Supp. X:** 206
"Six Years Later" (Brodsky), **Supp. VIII:** 26, 28
"Size and Sheer Will" (Olds), **Supp. X:** 206
Size of Thoughts, The: Essays and Other Lumber (Baker), **Supp. XIII: 52–53,** 55, 56
Sizwe Bansi Is Dead (Fugard), **Supp. VIII:** 330
Sjöwall, Maj, **Supp. XX:**87
"Skagway" (Haines), **Supp. XII:** 206
"Skaters, The" (Ashbery), **Supp. III Part 1:** 10, 12, 13, 18, 25
"Skaters, The" (Jarrell), **II:** 368–369
Skau, Michael, **Supp. XII:** 129, 130, 132, 134
Skeeters Kirby (Masters), **Supp. I Part 2:** 459, 470, 471
Skeleton Crew (King), **Supp. V:** 144
"Skeleton in Armor, The" (Longfellow), **Retro. Supp. II:** 168
"Skeleton's Cave, The" (Bryant), **Supp. I Part 1:** 157
Skelton, John, **III:** 521
Skepticisms (Aiken), **Supp. XV:** 298, 302
Sketch Book of Geoffrey Crayon, Gent., The (Irving), **II:** 295, 303, 304–308, 309, 311, 491; **Supp. I Part 1:** 155
Sketches of Art (Jameson), **Retro. Supp. II:** 58
Sketches of Eighteenth Century America (Crèvecoeur), **Supp. I Part 1:** 233, 240–241, 250, 251
"Sketches of Female Biography" (Rowson), **Supp. XV:** 245
Sketches of Switzerland (Cooper), **I:** 346
Sketches Old and New (Twain), **IV:** 198
"Sketch for a Job-Application Blank" (Harrison), **Supp. VIII:** 38
Sketch of Old England, by a New England Man (Paulding), **I:** 344
Skibell, Joseph, **Supp. XVII:** 48
"Skier and the Mountain, The" (Eberhart), **I:** 528–529
"Skin-Boats: 1830, The" (Bierds), **Supp. XVII:** 28
Skinker, Mary Scott, **Supp. IX:** 20
Skinny Island (Auchincloss), **Supp. IV Part 1:** 33
Skinny Legs and All (Robbins), **Supp. X:** 267, 273, **276–279**
Skin of Our Teeth, The (Wilder), **IV:** 357, 358, 369–372; **Supp. IV Part 2:** 586; **Supp. XX:**50
"Skins" (Wright), **Supp. V:** 340
Skins and Bones: Poems 1979–1987 (Gunn Allen), **Supp. IV Part 1:** 321, 331
"Skipper Ireson's Ride" (Whittier), **Supp. I Part 2:** 691, 693–694
"Skirmish at Sartoris" (Faulkner), **II:** 67
"Skirt" (Halliday), **Supp. XIX:** 90
Skirts and Slacks (Di Piero), **Supp. XIX:** 35, 36, 38, 45–47
Skloot, Floyd, **Supp. XX:**193–209

Skotheim, Robert Allen, **Supp. XVII:** 104
Skow, John, **Supp. V:** 213; **Supp. XVI:** 174
Skube, Michael, **Supp. XVIII:** 96
"Skunk Cabbage" (Bronk), **Supp. XXI:** 31
"Skunk Cabbage" (Oliver), **Supp. VII:** 235, 236
"Skunk Hour" (Lowell), **II:** 548–550; **Retro. Supp. II:** 188, 189; **Supp. XIV:** 269; **Supp. XX:**203
Sky, The Stars, The Wilderness, The (Bass), **Supp. XVI:** 19, 20
Sky Changes, The (Sorrentino), **Supp. XXI:** 228, 230, 231
"Sky Dance" (Leopold), **Supp. XIV:** 186
"Sky Line" (Taylor), **Supp. V:** 316
"Sky Line, The" (Mumford), **Supp. II Part 2:** 475
"Skyscraper" (Sandburg), **III:** 581–582
Sky's the Limit, The: A Defense of the Earth (Nichols), **Supp. XIII:** 268
"Sky Valley Rider" (Wright), **Supp. V:** 335, 340
Sky-Walk; or the Man Unknown to Himself (Brown), **Supp. I Part 1:** 127–128
"Slang in America" (Whitman), **IV:** 348
Slapstick (Vonnegut), **Supp. II Part 2:** 753, 754, 778
Slapstick Tragedy (T. Williams), **IV:** 382, 393
Slate, Lane, **Supp. IX:** 251, 253
Slattery, Mary Grace. *See* Miller, Mrs. Arthur (Mary Grace Slattery)
"Slaughterer, The" (Singer), **IV:** 19
Slaughterhouse-Five (Vonnegut), **Supp. II Part 2:** 755, 758–759, 760, 770, 772–776; **Supp. V:** 41, 244; **Supp. XIX:** 235
Slaughter Rule, The (film; Alex and Andrew Smith), **Supp. XIX:** 174
Slave, The (Baraka), **Supp. II Part 1:** 42, 44, 56
Slave, The: A Novel (Singer), **IV:** 13; **Retro. Supp. II:** 305–307
"Slave Canal" (Ray), **Supp. XVIII:** 193
"Slave Coffle" (Angelou), **Supp. IV Part 1:** 16
"Slave of the Sky" (P. N. Warren), **Supp. XX:**261
"Slave on the Block" (Hughes), **Supp. I Part 1:** 329
Slave Power, The: The Free North and Southern Domination, 1780–1860 (Richards), **Supp. XIV:** 48
"Slave Quarters" (Dickey), **Supp. IV Part 1:** 181
"Slave's Dream, The" (Longfellow), **Supp. I Part 2:** 409
Slave Ship: A Historical Pageant (Baraka), **Supp. II Part 1:** 47–49, 53, 56–57
"Slave-Ships, The" (Whittier), **Supp. I Part 2:** 687–688
Slaves in Algiers; or, A Struggle for Freedom (Rowson), **Supp. XV:** 236–237

Slavs! Thinking about the Longstanding Problems of Virtue and Happiness (Kushner), **Supp. IX:** 146

Sledge, Eugene, **Supp. V:** 250

Sleek for the Long Flight (Matthews), **Supp. IX:** 154, 155, **157–158**

Sleep (Dixon), **Supp. XII:** 154

"Sleep, The" (Strand), **Supp. IV Part 2:** 627

Sleeper (film; Allen), **Supp. XV:** 5

"Sleeper, The" (Poe), **III:** 411

"Sleeper 1, The" (Hay), **Supp. XIV:** 132–133

"Sleeper 2, The" (Hay), **Supp. XIV:** 132–133

"Sleepers, The" (Whitman), **IV:** 336

"Sleepers in Jaipur" (Kenyon), **Supp. VII:** 172

Sleepers in Moon-Crowned Valleys (Purdy), **Supp. VII:** 274, 275

Sleepers Joining Hands (R. Bly), **Supp. XXI:** 85

"Sleepers Joining Hands" (R. Bly), **Supp. IV Part 1:** 63, 73

Sleeping Beauty (Macdonald), **Supp. IV Part 2:** 474, 475

Sleeping Beauty, The (Carruth), **Supp. XVI:** 53, 57–58

"Sleeping Beauty Syndrome, The: The New Agony of Single Men" (Wasserstein), **Supp. XV:** 328

"Sleeping Fury, The" (Bogan), **Supp. III Part 1:** 58

Sleeping Fury, The: Poems (Bogan), **Supp. III Part 1:** 55–58

Sleeping Gypsy and Other Poems, The (Garrett), **Supp. VII:** 96–98

Sleeping in the Forest (Oliver), **Supp. VII:** 233

"Sleeping in the Forest" (Oliver), **Supp. VII:** 233–234

Sleeping in the Woods (Wagoner), **Supp. IX:** 328

Sleeping on Fists (Ríos), **Supp. IV Part 2:** 540

Sleeping on the Wing: An Anthology of Modern Poetry (Koch and Farrell, eds.), **Supp. XV:** 187–188

"Sleeping Standing Up" (Bishop), **Supp. I Part 1:** 85, 89, 93

"Sleeping with Animals" (Kumin), **Supp. IV Part 2:** 454

Sleeping with One Eye Open (Strand), **Supp. IV Part 2:** 621–624, 623, 628

Sleep in Thunder (Lacy), **Supp. XV:** 206

"Sleepless, The" (L.-Y. Lee), **Supp. XV:** 224

"Sleepless at Crown Point" (Wilbur), **Supp. III Part 2:** 561

Sleepless Nights (Hardwick), **Supp. III Part 1:** 193, 208–211

"Sleepless Nights" (Nelson), **Supp. XVIII:** 174

"Sleep-Walkers, The" (Gibran), **Supp. XX:** 118

Sleepy Lagoon Mystery, The (Endore), **Supp. XVII:** 60

"Sleepy People" (Lethem), **Supp. XVIII:** 140

Sleigh, Tom, **Supp. XIX:** 38, 40

Sleight, Ken, **Supp. XIII:** 12

Slick, Sam (pseudonym). *See* Haliburton, Thomas Chandler

"Slick Gonna Learn" (Ellison), **Retro. Supp. II:** 116; **Supp. II Part 1:** 237–238

"Slight Rebellion off Madison" (Salinger), **III:** 553

"Slight Sound at Evening, A" (White), **Supp. I Part 2:** 672

"Slim Graves Show, The" (Keillor), **Supp. XVI:** 172

"Slim Greer" series (Hayden), **Supp. II Part 1:** 369

"Slim in Hell" (Hayden), **Supp. II Part 1:** 369

"Slim Man Canyon" (Silko), **Supp. IV Part 2:** 560

"Slip, Shift, and Speed Up: The Influence of Robinson Jeffers's Narrative Syntax" (Jarman), **Supp. XVII:** 111, 112

"Slippery Fingers" (Hammett), **Supp. IV Part 1:** 343

Slipping-Down Life, A (Tyler), **Supp. IV Part 2:** 660–661

Sloan, Jacob, **IV:** 3, 6

Sloan, John, **I:** 254; **IV:** 411; **Retro. Supp. II:** 103

Sloane, John, **Supp. XV:** 295

"Slob" (Farrell), **II:** 25, 28, 31

Slocum, Joshua, **Supp. I Part 2:** 497

Slonim, Véra. *See* Nabokov, Véra

Slopen, Beverly, **Supp. XX:** 59

Slouching towards Bethlehem (Didion), **Supp. IV Part 1:** 196, 197, 200–201, 202, 206, 210

Slovic, Scott, **Supp. XVI:** 277

"Slow Child with a Book of Birds" (Levis), **Supp. XI:** 268

"Slow Down for Poetry" (Strand), **Supp. IV Part 2:** 620

"Slow Pacific Swell, The" (Winters), **Supp. II Part 2:** 790, 793, 795, 796, 799

Slow Parade (Kees), **Supp. XV:** 137

Slow Train Coming (album, Dylan), **Supp. XVIII:** 28

"Slum Church" (Espaillat), **Supp. XXI:** 110–111

"Slumgullions" (Olsen), **Supp. IV Part 1:** 54

Slumgullion Stew: An Edward Abbey Reader (Abbey), **Supp. XIII:** 4

Slung, Michelle, **Supp. XX:** 87

"S & M" (Komunyakaa), **Supp. XIII:** 114

"Small" (C. Frost), **Supp. XV:** 102

Small, Albion, **Supp. I Part 1:** 5

"Small, Good Thing, A" (Carver), **Supp. III Part 1:** 145, 147

Small, Miriam Rossiter, **Supp. I Part 1:** 319

Small Boy and Others, A (James), **II:** 337, 547; **Retro. Supp. I:** 235

"Small but Urgent Request to the Unknowable" (Karr), **Supp. XI:** 243

Small Ceremonies (Shields), **Supp. VII:** 312–315, 320

Small Craft Warnings (T. Williams), **IV:** 382, 383, 384, 385, 386, 387, 392, 393, 396, 398

"Small Fry" (Peacock), **Supp. XIX:** 206

Small Place, A (Kincaid), **Supp. VII:** 186–187, 188, 191

"Small Rain, The" (Pynchon), **Supp. II Part 2:** 620

Small Room, The (Sarton), **Supp. VIII:** 252, **255–256**

Smalls, Bob, **II:** 128

"Small Song for Andrew" (Weigl), **Supp. XIX:** 280

Small Time Crooks (film; Allen), **Supp. XV:** 11

Small Town, A (Hearon), **Supp. VIII:** **65–66**

"Small Vases from Hebron, The" (Nye), **Supp. XIII:** 283

"Small Vision, The" (Goldbarth), **Supp. XII:** 180

"Small Voice from the Wings" (Everwine), **Supp. XV:** 76

"Small Wire" (Sexton), **Supp. II Part 2:** 696

Small Worlds (A. Hoffman), **Supp. XVII:** 44

Smardz, Zofia, **Supp. XVI:** 155

Smart, Christopher, **III:** 534; **Supp. I Part 2:** 539; **Supp. IV Part 2:** 626

Smart, Joyce H., **Supp. XI:** 169

"Smart Cookie, A" (Cisneros), **Supp. VII:** 64

"Smashup" (Thurber), **Supp. I Part 2:** 616

Smedly, Agnes, **Supp. XIII:** 295

"Smell of a God, The" (Peacock), **Supp. XIX:** 199

"Smelt Fishing" (Hayden), **Supp. II Part 1:** 367

"Smile of the Bathers, The" (Kees), **Supp. XV:** 145

"Smile on the Face of a Kouros, The" (Bronk), **Supp. XXI:** 31

"Smiles" (Dunn), **Supp. XI:** 151

Smiles, Samuel, **Supp. X:** 167

Smiley, Jane, **Supp. VI: 291–309; Supp. XII:** 73, 297; **Supp. XIII:** 127; **Supp. XIX:** 54

Smith, Adam, **II:** 9; **Supp. I Part 2:** 633, 634, 639; **Supp. XVII:** 235

Smith, Annick, **Supp. XIV:** 223

Smith, Benjamin, **IV:** 148

Smith, Bernard, **I:** 260

Smith, Bessie, **Retro. Supp. I:** 343; **Supp. VIII:** 330; **Supp. XIX:** 147

Smith, Charlie, **Supp. X:** 177

Smith, Dale, **Supp. XV:** 136, 138, 139

Smith, Dave, **Supp. V:** 333; **Supp. XI:** 152; **Supp. XII:** 178, 198; **Supp. XIX:** 277, 282

Smith, David, **Supp. XIII:** 246, 247

Smith, David Nichol, **Supp. XIV:** 2

Smith, Dinitia, **Supp. VIII:** 74, 82, 83; **Supp. XVIII:** 162

Smith, Elihu Hubbard, **Supp. I Part 1:** 126, 127, 130

Smith, George Adam, **III:** 199

Smith, Hannah Whitall, **Supp. XIV:** 333, 334, 338

Smith, Harrison, **II:** 61

Smith, Henry Nash, **IV:** 210; **Supp. I Part 1:** 233

Smith, Herbert F., **Supp. I Part 2:** 423

Smith, Iain Crichton, **Supp. XVIII:** 196

Smith, James, **II:** 111

Smith, Jedediah Strong, **Supp. IV Part 2:** 602

Smith, Jerome, **Supp. IV Part 1:** 369

Smith, Joe, **Supp. IV Part 2:** 584

Smith, John, **I:** 4, 131; **II:** 296

Smith, John Allyn, **I:** 168

Smith, Johnston (pseudonym). *See* Crane, Stephen

Smith, Kellogg, **Supp. I Part 2:** 660

Smith, Lamar, **II:** 585

Smith, Mrs. Lamar (Marguerite Walters), **II:** 585, 587

Smith, Lane, **Supp. XIX:** 231

Smith, Larry David, **Supp. XVIII:** 22

Smith, Lee, **Supp. XII:** 311; **Supp. XVIII:** 195

Smith, Logan Pearsall, **Supp. XIV: 333–351**

Smith, Lula Carson. *See* McCullers, Carson

Smith, Mark, **Supp. XVIII:** 155

Smith, Martha Nell, **Retro. Supp. I:** 33, 43, 46, 47

Smith, Mary Rozet, **Supp. I Part 1:** 5, 22

Smith, Oliver, **II:** 586

Smith, Patricia Clark, **Supp. IV Part 1:** 397, 398, 402, 406, 408, 410; **Supp. IV Part 2:** 509; **Supp. XII:** 218

Smith, Patrick, **Supp. VIII:** 40, 41

Smith, Patti, **Supp. XII:** 136; **Supp. XIV:** 151

Smith, Porter, **III:** 572

Smith, Red, **II:** 417, 424

Smith, Robert McClure, **Supp. XV:** 270

Smith, Robert Pearsall, **Supp. XIV:** 333

Smith, Sarah A., **Supp. XVIII:** 99

Smith, Seba, **Supp. I Part 2:** 411

Smith, Sidonie Ann, **Supp. IV Part 1:** 11

Smith, Stevie, **Supp. V:** 84

Smith, Sydney, **II:** 295; **Supp. XIV:** 112

Smith, Thorne, **Supp. IX:** 194

Smith, Wendy, **Supp. XII:** 330, 335; **Supp. XVIII:** 89, 92

Smith, Wilford Bascom "Pitchfork", **Supp. XIII:** 168

Smith, William, **II:** 114

Smith, William Gardner, **Supp. XVI:** 142–143

Smith, William Jay, **Supp. XIII: 331–350**

"Smoke" (Di Piero), **Supp. XIX:** 38

Smoke (film), **Supp. XII:** 21

Smoke and Steel (Sandburg), **III:** 585–587, 592

"Smokehouse" (Offutt), **Supp. XIX:** 166, 167

"Smokers" (Wolff), **Supp. VII:** 340–341

Smokey Bites the Dust (film, C. Griffith), **Supp. XVII:** 9

"Smoking My Prayers" (Ortiz), **Supp. IV Part 2:** 503

"Smoking Room, The" (Jackson), **Supp. IX:** 116

"Smoky Gold" (Leopold), **Supp. XIV:** 186

Smolan, Sandy, **Supp. XVI:** 36

Smollett, Tobias G., **I:** 134, 339, 343; **II:** 304–305; **III:** 61; **Supp. XVIII:** 7

Smuggler's Bible, A (McElroy), **Supp. IV Part 1:** 285

Smuggler's Handbook, The (Goldbarth), **Supp. XII:** 181, 183

Smugglers of Lost Soul's Rock, The (Gardner), **Supp. VI: 70**

Smyth, Albert Henry, **II:** 123

Smyth, Jacqui, **Supp. XXI:** 215

"Snack Firm Maps New Chip Push" (Keillor), **Supp. XVI:** 168, 169

"Snail, The" (Hay), **Supp. XIV:** 124

"Snake, The" (Berry), **Supp. X:** 31

"Snake, The" (Crane), **I:** 420

"Snakecharmer" (Plath), **Supp. I Part 2:** 538

"Snakes, Mongooses" (Moore), **III:** 207

"Snakeskin" (Kooser), **Supp. XIX:** 123

"Snakes of September, The" (Kunitz), **Supp. III Part 1:** 258

"Snapshot of 15th S.W., A" (Hugo), **Supp. VI:** 141

"Snapshot Rediscovered, A" (X. J. Kennedy), **Supp. XV:** 170

"Snapshots in an Album" (Espaillat), **Supp. XXI:** 111

"Snapshots of a Daughter-in-Law" (Rich), **Supp. I Part 2:** 553–554

Snapshots of a Daughter-in-Law: Poems, 1954–1962 (Rich), **Supp. I Part 2:** 550–551, 553–554; **Supp. XII:** 255

Snaring the Flightless Birds (Bierds), **Supp. XVII:** 26

Sneetches and Other Stories, The (Geisel), **Supp. XVI:** 109

"Sneeze, The" (Chekhov), **Supp. IV Part 2:** 585

Snell, Ebenezer, **Supp. I Part 1:** 151

Snell, Thomas, **Supp. I Part 1:** 153

"Snob, The" (Shapiro), **Supp. II Part 2:** 705

Snobbery: The America Version (Epstein), **Supp. XIV:** 102, 114–115

Snodgrass, Kathleen, **Supp. XVI:** 42

Snodgrass, W. D., **I:** 400; **Retro. Supp. II:** 179; **Supp. III Part 2:** 541; **Supp. V:** 337; **Supp. VI: 311–328**; **Supp. XI:** 141, 315; **Supp. XIII:** 312; **Supp. XV:** 92, 153; **Supp. XVII:** 239

"Snow" (C. Baxter), **Supp. XVIII:** 19

"Snow" (Frost), **Retro. Supp. I:** 133

"Snow" (Haines), **Supp. XII:** 212

"Snow" (Sexton), **Supp. II Part 2:** 696

"Snow" (W. V. Davis), **Supp. XXI:** 89, 90, 93

Snow, C. P., **Supp. I Part 2:** 536

Snow, Hank, **Supp. V:** 335

Snow Ball, The (Gurney), **Supp. V:** 99

"Snow-Bound" (Whittier), **Supp. I Part 2:** 700–703

"Snow Bound at Eagle's" (Harte), **Supp. II Part 1:** 356

"Snowflakes" (Longfellow), **II:** 498

"Snow Goose, The" (Gallico), **Supp. XVI:** 238

Snow-Image and Other Twice Told Tales, The (Hawthorne), **II:** 237; **Retro. Supp. I:** 160

"Snowing in Greenwich Village" (Updike), **IV:** 226; **Retro. Supp. I:** 321

"Snow in New York" (Swenson), **Supp. IV Part 2:** 644

Snow Leopard, The (Matthiessen), **Supp. V:** 199, 207–211

"Snow Man, The" (Stevens), **IV:** 82–83; **Retro. Supp. I:** 299, 300, 302, 306, 307, 312; **Supp. XXI:** 60

"Snowmass Cycle, The" (Dunn), **Supp. XI:** 152

Snow: Meditations of a Cautious Man in Winter (Banks), **Supp. V:** 6

Snow Poems, The (Ammons), **Supp. VII:** 32–34

Snowshoe Trek to Otter River (Budbill), **Supp. XIX:** 11

Snow's Music, The (Skloot), **Supp. XX:** 196, **204–205**

"Snows of Kilimanjaro, The" (Hemingway), **II:** 78, 257, 263, 264; **Retro. Supp. I:** 98, 182; **Supp. XII:** 249

"Snows of Studiofiftyfour, The" (Plimpton), **Supp. XVI:** 245

"Snow Songs" (Snodgrass), **Supp. VI:** 324

"Snowstorm, The" (Oates), **Supp. II Part 2:** 523

"Snowstorm as It Affects the American Farmer, A" (Crèvecoeur), **Supp. I Part 1:** 251

Snow White (Barthelme), **Supp. IV Part 1:** 40, 47, 48–49, 50, 52; **Supp. V:** 39

"Snowy Egret" (Weigl), **Supp. XIX:** 280–281

"Snowy Mountain Song, A" (Ortiz), **Supp. IV Part 2:** 506

Snyder, Gary, **Supp. III Part 1:** 350; **Supp. IV Part 2:** 502; **Supp. V:** 168–169; **Supp. VIII:** 39, **289–307**; **Supp. XVI:** 283

Snyder, Mike, **Supp. XIV:** 36

"So-and-So Reclining on Her Couch" (Stevens), **IV:** 90

"Soapland" (Thurber), **Supp. I Part 2:** 619

Soares, Lota de Macedo, **Retro. Supp. II:** 44; **Supp. I Part 1:** 89, 94

"Sobbin' Women, The" (Benét), **Supp. XI:** 47

Sobin, Gustaf, **Supp. XVI: 281–298**

Sochen, June, **Supp. XXI:** 1

Social Ethics (Gilman), **Supp. XI:** 207

"Social Function of the Story Teller, The" (lecture, Murray), **Supp. XIX:** 153

"Socialism and the Negro" (McKay), **Supp. X:** 135

"Socialism of the Skin, A (Liberation, Honey!)" (Kushner), **Supp. IX:** 135

Social Thought in America: The Revolt against Formalism (White), **Supp. I Part 2:** 648, 650

"Society, Morality, and the Novel" (Ellison), **Retro. Supp. II:** 118, 123–124

"Sociological Habit Patterns in Linguistic Transmogrification" (Cowley), **Supp. II Part 1:** 143

"Sociological Poet, A" (Bourne), **I:** 228

Socrates, **I:** 136, 265; **II:** 8–9, 105, 106; **III:** 281, 419, 606; **Supp. I Part 2:** 458; **Supp. XII:** 98

Socrates Fortlow stories (Mosley), **Supp. XIII: 242–243**

So Forth (Brodsky), **Supp. VIII:** 32–33

"So Forth" (Brodsky), **Supp. VIII:** 33

"Soft Flame" (Skloot), **Supp. XX:**203

Soft Machine, The (Burroughs), **Supp. III Part 1:** 93, 103, 104

"Soft Mask" (Karr), **Supp. XI:** 243

Soft Side, The (James), **II:** 335; **Retro. Supp. I:** 229

"Soft Spring Night in Shillington, A" (Updike), **Retro. Supp. I:** 318, 319

"Soft Wood" (Lowell), **II:** 550–551

"So Help Me" (Algren), **Supp. IX:** 2

Soil and Survival: Land Stewardship and the Future of American Agriculture (C. Bly, J. Paddock and N. Paddock), **Supp. XVI:** 36–37

"Soirée in Hollywood" (H. Miller), **III:** 186

Sojourner, The (Rawlings), **Supp. X:** 233–234

"Sojourn in a Whale" (Moore), **III:** 211, 213

"Sojourns" (Didion), **Supp. IV Part 1:** 205

Sokolow, Jayme, **Supp. XIX:** 134

Solanus, Jane, **Supp. XVI:** 293

Solar Lottery (Dick), **Supp. XVIII:** 138

Solar Storms (Hogan), **Supp. IV Part 1:** 397, 410, 414–415

"Soldier, The" (Frost), **II:** 155

"Soldier Asleep at the Tomb" (Schnackenberg), **Supp. XV:** 262–263

Soldier Blue (film), **Supp. X:** 124

"Soldier of Fortune" (Wright), **Supp. XV:** 341

"Soldier's Home" (Hemingway), **Retro. Supp. I:** 189

Soldier's Joy (Bell), **Supp. X:** 7, **7–8**, 10, 11

Soldiers of the Storm (film), **Supp. XIII:** 163

Soldiers' Pay (Faulkner), **I:** 117; **II:** 56, 68; **Retro. Supp. I:** 80, 81

"Soldier's Testament, The" (Mumford), **Supp. II Part 2:** 473

"Soliloquy: Man Talking to a Mirror" (Komunyakaa), **Supp. XIII:** 116–117

"Solitary Confinement" (X. J. Kennedy), **Supp. XV:** 157

"Solitary Pond, The" (Updike), **Retro. Supp. I:** 323

So Little Time (Marquand), **III:** 55, 59, 65, 67, 69

"Solitude" (Maupassant), **Supp. I Part 1:** 223

Solo Faces (Salter), **Supp. IX: 259–260**

Solomon, Andy, **Supp. X:** 11

Solomon, Carl, **Supp. XIV:** 143, 150

Solomon, Charles, **Supp. VIII:** 82

Solomon, Deborah, **Supp. XXI:** 245

Solomon, Henry, Jr., **Supp. I Part 2:** 490

Solomons, Leon, **IV:** 26

So Long, See You Tomorrow (Maxwell), **Supp. VIII:** 156, 160, 162, **167–169; Supp. XVII:** 23

"So Long Ago" (Bausch), **Supp. VII:** 41–42

Solotaroff, Robert, **Retro. Supp. II:** 203

Solotaroff, Theodore, **III:** 452–453; **Retro. Supp. II:** 281; **Supp. I Part 2:** 440, 445; **Supp. X:** 79; **Supp. XI:** 340; **Supp. XII:** 291; **Supp. XIX:** 268

Solstice (Di Piero), **Supp. XIX:** 36

"Solstice" (Jeffers), **Supp. II Part 2:** 433, 435

"Solstice, The" (Merwin), **Supp. III Part 1:** 356

"Solus Rex" (Nabokov), **Retro. Supp. I:** 274

"Solutions" (McCarthy), **II:** 578

"Solving the Puzzle" (Dunn), **Supp. XI:** 152

Solzhenitsyn, Alexandr, **Retro. Supp. I:** 278; **Supp. VIII:** 241

"Some Afternoon" (Creeley), **Supp. IV Part 1:** 150–151

Some American People (Caldwell), **I:** 292, 294, 295, 296, 304, 309

"Some Ashes Drifting above Piedra, California" (Levis), **Supp. XI:** 264–265

"Some Aspects of the Grotesque in Southern Fiction" (O'Connor), **Retro. Supp. II:** 223, 224

"Some Birds on a Dun Field" (Bronk), **Supp. XXI:** 27

"Somebody Always Grabs the Purple" (H. Roth), **Supp. IX:** 234

Somebody in Boots (Algren), **Supp. IX:** 3, **5–7**, 12

Somebody's Darling (McMurtry), **Supp. V:** 225

Some Came Running (film), **Supp. XI:** 213

Some Came Running (Jones), **Supp. XI:** 214, 215, 220, **222–223**, 226, 227, 232

Some Can Whistle (McMurtry), **Supp. V:** 229

"Some Children of the Goddess" (Mailer), **Retro. Supp. II:** 204

Someday, Maybe (Stafford), **Supp. XI: 323–325; Supp. XIII:** 281

"Some Dreamers of the Golden Dream" (Didion), **Supp. IV Part 1:** 200

Some Faces in the Crowd (Schulberg), **Supp. XVIII:** 252

"Some Foreign Letters" (Sexton), **Supp. II Part 2:** 674

"Some General Instructions" (Koch), **Supp. XV:** 182

"Some Good News" (Olson), **Supp. II Part 2:** 575, 576, 577

"Some Grass along a Ditch Bank" (Levis), **Supp. XI:** 266

"Some Greek Writings" (Corso), **Supp. XII:** 130

Some Honorable Men: Political Conventions, 1960–1972 (Mailer), **Retro. Supp. II:** 208

Some Imagist Poets (Lowell), **III:** 511, 518, 520; **Supp. I Part 1:** 257, 261

"Some keep the Sabbath going to Church" (Dickinson), **Retro. Supp. I:** 30; **Supp. XVIII:** 301

"Some Laughed" (L. Michaels), **Supp. XVI:** 207

"Some Like Indians Endure" (Gunn Allen), **Supp. IV Part 1:** 330

"Some Like Them Cold" (Lardner), **II:** 427–428, 430, 431; **Supp. IX:** 202

"Some Lines from Whitman" (Jarrell), **IV:** 352

"Some Matters Concerning the Occupant" (Keillor), **Supp. XVI:** 167

"Some Musicians Play Chamber Music for Us" (Bronk), **Supp. XXI:** 27–28

"Some Negatives: X. at the Chateau" (Merrill), **Supp. III Part 1:** 322

"Some Neglected Points in the Theory of Socialism" (Veblen), **Supp. I Part 2:** 635

"Some Notes for an Autobiographical Lecture" (Trilling), **Supp. III Part 2:** 493, 497, 500

"Some Notes on French Poetry" (R. Bly), **Supp. IV Part 1:** 61

"Some Notes on Miss L." (West), **IV:** 290–291, 295; **Retro. Supp. II:** 322

"Some Notes on Organic Form" (Levertov), **Supp. III Part 1:** 272, 279

"Some Notes on Teaching: Probably Spoken" (Paley), **Supp. VI:** 225

"Some Notes on the Gazer Within" (Levis), **Supp. XI:** 270

"Some Notes on Violence" (West), **IV:** 304; **Retro. Supp. II:** 322, 323

"Some Observations Now" (Conroy), **Supp. XVI:** 75

Some of the Dharma (Kerouac), **Supp. III Part 1:** 225

"Someone Is Buried" (Salinas), **Supp. XIII:** 324

"Someone Puts a Pineapple Together" (Stevens), **IV:** 90–91

"Someone's Blood" (Dove), **Supp. IV Part 1:** 245

"Someone Talking" (Harjo), **Supp. XII:** 219–220

"Someone Talking to Himself" (Wilbur), **Supp. III Part 2:** 557

"Someone to Watch Over Me" (Stern), **Supp. IX:** 300

Someone to Watch Over Me: Stories (Bausch), **Supp. VII:** 53

Some People, Places, & Things That Will Not Appear in My Next Novel (Cheever), **Supp. I Part 1:** 184–185

"Some Poets' Criticism and the Age" (Yenser), **Supp. XV:** 113–114

Some Problems of Philosophy: A Beginning of an Introduction to Philosophy (James), **II:** 360–361

"Some Questions You Might Ask" (Oliver), **Supp. VII:** 238–239

"Some Remarks on Humor" (White), **Supp. I Part 2:** 672

"Some Remarks on Rhythm" (Roethke), **III:** 548–549

Somers, Fred, **I:** 196

Somerville, Jane, **Supp. IX:** 289, 296–297

"Some Secrets" (Stern), **Supp. IX:** 286, 287, 288, 289, 295

Some Sort of Epic Grandeur (Bruccoli), **Retro. Supp. I:** 115, 359

"Something" (Oliver), **Supp. VII:** 236

Something Happened (Heller), **Supp. IV Part 1:** 383, 386–388, 389, 392

"Something Happened: The Imaginary, the Symbolic, and the Discourse of the Family" (Mellard), **Supp. IV Part 1:** 387

Something in Common (Hughes), **Supp. I Part 1:** 329–330

Something Inside: Conversations with Gay Fiction Writers (Gambone), **Supp. XII:** 81

"Something Matters but We Don't " (Bronk), **Supp. XXI:** 32

"Something New" (Stern), **Supp. IX:** 290

Something Said (Sorrentino), **Supp. XXI:** 226, 227, 229, 235

"Something's Going to Happen" (Zinberg), **Supp. XV:** 196

"Something Spurious from the Mindinao Deep" (Stegner), **Supp. IV Part 2:** 605

Something to Declare (Alvarez), **Supp. VII:** 1, 2, 11, 17–19

Something to Remember Me By (Bellow), **Retro. Supp. II:** 32

"Something to Remember Me By" (Bellow), **Retro. Supp. II:** 32

Something Wicked This Way Comes (Bradbury), **Supp. IV Part 1:** 101, 110–111

"Something Wild . . ." (T. Williams), **IV:** 381

"Some Thoughts" (McNally), **Supp. XIII:** 207

"Some Thoughts on the Line" (Oliver), **Supp. VII:** 238

"Sometimes, Reading" (Stafford), **Supp. XI:** 314

"Sometimes It Just Happens That Way, That's All" (Hinojosa), **Supp. XIX:** 101

"Sometimes I Wonder" (Hughes), **Supp. I Part 1:** 337

Sometimes Mysteriously (Salinas), **Supp. XIII:** 311, **326–328**

"Sometimes Mysteriously" (Salinas), **Supp. XIII:** 328

Some Trees (Ashbery), **Supp. III Part 1:** 3–7, 12

"Some Trees" (Ashbery), **Supp. III Part 1:** 2

"Some Views on the Reading and Writing of Short Stories" (Welty), **Retro. Supp. I:** 351

"Somewhere" (Nemerov), **III:** 279–280

"Somewhere Else" (Paley), **Supp. VI:** 227

"Somewhere in Africa" (Sexton), **Supp. II Part 2:** 684–685

"Somewhere Is Such a Kingdom" (Ransom), **III:** 492

"Somewhere near Phu Bai:" (Komunyakaa), **Supp. XIII:** 123–124

Some Words (Bronk), **Supp. XXI:** 32

"Some Words with a Mummy" (Poe), **III:** 425

"Some Yips and Barks in the Dark" (Snyder), **Supp. VIII:** 291

Sommers, Michael, **Supp. IV Part 2:** 581

Sommers, William, **I:** 387, 388

"Somnambulisma" (Stevens), **Retro. Supp. I:** 310

"So Much Summer" (Dickinson), **Retro. Supp. I:** 26, 44, 45

"So Much the Worse for Boston" (Lindsay), **Supp. I Part 2:** 398

"So Much Water So Close to Home" (Carver), **Supp. III Part 1:** 143, 146

Son, Cathy, **Supp. X:** 292

"Son, The" (Dove), **Supp. IV Part 1:** 245

"Son and Father" (Pickering), **Supp. XXI:** 197

"Sonata" (Schnackenberg), **Supp. XV:** 259

"Sonata for the Invisible" (Harjo), **Supp. XII:** 228

Sonata for Two Pianos (Bowles), **Supp. IV Part 1:** 83

Son at the Front, A (Wharton), **II:** 183; **IV:** 320; **Retro. Supp. I:** 378

Sondheim, Stephen, **Supp. XII:** 260; **Supp. XVI:** 194

Son Excellence Eugène Rougon (Zola), **III:** 322

Song (B. Kelly), **Supp. XVII:** 123, **127–130**

"Song" (B. Kelly), **Supp. XVII:** 127

"Song" (Bogan), **Supp. III Part 1:** 57

"Song" (Bryant). *See* "Hunter of the West, The"

"Song" (Dunbar), **Supp. II Part 1:** 199

"Song" (Espaillat), **Supp. XXI:** 106–107

"Song" (Ginsberg), **Supp. II Part 1:** 317

"Song" (Kenyon), **Supp. VII:** 169

"Song" (Rich), **Supp. I Part 2:** 560

"Song" (Wylie), **Supp. I Part 2:** 729

"Song, A" (Creeley), **Supp. IV Part 1:** 145

"Song, The" (Gioia), **Supp. XV:** 117

Song and Idea (Eberhart), **I:** 526, 529, 533, 539

"Song: Enlightenment" (X. J. Kennedy), **Supp. XV:** 169

Song for My Father, A: A Play in Two Acts (Budbill), **Supp. XIX:** 3, **15–16**

"Song for Myself and the Deer to Return On" (Harjo), **Supp. XII:** 225

"Song for My Sixtieth Year" (Carruth), **Supp. XVI:** 54

"Song for Occupations, A" (Whitman), **Retro. Supp. I:** 394

"Song for Simeon, A" (Eliot), **Retro. Supp. I:** 64

"Song for the Coming of Smallpox" (Wagoner), **Supp. IX:** 329, 330

"Song for the End of Time" (Gioia), **Supp. XV:** 126–127

"Song for the First People" (Wagoner), **Supp. IX:** 328

"Song for the Last Act" (Bogan), **Supp. III Part 1:** 64

"Song for the Middle of the Night, A" (Wright), **Supp. III Part 2:** 594

"Song for the Rainy Season" (Bishop), **Supp. I Part 1:** 93–94, 96

"Song for the Romeos, A" (Stern), **Supp. IX:** 296

"Song for Woody" (song, Dylan), **Supp. XVIII:** 24

"Song from a Courtyard Window" (Gioia), **Supp. XV:** 119

"Song in the Front Yard, A" (Brooks), **Supp. XVIII:** 181

"Songline of Dawn" (Harjo), **Supp. XII:** 229

"Song: Love in Whose Rich Honor" (Rukeyser), **Supp. VI:** 285

"Song: Now That She Is Here" (Carruth), **Supp. XVI:** 59

"Song of Advent, A" (Winters), **Supp. II Part 2:** 789

"Song of a Man Who Rushed at the Enemy" (Wagoner), **Supp. IX:** 329, 330

"Song of Courage, A" (Masters), **Supp. I Part 2:** 458

Song of God, The: Bhagavad-Gita (Isherwood and Prabhavananda, trans.), **Supp. XIV:** 156, 157, 164

Song of Hiawatha, The (Longfellow), **II:** 501, 503–504; **Retro. Supp. II:** 155, **159–161,** 162, 163

"Song of Innocence, A" (Ellison), **Retro. Supp. II:** 126; **Supp. II Part 1:** 248

"Song of My Fiftieth Birthday, The" (Lindsay), **Supp. I Part 2:** 399

"Song of Myself" (Whitman), **II:** 544; **III:** 572, 584, 595; **IV:** 333, 334, 337–339, 340, 341, 342, 344, 348, 349, 351, 405; **Retro. Supp. I:** 388, 389, 395–399, 400; **Supp. V:** 122; **Supp. IX:** 131, 136, 143, 328, 331; **Supp. XIV:** 139; **Supp. XVIII:** 194, 304

Song of Napalm (Weigl), **Supp. XIX:** 278–282

"Song of Napalm" (Weigl), **Supp. XIX:** 276–277

Song of Russia (film), **Supp. I Part 1:** 281, 294; **Supp. XVII:** 60–61

"Song of Self" (Huncke), **Supp. XIV:** 138–139, 145

Song of Solomon (biblical book), **III:** 118; **IV:** 150

Song of Solomon (Morrison), **Supp. III Part 1:** 364, 368, 369, 372, 379; **Supp. XVIII:** 55

Song of Songs (biblical book), **II:** 538; **IV:** 153–154; **Supp. XV:** 221

"Song of the Answerer" (Whitman), **Retro. Supp. I:** 393, 399

Song of the Cardinal, The (Stratton-Porter), **Supp. XX:** 217, 218, 219

"Song of the Chattahoochee, The" (Lanier), **Supp. I Part 1:** 365, 368

"Song of the Degrees, A" (Pound), **III:** 466

"Song of the Exposition" (Whitman), **IV:** 332

"Song of the Gavilan" (Leopold), **Supp. XIV:** 189

"Song of the Gourd" (Wright), **Supp. XV:** 348–349

"Song of the Greek Amazon" (Bryant), **Supp. I Part 1:** 168

Song of the Lark, The (Cather), **I:** 312, 319–321, 323; **Retro. Supp. I:** 1, 3, 7, **9–11,** 13, 19, 20

"Song of the Open Road" (McGrath), **Supp. X:** 127

"Song of the Open Road" (Whitman), **IV:** 340–341; **Retro. Supp. I:** 400; **Supp. IX:** 265

"Song of the Redwood Tree" (Whitman), **IV:** 348

"Song of the Scullery" (McCarriston), **Supp. XIV:** 272

"Song of the Sky Loom" (traditional Tewa poem), **Supp. IV Part 1:** 325

"Song of the Son" (Toomer), **Supp. III Part 2:** 482–483; **Supp. IX:** 313

"Song of the Sower, The" (Bryant), **Supp. I Part 1:** 169

"Song of the Stars" (Bryant), **Supp. I Part 1:** 163

"Song of the Swamp-Robin, The" (Frederic), **II:** 138

"Song of the Vermonters, The" (Whittier), **Supp. I Part 2:** 692

"Song of Three Smiles" (Merwin), **Supp. III Part 1:** 344

"Song of Wandering Aengus, The" (Yeats), **IV:** 271; **Retro. Supp. I:** 342, 350

"Song of Welcome" (Brodsky), **Supp. VIII:** 32

"Song on Captain Barney's Victory" (Freneau), **Supp. II Part 1:** 261

"Song/Poetry and Language-Expression and Perception" (Ortiz), **Supp. IV Part 2:** 500, 508

"Song: 'Rough Winds Do Shake the Darling Buds of May' " (Simpson), **Supp. IX:** 268

Songs (Boyce), **Supp. XXI:** 9

Songs and Satires (Masters), **Supp. I Part 2:** 465–466

Songs and Sonnets (L. P. Smith), **Supp. XIV:** 341

Songs and Sonnets (Masters), **Supp. I Part 2:** 455, 459, 461, 466

"Songs for a Colored Singer" (Bishop), **Supp. I Part 1:** 80, 85

Songs for a Summer's Day (A Sonnet Cycle) (MacLeish), **III:** 3

Songs for Eve (MacLeish), **III:** 3, 19

"Songs for Eve" (MacLeish), **III:** 19

"Songs for My Father" (Komunyakaa), **Supp. XIII:** 128

"Songs for Two Seasons" (C. Frost), **Supp. XV:** 95–96

Songs from This Earth on Turtle's Back: Contemporary American Indian Poetry (Bruchac, ed.), **Supp. IV Part 1:** 320, 328

"Songs of a Housewife" (Rawlings), **Supp. X:** 221–222

"Songs of Billy Bathgate, The" (Doctorow), **Supp. IV Part 1:** 230

Songs of Innocence (Blake), **Supp. I Part 2:** 708

Songs of Jamaica (McKay), **Supp. X:** 131, 133

"Songs of Maximus, The" (Olson), **Supp. II Part 2:** 567

"Songs of Parting" (Whitman), **IV:** 348

Songs of the Sierras (J. Miller), **I:** 459

Songs of Three Centuries (Whittier and Larcom, eds.), **Supp. XIII:** 142

"Song to David" (Smart), **III:** 534

"Song to No Music, A" (Brodsky), **Supp. VIII:** 26

Soniat, Katherine, **Supp. XXI:** 245

Sonneschein, Rosa, **Retro. Supp. II:** 65

"Sonnet" (Rukeyser), **Supp. VI:** 284

"Sonnet Crown for Two Voices" (Bierds), **Supp. XVII:** 35

"Sonnets" (Carruth), **Supp. XVI:** 56

"Sonnets at Christmas" (Tate), **IV:** 135

Sonnets to Orpheus (Rilke), **Supp. XV:** 222

"Sonnet-To Zante" (Poe), **III:** 421

"Sonny's Blues" (Baldwin), **Retro. Supp. II:** 7, 8, 10, 14; **Supp. I Part 1:** 58–59, 63, 67; **Supp. XI:** 288

Son of Laughter, The: A Novel (Buechner), **Supp. XII:** 54

Son of Perdition, The (Cozzens), **I:** 359–360, 377, 378, 379

Son of the Circus, A (Irving), **Supp. VI:** 165, 166, **176–179**

"Son of the Gods, A" (Bierce), **I:** 202

Son of the Morning (Oates), **Supp. II Part 2:** 518, 519, 520–522

Son of the Morning Star: Custer and the Little Bighorn (Connell), **Supp. XIV:** 80, 82, 97

"Son of the Romanovs, A" (Simpson), **Supp. IX:** 273–274

Son of the Wolf, The (London), **II:** 465, 469

"Son of the Wolfman" (Chabon), **Supp. XI:** 76

"Sonrisas" (Mora), **Supp. XIII:** 216, 219

Sons (Buck), **Supp. II Part 1:** 117–118

Sons and Lovers (Lawrence), **III:** 27

Sontag, Kate, **Supp. XV:** 104

Sontag, Susan, **IV:** 13, 14; **Retro. Supp. II:** 279; **Supp. I Part 2:** 423; **Supp. III Part 2: 451–473; Supp. VIII:** 75; **Supp. XIV:** 14, 15, 95–96, 167; **Supp. XVI:** 201, 204, 206; **Supp. XX:** 205; **Supp. XXI:** 243

"Soonest Mended" (Ashbery), **Supp. III Part 1:** 1, 13

"Sootfall and Fallout" (White), **Supp. I Part 2:** 671

Sophocles, **I:** 274; **II:** 291, 385, 577; **III:** 145, 151, 152, 153, 159, 398, 476, 478, 609, 613; **IV:** 291, 363, 368, 370; **Supp. I Part 1:** 153, 284; **Supp. I Part 2:** 491; **Supp. V:** 97; **Supp. VIII:** 332; **Supp. XV:** 265, 266

"Sophronsiba" (Bourne), **I:** 221

Sorcerer's Apprentice, The: Tales and Conjurations (Johnson), **Supp. VI: 192–193,** 194

"Sorcerer's Eye, The" (Nemerov), **III:** 283

Sordello (Browning), **III:** 467, 469, 470

"Sordid? Good God!" (Williams), **Retro. Supp. II:** 334

"Sorghum" (Mason), **Supp. VIII:** 146

Sorokin, Pitirim, **Supp. I Part 2:** 679

Sorrentino, Christopher, **Supp. XVIII:** 148

Sorrentino, Gilbert, **Retro. Supp. I:** 426; **Supp. IV Part 1:** 286; **Supp. XII:** 139; **Supp. XXI: 225–241**

"Sorrow" (Komunyakaa), **Supp. XIII:** 119

Sorrow Dance, The (Levertov), **Supp. III Part 1:** 279–280, 283

"Sorrowful Guest, A" (Jewett), **Retro. Supp. II:** 137

Sorrows of Fat City, The: A Selection of Literary Essays and Reviews (Garrett), **Supp. VII:** 111

Sorrows of Young Werther, The (Goethe), **Supp. XI:** 169; **Supp. XX:** 234, 236

Sorrows of Young Werther, The (Goethe; Bogan and Mayer, trans.), **Supp. III Part 1:** 63

"Sorry Fugu" (Boyle), **Supp. XX:** 19

"Sorting Facts; or, Nineteen Ways of Looking at Marker" (Howe), **Supp. IV Part 2:** 434, 436

"Sort of Song, A" (W. C. Williams), **Supp. XVII:** 243

"S O S" (Baraka), **Supp. II Part 1:** 50

"So Sassafras" (Olson), **Supp. II Part 2:** 574

"So There" (Creeley), **Supp. IV Part 1:** 157

"So This Is Nebraska" (Kooser), **Supp. XIX:** 120

Sotirov, Vasil, **Supp. IX:** 152

Soto, Gary, **Supp. IV Part 2:** 545; **Supp. V:** 180; **Supp. XI:** 270; **Supp. XIII:** 313, 315, 316, 320, 323; **Supp. XV:** 73

"Soto Thinking of the Ocean" (Salinas), **Supp. XIII:** 321

"Sotto Voce" (Kunitz), **Supp. III Part 1:** 265

Sot-Weed Factor, The (Barth), **I:** 122, 123, 125, 129, 130, 131–134, 135

Soul, The (Brooks), **I:** 244

Soul and Body of John Brown, The (Rukeyser), **Supp. VI:** 273

Soul Clap Hands and Sing (Marshall), **Supp. XI:** 276, 278, **280–282**

Soul Expeditions (Singer). See Shosha (Singer)

Soul Gone Home (Hughes), **Retro. Supp. I:** 203; **Supp. I Part 1:** 328

"Soul inside the Sentence, The" (Gass), **Supp. VI:** 88

Soul Is Here for Its Own Joy, The (Bly, ed.), **Supp. IV Part 1:** 74

Soul of Man under Socialism, The (Wilde), **Supp. IX:** 134–135

"Soul of Spain, The \[In the manner of Gertrude Stein\]" (Hemingway), **Supp. XX:** 74

Soul of the Far East, The (Lowell), **II:** 513

"Soul on Bench" (Halliday), **Supp. XIX:** 91

Soul on Ice (Cleaver), **Retro. Supp. II:** 12, 13

"Souls Belated" (Wharton), **Retro. Supp. I:** 364

"Soul selects her own Society, The" (Dickinson), **Retro. Supp. I:** 37

Souls of Black Folk, The (Du Bois), **Supp. II Part 1:** 33, 40, 160, 168–170, 176, 183; **Supp. IV Part 1:** 164; **Supp. IX:** 305, 306; **Supp. X:** 133; **Supp. XIII:** 185, 238, 243

Souls of Black Folk. The (Du Bois), **Supp. XX:** 102

"Sound, The" (Olds), **Supp. X:** 214

Sound and Beauty (Hwang), **Supp. XXI:** 146

"Sound and Fury" (O. Henry), **Supp. II Part 1:** 402

Sound and the Fury, The (Faulkner), **I:** 480; **II:** 55, 57, 58–60, 73; **III:** 237; **IV:** 100, 101, 104; **Retro. Supp. I:** 73, 75, 77, 82, **83–84,** 86, 88, 89, 90, 91, 92; **Supp. VIII:** 215; **Supp. IX:** 103; **Supp. X:** 44; **Supp. XII:** 33; **Supp. XIV:** 12; **Supp. XVII:** 138; **Supp. XVIII:** 84

"Sound Bites" (Alvarez), **Supp. VII:** 11

Sound I Listened For, The (Francis), **Supp. IX: 78–79,** 87

"Soundless Trumpet, The" (Antin), **Supp. XX:** 12

"Sound Mind, Sound Body" (Lowell), **II:** 554

Sound of a Voice, The (Hwang), **Supp. XXI:** 146

"Sound of Distant Thunder, A" (Elkin), **Supp. VI: 42–43,** 44

"Sound of Light, The" (Merwin), **Supp. III Part 1:** 356

Sound of Mountain Water, The (Stegner), **Supp. IV Part 2:** 595, 596, 598, 600, 608

"Sound of Talking" (Purdy), **Supp. VII:** 270

Sounds of Poetry, The (Pinsky), **Supp. VI:** 236, 247, 248

Soupault, Philippe, **IV:** 288, 404; **Retro. Supp. II:** 85, 321, 324

Source (Doty), **Supp. XI:** 121, **134–137**

"Source" (Doty), **Supp. XI:** 136

"Source, The" (Olds), **Supp. X:** 211

"Source, The" (Porter), **III:** 443

Source of Light, The (Price), **Supp. VI: 262,** 266

"Sources of Soviet Conduct, The" (Kennan), **Supp. VIII:** 241

Sour Grapes (W. C. Williams), **Retro. Supp. I:** 418

"Sourwood Nocturne" (Skloot), **Supp. XX:** 202

"South" (Levis), **Supp. XI:** 266

"South" (Trethewey), **Supp. XXI:** 247, 256

"South, The" (Hughes), **Supp. I Part 1:** 321

South American Journey (W. Frank), **Supp. XX:** 79

"Southbound on the Freeway" (Swenson), **Supp. IV Part 2:** 643

South Dakota Guidebook, The (C. Baxter), **Supp. XVII:** 15

Southern, Terry, **Supp. IV Part 1:** 379; **Supp. V:** 40, 201; **Supp. XI: 293–310; Supp. XVI:** 230

Southern Cross, The (Wright), **Supp. V:** 332, 342

"Southern Cross, The" (Wright), **Supp. V:** 338

"Southerner's Problem, The" (Du Bois), **Supp. II Part 1:** 168

"Southern Girl" (Zelda Fitzgerald), **Supp. IX:** 71

"Southern Gothic" (Trethewey), **Supp. XXI:** 256

"Southern History" (Trethewey), **Supp. XXI:** 256, 257

"Southern Mode of the Imagination, A" (Tate), **IV:** 120

"Southern Romantic, A" (Tate), **Supp. I Part 1:** 373

"Southern Sojourn, A" (Hoffman), **Supp. XVIII:** 87

Southern Terry, **Supp. XIV:** 82

Southey, Robert, **II:** 304, 502; **Supp. I Part 1:** 154

"South Lingers On, The" (R. Fisher), **Supp. XIX:** 69–70

South Moon Under (Rawlings), **Supp. X: 225–226,** 229, 233

South Pacific Affair (Lacy), **Supp. XV:** 206

Southpaw, The (Harris), **II:** 424–425

"South Sangamon" (Cisneros), **Supp. VII:** 66

South to a Very Old Place (Murray), **Supp. XIX: 151–153**

Southwell, Robert, **IV:** 151

Southwick, Marcia, **Supp. XI:** 259

Southworth, E. D. E. N, **Retro. Supp. I:** 246

Souvenir of the Ancient World, Selected Poems of Carlos Drummond de Andrade (Strand, trans.), **Supp. IV Part 2:** 630

"Sow" (Plath), **Supp. I Part 2:** 537

"Sowing and Reaping in *Furors Die*" (Nostrandt), **Supp. XVIII:** 80–81

Soyinka, Wole, **Supp. XX:** 100

Space between Our Footsteps, The: Poems and Paintings from the Middle East (Nye, ed.), **Supp. XIII:** 280

"Space Quale, The" (James), **II:** 349

"Spaces Between, The" (Kingsolver), **Supp. VII:** 209

"Space Where Sex Should Be, The: Toward a Definition of the Black Literary Tradition" (Nelson), **Supp. XVIII:** 172

Spackman, Peter, **Supp. XVI:** 221

Spacks, Patricia, **Supp. XVI:** 251

"Spain" (Auden), **Supp. II Part 1:** 12–13, 14

"Spain in Fifty-Ninth Street" (White), **Supp. I Part 2:** 677

"Spanish-American War Play" (Crane), **I:** 422

Spanish Ballads (Merwin, trans.), **Supp. III Part 1:** 347

Spanish Bayonet (Benét), **Supp. XI:** 45, 47

Spanish Earth, The (film), **Retro. Supp. I:** 184

Spanish Papers and Other Miscellanies (Irving), **II:** 314

"Spanish Revolution, The" (Bryant), **Supp. I Part 1:** 153, 168

Spanish Student, The (Longfellow), **II:** 489, 506; **Retro. Supp. II:** 165

"Spanish Winter" (Egan), **Supp. XIX:** 52

Spanking the Maid (Coover), **Supp. V:** 47, 48, 49, 52

Spare Change (Parker), **Supp. XIX:** 186–187

Spargo, John, **Supp. I Part 1:** 13

"Spark, The" (Wharton), **Retro. Supp. I:** 381

"Sparkles from the Wheel" (Whitman), **IV:** 348

Sparks, Debra, **Supp. X:** 177

Sparks, Jared, **Supp. I Part 1:** 156

"Sparrow" (Berry), **Supp. X:** 31

Sparrow, Henry, **III:** 587

Sparrow, Mrs. Henry, **III:** 587

"Sparrow's Gate, The" (B. Kelly), **Supp. XVII:** 133

Spaulding, William, **Supp. XVI:** 106

"Spawning Run, The" (Humphrey), **Supp. IX:** 95

"Speak, Gay Memory" (Kirp), **Supp. XI:** 129

"Speak, Hoyt-Schermerhorn" (Lethem), **Supp. XVIII:** 148

Speak, Memory (Nabokov), **III:** 247–250, 252; **Retro. Supp. I:** 264, 265, 266, 267, 268, 277; **Supp. XVI:** 148

Speak, Memory (V. Nabakov), **Supp. XVII:** 47

Speaking and Language (Shapiro), **Supp. II Part 2:** 721

Speaking for Nature: How Literary Naturalists from Henry Thoreau to Rachel Carson Have Shaped America (Brooks), **Supp. IX:** 31

Speaking for Ourselves: American Ethnic Writing (Faderman and Bradshaw, eds.), **Supp. XIII:** 313

Speaking of Accidents (Everwine), **Supp. XV:** 75, 88

"Speaking of Accidents" (Everwine), **Supp. XV:** 88–89

"Speaking of Counterweights" (White), **Supp. I Part 2:** 669

Speaking of Literature and Society (Trilling), **Supp. III Part 2:** 494, 496, 499

"Speaking of Love" (Gioia), **Supp. XV:** 124–125

Speaking of Race, Speaking of Sex: Hate Speech, Civil Rights, and Civil Liberties (H. L. Gates, Griffin, Lively, and Strossen), **Supp. XX:** 111

Speaking on Stage (Kolin and Kullman, eds.), **Supp. IX:** 145

Speaking on Stage: Interviews with Contemporary American Playwrights (Balakian), **Supp. XV:** 327

"Speaking Passions" (Kitchen), **Supp. XV:** 215

Speak What We Feel (Not What We Ought to Say): Reflections on Literature and Faith (Buechner), **Supp. XII:** 57

Spear, Roberta, **Supp. V:** 180; **Supp. XV:** 73

"Special Kind of Fantasy, A: James Dickey on the Razor's Edge" (Niflis), **Supp. IV Part 1:** 175

"Special Pleading" (Lanier), **Supp. I Part 1:** 364

"Special Problems in Teaching Leslie Marmon Silko's *Ceremony*" (Gunn Allen), **Supp. IV Part 1:** 333

Special Providence, A (Yates), **Supp. XI:** 342, **344–345**

"Special Time, a Special School, A" (Knowles), **Supp. XII:** 236

Special View of History, The (Olson), **Supp. II Part 2:** 566, 569, 572

Specimen Days (Whitman), **IV:** 338, 347, 348, 350; **Retro. Supp. I:** 408

Specimens of the American Poets, **Supp. I Part 1:** 155

"Spectacles, The" (Poe), **III:** 425

Spectator Bird, The (Stegner), **Supp. IV Part 2:** 599, 604, 606, 611–612

Spector, Robert, **Supp. XIII:** 87

Spectra: A Book of Poetic Experiments (Bynner and Ficke), **Supp. XV:** 43

"Spectre Bridegroom, The" (Irving), **II:** 304

"Spectre Pig, The" (Holmes), **Supp. I Part 1:** 302

"Speculating Woman" (X. J. Kennedy), **Supp. XV:** 168

"Speech Sounds" (O. Butler), **Supp. XIII:** 61, **70**

"Speech to a Crowd" (MacLeish), **III:** 16

"Speech to the Detractors" (MacLeish), **III:** 16

"Speech to the Young" (Brooks), **Supp. III Part 1:** 79, 86

"Speech to Those Who Say Comrade" (MacLeish), **III:** 16

Speedboat (Adler), **Supp. X:** 171

Speed of Darkness, The (Rukeyser), **Supp. VI:** 274, 281

Speed-the-Plow (Mamet), **Supp. XIV:** 241, 246, 249, 250, 251

"Speedy Gonzales Was the Fastest Mouse in Mexico" (P. N. Warren as Kilina), **Supp. XX:**262

Speilberg, Steven, **Supp. XI:** 234

Speirs, Logan, **Supp. XIX:** 282

"Spell" (Francis), **Supp. IX:** 87

"Spell, The" (Peacock), **Supp. XIX:** 198, 200

"Spell for the Manufacture & Use of a Magic Carpet" (Hull), **Supp. XXI:** 132–133, 139, 141

Spelling Dictionary, A (Rowson), **Supp. XV:** 244

Spence, Thomas, **Supp. I Part 2:** 518

Spence + Lila (Mason), **Supp. VIII:** 133, **143–145**

Spencer, Edward, **Supp. I Part 1:** 357, 360

Spencer, Herbert, **I:** 515; **II:** 345, 462–463, 480, 483, 536; **III:** 102, 315; **IV:** 135; **Retro. Supp. II:** 60, 65, 93, 98; **Supp. I Part 1:** 368; **Supp. I Part 2:** 635

Spencer, Sharon, **Supp. X:** 185, 186, 195, 196

Spencer, Theodore, **I:** 433; **Supp. III Part 1:** 2

Spender, Natasha, **Supp. IV Part 1:** 119, 127, 134

Spender, Stephen, **II:** 371; **III:** 504, 527; **Retro. Supp. I:** 216; **Retro. Supp. II:** 243, 244; **Supp. I Part 2:** 536; **Supp. II Part 1:** 11; **Supp. IV Part 1:** 82, 134; **Supp. IV Part 2:** 440; **Supp. X:** 116

Spengler, Oswald, **I:** 255, 270; **II:** 7, 577; **III:** 172, 176; **Retro. Supp. II:** 324; **Supp. I Part 2:** 647

Spens, Sir Patrick, **Supp. I Part 2:** 404

Spenser, Edmund, **I:** 62; **III:** 77, 78, 89; **IV:** 155, 453; **Retro. Supp. I:** 62; **Supp. I Part 1:** 98, 152, 369; **Supp. I Part 2:** 422, 719

"Spenser's Ireland" (Moore), **III:** 211, 212

Sperry, Margaret, **Supp. IV Part 1:** 169

Spheres of Existence (C. L. R. James), **Supp. XXI:** 172

Sphere: The Form of a Motion (Ammons), **Supp. VII:** 24, 32, 33, 35, 36

"Sphinx" (Hayden), **Supp. II Part 1:** 373

"Spiced Plums" (Ríos), **Supp. IV Part 2:** 553

Spickard, Paul, **Supp. XXI:** 149

"Spider and the Ghost of the Fly, The" (Lindsay), **Supp. I Part 2:** 375

Spider Bay (Van Vechten), **Supp. II Part 2:** 746

"Spider Heart, The" (Peacock), **Supp. XIX:** 200

"Spiders" (Schwartz), **Supp. II Part 2:** 665

Spider's House, The (Bowles), **Supp. IV Part 1:** 87–89, 90, 91

Spider Woman's Granddaughters: Traditional Tales and Contemporary Writing by Native American Women (Gunn Allen, ed.), **Supp. IV Part 1:** 320, 326, 332–333; **Supp. IV Part 2:** 567

Spiegel, Sam, **Supp. XVIII:** 251, 252

Spiegelman, Art, **Supp. XVII:** 48

Spiegelman, Willard, **Supp. XI:** 126

Spielberg, Steven, **Supp. XXI:** 154

Spillane, Mickey, **Supp. IV Part 2:** 469, 472; **Supp. XV:** 200; **Supp. XVIII:** 236, 237

Spiller, Robert E., **I:** 241; **Supp. I Part 1:** 104

Spillers, Hortense, **Supp. XX:**109

"Spillikins: Gregor Mendel at the Table" (Bierds), **Supp. XVII:** 34–35

Spillway (Barnes), **Supp. III Part 1:** 44

Spingarn, Amy, **Supp. I Part 1:** 325, 326

Spingarn, Joel, **I:** 266; **Supp. I Part 1:** 325

Spinoza, Baruch, **I:** 493; **II:** 590, 593; **III:** 600; **IV:** 5, 7, 11, 12, 17; **Retro. Supp. II:** 300; **Supp. I Part 1:** 274; **Supp. I Part 2:** 643; **Supp. XVI:** 184

"Spinoza of Market Street, The" (Singer), **IV:** 12–13; **Retro. Supp. II:** 307

"Spinster" (Plath), **Supp. I Part 2:** 536

"Spinster's Tale, A" (Taylor), **Supp. V:** 314–315, 316–317, 319, 323

Spiral of Memory, The: Interviews (Coltelli, ed.), **Supp. XII:** 215

Spires, Elizabeth, **Supp. X:** 8

"Spire Song" (Bowles), **Supp. IV Part 1:** 80

Spirit and Flame: An Anthology of African American Poetry (Gilyard, ed.), **Supp. XXI:** 246

Spirit and the Flesh, The: Sexual Diversity in American Indian Culture (W. L. Williams), **Supp. IV Part 1:** 330

"Spirit Birth" (Cullen), **Supp. IV Part 1:** 168

Spirit Brides (Gibran). *See Nymphs in the Valley*

Spirit in Man, The (Jung), **Supp. IV Part 1:** 68

"Spirit in Me, The" (Hoffman), **Supp. XVIII:** 87

Spirit of Culver (West), **IV:** 287

Spirit of Labor, The (Hapgood), **Supp. XVII:** 96, 99, 101–102; **Supp. XXI:** 4

Spirit of Romance, The (Pound), **III:** 470; **Retro. Supp. I:** 286

Spirit of the Ghetto, The: Studies of the Jewish Quarter of New York (Hapgood), **Supp. XVII:** 96, 101, 103, 106

Spirit of Youth and the City Streets, The (Addams), **Supp. I Part 1:** 6–7, 12–13, 16, 17, 19

"Spirits" (Bausch), **Supp. VII:** 46–47

Spirits, and Other Stories (Bausch), **Supp. VII:** 46–47, 54

"Spirit Says, You Are Nothing, The" (Levis), **Supp. XI:** 265–266

Spirits Rebellious (al-Arwá&hudot; al-Mutamarrida) (Gibran), **Supp. XX:**115, 124, 125

Spiritual Adventures (Symons), **Supp. XX:**239

Spiritual Conflict, The (Scupoli), **IV:** 156

Spiritual Exercises, The (Loyola), **IV:** 151; **Supp. XI:** 162

"Spiritual Manifestation, A" (Whittier), **Supp. I Part 2:** 699

"Spirituals and Neo-Spirituals" (Hurston), **Supp. VI:** 152–153

Spits, Ellen Handler, **Supp. XII:** 166

"Spitzbergen Tales" (Crane), **I:** 409, 415, 423

Spitzer, Philip, **Supp. XIV:** 21

"Spleen" (Eliot), **I:** 569, 573–574

Spleen de Paris, Le (Baudelaire), **Supp. XIV:** 337

Splendid Drunken Twenties, The (Van Vechten), **Supp. II Part 2:** 739–744

Splendide-Hôtel (Sorrentino), **Supp. XXI:** 233

"Splinters" (Bukiet), **Supp. XVII:** 47

"Split Infinitive" (Pickering), **Supp. XXI:** 204

"Splitting an Order" (Kooser), **Supp. XIX:** 128–129

"Splittings" (Rich), **Supp. I Part 2:** 570–571

"Splitting Wood at Six Above" (Kumin), **Supp. IV Part 2:** 449

Spofford, Harriet Prescott, **Supp. XIII:** 143

Spoils of Poynton, The (James), **I:** 463; **Retro. Supp. I:** 229–230

Spoken Page, The (Nye), **Supp. XIII:** 274

"Spokes" (Auster), **Supp. XII:** 23

Spokesmen (Whipple), **II:** 456

Spook Sonata, The (Strindberg), **III:** 387, 392

Spooky Art, The: A Book about Writing (Mailer), **Retro. Supp. II:** 214

"Spoon, The" (Simic), **Supp. VIII:** 275

Spoon River Anthology (Masters), **I:** 106; **III:** 579; **Supp. I Part 2:** 454, 455, 456, 460–465, 466, 467, 471, 472, 473, 476; **Supp. IX:** 306; **Supp. XIV:** 282–283; **Supp. XIX:** 121

Sport and a Pastime, A (Salter), **Supp. IX:** 254–257; **Supp. XVI:** 237

Sporting Club, The (McGuane), **Supp. VIII:** 43

Sport of the Gods, The (Dunbar), **Supp. II Part 1:** 193, 200, 207, 214–217

Sports Illustrated Training with Weights (Parker and Marsh), **Supp. XIX:** 187

"Sportsman Born and Bred, A" (Plimpton), **Supp. XVI:** 241

Sportsman's Sketches, A (Turgenev), **I:** 106; **IV:** 277

Sportswriter, The (Ford), **Supp. V:** 57, 58, 62–67

"Spotted Horses" (Faulkner), **IV:** 260

Sprague, Morteza, **Retro. Supp. II:** 115

Spratling, William, **II:** 56; **Retro. Supp. I:** 80

Sprawl trilogy (W. Gibson), **Supp. XVI:** 117, 122, 124

"Spray, The" (Lethem), **Supp. XVIII:** 148

"Spray Paint King, The" (Dove), **Supp. IV Part 1:** 252–253

Spreading Fires (Knowles), **Supp. XII:** 249

Sprigge, Elizabeth, **IV:** 31

"Spring" (Kooser), **Supp. XIX:** 126

"Spring" (Millay), **III:** 126

"Spring" (Mora), **Supp. XIII:** 217

"Spring 1967" (Carruth), **Supp. XVI:** 55

Spring and All (W. C. Williams), **Retro. Supp. I:** 412, 418, **418–420,** 427, 430, 431

"Spring and All" (W. C. Williams), **Retro. Supp. I:** 419

Spring Awakening (Wedeking, trans. Franzen), **Supp. XX:**85

"Spring Break-Up" (Carruth), **Supp. XVI:** 56

"Spring Bulletin" (Allen), **Supp. XV:** 15

Springer's Progress (Markson), **Supp. XVII: 141–142,** 143, 146

"Spring Evening" (Farrell), **II:** 45

"Spring Evening" (Kenyon), **Supp. VII:** 173

"Springfield Magical" (Lindsay), **Supp. I Part 2:** 379

Spring in New Hampshire and Other Poems (McKay), **Supp. X:** 131, 135

"Spring Notes from Robin Hill" (Carruth), **Supp. XVI:** 48

"Spring Pastoral" (Wylie), **Supp. I Part 2:** 707

"Spring Pools" (Frost), **II:** 155; **Retro. Supp. I:** 137

"Spring Snow" (Matthews), **Supp. IX:** 160

"SPRING SONG" (Baraka), **Supp. II Part 1:** 60

Springsteen, Bruce, **Supp. VIII:** 143

"Spring Strains" (W. C. Williams), **Retro. Supp. I:** 416

Spring Tides (Morison), **Supp. I Part 2:** 494

Springtime and Harvest (Sinclair), **Supp. V:** 280

"Springtime for You" (Halliday), **Supp. XIX:** 87

Spruance, Raymond, **Supp. I Part 2:** 479, 491

"Spruce Has No Taproot, The" (Clampitt), **Supp. IX:** 41–42

"Spunk" (Hurston), **Supp. VI:** 150, 151–152

Spunk: The Selected Stories (Hurston), **Supp. VI:** 150

Spurr, David, **Supp. XV:** 183

Spy, The (Cooper), **I:** 335, 336, 337, 339, 340; **Supp. I Part 1:** 155

"Spy, The" (Francis), **Supp. IX:** 81

Spy, The (Freneau), **Supp. II Part 1:** 260

Spyglass Tree, The (Murray), **Supp. XIX: 155–156**

Spy in the House of Love, A (Nin), **Supp. X:** 186

Squanto, **Supp. I Part 2:** 486

"Square Business" (Baraka), **Supp. II Part 1:** 49

Square Root of Wonderful, The (McCullers), **II:** 587–588

"Squash in Blossom" (Francis), **Supp. IX:** 81

"Squatter on Company Land, The" (Hugo), **Supp. VI:** 133

"Squatter's Children" (Bishop), **Retro. Supp. II:** 47

"Squeak, Memory" (Bukiet), **Supp. XVII:** 47

Squeeze Play (Auster), **Supp. XII:** 21

Squires, Radcliffe, **IV:** 127; **Supp. XV:** 118

Squirrels (Mamet), **Supp. XIV:** 240

S.S. Gliencairn (O'Neill), **III:** 387, 388, 405

S.S. San Pedro (Cozzens), **I:** 360–362, 370, 378, 379

"Ssshh" (Olds), **Supp. X:** 215

"Stacking the Straw" (Clampitt), **Supp. IX:** 41

Stade, George, **Supp. IV Part 1:** 286

Staël, Madame de, **II:** 298

"Staff of Life, The" (H. Miller), **III:** 187

Stafford, Jean, **II:** 537; **Retro. Supp. II:** 177; **Supp. V:** 316

Stafford, William, **Supp. IV Part 1:** 72; **Supp. IV Part 2:** 642; **Supp. IX:** 273; **Supp. XI: 311–332; Supp. XIII:** 76, 274, 276, 277, 281, 283; **Supp. XIV:** 119, 123; **Supp. XX:**161; **Supp. XXI:** 246

"Stage All Blood, The" (MacLeish), **III:** 18

"Staggerlee Wonders" (Baldwin), **Retro. Supp. II:** 15

Stained White Radiance, A (Burke), **Supp. XIV:** 28, 31

Stalin, Joseph, **I:** 261, 490; **II:** 39, 40, 49, 564; **III:** 30, 298; **IV:** 372; **Supp. V:** 290; **Supp. XXI:** 164, 165, 167

"Stalking" (J. W. Miller), **Supp. XX:**167

"Stalking the Billion-Footed Beast: A Literary Manifesto for the New Social Novel" (Wolfe), **Supp. III Part 2:** 586

Stallman, R. W., **I:** 405

Stamberg, Susan, **Supp. IV Part 1:** 201; **Supp. XII:** 193

Stamford, Anne Marie, **Supp. XII:** 162

Stanard, Mrs. Jane, **III:** 410, 413

Stand, The (King), **Supp. V:** 139, 140–141, 144–146, 148, 152

"Standard of Liberty, The" (Rowson), **Supp. XV:** 243

"Standard of Living, The" (Parker), **Supp. IX: 198–199**

Stander, Lionel, **Supp. I Part 1:** 289

"Standing and the Waiting, The" (M. F. K. Fisher), **Supp. XVII:** 83

Standing by Words (Berry), **Supp. X:** 22, 27, 28, 31, 32, 35

Standing Fast (Swados), **Supp. XIX: 268–269**

"Standing Halfway Home" (Wagoner), **Supp. IX:** 324

"Standing In" (Caputo), **Supp. XIX:** 26

Stand in the Mountains, A (Taylor), **Supp. V:** 324

Standish, Burt L. (pseudonym). *See* Patten, Gilbert

Standish, Miles, **I:** 471; **II:** 502–503

Standley, Fred L., **Retro. Supp. II:** 6

Stand Still Like the Hummingbird (H. Miller), **III:** 184

"Stand Up" (Salinas), **Supp. XIII:** 315

Stand with Me Here (Francis), **Supp. IX:** 76

Stanford, Ann, **Retro. Supp. I:** 41; **Supp. I Part 1:** 99, 100, 102, 103, 106, 108, 109, 113, 117; **Supp. IV Part 2:** 637

Stanford, Charles Villiers, **Supp. XX:**228

Stanford, Donald E., **II:** 217

Stanford, Frank, **Supp. XV:** 338, 339, 341, 342–343, 343, 345, 348, 350

Stanford, Ginny (Crouch), **Supp. XV:** 339

Stanford, Leland, **I:** 196, 198

Stanislavsky, Konstantin, **Supp. XIV:** 240, 243

Stanley, Jodee, **Supp. XIX:** 52

"Stanley Kunitz" (Oliver), **Supp. VII:** 237

Stansell, Christine, **Supp. XVII:** 106; **Supp. XXI:** 4

Stanton, Frank L., **Supp. II Part 1:** 192

Stanton, Robert J., **Supp. IV Part 2:** 681

"Stanzas from the Grande Chartreuse" (Arnold), **Supp. I Part 2:** 417

Stanzas in Meditation (Stein), **Supp. III Part 1:** 13

Staples, Hugh, **Retro. Supp. II:** 187

Star, Alexander, **Supp. X:** 310

Starbuck, George, **Retro. Supp. II:** 53, 245; **Supp. I Part 2:** 538; **Supp. IV Part 2:** 440; **Supp. XIII:** 76
Star Child (Gunn Allen), **Supp. IV Part 1:** 324
"Star Dust" (Wrigley), **Supp. XVIII:** 296
Stardust Memories (film; Allen), **Supp. XV:** 1, 4, **8,** 9, 13
"Stare, The" (Updike), **Retro. Supp. I:** 329
"Starfish, The" (R. Bly), **Supp. IV Part 1:** 72
"Staring at the Sea on the Day of the Death of Another" (Swenson), **Supp. IV Part 2:** 652
Star Is Born, A (film), **Supp. IV Part 1:** 198; **Supp. IX:** 198; **Supp. XVIII:** 242, 243
Stark, David, **Supp. XII:** 202
"Stark Boughs on the Family Tree" (Oliver), **Supp. VII:** 232
Starke, Aubrey Harrison, **Supp. I Part 1:** 350, 352, 356, 360, 362, 365, 370, 371
Starkey, David, **Supp. XII:** 180, 181
Star Ledger (Hull), **Supp. XXI:** 129, **136–138**
"Star Ledger" (Hull), **Supp. XXI:** 136
"Starlight" (Levine), **Supp. V:** 188
"Starlight Scope Myopia" (Komunyakaa), **Supp. XIII:** 123, 124
Starnino, Carmine, **Supp. XVII:** 74
"Star of the Nativity" (Brodsky), **Supp. VIII:** 33
Starr, Ellen Gates, **Supp. I Part 1:** 4, 5, 11
Starr, Jean. *See* Untermeyer, Jean Starr
Starr, Ringo, **Supp. XI:** 309
Star Rover, The (London), **II:** 467
"Starry Night, The" (Sexton), **Supp. II Part 2:** 681
"Stars" (Frost), **II:** 153
Stars, the Snow, the Fire, The: Twenty-five Years in the Northern Wilderness (Haines), **Supp. XII: 199–201,** 206, 209
Star Shines over Mt. Morris Park, A (H. Roth), **Supp. IX:** 227, 236, **236–237**
"Stars of the Summer Night" (Longfellow), **II:** 493
"Stars over Harlem" (Hughes), **Retro. Supp. I:** 207
"Star-Spangled" (García), **Supp. XI:** 177, 178
Star-Spangled Girl, The (Simon), **Supp. IV Part 2:** 579
"Star-Splitter, The" (Frost), **Retro. Supp. I:** 123, 133
Stars Principal (McClatchy), **Supp. XII: 256–258**
"Star That Would Not Shine, The" (C. L. R. James), **Supp. XXI:** 160
"Starting from Paumanok" (Whitman), **IV:** 333
Starting Out in the Thirties (Kazin), **Supp. VIII: 95–97**
"Starved Lovers" (MacLeish), **III:** 19
Starved Rock (Masters), **Supp. I Part 2:** 465
"Starving Again" (Moore), **Supp. X:** 163, 172, 175

"State, The" (Bourne), **I:** 233
State and Main (Mamet), **Supp. XIV:** 241
"Statement of Principles" (Ransom), **III:** 496
"Statement: Phillipa Allen" (Rukeyser), **Supp. VI:** 283–284
"Statements on Poetics" (Snyder), **Supp. VIII:** 291, 292
"Statement with Rhymes" (Kees), **Supp. XV:** 139
"State of the Art, The" (Elkin), **Supp. VI:** 52
"State of the Arts, The" (Wasserstein), **Supp. XV:** 332
State of the Nation (Dos Passos), **I:** 489
"State of the Union" (Vidal), **Supp. IV Part 2:** 678
Static Element, The: Selected Poems of Natan Zach (Everwine, trans.), **Supp. XV:** 73, 75, **85–88**
"Statue, The" (Berryman), **I:** 173
"Statue and Birds" (Bogan), **Supp. III Part 1:** 50
"Statue of an Unkown Soldier, The" (Kooser), **Supp. XIX:** 124
"Statues, The" (Schwartz), **Supp. II Part 2:** 654, 659
"Status Rerum" (Pound), **Supp. I Part 1:** 257
Stavans, Ilan, **Supp. XI:** 190
"Stave Church" (W. V. Davis), **Supp. XXI:** 93, 94
"Staying Alive" (Levertov), **Supp. III Part 1:** 281
Staying Alive (Wagoner), **Supp. IX:** 324, **326**
"Staying at Ed's Place" (Swenson), **Supp. IV Part 2:** 648
Staying Put : Making a Home in a Restless World (Sanders), **Supp. XVI:** 274–275
Stay Me, Oh Comfort Me: Journals and Stories, 1933–1941 (M. F. K. Fisher), **Supp. XVII:** 92
Stayton, Richard, **Supp. IX:** 133
Steadman, Goodman, **IV:** 147
"Steak" (Snyder), **Supp. VIII:** 301
Steal Away: Selected and New Poems (Wright), **Supp. XV:** 337, 340, 348, 350–351
Stealing Beauty (Minot), **Supp. VI:** 205
Stealing Glimpses (McQuade), **Supp. IX:** 151
Stealing the Language: The Emergence of Women's Poetry in America (Ostriker), **Supp. XV:** 251
"Stealing the Thunder: Future Visions for American Indian Women, Tribes, and Literary Studies" (Gunn Allen), **Supp. IV Part 1:** 331
"Steam Shovel Cut" (Masters), **Supp. I Part 2:** 468
Stearns, Harold, **I:** 245; **Supp. XVII:** 106
Stedman, Edmund Clarence, **Supp. I Part 1:** 372; **Supp. II Part 1:** 192; **Supp. XV:** 115, 269, 273, 274, 282, 286
Steel, Sharon, **Supp. XIX:** 61
Steele, Margaret, **Supp. XXI:** 5

Steele, Max, **Supp. XIV:** 82
Steele, Sir Richard, **I:** 378; **II:** 105, 107, 300; **III:** 430
Steele, Timothy, **Supp. XV:** 251; **Supp. XVII:** 112
Steele, Wilbur Daniel, **Supp. XXI:** 5
Steelwork (Sorrentino), **Supp. XXI:** 227, 230, 231, 232
Steenburgen, Mary, **Supp. IV Part 1:** 236
Steeple Bush (Frost), **II:** 155; **Retro. Supp. I:** 140; **Retro. Supp. II:** 42
"Steeple-Jack, The" (Moore), **III:** 212, 213, 215
"Steerage" (Goldbarth), **Supp. XII:** 187
Steers, Nina, **Retro. Supp. II:** 25
Steffens, Lincoln, **II:** 577; **III:** 580; **Retro. Supp. I:** 202; **Retro. Supp. II:** 101; **Supp. I Part 1:** 7; **Supp. XVII:** 98, 101, 106–107; **Supp. XXI:** 2, 3, 5, 7, 10
Stegner, Page, **IV:** 114, 116; **Supp. IV Part 2:** 599
Stegner, Wallace, **Supp. IV Part 2: 595–618; Supp. V:** 220, 224, 296; **Supp. X:** 23, 24; **Supp. XIV:** 82, 193, 230, 233; **Supp. XVIII:** 192
"Stegner's Short Fiction" (Ahearn), **Supp. IV Part 2:** 604
Steichen, Edward, **III:** 580, 594–595
Steichen, Lillian. *See* Sandburg, Mrs. Carl (Lillian Steichen)
Steier, Rod, **Supp. VIII:** 269
Steiger, Rod, **Supp. XI:** 305
Stein, Gertrude, **I:** 103, 105, 476; **II:** 56, 251, 252, 257, 260, 262–263, 264, 289; **III:** 71, 454, 471–472, 600; **IV: 24–48,** 368, 375, 404, 415, 443, 477; **Retro. Supp. I:** 108, 170, 176, 177, 186, 418, 422; **Retro. Supp. II:** 85, 207, 326, 331; **Supp. I Part 1:** 292; **Supp. III Part 1:** 13, 37, 225, 226; **Supp. III Part 2:** 626; **Supp. IV Part 1:** 11, 79, 80, 81, 322; **Supp. IV Part 2:** 468; **Supp. V:** 53; **Supp. IX:** 55, 57, 62, 66; **Supp. XII:** 1, 139; **Supp. XIV:** 336; **Supp. XVI:** 187; **Supp. XVII:** 98, 105, 107; **Supp. XVIII:** 148; **Supp. XXI:** 7, 33
Stein, Jean, **Supp. XVI:** 245
Stein, Karen F., **Supp. XIII:** 29, 30
Stein, Leo, **IV:** 26; **Supp. XIV:** 336; **Supp. XV:** 298
Stein, Lorin, **Supp. XII:** 254; **Supp. XVIII:** 137, 139
Steinbeck, John, **I:** 107, 288, 301, 378, 495, 519; **II:** 272; **III:** 382, 453, 454, 589; **IV: 49–72; Retro. Supp. II:** 19, 196; **Supp. IV Part 1:** 102, 225; **Supp. IV Part 2:** 502; **Supp. V:** 290, 291; **Supp. VIII:** 10; **Supp. IX:** 33, 171; **Supp. XI:** 169; **Supp. XIII:** 1, 17; **Supp. XIV:** 21, 181; **Supp. XVII:** 228; **Supp. XVIII:** 90, 102, 254; **Supp. XIX:** 3
Steinbeck, Olive Hamilton, **IV:** 51
Steinberg, Saul, **Supp. VIII:** 272
Steinberg, Sybil, **Supp. XVII:** 165, 166
Steinem, Gloria, **Supp. IV Part 1:** 203

Steiner, George, **Retro. Supp. I:** 327; **Supp. IV Part 1:** 286; **Supp. XVI:** 230

Steiner, Nancy, **Supp. I Part 2:** 529

Steiner, Stan, **Supp. IV Part 2:** 505

Steinfels, Margaret, **Supp. XVII:** 170

Steinhoff, Eirik, **Supp. XVI:** 290

Steinman, Michael, **Supp. VIII:** 172

Steinmetz, Charles Proteus, **I:** 483

Steinway Quintet Plus Four, The (Epstein), **Supp. XII:** 159, **162–166**

Stekel, Wilhelm, **III:** 554

Stella (Goethe), **Supp. IX:** 133, 138

Stella (Kushner), **Supp. IX:** 133

Stella, Joseph, **I:** 387

"Stellaria" (Francis), **Supp. IX:** 83

Stelligery and Other Essays (Wendell), **Supp. I Part 2:** 414

Stendhal, **I:** 316; **III:** 465, 467; **Supp. I Part 1:** 293; **Supp. I Part 2:** 445

Stepanchev, Stephen, **Supp. XI:** 312

Stephen, Leslie, **IV:** 440

Stephen, Sir Leslie, **IV:** 440; **Supp. I Part 1:** 306

Stephen, Saint, **II:** 539; **IV:** 228

Stephen Crane (Berryman), **I:** 169–170, 405

Stephen King, The Second Decade: "Danse Macabre" to "The Dark Half" (Magistrale), *Supp. V:* 138, 146, 151

Stephen King: The Art of Darkness (Winter), **Supp. V:** 144

Stephens, Jack, **Supp. X:** 11, 14, 15, 17

Stephens, James, **Supp. XIX:** 204

Stephenson, Gregory, **Supp. XII:** 120, 123

"Stepping Out" (Dunn), **Supp. XI:** 140, 141

Steps (Kosinski), **Supp. VII:** 215, 221–222, 225

"Steps" (Nye), **Supp. XIII:** 288

Steps to the Temple (Crashaw), **IV:** 145

"Steps Toward Poverty and Death" (R. Bly), **Supp. IV Part 1:** 60

Stepto, Robert B., **Retro. Supp. II:** 116, 120, 123

Sterile Cuckoo, The (Nichols), **Supp. XIII:** 258, **259–263,** 264

Sterling, Bruce, **Supp. XVI:** 118, 121, 123, 124, 128–129

Sterling, George, **I:** 199, 207, 208, 209; **II:** 440; **Supp. V:** 286

Stern, Bernhard J., **Supp. XIV:** 202, 213

Stern, Daniel, **Supp. VIII:** 238

Stern, Frederick C., **Supp. X:** 114, 115, 117

Stern, Gerald, **Supp. IX: 285–303; Supp. XI:** 139, 267; **Supp. XV:** 211, 212

Stern, Madeleine B., **Supp. I Part 1:** 35

Stern, Maurice, **IV:** 285

Stern, Philip Van Doren, **Supp. XIII:** 164

Stern, Richard, **Retro. Supp. II:** 291

Stern, Richard G., **Retro. Supp. II:** 204

Stern, Steven, **Supp. XVII:** 42, 48, 49; **Supp. XX:**178

"Sterne" (Schwartz), **Supp. II Part 2:** 663

Sterne, Laurence, **II:** 302, 304–305, 308; **III:** 454; **IV:** 68, 211, 465; **Supp. I Part 2:** 714; **Supp. IV Part 1:** 299; **Supp. V:** 127; **Supp. X:** 324; **Supp. XV:** 232

Sterritt, David, **Supp. IV Part 2:** 574

Stetson, Caleb, **IV:** 178

Stetson, Charles Walter, **Supp. XI:** 195, 196, 197, 202, 204, 209

Steve Nelson, American Radical (Nelson), **Supp. XVIII:** 226

Stevens, Wallace, **I:** 60, 61, 266, 273, 462, 521, 528, 540–541; **II:** 56, 57, 530, 552, 556; **III:** 19, 23, 194, 216, 270–271, 272, 278, 279, 281, 453, 463, 493, 509, 521, 523, 600, 605, 613, 614; **IV: 73–96,** 140, 141, 332, 402, 415; **Retro. Supp. I:** 67, 89, 193, 284, 288, **295–315,** 335, 403, 411, 416, 417, 422; **Retro. Supp. II:** 40, 44, 326; **Supp. I Part 1:** 80, 82, 257; **Supp. II Part 1:** 9, 18; **Supp. III Part 1:** 2, 3, 12, 20, 48, 239, 318, 319, 344; **Supp. III Part 2:** 611; **Supp. IV Part 1:** 72, 393; **Supp. IV Part 2:** 619, 620, 621, 634; **Supp. V:** 337; **Supp. VIII:** 21, 102, 195, 271, 292; **Supp. IX:** 41; **Supp. X:** 58; **Supp. XI:** 123, 191, 312; **Supp. XIII:** 44, 45; **Supp. XV:** 39, 41, 92, 115, 250, 261, 298, 302, 306, 307; **Supp. XVI:** 64, 158, 202, 210, 288; **Supp. XVII:** 36, 42, 110, 129, 130, 240, 241; **Supp. XIX:** 7, 40, 86, 87; **Supp. XXI:** 19, 28, 60, 133

Stevens, Mrs. Wallace (Elsie Kachel), **IV:** 75

"Stevens and the Idea of the Hero" (Bromwich), **Retro. Supp. I:** 305

Stevens and the Interpersonal (Halliday), **Supp. XIX: 85–86**

Stevenson, Adlai, **II:** 49; **III:** 581

Stevenson, Anne, **Supp. XV:** 121; **Supp. XVII:** 74

Stevenson, Burton E., **Supp. XIV:** 120

Stevenson, David, **Supp. XI:** 230

Stevenson, Robert Louis, **I:** 2, 53; **II:** 283, 290, 311, 338; **III:** 328; **IV:** 183–184, 186, 187; **Retro. Supp. I:** 224, 228; **Supp. I Part 1:** 49; **Supp. II Part 1:** 404–405; **Supp. IV Part 1:** 298, 314; **Supp. VIII:** 125; **Supp. XIII:** 75; **Supp. XIV:** 40; **Supp. XVII:** 69; **Supp. XXI:** 204

Stevick, Robert D., **III:** 509

Stewart, Dugald, **II:** 8, 9; **Supp. I Part 1:** 151, 159; **Supp. I Part 2:** 422

Stewart, George, **Supp. XVIII:** 138

Stewart, Jeffrey C., **Supp. XIV:** 196, 209, 210

Stewart, Randall, **II:** 244; **Supp. XX:**164

Stewart, Robert E., **Supp. XI:** 216

"St. Francis of Assisi" (Di Piero), **Supp. XIX:** 43

Stickeen (Muir), **Supp. IX:** 182

"Sticks and Stones" (L. Michaels), **Supp. XVI:** 205

Sticks and Stones (Mumford), **Supp. II Part 2:** 475, 483, 487–488

Sticks & Stones (Matthews), **Supp. IX:** 154, 155, 157, 158

Stieglitz, Alfred, **Retro. Supp. I:** 416; **Retro. Supp. II:** 103; **Supp. VIII:** 98; **Supp. XVII:** 96; **Supp. XX:**74, 75

"Stigmata" (Oates), **Supp. II Part 2:** 520

Stiles, Ezra, **II:** 108, 122; **IV:** 144, 146, 148

Still, James, **Supp. XX:**163

Still, William Grant, **Retro. Supp. I:** 203

"Stillborn" (Plath), **Supp. I Part 2:** 544

"Still Here" (Hughes), **Retro. Supp. I:** 211

"Still Just Writing" (Tyler), **Supp. IV Part 2:** 658

"Still Life" (Hecht), **Supp. X:** 68

"Still Life" (Malamud), **Supp. I Part 2:** 450

Still Life (Pickering), **Supp. XXI:** 198

"Still Life" (Pickering), **Supp. XXI:** 198

"Still Life" (Sandburg), **III:** 584

"Still Life: Moonlight Striking up on a Chess-Board" (Lowell), **II:** 528

"Still Life Or" (Creeley), **Supp. IV Part 1:** 141, 150, 158

Still Life with Oysters and Lemon (Doty), **Supp. XI:** 119, 121, **133–134**

Still Life with Woodpecker (Robbins), **Supp. X:** 260, **271–274,** 282

"Still Moment, A" (Welty), **IV:** 265; **Retro. Supp. I:** 347

Stillness (Gardner), **Supp. VI:** 74

"Stillness in the Air" (Dickinson), **Supp. XV:** 261

Stillness of Dancing, The (Bierds), **Supp. XVII: 27–28**

"Still Small Voices, The" (Fante), **Supp. XI:** 164

Still Such (Salter), **Supp. IX:** 246

"Still the Place Where Creation Does Some Work on Itself" (W. V. Davis), **Supp. IV Part 1:** 68

Stimpson, Catharine R., **Supp. IV Part 2:** 686

Stimson, Eleanor Kenyon. *See* Brooks, Mrs. Van Wyck

"Stimulants, Poultices, Goads" (Wright), **Supp. XV:** 349

"Stings" (Plath), **Retro. Supp. II:** 255; **Supp. I Part 2:** 541

"Stirling Street September" (Baraka), **Supp. II Part 1:** 51

Stirner, Max, **II:** 27

"Stirrup-Cup, The" (Lanier), **Supp. I Part 1:** 364

Stitt, Peter, **Supp. IV Part 1:** 68; **Supp. IV Part 2:** 628; **Supp. IX:** 152, 163, 291, 299; **Supp. XI:** 311, 317; **Supp. XIII:** 87; **Supp. XV:** 98, 99; **Supp. XIX:** 121

Stivers, Valerie, **Supp. X:** 311

St. John, David, **Supp. XV:** 73, 253

St. Mark, Tyler, **Supp. XX:**260

Stock, Noel, **III:** 479

Stockton, Frank R., **I:** 201

Stoddard, Charles Warren, **I:** 193, 195, 196; **Supp. II Part 1:** 192, 341, 351

Stoddard, Elizabeth, **II:** 275; **Supp. XV: 269–291**

Stoddard, Richard, **Supp. I Part 1:** 372

Stoddard, Richard Henry, **Supp. XV:** 269, 271, 272, 273, 274, 278, 279, 286

Stoddard, Solomon, **I:** 545, 548; **IV:** 145, 148

Stoffman, Judy, **Supp. XVIII:** 97

Stoic, The (Dreiser), **I:** 497, 502, 508, 516; **Retro. Supp. II:** 95, 96, 101, 108

Stokes, Geoffrey, **Supp. XV:** 256

Stokes, Olivia Egleston Phelps, **Supp. XVIII:** 261

"Stolen Calf, The" (Dunbar), **Supp. II Part 1:** 196

Stolen Jew, The (Neugeboren), **Supp. XVI: 222–224,** 225

Stolen Past, A (Knowles), **Supp. XII:** 249

Stolen Words: Forays into the Origins and Ravages of Plagiarism (Mallon), **Supp. XIX: 134–135**

Stollman, Aryeh Lev, **Supp. XVII:** 49

Stolmar, Thomas, **Supp. XVIII:** 138

Stomping the Blues (Murray), **Supp. XIX: 158–159**

"Stone" (Ozick), **Supp. XVII:** 50

Stone, Edward, **III:** 479

Stone, Herbert S., **Supp. XXI:** 2

Stone, I. F., **Supp. XIV:** 3

Stone, Irving, **II:** 463, 466, 467

Stone, Oliver, **Supp. XIV:** 48, 316

Stone, Phil, **II:** 55

Stone, Richard, **Supp. XIV:** 54

Stone, Robert, **Supp. V: 295–312; Supp. X:** 1; **Supp. XIX:** 54

Stone, Rosetta (pseudonym). *See* Geisel, Theodor Seuss (Dr. Seuss)

Stone, Wilmer, **Supp. I Part 1:** 49

Stone and the Shell, The (Hay), **Supp. XIV:** 122, 123, 127, 130

"Stone Bear, The" (Haines), **Supp. XII:** 206–207, 212

"Stone City" (Proulx), **Supp. VII:** 251–253

Stone Country (Sanders), **Supp. XVI:** 271–272

Stone Diaries, The (Shields), **Supp. VII:** 307, 315, 324–326, 327

"Stone Dreams" (Kingsolver), **Supp. VII:** 203

Stone Harp, The (Haines), **Supp. XII: 204,** 205, 206, 207

Stonemason, The (McCarthy), **Supp. VIII:** 175, 187

"Stones" (Hoffman), **Supp. XVIII:** 86

"Stones" (Kumin), **Supp. IV Part 2:** 447

"Stones, The" (Plath), **Supp. I Part 2:** 535, 539

"Stones in My Passway, Hellhounds on My Trail" (Boyle), **Supp. VIII:** 15

Stones of Florence, The (McCarthy), **II:** 562

"Stone Walls" (Sarton), **Supp. VIII:** 259

"Stop" (Wilbur), **Supp. III Part 2:** 556

Stop-Loss (screenplay, Richard), **Supp. XIX:** 222

"Stop Me If You've Heard This One" (Lardner), **II:** 433

Stopover: Tokyo (Marquand), **III:** 53, 57, 61, 70

Stoppard, Tom, **Retro. Supp. I:** 189

"Stopping by Woods" (Frost), **II:** 154

"Stopping by Woods on a Snowy Evening" (Frost), **Retro. Supp. I:** 129, 133, 134, 135, 139

Stopping Westward (Richards), **II:** 396

"Stop Player. Joke No. 4" (Gaddis), **Supp. IV Part 1:** 280

Stop-Time (Conroy), **Supp. XVI: 63–71,** 72, 75, 76–77

Store, The (Stribling), **Supp. VIII:** 126

"*Store* and *Mockingbird:* Two Pulitzer Novels about Alabama" (Going), **Supp. VIII:** 126

Storer, Edward, **Supp. I Part 1:** 261, 262

Stories, Fables and Other Diversions (Nemerov), **III:** 268–269, 285

Stories: Elizabeth Stoddard, **Supp. XV:** 270

"Stories for Sale" (Kolba), **Supp. XVIII:** 257

Stories for the Sixties (Yates, ed.), **Supp. XI:** 343

Stories from Our Living Past (Prose), **Supp. XVI:** 251

Stories from the Italian Poets (Hunt), **Supp. XV:** 175

Stories from the Old Testament Retold (L. P. Smith), **Supp. XIV:** 342

Stories from World Literature, **Supp. IX:** 4

"Stories in the Snow" (Leopold), **Supp. XIV:** 183

Stories of an Imaginary Childhood (Bukiet), **Supp. XVII: 41–44,** 45

Stories of F. Scott Fitzgerald, The (Cowley, ed.), **Retro. Supp. I:** 115

Stories of F. Scott Fitzgerald, The (Fitzgerald), **II:** 94

Stories of Modern America, **Supp. IX:** 4

Stories of Stephen Dixon, The (Dixon), **Supp. XII:** 152

Stories of the Spanish Civil War (Hemingway), **II:** 258

Stories Revived (James), **II:** 322

Stories that Could Be True (Stafford), **Supp. XI: 325–327**

Stories Toto Told Me (Rolfe), **Supp. XX:**235

Storm, The (Buechner), **Supp. XII: 54–57**

"Storm, The" (Chopin), **Retro. Supp. II:** 60, 68; **Supp. I Part 1:** 218, 224

Storm, The (al-'Awásif) (Gibran), **Supp. XX:**116, 124, 125

"Storm Fear" (Frost), **II:** 153; **Retro. Supp. I:** 127

"Storm Ship, The" (Irving), **II:** 309

"Storm Warnings" (Kingsolver), **Supp. VII:** 207–208

"Stormy Weather" (Ellison), **Supp. II Part 1:** 233

"Story" (Everwine), **Supp. XV:** 89

"Story, A" (Jarrell), **II:** 371

Story, Julian, **Supp. XX:**232

Story, Richard David, **Supp. IV Part 2:** 575, 588

Story, William Wetmore, **Supp. XX:**228

"Story about Chicken Soup, A" (Simpson), **Supp. IX: 272–273**

"Story about the Anteater, The" (Benét), **Supp. XI:** 53

"Story About the Body, A" (Hass), **Supp. VI: 107–108**

"Story for Teddy, A" (Swados), **Supp. XIX:** 266–267

Story for Teddy, A—and Others (Swados), **Supp. XIX: 266–268**

"Story Hearer, The" (Paley), **Supp. VI:** 230, 231

"Story Hour" (Hay), **Supp. XIV:** 124

"Story Hour" (Jarman), **Supp. XVII:** 116

Story Hour: A Second Look at Cinderella, Bluebeard, and Company (Hay), **Supp. XIV:** 119, 124, 125, 132, 133

Story of a Country Town, The (Howe), **I:** 106

Story of a Lover, The (Hapgood), **Supp. XVII:** 99, 100, 104; **Supp. XXI:** 3, 5, 7

Story of an American Family, The: Letters of the Hapgood Family, 1648–1917 (Boyce), **Supp. XVII:** 97; **Supp. XXI:** 9, 14

"Story of an Hour, The" (Chopin), **Retro. Supp. II:** 72; **Supp. I Part 1:** 212–213, 216

Story of a Novel, The (Wolfe), **IV:** 456, 458

"Story of a Proverb, The" (Lanier), **Supp. I Part 1:** 365

"Story of a Proverb, The: A Fairy Tale for Grown People" (Lanier), **Supp. I Part 1:** 365

Story of a Story and Other Stories, The: A Novel (Dixon), **Supp. XII:** 155

Story of a Wonder Man, The (Lardner), **II:** 433–434

"Story of a Year, The" (James), **Retro. Supp. I:** 218

Story of G.I. Joe, The (film, Wellman), **Supp. XVII:** 61, 62

"Story of Gus, The" (A. Miller), **III:** 147–148

"Story of How a Wall Stands, A" (Ortiz), **Supp. IV Part 2:** 499, 507

Story of Mount Desert Island, Maine, The (Morison), **Supp. I Part 2:** 494

Story of My Boyhood and Youth, The (Muir), **Supp. IX: 172–174,** 176

Story of My Father, The: A Memoir (Miller), **Supp. XII:** 301

Story of O, The (Réage), **Supp. XII:** 9, 10

Story of Our Lives, The (Strand), **Supp. IV Part 2:** 620, 628–629, 629

"Story of Poppy Van Buster, The" (Briggs), **Supp. XVIII:** 8

Story of the Normans, The, Told Chiefly in Relation to Their Conquest of England (Jewett), **II:** 406

Story of the Telegraph, The (Briggs, and Maverick), **Supp. XVIII:** 4

"Story of Toby, The" (Melville), **III:** 76

"Story of To-day, A" (Davis). *See also Margret Howth*

"Story of To-day, A" (R. H. Davis), **Supp. XVI:** 88, 89

Story of Utopias, The (Mumford), **Supp. II Part 2:** 475, 483–486, 495

Story of Wine in California, The (M. F. K. Fisher), **Supp. XVII:** 88

Story on Page One, The (Odets), **Supp. II Part 2:** 546

Storyteller (Silko), **Supp. IV Part 2:** 558, 559, 560, 561, **566–570**

"Storyteller" (Silko), **Supp. IV Part 2:** 569

"*Storyteller:* Grandmother Spider's Web" (Danielson), **Supp. IV Part 2:** 569

"Storyteller's Notebook, A" (Carver), **Supp. III Part 1:** 142–143

Story Teller's Story, A: The Tale of an American Writer's Journey through His Own Imaginative World and through the World of Facts . . . (Anderson), **I:** 98, 101, 114, 117

"Story That Could Be True, A" (Stafford), **Supp. XI:** 326

"Stout Gentleman, The" (Irving), **II:** 309

Stover at Yale (Johnson), **III:** 321

Stowe, Calvin, **IV:** 445; **Supp. I Part 2:** 587, 588, 590, 596, 597

Stowe, Charles, **Supp. I Part 2:** 581, 582

Stowe, Eliza, **Supp. I Part 2:** 587

Stowe, Harriet Beecher, **II:** 274, 399, 403, 541; **Retro. Supp. I:** 34, 246; **Retro. Supp. II:** 4, 138, 156; **Supp. I Part 1:** 30, 206, 301; **Supp. I Part 2:** **579–601**; **Supp. III Part 1:** 154, 168, 171; **Supp. IX:** 33; **Supp. X:** 223, 246, 249, 250; **Supp. XI:** 193; **Supp. XIII:** 141, 295; **Supp. XV:** 278; **Supp. XVI:** 82, 85

Stowe, Samuel Charles, **Supp. I Part 2:** 587

Stowe, William, **Supp. IV Part 1:** 129

Strachey, Lytton, **I:** 5; **IV:** 436; **Retro. Supp. I:** 59; **Supp. I Part 2:** 485, 494; **Supp. XIV:** 342; **Supp. XVI:** 191

"Stradivari" (Bierds), **Supp. XVII:** 28

Straight Cut (Bell), **Supp. X:** 5, **6–7**, 10

Straight Man (Russo), **Supp. XII:** **335–339**, 340

Straits: Poems (Koch), **Supp. XV:** 184

Strand, Mark, **Supp. IV Part 2: 619–636;** **Supp. V:** 92, 332, 337, 338, 343; **Supp. IX:** 155; **Supp. XI:** 139, 145; **Supp. XII:** 254; **Supp. XIII:** 76; **Supp. XV:** 74

Strand, Paul, **Supp. VIII:** 272

Strandberg, Victor, **Supp. V:** 273

Strange, Sharan, **Supp. XXI:** 246

"Strange Beautiful Woman, A" (Nelson), **Supp. XVIII:** 173

Strange Bedfellows (Woods), **Supp. XXI:** 70

Strange Case of Dr. Jekyll and Mr. Hyde, The (Stevenson), **II:** 290

Strange Children, The (Gordon), **II:** 196, 197, 199, 211–213

Strange Commonplace, A (Sorrentino), **Supp. XXI:** 232, 237, 238

Strange Fire (Bukiet), **Supp. XVII:** 46

"Strange Fruit" (Harjo), **Supp. XII:** 224, 225

"Strange Fruit" (song), **Supp. I Part 1:** 80; **Supp. XVIII:** 228

Strange Interlude (O'Neill), **III:** 391, 397–398; **IV:** 61

Stranger, The (Camus), **I:** 53, 292; **Supp. VIII:** 11; **Supp. XV:** 352

"Stranger, The" (Rich), **Supp. I Part 2:** 555, 560

"Stranger, The" (Salinger), **III:** 552–553

"Stranger in My Own Life, A: Alienation in American Indian Poetry and Prose" (Gunn Allen), **Supp. IV Part 1:** 322

"Stranger in the Village" (Baldwin), **Retro. Supp. II:** 3; **Supp. I Part 1:** 54; **Supp. IV Part 1:** 10

"Stranger in Town" (Hughes), **Supp. I Part 1:** 334

"Strangers" (Howe), **Supp. VI:** 120

Strangers and Wayfarers (Jewett), **Retro. Supp. II:** 138

"Strangers from the Horizon" (Merwin), **Supp. III Part 1:** 356

Strangers on a Train (Highsmith), **Supp. IV Part 1:** 132

"Strange Story, A" (Taylor), **Supp. V:** 323

"Strange Story, A" (Wylie), **Supp. I Part 2:** 723

Strange Things (Atwood), **Supp. XIII:** 35

"Strato in Plaster" (Merrill), **Supp. III Part 1:** 328

Stratton-Porter, Gene, **Supp. XX:211–225**

Straus, Ralph, **Supp. XIII:** 168

Straus, Roger, **Supp. VIII:** 82; **Supp. XV:** 59

Strauss, Harold, **Supp. XV:** 137

Strauss, Johann, **I:** 66

Strauss, Richard, **IV:** 316

Strauss, Robert, **Supp. XI:** 141, 142

Stravinsky (De Schloezer), **III:** 474

Stravinsky, Igor, **Retro. Supp. I:** 378; **Supp. IV Part 1:** 81; **Supp. XI:** 133; **Supp. XV:** 265

"Stravinsky's Three Pieces 'Grotesques,' for String Quartet" (Lowell), **II:** 523

Straw, The (O'Neill), **III:** 390

"Strawberry Milkshake" (Halliday), **Supp. XIX:** 92, 94

"Stray Document, A" (Pound), **II:** 517

"Strays" (Richard), **Supp. XIX:** 210–211, 220

Streaks of the Tulip, The: Selected Criticism (W. J. Smith), **Supp. XIII:** 333, 334, 344, **347–348**

Streamline Your Mind (Mursell), **Supp. I Part 2:** 608

Strecker, Trey, **Supp. XXI:** 238

"Street, Cloud" (Ríos), **Supp. IV Part 2:** 549

Street, The (Petry), **Supp. XVIII:** 286

Streetcar Named Desire, A (T. Williams), **IV:** 382, 383, 385, 386, 387, 389–390, 395, 398; **Supp. IV Part 1:** 359

Street in Bronzeville, A (Brooks), **Retro. Supp. I:** 208; **Supp. III Part 1:** 74–78

"Street Moths" (X. J. Kennedy), **Supp. XV:** 170

"Street Musicians" (Ashbery), **Supp. III Part 1:** 18

"Street of Crocodiles" (Hull), **Supp. XXI:** 130

"Street off Sunset, A" (Jarrell), **II:** 387

"Streets" (Dixon), **Supp. XII: 145–146**

Streets in the Moon (MacLeish), **III:** 5, 8–11, 15, 19

"Streets of Laredo" (screenplay) (McMurtry and Ossana), **Supp. V:** 226, 230

Streets of Laredo (McMurtry), **Supp. V:** 230

Streets of Night (Dos Passos), **I:** 478, 479–480, 481, 488

Streitfield, David, **Supp. XIII:** 234; **Supp. XVI:** 63

Strength of Fields, The (Dickey), **Supp. IV Part 1:** 178

"Strength of Fields, The" (Dickey), **Supp. IV Part 1:** 176, 184–185

"Strength of Gideon, The" (Dunbar), **Supp. II Part 1:** 212

Strength of Gideon and Other Stories, The (Dunbar), **Supp. II Part 1:** 211, 212

"Strenuous Artistry" (Zagarell), **Supp. XV:** 281

Strether, Lambert, **II:** 313

Stribling, T. S., **Supp. VIII:** 126

Strickland, Barbara, **Supp. XIX:** 102

Strickland, Joe (pseudonym). *See* Arnold, George W.

"Strictly Bucolic" (Simic), **Supp. VIII:** 278

Strictly Business (O. Henry), **Supp. II Part 1:** 410

"Strike, The" (Olsen), **Supp. XIII:** 292, 297

Strike at Shane's, The (Skloot), **Supp. XX:216**

"Strikers" (Untermeyer), **Supp. XV:** 296

Strindberg, August, **I:** 78; **III:** 145, 165, 387, 390, 391, 392, 393; **IV:** 17; **Supp. XVII:** 100

"String, The" (Dickey), **Supp. IV Part 1:** 179

String Light (Wright), **Supp. XV:** **345–346**

"String Quartet, The" (Weigl), **Supp. XIX:** 278

"Strivings of the Negro People" (Du Bois), **Supp. II Part 1:** 167

Stroby, W. C., **Supp. XIV:** 26

Strohbach, Hermann, **Supp. XI:** 242

"Stroke of Good Fortune, A" (O'Connor), **III:** 344; **Retro. Supp. II:** 229, 232

Strom, Stephen, **Supp. XII:** 223

Strong, Anna Louise, **Supp. XVIII:** 238

Strong, George Templeton, **IV:** 321

Strong, Josiah, **Supp. XIV:** 64

"Strong Draughts of Their Refreshing Minds" (Dickinson), **Retro. Supp. I:** 46

Strong Motion (Franzen), **Supp. XX:85, 88–89,** 92, 95

Strong Opinions (Nabokov), **Retro. Supp. I:** 263, 266, 270, 276

"Strong Room of the House, The" (Bronk), **Supp. XXI:** 32

"Strong Women" (Dorman), **Supp. XI:** 240

Strout, Elizabeth, **Supp. X:** 86

Structure of Nations and Empires, The (Niebuhr), **III:** 292, 308

"Structure of Rime, The" (Duncan), **Supp. XVI:** 287

Structuring the Void (Klinkowitz), **Supp. XXI:** 233

Struggle, The (film; Griffith), **Supp. XVI:** 191

"Strumpet Song" (Plath), **Retro. Supp. II:** 246; **Supp. I Part 2:** 536

Strunk, William, **Supp. I Part 2:** 652, 662, 670, 671, 672

Strunsky, Anna, **II:** 465

"Strut for Roethke, A" (Berryman), **I:** 188

Strychacz, Thomas F., **Supp. XVI:** 69–70

Stuart, Dabney, **Supp. XVIII:** 79

Stuart, Gilbert, **I:** 16

Stuart, J. E. B., **III:** 56

Stuart, Jesse, **Supp. XX:**162–163, 165

Stuart, Michael, **Supp. XV:** 140

Stuart Little (White), **Supp. I Part 2:** 655–658

"Student, The" (Moore), **III:** 212, 215

"Student of Clouds" (Collins), **Supp. XXI:** 60

"Student of Salmanaca, The" (Irving), **II:** 309

"Student's Wife, The" (Carver), **Supp. III Part 1:** 141

Studies in American Indian Literature: Critical Essays and Course Designs (Gunn Allen), **Supp. IV Part 1:** 324, 333

Studies in Classic American Literature (Lawrence), **II:** 102; **III:** 33; **IV:** 333; **Retro. Supp. I:** 421

Studies in Short Fiction (Malin), **Supp. XVI:** 71

Studies in the Psychology of Sex (Ellis), **Supp. XX:**235

"Studs" (Farrell), **II:** 25, 28, 31

Studs Lonigan: A Trilogy (Farrell), **II:** 25, 26, 27, 31–34, 37, 38, 41–42

"Study in Orange and White" (Collins), **Supp. XXI:** 60

"Study of Images" (Stevens), **IV:** 79

"Study of Lanier's Poems, A" (Kent), **Supp. I Part 1:** 373

Study of Milton's Prosody (Bridges), **II:** 537

"Study of the Negro Problems, The" (Du Bois), **Supp. II Part 1:** 165

Stuewe, Paul, **Supp. IV Part 1:** 68

Stuhlmann, Gunther, **Supp. X:** 182, 184, 185, 187

Stultifera Navis (Brant), **III:** 447

Sturak, John Thomas, **Supp. XIII:** 162, 163, 165, 168

Sturgeon, Theodore, **Supp. XVIII:** 145

Sturgis, George, **III:** 600

Sturgis, Howard, **IV:** 319; **Retro. Supp. I:** 367, 373

Sturgis, Howard Overing, **Supp. XX:227–242**

Sturgis, Julian Russell, **Supp. XX:**228, 233, 238

Sturgis, Susan, **III:** 600

Sturm, Margaret. *See* Millar, Margaret

Stuttaford, Genevieve, **Supp. IX:** 279

Stuyvesant, Peter, **II:** 301

"Style" (Nemerov), **III:** 275

Styles of Radical Will (Sontag), **Supp. III Part 2:** 451, 459, 460–463

"Stylist, The" (Egan), **Supp. XIX:** 51, 52

Styne, Jule, **Supp. XVI:** 193

Styron, William, **III:** 40; **IV:** 4, **97–119,** 216; **Supp. V:** 201; **Supp. IX:** 208; **Supp. X:** 15–16, 250; **Supp. XI:** 229, 231, 343; **Supp. XIV:** 82; **Supp. XVI:** 235–236

Suares, J. C., **Supp. IV Part 1:** 234

Suarez, Ernest, **Supp. IV Part 1:** 175; **Supp. V:** 180

Suarez, Ray, **Supp. XXI:** 243

"Sub, The" (Dixon), **Supp. XII:** 146

Subjection of Women, The (Mill), **Supp. XI:** 196, 203

"Subjective Necessity for Social Settlements" (Addams), **Supp. I Part 1:** 4

"Subject of Childhood, A" (Paley), **Supp. VI:** 221; **Supp. XXI:** 118

"Submarginalia" (Howe), **Supp. IV Part 2:** 422

Substance and Shadow (James), **II:** 344

"Subterranean Homesick Blues" (song, Dylan), **Supp. XVIII:** 25

Subterraneans, The (Kerouac), **Supp. III Part 1:** 225, 227–231

"Subtitle" (Kees), **Supp. XV:** 139

Subtreasury of American Humor, A (White and White), **Supp. I Part 2:** 668

"Suburban Culture, Imaginative Wonder: The Fiction of Frederick Barthelme" (Brinkmeyer), **Supp. XI:** 38

Suburban Sketches (Howells), **II:** 274, 277

"Subversive Element, The" (Ryan as Quin), **Supp. XVIII:** 230

"Subverted Flower, The" (Frost), **Retro. Supp. I:** 139

"Subway, The" (Tate), **IV:** 128

"Subway Singer, The" (Clampitt), **Supp. IX:** 45

"Success" (Mora), **Supp. XIII:** 217

Successful Love and Other Stories (Schwartz), **Supp. II Part 2:** 661, 665

Succession, The: A Novel of Elizabeth and James (Garrett), **Supp. VII:** 104–107, 108

"Success is counted sweetest" (Dickinson), **Retro. Supp. I:** 30, 31–32, 38; **Supp. XV:** 126

Success Stories (Banks), **Supp. V:** 14–15

"Success Story" (Banks), **Supp. V:** 15

"Such Counsels You Gave to Me" (Jeffers), **Supp. II Part 2:** 433

Such Silence (Milburn), **Supp. XI:** 242

"Such Things Happen Only in Books" (Wilder), **IV:** 365

Suddenly, Last Summer (film) (Vidal), **Supp. IV Part 2:** 683

Suddenly Last Summer (T. Williams), **I:** 73; **IV:** 382, 383, 385, 386, 387, 389, 390, 391, 392, 395–396, 397, 398

Suder (Everett), **Supp. XVIII:** 54–55

Sudermann, Hermann, **I:** 66

Sugg, Richard P., **Supp. IV Part 1:** 68

"Suggestion from a Friend" (Kenyon), **Supp. VII:** 171

"Suicide" (Barnes), **Supp. III Part 1:** 33

"Suicide off Egg Rock" (Plath), **Supp. I Part 2:** 529, 538

Suicides and Jazzers (Carruth), **Supp. XVI:** 46

"Suicide's Note" (Hughes), **Retro. Supp. I:** 199

"Suitable Surroundings, The" (Bierce), **I:** 203

"Suitcase, The" (Ozick), **Supp. V:** 262, 264

"Suite for Augustus, A" (Dove), **Supp. IV Part 1:** 245

"Suite for Emily" (Hull), **Supp. XXI:** 139–140

"Suite for Lord Timothy Dexter" (Rukeyser), **Supp. VI:** 283, 285

"Suite from the Firebird" (Stravinsky), **Supp. XI:** 133

"Suitor, The" (Kenyon), **Supp. VII:** 164–165

Sukarno, **IV:** 490

Sukenick, Ronald, **Supp. V:** 39, 44, 46; **Supp. XII:** 139

Sula (Morrison), **Supp. III Part 1:** 362, 364, 367, 368, 379; **Supp. VIII:** 219

Sullivan, Andrew, **Supp. IX:** 135

Sullivan, Arthur, **Supp. XX:**228

Sullivan, Frank, **Supp. IX:** 201

Sullivan, Harry Stack, **I:** 59

Sullivan, Jack, **Supp. X:** 86; **Supp. XII:** 331

Sullivan, Noel, **Retro. Supp. I:** 202; **Supp. I Part 1:** 329, 333

Sullivan, Richard, **Supp. VIII:** 124

Sullivan, Walter, **Supp. VIII:** 168

"Sullivan County Sketches" (Crane), **I:** 407, 421

"Sumach and Goldenrod: An American Idyll" (Mumford), **Supp. II Part 2:** 475

Suma Genji (Play), **III:** 466

Sumerian Vistas (Ammons), **Supp. VII:** 34, 35

"Summa Lyrica" (Grossman), **Supp. XIX:** 86

"Summer" (Emerson), **II:** 10

Summer (Gioia), **Supp. XV:** 117

"Summer" (Lowell), **II:** 554

Summer (Wharton), **IV:** 317; **Retro. Supp. I:** 360, 367, 374, **378–379,** 382

Summer, Bob, **Supp. X:** 1, 5, 6, 42

Summer and Smoke (T. Williams), **IV:** 382, 384, 385, 386, 387, 395, 397, 398; **Supp. IV Part 1:** 84

Summer Anniversaries, The (Justice), **Supp. VII:** 115, 117

Summer Blue (Skloot), **Supp. XX:**196, **207–208**

"Summer Commentary, A" (Winters), **Supp. II Part 2:** 808

"Summer Day" (O'Hara), **III:** 369

"Summer Days, The" (Oliver), **Supp. VII:** 239

Summer Never Ends (W. Frank), **Supp. XX:**78

"Summer Night" (Hughes), **Supp. I Part 1:** 325

"Summer Night, A" (Auden), **Supp. II Part 1:** 8

"Summer Night—Broadway" (Untermeyer), **Supp. XV:** 296

"Summer Noon: 1941" (Winters), **Supp. II Part 2:** 811

"Summer of '82" (Merwin), **Supp. III Part 1:** 355–356

Summer on the Lakes in 1843 (Fuller), **Supp. II Part 1:** 279, 295–296

"Summer People" (Hemingway), **II:** 258–259

"Summer People, The" (Jackson), **Supp. IX:** 120

"Summer People, The" (Merrill), **Supp. III Part 1:** 325–326

"Summer Perdu" (Halliday), **Supp. XIX:** 89

"Summer Planning" (Halliday), **Supp. XIX:** 92

"Summer Ramble, A" (Bryant), **Supp. I Part 1:** 162, 164

Summers, Claude J., **Supp. IV Part 2:** 680–681; **Supp. XIV:** 161, 169

Summers, Robert, **Supp. IX:** 289

"Summer Solstice, New York City" (Olds), **Supp. X:** 207

"Summer's Reading, A" (Malamud), **Supp. I Part 2:** 430–431, 442

"Summer Storm" (Gioia), **Supp. XV:** 127

"Summer Storm" (Simpson), **Supp. IX:** 268

"'Summertime and the Living . . .' " (Hayden), **Supp. II Part 1:** 363, 366

Summertime Island (Caldwell), **I:** 307–308

"Summer: West Side" (Updike), **Retro. Supp. I:** 320

"Summer with Tu Fu, A" (Carruth), **Supp. XVI:** 55, 58

"Summit Beach, 1921" (Dove), **Supp. IV Part 1:** 249

Summoning of Stones, A (Hecht), **Supp. X:** 57, 58, **58–59**

"Summons" (Untermeyer), **Supp. XV:** 296

Summons to Memphis, A (Taylor), **Supp. V:** 313, 314, 327

Summons to the Free, A (Benét), **Supp. XI:** 47

Sumner, Charles, **I:** 3, 15; **Supp. I Part 2:** 685, 687

Sumner, John, **Retro. Supp. II:** 95

Sumner, John B., **I:** 511

Sumner, William Graham, **III:** 102, 108; **Supp. I Part 2:** 640

"Sumptuous Destination" (Wilbur), **Supp. III Part 2:** 553

"Sun" (Moore), **III:** 215

"Sun" (Swenson), **Supp. IV Part 2:** 640

"Sun, Sea, and Sand" (Marquand), **III:** 60

Sun Also Rises, The (Hemingway), **I:** 107; **II:** 68, 90, 249, 251–252, 260, 600; **III:** 36; **IV:** 35, 297; **Retro. Supp. I:** 171, **177–180**, 181, 189; **Supp. I Part 2:** 614; **Supp. XIII:** 263; **Supp. XVIII:** 74

"Sun and Moon" (Kenyon), **Supp. VII:** 168

"Sun and the Still-born Stars, The" (Southern), **Supp. XI:** 295

Sun at Midnight (Soseki; Merwin and Shigematsu, trans.), **Supp. III Part 1:** 353

"Sun Crosses Heaven from West to East Bringing Samson Back to the Womb, The" (R. Bly), **Supp. IV Part 1:** 73

"Sun Dance Shield" (Momaday), **Supp. IV Part 2:** 491

Sunday, Billy, **II:** 449

"Sunday Afternoons" (Komunyakaa), **Supp. XIII:** 127

Sunday after the War (H. Miller), **III:** 184

"Sunday at Home" (Hawthorne), **II:** 231–232

"Sunday Morning" (Stevens), **II:** 552; **III:** 278, 463, 509; **IV:** 92–93; **Retro. Supp. I:** 296, 300, 301, 304, 307, 313; **Supp. XV:** 120; **Supp. XVI:** 210; **Supp. XVII:** 42; **Supp. XIX:** 40; **Supp. XXI:** 28, 133

"Sunday Morning Apples" (Crane), **I:** 387

"Sunday Morning Prophecy" (Hughes), **Supp. I Part 1:** 334

"Sunday Morning with the Sensational Nightingales" (Collins), **Supp. XXI:** 60

"Sundays" (B. Kelly), **Supp. XVII:** 124–125

"Sundays" (Salter), **Supp. IX:** 257

"Sundays, They Sleep Late" (Rukeyser), **Supp. VI:** 278

"Sundays of Satin-Legs Smith, The" (Brooks), **Supp. III Part 1:** 74, 75

"Sundays Visiting" (Ríos), **Supp. IV Part 2:** 541

Sundial, The (Jackson), **Supp. IX:** 126–127

Sundog (Harrison), **Supp. VIII:** 46–48

Sun Dogs (R. O. Butler), **Supp. XII:** 64–65

Sun Do Move, The (Hughes), **Supp. I Part 1:** 339

Sundquist, Eric, **Supp. XIV:** 66, 71

"Sunfish" (C. Frost), **Supp. XV:** 100–101, 102

"Sunflower Sutra" (Ginsberg), **Supp. II Part 1:** 317, 321; **Supp. XV:** 215

Sunlight Dialogues, The (Gardner), **Supp. VI:** 63, **68,** 69, 70

"Sunlight Is Imagination" (Wilbur), **Supp. III Part 2:** 549

"Sunny Ridge, The" (Halliday), **Supp. XIX:** 92

Sun Out: Selected Poems, 1952–1954 (Koch), **Supp. XV:** 179

"Sunrise" (Lanier), **Supp. I Part 1:** 370

"Sunrise and the Bomb" (Halliday), **Supp. XIX:** 84, 85, 92

"Sunrise runs for Both, The" (Dickinson), **Retro. Supp. I:** 45

Sunrise with Seamonsters: Travels and Discoveries, 1964–1984 (Theroux), **Supp. VIII:** 311, 313, 323, 325

"Sun Rising" (Donne), **Supp. VIII:** 164

"Sunset" (Ransom), **III:** 484

"Sunset from Omaha Hotel Window" (Sandburg), **III:** 584

Sunset Gun (Parker), **Supp. IX:** 192

Sunset Limited (Burke), **Supp. XIV:** 32, 33

Sunset Limited (Harrison), **Supp. VIII:** 51

"Sunset Maker, The" (Justice), **Supp. VII:** 123

Sunset Maker, The: Poems, Stories, a Memoir (Justice), **Supp. VII:** 116, 118, 119, 123–124

Sunshine Boys, The (film), **Supp. IV Part 2:** 589

Sunshine Boys, The (Simon), **Supp. IV Part 2:** 575, 584–585

"Sunthin' in the Pastoral Line" (Lowell), **Supp. I Part 2:** 415–416

Sun to Sun (Hurston), **Supp. VI:** 154

Sun Tracks (Ortiz), **Supp. IV Part 2:** 499, 500

Sun Under Wood (Hass), **Supp. VI:** 103, 108–109

"Superb Lily, The" (Pinsky), **Supp. VI:** 250

"Super Goat Man" (Lethem), **Supp. XVIII:** 148

"Superman Comes to the Supermarket" (Mailer), **Retro. Supp. II:** 204

"Supermarket in California, A" (Ginsberg), **Supp. XI:** 135

"Supernatural Love" (Schnackenberg), **Supp. XV:** 257, 259–260

Supernatural Love: Poems 1976–1992 (Schnackenberg), **Supp. XV:** 253, 256, 260, 263

Suplee, Curt, **Supp. XVI:** 202

"Supper After the Last, The" (Kinnell), **Supp. III Part 1:** 239

"Supposedly Fun Thing I'll Never Do Again, A" (Wallace), **Supp. X:** 315

Supposedly Fun Thing I'll Never Do Again, A: Essays and Arguments (Wallace), **Supp. X: 314–316**

Suppressed Desires (Glaspell and Cook), **Supp. III Part 1:** 178; **Supp. XXI:** 6

Suppression of the African Slave Trade to the United States of America, 1638–1870 (Du Bois), **Supp. II Part 1:** 157, 162

Supreme Fiction, The (Stevens), **Supp. XVI:** 158

"Supremes, The" (Jarman), **Supp. XVII:** 115

Sure Hand of God, The (Caldwell), **I:** 297, 302

Sure Signs: New and Selected Poems (Kooser), **Supp. XIX:** 116, 117, **121–122**

"Surety and Fidelity Claims" (Stevens), **Retro. Supp. I:** 296, 309

Surface of Earth, The (Price), **Supp. VI:** 261–262

"Surfaces" (Ammons), **Supp. VII:** 36

Surfacing (Atwood), **Supp. XIII:** 20, 21, **22–23,** 24, 33, 35

"Surgeon at 2 A.M." (Plath), **Supp. I Part 2:** 545

Surmmer Knowledge (Schwartz), **Supp. II Part 2:** 662, 665

"Surprise" (Kenyon), **Supp. VII:** 173

Surprised by Sin: The Reader in Paradise Lost (Fish), **Supp. XIV:** 15

"Surround, The Imagining Herself as the Environment,/She Speaks to James Wright at Sundow" (Dickey), **Supp. IV Part 1:** 185
"Survey of Literature" (Ransom), **III:** 480
"Survey of the Literature, A" (Saunders), **Supp. XIX:** 235
"Surveyor, The" (H. Roth), **Supp. IX:** 233, 234
Survival (Atwood), **Supp. XIII:** 20, 22, 35
"Survival as Tao, Beginning at 5:00 A.M." (Carruth), **Supp. XVI:** 56
Survival of the Bark Canoe, The (McPhee), **Supp. III Part 1:** 301, 302, 308, 313
Survival This Way: Interviews with American Indian Poets (Bruchac), **Supp. IV Part 2:** 506
"Surviving Love" (Berryman), **I:** 173
Survivor (O. Butler), **Supp. XIII:** 62, 63
Susan and Anna Warner (Foster), **Supp. XVIII:** 265
Susan and God (film; Cukor), **Supp. XVI:** 192
Susanna Moodie: Voice and Vision (Shields), **Supp. VII:** 313
Susan Warner ("Elizabeth Wetherell") (A. Warner), **Supp. XVIII:** 259, 260
Suspect in Poetry, The (Dickey), **Supp. IV Part 1:** 177
"Sustained by Fiction" (Hoffman), **Supp. X:** 90, 92
"Susto" (Ríos), **Supp. IV Part 2:** 553
Sutherland, Donald, **IV:** 38, 44; **Supp. IX:** 254
Sutherland, Efua, **Supp. IV Part 1:** 9, 16
Sutherland-Smith, James, **Supp. X:** 211, 212
Sut Lovingood's Yarns (Harris), **II:** 70
Sutton, Roger, **Supp. X:** 266
Sutton, Walter, **III:** 479
Suttree (McCarthy), **Supp. VIII: 178–180,** 189
Suvero, Mark di, **Supp. IX:** 251
Svevo, Italo, **Supp. XIV:** 112
Swados, Harvey, **Supp. XI:** 222; **Supp. XIX: 255–271**
Swales, Martin, **Supp. XIX:** 183
Swallow, Alan, **Supp. X:** 112, 115, 116, 120, 123
Swallow Barn (J. P. Kennedy), **II:** 313
"Swamp Boy" (Bass), **Supp. XVI:** 20
Swan, Barbara, **Supp. IV Part 2:** 447
Swan, Jon, **Supp. IV Part 1:** 176
Swan Lake (Tchaikovsky), **Supp. IX:** 51
"Swan Legs" (Stern), **Supp. IX:** 299
Swann (Shields), **Supp. VII:** 315, 318–323, 326
Swann, Brian, **Supp. IV Part 2:** 500
Swanson, Gloria, **II:** 429
Swanson, Stevenson, **Supp. XIV:** 111
Swanton, John Reed, **Supp. VIII:** 295
Swan Watch (Schulberg), **Supp. XVIII:** 254
Swanwick, John, **Supp. XV:** 237
Swanwick, Michael, **Supp. XVI:** 128
"Swarm, The" (Plath), **Retro. Supp. II:** 255

"Sway" (Simpson), **Supp. IX:** 276
Sweat (Hurston), **Supp. VI:** 152
Swedenborg, Emanuel, **II:** 5, 10, 321, 342, 343–344, 396
Sweeney Agonistes (Eliot), **I:** 580; **Retro. Supp. I:** 64, 65; **Retro. Supp. II:** 247
"Sweeney Among the Nightingales" (Eliot), **III:** 4
"Sweeper, The" (Kooser), **Supp. XIX:** 125
Sweet, Blanche, **Supp. I Part 2:** 391
Sweet, Timothy, **Supp. IV Part 1:** 330
Sweet and Lowdown (film; Allen), **Supp. XV:** 11
Sweet and Sour (O'Hara), **III:** 361
"Sweet Armageddon" (Hoffman), **Supp. XVIII:** 85, 86
Sweet Bird of Youth (T. Williams), **IV:** 382, 383, 385, 386, 387, 388, 389, 390, 391, 392, 395, 396, 398; **Supp. IV Part 1:** 84, 89
Sweet Charity (musical), **Supp. IV Part 2:** 575
Sweet Flypaper of Life, The (Hughes), **Supp. I Part 1:** 335–336
"Sweetheart of the Song Tra Bong, The" (O'Brien), **Supp. V:** 243, 249
"Sweethearts" (Ford), **Supp. V:** 69
Sweet Hereafter, The (Banks), **Supp. V:** 15–16
Sweet Lorain (Weigl), **Supp. XIX:** 282
Sweet Machine (Doty), **Supp. XI:** 121, **131–132,** 135
Sweet Sue (Gurney), **Supp. V:** 105, 107–108
Sweet Sweetback's Baadasss Song (Peebles; film), **Supp. XI:** 17
Sweet Thursday (Steinbeck), **IV:** 50, 52, 64–65
Sweet Will (Levine), **Supp. V:** 178, 187, 189, 190
"Sweet Will" (Levine), **Supp. V:** 190
"Sweet Words on Race" (Hughes), **Retro. Supp. I:** 211
Sweezy, Paul, **Supp. I Part 2:** 645
"Swell-Looking Girl, A" (Caldwell), **I:** 310
Swenson, May, **Retro. Supp. II:** 44; **Supp. IV Part 2: 637–655; Supp. XIX:** 123
Swetman, Glenn R., **Supp. XXI:** 91
"Swift" (Schwartz), **Supp. II Part 2:** 663
Swift, Jonathan, **I:** 125, 194, 209, 441; **II:** 110, 302, 304–305, 577; **III:** 113; **IV:** 68; **Retro. Supp. I:** 66; **Supp. I Part 2:** 406, 523, 603, 656, 665, 708, 714; **Supp. IV Part 1:** 51; **Supp. IV Part 2:** 692; **Supp. XI:** 105, 209; **Supp. XII:** 276; **Supp. XV:** 258; **Supp. XVI:** 110; **Supp. XVIII:** 2, 12
"Swimmer" (Francis), **Supp. IX:** 82
"Swimmer" (Skloot), **Supp. XX:**199, 200
"Swimmer, The" (Cheever), **Supp. I Part 1:** 185, 187
"Swimmer, The" (Glück), **Supp. V:** 82
"Swimmers" (Untermeyer), **Supp. XV:** 300
"Swimmers, The" (Fitzgerald), **Retro. Supp. I:** 110, 111
"Swimmers, The" (Tate), **IV:** 136

"Swimming" (Harjo), **Supp. XII:** 218
Swinburne, Algernon C., **I:** 50, 384, 568; **II:** 3, 4, 129, 400, 524; **IV:** 135; **Retro. Supp. I:** 100; **Supp. I Part 1:** 79; **Supp. I Part 2:** 422, 552; **Supp. XIV:** 120, 344
"Swinburne as Poet" (Eliot), **I:** 576
Swinger of Birches, A: A Portrait of Robert Frost (Cox), **Retro. Supp. I:** 132
"Swinging an Arc Before Him As He Goes" (Espaillat), **Supp. XXI:** 108
"Swinging on a Birch-Tree" (Larcom), **Supp. XIII:** 147
Swiss, Tom, **Supp. XIX:** 40
Switch, The (Dixon), **Supp. XII:** 141
Swope, D. B., **Supp. IX:** 95
Sword Blades and Poppy Seed (Lowell), **II:** 518, 520, 522, 532
Sword of God, The: Jeanne D'Arc (Endore), **Supp. XVII:** 55
Sybil (Auchincloss), **Supp. IV Part 1:** 25
Sybil and Chryssa (S. and A. Warner), **Supp. XVIII:** 264
"Sycamore" (Stern), **Supp. IX:** 294
"Sycamore, The" (Moore), **III:** 216
"Sycamores, The" (Whittier), **Supp. I Part 2:** 699
Sylvester, Johnny, **Supp. I Part 2:** 438
Sylvester, Joshua, **I:** 178, 179; **II:** 18; **III:** 157; **Supp. I Part 1:** 98, 104, 114, 116
Sylvia (Gurney), **Supp. V:** 105
"Sylvia" (L. Michaels), **Supp. XVI:** 202, 213
"Sylvia" (Larcom), **Supp. XIII:** 144
"Sylvia" (Stern), **Supp. IX:** 297
Sylvia: A Fictional Memoir (L. Michaels), **Supp. XVI:** 202, 213
Sylvia Plath: Method and Madness (Butscher), **Supp. I Part 2:** 526
Sylvia Plath: Poetry and Existence (Holbrook), **Supp. I Part 2:** 526–527
"Sylvia's Death" (Sexton), **Supp. II Part 2:** 671, 684, 685
"Symbol and Image in the Shorter Poems of Herman Melville" (Dickey), **Supp. IV Part 1:** 176
Symbolist Movement in Literature, The (Symons), **I:** 50, 569; **Retro. Supp. I:** 55
Symonds, John Addington, **I:** 241, 242, 251, 259; **IV:** 334; **Supp. XIV:** 329, 335; **Supp. XX:**230
Symons, Arthur, **I:** 50, 569; **Retro. Supp. I:** 55; **Supp. XX:**239
Symons, Julian, **Supp. IV Part 1:** 343, 351
"Sympathy" (Dunbar), **Supp. IV Part 1:** 15
Sympathy of Souls, A (Goldbarth), **Supp. XII:** 175, 176, **186–187**
"Symphony, The" (Lanier), **Supp. I Part 1:** 352, 360–361, 364; **Supp. I Part 2:** 416
Symposium (Plato), **Retro. Supp. II:** 31; **Supp. IV Part 1:** 391
Symposium: To Kill a Mockingbird (Alabama Law Review), **Supp. VIII:** 127, 128

Symptoms of Being 35 (Lardner), **II:** 434
Synanon (Endore), **Supp. XVII:** 65
Synanon (film, Quine), **Supp. XVII:** 65
Synanon City (Endore), **Supp. XVII:** 65
Synge, John Millington, **I:** 434; **III:** 591–592; **Supp. III Part 1:** 34; **Supp. VIII:** 155
Synthetic Philosophy (Spencer), **II:** 462–463
"Syringa" (Ashbery), **Supp. III Part 1:** 19–21, 25
"Syrinx" (Clampitt), **Supp. IX:** 53
"Syrinx" (Merrill), **Supp. III Part 1:** 328
Syrkin, Marie, **Supp. XIV:** 279, 288, 291
"System, The" (Ashbery), **Supp. III Part 1:** 14, 15, 18, 21–22
System of Dante's Hell, The (Baraka), **Supp. II Part 1:** 39–41, 55
"System of Dante's Inferno, The" (Baraka), **Supp. II Part 1:** 40
"System of Doctor Tarr and Professor Fether, The" (Poe), **III:** 419, 425
System of General Geography, A (Brown), **Supp. I Part 1:** 146
Szaylay, Michael, **Supp. XXI:** 267
Sze, Mai-mai, **Supp. X:** 291
Szentgyorgyi, Tom, **Supp. IX:** 135, 136, 140, 141–142
Szulc, Tad, **Supp. XVI:** 154
Szymborka, Wislawa, **Supp. XI:** 267
Szymborska, Wislawa, **Supp. XVIII:** 29

T
"T-2 Tanker Blues" (Snyder), **Supp. VIII:** 294
Tabios, Eileen, **Supp. XV:** 214, 225, 226
"Table of Delectable Contents, The" (Simic), **Supp. VIII:** 276
Tabloid Dreams (R. O. Butler), **Supp. XII:** 70–72, 74
Tacey Cromwell (Richter), **Supp. XVIII:** 211, 215, 217
Tacitus, Cornelius, **I:** 485; **II:** 113
Tadic, Novica, **Supp. VIII:** 272
Taft (Patchett), **Supp. XII:** 307, 312, **314–317**
"Tag" (Hughes), **Supp. I Part 1:** 341
Taggard, Genevieve, **IV:** 436
Taggart, John, **Supp. IV Part 2:** 421
Tagore, Rabindranath, **I:** 383; **Supp. XX:** 117
"Taibele and Her Demon" (Singer), **Retro. Supp. II:** 307
Taibl, Erika, **Supp. XV:** 255
"Tailor Shop, The" (H. Miller), **III:** 175
"Tails" (Dixon), **Supp. XII:** 154
Taine, Hippolyte, **I:** 503; **II:** 271; **III:** 323; **IV:** 440, 444
"Tain't So" (Hughes), **Supp. I Part 1:** 330
"Taipei Tangle" (Halliday), **Supp. XIX:** 91
Takasago (play), **III:** 466
Take Away the Darkness (Bynner), **Supp. XV:** 51
Take Heart (Peacock), **Supp. XIX: 197–199,** 206
Take Me Back: A Novel (Bausch), **Supp. VII:** 41, 43–45, 46, 49

"Take My Saddle from the Wall: A Valediction" (McMurtry), **Supp. V:** 219
"'Take No for an Answer'" (Didion), **Supp. IV Part 1:** 203
"Take Pity" (Malamud), **Supp. I Part 2:** 427, 428, 435, 436, 437
"Takers, The" (Olds), **Supp. X:** 205
"Take the I Out" (Olds), **Supp. X:** 213
Take the Money and Run (film; Allen), **Supp. XV: 3–4,** 6
"Taking Away the Name of a Nephew" (Ríos), **Supp. IV Part 2:** 545–546
Taking Care of Mrs. Carroll (Monette), **Supp. X:** 153
"Taking of Captain Ball, The" (Jewett), **Retro. Supp. II:** 134
"Taking Off Emily Dickinson's Clothes" (Collins), **Supp. XXI:** 59, 60
"Taking Out the Lawn Chairs" (Karr), **Supp. XI:** 241
"Taking the Bypass" (J. Epstein), **Supp. XIV:** 110; **Supp. XVI:** 230
"Taking the Forest" (Howe), **Supp. IV Part 2:** 433
"Taking the Lambs to Market" (Kumin), **Supp. IV Part 2:** 455
Talbot, Daniel, **Supp. XIX:** 264
"Tale, A" (Bogan), **Supp. III Part 1:** 50, 51
Taleb-Khyar, Mohamed, **Supp. IV Part 1:** 242, 243, 244, 247, 257
"Tale of Jerusalem, A" (Poe), **III:** 411
Tale of Possessors Self-Dispossessed, A (O'Neill), **III:** 404
Tale of the Body Thief, The (Rice), **Supp. VII:** 290, 293–294, 297
Tale of Two Cities, A (film), **Supp. I Part 1:** 67
"Tale of Two Liars, A" (Singer), **IV:** 12
Tales (Baraka), **Supp. II Part 1:** 39, 55
Tales (Poe), **III:** 413
Tales and Stories for Black Folks (Bambara, ed.), **Supp. XI:** 1
Tales before Midnight (Benét), **Supp. XI:** 46, 53, 57
Talese, Gay, **Supp. XVI:** 273; **Supp. XVII: 199–211**
Tales of a Traveller (Irving), **II:** 309–310
Tales of a Wayside Inn (Longfellow), **II:** 489, 490, 501, 502, 504–505; **Retro. Supp. II:** 154, **162–165**
Tales of Glauber-Spa (Bryant, ed.), **Supp. I Part 1:** 157
Tales of Manhattan (Auchincloss), **Supp. IV Part 1:** 23
Tales of Men and Ghosts (Wharton), **IV:** 315; **Retro. Supp. I:** 372
Tales of Rhoda, The (Rice), **Supp. VII:** 288
Tales of Soldiers and Civilians (Bierce), **I:** 200–203, 204, 206, 208, 212
Tales of the Argonauts (Harte), **Supp. II Part 1:** 337, 348, 351
Tales of the Fish Patrol (London), **II:** 465
Tales of the Grotesque and Arabesque (Poe), **II:** 273; **III:** 412, 415; **Retro. Supp. II:** 270
Tales of the Jazz Age (Fitzgerald), **II:** 88; **Retro. Supp. I:** 105; **Supp. IX:** 57

Tales You Won't Believe (Stratton-Porter), **Supp. XX:** 217
"Talisman, A" (Moore), **III:** 195–196
Talisman, The (King), **Supp. V:** 140, 144, 152
"Talkin Bout Sonny" (Bambara), **Supp. XI:** 6–7
"Talking" (Merwin), **Supp. III Part 1:** 354
Talking All Morning (R. Bly), **Supp. IV Part 1:** 59, 60, 61, 62, 64, 65
Talking Dirty to the Gods (Komunyakaa), **Supp. XIII: 130–131**
Talking History (television program), **Supp. XXI:** 172
"Talking Horse" (Malamud), **Supp. I Part 2:** 435
Talking Soft Dutch (McCarriston), **Supp. XIV: 260–263,** 266, 270, 271
"Talking to Barr Creek" (Wagoner), **Supp. IX:** 328
"Talking to Sheep" (Sexton), **Supp. II Part 2:** 695
Talking to the Sun: An Illustrated Anthology of Poems for Young People (Koch and Farrell, eds.), **Supp. XV:** 188
"Talk of Heroes" (C. Bly), **Supp. XVI:** 34
"Talk of the Town" (*The New Yorker* column), **IV:** 215; **Supp. IV Part 1:** 53, 54
"Talk on Guadalcanal" (Wolfert), **Supp. XXI:** 264
Talk Talk (Boyle), **Supp. XX:** 24
"Talk with the Yellow Kid, A" (Bellow), **I:** 151
Tallent, Elizabeth, **Supp. IV Part 2:** 570
Tallman, Warren, **Supp. IV Part 1:** 154
TallMountain, Mary, **Supp. IV Part 1:** 324–325
Talma, Louise, **IV:** 357
Talmadge, Constance, **Supp. XVI:** 186, 187, 196
Talmadge, Norma, **Supp. XVI:** 186, 187, 196
Talmadge Girls, The (Loos), **Supp. XVI:** 186, 196
Talmey, Allene, **Supp. IV Part 1:** 197; **Supp. XIII:** 172
Talmud, **IV:** 8, 17
Taltos: Lives of the Mayfair Witches (Rice), **Supp. VII:** 299–300
"Tamar" (Jeffers), **Supp. II Part 2:** 427–428, 436
Tamar and Other Poems (Jeffers), **Supp. II Part 2:** 416, 419
Tambourines to Glory (Hughes), **Supp. I Part 1:** 338–339
"Tame Indians" (Jewett), **Retro. Supp. II:** 141
"Tamerlane" (Poe), **III:** 426
Tamerlane and Other Poems (Poe), **III:** 410
"Tammany Man, The" (Hapgood), **Supp. XVII:** 103
"Tam O'Shanter" (Burns), **II:** 306
Tamsen Donner: A Woman's Journey (Whitman), **Supp. XXI:** 246
Tan, Amy, **Supp. X: 289–300**
Tangential Views (Bierce), **I:** 209

"Tangier 1975" (Bowles), **Supp. IV Part 1:** 94

"Tankas" (McClatchy), **Supp. XII:** 266

Tanner, Laura E., **Supp. X:** 209; **Supp. XXI:** 217

Tanner, Obour, **Supp. XX:**281, 288

Tanner, Tony, **I:** 260, 261; **Retro. Supp. II:** 205; **Supp. IV Part 1:** 285; **Supp. XVI:** 65, 69

Tannhäuser (Wagner), **I:** 315

"Tan Ta Ra, Cries Mars...," (Wagoner), **Supp. IX:** 325

Tao of Physics, The (Capra), **Supp. X:** 261

Tao Teh Ching (Bynner, trans.), **Supp. XV:** 46, 47

Tapahonso, Luci, **Supp. IV Part 1:** 404; **Supp. IV Part 2:** 499, 508

Tape for the Turn of the Year (Ammons), **Supp. VII:** 31–33, 35

"Tapestry" (Ashbery), **Supp. III Part 1:** 22–23

"Tapiama" (Bowles), **Supp. IV Part 1:** 89–90

"Tapiola" (W. C. Williams), **Retro. Supp. I:** 429

Tappan, Arthur, **Supp. I Part 2:** 588

Tapping the White Cane of Solitude (F. Wright), **Supp. XVII:** 243

Taps at Reveille (Fitzgerald), **II:** 94, 96; **Retro. Supp. I:** 113

Tar: A Midwest Childhood (Anderson), **I:** 98, 115; **II:** 27

Tarantino, Quentin, **Supp. IV Part 1:** 356

Tarantula (Dylan), **Supp. XVIII:** 21, 29, **31–32**

Tar Baby (Morrison), **Supp. III Part 1:** 364, 369–372, 379; **Supp. IV Part 1:** 13

Tarbell, Ida, **III:** 322, 580; **Retro. Supp. II:** 101

"Target Practice" (Offutt), **Supp. XIX:** 171

"Target Study" (Baraka), **Supp. II Part 1:** 49–50, 54

Tarkington, Booth, **II:** 444; **III:** 70; **Retro. Supp. I:** 100; **Supp. XV:** 41

Tarnawsky, Yuriy (George) Orest, **Supp. XX:**259

Tarpon (film), **Supp. VIII:** 42

Tarr, Rodger L., **Supp. X:** 222, 224, 226

Tárrega, Francisco, **Supp. XXI:** 100

Tartt, Donna, **Supp. XVIII:** 135

Tartuffe (Molière; Wilbur, trans.), **Supp. III Part 2:** 560

Tarumba, Selected Poems of Jaime Sabines (Levine and Trejo, trans.), **Supp. V:** 178

Tarzan Finds a Son (film, Weismuller), **Supp. XX:**18

"Tarzan Is an Expatriate" (Theroux), **Supp. VIII:** 313

Tasis, Juan de, **Supp. XXI:** 104

Task, The (Cowper), **II:** 304

Tasker Street (Halliday), **Supp. XIX:** 82, **87–89**

Tasso, Torquato, **I:** 276

Taste of Palestine, A: Menus and Memories (Shihab), **Supp. XIII:** 273

Tate, Alan, **Supp. XV:** 141

Tate, Allen, **I:** 48, 49, 50, 67, 69, 381, 382, 386, 390, 396, 397, 399, 402, 441, 468; **II:** 197–198, 367, 536, 537, 542, 551, 554; **III:** 424, 428, 454, 482, 483, 485, 493, 495, 496, 497, 499, 500, 517; **IV:** **120–143**, 236, 237, 433; **Retro. Supp. I:** 37, 41, 90; **Retro. Supp. II:** 77, 79, 82, 83, 89, 176, 178, 179; **Supp. I Part 1:** 364, 371; **Supp. I Part 2:** 423; **Supp. II Part 1:** 90–91, 96, 98, 103–104, 136, 139, 144, 150, 151, 318; **Supp. II Part 2:** 643; **Supp. III Part 2:** 542; **Supp. V:** 315, 331; **Supp. X:** 1, 52; **Supp. XIV:** 2; **Supp. XXI:** 256

Tate, Mrs. Allen (Caroline Gordon). *See* Gordon, Caroline

Tate, Mrs. Allen (Helen Heinz), **IV:** 127

Tate, Mrs. Allen (Isabella Gardner), **IV:** 127

Tate, Benjamin Lewis Bogan, **IV:** 127

Tate, Greg, **Supp. XIII:** 233, 237

Tate, James, **Supp. V:** 92, 338; **Supp. VIII:** 39, 279; **Supp. XV:** 250; **Supp. XVII:** 242

Tate, John Allen, **IV:** 127

Tate, Michael Paul, **IV:** 127

Tate, Nancy, **II:** 197

Tattooed Countess, The (Van Vechten), **I:** 295; **Supp. II Part 2:** 726–728, 738, 742

Tattooed Feet (Nye), **Supp. XIII:** 274

"Tattoos" (McClatchy), **Supp. XII:** 266–267, 268

"Tattoos" (Wright), **Supp. V:** 335, 340

Tatum, Anna, **I:** 516

Tatum, James, **Supp. IV Part 2:** 684

Taupin, René, **II:** 528, 529; **Supp. III Part 2:** 614, 615, 617, 621

Tavano, John, **Supp. XXI:** 99

Tawney, Richard Henry, **Supp. I Part 2:** 481

Taylor, Bayard, **II:** 275; **Supp. I Part 1:** 350, 361, 362, 365, 366, 372; **Supp. XV:** 269

Taylor, Cora. *See* Howarth, Cora

Taylor, Deems, **III:** 138

Taylor, Edward, **III:** 493; **IV:** **144–166;** **Supp. I Part 1:** 98; **Supp. I Part 2:** 375, 386, 546

Taylor, Mrs. Edward (Elizabeth Fitch), **IV:** 147, 165

Taylor, Mrs. Edward (Ruth Wyllys), **IV:** 148

Taylor, Eleanor Ross, **Supp. V:** 317, 318

Taylor, Elizabeth, **II:** 588

Taylor, Frank, **III:** 81

Taylor, Frederick Winslow, **Supp. I Part 2:** 644

Taylor, Graham, **Supp. I Part 1:** 5

Taylor, Henry, **Retro. Supp. I:** 212; **Supp. XI:** 317; **Supp. XIII:** 333

Taylor, Henry W., **IV:** 144

Taylor, Jeremy, **II:** 11; **III:** 487; **Supp. I Part 1:** 349; **Supp. XII:** 45; **Supp. XIV:** 344, 345

Taylor, John, **IV:** 149

Taylor, Katherine, **Supp. VIII:** 251

Taylor, Kezia, **IV:** 148

Taylor, Nathaniel W., **Supp. I Part 2:** 580

Taylor, Paul, **I:** 293

Taylor, Peter, **Retro. Supp. II:** 179; **Supp. V: 313–329; Supp. XIV:** 3

Taylor, Raynor, **Supp. XV:** 238

Taylor, Richard, **IV:** 146

Taylor, Robert, **Supp. I Part 1:** 294; **Supp. XV:** 135, 138; **Supp. XVI:** 277

Taylor, Samuel A., **Supp. XX:**253

Taylor, Stephan, **Supp. XVI:** 203

Taylor, Thomas, **II:** 10

Taylor, William, **IV:** 145–146

Taylor, Zachary, **I:** 3; **II:** 433–434

Tchelitchew, Peter, **II:** 586

Tea and Sympathy (Anderson), **Supp. I Part 1:** 277; **Supp. V:** 108

"Tea at the Palaz of Hoon" (Stevens), **Retro. Supp. I:** 300, 302, 306

"Teacher's Pet" (Thurber), **Supp. I Part 2:** 605–606

"Teaching and Story Telling" (Maclean), **Supp. XIV:** 234

Teaching a Stone to Talk: Expeditions and Encounters (Dillard), **Supp. VI:** 23, 26, 28, 32, 33, 34–35

"Teaching Hanh the Blues" (Weigl), **Supp. XIX:** 287

Teachings of Don B., The (Barthelme), **Supp. IV Part 1:** 53

Teachout, Terry, **Supp. XIX:** 137

Teale, Edwin Way, **Supp. XIII:** 7

Teall, Dorothy, **I:** 221

Team Team Team (film), **Supp. IX:** 251

"Tea on the Mountain" (Bowles), **Supp. IV Part 1:** 90

"Tea Party, The" (MacLeish), **III:** 11

Tear and a Smile, A (Dam'a wa Ibtisáma) (Gibran), **Supp. XX:**116, 118, 124

"Tears, Idle Tears" (Lord Tennyson), **Supp. XIV:** 8

"Tears of the Pilgrims, The" (McClatchy), **Supp. XII:** 256

Teasdale, Sara, **Retro. Supp. I:** 133; **Supp. I Part 2:** 393, 707; **Supp. XIV:** 127; **Supp. XV:** 295, 297, 301, 305, 307, 308; **Supp. XVII:** 69, 75

"Tease" (Swados), **Supp. XIX:** 267

Tebeaux, Elizabeth, **Supp. IX:** 109

Technics and Civilization (Mumford), **Supp. I Part 2:** 638; **Supp. II Part 2:** 479, 493, 497

Technics and Human Development (Mumford), **Supp. I Part 2:** 638; **Supp. II Part 2:** 497

"Technology, The" (Egan), **Supp. XIX:** 61

"Teddy" (Salinger), **III:** 561–563, 571

"Te Deum" (Reznikoff), **Supp. XIV:** 281

Tedlock, Dennis, **Supp. IV Part 2:** 509

"Teeth Mother Naked at Last, The" (R. Bly), **Supp. IV Part 1:** 63, 68, 73

Teggart, Richard, **Supp. I Part 2:** 650

Tegnér, Esaias, **Retro. Supp. II:** 155

Teilhard de Chardin, Pierre, **Supp. I Part 1:** 314

Telephone, The (film), **Supp. XI:** 309

"Telephone Call, A" (Parker), **Supp. IX:** **202–203**

"Telephone Number of the Muse, The" (Justice), **Supp. VII:** 124–125

Telephone Poles and Other Poems (Updike), **IV:** 214, 215

"Television" (Beattie), **Supp. V:** 33

Teller, Edward, **I:** 137

"Telling" (Ortiz), **Supp. IV Part 2:** 509

"Telling It in Black and White: The Importance of the Africanist Presence in *To Kill a Mockingbird*" (Baecker), **Supp. VIII:** 128

Telling Secrets (Buechner), **Supp. XII:** 53–54

Telling Stories (Didion), **Supp. IV Part 1:** 197

"Telling Stories" (Didion), **Supp. IV Part 1:** 197

"Telling the Bees" (Whittier), **Supp. I Part 2:** 694–695

Telling the Little Secrets (J. Burstein), **Supp. XVII:** 44

Telling the Truth: The Gospel as Tragedy, Comedy, and Fairy Tale (Buechner), **Supp. XII:** 53

"Tell Me" (Hughes), **Supp. VIII:** 213

"Tell Me, Sir, ... What Is 'Black' Literature?" (H. L. Gates), **Supp. XX:** 108

Tell Me, Tell Me (Moore), **III:** 215

Tell Me Again How the White Heron Rises and Flies across the Nacreous River at Twilight toward the Distant Islands (Carruth), **Supp. XVI:** 56

Tell Me a Riddle (film), **Supp. XIII:** 295

Tell Me a Riddle (Olsen), **Supp. XIII:** 294, 296, **298–302,** 303, 305

"Tell Me a Riddle" (Olsen), **Supp. XIII:** 294, 297, 298, **300–302,** 305

"Tell Me a Story" (McDermott), **Supp. XVIII:** 177

Tell Me How Long the Train's Been Gone (Baldwin), **Retro. Supp. II:** 9, **11–12,** 14; **Supp. I Part 1:** 48, 52, 63–65, 67

"Tell Me My Fortune" (Epstein), **Supp. XII:** 163

Tell Me Your Answer True (Sexton), **Supp. II Part 2:** 683

Tell My Horse (Hurston), **Supp. VI:** 149, 156, 158

"Tell-Tale Heart, The" (Poe), **III:** 413, 414–415, 416; **Retro. Supp. II:** 267, 269, 270

"Tell the Women We're Going" (Carver), **Supp. III Part 1:** 138, 144

"Telluride Blues—A Hatchet Job" (Abbey), **Supp. XIII:** 10

Telushkin, Dvorah, **Retro. Supp. II:** 317

Temblor (Howe), **Supp. IV Part 2:** 431

Tempering of Eugene O'Neill, The (D. Alexander), **Supp. XVII:** 99

"Temper of Steel, The" (Jones), **Supp. XI:** 218

Tempers, The (W. C. Williams), **Retro. Supp. I:** 413–414, 415, 416, 424

Tempest, The (Shakespeare), **I:** 394; **II:** 12; **III:** 40, 61, 263; **Retro. Supp. I:** 61; **Supp. IV Part 2:** 463; **Supp. V:** 302–303; **Supp. XII:** 54–57; **Supp. XV:** 255, 256

Temple, Minnie, **II:** 323

Temple, The (Herbert), **IV:** 145, 153

Temple, William, **III:** 303

Temple House (E. Stoddard), **Supp. XV:** 273, **284–286**

Temple of My Familiar, The (Walker), **Supp. III Part 2:** 521, 527, 529, 535, 537; **Supp. IV Part 1:** 14

"Temple of the Holy Ghost, A" (O'Connor), **III:** 344, 352; **Retro. Supp. II:** 232

Templin, Charlotte, **Supp. V:** 116

Temporary Shelter (Gordon), **Supp. IV Part 1:** 299, 305–307

"Temporary Shelter" (Gordon), **Supp. IV Part 1:** 306

Temptation Game, The (Gardner), **Supp. VI:** 72

"Temptation of St. Anthony, The" (Barthelme), **Supp. IV Part 1:** 47

Temptations, The, **Supp. X:** 242

"Tenancy, A" (Merrill), **Supp. III Part 1:** 322, 323

"Tenant" (Hoffman), **Supp. XVIII:** 86

Tenants, The (Malamud), **Supp. I Part 2:** 448–450

Ten Commandments (McClatchy), **Supp. XII:** 262–265

Ten Days That Shook the World (Reed), **II:** 577; **Supp. X:** 136; **Supp. XVIII:** 225

Tendencies in Modern American Poetry (Lowell), **II:** 529

"Tender, Hilarious Reminiscences of Life in Mythical Lake Wobegon" (MacDougall), **Supp. XVI:** 174

Tender Buttons (G. Stein), **I:** 103, 105; **IV:** 27, 42–43; **Retro. Supp. II:** 331; **Supp. XV:** 347

"Tenderfoot" (Haines), **Supp. XII:** 209

Tender Is the Night (Fitzgerald), **I:** 375; **II:** 79, 84, 91, 95–96, 97, 98, 420; **Retro. Supp. I:** 105, 108, 109, 110–112, 114; **Supp. IX:** 59, 60, 61; **Supp. XV:** 197; **Supp. XXI:** 11

"Tenderloin" (Crane), **I:** 408

"Tenderly" (Dobyns), **Supp. XIII:** 86–87

'Tender Man, A" (Bambara), **Supp. XI:** 9–10

"Tenderness" (Dunn), **Supp. XI:** 149, 150

"Tender Offer, The" (Auchincloss), **Supp. IV Part 1:** 34

"Tender Organizations, The" (C. Bly), **Supp. XVI:** 40, 42

"Tenebrae" (Komunyakaa), **Supp. XIII:** 132

Tenenbaum, Joseph, **Supp. XX:** 253

"Ten Forty-Four" (Kingsolver), **Supp. VII:** 208

Ten Indians (Bell), **Supp. X:** 7, **12**

Tennant, Agnieszka, **Supp. XX:** 140

"Ten Neglected American Writers Who Deserve to Be Better Known" (Cantor), **Supp. IV Part 1:** 285

Tennent, Gilbert, **I:** 546

Tennessee Day in St. Louis (Taylor), **Supp. V:** 324

"Tennessee's Partner" (Harte), **Supp. II Part 1:** 345, 348–350

"Tennis" (Pinsky), **Supp. VI:** 241, 242

Tennis Court Oath, The (Ashbery), **Supp. III Part 1:** 7, 9, 12, 14, 26

Ten North Frederick (O'Hara), **III:** 361

Tennyson, Alfred, Lord, **I:** 587–588; **II:** 18, 82, 273, 338, 404, 439, 604; **III:** 5, 409, 469, 485, 511, 521, 523; **Retro. Supp. I:** 100, 325; **Retro. Supp. II:** 135; **Supp. I Part 1:** 349, 356; **Supp. I Part 2:** 410, 416, 552; **Supp. IX:** 19; **Supp. X:** 157; **Supp. XIII:** 111; **Supp. XIV:** 40, 120; **Supp. XV:** 275; **Supp. XVIII:** 78

"Tenochtitlan" (Bronk), **Supp. XXI:** 31

"Ten O'Clock News" (Ortiz), **Supp. IV Part 2:** 503–504

Ten Poems (Dove), **Supp. IV Part 1:** 244

Ten Poems of Francis Ponge Translated by Robert Bly and Ten Poems of Robert Bly Inspired by the Poems by Francis Ponge (R. Bly), **Supp. IV Part 1:** 71

"Tension in Poetry" (Tate), **IV:** 128, 129, 135

Tenth Muse, The (Bradstreet), **Supp. I Part 1:** 102, 103, 114

10,000 Days of Thunder: A History of the Vietnam War (Caputo), **Supp. XIX:** 29

"Tent on the Beach, The" (Whittier), **Supp. I Part 2:** 703

"Teodoro Luna Confesses after Years to His Brother, Anselmo the Priest, Who Is Required to Understand, But Who Understands Anyway, More Than People Think" (Ríos), **Supp. IV Part 2:** 552

Teodoro Luna's Two Kisses (Ríos), **Supp. IV Part 2:** 550–552, 553

"Tepeyac" (Cisneros), **Supp. VII:** 69

"Terce" (Auden), **Supp. II Part 1:** 22

Terence, **IV:** 155, 363; **Supp. I Part 2:** 405

Terkel, Studs, **Supp. IV Part 1:** 364

"Term" (Merwin), **Supp. III Part 1:** 356–357

"Terminal Days at Beverly Farms" (Lowell), **Retro. Supp. II:** 189

Terminating, or Sonnet LXXV, or "Lass Meine Schmerzen nicht verloren sein, or Ambivalence" (Kushner), Supp. IX: 132

"Terminations" (James), **Retro. Supp. I:** 229

"Terminus" (Emerson), **II:** 13, 19

"Terminus" (Wharton), **Retro. Supp. I:** 371

"Terms in Which I Think of Reality, The" (Ginsberg), **Supp. II Part 1:** 311

Terms of Endearment (film), **Supp. V:** 226

Terms of Endearment (McMurtry), **Supp. V:** 224–225

"Terrace, The" (Wilbur), **Supp. III Part 2:** 550

Terrarium (Sanders), **Supp. XVI:** 270

"Terrence McNally" (Bryer), **Supp. XIII:** 200

"Terrence McNally" (Di Gaetani), **Supp. XIII:** 200

Terrence McNally: A Casebook (Zinman), **Supp. XIII:** 209

"Terrible Peacock, The" (Barnes), **Supp. III Part 1:** 33

Terrible Threes, The (Reed), **Supp. X:** 241, 253

Terrible Twos, The (Reed), **Supp. X:** 241, **252–253**

"Terrific Mother" (Moore), **Supp. X:** 178

Territory Ahead, The (Morris), **III:** 228–229, 236

Terrorism (Wright), **Supp. XV:** 341, 342

"Terrorism" (Wright), **Supp. XV:** 341

Terry, Edward A., **II:** 128, 129

Terry, Rose, **Supp. I Part 2:** 420

Tertium Organum (Ouspensky), **I:** 383; **Supp. XX:**116

Tess of the d'Ubervilles (Hardy), **II:** 181; **Retro. Supp. II:** 100

"Testament" (Berry), **Supp. X:** 36

"Testament" (Carruth), **Supp. XVI:** 59

"Testament (Or, Homage to Walt Whitman)" (Jong), **Supp. V:** 130

"Testament of Flood" (Warren), **IV:** 253

Testament of François Villon, The (Pound, opera), **Retro. Supp. I:** 287

"Testament: Vermeer in December" (Bierds), **Supp. XVII:** 33

"Testimonia on the Question of Stesichoros' Blinding by Helen" (Carson), **Supp. XII:** 107

"Testimonies of a Roasted Chicken" (Jarman), **Supp. XVII:** 120

"Testimony" (Komunyakaa), **Supp. XIII:** 129

"Testimony of James Apthorp, The" (Kees), **Supp. XV:** 146

Testimony: The United States (1885–1890): Recitative (Reznikoff), **Supp. XIV:** 279, 280, 281, 285, **289–291**

Testimony: The United States (1891–1900): Recitative (Reznikoff), **Supp. XIV:** 291

Testing-Tree, The (Kunitz), **Supp. III Part 1:** 260, 263, 264, 267, 268

"Testing-Tree, The" (Kunitz), **Supp. III Part 1:** 269

Test of Poetry, A (Zukofsky), **Supp. III Part 2:** 618, 622

"Teutonic Scholar" (X. J. Kennedy), **Supp. XV:** 161

"Texas Moon, and Elsewhere, The" (McMurtry), **Supp. V:** 225

Texas Poets in Concert: A Quartet (Gwynn, ed.), **Supp. XIII:** 277

Texas Summer (Southern), **Supp. XI:** 309

Texasville (McMurtry), **Supp. V:** 228, 233

Thacher, Molly Day, **IV:** 381

Thackeray, William Makepeace, **I:** 194, 354; **II:** 182, 271, 282, 288, 316, 321, 322; **III:** 64, 70; **IV:** 326; **Retro. Supp. I:** 218; **Supp. I Part 1:** 307; **Supp. I Part 2:** 421, 495, 579; **Supp. IV Part 1:** 297; **Supp. IX:** 200; **Supp. XI:** 277; **Supp. XIV:** 306; **Supp. XX:**228

Thaddeus, Janice Farrar, **Supp. IV Part 1:** 299

"Thailand" (Barthelme), **Supp. IV Part 1:** 41

Thalberg, Irving, **Retro. Supp. I:** 109, 110, 114; **Supp. XVI:** 191, 192

Thales, **I:** 480–481

Thalia Trilogy (McMurtry), **Supp. V:** 220–223, 234

Tham, Claire, **Supp. VIII:** 79

"Thanatopsis" (Bryant), **Supp. I Part 1:** 150, 154, 155, 170

Thanatos Syndrome, The (Percy), **Supp. III Part 1:** 385, 397–399

"Thanks Can Be Named to Death" (Peacock), **Supp. XIX:** 199

"Thanksgiving" (Glück), **Supp. V:** 83

"Thanksgiving, A" (Auden), **Supp. II Part 1:** 26

"Thanksgiving for a Habitat" (Auden), **Supp. II Part 1:** 24

Thanksgivings (Traherne), **Supp. XVI:** 288

"Thanksgiving Spirit" (Farrell), **II:** 45

Thanksgiving Visitor, The (Capote), **Supp. III Part 1:** 116, 118, 119

"Thank You, Esther Forbes" (Saunders), **Supp. XIX:** 235

Thank You, Fog (Auden), **Supp. II Part 1:** 24

"Thank You, Lord" (Angelou), **Supp. IV Part 1:** 15

Thank You, Mr. Moto (Marquand), **III:** 57, 58

Thank You and Other Poems (Koch), **Supp. XV:** 180–181

"Thank You in Arabic" (Nye), **Supp. XIII:** 273, 281

"Thar's More in the Man Than Thar Is in the Land" (Lanier), **Supp. I Part 1:** 352–353, 359–360

"That Evening Sun" (Faulkner), **II:** 72; **Retro. Supp. I:** 75, 83

That Horse (Hogan), **Supp. IV Part 1:** 397, 404, 405

"That House, This Room" (W. V. Davis), **Supp. XXI:** 90

"That I Had the Wings" (Ellison), **Supp. II Part 1:** 238

That Night (McDermott), **Supp. XVIII:** 155, **158–160,** 162, 163, 166

"That's the Place Indians Talk About" (Ortiz), **Supp. IV Part 2:** 511

That Tantalus (Bronk), **Supp. XXI:** 31

"That the Soul May Wax Plump" (Swenson), **Supp. IV Part 2:** 650

"That the Universe Is Chrysalid" (Sobin), **Supp. XVI:** 284

"That Tree" (Porter), **III:** 434–435, 446, 451

That Was the Week That Was (television program), **Supp. XIV:** 125

"That Year" (Olds), **Supp. X:** 203

"Thaw" (C. Frost), **Supp. XV:** 93, 104, 105

Thaxter, Celia, **Retro. Supp. II:** 136, 147; **Supp. XIII:** 143, 153

Thayer, Abbott, **I:** 231

Thayer, Scofield, **I:** 231; **Retro. Supp. I:** 58

Thayer and Eldridge, **Retro. Supp. I:** 403

"Theater" (Toomer), **Supp. IX:** 309, 317–318

"Theater Chronicle" (McCarthy), **II:** 562

"Theater Problems? Call Dr. Chekhov" (Wasserstein), **Supp. XV:** 320

Theatricals (James), **Retro. Supp. I:** 228

The Blacker the Berry: A Novel of Negro Life (Thurman), **Supp. XVIII:** 281; **Supp. XIX:** 73

"Theft" (Porter), **III:** 434, 435

Theft, A (Bellow), **Retro. Supp. II:** 31–32, 34

The Harder They Fall (Schulberg), **Supp. XVIII:** **247,** 253

The Harder They Fall: Celebrities Tell Their Real-Life Stories of Addiction and Recovery (F. Wright), **Supp. XVII:** 240

Their Eyes Were Watching God (Hurston), **Supp. VI:** 149, 152, 156–157; **Supp. XX:**107

Their Heads Are Green and Their Hands Are Blue: Scenes from the Non-Christian World (Bowles), **Supp. IV Part 1:** 89

"Their Losses" (Taylor), **Supp. V:** 320

"Their Sleep" (W. V. Davis), **Supp. XXI:** 93

Their Wedding Journey (Howells), **II:** 277–278; **Retro. Supp. I:** 334

them (Oates), **Supp. II Part 2:** 503, 511–514

Theme Is Freedom, The (Dos Passos), **I:** 488–489, 492, 494

Theme Time Radio Hour (radio show, Dylan), **Supp. XVIII:** 28

"Theme with Variations" (Agee), **I:** 27

"Then" (Barthelme), **Supp. IV Part 1:** 48

"Then It All Came Down" (Capote), **Supp. III Part 1:** 125, 131

Theocritus, **II:** 169; **Retro. Supp. I:** 286

"Theodore the Poet" (Masters), **Supp. I Part 2:** 461

Theological Position, A (Coover), **Supp. V:** 44

Theophrastus, **I:** 58

"Theoretical and Scientific Conceptions of Race, The" (Locke), **Supp. XIV:** 209

"Theories of Time and Space" (Trethewey), **Supp. XXI:** 255

Theory and Practice of Rivers and Other Poems, The (Harrison), **Supp. VIII:** 47, 49

Theory of Business Enterprise, The (Veblen), **Supp. I Part 2:** 638, 641, 644

Theory of Flight (Rukeyser), **Supp. VI:** 272, 275, **277–278,** 284

"Theory of Flight" (Rukeyser), **Supp. VI:** 277–278

Theory of Moral Sentiments, The (A. Smith), **Supp. I Part 2:** 634

Theory of the Leisure Class, The (Veblen), **I:** 475–476; **Supp. I Part 2:** 629, 633, 641, 645; **Supp. IV Part 1:** 22

"There" (Taylor), **Supp. V:** 323

"There Are No Such Trees in Alpine California" (Haines), **Supp. XII:** 207

"There Goes (Varoom! Varoom!) That Kandy-Kolored Tangerine-Flake Streamline Baby" (Wolfe), **Supp. III Part 2:** 569–571

"There Have Been Changes" (Pickering), **Supp. XXI:** 202–203

"There Is a Lesson" (Olsen), **Supp. XIII:** 292, 297

"There is a Man" (Espaillat), **Supp. XXI:** 108–109

"There Is Only One of Everything" (Atwood), **Supp. XIII:** 34

There Is Something Out There (McNally). *See And Things That Go Bump in the Night* (McNally)

"There Must Be" (Peacock), **Supp. XIX:** 199

"There's a certain Slant of light" (Dickinson), **Retro. Supp. I:** 38

There's a Wocket in My Pocket! (Geisel), **Supp. XVI:** 111

Thérèse de Lisieux, Saint, **Supp. VIII:** 195

"There She Is She Is Taking Her Bath" (Anderson), **I:** 113, 114

"There Was a Child Went Forth" (Whitman), **IV:** 348

"There Was a Man, There Was a Woman" (Cisneros), **Supp. VII:** 70

"There Was an Old Woman She Had So Many Children She Didn't Know What to Do" (Cisneros), **Supp. VII:** 60

"There Was a Youth Whose Name Was Thomas Granger" (Olson), **Supp. II Part 2:** 558, 560, 563

There Were Giants in the Land (Benét), **Supp. XI:** 50

There You Are (Simpson), **Supp. IX:** 279–280

"There You Are" (Simpson), **Supp. IX:** 279

"Thermopylae" (Clampitt), **Supp. IX:** 43

Theroux, Alexander, **Supp. VIII:** 312

Theroux, Marcel, **Supp. VIII:** 325

Theroux, Paul, **Supp. V:** 122; **Supp. VIII: 309–327**

"These Are My People" (Hayden), **Supp. II Part 1:** 365

"These are the days when Birds come back" (Dickinson), **Retro. Supp. I:** 30

"These Days" (Olds), **Supp. X:** 215

"These Flames and Generosities of the Heart: Emily Dickinson and the Illogic of Sumptuary Values" (Howe), **Supp. IV Part 2:** 431

These Low Grounds (Turpin), **Supp. XVIII:** 283

"These saw Visions" (Dickinson), **Retro. Supp. I:** 46

These Thirteen (Faulkner), **II:** 72

These Three (film), **Supp. I Part 1:** 281

These Times (Untermeyer), **Supp. XV: 299–300,** 303

"These Times" (Untermeyer), **Supp. XV:** 300

"Thessalonica: A Roman Story" (Brown), **Supp. I Part 1:** 133

Thévenaz, Paul, **Supp. XV:** 42

Thew, Harvey, **Supp. XIII:** 166

"They Ain't the Men They Used To Be" (Farrell), **II:** 45

"They Burned the Books" (Benét), **Supp. XI:** 46

They Came Like Swallows (Maxwell), **Supp. VIII: 155–159,** 168, 169

"They Can't Turn Back" (Baldwin), **Supp. I Part 1:** 52

They Do Not: The Letters of a Non-Professional Lady Arranged for Public Consumption (Clements), **Supp. XVI:** 190

They Feed They Lion (Levine), **Supp. V:** 178, 179, 181, 184–185, 186

"They Feed They Lion" (Levine), **Supp. V:** 188

"They Lion Grow" (Levine), **Supp. V:** 184 185

"They're Not Your Husband" (Carver), **Supp. III Part 1:** 141, 143

They're Playing Our Song (musical), **Supp. IV Part 2:** 589

They Shall Inherit the Laughter (Jones), **Supp. XI:** 217, 218, 232

"They Shall Not Die" (Ryan as Quin), **Supp. XVIII:** 228–229

They Shoot Horses (film), **Supp. XIII:** 159

They Shoot Horses, Don't They? (McCoy), **Supp. XIII:** 159, **164–166,** 168, 171, 172, 174

"They Sing, They Sing" (Roethke), **III:** 544

They Stooped to Folly (Glasgow), **II:** 175, 186–187

They Were Expendable (film), **Supp. XVIII:** 247

They Whisper (R. O. Butler), **Supp. XII: 72–73**

They Who Knock at Our Gates: A Complete Gospel of Immigration (Antin), **Supp. XX:2–3, 10–11,** 12

Thidwick the Big-Hearted Moose (Geisel), **Supp. XVI:** 104

"Thief's Philosophy of Life, The" (Hapgood), **Supp. XVII:** 103

"Thief's Wife, The" (B. Kelly), **Supp. XVII:** 125–126

"Thieves" (Yates), **Supp. XI:** 349

Thieves of Paradise (Komunyakaa), **Supp. XIII:** 113, **128–130,** 132

"Thimble, The" (Kenyon), **Supp. VII:** 164

"Thing and Its Relations, The" (James), **II:** 357

"Things" (Haines), **Supp. XII:** 207

"Things" (Kenyon), **Supp. VII:** 169

"Things, The" (Kinnell), **Supp. III Part 1:** 246

Things As They Are (Stein), **IV:** 34, 37, 40

"Things Can Be Named to Death" (Peacock), **Supp. XIX:** 199

"Things Don't Stop" (Nye), **Supp. XIII:** 287

Things Gone and Things Still Here (Bowles), **Supp. IV Part 1:** 91

"Things of August" (Stevens), **Retro. Supp. I:** 309

Things of This World (Wilbur), **Supp. III Part 2:** 552–555

Things Themselves: Essays and Scenes (Price), **Supp. VI:** 261

Things They Carried, The (T. O'Brien), **Supp. V:** 238, 239, 240, 243, 248–250; **Supp. XVII:** 14; **Supp. XXI:** 122

"Thing That Killed My Father Off, The" (Carver), **Supp. III Part 1:** 143

Thingy World!: or, How We Got to Where We Are: A Satire in One Act (Budbill), **Supp. XIX: 13–14**

"Think about It" (Conroy), **Supp. XVI:** 75

Think Back on Us . . . (Cowley), **Supp. II Part 1:** 139, 140, 142

Think Fast, Mr. Moto (Marquand), **III:** 57, 58

"Thinking about Barbara Deming" (Paley), **Supp. VI:** 227

"Thinking about Being Called Simple by a Critic" (Stafford), **Supp. XI:** 328

Thinking about the Longstanding Problems of Virtue and Happiness: Essays, a Play, Two Poems, and a Prayer (Kushner), **Supp. IX:** 131, 134, 135

"Thinking about the Past" (Justice), **Supp. VII:** 123–124

"Thinking about Western Thinking" (Didion), **Supp. IV Part 1:** 204, 206

"'Thinking against Oneself': Reflections on Cioran" (Sontag), **Supp. III Part 2:** 459–460

"Thinking Back Through Our Mothers: Traditions in Canadian Women's Writing" (Shields), **Supp. VII:** 307–308

"Thinking for Berky" (Stafford), **Supp. XI:** 320

"Thinking like a Mountain" (Leopold), **Supp. XIV:** 188, 189

"Thinking of the Lost World" (Jarrell), **II:** 338–389

Thinking Out Loud (Quindlen), **Supp. XVII:** 167, **169–170**

Thin Man, The (film), **Supp. IV Part 1:** 342, 355

Thin Man, The (Hammett), **Supp. IV Part 1:** 354–355

"Thinnest Shadow, The" (Ashbery), **Supp. III Part 1:** 5

"Thin People, The" (Plath), **Supp. I Part 2:** 538, 547

Thin Red Line, The (film; Malick), **Supp. V:** 249; **Supp. XV:** 351

Thin Red Line, The (Jones), **Supp. XI:** 219, **224–225,** 229, 231, 232, 233, 234

"Thin Strips" (Sandburg), **III:** 587

"Third and Final Continent, The" (Lahiri), **Supp. XXI: 178–180**

"Third Avenue in Sunlight" (Hecht), **Supp. X:** 61

"Third Body, A" (R. Bly), **Supp. IV Part 1:** 71

Third Circle, The (Norris), **III:** 327

"Third Expedition, The" (Bradbury), **Supp. IV Part 1:** 103, 106

Third Generation, The (C. Himes), **Supp. XVI:** 135, **140–141**

Third Life of Grange Copeland, The (Walker), **Supp. III Part 2:** 520, 527–536

Third Mind, The (Burroughs), **Supp. XII:** 3

Third Rose, The (Brinnin), **IV:** 26

"Third Sermon on the Warpland, The" (Brooks), **Supp. III Part 1:** 85

"Third Thing That Killed My Father Off, The" (Carver), **Supp. III Part 1:** 144

Third Violet, The (Crane), **I:** 408, 417–418

Thirlwall, John C., **Retro. Supp. I:** 430

"Thirst: Introduction to Kinds of Water" (Carson), **Supp. XII:** 103

"13, 1977, 21" (Lethem), **Supp. XVIII:** 148

13 by Shanley (Shanley), **Supp. XIV:** 316

13 Seconds: A Look Back at the Kent State Shootings (Caputo), **Supp. XIX:** 29

Thirteen Hands: A Play in Two Acts (Shields), **Supp. VII:** 322–323

Thirteen O'Clock (Benét), **Supp. XI:** 46

Thirteen Other Stories (Purdy), **Supp. VII:** 278

Thirteen Stories and Thirteen Epitaphs (Vollmann), **Supp. XVII:** 226

"Thirteenth and Pennsylvania" (Stafford), **Supp. XI:** 324

Thirteenth Month, The (Pedersen; Nelson, trans.), **Supp. XVIII:** 179–180

"Thirteen Ways of Looking at a Blackbird" (Stevens), **IV:** 94; **Supp. IX:** 47; **Supp. XVII:** 130

"Thirteen Ways of Looking at a Blackbird" (W. Stevens), **Supp. XX:**110

Thirteen Ways of Looking at a Black Man (H. L. Gates), **Supp. XX:**102, 110

30/6 (poetry chapbook), **Supp. V:** 5, 6

"30. Meditation. 2. Cor. 5.17. He Is a New Creature" (Taylor), **IV:** 144

30: Pieces of a Novel (Dixon), **Supp. XII:** 152, **153–154**

"Thirty Bob a Week" (Davidson), **Retro. Supp. I:** 55

"Thirty Delft Tiles" (Doty), **Supp. XI:** 131

"35/10" (Olds), **Supp. X:** 206

"35,000 Feet—The Lanterns" (Goldbarth), **Supp. XII:** 182

31 Letters and 13 Dreams (Hugo), **Supp. VI:** 141–144

Thirty Poems (Bryant), **Supp. I Part 1:** 157, 158

Thirty-Six Poems (Warren), **IV:** 236, 239, 240

"33" (Alvarez), **Supp. VII:** 4

"3275" (Monette), **Supp. X:** 148, 159

Thirty Years (Marquand), **III:** 56, 60–61

Thirty Years of Treason (Bentley), **Supp. I Part 1:** 297

This, My Letter (Hay), **Supp. XIV:** 121, 122, 129, 131

"This, That & the Other" (Nemerov), **III:** 269

This Body Is Made of Camphor and Gopherwood (R. Bly), **Supp. IV Part 1:** 63–65, 66, 71; **Supp. XXI:** 85

This Boy's Life: A Memoir (T. Wolff), **Supp. VII:** 334–339, 340, 343; **Supp. XI:** 246, 247

"This Bright Dream" (Benét), **Supp. XI:** 55

This Coffin Has No Handles (McGrath), **Supp. X:** 117

"This Configuration" (Ashbery), **Supp. III Part 1:** 22

"This Corruptible" (Wylie), **Supp. I Part 2:** 727, 729

"This Crutch That I Love" (Nye), **Supp. XIII:** 288

"This Gentile World" (H. Miller), **III:** 177

"This Hand" (Wylie), **Supp. I Part 2:** 713

"This Hour" (Olds), **Supp. X:** 212

"This House I Cannot Leave" (Kingsolver), **Supp. VII:** 208

This Hunger (Nin), **Supp. X:** 185

"This Is a Photograph of Me" (Atwood), **Supp. XIII:** 33

"This Is a Poem, Good Afternoon" (Keillor), **Supp. XVI:** 167

"This Is It" (Stern), **Supp. IX:** 290

"This Is Just to Say" (W. C. Williams), **Supp. XI:** 328

"This Is My Heart" (Harjo), **Supp. XII:** 230

This Is Not a Novel (Markson), **Supp. XVII:** 145–146

"This Is Not Who We Are" (Nye), **Supp. XIII:** 285, 286

"This Is Us, Excellent" (Richard), **Supp. XIX:** 212

"This Is What I Said" (Salinas), **Supp. XIII:** 322

This Journey (Wright), **Supp. III Part 2:** 605–606

"This Lime-Tree Bower My Prison" (Coleridge), **Supp. XXI:** 52, 55

This Man and This Woman (Farrell), **II:** 42

"This Monkey, My Back" (Boyle), **Supp. XX:**17

"This Morning" (Kenyon), **Supp. VII:** 164

"This Morning, This Evening, So Soon" (Baldwin), **Supp. I Part 1:** 63

"This Morning Again It Was in the Dusty Pines" (Oliver), **Supp. VII:** 240

This Music Crept by Me upon the Waters (MacLeish), **III:** 21

This People Israel: The Meaning of Jewish Existence (Baeck), **Supp. V:** 260

"This Personal Maze Is Not the Prize" (Selinger), **Supp. XI:** 248

"This Place in the Ways" (Rukeyser), **Supp. VI:** 273–274

This Property Is Condemned (T. Williams), **IV:** 378

This Proud Heart (Buck), **Supp. II Part 1:** 119–120

This Same Sky: A Collection of Poems from around the World (Nye, ed.), **Supp. XIII:** 280

"This Sandwich Has No Mayonnaise" (Salinger), **III:** 552–553

This Shape We're In (Lethem), **Supp. XVIII:** 145

"This Shape We're In" (Lethem), **Supp. XVIII:** 148

This Side of Paradise (Fitzgerald), **I:** 358; **II:** 77, 80, 81, 82–83, 84, 85–87, 88; **Retro. Supp. I:** 99–100, **101–102**, 103, 105, 106, 110, 111; **Supp. XVIII:** 248

This Singing World: An Anthology of Modern Poetry for Young People (Untermeyer, ed.), **Supp. XV:** 306

This Strange Joy: Selected Poems of Sandro Penna (Di Perio, trans.), **Supp. XIX:** 34

This Stubborn Self: Texas Autobiographies (Almon), **Supp. XIII:** 288

This Thing Don't Lead to Heaven (Crews), **Supp. XI:** 112

This Time: New and Selected Poems (Stern), **Supp. IX:** 290–291, **299**

"Thistle Seed in the Wind" (Francis), **Supp. IX:** 81

"Thistles in Sweden, The" (Maxwell), **Supp. VIII:** 169

"This Tokyo" (Snyder), **Supp. VIII:** 298

This Tree Will Be Here for a Thousand Years (revised edition) (R. Bly), **Supp. IV Part 1:** 66

This Tree Will Be Here for a Thousand Years (R. Bly), **Supp. IV Part 1:** 65–66, 71, 72

This Very Earth (Caldwell), **I:** 297, 302

This Wheel's on Fire: Levon Helm and the Story of the Band (Helm), **Supp. XVIII:** 26

This Woman (di Donato), **Supp. XX:**33, **41–42**, 46

Thoens, Karen, **Supp. V:** 147

Thomas, Brandon, **II:** 138

Thomas, Debra, **Supp. XIII:** 114

Thomas, D. M., **Supp. VIII:** 5

Thomas, Dylan, **I:** 49, 64, 382, 432, 526, 533; **III:** 21, 521, 528, 532, 534; **IV:** 89, 93, 136; **Supp. I Part 1:** 263; **Supp. III Part 1:** 42, 47; **Supp. V:** 344; **Supp. VIII:** 21; **Supp. IX:** 114; **Supp. X:** 115; **Supp. XV:** 74; **Supp. XVII:** 135; **Supp. XX:**199, 204

Thomas, Edna Lewis, **Supp. XVIII:** 281

Thomas, Edward, **II:** 154; **Retro. Supp. I:** 127, 131, 132; **Supp. I Part 1:** 263; **Supp. II Part 1:** 4

Thomas, James, **Supp. XVI:** 268

Thomas, Joseph, **Supp. XVIII:** 183

Thomas, J. Parnell, **Supp. I Part 1:** 286; **Supp. XV:** 198

Thomas, Lewis, **Retro. Supp. I:** 323

Thomas, Rob, **Supp. XVIII:** 100, 101

Thomas, R. S., **Supp. XXI:** 83, 86–87, 93, 95, 96

Thomas, William I., **Supp. I Part 2:** 641

Thomas-a-Kempis, **Retro. Supp. I:** 247

Thomas and Beulah (Dove), **Supp. IV Part 1:** 242, 247–248, 249; **Supp. XVIII:** 174; **Supp. XXI:** 249

Thomas Aquinas (Saint), **I:** 13, 14, 265, 267; **III:** 270; **Retro. Supp. II:** 222; **Supp. IV Part 2:** 526

"Thomas at the Wheel" (Dove), **Supp. IV Part 1:** 248
"Thomas McGrath: Words for a Vanished Age" (Vinz), **Supp. X:** 117
Thomas Merton on Peace, **Supp. VIII:** 208
Thomas Merton Studies Center, The, **Supp. VIII:** 208
Thompson, Barbara, **Supp. V:** 322
Thompson, Cy, **I:** 538
Thompson, Dorothy, **II:** 449–450, 451, 453; **Supp. XV:** 307
Thompson, Edward, **Supp. XXI:** 172
Thompson, E. P., **Supp. X:** 112, 117
Thompson, Francis, **Retro. Supp. I:** 55
Thompson, Frank, **II:** 20
Thompson, George, **Supp. I Part 2:** 686
Thompson, Hunter S., **Supp. VIII:** 42; **Supp. XI:** 105; **Supp. XIII:** 1, 17; **Supp. XVII:** 95, 102, 228
Thompson, James R., **Supp. IV Part 1:** 217
Thompson, John, **Supp. V:** 323; **Supp. XXI:** 151
Thompson, Juliet, **Supp. XX:**117
Thompson, Lawrance, **II:** 508
Thompson, Lawrance Roger, **Retro. Supp. I:** 138, 141
Thompson, Morton, **Supp. XIII:** 170
Thompson, Theresa, **Supp. V:** 141
Thompson, William T., **Supp. I Part 2:** 411
Thomson, James, **II:** 304; **Supp. I Part 1:** 150, 151
Thomson, Virgil, **IV:** 45; **Supp. IV Part 1:** 81, 83, 84, 173; **Supp. XVI:** 195
"Thoreau" (Lowell), **Supp. I Part 2:** 420, 422
Thoreau, Henry David, **I:** 98, 104, 228, 236, 257, 258, 261, 305, 433; **II:** 7, 8, 13, 17, 101, 159, 224, 273–274, 295, 312–313, 321, 457–458, 540, 546–547; **III:** 171, 174, 186–187, 189, 208, 214–215, 453, 454, 507, 577; **IV: 167–189,** 191, 341; **Retro. Supp. I:** 51, 62, 122; **Retro. Supp. II:** 13, 96, 142, 158; **Supp. I Part 1:** 29, 34, 116, 188, 299, 358; **Supp. I Part 2:** 383, 400, 420, 421, 507, 540, 579, 580, 655, 659, 660, 664, 678; **Supp. III Part 1:** 340, 353; **Supp. IV Part 1:** 236, 392, 416; **Supp. IV Part 2:** 420, 430, 433, 439, 447; **Supp. V:** 200, 208; **Supp. VIII:** 40, 42, 103, 105, 198, 201, 204, 205, 292, 303; **Supp. IX:** 25, 90, 171; **Supp. X:** 21, 27, 28–29, 101, 102; **Supp. XI:** 155; **Supp. XIII:** 1, 17; **Supp. XIV:** 40, 54, 106, 177, 181; **Supp. XVIII:** 4; **Supp. XX:**116, 221; **Supp. XXI:** 203, 217
Thoreau, John, **IV:** 171, 182
Thoreau, Mrs. John, **IV:** 172
"Thorn, The" (Gordon), **Supp. IV Part 1:** 314
Thorne, Francis, **Supp. XII:** 253
"Thorn Merchant, The" (Komunyakaa), **Supp. XIII:** 119–120
Thornton, Billy Bob, **Supp. VIII:** 175
Thornton, Lionel, **III:** 291
"Thorofare" (Minot), **Supp. VI: 209–210**

"Thorow" (Howe), **Supp. IV Part 2:** 419, 420, 421, 431, 433–434
Thorp, Willard, **Supp. XIII:** 101
Thorslev, Peter L., Jr., **I:** 524
Thorstein Veblen (Dowd), **Supp. I Part 2:** 650
Thorstein Veblen (Qualey, ed.), **Supp. I Part 2:** 650
Thorstein Veblen: A Chapter in American Economic Thought (Teggart), **Supp. I Part 2:** 650
Thorstein Veblen: A Critical Interpretation (Riesman), **Supp. I Part 2:** 649, 650
Thorstein Veblen: A Critical Reappraisal (Dowd, ed.), **Supp. I Part 2:** 650
Thorstein Veblen and His America (Dorfman), **Supp. I Part 2:** 631, 650
Thorstein Veblen and the Institutionalists: A Study in the Social Philosophy of Economics (Seckler), **Supp. I Part 2:** 650
"Those before Us" (Lowell), **II:** 550
"Those Being Eaten by America" (R. Bly), **Supp. IV Part 1:** 62
Those Bones Are Not My Child (Bambara), **Supp. XI:** 1, 14, **20–22**
Those Extraordinary Twins (Twain), **IV:** 205–206
"Those Graves in Rome" (Levis), **Supp. XI:** 266
"Those of Us Who Think We Know" (Dunn), **Supp. XI:** 146
Those That Be in Bondage (Webber), **Supp. XXI:** 160
"Those Times . . ." (Sexton), **Supp. II Part 2:** 670, 684
"Those Various Scalpels" (Moore), **III:** 202
"Those Were the Days" (Levine), **Supp. V:** 190
"Those Who Don't" (Cisneros), **Supp. VII:** 60
"Those Who Thunder" (Hogan), **Supp. IV Part 1:** 406
"Thought, A" (Sarton), **Supp. VIII:** 262
Thought and Character of William James (Perry), **II:** 362
Thoughtbook of Francis Scott Key Fitzgerald (Fitzgerald), **Retro. Supp. I:** 99
"Thought Experiment" (Saunders), **Supp. XIX:** 235
"Thoughtful Roisterer Declines the Gambit, The" (Hecht), **Supp. X:** 63
"Thought of Heaven, The" (Stern), **Supp. IX:** 297
"Thoughts after Lambeth" (Eliot), **I:** 587; **Retro. Supp. I:** 324
Thoughts and Reflections (Lord Halifax), **II:** 111
Thoughts in Solitude (Merton), **Supp. VIII:** 207
"Thoughts on Being Bibliographed" (Wilson), **IV:** 435
"Thoughts on the Establishment of a Mint in the United States" (Paine), **Supp. I Part 2:** 512
"Thoughts on the Gifts of Art" (Kenyon), **Supp. VII:** 167

Thousand Acres, A (Smiley), **Supp. VI:** 292, **301–303**
"Thousand and Second Night, The" (Merrill), **Supp. III Part 1:** 324
"Thousand Dollar Vagrant, The" (Olsen), **Supp. XIII:** 292, 297
"Thousand Faces of Danny Torrance, The" (Figliola), **Supp. V:** 143
"Thousand Genuflections, A" (McCarriston), **Supp. XIV:** 266
Thousand-Mile Walk to the Gulf, A (Muir), **Supp. IX: 177–178**
"Thou Shalt Not Steal" (McClatchy), **Supp. XII:** 264
"Thread, The" (Merwin), **Supp. III Part 1:** 351
Three (film), **Supp. IX:** 253
3-3-8 (Marquand), **III:** 58
"Three Academic Pieces" (Stevens), **IV:** 90
"Three Agee Wards, The" (Morris), **III:** 220–221
"Three American Singers" (Cather), **Retro. Supp. I:** 10
"Three Around the Old Gentleman" (Berryman), **I:** 188
"Three Avilas, The" (Jeffers), **Supp. II Part 2:** 418
"Three Black Women Writers" (C. L. R. James), **Supp. XXI:** 172
Three Books of Song (Longfellow), **II:** 490
"Three Bushes" (Yeats), **Supp. I Part 1:** 80
Three Cantos (Pound), **Retro. Supp. I:** 290
Three Centuries of Harvard (Morison), **Supp. I Part 2:** 485
Three Circles of Light (di Donato), **Supp. XX:**33, **42–43,** 44, 46
Three Comrades (Remarque), **Retro. Supp. I:** 113
"Three Corollaries of Cultural Relativism" (Locke), **Supp. XIV:** 202
"Three-Day Blow, The" (Hemingway), **II:** 248
Three Essays on America (Brooks), **I:** 246
Three Farmers on Their Way to a Dance (Powers), **Supp. IX:** 211–212, **213–214,** 222
"Three Fates, The" (Benét), **Supp. XI:** 48–49, 50
"Three Generations of Secrets" (A. Finch), **Supp. XVII:** 73
"Three Gifts, The" (Gibran), **Supp. XX:**124
Three Gospels (Price), **Supp. VI:** 267
"Three Kings, The: Hemingway, Faulkner, and Fitzgerald" (Ford), **Supp. V:** 59
Three Lives (Auchincloss), **Supp. IV Part 1:** 25
Three Lives (Stein), **I:** 103; **IV:** 26, 27, 31, 35, 37–41, 42, 45, 46; **Supp. IX:** 306
"THREE MOVEMENTS AND A CODA" (Baraka), **Supp. II Part 1:** 50

Three One Act Plays (Riverside Drive, Old Saybrook, and *Central Park West)* (Allen), **Supp. XV:** 3

Three on the Tower: The Lives and Works of Ezra Pound, T. S. Eliot, and William Carlos Williams (Simpson), **Supp. IX:** 276

Three Papers on Fiction (Welty), **IV:** 261

Three-Penny Opera (Brecht), **I:** 301; **Supp. XIV:** 162

"Three Percent Own All the Wealth" (Ryan as Quin), **Supp. XVIII:** 231–232

Three Philosophical Poets (Santayana), **III:** 610–612

"Three Pigs in Five Days" (Prose), **Supp. XVI:** 257, 258

"Three Players of a Summer Game" (T. Williams), **IV:** 383

Three Poems (Ashbery), **Supp. III Part 1:** 2, 3, 14, 15, 18, 24–26

"Three Poems for my Daughter" (Di Piero), **Supp. XIX:** 40

"Three Pokes of a Thistle" (Nye), **Supp. XIII:** 281

Three Roads, The (Macdonald, under Millar), **Supp. IV Part 2:** 466, 467

"Three Silences of Molinos, The" (Longfellow), **Retro. Supp. II:** 169

Three Sisters, The (Chekhov), **Supp. XV:** 323

"Three Sisters, The" (Cisneros), **Supp. VII:** 64

Three Soldiers (Dos Passos), **I:** 477–478, 480, 482, 488, 493–494; **Supp. XXI:** 277

"Three Songs at the End of Summer" (Kenyon), **Supp. VII:** 169–170

"Three Steps to the Graveyard" (Wright), **Supp. III Part 2:** 593, 596

Three Stories and Ten Poems (Hemingway), **II:** 68, 263; **Supp. XVII:** 105

Three Taverns, The (Robinson), **III:** 510

"Three Taverns, The" (Robinson), **III:** 521, 522

Three Tenant Families (Agee), **I:** 37–38

Three Tenors, One Vehicle: A Book of Songs (X. J. Kennedy, Camp, and Waldrop), **Supp. XV:** 165

"Three Types of Poetry" (Tate), **IV:** 131

"Three Vagabonds of Trinidad" (Harte), **Supp. II Part 1:** 338

"Three Waterfalls, The" (Lanier), **Supp. I Part 1:** 350

"Three-Way Mirror" (Brooks), **Supp. III Part 1:** 69–70

Three Weeks in Spring (Parker and Parker), **Supp. XIX:** 187

"Three Women" (Plath), **Supp. I Part 2:** 539, 541, 544, 545, 546

Three Young Poets (Swallow, ed.), **Supp. X:** 116

Threnody (Emerson), **Supp. I Part 2:** 416

"Threnody" (Emerson), **II:** 7

"Threnody for a Brown Girl" (Cullen), **Supp. IV Part 1:** 166

"Threshing-Floor, The" (Baldwin), **Supp. I Part 1:** 50

Threshold (film), **Supp. IX:** 254

"Threshold" (Goldbarth), **Supp. XII:** 175

Threshold (Jackson), **Supp. IX:** 117

"Throat" (Goldbarth), **Supp. XII:** 177–178

Throne of Labdacus, The (Schnackenberg), **Supp. XV:** 260, **263–266**

Thrones (Pound), **Retro. Supp. I:** 293

Through Dooms of Love (Kumin), **Supp. IV Part 2:** 444

"Through the Black Curtain" (Kingston), **Supp. V:** 169

Through the Forest: New and Selected Poems, 1977–1987 (Wagoner), **Supp. IX: 330–331**

"Through the Hills of Spain" (Salinas), **Supp. XIII:** 315

"Through the Hole in the Mundane Millstone" (West), **Retro. Supp. II:** 321, 322

Through the Ivory Gate (Dove), **Supp. IV Part 1:** 242, 243, 251, 252, 253–254, 254

"Through the Kitchen Window, Chiapas" (Nye), **Supp. XIII:** 277

Through the Safety Net (C. Baxter), **Supp. XVII:** 17, 22

"Through the Smoke Hole" (Snyder), **Supp. VIII:** 299

"Thrush Relinquished, The" (Grossman), **Supp. XIX:** 83

Thucydides, **II:** 418; **IV:** 50; **Supp. I Part 2:** 488, 489, 492; **Supp. IV Part 1:** 391; **Supp. XIII:** 233

Thunderbolt and Lightfoot (film), **Supp. X:** 126

"Thunderhead" (MacLeish), **III:** 19

Thurber, James, **I:** 487; **II:** 432; **IV:** 396; **Supp. I Part 2: 602–627,** 653, 654, 668, 672, 673, 679; **Supp. II Part 1:** 143; **Supp. IV Part 1:** 349; **Supp. IX:** 118; **Supp. XIV:** 104; **Supp. XVI:** 167; **Supp. XVII:** 4

Thurber, Mrs. James (Althea Adams), **Supp. I Part 2:** 613, 615, 617

Thurber, Mrs. James (Helen Muriel Wismer), **Supp. I Part 2:** 613, 617, 618

Thurber, Robert, **Supp. I Part 2:** 613, 617

Thurber, Rosemary, **Supp. I Part 2:** 616

Thurber, William, **Supp. I Part 2:** 602

Thurber Album, The (Thurber), **Supp. I Part 2:** 611, 619

Thurber Carnival, The (Thurber), **Supp. I Part 2:** 620; **Supp. XIV:** 104

Thurman, Judith, **Supp. IV Part 1:** 309

Thurman, Wallace, **Retro. Supp. I:** 200; **Supp. I Part 1:** 325, 326, 328, 332; **Supp. IV Part 1:** 164; **Supp. X:** 136, 139; **Supp. XVI:** 135; **Supp. XVIII:** 279, 281; **Supp. XIX:** 78

"Thursday" (Millay), **III:** 129

"Thurso's Landing" (Jeffers), **Supp. II Part 2:** 433

"Thus Do I Refute Gioia" (Junker), **Supp. XV:** 116

"Thus Far by Faith" (Nelson), **Supp. XVIII:** 177

Thus Spake Zarathustra (Nietzsche), **II:** 463; **Supp. IV Part 1:** 110; **Supp. IV Part 2:** 519

Thwaite, Lady Alicia. *See* Rawlings, Marjorie Kinnan

Thy Neighbor's Wife (Talese), **Supp. XVII:** 204, 205–206, 207, 208, 210

"Tiara" (Doty), **Supp. XI:** 122

"Tibetan Time" (Prose), **Supp. XVI:** 255

Ticket for a Seamstitch, A (Harris), **II:** 424–425

Tickets for a Prayer Wheel (Dillard), **Supp. VI:** 22, 34

Ticket That Exploded, The (Burroughs), **Supp. III Part 1:** 93, 103, 104

Tickless Time (Glaspell), **Supp. III Part 1:** 179

Ticknor, George, **II:** 488; **Supp. I Part 1:** 313

Ticknor, William, **Supp. XVIII:** 258

"Ti Démon" (Chopin), **Supp. I Part 1:** 225

Tide of Time, The (Masters), **Supp. I Part 2:** 471

"Tide of Voices" (Hull), **Supp. XXI:** 132, 133–134, 136

"Tide Rises, the Tide Falls, The" (Longfellow), **I:** 498

"Tides" (Hoffman), **Supp. XVIII:** 86

Tidewater Blood (Hoffman), **Supp. XVIII: 82–83**

Tidyman, Ernest, **Supp. V:** 226

Tietjens, Eunice, **Supp. XV:** 47, 297

"Tiger" (Blake), **Supp. I Part 1:** 80; **Supp. VIII:** 26

Tiger (Bynner), **Supp. XV:** 42, 50

"Tiger, The" (Buechner), **Supp. XII:** 48

Tiger in the House, The (Van Vechten), **Supp. II Part 2:** 736

Tiger Joy (Benét), **Supp. XI:** 45

Tiger-Lilies (Lanier), **Supp. I Part 1:** 350–351, 357, 360, 371

Tiger Who Wore White Gloves, The: or, What You Are, You Are (Brooks), **Supp. III Part 1:** 86

Till, Emmett, **Supp. I Part 1:** 61

Tillich, Paul, **II:** 244; **III:** 291, 292, 303, 309; **IV:** 226; **Retro. Supp. I:** 325, 326, 327; **Supp. V:** 267; **Supp. XIII:** 74, 91

Tillie Olsen: A Study of the Short Fiction (Frye), **Supp. XIII:** 292, 296, 298, 299, 302

Tillman, Lynne, **Supp. XII:** 4

Tillotson, John, **II:** 114

Tillotson, Kristen, **Supp. XVII:** 23

Tillstrom, Burr, **Supp. XIV:** 125

Till the Day I Die (Odets), **Supp. II Part 2:** 530, 533–536, 552

Tilton, Eleanor, **Supp. I Part 1:** 317

Tilton, Theodore, **Supp. XVIII:** 4

Timaeus (Plato), **II:** 10; **III:** 609

Tim: A Story of School Life (Sturgis), **Supp. XX:** 227, 230, 232, **233–235**

Timber (Jonson), **II:** 16

Timberg, Scott, **Supp. XV:** 116

"Timberwolf" (Halliday), **Supp. XIX:** 91

Timbuktu (Auster), **Supp. XII:** 34, **35–36**

"Time" (Matthews), **Supp. IX: 165–166**

"Time" (Merrill), **Supp. III Part 1:** 325

"Time and Again" (Sanders), **Supp. XVI:** 269

Time and a Place, A (Humphrey), **Supp. IX:** 95, 98, **100–102**

"Time and the Garden" (Winters), **Supp. II Part 2:** 801, 809

"Time and the Liturgy" (Merton), **Supp. VIII:** 199

Time and Tide: A Walk through Nantucket (Conroy), **Supp. XVI:** 63, 71, **76–77**

"Time Exposure" (C. Baxter), **Supp. XVII:** 20–21

Time Exposures, by Search-Light (W. Frank), **Supp. XX:**75

Time in the Rock (Aiken), **I:** 65

Time Is Noon, The (Buck), **Supp. II Part 1:** 129, 130–131

Time & Money (Matthews), **Supp. IX:** 155, **165–167**

"Time of Friendship, The" (Bowles), **Supp. IV Part 1:** 90–91

"Time of Her Time, The" (Mailer), **III:** 37, 45; **Retro. Supp. II:** 200

Time of Our Time, The (Mailer), **Retro. Supp. II:** 213–214

Time of the Assassins, The: A Study of Rimbaud (H. Miller), **III:** 189

Time Out of Mind (album, Dylan), **Supp. XVIII:** 28

"Time Past" (Morris), **III:** 232

"Time Present" (Morris), **III:** 232

"Times" (Beattie), **Supp. V:** 31

"Times, The" (Emerson), **II:** 11–12

Times Are Never So Bad, The (Dubus), **Supp. VII:** 87–88

Time's Arrow (Amis), **Retro. Supp. I:** 278

"Time Shall Not Die" (Chandler), **Supp. IV Part 1:** 120

Times of Melville and Whitman, The (Brooks), **I:** 257

Times They Are A-Changin', The (album, Dylan), **Supp. XVIII:** 20, 25

"Times They Are A-Changin,' The" (song, Dylan), **Supp. XVIII:** 30

"Timesweep" (Sandburg), **III:** 595–596

Time to Act, A (MacLeish), **III:** 3

Time to Be Born, A (Powell), **Supp. XIX:** 143

Time to Go (Dixon), **Supp. XII:** 147

Time to Kill (film), **Supp. IV Part 1:** 130

Time to Speak, A (MacLeish), **III:** 3

Time Will Darken It (Maxwell), **Supp. VIII:** 159, **162–164**, 169

"Timing of Sin, The" (Dubus), **Supp. VII:** 91

Tim O'Brien (Herzog), **Supp. V:** 239

Timoleon (Melville), **III:** 93; **Retro. Supp. I:** 257

Timothy Dexter Revisited (Marquand), **III:** 55, 62, 63

Timothy Findley: Stories from a Life (Roberts), **Supp. XX:**53

Timrod, Henry, **Supp. XVIII:** 31, 33

Tin Can, The (W. J. Smith), **Supp. XIII:** 334, **Supp. XIII:** 336, 337

"Tin Can, The" (W. J. Smith), **Supp. XIII: 337–339**

Tin Can Tree, The (Tyler), **Supp. IV Part 2:** 659–660

Tinguely, Jean, **Supp. XV:** 187

Tinker, Chauncey Brewster, **Supp. XIV:** 12

Tintern Abbey (Wordsworth), **Supp. I Part 2:** 673, 675

Tiny Alice (Albee), **I:** 81–86, 87, 88, 94

"Tiny Mummies! The True Story of the Ruler of 43rd Street's Land of the Walking Dead" (Wolfe), **Supp. III Part 2:** 573, 574

Tip on a Dead Jockey and Other Stories (Shaw), **Supp. XIX:** 251

"Tip-Top Club, The" (Keillor), **Supp. XVI:** 172

"Tired" (Hughes), **Supp. I Part 1:** 331

"Tired and Unhappy, You Think of Houses" (Schwartz), **Supp. II Part 2:** 649

"Tiresias" (Garrett), **Supp. VII:** 96–97

'Tis (McCourt), **Supp. XII:** 271, **279–286**

Tisch (Dixon), **Supp. XII:** 141, **155–156**

Titan, The (Dreiser), **I:** 497, 501, 507–508, 509, 510; **Retro. Supp. II:** 94, 101, 102

Titian, **Supp. I Part 2:** 397, 714

"Tito's Goodbye" (García), **Supp. XI:** 190

To a Blossoming Pear Tree (Wright), **Supp. III Part 2:** 602–605

"To a Blossoming Pear Tree" (Wright), **Supp. III Part 2:** 604

"To Abolish Children" (Shapiro), **Supp. II Part 2:** 717

To Abolish Children and Other Essays (Shapiro), **Supp. II Part 2:** 703

"To a Caty-Did, the Precursor of Winter" (Freneau), **Supp. II Part 1:** 274–275

"To a Chameleon" (Moore), **III:** 195, 196, 215

"To a Conscript of 1940" (Read), **II:** 372–373, 377–378

"To a Contemporary Bunk Shooter" (Sandburg), **III:** 582

"To a Cough in the Street at Midnight" (Wylie), **Supp. I Part 2:** 727, 729–730

"To a Defeated Savior" (Wright), **Supp. III Part 2:** 593–594, 596

"To a Face in the Crowd" (Warren), **IV:** 239

"To a Fish Head Found on the Beach near Malaga" (Levine), **Supp. V:** 185

"To a Friend" (Nemerov), **III:** 272

"To a Friend Whose Work Has Come to Triumph" (Sexton), **Supp. II Part 2:** 683

To a God Unknown (Steinbeck), **I:** 107; **IV:** 51, 59–60, 67

"To a Greek Marble" (Aldington), **Supp. I Part 1:** 257

"To a Locomotive in Winter" (Whitman), **IV:** 348

"To a Military Rifle" (Winters), **Supp. II Part 2:** 810, 811, 815

"To a Mouse" (Burns), **Supp. IX:** 173

"To an Athlete Dying Young" (Houseman), **Supp. XVII:** 121

"To a Negro Jazz Band in a Parisian Cabaret" (Hughes), **Supp. I Part 1:** 325

"To an Old Philosopher in Rome" (Stevens), **III:** 605; **Retro. Supp. I:** 312

"To an Old Poet in Peru" (Ginsberg), **Supp. II Part 1:** 322

"To a Now-Type Poet" (X. J. Kennedy), **Supp. XV:** 161

"To Answer Your Question" (Jarman), **Supp. XVII:** 114–115

"To Any Would-Be Terrorists" (Nye), **Supp. XIII:** 285, 286

"To a Poet" (Rich), **Supp. I Part 2:** 571; **Supp. XIX:** 83

"To a Prize Bird" (Moore), **III:** 215

"To a Republican, with Mr. Paine's Rights of Man" (Freneau), **Supp. II Part 1:** 267

"To a Shade" (Yeats), **III:** 18

"To a Skylark" (Shelley), **Supp. I Part 2:** 720; **Supp. X:** 31

"Toast to Harlem, A" (Hughes), **Supp. I Part 1:** 338

"To Aunt Rose" (Ginsberg), **Supp. II Part 1:** 320

"To Autumn" (Keats), **Supp. IX:** 50

"To a Waterfowl" (Bryant), **Supp. I Part 1:** 154, 155, 162, 171

"To a Young Poet" (X. J. Kennedy), **Supp. XV:** 161

"To a Young Writer" (Stegner), **Supp. X:** 24

Tobacco Road (Caldwell), **I:** 288, 289, 290, 295–296, 297, 298, 302, 307, 309, 310; **IV:** 198

"To Be a Monstrous Clever Fellow" (Fante), **Supp. XI:** 167

"To Become Music or Break" (Jauss), **Supp. XXI:** 133

To Bedlam and Part Way Back (Sexton), **Retro. Supp. II:** 245; **Supp. II Part 2:** 672–678; **Supp. IV Part 2:** 441; **Supp. XI:** 317

"To Beethoven" (Lanier), **Supp. I Part 1:** 364

To Begin Again: Stories and Memoirs, 1908–1929 (M. F. K. Fisher), **Supp. XVII:** 92

Tobey, Mark, **Supp. X:** 264

To Be Young, Gifted, and Black: Lorraine Hansberry in Her Own Words (Nemiroff), **Supp. IV Part 1:** 372, 374

"To Big Mary from an Ex-Catholic" (Mora), **Supp. XIII:** 217, 224, 228

"Tobin's Palm" (O. Henry), **Supp. II Part 1:** 408; **Supp. XV:** 40

Tobit (apocryphal book), **I:** 89

"To Build a Fire" (London), **II:** 468

Toby Tyler: or, Ten Weeks with a Circus (Otis), **III:** 577

"To Change in a Good Way" (Ortiz), **Supp. IV Part 2:** 511

"To Charlotte Cushman" (Lanier), **Supp. I Part 1:** 364

"To Cole, the Painter, Departing for Europe" (Bryant), **Supp. I Part 1:** 157, 161

Tocqueville, Alexis de, **III**: 261; **IV**: 349; **Retro. Supp. I**: 235; **Supp. I Part 1**: 137; **Supp. I Part 2**: 659, 660; **Supp. II Part 1**: 281, 282, 284; **Supp. XIV**: 306, 312

"To Crispin O'Conner" (Freneau), **Supp. II Part 1**: 268

"To Da-Duh, In Memoriam" (Marshall), **Supp. XI**: 276

"TODAY" (Baraka), **Supp. II Part 1**: 55

"Today" (Ginsberg), **Supp. II Part 1**: 328

"Today Is a Good Day To Die" (Bell), **Supp. X**: 7

"Today Will Be a Quiet Day" (Hempel), **Supp. XXI**: 117, **Supp. XXI**: 118

Todd, Mabel Loomis, **I**: 454, 470; **Retro. Supp. I**: 33, 34, 35, 39, 47

"To Death" (Levertov), **Supp. III Part 1**: 274

"To Delmore Schwartz" (Lowell), **II**: 547; **Retro. Supp. II**: 188

"to disembark" (Brooks), **Supp. III Part 1**: 86

"To Dorothy on Her Exclusion from The Guinness Book of Records" (X. J. Kennedy), **Supp. XV**: 166

"To Dr. Thomas Shearer" (Lanier), **Supp. I Part 1**: 370

"To Earthward" (Frost), **II**: 154

"To Edwin V. McKenzie" (Winters), **Supp. II Part 2**: 801

"To Eleonora Duse" (Lowell), **II**: 528

"To Elizabeth Ward Perkins" (Lowell), **II**: 516

"To Elsie" (W. C. Williams), **Retro. Supp. I**: 419

"To Emily Dickinson" (H. Crane), **Retro. Supp. II**: 76

"To E. T." (Frost), **Retro. Supp. I**: 132

To Feel These Things (L. Michaels), **Supp. XVI**: 205, **213–214**

"To Feel These Things" (L. Michaels), **Supp. XVI**: 214

Toffler, Alvin, **Supp. IV Part 2**: 517

"To Fill" (Moore), **Supp. X**: 168, 169

"To Gabriela, a Young Writer" (Mora), **Supp. XIII**: 220

To Have and Have Not (film), **Supp. XV**: 347

To Have and Have Not (Hemingway), **I**: 31; **II**: 253–254, 264; **Retro. Supp. I**: 182, **183**, 187

"To Helen" (Poe), **III**: 410, 411, 427; **Retro. Supp. II**: 102

"To Hell With Dying" (Walker), **Supp. III Part 2**: 523

"To His Excellency General Washington" (Wheatley), **Supp. XX**:289

"To His Father" (Jeffers), **Supp. II Part 2**: 415

Toilet, The (Baraka), **Supp. II Part 1**: 37, 40–42

"To James Russell Lowell" (Holmes), **Supp. I Part 1**: 311

To Jerusalem and Back (Bellow), **Retro. Supp. II**: 29

"To Jesus on His Birthday" (Millay), **III**: 136–137

"To John Keats" (Lowell), **II**: 516

"To Judge Faolain, Dead Long Enough: A Summons" (McCarriston), **Supp. XIV**: 264–265

"To Justify My Singing" (Wright), **Supp. III Part 2**: 590

"To Kill a Deer" (C. Frost), **Supp. XV**: 102

To Kill a Mockingbird (film), **Supp. VIII**: 128–129

To Kill a Mockingbird (Lee), **Supp. VIII**: **113–129**; **Supp. XVI**: 259; **Supp. XIX**: 142

"To Kill a Mockingbird: Harper Lee's Tragic Vision" (Dave), **Supp. VIII**: 126

To Kill a Mockingbird: Threatening Boundaries (Johnson), **Supp. VIII**: 126

Toklas, Alice B., **IV**: 27; **Supp. IV Part 1**: 81, 91; **Supp. XVI**: 187

"Tokyo Story" (Wasserstein), **Supp. XV**: 328

"To Light" (Hogan), **Supp. IV Part 1**: 402

"To Live and Diet" (Wasserstein), **Supp. XV**: 328

Tolkien, J. R. R., **Supp. V**: 140

Tolkin, Michael, **Supp. XI**: 160

Toller, Ernst, **I**: 479

"To Lose the Earth" (Sexton), **Supp. II Part 2**: 684, 685

Tolson, Melvin, **Retro. Supp. I**: 208, 209, 210

Tolstoy, Leo, **I**: 6, 7, 58, 103, 312, 376; **II**: 191–192, 205, 271, 272, 275, 276, 281, 285, 286, 320, 407, 542, 559, 570, 579, 606; **III**: 37, 45, 61, 323, 467, 572; **IV**: 17, 21, 170, 285; **Retro. Supp. I**: 91, 225; **Retro. Supp. II**: 299; **Supp. I Part 1**: 2, 3, 6, 20; **Supp. IV Part 1**: 392; **Supp. V**: 277, 323; **Supp. IX**: 246; **Supp. XI**: 68; **Supp. XII**: 310, 322; **Supp. XIV**: 87, 97, 98; **Supp. XIX**: 241

"To Lu Chi" (Nemerov), **III**: 275

Tom (Cummings), **I**: 430

"Tom" (Oliver), **Supp. VII**: 232

"Tom, Tom, the Piper's Son" (Ransom), **Supp. X**: 58

"To M, with a Rose" (Lanier), **Supp. I Part 1**: 364

To Make a Prairie (Kumin), **Supp. IV Part 2**: 440, 441

"To Make Words Disappear" (Simpson), **Supp. IX**: 265–266

Tomás and the Library Lady (Mora), **Supp. XIII**: 216, 221

"Tomatoes" (Francis), **Supp. IX**: 82

"Tom Ball's Barn" (Kooser), **Supp. XIX**: 119

"Tom Brown at Fisk" (Du Bois), **Supp. II Part 1**: 160

Tom Brown's School Days (Hughes), **Supp. I Part 2**: 406

"Tomb Stone" (Dickey), **Supp. IV Part 1**: 185

"Tombstone Blues" (song, Dylan), **Supp. XVIII**: 30

Tomcat in Love (O'Brien), **Supp. V**: 238, 240, 243, 252–254

"Tomcat's Wife, The" (C. Bly), **Supp. XVI**: 40

Tomcat's Wife and Other Stories, The (C. Bly), **Supp. XVI**: 40–41

"Tom Fool at Jamaica" (Moore), **III**: 215

To Mix with Time (Swenson), **Supp. IV Part 2**: 637, 643–645, 645

Tom Jones (Fielding), **I**: 131; **Supp. V**: 127

Tomlinson, Charles, **Supp. XVI**: 284

Tommy Gallagher's Crusade (Farrell), **II**: 44

Tommyknockers, The (King), **Supp. V**: 139, 144

"Tommy's Burglar" (Henry), **Supp. II Part 1**: 399, 401

"Tommy Stames" (Budbill), **Supp. XIX**: 8

Tomo Cheeki (pseudonym). *See* Freneau, Philip

Tomorrow is Another Day (film, Feist), **Supp. XVII**: 62

"Tomorrow the Moon" (Dos Passos), **I**: 493

"Tom Outland's Story" (Cather), **I**: 325–326

Tompkins, Jane, **Supp. XVI**: 89; **Supp. XVIII**: 258, 259, 263

Tompson, Benjamin, **Supp. I Part 1**: 110, 111

"Tom-Rock Through Eels" (Hempel), **Supp. XXI**: 116, 118, **123–124**

Tom Sawyer (musical) (Gurney), **Supp. V**: 96

Tom Sawyer (Twain). *See Adventures of Tom Sawyer, The* (Twain)

Tom Sawyer Abroad (Twain), **II**: 482; **IV**: 19, 204

Tom Sawyer Detective (Twain), **IV**: 204

"Tom's Husband" (Jewett), **Retro. Supp. II**: 132, 141

Tom Swift (Stratemeyer), **III**: 146

"Tom Wolfe's Guide to Etiquette" (Wolfe), **Supp. III Part 2**: 578

"To My Brother Killed: Haumont Wood: October, 1918" (Bogan), **Supp. III Part 1**: 58

"To My Class, on Certain Fruits and Flowers Sent Me in Sickness" (Lanier), **Supp. I Part 1**: 370

"To My Father's Ghost" (Everwine), **Supp. XV**: 76

"To My Ghost Reflected in the Auxvasse River" (Levis), **Supp. XI**: 265

"To My Greek" (Merrill), **Supp. III Part 1**: 326

"To My Mother" (Berry), **Supp. X**: 23

"To My Small Son, at the Photographer's" (Hay), **Supp. XIV**: 121

"To My Small Son, on Certain Occasions" (Hay), **Supp. XIV**: 121

"To Name is to Possess" (Kincaid), **Supp. VII**: 194

Tone, Aileen, **I**: 21–22

"Tongue Is, The" (Komunyakaa), **Supp. XIII**: 113

"Tongue of the Jews" (Bukiet), **Supp. XVII**: 47

Tongues (Shepard and Chaikin), **Supp. III Part 2**: 433

Tongues of Angels, The (Price), **Supp. VI:** 265

Tongues Untied (Riggs; film), **Supp. XI:** 19, 20

"Tonight" (Lowell), **II:** 538

Tonight Is the Night of the Prom (Jarman), **Supp. XVII:** 110, **112–113**

"Tonight Is the Night of the Prom" (Jarman), **Supp. XVII:** 113

Tony Kushner in Conversation (Vorlicky, ed.), **Supp. IX:** 132

"Too Anxious for Rivers" (Frost), **II:** 162

"Too Blue" (Hughes), **Retro. Supp. I:** 207

"Too Damn Close: Thresholds and Their Maintenance in Rick Bass's Work" (Kerridge), **Supp. XVI:** 26

"Too Early" (Leopold), **Supp. XIV:** 186

"Too Early Spring" (Benét), **Supp. XI:** 53

"Too Far from Home" (Bowles), **Supp. IV Part 1:** 94–95

Too Far from Home: Selected Writings of Paul Bowles (Halpern, ed.), **Supp. IV Part 1:** 94, 95

Too Far to Go: The Maples Stories (Updike), **Retro. Supp. I:** 321

"Too Good To Be True": The Life and Art of Leslie Fiedler (Winchell), **Supp. XIII:** 94, 98, 99, 101

Toohey, John Peter, **Supp. IX:** 190

Toolan, David, **Supp. IV Part 1:** 308

Too Late (Dixon), **Supp. XII: 143–144**

"Too Late" (Pickering), **Supp. XXI:** 197

"Too-Late Born, The" (Hemingway), **III:** 9

Toole, John Kennedy, **Supp. XIV:** 21

"Toolless" (Pickering), **Supp. XXI:** 204

Toomer, Jean, **Retro. Supp. II:** 79; **Supp. I Part 1:** 325, 332; **Supp. III Part 2:** 475–491; **Supp. IV Part 1:** 16, 164, 168; **Supp. IX: 305–322; Supp. XIII:** 305; **Supp. XVIII:** 122; **Supp. XX:** 73

Toomer, Nathan Eugene Pinchback. *See* Toomer, Jean

Too Much Johnson (film), **Supp. IV Part 1:** 83

"To One Who Said Me Nay" (Cullen), **Supp. IV Part 1:** 166

"Tooth, The" (Jackson), **Supp. IX:** 122

Tooth and Claw (Boyle), **Supp. XX:** 20

Tooth of Crime, The (Shepard), **Supp. III Part 2:** 432, 441–445, 447

"Too Young" (O'Hara), **III:** 369

Topaz (film), **Supp. XX:** 253

Topaz (Uris), **Supp. XX:** 247, 248, **253**

"Top Israeli Official Hints at 'Shared' Jerusalem" (Nye), **Supp. XIII:** 287

"To P. L., 1916–1937" (Levine), **Supp. V:** 185

"To Please a Shadow" (Brodsky), **Supp. VIII:** 30

"Top of the Food Chain" (Boyle), **Supp. XX:** 20

"Top of the Hill" (Jewett), **II:** 406

"Topography" (Olds), **Supp. X:** 208

Topper (T. Smith), **Supp. IX:** 194

To Praise the Music (Bronk), **Supp. XXI:** 31, 32

Torah, **IV:** 19

"Torch Songs" (Wrigley), **Supp. XVIII:** 296

Torpedo 8: The Story of Swede Larsen's Bomber Squadron (Wolfert), **Supp. XXI:** 267

"Torquemada" (Bukiet), **Supp. XVII:** 44

"Torquemada" (Longfellow), **II:** 505; **Retro. Supp. II:** 164

Torrence, Ridgely, **III:** 507

Torrent and the Night Before, The (Robinson), **III:** 504

Torrents of Spring, The (Hemingway), **I:** 117; **II:** 250–251

Torres, Héctor A., **Supp. XIII:** 225

Torres, Louis, **Supp. IV Part 2:** 529, 530

Torres-Saillant, Silvio, **Supp. XXI:** 104, 105, 108, 109

Torsney, Cheryl, **Retro. Supp. I:** 224

Tortilla Curtain, The (Boyle), **Supp. VIII: 9–10; Supp. XX:28–29**

Tortilla Flat (Steinbeck), **IV:** 50, 51, 61, 64

Tortilla Flats (Steinbeck), **Supp. XX:** 28

Tory Lover, The (Jewett), **II:** 406; **Retro. Supp. II:** 144–145

"Toscana" (Dixon), **Supp. XII:** 154

"To Sir Toby" (Freneau), **Supp. II Part 1:** 269

"To Sophy, Expectant" (Mumford), **Supp. II Part 2:** 475

"To Speak of Woe That Is in Marriage" (Lowell), **II:** 550

"To Statecraft Embalmed" (Moore), **III:** 197

To Stay Alive (Levertov), **Supp. III Part 1:** 280–282

"Total Eclipse" (Dillard), **Supp. VI:** 28

Toth, Emily, **Retro. Supp. II:** 71

Toth, Susan Allan, **Retro. Supp. II:** 138

"To the Americans of the United States" (Freneau), **Supp. II Part 1:** 271

"To the Apennines" (Bryant), **Supp. I Part 1:** 157, 164

"To the Bleeding Hearts Association of American Novelists" (Nemerov), **III:** 281

"To the Botequim & Back" (Bishop), **Retro. Supp. II:** 51

To the Bright and Shining Sun (Burke), **Supp. XIV:** 22, 25

"To the Citizens of the United States" (Paine), **Supp. I Part 2:** 519–520

"To the Dandelion" (Lowell), **Supp. I Part 2:** 424

"To the End" (Haines), **Supp. XII:** 212–213

To the Ends of the Earth: The Selected Travels of Paul Theroux, **Supp. VIII:** 324

To the Finland Station: A Study in the Writing and Acting of History (Wilson), **IV:** 429, 436, 443–444, 446

"To the Governor & Legislature of Massachusetts" (Nemerov), **III:** 287

To the Green Man (Jarman), **Supp. XVII:** 110, 120–121

To the Holy Spirit (Winters), **Supp. II Part 2:** 810

"To the Keeper of the King's Water Works" (Freneau), **Supp. II Part 1:** 269

"To the Lacedemonians" (Tate), **IV:** 134

"To the Laodiceans" (Jarrell), **Retro. Supp. I:** 121, 140

To the Lighthouse (Woolf), **I:** 309; **II:** 600; **Retro. Supp. II:** 337; **Supp. VIII:** 155

"To the Man on Trail" (London), **II:** 466

"To the Memory of the Brave Americans Under General Greene" (Freneau), **Supp. II Part 1:** 262, 274

"To the Muse" (Wright), **Supp. III Part 2:** 601

"To the Nazi Leaders" (Hay), **Supp. XIV:** 121

"To the New World" (Jarrell), **II:** 371

"To the One of Fictive Music" (Stevens), **IV:** 89; **Retro. Supp. I:** 297, 300

"To the One Upstairs" (Simic), **Supp. VIII:** 283

"To the Peoples of the World" (Du Bois), **Supp. II Part 1:** 172

To the Place of Trumpets (B. Kelly), **Supp. XVII:** 123–127; 132

"To the Pliocene Skull" (Harte), **Supp. II Part 1:** 343–344

"To the Reader" (Baudelaire), **II:** 544–545

"To The Reader" (Jarman), **Supp. XVII:** 115

"To the Reader" (Levertov), **Supp. III Part 1:** 277

"To the Right Honourable William, Earl of Dartmouth" (Wheatley), **Supp. XX:** 278, 284, 287–288

"To the River Arve" (Bryant), **Supp. I Part 1:** 163

"To the Snake" (Levertov), **Supp. III Part 1:** 277

"To the Stone-Cutters" (Jeffers), **Supp. II Part 2:** 420

"To the Unseeable Animal" (Berry), **Supp. X:** 31

"To the Western World" (Simpson), **Supp. IX:** 269, 270

To the White Sea (Dickey), **Supp. IV Part 1:** 186, 190–191

"To the Young Who Want to Die" (Brooks), **Supp. III Part 1:** 85–86

"To Tlaoc of the Rain" (Everwine), **Supp. XV:** 77

"To Train a Writer" (Bierce), **I:** 199

"Touch, The" (Sexton), **Supp. II Part 2:** 687

Touch and Go (M. F. K. Fisher and D. Parrish), **Supp. XVII:** 84

"Touching the Tree" (Merwin), **Supp. III Part 1:** 355

Touching the World (Eakin), **Supp. VIII:** 167

Touch of Danger, A (Jones), **Supp. XI:** 226, **228–229**

Touch of the Poet, A (O'Neill), **III:** 385, 401, 404

Touchstone, The (Wharton), **Retro. Supp. I:** 365

"Touch-up Man" (Komunyakaa), **Supp. XIII:** 119

Tough Guys Don't Dance (Mailer), **Retro. Supp. II:** 211

"Tough People" (Offutt), **Supp. XIX:** 170–171

Toulet, Paul Jean, **IV:** 79

Tour (McNally), **Supp. XIII:** 197

"Tour 5" (Hayden), **Supp. II Part 1:** 381

To Urania (Brodsky), **Supp. VIII:** 22, 28–29

Tourgée, Albion W., **Supp. XIV:** 63

"Tour Guide" (Komunyakaa), **Supp. XIII:** 114

"Tourist Death" (MacLeish), **III:** 12

Tourmaline (J. Scott), **Supp. XVII:** 192–194, 195

Tour of Duty (Dos Passos), **I:** 489

Touron the Prairies, A (Irving), **II:** 312–313

Toussaint L'Ouverture, **Supp. XXI:** 166

Toussaint L'Ouverture (C. L. R. James), **Supp. XXI:** 167

Tovey, Donald Francis, **Supp. XIV:** 336

To Walk a Crooked Mile (McGrath), **Supp. X:** 117

Toward a New Synthesis (Begiebing), **Retro. Supp. II:** 210

"Toward Nightfall" (Simic), **Supp. VIII:** 277

Towards a Better Life (Burke), **I:** 270

"Towards a Chicano Poetics: The Making of the Chicano Subject, 1969–1982" (Saldívar), **Supp. IV Part 2:** 544

Towards an Enduring Peace (Bourne), **I:** 232

"Towards Morning" (Pedersen; Nelson, trans.), **Supp. XVIII:** 180

Toward the Blanched Alphabets (Sobin), **Supp. XVI:** 290

Toward the Gulf (Masters), **Supp. I Part 2:** 465–466

"Toward the Solstice" (Rich), **Supp. I Part 2:** 575–576

Toward Wholeness in Paule Marshall's Fiction (Pettis), **Supp. XI:** 276

"Tower" (Merwin), **Supp. III Part 1:** 343

"Tower Beyond Tragedy, The" (Jeffers), **Supp. II Part 2:** 429–430

Tower of Ivory (MacLeish), **III:** 3–4

Towers, Robert, **Supp. IX:** 259; **Supp. XVI:** 211

"To What Red Hell" (C. Himes), **Supp. XVI:** 137

"To Whistler, American" (Pound), **III:** 465–466

"To Wine" (Bogan), **Supp. III Part 1:** 57, 58

Town, Caren J., **Supp. XVIII:** 195, 199

Town, The (Faulkner), **II:** 57, 73; **Retro. Supp. I:** 74, 82

Town, The (Richter), **Supp. XVIII:** 207, 214–215, 217

Town and the City, The (Kerouac), **Supp. III Part 1:** 222–224; **Supp. XIV:** 143

"Town Crier" (Bierce), **I:** 193, 194, 195, 196

"*Town Crier* Exclusive, Confessions of a Princess Manqué: 'How Royals Found Me "Unsuitable" to Marry Their Larry' " (Elkin), **Supp. VI:** 56

Town Down the River, The (Robinson), **III:** 508

"Town Dump, The" (Nemerov), **III:** 272, 275, 281

Towne, Robert, **Supp. XI:** 159, 172, 174

"Townhouse Interior with Cat" (Clampitt), **Supp. IX:** 40

"Townies" (Dubus), **Supp. VII:** 86

Town in the Forest, The: Life Story of Richmond, New Hampshire (Boyce; Faust, ed.), **Supp. XXI:** 8

"Town of the Sound of a Twig Breaking" (Carson), **Supp. XII:** 102

"Town Poor, The" (Jewett), **Retro. Supp. II:** 138, 139, 143

Townsend, Alison, **Supp. XIII:** 222

Townsend, Ann, **Supp. V:** 77

"Towns in Colour" (Lowell), **II:** 523–524

Townsman, The (Sedges), **Supp. II Part 1:** 124–125

"To World War Two" (Koch), **Supp. XV:** 184

Toys in a Field (Komunyakaa), **Supp. XIII: 121–122**

"Toys in a Field" (Komunyakaa), **Supp. XIII:** 122

Toys in the Attic (Hellman), **Supp. I Part 1:** 289–290

Tracer (F. Barthelme), **Supp. XI:** 31–32, 33

Traces of Thomas Hariot, The (Rukeyser), **Supp. VI:** 273, 274, 283

"Tracing Life with a Finger" (Caldwell), **I:** 291

Tracker (Wagoner), **Supp. IX:** 329, 336–337

"Tracking" (Wagoner), **Supp. IX:** 329

"Track Meet, The" (Schwartz), **Supp. II Part 2:** 665

Tracks (Erdrich), **Supp. IV Part 1:** 259, 262–263, 269, 272, 273–274, 274, 275

"Tract" (W. C. Williams), **Retro. Supp. I:** 414

"Tract against Communism, A" (Twelve Southerners), **IV:** 125, 237

Tractatus (Wittgenstein), **Supp. XVII:** 143

Tracy, Benjamin, **Supp. XVIII:** 4

Tracy, D. H., **Supp. XVIII:** 178

Tracy, Lee, **IV:** 287, 288

Tracy, Steven, **Retro. Supp. I:** 195

"Trade, The" (Levine), **Supp. V:** 193

Trading Twelves (Callahan and Murray, eds.), **Retro. Supp. II:** 119

Trading Twelves: The Selected Letters of Ralph Ellison and Albert Murray (Murray and Callahan, eds.), **Supp. XIX:** 148, 158

" 'Traditional' Marriage: A Secular Affair" (P. N. Warren), **Supp. XX:**273

"Tradition and Industrialization" (Wright), **IV:** 489–490

"Tradition and Mythology: Signatures of Landscape in Chicana Poetry" (Rebolledo), **Supp. XIII:** 214

"Tradition and the Individual Talent" (Eliot), **I:** 441, 574, 585; **Retro. Supp. I:** 59, 286

Tragedies, Life and Letters of James Gates Percival (Swinburne), **Supp. I Part 2:** 422

Tragedy of Bees, A (P. N. Warren), **Supp. XX:**261

"Tragedy of Bees, A" (P. N. Warren), **Supp. XX:**272

Tragedy of Don Ippolito, The (Howells), **II:** 279

"Tragedy of Error, A" (James), **II:** 322; **Retro. Supp. I:** 218

Tragedy of Pudd'nhead Wilson, The (Twain), **IV:** 206–207

Tragic America (Dreiser), **Retro. Supp. II:** 95

"Tragic Dialogue" (Wylie), **Supp. I Part 2:** 724

Tragic Ground (Caldwell), **I:** 297, 306

Tragic Muse, The (James), **Retro. Supp. I:** 227

Traherne, Thomas, **IV:** 151; **Supp. III Part 1:** 14; **Supp. V:** 208; **Supp. XV:** 212; **Supp. XVI:** 282, 288, 295

"Trail, The" (W. J. Smith), **Supp. XIII:** 342

Trailerpark (Banks), **Supp. V:** 12

"Trailing Arbutus, The" (Whittier), **Supp. I Part 2:** 691

Trail of the Lonesome Pine, The (Fox), **Supp. XIII:** 166

"Train, The" (O'Connor), **Retro. Supp. II:** 225

"Train Rising Out of the Sea" (Ashbery), **Supp. III Part 1:** 22

"Trains" (Banks), **Supp. V:** 8

"Train Tune" (Bogan), **Supp. III Part 1:** 64

Train Whistle Guitar (Murray), **Supp. XIX: 153–155,** 157

"Traits of Indian Character" (Irving), **II:** 303

Trakl, Georg, **Supp. XVII:** 241

Tramp Abroad, A (Twain), **IV:** 200

Tramping With a Poet in the Rockies (S. Graham), **Supp. I Part 2:** 397

Tramp's Excuse, The (Lindsay), **Supp. I Part 2:** 379, 380, 382

"Transatlantic" (Toomer), **Supp. III Part 2:** 486

Transatlantic Sketches (James), **II:** 324; **Retro. Supp. I:** 219

"Transcendental Etude" (Rich), **Supp. I Part 2:** 576

"Transcontinental Highway" (Cowley), **Supp. II Part 1:** 141

"Transducer" (Ammons), **Supp. VII:** 28

"Transfiguration" (Jarman), **Supp. XVII:** 118, 119

"Transfigured Bird" (Merrill), **Supp. III Part 1:** 320–321

"Transformations" (Harjo), **Supp. XII:** 226

Transformations (Sexton), **Supp. II Part 2:** 689–691; **Supp. IV Part 2:** 447; **Supp. XIV:** 125

Transforming Madness: New Lives for People Living with Mental Illness (Neugeboren), **Supp. XVI:** 229

"Transit" (Conroy), **Supp. XVI:** 72

Transit to Narcissus, A (Mailer), **Retro. Supp. II:** 196

"Translation" (Espaillat), **Supp. XXI:** 107

"Translation and Transposition" (Carne-Ross), **Supp. I Part 1:** 268–269

"Translation of a Fragment of Simonides" (Bryant), **Supp. I Part 1:** 153, 155

"Translations" (Rich), **Supp. I Part 2:** 563

Translations of Ezra Pound, The (Kenner, ed.), **III:** 463

Translations of the Gospel Back into Tongues (Wright), **Supp. XV:** 342–343, 346

"Trans-National America" (Bourne), **I:** 229, 230

"Transparency" (X. J. Kennedy), **Supp. XV:** 159–160

"Transparent Itineraries: 1983" (Sobin), **Supp. XVI:** 287

"Transparent Itineraries: 1984" (Sobin), **Supp. XVI:** 287

"Transparent Itineraries: 1992" (Sobin), **Supp. XVI:** 289

"Transparent Itineraries" poems (Sobin), **Supp. XVI:** 290

Transparent Man, The (Hecht), **Supp. X:** 57, **69–71**

"Transparent Man, The" (Hecht), **Supp. X: 69–70**

Transparent Things (Nabokov), **Retro. Supp. I:** 266, 270, 277

"Transport" (Simic), **Supp. VIII:** 282

Transport to Summer (Stevens), **IV:** 76, 93; **Retro. Supp. I:** 309–312

Tranströmer, Thomas, **Supp. IV Part 2:** 648

"Traps for the Unwary" (Bourne), **I:** 235

Trash Trilogy (McMurtry), **Supp. V:** 225–226, 231

Traubel, Horace, **IV:** 350

"Travel: After a Death" (Kenyon), **Supp. VII:** 169

Travel Alarm (Nye), **Supp. XIII:** 277

"Traveled World, The" (Pickering), **Supp. XXI:** 203

"Traveler, The" (Haines), **Supp. XII:** 203–204, 210

"Traveler, The" (Stegner), **Supp. IV Part 2:** 605

Traveler at Forty, A (Dreiser), **I:** 515

Traveler from Altruria, a Romance A, (Howells), **II:** 285, 287

Traveler's Tree, The: New and Selected Poems (W. J. Smith), **Supp. XIII:** 332, 347

"Traveling" (Paley), **Supp. VI:** 230

"Traveling Light" (Wagoner), **Supp. IX:** 329

Traveling Mercies: Some Thoughts on Faith (Lamott), **Supp. XX:**132, **140–142**

"Traveling Onion, The" (Nye), **Supp. XIII:** 276

Traveling through the Dark (Stafford), **Supp. XI:** 311, 316, **318–321**

"Traveling through the Dark" (Stafford), **Supp. XI:** 318–320, 321, 323, 329

Travelling in Amherst: A Poet's Journal, 1931–1954, **Supp. IX: 88–89**

Travels in Alaska (Muir), **Supp. IX:** 182, 185–186

"Travels in Georgia" (McPhee), **Supp. III Part 1:** 293–294

"Travels in North America" (Kees), **Supp. XV:** 133–134

Travels in the Congo (Gide), **III:** 210

"Travels in the South" (Ortiz), **Supp. IV Part 2:** 506

Travels with Charley (Steinbeck), **IV:** 52

"Travel Writing: Why I Bother" (Theroux), **Supp. VIII:** 310

Travis, Merle, **Supp. V:** 335

Travisano, Thomas, **Retro. Supp. II:** 40

Treasure Hunt (Buechner), **Supp. XII:** 52

Treasure Island (Stevenson), **Supp. X:** 230

Treasure of the Humble, The (Maeterlinck), **Supp. XX:**116

"Treasure of the Redwoods, A" (Harte), **Supp. II Part 1:** 337

Treasury of Art Masterpieces, A: From the Renaissance to the Present Day (Craven), **Supp. XII:** 44

Treasury of English Aphorisms, A (L. P. Smith), **Supp. XIV:** 344

Treasury of English Prose, A (L. P. Smith, ed.), **Supp. XIV:** 341

Treasury of the Theatre, A (Gassner), **Supp. I Part 1:** 292

Treasury of Yiddish Stories, A (Howe and Greenberg, eds.), **Supp. I Part 2:** 432

Treat 'Em Rough (Lardner), **II:** 422–423

Treatise Concerning Religious Affections (Edwards), **I:** 547, 552, 554, 555, 557, 558, 560, 562

Treatise Concerning the Lord's Supper (Doolittle), **IV:** 150

"Treatise on Poetry" (Milosz), **Supp. VIII:** 20

Treatise on Right and Wrong, A (Mencken), **III:** 110, 119

"Treatise on Tales of Horror, A" (Wilson), **IV:** 438

Treatise on the Gods, A (Mencken), **III:** 108–109, 119

"Treatment" (Wright), **Supp. XV:** 343

Trece poetas del mundo azteca (León-Portilla), **Supp. XV:** 77

Tre Croce (Tozzi), **Supp. III Part 2:** 616

"Tree, a Rock, a Cloud, A" (McCullers), **II:** 587

"Tree, The" (Pound), **Retro. Supp. I:** 286; **Supp. I Part 1:** 255

"Tree, the Bird, The" (Roethke), **III:** 548

"Tree at My Window" (Frost), **II:** 155

Tree Grows in Brooklyn, A (B. Smith), **Supp. XVII:** 9

Tree Grows in Brooklyn, A (film; Kazan), **Supp. XVI:** 193

"Tree House at Night, The" (Dickey), **Supp. IV Part 1:** 179

Tree Is Older Than You Are, The (Nye, ed.), **Supp. XIII:** 280

"Tree of Laughing Bells, The" (Lindsay), **Supp. I Part 2:** 376

"Tree of Life, The" (Swados), **Supp. XIX:** 268

"Tree of Night, A" (Capote), **Supp. III Part 1:** 114, 120

Tree of Night and Other Stories, A (Capote), **Supp. III Part 1:** 114

"Trees, The" (Rich), **Supp. I Part 2:** 555

Trees, The (Richter), **Supp. XVIII:** 212–213, 220

"Trees Listening to Bach" (Merrill), **Supp. III Part 1:** 336

Tree That Came to Stay, The (Quindlen), **Supp. XVII:** 167

Tree Where Man Was Born, The (Matthiessen), **Supp. V:** 199, 203, 204

Trejo, Ernesto, **Supp. V:** 178, 180; **Supp. XIII:** 313, 316; **Supp. XV:** 73

Trelawny, Edward John, **Supp. I Part 2:** 721

"Trellis for R., A" (Swenson), **Supp. IV Part 2:** 647

Tremblay, Bill, **Supp. XIII:** 112

Tremble (Wright), **Supp. XV: 348–349**

"Trespass" (Frost), **Retro. Supp. I:** 139

Trespassing (Pickering), **Supp. XXI:** 202

"Trespassing" (Pickering), **Supp. XXI:** 202

Trethewey, Eric, **Supp. XXI:** 243, 244

Trethewey, Natasha, **Supp. XXI: 243–259**

"Tretitoli, Where the Bomb Group Was" (Hugo), **Supp. VI:** 138

Trevelyan, Robert C., **Supp. XIV:** 334

Trevor-Roper, Hugh, **Supp. XIV:** 348

Trial, The (Kafka), **IV:** 113; **Retro. Supp. II:** 20

"Trial, The" (Rukeyser), **Supp. VI:** 278

"Trial by Existence, The" (Frost), **II:** 166

Trial of a Poet, The (Shapiro), **Supp. II Part 2:** 710

Trial of the Hawk, The: A Comedy of the Seriousness of Life (Lewis), **II:** 441

Trials of the Human Heart (Rowson), **Supp. XV:** 237, 239

Tribal Secrets: Recovering American Indian Intellectual Traditions (Warrior), **Supp. IV Part 1:** 329

"Tribute" (A. Finch), **Supp. XVII:** 72, 73–74

"Tribute, A" (Easton), **Supp. IV Part 2:** 461

"Tribute, The" (Doolittle), **Supp. I Part 1:** 267

"Tribute (To My Mother)" (Cullen), **Supp. IV Part 1:** 166

Tribute to Freud (Doolittle), **Supp. I Part 1:** 253, 254, 258, 259, 260, 268

Tribute to the Angels (Doolittle), **Supp. I Part 1:** 272

"Trick on the World, A" (Ríos), **Supp. IV Part 2:** 553

"Tricks" (Olds), **Supp. X:** 203–204

"Trick Scenery" (F. Barthelme), **Supp. XI:** 26

Trifler, The (Masters), **Supp. I Part 2:** 459–460

Trifles (Glaspell), **Supp. III Part 1:** 175, 178, 179, 182, 186, 187; **Supp. X:** 46; **Supp. XXI:** 12

Trifonov, Iurii V., **Retro. Supp. I:** 278

Triggering Town, The: Lectures and Essays on Poetry and Writing (Hugo), **Supp. VI:** 133, 140

Trilling, Diana, **II:** 587, 600; **Supp. I Part 1:** 297; **Supp. XII:** 126; **Supp. XXI:** 271, 275

Trilling, Lionel, **I:** 48; **II:** 579; **III:** 308, 310, 319, 327; **IV:** 201, 211; **Retro. Supp. I:** 19, 97, 121, 216, 227; **Supp. III Part 2: 493–515; Supp. V:** 259; **Supp. VIII:** 93, 98, 190, 231, 236, 243; **Supp. IX:** 266, 287; **Supp. XIII:** 100–101; **Supp. XIV:** 280, 288–289; **Supp. XV:** 20, 140, 152

Trilogy (Doolittle), **Supp. I Part 1:** 271, 272

Trilogy of Desire (Dreiser), **I:** 497, 508; **Retro. Supp. II:** 94, 96, **101–102**

Trimberger, Ellen Kay, **Supp. XVII:** 96, 106; **Supp. XXI:** 12

Trimmed Lamp, The (O. Henry), **Supp. II Part 1:** 410

"Trinc" (McGrath), **Supp. X:** 127

Trinity (Uris), **Supp. XX:**243, 244, 245, 246, 247, 248, 253, **254–255**

Trio (Baker), **Supp. I Part 1:** 277

"Triolets for Triolet" (Nelson), **Supp. XVIII:** 179

"*Trip*" (F. Barthelme), *Supp. XI:* 26

Triple Thinkers, The: Ten Essays on Literature (Wilson), **IV:** 428, 431; **Supp. II Part 1:** 146

"Triplex" (Doolittle), **Supp. I Part 1:** 271

Tripmaster Monkey: His Fake Book (Kingston), **Supp. V:** 157, 158, 169, 170–173

Trippings in Authorland (Forrester), **Supp. XVIII:** 13

Trippings of Tom Pepper, The (Briggs), **Supp. XVIII:** 3, **13–14**

"Trip to Hanoi" (Sontag), **Supp. III Part 2:** 460–462

Trip to Parnassus, A; or, The Judgement of Apollo on Dramatic Authors and Performers (Rowson), **Supp. XV: 232–233**

"Triptych" (Eberhart), **I:** 522, 539

Tristan and Iseult, **Retro. Supp. I:** 328, 329, 330, 331

Tristessa (Kerouac), **Supp. III Part 1:** 225, 227, 229

Tristram (Robinson), **III:** 521, 522, 523

Tristram Shandy (Sterne), **I:** 299; **IV:** 465–466; **Supp. V:** 127; **Supp. XVIII:** 60

"Triumph" (C. L. R. James), **Supp. XXI:** 160

"Triumphal March" (Eliot), **I:** 580; **III:** 17; **Retro. Supp. I:** 64

Triumph of Achilles, The (Glück), **Supp. V:** 79, 84–86, 92

"Triumph of a Modern, The, or, Send for the Lawyer" (Anderson), **I:** 113, 114

"Triumph of the Egg, The" (Anderson), **I:** 113

Triumph of the Egg, The: A Book of Impressions from American Life in Tales and Poems (Anderson), **I:** 112, 114

Triumph of the Spider Monkey, The (Oates), **Supp. II Part 2:** 522

Triumphs of the Reformed Religion in America (Mather), **Supp. II Part 2:** 453

Trivial Breath (Wylie), **Supp. I Part 2:** 709, 722–724

Trivia; or, the Art of Walking the Streets of London (Gay), **Supp. XIV:** 337

Trivia: Printed from the Papers of Anthony Woodhouse, Esq. (L. P. Smith), **Supp. XIV:** 336, **337–340**

"Trivia Tea" (Skloot), **Supp. XX:**205

Trocchi, Alexander, **Supp. XI:** 294, 295, 301

Troilus and Criseyde (Chaucer), **Retro. Supp. I:** 426

Trois contes (Flaubert), **IV:** 31, 37

Trojan Horse, The: A Play (MacLeish), **III:** 21

"Trojan Women, The" (Maxwell), **Supp. VIII:** 169

Troll Garden, The (Cather), **I:** 313, 314–316, 322; **Retro. Supp. I:** 5, 6, 8, 14

"Trolling for Blues" (Wilbur), **Supp. III Part 2:** 563–564

Trollope, Anthony, **I:** 10, 375; **II:** 192, 237; **III:** 51, 70, 281, 382; **Retro. Supp. I:** 361

Trombly, Albert Edmund, **Supp. I Part 2:** 403

Trombold, John, **Supp. XVIII:** 111

"Trompe L'Oeil" (Collins), **Supp. XXI:** 60

"Troop Train" (Shapiro), **Supp. II Part 2:** 707

"Tropes of the Text" (Gass), **Supp. VI:** 88

Tropic of Cancer (H. Miller), **III:** 170, 171, 174, 177, 178–180, 181, 182, 183, 187, 190; **Supp. V:** 119; **Supp. X:** 187

Tropic of Capricorn (H. Miller), **III:** 170, 176–177, 178, 182, 183, 184, 187, 188–189, 190

"Tropic of Cuba" (di Donato), **Supp. XX:**45

Trotsky, Leon, **I:** 366; **II:** 562, 564; **IV:** 429; **Supp. XXI:** 161, 164, 165, 167, 168

Trotter, W., **I:** 249

Troubled Air, The (Shaw), **Supp. XIX: 249–250**

Troubled Island (opera; Hughes and Still), **Retro. Supp. I:** 203

Troubled Lovers in History (Goldbarth), **Supp. XII:** 176, **192–193**

Trouble Follows Me (Macdonald, under Millar), **Supp. IV Part 2:** 466

Trouble in July (Caldwell), **I:** 297, 304–305, 306, 309

Trouble Island (Hughes), **Supp. I Part 1:** 328

"Trouble of Marcie Flint, The" (Cheever), **Supp. I Part 1:** 186

Trouble with Francis, The: An Autobiography (Francis), **Supp. IX:** 76, 77, 82, **84–85**

Trouble with God, The (Francis), **Supp. IX:** 88

"Trouble with Poetry, The" (Collins), **Supp. XXI:** 57

Trouble with Poetry and Other Poems, The (Collins), **Supp. XXI:** 55, 57, 62

"Trouble with the Stars and Stripes" (Nye), **Supp. XIII:** 277

Trouillot, Michel-Rolphe, **Supp. X:** 14–15

Troupe, Quincy, **Retro. Supp. II:** 15, 111; **Supp. X:** 242

"Trout" (Hugo), **Supp. VI:** 135

Trout Fishing in America (Brautigan), **Supp. VIII:** 43

"Trouvée" (Bishop), **Retro. Supp. II:** 49

Troy (film), **Supp. XX:**273

"Truce of the Bishop, The" (Frederic), **II:** 139–140

"Truck Stop: Minnesota" (Dunn), **Supp. XI:** 145–146

True and False: Heresy and Common Sense for the Actor (Mamet), **Supp. XIV:** 241, 243

True Blood (television series), **Supp. XIX:** 174

Trueblood, Valerie, **Supp. XIII:** 306

True Confessions (Dunne), **Supp. IV Part 1:** 198

True Confessions (film), **Supp. IV Part 1:** 198

Trueheart, Charles, **Supp. XXI:** 238

True History of the Conquest of New Spain, The (Castillo), **III:** 13

True Intellectual System of the Universe, The (Cuddleworth), **II:** 10

"True Love" (Olds), **Supp. X:** 212

Trueman, Matthew (pseudonym). *See* Lowell, James Russell

"True Morality" (Bell), **Supp. X:** 13

"True Romance" (Everett), **Supp. XVIII:** 65

Truesdale, C. W., **Supp. XXI:** 246

True Stories (Atwood), **Supp. XIII:** 34–35

"True Stories" (Atwood), **Supp. XIII:** 34

"True Stories of Bitches" (Mamet), **Supp. XIV:** 246, 252

"Truest Sport, The: Jousting with Sam and Charlie" (Wolfe), **Supp. III Part 2:** 581–582

"True Vine" (Wylie), **Supp. I Part 2:** 723

True West (Shepard), **Supp. III Part 2:** 433, 441, 445, 447, 448

Truman, Harry, **III:** 3

Truman Capote: In Which Various Friends, Enemies, Acquaintances, and Detractors Recall His Turbulent Career (Plimpton), **Supp. XVI:**245

Truman Show, The (film), **Supp. XVI:** 271

Trumbo, Dalton, **Supp. I Part 1:** 295; **Supp. XIII:** 6; **Supp. XVII:** 63; **Supp. XX:**246; **Supp. XXI:** 45

Trumbull, John, **Supp. II Part 1:** 65, 69, 70, 268

Trump, Donald, **Supp. IV Part 1:** 393

Trumpener, Katie, **Retro. Supp. I:** 380

"Trumpet Player" (Hughes), **Supp. I Part 1:** 333

"Trumpet Player, 1963" (Halliday), **Supp. XIX:** 92

Trumpet Shall Sound, The (Wilder), **IV:** 356

Trumpet Unblown, The (Hoffman), **Supp. XVIII:** 71, **74–75**

Trunk Music (Connelly), **Supp. XXI:** 72, 75

"Truro Bear, The" (Oliver), **Supp. VII:** 234

Truscott, Lucian K., **Supp. IV Part 2:** 683

Trust (Ozick), **Supp. V:** 257–258, 259, 260–263, 270, 272

Trust Me (Updike), **Retro. Supp. I:** 322

"Trust Yourself" (Emerson), **II:** 10

"Truth" (Emerson), **II:** 6

"Truth, The" (Halliday), **Supp. XIX:** 87, 88, 94

"Truth, The" (Jarrell), **II:** 381–382

"Truth about God, The" (Carson), **Supp. XII:** 105–106

"Truth be told" (Trethewey), **Supp. XXI:** 255, 256

"Truthful James" (Harte), **IV:** 196

"Truth Is, The" (Hogan), **Supp. IV Part 1:** 401–402

"Truth Is Forced, The" (Swenson), **Supp. IV Part 2:** 652

"Truth of the Matter, The" (Nemerov), **III:** 270

Truth Serum (Cooper), **Supp. XI:** 129

"Truth the Dead Know, The" (Sexton), **Supp. II Part 2:** 681

"Trying to Evangelize a Cut Flower" (Peacock), **Supp. XIX:** 199

Trying to Find Chinatown (Hwang), **Supp. XXI:** 147

Trying to Save Piggy Sneed (Irving), **Supp. VI:** 19–165

"Trying to Talk with a Man" (Rich), **Supp. I Part 2:** 559

"Tryptich I" (Bell), **Supp. X:** 7

"Tryst, The" (Wharton), **Retro. Supp. I:** 378

"Try the Girl" (Chandler), **Supp. IV Part 1:** 125

"Ts'ai Chih" (Pound), **III:** 466

T. S. Eliot and American Philosophy (Jain), **Retro. Supp. I:** 58

T. S. Eliot's Silent Voices (Mayer), **Retro. Supp. I:** 58

Tsuji, Shizuo, **Supp. XVII:** 90

Tsvetayeva, Marina, **Supp. VIII:** 30

"Tuberoses" (E. Stoddard), **Supp. XV:** 282

Tucker, Benjamin R., **Supp. XXI:** 9

Tuckerman, Frederick Goddard, **IV:** 144

Tucker's People (Wolfert), **Supp. XXI:** 261, 262, 263, 267, **267–275**, 278

"Tuesday, November 5th, 1940" (Benét), **Supp. XI:** 46, 52

"Tuesday April 25th 1966" (Olson), **Supp. II Part 2:** 585

"Tuesday Night at the Savoy Ballroom" (Komunyakaa), **Supp. XIII:** 132

Tuffield, Aviva, **Supp. XVI:** 147, 148

"Tuft of Flowers, The" (Frost), **II:** 153; **Retro. Supp. I:** 126, 127

Tufts, James Hayden, **Supp. I Part 2:** 632

Tu Fu, **II:** 526; **Supp. XV:** 47

Tu Fu (Ayscough), **II:** 527

Tugwell, Rexford Guy, **Supp. I Part 2:** 645

"Tulip" (Hammett), **Supp. IV Part 1:** 356

"Tulip Man, The" (McCarriston), **Supp. XIV:** 261

"Tulips" (Nye), **Supp. XIII:** 281

"Tulips" (Plath), **Retro. Supp. II:** 252–253; **Supp. I Part 2:** 540, 542, 544

"Tulips" (Snodgrass), **Supp. VI:** 325

Tulips and Chimneys (Cummings), **I:** 436, 437, 440, 445, 447

Tully, Jim, **III:** 103, 109

Tumble Home (Hempel), **Supp. XXI:** 115, **124–125**

"Tumble Home" (Hempel), **Supp. XXI:** 115, 116, **124–125**, 126

Tumble Tower (Modarressi and Tyler), **Supp. IV Part 2:** 657

"Tuned in Late One Night" (Stafford), **Supp. XI:** 327–328

Tunnel, The (Gass), **Supp. V:** 44; **Supp. VI: 89–91**, 94

"Tunnel, The" (Strand), **Supp. IV Part 2:** 622

"Tunnels" (Komunyakaa), **Supp. XIII:** 123

Tuqan, Fadwa, **Supp. XIII:** 278

Tura, Cosimo, **III:** 474–475

Turandot and Other Poems (Ashbery), **Supp. III Part 1:** 3

Turco, Lewis, **Supp. XV:** 118

Turgenev, Ivan Sergeevich, **I:** 106; **II:** 263, 271, 275, 280, 281, 288, 319, 320, 324–325, 338, 407; **III:** 461; **IV:** 17, 277; **Retro. Supp. I:** 215, 222; **Supp. VIII:** 167

Turgot, Anne Robert Jacques, **II:** 103; **Supp. I Part 1:** 250

"Turkey and Bones and Eating and We Liked It" (Stein), **IV:** 44

Turman, Glynn, **Supp. IV Part 1:** 362

Turnbull, Dr. George, **II:** 113

Turnbull, Lawrence, **Supp. I Part 1:** 352

"Turned" (Gilman), **Supp. XI:** 207

Turner, Addie, **IV:** 123

Turner, Darwin, **Supp. I Part 1:** 339; **Supp. IV Part 1:** 165

Turner, Frederick Jackson, **Supp. I Part 2:** 480, 481, 632, 640; **Supp. IV Part 2:** 596

Turner, Nat, **IV:** 113–114, 115, 116, 117

Turner, Patricia A., **Supp. XIII:** 237; **Supp. XX:** 110

Turner, Russell. *See* Lacy, Ed

Turner, Victor, **Supp. IV Part 1:** 304

"Turning Away Variations on Estrangement" (Dickey), **Supp. IV Part 1:** 183

Turning Point, The (McCoy), **Supp. XIII:** 175

"Turning Thirty, I Contemplate Students Bicycling Home" (Dove), **Supp. IV Part 1:** 250

Turning Wind, A (Rukeyser), **Supp. VI:** 272–273, 279–280

Turn of the Screw, The (H. James), **Retro. Supp. I:** 219, 231; **Supp. IV Part 2:** 682

"Turn of the Screw, The" (H. James), **II:** 331–332; **Retro. Supp. I:** 228, 229, 231, 232; **Supp. XVII:** 143

Turns and Movies and Other Tales in Verse (Aiken), **I:** 65

"Turn with the Sun, A" (Knowles), **Supp. XII:** 237–238

"Turn Your Radio On" (J. W. Miller), **Supp. XX:** 169

Turow, Scott, **Supp. V:** 220; **Supp. XVII: 213–224**

Turpin, E. Walters, **Supp. XVIII:** 283

Turrinus, Lucius Mamilius, **IV:** 373

"Turtle" (Hogan), **Supp. IV Part 1:** 401

Turtle, Swan (Doty), **Supp. XI: 121–122**

"Turtle, Swan" (Doty), **Supp. XI:** 121–122

Turtle Island (Snyder), **Supp. VIII: 300–303**

Turtle Moon (Hoffman), **Supp. X:** 77, **87–88**, 89

"Turtle Shrine near Chittagong, The" (Nye), **Supp. XIII:** 277

Turturro, John, **Supp. XI:** 174

Tuscan Cities (Howells), **II:** 280

Tuskegee movement, **Supp. II Part 1:** 169, 172

Tuten, Frederic, **Supp. VIII:** 75, 76; **Supp. XIII:** 237, 249

Tuten, James, **Supp. XVIII:** 195

Tuthill, Louisa Cavolne, **Supp. I Part 2:** 684

"Tutored Child, The" (Kunitz), **Supp. III Part 1:** 264

Tuttleton, James W., **Supp. IV Part 1:** 166, 168

"T.V.A." (Agee), **I:** 35

Tvedten, Brother Benet, **Supp. IV Part 2:** 505

"TV Men" (Carson), **Supp. XII:** 105, 112

Twain, Mark, **I:** 57, 103, 107, 109, 190, 192, 193, 195, 197, 203, 209, 245, 246, 247–250, 255, 256, 257, 260, 261, 292, 342, 418, 469, 485; **II:** 70, 140, 259, 262, 266–268, 271, 272, 274–275, 276, 277, 280, 285–286, 287, 288, 289, 301, 304, 306, 307, 312, 415, 432, 434, 436, 446, 457, 467, 475, 476, 482; **III:** 65, 101, 102, 112–113, 114, 220, 347, 357, 409, 453, 454, 504, 507, 554, 558, 572, 575, 576; **IV: 190–213**, 333, 349, 451; **Retro. Supp. I:** 169, 194, 195; **Retro. Supp. II:** 123; **Supp. I Part 1:** 37, 39, 44, 247, 251, 313, 317; **Supp. I Part 2:** 377, 385, 393, 410, 455, 456, 457, 473, 475, 579, 602, 604, 618, 629, 651, 660; **Supp. II Part 1:** 193, 344, 354, 385; **Supp. IV Part 1:** 386, 388; **Supp. IV Part 2:** 463, 468, 603, 607, 693; **Supp. V:** 44, 113, 131; **Supp. VIII:** 40, 189; **Supp. IX:** 14, 171; **Supp. X:** 51, 227; **Supp. XII:** 343; **Supp. XIII:** 1, 17; **Supp. XV:** 41; **Supp. XVI:** 66, 208; **Supp. XVIII:** 1, 9, 13; **Supp. XXI:** 205

"Twa Sisters, The" (ballad), **Supp. I Part 2:** 696

Twelfth Night (Shakespeare), **Supp. IV Part 1:** 83; **Supp. IX:** 14

"12 O'Clock News" (Bishop), **Retro. Supp. II:** 48

Twelve Men (Dreiser), **Retro. Supp. II:** 94, 104

Twelve Moons (Oliver), **Supp. VII:** 231, 233–236, 238, 240

Twelve Southerners, **IV:** 125; **Supp. X:** 25

Twelve Years a Slave (Northup), **Supp. XIV:** 32

Twentieth Century Authors, **I:** 376, 527

"Twentieth Century Fiction and the Black Mask of Humanity" (Ellison), **Retro. Supp. II:** 118

Twentieth Century Pleasures (Hass), **Supp. VI:** 103, 106, 109

Twenty Drawings (Gibran), **Supp. XX:**116

"28" (Levine), **Supp. V:** 187, 191

"Twenty-Four Poems" (Schwartz), **Supp. II Part 2:** 646, 649

"2433 Agnes, First Home, Last House in Missoula" (Hugo), **Supp. VI:** 139–140

"Twenty Hill Hollow" (Muir), **Supp. IX:** 178

"Twenty Minutes" (Salter), **Supp. IX:** 260

"Twenty-One Love Poems" (Rich), **Supp. I Part 2:** 572–573

"Twenty-One Poems" (MacLeish), **III:** 19

Twenty Poems (Haines), **Supp. XII:** 204, **205–206**

Twenty Poems of Anna Akhmatova (Kenyon), **Supp. VII:** 165–166

Twenty Questions: (Posed by Poems) (McClatchy), **Supp. XII:** 254, **259–262**

27 Wagons Full of Cotton and Other One-Act Plays (T. Williams), **IV:** 381, 383

Twenty-seventh City, The (Franzen), **Supp. XX:**83–84, 84, 85, **86–88**, 88, 89, 91, 92, 95

Twenty Thousand Leagues under the Sea (Verne), **I:** 480; **Supp. XI:** 63

"Twenty Years Ago" (Lindsay), **Supp. I Part 2:** 384, 399

Twenty Years at Hull-House (Addams), **Supp. I Part 1:** 3, 4, 11, 16

Twersky, David, **Supp. XX:**244

Twice over Lightly: New York Ten and Now (Hayes and Loos), **Supp. XVI:** 195

Twice-Told Tales (Hawthorne), **I:** 354; **II:** 224; **III:** 412, 421; **Retro. Supp. I:** 154–155, 160

Twichell, Chase, **Supp. V:** 16; **Supp. XVII:** 110, 112

Twilight (Frost), **II:** 151

"Twilight's Last Gleaming" (Burroughs and Elvins), **Supp. III Part 1:** 93, 94, 101

Twilight Sleep (Wharton), **IV:** 320–322, 324–325, 327, 328; **Retro. Supp. I:** 381

"Twin, The" (Olds), **Supp. X:** 207

"Twin Beds in Rome" (Updike), **Retro. Supp. I:** 332

"Twins of Table Mountain, The" (Harte), **Supp. II Part 1:** 355

"Twist, The" (Olson), **Supp. II Part 2:** 570

Twitch and Shout (film), **Supp. XVIII:** 143

Twitchel-Waas, Jeffrey, **Supp. XVIII:** 99

Two Admirals, The (Cooper), **I:** 350

Two against One (F. Barthelme), **Supp. XI:** 32, 33, 36

"Two Boys" (Moore), **Supp. X:** 173

"Two Brothers, The" (Jewett), **Retro. Supp. II:** 132

Two-Character Play, The (T. Williams), **IV:** 382, 386, 393, 398

Two Citizens (Wright), **Supp. III Part 2:** 602–604

"Two Deer" (Bass), **Supp. XVI:** 24

"Two Domains, The" (Goldbarth), **Supp. XII:** 192

"Two-Eleven All Around" (Offutt), **Supp. XIX:** 170

"Two Environments, The" (Trilling), **Supp. III Part 2:** 510

"Two-Fisted Self Pity" (Broyard), **Supp. XI:** 348

Two for Texas (Burke), **Supp. XIV:** 25, 34

"Two Friends" (Cather), **I:** 332

"Two Gardens in Linndale" (Robinson), **III:** 508

Two Gentlemen in Bonds (Ransom), **III:** 491–492

Two: Gertrude Stein and Her Brother (Stein), **IV:** 43

"Two Ghosts" (Francis), **Supp. IX:** 87

"Two Hangovers" (Wright), **Supp. III Part 2:** 596

Two-Headed Poems (Atwood), **Supp. XIII:** 34

Two Hot to Handle (Lacy), **Supp. XV:** 206

Two Hours to Doom (Bryant), **Supp. XI:** 302

"Two Hundred Years in an Hour" (Boyce), **Supp. XXI:** 8

"Two Kitchens in Provence" (M. F. K. Fisher), **Supp. XVII:** 88, 91

"Two Ladies in Retirement" (Taylor), **Supp. V:** 320

Two Letters to the Citizens of the United States, and One to General Washington (Barlow), **Supp. II Part 1:** 80

"Two Lives, The" (Hogan), **Supp. IV Part 1:** 400, 402, 403, 406, 411

Two Long Poems (Stern), **Supp. IX:** 296

"Two Look at Two" (Frost), **Supp. XXI:** 26

"Two Lovers and a Beachcomber by the Real Sea" (Plath), **Supp. I Part 2:** 536

"Two Men" (McClatchy)", **Supp. XII:** 269

Two Men (E. Stoddard), **Supp. XV:** 272, 273, **283–284**

Two Men of Sandy Bar (Harte), **Supp. II Part 1:** 354

Twomey, Jay, **Supp. XVII:** 111

"Two Moods of Love" (Cullen), **Supp. IV Part 1:** 166

Two Moons (Mallon), **Supp. XIX:** 132, **138–141**

"Two Morning Monologues" (Bellow), **I:** 150; **Retro. Supp. II:** 20

"Two Nations of Black America, The" *(Frontline),* **Supp. XX:**99

Two-Ocean War, The (Morison), **Supp. I Part 2:** 491

"Two of Hearts" (Hogan), **Supp. IV Part 1:** 410

"Two on a Party" (T. Williams), **IV:** 388

"Two or Three Things I Dunno About John Cassavetes" (Lethem), **Supp. XVIII:** 148

"Two Pendants: For the Ears" (W. C. Williams), **Retro. Supp. I:** 423

"Two Poems of Going Home" (Dickey), **Supp. IV Part 1:** 182–183

"Two Portraits" (Chopin), **Supp. I Part 1:** 218

"Two Presences, The" (R. Bly), **Supp. IV Part 1:** 65

"Two Rivers" (Stegner), **Supp. IV Part 2:** 605

Tworkov, Jack, **Supp. XII:** 198

"Two Scenes" (Ashbery), **Supp. III Part 1:** 4

Two Serious Ladies (Jane Bowles), **Supp. IV Part 1:** 82

"Two Sisters" (Farrell), **II:** 45

Two Sisters: A Memoir in the Form of a Novel (Vidal), **Supp. IV Part 2:** 679

"Two Sisters of Persephone" (Plath), **Retro. Supp. II:** 246

"Two Songs on the Economy of Abundance" (Agee), **I:** 28

Two Sons, The (Boyce), **Supp. XXI:** 7, 13

"Two Tales of Clumsy" (Schnackenberg), **Supp. XV:** 258

"Two Temples, The" (Melville), **III:** 89–90

Two Thousand Seasons (Armah), **Supp. IV Part 1:** 373

Two Towns in Provence (M. F. K. Fisher), **Supp. XVII:** 91

Two Trains Running (Wilson), **Supp. VIII:** 345–348

"Two Tramps in Mudtime" (Frost), **II:** 164; **Retro. Supp. I:** 137; **Supp. IX:** 261

"Two Views of a Cadaver Room" (Plath), **Supp. I Part 2:** 538

"Two Villages" (Paley), **Supp. VI:** 227

"Two Voices in a Meadow" (Wilbur), **Supp. III Part 2:** 555

Two Weeks in Another Town (Shaw), **Supp. XIX:** 251

"Two Witches" (Frost), **Retro. Supp. I:** 135

"Two Words" (Francis), **Supp. IX:** 81

Two Worlds Walking: A Mixed-Blood Anthology (Glancy and Truesdale, eds.), **Supp. XXI:** 246

Two Years before the Mast (Dana), **I:** 351

"Tyger, The" (Blake), **Supp. XVII:** 128

Tyler, Anne, **Supp. IV Part 2: 657–675; Supp. V:** 227, 326; **Supp. VIII:** 141; **Supp. X:** 1, 77, 83, 85; **Supp. XII:** 307; **Supp. XVI:** 37; **Supp. XVIII:** 157, 195

Tyler, Royall, **I:** 344; **Retro. Supp. I:** 377

Tymms, Ralph, **Supp. IX:** 105

Tyndale, William, **II:** 15

Tyndall, John, **Retro. Supp. II:** 93

Typee: A Peep at Polynesian Life (Melville), **III:** 75–77, 79, 84; **Retro. Supp. I:** 245–246, 249, 252, 256

Types From City Streets (Hapgood), **Supp. XVII:** 103

"Typewriter, The" (D. West), **Supp. XVIII:** 279

Typewriter Town (W. J. Smith), **Supp. XIII:** 332

"Typhus" (Simpson), **Supp. IX:** 277

Tyranny of the Normal (Fiedler), **Supp. XIII: 107–108**

"Tyranny of the Normal" (Fiedler), **Supp. XIII:** 107–108

"Tyrant of Syracuse" (MacLeish), **III:** 20

"Tyrian Businesses" (Olson), **Supp. II Part 2:** 567, 568, 569

Tytell, John, **Supp. XIV:** 140

Tzara, Tristan, **Supp. III Part 1:** 104, 105

U

U and I (Baker), **Supp. XIII: 45–47,** 48, 52, 55

Überdie Seelenfrage (Fechner), **II:** 358

Ubik (Dick), **Supp. XVIII:** 136

Ubu Roi (Jarry), **Supp. XV:** 178, 186

Ueland, Brenda, **Supp. XVII:** 13

Uhry, Alfred, **Supp. XX:**177

Ukrainian Dumy (P. N. Warren as Kilina and Tarnawsky, trans.), **Supp. XX:**261

"Ulalume" (Poe), **III:** 427; **Retro. Supp. II:** 264, 266

Ulin, David, **Supp. XIII:** 244; **Supp. XVI:** 74

Ullman, Leslie, **Supp. IV Part 2:** 550; **Supp. XVIII:** 175

Ultimate Good Luck, The (Ford), **Supp. V:** 57, 61–62

Ultimate Punishment: A Lawyer's Reflections on Dealing with the Death Penalty (Turow), **Supp. XVII:** 220–221

Ultima Thule (Longfellow), **II:** 490; **Retro. Supp. II:** 169

"Ultima Thule" (Nabokov), **Retro. Supp. I:** 274

Ultramarine (Carver), **Supp. III Part 1:** 137, 138, 147, 148

Ulysses (Joyce), **I:** 395, 475–476, 478, 479, 481; **II:** 42, 264, 542; **III:** 170, 398; **IV:** 103, 418, 428, 455; **Retro. Supp. I:** 59, 63, 290, 291; **Retro. Supp. II:** 121; **Supp. I Part 1:** 57; **Supp. III Part 2:** 618, 619; **Supp. IV Part 1:** 285; **Supp. IV Part 2:** 424; **Supp. V:** 261; **Supp. IX:** 102; **Supp. X:** 114; **Supp. XIII:** 43, 191; **Supp. XV:** 305; **Supp. XVII:** 140, 227

"*Ulysses,* Order and Myth" (Eliot), **Retro. Supp. I:** 63

"*Umbrella, The*" (Peacock), **Supp. XIX:** 203–204

Unaccountable Worth of the World, The (Price), **Supp. VI:** 267

Unaccustomed Earth (Lahiri), **Supp. XXI: 176, 181–183,** 183, 188

"Unaccustomed Earth" (Lahiri), **Supp. XXI:** 186

Unamuno y Jugo, Miguel de, **III:** 310; **Supp. XV:** 79

"Unattached Smile, The" (Crews), **Supp. XI:** 101

"Unbelievable Thing Usually Goes to the Heart of the Story, The: Magic Realism in the Fiction of Rick Bass" (Dwyer), **Supp. XVI:** 16

"Unbeliever, The" (Bishop), **Retro. Supp. II:** 43

"Unborn Song" (Rukeyser), **Supp. VI:** 274

Unbought Spirit: A John Jay Chapman Reader (Stone, ed.), **Supp. XIV:** 54

Uncalled, The (Dunbar), **Supp. II Part 1:** 200, 211, 212

Uncentering the Earth: Copernicus and The Revolutions of the Heavenly Spheres (Vollmann), **Supp. XVII:** 226

Uncertain Certainty, The: Interviews, Essays, and Notes on Poetry (Simic), **Supp. VIII:** 270, 273, 274

Uncertainty and Plenitude: Five Contemporary Poets (Stitt), **Supp. IX:** 299

"Uncle" (Levine), **Supp. V:** 186

"Uncle Adler" (Kooser), **Supp. XIX:** 120

"Uncle Christmas" (Ríos), **Supp. IV Part 2:** 552

"Uncle Jim's Baptist Revival Hymn" (Lanier and Lanier), **Supp. I Part 1:** 353

"Uncle Lot" (Stowe), **Supp. I Part 2:** 585–586

"Uncle Moustapha's Eclipse" (McKnight), **Supp. XX:**148

Uncle Remus Tales (Harris), **Supp. II Part 1:** 201

"Uncle Tomitudes" (Briggs), **Supp. XVIII:** 14

Uncle Tom's Cabin (Stowe), **II:** 291; **Supp. I Part 1:** 49; **Supp. I Part 2:** 410, 579, 582, 589–592; **Supp. II Part 1:** 170; **Supp. III Part 1:** 154, 171; **Supp. IX:** 19; **Supp. X:** 246, 249, 250; **Supp. XIII:** 95; **Supp. XVI:** 82, 85, 88; **Supp. XVIII:** 14

Uncle Tom's Children (Wright), **IV:** 476, 478, 488; **Supp. II Part 1:** 228, 235; **Supp. XVIII:** 283

"Uncle Wiggily in Connecticut" (Salinger), **III:** 559–560, 563

"Unclouded Day, The" (Proulx), **Supp. VII:** 254–255

"Uncommon Visage" (Brodsky), **Supp. VIII:** 31

"Uncommon Woman: An Interview with Wendy Wasserstein" (Cohen), **Supp. XV:** 323

Uncommon Women and Others (Wasserstein), **Supp. XV:** 320–321, **322–323**

Uncompromising Fictions of Cynthia Ozick (Pinsker), **Supp. V:** 272

"Unconscious Came a Beauty" (Swenson), **Supp. IV Part 2:** 646

"Uncreation, The" (Pinsky), **Supp. VI:** 245

"Undead, The" (Wilbur), **Supp. III Part 2:** 556

"Undefeated, The" (Hemingway), **II:** 250; **Retro. Supp. I:** 180

Under a Glass Bell (Nin), **Supp. X:** 186

"Under Ben Bulben" (Yeats), **Supp. V:** 220

Undercliff: Poems 1946–1953 (Eberhart), **I:** 528, 536–537

Under Cover (Goldbarth), **Supp. XII:** 177, 180, 193

Undercover Doctor (film), **Supp. XIII:** 170

"Under Cygnus" (Wilbur), **Supp. III Part 2:** 558

"Under Forty" (Trilling), **Supp. III Part 2:** 494

Underground, The Story of a People (Tenenbaum), **Supp. XX:**253

Underground Man, The (film), **Supp. IV Part 2:** 474

Underground Man, The (Macdonald), **Supp. IV Part 2:** 474, 475

"Under Libra: Weights and Measures" (Merrill), **Supp. III Part 1:** 328

Under Milk Wood (D. Thomas), **III:** 21

"Undersea" (Carson), **Supp. IX:** 21

Understanding Cynthia Ozick (Friedman), **Supp. V:** 273

Understanding Drama (Brooks and Heilman), **Supp. XIV:** 12

Understanding E. L. Doctorow (Fowler), **Supp. IV Part 1:** 226

Understanding Fiction (Brooks and Warren), **IV:** 279; **Supp. XIV:** 11

Understanding Fiction (Brooks and Warren, eds.), **Supp. XIX:** 246

Understanding Flannery O'Connor (Whitt), **Retro. Supp. II:** 226

Understanding Nicholson Baker (Saltzman), **Supp. XIII:** 48

Understanding Poetry: An Anthology for College Students (Brooks and Warren), **IV:** 236; **Retro. Supp. I:** 40, 41; **Supp. XIV:** 4–5

Understanding Robert Bly (W. V. Davis), **Supp. XXI: 84–85,** 88

Understanding Tim O'Brien (Kaplan), **Supp. V:** 241

Understanding To Kill a Mockingbird: A Student Casebook to Issues, Sources, and Documents (Johnson), **Supp. VIII:** 127

Undertaker's Garland, The (Wilson and Bishop), **IV:** 427

Under the Banner of Heaven: A Story of Violent Faith (Krakauer), **Supp. XVIII:** 105, **114–116,** 117

"Under the Cedarcroft Chestnut" (Lanier), **Supp. I Part 1:** 364

"Under the Harbour Bridge" (Komunyakaa), **Supp. XIII:** 125
"Under the Influence" (Sanders), **Supp. XVI:** 274, 277
Under the Lilacs (Alcott), **Supp. I Part 1:** 42–43, 44
"Under the Maud Moon" (Kinnell), **Supp. III Part 1:** 246–247
Under the Mountain Wall: A Chronicle of Two Seasons in the Stone Age (Matthiessen), **Supp. V:** 202
Under the Red Flag (Jin), **Supp. XVIII:** 89, **94–95**
"Under the Rose" (Pynchon), **Supp. II Part 2:** 620
Under the Sea-Wind: A Naturalist's Picture of Ocean Life (Carson), **Supp. IX:** 19, **22–23**
Under the Shadow (Sorrentino), **Supp. XXI:** 236–237
Under the Sign of Saturn (Sontag), **Supp. III Part 2:** 451, 452, 458, 470–471
"Under the Sign of Saturn" (Sontag), **Supp. III Part 2:** 470
"Under the Sky" (Bowles), **Supp. IV Part 1:** 87
" 'Under the Umbrella of Black Civilization': A Conversation with Reginald McKnight" (Ashe), **Supp. XX:**154
Under the Volcano (M. Lowry), **Supp. XVII:** 135, 139, 140
"Under the Willows" (Lowell), **Supp. I Part 2:** 416
Under the Willows and Other Poems (Lowell), **Supp. I Part 2:** 424
"Undertow" (Boyce), **Supp. XXI:** 10
Underwood, Wilbur, **Retro. Supp. II:** 79
Underworld (DeLillo), **Supp. VI:** 2, 4–5, 6–7, 8, 9, 10, 11, **13–15; Supp. XI:** 68; **Supp. XX:**91
Underworld, The (Wolfert). *See Tucker's World* (Wolfert)
Undine (La Motte-Fouqué), **II:** 212; **III:** 78
Undiscovered Country, The (Howells), **II:** 282
"Undressing, The" (C. Frost), **Supp. XV:** 98
Uneasy Chair, The (Stegner), **Supp. IV Part 2:** 599
"Unemployed, Disabled, and Insane, The" (Haines), **Supp. XII:** 211–212
Unending Blues (Simic), **Supp. VIII:** **278–279**
"Unexpected Freedom" (Peacock), **Supp. XIX:** 199
"Unexpressed" (Dunbar), **Supp. II Part 1:** 199
"Unfinished Bronx, The" (Paley), **Supp. VI:** 228
"Unfinished Poems" (Eliot), **I:** 579
"Unfinished Song" (C. Frost), **Supp. XV:** 97
Unfinished Woman, An (Hellman), **Supp. I Part 1:** 292, 293, 294; **Supp. IV Part 1:** 12, 353–354; **Supp. IX:** 196, 200–201

Unforeseen Wilderness, The: An Essay on Kentucky's Red River Gorge (Berry), **Supp. X:** 28, 29, 30, 36
Unforgotten Years (L. P. Smith), **Supp. XIV:** 333, 334, 335, 336, 347
"Unfortunate Coincidence" (Parker), **Supp. IX:** 190
Unframed Originals (Merwin), **Supp. III Part 1:** 341
Ungar, Sanford, **Supp. XI:** 228
Ungaretti, Giuseppe, **Supp. V:** 337
Unguided Tour (Sontag), **Supp. III Part 2:** 452
"Unheimliche, Das" (The Uncanny) (Freud), **Supp. XVI:** 157–158
Unholy Sonnets (Jarman), **Supp. XVII:** 109, 110, **119–120; Supp. XVIII:** 178
"Unholy Sonnets" (Jarman), **Supp. XVII:** 118, 119–120
"Unidentified Flying Object" (Hayden), **Supp. II Part 1:** 368
"Unifying Principle, The" (Ammons), **Supp. VII:** 28
"Unimportant Man, An" (D. West), **Supp. XVIII:** 280
"Union" (Hughes), **Supp. I Part 1:** 331
"Union Street: San Francisco, Summer 1975" (Carver), **Supp. III Part 1:** 138
United States Army in World War II (Morison), **Supp. I Part 2:** 490
United States Constitution, **I:** 6, 283
United States Essays, 1951–1991 (Vidal), **Supp. IV Part 2:** 678, 687
"United States of Huck, The: Introduction to *Adventures of Huckleberry Finn*" (Saunders), *Supp. XIX:* 235
United States of Poetry, The (television series), **Supp. XIII:** 274
"Unity through Diversity" (Locke), **Supp. XIV:** 212, 213
Universal Baseball Association, Inc., J. Henry Waugh, Prop., The (Coover), **Supp. V:** 39, 41–42, 44, 46
Universal Passion (Young), **III:** 111
"Universe of Death, The" (H. Miller), **III:** 184
Universe of Time, A (Anderson), **II:** 27, 28, 45, 46, 48, 49
"Universities" (Emerson), **II:** 6
"Universities: A Mirage? " (Mora), **Supp. XIII:** 219
"University" (Shapiro), **Supp. II Part 2:** 704–705, 717
"University Avenue" (Mora), **Supp. XIII:** 216
"University Days" (Thurber), **Supp. I Part 2:** 605
"University Hospital, Boston" (Oliver), **Supp. VII:** 235
"Unknowable, The" (Levine), **Supp. V:** 195
"Unknown Girl in the Maternity Ward" (Sexton), **Supp. II Part 2:** 676
"Unknown Love, The" (Chandler), **Supp. IV Part 1:** 120
Unknown Rilke, The (Rilke; F. Wright, trans.), **Supp. XVII:** 244
"Unknown War, The" (Sandburg), **III:** 594

Unkown Constellations, The (Swados), **Supp. XIX:** 256
Unleashed (anthology), **Supp. XI:** 132
Unleashed: Poems by Writers' Dogs (Hempel and Shepard, eds.), **Supp. XXI:** 115
"Unlighted Lamps" (Anderson), **I:** 112
Unloved Wife, The (Alcott), **Supp. I Part 1:** 33
Unmarried Woman, An (film), **Supp. IV Part 1:** 303
"Unnatural Mother, The" (Gilman), **Supp. XI:** 207
"Unnatural State of the Unicorn" (Komunyakaa), **Supp. XIII:** 119
"Unparalleled Adventure of One Hans Pfaall, The" (Poe), **III:** 424
"Unpleasant Profession of Jonathan Hoag, The" (Heinlein), **Supp. XVIII:** 149
Unprecedented Era, The (Goebbels), **III:** 560
"Unprofitable Servant, The" (O. Henry), **Supp. II Part 1:** 403
Unpublished Poems of Emily Dickinson (Bianchi and Hampson, ed.), **Retro. Supp. I:** 35
Unpunished (Gilman), **Supp. XI:** 208
Unraveling Strangeness, The (Weigl), **Supp. XIX:** **287–288**
"Unreal City" (Eliot), **Supp. XV:** 218
"Unreasoning Heart" (Untermeyer), **Supp. XV:** 309
"Unsaid" (Gioia), **Supp. XV:** 129
"Unseen, The" (Pinsky), **Supp. VI:** 243–244
"Unseen, The" (Singer), **Retro. Supp. II:** 307
Unseen Hand, The (Shepard), **Supp. III Part 2:** 439, 445–446
Unselected Poems (Levine), **Supp. V:** 179
Unsettling of America, The: Culture and Agriculture (Berry), **Supp. X:** 22, 26, 29, 32, 33, 35; **Supp. XIV:** 177, 179
Unspeakable Gentleman, The (Marquand), **III:** 53–54, 60, 63
Unspeakable Practices, Unnatural Acts (Barthelme), **Supp. IV Part 1:** 39
"Unspeakable Things Unspoken: The Afro-American Presence in American Literature" (Morrison), **Supp. III Part 1:** 375, 377–379
"Untelling, The" (Strand), **Supp. IV Part 2:** 629
Unterecker, John, **I:** 386
Untermeyer, Jean Starr, **II:** 530; **Supp. XV:** 294, 295, 303, 307, 308, 310
Untermeyer, Louis, **II:** 516–517, 530, 532; **III:** 268; **Retro. Supp. I:** 124, 133, 136; **Supp. III Part 1:** 2; **Supp. IX:** 76; **Supp. XIV:** 119, 123; **Supp. XV: 293–318; Supp. XXI:** 277
Untimely Papers (Bourne), **I:** 218, 233
"Untitled" (C. Frost), **Supp. XV:** 103
"Untitled Blues" (Komunyakaa), **Supp. XIII:** 117
Unto the Sons (Talese), **Supp. XVII:** 199–200, **206–207,** 208, 209, 210

"Untrustworthy Speaker, The" (Glück), **Supp. V:** 86

"Unused" (Anderson), **I:** 112, 113

Unvanquished, The (Faulkner), **II:** 55, 67–68, 71; **Retro. Supp. I:** 84; **Supp. I Part 2:** 450

"Unvexed Isles, The" (Warren), **IV:** 253

"Unwedded" (Larcom), **Supp. XIII:** 144

"Unweepables, The" (Karr), **Supp. XI:** 243

"Unwelcome Guest, An" (Papernick), **Supp. XVII:** 50

Unwelcome Man, The (W. Frank), **Supp. XX:70,** 76

Unwelcome Words (Bowles), **Supp. IV Part 1:** 93, 94

"Unwelcome Words" (Bowles), **Supp. IV Part 1:** 94, 95

Unwin, T. Fisher, **Supp. XI:** 202

"Unwithered Garland, The" (Kunitz), **Supp. III Part 1:** 265

Unwobbling Pivot, The (Pound, trans.), **III:** 472

"Unwritten, The" (Merwin), **Supp. III Part 1:** 352

"Unwritten Law" (Glück), **Supp. V:** 91

Up (Sukenick), **Supp. V:** 39

Up Above the World (Bowles), **Supp. IV Part 1:** 82, 91, 92

"Up and Down" (Merrill), **Supp. III Part 1:** 328

Upanishads, **IV:** 183

Up Country: Poems of New England (Kumin), **Supp. IV Part 2:** 446, 447–448, 453

"Update" (Dunn), **Supp. XI:** 150–151

Updike, John, **I:** 54; **III:** 572; **IV: 214–235; Retro. Supp. I:** 116, **317–338; Retro. Supp. II:** 213, 279, 280; **Supp. I Part 1:** 186, 196; **Supp. IV Part 2:** 657; **Supp. V:** 23, 43, 95, 119; **Supp. VIII:** 151, 167, 236; **Supp. IX:** 208; **Supp. XI:** 65, 66, 99, 140; **Supp. XII:** 140, 296, 298, 310; **Supp. XIII:** 45–46, 47, 52; **Supp. XIV:** 79, 93, 111; **Supp. XVI:** 205, 207, 220; **Supp. XX:**17; **Supp. XXI:** 116, 226

Updike, Mrs. Wesley, **IV:** 218, 220

Up from Slavery (Washington), **Supp. II Part 1:** 169; **Supp. IX:** 19

Upham, Thomas Goggswell, **II:** 487

"Upholsterers, The" (Lardner), **II:** 435

"Up in Michigan" (Hemingway), **II:** 263; **Supp. XIX:** 241

Upjohn, Richard, **IV:** 312

"Upon a Spider Catching a Fly" (Taylor), **IV:** 161

"Upon a Wasp Child with Cold" (Taylor), **IV:** 161

"Upon Meeting Don L. Lee, in a Dream" (Dove), **Supp. IV Part 1:** 244

"Upon My Dear and Loving Husband His Going into England, Jan. 16, 1661" (Bradstreet), **Supp. I Part 1:** 110

"Upon Returning to the Country Road" (Lindsay), **Supp. I Part 2:** 382

"Upon the Burning of Our House, July 10th, 1666" (Bradstreet), **Supp. I Part 1:** 107–108, 122

"Upon the Sweeping Flood" (Taylor), **IV:** 161

"Upon Wedlock, and Death of Children" (Taylor), **IV:** 144, 147, 161

"Upset, An" (Merrill), **Supp. III Part 1:** 336

Upstairs and Downstairs (Vonnegut), **Supp. II Part 2:** 757

Upstate (Wilson), **IV:** 447

Upton, Lee, **Supp. X:** 209

"Upturned Face" (Crane), **I:** 423

Upward, Allen, **Supp. I Part 1:** 262

Upward, Edward, **Supp. XIV:** 159, 160

"Upward Moon and the Downward Moon, The" (R. Bly), **Supp. IV Part 1:** 71

Urania: A Rhymed Lesson (Holmes), **Supp. I Part 1:** 300

"Urban Convalescence, An" (Merrill), **Supp. III Part 1:** 322–324

"Urban Renewal" (Komunyakaa), **Supp. XIII:** 113

Urdang, Constance, **Supp. XV:** 74

"Urganda and Fatima" (Rowson), **Supp. XV:** 234

Urial Accosta: A Play (Reznikoff), **Supp. XIV:** 282, 288

Urich, Robert, **Supp. V:** 228

"Uriel" (Emerson), **II:** 19

Uris, Leon, **Supp. IV Part 1:** 285, 379; **Supp. XX:243–258**

Uroff, Margaret D., **Supp. I Part 2:** 542

"Us" (Sexton), **Supp. II Part 2:** 687

U.S. 1 (Rukeyser), **Supp. VI:** 272, 278, 283, 285

U.S.A. (Dos Passos), **I:** 379, 475, 478, 482–488, 489, 490, 491, 492, 493, 494, 495; **Retro. Supp. II:** 197; **Supp. I Part 2:** 646; **Supp. III Part 1:** 104, 105; **Supp. XIV:** 24

"U.S.A. School of Writing, The" (Bishop), **Retro. Supp. II:** 43

"U.S. Commercial Orchid, The" (Agee), **I:** 35

"Used-Boy Raisers, The" (Paley), **Supp. VI:** 218, 228

"Used Cars on Oahu" (Nye), **Supp. XIII:** 282

"Used Side of the Sofa, The" (Ríos), **Supp. IV Part 2:** 551

Useless Servants, The (Hinojosa), **Supp. XIX:** 98, 103, 104, **109–110**

Use of Fire, The (Price), **Supp. VI:** 265

"Use of Force, The" (W. C. Williams), **Retro. Supp. I:** 424

Use of Poetry and the Use of Criticism, The (Eliot), **Retro. Supp. I:** 65

Uses of Enchantment, The: The Meaning and Importance of Fairy Tales (Bettelheim), **Supp. XIV:** 126

Uses of Enchantment, The: The Meaning and Importance of Fairy Tales (Bettleheim), **Supp. X:** 77

"Uses of Hell, The" (E. Hoffman), **Supp. XVI:** 154

"Uses of Hell, The: An Exchange"(Novick, Katz, and Szulc), **Supp. XVI:** 154

Uses of Literacy, The (Hoggart), **Supp. XIV:** 299

"Uses of Poetry, The" (W. C. Williams), **Retro. Supp. I:** 412

"Uses of the Blues, The" (Baldwin), **Retro. Supp. II:** 8

"Use-Unuse of Us, The" (Bronk), **Supp. XXI:** 32

"USFS 1919: The Ranger, the Cook, and a Hole in the Sky" (Maclean), **Supp. XIV:** 230, 234

Ushant: An Essay (Aiken), **I:** 49, 54, 55, 56, 57

"Usher 11" (Bradbury), **Supp. I Part 2:** 622

"Using Parrots to Kill Mockingbirds: Yet Another Racial Prosecution and Wrongful Conviction in Maycomb" (Fair), **Supp. VIII:** 128

Ustedes y Nosotros: Nuevo Mensaje a Ibero-América (W. Frank), **Supp. XX:79**

Usual Star, The (Doolittle), **Supp. I Part 1:** 270

"Usurpation (Other People's Stories)" (Ozick), **Supp. V:** 268, 271

Utopia 14 (Vonnegut), **Supp. II Part 2:** 757

V

V. (Pynchon), **Supp. II Part 2:** 618, 620–622, 627–630; **Supp. IV Part 1:** 279

"Vacation" (Stafford), **Supp. XI:** 321, 322

"Vacation Trip" (Stafford), **Supp. XI:** 322

Vachel Lindsay: A Poet in America (Masters), **Supp. I Part 2:** 473, 474

"Vachel Lindsay: The Midwest as Utopia" (Whitney), **Supp. I Part 2:** 403

"Vachel Lindsay Writes to Floyd Dell" (Tanselle), **Supp. I Part 2:** 403

"Vacillation" (Yeats), **Supp. XV:** 253

Vadim, Roger, **Supp. XI:** 293, 307

"Vag" (Dos Passos), **I:** 487–488

Vagina Monologues, The (Ensler), **Supp. XIX:** 204–205

Valediction (Parker), **Supp. XIX:** 185

Valentine, Jean, **Supp. V:** 92

Valentine, Saint, **IV:** 396

Valentines (Kooser), **Supp. XIX:** 116, 123, **128–129**

Valentino, Rudolph, **I:** 483

Valéry, Paul, **II:** 543, 544; **III:** 279, 409, 428, 609; **IV:** 79, 91, 92, 428, 443; **Retro. Supp. II:** 187

"Valhalla" (Francis), **Supp. IX:** 77

Valhalla and Other Poems (Francis), **Supp. IX:** 76

Validity in Interpretation (Hirsch), **Supp. XIV:** 15

Valitsky, Ken, **Supp. XII:** 7

Vallejo, César, **Supp. V:** 332; **Supp. IX:** 271; **Supp. XIII:** 114, 315, 323; **Supp. XXI:** 132

"Valley, The" (Bass), **Supp. XVI:** 20, 22

Valley, The (Hinojosa), **Supp. XIX:** 97, 99, **100–101**

"Valley Between, The" (Marshall), **Supp. XI:** 278

Valley of Decision, The (Wharton), **IV:** 311, 315; **Retro. Supp. I:** 365–367

"Valley of the Monsters, The" (Peacock), **Supp. XIX:** 198

Valley of the Moon, The (London), **II:** 467, 481

"Valley of Unrest, The" (Poe), **III:** 411

Valli, Alida, **Supp. IV Part 2:** 520

"Valor" (Bausch), **Supp. VII:** 54

Valparaiso (DeLillo), **Supp. VI:** 4, 12

"Value of a Place, The" (Bass), **Supp. XVI:** 18

"Values and Fictions" (Toomer), **Supp. III Part 2:** 485–486

"Values and Imperatives" (Locke), **Supp. XIV:** 199, 202, 212

Values of Veblen, The: A Critical Appraisal (Rosenberg), **Supp. I Part 2:** 650

"Vampire" (Karr), **Supp. XI:** 241

Vampire Armand, The (Rice), **Supp. VII:** 290, 294–295

Vampire Chronicles, The (Rice), **Supp. VII:** 290

Vampire Lestat, The (Rice), **Supp. VII:** 290–292, 298, 299

Van Aalst, Mariska, **Supp. XIX:** 50, 51

Van Buren, Martin, **II:** 134, 312; **III:** 473

Vande Kieft, Ruth M., **IV:** 260

Vanderbilt, Cornelius, **III:** 14

Van Dine, S. S., **Supp. IV Part 1:** 341

Van Doren, Carl, **I:** 252–253, 423; **II:** 103, 111, 112; **Supp. I Part 2:** 474, 486, 707, 709, 717, 718, 727; **Supp. II Part 1:** 395; **Supp. VIII:** 96–97

Van Doren, Mark, **I:** 168; **III:** 4, 23, 589; **Supp. I Part 2:** 604; **Supp. III Part 2:** 626; **Supp. VIII:** 231; **Supp. IX:** 266, 268; **Supp. XV:** 152, 305, 307

Vandover and the Brute (Norris), **III:** 314, 315, 316, 320–322, 328, 333, 334

Van Duyn, Mona, **Supp. IX:** 269

Van Dyke, Annette, **Supp. IV Part 1:** 327

Van Dyke, Henry, **I:** 223; **II:** 456

Van Gogh, Vincent, **I:** 27; **IV:** 290; **Supp. I Part 2:** 451; **Supp. IV Part 1:** 284

Van Gogh's Room at Arles (Elkin), **Supp. VI:** 56

"Vanilla Dunk" (Lethem), **Supp. XVIII:** 139

"Vanisher, The" (Whittier), **Supp. I Part 2:** 691

Vanishing Point (Markson), **Supp. XVII:** 135, 137, 138, 145–146

"Vanishing Red, The" (Frost), **Retro. Supp. II:** 47

"Vanity" (B. Diop), **Supp. IV Part 1:** 16

Vanity Fair (Thackeray), **I:** 354; **II:** 91; **III:** 70; **Supp. IX:** 200

"Vanity of All Wordly Things, The" (Bradstreet), **Supp. I Part 1:** 102, 119

Vanity of Duluoz (Kerouac), **Supp. III Part 1:** 221, 222

"Vanity of Existence, The" (Freneau), **Supp. II Part 1:** 262

Van Matre, Lynn, **Supp. V:** 126

Vann, Barbara, **Supp. XV:** 187

Vanquished, The (Faulkner), **I:** 205

Van Rensselaer, Stephen, **I:** 351

Van Vechten, Carl, **I:** 295; **IV:** 76; **Supp. I Part 1:** 324, 327, 332; **Supp. I Part 2:** 715; **Supp. II Part 2:** 725–751;

Supp. X: 247; **Supp. XVI:** 135; **Supp. XVII:** 96, 97, 101, 104; **Supp. XVIII:** 123, 131, 132, 279, 280; **Supp. XIX:** 76; **Supp. XX:**69; **Supp. XXI:** 5, 8

Vanzetti, Bartolomeo, **I:** 482, 486, 490, 494; **II:** 38–39, 426; **III:** 139–140; **Supp. I Part 2:** 446, 610, 611; **Supp. V:** 288–289; **Supp. IX:** 199

"Vapor Trail Reflected in the Frog Pond" (Kinnell), **Supp. III Part 1:** 242–243

"Vapor Trails" (Snyder), **Supp. VIII:** 298

"Variation: Ode to Fear" (Warren), **IV:** 241

"Variation on a Sentence" (Bogan), **Supp. III Part 1:** 60

"Variation on Gaining a Son" (Dove), **Supp. IV Part 1:** 248

"Variation on Pain" (Dove), **Supp. IV Part 1:** 248

"Variations: The air is sweetest that a thistle guards" (Merrill), **Supp. III Part 1:** 321

"Variations: White Stag, Black Bear" (Merrill), **Supp. III Part 1:** 321

"Varick Street" (Bishop), **Supp. I Part 1:** 90, 92

Varieties of Metaphysical Poetry, The (Eliot), **Retro. Supp. I:** 65

Varieties of Religious Experience, The (William James), **II:** 344, 353, 354, 359–360, 362; **IV:** 28, 291; **Supp. IX:** 19

Variety (film), **Supp. XII:** 7

Variorum (Whitman), **Retro. Supp. I:** 406

Various Antidotes (J. Scott), **Supp. XVII: 188–189**

Various Miracles (Shields), **Supp. VII:** 318–320, 323, 324

"Various Miracles" (Shields), **Supp. VII:** 318–319, 324

Various Poems (Zach), **Supp. XV:** 86

"Various Tourists" (Connell), **Supp. XIV:** 79

"Varmint Question, The" (Leopold), **Supp. XIV:** 180–181

Varno, David, **Supp. XIX:** 205

Vasari, Giorgio, **Supp. I Part 2:** 450; **Supp. III Part 1:** 5

Vasquez, Robert, **Supp. V:** 180

Vassall Morton (Parkman), **Supp. II Part 2:** 595, 597–598

Vasse, W. W., **III:** 478

Vaudeville for a Princess (Schwartz), **Supp. II Part 2:** 661–662

Vaughan, Henry, **IV:** 151; **Supp. XV:** 251

Vaughn, Robert, **Supp. XI:** 343

"Vaunting Oak" (Ransom), **III:** 490

Vazirani, Reetika, **Supp. XIII:** 133

Veblen (Hobson), **Supp. I Part 2:** 650

Veblen, Andrew, **Supp. I Part 2:** 640

Veblen, Oswald, **Supp. I Part 2:** 640

Veblen, Thorstein, **I:** 104, 283, 475–476, 483, 498, 511; **II:** 27, 272, 276, 287; **Supp. I Part 2: 628–650; Supp. IV Part 1:** 22

Veblen, Mrs. Thorstein (Ellen Rolfe), **Supp. I Part 2:** 641

Veblenism: A New Critique (Dobriansky), **Supp. I Part 2:** 648, 650

"Veblen's Attack on Culture" (Adorno), **Supp. I Part 2:** 650

Vechten, Carl Van, **Retro. Supp. I:** 199

Vectors and Smoothable Curves (Bronk), **Supp. XXI: 24–26,** 32

Vedanta for Modern Man (Isherwood, ed.), **Supp. XIV:** 164

Vedanta for the Western World (Isherwood, ed.), **Supp. XIV:** 164

Vedas, **IV:** 183

Vega, Janine Pommy, **Supp. XIV:** 148

Vega, Lope de, **Retro. Supp. I:** 285; **Supp. III Part 1:** 341, 347

Vegetable, The (Fitzgerald), **Retro. Supp. I:** 105; **Supp. IX:** 57

Vegetable, The, or From President to Postman (Fitzgerald), **II:** 91

"Vegetable Love" (Apple), **Supp. XVII:** 4

"Vegetable Wisdom" (Halliday), **Supp. XIX:** 88

Veinberg, Jon, **Supp. V:** 180; **Supp. XIII:** 313; **Supp. XV:** 76–77, 86

Vein of Iron (Glasgow), **II:** 175, 186, 188–189, 191, 192, 194

Vein of Riches, A (Knowles), **Supp. XII:** 249

Vein of Words (J. W. Miller), **Supp. XX:**165

Velie, Alan R., **Supp. IV Part 2:** 486

Velocities: New and Selected Poems, 1966–1992 (Dobyns), **Supp. XIII:** 86–87, 87, 88

"Velocity" (Collins), **Supp. XXI:** 61

"Velorio" (Cisneros), **Supp. VII:** 66

"Velvet Gentleman, The (Skloot), **Supp. XX:**201

"Velvet Shoes" (Wylie), **Supp. I Part 2:** 711, 714

Venant, Elizabeth, **Supp. XI:** 343

Vencloca, Thomas, **Supp. VIII:** 29

Vendler, Helen H., **Retro. Supp. I:** 297; **Retro. Supp. II:** 184, 191; **Supp. I Part 1:** 77, 78, 92, 95; **Supp. I Part 2:** 565; **Supp. IV Part 1:** 245, 247, 249, 254, 257; **Supp. IV Part 2:** 448; **Supp. V:** 78, 82, 189, 343; **Supp. XII:** 187, 189; **Supp. XV:** 20, 184

"Venetian Blind, The" (Jarrell), **II:** 382–383

Venetian Glass Nephew, The (Wylie), **Supp. I Part 2:** 707, 709, 714, 717–719, 721, 724

Venetian Life (Howells), **II:** 274, 277, 279

Venetian Vespers, The (Hecht), **Supp. X:** 57, **65–69**

"Venetian Vespers, The" (Hecht), **Supp. X:** 65, **66–67**

Venice Observed (McCarthy), **II:** 562

Ventadorn, Bernard de, **Supp. IV Part 1:** 146

"Ventriloquists' Conversations" (Gentry), **Supp. IV Part 1:** 236

"Venus, Cupid, Folly and Time" (Taylor), **Supp. V:** 322–323

Venus and Adonis (film), **Supp. IV Part 1:** 82

Venus and Don Juan (C. Frost), **Supp. XV:** 93, **102–103,** 104, 107

"Venus and Don Juan" (C. Frost), **Supp. XV:** 103

Venus Blue (Sobin), **Supp. XVI:** 293–294, 294

Venus in Sparta (Auchincloss), **Supp. IV Part 1:** 25

"Venus Pandemos" (Halliday), **Supp. XIX:** 85, 89, 90, 93

"Venus's-flytraps" (Komunyakaa), **Supp. XIII:** 126, 127

"Veracruz" (Hayden), **Supp. II Part 1:** 371, 373

Verga, Giovanni, **II:** 271, 275

Verghese, Abraham, **Supp. X:** 160

Verhaeren, Emile, **I:** 476; **II:** 528, 529

Verlaine, Paul, **II:** 529, 543; **III:** 466; **IV:** 79, 80, 86, 286; **Retro. Supp. I:** 56, 62; **Retro. Supp. II:** 326

"Vermeer" (Nemerov), **III:** 275, 278, 280

Vermeer, Jan, **Retro. Supp. I:** 335

"Vermont" (Carruth), **Supp. XVI:** 54

Vermont Notebook, The (Ashbery), **Supp. III Part 1:** 1

"Vernal Ague, The" (Freneau), **Supp. II Part 1:** 258

Verne, Jules, **I:** 480; **Retro. Supp. I:** 270; **Supp. XI:** 63

Vernon, John, **Supp. X:** 15

Verplanck, Gulian C., **Supp. I Part 1:** 155, 156, 157, 158

Verrazano, Giovanni da, **Supp. I Part 2:** 496, 497

Verse (Zawacki), **Supp. VIII:** 272

"Verse for Urania" (Merrill), **Supp. III Part 1:** 329, 330

Verses (Wharton), **Retro. Supp. I:** 362

Verses, Printed for Her Friends (Jewett), **II:** 406

"Verses for Children" (Lowell), **II:** 516

"Verses Made at Sea in a Heavy Gale" (Freneau), **Supp. II Part 1:** 262

"Verses on the Death of T. S. Eliot" (Brodsky), **Supp. VIII:** 19

"Version of a Fragment of Simonides" (Bryant), **Supp. I Part 1:** 153, 155

Verulam, Baron. *See* Bacon, Francis

Very, Jones, **III:** 507

"Very Hot Sun in Bermuda, The" (Jackson), **Supp. IX:** 126

Very Old Bones (W. Kennedy), **Supp. VII:** 133, 148, 150–153

Very Persistent Gappers of Frip, The (Saunders), **Supp. XIX:** 229–230

"Very Proper Gander, The" (Thurber), **Supp. I Part 2:** 610

"Very Short Story, A" (Hemingway), **II:** 252; **Retro. Supp. I:** 173

"Vesalius in Zante" (Wharton), **Retro. Supp. I:** 372

Vesey, Denmark, **Supp. I Part 2:** 592

Vesey, Desmond, **Supp. XIV:** 162

"Vespers" (Auden), **Supp. II Part 1:** 23

"Vespers" (Glück), **Supp. V:** 88

Vestal Lady on Brattle, The (Corso), **Supp. XII:** 119, **120–121,** 134

Vested Interests and the Common Man, The (Veblen), **Supp. I Part 2:** 642

"Vesuvius at Home" (Rich), **Retro. Supp. I:** 42

"Veteran, The" (Crane), **I:** 413

"Veterans' Cemetery" (Gioia), **Supp. XV:** 117

"Veteran Sirens" (Robinson), **III:** 512, 524

"Veterinarian" (X. J. Kennedy), **Supp. XV:** 168

"Vetiver" (Ashbery), **Supp. III Part 1:** 26

"Via Dieppe-Newhaven" (H. Miller), **III:** 183

"Via Negativa" (Salter), **Supp. IX:** 257

Vicar of Wakefeld, The (Goldsmith), **I:** 216

Vicious Circle, The (film, Wilder), **Supp. XVII:** 62

"Vicissitudes of the Avant-Garde, The" (Gass), **Supp. VI:** 91

Vico, Giambattista, **Supp. XX:** 38

Victim, The (Bellow), **I:** 144, 145, 147, 149, 150, 151, 152, 153, 155, 156, 158, 159, 164; **IV:** 19; **Retro. Supp. II:** 21, 22, 34

"Victor" (Mumford), **Supp. II Part 2:** 476

Victoria (Rowson), **Supp. XV:** 231

Victorian in the Modern World, A (Hapgood), **Supp. XVII:** 95, 97, 100, 101, 103, 105, 106; **Supp. XXI:** 8

"Victoria's Secret" (Collins), **Supp. XXI:** 58–59

"Victories" (Untermeyer), **Supp. XV:** 300

"Victory at Sea" (television series), **Supp. I Part 2:** 490

"Victory comes late" (Dickinson), **Retro. Supp. I:** 45

"Victory of the Moon, The" (Crane), **I:** 420

Vida, Vendela, **Supp. XIX:** 49, 50, 53, 57, 58, 59, 61, 62

Vidal, Gore, **II:** 587; **IV:** 383; **Supp. IV Part 1:** 22, 35, 92, 95, 198; **Supp. IV Part 2: 677–696; Supp. IX:** 96; **Supp. X:** 186, 195; **Supp. XIV:** 156, 170, 338; **Supp. XIX:** 131, 132

Video Poems (Collins), **Supp. XXI:** 53

Viebahn, Fred, **Supp. IV Part 1:** 248

Viera, Joseph M., **Supp. XI:** 178, 186

Viereck, Peter, **Supp. I Part 2:** 403

Viertel, Berthold, **Supp. XIV:** 165

Viertel, Salka, **Supp. XVI:** 192

Viet Journal (Jones), **Supp. XI:** 230–231

Vietnam (McCarthy), **II:** 578–579

"Vietnam in Me, The" (O'Brien), **Supp. V:** 241, 252

Vie unanime, La (Romains), **I:** 227

"View, The" (Roussel), **Supp. III Part 1:** 15, 16, 21

View from 80, The (Cowley), **Supp. II Part 1:** 141, 144, 153

"View from an Institution" (F. Wright), **Supp. XVII:** 244

"View from the Backyard" (W. V. Davis), **Supp. XXI:** 96

View from the Bridge, A (A. Miller), **III:** 147, 148, 156, 158, 159–160

View of My Own, A: Essays in Literature and Society (Hardwick), **Supp. III Part 1:** 194, 200

"View of the Capital from the Library of Congress" (Bishop), **Retro. Supp. II:** 45

View of the Soil and Climate of the United States, A (Brown, trans.), **Supp. I Part 1:** 146

"View of the Woods, A" (O'Connor), **III:** 349, 351, 358; **Retro. Supp. II:** 237

"Views of the Mysterious Hill: The Appearance of Parnassus in American Poetry" (Strand), **Supp. IV Part 2:** 631

"Vigil" (Karr), **Supp. XI:** 241

"Vigil, The" (Dante), **III:** 542

"Vigil at Heiligenkreuz" (W. V. Davis), **Supp. XXI:** 93

"Vignette" (Trethewey), **Supp. XXI:** 253, 254

Vigny, Alfred Victor de, **II:** 543

Vildrac, Charles, **Supp. XV:** 50

Vile Bodies (Waugh), **Supp. I Part 2:** 607

Villa, Pancho, **I:** 210; **III:** 584

"Village Blacksmith, The" (Longfellow), **Retro. Supp. II:** 167, 168; **Supp. I Part 2:** 409

Village Hymns, a Supplement to Dr. Watts's Psalms and Hymns (Nettleton), **I:** 458

"Village Improvement Parade, The" (Lindsay), **Supp. I Part 2:** 388, 389

Village Magazine, The (Lindsay), **Supp. I Part 2:** 379–380, 382

Village Virus, The (Lewis), **II:** 440

"Villanelle at Sundown" (Justice), **Supp. VII:** 119, 122–123

"Villanelle of Change" (Robinson), **III:** 524

Villard, Oswald, **Supp. I Part 1:** 332

"Villa Selene" (Simpson), **Supp. IX:** 279

Villon, François, **II:** 544; **III:** 9, 174, 592; **Retro. Supp. I:** 286; **Supp. I Part 1:** 261; **Supp. III Part 1:** 235, 243, 249, 253; **Supp. III Part 2:** 560; **Supp. IX:** 116

"Villonaud for This Yule" (Pound), **Retro. Supp. I:** 286

"Vincenzo Tailor" (Di Piero), **Supp. XIX:** 38

Vindication of the Rights of Woman (Wollstonecraft), **Supp. I Part 1:** 126; **Supp. XI:** 203

Vines, Lois Davis, **Retro. Supp. II:** 261

Vintage Book of Amnesia, The (Lethem, ed.), **Supp. XVIII:** 138

"Vintage Thunderbird, A" (Beattie), **Supp. V:** 27

Vinz, Mark, **Supp. X:** 117

Viol de Lucrèce, Le (Obey), **IV:** 356

Violence (Bausch), **Supp. VII:** 48–49, 54

Violent Bear It Away, The (O'Connor), **III:** 339, 345–348, 350, 351, 354, 355, 356, 357; **Retro. Supp. II:** 233, **234–236**

Violent Hero, Wilderness Heritage and Urban Reality, The: A Study of the Private Eye in the Novels of Dashiell Hammett, Raymond Chandler and Ross Macdonald (Parker), **Supp. XIX:** 177

"Violent Vet, The" (O'Brien), **Supp. V:** 238

Violin (Rice), **Supp. VII:** 302

Viorst, Judith, **Supp. X:** 153

Viper Run (Karr), **Supp. XI: 248–251**

Virgil, **I:** 312, 322, 587; **II:** 133, 542; **IV:** 137, 359; **Retro. Supp. I:** 135; **Supp. I Part 1:** 153; **Supp. I Part 2:** 494; **Supp. IV Part 2:** 631

"Virgin and Child with Music and Numbers" (Bronk), **Supp. XXI:** 30

"Virgin and the Dynamo" (Adams), **III:** 396

"Virgin Carrying a Lantern, The" (Stevens), **IV:** 80

Virginia (Glasgow), **II:** 175, 178, 181–182, 193, 194

"Virginia" (Lindsay), **Supp. I Part 2:** 398

"Virginia Britannia" (Moore), **III:** 198, 208–209

"Virginians Are Coming Again, The" (Lindsay), **Supp. I Part 2:** 399

Virginia Reels (Hoffman), **Supp. XVIII:** 79, 86

Virgin Spain (W. Frank), **Supp. XX:**76

"Virgin Violeta" (Porter), **III:** 454

"Virility" (Ozick), **Supp. V:** 262, 265

Virtual Light (W. Gibson), **Supp. XVI:** 124, **129,** 130

Virtue of Selfishness, The: A New Concept of Egoism (Rand), **Supp. IV Part 2:** 527, 530–532

"Virtuoso" (Francis), **Supp. IX:** 82

Virtuous Woman, A (Gibbons), **Supp. X: 44–45,** 46, 50

Visconti, Luchino, **Supp. V:** 51

Viscusi, Robert, **Supp. XX:**46

Visible Saints: The History of a Puritan Idea (Morgan), **IV:** 149

"Vision, A" (Olds), **Supp. X:** 214

"Vision, A" (Winters), **Supp. II Part 2:** 785, 795

"Vision and Prayer" (D. Thomas), **I:** 432

"Visionary, The" (Poe), **III:** 411

Visionary Farms, The (Eberhart), **I:** 537–539

Visioning, The (Glaspell), **Supp. III Part 1:** 175–177, 180, 187, 188

Vision in Spring (Faulkner), **Retro. Supp. I:** 79

Vision of Columbus (Barlow), **Supp. I Part 1:** 124; **Supp. II Part 1:** 67, 68, 70–75, 77, 79

Vision of Sir Launfal, The (Lowell), **Supp. I Part 1:** 311; **Supp. I Part 2:** 406, 409, 410

"Vision of the World, A" (Cheever), **Supp. I Part 1:** 182, 192

Visions of Cody (Kerouac), **Supp. III Part 1:** 225–227

Visions of Gerard (Kerouac), **Supp. III Part 1:** 219–222, 225, 227, 229

"Visions of the Daughters of Albion" (Blake), **III:** 540

"Visit" (Ammons), **Supp. VII:** 28–29

"Visit, The" (Kenyon), **Supp. VII:** 169

"Visitant, The" (Dunn), **Supp. XI:** 147

"*Visitation, The*/La Visitación" (Mora), **Supp. XIII:** 217, 224, 228

"Visit Home, A" (Stafford), **Supp. XI:** 318

Visit in 2001, The (musical, McNally), **Supp. XIII:** 207

"Visiting My Own House in Iowa City" (Stern), **Supp. IX:** 300

"Visit of Charity, A" (Welty), **IV:** 262

"Visitors" (J. W. Miller), **Supp. XX:**167

"Visitors" (Salinas), **Supp. XIII:** 318

"Visitors, The/Los Visitantes" (Kingsolver), **Supp. VII:** 208

"Visits to St. Elizabeths" (Bishop), **Retro. Supp. II:** 47

"Visit to a Small Planet" (teleplay) (Vidal), **Supp. IV Part 2:** 682

Visit to a Small Planet: A Comedy Akin to Vaudeville (Vidal), **Supp. IV Part 2:** 682–683

"Visit to Avoyelles, A" (Chopin), **Supp. I Part 1:** 213

"Visit to Manafon, A" (W. V. Davis), **Supp. XXI:** 96

"Vissi d'Arte" (Moore), **Supp. X: 173–174**

Vistas of History (Morison), **Supp. I Part 2:** 492

"Vita" (Stafford), **Supp. XI:** 330

"Vita Brevis" (Hull), **Supp. XXI:** 138

Vital, David, **Supp. XVI:** 160

Vital Provisions (Price), **Supp. VI:** 262–263

"Vitamins" (Carver), **Supp. III Part 1:** 138

Vita Nova (Glück), **Supp. V:** 90–92

Vitruvius, **Supp. XVI:** 292

Vittorio, the Vampire (Rice), **Supp. VII:** 295–296

Viudas (Dorfman), **Supp. IX:** 138

"Viva Vargas!" (Allen), **Supp. XV:** 15

Viviparous Quadrupeds of North America, The (Audubon and Bachman), **Supp. XVI:** 10

Vizenor, Gerald, **Supp. IV Part 1:** 260, 262, 329, 404; **Supp. IV Part 2:** 502

Vladimir Nabokov: The American Years (Nabokov), **Retro. Supp. I:** 275

Vlag, Piet, **Supp. XV:** 295

"Vlemk, the Box Painter" (Gardner), **Supp. VI:** 73

"V-Letter" (Shapiro), **Supp. II Part 2:** 707

V-Letter and Other Poems (Shapiro), **Supp. II Part 2:** 702, 706

"Vocabulary of Dearness" (Nye), **Supp. XIII:** 284

"Vocation" (Stafford), **Supp. XI:** 312, 321

Vocation and a Voice, A (Chopin), **Retro. Supp. II:** 67, 72

"Vocation and a Voice, A" (Chopin), **Retro. Supp. II:** 72; **Supp. I Part 1:** 200, 220, 224, 225

Vogel, David, **Supp. XV:** 88

Vogel, Speed, **Supp. IV Part 1:** 390

"Vogue Vista" (Peacock), **Supp. XIX:** 200

"Voice" (F. Wright), **Supp. XVII:** 245

"Voice, The" (Dunn), **Supp. XI:** 152

Voiced Connections of James Dickey, The (Dickey), **Supp. IV Part 1:** 177

"Voice from the Wilderness" (Ray), **Supp. XVIII:** 202

"Voice from the Woods, A" (Humphrey), **Supp. IX:** 101

"Voice from Under the Table, A" (Wilbur), **Supp. III Part 2:** 553, 554

Voice of Reason, The: Essays in Objectivist Thought (Rand), **Supp. IV Part 2:** 527, 528, 532

"Voice of Rock, The" (Ginsberg), **Supp. II Part 1:** 313

Voice of the Butterfly, The (Nichols), **Supp. XIII:** 270

Voice of the City, The (O. Henry), **Supp. II Part 1:** 410

"Voice of the Mountain, The" (Crane), **I:** 420

Voice of the Negro (Barber), **Supp. II Part 1:** 168

"Voice of the Past, The" (Skloot), **Supp. XX:**207

Voice of the People, The (Glasgow), **II:** 175, 176

Voice of the Turtle: American Indian Literature 1900–1970 (Gunn Allen, ed.), **Supp. IV Part 1:** 332, 334

Voices from the Moon (Dubus), **Supp. VII:** 88–89

"Voices from the Other World" (Merrill), **Supp. III Part 1:** 331

Voices in the House (Sedges), **Supp. II Part 1:** 125

Voices of a Summer Day (Shaw), **Supp. XIX:** 251

Voices of the Night (Longfellow), **II:** 489, 493; **Retro. Supp. II:** 154, 157, 168

"Voices of Village Square, The" (Wolfe), **Supp. III Part 2:** 571–572

Voice That Is Great within Us, The (Caruth, ed.), **Supp. XIII:** 112

Void Moon (Connelly), **Supp. XXI: 73,** 74

Voigt, Ellen Bryan, **Supp. XIII:** 76

Voix humaine, La (Cocteau), **Supp. XX:**236

Volkening, Henry, **Retro. Supp. II:** 117; **Supp. XV:** 142

Vollmann, William T., **Supp. XIV:** 96; **Supp. XVII: 225–237; Supp. XX:**93

Volney, Constantin François de Chasseboeuf, **Supp. I Part 1:** 146

Voltaire, **I:** 194; **II:** 86, 103, 449; **III:** 420; **IV:** 18; **Retro. Supp. II:** 94; **Supp. I Part 1:** 288–289; **Supp. I Part 2:** 669, 717; **Supp. XV:** 258; **Supp. XX:**285

Voltaire! Voltaire! (Endore), **Supp. XVII:** 65

Volunteers, The (Rowson and Reinagle), **Supp. XV:** 238

Vonnegut, Kurt, **Retro. Supp. I:** 170; **Supp. II Part 2:** 557, 689, **753–784; Supp. IV Part 1:** 227, 392; **Supp. V:** 40, 42, 237, 244, 296; **Supp. X:** 260; **Supp. XI:** 104; **Supp. XII:** 139, 141; **Supp. XVIII:** 242, 252; **Supp. XXI:** 226

Vonnegut, Kurt, Jr., **Supp. XVII:** 41, 135; **Supp. XIX:** 223

"Voracities and Verities" (Moore), **III:** 214

Vore, Nellie, **I:** 199

Vorlicky, Robert, **Supp. IX:** 132, 135, 136, 141, 144, 147

Vorse, Mary Heaton, **Supp. XVII:** 99; **Supp. XX:**76; **Supp. XXI:** 5, 6, 9, 13

"Vorticism" (Pound), **Retro. Supp. I:** 288

Vosjoli, Philippe de, **Supp. XX:**253

Voss, Richard, **I:** 199–200

"Vow, The" (Hecht), **Supp. X:** 64

"Vowels 2" (Baraka), **Supp. II Part 1:** 51

Vow of Conversation, A: Journal, 1964–1965 (Merton), **Supp. VIII:** 206

Vox (Baker), **Supp. XIII:** 47–49, 50, 52, 53

"Voyage" (MacLeish), **III:** 15

Voyage, The (Caputo), **Supp. XIX:** 25, 27–28

"Voyage, The" (Irving), **II:** 304

Voyage, The, and Other Versions of Poems by Baudelaire (Lowell), **Retro. Supp. II:** 187

Voyage dans la Haute Pennsylvanie et dans l'état de New-York (Crèvecoeur), **Supp. I Part 1:** 250–251

Voyage of the Beagle (Darwin), **Supp. IX:** 211

Voyage Out, The (Woolf), **Supp. XV:** 65

"Voyager, The" (Everwine), **Supp. XV:** 75

"Voyages" (H. Crane), **I:** 393–395; **Retro. Supp. II:** 78, 80, 81

"Voyages" (Levine), **Supp. V:** 190

Voyages and Discoveries of the Companions of Columbus (Irving), **II:** 310

Voyage to Pagany, A (W. C. Williams), **IV:** 404; **Retro. Supp. I:** 418–419, **420–421,** 423

Voyaging Portraits (Sobin), **Supp. XVI:** 282, 287

"Voyeur, The" (Gioia), **Supp. XV:** 125

"Voz de America" (column, W. Frank), **Supp. XX:**80

Voznesensky, Andrei, **II:** 553; **Supp. III Part 1:** 268; **Supp. III Part 2:** 560

Vrbovska, Anca, **Supp. IV Part 2:** 639

V. S. Naipaul: An Introduction to His Work (Theroux), **Supp. VIII:** 314, 318

"V. S. Pritchett's Apprenticeship" (Maxwell), **Supp. VIII:** 172

"Vulgarity in Literature" (Huxley), **III:** 429–430

"Vultures" (Oliver), **Supp. VII:** 235

"V. V." (Alcott), **Supp. I Part 1:** 37

W

W (Viva) (Cummings), **I:** 429, 433, 434, 436, 443, 444, 447

Wabash (R. O. Butler), **Supp. XII:** 61, **68–69**

Wade, Grace, **I:** 216

"Wading at Wellfleet" (Bishop), **Retro. Supp. II:** 42, 43; **Supp. I Part 1:** 80, 85, 86

Wadsworth, Charles, **I:** 454, 470; **Retro. Supp. I:** 32, 33

Wagenknecht, Edward, **II:** 508; **Supp. I Part 2:** 408, 584; **Supp. IV Part 2:** 681

"Wages of Poetry, The" (Wright), **Supp. XV:** 337

Wagner, Erica, **Supp. XXI:** 117

Wagner, Jean, **Supp. I Part 1:** 341, 346; **Supp. IV Part 1:** 165, 167, 171

Wagner, Richard, **I:** 284, 395; **II:** 425; **III:** 396, 507; **Supp. IV Part 1:** 392

Wagner, Robert, **Supp. IX:** 250

"Wagnerians, The" (Auchincloss), **Supp. IV Part 1:** 23

"Wagner Matinee, A" (Cather), **I:** 315–316; **Retro. Supp. I:** 5, 8

Wagoner, David, **Supp. IX:** 323–340; **Supp. XII:** 178; **Supp. XX:**200

Wahlöö, Per, **Supp. XX:**87

Waid, Candace, **Retro. Supp. I:** 360, 372, 373

Waif, The (Longfellow, ed.), **Retro. Supp. II:** 155

"Waif of the Plains, A" (Harte), **Supp. II Part 1:** 354

Wain, John, **Supp. XIV:** 166

"Wait" (Kinnell), **Supp. III Part 1:** 250

"Waiting" (Dubus), **Supp. VII:** 87

Waiting (Jin), **Supp. XVIII:** 89, **96–97,** 99

"Waiting" (W. C. Williams), **Retro. Supp. I:** 418

"Waiting, The" (L.-Y. Lee), **Supp. XV:** 218

"Waiting, The" (Olds), **Supp. X:** 209

"Waiting between the Trees" (Tan), **Supp. X:** 290

"Waiting by the Gate" (Bryant), **Supp. I Part 1:** 171

Waiting for God (Weil), **I:** 298

Waiting for Godot (Beckett), **I:** 78, 91, 298; **Supp. IV Part 1:** 368–369

Waiting for Lefty (Odets), **Supp. I Part 1:** 277; **Supp. II Part 2:** 529, 530–533, 540; **Supp. V:** 109; **Supp. XIX:** 242

Waiting for the End of the World (Bell), **Supp. X:** 4–5, 11

"Waiting for the Ladies" (L. Brown), **Supp. XXI:** 44

Waiting for the Verdict (R. H. Davis), **Supp. XVI:** 85, 89, 90

"Waiting in a Rain Forest" (Wagoner), **Supp. IX:** 329

Waiting Room, The (Kees), **Supp. XV:** 133, 148

Waiting to Exhale (McMillan), **Supp. XIII:** 184, 185, **189–190,** 191

"Waiting to Freeze" (Banks), **Supp. V:** 5, 6

Waiting to Freeze: Poems (Banks), **Supp. V:** 6, 8

Waits, Tom, **Supp. VIII:** 12

Wait until Spring, Bandini (Fante), **Supp. XI:** 160, 161, 164, 165, **166–167**

Wait until Spring, Bandini (film), **Supp. XI:** 173

"Wake, The" (Dove), **Supp. IV Part 1:** 250

"Wakefield" (Hawthorne), **Retro. Supp. I:** 154, 159

Wakefield, Dan, **Supp. VIII:** 43; **Supp. XVI:** 220; **Supp. XIX:** 257, 258

Wakefield, Richard, **Supp. IX:** 323

"Wake Island" (Rukeyser), **Supp. VI:** 273

Wakeman, Frederic, **Supp. IX:** 247

Wake Up and Live! (Brande), **Supp. I Part 2:** 608

"Waking" (C. Frost), **Supp. XV:** 93

Waking, The (Roethke), **III:** 541

"Waking Early Sunday Morning" (Lowell), **II:** 552; **Retro. Supp. II:** 190

"Waking in the Blue" (Lowell), **II:** 547; **Retro. Supp. II:** 180

"Waking in the Dark" (Rich), **Supp. I Part 2:** 559

"Waking Up the Rake" (Hogan), **Supp. IV Part 1:** 415–416, 416

Wakoski, Diane, **Supp. V:** 79; **Supp. XII:** 184; **Supp. XV:** 252; **Supp. XVII:** 112

Walbridge, John, **Supp. XX:**125

Walcott, Charles C., **II:** 49

Walcott, Derek, **Supp. VIII:** 28; **Supp. X:** 122, 131; **Supp. XV:** 256

Walcott, Jersey Joe, **Supp. V:** 182

Wald, Alan, **Supp. XV:** 202; **Supp. XVIII:** 223; **Supp. XXI:** 261, 262, 271, 275–276, 277, 278

Wald, Lillian, **Supp. I Part 1:** 12

Walden (Thoreau), **Supp. XIV:** 177, 227; **Supp. XV:** 275; **Supp. XVIII:** 14, 80, 189

Walden, Daniel, **Supp. IV Part 2:** 584, 591; **Supp. V:** 272

Walden; or, Life in the Woods (Thoreau), **I:** 219, 305; **II:** 8, 142, 159, 312–313, 458; **IV:** 168, 169, 170, 176, 177–178, 179–182, 183, 187; **Retro. Supp. I:** 62; **Supp. I Part 2:** 579, 655, 664, 672; **Supp. VIII:** 296; **Supp. X:** 27, 101; **Supp. XIII:** 152

Waldman, Anne, **Supp. XIV:** 150

Waldmeir, Joseph, **III:** 45

Waldmeir, Joseph J., **Supp. I Part 2:** 476

Waldo (Theroux), **Supp. VIII:** 313, 314, **314–315**

Waldo Frank: A Study (Munson), **Supp. XX:**74

Waldron, Jeremy, **Supp. XVII:** 235

Waldrop, Keith, **Supp. XV:** 153, 165

Waley, Arthur, **II:** 526; **III:** 466; **Supp. V:** 340

"Walk, A" (Snyder), **Supp. VIII:** 297

Walkabout Year: Twelve Months in Australia (Pickering), **Supp. XXI:** 199, 200

"Walk at Sunset, A" (Bryant), **Supp. I Part 1:** 155

"Walk before Mass, A" (Agee), **I:** 28–29

Walker, Alice, **Retro. Supp. I:** 215; **Supp. I Part 2:** 550; **Supp. III Part 2:** 488, **517–540**; **Supp. IV Part 1:** 14; **Supp. VIII:** 141, 214; **Supp. IX:** 306, 311; **Supp. X:** 85, 228, 252, 325, 330; **Supp. XIII:** 179, 185, 291, 295; **Supp. XVI:** 39; **Supp. XVIII:** 200, 283; **Supp. XX:**84, 107, 108; **Supp. XXI:** 172

Walker, Cheryl, **Supp. XI:** 145

Walker, David, **Supp. V:** 189; **Supp. XVII:** 246

Walker, Franklin D., **III:** 321

Walker, Gue, **Supp. XII:** 207

Walker, Margaret, **Supp. XVIII:** 282; **Supp. XX:**106

Walker, Marianne, **Supp. VIII:** 139

Walker, Obadiah, **II:** 113

Walker, Scott, **Supp. XV:** 92

Walker in the City, A (Kazin), **Supp. VIII:** 93–95, 99

Walk Hard (Blum and Hill), **Supp. XV:** 194

Walk Hard-Talk Loud (Zinberg), **Supp. XV:** 194, 202

"Walking" (Hogan), **Supp. IV Part 1:** 416

"Walking" (Thoreau), **Supp. IV Part 1:** 416; **Supp. IX:** 178

"Walking Along in Winter" (Kenyon), **Supp. VII:** 167

"Walking around the Block with a Three-Year-Old" (Wagoner), **Supp. IX:** 331–332

"Walking at Noon Near the Burlington Depot in Lincoln, Nebraska" (Kooser), **Supp. XIX:** 122

"Walking Backwards into the Future" (R. Williams), **Supp. IX:** 146

Walking Down the Stairs: Selections from Interviews (Kinnell), **Supp. III Part 1:** 235, 249

"Walking Home" (Schnackenberg). *See* "Laughing with One Eye" (Schnackenberg)

"Walking Home at Night" (Ginsberg), **Supp. II Part 1:** 313

"Walking Is Almost Falling" (Peacock), **Supp. XIX:** 196, 197

Walking Light (Dunn), **Supp. XI:** 140, 141, 153

"Walking Man of Rodin, The" (Sandburg), **III:** 583

"Walking Sticks and Paperweights and Water Marks" (Moore), **III:** 215

Walking Tall (Dunn), **Supp. XI:** 140

Walking the Black Cat (Simic), **Supp. VIII:** 280, **282–284**

Walking to Martha's Vineyard (F. Wright), **Supp. XVII:** 240, 241, 245, 246

Walking to Sleep (Wilbur), **Supp. III Part 2:** 557–560

"Walking to Sleep" (Wilbur), **Supp. III Part 2:** 544, 557, 559, 561, 562

"Walking Wounded" (Shaw), **Supp. XIX:** 248

Walkin' the Dog (Mosley), **Supp. XIII:** 242

"Walk in the Moonlight, A" (Anderson), **I:** 114

Walk Me to the Distance (Everett), **Supp. XVIII:** 55–56, 57

Walk on the Wild Side, A (Algren), **Supp. V:** 4; **Supp. IX:** 3, **12–13**, 14

"Walks in Rome" (Merrill), **Supp. III Part 1:** 337

Walk to the River, A (Hoffman), **Supp. XVIII:** 77–78

Walk with Tom Jefferson, A (Levine), **Supp. V:** 179, 187, 190–191

"Wall, The" (Bronk), **Supp. XXI:** 31

"Wall, The" (Brooks), **Supp. III Part 1:** 70, 71, 84

Wall, The (Hersey), **IV:** 4; **Supp. XX:**251

"Wall, The" (Roethke), **III:** 544

"Wall, The" (Sexton), **Supp. II Part 2:** 696

Wallace, David, **Supp. XXI:** 277

Wallace, David Foster, **Retro. Supp. II:** 279; **Supp. X: 301–318; Supp. XVII:** 226; **Supp. XIX:** 223; **Supp. XX:**91, 93

Wallace, Henry, **I:** 489; **III:** 111, 475; **Supp. I Part 1:** 286; **Supp. I Part 2:** 645

Wallace, Jim, **Supp. XX:**143

Wallace, Mike, **Supp. IV Part 1:** 364; **Supp. IV Part 2:** 526; **Supp. XX:**102

Wallace, Richard, **Supp. XVIII:** 101–102

Wallace Stevens (Kermode), **Retro. Supp. I:** 301

Wallace Stevens: The Poems of our Climate (Bloom), **Retro. Supp. I:** 299

Wallace Stevens: Words Chosen out of Desire (Stevens), **Retro. Supp. I:** 297

Wallach, Eli, **III:** 161

Wallant, Edward Lewis, **Supp. XVI:** 220

Wallas, Graham, **Supp. I Part 2:** 643

"Walled City" (Oates), **Supp. II Part 2:** 524

Wallenstein, Anna. *See* Weinstein, Mrs. Max (Anna Wallenstein)

Waller, Edmund, **III:** 463

Waller, Fats, **IV:** 263

Walling, William English, **Supp. I Part 2:** 645; **Supp. XV:** 295

Wall of the Sky, the Wall of the Eye, The (Lethem), **Supp. XVIII:** 139

Walls Do Not Fall, The (Doolittle), **Supp. I Part 1:** 271, 272

Walls of Jericho, The (R. Fisher), **Supp. XIX:** 65, 67, 70, **72–77,** 78

"Wall Songs" (Hogan), **Supp. IV Part 1:** 413

Wall Writing (Auster), **Supp. XII:** 23–24

Walpole, Horace, **I:** 203; **Supp. I Part 2:** 410, 714

Walpole, Hugh, **Retro. Supp. I:** 231; **Supp. XX:**232

Walpole, Robert, **IV:** 145

Walsh, David M., **Supp. XV:** 5

Walsh, Ed, **II:** 424

Walsh, George, **Supp. IV Part 2:** 528

Walsh, Raoul, **Supp. XIII:** 174

Walsh, Richard J., **Supp. II Part 1:** 119, 130

Walsh, William, **Supp. IV Part 1:** 242, 243, 246, 248, 252, 254, 257

"Walt, the Wounded" (Di Piero), **Supp. XIX:** 37

"Walt and Will" (Apple), **Supp. XVII:** 6

Walter, Eugene, **Supp. XVI:** 230

Walter, Joyce, **Supp. XV:** 121

Walter Benjamin at the Dairy Queen: Reflections at Sixty and Beyond (McMurtry), **Supp. V:** 232

Walters, Barbara, **Supp. XIV:** 125

Walters, Marguerite. *See* Smith, Mrs. Lamar (Marguerite Walters)

"Walter T. Carriman" (O'Hara), **III:** 368

Walton, Izaak, **Supp. I Part 2:** 422

"Walt Whitman" (Kooser), **Supp. XIX:** 118

"Walt Whitman" (Masters), **Supp. I Part 2:** 458

"Walt Whitman at Bear Mountain" (Simpson), **Supp. IX:** 265

Walt Whitman Bathing (Wagoner), **Supp. IX: 331–332**

Walt Whitman Handbook (Allen), **IV:** 352

Walt Whitman Reconsidered (Chase), **IV:** 352

"Waltz, The" (Parker), **Supp. IX:** 204

"Waltzer in the House, The" (Kunitz), **Supp. III Part 1:** 258

Waltzing the Magpies: A Year in Australia (Pickering), **Supp. XXI:** 199, 200

Walzer, Kevin, **Supp. XII:** 202; **Supp. XV:** 118; **Supp. XVIII:** 174

Wambaugh, Joseph, **Supp. X:** 5; **Supp. XXI:** 67

Wampeters, Foma, & Granfalloons (Vonnegut), **Supp. II Part 2:** 758, 759–760, 776, 779

Wand, David Hsin-fu, **Supp. X:** 292

"Wanderer, The" (W. C. Williams), **Retro. Supp. I:** 414, 421

Wanderer, The: His Parables and His Sayings (Gibran), **Supp. XX:**116, **123–124**

"Wanderers, The" (Welty), **IV:** 273–274

"Wandering Jew, The" (Robinson), **III:** 505, 516–517

Wanderings of Oisin (Yeats), **Supp. I Part 1:** 79

Wang, Dorothy, **Supp. X:** 289

Wang Wei, **Supp. XV:** 47

Waniek, Marilyn Nelson, **Supp. IV Part 1:** 244. *See also* Nelson, Marilyn

"Wan Lee, the Pagan" (Harte), **Supp. II Part 1:** 351

"Want, The" (Olds), **Supp. X:** 210

Want Bone, The (Pinsky), **Supp. VI:** 236–237, 244–245, 247

"Wanted: An Ontological Critic" (Ransom), **III:** 498

"Wanting to Die" (Sexton), **Supp. II Part 2:** 684, 686; **Supp. XIV:** 132

"Wants" (Paley), **Supp. VI:** 219

Waples, Dorothy, **I:** 348

Wapshot Chronicle, The (Cheever), **Supp. I Part 1:** 174, 177–180, 181, 196

Wapshot Scandal, The (Cheever), **Supp. I Part 1:** 180–184, 187, 191, 196

"War" (Findley), **Supp. XX:**49

"War" (Jin), **Supp. XVIII:** 93

"War" (Kingston), **Supp. V:** 169

"War" (Simic), **Supp. VIII:** 282

"War, Response, and Contradiction" (Burke), **I:** 283

"War and Peace" (Sanders), **Supp. XVI:** 277

War and Peace (Tolstoy), **I:** 6, 7; **II:** 191, 205, 291; **IV:** 446; **Supp. V:** 277; **Supp. XI:** 68; **Supp. XIV:** 97

War and Remembrance (Wouk), **Supp. XX:**243

"War and the Small Nations" (Gibran), **Supp. XX:**127

War and War (F. Barthelme), **Supp. XI:** 25

"War Between Men and Women, The" (Thurber), **Supp. I Part 2:** 615

War Bulletins (Lindsay), **Supp. I Part 2:** 378–379

Ward, Aileen, **II:** 531

Ward, Artemus (pseudonym). *See* Browne, Charles Farrar

Ward, Douglas Turner, **Supp. IV Part 1:** 362

Ward, Henry, **Supp. I Part 2:** 588

Ward, Mrs. Humphry, **II:** 338

Ward, Leo R., **Supp. VIII:** 124

Ward, Lester F., **Supp. I Part 2:** 640; **Supp. XI:** 202, 203

Ward, Lynn, **I:** 31

Ward, Nathaniel, **Supp. I Part 1:** 99, 102, 111, 116

Ward, Theodora, **I:** 470; **Retro. Supp. I:** 28

Ward, William Hayes, **Supp. I Part 1:** 371

"War Debt, A" (Jewett), **Retro. Supp. II:** 138, 141

"War Diary" (Boyce), **Supp. XVII:** 104; **Supp. XXI:** 6

"War Diary, A" (Bourne), **I:** 229

War Dispatches of Stephen Crane, The (Crane), **I:** 422

"Ward Line, The" (Morris), **III:** 220

Warfel, Harry R., **Supp. I Part 1:** 366

War Games (Morris), **III:** 238

War in Heaven, The (Shepard and Chaikin), **Supp. III Part 2:** 433

War Is Kind (Crane), **I:** 409; **III:** 585

"War Is Kind" (Crane), **I:** 419

Warlock (Harrison), **Supp. VIII:** 45, **46**

Warm as Wool (Sanders), **Supp. XVI:** 269

"Warming" (Trethewey), **Supp. XXI:** 245

Warner, Anna, **Supp. XVIII:** 258–275

Warner, Charles Dudley, **II:** 405; **IV:** 198

Warner, Jack, **Supp. XII:** 160–161; **Supp. XVIII:** 249

Warner, John R., **III:** 193

Warner, Oliver, **I:** 548

Warner, Susan, **Retro. Supp. I:** 246; **Supp. XV:** 275; **Supp. XVIII: 257–275**

Warner, Sylvia Townsend, **Supp. VIII:** 151, 155, 164, 171

Warner, W. Lloyd, **III:** 60

Warner Family and the Warner Books, The (Baker), **Supp. XVIII:** 259, 267

"Warning" (Hughes), **Supp. I Part 1:** 343

"Warning" (Pound), **III:** 474

"Warning, The" (Creeley), **Supp. IV Part 1:** 150

"Warning, The" (Longfellow), **II:** 498

Warning Hill (Marquand), **III:** 55–56, 60, 68

"War of Eyes, A" (Coleman), **Supp. XI:** 93–94

War of Eyes and Other Stories, A (Coleman), **Supp. XI: 91–92**

War of the Classes (London), **II:** 466

"War of the Wall, The" (Bambara), **Supp. XI:** 15–16

"War of Vaslav Nijinsky, The" (Bidart), **Supp. XV:** 21–22, **27–29**

"War Poems" (Sandburg), **III:** 581

Warren, Austin, **I:** 265, 268, 271; **Supp. I Part 2:** 423

Warren, Earl, **III:** 581

Warren, Gabriel, **IV:** 244

Warren, Mercy Otis, **Supp. XV:** 230

Warren, Patricia Nell, **Supp. XX:259–276**

Warren, Robert Penn, **I:** 190, 211, 517; **II:** 57, 217, 228, 253; **III:** 134, 310, 382–383, 454, 482, 485, 490, 496, 497; **IV:** 121, 122, 123, 125, 126, **236–259**, 261, 262, 279, 340–341, 458; **Retro. Supp. I:** 40, 41, 73, 90; **Retro. Supp. II:** 220, 235; **Supp. I Part 1:** 359, 371; **Supp. I Part 2:** 386, 423; **Supp. II Part 1:** 139; **Supp. III Part 2:** 542; **Supp. V:** 261, 316, 318, 319, 333; **Supp. VIII:** 126, 176; **Supp. IX:** 257; **Supp. X:** 1, 25, 26; **Supp. XI:** 315; **Supp. XII:** 254, 255; **Supp. XIV:** 1, 2, 3, 4, 11, 14, 15; **Supp. XVIII:** 77, 78–79; **Supp. XIX:** 246; **Supp. XXI:** 256

Warren, Mrs. Robert Penn (Eleanor Clark), **IV:** 244

Warren, Rosanna, **IV:** 244; **Supp. XV:** 251, 261, 262, 263; **Supp. XIX:** 34

Warrington Poems, The (Ríos), **Supp. IV Part 2:** 540

Warrior, Robert Allen, **Supp. IV Part 1:** 329

"Warrior, The" (Gunn Allen), **Supp. IV Part 1:** 326

"Warrior: 5th Grade" (Olds), **Supp. X:** 214

"Warrior Road" (Harjo), **Supp. XII:** 217

Wars, The (Findley), **Supp. XX:53–54**

Warshavsky, Isaac (pseudonym). *See* Singer, Isaac Bashevis

Warshow, Robert, **Supp. I Part 1:** 51

Wars I Have Seen (Stein), **IV:** 27, 36, 477

Wartime (Fussell), **Supp. V:** 241

War Trash (Jin), **Supp. XVIII:** 89, **100–101**

"War Widow, The" (Frederic), **II:** 135–136

"Was" (Creeley), **Supp. IV Part 1:** 155

"Was" (Faulkner), **II:** 71

"Wash" (Faulkner), **II:** 72

Wash, Richard, **Supp. XII:** 14

"Washboard Wizard" (Nelson), **Supp. XVIII:** 182

"Washed in the Rain" (Fante), **Supp. XI:** 165

"Washing of Hands, A" (Kooser), **Supp. XIX:** 115

Washington, Booker T., **Supp. I Part 2:** 393; **Supp. II Part 1:** 157, 160, 167, 168, 171, 225; **Supp. XIV:** 198, 199, 201; **Supp. XVIII:** 121–122

Washington, D.C. (Vidal), **Supp. IV Part 2:** 677, 684, 686–687, 690

Washington, George, **I:** 453; **II:** 313–314; **Supp. I Part 2:** 399, 485, 508, 509, 511, 513, 517, 518, 520, 599

Washington, Mary Helen, **Supp. XVIII:** 119, 284

Washington Crossing the Delaware (Rivers), **Supp. XV:** 186

Washington Post Book World (Lesser), **Supp. IV Part 2:** 453; **Supp. VIII:** 80, 84, 241; **Supp. X:** 282

Washington Square (James), **II:** 327, 328; **Retro. Supp. I:** 215, 220, **222–223**

"Washington Square, 1946" (Ozick), **Supp. V:** 272

Washington Square Ensemble, The (Bell), **Supp. X:** 1, **3–4**

"Was Lowell an Historical Critic?" (Altick), **Supp. I Part 2:** 423

Wasserman, Earl R., **Supp. I Part 2:** 439, 440

Wasserman, Jakob, **Supp. I Part 2:** 669

Wasserstein, Wendy, **Supp. IV Part 1:** 309; **Supp. XV: 319–336**

Wasson, Ben, **Retro. Supp. I:** 79, 83

"Waste Carpet, The" (Matthews), **Supp. IX: 158–159**

Waste Land, The (T. S. Eliot), **I:** 107, 266, 298, 395, 396, 482, 570–571, 572, 574–575, 577–578, 580, 581, 584, 585, 586, 587; **III:** 6–8, 12, 196, 277–278, 453, 471, 492, 586; **IV:** 122, 123, 124, 140, 418, 419, 420; **Retro. Supp. I:** 51, 60, **60–62**, 63, 64, 66, 210, 290, 291, 299, 311, 420, 427; **Retro. Supp. II:** 85, 121, 190; **Supp. I Part 1:** 272; **Supp. I Part 2:** 439, 455, 614; **Supp. II Part 1:** 4, 5, 11, 96; **Supp. III Part 1:** 9, 10, 41, 63, 105; **Supp. IV Part 1:** 47, 284; **Supp. V:** 338; **Supp. IX:** 158, 305; **Supp. X:** 125; **Supp. XIII:** 341–342, 344, 346; **Supp. XIV:** 6, 284; **Supp. XV:** 21, 181, 261, 306; **Supp. XVI:** 204; **Supp. XVII:** 140–141, 144, 227; **Supp. XVIII:** 78, 79–80; **Supp. XIX:** 288

"Waste Land, The": A Facsimile and Transcript of the Original Drafts Including the Annotations of Ezra Pound (Eliot, ed.), **Retro. Supp. I:** 58

Waste Land and Other Poems, The (T. S. Eliot), **Supp. XV:** 305

Wat, Alexander, **Supp. XVI:** 155, 161

Watch, The (Bass), **Supp. XVI: 16–17**

"Watch, The, —" (Bass), **Supp. XVI:** 17

Watch and Ward (James), **II:** 323; **Retro. Supp. I:** 218, **219,** 220

"Watcher" (Trethewey), **Supp. XXI:** 247

"Watcher, The" (R. Bly), **Supp. IV Part 1:** 71

"Watcher by the Dead, A" (Bierce), **I:** 203

Watchfires (Auchincloss), **Supp. IV Part 1:** 23

"Watching Crow, Looking toward the Manzano Mountains" (Harjo), **Supp. XII:** 219

"Watching the Oregon Whale" (A. Finch), **Supp. XVII:** 77

"Watching the Sunset" (Coleman), **Supp. XI:** 92

Watch on the Rhine (Hellman), **Supp. I Part 1:** 276, 278, 279–281, 283–284; **Supp. IV Part 1:** 83

"Water" (Emerson), **II:** 19
"Water" (Komunyakaa), **Supp. XIII:** 132
"Water" (Lowell), **II:** 550
"Waterbird" (Swenson), **Supp. IV Part 2:** 651
"Water Borders" (Dillard), **Supp. VI:** 27
"Water Buffalo" (Komunyakaa), **Supp. XIII:** 122
"Watercolor of Grantchester Meadows" (Plath), **Supp. I Part 2:** 537
Water Cure, The (Everett), **Supp. XVIII: 64–66**
"Waterfall, The" (Clampitt), **Supp. IX:** 44
Waterfront (Schulberg), **Supp. XVIII: 251–252**
"Water Hose Is on Fire, The" (Simic), **Supp. XV:** 185
Waterhouse, Keith, **Supp. VIII:** 124
"Waterlily Fire" (Rukeyser), **Supp. VI:** 285, 286
Waterlily Fire: Poems 1935–1962 (Rukeyser), **Supp. VI:** 274, 283, 285
Watermark (Brodsky), **Supp. VIII:** 29
Water-Method Man, The (Irving), **Supp. VI:** 163, **167–179,** 180
Water Music (Boyle), **Supp. VIII:** 1, 3–5, 8, 14; **Supp. XX:20–22**
"Water Music for the Progress of Love in a Life-Raft Down the Sammamish Slough" (Wagoner), **Supp. IX:** 326
"Water People" (Burke), **Supp. XIV:** 21
"Water Picture" (Swenson), **Supp. IV Part 2:** 641
"Water Rising" (Hogan), **Supp. IV Part 1:** 400
Waters, Ethel, **II:** 587
Waters, Frank, **Supp. X:** 124
Waters, Muddy, **Supp. VIII:** 345
Watershed (Everett), **Supp. XVIII: 58–59,** 64
"Watershed" (Kingsolver), **Supp. VII:** 208
"Watershed" (Warren), **IV:** 239
"Watershed, The" (Auden), **Supp. II Part 1:** 5
Waters of Kronos, The (Richter), **Supp. XVIII:** 207, 208, **218–219,** 220
Waters of Siloe, The (Merton), **Supp. VIII:** 196, 208
Waterston, Sam, **Supp. IX:** 253
Water Street (Merrill), **Supp. III Part 1:** 321–323
"Water Walker" (Wilbur), **Supp. III Part 2:** 548, 560
Water-Witch, The (Cooper), **I:** 342–343
Waterworks (Doctorow), **Supp. IV Part 1:** 218, 222, 223, 231–233, 234
"Water Works, The" (Doctorow), **Supp. IV Part 1:** 234
Watkin, E. I., **Retro. Supp. II:** 187
Watkins, Floyd C., **IV:** 452
Watkins, James T., **I:** 193, 194
Watkins, Maureen, **Supp. XVI:** 188
Watkins, Mel, **Supp. X:** 330; **Supp. XIII:** 246
Watman, Max, **Supp. XX:92**
Watrous, Peter, **Supp. VIII:** 79
Watson, Brook, **Supp. XX:284**
Watson, Burton, **Supp. XV:** 47

Watson, James Sibley, Jr., **I:** 261
Watson, Jay, **Supp. XVIII:** 195; **Supp. XXI:** 46
Watson, J. B., **II:** 361
Watson, Richard, **Supp. I Part 2:** 516, 517
Watson, William, **II:** 114
Watt, Ian, **Supp. VIII:** 4
Watteau, Jean Antoine, **III:** 275; **IV:** 79
Watts, Emily Stipes, **Supp. I Part 1:** 115
Waugh, Evelyn, **I:** 480; **III:** 281; **Supp. I Part 2:** 607; **Supp. IV Part 2:** 688; **Supp. XI:** 305, 306; **Supp. XIX:** 131
"Wave" (Snyder), **Supp. VIII:** 299
Wave, A (Ashbery), **Supp. III Part 1:** 1, 4, 24–26
"Wave, A" (Ashbery), **Supp. III Part 1:** 9, 19, 24–25
"Wave, The" (MacLeish), **III:** 19
"Wave, The" (Untermeyer), **Supp. XV:** 300
"Wavemaker Falters, The" (Saunders), **Supp. XIX:** 225
"Waxwings" (Francis), **Supp. IX:** 82
Way, The (Steiner and Witt, eds.), **Supp. IV Part 2:** 505
"Way Down, The" (Kunitz), **Supp. III Part 1:** 263
"Way It Is, The" (Ellison), **Supp. II Part 1:** 245
"Way It Is, The" (Jones), **Supp. XI:** 229
Way It Is, The (Stafford), **Supp. XIII:** 274
"Way It Is, The" (Strand), **Supp. IV Part 2:** 627
"Wayland" (Sanders), **Supp. XVI:** 275
Wayne, John, **Supp. IV Part 1:** 200
Way of Chuang-Tzu, The (Merton), **Supp. VIII:** 208
"Way of Exchange in James Dickey's Poetry, The" (Weatherby), **Supp. IV Part 1:** 175
Way of Life According to Laotzu, The (Bynner), **Supp. XV:** 46, 48
Way Out, A (Frost), **Retro. Supp. I:** 133
Wayside Motor Inn, The (Gurney), **Supp. V:** 96, 105, 109
"Ways of Breaking: Lynda Hull's 'Ornithology' " (Jauss), **Supp. XXI:** 139
"Ways of Talking" (Jin), **Supp. XVIII:** 93
Ways of the Hour, The (Cooper), **I:** 354
Ways of White Folks, The (Hughes), **Retro. Supp. I:** 203, 204; **Supp. I Part 1:** 329, 330, 332
Way Some People Die, The (Macdonald), **Supp. IV Part 2:** 470, 471, 472, 474
Way Some People Live, The (Cheever), **Supp. I Part 1:** 175
"Way the Cards Fall, The" (Komunyakaa), **Supp. XIII:** 117
"Way the Luck Runs, The" (Wolfert), **Supp. XXI:** 265
"Way Things Are, The" (Turow, unpub.), **Supp. XVII:** 215, 218
Way to Rainy Mountain, The (Momaday), **Supp. IV Part 2:** 485–486, 487–489, 491, 493

Way to Wealth, The (Franklin), **II:** 101–102, 110; **Supp. XX:27**
Wayward and the Seeking, The: A Collection of Writings by Jean Toomer (Toomer), **Supp. III Part 2:** 478–481, 484, 487
Wayward Bus, The (Steinbeck), **IV:** 51, 64–65
"Way We Live Now, The" (Sontag), **Supp. III Part 2:** 467–468
"Way You'll Never Be, A" (Hemingway), **II:** 249
"W. D. Sees Himself Animated" (Snodgrass), **Supp. VI:** 327
"W. D. Sits in Kafka's Chair and Is Interrogated Concerning the Assumed Death of Cock Robin" (Snodgrass), **Supp. VI:** 319
"W. D. Tries to Warn Cock Robin" (Snodgrass), **Supp. VI:** 319
"We" (Alexander), **Supp. XVIII:** 185
Weaks, Mary Louise, **Supp. X:** 5
Weales, Gerald, **II:** 602
"Wealth," from *Conduct of Life, The* (Emerson), **II:** 2, 3–4
"Wealth," from *English Traits* (Emerson), **II:** 6
Wealth of Nations, The (A. Smith), **II:** 109
"We Are Looking at You, Agnes" (Caldwell), **I:** 309
We Are Still Married: Stories and Letters (Keillor), **Supp. XVI:** 176, 177
"We Are the Crazy Lady and Other Feisty Feminist Fables" (Ozick), **Supp. V:** 259
Weary Blues, The (Hughes), **Retro. Supp. I:** 195, 197, 198, 199, 200, 203, 205; **Supp. I Part 1:** 325
"Weary Blues, The" (Hughes), **Retro. Supp. I:** 198, 199; **Supp. I Part 1:** 324, 325
"Weary Kingdom" (Irving), **Supp. VI:** 163
Weasels and Wisemen: Ethics and Ethnicity in the Work of David Mamet (Kane), **Supp. XIV:** 250
Weather and the Women Treat Me Fair, The (Everett), **Supp. XVIII:** 66
Weatherby, H. L., **Supp. IV Part 1:** 175
Weather Central (Kooser), **Supp. XIX:** 116, **123–125**
"Weathering Out" (Dove), **Supp. IV Part 1:** 248
"Weather Within, The" (M. F. K. Fisher), **Supp. XVII:** 88, 91
Weaver, Harriet, **III:** 471
Weaver, James, **Supp. XVIII:** 72
Weaver, Michael, **Supp. XVIII:** 176, 177
Weaver, Mike, **Retro. Supp. I:** 430
Weaver, Will, **Supp. XVI:** 39
"Weaving" (Larcom), **Supp. XIII:** 142, **Supp. XIII:** 144–145, 150, 151
"Web" (Oliver), **Supp. VII:** 236
Web and the Rock, The (Wolfe), **IV:** 451, 455, 457, 459–460, 462, 464, 467, 468
Webb, Beatrice, **Supp. I Part 1:** 5
Webb, Mary, **I:** 226
Webb, Phyllis, **Supp. XX:56**
Webb, Sidney, **Supp. I Part 1:** 5

Webb, W. P., **Supp. V:** 225
Webber, A. R. F., **Supp. XXI:** 160
Weber, Brom, **I:** 383, 386
Weber, Carl, **Supp. IX:** 133, 138, 141
Weber, Max, **I:** 498; **Supp. I Part 2:** 637, 648
Weber, Sarah, **Supp. I Part 1:** 2
Weberman, A. J., **Supp. XVIII:** 27
Web of Earth, The (Wolfe), **IV:** 451–452, 456, 458, 464, 465
"Web of Life, The" (Nemerov), **III:** 282
Webster, Brenda, **Supp. XVI:** 157, 161
Webster, Daniel, **II:** 5, 9; **Supp. I Part 2:** 659, 687, 689, 690
Webster, John, **I:** 384; **Supp. I Part 2:** 422
Webster, Noah, **Supp. I Part 2:** 660; **Supp. II Part 1:** 77
Wector, Dixon, **II:** 103
Wedding, The (D. West), **Supp. XVIII:** 277, **287–289**
"Wedding, The" (Everwine), **Supp. XV:** 83
Wedding, The (television miniseries), **Supp. XVIII:** 277, 289
"Wedding Cake" (Nye), **Supp. XIII:** 283
"Wedding Dance, The" (Di Piero), **Supp. XIX:** 47
"Wedding in Brownsville, A" (Singer), **IV:** 15
Wedding in Hell, A (Simic), **Supp. VIII:** 280, **282**
"Wedding of the Rose and Lotus, The" (Lindsay), **Supp. I Part 2:** 387
"Wedding Supper, The" (Rowson), **Supp. XV:** 243
"Wedding Toast, A" (Wilbur), **Supp. III Part 2:** 561
Wedekind, Frank, **III:** 398; **Supp. XX:**85
Wedge, The (W. C. Williams), **Retro. Supp. I:** 424
"Wednesday at the Waldorf" (Swenson), **Supp. IV Part 2:** 647
"We Don't Live Here Anymore" (Dubus), **Supp. VII:** 78–79, 85
"Weed" (McCarriston), **Supp. XIV:** 259, 273
"Weed, The" (Bishop), **Supp. I Part 1:** 80, 88–89
"Weeds, The" (McCarthy), **II:** 566
"Weekend" (Beattie), **Supp. V:** 27
"Weekend" (Hempel), **Supp. XXI:** 124
Weekend, The (Cameron), **Supp. XII:** 80, 81, **86–88**
"Weekend at Ellerslie, A" (Wilson), **IV:** 431
Weekend Edition (National Public Radio), **Supp. IX:** 299; **Supp. XVII:** 240, 242
Week on the Concord and Merrimack Rivers, A (Thoreau), **IV:** 168, 169, 177, 182–183; **Supp. I Part 2:** 420; **Supp. XIV:** 227
Weeks, Edward, **III:** 64
Weeks, Jerome, **Supp. VIII:** 76
"Weeping Burgher" (Stevens), **IV:** 77
"Weeping Women" (Levertov), **Supp. III Part 1:** 282
We Fished All Night (W. Motley), **Supp. XVII: 155–158,** 159, **160**

We Fly Away (Francis), **Supp. IX: 79–80,** 84
We Happy Few (Hinojosa), **Supp. XIX:** 99, **111–112**
We Have Always Lived in the Castle (Jackson), **Supp. IX:** 121, 126, **127–128**
"We Have Our Arts So We Won't Die of Truth" (Bradbury), **Supp. IV Part 1:** 105
Weich, Dave, **Supp. XII:** 321; **Supp. XVIII:** 91
"Weighing In" (Espaillat), **Supp. XXI:** 111
"Weight" (Wideman), **Supp. X:** 321
"Weights" (C. Baxter), **Supp. XVII:** 16
Weigl, Bruce, **Supp. VIII:** 269, 274; **Supp. XV:** 342; **Supp. XIX: 273–290**
Weil, Dorothy, **Supp. XV:** 231
Weil, James L., **Supp. XXI:** 23, 31
Weil, Robert, **Supp. IX:** 236
Weil, Simone, **I:** 298; **Supp. XV:** 259
Weiland (C. B. Brown), **Supp. XIII:** 100
Weinauer, Ellen, **Supp. XV:** 270, 284
Weinberger, Eliot, **Supp. IV Part 1:** 66; **Supp. VIII:** 290, 292; **Supp. XVI:** 284
Weinfield, Henry, **Supp. XXI:** 24, 28, 33
Weininger, Otto, **Retro. Supp. I:** 416
Weinraub, Judith, **Supp. XXI:** 39
Weinreb, Mindy, **Supp. X:** 24
Weinreich, Regina, **Supp. XIV:** 22
Weinstein, Cindy, **Supp. XVIII:** 261
Weinstein, Hinda, **IV:** 285
Weinstein, Max, **IV:** 285
Weinstein, Mrs. Max (Anna Wallenstein), **IV:** 285, 287
Weinstein, Nathan. *See* West, Nathanael
Weinstein, Selma, **Supp. XXI:** 170
Weisheit, Rabbi, **V:** 76
Weismuller, Johnny, **Supp. X:** 264; **Supp. XX:**18
Weiss, David, **Supp. XVI:** 55
Weiss, Jane, **Supp. XVIII:** 267, 269
Weiss, Peter, **IV:** 117
Weiss, Theodore, **Supp. IV Part 2:** 440; **Supp. IX:** 96
Weist, Dianne, **Supp. X:** 80
Weithas, Art, **Supp. XI:** 231
Welch, Dave, **Supp. XXI:** 118
Welch, Don, **Supp. XIX:** 119
Welch, James, **Supp. IV Part 1:** 404; **Supp. IV Part 2:** 503, 513, 557, 562
Welch, Lew, **Supp. V:** 170; **Supp. VIII:** 303
"Welcome from War" (Rukeyser), **Supp. VI:** 286
"Welcome Morning" (Sexton), **Supp. II Part 2:** 696
"Welcome the Wrath" (Kunitz), **Supp. III Part 1:** 261
Welcome to Hard Times (Doctorow), **Supp. IV Part 1:** 218, 219–220, 222, 224, 230, 238
Welcome to Hard Times (film), **Supp. IV Part 1:** 236
"Welcome to New Dork" (Leonard), **Supp. XVIII:** 148
Welcome to Our City (Wolfe), **IV:** 461

Welcome to the Monkey House (Vonnegut), **Supp. II Part 2:** 758
Welcome to the Moon (Shanley), **Supp. XIV:** 318
Welcome to the Moon and Other Plays (Shanley), **Supp. XIV:** 315, **316–319**
Weld, Theodore, **Supp. I Part 2:** 587, 588
Weld, Tuesday, **Supp. XI:** 306
Welded (O'Neill), **III:** 390
"Welfare Worker, Disenchanted, Contemplates Friday Afternoon, The" (Trethewey), **Supp. XXI:** 246
"Well, The" (Momaday), **Supp. IV Part 2:** 483
"Well Dressed Man with a Beard, The" (Stevens), **Retro. Supp. I:** 297
Wellek, René, **I:** 253, 261, 282; **II:** 320; **Supp. XIV:** 12, 14
Weller, George, **III:** 322
Welles, Gideon, **Supp. I Part 2:** 484
Welles, Orson, **IV:** 476; **Supp. I Part 1:** 67; **Supp. IV Part 1:** 82, 83; **Supp. V:** 251; **Supp. VIII:** 46; **Supp. XI:** 169, 307
"Wellfleet Whale, The" (Kunitz), **Supp. III Part 1:** 263, 269
Wellfleet Whale and Companion Poems, The (Kunitz), **Supp. III Part 1:** 263
Wellink, Yvonne, **Supp. XVIII:** 257
Wellman, Flora, **II:** 463–464, 465
"Well Rising, The" (Stafford), **Supp. XI:** 318
Wells, H. G., **I:** 103, 226, 241, 243, 253, 405, 409, 415; **II:** 82, 144, 276, 337, 338, 458; **III:** 456; **IV:** 340, 455; **Retro. Supp. I:** 100, 228, 231; **Supp. XVI:** 190; **Supp. XXI:** 8
Wellspring, The (Olds), **Supp. X: 211–212**
Well Wrought Urn, The: Studies in the Structure of Poetry (Brooks), **Supp. XIV:** 1, **8–9,** 14, 15, 16
Welsh, Mary, **Supp. XIX:** 248. *See also* Hemingway, Mrs. Ernest (Mary Welsh)
Welty, Eudora, **II:** 194, 217, 606; **IV: 260–284; Retro. Supp. I:** 339–358; **Retro. Supp. II:** 235; **Supp. IV Part 2:** 474; **Supp. V:** 59, 315, 336; **Supp. VIII:** 94, 151, 171; **Supp. X:** 42, 290; **Supp. XII:** 310, 322; **Supp. XIV:** 3; **Supp. XV:** 338
Welty, Eurora, **Supp. XIX:** 151
Weltzien, O. Alan, **Supp. XVI:** 20–21, 28
"We miss Her, not because We see—" (Dickinson), **Retro. Supp. I:** 46
We Must Dance My Darlings (Trilling), **Supp. I Part 1:** 297
Wendell, Barrett, **III:** 507; **Supp. I Part 2:** 414; **Supp. XIV:** 197
Wendell, Sarah. *See* Holmes, Mrs. Abiel (Sarah Wendell)
Wendy Wasserstein: A Casebook (Barnett), **Supp. XV:** 323, 330
"Wendy Wasserstein's Three Sisters: Squandered Privilege" (Brewer), **Supp. XV:** 330

Wept of Wish-ton-Wish, The (Cooper), **I:** 339, 342, 350

Werbe, Peter, **Supp. XIII:** 236

"We Real Cool" (Brooks), **Supp. III Part 1:** 80

We're Back! A Dinosaur's Story (screenplay, Shanley), **Supp. XIV:** 316

"We're Friends Again" (O'Hara), **III:** 372–373

"Were the Whole Realm of Nature Mine" (Watts), **I:** 458

Werewolf (M. Sommers), **Supp. XVII:** 55

Were-Wolf, The (C. Housman), **Supp. XVII:** 55

Werewolf of Paris, The (Endore), **Supp. XVII:** 55–56

Werewolves in Their Youth (Chabon), **Supp. XI:** 66, **76–77**

Werlock, Abby, **Supp. XIII:** 293

Werthman, Michael, **Supp. V:** 115

"Wer-Trout, The" (Proulx), **Supp. VII:** 255–256

Wescott, Glenway, **I:** 288; **II:** 85; **III:** 448, 454; **Supp. VIII:** 156; **Supp. XIV:** 342; **Supp. XVI:** 195

"We Shall All Be Born Again But We Shall Not All Be Saved" (Matthews), **Supp. IX:** 162

West, Anthony, **Supp. IV Part 1:** 284

West, Benjamin, **Supp. I Part 2:** 511

West, Dorothy, **Supp. XIII:** 295; **Supp. XVIII:** 277–291; **Supp. XIX:** 72

West, James, **II:** 562

West, Nathanael, **I:** 97, 107, 190, 211, 298; **II:** 436; **III:** 357, 425; **IV: 285–307; Retro. Supp. II: 321–341; Supp. IV Part 1:** 203; **Supp. VIII:** 97; **Supp. XI:** 85, 105, 159, 296; **Supp. XII:** 173; **Supp. XIII:** 106, 170; **Supp. XVIII:** 251, 253, 254

West, Nathaniel, **Supp. XIX:** 223

West, Ray, **Supp. XV:** 142

West, Rebecca, **II:** 412, 445; **Supp. XVI:** 152, 153

Westall, Julia Elizabeth. *See* Wolfe, Mrs. William Oliver (Julia Elizabeth Westall)

"We Stand United" (Benét), **Supp. XI:** 46

"West Authentic, The: Willa Cather" (Stegner), **Supp. IV Part 2:** 608

"West Coast, The: Region with a View" (Stegner), **Supp. IV Part 2:** 608–609

"West Coast Waterfront: End of an Era" (Swados), **Supp. XIX:** 264

Westcott, Edward N., **II:** 102

"Western Association of Writers" (Chopin), **Supp. I Part 1:** 217

"Western Ballad, A" (Ginsberg), **Supp. II Part 1:** 311

Western Borders, The (Howe), **Supp. IV Part 2:** 424–425

Western Canon: The Books and Schools of the Ages (Bloom), **Supp. IX:** 146

Western Lands, The (Burroughs), **Supp. III Part 1:** 106

"Western North Carolina" (Halliday), **Supp. XIX:** 85

Western Star (Benét), **Supp. XI:** 46, 47, 57

"Westland" (C. Baxter), **Supp. XVII:** 18, 19

"West Marginal Way" (Hugo), **Supp. VI:** 131, 135

West of Eden: Writers in Hollywood, 1928–1940 (Fine), **Supp. XVIII:** 248

West of Yesterday, East of Summer: New and Selected Poems, 1973–1993 (Monette), **Supp. X:** 159

West of Your City (Stafford), **Supp. XI:** 316, **317–318,** 321, 322

Weston, Jessie L., **II:** 540; **III:** 12; **Supp. I Part 2:** 438

"West Real" (Ríos), **Supp. IV Part 2:** 539, 540

West-running Brook (Frost), **II:** 155; **Retro. Supp. I:** 136, 137

"West-running Brook" (Frost), **II:** 150, 162–164

"West Wall" (Merwin), **Supp. III Part 1:** 355

"Westward Beach, A" (Jeffers), **Supp. II Part 2:** 418

Westward Ho (Harrison), **Supp. VIII:** 51, 52

Westward the Course of Empire (Leutze), **Supp. X:** 307

"Westward the Course of Empire Takes Its Way" (Wallace), **Supp. X: 307–308**

"West Wind" (Oliver), **Supp. VII:** 246

"West Wind, The" (Bryant), **Supp. I Part 1:** 155

West Wind: Poems and Prose Poems (Oliver), **Supp. VII:** 243, 246–248

"Wet Casements" (Ashbery), **Supp. III Part 1:** 18–20

We the Living (film), **Supp. IV Part 2:** 520

We the Living (Rand), **Supp. IV Part 2:** 520–521

Wetherell, Elizabeth (pseudonym). *See* Warner, Susan

Wet Parade (Sinclair), **Supp. V:** 289

Wetzsteon, Ross, **Supp. XXI:** 12

"We've Adjusted Too Well" (O'Brien), **Supp. V:** 247

Wevill, David, **Retro. Supp. II:** 247, 249

"We Wear the Mask" (Dunbar), **Supp. II Part 1:** 199, 207, 209–210

Weybright, Victor, **Supp. XIII:** 172

Weyden, Rogier van der, **Supp. IV Part 1:** 284

Whalen, Marcella, **Supp. I Part 1:** 49

Whalen, Philip, **Supp. VIII:** 289

Whalen-Bridge, John, **Retro. Supp. II:** 211–212

"Whales off Wales, The" (X. J. Kennedy), **Supp. XV:** 163

"Whales Weep" (Boyle), **Supp. XX:** 19

"Whales Weep Not!" (D. H. Lawrence), **Supp. XVII:** 77

Wharton, Edith, **I:** 12, 375; **II:** 96, 180, 183, 186, 189–190, 193, 283, 338, 444, 451; **III:** 69, 175, 576; **IV:** 8, 53, 58, **308–330; Retro. Supp. I:** 108, 232, **359–385; Supp. IV Part 1:** 23, 31, 35, 36, 80, 81, 310; **Supp. IX:** 57;

Supp. XII: 308; **Supp. XIV:** 337, 347; **Supp. XVI:** 189; **Supp. XVIII:** 278; **Supp. XX:** 227, 229, 232, 239, 240

Wharton, Edward Robbins, **IV:** 310, 313–314, 319

"What" (Dunn), **Supp. XI:** 144

What a Kingdom It Was (Kinnell), **Supp. III Part 1:** 235, 238, 239

"What America Would Be Like without Blacks" (Ellison), **Retro. Supp. II:** 123

What Are Masterpieces (Stein), **IV:** 30–31

What Are Years (Moore), **III:** 208–209, 210, 215

"What Are Years?" (Moore), **III:** 211, 213

What a Way to Go (Morris), **III:** 230–232

"What a Wonder among the Instruments Is the Walloping Trombone!" (Carruth), **Supp. XVI:** 51

"What Became of the Flappers?" (Zelda Fitzgerald), **Supp. IX:** 71

"What Can I Tell My Bones?" (Roethke), **III:** 546, 549

"What Child Is This?" (Jarman), **Supp. XVII:** 113–114, 115

"What Do We Have Here" (Carson), **Supp. XII: 101**

"What Do We See" (Rukeyser), **Supp. VI:** 282

What Do Women Want? Bread Roses Sex Power (Jong), **Supp. V:** 115, 117, 129, 130

"What Do You Do in San Francisco?" (Carver), **Supp. III Part 1:** 143

What D'Ya Know for Sure (Zinberg), **Supp. XV:** 196

Whatever Happened to Gloomy Gus of the Chicago Bears? (Coover), **Supp. V:** 51, 52

Whatever Happened to Jacy Farrow? (Cleveland), **Supp. V:** 222

"What Every Boy Should Know" (Maxwell), **Supp. VIII:** 169

"What Feels Like the World" (Bausch), **Supp. VII:** 46

"What Fort Sumter Did for Me" (E. Stoddard), **Supp. XV:** 282

"What Girls Read" (Salmon), **Supp. XVIII:** 258

"What God Is Like to Him I Serve" (Bradstreet), **Supp. I Part 1:** 106–107

"What Happened Here Before" (Snyder), **Supp. VIII:** 302

"What Happened to Georgia" (Ray), **Supp. XVIII:** 194

What Have I Ever Lost by Dying? (R. Bly), **Supp. IV Part 1:** 71–72

What Have You Lost? (Nye, ed.), **Supp. XIII:** 280

"What I Believe" (Mumford), **Supp. II Part 2:** 479

"What I Call What They Call Onanism" (Goldbarth), **Supp. XII:** 175

What I Did Last Summer (Gurney), **Supp. V:** 96, 100, 107, 108

"What if God" (Olds), **Supp. X:** 208

What I Have Done with Birds: Character Studies of Native American Birds (Stratton-Porter), **Supp. XX:**218

"What I Have to Defend, What I Can't Bear Losing" (Stern), **Supp. IX:** 286, 287, 288, 298

"What I Knew" (Nelson), **Supp. XVIII:** 178

"What I Know about Being a Playwright" (McNally), **Supp. XIII:** 195, 207

"What I Mean" (Ortiz), **Supp. IV Part 2:** 497

"What Is an Emotion" (James), **II:** 350

What Is Art? (Tolstoy), **I:** 58

"What Is Civilization? Africa's Answer" (Du Bois), **Supp. II Part 1:** 176

"What Is College For?" (Bourne), **I:** 216

"What Is Exploitation?" (Bourne), **I:** 216

What Is Found There: Notebooks on Poetry and Politics (A. Rich), **Supp. XVII:** 74

"What Is It?" (Carver), **Supp. III Part 1:** 139

What Is Man? (Twain), **II:** 434; **IV:** 209

"What Is Poetry" (Ashbery), **Supp. III Part 1:** 19

"What Is Seized" (Moore), **Supp. X:** 164, 168, 169, 172, 175

"What Is the Earth?" (Olds), **Supp. X:** 213

"What Is This Poet" (Stern), **Supp. IX:** 295

What Is To Be Done? (Lenin), **Supp. XXI:** 164

"What I Think" (Hogan), **Supp. IV Part 1:** 406

What Maisie Knew (H. James), **II:** 332; **Retro. Supp. I:** 229, **230**; **Supp. XVIII:** 160

What Makes Sammy Run? (NBC broadcast, Schulberg and Schulberg), **Supp. XVIII:** 254

What Makes Sammy Run? (Schulberg), **Supp. XIII:** 170; **Supp. XVIII:** 241, **244–247,** 248, 249, 253

"What Makes Sammy Run?" (Schulberg), **Supp. XVIII:** 241

What Moon Drove Me to This? (Harjo), **Supp. XII: 218–220**

"What Must" (MacLeish), **III:** 18

What My Father Believed (Wrigley), **Supp. XVIII:** 298–300

"What My Father Believed" (Wrigley), **Supp. XVIII: 298–299**

What Price Hollywood? (film), **Supp. XVIII:** 243

"What Sally Said" (Cisneros), **Supp. VII:** 63

What Saves Us (Weigl), **Supp. XIX:** 282

"What's Happening in America" (Sontag), **Supp. III Part 2:** 460–461

"What's in Alaska?" (Carver), **Supp. III Part 1:** 141, 143

"What's in a Name" (H. L. Gates), **Supp. XX:**101

What's New, Pussycat? (film; Allen), **Supp. XI:** 307; **Supp. XV:** 1, 2, 14

"What's New in American and Canadian Poetry" (R. Bly), **Supp. IV Part 1:** 67

What's O'Clock (Lowell), **II:** 511, 527, 528

What's Up, Tiger Lily? (film; Allen), **Supp. XV:** 2, **3**

"What the Arts Need Now" (Baraka), **Supp. II Part 1:** 47

"What the Body Can Say" (Trethewey), **Supp. XXI:** 255

"What the Brand New Freeway Won't Go By" (Hugo), **Supp. VI:** 132–133

"What the Gypsies Told My Grandmother While She Was Still a Young Girl" (Simic), **Supp. VIII:** 283

"What the Prose Poem Carries with It" (R. Bly), **Supp. IV Part 1:** 64

"What They Wanted" (Dunn), **Supp. XI:** 151

What Thou Lovest Well (Hugo), **Supp. VI:** 140, 141

"What Thou Lovest Well Remains American" (Hugo), **Supp. VI:** 140, 141

What Time Collects (Farrell), **II:** 46, 47–48

What to Do? (Chernyshevsky), **Retro. Supp. I:** 269

What Use Are Flowers? (Hansberry), **Supp. IV Part 1:** 359, 368–369, 374

What Was Literature? (Fiedler), **Supp. XIII:** 96–97, **105–106**

What Was Mine (Beattie), **Supp. V:** 33, 35

What Was the Relationship of the Lone Ranger to the Means of Production? (Baraka), **Supp. II Part 1:** 58

"What We Came Through" (Goldbarth), **Supp. XII:** 179–180

"What Were the White Things?" (Hempel), **Supp. XXI:** 126

What We Talk About When We Talk About Love (Carver), **Supp. III Part 1:** 142–146

What We Talk about When We Talk about Love (Carver), **Supp. XII:** 139

"What Why When How Who" (Pinsky), **Supp. VI:** 244

What Will Suffice: Contemporary American Poets on the Art of Poetry (Buckley and Young, eds.), **Supp. XIII:** 313

What Work Is (Levine), **Supp. V:** 181, 187, 192–193

"What You Hear from Em" (Taylor), **Supp. V:** 314, 320, 324

"What You Want" (O. Henry), **Supp. II Part 1:** 402

"What You Would Do" (Weigl), **Supp. XIX:** 288

Wheatley, Phillis, **Supp. XIII:** 111; **Supp. XVII:** 74–75; **Supp. XX:**106, **277–291**

Whedon, Tony, **Supp. XXI:** 131, 132

Wheeler, David, **Supp. XVI:** 277

Wheeler, John, **II:** 433

Wheeler, Monroe, **Supp. XV:** 295

Wheelock, John Hall, **IV:** 461; **Supp. IX:** 268; **Supp. XIV:** 120; **Supp. XV:** 301

Wheel of Life, The (Glasgow), **II:** 176, 178, 179, 183

Wheelwright, Philip, **Supp. XV:** 20

"When" (Olds), **Supp. X:** 207

When Boyhood Dreams Come True (Farrell), **II:** 45

"When Death Came April Twelve 1945" (Sandburg), **III:** 591, 593

"When Death Comes" (Oliver), **Supp. VII:** 241

"When De Co'n Pone's Hot" (Dunbar), **Supp. II Part 1:** 202–203

"When God First Said" (Zach; Everwine trans.), **Supp. XV:** 87

"When Grandma Died—1942" (Shields), **Supp. VII:** 311

"When Howitzers Began" (Carruth), **Supp. XVI:** 55

"When I Buy Pictures" (Moore), **III:** 205

"When I Came from Colchis" (Merwin), **Supp. III Part 1:** 343

"When I Have Fears I May Cease to Be" (Keats), **Supp. XIX:** 92

"When I Left Business for Literature" (Anderson), **I:** 101

"When I Love You" (Peacock), **Supp. XIX:** 199

"When in Rome—Apologia" (Komunyakaa), **Supp. XIII:** 120

"When It Comes" (Olds), **Supp. X:** 213

"When It's Clear and Hot" (Trethewey), **Supp. XXI:** 246

"When I Was Seventeen" (Kincaid), **Supp. VII:** 181

"When I Was Twenty-five" (Talese), **Supp. XVII:** 202

When Knighthood Was in Flower (Major), **III:** 320

"\[When\] Let by rain" (Taylor), **IV:** 160–161

"When Lilacs Last in the Dooryard Bloom'd" (Whitman), **IV:** 347–348, 351; **Retro. Supp. I:** 406; **Supp. IV Part 1:** 16; **Supp. XV:** 215

"When Malindy Sings" (Dunbar), **Supp. II Part 1:** 200, 204–205

When Peoples Meet: A Study of Race and Culture (Locke and Stern), **Supp. XIV:** 202, 213

When She Was Good (P. Roth), **Retro. Supp. II:** 282, 283, 284; **Supp. III Part 2:** 403, 405, 410–413

"When Sue Wears Red" (Hughes), **Retro. Supp. I:** 195, 204

"When the Dead Ask My Father about Me" (Olds), **Supp. X:** 210

"When the Frost Is on the Punkin" (Riley), **Supp. II Part 1:** 202

When the Jack Hollers (Hughes), **Retro. Supp. I:** 203; **Supp. I Part 1:** 328

"When the Last Riders" (Zach; Everwine, trans.), **Supp. XV:** 75, 86

"When the Light Gets Green" (Warren), **IV:** 252

"When the Peace Corps Was Young" (Theroux), **Supp. VIII:** 314

When the Sun Tries to Go On (Koch), **Supp. XV:** 185

"When the Sun Tries to Go On" (Koch), **Supp. XV:** 179, 180

"When the World Ended as We Knew It" (Harjo), **Supp. XII:** 231

When Time Was Born (Farrell), **II:** 46, 47

"When We Dead Awaken: Writing as Re-Vision" (Rich), **Supp. I Part 2:** 552–553, 560

"When We Gonna Rise" (Baraka), **Supp. II Part 1:** 48

"When We Have To" (Salinas), **Supp. XIII:** 322–323

"WHEN WE'LL WORSHIP JESUS" (Baraka), **Supp. II Part 1:** 54

"When We Sold the Tent" (Espaillat), **Supp. XXI:** 102

"When we speak of God, is it God we speak of?" (J. Logan), **Supp. XVII:** 113

"When Women Throw Down Bundles: Strong Women Make Strong Nations" (Gunn Allen), **Supp. IV Part 1:** 328

"'When You Finally See Them': The Unconquered Eye in *To Kill a Mockingbird*" (Champion), **Supp. VIII:** 128

"When You Lie Down, the Sea Stands Up" (Swenson), **Supp. IV Part 2:** 643

"Where Blue Is Blue" (Richard), **Supp. XIX:** 221

Where Does One Go When There's No Place Left to Go? (Crews), **Supp. XI:** 103

"Where Go the Boats" (R. Stevenson), **Supp. XVII:** 69

Where Horizons Go (Espaillat), **Supp. XXI:** 99, 103, 104

"Where I Come from Is Like This" (Gunn Allen), **Supp. IV Part 1:** 319

"Where I'm Calling From" (Carver), **Supp. III Part 1:** 145

Where I'm Calling From: New and Selected Stories (Carver), **Supp. III Part 1:** 138, 148

"Where I Ought to Be" (Erdrich), **Supp. IV Part 1:** 265

Where Is My Wandering Boy Tonight? (Wagoner), **Supp. IX:** 335–336

"Where Is the Island?" (Francis), **Supp. IX:** 78

"Where Is the Voice Coming From?" (Welty), **IV:** 280; **Retro. Supp. I:** 355

Where Joy Resides (Isherwood), **Supp. XIV:** 156

"Where Knock Is Open Wide" (Roethke), **III:** 533–535

"Where My Sympathy Lies" (H. Roth), **Supp. IX:** 234

Where's My Money? (Shanley), **Supp. XIV:** 316, 328, **330–331**

Where the Bluebird Sings to the Lemonade Springs (Stegner), **Supp. IV Part 2:** 596, 597, 598, 600, 604, 606, 613

"Where the Bones Move" (W. V. Davis), **Supp. XXI:** 92

Where the Cross Is Made (O'Neill), **III:** 388, 391

Where the Sea Used to Be (Bass), **Supp. XVI:** 21

"Where the Sea Used to Be" (Bass), **Supp. XVI:** 20, 21

"*Where the Sea Used to Be:* Rick Bass and the Novel of Ecological Education" (Dixon), **Supp. XVI:** 21

"Where the Soft Air Lives" (Nye), **Supp. XIII:** 275

Where the Twilight Never Ends (Haines), **Supp. XII:** 211

Where the Wild Grape Grows: Selected Writings, 1930–1950 (D. West; Mitchell and Davis, eds.), **Supp. XVIII:** 283, 286

Where the Wild Things Are (Sendak), **Supp. IX:** 207

"Wherever Home Is" (Wright), **Supp. III Part 2:** 605, 606

Where Water Comes Together With Other Water (Carver), **Supp. III Part 1:** 147, 148

"Where We Crashed" (Hugo), **Supp. VI:** 138

"Where We Must Look for Help" (R. Bly), **Supp. XXI:** 84

"Where You Are" (Doty), **Supp. XI:** 131

Where You'll Find Me, and Other Stories (Beattie), **Supp. V:** 30–31

Whicher, Stephen, **II:** 20

"Which Is More Than I Can Say for Some People" (Moore), **Supp. X:** 177, 178

Which Ones Are the Enemy? (Garrett), **Supp. VII:** 98

"Which Theatre Is the Absurd One?" (Albee), **I:** 71

"Which Way to the Future?" (Rehder), **Supp. IV Part 1:** 69

While I Was Gone (Miller), **Supp. XII:** 290, **301–303**

"While Seated in a Plane" (Swenson), **Supp. IV Part 2:** 645

While the Messiah Tarries (Bukiet), **Supp. XVII:** 43, **46–47**

While We've Still Got Feet (Budbill), **Supp. XIX:** 5, 7, **10–11**, 15

Whilomville Stories (Crane), **I:** 414

"Whip, The" (Robinson), **III:** 513

Whipple, Thomas K., **II:** 456, 458; **IV:** 427

"Whippoorwill, The" (Francis), **Supp. IX:** 90

"Whip-poor-will, The" (Thurber), **Supp. I Part 2:** 616

Whirlpool (film, Preminger), **Supp. XVII:** 62

"Whispering Gallery, The" (Komunyakaa), **Supp. XIII:** 132

"Whispering Leaves" (Glasgow), **II:** 190

Whispering to Fool the Wind (Ríos), **Supp. IV Part 2:** 540–541, 544, 545

"Whispers in the Next Room" (Simic), **Supp. VIII:** 278

"Whispers of Heavenly Death" (Whitman), **IV:** 348

"Whispers of Immortality" (Eliot), **Supp. XI:** 242

Whistle (Jones), **Supp. XI:** 219, 224, **231–234**

"Whistle, The" (Franklin), **II:** 121

"Whistle, The" (Komunyakaa), **Supp. XIII:** 111, 126

"Whistle, The" (Welty), **IV:** 262

Whistler, James, **I:** 484; **III:** 461, 465, 466; **IV:** 77, 369

Whistler, James Abbott McNeill, **Supp. XIV:** 335–336

"Whistling Dick's Christmas Stocking" (O. Henry), **Supp. II Part 1:** 390, 392

Whistling in the Dark (Garrett), **Supp. VII:** 111

Whistling in the Dark: True Stories and Other Fables (Garrett), **Supp. VII:** 95

Whitcher, Frances Miriam Berry, **Supp. XIII:** 152

"White" (Simic), **Supp. VIII: 275–276**

White, Barbara, **Retro. Supp. I:** 379

White, E. B., **Retro. Supp. I:** 335; **Supp. I Part 2:** 602, 607, 608, 612, 619, 620, **651–681; Supp. II Part 1:** 143; **Supp. VIII:** 171; **Supp. IX:** 20, 32; **Supp. XVI:** 167

White, Elizabeth Wade, **Supp. I Part 1:** 100, 103, 111

White, Henry Kirke, **Supp. I Part 1:** 150

White, James L., **Supp. XI:** 123

White, Joel, **Supp. I Part 2:** 654, 678

White, Katharine. (Katharine Sergeant Angell), **Supp. I Part 2:** 610, 653, 655, 656, 669; **Supp. VIII:** 151, 171

White, Lillian, **Supp. I Part 2:** 651

White, Lucia, **I:** 258

White, Maria. *See* Lowell, Mrs. James Russell (Maria White)

White, Morton, **I:** 258; **Supp. I Part 2:** 647, 648, 650

White, Roberta, **Supp. XII:** 293

White, Stanford, **Supp. IV Part 1:** 223

White, Stanley, **Supp. I Part 2:** 651, 655

White, T. H., **III:** 522

White, T. W., **III:** 411, 415

White, Walter, **Supp. I Part 1:** 345; **Supp. XVIII:** 123, 127; **Supp. XIX:** 73

White, William, **Retro. Supp. II:** 326

White, William A., **I:** 252

White Album, The (Didion), **Supp. IV Part 1:** 198, 202, 205–207, 210

"White Album, The" (Didion), **Supp. IV Part 1:** 205, 206

"White Angel" (Cunningham), **Supp. XV:** 59

"White Apache" (Markson), **Supp. XVII:** 136

White Boys (McKnight), **Supp. XX:155–157**

"White Boys, The" (McKnight), **Supp. XX:155–157**

White Buildings (H. Crane), **I:** 385, 386, 390–395, 400; **Retro. Supp. II:** 77–78, **80–81,** 82, 83, 85

White Butterfly (Mosley), **Supp. XIII:** 237, 238, 240

White Center (Hugo), **Supp. VI:** 144–145

"White Center" (Hugo), **Supp. VI:** 144, 146

Whited, Stephen, **Supp. XI:** 135

White Deer, The (Thurber), **Supp. I Part 2:** 606

White Doves at Morning (Burke), **Supp. XIV:** 22–23, 32, 35–36

"White Eagle, The" (Chopin), **Retro. Supp. II:** 72

White Fang (London), **II:** 471–472, 481

Whitefield, George, **I:** 546; **Supp. XX:280**

White-Footed Deer and Other Poems (Bryant), **Supp. I Part 1:** 157
White Goddess, The (Graves), **Supp. IV Part 1:** 280
White-Haired Lover (Shapiro), **Supp. II Part 2:** 703, 717
Whitehead, Alfred North, **III:** 605, 619, 620; **IV:** 88; **Supp. I Part 2:** 554, 647
Whitehead, Mrs. Catherine, **IV:** 116
Whitehead, Colson, **Supp. XIII:** 233, 241
Whitehead, James, **Supp. XV:** 339
Whitehead, Margaret, **IV:** 114, 115, 116
Whitehead, William, **Supp. XX:** 50–51, 53
White Heat (Walsh), **Supp. XIII:** 174
"White Heron, A" (Jewett), **II:** 409; **Retro. Supp. II:** 17
White Heron and Other Stories, A (Jewett), **II:** 396
White Horses (Hoffman), **Supp. X:** 83–85, 90, 92
White House Diary, A (Lady Bird Johnson), **Supp. IV Part 1:** 22
White-Jacket; or, The World in a Man-of-War (Melville), **III:** 80, 81, 84, 94; **Retro Supp. I:** 248, 249, 254; **Supp. XVIII:** 7, 9
White Lantern, The (Connell), **Supp. XIV:** 97
"White Lies" (Trethewey), **Supp. XXI:** 244, 246, 251
"White Lights, The" (Robinson), **III:** 524
"White Lilies, The" (Glück), **Supp. V:** 88
White Man, Listen! (Wright), **IV:** 478, 488, 489, 494
"White Mulberry Tree, The" (Cather), **I:** 319; **Retro. Supp. I:** 7, 9, 17
White Mule (W. C. Williams), **Retro. Supp. I:** 423
"White Negro, The" (Mailer), **III:** 36–37; **Retro. Supp. II:** 202
"Whiteness of the Whale, The" (Melville), **III:** 84, 86
"White Night" (Oliver), **Supp. VII:** 236
"White Nights" (Auster), **Supp. XII:** 23–24
White Noise (DeLillo), **Supp. VI:** 1, 3–4, 5–7, 10, 11–12, 16; **Supp. XVIII:** 140; **Supp. XX:** 91
White Oxen and Other Stories, The (Burke), **I:** 269, 271
White Paper on Contemporary American Poetry (McClatchy), **Supp. XII:** 253, **259–260**
"White Pine" (Oliver), **Supp. VII:** 244
White Pine: Poems and Prose Poems (Oliver), **Supp. VII:** 243–246
White Sail (Sorrentino), **Supp. XXI:** 228
"White Silence, The" (London), **II:** 468
"White Silk" (Nye), **Supp. XIII:** 275
"White Snake, The" (Sexton), **Supp. II Part 2:** 691
"White Spot" (Anderson), **I:** 116
"White-Tailed Hornet, The" (Frost), **Retro. Supp. I:** 138
"White Trash Cowboys of *Father and Son*, The" (Bjerre), **Supp. XXI:** 41
Whitfield, Raoul, **Supp. IV Part 1:** 345
Whitfield, Stephen J., **Supp. XX:** 243, 244
Whitlock, Brand, **II:** 276

Whitman (Masters), **Supp. I Part 2:** 473, 475, 476
Whitman, George, **IV:** 346, 350
Whitman, Ruth, **Supp. XXI:** 246
Whitman, Sarah Wyman, **Retro. Supp. II:** 136
Whitman, Walt, **I:** 61, 68, 98, 103, 104, 109, 219, 220, 227, 228, 242, 246, 250, 251, 260, 261, 285, 381, 384, 386, 396, 397, 398, 402, 419, 430, 459, 460, 483, 485, 486, 577; **II:** 7, 8, 18, 127, 140, 273–274, 275, 289, 295, 301, 320, 321, 373, 445, 446, 451, 457, 494, 529, 530, 552; **III:** 171, 175, 177, 181–182, 189, 203, 234, 260, 426, 430, 453, 454, 461, 505, 507–508, 511, 528, 548, 552, 555, 559, 567, 572, 576, 577, 579, 584, 585, 595, 606, 609; **IV:** 74, 169, 191, 192, 202, **331–354**, 405, 409, 416, 444, 450–451, 457, 463, 464, 469, 470, 471; **Retro. Supp. I:** 8, 52, 194, 254, 283, 284, 333, **387–410**, 412, 417, 427; **Retro. Supp. II:** 40, 76, 93, 99, 155, 156, 158, 170, 262; **Supp. I Part 1:** 6, 79, 167, 311, 314, 325, 365, 368, 372; **Supp. I Part 2:** 374, 384, 385, 387, 389, 391, 393, 399, 416, 436, 455, 456, 458, 473, 474, 475, 525, 540, 579, 580, 582, 682, 691; **Supp. III Part 1:** 6, 20, 156, 239–241, 253, 340; **Supp. III Part 2:** 596; **Supp. IV Part 1:** 16, 169, 325; **Supp. IV Part 2:** 597, 625; **Supp. V:** 113, 118, 122, 130, 170, 178, 183, 277, 279, 332; **Supp. VIII:** 42, 95, 105, 126, 198, 202, 269; **Supp. IX:** 8, 9, 15, 38, 41, 44, 48, 53, 131, 292, 298, 299, 308, 320; **Supp. X:** 36, 112, 203, 204; **Supp. XI:** 83, 123, 132, 135, 203, 321; **Supp. XII:** 132, 185, 190, 256; **Supp. XIII:** 1, 77, 115, 153, 221, 304, 335; **Supp. XIV:** 89, 312, 334, 335, 338; **Supp. XV:** 41, 93, 181, 183, 212, 213, 218, 250, 275, 301, 302, 303, 309, 352; **Supp. XVI:** 209; **Supp. XVII:** 42, 71, 112, 133; **Supp. XVIII:** 4, 194, 196, 304; **Supp. XIX:** 118, 276; **Supp. XX:** 69, 115, 116, 221; **Supp. XXI:** 169, 217, 227, 256
"Whitman Pinch Hits, 1861" (Skloot), **Supp. XX:** 203
"Whitman: The Poet and the Mask" (Cowley), **Supp. II Part 1:** 143
Whitmarsh, Jason, **Supp. VIII:** 283
Whitmer, Peter, **Supp. X:** 264, 265
Whitney, Blair, **Supp. I Part 2:** 403
Whitney, Josiah, **Supp. IX:** 180, 181
Whitt, Margaret Earley, **Retro. Supp. II:** 226
Whittemore, Reed, **III:** 268; **Supp. XI:** 315
Whittier, Elizabeth, **Supp. I Part 2:** 700, 701, 703; **Supp. XIII:** 141, 142
Whittier, John Greenleaf, **I:** 216; **II:** 275; **III:** 52; **Retro. Supp. I:** 54; **Retro. Supp. II:** 155, 163, 169; **Supp. I Part 1:** 168, 299, 313, 317, 372; **Supp. I**

Part 2: 420, 602, **682–707**; **Supp. VIII:** 202, 204; **Supp. XI:** 50; **Supp. XIII:** 140, 145; **Supp. XV:** 246
Whittier, Mary, **Supp. I Part 2:** 683
"Whittier Birthday Speech" (Twain), **Supp. I Part 1:** 313
"Who" (Kenyon), **Supp. VII:** 174
"Who" (Sobin), **Supp. XVI:** 284–285
"Who Am I—Who I Am" (Corso), **Supp. XII:** 134
"Who Be Kind To" (Ginsberg), **Supp. II Part 1:** 323
"Whoever Was Using This Bed" (Carver), **Supp. III Part 1:** 148
"Whoever You Are Holding Me Now in Hand" (Whitman), **IV:** 342; **Retro. Supp. I:** 52
Who Gathered and Whispered behind Me (Goldbarth), **Supp. XII:** 181, 182
"Who in One Lifetime" (Rukeyser), **Supp. VI:** 276, 279
Who Is Witter Bynner? (Kraft), **Supp. XV:** 40, 52
"Who Is Your Mother? Red Roots of White Feminism" (Gunn Allen), **Supp. IV Part 1:** 329
Whole Hog (Wagoner), **Supp. IX:** 337–338
"Whole Mess…Almost, The" (Corso), **Supp. XII:** 135
"Whole Moisty Night, The" (R. Bly), **Supp. IV Part 1:** 69
Whole New Life, A (Price), **Supp. VI:** 265, **266,** 267
"Whole Self, The" (Nye), **Supp. XIII:** 275
"Whole Soul, The" (Levine), **Supp. V:** 192
"Whole Story, The" (Strand), **Supp. IV Part 2:** 622
Whole Town's Talking, The (Loos), **Supp. XVI:** 187
"Whole World Knows, The" (Welty), **IV:** 272; **Retro. Supp. I:** 343
Who'll Stop the Rain (film), **Supp. V:** 301
Who Lost an American? (Algren), **Supp. IX:** 15–16
Who Owns America? (symposium), **Supp. XIV:** 4
"Who Puts Together" (Hogan), **Supp. IV Part 1:** 403, 405, 412–413
"Whore of Mensa, The" (Allen), **Supp. XV:** 15
Whores for Gloria (Vollmann), **Supp. XVII:** 226, 230
Whorf, Benjamin Lee, **Supp. XVI:** 283
Who's Afraid of Virginia Woolf? (Albee), **I:** 71, 77–81, 83, 85, 86, 87, 94; **IV:** 230
Who Shall Be the Sun? Poems Based on the Lore, Legends, and Myths of the Northwest Coast and Plateau Indians (Wagoner), **Supp. IX:** 328, **329–330,** 337
"Whosis Kid, The" (Hammett), **Supp. IV Part 1:** 344
"Who Sit Watch in Daylight" (Wright), **Supp. XV:** 342
"Who's Passing for Who?" (Hughes), **Supp. I Part 1:** 330

"Who Speak on the Page?" (Sanders), **Supp. XVI:** 278

Who Will Run the Frog Hospital?: A Novel (Moore), **Supp. X:** 163, 165, 169, **175–177**

Why Are We in Vietnam? (Mailer), **III:** 27, 29, 30, 33, 34–35, 39, 42, 44; **Retro. Supp. II:** 205–206

"Why Bother?" (Franzen). *See* "Perchance to Dream" (Franzen)

"Why China?" (Egan), **Supp. XIX:** 51, 52

"Why Did the Balinese Chicken Cross the Road?" (Walker), **Supp. III Part 2:** 527

"Why Do the Heathens Rage?" (O'Connor), **III:** 351

"Why Do You Write About Russia?" (Simpson), **Supp. IX:** 277

"Why I Am a Danger to the Public" (Kingsolver), **Supp. VII:** 204

Why I Am Not a Christian (Russell), **Supp. I Part 2:** 522

Why I Came to Judevine (Budbill), **Supp. XIX:** 2, **7–8,** 15

"Why I Entered the Gurdjieff Work" (Toomer), **Supp. III Part 2:** 481

"Why I Like Laurel" (Patchett), **Supp. XII:** 309

"Why I Live at the P.O." (Welty), **IV:** 262; **Retro. Supp. I:** 345

"Why I Make Sam Go to Church" (Lamott), **Supp. XX:**141

"Why Is Economics Not an Evolutionary Science?" (Veblen), **Supp. I Part 2:** 634

"Why I Write" (Didion), **Supp. IV Part 1:** 201, 203

"Why I Wrote *Phil:* An Exclusive Essay for Amazon.com" (Saunders), **Supp. XIX:** 230–231

Why Johnny Can't Read: And What You Can Do About It (Flesch), **Supp. XVI:** 105

"Why Negro Women Leave Home" (Brooks), **Supp. III Part 1:** 75

Why Poetry Matters (Parini), **Supp. XIX:** 120, 129

"Why Resign from the Human Race?" (Swados), **Supp. XIX:** 265

"Why the Little Frenchman Wears His Hand in a Sling" (Poe), **III:** 425

"Why We Are Forgiven" (Weigl), **Supp. XIX:** 282–283

Why We Behave Like Microbe Hunters (Thurber), **Supp. I Part 2:** 606

Why We Were in Vietnam (Podhoretz), **Supp. VIII:** 241

"Why Write?" (Updike), **Retro. Supp. I:** 317

"Wichita Vortex Sutra" (Ginsberg), **Supp. II Part 1:** 319, 321, 323–325, 327

Wickes, George, **Supp. XIV:** 165

Wickford Point (Marquand), **III:** 50, 58, 64–65, 69

Wicks, Robert Russell, **Supp. XII:** 49

Wide, Wide World, The (S. Warner as Wetherell), **Supp. XV:** 275; **Supp. XVIII:** 257, 260, **262–264,** 265

"Wide Empty Landscape with a Death in the Foreground" (Momaday), **Supp. IV Part 2:** 492

Wideman, John Edgar, **Retro. Supp. II:** 123; **Supp. X:** 239, 250, **319–336;** **Supp. XI:** 245; **Supp. XIII:** 247; **Supp. XVIII:** 89; **Supp. XXI:** 246

Widener, Jeff, **Supp. XVIII:** 91

"Wideness" (Pickering), **Supp. XXI:** 203

"Wide Net, The" (Welty), **IV:** 266

Wide Net and Other Stories, The (Welty), **IV:** 261, 264–266, 271; **Retro. Supp. I:** **347–349,** 352, 355

Widening Spell of the Leaves, The (Levis), **Supp. XI:** 258, 259, 261, **268–269,** 271

"Wide Prospect, The" (Jarrell), **II:** 376–377

Wide Sargasso Sea (Rhys), **Supp. XVIII:** 131

"Widow" (Peacock), **Supp. XIX:** 206

"Widower" (Robison), **Supp. XXI:** 118

Widow for One Year, A (Irving), **Supp. VI:** 165, **179–181**

Widows of Thornton, The (Taylor), **Supp. V:** 320, 321

"Widow's Wish, The" (Briggs), **Supp. XVIII:** 15

Wieland; or, The Transformation. An American Tale (Brown), **Supp. I Part 1:** 128–132, 133, 137, 140

Wiene, Robert, **Retro. Supp. I:** 268

Wiener, John, **Supp. IV Part 1:** 153

Wieners, John, **Supp. II Part 1:** 32

Wiesel, Elie, **Supp. XVII:** 47, 48, 49

Wiest, Dianne, **Supp. XV:** 12

"Wife, Forty-five, Remembers Love, A" (Shields), **Supp. VII:** 310

"Wifebeater, The" (Sexton), **Supp. II Part 2:** 693

"Wife for Dino Rossi, A" (Fante), **Supp. XI:** 165

"Wife of His Youth, The" (Chesnutt), **Supp. XIV:** **63–66**

Wife of His Youth and Other Stories of the Color Line, The (Chesnutt), **Supp. XIV:** 62, 63

"Wife of Jesus Speaks, The" (Karr), **Supp. XI:** 250–251

"Wife of Nashville, A" (Taylor), **Supp. V:** 320

"Wife's Story, The" (R. H. Davis), **Supp. XVI:** 85, 91, 92–93

Wife's Story, The (Shields), **Supp. VII:** 316. *See also* Happenstance

"Wife-Wooing" (Updike), **IV:** 226

Wigan, Gareth, **Supp. XI:** 306

Wiget, Andrew, **Supp. IV Part 2:** 509

Wigglesworth, Michael, **IV:** 147, 156; **Supp. I Part 1:** 110, 111

Wilbur, Richard, **III:** 527; **Retro. Supp. II:** 50; **Supp. III Part 1:** 64; **Supp. III Part 2: 541–565; Supp. IV Part 2:** 626, 634, 642; **Supp. V:** 337; **Supp. VIII:** 28; **Supp. X:** 58, 120; **Supp. XII:** 258; **Supp. XIII:** 76, 336; **Supp. XV:** 51, 251, 256; **Supp. XVII:** 26; **Supp. XVIII:** 178; **Supp. XX:**199; **Supp. XXI:** 247

Wilcocks, Alexander, **Supp. I Part 1:** 125

Wilcox, Ella Wheeler, **Supp. II Part 1:** 197

Wilcox, Kirstin, **Supp. XX:**283, 284, 285

Wild, John, **II:** 362, 363–364

Wild, Peter, **Supp. V:** 5

Wild, Robert, **IV:** 155

"Wild, The" (Berry), **Supp. X:** 30

Wild 90 (film) (Mailer), **Retro. Supp. II:** 205

Wild and Woolly (film), **Supp. XVI:** 185

Wild Boy of Aveyron, The (Itard). *See* De l'éducation d'un homme sauvage

Wild Boys, The: A Book of the Dead (Burroughs), **Supp. III Part 1:** 106–107

Wild Card Quilt: Taking A chance on Home (Ray), **Supp. XVIII:** 189, 192, 193, 196, 198, **200–202,** 204

Wilde, Oscar, **I:** 50, 66, 381, 384; **II:** 515; **IV:** 77, 350; **Retro. Supp. I:** 56, 102, 227; **Retro. Supp. II:** 76, 326; **Supp. IV Part 2:** 578, 679, 683; **Supp. V:** 106, 283; **Supp. IX:** 65, 66, 68, 189, 192; **Supp. X:** 148, 151, 188–189; **Supp. XIV:** 324, 334; **Supp. XV:** 350

Wilder, Amos Parker, **IV:** 356

Wilder, Mrs. Amos Parker (Isabella Thornton Niven), **IV:** 356

Wilder, Billy, **Supp. IV Part 1:** 130; **Supp. XI:** 307

Wilder, Ingalls, **Supp. XXI:** 2

Wilder, Isabel, **IV:** 357, 366, 375

Wilder, Thornton, **I:** 360, 482; **IV: 355–377,** 431; **Retro. Supp. I:** 109, 359; **Supp. I Part 2:** 609; **Supp. IV Part 2:** 586; **Supp. V:** 105; **Supp. IX:** 140; **Supp. XII:** 236–237; **Supp. XX:**50

"Wilderness" (Leopold), **Supp. XIV:** 190

Wilderness (Parker), **Supp. XIX:** 177, **188–189**

"Wilderness" (Sandburg), **III:** 584, 595

Wilderness (Warren), **IV:** 256

"Wilderness, The" (Merwin), **Supp. III Part 1:** 340, 345

"Wilderness, The" (Robinson), **III:** 524

Wilderness of Vision, The: On the Poetry of John Haines (Bezner and Walzer, eds.), **Supp. XII:** 202

Wilderness Plots: Tales about the Settlement of the American Land (Sanders), **Supp. XVI:** 267–268, 269

Wilderness World of Anne LaBastille, The (LaBastille), **Supp. X:** **105,** 106

Wild Flag, The (White), **Supp. I Part 2:** 654

"Wildflower, The" (W. C. Williams), **Retro. Supp. I:** 420

"Wild Flowers" (Caldwell), **I:** 310

"Wildflowers" (Minot), **Supp. VI:** 208

"Wild Geese" (Oliver), **Supp. VII:** 237

"Wild Honey Suckle, The" (Freneau), **Supp. II Part 1:** 253, 264, 266

Wild in the Country (Odets), **Supp. II Part 2:** 546

"Wild in the Woods" (Skloot), **Supp. XX:**206

Wild Iris, The (Glück), **Supp. V:** 79, 87–89, 91

Wildlife (Ford), **Supp. V:** 57, 69–71

Wildlife in America (Matthiessen), **Supp. V:** 199, 201, 204

"Wildlife in American Culture" (Leopold), **Supp. XIV:** 190, 191

"Wild Light" (Skloot), **Supp. XX:** 200

Wild Man, The (P. N. Warren), **Supp. XX:** 260, **270–272**

"Wildness" (Sanders), **Supp. XVI:** 276

Wild Old Wicked Man, The (MacLeish), **III:** 3, 20

Wild Palms, The (Faulkner), **II:** 68–69; **Retro. Supp. I:** 85

"Wild Palms, The" (Faulkner), **II:** 68

"Wild Peaches" (Wylie), **Supp. I Part 2:** 707, 712

Wild Roses of Cape Ann and Other Poems (Larcom), **Supp. XIII:** 142, 147

Wild Seed (O. Butler), **Supp. XIII:** 62, 63

"Wild Swans at Coole, The " (W. B. Yeats), **Supp. XVI:** 48

"Wild Swans at Norfolk, The" (Carruth), **Supp. XVI:** 48

"Wild Thing" (L. Brown), **Supp. XXI:** 44

Wild Thorn (Hoffman), **Supp. XVIII:** **84–85**

Wild to the Heart (Bass), **Supp. XVI:** 16

"Wild Turkeys: Dignity of the Damned" (B. Kelly), **Supp. XVII:** 129

"Wildwest" (MacLeish), **III:** 14

Wiley, Craig, **Supp. VIII:** 313

Wilhelm Meister (Goethe), **II:** 291

Wilkes, John, **Supp. I Part 2:** 503, 519, 522

Wilkie, Curtis, **Supp. V:** 11

Wilkins, Roy, **Supp. I Part 1:** 345

Wilkinson, Alec, **Supp. VIII:** 164, 168, 171

Wilkinson, Max, **Supp. IX:** 251

Will, The (Swados), **Supp. XIX: 265–266**

Willard, Nancy, **Supp. XIX:** 138

Willard, Samuel, **IV:** 150

Willard Gibbs (Rukeyser), **Supp. VI:** 273, 283, 284

Willcutts, Tim, **Supp. XVII:** 239, 241, 246

Willett, Ralph, **Supp. XIV:** 27

Willey, Basil, **Retro. Supp. II:** 243

"William Butler Yeats Among the Ghosts" (Skloot), **Supp. XX:** 204–205

William Carlos Williams (Koch), **Retro. Supp. I:** 428

William Carlos Williams: An American Artist (Breslin), **Retro. Supp. I:** 430

William Carlos Williams and Alterity (Ahearn), **Retro. Supp. I:** 415

William Carlos Williams and the Meanings of Measure (Cushman), **Retro. Supp. I:** 430

William Carlos Williams: The American Background (Weaver), **Retro. Supp. I:** 430

William Faulkner: A Critical Study (Howe), **Supp. VI:** 119–120, 125

William Faulkner: Early Prose and Poetry (Faulkner), **Retro. Supp. I:** 80

William Faulkner: First Encounters (Brooks), **Supp. XIV:** 13

"William Faulkner's Legend of the South" (Cowley), **Supp. II Part 1:** 143

"William Faulkner: The Stillness of *Light in August*" (Kazin), *Supp. VIII:* 104

William Faulkner: The Yoknapatawpha Country (Brooks), **Supp. XIV: 12–13,** 16

William Faulkner: Toward Yoknapatawpha and Beyond (Brooks), **Supp. XIV:** 13

"William Humphrey, 73, Writer of Novels about Rural Texas" (Gussow), **Supp. IX:** 93

William Humphrey, Destroyer of Myths (Almon), **Supp. IX:** 93

William Humphrey. Boise State University Western Writers Series (Winchell), **Supp. IX:** 109

"William Humphrey Remembered" (Masters), **Supp. IX:** 96

William Humphrey. Southwestern Series (Lee), **Supp. IX:** 109

"William Ireland's Confession" (A. Miller), **III:** 147–148

William James and Phenomenology: A Study of the "Principles of Psychology" (Wilshire), *II:* 362

William Lloyd Garrison (Chapman), **Supp. XIV:** 46–51, 52, 53, 55

William Maxwell Portrait, A: Memories and Appreciations (C. Baxter, Collier, and Hirsch, eds.), **Supp. XVII:** 23

Williams, Annie Laurie, **Supp. IX:** 93

Williams, Blanch Colton, **Supp. XVIII:** 279

Williams, Cecil, **II:** 508

Williams, Charles, **Supp. II Part 1:** 15, 16

Williams, C. K., **Supp. XIII:** 114; **Supp. XVII:** 112

Williams, Cratis, **Supp. XX:** 163

Williams, Dakin, **IV:** 379

Williams, David Reichard, **Supp. XIII:** 162

Williams, Edward, **IV:** 404

Williams, Edwina Dakin, **IV:** 379

Williams, Eric, **Supp. XXI:** 166, 170, 171

Williams, Esther, **Supp. XII:** 165

Williams, Fannie Barrier, **Supp. XIV:** 201

Williams, George, **Supp. V:** 220

Williams, Henry Sylvester, **Supp. XXI:** 166

Williams, Horace, **IV:** 453

Williams, Joan, **Supp. IX:** 95

Williams, John A., **Supp. XVI:** 143

Williams, John Sharp, **IV:** 378

Williams, Kenny J., **Supp. XX:** 281, 286

Williams, Lyle, **Supp. XIV:** 22

Williams, Michael, **Supp. V:** 286

Williams, Miller, **Supp. XIV:** 126; **Supp. XV:** 339; **Supp. XVIII:** 177

Williams, Paul, **IV:** 404

Williams, Raymond, **Supp. IX:** 146

Williams, Roger, **Supp. I Part 2:** 699

Williams, Rose, **IV:** 379

Williams, Sherley Anne, **Supp. V:** 180

Williams, Solomon, **I:** 549

Williams, Stanley T., **II:** 301, 316; **Supp. I Part 1:** 251

Williams, Stephen, **IV:** 148

Williams, Ted, **IV:** 216; **Supp. IX:** 162

Williams, Tennessee, **I:** 73, 81, 113, 211; **II:** 190, 194; **III:** 145, 147; **IV:** 4, **378–401; Supp. I Part 1:** 290, 291; **Supp. IV Part 1:** 79, 83, 84, 359; **Supp. IV Part 2:** 574, 682; **Supp. IX:** 133; **Supp. XI:** 103; **Supp. XIII:** 331; **Supp. XIV:** 250, 315; **Supp. XVI:** 194

Williams, Terry Tempest, **Supp. XIII:** 16; **Supp. XVIII:** 189

Williams, Walter L., **Supp. IV Part 1:** 330, 331

Williams, William, **IV:** 404, 405

Williams, William Carlos, **I:** 61, 62, 229, 255, 256, 261, 285, 428, 438, 446, 539; **II:** 133, 536, 542, 543, 544, 545; **III:** 194, 196, 198, 214, 269, 409, 453, 457, 458, 464, 465, 591; **IV:** 30, 74, 75, 76, 94, 95, 286, 287, **402–425; Retro. Supp. I:** 51, 52, 62, 209, 284, 285, 288, 296, 298, **411–433; Retro. Supp. II:** 178, 181, 189, 250, 321, 322, 326, 327, 328, 334, 335; **Supp. I Part 1:** 254, 255, 259, 266; **Supp. II Part 1:** 9, 30, 308, 318; **Supp. II Part 2:** 421, 443; **Supp. III Part 1:** 9, 147, 239, 271, 275, 276, 278, 350; **Supp. III Part 2:** 542, 610, 613, 614, 615, 616, 617, 621, 622, 626, 628; **Supp. IV Part 1:** 151, 153, 246, 325; **Supp. V:** 180, 337; **Supp. VIII:** 195, 269, 272, 277, 292; **Supp. IX:** 38, 268, 291; **Supp. X:** 112, 120, 204; **Supp. XI:** 311, 328; **Supp. XII:** 198; **Supp. XIII:** 77, 90, 335; **Supp. XIV:** 280, 284, 285, 293; **Supp. XV:** 42, 51, 182, 250, 306, 307; **Supp. XVI:** 48, 282; **Supp. XVII:** 36, 113, 227, 243; **Supp. XIX:** 1, 42, 117, 119, 121; **Supp. XXI:** 226, 227, 230, 233

Williams, Mrs. William Carlos (Florence Herman), **IV:** 404

Williams, Wirt, **Supp. XIV:** 24

Williamson, Alan, **Retro. Supp. II:** 185; **Supp. XIX:** 91

Williamson, J. W., **Supp. XX:** 164

William Styron's Nat Turner: Ten Black Writers Respond (Clarke, ed.), **IV:** 115

Williams-Walsh, Mary Ellen, **Supp. IV Part 2:** 611

William the Conqueror, **Supp. I Part 2:** 507

William Wetmore Story and His Friends (James), **Retro. Supp. I:** 235; **Supp. XX:** 228

William Wilson (Gardner), **Supp. VI:** 72

"William Wilson" (Poe), **II:** 475; **III:** 410, 412; **Retro. Supp. II:** 269; **Supp. IX:** 105

"Willie" (Angelou), **Supp. IV Part 1:** 15

Willie Masters' Lonesome Wife (Gass), **Supp. VI:** 77, **84–85, 86–87**

"Willing" (Moore), **Supp. X:** 178

Willis, Bruce, **Supp. IV Part 1:** 236

Willis, Gordon, **Supp. XV:** 7

Willis, Mary Hard, **Supp. V:** 290–291

Willis, Nathaniel Parker, **II:** 313; **Supp. I Part 2:** 405; **Supp. XVIII:** 12

Williwaw (Vidal), **Supp. IV Part 2:** 677, 680, 681

"Willow Woman" (Francis), **Supp. IX:** 78

Wills, Garry, **Supp. I Part 1:** 294; **Supp. IV Part 1:** 355

Wills, Ridley, **IV:** 122

Wills, Ross B., **Supp. XI:** 169

"Will to Believe, The" (James), **II:** 352; **Supp. XIV:** 50

Will to Believe, The, and Other Essays in Popular Philosophy (James), **II:** 356; **IV:** 28

Will to Change, The: Poems, 1968–1970 (Rich), **Supp. I Part 2:** 551, 557–559

"Will We Plug Chips into Our Brains?" (W. Gibson), **Supp. XVI:** 117–118

Will You Please Be Quiet, Please? (Carver), **Supp. III Part 1:** 138, 140, 144

"Will You Please Be Quiet, Please?" (Carver), **Supp. III Part 1:** 137, 141

"Will You Tell Me?" (Barthelme), **Supp. IV Part 1:** 42, 47

Wilsdorf, Anne, **Supp. XVI:** 177

Wilshire, Bruce, **II:** 362, 364

Wilshire, Gaylord, **Supp. V:** 280

Wilson, Adrian, **Supp. XV:** 147

Wilson, Alexander, **Supp. XVI:** 4, 6

Wilson, Angus, **IV:** 430, 435

Wilson, August, **Supp. VIII: 329–353; Supp. XIX:** 132

Wilson, Augusta Jane Evans, **Retro. Supp. I:** 351

Wilson, Earl, **Supp. X:** 264

Wilson, Edmund, **I:** 67, 185, 236, 247, 260, 434, 482; **II:** 79, 80, 81, 86, 87, 91, 97, 98, 146, 276, 430, 530, 562, 587; **III:** 588; **IV:** 308, 310, **426–449; Retro. Supp. I:** 1, 97, 100, 101, 103, 104, 105, 115, 274; **Retro. Supp. II:** 321, 327, 329; **Supp. I Part 1:** 372; **Supp. I Part 2:** 407, 646, 678, 709; **Supp. II Part 1:** 19, 90, 106, 136, 137, 143; **Supp. III Part 2:** 612; **Supp. IV Part 2:** 693; **Supp. VIII:** 93, 95, 96, 97, 98–99, 100, 101, 103, 105, 162; **Supp. IX:** 55, 65, 190; **Supp. X:** 186; **Supp. XI:** 160; **Supp. XIII:** 170; **Supp. XIV:** 338; **Supp. XV:** 142, 308; **Supp. XVI:** 194; **Supp. XX:**76, 81

Wilson, Edmund (father), **IV:** 441

Wilson, E. O., **Supp. X:** 35

Wilson, Harriet, **Supp. XX:**105

Wilson, Henry, **Supp. XIV:** 48

Wilson, Reuel, **II:** 562

Wilson, Robert, **Supp. XI:** 144

Wilson, Sloan, **Supp. IV Part 1:** 387

Wilson, Thomas, **IV:** 153

Wilson, Tracy, **Supp. XVIII:** 101

Wilson, Victoria, **Supp. X:** 166

Wilson, Woodrow, **I:** 245, 246, 490; **II:** 183, 253; **III:** 105, 581; **Supp. I Part 1:** 21; **Supp. I Part 2:** 474, 643; **Supp. V:** 288

Wilton, David, **IV:** 147

Wiman, Christian, **Supp. XV:** 251, 253, 264; **Supp. XVII:** 74; **Supp. XVIII:** 173, 174

Wimberly, Lowry, **Supp. XV:** 136, 137

Wimsatt, William K., **Supp. XIV:** 12

Winchell, Mark, **Supp. VIII:** 176, 189

Winchell, Mark Royden, **Supp. VIII:** 241; **Supp. IX:** 97, 98, 109; **Supp. XIII:** 94, 98, 99, 101; **Supp. XIV:** 103, 106, 111

Winckelmann, Johann Joachim, **Supp. XII:** 178

Wind, Sand, and Stars (Saint-Exupéry), **Supp. IX:** 247

Wind Across the Everglades (film, Ray), **Supp. XVIII:** 253

Wind Chrysalid's Rattle (Sobin), **Supp. XVI:** 283

"Windfall" (B. Kelly), **Supp. XVII:** 132

Windflower Home Almanac of Poetry, The (Kooser, ed.), **Supp. XIX:** 119

Windham, Donald, **IV:** 382

"Windhover" (Hopkins), **I:** 397; **II:** 539; **Supp. IX:** 43

Winding Stair and Other Poems, The (Yeats), **Supp. XV:** 253

"Winding Street, The" (Petry), **Supp. XI:** 6

"Window" (Pinsky), **Supp. VI:** 237, 247

"Window, The" (Hull), **Supp. XXI:** 140–141

Windows (Creeley), **Supp. IV Part 1:** 157, 158

"Windows" (Jarrell), **II:** 388, 389

"Window Seat, A" (Goldbarth), **Supp. XII:** 185

Wind Remains, The (opera) (Bowles), **Supp. IV Part 1:** 83

"Winds, The" (Welty), **IV:** 265; **Retro. Supp. I:** 348, 350

"Winds and Clouds over a Funeral" (Jin), **Supp. XVIII:** 94

Winds of War (Wouk), **Supp. XX:**243

"Wind up Sushi" (Goldbarth), **Supp. XII:** 186–187

"Windy Day at the Reservoir, A" (Beattie), **Supp. V:** 33

Windy McPherson's Son (Anderson), **I:** 101, 102–103, 105, 111

"Wine" (Carver), **Supp. III Part 1:** 138

"Wine Menagerie, The" (H. Crane), **I:** 389, 391; **Retro. Supp. II:** 82

Wine of the Puritans, The: A Study of Present-Day America (Brooks), **I:** 240

"Wine of Wizardry, A" (Sterling), **I:** 208

Winer, Linda, **Supp. IV Part 2:** 580; **Supp. XV:** 332

Winesburg, Ohio: A Group of Tales of Ohio Small Town Life (Anderson), **I:** 97, 102, 103, 104, 105–108; **III:** 112, 113, 114, 116, 224, 579; **Supp. V:** 12; **Supp. IX:** 306, 308; **Supp. XI:** 164; **Supp. XVI:** 17

Winfrey, Oprah, **Supp. XIX:** 194, 204; **Supp. XX:**83, 93

Wing-and-Wing, The (Cooper), **I:** 350, 355

Winged Seed, The: A Remembrance (L.-Y. Lee), **Supp. XV:** 211, **220–223**

Winged Words: American Indian Writers Speak (Coltelli), **Supp. IV Part 2:** 493, 497

"Wingfield" (Wolff), **Supp. VII:** 341–342

"Wings, The" (Doty), **Supp. XI:** 124

Wings of the Dove, The (James), **I:** 436; **II:** 320, 323, 333, 334–335; **Retro. Supp. I:** 215, 216, 217, 232, **233–234; Supp. II Part 1:** 94–95; **Supp. IV Part 1:** 349

"Wink of the Zenith, The" (Skloot), **Supp. XX:**207

Wink of the Zenith, The: The Shaping of a Writer's Life (Skloot), **Supp. XX:**195, 196, **207**

"Winky" (Saunders), **Supp. XIX:** 228–229, 229

Winner Take Nothing (Hemingway), **II:** 249; **Retro. Supp. I:** 170, 175, 176, 181

"Winnie" (Brooks), **Supp. III Part 1:** 86

Winokur, Maxine. *See* Kumin, Maxine

Winslow, Art, **Supp. XVIII:** 102

Winslow, Devereux, **II:** 547

Winslow, Harriet, **II:** 552–553

Winslow, Ola Elizabeth, **I:** 547

Winslow, Warren, **II:** 540

Winston, Andrew, **Supp. XII:** 189

Winston, Michael R., **Supp. XIV:** 197

Winter, Douglas, **Supp. V:** 144

Winter, Johnny and Edgar, **Supp. V:** 334

Winter, Kate, **Supp. X:** 104

"Winter Branch, A" (Irving), **Supp. VI:** 163

"Winter Burial, A" (Clampitt), **Supp. IX:** 48

Winter Carnival (film), **Retro. Supp. I:** 113

"Winter Daybreak at Vence, A" (Wright), **Supp. III Part 1:** 249–250

Winter Diary, A (Van Doren), **I:** 168

"Winter Dreams" (Fitzgerald), **II:** 80, 94; **Retro. Supp. I:** 108

"Winter Drive, A" (Jewett), **Retro. Supp. II:** 147

"Winter Eden, A" (Frost), **Retro. Supp. I:** 137

"Winter Father, The" (Dubus), **Supp. VII:** 83, 87

Winter Hours: Prose, Prose Poems, and Poems (Oliver), **Supp. VII:** 230, 247

"Winter in Dunbarton" (Lowell), **II:** 547; **Retro. Supp. II:** 187

"Wintering" (Plath), **Retro. Supp. II:** 255

Winter Insomnia (Carver), **Supp. III Part 1:** 138

Winter in the Blood (Welch), **Supp. IV Part 2:** 562

"Winter Landscape" (Berryman), **I:** 174; **Retro. Supp. I:** 430

Winter Light (W. V. Davis), **Supp. XXI: 92,** 93

"Winter Light" (W. V. Davis), **Supp. XXI:** 90, 92

Winter Lightning (Nemerov), **III:** 269

Winter Morning Walks: One Hundred Postcards to Jim Harrison (Kooser), **Supp. XIX:** 116, **125–126**

Winter News (Haines), **Supp. XII:** 199, **201–204,** 207–208, 208

Winternitz, Mary. *See* Cheever, Mrs. John (Mary Winternitz)

Winter: Notes from Montana (Bass), **Supp. XVI:** 17–18

Winter of Our Discontent, The (Steinbeck), **IV:** 52, 65–66, 68

"Winter on Earth" (Toomer), **Supp. III Part 2:** 486

"Winter Piece, A" (Bryant), **Supp. I Part 1:** 150, 155

"Winter Rains, Cataluña" (Levine), **Supp. V:** 182

"Winter Remembered" (Ransom), **III:** 492–493

"Winter Roses" (W. V. Davis), **Supp. XXI:** 94

Winterrowd, Prudence, **I:** 217, 224

Winters, Jonathan, **Supp. XI:** 305

Winters, Yvor, **I:** 59, 63, 386, 393, 397, 398, 402, 471; **III:** 194, 498; **IV:** 153; **Retro. Supp. II:** 76, 77, 78, 82, 83, 85, 89; **Supp. I Part 1:** 268; **Supp. II Part 2:** 416, 666, **785–816; Supp. IV Part 2:** 480; **Supp. V:** 180, 191–192; **Supp. XIV:** 287; **Supp. XV:** 74, 341

"Winter Sacrament" (Bronk), **Supp. XXI:** 33

"Winter Scenes" (Bryant). *See* "Winter Piece, A"

Winterset (Anderson), **III:** 159

"Winter Shrub, A" (Bronk), **Supp. XXI:** 28

"Winter Skyline Late" (F. Wright), **Supp. XVII:** 245

"Winter Sleep" (Wylie), **Supp. I Part 2:** 711, 729

Winter's Night (Boyce), **Supp. XXI:** 7, **12–13**

Winter's Tale, The (Shakespeare), **Supp. XIII:** 219

Winter Stars (Levis), **Supp. XI:** 259, **266–268**

"Winter Stars" (Levis), **Supp. XI:** 267–268

Winter Stop-Over (Everwine), **Supp. XV:** 74, 76

"Winter Stop-Over" (Everwine), **Supp. XV:** 76

"Winter Swan" (Bogan), **Supp. III Part 1:** 52

Winter Thunder (X. J. Kennedy), **Supp. XV:** 167

"Winter Thunder" (X. J. Kennedy), **Supp. XV:** 169

"Winter Trees" (Pedersen; Nelson, trans.), **Supp. XVIII:** 180

Winter Trees (Plath), **Retro. Supp. II:** 257; **Supp. I Part 2:** 526, 539, 541

"Winter Walk" (W. V. Davis), **Supp. XXI:** 92

"Winter Weather Advisory" (Ashbery), **Supp. III Part 1:** 26

"Winter Wheat" (Hoffman), **Supp. XVIII:** 86, 87

"Winter without Snow, The" (C. Frost), **Supp. XV:** 96, 105–106

"Winter Words" (Levine), **Supp. V:** 192

Winthrop, John, **Supp. I Part 1:** 99, 100, 101, 102, 105; **Supp. I Part 2:** 484, 485

Winthrop Covenant, The (Auchincloss), **Supp. IV Part 1:** 23

"Wires of the Night, The" (Collins), **Supp. XXI:** 64

Wirt, William, **I:** 232

Wirth, Louis, **IV:** 475

Wisconsin Death Trip (Levy), **Supp. XIX:** 102

"Wisdom Cometh with the Years" (Cullen), **Supp. IV Part 1:** 166

Wisdom of the African World (McKnight, ed.), **Supp. XX:** 157–158

Wisdom of the Desert, The: Sayings from the Desert Fathers of the Fourth Century (Merton), **Supp. VIII:** 201

Wisdom of the Heart, The (H. Miller), **III:** 178, 184

Wise Blood (O'Connor), **III:** 337, 338, 339–343, 344, 345, 346, 350, 354, 356, 357; **Retro. Supp. II:** 219, 221, 222, 223, **225–228**

Wise Men, The (Price), **Supp. VI:** 254

"Wiser Than a God" (Chopin), **Retro. Supp. II:** 61; **Supp. I Part 1:** 208

Wishes, Lies, and Dreams: Teaching Children to Write Poetry (Koch), **Supp. XV:** 176, 189

"Wish for a Young Wife" (Roethke), **III:** 548

Wishful Thinking: A Theological ABC (Buechner), **Supp. XII:** 53

Wishing Tree, The: Christopher Isherwood on Mystical Religion (Adjemian, ed.), **Supp. XIV:** 164, 173

Wismer, Helen Muriel. *See* Thurber, Mrs. James (Helen Muriel Wismer)

Wisse, Ruth, **Supp. XII:** 167, 168

Wister, Owen, **I:** 62; **Retro. Supp. II:** 72; **Supp. XIV:** 39

Wit (Edson), **Supp. XVIII:** 35–36, 37, **38–51**

"Witchbird" (Bambara), **Supp. XI:** 11

"Witch Burning" (Plath), **Supp. I Part 2:** 539

Witchcraft of Salem Village, The (Jackson), **Supp. IX:** 121

"Witch Doctor" (Hayden), **Supp. II Part 1:** 368, 380

Witches of Eastwick, The (Updike), **Retro. Supp. I:** 330, 331

Witching Hour, The (Rice), **Supp. VII:** 299–300

"Witch of Coös, The" (Frost), **II:** 154–155; **Retro. Supp. I:** 135; **Retro. Supp. II:** 42

"Witch of Owl Mountain Springs, The: An Account of Her Remarkable Powers" (Taylor), **Supp. V:** 328

"Witch of Wenham, The" (Whittier), **Supp. I Part 2:** 694, 696

Witek, Terri, **Supp. XVII:** 117

"With a Little Help from My Friends" (Kushner), **Supp. IX:** 131

With Bold Knife and Fork (M. F. K. Fisher), **Supp. XVII:** 89, 91

"With Che at Kitty Hawk" (Banks), **Supp. V:** 6

"With Che at the Plaza" (Banks), **Supp. V:** 7

"With Che in New Hampshire" (Banks), **Supp. V:** 6

"Withdrawal Symptoms" (Mora), **Supp. XIII:** 216

"Withered Skins of Berries" (Toomer), **Supp. III Part 2:** 485; **Supp. IX:** 320

Withers, Harry Clay, **Supp. XIII:** 161

Witherspoon, John, **Supp. I Part 2:** 504

With Eyes at the Back of Our Heads (Levertov), **Supp. III Part 1:** 276–277

With Her in Ourland (Gilman), **Supp. XI:** 208–209

With His Pistol in His Hand (Paredes), **Supp. XIII:** 225; **Supp. XIX:** 98

"Within the Words: An Apprenticeship" (Haines), **Supp. XII:** 197

"With Kit, Age 7, at the Beach" (Stafford), **Supp. XI:** 323

"With Mercy for the Greedy" (Sexton), **Supp. II Part 2:** 680

With My Trousers Rolled (Epstein), **Supp. XIV:** 101, 105

Without a Hero (Boyle), **Supp. VIII:** 16; **Supp. XX:** 20

Without Feathers (Allen), **Supp. XV:** 3, 14, 15

Without Stopping (Bowles), **Supp. IV Part 1:** 79, 81, 85, 90, 91, 92

"Without Tradition and within Reason: Judge Horton and Atticus Finch in Court" (Johnson), **Supp. VIII:** 127

With Shuddering Fall (Oates), **Supp. II Part 2:** 504–506

"With the Dog at Sunrise" (Kenyon), **Supp. VII:** 170

With the Empress Dowager of China (Carl), **III:** 475

"With the Horse in the Winter Pasture" (McCarriston), **Supp. XIV:** 262

With the Old Breed: At Peleliu and Okinawa (Sledge), **Supp. V:** 249–250

"With the Violin" (Chopin), **Retro. Supp. II:** 61

"Witness" (Clampitt), **Supp. IX:** 42–43, 45, 46

"Witness" (Dubus), **Supp. VII:** 89

"Witness" (Harjo), **Supp. XII:** 227–228

Witness (McNally), **Supp. XIII:** 197

"Witness" (Nelson), **Supp. XVIII:** 186

"Witness, The" (Porter), **III:** 443–444

"Witness for Poetry, A" (Stafford), **Supp. XI:** 324

"Witness for the Defense" (Hay), **Supp. XIV:** 124

"Witnessing My Father's Will" (Karr), **Supp. XI:** 241

"Witnessing to a Shared World" (Sanders), **Supp. XVI:** 278

Witness to the Times! (McGrath), **Supp. X:** 118

Witness Tree, A (Frost), **II:** 155; **Retro. Supp. I:** 122, 137, 139

Wit's End: Days and Nights of the Algonquin Round Table (Gaines), **Supp. IX:** 190

Wits Recreations (Mennes and Smith), **II:** 111

Witt, Shirley Hill, **Supp. IV Part 2:** 505

Witte, John, **Supp. XX:** 200

Wittels, Anne F., **Supp. XV:** 59
Wittenberg, Judith Bryant, **Retro. Supp. II:** 146
Wittgenstein, Ludwig, **Retro. Supp. I:** 53; **Supp. III Part 2:** 626–627; **Supp. X:** 304; **Supp. XII:** 21; **Supp. XV:** 344, 346
Wittgensteins' Mistress (Markson), **Supp. XVII:** 135, 142, 143, 145
Wittliff, William, **Supp. V:** 227
"Witty War, A" (Simpson), **Supp. IX:** 268
"Wives and Mistresses" (Hardwick), **Supp. III Part 1:** 211–212
Wizard of Loneliness, The (Nichols), **Supp. XIII:** 259, 263, 264
Wizard of Oz, The (Baum), **Supp. IV Part 1:** 113
Wizard of Oz, The (film), **Supp. X:** 172, 214
Wizard's Tide, The: A Story (Buechner), **Supp. XII:** 54
"WLT (The Edgar Era)" (Keillor), **Supp. XVI:** 172
WLT: A Radio Romance (Keillor), **Supp. XVI:** 176
Wobegon Boy (Keillor), **Supp. XVI:** 177
Wodehouse, P. G., **Supp. IX:** 195; **Supp. XXI:** 204–205
Woiwode, Larry, **Supp. VIII:** 151; **Supp. XVI:** 206
Wojahn, David, **Supp. IX:** 161, 292, 293; **Supp. XXI:** 130, 131, 132, 138, 139, 141
Wolcott, James, **Supp. IX:** 259
Wolf, Christa, **Supp. IV Part 1:** 310, 314
Wolf, Daniel, **Retro. Supp. II:** 202
Wolf: A False Memoir (Harrison), **Supp. VIII:** 40, **41–42,** 45
Wolfe, Ben, **IV:** 454
Wolfe, Gregory, **Supp. XIV:** 307
Wolfe, James, **Supp. I Part 2:** 498
Wolfe, Linnie, **Supp. IX:** 176
Wolfe, Mabel, **IV:** 454
Wolfe, Thomas, **I:** 288, 289, 374, 478, 495; **II:** 457; **III:** 40, 108, 278, 334, 482; **IV:** 52, 97, 357, **450–473; Retro. Supp. I:** 382; **Supp. I Part 1:** 29; **Supp. IV Part 1:** 101; **Supp. IX:** 229; **Supp. X:** 225; **Supp. XI:** 213, 216, 217, 218; **Supp. XIII:** 17; **Supp. XIV:** 122; **Supp. XVIII:** 78; **Supp. XX:**163
Wolfe, Tom, **Supp. III Part 2: 567–588; Supp. IV Part 1:** 35, 198; **Supp. V:** 296; **Supp. X:** 264; **Supp. XI:** 239; **Supp. XV:** 143; **Supp. XVII:** 202; **Supp. XVIII:** 72, 117
Wolfe, William Oliver, **IV:** 454
Wolfe, Mrs. William Oliver (Julia Elizabeth Westall), **IV:** 454
"Wolfe Homo Scribens" (Cowley), **Supp. II Part 1:** 144
Wolfert, Ira, **Supp. XXI: 261–279**
Wolfert's Roost (Irving), **II:** 314
Wolff, Cynthia Griffin, **Retro. Supp. I:** 379; **Supp. IV Part 1:** 203
Wolff, Donald, **Supp. XIII:** 316, 317, 326
Wolff, Geoffrey, **Supp. II Part 1:** 97; **Supp. XI:** 239, 245, 246

Wolff, Tobias, **Retro. Supp. I:** 190; **Supp. V:** 22; **Supp. VII: 331–346; Supp. X:** 1; **Supp. XI:** 26, 239, 245, 246, 247; **Supp. XV:** 223; **Supp. XVI:** 39, 41, 63, 70, 77
Wolfreys, Julian, **Supp. XVIII:** 61
Wolfson, P. J., **Supp. XIII:** 172
"Wolf Town" (Carson), **Supp. XII: 102**
Wolf Willow: A History, a Story, and a Memory of the Last Plains Frontier (Stegner), **Supp. IV Part 2:** 595, 596, 597, 598, 599, 600, 601, 604, 606, 611, 613, 614
Wolitzer, Hilma, **Supp. XV:** 55
Wolitzer, Meg, **Supp. XV:** 65
Wollaston, William, **II:** 108
Wollstonecraft, Mary, **Supp. I Part 1:** 126; **Supp. I Part 2:** 512, 554
"Woman" (Bogan), **Supp. X:** 102
"Woman, I Got the Blues" (Komunyakaa), **Supp. XIII:** 117
"Woman, Why Are You Weeping?" (Kenyon), **Supp. VII:** 174–175
"Woman, Young and Old, A" (Paley), **Supp. VI:** 222, 225
Woman Aroused, The (Lacy), **Supp. XV:** 199–200
Woman at the Washington Zoo, The (Jarrell), **II:** 367, 386, 387, 389
"Womand and the Woman's Movement" (Briggs), **Supp. XVIII:** 14
"Woman Dead in Her Forties, A" (Rich), **Supp. I Part 2:** 574–575
"Woman Hanging from the Thirteenth Floor Window, The" (Harjo), **Supp. XII:** 216, 221
"Woman Hollering Creek" (Cisneros), **Supp. VII:** 70
Woman Hollering Creek and Other Stories (Cisneros), **Supp. VII:** 58, 68–70
"Womanhood" (Brooks), **Supp. III Part 1:** 77
"Woman in Rain" (X. J. Kennedy), **Supp. XV:** 168
Woman in the Dark (Hammett), **Supp. IV Part 1:** 343
"Woman in the House, A" (Caldwell), **I:** 310
Woman in the Nineteenth Century (Fuller), **Retro. Supp. I:** 156; **Supp. II Part 1:** 279, 292, 294–296; **Supp. XI:** 197, 203; **Supp. XVIII:** 3, 11
"Woman in the Shoe, The" (Ryan as Quin), **Supp. XVIII:** 231
Woman in White, The (Collins), **Supp. I Part 1:** 35, 36
"Womanizer, The" (Ford), **Supp. V:** 71, 72
"Woman Like Yourself, A" (C. Frost), **Supp. XV:** 107
Woman Lit by Fireflies, The (Harrison), **Supp. VIII: 50–51**
"Woman Loses Cookie Bake-Off, Sets Self on Fire" (R. O. Butler), **Supp. XII:** 72
Woman of Andros, The (Wilder), **IV:** 356, 363–364, 367, 368, 374
Woman of Means, A (Taylor), **Supp. V:** 319–320

Woman on the Edge of Time (Piercy), **Supp. XIII:** 29
Woman on the Porch, The (Gordon), **II:** 199, 209–211
"Woman on the Stair, The" (MacLeish), **III:** 15–16
"Woman's Dream, A" (E. Stoddard), **Supp. XV:** 278
Woman's Fiction: A Guide to Novels By and About Women in America, 1820–1870 (Baym), **Supp. XVIII:** 258
"Woman's Heartlessness" (Thaxter), **Retro. Supp. II:** 147
Woman's Honor (Glaspell), **Supp. III Part 1:** 179
"Woman Singing" (Ortiz), **Supp. IV Part 2:** 513
Woman's Place, A (C. L. R. James and Weinstein), **Supp. XXI:** 170
Woman's Share in Primitive Culture (Mason), **Supp. I Part 1:** 18
"Woman Struck by Car Turns into Nymphomaniac" (R. O. Butler), **Supp. XII:** 72
"Woman's Work" (Alvarez), **Supp. VII:** 4
"Woman Uses Glass Eye to Spy on Philandering Husband" (R. O. Butler), **Supp. XII:** 70, 72
Woman Warrior (Kingston), **Supp. IV Part 1:** 12; **Supp. V:** 157, 158, 159, 160–164, 166, 169; **Supp. X:** 291–292; **Supp. XIV:** 162
Woman Warrior, The (Kingston), **Supp. XV:** 220
Woman Who Fell from the Sky, The (Harjo), **Supp. XII: 226–228**
"Woman Who Fell From the Sky, The" (Iroquois creation story), **Supp. IV Part 1:** 327
Woman Who Owned the Shadows, The (Gunn Allen), **Supp. IV Part 1:** 320, 322, 326, 327–328
Woman Within, The (Glasgow), **II:** 183, 190–191
"Womanwork" (Gunn Allen), **Supp. IV Part 1:** 326
Women (Bukowski), **Supp. XI:** 172
"Women" (Didion), **Supp. IV Part 1:** 205
"Women" (Swenson), **Supp. IV Part 2:** 647
Women, The (Boyle), **Supp. XX:**24, **26–27**
Women, The (film), **Retro. Supp. I:** 113
Women, The (film; Cukor), **Supp. XVI:** 181, 192
"Women and Children First" (Prose), **Supp. XVI:** 254
Women and Children First: Stories (Prose), **Supp. XVI:** 254
Women and Economics (Gilman), **Supp. I Part 2:** 637; **Supp. V:** 284; **Supp. XI:** 200, **203–204,** 206
Women and Thomas Harrow (Marquand), **III:** 50, 61, 62, 66, 68, 69–70, 71
Women and Vodka (Markson as Merrill, ed.), **Supp. XVII:** 136
Women and Wilderness (LaBastille), **Supp. X:** 97, **102–104**

"Women as They Are" (Rowson), **Supp. XV:** 243

Women at Point Sur, The (Jeffers), **Supp. II Part 2:** 430–431

Women in Love (Lawrence), **III:** 27, 34

Women of Brewster Place, The: A Novel in Seven Stories (Naylor), **Supp. VIII:** 213, **214–218**

Women of Manhattan: An Upper West Side Story (Shanley), **Supp. XIV:** 315, **326–327**

"Women of My Color" (Coleman), **Supp. XI:** 88–89

Women of Trachis (Pound, trans.), **III:** 476

Women on the Wall, The (Stegner), **Supp. IV Part 2:** 599, 605, 606

Women Poets in English (Stanford, ed.), **Retro. Supp. I:** 41

"Women Reformers and American Culture, 1870–1930" (Conway), **Supp. I Part 1:** 19

"Women's Movement, The" (Didion), **Supp. IV Part 1:** 206

"Women Waiting" (Shields), **Supp. VII:** 320

"Women We Love Whom We Never See Again" (R. Bly), **Supp. IV Part 1:** 66

"Women We Never See Again" (R. Bly), **Supp. IV Part 1:** 66

Women with Men (Ford), **Supp. V:** 57, 71–72

"Wonder" (Olds), **Supp. X:** 210

Wonder Boys (Chabon), **Supp. XI:** 67, **73–75,** **Supp. XI:** 78; **Supp. XVI:** 259

Wonder Boys (film), **Supp. XI:** 67

Wonderful O, The (Thurber), **Supp. I Part 2:** 612

"Wonderful Old Gentleman, The" (Parker), **Supp. IX:** 197

"Wonderful Pen, The" (Swenson), **Supp. IV Part 2:** 650

Wonderful Words, Silent Truth: Essays on Poetry and a Memoir (Simic), **Supp. VIII:** 270

Wonderland (Oates), **Supp. II Part 2:** 511, 512, 514–515

Wonders Hidden (Sanders), **Supp. XVI:** 269

Wonders of the African World (television series), **Supp. XX:**99

Wonders of the Invisible World, The (Mather), **Supp. II Part 2:** 456–459, 460, 467

Wonder-Working Providence (Johnson), **IV:** 157

Wong, Hertha, **Supp. IV Part 1:** 275

Wong, Jade Snow, **Supp. X:** 291

Wong, Nellie, **Supp. XVII:** 72

Wong, Shawn, **Supp. XV:** 221

Wong, Timothy, **Supp. XVIII:** 94

"Wood" (Nye), **Supp. XIII:** 276

Wood, Audrey, **IV:** 381

Wood, Charles Erskine Scott, **Supp. XV:** 301

Wood, Clement, **Supp. XV:** 298

Wood, Clement Biddle, **Supp. XI:** 307

Wood, Mrs. Henry, **Supp. I Part 1:** 35

Wood, James, **Supp. XIV:** 95–96; **Supp. XIX:** 138

Wood, Mabel, **I:** 199

Wood, Michael, **Supp. IV Part 2:** 691

Wood, Norman Barton, **Supp. XIV:** 201

Wood, Susan, **Supp. XVI:** 123

Woodard, Calvin, **Supp. VIII:** 128

Woodard, Charles L., **Supp. IV Part 2:** 484, 493

Woodard, Deborah, **Supp. XIII:** 114

Woodberry, George Edward, **III:** 508

Woodbridge, Frederick, **I:** 217, 224

Woodbridge, John, **Supp. I Part 1:** 101, 102, 114

"Wood-Choppers, The" (Chopin), **Retro. Supp. II:** 72

Woodcock, George, **Supp. XIII:** 33

Woodcome, Beth, **Supp. XVII:** 240

"Wood Dove at Sandy Spring, The" (MacLeish), **III:** 19

"Wooden Spring" (Rukeyser), **Supp. VI:** 285

"Wooden Umbrella, The" (Porter), **IV:** 26

Woodhull, Victoria, **Supp. XVIII:** 4

"Woodnotes" (Emerson), **II:** 7, 19

"Wood-Pile, The" (Frost), **Retro. Supp. I:** 128; **Supp. IV Part 2:** 445

Woodrow, James, **Supp. I Part 1:** 349, 366

"Woods, Books, and Truant Officers, The" (Maclean), **Supp. XIV:** 221, 225

"Woods, New York, The" (Bronk), **Supp. XXI:** 27

Woods, Paula L., **Supp. XXI:** 70

Woods, Robert A., **Supp. I Part 1:** 19

Woods, The (Mamet), **Supp. XIV:** 241, 254–255

Woodswoman (LaBastille), **Supp. X:** 95, **96–99,** 108

Woodswoman III: Book Three of the Woodswoman's Adventures (LaBastille), **Supp. X:** 95, **106–107**

"Wood Thrush" (Kenyon), **Supp. VII:** 172

Woodward, C. Vann, **IV:** 114, 470–471; **Retro. Supp. I:** 75, 76; **Supp. XIX:** 152

"Woof: A Plea of Sorts" (Saunders), **Supp. XIX:** 235

"Wooing the Inanimate" (Brodsky), **Supp. VIII:** 32

Woolcott, Alexander, **Supp. IX:** 197

Wooley, Bryan, **Supp. V:** 225

Woolf, Leonard, **Supp. IX:** 95

Woolf, Virginia, **I:** 53, 79, 112, 309; **II:** 320, 415; **IV:** 59; **Retro. Supp. I:** 59, 75, 170, 215, 291, 359; **Supp. I Part 2:** 553, 714, 718; **Supp. IV Part 1:** 299; **Supp. V:** 127; **Supp. VIII:** 5, 155, 251, 252, 263, 265; **Supp. IX:** 66, 109; **Supp. XI:** 134, 193; **Supp. XII:** 81, 98, 289; **Supp. XIII:** 305; **Supp. XIV:** 341–342, 342, 343, 346, 348; **Supp. XV:** 55, 65; **Supp. XIX:** 134

Woollcott, Alexander, **IV:** 432; **Retro. Supp. II:** 327; **Supp. I Part 2:** 664; **Supp. IX:** 190, 194

Woollstonecraft, Mary, **Supp. XVI:** 184

"Woolly Mammoth" (X. J. Kennedy), **Supp. XV:** 163–164

Woolman, John, **Supp. VIII:** 202, 204, 205

Woolson, Constance Fenimore, **Retro. Supp. I:** 224, 228

Woolverton, Linda, **Supp. XXI:** 148

Wooster, David, **Supp. XX:**288

Worcester, Samuel, **I:** 458

Word and Idioms: Studies in the English Language (L. P. Smith), **Supp. XIV:** 343

"Word by Word" (column, Lamott), **Supp. XX:**140

Word of God and the Word of Man, The (Barth), **Retro. Supp. I:** 327

"Word out of the Sea, A" (Whitman), **IV:** 344

Words (Creeley), **Supp. IV Part 1:** 139, 150–153, 154, 155, 158

"Words" (Creeley), **Supp. IV Part 1:** 152

"Words" (Gioia), **Supp. XV:** 125

"Words" (Merwin), **Supp. III Part 1:** 352

"Words" (Plath), **Supp. I Part 2:** 547

"Words" (Shields), **Supp. VII:** 323

"Words, The" (Wagoner), **Supp. IX:** 326

"Words above a Narrow Entrance" (Wagoner), **Supp. IX:** 325

"Words for a Bike-Racing, Osprey-Chasing Wine-Drunk Squaw Man" (Gunn Allen), **Supp. IV Part 1:** 325

Words for Dr. Y (Sexton), **Supp. II Part 2:** 698

"Words for Hart Crane" (Lowell), **I:** 381; **II:** 547; **Retro. Supp. II:** 188

"Words for Maria" (Merrill), **Supp. III Part 1:** 327

"Words for the Unknown Makers" (Kunitz), **Supp. III Part 1:** 264

Words for the Wind (Roethke), **III:** 529, 533, 541, 543, 545

"Words for the Wind" (Roethke), **III:** 542–543

Words in the Mourning Time (Hayden), **Supp. II Part 1:** 361, 366, 367

"Words in the Mourning Time" (Hayden), **Supp. II Part 1:** 370–371

"Words into Fiction" (Welty), **IV:** 279

"Words Like Freedom" (Hughes), **Retro. Supp. I:** 207

"Words of a Young Girl" (Lowell), **II:** 554

Words under the Words: Selected Poems (Nye), **Supp. XIII:** 277

Wordsworth, Dorothy, **Supp. IX:** 38

Wordsworth, William, **I:** 283, 522, 524, 525, 588; **II:** 7, 11, 17, 18, 97, 169, 273, 303, 304, 532, 549, 552; **III:** 219, 263, 277, 278, 511, 521, 523, 528, 583; **IV:** 120, 331, 343, 453, 465; **Retro. Supp. I:** 121, 196; **Supp. I Part 1:** 150, 151, 154, 161, 163, 312, 313, 349, 365; **Supp. I Part 2:** 375, 409, 416, 422, 607, 621, 622, 673, 674, 675, 676, 677, 710–711, 729; **Supp. II Part 1:** 4; **Supp. III Part 1:** 12, 15, 73, 279; **Supp. IV Part 2:** 597, 601; **Supp. V:** 258; **Supp. VIII:** 273; **Supp. IX:** 38, 41, 265, 274; **Supp. X:** 22, 23, 65, 120; **Supp. XI:** 248, 251,

312; **Supp. XIII:** 214; **Supp. XIV:** 184; **Supp. XV:** 93, 250; **Supp. XIX:** 1; **Supp. XX:**108, 116; **Supp. XXI:** 131

" 'Word Which Made All Clear, The': The Silent Close of *The House of Mirth*" (Benstock), Supp. XX:240

Work (Alcott), **Supp. I Part 1:** 32–33, 42

Work (Dixon), **Supp. XII:** 141, **143**

"Work" (Halliday), **Supp. XIX:** 85

"Work" (Oliver), **Supp. VII:** 243

Work and Love (Dunn), **Supp. XI: 147–148**

"Worker" (Coleman), **Supp. XI:** 89

Working a Passage; or, Life on a Liner (Briggs), **Supp. XVIII:** 2, **9–10**

Working Class Movement in America, The (E. Marx and E. Aveling), **Supp. XVI:** 85

Working Papers: Selected Essays and Reviews (Carruth), **Supp. XVI:** 46

"Working Roots: A Collection of Poetry and Prose" (Trethewey), **Supp. XXI:** 245

"Working the Landscape" (Dunn), **Supp. XI:** 151

Workin' on the Chain Gang: Shaking Off the Dead Hand of History (Mosley), **Supp. XIII:** 247, 248

"Work Notes '66" (Baraka), **Supp. II Part 1:** 47

Work of Art (Lewis), **II:** 453–454

"Work of Shading, The" (Simic), **Supp. VIII:** 277–278

Work of Stephen Crane, The (Follett, ed.), **I:** 405

"Work on Red Mountain, The" (Harte), **Supp. II Part 1:** 339

"Workshop" (Espaillat), **Supp. XXI:** 105

Works of Love, The (Morris), **III:** 223–224, 225, 233

Works of Witter Bynner, The (Kraft, ed.), **Supp. XV:** 52

"World, The" (Bronk), **Supp. XXI:** 32

"World, The" (Simic), **Supp. VIII:** 282

World, the Worldless, The (Bronk), **Supp. XXI: 29–31**

World According to Garp, The (Irving), **Supp. VI:** 163, 164, **170–173,** 181

World and Africa, The: An Inquiry into the Part Which Africa Has Played in World History (Du Bois), **Supp. II Part 1:** 184–185

"World and All Its Teeth, The" (Nye), **Supp. XIII:** 282

"World and the Door, The" (O. Henry), **Supp. II Part 1:** 402

"World and the Jug, The" (Ellison), **Retro. Supp. II:** 112, 119, 123

"World as We Know It, The" (Barresi), **Supp. XV:** 100

World Authors 1950–1970, **Supp. XIII:** 102

World Below, The (Miller), **Supp. XII: 303–304**

World Below the Window, The: Poems 1937–1997 (W. J. Smith), **Supp. XIII:** 332, 340, 345

World Doesn't End, The (Simic), **Supp. VIII:** 272, **279–280**

World Elsewhere, A: The Place of Style in American Literature (Poirier), **I:** 239

"World Ends Here, The" (Harjo), **Supp. XII:** 227–228

World Enough and Time (Warren), **IV:** 243, 253–254

World Gone Wrong (album, Dylan), **Supp. XVIII:** 28

"World I Live In, The" (T. Williams), **IV:** 388

World I Never Made, A (Farrell), **II:** 34, 35, 424

World in the Attic, The (Morris), **III:** 222–223, 224

World in the Evening, The (Isherwood), **Supp. XIV:** 157, 164, 165, **166–167,** 170

World Is a Wedding, The (Schwartz), **Supp. II Part 2:** 643, 654–660

"World Is a Wedding, The" (Schwartz), **Supp. II Part 2:** 655–656, 657

"World Is Too Much with Us, The" (Wordsworth), **Supp. I Part 1:** 312

Worldly Hopes (Ammons), **Supp. VII:** 34

Worldly Philosophers, The (Heilbroner), **Supp. I Part 2:** 644, 650

World of Apples, The (Cheever), **Supp. I Part 1:** 191, 193

World of David Wagoner, The (McFarland), **Supp. IX:** 323

"World of Easy Rawlins, The" (Mosley), **Supp. XIII:** 234, 236

World of Gwendolyn Brooks, The (Brooks), **Supp. III Part 1:** 83, 84

World of H. G. Wells, The (Brooks), **I:** 240, 241, 242

World of Light, A (Skloot), **Supp. XX:**196, 205, **206–207**

"World of Light, A" (Skloot), **Supp. XX:**194, 207

World of Light, A: Portraits and Celebrations (Sarton), **Supp. III Part 1:** 62; **Supp. VIII:** 249, 253, 262

World of Our Fathers: The Journey of the Eastern European Jews to America and the Life They Found and Made (Howe), **Sup p. XIV:**104; **Supp. VI:** 113, 114, 116, 118, 119, **120–125**

"World of Pure Experience, A" (James), **II:** 356–357

World of Raymond Chandler, The (Spender), **Supp. IV Part 1:** 119

World of Sex, The (H. Miller), **III:** 170, 178, 187

"World of the Perfect Tear, The" (McGrath), **Supp. X:** 116, 118

World of the Ten Thousand Things, The: Selected Poems (Wright), **Supp. V:** 333

"World of Tomorrow, The" (White), **Supp. I Part 2:** 663

World of Washington Irving, The (Brooks), **I:** 256–257

World Over, The (Wharton), **Retro. Supp. I:** 382

World Revolution (C. L. R. James), **Supp. XXI:** 167

"Worlds" (Goldbarth), **Supp. XII:** 183, 189

World's Body, The (Ransom), **III:** 497, 499; **Supp. II Part 1:** 146

World's End (Boyle), **Supp. VIII: 11–12; Supp. XX:22–23**

World's End and Other Stories (Theroux), **Supp. VIII:** 322

"World's Fair" (Berryman), **I:** 173

World's Fair (Doctorow), **Supp. IV Part 1:** 217, 224, 227–229, 234, 236–237

World's Fair, The (Fitzgerald), **II:** 93

Worlds of Color (Du Bois), **Supp. II Part 1:** 185–186

"Worlds of Color" (Du Bois), **Supp. II Part 1:** 175

World So Wide (Lewis), **II:** 456

"World's Worst Boyfriends, The" (Wasserstein), **Supp. XV:** 328

"World-Telegram" (Berryman), **I:** 173

World to Come, The (D. Horn), **Supp. XVII:** 50

World View on Race and Democracy: A Study Guide in Human Group Relations (Locke), **Supp. XIV:** 205, 206

World within the Word, The (Gass), **Supp. VI:** 77

"World Without Objects Is a Sensible Place, A" (Wilbur), **Supp. III Part 2:** 550

"World Without Rodrigo, The" (Cisneros), **Supp. VII:** 68

"Worm Moon" (Oliver), **Supp. VII:** 234

"Worn Path, A" (Welty), **IV:** 262; **Retro. Supp. I:** 345–346

"Worsening Situation" (Ashbery), **Supp. III Part 1:** 17–18

"Worship" (Emerson), **II:** 2, 4–5

"Worship and Church Bells" (Paine), **Supp. I Part 2:** 521

Worster, Donald, **Supp. IX:** 19

Worthington, Marjorie, **Supp. XII:** 13

Wouk, Herman, **Supp. XX:**243

Wouldn't Take Nothing for My Journey Now (Angelou), **Supp. IV Part 1:** 10, 12, 14, 15, 16

"Wound" (Pedersen; Nelson, trans.), **Supp. XVIII:** 180

Wound and the Bow, The: Seven Studies in Literature (Wilson), **IV:** 429

Wounded (Everett), **Supp. XVIII:** 54, **64,** 65

Wounds in the Rain (Crane), **I:** 409, 414, 423

Woven Stone (Ortiz), **Supp. IV Part 2:** 501, 514

Woven Stories (Ortiz), **Supp. IV Part 2:** 503

"Wraith, The" (Roethke), **III:** 542

"Wrath of God, The" (Fante), **Supp. XI:** 160, 164

"Wreath for a Bridal" (Plath), **Supp. I Part 2:** 537

"Wreath for Emmet Till, A" (Nelson), **Supp. XVIII:** 177

Wreath for Emmett Till, A (Nelson), **Supp. XVIII:** 171, 173, 175, 181, **183–185**

Wreath for Garibaldi and Other Stories, A (Garrett), **Supp. VII:** 99–101

"Wreath of Women" (Rukeyser), **Supp. VI:** 280

Wreckage (Jin), **Supp. XVIII: 98–99**

Wreckage of Agathon, The (Gardner), **Supp. VI:** 63, **65–66**

Wrecking Crew (Levis), **Supp. XI: 259–260**

"Wreck of Rivermouth, The" (Whittier), **Supp. I Part 2:** 694, 696–697

"Wreck of the Deutschland" (Hopkins), **Supp. X:** 61

"Wreck of the Hesperus, The" (Longfellow), **Retro. Supp. II:** 168, 169

Wrestler's Cruel Study, The (Dobyns), **Supp. XIII: 82–83**

"Wrestler with Sharks, A" (Yates), **Supp. XI:** 341

Wright, Bernie, **I:** 191, 193

Wright, C. D. (Carolyn Doris), **Supp. XV: 337–355**

Wright, Charles, **Supp. V:** 92, **331–346;** **Supp. VIII:** 272; **Supp. XIII:** 114; **Supp. XVII:** 71; **Supp. XXI:** 95, 255

Wright, Chauncey, **II:** 344

Wright, Frank Lloyd, **I:** 104, 483

Wright, Franz, **Supp. XVII: 239–249**

Wright, George, **III:** 479

Wright, Harold Bell, **II:** 467–468

Wright, Holly, **Supp. VIII:** 272

Wright, James, **I:** 291; **Supp. III Part 1:** 249; **Supp. III Part 2:** 541, **589–607;** **Supp. IV Part 1:** 60, 72; **Supp. IV Part 2:** 557, 558, 561, 566, 571, 623; **Supp. V:** 332; **Supp. IX:** 152, 155, 159, 265, 271, 290, 293, 296; **Supp. X:** 69, 127; **Supp. XI:** 150; **Supp. XII:** 217; **Supp. XIII:** 76; **Supp. XV:** 79, 93, 212; **Supp. XVII:** 239, 241, 243, 244; **Supp. XIX:** 122, 273

Wright, Nathalia, **IV:** 155

Wright, Philip Green, **III:** 578, 579, 580

Wright, Richard, **II:** 586; **IV:** 40, **474–497; Retro. Supp. II:** 4, 111, 116, 120; **Supp. I Part 1:** 51, 52, 64, 332, 337; **Supp. II Part 1:** 17, 40, 221, 228, 235, 250; **Supp. IV Part 1:** 1, 11, 84, 374; **Supp. VIII:** 88; **Supp. IX:** 316; **Supp. X:** 131, 245, 254; **Supp. XI:** 85; **Supp. XII:** 316; **Supp. XIII:** 46, 233; **Supp. XIV:** 73; **Supp. XVI:** 135, 139, 141, 143; **Supp. XVIII:** 277, 282, 286; **Supp. XXI:** 169

Wright, Mrs. Richard (Ellen Poplar), **IV:** 476

Wright, Sarah, **Supp. IV Part 1:** 8; **Supp. XIII:** 295

Wright, William, **Retro. Supp. II:** 76, 77

Wrigley, Robert, **Supp. XVIII: 293–308**

"Writer" (Sanders), **Supp. XVI:** 277

"Writer, The" (Wilbur), **Supp. III Part 2:** 561, 562

"Writer as Alaskan, The" (Haines), **Supp. XII:** 199

Writer in America, The (Brooks), **I:** 253, 254, 257

Writer in America, The (Stegner), **Supp. IV Part 2:** 597, 599, 607

"Writers" (Lowell), **II:** 554

Writer's Almanac, The (Keillor, radio program), **Supp. XIII:** 274; **Supp. XVI:** 178

Writer's America, A: Landscape in Literature (Kazin), **Supp. VIII:** 106

"Writer's Bed, A" (Mirvis), **Supp. XX:**179

Writer's Capital, A (Auchincloss), **Supp. IV Part 1:** 21, 23, 24, 31

"Writer's Credo, A" (Abbey), **Supp. XIII:** 1, 17

Writer's Eye, A: Collected Book Reviews (Welty), **Retro. Supp. I:** 339, 354, 356

Writers in America (Schulberg), **Supp. XVIII:** 242, 243, 250, 254

Writers in Revolt (Southern, Seaver, and Trocchi, eds.), **Supp. XI:** 301

Writer's Life, A (Talese), **Supp. XVII:** 208–209, 210

Writer's Notebook, A (Maugham), **Supp. X:** 58

Writers on America (U.S. Department of State, ed.), **Supp. XIII:** 288

Writers on the Left (Aaron), **IV:** 429; **Supp. II Part 1:** 137

Writers on Writing (Prose), **Supp. XVI:** 259

"Writer's Prologue to a Play in Verse" (W. C. Williams), **Retro. Supp. I:** 424

"Writer's Quest for a Parnassus, A" (T. Williams), **IV:** 392

Writers' Workshop (University of Iowa), **Supp. V:** 42

"Writers Workshop, The" (Conroy), **Supp. XVI:** 76

"Writing" (Nemerov), **III:** 275

"Writing About the Universe" (Mosley), **Supp. XIII:** 247

"Writing American Fiction" (P. Roth), **Retro. Supp. II:** 279; **Supp. I Part 1:** 192; **Supp. I Part 2:** 431; **Supp. III Part 2:** 414, 420, 421; **Supp. V:** 45

"Writing and a Life Lived Well" (Patchett), **Supp. XII:** 308

"Writing and Writers: *Disjecta Membra*" (Sorrentino), **Supp. XXI:** 235

Writing a Woman's Life (Heilbrun), **Supp. IX:** 66

"Writing Between Worlds" (Mirvis), **Supp. XX:**177, 178, 179

Writing Brave and Free: Encouraging Words for People Who Want to Start Writing (Kooser and Cox), **Supp. XIX:** 116, 128

Writing Chicago: Modernism, Ethnography, and the Novel (Cappetti), **Supp. IX:** 4, 8

Writing Creative Nonfiction: The Literature of Reality (Talese and Lounsberry, eds.), **Supp. XVII:** 208

Writing Dylan: The Songs of a Lonesome Traveler (Smith), **Supp. XVIII:** 22

Writing from the Center (Sanders), **Supp. XVI:** 266, 275–276

"Writing from the Inside Out: Style Is Not the Frosting; It's the Cake" (Robbins), **Supp. X:** 266

"Writing here last autumn of my hopes of seeing a hoopoe" (Updike), **Retro. Supp. I:** 335

Writing in Restaurants (Mamet), **Supp. XIV:** 246

"Writing Lesson, The" (Gordon), **Supp. IV Part 1:** 306

Writing Life, The (Dillard), **Supp. VI:** 23, 31

"Writing of Apollinaire, The" (Zukofsky), **Supp. III Part 2:** 616, 617

"Writing of *Fearless Jones,* The" (Mosley), **Supp. XIII:** 242

Writing on the Wall, The, and Literary Essays (McCarthy), **II:** 579

Writings to an Unfinished Accompaniment (Merwin), **Supp. III Part 1:** 352

"Writing the Universe-Mind" (Tabios), **Supp. XV:** 225

Writing the World (Stafford), **Supp. XI:** 314

"Writing to Save Our Lives" (Milligan), **Supp. XIII:** 274

Writin' Is Fightin' (Reed), **Supp. X:** 241

"Writ on the Eve of My 32nd Birthday" (Corso), **Supp. XII:** 129–130

"Written History as an Act of Faith" (Beard), **Supp. I Part 2:** 492

"Written on the Land" (J. W. Miller), **Supp. XX:**170

"Wrong Man, The" (Larsen), **Supp. XVIII:** 124

"Wrong Notes" (S. Kauffmann), **Supp. XVI:** 74

"Wrought Figure" (McCarriston), **Supp. XIV:** 272

"Wunderkind" (McCullers), **II:** 585

Wunderlich, Mark, **Supp. XI:** 119, 132

Wundt, Wilhelm, **II:** 345

Wurster, William Wilson, **Supp. IV Part 1:** 197

WUSA (film), **Supp. V:** 301

Wuthering Heights (E. Brontë), **Supp. V:** 305; **Supp. X:** 89

WWII (Jones), **Supp. XI:** 219, 231

Wyandotté (Cooper), **I:** 350, 355

Wyatt, Robert B., **Supp. V:** 14

Wyatt, Thomas, **Supp. I Part 1:** 369

Wycherly Woman, The (Macdonald), **Supp. IV Part 2:** 473

Wych Hazel (S. and A. Warner), **Supp. XVIII:** 267, **268–269**

Wydra, Ewa. *See* Hoffman, Eva

Wyeth, Andrew, **Supp. XIX:** 117

Wyler, William, **Supp. XV:** 195

Wylie, Elinor, **IV:** 436; **Supp. I Part 2: 707–730; Supp. III Part 1:** 2, 63, 318–319; **Supp. XI:** 44; **Supp. XIV:** 127; **Supp. XV:** 307

Wylie, Horace, **Supp. I Part 2:** 708, 709

Wylie, Philip, **III:** 223

Wyllys, Ruth. *See* Taylor, Mrs. Edward (Ruth Wyllys)

"Wyoming Valley Tales" (Crane), **I:** 409

Wyzewa, Théodore de, **Supp. XIV:** 336

X

Xaipe (Cummings), **I:** 430, 432–433, 447

Xenogenesis trilogy (O. Butler), **Supp. XIII: 63–66,** 69

Xenophon, **II:** 105

X Factor, The: A Quest for Excellence" (Plimpton), *Supp. XVI:* 241

X Files (television series), **Supp. XVI:** 125

Xiaojing, Zhou, **Supp. XV:** 214

Xingu and Other Stories (Wharton), **IV:** 314, 320; **Retro. Supp. I:** 378

Xionia (Wright), **Supp. V:** 333

XLI Poems (Cummings), **I:** 429, 432, 440, 443

Y

Yabroff, Jennie, **Supp. XIX:** 50, 58, 61

Yacoubi, Ahmed, **Supp. IV Part 1:** 88, 92, 93

Yage Letters, The (Burroughs), **Supp. III Part 1:** 94, 98, 100

Yagoda, Ben, **Supp. VIII:** 151

Yamamoto, Isoroku, **Supp. I Part 2:** 491

Yancey's War (Hoffman), **Supp. XVIII:** 71, **75–76**

Yankee City (Warner), **III:** 60

Yankee Clipper (ballet) (Kirstein), **Supp. IV Part 1:** 82

Yankee in Canada, A (Thoreau), **IV:** 188

Yankey in London (Tyler), **I:** 344

"Yánnina" (Merrill), **Supp. III Part 1:** 329

"Yanosz Korczak's Last Walk" (Markowick-Olczakowa), **Supp. X:** 70

Yarboro, Chelsea Quinn, **Supp. V:** 147

Yardley, Jonathan, **Supp. V:** 326; **Supp. XI:** 67

"Yard Sale" (Kenyon), **Supp. VII:** 169

Yates, Richard, **Supp. XI:** **333–350**

"Year, The" (Sandburg), **III:** 584

Year at the Races, A (Parker and Parker), **Supp. XIX:** 187

"Year Between, The" (Neugeboren), **Supp. XVI:** 226

Year in Provence, A (Mayle), **Supp. XVI:** 295

Yearling, The (Rawlings), **Supp. X:** 219, **230–231**, 233, 234

"Year of Grace" (Swados), **Supp. XIX:** 262–263

Year of Happy, A (Goldbarth), **Supp. XII:** 180

"Year of Mourning, The" (Jeffers), **Supp. II Part 2:** 415

Year of Silence, The (Bell), **Supp. X:** 1, **5–6,** 7

"Year of the Double Spring, The" (Swenson), **Supp. IV Part 2:** 647

Year's Best Science Fiction, The (Merril, ed.), **Supp. XVI:** 123

Year's Life, A (Lowell), **Supp. I Part 2:** 405

"Years of Birth" (Cowley), **Supp. II Part 1:** 149

Years of Conscience: The Muckrakers: An Anthology of Reform Journalism (Swados, ed.), **Supp. XIX:** 264

Years of My Youth (Howells), **II:** 276

"Years of Wonder" (White), **Supp. I Part 2:** 652, 653

"Years Without Understanding, The" (Weigl), **Supp. XIX:** 282–283

Years With Ross, The (Thurber), **Supp. I Part 2:** 619

Yeats, Jack, **Supp. XVI:** 190

Yeats, Jack B., **Supp. XX:** 201

Yeats, John Butler, **III:** 458; **Supp. XX:** 69

Yeats, William Butler, **I:** 69, 172, 384, 389, 403, 434, 478, 494, 532; **II:** 168–169, 566, 598; **III:** 4, 5, 8, 18, 19, 20, 23, 29, 40, 205, 249, 269, 270–271, 272, 278, 279, 294, 347, 409, 457, 458–460, 472, 473, 476–477, 521, 523, 524, 527, 528, 533, 540, 541, 542, 543–544, 591–592; **IV:** 89, 93, 121, 126, 136, 140, 271, 394, 404; **Retro. Supp. I:** 59, 66, 127, 141, 270, 283, 285, 286, 288, 290, 311, 342, 350, 378, 413; **Retro. Supp. II:** 185, 331; **Supp. I Part 1:** 79, 80, 254, 257, 262; **Supp. I Part 2:** 388, 389; **Supp. II Part 1:** 1, 4, 9, 20, 26, 361; **Supp. III Part 1:** 59, 63, 236, 238, 253; **Supp. IV Part 1:** 81; **Supp. IV Part 2:** 634; **Supp. V:** 220; **Supp. VIII:** 19, 21, 30, 155, 156, 190, 239, 262, 292; **Supp. IX:** 43, 119; **Supp. X:** 35, 58, 119, 120; **Supp. XI:** 140; **Supp. XII:** 132, 198, 217, 266; **Supp. XIII:** 77, **Supp. XIII:** 87; **Supp. XIV:** 7; **Supp. XV:** 36, 41, 181, 186; **Supp. XVI:** 47–48, 159; **Supp. XVII:** 36; **Supp. XXI:** 61

Yee, Amy, **Supp. XVIII:** 93, 94

Yellin, Jean Fagan, **Supp. XVI:** 88, 89

Yellow Back Radio Broke-Down (Reed), **Supp. X:** 240, 242, **243–245**

"Yellow Dog Café" (Komunyakaa), **Supp. XIII:** 126

Yellow Face (Hwang), **Supp. XXI:** 143, 148, **154–156**

"Yellow Girl" (Caldwell), **I:** 310

Yellow Glove (Nye), **Supp. XIII:** 275, **276–277**

"Yellow Glove" (Nye), **Supp. XIII:** 276

"Yellow Gown, The" (Anderson), **I:** 114

Yellow House on the Corner, The (Dove), **Supp. IV Part 1:** 244, 245, 246, 254

"Yellow Raft, The" (Connell), **Supp. XIV:** **85–86**

"Yellow River" (Tate), **IV:** 141

"Yellow Violet, The" (Bryant), **Supp. I Part 1:** 154, 155

"Yellow Wallpaper, The" (Gilman), **Supp. XI:** **198–199,** 207; **Supp. XVI:** 84

"Yellow Woman" (Keres stories), **Supp. IV Part 1:** 327

"Yellow Woman" (Silko), **Supp. IV Part 2:** 567–568

Yelverton, Theresa, **Supp. IX:** 181

Yenser, Stephen, **Supp. X:** 207, 208; **Supp. XV:** 113–114

"Yentl the Yeshiva Boy" (Singer), **IV:** 15, 20

Yerkes, Charles E., **I:** 507, 512

Yerma (opera) (Bowles), **Supp. IV Part 1:** 89

Yertle the Turtle and Other Stories (Geisel), **Supp. XVI:** 109

"Yes" (Stafford), **Supp. XI:** 329

Yes, Mrs. Williams (W. C. Williams), **Retro. Supp. I:** 423

Yes, Yes, No, No (Kushner), **Supp. IX:** 133

"Yes and It's Hopeless" (Ginsberg), **Supp. II Part 1:** 326

Yesenin, Sergey, **Supp. VIII:** 40

"Yes: I Mean So OK–Love" (Bronk), **Supp. XXI:** 31

"Yes! No!" (Oliver), **Supp. VII:** 243–244

Yesterday and Today: A Comparative Anthology of Poetry (Untermeyer, ed.), **Supp. XV:** 309

Yesterday's Self: Nostalgia and the Immigrant Identity (Ritivoi), **Supp. XVI:** 148

Yesterday Will Make You Cry (C. Himes), **Supp. XVI:** 137

"Yet Another Example of the Porousness of Certain Borders" (Wallace), **Supp. X:** 309

"Yet Do I Marvel" (Cullen), **Supp. IV Part 1:** 165, 169

Yet Other Waters (Farrell), **II:** 29, 38, 39, 40

"Yevtushenko" (Kooser), **Supp. XIX:** 124

Yevtushenko, Yevgeny, **Supp. III Part 1:** 268

Yezzi, David, **Supp. XII:** 193

Yizkor Book, **Supp. XVI:** 154

...y no se lo tragó la tierra (Rivera), **Supp. XIX:** 99, 101

Y no se lo trago la tierra (And the Earth Did Not Cover Him) (Rivera), **Supp. XIII:** 216

¡Yo! (Alvarez), **Supp. VII:** 1, 15–17

"Yogurt of Vasirin Kefirovsky, The" (Apple), **Supp. XVII:** 3, 4

Yohannan, J. D., **II:** 20

"Yoke, The" (Bidart), **Supp. XV:** 33

Yonge, Charlotte, **II:** 174

"Yonnondio" (Whitman), **Supp. XIII:** 304

Yonnondio: From the Thirties (Olsen), **Supp. XIII:** 295, 295, **Supp. XIII:** 292, 296, **303–304,** 305

"Yore" (Nemerov), **III:** 283

York, Jake Adam, **Supp. XXI:** 257

York, Lorraine, **Supp. XX:** 51

"York Beach" (Toomer), **Supp. III Part 2:** 486

Yorke, Dorothy, **Supp. I Part 1:** 258

Yorke, Henry Vincent. See Green, Henry

"York Garrison, 1640" (Jewett), **Retro. Supp. II:** 141

Yosemite, The (Muir), **Supp. IX:** 185

"Yosemite Glaciers: Ice Streams of the Great Valley" (Muir), **Supp. IX:** 181

Yoshe Kalb (Singer), **IV:** 2

"You, Andrew Marvell" (MacLeish), **III:** 12–13

"You, Dr. Martin" (Sexton), **Supp. II Part 2:** 673

You, Emperors, and Others: Poems 1957–1960 (Warren), **IV:** 245

"You, Genoese Mariner" (Merwin), **Supp. III Part 1:** 343

"You, Reader" (Collins), **Supp. XXI:** 55

"You All Know the Story of the Other Woman" (Sexton), **Supp. II Part 2:** 688

You Are Happy (Atwood), **Supp. XIII:** 34

"You Are Happy" (Atwood), **Supp. XIII:** 34

"You Are in Bear Country" (Kumin), **Supp. IV Part 2:** 453, 455

"You Are Not I" (Bowles), **Supp. IV Part 1:** 87

"You Begin" (Atwood), **Supp. XIII:** 34

You Bright and Risen Angels (Vollmann), **Supp. XVII:** 225, 226

"You Bring Out the Mexican in Me" (Cisneros), **Supp. VII:** 71

You Came Along (film), **Supp. IV Part 2:** 524

"You *Can* Go Home Again" (TallMountain), **Supp. IV Part 1:** 324–325

"You Can Have It" (Levine), **Supp. V:** 188–189

You Can't Go Home Again (Wolfe), **IV:** 450, 451, 454, 456, 460, 462, 468, 469, 470

You Can't Keep a Good Woman Down (Walker), **Supp. III Part 2:** 520, 525, 531

You Can't Take It with You (Kaufman and Hart), **Supp. XIV:** 327

"You Can't Tell a Man by the Song He Sings" (P. Roth), **Supp. III Part 2:** 406

"You Don't Know What Love Is" (Carver), **Supp. III Part 1:** 147

You Don't Love Me Yet (Lethem), **Supp. XVIII:** 149–150

"You Have Left Your Lotus Pods on the Bus" (Bowles), **Supp. IV Part 1:** 91

You Have Seen Their Faces (Caldwell), **I:** 290, 293–294, 295, 304, 309

You Know Me, Al: A Busher's Letters (Lardner), **Supp. XVI:** 189

You Know Me Al (comic strip), **II:** 423

You Know Me Al (Lardner), **II:** 26, 415, 419, 422, 431

"You Know What" (Beattie), **Supp. V:** 33

"You Know Who You Are" (Nye), **Supp. XIII:** 275

You Might As Well Live: The Life and Times of Dorothy Parker (Keats), **Supp. IX:** 190

"You Must Relax!" (J. Scott), **Supp. XVII:** 189

You Must Revise Your Life (Stafford), **Supp. XI:** 312–313, 313–314, 315

"Young" (Sexton), **Supp. II Part 2:** 680

Young, Al, **Supp. X:** 240

Young, Art, **IV:** 436

Young, Barbara, **Supp. XX:** 119, 123

Young, Brigham, **Supp. IV Part 2:** 603

Young, David, **Supp. XIX:** 276

Young, Edward, **II:** 111; **III:** 415, 503

Young, Gary, **Supp. XV:** 88

Young, Mary, **Supp. XIII:** 236, 238, 239, 240

Young, Philip, **II:** 306; **Retro. Supp. I:** 172

Young Adventure (Benét), **Supp. XI:** 44

"Young America" (Brooks), **Supp. XV:** 298

"Young Child and His Pregnant Mother, A" (Schwartz), **Supp. II Part 2:** 650

Young Christian, The (Abbott), **Supp. I Part 1:** 38

"Young Dr. Gosse" (Chopin), **Supp. I Part 1:** 211, 216

Younger Choir, The (anthology), **Supp. XV:** 294

Younger Quire, The (Untermeyer), **Supp. XV:** 294, 297

"Young Folks, The" (Salinger), **III:** 551

Young Folk's Cyclopaedia of Persons and Places (Champlin), **III:** 577

"Young Girl's Lament, A" (Jin), **Supp. XVIII:** 99

"Young Goodman Brown" (Hawthorne), **II:** 229; **Retro. Supp. I:** 151–152, 153, 154; **Supp. XI:** 51; **Supp. XIV:** 48, 50

Young Harvard: First Poems of Witter Bynner (Bynner), **Supp. XV:** 41

Young Hearts Crying (Yates), **Supp. XI:** 348

"Young Housewife, The" (W. C. Williams), **Retro. Supp. I:** 415

Young Immigrants, The (Lardner), **II:** 426

"Young Lady's Friend, The: Verses, Addressed to a Young Lady, on Her Leaving School" (Rowson), **Supp. XV:** 234

Young Lions, The (Shaw), **Supp. XIX:** 248–249

Young Lonigan: A Boyhood in Chicago Streets (Farrell), **II:** 31, 41

Young Manhood of Studs Lonigan, The (Farrell), **II:** 31, 34

Young Men and Fire (Maclean), **Supp. XIV:** 221, 231–233

Young People's Pride (Benét), **Supp. XI:** 44

Young Poet's Primer (Brooks), **Supp. III Part 1:** 86

Youngren, J. Alan, **Supp. XVI:** 174

"Young Sammy's First Wild Oats" (Santayana), **III:** 607, 615

"Young Sor Juana, The" (Mora), **Supp. XIII:** 218

"Your Arkansas Traveler" (Schulberg), **Supp. XVIII:** 252

"Your Death" (Dove), **Supp. IV Part 1:** 250

You're Only Old Once! (Geisel), **Supp. XVI:** 111

"You're Ugly, Too" (Moore), **Supp. X:** 171

"Your Face on the Dog's Neck" (Sexton), **Supp. II Part 2:** 686

"Your Hand, Your Hand" (Hoffman), **Supp. XVIII:** 79

Your Job in Germany (film, Capra), **Supp. XVI:** 102

Your Job in Japan (film, Capra), **Supp. XVI:** 102

"Your Life" (Stafford), **Supp. XI:** 329

"Your Mother's Eyes" (Kingsolver), **Supp. VII:** 209

"You Take a Train through a Foreign Country" (Dobyns), **Supp. XIII:** 90

"Youth" (Hughes), **Supp. I Part 1:** 321

"Youth" (Huncke), **Supp. XIV:** 145

Youth and Life (Bourne), **I:** 217–222, 232

Youth and the Bright Medusa (Cather), **I:** 322; **Retro. Supp. I:** 14

"Youthful Religious Experiences" (Corso), **Supp. XII:** 117

Youth of Parnassus, and Other Stories, The (L. P. Smith), **Supp. XIV:** 336

Youth's First Steps in Geography (Rowson), **Supp. XV:** 243

You Touched Me! (Williams and Windham), **IV:** 382, 385, 387, 390, 392–393

"You Touch Me" (X. J. Kennedy), **Supp. XV:** 166

You Went Away (Findley), **Supp. XX:** 49

"You Who Sleep Soundly Through Our Bleakest Hour" (Espaillat), **Supp. XXI:** 110

Yurchenco, Henrietta, **Supp. XVIII:** 20

Yurka, Blanche, **Supp. I Part 1:** 67

Yutang, Adet, **Supp. X:** 291

Yutang, Anor, **Supp. X:** 291

Yutang, Lin, **Supp. X:** 291; **Supp. XVI:** 190

Yutang, Mei-mei, **Supp. X:** 291

Yvernelle: A Legend of Feudal France (Norris), **III:** 314

Y & X (Olson), **Supp. II Part 2:** 556

Z

Zabel, Morton Dauwen, **II:** 431; **III:** 194, 215; **Supp. I Part 2:** 721

Zach, Natan, **Supp. XV:** 75, 82, 85

Zagajewski, Adam, **Supp. XVII:** 241

Zagarell, Sandra, **Supp. XV:** 269, 270, 278, 281, 282

Zagarell, Sandra A., **Retro. Supp. II:** 140, 143

"Zagrowsky Tells" (Paley), **Supp. VI:** 229

Zakrzewska, Marie, **Retro. Supp. II:** 146

Zaleski, Jeff, **Supp. XI:** 143; **Supp. XIX:** 54

Zall, Paul, **Supp. XIV:** 156

Zaltzberg, Charlotte, **Supp. IV Part 1:** 374

"Zambesi and Ranee" (Swenson), **Supp. IV Part 2:** 647

Zamir, Israel, **Retro. Supp. II:** 303, 317

Zamora, Bernice, **Supp. IV Part 2:** 545

Zamoyski, Adam, **Supp. XV:** 257

Zangwill, Israel, **I:** 229; **Supp. XX:** 2

Zanita: A Tale of the Yosemite (Yelverton), **Supp. IX:** 181

Zanuck, Darryl F., **Supp. XI:** 170; **Supp. XII:** 165

Zapata, Emiliano, **Supp. XIII:** 324

"Zapatos" (Boyle), **Supp. VIII:** 15

Zapruder, Matthew, **Supp. XVI:** 55

Zarathustra, **III:** 602

Zawacki, Andrew, **Supp. VIII:** 272

"Zaydee" (Levine), **Supp. V:** 186

Zebra-Striped Hearse, The (Macdonald), **Supp. IV Part 2:** 473

Zechariah (biblical book), **IV:** 152

Zeidner, Lisa, **Supp. IV Part 2:** 453

"Zeitl and Rickel" (Singer), **IV:** 20

Zeke and Ned (McMurtry and Ossana), **Supp. V:** 232

Zeke Proctor, Cherokee Outlaw (Conley), **Supp. V:** 232

Zelda: A Biography (Milford), **Supp. IX:** 60

"Zelda and Scott: The Beautiful and Damned" (National Portrait Gallery exhibit), **Supp. IX:** 65
Zelig (film; Allen), **Supp. XV:** 4, 6, **8–9**
Zen and the Birds of Appetite (Merton), **Supp. VIII:** 205–206, 208
Zend-Avesta (Fechner), **II:** 358
Zeno, **Retro. Supp. I:** 247
Zero db and Other Stories (Bell), **Supp. X:** 1, 5, 6
"Zeus over Redeye" (Hayden), **Supp. II Part 1:** 380
Zevi, Sabbatai, **IV:** 6
Ziegfeld, Florenz, **II:** 427–428
Ziegler, Cyd, **Supp. XX:**273
Zigrosser, Carl, **I:** 226, 228, 231
Zilles, Klaus, **Supp. XIX:** 112
Zimmerman, Paul D., **Supp. IV Part 2:** 583, 589, 590
Zimmerman, Robert Allen. *See* Dylan, Bob
Zinberg, Leonard S. *See* Lacy, Ed
Zinman, Toby Silverman, **Supp. XIII:** 207–208, 209
Zinn, Howard, **Supp. V:** 289
Zinovyev, Grigory, **Supp. XXI:** 167
Zinsser, Hans, **I:** 251, 385

Zip: A Novel of the Left and Right (Apple), **Supp. XVII:** **4–5**
Zipes, Jack, **Supp. XIV:** 126
"Zipper, The" (L. Michaels), **Supp. XVI:** 214
"Zizi's Lament" (Corso), **Supp. XII:** 123
Zodiac, The (Dickey), **Supp. IV Part 1:** 178, 183–184, 185
Zola, Émile, **I:** 211, 411, 474, 500, 502, 518; **II:** 174, 175–176, 182, 194, 275, 276, 281, 282, 319, 325, 337, 338; **III:** 315, 316, 317–318, 319–320, 321, 322, 323, 393, 511, 583; **IV:** 326; **Retro. Supp. I:** 226, 235; **Retro. Supp. II:** 93; **Supp. I Part 1:** 207; **Supp. II Part 1:** 117
Zolotow, Maurice, **III:** 161
"Zone" (Bogan), **Supp. III Part 1:** 60–61
Zone Journals (Wright), **Supp. V:** 332–333, 342–343
"Zooey" (Salinger), **III:** 564–565, 566, 567, 569, 572
"Zoo Revisited" (White), **Supp. I Part 2:** 654
Zoo Story, The (Albee), **I:** 71, 72–74, 75, 77, 84, 93, 94; **III:** 281
Zorach, William, **I:** 260

Zuccotti, Susan, **Supp. XVI:** 154
Zuckerman Bound: A Trilogy and Epilogue (P. Roth), **Supp. III Part 2:** 423
Zuckerman Unbound (P. Roth), **Retro. Supp. II:** 283; **Supp. III Part 2:** 421–422
Zueblin, Charles, **Supp. I Part 1:** 5
Zuger, Abigail, **Supp. X:** 160
Zukofsky, Celia (Mrs. Louis), **Supp. III Part 2:** 619–621, 623, 625, 626–629, 631
Zukofsky, Louis, **IV:** 415; **Retro. Supp. I:** 422; **Supp. III Part 2:** **619–636**; **Supp. IV Part 1:** 154; **Supp. XIV:** 279, 282, 285, 286–287
Zukofsky, Paul, **Supp. III Part 2:** 622, 623–626, 627, 628
Zuleika Dobson (Beerbohm), **Supp. I Part 2:** 714
Zulus (Everett), **Supp. XVIII:** 54, **56–57**
"Zuni Potter: Drawing the Heartline" (Bierds), **Supp. XVII:** 26
Zverev, Aleksei, **Retro. Supp. I:** 278
Zwinger, Ann, **Supp. X:** 29
Zyda, Joan, **Retro. Supp. II:** 52

A Complete Listing of Authors in
American Writers

Abbey, Edward   Supp. XIII
Acker, Kathy   Supp. XII
Adams, Henry   Vol. I
Addams, Jane   Supp. I
Agee, James   Vol. I
Aiken, Conrad   Vol. I
Albee, Edward   Vol. I
Alcott, Louisa May   Supp. I
Algren, Nelson   Supp. IX
Allen, Woody   Supp. XV
Alvarez, Julia   Supp. VII
Ammons, A. R.   Supp. VII
Anderson, Sherwood   Vol. I
Angelou, Maya   Supp. IV
Antin, Mary   Supp. XX
Apple, Max   Supp. XVII
Ashbery, John   Supp. III
Atwood, Margaret   Supp. XIII
Auchincloss, Louis   Supp. IV
Auden, W. H.   Supp. II
Audubon, John James   Supp. XVI
Auster, Paul   Supp. XII
Baker, Nicholson   Supp. XIII
Baldwin, James   Supp. I
Baldwin, James   Retro. Supp. II
Bambara, Toni Cade   Supp. XI
Banks, Russell   Supp. V
Baraka, Amiri   Supp. II
Barlow, Joel   Supp. II
Barnes, Djuna   Supp. III
Barth, John   Vol. I
Barthelme, Donald   Supp. IV
Barthelme, Frederick   Supp. XI
Bass, Rick   Supp. XVI
Bausch, Richard   Supp. VII
Baxter, Charles   Supp. XVII
Beattie, Ann   Supp. V

Bell, Madison Smartt   Supp. X
Bellow, Saul   Vol. I
Bellow, Saul   Retro. Supp. II
Benét, Stephen Vincent   Supp. XI
Berry, Wendell   Supp. X
Berryman, John   Vol. I
Bidart, Frank   Supp. XV
Bierce, Ambrose   Vol. I
Bierds, Linda   Supp. XVII
Bishop, Elizabeth   Supp. I
Bishop, Elizabeth   Retro. Supp. II
Blackmur, R. P.   Supp. II
Bly, Carol   Supp. XVI
Bly, Robert   Supp. IV
Bogan, Louise   Supp. III
Bourne, Randolph   Vol. I
Bowles, Paul   Supp. IV
Boyce, Neith   Supp. XXI
Boyle, T. C.   Supp. VIII
Boyle, T. C.   Supp. XX
Bradbury, Ray   Supp. IV
Bradstreet, Anne   Supp. I
Briggs, Charles Frederick   Supp. XVIII
Brodsky, Joseph   Supp. VIII
Bronk, William   Supp. XXI
Brooks, Cleanth   Supp. XIV
Brooks, Gwendolyn   Supp. III
Brooks, Van Wyck   Vol. I
Brown, Charles Brockden   Supp. I
Brown, Larry   Supp. XXI
Bryant, William Cullen   Supp. I
Buck, Pearl S.   Supp. II
Budbill, David   Supp. XIX
Buechner, Frederick   Supp. XII
Bukiet, Melvin Jules   Supp. XVII
Burke, James Lee   Supp. XIV
Burke, Kenneth   Vol. I

Burroughs, William S.   Supp. III

Butler, Octavia   Supp. XIII

Butler, Robert Olen   Supp. XII

Bynner, Witter   Supp. XV

Caldwell, Erskine   Vol. I

Cameron, Peter   Supp. XII

Capote, Truman   Supp. III

Caputo, Philip   Supp. XIX

Carruth, Hayden   Supp. XVI

Carson, Anne   Supp. XII

Carson, Rachel   Supp. IX

Carver, Raymond   Supp. III

Cather, Willa   Vol. I

Cather, Willa   Retro. Supp. I

Chabon, Michael   Supp. XI

Chandler, Raymond   Supp. IV

Chapman, John Jay   Supp. XIV

Cheever, John   Supp. I

Chesnutt, Charles W.   Supp. XIV

Chopin, Kate   Supp. I

Chopin, Kate   Retro. Supp. II

Cisneros, Sandra   Supp. VII

Clampitt, Amy   Supp. IX

Coleman, Wanda   Supp. XI

Collins, Billy   Supp. XXI

Connell, Evan S.   Supp. XIV

Connell, Michael   Supp. XXI

Conroy, Frank   Supp. XVI

Cooper, James Fenimore   Vol. I

Coover, Robert   Supp. V

Corso, Gregory   Supp. XII

Cowley, Malcolm   Supp. II

Cozzens, James Gould   Vol. I

Crane, Hart   Vol. I

Crane, Hart   Retro. Supp. II

Crane, Stephen   Vol. I

Creeley, Robert   Supp. IV

Crèvecoeur, Michel-Guillaume Jean de   Supp. I

Crews, Harry   Supp. XI

Cullen, Countee   Supp. IV

Cummings, E. E.   Vol. I

Cunningham, Michael   Supp. XV

Davis, Rebecca Harding   Supp. XVI

Davis, William Virgil   Supp. XXI

DeLillo, Don   Supp. VI

Dickey, James   Supp. IV

Dickinson, Emily   Vol. I

Dickinson, Emily   Retro. Supp. I

Didion, Joan   Supp. IV

Di Donato, Pietro   Supp. XX

Dillard, Annie   Supp. VI

Di Piero, W. S.   Supp. XIX

Dixon, Stephen   Supp. XII

Dobyns, Stephen   Supp. XIII

Doctorow, E. L.   Supp. IV

Doolittle, Hilda (H.D.)   Supp. I

Dos Passos, John   Vol. I

Doty, Mark   Supp. XI

Douglass, Frederick   Supp. III

Dove, Rita   Supp. IV

Dreiser, Theodore   Vol. I

Dreiser, Theodore   Retro. Supp. II

Du Bois, W. E. B.   Supp. II

Dubus, Andre   Supp. VII

Dunbar, Paul Laurence   Supp. II

Dunn, Stephen   Supp. XI

Dylan, Bob   Supp. XVIII

Eberhart, Richard   Vol. I

Edson, Margaret   Supp. XVIII

Edwards, Jonathan   Vol. I

Egan, Jennifer   Supp. XIX

Eliot, T. S.   Vol. I

Eliot, T. S.   Retro. Supp. I

Elkin, Stanley   Supp. VI

Ellison, Ralph   Supp. II

Ellison, Ralph   Retro. Supp. II

Emerson, Ralph Waldo   Vol. II

Endore, Guy   Supp. XVII

Epstein, Joseph   Supp. XIV

Epstein, Leslie   Supp. XII

Erdrich, Louise   Supp. IV

Espaillat, Rhina P.   Supp. XXI

Everett, Percival   Supp. XVIII

Everwine, Peter   Supp. XV

Fante, John   Supp. XI

Farrell, James T.   Vol. II

Faulkner, William   Vol. II

Faulkner, William   Retro. Supp. I

Fiedler, Leslie   Supp. XIII
Finch, Annie   Supp. XVII
Findley, Timothy   Supp. XX
Fisher, M. F. K.   Supp. XVII
Fisher, Rudolph   Supp. XIX
Fitzgerald, F. Scott   Vol. II
Fitzgerald, F. Scott   Retro. Supp. I
Fitzgerald, Zelda   Supp. IX
Ford, Richard   Supp. V
Francis, Robert   Supp. IX
Frank, Waldo   Supp. XX
Franklin, Benjamin   Vol. II
Franzen, Jonathan   Supp. XX
Frederic, Harold   Vol. II
Freneau, Philip   Supp. II
Frost, Carol   Supp. XV
Frost, Robert   Vol. II
Frost, Robert   Retro. Supp. I
Fuller, Margaret   Supp. II
Gaddis, William   Supp. IV
García, Cristina   Supp. XI
Gardner, John   Supp. VI
Garrett, George   Supp. VII
Gass, William   Supp. VI
Gates, Henry Louis Jr.   Supp. XX
Geisel, Theodor Seuss   Supp. XVI
Gibbons, Kaye   Supp. X
Gibran, Kahlil   Supp. XX
Gibson, William   Supp. XVI
Gilman, Charlotte Perkins   Supp. XI
Ginsberg, Allen   Supp. II
Gioia, Dana   Supp. XV
Glasgow, Ellen   Vol. II
Glaspell, Susan   Supp. III
Goldbarth, Albert   Supp. XII
Glück, Louise   Supp. V
Gordon, Caroline   Vol. II
Gordon, Mary   Supp. IV
Gunn Allen, Paula   Supp. IV
Gurney, A. R.   Supp. V
Haines, John   Supp. XII
Halliday, Mark   Supp. XIX
Hammett, Dashiell   Supp. IV
Hansberry, Lorraine   Supp. IV

Hapgood, Hutchins   Supp. XVII
Hardwick, Elizabeth   Supp. III
Harjo, Joy   Supp. XII
Harrison, Jim   Supp. VIII
Harte, Bret   Supp. II
Hass, Robert   Supp. VI
Hawthorne, Nathaniel   Vol. II
Hawthorne, Nathaniel   Retro. Supp. I
Hay, Sara Henderson   Supp. XIV
Hayden, Robert   Supp. II
Hearon, Shelby   Supp. VIII
Hecht, Anthony   Supp. X
Heller, Joseph   Supp. IV
Hellman, Lillian   Supp. I
Hemingway, Ernest   Vol. II
Hemingway, Ernest   Retro. Supp. I
Hempel, Amy   Supp. XXI
Henry, O.   Supp. II
Hijuelos, Oscar   Supp. VIII
Himes, Chester Bomar   Supp. XVI
Hinojosa, Rolando   Supp. XIX
Hoffman, Alice   Supp. X
Hoffman, Eva   Supp. XVI
Hoffman, William   Supp. XVIII
Hogan, Linda   Supp. IV
Holmes, Oliver Wendell   Supp. I
Howe, Irving   Supp. VI
Howe, Susan   Supp. IV
Howells, William Dean   Vol. II
Hughes, Langston   Supp. I
Hughes, Langston   Retro. Supp. I
Hugo, Richard   Supp. VI
Hull, Lynda   Supp. XXI
Humphrey, William   Supp. IX
Huncke, Herbert   Supp. XIV
Hurston, Zora Neale   Supp. VI
Hwang, David Henry   Supp. XXI
Irving, John   Supp. VI
Irving, Washington   Vol. II
Isherwood, Christopher   Supp. XIV
Jackson, Shirley   Supp. IX
James, C. L. R.   Supp. XXI
James, Henry   Vol. II
James, Henry   Retro. Supp. I

James, William   Vol. II
Jarman, Mark   Supp. XVII
Jarrell, Randall   Vol. II
Jeffers, Robinson   Supp. II
Jewett, Sarah Orne   Vol. II
Jewett, Sarah Orne   Retro. Supp. II
Jin, Ha   Supp. XVIII
Johnson, Charles   Supp. VI
Jones, James   Supp. XI
Jong, Erica   Supp. V
Justice, Donald   Supp. VII
Karr, Mary   Supp. XI
Kazin, Alfred   Supp. VIII
Kees, Weldon   Supp. XV
Keillor, Garrison   Supp. XVI
Kelly, Brigit Pegeen   Supp. XVII
Kennedy, William   Supp. VII
Kennedy, X. J.   Supp. XV
Kenyon, Jane   Supp. VII
Kerouac, Jack   Supp. III
Kincaid, Jamaica   Supp. VII
King, Stephen   Supp. V
Kingsolver, Barbara   Supp. VII
Kingston, Maxine Hong   Supp. V
Kinnell, Galway   Supp. III
Knowles, John   Supp. XII
Koch, Kenneth   Supp. XV
Komunyakaa, Yusef   Supp. XIII
Kooser, Ted   Supp. XIX
Kosinski, Jerzy   Supp. VII
Krakauer, Jon   Supp. XVIII
Kumin, Maxine   Supp. IV
Kunitz, Stanley   Supp. III
Kushner, Tony   Supp. IX
LaBastille, Anne   Supp. X
Lacy, Ed   Supp. XV
Lahiri, Jhumpa   Supp. XXI
Lamott, Anne   Supp. XX
Lanier, Sidney   Supp. I
Larcom, Lucy   Supp. XIII
Lardner, Ring   Vol. II
Larsen, Nella   Supp. XVIII
Lee, Harper   Supp. VIII
Lee, Li-Young   Supp. XV

Leopold, Aldo   Supp. XIV
Lethem, Jonathan   Supp. XVIII
Levertov, Denise   Supp. III
Levine, Philip   Supp. V
Levis, Larry   Supp. XI
Lewis, Sinclair   Vol. II
Lindsay, Vachel   Supp. I
Locke, Alain   Supp. XIV
London, Jack   Vol. II
Longfellow, Henry Wadsworth   Vol. II
Longfellow, Henry Wadsworth   Retro. Supp. II
Loos, Anita   Supp. XVI
Lowell, Amy   Vol. II
Lowell, James Russell   Supp. I
Lowell, Robert   Vol. II
Lowell, Robert   Retro. Supp. II
Maclean, Norman   Supp. XIV
MacLeish, Archibald   Vol. III
Markson, David   Supp. XVII
McCarriston, Linda   Supp. XIV
McCarthy, Cormac   Supp. VIII
McCarthy, Mary   Vol. II
McClatchy, J. D.   Supp. XII
McCourt, Frank   Supp. XII
McCoy, Horace   Supp. XIII
McCullers, Carson   Vol. II
McDermott, Alice   Supp. XVIII
Macdonald, Ross   Supp. IV
McGrath, Thomas   Supp. X
McKay, Claude   Supp. X
McKnight, Reginald   Supp. XX
McMillan, Terry   Supp. XIII
McMurty, Larry   Supp. V
McNally, Terrence   Supp. XIII
McPhee, John   Supp. III
Mailer, Norman   Vol. III
Mailer, Norman   Retro. Supp. II
Malamud, Bernard   Supp. I
Mallon, Thomas   Supp. XIX
Mamet, David   Supp. XIV
Marquand, John P.   Vol. III
Marshall, Paule   Supp. XI
Mason, Bobbie Ann   Supp. VIII
Masters, Edgar Lee   Supp. I

Mather, Cotton   Supp. II
Matthews, William   Supp. IX
Matthiessen, Peter   Supp. V
Maxwell, William   Supp. VIII
Melville, Herman   Vol. III
Melville, Herman   Retro. Supp. I
Mencken, H. L.   Vol. III
Merrill, James   Supp. III
Merton, Thomas   Supp. VIII
Merwin, W. S.   Supp. III
Michaels, Leonard   Supp. XVI
Millay, Edna St. Vincent   Vol. III
Miller, Arthur   Vol. III
Miller, Henry   Vol. III
Miller, Jim Wayne   Supp. XX
Miller, Sue   Supp. XII
Minot, Susan   Supp. VI
Mirvis, Tova   Supp. XX
Momaday, N. Scott   Supp. IV
Monette, Paul   Supp. X
Moore, Lorrie   Supp. X
Moore, Marianne   Vol. III
Mora, Pat   Supp. XIII
Morison, Samuel Eliot   Supp. I
Morris, Wright   Vol. III
Morrison, Toni   Supp. III
Mosley, Walter   Supp. XIII
Motley, Willard   Supp. XVII
Muir, John   Supp. IX
Mumford, Lewis   Supp. III
Murray, Albert   Supp. XIX
Nabokov, Vladimir   Vol. III
Nabokov, Vladimir   Retro. Supp. I
Naylor, Gloria   Supp. VIII
Nelson, Marilyn   Supp. XVIII
Nemerov, Howard   Vol. III
Neugeboren, Jay   Supp. XVI
Nichols, John   Supp. XIII
Niebuhr, Reinhold   Vol. III
Nin, Anaïs   Supp. X
Norris, Frank   Vol. III
Nye, Naomi Shihab   Supp. XIII
Oates, Joyce Carol   Supp. II
O'Brien, Tim   Supp. V

O'Connor, Flannery   Vol. III
O'Connor, Flannery   Retro. Supp. II
Odets, Clifford   Supp. II
Offutt, Chris   Supp. XIX
O'Hara, John   Vol. III
Olds, Sharon   Supp. X
Oliver, Mary   Supp. VII
Olsen, Tillie   Supp. XIII
Olson, Charles   Supp. II
O'Neill, Eugene   Vol. III
Ortiz, Simon J.   Supp. IV
Ozick, Cynthia   Supp. V
Paine, Thomas   Supp. I
Paley, Grace   Supp. VI
Parker, Dorothy   Supp. IX
Parker, Robert B.   Supp. XIX
Parkman, Francis   Supp. II
Patchett, Ann   Supp. XII
Peacock, Molly   Supp. XIX
Percy, Walker   Supp. III
Pickering, Sam   Supp. XXI
Pinsky, Robert   Supp. VI
Plath, Sylvia   Supp. I
Plath, Sylvia   Retro. Supp. II
Plimpton, George   Supp. XVI
Podhoretz, Norman   Supp. VIII
Poe, Edgar Allan   Vol. III
Poe, Edgar Allan   Retro. Supp. II
Porter, Katherine Anne   Vol. III
Pound, Ezra   Vol. III
Pound, Ezra   Retro. Supp. I
Powers, Richard   Supp. IX
Price, Reynolds   Supp. VI
Prose, Francine   Supp. XVI
Proulx, Annie   Supp. VII
Purdy, James   Supp. VII
Pynchon, Thomas   Supp. II
Quindlen, Anna   Supp. XVII
Rand, Ayn   Supp. IV
Ransom, John Crowe   Vol. III
Rawlings, Marjorie Kinnan   Supp. X
Ray, Janisse   Supp. XVIII
Reed, Ishmael   Supp. X
Reznikoff, Charles   Supp. XIV

Rice, Anne   Supp. VII
Rich, Adrienne   Supp. I
Rich, Adrienne   Retro. Supp. II
Richard, Mark   Supp. XIX
Richter, Conrad   Supp. XVIII
Ríos, Alberto Álvaro   Supp. IV
Robbins, Tom   Supp. X
Robinson, Edwin Arlington   Vol. III
Robinson, Marilynne   Supp. XXI
Rodriguez, Richard   Supp. XIV
Roethke, Theodore   Vol. III
Roth, Henry   Supp. IX
Roth, Philip   Supp. III
Roth, Philip   Retro. Supp. II
Rowson, Susanna   Supp. XV
Rukeyser, Muriel   Supp. VI
Russo, Richard   Supp. XII
Ryan, Paul William   Supp. XVIII
Salinas, Luis Omar   Supp. XIII
Salinger, J. D.   Vol. III
Salter, James   Supp. IX
Sandburg, Carl   Vol. III
Sanders, Scott Russell   Supp. XVI
Santayana, George   Vol. III
Sarton, May   Supp. VIII
Saunders, George   Supp. XIX
Schnackenberg, Gjertrud   Supp. XV
Schulberg, Budd   Supp. XVIII
Schwartz, Delmore   Supp. II
Scott, Joanna   Supp. XVII
Sexton, Anne   Supp. II
Shanley, John Patrick   Supp. XIV
Shapiro, Karl   Supp. II
Shaw, Irwin   Supp. XIX
Shepard, Sam   Supp. III
Shields, Carol   Supp. VII
Silko, Leslie Marmon   Supp. IV
Simic, Charles   Supp. VIII
Simon, Neil   Supp. IV
Simpson, Louis   Supp. IX
Sinclair, Upton   Supp. V
Singer, Isaac Bashevis   Vol. IV
Singer, Isaac Bashevis   Retro. Supp. II
Skloot, Floyd   Supp. XX

Smiley, Jane   Supp. VI
Smith, Logan Pearsall   Supp. XIV
Smith, William Jay   Supp. XIII
Snodgrass, W. D.   Supp. VI
Snyder, Gary   Supp. VIII
Sobin, Gustaf   Supp. XVI
Sontag, Susan   Supp. III
Sorrentino, Gilbert   Supp. XXI
Southern, Terry   Supp. XI
Stafford, William   Supp. XI
Stegner, Wallace   Supp. IV
Stein, Gertrude   Vol. IV
Steinbeck, John   Vol. IV
Stern, Gerald   Supp. IX
Stevens, Wallace   Vol. IV
Stevens, Wallace   Retro. Supp. I
Stoddard, Elizabeth   Supp. XV
Stone, Robert   Supp. V
Stowe, Harriet Beecher   Supp. I
Strand, Mark   Supp. IV
Stratton-Porter, Gene   Supp. XX
Sturgis, Howard Overing   Supp. XX
Styron, William   Vol. IV
Swados, Harvey   Supp. XIX
Swenson, May   Supp. IV
Talese, Gay   Supp. XVII
Tan, Amy   Supp. X
Tate, Allen   Vol. IV
Taylor, Edward   Vol. IV
Taylor, Peter   Supp. V
Theroux, Paul   Supp. VIII
Thoreau, Henry David   Vol. IV
Thurber, James   Supp. I
Toomer, Jean   Supp. IX
Trethewey, Natasha   Supp. XXI
Trilling, Lionel   Supp. III
Turow, Scott   Supp. XVII
Twain, Mark   Vol. IV
Tyler, Anne   Supp. IV
Untermeyer, Louis   Supp. XV
Updike, John   Vol. IV
Updike, John   Retro. Supp. I
Uris, Leon   Supp. XX
Van Vechten, Carl   Supp. II

Veblen, Thorstein   Supp. I

Vidal, Gore   Supp. IV

Vollmann, William T.   Supp. XVII

Vonnegut, Kurt   Supp. II

Wagoner, David   Supp. IX

Walker, Alice   Supp. III

Wallace, David Foster   Supp. X

Warner, Susan   Supp. XVIII

Warren, Patricia Nell   Supp. XX

Warren, Robert Penn   Vol. IV

Wasserstein, Wendy   Supp. XV

Weigl, Bruce   Supp. XIX

Welty, Eudora   Vol. IV

Welty, Eudora   Retro. Supp. I

West, Dorothy   Supp. XVIII

West, Nathanael   Vol. IV

West, Nathanael   Retro. Supp. II

Wharton, Edith   Vol. IV

Wharton, Edith   Retro. Supp. I

Wheatley, Phillis   Supp. XX

White, E. B.   Supp. I

Whitman, Walt   Vol. IV

Whitman, Walt   Retro. Supp. I

Whittier, John Greenleaf   Supp. I

Wilbur, Richard   Supp. III

Wideman, John Edgar   Supp. X

Wilder, Thornton   Vol. IV

Williams, Tennessee   Vol. IV

Williams, William Carlos   Vol. IV

Williams, William Carlos   Retro. Supp. I

Wilson, August   Supp. VIII

Wilson, Edmund   Vol. IV

Winters, Yvor   Supp. II

Wolfe, Thomas   Vol. IV

Wolfe, Tom   Supp. III

Wolfert, Ira   Supp. XXI

Wolff, Tobias   Supp. VII

Wright, C. D.   Supp. XV

Wright, Charles   Supp. V

Wright, Franz   Supp. XVII

Wright, James   Supp. III

Wright, Richard   Vol. IV

Wrigley, Robert   Supp. XVIII

Wylie, Elinor   Supp. I

Yates, Richard   Supp. XI

Zukofsky, Louis   Supp. III

A 55

___

Supp 21